Reader's Guide to

LITERATURE

IN

ENGLISH

Reader's Guide to

LITERATURE IN ENGLISH

Editor

MARK HAWKINS-DADY

FD

LONDON • CHICAGO

FITZROY DEARBORN PUBLISHERS
70 East Walton Street
Chicago, Illinois 60611
USA

or

11 Rathbone Place
London W1P 1DE
England

British Library Cataloguing in Publication Data
Reader's guide to literature in English
1. English literature – History and criticism
I. Hawkins-Dady, Mark, 1962–
820.9

ISBN 1–884964–20–6

Library of Congress Cataloging in Publication Data is available.

First published in the USA and UK 1996

Typeset by Florencetype Ltd, Stoodleigh, Devon
Printed by Braun-Brumfield, Inc., Ann Arbor, Michigan

CONTENTS

EDITOR'S NOTE AND GUIDE TO USAGE

Aims, Scope and Selection of Entries

The aim of the *Reader's Guide to Literature in English* is to provide informed description and evaluation of the critical writing on a range of topics and writers in the literature of the British Isles, the United States, and the other major English-speaking traditions of the world.

In examining the published criticism of recent years, the *Reader's Guide* is a reflection of the increasing multiplicity in the field. On the one hand, new discourses and literary-theoretical perspectives have helped maintain the stream of publications on the "traditional" figures of the literary canon, and Shakespeare, as one essayist in the *Guide* writes, remains "the single most contested site of literary and theoretical skirmish in the English-speaking world". On the other hand, notions of a canon have had to become more flexible because of, among other developments, the reclamation of women writers in all genres, periods, and nationalities, the increasing attention to writers of ethnic minorities (most evidently in the United States), and the decline of the subsidiary term "Commonwealth Literature" in favour of the more assertively independent and plural "New Literatures".

In selecting entries for the *Guide* the views of the project's advisers (listed in the Acknowledgments), the contributing essayists, and other scholars and commentators were taken into account. Two principal criteria were borne in mind in choosing an entry: (a) the existence of a reasonably substantial body of discussion on the subject, particularly in book form, and (b) evidence of strong current interest in the subject. In most cases these two criteria were complementary. Writers and topics that do not receive their own entries – often because the amount of critical literature on them is small – frequently receive attention under more general entries: for example, while books on individual women writers of the Renaissance are few in number as yet, there are several general studies, which are here considered in the entry "Women Writers: Renaissance". (Citations of all individual writers discussed can be located via the General Index.)

The resulting selection includes entries about the literature on national traditions and periods (e.g., "British Literature: 18th Century" or "Canadian Literature"), genres and idioms (e.g., "Travel Literature" or "The Sonnet"), literary theory (e.g., "Deconstruction" or "New Historicism"), cultural contexts (e.g., "Film and Literature"), writing by women and ethnic minorities (e.g., "Women Writers to 1700" and "Native American Literature"), artistic schools and movements (e.g., "Black Mountain Poets" or "Beat Generation"), as well as entries on individual writers.

Arrangement of the Entries

Entries appear in alphabetical order: a complete list of them can be found in the **Alphabetical List of Entries** (p. xiii). An entry's heading is a broad indication of the level of specificity of the material to be discussed. Where there are several entries beginning with the same heading (as in those beginning "Drama . . .", "Novel . . .", "Poetry . . .", etc.) the order normally proceeds from the most general to the more particular, and from British to American, then to other national categories. Thus, for example, the "Poetry" entries begin with the very broad ones ("Poetry: Theory", "Poetry: General", etc.); these are followed by entries on British poetry (by period), American poetry (by period), and "Poetry: Australian" and "Poetry: Canadian".

While the arrangement of entries is alphabetical, there are several other means of access to the *Guide*'s contents. These are:

1. **Thematic List** (p. xix). Consult this if you want to know which entries in the *Guide* relate to a particular subject area, such as Victorian Literature, American Literature – 20th Century, etc.
2. **Booklist Index** (p. 891). Consult this if you want to find where the works of particular critics or scholars are discussed.
3. **General Index** (p. 937). Consult this if you want to know where a particular literary name (or other cultural figure) is discussed. This is particularly useful for locating writers who do not receive their own entries.

Format Within Entries

Each entry begins with a list of the books/articles – with appropriate publication information – discussed by the essayist. Dates of first publication and revised editions are normally given, though in most cases reprints are omitted. The books/articles have been selected by the contributors, within editorial guidelines.

In each essay, the citation of a critic's name in capital letters indicates the point at which his or her publication receives its principal commentary (though references to it might appear elsewhere in the essay). The essayists most commonly adopt either a chronological approach, tracing the development of criticism, or a thematic approach.

Acknowledgments

I should like to thank the following who have helped in the preparation of the *Reader's Guide*: all those who have written for the volume; Catherine Belsey, Malcolm Bradbury, Laurel Brake, Henry Claridge, Peter Hunt, Brian Matthews, Elizabeth Robertson, and Jeffrey C. Robinson, who all gave advice in the early stages; Barbara Archer; Kate Berney; Tony Germing; Lionel Kelly; and the staff of the British Library and London University Library. Especial thanks must go to two people at Fitzroy Dearborn: Daniel Kirkpatrick, who had the idea for the *Reader's Guide* and did much to enable its appearance; and Lesley Henderson for all her hard work.

ADVISERS AND CONTRIBUTORS

Edward A. Abramson
Chris Ackerley
Rosamund S. Allen
Misty G. Anderson
Katherine A. Armstrong
Mary Arseneau
Gwen McNeill Ashburn
Bob Ashley
Simon Baker
Victoria Bazin
Sandra J.Bell
Catherine Belsey
Stephen Bending
Lawrence I. Berkove
Anke Bernau
Delys Bird
David Blair
Christine Blake
J.D. Bone
Howard J. Booth
Roy J. Booth
Deborah C. Bowen
Malcolm Bradbury
Nicola Bradbury
Kevin P. Brady
Laurel Brake
Simon Brittan
Stephen W. Brown
Catherine Burgass
Tim Burke
Mark Thornton Burnett
Julie D. Campbell
Deborah Carlin
G.A. Cevasco
Karen Har-Yen Chow
Christine Christie
Henry Claridge
Carole Coates
John Coates
Katharine Mary Cockin
A.O.J. Cockshut
Catherine Wells Cole
Fiona M. Collins
Caroline M. Cooper
Daniel Cordle
D.T. Corker
Brian Corman
Ralph J. Crane
Jonathan Cutmore
Macdonald Daly
Tony Davenport
Alistair Davies
Paul Davies
Lloyd Davis
Brian J. Day
Paul W. DePasquale
R.P. Draper
Dawn E. Duncan
Steven Earnshaw
Siân Echard
Colin J. Edwards
Rainer Emig
Ruth Evans
Ian Fairley
Francis L. Fennell
Mac Fenwick
Alan Filewod
Susan Fremantle
Susan Frye
Eileen Chia-Ching Fung
Elizabeth Gardner
Julia Gasper
Davida Gavioli
Paola Gemme
Pamela K. Gilbert
Stuart Gillespie
John Goodridge
Val Gough
Trevor R. Griffiths
Andrew Hadfield
Andrew Hagiioannu
Martin Halliwell
Robin Hamilton
Susan Hancock

Lynne Hapgood
Margaret Harris
Oliver Harris
Donald M. Hassler
Heather A. Hathaway
Michael Herbert
Michael Hobbs
Philip Hobsbaum
Patrick Holland
David Holloway
Mark Houlahan
Derek Hughes
Peter Hunt
Philippa Hunt
Siv Jansson
Brian Jarvis
Debra Johanyak
Lawrence Jones
Mark Jones
Penelope Jowitt
Andrea J. Kaston
Dorothea Kehler
Lionel Kelly
Philippa Kelly
Ruth Kennedy
Tom Keymer
Pamela M. King
Jerome Klinkowitz
James D. Knowles
Edward A. Kopper Jr.
Elizabeth Kuhlmann
Jeremy Lane
Gillian Lathey
A. Robert Lee
Laurence Lerner
John Lingard
Margaret L. Llewellyn-Jones
Judith Lockyer
Michael Londry
Stephen Longstaffe
Bruce R.A. Lord
A.W. Lyle
Kevin McCarron
I.D. McCormick
Philip McGowan
Deborah L. Madsen
Willy Maley
Bryant Mangum
D.S. Marriott
Brian Matthews
Steven Matthews
Krista L. May
Laurence W. Mazzeno
Sarah Meer
Bruce Meyer
James A. Miller
Sara Mills
Susannah Milner
Philip Mingay
Radhika Mohanram
Robert A. Morace
Merritt Moseley
Julie Mullaney
Leonora Nattrass
Heather L.E. Neilson
Judie Newman
K.M. Newton
Shannon L. Nichols
Gerda S. Norvig
Jacqueline Nunn
George O'Brien
Michael J. O'Driscoll
Seiwoong Oh
Chidi Okonkwo
Barbara M. Onslow
Norman Page
Noel Peacock
Brian Pearce
John Peck
Jason R. Peters
Craig G. Peterson
Frank Piekarczyk
Jan Pilditch
Pat Pinsent
Carl Plasa
Jane Plastow
Roger Pooley
Chris Pourteau
Leslie K. Pourteau
Sarah Prescott
Joanna Price
R.E. Pritchard
Patrick J.M. Quinn
William Radice
Patricia Rae
Gay Raines
Trace Reddell
Penelope Reedy
Emma L.E. Rees
N.H. Reeve
Kimberley Reynolds
Alan Riach
Nigel Rigby
Pat Righelato
Adam Roberts
Margaret E. Roberts
Marie Mulvey Roberts
Elizabeth Robertson
Danny L. Robinson
Jeffrey C. Robinson
Mark Robson
Nicholas Rombes
Robert L. Ross
Antony Rowland
Susan Rowland
Nicholas Royle
Susan Rusinko
Raymond St-Jacques
D. Schauffer
William J. Scheick

Leah Scragg
David Seed
Peter J. Smith
Rakesh H. Solomon
Clara Elizabeth Speer
Charlotte Spivack
Jane Stabler
John Russell Stephens
Simon Stevens
Alan Stewart
Marjorie Stone
Gerald H. Strauss
Erin Striff
James T.F. Tanner
John Thieme
Peter Thoms
Richard C. Tobias
Marjorie Toone
George A. Tressider
Anna Tripp
Michael Trussler
Louise Tucker
Elizabeth A. Turner
Jonathan Veitch
Angela Vietto
Tony Voss
Nicola Vulpe
Diana Wallace
Elizabeth Porges Watson
Dianne Watt
Diane Looms Weber
Lynn S. Wells
Carolyn D. Williams
Don B. Wilmeth
Amy E.Winans
T.J. Winnifrith
Derek N.C. Wood
Thomas Woodman
Tim S. Woods
Ramona Wray
Charlotte M. Wright
Sue Zemka
William Zunder

ALPHABETICAL LIST OF ENTRIES

THEMATIC LIST

Entries by Category

African Literature

American Literature: Topics

New England Literature
Poetry: American – General
Poetry: American – 19th Century
Poetry: American – 20th Century
Proletarian Literature in America
Prose in America: Historical and Political
Prose in America: 19th Century
Puritan Literature: American
Realism in American Literature
Romanticism and Transcendentalism in America
Science Fiction
Short Fiction: American
Southern United States Literature: General
Southern United States Literature: 19th Century
Southern United States Literature: 20th Century
Vietnam War Literature
Women Writers: American – General
Women Writers: American – to 1900
Women Writers: American – 1900 to the Present
Women Writers: African-American

American Literature: Writers

Adams, Henry
Albee, Edward
Alcott, Louisa May
Anderson, Sherwood
Ashbery, John
Auden, W.H.
Baldwin, James
Baraka, Amiri [LeRoi Jones]
Barth, John
Barthelme, Donald
Bellow, Saul
Berryman, John
Bierce, Ambrose
Bishop, Elizabeth
Bradstreet, Anne
Brown, Charles Brockden
Burroughs, William S.
Carver, Raymond
Cather, Willa
Chandler, Raymond
Chopin, Kate
Cooper, James Fenimore
Crane, Hart
Crane, Stephen
Cummings, E.E.
Dickinson, Emily
Doolittle, Hilda [H.D.]
Dos Passos, John
Douglass, Frederick
Dreiser, Theodore
Du Bois, W.E.B.
Edwards, Jonathan
Eliot, T.S.
Ellison, Ralph
Emerson, Ralph Waldo
Erdrich, Louise
Faulkner, William
Fitzgerald, F. Scott
Franklin, Benjamin
Frost, Robert
Fuller, Margaret
Gaddis, William
Gilman, Charlotte Perkins
Ginsberg, Allen
Hawkes, John
Hawthorne, Nathaniel
Hearn, Lafcadio
Heller, Joseph
Hellman, Lillian
Hemingway, Ernest
Howells, William Dean
Hughes, Langston
Hurston, Zora Neale
Irving, Washington
Isherwood, Christopher
Jacobs, Harriet
James, Henry
James, William
Jeffers, Robinson
Jefferson, Thomas
Kerouac, Jack
Lewis, Sinclair
London, Jack
Lovecraft, H.P.
Lowell, Robert
McCullers, Carson
Mailer, Norman
Malamud, Bernard
Mamet, David
Melville, Herman
Millay, Edna St Vincent
Miller, Arthur
Moore, Marianne
Morrison, Toni
Nabokov, Vladimir
Norris, Frank
Oates, Joyce Carol
O'Connor, Flannery
Olson, Charles
O'Neill, Eugene
Paine, Thomas
Parker, Dorothy
Plath, Sylvia
Poe, Edgar Allan
Porter, Katherine Anne
Pound, Ezra
Pynchon, Thomas
Rich, Adrienne
Robinson, Edwin Arlington
Roethke, Theodore
Roth, Philip
Salinger, J.D.
Sandburg, Carl
Shepard, Sam
Simms, William Gilmore
Sinclair, Upton
Singer, Isaac Bashevis
Stein, Gertrude
Steinbeck, John
Stevens, Wallace
Stowe, Harriet Beecher
Styron, William
Taylor, Edward
Thoreau, Henry David
Twain, Mark
Updike, John
Vidal, Gore
Vonnegut, Kurt, Jr.
Walker, Alice
Warren, Robert Penn
Welty, Eudora
West, Nathanael
Wharton, Edith
Whitman, Walt
Wilder, Thornton
Williams, Tennessee
Williams, William Carlos
Wilson, Edmund
Wolfe, Thomas
Wright, Richard

American Literature: Ethnic Minorities

African-American Writers: General
African-American Writers: 20th Century
African-American Writers: Recent and Contemporary
Asian-American Literature
Baldwin, James
Baraka, Amiri [LeRoi Jones]
Douglass, Frederick
Du Bois, W.E.B.
Ellison, Ralph
Erdrich, Louise
Harlem Renaissance
Hughes, Langston
Hurston, Zora Neale
Jacobs, Harriet
Latino Writers
Morrison, Toni
Native American Literature
Walker, Alice
Women Writers: African-American
Wright, Richard

American Literature: to 1900

Adams, Henry
African-American Writers: General
Alcott, Louisa May
American Civil-War Literature
American Humor
American Literary Naturalism
American Literature: Early Period
American Literature: General
American Literature: 19th Century
American Renaissance
Bierce, Ambrose
Bradstreet, Anne
Brown, Charles Brockden
Children's Literature: American
Chopin, Kate
Cooper, James Fenimore
Crane, Stephen
Dickinson, Emily
Douglass, Frederick
Drama: American – General
Drama: American-19th Century
Edwards, Jonathan
Emerson, Ralph Waldo
Fiction: American – General
Fiction: American – 19th Century
Franklin, Benjamin
Fuller, Margaret
Gilman, Charlotte Perkins
Hawthorne, Nathaniel
Howells, William Dean
Irving, Washington
Jacobs, Harriet
James, Henry
James, William
Jefferson, Thomas
Melville, Herman
Native American Literature
New England Literature
Norris, Frank
Paine, Thomas
Poe, Edgar Allan
Poetry: American – General
Poetry: American – 19th Century
Prose in America: Historical and Political
Prose in America: 19th Century
Puritan Literature: American
Robinson, Edwin Arlington
Romanticism and Transcendentalism in America
Short Fiction: American
Simms, William Gilmore
Southern United States Literature: 19th Century
Stowe, Harriet Beecher
Taylor, Edward
Thoreau, Henry David
Twain, Mark
Whitman, Walt
Women Writers: American – General
Women Writers: American – to 1900
Women Writers: African-American

American Literature: 1900 to the Present

African-American Writers: General
African-American Writers: 20th Century
African-American Writers: Recent and Contemporary
Albee, Edward
American Literary Naturalism
American Literature: 20th Century
Anderson, Sherwood
Ashbery, John
Asian-American Literature
Auden, W.H.
Baldwin, James
Baraka, Amiri [LeRoi Jones]
Barth, John
Barthelme, Donald
Beat Generation
Bellow, Saul
Berryman, John
Bishop, Elizabeth
Black Mountain Poets
Burroughs, William S.
Carver, Raymond
Cather, Willa
Chandler, Raymond
Children's Literature: American
Crane, Hart
Crime Fiction
Cummings, E.E.
Deconstruction
Doolittle, Hilda [H.D.]
Dos Passos, John
Drama: American – 20th Century
Dreiser, Theodore
Du Bois, W.E.B.
Eliot, T.S.
Ellison, Ralph
Faulkner, William
Fiction: American – 20th Century
Fitzgerald, F. Scott
Frontier and Western Literature
Frost, Robert
Fugitives and Agrarians
Gaddis, William
Gilman, Charlotte Perkins
Ginsberg, Allen
Harlem Renaissance
Hawkes, John
Hearn, Lafcadio
Heller, Joseph
Hellman, Lillian
Hemingway, Ernest
Howells, William Dean
Hughes, Langston
Hurston, Zora Neale
Imagism
Isherwood, Christopher
James, Henry
Jeffers, Robinson
Jewish-American Writers
Kerouac, Jack
Latino Writers
Lewis, Sinclair
London, Jack
Lovecraft, H.P.
Lowell, Robert
McCullers, Carson
Mailer, Norman
Malamud, Bernard
Mamet, David
Millay, Edna St Vincent
Miller, Arthur
Modernism: Fiction
Modernism: Poetry
Moore, Marianne
Morrison, Toni
Nabokov, Vladimir
Native American Literature
New Criticism
Oates, Joyce Carol
O'Connor, Flannery
Olson, Charles
O'Neill, Eugene
Parker, Dorothy
Plath, Sylvia
Poetry: American – 20th Century
Porter, Katherine Anne
Pound, Ezra
Proletarian Literature in America
Pynchon, Thomas
Realism in American Literature
Rich, Adrienne
Robinson, Edwin Arlington
Roethke, Theodore
Roth, Philip
Salinger, J.D.
Sandburg, Carl
Shepard, Sam
Short Fiction: American
Sinclair, Upton
Singer, Isaac Bashevis
Southern United States Literature: 20th Century

Australian and New Zealand Literature

British and Irish Literature: Topics

British and Irish Literature: Writers

Addison, Joseph
Amis, Kingsley
Arnold, Matthew
Auden, W.H.
Austen, Jane
Bacon, Francis
Bale, John
Beckett, Samuel
Behn, Aphra
Bennett, Arnold
Blake, William
Boswell, James
Bowen, Elizabeth
Brontë, Charlotte
Brontë, Emily
Browning, Elizabeth Barrett
Browning, Robert
Bunyan, John
Burgess, Anthony
Burke, Edmund
Burney, Frances [Fanny]
Burns, Robert
Butler, Samuel
Byron, Lord
Carlyle, Thomas
Carroll, Lewis
Chapman, George
Chaucer, Geoffrey
Chesterton, G.K.
Churchill, Caryl
Clare, John
Coleridge, Samuel Taylor
Collins, Wilkie
Congreve, William
Conrad, Joseph
Cowper, William
Crabbe, George
Defoe, Daniel
Dekker, Thomas
De Quincey, Thomas
Dickens, Charles
Donne, John
Doyle, Arthur Conan
Drayton, Michael
Dryden, John
Dunbar, William
Durrell, Lawrence
Edgeworth, Maria
Eliot, George
Eliot, T.S.
Etherege, Sir George
Farquhar, George
Fielding, Henry
Fletcher, John
Ford, Ford Madox
Ford, John
Forster, E.M.
Fowles, John
Gaskell, Elizabeth
Gawain-Poet
Gibbon, Edward
Gissing, George
Godwin, William
Golding, William
Goldsmith, Oliver
Gower, John
Graves, Robert
Green, Henry
Greene, Graham
Greene, Robert
Hardy, Thomas
Harris, Wilson
Hazlitt, William
Heaney, Seamus
Herbert, George
Hobbes, Thomas
Hopkins, Gerard Manley
Housman, A.E.
Hughes, Ted
Huxley, Aldous
Isherwood, Christopher
James, Henry
Jhabvala, Ruth Prawer
Johnson, Samuel
Jonson, Ben
Joyce, James
Julian of Norwich
Keats, John
Kempe, Margery
Kingsley, Charles
Kipling, Rudyard
Lamb, Charles
Langland, William
Larkin, Philip
Lawrence, D.H.
Leavis, F.R.
le Carré, John
Lessing, Doris
Lewis, C.S.
Lewis, Wyndham
Locke, John
Lowry, Malcolm
Lyly, John
Macaulay, Thomas Babington
MacDiarmid, Hugh
MacNeice, Louis
Macpherson, James
Malory, Sir Thomas
Marlowe, Christopher
Marston, John
Martineau, Harriet
Marvell, Andrew
Massinger, Philip
Meredith, George
Middleton, Thomas
Milton, John
Moore, George
Moore, Marianne
More, Sir Thomas
Morris, William
Muir, Edwin
Murdoch, Iris
Newman, John Henry
O'Casey, Sean
Orwell, George
Osborne, John
Owen, Wilfred
Paine, Thomas
Pater, Walter
Peacock, Thomas Love
Pepys, Samuel
Philips, Katherine
Pinter, Harold
Pope, Alexander
Powys, John Cowper
Radcliffe, Ann
Ralegh, Sir Walter
Rhys, Jean
Richards, I.A.
Richardson, Dorothy
Richardson, Samuel
Rochester, Earl of
Rossetti, Christina
Rossetti, Dante Gabriel
Rushdie, Salman
Ruskin, John
Schreiner, Olive
Scott, Sir Walter
Shakespeare, William
Shaw, George Bernard
Shelley, Mary
Shelley, Percy Bysshe
Sheridan, Richard Brinsley
Sidney, Sir Philip
The Sitwells
Skelton, John
Smart, Christopher
Smollett, Tobias
Southey, Robert
Spark, Muriel
Spenser, Edmund
Steele, Sir Richard
Sterne, Laurence
Stevenson, Robert Louis
Stoppard, Tom
Swift, Jonathan
Swinburne, Algernon Charles
Synge, John Millington
Tennyson, Alfred, Lord
Thackeray, William Makepeace
Thomas, Dylan
Thomas, R.S.
Tolkien, J.R.R.
Traherne, Thomas
Trollope, Anthony
Vaughan, Henry
Walpole, Horace
Waugh, Evelyn
Webster, John
Wells, H.G.
West, Rebecca
Wilde, Oscar
Wilson, Angus
Wollstonecraft, Mary
Woolf, Virginia
Wordsworth, William
Wyatt, Sir Thomas
Wycherley, William
Yeats, W.B.
Yonge, Charlotte

British Literature: Old English and Medieval

British Literature: Renaissance

British and Irish Literature: Restoration

British and Irish Literature: 18th Century

Godwin, William
Goldsmith, Oliver
Gothic Fiction
Johnson, Samuel
Journalism and Literature in Britain
Literary Aesthetics: Romantic
Macpherson, James
Novel: 18th Century
Novel: Romantic Era
Paine, Thomas
Poetry: 18th Century
Poetry: Romantic
Pope, Alexander
Popular Literature in Britain
Grub Street and Popular Publishing
Prose and Journalism: 18th Century
Prose and Journalism: Romantic – Historical and Political
Radcliffe, Ann
Richardson, Samuel
Romanticism: British
Scottish Literature: 18th and 19th Centuries
Sentimentalism
Sheridan, Richard Brinsley
Smart, Christopher
Smollett, Tobias
Steele, Sir Richard
Sterne, Laurence
Swift, Jonathan
Topographical Poetry
Travel Literature: British – 18th and 19th Centuries
Walpole, Horace
Wollstonecraft, Mary
Women Writers: Restoration and 18th Century
Women Writers: British – 19th Century
Romantic Era

British and Irish Literature: Romantic Era

Austen, Jane
Blake, William
British Literature: 19th Century
Burns, Robert
Byron, Lord
Carlyle, Thomas
Clare, John
Coleridge, Samuel Taylor
Cowper, William
Crabbe, George
De Quincey, Thomas
Edgeworth, Maria
The Essay
Godwin, William
Gothic Fiction
Hazlitt, William
Historical Fiction
Keats, John
Lamb, Charles
Landscape and Literature in 18th-and 19th-Century Britain
Literary Aesthetics: Romantic
Novel: Romantic Era
Paine, Thomas
Peacock, Thomas Love
Poetry: Romantic
Prose and Journalism: Romantic – Historical and Political
Romanticism: British
Shelley, Mary
Shelley, Percy Bysshe
Southey, Robert
Topographical Poetry
Travel Literature: British – 18th and 19th Centuries
Walpole, Horace
Wollstonecraft, Mary
Women Writers: British – 19th Century
Romantic Era
Wordsworth, William

British and Irish Literature: Victorian

Arnold, Matthew
Biography and Autobiography: Victorian
British Literature: 19th Century
Brontë, Charlotte
Brontë, Emily
Browning, Elizabeth Barrett
Browning, Robert
Burney, Frances [Fanny]
Butler, Samuel
Carlyle, Thomas
Carroll, Lewis
Children's Literature: British – to 1900
Clare, John
Collins, Wilkie
Conrad, Joseph
Decadence, Aestheticism, and the 1890s
Dickens, Charles
Doyle, Arthur Conan
Drama: British – 19th Century
Drama: Irish
Eliot, George
Gissing, George
Hardy, Thomas
Hopkins, Gerard Manley
Housman, A.E.
James, Henry
Kingsley, Charles
Kipling, Rudyard
Landscape and Literature in 18th-and 19th-Century Britain
Macaulay, Thomas Babington
Martineau, Harriet
Melodrama
Meredith, George
Moore, George
Morris, William
Newman, John Henry
Novel: Victorian
Victorian Novel of Social Conscience
Pater, Walter
Peacock, Thomas Love
Poetry: Victorian
Popular Literature in Britain
Grub Street and Popular Publishing
Pre-Raphaelitism
Prose and Journalism: Victorian
Rossetti, Christina
Rossetti, Dante Gabriel
Ruskin, John
Schreiner, Olive
Scottish Literature: 18th and 19th Centuries
Shaw, George Bernard
Stevenson, Robert Louis
Swinburne, Algernon Charles
Synge, John Millington
Tennyson, Alfred, Lord
Thackeray, William Makepeace
Travel Literature: British – 18th and 19th Centuries
Trollope, Anthony
Victorian Literature: General
Victorian Literature and the City
Victorian Literature and Religion
Victorian Literature and Society
Victorian Literature, Science, and Evolutionary Theory
Wells, H.G.
Wilde, Oscar
Women Writers: British – 19th Century
Victorian
Yeats, W.B.
Yonge, Charlotte

British and Irish Literature: 20th Century

Canadian Literature

Drama

Melodrama
Middleton, Thomas
Miller, Arthur
Ngugi wa Thiong'o
O'Casey, Sean
O'Neill, Eugene
Osborne, John
Pinter, Harold
Reaney, James
Shakespeare, William
Shaw, George Bernard
Shepard, Sam
Sheridan, Richard Brinsley
Sinclair, Upton
Skelton, John
Soyinka, Wole
Steele, Sir Richard
Stein, Gertrude
Stoppard, Tom
Swinburne, Algernon Charles
Synge, John Millington
Tagore, Rabindranath
Tragedy: Theory
Tragedy: Renaissance
Tragedy: Restoration
Tragicomedy
Walcott, Derek
Webster, John
White, Patrick
Wilde, Oscar
Wilder, Thornton
Williams, Tennessee
Wycherley, William
Yeats, W.B.

Fiction: Topics

American Humor
American Literary Naturalism
Children's Literature: General
Children's Literature: 20th Century
Children's Literature: British – General
Children's Literature: British – to 1900
Children's Literature: British – 1900 to the Present
Children's Literature: American
Crime Fiction
Epistolary Novel
Fantasy Literature
Fiction: Theory
Fiction to 1700
Fiction: British – 20th Century
Fiction: American – General
Fiction: American – 19th Century
Fiction: American – 20th Century
Fiction: African
Fiction: Australian
Fiction: Canadian
Fiction: Indian
Fiction: New Zealand
Frontier and Western Literature
Gothic Fiction
Historical Fiction
Horror Literature
Modernism: Fiction
Narrative Theory
Novel: General
Novel: 20th Century
Novel: Recent and Contemporary
Novel: British – General
Novel: 18th Century
Novel: Romantic Era
Novel: Victorian
Victorian Novel of Social Conscience
Popular Fiction: General
Popular Fiction for Women
Popular Literature in Britain
Postmodern Literature
Proletarian Literature in America
Realism: General
Realism in American Literature
Romance
Romance Fiction
Science Fiction
Sentimentalism
Short Fiction: General
Short Fiction: British
Short Fiction: American
Utopian Literature
Victorian Literature and the City

Fiction: Writers

Achebe, Chinua
Alcott, Louisa May
Amis, Kingsley
Anand, Mulk Raj
Anderson, Sherwood
Atwood, Margaret
Austen, Jane
Baldwin, James
Baraka, Amiri [LeRoi Jones]
Barth, John
Barthelme, Donald
Beckett, Samuel
Behn, Aphra
Bellow, Saul
Bennett, Arnold
Bierce, Ambrose
Bowen, Elizabeth
Brontë, Charlotte
Brontë, Emily
Brown, Charles Brockden
Bunyan, John
Burgess, Anthony
Burney, Frances [Fanny]
Burroughs, William S.
Butler, Samuel
Carroll, Lewis
Carver, Raymond
Cather, Willa
Chandler, Raymond
Chesterton, G.K.
Chopin, Kate
Coetzee, J.M.
Collins, Wilkie
Conrad, Joseph
Cooper, James Fenimore
Crane, Stephen
Davies, Robertson
Defoe, Daniel
Dickens, Charles
Dos Passos, John
Doyle, Arthur Conan
Dreiser, Theodore
Du Bois, W.E.B.
Durrell, Lawrence
Edgeworth, Maria
Eliot, George
Ellison, Ralph
Erdrich, Louise
Faulkner, William
Fielding, Henry
Findley, Timothy
Fitzgerald, F. Scott
Ford, Ford Madox
Forster, E.M.
Fowles, John
Frame, Janet
Gaddis, William
Gaskell, Elizabeth
Gilman, Charlotte Perkins
Gissing, George
Godwin, William
Golding, William
Goldsmith, Oliver
Gordimer, Nadine
Graves, Robert
Green, Henry
Greene, Graham
Greene, Robert
Hardy, Thomas
Harris, Wilson
Hawkes, John
Hawthorne, Nathaniel
Hearn, Lafcadio
Heller, Joseph
Hemingway, Ernest
Howells, William Dean
Hughes, Langston
Hurston, Zora Neale

Huxley, Aldous
Irving, Washington
Isherwood, Christopher
James, Henry
Jhabvala, Ruth Prawer,
Jolley, Elizabeth
Joyce, James
Kerouac, Jack
Kingsley, Charles
Kipling, Rudyard
Laurence, Margaret
Lawrence, D.H.
le Carré, John
Lessing, Doris
Lewis, C.S.
Lewis, Sinclair
Lewis, Wyndham
London, Jack
Lovecraft, H.P.
Lowry, Malcolm
Lyly, John
McCullers, Carson
MacLennan, Hugh
Mailer, Norman
Malamud, Bernard
Malory, Sir Thomas
Malouf, David
Mansfield, Katherine
Martineau, Harriet
Melville, Herman
Meredith, George
Moore, George
Morris, William
Morrison, Toni
Munro, Alice
Murdoch, Iris
Nabokov, Vladimir
Naipaul, Sir V.S.
Narayan, R.K.
Newman, John Henry
Ngugi wa Thiong'o
Norris, Frank
Oates, Joyce Carol
O'Connor, Flannery
Ondaatje, Michael
Orwell, George
Parker, Dorothy
Pater, Walter
Peacock, Thomas Love
Plath, Sylvia
Poe, Edgar Allan
Porter, Katherine Anne
Powys, John Cowper
Pynchon, Thomas
Radcliffe, Ann
Rao, Raja
Rhys, Jean
Richardson, Dorothy
Richardson, Henry Handel
Richardson, Samuel
Roethke, Theodore
Ross, Sinclair
Roth, Philip
Rushdie, Salman
Salinger, J.D.
Schreiner, Olive
Scott, Sir Walter
Shelley, Mary
Simms, William Gilmore
Sinclair, Upton
Singer, Isaac Bashevis
The Sitwells
Smollett, Tobias
Spark, Muriel
Stead, Christina
Stein, Gertrude
Steinbeck, John
Sterne, Laurence
Stevenson, Robert Louis
Stowe, Harriet Beecher
Styron, William
Swift, Jonathan
Thackeray, William Makepeace
Thomas, Dylan
Tolkien, J.R.R.
Trollope, Anthony
Twain, Mark
Updike, John
Vidal, Gore
Vonnegut, Kurt, Jr.
Walker, Alice
Walpole, Horace
Warren, Robert Penn
Waugh, Evelyn
Wells, H.G.
Welty, Eudora
West, Nathanael
West, Rebecca
Wharton, Edith
White, Patrick
Wilder, Thornton
Williams, William Carlos
Wilson, Angus
Wolfe, Thomas
Woolf, Virginia
Wright, Judith
Wright, Richard
Yonge, Charlotte

Fiction: American

Alcott, Louisa May
American Humor
American Literary Naturalism
Anderson, Sherwood
Baldwin, James
Baraka, Amiri [LeRoi Jones]
Barth, John
Barthelme, Donald
Bellow, Saul
Bierce, Ambrose
Brown, Charles Brockden
Burroughs, William S.
Carver, Raymond
Cather, Willa
Chandler, Raymond
Children's Literature: American
Chopin, Kate
Cooper, James Fenimore
Crane, Stephen
Crime Fiction
Dos Passos, John
Dreiser, Theodore
Du Bois, W.E.B.
Ellison, Ralph
Erdrich, Louise
Fantasy Literature
Faulkner, William
Fiction: American – General
Fiction: American – 19th Century
Fiction: American – 20th Century
Fitzgerald, F. Scott
Frontier and Western Literature
Gaddis, William
Gilman, Charlotte Perkins
Harlem Renaissance
Hawkes, John
Hawthorne, Nathaniel
Hearn, Lafcadio
Heller, Joseph
Hemingway, Ernest
Horror Literature
Howells, William Dean
Hughes, Langston
Hurston, Zora Neale
Irving, Washington
Isherwood, Christopher
James, Henry
Kerouac, Jack
Lewis, Sinclair
London, Jack
Lovecraft, H.P.
McCullers, Carson
Mailer, Norman
Malamud, Bernard
Melville, Herman
Modernism: Fiction
Morrison, Toni
Nabokov, Vladimir
Norris, Frank
Oates, Joyce Carol
O'Connor, Flannery
Parker, Dorothy
Plath, Sylvia
Poe, Edgar Allan
Popular Fiction: General
Popular Fiction for Women
Porter, Katherine Anne
Postmodern Literature
Proletarian Literature in America
Pynchon, Thomas
Realism in American Literature
Roethke, Theodore

Romance Fiction
Romanticism and Transcendentalism in America
Roth, Philip
Salinger, J.D.
Science Fiction
Short Fiction: American
Simms, William Gilmore
Sinclair, Upton
Singer, Isaac Bashevis
Stein, Gertrude
Steinbeck, John
Stowe, Harriet Beecher
Styron, William
Twain, Mark
Updike, John
Vidal, Gore
Vietnam War Literature
Vonnegut, Kurt, Jr.
Walker, Alice
Warren, Robert Penn
Welty, Eudora
West, Nathanael
Wharton, Edith
Wilder, Thornton
Williams, William Carlos
Wilson, Edmund
Wolfe, Thomas
Wright, Richard

Fiction: British and Irish

Amis, Kingsley
Austen, Jane
Beckett, Samuel
Behn, Aphra
Bennett, Arnold
The Bloomsbury Group
Bowen, Elizabeth
Brontë, Charlotte
Brontë, Emily
Bunyan, John
Burgess, Anthony
Burney, Frances [Fanny]
Butler, Samuel
Carroll, Lewis
Chesterton, G.K.
Children's Literature: British – General
Children's Literature: British – to 1900
Children's Literature: British – 1900 to the Present
Collins, Wilkie
Conrad, Joseph
Defoe, Daniel
Dickens, Charles
Doyle, Arthur Conan
Durrell, Lawrence
Edgeworth, Maria
Eliot, George
Epistolary Novel
Fiction to 1700
Fiction: British – 20th Century
Fielding, Henry
Ford, Ford Madox
Forster, E.M.
Fowles, John
Gaskell, Elizabeth
Gissing, George
Godwin, William
Golding, William
Goldsmith, Oliver
Gothic Fiction
Graves, Robert
Green, Henry
Greene, Graham
Greene, Robert
Hardy, Thomas
Harris, Wilson
Historical Fiction
Horror Literature
Huxley, Aldous
Isherwood, Christopher
James, Henry
Jhabvala, Ruth Prawer
Joyce, James
Kingsley, Charles
Kipling, Rudyard
Lawrence, D.H.
le Carré, John
Lessing, Doris
Lewis, C.S.
Lewis, Wyndham
Lowry, Malcolm
Lyly, John
Malory, Sir Thomas
Mansfield, Katherine
Martineau, Harriet
Meredith, George
Modernism: Fiction
Moore, George
Morris, William
The Movement
Murdoch, Iris
Newman, John Henry
Novel: British – General
Novel: 18th Century
Novel: Romantic Era
Novel: Victorian
Victorian Novel of Social Conscience
Orwell, George
Pater, Walter
Peacock, Thomas Love
Popular Fiction for Women
Popular Literature in Britain
Postmodern Literature
Powys, John Cowper
Radcliffe, Ann
Rhys, Jean
Richardson, Dorothy
Richardson, Henry Handel
Richardson, Samuel
Romance Fiction
Rushdie, Salman
Satire: 18th Century
Science Fiction
Scott, Sir Walter
Sentimentalism
Shelley, Mary
Short Fiction: British
The Sitwells
Smollett, Tobias
Spark, Muriel
Sterne, Laurence
Stevenson, Robert Louis
Swift, Jonathan
Thackeray, William Makepeace
Thomas, Dylan
Tolkien, J.R.R.
Trollope, Anthony
Utopian Literature
Victorian Literature and the City
Walpole, Horace
Waugh, Evelyn
Wells, H.G.
West, Rebecca
Wilson, Angus
Woolf, Virginia
Yonge, Charlotte

Genres, Idioms, and Contexts

Allegory
Alliterative Tradition
American Civil-War Literature
American Humor
American Literary Naturalism
Apocalyptic Literature
Autobiography
The Ballad
The Bible and Literature
Biography: General
Biography: Renaissance
Biography and Autobiography: Victorian
Children's Literature: General
Children's Literature: 20th Century
Children's Literature: British – General
Children's Literature: British – to 1900
Children's Literature: British – 1900 to the Present
Children's Literature: American
Chronicle Literature
Comedy: Theory
Comedy: Renaissance
City Comedy
Comedy: Restoration
Crime Fiction
Decadence, Aestheticism, and the 1890s
Drama: Theory
Drama: British – General
Drama: Medieval
Cycle Plays
Morality Plays
Drama: Renaissance
Drama: Restoration
Drama: 18th Century
Drama: British – 19th Century
Drama: British – 20th Century
Drama: Irish
Drama: American – General
Drama: American-19th Century
Drama: American – 20th Century
Drama: Australian
Drama: Canadian
Dramatic Censorship
Dramatic Monologue
Dream-Vision Literature
Elegy and Poetry of Death
Epistolary Novel
The Erotic in Literature
The Essay
Exploration Literature
Fantasy Literature
Fiction: Theory
Fiction to 1700
Fiction: British – 20th Century
Fiction: American – General
Fiction: American – 19th Century
Fiction: American – 20th Century
Fiction: African
Fiction: Australian
Fiction: Canadian
Fiction: Indian
Fiction: New Zealand
Film and Literature
Frontier and Western Literature
Gay and Lesbian Literature
Gender and Literature
Georgian Poetry
Gothic Fiction
The Grotesque
Historical Drama
Historical Fiction
Horror Literature
Imagism
Irony
Journalism and Literature in Britain
Landscape and Literature in 18th- and 19th-Century Britain
Lyric in Medieval Literature
Madness and Literature
The Masque
Medicine and Literature
Melodrama
Metaphysical Poetry
Modernism: Fiction
Modernism: Poetry
Music and Literature
Mystical Literature
Novel: General
Novel: 20th Century
Novel: Recent and Contemporary
Novel: British – General
Novel: 18th Century
Novel: Romantic Era
Novel: Victorian
Victorian Novel of Social Conscience
Parody
Pastoral Literature
Poetry: Theory
Poetry: General
Poetry: 20th Century
Poetry: Recent and Contemporary
Poetry: British – General
Poetry: Old English
Poetry: Middle English
Poetry: Renaissance
Poetry: 18th Century
Poetry: Romantic
Poetry: Victorian
Poetry: British – 20th Century
Poetry: American – General
Poetry: American – 19th Century
Poetry: American – 20th Century
Poetry: Australian
Poetry: Canadian
Politics and Literature
Popular Fiction: General
Popular Fiction for Women
Popular Literature in Britain
Grub Street and Popular Publishing
Postmodern Literature
Pre-Raphaelitism
Proletarian Literature in America
Prose: Old English
Prose: Renaissance
Prose and Journalism: 18th Century
Prose and Journalism: Romantic – Historical and Political
Prose and Journalism: Victorian
Prose in America: Historical and Political
Prose in America: 19th Century
Puritan Literature: British
Puritan Literature: American
Realism: General
Realism in American Literature
Religion and Literature
Romance
Romance Fiction
Romanticism: British
Romanticism and Transcendentalism in America
Satire: General
Satire: 18th Century
Science and Literature
Science Fiction
Sentimentalism
Short Fiction: General
Short Fiction: British
Short Fiction: American
The Sonnet
Topographical Poetry
Tragedy: Theory
Tragedy: Renaissance
Tragedy: Restoration
Tragicomedy
Translation in the Middle Ages and Renaissance
Travel Literature: General
Travel Literature: British – 18th and 19th Centuries
Utopian Literature
Victorian Literature and the City
Victorian Literature and Religion
Victorian Literature and Society
Victorian Literature, Science, and Evolutionary Theory
Vietnam War Literature
Visual Arts and Literature
War and Literature

Historical and Political Literature

Achebe, Chinua
Adams, Henry
Addison, Joseph
American Civil-War Literature
Arnold, Matthew
Auden, W.H.
Autobiography
Baldwin, James
Baraka, Amiri [LeRoi Jones]
Bierce, Ambrose
Biography: General
Biography: Renaissance
Biography and Autobiography: Victorian
Brown, Charles Brockden
Burke, Edmund
Carlyle, Thomas
Chesterton, G.K.
Chronicle Literature
Coetzee, J.M.
Cooper, James Fenimore
Crane, Stephen
Defoe, Daniel
Dos Passos, John
Douglass, Frederick
Dramatic Censorship
Du Bois, W.E.B.
Emerson, Ralph Waldo
Equiano, Olaudah
The Essay
Franklin, Benjamin
Fuller, Margaret
Gibbon, Edward
Gilman, Charlotte Perkins
Godwin, William
Gordimer, Nadine
Graves, Robert
Harlem Renaissance
Hawthorne, Nathaniel
Historical Drama
Historical Fiction
Hobbes, Thomas
Hughes, Langston
Hurston, Zora Neale
Jacobs, Harriet
Jefferson, Thomas
Johnson, Samuel
Kipling, Rudyard
Locke, John
London, Jack
Macaulay, Thomas Babington
MacDiarmid, Hugh
Martineau, Harriet
Marxist Literary Theory
Milton, John
More, Sir Thomas
Morris, William
Naipaul, Sir V.S.
New Historicism
Ngugi wa Thiong'o
Novel: Victorian Novel of Social Conscience
Orwell, George
Owen, Wilfred
Paine, Thomas
Pater, Walter
Pepys, Samuel
Postcolonial Theory
Proletarian Literature in America
Prose and Journalism: 18th Century
Prose and Journalism: Romantic – Historical and Political
Prose and Journalism: Victorian
Prose in America: Historical and Political
Prose in America: 19th Century
Rushdie, Salman
Sandburg, Carl
Satire: 18th Century
Scott, Sir Walter
Shakespeare, William: Histories
Shaw, George Bernard
Shelley, Percy Bysshe
Sheridan, Richard Brinsley
Simms, William Gilmore
Sinclair, Upton
South African Literature: Black Writers
Southey, Robert
Soyinka, Wole
Steele, Sir Richard
Swift, Jonathan
The Thirties Generation
Utopian Literature
Victorian Literature and the City
Victorian Literature and Society
Vidal, Gore
Vietnam War Literature
Walker, Alice
War and Literature
The War Poets
Wells, H.G.
Wilson, Edmund
Wollstonecraft, Mary
Wright, Richard
Yonge, Charlotte

Literary Criticism and Theory

Arnold, Matthew
Coleridge, Samuel Taylor
Comedy: Theory
Deconstruction
Drama: Theory
Dryden, John
Eliot, T.S.
Feminist Literary Theory
Fiction: Theory
Forster, E.M.
Fugitives and Agrarians
Gender and Literature
Hazlitt, William
James, Henry
Johnson, Samuel
Lamb, Charles
Leavis, F.R.
Lewis, C.S.
Literary Aesthetics: Renaissance
Literary Aesthetics: Romantic
Literary Theory: General
Literary Theory: Postwar Approaches
Literary Theory: Contemporary Approaches
Marxist Literary Theory
Narrative Theory
New Criticism
New Historicism
Pater, Walter
Poe, Edgar Allan
Poetry: Theory
Postcolonial Theory
Postmodernist Literary Theory
Pound, Ezra
Psychoanalytic Literary Theory
Reader-Response Theory
Realism: General
Richards, I.A.
Semiotics
Short Fiction: General
Sidney, Sir Philip
Structuralism
Swinburne, Algernon Charles
Tragedy: Theory
Warren, Robert Penn
Wilson, Edmund
Woolf, Virginia
Yeats, W.B.

Modernism

Anderson, Sherwood
The Bloomsbury Group
Cather, Willa
Conrad, Joseph
Crane, Hart
Crane, Stephen
Cummings, E.E.
Doolittle, Hilda [H.D.]
Dos Passos, John
Drama: American – 20th Century
Before World War II
Dreiser, Theodore
Eliot, T.S.
Faulkner, William
Fiction: British – 20th Century
Before World War II
Fiction: American – 20th Century
Before World War II
Fitzgerald, F. Scott
Ford, Ford Madox
Forster, E.M.
Frost, Robert
Harlem Renaissance
Hemingway, Ernest
Hughes, Langston
Huxley, Aldous
Imagism
James, Henry
Joyce, James
Lawrence, D.H.
Leavis, F.R.
Lewis, Sinclair
Lewis, Wyndham
London, Jack
Mansfield, Katherine
Millay, Edna St Vincent
Modernism: Fiction
Modernism: Poetry
Moore, Marianne
O'Neill, Eugene
Poetry: British – 20th Century
Before World War II
Poetry: American – 20th Century
Before World War II
Pound, Ezra
Richards, I.A.
Richardson, Dorothy
Sandburg, Carl
Sinclair, Upton
The Sitwells
Stein, Gertrude
Stevens, Wallace
Wharton, Edith
Williams, William Carlos
Wolfe, Thomas
Woolf, Virginia
Yeats, W.B.

National and Regional Literature Surveys

African Literature: General
African Literature: East and Central
African Literature: West
African-American Writers: General
African-American Writers: 20th Century
African-American Writers: Recent and Contemporary
American Literature: General
American Literature: Early Period
American Literature: 19th Century
American Literature: 20th Century
Asian-American Literature
Australian Literature: General surveys
Australian Literature: Recent and Contemporary
British Literature: General
British Literature: Medieval
British Literature: 15th Century
British Literature: Renaissance
British Literature: Restoration
British Literature: 18th Century
British Literature: 19th Century
British Literature: 20th Century
Canadian Literature: General
Canadian Literature: Recent and Contemporary
Indian Literature
Irish Literature: General
Irish Literature: Literary Revival to the Present
Jewish-American Writers
Latino Writers
Native American Literature
New England Literature
New Literatures: General
New Zealand and South Pacific Literatures
Scottish Literature: Medieval and Renaissance
Scottish Literature: 18th and 19th Centuries
Scottish Literature: 20th Century
South African Literature: General
South African Literature: Black Writers
Southern United States Literature: General
Southern United States Literature: 19th Century
Southern United States Literature: 20th Century
Welsh Literature

New (Commonwealth) Literatures

Achebe, Chinua
African Literature: General
African Literature: East and Central
African Literature: West
Anand, Mulk Raj
Atwood, Margaret
Australian Literature: General surveys
Australian Literature: Recent and Contemporary
Baxter, James K.
Canadian Literature: General
Canadian Literature: Recent and Contemporary
Caribbean Literature
Coetzee, J.M.
Davies, Robertson
Drama: Australian
Drama: Canadian
Fiction: African
Fiction: Australian
Fiction: Canadian
Fiction: Indian
Fiction: New Zealand
Findley, Timothy
Frame, Janet
Fugard, Athol
Gordimer, Nadine
Harris, Wilson
Indian Literature
Jhabvala, Ruth Prawer
Jolley, Elizabeth
Laurence, Margaret
Lewis, Wyndham
MacLennan, Hugh
Malouf, David
Mansfield, Katherine
Munro, Alice
Naipaul, V.S.
Narayan, R.K.
New Literatures: General
New Zealand and South Pacific Literatures
Ngugi wa Thiong'o
Ondaatje, Michael
Poetry: Australian
Poetry: Canadian
Postcolonial Theory
Pratt, E.J.
Rao, Raja

Reaney, James
Rhys, Jean
Richardson, Henry Handel
Ross, Sinclair
Rushdie, Salman
Schreiner, Olive
South African Literature: General
South African Literature: Black Writers
Soyinka, Wole
Stead, Christina
Tagore, Rabindranath
Walcott, Derek
White, Patrick
Wright, Judith

Non-Fiction

Adams, Henry
Addison, Joseph
American Civil-War Literature
Arnold, Matthew
Autobiography
Bacon, Francis
Baldwin, James
Bale, John
Baraka, Amiri [LeRoi Jones]
The Bible and Literature
Bierce, Ambrose
Biography: General
Biography: Renaissance
Biography and Autobiography: Victorian
Brown, Charles Brockden
Burke, Edmund
Carlyle, Thomas
Chesterton, G.K.
Chronicle Literature
Coleridge, Samuel Taylor
Crane, Stephen
De Quincey, Thomas
Dos Passos, John
Douglass, Frederick
Du Bois, W.E.B.
Eliot, George
Eliot, T.S.
Emerson, Ralph Waldo
Equiano, Olaudah
The Essay
Exploration Literature
Forster, E.M.
Franklin, Benjamin
Fugitives and Agrarians
Fuller, Margaret
Gibbon, Edward
Gilman, Charlotte Perkins
Godwin, William
Goldsmith, Oliver
Gordimer, Nadine
Graves, Robert
Hazlitt, William
Hobbes, Thomas
Howells, William Dean
Hughes, Langston
Hurston, Zora Neale
Huxley, Aldous
Jacobs, Harriet
James, Henry
James, William
Jefferson, Thomas
Johnson, Samuel
Jonson, Ben
Journalism and Literature in Britain
Julian of Norwich
Kempe, Margery
Lamb, Charles
Lawrence, D.H.
Leavis, F.R.
Lewis, C.S.
Locke, John
Macaulay, Thomas Babington
MacDiarmid, Hugh
Mailer, Norman
Martineau, Harriet
Milton, John
More, Sir Thomas
Morris, William
Muir, Edwin
Murdoch, Iris
Mystical Literature
Nabokov, Vladimir
Naipaul, V.S.
Newman, John Henry
Ngugi wa Thiong'o
Oates, Joyce Carol
O'Connor, Flannery
Orwell, George
Paine, Thomas
Pater, Walter
Pepys, Samuel
Poe, Edgar Allan
Popular Literature in Britain
Grub Street and Popular Publishing
Pound, Ezra
Powys, John Cowper
Prose: Old English
Prose: Renaissance
Prose and Journalism: 18th Century
Prose and Journalism: Romantic – Historical and Political
Prose and Journalism: Victorian
Prose in America: Historical and Political
Prose in America: 19th Century
Puritan Literature: British
Puritan Literature: American
Richards, I.A.
Ruskin, John
Sandburg, Carl
Shaw, George Bernard
Shelley, Percy Bysshe
Sidney, Sir Philip
Simms, William Gilmore
Sinclair, Upton
The Sitwells
Southey, Robert
Soyinka, Wole
Steele, Sir Richard
Stevenson, Robert Louis
Stowe, Harriet Beecher
Swift, Jonathan
Swinburne, Algernon Charles
Tagore, Rabindranath
Thackeray, William Makepeace
Thoreau, Henry David
Travel Literature: General
Travel Literature: British – 18th and 19th Centuries
Twain, Mark
Updike, John
Vidal, Gore
Walker, Alice
Warren, Robert Penn
Waugh, Evelyn
Wells, H.G.
West, Rebecca
Whitman, Walt
Wilson, Edmund
Wollstonecraft, Mary
Woolf, Virginia
Wright, Richard
Yeats, W.B.
Yonge, Charlotte

Poetry: Topics

Allegory
Alliterative Tradition
The Ballad
Beat Generation
Beowulf
Black Mountain Poets
Decadence, Aestheticism, and the 1890s
Dramatic Monologue
Dream-Vision Literature
Elegy and Poetry of Death
The Erotic in Literature
Fugitives and Agrarians
Georgian Poetry
Imagism
Landscape and Literature in 18th- and 19th-Century Britain
Lyric in Medieval Literature
Metaphysical Poetry
Modernism: Poetry
The Movement
Pastoral Literature
Poetry: Theory
Poetry: General
Poetry: 20th Century
Poetry: Recent and Contemporary
Poetry: British – General
Poetry: Old English
Poetry: Middle English
Poetry: Renaissance
Poetry: 18th Century
Poetry: Romantic
Poetry: Victorian
Poetry: British – 20th Century
Poetry: American – General
Poetry: American – 19th Century
Poetry: American – 20th Century
Poetry: Australian
Poetry: Canadian
Puritan Literature: American
Satire: 18th Century
The Sonnet
The Thirties Generation
Topographical Poetry
The War Poets

Poetry: Writers

Arnold, Matthew
Ashbery, John
Atwood, Margaret
Auden, W.H.
Baraka, Amiri [LeRoi Jones]
Baxter, James K.
Behn, Aphra
Berryman, John
Bishop, Elizabeth
Blake, William
Brontë, Emily
Brown, Charles Brockden
Browning, Elizabeth Barrett
Browning, Robert
Burns, Robert
Byron, Lord
Carroll, Lewis
Chapman, George
Chaucer, Geoffrey
Clare, John
Coleridge, Samuel Taylor
Cowper, William
Crabbe, George
Crane, Hart
Cummings, E.E.
Dickinson, Emily
Donne, John
Doolittle, Hilda [H.D.]
Drayton, Michael
Dryden, John
Dunbar, William
Durrell, Lawrence
Edwards, Jonathan
Eliot, T.S.
Emerson, Ralph Waldo
Frost, Robert
Gawain-Poet
Ginsberg, Allen
Gower, John
Graves, Robert
Hardy, Thomas
Heaney, Seamus
Herbert, George
Hopkins, Gerard Manley
Housman, A.E.
Hughes, Langston
Hughes, Ted
Jeffers, Robinson
Johnson, Samuel
Jonson, Ben
Joyce, James
Keats, John
Kerouac, Jack
Kipling, Rudyard
Lamb, Charles
Langland, William
Larkin, Philip
Lawrence, D.H.
Lowell, Robert
MacDiarmid, Hugh
MacNeice, Louis
Macpherson, James
Malouf, David
Marlowe, Christopher
Marvell, Andrew
Melville, Herman
Meredith, George
Millay, Edna St Vincent
Milton, John
Moore, Marianne
Morris, William
Muir, Edwin
Oates, Joyce Carol
Olson, Charles
Ondaatje, Michael
Owen, Wilfred
Philips, Katherine
Plath, Sylvia
Poe, Edgar Allan
Pope, Alexander
Pound, Ezra
Powys, John Cowper
Pratt, E.J.
Ralegh, Sir Walter
Reaney, James
Rich, Adrienne
Robinson, Edwin Arlington
Rochester, Earl of
Rossetti, Christina
Rossetti, Dante Gabriel
Sandburg, Carl
Scott, Sir Walter
Shakespeare, William: Poetry
Shelley, Percy Bysshe
Sidney, Sir Philip
The Sitwells
Skelton, John
Smart, Christopher
Southey, Robert
Soyinka, Wole
Spenser, Edmund
Stein, Gertrude
Stevens, Wallace
Swift, Jonathan
Swinburne, Algernon Charles
Tagore, Rabindranath
Taylor, Edward
Tennyson, Alfred, Lord
Thomas, Dylan
Thomas, R.S.
Vaughan, Henry
Walcott, Derek
Warren, Robert Penn
Whitman, Walt
Wilde, Oscar
Williams, William Carlos
Wilson, Edmund
Wordsworth, William
Wright, Judith
Wyatt, Sir Thomas
Yeats, W.B.

Poetry: British and Irish

Allegory
Alliterative Tradition
Arnold, Matthew
Auden, W.H.
The Ballad
Behn, Aphra
Beowulf
Blake, William
Brontë, Emily
Browning, Elizabeth Barrett
Browning, Robert
Burns, Robert
Byron, Lord
Carroll, Lewis
Chapman, George
Chaucer, Geoffrey
Clare, John
Coleridge, Samuel Taylor
Cowper, William
Crabbe, George
Decadence, Aestheticism, and the 1890s
Donne, John
Dramatic Monologue
Drayton, Michael
Dream-Vision Literature
Dryden, John
Dunbar, William
Elegy and Poetry of Death
Eliot, T.S.
Gawain-Poet
Georgian Poetry
Gower, John
Graves, Robert
Hardy, Thomas
Heaney, Seamus
Herbert, George
Hopkins, Gerard Manley
Housman, A.E.
Hughes, Ted
Imagism
Johnson, Samuel
Jonson, Ben
Joyce, James
Keats, John
Kipling, Rudyard
Lamb, Charles
Landscape and Literature in 18th-and 19th-Century Britain
Langland, William
Larkin, Philip
Lawrence, D.H.
Lyric in Medieval Literature
MacDiarmid, Hugh
MacNeice, Louis
Macpherson, James
Marlowe, Christopher
Marvell, Andrew
Meredith, George
Metaphysical Poetry
Milton, John
Modernism: Poetry
Morris, William
The Movement
Muir, Edwin
Owen, Wilfred
Pastoral Literature
Philips, Katherine
Poetry: British – General
Poetry: Old English
Poetry: Middle English
Poetry: Renaissance
Poetry: 18th Century
Poetry: Romantic
Poetry: Victorian
Poetry: British – 20th Century
Pope, Alexander
Powys, John Cowper
Ralegh, Sir Walter
Rochester, Earl of
Romanticism: British
Rossetti, Christina
Rossetti, Dante Gabriel
Satire: 18th Century
Scott, Sir Walter
Shakespeare, William: Poetry
Shelley, Percy Bysshe
Sidney, Sir Philip
The Sitwells
Skelton, John
Smart, Christopher
The Sonnet
Southey, Robert
Spenser, Edmund
Swift, Jonathan
Swinburne, Algernon Charles
Tennyson, Alfred, Lord
The Thirties Generation
Thomas, Dylan
Thomas, R.S.
Topographical Poetry
Traherne, Thomas
Vaughan, Henry
The War Poets
Wilde, Oscar
Wordsworth, William
Wyatt, Sir Thomas
Yeats, W.B.

Poetry: American

Ashbery, John
Auden, W.H.
Baraka, Amiri [LeRoi Jones]
Beat Generation
Berryman, John
Bishop, Elizabeth
Black Mountain Poets
Bradstreet, Anne
Crane, Hart
Cummings, E.E.
Dickinson, Emily
Doolittle, Hilda [H.D.]
Edwards, Jonathan
Eliot, T.S.
Emerson, Ralph Waldo
Frost, Robert
Fugitives and Agrarians
Ginsberg, Allen
Harlem Renaissance
Imagism
Jeffers, Robinson
Kerouac, Jack
Lowell, Robert
Melville, Herman
Millay, Edna St Vincent
Modernism: Poetry
Moore, Marianne
Oates, Joyce Carol
Olson, Charles
Plath, Sylvia
Poe, Edgar Allan
Poetry: American – General
Poetry: American – 19th Century
Poetry: American – 20th Century
Pound, Ezra
Puritan Literature: American
Rich, Adrienne
Robinson, Edwin Arlington
Romanticism and Transcendentalism in America
Sandburg, Carl
Stein, Gertrude
Stevens, Wallace
Taylor, Edward
Warren, Robert Penn
Whitman, Walt
Williams, William Carlos
Wilson, Edmund

Popular Literature

American Humor
The Ballad
Bierce, Ambrose
Chandler, Raymond
Children's Literature: General
Children's Literature: 20th Century
Children's Literature: British – General
Children's Literature: British – to 1900
Children's Literature: British – 1900 to the Present
Children's Literature: American
Collins, Wilkie
Crime Fiction
Doyle, Arthur Conan
Fantasy Literature
Frontier and Western Literature
Gothic Fiction
Historical Fiction
Horror Literature
Journalism and Literature in Britain
Kipling, Rudyard
Lewis, C.S.
Melodrama
Poe, Edgar Allan
Popular Fiction: General
Popular Fiction for Women
Popular Literature in Britain
Grub Street and Popular Publishing
Romance Fiction
Science Fiction
Stevenson, Robert Louis
Tolkien, J.R.R.
Travel Literature: General
Twain, Mark

Religion and Literature

Allegory
American Literature: Early Period
Apocalyptic Literature
Bacon, Francis
Bale, John
The Bible and Literature
Blake, William
Bradstreet, Anne
Bunyan, John
Chesterton, G.K.
Cowper, William
Crabbe, George
Donne, John
Doyle, Arthur Conan
Drama: Medieval
General
Cycle Plays
Morality Plays
Dream-Vision Literature
Dunbar, William
Edwards, Jonathan
Elegy and Poetry of Death
Eliot, T.S.
Frost, Robert
Gower, John
Greene, Graham
Herbert, George
Hopkins, Gerard Manley
Julian of Norwich
Kempe, Margery
Langland, William
Lewis, C.S.
Lyric in Medieval Literature
Metaphysical Poetry
Milton, John
More, Sir Thomas
Mystical Literature
New England Literature
Newman, John Henry
O'Connor, Flannery
Poetry: Middle English
Prose: Renaissance
Puritan Literature: British
Puritan Literature: American
Religion and Literature
Rossetti, Christina
Scottish Literature: Medieval and Renaissance
Swift, Jonathan
Taylor, Edward
Thomas, R.S.
Traherne, Thomas
Vaughan, Henry
Victorian Literature and Religion
Yonge, Charlotte

Short Fiction

Achebe, Chinua
Anand, Mulk Raj
Anderson, Sherwood
Atwood, Margaret
Baldwin, James
Barth, John
Barthelme, Donald
Beckett, Samuel
Bellow, Saul
Bennett, Arnold
Bierce, Ambrose
Bowen, Elizabeth
Carver, Raymond
Chopin, Kate
Conrad, Joseph
Crane, Stephen
Dickens, Charles
Doyle, Arthur Conan
Dreiser, Theodore
Edgeworth, Maria
Faulkner, William
Findley, Timothy
Fitzgerald, F. Scott
Forster, E.M.
Frame, Janet
Gaskell, Elizabeth
Gordimer, Nadine
Greene, Graham
Hardy, Thomas
Hawkes, John
Hawthorne, Nathaniel
Hearn, Lafcadio
Hemingway, Ernest
Howells, William Dean
Hughes, Langston
Isherwood, Christopher
James, Henry
Jhabvala, Ruth Prawer,
Jolley, Elizabeth
Joyce, James
Kipling, Rudyard
Laurence, Margaret
Lawrence, D.H.
Lessing, Doris
London, Jack
Lovecraft, H.P.
McCullers, Carson
Mailer, Norman
Malamud, Bernard
Mansfield, Katherine
Melville, Herman
Moore, George
Munro, Alice
Nabokov, Vladimir
Narayan, R.K.
Oates, Joyce Carol
O'Connor, Flannery
Parker, Dorothy
Poe, Edgar Allan
Porter, Katherine Anne
Powys, John Cowper
Rhys, Jean
Richardson, Henry Handel

Twentieth-Century Literature: Topics

Twentieth-Century Literature: Writers

Achebe, Chinua
Albee, Edward
Amis, Kingsley
Anand, Mulk Raj
Anderson, Sherwood
Ashbery, John
Atwood, Margaret
Auden, W.H.
Baldwin, James
Baraka, Amiri [LeRoi Jones]
Barth, John
Barthelme, Donald
Baxter, James K.
Beckett, Samuel
Bellow, Saul
Bennett, Arnold
Berryman, John
Bierce, Ambrose
Bishop, Elizabeth
Bowen, Elizabeth
Burgess, Anthony
Burroughs, William S.
Carver, Raymond
Cather, Willa
Chandler, Raymond
Chesterton, G.K.
Chopin, Kate
Churchill, Caryl
Coetzee, J.M.
Conrad, Joseph
Crane, Hart
Cummings, E.E.
Davies, Robertson
Doolittle, Hilda
Dos Passos, John
Doyle, Arthur Conan
Dreiser, Theodore
Du Bois, W.E.B.
Durrell, Lawrence
Eliot, T.S.
Ellison, Ralph
Erdrich, Louise
Faulkner, William
Findley, Timothy
Fitzgerald, F. Scott
Ford, Ford Madox
Forster, E.M.
Fowles, John
Frame, Janet
Frost, Robert
Fugard, Athol
Gaddis, William
Gilman, Charlotte Perkins
Ginsberg, Allen
Golding, William
Gordimer, Nadine
Graves, Robert
Green, Henry
Greene, Graham
Hardy, Thomas
Harris, Wilson
Hawkes, John
Heaney, Seamus
Hearn, Lafcadio
Heller, Joseph
Hellman, Lillian
Hemingway, Ernest
Housman, A.E.
Howells, William Dean
Hughes, Langston
Hughes, Ted
Hurston, Zora Neale
Huxley, Aldous
Isherwood, Christopher
James, Henry
James, William
Jeffers, Robinson
Jhabvala, Ruth Prawer,
Jolley, Elizabeth
Joyce, James
Kerouac, Jack
Kipling, Rudyard
Larkin, Philip
Laurence, Margaret
Lawrence, D.H.
Leavis, F.R.
le Carré, John
Lessing, Doris
Lewis, C.S.
Lewis, Sinclair
Lewis, Wyndham
London, Jack
Lovecraft, H.P.
Lowell, Robert
Lowry, Malcolm
McCullers, Carson
MacDiarmid, Hugh
MacLennan, Hugh
MacNeice, Louis
Mailer, Norman
Malamud, Bernard
Malouf, David
Mamet, David
Mansfield, Katherine
Millay, Edna St Vincent
Miller, Arthur
Moore, Marianne
Morrison, Toni
Muir, Edwin
Munro, Alice
Murdoch, Iris
Nabokov, Vladimir
Naipaul, V.S.
Narayan, R.K.
Ngugi wa Thiong'o
Norris, Frank
Oates, Joyce Carol
O'Casey, Sean
O'Connor, Flannery
Olson, Charles
Ondaatje, Michael
O'Neill, Eugene
Orwell, George
Osborne, John
Owen, Wilfred
Parker, Dorothy
Pinter, Harold
Plath, Sylvia
Porter, Katherine Anne
Pound, Ezra
Powys, John Cowper
Pratt, E.J.
Pynchon, Thomas
Rao, Raja
Reaney, James
Rhys, Jean
Rich, Adrienne
Richards, I.A.
Richardson, Dorothy
Richardson, Henry Handel
Robinson, Edwin Arlington
Roethke, Theodore
Ross, Sinclair
Roth, Philip
Rushdie, Salman
Salinger, J.D.
Sandburg, Carl
Schreiner, Olive
Shaw, George Bernard
Shepard, Sam
Sinclair, Upton
Singer, Isaac Bashevis
The Sitwells
Soyinka, Wole
Spark, Muriel
Stead, Christina
Stein, Gertrude
Steinbeck, John
Stevens, Wallace
Stoppard, Tom
Styron, William
Synge, John Millington
Tagore, Rabindranath
Thomas, Dylan
Thomas, R.S.
Tolkien, J.R.R.
Updike, John
Vidal, Gore
Vonnegut, Kurt, Jr.
Walcott, Derek
Walker, Alice
Warren, Robert Penn
Waugh, Evelyn
Wells, H.G.
Welty, Eudora
West, Nathanael
West, Rebecca
Wharton, Edith
White, Patrick
Wilder, Thornton
Williams, Tennessee
Williams, William Carlos
Wilson, Angus
Wilson, Edmund
Wolfe, Thomas
Woolf, Virginia
Wright, Judith
Wright, Richard
Yeats, W.B.

Women's Writing

Alcott, Louisa May
Atwood, Margaret
Austen, Jane
Behn, Aphra
Bishop, Elizabeth
Bowen, Elizabeth
Bradstreet, Anne
Brontë, Charlotte
Brontë, Emily
Browning, Elizabeth Barrett
Burney, Frances [Fanny]
Cather, Willa
Chopin, Kate
Churchill, Caryl
Dickinson, Emily
Doolittle, Hilda [H.D.]
Edgeworth, Maria
Eliot, George
Erdrich, Louise
Feminist Literary Theory
Frame, Janet
Fuller, Margaret
Gaskell, Elizabeth
Gay and Lesbian Literature
Gender and Literature
Gilman, Charlotte Perkins
Gordimer, Nadine
Hellman, Lillian
Hurston, Zora Neale
Irish Literature: Women Writers
Jacobs, Harriet
Jhabvala, Ruth Prawer,
Jolley, Elizabeth
Julian of Norwich
Kempe, Margery
Laurence, Margaret
Lessing, Doris
McCullers, Carson
Mansfield, Katherine
Martineau, Harriet
Millay, Edna St Vincent
Moore, Marianne
Morrison, Toni
Munro, Alice
Murdoch, Iris
Oates, Joyce Carol
O'Connor, Flannery
Parker, Dorothy
Philips, Katherine
Plath, Sylvia
Popular Fiction for Women
Porter, Katherine Anne
Radcliffe, Ann
Rhys, Jean
Rich, Adrienne
Richardson, Dorothy
Richardson, Henry Handel
Romance Fiction
Rossetti, Christina
Schreiner, Olive
Shelley, Mary
The Sitwells (Edith)
Spark, Muriel
Stead, Christina
Stein, Gertrude
Stowe, Harriet Beecher
Walker, Alice
Welty, Eudora
West, Rebecca
Wharton, Edith
Wollstonecraft, Mary
Women Writers: General
Women Writers: 20th Century
Women Writers: Contemporary
Women Writers: British – General
Women Writers: Renaissance
Women Writers: Restoration and 18th Century
Women Writers: British – 19th Century
Romantic Era
Victorian
Women Writers: American – General
Women Writers: American – to 1900
Women Writers: American – 1900 to the Present
Women Writers: African-American
Woolf, Virginia
Wright, Judith
Yonge, Charlotte

A

Achebe, Chinua 1930–

Nigerian novelist, poet, and essayist

Carroll, David, *Chinua Achebe: Novelist, Poet, Critic*, New York: Twayne, 1970; revised editions, London: Macmillan, 1980, 1990

Gikandi, Simon, *Reading Chinua Achebe: Language and Ideology in Fiction*, London: James Currey, 1991; Portsmouth, New Hampshire: Heinemann, 1991

Innes, C.L., and Bernth Lindfors (eds.), *Critical Perspectives on Chinua Achebe*, Washington, D.C.: Three Continents Press, 1978; London: Heinemann, 1979

Innes, C.L., *Chinua Achebe*, Cambridge and New York: Cambridge University Press, 1990

Ojinmah, Umelo, *Chinua Achebe: New Perspectives*, Ibadan: Spectrum Books, 1991

Wren, Robert M., *Achebe's World: The Historical and Cultural Context of the Novels of Chinua Achebe*, Washington, D.C: Three Continents Press, 1980; London: Longman, 1981

Chinua Achebe has been widely acclaimed as the father of the African novel ever since the publication of *Things Fall Apart* in 1958. He is the most widely read of all African novelists, both on that continent and in the West, and has had a tremendous influence on subsequent African writers, particularly in his native Nigeria. Reflecting Achebe's stature in the African canon, he is one of the few African writers to have generated a substantial body of critical analysis. Early critics such as David Carroll (see below) and G.D. Killam (*The Novels of Chinua Achebe*, 1969) tended to concentrate on the themes and anthropology behind the novels, while more recent criticism has placed greater emphasis on narrative techniques and ideology.

CARROLL's update of an earlier version of this book provides a descriptive study of all five of Achebe's novels, the short stories, and the poetry. His work centres upon an attempt to understand the Igbo-ness of Achebe's writing. Carroll celebrates Achebe's flexible use of English to demonstrate Igbo modes of speech and thought. He also puts great emphasis on how Achebe values the role of the storyteller in explaining societies to themselves, and on the dualism of Igbo society, as demonstrated by the proverb "where something stands, there also something else will stand". The negative side to this emphasis is that it makes Achebe appear unduly parochial, and cannot easily accommodate the wider canvas of the later work, especially *Anthills of the Savannah*. Carroll is ultimately much more comfortable with Achebe as novelist-anthropologist than he is with the writer as contemporary political critic.

INNES and LINDFORS' 1978 collection of critical essays covers the first four novels and the poetry. The book brings together essays originally published in a wide variety of academic journals, and is an excellent introduction to both the major themes and the diversity of analysis of Chinua Achebe's work. Contributors include major critics of Achebe's writing, such as Carroll and Robert M. Wren, a number of Nigerians, and a powerful short essay from Ngugi wa Thiong'o on *A Man of the People*. Themes covered include linguistic studies, symbolism, ideology and politics, characterisation, historical vision, and comparative analysis.

INNES has produced a chronological study of Achebe's work, including the novels, short stories, poetry, and critical writing. In so doing he contextualises his subject's literary and political development as it has been affected by the vicissitudes of the Nigerian state. Expanding on the work of earlier critics, Innes examines how the four early novels are in many ways a critical response to Joyce Cary's stereotyped portrayals of Africans, and in particular a response to the characterisation of the eponymous hero of Cary's *Mister Johnson*. Central to this text is a challenge to the received wisdom – that Achebe writes realist novels. Instead, Innes argues that "Achebe's cool dispassionate style, his avoidance of the sensational, is comparable to the style of the epic theatre . . . it is above all his use of a variety of perspectives and his choice of narrative technique and structure which allows him to achieve effects similar to those aimed at by Brecht".

OJINMAH has chosen to analyse the canon of Achebe's work, not according to the chronology of publishing dates, but according to the order of historical time periods covered by the writing. He does this in order to highlight the central thesis of his book. This is that a major concern for Achebe is the abuse of power, and that whereas traditional Igbo societies had checks and balances to control the excesses of such as Okonkwo and Ezeulu, postcolonial Nigeria – and to some degree all Africa – has been betrayed by an uncontrolled élite, which assumed power after independence. Ojinmah emphasises Achebe's vision of the storyteller as social critic, and powerfully elucidates the novelist's growing anger with the African ruling classes.

GIKANDI looks at Achebe's novels in terms of the question of how ideology is inscribed in narrative structures. Like many commentators he is fascinated by the range of narrative voices

Achebe uses. Gikandi argues that this multiplicity is essential both to the author's attempt to re-inscribe African realities in opposition to colonial reductionist views of the continent's culture, and to his belief, in accordance with Igbo philosophy, that ambiguity and multiple viewpoints are necessary for the health of a balanced society. Gikandi draws extensively on Western linguistic theory and on relevant sociological theorists such as Edward Said and Frantz Fanon to develop his arguments. This is not a book for newcomers to Achebe's fiction, but it is a valuable contribution to the more advanced academic study of how the writer's ideology has developed through his complex use of language.

WREN explains that the starting point of his book was an attempt to come to a full understanding of all the connotations of the Igbo expressions used in Achebe's novels. This is developed into a fascinating exploration of the history of Achebe's home region from pre-colonial times to the present day. The historical material is used to bring a greater understanding to the context of the novelist's work than can be available in the texts themselves. The same investigative technique is applied to understanding Igbo culture. Wren's research is applied to the four early novels, and gives a most interesting extra dimension of understanding to the reader of the novels, which would not normally be available to any non-Igbo.

JANE PLASTOW

Adams, Henry 1838–1918

American writer of historical prose and fiction

Conder, John J., *A Formula of His Own: Henry Adams' Literary Experiment*, Chicago: University of Chicago Press, 1970
Harbert, Earl N., *The Force So Much Closer Home: Henry Adams and the Adams Family*, New York: New York University Press, 1977
Harbert, Earl N. (ed.), *Critical Essays on Henry Adams*, Boston: G.K. Hall, 1981
Jordy, William H., *Henry Adams: Scientific Historian*, New Haven, Connecticut: Yale University Press, 1952
Levenson, J.C., *The Mind and Art of Henry Adams*, Boston: Houghton Mifflin, 1957
Samuels, Ernest, *Henry Adams*, Cambridge, Massachusetts: Belknap Press of Harvard University Press, 1989

The literary reputation of Henry Adams is largely posthumous. Contemporary reviewers saw him as a scholarly, if rather conventional, historian who could afford to travel the world in pursuit of documentary sources; in the year of his death, T.S. Eliot, one of the first to review *The Education*, dismissed him as a "victim" of privilege. In recent decades, his belief in a scientific foundation to the movement of history and the impact of this belief upon his historical method have reopened interest in the complexities of his art and philosophy among political historians and literary critics alike. Although his nine-volume *History*, the biographies, and the sentimental non-fiction *Mont Saint-Michel and Chartres* established his professional reputation, the latter and his masterpiece *The Education of Henry Adams* – two works which Adams himself saw as a boxed set – have supported the critical literature since his death. His two novels, though not derivative, are remarkably like the American novels of Henry James, but have yet to generate more than passing interest, mostly as a stage in the development of his craft.

Biography is important to a rounded reading of most nineteenth-century non-fiction writers, who tended to pronounce on the world from within a uniquely nineteenth-century notion of the self, which inclined them to analyze with subjective abandon in both private and public forums. In Adams' particular case, the complex artistry and philosophizing of the autobiography, and the complicated psychological commentary that followed, would have begged a biographical layer to the criticism even without his famous family or his omission of 20 years in order to pass over the suicide of his wife. While Adams accepted the inescapability of his pedigree, the Adams narrative transcends mere racial memory, both the one he wrote and the one he actually lived.

Critics have almost universally agreed upon the originality of Adams' perspective upon American history in the nineteenth century. T.S. Eliot excepted, they have acknowledged the unique advantage afforded by access to the inner life of a great political family, and more importantly, to their papers. He enjoyed his greatest popularity in the 1960s and 1970s among formalist critics, who delighted in the near impossibility of finally uncovering the shape of Henry Adams' mind. Despite its diversity, there is little controversy in Adams criticism. He is not a man, even to biographers, but a speaking text, or perhaps a "mountain to be mined on all flanks for pure samples of human imagination" (R.P. Blackmur).

HARBERT (1981) has collected the important Adams criticism, choosing Mrs Humphrey Ward's response to *Democracy* as his starting point, followed by critical work from this century by R.P. Blackmur, Ernest Samuels, J.C. Levenson, and others. This collection deals primarily with *The Education*, but includes several essays on biographical context useful to those unwilling to read one of the several good Lives. His Introduction provides an overview of the entire career and the critical response, including Adams' first attempt at authorship, a travel piece much maligned in the British press, which was written with intended anonymity during his secretarial years in London. This critical incident has been detailed by all of Adams' biographers, possibly because it marked the beginning of a lifetime of professional shyness, which has an obvious counterpoise in the failure theme of *The Education*.

HARBERT's second volume listed here (1977) frames readings of Adams' major works with what he calls the "Adams heritage", an identifiable body of thought, conceptualized over four generations, which conditioned Adams to view himself as a public figure from early childhood, and which influenced, if it did not control, the mature Adams in the execution of his final and greatest work. This volume is an important contribution to a major segment of the criticism, which reads Adams' final work as the perfection of an Adams intellect under the historical-political-aesthetic conditions to which life exposed him.

SAMUELS has abridged his three-volume biography and critical study, the writing of which occupied nearly two decades, to provide an historical life to be read alongside the prevarications of *The Education*. On some points, particularly Adams' relationships with women, this work appears to go on in more detail than one expects in a scholarly biography, but the almost pathological third person impersonality in Adams' portrayal of his life probably suggested this approach to Samuels.

LEVENSON's critical biography portrays Adams as an American sage. In Adams' case, the life within his work is highly artificial – a caution to read Levenson as life framing art, and not vice versa. There is little overt evidence of ideological interconnection among Adams biographers, who rarely credit each other, but Levenson appears to have originated close reading of Henry Adams, the text. His biography is, structurally, a chronological reading of Adams' works, as the life, to Levenson, was a shadow of the works.

CONDER's is a formalist study. His argument centers upon the widely held belief that Adams systematically experimented with form throughout his literary life. His ability as a careful scholar, in combination with his drive to experiment formally in order to communicate interpretive history beyond the capacity of conventional historical narrative, is responsible for much of the complexity in the final product, in Conder's view. And Adams' final triumph, he continues, has been to be variously interpreted as an eccentric or a genius, depending upon whether accuracy or art is more cherished by the reader.

JORDY's is the most complete study to date of Adams' preoccupation with the scientific analysis of history, and includes clarifications of trends in scientific thought that were current in the late nineteenth century and early twentieth. As this century continues to fade, reading Henry Adams as an historian depends more and more upon guides such as Jordy's. While Jordy, like Adams, was operating within the limits of his time (1952), this work is still the most extensive discussion of Adams' interpretation of the role of science in history, and is still the standard source of detailed integration of the fragmented critical response to the serialized nine-volume *History*.

CLARA ELIZABETH SPEER

Addison, Joseph 1672–1719

English poet, dramatist, editor, and journalist

Bloom, Edward A., and Lillian D. Bloom, *Addison's Sociable Animal: In the Market Place, on the Hustings, in the Pulpit*, Providence, Rhode Island: Brown University Press, 1971

Bloom, Edward A., and Lillian D. Bloom, (eds.), *Addison and Steele: The Critical Heritage*, London and Boston: Routledge & Kegan Paul, 1980

Bloom, Edward A., Lillian D. Bloom, and Edmund Leites (eds.), *Educating the Audience: Addison, Steele, and Eighteenth-Century Culture*, Los Angeles: University of California William Clark Memorial Library, 1984

Elioseff, Lee A., *The Cultural Milieu of Addison's Literary Criticism*, Austin: University of Texas Press, 1963

Ketcham, Michael G., *Transparent Designs: Reading, Performance, and Form in the Spectator Papers*, Athens: University of Georgia Press, 1985

Lannering, Jan, *Studies in the Prose Style of Joseph Addison*, Uppsala, Sweden: A.-B. Lundequistska Bokhandeln, 1951; Cambridge, Massachusetts: Harvard University Press, 1951

McCrea, Brian, *Addison and Steele Are Dead: The English Department, Its Canon, and the Professionalization of Literary Criticism*, Newark: University of Delaware Press, 1990; London: Associated University Presses, 1990

Smithers, Peter, *The Life of Addison*, Oxford: Clarendon Press, 1954, revised 1968

Because Addison's literary reputation rests chiefly on his collaborations with Richard Steele (*q.v.*), and less attention has been devoted to the former's personal life than to Steele's, this entry includes some works that place equal emphasis on both writers.

LANNERING subjects Addison's style to minute analysis, traces its origins, and compares it with the work of contemporaries, notably John Dryden and Jonathan Swift. Nobody engaged in research on the development of English prose can afford to ignore this book.

ELIOSEFF makes an important contribution to the history of Addison criticism. In an effort to escape from the critical relativism of the 1950s, he argues that "if we cannot re-create all of the conditions under which a given work was written, we can discover what questions the critic was attempting to answer and what problems he was trying to solve". Addison's projects appear very adventurous. Elioseff shows him combining Longinian criticism with Christian doctrine to formulate his view of the sublime, applying John Locke's theory of the unstable self in his papers on *The Pleasures of the Imagination*, and trying unsuccessfully to use Aristotelian critical vocabulary to defend "Chevy Chase".

SMITHERS has written the standard biography of Addison – no easy task, since Addison "abhorred irrelevant self-revelation by authors, and was meticulous in his own avoidance thereof". His character was noted for "reticence and self-criticism": perhaps for this reason, few personal letters survive. Smithers often quarries *The Spectator* for evidence of Addison's personal responses – a strategy which Smithers defends by appealing to the steadfastness with which Addison "adhered to his opinions", and "the freedom with which" Addison used material he had written earlier, but not yet published. He emphasizes Addison's political career: "so fully rounded was his view of life that literary output became a byproduct, though a very important one, of a life well lived". Inevitably, there are occasions when the reader learns as much of Smithers' opinions as of Addison's, as in his critique of *Cato*: "his women possess a virtue which is not womanly, but that of men in women's clothes and subject to fainting". Smithers sees Addison as a social and moral crusader who succeeded too well for the good of his own reputation: "so fully did mankind endorse his teaching that many of his precepts came to be thought trite, axiomatic, or even presumptuous".

Working on the periodical and political writings, BLOOM and BLOOM (1971) expound Addison's economic, political, and religious views. The title recalls Addison's own adaptation of Aristotle's statement that man is a political animal. Because "political" in his own day "often meant the same as *factional*", Addison avoided trouble by using "sociable" to "connote one who properly discriminates between good and evil, just and unjust, indigent and idle". Bloom and Bloom argue that Addison's characteristic choice of the middle way was not dull or static, but dynamic, enterprising, and often risky. He wished merchants would exercise "daring individualism", rather than conservative methods that led to bankruptcy. In politics, he was a traditionalist who would always accept innovation if it seemed to offer greater stabililty. Readers are reminded that, in his lifetime, "the stability he wished for his country was not to be achieved". As for religion, the Anglican Church, which he always supported, "was fighting for its spiritual existence". Viewed against this turbulent background, Addison's reputation for complacency looks thoroughly outdated.

BLOOM and BLOOM (1980), writing for the *Critical Heritage* series, have compiled an invaluable collection of contemporary reactions to Addison's works. Sections on *The Tatler* and *The Spectator* are are followed by "Addison the Dramatist" and "Addison the Man and Writer". It is typical of Addison's demure character and august literary reputation that his contemporaries saw little need to separate his life from his writings. Some nineteenth-century responses are also included, culminating with Thomas Macaulay's near-apotheosis of Addison and William Thackeray's sceptical reaction, while subsequent developments are ably chronicled in the Preface. All aspects of Addison's creative output are covered, including his poems and other works that have received little recent attention.

BLOOM, BLOOM, and LEITES (1984) originally delivered their essays at a Clark Library Seminar. Bloom and Bloom defend Addison from the onslaughts of twentieth-century critics who have denounced him as "a liar, a timeserver, an expedientmonger, a homosexual, and worst of all, a Victorian". They depict Addison as an artist with a sense of public obligations, conscientiously fulfilling his responsibilities to his talent and to society. Leites surveys "the campaign of Steele and some of his contemporaries", including Addison, to "establish good humour as the temperament and mood appropriate to social life and marriage". It is a brilliant application of cultural history to literary criticism.

KETCHAM constructs a reading that arises from original and compelling observations on eighteenth-century notions of time and space. The only shortcoming is an occasional excess of complacency. Ketcham sees the "principle of synonymy" as characteristic of *The Spectator*, with such terms as "religion", "morality", and "Reason" coalescing peacefully in "a self-contained world where time is suspended by the forms of repetition which link essay to essay, just as a reader's coffee cup may be suspended in the air between his cheek and right ear". He pays too little attention to the possibility that this apparent lack of discrimination is politically charged: Addison and Steele were haunted by fears of the fanaticism and strife that arise when religion, morality, and reason part company.

McCREA's stimulating and controversial book is divided into two parts – "The Death of Joseph Addison and Richard Steele" and "The Making of the English Department". He combines his own analysis of Addison and Steele's journalism with an elegant study in the sociology of academic literary criticism to justify his claim that "we can learn much about the institutional situation and the social role of English professors by considering their neglect of Addison and Steele". He finds that the qualities which have led to this neglect are their commitment to clarity, and their concern with "literature's moral value and its role in improving the human character". He contrasts the current popularity of Swift, Alexander Pope, and other Scriblerians with their constant use of teasing irony and ambiguous personae. The future appearance of critical works on Addison and Steele will not invalidate McCrea's thesis: "Given the demands upon American university professors to get work out, Addison and Steele are unlikely to continue undiscovered: even Swift cannot generate enough controversies to employ all the eighteenth-century specialists". McCrea predicts Ketcham's book "will be followed by others, particularly since Ketcham has broached the subject of the transparency (I would say clarity) of Addison and Steele's work. I suspect subsequent writers will argue (misguidedly in my opinion) for complexity". Time will tell.

CAROLYN D. WILLIAMS

Aesthetícism *see* Decadence, Aestheticism, and the 1890s

African Literature: General

Writers, Regions, Movements, and Genres

Boyce Davies, Carole, and Anne Adams Graves (eds.), *Ngambika: Studies of Women in African Literature*, Trenton, New Jersey: Africa World Press, 1986

Chinweizu, Onwuchekwa Jemie, and Ihechukwu Madubuike, *Toward the Decolonisation of African Literature: African Fiction and Poetry and Their Critics*, Enugu, Nigeria: Fourth Division, 1980; Washington, D.C.: Howard University Press, 1983; London: KPI, 1985

Dathorne, O.R., *The Black Mind: A History of African Literature*, Minneapolis: University of Minnesota Press, 1974; Oxford: Oxford University Press, 1974; as *African Literature in the Twentieth Century*, London: Heinemann, 1976

Etherton, Michael, *The Development of African Drama*, London: Hutchinson, 1982

Klein, Leonard S. (ed.), *African Literature in the Twentieth Century: A Guide*, Harpenden, Hertfordshire: Oldcastle Books, 1986

Palmer, Eustace, *The Growth of the African Novel*, London: Heinemann, 1979

Schipper, Mineke, *Beyond the Boundaries: African Literature and Literary Theory*, London: Allison & Busby, 1989

Soyinka, Wole, *Myth, Literature and the African World*, Cambridge: Cambridge University Press, 1976

Wauthier, Claude, *The Literature and Thought of Modern Africa: A Survey*, London: Pall Mall Press, 1966

Wilkinson, Jane, *Talking with African Writers: Interviews with African Poets, Playwrights and Novelists*, London: James Currey, 1990

Critical writing on African literature is a rapidly growing area, which has developed from a rather Eurocentric standpoint in the 1960s, concerned mainly with presentation of theme and characterisation, into a much more diverse range of studies in recent years. This survey demonstrates the scope of different approaches, and deals with some of the more influential texts. It discusses attempts at a comprehensive analysis of the body of African literature in English, through to more polemical and personalised visions of the African literary scene. It also includes books that look at two particular aspects of African writing in depth – portrayals of women and a study of African drama.

DATHORNE's book covers an enormous range of material as he charts the evolution of sub-Saharan African literature from the beginning of the twentieth century to the late 1960s. This text deals with the three genres of the novel, drama, and poetry, in English, French, and Portuguese, and also includes a chapter on vernacular literatures. Because so many texts are covered there is often little space for critical analysis. Dathorne is primarily useful in telling us who wrote what, when, and in giving basic storylines and theme synopses. His analysis often appears dated, if not eccentric, as when he claims that Amos Tutuola is a superior writer to Chinua Achebe because he better reflects West African oral traditions. The central contention of the work is that early African writers act as spokesmen for their societies but actually write for a Western audience.

PALMER is one of the older generation of writers on the African novel (see also his *An Introduction to the African Novel*, 1972), and like most of these commentators his work centres on an examination of theme and character. When he does look at language and form he takes a conservative view, which tends to be critical of any experimentation moving far from standard English or a realist mode of expression. This book concentrates on the West African novelists. The only exceptions are studies of the Kenyans Ngugi wa Thiong'o and Meja Mwangi. Palmer includes the Francophone novelists Ousmane Sembène and Yambo Ouloguem; but the major part of this text is concerned with overview-essays about the major Anglophone West African novelists Cyprian Ekwensi, Achebe, and Wole Soyinka.

WAUTHIER's seminal text, first published in French in 1964, analyses what he calls "the cultural renaissance in black Africa at the moment of independence". This book looks not only at African literature, but also, more widely, at African letters as a whole, drawing on the work of anthropologists, lawyers, theologians, historians, and folklorists to present a contextualised vision of emergent nationalist Africa. Wauthier presents a broad view of culture, and gives a sympathetic overview of African intellectual vision at the time when the continent was, generally optimistically, seizing independence. Being French, Wauthier foregrounds the writing of French West Africa, and he is notably more sympathetic to the négritude movement than many Anglophone commentators. However, many important British, Portuguese, and Belgian writers are also given space. Above all Wauthier understands that culture and politics are vitally related in emergent African states, and that the small intellectual élites have exerted enormous influence over each other's writings in a wide variety of subject areas.

CHINWEIZU, JEMIE, and MADUBUIKE are three angry men. The summary of their argument is that:

> If African literature is not to become a transplanted fossil of European literature, it needs to burst out of the straight-jacket of anglomodernist poetry and of the "well-made novel", and it needs to find more ways of incorporating forms, treatments and devices taken from the African oral tradition.

The debate as to how far African literature has been dominated by the values of the European literary canon is indeed important. However, Chinweizu *et al.* choose to see the question as one influenced by a pernicious, conscious promotion of British imperialist policy. To bolster their argument they target particularly conservative critics and ignore many more recent, Afrocentric analysts. They also have a particularly Nigerian oriented viewpoint, which they apply in a reductionist manner to the entire African continent. Ultimately this is a rather tiresome book, containing much anger, a very simple message, but with an awful lot of words.

SCHIPPER has produced a most accessible investigation into the popular forms and the ideological imperatives that motivate African literature. She also examines the indigenous and foreign influences on that literature in considerable depth. Above all, Schipper demands that Eurocentric standards of judging African writing be challenged, both by properly valuing African world views and through careful intercultural literary analysis. Schipper's book contains essays on négritude, African realism, the importance of oral traditions, and censorship. This is an excellent critical study advocating sensitivity and modesty in any critic looking at a foreign culture.

SOYINKA's text is a very personal evaluation of African literature and theatre, demonstrating his proposition that there is a unique African worldview, based on a geocentric vision and the essential unity in humanity of mind, body, and spirit. The book is divided into four long essays, with an appendix that explicates what Soyinka calls the transitional zone between the realms of the unborn, the living, and the ancestors. The first two essays explain this African – or perhaps more specifically Yoruba (Soyinka's own ethnic group) – worldview primarily in the context of the medium of drama. The latter half of the work examines a range of African literature to demonstrate Soyinka's rejection of dualist Western ideologies in favour of what he calls a "social vision". Essential to this text is the rejection of any idea that African literature can only define itself in (a usually inferior) relationship to Western culture, plus an explanation of why Soyinka sees the négritude movement as a reductionist and Western-influenced philosophy.

KLEIN has edited a reference text, which gives general introductions to the literatures of 38 African nations, discussing both vernacular and metropolitan-language writing. There are also short essays on the work of the major writers from each nation, and bibliographies attached to each entry. This is a useful introductory guide, although some new writers, major texts, and rapidly developing national literatures have emerged since the time the book was published.

WILKINSON has conducted a series of fairly long and sympathetic interviews with 15 African writers from five nations – Ghana, Nigeria, Kenya, South Africa, and Zimbabwe. There have been previous volumes of interviews with African writers (see Duerden and Pieterse's *African Writers Talking*, 1972, and Brown's *Women Writers in Black Africa*, 1981), and to some extent any selection of interviewees has to be arbitrary. However, this book is particularly interesting, both because it is relatively recent, and because Wilkinson refrains from imposing her agenda unduly on her subjects. The interviewees include the giants of African literature – Achebe, Ngugi, and Soyinka – but there are also fascinating contributions from less well-known and less-published writers, such as Ghanaian playwright Mohammed ben Abdallah and the South African poet Mazisi Kunene. Younger voices are represented with contributions from Ben Okri and Tsitsi Dangerembga. This text allows us to hear directly what are the influences, concerns, and aesthetics of a representative range of African literary voices.

BOYCE DAVIES and ADAMS GRAVES have edited a series of essays illustrating how women are depicted in African literature. This book is a significant contribution to the still small, but growing, body of feminist criticism of African fiction. The introductory essay places the work in the context of African feminist theory. Subsequent contributions then examine both how female characters have often been used simply to illustrate facets of the characters of male protagonists, and also how many female writers, and a few men – notably Ngugi wa Thiong'o and Ousmane Sembène – have gone beyond the stereotypes of mother, virgin, and whore to examine the more complex realities of African women's lives. The works of Mariama Bâ, Flora Nwapa, and Buchi Emecheta are considered in several essays, and although the bulk of the essays deal with writing from Francophone and Anglophone West Africa, this book is unusual and interesting in that it also looks at the depiction of the often very circumscribed lives of women from North Africa.

ETHERTON looks at the area of African writing most commonly neglected in studies of the continent's literature – drama. This book is written with students in mind, and drama terminology is carefully explained throughout. Etherton does not seek to examine exhaustively published texts; instead he takes a range of examples, which point up the dichotomy between "art" or intellectual drama and the popular theatre that seeks to relate directly to the African masses. Since theatre lives primarily in performance, the debate as to whom African writers write for is obviously highlighted when we consider the communal activity of drama. Etherton sees intellectual drama as of dubious worth in Africa, and says: "I have constantly tried . . . to assert that the study of drama is primarily a study of its function in society". Among the major playwrights considered are Soyinka, Ola Rotimi, John Pepper Clark, Ama Ata Aidoo, Efua Sutherland, and Athol Fugard; but a host of lesser-known producers of theatre are also discussed in this valuable introductory text.

JANE PLASTOW

Decolonisation, Language Choice, and Politics

Chinweizu, Onwuchekwa Jemie, and Ihechukwu Madubuike, *Toward the Decolonisation of African Literature: African Fiction and Poetry and Their Critics*, Enugu, Nigeria: Fourth Division, 1980; Washington, D.C.: Howard University Press, 1983; London: KPI, 1985

Dabydeen, David (ed.), *The Black Presence in English Literature*, Manchester: Manchester University Press, 1985

Jan Mohamed, Abdul R., *Manichean Aesthetics: The Politics of Literature in Colonial Africa*, Amherst: University of Massachusetts Press, 1983

Jones, Eldred (ed.), *The Question of Language in African Literature Today: Borrowing and Carrying: A Review*, London: James Currey, 1991; Trenton, New Jersey: Africa World Press, 1991

Jones, Eldred (ed.), *Orature in African Literature Today: A Review*, London: James Currey, 1992

Ngugi wa Thiong'o, *Decolonising the Mind: The Politics of Language in African Literature*, London: James Currey, 1986; Porstmouth, New Hampshire: Heinemann, 1986

Pieterse, Cosmo, and Donald Munro (eds.), *Protest and Conflict in African Literature*, London: Heinemann, 1969

Tibble, Anne (ed.), *African-English Literature: A Short Survey and Anthology of Prose and Poetry up to 1965*, London: Peter Owen, 1965

Issues such as decolonisation, the relationship of the writer to oral poetic traditions, the questions of language choice, aesthetics, and ideology, and the stress on the issue of social committment in literature have been dominant critical concerns in recent writing on African literature.

TIBBLE's book contains both an anthology of poetry, fiction, and drama, and a critical Introduction. She outlines a national or regional model to account for cultural and "racial" differences within African literatures and draws on comparative studies to explain linguistic and cultural variations. The selection of poetry, fiction, and drama is both comprehensive and wide-ranging, and contains a valuable bibliography of African-English literature.

PIETERSE and MUNRO's collection contains discussions of a wide selection of writers – Achebe, Nadine Gordimer, Frantz Fanon, Soyinka, and Ngugi – within colonial and post-independence historical contexts. The theme of protest and conflict is a dominant preoccupation of all the commentators who discuss modern African literature in terms of social committment while disregarding questions of aesthetic or linguistic form, and one which has been criticised for being sometimes crudely empiricist.

DABYDEEN'S influential collection is concerned with "locating literary texts within social and historical contexts, and within patterns of popular and scientific ideas". To this end seventeenth-century racial hostility, as manifested in the racial edicts of Elizabeth I, is read into Shakespeare's representation of blacks in Renaissance drama; the ethnological imperialist novels of the late nineteenth century are related to social Darwinian ideas of scientific racism and ideologies of racial superiority; and postcolonial African novels are read as oppositional discourses to European representations of Africa as a "non-place" of civilisation, the dark continent of myth and fantasy. This book should be considered essential reading for readers interested in colonial discourse studies, and contains an excellent secondary bibliography.

JAN MOHAMED'S classic work has justifiably had a major influence on such studies. Drawing on a Lacanian psychoanalytic reading of colonial discourse and Fanon's existential Hegelianism, Jan Mohamed describes literary representations of the colonial encounter as a "Manichean struggle" between, on the one hand, the imaginary construction of the native as a negative image for the European and, on the other hand, the symbolic use of the native as mediator of European desires, fantasies, and myths – a rigid binarism that works to privilege European representations of Africa and to deny the native any agency unmediated by negation. Concentrating on texts by Joyce Cary, Isak Dinesen, Gordimer, Achebe, Ngugi, and Alex La Guma, Jan Mohamed explicates this Manichean allegory through close textual and theoretical analysis.

CHINWEIZU, JEMIE, and MADUBUIKE's influential study, in arguing for a distinctive African literature based on indigenous poetic traditions of folk tales and orature as against imported Western literary traditions and forms, has (as noted above) been criticised – for being ahistorical, chauvinistic, and for advocating a pseudo-tradition which neglects the inescapable political and cultural legacies of colonialism and its continued presence in contemporary Africa.

NGUGI's important study emphasises the political function of the writer in postcolonial Africa. If decolonisation is to take place, the contemporary African writer must be aware of the pervasiveness of European values and representations as enshrined in institutions, inherited élitism, and the English language. Ngugi's decision to write in Gikuyu rather than in English is an essential step in this "decolonising of the African mind". While this position has been criticised for its implicit essentialist view of language and culture, Ngugi's study raises important questions regarding the sociological implications of readership and literary production for the African writer in English.

JONES's 1991 critical anthology addresses a central preoccupation of many African writers writing in English, that is, how to appropriate and abrogate the idioms and vocabulary of a European language in order to express native cultural tradition and reflect the particular inflections of indigenous speech patterns. In the essays on Ayi Kwie Armah, Achebe, Tony Uchenna Ubesie, Wole Soyinka, Babafemi Adyemi Osofisan, John Pepper Clark, and Guillaume Oyono-Mbia, each of the contributors shows how these writers variously inflect English vocabulary with local cultural terms, distort English syntactical patterns to reflect native speech accents, and use pidgins and creoles to deviate from standard English orthography and morphology in order to represent their own linguistic cultures in their adopted tongue. The book should be considered a detailed explication of an important aspect of modern African writing, rather than a comprehensive approach to the literature as a whole.

JONES's second critical anthology (1992) addresses the turn to oral folk traditions in modern African writing in English. The attempt to reclaim pre-colonial oral traditions as secular rather than religious or ritualistic forms of communal expression is traced, in many of the essays, to a desire to counterpoise a tribal-based literature against modern urban forms of linguistic community. While the editorial Introduction describes the turn to ethnic tradition as a form of cultural nostalgia, prompted by the disappointments of decolonisation, others might view this reclamation of lost traditions as an attempt to redeem a tradition brutalised by colonialism. This turn to an African "orature" in poetry, drama, and prose is explored in various parts of the book. Excellent articles by Elimimian on Kofi Awoonor, and by Ogede on Armah make this collection a valuable contribution to African literary studies.

D.S. MARRIOTT

African Literature: East and Central

Gurr, Andrew, and Angus Calder (eds.), *Writers in East Africa*, Nairobi: East African Literature Bureau, 1974
Heron, G.A., *The Poetry of Okot p'Bitek*, London: Heinemann, 1976; New York: Africana, 1976
Killam, G.D. (ed.), *The Writing of East and Central Africa*, London: Heinemann, 1984
Roscoe, Adrian A., and Msiska Mpalive-Hangson, *The Quiet Chameleon: Modern Poetry from Central Africa*, London and New York: Hans Zell, 1992
Smith, Angela, *East African Writing in English*, London: Macmillan, 1989
Veit-Wild, Flora, *Teachers, Preachers, Non-Believers: A Social History of Zimbabwean Literature*, London and New York: Hans Zell, 1992

Literature in English in East and Central Africa was significantly later in developing than in the Southern or Western regions of the continent. Partly this was because of different colonial conditions and partly because the use of vernacular languages for developing national literatures, especially Kiswahali in East Africa, has often been a high priority for both writers and governments in the region. A significant body of writing in English dates only from the 1970s, and although some major voices have emerged in recent years, critical analysis in many areas is only just beginning to develop.

GURR and CALDER have edited a series of papers presented by writers working in Kenya for the 1971 Festival of East African Writing in Nairobi. Produced just as East African fictional writing in English was beginning to come into its own, the papers collectively provide a fascinating historical insight into the concerns of a region newly prepared to demand an Afrocentric literary agenda relevant to its own, as opposed to English cultural and political interests. The first half of the book consists of a series of papers discussing different kinds of writing emerging in Africa, and the problems and responsibilities of East African writers. The latter part of the work reflects the fact that the contributors were all attached to academic institutions. There is extensive discussion of the role of universities *vis à vis* literary production, of the ongoing language debate, and of the place of literature in English in East African societies.

KILLAM's book provides a thorough introduction to writing from East and Central Africa. The text is divided into three sections. Part One looks at the six countries under discussion – Kenya, Mauritania, Tanzania, Uganda, Zambia, and Zimbabwe – and gives an overview of national cultural and literary conditions. Part Two consists of five essays on major writers from the region – Ngugi wa Thiong'o, Okot p'Bitek, Taban lo Liyong, Meja Mwangi, and an especially perceptive critical analysis of the work of the Somalian novelist Nuruddin Farah. The final section looks at the standing of poetry, the novel, and playwriting on a regional basis. The standard of the essays varies, but this is generally an excellent book for anyone wishing to make acquaintance with a still under-researched part of Africa's literary scene. The only problem is that the book was published in 1984, and writing in this area is burgeoning so rapidly that several important new writers have appeared in the past ten years.

SMITH has produced a somewhat idiosyncratic review of selected East African writers. Her book is divided into sections on the novel, poetry, and drama, but the reasons for Smith's choice of writers in each category are not immediately clear. By far the greatest space is allotted to Ngugi wa Thiong'o as East Africa's most celebrated writer. The other novelists chosen are the populist Kenyan Meja Mwangi and Nuruddin Farah, who, as a Somali, actually comes from the Horn of Africa. In the chapter on poetry Smith looks at Okot p'Bitek, Taban lo Liyong, and Jack Mapanje, while for drama we return to Ngugi, with the only other playwright considered being Uganda's Mukotani Rugyendo. It becomes evident in the brief conclusion that the choice of writers in this survey has been dictated by Smith's desire to point up her idea that the common thread in East African writing is a desire for a "real" homecoming after the alienating experiences of both colonial and postcolonial life, which have driven many writers into spiritual or physical exile from their roots. Smith manipulates her material to serve her thesis and in the process leaves several significant writers and many viewpoints on East African writing undiscussed.

ROSCOE and MSISKA have produced the first overview of the work of the poets of Central Africa (here defined as Malawi, Zambia, and Zimbabwe) in English. The first, and by far the most compelling, half of the book is taken up with an analysis of the Malawian poetry scene. There are chapters on the work of Steve Chimombo, Frank Chipasula, Jack Mapanje, Felix Mnthali, and Edison Mpina. The writers obviously know Malawi well, and provide many insights into the work of a relatively unknown national poetry thriving in the face of massive political censorship and a constant fear of imprisonment for even the most minor of perceived insults to the former regime of Hastings Banda. Regrettably, coverage of Zimbabwe and Zambia is much weaker. There is a long essay on Zimbabwe's best-known poet, Musaemura Zimunya, but coverage of other poets is often pretentious and weak on critical insight. There is also much less understanding of the political and cultural conditions pertaining in Zambia and Zimbabwe. Read this book if you want to know about Malawi's poets, but put it down after page 93.

HERON's book is an in-depth study of the four songs that made Okot p'Bitek the best-known poet in East Africa. The central contention of the work is that the songs are primarily satiric assaults on various aspects of Acoli society, and that the voice behind each song should not be seen as that of a rounded individual but as a vehicle for expounding Okot's cultural ideologies. Heron's greatest strength is that he has lived among the Acoli and learned the language. This enables him to compare the Acoli and English versions of *Songs of Lawino*, to explain the Acoli oral traditions that have influenced the poet's writing, and to understand something of the cultural context from which Okot p'Bitek is speaking.

VEIT-WILD has written a social study of the evolution of black Zimbabwean writing. She divides her book into three sections, which look at the three generations of Zimbabwean writers, from the moralistic "teachers and preachers" of the 1950s and 1960s, to the disillusioned urbanites – the "non-believers" of the UDI generation – and on to the post-independence, international prize-winning novelists such as Shimmer Chindoya, Tsitsi Dangerembga, and Chengerai Hove. Veit-Wild uses extracts from fictional and autobiographical writings to chronicle the political and social lives of black Zimbabweans under white rule and, from 1980, the independence government. She does undertake extended literary-critical analysis of the major Zimbabwean authors, but this is primarily a social study, illustrated by a national literature.

JANE PLASTOW

African Literature: West

Dunton, Chris, *Make Man Talk True: Nigerian Drama in English since 1970*, London and New York: Hans Zell, 1992

Fraser, Robert, *West African Poetry: A Critical History*, Cambridge and New York: Cambridge University Press, 1986

Maja-Pearce, Adewale, *A Mask Dancing: Nigerian Novelists of the Eighties*, London and New York: Hans Zell, 1992

Nwoga, D.I. (ed.), *Literature and Modern West African Culture*, Benin City, Nigeria: Ethiope Publishing, 1978

Obiechina, Emmanuel, *Culture, Tradition and Society in the West African Novel*, Cambridge and New York: Cambridge University Press, 1975

Yoder, Carroll, *White Shadows: A Dialectical View of the French African Novel*, Washington, D.C.: Three Continents Press, 1991

Zabus, Chantal, *The African Palimpsest: Indigenization of Language in the West African Europhone Novel*, Amsterdam: Rodopi, 1991

Critical responses to West African literature in English began with introductory works on national literatures, designed primarily for a general and student readership. Region-wide surveys and theoretical works came much later.

NWOGA has edited a collection of conference essays on the definition and social functions of African literature, organised through such general themes as "The Writer and Commitment", "The Traditional Literary Artist and [the] Society", "The Writer and the West African Past", and "The Writer and the West African Present". Articles in each part either complement or interrogate one another. Thus, in Part One Ogungbesan's "The Modern Writer and Commitment", which advocates commitment to art, confronts Kalu Uka's "From Commitment to Essence", which favours *engagé* writing. In Part Four, Apronti's "The Writer in Our Society" contends that "the African writer . . . must take the rest of us by the hand and lead us to the promised land". Conversely, Omafume Onoge's "The Possibilities of a Radical Sociology of African Literature" continues the search for appropriate critical and aesthetic criteria for African literature.

An in-depth study of the socio-cultural and historical determinations of the West African novel is undertaken by OBIECHINA. Examining the convergence of socio-economic forces behind this, Obiechina reveals the influence of the Cambridge school of anthropology, Ian Watt's *The Rise of the Novel* (1957) and E.M. Forster's *Aspects of the Novel* (1927), and postulates debatable parallels between the socio-historical origin of the West African novel and the eighteenth-century

British novel. Part Two, "Domestication of the Novel in West Africa", discusses novelists' appropriation of the form by employing indigenous aesthetic codes and oral culture's modes of apprehending reality. Part Three focuses on literary themes of the late 1950s and 1960s. Considerable light is shed on the culturally specific dimensions of West African novelists' art.

Concentrating on post-World-War-II poetry, FRASER identifies a developmental pattern of "a sharp break with the traditions of oral verse, after which occurred a slow flirtatious reconciliation". The survey begins with the progression from oral to written poetry, and ends with "The Poetry of Dissent, 1970–80", with appropriate emphases on the cultural, historical, and literary forces that shaped the poetry. However, in discussing oral poetry in the first and last chapters, Fraser appears most at ease with Ghanaian traditions and gives inadequate attention to the rest of the region. Chapter 2 ("Ladies and Gentlemen") gives a stimulating account of the Victorian and Georgian legacies of Anglophone pioneer poetry. This is balanced with a study of the négritude movement and poetry in Chapter 3. Major poets like Christopher Okigbo, Gabriel Okara, and Wole Soyinka receive full-chapter scrutiny.

ZABUS explores the question: "how can a Europhone text incorporate in its linguistic and referential texture the languages autochthonous to West Africa?". The study is based mainly on novels written between 1960 and 1990 in Senegal, the Ivory Coast, Ghana, and Nigeria. Investigating "glottopolitics", or language politics, in Chapter 2, Zabus highlights the problematics of contesting foreign-language imperialism while competition among indigenous languages militates against formulating coherent language policies. Chapters 3, 4, and 5 describe various indigenization methods. She exaggerates the "glottopolitical" significance of Ken Saro-Wiwa's *Sozaboy* (1985). *Sozaboy*'s language is not new, for Onitsha Market writers employed it in mid-century, while Tunde Fatunde has experimented with it since 1985. In translating selected passages into meaningless syntax strings purportedly representing deep structures of African originals, her arguments are sometimes based on imaginary linguistic features.

Though YODER deals with Francophone novels, most of these have been translated into English, and the study is itself in English. Covering the pre-négritude period to the 1980s, the study is organised into "thesis", "antithesis", and "synthesis". The "Thesis" is the discourse of imperialism, which provoked the "Antithesis", or Africa's anti-colonialist discourse. The "Synthesis" is the post-independence text. This scheme is inconsistently followed, however. "The Denial of Négritude" in "Synthesis" logically belongs with "Négritude in the Novel" in "Antithesis", for the négritude controversies were concurrent with the movement's propagation of its philosophy, not phenomena of a later era. Moreover, Yoder's selection of incidents to scrutinise or emphasise subtly transforms the ideologies of the novels. This book's strength lies in its rigorous challenge to complacent readings, drawing attention to, for example, rarely noted weaknesses in Ousmane Sembène's *The Money Order* and René Maran's reproduction, in *Batouala*, of "the racist stereotypes [of Africans] propagated by the white writers".

The bulk of West African writing comes from Nigeria, and Maja Pearce and Dunton have produced panoramic studies of the Nigerian novel in the 1980s, and Nigerian drama since 1970, respectively.

MAJA-PEARCE contends that because "all Nigerian novelists in English" have an ambiguous response towards the language, "their novels are less interesting as *literature* than as a record of the dilemma of the Nigerian intellectual in the modern world". From this fashionable, but intellectually bankrupt, approach, his reading of Nigerian novels of the 1980s hardly penetrates the surface of plots and characters. Though his comments on particular novels are often appropriate, his need to justify his original thesis makes him surprisingly insensitive to irony and nuance whenever confronted with complex works. Okonkwo in *Things Fall Apart* becomes "a symbol for his community", Festus Iyayi's *Violence* "a long, sprawling, undisciplined novel". Maja-Pearce unfortunately offers gut reactions rather than systematic criticism.

Concentrating on ten university-educated dramatists who have become prominent after Soyinka and John Pepper Clark (-Bekederemo), DUNTON examines the relationship between their works and "currents of thought, of ideological patterning, in contemporary Nigerian society". Dunton provides "a degree of continuity in the book's argument" through a comparative approach, which constantly juxtaposes different dramatists' handling of common themes or aspects of stagecraft. Thus, Zulu Sofola's portrayal of the figure of the king in his *King Emene* is illuminated through comparison with Ola Rotimi's *The Gods are Not to Blame*, and Wale Ogunyemi's *The Vow*. Similarly, Kole Omotose's dramatisation of workers' struggle in *The Curse* is compared with that in Bode Sowande's and (Baba)Femi Osofisan's work.

CHIDI OKONKWO

African-American Writers: General

Baker, Houston A., Jr., *Singers of Daybreak: Studies in Black American Literature*, Washington, D.C.: Howard University Press, 1974

Baker, Houston A., Jr., *The Journey Back: Issues in Black Literature and Criticism*, Chicago: University of Chicago Press, 1980

Baker, Houston A., Jr., *Blues, Ideology and Afro-American Literature: A Vernacular Theory*, Chicago: University of Chicago Press, 1984

Bell, Bernard W., *The Afro-American Novel and Its Tradition*, Amherst: University of Massachusetts Press, 1987

Bone, Robert A., *The Negro Novel in America*, New Haven, Connecticut: Yale University Press, 1958

Bruce, Dickson D., Jr., *Black American Writing from the Nadir: The Evolution of a Literary Tradition 1877–1915*, Baton Rouge: Louisiana State University Press, 1989

Gates, Henry Louis, Jr. (ed.), *Black Literature and Literary Theory*, London and New York: Methuen, 1984

Gates, Henry Louis, Jr., *Figures in Black: Words, Signs, and the "Racial" Self*, New York and Oxford: Oxford University Press, 1987

Gates, Henry Louis, Jr., *The Signifying Monkey: A Theory of Afro-American Literary Criticism*, New York and Oxford: Oxford University Press, 1988

Petesch, Donald A., *A Spy in the Enemy's Country: The Emergence of Modern Black Literature*, Iowa City: University of Iowa Press, 1989

Stepto, Robert B., *From Behind the Veil: A Study of Afro-American Narrative*, Urbana: University of Illinois Press, 1979

Spanning the pre-Civil Rights era to the present, literary criticism on African-American poetry and fiction has explored the cultural dualism – what W.E.B. Du Bois termed "double consciousness" in *The Souls of Black Folk* – inherent in the struggle of creative expression in a racist environment. Earlier works of criticism tend to focus more on historical continuities and commonalities, while later works address themselves to the role that literary theory plays in the re-evaluation of African-American cultural and artistic contributions to a national literature.

BONE's important study stands as one of the first to break with the white liberal tradition (as evinced in Parrington and others) to treat African-American texts primarily as social documents. Bone treats major authors from the nineteenth and twentieth centuries in an effort to trace the literary history and aesthetic value of African-American writing. Early writers are treated socio-historically because, Bone contends, "the quality of these works does not justify literary analysis". Later works by Richard Wright and Ralph Ellison are examined as fully competent artistic productions and elicit thorough literary interpretations. Throughout, however, Bone keeps an eye toward what he terms "the conflicting loyalties of race and art", which he argues all African-American writers experience to some degree. While many of Bone's premises may seem outdated to the modern reader, his study was one of the first to argue that African-American literary production should be valued on its aesthetic merits, rather than dismissed as sociological studies slightly fictionalized.

One of BAKER's earliest books of criticism, *Singers of Daybreak* suggests the eclectic, associational, and brilliant logic that his subsequent critical productions have amplified. Baker organizes his essays around the:

> . . . several manifestations of the black creative spirit which have aided this process of cultural regeneration. They are concerned with writers, themes, and techniques that have helped to illumine the path for contemporaries and successors. James Weldon Johnson's *The Autobiography of an Ex-Colored Man*, for example, is analyzed as a prototype for Ralph Ellison's *Invisible Man*. The work of Paul Laurence Dunbar, the first black American poet of distinction, is re-evaluated, and the role of Jean Toomer's *Cane* in the black American tradition is assessed, in the longest essay in the volume. Similarly, Gwendolyn Brooks's poetical stance; the topic of justice in the black narrative; George Cain's novel of inner-city life and drug addiction; and the issues raised by a consideration of entertainment and instruction as critical criteria provide content for essays and point to some of the more lustrous aspirations and achievements of black American culture.

Like much of Baker's later work (see below), the essays in *Singers of Daybreak* offer brief, intense, and extraordinarily intelligent meditations on the links between culture and art.

STEPTO's work is a landmark in African-American literary criticism, for it is one of the earliest studies to chart theoretically what constitutes African-American literature, as well as how this literary tradition is shaped and articulated. Stepto organizes his study around the idea of what he terms "pregeneric myths – shared stories or myths that not only exist prior to literary form, but eventually shape the forms that comprise a given culture's literary canon". "The primary pregeneric myth for Afro-America", he claims, "is the quest for freedom and literacy". Throughout his work Stepto attempts to define how this myth becomes embodied in specific genres of narrative – autobiography, fiction, and historiography. Moreover, he claims that an identifiable African-American tradition in narrative exists not because of sheer numbers of texts produced, but because authors and texts are inextricably "bound historically and linguistically to a shared pregeneric myth". Beginning with slave narratives as "an umbrella term for many types of narratives", Stepto examines the writings of Booker T. Washington, Du Bois, James Weldon Johnson, Wright, and Ellison. This book has been widely influential in its treatment of a textually centered (rather than socio-political) literary tradition, and is essential reading for any scholar interested in African-American narrative.

Published one year after Stepto's groundbreaking work, BAKER's *The Journey Back* also examines how "black narrative texts written in English preserve and communicate culturally unique meanings". In it, Baker returns to eighteenth-century texts and nineteenth-century slave narratives in an effort to locate what he, after Kenneth Burke, calls "terms for order" in African-American literature, a "search for coherent arrangements of objects and events". In addition to his brilliant and allusive readings of early African-American literature, Baker also assesses African-American literature and criticism from 1954 to 1976. He concludes the study by stressing the importance of "the semantic levels of black culture", or the way in which literary texts exhibit how "blacks have attempted to order the disruption and chaos occasioned by their confrontation with the West through language".

Four years later, in his *Blues, Ideology, and Afro-American Literature*, BAKER returns to theoretical models as a gateway into "Afro-American expressive traditions". Employing the blues as a vernacular paradigm of American culture, Baker focuses on how the "material conditions of slavery in the United States and the rhythms of Afro-American blues combined and emerged from my revised materialistic perspective as an ancestral matrix that has produced a forceful and indigenous American creativity". As the preceding sentence indicates, Baker's own language in this work is consistently dense and frequently borders on the impenetrable. Readers tenacious enough to wade through Baker's prose, however, will be treated to his customary insightfulness and rewarded with the numerous connections between texts and genres that he makes throughout.

GATES' essay collection *Black Literature and Literary Theory* is grounded in poststructuralist theory and concerns itself "with the question of the formal relation between 'black' (African, Caribbean, Afro-American) literatures and Western literatures". Gates organizes the collection around the following questions:

> What is the status of the black literary work of art? How do canonical texts in the black traditions relate to canonical texts of the Western traditions? . . . Can the methods of explication developed in Western criticism be "translated" into the black idiom? How "text-specific" is literary theory, and how "universal" are rhetorical strategies? If every black canonical text is, as I shall argue, "two-toned" or "double-voiced", how do we explicate the signifyin(g) black difference that makes black literature "black"? And what do we make of the relation between the black vernacular tradition and the black formal tradition, as these inform the shape of a black text?

Stressing a diversity, rather than a uniformity of responses, Gates has collected essays from cutting-edge contemporary theorists, such as Anthony Appiah, Kimberly Benston, Barbara Johnson, Houston Baker, Mary Helen Washington, and Susan Willis, among others. Gates' project is to investigate how applicable contemporary theory is to African, Caribbean, and African-American traditions, and, with one or two exceptions, these essays suggest that theory can advance both understanding and appreciation of this wide body of literary production.

BELL's study, devoted specifically to the development of the African-American novel, manifests a more traditional, and less theoretical, approach. Spanning the period between 1853 and 1983, Bell surveys briefly more than 150 novels written by some 100 authors. Bell situates the novels within their historical, literary, cultural, and psychological contexts, and employs standard terms of literary categorization (realism, naturalism, etc.) both to group and to define certain strategies of representation. An alternative to the poststructuralism of both Baker and Gates, Bell's work is more of a comprehensive chronology, and might be most useful to those generally unfamiliar with the history and traditions of African-American literature.

GATES produced two books in the late 1980s that secured his reputation, along with that of Houston Baker, as one of the pre-eminent theorists working within African-American studies. The first of these studies, *Figures in Black,* constitutes Gates' plan to demonstrate the relevance and relationship of literary theory to African-American texts. The chapters consist of close readings of particular texts and authors (Phillis Wheatley, Frederick Douglass, Harriet Wilson, Jean Toomer, Sterling Brown), with an emphasis on the discursive practices these writers employ. This is an intelligent and accessible book of critical theory. One cannot, unfortunately, say the same thing about GATES' next book, *The Signifying Monkey.* In this work he explores the inheritance of African organizing myths within an African-American tradition, particularly that of the Yoruba trickster figure, Esu-Elegbara, and the Signifying Monkey so prevalent in African-American folklore. Though Gates' interpretation of this mythology is both original and important, his early chapters of theorizing may leave even the most critically sophisticated readers awash in a sea of theoretical jargon. More comprehensible are the later chapters, in which he elucidates his theories through the works of Zora Neale Hurston, Ishmael Reed, and Alice Walker.

BRUCE's study is more narrowly focused historically, and concerns itself with post-Reconstruction literary production in an intensely racist cultural, political, and social climate. Bruce locates certain prevalent "tensions and ambiguities" about race throughout the literature, and concludes that certain irresolvable contradictions, rather than answers, lie at the heart of this material. Bruce focuses on Paul Laurence Dunbar, Griggs, Charles W. Chesnutt, and James Weldon Johnson, situating his analyses within the cultural and racial discursive context in which they wrote and lived. One shortcoming of this study is its relative lack of attention to the important women writers of the period.

PETESCH's work returns to the issue of the canon, and the place of African-American literature within it. His concern is to broaden our understanding and definition of the canon by re-reading African-American literature through a literary lens of canonical terms and formulations, as well as in its historical and cultural context. Petesch identifies six predominant qualities in African-American literature, which, he argues, arose out of the conditions of slavery, and continued as racism persisted throughout the United States. These qualities consist of: "(1) a collective point of view; (2) the mimetic mode; (3) a sensitivity to the play of power; (4) a consciousness of the fragility of the self; (5) a predilection for the moral imperative; and (6) a recurrence of the tactic of masking". These focal points inform his selection of texts and his organization of chapters, occasionally bestowing a narrow feel to his discussions. This work would be most useful for beginning students of African-American literature and culture; more advanced scholars may find it a well-written rehashing of approaches long since established.

DEBORAH CARLIN

African-American Writers: 20th Century

Byerman, Keith E., *Fingering the Jagged Grain: Tradition and Form in Recent Black Fiction*, Athens: University of Georgia Press, 1985

Callahan, John F., *In the African-American Grain: The Pursuit of Voice in Twentieth-Century Black Fiction*, Urbana: University of Illinois Press, 1988; 2nd edition, as *In the African-American Grain: Call-and-Response in Twentieth-Century Black Fiction*, Middletown, Connecticut: Wesleyan University Press, 1990

Cooke, Michael G., *Afro-American Literature in the Twentieth Century: The Achievement of Intimacy*, New Haven, Connecticut, and London: Yale University Press, 1984

Davis, Arthur P., *From the Dark Tower: Afro-American Writers 1900 to 1960*, Washington, D.C.: Howard University Press, 1974

Dixon, Melvin, *Ride Out the Wilderness: Geography and Identity in Afro-American Literature*, Urbana: University of Illinois Press, 1987

Margolies, Edward, *Native Sons: A Critical Study of Twentieth-Century Negro American Authors*, Philadelphia: J.B. Lippincott, 1968

Criticism of twentieth-century African-American literature is diverse and eclectic. Early works tend to be historical surveys of basic themes, structures, and canonical writers. Later productions are more various, choosing instead to trace more narrowly focused tropes among select groups of writers, whose works reflect the critic's particular concerns.

MARGOLIES examines twentieth-century African-American literature in an effort to locate "the Negro's evaluation of his historical and cultural experience in this century: the Southern community, the continuing migration to the cities, the urban proletariat, miscegenation and interracial love, the Negro church, the expatriate point of view, the new nationalism, and so on". Such a broad range of inquiry necessarily results in a general history of letters, with an emphasis on the way in which literature addresses itself to contemporary cultural issues. Margolies is particularly interested in trying to pin down aspects of what he refers to as "Negro" identity, as a way, it would seem, of distinguishing African-American literature from Anglo-American literature produced in the twentieth century. Though Margolies does examine literary details and symbols, which might be helpful for first-time readers, his approach is outdated both in its condescending attitude toward the fiction, and in his reliance on "culture" as the interpretive basis from which to engage the novels.

DAVIS' work is intended, as he explains in his Introduction, to address "the classroom needs of Negro literature or black studies courses; indeed, it has grown out of the teaching of such courses". Organized chronologically by author, each section provides necessary biographical context, and offers brief, intelligent summations of the major themes in each work. Of far more use to beginning, rather than to advanced, students, the volume includes photographs of each writer discussed and ample bibliographies of both primary and secondary works. Also important is Davis's inclusion of several prominent women writers within his twentieth-century canonical formulation, including Zora Neale Hurston, Jessie Fauset, Nella Larsen, Alice Walker, Gwendolyn Brooks, Ann Petry, and Lorraine Hansberry.

COOKE is one of the earliest critics to examine the trope of "signifying" in African-American literature. He argues that signifying constitutes one of the hallmarks of African-American creativity and verbal expression in that it is "a way of using words that mean one acceptable thing to resonate with or *signify* another of a dangerous or insubordinate or forbidden character". Cooke's aim is to illuminate what he identifies as "the essential structure of Afro-American literature in our century", which is "the *intrinsic development* of this literature out of the secret matrix of signifying and the blues into successive conditions of (1) *self-veiling*, (2) *solitude*, (3) *kinship*, and (4) *intimacy*". This final category marks what Cooke envisions as the "achievement" of African-American literature, where specific fictions represent the "condition in which the Afro-American protagonist (male or female, pugilist or philosopher, activist or ascetic) is depicted as realistically enjoying a sound and clear orientation toward the self and the world". Cooke traces these antecedent developments of intimacy through the works of early twentieth-century writers, such as James Weldon Johnson, Jean Toomer, and Claude McKay, but he contends that it is not until the artistic production of Robert Hayden (with whom he pairs Alice Walker) that fully formulated representations of intimacy appear. Cooke's range of authors and interests in this work is sweeping, beginning with Charles W. Chesnutt and ending with the contemporary writers Ishmael Reed, David Bradley, and John Edgar Wideman. Though his argument is somewhat restricted by the paradigm of intimacy, this work is an illuminating reading of the ways in which twentieth-century African-American literature moves toward the goal of representing a fully grounded and creative self in a hostile and racist environment.

BYERMAN organizes his examination of contemporary African-American fiction through what he argues is an artistic rejection of the ideological inflexibility embodied by the political prescriptions of the Black Arts movement during the 1960s, in favor of the more syncretic imaginative approach evidenced in Ralph Ellison's *Invisible Man*. He suggests that what makes this novel "a crucial text for contemporary black fictionists is its combining of traditional Afro-American themes and devices with the stylistic and structural methods of modernist literature". Byerman contends that like Ellison, many of the most prominent contemporary writers – James Alan McPherson, Ernest J. Gaines, Toni Cade Bambara, Alice Walker, LeRoi Jones, Toni Morrison, Ishmael Reed, Leon Forrest, and Clarence Major – "have shaped a technically sophisticated body of literature by combining the methods of modern fiction making with the materials of folk culture". As a consequence, throughout his work Byerman focuses on this dialectic impulse in contemporary fiction, providing close readings informed by their resonance of cultural forms, attitudes, and conflicts.

DIXON's study examines "the ways in which Afro-American writers, often considered homeless, alienated from mainstream culture, and segregated in negative environments, have used language to create alternative landscapes where black culture and identity can flourish apart from any marginal, prescribed 'place'". His intent is "to show how images of journeys, conquered spaces, imagined havens, and places of refuge have produced not only a deliverance from slavery to freedom, but, more important, a transformation from rootlessness to rootedness for both author and protagonist". Dixon initially orients his argument in the lyrics of slave songs, and the perilous geography of the passage from slavery to freedom in the escape to the North chronicled in numerous slave narratives. Subsequent chapters investigate geography, both structurally and thematically in the works of Jean Toomer, Claude McKay, Richard Wright, Ellison, LeRoi Jones, Hurston, Walker, James Baldwin, and Morrison. Despite the far-reaching relevance of his thematic focus, many of Dixon's readings tend to be somewhat superficial, alluding to the significance of geography rather than demonstrating its centrality to the novels in question.

CALLAHAN's intriguing study chronicles the fundamental importance of voice in African-American narrative, especially the mode of call-and-response as "a distinctively African and African-American form of discourse in speech and story, sermons and songs". Beginning with his own history, as the ethnically ambiguous son of an Irish-American family, Callahan positions both himself and his work within a culture affected by the barriers, the boundaries, and the broad dimensions of language. Intrigued by the relationship between performer and audience, Callahan argues that in the necessarily distanced genre of fiction:

> ... African-American writers use the act of voice as a metaphor for the process of change. Alert to the participatory quality of oral storytelling, black writers imbue their fiction with the improvisatory energy and testamental ritual of the oral tradition. In their hands call-and-response evolves into a resilient literary device that persuades readers to become symbolic and then perhaps actual participants in the task of image-making, of storytelling. As a narrative technique adapted from the forms of music and storytelling, call-and-response opens up a potential relationship between writer and reader analogous to the human situation that exists between performers and their audience.

Examining individual novels by writers such as Toomer, Hurston, Ellison, Gaines, and Walker, Callahan advances rich, complex, skilfully argued, and well illustrated readings, which deftly balance their investigations of both art and politics.

DEBORAH CARLIN

African-American Writers: Recent and Contemporary

Bigsby, C.W.E., *The Second Black Renaissance: Essays in Black Literature*, Westport, Connecticut: Greenwood Press, 1980

Butler-Evans, Elliott, *Race, Gender, and Desire: Narrative Strategies in the Fiction of Toni Cade Bambara, Toni Morrison, Alice Walker*, Philadelphia: Temple University Press, 1989

Butterfield, Stephen, *Black Autobiography in America,* Amherst: University of Massachusetts Press, 1974

Byerman, Keith, *Fingering The Jagged Grain: Tradition and Form in Recent Black American Fiction*, Athens: University of Georgia Press, 1985

Callahan, John F., *In the African-American Grain: The Pursuit of Voice in Twentieth-Century Black Fiction*, Urbana: University of Illinois Press, 1988; 2nd edition, as *In the African-American Grain: Call and Response in Twentieth-Century Black Fiction*, Middletown, Connecticut: Wesleyan University Press, 1990

Christian, Barbara, *Black Women Novelists: The Development of a Tradition, 1892–1976*, Westport, Connecticut: Greenwood Press, 1980

Crouch, William J., *New Black Playwrights: An Anthology*, Baton Rouge: Louisiana State University Press, 1968

Evans, Mari (ed.), *Black Women Writers (1950–1980): A Critical Evaluation*, New York: Anchor Press, 1984

Gayle, Addison, Jr., *The Way of the New World: The Black Novel in America*, New York: Anchor Press, 1975

Harris, Norman, *Connecting Times: The Sixties in Afro-American Fiction*, Jackson: University Press of Mississippi, 1988

Henderson, Stephen (ed.), *Understanding The New Black Poetry: Black Speech and Black Music as Poetic References*, New York: William Morrow, 1973

Lee, A. Robert (ed)., *Black Fiction: New Studies in the Afro-American Novel,* London: Vision Press, 1980; New York: Barnes & Noble, 1980

Lee, A. Robert, *Black American Fiction since Richard Wright* (Pamphlets in American Studies, 11), London: British Association of American Studies, 1983

Melhem, D.H., *Heroism in the New Black Poetry*, Lexington: University Press of Kentucky, 1990

Pryse, Marjorie, and Hortense J. Spillers (eds.), *Conjuring: Black Women, Fiction, and Literary Tradition*, Bloomington: Indiana University Press, 1985

Willis, Susan, *Specifying: Black Women Writing The American Experience*, Madison: University of Wisconsin Press, 1987; London: Routledge, 1990

If, for America both black and white, the 1920s signified the era of "the New Negro" – the Harlem-centred flowering of African-American art, thought, and writing – so the postwar years are now thought to have given rise to the second black "renaissance". Here, across the literary spectrum, have been styles and voices to take up, and overlap with, the politics of Civil Rights and Black Power and its residues into the Clinton 1990s. Few accounts give a better early overview than BIGSBY, a wide-ranging estimate, which begins with Richard Wright, Ralph Ellison, and James Baldwin, covers a body of subsequent fiction from John A. Williams to Ishmael Reed, and maps the rise of a contemporary black autobiography along with black drama and poetry. This efflorescence Bigsby centres in the metaphor of a "risen Lazarus", a new embodiment of African-American feeling and expression.

HARRIS develops an essentially thematic view of key African-American texts which address the 1960s, above all "black involvement in Vietnam, the civil rights movement, and the black power movement". He analyzes "serial" war-fiction like John A. Williams's *Captain Blackman* (1972), a jazz-narrative like Wesley Brown's *Tragic Magic* (1978), a key political and Civil Rights novel like Alice Walker's *Meridian* (1976), and ideologically sophisticated "Black Power" texts like John McClusky's *Look What They Done to My Song* (1974) and John O. Killens's *The Cotillion, or, One Good Bull is Half the Herd* (1971). An epilogue is offered in a view of Ishmael Reed's "Neo-HooDoo" novel, *The Last Days of Lousiana Red* (1974), as developing an "anti-reductionist", syncretic view of African-American culture.

GAYLE established his name as a leading proponent of the "Black Aesthetic", black art to be judged by the black community and black political standards. His panoramic study, if marred by errors of plot-summary and dates, develops a full, "committed" view of the African-American novel. Awkwardnesses are frequent, symptomatically his judgement of Ralph Ellison's *Invisible Man* (1952) as "an otherwise superb novel" as he calls it, but whose "central flaw ... is ... attributable more to Ellison's political beliefs than to artistic deficiency". HENDERSON takes on postwar black poetry from generally shared assumptions, a critique/anthology aimed, even so, at particularizing the imaginative "blackness" of black poetry – whether blues or folklore, language or measure. MELHEM confirms how much cultural-political terms of reference have moved on, with interviews and evaluations of Gwendolyn Brooks, Dudley Randall, Haki R. Madhibuti (Don R. Lee), Sonia Sanchez, Jayne Cortez, and Amiri Baraka (LeRoi Jones) as a line of "heroic" poet-singers.

BYERMAN take his bearings from *The Invisible Man*, arguing for the influence on contemporary African-American writing of a historic legacy begun in slavery, of folklore, conjure, blues, jazz, spirituals – overall, as it were, the rich, necessary play of oral telling and texture. He offers careful diagnostic readings of James Alan McPherson, Ernest J. Gaines, Toni Cade Bambara, and Alice Walker, together with an account of the modernist/postmodernist turn of Gayl Jones, Toni Morrison, Ishmael Reed, Leon Forrest, and Clarence Major. My own (LEE's) 1980 collection amounts to 11 original essays offering re-evaluations of Richard Wright, Ralph Ellison, and James Baldwin, and moving into more composite readings of black womanist fiction, Harlem-centred novels, Baraka as activist-writer, Reed's "Neo-HooDooism" as aesthetic, "blackness' as itself a genre – a style of fabulation – and the emerging new cadre of black postmodern fiction writers. My (LEE's) 1983 pamphlet puts this achievement into shorter span, from "Richard Wright and the Wright Tradition" through to "The Line of Experiment". CALLAHAN, "an Irish-American writing about black American writers", seeks to decipher some of the "black" textual devices in fiction from Zora Neale Hurston to Alice Walker, techniques of call-and-response, oral-into-written "speechifying", and the gendering of narrative voice.

CHRISTIAN, after a Prologue outlining black women's writing from Frances Ellen Watkins Harper and Jessie Fauset to Zora Neale Hurston and Gwendolyn Brooks, develops a black-feminist (more accurately, in Alice Walker's term, a "black-womanist") anatomy of three pre-eminent contemporaries – Paule Marshall, Morrison, and Walker. The emphasis falls upon "womanism" as a continuity of a gendered wisdom and resource. The essay-collection put together by PRYSE and SPILLERS begins from slave narrative, tackles Fauset and other 1920s' black women writers, offers a shrewd "placing" of early moderns like Margaret Walker and Ann Petry, and concludes with close readings of Morrison, the science-fiction writer Octavia E. Butler, and Bambara's historical satire *The Salt Eaters* (1980). Two, more inclusive essays address the New World as a black sense of place (Hortense Spillers), and black fiction whose concern is both to refract and enact self-identity (Barbara Christian). A matching compendium of interpretations is to be found in EVANS, which consists of reprints of essays on poets from Margaret Walker to Maya Angelou, Gwendolyn Brooks to Nikki Giovanni. WILLIS takes a more historicist, and implicitly Marxian, view of African-American women's recent writing, a sequence of readings of Hurston, Marshall, Morrison, Walker, and Bambara, which emphasises the rites of passage from girlhood to womanhood, South to North, and the "journey home" to Dixie, the Caribbean, and Africa. For Willis the key lies in attitudes to work, capitalism, and the nature of black woman-centred community. BUTLER-EVANS, on the other hand, brings an array of deconstructive approaches to bear – Bambara, Morrison and Walker put under a "mix of semiotic, narrative, feminist and neo-Marxist theory".

The new black drama has a practitioner and critic-anthologist in CROUCH, his account of 1960s playwrights, theatres, and his selections of representative writing being a most useful starting point for looking at the renaissance that found its best-known instance in Baraka's *Dutchman* (1964). BUTTERFIELD does much the same for African-American autobiography, a line of black "first-person singular" writing from slave narrative to James Baldwin, Malcolm X, and Maya Angelou, seen as the "dialectic between what you wish to become and what society has determined you are".

A. ROBERT LEE

Agrarians *see* Fugitives and Agrarians

Albee, Edward 1928–

American dramatist

Bigsby, C.W.E., "Edward Albee", in *A Critical Introduction to Twentieth-Century American Drama, Volume 2: Tennessee Williams, Arthur Miller, Edward Albee*, Cambridge and New York: Cambridge University Press, 1984

Cohn, Ruby, *Edward Albee*, Minneapolis: University of Minnesota Press, 1969

Debusscher, Gilbert, *Edward Albee: Tradition and Renewal*, translated by Anne D. Williams, Brussels: American Studies Center, 1967

Kolin, Philip C., and J. Madison Davis (eds.), *Critical Essays on Edward Albee*, Boston: G.K. Hall, 1986

Roudané, Matthew C., *Understanding Edward Albee*, Columbia: University of South Carolina Press, 1987

Edward Albee's remarkable critical and popular renaissance in the mid-1990s – hailed by the *Village Voice* as "one of the happiest events in the history of American playwriting" and capped by the dramatist's third Pulitzer Prize (for *Three Tall Women*) – offers an excellent vantage point for reviewing more than three decades of Albee criticism.

DEBUSSCHER's short but influential study – the first book-length work on Albee – offers succinct analyses of the pre-1967 plays, including adaptations. Steeped in the contemporary critical debates that surrounded Albee's early offerings, the book nonetheless locates the plays within broad historical traditions: the Ibsen- and Strindberg-influenced modern American drama on the one hand, and the postwar French absurdist drama on the other. Debusscher lauds Albee for successfully synthesizing these traditions, for experimenting – like Eugene O'Neill – with numerous genres (naturalism, surrealism, expressionism, symbolism, farce, tragicomedy, and allegory), and for developing a dazzling theatrical style that fuses "minute observation . . . and wild invention". Yet Debusscher suspects Albee's moral intent. Echoing the now too-dated charge of early Albee critics – and drawing too heavily on scattered biographical details – Debusscher denounces Albee as a nihilist soaked in sexuality, impotence, and death, savaging society merely to validate his private obsessions. Some of Debusscher's views significantly color several later studies.

COHN's incisive and densely packed 48-page book – one of four Albee studies to appear in 1969 – remains the best introduction to the vision and craft of his early works up to *A Delicate Balance*. In these plays, Cohn finds "the existentialist view of an Outsider who suffers at the hands of the

Establishment – social, moral, or religious". Although, like most early critics, Cohn notes the affinities to the existentialists and absurdists, she emphasizes that Albee's central concern with demolishing the illusions that shield man from reality is distinctly different from the Europeans' focus on dramatizing the alogicality of that reality. Since facing mortality is equivalent to facing reality in Albee, Cohn reveals how a recurrent death motif darkens the plays. Yet she argues that, unlike O'Neill and Arthur Miller, Albee does not strain for tragedy, a testimony to his skill as a dramatist. Cohn praises Albee for creating "the most adroit dialogue ever heard on the American stage" (a subject developed fully in her *Dialogue in American Drama*, Bloomington: Indiana University Press, 1971) and unearths a wealth of allusions and patterns, which illuminate a dramaturgy forged out of a counterpoint of "interrogation and repetition, familiar phrase and diversified resonance, repartee and monologue, minute gesture and cosmic sweep, comic wit and a sense of tragedy".

BIGSBY paints a complex and finely etched portrait of Albee, extending and refining his previous assessments in *Albee* (Edinburgh: Oliver & Boyd, 1969) and *Edward Albee: A Collection of Critical Essays* (Englewood Cliffs, New Jersey: Prentice-Hall, 1975). Bigsby weaves analyses of Albee's biography, early unpublished verse and drama, and authorial commentary, as well as developments in American theatrical and cultural history, to present some of the most astute criticism of the major works through *The Lady from Dubuque*. Albee's enduring concern with man's "retreat from individuality and moral responsibility", Bigsby argues, approaches a metaphysical seriousness rarely equalled by other American dramatists. Rarely matched, too, according to Bigsby, are Albee's linguistic skills and his uncompromising insistence on experimentation, even at the cost of theatrical and critical attention. Still, Bigsby acknowledges the attenuation of Albee's moral concerns under pressure from a darkening mood and the consequent diminishment in immediacy and conviction in his later plays.

KOLIN and DAVIS present a remarkably comprehensive and representative picture of Albee's critical reception from *The Zoo Story* to *The Man Who Had Three Arms*, surpassing the range of the other four collections of essays on Albee to date. Kolin and Davis offer 16 reviews by such critics as Henry Hewes, Robert Brustein, John Gassner, Walter Kerr, Clive Barnes, and Brendan Gill, and they provide the first English translation of Albee's first two reviews. The bulk of the book consists of 20 essays by a cross-section of Albee scholars, who investigate broad issues like absurdism, language, and literary antecedents, as well as furnish exegesis of individual plays. The selections are rounded off by a new interview and a brief bibliography of interviews. Kolin and Davis augment their material with an extensive 40-page analysis of bibliographic resources, book-length studies, reviews, and essays. They conclude that while Albee reveals recurring themes, imagery, and techniques, "the major consistency and strength of his drama is a constant searching, changing, and evolving to find new modes of expression. Criticizing him for changing is like damning Picasso for not remaining a Cubist".

ROUDANÉ offers sensitive and finely nuanced readings of Albee's original works up to *The Man Who Had Three Arms*. Marshalling previous scholarship and examining the plays anew, he demonstrates that although Albee almost obsessively returns to such subjects as death, cruelty, and individual isolation, the dramatist's intent is profoundly compassionate – to jolt his audience into "catharsis, existential growth, and an ultimately affirmative, life-giving experience". While Roudané regards this as Albee's signal contribution, he also praises him for infusing fresh life into American drama through his brilliant dialogue, skilful blending of European and American dramatic conventions, dedicated experimentation, and, above all, his high moral seriousness. In Roudané's overview, Albee transcends O'Neill's deterministic vision and Miller's and Tennessee Williams's essentially naturalistic preoccupations. Linking aspects of biography, American society, and European artistic movements (especially existentialism and some elements of the "Theatre of Cruelty"), Roudané shows how personal, public, and aesthetic currents converge in Albee's plays.

RAKESH H. SOLOMON

Alcott, Louisa May 1832–1888

American novelist and short-story writer

Elbert, Sarah, *A Hunger for Home: Louisa May Alcott and "Little Women"*, Philadelphia: Temple University Press, 1984; revised edition, as *A Hunger for Home: Louisa May Alcott's Place in American Culture*, New Brunswick, New Jersey: Rutgers University Press, 1987

Fetterley, Judith, "*Little Women*: Alcott's Civil War", in *Feminist Studies*, 5, 1979

Marsella, Joy A., *The Promise of Destiny: Children and Women in the Short Stories of Louisa May Alcott*, Westport, Connecticut: Greenwood Press, 1983

Saxton, Martha, *Louisa May: A Modern Biography of Louisa May Alcott*, Boston: Houghton Mifflin, 1977; London: André Deutsch, 1978

Showalter, Elaine, "*Little Women*: The American Female Myth", in her *Sister's Choice: Tradition and Change in American Women's Writing*, New York: Oxford University Press, 1991; Oxford: Clarendon Press, 1991

Stern, Madeleine B. (ed.), *Critical Essays on Louisa May Alcott*, Boston: G.K. Hall, 1984

Strickland, Charles, *Victorian Domesticity: Families in the Life and Art of Louisa May Alcott*, University: University of Alabama Press, 1985

Until recently, literary critics have focused almost exclusively on the biographical and historical contexts of Alcott's writing and her most well-known work, *Little Women*. However, the discovery and reprinting of her pseudonymous sensation fiction in the mid-1970s, combined with a growing interest in nineteenth-century American women writers by a new generation of feminist scholars, has opened the way for more complex and wide-ranging analyses of her work. Much of the critical debate centres on the nature and extent of Alcott's feminism and the quality of her work. She has been read as both a conservative, seriously flawed writer who forfeited quality for a reliable income, and, alternatively, as a radical feminist whose works have been undervalued by the literary establishment. The truth probably lies somewhere in between, however, until more theoretical, in-depth readings of her adult and sensation fiction appear, any reassessment of Alcott's place in the American literary canon must remain provisional.

STERN's collection of essays is an invaluable overview of Alcott's changing stature and audience. Reprints of contemporary reviews, excerpts from early critical responses, and new essays on the entire range of Alcott's fiction give a comprehensive sampling of responses to Alcott's work. The volume also provides easy access to difficult-to-obtain historical material. Particularly useful are the articles on her pseudonymous sensation thrillers and little-known adult fiction. Organized chronologically, the volume reveals the experimental nature of much her work and suggests important areas for future critical work.

SAXTON's psychological biography and study of Alcott's fiction created a stir when it appeared in 1975. It is a largely unsympathetic treatment of both the author and her works. Saxton believes *Little Women* was "a regression for both the artist and the woman" after writing her overtly angry sensation fiction and her stormy first novel, *Moods*. According to Saxton, Alcott's failure to develop emotionally and her "bitterness" gave her later works an "obligatory quality". FETTERLEY also believes the commercial success of *Little Women* stunted Alcott's artistic growth, but argues that the tension between her naturally volatile nature and the pressure to conform to mid-nineteenth century expectations of female passivity gives *Little Women* its lasting power to charm readers. Alcott's inner conflicts create a "subliminal counterpoint" to the book's overt message of the importance for women of self-discipline and sacrifice.

SHOWALTER challenges earlier views that Alcott failed to fulfil her literary promise. According to Showalter, Alcott identified with both male and female literary traditions, and all of her writing expresses her ambivalence about marriage, sex, anger, and writing. Modern critics who demand a twentieth-century vision of the autonomous woman writer are naive, because the Romantic model has serious problems for women. Showalter suggests that in *Little Women* Jo learns to exchange the male model of "genius" for a more realistic feminine model – of authorship based on training, experimentation, professionalism, and self-fulfilment, with success of the product owing not to Romantic genius, but to hard work.

ELBERT's sensitive readings of Alcott's *oeuvre* are perhaps the best general discussion of the many complexities and ambiguities of her adult fiction. The chapters on *Little Women* are especially delightful. Tracing her intertextual ties to authors as diverse as Charles Dickens, Harriet Beecher Stowe, and Susan Warner, she puts Alcott's work in a literary landscape that earlier biographical-historical approaches have tended to ignore.

STRICKLAND, a social historian, reads Alcott's fiction in the light of Victorian American views on appropriate gender roles, marriage, and child-rearing. He claims that Alcott both shaped and was strongly influenced by the century's "sentimental revolution", a revolution that endorsed the doctrine of separate spheres, and that believed women were morally superior and innately nurturing. Unlike Marsella (see below), Strickland argues that Alcott's most radical feminism emerges in her juvenile fiction, where she depicts equitable, companionate marriages, and champions spinsterhood as a viable alternative to marriage without love. Well written and engaging, Strickland's study usefully situates Alcott's depictions of familial possibilities, which range from communities of sisterhood to old-fashioned rural families, within the cultural context of the period.

MARSELLA's is the only extended study of Alcott's children's short fiction. She examines the representations of women, children, and men in the six volumes of *Aunt Jo's Scrap-Bag*, generally treating these stories as cultural documents rather than literary works. She believes these "moral tales" for children are highly conservative, promoting an ethic of "labor, love, and hope" for her young readers. The stories focus on children's ordeals, their moral conversion from inappropriate behaviour, and their positive influence on those around them. In these tales, she sees women invariably presented as "the heart of the family" and exemplars of "domestic feminism". The major shortcoming of this volume is Marsella's tendency to ignore the manner in which issues of race and class often complicate these seemingly simple stories.

SHANNON L. NICHOLS

Allegory

Astell, Ann W., *"The Song of Songs" in the Middle Ages*, Ithaca, New York: Cornell University Press, 1990
Fletcher, Angus, *Allegory: The Theory of a Symbolic Mode*, Ithaca, New York: Cornell University Press, 1964
Huot, Sylvia, *"The Romance of the Rose" and Its Medieval Readers: Interpretation, Reception, Manuscript Transmission*, Cambridge and New York: Cambridge University Press, 1993
Lewis, C.S., *The Allegory of Love: A Study in Medieval Tradition*, Oxford: Clarendon Press, 1936
MacQueen, John, *Allegory*, London: Methuen, 1970
Matter, E. Ann, *The Voice of My Beloved: "The Song of Songs" in Western Medieval Christianity*, Philadelphia: University of Pennsylvania Press, 1990
Piehler, Paul, *The Visionary Landscape: A Study in Medieval Allegory*, London: Edward Arnold, 1971
Quilligan, Maureen, *The Language of Allegory: Defining the Genre*, Ithaca, New York: Cornell University Press, 1979
Tuve, Rosemond, *Allegorical Imagery: Some Mediaeval Books and Their Posterity*, edited by Thomas P. Roche, Princeton, New Jersey: Princeton University Press, 1966
Whitman, Jon, *Allegory: The Dynamics of an Ancient and Medieval Technique*, Oxford: Clarendon Press, 1987; New York: Oxford University Press, 1987

Study of medieval allegory has developed considerably since C.S. Lewis wrote his ground-breaking work in 1936. Although it continues to be quoted, Lewis's work is rooted in Greek philosophical distinctions between allegory and symbol which are not now considered relevant to the medieval period, where allegory had its roots in a discourse of religious meaning by which the created world and its recorded history were translated into the evolving plan of divine creativity. In this way, even monastic chroniclers were recorders of a symbolic meaning beyond historiography. However, the school of D.W.

Robertson took this too far in the 1960s by asserting that all medieval texts, even such wholly secular works as Chaucer's *fabliaux*, were to be interpreted in terms of allegories, whose underlying meaning demonstrated Augustine's division between *cupiditas* and *caritas*, love of this world and the next (see Robertson's "The Doctrine of Charity in Medieval Gardens: A Topical Approach Through Symbolism and Allegory", *Speculum*, 1951, pp. 24–49, reprinted in his *Essays in Medieval Culture*, 1980). This tendency is now much modified, and the best commentaries on secular allegorical texts such as the *Roman de la rose* emphasize the element of play in the application of scholastic techniques to mundane topics. As Tuve observed, the authors of the *Rose* do not copy explanations of charity from Augustine and Bernard, but the theologians clarify the comedy of love's folly in that text. Much critical commentary is currently directed to the biblical *The Song of Songs* as a source text for allegorical method and *topoi* in the Middle Ages. Following the work of Tuve, recent criticism is directed at the importance of image as index of allegorical meaning.

LEWIS's study follows Goethe's distinction between symbol and allegory: allegory makes concrete the intangible, such as human emotion, while symbol interprets the "real" world as a reflex of the supra-sensible world of ultimate reality. He therefore labours to justify allegory to a readership which, he assumes, favours the symbolic mode, locating the source of allegory within Latin rhetoric and the move from the fifth-century on to reappropriate pagan classical epic to Christian ideology by allegorizing texts such as *The Aeneid*. He briefly sketches the allegorical impulse from Prudentius and Martianus Capella through to the twelfth-century platonists of the School of Chartres, who influenced Guillaume de Lorris and Jean de Meun in the *Roman de la rose*. However, Lewis is blind to the erotic symbolism of, for example, the "garden of love" because of his naivety and his alignment with nineteenth-century Romantic criticism. His detailed interpretation of the *Rose* is innocent of the satire that modern critics identify in the work of both its writers. Modern criticism does not regard de Meun's method as "digressive" and does not, like Lewis, consider the encyclopedic nature of that poem a "fault fatal to [it]". Because Lewis grounds his discussion in courtly love, he seeks to identify in medieval allegory a blend of philosophical and courtly ethics where modern critics identify ironic counterplay between the two. Lewis's analysis of the works of Chaucer, John Gower, and Edmund Spenser attempts to isolate what he calls "radical allegory", which can be reduced to literal narration, and his lack of sympathy with the impetus of medieval allegory shows in his disapproval of much of the work he appraises: Gower nods, Chaucer can be clumsy, and in the fifteenth-century allegory comes "near death", reviving with Spenser's "nervously masculine" balancing of the homiletic and erotic modes (although Lewis deliberately ignores his political message). Lewis is master of the choice apophthegm and useful for narrative summaries of many minor allegorical texts, which the average reader may never expect to encounter.

MacQUEEN supplies a history of allegory from Graeco-Roman times, including biblical allegory and allegorical approaches to historiography. In the fourth of the six chapters the famous four-level medieval allegorical system is outlined, with lengthy quotations from Boccaccio, Bede, Aquinas, and Dante's Letter to Can Grande. Explanation of the application of such theories to secular works is not sufficient, and the brevity imposed by the restricted format of the series to which this book belongs means that the important discussion of pyschological allegory in Chapter 5 is very curtailed, while Chapter 6 on satire merely lists post-medieval writers and makes a brief nod in the direction of drama with Skelton's *Magnificence*.

FLETCHER fails to divest his study of the preoccupations of twentieth-century hermeneutics: his approach is profoundly scholarly, but ultimately rooted in Freudian psychology. He demonstrates the operation of allegory in modern, medieval, and Renaissance texts, and his study ranges across all periods from the ancient Greeks. Fletcher revives the term *kosmos* for the ornamental, linguistic, and verbal effects of the allegorical image. Like Lewis, he focuses on the literal narrative; as his assertion that "allegories are based on parallels between two levels of being that correspond to each other, the one supposed by the reader, the other literally presented in the fable" indicates, he is not alert to the witty allegory that deconstructs the gap between these supposed parallels (for example, Langland surprises the reader by shifting in and out of allegorical representation). His attempts to "explain" allegorical theory in terms of everyday experience and his conclusion that allegories are "monuments to our ideals" (and are currently manifest in film scores) seem simplistic beside more modern analyses.

The dilemma of the relationship between symbol and allegory is dextrously resolved by WHITMAN's study which, though it demonstrates ironical application of allegory in texts from Homer to Silvestris's *Cosmographia* in the mid-twelfth century, does not aim to present a history of allegory, but rather to explore its operation. The first chapter deftly resolves the symbolism/allegory polarity by defining two traditions of allegory, that of *interpretation*, which "claims to discover the truth hidden beneath a text", and that of *composition*, which "is essentially a grammatical or rhetorical technique" and largely operates through personification. In both types, there is an increasing divergence from the initial correspondence. Where this is not the case, the result is a feature of allegory that Fletcher termed its "anaesthesia". By the late twelfth century, the two types of allegory blend constructively "as if philosophy and rhetoric . . . were each developing by exploring the strategies of the other". The clarity of presentation make this work far less abstruse than its topic suggests, and it clarifies earlier writers such as Boethius and Martianus Capella and illuminates the essence of the twelfth-century renaissance as a whole.

QUILLIGAN defines allegory as a genre that codifies readers' expectations. She does not accept that all interpretation is allegory (as did Northrop Frye) but proposes that allegorical significance is often signalled by wordplay – not the literal, but the "letteral", meaning is the base level of allegory. This work is exciting because it correlates procedures in medieval and Renaissance works with those in modern ones, Spenser with Thomas Pynchon, Langland with Nathaniel Hawthorne and Herman Melville.

A vigorous and far from outmoded study of allegory in operation is TUVE's enjoyable and dextrous analysis of allegorical texts from the Middle Ages and Renaissance. These include

Frere Lorens' *Somme le Roi*, Guillaume de Digulleville's *Pélérinage de la vie humaine*, the *Roman de la rose*, and Spenser's *Faerie Queene*, to each of which a chapter is devoted. The wealth of detail in the analyses at times confuses, especially in the introductory chapter "Problems and Definitions". Tuve makes an important distinction between authorial allegory and "imposed allegory", the interpretation of later commentators, whose interpretations can be shown to be invalid. Her reading of de Meun's ironies is subtle and judicious.

Where Fleming attempts a Freudian reading of allegory, PIEHLER's is systematically Jungian. He modifies Lewis's distinction between allegory and symbol by claiming that allegory represents states of mind, while symbol represents an invisible world, or one in which our experience "is but the copy of an archetype". This archetype he traces back to the dawn of history and the "seminal images" of primitive religious rites. His exploration of landscape in the medieval allegories of Alain de Lille, Hanville, the *Rose*, Dante's *Commedia*, and the Middle English *Pearl* reveals the close association between "the inner and outer" worlds which was lost, with resulting "psychic dislocation" in later ages. This polemic is less persuasive than the critical reading of the texts themselves.

More profound than either Lewis's or Robertson's treatment of the *Roman de la rose* is HUOT's study of historically contemporary responses to the *Rose*, evidenced in the many medieval manuscripts, which reveal, in their rearrangements, excisions, interpolations, and illuminations, that contemporary readers recognized throughout the poem that its "play of registers – the sacred, the rational, the natural, the erotic" was essential to its poetics, so that the text "played an important part in the emergence of the very notion of French literature". This work, taking inspiration from a 1977 study of *Rose* iconography by Fleming, is not a study of the allegory of the poem as such, but offers a far more reliable interpretation of it than Lewis or Robertson.

ASTELL's and MATTER's studies of an important text in the tradition of biblical exegesis and the allegorical mode demonstrate the importance of *The Song of Songs* in yielding texts for medieval mariology, eschatology, and the piety of *imitatio Christi*, which deployed them allegorically in a development from rabbinical exegesis of *The Song*. These are extended and more sophisticated studies of a text which Robertson handled too inflexibly. Matter follows modern critical practice in extending inductively the Aristotelian categories of genre previously followed by Romantic criticism and the New Critics, and has a particularly good discussion of allegorical theory. Astell examines closely Richard Rolle's Latin and English works, *Pearl*, and the Middle English lyrics.

ROSAMUND S. ALLEN

Alliterative Tradition

Cable, T., *The English Alliterative Tradition*, Philadelphia: University of Pennsylvania Press, 1991
Duggan, H.N., "The Shape of the B-Verse in Middle English Alliterative Poetry", in *Speculum*, 61(3), 1986
Duggan, H.N., "Notes Towards a Theory of Langland's Meter", in *Yearbook of Langland Studies*, 1, 1987
Duggan, H.N., "Final -*e* and the Rhythmic Structure of the B-Verse in Middle English Alliterative Poetry", in *Modern Philology*, 86(2), 1988
Lawton, D., *Middle English Alliterative Poetry and Its Literary Background: Seven Essays*, Cambridge: D.S. Brewer, 1982
Oakden, J.P., *Alliterative Poetry in Middle English*, 2 vols., Manchester: Manchester University Press, 1930–35
Pearsall, Derek, "Alliterative Poetry", in his *Old English and Middle English Poetry* (Volume 1, Routledge History of English Poetry series), London and Boston: Routledge, 1977
Shepherd, G., "The Nature of Alliterative Poetry in Late Medieval England", in *Middle English Literature: British Academy Gollancz Lectures*, edited by J.A. Burrow, Oxford and New York: Oxford University Press, 1989
Turville Petre, Thorlac, *The Alliterative Revival*, Cambridge: D.S. Brewer, 1977; Totowa, New Jersey: Rowman & Littlefield, 1977
Turville Petre, Thorlac (ed.), *Alliterative Poetry of the Later Middle Ages: An Anthology*, London: Routledge, 1989

Much non-Chaucerian Middle English poetry is written in alliterating strong-stress metre. The major works are embodied in this rich and flexible tradition in which chronicle, epic, legend, lyric, dream-vision narrative, satire, elegy, and debate can all be found. The copious literary criticism is found almost entirely in works on the well-known individual texts, such as William Langland's *Piers Plowman*, *The Alliterative Morte Arthure,* and *Sir Gawain and the Green Knight*. In the case of undeservedly lesser-known works, such as *Susannah* and *St Erkenwald*, criticism is largely confined to academic journals, as are writings on such specialised but vital aspects as geographical and historical contextualisation, authorship and dating (though see Pearsall and Turville Petre, below). The origins, authorship, dating and provenance of the texts, and the specialised subject matter, diction, and collocations of the fourteenth-century "High Revival" have been researched and discussed throughout the century, with arguments about regionalism and whether the Revival was such, or a continuity of Old English verse form; but the emphasis in commentary on writings in the alliterative long line has recently shifted to metrical and theoretical studies, which attempt to account for the prosody of the long line. Recent hypotheses in this field have considerable implications for editorial practice, and the most prominent of these theorists are picked out here.

OAKDEN's large investigation, remarkable for its time, is the first comprehensive survey of the genre. It concentrates largely on dialect for the sake of geographical placing, and on discernible patterns of metre, alliterative diction, and collocations, many of which appear in lists and tables. Like much pioneering work, it makes enjoyable reading, but it is, sadly, no longer very serviceable because MS studies, lexicology, dialectology, and new critical editions have inevitably expanded knowledge, and also because new theories of the long line and provenance have been developed.

SHEPHERD's outstanding short lecture is fundamental to criticism of the tradition. It deals with the mnemonic nature of alliteration, problems of genre in the corpus, and the active memory of the alliterative poet. It is the most sophisticated and literary piece of generic criticism in this field.

PEARSALL's short, but rich, chapter is a scholarly and brilliantly sensible introduction to Middle English alliterative texts. It comprises 11 sections, three of which are on main texts (*Morte Arthure*, the *Gawain* poems, and *Piers Plowman*), and the others covering aspects such as origins, alliteration and rhyme, early poems of the Revival, techniques of alliterative verse, the "classic corpus", and historical, stanzaic, and other alliterative poems. Pearsall brings remarkable knowledge to the subject, and although the chapter purports to be merely an introduction to the material, it displays criticism of a high order.

TURVILLE PETRE's 1977 study is the first full-length reader's guide to the literature. Focusing on texts and their dates and provenances, as well as on language and metre, it remains the standard, full guide to the corpus, and is invaluable for understanding of the subject, as well as for its wide-ranging, bibliographical survey of texts. Turville Petre's studies in metricality and in alliterative patterning, undertaken in collaboration with Duggan, can be surveyed in their re-editing of *The Wars of Alexander* for the Early English Text Society (SS 10, Oxford, 1989) – an edition metrically emended according to hypotheses, particularly concerning metrical constraints in the second hemistich. The introduction to this edition is a very valuable digest of this work. TURVILLE PETRE's 1989 anthology has extremely useful, up-to-date, and accessible introductions to the fine selection of texts, and makes an excellent reader's introduction to the literature.

LAWTON's book marks an important advance in scholarship. It is a collection of speculative, very sound, academic essays on diverse aspects of the Middle English alliterative tradition. The authors – Angus McIntosh, Derek Pearsall, Rosalind Field, W.R.J. Barron, A.I. Doyle, and Anne Middleton – investigate the various contexts for the Revival in the literary culture of medieval England: the poems themselves, their metrical and historical background, their relation to their sources and to French and Anglo-Norman writing, the manuscripts in which they survive, and the public for which they were composed. Lawton furnishes a substantial Introduction, in which he suggests origins of the Revival in rhythmic prose, and he appends a most useful bibliography.

DUGGAN's work is available only in academic journals, but has been influential in the field of metrical analysis. His theses (particularly that poets who wrote in strong-stress metre had strong rhythmic aural templates for the second half line of alliterative long lines and that the scribes, not knowing these, deranged them) are largely based on computer analyses, and are still controversial, though accepted by many scholars. The main conclusion of Duggan's work – that a poem like *Sir Gawain and the Green Knight* exists only as a single witness, by default botched by a scribe and thus not analogous with the text – has clear implications for editorial practice. More recent essays have focused on Langland's metrics.

CABLE's is an extremely interesting and important book. Flying the flag of the "New Philology", it is a theoretical and technical study of metre and prosody, underpinned by his own and others' work on Old English, final *-e*, and broader linguistic theory. This immensely thoughtful work, with its broad prospects and evolving implications, will affect much scholarship and controversy in this field, and its ideas will be disseminated in future editions and in criticism of alliterative texts and English prosody.

RUTH KENNEDY

See also **Poetry: Middle English**

American Civil-War Literature

Aaron, Daniel, *The Unwritten War: American Writers and the Civil War*, New York: Knopf, 1973

Diffley, Kathleen, *Where My Heart is Ever Turning: Civil War Stories and Constitutional Reform, 1861–1876*, Athens: University of Georgia Press, 1992

Hutton, Paul Andrew (series ed.), *Eyewitness to the Civil War* series, New York: Bantam, 1992

Masur, Louis P. (ed.), "*. . . the real war will never get in the books": Selections from Writers During the Civil War*, New York and Oxford: Oxford University Press, 1993

Sweet, Timothy, *Traces of War: Poetry, Photography, and the Crisis of the Union*, Baltimore: Johns Hopkins University Press, 1990

Wilson, Edmund, *Patriotic Gore: Studies in the Literature of the American Civil War*, New York: Oxford University Press, 1962; London: André Deutsch, 1962; reprinted, London: Hogarth Press, 1987

AARON agrees with many scholars that the Civil War itself was an American epic tailor-made for a literary counterpart. Disdained by a readership of feminized tastes, however, the "real war" was never written. American writers were nevertheless deeply affected by the conflict, though few (Walt Whitman, perhaps, being the most notable exception) were able to construct meaning from the madness. By and large, this study looks at those writers that typically come to mind when we think of the era (Nathaniel Hawthorne, Herman Melville, Whitman, William Dean Howells, Henry Adams, Henry James, and Mark Twain) – though it also examines such "minor" writers as John W. De Forest, Henry Timrod, and Mary Chesnut – and the War's effect upon them. As Aaron points out, the voices of the latter writers, though perhaps less "lit'rary", as Twain would have said, nevertheless often provide more insightful, moving commentary than many of those we most often anthologize. His attempt to balance the perspective on the War between North and South is also laudable.

WILSON attempts to provide balance in his own perspective by choosing 30 authors from both the public and private spheres. He defends his choice of non-literary sources by asserting the value of multiple perspectives in giving us a total picture. Yet, Wilson's book is sorely dated by its naturalistic approach to US history and its underlying fear of nuclear annihilation. Wilson was writing when the Cold War was at its most volatile, during the Bay of Pigs disaster and the Cuban Missile Crisis, and his personal agenda skews an otherwise insightful reading of the War. "The difference between man and the other forms of life is that man has succeeded in cultivating enough of what he calls 'morality' and 'reason' to justify what he is doing in terms of what he calls 'virtue' and 'civilization'". War, then, is a means unto itself, and constructing meaning out of it is merely an exercise to validate ourselves as something other than animalistic. Despite the seeming contradictions when he declares himself divorced from moralizing, Wilson's reading of Civil-War literature provides a perceptive appreciation of the War, its possible meaning, and the writer's attempt to deal with it.

Taking his title from Whitman's assertion that ". . . the real war will never get in the books", MASUR adopts an interdisciplinary approach by looking at the literary, social, and political writings of the War. Instead of looking for a single American *Iliad*, he argues that one can construct it by synthesizing the various sources. Masur's brief biographical sketch preceding the sample of each writer's work provides just enough context for the pieces without getting in the way of the reader's own ability to interpret them for him- or herself. Again, in the interest of multiplicity, Masur offers a healthy scope of writers for us to examine – those who are still well-known today, those who were well-known during the War but have fallen into obscurity, and those who were neither popular in their day nor widely studied today but who, nevertheless, provide us with valuable insights

SWEET's work offers an interesting look at how photography and poetry represented Americans' attempts to explain their country's use of destruction to restore order. Its strengths are evident as it examines in a new light the value of photographs as artistic creations rather than as simple illustrations. His insights into the use of pastoralism, particularly by Whitman, and its disdain, specifically by Melville, prove useful in assessing the impact of war on art and vice versa. Yet, there marches throughout Sweet's work a disturbing trend of "political correctness"; there is, in his perspective, a "right" way to view the War and a "wrong" way. Too often Sweet's ideological framework weighs down what might otherwise be a refreshing examination of the War's artistic representations, so much so that those unfamiliar with it will have great difficulty wading through his book.

DIFFLEY's study, the first in a three-volume series, offers a refreshing look at the long-neglected field of popular literature. By not limiting herself merely to authorial purpose, she is able to describe a more accurate cross-section of mid-nineteenth-century America. Indeed, the daily demands of the popular press became more important than authorial intent: "under the auspices of production conventions . . . popular narratives helped to codify the events of significant social drama for a growing audience and thereby oriented the normative culture that was taking shape". By sampling magazines across the United States, Diffley balances her study well, and sets each chapter in a historical context by assessing the political debates of the time.

HUTTON's series, though not an endeavor in "literary criticism," is a recommendation not out of place here. If we trace the history of literary criticism of this period, we can see a movement away from the assumption that the "great writers" of the day could provide the greatest insights into the War and toward the realization that those most affected by it – the soldiers, the ordinary people – were those best able to impart its significance (and the least heard for many decades). This series provides readily accessible paperback reprints of the memoirs of several of the key participants in the conflict. For an example of the value of the series, take one passage from J.L. Chamberlain's *The Passing of the Armies*: the moment when Confederate General John B. Gordon realizes that Chamberlain (charged by Grant himself with accepting the Confederate colors in surrender) is offering Gordon, his men, and their valor respect by means of a salute. Chamberlain's description of that moment is as sublime and affecting as any image in Whitman's poetry.

CHRIS POURTEAU

American Humor

Blair, Walter, *Native American Humor (1800–1900)*, New York: American Book Company, 1937; revised edition, as *Native American Humor*, San Francisco: Chandler, 1960

Blair, Walter, *Horse Sense in American Humor: From Benjamin Franklin to Ogden Nash*, Chicago: University of Chicago Press, 1942

Blair, Walter, and Hamlin Hill, *America's Humor: From Poor Richard to Doonesbury*, New York and Oxford: Oxford University Press, 1978

Clark, William Bedford, and W. Craig Turner (eds.), *Critical Essays on American Humor*, Boston: G.K. Hall, 1984

Gale, Steven H. (ed.), *Encyclopedia of American Humorists*, New York: Garland, 1988

Inge, M. Thomas (ed.), *The Frontier Humorists: Critical Views*, Hamden, Connnecticut: Archon Books, 1975

Rourke, Constance, *American Humor: A Study of the National Character*, New York: Harcourt, Brace & Co., 1931

Rubin, Louis D., Jr., *The Comic Imagination in American Literature*, New Brunswick, New Jersey: Rutgers University Press, 1973

Yates, Norris, *The American Humorist: Conscience of the Twentieth Century*, Ames: Iowa State University Press, 1964

Criticism of American humor has been afflicted and restricted, from the beginning, by a suspicion that humor is unimportant or trivial or embarrassing: by the thought that, in Woody Allen's words, "when you're writing humor, you're not sitting at the grownup table". Critical disdain may be explained by the Puritan roots of American culture, inculcating a fear of levity and playfulness; by a self-conscious worry about how American letters appeared to outsiders, particularly the British; and by unease with the generally unlettered and/or anti-intellectual tone of much early American humor. "Southwestern humor" usually recounted the uncouth doings of backwoodsmen; the "literary comedians" built much of their humor on their own pretended illiteracy. Neither gave much cause for pride to the nationalistic American literary observer.

English critics were among the first to recognize the virtues of native American humor; not surprisingly, the first essay in Clark and Turner's collection, "Slick, Downing, Crockett, Etc.", appeared in the *London and Westminster Review*. Mark Twain and Artemus Ward were appreciated much more and much earlier in England than in the United States.

Though Mark Twain published anthologies of American humor and wrote sagely about it, claiming for instance that the comic story is English, the witty story French, and the humorous story American, important native criticism of American humor really began to appear between the world wars, perhaps as a response to growing American dominance in political and economic affairs. ROURKE is a key document in this change, and study of humor is now a large and respected branch of literary criticism. Rourke announces her theme in the Foreword:

> There is scarcely an aspect of the American character to which humor is not related, few which in some sense it has not governed. It has moved into literature, not merely as an occasional touch, but as a force determining large patterns and intentions. It is a lawless element, full of surprises. It sustains its own appeal, yet its vigorous power invites absorption in that character of which it is a part.

In her early chapters she traces the appearance and development of familiar comic types – the Yankee, the tall-tale figure of the frontiers (of whom the real-life David Crockett made himself a supreme example), the comic black figure – and comic genres: burlesque theatre, comic poetry, the literary comedy of the likes of Petroleum V. Nasby. Rourke insists that humor is at the heart of American culture, and demonstrates powerfully the connections between this forceful demotic element and the "high culture" of Ralph Waldo Emerson, Herman Melville, and Walt Whitman.

BLAIR is one of the major names in the study of American humor, and his 1937 book is one of the groundbreaking works in its serious study. It begins with 180 pages of critical survey and definition, including the definition of "the requisites for 'American humor'" in both subject matter and technique. He focuses on the American character, or more properly, American types, and on such techniques as exaggeration and burlesque. The remaining nearly 400 pages contain selections from American humorous writings, beginning with "Down East Humor" (i.e., of New England, particularly Maine) in around 1830, and ending with Mark Twain. There is much unexpected and genuinely funny material here; and there is also a selected bibliography, an index of humorous writers, and a useful list of identifiable pseudonyms.

BLAIR (1942) is also a history of American humor, but with a particular thesis, that "horse sense" helps to define a particularly American brand of humor. The author defines horse sense as "the same thing as common sense, homespun philosophy, pawkiness, cracker-box philosophy, gumption, or mother-wit". Clearly Blair is defining as a virtue the very traits that made many nineteenth-century Americans dubious about their own humor. He follows his short theoretical Introduction with a chronological survey, touching on most of the usual figures and groups, including both fictional creations like "Mr. Dooley" and "Jack Downing" and real people like Benjamin Franklin, Abe Lincoln, and Davy Crockett. He brings his survey up to the twentieth century with Will Rogers and James Thurber.

YATES's book differs from most of those discussed here, in being focused on a smaller portion of the whole story of American humor – the twentieth century. He also has a more tightly focused thesis: that the humorist is an embodiment of ethical ideals. He identifies three common character types found in American humor – the rustic sage, the respectable citizen, and the worried "little man". More controversially, he argues that "these three types represent the ethical élite, those who think and who try to be 'good' men, in contrast to the hypocritical and unthinking masses". After a brief overview of the humor of the end of the nineteenth century, Yates uses his three types as a template for his survey of twentieth-century humorists, such as "crackerbarrel survivals" George Ade, Mr. Dooley, and Will Rogers, skeptics like H.L. Mencken and Ring Lardner, and "little man" humorists like Robert Benchley, Dorothy Parker, and S.J. Perelman.

The overlap between the first category and Walter Blair's "horse sense" school, and between the third category and Blair and Hill's extensive chapters (in their 1978 book) on *The New Yorker* is obvious. Yates's second category, that of the sophisticated skeptics, is the least persuasive, especially with regard to writers like Lardner and Don Marquis.

RUBIN's collection arises from a series of talks broadcast to overseas audiences over Voice of America radio. Thus, they are clearly introductory and, unlike most other titles in this list, aimed at explaining American humor to non-Americans. The 32 chapters cover, lightly, such familiar territory as Benjamin Franklin, southwestern humor, Mark Twain, and *The New Yorker*; there are also useful essays on Jewish humor, Edgar Allan Poe, Nathaniel Hawthorne, and Melville (not usually included in surveys of humor), light verse, Eudora Welty, and the Harlem Renaissance. This is a very miscellaneous collection, necessarily broader than it is deep, but the essays are written by major scholars in the study of American literature, and their standard is high.

INGE's book is dedicated to the humor of the "old Southwest" – i.e. the southeastern United States, Georgia, Tennessee, Mississippi, etc. – and to such major figures as Augustus Baldwin Longstreet, William Tappan Thompson, George Washington Harris, and Joseph Glover Baldwin, who are, basically, Mark Twain's predecessors. There are generous sections on each of the men named, folk figures – e.g., Davy Crockett – and then a section on "Impact on American Literature", including Twain, William Faulkner, and others. There is a lengthy checklist and a useful Introduction by Inge, giving overview, tracing influences on Twain and others up to the present, and (most surprising) indicating the reception of southwestern humor in Europe, including expressions of admiration by William Makepeace Thackeray, frequent reprinting in *Bentley's Miscellany*, and imitation and adaptation of southwestern tales by Charles Dickens and Thomas Hardy.

BLAIR and HILL (1978) are the joint authors of another historical book, more comprehensive than Rourke's or Blair's earlier works. The authors set themselves the task of tracing American humor, in all its varieties, from colonial times to the mid-1970s. They provide two interesting rationales for the importance of studying American humor: 1) as probably the most popular creative achievement of Americans, humor reveals a great deal about America's history, and 2) much of it, whether forgotten or still admired, is fine enough as literature to justify critical analysis. There are large sections devoted to Twain (Hamlin Hill is the author of a fine Twain biography) and sections carefully doing justice to Davy Crockett, the Yankee stereotype, and urban humorists. Roughly the last third of the book, however, gets beyond this relatively familiar, even exhaustively documented, material and concentrates on the twentieth century, with important chapters on *The New Yorker*, underground comedy, and films. It ends with discussion of taste and subversion in American humor – in the television series *All in the Family*, the cartoon strip *Doonesbury*, and comedian Lenny Bruce.

CLARK and TURNER's is a valuable collection, which includes both historical items, like the 1839 *London and Westminster Review* article (mentioned above), which argues that the books of humor under review "show that American literature has ceased to be exclusively imitative", and modern essays by leading figures like Walter Blair, Sanford Pinsker, and Hamlin Hill. There is some effort at correction of common mistakes – for instance, in Robert Micklus's "Colonial Humor: Beginning with the Butt", which attempts to correct the neglect of colonial humor by people like Walter Blair and Constance Rourke, focusing on such early works as Nathaniel Ward's "The Simple Cobler of Agawam", Thomas Morton's *New England Canaan*, and Ebenezer Cook's *The Sot-Weed Factor*. There is a good chapter on the literary comedians – Artemus Ward, Bill Arp, Petroleum V. Nasby, and others – and a good essay by Hamlin Hill on "The Future of American Humor: Through a Glass Eye, Darkly".

GALE's reference book brings together entries on 135 American and Canadian humorists, each of which contains "Biography", "Literary Analysis", "Summary", and "Bibliography". The approach is very catholic; unlike most other books on American humor, this one not only includes Canadians but also makes room for a wide range of humorists in various media, such as popular essayist and television commentator Andy Rooney, playwright Murray Schisgal, songwriter Tom Lehrer, novelist Ishmael Reed, screenwriter Terry Southern, and publisher/television personality Bennett Cerf. There are odd omissions – no entry for Artemus Ward, for instance – but this remains a useful book of reference on a large variety of humorous writers. It is arranged alphabetically rather than chronologically, and by authors' real names, with pseudonyms supplied in a separate table.

MERRITT MOSELEY

American Literary Naturalism

Conder, John, *Naturalism in American Fiction: The Classic Phase*, Lexington: University Press of Kentucky, 1984

Howard, June, *Form and History of American Literary Naturalism*, Chapel Hill: University of North Carolina Press, 1985

Michaels, Walter B., *The Gold Standard and the Logic of Naturalism: American Literature at the Turn of the Century*, Berkeley: University of California Press, 1987

Mitchell, Lee C., *Determined Fictions: American Literary Naturalism*, New York: Columbia University Press, 1989

Walcutt, Charles C., *American Literary Naturalism: A Divided Stream*, Minneapolis: University of Minnesota Press, 1974

Literary criticism of American naturalism is increasingly showing a healthy respect for a genre that was traditionally seen as over-preoccupied with the sensational, the scandalous, and lacking those qualities of "literariness" that distinguished its high-cultural counterparts.

WALCUTT's book was one of the first sustained analyses of American literary naturalism. He proposes to reconcile the three dominant critical views of naturalism – that it expresses an optimistic social purpose; that it reveals a pessimistic determinism, a philosophy of gloom and despair; and that it is incomprehensibly, hopelessly contradictory – by distinguishing between the literary work and the ideas that inform it. The key to this puzzle, he suggests, is that despite naturalism's philosophical pessimism, the novelist is equally committed to both science and reform; what this "scientist-informer" produces – a work of art – is itself, Walcutt argues, a victory, which holds out the possibility of improving the human condition. The determinism-reformism contradiction becomes the main structuring motif of the genre, albeit one of dynamic opposition rather than a concept of unity. As Walcutt argues, both of these polar terms are a part of the "meaning" of a naturalistic novel, and the antinomies between fate and hope, determinism and human will, are not only implicit in the programme of naturalism but are also repeatedly dramatised in the action of the novels. Walcutt then proceeds to illustrate this thesis with reference to Harold Frederic, Hamlin Garland, Stephen Crane, Jack London, Frank Norris, Theodore Dreiser, and James T. Farrell.

CONDER interrogates the question of whether naturalism is a meaningful term. With chapters on Crane, Norris, Dreiser, John Dos Passos, John Steinbeck, and even William Faulkner, Conder's theory is a response to a perennial problem discussed by naturalist critics: on the one hand, naturalists depict a deterministic world in which the individual is governed by nature and society; on the other hand, they examine notions of morality and the need for self-realization, both of which seem impossible in a deterministic world. For Conder, though, the perceived fact of determinism does not necessarily eradicate all allegiances to the idea of freedom – even if an author knows it to be illusory in the end. Naturalism is the school in which fiction-writers wrestle with the determinism-freedom dialectic, coming to rather sombre conclusions as expressed by Conder's canon of writers. But, as Conder argues, it is also a movement that finally discovered the means to have it both ways through its later writers, such as Faulkner and Steinbeck, who found ways for "determined-man" to become conscious of a "second-self" providing freedom. The positing of group consciousness in Steinbeck's *Grapes of Wrath*, and a consciousness of the Bergsonian "durational self" in Faulkner's *Sound and the Fury*, allow naturalistic man to be both determined and free simultaneously, thus resolving the dilemma encountered and lamented by previous naturalists. However, problems remain in Conder's attempt to broaden the canon of naturalism. A corpus of texts that includes works by writers such as John Keats, Ralph Waldo Emerson, Henry David Thoreau, Walt Whitman, and W.B. Yeats, along with writings by authors more usually classified as naturalistic, suggests that naturalism itself is no longer Conder's topic.

HOWARD focuses on naturalist writing published between 1893 and 1909, discussing not only Dreiser but also Norris and London. To a lesser extent, she draws upon the fiction of Crane and Upton Sinclair. Howard argues that genre criticism cannot be considered in purely aesthetic terms, but must consider, as well, the relation between literary form and history, and of naturalism and American naturalism. The book is offered as "a contribution to a revitalized literary history". Each of her chapters analyses a matter central to the genre of naturalism: these include detailing the relationship between mimesis and naturalism; analysing the tension between free will and determinism, the conflict between reformism and a world immune to man's efforts to change it; discussing the role of ideology in naturalism, how the genre "is shaped by and imaginatively reshapes a historical experience"; and an explication of naturalism's narrative strategies by detailing "the fluid distinction between fiction and non-fiction" in this genre. Drawing upon literary theory, and social and political history, she discusses naturalism not in terms of Charles Darwin and Herbert Spencer, but rather in light of Jacques Derrida, Louis Althusser, and Fredric Jameson. To Howard's credit, this book informs the reader not only about naturalism but also about our current critical values.

MITCHELL plays close attention to what he calls "the narrative effects of determinism". He demonstrates that the very qualities of naturalist novels traditionally singled out as unsatisfactory – their creation of characters who are implausibly and repulsively limited and their apparently ungainly style – are integral to narratives based on philosophical determinism. He goes on to argue provocatively that they constitute a challenge to "the assumptions we hold about the coherent self", disrupting "the habitual and powerful process by which we create not only ourselves but each other as responsible agents" – that, in other words, the naturalists anticipate the contemporary poststructuralist critique of the human subject. Mitchell's approach produces subtle and powerful results in his chapters on London's "To Build a Fire" and Crane's *The Red Badge of Courage*. The detail and conviction of Mitchell's demonstration of the effects of determinism and his series of sustained analyses of naturalist style are persuasive. At times, however, his analysis tends to be reductive, attending only in passing to what he calls "the medley of contradictory voices" found in naturalist novels. As such, he refuses to attend to the undoing of the consistencies he proposes or to the way in which the freedom and lack of freedom of naturalist characters depend on their position in hierarchies of class, which ascribe different levels of self-determination to different individuals.

MICHAELS' book has made a powerful impact on the redefinition of naturalism and the profession's current fascination with literature and the market. In contrast to much recent criticism, in which the economic or the historical becomes the previously repressed level of a text's meaning, Michaels refuses this allegorical mode of explication. For example, Norris's works, according to Michaels, are not *about* the gold standard. Instead, a text such as *Vandover and the Brute* exemplifies conflicting ideas of representation, which structure the dispute over the gold standard. The connection between the gold standard and the cultural logic of naturalism is for Michaels one of structural homology, not mechanical causality. As such, the structural homologies between literature and other discursive practices allow Michaels to shift the focus of his analysis from the level of the individual text or author to structures, whose effect may be of greater determination than either of these.

The structure that most interests Michaels is that of "internal difference" as it manifests itself in all literary discourse. Michaels anchors this in a particular historical moment – the rise of consumer capitalism in turn-of-the-century America. For Michaels, the discourse of naturalism is "above all obsessed with the manifestations of internal difference, or what comes to the same thing, personhood. Continually imagining the possibility of identity without difference, it is provoked by its own images into ever more powerful imaginations of identity by way of difference". Michaels proceeds to trace this particular logic as it manifests itself in each text under analysis. The author thus constructs some fascinating readings with this methodology. For example, Dreiser's fiction, often seen as critical of or resistant to capitalism, is shown to be absorbed by the speculative logic of the capitalist marketplace; there is no space outside the capitalist economy from which naturalist literature can reflect or resist capitalism. Instead, like all cultural practices, it cannot escape the logic of the capitalist economy, which thoroughly pervades its representational structures.

This theoretical model does create problems however. Michaels' emphasis on internal difference risks ignoring differences within history and culture, structured as they are by the unequal distribution of power across the fracture-lines of class, race, and gender. Rather than describing *the* logic of naturalism, Michaels might be wiser to note competing logics if the possibilities of an oppositional cultural criticism are to be realized.

FRANK PIEKARCZYK

American Literature: General

Bercovitch, Sacvan, *The Rites of Assent: Transformations in the Symbolic Construction of America*, New York: Routledge, 1993

Conn, Robert, *Literature in America: An Illustrated History*, Cambridge and New York: Cambridge University Press, 1989

Hart, James D. (ed.) *The Oxford Companion to American Literature*, 5th revised edition, New York and Oxford: Oxford University Press, 1983

Kirkpatrick, D.L. (ed.), *Reference Guide to American Literature*, Chicago and London: St James Press, 1987; revised edition, edited by Jim Kamp, Detroit and London: St James Press, 1994

Morey, Ann-Janine, *Religion and Sexuality in American Literature*, Cambridge and New York: Cambridge University Press, 1992

Reising, Russell J., *The Unusable Past: Theory and the Study of American Literature*, New York and London: Methuen, 1986

Ruland, Richard, and Malcolm Bradbury, *From Puritanism to Postmodernism: A History of American Literature*, London and New York: Routledge, 1991

Ruoff, A. LaVonne Brown, and Jerry W. Ward Jr. (eds.), *Redefining American Literary History*, New York: MLA, 1990

Salzman, Jack, *et al.* (eds.), *The Cambridge Handbook of American Literature*, New York and Cambridge, Cambridge University Press, 1986

Scholnick, Robert J. (ed.), *American Literature and Science*, Lexington: University Press of Kentucky, 1991

Spengemann, William C., *A Mirror for Americanists: Reflections on the Idea of American Literature*, Hanover, New Hampshire: University Press of New England, 1990
Sundquist, Eric J., *To Wake the Nations: Race and the Making of American Literature*, Cambridge, Massachusetts: Belknap Press of Harvard University Press, 1991
Tanner, Tony, *The Reign of Wonder: Naivety and Reality in American Literature*, Cambridge: Cambridge University Press, 1965
Walker, Marshall, *The Literature of the United States of America*, London: Macmillan, 1983, 2nd edition, 1988

There are several very useful general surveys of, or guides to, American literature, each of which serves different needs and readerships. The standard reference guide to American literature must be HART's, which is addressed to students and general readers. This is an extensive book, at almost 900 pages, and includes a comprehensive listing of American authors, texts, genres, and literary movements, as well as key non-literary aspects of American culture that are important for an understanding of American literature – trends, events, and individuals – such as religious sects, Indian tribes, wars, laws and legal documents, educational institutions, cities and regions, popular songs, all of which are crucial to social history, and all of which have important relationships with literature. Only literary terms with specifically American significance are included – "local-color" fiction and the "tall tale", for example. Authors of nationalities other than American are included, but only in relation to their importance for American writers and texts. Each author-entry includes a brief biography and a bibliography, with a summary of the works; important texts are summarized in their own entries.

KIRKPATRICK's guide to American literature differs particularly in the length of each entry. Where Hart favors short and concise entries, Kirkpatrick's book offers a signed critical essay on each author, which is preceded by a biography, an extensive publication list of the author's works, and a selected bibliography. The most recent collections and only authoritative editions are cited. In the section devoted to "Works:, a selection of essays on the best-known works of American literature and texts of historical importance appear: each entry provides a description of the plot and the significance of the text within the context of the writer's work specifically, and American literature generally. A chronology of literary and social history and a title index make this an extremely valuable resource for more specialist readers. The 1994 revision, edited by Kamp, updates the lists of primary and secondary works, revises some of the essays, and follows the advice of its advisory consultants in expanding the coverage to include a greater number of contemporary writers, particularly from ethnic minorities.

SALZMAN has focused on the needs of much more general readers in this very compact guide (less than 300 pages). Here, the main tradition of American literature provides the basic structure, with no space allowed for information about the social and cultural movements that are deemed peripheral to the literature. Writers, works, and literary movements are the basic categories surveyed, and the canon is represented at the expense of the minority writers (women, popular authors, ethnic writers) so generously represented by Hart and Kirkpatrick/Kamp.

Surveys which are presented in continuous prose, rather than short entries, and represent an evaluation instead of a description of American literature include those by Conn, Ruland and Bradbury, Walker, and Ruoff and Ward. CONN's is the most impressive work of this type. His purpose is threefold: to describe American literary movements within a chronological framework, to suggest links between texts and their historical contexts, and to define and exemplify the work of a large cross-section of writers. So, the discussion represents both the high points and the diversity of American literary achievement. This is emphatically an illustrated guide, with nearly 200 pictures to assist the representation of literary themes and movements and to emphasize the embeddedness of the texts in cultural history. All the periods of literary activity are covered: from the colonial through the nationalist eras, Transcendentalism, realism, regionalism, naturalism, modernists and muckrakers, the Harlem Renaissance, the Depression and proletarian writing. Southern literature, and contemporary experimentation. Attention is given not only to the principal genres (poetry, fiction, and drama) but also to peripheral forms, such as early sermons, diaries, letters, autobiographies, and histories. This really is an excellent introduction for novices, and an entertaining narrative for the more advanced reader. Conn also includes a list of recommended critical studies of American literature and a very useful pair of chronologies – one outlining the events of literary history, the other detailing significant American events.

RULAND and BRADBURY do not provide bibliographical guides or supporting factual apparatus. Their focus is upon the processes by which an American national literature was created, with profound roots in the European literary tradition, but with an equally profound striving for cultural independence and uniqueness. Beginning with the Puritan legacy, they discuss the various images of America represented by writers through the colonial and nationalist periods into the American Renaissance to the modernist era, which then becomes the basis for an assessment of postmodern responses and speculations about the future shape of American literature. They argue that American literature has always been peculiarly responsive to historical and political pressures, and that, above all, American literature has always been essentially "modern" – the expression of the modern age.

WALKER's book is designed less for the general reader than for the student, including, as it does, an informative chronology and suggestions for further reading. Walker is also more select in his coverage, and his book is consequently much shorter than those by Conn and Ruland/Bradbury. However, Walker does cover the ground in an engaging and informative style, moving from a discussion of tradition and what that might mean in the context of American literature, through the major periods of colonialism, nationalism, the American Renaissance, realism, and modernism, concluding with an account of the diversity of contemporary literary production.

RUOFF and WARD provide a revisionary account of American literary history. This book could be seen as an expression of recent controversy over the whole concept of the American literary canon, and it is very informative in terms of filling in the blanks created by conventional accounts of American literature. The contributors to this volume address the history of oral expression and its relationships with ethnic writing and with Anglo-American culture; they recount the histories of Asian-American, African-American, Hispanic, and Native American literatures; and they provide comprehensive bibliographical listings of primary and secondary works relating to these long-neglected aspects of American literary history. This book serves as an excellent corrective to the view of American literature proposed by the other surveys reviewed above.

SUNDQUIST's mammoth study also argues powerfully for a revisionist view of American literary history; but where Ruoff and Ward treat ethnicity liberally in relation to the literatures of the Americas, Sundquist focuses exclusively on African-American writing. Drawing on such studies of the hidden black presence in American literature as Toni Morrison's *Playing in the Dark*, Sundquist shows how, in the formative period of 1830–1930, the writings of white and black Americans were inseparable, and form a single continuous tradition. The place of black literature in relation to white culture – the distinct function, textures, and shapes of texts seen in their ethnic dimension – is an important and correspondingly difficult issue, and Sundquist's treatment of this question is scholarly, intelligent, and sensitive. He discusses each text within a sophisticated cultural context comprised of history, law, music, politics, religion, and folklore. He begins with Nat Turner, Frederick Douglass, and the American Renaissance (specifically Herman Melville) and concludes with W.E.B. Du Bois and the Pan-African movement, having in between considered the racial context of the writings of Mark Twain and Charles Chesnutt. This is a major contribution to the current debate concerning American literary history and the issue of race.

Analyses of American literature that survey the history in order to propose some particular kind of coherence explaining its "Americanness" include the work of Sacvan Bercovitch and Tony Tanner, while critics such as Spengemann and Reising take issue with the whole enterprise of theorizing American literature in this way.

BERCOVITCH is perhaps the most influential analyst of American literature and its relationship with the mythology that invigorates American culture. In his earliest books he described the Puritan inheritance, especially the contradictory demands of individualism and consensus, and its influence upon American public life in all its expressions. The relationship between self-knowledge and cultural knowledge (the American self) lends Bercovitch an access to the symbolic logic that unifies the periods, writers and major texts of American literary history. This symbolic logic is otherwise known as ideology: the role of ideology in the creation of a national past and a hegemonic definition of America matching American imperialist ambitions provides one half of a complex dialectic, which moves from these broad cultural definitions to private concepts of the self via the medium of (among other forms of expression) American literature to create the great American subject, as Bercovitch sees it – the American Self. Bercovitch's work is subtle yet profound, informed and informative, and of crucial importance to the development of American literary studies.

TANNER's book, written nearly 30 years before Bercovitch's, is among the best of the old-fashioned kind of analysis against which Bercovitch reacts. Tanner identifies as peculiarly American, and inherited from the Puritan colonists, a sense of wonder in the presence of nature. Tanner develops an argument based upon his reading of Ralph Waldo Emerson and American Romanticism, which extends to include all American literature. American writers have always struggled to account for the vast new continent they inhabit, and "wonder" is Tanner's concept for the preferred imaginative reaction, which incorporates all that is distinctively American and gives that national identification literary expression. Tanner belongs to a group of critics, including F.O. Matthiessen, Charles Feidelson, Leslie Feidler, and Richard Poirier, who seek to identify as peculiarly American elements of Puritan culture sustained throughout American literary history.

MOREY's work belongs in this critical tradition. She shows how the twin themes of religion and sexuality have come to characterise American literature by identifying a recurring pattern of thematic and formal concerns in American fiction from Nathaniel Hawthorne to John Updike. Thus, the "classic" texts of the American literary canon again and again engage with this issue – the connection between religion and sexuality. Morey uses a sophisticated theoretical approach based upon the insights of deconstruction, feminism, and postmodernism to analyse the function of metaphor as a uniquely American device used to dramatize the intimate relationship between language and physical life, body, and spirit.

REISING's book analyses the work of such, and other, critics and places them within an historical and political context. He suggests ways in which these theories of American literature have constrained thinking about the field by falsely unifying diverse literary texts and marginalizing all imaginative works that do not fit prescribed patterns. SPENGEMANN also questions the ways in which American literary traditions are constructed, but he is less interested in deconstructing previous critics' work than in exploring the whole notion of "American literature" as an object of study. He begins by asking whether this category is purely a discursive creation, or whether it names some external reality and, if the latter, how we can identify a given text as "American". Spengemann is obviously concerned with the current debates about the literary canon and the controversy over exclusions and gaps, which appear to be political rather than literary. He provides no easy answers, but he does raise important issues in a stimulating and constructive spirit.

The essays edited by SCHOLNICK put into question the whole concept of "literary" discourse in relation to that of science and technology. Rather than maintain an opposition to science, to which some Romantics and their modernist heirs were committed, and which was developed by such theoretical schools as structuralism, formalism, and reader-response criticism, these essays demonstrate that the history of American literature reveals a sustained and complex interplay between the two kinds of discourse. Essay subjects range chronologically from Edward Taylor, Benjamin Franklin, and Thomas Jefferson to postmodernism and cyberpunk; in the course of such a wide-ranging exploration, the constantly changing conception of science and its relations with the arts becomes apparent. This book provides a stimulus for a reconsideration of cross-disciplinary relationships involving American literary history.

DEBORAH L. MADSEN

American Literature: Early Period

Bercovitch, Sacvan, *The Puritan Origins of the American Self*, New Haven, Connecticut: Yale University Press, 1975

Franklin, Wayne, *Discoverers, Explorers, Settlers: The Diligent Writers of Early America*, Chicago: Chicago University Press, 1979

Greenblatt, Stephen, *Marvelous Possessions: The Wonder of the New World*, Chicago: University of Chicago Press, 1991; Oxford: Clarendon Press, 1991

Kibbey, Ann, *The Interpretation of Material Shapes in Puritanism: A Study of Rhetoric, Prejudice, and Violence*, Cambridge and New York: Cambridge University Press, 1986

Shuffelton, Frank (ed.), *A Mixed Race: Ethnicity in Early America*, New York: Oxford University Press, 1993

Williams, Jerry M., and Robert E. Lewis (eds.), *Early Images of the Americas: Transfer and Invention*, Tucson: University of Arizona Press, 1993

Until fairly recently, discussions of the colonial era were primarily limited to a consideration of the Puritan errand in the New World. Today, this Anglicized version of the colonial enterprise is under massive revision. Not only are differences between the northern, Middle Atlantic, and southern colonies more apparent than they were previously, but the presence of representatives from other European nations (such as France and Spain) is considered more important now than formerly. And even beyond these two areas of recovery, major interest has emerged concerning issues of ethnicity during the colonial period, particularly regarding Native Americans and African Americans.

BERCOVITCH concludes that the chronicles of Cotton Mather and others anticipated the American development of a hybrid sense of history, which insisted on secular details as well as on an allegorical ideal framework. In contrast to the English sense of only a temporary conjunction of sainthood and nationality, Americans insisted on this correlation, so much so that their histories read like spiritual autobiographies. Bercovitch's study requires a little qualification now and then – such as his assertions concerning the Puritans' repudiation of returning to England – but overall his book provides a learned and cogent reading of a meta-structure of early American culture.

FRANKLIN delineates three modes of perception in the New World travel documents of the sixteenth through the eighteenth centuries. The first is the discovery mode, which records either the atemporal stare or the emotional paralysis of the ravished observer, and which presents descriptive set-pieces in lieu of narrative action. The second is the exploratory mode, which emphasizes physical or linguistic activity, and which presents a vision of an ideal future colony. The third is the settlement mode, which recognizes disagreeable facts and relies on an ironic perception of the colonist as a pawn of large forces. Franklin singles out passages rather than treats entire texts, a procedure of decontextualization that raises questions concerning the overall reliability of his taxonomy when he generalizes about authors. Nevertheless, his elegantly written, richly illustrated book is a mature investigation worthy of debate.

KIBBEY's feminist interpretation focuses on Puritan spoken words and sacramental rituals as material signifiers of, and substitutes for, an absent deity. This emphasis, contrary to explicit Calvinistic belief, amounts to a furtive reverence for icons, a reverence extended by men to men, who are represented as living icons. Women were the scapegoats of this covert reverence. Designated as profane icons of the imagination, women were culturally threatened with defacement and violence. Women's lives were implicitly threatened in Puritan attacks on Roman Catholics and Native Americans. Kibbey's argument raises several pertinent questions about Puritan responses to women, but it also often distractingly forces dubious connections and asserts outlandish conclusions.

GREENBLATT features early narratives of negotiation, which he terms "mimetic capital". This phrase refers to a stockpile of images, accumulated in various cultural ways, and which were commonly shared by most explorers of the New World. Circulated widely, these images were applied to whatever was new in such a way that the new was appropriated to reinforce the old. For example, Columbus relied on a rhetoric of binary opposition when he reported on the wonders of the western hemisphere. Because Columbus was an agent of cultural imperatives, which he could not help but represent, his language worked to "colonize" (normalize) whatever was resistantly anomalous in his New World encounters. Greenblatt's book, which represents the direction of current investigations of the colonial era, is written from deep within New-Historicist discourse, and so some readers may experience difficulty in following its argument.

WILLIAMS and LEWIS offer an anthology of 12 essays on the Spanish response to the New World. Included are: a review of how early reports of Native Americans departed from the noble-savage idea and suggested some objectivity in viewpoint; an analysis of the use of two ritual signs as a means of incorporating Native American lands within the coded space of colonial expectations; and a consideration of the English reliance upon the form and substance of medieval papal bulls as a means to legitimate their control of territory, in contrast to Spanish emphasis on control of Native American people. Although limited in focus and range, this volume contributes to our understanding of the Spanish approach and reaction to the New World.

SHUFFELTON's anthology of 13 articles provides fairly comprehensive coverage of the idea of race in early American thought. Chief among its discussions are considerations of rape accounts and captivity narratives, both emphasizing ethnicity as alien. Included are Native Americans, African Americans, Jews, French settlers, and Pennsylvania Germans. While mainly predictable in its overall configuration, this volume enhances our understanding of the place of ethnicity in the early American imagination.

William J. Scheick

See also **Puritan Literature: American**

American Literature: 19th Century

Elliott, Emory (general ed.), *Columbia Literary History of the United States*, New York: Columbia University Press, 1988

Herreshof, David Sprague, *Labor into Art: The Theme of Work in Nineteenth-Century American Literature*, Detroit: Wayne State University Press, 1991

Kelley, Mary, *Private Woman, Public Stage: Literary Domesticity in Nineteenth-Century America*, 1984

Lewis, R.W.B., *The American Adam: Innocence, Tradition and Tragedy in the Nineteenth Century*, Chicago: University of Chicago Press, 1955

Martin, Ronald E., *American Literature and the Destruction of Knowledge in the Age of Epistemology*, Durham, North Carolina: Duke University Press, 1991

Pizer, Donald, *Realism and Naturalism in Nineteenth-Century American Literature*, Carbondale: Southern Illinois University Press, 1966, revised 1984

Sundquist, Eric J., *Home As Found: Authority and Genealogy in Nineteenth-Century American Literature*, Baltimore: Johns Hopkins University Press, 1979

Of the numerous surveys of nineteenth-century American literature, those discussed here have attracted most attention in recent years. But the reader is reminded that this listing is necessarily partial and highly selective.

LEWIS's study traces the nineteenth-century image of the authentic American as a figure of heroic innocence and vast potentialities, poised at the start of a new history, i.e., the eternal, recurring Adam – Adam before the Fall, without the sense of guilt, and eager to celebrate his existence. The indestructible vitality of the Adamic vision is traced in selected texts of Oliver Wendell Holmes, Walt Whitman, Henry James, Charles Brockden Brown, James Fenimore Cooper, Nathaniel Hawthorne, and Herman Melville. For better or worse, according to Lewis, each new generation of Americans must start all over again in reconstructing the culture; the past, therefore, is held to be of little account and tradition goes by the board.

SUNDQUIST's work is a Freudian interpretation of the conflict between authority and desire as reflected in nineteenth-century American literature. The struggle between the individual's desire to fulfil himself and society's insistence upon imposing conventional regulations is traced in individual literary works by Cooper, Henry David Thoreau, Hawthorne, and Melville. Individual chapters are "Incest and Imitation in Cooper's *Home As Found*", "Cultivation and Grafting in Thoreau and the *Week*", "Representation and Speculation in Hawthorne and *The House of the Seven Gables*", and "Parody and Parricide in Melville's *Pierre*". Works by Whitman, Emily Dickinson, Emerson, and Edgar Allan Poe are not included because, as the author observes in his Introduction, they do not fit the general thesis of the study.

KELLEY studies the paradoxical ambition of literary domesticity in nineteenth-century America. The book "attempts to answer the question of how the literary domestics could have been so visibly onstage in their own time and yet remain invisible to the historical audience". The book is, therefore, an excellent introduction to a group of writers currently being re-examined in terms of canon reform. Readers are introduced to Fanny Fern, Catharine Maria Sedgwick, Susan Warner, Augusta Evans Wilson, E.D.E.N. Southworth, Roxana Beecher, Harriet Beecher Stowe, Sara Josepha Hale, Mary Jane Holmes, and others – all best-sellers in their own day, but forgotten in the present day. Since most of these writers were female, this work is an important feminist document.

PIZER's study attempts to differentiate between realism and naturalism in late nineteenth-century American literature. In his Introduction the author states: "this book attempts to answer two major questions: how can one best describe realism and naturalism in nineteenth-century American fiction, and what is the relation between the literary criticism of the age and the emergence and nature of realism and naturalism?". Writers covered are Frank Norris, Theodore Dreiser, William Dean Howells, Hamlin Garland, Stephen Crane, and Jack London.

ELLIOTT's work is clearly the most ambitious general survey of United States literature attempted since Robert E. Spiller and his co-editors completed the *Literary History of the United States* in 1948. A new general survey is required, according to the editors of this work, because of "events such as the Cold War, the war in Vietnam and the protests against it, the civil rights movement, the women's movement, and the struggles of various minority groups to achieve equity in American society". All these and other events "have reformed the way many Americans view their nation and thereby their national literature and culture". This new history, say the editors:

> . . . is modestly postmodern: it acknowledges diversity, complexity, and contradiction by making them structural principles, and it forgoes closure as well as consensus. Designed to be explored like a library or an art gallery, this book is composed of corridors to be entered through many portals intended to give the reader the paradoxical experience of seeing both the harmony and the discontinuity of materials.

The nineteenth century is fully treated here. The canonical figures are given ample space, and the popular writers, ethnic minorities, feminists, and subversives finally come into their own in this new survey.

HERRESHOF discusses what five American writers made of the theme of work. The relationship between making a living and human character, the question of whether to endure or celebrate the workplace and human labor, how to make use of leisure – all these and other questions are developed fully in the body of the essay. Writers dealt with are Thoreau, Melville, Dickinson, Frederick Douglass, and Whitman.

In his Preface, MARTIN observes that:

> . . . this book is a study of the literature produced by a number of nineteenth-century American authors who acted on the deep conviction that the principal obstacles to real understanding . . . were the culture's certified knowledge and the habits and techniques by which that knowledge was customarily produced . . . . Their assault was on nothing less than the linguistic order of their world.

In pursuing this view, Martin's study links Melville, Emerson, Whitman, and Dickinson (as well as several twentieth-century authors) to a cultural tradition that casts doubt on the possibility of knowledge itself.

JAMES T.F. TANNER

American Literature: 20th Century

Cunliffe, Marcus (ed.), *American Literature since 1900*, London: Barrie & Jenkins, 1973; as Volume 9 of the *Sphere History of Literature in the English Language* series London: Sphere Books, 1975; New York: P. Bedrick Books, 1987

Jones, Howard Mumford, and Richard M. Ludwig, *Guide to American Literature and Its Backgrounds since 1890*, Cambridge, Massachusetts: Harvard University Press, 1972, 4th, revised edition, 1972

Massa, Ann, *American Literature in Context: 1900–1930*, London: Methuen, 1982

Schorer, Mark, *The Literature of America: Twentieth Century*, New York: McGraw-Hill, 1970

Tallack, Douglas, *Twentieth-Century America: The Intellectual and Cultural Context*, London: Longman, 1991

Thorp, Willard, *American Writing in the Twentieth Century*, Cambridge, Massachusetts: Harvard University Press, 1960

CUNLIFFE's volume of essays covers the twentieth century up to the 1970s, and includes American literature of all genres. The editor has consciously avoided the creation of a uniform tone and a set of common presuppositions among the essays, so that the volume as a whole reflects some of the controversies that characterize the criticism of modern American writing. Malcolm Bradbury and David Corker discuss modernism and the "new arts" in relation to nineteenth-century inheritances and later developments. Dennis Welland accounts for fiction between the world wars; David Morse surveys theatre in the age of Eugene O'Neill; poetry before World War II is described by Geoffrey Moore, and post-1945 poetry by Aleksandar Nejgebauer; developments in literary criticism are discussed by Marshall van Deusen; Ursula Brumm describes trends in Southern writing; and Irving Wardle surveys postwar theatre. The period since the 1960s is covered in a number of essays: Eric Mottram surveys the variety of poetic practices; Arnold Goldman discusses minority writers; and Leslie Fiedler, in what is now a classic essay, confronts the phenomenon of postmodernism. In his conclusion, Marcus Cunliffe considers the relationships and dynamics that exist between literature and society.

MASSA's contribution to the "American Literature in Context" series covers the early part of the century (1900–30). In conformity with the series, each chapter is prefaced by an extract which serves as the basis for the subsequent analysis of the writer's characteristic interests and techniques and the broader discussion of the cultural context of that writer and that text. Issues of cultural relevance include nationalism and expatriatism, the rise of science and technology, the decline of religion and the increasing influence of psychology or psychoanalysis, and events like World War I and the Great Depression. The Introduction, which usefully, if briefly, surveys the range of literary expression during the period, is followed by detailed analyses of Edith Wharton, Henry Adams, Henry James, Gertrude Stein, Wallace Stevens, Ezra Pound, Sherwood Anderson, Sinclair Lewis, Jean Toomer, H.L. Mencken, F. Scott Fitzgerald, Ernest Hemingway, Eugene O'Neill, and William Faulkner.

The "Longman Literature in English" series includes an extremely informative and comprehensive account of twentieth-century American intellectual culture which, while it does not deal directly with American literature, is enormously helpful in making accessible some of the more difficult texts that have been written in this century. TALLACK's achievement is very considerable in writing such a well-informed, detailed, and yet wide-ranging account of twentieth-century American thought. The organizing principle, which lends coherence to this mass of information, is the relationship between modernity and postmodernity. The forces of modernity are viewed in terms of the impact created upon various forms of artistic expression, such as cinema, painting, and architecture. Such intellectual movements as pragmatism, Agrarianism, feminism, the Civil Rights Movement, and black activism are explained and elucidated in detail. The concluding chapter discusses the rise of postmodernism, giving account of the emergence of the term and the major figures in the postmodernism debate. The book includes a set of extremely valuable appendices – a chronology, a general bibliography, and bibliographies of individual authors.

THORP provides a very useful guide to twentieth-century American literature from 1900 to the literary "Renaissance" following World War II. The book is divided into sections dealing with: fiction, 1900–14 and 1912–22; drama, 1915–40; the novel, 1920–50; naturalism and the novel; and poetry, 1920–1950. Regional movements, such as the Southern Renaissance, are covered, and the text concludes with a survey of critical work on twentieth-century literature. The approach to the subject is primarily descriptive rather than evaluative, and the coverage focuses heavily on the first half of the century; nevertheless, it is an informative guide for a beginner.

SCHORER's survey takes the form of an annotated anthology, comprised mainly of selections and excerpts. The book is organized chronologically rather than in a fashion that would reflect changing literary movements, schools, or artistic or intellectual emphases. The primary divisions are made between pre-World-War-I writing, literature between the wars, and post-World-War-II writing. However, the general Introduction explains usefully the major trends and innovations of modern American literature – for example, modernism, naturalism, realism, the influence of little magazines, and the like. The entry for each author is prefaced with a biographical sketch, a description of characteristic themes, techniques, and interests, with a bibliography of further reading. The coverage is more comprehensive than Thorp was able to achieve ten years earlier: Schorer includes writers from Henry Adams to Donald Barthelme. The mass of information included in this book is made easily accessible by indexes of authors, titles, and first lines of poems.

Tallack's guide to American culture could be seen as updating and generalizing the earlier work of JONES and LUDWIG, who provide a more purely artistic context for twentieth-century American literature. They list an extensive bibliography of authors and literary texts for the periods 1890–1919 and 1920–72. Obviously the coverage stops short of Tallack's very contemporary account of the cultural contexts of American literature, but the amount of information about modern literary history and the specifics of various artistic movements included by Jones and Ludwig is impressive. Literary histories are recounted according to literary genre; influential literary magazines are listed; cultural trends, such as those in the fine arts, popular arts, and intellectual history, are described; and important historical events between 1890 and 1971 are listed. Also very useful is the extensive account of critical work published on modern American literature: general guides, general reference works, and general histories for each decade, are listed separately. The sheer volume of factual information gathered in this book ensure its continuing relevance and importance for students of American literature.

DEBORAH L. MADSEN

American Renaissance

Bercovitch, Sacvan, and Myra Jehlen (eds.), *Ideology and Classic American Literature*, Cambridge and New York: Cambridge University Press, 1986

Bewley, Marius, *The Eccentric Design: Form in the Classic American Novel*, New York: Columbia University Press, 1959

Carton, Evan, *The Rhetoric of American Romance: Dialectic and Identity in Emerson, Dickinson, Poe, and Hawthorne*, Baltimore: Johns Hopkins University Press, 1985

Feidelson, Charles, Jr., *Symbolism and American Literature*, Chicago: University of Chicago Press, 1953

Fussell, Edwin S., *Frontier: American Literature and the American West*, Princeton, New Jersey: Princeton University Press, 1965

Leverenz, David, *Manhood and the American Renaissance*, Ithaca, New York: Cornell University Press, 1989

Lewis, R.W.B., *The American Adam: Innocence, Tragedy and Tradition in the Nineteenth Century*, Chicago: University of Chicago Press, 1955

Matthiessen, F.O., *American Renaissance: Art and Expression in the Age of Emerson and Whitman*, London: Oxford University Press, 1941

Reynolds, David S., *Beneath the American Renaissance: The Subversive Imagination in the Age of Emerson and Melville*, New York: Knopf, 1988

Slotkin, Richard, *Regeneration Through Violence: The Mythology of the American Frontier 1600–1860*, Middletown, Connecticut: Wesleyan University Press, 1973

Steele, Jeffrey, *The Representation of the Self in the American Renaissance*, Chapel Hill: University of North Carolina Press, 1987

MATTHIESSEN's pioneering achievement, at a time when American literature had little status on either side of the Atlantic, was to present a period, 1850–55, as the point at which the national culture "came of age", in the sense that during this short period five major writers all published what could be claimed to be their greatest work, ranging from Nathaniel Hawthorne's *The Scarlet Letter*, Ralph Waldo Emerson's *Representative Man*, and Henry David Thoreau's *Walden* to Herman Melville's *Moby-Dick* and Walt Whitman's *Leaves of Grass*. Matthiessen claimed that these works, and others, expressed the profundity and idealism of American identity in ways that sought to unite the individual and the collective in a common, but self-critical, sense of purpose. His close analyses of the ways in which these works came into being stress the authors' struggles to overcome doubt and rejection in order to hold a mirror up to their contemporaries, one in which they could find "a culture adequate to our needs". This vision expressed its author's faith in America's mission to be a world cultural leader as well as the major economic and military power.

FEIDELSON's remarkable work gave intellectual seriousness to the writers of this time, particularly to Emerson, by claiming that they were writing in a symbolist tradition, which, beginning with the Romantics, persisted in France in the nineteenth century until it re-entered American literature via Henri Bergson and T.E. Hulme with the Imagist movement. The underlying belief of this tradition is that "there is in nature a parallel unity which corresponds to the unity in the mind and makes it available" (Emerson), and that the imagination seizes upon aspects of nature to serve as symbols of this otherwise invisible substratum. Melville, in this account, comes to doubt the existence of such a benign unity, but, nonetheless, Lewis argues, his work needs to be read in the light of this on-going philosophical and aesthetic debate.

LEWIS, while sharing Feidelson's faith in the seriousness of American literature, stressed the conflicts in the period between traditionalists, who feared the anarchic consequences of Jacksonian democracy, and the optimists, who placed their faith in the new "Adam" – the American representing a new beginning, free from Old-World errors and guilt. Lewis analyses a wide variety of writers, including historians and religious thinkers, such as Francis Parkman, George Bancroft, Theodore Parker, and Orestes Brownson, as well as poets and novelists, in order to demonstrate the debates between the parties of "Hope" and "Memory", culminating in a third voice – that of "Irony", whereby writers could, if only in the work of art, confront both the innocence and the tragic past of the American experience: "history recovered in the individual imagination". The analyses of Hawthorne's *The House of Seven Gables* and *The Marble Faun* are particularly noteworthy, as is the section on Melville's *Billy Budd*.

BEWLEY's book deserves mention because of its brave, and largely ignored, attempt to relate the form and content of works by such writers as James Fenimore Cooper, Hawthorne, and Melville to their contemporary political and economic issues, especially Alexander Hamilton's financial reforms and the controversy surrounding the National Bank, thus picking up Lewis's insights into the influence of the struggle to generate economic structures necessary, in Bewley's words to "meet the needs of the new capitalist enterprises".

FUSSELL's book opened up an entirely new focus of attention by concentrating upon the frontier as the place – largely in the imagination, rather than in the West as such – in which the savage and the civilised meet, and hence as a space in which the assumptions of modernity become exposed and subject to critique. Examining the portrayal of the Native American in the writings of Cooper, Thoreau, and Melville, as well as looking at Hawthorne, Edgar Allan Poe, and Whitman, Fussell traces the conflict between the apparent spontaneity, freedom, and vigour of the "savage" with the uncertainties and decadence of the literate, intellectual whites. The frontier becomes a testing ground where these polarities can be reconciled, at least temporarily, to enable individual, and perhaps, cultural recognition to take place, but only within this "neutral territory". The end product is not therefore affirmation, but paradox and irony. SLOTKIN develops this theme by examining the image of the frontiersman from the captivity narratives of the seventeenth century to the writings of Catharine Maria Sedgwick, Cooper, and the popular mythology of Daniel Boone and Davy Crockett. As hunters and frontiersmen, these figures act as a link to the "hidden or dark sources of our personal and collective past – factors which limit our power to aspire and transcend", but which we can utilise by descending into them in a cycle of initiation, exorcism, sacrifice, and rebirth. The obsessive rationalism of Western culture can thus be corrected by such an acknowledgement of the "primitive" within us all.

A masterly deconstructionist account of the dialectical tensions between conflicting views of nature in the American romance is given by CARTON. He demonstrates the irresolvable contradictions in Emerson, Emily Dickinson, Poe, and Hawthorne as they struggled with the Puritan conception of Nature as a fallen world, redeemable by moral labour into knowledge, Romantic beliefs concerning the evidence of divinity within nature, and more modern doubts about the intelligibility of nature in any human terms at all.

BERCOVITCH and JEHLEN collect together an excellent collection of essays, the central theme of which is a critique of the ways in which American literature has been read as an expression of national confidence, and of concern for universal human experience, rather than as the exploration of those specific economic and historical factors that have shaped the nation, particularly the phases of the development of Western capitalism and the triumph of the market revolution. The classic American writers, products of a "pre-capitalist worldview", "sustained the pastoral vision through the country's industrial transformation" and thereby formed a radical opposition to the pieties of their age.

REYNOLDS's book breaks down the high-culture/low-culture distinction by demonstrating the extent to which the major writers were aware of, and responded to, the forms of popular fiction and tract, whether sensationalistic, scurrilous, or moralistic. Carnivalesque figures and stereotypes can be recognised in the poems of Dickinson as well as in Emerson, Melville, and Whitman. The image of the frontiersman becomes here a source of linguistic and emotional energy, deflating the pomposities of the bourgeoisie and its "genteel tradition", and leading the way to stylistic and cultural innovation.

STEELE and LEVERENZ present much more sceptical and debunking perspectives, both being particularly harsh on Emerson. Steele sees all attempts at self-presentation as mere rhetorical devices, designed to appeal to the writers' audiences' needs for certainty, assurance, and faith. Emerson's view of the self is seen to depend "upon a masculine conception of the spirit", whereas Margaret Fuller's is a "feminised model of psychic energy and its expression". Leverenz continues this critique of what he sees as gender stereotypes by claiming that Emerson's "politics of man-making . . . trivialises women and feelings". The problem with these recent approaches is that they trivialise the writers which they so smugly condemn from a position of assumed wisdom and hindsight, instead of seeing that these writers were themselves engaged in the work of cultural critique.

D.T. CORKER

Amis, Kingsley 1922–1995

English novelist, short-story writer, essayist, and poet

Bradford, Richard, *Kingsley Amis*, London and New York: Edward Arnold, 1989
Gardner, Philip, *Kingsley Amis*, Boston: Twayne, 1981
Fussell, Paul, *The Anti-Egotist: Kingsley Amis, Man of Letters*, New York: Oxford University Press, 1994
McDermott, John, *Kingsley Amis: An English Moralist*, London: Macmillan, 1989; New York: St Martin's Press, 1989
Moseley, Merritt, *Understanding Kingsley Amis*, Columbia: University of South Carolina Press, 1993
Salwak, Dale (ed.), *Kingsley Amis in Life and Letters*, London: Macmillan, 1990
Salwak, Dale, *Kingsley Amis: Modern Novelist*, Hemel Hempstead, Hertfordshire: Harvester Wheatsheaf, 1992; Lanham, Maryland: Barnes & Noble, 1992

From the beginning, critical commentary on Kingsley Amis has been complicated by political factors – in his early years, his apparent Leftism, in later years, his reactionary views – by the spectacular success of his first novel *Lucky Jim*, and by the journalistic need to find a "school" or niche to which he could be assigned. Thus, much early criticism is about "Anger" – the supposed hallmark of England's mid-1950s' Angry Young Men – and the success or failure of Amis's books in demonstrating this quality. Various other convenient assumptions, for instance that Amis is a high-spirited comic writer and little more, or that he has something in common with America's Beat poets, have made the early periodical criticism wear poorly. Perhaps it is fortunate that he had been publishing books for 17 years and had a substantial body of fiction in print before a critical book on him appeared, though since then Amis has been fortunate in his critics, who have largely done justice to his versatility and range without loss of acuity.

GARDNER's book is, like most of these, an overview, with an introductory section on Amis's life and career. It covers the books through *Jake's Thing* (1978). The organization is both chronological and thematic; for instance, one chapter, entitled "Alternate Worlds of Youth", is about the books of the 1970s, but focuses specifically on the ways in which Amis combines his interest in genre fiction with the subject of childhood and adolescence in *The Riverside Villas Murder* and *The Alteration*. Gardner recommends care "in trying to sum up a writer in whom irony, satire, comedy, and indirection . . . vie with a wish to believe in, and to assert, quite straightforward and traditional notions of decent feeling and behavior", and he aims to balance the interest in Amis as "entertainer" and "debunker" with what he insists is the author's more serious side. Gardner's book has a selected bibliography with some intelligent annotation. It is a good example of the Twayne series – aimed at students and general readers, yet doing justice to the author's work.

BRADFORD has a greater "edge" and a less comprehensive remit, though he discusses all the novels. He begins with a useful chapter on "Amis and the Critics" and follows with three groupings – "The Early Novels", "The 'Experiments'", and "The Realist Tendency". The book ends with Amis's 1988 *Difficulties with Girls*. The purpose of the book is more openly polemical, attempting to address both some misunderstandings of Amis and some shortcomings of contemporary criticism in dealing with contemporary fiction, particularly of a non-modernist sort. Bradford takes on the critics who have labeled several of Amis's late novels as misogynist or otherwise bigoted, and declares that these novels "mix satire, black humour, vivid reality and compassion in a way that has rarely been achieved since Swift".

McDERMOTT has written the most substantial study of Amis. Longer and more thorough than most of these books, it is well-written, subtle, and persuasive. He pays attention to Amis's poems, short stories, and non-fiction, as well as the novels up through *The Old Devils* and *The Crime of the Century* (both 1987). McDermott's particular emphasis is on Amis as a moralist; in his discussion of *Take a Girl Like You*, one of the first Amis novels in which readers are required to readjust their prejudices about "Anger" and "knockabout comedy", he corrects some obtuse readings and insists that the "large theme" of this novel (and most of Amis's work, in fact) is that "nothing matters more than what you do". McDermott is also good on Amis as an experimental novelist – a distinction Amis has claimed while denouncing modernist obscurity. McDermott writes:

> The "linguistic and formal daring" advanced as a necessary element in this programme [of radical experiment] is to be found in Amis, but without the barricade-storming flamboyance suggested by words like "radical". Innovation is, for Amis, a matter rather of adjustment than of revolution.

SALWAK's 1990 collection is a very mixed book. It has the look of being a by-product of Salwak's work for his 1992 book (see below). It brings together some contributions by people who knew Amis well (for instance, Paul Fussell, Robert Conquest, and Anthony Powell); others by relatively well-known people who did not know Amis very well; some questionable reports, for instance on Amis's politics in his year in residence at Vanderbilt University; and traditional literary criticism, including some which focuses on science fiction and one heavy-duty linguistic analysis of Amis's diction. It seems an uneasy mixture of anthology of literary criticism and *Festschrift* of tributes to a retiring colleague. There are a number of photographs.

SALWAK's 1992 study is a substantial, thorough book. It is a study of the writer's works, but includes much more biography than the other books here reviewed. It also contains photographs, is solidly grounded in collections of Amis materials at the University of Texas and the Huntington Library, and was written with the co-operation of Amis and his family. Salwak sees a clear outline of the Amis career, which identifies an arc of disillusionment and darkening vision; he argues that "Amis's view of life has grown increasingly pessimistic until he ultimately arrives at a fearfully grim vision of a nightmare world characterized by hostility, violence, sexual abuse and self-destruction"; but it is a tribute to the author's wit and style that though "at times his vision is bleak, his novels rarely make for bleak reading". This is the most scholarly book yet published on Amis.

My own (MOSELEY's) book is part of a series on "Understanding Contemporary British Literature". I argue that understanding Amis is not problematic in the same way that understanding, say, James Joyce is, since Amis has always stood for clarity and against any of what he considers willful obfuscation in the name of experiment; however, proper understanding of Amis may be impeded by false expectations and by blindness to the moral seriousness that coexists with comedy in his work. Included are discussions of Amis's non-fiction, short stories, and poems, but the concentration is mostly on the novels, up through *The Folks That Live on the Hill*.

FUSSELL has the virtue of taking the most unusual approach to Amis, who was a longtime friend: he almost completely ignores the novels, which are the main subject of all the other books here. He explains:

> My focus is on his non-fiction and his literary learning, his performance as a critic, a learned anthologist, a memoirist, a teacher, and a poet – in short, a man of letters in the old sense, a writer conspicuous for complex literary knowledge and subtle taste as well as for vigorous views on politics and society.

This is an entirely salutary undertaking; though other commentators have given some notice to the non-novel-writing parts of Amis's career, and quoted with agreement his own assessment of himself as a man of letters in the nineteenth-century vein, only Fussell has given this sort of scrutiny, especially to activities like Amis's poetry column in the *Daily Mirror*, his interest in soldiers and enlisted men in his fiction, and his work as a restaurant critic, a critic of the language, and an anthologist. Fussell faces the question of Amis's reactionary political views squarely and forcefully. This is a badly needed and triumphant demonstration of Amis's versatility and his importance as a writer who did much more than write novels.

MERRITT MOSELEY

Anand, Mulk Raj 1905–

Indian novelist, short-story writer, essayist, and children's writer

Cowasjee, Saros, *So Many Freedoms: A Study of the Major Fiction of Mulk Raj Anand*, New Delhi and Oxford: Oxford University Press, 1977

Dhawan, R.K. (ed.), *The Novels of Mulk Raj Anand*, New Delhi: Prestige, 1992

Fisher, Marlene, *The Wisdom of the Heart: A Study of the Works of Mulk Raj Anand*, New Delhi: Sterling, 1985

Mukherjee, Arun P., "The Exclusion of Postcolonial Theory and Mulk Raj Anand's *Untouchable*: A Case Study", in *Ariel: A Review of International English Literaure*, 22(3), July 1991

Niven, Alastair, *The Yoke of Pity: A Study of the Fictional Writings of Mulk Raj Anand*, New Delhi: Arnold/Heinemann, 1978

Sharma, K.K. (ed.), *Perspectives on Mulk Raj Anand*, Ghaziabad: Vimal, 1978

Sinha, Krishna H. Nandan, *Mulk Raj Anand*, New York: Twayne, 1972

Mulk Raj Anand is universally recognised – along with Raja Rao and R.K. Narayan – as one of the big three founding fathers of the Indian novel in English. A prolific, versatile, and at times controversial writer, his work has received a mixed critical reception. Recent criticism is now tending to reassess Anand's work in the light of postcolonial theory and question the views of much earlier criticism, which focused on Anand's humanism and realism.

SINHA's book, though now over 20 years old, remains a useful introduction to Anand's earlier work up to *Morning Face* (1968). Treating the novels and short stories in chronological order, he presents Anand as a committed humanist, whose fiction delineates, in a realist mode, the lives and experiences of India's masses.

COWASJEE's book, one of the major studies of Anand's fiction, is a detailed critical analysis of all the novels (including the three autobiographical ones) from *Untouchable* (1935) to *Confession of a Lover* (1976). His reassessment of *Private Life of an Indian Prince* (1953, revised 1970) in the chapter entitled "Princes and Proletarians", which he places in the wider context of a discussion of the treatment of the Indian princes in English fiction and the political background of the princely states, is of particular interest. Cowasjee sees this novel, which had been received in very lukewarm fashion by many Indian critics, as both the climax and end of Anand's career as a novelist. The later novels and fictional autobiographies, which he sees as failures, are only dealt with in order "to place Anand's achievements in proper perspective". The still-helpful bibliography provides a list of primary and significant secondary sources to 1976.

NIVEN has written a useful short study of Anand's major fiction up to *Confession of a Lover*. In contrast to Cowasjee, he sees the fictional autobiographies, which he believes are likely "to rank with Anand's foremost achievements", as essential to the rest of Anand's *oeuvre*. In order to emphasise the centrality of these works, he takes the unusual step of commencing his study with a chapter on the autobiographical novels. There is also a particularly interesting chapter on three stories, which he thinks bridge the gap between the largely peasant-orientated work and *Private Life of an Indian Prince*. Niven suggests that after this novel Anand's work separates into two strands – the autobiographical fiction and the fable-like, folk-art stories and novellas.

SHARMA's book is a somewhat uneven, but nevertheless substantial, collection of criticism. It brings together 16 essays from India and elsewhere, which approach Anand's fiction from a variety of critical stances. M.K. Naik's essay on the short stories is especially important, as Anand's stories are often overlooked by the authors of full-length studies of his fiction. With reference to the influences of traditional Indian tales, his mother, and various Western writers, Naik discusses the social satire, humour, and acute psychological perception present in the stories. Among the essays on the novels, Dieter Riemenschneider's socio-literary discussion of Anand's Marxist-socialist understanding of human labour provides an interesting context for analysis of some of the early novels.

FISHER sets out "to introduce Mulk Raj Anand to audiences and potential readers of his works to whom he is unknown or little known". The strength of the work lies in its biographical approach and it is best seen as a study of the influence of Anand's life on his work rather than as a critical study of the works themselves. The final chapters, which deal with Anand's founding and editing of the art magazine *Marg*, are particularly noteworthy as they cover ground only touched on by most of the critical studies, which focus on his fiction.

MUKHERJEE, conscious of the failings of postcolonial theory always to question the validity of the voice of postcolonial writers, applies a "hermeneutic of suspicion" to Anand's first and probably best-known novel, *Untouchable*. She analyses Anand's novel in terms of its "absences" and "strategies of containment" to produce a reading that is radically different from earlier humanist or socio-literary readings. In particular, she reminds us that "*Untouchable* represents the untouchables as they appear to the gaze of an upper class, upper caste *kshatriya* Hindu". The article invites similar re-readings of Anand's other works, as well as works by other postcolonial writers.

DHAWAN's book contains 31 short pieces on Anand's fiction, which offer perspectives on a selection of texts up to *Little Plays of Mahatma Gandhi* (1991). Although it lacks editorial direction (there is no Introduction), it is useful for the number of essays and disparate views it gathers together. The section comprising five pieces under the heading "Themes and Techniques" includes an interesting comparative essay by Shyam Asnani, which considers Anand's novel *The Old Woman and the Cow* (1960), which has a female central character, alongside early novels by Anita Desai and Nayantara Sahgal.

RALPH J. CRANE

Anderson, Sherwood 1876–1941

American novelist, short-story writer, and essayist

Anderson, David D., *Sherwood Anderson: An Introduction and Interpretation*, New York: Holt, Rinehart & Winston, 1967

Burbank, Rex James, *Sherwood Anderson*, New York: Twayne, 1964

Carabine, Keith, *Sherwood Anderson's Novels: "An Excessive Waste of Faith"*, Charleston, North Carolina: *Mark Twain Journal*, 1983

Crowley, John W. (ed.), *New Essays on "Winesburg, Ohio"*, Cambridge and New York: Cambridge University Press, 1990

Howe, Irving, *Sherwood Anderson*, London: Methuen, 1951

Kazin, Alfred, "The New Realism: Sherwood Anderson and Sinclair Lewis", in his *On Native Grounds: An Interpretation of Modern American Prose Literature*, New York: Harcourt, Brace & Co., and Reynal & Hitchcock, both 1942; London: Jonathan Cape, 1943

Rideout, Walter B. (ed.), *Sherwood Anderson: A Collection of Critical Essays*, Englewood Cliffs, New Jersey: Prentice-Hall, 1974

Townsend, Kim, *Sherwood Anderson*, Boston: Houghton Mifflin, 1987

Trilling, Lionel, "Sherwood Anderson", in his *The Liberal Imagination: Essays on Literature and Society*, Garden City, New York: Doubleday, 1950; London: Secker & Warburg, 1951

Weber, Brom, *Sherwood Anderson*, Minneapolis: University of Minnesota Press, 1964

White, Ray Lewis (ed.), *The Achievement of Sherwood Anderson: Essays in Criticism*, Chapel Hill: University of North Carolina Press, 1966

Williams, Kenny J., *A Storyteller and a City: Sherwood Anderson's Chicago*, DeKalb: Northern Illinois University Press, 1988

Sherwood Anderson's critics have righly recognized the very important place that he occupies in any history of American fiction in the early years of the twentieth century and, indeed, his pre-eminent position in the emergence of American modernism, both in respect of his writings and his encouragement of other writers. His own merits as a writer, however, remain a matter of debate and, broadly speaking, his critics maintain that his failings as a novelist are compensated for by his strengths as a short-story writer. As a whole, his work has been eclipsed by that of his now more famous contemporaries, particularly William Faulkner, F. Scott Fitzgerald, and Ernest Hemingway, and critical commentary on him has, it must be said, reached something of an impasse.

KAZIN's essay on "The New Realism" argues that *Winesburg, Ohio* and Sinclair Lewis's *Main Street* are, in effect, essays of cultural and social emancipation, revolts "against small-town life in the Middle West", notable both for their dramatization of "common experience" and their contributions to the more general "struggle for realism". Kazin emphasises Anderson's indebtedness to European models of modernist fiction, particularly those of Dorothy Richardson, Virginia Woolf, and James Joyce, and their treatment of the unconscious, though he suggests that what interested Anderson was "sex as a disturbance in consciousness, the kind of disturbance that drove so many of his heroes out of the world of constraint" and the resulting loneliness, which gives his characters significance. Kazin's argument is best understood in its applicability to the characters in *Winesburg, Ohio*, but the essay is a general treatment of Anderson's work and, though brief, is frequently illuminating.

HOWE's book is one of the earliest extended commentaries on his work. The guiding thesis is that "what has been distinctive in American literature is a tradition of gifted figures who managed only once or twice to realize their talent". Anderson is a minor figure, who is important more for his "place" (notably his encouragement of others and his central role in the assault on the "genteel tradition") in American letters than for individual works of high literary merit. Howe's reading of *Winesburg, Ohio* is particularly interesting for the emphasis it places on the influences of George Borrow and Ivan Turgenev, the former as a guide to how the writer might live, the latter as to how he might write. A concluding chapter on "An American as Artist" intelligently raises questions about the effects of the "absence of an ample sense of tradition" on the developments of literary talent in the United States, and Anderson is seen, finally, as a "dramatic instance of a gifted writer impoverished by a constricting culture".

TRILLING's essay is now over half a century old, but it contains some of the most trenchant criticism of the limitations of Anderson's fiction yet written. Trilling accuses the fiction of "an inadequate representation of reality": "there are very few sights, sounds, and smells, very little of the stuff of actuality", and his characters have "not only no wit, but no idiom". Anderson is, for Trilling, a writer who speaks in "visions and mysteries and raptures", but these traits, and the characters in whom Anderson seeks to embody them, are not sufficient "to make an adequate antagonism to the culture which Anderson opposed". Though this essay says virtually nothing about individual works, it is both challenging and perceptive, and those who seek to appreciate Anderson's works must of necessity try to answer Trilling's objections.

BURBANK's book (in Twayne's "United States Authors" series) provides both a brief biographical overview and critical commentary on all the major works. Burbank's argument rests on what he sees as Anderson's particular vantage point: he was "admirably equipped, in range and variety of experience, to explore the possibilities and limitations of Midwestern American life". Burbank is insistent on what he calls Anderson's "populist temper", evident especially in his first two novels, a "strange amalgamation of Jeffersonian agrarian primitivism and secular Calvinism that made up the 'folklore of Populism' which was . . . a powerful ideological force in Anderson's Midwest". This, in part, Burbank suggests, accounts for the "itinerary" of many of Anderson's heroes, frequently moving from small towns to the larger world, where they come into contact with more complex, often duplicitous, values. Burbank's book is notable for the extended consideration he gives to the "minor" novels and the short stories written after *Winesburg, Ohio*.

WEBER's brief study (in the University of Minnesota "Pamphlets on American Writers" series) is a serviceable introduction to Anderson's work, combining biography and critical commentary. Weber is alert to the failings of the novels (they are frequently "structurally flawed" and "uneven" in character) but he argues that, ironically, "his alleged weaknesses . . . have become strengths", for though Anderson wrote in an age "which believed it could master the disorder of existence with patterns of order derived from myth and ideologies of the past or else with descriptions of objects and behavior that possessed the irreducible precision of scientific writing", he rejected both these "solutions". This, for Weber, makes him "modern".

WHITE's collection, the first of its kind on Anderson, drew together most of the important writing on Anderson that had appeared to date. The volume as a whole is dedicated to White's sense of that "distinctive position" Anderson occupies in the history of American letters: a writer who revitalized the "stream of literary naturalism by demonstrating a concern with inward, psychological reality", a writer who brought European developments in the arts and psychology to the attention of the American reading public, and a writer who "influenced the development of the American short story more strongly than anyone else except, possibly, Edgar Allan

Poe". Lewis reprints the influential essays of Waldo Frank and Lionel Trilling, William Faulkner's "Appreciation", and critical essays by Irving Howe, Charles Child Walcutt, Frederick J. Hoffman (from his book *Freudianism and the Literary Mind*), and David D. Anderson, among others. This is an important collection.

David ANDERSON's short book combines a useful biographical summary with more-extensive critical commentary on the major works. He argues that to see Anderson primarily as a writer of short stories is to misrepresent his achievement as a writer, and there is a concerted, if finally unpersuasive, effort here to make a case for the novels. He recognizes the weaknesses of *Windy McPherson's Son*, but insists firmly on the virtues of later novels, such as *Poor White*. He takes issue with those who wish to see Anderson, somewhat reductively, as a critic of small-town America, and suggests that there is greater ambiguity in his treatment of the small town than might first meet the eye. This is a useful introduction to Anderson's life and writing.

RIDEOUT's is a most valuable anthology of Anderson criticism, though there is some overlap with the collection edited by Lewis (see above). Included here are Waldo Frank's 1916 essay in praise of Anderson's "emerging greatness", the reviews by Ernest Hemingway and Gertrude Stein of *A Story Teller's Story*, Malcolm Cowley's perceptive introduction to *Winesburg, Ohio*, Faulkner's "Appreciation", Trilling's essay (see above), and essays by Rex Burbank, T.K. Whipple, and Irving Howe, among others. This is certainly a useful starting-point for the beginning student of Anderson.

CARABINE's brief study (in the *Mark Twain Journal* monograph series) is well worth reading for its trenchant criticism of Anderson's failure as a novelist. He argues that claims for Anderson's accomplishments are "untenable because they fail to recognize that Anderson's inability to handle narrative continuity, point of view and character radically undermines any 'case' for his status", and that it is the "loose form" of *Winesburg, Ohio* that better exploits his talents as a writer and his particular vision of life. This thesis is argued through close readings of sequences from *Windy McPherson's Son* and *Poor White*, sequences that demonstrate failures of intelligence and execution, and reveal a novelist whose "sensibility was generous but also crude and diffused". Carabine shows how the stress on individual lives in *Winesburg, Ohio*, and the presentation of fragments of experience, enables Anderson to "bypass" those difficulties he encounters when writing extended narratives.

TOWNSEND's recent biography is up-to-date, scholarly, and readable. The stress is on a man who never quite "fitted in" to whatever world it was in which he moved – small Ohio town or big city – and whose life was characterized by a struggle for sexual maturity and identity, so much so that his boyhood came to seem, in retrospect, the climax of his life. The value of this biography is the extensive use Townsend makes of the literary works, the fiction being mined for biographical evidence without any disservice done to its imaginative integrity.

WILLIAMS's detailed account of the role that the city of Chicago played in Anderson's literary career is both an important contribution to an understanding of his work and, more generally, to an understanding of what literary historians call "the Chicago School" of writing. The two Chicago novels, *Windy McPherson's Son* and *Marching Men*, are seen as questioning the kind of realism associated with William Dean Howells and the "success formula" novel of the late nineteenth century. *Winesburg, Ohio* is read as a unified modernist work, mainly through what Williams sees as a complex pattern of imagery, metaphors, and motifs. The overarching argument is that Chicago functions as a symbolic point of reference in many of Anderson's works. Though this book has a somewhat specialised compass, it offers one of the most informed accounts we have of the literary, cultural, and social milieu in which Anderson wrote.

CROWLEY's collection draws together four newly-commissioned essays on *Winesburg, Ohio* and an introductory essay by the editor. David Stouck writes on the link between Anderson's prose style and techniques in expressionist art, particularly in painting, arguing that Anderson's task was to give "outward expression to the intense private feelings of both the artist and the characters he created". In "*Winesburg, Ohio* and the Autobiographical Moment" Marcia Johnson considers the work as "a complex autobiographical fiction", a "meditation on autobiographical issues and an exploration of the relationship between past and present selves". Clare Colquitt explores continuities in the treatment of "motherlove" between *Winesburg, Ohio* and Sarah Orne Jewett's *The Country of the Pointed Firs*, despite what she calls "the ultimately conceptual gulf that separates Anderson's and Jewett's disparate portraits of the artist". The final essay, by Thomas Yingling, entitled "*Winesburg, Ohio* and the End of Collective Experience", suggests that Anderson's stories often enact a confrontation between collectivity and separation, usually seen through a "number of ritualized moments when the town exists as a single social unit"; Yingling's approach emphasises Marxist models of social decline, specifically alienation from social relations and the commodification of culture.

HENRY CLARIDGE

Anglo-Irish Literature *see* Irish Literature

Anglo-Welsh Literature *see* Welsh Literature

Apocalyptic Literature

Emmerson, Richard K., and Bernard McGinn (eds.), *The Apocalypse in the Middle Ages*, Ithaca, New York: Cornell University Press, 1992

Frye, Northrop, *The Great Code: The Bible and Literature*, Toronto: Academic Press Canada, 1982; New York: Harcourt Brace Jovanovich, 1982; London: Routledge & Kegan Paul, 1982

Kermode, Frank, *The Sense of an Ending: Studies in the Theory of Fiction*, London and New York: Oxford University Press, 1966

O'Leary, Stephen D., *Arguing the Apocalypse: A Theory of Millennial Rhetoric*, Oxford and New York: Oxford University Press, 1994

Patrides, C.A., and Joseph Wittreich (eds.), *The Apocalypse in English Renaissance Thought and Literature: Patterns, Antecedents, and Repercussions*, Ithaca, New York: Cornell University Press, 1984; Manchester: Manchester University Press, 1984

Stocker, Margarita, *Apocalyptic Marvell: The Second Coming in Seventeenth-Century Poetry*, Athens: Ohio University Press, 1986; Brighton, Sussex: Harvester Press, 1986

"Apocalypse" derives from a Greek word meaning revelation; by far the most influential apocalypse in Western literature is John of Patmos's Book of Revelation, the last book in the Christian Bible. This reveals the things that will come to pass at the end of Christian time – the final vanquishing of the Antichrist and Babylon the Great, and the establishment of New Jerusalem, the Kingdom of the saved. It predicts global catastrophe as well as cosmic renewal. Apocalyptic literature since the Book of Revelation, then, is preoccupied with the timetabling of the end of the world as well as with depicting disasters, which will precede the coming of ultimate peace. Scholarship on apocalyptic literature is divided between works that trace the history of the exegesis of apocalypse in relation to both the Bible and more secular works, and those that reflect upon the influence on literature of Revelation's "fictive" structures, themes, images, and narrative frames.

EMMERSON and McGINN's anthology presents the authoritative current version of medieval readings of apocalypse. A series of essays covers the apocalypse in medieval thought, art, and culture, and each section is prefaced by a brief and helpful introduction. Emmerson and McGinn emphasise the conservatism of medieval readings of apocalypse, governed by Saint Augustine's claim in his *City of God* that Revelation's time scheme was not to be read literally but rather to be understood poetically as a figure for the fullness of earthly time. They trace Joachim of Fiore's deconstruction of Augustine, with his three ages of the Father, the Son, and the Spirit. Building on the seminal work of Marjorie Reeves, they show how, though he himself was not a prophetic enthusiast, Joachim's claims could provoke millennial excitement and civic unrest in the hands of less ironic spirits than Joachim himself. Various essays then amplify these introductory comments; most useful are those which discuss visual art, sculpture, or written texts. The whole makes an excellent companion to PATRIDES and WITTREICH's book on Renaissance apocalypse. This volume also contains material by the main authorities in the field. Their editors' brief is far wider than the title suggests. They situate the Renaissance amid discussions of apocalypse since the time of John of Patmos and developments up to, and including, the twentieth century. Effectively, the book is a history of apocalypse in the English-speaking world. It includes a massive bibliography of commentaries on, and versions of, apocalypse. Its main focus, however, is the centrality of apocalypse in English Renaissance literature, with essays on Edmund Spenser's *The Faerie Queene*, Shakespeare's *King Lear*, and Milton's *Paradise Lost*. Necessarily these are schematic, sacrificing detail for the sake of overview: zeal for apocalypse frequently crowds out human details. Nevertheless, given the authority and sweep of its coverage, this is the single most useful reference work available on the subject of apocalyptic literature.

STOCKER's study is much more restricted in focus. She covers a single poet, Andrew Marvell, and a single epoch – the middle of the seventeenth century. Nevertheless, as Patrides and Wittreich show, this was a crucial period in the history of apocalyptic exegesis, for the disconfirmation of mid-seventeenth century prophecies eventually gave rise to the more allegorical and psychological applications of apocalypse that have become the norm in the modern period. Stocker surveys all of Marvell's texts. Her vision of him is provocative: she holds him to have been a true believer in the Apocalypse, rapturously awaiting the final days, in which his hero, Oliver Cromwell, seemed destined to play a large, perhaps even messianic part. Stocker is deeply learned in seventeenth century commentaries on apocalypse, and she makes many astute and original points. Despite this, her enthusiasm leads her to push the case too far, and to neglect the complex textures of Marvell's verse. As well as a study of Renaissance apocalypse, her book would be useful for anyone wishing to learn the profit, as well as the pitfalls, of reading literary texts in an apocalyptic light.

This approach is KERMODE's self-appointed task also, though he is too sceptical a humanist to fall into the poetic dogma Stocker promotes. For Kermode, the Apocalypse becomes part of his ongoing inquiry into the shape of our fictions and the dangerous pleasures of decoding them. He takes the Revelation as paradigm for all our fictions – stories which have beginnings and endings. A story which begins so promisingly in the Book of Genesis is thus wound up, not without some travail, in the last chapters of Revelation. Kermode subverts the demands of dogma. He insists we recognise the power that the fictions of apocalypse – the ultimate "sense of an ending" – have over us, but that we not mistake this power for reality, and convert the fiction into reified myth. Kermode elegantly shows how and why agnostics and atheists must concern themselves with biblical fictions, to rescue them for literature from their more fundamentalist interpreters.

Whereas Kermode's interest is in the psychology of narrative, FRYE's is on the psychology of mythic structure. The Bible is still one of our master narratives, and underpins most secular narratives. His luminous work places the Apocalypse within the overarching structure of the Bible, leading from Creation through to Apocalypse in a single sequence. Frye thinks it possible also to "freeze-frame" the entire Bible, to see it as one gigantic image. From that perspective, the Apocalypse is the epitome of all the Bible has to say, a full grammar of all its images. Those images, in turn, are the poetic epitome of human aspirations, at least in the Christian West, so the Apocalypse, and literature deriving from it "is the way the world looks after the ego has disappeared". Frye's vision of Apocalypse derives from William Blake: he transformed Apocalypse into a prophetic myth of internal transformation which, once achieved, would transform the external cosmos. It is not at all clear what this may eventually mean, and Frye's work is certainly not for the uninitiated; yet his Apocalypse has something of the sweep of the original text, and his witty and riddling rhetoric make this a profound modern commentary on what apocalypse might yet mean.

O'LEARY's work signals that apocalypse will continue to preoccupy many readers up to and beyond the year 2000. His work is a useful contrast to Kermode and Frye. O'Leary focuses on Apocalypse's persuasive power rather than narrative or imagery. Why is it that, time and again, people can be convinced of the accuracy of prophecy? When prophecy is disconfirmed, how can people relocate their aspirations without losing faith in the eventual Apocalypse itself? O'Leary's answer to these questions relies on the structure of argument in Apocalypse. Its power is the solution it offers to the problem of evil in time: in time, evil will eventually be cast down, by a final authority. O'Leary briefly surveys the history of reading the Apocalypse, before examining in exhaustive detail William Miller's nineteenth-century lectures on prophecy, and Hal Lindsey's best-selling linkages of Revelation's imagery with the invention of the atom bomb and the creation of Israel: both events hold out the promise of a final battle for the Holy Land and for the world as a whole. O'Leary deftly shows how shrewd Lindsey's rhetoric is, and how persuasive his twentieth-century apocalypse can seem. Though O'Leary focuses on populist commentators, his paradigms would be of use to anyone reading apocalyptic texts. His own writing is conspicuously graceless; yet his study will be useful to keep on hand, a Hemingwayesque "bullshit detector", as the tide of prophecy rises – as it seems it must – as this millennium wanes.

MARK HOULAHAN

Arnold, Matthew 1822–1888

English poet, essayist, and critic

apRoberts, Ruth, *Arnold and God*, Berkeley: University of California Press, 1983

Bloom, Harold (ed.), *Matthew Arnold*, New York: Chelsea House, 1987

Buckler, William E., *On the Poetry of Matthew Arnold: Essays in Critical Reconstruction*, New York: New York University Press 1982

Collini, Stefan, *Arnold*, Oxford and New York: Oxford University Press, 1988

Culler, A. Dwight, *Imaginative Reason: The Poetry of Matthew Arnold*, New Haven, Connecticut: Yale University Press, 1966

DeLaura, David J., *Hebrew and Hellene in Victorian England: Newman, Arnold, Pater*, Austin: University of Texas Press, 1969

Honan, Park, *Matthew Arnold: A Life*, London: Weidenfeld & Nicolson, 1981; New York: McGraw-Hill, 1981

Miller, J. Hillis, *The Disappearance of God: Five Nineteenth Century Writers*, Cambridge, Massachusetts: Belknap Press of Harvard University Press, 1963, 2nd edition, 1975

Riede, David G., *Matthew Arnold and the Betrayal of Language*, Charlottesville: University Press of Virginia, 1988

Roper, Alan, *Arnold's Poetic Landscapes*, Baltimore: Johns Hopkins University Press, 1969

Schneider, Mary W., *Poetry in the Age of Democracy: The Literary Criticism of Matthew Arnold*, Lawrence: University Press of Kansas, 1989

Trilling, Lionel, *Matthew Arnold*, New York: Norton, 1939; London: Allen & Unwin, 1939; 2nd edition, New York: Columbia University Press, 1949

Critics approaching Arnold generally decide whether they want to concentrate on Arnold the poet, or Arnold the critic, and studies that combine the two approaches are rare. TRILLING's venerable biographical-critical study still has its uses. The straightforward readings of the poetry (as a poetry of loss) and the valuable account of the prose writings do combine to provide a coherent account of Arnold's development, and Trilling nicely elaborates what he calls "the complex unity" of his whole career. HONAN's biography is the only English-language one in print (Arnold asked in his will that there be no biographies), and it manages the task of integrating Arnold's poetry and prose well enough, while accumulating an impressive amount of detail. A more manageable, and in ways more useful, introduction is provided by COLLINI's brief but fertile study. The emphasis is more on Arnold as a literary and cultural critic, and the chapter on the poetry is good but brief; but notwithstanding the limitations of so short a work, this is an intelligent and cogent place to begin study of Arnold. Not least among its virtues is a dry and witty prose style, which would certainly have gained Arnold's approval.

BLOOM's book is part of an extensive series of collected essays, "Modern Critical Views", all chosen and introduced by Bloom; the standard of individual volumes can be rather hit-and-miss, but this one, on Arnold, is better than many. Bloom's Introduction articulates his thesis that "Arnold is a Romantic poet who did not wish to be one, an impossible conflict which caused him finally to abandon poetry for literary criticism and prose prophecy". The essays that follow explore various aspects of this theme, including excerpts from classic studies by Hillis Miller, Geoffrey Tillotson, and Ruth apRoberts. The collection concludes with an interesting essay on *Empedocles on Etna* by Sara Sulieri, only available in this volume.

Several specialist studies of Arnold's poetry are of particular merit. MILLER's chapter on Arnold remains vital. In step with the argument Miller advances in the book as a whole – that a consciousness of God's withdrawal from the world directly shaped the major Victorian writers – Arnold is praised for the courage and consistency with which he recognises the immensely painful (for him) fragmentation of experience, and the impermanence and instability of his aesthetic. For Miller, Arnold is a key figure in Victorian literature "in the subversions of his irony, and in his courageous recording of what was most negative in his spiritual experience". He does run the risk, in withdrawing from the present, of attempting to embalm a dead past: but "in the end Arnold no longer faces toward the lost past, but toward the future return of the divine spirit, a return which he can almost see".

CULLER traces what he calls the "poetic or imaginative world" of Arnold's verse, seeing in the deployment of certain symbolic features (the "River of Life", the "Darkling Plain", and the "Forest Glade") elements of an ultimately unified vision. Culler uses these figures to examine Arnold's relationship with his Romantic predecessors, and his attempts to create a distinctive, post-Romantic poetry. He argues that it is in Arnold's elegies that we find his crowning achievement, and in particular in the way Arnold re-casts traditional elegiac forms to allow himself space for creative self-transformation. Some of Culler's readings do appear overly schematic, but the cumulative effect of his study is convincing.

ROPER's work is a study of the recurrence of descriptions of landscape in Arnold's poetry: "landscape features rarely operate in Arnold's poems as mere decorative backdrop, but are again and again the source and correlative of a mood and a representation of a kind of life". Roper asserts that Arnold, as poet, worked and reworked elements of "what is recognizably the same landscape", and he sets out to map the fluid symbolic and metaphorical significances of that landscape. After an opening chapter on Arnold's poetics, there are various chapters on landscape in different poems, as well as chapters dealing with recurring landscape features (Mount Etna, the Cumnor Hills).

BUCKLER's study seeks a reappraisal of the "more or less benign interpretive myths" that (he argues) have grown up around Arnold's poetry. He begins by stating what he sees as the threefold traditional view – that Arnold was an autobiographical poet, whose poetic mode consisted of the making of straightforward statements, and who was the creator of a fragmented, centerless poetry. In place of this, Buckler sets out to read Arnold as a "dramatic or personative poet" (although closer in this respect to Thomas Hardy than to Robert Browning), whose work is centered on an "acutely conscious literariness". The reading is subtle and persuasive, and it stresses the ironic and suggestive possibilities or Arnold's poetry.

Certain aspects of Arnold's long career as a writer of prose have come under critical scrutiny, although it has to be said that many important areas remain unexplored. DeLAURA treats Arnold's thought at some length, particularly in its relationships to that of John Henry Newman and Walter Pater. This study sees Arnold's distinction (made in *Culture and Anarchy*) between Hebrew and Hellene, religious and secular, as a dialectic "concerned with nothing less than the total 'vision' of Arnold". Arnold, J.S. Mill, and Pater were all directly concerned with the relationship between traditional religion and with "Culture" in the broader sense.

ApROBERTS's large and impressive study of Arnold's religion (in which "religion" is taken broadly as, in Carlyle's phrase, "a man's relationship to the Eternities and Immensities") remains one of the best analyses of Arnold's thought we have. Even after ten years it is difficult to deny apRoberts's main point – that most studies of Arnold shy away from exploring his writings on religious subjects, and that the result of this is "a notably incomplete view of Arnold" in which "the chief fact, which makes sense of the whole, is missing". She convincingly demonstrates that Arnold's central aesthetic/political concept – "Culture" – subsumed religion just as much as it subsumed literature and art, and that we need to address Arnold's religious writings head-on if we wish to comprehend his work.

RIEDE sees the crisis at the heart of Arnold's writings as having less to do with belief in God, and more with concern over language. "Language itself", he says, "was in a state of 'wandering', of perpetual errantry in error". He examines Arnold's (admittedly amateur) philological interests, and connects theories of language (both Victorian and modern-day) with Arnold's poetry and prose. Briefly, language "betrays" Arnold in the way it refuses to allow him to believe in a transcendental word, a language in which "word" = "thing".

SCHNEIDER attempts, quite refreshingly, to correct readings of Arnold as an "élitist" cultural theorist by careful attention to the literary criticism and other prose writings. Arnold's belief in democracy is shown as modelled on the sort of participatory models of Ancient Greece, and Arnold possessed a genuine hope that modern society could emulate that paradigm. The key was education, and Schneider places particular emphasis on Arnold's writings on that subject.

ADAM ROBERTS

Ashbery, John 1927–

American poet

Bloom, Harold (ed.), *John Ashbery*, New York: Chelsea House, 1985

Lehman, David (ed.), *Beyond Amazement: New Essays on John Ashbery*, Ithaca, New York: Cornell University Press, 1980

Perloff, Marjorie, *The Poetics of Indeterminacy: Rimbaud to Cage*, Princeton, New Jersey: Princeton University Press, 1981

Shapiro, David, *John Ashbery: An Introduction to the Poetry*, New York: Columbia University Press, 1979

Ward, Geoff, *Statutes of Liberty: The New York School of Poets*, New York: St Martin's Press, 1993; London: Macmillan, 1993

Often regarded – along with such writers as Frank O'Hara and Kenneth Koch – as a poet of the "New York School", John Ashbery's first major critical acclaim came when W.H. Auden selected his manuscript of *Some Trees* for the Yale Younger Poets Prize in 1956. His reputation then grew quietly until it received sudden consolidation in 1975, when his volume *Self-Portrait in a Convex Mirror* won the three most prestigious book prizes in America – the Pulitzer, the National Book Award, and the National Book Critics Circle Award. Though unquestionably a prominent poet, now appearing on the syllabi of many university English courses, Ashbery remains controversial. Regarded by some as a writer of gratuitously difficult or even largely unintelligible verse, Ashbery is hailed by others as America's most important living poet. Ashbery's poetry is often described as "abstract", and he himself has likened it to non-representational, non-literary art forms:

> I feel I could express myself best in music. What I like about music is its ability of being convincing, of carrying an argument through successfully to the finish, though the terms of this argument remain unknown quantities. What remains is the structure, the architecture of the argument, scene or story. I would like to do this in poetry.
>
> (Biographical Note, *A Controversy of Poets*, 1965)

Broadly, critics have tended to see Ashbery's poetry as primarily either referential or non-referential: a poetry that is – despite its surface oddness – determinably "about" things, or, on the other hand, a poetry that radically emphasizes process over content, rhythm and image over denotative meaning. Somewhat parallel is the tendency to regard Ashbery as primarily either "American" or "French" in poetic lineage and temperament.

SHAPIRO, himself a talented poet who is sometimes regarded as belonging to a "second generation" of the New York School, wrote this first book-length study of Ashbery almost two decades ago. The theoretical framework of the book resonates strongly with the brand of deconstructionism that Sextus Empiricus would surely have diagnosed as academic skepticism. Shapiro begins by applauding Ashbery as a "master of those who do know they do not know", and concludes that "Ashbery's poignant privacies affirm our elaborated sense of the certainty of uncertainty". Yet, despite Shapiro's programmatic emphasis on radical opacity – which would seem implicitly to deny the possibility of insight – his readings of the poems are often revealing. He is especially adept at proposing possible intertextualities in allusions, influences, and analogues. His study is valuable also for its substantial biographical material – culled from personal discussion and correspondence with Ashbery – which is available nowhere else.

LEHMAN opens his book with an excellent concise history of Ashbery's critical reception – large-heartedly quoting from Ashbery's "detractors" as well as his champions – and also provides helpful synopses of the essays he collects. The articles cover an impressive range of topics. Lawrence Kramer and Leslie Wolf, for example, explore Ashbery's affinities with music and the visual arts respectively. Seeing a political agenda in the poetry, Keith Cohen argues that "Ashbery aims consistently at the glibness, deceitfulness, and vapidity of bourgeois discourse". Fred Moramarco offers a favourable re-evaluation of Ashbery's most maligned book, *The Tennis Court Oath* (1962), a volume Harold Bloom (see below) had censured as "a bog" and "a great mass of egregious disjunctiveness". As one of only two existing anthologies of essays on Ashbery to date, this is an important volume.

PERLOFF's influential book argues that we cannot "really come to terms with the major poetic experiments of our time" without gaining a better understanding of what she calls "the French connection". For Perloff, Ashbery is a chief figure in this "other tradition":

> Not *what* one dreams but *how* – this is Ashbery's subject. His stories "tell only of themselves," presenting the reader with the challenge of what he calls "an open field of narrative possibilities". For, like Rimbaud's, his are not dreams "about" such and such characters or events; the dream structure is itself the event that haunts the poet's imagination.

Wisely delimiting the range of interpretive possibilities, Perloff assures us that Ashbery's indeterminacy does not entail that his "poetry is merely incoherent, [or] that anything goes". Reading a representative poem closely, she concludes that "however open the meaning of individual lines or passages may be, images do coalesce to create, not a coherent narrative with a specific theme, but a precise tonality of feeling".

BLOOM's reading of Ashbery is heavily informed by his own theory of poetry, first outlined in *The Anxiety of Influence* (1973). Downplaying Ashbery's associations with both the French surrealists and the label "New York School", Bloom prefers to see him as a unique individual who produces his best poetry chiefly when struggling with the influence of his American precursors, particularly Walt Whitman and Wallace Stevens. Though Bloom's view of Ashbery is controversial, there is much perceptiveness in the articles he collects (including the three he wrote himself): Bloom's characterizing of the poetry, for instance, as offering a "curious radiance" and "qualified epiphanies" is excellent. Also worth special note is Richard Howard's treatment of Ashbery's first six books, as well as David Kalstone's discussion of *Self-Portrait in a Convex Mirror*. In another important article, Helen Vendler places Ashbery – as Bloom does – firmly within the Anglo-American tradition of poetry; yet, while even Bloom admits to being occasionally puzzled by an Ashbery poem, Vendler downplays Ashbery's difficulty, claiming "it is possible to explain his 'hard' parts, too, given time, patience, and an acquaintance with his manner". Of all Ashbery critics, Vendler has the strongest faith in his referentiality: while discussing the "short lyrics" in *As We Know*, Vendler claims they "are all 'about' something", and lists Ashbery's main topics as "love, or time, or age".

WARD's is a continually incisive and lucidly written study of the New York School, with an excellent long chapter on "Ashbery and Influence". He helpfully discusses the continuing British puzzlement over Ashbery, which contrasts with Ashbery's powerful influence on the American so-called "Language Poets", some of whom are inspired especially by Ashbery's volume *The Tennis Court Oath*. Ward reads Ashbery closely and well, and his interpretations are informed by a thorough familiarity with several relevant contexts – political, sexual, literary-historical, and biographical. Except for its largely ignoring Kenneth Koch's work, Ward's study is one of the most balanced and discerning treatments of New York School poetry to date.

MICHAEL LONDRY

Asian-American Literature

Cheung, King-Kok, *Articulate Silences: Hisaye Yamamoto, Maxine Hong Kingston, Joy Kogawa*, Ithaca, New York: Cornell University Press, 1993

Chin, Frank, Jeffrey Paul Chan, Lawson Fusao Inada, and Shawn Wong (eds.), *AIIIEEEEE!: An Anthology of Asian American Writers*, Washington, D.C.: Howard University Press, 1974; 2nd edition, New York: Mentor Press, 1991

Hongo, Garrett (ed.), *The Open Boat: Poems from Asian America*, New York: Doubleday, 1993

Houston, Velina Hasu, *The Politics of Life: Four Plays by Asian American Women*, Philadelphia: Temple University Press, 1993

Kim, Elaine, *Asian American Literature: An Introduction to the Writings and Their Social Context*, Philadelphia: Temple University Press, 1982

Lim, Shirley G., and Amy Ling, *Reading the Literatures of Asian America*, Philadelphia: Temple University Press, 1992

Sumida, Steven, *And the View from the Shore: Literary Traditions from Hawai'i*, Seattle: University of Washington Press, 1991

Wong, Sau-Ling, *Reading Asian American Literature: From Necessity to Extravagance*, Princeton, New Jersey: Princeton University Press, 1993

Asian-American literature has had a dynamic, continuously changing definition since the term and genre arose when a body of work was claimed as such by writers and members of CARP (Combined Asian Resources Project) in the early 1970s. A myriad of texts can claim inclusion in the genre, based on their themes (issues of Asian American historical, political, sociological, and psychological experiences), aesthetics (marked by attempts to define ethnic poetics and aesthetics of the genre), or identity politics (of writers who claim an Asian-American identification in their heritage, which somehow defines their work). In fact, a history of such literature dates as far back as the late 1800s, with Yan Phou's autobiography.

"Asian-American literature" can also refer to literature which, thematically, can be located in texts penned in languages other than English: an example would be the Chinese poems published in Mark Him Lai and Judy Yung's *Island Poetry and History of Chinese Immigration* (1980). The poems here describe immigration experiences, and were composed and carved on barrack walls during 1910–40 by immigrant Chinese men detained on Angel Island, the detention center off the coast of northern California. And literature such as David Mura's autobiographical novel *Turning Japanese* (1988), about his experiences as a third-generation Japanese American in Japan, may be described as "Asian-American", even though it is not about life in the United States.

LIM and LING's book is a collection of essays, which attempts to "read" Asian-American literatures across the terrains of boundaries (both geographical and cultural), race, gender, and identity (of "other" and of the self). Lim opens this penetrating collection with a sharp investigation of American identity, introducing it as one of ambivalence. In the hands of minority writers, this ambivalence acquires a doubled or multiple perspective. George Uba's essay is interesting for its focus on Asian-American activist poets, a marginal group within the already marginalized group of Asian-American poets. Other essays cover other critically little-explored subjects: Korean-American literature, sexuality in Chinese immigrant literature, Vietnamese-American literature, Asian-American drama, American orientalist discourse, and Chinese-American literary traditions, to name just a few. If this collection has a weakness, it is that the essays seem to have little connection with one another. However, as the Introduction admits, "the diversity and range of subjects, critical stances, styles, concerns and theoretical grids compellingly demonstrate the heterogeneous, multiple, divergent, polyphonic, multivocal character of Asian American cultural discourse".

CHIN, CHAN, INADA, and WONG's anthology is an important critical resource, being the seminal text of Asian-American literature. Prior to its publication, there was no recognized body of work referred to as "Asian-American literature". Although most of the texts included here are now well-known and back in print, this anthology continues to be important and controversial for its lengthy Introduction, which attempts not only to claim a place in mainstream American literature for this body of work, but also to define an authentic, versus an inauthentic or "fake", Asian-American literary tradition. Urgent in tone, and compelling in its argument against the myth that persons of Asian descent are perpetual "foreigners" in America, the Introduction continues to reflect controversies of identity and artistic responsibility concerning Asian-American writers and literary critics. In addition, the editors continue to hone their visions of Asian-American literature in the expanded anthology *The Big AIIIEEEEE!* (1990), as well as in "AIIIEEEEE! Revisited", the added Preface to the 1991 edition of the original anthology.

KIM's book is another seminal text of Asian-American literature, as it is the first critical survey of the literature. Though Kim's text is now dated, particularly in its inclusion of texts written in English by a limited number of ethnic groups (Japanese-, Chinese-, Korean-, and Filipino-Americans), it is interesting as a historical marker of the development of Asian-American literary studies, as well as of the growth in the number of texts in the genre itself. The popularity and publication of Asian-American literature expanded rapidly in the 1980s and 1990s. At this time of writing, a revised edition of the volume is expected.

HOUSTON's book, although not the first-published anthology of Asian-American drama (Misha Berson's *Between Worlds: Contemporary Asian American Plays*, 1990, claims that honor), is one of two ground-breaking anthologies devoted to works by women playwrights: the other, larger anthology, edited by Roberta Uno and titled *Unbroken Thread* (1993), emerged the same year, but Houston's Introduction is lengthier and more informative in describing how Asian-American theatre and playwrights differ from "mainstream" American counterparts. Of the three anthologies, hers also gives the most comprehensive historical background of the development of Asian-American theatre, delineating two "generations" of playwrights.

HONGO's anthology of Asian-American poetry is notable for its stimulating Introduction by editor and eminent poet Hongo. The theme of "crossing" defines the aim of this anthology, one which represents the Asian immigrant experience of leaving homelands to forge a new life in America, but also marks a "crossing" of the sea of literary intolerance to embrace a diverse multitude of Asian-American poets. Hongo locates this intolerance not only in vanguards of a Eurocentric canon of American poetry, but also in literary critics "who have engaged in the ideological practice of judging the cultural pertinence of a given literary work by employing a litmus test of ethnic authenticity". In short, Hongo argues for a validation of Asian-American artists based not on the political tones in their work but on artistic merits. Although, in its selectivity, an anthology like his contributes to the creation of a "canon" (which Hongo ostensibly is against), the diversity of the 31 poets represented here does succeed in at least expanding the Asian-American poetic canon. His eloquent presentation of the fine distinction between, on the one hand, assessing critically the poetic voice and vision, and on the other proscribing literary style or perspective to uphold an Asian-American thematic will be one which Asian-American poetry will grapple with for some time.

WONG's work is one of a growing number of book-length literary studies of particular kinds of Asian-American text. Wong's dense but deft investigation deals with prose narratives (novels, novellas, autobiographies, and short stories); her project is to clarify the writers' "claiming" of America through a differentiation of Asian-American symbolic configurations from those considered "mainstream American". In particular, in Chapter 1 she looks at the ways in which writers use images of eating and food to examine issues of economic and cultural survival. The second chapter is devoted to the figure of the double, or *Doppelgänger*, as an identifiable mechanism in Asian-American literature to reflect the tension resulting from a culturally reinforced psychological suppression of ethnic identity. A third chapter explores "'unfettered' mobility, a key component of American ideology", and how it is negotiated in the literature, even as it is a historically unfulfilled myth for Asian Americans, limited as they have been by legal and social restraints. Wong's final chapter is devoted to looking at the writers' negotiation of aesthetics and cultural representation, which Wong asserts is expressed through the writers' adoption of a stance of "interested disinterestedness" towards artistic representation in minority communities.

SUMIDA's work makes room in the Asian-American canon for the literature of Asian Pacific Islanders. His work points to the importance of looking at geographical diversity not only in the national and cultural origins of Asian Americans, but also in the diversity across the whole of American territory itself.

CHEUNG's book focuses on the symbolism of silence and articulation in texts by three Asian American women writers – Maxine Hong Kingston, Joy Kogawa, and Hisaye Yamamoto. Cheung traces a feminist resistance and strength to be found in literary trope of silence. She asserts that these writers challenge Eurocentric, logocentric notions of feminism, which value speech and assertiveness over silence. For instance, with regard to Kingston's *Woman Warrior*, Cheung discusses how Kingston subverts the silence of the narrator's first-generation immigrant parents by using it as artistic license to produce a panoply of immigrant Chinese narratives, thereby creating "a national epic" of Chinese-American immigration. With Kogawa's novel *Obasan*, Cheung explores how silence is portrayed as a healing kind of non-verbal communication exemplifying vigilance and grace, especially for first-generation immigrant (Issei) Japanese Canadians, who experienced the pain of family separation and property loss through forced evacuation during World War II. Finally, Cheung looks at silence in the short stories of Yamamoto as a "rhetorical silence", which acts to engage the reader in not only sympathizing with mute characters but also in questioning how masculine, as well as xenophobic, anxiety can lead to a socially and politically enforced silencing of Japanese-American women. Underlying Cheung's careful unravelling of silence in all of these narratives is Trinh T. Minh-ha's notion of the "double oppression" that women of color face, both as women in patriarchal Asian and American societies, and as ethnic minorities in the racialized terrain of North America.

KAREN HAR-YEN CHOW

Atwood, Margaret 1939 –

Canadian novelist, poet, and critic

Davey, Frank, *Margaret Atwood: A Feminist Poetics*, Vancouver: Talonbooks, 1984

Grace, Sherrill E., *A Violent Duality: A Study of Margaret Atwood*, Montreal: Véhicule Press, 1980

Nicholson, Colin E. (ed.), *Margaret Atwood: Writing and Subjectivity: New Critical Essays*, London: Macmillan, 1994; New York: St Martin's Press, 1994

Rigney, Barbara Hill, *Margaret Atwood*, London: Macmillan, 1987; Totowa, New Jersey: Barnes & Noble, 1987

Rosenberg, Jerome H., *Margaret Atwood*, Boston: Twayne, 1984

Van Spanckeren, Kathryn, and Jan Garden Castro (eds.), *Margaret Atwood: Vision and Forms*, Carbondale: Southern Illinois University Press, 1988

The difficult theoretical implications and the sheer diversity of Atwood's work pose considerable problems for the critic; as Rosenberg notes:

> Reviewers of Atwood's work have attempted to place her in many different categories: she has been called a feminist writer, for her incisive commentaries on sex roles; a religious writer, for her visions of spiritual ecstasy; a gothic writer, for her images of grotesques, misfits, and surreal disorientations of the psyche; a writer of the Canadian wilderness; a nationalist writer; a regionalist.

Atwood explores to great effect in both poetry and prose the limitations of dualistic categories and identities, both gender and national. Atwood's work poses other dilemmas for the critic. Some studies attempt to be comprehensive without being reductive, examining her work in the novel, poetry, the short story, and criticism. Others attempt, often in vain, to keep up with Atwood's prolific output.

GRACE's accessible and informative study succeeds as "an interpretive guide to form and theme" in its comprehensive and selective analyses of "the central Atwood canon". It claims to be formalist rather than "theoretical" as regards feminism or structuralism; in spite of this, it acknowledges Atwood's formal diversity and is attentive to the epistemological questions raised by the recurring theme of duality. The formal characteristics of Atwood's work are regarded as developments from her exploration of identity: "Atwood's fiction is written in . . . a mixed style combining realist and romance elements. It is a style well suited to the exploration of the contingency of life, the nature of language and the duplicity of human perception". The "mixed style" and the "sense of pervasive duality in her art" are related to Atwood's contention that the "self is a place not an ego". Although Grace disclaims a feminist approach, she produces perceptive analyses of Atwood's approach to gender.

DAVEY's study contrasts with Grace's in several respects. Subtitled "*A Feminist Poetics*", it is, in fact, formalist rather than feminist. Grace argues that Atwood actively engages with the epistemological problem of duality, asserting "it is not duality but polarity that is destructive". For Davey the dichotomies of Western thought are reversed rather than destabilised by Atwood, and this is detrimental to her work. This argument is particularly evident in Davey's analysis of *Lady Oracle*. Here Atwood is said to emulate rather than parody "male patterns" of quest. Furthermore, Davey's expressive-realist approach discovers many troublesome indeterminacies in Atwood's poetic voice:

> Atwood's recurrent use of personae in these early poems means that the critic can never be sure that Atwood is speaking in her own voice (i.e. out of her own biography or beliefs) and wishes to be held responsible for the implications of a given statement or image. In some cases he cannot be sure about the sex of the speaker.

Davey seems to argue that Atwood's aesthetic is ultimately contradictory. If Atwood ascribes the creative/irrational to the female and the political/rational to the male, her work can be successful neither as "feminist" nor as "creative" in Davey's terms.

Such a critical impasse does not confront RIGNEY, whose study of Atwood, in the "Women Writers" series, is explicitly feminist. Atwood is placed in a (white, Western) female literary tradition, which makes more sense of the serious humour underlying her conflation of styles and forms. For Rigney, Atwood's is a "radical humanism" in which the "morality of language" and the "responsibility of the artist" redefines "humanism" to include, rather than elide, women. Atwood's work is therefore feminist and deconstructive: the apparent conflict between humanism and poststructuralism is a productive tension, reflecting on the problem that gender poses for both of these critical approaches. Like Grace, Rigney identifies an aesthetic consistency in Atwood's poetry and prose: they are therefore analysed together.

ROSENBERG, by contrast, discusses Atwood's poetry, fiction, and non-fiction separately. The historically changing contexts for Atwood's writing are examined in useful detail. Since Atwood's work is controversial it has often met with a hostile critical reception, exemplified by the furore surrounding her *Survival: A Thematic Guide to Canadian Literature* (1972). Particularly illuminating therefore is Rosenberg's assessment of Atwood's relationship with the masculine literary/critical tradition, in which Davey emerges as "one of [Atwood's] more tenacious critical adversaries".

VAN SPANCKEREN and CASTRO edited "a new, comprehensive critical collection encompassing Atwood's recent work". This volume in Sandra M. Gilbert's series "Ad Feminam: Women and Literature" foregrounds the "eclectic" critical approaches selected. The anthology emphasises the diversity of feminist criticism, and treats Atwood's work as cultural practice. The collection breaks disciplinary boundaries and in this respect it is perhaps one of the most comprehensive studies of Atwood's work to date. Critical essays on fiction and poetry are placed alongside an interview with, and an autobiographical piece by, Atwood, a report of a critical "Conversation" between Atwood and a group of students, and colour reproductions of some of "Atwood's rich and disturbing original watercolours".

While NICHOLSON's anthology may not have succeeded in representing the formal diversity of Atwood's work it does succeed in representing its complexity. For some critics *Survival* has proved to be Atwood's most limited work, but for Nicholson it has profound insight into the problems of identity. It "establishes parameters, in substance if not in terminology, for much of the recent theorising of post-colonial representations of literary subjectivity, whether Indian, African, Caribbean or Australian". Nicholson's anthology of post-colonialist, poststructuralist essays on Atwood's "Writing and Subjectivity" expects gender and national identities to be complex and inevitably overlapping. Earlier studies were often bemused or frustrated when Atwood's writing defied the coherence of the autonomous subject presumed by expressive realism. Atwood's treatment of gender and national identities is complex. Her contrariness – in combining the gravely political with the humorously playful, in deconstructing realism through fusion with the gothic, the mythic, the unconscious – finds a home of sorts in postmodernity.

KATHARINE MARY COCKIN

Auden, W.H. 1907–1973

English poet, dramatist, and essayist

Bahlke, George W., *The Later Auden: From "New Year Letter" to "About the House"*, New Brunswick, New Jersey: Rutgers University Press, 1970

Bahlke, George W., (ed.), *Critical Essays on W.H. Auden*, Boston: G.K. Hall, 1991

Beach, Joseph Warren, *The Making of the Auden Canon*, Minneapolis: University of Minnesota Press, 1957

Carpenter, Humphrey, *W.H. Auden: A Biography*, London: Allen & Unwin, 1981, revised 1983; Boston: Houghton Mifflin, 1981

Fuller, John, *A Reader's Guide to W.H. Auden*, London: Thames & Hudson, 1970; New York: Farrar, Straus, Giroux, 1970

Hoggart, Richard, *Auden: An Introductory Essay*, London: Chatto & Windus, 1951; New Haven, Connecticut: Yale University Press, 1951

Mendelson, Edward, *Early Auden*, London: Faber & Faber, 1981; New York: Viking Press, 1981

Replogle, Justin, *Auden's Poetry*, London: Methuen, 1969; Seattle: University of Washington Press, 1969

Smith, Stan, *W.H. Auden*, Oxford and New York: Blackwell, 1985

W.H. Auden has been the focus of critical debate from the early 1930s onwards. His topicality, sharp intelligence, and wide-ranging reading, in science and philosophy as well as literature, have made him in some ways *the* representative twentieth-century poet, and, as a result of his controversial emigration to New York in 1939, as much a part of the American as of the British scene. Much discussion has also been focused on his – to many – surprising shift from Freudian-cum-Marxist themes in the 1930s (which led to his being frequently grouped with other Oxford left-wing friends of the time, such as Stephen Spender and Cecil Day Lewis) to Kierkegaardian Christianity in the 1940s and later. To some critics he was a better poet in the 1930s than afterwards; and some strongly disapprove of his habit of seeking to suppress, or even rewrite, in later editions of his work, earlier poems expressing views which he had come to regard as foolish, or even wicked. Few, however, deny the technical virtuosity of his "Christian" poetry, and to many it is his supreme achievement.

HOGGART'S book, written at the time when Auden was in America, is something of a report on work in progress. Aimed at the general, rather than the specialist, reader, it still provides an excellent introduction to Auden's themes, style, and social preoccupations. It also includes useful commentaries on representative works, such as *The Wanderer*, "Our hunting fathers", "May with its bright behaving", and an extract from *The Sea and the Mirror*. The various experiments engaged in by the "American" Auden leave Hoggart uncertain whether they are evidence of growth or decline; but his provisional judgement is that Auden is "one of those who play out in themselves, with unusual and revealing clarity, struggles to which, whether we recognise it or not, we are all committed".

BEACH is particularly concerned with Auden's habit of revising his own earlier work from the standpoint of his later, changed attitudes and beliefs. The reader becomes uneasy "as he compares the original texts with those of 1945 and 1950, where so many relatively unambiguous poems are translated into the terms of Auden's later thinking, only to find themselves rather shockingly out of place". Beach demands of the highest art an overall unity despite diversity and conflicting positions, and this is a standard by which he also finds Auden lacking.

REPLOGLE's book has four chapters. Chapter 1, "The Pattern of Ideas", examines Auden's debt to the "Germanic intellectual stream" and, in particular, the work of Marx, Freud and Kierkegaard. Chapter 2, "The Pattern of Personae", is concerned with the conflict between the aesthetically dedicated "Poet" and the iconoclastic "Antipoet", which, however, is also presented as an essentially complementary, dialectical process. Chapter 3, on "Style", adeptly characterises the special nature of Auden's abstract, non-incantatory, yet highly figurative, language; and the final chapter, "Comedy", argues that Auden's distinctive quality, above all in the later work, is as a comic poet. This is an excellent introduction to the intellectual development of a highly intelligent and self-conscious poet, but one that is also fully aware of the interaction between Auden's thought and his language.

FULLER's aim is to provide "a commentary on Auden's poetry and drama, taken in their chronological sequence ... [and] to help the reader with difficult passages and to trace some of the sources and allusions". He also makes some useful comments on Auden's alterations and omissions. Though at times rather pedestrian in its explicatory manner, this is a helpful companion to Auden's work, to be consulted rather than read through from beginning to end.

As his title indicates, BAHLKE'S 1970 study focuses exclusively on the later Auden, covering the work from *New Year Letter* (1941) to *About the House* (1965). Like Replogle, he finds comedy, both in the sense of the humorous and the Dantesque happy ending, to be the keynote of this Kierkegaardian phase in Auden's development, and for him it encompasses language that is seemingly flippant but co-existently serious. BAHLKE's more recent collection of essays (1991) provides a useful sampling of all the major critics of Auden, from Randall Jarrell to Stan Smith, along with important essays and reviews by Babette Deutsch, Harry Levin, Cleanth Brooks, Christopher Isherwood, Stravinsky, and Stephen Spender. This usefully represents the extant range of critical opinion on Auden.

CARPENTER's biography is the standard life of Auden, and also a perceptive work of literary criticism. It is packed with detail on every aspect of Auden's career, including his family background, his wide range of intellectual interests, his literary associates, and his homosexual relationships. It makes extensive use of quotation from Auden's essays, letters, and notebooks: an illuminating and highly readable book.

MENDELSON'S "early" Auden runs from 1927 to 1939, and is also the *English Auden* of his anthology of that name. This is a full and detailed study of these years, tracing the emergence of Auden from his vatic, modernist poetry of 1927–33 to a more didactic, moral, and historically minded poetry in the mid-1930s. Mendelson is in very close touch with his subject, and at the same time aware of critical tendencies in the 1960s and 1970s, which give a new perspective to Auden's work, and which some of Auden's own pronouncements anticipate. This is a major contribution to Auden studies, and an indispensable aid to understanding his work in the 1930s.

SMITH undercuts the usual distinction between a radical Auden of the 1930s and a more conservative postwar Auden by exploring the verbal and mental habits of provisionality, which underlie the entire span of his work. Viewing him from a left-wing standpoint, and using ideas drawn from modern literary theory, Smith suggests that there is an inherently elusive principle to be found "in the provisional and speculative, the play of signifiers that constantly subvert their own tendency to settle into platitudes". Despite its occasional pretentiousness and over-elaboration, this book offers an interestingly different approach to Auden's language, especially of his later work, which reveals him as consistently a radical – consistent even in his seeming inconsistencies.

R.P. DRAPER

Augustan Literature *see* British Literature: 18th Century

Austen, Jane 1775–1817

English novelist

Grey, J. David (ed.), *The Jane Austen Companion*, New York: Macmillan, 1986; as *The Jane Austen Handbook*, London: Athlone Press, 1986

Harris, Jocelyn, *Jane Austen's Art of Memory*, Cambridge and New York: Cambridge University Press, 1989

Kirkham, Margaret, *Jane Austen: Feminism and Fiction*, Brighton, Sussex: Harvester Press, 1983; Totowa, New Jersey: Barnes & Noble, 1983

Lascelles, Mary, *Jane Austen and Her Art*, Oxford: Clarendon Press, 1939, revised 1941

McMaster, Juliet, *Jane Austen on Love*, Victoria, British Columbia: University of Victoria, 1978
Page, Norman, *The Language of Jane Austen*, Oxford: Blackwell, 1972
Roberts, Warren, *Jane Austen and the French Revolution*, London and New York: Macmillan, 1979
Southam, Brian (ed.), *Critical Essays on Jane Austen*, London: Routledge & Kegan Paul, 1968
Southam, Brian (ed.), *Jane Austen: The Critical Heritage*, 2 vols., London: Routledge & Kegan Paul, 1968–87; New York: Barnes & Noble, 1968–87
Tanner, Tony, *Jane Austen*, London: Macmillan, 1986; Cambridge, Massachusetts: Harvard University Press, 1986
Trilling, Lionel, "*Mansfield Park*", in his *The Opposing Self: Nine Essays in Criticism*, New York: Viking Press, 1955; London: Secker & Warburg, 1955

Significant nineteenth-century criticism of Jane Austen is relatively sparse and tends to accept, if only by implication, the now outmoded view that her fiction suffers from damaging limitations. The exceptions, which include essays by Sir Walter Scott (1816), G.H. Lewes (1874, and subsequently), and Richard Simpson (1870), are excerpted in the first of Southam's *Critical Heritage* volumes. Early twentieth-century criticism by A.C. Bradley, Virginia Woolf, E.M. Forster, and others is for the most part appreciative rather than incisive. There is a notable increase in the amount of critical attention paid to Austen after the commemoration in 1975 of the bicentenary of her birth. Major developments in Austen criticism in recent years have included detailed analyses of her language, style, and narrative technique, and greatly increased attention to the historical, social, political, and ideological context of her work. Understandably, feminist critics in particular have found Austen's writings a rewarding field for investigation.

LASCELLES's is the earliest of the book-length studies that still repays careful attention and, in its time, provided a model for further work in several directions. As well as providing the biographical background, it covers Jane Austen's response to her reading, though the larger part of the book is concerned with issues relating to style and narrative technique. Lascelles refreshingly refuses to discuss the novels as separate entities, favouring a synthesising approach, which permits a wide range of close references to the texts (the letters and minor writings as well as the major novels). This major pioneering study was one of the first to use the evidence of Austen's surviving manuscripts. Lascelles is also one of the first critics to draw attention to the subtlety and flexibility of Austen's style and technique ("command of a variety of tones"), especially in her later novels, whereby shifts in feeling or relationships can be delicately registered.

TRILLING's essay, though ostensibly confined to a single novel, raises issues relevant to Austen's work as a whole. He stresses the central importance of irony in her work, while suggesting that in *Mansfield Park* "the characteristic irony seems not to be at work. Indeed, one might say of this novel that it undertakes to discredit irony and to affirm literalness". He also suggests that religious ideas are of vital importance to the novel (Fanny Price is "a Christian heroine"). In these and in other respects, *Mansfield Park* appears to constitute an exception in Austen's work as a whole, and therefore challenges our view of her. She can be regarded as one of the first modern novelists, but "there is scarcely one of our modern pieties" that is not offended by this particular novel. Trilling's provocative and influential essay may help to explain why *Mansfield Park* has in the last generation or so been the most widely discussed of Austen's novels.

SOUTHAM's two *Critical Heritage* volumes, the first of which covers the period from Austen's lifetime to 1870, document the contemporary reception and subsequent critical history of her work through a series of extracts from reviews, periodical articles, and critical books and essays. Though much of the earlier criticism is not very penetrating – and Southam is the first to admit that "in many respects the birth and growth of Jane Austen's critical reputation was a dull and long-drawn-out affair" – it highlights the shifts in the reputation of a writer who, at different times, has been valued for widely disparate reasons. Thus, to read through these chronologically arranged extracts is to receive a strong sense of the revolution that has taken place in Austen criticism, especially in the past half century. Possibly no other great English novelist is now regarded in such radically different terms from those in which her earlier readers and critics viewed her.

The 1968 collection of essays also edited by SOUTHAM illustrates the diversification of Austen criticism that had been accomplished a generation after Lascelles's book. Important items here include D.W. Harding on character and caricature, Gilbert Ryle on "Jane Austen and the Moralists", and Rachel Trickett on Austen's comedy in its nineteenth-century context. Revealingly, the only novel to receive separate attention is *Mansfield Park* (essays by Denis Donoghue and Tony Tanner), which by this time had been widely recognized as the most problematic and difficult to "place" of the novels. Other contributors include John Bayley and Angus Wilson.

My own (PAGE's) study is an attempt to chart the distinctive qualities of Austen's style through an examination of her attitudes to language and through analysis of such features as vocabulary, syntax, and dialogue. Its main argument is that Austen represents a transition between Augustan and modern ideas of the nature and possibilities of prose, especially fictional prose: her early style is heavily Johnsonian (for example, in its use of balance and antithesis) and her diction is that of the eighteenth-century essayists and moralists; but in her later work there are distinctively innovative and experimental elements, which look forward to such later novelists as Henry James and Virginia Woolf; her individuation of characters through varieties and eccentricities of speech led early critics to compare her to Shakespeare; and she has a particular interest in the ways in which the stability and precision of the language were threatened in her lifetime by social change, and dramatises this phenomenon in her many portrayals of characters who are socially aspiring but irredeemably vulgar. Though a number of passages are analyzed in detail, the primary purpose of the book is not linguistic analysis or a consideration of the place of Austen's work in the history of the language, but consideration of the way in which her profound concern with language informs her morality and her literary art.

The purpose of McMASTER's book is to present a Jane Austen somewhat different from the satirist and writer of comedy she is universally acknowledged to be. The emphasis is, instead, on her interest in depicting feelings, especially romantic and sexual feelings: she is, according to McMaster, "acutely awake to sex, and quite able to convey sexual feeling even though she may not take us into bedrooms". Since all the novels are love stories, there is no shortage of material for the critic who confronts this theme seriously, and this short study examines the presentation of different stages of love, from falling in love to marriage, the institutionalization of love in society, and – since many of Austen's male lovers occupy a kind of "tutorial" role, often representing maturity in contrast to the heroine's immaturity – the relationship of love and pedagogy.

ROBERTS's deliberately challenging title – for many might entertain initial doubts whether there is any connection between Austen and the French Revolution – prepares us for a book in which the emphasis is on Austen's relationship to contemporary history and ideologies. Its four long chapters deal with politics, war, religion, and women and the family. Roberts notes that Austen has received little attention from historians, and questions the validity of the then traditional approach to her work, which largely ignored the contemporary context and treated the novels as if they were "timeless". He argues, for instance, that *Persuasion* "could only have been written by someone whose life was deeply affected by the Revolutionary and Napoleonic Wars". The effect of his arguments, as with those of many other critics of the last 20 years, is to discredit earlier judgements of the narrowness of Austen's interests as a novelist and the claustrophobic quality of the social and intellectual world she depicts.

KIRKHAM's study, though more specifically feminist, is similarly grounded in the conviction that Austen can only be fully understood in relationship to the history and ideologies – and specifically the feminist ideologies – of her day. In this respect, the book is representative of a major development in recent Austen criticism. Kirkham provides first a sketch of the history of women's writing in the century that preceded Austen's working life, paying attention to women writers from Mary Astell and Catharine Macaulay to Mary Wollstonecraft, and also considering the relevance of Samuel Richardson's *Sir Charles Grandison*. A further introductory chapter deals with the publication and reception of Austen's books. This is followed by extended discussion of the six major novels and the fragment *Sanditon*. Kirkham takes issue with F.R. Leavis's placing of Austen in his "Great Tradition" of English novelists, and maintains that Austen's "moral interest was a feminist one".

GREY's wide-ranging volume contains more than 60 sections dealing with the novels and their background. It can be usefully treated as a work of reference and a source of information on such factual matters as genealogy, topography, and the chronology of the action within the novels, and there are informative sections on such aspects of contemporary social life as dress and fashion, food and drink, music, houses, gardens, travel and transportation, postal services, and military life. There are also useful plot-summaries, outlines of the history of Austen criticism, discussions of the novels (including the minor works), and a substantial dictionary of Austen's life and works.

TANNER's volume consists of an Introduction and novel-by-novel discussion of individual works. In many respects this penetrating but accessible study brings together the results of recent developments in Austen criticism. For Tanner, Austen did not simply record and reflect contemporary realities but was "in many profound ways" deeply critical of the society she lived in, and the novels expose and offer a critique of the basic ideologies of that society. He suggests that a concern with education, in the broadest sense of the word, is central to all her work. A further theme of his study is Austen's "moral relation to language": she "enacts and dramatises the difficulties, as well as the necessity, of using language to proper ends". These issues are related to discussions of the individual novels, which are consistently incisive and invigorating.

In another study emphasizing the importance of "context", this time of a more strictly literary nature, HARRIS provides a thoroughly documented exploration of Jane Austen's reading. She goes beyond a preoccupation with "sources" and "influences" to demonstrate that Austen not only read widely and deeply but effected creative transformations of her reading, with the result that her novels are, in a sense, rewritings of certain classic texts by Chaucer, Shakespeare, John Locke, Richardson, and others. *Sense and Sensibility*, for instance, may be regarded as, to a significant extent, a rewriting of Richardson's *Clarissa*, with additional ideas being derived from other novels by Richardson and from Milton's *Paradise Lost*. More unexpectedly, the influence of Chaucer is detected in *Persuasion*, and the ensuing argument is cogent and persuasive. Harris's method often produces some valuable comparative criticism, so that when she is suggesting the affinity between *Pride and Prejudice* and Richardson's *Sir Charles Grandison*, she is able to show that in the process of borrowing Austen transforms "story" into "plot". As Harris points out, her procedure is, in effect, to apply to fiction some of Harold Bloom's ideas concerning "the anxiety of influence", which have hitherto been mainly applied to poetry. Though at first sight some of her claims seem startling, they are in general persuasively argued, and the outcome is a view of Jane Austen as being very far from the "unlearned female" of legend – a legend, it should be said, that was partly self-propagated.

NORMAN PAGE

Australian Literature: General

Barnes, John (ed.), *The Writer in Australia: A Collection of Documents 1856 to 1964*, Melbourne: Oxford Unversity Press Australia, 1969

Docker, John, *Australian Cultural Elites: Intellectual Traditions in Sydney and Melbourne*, Sydney: Angus & Robertson, 1974

Dutton, Geoffrey (ed.), *The Literature of Australia*, Ringwood, Victoria, and Harmondsworth, Middlesex: Penguin, 1964, revised 1976

Duwell, Martin, and Laurie Hergenhan, *The "ALS" Guide to Australian Writers: A Bibliography 1963–1990*, St Lucia: University of Queensland Press, 1992

Goodwin, Ken, *A History of Australian Literature*, London: Macmillan, 1986; New York: St Martin's Press, 1986

Green, H.M., *A History of Australian Literature*, Sydney: Angus & Robertson, 1961, revised by Dorothy Greeen, 1984
Hadgraft, Cecil, *Australian Literature: A Critical Account to 1955*, London: Heinemann, 1960
Hergenhan, Laurie, *et al.* (eds.), *The Penguin New Literary History of Australia*, Ringwood, Victoria, and New York: Penguin, 1988
Kramer, Leonie (ed.), *The Oxford History of Australian Literature*, Melbourne, Oxford, and New York: Oxford University Press, 1981
McLaren, John, *Australian Literature: An Historical Introduction*, Melbourne: Longman Cheshire, 1989
Phillips, A.A., *The Australian Tradition: Studies in a Colonial Culture*, Melbourne: F.W. Cheshire-Lansdowne, 1958, revised 1966 (reprinted, Longman Cheshire, 1980)
Ross, Robert, *Australian Literary Criticism 1945–1988: An Annotated Bibliography*, New York: Garland, 1989
Serle, Geoffrey, *From Deserts the Prophets Come: The Creative Spirit in Australia 1788–1972*, Melbourne: Heinemann, 1973
Ward, Russell, *The Australian Legend*, Melbourne: Oxford University Press, 1958
Wilde, William H., Joy Hooton, and Barry Andrews (eds.), *The Oxford Companion to Australian Literature*, Melbourne, Oxford, and New York: Oxford University Press, 1985, with corrections, 1991, 2nd edition, 1994
Wilkes, G.A., *Australian Literature: A Conspectus*, Sydney: Angus & Robertson, 1969
Wilkes, G.A. *The Stockyard and the Croquet Lawn: Literary Evidence for Australian Cultural Development*, Melbourne and London: Edward Arnold, 1981

There are two useful overviews of the development of Australian literary criticism. Harry Heseltine's entry "Criticism" in the *Oxford Companion to Australian Literature* (see Wilde *et al.*, below) points out that the beginnings are inextricably linked with the development of journals in Australia from 1821 onwards. He gives a full and careful account of nineteenth-century and twentieth-century material in chronological order. Peter Pierce's "Forms of Literary History", in *the Penguin New Literary History* (see Hergenhan *et al.*, below), is less clear, jumping around a number of themes, acting chronologically only within each theme. Starting from the work of Frederick Simnett, in 1856, he identifies criticism devoted to "cataloguing absences", that adopting the organic metaphors of the land and growth, that revealing political splits between nationalists and universalists, that which is essentially melodramatic, and the general tendency of Australian critics to work in dualistic or antagonistic modes. His clearest stand is, however, on the seminal nature of H.M. Green's 1930 *Outline of Australian Literature*, which insisted on the close relationship between Australian national characteristics and Australian literature.

WARD's book, which has had a continuing influence on subsequent criticism, argued that personal qualities developed by pioneer life in the bush are dominant in the idea of Australian character, which is clearly discernible in Australian literature. In the same year PHILLIPS' book, examining issues which might condition the shaping of an Australian literary tradition, republished his 1950 essay "The Cultural Cringe". This phrase, indicating tendencies in Australian critics to deprecate their own tradition in comparison with European and American literature, evident also in Australian creative writing, has had a continuing and active life ever since, in spite of Phillips' own attempt to kill it off, as by then no longer relevant in contemporary criticism, in his "Death to the Cringe" (*The Age Monthly Review*, 3(2), 1983).

HADGRAFT's book is sympathetic to the work of both Phillips and Ward, and goes further, attempting to identify the main works of an Australian tradition, up to 1955, suggesting a kind of "canon of the broad view". GREEN's two-volume work is as sensible and uncontentious as Hadgraft's, but it does not offer any kind of canon. Its distinctive contribution is the detailed recording of a full and comprehensive knowledge of a wider development, of all the different forms of Australian literature. Although later revised by Dorothy Green, its strength remains in its coverage of the period up to, and including, World War II.

DUTTON's essay collection, by marshalling a number of scholars, achieves similar coverage but has less cohesion. The first half of the book has items on the social setting, poetry to 1920, poetry since 1920, fiction to 1920, fiction since 1920, and drama. It is a pity that the important genre – in this "new" literature as in others – of the short story was not given a separate essay instead of being scrambled in bits and pieces through treatments of seemingly more important novel writing. Part II has essays on ballads and popular verse, and on *The Bulletin*, followed by individual essays on the canon of the time: Henry Lawson, Joseph Furphy, Christopher Brennan, Henry Handel Richardson, Kenneth Slessor, Judith Wright, A.D. Hope, Douglas Stewart, James McAuley, Patrick White, Christina Stead, Francis Webb, and Martin Boyd. The book has balance, from its spread of views, and the individual essays are still sound and useful, but this canon is no longer representative. The Bibliography, which is Part III, is, of course, of only limited value now.

WILKES' *Conspectus*, in 1969, attempted to make the different phases of development clearer, writing about the "Colonial Period", the "Nationalist Period", and the "Modern Period". He also tried to modify the "Legend of the Nineties". This had been generally and somewhat uncritically absorbed from a rather scrappy 1954 book of Vance Palmer's, with that title, which promoted a sentimental view of *Bulletin*-school writers as the real producers of a new national literature. The 1890s have continued to retain a special place in critical accounts of Australian literature, nevertheless. BARNES' collection of literary documents from 1865 to 1964 was a timely use of actual scholarly materials in the attempt to achieve definition, more precisely here, of the emergence of Australian writers' awareness of their task. It remains a useful seminal reference volume 25 years on.

During the 1970s there was a discernible movement away from focusing on a developing tradition of Australian writing towards examining it in terms of general social or cultural history. SERLE's book aims "to bridge the gap between general historians and historians of the arts", to examine the difference between national- and international-oriented art, and to sketch a theory of the development of culture in "new" countries. The brief is wide and the book is not over-long.

The chapter "Literature and the National Problem" gives undue space and status to Vance Palmer and typifies the kind of generalisations Serle has to draw on to project his conception. But it is a first, and challenging, effort to put Australian literature into this larger perspective. In the course of it Serle indicates differences between the cultural outputs of Sydney and Melbourne, the literary aspects of which are examined in greater detail in DOCKER's book. After decades of critical attempts to establish a unified identity for Australian literature, Docker, in the 1970s, was able to challenge the monolith and argue that the European inheritance had been mediated in fundamentally conflicting ways in the differing literary traditions of Sydney and Melbourne. Parochialism, sexism, and racism he can see in all Australian writing, but Sydney writers (Christopher Brennan, Norman Lindsay, Kenneth Slessor, A.D. Hope, Patrick White), he argues, are philosophically apart from society, while Melbourne writers, those encouraged by the journal *Meanjin*, its guru Vance Palmer, and its longstanding editor Clem Christesen, assume intellectual issues are central to Australian society.

WILKES' criticism also moved in a similar direction. His 1981 book set out to examine "the connections between social and literary histories of Australia". He aligns cultural development with the developing sense of nationhood, and sees the process as one of continual tension between "the genteel and the robust", the "refined and the crude", and "the old world and the new" – in short between "the stockyard and the croquet lawn".

KRAMER collects genre surveys – "Fiction", by Adrian Mitchell, "Poetry" by Vivian Smith, and "Drama" by Terry Sturm. Though substantial and detailed, they are largely descriptive. Her own Introduction protests against the "protectionism" of much Australian criticism, and dares to set Australian literature in the context of world literature. Much more impressive, and the one consistently useful, full, and substantial reference work, is WILDE, HOOTON, and ANDREWS' *Oxford Companion*. Its 760 pages embrace "broad definitions" of both "author" and "literary work", and include entries on literary, cultural, and historical contexts in which authors lived and worked. Significant entries by other hands have been included, such as Harry Heseltine's on "Criticism", John Laird's on "War Literature", and Bruce Moore's on "Aboriginal Song and Narrative in Translation".

After so much larger-than-literary and multiple-voiced material, GOODWIN's book, without ignoring contextual matters, focuses unashamedly on the literature itself – authors and particular books – and its development, and from his own coherent and energetic viewpoint. Further to the three periods identified in Wilkes' *Conspectus*, Goodwin distinguishes ten periods, extending up to "The Generation of the 1960s" and has a final chapter on "Recent Writing", which includes Aboriginal and newly emerging writers of non-English-speaking backgrounds. Throughout, Goodwin notes recurring themes of the search for identity by the wanderer or explorer, the urge to settle the land or tame a frontier, the quest to recover the past, the experience of being an outcast, and, always, the subliminal threat of violence. Instead of a bibliography there is a short list of "Further Reading" and an extensive and very useful "Chronological Table of Authors, Titles and Events from 1770 to 1984".

HERGENHAN returns to the multiple-voiced history, the insistence on cultural contexts, and attempts to instil into the project of presenting a history a contemporary dimension of postmodern deconstruction. Timed to coincide with the Australian Bicentenary, it lays claim to the role of reinterpreting the tradition at the crossroads suggested by the calendar. But it does not offer a graspable account. History is not a record of what happened, argues Hergenhan; rather it involves competing recounted versions of the past. The actual writing of literary histories needs to be reconceived to reflect this, and that is what is attempted here. The book is organised to prevent its readers perceiving arbitrary divisions. Comments on a writer "will be found not in any one place but in a number of contexts". There are chapters on "Colonial Transformations", "Changing Perceptions of Australia", "Production of Literature", "Marketing the Imagination", "Publishing, Censorship, and Writers' Incomes", with a handful of chapters on "War Literature", "Poetry", "Short Fiction", or "The Novel" scattered unevenly among them. The same authors are allowed to come up in numerous disjointed contexts in a way that disperses perception of them rather than renders the grasp of them more complex. A brave and big undertaking, it achieves something of the aim its editor outlines. But should the main purpose of a history of literature be to imitate the processes of history? Shouldn't its prime focus be the literature? The book demonstrates that its conceivers and contributors are aware of the most recent theoretical developments, and that awareness does need to infiltrate general accounts of Australian literature. But this attempt, though fascinating to browse in, nevertheless confuses and disorientates the reader overall, revealing the dangers of the task.

McLAREN does not try to problematize or deconstruct his firm sense of his subject. He homes in clearly on the authors he believes are important, evaluating them in the light of his declaration that properly Australian literature is that writing which brings the forces that shaped the inherited world most forcefully into encounter with the new place and its new ways of life. As an addition to the body of criticism, McLaren's study was welcomed by Harry Heseltine as marked by integrity, constancy, and clarity, not words usually applicable to other poststructural accounts.

Lastly, two bibliographical books in easily usable forms facilitate access to Australian criticism. ROSS's is particularly useful in its general sections, and his short annotations are a helpful preliminary guide in sorting out the books a researcher wants. DUWELL and HERGENHAN's listing of articles published on individual authors in the pre-eminent journal of Australian literary criticism, *Australian Literary Studies*, is presented in alphabetical order for easy access. But the listings under each author-heading are in chronological order so that in following them through it is possible to experience the development of critical argument about an author over nearly three decades of dynamic discussion.

GAY RAINES

Australian Literature: Recent and Contemporary

Docker, John, *In a Critical Condition: Reading Australian Literature*, Melbourne: Penguin, 1984
Ferrier, Carole (ed.), *Gender, Politics and Fiction: Twentieth Century Australian Women's Novels*, St Lucia: University of Queensland Press, 1985
Gunew, Sneja, and Kateryna O. Longley, *Striking Chords: Multicultural Literary Interpretations*, Sydney: Allen & Unwin, 1992
Hodge, Bob, and Vijay Mishra, *Dark Side of the Dream: Australian Literature and the Postcolonial Mind*, Sydney: Allen & Unwin, 1991
McLaren, John, *New Pacific Literatures: Culture and Environment in the European Pacific*, New York: Garland, 1993
Shoemaker, Adam, *Black Words, White Page: Aboriginal Literature 1929–1988*, St Lucia: University of Queensland Press, 1989

Several histories of Australian literature from the colonial period onward have appeared in recent years, as have studies on individual writers and genres in the post-World-War-II period. Lacking, however, are general examinations of this significant era that show the relationships between the overall development of fiction, poetry, and drama. Instead, Australian critics have tended to examine the contemporary period by taking up more specific subjects, such as critical reception, gender, Aboriginal writing, postcolonialism, and multiculturalism.

DOCKER examines the way Australian literature has been received and discussed by critics and literary historians. While primarily concerned with Australian-written criticism, Docker offers a lively survey of a time when Australian writing was first being taken seriously, especially in the academy. He finds fault with much of the critical response, in particular that based on the "New Criticism", and prescribes a method that will embrace the cultural aspects from which the writing grew. Although helpful as an introduction to one aspect of the contemporary period, the book is sometimes limited by its vitriolic tone and its tendency to view the country's literature as a body of work understandable only to Australians.

FERRIER, in her Introduction, notes that this collection of essays "brings together a range of new readings of twentieth-century Australian women's fiction from socialist and/or feminist standpoints". Following Ferrier's succinct history of the development of feminist criticism in Australia, essays on writers such as Miles Franklin and Christina Stead appear, along with chapters on migrant women writers, literary reception, and Australian women novelists of the 1970s. Unfortunately heavy-handed at times, the collection does offer an accessible overview of a field that Ferrier insists has been critically "limited and deficient".

Although SHOEMAKER's book is subtitled "*Aboriginal Literature, 1929–1988*", the main focus is the period from 1963 when a written literature in English by Aborigines first began to develop fully and to be recognized. Although, in a sense, the book was outdated the day it appeared, it remains a valuable guide to a burgeoning literature coming from what Shoemaker calls the "Fourth World", which he says "will define itself and demand both artistic and political recognition through its creative literature". The work sets the stage for its critical analyses by surveying the political and historical environment from which the literature grew. At the same time its examination of the way fiction, poetry, and drama developed illustrates how the writing reflects Aboriginal sensibility.

While books on the Australian search for identity through literature abound, HODGE and MISHRA have approached the topic in a new and original way by viewing it in the light of postcolonial theory. The critics propose that Australia's attempt to construct a national identity mistakenly relied on "the unjust act of an imperial power", which led to the bush myth. Long seen by many critics and literary historians as the essence of Australian-ness, the bush myth, according to Hodge and Mishra, is actually sexist, racist, and imperialist. The writers examine texts both outside of and within the mainstream of Australian writing, and conclude that the culture is "paranoiac" because of its historical background and its reliance on a deficient mythology. Although open to debate, the ideas presented challenge much of what has been written about the never-ending search for a "national identity", and takes a refreshing look at this perennial quest.

Hodge and Mishra introduce the topic of multiculturalism in literature, a field that has recently received attention in what some critics have considered as an Anglo-Celtic dominated literature. Editors GUNEW and LONGLEY expand on this subject by making a case, in their Introduction to this essay collection, for those Australians "who write from other than English or Irish cultural antecedents and languages". Following this discussion of "exclusion" are essays on "theoretical perspectives" of multicultural aesthetics, omissions in Australian literary histories, author studies, "subversive re-readings", and "re-writings". Written by major writers and critics from Australia – whose names reveal that they are not Anglo-Celtic – the entries present a diversity of viewpoints, some more accessible than others. On the whole, the collection provides an excellent introduction to an emerging area of contemporary Australian writing.

McLAREN embarks on a rare project for Australian critics – that is, a comparative study. Although he focuses on writing from the Pacific for the most part, the wide-ranging discussion touches on an impressive number of what he calls the "new literatures", including Canadian and African. McLaren works from the premise that the history of the literature that developed from the British Empire, a history he presents clearly and concisely, contains a record of mutual destruction. First the imperial powers destroyed native values, and then the new environments brought about "the frustration and perversion of imperial hopes". To illustrate this thesis, McLaren gives close readings of numerous works by both indigenous and settler authors. The study places Australian literature in a larger framework than is usually the case, thereby broadening the perspectives of Australian writing as well as offering an overview of the "new literatures".

ROBERT L. ROSS

Autobiography

Brodzki, Bella, and Celeste Schenck (eds.), *Life/Lines: Theorising Women's Autobiography*, Ithaca, New York: Cornell University Press, 1988

Jay, Paul, *Being in the Text: Self-Representation from Wordsworth to Roland Barthes*, Ithaca, New York: Cornell University Press, 1984

Jelinek, Estelle C. (ed.), *Women's Autobiography: Essays in Criticism*, Bloomington: Indiana University Press, 1980

Olney, James (ed.), *Autobiography: Essays Theoretical and Critical*, Princeton, New Jersey: Princeton University Press, 1980

Olney, James (ed.), *Studies in Autobiography*, New York and Oxford: Oxford University Press, 1988

Stanton, Domna, *The Female Autograph: Theory and Practice of Autobiography from the Tenth to the Twentieth Century*, Chicago: University of Chicago Press, 1987

Weintraub, Karl J., *The Value of the Individual: Self and Circumstance in Autobiography*, Chicago: University of Chicago Press, 1978

During the last 30 years, and more particularly during the last ten, books and articles about autobiography have appeared at an increasing rate.

WEINTRAUB's interesting study offers a coherent history of the emergence, in the seventeenth and eighteenth centuries, of the elements and types of autobiography. At the same time, it analyses the historical and cultural conditions that made that emergence possible. Rather than steer his 1980 collection in a unitary critical direction, OLNEY provides a forum for different and occasionally conflicting voices. Essays include the fascinating "Malcolm X and the Limits of Autobiography" by Paul John Eakin and the provocative "Recovering Literature's Lost Ground Through Autobiography", in which James Cox argues that in writing the autobiography of the American nation (the Declaration of Independence) Thomas Jefferson also wrote the script of its subsequent history. Valuable reprints include Georges Gusdorf's seminal essay "Conditions and Limits of Autobiography" – probably the first essay to subject autobiography to a systematic literary analysis – and William L. Howarth's "Some Principles of Autobiography". The Introduction usefully situates such work by sketching the history and shifting preoccupations of theoretical and critical writing on autobiography, introducing the reader to many of the main issues *en route*. Autobiographies by women and minorities are highlighted, albeit in relation to various "studies" – American, African-American, and African, for which Olney believes autobiography offers a means of exploring an experience. Also included in the Introduction are some interesting speculations about the appeal of autobiography to the modern-day critic.

JELINEK's now rather dated collection was the first to postulate the existence of a distinct female autobiographical tradition. The collection concentrates wholly on English and American autobiographies, with most essays treating now "canonised" writers such as Gertrude Stein, Elizabeth Cady Stanton, Kate Millett, Maya Angelou, and Anaïs Nin. Several essays cover a number of autobiographies during a given historical period. Particularly interesting is Pomerleau's analysis of autobiography as an emerging genre during the seventeenth century. However, the collection as a whole gives predominant attention to life studies published during the last decade. The final impression yielded by the essays confirms Jelinek's thesis that women "write in discontinuous forms and . . . emphasise the personal over the professional". The thesis may often be true but, as a general statement, it both neglects and elides the complex differences between women's autobiographical forms.

JAY, in a judiciously Derridean reading of self-reflexive forms of writing, gives an incisive history of (masculine) autobiography. Beginning with Augustine's reflection and reification of "a particular philosophical conception of the subject", he goes on to trace the undermining of this ideology in twentieth-century works "whose preoccupations are more philosophical than biographical and whose subjects are represented in fragmented discursive forms that seek by their fragmentation to mirror what modern criticism has come to call . . . the divided self". Jay argues eloquently with reference to texts which range from Thomas Carlyle to T.S. Eliot. For Jay the tradition climaxes with Roland Barthes and the first deliberate undoing of time, continuity, coherence, and selfhood.

STANTON points out the theoretical limitations of the assumed model of difference prevalent in many discussions of women's autobiography, observing that it is predicated "on a preselected corpus of male autobiographies and a preestablished set of common traits". What is often hypothesised "as a fundamental female quality", she suggests, is in fact the product of "cultural norms". Drawing upon French theory, she investigates women's non-traditional literature in a pluralistic, comparative, and highly self-conscious manner. Her strategy is to undermine the generic boundaries that have plagued studies of autobiography by assembling a "collage of pieces" from different fields, modes, cultures and eras. Her retrospective assessment of her own collection, however, is that "issues of class, race, and sexual orientation have only been sporadically addressed".

BRODZKI's collection as a whole illustrates the thesis that women's autobiographies centre on relationships and interconnectedness. Mary Mason's now famous essay "The Other Voice: Autobiographies of Women Writers", reprinted here, eloquently sums up this position. Mason argues that where men stress their individualism in their autobiographies, women define their identities in terms of their relationship with others, a view that has gained widespread popularity. Brodzki's critical and political stance plots a course somewhere in between Jelinek and Stanton's polarities. Her aim is "to maintain female specificity and articulate female subjectivity without either falling back into the essentialism that has plagued both American feminist criticism and écriture feminine of France or retreating into a pure textuality that consigns woman to an unrecoverable absence". Editorial policy enforces this mediating position. The book gathers a range of widely varying feminist critical perspectives in its readings of texts, which span the medieval to modern periods. Ethnic and political diversity is one of the hallmarks of the collection. The broad scope of the book in terms of orientation and choice of material has as one of its concomitant effects a realisation about the hazards of generalising about female experience.

OLNEY's second collection (1988) emphasises the increasing sophistication of critical writing on autobiography. It is usefully divided into four sections – "The Interpretation of Autobiography", "Ethnic and Minority Autobiography", "Autobiography as Cultural Expression", and "Women's Autobiography", indicating the current scope of study. The arrangement of essays in each section consciously generates a symposium/discussion effect, with the principal essays establishing large, general positions which are then elaborated, contradicted, or just responded to by the articles that follow. Read alongside Olney's earlier collection, this book provides an excellent introduction to the field.

RAMONA WRAY

B

Bacon, Francis 1561–1626

English prose writer

Jardine, Lisa, *Francis Bacon: Discovery and the Art of Discourse*, London & New York: Cambridge University Press, 1974

Martin, Julian, *Francis Bacon, the State, and the Reform of Natural Philosophy*, Cambridge and New York: Cambridge University Press, 1992

Pérez-Ramos, Antonio, *Francis Bacon's Idea of Science and the Maker's Knowledge Tradition*, Oxford: Clarendon Press, 1988; New York: Oxford University Press, 1988

Quinton, Anthony, *Francis Bacon*, Oxford, Toronto, and Melbourne: Oxford University Press, 1980; New York: Oxford University Press/Hill & Wang, 1980

Sessions, William A. (ed.), *Francis Bacon's Legacy of Texts: "The Art of Discovery Grows with Discovery"*, New York: AMS Press, 1990

Stephens, James, *Francis Bacon and the Style of Science*, Chicago: University of Chicago Press, 1975

Vickers, Brian, *Francis Bacon and Renaissance Prose*, Cambridge: Cambridge University Press, 1968

Vickers, Brian (ed.), *Essential Articles for the Study of Francis Bacon*, Hamden, Connecticut: Archon Books, 1968; London: Sidgwick & Jackson, 1972

Whitney, Charles, *Francis Bacon and Modernity*, New Haven, Connecticut, and London: Yale University Press, 1986

Reflecting his ambition to take all knowledge as his terrain, Francis Bacon inspires comment in many disciplines – history of science, literary criticism, history, theology, political philosophy, law, ethics, and so on – with each of these critical traditions remaining impervious to the findings of the others. In recent years, however, the most vital work on Bacon has come through interdisciplinary considerations of his work and thought. All of the above tend to ignore the most relentlessly productive tradition, which continues to maintain that Bacon was the son of Queen Elizabeth and that he wrote Shakespeare's works (for which see Alfred Dodd, *Francis Bacon's Personal Life-Story*, 2 vols., London: Rider & Co., 1986).

VICKERS' *Essential Articles* collection gathers 14 valuable articles dating from 1923 to 1964, covering Bacon's contribution to science, law, politics, and history, and his work as a writer. Vickers provides a lucid introduction to the field of Bacon studies as of 1968, and suggests areas for its future development. In addition to useful contextualisations of the historical context for Bacon's scientific ideas and the humanist debate, the essays include accounts of his debt to contemporary encylopedists, considerations of his philosophy of science, his theory of jurisprudence, his parliamentary oratory, his psychology of history, and his concept of the nature and function of poetry, as well as original readings of *De Sapientia Veterum* and the *Essays*.

Arguing that "the disparity between the meagre, confused and inaccurate contents of his scientific programme and its overwhelming effect can only be explained by his mastery of style", VICKERS' *Francis Bacon and Renaissance Prose* examines this style in the organisation of Bacon's writing (through a discussion of *partitio*), his use of the aphorism, and "syntactical symmetry". He further argues for analogy as a method of scientific discovery, and examines the recurrence of certain image patterns throughout Bacon's *oeuvre*. Carefully setting each discussion in its classical and contemporary contexts, Vickers draws primarily on *Advancement of Learning* and the *Essays*, and uses their revisions as a test-case. The study concludes with a survey of critical judgments of Bacon's style since the early seventeenth century.

JARDINE examines Bacon's works against a background of sixteenth-century dialectic handbooks, reconstructing his intellectual background to demonstrate the originality and ingenuity of his solutions to dialectical problems. Through readings of the *Novum Organum*, *De Sapientia Veterum*, and the *Essays*, she shows "how an uneasy alliance between Aristotelian dialectic and experimental science produced a logic of scientific discovery", demonstrates the intimate relationship between his "scientific" and "literary" works, and presents Bacon as "a well-educated English gentleman with a good (but not scholarly) grounding in the curriculum subjects, and with a remarkably clear grasp of precisely the limitations of that education as the basis for any growth of understanding of the natural world".

STEPHENS focuses on Bacon's ongoing concern, from *The Masculine Birth of Time* to *New Atlantis*, with the subject of communication among intellectuals, how science can exchange information, in "an effort to follow Bacon's mind as it moves through 'progressive stages of certainty' to a clear and defensible theory of the philosophical style". Stephens pays particular attention to Bacon's debts to Aristotle, the uniting of science and style in practical experience, and to the use of the aphorism and the acroamatic in Bacon's own style.

QUINTON provides a brief, accessible introduction to Bacon's philosophical work (specifically *The Advancement of Learning* and *Novum Organum*), with chapters devoted to his biography and intellectual background, the Great Instauration, his critique of false systems (especially the "idols of the mind"), the classification of the sciences, the new method of "Baconian induction", and human philosophy, concluding with a survey of "followers and critics". Other works are not dealt with in any detail.

Bacon as "both a test case for conflicting views of modernity and a modern whose insights and innovativeness are especially pertinent today" is the focus of WHITNEY's book. Rather than placing Bacon with either the ancients or the moderns, Whitney identifies a struggle in his work (and in the nature of "instauration") between innovation and tradition, and argues that Bacon's case "suggests an unresolved modernity, a self-contradictory condition of emergence" – innovation as both reform and revolution. Whitney also restores the centrality of Bacon's profession of Christianity in an important discussion of prophecy and secularisation.

PÉREZ-RAMOS provides a thorough and learned investigation into the key notions which, he claims, make up Bacon's idea of science – *forma*, *opus*, and *inductio* – arguing that *inductio* "could be more profitably seen as Bacon's attempt to prescribe (or perhaps describe) a 'logic of scientific discovery' in his own terms". He also includes useful surveys of both the historiographic background customarily associated with Bacon's philosophy and the ways in which Bacon's proposals may have concretely influenced Western science.

To reinforce his contention that Bacon's aim was "the reform of human epistemology itself", SESSIONS brings together 16 essays from a range of disciplines and an international set of scholars. The first section dwells on issues such as Bacon's methodology and its context, his influences and borrowings, and theological interpretations, while the more specialised second section includes discussions of Bacon's use of theatrical imagery, his early drama, classical literary patterns, his technique of inquisition, and the transmission of his texts. There is a useful bibliography of recent Bacon scholarship to 1988.

MARTIN provides an historical explanation as to why Bacon, a politician, devoted his energies to proposing the reform of natural sciences. He argues that this reform was a central part of an audacious programme on the part of a conservative and élitist Bacon to strengthen the powers of an imperial Crown in the state. Martin focuses particularly on the 1590s to show how Bacon's concern with political philosophy and the common law fed into the formulation of this reform, in effect "the natural philosophy of a late Elizabethan statesman".

ALAN STEWART

Baldwin, James 1924–1987

American novelist, essayist, dramatist, and short-story writer

Bloom, Harold (ed.), *James Baldwin*, New York: Chelsea House, 1986
Burt, Nancy V., and Fred L. Standley (eds.), *Critical Essays on James Baldwin*, Boston: G.K. Hall, 1988
Campbell, James, *Talking at the Gates: A Life of James Baldwin*, London: Faber & Faber, 1991; New York: Viking Press, 1991
Eckman, Fern M., *The Furious Passage of James Baldwin*, New York: M. Evans, 1966
Harris, Trudier, *Black Women in the Fiction of James Baldwin*, Knoxville: University of Tennessee Press, 1985
Kinnamon, Keneth (ed.), *James Baldwin: A Collection of Critical Essays*, Englewood Cliffs, New Jersey: Prentice-Hall, 1974
Leeming, David, *James Baldwin: A Biography*, London: Michael Joseph, 1994; New York: Knopf, 1994
Troupe, Quincy (ed.), *James Baldwin: The Legacy*, New York: Simon & Schuster, 1989
Weatherby, W.J., *James Baldwin: Artist on Fire: A Portrait*, New York: D.I. Fine, 1989; London: Michael Joseph, 1990

Early 1950s' critical reaction to James Baldwin tended to present him primarily as a spokesman on "race relations" rather than a writer concerned with issues of morality and religion, love and personal identity. With Baldwin's active participation in the Civil Rights movement, critical reaction continued this paradigm, presenting Baldwin as the prophet of the deepening racial crisis in 1960s' America, alternatively downplaying or ignoring Baldwin's focus on gender, sexuality, and interracial desire, and misinterpreting his deconstruction of cultural fictions of racial authenticity as a lyrical search for a sense of self. As the scope of Baldwin's literary corpus broadened in the 1970s to embrace a wide variety of genres, so the range and quantity of criticism grew, reflecting a growing awareness of Baldwin's stature as a major writer. Baldwin's interest in the moral and social responsibility of the writer has tended to divide critics into admirers of his prophetic stance, indifferent to his stylistic lapses, and detractors, who dismiss his political ideas on interracial conflict and interracial love as naive, and bemoan the sacrifice of literary form for the polemical exhortation and inflated rhetoric of later works such as *The Evidence of Things Not Seen*.

ECKMAN's early study focuses upon Baldwin as prophet, performing moral surgery on the "wounds of the nation's conscience". While recognising Baldwin's dual role as both writer and civil rights campaigner, she also includes extensive personal accounts and biographical data, which provide illuminating insights of Baldwin the man as well as Baldwin the author. KINNAMON's 1970s' collection of 13 essays, reviews, a chronology of dates, and a highly selective bibliography offers a broad and comprehensive approach to Baldwin's diverse concerns. Insisting that "a proper understanding of Baldwin and his work must take into account a complicated amalgam of psychological and social elements sometimes thought to be antithetical", the editorial selection ensures Baldwin's multiplicity of themes – a quest for love, sexual and personal identity, the social responsibility of the writer, black religious faith, culture and community – are understood in terms of their mutual interaction.

LEEMING's biography argues that this multiplicity, from the beginnings of Baldwin's writing career through to the end, may be best understood as a prophetic form of witnessing or calling, the harsh demands of which condemned Baldwin to loneliness and social isolation. Leeming's inability to distinguish between the myth and the man often results in a critical myopia in which the frailty, shortsightedness, and self-serving narcissism displayed at times by Baldwin are explained away as signs of his higher redemptive purpose.

Also biographical in approach, WEATHERBY's portrait is a primarily reportorial account of Baldwin's life treating him as a representative figure of a turbulent moment in American social, political, and intellectual history. The result is often a skewed reading of the relationship between the life and the creative work, but one redeemed by the many-layered and complex readings of the intellectual and social milieux in which Baldwin found himself. CAMPBELL's biography has an unusually skeptical bias towards its subject, suggesting that Baldwin's calling as a writer was sadly superseded by interventions in various socio-political "causes", which undermined his impartial moral authority as an imaginative witness. This approach presents Baldwin's concern with social change and the moral responsibility of the individual as somehow extrinsic or antithetical to his art, despite Baldwin's repeated statements to the contrary (those writings in which Baldwin talks of his wish to make the creative self and social actor interact in a state of moral coherence).

More recent volumes of essays than Kinnamon's are Bloom's, Burt and Standley's, and Troupe's. BLOOM's collection presents Baldwin as polemical novelist-essayist, showing how the writer of the early novels – *Go Tell It on the Mountain* and *Another Country* – emerges through an intimate exploration of a metaphysics of self as articulated in race, religion, and cultural community. The formal dissolution of the later fictional and critical work is thus contrasted to the rigoristic and far-reaching meditation on the links between race, community and sexuality in Baldwin's early autobiographical writings. BURT and STANDLEY's collection provides an evolutionary survey of 1970s' and 1980s' Baldwin criticism, with essays on general themes, fiction, non-fiction, and drama. As such, Baldwin is presented in all his guises: the humanist exploring racial, sexual and familial intimacy as against the apocalyptic polemicist of *The Fire Next Time*; the exquisite stylist and weaver of Jamesian narrative fictions as against the platitudinous political journalist; the explorer of interracial fear and desire as against the racial bigot. This collection presents a major and balanced appreciation of Baldwin's stature as a writer, and includes a wide-ranging bibliography. TROUPE's major anthology of recollections, tributes, interviews, and criticisms of Baldwin by contemporary black writers is an attempt both to summarise Baldwin's literary legacy and to place him in his intellectual and cultural context. Baldwin's role as the "conscience of a generation" of black writers and artists, his subtle analyses of emotional ambiguities in personal and social interracial relationships, his turn to, and reconstitution of, black American culture and history, in addition to his ethical questioning of political and sexual choices, and his own homosexuality, are all discussed in tightly argued and insightful readings, which include both the fictional and non-fictional works.

HARRIS's pioneer study provides a careful examination of the fiction in order to explicate the roles women play and the significance of their characters in Baldwin's many writings. She charts how Baldwin's characterisation of women moves from a moralistic portrayal to a greater complexity of personality, despite the fact that, overall, Baldwin tends to place them in subordinate relations to his male characters.

D.S. MARRIOTT

Bale, John 1495–1563

English dramatist, historian, and prose writer

Blatt, Thora B., *The Plays of John Bale: A Study of Ideas, Technique and Style*, Copenhagen: G.E.C. Gad, 1968

Davies, William T., "A Bibliography of John Bale", in *Proceedings and Papers of the Oxford Bibliographical Society*, 5, 1940

Fairfield, Leslie P., *John Bale: Mythmaker for the English Reformation*, West Lafayette, Indiana: Purdue University Press, 1976

Hadfield, Andrew, "John Bale and the Time of the Nation", in his *Literature, Politics and National Identity: Reformation to Renaissance*, Cambridge: Cambridge University Press, 1994

Haller, William, *Foxe's Book of Martyrs and the Elect Nation*, London: Jonathan Cape, 1963

Harris, Jessie W., *John Bale: A Study in the Minor Literature of the Reformation*, Urbana: University of Illinois Press, 1940

King, John N., *English Reformation Literature: The Tudor Origins of the Protestant Tradition*, Princeton, New Jersey: Princeton University Press, 1982

McCusker, Honor, *John Bale: Dramatist and Antiquary*, Bryn Mawr, Pennsylvania: Bryn Mawr University Press, 1942

John Bale has always been a difficult writer to pigeon-hole, partly because of his vast and varied output – plays, pamphlets, literary histories, theological texts, biblical commentaries, polemics, satires – and partly because he employed a more inclusive definition of "literature" than is now acceptable, in his massive literary history, *Scriptorum Illustrium Majoris Brytanniae Catalogus* (1557). Despite his crucially important role in the history of English literature, particularly in his rescuing of numerous manuscripts and works from obscurity and playing a major role in the development of a native English drama, Bale has all too often been damned with faint praise – as the title of Harris indicates – or studied as the precursor of more interesting authors.

DAVIES is still the best account of Bale's life, and provides a bibliography of Bale's extant works (a recent bibliography of secondary material is provided by Peter Happé in "Recent Studies in John Bale", *English Literary Renaissance*, 17, 1987). Davies points out that Bale's plays "were directly inspired by Thomas Cromwell's policy of making the State, as represented by the King, the supreme authority in the national church", a political form of Protestantism that was to become antiquated towards the end of his long life. He also sorts out some intricate textual problems, especially regarding the two versions of *King John*.

HARRIS's study is solid but uninspiring. It does usefully catalogue Bale's intellectual debt to Lutheranism and his role in preserving the contents of the libraries of the recently dissolved monastic orders after the mental breakdown of another of his mentors, John Leland (?1506–52).

This latter theme is more exhaustively chronicled in McCUSKER, a study which has been criticised for its partiality in presenting Bale as simply an antiquarian, ignoring his active participation in vigorous theological debate and propaganda and his penchant for spiteful invective. McCusker shows that Bale was the most voluminous early modern English book collector apart from Leland and Archbishop Matthew Parker (1504–74), and laments the dispersal of his library in Ireland after Bale's disastrous tenure as Bishop of Ossory (1552–53).

HALLER's influential book has been heavily criticised by recent historians of the English Reformation for arguing that either Bale or John Foxe (1516–87) had a clear notion of the English as an elect nation in their interpretations of English history. Haller argues that in his plays and works such as the commentary on Revelation, *The Image of Both Churches* (1548), which went on to form the basis for the marginal comments in *The Geneva Bible* (1560), Bale attempted to foster a national consciousness. According to Haller, Bale conceived of history as a struggle between believers in the word of God – Protestants – and wordly opponents, specifically Catholics. The primitive British Church had successfully resisted the attempts of the over-mighty Roman Church to bring all churches under its suzerainty, and so served as a beacon for other European Protestants to follow. Henry VIII's break with the papacy and the subsequent progress of the Reformation in Britain meant that Britain had once again assumed this special role.

FAIRFIELD expands and substantiates much of Haller's thesis, illustrating how much of Bale's output depends upon a reading of Revelation. Bale was more of a millenarian thinker than a chiliast, having no real faith in direct political action to bring about the last days and the return of Christ, but believing that an inner, not an outer, peace would be the reward of God's elect. Throughout his life Bale stressed the need for the monarch to rule as God's annointed leader and was unable to comprehend the more radical political theories of some of the younger reformers. According to Fairfield, Bale's originality lies in his application of the historical schema of Revelation to the events of English history. Bale divided English history into six ages, the first starting with the missionary voyage of Joseph of Arimathea, and the sixth and last with the current overthrow of the papacy. Patriotism was never an end in itself, but led to spiritual rejuvenation.

KING's massive volume catalogues the neglected body of English literature from the middle years of the sixteenth-century, demonstrating Bale's crucial role in the development of a specifically Protestant tradition, despite the extreme hostility shown towards his work from the 1580s onwards. King shows how Bale's conception of literature stems from the belief in apostleship as the highest category of authorship.

BLATT provides a competent but somewhat dull analysis of Bale's plays, adding little to the historical and theological readings outlined above. However, there is a useful chapter on Bale's style and use of rhetoric.

My own (HADFIELD's) piece examines the inherent paradoxes within Bale's writings, especially the uncomfortable clash between a universal faith and a native Christianity. Bale's stress upon the need for the Bible to be read by the faithful required him to demand its translation into a specific language – English – and, therefore, to take on a national rather than an international form. Similarly, in concentrating his writing of history on the persons of the monarchs, Bale's narratives are "inexorably metonymic and nationalistic". Bale further suffered from the classic dilemma of early Protestants: how should the godly act if the monarch is ungodly? This was a personal struggle dramatised in his spiritual autobiography, *The Vocacyon of Johan Bale to the Bishopricke of Ossorie* (1553).

ANDREW HADFIELD

The Ballad

Bold, Alan, *The Ballad*, London and New York: Methuen, 1979

Dugaw, Dianne, *Warrior Women and Popular Balladry, 1650–1850*, Cambridge and New York: Cambridge University Press, 1989

Fowler, David C., *Literary History of the Popular Ballad*, Durham, North Carolina: Duke University Press, 1968

Friedman, Albert B., *The Ballad Revival: Studies in the Influence of Popular on Sophisticated Poetry*, Chicago: University of Chicago Press, 1961

Gerould, Gordon H., *The Ballad of Tradition*, Oxford: Clarendon Press, 1932; New York: Oxford University Press, 1932

Harker, Dave, *Fakesong: The Manufacture of British "Folksong" 1700 to the Present Day*, Milton Keynes, Buckinghamshire: Open University Press, 1985

Harris, Joseph (ed.), *The Ballad and Oral Literature*, Cambridge, Massachusetts: Harvard University Press, 1991

Muir, Willa, *Living with Ballads*, London: Hogarth Press, 1965

Würzbach, Natascha, *The Rise of the English Street Ballad, 1550–1650*, translated by Gayna Walls, Cambridge and New York: Cambridge University Press, 1990

The definition of "ballad" is ambiguous: it is commonly held to be a stanzaic narrative poem, intended for singing; but some of them may have been spoken. The history of ballad scholarship contains much controversy over the form's origin, history, and influence: "communalists" believed that ballads, or the more ancient folksongs from which they evolved, were composed as the result of spontaneous group activity; "individualists" believed every ballad originally had a single author, and any deviation from the first version was a corruption. Distinctions have been drawn between "traditional" ballads, often perceived as genuine "folk" compositions, transmitted orally by generations of amateurs, and "broadside", "street", or "stall" ballads, designed for publication, and regarded by many collectors and critics as inferior hack-work. This attitude has undergone major modifications; significantly, the term "popular" has been applied to both kinds of ballad.

GEROULD, in one of the earliest full-length examinations of the ballad's literary qualities, concentrates mainly on English and Scottish works, but deploys extensive knowledge of folksong in other cultures: Poles and Ojibway Indians are equally likely to provide appropriate analogies. His views are well-considered and deservedly influential, particularly his perception that William Wordsworth was affected mainly by broadsides, while Samuel Taylor Coleridge owed more to traditional ballads. He demolishes the excesses of communalists and individualists with even-handed discretion. Nevertheless, he displays occasional naivety: narrative inconsistencies are cited as evidence of confused belief systems, whereas later critics would tend to consider their poetic effects.

FRIEDMAN's chief concern is the influence of ballads on literature and criticism in the eighteenth and nineteenth centuries, but his argument embraces many interactions between written and oral culture, from Old Testament and Homer scholarship to jazz rhythms in twentieth-century poetry. He is the first to relate Joseph Addison's epoch-making essays on "Chevy Chase" to his neoclassical hostility to over-elaborate "false wit". Although Friedman writes with conspicuous verve, he knows when to let historical ironies speak for themselves. He cites without comment the communalist Johann Gottfried von Herder's theories: "each race had a special mission to perform in moving humanity toward the distant era of universal peace .... The *Volkslied* was, thus, one of several touchstones by which the community could measure its approach to, or declension from, purity". Friedman implicitly discredits communalism by associating it with the genocidal Nazism that flourished a century after Herder's death.

MUIR offers a unique combination of personal testimony and scholarly analysis. Starting from her childhood experience of oral poetry in the playgrounds and countryside of Scotland, she moves on to investigate ballads in general, and Scottish ballads in particular. Songs still sung in the twentieth century are related to ancient legends of many lands, including the Babylonian epic of Gilgamesh. Especially valuable is her shrewd account of the role played by Robert Burns and other lowlanders in creating and marketing the myth of the glamorous wild highlander.

For the serious student of ballads, equipped with some knowledge of medieval English, FOWLER is essential. He works on the revolutionary principle that "a given ballad took the particular shape it has about the time it was written down, unless there is specific evidence to the contrary". He defines the ballad as "a new type of narrative song", which developed with "the coming together of traditional song and medieval minstrelsy in the fifteenth and sixteenth centuries". His arguments that not all ballads were intended for singing, and his insistence on the creative contribution of the men and women who performed them, typify his vision of the variety and dynamism of ballad tradition.

BOLD's contribution to Methuen's "Critical Idiom" series provides a clear and comprehensive introduction to ballad history, criticism, and composition, from the Middle Ages to the twentieth century. He pours contempt on the communalists, cites hilariously terrible instances of how bad early nineteenth-century broadsides could be, and neatly sums up ballads' distinctive formal characteristics as devices to aid memory: "to survive they had to be unforgettable".

First published in German as *Die Englische Strassenballade (1550–1650)*, WÜRZBACH's study is a thorough investigation of Elizabethan and early Stuart broadside ballads. Paying comparatively little attention to melody, but aware of ballads as performance art, Würzbach applies a wide range of critical techniques to an impressive array of information. Communication theory and speech-act theories reveal "the close relationship between texts and socio-cultural environment". Selected ballads run the gauntlet of diagrams, genre-theory categories, and statistical analysis of themes and rhymes. Although inflexible use of these methods sometimes obfuscates issues and blunts the edge of critical response, these are small caveats and do not detract from the overall value of Würzbach's material.

HARKER believes "even intellectuals interested in culture have their part to play" in the struggle for workers' power. His substantial, passionately engaged, history of "the *mediation* of songs" reveals the multifarious links between ballads and politics, showing how their transmission was affected by the attitude of collectors. The process emerges as manipulation and censorship of popular songs by and for the bourgeoisie. Harker believes "concepts like 'folksong' and 'ballad' are intellectual rubble which needs to be shifted so that building can begin again".

DUGAW focuses on tales of early-modern women serving as soldiers and sailors in male disguise. Concentration on this relatively limited topic enables her to cover every aspect, from the evolution of melodies to sexual discrimination (or lack of it) in the working classes. Although she makes no reference to Würzbach, Dugaw employs similar techniques, but in a manner which never impedes sensitive reading or clear presentation. She brilliantly demonstrates the use of ballads to illuminate other disciplines: in this case, gender studies.

Finally, HARRIS has assembled a collection of stimulating, scholarly essays with an international range of interests. For example, Faroese ballads are compared with Greek choral lyrics, and Homeric epic devices with Anglo-Saxon poetry. Harris places ballads in the broader context of all "oral literature" – an apparently self-contradictory phrase, which "ought to be savored as a reminder of the problematics of literature itself and of the relationships of the oral to the literate".

CAROLYN D. WILLIAMS

Baraka, Amiri [LeRoi Jones] 1934–

American poet, dramatist, and prose writer

Benston, Kimberly W., *Baraka: The Renegade and the Mask*, New Haven, Connecticut: Yale University Press, 1976

Brown, Lloyd W., *Amiri Baraka*, Boston: Twayne, 1980

Harris, William J., *The Poetry and Poetics of Amiri Baraka: The Jazz Aesthetic*, Columbia: University of Missouri Press, 1985

Hudson, Theodore R., *From LeRoi Jones to Amiri Baraka: The Literary Works*, Durham, North Carolina: Duke University Press, 1973

Lacey, Henry C., *To Raise, Destroy and Create: The Poetry, Drama, and Fiction of Imamu Amiri Baraka (LeRoi Jones)*, Troy, New York: Whitston, 1981

Sollers, Werner, *Amiri Baraka/LeRoi Jones: The Quest for a "Populist Modernism"*, New York: Columbia University Press, 1978

The main themes of Baraka criticism were established in the 1970s, and have continued to shape discussion of this prolific and influential writer, even as his art and politics still resist easy classification. From the beginning, critics noted the restless motion of Baraka's life, poetics, and politics, a tension that has often expressed itself in abrupt and radical shifts in his performance and point of view – often played out in public arenas.

HUDSON's work, the first attempt to offer a comprehensive view of Baraka's life and art, surveys his non-fictional prose, fiction, poetry, and drama through his black, cultural, nationalist periods – concluding with works like *It's Nation Time*, *A Black Value System*, and *Strategy and Tactics of a Pan-African Nationalist Party*. Hudson combines biography with literary exegesis, often providing valuable biographical details on which subsequent critics would build. Although many of his judgments have been superseded by Baraka's subsequent shifts in political and ideological allegiances, his study remains a pioneering work.

BENSTON undertakes a systematic analysis of the philosophical, aesthetic, and ideological underpinnings of Baraka's poetry, prose, and political manifestos, culminating in a detailed examination of his drama through *Slave Ship*. Tracing Baraka's journey from the avant garde of Euro-American literary traditions to his position at the forefront of African-American revolutionary art, Benston's study adeptly captures one of the fundamental sources of tension in Baraka's early artistic career. It remains one of the most durable accounts of Baraka's restless search for the artistic and political forms appropriate for his vision of African-American life.

SOLLERS, like Benston, locates Baraka at the intersection of Euro-American and African-American artistic and cultural traditions. Sollers sees one constant, however, which links the various shifts and turns of Baraka's often turbulent public life: the quest for a "populist modernism", by which he means Baraka's attempts to join modernist literature with populist politics. Sollers carefully and systematically examines this dualism in Baraka's life and work, from his early involvement with the Beat poets through his ideological re-alignment to Marxist-Leninist-Maoist thought in the mid-1970s. His work concludes with excerpts from an interview Sollers conducted with Baraka in 1976. Like Benston's study, Sollers's work is a seminal text in Baraka criticism, and an excellent account of the trajectory of Baraka's career through the late 1970s.

BROWN's study, consistent with the format of Twayne's "United States Authors" series, offers a lucid and comprehensive overview of Baraka's writing through the late 1970s. Although Brown points to a certain political and intellectual flabbiness in Baraka's work since the mid-1970s, his survey of Baraka's life and work is generally balanced and judicious, and his easily accessible style makes this work an excellent introduction for general, non-specialist readers.

LACEY works within the broad terrain defined by Benston and Sollers, charting Baraka's development from his "Beat" period though his transition from Greenwich Village to Harlem, to his rebirth as "Imamu", and concluding with a consideration of his fiction. Lacey is particularly insightful in his close readings of Baraka's poetry at various stages of his career, but seems relatively uninterested in exploring the intersection between art and politics in his work since the mid-1970s. Lacey, in short, argues that Baraka's work can, and should, be read for its own sake, and his readings of selected works are designed to correct the critical imbalance that, in his judgment, stresses social values over artistic ones.

HARRIS invokes the jazz aesthetic to signify several levels of transformation in Baraka's life and work: of avant-garde poetics into African-American poetics, of jazz forms into literary forms, of white liberal politics into black nationalist and Marxist politics. Attentive to both the formal and sociopolitical dimensions of the jazz aesthetic, Harris proposes black music as the paradigm for Baraka's art. He draws on the insights of earlier critics to offer a systematic exposition of Baraka's relationship to the white, radical avant garde, his growing sense of the failure of this movement, and his transformation of these traditions into art forms that more fully served his own vision of black revolution. Harris's study concludes with a consideration of Baraka's influence, as both theoretician and practitioner, on the Black Arts Movement, with an interview conducted in 1980, a selection from Baraka's work-in-progress, and a long poem entitled *Wise/Whys*. Its careful attention to Baraka's poetry makes Harris's work a particularly valuable contribution to Baraka criticism.

JAMES A. MILLER

Barth, John 1930–

American novelist

Fogel, Stan, and Gordon Slethaug, *Understanding John Barth*, Columbia: University of South Carolina Press, 1990

Harris, Charles, *Passionate Virtuosity: The Fiction of John Barth*, Urbana: University of Illinois Press, 1983

Schulz, Max F., *The Muses of John Barth: Tradition and Metafiction from "Lost in the Funhouse" to "The Tidewater Tales"*, Baltimore: Johns Hopkins University Press, 1990

Stark, John O., *The Literature of Exhaustion: Borges, Nabokov, and Barth*, Durham, North Carolina: Duke University Press, 1974

Tharpe, Jac, *John Barth: The Comic Sublimity of Paradox*, Carbondale: Southern Illinois University Press, 1974

Tobin, Patricia, *John Barth and the Anxiety of Influence*, Philadelphia: University of Pennsylvania Press, 1992

Self-consciously styling himself a postmodern novelist, John Barth has sought to test the very structures and limits of conventional literary articulation. Consequently, casting around for an appropriate form of explanation and understanding, the early criticism of Barth's writings took its critical discourse from the terminology of Barth's own critical writings. However, the entry of poststructuralist thought into literary-critical discourse has provided a "postmodern" conceptual apparatus, which has enabled a more sophisticated articulation of Barth's fictional experimentation.

STARK's book argues that Barth's essay "The Literature of Exhaustion" provides the rationale for a new breed of writers who use as a theme for their fiction "the agonising hypothesis that literature is finished". Comparing the fiction of Jorge Luis

Borges and Vladimir Nabokov, and Barth's first six novels, Stark argues that these writers develop techniques that reinvigorate fiction by using new forms and by making "reality" problematic. Focusing on the ramifications of such techniques on ideas of space and time, Stark thus perceives Barth to be part of a concerted attack on literary realism.

THARPE's work begins with a general orientation to "Barth's universe", and then proceeds to examine individual works, before concluding that in the fiction "ultimately, Barth says nothing – positively. There is nothing positive to say. No truth to tell. All one can do is tell the story". Focusing on Barth's early novels up to *Chimera*, this study regards Barth's work as philosophical in bearing, dealing with ethics, existentialism, the history of philosophy, ontology, and aesthetics. The conclusion is that as the stories create their own universe, Barth's works gradually emerge as paths to a linguistic Babel. Incorporating a useful bibliography, this claims to be the first full-length study of Barth.

In a more sophisticated if somewhat formalist approach, HARRIS argues that Barth's aesthetic forms a mythopoeic fiction. Tracing the structural and thematic concerns through Barth's first seven books, he suggests that Barth's continual problematic within his continually expanding mythopoeic imagination is how to translate ineffable mythic intentions into a language that can convey the inexpressible. Reading each novel as a qualification and alteration of the previous novel's limits, all the novels "achieve the effect of a constant grasping for meaning, on the one hand, balanced by the realisation that all meaning is *projected* – invented, rather than discovered, and therefore relative and contingent". Barth's ideas of sex, death, comedy, language, and doubles, are developed here in tandem with a matrix of theoretical developments from (post)structuralism, phenomenology, and psychology.

In a far more introductory approach to Barth's fiction, FOGEL and SLETHAUG attempt to situate it within the general context of postmodernism. Looking at Barth's processes of fictive self-reflexiveness, parody, unstable subjectivity, and self-negation, the novels are regarded as violating and denying conventional expectations regarding fiction at every turn. The study analyses how each series of books engages a genre, then explores, questions, and subverts it. This is a straightforward analysis, which acts as solid introduction to Barth's writings.

SCHULZ's focus falls principally on those novels after *Giles Goat-Boy*, regarding them as Barth's principal achievement. In a detailed argument, Schulz is concerned with how Barth resuscitates the novel by utilising a heterogeneity of fictive forms and structural modes. Barth's experiments with numerological and structural patterns are scrutinised closely, and he argues that Barth seeks a form "that accommodates realist assumptions about the alliance of words and things with poststructuralist theories of history (and fact) and myth (and fiction)". *Lost in the Funhouse* and *Letters* are the key texts of this focus, as Schulz details how Barth uses the narrative conventions of the "Great Tradition" "to establish on its own terms a fusion of the American experience and the Anglo-European epistemology and confessional novel tradition".

TOBIN adopts a chronological progression through all the novels, and argues that the creativity in each is born out of an antithetical and revisionary stance towards its precursor. Each chapter is structured on the basis of an aspect of Harold Bloom's model of the "anxiety of influence", although it is acknowledged that Barth's artistic development does not always bow to Bloomian schema. However, in a study that embraces a variety of psychoanalytic and poststructuralist approaches, Tobin argues that Barth's writing becomes marked by "creative revisions" of his previous work, and in this perpetual reinvention of himself Barth thereby revises Bloom, producing an "anxiety of continuance". This book is complex and stimulating in its ideas, yet perhaps also rather too rigid in its conception.

TIM S. WOODS

Barthelme, Donald 1931–1989

American novelist and short-story writer

Couturier, Maurice, and Régis Durand, *Donald Barthelme*, London and New York: Methuen, 1982
Gordon, Lois, *Donald Barthelme*, Boston: Twayne, 1981
Klinkowitz, Jerome, *Donald Barthelme: An Exhibition*, Durham, North Carolina: Duke University Press, 1991
McCaffery, Larry, *The Metafictional Muse: The Works of Robert Coover, Donald Barthelme, and William H. Gass*, Pittsburgh: University of Pittsburgh Press, 1982; London: Feffer & Simons, 1982
Molesworth, Charles, *Donald Barthelme's Fiction: The Ironist Saves from Drowning*, Columbia: University of Missouri Press, 1982
Stengel, Wayne B., *The Shape of Art in the Short Stories of Donald Barthelme*, Baton Rouge: Louisiana State University Press, 1985
Trachtenberg, Stanley, *Understanding Donald Barthelme*, Columbia: University of South Carolina Press, 1990

Donald Barthelme's fascination with the role of language in human experience identified him from the beginning with the innovative fiction being written by Kurt Vonnegut, Grace Paley, Ishmael Reed, Ronald Sukenick, and others who, from the 1960s onwards, had been disrupting conventions of representational realism. His background as an art museum director and art magazine editor allowed him to infiltrate areas of high culture otherwise resistant to such disruptions; as a result his regular appearance in *The New Yorker* magazine introduced a whole new readership to a style of fiction that had previously been more apparent in less traditional venues.

GORDON's introductory study reflects attitudes about Barthelme's work expressed by the authors of reviews, essays, and chapters in books during the 1970s: that rather than literature reflecting life, the lives in his fiction "have in great part become the media, the art and the slogans – the words – about them". Anticipating the rejections of mimetic tradition that characterize postmodernism, Gordon does not use postmodern theory to explain the consequences of this orientation, but suggests instead that "Barthelme had pushed the existential position to its furthest limits", having his characters embrace roles (whether from television, advertising, or philosophy itself) and play them out as if they were authentic, even though they are not.

McCAFFERY is most emphatic in drawing Barthelme's work into the canon of innovation being established by the other figures in his study, Robert Coover and William H. Gass, as well as by such more radical figures as Sukenick and Raymond Federman (who are cited frequently as measures for comparison). The critic's term for such work is "metafiction", meaning fiction whose substance consists in the exploration of its own making, and in Barthelme's work he sees it as a thematic as well as technical interest, consisting in "the difficulties of expressing a total vision of oneself in a fragmenting universe, the failure of most of our social and linguistic systems, the difficulties of making contact or sustaining relationships with others". Above all, Barthelme is cast as a student of language, studying the symbol-making activities of persons living not so much in contemporary times as within the signs of those times.

It is COUTURIER and DURAND who bring postmodern theory (albeit with a light touch) to bear on Barthelme's fiction. "Signs are signs", they quote from the author's short story "Me and Miss Mandible", and concur with the story's narrator that "some of them are lies". Deconstruction, as practised by Jacques Derrida and dedicated to exposing the otherwise unquestioned assumptions behind conventional beliefs and decisions, is offered as a clue to understanding Barthelme's motives. In story after story the author is seen as making problematic "not simply the failure to decipher and narrate the subject or referent . . . but the activity of reference itself, the possibility of situating any referent of a discourse". Because the fiction does not become self-referential itself, Barthelme escapes what the critics call "the confident irony of modernism"; instead, he creates a postmodern text, which "resolves nothing, and denies self-sufficiency and autonomy", leaving the reader "suspended" between meanings in a way that questions "the symbolic process itself".

A step backwards is taken by MOLESWORTH, who tries to establish that Barthelme is just the ironist (and hence modernist) that previous critics said he was not. Molesworth's strategy is to favour the author's penchant for satire and parody and the essential self-referentiality of such work, whereby "the parodic centre is itself parodied". It is a strongly thematic and even moralistic reading that Molesworth provides, at the cost of dismissing work that does not fit his thesis, such as the dialogue stories in *Great Days*. "What Barthelme's parody of realism suggests", the critic believes, "is that if people are overmastered by something from within, that 'something' is a lack, an absence, an awareness of their own frustrated desires".

STENGEL corrects Molesworth's misapprehension by organizing the author's stories according to how they handle what realistically-inclined critics argue are overwhelming thematic concerns. Thus is identity resolved by a license for play, dialogue empowered by strategies of epistemology, society as authority undercut by devices of repetition, and objectivation effaced by a new emphasis on creation. Barthelme does indeed want the formal elements of his fiction to take precedence over referential concerns, Stengel argues, suggesting that the author's attempt "to remake the world" derives its "buoyant optimism and gaiety" from "the dramatization of the artist's personality in his art".

TRACHTENBERG reconciles much of the representational/anti-representational debate by considering how "though straining, at least in part, toward the world, whose modalities it faithfully records often in recognizable speech patterns or in objects drawn from popular culture, Barthelme's fictions are far from realistic". Yet neither are they as destructive of referential centres as the novels and stories of the author's more innovative contemporaries. Never do Barthelme's fictions confuse "the absence of meaning with the absence of a reality outside that of the text" or confine that reality "to the activity or process of writing through which it is structured". Instead, the author's works "attempt to exploit the informational ellipses to confirm the existence of an experiential world, particularly in its more ephemeral or popular forms".

My own study (KLINKOWITZ's), written after Barthelme's death and the publication of his final work, organizes the author's career in three stages: the radical attack on established conventions of fiction in his early stories and first novel, *Snow White*; his composition of an unimpeded postmodern novel, *The Dead Father*, within the space cleared by his earlier experiments; and ultimately, his re-embrace of referential materials from a new position independent of the hierarchal dictates of realism.

JEROME KLINKOWITZ

Baxter, James K. 1926–1972

New Zealand poet and dramatist

Doyle, Charles, *James K. Baxter*, Boston: Twayne, 1976
McKay, Frank, *The Life of James K. Baxter*, Auckland: Oxford University Press, 1990
Oliver, W.H., *James K. Baxter: A Portrait*, Sydney: Allen & Unwin, 1983
O'Sullivan, Vincent, *James K. Baxter*, Wellington: Oxford University Press, 1976
Weir, J.E., *The Poetry of James K. Baxter*, Wellington: Oxford University Press, 1970

Much of the early critical writing on Baxter's poetry tends to focus on his literary influences and his incorporation of European myths into his specifically New Zealand poems. The later criticism usually incorporates these issues into more general evaluations of Baxter's work, which also consider his keen interest in Maori culture and language, and the significance to his poetry of his conversion to Catholicism. Baxter's critics are often divided into those who admire the variety of his considerable output and those who point to a certain glibness in his work.

WEIR's book is short and accessible, opening with concise biographical information, and containing a good bibliography of Baxter's principal publications. He focuses on, in particular, the three most important themes he discerns in Baxter's poetry – myth, nature, and religion – while also noting the centrality of Baxter's love poems to his extensive body of work. Although clearly an admirer of Baxter, Weir often draws his reader's attention to his faults, noting, for example, the preponderance of various myths in the early work: "Sometimes the structure of the poems is swamped by their imposition so that the verse loses coherence and is reduced to a series of multiple images. At its best, however, especially when the poetry is strongly rooted in the New Zealand scene, this practice creates a genuine universality".

DOYLE's book is prefaced with a very useful chronology of Baxter's life, intertwining the dates of significant publications with important events in the poet's life. The book begins with biographical details, and throughout Doyle relates the life to the work. This is a comprehensive study, beginning with assessments of the early collections (*Beyond the Palisade*, *Blow, Wind of Forgetfulness*) and concluding the evaluation of the poetry with particularly close readings of many of the poems in *Jerusalem Sonnets* and *Pig Island Letters*, noting how serviceable Baxter found the two-line unrhymed stanza. Doyle's thorough research is evident in the sections that consider Baxter's own reading, and he also devotes considerable time to gauging the importance of a number of Baxter's poetic influences. Doyle stresses the complexity of Baxter's work, and his life, noting that it is difficult confidently to label him. He writes, for example, that "a poet of varied moods, modes, and approaches, Baxter, by and large, is subjective, expressionistic; but he is not merely confessional". Although Doyle does not discuss all of Baxter's plays, and reads the ones he does cover primarily for the light they shed on the poetry, the consideration of this usually neglected aspect of Baxter's work remains useful.

O'SULLIVAN, himself a well-known New Zealand writer, begins his brief study with Baxter's biographical details, but swiftly moves on to a detailed assessment of *Beyond the Palisade* (1944), noting that in this first book the majority of the poet's life-long preoccupations can be found – myth, love, nature, and death. The second half of his book concentrates on Baxter's developing interest in religion. O'Sullivan stresses the complexity of Baxter's relationship with the established order, noting that while Baxter was politically active in his private life, throughout his career he was technically conservative, with virtually no interest in formal experimentation. Baxter is, for O'Sullivan, a specifically New Zealand poet: "that is the proportion of Baxter's achievement – the most complete delineation yet of a New Zealand mind. The poetic record of its shaping is as original an act as anything we have".

OLIVER's book is unusual in that while it is a critical biography, it contains a very large number of photographs, not just of Baxter and other New Zealand writers but also of New Zealand's landscape: an appreciation of the latter, Oliver argues, is crucial to any understanding of Baxter's poetry. Some of the photographs of drab and colourless New Zealand cities in the 1950s and the early 1960s might also convey, better than any critical argument, Baxter's powerful desire to assault convention. Much of the book finds connections between events in Baxter's life and specific poems, and within this limitation the readings are persuasive. Oliver makes interesting observations on Baxter's use of the ballad form and the ways in which this demotic medium suited a poet who always wished to be seen as a man of the people.

McKAY's book is also a critical biography, but a considerably more conventional one than Oliver's. This book is particularly useful regarding background information on New Zealand society in the 1940s–60s, and especially interesting for its portrayal of the role of the artist in New Zealand society. At times McKay's style is somewhat arch ("Venus, so long delayed and looked for, showed up at last in the person of Jane Alymer, a medical student at Otago University"). The biography is conventionally structured, beginning with the arrival of Baxter's ancestors in Otago and ending with the poet's death, and McKay, wherever possible, links the life and the work. Each of Baxter's important publications is discussed, and a survey of the critical response to each volume is included. The book is impressively researched, and McKay demonstrates great familiarity not only with Baxter's poetry but with New Zealand poetry in general. He also has a comprehensive understanding of the importance Maori language and culture had for Baxter, particularly in his later years. Perhaps the book's most significant contribution to Baxter studies is its evaluation of the poet's alcoholism and his conversion to Roman Catholicism, both of which McKay sees as powerful themes in Baxter's poetry.

KEVIN MCCARRON

Beat Generation

Bartlett, Lee (ed.), *The Beats: Essays in Criticism*, Jefferson, North Carolina: McFarland, 1981

Cook, Bruce, *The Beat Generation*, New York: Scribner, 1971; 2nd edition, New York: William Morrow, 1994

Nicosia, Gerald, *Memory Babe: A Critical Biography of Jack Kerouac*, New York: Grove Press, 1983; Harmondsworth, Middlesex: Viking Press, 1985

Parkinson, Thomas (ed.), *A Casebook on the Beat*, New York: Thomas Y. Crowell, 1961

Stephenson, Gregory, *The Daybreak Boys: Essays on the Literature of the Beat Generation*, Carbondale: Southern Illinois University Press, 1990

Tytell, John, *Naked Angels: The Lives and Literature of the Beat Generation*, New York: McGraw-Hill, 1976

The Beat Generation has never been amenable to single or stable definition, and the history of its documentation and criticism has been one of parallel, often mutually exclusive, constructions. In broad terms, interpretations have stressed a different dominant out of two elements: viewing the "Generation" as a sociological phenomenon of the 1950s with literary roots, or seeing "the Beats" as a literary circle that had social and cultural impact. The main area of revision and contest has been the continual dispute over inclusion or exclusion of authors, reflected in the protean anthologies of Beat writing.

Aside from its documentary value, the importance of PARKINSON's collection of primary materials and commentaries is principally its influential combination of range and approach. The first half brings together Allen Ginsberg, Jack Kerouac, Gregory Corso, William S. Burroughs, Lawrence Ferlinghetti, Gary Snyder, Philip Whalen, Michael McClure, and John Wieners. These literary figures are not presented as definitive – Parkinson offers no editorial or Introduction in which to argue any claims – but the significance is in the sequence itself. Later critics tacitly used the emphasis given to the more recognisably major writers to advance the case for the Beats as a serious artistic movement. Parkinson therefore avoids the problem of a definition-led selection, which might promote lesser writers. However, a problem of another order emerges: it is hard to reconcile such anomalous items as Burroughs' minor collage piece with either the texts adjacent to it, or with the commentaries that constitute the second half of the volume. Of these essays, the most significant remains the most hostile, Norman Podherotz's "The Know-Nothing Bohemians", a vitriolic attack on Jack Kerouac. More than any promoter of the Beats, Podhoretz effectively identified their challenge to the cultural and political orthodoxy of the Cold War. Next to his revealing hysteria, such partisan items as the selection from Lawrence Lipton's *The Holy Barbarians* seem merely dated period pieces. The mismatch between the two halves of Parkinson's collection is evidence of an unresolved confusion between the enduring values of the literary phenomenon and the transience of a sociological one.

COOK, in the first full-length treatment of the Beat Generation, constructs a more coherent relationship between these conflicting elements. With the advantage of hindsight, he is able to distinguish the Beats, as writers, from the Beatniks, the youth culture they inspired, and which the media sensationalized. His personalized tone – identifying the Beats as "my generation" – establishes the nature of his approach, which, in his Preface to the 1994 edition, he acknowledges as "literary journalism" rather than literary criticism. His book thus combines interviews, impressionistic anecdotal material, biographical sketches, and cultural essays.

Cook's predominantly sociological analysis focuses on the Beat Generation as a counter-cultural movement: he explores both the immediate context of the 1950s and also the "long, rich, and deeply American tradition" that they inherited. In this latter field, Cook aligns Ginsberg with Walt Whitman, and Snyder with Henry David Thoreau, while viewing Kerouac and Corso as heirs to the same lineage of American nonconformity. As for Burroughs, Cook gives him the opportunity for a parodic McCarthyite denial: "I am not now, nor have I ever been, a member of the Beat Generation". Tacitly, Cook here admits the difficulty that association caused, namely that its effect was to periodize writers and deter wider critical recognition with the tag of controversy. Concluding that the Beats accelerated the process of social, cultural, and hence political, change, Cook's final chapters deal with the hippy generation, culminating in the Woodstock Festival and the conversion of Beat revolt into bohemian style.

TYTELL structures his book in keeping with the balance of his subtitle, and the result is a work of narrower focus but significantly greater depth. Writing with a forceful style and discriminating intelligence, he limits his range to Burroughs, Kerouac, and Ginsberg, and follows biographical portraits with literary analysis. Although his range of reference and critical approach was soon to be surpassed by specialist studies, the usefulness of Tytell's work as an introduction remains strong. It also has the value of an incisive introductory chapter on the Cold War, which allows him to argue that the major works of Burroughs, Kerouac, and Ginsberg are "the creative soul of the fifties" and keys to the "cultural disorder" of the era.

BARTLETT's collection of essays declares itself an extension and updating of Parkinson's of 20 years earlier. In the same vein, it makes no claims to definition, although the range certainly implies one. It emphasizes the literary group over the social or political movement, gives space to more poets – such as Bob Kaufman – and includes two articles on the marginal figure of William Everson, a mystical Catholic also known as Brother Antonius. The result is a collection that promotes spiritual values without making them a principle of cohesion. This difficulty is compounded by the lack of essays dealing with later works by the main writers. For example, neither essay on Ginsberg or Burroughs goes in any significant way beyond 1960.

NICOSIA's critical biography of Kerouac merits brief inclusion here, on the grounds that its exhaustive and exemplary scholarship provides a much-needed corrective to the generalisations so widespread in the field. This can be attributed to the centrality of Kerouac to any construction of the topic, itself a consequence of his early death, which may have denied him the opportunity of major development evident in the work of Burroughs and Ginsberg.

STEPHENSON offers a distinctive approach, seeing the unity of the Beat Generation in a "shared sense of quest", a "journey from darkness to light". He argues for a common narrative of personal and human liberation, informed by a strong sense of spiritual mission: for Stephenson, Beat writing entails "both a species of exorcism and an alchemical transmutation of the base to the precious". His selection of authors offers only one surprise – Richard Farina, presented as a "second generation" Beat – although he does devote a section to Neal Cassady, usually treated along with Kerouac. Devotion is, in fact, the characteristic tone of Stephenson's writing, and his book reads at times like an exegetical commentary on a series of sacred texts, or, as with Cassady, like hagiography. Thus the major weakness is less distortion – his line of interpretation is cogent and well-supported – but rather a lack of critical distance, a failure to dispute claims and pay attention to evident problems.

OLIVER HARRIS

Beaumont, Francis *see* Fletcher, John

Beckett, Samuel 1906–1989

Irish dramatist, fiction writer, and poet

Acheson, James, and Kateryna Arthur (eds.), *Beckett's Later Fiction and Drama: Texts for Company*, London: Macmillan, 1987

Bair, Deirdre, *Samuel Beckett: A Biography*, London: Jonathan Cape, 1978; New York: Harcourt Brace Jovanovich, 1978

Connor, Steven, *Samuel Beckett: Repetition, Theory and Text*, Oxford and New York: Blackwell, 1988

Doherty, Francis, *Samuel Beckett*, London: Hutchinson, 1971

Fitch, Brian T., *Beckett and Babel: An Investigation into the Bilingual Work*, Toronto and Buffalo, New York: University of Toronto Press, 1988

Friedman, Alan Warren, Charles Rossman, and Dina Sherzer (eds.), *Beckett Translating/ Translating Beckett*, University Park: Pennsylvania State University Press, 1987

Gontarski, S.E., *The Beckett Studies Reader*, Gainesville: University Press of Florida, 1993
Hill, Leslie, *Beckett's Fiction: In Different Words*, Cambridge and New York: Cambridge University Press, 1990
Kalb, Jonathan, *Beckett in Performance*, Cambridge and New York: Cambridge University Press, 1989
Kennedy, Andrew K., *Samuel Beckett*, Cambridge and New York: Cambridge University Press, 1989
Knowlson, James (general ed.), *The Theatrical Notebooks of Samuel Beckett* series (published to date: *Krapp's Last Tape*, edited by Knowlson & Dougald McMillan; *Waiting for Godot* edited by Knowlson; *Endgame* edited by S.E. Gontarski), London: Faber & Faber, 1992–
Krance, Charles (ed.), *Samuel Beckett's "Company/ Compagnie" and "A Piece of Monologue/Solo"*, bilingual variorum edition, New York: Garland, 1993
Miller, Lawrence, *Samuel Beckett: The Expressive Dilemma*, New York: St Martin's Press, 1992; London: Macmillan, 1992
Pilling, John (ed.), *The Cambridge Companion to Beckett*, Cambridge and New York: Cambridge University Press, 1994
Pilling, John, and Mary Bryden (eds.), *The Ideal Core of the Onion: Reading Beckett Archives*, Reading, Berkshire: Beckett International Foundation, 1992
Rabinovitz, Rubin, *Innovation in Samuel Beckett's Fiction*, Urbana: University of Illinois Press, 1992
Ricks, Christopher, *Beckett's Dying Words: The Clarendon Lectures*, Oxford and New York: Oxford University Press, 1993

The writings of Samuel Beckett have probably generated more critical responses than those of any other twentieth-century author, and yet it is not unfair to suggest that until recently he had fewer scholars than critics (that ultimate insult in the flyting of *Godot*). Yet that situation is changing. Beckett has attracted fine editors, and he has been well served by many excellent recent studies, with yet others in the offing. The following constitutes but a tiny selection from the literally hundreds available.

BAIR's biography remains controversial. Too often naive, unreliable on points of detail, and not incisively written, it nevertheless broke new ground, and was for many readers the first glimpse of the man behind the masks. Bair succeeds in relating the author to his works, and in providing a poignant context for the writing. Her study will be superseded by that of James Knowlson, authorised by Beckett shortly before he died, but for many years has been the standard account, and one of greater value than many reviewers were prepared to admit.

A more recent overview of the range of Beckett's achievement is given in PILLING's 1994 *Companion*. The title is a little misleading, for what Pilling offers is a selection of essays by eminent scholars who survey the current trends in their chosen field and provide extensive bibliographies for further reading. The quality is variable, but the collection as a whole achieves its stated aims of overviewing the recent expansion of critical perspectives, and directing the student of Beckett towards the more valuable secondary materials. More specialised is the edition by PILLING and BRYDEN (1992), for the essays therein are based specifically upon the holdings of the Beckett archives at the University of Reading. Pilling on the *Murphy* Notebook is particularly rewarding for his insights into Beckett's early reading; Mary Bryden gives a provocative account of one of Beckett's intricate doodles; most of the other essays offer insights into the later plays (the strength of the holdings). With the Reading archives likely to become the future "core" of Beckett studies, this collection alerts scholars to the range of invaluable materials held there.

As an introduction to Beckett's early fiction and the way that the drama rose directly from those roots, DOHERTY's little book remains instructive. Attentive to detail, incisive in expression, Doherty does justice to the complexities of Beckett's concerns without ever losing sight of their essential simplicity. This cannot be said of the more recent study by RABINOVITZ. Although impressive in his range of references and his general understanding, Rabinovitz tends to be unsure of the tonalities of Beckett's fundamental sounds and somewhat vague about the "deeper meanings" he sees the innovative structures hinting at. For instance, as a means of gaining insight into Beckett's metaphorical structures, he offers an intriguing analogy with a neural network; yet the configuration and its concommitant sense of deeply layered meaning is rendered suspect by the simple fact that the manuscripts of the Trilogy reveal that Beckett did not compose this text in his usual schematic way. Rabinovitz is comprehensive and clear, and rightly suspicious of truisms; yet his account, for all its considerable merits, remains less than penetrating.

More complex is the work by HILL. The superb pun of his subtitle ("in different words") initiates a study of the fiction in which the notion of *différance* is itself deconstructed to lead to the still turbulence at the centre of Beckett's language and negativity. Hill is compelling on the rhetoric of purgatory in *Murphy*, the metaphor of incarnation in *Watt*, and the logic of aporia in the Trilogy; and his exploration of the later "fizzles" in terms of the language of the body invests that contemporary cliché with the dynamics of immediate experience. The rhetoric of aporetic indifference, as defined by Hill, leads to illuminating insights.

MILLER seeks to define the expressive dilemma by focusing upon the Trilogy as the inconclusive centre of Beckett's writing, and to see that work as a sustained investigation of voice, words, and writing. He sees Beckett's importance as lying, paradoxically, in the failure to solve the problems of artistic expression, yet he has a sure sense of the central significance of the novel(s) in the context of the postmodernist movement, emphasising the experience of reading the Trilogy as a way of rethinking literary history. Although he presents rather too readily the spectre of Beckett hovering over the ruins of modernism, Miller makes a powerful case for seeing in Beckett's most sustained work both the rejection of an expressive theory of art and the recognition that the goal of expression cannot be easily abandoned.

Two volumes, from the many available, illustrate opposite approaches to the range of Beckett's work, particularly the middle drama. KENNEDY's is an introductory critical study, which says sensible things sensibly, and places the innovations of *Waiting for Godot* and *Endgame* appropriately within both Beckett's *oeuvre* and the developments of twentieth-century theatre. It is an excellent beginner's study, though not challenging to the experienced reader. CONNOR, conversely, draws upon poststructuralist theory to examine how repetition functions within Beckett's discourse to assert (that is, to question) essence and identity. His examination of repetition in terms of *différance* is provocative, as is his discussion of *Godot* as "theatre of presence", and *Endgame* as constantly deferring the consummation of its ending: Connor uses the current critical idiom playfully, but to effect (though exactly what effect may yet be debated).

GONTARSKI's collection of essays is full of variety. Gontarski is editor of *The Journal of Beckett Studies*, which in its revival has become the central forum of Beckett scholarship. His criterion of selection was to choose from past issues essays likely to remain significant but which have not reappeared elsewhere. The outcome is a valuable compendium of the best of 15 years, including such fine studies as John Pilling on *Proust*, Heath Lees on the music of *Watt*, and J.D. O'Hara's account of the Jungian dimensions of *Molloy* (anticipating his forthcoming study of Beckett's psychological reading, a work likely to be both controversial and definitive).

The essays edited by ACHESON and ARTHUR provide a good introduction to the variety of Beckett's later writings. Robert Wilcher gives a fine account of the radio plays, Katharine Worth of the tendency towards minimalism in the stage plays, Martin Esslin of a similar impulse leading to the plays for television. Acheson's essay rather overstresses the parallels with William Wordsworth in *That Time* and with T.S. Eliot in *Footfalls,* while Arthur strives too much for effect in her account of "scripsophrenia"; but their assembling of essays on this late period of creativity induces a significant evaluation of some complex and provocative material. There is also a grimly amusing account of a 1984 production of *Godot* incorporating many changes insisted on by Beckett, leading Colin Duckworth to wonder if authors should be let loose on their plays 30-odd years after writing them.

The approach taken by KALB is a practical one. From a lifetime of experience in theatre, Kalb has brought together a provocative account of the intrinsic problems that arise in producing Beckett's work for the stage. He covers the range and variety of Beckett's drama, and includes photos of performances, interviews with actors and directors (including Beckett himself), with full details of important productions. The result is an imporant contribution to the history of Beckett in the theatre.

There has been considerable interest recently in problems of translation, and FRIEDMAN's collection of essays is a good introduction to Beckett's bilingualism and the "conceptual transmutations" arising from the invention of specific metaphors to translate metaphysical concepts. If the collection has a weakness, it is perhaps the extension of the idea of "translation" to Beckett's manipulation of genre conventions and to the consideration of other creative writers who have taken their inspiration from Beckett, when the central issue of bilingualism itself requires further exploration.

One of the contributors to Friedman, FITCH, goes further in his own study, assessing Beckett's achievement as a bilingual writer and analysing the complexities posed by the status of "second" versions of the works. He discusses the shifts of perspective brought about by the discrepancies between the French and English versions of the "same" work, two fictive universes but each corresponding to a different text. The outcome is a fascinating account, which raises intricate philosophical and aesthetic questions without, however, losing sight of the fiction and drama that generates them.

The edition by KRANCE of Beckett's *Company/Compagnie* is the initial volume in a series of bilingual variorum editions aiming to give virtual definition to problematic and multilingual texts, following them through the first holograph drafts to the final typescripts and proofs. The result is a model of scholarship, the text as definitive as possible, and, thanks to the evolution of a sophisticated critical apparatus, a compendium of manuscript variants that is all-inclusive.

The final word should be reserved for the magnificent series of *Theatrical Notebooks* brought out by different scholars under the general editorship of James KNOWLSON. They offer not so much definitive texts (the production history of Beckett's plays makes that impossible), but come as close as possible to what Beckett wanted his plays to be. They include revisions, textual notes, explanatory material, facsimiles of Beckett's notebooks, the author's own manuscript notes, and comprehensive biographies relating to performance as well as critical history. In this series, Beckett's drama has found scholars worthy of its merits, and the outcome is a most satisfactory balance between theatrical production, textual history, and critical response.

An epigraph: the finest tribute to Beckett after his death came from RICKS, whose 1990 Clarendon lectures scrutinised Beckett's dying words. Ricks considers the motif of death throughout Beckett's *oeuvre*, defining what he calls a syntax of weakness, and showing why Beckett's clichés will not stay dead. Ricks's genius is his command of detail and precise rhetorical analysis; indeed, he is contemptuous of the recent trend towards deconstruction, affirming unequivocally that far from saying Nothing ("language is all that remains"), Beckett incarnates the reality of human suffering in words that are articulate and will endure. If Doherty makes a good beginning to the study of Beckett, then Ricks is an appropriate end. In a paradox that Beckett might not have found displeasing, two scholars with something significant to say have done so in very few words.

CHRIS ACKERLEY

Behn, Aphra c.1640–1689

English novelist, dramatist, and poet

Ballaster, Ros, "New Hystericism: Aphra Behn's *Oroonoko:* The Body and the Text", in *New Feminist Discourses: Critical Essays on Theories and Texts*, edited by Isobel Armstrong, London and New York: Routledge, 1992

Duffy, Maureen, *The Passionate Shepherdess: Aphra Behn 1640–89*, London: Jonathan Cape, 1977

Goreau, Angeline, *Reconstructing Aphra: A Social Biography of Aphra Behn*, New York: Dial Press, 1980

Hutner, Heidi (ed.), *Rereading Aphra Behn: History, Theory, and Criticism*, Charlottesville: University Press of Virginia, 1993

Jones, Jane, "New Light on the Background and Early Life of Aphra Behn", in *Notes and Queries*, 37(3), 1990

Mendelson, Sara Heller, *The Mental World of Stuart Women: Three Studies*, Brighton, Sussex: Harvester Press, 1987; Amherst: University of Massachusetts Press, 1987

Pearson, Jacqueline, "Gender and Narrative in the Fiction of Aphra Behn", in *Review of English Studies*, 42(165), February 1991, and 42(166), May 1991

Schofield, Mary Anne, and Cecilia Macheski (eds.), *Curtain Calls: British and American Women and the Theatre, 1660–1820*, Athens: Ohio University Press, 1991

Todd, Janet, *The Sign of Angellica: Women, Writing and Fiction 1660–1800*, London: Virago,1989; New York: Columbia University Press, 1989

Todd, Janet, *Gender, Art and Death*, Cambridge: Polity Press, 1993; New York: Continuum, 1993

The sheer enigma that is Aphra Behn's life led many early critics to concentrate on biography at the expense of analysis. However, in more recent years, much critical work on her writing has emerged, as has a new edition of her complete works compiled by Janet Todd. Owing to such research, most commentators now recognise Behn, probably the first professional woman writer in English, as being central to any discussion of late seventeenth-century literature and culture. Inevitably, perhaps, in view of Behn's anomalous literary and historical position, much criticism of her writing has had an accent on gender issues. This is particularly true of collections of essays about her.

TODD's 1989 study derives its very title from the self-advertisement of the prostitute Angellica Bianca in Behn's 1677 play *The Rover*. Such a title thereby unequivocally places Behn at the core of this work, which investigates the emergence of English women writers in the late seventeenth, and eighteenth centuries. Having provided a thorough and readable historical context for her study, Todd devotes her fourth chapter, "An Honour and Glory to Our Sex", to an assessment of Behn's work. Todd evaluates Behn's creativity from a resolutely historicist perspective, locating her firmly within the peculiar socio-political circumstances of the period. She argues that Behn, in her prose writing, develops a complex narrative voice which speaks as eye-witness or participant, thus almost becoming a character in its own right, while simultaneously resisting an absolute, and "masculine", authoritativeness. What the ensuing combination of fact and fiction, reportage and invention, can lead to, Todd avers, is a "common lack of moral placing that shocks a modern reader. People perpetrate the most frightful crimes without necessarily being the worse for them". Further, she highlights Behn's sometimes unconventional approach to sexuality and heroism thus: "brutality crashes through Arcadia and yawns interrupt romance". The concluding pages of Todd's chapter on Behn concentrate on her *Love-Letters Between a Nobleman and His Sister*. Overall, Todd's work on Behn is fresh and original, typified by detailed and yet never tedious research.

This is also true of TODD's 1993 group of essays, several of which focus on Behn's drama, poetry, and prose. Particularly intriguing is Todd's reading of Behn's *Oroonoko*, the story of a noble slave in Surinam, where the overarching elements of gender, art, and death unite. She demonstrates how Oroonoko is fundamentally a flawed hero in the classical Roman mode, whose self-perception differs startlingly from the reality of events around him. The imperfections of the identity he created for himself have direct and grotesquely tragic consequences for his wife, and ultimately for himself, as he dies a death which Todd sets up in comparison with that of Behn's revered Charles I. In the narrative, the reader is subject to the "relation between fiction and fact, fiction and faction, fact and faction, literary faction and political faction". Todd offers a fascinating and ground-breaking interpretation. Also of note is the deeply poignant and yet historically acute analysis of Behn's "Pindaric Poem to the Reverend Doctor Burnet", written in 1689, and published just before her death. Here Todd movingly delineates the stoic integrity of the female artist who "considered the cost of compliance too high".

BALLASTER's essay offers an alternative, New-Historicist approach to *Oroonoko*, acting as an imaginative counterpoint to Todd's thesis. The papers edited by HUTNER also have in common a New-Historicist literary-critical approach. Hutner's collection contains some important essays on Behn, like Gallagher's influential "Who Was That Masked Woman? The Prostitute and the Playwright in the Comedies of Aphra Behn". Gallagher connects publication with self-publicity which, for a seventeenth-century woman, had sexual implications. She forges this connection unequivocally in her discussion of Behn's Prologue to *The Forced Marriage*, commenting:

> . . . the prostitute is she who stands out by virtue of her mask. The dramatic masking of the prostitute and the stagey masking of the playwright's interest in money are exactly parallel cases of theatrical unmasking in which what is revealed is the parallel itself: the playwright is a whore.

The image of the whore as a model of femininity also features in Hutner's own contribution, "Revisioning the Female Body: Aphra Behn's *The Rover*, Parts I and II", a quasi-Foucauldian reading of that play. The most accessible offering in the collection is "The History of *The History of the Nun*", in which Pearson concentrates on needlework's actual and metaphorical operations as a specifically female discourse to which male characters have little access. As Pearson argues, "Behn typically places a time bomb under the conventionally repressive metaphor of sewing". Also by PEARSON, and worthy of note for its important and original research, is her 1991 work, which focuses especially on *Oroonoko*, and on the relationship between authority and the private and political worlds of *Love-Letters Between a Nobleman and His Sister*. Along the way, Pearson's investigations into the relationship between gender and narrative in Behn's work leads her to conclude that:

> Behn's tales . . . proliferate images of female authors and narrators and male readers, and thereby create complex paradoxes about female power and powerlessness. More important, Behn creates narrators who either speak with a consciously ironic voice to reveal the contradictions in the received orthodoxies of gender, or unconsciously reveal themselves as victims of these very contradictions.

Pearson's contribution to Behn studies is ingenious, methodical, and of great value.

SCHOFIELD and MACHESKI's volume is a competent collection of essays, most of which deal with aspects of Behn's writing. Once again Behn's treatment of gender is at issue, for example in Munns's "'I by a Double Right Thy Bounties Claim': Aphra Behn and Sexual Space". Munns compares Behn's approach to gender with that of her male contemporaries, arguing that "Behn is less concerned than a male dramatist with confusions in male identity than with asserting that there are no territories marked off from her fe/male access". This relationship between Behn and other playwrights is also central to Cotton's "Aphra Behn and the Pattern Hero". Cotton maps a series of similarities between Etherege, Wycherley, and Behn – they shared political allegiances and acquaintances, for example – in her demonstration that in the 1670s they wrote pattern hero plays. This allows her to draw comparisons between Behn's Willmore and Etherege's Dorimant, concluding that "Behn found the masculinist preoccupations of manners comedy uninteresting and preferred to use romantic comedy to pursue her own interest in unhappy and forced marriage as a trap for women". In all, the works selected by Schofield and Macheski are useful and challenging, with their concentration on gender issues, but discussion does focus repeatedly on *The Rover*, making the collection less an overview than a specific – and critically advanced – study.

An attempt to ascertain particulars about Behn's life is the task of Duffy, Jones, Goreau, and Mendelson, each of whom takes a slightly different approach from the others, and, in the absence of much reliable historical information, develops diverse conclusions about Behn's origins.

DUFFY's hypothesis is rarely elevated above the level of speculation, but she does provide for future biographical scholarship – which has been continued by JONES, who establishes with more certainty Duffy's speculation concerning Behn's lowly background and early life. Duffy's literary analysis lacks the immediacy of, for example, Todd's, but she does provide a good introductory overview.

GOREAU, like Todd, maintains that Behn developed an effective means of transforming her actual experiences into fiction, situating Behn's influential contribution to the shift away from historical romance to a more realistic novel form. *The Fair Jilt*, for example, marks a combination of elements from romance and journalistic claims for veracity. Goreau further emphasises Behn's overall concentration on "love, marriage, and the contingent negotiation of both between the sexes".

MENDELSON, in addition to her study of Behn, examines two Stuart contemporaries, Margaret Cavendish, Duchess of Newcastle, and Mary Rich, Countess of Warwick, in her attempt to provide an insight into:

> . . . prototypical feminine themes of the seventeenth century: female life stages, patriarchalism in theory and practice, the control of female sexuality, the limitations inherent in women's conventional role and the reactions provoked by those who sought to challenge them.

Mendelson's real strength is in construing how Behn used her writing as a vehicle for the expression of often fervent political sentiments. Overall Mendelson presents a good balance between personal detail of Behn's life, her work, and her location within the social and cultural milieux of the seventeenth century. She fulfils her aim, which is to show how a "tiny minority [of Stuart women] who had the means and leisure might profit from a certain blurring of sexual boundaries in the intellectual realm", presenting a study that is a good introduction to Behn, and which could profitably be read before moving onto the more focused and specific work as detailed above.

EMMA L.E. REES

Bellow, Saul 1915 –

Canadian-born American novelist and short-story writer

Bach, Gerhard (ed.), *Saul Bellow at Seventy-Five: A Collection of Critical Essays*, Tübingen, Germany: Gunter Narr, 1991

Clayton, John J., *Saul Bellow: In Defense of Man*, Bloomington: Indiana University Press, 1968, 2nd edition, 1979

Cronin, Gloria L., and L.H. Goldman (eds.), *Saul Bellow in the 1980s*, East Lansing: Michigan State University Press, 1989

Fuchs, Daniel, *Saul Bellow: Vision and Revision*, Durham, North Carolina: Duke University Press, 1984

Hyland, Peter, *Saul Bellow*, London: Macmillan, 1992; New York: St Martin's Press, 1992

Newman, Judie, *Saul Bellow and History*, London: Macmillan, 1984; New York: St Martin's Press, 1984

Pifer, Ellen, *Saul Bellow: Against the Grain*, Philadelphia: University of Pennsylvania Press, 1990

More Die of Heartbreak, special issue of *Saul Bellow Journal*, 11(1), 1992

HYLAND has written an up-to-date and useful overview of the work of Saul Bellow, which can be recommended to students coming fresh to the work of the most important of American postwar novelists. Although essentially introductory, the volume has its own distinctive approach, arguing that Bellow's work is marked by an intimate awareness of the intellectual currents of the time, and a persistent engagement with the movement of contemporary history. For Hyland it is Bellow's eclecticism, the manner in which he draws on a wide range of cultural fields and traditions – not merely as an intellectual foundation for his fiction, but also as a means to examine the polyglot nature of modern American experience – that forms the basis of his popular appeal.

Something of this eclecticism is indicated in the work of three very different critics. CLAYTON takes a strongly psychoanalytic view, discovering within the works a psychic pattern based on Oedipal conflicts and the fear of deserved death. First published in 1968, with a second edition in 1979, it remains a cogent and persuasive reading, particularly in relation to *The Victim* and *Herzog*, and in its discussion of Jewish cultural traditions. My study (NEWMAN), on the other hand, reads Bellow as deeply engaged with Nietzsche's "sixth sense", the sense of history. Contesting an early critical consensus, which presented Bellow as more interested in the universal than the particular, the transcendent rather than the temporal, I argue that the engagement with history pervades the major novels, and governs the dynamics of plot, character, and theme. The study deals with the influence on Bellow of Hegel, Freud, Julia Ortega, and Nietzsche, among other thinkers about history. PIFER's essential views are: that each of Bellow's protagonists is polarized between the alternative claims of reason (in the loser's corner) and faith (emerging triumphant), that Bellow's development reflects a deepening commitment to articulating the reality of the soul, and that his opposition to the ruling orthodoxies of secularism makes him a radical writer. Squarely in the Emersonian camp, Pifer tends to underestimate the darker side of Bellow, particularly in relation to the Holocaust, a special focus for Hyland (*The Victim*) and Newman (*Mr Sammler's Planet*).

Less polemically, FUCHS provides a detailed and scholarly account of Bellow's unpublished manuscripts, from which he has sole permission to quote. (They include 6,000 pages for *Humboldt's Gift* and 20 versions of *Herzog*.) With a detailed study of the processes of revision, Fuchs offers a judicious evaluation of Bellow's relation to modernism as well as his intellectual evolution and the development of the fiction.

Three volumes concern themselves with the later work. CRONIN and GOLDMAN have collected 18 important essays from the 1980s, both general and specialised. The essays tend to be innovative in their topics, and cover subjects of central importance to Bellow's work. BACH focuses on the middle and later fiction, from *Mr Sammler's Planet* to the recent novellas, with contributions from established scholars (Malcolm Bradbury, Fuchs, Newman, Cronin) and a host of impressive younger ones. Based on a symposium in Heidelberg in 1990, the volume includes a considerable number of European critics, and deals with, among other topics, the adaptation of the novels in music and film, the Holocaust, Eastern Europe, Carl Jung, feminism, anthropology, and structuralism.

Founded in 1981, the *Saul Bellow Journal* includes essays, reviews, short notes and an annual annotated bibliography. Its special issue on *More Die of Heartbreak*, the product of a symposium in Mexico in 1991, offers the best introduction to a novel that has given readers particular difficulties. Topics discussed include the influence of Jung, Edgar Allan Poe, Alfred Hitchcock, the Addams Family, William Blake, Allan Bloom, Greco-Roman antecedents, misogyny, and the arcane. The contributors evaluate the novel against Bellow's previous achievements and offer multiple and eclectic readings. As the different contributors recognise, in a long career – from the fledgling author who received a fan letter from H.G. Wells to the Nobel Prize winner who debated the condition of American culture on television with Toni Morrison – Bellow still has the capacity to surprise and delight his readers.

JUDIE NEWMAN

Bennett, Arnold 1867–1931

English novelist, short-story writer, dramatist, and essayist

Allen, Walter, *Arnold Bennett*, London: Home & Van Thal, 1948

Darton, F.J. Harvey, *Arnold Bennett*, New York: Henry Holt & Co., 1915

Drabble, Margaret, *Arnold Bennett: A Biography*, London: Weidenfeld & Nicolson, 1974; New York: Knopf, 1974

Hepburn, James G., *The Art of Arnold Bennett*, Bloomington: Indiana University Press, 1963

Lucas, John, *Arnold Bennett: A Study of His Fiction*, London and New York: Methuen, 1974

Pound, Reginald, *Arnold Bennett: A Biography*, London: Heinemann, 1952; New York: Harcourt Brace Jovanovich, 1953

Roby, Kinley E., *A Writer at War: Arnold Bennett, 1914–1918*, Baton Rouge: Louisiana State University Press, 1972

Woolf, Virginia, "Character in Fiction", in *Criterion*, July 1924

Wright, Walter F., *Arnold Bennett: Romantic Realist*, Lincoln: University of Nebraska Press, 1971

Arnold Bennett's literary reputation has suffered a worse fate than those of most of his Edwardian colleagues; his work is largely unread by the high-brow public because Bennett has never recovered from Virginia Woolf's attack on what she saw as his out-moded style and common subject matter. The so-called "low-brow" readers avoid him because of his supposed betrayal of his class and the (unfounded) accusations that he was a materialist, encouraged by the satirical depiction of him as Mr Nixon in Ezra Pound's *Hugh Selwyn Mauberley*. But when Bennett was writing at his peak, he was able to create novels of great power and worth: *The Old Wives' Tale*, *Clayhanger*, *Riceyman Steps*, and his short story collection *The Grim Smile of the Five Towns* are all classics in the realistic mode. Unfortunately for Bennett, he was a realist in a period when change was in the air, and his work was criticised for its lack of psychological insight and laborious descriptiveness. More recent critics have praised his humour, valued his infusion of French realism into English letters, and admired the skill with which he presented the mystery of the everyday life of the common tradesman or servant.

DARTON's study of Bennett was the first of any critical importance. Darton gives an overview of Bennett's Five Towns novels, the Fantasias, the Philosophies, and the plays, along with a detailed study of the Potteries (map included). Darton claims that Bennett's greatest contribution to literature was his purely middle-class vision of life: that Bennett's novels celebrate the romance of business and realism of daily existence in the industrial wastelands of the English Midlands. Darton felt that Bennett was ushering in "a new spirit of English fiction".

WOOLF's essay, a largely revised version of an article which she had published in the "Nation and Athenaeum" (1923) on Bennett's style of characterisation, was an attack on one of the two distinct visions of the twentieth-century novel. Woolf's essay is concerned with the superiority of art, which she practiced in her novels, over the realistic depiction of ordinary life, as in Bennett's works. Woolf's argument is founded upon the contention that in 1910 or thereabouts human character changed significantly, and that consequently the contemporary novelist's task was to discover new methods of characterisation to exhibit this change. For Woolf, Bennett's externalised depiction of character somehow missed the essential element of psychological motivations, which lies within the essence of these new characters. She argues that Bennett's depiction of character is photographic and one-dimensional. The article has had considerable influence as a criticism of Bennett's realistic technique.

ALLEN's book is comprised one-third of biographical information and two-thirds of plot summary and the occasional reference to influences on Bennett, like French naturalism and Elizabeth Gaskell. Allen sees Bennett as a realist who dedicated himself to re-creating the life of the common person with scrupulous fidelity and honesty, a rather narrow view of Bennett's art which is given some credence by Allen's rather superficial rendering of the final decade of Bennett's literary life: his chapter on Bennett's final novels contains fewer than ten pages.

The first of Bennett's biographers, Reginald POUND, wrote a biography that Bennett might himself have wished to write. Pound's biography offers great observation of detail concerning the latter half of Bennett's life, but gives very little in the way of literary criticism. However, Pound's contention, that Bennett's decision to leave Burslem at 21 and purposely to sever himself from his restrictive home environment gave him the freedom to become a novelist, is a useful starting point for examining Bennett's Five Town novels. Ironically, though, Pound felt that by leaving his Midland roots, Bennett stifled his personal development.

HEPBURN introduced a new perspective on Bennett through his close scrutiny of Bennett's works. He suggests that Bennett should be taken seriously as an intentional artist and that he was far less journalistic or sociological than his reputation as a realist might suggest; consequently, he explores "the broader path that his art actually took". Hepburn demonstrates that Bennett's work lent itself quite remarkably to structural analysis, and particularly in regard to image patterns and symbolism. He carries further earlier suggestions concerning Bennett's "psychological understanding". Furthermore, Hepburn demonstrates that Bennett was more interested in beauty than in realism, more interested in character than in sociology, more interested in technique than in undifferentiated facts of life. Bennett's use of symbolism was a deliberate and elaborate technique used to disclose character and to discover beauty. Hepburn scrutinises the structure of *The Pretty Lady*, for example, and exposes the careful craftsmanship in the construction of the novel. In the detailed discussion of the cave symbolism in *The Old Wives' Tale* or in the discourse concerning the sexual imagery in the scene where Sam Povey's teeth are removed, Hepburn offers proof of Bennett's intentional artistic skill.

WRIGHT opens by considering Bennett's personal philosophy, literary criticism, and his intentions and methods as a novelist. Moreover, he examines the novels as they reflect a duality between romantic and realistic modes. Using Henry James' definition of romantic and realistic in his preface to *The American* as a starting point, Wright considers both of these impulses in Bennett's writing, and concludes that in spite of the death and decay which saturate Bennett's novels they offer "a sense of wonder – that men and women do bear up and live with decorum and personal dignity in a universe whose values they cannot comprehend". In Wright's view, this blending of the realistic with the romantic gave Bennett his peculiar literary vision.

ROBY chronicles Bennett's creative, marital, and financial problems during the period 1913–19. The mixture of rare manuscript sources with published sources presents an interesting insight into Bennett's creative struggles during World War I. Roby perceives that the unhappiness of Bennett's private life – largely as a result of his marriage to Marguerite Soulie – prompted Bennett to investigate the stresses imposed on married couples by their being forced to live together in spite of temperamental difficulties. Roby sees Bennett's inquiry into the relationship of younger women with older men in *The Lion's Share*, *Lord Raingo*, and *The Pretty Lady* as an examination of his own personal concerns.

LUCAS's study dissects each of Bennett's works chronologically, volume by volume. This method exposes what is both positive and poor in Bennett's output. The importance of Lucas's treatment is its thoroughness, for it examines the entire corpus of Bennett's work, and, as an introductory view of Bennett's work, it still stands alone. Lucas's strength is his careful attention to detail; he meticulously outlines characters and situations, occasionally alights on a seldom-discussed masterpiece such as *Whom God Hath Joined*, and offers insights into Bennett's realistic methods. Through his discussion of *Clayhanger*, which Lucas feels is a stunningly rich novel of provincial family life, he places Bennett squarely in the realist camp. The final question with which Lucas grapples is whether Bennett's competence in being able to portray real life with integrity is enough to make him a great artist. Ultimately, Lucas concludes that Bennett's art fell short of greatness.

Perhaps on account of her own experiences growing up in the Five Towns, DRABBLE is able to pinpoint with accuracy and with flair the tensions and dilemmas of Bennett's life. Drabble's skill lies in her ability to focus on those elements that formed the core of life in the Five Towns: religion, the family, and the values. Her study demonstrates how carefully Bennett drew on his precise memories and observations of his childhood and youth to bring the lives of the Baines, the Clayhangers, and Hilda Lessways alive. Drabble's study is seldom critical of Bennett the man or Bennett the writer, but it offers an up-to-date biography and utilises quotations from Bennett's journals very effectively.

PATRICK J. M. QUINN

Beowulf

Old English poem

Clark, George, *Beowulf*, Boston: Twayne, 1990

Hasenfratz, Robert J., *"Beowulf" Scholarship: An Annotated Bibliography 1970–1990*, New York: Garland, 1993 (supplement to Short, see below)

Irving, Edward B., Jr., *Rereading "Beowulf"*, Philadelphia: University of Pennsylvania Press, 1989
Niles, John D., *Beowulf: The Poem and Its Tradition*, Cambridge, Massachusetts: Harvard University Press, 1983
Ogilvy, J.D.A., and Donald C. Baker, *Reading "Beowulf": An Introduction to the Poem, Its Background, and Its Style*, Norman: University of Oklahoma Press, 1983
Shippey, T.A., *Beowulf*, London: Edward Arnold, 1978
Short, Douglas D., *"Beowulf" Scholarship: An Annotated Bibliography*, New York: Garland, 1980

Surviving in a unique early eleventh-century manuscript, and written in the West Saxon dialect of Old English, the anonymous poem *Beowulf* is set in sixth-century Sweden, Denmark, and Frisia, where small enclaves of Germanic civilization cling precariously to existence in the face of dynastic struggles, tribal warfare, and the violence of the blood-feud. In this world, dominated by the all-encompassing force of *wyrd*, the Geat warrior (and later king) Beowulf battles those men and monsters that embody the forces inimical to heroic values and to a stable society. Successful in his youth in destroying a giant troll and its mother, which were ravaging the Danish kingdom of King Hrothgar, Beowulf in later life ascends the Geatish throne. When he is advanced in age, King Beowulf destroys a fire dragon ravaging his kingdom, thereby winning the dragon's treasure hoard for his people, but he dies from poisonous wounds received in the fight. Although the final words of the poem praise Beowulf, an ominous note has already been sounded by an allusion to the age-old strife between Swedes and Geats and by the suggestion of the likelihood of Swedish domination now that Beowulf, protector of the Geats, is dead.

SHORT's bibliography is divided into two sections, the first containing annotations for 200 works of Beowulfian scholarship published between 1705 and 1949 which were still being cited by other scholars at the end of the 1970s. A second section lists in chronological order and annotates some 900 scholarly works published between 1950 and 1978. The full and correct annotations are meant to be more informative than critical, but Short identifies selected book reviews where the reader can gauge scholarly reception of a given work, and he cross-references many entries to identify specific exchanges in ensuing scholarly debates. His subject index provides a quick list of references to scholarship concerning major characters, events, and themes. Short's bibliography is continued to 1990 by HASENFRATZ, but with two additional useful indices on individual words and lines.

For readers who will limit their reading of *Beowulf* to one of many fine translations, OGILVY and BAKER offer much useful information, including chapters on the manuscript, date, analogues, versification, and formulaic style. A chapter on current interpretations and criticism is supported by an annotated bibliography. The authors include a detailed summary of the story with accompanying commentary, but too great reliance on this may persuade the reader to see *Beowulf* as realistic fiction, which it is definitely not, and to lose sight of the poem's thematic, linguistic, and structural complexities, which make of it a rich yet perplexing work of art.

SHIPPEY's main purpose is to warn against the error of reading *Beowulf* through a twentieth-century cultural filter, resulting in ethnocentric critical judgments; while some of the poet's beliefs and biases will be familiar to today's readers and others will yield to analysis, some knowledge implicit for the author and his Anglo-Saxon audience must now be made explicit. To help define more clearly the basic cultural and poetic framework within which the poem must be situated before the finer literary details are approached, Shippey divides his work into chapters on the world of the poem, on the poem's structure, and on poetry and its functions. Each chapter contains a series of crisp, illuminating notes about particular themes, structural elements, or literary devices, such as: characters and emotions; money, worth, and prestige; balance and interlace; implications of digressions; and the gnomic voice. His Afterword reminds us of the centrality of the poem's originally oral nature and points out the dangers of both an exclusive allegorical reading and of the modern critical preference for multiple meanings and non-didacticism.

Of those who have embraced the oral-formulaic approach, NILES presents the most thorough and convincing demonstration that the poem should be read as a Germanic *scop*'s (poet-singer's) oral performance for an aristocratic audience. He begins by rejecting any direct influence on the poem's form and content of Latin epics or of the writings of the Christian Fathers. He then devotes a section to a rigorous application of oral-formulaic structures to individual passages, finding that such systems underlie as many as 60% of the poem's verses; readers will need a good grounding in Old English grammar and versification to appreciate the value of this section. In a concluding interpretative section, Niles locates *Beowulf*'s controlling theme in "community: its nature, its occasional breakdown, and the qualities necessary to maintain it". He does not find in Beowulf, the epitome of these qualities, the fatal flaw many recent interpreters claim exists; although Niles does not disprove these views convincingly, he does establish in detail his own view that Beowulf dies triumphant and blameless, having won a magnificent hoard for his people and having destroyed the dragon while living up to his pledge not to flee one foot from the dragon's barrow.

Although 20 years earlier he had written one of the most cogent and thorough New-Critical analyses of *Beowulf*, IRVING, too, has felt the attraction of oral theory and is now challenging many of his own earlier views. He now holds that oral style could couch its characters only in predictable and conventional terms, any complexity of characterization in that poetic medium being "unfamiliar and oblique". He rejects New-Critical organic unity in favor of other oral methods of structural and thematic unification; in *Beowulf*, a single dominant image, the hall, serves this purpose. He also attempts to translate into oral terms such as alliteration, enjambement, juxtaposition, and contrast, the interlace patterns and carpet pages of Anglo-Saxon illuminated manuscripts. While Irving forcefully defends his theoretical model, many of his best insights derive less from the model than from his own appreciative critical meditations on the poem's wonders over the years.

More eclectic in his critical approach, CLARK looks back to J.R.R. Tolkien's work as underlying much of later criticism; but he challenges several of Tolkien's views, finding that the horrors and significance of the fight with Grendel's mother are greater than Tolkien allowed (Chapter 4) and that the dragon is not a symbol of evil but rather "a part of nature or things as they are – at once demanding and defying explication" (Chapter 5). Also, apparently rejecting more recent views on the polysemous nature of the poem, he reads the concluding description of Beowulf as positive not in any Christian sense but in "specifically secular and even heroic meanings". Although Clark's work is balanced, generally critically sound, and often fresh, his discussion of the date and place of original oral compositions underlying the poem as we have it (Chapter 2) has little scholarly support and should be treated cautiously.

RAYMOND ST-JACQUES

Berryman, John 1914–1972

American poet and literary critic

Bloom, Harold (ed.), *John Berryman*, New York: Chelsea House, 1989
Bloom, James D., *The Stock of Available Reality: R.P. Blackmur and John Berryman*, Lewisburg, Pennsylvania: Bucknell University Press, 1984; London: Associated University Presses, 1984
Haffenden, John, *John Berryman: A Critical Commentary*, London: Macmillan, 1980; New York: New York University Press, 1980
Halliday, E.M., *John Berryman and the Thirties: A Memoir*, Amherst: University of Massachusetts Press, 1987
Kelly, Richard J. (ed.), *We Dream of Honour: John Berryman's Letters to His Mother*, New York: Norton, 1988
Matterson, Stephen, *Berryman and Lowell: The Art of Losing*, London: Macmillan, 1988
Simpson, Eileen, *Poets in Their Youth: A Memoir*, New York: Random House, 1982; London: Faber & Faber, 1982
Thomas, Harry (ed.), *Berryman's Understanding: Reflections on the Poetry of John Berryman*, Boston: Northeastern University Press, 1988

An accomplished scholar and brilliant literary critic, Berryman is best known as a poet. His early poetry won immediate recognition, and his status as a major mid-twentieth century poet seemed assured with the completion of his epic sequence of 385 poems known as *The Dream Songs*, finished in 1969. He has been categorised as one of the American school of "Confessional" poets of the 1950s and 1960s, and a good deal of his work is autobiographical in kind, as in *Berryman's Sonnets* (1967), a sequence of 115 Petrarchan sonnets telling of a summer love affair, and the late religious poems of *Love and Fame* (1970) and *Delusions, Etc*. Berryman, though, hated the "Confessional" label and refused to discuss its relevance to his work. His reputation has waned somewhat in recent years, and there has been no major study of his work over the past several years. Much of the best critical writing on him is reissued in the two anthologies of essays reviewed below (Harold Bloom and Thomas).

Simpson's, Kelly's, and Halliday's books provide useful biographical and contextual material. SIMPSON was Berryman's first wife, and this memoir of the poet and his intellectual milieu is required reading for those interested in the poet's life. This is an absorbing chronicle of a whole generation of American writers and of Berryman's relations with them, especially in his important friendship with the influential critic R.P. Blackmur, and his fellow poets and writers Robert Lowell, Randall Jarrell, Delmore Schwartz, and Jean Stafford.

KELLY's edition of the correspondence between Berryman and his mother is another indispensable contribution to our knowledge of the poet. His relations with his formidable mother were complex and frequently combative in tone. His letters to her from Cambridge, England (in the late 1930s), where he studied for two years, chart his intellectual awakening to the traditions of British poetry and express his earliest endeavours to discover his own poetic voice. The later letters provide an intimate account of the difficulties of this relationship, bounded as it was by his love for her and his need for her approval, set against her possessiveness, which was as much intellectual as physical. Kelly's linking commentary on the letters is very helpful in completing this picture of the relationship between an equally difficult and ambitious mother and son.

HALLIDAY tells the story of his friendship with Berryman, whom he met in 1933, and of their relationship through their university years until the early 1940s when they went their separate ways. Though this memoir is largely concerned with the social intimacies of their friendship, it prints extensive passages from Berryman's letters to Halliday written over that decade in which his poetic and scholarly ambitions took shape through the expansion of his physical and intellectual horizons. The picture Halliday gives of Berryman in that period is of a fun-loving and genial companion, though it ends with an account of the severance of their friendship brought about by a shared sense of betrayal.

HAFFENDEN's critical commentary on the poems is a source of both deep pleasure and irritation to the reader of Berryman. Haffenden has had unrivalled access to the poet's papers and manuscripts, and his commentary is indispensable for the information it gives about many of the puzzling references and allusions we encounter in reading Berryman. He makes an important point about how *The Dream Songs* work through the immediacy and complexity of Berryman's response to experience, rather than through some preconceived plan, which the poem is then made to fit, so that its compositional imperative is processive rather than architectural. But there is a sense in which this study promises more than it delivers, for the annotations to the poems, especially to *The Dream Songs*, are frequently incomplete or non-existent, particularly where one feels the reader needs most help. Despite this, Haffenden's study remains essential reading for the serious student. Haffenden has also written the definitive biography of Berryman (*The Life of John Berryman*, 1982), which is highly recommended.

Harold BLOOM's gathering prints three pieces which also appear in Thomas (see below) – those by William Wasserstrom, Denis Donoghue, and John Bayley – but they bear repeated printing since they represent some of the best commentary on this poet. Wasserstrom's essay dates from 1968, before the completed publication of *The Dream Songs*, and makes serious claims for the high quality and durability of the sequence. He writes of Berryman as a contemporary "medicine man", a "shaman" or prophetic speaker who uses the conventions of black minstrelsy to utter his revelatory vision of contemporary America: he argues that the comedic voices of the tradition of minstrelsy fuse with an ironic perspective on experience to overcome the difficulties of speaking for a nation whose values Berryman can barely tolerate. Wasserstrom accords *The Dream Songs* a kind of mythic authority through Berryman's use of a vernacular or common idiom of speech, used to reflect the dubious politics and complex social psychology of mid-twentieth-century American society, a feat that Wasserstrom believes elevates Berryman above all his contemporaries. This remains a seminal essay on the poem. Donoghue, one of the best non-American critics of American poetry, finds a Wordsworthian strain in the completed version of *The Dream Songs*, with Berryman ultimately celebrating his own sensibility, a formal egotism redeemed by the accomplished fusion of passion and perception in the very last poems of the sequence. Bayley writes on the heroic enterprise of Berryman, and others, in the struggle to become a great poet in a culture increasingly alien to poetry and the poet, even though the struggle is "ruinously hard". Elizabeth Kaspar Aldrich's essay on *Homage to Mistress Bradstreet* should be read in conjunction with that of Stanley Kunitz in Thomas, for like Kunitz she sees this poem as the "break-through" in Berryman's search for his own poetic voice, but sees it as a poem that "celebrates impossibilities", the impossibility of creating such work "in the faithless void of the present time".

James D. BLOOM writes on the poetic and critical relationship between R.P. Blackmur and Berryman, which centres, for him, on their attitude towards the American past and to the problematics of creative influence where Harold Bloom's theories of the "anxiety of influence" prevail. The focus of this book is on these writers' relationship to the orthodoxies of New Criticism, featured in their attention to Milton, John Keats, W.B. Yeats, T.S. Eliot, and Wallace Stevens, and in their strivings for a contemporary expression of the "American Sublime", which led them to reject Eliot's modernist theory of creative impersonality and to relocate the poet in a belated post-Romantic context.

MATTERSON argues that if the early poetry of Berryman and Lowell was what he calls a "poetics of recovery and restitution" learned from the examples of Yeats, Allen Tate, and John Crowe Ransom, then both poets turned from this mode to a "poetics of loss", in which the ornate complexity of their first styles was displaced by what Lowell called a "rhetoric of destitution". In the case of Berryman, the point of this argument is to show how he developed his own voice in his struggle to overcome the influence of Yeats, and how the development of this creative identity is evident in those idioms of language that come to characterize his major work, and through his innovatory form in *The Dream Songs*. Matterson is unconvinced by the spiritual ambition of the late books *Love & Fame*, and *Delusions Etc.*, and finds their dominant mood one of hysteria and despair, rather than one of consoling expressions of a late recovery of faith.

THOMAS has collected a variety of tributes and critical assessments that have appeared over the last 30-odd years, offering what he calls a "choral homage" to the poet. The most recent essay is Michael Heffernan's 1984 piece on "The Poetics of Martyrdom", which provides a counter-view to Matterson's reading of *Love & Fame* and *Delusions Etc.*, in which he argues that even in the extremes of personal despair, towards the end of his life, Berryman found poetry a source of survival and a means of belief in the "ongoing life for the soul" despite the body's decrepitude. Stanley Kunitz's reading of *Homage to Mistress Bradstreet* is one of the better discussions of the poem: Kunitz compares it to Hart Crane's *The Bridge*, and sees it as Berryman's sustained attempt to relate himself to the American past "through the discovery of a viable myth" and a means of creating a vehicle for his "grand and exalted language, a language of transfiguration". Most of the critical essays herein were first published in the 1960s and 1970s (including the important essays by William Wasserstrom, John Bayley, and Denis Donoghue, also given in Harold Bloom's volume). This valuable collection includes the *Paris Review* interview with Berryman of 1971, the *Harvard Advocate* interview of 1969, and memoirs by Eileen Simpson, Robert Lowell, Saul Bellow, and William Meredith.

LIONEL KELLY

Bestsellers *see* Popular Fiction

The Bible and Literature

Alter, Robert, *The Art of Biblical Narrative*, New York: Basic Books, 1981; London: Allen & Unwin, 1981

Alter, Robert, *The Art of Biblical Poetry*, New York: Basic Books, 1985; Edinburgh: T. & T. Clark, 1990

Alter, Robert, and Frank Kermode (eds.), *The Literary Guide to the Bible*, Cambridge, Massachusetts: Belknap Press of Harvard University Press, 1987; London: Collins, 1987

Frye, Northrop, *The Great Code: The Bible and Literature*,Toronto: Academic Press Canada, 1982; New York: Harcourt Brace Jovanovich, 1982; London: Routledge & Kegan Paul, 1982

Hammond, Gerald, *The Making of the English Bible*, Manchester: Carcanet, 1982; New York: Philosophical Library, 1983

Jeffrey, David Lyle (ed.), *A Dictionary of Biblical Tradition in English Literature*, Grand Rapids, Michigan: W.B. Eerdmans, 1992

Norton, David, *A History of the Bible as Literature*, 2 vols., Cambridge and New York: Cambridge University Press, 1993

In an essay on the literary impact of the Authorised Version of the Bible, C.S. Lewis argued that reading the Bible as literature meant reading it against the grain, against its principal purpose as a sacred text. There is less worry about this apparent tension now. In recent years there has been a revival of interest, as much among theologians as literary scholars, in applying modern habits of reading to the Bible. This has been more marked in the USA, which has a higher proportion of churchgoers than the UK; so reading the Bible "as literature" is not in any simple way a replacement for reading it "as the Word of God".

ALTER's twin studies (1981 and 1990) are the work of a distinguished critic of fiction who is also a Jew; for him the Bible is the Hebrew Old Testament. A major strength of his work is the combination of alertness to the language of biblical Hebrew with a sense of the usefulness and limitations of literary categories and procedures. For example, in a chapter on "Sacred History and the Beginnings of Prose Fiction" he is able to identify a "theologically intent" shaping of narrative, which nonetheless exhibits an element of imaginative play. He identifies the complexities of a narrative technique that is more obviously "an art of reticence" in terms of characterisation and realistic detail. The excitement of the first book comes from a sense of discovery, of new insights and new methods. *The Art of Biblical Poetry* is a more focused formal study, starting from a reworking of parallelism as a prosodic feature, and moving outwards towards ever more complex "structures of intensification" in the Psalms, Job, and the Song of Songs.

ALTER and KERMODE's *Guide* is a substantial reference text which has much of the readability of a collection of essays. There is a chapter on most of the major books or groupings in the Bible. By and large, the Old Testament section is the more successful. The New Testament essays seem more tentative. There are also a number of general essays on the contexts of the Bible, the canon, translation, poetry, and Midrash. Many of these chapters give the reader the opportunity to sample ideas developed at book length elsewhere – Alter himself on Hebrew poetry, for example, or Francis Landy on the Song of Songs. The collection also provides a repertoire of literary approaches to the Bible because of the sheer variety of contributors.

HAMMOND contributes an essay on translation to Alter and Kermode. His own book concentrates on the English tradition from William Tyndale to the Authorized Version, with a few unflattering comparisons with modern translations such as the New English Bible. It is a sustained defence of the method as well as the results of the early modern English translators, who, by being faithful to the form of biblical expression, remained faithful to its imaginative and spiritual dimensions, too. It is full of illuminating examples, drawing on the Greek and Hebrew originals as well as a variety of translations.

FRYE's book was originally designed as part of a pair, the second of which did not appear. The title derives from William Blake, who wrote that the Old and New Testaments were "the great code of art". In a series of paired chapters on language, myth, and typology, Frye attempts to lay out that code. The book moves easily and confidently among biblical, Greek, and European material, though the focus is on the Bible and its method – what happens when its distinctive literary qualities (conceived as a progression rather than a unity) are interpreted, for example, into a theological concept of "creative time". Typology is perhaps the key term in his argument; though the traditional idea of analogous characters is extended into repeating patterns, such as Exodus followed by law-giving. Frye is admirably suggestive in tackling big questions.

NORTON's two-volume work is vast in its scope – covering antiquity to the present day, and focusing on what we would now call the literary qualities of the Bible and (more briefly) its literary impact in English. Not the least of its virtues is that it becomes an alternative history of "the literary". While the two volumes overlap with many of the studies listed here, as well as with numerous critics on individual authors, they can always be relied on for judicious formulation and scholarly accuracy. Because Norton began with a different set of questions, including how the Authorized Version came to be regarded as a great work of literature, he has a fresh angle on familiar material, and links it with the less familiar. The books function both as a study that can be read through, or as a reference resource for, for example, the Romantics and the Bible, or the discovery of parallelism.

On a scale of usefulness, JEFFREY's *Dictionary* must rate very highly. The bulk of the book (it runs to 960 double-column pages) is a series of articles on words, phrases, and names from the Bible, plus a few Christian ideas that link biblical themes. In each entry there first comes an explanation of its use in the Bible, then (usually) its principal Christian formulators, and finally, and selectively, its appearance in English and American literature. For example, the section on "madness" draws on St John Chrysostom and Kierkegaard as interpreters of the concept, before heading on to *King Lear*. Each article has a bibliography; and there are substantial general and author bibliographies at the end, and plenty of cross-referencing (but no index). This is not a book that engages with theoretical issues, but it will become increasingly useful as biblical references once taken for granted by authors become obscure and forgotten.

ROGER POOLEY

Bierce, Ambrose 1842–1914

American short-story writer and essayist

Berkove, Lawrence I. (ed.), *Skepticism and Dissent: Selected Journalism, 1898–1901* by Bierce, Ann Arbor, Michigan: Delmas, 1980; revised edition, Ann Arbor, Michigan: UMI Research Press, 1986
Davidson, Cathy N. (ed.), *Critical Essays on Ambrose Bierce*, Boston: G.K. Hall, 1982
Davidson, Cathy N., *The Experimental Fictions of Ambrose Bierce: Structuring the Ineffable*, Lincoln: University of Nebraska Press, 1984
Fatout, Paul, *Ambrose Bierce and the Black Hills*, Norman: University of Oklahoma Press, 1956
Grenander, M.E., *Ambrose Bierce*, New York: Twayne, 1971
McWilliams, Carey, *Ambrose Bierce: A Biography*, New York: A & C Boni, 1929; reprinted, with new Introduction, Hamden, Connecticut: Archon Books, 1967
O'Connor, Richard, *Ambrose Bierce: A Biography*, Boston: Little Brown, 1967; London: Victor Gollancz, 1968

Ambrose Bierce has been particularly ill-served by criticism. Literary histories have done a notoriously poor job by pigeonholing him, and far too many have "discovered" him and dealt glibly and superficially with his fiction (usually his most famous story, "An Occurrence at Owl Creek Bridge"), his *Devil's Dictionary*, or some aspect of his life. There are some notable exceptions, but most literary scholarship has followed one of two unsatisfactory approaches: inquiry into why Bierce was so "bitter", cynical, misanthropic, pessimistic, etc.; or "discovery" of how Bierce anticipated some later literary or cultural development, e.g., black humor, Freudianism, postmodernism, etc. The first approach gives excessive emphasis to the man over the author, and then treats the man reductively. The second is ahistorical in not dealing with Bierce in terms of his own time and place, and in warping some facet of Bierce's style to suit a subsequent fad.

McWILLIAMS's biography is one of the earliest and is still the best. In preparing it, McWilliams thoroughly immersed himself in his subject: he read all of Bierce's books and most of his uncollected journalism; he interviewed members of his family as well as people who knew Bierce personally; and he read and assimilated a great deal of background material. No other biography has, or will have, such authority, based as it is on access to information that has been subsequently lost. The result is a painstakingly researched and intelligently balanced book. Its main shortcoming, acknowledged by McWilliams in his valuable Introduction to the 1967 reprint, is its underestimation of Bierce's literary skill.

FATOUT focuses on a four-month episode in the life of Bierce – his superintendency of a gold-mining operation in the Black Hills of South Dakota in 1880. The book is based on a collection of Bierce's letters and records that relate to this employment, and is soundly supplemented by extensive background research. It brings to light important facets of Bierce's character and abilities that would otherwise be insufficiently known – his integrity, resolve, managerial ability, and resourcefulness.

O'CONNOR has written a popular biography, readable but not searching and not up to the standard of the McWilliams work. To O'Connor, Bierce is primarily of interest as a sardonic personality and as a precursor of black humour. The book uses familiar biographical information, but it is seriously lacking in literary judgement. It underestimates Bierce's literary importance and downplays his fiction, mentioning it only in passing.

GRENANDER's book is the best full-length study of Bierce after McWilliams. Following the format of the Twayne "United States Authors" series, it is divided between biography and literary criticism. At the time of its publication, it did an excellent job of summarizing what was known about Bierce, and its interpretations of Bierce's literary output were, and remain, considerable. The book also contains a still-useful critical bibliography.

DAVIDSON (1982) has gathered a fine selection of essays, which reflect insightful, as well as typical, Bierce criticism from its beginnings to 1980. Many of the essays in the book are difficult to obtain in all but the best of American libraries, so it is doubly worthy, both in its range and in its making accessible works that would otherwise be overlooked. DAVIDSON's 1984 study of Bierce's fiction is a disappointing sequel. It sets out to prove that Bierce is "the pre-modern precursor of post-modern fiction", and that his fiction represents the radical uncertainty of life, by arguing that Bierce was influenced in the development of his method of perceiving reality by his philosophical contemporary C.S. Peirce. The book begins by "eschewing biographical as well as historical criticism", and then cannot provide evidence that Bierce ever even mentioned Peirce. Although the book is radically flawed by this lack of evidence, and by biographical inaccuracies, it does offer some interesting close readings of Bierce stories, the best of which is its persuasive argument that the problematic story "The Death of Halpin Frayser" is a hoax.

My (BERKOVE's) edition of Bierce's previously uncollected journalism from the vintage years 1898–1901 includes material revealing valuable – and surprising – insights into the author, such as his informed and qualified criticisms of the Spanish-American War, the Philippine Insurrection, US confrontation with Britain and Germany over Samoa, and the Boxer Rebellion, and his attitudes to the Boer War and war in general. The Introduction provides a historical and literary context for the selections.

LAWRENCE I. BERKOVE

Biography: General

Aaron, Daniel (ed.), *Studies in Biography*, Cambridge, Massachusetts: Harvard University Press, 1978

Epstein, William H. (ed.), *Contesting the Subject: Essays in the Postmodern Theory and Practice of Biography and Biographical Criticism*, West Lafayette, Indiana: Purdue University Press, 1991

Farran, Denise, Sue Scott, and Liz Stanley (ed.), *Writing Feminist Biography*, Manchester: Manchester University Press, 1986

McCann, Graham, "Biographical Boundaries: Sociology and Marilyn Monroe", in *The Body: Social Process and Cultural Theory*, edited by Mike Featherstone, Mike Hepworth, and Bryan S. Turner, London: Sage Publications, 1991

Ramelb, Carol (ed.), *Biography East and West: Selected Conference Papers*, Honolulu: University of Hawaii Press, 1989

Shelston, Alan, *Biography*, London and New York: Methuen, 1977

Biography remains a marginal form, despite its popularity among writers and readers. Critical attention has tended to focus on literary biography, and much might be better termed "biographical criticism" rather than criticism of biography as a genre. The increasing psychologization of biography, both in its writing and in criticism, has done little to correct this emphasis on the famous individual. Some work, however, has recognized the significance of individual lives for the analysis of cultures and societies, perhaps belatedly influenced by Ralph Waldo Emerson's proposition that "there is properly no history, only biography".

SHELSTON, in a slim volume which surveys attitudes towards biography from Sir Thomas North's translations of Plutarch via Bloomsbury to the work of Leon Edel and James Clifford, suggests that "objectivity is not the only standard by which the success of a biographer may be measured". Considering the "truth of fact" and the "truth of fiction", Shelston provides a brief but informative introduction to some of the central issues in relation to biography, although the title of his opening chapter, "Some Problems of the Form", strikes a defensive note which the book never quite loses. Biography is considered as moral exemplum, as personal testimony to another's life, as an index of Victorian discretion, and as a twentieth-century art form in its own right. Shelston's chronological survey contains many valuable references, but its limits are its focus on literary biography, and that the bulk of its quotation comes from the last two centuries.

AARON's collection includes discussions of critical issues pertinent to biography, and opens with an essay by Kaplan, which discusses the manipulation of the biographical archive (including the destruction of documents) by the subject, taking as examples Mark Twain and Walt Whitman. Mendelson explores the ethical consequences of the post-Romantic psychologization of biography, beginning with his own decision *not* to write an authorized life of W.H. Auden, and Clive laments the failure of "cliographers" to capture the essence of the historical imagination in the lives of great historians. In the most theoretically interesting essay in the volume, James Clifford argues for an "ethnobiography", informed by structuralism and psychoanalysis, able to account for the conjunction of individual identity and culture. There are also essays on Samuel Johnson, James Boswell, Emerson, Thomas Carlyle, and others, and the book is dominated by America and the nineteenth century. Due to the age of the collection, many of the critical positions espoused have dated rather badly.

The series of papers gathered by FARRAN *et al.* are unusual in that they challenge the notion of biography as necessarily concerned with the illustrious (and usually male) individual. Arguing that such a concentration is at odds with much feminist thought, which is often interested in the individual as representative of wider social movements, Hannan discusses the exclusion of women from labour history. Stanley resists the urge to reduce the complexity of the biographical subject in the name of the construction of a portrait of a "real" life, recognizing objectivity as an ideological construct, and showing how it is possible to learn (not least about feminism and power) from the diaries of "ordinary" women through reading the "intellectual autobiography" in which the writer reveals how she understands her world. Mulford explores her own subjectivity and use of fictive elements in her work as a biographer, emphasizing the frustrations and revelations of her own experience of the process of research, and Farran opposes the common representation of non-feminist women as powerless and passive. Wise encounters the traumas of being a feminist and an Elvis fan, questioning the relationship of the biographer to her subject, while Cline explores discretion and disclosure in writing, and Wayte looks at the use of biography in the socialization of Fine Art students. Most papers are followed by transcriptions of discussions which further explore the issues raised.

The 25 contributions which make up RAMELB's work are divided thematically and geographically, and cover work on neuroscience, visual perception, intuition, and psychoanalysis, as well as the more expected issues of representation and translation. The papers are summarized at the beginning of the book, but these abstracts are occasionally misleading, as in the disguise of Halperin's viciously ignorant attack upon poststructuralist theorists through the most dubious form of biographical criticism as a reasonable piece. Caramagno's response is judicious. Papers on China, India, and Japan, supplemented by others on European experiences of the East, usefully address cultural and historical difference in the writing of biography, and allow the discussion of figures such as Mahatma Gandhi, Bertolt Brecht, André Malraux, and Emperor Hirohito.

McCANN's article is at once a meditation on theories of biography, and on the significance of those theories for McCann's discipline, sociology. Taking account of recent critical theory, McCann argues that "no biographer merely records a life; every biographer, no matter how objective she declares herself, interprets a life. How the biographer expresses the life becomes, to some extent, the real subject of the biography". McCann's important question, "why should we need more than one life of an individual?", prompts a recognition that the inescapable subjectivity of the biographer leads to the framing of the subject's life within an aesthetic construct that will in part be determined by the cultural and historical situation of the biographer. McCann's subtle and persuasive essay attempts to demythologize biography, while accepting that an uncritical approach will simply remythologize the genre in a different form.

EPSTEIN's collection opens with a bravura defence by the editor of the study of the biographical from a postmodern perspective:

> . . . the narratives of biography and biographical criticism are "life-texts", powerful and influential discourses precisely and strategically situated at the intersections of objectivity and subjectivity, body and mind, self and other, the natural and the cultural, fact and fiction, as well as many other conceptual dyads with which Western civilization has traditionally theorized both the practices and the representations of everyday life.

Such diversity within the field of biographical study, and the consequent cultural investment, is reflected in the essays that follow. Articles by Stanley Fish, Cheryl Walker, and Epstein himself are particularly recommended, as the "subject" of biography – in all its connotations – is contested. Alive to the consequences for biography and biographical criticism of poststructuralisms, psychoanalysis, Marxism, feminisms, and institutional pressures, this is a stimulating and provocative collection, which reveals the poverty of so much of the thinking concerned with the biographical.

MARK ROBSON

Biography: Renaissance

Anderson, Judith H., *Biographical Truth: The Representation of Historical Persons in Tudor-Stuart Writing*, New Haven, Connecticut: Yale University Press, 1984

Clifford, James L. (ed.), *Biography as an Art: Selected Criticism 1560–1960*, London and New York: Oxford University Press, 1962

Crewe, Jonathan V., *Trials of Authorship: Anterior Forms and Poetic Reconstruction from Wyatt to Shakespeare*, Berkeley: University of California Press, 1990

Lewis, C.S., *Oxford History of English Literature: English Literature in the Sixteenth Century, Excluding Drama*, Oxford: Clarendon Press, 1954
Stauffer, Donald A., *English Biography Before 1700*, Cambridge, Massachusetts: Harvard University Press, 1930
White, Helen C., *Tudor Books of Saints and Martyrs*, Madison: University of Wisconsin Press, 1963

Biography in the early modern period should perhaps be more accurately described as life-writing. The term "biography" did not enter the English language until around 1660, reflecting the generic instability of the form. Occupying an uneasy position between the "fact" of history and the "fiction" of poetry, "lives" developed from a chronicle of the deeds of the famous into the more rounded psychological portraits with which we are familiar. As such, the writing of lives may be seen to respond to changing conceptions of truth and ethics, and to an increasing concentration upon the individual. The exemplary status of much (if not all) life-writing reveals cultural sensitivities to particular kinds of individuals who are used as positive or negative role-models. Despite this, Renaissance biography has been neglected as a form.

For STAUFFER, "the highest aim of biography" is "the reconstruction of a personality in thought and actions". Using this definition in charting the movement from the "life and times" model of medieval biography to something more easily reconciled with modern conceptions of the form, Stauffer identifies Sir Thomas More's *Richard III* (1513) as the text that marks this transition. Stauffer's text covers the medieval period (700–1500) through to the seventeenth-century works of those such as Izaak Walton. Stauffer's work contains many interesting and useful observations on the changing role of the biographer, relating biography to historiography and other genres, but also possesses some idiosyncrasies, for example his claim that controversial lives are unimportant in the history of biography because of their obvious bias. Most useful, perhaps, is the extensive bibliography of early lives, and Stauffer's text remains a significant one in any study of biography.

LEWIS's survey is divided into three sections, the last two of which – "Drab" and "Golden" – concern us here. Of the two, it is the Drab part which contains the most relevant material, featuring comments on works by William Roper, Nicholas Harpsfield, George Cavendish, John Foxe, John Lyly, and Sir Thomas North, as well as a mention of a *Life of Fisher* (which in the Early English Text Society edition is attributed to Richard Hall). Lewis's judgmental prose is exemplified in the following, typically value-laden, statement: "most authors in this period can be classified either as 'plain' or as 'literary', and there is something to dislike in each class; Harpsfield unhappily shares the faults of both". In the Golden period – the last quarter of the sixteenth century – Lewis asserts there was a marked improvement in the quality of prose. Unfortunately for us, and perhaps not coincidentally, he makes no mention of life-writing, unless we are to count *A Mirror for Magistrates*. Lewis's own prose quickly becomes tiresome, saturated as it is with opinion in place of the analysis that would have been more enlightening.

CLIFFORD's work begins with an interesting Introduction, in which the editor traces the changing extent of biographers' self-consciousness about, and theorization of, their own practice, from the early hagiographers to the present. Although most of the contents of the book fall outside the early-modern period, there are useful excerpts from Thomas Wilson and Francis Bacon. Wilson gives a guide to the praising of a noble personage through a prose portrait, delineating precisely the elements that should be included in such praise, whereas Bacon laments the lack of written testaments to the excellent men of the age. Clifford's excerpts are brief and frequently edited, but provide a useful resource for tracing changing attitudes to life-writing.

Chapters in WHITE on the literary type of the saints' legend and its subsequent transformations through the *Golden Legend*, representations of the lives of Catholics martyred under Henry VIII, works by Protestants such as Foxe, and by the Jesuits and recusants of the late sixteenth century, show the preoccupations of the author. Despite an apparent Catholic bias in the book – perhaps reflecting the material available – White gives reasonable space to Protestant martyrdoms, and her conclusion gives voice to what would seem to be her real concern:

> With all that we know today of the often shabby maneuverings of greed and ambition behind so many of the religious controversies and struggles of the period, it is well to be reminded that there were also men on both sides for whom the religious issue was the only one that mattered.

Covering numerous lives of More, as well as saints John Fisher, Robert Southwell, Edmund Campion, and others, and stressing issues such as witnessing and the conflict between the demands of history and the desires of the creators of legends, White reveals the roots of biography in the saint's life.

ANDERSON maps the relationship of factual truth to fictional truth in the writing of biography, drama, and history in the early-modern period. Chapters on Bede, Cavendish's *Wolsey*, Roper's *More*, Walton, More's *Richard III*, Shakespeare's *Richard III* and *Henry VIII*, and Bacon's *Henry VII* examine the self-reflexive fashioning of identities. Anderson offers a number of useful insights, emphasizing the processes of selection, editing, and structuring that were involved in the creation of meaning in these works. Concepts such as "retrospective shading", in which details introduced early in a text attain significance as subsequent events unfold, and her recognition of the importance of meta-language and of the juxtaposition of events demonstrate Anderson's careful readings of the works discussed. However, much remains questionable in Anderson's theoretical framework, and the interpretations clearly have a religious dimension, which may trouble some readers.

Certainly CREWE feels some discomfort at what he perceives to be Anderson's Catholic bias, and his readings are avowedly "parallel" but oppositional. In his chapters on Roper's *More* and Cavendish's *Wolsey*, Crewe suggests formal alternatives to uncomplicatedly hagiographical interpretations. Making a link to Erasmus and to More's *Utopia*, Roper's text is read as an example of an *encomium moriae*, and Cavendish is shown to be establishing a paradigm of life-writing which recognizes the theatrical nature of Renaissance culture. In both chapters, Crewe stresses the roles of the authors as witnesses within the biographies, asking whose "lives" the texts represent: More and Wolsey, or Roper and Cavendish? Influenced by New Historicism and psychoanalysis, Crewe produces readings that are deliberately unsettling, and this book offers many insights into the current state of Renaissance studies.

MARK ROBSON

Biography and Autobiography: Victorian

Aaron, Daniel (ed.), *Studies in Biography*, Cambridge, Massachusetts: Harvard University Press, 1978

Cockshut, A.O.J., *Truth to Life: The Art of Biography in the Nineteenth Century*, London: Collins, 1974; New York: Harcourt Brace, 1974

Cockshut, A.O.J., *The Art of Autobiography in 19th and 20th Century England*, New Haven, Connecticut, and London: Yale University Press, 1984

Edel, Leon, *Literary Biography*, London: Rupert Hart-Davis, 1957; Bloomington: Indiana University Press, 1973

Johnson, E., *One Mighty Torrent: The Drama of Biography*, New York: Stackpole Sons, 1937; 2nd edition, New York: Macmillan, 1955

Meyers, Jeffrey (ed.), *The Biographer's Art: New Essays*, London: Macmillan, 1989

Olney, James, *Metaphors of Self: The Meaning of Autobiography*, Princeton, New Jersey: Princeton University Press, 1972

Pascal, Roy, *Design and Truth in Autobiography*, London: Routledge & Kegan Paul, 1960; Cambridge, Massachusetts: Harvard University Press, 1960

Peterson, Linda H., *Victorian Autobiography*, New Haven, Connecticut, and London: Yale University Press, 1986

JOHNSON's work, published originally in 1937, was a pioneering effort, since biographies had generally been read much more for the interest in the subject than for the art of the writer. Thomas Macaulay's dictum that if James Boswell had not been such a great fool he could not have been such a great writer contained the assumption that the biographer was a simple recorder of facts, and that his success depended on the inherent interest of these facts. Boswell's art was hidden even from those who most enjoyed his book. Similarly, another great biography, J.A. Froude's *Carlyle*, was criticized for irreverence, but hardly assessed for literary art until the twentieth century was well advanced. Johnson's book is a full survey, which includes sixteenth- and seventeenth-century work. This attempt to be so inclusive led to hasty judgements. When he imagines that he detects panegyric in Thomas Carlyle's *Sterling*, it becomes obvious that he had not read it attentively; and he is often content with summaries, which evade critical questions. It evidently did not strike him that Lytton Strachey and Stalin were liars, and he shows uncritical admiration of both.

EDEL's book is interesting for containing the reflections of a distinguished biographer on the problems of his art. Confronted with the immense volume of surviving documents relating to Henry James, he describes the modern biographer as an "unwilling glutton", who longs for a leaner diet. His stance as biographer, rather than critic of biography, is noticed again when he says that in Arthur Symons's *Quest for Corvo* the account of the enquiry is more interesting than its subject. Though it does not go deep, it will remain a useful starting-point for those embarking on biographical labours.

In my (COCKSHUT's) 1974 work I tried to rehabilitate those long Victorian biographies, crammed with facts and letters, and reticent about some aspects of life, which many people seemed to have condemned unread. The case of Cromwell was used to show how the same facts could be used for bewilderingly different conclusions; in a study of Samuel Smiles as biographer I aimed at showing how unconscious assumptions would affect interpretation. The most detailed study is reserved for Froude's *Carlyle*.

Daniel AARON's introduction to a wide-ranging collection claims that "biography fulfils the need once supplied by fiction, poetry, criticism and history", because "it is less in danger than these genres . . . of becoming dehumanized by a surfeit of theory". The aim is to find new insights by a fresh look at familiar examples, such as Samuel Johnson's *Savage*, Boswell's *Johnson*, and biographies of Carlyle and Ralph Waldo Emerson. John Clive, the biographer of Macaulay, has a valuable piece on historians as biographical subjects.

PASCAL was a pioneer in the study of autobiography, as Johnson had been in biography; But he is more thoughtful, more selective, and more satisfying than Johnson. His fruitful distinction between autobiography and memoir, with his insistence that only those who meditate on the pattern of their life and the formation of their characters are truly autobiographers, limits the discussion to books that can usefully be judged by aesthetic standards. He sees autobiography as an "interplay, a collusion between past and present". His ranging over many languages and cultures does not make the book indigestible, because he is always aiming to extract a general critical truth from his examples.

James OLNEY's study asks "'How Shall I Live?' If autobiography can advance an understanding of that question, and I think it can, then it is a very valuable literature indeed". Accordingly, he is always searching in the particular for guides to general wisdom. This leads him to range more widely than the strict boundaries of autobiography. Montaigne's *Essais* and T.S. Eliot's *Four Quartets* are pressed into service. But abstraction does not lead him to neglect the specific, and in dealing with John Henry Newman, J.S. Mill, and Charles Darwin he shows awareness of their differing aims and contrasting milieux. His likening of the link between Newman's Anglican quotations and his Catholic conclusion to that between seeds and ripened fruit illustrates his awareness of each book and personality as forming a coherent whole; and we realize that it is the absence of this awareness in many inferior discussions of autobiography that makes them trivial. This is a distinguished work.

In my second study (COCKSHUT, 1984), I attempted to group autobiographies, without reference to chronology, into categories of people defined by the world, those making a secular quest, and religious converts. The stress was thus more on similarities of character-type than on social influences and changing fashions. A large part of the book was devoted to the re-creation of childhood. Each section is introduced by a series of quotations from autobiographies or students of autobiography.

PETERSON relates spiritual autobiography to biblical hermeneutics, and places John Bunyan's *Grace Abounding* as a marker against which Victorian successors may be measured. Her examples are Carlyle (in *Sartor Resartus*, not a genuine autobiography), Newman, John Ruskin, Harriet Martineau, and Edmund Gosse. She sees all her authors as self-conscious literary artists, aware of tradition and shaping it creatively for their own ends.

Jeffrey MEYERS' collection is a wide-ranging set of specialist studies, mostly by American authors, which begins with Johnson's *Savage*, and ends with Leon Edel's *Henry James*. The book is a sequel to the same editor's *The Craft of Literary Biography* (1985). In his Introduction, Meyers comments wittily on the repeated frustration of the desire of eminent authors for posthumous privacy. These recent works, together with many others not noticed here, testify to the rapid development in the last 25 years in biography and autobiography as literary forms.

A.O.J. COCKSHUT

Bishop, Elizabeth 1911–1979

American poet

Bloom, Harold (ed.), *Elizabeth Bishop*, New York: Chelsea House, 1985

Costello, Bonnie, *Elizabeth Bishop: Questions of Mastery*, Cambridge, Massachusetts: Harvard University Press, 1991

Goldensohn, Lorrie, *Elizabeth Bishop: The Biography of a Poetry*, New York: Columbia University Press, 1992

Harrison, Victoria, *Elizabeth Bishop's Poetics of Intimacy*, Cambridge and New York: Cambridge University Press, 1993

Kalstone, David, *Becoming a Poet: Elizabeth Bishop with Marianne Moore and Robert Lowell*, New York: Farrar, Straus, Giroux, 1989; London: Hogarth Press, 1989

McCabe, Susan, *Elizabeth Bishop: Her Poetics of Loss*, University Park: Pennsylvania State University Press, 1994

Millier, Brett C., *Elizabeth Bishop: Life and the Memory of It*, Berkeley: University of California Press, 1993

Parker, Robert Dale, *The Unbeliever: The Poetry of Elizabeth Bishop*, Urbana: University of Illinois Press, 1988

Schwartz, Lloyd, and Sybil P. Estess (eds.), *Elizabeth Bishop and Her Art*, Ann Arbor: University of Michigan Press, 1983

Travisano, Thomas J., *Elizabeth Bishop: Her Artistic Development*, Charlottesville: University Press of Virginia, 1988

Even before the publication of her first volume, *North and South*, in 1946, Bishop had an exclusive group of admirers in her poetic peers, including Marianne Moore and Robert Lowell. Contemporary reviews were respectful of her reticences and admiring of her ability to combine cool artistry with truth of perception: "all her poems have written underneath, *I have seen it*" (Randall Jarrell, *Partisan Review*, 13[4], 1946). Critical appreciation has grown steadily since her death, in a flow of high quality monographs drawing on archival material. Criticism of the early 1980s emphasized Bishop's modernist origins; in the 1990s her poetry has more often been interpreted as postmodern in sensibility, and the general tenor has been towards more biographical revelation.

SCHWARTZ and ESTESS have assembled an excellent collection of material in three sections. The first part consists of critical essays, all distinguished, including contributions from Helen Vendler, Robert Pinsky, and David Kalstone. Part Two, "A Chronology", is an invaluable record of contemporary reviews, interviews, and memorial addresses. Part Three, "In Her Own Words", comprises extracts from Bishop's own prose about writers and writing. There is also a useful bibliography, which includes the poet's uncollected work and secondary material.

BLOOM's chosen 16 critical essays, mainly written in the early 1980s, replicate eight from Schwartz and Estess, but also include important essays by Jerome Mazzaro on memory, Joanne Feit Diehl on the sublime, and David Bromwich on "Dream-Houses". The collection, accessible and varied, is a good introduction for students, although it does not convey the sense of the poet working and thinking with her contemporaries, which is a feature of Schwartz and Estess.

TRAVISANO provides the first developmental account of Bishop's work from "Prison", the first modernist phase of sealed imaginary worlds, through the precise observations of the external world in the middle phase, "Travel", to the challenges of the public and private realms in the last phase, "History". This is a traditional study, with detailed commentary on some of the major poems.

PARKER presents Bishop not as reticent and controlled, but as driven by anxiety in relation to her poetic contemporaries and predecessors. The basis of this study is comparative: it begins with, for example, an analysis of "The Weed" which cites Samuel Taylor Coleridge, Walt Whitman, and Emily Dickinson among others, but only passingly George Herbert whose "Love-unknowne" Bishop herself cited as a source for the poem. Parker's address has the merits of a good seminar mode of discussion, although his broad-ranging comparisons are too arbitrary and unfocused to be more than intermittently illuminating.

KALSTONE was a friend of Bishop and his enthusiasm for her work set academic criticism in motion. This study illuminates the artistic and human value of her relationships with Moore and Lowell. Bishop sought out Moore as her mentor and, with Lowell, brilliant and often self-destructive like herself, she had stimulating exchanges about the struggle to write their very different kinds of poetry. Kalstone's unobtrusive deployment of source material shows how lives and poems were interwoven. This is an ideal introduction and a meditation on the making of poetry to which the reader is likely to return.

COSTELLO's study, the first to engage seriously with Bishop's visual poetics, argues that the poet has the early postmodern desire to create pattern without stasis, a poetry of "looks", which dismantles Romantic and transcendental notions of "vision" and mastery. This is a subtle and sophisticated analysis of how the contemplative stance can be alive with change, and free of the desire to dominate.

GOLDENSOHN's first three chapters concentrate on Brazil, her own retracing of Bishop's steps, and exhilaration in the discovery of an unpublished love poem, "It is marvellous to wake up together". Thereafter the book offers a developmental account, with an awareness of gender issues, from the surrealist spatializing allegories of early work such as "The Man-Moth" through to the enlargement of scope in the ability to deal more directly with personal experience in the later poems. The enthusiasm and energy of Goldensohn's quest to discover the pattern of this evolution justifies the emphasis of the title, a "biography" not of an individual, but of "a poetry".

HARRISON is explicit about the theoretical perspectives, postmodern and pragmatic, informing her readings, particularly of the Brazilian poems (based on the politics of gender and ethnicity). The insights derived from the methodology of Gayatri Spivak, Teresa de Lauretis, and the cultural anthropologist Clifford Geertz, are unevenly handled, yet always thought-provoking about Bishop's mobile questionings of how she was culturally "situated". The core of this important book – which is for the Bishop devotee rather than the beginning student – is in the chapters that cover the manuscript drafts, of the attempts to write about childhood and the unpublished love poems. The harrowing process of reworking memory is revealed in these drafts so that the poetry comes to seem not reticent but, as Bishop expressed it in "Poem", "life and the memory of it so compressed/ they've turned into each other".

MILLIER, in this indispensable critical biography, is frank about the difficulties with asthma, alcohol, and depression that Bishop faced, and combines details of the poet's income with a sympathetic account of "her existence as a chronically displaced person". But in revealing the stumblings of the life, Millier brilliantly succeeds in illuminating the pattern of the poems, "opening out private meaning from apparently objective description".

McCABE's account of the poetry, as premised on loss, and undermining the notion of an integrated selfhood, is the first book-length study informed throughout by a postmodern interpretation of gender, drawing on Jacques Lacan and Freud, in a synthesis of French and Anglo-American feminist theory. To theorize Bishop's sense of loss and her privileging of the "home-made" seems no great gain; Harrison and Goldensohn are more insightful in their meticulous use of source material. But, for better or worse, McCabe's book puts Bishop squarely in the feminist frame of reference, a positioning the poet herself would have resisted.

PAT RIGHELATO

Black Mountain Poets

Allen, Donald, and Warren Tallman (eds.), *The Poetics of the New American Poetry*, New York: Grove Press, 1973

Beach, Christopher, *ABC of Influence; Ezra Pound and the Remaking of American Poetic Tradition*, Berkeley: University of California Press, 1992

Bertholf, Robert, Don Byrd, and Ian Reid, *Robert Duncan: Scales of the Marvelous*, New York: New Directions, 1979

Butterick, George (ed.), *Charles Olson and Robert Creeley: The Complete Correspondence*, 9 vols.(to date), Santa Barbara, California: Black Sparrow Press, 1980 –

Clark, Tom, *Charles Olson: The Allegory of a Poet's Life*, New York: Norton, 1991

Edelberg, Cynthia Dubin, *Robert Creeley's Poetry: A Critical Introduction*, Albuquerque: University of New Mexico Press, 1978

Géfin, Laszlo, *Ideogram: History of a Poetic Method*, Austin: University of Texas Press, 1982; Milton Keynes, Buckinghamshire: Open University Press, 1982

Marriott, D.S., "A Note on Olson's Projective Prosody", in *Parataxis: Modernism and Modern Writing*, 6, Spring–Summer 1994

Wesling, Donald (ed.), *Internal Resistances: The Poetry of Edward Dorn*, Berkeley: University of California Press, 1985

The term "Black Mountain poets" refers to a group of poets who first came together in the 1950s at Black Mountain College, North Carolina. The poetry written by the group – which includes Charles Olson, Robert Creeley, Robert Duncan, and Edward Dorn – is renowned for its "open field" or "projective" formal experimentation with the typographical positioning of words, lines, and strophes on the page rather than the "closed" abstract formulae of traditional prosodic meters and rhyme. Since the 1970s the scope of the group has extended to embrace a wide diversity of styles in succeeding generations of American and British writers. The selection discussed below begins with general studies of the Black Mountain phenomenon before considering items focused on particular poets.

ALLEN and TALLMAN's poetics anthology should be read as a complement to Allen's groundbreaking anthology, *The New American Poetry, 1945–1960*. It includes Olson's influential "Projective Verse" essay, Duncan's "Notes on Poetics", and Dorn's "What I See in *The Maximus Poems*". The revival of Poundian modernism for these poets consisted in an attempt to represent objectively the dynamics of phenomena unmediated by the subjective lyric ego of the poet. These ideas receive their most trenchant expression in the three essays above. The anthology remains an important source book for any readers interested in postwar American experimental poetry.

GÉFIN's study identifies an "ideogrammatic or paratactic tradition", claiming Pound as its founder and continued in the work of the Black Mountain poets. The rejection of previous prosodic categories or metrical norms as "closed" is linked to an entirely new epistemology of poetic form as an ideogrammatic or visual registration of the perceptual, mental, and spoken process that brought it into being. Black Mountain poetry is thus based on paratactic and typographical "measures" rather than on grammar or syntactical linearity, on "breath" rather than metric feet, on kinetic energy or rhythm rather than on cognitive process or intellection. As a formal history of stylistic traits in new American poetry, Géfin's book fails to contextualise the poetry, but contains close textual analysis.

BEACH's study situates Olson, Duncan, and Dorn in terms of poetic influence in social, historical, political, institutional, and interpersonal contexts. The influence of Pound, especially the greater formal experimentation of the later *Cantos*, is crucial, especially for an understanding of Olson's "historical method" and Duncan's "collage" technique and ideogrammatic method. Although some of the detail of Beach's readings is open to question, his emphasis on larger historical contexts is an important one.

CLARK's biography of Olson, being the first, presents a fascinating glimpse of both the man and his milieu at Black Mountain College. The importance in Olson's life and work of the writer Frances Boldereff is a genuine surprise of the book, as is Clark's portrayal of Olson himself – as an overbearing, self-righteous, and self-justifying autodidact, who was ruined through self-abuse and the abuse of others. However, what receives less thorough investigation is Olson's life as a poet. This is to be regretted in a self-consciously intellectual poet who interpreted his own life as a dialectical multiplicity of ideas struggling for systematic presentation in his major works.

BUTTERICK's edition of the Olson-Creeley correspondence provides intriguing insights into the evolution of the Black Mountain aesthetic, especially Olson's search for a viable historical methodology for his own postmodernist poetic project, *The Maximus Poems*. In the letters Olson writes to Creeley from the Yucatan Peninsula he sets out his rethinking of the ontological status of history and the method of historical understanding in Pound's *The Cantos* and William Carlos Williams's *Paterson*. These letters show him exploring palaeolithic archaeology, cultural geography, and mythology in an effort to "repossess man of his dynamic". This collection is essential reading for anyone interested in Black Mountain poetry.

My own (MARRIOTT's) article aims to show how Olson's projectivism involves a rejection of regular rhyme and lineal closure; the displacement of traditional prosodic measures by the "cadence" and "breath pause" is directly related to Olson's interest in the spatial and prehensive relations between syllables and words (which he derived from Reimann's projective geometry and post-Einsteinian relational theories of space-time). The philosophical dimension underlying Olson's projective epistemology is thus shown to be intimately linked to his poetics.

EDELBERG's study is a comprehensive survey of Creeley's roles as editor (of *The Black Mountain Review*), correspondent, and poet. She identifies Creeley's main poetic mode as an intense "condensation" of the connotative properties of words in a search for a "literal transmission" of experience in lines stressed and shaped by actual speech patterns. In Creeley's use of short, enjambed lines the influence of Williams' triadic stanza is also pointed out. The book is a useful introduction to the patterns of organisation and stylistic techniques employed in Creeley's poetry.

BERTHOLF, BYRD, and REID's collection of articles and essays attempts to define Duncan's incorporation of a post-Romantic spiritual sensibility within the framework of open-field poetry. Essays by Davidson and Byrd excellently describe Duncan's struggle to represent a mystical evocation of desire and spirituality within the Poundian virtues of precision, workmanship, and open form. Accessible while also erudite and wide ranging, this book is an excellent introduction to Duncan criticism.

WESLING's collection of essays seeks to explain Dorn's geographical imagination as an inner, imaginative landscape rather than a treatment of "place" or sentimental regional localism as in Olson's *Maximus Poems*. Excellent essays by Wesling and Von Hallberg explore the interrelationship between language and migration in Dorn's geopolitical poetics of travel and the consequent deconstruction of Black Mountain poetics of place in *Slinger*. This thesis is an important one, and shows the extent to which Black Mountain poetics have changed and adapted since Olson's death in 1971.

D.S. MARRIOTT

Blake, William 1757–1827

English poet, painter, and illustrator

Damon, S. Foster, *A Blake Dictionary: The Ideas and Symbols of William Blake*, Providence, Rhode Island: Brown University Press, 1965; London: Thames & Hudson, 1973; revised edition, Hanover, New Hampshire: University Press of New England, 1988

De Luca, Vincent Arthur, *Words of Eternity: Blake and the Poetics of the Sublime*, Princeton, New Jersey: Princeton University Press, 1991

Erdman, David V., *Blake, Prophet Against Empire: A Poet's Interpretation of the History of His Own Time*, Princeton, New Jersey: Princeton University Press, 1954, 3rd, revised edition, 1977

Essick, Robert N., and Joseph Viscomi (eds.), *"Milton a Poem" and the Final Illuminated Works: "The Ghost of Abel," "On Homer's Poetry," "On Virgil", Laocoön"* (Volume 5, *Blake's Illuminated Works*), Princeton, New Jersey: Princeton University Press/William Blake Trust, 1993

Esterhammer, Angela, *Creating States: Studies in the Performative Language of John Milton and William Blake*, Toronto: University of Toronto Press, 1994

Frye, Northrop, *Fearful Symmetry: A Study of William Blake*, Princeton, New Jersey: Princeton University Press, 1947

Glen, Heather, *Vision and Disenchantment: Blake's "Songs" and Wordsworth's "Lyrical Ballads"*, Cambridge and New York: Cambridge University Press, 1983

Hilton, Nelson, *Literal Imagination: Blake's Vision of Words*, Berkeley: University of California Press, 1983

Larrissy, Edward, *William Blake*, Oxford and New York: Blackwell, 1985

Mee, Jon, *Dangerous Enthusiasm: William Blake and the Culture of Radicalism in the 1790s*, Oxford: Clarendon Press, 1992; New York: Oxford University Press, 1992

Mitchell, W.J.T., *Blake's Composite Art: A Study of the Illuminated Poetry*, Princeton, New Jersey: Princeton University Press, 1978

Norvig, Gerda S., *Dark Figures in the Desired Country: Blake's Illustrations to "The Pilgrim's Progress"*, Berkeley: University of California Press, 1993

Ostriker, Alicia, "Desire Gratified and Ungratified: William Blake and Sexuality", in *Essential Articles for the Study of Blake, 1970–1984*, edited by Nelson Hilton, Hamden, Connecticut: Archon Books, 1986

Shaviro, Steven, "'Striving with Systems': Blake and the Politics of Difference", in *Essential Articles for the Study of Blake, 1970–1984*, edited by Nelson Hilton, Hamden, Connecticut: Archon Books, 1986

In the first half of the twentieth century, criticism of Blake focused on mapping the territory of his extensive, but at that time still unfamiliar, canon of poetry, visual designs, and intellectual commentary. Untying the interpretive knots of his vastly allusive and apparently monolithic symbolic "system" occupied many who sought to place his abstruse writings in coherent relation to the influential aesthetic, literary, spiritual, philosophical, and socio-political traditions of his time. In partial reaction against this totalizing trend, yet in conformity with the hagiographic tone of the early criticism, a spate of subjective close readings in the New-Critical mode followed. This phase of the reception of Blake's work culminated in the 1960s, when he became something of a cult figure. His radical politics, his visionary enthusiasm, his psychedelic playfulness with what he named the "minute particulars" of his art all made him a literary hero of the progressive Left. During the last two decades, however, after an intense exploration of the semiotic complexities of his verbal and pictorial language, a more suspicious approach has dominated critical commentary on the man and his work. Fed by interest in such poststructural theoretical models as cultural materialism, deconstruction, feminism, and Lacanian psychoanalysis, critics today – whether formalist or historicist in orientation – tend to cite those places in Blake's illuminated poems where cracks in the biographical and representational systems surface. Still, whether riding the crest of antithetical criticism or not, all the books discussed below present detailed analyses of the most significant elements of Blake's transformative poetic agenda.

FRYE can justifiably be called the dean of twentieth-century Blake studies. His magisterial book of the late 1940s, though very much a text of its time in its essentializing, apocalyptic views of psyche, and history and myth (and history *as* myth), still constitutes the most exciting introduction there is to a reading of Blake's entire corpus. A sweeping exposition of Enlightenment epistemology and of Blake's detailed objections to it, Frye's book provides a chronological treatment of the poems and prose writings that weaves a picture of Blake as a consistently utopian champion of the liberal imagination.

Another mid-century classic in its first edition is ERDMAN's descriptive analysis of Blake's poetic "interpretation of the history of his own time". Crammed full of detailed, often eccentric, historical facts and documentary discourses, which are shown to have significantly impinged on every one of Blake's works, the study proves how steeped Blake was in the social controversies of late eighteenth- and early nineteenth-century England. No subsequent book on Blake as a social and political animal has escaped a profound debt to this work of Erdman's.

DAMON's dictionary remains still another good tool for the beginner who craves a clear "map" to guide him or her through the wild territories of Blake's odd vocabularies, confusing narrative structures, and mythic, historical, or biblical allusions. An important *caveat* for the critical reader, however, is that Damon's definitions nourish the desire to stabilize prematurely the "meanings" of certain words and signs which in practice gain their effects from their indeterminacy. One should therefore use this dictionary with some caution, and question both its particular definitions and its underlying assumption that fixing meanings and following themes are the keys to understanding Blake.

HILTON's work is perhaps the most important swing away from either a purely interpretive or purely socio-historical reading of Blake. His rigorous study of Blake's semantic inventiveness reveals surprising gems of meanings within meanings. Through a subtle exploration of Blake's purposeful overdetermination of signs, Hilton helps the reader see how essential the "literal" ground of metaphor becomes in texts as various as *The Four Zoas*, *Songs of Innocence and of Experience*, *Milton*, *Jerusalem*, and "Auguries of Innocence". More than a study of semiotic multi-dimensionality (although it is that), this book focuses on verbal and visual puns, which disturb the surface meanings of the very words and images we orient ourselves by. Besides demonstrating Blake's drive to probe the limits of what is possible for the imagination to say, Hilton's book communicates a respect for the materiality of Blakean texts and the cultural contexts of their production.

Like Hilton's study, but more intensely focused on a philosophical hermeneutic, SHAVIRO's essay is exemplary of the critical application of poststructuralist theory to a reading of Blake's methods and intentions. After a densely argued opening section, which explains Blake's strategic use of conceptual contradictions, Shaviro takes as his case study "The Tyger", Blake's famous dramatic lyric from *Songs of Experience*. Here he demonstrates how Blake's "doctrine of contraries", put into practice as a thematic, structural, and audience-response device, differs fundamentally from both Derridean deconstruction and Hegelian dialectics. The reading of the poem that this approach yields is rich and rewarding. Shaviro's essay anticipated a rash of articles and books that argue the applicability of the deconstructive turn in critical theory to Blake.

Taking a different, more historically based approach to the poet's own theories of creative expression, De LUCA examines Blake's writings in the framework of both neoclassical and Romantic discussions of the sublime. His book shows how deeply the epistemological, psychological, and moral elements of Blake's aesthetic concerns are conditioned by dynamically opposed discourses of the sublime. Embracing the values at once of the definite and the infinite, Blake positions himself between the competing perspectives, De Luca explains, and so creates a nearly postmodern world view that critiques the limits of each standpoint. Part intellectual history, part textual explication, De Luca's book applies cultural theories then and now to excellent discussions of all the "grand" epics, including *Vala* and its transformation into *The Four Zoas*, *Milton*, and *Jerusalem*.

ESTERHAMMER uses the surprisingly flexible lens of a revisionist speech-act theory to look afresh at the speakerly effects of many key Blakean narratives. Her goal is to re-invent the notion of a visionary poetics in both Milton and Blake by specifying its performative, rhetorical components and by identifying its socio-political and phenomenological character. In the process she offers energetic new readings of some particularly vexing passages from the *Songs*, *The Book of Urizen*, and *Jerusalem*. In all of these interpretive commentaries, furthermore, she shows how both the formalist and historical contexts of Blake's poetic strategies play into a quasi-postmodern view of issues of identity and the construction of subjectivity.

LARRISSY's book is a sophisticated Blake primer, alive to the most pressing cultural, philosophical, and literary questions of our day. It is by far the best short introduction to Blake's early work that has been written in the past 40 years. He has fine discussions of Blake's foundational "Religion" tracts, the *Songs*, the Lambeth prophecies, *The Marriage of Heaven and Hell*, and *The Book of Urizen*. Although he makes use of contemporary theorists such as Jacques Derrida, Jacques Lacan, and Michel Foucault, he does so in the clearest manner possible, avoiding the postmodern affectation that so often accompanies such references. In like manner, Larrissy introduces the reader to the subtleties and complexities of the Blakean method without either over-elaborating or settling for reductive explications. This is a powerful, intellectually challenging survey of the hardest questions posed by the most accessible works in the Blakean canon.

By placing Blake's *Songs* (1794) in dialectical relation to Wordsworth's *Lyrical Ballads* (1798), GLEN lucidly pinpoints the uniqueness of each poet's project. The main thrust of her argument is that despite profound differences in political and class allegiances, both authors chose to articulate their distinct social and aesthetic visions by radically transforming popular generic traditions. In Blake's case this included a bold manipulation of the forms of conventional children's literature and an implicit critique of its cultural assumptions and moral purposes. Glen's is one of the best of an ever-growing list of comparative studies that interpret intertextual relations between Blake and such writers as James Joyce, D.H. Lawrence, Goethe, Milton, John Bunyan, Dante; philosophers Derrida, Søren Kierkegaard, Nietzsche, Hegel, John Locke, and Jakob Böhme; psychologists Lacan, Carl Jung, Otto Rank, and Freud; and scientists Charles Darwin, Isaac Newton, Descartes, etc. In Glen's case, the question of direct influence is not at issue (Wordsworth never knew Blake, and Blake read only a little of Wordsworth's poetry). Instead, Glen highlights salient parallels in the formal strategies of these two great Romantic writers, while providing wonderfully fresh, antithetical readings of many of their most compelling lyrics.

With MEE's study of Blake's indebtedness to the language of radicalism in late eighteenth-century England, a postmodern trend toward theoretical eclecticism in Blake studies takes center stage. To begin with, Mee's book traces the way Blake himself, like other radicals of the period, deliberately drew on the contrasting discourses of religious enthusiasm and rational skepticism to form what Mee (after Claude Lévi-Strauss) calls a "bricolage" of strange theoretical bedfellows. By breaking discursive boundaries and re-combining what had been seen as contradictory realms of thought, these writers could in one stroke revise old concepts and create new ones. Mee shows how the ironies of this method permeate the full range of Blake's poetic utterances, from the simplest aphorism to the most inflated rhetoric of the visionary epics. One great value of this New-Historicist study is that it exposes the shortsightedness of faulting Blake for the kind of conceptual inconsistencies that, in fact, were a conscious hallmark of the English radical style proudly embraced by Blake. At the same time, Mee's own method of analysis reflects the eclecticism he discusses, in that he happily combines the practices of formalism, discourse theory, cultural materialism, and historicist approaches to give elegant interpretations of Blake's texts in their social contexts.

Feminist commentary – another new direction in Blake criticism – is well represented by OSTRIKER's introductory article on themes of gender and sexuality throughout Blake's writings. Except for some questionable assumptions about the general development of Blakean thought, this essay raises all the important points on which further exploration of gender issues in Blake's work must be based. Ostriker identifies four mutually contradictory attitudes toward gender, which are endorsed by key speakers in the poems, early and late, and she clearly sets forth their pro- and anti-feminist implications. Far from being a tirade against Blake's sexism, Ostriker's piece judiciously balances moments in the texts that celebrate women's liberation against those that either consciously or unconsciously recycle patriarchal patterns of oppression.

A final category of Blake criticism with a long tradition centers on the relationship between his writing and his painting, drawing, and engraving. MITCHELL's study of Blake's mixed-media process, for example, is a book that broke new ground by stressing the importance of learning to read the linguistic and pictorial elements of the illuminated texts together as a single, "composite" art form. Like antiphonal voices, verbal imagery, visual iconography, poetic theme, and pictorial style are all shown to interact and comment upon one another in highly complex and dynamic ways. Taking the engraved plate as Blake's principal unit of meaning, Mitchell taught readers (including most subsequent critics) how to look for structural resonances and thematic tensions both within the design of individual pages and across plate sequences. Since Mitchell, few serious Blake critics have written about the illuminated texts without including pointed analyses of the mixed-media effects. Mitchell's most enduring contribution, however, lies in the way he brings his concept of Blake's composite art home through stunning, exemplary interpretations of *The Book of Thel*, *The Book of Urizen*, and portions of *Jerusalem*.

Because the structure of the printed page has such semantic salience in Blake's work, excellent sources of critical commentary often appear in the Introductions and notes to facsimile editions of specific poems. Continuing their mission to reproduce a full color example of every one of Blake's texts, the William Blake Trust has sponsored a new series of photographic facsimiles with up-to-date critical discussions in every volume. ESSICK and VISCOMI's edition of *Milton* exemplifies the value of this critical format. Besides giving a succinct and penetrating summary of the critical questions raised by the verbal and visual components of the text, these authors also elucidate the poem's underlying mythography, its narrative line, and keys to its socio-political and cultural allusions. In addition they lucidly discuss those all-important matters of material production, which directly and visibly affect the finished work.

My own book (NORVIG's) is one of many that have set out to examine the way in which Blake's serial illustrations to the work of other writers function as a form of literary criticism. Blake commented extensively in this cross-media way on the poetry of, among others, Thomas Gray, Milton, Dante and the Bible. The study explores the critical implications of his set of 24 watercolor drawings for Bunyan's *The Pilgrim's Progress*. In addition to charting the growing importance Blake placed on the archetypal dimensions of the *Progress* theme in his own poetic enterprise, it seeks to show how these drawings critique the moral focus and interpretive narrowness of previous Bunyan illustrators. (Color reproductions of all of Blake's Bunyan drawings and many black-and-white photographs here demonstrate significant variations in the popular illustrative convention he inherited.)

GERDA S. NORVIG

The Bloomsbury Group

Bell, Quentin, *Bloomsbury*, London: Weidenfeld & Nicolson, 1968; New York: Basic Books, 1969

Edel, Leon, *Bloomsbury: A House of Lions*, Philadelphia: J.B. Lippincott, 1979; London: Hogarth Press, 1979

Johnstone, J.K., *The Bloomsbury Group: A Study of E.M. Forster, Lytton Strachey, Virginia Woolf and Their Circle*, London: Secker & Warburg, 1954; New York: Noonday Press, 1954

Nicolson, Nigel, "Bloomsbury: The Myth and the Reality" in *Virginia Woolf and Bloomsbury: A Centenary Celebration*, edited by Jane Marcus, London: Macmillan, 1987; Bloomington: Indiana University Press, 1987

Rosenbaum, S.P., *The Early Literary History of the Bloomsbury Group*, 2 vols., London: Macmillan, 1987–94

Shone, Richard, *Bloomsbury Portraits: Vanessa Bell, Duncan Grant and Their Circle*, Oxford: Phaidon Press, 1976, revised 1993; New York: Dutton, 1976

While early studies of Bloomsbury tend to emphasise a collective Bloomsbury identity, later accounts more easily accommodate difference and diversity in their portrayals. Across the body of Bloomsbury criticism there remains considerable variation of opinion as to the membership and precise nature of the group.

JOHNSTONE's study sets the tone of many later accounts by distinguishing the Bloomsbury Group through a set of shared first principles and ultimate values. They depended, says the author, on intuition and mysticism, but they subjected the findings of intuition to a rigorous intellectual examination. G.E. Moore's *Principia Ethica* and the Cambridge humanism of Goldsworthy Lowes Dickinson, John Ellis McTaggart, and Leslie Stephen, is viewed as the central influence on Bloomsbury philosophy, while Bloomsbury aesthetics are shown to owe most to Roger Fry. The study's major focus is upon the literature of Virginia Woolf, E.M. Forster, and Lytton Strachey, among whom Johnstone sees an "essential agreement". For Johnstone the Bloomsbury Group's significance cannot be underestimated, being "a nucleus from which civilisation has spread outwards".

BELL's chronological account examines three phases of Bloomsbury: before 1914, during World War I, and after 1918. Written from an overtly partisan perspective – "I was born and bred in Bloomsbury; writing about it I must write about my friends and relations" – its stated purpose is as a history of ideas, not an airing of Bloomsbury linen, "whether clean or dirty". Consequently its focus is upon the main events within and outside the Bloomsbury Group affecting its development, and the shared attitude to life – rationalism and scepticism – which Bell sees as constitutive of the group. The study's strength lies in its contextualisation of Bloomsbury's ideas, aesthetics, and politics, and its even-handed assessment of charges of snobbery, élitism, and ruthlessness levelled against the Group. Bell's emphasis on rationalism means that the internal differences of the Group and the emotional and sexual lives of its members are not addressed.

EDEL's book takes a psychological approach, charting the development of Bloomsbury by focusing on the lives of nine main "characters". Because his aim is "to tell the unfolding of their lives, in biographical form, as if it were a novel", Edel's study is openly a mixture of fact and interpretation. Its strength lies in its portrayal of Bloomsbury both as a set of individual personalities and as a closely knit group.

NICOLSON laments that "Bloomsbury is regarded in England as fair game for abuse", comparing unfavourably the hostility and indifference of British academia with the flourishing scholarly interest of America. But he also warns against a too-enthusiastic reverence for Bloomsbury and its intellectual significance. The essay highlights the mythological nature of Bloomsbury, asking "did Bloomsbury invent Bloomsbury?". Nicolson paints a different picture from the rationalism emphasised elsewhere, and warns against reading Bloomsbury's letters, diaries, and memoirs too much at face-value. This is a short but invaluable essay in its evocation of atmosphere, its debunking of too-reverent myths, and its challenge to the notion of a shared system of Bloomsbury aesthetics and philosophy.

ROSENBAUM's two-part literary history of the group begins with his 1987 study of *Victorian Bloomsbury* and its influences. His aim is to describe a historical sequence of Bloomsbury's early interconnected texts in order to interpret them analytically and comparatively, taking as his motto Forster's epigraph for *Howards End*: "only connect". The book examines the intellectual, family, and Cambridge origins of the group, focusing particularly on autobiographical and undergraduate writings. Cambridge necessarily figures highly in this scholarly and significant study, setting the direction of attention of later accounts. Volume 2, *Edwardian Bloomsbury* (1994), continues the view of Bloomsbury as a distinct and coherent group with a delineable ideology, aesthetic, and style. The unifying features located include the desire to "extend the boundaries of literature", "deep similarities in moral outlook", and an emphasis upon "the timeless moment". Depicted here is a male, Cambridge-dominated Bloomsbury, influenced above all by G.E. Moore, the Cambridge Apostles, the eighteenth century, and French culture, much in the tradition of Bell's earlier account. Because of the book's parameters of 1903 to 1910, Forster's first four novels command most attention as representative of a "Bloomsbury Literature". The book's examination of early and minor works is valuable. By showing that imperialism was "perhaps the central concern of Bloomsbury's criticism of English life", and by providing an excellent journalistic context for Bloomsbury writing, Rosenbaum's study adds significantly to work on this subject.

SHONE's reissued volume includes 80 superlative colour illustrations, and valuable bibliographies and chronologies, which underpin a comprehensive account of the artists, their development, and their relations with British colleagues and French counterparts. A last chapter deals with the declining years of Vanessa Bell and Duncan Grant.

VAL GOUGH

Boswell, James 1740–1795

Scottish biographer, essayist, and poet

Clingham, Greg (ed.), *New Light on Boswell: Critical and Historical Essays on the Occasion of the Bicentenary of the "Life of Johnson"*, Cambridge and New York: Cambridge University Press, 1991

Clingham, Greg, *James Boswell: The Life of Johnson*, Cambridge and New York: Cambridge University Press, 1992

Dowling, William C., *The Boswellian Hero*, Athens: University of Georgia Press, 1979

Dowling, William C., *Language and Logos in Boswell's "Life of Johnson"*, Princeton, New Jersey: Princeton University Press, 1981

Ingram, Allan, *Boswell's Creative Gloom: A Study of Imagery and Melancholy in the Writings of James Boswell*, Totowa: Barnes & Noble, 1982; London: Macmillan, 1982

Schwartz, Richard B., *Boswell's Johnson: A Preface to the "Life"*, Madison: University of Wisconsin Press, 1978

Vance, John (ed.), *Boswell's "Life of Johnson": New Questions, New Answers*, Athens: University of Georgia Press, 1985

> In worth as a Book we have rated it beyond any other product of the eighteenth century: all Johnson's own Writings, laborious and in their kind genuine above most, stand on a quite inferior level to it: already, indeed, they are becoming obsolete for this generation; and for some future generation may be valuable chiefly as Prolegomena and expository Scholia to this *Johnsoniad* of Boswell.
>
> (Thomas Carlyle)

Johnson's works may not themselves have been eclipsed by Boswell's monumental *Life*, as Carlyle famously predicted in 1832, but the same cannot be said of the miscellaneous other writings of Boswell himself. Despite the existence of *An Account of Corsica*, his essays as "The Hypochondriack" in *The London Magazine*, his *Journal of a Tour to the Hebrides* and other writings (and not to mention the gradual post-war publication of Boswell's voluminous journals and private papers), critical attention remains focused above all on the *Life*.

INGRAM's eccentric study is one exception, reading patterns of imagery throughout Boswell's writings in relation to eighteenth-century attitudes to melancholy and more recent psychoanalytic theories. Ingram concludes, nonetheless, that pride of place must remain with the *Life of Johnson*, even from this point of view:

> . . . it was Boswell's conscious artistry and integrity, his willingness to accept in all its implications his role as an author, that made it possible for him to carry to the *Life* the subjective truth of his journals, and yet also to prune that truth of the self-obsession which unbalanced the whole of his life.

An interesting study in the rapid change of critical fashions is provided by DOWLING's two monographs, the first of which (1979) also gives due attention to the *Account of Corsica* and the *Journal of a Tour to the Hebrides*. Here too a melancholy preoccupation is found throughout these various texts, focused this time on the inevitable isolation of the heroic individuals constructed by Boswell within the post-heroic environments he finds them to inhabit. At the end of the *Life of Johnson*, Dowling argues, Johnson's death seems to symbolize the passing of an age; "yet the full meaning of Boswellian narrative lies beyond this conventional truth, for Boswell has given us the image of a world that cannot survive its hero, a separate world of moral stability in the midst of moral chaos, born out of a heroic conflict with the age".

The methodological self-consciousness increasingly evident towards the end of Dowling's *The Boswellian Hero* comes to the fore in DOWLING's (1981) book. This second study attempts to recuperate the formalist methods of his earlier book within the framework of deconstruction, arguing "that these assumptions are not really irreconcilable with the newer assumptions of Derrida and the Yale critics". The result is that Dowling here treats Boswell's text mainly as the means to a somewhat paradoxical (if not actually untenable) theoretical end. As a reading of the *Life*, the book is locally illuminating, and it is always lucidly written. But it makes very heavy weather of demonstrating that here is an interestingly discontinuous, polyphonic and fragmented text in which the organicist criteria of 1950s' New Criticism, unsurprisingly, are not observed.

Two introductory studies are to be noted. SCHWARTZ unabashedly takes on the role of critic in the Johnsonian sense ("a man skilled in the art of judging of literature; a man able to distinguish the faults and beauties of writing"). Declaring himself to share the current admiration for Boswell's craft while thinking it "somewhat exaggerated", he argues in particular that the *Life* fails to see beyond the limits of its author's personal perspective: "Boswell's sense of Johnson is too superficial and overlooks (along with much modern scholarship) Johnson's Johnson, the image which emerges in the self-portraits sprinkled throughout Johnson's works". CLINGHAM (1992) is more wary of evaluation – and more sceptical, too, about the consistency or coherence of Boswell's subject. His ambitious contribution to the Cambridge University Press "Landmarks of World Literature" series goes beyond the limits of mere survey, to make an eloquent case for the *Life* as a work that is "not primarily documentary . . . but imaginative and recreative". Patiently disentangling the chronological, thematic, and symbolic structures of the *Life*, Clingham reads it as a perpetually provisional kind of analysis in which, "because Boswell's vision of Johnson is artistic and not merely documentary, his portrait of Johnson's character paradoxically both precedes and results from the act and experience of writing the biography".

Two collections of essays contain important material. VANCE gives an overview of criticism to 1985, and his book reprints influential essays by Ralph W. Rader, Frederick A. Pottle, and Donald Greene, all of whom deal, in various ways, with the rival demands on Boswell of documentary fidelity and literary shaping. Several new essays in the volume engage with similar issues, and there are also discussions of particular moments or figures in the *Life*, such as the deathbed scene and the presentation of Goldsmith. CLINGHAM's more recent collection of essays (1991), published on the bicentenary of the *Life*, concentrates attention on the Scottish contexts of Boswell's writing in essays by Thomas Crawford, Richard B. Sher, Pat Rogers, Joan H. Pittock, Gordon Turnbull, Richard B. Schwartz, and Susan Manning. Further essays discuss formal or thematic features of the *Life*: Paul J. Korshin is especially good on Johnson's conversation.

TOM KEYMER

Bowen, Elizabeth 1899–1973

Anglo-Irish novelist and short-story writer

Austin, Allan E., *Elizabeth Bowen*, New York: Twayne, 1971
Bennett, Andrew, and Nicholas Royle, *Elizabeth Bowen and the Dissolution of the Novel: Still Lives*, London: Macmillan, 1995
Bloom, Harold (ed.), *Elizabeth Bowen*, New York: Chelsea House, 1987
Heath, William, *Elizabeth Bowen: An Introduction to Her Novels*, Madison: University of Wisconsin Press, 1961
Hoogland, Renée C., *Elizabeth Bowen: A Reputation in Writing*, New York: New York University Press, 1994
Kenney, Edwin J., *Elizabeth Bowen*, Lewisburg, Pennsylvania: Bucknell University Press, 1975; London: Associated University Presses, 1975
Lee, Hermione, *Elizabeth Bowen: An Estimation,* London: Vision Press, 1981; New York: Barnes & Noble, 1981
Lassner, Phyllis, *Elizabeth Bowen*, Savage, Maryland: Barnes & Noble, 1989; London: Macmillan, 1990

Elizabeth Bowen remains a remarkably undervalued twentieth-century writer. Various factors may explain this. First, her work has been pigeon-holed through being compared with others' (above all, Henry James and Virginia Woolf) and found wanting. Second, it has suffered from being identified (rightly *and* wrongly) with the values of gentrified, upper-middle-class English or Anglo-Irish life. Third, Bowen's novels were published over a long period (*The Hotel* in 1927, *Eva Trout* in 1968): her work tended to shift ahead of its critics, so that earlier criticism especially maintained its allegiances to the Elizabeth Bowen of, say, *The Death of the Heart* (1938) rather than the Elizabeth Bowen of *The Little Girls* (1963) or *Eva Trout*. It can indeed be said that Bowen's work has not been well served by critics, even by its admirers. In particular, her novels have consistently been seen in author-centred terms, as revelations of "Miss Bowen's sensibility" rather than, say, of what she calls "the strange eventfulness of writing" itself. Even in spite of itself, however, most Bowen criticism betrays something of the deranged and deranging qualities of her work.

HEATH's is the earliest full-length study of Bowen's fiction. He sees her work as primarily concerned with the opposition of innocence and experience and with exploring the idea of a "saving pattern". Heath takes issue with the view that Bowen's work is romantic in any sentimental sense, arguing that "Elizabeth Bowen's fiction at its best is conscious, intelligent, even austere". He refers to his subject, with appropriate decorum, as "Miss Bowen". Heath's study is inevitably limited by the fact that at the time of its appearance Bowen's final novels had not yet been published.

AUSTIN also belongs to the "Miss Bowen" school of criticism. His book opens with a biographical focus on what he calls "The Bowen World", then proceeds to give a chronological survey of her ten novels, a chapter on the short stories, and a concluding chapter on Bowen criticism. Austin's overall judgments of the novels represent what probably remains a critical consensus: *The Death of the Heart* and *The Heat of the Day* are "the twin peaks of her work". Austin has some interesting things to say, but he appears to register intriguing facts without then knowing quite what to do with them. Thus he acknowledges that *A World of Love* (1955) is "an experiment", that *The Little Girls* is Bowen's "most challenging book", and that *Eva Trout* is "her weirdest and darkest", but tends to dismiss them for their strangeness rather than reflect on what the different kinds of critical procedures they might call for.

KENNEY, too, offers a biographically focused opening chapter followed by a chronological survey of the novels. His account suffers from the author-centred limitations noted above, as well as from a strong investment in the traditional values of novelistic realism. Thus, *The Death of the Heart* is "the finest of her novels, and a significant achievement in modern fiction" because it is "a triumph of the 'well-made' realistic novel". Like Austin, Kenney registers the fact that Bowen's work is dark, as well as terribly funny, but does not try to pursue this beyond what are, in effect, rudimentary observations. Kenney recognizes the fundamental and destabilizing stress on "fiction", noting "the importance of fictive concords to overcome the fragmentariness of life and the self" in her novels, but does little to elaborate. Of *Eva Trout* he writes: "what this novel, with its black humor, mischievous puns, and its own imperious willingness to ignore the conventional expectations for the realistic novel, conveys is that identity is energy". The proposition that "identity is energy" does not take us very far, though it constitutes the conclusion to his book.

LEE offers a much fuller and more satisfactory account than Austin, Kenney, or any other earlier criticism. She provides quite thorough coverage not only of the novels, but of the short stories and other prose writings. Lee regards Bowen as "an exceptional English novelist because she fuses two traditions – that of Anglo-Irish literature and history, and that of a European modernism indebted to Flaubert and James".

She gives a good sense of the broadly political dimensions of Bowen's work, asserting that "the personal, emotional concerns of her novels and stories are consistently deployed for a critique of the English middle-classes". She also provides a valuable delineation of Bowen's work in relation to what she calls "the modernist paradox – the application of elaborately formal methods to chaotic, inexpressible experience". Lee's account has its limitations. It is in many respects highly traditional, not least in its author-centredness. To declare, for example, that Bowen's "last novels confirm her lifelong attitudes to existence" suggests the extent to which Lee's reading privileges a sense of the authorial presence presiding beyond the work rather than seeks to inhabit the strange world of the words on the page. Nevertheless Lee makes a balanced and persuasive case for Bowen's importance. Indeed she argues that Bowen "deserves consideration as a short story writer alone", noting that "it is here that her careful effects, her mannered emphases, her exact detailing of atmosphere, and the disconcerting suggestiveness produced by these techniques are most immaculately and resonantly employed".

BLOOM too, in his Introduction to the "Modern Critical Views" collection of essays, indicates a preference for the short stories, proposing that "after James Joyce and D.H. Lawrence, Bowen may be the most distinguished British writer of short stories in our time". Bloom's book brings together a good range of earlier critical essays, of which perhaps the most valuable are Barbara Bellow Watson's "Variations on an Enigma: Elizabeth Bowen's War Novel", which gives an eloquent and thoughtful account of *The Heat of the Day*, and Harriet S. Chessman's "Women and Language in the Fiction of Elizabeth Bowen", which sees Bowen's work in terms of a recurring kind of schizophrenic structure involving "two primary female characters" who are "storyteller and object of the story, 'insider' and 'outsider'".

LASSNER's is the first full-length study to attempt to situate Bowen's work in terms of feminism. While sensitive to the fact that Bowen herself dismissed the label of "feminist", Lassner is concerned to explore the general argument that "readers cannot ignore the persistence of female characters in Bowen's work who struggle with autonomy, dependence and self-expression in circumstances always defined by traditional family values". Her account is somewhat uneven: some novels receive extensive treatment, others (especially *The Hotel*, *A World of Love* and *The Little Girls*) scarcely any. Unusual and insightful suggestions – for instance, about the ways in which *The Heat of the Day* "undermines the interpretive strategies of both characters and readers" – jostle alongside frustratingly unsupported claims – for instance, that *Eva Trout* is, simply, "problematic in many ways". Nevertheless, Lassner's is a useful contribution to the modernisation (or, perhaps, postmodernisation) of Bowen criticism.

HOOGLAND takes up the postmodern gauntlet with something of a vengeance. Her study is extraordinarily ambitious in many respects, and provides what is undoubtedly the most intensively and explicitly theoretical account of Bowen's work to date. Hoogland gives extensive attention to the eccentric, or more precisely the "ex-centric", characteristics of Bowen's writing, both in its reworkings of fiction/reality distinctions and in its displacements of conventional notions of sexual identity. Written from a specifically lesbian feminist perspective, Hoogland's book contains many acute and valuable observations – not least in its account of earlier Bowen criticism. Its chief drawbacks are, firstly, that (despite being some 370 pages long) it is almost entirely focused on *The Last September* and *Eva Trout*; and secondly, that it tends to sag in some respects under its own theoretical weight. Too much space is devoted to lengthy expositions of semiotics, narratology, and psychoanalysis, even if Bowen's work does indeed seem to call for these kinds of critical thinking. Hoogland's book must, however, be appreciated on its own terms: it is itself admirably ex-centric.

Finally, BENNETT and I (ROYLE) have recently produced a book which tries to stage "the strange eventfulness" of Bowen's writing somewhat differently. Emphasizing the ways in which her novels are concerned with haunting and dissolution, these readings for the most part take their terms of reference from the novels themselves rather than from any theoretical discourse. The aim here is to show that the world of Bowen's novels is itself as complex and provocative as any "theory".

NICHOLAS ROYLE

Bradstreet, Anne c.1612–1672

English-born American poet

Martin, Wendy, *An American Triptych: Anne Bradstreet, Emily Dickinson, Adrienne Rich*, Chapel Hill: University of North Carolina Press, 1984

Piercy, Josephine K., *Anne Bradstreet*, New York: Twayne, 1965

Rosenmeier, Rosamond, *Anne Bradstreet Revisited*, Boston: Twayne, 1991

Stanford, Ann, *Anne Bradstreet, The Wordly Puritan: An Introduction to Her Poetry*, New York: Burt Franklin, 1974

White, Elizabeth Wade, *Anne Bradstreet: "The Tenth Muse"*, New York: Oxford University Press, 1971

Early critical responses to Anne Bradstreet emphasized the fact that she was the first published American female poet. The fact of her being first and the nature of Renaissance influences on her writing mattered more than the verse itself, which was frequently damned by faint praise. Over time Bradstreet's poetry assumed more importance as critics began to appreciate better what it recorded about the poet: her intense feelings for her husband and the material world in general, her various tensions between emotion and doctrine, and her anticipation of certain elements of a future feminist sensibility. This interest in Bradstreet's feminist proclivities, the subject of many essay-discussions of the poet, highlights various modes of resistance found in her writings. This resistance includes the poet's understated use of irony, her subtle subversion of verse genres, and her careful management of gender identity. Today there is general agreement that "Contemplations" is her best poem.

PIERCY suggests that early in her career Bradstreet sublimated her rebellious feelings through imitative verse. Her domestic poems reveal these religious conflicts, especially in treatments of her burned home, her dead relatives, and her absent husband. Late in her career, however, she records greater peace of mind concerning religious matters. Piercy's slim volume has been seminal to the current appreciation of Bradstreet.

WHITE, building on Piercy's book, reads Bradstreet's prose and verse in an effort to construct her biography. White, too, documents how the poet's studies were influential on her work. The 13 personal lyrics Bradstreet wrote between 1632 and 1670 are the most important of her verse, because in them the woman and the poet come together. After her poems were published by her relatives, Bradstreet became more private and more contemplative in her verse. Although White is not very helpful in critically assessing Bradstreet's poetry, she has written the fullest life-and-times biography of the poet that is currently possible.

STANFORD, with more success than Piercy, offers a bio-critical approach to Bradstreet. She delineates various changes in the poet, including the transformation of her initial rejection of New England into acceptance of her experiences there. Among other conflicts, as seen especially in her dialogue verse, the poet mentally wrestled with an emotional enjoyment of the material world in conflict with her rational, doctrinally tutored repudiation of the secular. In her later years, reason supplanted emotion. As expressed in her verse, this conflict records a personal voice that contrasts with the impersonal quality of so many of the other documents of Bradstreet's time. Stanford's useful volume includes a chronology of Bradstreet's works and a frequency list of her images.

MARTIN extends the findings of Piercy, White, and Stanford by converting Bradstreet into a self-conscious feminist. The poet, according to Martin, commenced by relying on male literary models, but eventually derived from her personal experiences a firm sense of self-definition. At this later time, too, Bradstreet associated spiritual matters with men, and natural matters with women, and then preferred the natural. Moreover, Bradstreet substituted an appreciation of female nurture and co-operation for the male valuation of societal and domestic dominance. The poet, therefore, resisted the Puritan patriarchal repudiation of life and, instead, relished female experience. Martin's interpretation appropriates Bradstreet on behalf of the feminist cause, a project that sometimes succeeds and at other times does not, such as when she claims that the poet's self-deprecating statements are always ironic.

ROSENMEIER exceeds even Martin in her discussion of Bradstreet's feminist consciousness. Rosenmeier highlights the poet's awareness of being in the midst of cosmic change (the looming Apocalypse), which in her verse is likened to an alchemical transmutation. One feature of Bradstreet's awareness is the recovery of the role of Wisdom, a figure hidden within her poem on Queen Elizabeth. For the poet, Wisdom emphasizes the feminine aspect of divinity, and is therefore operative in the ongoing cosmic revolution, just as Wisdom had a role in creation. With this understanding of creation, Bradstreet celebrates a sexuality that resonates with the divine, for she believed the body to be suffused with the presence of Christ. This, like much in Rosenmeier's book, amounts to an extreme and improbable reading of a Congregationalist poet whose writings do not anywhere explicitly reveal such heretical postures. Indeed, such a view would have shocked Bradstreet and her immediate contemporaries, those astute students of Origin and other Church fathers who specifically refuted such notions of Christian gnosticism. The value of Rosenmeier's book lies in its stress on a number of Bradstreet's interests, including her knowledge of alchemy.

William J. Scheick

British Literature: General

Adams, Robert M., *The Land and Literature of England: A Historical Account*, New York and London: Norton, 1983

Baugh, Albert C. (ed.), *A Literary History of England*, London: Routledge & Kegan Paul, 1948; revised edition, New York: Appleton-Century-Crofts, 1967

Coote, Stephen, *The Penguin Short History of English Literature*, New York: Penguin, 1993

Daiches, David, *A Critical History of English Literature*, London: Secker & Warburg, 1960; 2nd edition, New York: Ronald Press, 1970

Fowler, Alastair, *A History of English Literature: Forms and Kinds from the Middle Ages to the Present*, Oxford: Blackwell, 1987, revised 1989; Cambridge, Massachusetts: Harvard University Press, 1987

Quennell, Peter, and Hamish Johnson *A History of English Literature*, London: Weidenfeld & Nicolson, 1973; Springfield, Massachusetts: G. & C. Merriam, 1973

Rogers, Pat (ed.), *The Oxford Illustrated History of English Literature*, Oxford and New York: Oxford University Press, 1987

Sampson, George, *The Concise Cambridge History of English Literature*, Cambridge: Cambridge University Press, 1941, 3rd, revised edition, 1969

Sanders, Andrew, *The Short History of English Literature*, Oxford and New York: Clarendon Press, 1994

Tibble, Anne, *The Story of English Literature: A Critical Survey*, London: Peter Owen, 1970

Major multi-volume editions like the *Oxford History of English Literature* (1945–), the *Cambridge History of English Literature* (1907–16, reprinted 1932–33), the *[Sphere] History of Literature in English* series (1969 –), the *New Pelican Guide to English Literature* (revised edition, 1982–88), and the *Longman Literature in English* series (1985–) are filled with authoritative commentary. In addition, there are numerous encyclopedic "companions" to British literature, handbooks, casebook series, and general bibliographic collections. However, few people read such series or reference works all the way through, and therefore this essay will discuss those shorter literary surveys that offer readable and, in some cases, even entertaining general accounts of British literature.

Early surveys, of the 1870s, compiled facts and charts, providing students with as much biographical, historical, and bibliographical materials as possible. Then came another breed of surveys, which did not hesitate to pass judgment on the literary merit of individual writers. In the early part of the twentieth century, surveys now contained political and intellectual history, to explain the causes and effects of the changes in literary productions. Surveys published from the mid-twentieth century emphasized sources, composition, publication and performance dates, literary and philosophical influences, biography, history, cultural background, genre, and critical evaluations. Added in more recent surveys are illustrations, extensive quotations, and introductions to the recent developments in literary theory and canon debates. Unless otherwise noted below, the surveys discussed here are arranged according to the traditional division of periods: Anglo-Saxon, Medieval, Renaissance, Restoration and Enlightenment, Romantic, Victorian, Modern, and Postmodern.

BAUGH's study (it has appeared as one volume and in four volumes), which remains a reliable old friend to students of literature, is a collaboration by five prominent American scholars, Kemp Malone, Albert C. Baugh, Tucker Brooke, George Sherburn, and Samuel C. Chew. The first edition of 1948 became an instant classic. Chapters are divided according to periods and genres, but important literary figures are dealt with in separate chapters. Particularly helpful are the additional chapters offering succinct information on culture, religion, science, art, and music related to the period under discussion. Footnotes generously cite standard editions and significant biographical and critical works. The running index within the pages is a time-saving measure when students wish to look up certain writers or works of literature. The second edition updates the first by adding factual and bibliographical information, mostly in the Supplement.

SAMPSON compresses and partly rewrites the 15 volumes of *The Cambridge History of English Literature* into a readable, brief, well-balanced, and accurate desk reference. Thanks to the succinctness and precision of Sampson's prose, much of the parent work has been preserved, except for matters relating to sources and foreign affiliations. The third edition, revised by R.C. Churchill, updates the volume and adds a chapter on the literature of the United States from the colonial period to Henry James, another chapter on the mid-twentieth-century literature of the English-speaking world, including the West Indies and the new African states.

TIBBLE's non-technical account is an introductory outline of English literature suitable and recommendable for uninitiated readers who want a quick overview of English literary history. Tibble frequently explains the historical and cultural background before introducing the literary works of an era. Up to Chaucer, prose and poetry quotations are accompanied by translations.

DAICHES, a writer of numerous useful books on literature, sets out to write his own version of the history of English literature, intended not "to be looked up, but to be read". The result is a well-balanced, lucid, and lively account of English literature, but without bibliography or footnotes for further reference. The two-volume history is arranged by periods and genres, with Chaucer, Shakespeare, and Milton treated in separate chapters. Unlike some scholars who believe that English literature actually began with what Chaucer imported from the Mediterranean, Daiches emphasizes the continuity of the Old English tradition in medieval prose and verse. Because of the author's own areas of expertise, the chapters on Shakespeare, Milton, and Scottish literature are more impressive than those on the Restoration, Victorian, and post-Victorian periods.

QUENNELL, who wrote biographies of Shakespeare, Samuel Johnson, Alexander Pope, and Byron, offers an English literary history filled not only with illustrations, portraits, and quotations, but also with entertaining anecdotes and interesting biographical information. Appropriate as a reference book for general readers, it does not propose any theory or make exclusive judgment on literary works; rather, the book assembles reliable facts and introduces views by noted scholars on literary figures.

ADAMS' book is a witty and concise historical narrative of England from 1500 BC to the 1950s. The narrative offers very brief introductions to the major literary works. Most of the space is devoted to explaining the cultural atmosphere in which the works were produced: historical events, types of audiences for the writers, literary trends, patterns of patronage, the nature of printing and book sales, and the original staging of early plays. Literary judgments are rare, but there are plenty of maps and illustrations as well as an annotated bibliography. Particularly useful for non-British students are the appendices on British money, measures of distance, baronage, and Anglican ecclesiastical offices. (In fact, the book is intended as "background material for a one-year introduction to English literature".)

ROGERS' volume covers the period from 700 to 1980 and excludes writing in English outside Britain. As the title suggests, pictures are aplenty, including portraits, frontispieces, maps, and artistic renderings of literary characters and scenes. The whole volume is divided into nine chapters, each dealing with a different period – with the exception of a separate chapter on Shakespeare – and each written by a different scholar. Eight of the nine chapters are conservative and traditional in approach; one chapter, however, on Tudor literature, offers new and provocative interpretations informed by recent critical theory.

FOWLER's excellent book is unique among literary surveys in that it has little to say about historical events or the cultural and intellectual atmosphere from which literature has grown. The author, instead, focuses on forms and types of British literature. In that context, the fact that four out of the 15 chapters are devoted to British Renaissance literature is justified; after all, the Renaissance is a period in which writers, professional or not, experimented with, and diversified, literary genres. Also, unlike others of the similar kind, Fowler's survey begins with Chaucer, with "works that can still be read with pleasure and without translation". Fowler's book is accessible, because all technical terms are explained, and lively, because Fowler offers plenty of sound evaluative commentary on writers and their works. Despite the lack of notes and bibliography, the book is recommendable for readers who are already familiar with English literature and who want to re-acquaint themselves with aspects of it.

COOTE, an expert on Chaucer, Byron, and T.S. Eliot, has written a long but readable historical narrative. In discussing Anglo-Saxon literature, Coote provides translations rather than the original; with medieval literature, most quotations are accompanied by translations. Evaluations are subtly incorporated into plot summaries of major works, and short, well-known poems are quoted in full. His views are traditional: important literary figures are accorded their usual importance, although some female writers are carefully introduced. The text is not documented, but the book does end with a helpful annotated bibliography for further reading.

SANDERS begins his book with a long, comprehensive history of the controversy over the literary canon, following with ten chapters arranged in traditional chronological divisions. The volume opens with the Germanic tribes and ends with the discussion of "The New Morality", which explores the 1970s and 1980s, with a few lines on Kazuo Ishiguro and a quotation from Bob Dylan. Besides being very much more up-to-date than many of the other surveys, Sanders' book differs from previous studies in the author's conscious efforts to include women writers, as seen in such innovative essays as "Women's Writing in the Restoration". The author has included Irish, Scottish, and Welsh writers, because they "cannot easily be separated from the English tradition or from the broad sense of an English literature which once embraced regional, provincial, and other national traditions within the British isles". With its reliable facts, accurate historical information, detailed analyses, and well-informed evaluation, the book is recommendable for all students of literature.

SEIWOONG OH

British Literature: Medieval

Aers, David, *Community, Gender, and Individual Identity: English Writing, 1360–1430*, London and New York: Routledge, 1988

Boitani, Piero, *English Medieval Narrative in the Thirteenth and Fourteenth Centuries*, translated by Joan Krakover Hall, Cambridge and New York: Cambridge University Press, 1982

Boitani, Piero, *The Tragic and Sublime in Medieval Literature*, Cambridge and New York: Cambridge University Press, 1989

Carruthers, Mary J., *The Book of Memory: A Study of Memory in Medieval Culture*, Cambridge and New York: Cambridge University Press, 1990

Coleman, Janet, *Medieval Readers and Writers: 1350–1400*, New York: Columbia University Press, 1981

Coleman, Janet, *Ancient and Medieval Memories: Studies in the Reconstruction of the Past*, Cambridge and New York: Cambridge University Press, 1992

Copeland, Rita, *Rhetoric, Hermeneutics, and Translation in the Middle Ages: Academic Traditions and Vernacular Texts*, Cambridge and New York: Cambridge University Press, 1991

Minnis, A.J., *Medieval Theory of Authorship: Scholastic Literary Attitudes in the Later Middle Ages*, London and Philadelphia: Scolar Press, 1984; revised edition, Aldershot, Hampshire: Wildwood, 1988

Morse, Ruth, *Truth and Convention in the Middle Ages: Rhetoric, Representation and Reality*, Cambridge and New York: Cambridge University Press, 1991

Patterson, Lee, *Negotiating the Past: The Historical Understanding of Medieval Literature*, Madison: University of Wisconsin Press, 1987

Stock, Brian, *The Implications of Literacy: Written Language and Models of Interpretation in the Eleventh and Twelfth Centuries*, Princeton, New Jersey: Princeton University Press, 1983

Sturges, Robert S., *Medieval Interpretation: Models of Reading in Literary Narrative, 1100–1500*, Carbondale: Southern Illinois University Press, 1991

The study of medieval literature, like most branches of literary study today, dissolves many of the traditional boundaries between national literatures and academic disciplines. Points of departure for studies which influence how we read medieval literature include medieval ideas about memory, the physical and social contexts of medieval literature, and the Latin scholastic background to medieval literary and academic culture. Many of the most significant books for the study of medieval literature are now works belonging to the tradition of the history of ideas. Cultural histories of literacy and reading practice are particularly important. There are a few useful introductory surveys along more traditional lines, and those will be dealt with first; but the rethinking of the medieval literary tradition requires the reader to range far beyond such works.

The prolific Piero BOITANI has provided two of the introductory surveys described here. His 1982 book describes the literary tradition of England in the thirteenth and fourteenth centuries through chapters on the religious tradition, the comic tradition, romance, dream- and vision-literature, narrative collections, and John Gower and Chaucer. The divisions are not always perfect: *Sir Gawain and the Green Knight* is presented as an exception in the chapter on romance, largely because of its ethical concerns. These concerns suggests that the work would fit nicely into the chapter on "religious" writing, with its focus on didacticism and the *exemplum*. This is nevertheless an accessible survey, which describes a wide range of works.

BOITANI's 1989 work is a collection of nine essays, ranging beyond English literature, and indeed beyond the Middle Ages, to explore the related ideas of tragedy, here an Aristotelian notion, and the sublime, here characterized as a response of "supreme elation" to a text. If these terms are not always as precise or as precisely delineated as one might wish, Boitani's texts, which include the Bible, Virgil, Petrarch, Dante, Chaucer, Shakespeare, William Wordsworth, and Ernest Hemingway, nevertheless offer ample testimony to the sheer range of the book. The focus through Dante produces some of the most stimulating readings and is entirely appropriate when one considers Dante's significance to the medieval literary tradition (as well as to the author's own).

Another accessible survey is COLEMAN's 1981 study of fourteenth-century literature in Anglo-Norman, Latin, and Middle English. While Boitani's work concentrates on describing specific literary works, Coleman's book considers the social background of her literary texts. She offers a useful introduction to the crucial ideas of literacy, education, audience, and the implications of the transition from memory to print, before exploring the literature that recorded and reinforced the role of the expanding middle class. This focus allows her to discuss complaint literature, preaching, translation and theological writing alongside more familiar genres, such as romance. The literature of fourteenth-century England is, she argues, characterized by "the active, reforming character of a socially mobile and increasingly literate fourteenth-century English society that saw itself mirrored in the literature of its own time".

Like Coleman, AERS takes as his point of departure a re-creation of the social and historical circumstances of his texts; his is the historicist position, which holds that any attempt to read a text "must include an attempt to relocate it in the web of discourses and social practices within which it was made and which determined its horizon". The anxieties which Aers exposes in his texts are related to the situation of late medieval England; they also have considerable resonance for (post)modern readers, as Aers focuses on the struggle between individual identity and communally assigned or ratified roles. Aers explores *Piers Plowman*, the writing of Margery Kempe, Chaucer's *Troilus and Criseyde*, and *Sir Gawain and the Green Knight*, in each case in terms of the text's exposure of and responses to prevailing ideologies. In *Piers*, attitudes towards poverty and the poor are the focus; the gendered construction of identity is at issue for both Margery and Troilus; and *Gawain* is read as an attempt to affirm the values of an endangered ruling class. This last chapter fails to engage fully the common critical conviction that *Gawain* is ironic in its portrayal of knightly culture, but there is much in this book to stimulate and enlighten.

PATTERSON, like Coleman and Aers, stresses historical awareness. He opens with a survey of the nineteenth- and twentieth-century reception of medieval literature. He then ranges through such subjects as twentieth-century editors of *Piers Plowman*, fifteenth-century readers of Chaucer, and medieval responses to history and to the historiographical models of classical texts; *The Alliterative Morte Arthure* is one of the texts explored in this section. Each study contextualizes its subject in terms both of its historical circumstance and of the circumstances which produced the criticism of it.

The works examined thus far have as their primary purpose the elucidation of particular literary texts. The next group to be considered is more purely theoretical. These texts are important, indeed central, to the understanding of medieval literature, but it is their role to provide the interpretative frameworks within which criticism of individual texts can function.

STOCK's 1983 study of literacy in the eleventh and twelfth centuries explores how the rise in literacy changed the ways in which people reacted to, and interacted with, both text and experience. Texts, he argues, became "a reference system both for everyday activities and for giving shape to many larger vehicles of explanation", and even when texts were not present, "people often thought or behaved as if they were": orality itself began to function within the universe of text. Stock's first two chapters, "Oral and Written" and "Textual Communities", have the most obvious relevance for literary studies. In the first, Stock deals with questions such as the relative status of written and oral modes of knowledge, and Latin and vernacular modes of expression. The second explores the rise in heresy in the eleventh century through the period's emergent "textual communities", groups which made use of a text, not necessarily present but rather interpreted for the group by an individual, to reform the group's thought and action. Other chapters on "Language", "Texts and Reality", or "Rituals, Symbols, and Interpretations" further contribute to the book's exposition of the revolution brought about by literacy:

> Sets of rules, that is, codes generated from written discourse, were employed not only to produce new behavioural patterns but to restructure existing ones. Literacy thereby intersected the progress of reform. At an individual level, a change was brought about in the means by which one established a personal identity, both with respect to the inner self and to external forces. And the writing down of events, the editing so to speak of experience, gave rise to unprecedented parallels between literature and life: for, as texts informed experience, so men and women began to live texts.

Stock's interest in questions of textuality and authority ranges through literary, social, and religious realms; MINNIS gives the question a more specifically literary focus in his book. He starts from the twelfth-century academic prologue, an introduction to the works of a canonical author, and traces the development of the prologue through the thirteenth century, where interest in the form of the text merged with a new focus on the human author as agent of the text. From these prologues, Minnis recovers a literary-critical vocabulary that addresses both the nature of authorship and the technical aspects of a literary work. This vocabulary was applied to both sacred and profane texts; writers such as Jean de Meun, Chaucer, and Gower thus found room to define themselves through this terminology as *auctores*. Such a definition raised the status of vernacular literature and its producers.

COPELAND and Morse both operate within the critical framework established by works such as Stock's and Minnis's; that is, each attempts to use medieval attitudes towards text and its production to explicate medieval literary artefacts. Copeland's focus is on *interpretatio*, an activity which in the Middle Ages involved both translation and interpretation. Her attention to the interpretative aspects of vernacular translation allows us to see medieval vernacular translation as successor to the Latin commentaries on *auctores* studied by Minnis. She traces the classical, rhetorical roots of medieval ideas on translation, noting that Cicero said that the orator is one who produces ideas and forms of thought rather than rendering his original word for word. The medieval commentary tradition is similarly substitutive, as the second text re-invents and rewrites the first. Chaucer's translation of Boethius is both a response to, and a replacement of, Latin and French canonical traditions. The rhetorical terms *interpretatio*, *conversio*, and *translatio* are shown to be closely connected, so that the interpretation of allegorical texts functions in a way similar to the vernacular translation of Latin text. There are obvious implications for vernacular literature, and Copeland argues that Chaucer's *Legend of Good Women* and Gower's *Confessio Amantis* contain their own exegeses, thus conferring authorial status on the vernacular authors.

MORSE also starts with rhetorical theory, in this case to explore the representation of the past in the Middle Ages. There are chapters on the function of translation, glosses, and commentary, on biography as encomium, and on the reception and manipulation of the Troy story, among others. Clearly there are many points of contact here with the work of Copeland and Minnis, although Morse's work is much more general and less fully articulated than these.

More theoretically satisfying is STURGES's work on reading and interpretation in medieval narrative. His particular focus is on language; he shares Eugene Vance's conviction that language is a central and abiding interest for medieval writers. Sturges traces a movement from a certainty about language in early medieval texts to a profound pessimism about the reliability of language and the possibilities of meaning in later medieval works. Like Morse, Sturges explores truth-claims and the ways in which they are explored and exposed in texts like Guillaume de Machaut's *Voir dit*. This indeterminacy of meaning is then explored through readings of Chaucer and Malory. Deeply informed by the author's knowledge of both medieval and modern theoretical systems, this book is an important one for all readers of medieval literature.

CARRUTHERS and COLEMAN (1992) are both concerned with medieval memory, and their treatment of the subject combines many of the perspectives and sources of information examined thus far. Carruthers stresses the close association between memory and writing in both classical and medieval culture. It is a commonplace to say that the movement from oral to textual culture led to a loss of memory. Carruthers, however, points out that there was a strongly mnemonic aspect to textual culture. Manuscripts were designed with memory in mind, so that the layout of the page becomes a guide to remembering its contents (Malcolm Parkes has suggested that the *ordinatio* of a medieval manuscript functions like punctuation, facilitating a text's use by its reader). Thus the medieval memory becomes what Carruthers calls "a library of texts, and a thoroughly catalogued and indexed one at that". Carruthers also discusses how medieval readers approached their texts, moving from the understanding of the literal sense of the text to its *ruminatio*, the "chewing over" of the text in order to draw out the relevance to oneself. The popular medieval figure of "eating the book" suggests the pervasiveness of this model of knowledge and the close connection between memory and reading.

Coleman uses memory theory to open a discussion of medieval theories of mind and of language, and she too draws on rhetoric, historiography, and medieval ideas about the creation and reception of text. Concern over the basis of knowledge permeates the late-antique and medieval theories of memory she treats. Memory and historiography intersect, whether it be in the deliberately communal memory of monastic culture or in the attempts of twelfth-century historians to engage with the past. Like all the works of intellectual history explored here, Coleman's book provides a necessary theoretical basis for the discussion of medieval writing in all its forms.

SIÂN ECHARD

British Literature: 15th Century

Bennett, H.S., *Oxford History of English Literature: Chaucer and the Fifteenth Century*, Oxford: Clarendon Press, 1947

Blake, Norman, *Caxton and His World*, London: André Deutsch, 1969

Boffey, Julia, and Janet Cowen (eds.), *Chaucer and Fifteenth-Century Poetry*, London: King's College Medieval Studies, 1991

Chambers, E.K., *Oxford History of English Literature: English Literature at the Close of the Middle Ages*, Oxford: Clarendon Press, 1947

Ebin, Lois A., *Illuminator, Makar, Vates: Visions of Poetry in the Fifteenth Century*, Lincoln: University of Nebraska Press, 1988

Green, Richard Firth, *Poets and Princepleasers: Literature and the English Court in the Late Middle Ages*, Toronto and Buffalo, New York: University of Toronto Press, 1980

Kratzmann, Gregory, *Anglo-Scottish Literary Relations 1430–1550*, London and New York: Cambridge University Press, 1980

Scattergood, V.J., *Politics and Poetry in the Fifteenth Century*, London: Blandford Press, 1971; New York: Barnes & Noble, 1972

Fifteenth-century literature has been dramatically recuperated in the late twentieth century. The period between Chaucer and Sir Thomas More is now valued for the distinctiveness of its culture and for the radical changes, such as the introduction of the printing press, which impacted on its literary production.

BENNETT's and CHAMBERS' companion volumes, though outmoded in attitude, set up literary categories which remain largely unassailed: Chaucerian poetry, drama, lyric, narrative poetry, and prose. Bennett establishes Chaucer's death in 1400 as a significant point of departure for his attempt to account for a "lack of great literature" of the period. Chaucerian poetry was emulated, but was "lifeless and empty" with the exception of the distinctive work of Scots Robert Henryson and William Dunbar. The period is more to be valued for laying the foundations of English prose style, chiefly through works of translation. Chambers alerts readers to the difficulties of definitive dating in exploring the characteristic genres of late medieval writing. His critical conspectus broke the new ground made accessible by, for example, the recent indexing and anthologising work of Carleton Brown and R.H. Robbins. His chapter on Malory, as opposed to Caxton's Malory, is an early study of the manuscript discovered in 1934 and predates the appearance of Vinaver's edition.

SCATTERGOOD, evading the problematic of the fifteenth-century canon, gathered verse of variable quality to construct a valuable study of contemporary ideas and opinions on political and social issues. Radical for its time in its historicising agenda, this book alerts its readers to the social situation of poets and to the patronage system. Significant political crises and polarising events are the organising principle where biographical information about the poets gives out. Scattergood's imposed distinctions between verse – of little direct influence – and documentary sources is based on premises that New Historicists might now question.

GREEN considers writing as just one facet of the distinctive aesthetic tastes that developed in the socially complex court structures of fifteenth-century England and lowland Scotland. He meticulously explores the spread of the use of the vernacular, commonly seen as characterising the period, using a wide variety of textual material – e.g., private letters and accounts – to reconstruct a complex social life in which English literary activity flourished. For instance, a group of poet-secretaries is identified, including John Shirley (Chaucer's "publisher") and Richard Holland (author of the *Buke of the Howlat*), and the increased poetic output of aristocrats is associated with the Lancastrian throne's preference for lay, rather than clerical, tutors for their children. The revival and transformation of the poetry of chivalry is reviewed, as well as the "mirror for princes", in the context of a court where poetry in particular had become the business of the leisured amateur rather than the hired professional.

EBIN draws on growing critical consensus about the new reading public, new means of production, and a new status for the vernacular of the fifteenth century to reconstruct from fragmentary evidence the "poetics" of the age. Though still using Chaucer as a benchmark, she moves beyond simple comparison to observe broad humanist trends in poetry, away from the search for divine truth, towards secular ethics and politics which anticipate Edmund Spenser and Milton. The work sets out to observe and articulate shared assumptions about the poetic process rather than individual difference, and therefore ends with John Skelton's perceived refusal to conform stylistically or formally. Ebin's argument may appear to impose synthesis on an arbitrarily designated period of poetic production, but its detailed observations are finely judged.

BOFFEY and COWEN's collection of essays originated in a series of undergraduate lectures. As such, it offers a conspectus of current views applied to individual texts in some detail. Both James Simpson's astute examination of intertextuality evident in Thomas Hoccleve's social and poetic alienation, and Julia Boffey's essay on "Chaucerian Prisoners", real and metaphorical, draw out one of the collection's main foci – the fifteenth-century overlap between lives and texts. Two essays on Henryson reread his major poems against their Chaucerian originals. Other contributions consider the self-conscious reworking of Chaucerian poetic models, poetic theory, favoured themes (bird lore) and exempla (women) from developmental perspectives.

KRATZMANN also deals with the subject of literary influence, in a study focused on fifteenth-century Scottish literary production. English influence on Scots literature begins here with the accident of literary history which brought James I, author of the *Kingis Quair*, as a prisoner to England. Particularly interesting are the comparison of Gavin Douglas's *Palice of Honour* and Chaucer's *Hous of Fame*, and Kratzmann's fresh reading of Henryson's *Testament of Cresseid* in relation to Chaucer's *Troilus and Criseyde*. Influence does not run always one way, however, and the Earl of Surrey's debt to Douglas as translator of the *Aeneid* is explored, as is Sir Thomas Wyatt's debt to Henryson. Wyatt in turn influenced many sixteenth-century Scots lyricists. The book probes the significance of the Anglo-Scottish border country as a significant cultural barrier, acknowledging the existence of an independent Scottish vernacular tradition. The early chapter on influences and perspectives is an excellent exercise in historical and literary orientation.

BLAKE's work offers a rather different perspective on the issues available in the general works about fifteenth-century literature. In considering Caxton, one is forced to see one man as both a product of his age and a significant agent in its change. Organised not as literary criticism but as a biographical narrative about the man who neither invented printing nor wrote "anything of note", Blake's work draws on Caxton's reflective and discursive prologues and epilogues, his commissioned translations and editions, and his speculative publishing ventures to invite further discussion of the dissemination of works of literature and literary taste in the period. All studies discussed here also consider to some extent the relationship between English literature of the period and contemporary developments in Continental Europe: Caxton's retrievable life history reinforces the importance of this aspect of fifteenth-century studies.

PAMELA M. KING

British Literature: Renaissance

Ford, Boris (ed.), *The Pelican Guide to English Literature: The Age of Shakespeare*, Harmondsworth, Middlesex: Penguin, 1955, revised, 3rd edition, 1982

Greenblatt, Stephen J., *Renaissance Self-Fashioning: From More to Shakespeare,* Chicago: University of Chicago Press, 1980

Krontiris, Tina, *Oppositional Voices: Women as Writers and Translators of Literature in the English Renaissance*, New York and London: Routledge, 1992

Lewalski, Barbara, *Writing Women in Jacobean England*, Cambridge, Massachusetts: Harvard University Press, 1993

Lewis, C.S., *Oxford History of English Literature: English Literature in the Sixteenth Century, Excluding Drama*, Oxford: Clarendon Press, 1954

Sinfield, Alan, *Literature in Protestant England 1588–1660*, London: Croom Helm, 1983; Totowa, New Jersey: Barnes & Noble, 1983

Earlier this century criticism argued for the literary text as a unified, organic creation reflecting the views of its author or the dominant philosophical assumptions of its age. What E.M.W. Tillyard termed the "Elizabethan World Picture" – a philosophical conglomerate, supposedly accepted by all Elizabethans, that the universe was a divinely-created organism, characterised by unity, concord, and hierarchy – was widely seen as expressed in the period's literature. Such a reading has been increasingly questioned in the last 20 years, because the influence of critical theory in general, and of New Historicism, cultural materialism, and feminism in particular. Recent enquiry into the Renaissance has tended to find the reverse of Tillyard's views – disorder rather than order, contention and subversion rather than consensus. Lying central to such work are topics such as censorship, subversion, power and authority, the conditions of patronage, and the nature of individual identity. The following discussion considers two traditional approaches (Ford and Lewis) along with a selection of significant studies adopting the newer perspectives.

FORD's collection is probably best now approached with caution. The emphasis of the revised edition remains stringently Leavisite (the Introduction declares its objective "to help validate as firmly as possible a feeling for a living literature and for the values it embodies"). Taking Shakespeare's lifetime as its chronological timeframe, the guide includes 20 essays considering the work and importance of individual dramatists, poets, and prose writers. Emphasis is firmly on the dramatists, about whom the editor avers "this was their age". As the perceived major dramatist, Shakespeare occupies a privileged place – five essays are devoted to his plays alone, illustrating Ford's rather limited conception of what constitutes "Renaissance literature". But the *Guide*'s most serious shortcoming is betrayed in its title – it is generally accepted now, given the relationship of writing and history, that it was certainly not "Shakespeare's age". This supposed concern only with literary values is indicative of the collection as a whole. Even the addition of new essays on Philip Sidney and Edmund Spenser, by J.C.A. Rathmell and W.W. Robson respectively, change the direction only slightly.

LEWIS's lively and magisterial account deals very thoroughly with much of the period's prose and poetry, including some (usually neglected) Scottish texts. Lewis divides the mass of the century's literature into three "ages" – "Late Mediaeval", the "Drab Age", and the "Golden Age" – terms which he ingeniously asserts are not qualitative but descriptive. Literature in the "Late Mediaeval" period is characterised as "dull, feeble and incompetent", that in the "Drab Age" as "monotonous, clumsy and garrulous"; however:

> Then in the last quarter of the century, the unpredictable happens. With startling suddenness we ascend. Fantasy, conceit, paradox, colour, incantation, return. Youth returns. The fine frenzies of ideal love and ideal war are readmitted. Sidney, Spenser, Shakespeare, Hooker display what is almost a new culture: that culture which was to last through most of the seventeenth century and to enrich the very meanings of the words "England" and "Aristocracy".

Lewis's account remains very readable, remarkably provocative and, for modern readers, sometimes diverting in the extreme.

GREENBLATT's book, often regarded as an early manifesto of New Historicism, studies the interplay between culture and selfhood in the lives and works of five Tudor writers. Partly seeing himself as a historian responding to new processes advanced by anthropologists for the understanding of culture, Greenblatt argues against the earlier critical commonplace that saw in the period a growing ability for some individuals to shape their own lives. For Greenblatt, Renaissance texts were not celebrating human autonomy and unfettered subjectivity, nor did they mark out an expression that could somehow break free of the culture in which they were produced. Texts were inevitably part of culture, as were the individuals who wrote them under the determining constraints of state, family, and religion. Provocative studies of Thomas More, William Tyndale, Sir Thomas Wyatt, Spenser, Christopher Marlowe, and Shakespeare's *Othello* eloquently develop this thesis. *En route* Greenblatt explodes the idea of a culture that can be apprehended only in terms of its selected artistic artifacts, problematising ideas about the ways in which culture is constituted and disseminated. Essential reading for any student of the period, the book's crucial importance can be gauged by the fact that many of its theoretical and methodological procedures are now an accepted part of the critical establishment.

SINFIELD argues that a fundamental strand of literature in England between 1550 and 1650 is the working out of the contradictions inherent in Protestant religion. Consequently, he argues, cultural practices, seemingly inconceivable in the early sixteenth century, were increasingly able to find space and expression in later periods, to the extent that they transformed the whole society. Gary Waller has argued elsewhere that such a view omits a consideration of the continuation of Catholic ways of thinking, some of which are adapted in Protestant poetry, or which emerge in Catholic poets. But Sinfield's overall thesis remains persuasive, his writing vibrant, self-conscious, and crystal-clear. As an early document of cultural materialism, the book's importance lies not only in its conclusions about Renaissance culture, but also in its highly suggestive methodology. Chapter 1 usefully elaborates Sinfield's theoretical orientation.

KRONTIRIS's work fuses together many recent developments in cultural-materialist and feminist criticism. Focusing on the writings of Isabella Whitney, Margaret Tyler, Mary Sidney Herbert, Elizabeth Cary, Aemelia Lanyer, and Mary Sidney Wroth, she explores the means by which women writers voiced opposition to dominant gender ideologies. Intelligent and enlightening chapters offer examples of women "employing, consciously or unconsciously, strategies of appropriation, accommodation, and modification" in order to voice their critique. Mary Herbert for example "indirectly counters the stereotype of women as whore and seductress" and Mary Wroth "exposes the binds that women are placed in by tyrannical fathers on the one hand and inconstant lovers on the other". However, Krontiris is careful to insist that such verbal opposition constitutes a highly "circumscribed" resistance. Krontiris is acute on the important gaps that existed in Renaissance society between ideologies oppressive to women and women's actual behaviour, although just occasionally her study tends to conflate "women" and "women writers": the privileged status of the women writers she considers means it is risky to take their textual depictions of their experiences as representative of "female experience" in general.

LEWALSKI's lengthy book is an ideal introduction to the field, as it eloquently reviews what previous literary historians and feminist scholars have uncovered, while also offering many original and often brilliant insights. Meticulously researched chapters discuss the lives and works of nine exceptional women who were "actively involved in cultural production in Jacobean England" and who "rewrote the major discourses of their era in strikingly oppositional terms". Each chapter shows an oppressed woman using her social and verbal skills to allow the "emergence of a female self able to resist existing norms and to struggle for certain . . . rights". The book explores historical links among these women as well as common concerns, although in doing so it somewhat overlooks the considerable social and religious differences that divide them. And again, as in Krontiris's book, it seems problematic to define possibility on the basis of a historical record inherited through literate persons and élite institutions.

RAMONA WRAY

Tudor and Elizabethan

Beilin, Elaine V., *Redeeming Eve: Women Writers of the English Renaissance*, Princeton, New Jersey: Princeton University Press, 1987
Crewe, Jonathan V., *Trials of Authorship: Anterior Forms and Poetic Reconstruction from Wyatt to Shakespeare*, Berkeley: University of California Press, 1990
Kinney, Arthur F., *Humanist Poetics: Thought, Rhetoric and Fiction in Sixteenth-Century England*, Amherst: University of Massachusetts Press, 1986
Lewis, C.S., *Oxford History of English Literature: English Literature in the Sixteenth Century, Excluding Drama*, Oxford: Clarendon Press, 1954
Norbrook, David, *Poetry and Politics in the English Renaissance*, London and Boston: Routledge & Kegan Paul, 1984
Peterson, Douglas D., *The English Lyric from Wyatt to Donne: A History of the Plain and Eloquent Styles*, Princeton, New Jersey: Princeton University Press, 1967; 2nd edition, East Lansing: Colleagues Press, 1990
Waller, Gary F., *English Poetry of the Sixteenth Century*, London: Longman, 1986, revised 1993

C.S. LEWIS's literary history, sometimes described as "magisterial", remains, despite its age, the general study that others must be measured against. Scholarship has moved on (we know more about what is going on in John Skelton or Thomas Nashe, for example), as has critical sophistication and taste (he's disappointing on Sir Thomas Wyatt and knows no women writers), but there is impressive breadth (including the obscure and unfashionable, religious prose, controversy, poetic theory) and remarkable confidence of taste, with a valuable emphasis on the fundamental importance of literary quality: "we are to consider what men wrote, and our judgement on it must, of course, attempt to be literary, not theological" – nor, he might have added now, derived from political, historical, or gender concerns: such issues figure little here. Most famous, or notorious, is his division of sixteenth-century writing into the "Drab" and "Golden" – not, he insists, evaluative, but descriptive, terms, the former characteristically plain in statement, rhythm, and morality, the latter "innocent or ingenious, idealistic, mellifluous"; the scheme is ahistorical and insufficiently developed, but has given useful critical leverage. The volume's breadth, vigour, and independence make it, despite its deficiencies of theory, almost more valuable today than when it first appeared.

PETERSON's influential study of the lyric redefines "Drab" and "Golden" as the "native plain" and "eloquent". The former tradition, of direct statement, dominant rhythm, and moralist suspicion of courtly values, is traced from the late Middle Ages through Wyatt and George Gascoigne to Sir Walter Ralegh and Fulke Greville. The latter, associated with courtly values, is dominant later in the century; Sir Philip Sidney, Edmund Spenser, and Shakespeare are associated with this, though Peterson has to acknowledge their having qualities of the other tradition; John Donne and Ben Jonson are seen as anti-courtly (which doesn't seem wholly satisfactory). Despite usefully demonstrating the strengths of some undervalued writers, stylistic continuities and developments throughout the century, the relation of poetic practice to rhetorical theory, and the links between style and (political) values, Peterson's original (1967) scheme seems somewhat cramping; the second edition benefits from introducing a third category, the "classical plain style", where metre is subordinated to syntactical requirements and speech effects, as exemplified by Donne and then Jonson.

Rejecting "the narrowingly literary approach", NORBROOK seeks "to politicise aesthetics" (from a Left-sympathetic standpoint), showing little interest in literary techniques or qualities, concentrating on related selected texts, from Sir Thomas More, to Milton's 1645 volume, to contemporary political issues, and emphasising the values and importance of radical Protestantism. Thus, he largely ignores the ironies of More's *Utopia* to concentrate on political issues and humanist élitism; he is happier with largely forgotten mid-century radicals such as Luke Shepherd and Robert Crowley (where literary criticism is ignored in favour of their social criticism). He is very selective with Spenser, concentrating on the political allegories in *The Shepheardes Calender*, and Books 1, 5, and 6 of *The Faerie Queene* (Protestant apocalyptic, policies in Ireland and the Netherlands, and doubts about courtly values, respectively). Likewise, the political and Protestant in Sidney's *Arcadia* are emphasised (and the courtly disapproved of), and Fulke Greville regarded more favourably as a radical critic of the court, with republican sympathies. The study is generally better on political analysis than on the literary, especially of the more complex, sophisticated texts.

KINNEY's book is a weighty and instructive study, rather sound-textbook-scholarly in effect, of sixteenth-century humanist prose, relating it usefully to (often classical) sources and models, and Continental analogues. The first section proposes an early humanist "poetics of wordplay", illustrated by Erasmus, *Utopia*, and Gascoigne's *Master F.J.*, emphasising wit and irony. Then comes a "poetics of eloquence", with Castiglione preceding John Lyly's courtly *Euphues*, Robert Greene's popular romances, and Sidney's *Arcadia*, stressing moral exploration and "the explored inconsistencies and paradoxes at the heart of humanist philosophy". Finally comes "the twilight of humanism", related partly to economic and political anxieties, partly to ontological doubts, illustrated by *Lazarillo de Tormes*, Nashe, and Thomas Lodge, with unpleasant (if entertaining) tales of rogue and beggar. A final, uneasy chapter considers the unsettling effect of post-humanist scepticism both then, as in Montaigne and Francis Bacon, and now, in recent critical theory.

Probably the most useful general introduction to English women's writing of the time, BEILIN's volume covers the period 1521 to 1623. The first section establishes the cultural setting (particularly assumptions regarding women's nature and place) and examines the tradition of pious writing, including Margaret More Roper and Anne Askew, before discussing the early Elizabethans such as Isabella Whitney, though Queen Elizabeth's poems are, curiously, ignored. The next section discusses better-known writers, notably Mary Sidney Herbert, Elizabeth Cary, Aemilia Lanyer, and Mary Sidney Wroth, and the third section reviews early seventeenth-century non-literary writing. Achievements seem rather overrated, and analysis of literary qualities is not the prime concern (whether the limitations of some mid-century writers or the skills of Herbert or Wroth); a somewhat oppressive coherence is given by a theme of women writers virtuously presenting the figure of the virtuous woman (hence "redeeming Eve").

Conversely, CREWE provides a subtle, provocative, and entertaining post-Freudian account of the construction and anxieties of masculine authorship in the period. Wyatt's "crafty" "doubleness" creates and subverts form and identity; the Earl of Surrey's poetics are "suicidal" (with a homosexual undertone); William Roper's "Life of More" is a destructive hagiography driven by Oedipal and incestuous energies, while George Cavendish's *Life* of Cardinal Wolsey creatively deconstructs an oppressive father-figure. Subtle readings of Gascoigne expose a hopeless quest for masculine subject-hood in "the specifically Elizabethan culture-and-gender context", and even Shakespeare gets it in the end when his Lucrece is revealed as fronting for Shakespeare himself. This is not a "sound" orthodox volume – but stimulating.

The second, revised edition of WALLER is as up-to-date as possible, constituting a lively, readable *bricolage* of current trends, skilfully synthesising New-Historicist, cultural-materialist, feminist, and psychological theories. Althusserian theory underlies references to "cultural apparatuses", as poetry is viewed as the product, *via* "shattered, decentred subjects" (i.e., individual writers) of dominant ideologies, though, being characterized by "fascinating fissures, contradictions, and repressions", most poetry typically questions and subverts most orthodoxies. Coverage is reasonable if uneven, with a fuller account of "Petrarchism as perversion" than of religious concerns (generally *terra incognita* to the modern student). The emphasis is on court literature, with particular attention paid to the Sidneys, including Mary Sidney Wroth, whose 1621 sonnet-sequence dominates the chapter "Women's Poetry, Gay Voices". The early Donne shares a chapter with Shakespeare, whose sonnets' power "rests on the seemingly fragile basis not of Shakespeare's but their readers' shifting and unpredictable experiences". The account of *The Faerie Queene* emphasises the contradictions of a poem "to which readers can return endlessly because it is an encyclopedia of the ways ideology and textuality interact" – though it is hard to imagine anyone who actually enjoys reading it for such reasons. The modern student, for whom the book is intended, should find it – and its extensive bibliographies – useful.

R.E. PRITCHARD

British Literature: Restoration

Keeble, N. H., *The Literary Culture of Nonconformity in Later Seventeenth-Century England*, Leicester: Leicester University Press, 1987
Love, Harold (ed.), *Restoration Literature: Critical Approaches*, London: Methuen, 1972
Malekin, Peter, *Liberty and Love: English Literature and Society 1640–88*, London: Hutchinson, 1981
Miner, Earl, *The Restoration Mode from Milton to Dryden*, Princeton, New Jersey: Princeton University Press, 1974
Sutherland, James, *Oxford History of English Literature: Restoration Literature 1660–1700: Dryden, Bunyan, and Pepys*, Oxford: Clarendon Press, 1969

The Restoration period in English literature – usually taken to mean the years 1660–1700 – has, in the twentieth century, often been thought something of an oddity. Its writing was clearly moving away from the genres, styles, and preoccupations of the Renaissance (though Milton's *Paradise Lost* was first published in 1667), yet it was not altogether consonant with those of the eighteenth century. Among critics, prejudices about the supposed "licentiousness" of the age and Whiggish interpretations of its history have become entrenched, and have been obstacles to the appreciation of its poetry and drama. Nevertheless, it has usually been recognized that the period is historically crucial, for example in the development of the heroic couplet, the beginnings of "Augustanism", and – as has been shown more recently – the rise of the woman writer. The energy, diversity, and innovativeness of its literature are now beginning to receive fairer recognition.

SUTHERLAND's volume appeared in the "Oxford History of English Literature" series, and so gives a narrative overview of the period, organized generically and thematically, as well as providing reference material. The three longest chapters, two on the drama and one on religious literature, are meant to indicate "where the main emphasis of this curiously divided period really fell"; it does not follow that modern criticism should also place its emphases here. The volume now looks dated in omitting, for example, several women writers whose work has come to the fore subsequently, and in underrating other writers, such as Andrew Marvell. But it still has something to offer in surveys of background material (science, philosophy, economics) and of genres such as biography and travel writing. The author-bibliographies are out of date for criticism, but still useful for primary works, especially as regards minor writers.

LOVE's essay-collection ranges widely over the period's drama and poetry, and also includes a contribution on the prose writers Gilbert Burnet and George Halifax, but no general essays are provided. Instead, the contributions mostly address individual authors, especially poets – Milton, Samuel Butler, Thomas Traherne, the Earl of Rochester, John Oldham, and John Dryden. The first essay, "Restoration Comedy and the Provok'd Critic", reviews and takes issue with the hostile critical tradition on this literature; one further contribution engages with Restoration comedy, and one with tragedy, especially Dryden's. Harold F. Brooks's essay on Oldham is a useful short introduction to that poet. The best of the Dryden contributions is William J. Cameron's judicious account of his political stance, "John Dryden's Jacobitism".

MINER deals almost exclusively with poetry. The two guiding spirits are Milton and Dryden, both seen as public poets, whose "selves are premised on the historical existence and public validity of the world outside their own consciousness". Their way of regarding the self and the world is distinctive to what Miner calls the "Restoration mode", and can also be found in work by, among others, Butler, Abraham Cowley, and Rochester. Miner's panoramic survey of all this poetry is individualistic, occasionally even eccentric, but full of ideas, some of which have subsequently taken hold. Again, there is a mass of information here, and Miner draws together the works he discusses in interesting ways; but the discussion can tend to superficiality, so vaguely defined is its scope.

MALEKIN aims his treatment of life and literature in the Interregnum and Restoration at the general reader rather than the specialist. Part One, on "Liberty", discusses Marvell, Milton, Restoration satirists, and others in the light of political thought up to the time of John Locke. Part Two treats the historical role of women in conjunction with love poetry, Milton again, and Restoration comedy. Malekin's setting of the literary texts he discusses into social or intellectual contexts is welcome, especially with works such as Restoration comedies, which rely on the reader's awareness of contemporary circumstances. This is an enthusiastic and readable attempt to link together some of the literature with some of the history of the era.

KEEBLE's volume deals primarily with the Restoration period, but, like its subject, has its roots in the Interregnum. It deserves inclusion here not as a standard treatment of Restoration literature, but as a cogent argument for a different set of emphases within it. As Keeble observes, the "Caroline rule" dictates that we see wit and licentiousness as the period's hallmarks, and the Nonconformists Milton and Bunyan appear exceptions. If, however:

> . . . we shift the rule, Milton and Bunyan appear as what they truly were, the surpassing representatives of a large and neglected body of writing which made a distinctive contribution to our literary history precisely because it was the product of a movement accommodating itself to the experience of defeat, repression and ridicule.

Thus, Keeble's volume not only contextualizes the masterpieces of this literature – Milton's later poems and Bunyan's fictional works – but also describes the neglected writing (most often autobiographical prose) of others, such as George Fox, Lucy Hutchinson, and William Penn. Its thematic organization makes the book hard to use, except by reading as a whole, and in general it will appeal most strongly to specialized students; but it is one of few recent attempts to question radically the established assumptions about the literary history of this period.

STUART GILLESPIE

British Literature: 18th Century

Butt, John, completed by Geoffrey Carnall, *The Oxford History of English Literature: The Mid-Eighteenth Century*, Oxford: Clarendon Press, 1979; New York: Oxford University Press, 1979

Damrosch, Leopold, Jr. (ed.), *Modern Essays on Eighteenth-Century Literature*, New York and Oxford: Oxford University Press, 1988

Dobrée, Bonamy, *The Oxford History of English Literature: English Literature in the Early Eighteenth Century*, Oxford: Clarendon Press, 1959; New York: Oxford University Press, 1959

Doody, Margaret Anne, *The Daring Muse: Augustan Poetry Reconsidered*, Cambridge and New York: Cambridge University Press, 1985

Nussbaum, Felicity, and Laura Brown (eds.), *The New Eighteenth Century: Theory, Politics, English Literature*, London and New York: Methuen, 1987

Redford, Bruce, *The Converse of the Pen: Acts of Intimacy in the Eighteenth-Century Familiar Letter*, Chicago: University of Chicago Press, 1986

Sambrook, James, *The Eighteenth Century: The Intellectual and Cultural Context of English Literature, 1700–1789*, London: Longman, 1986, 2nd edition, 1993

Sherburn, George, and Donald Bond, "The Restoration and Eighteenth Century", in *A Literary History of England*, edited by Albert C. Baugh, London: Routledge & Kegan Paul, 1948; revised edition, New York: Appleton-Century-Crofts, 1967

Spencer, Jane, *The Rise of the Woman Novelist: From Aphra Behn to Jane Austen*, Oxford and New York: Blackwell, 1986

Spender, Dale, *Mothers of the Novel: 100 Good Women Writers Before Jane Austen*, London: Pandora, 1986; New York: Routledge & Kegan Paul, 1986

Todd, Janet, *The Sign of Angellica: Women, Writing and Fiction, 1660–1800*, London: Virago, 1989; New York: Columbia University Press, 1989

Watt, Ian, *The Rise of the Novel: Studies in Defoe, Richardson and Fielding*, London: Chatto & Windus, 1957; Berkeley: University of California Press, 1957

Yolton, John W., Roy Porter, Pat Rogers, and Barbara Maria Stafford (eds.), *The Blackwell Companion to the Enlightenment*, Oxford: Blackwell, 1991

At one time literary historians portrayed the eighteenth century in English literature as the Age of Reason, of neoclassicism, of the essay, and of poetry as statement. Those comfortable labels no longer apply. Criticism since the 1950s has increasingly portrayed eighteenth-century literature in more paradoxical terms. For one thing, the eighteenth century is now recognized as the period that gave rise to feminism, a turbulent age of change and multiplicity in which issues of gender and class come to be prominent, a period of great literary diversity, which generated two significant new kinds of prose writing in the novel and in journalism. The impact of science and empirical philosophy on eighteenth-century thought made the literature of the period sceptical and realistic; satire and the rise of the novel are evidence of that literature's critical fascination with society. London and Edinburgh became mature cities during the eighteenth century, and produced a culture that was remarkable for its urban character, one that reflected the psychological and sociological advantages and disadvantages of modern life.

SHERBURN and BOND are still solid and trustworthy guides to the issues and achievements of eighteenth-century British literature. As a traditional source, their work describes the classicism of the era, beginning with the rise of literary criticism as a science and emphasizing the role of classical aesthetics in the development of the heroic and Augustan styles in drama and poetry. Sherburn and Bond are at their best discussing the canonical figures of the age, and assume that the eighteenth century was a period of rationalism and enlightened optimism. Their 400-page study is strong on definition and emphasizes analytical prose, especially the essay in its various forms. Well indexed and clearly subdivided into useful topics of discussion, this is a good source to turn to for an introduction to the eighteenth century.

DOBRÉE is in the same tradition as Sherburn and Bond, and may be even more conventional. His study is strong on drama and poetry, weaker on the discussion of the novel and of the philosophical issues that shored up, but eventually eroded, Augustan literature. The volume can be faulted for its exclusive focus on individual authors: by structuring the survey around the "greats" (Daniel Defoe, Jonathan Swift, Joseph Addison, Alexander Pope, James Thomson, and Samuel Johnson) Dobrée neglects, and even ignores, the so-called minor figures, especially women writers. The study is also light in its discussion of genre, particularly the impact of journalism. Still, in its presentation of classical Augustan ideals, Dobrée's book is accessible and consistently representative of the standard notion that the early eighteenth-century was a period of masculine and assured literary achievement. It is not a reflective or a critical survey.

BUTT and CARNALL's work in the same series, the "Oxford History of English Literature", is more modern in its critical sensibility. Their study is concerned with genre rather than author and they effectively explore the many new kinds of writing that matured in the mid-eighteenth century – travel writing, memoirs, biographies, histories, and the novel. Again, they are not strong on journalism, but do discuss Scottish writing in some detail, a feature lacking in some surveys. While women's writing is much more in evidence here than in Dobrée, it is still treated marginally, and one must be warned that Butt and Carnall do not represent current views on who should be included in the canon of eighteenth-century British writing. As in Dobrée's survey, this volume contains a useful chronology of publication dates and historical events, and remains an essential, if incomplete, reference guide to the period.

YOLTON's survey explores the context of ideas that shaped eighteenth-century literature. While his study includes all of European literature in its examination of critical issues and noteworthy figures of the Enlightenment, it is widely and stimulatingly concerned with the place of British writing. It is crucial that English literature of the period be understood in its European contexts, and Yolton is the single best source for an appreciation of this aspect. The work comprises a multitude of concise essays, ranging in length from a few hundred to several thousand words, contributed by international scholars on topics ranging from the Encyclopaedia movement to women's authorship, from new ideas in medicine and philosophy to discussions of the political and religious controversies of the day. Succinct biographies of several hundred authors and other prominent figures are included, and each essay concludes with a brief and informed bibliography. The index is extensively cross-referenced. This is a survey that is cognizant of recent critical trends and approaches in eighteenth-century scholarship. It is the best single-volume guide to the ethos of eighteenth-century literature.

SAMBROOK gives the reader a survey that concentrates on the intellectual milieu of the eighteenth century. His book divides into long chapters on science, religion, philosophy, politics and history, aesthetics, and the visual arts. He effectively dismisses clichés about the period, especially the label "Age of Reason", and in a quite original last chapter explores the influences and sources, the ideals and obsessions of the eighteenth century – the Roman, the Greek, the Gothic, the Oriental, and the Savage. Sambrook provides an excellent chronology and a series of precise thematically selected bibliographies. This is both a fine compliment to, and antidote for, the more traditional work of Sherburn and Dobrée.

WATT's book remains the most influential study of the origins of the novel in the eighteenth century. Its thesis brings together social change, especially the rise of the middle class and an expanding female readership, with the genesis of realism as the sources for the novel's development and success in the eighteenth century. Watt refers in passing to women writers but concentrates his discussion on Defoe, Samuel Richardson, and Henry Fielding, a strategy which severely limits the study. Nonetheless, this remains the place from which to begin any survey of eighteenth-century fiction, particularly so for its examination of the period's reading public. Watt details, without jargon, the essentially political nature of the novel in both its form and content by illustrating that the novel attracted its readership through a "serious concern with the daily lives of ordinary people" and with its insistence that "society must value every individual".

Both Spender and Spencer continue Watt's sociological and political analysis but extend it to embrace the vast area of women's writing in fiction. SPENDER's is a bifocal study, concerned first with literary origins and establishing the woman novelist's seventeenth-century pedigree and then moving on to an examination of the politics of women's writing in the eighteenth century. Most useful is her chronology of 100 women novelists before Jane Austen, a list that contains the publication dates of all of their works. Spender successfully argues for the political authority of women's writing. Her work is essential to all subsequent discussions of the novel. SPENCER's is, however, a better-written survey, more thoroughly researched and more thoughtful. She attributes much of the strength of women's writing to self-portraiture, especially in the examples of Aphra Behn, Mary Manley, and Jane Barker. Spencer treats in a balanced way the lesser-known writers, like Eliza Haywood, along with the obvious successes of the era, Frances Burney and Jane Austen. Through an exhaustive appreciation of the social and historic circumstances that affected the rise of the woman novelist, Spencer demonstrates how women writers moved from comic realism in Behn, Haywood, and Burney, to the gothic sensibility of Charlotte Lennox, Maria Edgeworth, and Ann Radcliffe, finding in romance a language to "express the fears and anger that could not openly be acknowledged".

TODD's is perhaps the most useful survey of eighteenth-century women's writing. Her focus is primarily on fictional prose, but forays into the drama and poetry expand her field of study at appropriate points. The role of sincerity and the radical movements of the late century are treated with particular care, and Todd highlights work by Frances Sheridan and Frances Brooke that is seldom dealt with in much detail in other surveys of the period, despite the significance of both writers. The analyses of Aphra Behn and of female sexuality are especially useful.

There are a great many surveys of eighteenth-century poetry but the most incisive and critically innovative is DOODY's.

While concentrating on Augustan poets, this study takes a thematic approach that is appropriately sensitive to the political origins and implications of the persona of the poet in the eighteenth century. That source of the Augustan spirit, Doody argues, accounts for what she calls the "excitement of the works and their strangeness". The poetic voice of the eighteenth century is characterized "by stylistic versatility, generic self-consciousness and distrust of set forms"; it is for Doody a poetry charged by the "energies of transformation." This is a serious scholarly revaluation, which challenges the conventional assumptions of earlier surveys.

REDFORD examines the eighteenth-century familiar letter, arguing that this genre was the particular means by which concepts of the self, both private and public, were constructed and explored in the period. For Redford, correspondence was peculiarly adapted by the best writers at the time to make of the epistolary form a speech act of a conversational kind. Letter-writing is certainly a distinctive activity of the eighteenth century and Redford's is both the most speculative and the most scholarly of the critical works that examine this genre. Redford discusses in detail Lady Mary Wortley Montagu, William Cowper, Thomas Gray, Horace Walpole, James Boswell, Samuel Johnson, and Hester Thrale, finding in the best letter-writers a tone of intimacy that is a "moral parody" of the essay form.

DAMROSCH has brought together essays by the leading scholars of eighteenth-century studies from three successive generations. He offers Irvin Ehrenpreis on Pope, William Wimsatt on Swift, Ian Donaldson on John Gay, Richard Lanham on Laurence Sterne, Lawrence Lipking on Johnson, and Michael McKeon on the novel, among other distinguished essays. Damrosch provides a comprehensive range of critical and theoretical approaches, including revisionary points of view, with, however, the balance tipped toward scholarship and tradition. The essays deal with individual authors and works as well as presenting more general thematic analyses. There is only a limited discussion of women's writing: just one of the 20 essays deals exclusively with a woman author.

NUSSBAUM and BROWN have concentrated on radical and innovative revaluations in their suvey. Contributors to this volume take often extreme and always challenging positions, espousing postmodern values in their re-reading of the century. The authors and texts examined here are often not canonical, and there is considerable space given to feminist and Marxist interpretations. Nussbaum intends this collection as a challenge to convention, which "calls attention to the resistance to contemporary theory . . . [in] the study of 18th-century English literature". Of special note are the essays by John Richetti on Fielding and Tobias Smollett, Donna Landry on Mary Collier, Nussbaum on life-writing, and Terry Castle on Radcliffe. (Michael McKeon is the only critic to appear in both Nussbaum's and Damrosch's collections.) Together these two anthologies of recent criticism provide a comprehensive survey of critical approaches and theoretical positions on eighteenth-century British literature.

STEPHEN W. BROWN

British Literature: 19th Century

Blake, Kathleen, *Love and the Woman Question in Victorian Literature: The Art of Self-Postponement*, Brighton, Sussex: Harvester Press, 1983; Totowa, New Jersey: Barnes & Noble, 1983

Buckley, Jerome H., *The Victorian Temper: A Study in Literary Culture*, Cambridge, Massachusetts: Harvard University Press, 1951; London: Allen & Unwin, 1952

Chew, Samuel C., and Richard D. Altick, "The Nineteenth Century and After", in *A Literary History of England*, edited by Albert C. Baugh, London: Routledge & Kegan Paul, 1948; revised edition, New York: Appleton-Century-Crofts, 1967

Daiches, David, *A Critical History of English Literature: Volume 2*, London: Secker & Warburg, 1960; New York: Ronald Press, 1960

Ford, Boris (ed.), *The New Pelican Guide to English Literature: From Blake to Byron* (revised edition), Harmondsworth, Middlesex, and New York: Penguin, 1982

Ford, Boris (ed.), *The New Pelican Guide to English Literature: From Dickens to Hardy* (revised edition), Harmondsworth, Middlesex, and New York: Penguin, 1983

Fraser, Hilary, *Beauty and Belief: Aesthetics and Religion in Victorian Literature*, Cambridge and New York: Cambridge University Press, 1986

Gilbert, Sandra M., and Susan Gubar, *The Madwoman in the Attic: The Woman Writer and the Nineteenth-Century Literary Imagination*, New Haven, Connecticut, and London: Yale University Press, 1979

Gurney, Stephen, *British Poetry of the Nineteenth Century*, New York: Twayne, 1993

Levine, George, *The Realistic Imagination: English Fiction from "Frankenstein" to "Lady Chatterley"*, Chicago: University of Chicago Press, 1981

Miyoshi, Masao, *The Divided Self: A Perspective on the Literature of the Victorians*, New York: New York University Press, 1969

Saintsbury, George, *A History of Nineteenth Century Literature 1780–1895*, London: Macmillan, 1896

Willey, Basil, *Nineteenth Century Studies: Coleridge to Matthew Arnold*, London: Chatto & Windus, 1949; New York: Columbia University Press, 1949, reprinted 1977

Willey, Basil, *More Nineteenth Century Studies: A Group of Honest Doubters*, London: Chatto & Windus, 1956; New York: Columbia University Press, 1956, reprinted 1977

Williams, Merryn, *Women in the English Novel 1800–1900*, London: Macmillan, 1984; New York: St Martin's Press, 1984

One of the earliest comprehensive assessments of nineteenth-century literature, SAINTSBURY's volume is of special interest to the literary historian, as much for what is left out as for what is contained. A recognized giant among his contemporaries, Saintsbury was well read and sensitive to literary trends, but even he admits in his Preface that it is sometimes difficult to offer an objective analysis of the works of living writers.

Nevertheless, his account is an attempt to fix the relative value of authors from the late eighteenth century – the writers now canonized as the Romantics – and those of Saintsbury's own age. As one might expect, his judgments have not all been upheld by his successors; for example, he pays slight attention to William Blake, considerably more to Robert Southey. Remarkably, however, he is more often correct in designating those writers of the century who would stand the test of time. Additionally, he writes with clarity and is not afraid to make judgments – qualities not always apparent in the works of later critics.

CHEW and ALTICK's highly detailed account of the literature produced in England during the nineteenth century is one of those rare compendiums whose value as a reference tool continues long after many of its critical pronouncements have become outdated. Nearly two dozen writers are the subjects of separate chapters, including such figures as William Wordsworth, Samuel Taylor Coleridge, Alfred Lord Tennyson, William Morris, and Thomas Hardy. Additionally, the authors include accounts of various literary movements (e.g., Aestheticism and Decadence) and important extra-literary topics (the French Revolution, the religious revival in England), summary chapters on the various genres, and background information on each of the major periods into which the literary history of the century may be divided. Of special significance is the attention given to minor figures; hundreds are mentioned, and brief summary judgments of their work are provided. The text is well documented, making the volume most useful in identifying sources of scholarship published before 1965.

In a similar vein, DAICHES' illuminating and insightful study goes beyond analysis of major works to give a sense of the vitality of literary activity in the century. Part of a larger survey, Daiches' work is most helpful to readers wishing to see how earlier works influenced the writings of the Romantics and Victorians, and how nineteenth-century poets, novelists, dramatists, and non-fiction writers shaped the productions of their successors. Daiches is particularly good at offering succinct analyses of individual works while maintaining a focus on the general contributions of writers to the national tradition. Like most critics writing at mid-century, he pays more attention to male writers and to those whose works have traditionally been judged important. He includes an informative chapter on Scottish literature, and one on drama, which attempts to make sense of a genre that attracted few distinguished practitioners in the century.

WILLEY assembles a collection of essays in two highly useful volumes, which give readers a sound understanding of the century and its literature. Concentrating on the ideas and issues that occupied writers of every genre, he begins with an analysis of Coleridge's aesthetic and religious theories. He follows with insightful commentary on the works of John Henry Newman, Thomas Carlyle, J.S. Mill, George Eliot, and Matthew Arnold. In the second volume, Willey examines the values held by the Victorians as they are revealed in the writings of key figures who fell away from traditional Christian religious faith in the face of scientific discoveries. Of particular value is his discussion of Tennyson's *In Memoriam*, the poem that has come to serve as a paradigm of the Victorians' struggle between faith and doubt.

For over 30 years FORD has been working to provide readers with a single source for examining the accomplishments and concerns of British writers in a multi-volume series which combines excellent analysis by dozens of scholars with careful selection of topics and authors. First issued in the 1960s, Ford's revised series includes two volumes devoted to criticism of the Romantics (*From Blake to Byron*) and the Victorians (*From Dickens to Hardy*). The format of the series allows contributors to be detailed in their assessments of individual authors and works, and the expansion of the revised edition has afforded the editor an opportunity to include commentary on figures not covered adequately, or at all, in the original publications.

BUCKLEY is among the first scholars to attempt a systematic analysis of the Victorians aimed at restoring a balance to the skewed, negative (and sometimes vituperative) assessments that dominated criticism for near a half-century after Queen Victoria's death. Though he claims his is not a rigorous intellectual or social history, his focus nevertheless is on exploring some common traits which bound disparate Victorian writers. Arguing that "Victorian taste" is "in large measure, necessarily, the product of a diverse culture, of attitudes social and moral which helped shape its values", he charts for readers "the impulses that prompted and the forces that shaped a manifold creative expression". His introductory chapter provides a succinct definition (and defense) of "Victorianism" – something necessary at the time Buckley's study was originally published. His analyses of individual authors remain useful as a critical introduction to the thought and writing of diverse figures such as Tennyson, Charles Kingsley, John Ruskin, and Oscar Wilde.

Despite his title, MIYOSHI surveys literature of the entire nineteenth century to uncover a theme familiar to many critics of Victorians. Concerned with "the ways in which Victorian men of letters experienced the self-division endemic of the times and gave expression to it in their writing", he selects from the thousands of texts written during the period a generous handful, which illustrates formally, ideologically, or biographically an author's concern over "the crisis of self division". Beginning with an analysis of the gothic and Romanticism, Miyoshi discusses the pervasiveness of the romance tradition, which ran parallel with the more dominant strain of realism during the century. Dividing his study neatly into periods of approximately 20 years, he remarks on the works of the major Victorians (Tennyson and Arnold receive special attention) and their inheritors, and comments on writers of the *fin de siècle*, who saw in "the High Victorian commitment little else than self-delusion and hypocrisy". Steeped in the vocabulary of Freudian psychology and formalist criticism, Miyoshi rewards readers with important psychological insights into the lives and works of those he studies, and reveals, in the process, a sound understanding of one of the dominant problems of the age.

Although the principal focus of their important work on feminist criticism is on a few significant women writers, GILBERT and GUBAR's wide-ranging assessment of the background that led to the production of the works they examine provides a distinct way of viewing all literature written during the century. Struck by the similarities that unite women writers, regardless of the genres in which they worked, the authors explain with considerable erudition the "common, female impulses to struggle free from the social and literary confinement" imposed on women by a patriarchal society, "through strategic redefinition of self, art, and society". Not only are their commentaries on individual works provocative and enlightening, the authors' theoretical introductory chapter, "Towards a Feminist Poetics", provides a revisionist view of the entire art of criticism and a methodology for reading the work of all women authors of the nineteenth and other centuries.

The feminist approach to nineteenth-century literature is also well represented in BLAKE's examination of a theme common to both female and male writers of the period. Blake is interested in exploring "the woman question" by concentrating on the phenomenon she calls "self-postponement", a form of self-sacrifice which often led women to defer satisfying their desires, especially those involving love, in favor of what they and others would consider some more noble goal. Blake examines works in which such self-sacrifice is looked upon favorably, and those that protest against the practice. Relying heavily on feminist critical theory, but not bound slavishly to its radical political agenda, Blake presents sensible, detailed readings of the works of major women writers such as Christina Rossetti, Charlotte Brontë, and George Eliot; men such as Hardy and George Gissing; and less-studied authors, such as Olive Schreiner and a number of the "too much neglected women poets". Her study indicates what may be done by bringing to bear on an examination of nineteenth-century literature a sound understanding of feminist thinking.

Thematic studies of the literature of any period are often useful for developing an understanding of the bonds that joined authors with their contemporaries and set them apart from their predecessors. FRASER's examination of the Victorians' "all-pervasive, deliberate, and rather self-conscious concern with the relationship between religious and aesthetic experience" is just such a work. Taking her cue from T.S. Eliot's remark that the dissociated sensibility of Victorian writers is often masked by "chimerical attempts to effect synthesis" between art, politics, philosophy, and religion, Fraser traces what she calls the "Romantic legacy" of Hegel, Wordsworth, and Coleridge through the works of essayists, critics, and poets. Though focusing on figures notably involved with religious issues (the Oxford Tractarians, Gerard Manley Hopkins, Arnold, Ruskin), she includes observations on a number of others who transformed art into "a legitimate medium of aesthetic instruction" in which the work became a means of promoting morality – or, eventually, a substitute for it. Fraser's study makes clear the reasons for nineteenth-century writers' fascination with – some might say fixation on – religious topics.

In a similar topical study, WILLIAMS traces attitudes toward women as they are exhibited in novels written by both men and women during the century. She focuses on the many frustrations women felt as second-class citizens in English society, despite the advances toward emancipation that occurred during Victoria's reign. In an attempt to be widely inclusive, she provides brief assessments of a number of women writers traditionally designated "minor", while devoting considerably more attention to figures such as Jane Austen, George Eliot, and Schreiner. Her sensitive analyses are clearly stated and convincing. In light of this, it is not surprising that many will find her conclusion about the fate of fictional women demoralizing: Williams claims that the heroines of late-century novels resemble more closely Sir Walter Scott's "hysteric" Bride of Lammermoor than the sensible heroines of Austen's work.

The nineteenth century saw the eventual rise and dominance of realistic fiction. LEVINE examines this phenomenon in an important and well-researched study, which challenges the assertions of poststructuralist critics who hold that "realism" is simply another fiction, a set of conventions prevalent in the nineteenth century but no longer accepted by writers after World War I. Levine argues that the great novelists of the century were engaged in a process "intimately and authoritatively connected to the modernist position". Aimed at subverting the conventions of romance, realism became a way for authors to control the chaos of surface impressions and assert the permanence of society and its values. Levine's opening chapters describe the theory he sees underlying the works of the great novelists of the century; in his middle chapters, he examines in detail novels by Scott, Charles Dickens, George Eliot, William Makepeace Thackeray, and Hardy, as well as lesser-known works by less-read writers. Well versed in disciplines other than literature, Levine ranges into philosophy, history, psychology, and science to explain how writers of fiction drew upon the thoughts and reflected the concerns of their contemporaries in the intellectual community.

In a similar vein, GURNEY surveys the poetry of the century to explain how writers from Blake to A.E. Housman are connected with the writers of the twentieth century, and how they reflect concerns that extend beyond their own age. Arguing that "the study of the past has an intrinsic value inasmuch as it enables us to rise above the restrictive or reductive vantage point of our present moment", Gurney sketches the accomplishments and outlines the legacy of every figure included in the traditional canon of Romantic and Victorian poets. His chapters on "The Romantic Ethos" and "The Victorian Ethos" give readers a sound appreciation of the essential differences between writers of the early and later decades of the century. Like most books published by Twayne, the volume contains a useful chronology of major literary events.

LAURENCE W. MAZZENO

British Literature: 20th Century

Bergonzi, Bernard (ed.), *The Twentieth Century*, London: Barrie & Jenkins, 1970

Blamires, Harry, *Twentieth-Century English Literature*, London: Macmillan, 1982, revised 1986; New York: Schocken Books, 1982

Brower, Reuben A. (ed.), *Twentieth-Century Literature in Retrospect*, Cambridge, Massachusetts: Harvard University Press, 1971

Dodsworth, Martin (ed.), *The Penguin History of Literature: The Twentieth Century*, Harmondsworth, Middlesex: Penguin, 1994

Ford, Boris (ed.), *The New Pelican Guide to English Literature: From James to Eliot*, revised edition, Harmondsworth, Middlesex: Penguin, 1983

Ford, Boris (ed.), *The New Pelican Guide to English Literature: The Present*, revised edition, Harmondsworth, Middlesex: Penguin, 1983

Fraser, G.S., *The Modern Writer and His World*, London: Derek Verschoyle, 1953; revised edition, London: André Deutsch/Penguin, 1964; New York: Praeger, 1965

The definitions of "twentieth century" assumed by the writers of the surveys discussed below inevitably vary according to both the focus of a particular study and its date of publication (Bergonzi's century, for example, being almost 25 years younger than Dodsworth's).

FRASER's book was an innovative work when first published, and, although some of its ideas have dated it remains a very useful introduction to the relations between literary production and the background of ideas out of which it emerged. The book covers all genres of writing, including criticism, and in three parts gives reasonably comprehensive histories of each genre across the century – histories that are concerned also to make links back to the writing being produced at the end of the nineteenth century. In the opening section there are discussions – concise and forceful – of the "Background of Ideas" drawn upon by the writers. The historical sense of "modernity" leads into chapters on realism, psychology and experiment in novels, complexity, allusion and irony in poetry, and conceptions of "modernity" in the drama. This "Background" is continually drawn upon in the surveys in the rest of the book. What emerges is a dense and comprehensive discussion of the relations between the individual writer and the literary and philosophical thought of the age, which has not lost its insight and value in the years since the book appeared.

BERGONZI's collection of essays combines criticism of single authors with more general survey pieces on the novel, poetry, and drama. The collection ends with some interesting work by Andrew Bear on popular reading, and by David Lodge on literary criticism. In the essays on single authors, a survey approach is also adopted, with the careers of W.B Yeats, James Joyce, D.H. Lawrence, and T.S. Eliot being treated very much in chronological order. This introduces a certain rigidity into the readings while having the advantage of providing a useful précis of the works and the developing artistic ideas of their subjects. Perhaps most impressive in the book is the opening essay, by the editor himself, on "The Advent of Modernism 1900–1920", which provides an admirable synthesis of the ideas behind modernist experimentalism and discusses them alongside works by more "realist" writers of the age like Arnold Bennett, Ford Madox Ford, and Rudyard Kipling.

BROWER's collection contains essays by leading critics from Britain and America, including Helen Gardner, Frank Kermode, Louis L. Martz, Richard Poirier, F.R. Leavis, and Christopher Ricks. The book is divided into two sections. The first, on "Writers and Critics", offers reappraisals of some of the key ideas, authors, and texts in the earlier part of the period, from Joyce's *Dubliners* to T.S. Eliot and Yeats. There is an interesting essay by John Paul Russo on the crucial influence I.A. Richards had on later thinking about the literature of the century. In the second section, Brower has adopted the novel tack of including essays on the re-readings of earlier literature by twentieth-century writers. The reconsideration of Shakespeare in the work of Eliot is discussed in one essay, and there are pieces on John Donne, Milton, Alexander Pope, and the Metaphysical poets as viewed by later writers. By adopting this approach, Brower establishes this century's literature as one in which complex allusion is to the fore, and in the process the book raises some pertinent questions about the importance of poetic influence.

BLAMIRES' book is concerned to read the literary history of the century alongside the processes of historical development and change. The century is broken up into 20-year periods, each of which are provided with an Introduction to the historical events that took place at that stage. The book is also consistently concerned to take account of the literature produced in all parts of the British Isles, and has sub-sections on English, Welsh, Scottish, and Irish writers. It is remarkable for Blamires' sheer breadth of reference, which provides useful bibliographical information on the authors under discussion while allowing also for a brief critical account of their work. Blamires' concern throughout to discuss the work of lesser-known writers alongside that of the canonical "greats" leads to an illuminating historicization and sense of the dynamics of the century's literature. The sub-sections in each period tend to operate generically and lead to some intriguing juxtapositions of information and critical discussion in, for example, the section on "Dominant Novelists" in the 1930s and 1940s, which includes the work of Evelyn Waugh, Graham Greene, Ivy Compton-Burnett, Anthony Powell, and George Orwell. The only slight problem with the book is its comparative neglect of drama throughout.

The guides to the period edited by FORD have in many ways become the standard surveys of the century's literature. Ford's original volume, *The Modern Age* (1961), is now updated, expanded, and divided into the two present volumes. In *From James to Eliot* two introductory sections deal with "The Social and Intellectual Background" and "The Literary Scene". Though written by different authors, both sections are strikingly preoccupied with the crisis in values, both literary and ethical, in the century. Part III of the volume is taken up by essays on either major figures or more general subjects, such as "Criticism and the Reading Public" and "Mass Communications in Britain" (the latter a lively piece by Richard Hoggart, following up his earlier enquiry into literacy in modern Britain). The period is then elaborated by general essays mapping the state of the novel, poetry, and drama. These essays are a rag-bag mixture of close yet contextual readings – for example, those essays on Ezra Pound's *Hugh Selwyn Mauberley* or D.H. Lawrence's *Women in Love* – with broader surveys of various writers' careers. The essays in the collection are of a somewhat uneven quality, but the volume nevertheless provides an impressive starting point for exploring the period's literature, and includes discussion of all the major figures. The succeeding volume, *The Present*, continues in a similar vein. It also begins with two contextual chapters, discussing cultural and critical developments, before launching into a series of essays on selected British authors (George Orwell, Anthony Powell, Angus Wilson, Iris Murdoch, Doris Lessing, Ted Hughes, Philip Larkin, and others), several Commonwealth writers, and selected topics (including "Literature for Children", "The Book Market", "Autobiography: Quest for Identity", and "The English Stage Company and the

Dramatic Critics"). The "present" under discussion here means, in effect, the postwar period up to the 1970s.

The most recent of these surveys, DODSWORTH's, is arranged chronologically according to genre, and gives an energetic sense of the changes and developments within each genre across the century. Dodsworth is convinced of the central importance of World War I for later social and literary developments, and so includes an essay on the War poets, alongside the concentrated discussion of formal generic issues. One major disappointment in this history is that more recent writing is gathered in the broad category of literature "Since 1950" – a surprisingly long period given the book's date of publication. The result is a hasty and highly selective treatment of writers from the latter half of the century; even those who are included can only be allowed a page of discussion, for what have been in some cases lengthy careers. So, the essays on the generic experiments and questionings in the earlier part of the century remain the most revealing and innovative.

STEVEN MATTHEWS

Brontë, Charlotte 1816–1855

English novelist

Alexander, Christine, *The Early Writings of Charlotte Brontë*, Oxford: Blackwell, 1983
Barker, Juliet, *The Brontës*, London: Weidenfeld & Nicolson, 1994
Craik, W.A., *The Brontë Novels*, London: Methuen, 1968
Ewbank, Inga-Stina, *Their Proper Sphere: A Study of the Brontë Sisters as Early Victorian Female Novelists*, London: Edward Arnold, 1966; Cambridge, Massachusetts: Harvard University Press, 1966
Fraser, Rebecca, *Charlotte Brontë*, London: Methuen, 1988
Gérin, Winifred, *Charlotte Brontë: The Evolution of Genius*, Oxford: Clarendon Press, 1967; New York: Oxford University Press, 1967
Gilbert, Sandra M., and Susan Gubar, *The Madwoman in the Attic: The Woman Writer and the Nineteenth-Century Imagination*, New Haven, Connecticut, and London: Yale University Press, 1979
Gordon, Lyndall: *Charlotte Brontë: A Passionate Life*, London: Chatto & Windus, 1994; New York: Norton, 1995

Much of the interest in Charlotte Brontë has been biographical. Following the publication of Elizabeth Gaskell's famous biography in 1857, writers have been eager – perhaps too eager – to trace links between Brontë's books and her life. In the first half of the twentieth century, when biographical criticism became unfashionable, the novels fell into critical disrepute, being attacked for their lack of realism and for their melodramatic coincidences. Gérin's biography coincided with a series of critical studies, which re-established Brontë's reputation as an original and poetic writer, linking the various episodes of the novels by a web of poetic images. Feminist criticism found much to admire in *Shirley* and *Villette* as well as *Jane Eyre*, and recent biographers have tended to paint Brontë as rebelling against her woman's lot.

EWBANK's book, in spite of its title, is a pre-feminist study of all three Brontë sisters. She begins with a general discussion of the woman writer in the 1840s, and shows how pioneering the Brontës were in an age when women as well as men believed that it was only right for man to command, woman to obey. In her chapter on Charlotte, Ewbank stresses the importance of independence in all four novels, and explores the concept of imaginative truth. *The Professor*, with its rather feminine hero, and *Shirley*, with its masculine heroine, receive, for obvious reasons, some attention, although the passion of Jane Eyre and the psychological struggles of Lucy Snowe are acknowledged to be more interesting. Ewbank on the whole eschews the biographical approach, but is careful to give the appropriate Victorian background; her analysis, though historically correct, may seem outdated to those accustomed to looking at Brontë through modern spectacles.

GÉRIN wrote biographies of all four Brontë children. Her book on Charlotte is much the longest, but she shows remarkable skill in not repeating her material and in capturing the spirit of the Brontë legends that have grown up over the years. On fact she is weaker. She relies too heavily on imperfectly edited versions of the Brontë letters, poems, and juvenilia. Her chronology is unreliable, and she shows little knowledge of Victorian religion or social history. Her discussion of the novels is vitiated by the assumption that the Brontës were unable to write fiction without reproducing fact, an assumption made worse by drawing on the fiction for an account of the facts. Thus, Charlotte's stay in Brussels is discussed largely from the pages of *Villette* as if she had visited Belgium on her own as a complete stranger, as if M. Heger had been unmarried, and as if she were able and willing nine years after the event to give a literal account of her painful experiences. It is a pity that these faults spoil the effect of much patient and interesting research.

CRAIK's book, like Ewbank's, includes discussions of all three Brontë sisters, with little consideration of biography and some rather kind remarks about Anne. There are chapters on all four of Charlotte's novels, although *Jane Eyre* and *Villette* receive much the fullest treatment, *Shirley* being dismissed as having technical skill and some memorable scenes, but wrongly conceived, while *The Professor* is said to be the work of a beginner. The juvenilia are largely ignored. *Jane Eyre* is seen as achieving a proper balance between the real and the true, and there are some accurate appreciations of the different voices in the novel, with distinctions drawn between the youthful Jane, the mature Jane, and the authorial voice of Charlotte. Charlotte's comic touches in the house-party scenes and her use of the different places in the novel are seen as strengths rather than weaknesses, as some critics have regarded them. Craik thinks Lucy Snowe a more impressive character than Jane Eyre, and calls Paul Emanuel a most successful creation. She is a little too kind to the use of coincidence as a plot device.

GILBERT and GUBAR'S provocative opening sentence, "Is the pen a penis?", opens a new path in Brontë studies, a path clearly signposted by their title, referring to the first Mrs Rochester. Allusive, learned, covering a vast range of female authors, and full of subtle wordplay, this book seems determined to redraw the map of nineteenth century literature. Thus, George Eliot gets little attention, Jane Austen's Mrs

Norris is a much maligned woman, and Jane Eyre is the mirror image of Bertha Mason. And in a way she is, although in spite of the presence of mirrors and images of imprisonment in the novel it is not always easy to trace the likeness between the small chaste Jane and larger more licentious figures in the Brontë novels. Gilbert and Gubar have rightly been regarded as pioneers in Brontë criticism, but they should not be regarded as holy writ.

ALEXANDER's book is an excellent introduction to Brontë's juvenilia, which she is also editing in a scholarly fashion. Such a work is indispensable for the study of Brontë's life, and helpful to the study of her novels. We are able to see the prototypes of Jane Eyre and Rochester in characters like Mina Laury and Zamorna, conceived before the visit to Belgium, where Heger, as well as providing an extra model for a masterful hero, also taught the importance of realism. Alexander does not make the mistake of overestimating the literary value of the juvenilia, and their rather tawdry nature does emerge from her succinct plot summaries. At times she does seem too eager to show links between characters in the juvenilia and characters in the novels; nor does she quite sufficiently stress the fact that adulterous relationships, so common in the juvenilia, are frowned upon in the novels, written after the Belgian visit and Branwell's disgrace.

FRASER's elegantly written biography was able to take account of more scholarly work on primary sources like the juvenilia. Her generous acknowledgment of the work of other writers is welcome in a field where there has been too much sniping. She is equally generous and fair in her account of the main characters in Brontë's life, although Branwell gets rather short shrift. The abortive love affair with Heger is handled at length, and with compassion for all parties, including Heger. George Smith receives slightly less emphasis. Criticism of the novels is sensible and not too closely wedded to the biography. Oddly, in spite of the kindly and sympathetic note that this biography strikes, the principal figure in it emerges as rather more rebellious, bitter, and stridently feminist than in previous studies.

GORDON's book, though quirky on individual facts (such as the date of the composition of *Shirley*), is the best study of Brontë's inner life and the workings of her mind as a novelist. She perhaps exaggerates the role of George Smith in the composition of *Villette*, drawing upon some hitherto unpublished letters between Brontë and her publisher, hinting at an unreciprocated love (although making clear that both parties in real life behaved honourably). Sometimes she blurs the distinction between Smith and John Brieton in *Villette*. On the other hand, the problem of Heger, a married Belgian schoolteacher, is discussed very sensibly in relation to the novels, with their heroes married men, or Belgians, or schoolmasters. Unlike Gérin, Gordon is able to see that Brontë was a creative artist able to make her rather sad, drab life into great art.

BARKER's long history of all the Brontës is the latest and best attempt to put them in their historical context, and to clear away some of the myths surrounding them. At times, especially in the extremely long footnotes, the author appears to be moving from the realm of literature to that of social history. Mr Brontë emerges as a kindly and normal pastor in spite of his burden of loneliness and grief, and Branwell as an ordinary young man (although there are speculations about an illegitimate child). In contrast, Charlotte is shown as self pitying, neurotic, and over-sensitive, possibly suppressing a second novel by Emily on the grounds that it was too shocking. There is a great deal of useful and relevant historical material in this work, in which literary criticism takes second place. The bleak and depressing view of Charlotte's personality does tend to spill over into the discussion of her novels.

T.J. WINNIFRITH

Brontë, Emily 1818–1848

English novelist and poet

Cecil, David, *Early Victorian Novelists: Essays in Revaluation*, London: Constable & Co., 1934; Indianapolis, Indiana: Bobbs-Merrill, 1935

Chitham, Edward, *A Life of Emily Brontë*, Oxford and New York: Blackwell, 1987

Davies, Stevie, *Emily Brontë*, Brighton, Sussex: Harvester Press, 1988; Bloomington: Indiana University Press, 1988

Eagleton, Terry, *Myths of Power: A Marxist Study of the Brontës*, London: Macmillan, 1975, 2nd edition, 1988; New York: Barnes & Noble, 1975

Frank, Katherine, *A Chainless Soul: A Life of Emily Brontë*, Boston: Houghton Mifflin, 1990; as *Emily Brontë: A Chainles Soul*, London: Hamish Hamilton, 1990

Hewish, John, *Emily Brontë: A Critical and Biographical Study*, London: Macmillan, 1969; New York: St Martin's Press, 1969

Kermode, Frank, *The Classic: Literary Images of Permanence and Change*, London: Faber & Faber, 1975; New York: Viking Press, 1975

Winnifrith, T.J., *The Brontës and Their Background: Romance and Reality*, London: Macmillan, 1973, revised 1988

Emily Brontë's reputation has not followed the same pattern as that of her elder sister, Charlotte. There is a dearth of primary biographical information, and attempts at a definitive biographical study have suffered through too much guesswork and the fact that what little we know of the life of Brontë seems very different from the wild world of *Wuthering Heights*. This novel was unpopular in Victorian times, but twentieth-century critics were able to prove its precision as well as its passion. Emily was seen as superior to Charlotte by critics as diverse as Virginia Woolf in 1919 and F.R. Leavis in 1948. Recent interest in Charlotte through new critical approaches has not diminished the appreciation of her younger sister, but these same approaches have been less successful with *Wuthering Heights*, always seen as a novel operating on many different levels.

CECIL'S work has an authoritative air, firmly placing Emily as a superior writer to Charlotte, and insisting that *Wuthering Heights* is an aesthetic masterpiece with no moral overtones. The world of the Earnshaws at Wuthering Heights is not superior or inferior to that of the Lintons at Thrushcross Grange; rather the two worlds of storm and calm are just different, hopelessly incompatible until the second generation issuing from mixed marriages, which blend storm and calm, arrive to resolve the issue. Cecil is perhaps too schematic. He does not really explain why Linton Heathcliff in the second generation should be so different from Catherine Linton, although he does say that one is the child of hate and the other the child of love. Nor does he show why the elder Catherine always, and the younger Catherine sometimes, finds Wuthering Heights more attractive, or indeed why the general reader is similarly drawn to the bracing, often violent, but always lively and passionate world of the Heights, and tends to reject the coldly formal and slightly effete world of the Grange.

HEWISH's book consists of a section on biography, a section on *Wuthering Heights*, and a disappointingly short chapter on "Public and Critics". Extensive and sensible use is made of Brontë's poetry, both to provide a background to her life and as a help in interpreting *Wuthering Heights*. There are no startling biographical discoveries, and the discussion of *Wuthering Heights* contains rather more literary history than literary criticism. Sources for the novel are investigated, and there is some exploration of contemporary reviews, though very little explanation for the rehabilitation of Brontë in the twentieth century. The possibility of a second novel is mentioned briefly, and there is a surprisingly lengthy argument about a possible incestuous relationship between Catherine and Heathcliff, an unusual feature of a cautious and careful book.

My own (WINNIFRITH's) study of all three Brontë sisters aims to set them in their contemporary background and to show how they both reflected and rejected early Victorian attitudes to sexuality, religion, and snobbery. Emily is seen as the most outspoken in her rejection of conventional views on eternal damnation, in her freedom from the restrictions imposed by class barriers, and in her refusal to condemn the love of Catherine and Heathcliff. At the same time Emily's novel and poetry are seen to have a universal appeal rather than one restricted to the middle of the nineteenth century. A somewhat longer account than Hewish's of contemporary reviews and possible sources for *Wuthering Heights* is included. There is also a lengthy examination of the way in which all Brontë texts need more careful editing than has hitherto been accorded to them.

EAGLETON'S work on the Brontës, revised in 1987, provides an interesting insight into the contemporary preoccupations of literary criticism. A Marxist attitude in the first edition is reinforced by a theoretical Preface in the second. Readers not totally committed to theory or Marxism will nevertheless be encouraged by the sensible and sensitive study of the novels of all three sisters. In the case of *Wuthering Heights,* Eagleton expresses a distinct preference for the real world of the Heights as opposed to the artificial world of the Grange. His explanation of how the values of Wuthering Heights are in the end subordinated to the preoccupations of Thrushcross Grange is not wholly convincing. He sees the digging up of blackcurrant bushes by the younger Cathy and Hareton and their replacement with flowers as the victory of capitalism over yeoman feudalism, not apparently noticing that Heathcliff orders the blackcurrants to be restored to their original place.

KERMODE's chapter on *Wuthering Heights* is part of his thesis that a classic work, widely read more than a century after its author's death, is capable of many levels of interpretation and not, as structuralist critics would have it, essentially naive. He points to the mysterious significance of the name Hareton Earnshaw and the date 1500 over the door of Wuthering Heights in a novel that ends with Hareton leaving his ancestral home for Thrushcross Grange. He examines the baffling nature of Lockwood's dreams and the way in which the names Catherine Earnshaw, Catherine Heathcliff, and Catherine Linton reflect the fates of both generations. Heathcliff is seen as the centre of the novel, the door through which the other characters have to pass, and this explains his ambiguous position as hero and villain, worker and capitalist, arousing pity and fear. Kermode is the first and best of many critics to explore the richness of possible interpretations in *Wuthering Heights*; later critics have tended either to concentrate on one aspect of the book, or to maintain rather negatively that the book has no meaning.

CHITHAM's biography is the fullest and most sensible available, although he has to make do with a number of conjectures in view of the paucity of primary evidence. His use of Brontë's poetry in trying to establish key events in her life is open to criticism, but he has done much patient work in, for instance, establishing the date of her visit to Law Hill and her use of the nearby Sunderland Hall as well as Ponden House in *Wuthering Heights*. He is also convincing in his account of the last years of Emily's life, suggesting that she and Anne had quarrelled over the immoral nature of *Wuthering Heights*, and that she may have been engaged in lengthening her novel from what was originally only one volume. Critical insights into *Wuthering Heights* are comparatively pedestrian, and though there is much discussion of the poetry and the mysterious imaginary realm of Gondal, some of this is far-fetched. The idea that Brontë was inspired by Shelley is not convincing.

DAVIES, though writing from a feminist viewpoint, is at pains to stress the power and the energy of Brontë rather than her repression in a patriarchal world. She notes the absence of normal adult conduct in *Wuthering Heights* and a hostility to conventional religion shown when the elder Catherine states that she woke up sobbing for joy when flung out of heaven, which did not seem to be her home. She sees this as a statement of the importance of primitive, childish emotions untrammelled by the rules and regulations of the moral adult world. This thesis is powerfully stated, although Davies is not particularly sound on Brontë's own background or religious views, making for instance the common mistake of believing that Miss Branwell was a Calvinist.

FRANK's book is written in a less dry style than Chitham's, has a fashionable feminist slant, and seizes on the contemporary scourge of anorexia as the clue linking Emily's life and her novel. But this thesis and the whole book should be treated with caution. Heathcliff refused food before his death, Brontë's own death is mysterious, and when away from Haworth she suffered from loneliness and homesickness. But there is not a great deal of evidence for anorexia, and Frank, like many Brontë biographers, is too anxious to find links between fact and fiction, thus underestimating the author's creative genius. The references in this biography are unscholarly and there are some errors of chronology. Critical insights into *Wuthering Heights* are passionate rather than perceptive.

T.J. WINNIFRITH

Brown, Charles Brockden 1771–1810

American novelist and short-story writer

Christophersen, Bill, *The Apparition in the Glass: Charles Brockden Brown's American Gothic*, Athens: University of Georgia Press, 1993
Grabo, Norman S., *The Coincidental Art of Charles Brockden Brown*, Chapel Hill: University of North Carolina Press, 1981
Kimball, Arthur, *Rational Fictions: A Study of Charles Brockden Brown*, McMinnville, Oregon: Linfield Research Institute, 1968
Levine, Robert S., *Conspiracy and Romance: Studies in Brockden Brown, Cooper, Hawthorne, and Melville*, Cambridge and New York: Cambridge University Press, 1989
Rosenthal, Bernard (ed.), *Critical Essays on Charles Brockden Brown*, Boston: G.K. Hall, 1981
Warfel, Harry R., *Charles Brockden Brown: American Gothic Novelist*, Gainesville: University of Florida Press, 1949; reprinted, New York: Octagon Books, 1974
Watts, Steven, *The Romance of Real Life: Charles Brockden Brown and the Origins of American Culture*, Baltimore: Johns Hopkins University Press, 1994

Although critical interest in Brown has always remained high, recent scholarship has been reinvigorated by newer methodologies. Brown, unlike some other canonical figures, seems to have weathered the "methodoligical storms" fairly well. To some he is a proto-feminist, to others a cultural critic, to yet others a forerunner of postmodern skepticism. Indeed, his novels have proved fruitful for postmodern critics, as his writings resist closure and are energized by the instability of language. In our age, where we are called on to notice how appearances aren't what they seem, Brown's novels of deception are still compelling.

WARFEL's book is perhaps the finest of the "early" biographies, and is of special interest to students of Brown's literary works because Warfel writes knowledgeably about Brown's major and less-known texts. Warfel contends that Brown's "outstanding contribution to fiction . . . is not his ideas nor his Gothicism, but his psychological probing into the minds of people under various kinds of tension". Detailed and historically meticulous, Warfel's book, though in some ways superseded by Watts's biography (see below), nonetheless remains an important book in Brown studies.

KIMBALL's book is a kind of "cult classic" in Brown studies. Its dissertation-like binding and print quality are deceptive; between the covers is a careful and deliberate study, which convincingly explores Brown's writings in the light of Lockean pyschology, "Common Sense" philosophy, and eighteenth-century assumptions about the nature of madness. In some ways predicting later cultural studies of Brown, Kimball's book places Brown at the dark edges of the Enlightenment. Kimball also treats some of Brown's neglected fiction and non-fiction.

Although LEVINE only devotes one chapter to Brown, that chapter is a persuasive and eloquent one, situating Brown's novel *Ormond* and other writings amid the Illuminati "conspiracies" of the late 1790s. Drawing on a wide range of historical documents as well as the work of eminent social and cultural historians, Levine contends that in his writing Brown explores "the problem of subversion of self in the postrevolutionary age", astutely noting that Brown paradoxically imagines himself both as "concerned citizen unmasking conspiracy" and a "bold and energetic subversive".

GRABO offers what is still one of the finest close readings of Brown's work yet, providing an insightful psychological portrait of Brown's characters. Specifically, Grabo focuses on Brown's use of the "double", suggesting that Brown's complex plots and seemingly unmotivated characters reveal his craftsmanship.

ROSENTHAL's valuable collection of essays includes a section entitled "Reviews and Early Criticism", which reprints assessments of Brown by authors such as Margaret Fuller and John Greenleaf Whittier, and a section entitled "Original Essays", which includes nine original critical essays by scholars such as Cathy N. Davidson, Emory Elliott, and Sydney J. Krause. This is a significant and impressive collection of well-researched and well-written essays.

WATTS calls his book a "cultural biography", which aims to connect Brown's works to the culture in which they were written. Although not the first to attempt this approach (Warfel adopted a similar approach) Watts's book is different in a few significant ways. First, the book openly parades its quasi-Marxist politics, as it explores Brown's complicated agency in "the hegemony of liberal capitalism". Second, the book examines and treats seriously some of Brown's previously neglected writings, such as his *Historical Sketches,* although it neglects to examine other little-studied writings, such as some of Brown's short stories. Third, the book is the first on Brown to be informed by recent developments in critical and cultural theory, as it displays an awareness of how politics, language, and power are all interconnected. This significant book also contains a very useful and current "Bibliographic Essay".

CHRISTOPHERSEN focuses primarily on Brown's four major novels – *Wieland*, *Ormond*, *Arthur Mervyn*, and *Edgar Huntly*. Christophersen usefully situates Brown's writings amid the social, political, and cultural turmoil of the 1790s, noting that "at the same time we attend to the minutiae of these tales, we must also be willing to consider them as fables, stripping away circumstantial gratuities . . . and retrieving their cultural contexts". Although lacking the element of cultural critique characteristic of New-Historicist approaches, Christophersen's book, like Watts's, reads Brown's writings as social and political allegories rather than as disembodied works of art.

NICHOLAS ROMBES

Browning, Elizabeth Barrett 1806–1861

English poet

Barnes, Warner, *A Bibliography of Elizabeth Barrett Browning*, Austin: University of Texas Press, 1967
Cooper, Helen, *Elizabeth Barrett Browning: Woman and Artist*, Chapel Hill: University of North Carolina Press, 1988
Donaldson, Sandra, *Elizabeth Barrett Browning: An Annotated Bibliography of Commentary and Criticism, 1826–1990*, New York: G.K. Hall, 1993; Toronto: Maxwell Macmillan, 1993

Forster, Margaret, *Elizabeth Barrett Browning: A Biography*, London: Chatto & Windus, 1988; New York: Doubleday, 1989

Hayter, Alethea, *Mrs Browning: A Poet's Work and Its Setting*, London: Faber & Faber, 1962; New York: Barnes & Noble, 1963

Kaplan, Cora (ed.), *"Aurora Leigh", with Other Poems* by Browning, London: Women's Press, 1978

Karlin, Daniel, *The Courtship of Robert Browning and Elizabeth Barrett*, Oxford: Clarendon Press, 1985; New York: Oxford University Press, 1985

Leighton, Angela, *Elizabeth Barrett Browning*, Brighton, Sussex: Harvester Press, 1986; Bloomington: Indiana University Press, 1986

Markus, Julia (ed.), *Casa Guidi Windows* by Browning, New York: Browning Institute, 1977

Mermin, Dorothy, *Elizabeth Barrett Browning: The Origins of a New Poetry*, Chicago: University of Chicago Press, 1989

Porter, Charlotte, and Helen A. Clarke (eds.), *The Complete Works of Elizabeth Barrett Browning*, 6 vols., New York: Thomas Crowell, 1900; reprinted, New York: AMS Press, 1973

Reynolds, Margaret (ed.), *Aurora Leigh*, by Browning, Athens: Ohio University Press, 1992

Stephenson, Glennis, *Elizabeth Barrett Browning and the Poetry of Love*, Ann Arbor, Michigan: UMI Research Press, 1989

Stone, Marjorie, *Elizabeth Barrett Browning*, London: Macmillan, 1995; New York: St Martin's Press, 1995

Taplin, Gardner B., *The Life of Elizabeth Barrett Browning*, New Haven, Connecticut: Yale University Press, 1957; London: John Murray, 1957

Until the close of the nineteenth century, Elizabeth Barrett Browning was widely regarded as a major English poet, whose works were read and appreciated in a number of countries, including France, Italy, Russia, and the United States. But from the turn of the century up to 1970, her poetical works – with the notable exception of the *Sonnets from the Portuguese* – were dismissed by critics who focused chiefly on her life, her letters, and her role as Robert Browning's wife. The cultural transformations effected by Second-Wave feminism led to her recovery as a major nineteenth-century writer, and to renewed interest in her greatest work, *Aurora Leigh*, a novel-in-verse that has been described as the first full-length portrait of the woman writer in English poetry. Since 1970, a number of feminist reinterpretations of her works have appeared, but great deal of work is still in progress – evinced by a conference at Baylor University in November of 1993 that attracted a great number of submissions.

TAPLIN's biographical study is representative of the critical assumptions prior to 1970 that transformed Elizabeth Barrett Browning the poet into a woman notable chiefly for her life and her relationship with Robert Browning. Although this study remains a useful source, it does little to illumine Browning's poetical achievement. Constructing "Elizabeth" as an emotional, undisciplined woman, and a diffuse, sentimental writer, Taplin treats her poetry despairingly and often in passing. Through selective quotation of Victorian reviews, he also creates the misleading impression that she was merely a popular, rather than a critical, success in her own time.

HAYTER, unlike Taplin, focuses on Browning's poetical works and on her craft, not on her life. While Hayter tends to be dismissive of works such as the ballads, which now attract a high degree of interest, she does comprehensively investigate Browning's achievement in a range of poetical and prose forms, including her innovative work as a scholar and critic in her essays on the Greek Christian poets. She also gives close attention to Browning's experiments with poetic technique, and her chapter on this subject remains the most detailed analysis to date of the poet's innovative use of double rhymes, metrical variations, *enjambement*, artfully varied refrains, and differing forms of syntactical ellipsis and compression. In her closing chapter, Hayter calls for a reassessment of Browning's work as a poet; but the cultural context in 1962 was not receptive to such a call.

KAPLAN's Women's Press edition of *Aurora Leigh* marks the critical recovery of Browning's reputation, which accompanied the women's movement of the 1970s. In her critical Introduction, the most penetrating and comprehensive analysis of *Aurora Leigh* to appear in over a century, Kaplan shows how Browning's novel-epic challenged and subverted the gender ideologies of its time, in part through the overlapping series of debates it carried on with a range of other texts, among them Madame de Staël's *Corinne*, Charlotte Brontë's *Jane Eyre*, Tennyson's *The Princess*, Charles Kingsley's *Alton Locke*, and works by Elizabeth Gaskell and Arthur Hugh Clough. Writing from a Marxist feminist perspective, Kaplan is more critical than others of Browning's representation of mid-Victorian class conflicts.

KARLIN offers a subtle analysis of the myths surrounding the Brownings' courtship, and of the celebrated courtship letters themselves. Browning has long been praised as an artful and witty letter-writer, but Karlin's study reveals how much her complex textual exchanges with Robert Browning focused on issues of artistic identity and authority. He also elucidates the often baffling play of paradox in the "sphinxine" discourse of these letters.

LEIGHTON's 1986 study, drawing on feminist and Lacanian theoretical perspectives, was the first full-length revaluation of Browning's poetical achievement to appear since Hayter's. It perceptively explores the poet's difficulties as a woman in finding a muse figure, and argues that throughout her career her father remained her most important muse, despite the gulf that divided her from him after her elopement with Robert Browning. Although sophisticated, Leighton's Lacanian reading of *Aurora Leigh* as Browning's hidden last quest for the father tends to recuperate traditional biographical interpretations. Her analysis of the subtle, paradoxical negotiations of sexual politics in the *Sonnets from the Portuguese* is a more groundbreaking reinterpretation in its consideration of Browning's revision of courtly love conventions.

COOPER's study focuses on Browning's evolution as both woman and poet towards the gynocentric perspectives and politics that dominate her later works. Demonstrating how the poet overcame the silence imposed upon her as a female "Other" in a predominantly male poetical tradition, Cooper traces the emergence of a subversive, rebellious voice in the ballads, culminating in the radical defiance of "The Runaway

Slave at Pilgrim's Point". In contrast to Leighton, she sees Browning as breaking free from the authority of her father, and of poetical father figures in general, by 1846, in part through reconciling her identity as a woman with her identity as a poet in the first-person perspective of the *Sonnets from the Portuguese*. Cooper also presents a close analysis of the intricate structure of *Aurora Leigh*, and a particularly illuminating discussion of *Casa Guidi Windows*, a work that has remained under-appreciated despite Julia MARKUS's work in both recovering the poem and elucidating its political context.

STEPHENSON engages in close and perceptive readings of Browning's ballads, sonnets, love lyrics, and dramatic monologues, with particular attention to both the subtle gender conflicts that inform many of these works and the poet's adaptation of the conventions of love poetry. In contrast to most other critics, Stephenson provides a full discussion of Browning's *Last Poems*, which she reads as complex portrayals of possessive love.

MERMIN combines literary biography with analyses of poems, letters, and essays written throughout Browning's career in the most comprehensive and invaluable study to date. Drawing extensively, as FORSTER does, on the new material appearing in the many volumes of *The Brownings' Correspondence*, Mermin focuses much more than Forster on Browning's artistic development and achievement. Almost all of the works in Browning's canon receive illuminating attention in this study, though Mermin tends to be somewhat dismissive of the ballads, even as she examines their subversive representations of sexual politics. Mermin also relates Browning's evolution as a woman poet to the larger traditions and developments in nineteenth-century literary history through comparisons with other Victorian writers, threaded throughout her study.

My own book (STONE) focuses in its earlier chapters on aspects of Browning's poetical development revealed by her manuscripts, on her connections with a matrix of women writers, and on her affiliations with the Romantic poets, in particular Byron, Shelley, and Keats. Emphasizing the audacity of authorship evident in Browning's revisionary impulse, I analyse neglected works in the 1844 *Poems*, including *A Drama of Exile* and "A Vision of Poets". Browning's ballads are approached in the context of the Romantic ballad revival, and related to works by Wordsworth, Coleridge, Bishop Percy, and Sir Walter Scott, while *Aurora Leigh* is analysed as a work that enters and subverts the tradition of Victorian sage discourse, and as a text that reveals Browning's close ties with the Langham Place group of women's rights activists. A final chapter surveys the reception of Browning's works from the time of her death in 1861 up to the 1980s.

DONALDSON's comprehensive bibliography provides very helpful summaries of all of the reviews and critical assessments of Browning appearing between 1826 and 1990. REYNOLDS's annotated critical edition of *Aurora Leigh* is clearly the definitive one, incorporating a consideration of all of the extant manuscripts and textual variants. Reynolds includes an editorial Introduction that casts much new light on the composition of Browning's greatest work, and a critical Introduction that reveals its narrative sophistication and structural complexity. Many of Browning's other works, however, remain available only in turn-of-the-century editions, the best of which is PORTER and CLARKE's annotated edition. Even this is, unfortunately, incomplete, as BARNES's bibliography reveals, which itself does not include some works subsequently discovered or attributed to Browning.

MARJORIE STONE

Browning, Robert 1812–1889

English poet

Cook, Eleanor, *Browning's Lyrics: An Exploration*, Toronto: University of Toronto Press, 1974

DeVane, William Clyde, *A Browning Handbook*, London: John Murray, 1935; New York: F.S. Crofts, 1935; 2nd edition, New York: Appleton-Century-Crofts, 1955

Erickson, Lee, *Robert Browning: His Poetry and His Audiences*, Ithaca, New York: Cornell University Press, 1984

Gibson, Mary Ellis (ed.), *Critical Essays on Robert Browning*, New York: G.K. Hall, 1992

Gridley, Roy E., *Browning*, London and Boston: Routledge & Kegan Paul, 1972

Langbaum, Robert, *The Poetry of Experience: The Dramatic Monologue in Modern Literary Tradition*, Chicago: University of Chicago Press, 1957; London: Chatto & Windus, 1957; reprinted, Harmondsworth, Middlesex: Penguin, 1974

Martin, Loy D., *Browning's Dramatic Monologues and the Post-Romantic Subject*, Baltimore: Johns Hopkins University Press, 1985

Shaw, W. David, *The Dialectical Temper: The Rhetorical Art of Robert Browning*, Ithaca, New York: Cornell University Press, 1968

Slinn, E. Warwick, *Browning and the Fictions of Identity*, London: Macmillan, 1982; Totowa, New Jersey: Barnes & Noble, 1982

Tucker, Herbert F., Jr., *Browning's Beginnings: The Art of Disclosure*, Minneapolis: University of Minnesota Press, 1980

While the enthusiasts of the Browning Society have almost disappeared, and while the poet is no longer regarded as something of an oracle, Browning's poetry remains the focus of interest for a large group of attentive readers and critics. The late Victorian tendency to read Browning for his "teachings" gave way early in the twentieth century to an interest in Browning the man; the middle part of the century had its own characteristic interests, especially the close reading of selected works and an emphasis on the characters revealed through the dramatic monologues; and since the 1970s the poet has been read in the light of certain reigning criticial methodologies.

Readers who want background information on any of the poems can do no better than turn to DeVANE's handbook. Though it is one of the older works on Browning, DeVane's volume is still a treasure-trove, full of relevant information. For each poem DeVane discusses its genesis, sources, publication history, textual and interpretive problems, and provides a short "after-history" of the poem's reception. The book is organized chronologically, and the length of each poem's treatment is roughly in proportion to DeVane's estimation of its importance. A helpful brief biography of Browning is also included.

Several good introductions to Browning have been published. Perhaps the most useful is GRIDLEY's, because it offers the most detailed explications of the major poems and gives the most extensive treatment of the poet's social and historical contexts. After a summary of Browning's early life, the book moves chronologically through each of the decades of the poet's career. Each chapter opens with an account of "the times", and then locates Browning's major achievements in that historical framework. A final chapter assesses the poet's influence on such later poets as Thomas Hardy, W.B. Yeats, Ezra Pound, and T.S. Eliot.

The seminal work in postwar Browning criticism is LANGBAUM's analysis of the dramatic monologue. While not limited solely to Browning, this study makes considerable use of him, advancing a process-oriented method of reading his poetry. Langbaum argues that the ideal reader, when fully informed about the conventions of the dramatic monologue sub-genre, should bring to his/her reading of the form both a sympathetic response and a certain wariness or reservation. While the emphasis on process may seem to anticipate later reader-response criticism, Langbaum is firm in his belief that the poems offer clear indications about how, ultimately, we should understand and judge their characters, and he therefore offers an interpretation against which many later critics feel compelled to argue.

SHAW studies Browning as a rhetorician, and sees in his work a prescient grasp of our "modern sense of the relative, the partial and the unknown". Shaw reflects, too, the tendency of an earlier era of critics to privilege the relativistic monologues at the expense of the other poetry, so that Browning's career is seen as an ascent – from the relative failures of the Shelleyan subjectivity in *Pauline* and *Sordello*, through the objective monologues, which are "the dialectival weapon[s] of a comic philosopher", to the triumphant *The Ring and the Book*, in which the poet combines subjectivity and objectivity in a uniquely authoritative personal voice. The argument proceeds by means of lengthy explications of the major poems.

In contrast, COOK prefers to focus on the lyrics rather than the monologues; indeed, hers is the only major critical work to do this. Part handbook on the lyrics, part analysis of imagery, and part discussion of Browning's poetics, her book shares with Shaw's a chronological arrangement, a methodological preference for close reading, a conviction that Browning has explicit intentions as regards his readers, and a belief that Browning's career evidences a clear and coherent trajectory. Perhaps the most valuable contribution Cook makes is her discussion of imagery, especially those images associated with enclosure (house, wall, cave), and others such as rose, gold, magus, and prophet.

If Langbaum, Shaw, and Cook demonstrate the interests and methodologies characteristic of many of the critics who came of age during the postwar years up to the 1970s, TUCKER inaugurates the new, poststructuralist ways of reading Browning. The "beginnings" of his title refer to the poet's continuous re-invention of his poetic self, but more importantly to his deep and inveterate resistance to closure in his work. By practicing "an art that resists its own finalities", Browning, according to Tucker, illustrates Jacques Derrida's theory of the indefinite postponement of meaning (through *différance*) and Derrida's conviction that "all experience is textual and is constituted in the play of an anarchic and atelic tissue of signs". Greater emphasis than in previous criticism is placed on close readings of the earlier poems and plays, as inscriptions of the poet's appetite for the future, for anticipation rather than retrospection. This preference, with its obvious analogs in Browning's own theory of the imperfect, has both moral an aesthetic components. Furthermore, Tucker feels, while sustaining Browning's career, despite vicissitudes that might have daunted earlier Romantics, it has made Browning's a remarkably modern poetic voice.

Building on such a poststructuralist approach, SLINN proposes to reinterpret earlier topics of Browning criticism, such as "character" and "action", in ways that demonstrate the poet's determination "to explore man as the product of a self-reflexive use of language". Browning's characters create fictitious selves, they dramatize, they resist definition and interpretation; thus, Slinn argues against Langbaum's claim that the poems offer explicit clues for the reader's interpretation of character. The artificiality of language guarantees that these characters "become trapped in their own hermeneutic cycle", and helps to deconstruct any objective ideas about their identities. Slinn offers a sympathetic portrait of Browning's monologuists as engaged in "a tightrope walk" between "a multitudinousness which threatens to fragment and diffuse experience" and "the self-determined fiction of a controlled solipsism". The book evidences a cross-fertilization between literary theory and personality theory, but it remains accessible to non-specialists.

Another important trend in recent criticism, reader-response theory, has relevance for ERICKSON, who aims to demonstrate how Browning's "need for his audiences' recognition affected his poetic strategies". (Erickson credits Stanley Fish for his critical method.) The focus here is on the auditors of the monologues: what does it mean for the reader to know, for example, that Andrea del Sarto "speaks" to his faithless wife, Lucrezia? Certainly a knowledge of auditors determines how we understand the speakers themselves, because the "process of self-realization requires the active participation of others, for the speakers gain their self-consciousness by being recognized by their audiences". Therefore what is true for Browning's speakers was, implicitly, true for the poet as well in his need for the reading public.

Still another significant trend in recent criticism is the so-called "New Historicism", a term associated with Marxist-inspired studies of works as ideological and cultural products. MARTIN regards the dramatic monologue as just such a product, one which "provides its reader (consumer) with a formal alternative to literary forms previously produced and largely abandoned". His interest is not so much in explicating particular poems, and rather more in showing the dialectical tensions at work in both the poet, as constructor of the monologues, and in the monologues themselves. Thus, Martin finds in Browning "not only the desire for reconnection and disalienation, but the competing desire for individual autonomy as well", a tension manifested also in the speakers of the monologues, themselves in turn reflecting such tensions between impulses towards community and autonomy in Victorian society at large.

Many good collections of essays on Browning have been published over the years, among which GIBSON's will give the reader the best idea of some of the principal strands of recent critical approaches. She has gathered 13 essays, 12 of which were previously published in the years since 1982, and one of which is newly commissioned for the volume. With five essays concerned with genre and "accounting for forms culturally and theoretically", and eight targeted at the cultural context of the poems, this collection makes plain its overarching critical perspective, in its alignment with the school that percieves Browning's poetry as cultural products.

FRANCIS L. FENNELL

Bunyan, John 1628–1688

English writer of religious prose, poetry, and fiction

Hill, Christopher, *A Turbulent, Seditious, and Factious People: John Bunyan and His Church, 1628–1688*, Oxford: Clarendon Press, 1988; as *A Tinker and a Poor Man: John Bunyan and His Church, 1628–1688*, New York: Knopf, 1989

Keeble, N.H. (ed.), *John Bunyan: Conventicle and Parnassus: Tercentenary Essays*, Oxford: Clarendon Press, 1988; New York: Oxford University Press, 1988

Laurence, Anne, W.R. Owens, and Stuart Sim (eds.), *John Bunyan and His England, 1628–1688*, London: Hambledon Press, 1990

Newey, Vincent (ed.), *The Pilgrim's Progress: Critical and Historical Views*, Liverpool: Liverpool University Press, 1980; Totowa, New Jersey: Barnes & Noble, 1980

Sharrock, Roger, *John Bunyan*, London: Macmillan, 1954, revised 1968; New York: St Martin's Press, 1968

Swaim, Kathleen M., *Pilgrim's Progress, Puritan Progress*, Urbana: University of Illinois Press, 1993

Though Bunyan wrote some 60 books of theology, controversy, poetry, and fiction, his reputation and readership depend largely on the great allegories *The Pilgrim's Progress*, *The Holy War*, and *The Life and Death of Mr Badman*, and the autobiographical *Grace Abounding to the Chief of Sinners*. Even now there are a number of devotional commentaries on Bunyan available; and recent studies remind us that a certain theological knowledge is still an important tool in fully understanding him. Two, more general, hostile studies of Calvinism and literature, John Stachniewski's *The Persecutory Imagination* (1991) and Stuart Sim's *Negotiations with Paradox* (1991), are important here, as well as Richard Greaves' 1969 study of Bunyan's theology, where the influence of Luther figures more prominently. More recent work reflects a different awareness of Bunyan's historical situation, as representative of the changes in Puritanism as it became Nonconformity after the Restoration.

SHARROCK did most for the modern study of Bunyan, as editor and critic. His study begins with biography and an introduction to the Puritan movement. The heart of the book is in the two central, linked chapters on *Grace Abounding* as a source for the first part of *The Pilgrim's Progress*. His critical views on *Mr Badman* and *The Holy War* here should be supplemented by the Introductions to his later editions of those works. He acknowledges that Bunyan's work has a life independent of "literature", while giving due weight to the literary qualities, and longeurs, of the major works.

NEWEY's collection contains 14 essays giving a wide range of literary approaches within a traditional methodology – comparing *The Pilgrim's Progress* with John Dryden, William Langland, and popular fiction and folktale, and assessing the relationship between the two parts, the theology and the central metaphors. James Turner's perceptive chapter on "Bunyan's Sense of Place" draws attention to questions of authority and control, and is seminal to Hill's study.

The contributors to KEEBLE's collection take on a much wider selection of Bunyan's works, partly as a result of the edition of the *Miscellaneous Works*, which was then in full swing. It is probably the best reference source for the context of Bunyan's works, historical and theological. There are two lively critical chapters as well: by Newey, on the relation between experience and interpretation, particularly in *Grace Abounding*, and by Valentine Cunningham on allegory, which engages with the poststructuralist critique of logocentrism, and how that might affect the reading of a Christian, biblical author like Bunyan.

HILL's study, which appeared in the same tercentenary year, is like an extended biography of Bunyan and his Church, drawing on the author's unrivalled historical knowledge. The English title reflects Hill's polemic concern to recover the radical political impact of Puritanism, a corrective to earlier readings, which had seen Bunyan's long imprisonment as an essentially religious act of persecution. It is instructive to compare Hill's political reading of Bunyan with that of another distinguished historian of Nonconformity, Richard Greaves, most easily available in Keeble. For all its polemical intent, this book has undoubtedly become the standard biography of Bunyan. It is full of, not to say clogged with, fascinating information, though the chapter on *The Pilgrim's Progress* itself is curiously muted.

The collection edited by LAURENCE, OWENS, and SIM demonstrates that Bunyan can be a focus for a whole range of historical and cultural discussions; the book is notable for its gathering of historians as well as critics, and its focus away from *The Pilgrim's Progress* in favour of *Grace Abounding* and the minor works. There is important material on Bunyan's army service, his experience of persecution, and the portrayal of the feminine.

SWAIM's book centres on both parts of *The Pilgrim's Progress* as forming an artistic achievement and "as a mirror of late seventeenth-century Puritan culture". This latter aim is fulfilled by drawing on the recent revival of Bunyan scholarship, and the book confidently negotiates the differences between Puritanism and Restoration Nonconformity, while advancing an interesting thesis about Bunyan's gradual abandonment of Calvinism for something more dispersed and modern in the 1680s. This is particularly evident in her reading of Part II of *The Pilgrim's Progress* as a feminisation of Bunyan's concerns.

ROGER POOLEY

Burgess, Anthony 1917–1993

English novelist, critic, and essayist

Aggeler, Geoffrey, *Anthony Burgess: The Artist as Novelist*, University: University of Alabama Press, 1979
Aggeler, Geoffrey (ed.), *Critical Essays on Anthony Burgess*, Boston: G.K. Hall, 1986
Bergonzi, Bernard, *The Situation of the Novel*, London: Macmillan, 1970, 2nd edition, 1979
DeVitis, A.A., *Anthony Burgess*, New York: Twayne, 1972
Dix, Carol M., *Anthony Burgess*, London: Longman, 1971
Mathews, Richard, *The Clockwork Universe of Anthony Burgess*, San Bernardino, California: Borgo Press, 1978
Morris, Robert K., *The Consolations of Ambiguity: An Essay on the Novels of Anthony Burgess*, Columbia: University of Missouri Press, 1971

Criticism of Burgess has broadly welcomed his experimental vitality and imaginative energy, especially his verbal inventiveness, often expressed in comic mode, though sometimes there has been anxiety that his prolific output may indicate mere prolixity or lack of seriousness.

In his survey of the postwar British novel, BERGONZI locates Burgess among the writers in mid-twentieth-century Britain tensely and ambivalently situated between nostalgia and dystopian nightmare. He greets him as the most exciting and innovative of these, and finds in his work a powerfully satirical imagination informed by an Augustinian religious pessimism.

DIX's introductory essay in the British Council "Writers and Their Work" series is appreciative but not uncritical. Appearing about halfway through Burgess's career, it notes, like most criticism, his polymath interests (music, philosophy, languages) and immense output, relating the writing to the life. Treatment of the novels, largely expository, falls under three headings: social realism and satire, philosophy, and language. Echoing Bergonzi, Dix emphasises the romantic pessimism of Burgess the lapsed Catholic, his innovative verbal vigour, and his creative and critical energy.

MORRIS, in his engagingly personalised monograph, also stresses Burgess's protean powers, noting, but dismissing, the worry that he may be "too prolific", emphasising the writer's rhetorical and linguistic exuberance, and seeing his fiction as fundamentally concerned with the modern human comedy and condition, where acceptance of imperfection and ambiguity is ultimately necessary and consoling. Seen here as expressing not romantic pessimism but, on the contrary, humanely existential and ironised optimism, Burgess's fiction is given lucid, perceptive, and discriminating readings, in one of the most fluent and shrewd of the earlier studies.

The first book-length study, by DeVITIS, analyses the novels thematically, emphasising interrelations among them, and focusing on the theological and eschatological issues given fictional, and often comic or ironic, treatment – in particular the antithesis of Pelagian optimism and Augustinian pessimism explicitly informing several of them. Though occasionally too insistently allegorising, its approach is, if partial, often illuminating, setting Burgess helpfully in a wider context of twentieth-century fiction.

MATHEWS' brief but adulatory study affirms Burgess's cosmopolitan, and indeed universal, quality, placing him unabashedly among the great moderns. The metaphor of clockwork, connecting the ten novels discussed, is perhaps somewhat obsessively pursued, but this critique – enthusiastic and well-informed, if inclined at times to swamp the argument in detail and insistent symbolistic interpretation – contributes usefully to appreciation of the novelist, who, often seen as strongly influenced by James Joyce, might be said to invite such approaches.

AGGELER's 1979 book (though it predates Burgess's ambitiously Faustian novel *Earthly Powers*) is the most substantial treatment of the writer to date, incorporating biography and criticism. It treats the novels in mainly chronological order, though also groups them thematically in terms of their author's religious and aesthetic preoccupations, his Manichean, dualistic vision, and his concern with the artist. Enthusiastic and perceptive, it welcomes Burgess's fecundity and dynamic energy, and shows close knowledge and appreciation of the whole range of his achievement to date. AGGELER, perhaps Burgess's most assiduous critical champion, is also editor of, and contributor to, a later collection of essays (1986), which is well chosen and includes excerpts from some of the criticism noted above. It engages appreciatively and fairly comprehensively with Burgess's prolific output, with three novels commanding particular attention – *A Clockwork Orange*, the less well-known *Tremor of Intent*, and the "musical novel" *Napoleon Symphony*. A revealing interview is also included, and Burgess's career and critical reception are capably outlined in the editorial Introduction, with brief synopses of the major novels.

JEREMY LANE

Burke, Edmund 1729–1797

Irish prose writer

Blakemore, Steven (ed.), *Burke and the French Revolution: Bicentennial Essays*, Athens: University of Georgia Press, 1992
Conniff, James, *The Useful Cobbler: Edmund Burke and the Politics of Progress*, Albany: State University of New York Press, 1994
Freeman, Michael, *Edmund Burke and the Critique of Political Radicalism*, Oxford: Blackwell, 1980
Gandy, Clara I., and Peter J. Stanlis, *Edmund Burke: A Bibliography of Secondary Studies to 1982*, New York: Garland, 1983
Kramnick, Isaac, *The Rage of Edmund Burke: Portrait of an Ambivalent Conservative*, New York: Basic Books, 1977
Reid, Christopher, *Edmund Burke and the Practice of Political Writing*, Dublin: Gill & Macmillan, 1985; New York: St Martin's Press, 1985
Ritchie, Daniel E. (ed.), *Edmund Burke: Appraisals and Applications*, New Brunswick, New Jersey: Transaction, 1990

Unlike other political writers of his generation, whose stock tends to rise during periods of political instability, interest in

Edmund Burke has remained steady in the 200 years since his death. Though his theoretical works are unquestionably representative of eighteenth-century conservative political thought, the exact nature of his conservatism, made occasionally obscure by the wealth of possible intentions behind his rhetoric, has been interpreted in a bewildering variety of ways. To the nineteenth century he was a practical politician-philosopher associated loosely with early Utilitarianism, which effectively threw a veil over his aesthetic theories for over a century. During the twentieth century, especially since World War II, he has been associated more closely with natural-law philosophy, which restored critical light to his aesthetic theory, but tended to confine his texts to historical studies. In recent years, interest has centered on analysis of Burke's rhetorical skill, his display of a substantial intellect, and to the numerous cases in which he appears to have been contending with himself through half a century of social and political flux. Burke was never uncontroversial in his conservatism, and the literature on him (listed in GANDY) is equally polemical.

All interpretations of Burke sustain interest in his theoretical works as secondary texts in the study of Romantic and Victorian literature – aesthetically, socially, psychologically, and politically. Literary criticism of Burke, a considerably smaller body of work than that produced by political scientists who continue to own him as a subject, concerns itself with his rhetoric – most notably, but not exclusively, his well-known challenge to the radicals – and his aesthetic theory, which is systematically articulated in the *Enquiry*.

CONNIFF, although he is a political scientist and unconcerned with the excellencies of Burke's rhetoric, provides the most up-to-date account of previous interpretations of Burke's political philosophy, and a comprehensive discussion of the complexities of British politics during Burke's tenure. His work is useful as a readable explanation, for the non-specialist, of the complex influences on Burke, and he provides a useful index to aid the process.

KRAMNICK "stands Burke on his head" by reading the public Burke simultaneously with the private one, in one of the few psychoanalytical readings of Burke's much-commented-on public displays of private bitterness. The occasional vehemence of Burke's attack on political radicalism and of his defense of the established order, according to Kramnick, begins with Burke's family dynamics and youthful relationships. His is more than a psychoanalytical reading of Burke, however, as his work is founded in, and answerable to, historical method, and his career interest has been in the larger political framework within which Burke's political thought formed itself. This work is useful for the balance with which Kramnick interprets Burke as something more than the "patron saint of conservatism", and enriches an understanding of the rhetorical stances apparent in Burke's texts, but not always clear to the twentieth-century reader.

FREEMAN begins with the relevance of revolution to this century, and argues for Burke's analysis as the best philosophical articulation of a timeless theory of counter-revolution. This is a critique of Burke's philosophy rather than of individual texts, and his interpretation of Burke has been strenuously argued against elsewhere. The isolation of Burke from his numerous other political interests, however, makes this work an accessible source of commentary on his counter-revolutionary position for those who are interested in Burke primarily for his opposition to the radical rhetoric of the 1790s.

The French Revolution is also the focus of the collection of essays in BLAKEMORE. Burke's *Reflections* – long read as a monument, at best, to personal integrity, and as withstanding the tide of public opinion as the last great defender of "reactionary high culture" at worst – are discussed in this volume. The essays here represent the currently popular view that Burke's strong theatrical theme in the *Reflections* is rather a synthesis of his aesthetic and political thought. He was, as Blakemore notes in his concluding essay, "problematically complex".

RITCHIE has brought together an anthology of criticism on Burke, beginning with Samuel Taylor Coleridge, who commented, often effusively, on all the central players in the revolutionary debate. It is an impressive collection, divided by subject matter rather than chronology, and represents a broad range of interests and disciplines.

REID, who also contributed to the collections above, reads Burke through his language rather than through content or context. Sharply contradicting the fairly large body of work that celebrates integrity as the single most important influence on Burke as he railed against his political foes, it is convention, according to Reid, put into the service of a keen sense of history, that consistently explains Burke's rhetorical choices. While Reid's detailed explanations of the literary-historical contexts of Burke's extensive political writings exceed most literary interests in Burke, his early chapters, especially his introductory discussion of the place Burke holds in critical studies, make this work particularly valuable.

CLARA ELIZABETH SPEER

Burney, Frances [Fanny] 1752–1840

English novelist, playwright, and diarist

Cutting-Gray, Joanne, *Woman as "Nobody" and the Novels of Fanny Burney*, Gainesville: University Press of Florida, 1991

Devlin, D.D., *The Novels and Journals of Fanny Burney*, London: Macmillan, 1987; New York: St Martin's Press, 1988

Doody, Margaret, *Frances Burney: The Life in the Works*, Cambridge: Cambridge University Press, 1988; New Brunswick, New Jersey: Rutgers University Press, 1988

Epstein, Julia, *The Iron Pen: Frances Burney and the Politics of Women's Writing*, Bristol: Bristol Classical Press, 1989; Madison: University of Wisconsin Press, 1989

Rogers, Katharine M., *Frances Burney: The World of "Female Difficulties"*, Hemel Hempstead, Hertfordshire: Harvester Wheatsheaf, 1990

Straub, Kristina, *Divided Fictions: Burney and Feminine Strategy*, Lexington: University Press of Kentucky, 1988

The act of naming in Burney studies suggests an author's critical position prior to the actual critical text. The difference between "Fanny" and "Frances" Burney indicates more than just differences in critical generations; those who see her as a conservative, youthful writer who offers a mirror to the manners of her times tend to prefer "Fanny", while "Frances" becomes a banner for critics who emphasize the political dimension of her writing and who argue for her significance as a late eighteenth-century writer. Critical interest in Burney is reflected in the reprinting of her four complete novels and two comedies during the last ten years, with the promise of more plays to come. Burney's youthful start at 26, with *Evelina*, has helped to perpetuate the image of Burney the writer as a naive intellect observing whirling society of late eighteenth-century London and its environs; but it is important to remember that her last novel, *The Wanderer*, was published in 1814 when Burney was 61, and that she wrote her *Memoirs of Doctor Burney* at close to 80.

CUTTING-GRAY's study of the four complete novels takes as its point of departure Burney's observation in her early journals that she is writing for nobody, which is to say for herself. Cutting-Gray theorizes this space of "nobody" as a performance of the "otherness" and nothingness of woman. She proposes an intersubjective model of authorship for Burney, which marks a difference from the masculine construct of "author-as-source". The model allows her to examine the relation between Burney's role as a writer and the cultural definitions of femininity with which she had to contend. Her approach, although it lacks the critical rigor of Straub's argument or the wealth of information that Doody's study marshals, shows the applicability of feminist and poststructuralist criticisms to Burney's work.

DEVLIN's argument opens and closes with the proposition that "the dates of Fanny Burney's novels are important", but illuminates a more complex and fluid relation between fiction and fact in Burney's development as an artist. Devlin works through a strong connection between Burney's journals, letters, and personal experiences on the one hand, and the novelistic fiction she produced on the other. Although this approach reflects a traditional privileging of the journals, which characterizes more anecdotal studies of Burney's writing, Devlin's analysis integrates a wealth of historical material, particularly details of the French Revolution and the influence of conservative writer Hannah More and the more radical Mary Wollstonecraft on Burney's political horizons. He sees her novels as intuitive yet skilled and disciplined through the creative composition of memories in her journals and letters.

DOODY brings together a wealth of biographical and textual research with insightful readings of Burney's works. Biography in her account serves not to supplant the aesthetic value of Burney's texts, but to provide a complex psychological narrative of female development, which explores the sources of Burney's so-called "conservatism" as well as her moments of departure from social expectations and even realism. Her study is the most comprehensive available, taking up the novels, the journals, and the plays as well as the abandoned MS of "Clarinda", parts of which were revived in *Camilla*. Doody's emphasis on the policing roles of Dr. Charles Burney and Samuel Crisp offers an argument for the emotional and social pressures on her writing as well as a biographical explanation for contrast between the prominence of the novels and the suppression of the stage comedies.

EPSTEIN's study looks at the conflict between the predominant image of Burney as shy and prudish and "the masked simmering rage of a conflicted but self-conscious social reformer". Epstein takes up the issues of violence and hostility, which explode at telling moments in Burney's texts, as means to explain the relationship between women writers and the literary marketplace in late eighteenth- and early nineteenth-century England. The ideological limitations of literary criticism, according to Epstein, have inhibited readings of Burney's aggression, and an understanding of the material conditions and social divisions in which Burney wrote is necessary to read beyond traditional Burney criticism. Her emphasis on *Camilla* and *The Wanderer* underscores the break with critical tradition, which until recently has focused on the first two novels. Instead of portraying the innocent writer in the image of the innocent heroine, Epstein's approach reveals strategies of social challenge and creative revision in Burney's novels.

ROGERS' work on Burney is singular as a structurally feminist approach to Burney that is not sympathetic to the proto-feminist view of Burney in studies such as Epstein's and Straub's. Her reading of Burney's personality, her timidity and repressed emotions, leads her to conclude that the works remain imperfect, marred by Burney's own divided state. Although most Burney scholars would agree with her statement that "even in the eighteenth-century context, Burney's subduing of self in the interests of feminine propriety was excessive", the conclusion that her individual prudishness constitutes the truth of her novels is hardly foregone. Rogers' study provides an important balance to the studies that focus on Burney's exploration, wittingly or not, of the limitations and contradictions of cultural femininity in late eighteenth-century England.

STRAUB's investigation shares some aspects of Epstein's, in that she sees Burney's writing in terms of ideological rifts revealing her desire to be both woman and writer, a contradiction according to the definitions available to her. In order to read this tension as telling and informative, Straub openly rejects notions of aesthetic unity and timelessness that have informed definitions of aesthetic of worth, rather seeing them as politically expedient instead of as literary truths. The influence of Alexander Pope and Jonathan Swift, as well as moralists like Fordyce and Reeve, provides a context for the conflicts Straub sees in Burney's work over issues of love, work, writing, and femininity.

MISTY G. ANDERSON

Burns, Robert 1759–1796

Scottish poet

Brown, Mary Ellen, *Burns and Tradition*, London: Macmillan, 1984

Crawford, Thomas, *Burns: A Study of the Poems and Songs*, Edinburgh and London: Oliver & Boyd, 1960

Daiches, David, *Robert Burns*, London: G. Bell & Sons, 1952

Jack, R.D.S., and Andrew Noble (eds.), *The Art of Robert Burns*, London: Vision Press, 1982; Totowa, New Jersey: Barnes & Noble, 1982

Lindsay, Maurice, *The Burns Encyclopedia*, London: Hutchinson, 1959; 3rd, revised edition, London: Robert Hale, 1980; New York: St Martin's Press, 1980

Low, Donald A. (ed.), *Robert Burns: The Critical Heritage*, London and Boston: Routledge & Kegan Paul, 1974
Low, Donald A. (ed.), *Critical Essays on Robert Burns*, London and Boston: Routledge & Kegan Paul, 1975
MacDiarmid, Hugh, *Burns Today and Tomorrow*, Edinburgh: Castle Wynd, 1959
MacDiarmid, Hugh, "The Last Great Burns Discovery" and "The Burns Cult", in his *Selected Prose*, Manchester: Carcanet Press, 1992
McGuirk, Carol, *Robert Burns and the Sentimental Era*, Athens: University of Georgia Press, 1985
Montgomerie, William (ed.), *New Judgements: Robert Burns: Essays by Six Contemporary Writers*, Glasgow: William MacLellan, 1947
Walker, Marshall, *Robert Burns: The Myth and the Gift*, Hamilton, New Zealand: University of Waikato Scottish Studies Association Avizandum Editions, 1995

Though Glasgow's Mitchell Library holds over 3,500 books in its Burns collection, good literary introductions to the poet's work are rare, partly because of the strictly non-literary fate that overtook him. Lionized by a literary élite, Burns was also genuinely popular, and through the nineteenth century his democratic sentiments were quoted throughout Europe and the United States. Walt Whitman sang his praises, and in the twentieth century Soviet Russia put him on a postage stamp. A "personality cult" developed: Burns clubs were formed and "Burns Suppers" became an annual event both in Scotland and throughout the Scots diaspora. Literary critics, however, have been uncomfortable with Burns partly because his irreverent immediacy undermines the solemnity of extensive exegesis, and partly because his work needs to be understood not only in the international historical context of the late eighteenth century and the rise of the Romantic movement, but also in the context of Scottish literature and culture – and modern Anglo-American literary criticism has frequently neglected the distinctive traditions of Scottish literature. Burns is the peer of William Blake, and along with Sir Walter Scott one of the most widespread influences on nineteenth-century sensibilities internationally.

Any understanding of Burns will require both a sense of his work itself and a sense of its phenomenal reception. LOW's *Critical Heritage* volume (1974) collects the early responses to Burns's first published poems, from the Scottish literati who were his first readers, the English Romantics, including the Wordsworths, Samuel Taylor Coleridge, Charles Lamb, Robert Southey, and Thomas Moore, to Burns's fellow-Scots Byron and Scott himself. The Introduction gives a brief summary of critical responses to Burns in the twentieth century, and Burns's reception in America in the nineteenth century is discussed in an appendix.

One of the results of recent scholarship is BROWN's study. The first three chapters deal with Burns's use of tradition, his understanding of folklore, traditional wisdoms, and colloquial forms of diction and attitude. Brown examines the ways in which Burns collected folk-songs and transformed them into songs, which became popular both in the bothy (cottage) and the drawing-room, and points out how this was effective as a nationalist gesture, constructing a coherent hinterland of song. The next three chapters deal with "Tradition's Use of Burns", illustrating the ways in which Burns's work and his personality have passed into legendary tradition and become part of "calendar custom". This is as much a sociological analysis as it is a literary study, but it is a significant attempt to understand Burns historically. A final chapter discusses some important literary connections with Hugh MacDiarmid, Lewis Grassic Gibbon, Jane Austen, George Douglas Brown, and Woody Guthrie.

McGUIRK also attempts to locate Burns historically, but limits her study to "the sentimental era" – the late eighteenth century. McGuirk examines the myth of the "heav'n-taught ploughman" in the context of the psychological and literary dynamics of the period in which Burns wrote and was first read, and in terms of the Anglo-Scottish and English authors he most admired: Henry Mackenzie, James Thomson, "Ossian" Macpherson, Laurence Sterne, Alexander Pope, and William Shenstone. An understanding of Burns's inclination to the sentimental emerges, but there is less sense of the saturnine, the suppressed savage force and wildness that is its corollary.

For that, one must return to MacDIARMID, who did more to make possible a modern reassessment of Burns's literary worth than anyone else in the twentieth century. The two items in his *Selected Prose* are attacks upon Burns idolatry, whose purpose, in MacDiarmid's view, is "to deny that Burns was Burns". The Burns cult, he claims, has "denied his spirit to honour his name. It has denied his poetry to laud his amours. It has preserved his furniture and repelled his message". MacDiarmid criticizes Burns himself in his 1949 book, for devoting inordinate energy to songs and the preservation of folk-music, and denying his own most demonic creative energies. Yet he recognises the significance of Burns's international popularity and his use of the Scots language as a literary medium.

MONTGOMERIE's 1947 collection gathers essays by various twentieth-century writers who had developed their ideas in MacDiarmid's wake, including Edwin Muir (on the Burns myth), George Bruce, and J.F. Hendry. A spirit of iconoclasm pervades the volume and the results are beneficial, consisting of independently minded enquiries. Montgomerie himself is acute to point out that Burns, writing after Allan Ramsay and Robert Fergusson, eliminated the potentialities of all the urban elements that might have developed in Scottish poetry, and left it "bogged for over a century in rural and Ayrshire Scotland". But the first major critical book devoted to Burns was DAICHES's erudite, chronological, detailed reading of his poetic achievement. Biographical information sustains the shape of this study, but it is primarily a critical exposition of the poems along the lines of New Criticism. An invaluable introductory chapter entitled "The Scottish Literary Tradition" gives Burns's work the context it requires and concisely brings together the national and international contexts.

CRAWFORD's magisterial survey is occasionally overbearing, whereas Daiches retains a lightness of touch; nevertheless, Crawford is extensive and indefatigable. His desire to see Burns in a comparative literary context is laudable, but leads to occasional excesses, as when "The Cottar's Saturday Night" is compared to *King Lear* and *The Oresteia*. Crawford is sensitive to the aesthetic distinctions in Burns's work, but he is less alert to Burns's quickness than to his emotional resonance. In comparing a song with a passage from Joseph Conrad's *Nostromo*, he mistakes delicate strength for durable weight. Nevertheless, Crawford is learned about Burns's musicality.

LINDSAY's *Burns Encyclopedia* is clearly a labour of love and a storehouse of information about Burns's references to people, places, legends, and lore. There are individual entries on Burns's fellow poets, the poems and songs themselves, and his contemporaries and acquaintances. Copiously illustrated, the book supplies in a readily accessible way essential information on the allusions to the contemporary world of Burns's poetry.

In the essay collection edited by JACK and NOBLE the most valuable contributions are by Iain Crichton Smith, writing on Burns as a lyric poet, R.D.S. Jack, on Burns's bawdy poems *The Merry Muses* (which more genteel commentators usually overlook), K.G. Simpson, comparing the sharp wit of Burns and Sterne, and Andrew Noble, discussing the context and dynamics of "Romantic Revolt". LOW's 1975 essay collection includes a rounded "self portrait" edited from Burns's journals and letters by G.Ross Roy, a consideration of Burns's language by David Murison, the editor of the *Scottish National Dictionary*, and three essays on Burns and music by James Kinsley, David Daiches, and Cedric Thorpe Davie – the latter a composer of distinction.

For a recent and readily accessible introduction to the poet's achievement, WALKER's small book is impeccably poised between keen recognition of Burns's popular aspect and his literary uniqueness. Freshness and exuberance colour Walker's reading, but more of the energy of Burns's low humour and high sentiment is caught here than in anything more weighty. The misreadings of others (including Carlyle's wayward sense of "Tam o' Shanter" as a failed tragedy) are sidelighted as an overview of Burns's life and a rich yet intuitive reading of his poetry combine. This is, perhaps, the only study of Burns that, while it invites us to share the poignancy of the love-songs and the scathe of the satires, is also completely in tune with Burns's anarchic sense of humour – the most difficult of all things to write about well.

ALAN RIACH

Burroughs, William S. 1914 –

American fiction writer

Goodman, Michael B., *Contemporary Literary Censorship: The Case History of Burroughs' "Naked Lunch"*, Metuchen, New Jersey: Scarecrow Press, 1981

Lydenberg, Robin, *Word Cultures: Radical Theory and Practice in William S. Burroughs' Fiction*, Urbana: University of Illinois Press, 1987

Lydenberg, Robin, and Jennie Skerl (eds.), *William S. Burroughs at the Front: Critical Reception, 1959–1989*, Carbondale: Southern Illinois University Press, 1991

Mottram, Eric, *William Burroughs: The Algebra of Need*, Buffalo, New York: Intrepid Press, 1971; London: Marion Boyars, 1977; revised edition, as *Algebra of Need: William Burroughs and the Gods of Death*, London and New York: Marion Boyars, 1992

Skerl, Jennie, *William S. Burroughs*, Boston: Twayne, 1985

Tanner, Tony, *City of Words: American Fiction, 1950–1970*, New York: Harper & Row, 1971; London: Jonathan Cape, 1971

The critical reaction to William Burroughs has been problematic: three decades of exceptionally heated debate have generated very little light, and produced a mass of diversely focused articles but few substantial studies. Burroughs has therefore remained a figure of recognised cultural influence, but also a controversial writer who resists canonical status. The quantity and quality of academic engagement has clearly been affected by the absolute division of critics, emotionally expressed as repulsion (most famously in the "UGH" review of *Naked Lunch* in the *Times Literary Supplement*, 23 January 1964: "Glug glug. It tastes disgusting") or reverence (see Skerl, below). Extra-literary factors (drug-addiction, shooting his wife, role in the Beat Generation) contributed to the early polarisation of critics on moral grounds; but, finally, the response of the critical world may be only as Manichean as Burroughs' writing has demanded. For what unites his work is the most extreme ambivalence, both emotional and ideological, about the power of the word itself (to determine the subject, its relations, the construction of reality). Critics have tended to celebrate or condemn his obscenity, anti-humanist humour, experimentalism, or radical theories, but they have not been able to match and make cohere the writer's own singularity. As a result of such partisanship and fragmentation, criticism has yet to bring together Burroughs the 1950s' "Beat", 1960s' avant-gardist, 1970s' space-age mythographer, and 1980s' postmodern iconoclast, let alone make a place for him in the literary canon.

TANNER's chief value has been to situate Burroughs successfully in an influential survey of modern American fiction; in doing so, he was the first major critic to go beyond the approach of the 1960s, which treated Burroughs as an outraged voice of spiritual protest. Focusing on his 1960s' language experiments, Tanner persuasively identifies Burroughs' main field of action as the central theme of American fiction: the conflict between a dream of autonomy and a dread of conditioning and control. Tanner's achievement is to interpret Burroughs' writing alongside that of less anomolous novelists, such as Thomas Pynchon, Kurt Vonnegut, and Norman Mailer, without denaturing it.

MOTTRAM, whose work was the first full-length study, pioneered and maintained the serious academic claims for Burroughs in English (significant treatments appeared in French, reflecting early European acceptance of Burroughs). Contextualising his work in a tradition of dissident thought and radical social satire, Mottram deals with the whole Burroughs *oeuvre*, explicating it as a scathing critique of Western religious and sexual power-structures. While groundbreaking and fully abreast of its subject, Mottram's analysis has, as a whole, not proved fruitful: the structural obscurity of his book and the encyclopedic erudition of his writing has limited its accessibility for readers, while critics have found it difficult to build on.

GOODMAN constructs an often fascinating account narrating the protracted writing, publication history, and censorship trials of *Naked Lunch*. He recognises the 1966 court case as a landmark in legal and literary relations, which freed *Naked Lunch* and all other such works from the dubious fate of the *cause célèbre*. Although narrow in scope and lacking in interpretive analysis, Goodman's scholarship is valuable for making significant documentary material available in coherent form for the first time.

SKERL's 1985 book, in contrast, is especially weak in its material base, while its arguments prove generally reductive. In effect, her analysis confirms the liability of treating Burroughs within the conventions of a critical guide, as if he were a traditional novelist. Skerl admits the difficulty early on, conceding that a chronological approach partially "falsifies the nature of his work". Her justification – that it permits access to Burroughs' development – would require analysis supported by a knowledge that is not evident here. Her treatment is marred by crucial lacunae and large but banal claims. Such weaknesses are only compounded by Skerl's starting point, which is that she writes "out of admiration" for Burroughs, and her conclusion, where she recognizes that his work should properly "be compared to that of other avant-garde artists". The book is not without important merits – for example, Skerl makes a strong case for Burroughs' radical use of popular-cultural materials – but perhaps its real significance is simply that, with all its factual and interpretive inadequacies, it was, 25 years after publication of *Naked Lunch*, the first book-length treatment of Burroughs by a fellow American.

LYDENBERG (1987) has not only written by far the most successful study; she has proved that Burroughs *is* amenable to criticism – of the appropriate kind. She argues that: "the inability of humanistic literary criticism to account for a novel like *Naked Lunch* stems from the fact that such an approach is based on the very structures of metaphor and morality which Burroughs attacks". Lydenberg's methodology fulfils the logic of this premise. Her first section deals with the works (*Naked Lunch* and the cut-up trilogy of the early 1960s), making exemplary close readings of texts previously viewed as all but unreadable; her second section performs an "analytical experiment", by relating Burroughs to poststructuralist critical theory. She lucidly demonstrates what others have merely suggested: that Burroughs' assault on the logocentric tradition fully anticipates deconstructionism, which in turn offers the necessary theoretical framework for reading him. Lydenberg's work has its flaws – chiefly narrowness of focus (in effect 1959–64), and misreadings, which derive from failure to consider the actual *practice* of the cut-up methods – but its major strengths should ensure that Burroughs' most experimental texts are now seen as rigorous avant-garde explorations rather than lazy and reckless follies.

LYDENBERG and SKERL (1991) have produced an essential collection of criticism spanning three decades, and have provided an excellent overview in their Introduction. They include early classic articles by Alan Ansen, Mary McCarthy, and Marshall McLuhan, and selections from major critics such as Mottram, Tanner, Ihab Hassan, and David Lodge. But equally notable are less well-known essays by Frank D. McConnell on addiction and Romanticism, and by Cary Nelson on the effects of non-linear prose. Also of note are the selections from 1980s' criticism and scholarship: Nicholas Zurbrugg's essay on Samuel Beckett, Marcel Proust, and Burroughs the "wicked uncle of postmodernism", and my own account of Burroughs' "settling of scores" against literature through the material and technological possibilities of collage.

OLIVER HARRIS

Butler, Samuel 1835–1902

English novelist and prose writer

Furbank, P.N., *Samuel Butler, 1835–1902*, Cambridge: Cambridge University Press, 1948; 2nd edition, Hamden, Connecticut: Archon Books, 1971

Holt, Lee E., *Samuel Butler*, New York: Twayne, 1964, revised (Boston) 1989

Jeffers, Thomas L., *Samuel Butler Revalued*, University Park: Pennsylvania State University Press, 1981

Knoepflmacher, U.C., *Religious Humanism and the Victorian Novel: George Eliot, Walter Pater and Samuel Butler*, Princeton, New Jersey: Princeton University Press, 1965

Norrman, Ralf, *Samuel Butler and the Meaning of Chiasmus*, London: Macmillan, 1986

Raby, Peter, *Samuel Butler: A Biography*, London: Hogarth Press, 1991

Writers on Butler have to choose whether to stress his importance as a novelist and *The Way of All Flesh* as a seminal twentieth-century text waiting, from its completion by 1884 until its posthumous publication in 1903, to "blow up the Victorian family and with it the whole great pillared and balustraded edifice of the Victorian novel" (as V.S. Pritchett expressed it), or as a social and scientific controversialist, mediating between Charles Darwin's theory of evolution and modern theories of psychology, or as a challenging biographical case-history to be diagnosed and interpreted. Since the publication of Henry Festing Jones's two-volume *Butler: A Memoir* (1919), the temptation to read *The Way of All Flesh* as self-catharsis, and to write about Butler as Ernest Pontifex, has been difficult to resist, and critical discussion has often been essentially an attack on, or a defence of, his attitudes and inconsistencies towards family, religion, academe, his friends, and to life in general.

The attack most often quoted, Malcolm Muggeridge's *The Earnest Atheist* (1936), undermines Butler by seeing him not as a modern iconoclast but as the "Ultimate Victorian", a money-obsessed snob, a timid homosexual, motivated by "hate at its worst, because love [had] gone rancid". FURBANK combats Muggeridge's antagonism by focusing on positive themes: the savage strength of Butler's satirical vein in *Erewhon* (compared, say, to the tameness of William Morris's *News from Nowhere*), or the major emotional experience communicated in *The Way of All Flesh*, seen as a novel about conversion and the establishment of what is one's own in life. Butler's obsessive need for intellectual possession of the objects of his enthusiasm, and his glee in confuting academic expertise may count against him, but he did find some fair targets. Using quotations from the *Notebooks*, Furbank displays the enlightened hedonism that runs through Butler's work.

KNOEPFLMACHER also takes Butler seriously, treating him as one of a group of nineteenth-century novelists who sought to express the search for new ethical principles with which to face an alien evolutionary world. Two chapters trace the steps by which Butler came to terms with his own loss of faith and his reactions to Darwin, so that he formulated "his own hopeful belief in a power which can bequeath strength, beauty, and wealth to those who are conscious of their weakness, ugliness, and financial dependence". Ernest is the bridge-builder between "Victorian dissent and modern alienation", the culmination of the period's attempts to revitalize religion in fiction.

JEFFERS' revaluation sets Butler in the historical contexts of classical ethics and English moral philosophy; David Hume is the main point of reference, with glances also at John Locke, the Earl of Chesterfield, William Cobbett, *et al.*, and ample quotation from George Bernard Shaw as younger contemporary and inheritor of influence. Jeffers is resisting Leavis's characterisation of *The Way of All Flesh* as "morbidly egotistic, self-ignorant and Pharisaical ... small-minded, blind and odiously complacent" as much as Muggeridge's view, and does so by insisting on Butler's intelligence, his "evangelizing on behalf of the mind", and by demonstrating the strain of magnanimity in Overton, Alethea, and Ernest, which enlightens the ethics of the novel. After reading *The Origin of Species* it was inevitable that Butler would treat ethics empirically, deriving norms not from theory but from observed experience; he follows Hume's ethics of the articulation of commonsense conclusions.

NORRMAN renews the attack, seeing Butler as a relativist, full of morbid self-blame for imbalance in his relationships (with Miss Savage, for instance). This is part of a view extending the rhetorical figure of "chiasmus" to include all forms of symmetry, inversion, and reciprocity – all dualistic in nature, and leading to the repetitive, obsessive use by the pronounced chiasticist (as Norrman sees Butler) of such stylistic features as dramatic self-division, antithesis, balancing, dialogue, parallelism, and zigzag thinking and plotting. Butler's "ambilateralism" is a state of mind running through his style, his outlook, and the events of his life: always placing himself in opposition, he does not seek solutions – confirmed dualists want the problems only. Butler's self-contradictions are, despite witty effects, disastrous: his obsession with symmetry of style, evidenced most obviously in his fondness for inverted proverbs, corresponds, in Norrman's view, to the larger emotional limitations of life and outlook.

HOLT's summation of Butler's career and of critical views of his work contains little original criticism, but is a sound chronological account of life and works, with useful bibliography, giving sufficient stress to Butler's other major works, *Erewhon*, *The Fair Haven*, and *Erewhon Revisited*, as well as reminding the reader of forgotten writings, such as the "Earnest Clergyman" letters (1879). Holt emphasises the energy, strength, and variety of Butler's output, characterising him both as a challenger, demanding candour and openness in the reader, and one of the last "universal men", who tried in his life to realise what a human being is capable of, as artist, scientist, musician, poet, and philosopher. The clear directness of Butler's style, in contrast to the purple prose of John Ruskin or Walter Pater, and the deeper intimations, such as the "virtuoso attack on human reason" in *The Fair Haven*, which out-distance any mere riding of hobby horses, win Holt's admiration.

RABY's biography stresses Butler's intellectual, controversialist nature, is frank about his sexuality, his pettinesses, and mistakes, but positive about his enthusiasms and affections. Butler's intellectual stance emerges as that of a leveller, a demythologiser, intransigent and exasperating, but with unblinking awareness of his own deficiencies. Major works are interestingly assessed: *The Fair Haven*, *The Authoress of the Odyssey*, and *Shakespeare's Sonnets Reconsidered* are seen as "novels in disguise"; *Erewhon* is a composite presentation of "a development of Western civilisation, a reversal of it, and an aberration from it", producing sufficient depth in its series of distorting mirrors and its double-edged views of law, church, and education to make significant valid statements; and *The Way of All Flesh* is seen as combining "the deceptive simplicity of domestic melodrama, or, perhaps, of subtle parody" with illustration of Butler's theory of unconscious memory – the optimism of the theory mocked by the contrivances of the plot. Raby sees Butler as "one of the first Victorian novelists to embrace the negative".

TONY DAVENPORT

Byron, Lord 1788–1824

English poet and dramatist

Barton, Anne, *Byron: Don Juan*, Cambridge and New York: Cambridge University Press, 1992
Beatty, Bernard, *Byron's "Don Juan"*, London: Croom Helm, 1985; Totowa, New Jersey: Barnes & Noble, 1985
Beatty, Bernard, and Vince Newey, (eds.), *Byron and the Limits of Fiction*, Liverpool: Liverpool University Press, 1988
Christensen, Jerome, *Lord Byron's Strength: Romantic Writing and Commercial Society*, Baltimore and London: Johns Hopkins University Press, 1993
Cooke, Michael G., *The Blind Man Traces the Circle: On the Patterns and Philosophy of Byron's Poetry*, Princeton, New Jersey: Princeton University Press, 1969
Elledge, W. Paul, *Byron and the Dynamics of Metaphor*, Nashville, Tennessee: Vanderbilt University Press, 1968
Franklin, Caroline, *Byron's Heroines*, Oxford: Clarendon Press, 1992; New York: Oxford University Press, 1992
Hoagwood, Terence Allan, *Byron's Dialectic: Skepticism and the Critique of Culture*, Lewisburg, Pennsylvania: Bucknell University Press, 1993; London: Associated University Presses, 1993
Joseph, M.K., *Byron the Poet*, London: Victor Gollancz, 1964
Kelsall, Malcolm, *Byron's Politics*, Brighton, Sussex: Harvester Press, 1987; Totowa, New Jersey: Barnes & Noble, 1987
McGann, Jerome J., *"Don Juan" in Context*, London: John Murray, 1976; Chicago: University of Chicago Press, 1976
Watkins, Daniel P., *Social Relations in Byron's Eastern Tales*, Rutherford, New Jersey: Fairleigh Dickinson University Press, 1987; London: Associated University Presses, 1987

The trigger for the reawakening of interest in Byron's work in the United Kingdom – always remembering that Byron has been second only to Shakespeare in cultural interest on the Continent, more or less without break since his death – has been the shift of interest from the early to the late poems, and the seemingly decisive revaluing of the *ottava rima* works, *Beppo*, *Don Juan*, and *Vision of Judgement*, as *his* major, and *a* major, contribution to literature. Within this shift – indeed the key to its operating mechanisms – there are two somewhat contradictory lines of thought: one stressing the self-reflexive, in extreme cases ludic, qualities of the late poetry, and linking their view of reality to a very postmodernist reality-as-text outlook; the other stressing rather their anti-Romantic concern with the nuts and bolts of social criticism, and positively evaluating what had earlier been seen negatively as Byron's retreat from Romanticism to the eighteenth-century world of satire. Interesting work by Susan Wolfson, Kathy Kernberger, and Amanda Gilroy, among others, has begun to illuminate the feminine in Byron's text. Two major editorial achievements have dominated the field – Leslie Marchand's edition of *Byron's Letters and Journals* (London: John Murray, 1973–82) and J.J. McGann's edition *Lord Byron: Complete Poetical Works* (Oxford: Clarendon Press, 1980–93). We should also note Andrew Nicholson's *Lord Byron: Complete Miscellaneous Prose* (Oxford: Clarendon Press, 1991).

JOSEPH's study was one of the first to indicate a return of serious academic interest to Byron. It is a lucid and reliable introduction, though now perhaps somewhat dated. In taking up the question of voice in *Childe Harold's Pilgrimage* it hints at the way in which the idea of a voice floating free of a personality was to become a central concern of Byron criticism from the mid-1970s onwards.

ELLEDGE's study is notable for the way in which, particularly in his discussion of *Manfred*, he emphasises the mind/matter, inner/outer, tension in works up to the 1816 period. This again prepares the way for later developments. Elledge's view of Manfred "triumphing in the vacuum of his selfhood" represents an extreme "romantic" view of Byron's hero, and a reading of the play that was to be much disputed.

COOKE, though not at all at this point a postmodernist critic, produced a view of Byron that is in many ways sympathetic to later critics working broadly in this tradition, picking up as he does the distinction between cynicism and radical scepticism. Although Byron is radically sceptical of all systems of belief, this does not mean, in his view, that man cannot construct provisional values by which to live. Cooke's claim produces a decidedly late-twentieth-century Byron.

McGANN's study of *Don Juan* came early on in what was to become his development as the champion of New Historicism in Romantic studies, but significantly after his earlier study *Fiery Dust: Byron's Poetic Development* (1968). In many ways McGann is, one suspects, probably going to be most highly valued as a historicist, rather than as an ideological critic or theorist. What his edition of the *Poetical Works* also stresses is the immense richness to be gained from firmly placing Byron in his historical context, and the complexity of that context. It is later that McGann will stress the importance of realising how much of our view of historical context is conditioned by the way in which we are still part of a cultural web itself conditioned by that very context.

WATKINS' study of the understudied Turkish Tales (particularly neglected in the early part of the twentieth-century revival) is a fairly extreme example of the New-Historicist readings of Byron, enabled by McGann's later views. Here Byron the Romantic vanishes under the revelation of political relevance of a very precisely defined kind, tightly bound to the actualities of Byron's day.

BEATTY's 1985 study could not be further removed from Watkins. Though very much a study of the voice of *Don Juan* and of its existence as verbal texture, Beatty's argument probably has to be characterised in the end as metaphysical, with the poem seen as an organic development towards a goal (rather than a picaresque tale), whose emblem is the character Aurora Raby. It is a curious and beguiling mixture of the religious and what it is too crass to call the "postmodernist". BARTON's short book on *Don Juan* goes much further than being the best introduction to the poem. Combining close reading, a sense of the poem's literary background, and the realities of the poem's audience, this short study is a model of critical pragmatism. Although there is more to be said on the English Cantos surely, Barton's account of the Adeline/Aurora nexus is more centred than that of Beatty.

BEATTY and NEWEY's anthology, titled to suggest a "Byron-as-text" view, also includes a firmly New-Historicist piece by Marilyn Butler, which represents a more middle-of-the-road approach to *The Giaour* than others, Watkins' for example. An essay of my own here might be taken to represent the opposite camp, reading *Beppo* for the pleasures and sadnesses of its verbal texture, rather than for any "underlying" meaning.

KELSALL's book is by far the most satisfying on Byron's politics from a straightforward historical perspective. Rather than as a revolutionary, Byron emerges as a progressive Whig, with all the instincts for checks and balances that his political background bred into him. There is a particularly illuminating chapter on *Vision of Judgement*.

CHRISTIANSEN's is a difficult book, and perhaps overlong; but it offers an intriguing tangent on the New-Historicist/textualist debate. He announces that "empiricism reduced strength to mere cause; industrialism disciplined cause to mass production; commercialism subordinated production to . . . pervasive . . . demand. . . . This book conducts a Romantic argument with political economy and with functionalist accounts of poetry". In many ways, perhaps paradoxically in view of its own difficulty, this study seeks to place Byron's strength in the community of writer and reader, though the idea of that community is a highly sophisticated one.

FRANKLIN's study is a straightforwardly historicized account of the role of women in Byron's poetry, and, by the by, of the role of women more generally in Regency verse romances and dramas. It is not perhaps at the cutting edge of feminist theory, but is, in its scholarship, much more than an introduction to an expanding area of interest.

HOAGWOOD's is a particularly clear-cut example of Byron as postmodernist sceptic, with well-controlled nostalgia. For all that, it does not renounce context as a way of making its point, and is particularly interesting on prose writers who lie behind Byron's scepticism. In many ways its singlemindedness provides an odd point of contact with the very different content of Watkins' study.

J.D. BONE

C

Canadian Literature: General

Atwood, Margaret, *Survival: A Thematic Guide to Canadian Literature*, Toronto: Anansi, 1972
Bayard, Caroline (ed.), *100 Years of Critical Solitudes: Canadian and Quebeçois Criticism from the 1880s to the 1980s*, Toronto: ECW Press, 1992
Frye, Northrop, *The Bush Garden: Essays on the Canadian Imagination*, Toronto: Anansi, 1971
Howells, Coral Ann, and Lynette Hunter (eds.), *Narrative Strategies in Canadian Literature: Feminism and Postcolonialism*, Milton Keynes, Buckinghamshire: Open University Press, 1991
Keith, W.J., *An Independent Stance: Essays on English-Canadian Criticism and Fiction*, Erin, Ontario: Porcupine's Quill, 1991
Klinck, Carl F., *Giving Canada a Literary History: A Memoir*, edited by Sandra Djwa, Ottawa: Carleton University Press, 1991
Lecker, Robert (ed.), *Canadian Canons: Essays in Literary Value*, Toronto: University of Toronto Press, 1991
Staines, David (ed.), *The Canadian Imagination: Dimensions of a Literary Culture*, Cambridge, Massachusetts: Harvard University Press, 1977

Canadian literature acquired status as a subject for serious attention only in 1967, the centennial year of Canadian confederation. In the three decades since, it has called forth an increasing body of commentary and theory, of which the titles listed above – mainly essay collections – can claim, at best, to be representative.

FRYE's retrospective collection of essays represents a turning-point in Canada's criticism of its own literature, in that it places all the writing it considers in a historical perspective, and also views it as part of the larger story of "the Canadian imagination". Defining this national imagination was a major project of the years surrounding the confederation centenary, and Frye did much to establish the terms of the debate. His notion of Canada as "practically the only country left in the world which is a pure colony", imaginatively characterized by a "garrison mentality", remained influential into the 1980s. The most useful section contains Frye's annual surveys of poetic production in Canada, published in the *University of Toronto Quarterly* during the 1950s. Although he avoided evaluative judgments, Frye conveyed a sure sense of what was significant and what was peripheral. The reader of this section obtains a good sense of what characterized emerging modernism in Canada, and who were its most significant practitioners. The other notable item of the collection is Frye's essay concluding the *Literary History of Canada* (1965, edited by Carl F. Klinck), in which he engages with the relation of Canadian culture to the country's history and geography. He deals with issues of identity and unity, fleshing out his conception of Canada as garrison, and placing emphasis on literature as regional and structurally mythopoeic. Frye's study remains a useful starting-point for investigating Canadian literature from modernist and postmodern perspectives.

KLINCK's memoir, nurtured and edited by Sandra Djwa, records the education and career of the person who "became the principal architect of the new, systematic, historically based scholarship that emerged in Canada in the early sixties", and who instigated and carried through to fruition the most ambitious project in Canadian literary history. Klinck throws light not only on the literary history of Canada, but, more importantly, on what was involved in the process of justifying a national literature: defining the purpose and scope of historical scholarship, establishing institutional instruments such as university courses, and providing materials like anthologies, series, and library holdings to enable study and research. This memoir supplements Frye's essays in that it reveals the importance of scholarship as a basis for criticism and commentary, and shows how and why the 1960s were so important in the development of Canadian literature as a field of study. Klinck's book is also related to Lecker's collection of essays on canon formation and revision.

ATWOOD's now classic study is in the mythopoeic tradition of Frye rather than the scholarly-historical tradition of Klinck. Her starting point is Frye's reformulation of the identity question as "where is here?". She also treats Canadian writing as a collective cultural construct, not as a collection of works by individual authors: writers participate in a shared cultural community, albeit one without tools to recognize itself. In short, for Atwood, as for Frye, Canada is a colony. Atwood's identification of "survival" as the key Canadian thematic extends to a comprehensive treatment of Canadian topics in terms of a victor-victim model. Such a model organizes discussions of nature, animals, Native Canadians, explorers and settlers, immigrants, heroes and martyrs, women, the family, and Quebec. The argument is that only by recognizing our entrapment within the victor-victim pattern can we change it. Atwood's book has been tremendously influential for both writing and criticism, and it was probably the first to acknowledge how much of Canadian cultural perception has depended on ambivalence about margins and boundaries. Although discussions about individual authors and works in *Survival* are brief, Atwood's choice of passages for quotation is telling. Written accessibly and with considerable wit, this is still the best introduction to Canadian writing in English up to the late 1960s.

The collection of essays edited and introduced by STAINES is the literary product of his introduction of a course on Canadian literature in the Department of English at Harvard University in 1976. Its contributors include such distinguished and widely reflective writers and critics as Frye, Atwood, George Woodcock, and Marshall McLuhan. Most of the essays address themselves specifically to an American audience, and are concerned with drawing a contrast between the cultural situations of the United States and Canada. They also reflect the general cultural stance formed during the 1960s and described above: individual voices are subordinated to a questioning (and often querulous) cultural voice; Canadian identity is conflicted, given that Canada, a "mosaic" and a "dialectic of regional and ethnic tensions", lacks unity. Essay titles express a sense of incompletion: "Haunted by Lack of Ghosts" (Frye), "Canada: The Borderline Case" (McLuhan), and "Is There a Canadian Drama?" (Parker). The volume contains a useful essay on Canadian fiction by George Woodcock, and Staines' Introduction ("Canada Observed") contextualizes the various discussions of writing within issues of unity and identity established as major categories in the 1960s and 1970s.

Those categories are far less relevant to the essay collection edited by HOWELLS and HUNTER; "*Strategies*" is as significant as "*Canadian*" in the title. The ten essays have been written for British students and teachers of Canadian literature, and are less concerned with generalizing Canadian experience than with offering up-to-date commentary on, and analysis of, Canadian works in a changed theoretical environment. Yet although the volume is subtitled *Feminism and Postcolonialism*, those categories are in fact peripheral to most of the essays. Major contemporary writers dealt with here include Michael Ondaatje, Daphne Marlatt, Alice Munro, and Margaret Atwood. Andrew Gurr's opening essay on the genre of linked short stories uncharacteristically argues that Canadian literature, far from being postmodern or even modernist, is regional and *pre*modernist. On the subject of short fiction, so pervasive a genre in contemporary Canadian writing, Stephen Regan's concluding piece on modernism and postmodernism is well argued and compelling. Although this collection includes essays on Margaret Laurence and Marian Engel, the emphasis is on still-active major writers to whose work it serves as useful, if uneven, introduction.

KEITH offers an annotated selection of his own articles, papers, and reviews, dealing both with topics within criticism and with individual writers and works. A recurrent note in his work is a call for a return to evaluative criticism. He criticizes both the mythopoeic/cultural procedures of Frye and his followers, and the scholarly/historical procedures involved in the production of Klinck's *The Literary History of Canada*, hence his claim to an "independent stance". That independence is, however, compromised by his frequent invocation of English critic F.R. Leavis as against Canadian critics who take a "thematic" or a "patriotic" approach. Keith is equally resistant to emergent critical paths like poststructuralism and postmodernism, insisting that attention to them inhibits the possibility of *true* criticism. Keith's positions are certainly provocative and critically unfashionable. Part of his book's value lies in its treatment of figures neglected in other studies. There is an essay on Louis Dudek as poet and critic, essays on Frederick Philip Grove, Ethel Wilson, and Hugh MacLennan from earlier generations, and a number of essays on Jack Hodgins, which privilege the realist pole of the label "magic realism". The somewhat reactionary, polemical tone and points of view of the essays give Keith's collection unity and a sense of critical purpose.

BAYARD, a completely bilingual critic, has edited a collection of essays, in English-French language pairs, which attempts a comparativity rare in Canadian literary discourse. Her book is, however, valuable even for readers whose interest is solely in English-Canadian literary and critical production. While the essays' emphases are on literary theory and critical procedures, these are seen as inseparable from works of literature, for they fashion audiences and ways of reading. Bayard claims that "the most original contribution to theory in English Canada was Northrop Frye's work on archetypes", and the volume's contributors are therefore interested in different critical paths as these have flourished and are just emerging: biographical criticism, historical criticism, thematic/sociological criticism, psychoanalysis, semiotics, and poststructuralism. Most of the contributors are well-known critics, and the essays are both informative and searching. This is a particularly valuable book for readers interested in the gap, in Canada, between its two literatures and critical traditions.

In LECKER's recent collection, the focus shifts from both literary works and critical schools in themselves to a question that is as much institutional as formal: who decides what makes up "Canadian literature", and how are such decisions made? These issues of canonicity are generally passed over; some writers, like Atwood, appear to assume that a work becomes canonical when it embodies deep, culturally determined, mythic structures, while others, like Keith, might argue that some intrinsic and self-evident literary quality gets a work into the canon. Lecker's controversial collection highlights the canonical issue as a political site where individuals and institutional groups contest field formation. The various essays in Lecker's compilation – by, on the whole, younger writers – deal with every major genre, with history and culture, and with different and conflicting schools. As a whole, this is a provocative book, which succeeds in denaturalising "Canadian literature".

PATRICK HOLLAND

Canadian Literature: Recent and Contemporary

Atwood, Margaret, *Survival: A Thematic Guide to Canadian Literature*, Toronto: Anansi, 1972

Davey, Frank, *Surviving the Paraphrase: Eleven Essays on Canadian Literature*, Winnipeg, Manitoba: Turnstone Press, 1983

Davidson, Arnold E. (ed.), *Studies on Canadian Literature: Introductory and Critical Essays*, New York: Modern Language Association of America, 1990
Frye, Northrop, *The Bush Garden: Essays on the Canadian Imagination*, Toronto: Anansi, 1971
Hutcheon, Linda, *The Canadian Postmodern: A Study of Contemporary English-Canadian Fiction*, Toronto, New York, and Oxford: Oxford University Press, 1988
Kroetsch, Robert, *The Lovely Treachery of Words: Essays Selected and New*, Toronto, New York, and Oxford: Oxford University Press, 1989
Moss, John, *Patterns of Isolation in English Canadian Fiction*, Toronto: McClelland & Stewart, 1974
New, W.H. (ed.), *Canadian Writers since 1960: First Series* and *Canadian Writers since 1960: Second Series* (Volumes 53 and 60, *Dictionary of Literary Biography*), Detroit: Gale Research, 1986–87
Staines, David, *Beyond the Provinces: Literary Canada at Century's End*, Toronto: University of Toronto Press, 1995

In his Preface to Volume 53 of the *Dictionary of Literary Biography*, New describes the years since 1960 as "unparalleled in Canadian literary history for the sheer amount of work published and the extraordinary liveliness of literary activity". The establishment of the Canada Council in 1958, with a mandate and a budget to encourage artistic endeavors, led swiftly to rapid growth in Canadian publishing, bookselling, theater production, journal production, and university course development. Initially, within the climate of militant cultural nationalism leading up to the 1967 centennial celebrations of Canadian confederation, there was a spirited turn away from previously received (largely British) conventions, and a growing awareness of the political nature of language in the cultural development of a diverse community.

NEW himself has contributed a number of books to the tide of recent critical literature (he is, for instance, editor of four other Canadian volumes of the *Dictionary of Literary Biography*, and of Volume IV [1990] of Carl F. Klinck's monumental *Literary History of Canada* [1965, revised 1976]; he has also written his own *History of Canadian Literature* [1989]). The two volumes of *Canadian Writers since 1960* aim to provide "career biographies" of both major and minor literary figures, and appraisals of them by scholars, most of whom are faculty at Canadian universities. Volume 53 covers 67 writers, and Volume 60 covers 82 writers; a third or more of these are French-speaking. The entries range from two pages in length for an author considered minor, to 15 or more pages for major writers like Margaret Atwood and Robert Kroetsch. Each entry includes a bibliography of primary works and critical material; most have authorial photographs and reproductions of original book-jackets and/or manuscript pages. These volumes are indispensable as introductory reference tools for recent Canadian literature.

Although best-known internationally for his reading of biblical mythology as the basis for Western literature, FRYE has also produced a considerable body of criticism on Canadian literature and culture. In *The Bush Garden*, whose essays cover a 30-year period, he advocated (though he seldom adopted) a primarily cultural-historical and non-evaluative view of Canadian writing, understood as an inferior, though nationally interesting, product. In fact half the essays in the book are evaluative reviews of Canadian poetry, which Frye contributed annually to *The University of Toronto Quarterly* from 1950 to 1959. These provide fascinating first readings of new poetry by, for instance, Irving Layton, Phyllis Webb, Raymond Souster, Miriam Waddington, Eli Mandel, P.K. Page, Dorothy Livesay, and Leonard Cohen; in the Preface, Frye describes these reviews as "field work" undergone while he was working out his "comprehensive critical theory" of myth as the structural principle of a poem and literature as "conscious mythology". Frye consistently asserts the importance to poetry of regionalism – "the sense of a specific environment as something that provides a circumference for an imagination". Included are important papers on Canadian narrative poetry and on E.J. Pratt, and Frye's influential "Conclusion" to Klinck's 1965 *Literary History of Canada*. Here Frye argues that the small communities of early white Canadian settlement, confronted with "a huge, unthinking, menacing, and formidable physical setting", were bound to develop the conservative and defensive stance of a "garrison mentality" whose literature would be largely rhetorical illustration of conventional social attitudes. The thematic tradition in Canadian criticism thus effectively begins with Frye's positing of landscape as the generative principle of literature in Canada. Frye's revised conclusion to the second (1976) edition of Klinck (anthologized in *Divisions on a Ground* [1982]) documents the rapid development since 1960 of a Canadian literature now "professional" in its concern with craft and tradition over rhetoric, no longer in need of cultural-historical, rather than evaluative, reading, and having moved from garrison to library for inspiration.

Frye's concept of the garrison has obvious affiliations with the survival thesis developed by his student Margaret ATWOOD. (Influence in the opposite direction is evident in Frye's title *The Bush Garden* – a phrase he borrowed from Atwood's *The Journals of Susanna Moodie*). Hers has undoubtedly been one of the most influential books of Canadian criticism, partly because of its accessible "reader-friendly" style, and partly because of the alluring simplicity of its message. Arguing that literature is "a geography of the mind" and that "every country or culture has a single unifying and informing symbol at its core", Atwood proposes that, for Canada, survival is such a symbol. This central idea generates "an almost intolerable anxiety" which Atwood proceeds to discover in all the literature that she discusses (and, in fact, to demonstrate in the fiction and poetry that she herself produces). Because Canada as colony is in the victim position, Canadian literature exhibits a superabundance of victims, failed explorers, doomed settlers, and crippled artists. Atwood's thematic cultural poetics initially generated considerable critical activity, but has lately fallen into disrepute because of its perceived central-Canadian bias, its selectivity of textual reference, its privileging of thematic content over literary merit, and its tendency to canonize works that fit the paradigm.

Another influential "thematologist" is MOSS, although in *Patterns of Isolation* he is at pains to distinguish his version of thematic criticism from what he sees as the over-exclusive thematizing of Frye and Atwood. However, he does align his interests with those of cultural nationalism in asserting that, while other patterns might well be traced, an investigation of the common patterns of isolation in the themes, imagery, and incidents of Canadian literature will best display "the indigenous character of our Canadian community" and "reflect the progress of the Canadian imagination towards a positive identity". He suggests that these patterns may describe different versions of the dislocation of exile, corresponding to the four distinct historical phases of garrison, frontier, colonial, and immigrant experience; or such patterns may express a moral vision in response to the geophysical nature of a particular region; or they may arise out of ironic conflicts between the individual and societal norms. Under each of these headings, Moss offers stimulating readings of various (mainly recent) Canadian fictions; these readings are more critically suggestive than those of his later book *The Ancestral Present: Sex and Violence in the Canadian Novel* (1977), which he vainly protests is not thematic but descriptive of structure. Moss makes available a much greater diversity of approach as editor of two volumes of critical essays by other scholars – *The Canadian Novel: Here and Now* (1978) and *The Canadian Novel: Present Tense* (1985).

DAVEY writes to provide a corrective to the hegemony of thematic criticism as both method and ideology. One of a number of contemporary poet-critics in Canada, he advocates a postmodern, ideologically self-conscious and linguistically constructionist textual analysis, and suggests a number of non-evaluative approaches (historical criticism, phenomenological criticism, genre studies, linguistic analysis, regional criticism). His own criticism, however, which occupies a major portion of this study, does not generally maintain a neutrally descriptive stance, but instead offers first-rate and openly evaluative close readings of form, imagery, and technique in such writers as E.J. Pratt, Robert Stead, Sinclair Ross, and Atwood herself, on whom he has also written a full-length book. As in his earlier *From There to Here* (1974 – a somewhat triumphalistic guidebook to 60 recent Canadian writers, and one whose apparent authority Davey later deconstructs in *Reading Canadian Reading* [1988]), Davey foregrounds his western-Canadian bias, his interest in postmodern poetry, and his non-referential understanding of literature, in contradistinction to the central-Ontarian, monolithic, and referential criticism that he sees as still dominant.

Undoubtedly the foremost postmodernist critic in Canada is poet and novelist KROETSCH. In his playfully idiosyncratic collection of essays, ranging over 20 years, he moves between personal musings and rigorously intellectual critiques, eliding the boundaries between the two through a constant foregrounding of the materiality of his words and the process of writing. Kroetsch demonstrates his simultaneous indebtedness to, and difference from, Frye in asserting that "Frye, in his decent and quiet and radical way, tells the Canadian poet to be anti-colonial . . . by the act of retelling we can tell ourselves both out of and into story". In Kroetsch's terms, Canadian writers must "uninvent the world" in order to rewrite it as authentically their own; this involves what, following Michel Foucault, he calls archaeology rather than history, and leads to a writing of fragments, traces, and discontinuities. Kroetsch understands the "metanarrative" of Canadian literature, its "strategy for survival", to be precisely its distrust of metanarrative and its insistence on remaining "multiple". He discusses the characteristic silences and absent centers in writing by, for instance, Sinclair Ross, Sheila Watson, Ernest Buckler, Margaret Laurence, Rudy Wiebe, Michael Ondaatje, and Atwood herself; he proposes a reading of ethnic narrative as a rewriting of myth; and he speculates on the suggestive tendency of major Canadian fictional characters to have no names: "at its best, the threat of anonymity generates story".

Appropriately, Kroetsch gets both the first and the last word in HUTCHEON's book: she labels him "Mr Canadian Postmodern". Arguing that postmodernism both confronts and goes beyond the problematics of colonial dependency, and that "the postmodern 'different' . . . is starting to replace the humanist 'universal' as a prime cultural value", Hutcheon gives readings of a number of contemporary Canadian writers (Cohen, Ondaatje, Audrey Thomas, Atwood, Timothy Findley, Kroetsch) who make use of the parodic or ironic as a way simultaneously to inscribe and subvert the authority of traditional realism. She sees in postmodern Canadian writing major new forms of the embodiment of ethnicity and the female, and major refigurations of the "realist regional" into the "postmodern different". One chapter deals with the relationship of the dynamic to the static in writing, orality, and photographic imaging; another discusses fiction and non-fiction as two traditional genres of discourse whose interpenetration is the subject of Canadian "historiographic metafiction". Hutcheon reads Atwood's fictions as "the epitome of [the] postmodern contradiction" between process and product.

An earlier version of Hutcheon's introduction appears as "The Canadian Postmodern" in DAVIDSON's edition of critical essays, published by the Modern Language Association of America, and valuable specifically for its orientation to the newcomer to Canadian literature and criticism. Davidson explains that this volume has been composed in response to "the arrival of a national literature on the international stage" and that the essays included are intentionally very diverse, partly in order to avoid any suggestion of univalency in Canadian literature. Eight consider Canadian writing in English, a further eight Canadian writing in French, and four cross this linguistic divide; each offers a substantial bibliography. Davidson envisages the book being used in courses looking at Canadian studies, comparative literature, and a variety of critical and theoretical concerns, such as cultural imperialism, canonization, and issues of genre and form, ethnicity and postcolonialism. Of particular interest are papers by: Shirley Neuman on "English-Canadian Poetry since 1960", in which she questions the exclusoriness of the label "postmodern"; Terry Goldie on the native as "semiotic pawn" in Canadian literature; and Barry Cameron on the process of literary institutionalization, which has also involved "English Critical Discourse in/on Canada".

STAINES's book is the published version of his 1994 F.E.L. Priestley Lectures in the History of Ideas at the University of Toronto, and provides a timely overview of Canadian literature and criticism at the end of the twentieth century. The three chapters trace the movement over the century from a colonial mentality in literature to "the quiet assertion of selfhood"; the finding of literary independence from the United States in the corrective perspective of Canadian as "other"; and the development in criticism of a distinctly Canadian stance, no longer of thoughtless praise or disdainful debunking, but of "dispassionate witness" – a stance that Staines himself demonstrates. Noting that none of the first four novels of the 1990s to win the Governor General's Award for Literature makes much, if any, direct reference to Canada, and yet none of them has been questioned as to its Canadianness, Staines suggests that the time for assertions of national identity and definition is past. Now Canadian literature involves "a balancing of voices in a global village whose citizens and their works are at once native and naturalized".

DEBORAH C. BOWEN

Caribbean Literature

Baugh, Edward (ed.), *Critics on Caribbean Literature*, London: Allen & Unwin, 1978; New York: St Martin's Press, 1978

Brathwaite, Edward Kamau, *History of the Voice: The Development of Nation Language in Anglophone Caribbean Poetry*, London: New Beacon, 1984

Brown, Lloyd W., *West Indian Poetry*, Boston: Twayne, 1978; 2nd edition, London: Heinemann, 1984

Chamberlin, J. Edward, *Come Back to Me My Language: Poetry and the West Indies*, Urbana: University of Illinois Press, 1993; Toronto: McLelland & Stewart, 1993

Dance, Daryl Cumber (ed.), *Fifty Caribbean Writers: A Bio-Bibliographical Critical Sourcebook*, Westwood, Connecticut: Greenwood Press, 1986

Gilkes, Michael, *Wilson Harris and the Caribbean Novel*, Trinidad and London: Longman, 1975

Gilkes, Michael, *The West Indian Novel*, Boston: Twayne, 1981

Herdeck, Donald (ed.), *Caribbean Writers: A Bio-Bibliographical-Critical-Encyclopedia*, 4 vols., Washington, D.C.: Three Continents Press, 1979

Hill, Errol, *The Jamaican Stage: 1655–1900: Profile of a Colonial Theatre*, Amherst: University of Massachusetts Press, 1992

James, Louis (ed.), *The Islands in Between: Essays on West Indian Literature*, London: Oxford University Press, 1968

King, Bruce (ed.), *West Indian Literature*, London: Macmillan, 1979; Hamden, Connecticut: Archon Books, 1979

McWatt, Mark (ed.), *West Indian Literature in Its Social Context*, St Michael, Barbados: University of the West Indies English Department, 1985

Ramchand, Kenneth, *The West Indian Novel and Its Background*, London: Faber & Faber, 1970; 2nd edition, London: Heinemann, 1983

Ramchand, Kenneth, *An Introduction to the Study of West Indian Literature*, Sunbury-on-Thames, Surrey: Nelson Caribbean, 1976

Though by no means the first critical book on Anglophone Caribbean literature, JAMES's collection provides an excellent guide to writing from the region during the two decades prior to publication. Individual essays offer valuable introductions to the early work of some of the major figures of Caribbean literature – V.S. Naipaul, Derek Walcott, George Lamming, and Wilson Harris – and fine discussions of writers such as Andrew Salkey, John Hearne, and V.S. Reid. James's 50-page Introduction remains a first-rate prolegomenon to Caribbean writing, and is notable for its succinct sketching in of the social and historical background and useful short discussions of Denis Williams's *Other Leopards*, Creole verse, and calypso.

RAMCHAND attacked James's study for "compound[ing] the metaphor of [an] explosion or sudden growth" in Caribbean writing in the 1950s (*Journal of Commonwealth Literature*, 9, 1970) and his own 1970 study establishes a longer genealogy. It is a scholarly work, which offers insights into some of the social contexts from which the West Indian novel emerged earlier this century. Ramchand is particularly good on the problems facing local publishing and the development of Jamaican writing in the first half of the century; and in coining the term "cultural absenteeism" – the suggestion is that the region's Eurocentric orientation, a correlative of the physical absenteeism of many of the planter class, created a "cultural void" – he helped develop a key concept. The book also discusses the language situation in the Caribbean, and includes chapters on the novel of boyhood, literary interest in Africa, and white West Indian fiction. It remains essential reading, even though the subsequent impact of New Historicist approaches makes its sociological apparatus seem somewhat outmoded now.

RAMCHAND's 1976 book is primarily directed towards an undergraduate audience, and has chapters on nine novels and the regions' two most highly acclaimed poets, Derek Walcott and Edward Kamau Brathwaite. It is at its best when relating writers to their backgrounds and when offering close readings of particular passages.

BAUGH's collection contains extracts from 18 previously published essays, dividing them into four sections. The first, "Contexts for Criticism", reprints seminal pieces by writer-critics – Harris, Walcott, Lamming, and Sylvia Wynter – as well as part of Gordon Rohlehr's fine discussion of "The Folk in Caribbean Literature". The other sections – "From Colonialism to Independence", "Relationships: Individual, Community, Mankind", and "A Language of One's Own" – all tackle subjects of central importance in Caribbean writing. The general level of quality is high, though the section on language, while notable for making another section of Rohlehr's "Folk" essay available to a wider audience, seems dated after the appearance of articles that devoted more sophisticated attention to the subject in the 1980s.

KING's collection is made up of newly written essays – five general pieces on the background to, and particular periods of, West Indian writing, which are notable for their concise, though sometimes uncritical, provision of information; and chapters on the same major figures as in James, as well as Edgar Mittelholzer, Sam Selvon, Jean Rhys, and Brathwaite. In the absence of a comprehensive history of Anglophone Caribbean literature, this remains a useful primer for the pre-1980 period.

GILKES's two books are closer in approach than their titles suggest: the Introduction to the 1975 Wilson Harris volume ranges widely across a range of Caribbean fiction, making it far more than a study of a single author; in contrast the 1981 work offers a less comprehensive survey than its title and the Twayne format lead one to expect. In the earlier book Gilkes explores the theme of psychic reconstruction in Harris's work, demonstrating the urgency of attaining "unity of being" in a society that has suffered from the negative aspects of cultural schizophrenia. Jungian in conception, the study explores the mythopoeic aspects of Harris's imagination, making productive use of such thinkers as Mircea Eliade and Joseph Campbell. The Introduction provides a context for Harris by examining responses to psychic fragmentation in the work of Mittelholzer, Lamming, Naipaul, and Walcott. In the Twayne volume, after providing an "aeriel" view of the beginnings of the Caribbean novel, Gilkes focuses on four aspects: novels by "pioneers" (H.G. De Lisser, C.L.R. James, Roger Mais, and Mittelholzer); the major work of three later "exiles" (Lamming, Naipaul, and Garth St Omer), each of whom is seen as rejecting "the stereotype of 'West Indian' character and society . . . for the truth of personal experience and private sensibility"; two classics of "growing up" (Reid's *New Day* and Lamming's *In the Castle of My Skin*); and novels of shamanistic journeying (W.H. Hudson's *Green Mansions*, as well as works by Denis Williams, and, again, Wilson Harris). The latter section apart, the most distinctive element of the book is its discussion of Mittelholzer's fiction. Occupying over a quarter of the text, this is accorded a disproportionate emphasis, but makes a major contribution to criticism of his work.

BROWN's study follows earlier poetry surveys, such as Baugh's 1970 monograph *West Indian Poetry 1900–1970: A Study in Cultural Decolonisation*, in tracing the evolution of a local consciousness in Anglophone Caribbean verse with reference to articulations of West Indian identity and the search for a distinctively Caribbean poetic voice. He detects Eurocentricity in James's collection, and sets out to provide a different approach, but, in choosing to devote more than half his space to pre-1960 poetry and taking cultural emancipation as his theme, he locks himself into the very agendas he sets out to contest. His discussion of early Caribbean poetry traverses ground already covered more illuminatingly in Brathwaite's "Creative Literature of the British West Indies During the Period of Slavery" (in *Savacou*, 1, 1970), which, like Baugh's monograph, is missing from his bibliography. Nevertheless, as the first full-length book on Caribbean poetry this is a significant landmark, which does offer useful discussions of pioneers like Claude McKay and Louise Bennett. BRATHWAITE's monograph, originally delivered as an "electronic lecture", makes no claim to comprehensiveness. It is rather a manifesto for a certain kind of linguistic and poetic practice. Coining the term "nation language" as a preferred alternative to "dialect", Brathwaite provides a stimulating introduction to its usage in Caribbean poetry.

CHAMBERLIN offers a more detailed examination of the politics of language in Caribbean poetry. After two chapters devoted primarily to providing historical and social background, he discusses more than 30 poets in a context of post-Whorfian linguistic relativity, and with reference to the Jakobsonian concept of "code-switching", which is particularly appropriate for charting the varieties of "English" that exist within Caribbean linguistic continua. His study addresses key issues and employs numerous theoretical reference-points, but is stronger on exposition than in-depth analysis of the linguistic dynamics of particular poems.

HERDECK's four-volume encyclopedia is an indispensable research aid: Volume 1 is devoted to Anglophone Caribbean writing; other volumes concern themselves with Francophone and Hispanophone writing and literature from the Netherlands Antilles and Surinam. The Anglophone volume has entries on virtually every writer of any significance who had emerged by the late 1970s, and includes figures born outside the region who have made significant contributions to West Indian writing, such as the British-born "Jamaican" folklorist Walter Jekyll and "Guyanese" historian James Rodway. It also offers useful bibliographies. But its main strength is its 200-plus pages of alphabetical entries, which make it the most valuable sourcebook for Anglophone Caribbean literary biography.

DANCE follows Herdeck in mixing biography and criticism, but is more selective in approach, thus allowing her contributors to offer fuller, and generally more incisive, critical appraisals of the 50 writers included. Each author is treated under the headings of biography, major works and themes, critical reception, and honours and awards (where relevant); and there are primary and secondary bibliographies. The majority of the contributors are from the Caribbean, and the general level is high. The entries on major writers provide guidance on where to look for further information; those on less well-known figures – such as Marion Patrick Jones, Anthony McNeill and Eric Walrond – are often key sources of information in themselves.

McWATT's collection is the proceedings of a 1984 conference held in Barbados. General pieces include his own discussion of positive and negative aspects of the El Dorado myth and a complementary essay by Subramani, which contrasts Naipaul's "radical parody of the paradise myth" with Harris's treatment of the same subject. A section on "Naipaul and Sexuality" has pieces on Naipaul and the sexuality of power, psycho-sexual aspects of his women characters, and "the woman as whore" in his novels, together with a discussion that links his representation of women with his failure to reconcile an idealized notion of cultural purity and the actuality of experience. There are also useful essays on De Lisser, Ralph de Boissière, and popular fiction in the West Indies.

Caribbean drama has not been as well served as work from the region in other genres, but HILL provides as comprehensive a history of the pre-twentieth-century Jamaican theatre and related performance modes as one could reasonably expect. He gives a detailed account of theatres, plays, players, and playwrights in the pre- and post-Emancipation eras; he chronicles the visits of touring professionals; and, most interestingly, he examines performance elements in the folk culture. The strengths and weaknesses of his method go hand-in-glove. This is a minutely detailed book on a neglected subject, and hence a major contribution to the study of nineteenth-century Caribbean culture; at the same time its accretive approach often leads to a rehashing of its meticulously garnered material without adequate analysis.

JOHN THIEME

Carlyle, Thomas 1795–1881

Scottish writer of historical, social, and political prose

Cumming, Mark, *A Disimprisoned Epic: Form and Vision in Carlyle's "French Revolution"*, Philadelphia: University of Pennsylvania Press, 1988

Goldberg, Michael K., Joel J. Brattin, and Mark Engel (eds.), *On Heroes, Hero-Worship, and the Heroic in History* by Carlyle, Berkeley: University of California Press, 1993

Harrold, Charles Frederick, *Carlyle and German Thought: 1819–1834*, New Haven, Connecticut: Yale University Press, 1934; London: Oxford University Press/Humphrey Milford, 1963

Kaplan, Fred, *Thomas Carlyle: A Biography*, Ithaca, New York: Cornell University Press, 1983

Le Quesne, A.L., *Carlyle*, Oxford and New York: Oxford University Press, 1982

Rosenberg, John D., *Carlyle and the Burden of History*, Cambridge, Massachusetts: Harvard University Press, 1985; Oxford: Clarendon Press, 1985

Rosenberg, Philip, *The Seventh Hero: Thomas Carlyle and the Theory of Radical Activism*, Cambridge, Massachusetts: Harvard University Press, 1974

Tennyson, G.B., *Sartor Called Resartus: The Genius, Structure, and Style of Thomas Carlyle's First Major Work*, Princeton, New Jersey: Princeton University Press, 1965

Vida, Elizabeth, *Romantic Affinities: German Authors and Carlyle: A Study in the History of Ideas*, Toronto and Buffalo, New York: University of Toronto Press, 1993

Williams, Raymond, "Thomas Carlyle", in his *Culture and Society, 1780–1950*, London: Chatto & Windus, 1958; New York: Columbia University Press, 1958

The student of Carlyle should be aware that a new, eight-volume edition of the *Writings of Thomas Carlyle* is currently being prepared, although to date only the first volume, *On Heroes, Hero-Worship, and the Heroic in History*, edited by GOLDBERG, BRATTIN and ENGEL, has been published. Based on the quality of this first volume, the Norman and Charlotte Strouse Edition promises to be a highly accurate and richly annotated edition of Carlyle's major works.

KAPLAN's biography never fails to keep the reader's interest. Although it explicitly refrains from the "life and works" approach, electing instead to tell a story of Carlyle's life without journeying into critical assessments of his writings, it is still a valuable aid to students who may wish to see how his ideas unfolded under the pressure of historical and personal events. Also of interest is Kaplan's even-tempered version of Carlyle's relationship with his wife, Jane Welsh Carlyle. On the topic of the Carlyle marriage, certainly the most vexed issue in Carlyle biography, Kaplan strives to give a fair and persuasive assessment of what was by all accounts a beleaguered but in some sense necessary union.

One topic that receives little attention in Kaplan's biography is Carlyle's indebtedness to German philosophy and literature. This subject has received ample attention elsewhere, notably in HARROLD's classic study, and more recently in the work by VIDA. Harrold endeavors to specify where Carlyle understood his German authors and where he misunderstood them; it is a finely nuanced analysis, attentive to signs of Carlyle's manipulations of Fichte and Kant, but decidedly opposed to the view that Carlyle's knowledge of such thinkers was flawed and superficial. Vida presses farther the defense of Carlyle's Germanicism, arguing that he had a sophisticated understanding of his German influences, and was not, as she puts the opposite case, an "ignoramus" unsuited to the intellectual challenges of the German Romantic tradition. Harrold's work is largely interested in philosophical and spiritual ideas; Vida adds to this set of concerns an appreciation for the German critical methods and literary techniques that permeated Carlyle's style.

Most book-length studies of Carlyle's writings limit themselves to examining the output that preceded the alienating excesses of "Occasional Discourse on the Nigger Question" and the *Latter-Day Pamphlets*. TENNYSON's work demonstrates why, and how, Carlyle has become a figure primarily of interest to literary scholars. Focusing on the inception and structure of *Sartor Resartus*, Tennyson manages an exhaustive formalist analysis of the text, one that remains indispensable to Carlyle scholarship. CUMMING examines Carlyle's other masterwork, *The French Revolution*. The structural complexity of this fictional history Cumming understands as a register of Carlyle's similarly complex attitudes towards history and politics. Every bit as unwilling to commit himself to one genre as he was unwilling to commit himself to a political stance or a version of the past, Carlyle assimilated various literary traditions as a means of forcing the reader to entertain several versions of history at once. In this way, Cumming argues, *The French Revolution* is a "disimprisoned epic", an attempt to supersede, via an iconoclastic pastiche, the limitations of genre, history, and politics.

Other works take as their subject several of Carlyle's texts. LE QUESNE provides a well-informed introductory overview of Carlyle's career, and does not shy away from the frequently offensive writings of the late 1840s. Attempting to assess Carlyle's place in literary and intellectual history, Le Quesne makes no grandiose claims, arguing instead that Carlyle's prophetic function was, as he intended it to be, specific to the social and political climate of the early Victorian age. Philip ROSENBERG's 1974 study traces a development from Carlyle's introspective meditations on the nature of selfhood to his belief in the importance of political action. Carlyle's philosophy of hero-worship the author defines in attractive terms as a movement that, properly understood, leads to a heroism of one's self, to an internalization of the dignity that has thus far been realized only in certain visionary individuals. While persuasive, Rosenberg's mostly sympathetic picture of Carlyle is to some extent assisted by the fact that he focuses only on the writings up to *Past and Present* (1843). But it is a compelling study, in part because of the author's willingness to reflect upon his historical predicament as a scholar working on Carlyle's politics in the wake of the North American radical activism of the 1960s. John D. ROSENBERG approaches his selections from Carlyle's corpus in terms of the growing cloud that history cast over his philosophical vision. Rosenberg's Carlyle is at once preoccupied with the seemingly superior social orders of the past and with his own inability to render this past in forms untainted by fictionalization. Hence the Carlyle uncovered in these pages is relevant, by implication, to recent theoretical concerns with the metaphorical bases of factual representations. The linchpin of this study is the author's treatment of *The French Revolution*, but Rosenberg also addresses some of Carlyle's frequently neglected writings, such as *Cromwell* and *Frederick the Great*.

Finally, one of the most moving engagements with Carlyle is still the brief study that appears in WILLIAMS. This work gives us a sense of both the promise and the disappointment that Carlyle held for British radicals of his own day as well as of this century.

SUE ZEMKA

Carroll, Lewis 1832–1898

English poet and children's writer

Bloom, Harold (ed.), *Lewis Carroll*, New York: Chelsea House, 1987

Gardner, Martin, *The Annotated Alice*, revised edition, Harmondsworth, Middlesex: Penguin, 1970

Guiliano, Edward, *Lewis Carroll: A Celebration; Essays on the Occasion of the 150th Anniversary of the Birth of Charles Lutwidge Dodgson*, New York: Clarkson N. Potter, 1982

Hancher, Michael, *The Tenniel Illustrations to the "Alice" Books*, Columbus: Ohio State University Press, 1985

Lecercle, Jean-Jacques, *The Philosophy of Nonsense: The Intuition of Victorian Nonsense Literature*, London and New York: Routledge, 1994

The two *Alice* books have received, and continue to receive, most critical attention in discussions of Carroll. "The Hunting of the Snark" has also been popular, but work done on the *Sylvie and Bruno* books has been minimal, and attention paid to Carroll's mathematical output and photography, which is sometimes found alongside the literary criticism, has been more for the sake of comprehensiveness than illumination. The man behind the pseudonym, Charles Lutwidge Dodgson, has proved a fertile hunting ground for psychological critics, most obviously in his fondness for children. This kind of approach is often conjoined with analysis of his literature, but is usually the least profitable line of enquiry. The linguistic issues raised by the *Alice*s have been explored in detail, but are more for the benefit of linguists than those interested in the literature itself. Similar in vein, but less dry, is the work done by those concerned with the philosophical interests of the literature. Approaches most able to do justice to the books focus on their place within Victorian literature and society, their status as "nonsense", and their functioning as "quest narrative". There has also been an industry in attempting to find the allegorical meaning behind Carroll's work (conclusions ranging from finding it to be "a secret history of the Oxford Movement" to a companion volume for Judaic scripture), but this remains highly speculative, rather in the manner of psychoanalytical criticism. Carroll's work has benefited from the recent upsurge in interest in children's literature.

BLOOM's collection of essays brings together some of the best critics writing on Carroll, and demonstrates the range of interpretative possibilities available. The connections between the child Alice and the Victorian child in general are explored by Jan B. Gordon and Nina Auerbach. Gordon's essay links the image of "the orphan" in Victorian novels to Alice, and provides a very interesting social/contextual analysis of the child in Victorian society. Auerbach's essay is equally interesting, if more psychological in approach, bringing in details of Dodgson's life as "evidence". Peter Heath gives us "the philosopher's *Alice*" and argues that Carroll was not a writer of nonsense but of the absurd, an existential outlook that is commented on by others (Gardner and Guiliano for example), and given as an explanation for his congeniality for twentieth-century thinking. A couple of essays involve themselves in literary-theoretical freeplay in an unhelpful manner; but in the main this is an excellent collection.

GARDNER's work reprints the original *Alice* texts with his own commentary running alongside, explaining jokes, allusions, and interpretations. Undoubtedly this is not the kind of approach to everyone's taste, since the critical apparatus could be said to detract from the literature. However, for anyone curious enough to go further with the *Alice* books, this is a real boon and has the advantage of not being a critique abstracted from the work. There is a more recent companion to this book, but it is very much an addition rather than a replacement.

Not on a par with Bloom's collection in terms of theoretical sophistication, GUILIANO's collection of various critics' essays on Carroll nevertheless has a number of angles not covered in Bloom's volume. Some of the essays discuss the relationship of Tenniel's illustrations, the writing, and Carroll. Other essays look at genre, form, Carroll as surrealist, the use of Carroll by James Joyce, and Morton N. Cohen's essay about Carroll's relationship with the actress Ellen Terry provides biographical details of Carroll's Victorian moral outlook in a tangential but fascinating manner.

For some, a book devoted to Tenniel's illustrations in the *Alice* books might be nothing more than secondary to commentary on the literature; but HANCHER's work in this area, particularly on the precursors of the *Alice* characters in Tenniel's work for *Punch*, creates a useful extra dimension. It also serves to contextualise the possible Victorian audience reaction to the work, and makes explicit just how connected the material as a whole was to Victorian society. Readers would have been familiar with *Punch* cartoons, and so the *Alice* drawings would be seen as echoes of these more politically oriented outpourings.

Carroll's work provides an opportunity for LECERCLE to muse on the nature of language and meaning from whichever angle takes his fancy. Thus, we get statements such as: "a portmanteau word is . . . both, contradictorily, entirely meaningless and infinitely meaningful". As usual, Carroll's "nonsense" literature is seen almost to predict the work of twentieth-century linguists, from Ferdinand de Saussure to J.L. Austin, H.P. Grice, and Noam Chomsky, although, to be fair to Lecercle, he does not find these to be adequate accounts. Jürgen Habermas's theory of "communicative action" also gets a look in, and even Heidegger is enlisted when some of the focus is placed upon Edward Lear's nonsense verse. There are some interesting insights in this book, but it is necessary to wade through some material that can be quite indigestible.

STEVEN EARNSHAW

Carver, Raymond 1938–1988

American short-story writer and poet

Campbell, Ewing, *Raymond Carver: A Study of the Short Fiction*, New York: Twayne, 1992
Chénetier, Marc, "Living On/Off the 'Reserve': Performance, Interrogation, and Negativity in the Works of Raymond Carver", in *Critical Angles: European Views of Contemporary American Literature*, edited by Chénetier, Carbondale: Southern Illinois University Press, 1986
Clarke, Graham, "Investing the Glimpse: Raymond Carver and the Syntax of Silence", in *The New American Writing: Essays on American Literature since 1970*, edited by Clarke, London: Vision Press, 1990; New York: St Martin's Press, 1990
Gentry, Marshall Bruce, and William L. Stull (eds.), *Conversations with Raymond Carver*, Jackson: University of Mississippi Press, 1990
Runyon, Randolph Paul, *Reading Raymond Carver*, Syracuse, New York: Syracuse University Press, 1992
Saltzman, Arthur M., *Understanding Raymond Carver*, Columbia: University of South Carolina Press, 1988
Trussler, Michael, "The Narrowed Voice: Minimalism and Raymond Carver", in *Studies in Short Fiction*, 31, Winter 1994

Raymond Carver's writing has generated considerable controversy. Neo-conservative reviewers have censured its negative portrayal of America, whereas literary critics on the Left – through an appeal to poststructuralist theories of referentiality – have often attacked Carver's supposedly naive use of language. Scholars sympathetic to Carver's work either ignore this turmoil or attempt to place the "minimalist" fiction within the context of postmodern literature. Critical acclaim began with *Will You Please Be Quiet, Please?* (1978). Carver's reputation as a master of the short story became assured when *What We Talk about When We Talk about Love* was published in 1982.

GENTRY and STULL's collection of interviews with Carver is indispensable. Containing 25 interviews, which extend over the range of his career, a detailed chronology, and a useful Introduction by the editors, the book brings together Carver's views on his own writing and poetics with revelations concerning the genesis of several of the most important short stories. While there is some overlap in the topics covered, the editors have assembled an invaluable resource.

CHÉNETIER's essay reacts to the initial critical emphasis on thematics by bringing an informed discussion of Wolfgang Iser's reception theory and Roland Barthes' conceptions of narrative to the fiction. Observing Carver's structural strategies of omission and idiosyncratic use of deictics, Chénetier posits that what "mimetic dimensions the texts retain have to do with . . . the radical 'béance' or gap that yawns at the heart of experience, in the presentation, rather than the representation, of a world of fractures". Chénetier cites numerous stories, both early and late, while also streamlining his argument with references to the poetry.

SALTZMAN's introductory survey examines mainly the fiction, but also contains a brief chapter on Carver's poetry, and an annotated bibliography. Entailing considerably more interpretative analysis than the plot-summary format normally associated with such studies, the book investigates narrative voice, techniques of closure, and Carver's particular use of framing devices. Saltzman clarifies Carver's contributions to the "maximalist-minimalist" debate by relating his "suspicion of language" to such writers as Franz Kafka, William Carlos Williams, and Harold Pinter. Despite an occasional lapse into too close an identification with Carver's characters, in which he expresses perplexed consternation as to their motives and desires, Saltzman provides a useful overview of Carver's writing and its position in contemporary American literature.

CLARKE positions Carver's short fiction and essays within the overall postmodern critique of modernist literature and ideology. Beginning with an astute analysis of the photograph discussed in the essay "My Father's Life", Clarke contrasts Ernest Hemingway's "Big-Two Hearted River: II" with Carver's fiction to elucidate how the latter not only reveals "the contingencies of American myth" but "exposes the extent to which the Hemingway code is dependent upon it". Clarke's most incisive remarks pertain to his Baudrillardian reading of Carver's treatment of the media in general, but television specifically. Relating the stories to the visual arts as well, Clarke's essay valuably locates Carver's writing within the context of contemporary theory and American culture.

CAMPBELL's discerning critique is perhaps the study to which dedicated scholars will most profitably turn. Containing one of Carver's own essays and the important McCaffery/Gregory interview, plus reprinted articles by three other critics, Campbell's book not only renders an evenhanded account of the minimalist debate, but seriously addresses the textual problems created by Carver's tendency to publish numerous revised versions of given stories. While many have noticed Carver's debts to Hemingway and Anton Chekhov, Campbell demonstrates Carver's persistent reassessment of the meaning of Joyce's techniques in *Dubliners*. Campbell's analysis of *Cathedral*, which draws on Vladimir Nabokov and Isak Dinesen, contributes greatly to our understanding of Carver's *oeuvre*; arguing that the "mature" Carver repudiated his earlier realism, Campbell convincingly elucidates how Carver learned to "exploit the melodrama . . . of daytime television . . . and the convictions of a culture's assimilated lessons" in order to create a more redemptive, allegorical mode of fiction.

My own (TRUSSLER's) essay, building on the work of Clarke and Chénetier, focuses on an exegesis of "Why Don't You Dance?" to investigate how the story's inversion of everyday order emphasizes "the manner in which narration may serve to splinter narrators from themselves, their narratees and often from the experience that occasioned the narrative". Arguing that Carver's work confronts the problematic relation between the construction of narrative and the perception of history, my approach is to contrast the story with Thoreau's *Walden* before reading the fiction through the context of Ihab Hassan's "anti-style", Louis Marin's critique of "ordinary language", and Edward Said's analysis of "verbal intention".

RUNYON argues that critics, by isolating various stories for interpretation, have failed to perceive the underlying patterns, and recurrent narrative situations and images that metamorphose throughout the fiction as a whole. Maintaining that the boundaries separating individual texts are semi-permeable, the book suggests that the reader does well to observe "the interstices *between the stories*". Runyon's is a remarkably assiduous reading, which goes far beyond simply itemizing the numerous details that traverse the collections, however. Drawing on the archetypal imagery explained by Freud in his essay "Medusa's Head", Runyon theorizes that the stories engage psychic dilemmas and conflicts which, roving from story to story, together form an overall gestalt. Runyon's accomplishment is that he allows us to rethink Carver's surface "minimalism" by perceiving the ways in which the stories respond to each other, provisionally filling in (what previously have been seen as) textual gaps and omissions.

MICHAEL TRUSSLER

Cather, Willa 1873–1947

American novelist and short-story writer

Arnold, Marilyn, *Willa Cather's Short Fiction*, Athens: Ohio University Press, 1984
Carlin, Deborah, *Cather, Canon, and the Politics of Reading*, Amherst: University of Massachusetts Press, 1992
Lee, Hermione, *Willa Cather: Double Lives*, New York: Pantheon, 1989; as *Willa Cather: A Life Saved Up*, London: Virago, 1989
O'Brien, Sharon, *Willa Cather: The Emerging Voice*, New York: Oxford University Press, 1987
Rosowski, Susan J., *The Voyage Perilous: Willa Cather's Romanticism*, Lincoln: University of Nebraska Press, 1986
Skaggs, Merrill Maguire, *After the World Broke in Two: The Later Novels of Willa Cather*, Charlottesville: University of Virginia Press, 1990
Slote, Bernice (ed.), *The Kingdom of Art: Willa Cather's First Principles and Critical Statements, 1893–1896* by Cather, Lincoln: University of Nebraska Press, 1966
Stouck, David, *Willa Cather's Imagination*, Lincoln: University of Nebraska Press, 1975
Woodress, James, *Willa Cather: A Literary Life*, Lincoln: University of Nebraska Press, 1987

Early critical attention paid to Willa Cather centered on the identification of Cather's dominant themes and symbols, focusing on Cather as a regional writer who was concerned with the realities of existence on the plains. The resurgence in Cather studies, which began in the mid-1980's, argues for a more complicated Cather, who frequently defies critical attempts to label her work. Contemporary approaches to Cather are wide-ranging; consequently, Cather is viewed through many lenses: biographical, historical, psychoanalytical, gender-based, narratological, and in connection with literary movements.

In many ways Cather scholarship begins with SLOTE. In her first chapter, "Writer in Nebraska", she presents biographical information about the formative years in Cather's literary life, arguing that Cather's work as a drama critic and editor helped her to define her relation to art and criticism. In the second chapter, "The Kingdom of Art," Slote lays the groundwork for Cather research in her identification of Cather's literary influences as well as her recurring themes, metaphors, and symbols. Slote continually makes connections between Cather's early critical pieces and her short stories and novels to argue that "what was constant in her from those earliest years" is present in her later works as well. Slote's own essays here, and the collection as a whole, remain an important resource for Cather scholars.

STOUCK's work explores "the unusual range and depth of Willa Cather's imagination". Stouck demonstrates that Cather incorporates traditional literary forms – epic, pastoral, and satire – into her novels, while he points to the "archetypal imaginative pattern which adheres in these American narratives". Stouck is one of the first critics to span the author's entire oeuvre, from *Alexander's Bridge* to the posthumous collection *The Old Beauty and Others*. Like Slote, Stouck argues powerfully for the thematic and structural complexities of Cather's novels.

ARNOLD's study is one of two devoted exclusively to the interpretation of Cather's body of 62 short stories. Arnold organizes her work chronologically, while identifying common themes among the stories. The entries are a combination of plot synopsis and interpretation, making this study a valuable source for those readers interested in the short stories.

ROSOWSKI delivered one of the first book-length studies to lead the recent surge of Cather scholarship. According to Rosowski, Cather formed her own principles of art in the Romantic tradition, defined as an historical movement that began in the late eighteenth century. Rosowski's refined thesis is that "Cather early took up the romantic challenge to vindicate imaginative thought in a world threatened by materialism and pursued it with remarkable consistency throughout her career". Like Stouck's, Rosowski's study considers some of Cather's stories and each of her novels.

WOODRESS's literary biography seeks to place the author's work within the context of her life. A model of scholarly biography, Woodress's study is a detailed consideration of Cather's entire literary *oeuvre*. Each chapter begins with a description of the people and events in Cather's life at the time she was writing a given novel, followed by a brief plot synopsis; then Woodress blends biography and interpretation to draw parallels between Cather's life and work, considering Cather's questions about the changing world around her and establishing patterns of themes, symbols, and images. Along with Rosowski's, Woodress's work ushered in a new wave of Cather criticism. This biography is invaluable to serious Cather scholars, yet it also remains accessible to those who simply want to learn about the author's life and works.

O'BRIEN uses a range of methods – biographical, historical, psychoanalytical, literary – to draw connections between Cather's life and fiction. O'Brien concentrates on issues of gender identification, for she reads Cather as a "woman writer", who struggled with culturally imposed contradictions between femininity and creativity. O'Brien asks questions about how Cather established her identity as a woman and as a woman writer, beginning her study by considering Cather at birth and ending with the publication of *O Pioneers!* O'Brien's work is important to Cather scholars because it was the first book-length study to address issues of gender and sexuality and their connection to creativity.

LEE's study explores the nature of duality and paradoxes in Cather's literature and life. While approaching Cather's work chronologically, Lee organizes her interpretation around central themes, including feeling and memory, the personal and the objective, escape and return, language and silence, the private and the public, feminine and masculine. Lee illuminates Cather's works in new ways as she effectively argues that the theme of "doubleness" reflects Cather as an individual and an author.

SKAGGS examines Cather's novels published after 1922, the year in which, according to Cather, the world broke in two. Beginning with a consideration of Cather's recurring themes and literary techniques, Skaggs demonstrates that Cather's fiction is "inexhaustible": it is capable of sustaining multiple interpretations. Skaggs' focus on the later novels, works that have received less scholarly attention than Cather's earlier ones, is one of the many reasons why scholars will want to become familiar with her study.

CARLIN also focuses on the later works. Her Introduction – an overview of Cather literary scholarship – considers Cather's place in the literary "canon(s)". Carlin focuses on the subject of "reading" and "the reading process" to suggest why Cather's later novels prove to be so challenging. Carlin's study is a combination of narratology, feminism, and deconstruction, which examines the act of narration and narrative structures, thus bringing the field of Cather scholarship into new theoretical arenas.

ELIZABETH A. TURNER

Chandler, Raymond 1888–1959

American novelist, short-story writer, and screenwriter

Gross, Miriam (ed.), *The World of Raymond Chandler* London: Weidenfeld & Nicolson, 1977; New York: A & W, 1978

Luhr, William, *Raymond Chandler and Film*, New York: Frederick Ungar, 1982, 2nd edition, 1991

MacShane, Frank, *The Life of Raymond Chandler*, London: Jonathan Cape, 1976; New York: Dutton, 1976

Marling, William, *Raymond Chandler*, Boston: Twayne, 1986

Newlin, Keith, *Hardboiled Burlesque: Raymond Chandler's Comic Style*, San Bernardino, California: Borgo Press, 1984

Speir, Jerry, *Raymond Chandler* New York: Frederick Ungar, 1981

Despite early appreciative comments by such writers as W.H. Auden, the critical recognition of Raymond Chandler was delayed until the detective genre had gained critical acceptance. It was in the 1970s that essays on Chandler began to appear regularly in anthologies on detective and popular fiction, and also articles on films based on his novels.

MacSHANE's Chandler biography was one of the first to appear, and has remained among the best for its combination of scholarly research and critical insight. At every stage of his discussion MacShane quotes from a wealth of unpublished material. He draws a complex picture of Chandler as an Anglophile whose outlook was moulded by his years at Dulwich College, London. He recounts Chandler's beginnings as a writer in periodicals like *Black Mask*, but argues that he had an inclination right from the start towards full-length novels and burlesque. His period in Hollywood during the 1940s was an uneasy one, where high wages did nothing to stifle Chandler's doubts about the Hollywood system. The MacShane biography remains a mine of information about Chandler's serious commitment to the craft of writing.

GROSS's anthology is a very miscellaneous volume indeed, containing comments by fellow writers, memoirs of his wife, and a brief essay by T.J. Binyon explaining why Chandler's influence on subsequent writers was so minimal. One of the best essays is Eric Homberger's finely poised analysis of Chandler's two careers: as a man of letters in London, and then as a writer of detective fiction. Chandler was subsequently embarrassed by the precious tone of his early essays, and Homberger argues that he was comfortable in neither literary context. Hence "his cultural ambivalence appears in the novels as self-consciousness and irony". Julian Symons, by contrast, reads Chandler more straightforwardly as a "romantic aesthete". Of the other outstandingly useful essays in the volume, Philip French surveys the film adaptations of Chandler's novels, and Michael Mason examines Chandler's depiction of women, an issue that has cropped up repeatedly in more recent articles. He finds that Chandler's moral scheme is skewed heavily towards men at the expense of women, and begins to speculate tentatively on the feminine aspects of Marlowe himself.

SPEIR gives a detailed reading of the main novels which is rather clogged in the first chapters by lengthy summary. In spite of this he usefully points out the "calculated pacing" of *The Big Sleep* and Chandler's use of parallels, plot disruptions, and the *deus ex machina*. He insists that, contrary to some Chandler critics, the chivalric and Arthurian allusions in the Marlowe stories are ironic and should not be taken at face value. Among many other points he stresses the prominence of queries in *The Long Goodbye*, which foreground the act of investigation. In many ways the last three chapters of Speir's study are the better ones. He examines Marlowe, locating a "dualism of mind", a "split between an idealistic longing and an imperfect present". And he too touches on the issue of whether or not Marlowe will form any relations with women. Next, Speir's survey of the hallmarks of Chandler's style points up the prominence of wisecracks and, less predictably, notes how Chandler uses colour symbolism to refer to emotions. Finally, he considers Chandler's "vision", stressing the narrative tension between expectation and fact.

LUHR's study of Chandler and film nicely complements the critical discussions of Chandler's fiction. It is impossible for any reader to blank out of their consciousness the visual images of film adaptations of Chandler's novels, and these are discussed in considerable detail in Luhr's final section. His study also gives us an account of Chandler's brief career as a screenwriter, concluding, like MacShane, that Chandler could not reconcile the demands of the two media. Luhr analyzes Chandler's part in the composition of *Double Indemnity* and also *The Blue Dahlia*, where loss of memory becomes a major threat to the individual's identity. More generally Luhr suggestively notes similarities between Chandler's fiction and the film-noir genre of the late 1940s, with its complicated twists of plot.

NEWLIN's analysis of Chandler's style is brief but nevertheless one of the best to date. He identifies three phases in Chandler's career as a writer of detective fiction. Initially Chandler was heavily influenced by Dashiell Hammett, and then Ernest Hemingway led him towards a tersely laconic style. But even in his early stories, Newlin argues, Chandler was beginning to burlesque such clichés of the genre as coincidence or the lucky shot device. In the early 1940s Chandler achieved a comic poise stylistically distinguished by the self-parodic wisecrack. From *The Little Sister* (1949) onwards Chandler's style then declined into sentimentality.

MARLING brings together the insights of some of these earlier critics in his volume on Chandler for the Twayne "United States Authors" series. He suggests that Chandler in his early English essays was searching for a style or stance. He rightly stresses the impact of Hammett since, in Chandler's own words, "he demonstrated that the detective story can be important writing". Marling discusses the origin of the detective genre, Chandler's use of the California setting, and stresses the recurrence of blackmail and kidnapping in the stories of the 1930s. A key work here, he argues, is "Killer in the Rain" (1935), where Chandler tries out the use of the first-person perspective that he was to develop at length in the Marlowe novels. In his discussion of these novels Marling examines once again the Arthurian allusions and the use of metaphor which, he suggests, can be either oral or a device to help the reader to understand key scenes. He also suggests shrewdly that "tough talk is aggressive metaphor". For its breadth and thoroughness, Marling's study is one of the best surveys of Chandler's work.

DAVID SEED

Chapman, George c.1560–1634

English poet and dramatist

Bement, Peter, *George Chapman: Action and Contemplation in His Tragedies*, Salzburg: Institut für Anglistik und Amerikanistik (University of Salzburg), 1974

Bradbrook, M C., *George Chapman*, London: Longman, 1977

Braunmuller, A.R., *Natural Fictions: George Chapman's Major Tragedies*, Newark, Delaware: University of Delaware Press, 1992; London: Associated University Presses, 1992

MacLure, Millar, *George Chapman: A Critical Study*, Toronto: University of Toronto Press, 1966; London: Oxford University Press, 1966

Rees, Ennis, *The Tragedies of George Chapman: Renaissance Ethics in Action*, Cambridge, Massachusetts: Harvard University Press, 1954

Snare, Gerald, *The Mystification of George Chapman*, Durham, North Carolina: Duke University Press, 1989

Spivack, Charlotte, *George Chapman*, New York: Twayne, 1967

Although unpopular with some modern readers for being too philosophical, moral, and obscure, Chapman's works – his best known tragedy, *Bussy D'Ambois*, in particular – have drawn a considerable amount of critical attention. The focus of attention has been on how much, and how well, Chapman's moral philosophy finds its expression in his poetry and drama.

REES discovers in Chapman's poems ideas of a Christian humanist drawn deeply into Stoicism and neo-Platonism. Rees then applies his findings to reading the plays – by measuring the tragic heroes against Chapman's ideal man, a learned man whose reason firmly controls his passion. According to this reading, Bussy and Byron represent highly gifted but uncontrolled individuals; and Cato, Clermont, and Chabot are ideal men who have, through learning, refined their crude, natural selves to be close to God's image. Rees's interpretive strategy has been criticized for being too simple and also for falsely assuming that Chapman had held the same interest and principle throughout his writing career.

MacLURE's erudite, witty, and comprehensive study refutes such assumptions by Rees and other earlier critics. However, MacLure does find in all Chapman's writing the consistent self-dramatization of the lonely figure who draws confidence from within against the corrupt and hostile outside world. Arguing that Chapman's obscurity springs from "the complexity of imperfection rather than of profundity", MacLure detects an unevenly gradual and complicated transition from Bussy and Byron to Clermont. The comedies, although often poorly structured, have stylistic grace and effective humor. Tragedies are eminently dramatic in conception, but they are at times impaired by a "pedantic insistence upon preconceived propositions". Among his contemporaries, Chapman had "the finest imagination of them all, but he was possessed . . . by a body of ideas", or "philosophical conceits" as Chapman called them. Three decades later, MacLure's study remains the best comprehensive study of Chapman.

SPIVACK, following the usual format of the Twayne series, offers a brief biography, a chapter on the poems, two chapters on the comedies, and another two on the tragedies, followed by a summary of critical history. More introductory than argumentative, Spivack's book provides typically sound interpretations of the works and the formulaic analyses of them in terms of plot, sources, and character. For Spivack, Chapman wrote with "exceptional clarity", and his works show a "definite but complex pattern of development, both technical and philosophical", a sign of both a "progression and deepening in the author's interpretation of life". BRADBROOK's small volume of some 50 pages is a quick read. The author rarely engages in dispute, but rather introduces the author and his individual works, arranged much like Spivack's Twayne volume. For Bradbrook, Chapman was an Elizabethan writing in Jacobean times; like Christopher Marlowe, Chapman attempted to face an "age of growing internal tension".

BEMENT's book, a revised version of his doctoral thesis, forwards a thesis that Chapman's interest in neo-Platonism dominated his early works, but was later largely replaced by Stoicism, which is reflected in the tragedies after *Bussy D'Ambois*. Bement finds the conflict between action and contemplation – in tragedies, more specifically between virtue and Fortune – as "the great unifying theme" in Chapman's work as a whole. According to Bement, the philosophical elements in Chapman's works exist in "shifting perspective, and are constantly being disposed in new patterns which lead to new conclusions as his work progresses". As for *Bussy D'Ambois*, the play offers "no dogmatic philosophic conclusions whatever, and remains in temper essentially an experiment, an unresolved intellectual endeavor".

SNARE accuses earlier critics of unnecessarily mystifying Chapman's poems and of forcing them to submit to ethical or philosophical categories. By offering evidence from *Hero and Leander*, *Ovids Banquet of Sense*, and *The Shadow of Night*, Snare argues that Chapman's poems are neither obscure nor difficult, and that his random borrowings from various authors are "simple material for invention", and not a coherent intellectual program with didactic ends.

BRAUNMULLER, well-informed by such recent critical approaches as deconstruction, reader-response theory, and New Historicism, examines the four major tragedies based on French history. Placing Chapman in a broad historical, political, and literary context, Braunmuller argues that the well-paid, popular playwright began his career as a tragic dramatist with a highly developed theory of art, but that with each successive tragedy he lost confidence in his poetic theory – the theory that poetry could accommodate and "reshape mundane experience into transcendent meaning":

> With *Hero and Leander*, Chapman managed an almost perfect balance between his competing views of the poet and the tensions within his own theory and practice. *Bussy D'Ambois* nearly achieves a dramatic equilibrium of the same sort, but the rifts become very plain in the *Byron* plays, and *Chabot* concedes defeat.

The book ends with a useful collection of Chapman's comments on various literary topics and an updated bibliography.

SEIWOONG OH

Chauncer, Geoffrey c.1340–1400

English poet

Aers, David, *Chaucer, Langland and the Creative Imagination*, London and Boston: Routledge & Kegan Paul, 1980

Barney, Stephen A. (ed.), *Chaucer's Troilus: Essays in Criticism*, London: Scolar Press, 1980; Hamden, Connecticut: Archon Books, 1980

Benson, C. David, *Chaucer's Drama of Style: Poetic Variety and Contrast in the "Canterbury Tales"*, Chapel Hill: University of North Carolina Press, 1986

Benson, C. David, *Chaucer's "Troilus and Criseyde"*, London and Boston: Unwin Hyman, 1990

Benson, C. David (ed.), *Critical Essays on Chaucer's "Troilus and Criseyde" and His Major Early Poems*, Milton Keynes, Buckinghamshire: Open University Press, 1991

Benson, C. David, and Elizabeth Robertson (eds.), *Chaucer's Religious Tales*, Cambridge: D.S. Brewer, 1990

Benson, Larry D., et al. (eds.), *The Riverside Chaucer*, 3rd edition, Boston: Houghton Mifflin, 1987; Oxford: Oxford University Press, 1987

Chute, Marchette, *Geoffrey Chaucer of England*, New York: Dutton, 1946; London: Hale, 1951

Crane, Susan, *Gender and Romance in Chaucer's "Canterbury Tales"*, Princeton, New Jersey: Princeton University Press, 1994

Dinshaw, Carolyn, *Chaucer's Sexual Poetics*, Madison: University of Wisconsin Press, 1989

Donaldson, E. Talbot, *Speaking of Chaucer*, London: Athlone Press, 1970; New York: Norton, 1972

Ferster, Judith, *Chaucer on Interpretation*, Cambridge and New York: Cambridge University Press, 1985

Fyler, John, *Chaucer and Ovid*, New Haven, Connecticut: Yale University Press, 1979

Green, Richard Firth, *Poets and Princepleasers: Literature and the Court in the Late Middle Ages*, Toronto and Buffalo, New York: University of Toronto Press, 1980

Hansen, Elaine Tuttle, *Chaucer's Fictions of Gender*, Berkeley: University of California Press, 1992

Howard, Donald, *Chaucer: His Life, His Works, His World*, New York: Dutton, 1987

Knapp, Peggy, *Chaucer and the Social Contest*, New York and London: Routledge, 1990

Kolve, V.A., *Chaucer and the Imagery of Narrative: The First Five Canterbury Tales*, Stanford, California: Stanford University Press, 1984

Leicester, Marshall H., *The Disenchanted Self: Representing the Subject in the Canterbury Tales*, Berkeley: University of California Press, 1990

Mann, Jill, *Chaucer and Medieval Estates Satire: The Literature of Social Classes and the General Prologue to the "Canterbury Tales"*, Cambridge: Cambridge University Press, 1973

Mann, Jill, *Geoffrey Chaucer*, Hemel Hempstead, Hertfordshire: Harvester Wheatsheaf, 1991; Atlantic Highlands, New Jersey: Humanities Press, 1991

Martin, Priscilla, *Chaucer's Women: Nuns, Wives, and Amazons*, Iowa City: University of Iowa Press, 1990; London: Macmillan, 1990

Muscatine, Charles, *Chaucer and the French Tradition*, Berkeley: University of California Press, 1957

Nolan, Barbara, *Chaucer and the Tradition of the Roman Antique*, Cambridge and New York: Cambridge University Press, 1992

Patterson, Lee, *Chaucer and the Subject of History*, London and New York: Routledge, 1991

Pearsall, Derek, *The Canterbury Tales*, London and Boston: Unwin Hyman, 1985

Pearsall, Derek, *The Life of Geoffrey Chaucer: A Critical Biography*, Oxford and Cambridge, Massachusetts: Blackwell, 1992

Robertson, D.W., *A Preface to Chaucer: Studies in Medieval*

Perspectives, Princeton, New Jersey: Princeton University Press, 1962
Ruggiers, Paul G., *Editing Chaucer: The Great Tradition*, Norman, Oklahoma: Pilgrim Books, 1984
Salter, Elizabeth, *Chaucer: "The Knight's Tale" and "The Clerk's Tale"*, London: Edward Arnold, 1962
Spearing, A.C., "Chaucer's Clerk's Tale as a Medieval Poem," in his *Criticism and Medieval Poetry*, London: Edward Arnold, 1964, 2nd edition, 1972; New York: Barnes & Noble, 1964
Spearing, A.C., *Medieval Dream Poetry*, Cambridge and New York: Cambridge University Press, 1976
Spearing, A.C., *The Medieval Poet as Voyeur: Looking and Listening in Medieval Love-Narratives*, Cambridge and New York: Cambridge University Press, 1993
Strohm, Paul, *Social Chaucer*, Cambridge, Massachusetts: Harvard University Press, 1989
Wallace, David, *Chaucer and the Early Writings of Boccaccio*, Woodbridge, Suffolk: D.S. Brewer, 1985
Waswo, Richard, "The Narrator of Troilus and Criseyde", in *English Literary History*, 50, 1983
Wetherbee, Winthrop, *Chaucer and the Poets: An Essay on "Troilus and Criseyde"*, Ithaca, New York: Cornell University Press, 1984
Windeatt, B.A., *Geoffrey Chaucer: "Troilus & Criseyde": A New Edition of the Book of Troilus*, London and New York: Longman, 1984

Readers interested in Chaucer and Chaucer criticism should turn to The Riverside Chaucer, both for the most up-to-date text of Chaucer and for useful summaries of major criticism and textual scholarship on each work. In addition, readers can consult the two most prominent journals in the field of Chaucer studies, *Chaucer Review* and *Studies in the Age of Chaucer*. The latter includes articles, reviews, and a yearly annotated bibliography. Those interested in textual matters as well as up-to-date bibliographies on individual works should also consult the Variorum editions of Chaucer. (A small percentage of Chaucer's works have been edited in this series, but the series is in progress.) A useful introduction to the variety of issues confronted by the editor of Chaucer can be found in RUGGIERS's collection of essays.

The biography of Chaucer that used to be the most popular, and is still very readable, is CHUTE's, which has now been superseded by two major biographies. HOWARD's biography is thorough and imaginative; indeed, some have found it too fanciful, as Howard assigns thoughts, responses, and even experiences to Chaucer for which there is no evidence. PEARSALL's biography (1992) is equally thorough, but more cautious and scholarly in its approach. Pearsall places Chaucer within the context of the turbulent reign of Richard II, and, using the life documents remaining about Chaucer, describes Chaucer's multiple careers as diplomat, government official in many different capacities, and poet. Pearsall demonstrates his keen understanding of Chaucer's poetry, which he weds to the biography.

Twentieth-century criticism on Chaucer has flourished, and these notes will concentrate on the most recent work of the last two decades. For further information on the many important books and articles of this century, the reader should consult one of the many bibliographies on Chaucer. Since the late 1950s, Chaucer criticism in America has been dominated by two major schools, the exegetical school, established by D.W. Robertson, and the humanist/formalist school, which argued for the primacy of close textual readings of Chaucer. The primary figures of this latter school were Donaldson, who published numerous ground-breaking articles and books, and Muscatine. MUSCATINE (1957) argued that Chaucer's poetry should be studied for its literary self-consciousness and especially in relationship to the other French poets Chaucer read. Adherents of the exegetical school, which was fully articulated by ROBERTSON (1962), believe that Chaucer's work is profoundly shaped by, if not written with direct reference to, major doctrinal and exegetical writing, particularly that of St. Augustine. Robertsonian readings tend to reveal Chaucer's moral didacticism. A recent very useful work in the Robertsonian tradition is by KOLVE, who explains the primacy of visual imagery and memory in the period, and studies the controlling imagery of the first five Canterbury Tales in terms of Chaucer's use of received iconographic traditions. The book includes 175 illustrations, which are a wonderful introduction to the age. DONALDSON, in numerous articles and books (including his lively and enjoyable 1972 volume, a collection of essays that explores both individual tales and larger medieval topics such as courtly love, and the question of exegetical criticism itself in an essay called "Patristic Exegesis in the Criticism of Medieval Literature: The Opposition") considers how Chaucer engages the reader with his works and celebrates Chaucer as a witty and self-ironical humanist.

Most major critics of Chaucer since these two dominant schools were established were students of one or more of these figures and have followed their critical approaches closely. For example, BENSON (in his 1986 *Chaucer's Drama of Style*), following Donaldson and Muscatine, critiques the long-standing "dramatic theory" of Chaucer established by Kittredge and Lumiansky. Rather than focus on the teller to the exclusion of the tale, an approach prominent in earlier criticism and still quite popular, Benson argues for, and demonstrates, in-depth stylistic analysis of each tale.

Until recently, when many Chaucer critics from England moved to the United States, English Chaucer criticism had its own tradition led by figures who (with the exception of Salter, whose untimely death marked a tragic loss to the field) are still major Chaucer critics. PEARSALL is not only Chaucer's most renowned biographer and a superb textual scholar, but also a thorough and measured critic. His book on *The Canterbury Tales* (1985) is an extremely useful guide for the beginning reader of the *Tales*, for it includes important summaries of debates about the date and manuscripts of the poem, the controversies about the order of the *Tales*, and a discussion of audience and reception, as well as summaries of critical responses to each tale grouped under the headings of the "Portraits", the "Romances", "Comic Tales and Fables", and the "Religious Tales". These short essays not only describe, but also carefully assess, the merits and weaknesses of the most significant critical treatments of Chaucer's work.

SALTER's essays and introductions to medieval poetry are similarly paradigmatic. For example, her classic essay on "The Clerk's Tale" must be read by anyone trying to come to terms with this deeply troubling story of a young wife forced to give up her children apparently to a cruel death simply because she has promised obedience to her husband. Considering the problem of religious meaning and secular illustration, Salter argues that the "human sympathies evoked by the sight of unmerited suffering form, ultimately, a barrier to total acceptance of the work in its original function" as a religious parable about the merits of human constancy and patience before God. She concludes that Chaucer was not fully in control of his material and that here he inadvertently betrays his ambivalent feelings about his source. SPEARING, in his equally classic essay "Chaucer's Clerk's Tale as a Medieval Poem" (1972), considers Chaucer's use of Petrarch and a French version of the story of patient Griselda in order to show how Chaucer deliberately makes it impossible for readers to glean the simple Petrarchan message that Griselda is a model of human constancy before God. The clerk, he demonstrates, is an adversely critical commentator on his source. Responding to Salter, Spearing argues that Chaucer chose his source specifically because the poem illustrated a contrast between two perspectives, the one absolute and symbolic, and the other relative and realistic, and further that Chaucer deliberately set out to tell a tale of disharmony. Disharmony and tension are crucial features of medieval religion, and it is this problematic religion that is at the heart of the tale, he concludes.

SPEARING is also the author of the only major book on Chaucer's dream visions (1976). Here he provides an excellent background to the late-medieval dream poem by explaining the genre's sources in scriptural and classical visions. He describes and explains the influence on Chaucer of Macrobius's *Commentary of the Dream of Scipio Scipionis*, *The Romance of the Rose*, and other fourteenth-century French dream poems. The book also includes extensive analyses of each one of Chaucer's dream visions, which focus especially on the self-reflexivity of each poem. The remainder of the book considers dream visions contemporary to Chaucer. SPEARING's recent book (1993) also treats a number of Chaucer's poems in terms of the voyeurism of many characters inscribed within the poems and of the poet.

MANN (1973) was among the first to establish Chaucer as a self-conscious literary poet rather than a poet of "real life". She describes the distinguishing features of the genre of estates satire, poems that criticized members of the various classes in society (the three major estates in the Middle Ages were those who ruled, those who worked, and those who prayed) thereby exposing the limitations of those individuals who failed to uphold the responsibilities to their estate. Mann argues that Chaucer modelled his Canterbury pilgrims less on real people than on the conventions of the genre, and further that he complicated the genre by refusing to judge characters while providing sufficient evidence to tempt the reader to do so.

AERS was for a long time a sole voice arguing for the consideration of Chaucer within historical contexts in numerous articles and books. In his book he demonstrates Chaucer's engagement with social, theological, and ecclesiastical issues, arguing that Chaucer affirms his culture while exposing its contradictions and tensions. Arguing against Robertsonianism, he posits that Chaucer and William Langland "engage in a critical dialectic with traditional ideologies and social practices". In this book, and in much of his recent work, he has urged critics not to use Chaucer as the paradigm of the age, but rather to include Langland in our studies in order to gain a richer and more complex understanding of the period. His work, and especially his recent articles, have been taken up by critics of the last decade.

Drawing on English literary and textual criticism, recent criticism has reassessed the two dominant American schools arguing against a general formalist trend and for the inclusion of larger contexts of various sorts. PATTERSON revised Robertson (in his 1987 *Negotiating the Past*) by arguing that while Robertson was wrong about exegetics, he was right to situate Chaucer within the historical concerns of his own time. His major book (1991) addresses Chaucer's construction of the subject within medieval literary tradition and historical event. Patterson turns his attention first to "Anelida and Arcite" and *Troilus and Criseyde*, and considers Chaucer's contention with the classical tradition as Chaucer developed his own idea of history and further explored history as a subject for poetry. In the remaining chapters, Patterson considers Chaucer's abandonment of the classics in favor of contemporary subjects in major Canterbury Tales including the Knight's, Miller's, Wife of Bath's, Merchant's, Shipman's, and Pardoner's. Patterson considers these tales as responses to a variety of urgent contemporary issues including the crisis of governance and chivalry, emergent bourgeois identity, and social pressures such as the English Rising. This comprehensive study not only brings to bear on Chaucer studies a wide variety of historical materials, but also gathers together most of the major Chaucer criticism of the past two decades.

STROHM, also in the historicist school, describes Chaucer's social milieu, his position as a court poet, and his marginal status as an "esquire en service", that is, a squire who earned rather than inherited the right to bear arms. He goes on to illustrate the effect Chaucer's social standing had on the implied and fictional audiences of his work. GREEN also considers Chaucer with other poets in the late Middle Ages as a court poet, while KNAPP views Chaucer in relation to larger social issues of the fourteenth century.

Recent work has looked at Chaucer's work from a variety of poststructuralist theoretical and interdisciplinary perspectives. FERSTER was among the first to consider Chaucer in terms of contemporary literary theory. She argues that interpretation is of central concern to Chaucer, and demonstrates how modern phenomenological hermeneutics can help us understand Chaucer's hermeneutics. LEICESTER, focusing exhaustively on the Pardoner's, Wife of Bath's, and Knight's tales, delves deeply into the question of the nature of Chaucer's representation of the subject. Drawing on psychoanalytic and poststructuralist theory, Leicester revises the older Kittredgian "dramatic theory" of the *Canterbury Tales* by arguing that they create "impersonated artistry" in which voicing rather than self-expression is critically important: through voicing, pilgrims create themselves from moment to moment in varied responses to institutional pressures. This work is sensitive to gender issues as well as to philosophical and poststructuralist debates about the nature of the subject and its representation in literature.

BENSON (C. David) and I (ROBERTSON) argue, in our edited collection (1990) on Chaucer's religious tales, for a consideration of Chaucer's religion from a non-exegetical perspective. This collection includes essays devoted to a survey of criticism on each religious tale and critical essays on the tales themselves. In addition, it contains general essays on religious issues, including the important piece by Linda Georgianna, "The Protestant Chaucer", which argues that criticism has been dominated by a Protestant bias which misrepresents and misunderstands Chaucer's Catholic beliefs.

Most neglected until recently was the issue of the representation of women in Chaucer, and feminist criticism of Chaucer has flourished in the past ten years. The most important works have been Dinshaw's and Hansen's studies. Both critics bring a variety of theory to bear on Chaucer but generally expose Chaucer's inevitable participation in the misogyny of his age despite his unusual sensitivity to the effects of this misogyny. DINSHAW establishes first that writing itself was understood in the Middle Ages as a patriarchal act upon the feminine surface of the page, and that Chaucer both practiced such an act while at the same time being aware of its limitations. Her work provides brilliant readings of understudied works such as "The Legend of Good Women" and very well-studied texts such as the "Wife of Bath's Tale", where she offers an Irigarayan reading of the prologue as a liberating act of mimicry of the discourses that entrap and attempt to control her voice. HANSEN criticizes Chaucer more forcefully for his misogyny in far-reaching analyses of works, including the dream visions and the *Canterbury Tales*. Hansen demonstrates first that Chaucer criticism has been dominated by a celebration of Chaucer as a humanist and that the humanist tradition is based on the exclusion of the feminine. In each analysis she shows how women are excluded, repressed, or silenced, whatever their social classes or the genre of the poem in which female characters appear. In her study of the first fragment, for example, she demonstrates how the women characters of the works – Emelye, Alisoun, Symkyn's unnamed wife and daughter, Malyn, and even the prostitute wife of the "Cook's Tale" – are all constructed in the same way, as subordinate to male desire and caught within a homosocial discourse in which women are used to enhance the goals of male competition. MANN, in her feminist study of Chaucer (1991), takes the opposite point of view arguing instead in her readings of many of the Canterbury tales and *Troilus and Criseyde* for Chaucer's sensitivity to the misogyny of the age and to his celebration of "femininity" as a redeeming quality, which can be exhibited by male (such as Troilus) and female characters alike. MARTIN similarly argues for Chaucer's positive understanding and representation of women. CRANE reconsiders Chaucer's reaction to the romance genre from a feminist perspective. Arguing against the critical cliché that Chaucer had an aversion to the romance genre, Crane posits, on the contrary, that the romance genre deeply informed Chaucer's work because of its overt exploration of the ever-shifting social construction of male and female identity. Furthermore, she demonstrates how the genre of romance is peculiarly suited to a demonstration that the categories of male and female determine, inform and challenge each other.

Troilus and Criseyde has been considered by these critics in numerous articles and in chapters of their books, and has spawned a critical tradition of its own. The major critical edition, and one of the most acclaimed editions of any Chaucerian work, is by WINDEATT. BARNEY and BENSON, in each of their edited collections of essays on the poem, bring together classic essays, such as those by Kittredge and Lewis, and major new essays. Benson's collection includes Mann's important essay "Troilus's Swoon", in which she argues that it is indeed true that Criseyde has been victimized by the machinations of Pandarus and Troilus until the point of Troilus's swoon, but then explains how this faint changes the power dynamics of the poem and paves the way for the celebration of mutual love presented in Book III. Another equally important (although unanthologized) essay, by WASWO, demonstrates how Chaucer's marginal position in the court is reflected both in his ambivalent view of court life presented in the poem and in the character of Pandarus. An important book of the 1970s on the *Troilus* was WETHERBEE's, which considers Chaucer's use of Virgil, Ovid, Statius, Dante, and *The Romance of the Rose*. The only full-length treatment of Chaucer's use of Ovid is FYLER's. WALLACE studies Chaucer's relationship to the early writings of Boccaccio. C. David BENSON (1991) has published the most recent complete book on the *Troilus* at the time of writing; in this lively introduction to the complexities of the poem, Benson presents Chaucer's techniques in terms of reader-response theory. Wallace's is among the few studies to consider Chaucer in relationship to the Italians. Barbara NOLAN studies *Troilus and Criseyde* and "The Knight's Tale" in relation to Continental sources, which similarly treat classical subjects known as the *romans antiques*.

Major books on textual issues and of literary criticism relating to Chaucer appear yearly, and readers should be careful to check for the most recent bibliography.

ELIZABETH ROBERTSON

Chesterton, G.K. 1874–1936

English essayist, novelist, poet, and short-story writer

Boyd, Ian, *The Novels of G.K. Chesterton*, London: Paul Elek, 1975; New York: Barnes & Noble, 1975

Canovan, Margaret, *G.K. Chesterton, Radical Populist*, New York: Harcourt Brace Jovanovich, 1977

Coates, John, *Chesterton and the Edwardian Cultural Crisis*, Hull, Humberside: University of Hull Press, 1984

Conlon, Denis, G.K. *Chesterton: The Critical Judgements: A Study in Art and Propaganda*, Antwerp: Universitaire Faculteiten Sint-Ignatious (University of Antwerp), 1976

Ward, Maisie, *Gilbert Keith Chesterton*, London and New York: Sheed & Ward, 1944

Wills, Garry, *Chesterton: Man and Mask*, New York: Sheed & Ward, 1961

A brilliant and distinctive stylist, strikingly original as a critic of Robert Browning and Charles Dickens and as a writer on religion in *Orthodoxy* and *The Everlasting Man*, a master of the philosophical novel in *The Man Who Was Thursday* and *The Ball and the Cross*, one of the finest of English essayists, one of the most popular of detective-story writers, still widely read and often quoted, Chesterton receives relatively little attention from academic literary critics. The problems of his work include the bulk and uneven quality of his over-100 books, his distinctive political views, which are often misrepresented as reactionary, and his strongly religious position in a somewhat intolerant secularised culture. Chesterton criticism has not always addressed these problems, and the writing on Chesterton includes a disproportionate amount of cosy biography and sentimental reminiscence.

WARD's life is an excellent first-hand account by a friend, corresponding to John Forster's *Life of Dickens*, a valuable primary source for facts about Chesterton, drawing on his notebooks and letters. While certainly not hagiography, it is by a co-religionist. It has not been superseded by any subsequent biography of Chesterton.

WILLS does for Chesterton what the best twentieth-century scholarship has done for Samuel Johnson. He discovers the subtleties and half-tones behind the *persona* of the robust, downright controversialist and "character". Exploring the conflict of "realism" and solipsism in Chesterton's work, this study gives a particularly persuasive and intelligent account of symbol in the poetry.

BOYD offers a careful reading of 11 of Chesterton's novels, showing how they work in themselves, and how they mediate a distinctive political and social attitude. This lucid and detailed book is a useful corrective to the common schematic division of Chesterton's work into "art" and "propaganda".

CONLON has brought together a valuable collection of first reviews of Chesterton's work, which makes it possible to estimate much more accurately the cultural and intellectual climate in which Chesterton wrote and the types of reader-expectations his writings delighted or provoked. This book also offers a useful picture of the way in which Chesterton became a public personality and a "myth".

CANOVAN gives a brief but interesting account of Chesterton's political beliefs. Often incorrectly seen as right-wing, he was, in fact, a radical populist firmly supporting social justice and the redistribution of wealth, but opposed to socialism. This study cogently removes some very widespread misconceptions about Chesterton.

My (COATES's) study attempts to place Chesterton in the context of the battle of ideas of his time. The waning of religious belief left intellectuals of the day vulnerable to various superficially opposed ideologies which saw the melting of the individual into some "higher" unity as the cure for life's sorrow and futility. This Chesterton steadily opposed in his day-to-day activity as a journalist.

JOHN COATES

Chicano Literature *see* Latino Writers

Children's Literature: General

Chambers, Aidan, *Booktalk: Occasional Writing on Literature and Children*, London: Bodley Head, 1985; New York: Harper & Row, 1985

Hunt, Peter (ed.), *Children's Literature: The Development of Criticism*, London and New York: Routledge, 1990

Hunt, Peter, *Criticism, Theory and Children's Literature*, Oxford: Blackwell, 1991

Hunt, Peter (ed.) *Literature for Children: Contemporary Criticism*, London: Routledge, 1992

Lesnik-Oberstein, Karín, *Children's Literature: Criticism and the Fictional Child*, Oxford: Clarendon Press, 1994; New York: Oxford University Press, 1994

Nodelman, Perry, *Words about Pictures: The Narrative Art of Children's Picture Books*, Athens: University of Georgia Press, 1988

Rose, Jacqueline, *The Case of Peter Pan; or, The Impossibility of Children's Fiction*, London: Macmillan, 1984, revised 1993

Stephens, John, *Language and Ideology in Children's Fiction*, London: Longman, 1992

Wall, Barbara, *The Narrator's Voice: The Dilemma of Children's Fiction*, London: Macmillan, 1991

Critical theory of, and for, children's literature is still in its infancy. Dealing with one of the few literatures defined in terms of its audience, it has been preoccupied with defining both a range of reference and the concept of the reading child. Because of the power structure implied in the adult-child relationship, the criticism of children's literature is much concerned with affect – largely in educational and ideological, rather than traditional "literary", terms. It has its roots – and its primary audience – in education and librarianship rather than literary criticism, and it has a wide non-academic readership. What has emerged has been a criticism divided between the academic exploitation of the subject, and one that attempts to be accessible and balance the demands of theory and practice.

ROSE, in an academic study, confronts some of the basic dilemmas inherent in children's literature in her exploration of the "unstable" text of *Peter Pan*. Her book "closes down" the enterprise of children's literature criticism, pointing out that:

> There is . . . no body of literature which rests so openly on an acknowledged difference, a rupture almost, between writer and addressee. Children's fiction sets up the child as an outsider in its own process, and then aims, unashamedly, to take the child in.

This view has been widely disputed, although Rose's argument that the endorsement by children's literature critics of the classic realist novel is ideologically suspect is very persuasive. The "Peter Pan" story, in its various forms, is seen as a paradigm for this uneasy relationship, and illustrates her thesis that the identification of the child/subject in language needs to be carefully attended to.

LESNIK-OBERSTEIN offers an extensive examination of Rose. She argues that children's literature criticism is based on the premise of the "real child" within the meaning-making process and therefore cannot, like other criticism, abandon its audience. All children's-book criticism/theory "constructs" a – or, better, the – child, and Rose's construction "exists as a Freudian unconscious child sexuality [which] need not exist outside the unconscious of the adult at all". As it commonly operates, then, children's literature criticism is a nonsense: "in making judgements and criticisms on behalf of a 'real child' who does not exist, its writings are useless to the fulfilment of its own professed aims". To find a way out of this impasse, Lesnik-Oberstein suggests that an understanding of child psychotherapy may be an answer: "the book gains whatever importance it may have for any reader at any time precisely by allowing the reader the space to inscribe the text in his own way into his narrative of emotional meaning".

My (HUNT's) 1991 book stands accused by Lesnik-Oberstein of constructing a romantic image of a liberated, anarchic child reader. Other critics have pointed out the paradox between the acknowledgement of the social construction of readers, and their supposed freedom. These difficulties stem from the basic attempt in that book to mediate both the problems of children's literature/criticism and a practical critical approach to a non-specialist audience. I argue that not only are canonical literary standards irrelevant to children's books, but they are also subtly divisive, lying unconsciously behind many confused value judgements. The concept of "child*ist*" criticism – trying to understand the possible meaning made by the (or a) child reader – is an attempt to force adults to understand the true basis (and, frequently, the irrelevance) of their own judgements of children's books.

WALL avoids at least some of these philosophic pitfalls by concentrating on "objective" stylistic differences in texts. She distinguishes between "single", "double", and "dual" modes of address, arguing that least admirable are those books with "double" address, which patronisingly address the adult "over the head of" the child. (A.A. Milne's *Winnie-the-Pooh* is a classic example). Her wide-ranging history suggests that there has been a move in the twentieth century towards what she sees as the more acceptable "dual" mode, of which adults and children can partake according to their capacities. Whether her "single" address – purely to the child – is actually achievable, may be debated. One of her many generally applicable points is that the less a children's book looks like a children's book (that is when "the narrator [who] addresses the child narrates so circumspectly that adult readers are not forced to acknowledge their existence") the greater that book's status.

STEPHENS, another Australian, comprehensively mobilises linguistic and stylistic theory in considering the ideologies embedded in texts "for children", in terms of, for example, text, perception and power, story and discourse, and macro- and micro-discourses. His view is that every stylistic and narrative feature of a text encodes ideology, and his text is centred on virtuoso close readings of texts – how they work, rather than, as in Hollindale's article (see below), on the external influences themselves. However, he notes that the concept of a world "outside" the text must be treated cautiously "since language does not merely reflect the world but is crucial to the very constitution of the world". The question of *whose* world is being constituted is not directly approached.

One of the topics that Stephens considers is that of the picture-book, an area where children's literature has made a unique contribution, and this is explored with similar virtuosity – although with rather more attention to reader-response theory – by NODELMAN. Readers who might be inclined to underestimate the complexity of books apparently designed for inexperienced readers might find their opinion altered by Nodelman's examination of such topics as the picture and the implied viewer, format, design, contextual meanings of visual objects, visual weight and directed tension, and so on. His overall critical conclusion, that "good picture books . . . offer us what all good art offers us: greater consciousness", is both intricately demonstrated while being traditionally based.

If Wall, Stephens, and Nodelman are on the whole inward-looking, text-orientated, CHAMBERS represents the more empirical school of writers, which deals with books in children's lives. Chambers was one of the earliest commentators to relate critical ideas to children's literature, and this book contains, among other essays, his seminal application of Wolfgang Iser's work on reader-response theory – "The Reader in the Book". Chambers' criticism is based on his work as teacher, editor, and experimental author, and a recurring theme is the importance of literature for the development of children (as in "Axes for Frozen Seas"). Wayne Booth is a major influence in humanistic terms, and Chambers is not in the business of challenging conventional concepts of literariness: "if we are shown only a narrow range of literature, then we become readers of that restricted kind of writing". One of his major contributions here is his report on eliciting and analysing responses from children – "Tell Me: Are Children Critics?". Chambers, at once evangelical, accessible, and scholarly, can be seen as the best of one side of children's literature criticism.

I have sought to gather many of the most influential essays on the subject, with linking commentary and other material, in my (HUNT's) 1990 and 1992 collections. The 1990 volume argues for the innovativeness of the field, and reprints two seminal articles: William Moebius's "Introduction to Picture Book Codes" and Lissa Paul's "Enigma Variations: What Feminist Theory Knows about Children's Literature". As Paul writes, "there is good reason for appropriating feminist theory to children's literature. Both women's literature and children's literature are devalued and regarded as marginal or peripheral by the literary and educational communities . . . it is almost inconceivable that women and children have been invisible and voiceless for so long". The 1992 volume explores the process by which the subject of children's literature – rather in the manner of postcolonial literatures – is escaping the hegemony of "Eng. Lit.". It reprints Peter Hollindale's "Ideology and the Children's Book", a highly influential relocating of children's literature, and seeks to demonstrate the links between children's literature and (among other things) metafiction, psychology, and the New Historicism.

PETER HUNT

Children's Literature: 20th Century

1. British and American Writing

Butts, Dennis (ed.), *Stories and Society: Children's Literature in its Social Context*, London: Macmillan, 1992; New York: St Martin's Press, 1992

Nodelman Perry (ed.), *Touchstones: Reflections on the Best in Children's Literature*, 3 vols., West Lafayette, Indiana: Children's Literature Association, 1985–89

Rees, David, *The Marble in the Water: Essays on Contemporary Writers of Fiction for Children and Young Adults*, Boston: Horn Book, 1980

Rees, David, *Painted Desert, Green Shade: Essays on Contemporary Writers of Fiction for Children and Young Adults*, Boston: Horn Book, 1984

Rees, David, *What Do Draculas Do? Essays on Contemporary Writers of Fiction for Children and Young Adults*, Metuchen, New Jersey: Scarecrow Press, 1991
Swinfen, Ann, *In Defence of Fantasy: A Study of the Genre in English and American Literature since 1945*, London and Boston: Routledge & Kegan Paul, 1984

One could say that American and British children's literature complement each other, but in some of the following texts the linking together of the two countries highlights differences as well as similarities.

BUTTS has used authors from both sides of the Atlantic to discuss ideology and social context in relation to specific genres. The school story, the adventure story, the family story, and fantasy are all discussed. Books referred to are mainly set in the modern era, but as in the case of Gillian Avery's article on the nineteenth-century family story, reference is made to books written in an earlier period. In relation to the school story Jeffrey Richards gives a detailed development of this genre from Thomas Hughes's *Tom Brown's Schooldays* to Phil Redmond's contemporary *Grange Hill*. Throughout he relates the stories to society, Butts argues in his introduction that children's literature is not just a reflection of the ideology of the time in which it was written, but is an example of authors struggling to show problems they perceive in the world, and one could argue that Richards is doing just that in relation to British comprehensive schools. By contrast, in the following chapter, Perry Nodelman discusses the violence and guilt present in Robert Cormier's *The Chocolate War* and leads the reader onto thinking about human cruelty as a whole.

SWINFEN in her work on fantasy in British and American literature looks at the genre from 1945, in its broadest sense. From the beginning of the book she argues that J.R.R. Tolkien made fantasy, as a genre, "respectable", and that since the end of World War II it has developed widely in both countries. Swinfen examines different aspects of the genre, from worlds in parallel, secondary worlds, and talking animals, to the different "idealisms" present in the stories. Fantasy, as Swinfen argues, is a form that modern writers use to outline or present ideas relating to religious, political, and social aspects of the world. She discusses C.S. Lewis's *The Chronicles of Narnia* in relation to religious idealism, and says that the *Chronicles* are "the archetypical Christian battle between good and evil, the Holy War". Lastly, she argues that far from being a form of escapism, fantasy is a way of evaluating and discussing the world as the author sees it.

REES, in his three books on contemporary children's authors, discusses established children's writers of the period since the 1950s. In *The Marble in the Water* (1980) Rees compares the work of American and British authors, while in *Painted Desert, Green Shade* (1984) he tries to combine his discussion on a particular author with wider issues, such as linking the article on Katherine Paterson to the questions of why, and how, literary awards are given. However, through the trilogy of books Rees draws attention to the similarities and differences in British and American writing. He poses such questions as "why is it that British authors do not rival the Americans in the realistic depiction of everyday life?" (an issue taken up by Gillian Avery in *Stories and Society*), asks why Americans authors use the first person so often, and what makes authors like Ursula Le Guin and Philippa Pearce popular on both sides of the Atlantic. In the third book of the series, *What Do Draculas Do?* (1991), Rees speaks of the second golden era in writing for children, of writers who started writing in the 1950s–60s, and wrote their best books in the 1970s. All three studies are extremely useful in looking at the wealth of children's writers in both countries.

In Volume 1 of *Touchstones*, NODELMAN has collected together articles that discuss the best of children's literature. "Touchstones" is a metaphor first used by Matthew Arnold and relates to something that is truly excellent, and within this collection each essayist tries to explain why a particular book can be termed a "touchstone" and why we, as readers, may judge one book against another. The list includes books mainly written in the last 100 years or so, and by his own acknowledgement Nodelman states that the selection has faults and omissions. However, it does cover a variety of books from A.A. Milne's *Winnie the Pooh* to Madeleine L'Engle's *A Wrinkle in Time* and L.M Montgomery's *Anne of Green Gables*. Only two originally non-English-language books are included – Johanna Spyri's *Heidi* and Carlo Lorenzini's ("Collodi's") *Pinocchio* – and this limitation could, of course, be seen as one of the failings of the list. But generally the articles are informative and useful.

FIONA M. COLLINS

2. Translation into English

Bell, Anthea, "Translator's Notebook", in *The Signal Approach to Children's Books: A Collection*, edited by Nancy Chambers, Harmondsworth, Middlesex: Kestrel, 1980; Metuchen, New Jersey: Scarecrow Press, 1981
Cott, Jonathan, *Pipers at the Gates of Dawn: The Wisdom of Children's Literature*, New York: Random House, 1983; Harmondsworth, Middlesex: Viking, 1984
Hazard, Paul, *Books, Children and Men*, translated by Marguerite Mitchell, Boston: Horn Book, 1944, 5th edition, 1983
Hürlimann, Bettina, *Three Centuries of Children's Books in Europe*, edited and translated by Brian W. Alderson, London: Oxford University Press, 1967

HAZARD, in his comparative study of European children's literature, claims that children's literature may be regarded as truly international, promoting the "universal republic of childhood". The classics of British children's literature rapidly achieved a worldwide readership, a trend continued by the publication in many countries of contemporary literature translated from English. However, the number of children's books translated *into* English in recent decades is steadily declining. Critical studies of major European authors of the modern era whose work has been translated into English are limited to journal articles and chapters within general studies on children's literature.

HÜRLIMANN's survey of European literature traces cross-cultural developments, setting the sociological and literary contexts for the books cited. In a chapter entitled "Fantasy and Reality" she points to the imaginative inventiveness of Tove Jansson's *Moomin* series and Astrid Lindgren's *Pippi Longstocking*, categorising these narratives as carefully crafted "nonsense" to distinguish them from the aura of unreality present in many traditional tales. Saint-Exupéry's equally fantastic illustrated story *The Little Prince* is characterised as a delicate moral tale introducing children to transcendental values. A chapter devoted to Jean and Laurent de Brunhoff commends the *Babar* picture books as a high point of modern graphic art.

COTT discusses the subversion of bourgeois conventions and manners by Astrid Lindgren's eternally youthful and uncompromising Pippi, representing as she does a break with the tradition of female characters in children's literature who are either submissive and well-behaved or whose independent spirit is ultimately tamed.

BELL offers detailed and witty insights into the complexity of the translation process itself in an account of the gestation of the English version of Goscinny and Uderzo's *Asterix in Corsica*. *Signal*, the journal in which this essay first appeared, is a useful source of occasional articles on contemporary European authors translated into English.

GILLIAN LATHEY

3. Picture Books

Doonan, Jane, *Looking at Pictures in Picture Books*, Stroud, Gloucestershire: Thimble Press, 1993

Moss, Elaine, *Picture Books for Young People*, Stroud, Gloucestershire: Thimble Press, 1981, revised 1992

Nodelman, Perry, *Words about Pictures: The Narrative Art of Children's Picture Books*, Athens, Georgia: University of Georgia Press, 1988

Whalley, Joyce, and Tessa Chester, *A History of Children's Book Illustration*, London: John Murray/Victoria and Albert Museum, 1988

Perhaps the most important development in children's picture books since 1960 has been the transformation in the role of illustration. WHALLEY and CHESTER trace the history of illustration from its subsidiary, supportive function (focusing on a seventeenth-century edition of Aesop's *Fables*) to its current situation, where "harmonious integration of word and picture is now recognised as the ultimate requirement of picture book illustration". They distinguish clearly between book illustration in its interpretive function of "enhancing the narrative" without overwhelming or contradicting it, and the modern picture book "as a whole, produced by a combination of finely balanced verbal and visual qualities". While their study chronicles mainly the historical aspects of illustration for children, the final chapter discusses modern picture books, which they see as largely products of the explosion of colour printing, which occurred in the early 1960s as a result of new technology. They are critical of what they feel is the current over-production of picture books because of (largely) commercial pressures, and consider there to be a "plethora of mediocre work . . . with little concern for excellence in word or picture" in contrast to the higher quality of books in the 1960s and 1970s.

NODELMAN focuses on the ways in which picture books communicate meaning, in the sense of their "unique rhythms, unique conventions of shape and structure [and their] unique body of narrative techniques". He includes an in-depth examination of the relationship between the "narrative information in pictures and the viewer's acquaintance with learned assumptions and codes of signification". Books and pictures constituting unified works, details within pictures, and relationships between pictures alone on the one hand and pictures with text on the other – these subjects are also examined. Having countered various arguments against the practice of illustration, Nodelman indicates how important he considers the role of picture books in children's lives to be. By telling of "the same event by means of two different media and therefore in two quite different ways . . . it [the picture book] mirrors the process by which human beings come to know their world, better than does any other imaginative experience". He claims that it is the "objective awareness [of art] based on a deep understanding that allows us first to know the world and then to love the world we know": such power he attributes to the picture book, and his work is primarily, though not exclusively, a detailed analysis of its semiotics.

Children, as well as adults in their roles as mediators, need to understand how picture books "work", in order to gain from them. DOONAN's is a resource book to help adults aid children in appreciating picture books in all their depth and variety. After three chapters about the issues and practice of close reading, supported by detailed analysis of two picture books, and with reference to many others, she offers her own practical approaches to the development of this kind of close scrutiny. MOSS was the first to publicise the potential of the modern multi-layered picture book, with its social, political, and environmental overtones, to be serious literature for older readers. This publication is an annotated bibliography, which supplies titles to enthuse older readers, even adults.

SUSAN FREMANTLE

Children's Literature: British – General

Avery, Gillian, and Julia Briggs (eds.), *Children and Their Books: A Celebration of the Work of Iona and Peter Opie*, Oxford: Clarendon Press, 1989; New York: Oxford University Press, 1989

Carpenter, Humphrey, and Mari Prichard, *The Oxford Companion to Children's Literature*, Oxford and New York: Oxford University Press, 1984

Darton, F.J. Harvey, *Children's Books in England: Five Centuries of Social Life*, Cambridge: Cambridge University Press, 1932; 3rd revised edition, edited by Brian Alderson, London and New York: Cambridge University Press, 1982

Eyre, Frank, *20th-Century Children's Books*, London: Longman, 1952; Boston: Bentley, 1953; revised edition, as *British Children's Books in the Twentieth Century*, Longman: 1971; New York: Dutton, 1973

Fisher, Margery, *Who's Who in Children's Books: A Treasury of the Familiar Characters of Childhood*, London: Weidenfeld & Nicolson, 1975; New York: Holt Rinehart, 1975

Hunt, Peter, *An Introduction to Children's Literature*, Oxford and New York: Oxford University Press, 1994
Reynolds, Kimberley, *Children's Literature in the 1890s and the 1990s*, Plymouth, Devon: Northcote House, 1994
Stephens, John, *Language and Ideology in Children's Fiction*, London: Longman, 1992
Townsend, John Rowe, *Written for Children: An Outline of English Children's Literature*, London: J. Garnet Miller, 1965; New York: Lothrop, 1967; 4th, revised, edition, as *Written for Children: An Outline of English-Language Children's Literature*, Harmondsworth, Middlesex: Penguin, 1987; New York: Harper, 1988

The earliest study considered here, DARTON's, is an informative account of the historical development of children's books up until the end of the nineteenth century. (He does touch on early twentieth-century works but produces only a rather sketchy summary.) The third edition is particularly useful, having been enhanced by Brian Alderson's scholarly revision in 1982. Alderson, acutely perceiving the particular strengths and weaknesses of the first edition, was able to make the numerous necessary factual corrections, without interfering with the flow of this eminently readable text.

Darton concentrates on "printed works produced ostensibly to give children spontaneous pleasure", tracing the roots of his subject back to the fables and the chivalric romances of the Middle Ages. He examines contributions made to the development of the field by seventeenth-century chapbooks and (at the other end of the spectrum) the Puritans' "Good Godly Books". Although Darton does comment on writing styles and on stories which he regards as "unfailingly readable", he concentrates on changes in form and content over time, with particular emphasis on the social, philosophical (John Locke and Jean-Jacques Rousseau) and commercial influences at work.

In terms of time span, EYRE continues where Darton left off. His revised edition effectively covers the first 69 years of the twentieth century. Eyre begins with a brief historical survey, then moves on to a closer examination of genre groupings. For each type and period, he discusses those texts he regards as the "more significant books". Eyre is clearly as much concerned with evaluating what is on offer to child readers as with providing an historical survey. His analysis consists mainly of plot summaries and somewhat subjective assessments of quality of writing; he offers infectiously enthusiastic support for what he regards as original creative work.

The study includes useful appendices on regional writing and award winners, and a bibliography of books about children's literature. However, there is an unfortunate lack of attention given, in the body of the work, to the provision of publication dates for many of the books cited, and no bibliography of primary sources.

TOWNSEND brings together the periods covered by Darton and Eyre into one volume and, in his latest revised edition, takes discussion of the field into the 1980s. Townsend's work is organised chronologically, with early chapters broadly following Darton's account and later chapters devoted to the examination of genre groupings, within each of the periods surveyed.

The twentieth-century texts discussed by Townsend have been chosen on the basis of a personal, qualitative assessment of literary merit, eliminating discussion of some popular commercial successes (such as Enid Blyton's books), which may have social or historical significance, but fall short, in his view, of the highest literary standards. As Townsend emphasizes, "this is a study of children's literature, not of children's reading matter. It seeks to discriminate". He is also clearly concerned for the welfare of child readers and includes discussion of moral issues in his treatment of individual works. For example, Townsend labels Rudyard Kipling as a "morally obtuse" writer for children. The study does however provide many substantial quotations in support of particular points, giving readers the chance to examine the primary material on which Townsend's judgements are based.

A more problematic element of the degree of personal selectivity exercised by Townsend arises from omissions. For example, he talks at some length about school stories for boys, but fails to give similar treatment to equally well-known books for girls. Writers such as L.T. Meade, Angela Brazil, Elsie J. Oxenham, and Elinor Brent-Dyer are not mentioned.

HUNT provides the most up-to-date of the historical surveys. He also includes some discussion of the ways in which critical attention to the subject has developed over recent years, and puts forward his own views on the direction this should take in the future. Hunt warns against the application of literary theory to children's books, and seeks to distance the study of children's literature from more general literary studies. Readers may be surprised to find that Hunt seems to regard literary studies as still primarily consisting of efforts to rearrange texts into some eternal form of canon, and be disappointed that he does not open out into discussion of the possible relevance of, say, feminist, Marxist, or psychoanalytical criticism to the field. Hunt's earlier essay collections, *Children's Literature: The Development of Criticism* (1990) and *Literature for Children: Contemporary Criticism* (1992) are to be preferred in this respect. Hunt's subsequent "whistle-stop" presentation of individual books relies heavily on examination of narrative "tone of voice" and study of the "implied reader". The result, possibly due to the large number of books examined, is a rather disappointing and cursory dismissal of many texts.

FISHER's material is organised into an alphabetical reference work, covering fictional works from the eighteenth, nineteenth, and twentieth centuries. Her entries, as the title of the book implies, are the names of fictional characters, but reference to particular works can also be traced from the invaluable alphabetical listings of authors and book titles at the back of the book. The work is further enhanced by numerous reproductions of relevant illustrations, including some colour plates. Entries give plot summaries and also Fisher's own comments on the merits of individual works. Successful character delineation is highly regarded by Fisher, who sees it as "a tremendous, complicated conjuring-trick". Because of her emphasis on character, rather than on individual texts or authors, Fisher is able to refer, on occasion, to relevant film interpretations of well-known fictional characters and to develop her individual entries to include related characters, as when she discusses E.B. White's *Stuart Little* and Hans Christian Andersen's *Thumbelina* under the entry on Gulliver. For those looking for the most up-to-date references, it is disappointing that Fisher's work was published as early as 1975, thus missing the many interesting characters that have been created since then. On the other hand, there are entries relating to (then) contemporary books that have disappeared from later studies, and this makes Fisher's a particularly interesting historical reference work in relation to mid-twentieth-century texts (in particular those of the 1960s and 1970s).

The more recent reference work by CARPENTER and PRICHARD includes entries on writers, illustrators, publishers, individual books, and almost anything else one might think of with relevance to the subject. Covering all periods up until its publication in 1985, it must be regarded as the essential reference work in the field, with its concise informative entries. There is a certain amount of critical evaluation (particularly in relation to recent works); this is often balanced by the provision of bibliographical details for further reading on the particular book, writer or topic under discussion. Because of the sheer volume of material contained here, it is difficult for any writer, involved in a general survey of this vast subject area, to focus in depth on any individual author or work. The next two studies to be discussed have engaged with this problem and have come up with two differing, yet equally effective, strategies for dealing with it.

AVERY and BRIGGS have drawn together a book that consists of 20 essays, each offering an interesting perspective on some aspect of the general subject area. The essays are wide-ranging, exploring such diverse topics as book collecting, the behaviour of children in early-modern England, the work of individual writers for children, the work of an influential children's bookseller, and many more. Varied as these studies are, when taken together in one volume they stress, most effectively, the broad range of the field under examination. Yet the format allows individual contributors the freedom to develop a critical argument relating to a particular writer, text, or historical moment, so that discussion can move from the lightning personal assessment of all-inclusive surveys into a more balanced and scholarly concentration on interesting aspects of the work covered.

REYNOLDS, despite the title of her work, is not solely concerned with texts of the 1890s and 1990s, looking also at the possible influences of mid-century texts on those children who were to become the parents and writers of the 1990s. This imaginative approach allows for wide-ranging discussion on a selection of key texts from both centuries. Free from the "overload" of an all-embracing survey, Reynolds is able to undertake a fascinating, scholarly examination of the dialectical relationship between children's literature and attitudes towards children and childhood, without neglecting detailed critical work on individual texts. The reader is offered the chance to engage fully with the critical argument, being given ample quotations from primary texts and details of numerous other critical and historical studies for further reading.

Finally, for those wishing to study books published during the 1960s, 1970s, and 1980s, STEPHENS offers an entirely different approach from that of Eyre, Townsend, and even Hunt, reflecting increased contemporary interest in a more rigorous approach to critical analysis. The main thrust of Stephens' study is to reveal the ideological presuppositions that pervade fiction for children, and he points to the social relevance of such an analysis, commenting that "children's fiction belongs firmly within the domain of cultural practices which exist for the purpose of socializing their target audience". Like Reynolds, Stephens includes detailed quotations which illustrate the points he makes. This is a study that should not be missed by those with a keen interest in critical approaches to the field.

SUSAN HANCOCK

Children's Literature: British – to 1900

Avery, Gillian, *Behold the Child: American Children and Their Books 1621–1922*, London: Bodley Head, 1994; Baltimore: Johns Hopkins University Press, 1994

Avery, Gillian, and Julia Briggs (eds.), *Children and Their Books: A Celebration of the Work of Iona and Peter Opie*, Oxford: Clarendon Press, 1989; New York: Oxford University Press, 1989

Bratton, J.S., *The Impact of Victorian Children's Fiction*, London: Croom Helm, 1981; Totowa, New Jersey: Barnes & Noble, 1981

Muir, Percy, *English Children's Books 1600 to 1900*, London: Batsford, 1954

Reynolds, Kimberley, *Girls Only? Gender and Popular Children's Fiction in Britain, 1880–1910*, Hemel Hempstead, Hertfordshire: Harvester Wheatsheaf, 1990; Philadelphia: Temple University Press, 1990

Reynolds, Kimberley, *Children's Literature in the 1890s and 1990s*, Plymouth, Devon: Northcote House, 1994

Sommerville, John C., *The Discovery of Childhood in Puritan England*, Athens: University of Georgia Press, 1992

F.J. Harvey Darton's *Children's Books in England* (1958) set the pattern and provided the factual basis for twentieth-century studies of British children's literature and those who wrote it. Of particular significance was Darton's recognition that children's books must be understood as part of social history, and need to be considered in the light of their intended audience.

MUIR continues the work begun by Darton, though focusing primarily on works of entertainment and providing more bibliographical detail (bibliography, he claims, is the "anatomy" of the book). Generously illustrated with many full-colour plates, the book usefully combines visual evidence with historical detail and provides a rapid overview of books read by children (as distinct from those specifically published for young readers) between the seventeenth and twentieth centuries. Like Darton, Muir provides information about the earliest examples of books for children, including chapbooks, fables, and fairytales, before moving on to stories of adventure, books for girls, nonsense, and verse. Little is provided in the way of a thesis, most discussions of books and authors are limited, and Muir is at times overly subjective; nonetheless, his is a valuable introduction to the field.

SOMMERVILLE confines his study to the Puritan movement of the seventeenth century. While the primary focus of this work is not those who wrote for children, because Sommerville constructs his history of Puritan childhood largely through literature for and about children (children's books, child-rearing manuals, biographies, catechisms, and educational and theological treatises), he necessarily discusses them in some depth. The Puritans are largely credited with having invented literature for children, and this work considers the impetus behind their decision to produce and distribute stories and books for young readers. Sommerville's is a thoughtful and ground-breaking study, which asks that long-held assumptions about the Puritans and their attitudes to children be reconsidered. For instance, in his discussion of works of entertainment, Sommerville argues that the Puritans used humour both to get closer to children, and to provide young people with a defence against social hostility and mockery. The book provides many fascinating and surprising anecdotes and examples, and some useful descriptions and analyses of Puritan texts read by children. The discussion of John Bunyan and other Dissenters, who between them revolutionised the Puritan concept of childhood, is particularly fine.

AVERY too looks at the influence of the Puritans in her 1994 study, which combines social history with a history of publishing for children. She compares British and American writers for children, and though her interest is primarily in what American children read between 1621 and 1922, she also provides detailed discussions of prominent British writers such as Bunyan, John Newbery, James Janeway, Isaac Watts, Maria Edgeworth, and Charlotte Yonge. The perspective she gains by looking back at British children's books from America provokes some useful insights. For instance, British readers were taught to do their duty in the state of life in which God had placed them, while Americans were exhorted to strive to improve themselves; British fiction celebrated leisure, American stories were preoccupied with industry, and readers in the New World were encouraged to reject fairytales as "relics of a credulous past". Avery's conclusion, that American and British girls could successfully share their fiction while the patriotic sentiments characteristic of books for boys inhibited this kind of exchange, is helpful, as are her thoughtful discussions of the treatment of childhood death and motherhood.

In their 1989 collection of essays, AVERY and BRIGGS have included several pieces by distinguished scholars on writing for children before 1900. Among these are Keith Thomas's essay on "Childhood in Early Modern England (1500–1800)", which attempts to distinguish between the history of children and the history of the treatment of children by adults on the basis of imaginative literature for children, schoolboy diaries, children's letters, and adults' observations. Thomas argues that children "tended to behave in a way which was inconsistent with the values of adult society". Elsewhere in the collection Julia Briggs looks at the history of women writers for children. This important essay suggests that women found ways of using children's literature to articulate their dissatisfactions with society and to mock the patriarchs who ran it. *Children and Their Books* provides a wide range of informative and stimulating discussions.

BRATTON sets out "to describe and attempt to evaluate the flood of fiction for children written during the nineteenth century with the intention of conveying moral instruction". Throughout this slim but elegantly argued book, information about the juvenile publishing industry is placed in its historical context. Readers are encouraged to think about the commercial and social factors that shaped writing for children – a practice that is particularly helpful for understanding both the operations of the huge Evangelical publishing houses and the perceived links between literacy and morality. Bratton introduces a number of writers whose work is now little read, and provides good plot summaries. Her observations about publishing and educational strategies (including books given as prizes) based on sex, class, and age have prompted a number of further studies of children's reading in the nineteenth century.

My own (REYNOLDS's) studies of pre-1900 children's literature have focused on the history of childhood and children's reading. In the 1990 title, feminist, structuralist, and psychoanalytic theories are used to offer an explanation for the emergence of separate literatures for girls and boys in late Victorian and Edwardian England, and ask what the significance of segregated reading may be. A particular interest of the study is how reading shapes gender constructions and the role played by gendered reading in maintaining patriarchy. The history of book publishing, educational practices, and popular culture are also considered. In the 1994 volume I look at changing images of childhood in *fin-de-siècle* writing for children, and the way these both reflect and shape thinking about children. Fear of children, nostalgic fantasies of childhood, and fashions in child-rearing are discussed in relation to explicit and implicit ideological constructions of the child in children's books.

KIMBERLEY REYNOLDS

Children's Literature: British – 1900 to the Present

Cadogan, Mary and Patricia Craig, *You're a Brick, Angela! A New Look at Girls' Fiction from 1839 to 1975*, London: Victor Gollancz, 1976

Chambers, Aidan, *Booktalk: Occasional Writing on Literature for Children*, London: Bodley Head 1985; New York: Harper & Row, 1985

Fox, Geoff, *et al.* (eds.), *Writers, Critics and Children: Articles from "Children's Literature in Education"*, London: Heinemann, 1976; New York: Agathon Press, 1976

Hunt, Peter, *Criticism, Theory and Children's Literature*, Oxford and Cambridge, Massachusetts: Blackwell, 1991

Meek, Margaret, Aidan Warlow, and Griselda Barton (eds.), *The Cool Web: The Pattern of Children's Reading*, London: Bodley Head 1977; New York: Atheneum, 1978

Rustin, Michael, and Margaret Rustin, *Narratives of Love and Loss: Studies in Modern Children's Fiction*, London: Verso, 1987

Styles, Morag, Eve Bearne, and Victor Watson (eds.), *After Alice: Exploring Children's Literature*, London: Cassell, 1992

Wall, Barbara, *The Narrator's Voice: The Dilemma of Children's Fiction*, London: Macmillan, 1991

The status of children's literature as the focus of serious study is relatively recent. Indeed the definition of what constitutes a children's literature has been a subject of debate.

HUNT sets out to investigate the relationship between literary criticism and children's literature. In his opening chapters he defines his field of study by examining the relationship between children's literature and contemporary aspects of literary theory. He goes on to consider the state of children's literature and discusses some current definitions. In doing so he acknowledges the problematic area of the interrelatedness of the concept of quality with that of the intended audience for any work of literature, and emphasises a central premise of his argument: that "literature" tends to be writing whose worth is sanctioned by a powerful minority of academics; therefore if literature for children is to receive serious attention it must either be recognised as part of the canon, or the modes of criticism must change. If, as a genre, it is accorded a low status, that in part derives from the views of children and childhood currently held by society at large. Hunt develops these ideas not through detailed analysis of specific texts but through an exploration of how the child-reader makes meaning from the text. Later chapters deal with the child's concept of narrative, politics and ideology in children's literature, and aspects of criticism. Hunt's is also one of the few academic studies to consider institutional aspects of children's publishing, in a chapter on the production of children's books.

By contrast, RUSTIN and RUSTIN set out to develop a series of detailed readings of key texts in postwar children's fiction. Because their chief interest is in the emotional and imaginative development of the child, their examples are drawn largely from the genre of fantasy. While the works of E. Nesbit, Philippa Pearce, and Mary Norton are widely regarded as part of an acknowledged canon of children's literature, the inclusion of Lynne Reid Banks and Russell Hoban, whose works are possibly less familiar and who are equally well known for their writing for an adult audience, is illustrative of the areas of controversy indicated by Hunt about the status and definition of children's literature. While Hunt suggests institutional factors may be paramount in defining what it is that delineates children's fiction, the Rustins argue that their selection has been guided by the "poetic realism" that distinguishes the best writing for children. They develop a triangular framework for their detailed investigation of individual texts, drawing on the disciplines of psychoanalysis, sociology, and literary criticism.

WALL also introduces her study by posing the question "is it really a children's book?". Unlike the Rustins, who derive their conclusions from the subject matter and deep structures of metaphor, she sets out to answer this question by drawing on developments in the field of narratology. She bases her study on the concepts of the "implied author" and the "implied reader" of any given text. Her analysis concludes that such popular twentieth-century authors as C.S. Lewis, Enid Blyton, and Roald Dahl have a direct descent from the authorial narrator familiar in nineteenth-century writing. It provides the basis for a fresh appraisal of several acknowledged classics, such as the work of Nesbit and Norton. Of particular interest is her chapter on the ironic narrative stance in fiction addressed to young children and her account of the work authors such as Jane Gardam and Penelope Lively, known equally for their writing for an adult audience. The understanding that permeates the work is that "it is not what is said, but the way that it is said, and to whom it is said, which marks a book for children".

The study of girls' fiction by CADOGAN and CRAIG is representative of two further identifiable features of writing for children: that the most popular writing is frequently regarded as ephemeral or non-quality, and that much writing for children and young people is specifically aimed at a readership of one gender. Drawing on the nineteenth-century context of the evolution of the New Woman, they track the career of the New Girl in a literary history of twentieth-century writing for girls. They offer an often entertaining overview, with some detailed consideration of individual texts. Successive chapters discuss genres – notably school stories (including such noted exponents as Angela Brazil and Elinor Brent-Dyer) – the middle-class bias in much of the material discussed, the influence of social change, and the development of comics and magazines. In their final chapter they address future developments in children's literature. This is a distinctive account of the field, though their conclusion, that at the end of the twentieth century girls' fiction is "almost redundant as a genre", is highly questionable.

Clearly a key theme in any discussion of children's literature is its practical application in an educational context. The original purpose of FOX *et al.* was to gain a wider audience for some of the most interesting articles published during the first six years of the influential journal *Children's Literature in Education*. The book is aimed at teachers, student teachers, librarians, and parents whose concern is to bring children and literature together. Although some of the pieces may now seem dated there is much of value in this collection. For example, in the "Writers" section, Nina Bawden and Joan Aiken, both popular and prolific children's authors, add their views on the complicated issue of what, if anything, makes writing for children different from works aimed at an adult audience; the "Critics" section has some of the most memorable pieces, including Ted Hughes' powerful article "Myth and Education"; while pedagogy is central in the final section, entitled "Children". No attempt is made to link the pieces or give a theoretical framework for their inclusion beyond the desire to spread the good word that children's literature is a serious and valuable area of interest.

MEEK, WARLOW, and BARTON, on the other hand, have much more ambitious aims, although they too are concerned to address those who are involved in bringing children and story together. Published in 1977, it was prepared in 1975 to expand on ideas about literacy raised in the educational Bullock Report. It shares with that publication "the recurrent interests in offering a contribution to the theoretical study of the place of literature in literacy". This wide-ranging collection of 50 essays by distinguished authors, critics, and others aims to illustrate the truth of the statement that stories of all kinds are central to the experience of both children and adults. The editors realised that there was still a need to raise the status of children's literature, but their concern went beyond consideration of the adult's perception. They wanted to examine what children get out of reading and were keen to consider more than a conventional view of literature. As Margaret Meek says, "we wanted to distinguish 'storying' –

the writer's narrative habit – from Story, the art form". There are four main sections – "The Reader", "What the Authors Tell Us", "Approaches to Criticism", and "Ways Forward". Most of the contributions are short and are prefaced by a commentary from the editors. The final part is a bibliography of useful articles and books on the subject, and although it needs updating, interested readers will still find it helpful for reference.

STYLES, BEARNE, and WATSON also address children's literature from the perspective of educators; but this collection of seminar papers shows the development in thinking about readers in the years since Meek *et al.* Margaret Meek, to whom this book is dedicated, says that at the time of *The Cool Web*, people were inexperienced in writing about "varieties of discourse", the different rhetorics or ways of telling stories. Now the child reader is not only pre-eminent, but the manner in which children read texts of all kinds is discussed in many of the articles. As with Fox and Meek, Styles *et al.* give a place for children's authors to discuss their views on writing for the young; but a large part of the book examines the children's experiences of the texts they are given, and the different ways in which the texts can be interpreted. The second section, "Children Constructing Texts", moves right away from the texts adults provide and looks at the stories children themselves create. Much of the pedagogy described is based on the experiences of working with children who are in their first few years of schooling.

Unlike the other compilations discussed here, CHAMBERS contains only one person's voice, but, in his many different roles, his contribution to the debate about literature and children has been enormous over the last 20 years. He brings together in this collection some of his lectures, articles, and essays, and, at the centre of most of them, is his preoccupation with discussion about reading as a literary and an educational activity. As a children's author, he is keen to explore his intended audience's reactions to his books as well as explain and justify his own particular ways of telling. He also includes detailed accounts of his work with teachers, showing how together they attempted to elicit pupils' responses to a range of literature. His own views of several children's authors and their books are included.

PHILIPPA HUNT AND JACQUELINE NUNN

Children's Literature: American

Avery, Gillian, *Behold the Child: American Children and Their Books 1621–1922*, London: Bodley Head, 1994; Baltimore: Johns Hopkins University Press, 1994

Butler, Francelia, and Richard Rotert (eds.), *Triumphs of the Spirit in Children's Literature*, Hamden, Connecticut: Library Professionals Publications, 1986

Dizer, John T., Jr., *Tom Swift and Company: "Boys' Books" by Stratemeyer and Others*, Jefferson, North Carolina: McFarland, 1982

Griswold, Jerome, *Audacious Kids: Coming of Age in America's Classic Children's Books*, New York: Oxford University Press, 1992; as *Audacious Kids: America's Favourite Books from the Golden Age* (credited to Jerry Griswold), 1993

Johnson, Dianne, *Telling Tales: The Pedagogy and Promise of African American Literature for Youth*, New York: Greenwood Press, 1990

Kensinger, Faye Riter, *Children of the Series and How They Grew, or, A Century of Heroines and Heroes, Romantic, Comic, Moral*, Bowling Green, Ohio: Bowling Green State University Popular Press, 1987

Lindgren, Merri V. (ed.), *The Multicolored Mirror: Cultural Substance in Literature for Children and Young Adults*, Fort Atkinson, Wisconsin: Highsmith Press, 1991

Lystad, Mary, *At Home in America: As Seen Through Its Books for Children,* Cambridge, Massachusetts: Schenkman, 1984

MacCann, Donnarae, and Gloria Woodard (eds.), *The Black American in Books for Children: Readings in Racism*, Metuchen, New Jersey: Scarecrow Press, 1972, revised 1985

MacLeod, Anne Scott, *American Childhood: Essays on Children's Literature of the Nineteenth and Twentieth Centuries*, Athens: University of Georgia Press, 1994

Children's books have been read as literature only recently in the American academy. Prior to the 1970s their study was confined almost exclusively to the fields of education and library science. Thus, despite increasing attention from literature departments, children's literature criticism in America today remains interdisciplinary. Theory, pedagogy, history, psychology, and multiculturalism all play varying roles in critical texts, depending on the perspective of the particular critic. The following overview represents the related but not always coalescing nature of these discussions.

Surveying the evolution of children's books in America since the seventeenth century, AVERY gives detailed attention to both an impressive number of individual texts and their publishing history. The most notable aspect of this study is Avery's cross-cultural focus: she consistently reads American children's books against their British counterparts on the grounds that they were often mutually influential. This is at once her work's best and most problematic quality. It enables insightful observations, as Avery demonstrates the historical continuity of the ideal American child – independent, energetic, resourceful, and integral to the family's daily operation. Yet while Avery traces the permutations of this self-sufficient and self-improving child, she does not address issues such as class, race, and/or gender, which make the concept of a single "ideal American child" problematic. Furthermore, her background in British children's literature yields brief and pointed reflections on British children's books or movements, yet she is repeatedly less precise – making broad claims that something is "American through and through" for example – on her ostensible subject-matter. Although this book is more history than theory, it is remarkably wide-ranging and thorough in its coverage, and provides a resource unmatched by earlier efforts to contextualize American children's books.

LYSTAD's work has a similarly broad timeline (1700–1980), but takes a socio-historical approach, exploring the evolving socialization of children and the structure of the family in America. Her study traces an increasing degree of egalitarianism, self-expression, and freedom of choice allowed to all family members. She describes each of these three measures of family life in an historical and sociological context, which demonstrates the ways in which children's books often contain adult visions of society's potential rather than revealing society's actualities. More quantifying than theoretical, her study is provocative in its use of children's books as historical documents to reveal social roles within the family and societal views of the family structure.

MacLEOD has a narrower historical focus than Avery or Lystad, and is more theoretically complex. She concentrates on what she calls the "family story" – one that both has a domestic setting and is intended to impart a good example. She explores the gender socialization that occurs within, and through, children's books, and examines its realtionship to national consciousness. Expanding on the success-story motif, which other critics have observed, MacLeod emphasizes the ways in which obedience, moral selflessness, and hard work were not simply a means to personal success, but were key virtues for members of a young republic. Her book thus negotiates the two primary trends in the historicization of American children's books – (1) analyzing and celebrating the independent, American-Dream-seeking child, and (2) reading the child-as-America, drawing on nineteenth-century notions of Republican motherhood. Remarking on the absence of overt politics in early children's books, MacLeod convincingly pursues issues of nationalism and identity by linking them to the senses of belonging and usefulness that characterize the American child. Reading children's books as a form of wish-fulfillment for the culture, MacLeod reveals their growing politicization and shift to a child-centered consciousness.

Influenced by folklore theory, GRISWOLD's work provides a psychological reading of the self-sufficient American youth. He identifies an archetypal story pattern, the "Three Lives of the Child-Hero", in which one matures and negotiates identity. Reading 12 "classics", he theorizes that American children's literature (and thus Americans in general, he presumes) are drawn to this ur-story through the republican metaphors of America-as-child and children-as-America. This premise allows him to psycho-historicize, that is, to psychoanalyze relationships within these books and then contextualize them within contemporary politics to explore cultural concerns. Such concerns range from English-American relations, to teaching republicanism, to coping with divorce and drug gangs. Where MacLeod reads books as contradicting rather than reflecting social trends (as people gain freedoms, emphasis on self-control increases, for example), Griswold sees parallels in the personal and political implications of these stories. His psychoanalytic readings emphasize the "landscape leading inward" and the notion of fiction legitimating self-identity, both of which he finds characteristic of American children's books.

The issue of gender is raised in some form in almost every recent study of children's texts. In this light, the so-called "girls' books" and "boys' books" of the nineteenth century have received considerable attention, although there are few book-length studies of the gendered series genre. DIZER's text is primarily a defense of series books, which for many years were impugned as pulp fiction containing immoral models of behavior, poor quality of writing, and thin storylines. Dizer hopes to recuperate these books by suggesting that they have retained their intense popularity among readers because they reflect American values of action, ingenuity, and heroism. In addition, he provides a detailed history of the Stratemeyer syndicate and the rise of boys' serial fiction, as well as of the adult antagonism toward these books. Yet his thinly veiled attacks on the library and educational circles and his cataloguing of plot devices are often tiresome.

KENSINGER's study, on the other hand, contains less straight history and more complex readings of series books. She looks at both boys' and girls' books and the role models contained therein, claiming that while heroes and heroines were shaped to suit the culture's changing attitudes, the series offered at least two benefits – a model of a child protagonist who was resourceful enough to emerge victorious from any struggle, and a ready supply of affordable reading material for real children. While romanticizing the process of reading somewhat, Kensinger nevertheless addresses a range of issues surrounding series books – from orphanhood to morality to style – in their historical contexts, and with numerous and thorough examples.

Although some of the studies above acknowledge that children's books have historically adopted a single vision of the American child as a white Protestant, none of them address the issue of ethnicity or its erasure at any length. While the BUTLER and ROTERT collection does not sustain such an enquiry, a number of its essays retain more diverse notions of American culture. The authors explore nineteenth- and twentieth-century books, archetypes and myth patterns, and more modern problems with which children cope and have coped. The essays are brief, highly varied, and not overly theoretical. Psychological and socio-historical insights reveal that children's books often demonstrate the indominatable spirits of children in the face of adversities. From racism to dust-bowl poverty, to dysfunctional families, the collection's concerns suggest that contemporary children's literature attempts to bring to the fore the thornier issues and diversity of America that earlier books (often offensively) side-stepped.

With a narrower focus, MacCANN and WOODARD's collection operates from the premise that African-American children and minorities in general need special attention to help them grow up with positive self-images. Calling for an increased "black perspective" in children's books, and citing numerous examples of the problems of negative portrayals of ethnicity, this collection of essays explores the African-American perspective and aesthetic, and the problem of choosing positive and enlightening books for children. The majority of its essays (written originally in the 1960s), however, are more intent on consciousness-raising than on exploring the more complicated interrelation of subjectivity and ethnicity. Thus, while the historical overview provided is particularly detailed, the book (revised in 1985) lacks more recent perspectives.

JOHNSON's study takes the next step, celebrating literature for African-American children. Exploring The Brownies' Book, the "legacy" of Langston Hughes and Arna Bontemps, and Lucille Clifton's picture books, Johnson considers the pedagogical implications of the evolution of writing for African-American children. Her study examines the interplay of cultural forces, book production, and perspectives of new generations, insisting throughout that to write effectively for an African-

American child one must know that position intimately. Johnson's examination of the teaching and learning that goes on through these books centers on the question of "the relationship between Black Americans and the 'American Dream'". Ultimately, her study illustrates the power of positive images and models.

LINDGREN's collection similarly moves toward action rather than condemnation of poor role models. Like MacCann and Woodard's collection, it provides a history of the African-American perspective and children's literature. Furthermore, its essays address a *variety* of American cultural positions by contrasting their historical representations and their realities. Rather than analyzing children's books, the primary aim of this collection is pedagogical. Its essays cover texts and politics in detail, in the interest of improving the use of children's books. Personal testimony and teaching suggestions are combined with lists of recommended books which offer enlightened portrayals of the diversity of American culture.

ANDREA J. KASTON

Chopin, Kate 1851–1904

American novelist and short-story writer

Ammons, Elizabeth, *Conflicting Stories: American Women Writers at the Turn into the Twentieth Century*, New York and Oxford: Oxford University Press, 1991, revised 1993

Boren, Lynda S., and Sara de Saussure Davis (eds.), *Kate Chopin Reconsidered: Beyond the Bayou*, Baton Rouge: Louisiana State University Press, 1992

Culley, Margo (ed.), *The Awakening: An Authoritative Text, Biographical and Historical Contexts, and Criticism*, New York: Norton, 1994

Elfenbein, Anne Shannon, *Women on the Color Line: Evolving Sterotypes and the Writings of George Washington Cable, Grace King, Kate Chopin*, Charlottesville: University Press of Virginia, 1989

Ewell, Barbara C., *Kate Chopin*, New York: Frederick Ungar, 1986

Gilbert, Sandra M., and Susan Gubar, *No Man's Land: The Place of the Woman Writer in the Twentieth Century, Volume II: Sexchanges*, New Haven, Connecticut, and London: Yale University Press, 1989

Koloski, Bernard (ed.), *Approaches to Teaching Chopin's "The Awakening"*, New York: Modern Language Association of America, 1988

Martin, Wendy (ed.), *New Essays on "The Awakening"*, Cambridge and New York: Cambridge University Press, 1987

Skaggs, Penny, *Kate Chopin*, Boston: Twayne, 1985

Toth, Emily, *Kate Chopin*, New York: William Morrow, 1990; London: Century, 1991

Walker, Nancy A. (ed.), *The Awakening: Complete, Authoritative Text, with Biographical and Historical Contexts, Critical History, and Essays from Five Contemporary Criticial Perspectives*, Boston: Bedford Books, 1993; London: Macmillan, 1993

Kate Chopin's stories of the Creole and Cajun communities of late nineteenth-century Louisiana won a reputation for her skill in the idiom of "local-color" writing. Nourished by the influence of the French realists such as Émile Zola and Guy de Maupassant, Chopin's first two collections of stories, *Bayou Folk* (1894) and *A Night in Acadie* (1897), show an extraordinary intimacy with the modes of life and sensibilities of the Creole and Cajun peoples, mediated through an impersonal narrative in which the characters of her stories speak for themselves, while the landscapes, houses, and social customs of this world are realised through Chopin's intense feel for location and manners. In 1899 she published her second novel, *The Awakening*, a stunning account of a young wife and mother's sexual and psychological self-discovery. In this book Chopin was far ahead of the taste of her time, and the novel was widely condemned as vulgar in treatment and sordid in theme because of its treatment of extra-marital sexual relations. *The Awakening* is now established as one of the classics of American fiction, and is a remarkable achievement by any standards. Editions of it now proliferate and Chopin is to be found centre-stage in most discussions of late nineteenth-century fiction, especially in writings by feminist scholars. However, much of the best commentary on her is in essays, and though she is well served by her biographers, and her texts are now scrupulously edited, there are not many book-length studies devoted to her.

EWELL's book in an American "Literature and Life" series is valuable for her account of the whole of Chopin's work, and especially for what she writes about the first novel, *At Fault*, which is often disregarded in the light of Chopin's achievement in *The Awakening*; Ewell's attention to this earlier work will certainly encourage readers to approach it. This is an excellent introductory study to Chopin's *oeuvre*, which opens with a biographical sketch, critical synopses of the novels and stories, and commentary on Chopin's poetry. In addition, Ewell gives us other aspects of the writer through her letters, journals, diaries, public talks, and essays.

SKAGGS, in another general introduction to Chopin, disputes the critical consensus that treats Chopin's work from realist and feminist perspectives, and wants to see her achievement in universalised terms: she writes of the way Chopin transcends the literary and social history she emerges from, yet at the same time the drive of Skaggs' criticism necessarily attends to the ways in which Chopin persistently pictures the world from "a woman's point of view". In a further contradiction, Skaggs writes well on Chopin's regionalism, which necessarily re-centres her work within the frame of the literary and social history of the Cajun communities in the last quarter of the nineteenth century. Thus, Skaggs writes intelligently of *The Awakening*, yet persists in dislocating the novel from its regional and historical context. Therefore this is a study of mixed quality, but worth reading for the good things in it.

ELFENBEIN writes of Chopin and two of her contemporary "local colorists", George Washington Cable and Grace King, specifically in relation to the figure of the female "octoroon", whose history is said to embody the oppression inherent in the private and social lives of a great many American women in the nineteenth and twentieth centuries. She provides a detailed history of the literary representations of this figure, from Richard Hildreth's anti-slavery novel *The*

Slave (1836) through to the end of the century. On Chopin she considers *The Awakening* and four of the most famous stories, "Désiree's Baby", "La Belle Zoraide", "At the 'Cajun Ball'", and "The Storm". Elfenbein's book is valuable for historicising the women who feature in Chopin's work, and for the subtlety of some of her interpretations, especially of "Désiree's Baby".

TOTH's is the third biography of Chopin, and the most extensive in its coverage and authority. She provides important new information about Chopin's life, and challenges several popular myths, which have gathered around her. In particular Toth shows that while Chopin was deeply distressed by contemporary responses to *The Awakening*, she did not abandon her work then, but continued to write through to the end of her life. Nor was the novel banned or withdrawn from St Louis libraries, nor was Chopin's social life markedly disrupted by the furore over the novel. Toth's primary concerns are biographical rather than critical, but she provides much useful bibliographical information about the short stories and the magazines to which they were sent, making this work a valuable research source for students of Chopin.

GILBERT and GUBAR open this book with a section on "Feminism and Fantasy", where they discuss the image and role of the "femme fatale" and that of the "new woman" of earlier twentieth-century writing and social history, one opposed to the cultural icon of the woman as temptress in her appropriation of a self-conscious sexuality, socially expressed, which is conceived as her's by right, and not by the culturally imposed performance of an idea of the sexually available woman. In the later passages of this section they write persuasively of Chopin and her revolutionary demand for an equal representation of women's desire in literature.

AMMONS' work on Chopin is highly regarded and often reprinted from this study of women writers from 1890 to the late 1920s, where she considers the work of 17 writers in some detail. In her treatment of Chopin, Ammons writes of "women of color" in *The Awakening*, those "nameless, faceless black women" whose labour in one context or another, either as domestic menials or as prostitutes, makes Edna Pontellier's "liberation" possible by freeing her to pursue her self-centred concerns. Ammons' point is that Chopin cannot entirely control the social or sexual politics of this situation, and that in a novel about "liberation", Edna's freedoms are "purchased on the backs of black women", a social, political and cultural situation which the novel barely addresses, given its dominant preoccupation with Edna's destiny.

BOREN introduces this collection of essays with a good account of Chopin's regionalism, and provides a helpful survey of the present state of Chopin studies. The first section of the book covers biographical issues, and includes an essay by Emily Toth, while Jean Bardot gives a history of Oscar Chopin's French-American family in its Louisiana parish of Natchitoches. Thereafter this collection is mostly taken up with essays on *The Awakening* from a variety of feminist perspectives, attending to issues of sex, female selfhood, the female body, and so on. In addition, Katherine Joslin provides a comparative study of the representation of the domestic life in *The Awakening* with that in Willa Cather's *The Professor's House*; and in the last section some attention is given to the role of music in Chopin's work.

The remaining books to be considered here – Culley, Koloski, Martin, and Walker – all focus on *The Awakening* exclusively.

CULLEY's Norton critical edition of the novel will give most readers all they want of commentary on it, for it not only provides an authoritative text but, in common with the rest of this series, gives a great deal of biographical and historical contextual information about the writer, her writing career, the making of the novel, and its reception. The history of the novel's reputation is covered by a tranche of contemporary reviews reprinted from journals and newspapers of 1899, and a splendid collection of modern critical commentary from 1909 to 1989. This latter section includes seminal essays by Larzer Ziff, Per Seyersted, Cynthia Griffin Wolff, Nancy Walker, Sandra M. Gilbert, Elizabeth Ammons, Elaine Showalter, and others, providing a showcase of intelligent commentary across the whole spectrum of literary-critical practices, especially over the past 30 years.

KOLOSKI's teaching guide to *The Awakening* provides a whole battery of useful documents about the novel, including lists of background studies, critical studies, editions, and further aids to teaching it. However, the major part of this compilation consists of excerpts from a wide range of critical essays, which deal with the novel through the perspective of "women's experience", the historical and regional context of its setting, its place in the larger narrative of late nineteenth-century American literature, and from various formalist readings in relation to matters of style, character, setting, symbolism, and myth. This is an excellent and instructive collection of materials, of great help to the general reader as well as to the teachers and students to whom it is addressed.

MARTIN's collection has four extensive essays, which all promise radical readings of the novel, promises not always fulfilled. Elaine Showalter sees it within a transitional phase of women's writing in the later part of the nineteenth century, though she also holds that Edna Pontellier's death at the end of the novel belongs to traditional narrative endings of self-destruction, because Chopin could find no alternative tradition of endings that might have better served her ethical concerns. (On the contrary, most readers will find Edna's death, and the manner of it, inevitable and impressively realised.) Michael T. Gilmore sees the novel as (ur-)modernist in its analysis of Southern culture, and a foreshadowing of postmodernist preoccupations in its commitment to the processes of "female awakening". If Gilmore's placing of the novel just within the frame of modernism is tenable, the argument about its postmodern foreshadowings is less convincing, though ambitious. Andrew Delbanco provides a thorough-going analysis of the novel's scrutiny of male and female identity, and, clearly, these concerns are central to a substantial part of it. Christina Giorcelli looks at Edna as a figure of "liminal consciousness", one who exists on the borders between conditions – the wife who is not a wife, the mother who abandons motherhood, the lover who is not a lover, and who fatally crosses the borderline between land and sea as she goes to her death.

WALKER's edition of *The Awakening* is accompanied by five essays from particular critical perspectives, and is directed at a student market. It shows how this novel lends itself to a multiplicity of interpretations. It includes Elaine Showalter's essay (also in Martin) expressive of "A Feminist Perspective" on the novel, to go with the New-Historicist, psychoanalytic, deconstructionist, and reader-response pieces by the other contributors, thus meeting the format prescriptions of the series in which this book appears. The New-Historicist approach is by Margit Stange, who writes on concepts of personal property in the novel in relation to ideas of "Exchange Value and the Female Self"; Cynthia Griffin Wolff's psychoanalytic essay, "Thanatos and Eros", which originally appeared in 1973, has had a powerful influence on studies of the novel, and is widely disseminated in a variety of contexts; a deconstructive approach is given in Patricia S. Yaeger's 1987 essay on the language of the novel in relation to its handling of concepts of emancipation; and Paula S. Treichler's reader-response essay, first published in 1980, addresses the problem of language in the novel in relation to Edna Pontellier's "struggle to define herself as an active subject, and to cease to be merely the passive object of forces beyond her control". These are all impressive responses to the novel, very much worth reading, though whether they need these contemporary theoretical alignments in defence of their approaches is open to debate.

LIONEL KELLY

Chronicle Literature

Albano, Robert A., *Middle English Historiography*, New York: Peter Lang, 1993

Clanchy, Michael, *From Memory to Written Record: England 1066–1307*, Cambridge, Massachusetts: Harvard University Press, 1979; London: Edward Arnold, 1979; revised edition, Oxford and Cambridge, Massachusetts: Blackwell, 1993

Edwards, A.S.G., "John Trevisa", in *Middle English Prose: A Critical Guide to Major Authors and Genres*, edited by Edwards, New Brunswick, New Jersey: Rutgers University Press, 1984

Hanning, R.W., *The Vision of History in Early Britain: From Gildas to Geoffrey of Monmouth*, New York: Columbia University Press, 1966

Johnson, Lesley, "Robert Mannyng's History of Arthurian Literature", in *Church and Chronicle in the Middle Ages: Essays Presented to John Taylor*, edited by Ian Wood and G.A. Loud, London and Rio Grande, Ohio: Hambledon Press, 1991

Kennedy, E.D., *Chronicles and Other Historical Writing* (Volume 8, *A Manual of Writings in Middle English, 1050–1500*, general editor: A.E. Hartung), New York: Modern Language Association of America, 1989

Le Saux, Françoise, *Laȝamon's "Brut": The Poem and Its Sources*, Cambridge: D.S. Brewer, 1989

Matheson, Lister, "Historical Prose", in *Middle English Prose: A Critical Guide to Major Authors and Genres*, edited by A.S.G. Edwards, New Brunswick, New Jersey: Rutgers University Press, 1984

Taylor, John, *English Historical Literature in the Fourteenth Century*, Oxford: Clarendon Press, 1987; New York: Oxford University Press, 1987

The excellent surveys of chronicle literature by Matheson and Kennedy are essential preliminaries for study. Unlike the *Anglo-Saxon Chronicle*, the literary qualities of the fourteenth-century English chronicles have only fairly recently been examined. Current research is particularly concerned with the English translations of the French prose *Brut* (c.1400) and of John Trevisa's Latin *Polychronicon*, especially with the bias exhibited by the writers through the demands of patrons or political affiliation. John Taylor has produced the most extensive and authoritative work on medieval Latin and vernacular (i.e., French and English) chronicles to date, while Michael Clanchy analyses the impulse to record the history that lies behind the actual texts.

CLANCHY's book signalled a new departure in medieval studies when the first edition appeared in 1979, alerting modern readers to the changes in social identity with the steady shift from collective memory to written documentation. He shows that the spread of literacy owed more to the dissemination of Christianity (with its basis in a written text) than to a humanist emphasis on Latin and Greek. Of interest to students of history at undergraduate level, and essential students of literature at postgraduate level and above, Clanchy's survey outlines many types of record, including charters, certificates, chronicles, and year books, and appraises the technology and the languages of record, and the use of documents. Part II is most relevant to students of literature, and explains the function of charters (even forged ones) and chronicles for identifying the historical rights of monastic and larger communities to their current possessions and as evidence for posterity of local and national events. The revised edition has substantial additions to the introductions to both parts, and to eight chapters and the bibliography. It takes account of much that has been written under the inspiration of Clanchy's 1979 edition (e.g., W.J. Ong's *Orality and Literacy: The Technologizing of the Word*, 1982). This book is essential for understanding the nature and function of literacy in the Middle Ages, and how medieval society related to its past.

The Latin historical texts discussed by HANNING form an indispensable prelude to the Middle English chronicles, and Hanning's study of attitudes to history in the early Middle Ages is a seminal work. By examining the two main Christian approaches to history from the New Testament on, Hanning shows that Eusebius's (born c.263) literal interpretation of events as manifestation of God's providence in history prevailed over Augustine's allegorical reading. The historical accounts of Gildas, Bede, and Nennius' *Historia Brittonum* are considered in relation to contemporary theory: each demonstrates increasingly the influence the individual can have on national affairs. The culminating work in the "fall of Britain" tradition is Geoffrey of Monmouth's, which rejects divine providence and exploits the belief, developing since the twelfth century, in secular, political history; but Geoffrey represents the divide between history as fact and history as romance.

The first Middle English chronicle poem is Laȝamon's *Brut*, a rendering of Wace's French translation of Geoffrey of Monmouth's *Historia Regum Britanniae*, a twelfth-century pseudo-history of Britain. Laȝamon (also called "Layamon" and "Lawman") added detail from other Latin and French and possibly Welsh sources, as LE SAUX demonstrates in a sympathetic and lively study of the poem's sources, structure and diction, and its political affiliation. Le Saux regards Laȝamon as a priest concerned with the moral message of his material and with the agents (messengers, the knights of the Round Table) who contribute to the fame of the great men of the (legendary) past.

MATHESON and KENNEDY both survey the Middle English chronicles, their sources, and the use subsequently made of them within and beyond the medieval period. Kennedy discusses the content, manuscript attestation, and authorship, where known, of both prose- and verse-chronicles. He supplies a summary of the plots of the literary "chronicles", especially those in verse, and briefly outlines their literary quality and the tenor of their content. A complete bibliography is supplied, which includes even brief mentions of the texts or their manuscripts. Significant among the *Brut* chronicles treated are Laȝamon's, Robert of Gloucester's, Robert Mannyng's *The Story of England*, the prose *Brut*, and the Chronicle of John Hardyng; most important of the universal chronicles are Trevisa's translation of Ranulf Higden's *Polychronicon*, the Chronicle of Nicholas Trevet (which was used by Chaucer and Gower for the story of Constance), and John Capgrave's *Abbreviacion of Chronicles*; those covering Scottish history are John Barbour's *Bruce*, Andrew of Wyntoun's *Orygynale Cronykil of Scotland* and Blind Harry's *The Wallace*. Matheson's survey of prose chronicles critiques literary, historical, and textual studies of the chronicles, with a comprehensive bibliography, as does EDWARDS' study of work on Trevisa, which is not confined to the *Polychronicon*; both take stands in assessing critics' opinions, and helpfully suggest texts and topics where work remains to be done, notably in establishing the quality of Trevisa's translation, and study of the manuscripts and language of the prose *Brut*.

ALBANO begins his study of four fourteenth-century chronicles with a discussion of modern theories of historiography. The focus is on early fourteenth-century Scotland. This study is often difficult to follow, is sometimes inaccurate in expression (e.g. the apparent assertion that the entire *Anglo-Saxon Chronicle* was composed in the ninth century), and has not been sufficiently adapted from its original dissertation form. However, it is important as a study of the influence of culture on the content and style of medieval chronicles. The prose *Brut*, Trevisa's *Polychronicon*, Barbour's *Bruce*, and Wyntoun's *Orygynale Cronykil of Scotland* are each accorded a full chapter and examined in detail. A final chapter deals with the political poems of Laurence Minot. These texts are usefully examined against a modern reconstruction from other records of the events depicted in these accounts. The chroniclers' choice of emphasis, and suppression of details and even whole incidents to serve their purposes of eulogy or detraction, are well demonstrated.

JOHNSON's study is an important consideration of a hitherto neglected text, which is beginning to receive its due critical acclaim. This is an authoritative literary survey of part of Robert Mannyng of Brunne's *Chronicle of England*. Mannyng, basing his text on Wace and Langtoft, considered the different types of source for British historiography and the significance of French chivalric treatments of Arthur; his comparison of literary traditions in the early fourteenth century forms an important cultural and linguistic testimony of the period.

TAYLOR's work is more historical in basis, but his chapters on universal history (Chapter 5), on the development and translation of the French prose *Brut* (Chapter 6) and the *Anonimalle Chronicle* are important for literary students as evidence of a growing command of vernacular prose. Chapter 8 outlines "Chivalrous Histories", especially those of Jean Froissart and Jean le Bel, and shows how Froissart steadily outgrew his use of material from Le Bel as his greater narrative skill steadily surpassed his partial source. The Chandos Herald and Sir Thomas Gray also present a chivalric interpretation of history, of limited value historically but important as a supplement to fourteenth- and fifteenth-century literary narratives. The chapter on "Letters" (Chapter 11) is primarily taxonomic, but that on "Political Poems and Ballads" (Chapter 12) has a literary basis, and provides an important discussion on the literature of social complaint in French and Latin, while concluding that it is the English texts that express more fully the native genius for satire and point significantly to the future.

ROSAMUND S. ALLEN

Churchill, Caryl 1938–

English dramatist

Case, Sue-Ellen, *Performing Feminisms: Feminist Critical Theory and Theatre*, Baltimore: Johns Hopkins University Press, 1990

Cousin, Geraldine, *Churchill the Playwright*, London and Porstmouth, New Hampshire: Methuen, 1989

FitzSimmons, Linda (ed.), *File on Churchill*, London: Methuen, 1989

Goodman, Lizbeth, *Contemporary Feminist Theatres: To Each Her Own*, London and New York: Routledge, 1993

Griffiths, Trevor R., and Margaret Llewellyn-Jones, *British and Irish Women Dramatists since 1958: A Critical Handbook*, Milton Keynes, Buckingham: Open University Press, 1993

Keyssar, Helen, *Feminist Theatre: An Introduction to Plays of Contemporary British and American Women*, London: Macmillan, 1984; New York: St Martin's Press, 1984

Kritzer, Amelia Howe, *The Plays of Caryl Churchill: Theatre of Empowerment*, London: Macmillan, 1991; New York: St Martin's Press, 1991

Llewellyn-Jones, Margaret L., "Spectacle, Silence, and Subversion: Women's Performance Language and Strategies", in *Contemporary Theatre Review* (Switzerland: Harwood Academic), 2(1), 1994

Randall, Phyllis R., *Caryl Churchill: A Casebook*, New York: Garland, 1988

Thomsen, Christian, "Three Socialist Playwrights", In *Contemporary British Drama* (Stratford-upon-Avon Studies series), edited by Malcolm Bradbury and David Palmer, London: Edward Arnold, 1981

Wandor, Michelene, *Carry on Understudies: Theatre and Sexual Politics*, London and New York: Routledge and Kegan Paul, 1981; revised edition, as *Understudies*, 1986

Although Caryl Churchill, who has been writing plays since her student days at Oxford in the late 1950s, could be considered one of the best, if not the most innovative, of contemporary British dramatists, it was not until 1988–89 that the first critical books devoted entirely to her work were published. As the bibliographies in these indicate, there was, from the beginning, a steady output of academic and professional interest in her, varying from articles within theatre journals in England, Europe, and America, to conference papers, interviews, and sections within general books on British contemporary drama. Churchill, when questioned about whether she sees herself as a "woman writer", has responded:

> Sometimes. Originally, not. During the 1970s there was a context for thinking of myself as a woman writer. . . . If . . . a critic thinks of you as one of the best women writers, and you feel there's any possibility that he thinks of that as a *lesser* category, you resent the use of it as a term. If it means that women themselves thinking about things they haven't thought about before, then you can actually feel very positive about the idea of being a woman writer.
>
> (FitzSimmons, 1989)

Despite this ambivalence, Churchill's position as a successful woman writer has encouraged readings that place aspects of her plays within a feminist, as well as a socialist, context. Some provide a relatively straightforward appraisal of content and performance elements, others examine her work from a more complex theoretical perspective, drawn from psychoanalysis and French feminism.

Earlier articles, such as THOMSEN's, which links Churchill with the methodology and concerns of playwrights John McGrath of the 7:84 theatre company and Trevor Griffiths, emphasise the post-Brechtian aspects of her approach. The historical plays are valorised for their commitment to cultural criticism and their absence of a party line, and Thomsen predicts that Churchill, an "intellectual farceur", will continue in a more experimental vein. WANDOR weighs up the extent to which Churchill's mix of styles and forms relates dynamically to bourgeois, socialist, or radical feminism, in the contemporary context of the two developmental waves of women's theatre.

FITZSIMMONS's compilation follows the house style format of this series – a brief chronology; play summaries and production details with a range of contemporary reviews, interviews, and comments; quotations from the writer on her work; and a bibliography. Simon Trussler's Introduction indicates some points of potential controversy, especially the debate around the relationship of gender to particular dramatic forms, and the effect of a special creative process such as the Joint Stock method. These remarks frame a particularly judicious selection of material, usually placed without sub-headings or further editorial comment, within the sections indicated above. This method forces the student or general reader to form their own conclusions, for instance about contradictory reviews or judgements on a specific play – and hence, like Churchill's plays, enables more open-ended responses. The book includes illuminating material, such as the reviews and letters about the unsuccessful German production of *Top Girls*, and alterations to *Cloud Nine* for the American market, and the possible relationship of her work to socialist, rather than bourgeois, feminism. Thus, the material speaks for itself about the plays' reception, revealing, for example, the significance of gender difference in appreciation of Churchill's stylistic fragmentation. Although the play summaries are sometimes over-compact, especially for less well-known work, they at least alert the reader to the basic content. This is a very useful sourcebook, which prompts further inquiry.

COUSIN's book gives a comprehensive account of Churchill's plays up to 1988. Despite the useful chronological table, her critical approach, as she herself acknowledges, is circuitous, giving the impression of a web of interrelated themes and linked formal concerns, such as the fluid nature of time. This kind of grouping is most useful where work with similar methods but different concepts can be drawn together, for example, in the plays created with the Joint Stock theatre company. Where the creative process is described in most detail, and where she draws upon Churchill's notebooks, Cousin's exposition is the most perceptive. Inevitably there is an unevenness of approach when text rather than performance is the basis for commentary; but in responses to major plays such as *Light Shining in Buckinghamshire*, *Fen*, *Top Girls*, and *Cloud Nine* Cousin conveys the innovative quality of Churchill's dramaturgy. A careful account of lesser-known work, particularly the radio and television plays, provides evidence of the way Churchill returns to explore key issues. The conclusion lists these major themes, such as the organic relationship of the past and present, the need for change, the relationship between the inner and the public self, issues of gender and violence, then recalls predominant dramatic strategies, such as the fragmenting of linear narrative and the use of overlapping dialogue. However, Cousin's relatively descriptive approach does not really engage with theoretical issues associated with the kinds of structural and theatrical devices used by Churchill, which some feminists would wish to discuss as potentially indicative of a theatrical "*écriture feminine*". More could also be made of the varied audience responses to the ideological challenge implicit in some plays – particularly the potentially recuperative reading of *Serious Money*. Unavoidably, the publication date precludes discussion of the more recent work, such as *Lives of the Great Poisoners* (1991) and *The Skriker* (1994), both collaborations with the choreographer Ian Spink and others, which would further extend Cousin's point about the growing significance of the visual in Churchill's work (a topic also considered in my [LLEWELLYN-JONES's] 1994 article, in relation to Churchill's *Mouthful of Birds*). This book does, though, provide an accessible introductory survey with significant insights woven into the more detailed sections.

RANDALL's Introduction to her collection of essays, grouped according to play chronology, emphasises content rather than theoretical perspectives, though her bibliography's useful summaries of critical studies does engage more fully with feminist theory. Among the range of essays, Selmon's semiotically grounded analysis of Churchill's politically motivated exploration of signifying practices and Keyssar's comparison of *Mouthful of Birds* and *Serious Money* in terms of transformative practice and ideological effect are the most productive. KRITZER's book draws ideological themes and aesthetic experiment together more effectively. From the conceptualised methodology of her Introduction – which indicates the potential relationship between the grammar of theatrical production and the psychoanalytic readings of the construction of the self within patriarchy and capitalism – she proceeds to a detailed analysis of the plays, which are grouped according to issues related to power rather than to creative method. Within this well-informed analysis of the transforming, and potentially empowering, effect of Churchill's "theatre of process", the theoretical strands are integrated rather than heavily imposed, although more consideration of performance would have been welcome.

Survey works such as GOODMAN, KEYSSAR, and GRIFFITHS & LLEWELLYN-JONES set a contemporary context for Churchill's plays, providing points of comparison in terms of content, style, form and creative process with work by other women, as well as introductory indications of potential reading positions. CASE's theoretical collection contains two key appraisals of Churchill: Diamond, using French feminism, compares her deconstruction of identity with the theatre of Marguerite Duras and Simone Benmussa, while Herrmann contrasts her use of transvestism with that of Shakespeare and Bertolt Brecht – especially the tension between signification of clothes and body.

MARGARET L. LLEWELLYN-JONES

Clare, John 1793–1864

English poet

Barrell, John, *The Idea of Landscape and the Sense of Place, 1730–1840: An Approach to the Poetry of John Clare*, London: Cambridge University Press, 1972

Chilcott, Tim, *"A Real World & Doubting Mind": A Critical Study of the Poetry of John Clare*, Hull, Humberside: Hull University Press, 1985

Clare, Johanne, *John Clare and the Bounds of Circumstance*, Montreal and Kingston, Ontario: McGill-Queen's University Press, 1987

Deacon, George, *John Clare and the Folk Tradition*, London: Sinclair Browne, 1983

Haughton, Hugh, Adam Phillips, and Geoffrey Summerfield (eds.), *John Clare in Context*, Cambridge and New York: Cambridge University Press, 1994

Mabey, Richard, Jonathan Bate, John Coletta, *et al.*, "Clare and Ecology" issue of *John Clare Society Journal*, 14, 1995

Pearce, Lynn, "John Clare's 'Child Harold': A Polyphonic Reading", in *Criticism*, 31(2), Spring 1989

Strang, Barbara M.H., "John Clare's Language", in *The Rural Muse* by Clare, edited by R.K.R. Thornton, 2nd edition, Ashington, Northumberland, and Manchester: Mid-Northumberland Arts Group/Carcanet New Press, 1982

The contemporary revival in Clare's fortunes has its origins in the project to transcribe and edit his voluminous manuscripts faithfully and comprehensively, initiated by Geoffrey Summerfield and others. The new texts began to appear in 1964, and their critical first-fruit was BARRELL's study (for earlier criticism see Mark Storey's useful *John Clare: The Critical Heritage*, 1973). Barrell begins with eighteenth-century ways of seeing the landscape, governed by "improvement" mentality, which he examines with great thoroughness, setting the context for a reading of Clare that considers the poet's struggles, both with the poetics of improvement, and to develop his own ways of describing the unenclosed landscape and the changes wrought by enclosure. Ultimately Clare was true to the integrity and "localism" of his vision, but at the cost of "writing himself out of the mainstream of European literature". Barrell's study remains a model of historical literary scholarship and serious criticism of Clare, though its conclusions have sometimes been challenged.

STRANG's influential essay is a ground-clearing exercise in the vital area of language. Seeking to break the logjam of often unsupported arguments over Clare's alleged "provincialisms", literary borrowings, etc., Strang argues for recognition that Clare's linguistic register is both eclectic and unique. Her statistical and "cluster"-based analysis of the language of *The Rural Muse* and *The Midsummer Cushion* reveals many facets to this uniqueness, including "archaic" qualities, and a tendency for the poet to use clusters of linked words. DEACON's book, also seminal, considers Clare's extensive work in recording folk-songs, tunes, and customary activities, and is an essential reference book in these areas. Its critical significance lies in its mapping of the sheer range of folk influences on Clare.

CHILCOTT brings a boldly formalistic perspective to an author whose critics have usually been strongly historicist in approach. The tensions between "the real world" and Clare's "doubting mind" give a guiding theme to a well-ordered chronological (and refreshingly omnivorous) reading of the poetry, one which both reads Clare on his own terms and alertly contextualises him in relation to his Romantic contemporaries and the general sweep of literary movements and ideas. Johanne CLARE's study, by contrast, follows more familiar social-historical themes, though to equally useful effect. Clare may be trapped by the "bounds of circumstance" (both in his own time and by later critics), but such "bounds" also produced his art, with its characteristic movement towards unboundedness. The study of Clare's "sociological formation" as a poet can thus be productive, as indeed it is here, yielding a rich and unreductive reading of his art. Although it excludes the asylum poetry, this study is also helpful in mapping several intellectually coherent areas in Clare's poetry beyond the usual "nature poetry" tag; and Johanne Clare's term "enclosure elegies" has now been more widely adopted in discussions of the poet.

Recent theoretically alert approaches are well exemplified by PEARCE's essay, which draws on Bakhtinian ideas to make a rich "polyphonic" reading of a text that earlier biographical approaches had failed to comprehend adequately. The same critic has outlined a feminist critique of Clare (in *Feminist Criticism*, edited by Susan Sellers, 1991 – also taken up by Helen Boden in *The Independent Spirit*). Among other recent theory-oriented readings, Juliet Sychrava recruits Clare for her exploration of idealism in aesthetics, in *Schiller to Derrida* (1989), and Jean Paira-Pemberton draws on Jacques Lacan and others (*Recherches Anglaises et Nord-Americaines*, 27, 1994).

Introducing their collection, HAUGHTON and PHILLIPS lament the poet's continued exclusion from the mainstream of critical debate, and argue for a greater diversity in textual approaches to Clare, so that more accessible versions of his texts may compete with the orthographic starkness of recent editions. Theirs has been the best-received of three essay collections published to mark Clare's bicentenary (the others are *John Clare: A Bicentenary Celebration*, edited by Richard Foulkes, Northampton, 1994, and *The Independent Spirit*, edited by me [Goodridge], Helpston, Cambridgeshire, 1994), and reviewers have noted the range of contexts offered and the high quality of many essays. Seamus Heaney, for example, places Clare alongside some of the modern and postcolonial poets, rather than in the more familiar Romantic contexts, reading Clare's poetry as the trumpet of a multicultural prophecy, the "dream of a world culture".

Heaney's eloquent essay reminds us that Clare has been well served by his fellow poets. It also exemplifies the general tendency, among these essays and in other recent work, to see Clare as a transgressive, even a radical figure, a poet whose exclusion from mainstream contexts may be an injustice but is also a possible source of strength. In the role of outsider, transgressor, trespasser, Clare is seen to offer a powerful critique of society. His recent adoption as a significantly "green" poet, notably by MABEY *et al.*, exemplifies this trend well, and gives a new energy to the more familiar idea of Clare as (in Tom Paulin's words) "quite simply the greatest English nature poet".

JOHN GOODRIDGE

Coetzee, J.M. 1940–

South African novelist

Attridge, Derek, "Oppressive Silence: J.M.Coetzee's *Foe* and the Politics of the Canon," in *Decolonizing Tradition: New Views of Twentieth-Century "British" Literary Canons*, edited by Karen Lawrence, Urbana: University of Illinois Press, 1992

Attwell, David (ed.), *Doubling the Point: Essays and Interviews*, by Coetzee, Cambridge, Massachusetts: Harvard University Press, 1992

Attwell, David, *J.M. Coetzee: South Africa and the Politics of Writing*, Berkeley: University of California Press, 1993; Cape Town: David Philip, 1993

Dovey, Teresa, *The Novels of J.M. Coetzee: Lacanian Allegories*, Craighall, South Africa: Ad Donker, 1988

Gallagher, Susan Van Zanten, *A Story of South Africa: J.M. Coetzee's Fiction in Context*, Cambridge, Massachusetts: Harvard University Press, 1991

Moses, Michael Valdez (ed.), "The Writings of J.M. Coetzee" issue of *The South Atlantic Quarterly*, 93(1), 1994

Penner, Dick , *Countries of the Mind: The Fiction of J.M. Coetzee*, Westport, Connecticut: Greenwood Press, 1989

Waiting for the Barbarians issue of *Commonwealth*, SP3, 1992

Writing in 1988, J.M. Coetzee inveighed against the tendency in South Africa to subsume fiction under history, to read novels as imaginative investigations of real historical circumstances, and to treat those that do not perform such investigations as lacking in seriousness. While some critics have agreed with him, others have defined Coetzee's apparent distance from his immediate socio-political situation as a weakness.

As his title suggests, PENNER is very much an ethical universalist, advancing the case that Coetzee's fictions maintain their significance apart from a South African context, because of their artistry and because they transform urgent social questions into more universal topics (the nature of colonialism, the relations of master to slave, or between cultures and individuals). For him, there is a distinction between Coetzee as ethical individual and Coetzee as teller of tales. The study is none the less accessible, carefully researched, and a good starting point for the student and general reader. The same cannot be said of DOVEY's Lacanian psychoanalytical reading, which is specialised to the point of monocausality. Dovey argues that each of the novels constitutes a psychoanalytic allegory of the act of narration, while deconstructing the subgenres of the white South African novelistic tradition. Although a detailed and careful piece of work, the volume rather preaches to the Lacanian converted, admittedly a sizeable congregation today. Unbelievers may have reservations, not least because it is never clear whether it is the novelist or his critic who is the Lacanian.

Historicist critics enter the field with GALLAGHER, who investigates the South African literary and historical contexts (two chapters on Afrikaner society's myths and modes of discourse), and follows with individual chapters on the models and background to each novel (e.g., *Waiting for the Barbarians* in relation to torture, deaths in custody, and the ineffectuality of magistrates). Although the recognition of the novel as a worldly event, a part of history, is compelling, there are points where Gallagher forces her thesis, overstretching the connections between fiction and history.

Gallagher's account was described by the reviewer for *Modern Fiction Studies* as likely to become "the standard contextual study of Coetzee's writing for some years to come". Two years later ATTWELL (1993) disputed that claim with a very fine study indeed, and one which consistently opens up the novels to fresh debate. Despite his postmodernist qualities, Attwell discerns an intensely ethical writer in Coetzee, in a volume that charts the evolution of the fiction from the subject's entrapment in forms of subjectivity imposed by history to preoccupation with the limitlessness of textuality.

Attwell places *Waiting for the Barbarians* at the midpoint of this development, and highlights its return to a modified form of realism. Eight specially commissioned articles are devoted to the novel in a special issue of *Commonwealth*, which also includes a useful bibliography. Essays engage with such topics as dreams, intertextuality, allegory, time, and the body. The essays are also interesting as evidence of the European reception of Coetzee: contributors are from France, Spain, and Britain. A second special issue of *The South Atlantic Quarterly*, guest-edited by MOSES, brings together an excerpt from *The Master of Petersburg*, plus eight essays from American and South African critics. Contributions are highly theorised and concern themselves with Coetzee's reception, influences (Samuel Beckett, Jean-Jacques Rousseau, the pastoral), and politics. Derek Attridge's close textual analysis of *Age of Iron* deserves to be singled out for the intelligent clarity of its sophisticated literary and ethical analysis.

ATTRIDGE also provides one of the best essays on Coetzee in general, and on *Foe* in particular, arguing that the intertextuality of the novels – a crucial critical focus – is not an implicit claim to a place in a metropolitan canon, but a means of drawing attention to the way in which any text is manufactured from within the resources of a particular culture, any representation is mediated through the discourses that that culture provides.

Finally, ATTWELL's 1992 collection is invaluable in the wealth of material provided, both in Coetzee's own essays, and in the interviews (with Attwell), which precede them and lead into their central concerns. Unusually and subtly organised, the volume comes close to constituting an intellectual autobiography of its subject.

JUDIE NEWMAN

Coleridge, Samuel Taylor 1772–1834

English poet, critic, and writer of philosophical prose

Barfield, Owen, *What Coleridge Thought*, Oxford: Oxford University Press 1977; Middletown, Connecticut: Wesleyan University Press, 1978

Beer, John, *Coleridge's Poetic Intelligence*, London: Macmillan, 1977

Fulford, Tim, *Coleridge's Figurative Language*, London: Macmillan 1991

Goodson, A.C., *Verbal Imagination: Coleridge and the Language of Modern Criticism*, New York: Oxford University Press, 1988

Hamilton, Paul, *Coleridge's Poetics*, Oxford: Blackwell, 1983

Holmes, Richard, *Coleridge*, Oxford and New York: Oxford University Press, 1982

Holmes, Richard, *Coleridge: Early Visions*, London: Hodder & Stoughton, 1989; New York: Viking Press, 1990

Jasper, David, *Coleridge as Poet and Religious Thinker: Inspiration and Revelation*, London: Macmillan, 1985; Allison Park, Pennsylvania: Pickwick, 1985

Lowes, John Livingston, *The Road to Xanadu: A Study in the Ways of the Imagination*, Boston: Houghton Mifflin, 1927, revised 1930; London: Constable, 1940

Marks, Emerson R., *Coleridge on the Language of Verse*, Princeton, New Jersey: Princeton University Press, 1981

Mileur, Jean-Pierre, *Vision and Revision: Coleridge's Art of Immanence*, Berkeley: University of California Press, 1982

Raine, Kathleen, *Coleridge*, London: Longman, 1954

Richards, I. A., *Coleridge on Imagination*, London: Kegan Paul, 1934; New York: Harcourt Brace, 1935; 2nd edition, New York: Norton, 1950

Watson, Jeanie, *Risking Enchantment: Coleridge's Symbolic World of Faery*, Lincoln: University of Nebraska Press, 1990

Wylie, Ian, *Young Coleridge and the Philosophers of Nature*, Oxford: Clarendon Press, 1989; New York: Oxford University Press, 1989

Students of Coleridge do well to familiarise themselves with his life. The two of HOLMES' books together – a short Oxford "Past Masters" guide to the life and works (1982), and an extended literary biography of Coleridge's early and middle years (1989) – are indispensable: they are highly readable, and ideally complement the more strictly literary critical accounts. (A sequel to *Early Visions* is expected.) Holmes offers a balance between dispassionate assessment and the fascination needed for both writer and reader to maintain interest in the subject. Also recommended is RAINE's short study for the British Council "Writers and Their Work" series.

Already in the 1930s a Coleridge critical establishment existed. RICHARDS began his book by remarking:

> Coleridge has been treated sufficiently often as a human contradiction and as a biographers' puzzle. He has been pitied and patronised, condemned and defended, enough. The literature on his case must now be nearly as voluminous as his own writings. I do not propose to add to it.

Add he does, however. But he also foresees the industrious future of Coleridge studies, limiting his agenda to "extracting from the vast confusing network of Coleridge's speculations and observations those hypotheses which seem most likely to be useful in other hands", and does not claim universal validity for his interpretation: "every theoretical contribution must sooner or later be wronged if it is successful in aiding further development". For Richards, the key quality of Coleridge's work is that it "requires us, if we are to study it seriously, to reconsider our most fundamental conceptions of man's being, the nature of his mind, and its knowledge. It is no defect that he forces us to do so more evidently than other critics".

LOWES produced in 1927 perhaps the all-time classic of Coleridge criticism, a ground-breaking scholarly study and literary detective story. Lowes' governing intention is striking: "this is not a study of Coleridge's theory of the imagination; it is an attempt to get at the workings of the faculty itself". And again: "Coleridge's most precious contribution to our understanding of the imagination lies not in his metaphysical lucubrations on it after it was lost, but in the implications of its practice while he yet possessed the power." The style may be dated, and sometimes rambling, but the multiple lines of the story and its interest remain untarnished. "To follow Coleridge through his reading", which Lowes does, "is to retrace the obliterated vestiges of creation". First and foremost this book is a study of the genesis of Coleridge's imagery, but it is essential reading. "The road to Xanadu, as we have traced it, is the road of the human spirit, and the imagination voyaging through chaos and reducing it to clarity and order is the symbol of all the quests which lend glory to our dust". Despite its bulk, it is an easy book to use, with an excellent index and the voluminous footnotes "securely kenneled in the rear". Among Lowes's many attractions is that he can offer 500 pages on two major poems alone and still have most readers spell-bound.

The spell-bound child is a well-known Coleridgean theme, but rarely more interestingly handled than by WATSON's study of enchantment in Coleridge's poetry. It is rooted in the tradition of the fairy tale and in the analysis of the intermediary world between sense and spirit, which is called faery by such as J.R.R. Tolkien (in his celebrated essay "On Fairy Stories") and others. "Faery is a realm entered through as an act of the symbolic imagination". Watson's is a convincing and persuasive account of Coleridge's psychology as well as of his poems; all the major poems and many of the minor ones receive full attention. The charge of escapism is well met: "like all fairy tales, Coleridge's are concerned in a very fundamental way with the realities of existence. Elves and fairies and witches are merely a way of talking about these realities". The book argues the following five points which the author regards as axiomatic to an understanding of Coleridge's work as a whole:

> . . . i) the burden of Coleridge's poetry, early and late, is an exploration of the possibilities available to the human spirit for intuitive spiritual knowledge and for participation in the Reality of Spirit – possibilities that must inevitably be played out within the limitations imposed by the fallen world; ii) the world is by nature consubstantial with spirit and therefore symbolic; iii) the symbolic character of existence is communicated in Coleridge's poetry through symbolic metaphor/symbolic story; iv) the concept of faery is one of these metaphors, and a fairy tale one of these stories; v) Coleridge uses these – whether they occur as brief moments of spiritual encounter or as entire narratives – as appropriate vehicles for exploring the possibilities of participation in spirit which he sees as the soul's task in the world.

Watson usefully emphasises Coleridge's "childhood response to reading imaginative literature and the certainty behind the early connections he makes between those experiences and the spiritual realities of the universe". Besides this, detailed discussion of androgyny in Coleridge and in fairy tales is offered, along with interesting material, drawing on Bruno Bettelheim, on fairy tale mother/daughter relationships relevant to the poetry.

BARFIELD offers a still-unequalled account of Coleridge's elusive philosophy, attempting to give it a structure where Coleridge despaired of one himself. Barfield's claim, both modest and bold, to function as Coleridge's midwife is arguably met. Here is probably the definitive account of the subtleties of the famous distinction between imagination and fancy. JASPER, while not Barfield's equal in discussing the imagination, does a similar job in "bridging the schism" of those who read Coleridge as a religious writer and those who treat him as a poet and literary critic. His interesting study grows out of "Coleridge's belief that art and aesthetics can illuminate and refresh the religious life" and conversely the idea that "theology may be the conserving source for a theory of the almost limitless freedom of the artist as inspired creator". While the book is the work of a theologian, it is critically acute. Chapter 4 is a study of "Kubla Khan", the "Rime of the Ancient Mariner", and "Dejection: An Ode".

The title of FULFORD's book refers to "a language, a discourse which embraced conceits, allusions, puns [e.g. Coleridge's transliterated signature in Greek ESTEESE] and even verbal slips as well as metaphor and symbol". This large ambit is Fulford's principal theme – all Coleridge's private and public life and work is covered, the poetic, the religious, the political, the private notes, and the letters. Useful sections discuss "spiritual politics" and Coleridge's relation to the Hebrew esoteric tradition and the European Cabala, the Bible, orthodox Christianity, and the Christian inner tradition (instanced for Coleridge in Jakob Böhme). Studies of the "Rime of the Ancient Mariner", "Christabel", and "Dejection: An Ode", as poetry of isolation, are as far as the poetry is taken. Perhaps the account in total marginalises the poems or makes them seem peripheral, but given the convincingness of the rest of Fulford's case on Coleridge's *oeuvre*, that might now be one way assessments may properly tend. "Coleridge's writing took private forms: the public exposition of ideas tested in notebook, manuscript and letter was often incomplete". This remark typifies another presupposition of this study, along with the claim that Coleridge's "linguistic attack on post-Kantian dualism uncannily anticipated the major philosophical debates of the 20th Century".

MARKS, likewise, offers a picture of Coleridge the intellectual ancestor and presager of structuralism, who "directed his superb analytical powers on language itself as an artistic medium". Marks is motivated by "the successive efforts of poets, critics and philosophers to solve what many of them regard as the enigma of poetic utterance". He pays special attention to Coleridge's interest in verbal style, and to his lifelong preoccupation with the distinction between prose and verse, and the poetic and the prosaic. Attribute here does not always go hand in glove with genre, and for Coleridge, we learn, many a poem is prosaic and many a piece of prose poetic. "Coleridge's ultimate concern", however, "was with language as it functions in poetry". Marks concludes as he began, with the thought that "Coleridgean discoveries have since become theoretical commonplaces", and that Coleridge's is "a poetics which further investigation dare not ignore".

GOODSON takes as his subject Coleridge's fortunes in the stormy seas of English and American criticism of the twentieth century, represented by, among others, T.S. Eliot, F.R. Leavis, I.A. Richards, William Empson, Raymond Williams, Allen Tate, R.P. Blackmur, Yvor Winters, and Irving Babbitt. Goodson notes that:

> Coleridge remains one of our exemplary readers, an enduring model of response . . . Influential opinion since Leavis has discounted Coleridge's defence of poetry along with his metaphysical aspiration, abandoning also the example of his responsive reading. The quality of Coleridge's commitment remains worth considering for what it offers modern reading.

Like his subject, Goodson demands and rewards careful study. "The comparison of an original defence of poetry, that is, Coleridge's, with its rehabilitation for academic purposes exemplifies the difference between Romantic and modern reading": from this starting point and other remarks, a comparison emerges between Coleridge's clerisy and Leavis's reading public. Goodson feels Coleridge is at the root of Cambridge English, in fact, and not only for I.A. Richards: "formed by Cambridge English but inspired by a Coleridge it had not recognised, Raymond Williams represents a singular convergence of the most important thinking about literature in the language". In view of this, it is odd that Goodson does not discuss *On the Constitution of the Church and State*, Coleridge's exposition of the clerisy principle (of a literate and culturally aware class), which Leavis's mission later strove to realise. The conclusion is that "language and mind, a leitmotif of Coleridge's mature reflection, was as important to his critical enterprise as was his more celebrated search for the wellsprings of imagination, and it has proved nearly as influential for modern thinking".

HAMILTON, in a book which "studies the place of poetry in Coleridge's thought", offers a similar emphasis to Goodson in terms of Coleridge's formative place in the history of post-Romantic literary criticism: "we need a criticism which can explain the educative importance of literature, and Coleridge, for all his weaknesses, gives the English tradition the modern formulation of the problem". Hamilton also demonstrates that "the importance of Coleridge, historically understood, is to show that the theory and the practice of criticism are not alternatives, but only fully comprehended in one another".

The title of BEER's study says something essential about it, in that it conceives Coleridge's entire work as informed by a poetic, creative intelligence and action, and assumes, like Richards and Marks, that the prose work is as much informed by it as the poetry is. As a collection of loosely connected studies it works very well, offering an interpretation of the "Rime of the Ancient Mariner" in Chapter 7, and of "Christabel" in Chapter 8, studying the poems by relating them to events in Coleridge's life contemporaneous with their writing (this method is also followed in Beer's excellent 1993 Everyman edition of the poems, with its critical and biographical interpolations). Other matters of interest rarely covered by other critics include Coleridge's recurrent interest in vortical forms of movement such as eddies, springs, whirlwinds, coils – Beer mentions contemporary precursors of the discovery of the DNA helix and the observations made by scientists, Goethe included, of spiral forms in plants. There are also various suggestions that "set his drug-taking in the realm of his intellectual interests and even offer it a possible moral support". And an interesting final chapter is devoted to Coleridge's influences. The discussion of the possible contacts and actual evidence of contact between Coleridge and Blake is a case in point; Beer reviews the evidence and circumspectly adds "or they may have come to the same paradigms independently". This is a salutary treatment of the vexed question of influence among the Romantics. Beer's is a rewarding book, its hallmark his knack of identifying a seemingly marginal theme and relating major aspects of Coleridge's major works to it, making it seem much less marginal in the process and giving Coleridge even more credit for an astonishing breadth of interests. After reading Beer we can see that when Coleridge is viewed sympathetically, his intelligence "not stretched on the rack of a criminal indictment, but seen flowering in its own original setting, the reasons for his extraordinary impact on his contemporaries becomes more comprehensible".

WYLIE's book is rich in demonstration and documentation, though weaker in argument. Coleridge's 1810 jotting "I wish much to investigate the connection of the imagination with the Bildungstrieb [generative principle] is not there a link between physical imitation and imagination?" prompts Wylie to introduce one of the most detailed, if eccentric, descriptions available of Coleridge's relationship to science. Wylie's study bridges ancient and modern influences on Coleridge, and argues on the basis of a continuity between ancient and modern thought that existed at the end of the eighteenth century. The study generally derives advantage from focusing on one point of Coleridge's life. The early part of it is seminal, conspicuously so when examined on its own. There is a good Introduction, which orientates the study and rejects the polarization of art and science, and Wylie is throughout as disciplined a philosopher as he is literary critic.

MILEUR tackles head-on, generally and in particular, Coleridge's inability, refusal, or hesitation to finish work. About revision, in deconstructionist tradition, this book gives great emphasis to Coleridge's insertion of glosses, introductions, prefaces, postfaces, parentheses; it admits frankly, and tries to explain the obliqueness and often manifest irrelevancy of, Coleridge's self-explanations – a good instance is Mileur's long discussion of the final part of "Christabel". Interestingly addressed are Coleridge's biblical interests and their relation to Word and Scripture, and in turn to poetic production. Mileur's emphasis on psychological contingency and Coleridge's reliance on it is characteristic of postmodern commentary, but very relevant to Coleridge's noting of the "secondariness inherent in our condition" in its psychological and literary implications. Conclusions suggest that Coleridge, even if "he does not understand his own poetry" nevertheless "refutes the preemptive conceptions of self and of his work that had plagued him throughout his career".

PAUL DAVIES

Collins, Wilkie 1824–1889

English novelist and dramatist

Heller, Tamar, *Dead Secrets: Wilkie Collins and the Female Gothic*, New Haven, Connecticut: Yale University Press, 1992

Lonoff de Cuevas, Sue, *Wilkie Collins and His Victorian Readers: A Study in the Rhetoric of Authorship*, New York: AMS Press, 1982

Marshall, William H., *Wilkie Collins*, New York: Twayne, 1970

O'Neill, Philip, *Wilkie Collins: Women, Property and Propriety*, London: Macmillan, 1988

Taylor, Jenny Bourne, *In the Secret Theatre of Home: Wilkie Collins, Sensation Narrative, and Nineteenth-Century Psychology*, London and New York: Routledge, 1988

Thoms, Peter, *The Windings of the Labyrinth: Quest and Structure in the Major Novels of Wilkie Collins*, Athens: Ohio University Press, 1992

Until recently, Wilkie Collins's extraordinary skills as a plotter of suspenseful narratives have discouraged rather than encouraged serious consideration of his fiction. Indeed, the tag of popular storyteller – implying that the novels do not repay the efforts of close reading – seems partly responsible for the strong *biographical* interest in Collins studies. While the fiction itself might not seem to merit sustained attention, Collins the man, with his unconventional private life, his friendship with Charles Dickens, and his lengthy novelistic career, clearly presented an intriguing subject for investigation and analysis. Since the publication in 1951 of Kenneth Robinson's superb *Wilkie Collins*, five additional biographies have appeared, the most recent being Catherine Peter's fine study, *The King of Inventors: A Life of Wilkie Collins* (1991).

MARSHALL's study is (its author states) "the first attempt to deal extensively and exclusively with the literary art of Wilkie Collins and the part that it played in the development of the English novel". Although he does not examine any text in great detail, Marshall's chronological survey offers a useful introduction to Collins's fiction. Marshall argues that Collins was torn "between the two opposing demands, the intellectual and the popular, that his epoch placed upon his art", and that often, as a consequence, his fiction suffered. As prime examples of this problem, Collins's endings are cited, which Marshall views as contrived and happy, concessions to popularity that conflict with the intellectual, realistic, and more complex content contained in the main bodies of the novels.

LONOFF insightfully examines Collins's relationship with his British readers and its influence upon his novels. Collins desired popularity; "he was always concerned with his effect upon his audience, and that concern permeates his fiction". Echoing Marshall's opposition of the "intellectual and the popular", Lonoff asserts that while Collins wished to please, he concurrently possessed rebellious urges to disturb his readers by introducing controversial content. That mixture of the pleasing and the upsetting, she contends, "gives his work more complexity and meaning than it is generally thought to possess". Lonoff's accessible and engaging study begins with considerations of Collins's "own remarks about works of fiction and the reading public", and "the influence of his family and various members of his audience". Then, for the bulk of the book, she focuses on Collins's writing, providing discussions of such topics as game-playing in the fiction and the portrayal of women, and concluding with a lengthy chapter on *The Moonstone*.

O'NEILL's central topic is Collins's representation of women: "Collins sees the situation of women as both symptomatic of, and supportive to, bourgeois patriarchy. Women cannot be discussed in Collins in isolation from the authority exercised by property and mediated through the sense of propriety". Although O'Neill's arguments are not always sharply focused, he seizes upon an important area of investigation (particularly given recent interest in the subversive Collins and his criticism of Victorian society); and he offers, in addition to discussions of the major novels, criticism of the neglected *Man and Wife* and *The Fallen Leaves*.

TAYLOR, in a difficult and demanding book, considers how nineteenth-century psychological discourses inform the writing and understanding of Collins's fiction. In attempting to examine Collins's work within "its historical and discursive context", Taylor considers how Collins in his fiction is "assimilating and resisting a contradictory set of contemporary discourses" about "consciousness and identity, about the social formation of the self, about the workings of the unconscious and the interlinking of the mind and the body, about the problematic boundaries between sanity and madness". After opening chapters on Collins and sensation fiction, and on nineteenth-century psychology, Taylor examines, successively, *Basil*, the four novels of the major decade, and, in a final chapter, some of the novels of Collins's decline.

My own (THOMS's) study argues that Collins's highly plotted novels are, in fact, about plotting; they dramatize the formation of narrative patterns through their depictions of protagonists who, in resisting the oppressive plots that constrain them, attempt to define their own independent stories. After briefly charting the development of this quest for self-expression in *Basil*, *Hide and Seek*, and *The Dead Secret*, I offer readings of *The Woman in White*, *No Name*, *Armadale*, and *The Moonstone*, portraying the struggle for self-determination and the novels' increasing scepticism of the designs that the protagonists construct.

HELLER, in a sophisticated feminist study, offers chapters on *The Woman in White*, *The Moonstone*, the important early novel *Basil*, and the short-story collection *After Dark*, and discussions of lesser-known works such as *Antonina* and *Memoirs of the Life of William Collins*. Linking Collins to the "Gothic writing by women known as the female Gothic", Heller considers how this tradition gives Collins "a way of being a social critic, and of writing about his often liberal views on social issues, including gender, while also offering him an avenue for portraying types of alienation and subversion". Yet Collins, she contends, is unable to endorse fully a feminist perspective; the rebellious and "feminized" strains of the gothic conflict with – and are harnessed by – Collins's conservative desire to identify himself as a professional, and hence "masculine", writer.

PETER THOMS

Comedy: Theory

Charney, Maurice, *Comedy High and Low: An Introduction to the Experience of Comedy*, Oxford and New York: Oxford University Press, 1978
Nelson, T.G.A., *Comedy: An Introduction to Comedy in Literature, Drama and Cinema*, Oxford and New York: Oxford University Press, 1990
Palmer, D.J. (ed.), *Comedy: Developments in Criticism*, London: Macmillan London, 1984
Potts, L.J., *Comedy*, Hutchinson: London, 1948
Sorell, W., *Facets of Comedy*, New York: Grosset & Dunlap, 1972
Torrance, R.M., *The Comic Hero*, Cambridge, Massachusetts: Harvard University Press, 1978

POTTS's endearing very early study has the advantage of approaching the texts face-to-face, rather than filtered through a wash of theory. Many would disagree with his attitudes, which depend largely on theories of humour or comic relief, but his view of comedy as a "mode of thought" is still extremely helpful.

CHARNEY's book is a very useful introduction, not only because it is wittily written and furnished with 20 hilarious illustrations (cartoons and film-shots), but also on account of its clear and sensible structure. We commence with a very full account of the language of comedy with good examples of irony, nonsense, and popular humour. This is complemented with a dazzling array of puns, jokes, malapropisms, spoonerisms, and graffiti. Charney then proceeds to give a finely-articulated study of conventional comic characters, emphasising stereotypes and caricatures with a wide range of examples from Shakespeare to the television series *Monty Python's Flying Circus*. "The greatest vice in comedy is hypocrisy", says Charney, and he goes on to demonstrate this with an admirable array of examples. The succeeding analysis of the structure of comedy is perhaps more predictable, but the treatment of repetition is very enlightening. Subsequent sections deal with farce, burlesque, satiric comedy, and other important forms, including the festive mode with its stress on what Mikhail Bakhtin called the base bodily stratum. In a completely different approach from Torrance, Charney goes on to analyse the seven key aspects of the comic hero, ranging from Shakespeare's Falstaff to Buster Keaton, including, helpfully, satirical aspects. The "Reading List", though inevitably dated, is still useful.

NELSON's study attempts a vaguely generic approach, reconciling the dual aspects of comedy as laughter and comedy as structure. He also usefully demonstrates how even laughter can be vindictive. There is considerable use made of Aristotle, Freud, and Lane Cooper – not always well-organised, but helpful in providing a wide spectrum of comedic theory. The examples drawn from films are also very well chosen. In Chapter 2 Nelson deals with the relation of comedy to other forms – even tragedy. This is highly suggestive, but probably attempts to cover too much ground, although the use of Bakhtin is admirable. Chapter 3 is far too vague, with its mixture of Freud, Helen Gardner, Jacques Lacan, and Oscar Wilde. Further chapters deal with procreation, death, tricksters, fools, and the language of comedy. The range of examples provided is impressive, but the text (admirable as it is) should really be twice the length it is to enable Nelson to develop his ideas further. The bibliography, though, is full and up to date.

TORRANCE's study is a diachronic view ranging (rather dauntingly) from *The Odyssey* to Thomas Mann's *Felix Krull*, but what distinguishes this text is the way the author selects from each period a representative comedic figure, such as "Jackanapes", "Renegade", "Rake", and "Stumblebum". Also notable is his stress on the idea of the comic hero, while most other texts concentrate on the comic characters as fools or butts.

After an introduction outlining these ideas, incorporating a useful critique of Henri Bergson, Torrance points how characters like Till Eulenspiegl or Hašek's the Good Soldier Schweik always manage to defeat authority and emerge (at least temporarily) as victors. He points out too how, in contrast to the usual satirical conception, philosophers like Susanne Langer have concentrated on how comedy expresses the "elemental strains" and "animal drives" of human nature. This is followed by a detailed treatment of Odysseus as the opposite of the tragic hero Achilles in *The Iliad*, yet still a hero in a very different way. A subsequent chapter on Aristophanes proceeds along the same lines, emphasising the way Old Comedy demonstrates how spiritual and physical release are the comedic results of eliminating social constraints. He then deals with Plautus and Lucius, before showing that, even in the repressive austerity of medieval Christianity, the Goliards, the writers of *fabliaux*, and above all the saga of Reynard the Fox, with its profanation of love and religion, kept the comic spirit alive. Perhaps in these times only an animal could he a hero! Equally cogent is Torrance's treatment of parody and social satire in the period. Courtly love, as he rightly points out, is "brought down to its animal underpinnings".

The fifth chapter focuses on Falstaff as opponent of majesty and even figure of innocence against the "sickened perfidy of the political world of the play". Subsequent chapters deal with Cervantes' *Don Quixote* as parody (less convincing perhaps on the idea of the "addle-brained hidalgo" as comic hero) and the plays of Ben Jonson and Molière (eliminated because they contain no true comic heroes – though one could make a case for Jonson's Volpone). Torrance then turns to Henry Fielding's Tom Jones, Denis Diderot, and Beaumarchais. One might feel that the analysis of Lord Byron in Chapter 8 is stretching the idea of the comedic to its absolute limits, and the saturation bombing on Charles Dickens, Mark Twain, Henrik Ibsen, and Gustave Flaubert might very well confuse rather than enlighten the novitiate reader. On the other hand, the concluding analyses of James Joyce's *Ulysses* and *Felix Krull* are admirable. Not the least of the virtues of this study are the meticulously scholarly notes. There is no bibliography.

PALMER's *Casebook* follows the traditional Macmillan format of having three diachronic sections. The first set of extracts covers classical and medieval material from Plato to Dante, with a useful but too attenuated passage from the otherwise hard-to-obtain Evanthius; the second selection has all the traditional material from Nicholas Udall to Henri Bergson (though the extract from *Le Rire* is far too short); and the third group provides a suggestive survey of twentieth-century views. There are some classic studies excerpted here – notably Northrop Frye on the argument of comedy, Walter Kaiser on the wise fool, Bakhtin on the carnivalesque aspect of comedy, and Ian Donaldson on the world upside down. A final section dealing with comic form deals with Susanne Langer's incisive remarks on comedic rhythm and Eric Bentley's discussion of the relationship between tragedy and comedy. This is clearly an anthology aimed at undergraduates, and, while one might feel that the extracts are too brief, it could be argued that this very fact, combined with their well-chosenness, might stimulate readers to go back to the original texts. The bibliography is eclectically irrational; the index is full and helpful.

SORELL's little-known but excellent book is slanted much more towards humour in comedy, though it is wide-ranging enough to include such topics as political satire, Irish eloquence, Molière, and melancholy. As a glance at the index will prove, this text covers more comedic material than other work reviewed here, including almost unknown (in England) Hungarian writers (e.g., Ladislav Bus-Fekete) or epigramaticists like Karl Kraus. Sorel provides us with what he considers the seven fundamental features of comedy and a laughter-scale, from horseplay to satire: on this basis he erects a useful theory of the scope of comedy, embracing wit, parody, irony, caricature, and other modes.

Further chapters deal with comic types (such as the *miles gloriosus*), with political satire (as in Aristophanes, Jonson, and Christian Dietrich Grabbe, and with the comedy of ideas (exemplified in the plays of George Bernard Shaw). Sorell then moves on to farce, burlesque, and *commedia dell'arte* (a particularly finely-detailed analysis). The sections on Molière are comprehensive and convincingly demonstrate the essential conservatism of satiric comedy – a useful complement to Bakhtin's stress on the carnivalesque or Langer's preoccupation with biological drives.

The discussion of Restoration comedy is a rather disappointing series of plot summaries; and Chapter 10 focuses too heavily on Russian literature, which is really rather tangential to the "melancholy" the chapter heading promised us. After a somewhat pretentious comparison between "Renaissance Man" and "Twentieth-Century Man", Sorell provides a sort of interlude, contrasting comedy and tragedy and asserting (with George Steiner) the death of the latter in the twentieth century: comedy, however, is not dead – it has simply become black, negative, and absurd. He then reverts to Wilde and drawing-room comedy, surveys the work of W. Somerset Maugham and Jean Giraudoux, and in a series of rather chaotically organised final chapters gives us a comprehensive sociological analysis of the 1960s, the Theatre of the Absurd, Brechtian epic drama, "dark comedy", and Luigi Pirandello.

The value of this study lies not so much in any theoretical approach to comedy or in any rigorous order of treatment as in the author's infectious enthusiasm for his subject and the astonishing number of examples drawn from all countries that he manages to include. The bibliography is very dated, but the index is excellent.

A.W. LYLE

Comedy: Renaissance

Bristol, Michael D., *Carnival and Theater: Plebeian Culture and the Structure of Authority in Renaissance England*, New York and London: Methuen, 1985

Farley-Hills, David, *The Comic in Renaissance Comedy*, London: Macmillan, 1981

Gibbons, Brian, *Jacobean City Comedy: A Study of Satiric Plays by Jonson, Marston and Middleton*, London: Methuen, 1968; Cambridge, Massachusetts: Harvard University Press, 1968; revised edition, London and New York: Methuen, 1980

Laroque, François, *Shakespeare's Festive World: Elizabethan Seasonal Entertainment and the Professional Stage*, translated by Janet Lloyd, Cambridge and New York: Cambridge University Press, 1991

Leggatt, Alexander, *Citizen Comedy in the Age of Shakespeare*, Toronto and Buffalo, New York: University of Toronto Press, 1973

Weld, John, *Meaning in Comedy: Studies in Elizabethan Romantic Comedy*, Albany: State University of New York Press, 1975

Earlier studies of Renaissance comedy tended to enumerate generic dimensions without an overarching theoretical framework; more recently, however, critics have attempted to relate comic forms to broader social and methodological imperatives, expanding definitions and deepening an awareness of dramatic diversity and possibility.

Addressing the drama of Thomas Dekker, Thomas Heywood, Ben Jonson, John Marston and Thomas Middleton, LEGGATT defines "Citizen Comedy" as a dramatic mode that, moving away from representations of the aristocracy and the court, is mainly concerned with the middle classes and lower social levels. This does not mean that the plays he discusses catered to exclusive commercial groups: one of the chief virtues of Leggatt's study is the argument that the theatre staged realizations *about* the middle classes rather than *for* their particular tastes and interests. The focus of Leggatt's account is the treatment of contemporary social situations, and to this end he details attitudes towards money, sex, and marriage; explores class satire; charts the versatility of the intrigue plot; and attends to the charged place occupied by the citizen hero and the witty, attractive rogue. While some of Leggatt's perspectives (the elaboration of moral judgements and the importance accorded to aesthetic features, for example) have now been superseded, his study is valuable for its identification of the increasing complexity of generic experimentation undertaken by dramatists, and for its survey of a range of pressing social issues and questions.

The rather slighter volume by WELD concentrates on Renaissance comedy written before 1597, which provides the book with a specifically Elizabethan aspect. In the first part of the book, Weld outlines the dramatic tradition in which the audiences of John Lyly, Robert Greene, and Shakespeare's early plays had been schooled. Costume, theatrical devices, the uses of metaphor and allegorical features are the chief areas of concern in these early sections of the book. Part Two is devoted to romantic comedy, and as well as describing the distinctive flavour of such plays as Greene's *Friar Bacon and Friar Bungay*, and Shakespeare's *The Comedy of Errors*, *The Taming of the Shrew*, *A Midsummer Night's Dream*, and *The Merchant of Venice*, Weld offers a contextual reading of early satiric comedies, highlighting their exploration of new comic concepts: dramatists such as Lyly, Weld argues, entertained "the notion of man as comic in his very nature as opposed to the notion of man as comic in his correctable or reformable vice and folly".

While Weld is not primarily interested in comedy and its contextual relations, GIBBONS makes available two finely nuanced chapters on the social and economic background to dramatic production in the Jacobean period. He goes on to investigate the self-conscious formation of a new dramatic genre (by Jonson, Marston, and Middleton) in which images of gullibility and stupidity in court and city are given an ironic twist. As the genre developed, Gibbons argues, the role of contemporary London expanded, reflecting no original social theories, but displaying a shrewd engagement with the forces of instability and change, which were transforming the early seventeenth-century English landscape.

In contrast, FARLEY-HILLS takes an arguably ahistorical approach in his analysis of English Renaissance comedy, claiming that the "critic is concerned with the viability of literature as a living experience". One might choose to question this methodological outlook, but the book is still helpful for its distinctions between "comedy" and "comic", for its generic definitions, and for its discussion of a double or multiple dramatic structure. The individual chapters light upon Jonson's *The Alchemist*, Middleton's *A Mad World, My Masters*, Dekker's *The Shoemaker's Holiday*, Richard Brome's *A Jovial Crew*, and Shakespeare's *The Taming of the Shrew* for assessment, and there are informed appreciations of Jonson's satirical techniques (such as deft maintenance of various levels of sympathy), of the moral values that Middleton hints at but never celebrates in a broadly Calvinistic view of the world, of

Dekker's affirmation of the multiplicity of God's divine bounty, of Brome's discovery of pleasure and enjoyment in uncertainty, and of Shakespeare's resolution of tensions in the laughter of acceptance. If this is a study to question for its emphasis on the integrity of the text, it is also one to bear in mind for its breadth of endeavour and its full readings of a select dramatic sampling.

Where Farley-Hills privileges the aesthetic qualities of the dramatic experience, BRISTOL is more concerned with the theatre as social institution and potential site of political conflict. For Bristol, popular carnival manifestations are an integral part of the operations of the playhouse, and in pursuing this theme he draws upon a number of recent theoretical models, pointing up issues of authority and resistance, and the intersection of stage representations and forms of popular culture. In electing to discuss a number of familiar and non-familiar materials, Bristol casts his generic net widely; his study is germane to the topic of comedy, however, in that it establishes provocative discursive relations and reveals the materialist underside to such texts as the anonymous *The Merry Devil of Edmonton*, and Shakespeare's *A Midsummer Night's Dream* and *Twelfth Night*.

Bristol's account acts as a prelude for the more rigorous and magisterial study by LAROQUE. With a commanding range of documentation (travellers' journals, diaries, and royal pronouncements), Laroque surveys the field, describing the agricultural provenance of seasonal entertainments, the activities of youthful fraternities, and the relative popularity of secular and religious observances. In the latter part of the book, Laroque chases the ramifications of festive ideas in Shakespeare's plays: he favours inexact refractions and echoes rather than easy reflections, a procedure which enables him to find vestiges of mummers' plays in *The Merry Wives of Windsor*; an alternation between celebration and war in *Much Ado about Nothing*; a carnivalesque dispute between courtship and abstemious academicism in *Love's Labour's Lost*; and a manipulation of Hocktide practices in *The Taming of the Shrew*. No less pertinent in his treatment of parodic elements in the tragedies, Laroque convincingly demonstrates the ways in which Shakespeare reinvigorated faded or discarded traditions, thus ensuring an impact for his plays in the theatre.

MARK THORNTON BURNETT

City Comedy

Butler, Martin, *Theatre and Crisis 1632–1642*, Cambridge and New York: Cambridge University Press, 1984

Gibbons, Brian, *Jacobean City Comedy*, London: Methuen, 1968; Cambridge, Massachusetts: Harvard University Press, 1968; revised edition, London and New York: Methuen, 1980

Griswold, Wendy, *Renaissance Revivals: City Comedy and Revenge Tragedy in the London Theatre, 1576–1980*, Chicago: University of Chicago Press, 1986

Leggatt, Alexander, *Citizen Comedy in the Age of Shakespeare*, Toronto and Buffalo, New York: University of Toronto Press, 1973

Leinwand, Theodore B., *The City Staged: Jacobean Comedy, 1603–1613*, Madison: University of Wisconsin Press, 1986

Mullaney, Steven, *The Place of the Stage: License, Play, and Power in Renaissance England*, Chicago: University of Chicago Press, 1988

Paster, Gail Kern, *The Idea of the City in the Age of Shakespeare*, Athens: University of Georgia Press, 1985

The term "city comedy" designates a wide range of entertaining and provocative plays written and performed in London from the late 1590s until the closing of the theatres in 1642. Usually, though not always, set in contemporary London, they describe the strains of living in the early-modern metropolis, celebrating, as much as denigrating, the greed and Machiavellian energy required to survive and flourish there. Scholarship on the genre tends to focus either on the literary background and the formal properties of the genre, or attempts to trace connections between the rise of the genre and the explosive growth London experienced in the early decades of the seventeenth century.

PASTER's focus is on the literary side of this ledger. She deals at length with the city comedies of Ben Jonson and Thomas Middleton: like most critics she sees these two as the chief exponents of the genre. She places their plays within the context of Renaissance ideas about cities, inherited in large measure from Europe's classical and Christian past. Writing about the city necessitates drawing on classical Roman sources, especially the excoriating satires of Juvenal, as well as on biblical representations of the city. In particular, urban literature is haunted by the twin cities of the Book of Revelation, Babylon the Great, the cynosure of material desire, and the dream city, New Jerusalem. Like Northrop Frye, Paster sees the latter as the epitome of human ideals, depicted in urban form. City comedy draws on both these traditions; thus Jonson and Middleton present the city as predator in their comedies, and then, in their civic masques and pageants, present "the city as an ideal form of social organization". Paster is a lucid and well informed guide to the idea of the city in this form of comedy.

GIBBONS's study is more generic than ideological. He traces the growth of the genre, from Jonson's "comicall satyres" of the 1590s, which depict the flawed "humours" of galleries of urban dwellers, through to its development by Marston, Jonson, and Middleton, until its apotheosis in Jonson's *Bartholomew Fair* (1614) and *The Devil is an Ass* (1616). These comedies blend medieval morality with the verse satires of the 1590s. The resultant hybrid combines realism with a satiric criticism that is deeply moral, focused not so much on contemporary materialism as on deeper "sources of conflict and change". Gibbons's formalist approach is still valuable, but needs now to be balanced by the more recent consideration of the connections between Jacobean city comedy and the specifics of power relations in early-modern London.

Of these tensions LEGGATT is also blithely unaware; but his is the more engaging introduction to the formal properties of the genre. His boundaries are more elastic than Gibbons's: for Leggatt the genre encompasses "the satiric, the didactic, and the simply amusing". Like Gibbons, Leggatt sees Marston, Middleton, and Jonson as the chief practitioners of the genre, but he finds room also for the exuberant celebrations of Thomas Dekker's *The Shoemaker's Holiday* (1599), with its "glorification of citizen life". Leggatt emphasises both the realism of city-comedy settings, firmly anchored in prosaic streets and shops, familiar to the original audiences for these plays, and the pragmatic nature of city-comedy characters, concerned with the getting and spending of money as well as the getting and keeping of wives. Both Leggatt and Gibbons see city comedy as inherently conservative, its anarchic energies as a safety valve, eventually promoting stability and bourgeois decorum.

GRISWOLD takes a longer view, though like Gibbons or Leggatt she sees city comedy as a vehicle for "soothing social anxieties". She tracks the pattern of revivals of city comedy over the last 300 years against the background of a compact summary of the formal attributes of city comedy; and she speculates, as well, as to the appeal of city comedy for both its initial and subsequent audiences. In her analysis she attempts to be both "social scientist" and "humanist", drawing on Weberian sociology to construct a "cultural diamond", in which the shape of the plays is dictated by the balance between four forces – the nature of London in the 1600s, the nature of the audience, the disposition of the artist, and finally the art object itself. Her diamond is perhaps too elegant to be plausible, especially when dealing with such a rousingly material form as city comedy; but her description of the genre is the most effective currently available, and her discussion of the patterns of revivals of city comedies presents material that would otherwise be very difficult to find.

In the 1980s, New Historicists have frequently been more interested in city comedy's relationship with the turbulent politics of seventeenth-century London than in its formal properties. These critics provide a useful ideological corrective to the more exclusively formal readings of the 1960s and 1970s.

MULLANEY places city comedy within his overall theory of the place of Renaissance drama in the life of early-modern London. He uses Victor Turner's anthropology of liminality to reinvent the place of the stage. Outside the medieval walls of the city, theatre took place in the Liberties, where ideas and images could be rehearsed which inside the city would not be allowed. Yet these liberties were symbiotically attached to the city; and the images were offered to its citizens. Thus city comedy's scurrilous reworking of the city as a place of greed and conspicuous consumption is a refracted mirror held up for the city to see itself and to frame in turn the nature of power within the city. Mullaney's vision of early-modern London has been influential, partly because his plague-ridden metropolis speaks so piercingly to our own (metaphorically and in some ways literally) plague-ridden times. His comedies are persistently "cheerless dark and deadly", and should probably be balanced by the sunny enthusiasm of Leggatt or Gibbons.

LEINWAND returns the focus to city comedies themselves, but his reading of them reproduces the sombreness which is the hallmark of New-Historicist readings, a legacy of its Foucauldian scepticism about the workings of power. He rejects attention to the form of city comedy, and insists that instead we see it as "informed by the social and economic reality in which playwrights found themselves". Their plays, in turn, depict the tensions inevitable in a "status society itself under pressure". With this model in mind, Leinwand studies merchants, wives, whores, widows, and maids, comparing their history with their representations, especially in Middleton's plays. Leinwand lacks Mullaney's dark, poetic vision, but his readings are well informed and accomplished. He presents fairly the new orthodoxy in city-comedy scholarship.

BUTLER's is the most important and influential of these new accounts. He extends city comedy well beyond its normal Jacobean boundaries, using the term to cover the comedies of urban manners written by Philip Massinger, Richard Brome, and James Shirley during the 1630s. This forms part of his ground-breaking rewriting of the theatrical history of that decade. In his view, Caroline drama reacts to, and meditates upon, the growing political crisis, especially the growing estrangement of Charles I from his politically active subjects. City comedies of the 1630s reflect the new growth of the metropolis in this period. In particular they record the presence of a new group in London, "the town", separate from the city of London or the court, a gentry audience establishing a permanent presence in London with its own places of recreation, such as Covent Garden or Hyde Park, both of which were celebrated in comedies in the 1630s. These plays were not simply entertainments; they presented "manners, morals and politics" as parts of a whole, through which "the town" put its case for the balanced reformation of the city, the court, and the country. Butler's readings are politically astute, and his attention to context dense and exemplary. He has assured a renewed critical life for the complex and elegant city comedies he celebrates.

MARK HOULAHAN

Comedy: Restoration

Birdsall, Virginia Ogden, *Wild Civility: The English Comic Spirit on the Restoration Stage*, Bloomington: Indiana University Press, 1970

Brown, John Russell, and Bernard Harris (eds.), *Restoration Theatre* (Stratford-upon-Avon Studies series), London: Edward Arnold, 1965; New York: St Martin's Press, 1965

Burns, Edward, *Restoration Comedy: Crises of Desire and Identity*, London: Macmillan, 1986

Dobrée, Bonamy, *Restoration Comedy 1660–1720*, Oxford: Clarendon Press, 1924

Hirst, David, *The Comedy of Manners*, London and New York: Methuen, 1979

Holland, Peter, *The Ornament of Action: Text and Performance in Restoration Comedy 1660–1720*, Cambridge and New York: Cambridge University Press, 1979

Hume, Robert D., *The Rakish Stage: Studies in English Drama 1660–1800*, Carbondale: Southern Illinois University Press, 1983

Loftis, John (ed.), *Restoration Drama: Modern Essays in Criticism*, New York: Oxford University Press, 1966

Nicoll, Allardyce, *A History of Restoration Drama 1660–1700*, Cambridge: Cambridge University Press, 1923, 3rd edition, 1940

Styan, J.L., *Restoration Comedy in Performance*, Cambridge and New York: Cambridge University Press, 1986

Restoration comedy, taking its designation from Charles II's restoration to the throne in 1660, has engendered lively twentieth-century critical controversy. Although questions about its moral, aesthetic, and theatrical value have been settled – very much in its favour – its definition, nature, purpose, and origins are still in dispute. In the past generation, critics have profited from intensified research into the practicalities of seventeenth- and eighteenth-century theatrical production, as well as frequent modern revivals.

DOBRÉE sees Restoration comedy as the product of an unsettled age when "men and women were experimenting in social things; they were trying to rationalize human relationships". He acknowledges and justifies the presence of "Impurity" (often discounted or condemned by previous critics), arguing that the dramatists turned "the common facts of life into art". This was "Comedy of Manners", descended from English humours comedy and characterised by "verbal pyrotechnics" and attacks on "acquired follies". Briefly, but perceptively, he describes the careers and principal comedies of Sir George Etherege, William Wycherley, John Dryden, Thomas Shadwell, William Congreve, Sir John Vanbrugh, and George Farquhar.

NICOLL's magisterial study combines the encyclopedic inclusiveness of a survey with shapely development and incisive argument. Beginning, in exemplary fashion, with a study of Restoration theatrical conditions, he proceeds to discuss tragedy, then the various forms of comedy. The Appendices include a "History of the Playhouses: 1660–1700", fascinating contemporary documents, and an invaluable "Hand-List of Restoration Plays".

LOFTIS reprints a collection of previously published material, which not only suggests "the current state of literary scholarship on the subject", but encapsulates the critical history of Restoration drama since World War I. L.C. Knights' notorious proposition that Restoration comedies are "trivial, gross and dull" joins F.W. Bateson's counterblast, G. Montgomery's defence of comedy's "human significance", and Dobrée's impassioned revelation of Congreve's emotional power. Two other epoch-making papers are B.H. Bronson's "*The Beggar's Opera*" and P.E. Parnell's "The Sentimental Mask". Attention is also paid to the political and philosophical background, while A.S. Downer's essay on eighteenth-century acting illuminates the theatrical foreground. In another essay-collection, BROWN and HARRIS guided nine chosen authors "towards topics familiar and unfamiliar" in order to cast more light on a period "known uncertainly as well as patchily". This useful, well-balanced volume has chapters on Etherege, Dryden, Wycherley, and Congreve, as well as on broader topics such as comic language from Etherege to Vanbrugh, the satirical literary background, a comparison with Molière's comedies, and – showing salutary concern with the plays in performance – Restoration acting style.

BIRDSALL traces Restoration comedy's roots to medieval morality plays, with the "Rake-hero" as a descendant of the deplorably wicked, but irresistibly comic, "Vice". Both contribute generously to the audience's enjoyment through "a seemingly inexhaustible talent for improvisation". She portrays Etherege, Wycherley and Congreve as champions of nature, humanity, and wholesome liberty, who often associate in their plays conventional morality with oppression, hypocrisy, and perversion of healthy instincts. Her analyses are sensitive and compelling, but carry most conviction when comic liberty coincides with recognisably correct morality, as in Congreve's *The Way of the World*.

HIRST observes that "Restoration comedy and comedy of manners have become virtually synonymous", but argues that applying the term "Restoration" to comedy covering 50 years, including the reigns of monarchs whose political policies and lifestyles differed greatly from those of Charles II, is "absurd". Comedy of manners' chief subject is "the way people behave, the manners they employ in a social context"; the characters' chief concerns are "sex and money"; the style is distinguished by "wit". Hirst's brief study locates such comedy in various periods; his supreme examples are *The Way of the World*, Oscar Wilde's *The Importance of Being Earnest*, Noel Coward's *Design for Living*, Joe Orton's *Loot*, and Harold Pinter's *The Homecoming*. He draws a convincing genealogy of wit, using evidence from modern performances as well as more traditional scholarship.

BURNS believes Restoration dramatists utilised "ironic explorations" of "courtly pastoral", a theme which he pursues with admirable critical acumen through the comedies of Abraham Cowley, Etherege, James Howard, Robert Howard, Wycherley, Dryden, Shadwell, John Crowne, Thomas Otway, Colley Cibber, Southerne, Vanbrugh, Congreve, Farquhar, Susanna Centlivre, and Sir Richard Steele, before coming to rest with that "Newgate Pastoral", John Gay's *The Beggar's Opera*.

The final three studies pay considerable attention to the performance aspects of the drama.

HOLLAND investigates "the relationship of performance to published text, in terms of the physical conditions of English theatre between 1660 and about 1705 and the force of those conditions on comedy". After superb general studies of text and audience, theatre design and scenery, actors and casting, and the relationship between performance and published text, Holland provides detailed examination of comedies performed from 1691 to 1693 (including Thomas Southerne's *The Wives' Excuse*), Wycherley's *The Plain-Dealer*, and Congreve. He argues that most "attributes of the representation – though not the quarrels in the pit – can be an essential part of the play's communication of its meaning". This book is indispensable for serious students of Restoration comedy.

HUME also triumphantly fuses literary criticism with theatre history. He continually challenges conventional wisdom by appealing to fresh evidence, or by setting familiar material in a new light. His chapter on "'Restoration Comedy' and Its Audience, 1660–1776", co-written with Arthur H. Scouten, is particularly important, both for its demolition of the myth that Restoration comedy was unsuccessful on the eighteenth-century stage, and for its denial that Restoration comedy is an ideologically uniform comedy of manners.

STYAN goes further than Holland. His imaginative integration of scripted performance with audience experience is so complete that even fights in the pit might become part of the act. "Lack of decorum" in the auditorium could be "the ultimate sign of a theatre of non-illusion", whose audience "has completely accepted its own participatory role in the business of playmaking". Meticulously researched and lavishly illustrated, using evidence from Restoration and modern productions, as well as the history of costume, dance, and etiquette, this book brings Restoration comedy to life for readers, and abounds with useful advice for actors and directors.

CAROLYN D. WILLIAMS

Commonwealth Literature *see* New Literatures

Congreve, William 1670–1729

English dramatist

Holland, Norman N., *The First Modern Comedies*, Cambridge, Massachusetts: Harvard University Press, 1959
Love, Harold, *Congreve*, Oxford: Blackwell, 1974
Markley, Robert, *Two-Edg'd Weapons: Style and Ideology in the Comedies of Etherege, Wycherley and Congreve*, Oxford: Clarendon Press, 1988; New York: Oxford University Press, 1988
Novak, Maximillian E., *William Congreve*, New York: Twayne, 1971
Peters, Julie Stone, *Congreve, the Drama, and the Printed Word*, Stanford, California: Stanford University Press, 1990
Thomas, David, *William Congreve*, London: Macmillan, 1992
Van Voris, W.H., *The Cultivated Stance: The Designs of Congreve's Plays*, Dublin: Dolmen Press, 1965; London: Oxford University Press, 1965
Williams, Aubrey L., *An Approach to Congreve*, New Haven, Connecticut, and London: Yale University Press, 1979

HOLLAND's book provides the first close, analytic reading of Congreve with the techniques of modern criticism. He reacts against the traditional concentration on manners, and the traditional charges of intellectual triviality and sexual immorality, linking Restoration comedy to the birth of the modern world-outlook, when a mechanistic cosmos replaced a divinely animated one, and when sensory appearances were no longer held directly to disclose the nature of objects. The discussions of Congreve are too repetitively concerned with the conflict of appearance and nature, and with identifying right and wrong ways of life; but Holland does demonstrate the intricacy of Congreve's imagery and craftsmanship, and highlights his concern with the reform of repressive social structures.

Whereas Holland sees Congreve as valuing the natural and essential above social artifice, VAN VORIS argues that he treats artifice as a necessary defence against the chaos and essential unknowability of experience, and the corroding influence of time. In *The Old Bachelor* festivity provides illusory perpetuation of the moment, but the remaining plays are concerned with imposing new forms of stability on disintegrating societies, though the new forms are themselves only serviceable fictions. Congreve's debt to John Locke's political theories is repeatedly emphasized.

Far more fully than his predecessors, NOVAK presents Congreve "specifically in terms of English art and society after the Glorious Revolution of 1688" (Preface) – as the product of a culture quite different from that of William Wycherley and Sir George Etherege. Libertinism, for example, had changed from a creed of ferocious sensuality to "a genteel and retired love of pleasure". Novak sees Congreve as resolutely un-Christian, arguing (for example) that the celestial imagery in *Love for Love* locates Heaven purely in the present life, and he uses exceptional learning to illuminate both Congreve's cultural debts and his originality.

LOVE describes the theatrical contexts of Congreve's work, and rebuts the enduring misconception that the Restoration audience consisted solely of aristocratic layabouts. The chapter on *The Old Bachelor* analyses its different forms of wit, showing that they are dramatically functional rather than decorative, in that they reveal mental isolation and express differences in power and self-assurance. In *The Double-Dealer*, the primary emphasis is on structural integrity rather than verbal display, for the leading characters have matured beyond wit, though its residue survives among the malicious fools. The discussions of *Love for Love* and *The Way of the World* concentrate rather narrowly on characters and their interaction, but nevertheless provide illuminating comment, especially on the interdependence of courtesy and hostility. In the concluding chapter, Love surveys the critics who have disparaged Congreve, and vigorously slaughters the Philistines.

WILLIAMS dissents sharply from Novak's view of Congreve as a religious sceptic: as a member of a predominantly Christian society, Congreve would have shared its views, and written works celebrating divine Providence. This argument exaggerates the unanimity of Christian belief in the late seventeenth century, and in any case a writer will not automatically speak for the moral majority. Williams even misunderstands the Christian homilists on whom he relies, ignoring their caveats that Providence should not be expected to intervene in domestic affairs in the way that it does in great national events. And there are many strained interpretations: in the chapter on *The Double-Dealer*, for example, the stage direction that Cynthia and Lord Touchwood "*abscond*" (hide) is, astonishingly, taken as an allusion to Pascal's *deus absconditus*. Williams imagines that the word "abscond" is ostentatiously unusual, but it is not, and it crops up in some very untheological contexts. (In Ravenscroft's *The London Cuckolds* a witty and wanton wife *absconds* while a rustic *ingenue* is bullied by her husband, and then emerges to give a demonstration of how husbands should be handled.)

MARKLEY examines the relationship between comic style and the ideology of the aristocracy (a term freely used to describe the gentry). His inquisitorial inflations and misrepresentations of class motive are often wearisome: even Thomas Sprat's famous prescriptions for scientific discourse in the *History of the Royal Society* are, "for all his talk about science and prose style", an expression of "upper-class ideology", his explicit preference of the language of artisans and countrymen being an "improbable fiction". Nevertheless, Markley provides an unprecedentedly sophisticated account of the forms and varieties of verbal wit. Congreve, he argues, reacted against his chief predecessors by restoring a relationship between language and morality. In *Love for Love* the language of wit is morally, and epistemologically, inadequate, and Congreve finally creates "a mode of expression to replace and transcend" it. In *The Way of the World* "the forms of wit are shared by fools and villains as well as by men of sense", and true decorum therefore "becomes a matter of the heart rather than of the tongue".

PETERS examines the place of the dramatist in a culture increasingly dominated by the printed book. There are many good passages (for example, the analyses of Congreve's explicit references to print), but also some intellectual laxity. She is very arbitrary in identifying the manifestations of print culture (even Millamant's love-letters count as honorary print). And, although contrast between Congreve's age and the past is central to her argument, she displays little knowledge of that past, falling back on vague and unsupported comparisons such as the statement that the classical world was becoming "less sacred" in Congreve's time.

THOMAS's book provides a good introductory survey, though in some peripheral respects it is out of touch with recent scholarship: for example, Lockean contract theory, though useful for elucidating Congreve himself, is no longer seen as the dominant political philosophy of the 1690s, and sentimental comedy did not swamp laughing comedy in the mid-eighteenth century. Thomas discusses the structure and characters of the plays, explains their political implications, and provides short chapters on theatre in the 1690s, and on the production history and critical reception of Congreve's works. Whereas Markley sees Congreve's women as linguistically and domestically underprivileged in a patriarchal world, Thomas (without mentioning Markley) argues that, in the proviso scene with Millamant, Mirabell renounces "most of the accepted signs of patriarchal control".

DEREK HUGHES

Conrad, Joseph 1857–1924

Polish-born English novelist and short-story writer

Achebe, Chinua, "An Image of Africa: Racism in Conrad's *Heart of Darkness*", in *Massachusetts Review*, 18, 1977

Erdinast-Vulcan, Daphna, *Joseph Conrad and the Modern Temper*, Oxford: Clarendon Press, 1991; New York: Oxford University Press, 1991

Fleishman, Avrom, *Conrad's Politics: Community and Anarchy in the Fiction of Joseph Conrad*, Baltimore: Johns Hopkins University Press, 1967

Guerard, Albert J., *Conrad the Novelist*, Cambridge, Massachusetts: Harvard University Press, 1958

Hawthorn, Jeremy, *Joseph Conrad: Narrative Technique and Ideological Commitment*, London and New York: Edward Arnold, 1990, revised 1992

Karl, Frederick R., *A Reader's Guide to Joseph Conrad*, New York: Noonday Press, 1960; London: Thames & Hudson, 1960

Leavis, F.R., *The Great Tradition: George Eliot, Henry James, Joseph Conrad*, London: Chatto & Windus, 1948; New York: G.W. Stewart, 1948

Najder, Zdzislaw, *Joseph Conrad: A Chronicle*, New Brunswick, New Jersey: Rutgers University Press, 1983; Cambridge: Cambridge University Press, 1983

Parry, Benita, *Conrad and Imperialism: Ideological Boundaries and Visionary Frontiers*, London: Macmillan, 1983

Sherry, Norman, *Conrad's Eastern World*, Cambridge: Cambridge University Press, 1966

Watt, Ian, *Conrad in the Nineteenth Century*, Berkeley: University of California Press, 1979; London: Chatto & Windus, 1980

White, Andrea, *Joseph Conrad and the Adventure Tradition: Constructing and Deconstructing the Imperial Subject*, Cambridge and New York: Cambridge University Press, 1993

Joseph Conrad is generally acclaimed as one of the most important fiction writers of the modern era, and attention to his work has increased exponentially since writers acknowledged his centrality in the 1940s. While earlier studies tended to work within New-Critical and formalist frameworks, subsequently biographical, historical, and political studies have mined the fiction in order to unearth other meanings. Recently, a post-colonial critical context has emerged as significant in Conrad studies.

LEAVIS's classic essay on Conrad aimed to change the perception of Conrad as a spinner of sea stories. He also criticized the tendency to emphasize Conrad's debts to French nineteenth-century novelists, since he wanted to claim Conrad for his "Great Tradition" of the English novel, along with George Eliot and Henry James. Leavis dismisses Conrad's early fiction, and is particularly harsh on *Heart of Darkness* and *Lord Jim*, two works especially valued by many readers, teachers, and critics. Leavis promoted *Nostromo* as Conrad's first great novel, in which his attention to French writers like Gustave Flaubert, along with intense work on fiction as craft, shows him to be a fully professional writer. Leavis then selects the novels of the middle period for examination, and on their basis claims that Conrad is "among the very greatest novelists in the language". Leavis's study was instrumental in initiating the first phase of Conrad scholarship and criticism.

Where Leavis places the writer in an English tradition, GUERARD linked Conrad with Thomas Hardy, André Gide, and William Faulkner. Guerard's was the first major American study of Conrad and, like Leavis's, it has become a classic. It is very interested in Conrad's relation to modernism, and thus in privileging themes like individualism and isolation, techniques like impressionism, and psychological modes of interpreting character. These concerns are set within a modernist critical context which assumes universalism as an unquestioned value, and adopts close study of the text to establish a work's literary integrity. Guerard follows Leavis in focusing on works of Conrad's middle period, but his estimates of the works differs: where Leavis dismisses *Heart of Darkness* and *Lord Jim*, Guerard treats the latter as centrally significant, is guarded in his praise of *Nostromo*, and asserts that "the time has come to drop *Victory* from the Conrad canon". Guerard's study remains a useful, serious introduction to Conrad's work.

KARL's *Guide* remains a useful starting-point for study of Conrad. Beginning with an account of how Conrad fell from critical favour after his death, and was subsequently recognized as an important twentieth-century writer by Leavis, Guerard, and others, Karl proceeds to claim Conrad as a modernist master in the ranks of Gide, Marcel Proust, D.H. Lawrence, James Joyce, Virginia Woolf, and Faulkner. He underlines also technical lessons taken from the French nineteenth-century novel. Karl announces his own approach as "new critical", involving emphasis on symbolic ordering in the fiction. Three useful chapters devoted to Conrad's aesthetic pronouncements (in which Conrad's Notes are compared to James's Prefaces), his "practice" (where Conrad is contextualized with French writers Guy de Maupassant and Flaubert, and with his occasional collaborator Ford Madox Ford), and his innovative use of time, are followed by chapters devoted to the major periods and novels. Karl, known for his work as Conrad editor and biographer, reclaims the writer as a significant modernist who established the novel as a major medium in formal terms, one able to engage with life from complex modern perspectives.

WATT's long, thorough study concentrates on Conrad's personal life up to 1894, and his writing life to 1900. Watt believed that his predecessors had not dealt adequately with questions of literary and intellectual history, and he seeks to remedy this lack while giving detailed interpretations of *Almayer's Folly*, *The Nigger of the "Narcissus"*, *Heart of Darkness*, and *Lord Jim*. Conrad, Watt believes, is a special case since the relation between his personal and writing life is so complex. Watt, therefore, looks closely at a number of issues, including Conrad's Polish history, the Romantic movement, traditions of the novel, impressionist and symbolist movements, and the treatment of time. Watt's study demonstrates how any consideration of Conrad as a pivotal modernist will be inaccurate unless it takes seriously his nineteenth-century heritage.

HAWTHORN presents a writer whose innovations in technique remain subordinated to a "view of the whole", a vision of human agents living and acting within a *moral* universe, so that Conrad's much-vaunted technical flexibility must be seen in relation to his commitment to order. Hawthorn maintains that Conrad was predominantly a materialist, so that his attitudes towards the world, as a moral universe, remained reasonably stable and unshakable. Hawthorn therefore rejects the contemporary tendency to re-evaluate Conrad's work in terms of relativism and contingency. Giving close attention to works representing every phase of Conrad's career, Hawthorn engages with ideologically weighted issues like race, class, gender, and imperialism, and concludes with the more traditional category of "imagination".

ERDINAST-VULCAN's study is representative of recent critical engagement with Conrad; in moving beyond formalist analysis, it seeks to relate Conrad to the post-Nietzschean crisis of modernity, which has radically relativized issues of epistemology, ethics, and aesthetics. Erdinast-Vulcan's Conrad is a figure of conflicts, recognizing his existence in a Copernican universe but – in his fiction – attempting to recover a Ptolemaic order of things. While she charts the course of Conrad's disillusionment with, respectively, myth, metaphysics, and textuality, she disavows the possibility of periodizing the fictional sequence. Acknowledging debts to such writers as Mikhail Bakhtin and Jacques Derrida, Erdinast-Vulcan finds Conrad to have been a "proto-deconstructionist"; consequently, the unevenness that several critics have noted in the novels is not symptomatic of aesthetic failure, but constitutes a principle of structure. Because *The Secret Agent* is artistically flawless, then, there is no discussion of that novel in the study. The modes and phases of Conrad's writing career are examined in close study of *Lord Jim*, *The Rescue*, *Nostromo*, *Heart of Darkness*, *Under Western Eyes*, *The Shadow-Line*, *Chance*, *Victory*, and *The Arrow of Gold*. This useful study relates Conrad's acute consciousness of the crisis of modernity to his self-awareness as an exiled figure, both actually and metaphorically.

FLEISHMAN establishes the importance of locating Conrad's politics in order to proceed to full interpretation of the fiction. He carefully takes into account Conrad's Polish birth and upbringing, his familiarity – through his Merchant Service career – with the processes and sites of European imperialism in the late nineteenth century, and his subsequent British affiliation. Fleishman insists on recognizing the complexity of, and contradictory elements in, Conrad's political thinking, but ultimately identifies his dominant philosophy as organicist, resistant to any formation making for anarchy: his "ideal society [is] a genuine community". Fleishman's study can be seen in the context of subsequent studies that have engaged in reassessing Conrad's Polish heritage on the one hand and his imperial and colonial involvements on the other. Fleishman pays more attention to the Malayan Archipelago ("Lingard") trilogy (*Almayer's Folly*, *An Outcast of the Islands*, and *The Rescue*) than previous critics, and devotes major chapters to each of *Nostromo*, *The Secret Agent*, and *Under Western Eyes*; *Nostromo*, he believes, "marks the fulfillment of Conrad's political imagination". This is an excellent text with which to begin a study of Conrad's extraordinarily complex politics.

ACHEBE's essay – a public university lecture in its original form – was instrumental for the emergence of work on Conrad from a postcolonial perspective. Achebe protests at the then predominant approach to *Heart of Darkness* as a metaphysical text, in which Africa figures only as backdrop for the degradation of European man, and Africans only as subhumans. He goes so far as to call Conrad a "bloody racist", and on that ground asserts that Conrad's most famous novella cannot be considered great literature. Achebe's essay has served as a critical provocation. It continues to haunt those subsequent studies that have turned from a universalist approach to one that situates Conrad's work, up to *Nostromo*, in the context of imperialism.

Although SHERRY's study of the Eastern seas, the archipelago world whose centre was Singapore, is not useful for help in theorizing Conrad's attitudes to imperialism and colonialism, it does offer the fruits of his research on this region and period in the novelist's life, and shows how Conrad translated hearsay, observation, experience, and reading into a rich body of fiction. His important study is "an attempt to recreate the world Conrad knew as a seaman in the East of the 1880s". Sherry's literary detective work is particularly relevant to study of *Lord Jim*, the Lingard trilogy, *The Shadow Line*, and a number of the stories. Sherry follows Conrad in not exaggerating elements of extraordinary adventure in the Eastern experience.

PARRY has produced a study which, like Achebe's essay, reacts against the dominant stream of work on Conrad, which has emphasized its literary qualities, psychological profundity, relation to modernism, and universal significance. She therefore insists on Conrad's historicity and specificity, and takes as context "the literary subculture of imperialism". Her study examines the early fiction up to, and including, *Nostromo*, with a particularly valuable chapter on *The Rescue*, not completed until late in Conrad's career. Parry asserts that Conrad endorsed the ideology of imperialism – the assumption of the superiority of the West. However, Conrad's fiction questions several of imperialism's leading assumptions, and reverses its representations, before recuperating it as normative and just. Conrad's subversion of imperial fiction went largely unrecognized by contemporary readers because it ultimately confirmed the doctrine that Europe as imperial centre was inherently morally superior to its colonial peripheries. Parry's study is careful, thorough, and well-organized; and she underlines the relation of her own work to the significant Conrad criticism that preceded her work.

WHITE's study throws light on some of Conrad's early fiction, particularly *Almayer's Folly*, *An Outcast of the Islands*, and *Heart of Darkness*, by exploring its relation to "imperial discourse" in the form of popular British adventure fiction of the nineteenth century's second half. White argues that the adventure stories of such writers as G.A. Henty, Charles Kingsley, H. Rider Haggard, and Robert Louis Stevenson were instrumental in characterizing the British imperial adventurer as normative hero for readers. While their imperial narratives provided a literary context for Conrad's earlier work, their assumptions were challenged by him; his questing adventurers are not motivated by patriotism, but by greed, and, far from achieving glory, they experience defeat and disillusionment in far-flung, exotic places. White, using Bakhtin's theory of monologic and dialogic discourses, claims that Conrad not only questions the imperialist's authority, but also gives a limited voice to his fictions' native characters and cultures. Conrad, therefore, subverts the adventure tradition along with its ideology of Eurocentric superiority, bringing inevitable progress to colonized outposts of empire.

The importance of NAJDER's biography is that it is the work of a leading Conrad scholar who, like his subject, became a Polish exile, and who recognizes how crucial an understanding of Conrad's Polish background, and his exceptional alienation, is to a reading of his works. Najder does not attempt to mix his biographical aims with the roles of literary critic or historian, nor does he believe that biography is necessarily important to forming an understanding or appreciation of literary works; but Conrad is, after all, a special case. Although Najder foregrounds Conrad's double status as Anglo-Pole, he gives his attention to the whole of his subject's life and career, and makes extensive use of quotation in building the life. Najder's substantial biography has both responded to, and stimulated recent interest in, Conrad as Pole and as "split subject".

PATRICK HOLLAND

Cooper, James Fenimore 1789–1851

American writer of novels, tales, and travel sketches

Darnell, Donald, *James Fenimore Cooper: Novelist of Manners*, Newark: University of Delaware Press, 1993; London: Associated University Presses, 1993

Dekker, George, *James Fenimore Cooper: The Novelist*, London: Routledge & Kegan Paul, 1967

House, Kay Seymour, *Cooper's Americans*, Columbus: Ohio State University Press, 1965

Ringe, Donald A., *James Fenimore Cooper*, New York: Twayne, 1962, revised (Boston) 1988

Spiller, Robert E., *Fenimore Cooper: Critic of His Times*, New York: Minton, Balch & Co., 1931; reprinted, New York: Russell & Russell, 1963

Wallace, James D., *Early Cooper and His Audience*, New York: Columbia University Press, 1986

Cooper critics emphasize his talent for writing frontier romances and maritime adventure stories, while noting his penchant for Americanizing both male and female characters as well as plots and settings. Cooper perceived the new Republic as an opportunity for giving humanity a second chance in the newly settled land of opportunity, a theme utilized by many of Cooper's contemporaries. Earlier critics define Cooper's role in, and contributions to, American literary culture, while later reviewers examine the development of his style as it either reflects or affects the growing young Republic.

SPILLER, in the earliest study discussed here, explores Cooper's role as social critic in contributing to his culture's "mental independence". Three stages of Cooper's development are noted: 1) pioneer society – Cooper reacted to polarities of aristocracy and democracy within and about him; 2) European residence – seven years abroad helped Cooper understand European corruption and prejudices; 3) American civilization after 1833 – when Cooper became dismayed by the discrepancy between the ideal and the real. Each of these periods is viewed as contributing to the development of Cooper's mature writing style.

HOUSE suggests that Cooper's characters represent the many "possibilities of American life", especially as they reflect his views as one of America's earliest Romantic historians. House recognizes over 400 clearly distinct American characters in Cooper's works, "subdivided into two general types". Most of his characters are representative; they interact with various moral and historical conflicts. Several sub-groups emerge, including women, Indians, Negroes, the Dutch, gentry, Yankees, and seamen. The second and third parts of his study follow the chronology of Cooper's novels.

DEKKER conducts a critical study of Cooper's fiction with attention to Cooper's politics, on the one hand, and to his "assimilation and development of the historical novel as first perfected by Sir Walter Scott", on the other. Dekker makes the point that Cooper's roles as social critic and as romancer "were not always at odds with each other". This study attempts to reconcile the potentially conflicting aspects of Cooper's life, which were reflected more or less harmoniously in his writing.

WALLACE analyzes reasons for Cooper's ready acceptance by examining the American literary context that prepared readers for Cooper's work: "in a surprisingly short time, Cooper succeeded in transforming both his art and his audience from awkward imitations of the English into something triumphantly American". In doing so, Cooper paved the way for his Romantic contemporaries and later realistic successors, who would continue to write for the audience that Cooper had in large part shaped, by acknowledging a relationship between reader, writer, and the publishing economics of his time. In attempting to improve his readers' tastes, he indirectly served the nation's developing cultural needs.

RINGE considers Cooper a moralist "whose work is the coherent expression of his fundamentally religious vision of life". The book suggests that Cooper's later work adopts an increasingly religious tone, and Ringe attempts to counter misunderstandings about Cooper by critics from Mark Twain through the mid-point of the twentieth century, emphasizing that Cooper's fundamentalist leanings enhance his style rather than diminish it.

DARNELL's book is devoted to the theme of manners as a significant aspect of Cooper's time, which has received scant critical attention either in his period, or since. Reviewing this theme in 15 of Cooper's works, including his first, *Precaution*, and his last, *The Ways of the Hour*, Darnell argues three main ideas: 1) Cooper balances serious or didactic motives with his social purpose to "satirize inappropriate behaviour and attitudes"; 2) the manners theme is central, not marginal, to Cooper's work; and 3) Cooper's "upper-class" characters instruct by example and admonition, as evidenced in the inextricable relations between money, manners, and morals in *Lionel Lincoln*. The influence of the manners theme in areas like patriotism, social status, class pride, and moral innocence are also explored.

DEBRA JOHANYAK

Corpus Christi Plays *see* Drama: Medieval

Cowper, William 1731–1800

English poet

Cecil, David, *The Stricken Deer, or, The Life of Cowper*, London: Constable, 1929; Indianapolis, Indiana: Bobbs-Merrill, 1930
Feingold, Richard, *Nature and Society: Later Eighteenth-Century Uses of the Pastoral and Georgic*, Hassocks, Sussex: Harvester Press, 1978; New Brunswick, New Jersey: Rutgers University Press, 1978
Hutchings, Bill, *The Poetry of William Cowper*, London and Canberra: Croom Helm, 1983
Newey, Vincent, *Cowper's Poetry: A Critical Study and Reassessment*, Liverpool: Liverpool University Press, 1982
Nicholson, Norman, *William Cowper*, London: John Lehmann, 1951
Priestman, Martin, *Cowper's Task: Structure and Influence*, Cambridge and New York: Cambridge University Press, 1983
Thomas, Gilbert, *William Cowper and the Eighteenth Century*, London: Nicholson & Watson, 1935; revised edition, London: Allen & Unwin, 1948
Spacks, Patricia Meyer, *The Poetry of Vision: Five Eighteenth-Century Poets*, Cambridge, Massachusetts: Harvard University Press, 1967

As Vincent Newey has remarked, William Cowper's early and substantial reputation rested more upon "his Evangelicalism, conservative morals and peculiar 'Englishness' than in a response to his strictly literary or intellectual qualities". One result of this has been that much twentieth-century criticism has been content to enlist Cowper's poetry simply to portray a quirky but lovable personality, a quintessentially domestic English spirit.

In the 1920s CECIL was already pointing to a tradition of Cowper scholarship that was largely biographical, beginning with the work of Hayley and others early in the nineteenth century; his own concern was to map such biographical information against "the trend and fluctuation of [Cowper's] solitary thought". For Cecil, in perhaps the most well-known study of the poet, Cowper is "the epitome of his environment", a poet of provincial domesticity; but he is also a poet of duality, for such domestic happiness is constantly challenged by religious madness, horror, and despair. Drawing largely upon the correspondence for this analysis, Cecil makes use of the poetry largely as versified letters, representing Cowper's imagination as rarely creative except when under the stress of intense emotional pressure. If his study now seems outdated, it remains useful as itself epitomising an extremely strong tradition of Cowper criticism.

THOMAS seeks to set Cowper specifically within the context of eighteenth-century Evangelicalism, which he argues is the dominant influence in the poet's life. Accordingly, Cowper's major poem, *The Task*, while marked by the personality of the poet, is "in its essential aim, scope, and sense of values, both a reflection and a product of the Methodist Revival". While the poem is recognized as manifestly contradictory, such contradictions are those of the "age" in which he lived. But Thomas's biographical approach also draws Cowper into the debates of the 1930s, claiming him for a contemporary English spirituality apparently beset by the pessimism of modern intellectuals; and if Cowper's poetry draws upon Evangelicalism, Thomas's reading of those poems becomes the defence of such a tradition.

NICHOLSON's study also recognizes the importance of the Evangelical Revival in Cowper's poetry, but seeks to draw a distinction between the early works, the *Olney Hymns* and the Moral Satires, and the later poems, most notably *The Task*, which he sees as part of a broader "Romanticism" in the later eighteenth century. There is much of use in Nicholson's work, including his account of the Hymns in relation to Isaac Watts and John Wesley, his discussion of the Homer translation (ignored by many critics), and his extensive treatment of *The Task*. In the latter he traces with great clarity Cowper's concern for the countryside in terms of God's revealed wisdom, but stresses also its function as a means of retreat from spiritual torment.

While Nicholson deals with Cowper's topography and the picturesque to some degree, that subject is taken up more fully by other critics. One such is PRIESTMAN, who concentrates specifically on *The Task*. Priestman's concern is to explore the structural design of the poem, partly with the aim of demolishing the myth that the poetry cannot be separated from the man. Instead, he suggests that this sense of authorial presence is quite deliberately exploited within the poem as a knowing and challenging "conundrum". With this in view he questions also the common emphasis upon Cowper's social realism, usefully exploring the extent to which such apparent objectivity is a function of the authorial self and its changing needs at different points within the poem. Having considered Cowper's debt to Horace in the central books of the poem, Priestman points in turn to Wordsworth's debts to Cowper in *The Prelude*, the poem that for many was to eclipse Cowper's major work.

HUTCHINGS' study of Cowper is very much an introductory survey of the poet's work, with chapters not only upon *The Task*, the *Hymns*, and the Satires, but also on many of the shorter poems. It is written with those new to both Cowper and the eighteenth century in mind and leads us through many of the basic issues. There are detailed readings of many of the poems along with helpful contextual material upon both the traditions from which Cowper drew and the literary environment in which he worked.

SPACKS' account of Cowper seeks to place him within a tradition of "poets of sensibility", along with James Thomson, Thomas Gray, William Collins, and Christopher Smart, and she admirably demonstrates the value of considering his work "in the light of the critical theory and the poetic conventions of [his] time" in conjunction with the expectations of close reading in our own. In particular, she explores "the visual and the visionary" in Cowper's writing, setting herself the task of examining the source and nature of his poetic effects. For Spacks, *The Task* in particular is a poem of "detail", offering a series of different ways of "seeing", which finally lead to the assertion that true perception is "a product of man's right relationship with God".

Like Spacks, FEINGOLD presents a series of close readings of Cowper's poetry but is concerned specifically with that poetry's more public expressions and with the georgic and pastoral contexts with which they engage. Concentrating once again upon *The Task*, Feingold suggests Cowper's poetry of apparent retreat is not "a mystification of capitalism" but rather "a prescient approach towards and bewildered withdrawal from the larger phenomenon of which capitalism is a part – the secularization of life, the divorce between ethics and politics, and the need for these to be acknowledged, named, envisioned, and interpreted".

In a series of eloquent and fruitful essays, NEWEY, like a number of recent critics, seeks to move away from an overly restrictive biographical approach to a limited group of Cowper's works and stresses instead both the range of the poet's work and the sense in which his poetry represents and explores a "dynamic centre of consciousness". This he aligns with both a Romantic and modernist attempt actively to create a "self" as a defence against a threatening universe: the necessity of repeated attempts and necessarily limited successes is, Newey argues, what makes Cowper part of a distinctly modern tradition.

STEPHEN BENDING

Crabbe, George 1754–1832

English poet

Bareham, Terence, *George Crabbe*, London: Vision Press, 1977; New York: Barnes & Noble, 1977

Edgecombe, Rodney Stenning, *Theme, Embodiment and Structure in the Poetry of George Crabbe*, Salzburg: Institut für Anglistik und Amerikanistik (Salzburg University), 1983

Edwards, Gavin, *George Crabbe's Poetry on Border Land*, Lewiston, New York, Queenstown, Ontario, and Lampeter, Dyfed: Edwin Mellen Press, 1990

Haddakin, Lilian, *The Poetry of Crabbe*, London: Chatto & Windus, 1955

Hatch, Ronald B., *Crabbe's Arabesque: Social Drama in the Poetry of George Crabbe*, Montreal and London: McGill-Queen's University Press, 1976

McGann, Jerome J., "The Anachronism of George Crabbe", in *English Literary History*, 48(3), 1981

New, Peter, *George Crabbe's Poetry*, London: Macmillan, 1976

George Crabbe is a poet who steadfastly resists period classification. His poetic career (albeit lengthened considerably by a 22 year hiatus from the composition of verse) bridged the eighteenth and nineteenth centuries: Crabbe earned fame with *The Village* (1783) in the Age of Johnson, but produced his best work, including *The Borough* (1810), as a contemporary of the English Romantic poets. Throughout his career Crabbe wrote in the heroic couplet but employed it to explore moral, social, and psychological themes in a decidedly post-Augustan manner. He was such an accomplished exponent of verse narrative that passages in some of his work appear to anticipate the development of realism later in the nineteenth century. This body of critical work illustrates the difficulties inherent to the assessment of a poet who belongs to no single period of English literature.

HADDAKIN redresses both the scant critical attention Crabbe commanded in the first half of the twentieth century and his few critics' overwhelming preoccupation with his poetry's social realism. She accomplishes this by scrutinising nineteenth-century critical assessments of the poet, revealing that Crabbe was not primarily thought of as an upholder of the eighteenth-century poetical tradition but rather as an "original" poet, whose propensity for rendering his subjects in minute detail facilitated a psychological – not sociological – analysis of human character. Demonstrating how Crabbe invites his readers to apply their own personal moral standards to the characters and situations depicted in his work, Haddakin argues that it is the "forcible spareness of expression" that is the distinctive quality of his poetic mode. It is in the later poems, notably *Tales of the Hall*, that Crabbe best achieves interaction between subject matter and expression. Despite its age, Haddakin's study is still a useful critical introduction to Crabbe's work.

Each of the three major studies published in the mid-1970s interrogate Crabbe's poetic accomplishment from an historical perspective. NEW adopts a chronological approach to explicate the literary and ethical contexts of Crabbe's poetry. Although he was a champion of the "old aesthetic of imitation", who consciously rejected the Romantic notion of "creative Imagination", Crabbe was nevertheless "poised between characteristically eighteenth- and nineteenth-century views of the moral effect of literature". Utilising Crabbe's correspondence and sermons, New convincingly demonstrates that Crabbe's religious conservatism was grounded in a belief that the world was governed by moral laws that were absolute, a world the individual navigated according to his conscience. In Crabbe's poetry society and the individual are represented as inseparable spheres of human existence.

HATCH's Crabbe is a complex figure. He is a natural heir of Jonathan Swift, Laurence Sterne, and Tobias Smollett in terms of his engagement with social, moral, and religious issues, but reveals his post-Augustan credentials by producing verse that embodies several, antithetical visions of the world and rejects the eighteenth-century belief in a providentially ordered universe. Crabbe's development of dramatic structures led him from the single-narrator, omniscient point of view typical of his early poems to the multiple narrators and conflicting points of view that characterise his later verse. In Hatch's estimation, *Tales of the Hall* is Crabbe's consummate artistic achievement because he created a dramatic structure that expressed the various dimensions of his own ambivalence of feeling. This work contains a useful select bibliography listing critical studies of Crabbe.

BAREHAM employs an historicist approach to examine Crabbe's verse in the contexts of the church he served as an ordained minister for 50 years, the political and social upheavals of the Regency, and the poet's interest in his age's scientific investigation of the human mind. Crabbe emerges in this study as a poet who wrote as a spiritual counsellor, displayed individualistic, liberal thinking, which placed him above party and creed, and who became increasingly fascinated by the "processes of liberation or dislocation of the psyche" associated with madness. Bareham surveys Crabbe's letters, notebooks, and fascicles for evidence of the poet's practice of self-criticism.

More recent studies primarily engage Crabbe in terms of the issues established by earlier critics. EDGECOMBE's is the exception: his study assesses Crabbe first and foremost as a poet, thus redressing critical appraisals of Crabbe that have privileged his roles as social critic, moralist, and storyteller. A synchronic approach in the first two chapters allows Edgecombe to examine Crabbe's major themes and poetic techniques, especially modes and tropes such as allegory, personification, and syllepsis. In the third and final chapter a diachronic approach is utilised to chart the evolution of Crabbe's themes and their poetic embodiment. A very good bibliography is a definite asset of this work.

McGANN seeks to rescue Crabbe from a critical tradition of polemical comparisons with the Romantics. Where Crabbe conceived of poetry in terms of the human, the social, and the historical, his Romantic contemporaries did so in terms of the divine, the inspirational and the transcendent. Crabbe's functional notions of poetry separate him from the Romantics – especially Wordsworth, who wrote poetry to impart theoretical solutions to problems based on the aesthetic of universal sympathy – because his verse taught readers critical and exploratory observation. McGann credits Crabbe with developing a new aesthetic: "his was a poetry of discovery and investigation, of empirical research whose initial limits would be set in scientific rather than in ideological terms".

EDWARDS is influenced by post-Saussurian literary theory's refusal to accept "realism" on its own terms. He argues that Crabbe's poetry "participated in, and illuminates for us, certain tensions in the relationship between existence and its formal representation", or "real" life and its "narrative organisation" (Life). The complex relationship between text and historical context in Crabbe's poetry is illustrated by his ambivalent attitude to narrative representation (most notably in his attitude towards "naming") and the deliberate formality of ritual, especially the rites of passage – baptism, marriage, and funeral – marking the transitional stages of the human life-cycle. "On border land" is the phrase Edwards coins to define those poetic narratives (such as *The Parish Register*) that interrogate instances when people fail to make the transition represented by a rite of passage, particularly the transition from the service-to-a-master relationship to the service-to-an-equal one demarcated by marriage. Crabbe displays an "insecure commitment to a narrative idea of life . . . linked, at every point, to his equally insecure commitment to the patriarchal language of 'service'". Edwards's study raises a number of pertinent issues that warrant investigation by future critics of Crabbe's verse.

GEORGE A. TRESSIDER

Crane, Hart 1899–1932

American poet

Berthoff, Warner, *Hart Crane: A Re-introduction*, Minneapolis: University of Minnesota Press, 1989

Dickie, Margaret, *On the Modernist Long Poem*, Iowa City: University of Iowa Press, 1986

Gelpi, Albert, *A Coherent Splendor: The American Poetic Renaissance 1910–1950*, Cambridge and New York: Cambridge University Press, 1987

Giles, Paul, *Hart Crane: The Contexts of "The Bridge"*, Cambridge and New York: Cambridge University Press, 1986

Smith, Ernest, *"The Imaged Word": The Infrastructure of Hart Crane's "White Buildings"*, New York: Peter Lang, 1990

Woods, Gregory, *Articulate Flesh: Male Homo-Eroticism and Modern Poetry*, New Haven, Connecticut, and London: Yale University Press, 1987

Yingling, Thomas E., *Hart Crane and the Homosexual Text: New Thresholds, New Anatomies*, Chicago: University of Chicago Press, 1990

Crane's reputation is based on his two major publications, *White Buildings* (1926) and *The Bridge* (1930). His *Collected Poems* appeared posthumously in 1933, incorporating previously unpublished work. While the lyric power and passionate density of the poems of *White Buildings* continues to be celebrated, *The Bridge* has frequently been written about in paradoxical terms as a brilliant failure. Crane intended it as an "epic of modern consciousness" and a mystical synthesis of the American past, present, and future, in which the central symbol of the poem, Brooklyn Bridge, is read both as a triumph of modern science and technology and as a symbol of America's "constructive future". Crane sought to infuse his poem with an optimistic faith in the spiritual possibilities of America in the 1920s, to repudiate American materialism and what he read as the spiritual negation of T.S. Eliot's vision in *The Waste Land*. The common view is that while *The Bridge* fails in its visionary ambition it stands as an important record of human spiritual aspirations. Recent studies of Crane show a new willingness to address the fact of his homosexuality sympathetically, and to see this as a crucial factor in his work.

DICKIE's study of the American long poem in this century is a collection of essays predominantly on T.S. Eliot, William Carlos Williams, Ezra Pound, and Crane. In her account of *The Bridge*, Dickie addresses what have always been seen as central problems – its organizational principle and its method of construction. Dickie traces the discrepancies between "the poem he imagined and the one he was able to write", and if she finally rejects the view that its organizing principle is sustained, she finds virtue in the sense that, while the poem degenerated in vision and in verbal power over the long process of its composition, it actually grew in strength through its representation of degeneration as an instrument of expressive form. This is a subtle reading of *The Bridge*, and this book as a whole offers an assured introduction to the twentieth-century American long poem. Dickie's study *Hart Crane: The Patterns of His Poetry* (1974) is one of the standard earlier commentaries.

GELPI's survey of 40 years of American modernist poetry includes a useful account of the creative and intellectual relationship between Crane and Allen Tate. In this book Gelpi argues that much modernist poetry is Janus-faced, in that its forward-looking revolutionary modernism is persistently, if often covertly, accompanied by a backward-looking appeal to the aesthetics of Romanticism. This argument is shown to particular effect in his reading of the Tate-Crane relationship, for while Tate thought Crane had written some of the best poems of the 1920s, he finally saw Crane as a poet trapped in a Romantic consciousness and unable to fulfil his ambitions in *The Bridge*. In his turn, Gelpi offers a persuasive defence of *The Bridge* in what he calls an "archetypal reading", where he pays particular attention to Crane's psychology and the conflictual expression of the masculine and feminine aspects of Crane's sense of his identity as these are mediated through the poem. Gelpi cannot entirely dissent from earlier sceptical views of *The Bridge*, and finally sees Crane's "Modernist masterpiece" as a "Romantic failure". Despite this, the value of Gelpi's chapter on Crane lies in his lucid statement of the problems critics have found with this work, and the arguments that can be made on Crane's behalf.

The subject of the verbal pun is at the centre of GILES's absorbing study of *The Bridge*, a poem he sees constructed out of a series of puns and paradoxes. In addition, Giles sets out the social and cultural contexts in which the poem should be seen, such as the historical moment of the poem's making, and its relation to its own period, which was (among other things) the Prohibition era, "when disguise and deception were all the rage". These contexts – which include the significance of contemporary American capitalism, cultural surrealism, ideas of relativity as informed by Einstein's theories, the advent of psychoanalysis, and the representation of eroticism – are all held to play their part in Crane's realisation of his version of modern American consciousness. Giles's attention to the pun as a functional conceit in the poem depends upon an understanding of the pun as an essentially subversive instrument of language, always in opposition to the conventional vocabulary of social relations and meaning as we ordinarily understand them. This is a clever and innovative study of *The Bridge*.

Though BERTHOFF's study is subtitled "*A Re-introduction*", this is a sophisticated reading of Crane, one of the best of recent years. Berthoff disputes Allen Tate's view of *The Bridge* as a poem incapable of realization because its "sublime subject" could not be "structurally clarified". Berthoff argues that Crane was a master of the formal lyric stanza, and holds that line and stanza became "acts of life" as well as acts of poetic faith for Crane. Thus he finds Crane's virtues in the local and particular where line and stanza are the primary expressive units, the elements that constitute his poems' authority for his readers and give the greatest pleasure. Berthoff makes good use of Crane's letters about the relationship between idea and poetic composition, and sees in these letters a "notable objectivity in self-judgment" at odds with the standard depiction of Crane as a Romantic agonist. In his reading of *The Bridge* Berthoff celebrates the "displayed inventiveness of its successive parts, the autonomy and form of their separate execution" rather than "any fully constituted and sustained action or theme". Thus *The Bridge* is read not as an example of modernist epic but as an intense lyric apostrophe, which yet embraces "the collective and historical".

SMITH shares Berthoff's conviction that Crane's achievement in *White Buildings* has been unduly overshadowed by *The Bridge*, and seeks to read the poems of the earlier volume as more than Crane's "lyric phase". He sees the poetics of *White Buildings* as impelled by a "logic of metaphor", in which images and units of phrasing echo each other connotatively throughout, establishing "associational meanings", which connect poem to poem through the attendant emotional dynamics of each image. Smith follows the final ordering of the poems in *White Buildings* against the early manuscript version to illustrate how Crane's "logic of metaphor" developed from a compositional technique within an individual poem to a structural device for the whole volume. Smith is less interested in *The Bridge*, and is content to rest his claims for Crane on *White Buildings*' "anguished but spirited resistance" to the denunciations of the modern. This is a very accessible account of Crane's earlier work, in which Smith's critical approach is largely determined by an aesthetic vocabulary taken from Crane's own account of his compositional methods, as given in his letters.

The homoerotic dimension of Crane's work is eloquently and sympathetically anatomised by WOODS in his major study of homoeroticism in modern poetry, in which he pays particular attention to the work of D.H. Lawrence, W.H. Auden, Allen Ginsberg, and Thom Gunn, as well as Crane. Woods seeks to redress the ambivalent treatment of Crane's homosexuality, and its impact on his poems, in the majority of his critics until very recently, and works through an insistent scrutiny of Crane's images and vocabulary from the earliest poems through to *White Buildings* and *The Bridge*. Woods's readings are brilliant and persuasive, and no student of Crane can afford to ignore this study.

Like Woods, YINGLING is a passionate critic of the failures and evasions of earlier criticism of Crane in its handling of his homosexuality, though in Yingling's work this argument has a wider focus. Yingling believes that homosexuality has been customarily erased from the canonical discussions of American poetry in favour of what he calls "myth criticism", a mode of commentary that sees literary production in America "under a series of national mythic terms such as the frontier, the self, the Edenic or Adamic", terms that have established an individual and national, validatory authority. In this book Yingling reads Crane within "a sexual-critical matrix that highlights the problem of sexual identity and practice rather than allowing it to be glossed in a national-cultural matrix in which the issue disappears". Yingling's account of the critical reception of Crane's work is very impressive in the way it anatomizes the pervasive view that Crane's talent was imperilled by his alcoholism and homosexuality, and his counter-argument for a re-orientation of criticism, to take Crane's homosexuality as a central feature of his creative life and achievement, now seems unarguably right. This is an important revisionary study of both Crane and, more generally, the homosexual writer in American culture.

LIONEL KELLY

Crane, Stephen 1871–1900

American novelist, short-story writer, poet, and war correspondent

Ahnebrink, Lars, *The Beginnings of Naturalism in American Fiction: 1891–1903: A Study of the Works of Hamlin Garland, Stephen Crane and Frank Norris*, Uppsala, Sweden: Lundequistska, 1950; reprinted, New York: Russell & Russell, 1961

Benfey, Christopher, *The Double Life of Stephen Crane*, New York: Knopf, 1992; London: André Deutsch, 1993

Bergon, Frank, *Stephen Crane's Artistry*, New York: Columbia University Press, 1975

Berryman, John, *Stephen Crane*, New York: William Sloane, 1950; London: Methuen, 1950

Fried, Michael, *Realism, Writing, Disfiguration: On Thomas Eakins and Stephen Crane*, Chicago: University of Chicago Press, 1987

Halliburton, David, *The Color of the Sky: A Study of Stephen Crane*, Cambridge and New York: Cambridge University Press, 1989

Katz, Joseph, (ed.), *Stephen Crane in Transition: Centenary Essays*, DeKalb: Northern Illinois University Press, 1972

Mitchell, Lee Clark (ed.), *New Essays on "The Red Badge of Courage"*, Cambridge and New York: Cambridge University Press, 1986

Pizer, Donald (ed.), *"The Red Badge of Courage": An Authoritative Text; Backgrounds and Sources; Criticism*, 3rd edition, New York: Norton, 1994

Stallman, Robert Wooster, *Stephen Crane: A Critical Bibliography*, Ames: Iowa State University Press, 1972

STALLMAN's bibliography, an essential reference work, which provides multiple sources for the study of Crane, is divided into six sections: the first three are a descriptive bibliography of Crane's books; the fourth catalogues contemporary reviews and parodies from the period 1893–1904; the fifth arranges Crane's works, manuscripts, and typescripts in alphabetical order; and the last lists, alphabetically and chronologically, critical writings on Crane from 1888 to 1970. Jean Cazemajou's Introduction explains the need for such a comprehensive volume in order to counteract Thomas Beer's *Stephen Crane: A Study in American Letters* (New York, 1923), a work which "contributed more to the literature of devotion than to a correct assessment of Crane's achievement".

KATZ presents his collection as an attempt to deconstruct the Crane legend so as to reconstruct his reputation as a writer and to transform Crane criticism "from worshipful amateurism to respectful professionalism". Katz's Afterword provides details of manuscripts, Crane library collections, and summaries of bibliographies and biographies, while suggesting areas for further Crane research. In an earlier essay Katz analyses the writings and the fluctuating critical reactions to Crane of his contemporary Theodore Dreiser, both before and after Crane's premature death. Also of note is Bernard Weinstein's discussion of Crane's journalism which, while paralleling his literary career, "reflects the several stages of his philosophical and artistic development and offers perhaps the best barometer of his attitude toward man and his place in the universe". Weinstein discovers a growing celebration of man's heroism and endurance in the face of nature's extremes, and believes that Crane's war journalism displays "a lean and stoic masculinity" suggestive of Hemingway. Other essays include: Cazemajou's situating of *The Red Badge of Courage* within a context of conflict, which he traces through Crane's other writings; Bruccoli's exploration of Crane's market value at sales and auctions since his death; and Colvert's discussion of Crane's personal vision and construction of realism, in which he quotes Crane's dual approach to poetry and fiction – "my aim was to comprehend in [the poetry] the thoughts I have had about life in general, while 'The Red Badge' is a mere episode in life, an amplification".

The five essays dealing specifically with *The Red Badge* contained in MITCHELL's book discuss Crane's novel as a novel of war (Delbanco); as intended ironic statement about both Henry Fleming's heroism and the ability to write a comprehensive war novel (Brooke-Rose); as a work based on a set of binary oppositions and double perspectives, which undermine Fleming's character and any possibility of a simple resolution (Horsford); as a book that was edited and revised to suit contemporary public attitudes and to accommodate market forces (Parker); and as a study reflective of the growing street violence of the nineteenth-century American cities and of the increased militarism of the age on both sides of the Atlantic (Kaplan). Kaplan's essay, which also appears in Pizer's study, importantly re-views the depicted battle scenes as spectacle, while accepting Crane's deliberate decontextualizing of the conflict as a specific moment in the American Civil War. Kaplan also notes Crane's reduction of history and the historical novel in a work about social change and "the transition not only from internecine to international conflict or from preindustrial to mechanized forms of warfare, but also from traditional to modern views of representation".

For a detailed study of the text of *The Red Badge*, of its background, sources, revisions, and critical appraisals,

PIZER's volume, which includes the short story sequel "The Veteran" as well as selected Crane letters and unpublished passages of the novel, is invaluable. Among the essays, Fraser and Cox discuss the work's war context; Rechnite and Henderson focus on the role of history in Crane's narrative, and the manner in which he employs differing versions of history – the narrator's, Fleming's, other soldiers – to provide an ironic context for Fleming's "growth", as well as alternate perspectives which displace the notion of any one true history; Walcutt and Nagel argue opposing views of Crane's naturalistic/impressionistic mode of representation; and Pizer concentrates on Crane's deliberately ambivalent characterization and contextualization of Fleming which, he argues, survives despite editorial excisions and textual differences between early editions of the novel.

BERRYMAN's biography, dependent on Beer's earlier work, attempts to correlate Crane's life and those of his characters with recourse to Freudian and psychoanalytic readings of the texts. Despite his personal agenda, Berryman produces one writer's stimulating appreciation of another, whom he considers to be a "genius". Believing Crane not to be a naturalist, Berryman maintains that he was a writer "alone in a room with the English language, trying to get human feelings right", trying to explain his vision and version of the world without losing sight of the nature of humanity. For Berryman, Crane's works are experimental pieces populated not by traditional fleshed-out characters but by brief sketches and outlines of individual human traits and emotions at the mercy of the workings of fate. What Crane produced as a result "is a series of extremely formidable, *new*, compact, finished, and distressing works of art".

The main focus of BENFEY's work is also biographical, though he avoids the unreliable Beer material. By providing the basic details of the family's religious background, as well as citing Crane's mother's Temperance work, Benfey established a backdrop against which to reassess Crane's own somewhat bohemian lifestyle in conjunction with the characters that he created. Although he seeks to draw parallels between Crane's real and fictive worlds, Benfey raises some important points in relation to the writings, which he observes, are "notable for their absent fathers, their harassed and difficult mothers", possibly because of Crane's father's death when the writer was only eight years old. Benfey promotes a link, both within Crane's mind and his work, between language and bereavement – "words filled a space where people once breathed" – and he correctly asserts that the characters are continually presented in exposed and vulnerable states.

AHNEBRINK's study focuses on the growth of naturalism in the fictions of Crane, Frank Norris, and Hamlin Garland. With reference to Crane, he analyses the writings with regard to influences from French naturalists (Zola) and Russian fatalists (Tolstoy). Ahnebrink, in outlining the late nineteenth-century shift in American writing – towards forms of realism, capable of presenting truer accounts of the developing country and its cities, and away from the idealistic romanticism of previous decades – sees in Crane's works an effort to fuse attention to realistic detail with deterministic notions of human fate. He judges characters such as Crane's Maggie to be victims of both a malevolent universe and of a brutal, male-structured world, while Fleming and the soldiers in *The Red Badge* are degraded and dehumanised by the circumstances of war and by the manoeuvrings of the opposing side's generals.

FRIED focuses on what he terms the "problematic of the materiality of writing as that materiality enters Eakins's paintings and Crane's prose". In his Crane section, he extends the metaphor of the recurring upturned faces in Crane's writings as reflective of the blank canvas of the page and of its gradual covering-over and ultimate burial by ink and words. In addition, he discusses a recurring theme in Crane criticism, that of the emphasis on the importance of seeing and observation on the part of the characters, readers, and author alike.

HALLIBURTON's close commentary on Crane texts, while concerning itself with the author's perception and presentation of characters, colours, and images, and providing interesting viewpoints on areas of works such as *Maggie* and a selection of the short stories, undermines such points of note with dubious conclusions as to authorial intent. Halliburton is correct in viewing the Bowery district as a characteristically violent place in which excesses of alcohol led to familial unrest and domestic abuse, and he highlights how the characters, in this state of violent inertia, become mere consumers; but he misreads such depictions of alcohol-related discord as evidence of Crane being "as clear as any reformed" on this issue. Further, when he claims that Maggie, an abused girl forced to become a prostitute, finds in her destitution "a positive sense of the propriety of her appearance", he has confused a victimised female's compliance with the whims of the sordid male-oriented marketplace for an expression of a new-found freedom and self-confidence.

The central thrust of BERGON's argument is that Crane – through the use of "nameless, fragmented, depersonalized" characters, a segmented prose style which depends upon an episodic structure, a recurring "indefiniteness of statement", and a refusal to provide a single vision – deliberately implicates the reader in an uncomfortable participation with the literary text. Easy resolutions and simple readings are disallowed in Crane's panoramic representations of human situations. Again, acts of seeing and perception are seen to lie at the centre of Crane's art, with the reader not on the outside as a passive observer, but on the inside, with the narrator, actively perceiving and figuring the surrounding world.

PHILIP MCGOWAN

Crime Fiction

Baker, Robert A., and Michael T. Neitzel, *"Private Eyes: One Hundred and One Knights": A Survey of American Detective Fiction, 1922–1984*, Bowling Green, Ohio: Bowling Green State University Press, 1985

Bell, Ian A., and Graham Daldry (eds.), *Watching The Detectives: Essays on Crime Fiction*, London: Macmillan, 1990

Binyon, T.J., *"Murder Will Out": The Detective in Fiction*, Oxford and New York: Oxford University Press, 1989

Docherty, Brian (ed.), *American Crime Fiction: Studies in the Genre*, London: Macmillan, 1988; New York: St Martin's Press, 1988

Klein, Kathleen Gregory, *The Woman Detective: Gender and Genre*, Urbana: University of Illinois Press, 1988
Symons, Julian, *Bloody Murder: From the Detective Story to the Crime Novel: A History*, London: Faber & Faber, 1972; as *Mortal Consequences: A History from the Detective Story to the Crime Novel,* New York: Harper & Row,1972; 4th revised edition, London: Pan Books, 1994
Tani, Stefano, *The Doomed Detective: The Contribution of the Detective Novel to Postmodern American and Italian Fiction*, Carbondale: Southern Illinois University Press, 1984
Winks, Robin W. (ed.), *Detective Fiction: A Collection of Critical Essays*, Englewood Cliffs, New Jersey: Prentice-Hall, 1980; revised edition, Woodstock, Vermont: Countryman Press, 1988

Crime fiction, which certain critics claim to be a descendant of the Oedipus myth and the Grail legend, accommodates various sub-categories, such as the police novel and the spy novel; the eight books reviewed here provide introductory approaches to the study of each of these. The exploits of the earliest (self-conscious) fictional detective, Edgar Allan Poe's Auguste Dupin, have been adapted and expanded upon by generations of writers who have produced novels and short stories that either revel in pure detection in remote and unreal locations, or attempt to produce works that realistically display the crime-ridden landscapes of Western society.

SYMONS provides a chronological history of the development of the detective story from its earliest incarnations in the *Oedipus* trilogy and novels such as William Godwin's *Caleb Williams* and Charles Dickens's *Bleak House* up to the work of more recent practitioners – Paul Auster, Colin Dexter, Umberto Eco, and Elmore Leonard. Regarded as a benchmark text, this work analyses how the detective story's popularity increased due to the writings of Arthur Conan Doyle, Agatha Christie, Georges Simenon, and Ellery Queen, and offers comparisons between the "Golden Age" of British crime writers and their American "hard-boiled" counterparts Dashiell Hammett and Raymond Chandler. Discussing the genre in relation to the fluctuating relationship between the short story and the novel, Symons includes brief references to an extensive list of lesser names in the field.

WINKS's collection gathers together over 50-years worth of essays from both crime writers and critics, which seek to provide an historical explanation for the genre's existence and an analytical reason for its continuing success. Beside the conservative contributions of W.H. Auden, Dorothy L. Sayers, and Ronald Knox, which promote detective fiction as a formulaic mode of writing, are placed essays focusing on the genre's ability, especially in America, to become a subversive form of fiction. George Grella's two essays detail the British pure-puzzle stories in opposition to the efforts of the American writers to provide a more realistic fiction, which depicts society as essentially evil and corrupt, with the detective as a lone hero defending the weak. In conjunction with this, Ross Macdonald's discussion of Hammett's, and especially Chandler's, legacy to the genre is of particular interest.

BAKER and NIETZEL's at times amusing survey of American private-eyes and BINYON's history of the fictional character of the detective both offer exhaustive listings of writers and their heroes and are essential reference works for those intent on tracing the genre's progress in the hands of now-famous writers and among the ranks of perhaps more obscure authors.

The 11 essays in BELL and DALDRY's book aim to reassess the work of canonical detective-fiction writers such as Poe, Christie, Chandler, and John le Carré, while also examining the work of Patricia Highsmith, George V. Higgins, William McIlvanney, and other writers who have received less critical attention. Lyn Pykett's essay reveals how female writers have been unable to subvert the conservative male values of detective fiction despite attempts at feminising the central character, while the articles by Richard Ireland and John Simons correlate the crime fiction of authors with the factual accounts of pathologists and criminologists.

A more theoretical approach to the study of crime fiction, with essays seeking to provide psychoanalytical, semiotic, linguistic, cultural, and Marxist analyses of the texts of Poe, Hammett, Chandler, Mickey Spillane, Jack Higgins, James M. Cain, and Jerome Charyn, is the aim of DOCHERTY's collection of nine essays. Peter Humm and Gary Day's contributions, which focus on the hard-boiled writers' use of a realistic narrative style to portray a real world of gangsters and Prohibition, are of note, while Christopher Rollason's re-reading of Jacques Lacan's and Jacques Derrida's interpretations of "The Purloined Letter" explains the intricate double nature of Poe's detective Dupin as essential for his solving of the mystery.

KLEIN traces the growth of the female detective from Andrew Forrester's Mrs Gladden in 1864 forward to the heroines in the fictions of Sue Grafton, Sara Paretsky, Marcia Muller, and Susan Steiner. By mapping this character's development on both sides of the Atlantic in relation to more than a century of social issues that have affected the position of the female within Western society, she discovers that crime fiction, "especially in its action stories and even in its classical form, encodes gender-based structures of power" which seek to undercut the female detective's role and portray her as a subversive threat to the male hegemony: "like a spy, she is an intruder into the public realm controlled by masculinist, patriarchal power".

TANI, who includes a comprehensive bibliography, furnishes an analysis of the genre that departs from the more orthodox historical approaches of most critics of crime fiction. Dismissing the British "Golden Age" as productive of "essentially novels-of-manners", Tani reveals that his interest centres partly on the tough-guy heroes of Hammett and Chandler but, more significantly, on postmodernist formulations of "anti-detective" fiction which, although initially employing the conventions of the genre, disappoint the reader by not solving the mystery. These thereby subvert the traditional and highly conservative rationale of detective fiction, in which the detective restores social order and the criminal is brought to justice. Tani identifies three strains of anti-detective fiction – the "Innovative Anti-Detective Novel", the "Deconstructive Anti-Detective Novel", and the "Metafictional Anti-Detective Novel" – and discusses these in relation to Italian and American authors, such as Umberto Eco, Leonardo Sciascia, Italo Calvino, John Gardner, and Thomas Pynchon. In each of these three phases, the puzzle and detection become decreasingly important and the conventional elements of the genre are mostly removed from the text: "the detective is the reader making sense out of an unfinished fiction that has been distorted or cut short by a playful and perverse 'criminal', the writer".

PHILIP MCGOWAN

Critical Theory *see* Literary Theory

Cultural Materialism *see* New Historicism

Cummings, E.E. 1894–1962

American poet

Dumas, Bethany K., *E.E. Cummings: A Remembrance of Miracles*, New York, Barnes & Noble, 1974; London: Vision Press, 1974

Fairley, Irene R., *E.E. Cummings and Ungrammar: A Study of Syntactic Deviance in His Poems*, Searingtown, New York: Watermill, 1975

Friedman, Norman, *E.E. Cummings: The Art of His Poetry*, Baltimore: Johns Hopkins University Press, 1960; London: Oxford University Press, 1960

Friedman, Norman, *E.E. Cummings: The Growth of a Writer*, Carbondale: Southern Illinois University Press, 1964

Kennedy, Richard S., *Dreams in the Mirror: A Biography of E.E. Cummings*, New York: Liveright, 1980

Kennedy, Richard S., *E.E. Cummings Revisited*, New York: Twayne, 1994; Oxford: Maxwell Macmillan, 1994

Lane, Gary, *I Am: A Study of E.E. Cummings' Poems*, Lawrence: University Press of Kansas, 1976

Marks, Barry, *E.E. Cummings*, New York: Twayne, 1964

Norman, Charles, *The Magic Maker: E.E. Cummings*, New York: Macmillan, 1958; revised edition, New York: Duell, Sloan, and Pearce, 1964

NORMAN's rather uncritical account of Cummings' life and work is less an analysis of the poet's achievement and influences than simply a collection of letters, anecdotes, recollections and apologies. Written after a 32-year friendship with the artist, and with Cummings' co-operation and approval, the book contains numerous previously unpublished letters, personal reminiscences of both the author and the artist, a description of Cummings' relationship with other artists and publishers, and some account of the early critical response to Cummings' work. Published in 1958, it is the first account of Cummings' early life. Undoubtedly a useful source for later, more critical studies, this book lacks the focus and perspective necessary for a balanced account of Cummings' achievement.

FRIEDMAN's book, published only two years after Norman's, is a much more useful work for one who welcomes a little assistance in making sense of Cummings' unusual techniques as well as his poetic voice, vision and general development. Although it, too, was written with the co-operation of Cummings, the book has a straightforward critical tone. Friedman is not concerned with biography, psychology, or even the telling anecdote; his concern is the poetry, with the "qualities of imagination and sensibility" that it reveals and elicits from the reader. He notes early on that "it is the right of any poet to be evaluated in terms of what he does rather than in terms of what he should do", and he points out that the critical reception of Cummings' work was sometimes misguided. Friedman presents, with considerable success, a fuller analysis of the whole body of Cummings' work as well as individual poems or techniques. He devotes much of the book to discussing Cummings as a visionary, a moralist, and a craftsman. He attempts to make sense of Cummings' approach to poetic language and style, his "calculated dislocations", which the poet himself termed "carnalized metaphysics; or abstraction raised to the power of the concrete". The final chapters are devoted to a detailed analysis of the numerous revisions of a single poem and a spirited defense of Cummings' artistic growth from his earliest publications to *95 Poems* (1959).

MARKS' brief book is the first of two on Cummings that Twayne commissioned (the other, by Kennedy, appeared in 1994 – see below). In his Preface, Marks notes his approach of analyzing a few poems thoroughly rather than touching on many or tracing the growth of the author's ideas or his development as an artist. It means, Marks notes, "sacrificing comprehensiveness in the interest of concentration". Yet, in 123 pages the book also tackles Cummings as art critic, his relationship to other artists and traditions, his quintessential American qualities, his "esthetics of realism", and other topics. There are some useful readings of individual poems, and interesting observations of Cummings' use of children and of sexuality to startle and engage his readers.

FRIEDMAN's second book (1964) is an assessment of all of Cummings' writings, the plays and lectures as well as the poetry, in order to chart the poet's artistic growth. He begins with an introductory chapter on Cummings' "transcendental vision" of Nature, human nature, and art. It is a vision that emphasizes truth over facts, intuition and insight over reason and knowledge. It is a vision, as Cummings noted in his final lecture, that "affirms that love is the mystery-of-mysteries, and that nothing measurable matters". Friedman is careful to distinguish Cummings' work from that of mere romantic sentimentalism. That Cummings' art is grounded in poetic tradition is what makes his innovations interesting and largely successful. Although generally appreciative, Friedman makes no claim that Cummings' experiments in his poetry and plays are uniformly successful. Cummings, he notes on several occasions, can be both heavy-handed and obscure. Yet in terms of Cummings' overall achievement – his bold efforts to escape categorization, to capture the power and fluidity of the present while focusing on the transcendental, to stretch the imagination through creative use of language and form – he was remarkably effective. Friedman divides the work by decades, in order to analyze both the intent and achievement at various stages of the artist's life. He insists that Cummings' theories of art must be understood in order for us to appreciate fully his work.

DUMAS' book is one of several volumes in the Barnes & Noble "Critical Studies" series. It is a brief, 140-page study, designed as an introduction to readers unfamiliar with Cummings or the criticism on him. Thirty-five pages are devoted to biography, 56 to the poetry, 26 to the prose, and 16 to the drama. She relies heavily on Friedman's work, and offers little that is new or noteworthy. She does, though, sum up Cummings nicely in her final sentence, noting that "he was the most traditional of innovators and the most innovative of traditionalists".

LANE's short study of Cummings' themes and techniques is a persuasive, crisp, to-the-point analysis of the poet's unique contribution to twentieth-century poetry. Although the novice will find it very readable and useful, the book's references to T.S. Eliot, W.B. Yeats, Robert Frost, Wallace Stevens, Robert Lowell, Theodore Roethke, and other contemporaries – as well as the Romantic poets, Shakespeare, and mythology – are helpful for those who wish to have some sense of Cummings *vis-à-vis* other poets. Lane notes that the price of being an experimental writer is often failure, and many of the poems are "thematically and technically repetitious". Some traits, such as Cummings' relentless subjectivity, his insistence on "the sanctity of his personal private vision", and the intransigence of his idealism, were the source for both trival verse and for powerful poems that will remain "permanently interesting". Lane's explication of numerous poems reveals the strength of his case that the poet had "a firm and affirmative vision, structural discipline, and the magical power to make language 'stir and squirm'".

FAIRLEY's study of Cummings' "ungrammar" provides a fresh approach to the poet's use of poetic language and form. Except for Friedman's, all earlier books are rather general introductions aimed primarily at the novice and the reader who balks at, or resents, Cummings' unusual style. Subtitled *A Study of Syntactic Deviance in His Poems*, the book is a carefully focused linguistic analysis of Cummings' style, especially his irregular word order. She applies the theoretical insights and vocabulary of linguistics in an attempt to explain what Cummings was doing with language: how his unusual syntax, orthography, compounding, adverb and adjective displacement, etc. are an integral part of a poem's structure and meaning, often creating unexpected and intriguing ambiguities and alternative readings. Cummings' poems, she notes, "raise questions that underlie all poetic language". She examines how specific words and phrases function in particular poems in order to understand how Cummings is able "to transgress rules without tipping the scales, by experimenting with certain levels and keeping others very much in check". This is an informed analysis of the poet's linguistic acrobatics, suggesting possibilities for further study.

KENNEDY's 1980 volume, the first book-length biography of the poet, is a well-documented, perceptive, and balanced study of the events and personalities that influenced Cummings. Kennedy makes excellent use of a great deal of material, especially that concerning Cummings' childhood and adolescence, which was not previously available. In his detailed account of the love, coddling, concern, and high expectations that surrounded the youthful poet, the biographer shows us the seeds of many of the traits of Cummings' poetry and personality, which were to flower many years later. The different sides of his nature did not always blend harmoniously. His individualism could be both inspiring and, at times, narrowly self-serving. His idealism resulted in highly original poems celebrating the spiritual over the material; yet it could also appear as self-righteous self-satisfaction. Here we find the loyal friend and devoted son, the rebel, the immature husband and father, the conservative iconoclast, and the devoted artist who spent a lifetime crafting a unique style against formidable odds. A fuller discussion of the poetry itself, and its place *vis-à-vis* his contemporaries and poetic tradition, would have made this informed and informative book complete.

KENNEDY's 1994 volume for the Twayne series is a critical study of the poetry and prose, with only minimal biographical detail. It is addressed, as the Preface notes, "to the general reader, especially the college student who is interested in modern poetry". As such, it is a general introduction, which attempts to highlight Cummings' growth as an artist, the uneven success of his linguistic experiments, and some of his contribution to modern verse. Kennedy includes a variety of poems from different periods in Cummings' career to give the reader a sense of how this artist "often tumbled", but at times achieved a "unique quality", which has had a "lasting impact" on twentieth-century literature.

DANNY L. ROBINSON

D

Davies, Robertson 1913–1995

Canadian novelist, dramatist, and critic

Buitenhuis, Elspeth, *Robertson Davies*, Toronto: Forum House, 1972

Davis, J. Madison (ed.), *Conversations with Robertson Davies*, Jackson: University Press of Mississippi, 1989

Grant, Judith Skelton, *Robertson Davies*, Toronto: McClelland & Stewart, 1978

Lawrence, Robert G., and Samuel L. Macey (eds.), *Studies in Robertson Davies' "Deptford Trilogy"*, Victoria, British Columbia: University of Victoria Press, 1980

Monk, Patricia, *The Smaller Infinity: The Jungian Self in the Novels of Robertson Davies*, Toronto and Buffalo, New York: University of Toronto Press, 1982

Morley, Patricia A., *Robertson Davies*, Agincourt, Ontario: Gage Educational, 1977

Peterman, Michael, *Robertson Davies*, Boston: Twayne, 1986

Stone-Blackburn, Susan, *Robertson Davies, Playwright: A Search for the Self on the Canadian Stage*, Vancouver: University of British Columbia Press, 1985

Robertson Davies emerged over the years as one of Canada's most popular writers. For the most part, criticism of his work has been thoughtful and engaging, although mainly confined to Canadian scholarship and to his fiction rather than his plays. However, the critical approaches are wide and varied, reflecting the abundance of facts, themes, and ideas in Davies's work. Davies's novels are parts of trilogies, a point that is inescapable when examining them in any detail. Similarly, Davies's fascination with the work of psychologist Carl Jung – particularly in *The Deptford Trilogy* – has caused much discussion and debate. At the centre of these debates is the complexity of Davies's characters as they struggle to come to a sense of a self in an increasingly complex world.

BUITENHUIS's brief but informative book is one of the initial attempts to examine Davies's work. Examining both his plays and his fiction up to *Fifth Business* (1970), Buitenhuis's analysis concentrates on the satirical and romantic elements of his novels. Claiming he is the only writer of the "satirical romance", she traces how satire continually undercuts the world of romance, forcing his novels to "walk a tightrope between two forms which are at opposite ends of human experience". However, the study is lacking in depth because of its publication date, before the completion of *The Deptford Trilogy*.

Another brief book aimed at the general reader is MORLEY's. Morley provides plot summaries of most of Davies's plays up to *Question Time* (1975), followed by brief analyses. Best suited to undergraduate students, Morley's study is restricted to Davies's drama; however, she does note that the study of Davies's drama casts light on his fiction, and vice versa, and she points out how they both contribute to the forging of a national literature. She also aptly notes that Davies abhors sentimentality, and that "the special quality of his comedies lies in their being romantic without being sentimental, or romantic and satiric at once". The blending of these comedic qualities is examined in detail in each play. Of particular interest to scholars of Canadian drama is STONE-BLACKBURN's study. She believes that "the story of Robertson Davies, playwright, is part of the larger story of the growth of Canadian drama". As a result, her book contributes much of the rise of modern Canadian drama to the efforts of Davies.

GRANT sees the progression of the protagonists in Davies's works as conceived out of his love for information, and refined over time. She believes Davies's protagonists "live life in relation to ideas learned", with these ideas emerging from numerous sources, but rooted essentially in myth and philosophy. Although Grant has a tendency to lapse into simple admiration for Davies's work, she is thorough in her thesis.

The collection of nine essays by Canadian critics in LAWRENCE's text is varied in its subject matter, and includes an important essay by Davies himself on "*The Deptford Trilogy* in Retrospect". Also of note is Macey's essay on "Time, Clockwork, and the Devil in Robertson Davies", in which he connects the history of horology with the characters' obsessions with time and their relationship to Western civilization. Other essay topics include: *The Salterton Trilogy*, folklore in *The Deptford Trilogy*, public figures, autobiography, Jung, the law, archaeology, and Canadian theatre.

MONK's book details the influence of Jung on both Davies and his novels up to and including *World of Wonders* (1975). It is an ambitious undertaking, and Monk begins by examining early evidence of Jungian influence, such as journalism pieces and interviews. Although Monk is thorough, she has been accused – by Peterman (see below), for example – of attaching too much importance to Jung's influence on Davies's personal pyschology, particularly when analysing the ambiguous character of Samuel Marchbanks. However, Monk is aware of the pitfalls of her thesis, and concludes by stating that "Davies eventually moves beyond his affinity with Jung to a more impartial assessment of Jungianism as simply one way of looking at the universe".

PETERMAN's book is a critically sound survey of Davies's fiction and drama up to *The Rebel Angels* (1981). It contains an informative biography, and an annotated bibliography. Like Buitenhuis, Grant, and Morley, Peterman attempts to cover a lot of ground, as he focuses on Davies's obsession with the self in the modern world. However, Peterman's book is more critically informed, utilizing the wealth of scholarly criticism on Davies's work that has emerged over the years. Keenly aware of Davies's status as an international writer of Canadian origin, this is one of the most informative books on Davies.

DAVIS's collection of 28 interviews, which took place between 1963 and 1988, is a useful and necessary book. It includes previously unpublished interviews, as well as transcripts from interviews recorded by the Canadian Broadcasting Corporation. If read chronologically, it gives the reader an opportunity to follow the creative process of Davies as his career developed. Also of interest are his frequent responses to the "Englishness" of his work, and how it affected his position as a Canadian author.

PHILIP MINGAY

Decadence, Aestheticism, and the 1890s

Cevasco, G.A. (ed.), *The 1890s: An Encyclopaedia of British Literature, Art and Culture*, New York: Garland, 1993

Dowling, Linda, *Language and Decadence in the Victorian Fin de Siècle*: Princeton, New Jersey: Princeton University Press, 1986

Jackson, Holbrook, *The Eighteen Nineties: A Review of Art and Ideas at the Close of the Nineteenth Century*, London: Grant Richards, 1913; New York: Knopf, 1927; reprinted, London: Cresset Library, 1988

Nordau, Max, *Degeneration*, London: Heinemann, 1895; New York: Appleton, 1895; reprinted, Lincoln: University of Nebraska Press, 1993

Praz, Mario, *The Romantic Agony*, translated by Angus Davidson, London: Oxford University Press, 1933, 2nd edition (also New York), 1951, with new Foreword, 1970

Showalter, Elaine, *Sexual Anarchy: Gender and Culture at the Fin de Siècle*, New York: Viking Press, 1990; London: Bloomsbury, 1991

Stokes, John (ed.), *Fin de Siècle/Fin du Globe: Fears and Fantasies of the Late Nineteenth Century*, London: Macmillan, 1992; New York: St Martin's Press, 1992

Thornton, R.K.R., *The Decadent Dilemma*, London: Edward Arnold, 1983

Late nineteenth-century writing that proclaimed itself "Decadent" soon begot a critical literature concerned with its diagnosis. This literature continues to exert its own fascination, testified to by the periodic reissue of, most famously, Nordau's *Degeneration* – a curiously symbiotic indictment of its subject – and JACKSON's celebrated commemoration of *The Eighteeen Nineties* as a decade legendary in its own lifetime. The retrospect of the latter is sufficiently distant to furnish a conspectus rare in the many works of memoir and mythology generated by the period. Yet the book endures through its quality of witness and familiarity of reference to a network of individuals, movements, ideas, and aspirations. Its critical value lies in the recognition that 1890s' culture was most vitally engaged in the realisation of "possibility". In this variously utopian concern Jackson discerns a convergence of otherwise diverse projects from the New Hedonism of Oscar Wilde's Lord Henry Wotton to Rudyard Kipling's "new imperialistic patriotism" and the communitarian aims of those who answered to John Ruskin's vision of art as an instrument of social praxis.

Jackson locates Decadence within a broader 1890s' renaissance "far more concerned with art for the sake of life than with art for the sake of art". If an aberrant aestheticism is lamented, it is also acknowledged as a critical symptom of its time: decadent art proposes not only its own impossibility but that of the world which it refuses. NORDAU cannot concede any such perversely positive evaluation. Blindness to the paradoxes of Decadence is a condition of his work's many insights. His study, first published in German in 1892, takes Decadent writing at its word, reading it as uncritically symptomatic of the greater malaise it is held to embody. This catalogue of denunciation in turn reads as unusually faithful to the phenomenon it abhors; heeding the letter rather than the spirit of its chosen texts, *Degeneration* is subject to the paradoxes it ignores. Nordau discusses modern literature under the categories of "mysticism" (affliction of the Pre-Raphaelites), "ego-mania" (typical of Decadents and Aesthetes) and the misconceived "realism" of the naturalist school; his aetiology of Decadence sets the agenda for later genealogies drawn to its disillusioned hybrid of social-Darwinist discourse.

THORNTON's book records at its outset that degeneration was itself predicted by evolutionary theory in both the natural and the social sciences. More telling (and bewildering) still is the report that Wilde instanced Nordau's analysis when appealing for clemency after his trial in 1895. Wilde's imprisonment marks the end of English Decadence for many commentators, and for some the end of the mythic ("naughty", "yellow", etc.) 1890s. Thornton's early chapters describe the formation of an English Decadence through meticulous attention to the statements of its principal advocates and arbiters; but, as he records, commentors such as Arthur Symons became increasingly concerned to dissociate themselves from the Decadence they had publicised. This ambivalence contributes to the "decadent dilemma" as Thornton understands it, where Decadence is viewed as parasitic upon the modernity whose ruin it enacts. Decadent writing is read as committed – ironically or not – to its own failure; but this granted, Thornton follows Symons in evaluating that literature chiefly in terms of its stylistic innovations, to some degree raising aesthetic virtue above Decadent vice. There follows a series of chapters exemplary in their attention to the verse of, in particular, Ernest Dowson, Lionel Johnson, and Symons himself.

The modernity attributed to these poets is informed by T.S. Eliot's acknowledgement of Dowson's example and the precedent of Yeats' *Oxford Book of Modern Verse* (1936). The

1890s confound beginning and ending, exhaustion and innovation, and in crossing this territory literary critics and historians have deemed it wise to look both ways. The progenitor of much of this inquiry is PRAZ's classic study. Its subject is, as Frank Kermode notes in his Foreword to the 1970 edition, "The Pathology of Romanticism", of which Decadence is considered a development. Praz's disinterested attention to "erotic sensibility" is intended as a corrective to Nordau's "literary nosology", and the originality of his book is at one with its primary endeavour to envisage its field. Praz places English writing largely in the company of French and Italian, and takes a thematic and motivic approach to its material, discussing later nineteenth-century literature in the closing chapters – "La Belle Dame Sans Merci" and "Byzantium" – and in an appendix on "Swinburne and 'Le Vice Anglais'". Because Praz is concerned with affinities across both geographic and historical borderlines, he encourages us to anticipate the relation of Decadence to modernism and beyond in our own century. He contributes to our understanding of the *agon* of indebted rejection and ironic engagement which informs James Joyce's portrayal of Stephen Dedalus and Ezra Pound's Hugh Selwyn Mauberley.

DOWLING grounds this inquiry in linguistic terrain, proposing that "Literary Decadence, one might say, is Romanticism demoralized by philology". He charts the nineteenth-century decline of an organic model of (literary) language against the ascendancy of neogrammarian theories of impersonal linguistic system. Its central chapter interprets Walter Pater's *Marius the Epicurean* and his essay on "Style" as at once conceding the claims of philology while resisting its most destructive implications. Where the latter prefers living (mutating) speech over petrified writing, Pater seeks to establish euphuism as a written dialect capable of regenerating the Coleridgean ideal of a *lingua communis*. Yet the more vitally recondite this language, the more narrowly cloistered is its community. Dowling reads the "disembodied" – consciously or parodically occult – voice of much 1890s' writing as a response, in both its quietism and abandon, to the Paterian impasse: the style of decadent writing is here returned to its subject as described by Praz. Dowling then evaluates the attempt to recover a living form of literary language in the 1890s' ballad revival and sometime imitation of "folk" speech. A final and no less fascinating chapter discusses Yeats' passage through these various possibilities to an "embodied" and new-made idiom of his own.

As Dowling reminds us, Yeats was disinclined to see Decadence "as any sort of final 'end'". In the 1990s, this stress has received a new, postmodern inflection marked by a pluralism of interests and alliances. Thus, in the Introduction to his superb encyclopaedia, CEVASCO emphasises the variety of a period chiasmically preoccupied "with high culture and low, as interested in serious drama as in the frivolity of the music hall". The book's conception of "British culture" is refreshingly free of evaluative hierarchy, encouraging the reader to map that topos in any number of ways through its cross-referencing of articles and an extensive general index. Entries on "The Aesthetic Movement" and "Decadence" are notably cautionary: the former, we are told, "had neither a clear philosophy, nor strong leaders, nor strict adherents"; while our understanding of the latter has been "burdened by associations with the Latin *decadere*, a falling away, a decline or sinking".

Recognition of the constitutive pose of Decadence – its strategic cultivation of a *mythos* by analogy – likewise informs SHOWALTER's analysis of its significance. Showalter aims to recover the generative concerns of modern feminism in the work of late-Victorian women writers (most importantly Olive Schreiner), and to evaluate a series of mutually determining representations of disruptive femininity and masculinity in the period. Showalter further describes how certain narratives – Robert Louis Stevenson's *Doctor Jekyll* and Bram Stoker's *Dracula* among them – have been reworked in film and fiction, arguing that the politics of these revisions are continuous with the energies of their original. Decadence is, in this context, largely (and perhaps narrowly) viewed as an "aestheticization of homosexuality", ambivalent towards femininity and ambiguous for feminism, a reading most vigorously pursued in relation to the androgyny of Wilde's *Salome*. Showalter translates *fin-de-siècle* anxiety to a present shaped by AIDS. Equally aware of convergence and conflict between gay and feminist politics, she nonetheless suggests that apparent "sexual anarchy" may augur "the birth throes of new sexual equality".

Here we return, in markedly rhetorical fashion, to the *topos* of beginnings and endings which so concerned the literature of the 1890s. The propensity of Showalter to reproduce as much as analyse its subject is also occasionally evident in a number of recent symposia on Decadence and Aestheticism. This is not, however, the case with one of the finest of these collections, STOKES' *Fin de Siècle/Fin du Globe*, which undertakes to reassess "the eschatological thought of the 1890s in the light of the critical thought of the 1990s". At its best, this volume offers an energetic and sceptical engagement with the myth-making of the 1890s in a range of textually and historically particular studies, among them John Goode on utopian "Writing Beyond the End" and Chris Snodgrass on Aubrey Beardsley's "Decadent Parodies". We may doubtless anticipate a burgeoning literature with the *fin de siècle* as its theme and the millenium as its deadline.

IAN FAIRLEY

Deconstruction

Arac, Jonathan, Wlad Godzich, and Wallace Martin (eds.), *The Yale Critics: Deconstruction in America*, Minneapolis: University of Minnesota Press, 1983

de Man, Paul, *Allegories of Reading: Figural Language in Rousseau, Nietzsche, Rilke, and Proust*, New Haven,Connecticut, and London: Yale University Press, 1979

Derrida, Jacques, "Letter to a Japanese Friend", translated by Andrew Benjamin, in *Derrida and Différance*, edited by David Wood and Robert Bernasconi, Coventry: Parousia Press, 1985; Evanston, Illinois: Northwestern University Press, 1988

Derrida, Jacques, *Acts of Literature*, edited by Derek Attridge, New York and London: Routledge, 1992

Elam, Diane, *Feminism and Deconstruction: Ms. en Abyme*, New York and London: Routledge, 1994

Jay, Gregory S., *America the Scrivener: Deconstruction and the Subject of Literary History*, Ithaca, New York: Cornell University Press, 1990

Johnson, Barbara, *A World of Difference*, Baltimore: Johns Hopkins University Press, 1987

Spivak, Gayatri Chakravorty, *In Other Worlds: Essays in Cultural Politics*, New York and London: Methuen, 1987

Addressing the problem of translating the word "deconstruction", Jacques DERRIDA's 1983 letter also explores the difficulty any commentator, including himself, faces when attempting to define deconstruction. Deconstruction is not just one thing, since the term does not describe a critical method that can be abstracted from Derrida's works or the other conversations in which deconstruction takes part. Derrida insists that deconstruction is not a method but, rather, an event. Thus, for Derrida, deconstruction is not simply a critical strategy employed by a reading subject. Instead, he emphasizes that deconstruction happens without dependence on subjective agency and that deconstruction happens everywhere. The "text" with which deconstruction concerns itself is not limited simply to written language but instead includes the discursive structuring of subjectivity, experience, reality.

Similarly, DE MAN makes clear that his deconstructive interest in rhetorical tropes and figures is not a concern simply confined to literature. He begins his discussion with a challenge to the inside/outside opposition that governs both formalist insistence on limiting interest to what is in the text and cultural critique that locates importance in what is outside the text. As he moves through engagements with Proust, Rilke, Nietzsche, and Rousseau, de Man's discussion moves from problems posed by a rhetorical question or the privilege of metaphor over metonymy, and leads to a discussion of ethics and politics.

Thus, deconstruction's concern with language necessarily leads to a concern with other things – structures of knowledge, institutions, etc. Because deconstruction happens everywhere, writers interested in deconstruction and the discussions it generates pursue deconstruction in its conversations with many other concerns, including literature, philosophy, history, and feminism.

For those new to deconstruction, ARAC, GODZICH, and MARTIN's book is interesting primarily for its account of the history of deconstruction's first decade as an influence in American literary criticism and literature departments. This collection of essays addresses the work of the "Yale Critics" – Harold Bloom, Geoffrey Hartman, Paul de Man, and J. Hillis Miller – the group of American critics often connected with deconstructive literary criticism in the 1970s. The essays in this collection attempt to consider the Yale Critics as individual theorists with often widely varying approaches, rather than as a single school of deconstructive thought, while also addressing the question of their relation to the works of Derrida. Many of these essays share an interest in exploring the relation between the New-Critical tradition – prevalent in literature departments at the time of deconstruction's "arrival" – and the tradition of Continental philosophy, to which deconstruction is both an heir and a response.

Of particular interest to readers concerned with literature is Attridge's 1992 collection of DERRIDA's works that focus primarily on "questions of literature as an institution and literary writing as a practice". The collection includes essays, excerpts from longer works, an original interview with Derrida, as well as Attridge's useful introductory essay and headnotes. Despite the collection's focus on literature, Attridge's Introduction makes clear that he is not choosing a side in a common division between those who insist on reading Derrida as either "sternly philosophical" or "playfully literary". Rather, deconstruction is interested in the unstable distinction between philosophy and literature; it is the discussion of this boundary and that between other opposed metaphysical concepts that generate many of Derrida's most important terms – supplement, hymen, pharmakon, trace, parergon, différance, etc.

JAY's discussion is primarily concerned with the "triple play" of history, subjectivity, and literariness. For Jay, deconstruction's challenge to the "subject of history" is not antithetical to politics or ethics, but instead offers the possibility of a "speculation on alternative modes of knowing and of acting". He argues for an understanding of deconstructive "play" that can counter a tendency that he sees "across the spectrum of the human sciences", which "stems from a conventional reading of literary and cultural history, a reading that narrates fragmentation, plurality, difference, and dissemination as variations of the Fall". He pursues these issues through discussions of critics writing about American literary history and of canonical American authors, including Henry David Thoreau, Herman Melville, Edgar Allan Poe, Ralph Waldo Emerson, Frederick Douglass, Henry James, and William Faulkner.

JOHNSON describes her project as an attempt to take deconstructive analyses of difference into the "real world", but she also makes clear that the institutional boundary suggested by the "theory"/"real world" opposition is among those that her project will critique. Particularly concerned with issues of sexual and racial difference, her book is an engagement with questions such as "what are the political consequences of the fact that language is not a transparently expressive medium?" and "how can the study of suppressed, disseminated, or marginalized messages within texts equip us to intervene against oppression and injustice in the world?" Johnson pursues these questions through a series of essays that discuss literary texts – among them works by Mallarmé, Thoreau, Poe, Mary Shelley, Zora Neale Hurston, Gwendolyn Brooks, and Adrienne Rich – as well as deconstruction's relation to feminism and institutional questions raised by its reception in the academy.

ELAM takes the encounter between feminism and deconstruction as her central concern, and in the course of arguing for their relevance to each other offers a detailed discussion of previous considerations of this sometimes troubled relationship. She also pursues questions raised by the institutional and disciplinary placement of both feminism and deconstruction. Elam argues that feminism and deconstruction ask questions that allow a rethinking of the political, and goes on to argue that "the ethics of deconstruction and feminism is an ethical activism which requires that judgments be made, yet which does not supply the means of legitimating those judgments. No recourse to self-present subjects, natural rights, or transcendental truths . . .". For literary study, this encounter between deconstruction and feminism is important because both feminism and deconstruction challenge the assumption that literature's importance lies in its ability to reflect universal truths of experience. Elam's discussion of an ethics not predicated on transcendental truths suggests possible avenues for a reconsideration of literature and reading.

SPIVAK's book is a collection of essays which address a wide range of topics. These apparently disparate concerns include: feminist criticism of canonical literature in English, such as William Wordsworth's *Prelude* and Virginia Woolf's *To the Lighthouse*; reconsiderations of literary institutions and theoretical discourses, such as French feminism, Marxism, and postcolonial studies; discussions of the Subaltern Studies Group's revision of the practice of history; and translations and readings of stories by Mahasweta Devi. Deconstruction connects these interests in "its disclosure of complicities where a will to knowledge would create oppositions; its insistence that in disclosing complicities the critic-as-subject is herself complicit with the object of her critique". This disclosure of complexity constitutes an insistence on the impossibility of occupying a masterful critical position external to the object of discussion. Spivak pursues her concern with critics' implication in, and construction of, their subjects of inquiry, whether that subject is literary, cultural, or political.

ELIZABETH KUHLMANN

Defoe, Daniel 1660–1731

English novelist and journalist

Backscheider, Paula R., *Daniel Defoe: His Life*, Baltimore: Johns Hopkins University Press, 1989

Blewitt, David, *Defoe's Art of Fiction: "Robinson Crusoe", "Moll Flanders", "Colonel Jack" and "Roxana"*, Toronto: University of Toronto Press, 1979

Flynn, Carol Houlihan, *The Body in Swift and Defoe*, Cambridge and New York: Cambridge University Press, 1990

Furbank, P.N., and W.R. Owens, *The Canonization of Daniel Defoe*, New Haven, Connecticut, and London: Yale University Press, 1988

Novak, Maximillian E., *Economics and the Fiction of Daniel Defoe*, Berkeley: University of California Press, 1962

Seidel, Michael, *"Robinson Crusoe": Island Myths and the Novel*, Boston: Twayne, 1991

Starr, G.A., *Defoe and Spiritual Autobiography*, Princeton, New Jersey: Princeton University Press, 1965

Watt, Ian, *The Rise of the Novel: Studies in Defoe, Richardson and Fielding*, London: Chatto & Windus, 1957; Berkeley: University of California Press, 1957

Contemporary responses to Defoe were overwhelmingly hostile, giving little or no consideration to his artistic merits, and attacking him purely on political and class grounds. The enduring popularity of *Robinson Crusoe* (1719) ensured a place for its author in literary history, but, as Virginia Woolf pointed out in a bicentennial essay ("The Novels of Defoe", in the *Times Literary Supplement*, 24 April 1919), nineteenth- and twentieth-century sensibilities were so offended by *Moll Flanders* and *Roxana* that they, and many of Defoe's other works, fell from view. In recent decades Defoe's critical fortunes have steadily improved, owing partly to the labours of his bibliographer, J.R. Moore, and partly to the prominence given to Defoe by Ian Watt in *The Rise of the Novel*. Recent criticism has focused on contextualizing Defoe and on exploring his non-fiction, though, for a writer so adept at impersonation, terms such as "non-fiction" and "fiction" are of limited usefulness.

WATT made a significant contribution to Defoe's critical recognition by stressing his role in the development of the English novel. Watt regarded Robinson Crusoe as the type of early capitalist man, not least in his Protestant self-consciousness, while Moll Flanders is an equally assiduous if less reflective example of the economic individualist. Both novels illustrate Defoe's extraordinary realism, which Watt regarded as his most important formal innovation.

NOVAK voiced the critics' perennial complaint that Defoe's opinions are bewilderingly self-contradictory; nonetheless, he firmly identified him as an old-fashioned mercantilist economist who favoured state regulation of trade and its centralization in London. Novak was sceptical of Watt's interpretation of *Robinson Crusoe* as a study of economic individualism; whereas Watt had viewed Crusoe as the embodiment of capitalist values, Novak pointed out that his story is a warning against speculation and selfish accumulation.

In exploring the impact of English Protestantism on Defoe, STARR, too, was influenced by Watt, though his emphasis was on the religious dimension of *Robinson Crusoe* rather than on its concern with the capitalist ethic. For Starr, *Robinson Crusoe* imitated the spiritual autobiographies of the seventeenth century, reflecting their preoccupations with self-examination, Grace, and salvation. Like Novak, Starr argued that Crusoe's story is a moralistic warning to the restlessly acquisitive: Crusoe's minutely documented conversion is painfully achieved.

BLEWITT offered detailed and illuminating readings of three other novels in addition to *Robinson Crusoe* – *Moll Flanders*, *Colonel Jack*, and *Roxana* – and demonstrated the importance of reading them in relation to their social and political backgrounds. Blewitt also insisted on the need to remain alert to Defoe's deliberate irony when he deals with topics such as gentility. Colonel Jack's social ambitions, for example, should not be regarded as a thinly disguised expression of Defoe's own yearnings for success but as an oblique comment on the ruthless scheming and self-importance he associated with the Jacobites.

BACKSCHEIDER's 1989 critical biography is the most comprehensive available, drawing on some new primary sources and an extensive range of secondary ones. It is subdivided into three parts, with sections on: Defoe's early career as a merchant and his subsequent bankruptcy and disgrace; his work as an agent and political pamphleteer; and the even more productive years of his old age, when he produced his most famous works and yet experienced financial hardship once more. In an earlier critical work (*Daniel Defoe: Ambition and Innovation*, Lexington: University Press of Kentucky, 1986) Backscheider dealt with his literary output at greater length. While her view of him as a versatile, open-ended writer who worked outside the literary establishment is a conventional one, her critique is well-informed and encompasses Defoe's entire *oeuvre*.

In 1988 FURBANK and OWENS unsettled the world of Defoe scholarship with their sceptical account of Defoe's treatment at the hands of successive biographers and bibliographers. Furbank and Owens raised substantial objections to many accepted attributions. They also showed how the desire to make ever more additions to the Defoe canon and the idea of Defoe's protean willingness to write on any side of a question have been mutually reinforcing. Furbank and Owens promise to provide a more conservative canon for Defoe in the latest edition of the *New Cambridge Bibliography of English Literature*.

FLYNN's book broke new ground by applying the insights of "body criticism" to Jonathan Swift and Defoe, both of whom struggle with the problems of materiality for their post-Lockean world. Flynn discusses *A Journal of the Plague Year* and *Conjugal Lewdness*, as well as *Robinson Crusoe* and *Moll Flanders*, in the context of eighteenth-century epistemology, and discovers interesting parallels between Defoe, Swift, and their contemporaries (e.g., Samuel Johnson, Montesquieu). Her work is of particular value in foregrounding issues of gender in reading Defoe, and in tracing ideas of consumption and urban expansion in his work.

SEIDEL's study of *Robinson Crusoe* in the Twayne "Masterworks" series is traditionalist in its narrow focus on Defoe's best-known book, but it usefully draws on the work of many writers on his economic and political backgrounds, and is a lively and accessible introduction to Defoe. Seidel reflects the current trend among critics to recognize the consistency of Defoe's views on issues such as Jacobitism, colonization, and trade. This trend is, perhaps, a reaction against previous characterizations of him as either a shrewd political trimmer or an unscrupulous hack.

KATHERINE A. ARMSTRONG

Dekker, Thomas c.1572–1632

English dramatist and prose writer

Berger, Thomas Leland (ed.), *A Critical Old-Spelling Edition of Thomas Dekker's "Blurt, Master-Constable"*, Salzburg: Institut für Anglistik und Amerikanistik (Salzburg University), 1979

Blow, Suzanne K., *Rhetoric in the Plays of Thomas Dekker*, Salzburg: James Hogg/Salzburg University, 1972

Bose, Tirthankar, *The Gentle Craft of Revision in Dekker's Last Plays*, Salzburg: Institut für Anglistik und Amerikanistik (Salzburg University), 1979

Champion, Larry S., *Dekker and the Traditions of English Drama*, New York: Peter Lang, 1985

Conover, James H., *Thomas Dekker: An Analysis of Dramatic Structure*, The Hague and Paris: Mouton, 1969

Gasper, Julia, *The Dragon and the Dove; The Plays of Thomas Dekker*, Oxford: Clarendon Press, 1990; New York: Oxford University Press, 1990

Gregg, K.L., *Dekker: A Study of Economic and Social Backgrounds*, Seattle: University of Washington Publications, 1924

Hoy, Cyrus, *Introductions, Notes and Commentaries to Texts in the Dramatic Works of Thomas Dekker*, 4 vols., Cambridge and New York: Cambridge University Press, 1980–81

Lawrence, W.J., "Dekker's Theatrical Allusiveness", in *Times Literary Supplement*, 30 January 1937

McLuskie, Kathleen E., *Dekker and Heywood: Professional Dramatists*, London: Macmillan, 1994; New York: St Martin's Press, 1994

Shirley, Peggy F., *Serious and Tragic Elements in the Comedy of Dekker*, Salzburg: Institut für Anglistik und Amerikanistik (Salzburg University), 1975

Waage, Frederick O., *Dekker's Pamphlets, 1603–1609, and Jacobean Popular Literature*, 2 vols., Salzburg: Institut für Anglistik und Amerikanistik (Salzburg University), 1977

Despite some Victorian admirers, Dekker's reputation in the early twentieth century was, in general, rather low. The works discussed below, together with those of other critics (such as, M.-T. Jones-Davies), have, however, given Dekker a far higher place in critical esteem now than he held 30 or 40 years ago.

GREGG's study asserted that Dekker was a Puritan, yet concluded that he supported the "Anglican establishment". She argued that the ethics of the theatre necessarily clashed with Dekker's Puritanism, but while she referred to much historical material she rarely managed to link this closely with the texts. LAWRENCE's perceptive short article reveals one of Dekker's idiosyncrasies – his habit of making characters in one play allude jestingly to passages in others. This sheds light on problems of date and authorship.

CONOVER defends many of Dekker's plays from previous charges of careless construction, proving they are coherent. This differs from the conclusion of L.M. Manheim, whose unpublished Ph.D thesis of 1960 argues that Dekker's plays have a "thematic structure" rather than "'cause-and-effect' logic".

BLOW's study is a straightforward demonstration of Dekker's use of rhetorical devices such as *metastasis*, *pysma*, *philophronesis*, etc., which were expounded in Renaissance works by Henry Peacham, Thomas Wilson, Richard Sherry, and others. This apparently dry approach actually increases one's sense of the freshness and liveliness of the text.

SHIRLEY's study pinpointed a key problem for Dekker scholars – that so many of his works pose problems of genre. Even *The Shoemaker's Holiday* has sombre elements which are unresolved by its comic ending, while *Old Fortunatus* actually fulfils all Aristotle's criteria for tragedy, yet is written in a comic vein. Shirley's close readings of these and of *If This Be Not a Good Play* are valuable and sensitive. She concludes that by violating genre, Dekker gave a more complete picture of human life.

WAAGE has produced the most in-depth study of Dekker's prose, using intertextual comparison and a wide range of critical concepts to produce impressive readings which overturn accepted views. For instance, Waage compares *The Wonderful*

Year to works on the Plague by authors including Martin Luther, Francis Bacon, and Jeremy Taylor, concluding that Dekker's ideas on plague, far from being conventional, were actually "eccentric". Waage explores Dekker's political allegiance and proves that he was a friend of supporters of the Essex rebellion, an "oppositional" faction, but concludes that Dekker's politics and his theology were not consistent, because in *Work for Armourers* (which Waage reads as a satire on James I's government) Dekker advocates warfare.

BOSE is concerned with authorship problems in several of Dekker's late plays, and also with accounting for the apparent rewriting of *The Noble Spanish Soldier*. He uses internal evidence from parallel passages, favourite imagery, etc., to argue that this play and *The Wonder of a Kingdom* are wholly or mainly Dekker's work and were the source for John Day's *Parliament of Bees*, not vice versa (a conclusion arrived at also by me, in the *Durham University Journal*, June 1987). BERGER's Introduction collects evidence, almost all internal, that this play is by Dekker, despite being excluded from Bowers' edition, and provides a useful summary of Dekker's and Thomas Middleton's stylistic pointers, e.g., the contractions or synonyms each preferred.

HOY's commentaries are intended as a companion to Bowers' edition of the plays. Essentially a compilation of earlier criticism, leaning heavily towards work published in the United States, Hoy tends to explain the obvious, while passing over genuinely obscure passages in silence. Dekker's Latin is not translated. He pays scant attention to the later works, and has a patronising attitude to Dekker.

CHAMPION asserts that Dekker was an experimental dramatist who interacted with, rather than merely imitated, other writers. But this book brings few new insights into the texts and is unsympathetic to Dekker's most experimental works, such as *The Whore of Babylon*.

My own study (GASPER) reconstructs Dekker's world-picture as revealed in his plays, arguing that he was a "militant Protestant", which involved him in persistent opposition to the royal absolutism. This book and Waage's complement each other, being consistent in their analyses of Dekker's political position. *The Whore of Babylon* is advanced as Dekker's central work and a successful example of its peculiar genre, the apocalyptic comedy, while Dekker's late play *The Noble Spanish Soldier*, I argue, shows that he was capable of contemplating regicide as a solution to tyranny.

The pairing of Dekker with Thomas Heywood in McLUSKIE is reasonable, as they have much in common; but McLuskie's definition of them as "commercial" writers who aimed to "please the widest possible market" is not very perceptive, as the same could be said of most, if not all, Elizabethan dramatists who are read today. McLuskie's approach is a combination of feminist and New-Historicist angles, strongest on the comedies and their sexual politics; but this is a very poorly produced book, full of misprints, and it does not always credit its sources.

JULIA GASPER

De Quincey, Thomas 1785–1859

English journalist, essayist, and critic

Barrell, John, *The Infection of Thomas De Quincey: A Psychopathology of Imperialism*, New Haven, Connecticut, and London: Yale University Press, 1991

Davies, Hugh Sykes, *Thomas De Quincey*, London: Longmans, Green & Co., 1964

Devlin, D.D., *De Quincey, Wordsworth and the Art of Prose*, London: Macmillan, 1983; New York: St Martin's Press, 1983

Jordan, John E., *Thomas De Quincey, Literary Critic: His Method and Achievement*, Berkeley: University of California Press, 1952

Leighton, Angela, "De Quincey and Women", in *Beyond Romanticism: New Approaches to Texts and Contexts 1780–1832*, edited by Stephen Copley and John C. Whale, London and New York: Routledge, 1992

Lindop, Grevel, *The Opium-Eater: A Life of Thomas De Quincey*, London: Dent & Sons, 1981; New York: Taplinger, 1981

McDonagh, Josephine, *De Quincey's Disciplines*, Oxford: Clarendon Press, 1994; New York: Oxford University Press, 1994

Whale, John C., *Thomas De Quincey's Reluctant Autobiography*, London and Sydney: Croom Helm, 1984

The scope of Thomas De Quincey's writing has provided material for every variety of late twentieth-century theoretical approach, from the interest in visionary drug literature in the 1960s, through deconstructive play in the 1970s, to the critiques of empire and orientalism of the 1980s and 1990s. Through the changing contexts of debate, however, the reader can detect a recurrent post-Romantic critical desire to unify De Quincey's various achievements.

DAVIES supplies a lucid introduction to the many subjects of De Quincey's periodical writing. After foregrounding the presence of autobiography in what he judges to be De Quincey's most powerful work, Davies reads the values of De Quincey's criticism back into his prose discovering a "deep-seated duality of feeling" between "the humdrum domesticity of his outward life, and the exotic violence of his inner world". The brevity of the guide precludes detailed discussion, but Davies successfully conveys the digressive complexities of De Quincey's prose over "a fundamental coherence . . . not of logical structure, but of emotion and of recollection".

JORDAN's study is divided between analysis of De Quincey's critical method and estimation of its value. Focusing on De Quincey's appraisals of canonical poets, Jordan allows the objects of De Quincey's attention to reveal the strengths and inadequacies of his discursive techniques. Integrated with the then dominant critical voices of W.K. Wimsatt, Monroe Beardsley, Allen Tate, and John Crowe Ransom – Jordan's view that De Quincey overrated gothic fiction and the work of Ann Radcliffe, Elizabeth Inchbald, and Harriet Lee now suggests some of the limitations of his own critical stance. Nevertheless, this is an engrossing, labyrinthine account of De Quincey's place in critical history, concluding with a *loci critici* keyed to the Masson edition.

LINDOP's bibliographic, critical, and editorial scholarship on De Quincey enhances this biography, covering the whole life but centring on the Grasmere years and De Quincey's close personal and textual relationships with Coleridge and the Wordsworth family. Wide-ranging attention to De Quincey's writing brings perceptive analysis, for example: "might not the lion-dream, and the failure of will it symbolized, point to a kind of original sin, a self-betrayal first suffered in infancy?". Lindop's study is full of such insights and provocative suppositions (did De Quincey possess an early manuscript of *The Prelude*?), drawing the reader through a mass of material, but admitting *lacunae* which disturb the narrative. Helpfully indexed, this offers a general survey of the social entanglements treated more theoretically by New Historicists.

DEVLIN's line is that De Quincey is a "disappointing critic of Wordsworth", but that his responses to Wordsworth are revealed indirectly in comments on his own impassioned prose:

> Wordsworth by implication and example gave De Quincey a body of critical theory and value which De Quincey's generalising power and logical skill could shape into a critical position so subtly consistent that it made of forty years of critical essays and articles and notes a great intellectual achievement.

Treating Wordsworth as De Quincey's source of energy, Devlin focuses on the relationship between Wordsworth's spots of time and De Quincey's "involutes", arguing that Wordsworth's theory of language as incarnation pervades De Quincey's writing about the literature of power.

WHALE uses autobiographical paradigms, aesthetic theory, and textual analysis to approach De Quincey's "dramatic enactment" of personality. Beginning with the pressures of journalistic context, Whale differs from Devlin by suggesting that De Quincey's prose foregrounds the difficulties of translating private experience for a large and demanding audience. A tension is identified between Romantic autobiographical calls for sympathy and more aggressive forms of Victorian cultural commentary. This allows Whale to define different types of readerly involvement in De Quincey's most well-known compositions. Whale's book is a useful alternative to readings like Devlin's, which concentrate on De Quincey's apocalyptic vision.

BARRELL's psychoanalysis of De Quincey posits two processes of displacement in De Quincey's writing whereby fear of the working class and guilt about his sister's death are figured in a hatred of Orientals. De Quincey's autobiographical writing, Barrell argues, creates a mythic melodrama:

> . . . from an orientalised East End to a demonised Far East; behind every palm-tree lurks an eastern assassin, human, animal or microbiological. The cast are all members of De Quincey's own family, some appearing as the terrified victims of the Orient, and some as its terrifying embodiment.

Barrell watches as recurring surrogates of Elizabeth arise in De Quincey's "involutes", linking Victorian domestic and imperial fantasies. Acknowledging its own excesses, the study makes compulsive reading.

LEIGHTON's essay argues that the surface sentimentality of De Quincey's repeated narratives of victimised females conceals more complex attitudes and ultimately a critique of Victorian patriarchy. The polarities of deconstructive and historical criticism are brought into dialogue by Leighton's suggestion that these two kinds of discourse "fret" against each other in De Quincey's later writing. Leighton's argument is theoretically informed, but her freedom from burdensome apparatus and theoretical piety is demonstrated when she identifies De Quincey's "movement of substitution as more delicate and memorable than any in Derrida". Sensitive, sceptical, and readable, Leighton's essay summarises many of the insights disclosed by gender-oriented approaches to De Quincey.

McDONAGH has given detailed attention to the political commentaries, translation of German philosophy, treatise on economics, and lesser-known essays that De Quincey produced in the 1830s and 1840s. The focus of her study is De Quincey as a populariser and disseminator of work from diverse fields of knowledge. Using Michel Foucault's analysis of power relations, McDonagh develops Barrell's reading of De Quincey, seeing him less as extraordinary individual and more as "representative Victorian". McDonagh explores De Quincey's complex participation (as addict and debtor) in discursive and market economies based on consumption. Aligned with McGann's revision of Romanticism, McDonagh concludes that De Quincey's "frequently unnoticed legacy in the history of English literature is the deeper inscription of forms of social violence in an ostensibly disinterested aesthetic".

JANE STABLER

Dickens, Charles 1812–1870

English novelist, journalist, and dramatist

Ackroyd, Peter, *Dickens*, London: Sinclair-Stevenson, 1990; New York: HarperCollins, 1990
Armstrong, Frances, *Dickens and the Concept of Home*, Ann Arbor, Michigan: UMI Research Press, 1990
Butt, John, and Kathleen Tillotson, *Dickens at Work*, London: Methuen, 1957; Fair Lawn, New Jersey: Essential Books, 1958
Chesterton, G.K., with F.J. Kitton, *Charles Dickens*, London: Hodder & Stoughton, 1903
Collins, Philip, *Dickens and Crime*, London: Macmillan, 1962, 2nd edition, 1964; New York: St Martin's Press, 1962, 2nd edition, 1964
Collins, Philip, *Dickens and Education*, London: Macmillan, 1965; New York: St Martin's Press, 1965
Flint, Kate, *Dickens*, Brighton, Sussex: Harvester Press, 1986; Atlantic Highlands, New Jersey: Humanities Press, 1986
Ford, George, *Dickens and His Readers: Aspects of Novel-Criticism since 1836*, Princeton, New Jersey: Princeton University Press, 1955
House, Humphrey, *The Dickens World*, Oxford: Oxford University Press, 1941

Ingham, Patricia, *Dickens, Women and Language*, Toronto: University of Toronto Press, 1992; Hemel Hempstead, Hertfordshire: Harvester Wheatsheaf, 1992
Johnson, Edgar, *Charles Dickens: His Tragedy and Triumph*, Boston: Little Brown, 1952; London: Victor Gollancz, 1953
Lucas, John, *Charles Dickens: The Major Novels*, Harmondsworth, Middlesex: Penguin, 1992
Marcus, Steven, *Dickens from Pickwick to Dombey*, London: Chatto & Windus, 1965; New York: Basic Books, 1965
Miller, D.A., *The Novel and the Police*, Berkeley: University of California Press, 1988
Miller, J. Hillis, *Charles Dickens: The World of His Novels*, Cambridge, Massachusetts: Harvard University Press, 1958
Morgan, Nicholas H., *Secret Journeys: Theory and Practice in Reading Dickens*, Rutherford, New Jersey: Fairleigh Dickinson University Press, 1992; London: Associated University Presses, 1992
Orwell, George, "Charles Dickens", in his *"Inside the Whale" and Other Essays*, London: Victor Gollancz, 1940; reprinted in *Dickens, Dali, and Others*, New York: Harcourt, Brace & World, 1963
Price, Martin (ed.), *Dickens: A Collection of Critical Essays*, Englewood Cliffs, New Jersey: Prentice-Hall, 1967
Sadrin, Anny, *Parentage and Inheritance in the Novels of Charles Dickens*, Cambridge and New York: Cambridge University Press, 1994
Stewart, Garrett, *Dickens and the Trials of Imagination*, Cambridge, Massachusetts: Harvard University Press, 1974
Slater, Michael, *Dickens and Women*, London: Dent 1983; Stanford, California: Stanford University Press, 1983
Wall, Stephen (ed.), *Charles Dickens: A Critical Anthology*, Harmondworth, Middlesex: Penguin, 1970
Welsh, Alexander, *The City of Dickens*, Oxford: Clarendon Press, 1971
Wilson, Edmund, "Dickens: The Two Scrooges", in *The Wound and the Bow: Seven Studies in Literature*, Boston: Houghton Mifflin, 1929; London: Secker & Warburg, 1942

There is a wealth of critical and biographical material about Dickens. The following discussion examines many of the principal studies, beginning with G.K. Chesterton's early work and progressing to the recent studies of the 1990s.

CHESTERTON's lively, insistent, paradoxical style delights some and infuriates others. He batters the reader with wild and dogmatic generalisations, and uses Dickens to illustrate his own noisy brand of Christian optimism: the result is a stimulating book, which does not pause to look closely at the texts of the novels, though it is obviously by an enthusiast who knows his Dickens intimately. The central question it asks is "how did a man of such a coarse mind become a master of his art?". Chesterton finds – and loves – in Dickens "a joy so vital and violent that only impossible characters can express it". A few of his generalisations will give the flavour of the book better than any summary: "Dickens had all his life the faults of the little boy who is kept up too late at night"; "this is the first and last dignity of Dickens: that he was a creator. He did not point out things, he made them"; "here . . . is the last and deepest lesson of Dickens. It is in our daily life that we are to look for the portents and the prophecies".

WILSON's long essay (almost a short book), however, inaugurates modern criticism of Dickens: it uses Marxist and Freudian ideas, and sees Dickens as a far more complex figure than any earlier critic had done; it also pays far more attention to the later novels (the shift from early to late Dickens is probably the most important difference between nineteenth- and twentieth-century Dickens criticism), though in Wilson's case this shift is prompted more by psychological and political interest than by aesthetic preference. Indeed, he repeats many of the standard nineteenth-century preferences, including the very questionable view that the later comic characters are often "mechanical and boring". (Flora Finching and Mr Finching's Aunt in *Little Dorritt* are surely among the funniest characters Dickens ever created).

Wilson approaches the novels through the biography: "it is necessary to see him as a man in order to appreciate him as an artist". The man he depicts is not the simple exuberant figure beloved of earlier readers, but is shown as disturbed and as psychologically dependent on his public: "a falling off in the popularity of his monthly instalments would plunge him into anxiety and depression". He is also shown as more subversive than earlier critics had thought: "of all the great Victorian writers he was possibly the most antagonistic of the Victorian age itself".Though many (not all) of Wilson's insights are now widely accepted, he states them with a force and succinctness seldom attained by later critics.

ORWELL's enormously influential essay discusses the political implications of Dickens's work: it is vigorously argued, commonsensical, unsubtle, and free of jargon. It maintains that Dickens's criticism of society is almost exclusively moral, and shows no real understanding of the political roots of the social evils he attacks:

> In the last resort there is nothing he admires except common decency. Science is uninteresting, and machinery is cruel and ugly . . . Business is only for ruffians like Bounderby. As for politics – leave that to the Tite Barnacles. Really there is no objective except to marry the heroine, settle down, live solvently and be kind.

HOUSE sets out to show "the connection between what Dickens wrote and the time in which he wrote it, between reformism and some of the things he wanted reformed, between the attitude to life shown in his books and the society in which he lived". He examines political discussion in the nineteenth century, including arguments about progress, reform, and self-help, and relates these to some of Dickens's informing concepts, such as benevolence, snobbery, and attitudes to money. Informative and readable, this is the best short introduction to a historical study of Dickens.

JOHNSON's is the standard scholarly biography, extremely detailed, lavishly illustrated, and meticulously documented. The interspersed critical discussions of the novels are less valuable than the biographical material, which is very thorough indeed. No serious study of Dickens's life is possible without this book.

FORD's study of Dickens's readers is also a book about Dickens himself. With a novelist so deeply embroiled in his own culture as Dickens was, this is perhaps inevitable; and Ford moves with great skill between discussion of the novels and discussion of their reception. He is particularly illuminating on the question of sentimentality, and the issues raised for the modern reader by contemporary enthusiasm for Dickens's sentimental death-scenes; and on Dickens's characterisation: "the static characters tend to crowd the developing characters off the stage".

BUTT and TILLOTSON are concerned with the process of writing the novels rather than the result: they "examine several of Dickens's novels in the light of the conditions under which he wrote them". Their pioneering study makes careful use of Dickens's number plans and his revisions in proof in order to recover a view of Dickens as a writer of periodical novels, showing how he modified his original plans while writing, and how later episodes of a novel included responses to the reception of its earlier parts by the public. Their book casts light on the relationship between the novelist and his audience, as well as showing how the books developed. The chapter on *Little Dorrit*, for instance, documents Dickens's original intention to call the book "Nobody's Fault", and his gradual abandonment of this title as his interest shifted from the topical political theme to the personal. There is material in this study for much fuller and more varied investigations than the authors actually conduct.

Hillis MILLER's declared aim is to "assess the specific quality of Dickens's imagination". A brief Introduction and conclusion frame a chapter-by-chapter treatment of each novel separately, but the book is held together by a small number of unifying themes. All the novels show "the theme of the search for a true and viable identity"; the multitudinousness, the proliferation of characters, is Dickens's way of "absorbing the city into his imagination", and within that world he shows the usual vain attempts to achieve true selfhood by characters who are isolated, and who, in their isolation, are "without substance, hollow". The great comic grotesques of Dickens show that "in this universe of the moment and of the idiosyncratic, nothing can have a significant existence because nothing can be related to everything else". He notes that "in Dickens's world, as in Conrad's, people exist in the exact degree that they exist in other people's eyes". Miller, who subsequently became well known as a deconstructionist, here writes as a thematic critic, exploring with great subtlety a small number of abstract ideas and symbols, along with complexities of motive and the conflicts that they lead to. Dickens emerges not as a great comic, but as a deeply tragic writer.

MARCUS, although he accepts the modern tendency to prefer the later Dickens, claims that the later novels can be better understood if we look carefully at the earlier ones. His book relates the first seven novels "to each other, to the course of Dickens's life and thought, and to the culture in which they belong". Marcus's strong interest in Victorian culture and its tensions leads him to place the novels in their political and ideological contexts, but never distracts him from the question of their literary quality, and he discusses the striking disparity between the brilliance of Dickens's best writing and the appalling badness of his sentimental and melodramatic scenes: "no writer of comparable genius has ever been so wayward". Dickens's art at its best shows us that the "free aesthetic life" (Henry James's expression) found in such abundance in his novels is compatible with unity of conception. This is one of the most balanced and perceptive books on Dickens.

COLLINS's two books situate Dickens historically by relating his opinions and his fiction to two important and far-reaching political issues. *Dickens and Crime* deals with nineteenth-century criminology and the controversy about how prisons should run, and shows how closely Dickens was in touch with contemporary thinking, and how forcefully he entered into the arguments in his journalism, and even in practical life; in discussing the fiction Collins pays particular attention to the treatment of the police, and to murder. *Dickens and Education* performs a parallel task, including an account of how Dickens had his own children educated. Since almost all the novels contain at least one school or some other account of how a child is educated, this study ranges through almost the whole of Dickens's work. Collins challenges the old-fashioned simplistic view that "Dickens did a great deal of good", and accepts at least in part the "tortured necrophilic, aggressive Dickens who has proved more congenial to a generation somewhat cool towards novelists alleged to have done good".

PRICE's collection of critical essays include extracts from the books by Ford, Marcus, and Hillis Miller. Among the other essays, the following are particularly to be recommended: Dorothy Van Ghent on "The Dickens World: A View from Todger's" (about the animation of inanimate objects), W.H. Auden on "Dingley Dell and the Fleet" (about Mr Pickwick's loss of innocence: "the real theme of *Pickwick Papers* is the Fall of Man"); and "Little Dorrit" by Lionel Trilling (on the theme of imprisonment, and Dickens's personal involvement with the novel).

WELSH's brilliant book begins by looking at traditional literary representations of the city, and asks how they were modified in the nineteenth century by social change, in particular by industrialism. Satire views its subject ironically: but "to an engineer, an irony is a problem to be solved". He then relates these concerns to the other-worldliness that rejects the earthly for the heavenly city, and finally studies the Victorian heroine as angelic and unworldly, and marriage as a fictional equivalent of death. The first part, which deals with the comic and grotesque elements in Dickens, is more likely to appeal to the modern reader than the third part, on the Bride of Heaven, which deals with the sentimental and idealising elements so out of favour nowadays; but the whole book is rich with insights.

STEWART's book is a study of Dickens's style, theoretically sophisticated, often difficult, but at the same time closely aware of, and filled with enthusiasm for, the particularities of the text. Its special concern is "to examine style mainly when with peculiar directness it oversees or enacts the trials of imagination", and he explains that "trials" is here an intentional pun, referring both to experiments and to ordeals. The influence of poststructuralist theory no doubt lies behind Stewart's interest in how style can explore "the poetic impulse itself from which language springs", though he concedes that Dickens is not one of the writers whose prose "takes itself as its subject".

The special experiences attributed by the Romantic poet to the extraordinary imagination of a gifted few are extended in the nineteenth-century novel to ordinary people, and Stewart sets out to show this taking place in Dickens. His "only methodology" is "a watchful interest in those scenes that become invested with meanings by their own advance scenarios, beyond plan or plotting", which "summon . . . the complex surrounding drama which they so unsuspectingly mirror". The two crucial figures in his argument, from the beginning and end of Dickens's career, are Sam Weller (*Pickwick Papers*) and Jenny Wren (*Our Mutual Friend*): both of them ratify belief in the imagination – Sam "with miraculous ease and finesse", Jenny "wearied by pain and remorseless threats of disillusionment".

SLATER sets out not only "to provide a fuller and juster account of Dickens's actual relations with, and ideas about, women than has yet been offered to the world, but also to further the critical rehabilitation of his fictional women". The sharp focus of his study enables him to produce one of the most successful of literary biographies. There are three parts: first, a very well documented account of the women in Dickens's life – his mother, Maria Beadnell, the three Hogarth sisters, and Ellen Ternan; second, a discussion of the female characters in the novels; and third, an account of what Dickens wrote or said about women. Dickens's explicit views of women and on domesticity were conventional in the extreme, but the novels are often richer and more complex than his opinions. Thus, despite his orthodox veneration for the angel in the house, the fiction devotes at least as much space to showing disruptions of the domestic ideal. When the ideal is ruined by male brutality or weakness, the treatment is comic. The three types of young woman to whom Dickens is always responsive are the Fairy or Angel, the Good Sister, and the Kitten. Slater is particularly interesting on the strategies for minimising the elements of sexuality in the depiction of young women, and the indications of Dickens's "basic hostility to women asserting themselves as sexual beings".

FLINT's book provides an interesting supplement to House. It too relates the novels to Victorian society, especially in the treatment of social change, industrialism, class and gender, while at the same time using structuralist, Bakhtinian, and deconstructive methods to show the centrality of contradictions and ambivalences in the representation of character and social problems (she suggests replacing the concept of "character" by A.J. Greimas's term "actant"). Her constant aim is to show the apparent unity of the novels is a chimera, that they "admit and present unresolvable differences and points of view".

D.A. MILLER's book is a general study of the novel, but Dickens plays a major role in it. Its opening discussion of the novel and the police, in which *Oliver Twist* looms large, develops a Foucauldian argument, that despite recent deconstructive theories about the wild, lawless, and rebellious elements in the novel, it is actually complicit with the police procedures it seems to criticise, in a way similar to the operation of discipline in modern society. Its chapter on *Bleak House* contrasts the anonymity and constant delay of the law with the efficacy of the police, in which priority is given to personal agency, and compares the former to deconstructive, and the latter to Marxist, criticism, claiming that each implies a need for the other. This is probably the most rewarding New-Historicist study of Dickens.

ACKROYD's is the one recent biography on a scale to compare with Johnson's. There are two striking contrasts between them. First, Ackroyd's writing is more lively, and his psychology more modern and complex: his Dickens is ravaged by contradictory feelings and self-doubts, and is less morally confident than Johnson's. And second, Ackroyd has no footnotes, and is sparing of dates, so that it is almost impossible to find out from his book just when any particular episode happened.

ARMSTRONG begins with a historical survey of the idea of home in English culture before, and contemporary with, Dickens, quoting (in an informative first chapter) a number of Victorian poems and essays to illustrate its religious and psychological function. She then proceeds to a meticulous examination of the idea in all of Dickens's novels. There are occasional shrewd general comments ("the religion of home not being acknowledged as a religion, its implications are never examined"), but her treatment of the novels is uncritical: all examples are treated as uniformly successful, even those plasterboard saints Kate Nickleby and Agnes Wickfield. But for this very reason, the book gives an excellent account of Dickens's intentions.

INGHAM's book invites comparison with Slater's, from which it differs strikingly and explicitly in method: it addresses itself to an examination of the language in which women are constructed in the novels, and not to the social conditions that lie behind them: indeed, she explicitly attacks biographical criticism as necessarily tautological. Five main stereotypes (or, as she calls them, "signs") of women are discussed: mobile girls, fallen girls, excessive females ("garrulous inconsequentiality" is seen as the hallmark of women speaking), passionate women (though they do not actually commit adultery, the "not" functions more as a positive than a negative: Freud's dream-interpretation is invoked as justification for this reasoning), and true mothers (who are almost never the biological mothers). This is a book full of perceptive insights, valuable even to those who may not share its feminist-structuralist approach.

MORGAN begins with a chapter on "Critical Issues", which attempts "to escape both the Scylla of the radical instability of language and the Charybdis of too narrowly restricting [the critic's] task", is a serious and helpful attempt to learn from recent critical theories without abandoning traditional interpretations. The use of psychoanalysis, for instance, leads to "archaeological" discoveries about what is buried, "the hidden engine that drives a novel", but it must be balanced by a teleology, an exploration of the intended meaning of the literary work. This dialectical approach is then used in four illuminating essays on *The Old Curiosity Shop*, *David Copperfield*, *Little Dorrit*, and *Great Expectations*.

LUCAS's book is perceptive though one-sided. It is based on a well-informed awareness of the tensions of Victorian society, and explores Dickens's intervention in social and political conflict: his writing is described as "an offence against refinement", his subject as "the cost of class-consciousness". All the novels are seen as engaging with "Dickens's deep fears about the emergent society of industrial commercial capitalism". The result is some very illuminating insights into the fiction, especially *Bleak House*, but always from a relentlessly materialist viewpoint, so that personal and spiritual issues are constantly subordinated to questions of class and power, and Dickens is regarded not as deeply ambivalent about politics, but steadily as a radical. It is nevertheless more perceptive than many a better-balanced study.

SADRIN's book is more wide-ranging than its narrowly focused title suggests. It treats the themes of paternity and inheritance as a way of finding interest in even the most conventionally melodramatic aspects of Dickens's plots. The handing over of both the father's money and the father's name is seen as central to much of Dickens's fictive world: "the father's death is vital, necessary to the self-fulfilment of the son, whose bereavement is his true birth". Careful analysis of plots is supplemented by a discriminating use of Freud on gender-asymmetry in the language – "patrimony" has a financial meaning that "matrimony" has not. The book concludes with a speculation on the connection between the figures of Oedipus and Telemachus – the son who murders and the son who obeys his father – as a way of representing the ambivalence of Dickens's treatment of fathers and sons.

LAURENCE LERNER

Dickinson, Emily 1830–1886

American poet

Bennett, Paula, *Emily Dickinson: Woman Poet*, Hemel Hempstead, Hertfordshire: Harvester Wheatsheaf, 1990; Iowa City: University of Iowa Press, 1990

Cameron, Sharon, *Choosing Not Choosing: Dickinson's Fascicles*, Chicago: University of Chicago Press, 1993

Dickie, Margaret, *Lyric Contingencies: Emily Dickinson and Wallace Stevens*, Philadelphia: University of Pennsylvania Press, 1991

Diehl, Joanne Feit, *Women Poets and the American Sublime*, Bloomington: Indiana University Press, 1990

Dobson, Joanne, *Dickinson and the Strategies of Reticence: The Woman Writer in Nineteenth-Century America*, Bloomington: Indiana University Press, 1989

Farr, Judith, *The Passion of Emily Dickinson*, Cambridge, Massachusetts: Harvard University Press, 1992

Juhasz, Suzanne, and Cristanne Miller (eds.), *Emily Dickinson: A Celebration for Readers*, New York and London: Gordon & Breach, 1989

Knapp, Bettina L., *Emily Dickinson*, New York: Continuum, 1989

Lease, Benjamin, *Emily Dickinson's Readings of Men and Books: Sacred Soundings*, London: Mamillan, 1990; New York: St Martin's Press, 1990

Loving, Jerome, *Emily Dickinson: The Poet on the Second Story*, Cambridge and New York: Cambridge University Press, 1986

McHugh, Heather, *Broken English: Poetry and Partiality*, Middletown, Connecticut: Wesleyan University Press, 1993; Hanover, New Hampshire: University Press of New England, 1994

McNeil, Helen, *Emily Dickinson*, London: Virago Press, 1986; New York: Pantheon, 1986

Miller, Cristanne, *Emily Dickinson: A Poet's Grammar*, Cambridge, Massachusetts: Harvard University Press, 1987

Phillips, Elizabeth, *Emily Dickinson: Personae and Performance*, University Park: Pennsylvania State University Press, 1988

Smith, Martha Nell, *Rowing in Eden: Rereading Emily Dickinson*, Austin: University of Texas Press, 1992

Two circumstances affect all commentary on Dickinson. First, only a handful of her poems were published in her lifetime, and her response to the ways magazine editors mishandled her work was to renounce publication entirely. Therefore, no editions of her poems exist which have her authority. (They were known in her lifetime because they were circulated among her family and wide circle of friends and correspondents, and she often included poems in her letters.). After the first – and not dependable – edition of 1890, several other editions followed over the first 30 years of this century; but the first scholarly edition was done in 1955 by Thomas H. Johnson, and this edition is the text which all subsequent ones follow. The major exception to this is R.W. Franklin's *The Manuscript Books of Emily Dickinson* (1981), a two-volume edition of the manuscripts of the poems in facsimile, which reproduce the "fascicles" – the loosely bound gatherings of her poems, which Dickinson made. All recent critical commentary now refers to Johnson's and Franklin's editions, frequently citing Franklin's text as a better authority than Johnson's, and this is especially true of the recent wave of feminist commentary on Dickinson.

The second major circumstance that affects commentary on Dickinson has to do with a psychological trauma she suffered in the late 1850s and early 1860s. In the aftermath of this, Dickinson withdrew from all normal forms of social intercourse, and was rarely seen thereafter by anyone other than close members of her family and some few friends. The cause of this trauma remains unknown – possibly a fear of blindness due to certain eye-illnesses she suffered at that period – although most commentators tend to interpret it as emotional despair at rejection by a lover or lovers, an argument supported by the existence of three letters known as "the Master letters", written between 1858 and 1861 and addressed to an unidentified "Master", which are deeply painful expressions of ardent love and emotional subjection. Though these letters exist in manuscript, we have no means of knowing whether they were sent, or to whom. The Master letters are a major irritant to feminist critics, some of whom dispute their centrality to a full understanding of Dickinson's work. Increasingly feminist critics argue, with some justice, that the central emotional relationship in Dickinson's life was with her sister-in-law, Sue Gilbert.

In addition, Dickinson's poems repeatedly express crises of religious faith, and some argue that the central concern of her work is succinctly expressed in her question to a correspondent – "does eternity exist?"

These circumstances determine the approaches critics make to Dickinson's work, and lead some writers into psychobiographical readings. Thus, the labour to identify the addressee of the Master letters has been one dominant branch of Dickinson commentary. The most important recent commentary on her is by women, not all of them ideological feminists.

She is now regarded as one of the two greatest American poets (the other is Walt Whitman), and one of the greatest women poets of all time. She wrote exclusively in the lyric form, using an idiosyncratic punctuation and a remarkably exotic vocabulary in which she addresses the fundamental concerns of human experience. The emotional and intellectual strength of her poems is evident both in her short passionate love lyrics and in her intense, cerebral meditations on death, faith, and God.

BENNETT exemplifies the virtues and the extreme partisanship of feminist criticism in what is generally one of the best introductory studies of Dickinson available. This short, trenchant study has at its centre the argument that the sources of Dickinson's creativity are cliterocentric, that much of her work celebrates same-sex love, and that she makes a virtue of smallness. Bennett proposes that Dickinson embraced smallness both as the given condition of the female in sexual terms (the female organ of sexual pleasure, the clitoris, being small by comparison with the male phallus) and in relation to the wider cultural status of women in the second half of nineteenth-century America; but far from bemoaning this condition, Dickinson celebrated it and associated it with women's strengths and their challenge to the phallocentric sexual and social power of the dominant male culture. If this description suggests an aridly ideological reading of Dickinson, the truth is that Bennett's book is lively and provocative in the best ways, and the issue of Dickinson's cliterocentric creativity is but one part of her concerns. She has instructive chapters on Dickinson's metaphysics (her questioning response to the nature of being), on religion, nature, and the poet's psychology. In addition, Bennett is one of those critics who particularly challenge the authority of Johnson's edition of the poems, and she argues for an edition that will reflect what she thinks to be Dickinson's condition of creative undecidability in relation to variant words, lines and punctuation in particular poems as these may be seen in Franklin's facsimile edition of the manuscripts.

McNEIL's introductory study reads Dickinson's refusal of publication, and her social reclusiveness from her early thirties, as strategies for asking questions about her society and its beliefs and values, questions not generally considered appropriate topics for women writers in nineteenth-century America. This is one possible way of dealing with the poet's withdrawal from the social world, and a way that seeks to demystify it, and give Dickinson's choices an intellectual and a spiritual authority denied her in some other readings. This is a sophisticated yet accessible study of particular value for new readers of Dickinson who are unfamiliar with her American contexts.

KNAPP's study comes in a series of introductory accounts of American writers, though this reading of Dickinson is wide ranging and thorough. Her criticism has a tendency to overemphasize the extent to which Dickinson may be read as an examplar of modernist writing, through the ways in which her poems suggest a spirit alienated from the intellectual culture to which she belonged. This is simply a matter of emphasis and degree, because there is no doubt that the impassioned introspective self-scrutiny we find in Dickinson's work makes a powerful appeal to the mid-twentieth-century reader. One of the particular virtues of Knapp's study is in the instructive close reading she gives of a wide range of poems, many of them not usually examined in Dickinson criticism. This is a very valuable study for students.

CAMERON's concern is with the fascicles of the poems and the interactive relationship of context and meaning revealed by reading poems grouped within the same fascicle, a way of reading Dickinson not possible using Johnson's edition. Ideally Cameron looks for the ways in which these conjunctions of poems yield new interpretative possibilities, though she is just as interested where these placings seem to defeat inquiry into the relatedness of theme, idea, and modes of figuration. In addition, Cameron looks at the way these fascicle groups seem to defeat our conventional understanding of the boundedness, or the "limit of the frame", of the lyric form. This approach to the poems destabilises the assumed relationship between the speaking voice of a poem, its subject, and its meaning, which must remain potential rather than realised, as is suggested by Dickinson's practice of including variant words and lines in the fascicle text of many poems, as though holding out the possibility of other ways of reading them. This complex study is not for beginners, but for those familiar with the debate about the status of the fascicles and the possibilities of reading the poems grouped within them as bound by common preoccupations.

SMITH, like Cameron, chooses the fascicles (and the poet's letters) as the best text of her work: she works with them rather than Johnson's edition, because she believes in them as a "performance script" ever open to new possibilities of interpretation and response. She looks at the Master letters and the letters to Sue Gilbert to explore the potential relationship between text and reader, which she sees as at the heart of Dickinson's work. Of the Master letters Smith challenges the belief that they were intended for a single reader, and argues instead that they are the site of Dickinson's creative negotiations of the self within a literary framework, rather than confessional admissions of emotional dependence. Smith writes in the recent tradition of homoerotic readings in looking at the poems for, and letters to, Sue Gilbert in an endeavour to challenge the gender biases of Dickinson's early editors and commentators in their desire to erase or conceal the lesbian context of the poet's feelings for her sister-in-law. Finally, Smith wants the poems and letters seen as occasions for interactive engagements – between Dickinson herself and her texts, between text and reader, and between reader and author. This is an important revisionary reading of the poet, and one that argues cogently for the priority of the manuscripts over the printed versions of the work.

PHILLIPS takes to heart Dickinson's cautionary words to Higginson that her poems were about a "supposed self", a warning against reading them as concealed expressions of her own biography. As a result Phillips' study is a welcome relief from those psychobiographical studies of Dickinson in which there is as much invention about the poet and her life and times as there is intelligent commentary. Furthermore, Phillips has good chapters on Dickinson's creative engagement with other writers, such as the Brontë sisters, George Eliot, and the Brownings, and she writes instructively of Dickinson's response to the American Civil War. Phillips disputes the presentation of the poet as the psychologically damaged recluse of popular legend, and gives us a version of Dickinson as a robust and confident figure in her creative and social contexts.

LEASE sees Dickinson's creativity as intimately bound up with her relationship to certain key men in her life, notably the Reverend Charles Wadsworth (often cited as the addressee of the Master letters, without any hard evidence) and Thomas Wentworth Higginson, the first outsider to whom she sent her poems for scrutiny. In addition, Lease argues for Dickinson's imaginative relationship with a series of "sacred texts", Shakespeare, the Bible, Isaac Watts's hymns, and the devotional poetry and prose of the seventeenth century. Lease's arguments about the importance of Wadsworth and Higginson are conventional, as is his account of the intensity of Dickinson's reading of, and intimacy with, the writers listed: what is original in his book is his final chapter on the burgeoning movement of Christian Spiritualism in America in the 1850s and its scientific and psychological expression through telegraphy and mesmerism, all of which lends support to his view of Dickinson's involvement with the language and imagery of the occult.

FARR has written the best recent biographical-critical study of Dickinson, in which she confidently identifies Samuel Bowles as the addressee of the Master letters, and argues for Sue Gilbert as both the focus of the poet's unceasing, if unrequited, love and the best contemporary reader of Dickinson's poems. In addition, Farr reads Dickinson's relationship to a vocabulary of visual imagery drawn from two contemporary schools of American painting, the Hudson River School and the Luminists, whose moralizing versions of the American landscape provide a context for the poet's vocabulary of desire and loss in both her passional and metaphysical contexts. Farr has anatomized those poems, which can be confidently described as written to, or for, either Bowles or Gilbert, and has uncovered the coded language Dickinson used to speak of both these figures. Bowles, a journalist and editor of considerable renown, was an intimate friend of the poet's father and brother, and thus a familiar of the Dickinson household, and the argument Farr makes for him as the unacknowledged Master is difficult to refute. Equally, Farr's account of the poet's passionate feelings for Sue Gilbert, and the consequential difficulties of that relationship, are entirely convincing. Farr here makes a major contribution to our understanding of Dickinson's work in its most private and troubling contexts, ably supported by her placement of Dickinson's use of a moral and ethical vocabulary drawn from the world of the visual arts in nineteenth-century America.

DIEHL reads Dickinson in relation to four twentieth-century American women poets – Marianne Moore, Elizabeth Bishop, Sylvia Plath, and Adrienne Rich – in an argument that sees Dickinson as the instigator of a feminine tradition of the "sublime", which runs counter to that of Ralph Waldo Emerson, the orthodox spokesman for American Transcendentalism, and his creative successor Whitman, together the two nineteenth-century male American writers widely regarded as the originators of a mode of writing that speaks optimistically of the deep spiritual potential of the American experience. Diehl uses Dickinson and these other women poets as feminine voices equal to their male counterparts in their expression of sublime potential and experiential difficulty. In particular, Diehl's reading of what she calls the "glowing austerity" of Dickinson's argument with Emerson constitutes a brilliant analysis of the expressive strategies of Dickinson's work, in which Emerson's spiritual idea of "self-reliance" becomes subordinate to Dickinson's empowering of her own consciousness as the centre of a self-made world. This very impressive scholarly book will appeal particularly to readers familiar with the canonical placement of Emerson and Whitman at the centre of the American nineteenth-century renaissance of creative thought, and its great virtue has to do with the way it argues for Dickinson as a creative artist equally at the centre of that world, who becomes a powerful model for later women writers.

DOBSON pays close attention to the formal difficulties of interpreting the poems, and to their textual ambiguities, though she is equally concerned to read them in the social context and intellectual temper of Dickinson's life and times. She argues that the poetry reflects Dickinson's response to the contemporary ideology of womanhood to which she both assents and dissents, and that these opposed responses generate the essential dynamics of the poems. This is an impressive scholarly study which moves persuasively between close focus on particular poems to the wider frame of the cultural ambience and its pressures as they are registered in Dickinson's work.

JUHASZ and MILLER's collection of essays by delegates to a conference on Dickinson gives a useful insight into the nature of the contemporary debates about Dickinson's work among American feminist scholars. The sections of this book reflect the "workshops" at which individual poems were analyzed from a variety of feminist perspectives by different speakers, whose readings were then debated by the workshop as a whole. This is a helpful book for students, in that it opens a window on the ways in which their teachers strive to understand Dickinson's work, and some of the individual contributions here offer persuasive interpretations of some particularly difficult poems.

LOVING takes what he calls Dickinson's "slant" or peculiarly angled view of life in pursuit of what he calls an "interiorized" view of the "echo chamber of her metaphors" through which her work achieves its extreme intensity of expression. In Loving's version, Dickinson is a proto-modernist writer whose art enables her to survive both the daily failures of social experience and the spiritual crises of unbelief. Despite its agonistic expression of anxiety and religious scepticism, Dickinson's work is seen by Loving as an instrument of survival, and he gives a version of the poet who deals in the mess of human circumstances rather than in the ecstasy of origins and conclusions. He writes persuasively of the poet's refusal of Emersonian optimism, and is a good reader of the deliberate incivility of tone that marks much of Dickinson's work and gives it its characteristically challenging flavour. He argues plausibly that Dickinson refused to publish her work as a way of preserving it as her own "psychological property", and while he toys with some of the biographical materials of Dickinson's life, his version of her rather dislocates her from her social and cultural context, and gives us a wilfully isolated and withdrawn artist. This is not a book for beginners, but is an intelligent reading of Dickinson for those familiar with the psychobiographical accounts of her.

McHUGH is a poet whose critical engagement with other poets is from a shared creative impulse. This recent gathering of her critical essays includes a brilliant account of Dickinson's punctuation, read as an index of her creative power in opening up the most simple-seeming poem to a wide variety of interpretations. The essay "What Dickinson Makes a Dash For: Interpretive Insecurity as Poetic Freedom" confronts the paradox that terms like "book", "sentence", and "pen" are not only those of artistic freedom, but also those of penal containment, and she plays dramatically with the confluence of meanings of simple terms in a series of spirited readings of some poems by Dickinson. This is the work of a clever writer paying homage to a like mind, and is wonderfully instructive in what she shows us of the potential for meaning inherent in some of the barest of Dickinson's lyrics.

DICKIE's comparative study of lyric form in Dickinson and Wallace Stevens is unusual in that it is one of the few studies of Dickinson to maintain this comparative approach with a male poet. Dickie is interested in the relationship between the lyric voices of these poems and the questions of audience such poetry entails, for the lyric form invites an intimacy between poem and reader, yet here that intimacy is repeatedly occluded or made problematic by the unyieldingly complex and abstract ways Dickinson and Stevens find to articulate their concerns.

MILLER's book is of seminal importance because of her persistent concern with the poet's grammar: she is more interested in Dickinson's rhetoric than in her biography, that is to say in all the devices of writing which the poet used to structure and develop her poems. Miller addresses the tension between "this poet's partially articulated desire to speak to an audience . . . and her largely inarticulated decision to write the riddling elliptical poetry she does". Her central chapter analyses Dickinson's use of compression, disjunction, repetition, syntax, and speech, each of these concerns subdivided into issues such as the play of parataxis and hypotaxis, punctuation, capitalization, negation, and contrast. Though Miller's book sounds dauntingly technical in her concern with Dickinson's grammatical forms, her approach is lively and engaging, and is accessible to readers of all kinds. In this book, Miller's proto-feminist reading of Dickinson is rather half-hearted, but this is a matter of emphasis only, and other readers may respond more positively to this aspect of what is generally an excellent study of Dickinson.

LIONEL KELLY

Donne, John 1572–1631

English poet and sermon writer

Bald, Robert Cecil, *John Donne: A Life*, completed and edited by Wesley Milgate, Oxford: Clarendon Press, 1970; New York: Oxford University Press, 1970

Carey, John, *John Donne: Life, Mind and Art*, London and Boston: Faber & Faber, 1981

Larson, Deborah Aldrich, *John Donne and Twentieth-Century Criticism*, Rutherford, New Jersey: Fairleigh Dickinson University Press, 1989

Leishman, J.B., *The Monarch of Wit: An Analytical and Comparative Study of the Poetry of John Donne*, London: Hutchinson, 1951; New York: Harper & Row, 1965

Marotti, Arthur F., *John Donne, Coterie Poet*, Madison: University of Wisconsin Press, 1986

Marotti, Arthur F. (ed.), *Critical Essays on John Donne*, New York: G.K. Hall, 1994

Martz, Louis L., *The Poetry of Meditation: A Study in English Religious Literature of the Seventeenth Century*, New Haven, Connecticut: Yale University Press, 1954, revised 1962; London: Oxford University Press, 1954

Roberts, John R. (ed.), *Essential Articles for the Study of John Donne's Poetry*, Hamden, Connecticut: Archon Books, 1975

The poems and other writings of John Donne command continuing critical attention. He has been claimed by modernism, by being read as a twentieth-century poet (the colloquial/dramatic/abrupt Donne), but is as often rehistoricized, particularly by those critics who look at the poetry as it was initially divulged to its coterie readers. The critic on Donne faces the inescapable doom of being found less brilliant than the poet. Much of Donne's effect depends on ingenuities, which can be laborious when expounded, while an honest attempt to explain what Donne thought about things can transmute glittering show into leaden substance. Only Carey's bravura performance matches the *brio* of the author. Those who read the poetry first, and well, will know how hard it is to guess what lay behind this poetry of stances: psycho-biographical theories abound, assigning to Donne every kind of complex. Larson's book (see below) is a study of the accumulated studies.

MARTZ's study (*q.v.* "Metaphysical Poetry" entry) has had a pervasive influence on studies of Donne, especially those focusing on the *Anniversaries* and *Divine Poems*. Martz argues that Donne's true subject was not Elizabeth Drury, but meditation on the world's decay using methods taken from the devotional exercises of Ignatius Loyola. A five-part structure is discerned in the "First Anniversary", a composition judged to fail because Donne cannot unify the purposes of meditation and eulogy. The "Second Anniversary" is judged a more successful poem. The implications of Martz's study were far reaching for Donne scholarship, and thereafter he continued to amplify and support his thesis. Barbara Lewalski's study *Donne's Anniversaries and the Poetry of Praise* (1973) was the most thorough reply, and Martz has subsequently conceded the importance of the Protestant tradition of sermon and meditation she describes. There is a useful discussion of Martz's impact on scholarship and a bibliography of it in Larson, while Carey delivers a characteristically brusque dismissal of the meditative tradition as Martz supposed it to function in the more intense Holy Sonnets.

Reviewed by Dame Helen Gardner under the simple and admiring title "All the Facts", BALD's *Life* scrupulously avoids the kind of autobiographical inferences and subjective interpretations which feature so large in the criticism. Its massive scholarship and detail (in 627 pages) reminds us of how much we do know factually, not inferentially, about Donne and his friends, patrons, and contacts. Most historicizing scholarship starts with this volume, whose sobriety is a good corrective for any reader after considering those who enlarge upon conjectures. Real life happens for poets too: here is Donne and his family, or Donne as Dean of St Paul's (the organisational structure of the Cathedral and the modest reforms to public decorum in the building that Donne made are all interestingly described). Penny-plain to Carey's tuppence- coloured, Bald is fair and measured on Donne's religious life. Perhaps the life tends towards the style of the nineteenth-century hero-worshipping biography, but doing Donne credit as a man of conscience is positively unusual. The full portraiture is included and discussed.

CAREY's book is the outstanding critical work on Donne. Compellingly written, the study takes a pyscho-biographical approach to the author, moving without hesitation between "Life", "Mind" and "Art". Carey's mastery of all the writings – poems, prose, sermons – and acute gift for quotation combine with acerbic reactions to other critics and a penchant for distressing or hilarious backgound information. The total effect undeniably informs and animates the reader's response to the writings, but there is in Carey a shade too much of the prosecuting counsel. The subject under dissection is Donne's personality, and to Donne is ascribed an ambitiousness and will-worship that can finally seem mean-spirited. Rigorously unsentimental, the study tends to deny Donne all higher motives – any spiritual impulse, any chance of an ideal in love is slighted. Carey's treatment of Elegie XIX, "To His Mistress: Going to Bed", has become notorious, and the second edition of this study does show signs of a slight softening (the "girls" in the amatory poems become "women", which tilts the poems back a little towards mutuality. Readers should note Carey's rhetoric performance as carefully as Donne's own: for instance, the quick progress from the poet's "oppressed shoes" in Elegie IV to the martyrdom of Margaret Clitheroe. The contentions (that Donne projects onto his inconstant female partners his own apostatic unfaithfulness to the Catholic God) may either suggest much, or seem like lecture-theatre brilliancies. Some of the critical readings (e.g., of "Death Be Not Proud") are so well honed, so unexpectedly expressed, that they seem to invite bursts of applause – and to deserve them too. Carey is far too intelligent and informed ever to be demonstrably wrong, and far too provocative to be unobjectionable. His advocacy of certain poems, particularly of "Metempsychosis", does Donne a great service. An associated study, "Donne and Coins", appeared in a *Festschrift* volume, *Renaissance Essays Presented to Dame Helen Gardner*, edited by Carey himself.

LARSON does more than her title promises. She first gives an account of the early critical heritage, looks at biographical criticism (including Carey), then the refashioning of Donne post-Eliot by the New Critics, surveys attempts to align Donne with, or set him in contrast to, various literary traditions, and looks at critics on Donne's views of women, religion, and science. Larson is assiduous and even-handed, but evidently prefers studies that depend on biographical, historical, and textual facts.

LEISHMANN's book, many times reprinted, perhaps by now owes its place on bibliographies to longevity and the author's wit in getting first to Thomas Carew's elegy to supply this book's memorable and effective title. The work itself is intended as an introduction, and often reads like written-up lectures. Leishmann tends to quote whole poems. He warns that the more "outrageous" songs and sonnets are not autobiographical (retiring "The Indifferent" to behind its Ovidian model, for example). Conversely, he is willing to suppose that the "serious" songs and sonnets do deal with Donne's own feelings: the "Valediction Forbidding Mourning" is "surely . . . the language of the heart". Prone to such biographical suppositions, Leishmann arranges the poems into different classes, from the most cynical to the most earnest. Diffuse and undemanding, this was the best introduction written at its time, and has had many readers. It now reads like an example of what criticism once was like.

MAROTTI (1986) claims that "virtually all the basic features of Donne's poetic art are related to its coterie character". His important study of Donne's output in relation to the main cultural environments of Donne's life (The Inns of Court, the courts of Elizabeth and James, the reduced world of the social exile) is perhaps most valuable when contextualising the early and mature verse epistles, poems to friends and partronesses. On other works, Marotti can be unsurprising; in search of excitement he ventures away from his initial project and into psychologising. That Donne didn't publish his poems in a conventional way is undeniably the basic fact to be impressed upon new students, but Marotti inconsistently takes his texts from modern editions, rather than from the early manuscript collections he describes. The idea of a particular audience is pressed too far: Donne often punned upon his own name, but that his use of the word "more" is conditioned by his wife's maiden name will only be allowed by those who can imagine that an ego as big as Donne's could think of his wife as anything other than Ann Donne.

In the "Critical Essays on British Literature" series, MAROTTI (1994) edits and introduces a collection of seven essays by respected critics, one commissioned for the volume, the others recently published elsewhere. The subject matter is contemporary. Annabel Patterson on the politics of Donne's writing is arguably the most substantial piece in the collection: it asks us to rethink the notion of Donne as unqualified in his allegiance to King James; Aers and Kress discuss Donne as "alienated intellectual"; Janet Mueller writes on "Women among the Metaphysicals". The conclusions are less radical: that Donne was both a subtle sycophant and critical troublemaker, that the love poems may "imagine equality, but inscribe at key points asymmetry of outlook and sexual role" (Mueller). The newness is sometimes carried too far: Richard Halpern writes of Donne writing "difficult poems, full of cybernetic noise", and Achsah Guibbory, writing on the politics of love in Donne's *Elegies*, suggests that their misogyny is a reaction to threats posed to Donne's notions of masculine superiority by a female monarch, looks like a determined attempt to get some politics into the poems. Donne's reservations about the emotional forcefulness of women and the desire they provoke are interesting enough without unevidenced suppositions about Donne's "Greatest and Fairest Empress". Richard Corthell contributes to this volume a psychoanalytic study of the *Anniversaries*. The divine poems are only discussed in Marotti's own contribution to the volume, which is, disappointingly, an extract from his 1986 volume (discussed above).

ROBERTS's collection has a generous 474 pages, with another 80 pages of notes, and divides into eight sections: Donne's reputation; Donne and the development of English poetry; Donne's use of tradition; prosody; love poetry; religious poetry; the *Anniversaries*; and miscellaneous poems. The articles and extracts range from the grand claim (Martz) to the knotty point (Murray on "What Was the Soul of the Apple?"), and feature classic essays and classic disagreements (Kermode and Bateson versus Eliot's dissociation of sensibility,

Harold Love against Martz on the *Anniversaries*). Pre-feminist and pre-New-Historicist, the editor misses little that was important (particularly in American scholarship) up to its time of publication.

ROY J. BOOTH

Doolittle, Hilda 1886–1961

Known as "H.D." American poet and novelist

Buck, Claire, *H.D. and Freud: Bisexuality and a Feminine Discourse*, Hemel Hempstead, Hertfordshire: Harvester Wheatsheaf, 1991; New York: St Martin's Press, 1991

DuPlessis, Rachel Blau, *H.D.: The Career of That Struggle*, Bloomington: Indiana University Press, 1986; Brighton, Sussex: Harvester Press, 1986

Friedman, Susan Stanford, *Psyche Reborn: The Emergence of H.D.*, Bloomington: Indiana University Press, 1981

Friedman, Susan Stanford, *Penelope's Web: Gender, Modernity, H.D.'s Fiction*, Cambridge and New York: Cambridge University Press, 1990

Guest, Barbara, *Herself Defined: The Poet H.D. and Her World*, Garden City, New York: Doubleday, 1984; London: Collins, 1985

Robinson, Janice S., *H.D.: The Life and Work of an American Poet*, Boston: Houghton Mifflin, 1982

Arguably the most significant and pioneering analytical work on H.D.'s *oeuvre* to date has been done by Susan Friedman. FRIEDMAN (1981) argues that "H.D.'s experience as an analysand with Sigmund Freud and her exploration of esoteric tradition provided her with an interrelated framework of quest that nourished the explosion of a new kind of poetry and prose during the forties and fifties". Consequently, the two sections of the book focus on the function of psychoanalysis and esoteric religion in H.D.'s work, as well as considering these as part of a larger debate within modernism about the differences between scientific and artistic modes of creating meaning. Part One discusses the impact of Freud on her ideas, and her disagreement with his methods, in her search to "overturn Freud's misogyny and develop an authentic female voice". Part Two examines H.D.'s interest in occult and esoteric religions, and explores the manner in which she utilizes myths and religious traditions in her re-vision of patriarchal traditions. The book seeks to liberate H.D from people's narrow definition of her as an Imagist, and the "concomitant 'phallic criticism' that has plagued her woman-centered mythmaking".

Building on her earlier work, FRIEDMAN (1990) turns to H.D.'s fiction and "examines the weave of H.D.'s modernity as it is patterned by gender, genre, and history in the discourse of her prose". Friedman sees the fiction anticipating much post-structuralist theory of the feminine, although her book resists becoming an "illustrative praxis" for proving of the new French feminist theory. Focusing on H.D.'s self-conscious construction of self-identity, the predominant metaphor of the text is H.D.'s own adopted figure of Penelope, a writer weaving an entangled, palimpsetic text. After placing H.D.'s prose *oeuvre* within the context of modernity, the text considers the relation of H.D.'s prose fiction to Imagist lyrics, its autobiographical telos, and its poststructuralist stylistics. Subsequent chapters examine "the textualized selves H.D. constructed as she reflected on her various pasts in her prose fictions and memoirs". In a series of sensitive, patient, and detailed readings, Friedman's avowed aim is "to explore the *difference* of H.D.'s prose oeuvre: its difference from her poetry, its difference from male modernism as the Penelopean Other enacting its own agency, and the difference it makes to a literary history of modernity". Friedman concludes that an endless desire for, and resistance to, a bridge between the poetry and prose is evident: and through this oscillation between H.D.'s poetry and prose, a symbiotic relationship, a hybridization, emerges.

Two complementary analytical, literary biographies of H.D.'s life and work have been written. GUEST traces H.D.'s life and its intersections with what H.D. called her "initiators" – men who directed and shared her work and life – and her relations with women who variously admired and adored her. Guest's focus falls on H.D.'s preoccupation and obsession with "the definition of self, the penetration of self". Symptomatic of her "surfacing narcissism", Guest regards this necessity to define herself as indicative of her reclusiveness, loneliness, and exile: "she was separated by a kind of homelessness of self, from the self who hypnotized her". ROBINSON tends to integrate the life with the writings more fully. With copious illustrations, she also provides a full bibliography of primary and secondary sources, and a chronology of H.D.'s life. Seeking to illuminate the autobiographical aspects of the poetry and novels, the book "presents H.D. within the literary context within which she wrote", and hence there is a stress on the work of other writers, such as Ezra Pound, Richard Aldington, D.H. Lawrence, and Bryher. Among the general discussions of twentieth-century modernisms, there are a series of good chapters on Imagism, contextualizing her poetics within the general development of the Imagist movement. Altogether, these two biographies provide a very comprehensive treatment of the writer's life and work.

A feminist analysis of H.D.'s *oeuvre* initiates DuPLESSIS's work, relating biographical information to "material conflicts, issues and resolutions inscribed or encoded in individual texts". The study pivots on the isolation of four types of authority evident in her work – "cultural authority", "authority of otherness/marginality", "gender authority", and "sexual/erotic authority". In focusing on "cultural authority", DuPlessis argues that H.D.'s treatment of classicism in her early life often put "woman at the centre of inquiry, and [asked] about the inscription of gender and the female in traditional culture". The second focus, on the types of otherness that preoccupied H.D.'s writing, looks at her various groups of novels and films, and scrutinizes the politics of the sexuality and textuality of feminine "otherness". The third focus falls on the period of analysis with Freud and the writing sparked by the two world wars, during which, it is argued, H.D. sought to rupture the universalization of male experience and authority embedded in the Western philosophical and psychological tradition. Finally, the book considers H.D.'s experiments with various kinds of female desire at the heart of narrative and language, as she repeatedly confronted "the dilemmas which gender poses and

. . . claim[ed] the authorities that one's gender offers for female creativity".

Acknowledging her debt to Friedman and DuPlessis, BUCK explores a slightly different tack, investigating the "model or models of the self she creates; from where she derives the models of subjectivity and sexuality which her work deploys, and . . . their relationship to sexual difference, sexuality and textuality". Although refraining from using psychoanalytic theories as a "master" discourse to *explain* H.D.'s writing, Buck works on four central themes in her study – subjectivity as sexuality, myth as an alternative model of the self and sexual difference, translation, and reading. Predicating a reading of H.D.'s fiction and prose on the basis of the structural use H.D. makes of bisexuality, Buck argues that H.D. persistently questions the terms of subjectivity itself rather than achieves a new mode of identity or femininity. In a series of sophisticated, well-informed, and detailed feminist and psychoanalytical readings, Buck finally concludes that H.D. defines "the knowledge of women as something you can know by knowing that you do not know it".

TIM S. WOODS

Dos Passos, John 1896–1970

American novelist, dramatist, and essayist

Colley, Iain, *Dos Passos and the Fiction of Despair*, London: Macmillan, 1978; Totowa, New Jersey: Rowman & Littlefield, 1978

Davis, Robert Gorham, *John Dos Passos*, Minneapolis: University of Minnesota Press, 1962

Hook, Andrew (ed.), *Dos Passos: A Collection of Critical Essays*, Englewood Cliffs, New Jersey: Prentice-Hall, 1974

Rosen, Robert C., *John Dos Passos: Politics and the Writer*, Lincoln: University of Nebraska Press, 1981

Wagner, Linda W., *Dos Passos: Artist as American*, Austin: University of Texas Press, 1979

Wrenn, John H., *John Dos Passos*, New York: Twayne, 1961

For a long time John Dos Passos was eclipsed in importance by his more famous literary contemporaries, notably William Faulkner, F. Scott Fitzgerald, and Ernest Hemingway. In the past quarter of a century or so, however, his place in any canonical account of early twentieth-century literature has become established. Criticism of him tends to veer between two connected, but uncomplementary, poles: some read his major fiction as an extreme manifestation of literary naturalism, seeing it as part of a tradition that extends back to Stephen Crane, Theodore Dreiser, and Frank Norris; others see it as one of the distinctive, and formative, achievements of American modernism. Both poles, nevertheless, emphasise the importance of reading Dos Passos's major work in the light of what might be called his sociological history of American life in the first half of this century.

WRENN's book is the first important attempt to resurrect Dos Passos from the relative obscurity into which he had fallen at the end of the 1950s, a consequence, Wrenn claims, of the "stereotyping" of his work. His approach is both biographical and critical, since, as he argues in his Preface, in Dos Passos's case it is particularly difficult to separate the man and his work when the work (especially *U.S.A.*) is presented as both personal and historical chronicle. Wrenn provides a detailed account of the influences that came to bear on Dos Passos in his formative years, and is one of the few critics to address intelligently the manner in which Dos Passos's decision to study architecture in Spain after graduating from Harvard evinces his concern with the social responsibility of the artist. The one real weakness of this otherwise very readable book is the very cursory treatment given to the late (i.e., post-*U.S.A.*) fiction.

DAVIS's brief study (in the University of Minnesota "Pamphlets on American Writers" series) is a serviceable introduction to Dos Passos's work. Davis provides a short biographical account of Dos Passos and some intelligent commentary on the way in which his sensibility was shaped by the intellectual and moral climate of World War I. This commentary directly influences Davis's reading of the political character of the early major novels, notably *Manhattan Transfer*.Several pages are given to a reading of the *U.S.A.* trilogy, but it is one of the merits of Davis's book that he offers an overview of those later novels that Dos Passos's critics all too frequently neglect (though it should be remembered that this study was published eight years before Dos Passos died).

HOOK's collection of critical essays (from the Prentice-Hall "Twentieth-Century Views" series) is particularly valuable since it gathers together more or less all the major essays on Dos Passos published during his lifetime. As Hook notes, his collection "embodies a selection from a modest critical harvest rather than a bumper crop", but included here are the excellent essays by Granville Hicks and Edmund Wilson on Dos Passos as a social and political novelist, the influential assessments of individual novels by Jean-Paul Sartre and F.R. Leavis (the former writing on *1919*, the latter on *The 42nd Parallel*), and other significant essays by Lionel Trilling, Alfred Kazin, John William Ward, Marshall McLuhan, Arthur Mizener, and Richard Chase. The student interested in a conspectus of perceptive critical commentary on Dos Passos can do no better than start here.

COLLEY's book, the first full-length study by an English critic, focuses on Dos Passos as a novelist of failure, despair, and alienation, its central argument being that where "the fiction of John Dos Passos ceases to draw energy from a nexus of alienation and doubt it loses artistic cohesion". Colley concentrates on the major novels, particularly *Manhattan Transfer* and *U.S.A.* (indeed, almost a third of the book is given over to *U.S.A*), and the emphasis in his criticism falls very much on Dos Passos's treatment of social and political polarities, with rather less time spent on a consideration of fictional technique. The concluding chapter looks, in somewhat summary fashion, at the post-*U.S.A.* fiction, with Colley tending to criticise it for a failure of political vision rather than for artistic defects.

WAGNER reads Dos Passos for what she calls his "deep involvement with American culture and the literature it might be expected to produce", and she tries to show, through a chronological reading of the major fiction, how Dos Passos "engages" with America, and how his changing political stances and changing narrative techniques reflect stages in his understanding of, and "interpretation" of, American life. Unlike Colley, she gives extensive treatment to the post-*U.S.A.* fiction, notably *District of Columbia* and *Midcentury*.

ROSEN's book remains the best study of Dos Passos' politics and their relationship to his writing, and in this respect he is not narrowly concerned with the fiction, for he makes considerable use of Dos Passos's journalism and his historical prose. The stages in Dos Passos's political itinerary – "a youthful pacifist rebel, a libertarian socialist, a Jeffersonian democrat, and finally a conservative Republican" – are all afforded a detailed exegesis, which locates each "guise" in American political and social history, while at the same time addressing "the complex relationship between Dos Passos's political thinking and his art".

HENRY CLARIDGE

Douglass, Frederick 1818–1895

American autobiographer, essayist, and journalist

Andrews, William (ed.), *Critical Essays on Frederick Douglass*, Boston: G.K. Hall, 1991
Bloom, Harold (ed.), *Frederick Douglass's "Narrative of the Life of Frederick Douglass"*, New York: Chelsea House, 1988
Martin, Waldo E., Jr., *The Mind of Frederick Douglass*, Chapel Hill: University of North Carolina Press, 1984
Preston, Dickson J., *Young Frederick Douglass: The Maryland Years*, Baltimore: Johns Hopkins University Press, 1980
Rowe, John Carlos, "Between Politics and Poetics: Frederick Douglass and Postmodernity", in *Reconstructing American Literary and Historical Studies*, edited by Günter H. Lenz, Hartmut Keil, and Sabine Bröck-Sallah, Frankfurt: Campus, 1990
Sundquist, Eric J. (ed.), *Frederick Douglass: New Literary and Historical Essays*, Cambridge and New York: Cambridge University Press, 1990

After generations of critical neglect by white academics, Frederick Douglass has been one of the major beneficiaries of the recent explosive proliferation of African-American studies. While much Douglass scholarship has gravitated towards his 1845 *Narrative of the Life of Frederick Douglass*, there has of late been a steady increase in attention to his other autobiographical works, as well as to "The Heroic Slave", various orations, political essays, newspaper articles, and letters. To date, however, academic commentary has been dominated by biographies and collections of essays, with no single-author extended analyses of the Douglass *oeuvre*.

BLOOM has brought together a representative sample of critical readings of the *Narrative*. The essays in this volume are arranged in the chronological sequence of their original publication between 1973 and 1986, and this provides a good opportunity to survey the development and range of responses to one of the key texts in African-American history. Several of the contributions are concerned with establishing the generic status of the text by exploring its relationship with both black and white linguistic codes (the slave narrative and autobiography, the black sermon and jeremiad, tribal and oral traditions, sentimental fiction, abolitionist propaganda, and the picaresque novel). Alongside these formal investigations there are noteworthy studies of Douglass's sensitivity to the economic and erotic imperatives of slavery and the significance of literacy and narrative to the African-American community. The variety of theoretical perspectives employed and the quality of much of the writing make this a useful introduction to criticism of the *Narrative*.

SUNDQUIST has compiled a collection of original essays by critics from a variety of disciplinary backgrounds. In addition to readings of the *Narrative* this volume contains material on *Life and Times* and "The Heroic Slave", as well as assessments of Douglass's achievements in the fields of journalism, oratory, and political activism. One of the focal points for this work is the nature of Douglass's sexual politics, and in "From Wheatley to Douglass: The Politics of Displacement" Henry Louis Gates, Jr., one of the foremost Douglass scholars, reiterates and expands on the objection, made by some black feminists, that the canonisation of work by African-American men has exacerbated the marginalization of writing by black women. Also worthy of mention are David Van Leer's piece on the "anxiety of ethnicity" produced by the *Narrative* for non-black readers, and Waldo E. Martin Jr.'s survey of Douglass's presence as a pivotal icon in the struggle for black rights, from the mid-1950s to the early 1970s. The strengths of this stimulating collection include its interdisciplinary scope, the originality of the subjects addressed, and the effort made by the contributors to sustain a genuinely critical engagement with Douglass and his writing.

ANDREWS has edited a comprehensive collection of essays, which brings together contemporary reviews of Douglass's autobiographies, reprinted articles, and some newly commissioned material. Two of the original essays focus on the subject of language and power in relation to the *Narrative*. Thad Ziolkowski investigates the dilemma confronted by the black writer who seeks to challenge white power from within the confines of the oppressor's language. In "The Antilanguage of Slavery", Ann Kibbey and Michele Stepto combine Marxist critical theory with linguistics to examine the alienation from self and language within the plantation economy, which Douglass struggles, in his writings, to overcome. In the most challenging and provocative contribution to this volume, Deborah McDowell offers a feminist reading of both the *Narrative* and *My Bondage and My Freedom*, and of Douglass's assimilation into the intellectual establishment. McDowell's critique of the gendered subjectivity that informs both Douglass's writing and its contemporary canonisation needs to be considered by all those with an interest in African-American cultural history.

In an article that represents a significant contribution to the debate on language and power in this field, ROWE proposes that the *Narrative* testifies to Douglass's acute awareness of the semiotics of slavery – the power-struggle taking place between the definers and the defined within both the systems of Southern feudalism and Northern capitalism. According to this thesis, Douglass managed to sequester the economic and religious discourses of the dominant culture and subvert them from within. Consequently, Rowe contends, the labels that are traditionally applied to this text – such as "autobiography" and "*Bildungsroman*" – constitute a distraction from its essential political imperatives, and are an academic embodiment of the "liberal racism" that Douglass had to contend with throughout his life. Rowe also argues that Douglass's recognition of the importance of control over information in the *Narrative* anticipates developments towards the commodification of knowledge in a post-industrial society. Although this and other parts of his thesis remain rather conjectural, Rowe's essay is undoubtedly a significant contribution to Douglass scholarship.

PRESTON's work was the first major biography of Douglass to appear since the 1940s. His major concern is with Douglass's formative years in the period before his escape from bondage in 1838. The exhaustive documentation of the details of black history in Talbot County make this a useful companion to close study of Douglass's autobiographies. Henry Louis Gates has suggested that the range and depth of Preston's biography enables scholars to move beyond essentialist readings of black autobiography towards a more sophisticated understanding of both Douglass's position in history and his rhetorical performances.

MARTIN's biography traces the full span of Douglass's career from the Maryland years right through to his death and subsequent legacy. The sections on Douglass's involvement in social reform, feminism, and changes in the ruling definitions of race and national identity will be of particular interest to students of his writing.

BRIAN JARVIS

Doyle, Arthur Conan 1859–1930

Scottish novelist, short-story writer, dramatist, and essayist

Hall, Trevor H., *Sherlock Holmes and His Creator*, London: Duckworth, 1978; New York: St Martin's Press, 1978

Harrison, Michael, *A Study in Surmise: The Making of Sherlock Holmes*, Bloomington, Indiana: Gaslight Publications, 1984

Jaffe, Jacqueline A., *Arthur Conan Doyle*, Boston: Twayne, 1987

McQueen, Ian, *Sherlock Holmes Detected: The Problems of the Long Stories*, New York: Drake, 1974; Newton Abbot, Devon: David & Charles, 1974

Payne, David S., *Myth and Modern Man in Sherlock Holmes: Sir Arthur Conan Doyle and the Uses of Nostalgia*, Bloomington, Indiana: Gaslight Publications, 1992

Shreffler, Philip A.(ed.), *The Baker Street Reader: Cornerstone Writings about Sherlock Holmes*, Westport, Connecticut: Greenwood Press, 1984

Sherlock Holmes is Arthur Conan Doyle's most famous creation, and most of the criticism written about Doyle revolves around his heroic consulting detective, who first appeared in *A Study in Scarlet* (1887). Since that time "the whole phenomenon of Sherlock Holmes has taken on its own life" (Shreffler), leaving the rest of Doyle's considerable literary accomplishments somewhat obscured.

McQUEEN applies his "tongue-in-cheek" theory that "Holmes and Watson were only *pretending* to be characters of fiction and had employed Conan Doyle to edit their scripts and have them published as if they were only stories". McQueen applies this premise while thoroughly examining various aspects of the canon, as well as biographical and chronological topics in the four longer stories. His novel approach suggests another way of viewing and investigating the "Holmesian saga".

HALL, who was responsible for all but two of the essays in this collection, investigates a broad spectrum of issues involving Doyle. These exercises in literary inquiry delve into the relationship between the work of Doyle and that of T.S. Eliot, Maurice Leblanc, Fritz Lang, and Sax Rohmer, and discusses Doyle's considerable influence upon them. Hall then moves to discuss the conflicting theories that led to Doyle's *A Study in Scarlet*, the starting point of our knowledge about Holmes. The longest essay deals with Doyle's obsessive interest in spiritualism and the numerous books he wrote on the subject, including the most notable, *History of Spiritualism* (1926).

HARRISON describes himself as a detective searching for the original inspiration for Doyle's Sherlock Holmes. Unlike most critics who accept Doyle's assertion that his famous detective was patterned after his former teacher, Harrison disagrees: "of all the many real-life characters who have 'added up' to that composite fictional character known as Sherlock Holmes, Dr Joseph Bell has probably made the least contribution of all". Harrison explores numerous other influences, and comes to the conclusion that the 1881 disappearance of a German baker named Strange was the most pivotal, as it "made Doyle wonder what would have happened if a professionally competent detective had been given the case?"

SHREFFLER presents a text designed to acknowledge the 50 previous years' research into the phenomenon of Sherlock Holmes and the existence of the Baker Street Irregulars and numerous other similar organizations. The volume begins with an article by Conan Doyle, and continues with articles and letters by such enthusiasts as T.S. Eliot, Mark Van Doren, Rex Stout, and Franklin D. Roosevelt: the "High Criticism" type of scholarship practised by devotees of Doyle and Holmes either deals with questions of the literal existence of Holmes and Watson, or seeks to define the place Holmes holds in popular culture.

JAFFE refers to Doyle as a "representative figure of his age . . . many of his own contemporaries found in him the very embodiment of the best of the Victorian spirit . . . A serious artist who involved himself fully in the concerns of his time". Her professed desire is to see Doyle awarded the respect due him as a literary figure. Unfortunately the great success of Sherlock Holmes is seen to overshadow his historical romances, scientific novels, poems, plays, essays, pamphlets, non-Holmesian short stories, and his non-fiction works dealing with history and spiritualism.

PAYNE discusses how "By the canon's end, the complete rationalist [Holmes] has become the complete human being", and then continues, "this transformation is absolutely essential to the enigma of Holmes's singularly continuous hold upon the world's imagination". It is the hold Holmes has on readers that Payne investigates, as he examines how this larger-than-life character has provided a sense of reassurance in an unstable time, as people have nostalgically looked back to what has appeared to be a simpler era.

DIANE LOOMS WEBER

Drama: Theory

Aston, Elaine, and George Savona, *Theatre As Sign System: A Semiotics of Text and Performance*, New York and London: Routledge, 1991
Aston, Elaine, *An Introduction to Feminism and Theatre*, London and New York: Routledge, 1995
Beckerman, Bernard, *Theatrical Presentation, Performer, Audience and Act*, London and New York: Routledge, 1990
Bennett, Susan, *Theatre Audiences: A Theory of Production and Reception*, London and New York: Routledge, 1990
Bentley, Eric, *The Life of the Drama*, New York: Atheneum, 1964; London: Methuen, 1965
Bentley, Eric (ed.), *The Theory of the Modern Stage*, Harmondsworth, Middlesex: Penguin, 1968
Bharucha, Rustom, *Theatre and the World: Performance and the Politics of Culture*, London and New York: Routledge, 1993
Birch, David, *The Language of Drama: Critical Theory and Practice*, London: Macmillan, 1991
Birringer, Johannes, *Theatre, Theory, Postmodernism*, Bloomington: Indiana University Press, 1993
Blau, Herbert, *To All Appearances: Ideology and Performance*, London and New York: Routledge, 1992
Braun, Edward, *The Director and the Stage: From Naturalism to Grotowski*, London: Methuen, 1982
Brownsteen, Oscar L., and Darlene M. Daubert, *Analytic Source Book of Concepts in Dramatic Theory*, Westport, Connecticut: Greenwood Press, 1981
Carlson, Marvin, *Theatre Semiotics: Signs of Life*, Bloomington: Indiana University Press, 1990
Elam, Keir, *The Semiotics of Theatre and Drama*, London and New York: Methuen, 1980
Esslin, Martin, *The Field of Drama*, London and New York: Methuen, 1987
Llewellyn-Jones, Margaret L. (ed.) "Women's Performance Languages and Strategies", issue of *Contemporary Theatre Review*, 2(1), 1994
Melrose, Susan, *Semiotics of the Dramatic Text*, London: Macmillan, 1994
Mitter, Shomit, *Systems of Rehearsal: Stanislavsky, Brecht, Grotowski and Peter Brook*, London and New York: Routledge, 1992
Page, Adrian (ed.), *The Death of the Playwright? Modern British Drama and Literary Theory*, London: Macmillan, 1992
Pavis, Patrice, *Languages of the Stage: Essays in the Semiology of the Theatre*, New York: PAJ Publications, 1982
Pavis, Patrice, *Theatre at the Crossroads of Culture*, translated by Loren Kruger, London and New York: Routledge, 1992
Pfister, Manfred, *The Theory and Analysis of Drama*, translated by John Halliday, Cambridge: Cambridge University Press, 1988
Reinelt, Janelle G., and Joseph G. Roach (eds.), *Critical Theory and Performance*, Ann Arbor: University of Michigan Press, 1992
Schechner, Richard, *Essays on Performance Theory*, New York: Drama Books Specialists, 1977; revised edition, as *Performance Theory*, New York and London: Routledge, 1988
Schmidt, Herta, and Aloysius van Kesteven (eds.), *Semiotics of Drama and Theatre: New Perspectives in the Theory of Drama*, Amsterdam: Benjamins, 1984
States, Bert O., *Great Reckonings in Little Rooms: On the Phenomenology of the Theater*, Berkeley: University of California Press, 1985
Styan, J.L., *Drama, Stage and Audience*, Cambridge: Cambridge University Press, 1975
Vanden Heuvel, Michael, *Performing Drama/Dramatizing Performance: Alternative Theater and the Dramatic Text*, Ann Arbor: University of Michigan Press, 1991
Whitmore, John, *Directing Postmodern Theatre: Shaping Signification in Performance*, Ann Arbor: University of Michigan Press, 1994

The academic study of drama was transformed in the 1980s by the explosive development of critical theory within university English Literature departments and the growth of cultural and media studies, and these methods of inquiry have impinged upon the problematics of drama and performance. While the relationship between theory, drama, and performance is a dynamic one, a distinction – albeit a fine one – for our purposes can be made between, on the one hand, studies of dramatic texts in relation to their performance possibilities and circumstances, and, on the other hand, studies of theatrical practice, practitioners, and the very nature, function, and definition of performance. Nevertheless, it is in the nature of the books discussed below to range widely in their frames of reference.

The Dramatic Text and Its Performance: Structure, Language, Semiotics

The opening lines of BENTLEY's *Life of the Drama* (1964), evoking "the living experience of a play . . . [as] . . . a river of feeling within us", indicate both his easily read style and his rather Leavisite approach. Dividing his book into two sections – "Aspects of a Play" and "Different Kinds of Plays" – Bentley discusses dramatic form, technique, and genres with reference to philosophies of theatre by Nietzsche and Freud, and using examples from plays and practitioners. Concerned with the relationship between life and art, he does not much consider that between text and performance, though he cites Erving Goffman on the sociology of self-presentation and the question of Brechtian efficacy.

STYAN's book acknowledges that the words of a text "are merely signals for communication in which (heresy, still, to some) the unspoken can be as important as the spoken". Although his choice of texts tends towards the canonical, Styan sees the text as a coded pattern of signals further encoded by the performer. Thus he is concerned to analyse the dynamic between stage and audience, providing communication models for this process. Drawing upon theatre practitioners, he also considers the possibility of effecting social and moral change through the audience.

BROWNSTEEN and DAUBERT functions most effectively as a source for definitions of categories which have been traditionally associated with theories of drama – such as decorum, poetic justice, the unities – from Aristotle to Bertolt Brecht and T.S. Eliot. Since the latter is the latest cited author in a list which starts with the sixteenth century, the book's canonical scope takes no account of the more recent theories.

SCHMIDT and KESTEVEN's volume contains some essays in languages other than English, and an extensive bibliography, but is significant as a relatively early call for systematic methodology and a common language for theatre research as a discipline, within a framework of five sub-fields. Their documentation question – whether a performance can be reconstructed from a text which operates like a music score – is still of prime interest, and many of the essays reveal the foundation of current academic practice especially in semiotics.

Other earlier work in this field varies between the extremes of complexity and simplicity. ELAM's book, the earliest in English on theatre semiotics, can seem over-dense to a beginner, but it provides a historical context for this approach, presenting communication models and tabular classifications of performance sub-codes. Although some of the latter may seem to over-fragment aspects such as dramatic discourse into minutiae which obscure the performance effect, Elam does draw upon a range of dramatic texts as well as linguistic and reception theories. ESSLIN, on the other hand, sometimes glides over potential complexities, because not only does he cover stage, film, and television without enough attention to their specificity, but he insists on accessibility before terminology. After chapters assigned to theatrical sign systems, with reference to the work of Umberto Eco and C.S. Peirce, he then dismisses formalist analysis as reductive, examining the role of other structural signifiers in performance, including rhythm and pace. Although Esslin looks at the role of social conventions in the act of decoding, his references to texts are not organised within definitions of specific theatrical modes. In contrast, ASTON and SAVONA offer a lucid introduction to the methodological implications of major elements in semiotics and structuralist theories through defining three categories of theatre practice – classical, bourgeois, and radical. This approach includes detailed examples, such as the function of stage picture or the application of basic speech-act theory to specific scenes from plays in the three modes. It is accessible to undergraduates but without over-generalising simplification, and aims to analyse the transformative process from page to stage. However, from the practitioner's perspective, WHITMORE shows more thoroughly how a knowledge of semiotics can positively inform a director in his deployment of the various communication systems in production. Unlike Aston and Savona, Whitmore does not give the philosophical roots of these theories, but his reference to postmodern directors and his own work with students gives his book a creative rather than a critical quality.

The semiotics of the socio-physical context of performance is explored within CARLSON's essays. He studies the London Old Vic theatre in both the past and present, as well as the iconic identity of other performance spaces. Carlson also considers the role of audience reception, a theme efficiently extended in BENNETT's work, which embraces reader-response approaches as well as semiotics. Her work on the audience as community is also contextualised in terms of notions of culture, and of specific examples of the effects of venue and publicity. Two further, more abstract and complex, works in the field of semiotics are Pavis and Melrose. PAVIS, famous for his original questionnaire for theatre analysis, reviews the current state of semiotics, discusses theatre practitioners from the classical to the avant-garde in *Languages of the Stage* (1982), and questions the task and nature of dramatic criticism, including the role of *mise-en-scène*. MELROSE interrogates the nature of semiotics in the light of new departures in the practices of linguistics and in everyday life, as theorised by Halliday and de Certeau. In search of the logic of theatre practice, she draws upon particular productions as the basis for her in-depth analysis of what is actually in process during performance; but the level of her debate is highly specialised.

STATES is aware of semiotics, which disturbs him for its "almost imperialistic confidence . . . that you have exhausted a thing's interest when you have explained how it works as a sign". He feels that phenomenology provides a useful balance in focusing on how theatre creates itself from its various material processes. States divides his book into sections on "The Scene" and "The Actor". Within the first, he distinguishes between the illusionary techniques of Shakespearean and naturalistic drama and those of expressionism and after – drawing on, among other elements, Roman Jakobson's distinction between metaphor and metonymy, and its relationship to a shift in both the function of art and performance style. States questions notions of estrangement and empathy in the context of theatre as "flirtation with the psychical distance between stage and audience". The phenomenological relationship of acting event and acted event is interestingly related to speech-act theory and the triadic relationship of actor, audience, and character. States' clear exposition is grounded in reference to plays, practitioners, and contemporary theoreticians.

PFISTER's Contents page is broken down into such small components that the reader anticipates an over-schematic approach. However, this readable book attempts to bridge the gap between the literary text and enactment, while devising a model "for a coordinated analysis of the various levels of verbal and non-verbal communication in a dramatic text performed on stage". While acknowledging the existence of semiotics, Pfister eschews that kind of technical approach, preferring to devise some useful communication models and diagrams, which he uses to demonstrate, for example, the configuration of figures in the drama. With reference to plays and practitioners across historical periods he usefully discusses concepts such as the open and closed uses of time and space, including semantic interpretations and dramatic function of these concepts. Although concerned with the internal, textual web of dramatic structures, Pfister is also at pains to relate these to the wider institutional context of the theatre in terms of history, "authorial intentions, and audience expectations, and of social conditions and frames".

BIRCH's theory of dramatic practice is linked to a social theory of language based on conflict rather than co-operation, and his central concern is the role of ideology. Embracing television, film, photography, and classroom practice, as well as the role of director, actor, and writer, his analysis centres on the potential of dramatic language as a means of effecting institutional action and change. Performance is thus "a struggle for the control of meaning". References to largely contemporary texts across cultures are woven into Birch's discussion, which ranges across the multiplicity of discursive meanings, the function of linguistic instability in creating change, the ideological import of grammatical structures, roles and the nature of subjectivity, and the carnivalesque.

Also theoretically comprehensive and accessible are the collections of Reinelt and Roach (see below) and PAGE. The essays that follow Page's introduction on the "Death of the Author" effectively demonstrate methodologies born of contemporary critical theory in action. Including feminism, speech-act theory, psychoanalysis, the ideas of Mikhail Bakhtin, Michel Foucault, and Jacques Derrida, these readings indicate the multiplicity of interpretations possible for a theatre production: "a multi-dimensional space . . . in which a variety of writings, none of them original, blend and clash". Contributors examine a spectrum of contemporary texts and performances from television to political drama, including reference to key practitioners such as Brecht and Antonin Artaud. The book also usefully indicates how new approaches differ from past liberal humanism. Coverage of some of the issues that recur throughout critiques discussed elsewhere – for instance, audience response, desire and the gaze, efficacy and ideology, postmodernism, the nature of enactment – is clearer in Page than elsewhere. Paradoxically, the opportunity of reading a range of essays which apply some of the same techniques and terms in different contexts seems more illuminating than reading single voiced explication. However, Whitmore (above) perhaps best indicates the creative possibilities of theatre practice in dynamic relation to critical theory.

Performance Theories: Directors, Alternative Theatre, Intercultural Performance

Whereas earlier work, such as Bentley's *Theories of the Modern Stage* (1968), tends to expound in a relatively straightforward way the ideas of key practitioners of the modern period, more recent performance theorists question the nature and function of performance, for example contextualising it within postmodernism, or considering issues such as efficacy, ideology, and intercultural transfer. Assuming that readers can easily obtain the standard works of such well-known practitioners as Artaud, Brecht, Peter Brook, and Jerzy Grotowski, this essay will focus both on critiques that assume knowledge of their work, and on more recent developments in performance theory.

The first section of BENTLEY's 1968 book covers "Ten Makers of Modern Theatre" and consists mostly of extracts from significant practitioners, including Adolphe Appia, Artaud, Brecht, Edward Gordon Craig, and Stanislavsky, as well as writers such as Bernard Shaw, W.B. Yeats, and Émile Zola. Essays in the second section provide a historical overview, and include a theoretically useful piece by Georg Lukács. Bentley's Introduction defends his omission of Anton Chekhov, Henrik Ibsen, and August Strindberg, suggesting the two former are writers rather than theoreticians, and that notions of naturalism are better represented by Zola than Strindberg. As the selection was based on a consensus choice, related to naturalism and epic theatre as two major movements in modern theatre-practice – but without any throughline of argument – this book is essentially a primer for beginners. More informative in terms of contextualising the theatre practice of major directors is BRAUN's book, although it is descriptive rather than theoretical. MITTER's more recent work analyses the theories of Stanislavsky, Brecht, and Grotowski, through a close comparative examination of their rehearsal and workshop practices. Despite apparent differences between the ideas of these three, he perceptively traces the extent to which Brook has assimilated aspects from the beliefs and methodologies of each. Mitter's experiences in Brook's workshops have contributed to the way this book attempts to bridge theory and practice, although his emphasis on the role of somatic exercises is perhaps overplayed. He does permit criticism of his mentor's ambivalent attitude to questions of audience participation, yet his sympathy defends Brook against the charge of cultural imperialism.

Two works which problematise the nature of performance itself, while drawing upon a wide range of different kinds of presentation from plays to vaudeville and street theatre, are those of Vanden Heuvel and Beckerman. VANDEN HEUVEL is concerned to challenge the traditional notion that performance merely restages the literary artefact, and is particularly interested in experimental work, especially how performance "which can be ludic, liminal and liberating" functions in a variety of contexts. While referring to work as apparently diverse as that of Samuel Beckett, Sam Shepard, Robert Wilson, and the Wooster Group, Vanden Heuvel gives an overview of the period from the 1960s to the 1980s, which looks at the oscillating relationship between a flight from, and return to, textuality in contemporary alternative performance. Apart from a frustrating tendency towards using metaphors from chaos theory and fractal geometry, this book shrewdly explores the fate of new types of dramatic language in their resistance to the "recuperative mechanisms of late capitalist culture" which absorb them into mainstream practice. BECKERMANN's work investigates the nature of both the "show" and the unique quality of projective performance energy which "simultaneously links . . . the earthly and overreaching aspects of humanity" while infusing a role with "the appearance of a fictional energy". Despite this apparently transcendental element, his argument is well grounded in a wide range of different types of dramatic presentation, from the classical to the avant-garde, and provides effective analysis of the juxtapositions associated with the different aspects of presentation – "performer and audience, performer and performer, performer and environment, performer and self". Although requiring a theatrically informed reader, the fluent style of this book makes the more philosophical passages accessible.

Conflicting attitudes to the ideological implications of intercultural performance, mentioned by Mitter, are more central to Schechner, Pavis, and Bharucha.

The revised version of SCHECHNER's book demonstrates his 20-year relationship with the theatre anthropology movement. He is concerned to define theatre as only one aspect of performance, a term which embraces animal and human social activities from greeting routines through to play, sports, and ceremonies. Including photographs and the figurative diagrams typical of his approach, which values action above textual analysis, Schechner explores the nature of performance/event in different physical and cultural environments. He examines the role of ritual and psychical significance for audience and performer – especially in terms for the latter of psycho-physical transformations of self. Notions of entertainment or efficacy, aesthetic or social drama are considered through references that do include some more conventional play texts; but greater space is given to anthropological exposition, the activities of Schechner's Performance Group, and notions of macrodrama. Schechner's enthusiasm to embrace almost every aspect of human life within his notion of performed behaviour rather unproblematically assumes that intercultural exchange is equal and that "the human community taken as a whole is entering a post-modern phase where the construction of intercultural aesthetics and ritual is essential".

PAVIS (1992), on the basis of a semiotic model of performance production and reception, studies the process of transference from a source to a target culture, especially through *mise-en-scène* as a site of confrontation between two semiotic systems rather than a transformation of text into performance. Proceeding from different definitions of culture, an investigation into the role of theory, and productions, including those of Eugenio Barba, Brook, Robert Wilson, and Ariane Mnouchkine, Pavis claims that postmodern and intercultural theatre are parallel developments. He suggests that "our western guilty conscience" partly influences these quests for either the culture of abstraction or the culture of sensuality. Pavis is concerned that a dichotomy may be developing between an almost clandestine audience for élite "radical and irreducible culture" and mass-audience access to a bland, undifferentiated "all purpose culture".

BHARUCHA is indignant about the unacknowledged power base that underlies "the seemingly altruistic processes of intercultural exchange". Acknowledging the influence of Artaud, Barba, and Grotowski, he accuses Schechner and the American avant garde of a "naive and unexamined ethnocentricity" in their claim to celebrate other cultures, considering their interculturalism to be "a continuation of colonialism". Further, he challenges Brook's *Mahabharata* project, not only as a "glorious trivialisation of our epic", but also as an exploration of his own intercultural academic research and practical theatre projects, on which he worked in different parts of the world before returning to India. His book provides a significant counterview to much almost canonical performance theory.

REINELT and ROACH have collected contributions under eight sectional headings – "Cultural Studies", "Semiotics and Deconstruction", "After Marx", "Feminism(s)", "Theatre History & Historiography", "Hermeneutics and Phenomenology", "Psychoanalysis", and "Critical Convergence". Each section is helpfully introduced by one of the editors. The book emphasises the extra-literary elements of performance, but although no essays centre upon traditional dramatic texts *per se*, performances discussed range from a Kathakhali *King Lear* to cross-dressing and sharp-shooting. It sets the agenda within an approach to postmodernism, seen as a condition in which a "positive stimulus to creative work, an opening out and up of imaginative esoteric, the local and the global can come into play". This impressive book provides a full spectrum of sometimes conflicting perspectives, including controversial and popular issues such as interculturalism, liminality, carnival, re-presentation of the body, and performance as "the meeting between history and desire". Although the essays vary in complexity, this book provides comprehensive and worthwhile access to the major concerns in the field.

Blau and Birringer embrace some of the same concerns and theoretical tools, but because each has a particular central thesis, the result is perhaps generally less illuminating for the reader than the scope of Reinelt and Roach.

BLAU's work, a development of his contribution to Reinelt and Roach, is philosophically dense in its investigation into the slippage among definitions of ideology, performance, and appearance, in part prompted by the apparent world-wide failure of ideology. A knowing reader – aware of the views of key practitioners, a wide spectrum of world theatre history and performance, and a familiarity with the ideas of Roland Barthes and Jacques Derrida – would find this a fertile and thought-provoking book, with an ultimately utopian concept of theatre, maintained despite Blau's critique of the corrosive interaction of power, illusion, and language.

The illustrations in BIRRINGER's book are typical of his more physically detailed references to performances – including some to which Blau alludes – and help to make his approach more accessible. Birringer is also concerned with the shifting nature of representations in relation to possible ideological challenge, and whether "performances can speak across the boundaries of culture", with reference to experiments which "question the familiar territories and 'closed circuits' of the theatre's system of representation". He places the debate firmly within the postmodern cityscape and media technology, while considering how, for example, the "architectonic-technological brilliance" of Robert Wilson's interpretation of the work of Heiner Müller may be "sucking the political thought out of the images". Challenging some of Blau's ideas, he feels that the "radical impoverishment of post-modern culture" can in some way be redressed by re-presentation of the postmodern body in performance, hence his detailed account of work varying from Pina Bausch to Laurie Anderson and Karen Finley. Though drawing upon some of the same poststructural theorists as Blau, sometimes with caution, Birringer's book is generally less obscure than some of Blau's.

All the more recent works listed have extensive footnotes and bibliographical reference although there could have been more extensive coverage on the debate about women's performance language and strategies, which is acknowledged in the "Feminism(s)" section of Reinelt and Roach, but not fully explored elsewhere. Contributors to my (LLEWELLYN-JONES') volume of *Contemporary Theatre Review* suggest the theoretical and practical dimensions of this significant and controversial performance issue. ASTON's book provides a comprehensive and accessible theoretical overview of the development of feminist theatre practice, with reference to performance case studies and teaching.

MARGARET L. LLEWELLYN-JONES

Drama: British – General

Banham, Martin (ed.), *The Cambridge Guide to World Theatre*, Cambridge and New York: Cambridge University Press, 1988, revised 1992

Chambers, E.K., *The Mediaeval Stage*, 2 vols., Oxford: Clarendon Press, 1903, 3rd edition, 1948

Craik, T.W., Clifford Leech, and Lois Potter (general eds.), *The Revels History of Drama in English*, 8 vols. (*Medieval Drama*, *1500–1576*, *1576–1613*, *1613–1660*, *1660–1750*, *1750–1880*, *1880 to the Present Day*, and *American Drama*), London and New York: Methuen, 1975–83

Hartnoll, Phyllis, *A Concise History of the Theatre*, London: Thames & Hudson, 1968; New York: Abrams, 1968

Hartnoll, Phyllis, *The Concise Oxford Companion to the Theatre*, Oxford and New York: Oxford University Press, 1972, revised with Peter Found, 1992

Nicoll, Allardyce, *A History of English Drama, 1660–1900*, 5 vols. (*Restoration Drama, 1660–1700*; *Early Eighteenth Century Drama, 1700–1750*; *Late Eighteenth Century Drama, 1750–1800*; *Early Nineteenth Century Drama, 1800–1850*; *Late Nineteenth Century Drama, 1850–1900*), Cambridge: Cambridge University Press, 1923–46; revised edition, 1952–59, supplemented with *Short-Title Alphabetical Catalogue of Plays Produced or Printed in England from 1660 to 1900*, 1959, and *English Drama, 1900–1930: The Beginning of the Modern Period*, 1973

Nicoll, Allardyce, *British Drama: An Historical Survey from the Beginnings to the Present Time*, London: Harrap, 1925; 6th edition, revised by J.C. Trewin, 1978

Ricks, Christopher (ed.), *English Drama to 1710* (Sphere History of Literature in English series), London: Barrie & Jenkins/Sphere, 1971; New York: Bedrick, 1987

Thompson, John Cargill, *A Reader's Guide to Fifty British Plays 1660–1900*, London: Heinemann, 1980; Totowa, New Jersey: Barnes & Noble, 1980

Trussler, Simon, *The Cambridge Illustrated History of British Theatre*, Cambridge and New York: Cambridge University Press, 1994

Ward, Adolphus William, *A History of English Dramatic Literature to the Death of Queen Anne*, 2 vols., London: Macmillan, 1875, revised (3 vols.) 1899

WARD's first volume describes the development of English drama from the Middle Ages to Shakespeare's predecessors, concluding with a chapter on the history of Shakespearian publication and criticism. Volume II covers Shakespeare and the "Late Elizabethans" (whom we today would describe as "Jacobeans"), paying particular attention to Ben Jonson, and Francis Beaumont and John Fletcher. Volume III goes from Philip Massinger in the 1620s to Colley Cibber and Susanna Centlivre at the beginning of the eighteenth century, finishing with a general index to the whole work. By present-day standards, Ward's critical views are excessively influenced by a rather simplistic morality: dramatists are rebuked for depicting sexual impropriety or neglecting poetic justice. Nevertheless, his text and footnotes are a mine of information.

CHAMBERS pays meticulous attention to a wide variety of dramatic and quasi-dramatic activities, and their interactions with Church, court, township, and countryside, as well as to surviving scripts. The origins of medieval drama are found in classical theatre, Christian liturgy, and primitive fertility rituals; its influence is followed through to the revels of Elizabeth I and Charles II. Volume I covers "Minstrelsy" and "Folk Drama". Volume II deals with "Religious Drama" and "The Interlude", ending with 24 appendices, which range from medieval account-books and play-texts to descriptions of eighteenth-century sword dances in Shetland. A monument of exhaustive scholarship, humane common sense, and unquenchable enthusiasm, this is essential reading for students of medieval drama.

NICOLL's *A History of English Drama* is still, in many ways, the standard work for the period 1660–1900. Each of the first five volumes begins with an examination of theatrical conditions, then proceeds to discussions of dramatists and their works, paying due attention to sources, influences, and interrelationships. His habit of grouping plays by category may strike some readers as excessively arbitrary, but it counteracts the danger of mechanical, chronological cataloguing that besets all surveys. Each volume concludes with a bibliography, appendices which further enhance theatrical background knowledge, an index, and a hand-list of plays, including (for each title) author(s), type of play, and date and location of first performance. Volume VI is a comprehensive alphabetical index of plays in the whole series: there are various omissions from this volume, including material in foreign languages, but these are conscientiously acknowledged and abundantly justified by the introduction of a cross-referencing system that includes alternative titles. Nicoll's original scope (to 1900) was extended in his 1973 supplementary volume, *1900–1930*. He argues that "the thirty years from 1900 to 1930, besides establishing the foundation for all that was to follow later, had been possessed by a spirit characteristically its own". He discusses theatrical developments, popular entertainments (including musical plays and melodrama), "established" drama and "the play of ideas", as well as numerous experimental and innovative forms. A copious index and a 600-page hand-list of plays bear witness to his interest in the unprecedentedly multifarious theatrical activity of the period.

HARTNOLL (1968) provides an excellent general introduction to theatre history, beginning with a chapter on "The Greek and Roman Theatre" and concluding in the 1960s with such diverse productions as *Ubu Roi*, *Who's Afraid of Virginia Woolf?*, and *My Fair Lady*. This is not exclusively a history of British theatre, but it reflects a history of mutual influence between Britain and other countries, showing first Western drama and now the drama of the world developing as a complex but unified whole. With 262 illlustrations, 34 coloured, and all scrupulously annotated, this book is equally instructive and delightful.

RICKS intends to give a modern reader a sense of "the many contexts in which literature – in this case, drama – exists". A chronological table of theatrical, historical, and literary events is followed by Glynne Wickham's survey of "Stage and Drama till 1660". Brian Morris' survey of "Elizabethan and Jacobean Drama" provides an overall context for other writers' detailed discussions of Christopher Marlowe, Ben Jonson, the Jacobean dramatists, and various aspects of Shakespeare. According to Ricks, Shakespeare is the core of the volume, "just as he is the core not only of dramatic achievement in English but of all literary achievement". Stephen Orgel's chapter on "The Masque" marks a new departure in dramatic criticism. Glynne Wickham's brief account of "The Restoration Theatre" precedes John Barnard's survey of "Drama from the Restoration till 1710", which traces its subject's affinities with the "Renaissance romance and drama" of an earlier period, and the growing "bourgeois sentimentality", which that was to find its fullest expression in the novel. Each chapter is followed by a bibliography. NICOLL (1925, 6th edition 1978) is an excellent one-volume introduction to the history of drama from the middle ages to the twentieth century. He concentrates on Britain more than Hartnoll does, but takes account of foreign influences when circumstances require it.

Every volume in CRAIK, LEECH, and POTTER's *Revels History* series begins with a chronological table of historical and theatrical events, non-dramatic literary events, first performances of "notable" plays written in English, births and deaths of playwrights, and theatrical events outside Britain – or, in Volume VIII, outside the United States of America. The bulk of each book comprises surveys of "The Social and Literary Context", "Actors and Theatres", and "Dramatists and Plays", balancing literary criticism, theatrical sense, and social history. There are also illustrations, an index, and a bibliography which provides thorough coverage of current research and critical opinion. The series is packed with information: even the end-papers are specially selected to exemplify some aspect of the relevant period. Within this framework, authors of the survey sections have been allowed to use their own discretion, selecting and emphasising the developments which they consider particularly important, rather than following some inflexible formula. The presence of the chronological tables leaves the reader free to enjoy the fascinating historical and critical essays, confident that nothing vital has been unaccounted for.

The *Revels History* is the most comprehensive survey of English drama in general; nothing matches its combination of broad scope and detailed coverage across the full historical range, though shorter periods may have been more fully covered elsewhere. Some questions might be raised, however, about the validity of its specifications. As the dates on the title-pages indicate, a great deal of attention is devoted to the late sixteenth and early seventeenth centuries. If the length of time involved or the amount of theatrical activity undertaken is considered, this is disproportionate. Of course, it could be argued that, since this is the age of Shakespeare and other great Elizabethan and Jacobean dramatists, this extravagance can be justified by the drama's superior quality, lasting appeal in the national repertoire, and the enormous amount of scholarly and critical interest generated by the subject. It is harder to justify the series' implication that no "Drama in English" worth recording occurred outside Great Britain and the United States of America. Equally overdue for examination is the assumption that "drama" means only "live theatre". Omitting all but the most perfunctory references to cinema and television helps to keep Volumes VII and VIII within their allotted bounds, but gives a distorted and limited picture of a period when relationships between various media have been complex and fruitful.

THOMPSON objects to "our unbalanced approach to the study of Elizabethan theatre", and demands "a more objective appraisal of the vast amount of work produced after the Restoration". He provides accounts of 50 plays, from *The Tempest* (1667) by William D'Avenant and John Dryden to Arthur Wing Pinero's *Trelawney of the "Wells"* (1898). Every chapter contains a brief biographical introduction, cast list, plot summary, and critical commentary. There is also a useful bibliography, a well-argued Preface, and an introductory chapter on "Audience and Taste", which defends Thompson's thesis that an evolving theatre tradition, rather than the genius of individual dramatists, is "our strongest asset". Thompson's insights are fresh and stimulating; he responds to each play on its own terms, placing it securely in its literary and theatrical context.

HARTNOLL and FOUND's revised *Concise Oxford Companion* aims at "world coverage, though with a discernible bias towards the British and US theatre". Their work, "while basically mainstream, takes cognizance of the Fringe and avant-garde," though "newcomers under forty" have been excluded to save space. They cover every aspect of theatre, from first productions and revivals to actors, producers, and even such humble technicalities as sound effects. An efficient cross-indexing system enables a work of encyclopaedic scope to be crammed into one volume. Inevitably, some statements have already been overtaken by circumstances, but it is still an extremely useful reference work. More up to date however is BANHAM's guide, which has an even wider-ranging world-wide breadth, some useful and striking illustrations, and, without a ban on entrants under 40, a greater concentration on the present day. This is an indispensable work of reference and criticism for anyone interested in British Theatre alone (inevitably its most thorough coverage) or in its relations with theatrical traditions from around the world.

TRUSSLER provides the best and most up-to-date single-volume guide to British theatre currently available. Beginning with "Roman Britain and the Early Middle Ages 44–950", and working its way through every subsequent twist and turn of British theatrical history until it reaches "Theatre and the Marketplace 1979–1990", it is rich in essential detail, but never loses its sense of direction. Everything in this "radical" history is related to artistic, historical or political context: Trussler is never content to record a fact without explaining its significance. Nor is he afraid to be original or controversial in his views and emphases. His refusal to devote a separate chapter to Shakespeare, and his insistence on examining various forms of popular, "unofficial" theatre, from Elizabethan jigs to 1990s' karaoke, are most refreshing. The book is equipped with a chronology, glossary, "Who's Who", select bibliography, and index, as well as a lavish array of stunningly attractive, and extremely informative, illustrations.

CAROLYN D. WILLIAMS

Drama: Medieval

1. General

Axton, Richard, *European Drama of the Early Middle Ages*, London: Hutchinson, 1974; Pittsburgh: University of Pittsburgh Press, 1975

Beadle, Richard (ed.), *The Cambridge Companion to Medieval English Theatre*, Cambridge and New York: Cambridge University Press, 1994

Cawley, A.C., Marion Jones, Peter F. McDonald, and David Mills (eds), *The Revels History of Drama in English, Volume 1: Medieval Drama*, London and New York: Methuen, 1983

Chambers, E.K., *The Mediaeval Stage*, 2 vols., Oxford: Clarendon Press, 1903

Davidson, Clifford, C.J. Gianakaris, and John H. Stroupe, *The Drama of the Middle Ages: Comparative and Critical Essays*, New York: AMS Press, 1982

Gibson, Gail McMurray, *The Theater of Devotion: East Anglian Drama and Society in the Late Middle Ages*, Chicago: University of Chicago Press, 1989

Happé, Peter (ed.), *Medieval English Drama: A Casebook*, London: Macmillan, 1984

Harris, John Wesley, *Medieval Theatre in Context: An Introduction*, London and New York: Routledge, 1992

Tydeman, William, *The Theatre in the Middle Ages: Western European Stage Conditions, c.800–1576*, Cambridge and New York: Cambridge University Press, 1978

Until the middle of the twentieth century, medieval English drama was invariably presented as a simple developmental process. Recent criticism has radically questioned this assumption as, chiefly thanks to the Records of Early English Drama (REED) project, significant new sources have come to light. The study of medieval plays is now considered inseparable from what is known of the physical circumstances of their production.

CHAMBERS did not have the benefit of systematically investigated records, so constructed his discursive, deeply causal history from a few well-known documents and, principally, surviving play texts. The result, while rich in individual instances, is a confidently coherent picture of an evolving tradition. The account moves from the fall of the late antique theatre, through the minstrel tradition and local seasonal customs, to the liturgical plays of the twelfth-century monastic Renaissance, which are then secularized as the mystery cycles of the urban guilds. The morality plays, which followed, prepared the way for the Tudor interludes, which in turn made way for the revival of classical forms on the Shakespearean stage.

AXTON was among the first to revise Chambers' narrative while still attempting a unified history. He asserts that English medieval drama cannot be isolated from pan-European developments. England is, therefore, approached first from a generic investigation of traditional playing – mimicry, combat, dancing-game, and church ceremony. The Latin liturgical tradition is presented as a distinct and parallel development, alongside vernacular plays from Europe, particularly the flourishing tradition of playing in Arras in the thirteenth century. English drama is linked here with the Anglo-Norman of the Angevin kings, its late development attributed to accidents in the development of urban organisation and linguistic divisions. It is also suggested that popular and secular drama "accommodated the Christian story" rather than the reverse, as England had few liturgical plays.

TYDEMAN also begins by considering ritual survivals, but his study is focused specifically on stage conditions. What is established is the collaborative, as opposed to entrepreneurial, character of medieval theatrical enterprise, in a discussion that is geographically and chronologically specific, and attentive to suitably illustrated physical detail. Debates over the distinctive processional performance of English mystery plays are contextualised with other forms of street theatre, such as the royal entry. Moralities and saints' plays are not generically separated, but considered according to the auspices of the individual text alongside other place-and-scaffold productions or court interludes. Chapters are also devoted to theatrical effects, performers, and finance.

DAVIDSON *et al.* and HAPPÉ present two indispensable collections of previously published journal articles on medieval English drama from both sides of the Atlantic, too numerous to cite individually here. The first draws on the journal *Comparative Drama* for articles on iconography, narrative biblical cycles in drama and art, articles which all deal with specific plays alongside much wider issues such as play/audience relations, characterisation, and anti-semitism. Each article draws on a specific body of textual material, putting it in a larger theoretical or comparative context. HAPPÉ opens with extracts from contemporary witnesses of medieval drama, before moving on to articles of modern criticism of mystery cycles, morality plays, interludes, and aspects of performance. The last section includes material on Cornish drama and on modern reconstructions.

CAWLEY *et al.* is also a collection of the work of many scholars, but is set out as a developmental narrative prefaced by a detailed chronological table. The format of the volume, however, permits that the polyvalency and diffuseness of the history it documents may be acknowledged, as each section aims to be a conspectus of the variety of medieval staging, of the drama of religious ceremonial, and of early moral plays and secular interludes. Within each section, too, each essay has a different focus, from manuscripts, through style, rhetoric, music, allegory, and the economics of performance, to mythology and folk ritual.

GIBSON's scope is much more specific, but this book has a more ambitious intellectual agenda than its central aim – to study the habits of mind which shaped the East Anglian N-town Cycle – suggests. Importantly it questions the premise that so-called English medieval drama had any real existence in the thirteenth and fourteenth centuries, claiming rather that it must be studied as integral to the cultural circumstances of the period from which its textual evidence survives – that is the fifteenth and early sixteenth centuries. What follows is a recuperation of the cultural distinctiveness of fifteenth-century East Anglia and a methodology for the painstaking reconstruction of the material circumstances that give a new intelligibility to medieval dramatic texts.

HARRIS returns to general history with yet a different focus, this time the drama's relationship with contemporary secular and ecclesiastical society, attempting to make accessible a coherent picture of the culture in which this plural tradition evolved, and with which it interacted. In an early chapter, the influence of the pagan legacy, in particular of farce, on medieval religious plays is explored. Later chapters look at units of social organisation, from village to court, and their customary forms of celebration. The interaction of theatre and church ceremony, as well as underlying ethical beliefs, is re-examined, and the volume ends with a reconsideration of the social trends that proved terminal for the great mystery cycles.

BEADLE's is, to date, the most recent of the collections of essays to circumscribe the whole field. And the editor claims it is "something of an interim report on a field of knowledge and interpretation which has changed out of all recognition over the last two decades". Each essay aims to summarise the current scholarly position in one area. The volume includes essays on theatricality, on each of the York, Chester, Towneley, and N-town plays, on East Anglian non-cycle plays, on the Cornish tradition, morality plays, and saints plays. The collection concludes with a consideration of modern productions of medieval English plays and a survey of recent criticism.

PAMELA M. KING

2. Cycle Plays

Beadle, Richard (ed.), *The Cambridge Companion to Medieval English Theatre*, Cambridge and New York: Cambridge University Press, 1994

Coletti, Theresa, "Purity and Danger: The Paradox of Mary's Body and the En-Gendering of the Infancy Narrative in the English Mystery Cycles", in *Feminist Approaches to the Body in Medieval Literature*, edited by Linda Lomperis and Sarah Stanbury, Philadelphia: University of Pennsylvania Press, 1993

Kolve, V.A., *The Play Called Corpus Christi*, Stanford, California: Stanford University Press, 1966

Stevens, Martin, *Four Middle English Mystery Cycles: Textual, Contextual, and Critical Interpretations*, Princeton, New Jersey: Princeton University Press, 1987

Travis, Peter W., *Dramatic Design in the Chester Cycle: Essays and Documents*, Chicago: Chicago University Press, 1982

Woolf, Rosemary, *The English Mystery Plays*, London: Routledge & Kegan Paul, 1972; Berkeley: University of California Press, 1972

Four extant medieval plays can be grouped under the rubric of cycle drama: Wakefield (or Towneley), York, Chester, and N-Town (whose status as a true cycle is contested). Seen by critics in the first half of this century as naive forerunners of Shakespearean drama, their appearance as major urban rituals in the late fourteenth century was explained as a seamless evolutionary development from the Latin liturgy. Influential modern studies like those by Kolve, Woolf, and Travis not only knocked the evolutionary theory on the head, but enhanced the critical standing of the cycles. Though chiefly acknowledged as vehicles of spiritual instruction for their medieval audiences, to a lesser extent they are now also recognised as channels for social meanings. Two areas of criticism deserve special mention: first, anthropological and New-Historicist approaches, which consider the plays' function within the festival of Corpus Christi; second, the painstaking scholarly recovery from local historical records of information about original circumstances of production, being done on a rolling programme under the aegis of the Toronto-based REED (Records of Early English Drama). Critical fascination with this undertaking has occasionally seemed to stall the project of producing new literary readings.

KOLVE's classic and influential study is the first to take the plays seriously, as examples of "the most truly popular drama England has ever known", worthy of comparison with the work of Bertolt Brecht, Eugène Ionesco, and Samuel Beckett. His innovation is a formalist account of the four cycles, isolating a "protocycle" – an irreducible common core structure, made up of selected key episodes from biblical history. The choice of episodes, he argues, was determined by typology (the foreshadowing of meanings in the events and persons of the Old Testament), according to primary (doctrine of figures) and secondary (seven ages of the world) principles of selection. In this light he discusses the plays' representations of time and place; their comic visions; the representations of the Passion; humankind's postlapsarian relationship to God; and the figurings of humankind's possibilities for goodness. By identifying on a much wider scale than before the processes of typology at work in the drama, the study moves away refreshingly from traditional "character" criticism, but also loses sight of the specific characteristics of the individual cycles.

WOOLF plays down allegorical and typological interpretations. She offers broadly literary-critical judgements of the cycles as a whole and of single pageants, illuminating their meanings by reference to a wealth of scholarly material (apocryphal, patristic, and liturgical traditions; non-cycle and Continental analogues). For her, the plays are satisfying aesthetic and theatrical works, deriving their artistic coherence from their status as sacred drama. Less concerned than Kolve with establishing common structural principles (though she notes the centrality of the Nativity, and especially of the Passion), she is attentive chiefly to *differences* between the cycles. She divides the narrative sequences of the four cycles into five groups of pageants, offering detailed comparisons and contrasts between the individual dramatists' treatment of similar themes.

TRAVIS's admired study of the Chester Cycle manoeuvres elegantly between the individual pageants and the grand design of the play, identifying six discrete pageant-groups, exemplifying different aspects of the dramatic dynamics of this larger unit. These include the Cycle's understanding of ritual and Christian time, its non-illusionism, and its semiotic and interpretative modes. He characterises Chester by its austere Christology, its nominalist theology, and its unique credal design. Although not primarily a theoretical or polemical book, its importance lies in its attention to the distinctive character of a single cycle (one that is often neglected), and its finely nuanced understanding of the cultural forces at work in the dramatic presentation of sacred matter, especially those that inhere in the meanings of the Body of God. Travis's approach is broadly New-Critical and expository, but his exposition is informed by a range of critical methods, including anthropology and traditional historical scholarship. This is one of the best advanced introductions to the subject.

STEVENS's study is the most substantial new reading of all four cycles. Controversially, he argues that each play-text must be seen as "an entity separate from the text's performance history"; his major premise is that the individual cycles have their own "unique artistic coherence" and that each is the work of a single playwright. Thus, York is characterised by its self-conscious concern with its own status as a city, Wakefield by its sophisticated authorial voice, Chester by its "sense of endings", and N-Town by its elaborate and singular formal organisation, such as its unique deployment of the "double main plot". Stevens's work is not consistently informed by a theoretical vision, though he proposes a Bakhtinian carnival reading of the York cycle. Despite the reiterated insistence on reading the texts as literary works, there are some extensive, though positivist, reinterpretations of archival evidence.

COLETTI's sophisticated feminist essay contests the traditional idealist view that comic elements in the plays are finally recuperated within the larger scheme of salvation history. In noting how Mary's body becomes a focus for domestic and social conflict in the Infancy pageants, Coletti argues that the plays are sites where social relations are explored, and where differences, especially of gender, but also of class, are negotiated. Her historicist reading of Mary's paradoxically virginal body as "an ambiguous site of purity and pollution" extends anthropological readings of the drama, and convincingly demonstrates how the scriptural narrative does not simply uphold the late medieval sex-gender, system but exposes its contradictions. After Coletti, the boundaries between theological and social meanings appear radically intertwined.

BEADLE's substantial survey volume includes an essay on each of the four cycles, written by established scholars in the field. There is also a general introductory essay by William Tydeman, one on dramaturgy by Meg Twycross, a very full bibliography, and a critical guide by Peter Happé, which disappointingly does not refer to recent stimulating theoretical work. The focus is on dramaturgical aspects (staging, costumes, properties, stage directions, performance), on meticulous textual scholarship, and on editorial problems (Fletcher's lively essay on N-Town proposes a new localisation of the text in East Harling). The volume tends towards standard interpretations of the plays' meanings, but has a useful emphasis on local identity, the result of the importance given to reading the dramatic records as indispensable intertexts. Student readers may find the volume lacks sufficient literary-interpretative discussion, though Beadle offers a close reading of the York *Crucifixion*, *Christ Before Pilate*, and *Death of Christ* pageants.

RUTH EVANS

3. Morality Plays

Bevington, David M., *From "Mankind" to Marlowe: Growth of Structure in the Popular Drama of Tudor England*, Cambridge, Massachusetts: Harvard University Press, 1962

Davenport, W.A., *Fifteenth-Century English Drama*, Cambridge: D.S. Bewer, 1982; Totowa, New Jersey: Rowman & Littlefield, 1992

Davidson, Clifford, *Visualizing the Moral Life: Medieval Iconography and the Macro Morality Plays*, New York: AMS Press, 1989

Gilman, Donald (ed.), *"Everyman" and Company: Essays on the Themes and Structure of the European Morality Play*, New York: AMS Press, 1988

Kelley, Michael R., *Flamboyant Drama: A Study of the "Castle of Perseverance", "Mankind", and "Wisdom"*, Carbondale: Southern Illinois University Press, 1979

MacKenzie, W.R., *The English Moralities from the Point of View of Allegory*, Boston and London: Ginn & Co., 1914

Miyajima, Sumilo, *The Theatre of Man: Dramatic Technique and Stagecraft in the English Medieval Morality Plays*, Clevedon, Avon: Six Ways, 1977

Potter, Robert, *The English Morality Play: Origins, History, and Influence of a Dramatic Tradition*, London and Boston: Routledge & Kegan Paul, 1975

The twentieth century has shown renewed interest in the long-scorned medieval morality play, as the texts discussed below will show.

MACKENZIE's pioneering work on the moralities remains a classic study of the genre, with its definition still the one most frequently cited: "a Morality is a play, allegorical in structure, which has for its main object the teaching of some lesson for the guidance of life, and in which the principal characters are personified abstractions or highly universalized types". After so defining his subject, the author proceeds to classify and discuss specific plays according to their content, focusing on those dealing with the conflict between virtues and vices, those illustrating a particular text, those dealing with the summons of death, and those dealing with religious and political controversy. He concludes by assessing the theatrical potential of these works, which are generally neglected by modern readers, but which had considerable popularity in performance for their contemporary audiences. MacKenzie's study is both historically sound and eminently sensible, and has not been superseded but only supplemented by more recent works dealing with the same subject.

BEVINGTON argues the significance of the native morality-play tradition in producing the dramatic achievement of the Elizabethan-Jacobean stage. He is especially concerned with staging conditions and with the practice of doubling in popular performance, a way of achieving a "maximum of scope with a minimum of means". He also traces the movement from moral and social abstractions to specific historical personalities in the plays considered. Particularly useful are the final chapters, which offer analyses of Christopher Marlowe's major tragedies from the perspective of the morality-play structure.

POTTER regards the moralities as "repentance plays", comic in the Dantean sense, for they typically end with the repentance and salvation of the protagonist. He takes issue with the prevailing idea of the central conflict of virtue and vice, arguing that these personifications do not represent such a battle but rather ritualistically demonstrate the forgiveness of sins. More than half of the book is concerned with post-medieval drama, when the moralities became predominantly political in subject matter and intention. He examines early Elizabethan plays, which inherited certain features from the morality tradition. In conclusion, he discuses the influence of the didactic genre on such modern playwrights as Bertolt Brecht. This book is ambitious in range of reference, but limited by its focus on repentance.

MIYAJIMA defines moralities as a genre of "dramatic allegory employing the personification of abstract qualities for religious ends and performed by actors (who may be clerics but are predominantly lay or wholly professionals) on a fixed stage in the open air or indoors". A chapter on background and tradition considers the genre in relationship to fifteenth-century English life, noting details of costume and music. He rejects the popular theory of the medieval theatre-in-the-round as "misconceived and misleading". He analyzes five plays – *The Castle of Perseverance*, *Wisdom*, *Mankind*, *Pride of Life* and *Everyman* – with emphasis on stagecraft and dramatic techniques. A chapter on characterization deals with the double nature of man as protagonist, and one on idea and form stresses the principle of dualism as a key to structure. More in-depth than most, this is an excellent and sophisticated study of the neglected genre.

KELLEY's approach is based on a term from art history, referring to the duality of symbolism and realism characteristic of fourteenth- and fifteenth-century architecture. The morality plays combined the two modes by mixing allegory with concrete detail. Kelley then views the three Macro plays as examples. *The Castle of Perseverance* blends ornate rhetoric with homely realism and has a dual plot combining linearity and circularity. *Mankind* is also distinguished by verbal decoration in the flamboyant style: indeed, this play is described as "flamboyance gone wild". Finally, *Wisdom* is seen as a more intellectual play but enlivened by flamboyantly decorative language and richly detailed costumes. Concluding with a chapter on art as design in the Middle Ages, he observes that the Macro plays are "microcosmic mirrors of the medieval cosmos". Well-researched, this book offers an original view of the genre by relating it to the art and architecture of its time.

DAVENPORT devotes each of four chapters to one morality, dealing with *Pride of Life*, *Mankind*, *Wisdom*, and *The Castle of Perseverance*. In *Pride of Life*, he finds a pattern of tragedy, which resembles that in both *Everyman* and *Magnificence*. In contrast, *Mankind* is a comic play which imaginatively turns the formula of innocence, sin, then redemption into vigorous stage action, as similarly happens in some of the mystery plays. *Wisdom* is seen as a drama of ideas, literary and sophisticated but traditionally underrated. *The Castle of Perseverance* follows the typical medieval tendency to comprehensiveness, neither tragic nor comic but instead epic, with its large-scale setting and its handling of supernatural warfare. Although the individual analyses are effective, the book is weakened by the author's reluctance to define the genre.

GILMAN's work is a comparative study, dealing with several national literatures. The essays cover a range of subjects: (1) the development of the hero in French moral plays; (2) the political contexts of the Spanish moralities; (3) the Susanna story in Reformation Germany; (4) salvation and damnation plays which develop into homiletic tragedies; (5) rhetoric in Dutch moral drama; (6) a broad view of methods and modes as they developed in the moral drama; (7) and four Florentine plays, which move away from allegory toward concrete representation of character. One of the most valuable features is the extensive bibliography (129 pages), which includes both primary and secondary materials in several languages.

DAVIDSON argues that the Macro moralities represent a kind of allegory that is distinguished by its iconography, which in turn is based on phenomenological considerations. One chapter is devoted to each of the Macro plays, which are discussed in terms of concrete visual images. In *Mankind* the tilling of the ground and planting of seeds is the central image, as Mankind symbolically re-enacts the expulsion from the Garden. The circular stage of *The Castle of Perseverance* suggests the vicissitudes of life, moving from devotion, to the religious ideal, to alienation from it. *Wisdom*, a more spiritual play, is focused on the transcendental image of its title character. The final chapter deals with the subject and iconography of death, central to all of the moralities. The book calls attention to the complex iconography of the moralities, which has been largely neglected by critics.

CHARLOTTE SPIVACK

Drama: Renaissance

1. General

Braunmuller, A.R., and Michael Hattaway (eds.), *The Cambridge Companion to English Renaissance Drama*, Cambridge and New York: Cambridge University Press, 1990

Bushnell, Rebecca W., *Tragedies of Tyrants: Political Thought and Theatre in the English Renaissance*, Ithaca, New York: Cornell University Press, 1990

Butler, Martin, *Theatre and Crisis 1632–1642*, Cambridge and New York: Cambridge University Press, 1984

Dutton, Richard, *Mastering the Revels: The Regulation and Censorship of English Renaissance Drama*, London: Macmillan, 1991

Kastan, David Scott, and Peter Stallybrass (eds.), *Staging the Renaissance: Reinterpretations of Elizabethan and Jacobean Drama*, New York and London: Routledge, 1991

McMullan, Gordon, and Jonathan Hope (eds.), *The Politics of Tragicomedy: Shakespeare and After*, London and New York: Routledge, 1992

Mulryne, J.R., and Margaret Shewring (eds.), *Theatre and Government under the Early Stuarts*, Cambridge and New York: Cambridge University Press, 1993

Over the last decade, critical assessment of English Renaissance drama has undergone a series of startling transformations. The current emphasis has shifted attention away from stylistic and formal properties towards an appreciation of the historical and ideological aspects of the theatrical experience.

BRAUNMULLER and HATTAWAY's *Companion* collection covers the entire period, from 1580 to 1642. In a range of carefully chosen pieces, the essays broach such questions as the relationship between social and cultural conditions and the theatrical repertoire, the diversity of genres, and the particular political inflections that plays reveal. While established figures – such as Christopher Marlowe, Thomas Middleton, Shakespeare, and John Webster – are discussed, space is reserved equally for a consideration of less well-known writers and works; the volume as a whole is complemented by a full bibliography and a chronological list, which parallels the composition of plays with key historical events.

In contrast, BUSHNELL takes a more selective approach to its chosen theme – the languages and modes of representation shared by the drama and the political prose. Drawing upon an intimate knowledge of classical convention and political treatises, Bushnell charts the ways in which tyranny was defined in terms of morality, monstrosity, theatricality, and the feminizing threat to masculinity. In three major sections, she argues that early sixteenth-century plays demonstrate the instability of the discourse of statecraft; that Ben Jonson and Shakespeare exposed the ideological basis of the legitimization of power in their plays; and that Stuart drama recognized the theatre's role in fashioning both the image of the tyrant and claims to absolutist authority.

The political dimensions of dramatic activity also occupy DUTTON in his stimulating critique of Masters of the Revels and dramatic censorship in the 1581–1626 period. Dutton traces the development of the censor's office and the expansion of the public theatres, arguing that the ideology of monarchy was shifting, contradictory, and diverse. The analysis of plays that occasioned controversy (Shakespeare's *Richard II* and the collaborative *Sir Thomas More*, for example) forms part of Dutton's thesis that different patrons entertained competing agendas, and that the Master of the Revels did not suppress all debate. His authority permitted rather than prohibited a complexity of dramatic expression, which throws into doubt the view that the period was wholly conformist in its tendencies.

The recent collaborative volume, MULRYNE and SHEWRING's, combines a number of interpretive approaches: Richard Dutton highlights Jonson's covert dramatic criticisms; Kathleen McLuskie theorizes the oppositional character of theatrical self-consciousness; Margot Heinemann discovers in Philip Massinger's plays debates about England's military policies; Martin Butler and Graham Parry unpick the questioning intricacies of masque entertainments; James Knowles rehearses the social contexts of civic rituals; and Julia Gasper outlines the theological and ideological impact of Reformation drama. The essays gain much from Simon Adams' judicious appraisal of the Stuart political scene, which places the authors' efforts in an admirably nuanced and illuminating perspective.

Plays composed and staged during the 1632–1642 period are the subject of BUTLER's rigorously contextual study, and the author persuasively demonstrates the radically critical impulses of neglected dramatists such as Richard Brome, Massinger, and James Shirley. The book works well as a re-evaluation of the political embeddedness of the Caroline stage, stressing the tradition of presenting unorthodox drama at court and establishing connections between theatrical concerns and the extreme sectarian and millenarian views marking the Civil War. Butler's study is distinctive in that it complicates previous judgements about the composition of audiences: far from reinforcing the idea of a unitary Caroline audience, Butler finds a substantial gentry element in contemporary playhouses.

Elaborating recent reconfigurations of the theatre and its political environment, KASTAN and STALLYBRASS assemble a variety of interdisciplinary work in their edited volume. Anti-theatrical polemic, the owner of the theatrical script, homoeroticism on stage, and women spectators – these and related subjects are explored by the 23 contributors. A discussion of the plays themselves follows upon a survey of the theatre's contexts, and canonical and non-canonical instances are investigated: the most fruitful essays tie dramatic concerns to anxieties about carnival, riot, and violence. A comparable compendium of contextual essays is McMULLAN and HOPE's, although this volume displays a mainly British rather than an American perspective. Individual studies attend to the complex political stance adopted by *The Tempest*, to pre-revolutionary criticisms in *Cymbeline*, to the topicality of *The Two Noble Kinsmen*, to questions of gender and consumption in John Fletcher's plays, to popular festive traditions in the theatre, to the contradictory courtly aesthetic of Jonson's late drama, and to the rise of the actress. In so doing, they furnish a powerful means of understanding a literary mode sometimes dismissed for its idealizing distance from material urgencies.

MARK THORNTON BURNETT

See also **Comedy: Renaissance, Tragedy: Renaissance**

2. Elizabethan

Altman, Joel E., *The Tudor Play of Mind: Rhetorical Inquiry and the Development of Elizabethan Drama*, Berkeley: University of California Press, 1978

Bevington, David, *From "Mankind" to Marlowe: Growth of Structure in the Popular Drama of Tudor England*, Cambridge, Massachusetts: Harvard University Press, 1962

Braunmuller, A.R., "The Arts of the Dramatists" in *The Cambridge Companion to English Renaissance Drama*, edited by Braunmuller and Michael Hattaway, Cambridge and New York: Cambridge University Press, 1990

Dollimore, Jonathan, *Radical Tragedy: Religion, Ideology and Power in the Drama of Shakespeare and His Contemporaries*, Brighton, Sussex: Harvester Press, 1984, 2nd edition, 1989; Chicago: University of Chicago Press, 1984

Greenblatt, Stephen J., *Renaissance Self-Fashioning: From More to Shakespeare*, Chicago: University of Chicago Press, 1980

Gurr, Andrew, *The Shakespearean Stage, 1574–1642*, Cambridge and New York: Cambridge University Press, 1970, 3rd, revised, edition, 1992

Gurr, Andrew, *Playgoing in Shakespeare's London*, Cambridge and New York: Cambridge University Press, 1987

Hattaway, Michael, *Elizabethan Popular Theatre: Plays in Performance*, London and Boston: Routledge & Kegan Paul, 1982

Hellenga, Robert R., "Elizabethan Dramatic Conventions and Elizabethan Reality", in *Renaissance Drama*, new series, 12, 1981

Hunter, G.K., "The Beginning of Elizabethan Drama: Revolution and Continuity", in *Renaissance Drama*, new series, 17, 1986
McMillin, Scott, *The Elizabethan Theatre and "The Book of Sir Thomas More"*, Ithaca, New York: Cornell University Press, 1987
White, Paul Whitefield, *Theatre and Reformation: Protestantism, Patronage and Playing in the Tudor Period*, Cambridge and New York: Cambridge University Press, 1993
Wilson, F.P., *The Oxford History of English Literature: English Drama, 1485–1585*, edited by G.K. Hunter, Oxford: Clarendon Press, 1968; New York: Oxford University Press, 1968

Few studies offer an overarching survey of Elizabethan drama. But two that have been especially influential during the last thirty years are Bevington and Wilson. BEVINGTON explores the variety of structural principles underlying the morality-play and popular traditions of the later medieval and Tudor eras, and considers the limitations imposed by the size and organisation of theatrical troupes. In particular the study seeks to counter the misapplication of overly-rigid classical rules to the varied forms of morality and homiletic theatre throughout the period, giving examples of the developments within the forms and the manner in which these shaped later drama. In contrast WILSON offers a more traditional historical approach to literary texts, with discrete chapters on modes of writing (such as "The Earlier Tudor Morality" and "Interlude" or "Sacred Drama"), and a focus on the period 1485–1585. The generic approach allows Wilson to emphasise classical and medieval antecedents, models, and forms, as well as particular works of certain dramatists. The study now requires considerable revision (a process being undertaken by G.K. Hunter, who edited Wilson's original text), especially in the account of the interaction of theatre and Protestantism. WHITE, although largely focused on the Tudor drama, provides valuable correctives to earlier studies, showing how many Protestants utilised theatre as a weapon to spread their ideology. The study moves beyond simply discussing texts, to examine the personnel, companies and patrons who fostered early Protestant reformations of medieval Catholic drama. White then engages in an examination of the later Elizabethan Protestant response to didactic theatre and to aesthetic production in general. HUNTER's article also illustrates advances in our understanding of the relation between theology and theatre, rewriting the history of the University Wits to argue that their innovations were not only the importation of classical forms and styles, but also their theology, which brought a new individualism, fostered by Protestantism, to the fore.

A particularly fruitful approach to Elizabethan theatre has come through the study of the material conditions of its production. GURR (1970, revised 1992) studies the history of companies, theatres, and the nature of acting in the period to illuminate the performance conditions and possibilities of a wide range of texts. The most recent edition takes in the new archaeological evidence found at the Rose Theatre. His other key book (GURR 1987) illuminates audience response in the period, and so starts to explore the intellectual structures through which theatre was perceived, as well as detailing shifts in audience taste across the Elizabethan and Jacobean periods and their relation to commercial and theatrical innovations. HATTAWAY also follows such an approach, but with a specific concentration upon the "popular", looking at "hit" plays such as Thomas Kyd's *Spanish Tragedy*, Christopher Marlowe's *Doctor Faustus* and *Edward II*, and the unattributed *Mucedorus* using reconstructions of the theatres, props, acting styles, and so on to illuminate the performance possibilities of these texts. Hattaway combines traditional theatre history with a more radical sense of performance drawn from Brechtian theory. McMILLIN's study of *Sir Thomas More*, although centred on one text, supplies an extensive historical analysis, which supplements Hattaway's work. McMillin illuminates the repertoire, staging techniques, and company structure of theatre in the early 1590s, a particularly murky period, and so provides important evidence about the kind of theatre that Shakespeare encountered upon his arrival in London.

Formalist criticism of Elizabethan theatre has shown the impact of rhetorical technique in the theatrical repertoire. ALTMAN studies the Ciceronian theory of arousing and expressing wonder and the way in which it influenced drama. In particular, Altman emphasises the combination of elements in rhetoric (the arousal of passion, the investigation of truth, and the persuasion of the audience), while showing how these explorative qualities are centred on the presentation of both sides of a debate, a technique that lay at the core of sixteenth-century humanist training. A particularly useful survey, again designed for undergraduates but of wider applicability, can be found in BRAUNMULLER, who studies the changing use of rhetoric in the Elizabethan and Jacobean eras, and shows how actors approached the technical problems surrrounding impersonation (the creation of dramatic figures) or problems of how action might be represented (symbolically, naturalistically, etc.). HELLENGA considers these issues in greater depth, using debates about form and style in Elizabethan theatre to pose fundamental questions about the nature of selfhood and the relations of dramatic conventions with social reality. The emphasis on the radical difference of the Elizabethan era, and on the manner in which historical understanding of the interconnection of childhood, privacy, and autonomy in the creation of selfhood should all shape our aesthetic responses to Elizabethan drama, is productive and points forward to the more radical work of the cultural materialists and New Historicists.

Recent criticism of Elizabethan theatre has concentrated on such issues as self-fashioning and selfhood (sometimes called "subjectivity"), the relationship between drama and political power, and issues of gender and sexuality. GREENBLATT offers a powerful new methodology, combining historical background, close textual detail, and theoretical insight, an approach now known as New Historicism. Greenblatt focuses, in particular, on the implications of self-conscious self-construction through the literature of the period to consider how far this can be seen as autonomous or socially/politically determined. Marlovian theatre becomes, for Greenblatt, the test case, its radicalism embodied in its seemingly unending desire for unattainable self-determination, a pattern which the desire for geographical liberation encapsulates, even as conquest and discovery actually reduce the world to a mere map.

This paradox becomes the paradigm for Greenblatt's version of Renaissance culture. In contrast DOLLIMORE, who established the agenda for much theoretically oriented criticism during the 1980s by extending Althusserian ideas about subjectivity, presents a much more consciously determinist stance. For Dollimore, terms such as "human will" or "consciousness" merely represent the ways in which power in all its forms – political, economic and cultural – determines our lives. Greenblatt and Dollimore offer views of Marlovian theatre that differ radically in their implications, and which have important ramifications for the study of Elizabethan theatre as a whole. Greenblatt offers an account that identifies a fascination with the alien, a sense of "transcendental homelessness" and restlessness, but which ultimately binds figures like Faustus closer to the orthodoxies he apparently rejects. In contrast, Dollimore, although he works within a more explicitly determinist framework, argues that the *form* of Marlovian theatre is crucial, because by staging Faustian struggles within a morality-play convention and ideology a subversion is thus achieved of both form and ideology. It could be said that if Greenblatt offers subversion with containment, Dollimore argues for subversion and transgression – both models that have become dominant in recent discussions of Elizabethan theatre.

JAMES D. KNOWLES

3. Jacobean and Caroline

Brooke, Nicholas, *Horrid Laughter in Jacobean Tragedy*, London: Open Books, 1979; New York: Harper & Row, 1979

Butler, Martin, *Theatre and Crisis 1632–1642*, Cambridge and New York: Cambridge University Press, 1984.

Champion, Larry, *Tragic Patterns in Jacobean and Caroline Drama*, Knoxville: University of Tennessee Press, 1977

Clark, Ira, *Professional Playwrights: Massinger, Ford, Shirley and Brome*, Lexington: University Press of Kentucky, 1992

Dollimore, Jonathan, *Radical Tragedy: Religion, Ideology and Power in the Drama of Shakespeare and His Contemporaries*, Brighton, Sussex: Harvester Press, 1984, 2nd ed., 1989; Chicago: University of Chicago Press, 1984

Ellis-Fermor, Una, *Jacobean Drama*, London: Methuen, 1936, 4th revised edition, 1958

Farley-Hills, David, *Jacobean Drama: A Critical Survey of the Professional Drama 1600–25*, London: Macmillan, 1988; New York: St Martin's Press, 1988

Freer, Coburn, *The Poetics of Jacobean Drama*, Baltimore: Johns Hopkins University Press, 1981

Hall, Joan Lord, *The Dynamics of Role-Playing in Jacobean Drama*, New York and London: Macmillan, 1991

Harris, Anthony, *Night's Black Agents: Witchcraft and Magic in Seventeenth-Century English Drama*, Manchester: Manchester University Press, 1980; Totowa, New Jersey: Rowman & Littlefield, 1980

Kirsch, Arthur C., *Jacobean Dramatic Perspectives*, Charlottesville: University Press of Virginia, 1972

Knights, L.C., *Drama and Society in the Age of Jonson*, London: Chatto & Windus, 1937; New York: G.W. Stewart, 1937

Leinwand, Theodore B., *The City Staged: Jacobean Comedy, 1603–1613*, Madison: University of Wisconsin Press, 1986

McMullan, Gordon, and Jonathan Hope (eds.), *The Politics of Tragicomedy: Shakespeare and After*, London and New York: Routledge, 1992

Ornstein, Robert, *The Moral Vision of Jacobean Tragedy*, Madison: University of Wisconsin Press, 1960

Putt, S. Gorley, *The Golden Age of English Drama*, Totowa, New Jersey: Rowman & Littlefield, 1981; Cambridge: D.S. Brewer, 1981

Ribner, Irving, *Jacobean Tragedy: The Quest for Moral Order*, London: Methuen, 1962; New York: Barnes & Noble, 1962

Wymer, Rowland, *Suicide and Despair in the Jacobean Drama*, Brighton, Sussex: Harvester Press, 1986

Modern criticism of Jacobean-Caroline drama is distinguished by the variety of innovative approaches to the subject.

KNIGHTS in his pioneering work investigates the social and economic bases of early seventeenth-century culture in England, with emphasis on the influence of developing capitalism on the drama. The first half of the book is a study of economic changes taking place at that time, and the second half approaches the major playwrights from that point of view. Ben Jonson's satiric focus is on acquisition; Thomas Heywood and Thomas Dekker are concerned with stabilizing social values in this period of capitalist expansion; Thomas Middleton depicts the newly emerging social classes, usually with a satiric bias; Philip Massinger is derivative, but his comedies reflect the vitality of the Jonsonian tradition. In a brief appendix on seventeenth-century melancholy, Knights cites economic causation, particularly poverty, as a prime factor. An early work, this book is still useful for its insight into the economic conditions which affected the drama of the time.

ELLIS-FERMOR's book is also early, a classic study which has often been supplemented but never superseded. She probes the effect of the disillusioned mood of the Jacobean period on the dramaturgy, with especial attention to ten playwrights (George Chapman, John Marston, Jonson, Dekker, Middleton, Cyril Tourneur, John Webster, Fulke Greville, John Ford, Francis Beaumont, and John Fletcher) in addition to Shakespeare. One of the first critics to elucidate the distinction between the Elizabethan and Jacobean modes of drama, she also explores the relationship between the visual arts and stage representation.

RIBNER argues that the major Jacobean tragedians sought moral meaning in spite of the prevailing pessimism and melancholy of their time. He deals with six writers as examples. Chapman's search for moral order led him to failure and resignation in spite of his philosophical commitment to stoicism. In contrast Heywood was the apostle of "cosmic optimism", but less effective as a dramatic artist. Tourneur (to whom he attributes *The Revenger's Tragedy*) echoed a medieval vision of evil in his portrayal of corrupt humanity. In Webster's tragedies the author finds the search for moral order to be "agonized", reflecting the chaotic world of Jacobean scepticism. Middleton is seen as a Christian writer with an emphasis on damnation, and Ford as a playwright whose search can "only resolve itself in paradox". Although the focus on moral order may seem old-fashioned, Ribner's treatment of individual plays is not simplistic but acknowledges the complexities of the Jacobean mentality.

ORNSTEIN's work is also a classic study of Jacobean drama, with analyses of nine major playwrights, including Shakespeare. In an introductory chapter, he discusses the background of the period, looking at politics, moral philosophy, dramatic tradition, and religious belief, concluding that although we "cannot generalize" about the moral vision of Jacobean tragedy, we can appreciate the "vitality and immediacy" of the plays. Citing Marston as prologue and Beaumont and Fletcher as epilogue to the tragedies of the period, he concentrates on Chapman, Jonson, Tourneur, Middleton, Webster, and Ford, with a final chapter devoted to Shakespeare. Ornstein's style is engaging, as when he sums up the objective nature of Middleton's tragedies with a metaphor: "even when his plays blaze like diamonds, they are cold to the touch".

KIRSCH finds the distinctive character of Jacobean drama largely the result of three influences: the rise of satiric plays, the popularity of tragicomedy, and the private theatre. Jonson was the major exemplar of satire; Beaumont and Fletcher were the prime examples of tragicomedy; Marston was a private-theatre writer who exploited the theatrical self-consciousness of the boys' companies who acted there. These three developments were ultimately symptoms of the early seventeenth-century loss of faith, which in turn resulted in the virtual disappearance of providence from the drama.

CHAMPION's purpose is to examine how dramatic tragedy reflected the complex and changing political thought of the time, finding the tragedy in this period of spiritual uncertainty to be "pervasively ambivalent". He sees Shakespeare's final tragedies as closely akin to those of his contemporaries, all dealing with the plight of the individual in a "physically corrupt and a metaphysically uncertain world". Consequently there was a trend toward a societal perspective in tragedy. The resulting moral ambivalence was greatest in the late tragedies of Ford, but it is also present in the plays of Jonson, Tourneur, Webster, and Middleton.

BROOKE begins with the generally accepted idea that laughter does not become tragedy, a serious and solemn genre. He proceeds to argue, through analysis of six Jacobean and Caroline plays, that "horrid" laughter was an important part of the perception of human experience in the tragedy of that time. In *The Revenger's Tragedy* the "cackle of skulls" is essential to the grotesque action. Similarly, in both of Webster's tragedies laughter is a part of the imaginative mode of perception. The laughter in the comic subplot of Middleton and William Rowley's *The Changeling*, in the final masque in Middleton's *Women Beware Women*, and in the comic suitor in Ford's *'Tis Pity She's a Whore* is not so wildly disturbing as it is in the earlier plays. Although the author insists that the "horrid" laughter in these plays is "essential to their tragic form", he does not offer any explanations for its origin or development.

FREER argues that our understanding of the plays involves listening to the poetry and becoming aware of them as poetic structures. He stresses the difference between dramatic speeches and separate poems. The Stuart audience could hear the poetry and believed in the affective power of verse. He chooses five plays for analysis. First is *The Revenger's Tragedy*, where the protagonist Vindice illustrates a wide range of stylistic variation in his speech, beginning with "nervous" and ending with "derisive". Then he turns to Shakespeare's romance *Cymbeline*, where the villain Iachimo tries on one voice after another. In both of Webster's tragedies the poetic language offers a "double reality", poetry growing out of the dramatic moment and poetry taken from the library. Finally in Ford's *The Broken Heart* the formality of the language is significant, for the characters are all caught in rigid attitudes. This book is valuable in showing how the dramatic poetry penetrates the other elements in the plays.

PUTT's intention is for this book to serve as "merely an introduction to its vast subject" rather than to offer any new scholarly material. After a brief look at the earlier drama, he focuses on the major Jacobean dramatists, Marston, Chapman, Middleton, Webster, Ford, and Beaumont and Fletcher. Throughout this engagingly written book, the author argues for both an appreciation of the power of the Jacobean drama and for the many parallels between the Jacobean age and our own, which should make modern audiences responsive to these plays from the past. He reaches no conclusions but rejects the various "-isms" and "-ologies" of critics. His so-called "anti-conclusion" expresses his approach: "it was providential, if you like, that at the very moment when the language of England had reached its highest point of richness, a new, lusty, young popular theatre could act like a crucible for all the laughter, politics, agonies, raptures, brutalities, news items, sheer nonsense and old wives' tales tossed into it".

DOLLIMORE's influential study deals with, as the subtitle explains, "the religion, ideology, and power in the drama of Shakespeare and his contemporaries". Part I concerns the religious and political contexts of the early seventeenth century and the emergence of a new radically subversive drama, distinguished by discontinuous identity in character as well as other radical ideas. Part II deals with structure, mimesis, and providence, tracing through several plays the disintegration of the traditional providentialist belief. Part III focuses on man decentred, as exemplified in the rejection of essentialist humanism in several plays. Part IV focuses on subjectivity, reviewing his argument for the emergence in the Renaissance of a "conception of subjectivity legitimately identified in terms of a materialist perspective rather than one of essentialist humanism". This provocative book is itself exemplary of the subversiveness it studies.

FARLEY-HILLS offers a survey of the "Professional Drama 1600–25", "the most brilliant and dynamic the world has seen". After a quick look at lesser writers, he concentrates on the major figures. Jonson is seen as the supreme comic satirist; Marston, who wrote exclusively for the boys' companies, combined entertainment with serious moral comment; Chapman, who has been underrated, wrote effective tragedies and comedies, which deserve reading; Middleton, in contrast, was virtually unrecognized in his own time but now has the stature of a major playwright. In analyzing Webster's two great tragedies, the author focuses on the complex characterization. Finally, the work of Fletcher and his collaborators is discussed as tragicomedy. This book is a persuasive argument for appreciation of Shakespeare's relatively neglected contemporaries.

CLARK deals with four largely neglected Caroline dramatists. His book is revisionist, arguing against the prevailing view of these four as decadent and escapist. Instead he calls attention to their treatment of sociopolitical issues and to their original handling of traditional dramatic conventions. For each of the four Clark first describes his social circle, then analyzes both his sociopolitical ideas and his dramatic technique. For each he also discusses in depth one representative play. Massinger's *The Picture*, Ford's *The Broken Heart*, Shirley's *Hyde Park*, and Brome's *The Antipodes* receive detailed commentary. This is a useful work in demonstrating the concern these playwrights show about the social issues of their time. Another revisionist, and influential, account of Caroline drama is BUTLER's. He concentrates on the comedies of Massinger, Brome, and Shirley, exploring the ways in which they reflected the perspectives of a developing gentry class, thereby modifying the usual view of the period's drama as being created primarily with a court or city audience in mind.

McMULLAN and HOPE regard tragicomedy as "the most important dramatic genre of the period 1610–50". The essays here take a variety of exploratory approaches to the subject with an attempt to ascertain its political impact on its audiences. Topics include the interrelations of utopia and language, sex as commodity, women in pre-revolutionary drama, and the effect of the introduction of the actress into Caroline culture. One essay explains the typical utopian ending of tragicomedy as a way of balancing the harsh social criticism which precedes it in the plays. These essays represent widely divergent attitudes in the tragicomedies and raise important questions about the relationship of drama to the culture of its time.

More specialized than the other studies discussed here are the books by Harris, Wymer, and Hall.

HARRIS explores the relationship between the actual practices of the attitudes toward witchcraft in the Renaissance and their representation on the stage of the time. After reviewing many contradictory points of view on witchcraft, he gives a brief account of the subject in poetry before turning to the stage. He then deals with the Weird Sisters in *Macbeth* and three plays which were influenced by them, Marston's *Sophonisba*, Jonson's *Masque of Queenes*, and Middleton's *The Witch*. In contrast to these plays, Dekker, Ford, and Rowley's *The Witch of Edmonton* was based on the actual trial of a woman who, as protagonist, is treated with sympathy and understanding. A very interesting chapter is devoted to the theatrical realization of supernatural scenes in this useful survey of the staging of magic and witchcraft.

WYMER assumes an intentionalist approach in this study of suicide as a dramatic convention. His thesis is that the playwrights manipulated the culturally problematic status of suicide for dramatic effect. He deals with classical and medieval backgrounds with their conflicting attitudes towards suicide in terms of honour and despair, then analyzes several plays in which the patterns of suicidal behaviour are based on retribution and repentance as well as on love, including Shakespeare's *Romeo and Juliet*, and on stoicism, including Shakespeare's *Julius Caesar*. He finds that in the tragedies the convention of suicide becomes tragic only when there is "a balancing of opposed implications", such as dignity and despair, implying a dynamic view of human nature as a "meeting-point between polarities". This is a thoughtful and insightful work.

HALL investigates what happens to dramatic characters when they engage in role-playing, with both potentially creative and destructive results. Role-playing was a preoccupation of the Renaissance, both celebrating humanity's creative diversity and warning of the dangerous consequences. In most instances of Jacobean tragedy "adopting new personae leads to degeneration". Two tragedies of Middleton, and Jonson's *Volpone*, are studied as examples of the negative consequences. The author also devotes chapters to examples in revenge tragedy and in tragicomedy. Webster and Ford offer more creative possibilities. Bosola's many assumed roles in *The Duchess of Malfi* further his own self-discovery, and in *The Broken Heart* the central figures assume roles in order to find "a decorous way of conducting themselves". This book offers intriguing new insights into the old subject of role-playing and selfhood.

CHARLOTTE SPIVACK

Drama: Restoration

Brown, Laura, *English Dramatic Form 1660–1760: An Essay in Generic History*, New Haven and London: Yale University Press, 1981

Hotson, Leslie, *The Commonwealth and Restoration Stage*, Cambridge, Massachusetts: Harvard University Press, 1928; reprinted New York: Russell & Russell, 1962

Hume, Robert D., *The Development of English Drama in the Late Seventeenth Century*, Oxford: Clarendon Press, 1976; New York: Oxford University Press, 1976

Hume, Robert D., *The Rakish Stage: Studies in English Drama 1660–1800*, Carbondale: Southern Illinois University Press, 1983

Loftis, John, Richard Southern, Marion Jones, and A.H. Scouten, *The Revels History of Drama in English, Volume 5: 1660–1750*, London: Methuen, 1976

Powell, Jocelyn, *Restoration Theatre Production*, London and Boston: Routledge & Kegan Paul, 1984

Criticism of Restoration drama ranges from the general – such as Loftis's volume – to the specific – for example, that by Brown. The field is dominated, justifiably, by the highly readable and well-researched work of Hume, with his strongly historicist approach and challenging conceptions. Overall, and perhaps unsurprisingly given the nature of the extant plays themselves, there is more critical concentration on the comedy of the age than on other Restoration dramatic genres.

LOFTIS *et al.*'s volume provides perhaps the best introductory overview of drama of the period. The first section, written by Loftis himself, gives a valuable historical and cultural context for the studies that follow. The second section, "Theatres and Actors", is divided into two parts, one by Southern, concentrating on innovations like scenery, and one by Jones, in which she vividly recreates the lives and circumstances of repertory actors. It is Scouten's section, however, the first part of which is most relevant here, which really stands out in its scope, organisation, and style. "Plays and Playwrights", Scouten's contribution, traces the development of

Restoration drama, investigating "the new dramatists" John Dryden, George Etherege, William Wycherley, and others, and "the later comic dramatists" along the way. He devotes separate sections to farce and burlesque, tragedy, and dramatic opera. The overall effect is one of a comprehensive, well-written and researched, and entertaining study. The extensive thematic bibliography, the wide-ranging chronological table, and the general quality and depth of the contributions combine to make the entire work indispensable as a starting-point for any student of the period.

HUME's 1976 book, as the title suggests, is an attempt to trace the chronological development of the drama, thereby placing plays in categories. The study exists as a response to the fact that the "history of drama, closely considered, is infuriatingly untidy", and in his opening pages Hume warns against too cursory a grouping-together of "Restoration plays" – after all, he reminds his reader, some 17 years separate the last plays of Wycherley and Etherege from the first of William Congreve. At times his study veers towards the schematic, such as his categorisation of female characters into ten types, ranging from romantic lead, to whore, to abused wife; but overall it is extremely useful as an introductory work that places the drama within a social and cultural context – in, for example, the useful reminder that "ten consecutive performances constituted a smash hit" – and will enable students to get a handle on the plays.

The later collection of essays, which make up HUME's 1983 volume, have in common a different emphasis, concentrating equally on text – that is, the plays – and audiences. In his Preface to this collection, Hume explains how it contains essays that can roughly be divided into three types – "Generic Study", "Critical Analysis", and "Contextual Study". The first of these, "Generic Study", is more concerned with the eighteenth century than the other two, and "Critical Analysis" with investigating work by Thomas Otway, Nathaniel Lee, and John Gay. The most complex of the three, "Contextual Study", constitutes perhaps also the most interesting approach in the volume, investigating "the plays' values, ideology, and subject matter, but also studies of the plays' relationship to changing audiences and to the theatrical context in which they were produced". His opening chapter on "Content and Meaning in the Drama" is a convincing and audacious response to prevailing ways of "reading" the plays, and should be read by anyone setting out to study the period. As for the rest of the volume, especially illuminating is Hume's chapter on "The Myth of the Rake in 'Restoration Comedy'", in which he answers modern critics who have made twentieth-century assumptions about the figure of the libertine, and his propensity, or otherwise, to "reform". He argues that "late seventeenth-century comedies contain plenty of sex, and even smut, but the values which emerge after a balanced reading are by no means libertine values". He challenges prevalent theories about Restoration drama, including his own, and provides fresh and innovative interpretations in an engaging style, which most readers should find accessible.

HOTSON's study is viewed as an important work, not least on account of its unprecedented investigation of the London stage during the Commonwealth years. Hotson divides his study of the Restoration stage into chapters dealing with each of the dramatic companies of the time – the Duke's, the King's, and the United – with a concluding chapter on rival companies. This division leads to a dull and overtly schematic overall approach, replete with documented information, but lacking entertainment or levity. The work was originally published in 1928, leading it to appear very outdated in places where it has long since been overtaken by other research.

The work by BROWN is altogether more advanced and focused in its critical scope, being an attempt "not to seek to imitate the extensive theatrical and repertorial studies of Restoration and eighteenth-century drama. . . . It does not document debt or influence. It is a history neither of the theater, of the repertory, nor of dramatic taste. It is an essay in generic history, narrowly defined by the evolution of dramatic form". It comprises three parts, the first two of which – "Social Forms, 1660–1677" and "Transitional Forms 1677–1707" – are of particular import here. This emphasis on form leads the author to attempt a negotiation of the often complex or ambiguous relationship between literature and social, or historical, context – this latter being the "source" of the author's "conceptualization of the whole trajectory of this generic history". This trajectory starts in the early seventeenth century with forms whose actions are governed by "a social standard of assessment" – that is, heroic drama and social satire – and ends in the eighteenth century with a dramatic structure within which actions are judged on moral worth, a structure closely linked with the rise of the novel. Brown finds much evidence in support of her thesis, presenting it with considerable depth and clarity. Especially illuminating is her analysis of Etherege's *Man of Mode*, which she convincingly – and, on the face of it, surprisingly – avers has the same "formal ends" as Dryden's *Conquest of Granada*. In all, Brown's is a daring and refreshing study, whose very specific theoretical aims are cogently realised.

An immediate sense of the layout and atmosphere of the Restoration playhouse is vividly conveyed in POWELL's work, and thus the reader can appreciate the analyses of the plays in their original historical and cultural context. The author communicates how the theme of disguise, so common in the drama, actually found expression in the playhouse itself, where a social facade of cultured wealth overlay a depth of violence and poverty. Of note in the study overall is Powell's investigation of Wycherley's *Country Wife*, particularly his original and sensitive reading of the women's drinking scene. In the analysis of the play as a whole, the complex relationship of comedy and violence is carefully negotiated, as is the character of Horner, whom Powell regards as almost mock-heroic. The writer identifies and explores a series of oppositions – between town and country, jealousy and complacency, love and lust – present in the play's structure, and brings out well the theatrical self-referentiality central to much of the play's action. The conclusion arrived at is that *The Country Wife*, despite its realistic elements, is essentially fantastic, and within it a "desire for the successful fulfilment of the basest wishes competes with an awareness of the essential absurdity of those wishes when fulfilled. This dialectic of response forms the moral and theatrical centre of the play". This capacity for a neat turn-of-phrase employed to encapsulate a complex idea is also in evidence in Powell's analysis of the play's epilogue, which "gives the whole a neat frame, demonstrating the social and moral paradox that a man's honour is a woman's shame". In sum, this work is an adept and serviceable contribution to the criticism of Restoration drama.

EMMA L.E. REES

See also **Comedy: Restoration, Tragedy: Restoration**

Drama: 18th Century

Boas, Frederick S., *An Introduction to Eighteenth-Century Drama, 1700–1780*, Oxford: Clarendon Press, 1953

Brown, Laura O., *English Dramatic Form 1660–1760: An Essay in Generic History*, New Haven, Connecticut, and London: Yale Unversity Press, 1981

Hume, Robert D. (ed.), *The London Theatre World 1660–1800*, Carbondale: Southern Illinois University Press, 1980; London: Feffer & Simons, 1980

Hume, Robert D., *The Rakish Stage: Studies in English Drama 1660–1800*, Carbondale: Southern Illinois University Press, 1983

Loftis, John, *Comedy and Society from Congreve to Fielding*, Stanford, California: Stanford University Press, 1959

Nicoll, Allardyce, *A History of English Drama: Early Eighteenth Century Drama 1700–1750*, Cambridge: Cambridge University Press, 1925, 3rd revised edition, 1952

Nicoll, Allardyce, *A History of English Drama: Late Eighteenth Century Drama 1700–1800*, Cambridge: Cambridge University Press, 1927, 3rd revised edition, 1952

Pearson, Jacqueline, *The Prostituted Muse: Images of Women and Women Dramatists, 1642–1737*, Brighton, Sussex: Harvester, 1988; New York: St Martin's Press, 1988

Price, Cecil, *Theatre in the Age of Garrick*, Oxford: Blackwell, 1973; Totowa, New Jersey: Rowman & Littlefield, 1973

Richards, Kenneth, and Thomson, Peter (eds.), *The Eighteenth-Century English Stage*, London: Methuen, 1972

Van Lennep, William, Emmett L. Avery, Arthur H. Scouten, George W. Stone, and Charles B. Hogan, *The London Stage 1660–1800: A Calendar of Plays, Entertainments, and Afterpieces, Together with Casts, Box-Receipts, and Contemporary Comment Compiled from the Playbills, Newspapers, and Theatrical Diaries of the Time*, 5 parts in 11 vols., Carbondale: Southern Illinois University Press, 1965–68

Writers on eighteenth-century drama divide their attention between the literary criticism of scripts ("drama") and investigation of the conditions in which they were performed ("theatre"). The latter pursuit is sometimes perceived as more rewarding than the former, because eighteenth-century plays are often considered inferior to those of other periods. This view has been attributed to a growing eighteenth-century taste for sentimentalism, but the existence and nature of this connection are controversial.

VAN LENNEP *et al.* is an indispensable reference book for anyone who wishes to know what was actually happening in London theatres at any given time. It has absorbed and superseded all previous research.

NICOLL (1925) is equally concerned with "drama" and "theatre". He paints a grim picture of the plays: "as we watch the drama progressing from 1610 to the end of the eighteenth century, we see in general only a retrograde movement". Between 1700 and 1750 he values dramatists mainly for their connection with other contemporary literature, or their later influence: Henrik Ibsen is "the direct descendent of George Lillo". He investigates many aspects of theatre conditions, compiling a hand-list of all new plays and their subsequent performances. He hopes, justifiably, that the latter "may prove of value to later workers on this period". Nicoll's critical judgements have fared less well. Objections have been raised to his classification of plays as "Heroic Drama", "Pseudo-Classic Tragedies", "Comedies of Manners", "Comedies of Intrigue", "Comedies of Sensibility", etc.. Are these categories appropriate, or even necessary? Categorisation, however, reflects Nicoll's careful attention to the individual characteristics of each play, especially the features that would strike a chord with a contemporary eighteenth-century audience. NICOLL (1927) proceeds more cheerfully to 1800: he has successfully produced five plays of the period, proving that "the final and only sure test of dramatic excellence lies in the playhouse".

BOAS concentrates on "drama". His selective survey gives bland commentaries, usually accompanied by plot summaries and substantial quotations, on the work of 26 playwrights, ranging from familiar figures like George Farquhar, John Dennis, and Nicholas Rowe, to the lesser-known W.R. Chetwood and Edward Moore. Susanna Centlivre is the only woman included. Readers can decide which plays to study for themselves.

LOFTIS argues that early eighteenth-century plays reflect changing relationships between the moneyed bourgeoisie and the aristocratic landed classes, with increasingly favourable portrayals of merchants. He rejects the view that the adoption of bourgeois values encouraged the fashion for sentimentalism, which he attributes to snobbish critics who thought that the (supposedly unsentimental) aristocrats had better taste. Few critics today would endorse his firm division between "the history of thought" and "the history of society". But he has laid factual and conceptual foundations for much subsequent research.

Although mainly "theatrical" in orientation, the collection of brief essays edited by RICHARDS and THOMSON also deals with texts. Appropriately, it begins with a study of moral and aesthetic aims: Malcolm Kelsall shows how Sir Richard Steele adapted Terence to create a new sort of comedy that would "re-establish humane values" by exorcising the spirit of the rapacious Restoration rake. Equally appropriately, it ends with technical means: Graham Barlow's study of James Thornhill's set designs for the Theatre Royal, Drury Lane, in 1705, with illustrations and measurements. The intervening chapters on actors, managers, music, stage directions, and landscape scenery are all sufficiently self-contained to assist a reader in search of instant enlightenment, while opening fascinating avenues to further research for those who wish to study in more depth.

PRICE also offers an impressive variety of information, clearly set and out vividly illustrated, in a small space. Working on his own, he follows a more coherent plan than Richards and Thomson, and he even manages to include a chapter on audiences: an important topic that the former leave out. Both books, however, are self-explanatory enough to be useful to absolute beginners, while containing enough original findings to please more experienced scholars.

HUME (1980) contains essays that cover much the same ground as the two previous books, but in much more detail and at greater length. It is equally free from the effects of financial corner-cutting and intellectual concessions: the contributors have been concerned solely with giving the best possible account of their subjects, even when that required the inclusion of facts or figures that could not be absorbed at first reading. The result of this academic integrity is a substantial, authoritative volume that will be frequently consulted by grateful scholars.

BROWN's brilliantly innovative study applies generic history to drama from 1660 to 1760. She traces its evolution from "Social Forms" ("Heroic Action" and "Social Satire") through "Transitional Forms" ("Affective Tragedy" and "Transitional Comedy") to "Moral Forms" ("Dramatic Moral Action"). In social forms, characters are assessed by their ability to conform to aristocratic standards of honour or "witty decorum". In more sentimental, bourgeois forms, characters are judged by their inner worth. (No aesthetic class distinction is implied: Brown believes the aristocracy had embraced bourgeois standards.) Her final chapter, "Novelistic Moral Action", argues that novelists, unlike dramatists, were not hampered by conflicting emotional demands and outdated formal constraints.

HUME (1983) devastatingly combines theatre and drama criticism. He begins with a chapter designed "not to spoil the fun of those critics hell-bent on finding tidy themes and meanings in the drama (I only wish I could), but rather in the hope of encouraging more serious and careful use of content in interpretation". In "'Restoration Comedy' and Its Audiences, 1660–1776", a collaboration with Arthur H. Scouten, Nicoll and his successors are rebuked for neglecting revivals of seventeenth-century plays in the eighteenth-century repertory. He ends by dismissing as "bunk" the conventional view that Oliver Goldsmith and Richard Brinsley Sheridan were anti-sentimental revolutionaries.

PEARSON reads exhaustively, examines texts microscopically (even counting the lines given to every character), and maintains sufficient theatrical sense to spot a dozen neglected masterpieces. The first half of her book deals with women writers, actresses, women in theatre management and in audiences, and the treatment of women in plays and other writings by men. She then examines the treatment of women by female dramatists, covering the double standard, "Amazons", transvestites, "learned ladies", rape victims, women who refuse marriage, and women's language. Her method is a model for all gender studies.

CAROLYN D. WILLIAMS

Drama: British – 19th Century

Booth, Michael R., *Prefaces to English Nineteenth-Century Theatre*, Manchester: Manchester University Press, 1980
Booth, Michael R., *Theatre in the Victorian Age*, Cambridge and New York: Cambridge University Press, 1991
Donohue, Joseph, *Theatre in the Age of Kean*, Oxford: Blackwell, 1975; Totowa, New Jersey: Rowman & Littlefield, 1975
Emeljanow, Victor, *Victorian Popular Dramatists*, Boston: Twayne, 1987
Jenkins, Anthony, *The Making of Victorian Drama*, Cambridge and New York: Cambridge University Press, 1991
Nicoll, Allardyce, *The History of English Drama IV: Early Nineteenth Century Drama, 1800–1850*, Cambridge: Cambridge University Press, 1930, revised 1955
Nicoll, Allardyce, *The History of English Drama V: Late Nineteenth Century Drama, 1850–1900*, Cambridge: Cambridge University Press, 1946, revised 1959
Reynolds, Ernest, *Early Victorian Drama (1830–1870)*, Cambridge: W. Heffer & Sons, 1936; reprinted, New York: Benjamin Blom, 1965
Rowell, George, *The Victorian Theatre*, Oxford: Oxford University Press, 1956; 2nd edition, as *The Victorian Theatre, 1792–1914: A Survey*, Cambridge and New York: Cambridge University Press, 1978
Watson, Ernest Bradlee, *From Sheridan to Robertson: A Study of the Nineteenth-Century London Stage*, Cambridge, Massachusetts: Harvard University Press, 1926

Theatre in the nineteenth century was arguably the most vigorous and colourful of any era, though until the mid 1970s, with the exceptions noted below, the drama tended to be represented as largely unworthy of significant critical attention. A handicap, which still applies but to noticeably lesser extent, has been the lack of easily accessible play texts, outside a few mainstream authors. But the appreciation of the indissoluble link between text and performance – that to study the drama is not to study text alone, but text and performance conditions together (perhaps more true of this period than of any previous) – has helped to confirm the place of the drama in the study of literature and nineteenth-century society.

Most writing on nineteenth-century or Victorian drama is fairly conventional in approach. On the whole poststructural and deconstructive theory has made little direct impact; but it has perhaps reinforced the importance of the study of popular culture represented by theatre in all its guises, from the classical repertoire of the royal theatres and the respectability of middle-class West End social drama to the penny shows of bustling "minor" theatres further south and east. While critical interest still tends to stress the post-T.W. Robertson era and "literary" dramatists like Oscar Wilde and George Bernard Shaw (and to a lesser degree Henry Arthur Jones and Arthur Wing Pinero), discussion of writers such as Edward Fitzball, Douglas Jerrold, Dion Boucicault, and Sydney Grundy, most of whom have traditionally lain outside literary boundaries, is now more common.

There are several older studies still worth reading. WATSON sets the scene and to some extent the context for the study of Victorian theatre and its drama. The genre was deeply unfashionable in 1926, yet he gives it serious scholarly attention, stressing the shape and colour of theatre, and the significance of the acting styles and traditions that developed from c.1770 to 1870 in ways that assist understanding of the nature and quality of the drama.

Without NICOLL the academic study of the period's drama would be seriously limited. He provides its essential framework in the two volumes covering the nineteenth century, which are monuments to Nicoll's scholarship and energy. He explores essential and distinctive issues like copyright, the patent-theatre monopoly, and the place of the theatre in society. Although the critical material on the plays, divided by genre, is now in some ways outdated (indeed it was never the strongest element in Nicoll's work), the two "Hand-Lists" of plays listing all known plays by author, with records of performance and publication, are still indispensable. In the revised editions, much new work on author identification, performance, and printing data was incorporated. Nicoll's scholarship is constantly being added to, but his endeavour has never been equalled.

To the above may be added REYNOLDS' pioneering academic study from 1936, representing an early attempt to discuss Victorian dramatic literature. Avoiding the artificial divide of the century at 1850 later perpetrated by Nicoll, it is a brief, though well-documented, critical discussion of the broad genres of comedy and farce, tragedy and melodrama, in which several important Victorian playwrights are selected for special attention. It is perhaps noteworthy for early recognition of the quality of the extravaganzas of James Robinson Planché.

The revised 1978 edition of ROWELL, in which the main text was untouched but supplemented by an Afterword and extended bibliography, has helped maintain this work as the standard survey of the field for over 30 years. Rowell elegantly handles general issues tackled by Nicoll, such as stage conditions, audiences, authors' incomes, acting styles, and the like, alongside useful, if necessarily brief, analyses of important playwrights, including valuable chapters on Robertson and on the society drama of the 1890s. Rowell's eccentric use of 1792 as a starting point for his discussion is defended on the grounds that Victorian drama has its roots in the years well before Victoria's accession. DONOHUE covers the often neglected period of 1790 to the late 1830s. Helpful on dramatic literature (and acting) generally between these dates, it is especially useful for a succinct discussion of the rise of melodrama.

Booth, represented here by two essential works, has continually stressed the need to look beyond the usual preoccupations with established genres like tragedy and comedy (neither of which was particularly strong in the period), beyond West End conventions, to the often livelier "minor"-theatre traditions in order to investigate the astonishing variety of Victorian theatre, expressed through not only melodrama (see his standard work *English Melodrama*, London: Herbert Jenkins, 1965), but also burletta, pantomime, farce, and extravaganza. Apart from a new retrospective Foreword and a bibliographical essay, BOOTH's *Prefaces* are reprints of material from his Clarendon edition of *English Plays of the Nineteenth Century* (5 vols., Oxford: Oxford University Press, 1969–76), which provides reliably edited texts of important plays drawn from the above-mentioned genres. Detached from their accompanying play texts, these essays read slightly oddly, but they are nevertheless useful and perceptive accounts of a number of both well-known and less familiar plays of the period. His knowledge of the period, and his handling of literary and non-literary material, is impressive, though even here the almost inevitable bias towards West End drama is still evident. This is to some extent redressed in BOOTH's 1991 book, which has few pretensions to original research but is a balanced survey, incorporating the latest scholarship, and attempts to give rather more weight than formerly to the socio-economic context that shaped the Victorian theatre and its drama. It is effectively a Rowell for the 1990s.

On a more specific level, EMELJANOW, though devoting a fair amount of space to plot outlines, writes refreshingly directly about dramatic literature, and offers new perspectives on playwrights like Tom Taylor and Jerrold as well as the more familiar figures of Robertson and Jones.

Finally, JENKINS, while not ignoring conditions of performance, examines seven Victorian playwrights, beginning with Edward Bulwer-Lytton through to Jones and Shaw, in order to determine the ways in which topical issues such as reform, revolution, and (most strikingly) the New Woman found theatrical foci. It is a well-argued attempt to blend conventional dramatic criticism with politics, and social and theatrical history.

JOHN RUSSELL STEPHENS

Drama: British – 20th Century

1. General

Bull, John, *Stage Right: Crisis and Recovery in British Contemporary Mainstream Theatre*, London: Macmillan, 1994

Cave, Richard Allen, *New British Drama in Performance on the London Stage 1970–1985*, Gerrards Cross, Buckinghamshire: Colin Smythe, 1987; New York: St Martin's Press, 1988

Chambers, Colin, and Mike Prior, *Playwrights' Progress: Patterns of Postwar British Drama*, Oxford: Amber Lane, 1987

Clarke, Ian, *Edwardian Drama*, London: Faber & Faber, 1989

Cohn, Ruby, *Retreats from Realism in Recent English Drama*, Cambridge and New York: Cambridge University Press, 1991

Davies, Andrew, *Other Theatres: The Development of Alternative and Experimental Theatre in Britain*, London: Macmillan, 1987

Elsom, John, *Post-War British Theatre*, London and Boston: Routledge & Kegan Paul, 1976, revised 1979

Griffiths, Trevor R., and Margaret L. Llewellyn-Jones (eds.), *British and Irish Women Dramatists since 1958*, Milton Keynes, Buckinghamshire: Open University Press, 1992

Hinchliffe, Arnold P., *British Theatre 1950–1970*, Oxford: Blackwell, 1974; Totowa, New Jersey: Rowman & Littlefield, 1974
Hunt, Hugh, Kenneth Richards, and John Russell Taylor, *The Revels History of Drama in English: Volume VII, 1880 to the Present Day*, London and New York: Methuen, 1978
Innes, Christopher, *Modern British Drama 1890–1990*, Cambridge and New York: Cambridge University Press, 1992
Itzin, Catherine, *Stages in the Revolution: Political Theatre in Britain since 1968*, London: Methuen, 1980
Marshall, Norman, *The Other Theatre*, London: John Lehmann, 1947
Stowell, Sheila, *A Stage of Their Own: Feminist Playwrights of the Suffrage Era*, Manchester: Manchester University Press, 1992; Ann Arbor, Michigan: UMI Research Press, 1992
Taylor, John Russell, *Anger and After: A Guide to the New British Drama*, London: Methuen, 1962, revised 1969; as *The Angry Theatre: New British Drama*, New York: Hill & Wang, 1962
Taylor, John Russell, *The Second Wave: British Drama for the Seventies*, London: Methuen, 1971; New York: Hill & Wang, 1971
Trewin, J.C., *The Gay Twenties*, London: Macdonald, 1958
Trewin, J.C., *The Turbulent Thirties*, London: Macdonald, 1960
Trussler, Simon, *The Cambridge Illustrated History of British Theatre*, Cambridge and New York: Cambridge University Press, 1994
Woodfield, James, *English Theatre in Transition 1881–1914*, London: Croom Helm, 1984
Worth, Katharine J., *Revolutions in Modern English Drama*, London: Bell, 1973

Drama is, by its nature, a public art, directly susceptible to the vagaries of social, economic, and political forces, which makes the task of creating a general survey of drama particularly demanding. When the further complexities of covering the contemporary period are added, with all the difficulties inherent in attempting to discern the underlying trends beneath a mass of contingent data, it is not surprising that there are relatively few such overall surveys of the modern era. Of those that do exist, some cover only drama in the sense of plays and playwrights, others attempt the more difficult task of placing the drama in the wider theatrical and socio-economic context.

By far the best survey in terms of its handling of the wider issues is TRUSSLER's discussion of the twentieth century in his general study of British theatre, which is exemplary in its coverage, concision, wit, and perception, and aided by a selection of illuminating photographs of major productions. Trussler is fully conversant with modern scholarship, so that his historical account is informed by a knowledge of both alternative theatre ventures and modern critical theory, and he is also admirably clear about his own critical standpoints. His treatment of the twentieth century is only part of a much wider historical project, so that he does not have room to discuss any playwrights in great depth (even George Bernard Shaw gets only just over a page), although some of his almost throw-away judgments are as incisive and illuminating as anything one might find in a far lengthier discussion.

Trussler supersedes all previous works in terms of its overall grasp of theatre as an aesthetic and social phenomenon. However, there is still value in HUNT, RICHARDS, and TAYLOR's volume in the *Revels History* series, which offers decade-by-decade overviews of the socio-political and aesthetic contexts of the period, which it usefully defines as "1880 to the Present" (which is the mid-1970s). Hugh Hunt provides a lengthy account of "The Social and Literary Context", which deftly summarises a wide range of factors influencing the development of British drama and theatre, although it now needs qualification in terms of the kinds of recent scholarship and theatrical rediscovery that inform Trussler. Kenneth Richards contributes a section on "Actors and Theatres 1880–1918", and Hunt continues the story to the opening of the National Theatre in 1976; but the most important contribution is John Russell Taylor's survey of "Dramatists and Plays since 1880", again on a decade-by-decade basis. Russell Taylor draws on his own *Anger and After* (see below) and *The Rise and Fall of the Well-Made Play* (1967) to analyse the relationship between dramatic form and artistic achievement without ever degenerating into mere list-making.

The most substantial survey concentrating on twentieth-century plays and playwrights is INNES. He takes 1890 as his starting point and ends in 1990, so he is able to cover more recent developments and to refer to such enterprises as the Actress's Franchise League which have only been rediscovered relatively recently. He concentrates almost entirely on interpreting dramatists and plays rather than discussing wider social and intellectual contexts. He also adopts a thematically based approach within broader chronological parameters, which allows him greater freedom to follow up a debate than the strictly decade-based approach adopted in the *Revels* book. Like Russell Taylor he sees Shaw as exerting an enormous influence over the theory and practice of British drama in the first half of the century, thus accounting for the relative neglect of those Continental influences that only made their full impact from the mid-1950s. Innes rightly draws attention to the dangers of a single linear account of developments in British drama, emphasising the links between the post-1968 "political dramatists" and the agitprop theatre of the 1930s, and between the so-called "kitchen sink" realists of the 1950s and the work of such predecessors as Shaw, John Galsworthy, D.H. Lawrence, and Harley Granville Barker. However, his wariness of straight chronological narrative leads him to approach his subject under the three headings of "Realism", "Comedy", and "Poetic Drama", which he regards as "defined equally by stylistic approach and thematic focus". This does impose its own straitjacket, in that Innes has to adopt Procrustean methods to fit some of his writers into his categories; and the choice of the heading "Present Tense – Feminist Theatre" to cover recent feminist drama seems indicative of a tension in the work itself in dealing with some of the most recent theatrical activity.

Of the three general studies considered above, Trussler offers the fullest sense of theatre as whole and is the most up to date, whereas the *Revels History* perhaps covers more ground in terms of offering helpful starting points for considering individual plays and playwrights in the context of their contemporaries, and Innes has room to make some interesting comparative judgments and is informed by an awareness of somepreviously overlooked work.

The accounts offered by the general histories may be supplemented by some significant studies of discrete periods or themes in dramatic and theatrical activity (and for a more detailed description of some of these books, see the other entries on twentieth-century British drama). These include: CLARKE's deft and succinct account of Edwardian drama, particularly as practised by Shaw, Barker, Galsworthy, Henry Arthur Jones, and Arthur Wing Pinero; WOODFIELD's account of aspects of the "alternative theatre" movements of the earlier part of the period; and STOWELL's corrective to the gender gaps left by more traditional accounts. In the absence of more recent studies, TREWIN's books (1958 and 1960) remain the best overview of the mainstream in the interwar years, while MARSHALL remains an important first-hand source for "alternative theatre" in the 1920s and 1930s. WORTH takes a long view, placing her "Revolutions" in the context of the dramaturgy of the interwar years – that of Shaw, Sean O'Casey, W.H. Auden and Christopher Isherwood, James Joyce, Samuel Beckett, and T.S. Eliot. She is particularly concerned with issues of realism, epic, and subtext, and her work benefits from her strong sense of the continuities and shared preoccupations of the writers she chooses to address.

HINCHLIFFE and ELSOM each provide a general introduction to the postwar period up to the early 1970s, with coverage of wider aesthetic and social contexts as well as the new playwriting of the period. Hinchliffe has more on the immediate postwar years and the early 1950s, and on the role of the director; Elsom has more to say about the economics and the cultural politics of funding and organisation in general. The classic study of the John Osborne generation is TAYLOR (1962), which sets the scene both in terms of its coverage and its concentration on surveying individual dramatists rather than attempting to cover broader socio-political or aesthetic contexts. TAYLOR's similar study of *The Second Wave* of dramatists to emerge after 1956 remains an important account of a particular phenomenon at a particular historical moment, defining a period and a stance. DAVIES offers a good introductory overview of alternative-theatre developments up to the mid-1980s, while ITZIN traces the growth of a "political theatre" in Britain from 1968 to 1978 in some detail. CHAMBERS and PRIOR's focus is the various kinds of working-class and political theatre (including issues of gender and sexual orientation) and their contexts, while CAVE is more concerned with the politics of cultural production than with the texture of individual performances and aesthetics of actual productions of some of the major dramatists during the 1970–85 period he discusses. COHN examines a wide range of examples of the ways in which British theatrical practice has explored non-realistic dramatic and theatrical strategies in the period 1956–90, while BULL shows how the "West End" theatre has reacted to, and in part absorbed, some of the dramaturgical and theatrical innovations of the 1960s and 1970s.

My (GRIFFITHS) and LLEWELLYN-JONES's book attempts to redress the inherently male preoccupations of most surveys of dramatic activity in the last 40 years by concentrating on recording and analysing the work of women dramatists in the mainstream and on the fringe, in England, Scotland, Wales, and Ireland, with particular consideration of lesbian and ethnic-minority writers.

TREVOR R. GRIFFITHS

2. Before World War II

Dietrich, Richard F., *British Drama 1890–1950: A Critical History*, Boston: Twayne, 1989

Innes, Christopher, *Modern British Drama 1890–1990*, Cambridge and New York: Cambridge University Press, 1992

Leeming, Glenda, *Poetic Drama*, London: Macmillan, 1989; New York: St Martin's Press, 1989

McDonald, Jan, *The "New Drama" 1900–1914: Harley Granville Barker, John Galsworthy, St John Hankin, John Masefield*, London: Macmillan, 1986; New York: Grove Press, 1986

Nicoll, Allardyce, *English Drama 1900–1930: The Beginnings of the Modern Period*, Cambridge and New York: Cambridge University Press, 1973

Sidnell, Michael J., *Dances of Death: The Group Theatre of London in the Thirties*, London and Boston: Faber & Faber, 1984

Trewin, J.C., *The Edwardian Theatre*, Oxford: Blackwell, 1976; Totowa, New Jersey: Rowman & Littlefield, 1976

Criticism of British drama in the first half of this century falls into three categories: general surveys; studies of Edwardian drama; and studies of poetic drama. Differences of approach within each category will depend on two factors: selectivity – in other words, the number of plays and playwrights selected for discussion; and the degree to which an author follows a particular theory of genre or reveals a distinct prejudice about what does or does not work in the theatre. As far as development is concerned, there has been an encouraging trend in recent studies of this period, away from condescension or parochial enthusiasm, and towards an appreciation of its uniqueness and intrinsic value.

For DIETRICH, the death of Dion Boucicault in 1890 and George Bernard Shaw's lectures on Ibsenism from the same year represent a "Dionysian" ritual of death and rebirth to usher in the second great flowering of British drama. He goes on to argue that our concept of "the new Drama" should be enlarged to embrace non-realistic plays as well as the well-made problem-play associated with Henry Arthur Jones and Arthur Wing Pinero. These ideas help him to unify his history and develop a fresh approach to such diverse writers as J.M. Barrie, John Galsworthy, and J.M. Synge; but they also lead him to some rather arbitrary value judgements: that R.C. Sherriff's *Journey's End*, for example, is "slight and sentimental"; and that J.B. Priestley and Terence Rattigan were simply "waiting for Beckett". Moreover, so much space is devoted to Shaw that a serious imbalance is created. This is an interesting but too-subjective study of the period, which has been replaced by Innes's more reliable survey.

As his publishers claim, INNES has provided the first one-volume analysis of British drama from the late nineteenth to the late twentieth century. He focuses on three dramatic types

– social realism, comedy, and poetic drama – and traces the development of each through a discussion of individual playwrights. The result is an intelligent fusion of the generic and the chronological, which gives the reader a clear and detailed introduction to the period. He is generous and perceptive in his evaluation of critically neglected figures, such as Noel Coward, Priestley, and Rattigan; his re-appraisal of major dramatists – Shaw, Synge, and Sean O'Casey, for example – never lapses into the routine; and his more negative criticism, of W.B. Yeats, W.H. Auden, and Christopher Isherwood, especially, is always cogently argued. Enhanced by well-chosen photographs, as well as being meticulously cross-referenced and indexed, this book is clearly the outstanding study of its kind.

TREWIN notes that his survey of Edwardian drama "takes in the last eighteen months of Queen Victoria's reign and, later, the early Georgian period to the outbreak of the first world war". His organizing metaphor is the Edwardian house, which was reflected in the architecture and social structure of the Edwardian theatre: the well-made problem-plays of Jones and Pinero are found in the drawing room; the "Theatre of Ideas" created by Shaw and Harley Granville Barker is located in the study; poetic drama in the music room; and all lighter forms of "the Theatre Theatrical" – from comic opera to Ruritanian melodrama – take place in the play-room. Trewin does not so much offer analysis as capture the tone of different dramatists through epitomizing quotation and vignette, an approach that enables him to introduce a surprisingly large number of dramatists without giving the impression of a simple catalogue. There is an archness, even an air of back-stage gossip, about his writing, which makes his book less scholarly than McDonald's or Nicoll's studies, but this fault is offset by a broad and intimate knowledge of the period.

McDONALD defines the philosophy of the New Drama as "a belief in the importance of the theatre as a social force rather than as a social event". Her choice of only four dramatists to illustrate the genre might seem limiting, but it does permit detailed analysis of individual plays as well as a useful discussion of the theatre companies enterprising enough to produce them. The chapters on Harley Granville Barker and Galsworthy are clearly the most rewarding, and include valuable commentary on the relation between staging and social idea: witness the parade of fashion models in Granville Barker's *The Madras House*, or the solitary confinement scene in Galsworthy's *Justice*. The author also provides precise summaries of critical reaction to the plays in the premieres and revivals, as well as some interesting photographs. She is somewhat tentative in her claims for St John Hankin as a significant dramatist, and John Masefield does seem odd company in the context of this distinctly Ibsenite tradition. Nonetheless this is a perceptive study which makes the reader eager for a chance to see these unjustly neglected works in new productions.

NICOLL argues that the first three decades of this century make up an integral unit in the history of English drama, and that 1930 marked "the termination of an old journey . . . and the start of another". He discusses three types of drama: popular entertainment; minority drama, especially religious plays and plays in verse; and what he calls the "general" drama, which includes the work of Pinero, Shaw, Somerset Maugham, and Coward, as well as that of interesting and largely forgotten figures such as David Sutro and A.A. Milne. The second part of this 1,000-page book is given over to a hand-list of plays. Almost inevitably, given the large number of writers he has chosen to include, the author is forced to replace analysis with brief plot-summary, representative quotation, and value judgement. No one, however, does this kind of thing more expertly, and his book remains a highly readable and informative introduction to modern English drama.

LEEMING examines British and Irish verse drama from Yeats to John Arden. She devotes two chapters each to Yeats and T.S. Eliot, and a substantial chapter to Christopher Fry. There is a separate discussion of experimental drama in the 1930s, together with a conclusion on new directions in poetic drama. The book is illustrated with eight production photographs. The author lifts her work above the simple survey level by a persistent focus on the tension between the greater potentialities of verse as a theatre language and what might be called the vortex of realism. She demonstrates, for example, how Eliot watered down poetic expression and the supernatural in his later plays, and how the dramatic work of Auden and Isherwood tends to flounder between verse and prose. The author can be faulted for allowing her three major playwrights to crowd out interesting minor figures such as Gordon Bottomley and Ronald Duncan, who are only given passing reference; but this is otherwise the most recommendable introduction to the genre.

The Group Theatre described by SIDNELL enjoyed a lively, if precarious, existence from 1932 to the outbreak of World War II. It was dedicated to experimental drama – in practice this meant verse drama – and attracted a number of prominent writers, notably Auden, Eliot, Isherwood, Louis MacNeice, and Stephen Spender. The author offers both a fascinating history of the Group against the politically darkening backdrop of the 1930s, and an expert analysis of its repertoire, especially Auden's *The Dance of Death*, Eliot's *Sweeney Agonistes*, Auden and Isherwood's *The Ascent of F6*, MacNeice's *Out of the Picture*, and Spender's *Trial of a Judge*. He demonstrates how the form and content of these plays were shaped by a fear of European fascism, a somewhat naive attraction to Stalin's Soviet Union (Eliot is the exception here of course), and a general desire to "shake up" the English stage. There are some useful production photographs, which underline the author's point that it is unusually hard to judge these works from the texts alone, so dependent as they were on music, dance, costume, and stage design. This is a stimulating introduction to non-realistic British drama.

JOHN LINGARD

3. Postwar Period (to 1960s)

Anderson, Michael, *Anger and Detachment: A Study of Arden, Osborne and Pinter*, London: Pitman, 1976

Elsom, John, *Post-War British Theatre*, London and Boston: Routledge & Kegan Paul, 1976, revised 1979

Hinchliffe, Arnold P., *British Theatre 1950–1970*, Oxford: Blackwell, 1974; Totowa, New Jersey: Rowman & Littlefield, 1974

Marowitz, Charles, Tom Milne, and Owen Hale (eds.), *New Theatre Voices of the Fifties and Sixties*, London: Methuen, 1965, with new Introduction, 1981
Taylor, John Russell, *Anger and After: A Guide to the New British Drama*, Methuen, 1962, revised 1969; as *The Angry Theatre: New British Drama*, New York: Hill & Wang, 1962
Taylor, John Russell, *The Second Wave: British Drama for the Seventies*, London: Methuen, 1971; New York: Hill & Wang, 1971

This essay concentrates particularly on studies of the drama of the late 1950s and 1960s. This focus does reveal the striking omission of any extended consideration of women's dramatic output during the period (though this is being remedied in more recent work) and the dearth of serious studies of the pre-Osborne period in its own right. Although the first performance of John Osborne's *Look Back in Anger* in 1956 is widely taken as heralding a rebirth of serious British drama, most studies of the period take in the preceding years, however, in order to give a context to the changes wrought by Osborne, Bertolt Brecht, and Samuel Beckett in British theatrical practice and dramaturgy.

HINCHLIFFE and ELSOM both provide general introductions to the period up to the early 1970s, with coverage of wider aesthetic and social contexts as well as the new playwriting of the period. As part of their attempts to present a full picture of theatrical activity, each deals with European influences, particularly Brecht and the "Theatre of the Absurd", and also with the vogue for verse drama, the Royal Court, the Royal Shakespeare Company, and the National Theatre. Hinchliffe has more on the immediate postwar years and the early 1950s in Britain, and on the role of the director; Elsom has more to say about the economics and the cultural politics of funding and organisation in general. Both are very valuable as historical records of how the situation looked from the mid-1970s, without the benefit of too much hindsight, and they remain more than useful guides to the period.

The classic study of the Osborne generation is TAYLOR's *Anger and After*, which sets the scene both in terms of its coverage and its concentration on surveying individual dramatists rather than attempting to cover broader socio-political or aesthetic contexts. Taylor deals with the output of the Royal Court Theatre and the Theatre Workshop in some depth, and he devotes his most substantial coverage to John Osborne, Arnold Wesker, and Harold Pinter. Some of his divisions seem logical enough: he considers Osborne, N.F. Simpson, Ann Jellicoe, and Arden as well as other writers who made their debut at the Court in the late 1950s, while in the context of the Theatre Workshop he considers Brendan Behan, Shelagh Delaney, and "Wolf Mankowitz and the Cockney Improvisers". Other sections seem more arbitrary: Wesker, Bernard Kops, and David Turner are grouped together on the basis of having been produced outside London; and Alun Owen, Clive Exton, John Mortimer, and Peter Shaffer are seen as recruits from radio and television. In all, he names 19 writers in his chapter headings, and includes very brief references to several more. His concluding predictions are a fair indication of the difficulty of trend-spotting, since they did not all prove to be accurate:

> . . . the Theatre Workshop dramatists will go to pieces if Joan Littlewood does not continue to guide them, Osborne will develop . . . into a good reliable commercial dramatist, Arden will at last achieve his long-deferred success with the public . . . David Campton will finally make his mark in the West End, and the long-term staying power will be in the hands of Arden, Owen, Exton, and Pinter.

Although Taylor did not see Peter Shaffer's potential to achieve what he imagined Osborne might turn into, his pioneering survey remains an important contemporary guide to the first wave of the "new dramatists", and includes material on many writers who seemed promising at the time.

In 1971 TAYLOR followed up *Anger and After* with a similar study of *The Second Wave* of dramatists to emerge after 1956. His method remained broadly similar, with individual attention being given to Peter Nichols, David Mercer, Charles Wood, Edward Bond, Tom Stoppard, Peter Terson, Joe Orton, and David Storey, with briefer consideration of another 22 dramatists under the headings "Three Farceurs" (Alan Ayckbourn, David Cregan, Simon Gray), "Three Social Realists" (John Hopkins, Alan Plater, C.P. Taylor), "The Legacy of Realism" (William Corlett, Kevin Laffan, Christopher Hampton, Barry England, Anthony Shaffer, Robert Shaw, David Caute), and "The Dark Fantastic" (Peter Barnes, Colin Spencer, David Pinner, David Selbourne, David Hare, Roger Milner, David Halliwell, Howard Brenton, Heathcote Williams). Once again, this study remains an important account of a particular phenomenon at a particular historical moment, defining a period and a stance.

ANDERSON also provides a useful overview of a particular moment. Writing, like Elsom, in 1976, he concentrates on the work of three of the dramatists to emerge from the late 1950s – Arden, Osborne, and Pinter – surveying their individual output separately and tracing their development through individual discussions of the plays and their authors' dramatic strategies.

Finally, MAROWITZ, MILNE, and HALE have selected a variety of articles – play reviews and short essays, many by leading theatre practitioners on their own and others' work – from *Encore* magazine, originally published between 1956 and 1963. These reprints form an interesting contemporary backdrop for the period's drama and a context for the books discussed above.

TREVOR R. GRIFFITHS

4. Recent and Contemporary

Bull, John, *New British Political Dramatists*, London: Macmillan, 1984
Bull, John, *Stage Right: Crisis and Recovery in British Contemporary Mainstream Theatre*, London: Macmillan, 1994
Cave, Richard Allen, *New British Drama in Performance on the London Stage 1970–1985*, Gerrards Cross, Buckinghamshire: Colin Smythe, 1987; New York: St Martin's Press, 1988
Chambers, Colin, and Mike Prior, *Playwrights' Progress: Patterns of Postwar British Drama*, Oxford: Amber Lane, 1987

Cohn, Ruby, *Retreats from Realism in Recent English Drama*, Cambridge and New York: Cambridge University Press, 1991
Itzin, Catherine, *Stages in the Revolution: Political Theatre in Britain since 1968*, London: Methuen, 1980
Wandor, Michelene, *Look Back in Gender: Sexuality and the Family in Post-War British Drama*, London and New York: Methuen, 1987

The majority of studies of recent and contemporary drama have concentrated on the period since 1956 and on dramatic practices which have been seen as in some way challenging the cultural values associated with commercial theatre. There is as yet no full-length comprehensive overview that considers the period in terms of the often complex relationships between commercial and subsidised theatres, and the impact of political changes upon funding and upon dramatic practice, though all the studies considered here touch on such issues in greater or lesser detail.

ITZIN traces the growth of a "political theatre" in Britain from 1968 to 1978, devoting a section to each year, prefacing consideration of particular themes, companies, institutions, or writers with her own overview of the year. It remains an absolutely essential source book, valuable for lengthy extracts from interviews with the actual protagonists as much as for the chronology of productions and the author's own evaluations. Itzin closes with a Postscript dealing with the immediate impacts of the election of a Conservative government in 1979, so that she is able to cover both the flowering of a self-consciously "political" theatre and the beginnings of its demise. Within her compass she includes both political companies and political dramatists.

Itzin's account is usefully supplemented and expanded by BULL's two studies: in *New British Political Dramatists* he deals with the work of four major writers (Howard Brenton, David Edgar, Trevor Griffiths, and David Hare) in the context of the ways in which they both built on and challenged the bases of a politically aware theatre established by their immediate predecessors. In *Stage Right* he shows how the "West End" theatre has responded to, and in part accommodated, some of the dramaturgical and theatrical changes pioneered in the 1960s and 1970s. As well as considering individual dramatists (Alan Ayckbourn, Alan Bennett, Michael Frayn, Simon Gray, Peter Nichols, and Tom Stoppard), he offers an illuminating discussion of how the English theatre coped with the impact of both Bertolt Brecht and the "Theatre of the Absurd", which very usefully charts the actual scale of their influences in the 1950s–60s.

WANDOR's focus is, as her subtitle explains, "*Sexuality and the Family in Post-War British Drama*". She draws on examples from a wide range of dramatists to pursue her investigations, before arriving at the conclusion that one of the impacts of Brecht's concern with the political sphere had been a sharp reduction in the presence of the family in overtly political plays. Paradoxically, this remained the case despite the impact of feminisms and the idea that the personal is political, although the family remained a staple of those dramatists whom Bull would later deal with (in *Stage Right*).

CHAMBERS and PRIOR share the usual interest in discussing non-commercial theatre from a broadly socialist perspective. They briefly survey the socio-political context before considering issues associated with the presentation of the working class, the broad theme of varieties of political theatre, state-of-the-nation plays, and the presentation of gender and sexual orientation, as well as discussing major dramatists (John Osborne, Arnold Wesker, John Arden and Margaretta d'Arcy, Edward Bond, Howard Brenton, David Hare, and Caryl Churchill receive individual attention). Although his work was published in the same year as Chambers and Prior's, CAVE takes a different view of who the major figures of his, admittedly narrower, period actually are, with only Bond and Hare receiving individual consideration in both studies. Otherwise Cave concentrates on Harold Pinter, Alan Ayckbourn, Tom Stoppard, Samuel Beckett, David Storey, and Trevor Griffiths, and he is less concerned with the politics of cultural production than with the texture of individual performances and productions.

COHN takes the period 1956 to 1990 as the subject of her book, in which she examines a wide range of examples of the ways in which British theatrical practice has explored non-realistic dramatic and theatrical strategies. This is an incisive study of some of the key ways in which an unthinking adherence to the values of quasi-photographic recreation of everyday life has been successfully challenged over the period. Although the use of "*Retreats*" in the title might suggest a certain dismissiveness or antipathy towards these phenomena, Cohn is in fact enthusiastic about these changes. Her work benefits from her decision to treat the material thematically rather than in an author-by-author division, so that she is able to range historically when considering such topics as the state-of-the-nation play, the competing appropriations of Shakespeare, the use of verse and meta-theatre, and the staging of the unconscious and history.

TREVOR R. GRIFFITHS

Drama: Irish

Genet, Jacqueline, and Richard Allen Cave (eds.), *Perspectives on Irish Drama and Theatre*, Savage, Maryland: Barnes & Noble, 1991
Hogan, Robert, *After the Irish Renaissance: A Critical History of the Irish Drama since "The Plough and the Stars"*, Minneapolis: University of Minnesota Press, 1967
Hunt, Hugh, *The Abbey: Ireland's National Theatre, 1904–1978*, Dublin: Gill & Macmillan, 1979; New York: Columbia University Press, 1979
Krause, David, *The Profane Book of Irish Comedy: An Irreverent Look at Fourteen Irish Dramatists*, Ithaca, New York: Cornell University Press, 1982
Malone, Andrew E., *The Irish Drama*, London: Constable, 1929; reprinted, New York: Benjamin Blom, 1965
Maxwell, D.E.S., *A Critical History of Modern Irish Drama, 1891–1980*, Cambridge and New York: Cambridge University Press, 1984
Worth, Katharine, *The Irish Drama of Europe from Yeats to Beckett*, London: Athlone Press, 1978

Irish drama, as an entity distinct from the English dramatic tradition, is generally defined as beginning at the turn of the twentieth century with the foundation of the Irish National Theatre group under the leadership of W.B. Yeats and Lady Gregory. In this century of development, playwrights have moved from a romantic nationalism to a postcolonial concern with post-nationalism, and scholars have learned to shift their perceptions accordingly.

MALONE surveys the first 25 years of Irish drama with authority as one who saw every play presented by the National Theatre group during those years. He discusses the need for, and development of, a specifically Irish drama, and provides portraits of the personalities, playwrights, and performers who led the way. Especially helpful are the appendices, which provide the number of productions per year, a chronological list of openings, and a list of playwrights and their works.

HOGAN picks up where Malone leaves off, introducing "about thirty or forty valuable playwrights" working in Ireland from 1926 to 1966. Because both men lived in exile, Sean O'Casey is given only one chapter and Samuel Beckett no mention outside the Introduction: contemporary critics might question Hogan's assertion that "Beckett's plays are not really Irish in subject matter". A substantial portion of the book deals with Abbey Theatre playwrights, though Hogan does turn his attention to the Gate Theatre, experimental theatres, and festivals. He singles out for particular discussion Paul Vincent Carroll, M.J. Molloy, Denis Johnston, George Fitzmaurice, Brendan Behan, and John B. Keane.

HUNT places the Abbey Theatre at center stage, having been both an Abbey playwright and director, in a study of the first 75 years of Irish drama. Hunt credits the longevity of the theatrical movement to the "union of Irish playwrights and players", which superseded any narrow dimensions of language or political nationalism. In the first two chapters, he details the development of the Irish National Theatre, its playwrights, and its performers. Each following chapter provides glimpses and explanations of the personalities, problems, and successes that make up the history of the Abbey. Hunt also includes a list of plays produced by the National Theatre for the titular years, arranged according to opening dates.

WORTH places Yeats at the head of an Irish dramatic movement which, she claims, is European in nature, showing the influence of French symbolism in general and specifically of Maurice Maeterlinck (notably on Yeats's interior drama). She credits Yeats with responding by inventing a "modern syntax" for the theatre, which preceded other European dramatists by some 50 years. Worth includes Oscar Wilde, J.M. Synge, O'Casey, and Beckett in her analysis of Irish European drama. One might question Worth's insistence on the Europeanness of Irish drama, but she makes a strong case for the French-Irish connection and avoids problems of nationalism.

GENET and CAVE edit a collection of essays resulting from lectures given at the 1987 meeting of the International Association for the Study of Anglo-Irish Literature. With the intent of giving "a comprehensive view of the Irish drama", the editors have included essays by some of the foremost contemporary scholars working in the field. The editors have generally accomplished their aims, providing essays that cover two centuries of Irish drama, looking back, as well as forward, from the foundational movement, and which comment upon such important issues as myth/history, language and identity, and the political and social implications of these issues as they converge in postmodernity.

KRAUSE makes some provocative suggestions about Irish dramatic comedy and the rebellion against "whatever is too sacred in Ireland" by 14 specific playwrights. He takes a Freudian twist, examining the use of laughter as a release from repression, while connecting the central comic heroes to barbarous or satanic rebels who range across myths. Synge and O'Casey emerge as "the seminal figures" among these profane playwrights. While his knowledge of myth is impressive, as is his understanding of Irish history, his interpretation of the works of such playwrights as Carroll and Yeats might well be questioned, both playwrights perhaps embracing, and affirming with humor, a kind of religious experience that provides for universal toleration, Christian or otherwise. Still, the study is worth review for its provocative argument and insight into the manner in which Irish comedies have developed and been interpreted.

MAXWELL studies Irish dramatists since the inception of the National movement up to 1980, from Douglas Hyde, Lady Gregory, and Yeats through Beckett to Brian Friel and his contemporaries. Maxwell gives special attention to Yeats, Synge, O'Casey, Johnston, Beckett, and Friel, with numerous others earning honorable mentions, such as Edward Martyn, M.J. Molloy, Behan, Austin Clarke, and Carroll. A chronology provides an historical framework, and there are bibliographical lists of general works, plays by the dramatists discussed, and critical studies of these writers. In his Introduction, Maxwell fairly reviews the precursors to his own study – including Ernest Boyd (1918), A.E. Malone (1929), Peter Kavanagh (1950), Lennox Robinson (1951), Una Ellis Fermor (1954), Gerald Fay (1958), and Worth and Hunt (discussed above) – pointing out especial merits and weaknesses. He then encapsulates the arguments he sets forth in the succeeding chapters: that Irish drama owes a debt to Yeats more for his dream, a "partial theory", than for his plays; that Yeats's dream, combined with Synge's "passionately poetic language" and "realist representations" of Irish people, provides "a draft" for the Abbey Theatre's continuing policy; that O'Casey extravagantly "engages realist theatre in poetic transformation"; that Johnston endows European forms – particularly German expressionism – with "a peculiarly Irish character"; and that within Beckett's plays "the unevicted host is his Irish background". In the closing chapter, which Friel shares with Beckett – the link being language play and its postcolonial importance – Maxwell identifies Friel as having written "the most substantial and impressive body of work in contemporary Irish drama", which, like the work of some of his contemporaries, reflects both the dreams and the realities of Irish past and present. Other contemporary writers discussed, though in less detail, are Thomas Kilroy, Hugh Leonard, Bill Morrison, and Graham Reid.

DAWN E. DUNCAN

Drama: American – General

Adler, Thomas P., *American Drama 1940–1960: A Critical History*, New York: Twayne, 1994
Bordman, Gerald, *American Theatre: A Chronicle of Comedy and Drama, 1869–1914*, New York and Oxford: Oxford University Press, 1994
Henderson, Mary C., *Theater in America: 200 Years of Plays, Players, and Productions*, New York: Abrams, 1986
Magill, Frank N. (ed.), *Critical Survey of Drama*, 7 vols., Englewood Cliffs, New Jersey: Salem Press, 1985; revised edition, Pasadena, California: Salem Press, 1994
Meserve, Walter J., *An Outline History of American Drama*, Totowa, New Jersey: Littlefield Adams, 1970; 2nd edition, New York: Feedback Theatrebooks/Prospero Press, 1994
Miller, Jordan Y., and Winifred L. Frazer, *American Drama Between the Wars: A Critical History*, Boston: Twayne, 1991
Mordden, Ethan, *The American Theatre*, New York: Oxford University Press, 1981
Quinn, Arthur Hobson, *A History of the American Drama: From the Beginning to the Civil War*, New York: Harper & Bros.,1923; 2nd edition, New York: Appleton-Century-Crofts, 1943
Quinn, Arthur Hobson, *A History of the American Drama: From the Civil War to the Present Day*, New York: Harper & Bros, 1927; revised edition, New York: F.S. Crofts & Co., 1936; London: Pitman & Sons, 1937
Richardson, Gary A., *American Drama from the Colonial Period Through World War I: A Critical History*, New York: Twayne, 1993
Williams, Henry B., *The American Theatre: A Sum of Its Parts*, New York: Samuel French, 1971
Wilmeth, Don B., and Tice L. Miller (eds.), *The Cambridge Guide to American Theatre*, New York and Cambridge: Cambridge University Press, 1993
Wilson, Garff B., *Three Hundred Years of American Drama and Theatre: From "Ye Bare and Ye Cubb" to "Chorus Line"*, Englewood Cliffs, New Jersey: Prentice-Hall, 1973, 2nd edition, 1982

American drama has been marginalized in most critical histories of American literature; consequently several works are needed to piece together a survey of American drama from its beginnings in the eighteenth century to the present.

MESERVE's outline is a good starting place for an overview of the full spectrum of drama over a 300-year period. He reinforces the opening statement above, adding that no scholar as yet has tried to impose any critical order on the drama's development (there are strong efforts in this direction for twentieth-century American drama however). This outline history provides sensible summaries of plays and historical periods, basic critical judgements, and useful bibliographies at the end of each of six sections.

QUINN's two-volume history remains a standard source, but the assessments are dated (ending with the 1930s) and provide insights that are conservative and limited. Although Quinn places his survey of plays and playwrights within the context of the drama as staged, he fails to provide a more general cultural or social context, thus dealing with the drama and theatre as isolated phenomena. Both volumes provide useful, though also dated, bibliographies; more helpful are checklists of plays with relevant data (places and dates of first performances, and, in some instances, publication information).

More up-to-date and informed by today's critical, theoretical, and historiographical strategies is a series of books collectively identified as "Twayne's Critical History of American Drama". To date, three volumes – by Richardson, Miller and Frazer, and Adler – under the general editorship of Jordan Y. Miller have been published; a final volume by Matthew Roudané is planned for late 1996. Each volume has some features in common – a chronology of drama and national events, extensive notes, and excellent bibliographies. When all four volumes are published, this will be the most comprehensive history available (Meserve has projected a six-volume history, of which only two have been published to date).

RICHARDSON's volume on early American drama provides an excellent critical survey of the period known least by most readers; though more selective than other specialized volumes on this time period, the book foregrounds what is truly significant during the most formative period in American theatre history, and proffers carefully contextualized readings of key plays. MILLER and FRAZER's volume follows a pattern similar to Richardson, although it is even less a survey history of American theatre and more a critical overview of texts. For each of nine key chapters the authors provide brief introductions and background. The period between World War I and World War II is one of the most dynamic and exciting in the history of the American theatre, and this study divides its coverage into: a prologue, which explores a new spirit in drama (1912–20); revolt against tradition (which reincorporates key women playwrights of the 1910s and 1920s); realism, naturalism, and expressionism; the early work of Eugene O'Neill; groups and political drama of the 1930s; variations on realistic themes; American comedy; writers of fantasy; folk drama; and a final summary epilogue. ADLER's contribution to the series focuses more specifically on dominant voices as central foci of chapters, though there is general discussion of more marginal figures as well. Using the notion that many plays from 1940–60 examine the price paid by the human soul for the purchase of the American Dream, Adler gives sensitive insights into the work of Eugene O'Neill, Lillian Hellman, Arthur Miller, William Inge, Lorraine Hansberry, Edward Albee, and Tennessee Williams, with a clear bias for the work of the latter.

Though the number is small, several books published in the past 15 years attempt to survey the history of American theatre, including the playtext. WILSON's book is designed as an undergraduate textbook, yet is the only "comprehensive" history currently in print. The second edition is actually a somewhat condensed version of the superior first edition, although it is updated to the early 1980s. Much space is consumed with "imagery visits" to the theatres of each era. The major weakness of the work, especially the newer edition, is that too much is crammed into 350 pages, thus giving short shrift to most topics, although some effort is made to relate the theatre to other societal elements. Ten chapters out of 21 are devoted primarily to plays and playwrights, with fairly standard critical commentary. Even less even in its coverage, and far more idiosyncratic, is MORDDEN's book, which is neither scholarly, documented, nor intended as a serious history. As a straight chronological treatment, the slight given to pre-twentieth-century drama is painfully obvious. The balance of the coverage does privilege the dramatic text, however, with the author's very personal interpretation of the importance of the various plays chosen for discussion.

HENDERSON's approach is far more valuable in isolating the playwright from other theatre artists. Her structure favors seven chapters, on producers, playwrights, directors and choreographers, actors, designers, architects, and theatre beyond Broadway. Unfortunately, there is unavoidable overlap and little effort to provide connections or conclusions. Nevertheless, she is a sound critic and historian, offering a good sense of progression and succinct analyses of select specific plays. A beautifully-produced volume, this book has the best illustrations of any available history, with much of the important text in captions.

Though a dated overview, WILLIAMS's edited volume of essays by major authorities of the 1960s is nevertheless worth consulting for its specific essays on playwrights. There is an essay that covers the timeframe 1860–1920, plus separate chapters on musical theatre (beginnings to 1900, and 1900–69), popular theatre, and black theatre. Although the choices do not give adequate balance, and the coverage ends at the beginning of the 1970s, thus offering what now seems like often naive and shortsighted perspectives, the essays nonetheless offer commentary by some of the most respected scholars in the field of theatre study during the first half of this century.

BORDMAN's encyclopedic chronicle, is, as the title suggests, a season-by-season summary of all plays (primarily produced at first-class theatres in New York City) from the start of the 1869–70 season until the eruption of World War I. It is divided into five sections – 1869–79, 1879–92, 1892–99, 1899–1906, and 1906–14. As a reference book it is an invaluble source for production data and hundreds of play synopses during this almost 50-year period, with select critical comments extracted from contemporary reviews. Other than brief introductions to each section, however, Bordman provides none of his own critical commentary. Bordman's intent is to supply similar volumes that will cover the whole of American theatre; as of the publication date of this first volume, he was dealing with a volume on drama and comedy from mid-1914 to the present, and a final volume is envisioned for the colonial and pre-Civil-War stage. As is true with most of Bordman's numerous reference works, there are no source citations or a bibliography of authorities to valorize his effort, both unfortunate exclusions.

Finally, two recent reference sources are especially good for locating basic information and, in some cases, critical commentary on specific American plays and playwrights from the beginning to the present. MAGILL's seven-volume survey of drama, though not limited to American writers or plays, nonetheless covers a wide-range of American examples, written by a large number of contributors. Each entry includes critical commentary and a bibliography; Volume 7 includes a sketchy overview essay on American drama. In contrast, my (WILMETH) and MILLER's guide is focused more on the play as performed; still, of its 2,300 entries many are on plays or playwrights. In addition to a potted history of American theatre, which serves as the book's Introduction, there are also entries on such issues of current interest as African-American theatre, Asian-American theatre, Chicano theatre, dramatic theory, feminist theatre, gay and lesbian theatre, musical theatre, and Yiddish theatre. The volume concludes with an extensive bibliography and a biographical index to those individuals mentioned who do not have their own entries. There is an attempt in the play entries to provide a sense of theme, significance, and production history, while plot summaries are de-emphasized. (An expanded and updated paperback edition is scheduled for 1996.)

DON B. WILMETH

Drama: American – 19th Century

Grimsted, David, *Melodrama Unveiled: American Theater and Culture 1800–1850*, Chicago: University of Chicago Press, 1968

McConachie, Bruce A., *Melodramatic Formations: American Theatre and Society, 1820–1870*, Iowa City: University of Iowa Press, 1992

Mason, Jeffrey D., *Melodrama and the Myth of America*, Bloomington: Indiana University Press, 1993

Meserve, Walter J., *An Emerging Entertainment: The Drama of the American People to 1828*, Bloomington: Indiana University Press, 1977

Meserve, Walter J., *American Drama to 1900: A Guide to Information Sources*, Detroit: Gale Research, 1980

Meserve, Walter J., *Heralds of Promise: The Drama of the American People in the Age of Jackson, 1829–1849*, New York: Greenwood Press, 1986

Moody, Richard, *America Takes the Stage: Romanticism in American Drama and Theatre, 1750–1900*, Bloomington: Indiana University Press, 1955

Richardson, Gary A., *American Drama from the Colonial Period Through World War I: A Critical History*, New York: Twayne, 1993

Since the late 1970s, nineteenth-century American drama has undergone a much-needed reassessment, especially in terms of its historical and cultural context; yet there is still no comprehensive critical overview of the entirety of the drama of the century.

MOODY's important study, though dated in its critical approach, was an early effort to deal with identifiable American stereotypes as dramatized for the stage. Covering the whole century, Moody provides insights into the Romantic Movement as reflected in American theatre (acting, scene design, as well as plays). Most germane to drama is his lengthy chapter on native themes and characters, including the black character (both as depicted in "Negro" minstrelsy and in more conventional plays), the Yankee, Indian, and frontiersman. He also analyzes the impact of wars on the drama, including the War of Independence, wars against the Barbary States, the War of 1812, the Mexican War, and the American Civil War. Though more recent studies reflect greater sophistication in analysis, Moody's study, written with great clarity, remains a useful standard source.

The various works of Walter J. Meserve, one of the major active US scholars in the field, focus more specifically on the drama than any other (most contemporary sources devote considerable attention to the performative aspects of the subject, choosing not to separate text from production and the role of the audience). MESERVE's *American Drama to 1900* provides a selective bibliography of sources keyed to material on major plays and playwrights as well as general sources on the subject of drama as text (as opposed to theatre). A total of 1,494 sources are succinctly annotated by Meserve.

More significant are Meserve's two books on discrete periods in the nineteenth century. These critical and historical surveys represent the first in a series of studies projected by Meserve that would cover the whole of American drama, usurping the standard, but now dated, efforts by Arthur Hobson Quinn. MESERVE's *An Emerging Entertainment* covers in great detail virtually all drama, both produced and unproduced, from the Colonial period until 1828. His purpose is to explore all types of drama in this period and to relate the drama to the cultural and historical progress of the country, to analyze drama as a literary genre, and to provide the reader with biographical material on important playwrights, as well as historical data on relevant plays. Key chapters focus on the period 1801–14 and 1815–28. Meserve's strength is his broad range, though it is consequently difficult to extract what is truly important in the development of American drama during this rather narrow time period. In *Heralds of Promise*, MESERVE continues his overview, covering 1829–49, a period of great potential in an atmosphere hostile to the development of an indigenous drama. Like the first volume, the second is full of specifics, including useful lists of plays and playwrights. Both volumes reflect prodigious research and reflection; each includes copious notes and bibliographies; both suffer from a lack of foregrounding of major examples of American drama.

RICHARDSON's book, in contrast to Meserve's attempt at comprehensiveness, offers a more selective historical survey and critical overview. The readings of key plays is sensitive, insightful, scholarly, yet clear and thoughtfully contextualized historically. Especially useful for students, Richardson's book is informed by much of the scholarship on nineteenth-century drama of the past 20 years, and attempts to apply contemporary critical perspectives. The result is a survey that provides a greater understanding of the plays' impact upon their original audiences, a clearer sense of the achievements of the major authors, and a much overdue recovery of a central part of America's heritage. Playwrights given central attention are Royall Tyler, William Dunlap, James Nelson Barker, John Howard Payne, R.M. Bird, George Henry Boker, James K. Paulding, John Augustus Stone, J.S. Jones, George Aiken, Dion Boucicault, Augustin Daly, David Belasco, Joaquin Miller, Bronson Howard, William Dean Howells, Steele MacKaye, James A. Herne, William Gillette, Langdon Mitchell, Clyde Fitch, William Vaughn Moody, Edward Sheldon, Rachel Crothers, and Susan Glaspell.

Three central studies in recent years focus on America's dominant form of drama, the melodrama. Though there are unavoidable overlaps, the three offer unique foci and complement one another. Together they represent the best of scholarship in the field and provide new insights into melodrama in its cultural, social, political, and economic contexts.

GRIMSTED's study is the oldest of the three, and covers the earliest period, 1800–50. His object is to use early melodrama to explore the form as social reflector of external tensions. Although he frequently denigrates the plays, he is the first major writer to take American melodrama seriously, looking at the plays as part of America's social history. In addition to chapters on the plays and playwrights, Grimsted provides sections on theatres and actors, critics, the structure of the nineteenth-century theatre, and a useful analysis of melodramatic dramaturgy and vision.

McCONACHIE's book reflects his well-known interest in class and audience, and is conditioned by his Marxist critical point of view, though he is not a slave to this ideology. His coverage is 1820–70, a time of dynamic change, in which the theatre played an important role in the formation of American cultural and social history. McConachie, more than Grimsted or Mason (see below), provides an interdisciplinary approach. Although his conclusions sometimes seem to be based on inadequate evidence (especially as regards audience demographics), he nonetheless gives the reader a challenging and thought-provoking interpretation of various forms of melodrama and the theatre's place in three distinct but contiguous phases of American society. What is most unique in McConachie's historiographical approach is his demonstration of the interaction of general society and the creation of a theatrical culture, or as he calls it, a "formation". Without doubt, this is one of the most significant studies of nineteenth-century American drama to appear in the past two decades.

MASON's book appeared shortly after McConachie's, but owes nothing directly to it, though Mason does acknowledge some of McConachie's published essays. Mason, who ranges over the entire century, differs from Grimsted and McConachie in several other respects. He is more interested in how American popular melodrama has, based on five key examples, contributed to the construction of an American ideology – or "myth" (which he uses synonymously with continuity). With a great deal of historical, literary, social, and political background, Mason provides fascinating analyses of plays that illustrate aspects of the American experience while, at the same time, creating mythical, usually simplistic, sentimental, and often skewered interpretations of reality.

DON B. WILMETH

Drama: American – 20th Century

1. Before World War II

Abramson, Doris E., *Negro Playwrights in the American Theatre, 1925–1959*, New York: Columbia University Press, 1969

Berkowitz, Gerald M., *American Drama of the Twentieth Century*, London: Longman, 1992

Bigsby, C.W.E., *A Critical Introduction to Twentieth-Century American Drama, Volume 1: 1900–1940*, Cambridge and New York: Cambridge University Press, 1982

Broussard, Louis, *American Drama: Contemporary Allegory from Eugene O'Neill to Tennessee Williams*, Norman: University of Oklahoma Press, 1962

Craig, E. Quita, *Black Drama of the Federal Theatre Era: Beyond the Formal Horizons*, Amherst: University of Massachusetts Press, 1980

Dukore, Bernard F., *American Dramatists 1918–1945*, London: Macmillan, 1984; New York: Grove Press, 1984

Gardner, R.H., *The Splintered Stage: The Decline of the American Theater*, New York: Macmillan, 1965; London: Collier-Macmillan, 1965

Goldstein, Malcolm, *The Political Stage: American Drama and Theater of the Great Depression*, New York: Oxford University Press, 1974

Himmelstein, Morgan Y., *Drama Was a Weapon: The Left-Wing Theatre in New York, 1929–1941*, New Brunswick, New Jersey: Rutgers University Press, 1963

Krutch, Joseph Wood, *The American Drama since 1918: An Informal History*, New York: Random House, 1939; revised edition, New York: George Braziller, 1957; London: Thames & Hudson, 1957

Meserve, Walter J. (ed.), *Discussions of Modern American Drama*, Boston: D.C. Heath, 1966

Sievers, W. David, *Freud on Broadway: A History of Psychoanalysis and the American Dream*, New York: Hermitage House, 1955

Smiley, Sam, *The Drama of Attack: Didactic Plays of the American Depression*, Columbia: University of Missouri Press, 1972

Tyson, Lois, *Psychological Politics of the American Dream: The Commodification of Subjectivity in Twentieth-Century American Literature*, Columbus: Ohio State University Press, 1994

Despite a great deal of energy poured into recognising the achievement and significance of forgotten and ignored playwrights such as Susan Glaspell, black writers of the Harlem Renaissance and beyond, and radical dramatists of the 1930s, as well as resurrecting the forgotten plays and melodramas of the nineteenth century, American drama is an area not so much overlooked as patronised by critics. These commentators rarely get beyond analyses based on biographical material, simple plot summaries, and moralising homilies on the failures of the writers to offer resolutions to contemporary moral, social, or political conflicts.

Robert Brustein, in a semi-humorous article written for *Harper's* in 1959, and reprinted in MESERVE, put his finger on the root of the problem by pointing out that dramatists, unlike poets or novelists, are not regarded as intellectuals, or as sophisticated and self-aware artists, but rather as craftsmen, artisans of the demi-monde that is the theatre. Speaking of postwar dramatic criticism he states that, according to this state of affairs, American drama has developed "in a cheerful isolation from a central literary tradition", "far removed, if not completely cut off from the mainstream of intellectual and literary discourse". The snobbery of this view, which dismisses these plays as "lacking intelligence and restraint" and as the "most mindless form of legitimate culture", is still visible even in the best surveys of recent years. In the same collection Mary McCarthy unwittingly confirms Brustein's view when she describes realism in the theatre as a "deprecation of the real" and attacks Tennessee Williams as being "fascinated by the refinements of cruelty" and as playing sadistic games with the audience, not purposefully [a view that I would endorse] but only "to titillate society like a peepshow".

SIEVERS opened up a potentially very useful mode of analysis in his study of the prevalence of psychological material in modern plays, and of the way psychoanalysis had been appropriated by these writers, beginning right at the turn of the century with Clyde Fitch, Augustus Thomas, and Hutchins Hapgood, as well as Alice Gerstenberg of the Chicago Little Theatre. His account continues through the plays of Eugene O'Neill and the popular psychodramas of Philip Barry in the late 1920s, to the plays of Tennessee Williams. This otherwise thorough and systematic work is marred by a mechanistic and disparaging view of psychoanalysis, which results in a belief that the writers are merely re-hashing second-hand and sensationalist Freudian clichés. Hence he parades a succession of hysterical women, "psychologically damaged or perverse" characters. Psychopathology pulls in the audiences and creates powerful parts for actors, for playwrights are "tailors who cut their cloth to fit the great stars of the stage".

KRUTCH's book, although an earlier one, at least gives a sympathetic and intelligent account of drama, because, as a cultural critic who had confronted the problems of modernity since the 1920s and who was therefore a contemporary of these writers, Krutch recognised the sincerity of the feelings that they expressed and the reality of the issues they faced. O'Neill he sees as a social critic with an "unwillingness to accept defeat for [his] desires".

GARDNER's response was far more characteristic of attitudes to American drama in general. He bemoans the "decline of the American Theatre" and blames the "socio-psychological frame" for shifting responsibility from the individual to society, so that the hero "is regarded as a victim of social and psychological forces beyond his control". As a result, the contemporary theatre has an "atmosphere of depravity and despair", and instead of the ennobling effects of tragedy, we are given only absurdism and "senselessness". A great proportion of the criticism to date has circled endlessly around this sterile debate between self and society, as if they were opposed and the issue was always to apportion blame between them.

BROUSSARD's work on allegory and expressionism in the American theatre was another promising opening. He proposes that the influence of August Strindberg has been much stronger than normally supposed, and "expressionism", in which the protagonist becomes a representative of a class – a collective figure engaged in and illuminating struggles between revolt and submission, justice and energy, and so on – is the appropriate label for much American drama. In the plays of this tradition, such as those by O'Neill, Clifford Odets, and Elmer Rice, the modern everyman goes "in search of values to replace the traditions no longer conclusive". O'Neill, in particular, is fruitfully seen to be engaged in a dialogue with Freud, Jung, Nietzsche, and Henri Bergson. Unfortunately, even the writers own protestations that they were challenging the parameters of realism have not prevented their plays from being interpreted as being firmly rooted in a realist mode of representation.

HIMMELSTEIN's book emerged at the same time as a 1960s' resurgence of interest in the radical playwrights of the

1930s. The book was an attempt to exonerate the majority of writers from any real engagement with communist beliefs, but, instead, to see them as at odds with the attempted take-over of the stage by the Communist Party via its organ in the United States, *The New Masses*, and its editor Mike Gold. Whereas they were supposed to interpret events through the lens of economic determinism, playwrights such as Odets, Paul Peters, and George Sklar were more interested in democratic values, in defending justice and liberty and in attacking racism. Himmelstein argues that one major problem of radical playwrights was their failure to understand the Aristotelian principle of catharsis, whereby drama tends towards discharging emotions rather than storing them up to be used for political action. No theory of political drama is suggested, nor any means whereby a dramatist could subvert the audience's assured beliefs and common-sense.

SMILEY similarly picks up the conflict between the functions of mimesis and didacticism, but is much more sympathetic to attempts to persuade and to mobilise the audience's sympathies against the "Hydra" of totalitarianism. Hence he can accept the use of melodrama and allegory, humour and absurdism, as means to these ends. The result is a much more useful account of the writers of the Federal Theatre Project, especially the "leading dramatic theorist of leftist theatre" John Howard Lawson, as well as the work of Odets, Sklar, and Irwin Shaw.

GOLDSTEIN has excellent chapters on the New Playwrights, The Theatre Guild, and the Theatre Union, but mainly from the perspective of the conflicts and collaborations between writers, producers, and directors. His comments on the plays reinforce his belief in a general shift from "social message drama to plays of the secret self". O'Neill in particular is granted the status of "the first modernist playwright", interested not in "social rebellion" but in an exploration of "the human personality" (whatever this oxymoron might be). He thus backs off from the issues raised by these writers, and reinstates the mistaken polarity between committed writing and that devoted to supposedly "universal" truths.

CRAIG's book gives black playwrights a much more thorough treatment than they get in ABRAMSON's work, where they are seen as primarily perpetuating stereotypes of blacks and whites. Craig's book utilises the "lost" archives of the Federal Theater Project, which were opened up in Baltimore in 1974. By interpreting the plays as contributions to, and a commentary on, the contemporary life of the black communities of the 1930s, and utilising the oral African-American traditions of story-telling, allegorical figures, and mythical patterns of action, Craig overcomes oppositions of self and society, of universalist and propagandist concerns. Thus Craig is able to reveal the rich interaction between community and artist that gives these plays a density of meaning, using the "coded grapevine or dual communication system" to enable the plays to carry a multiplicity of messages but to remain within the understanding of their audiences. Such a technique could, with profit, be employed in analysing the works of white playwrights as well. The only real drawback of this book is its romanticised view of African belief-systems, culture, and art, which are portrayed as being in harmony with each other unlike the fallen world of the West.

BIGSBY's three-volume magnum opus, of which Volume 1 is relevant here, has become – with its wealth of information from the Provincetown Players and the Little Theatre onwards, and its cool, lucid style – the standard work on American drama. Its tone, unfortunately, remains magisterial throughout, in the tradition of the earlier critical writing surveyed here. The twentieth century is analysed primarily in terms of alienation consequent on a loss of faith, and every writer is seen in these terms to dash themselves to pieces against the unyielding logic of nihilism. Playwrights respond to "a time of crisis", in which "language itself was in decay", but their proffered solutions were seldom "rooted in a practical perception of social realities". O'Neill especially "had no very clear social view" and he employed "partially digested Freudianism". The writers are never seen to be engaging in a dialogue with the major figures of our intellectual tradition, and the result is that they come to be seen as bumbling amateurs. Plays are seen as statements rather than as provocations or as devices for challenging received wisdom or complacent belief, and all, as a result, can be found guilty of not giving us the solutions to our difficulties. Specific analyses of cultural contradictions or of social abuses tend to be downplayed as the results of the metaphysical absence, which is the over-arching interpretive framework.

BERKOWITZ similarly repeats the clichés of earlier critics, especially the "return to domestic realism" he locates as the dominant feature of American drama from the 1930s onwards, a belief that leads him to play down the expressionist or subversive aspects of the drama. Instead he defines the purpose of drama as the mimetic one: "to reflect and illuminate the world of reality to its inhabitants". Recognising that many American plays are about the urban middle class, whose patronage is so vital to the commercial vitality of the theatre, Berkowitz never imagines that O'Neill, for example, could be criticising his audience, but settles for statements, such as that *The Iceman Cometh* is about "the need for fantasy" and that *Long Day's Journey into Night* has characters who cannot help their actions for "the past had programmed them to behave this way", as if the plays offered no commentary on these mindsets or engagement with the issues surrounding agency, guilt, and temporality. Even a playwright as clearly involved in social commentary as Arthur Miller is scolded for his naivety, for while he "accuses American society of destroying life and dignity" and therefore claims the status of tragic hero for Willy Loman, "few theatre-goers are likely to share that specialised definition of tragedy".

TYSON offers one promising way out of these impasses of critical arrogance and condescension. In her chapter on Miller's *Death of a Salesman* she attempts to evolve a dialectical conception of the relationship between social and individual identity and to see Willy in this light, as a protagonist who embodies and exposes the sexual, psychological, and economic conflicts in which we are all enmeshed. It is testimony to the power of the form, then, and to the power of the playwright's unconscious, which this form taps, that the play tells the truth about commodity psychology and the American Dream despite the desire of Miller and his critics to hide it.

D.T. CORKER

2. Postwar Period (to 1960s)

Adam, Julie, *Versions Of Heroism in Modern American Drama: Redefinitions By Miller*, Williams, O'Neill and Anderson. London: Macmillan, 1991
Bigsby, C.W.E., *Confrontation and Commitment: A Study of Contemporary American Drama 1959–1966*, Kansas City: University of Missouri Press, 1967
Bigsby, C.W.E., *A Critical Introduction to Twentieth-Century American Drama, 2: Williams, Miller, Albee*, Cambridge and New York: Cambridge University Press, 1984
Bigsby, C.W.E., *Modern American Drama 1945–1990*, Cambridge and New York: Cambridge University Press, 1992
Broussard, Louis, *American Drama: Contemporary Allegory from Eugene O'Neill to Tennessee Williams*, Norman: University Of Oklahoma Press, 1962
Davis, Walter A., *Get the Guests: Psychoanalysis, Modern American Drama, and The Audience*, Madison: University of Wisconsin Press, 1994
Greenfield, Thomas Allen, *Work and the Work Ethic in American Drama 1920–1970*, Columbia: University of Missouri Press, 1982
Hughes, Catharine, *American Playwrights 1945–75*, London: Pitman, 1976
Kolin, Philip C. (ed.), *American Playwrights since 1945: A Guide to Scholarship, Criticism and Performance*, Westport, Connecticut: Greenwood Press, 1989
Parker, Dorothy (ed.), *Essays on Modern American Drama: Williams, Miller, Albee and Shepard*, Toronto and Buffalo, New York: University of Toronto Press, 1987
Porter, Thomas E., *Myth and Modern American Drama*, Detroit: Wayne State University Press, 1969
Pradham, N.S., *Modern American Drama: A Study in Myth and Tradition*, New Delhi: Arnold-Heinemann, 1978
Scharine, Richard G., *From Class to Caste in American Drama: Political and Social Themes since the 1930s*, Westport, Connecticut: Greenwood Press, 1991
Studies in American Drama 1945–Present (journal): 1986–
Weales, Gerald, *American Drama since World War Two*, New York: Harcourt Brace, 1962

Two reference sources are useful in considering this period. HUGHES' short text contains general overviews of a variety of playwrights and listings of their work in the period 1945–75. KOLIN's collection contains evaluations of 40 US playwrights by various critics. The major names – Arthur Miller, Tennessee Williams, Edward Albee, Sam Shepard, etc. – are, of course present; however, it also provides sources and information on writers such as Paddy Chayefsky, Israel Horovitz, Beth Henley, Robert Lowell, Carson McCullers, and Terrence McNally. This is a very valuable guide and overview: its aim is not particularly to distinguish overall trends and movements, but to focus on the playwrights themselves. The Introduction gives the guidelines which contributors followed, which were to include: "A brief assessment/ A list of works/ Films (where relevant)/ Interviews/ Essays/ Production history/ Bibliography/ Biographies/ Influences/ General Studies/ Analyses of Individual Productions/ Future Research Opportunities/ Secondary Sources". Kolin's book doesn't pretend to offer in-depth readings, but is hugely informative and indispensable as a reference guide.

The key to BROUSSARD's book is the theme of expressionism, and he reads certain texts with reference to this. The intention of the book is to "establish the attitude of American drama toward contemporary man and his problems as it traces the evolution of the allegorical play in America, to suggest the influences which went into its creation, and to relate the example in question to other works by the same author and to other forms of contemporary expression with the same theme". Obviously, it can, therefore, only examine writers who slot into this thesis – including Eugene O'Neill, Williams, and Miller – and excludes writers such as Maxwell Anderson and Clifford Odets, for example. These limitations accepted, it is worth looking at, and contains a relevant exploration of the "journey" of character in American drama.

WEALES' book is a general overview, which covers Miller and Williams, as well as having sections on adaptations, musical theatre, film, off-Broadway, and "poets and novelists" on stage. He has some worthwhile analyses, and is useful for historical perspectives and factual information. He goes into more depth when he looks at specific writers, but the book operates more as a wide-ranging assessment than as detailed scholarship on any particular author or issue.

Bigsby's work on American drama has been both comprehensive and invaluable, and three of his texts merit discussion in this section. BIGSBY's *Confrontation and Commitment* is divided into two sections, and explores what the author sees as the willingness to experiment on the part of playwrights of the late 1950s/early 1960s. It reflects the American equivalent of the English "Angry Young Man" theatre of post-1956, and Bigsby mixes considerations of major playwrights with those of slightly less well-known figures, such as Lorraine Hansberry and LeRoi Jones; he also includes observations on surrealism, the Living Theatre, and the theatre of commitment. BIGSBY's *Modern American Drama 1945–90* was, as the author puts it in the Preface, an "accidental study", which grew out of another project. It covers some familiar ground on O'Neill, Williams, Miller, and Albee, looks at Shepard and David Mamet, and contains interesting general chapters on the "absent voice" of the American drama critic, the performing self, and politics, race and gender. Essential reading is the second volume of BIGSBY's *A Critical Introduction to Twentieth-Century American Drama*, which is an indispensable guide to the history, context, and interpretation of the period. This volume concentrates on Williams, Miller, and Albee, offering detailed readings and examination. Bigsby's work is clear and thorough: he provides biographical background on his subjects, as well as critical interpretation, and the depth of exploration is impressive, even on three authors so heavily researched.

PORTER's book contains chapters on a number of major texts plus examination of some lesser-known ones, such as *JB* by Archibald MacLeish, and *Detective Story* by Sidney Kingsley. Generally, Porter offers close readings of his chosen plays, with the intent of assessing plot structure, character, and setting in relation to cultural milieu. These are straightforward readings, but Porter offers some useful observations.

PARKER's collection comprises essays originally published in the journal *Modern Drama*, and usefully assembled here under their relevance to the four authors mentioned in the title. This is an accumulation of some provocative and sparkling work, which lies at the forefront of American drama criticism. It's also good to see some relatively neglected plays being discussed, such as Miller's *Incident At Vichy* and Albee's *Tiny Alice* and *All Over*.

The other books, discussed below, focus on particular aspects of, or have particular theses about, postwar drama.

PRADHAM's text, which reads American drama with close reference to the creation myth, heading chapters with titles such as "Eden", "The Fall", and "Innocence". Pradham's thesis – that "the loss of innocence and its tragic implications . . . are a peculiarly American phenomenon" is, clearly, an important theme for American drama, and Pradham explores it well.

GREENFIELD's book looks at the issue of the work ethic in American drama: although half of it is devoted to the prewar period, it contains chapters on World War II, readings of Miller's *Death of a Salesman* and *All My Sons*, and Williams's *The Glass Menagerie*, together with a look at the 1960s. The author states in the Introduction that "of the several themes that recur in the sixty years of modern American drama, perhaps the most prevalent and most intriguing is the one surrounding the American and his work, involving conflicts that occur 'on the job' and problems that arise in his attitude toward work itself", and its premise is well backed up.

ADAM's book looks at plays by Miller, Williams, Anderson, and O'Neill in terms of four different "types" of heroism: idealism, martyrdom, self-reflection, and survival. In her first chapter, Adam considers what she terms the "debate on tragedy", which has been conducted by various earlier critics, such as Joseph Wood Krutch and Francis Fergusson, and then states that her aim is to "situate the playwrights in these discussions and define their ideas of tragedy and of heroism in the face of the 'death of tragedy' debate". Adam groups her material in terms of these differing definitions and presents the argument that "specific forms of heroism constitute the tragic experience in these plays and that tragedy is most often interpreted as a dramatization of heroism". She focuses on plays from the 1940s to the 1960s, and offers some thought-provoking considerations of many "classic" texts, within the limitations of her thesis.

SCHARINE's exploration of politics and society in American theatre is essential reading. Well-written, enormously accessible, wide-ranging, and excellent for historical background, it assembles material under headings of themes and issues, rather than under playwrights: examples are "The Cold War", "Vietnam", and "Civil Rights". This is an excellent companion to the more playwright-centred works, and because of Scharine's coverage of less-researched, and sometimes more overtly political authors, offers an additional dimension to perspectives on the more mainstream writers. The book provides a clear and cogent location of American drama within the unfolding of powerful issues, and displays a solid knowledge of the plays and their contexts.

DAVIS offers a complex and detailed psychoanalytic reading of five classic plays, including O'Neill's *The Iceman Cometh* and Miller's *Death of a Salesman*. The introductory chapters are overly complex, and the book may be too demanding for students, being better suited to scholars and specialists. The author states that his intention is "to engage the being of the critic by showing how drama subjects its audience to a process which exposes the arrested drama of their own psyche". However, once the reader is past the complicated terminology, and Davis starts to discuss the plays, the text clarifies and becomes detailed and explanatory, offering a particularly interesting look at Albee's *Who's Afraid Of Virginia Woolf?*

Finally, mention should be made of the journal *Studies in American Drama 1945–Present*, which provides a platform for current scholarship on postwar American drama and theatre.

SIV JANSSON

3. Recent and Contemporary

Bigsby, C.W.E., *Modern American Drama 1945–1990*, Cambridge and New York: Cambridge University Press, 1992

Bigsby, C.W.E., *A Critical Introduction to Twentieth-Century American Drama, 3: Beyond Broadway*, Cambridge and New York: Cambridge University Press, 1985

Cohn, Ruby, *New American Dramatists 1960–1980*, London: Macmillan, 1982, revised as New American Dramatists 1960–1990, 1991

King, Bruce (ed.), *Contemporary American Theatre*, London: Macmillan, 1991

Robinson, Marc, *The Other American Drama*, Cambridge and New York: Cambridge University Press, 1994

Shank, Theodore, *American Alternative Theatre*, London: Macmillan, 1982

Until the 1960s American drama meant Broadway: Eugene O'Neill, Arthur Miller, and Tennessee Williams all found success there. After the social and political upheavals in the 1960s and early 1970s, however, American theatre became much more varied. Exciting theatre began to originate off-Broadway, off-off-Broadway, and in regional and street theatres. Contemporary American drama can no longer be summed up by the works of a few well-known playwrights. Critics must instead reflect the works of many different writers, as well as disparate styles of theatre and performance.

SHANK limits his work to alternative performance inspired by political and social protest in the 1960s. He defines this theatre as "an alternative to the theatre of the dominant complacent middle-class society which tended to perpetuate the status quo in its aesthetics, politics, working methods and techniques". This theatre was often visual, as opposed to textual, developed in workshops, and concerned with the political issues of the day. Shank devotes chapters to such theatre groups as the Living Theatre, the Performance Group, and the San Francisco Mime Troupe, tracing their histories and explaining their intentions. He also discusses performances, ranging from the autobiographical work of Spalding Gray to the technological extravaganzas of Robert Wilson. This volume is most useful as a history of alternative theatre in America, and as documentation of performances that were largely ephemeral.

BIGSBY's 1985 volume covers many of the same alternative theatre groups as Shank's work, but includes studies of individual playwrights as well. Constantly putting performance into a historical framework, he documents the change in

American theatre after the 1960s: "institutionally, aesthetically, socially and politically it began to fragment. Theatricality itself became a major concern, the writer was demoted, language distrusted, character disassembled and the relationship between performer and audience redefined". Bigsby traces the rise of off-Broadway theatre, once Broadway had failed to represent the needs of a more complex society. He discusses in great detail the modern-day myths of Sam Shepard and David Mamet's broken American Dream. The last section of the book is entitled "Theatre of Commitment" and deals briefly with works by women, gays, and ethnic minorities. Cursory introductions to lesser-known playwrights such as Ntozake Shange, Ed Bullins, and David Rabe are also provided.

COHN's 1982 work, expanded in 1991, is a basic summary of contemporary theatre, discussing many playwrights in a short period of time. She concerns herself with Broadway, off-Broadway, and alternative theatre since the 1960s. Cohn excludes anything which is not based on a set script, such as performance art. Sections are devoted to a wide variety of playwrights, including Neil Simon, Tina Howe, and David Henry Hwang. No playwright is discussed in particular detail, except in the final chapter, which she devotes to Mamet and Shepard. This book seems to be written for those with no prior knowledge of recent American drama, and Cohn therefore spends much of her time summarising the plots of important plays.

KING's collection is an excellent introduction to contemporary theatre since the 1970s, which is broad in scope without over-simplification. King has collected essays from writers who are academics, theatre critics, and dramatists themselves. This book provides useful introductions to lesser-known styles of American performance, such as dance theatre and performance art, and assessments of the work of mainstream playwrights, including Marsha Norman and Lanford Wilson. The collection in no way limits itself to text-based or mainstream theatre, and neither does it ignore the current influence of Broadway. One chapter provides a good summary of American feminist theatre, and another looks closely at mainstream black theatre. This is an indispensable introductory work on the state of contemporary performance, and strikes a balance between the alternative and the more popular styles of American theatre.

BIGSBY's 1992 volume deals with contemporary theatre as well as earlier postwar American drama. He discusses recent works of Arthur Miller and Edward Albee, who are often only considered in terms of the plays they wrote early in their career. Bigsby also deals with the current state of Broadway and how it fails to provide a suitable venue for many contemporary playwrights. As he does in his 1985 book, he focuses on the works of Shepard, Mamet, and alternative performance in the 1960s and 1970s. Political, feminist, and minority theatre-forms are summed up in a separate chapter. This volume provides only a brief introduction to lesser-known contemporary dramatists, concentrating instead on the key figures in twentieth-century American dramatic writing.

ROBINSON's book was written largely in response to surveys of American drama that neglect "alternative" plays. He devotes a chapter each to playwrights María Irene Fornés and Adrienne Kennedy, who, in most books on contemporary American drama, are summed up in a few paragraphs. Robinson is most interested in playwrights who do not write in conventional narrative terms, and this is evident in his treatment of Shepard, whose early, more experimental works Robinson greatly admires. This is an in-depth look at a few writers who have tried to use theatre as a platform for new ideas. Although other works on contemporary theatre may cover a greater number of playwrights, this volume gives a sense of the more vital and experimental theatre that has come out of America in recent years.

ERIN STRIFF

Drama: Australian

Australasian Drama Studies (journal), St Lucia: University of Queensland Press, 1982 –

Brisbane, Katharine, "Australian Drama", in *The Literature of Australia*, edited by Geoffrey Dutton, Ringwood, Victoria, and Harmondsworth, Middlesex: Penguin, 1964, revised 1976

Brisbane, Katharine (ed.), *Entertaining Australia: An Illustrated History*, Sydney: Currency Press, 1991

Fitzpatrick, Peter, *After "The Doll": Australian Drama since 1955*, Melbourne and London: Edward Arnold, 1979

Fotheringham, Richard, *Sport in Australian Drama*, Cambridge, Melbourne, and New York: Cambridge University Press, 1992

Holloway, Peter (ed.), *Contemporary Australian Drama: Perspectives since 1955*, Sydney: Currency Press, 1981, revised 1987

Kiernan, Brian, *David Williamson: A Writer's Career*, Port Melbourne, Victoria: Heinemann, 1990; as David Williamson, London: Heinemann, 1990

Radic, Leonard, *The State of Play: The Revolution in the Australian Theatre since the 1960s*, Ringwood, Victoria: Penguin, 1991

Rees, Leslie, *The Making of Australian Drama: A Historical and Critical Survey from the 1830s to the 1970s*, Sydney: Angus & Robertson, 1973, revised as *A History of Australian Drama*, 2 vols., 1978

Saunders, Justine (ed.), *Plays from Black Australia*, Sydney: Currency Press, 1989

Waterhouse, Richard, *From Minstrel Show to Vaudeville: The Australian Popular Stage 1788–1914*, Kensington: New South Wales University Press, 1990

Webby, Elizabeth, *Modern Australian Drama*, South Melbourne: Sydney University Press/Oxford University Press, 1990, revised 1993

Drama is the genre least developed in the New Literature of Australia. It has been unfairly perceived as being non-existent save for one or two memorable plays such as Ray Lawler's *Summer of the Seventeenth Doll* and Alan Seymour's *One Day in the Year*.

Commentaries on the earliest drama in Australia are, inevitably, historical and social rather than critical. BRISBANE's 1991 book is the most substantial, all-embracing volume. Based on the contributions of 138 scholars, it anticipates Currency Press's promised series of *Companions to Australian Film, Radio and Television*, *Music in Australia*, and *Theatre in*

Australia, and presents the material chronologically. In her introductory chapter Brisbane examines the emerging currents of taste and custom in the performing arts in Australia, some derived from international culture, merging to produce a culture "cosmopolitan and unique to Australia". Three sections – "Origins of a Colonial Culture", "Moving Pictures in the Theatre", and "Moving Pictures in the Home" – each with an overall Introduction followed by a series of individual entries, form the body of the book, and Brisbane's conclusion focuses on the trends in the 1980s and the future for the 1990s. WATERHOUSE's book is similarly historical and cultural in bias, but focuses on a smaller area – the popular stage from 1788 to 1914. He argues that failure to explore the role of imported stage entertainment distorted the understanding of Australia's theatrical past. Vaudeville became an important conduit of American, as well as British, cultural values, facilitating a shift from Anglophile outlooks after 1914 and, though class structures are still inclined to affect what goes on in Australian theatres, it made the popular stage an "institution which established a set of cultural values asserted from below rather than imposed from above".

REES has done the most work towards outlining a tradition while focusing on particular playwrights. From his first book on the subject (1953), he maintained that an Australian play, for him, had to be written about Australian life. *The Making of Australian Drama: A Historical and Critical Survey from the 1830s to the 1970s* (1973) describes plays and authors with care, and develops his argument to the point of suggesting that playwrights have the responsibility of creating Australian identity. The second revision and update of his work (1978) is divided into two volumes, one covering the period up to the 1960s, and the other devoted to the 1970s, including the work of Jack Hibberd, David Williamson, and Dorothy Hewett, and others who were part of the local flowering in Australian drama, nurtured by "alternative" theatres. BRISBANE's 40-page essay (1964, revised 1976) combines a brisk pace with attention to detail, and is the clearest outline available, covering the same ground as Rees, and emphasising throughout that working-class values have been an overriding influence, and that there has been a recurrent expression of alienation and defeat in Australian theatre. Selected bibliographies of individual playwrights are given by Brisbane, while Rees gives chronological lists of stage, radio and television dramas.

Most studies of Australian drama concentrate on the twentieth century. WEBBY's is a small "handbook" study, but useful in devoting itself to commenting directly on the text of six plays written between 1912 and 1986: Louis Esson's *The Time is Not Yet Ripe*, Ray Lawler's *Summer of the Seventeenth Doll*, Peter Kenna's *A Hard God*, John Romeril's *The Floating World*, Patrick White's *Signal Driver*, and Michael Gow's *Away*. Webby does comment on performance aspects such as sets, costumes, and music, but her approach is that of a literary critic making connections between nineteenth- and twentieth-century material, and to the drama of other countries as well. HOLLOWAY's book should be regarded as the standard reference text for modern Australian drama. The Introduction to the first edition is a useful outline of the development of Australian drama and of the formal commentary on it. Part I – "Historical Perspectives" collects the 15 best essays on the four decades from the 1950s to the 1990s. Part II – "Critical Perspectives" – presents 34 of the best essays on 15 different playwrights. Appendices contain a very full bibliography, lists of archives and theses, and biographical details of 72 playwrights at work in contemporary Australian theatre. This book in itself presents the case for the existence of a substantial Australian drama, even though so little of it penetrates the international commercial scene. FITZPATRICK's discussion of the period after 1955 distinguishes a phase of playwriting rich in the use of vernacular language, encouraged by the alternative theatre (in authors like Jack Hibberd and Barry Oakley) and a more recent phase (in authors like Louis Nowra and Stephen Sewell), which seems now to be free of preoccupation with the way in which Australian language is culturally defining. RADIC's book examines the work of "alternative" theatre companies – La Mama and the Pram Factory in Melbourne, and Nimrod in Sydney – where, in the 1960s, young writers, often fresh out of university, first determined to turn their backs on London and New York and produce a new, home-grown Australian drama. A playwright himself, and drama reviewer for *The Age*, Radic has written an account that is full, close, lively, and familiar as well as authoritative on this particular period.

Three books looking at more specific aspects of Australian drama are worthy of attention. SAUNDERS' anthology of plays, to which she writes an Introduction, is important as being the first to give access to the work of the Aboriginal playwrights Jack Davis, Eva Johnson, Richard Walley, and Bob Maza. FOTHERINGHAM studies in detail the links between sport and drama in Australia, from the earliest days when theatre tours had to be linked to race meetings to survive, and when the entrepreneurs of both learned to work together. Popular sporting narratives evolved in the nineteenth century, and entered legitimate drama, helping to establish some of the myths of the Australian character. KIERNAN's mid-career biography of Australia's most notable playwright, David Williamson, is an in-depth study of the man, the changing theatre of his times, and the individual plays. It is the only study of its kind in Australian drama criticism to date: perhaps only David Williamson is of the stature to reward such attention, but it is sad that this is a solitary beacon. It should be read by any student in the field.

Finally, essential to the study of Australian drama is the journal *Australasian Drama Studies* (whose coverage also includes New Zealand), the principal source for current drama criticism and first printing of new material. Originally edited by Katharine Brisbane, and now by Veronica Kelly and Richard Fotheringham, it is published by the Department of English in the University of Queensland.

GAY RAINES

Drama: Canadian

Benson, Eugene, and L.W. Conolly (eds.), *The Oxford Companion to Canadian Drama and Theatre*, Toronto, Oxford, and New York: Oxford University Press, 1989

Bessai, Diane, *Playwrights of Collective Creation*, Toronto: Simon & Pierre, 1992

Brask, Per (ed.), *Contemporary Issues in Canadian Drama*, Winnipeg, Manitoba: Blizzard, 1995
Massey, Vincent, "The Prospects of a Canadian Drama", in *Queen's Quarterly*, 30, December 1922
Much, Rita (ed.), *Women on the Canadian Stage: The Legacy of Hrotsvit*, Winnipeg, Manitoba: Blizzard, 1992
Parker, Gerald D., *How to Play: The Theatre of James Reaney*, Toronto: ECW Press, 1991
Wallace, Robert, *Producing Marginality: Theatre and Criticism in Canada*, Saskatoon, Saskatchewan: Fifth House, 1990
Wallace, Robert, and Cynthia Zimmerman, *The Work: Conversations with English-Canadian Playwrights*, Toronto: Coach House Press, 1982

Critical studies of Canadian drama have only recently appeared, ancillary to the postwar development of a professional theatre industry, which has produced a substantial canon of plays. Whereas 70 years ago Massey could write (albeit incorrectly) that the body of Canadian drama consisted of "no more than twelve or fifteen plays", it now numbers in the thousands.

Critical discussion of Canadian drama tends to recognize two broad periods of development. Most narratives dismiss (perhaps too quickly) the hundreds of plays written before the 1950s as dated and amateurish for the most part, a consequence of the fact that for almost a century Canadian theatres were built to house touring American and British troupes. The onset of public funding in the arts in the 1950s brought about a remarkable material change, as Canadian playwrights found – and founded – professional theatres committed to the development of Canadian drama. This resulted in a renaissance of dramatic writing, and a large body of popular, stageworthy plays. Although there is as yet no single survey of this literature, a growing collection of more selective studies reveals the emergence of a critical orthodoxy in the 1980s, which is now subject to revision by more theoretically sophisticated scholarship.

MASSEY proposed that a canon of Canadian drama should refute "artificial Canadianism" to recognize that Canada is a diverse and plural society. His article is particularly important as an early formulation of the ideas that the young diplomat would later enact in Canadian cultural policy as chairman of the Royal Commission on National Development in the Arts, Letters and Sciences, 1949–51. As the foundation document for the establishment of the Canada Council in 1957 and the introduction of public subsidies in the arts, the *Massey Report* made possible the theatrical renaissance of the postwar decades. In 1951, Canada had almost no professional theatre; four decades later, the Canada Council was funding more than 200 theatre companies.

The pace of that development is apparent in WALLACE and ZIMMERMAN's 1982 collection of interviews with 26 leading playwrights, all of whom launched professional careers in the 1970s. Although not the first such collection, this was the first to examine closely the interconnection of the craft of the dramatist with the changing material structures of the Canadian theatre industry. It remains useful today, mainly because of its conversations with several first-rank playwrights (Sharon Pollock, George F. Walker) at early stages in their respective careers.

The establishment of a scholarly discipline of research in Canadian drama was advanced substantially by the 1989 publication of BENSON and CONOLLY's *Companion.* It represents the major effort, to date, to compile historical and contemporary information and assessment, although by its nature it lacks critical argument. The pages of this volume do offer, however, a meta-narrative, which locates the rise of playwriting in Canada in the postcolonial recuperation of the theatre. It also provides useful individual entries on major playwrights and plays.

For reasons that may have more to do with the economics of the publishing industry than with scholarly interest, few books have been written about individual Canadian playwrights. In one of the most useful studies, PARKER shows clearly that James Reaney, the theatrical fabulist whose work mixes mythic lyricism, ribald physicality, puppetry, and lavish melodrama, may justifiably be ranked among the best playwrights in the English language today. BESSAI's study of a group of influential playwrights whose roots lie in the practice of collective creation follows several earlier studies by theatre historians less interested in literary value. Bessai offers an accessible introduction to (and reconsideration of) the dramaturgy of a movement that many claim to be the formative influence on modern Canadian playwriting.

Both Bessai and Parker approach their subject with a narrative analytical approach derived from New Criticism. The more radical critical attitudes that have defined theatre research over the past decade are exemplified in WALLACE's groundbreaking study. His examination of how ideological structures govern the production and reception of theatre practice (including, but not restricted to, playtexts) challenges the ethnic, gender, and class assumptions inscribed in most previous writing. In a series of essays, which examine the material and cultural growth of the theatre through the 1970s and 1980s, Wallace proposes a theoretical framework to examine the crucial importance of feminist, gay, and other marginalized voices in Canadian drama.

MUCH's more recent collection of essays by leading women academics and playwrights (including Judith Thompson and Sharon Pollock) reveals the diversity of critical and thematic approaches produced by feminist analyses in the multicultural 1990s. For the same publisher, BRASK has compiled the most up-to-date and provocative anthology of essays yet available. His collection, prepared with an eye to the undergraduate market, displays a range of contemporary critical strategies, mapped across a thematic and regionalist structure. It is perhaps the most accessible and representative introduction to the subject.

It is because the development of a canon has been an integral function of the postcolonial theatre industry that critical studies of Canadian drama have focused on performance conditions and theatrical provenance as well as literary value. The disciplines of dramatic criticism and theatre history have by necessity converged; both are now contained in the term "theatre research". This move recognizes as well that the imagistic theatricality that has characterized the new dramatic forms of the last 30 years requires an analytical approach, which appreciates performance as a form of textuality.

ALAN FILEWOD

Dramatic Censorship

Clare, Janet, *"Art Made Tongue-Tied by Authority": Elizabethan and Jacobean Dramatic Censorship*, Manchester: Manchester University Press, 1990

Conolly, L.W., *The Censorship of English Drama 1737–1824*, San Marino, California: Huntington Library, 1976

Findlater, Richard, *Banned! A Review of Theatrical Censorship in Britain*, London: MacGibbon & Kee, 1967

Fowell, Frank, and Frank Palmer, *Censorship in England*, London: Frank Palmer, 1913

Johnston, John, *The Lord Chamberlain's Blue Pencil*, London: Hodder & Stoughton, 1990

Stephens, John Russell, *The Censorship of English Drama 1824–1901*, Cambridge and New York: Cambridge University Press, 1980

George Bernard Shaw, an arch-opponent of censorship, wrote that "all censorships exist to prevent anyone from challenging current conceptions and existing institutions". Censorship is always a contentious issue and it is perhaps to be expected that the writing on this topic is often less than dispassionate. A number of studies, including the first two discussed here, have arisen out of special historical circumstances of their day as elements in the continuing public debate on censorship.

FOWELL and PALMER's book was published four years after the 1909 Joint Select Committee "Report" (*British Sessional Papers*, VIII), when it had become clear that its recommendation to abolish pre-production censorship and replace it by a voluntary system was not to be implemented. Although lacking adequate references, it is still the fullest survey of dramatic censorship from its origins in the sixteenth century up to 1912, and especially strong on the immediate events of the Edwardian period.

FINDLATER's survey helped reinforce the increasingly vociferous anti-censorship lobby of the late 1960s for the appointment of a new parliamentary investigation into dramatic censorship. (Such a committee, in the event, recommended abolition, which duly took place in September 1968.) For the pre-1912 period his main source is Fowell and Palmer; but the second half of the book concentrates on newer twentieth-century material, including some of the most recent victims of censorship like John Osborne and Edward Bond. He concludes by outlining the arguments against censorship, and defends his belief that no stable and ostensibly liberal society should have any need for the special protection of censorship. Findlater revels in the inconsistencies, caprice, and absurdity (and hence the humour) uncovered in the procedures of a censorship run for the government by the chief of the royal household residing in St James's Palace.

Dramatic censorship in Britain was originally the prerogative of the Court, initially under the Master of the Revels. This early period is discussed by CLARE, who considers the censorship under which Shakespeare wrote (e.g., the loss of the deposition scene from *Richard II*), that endured by George Chapman and Ben Jonson (both of whom were temporarily imprisoned for scurrilous attacks on the court of James I), and, at the end of the period under review, Thomas Middleton. Through a broadly historical approach, the notions that censorship of the period up to about 1630 posed "no serious threat" or, conversely, was "consistently repressive and menacing" are dismissed as equally inaccurate.

Official censorship under parliamentary statute began in 1737 with the Stage Licensing Act, hurried into effect to prevent the use of the stage as a means of attacking the government. CONOLLY provides a scholarly and impressively detailed account of censorship from the implementation of the Act to the death of John Larpent (Examiner of Plays) in 1824. This is a pioneering study, using MS material from the Larpent Collection of playscripts in the Huntington Library. Of the six chapters, those on political censorship, including personal satire, are especially revealing. My study (STEPHENS) begins where Conolly ends, and continues down to the end of the Victorian era, which at the time of publication was the terminal date for the availability of the papers of the Lord Chamberlain's Office. Drawing substantially on this major resource, I attempt to chart the character and dynamics of official censorship, and its relation to public opinion, through the individuals who administered it and through discussion of the censors at work. Political, moral, religious censorship is discussed, as well as violence and the presence of undesirable role-models in crime drama (which, because of fears about the rise in juvenile crime in mid-century, was a particularly active area for censorship). Discussed also are the tensions between theatre and censorship in the 1890s, when the "advanced drama" attempted to extend the traditional boundaries, particularly in issues of sexual morality.

JOHNSTON is of interest almost exclusively for its post-1900 material. As Assistant Comptroller of the Lord Chamberlain's Office from 1964 to 1968, the author had direct experience of (and sometimes actively participated in) the operation of censorship in its final phase. This gives the work the unique distinction of being a book on censorship written by a censor, though it is not by any means an official account. In its insider's view lies both its value and its limitation. Not devoid of humour and an ability to laugh at some of the more bizarre examples of censorship, Johnston also suggests that the censor was too hard on religious drama and (more surprisingly) on portrayal of the royal family. But opportunities for rather more comprehensive analyses of events are lost. Edward Bond, for instance, is seen only from the official viewpoint rather than in terms of his wider challenge to the establishment through such plays as *Saved* and *Early Morning*. There is a useful set of appendices, including statistics on plays refused a licence between January 1900 and September 1968. However, the general absence of specific references is annoying, though it is made clear that the official archives are the main source. This rather tends to confirm the overall impression of the book, as, in tone and manner, rather like a set of loosely put together theatrical reminiscences, fascinating though the glimpses of the work of modern censors are. The standard work on dramatic censorship in this century is still to be written.

JOHN RUSSELL STEPHENS

Dramatic Monologue

Culler, A. Dwight, "Monodrama and the Dramatic Monologue", in *PMLA* [*Publications of the Modern Language Association*], 90, 1975

Faas, Ekbert, *Retreat into the Mind: Victorian Poetry and the Rise of Psychiatry*, Princeton, New Jersey: Princeton University Press, 1988

Hobsbaum, Philip, "The Rise of the Dramatic Monologue", in *Hudson Review*, 28, 1975

Hughes, Linda, *The Manyfaced Glass: Tennyson's Dramatic Monologues*, Athens: Ohio University Press, 1987

Langbaum, Robert, *The Poetry of Experience: The Dramatic Monologue in Modern Literary Tradition*, Chicago: University of Chicago Press, 1957; London: Chatto & Windus, 1957

Martin, Loy D., *Browning's Dramatic Monologues and the Post-Romantic Subject*, Baltimore: Johns Hopkins University Press, 1985

Mason, Michael, "Browning and the Dramatic Monologue", in *Robert Browning*, edited by Isobel Armstrong, London: Bell, 1974; Athens: Ohio University Press, 1975

Rader, Ralph, "Notes on Some Structural Varieties and Variations in Dramatic 'I' Poems and Their Theoretical Implications", in *Victorian Poetry*, 22, 1984

Sessions, Ida Beth, "The Dramatic Monologue", in *PMLA* [*Publications of the Modern Language Association*], 62, 1947

Sinfield, Alan, *The Dramatic Monologue*, London: Methuen, 1977; New York: Barnes & Noble, 1977

Definitions of the dramatic monologue vary significantly, but most critics agree on the following features: the dramatic monologue is a poetic genre presenting the imaginary utterance of a single speaker who is someone other than the poet concerned; the speaker often interacts with an identifiable though silent listener at a dramatic moment in the speaker's life; in the process, the speaker reveals significant aspects of character or the flow of consciousness. Poems by Robert Browning such as "My Last Duchess" are the usual examples of the form.

Unfortunately, many attempts to define the dramatic monologue rely on circular reasoning: critics derive a definition of the genre from a limited selection of poems by Robert Browning (and sometimes Tennyson), and then prescriptively apply this definition as a test of the genre itself. SESSIONS, for example, defines the "perfect" dramatic monologue as a poem having the "definite characteristics of speaker, audience, dramatic action, interplay between speaker and audience, dramatic action, and action which takes place in the present". More interesting studies take a broader approach, relating generic practices associated with the form to historical and cultural developments.

LANGBAUM's highly influential study argues for the importance of the dramatic monologue as a predominant Victorian and modern poetical form growing out of the Romantic epistemological shift to a "poetry of experience". According to Langbaum, poetry since the Romantic period has tended to present the poet's subjective experience of phenomena by fusing the perceiving subject and the world. This perspective elicits the reader's sympathy because the poet's experience is dramatized as an event rather than formulated as an idea with which the reader may agree or disagree. Langbaum emphasizes the continuity between Romantic lyrics like William Wordsworth's "Tintern Abbey" and Victorian dramatic monologues, interpreting both as the "poetry of experience". In the case of the dramatic monologue, however, the reader's sympathy for the speaker exists in a state of tension with moral judgment of ethically questionable motives and actions, as in the case of the Duke who is the speaker in "My Last Duchess". Many critics have questioned or modified Langbaum's formulation of the dialectic of sympathy and judgment, but it has remained widely influential. Still others have questioned his historical account of the origins of the dramatic monologue.

CULLER was one of the first to critique the historical metanarrative Langbaum constructs. Noting that the term "dramatic monologue" was not used before 1857, and not widely used until the end of the century, Culler emphasizes that poems with a single dramatic speaker followed several different models in the early nineteenth century. He disputes Langbaum's contention that they arose out of the Romantic lyric of experience, and points to two other lines of development instead, one arising out of *prosopopoeia* or impersonation, a standard exercise in classical rhetoric, and the other out of Romantic monodrama, a form in which a single speaker (often a classical heroine) articulates a series of passions, either accompanied by, or in alternation with, music. The influence of monodrama is particularly apparent in works by Tennyson, such as *Maud*.

SINFIELD, like Culler, takes a broader historical view of the development of the dramatic monologue, finding precursors for the form in the complaint, the epistle, and the humorous colloquial monologue – poetic forms of impersonation, which that he traces back to Theocritus and Ovid. Sinfield argues that Victorian poets turned increasingly to the opportunities for oblique self-expression that the dramatic monologue offered in order to escape the burdens placed on them by Romantic concepts of poetic subjectivity. Considering modernist as well as Victorian forms of the dramatic monologue, Sinfield questions the tendency to privilege examples of the genre by Browning, which that reproduce the effects of actual speech. In Tennyson's, as opposed to Browning's, dramatic monologues, dramatic speech tends to be rhetorical and lyrical, not casual and colloquial. Lyrical modes also predominate in modernist examples of the genre, like T.S. Eliot's "The Love Song of J. Alfred Prufrock", because modernist writers undermine naturalistic conceptions of character.

RADER attempts to distinguish dramatic monologues proper from other categories of poems with first speakers, including the dramatic lyric, the mask lyric, and the expressive lyric. In the expressive lyric (for example, Wordsworth's "Tintern Abbey"), we identify the speaker as the poet, and interpret the lyric as the poet's reponse to a scene or situation. In the mask lyric (for example, Tennyson's "Ulysses" or Eliot's "Prufrock"), the poet uses an "artificial personage" as a vehicle of lyrical expression in order to represent his or her own subjective situation. As a result, the reader experiences the speaker from the "inside out", seeing the scene or situation the poem presents through the speaker's eyes. In the dramatic monologue proper, on the contrary, the reader perceives the speaker from the "outside in", as an "other" with an outward presence, like the Duke in "My Last Duchess".

HOBSBAUM and MASON explore the connections between the dramatic monologue and changing theories and practices associated with the drama. Hobsbaum links the rise of the dramatic monologue to the late eighteenth-century and early nineteenth-century tendency to extract dramatic soliloquies from their contexts and to reprint them in elocutionary handbooks and in anthologies such as Charles Lamb's *Specimens of English Dramatic Poetry*. Mason demonstrates how Browning's experiments with the drama and the dramatic monologue were shaped by Romantic "anti-theatrical" attitudes privileging poeticity over action, written text over production, and the authority of the author over the interpretation of directors. (Langbaum similarly considers how the decline of traditional stage drama into psychologizing and lyricizing fragments contributed to the rise of the dramatic monologue.)

FAAS provides an illuminating account of the connections between early psychology or nineteenth-century "mental science" and the rise of the dramatic monologue. Drawing extensively on Victorian periodical literature, he demonstrates that nineteenth-century reviewers clearly approached the dramatic monologue as a new form of psychological poetry. Faas is also unusual in considering a wide range of nineteenth-century authors of dramatic monologues, including some women authors.

MARTIN develops a poststructuralist paradigm of the dramatic monologue as a form that denies the homogeneity of the subject. Whereas Langbaum emphasizes the continuity between Romantic expressive lyrics and Victorian dramatic monologues as alternative forms of the "poetry of experience", Martin argues to the contrary that the dramatic monologue manifests a split between the Romantic and the post-Romantic subject. According to Martin, the dramatic monologue is a form that powerfully expresses the desire for the unity of the perceiving subject, while it simultaneously denies such a possibility in its formal conventions. Although Martin attempts to deploy a Marxist approach in relating the rise of the dramatic monologue to changing conditions of poetic production, he gives very little attention to authors other than Browning.

HUGHES provides one of the most serviceable models to date, both of the diversity of the dramatic monologue form and of its dynamics. She demonstrates how Victorian dramatic monologues are built upon a complex array of overlapping and interacting relationships among the poet, the speaker, the inscribed or implied auditor, and the reader. Like Sinfield, Hughes questions the tendency to privilege as ideal types of the genre certain of Browning's dramatic monologues, in which the speaker is naturalistically presented. Hughes observes that, whereas Browning typically presents the "personality" of his speakers from an exterior vantage point, Tennyson typically presents the "consciousness"of his speakers from an interior perspective, using lyrical and rhetorical rather than naturalistic dramatic modes.

Like almost all of the studies summarized here, however, Hughes relies chiefly on dramatic monologues by Tennyson and Browning in developing a theory of the form. What remains to be written are comprehensive histories of the form, which consider the many other authors who experimented with, or employed variants on, the dramatic monologue, including the women writers that research since the 1970s has started to recover. Accounts of the dramatic monologue have also not yet adequately considered how variables such as gender, race, and class enter into the dynamics of the form in relation to poet, speaker, implied or inscribed auditor, and reader.

MARJORIE STONE

Drayton, Michael 1563–1631

English poet

Berthelot, Joseph A., *Michael Drayton*, New York: Twayne, 1967
Brink, Jean R., *Michael Drayton Revisited*, Boston: Twayne, 1990
Elton, Oliver, *Michael Drayton: A Critical Study*, London: Constable & Co., 1905
Guffey, George Robert (ed.), *Samuel Daniel, 1942–1965; Michael Drayton, 1942–65; Sir Philip Sidney, 1941–1965* (Elizabethan Bibliographies Supplements VII), London: Nether Press, 1967
Hardin, Richard F., *Michael Drayton and the Passing of Elizabethan England*, Lawrence: University Press of Kansas, 1973
Harner, James L., *Samuel Daniel and Michael Drayton: A Reference Guide*, Boston: G.K. Hall, 1980
Jafri, S. Naqi Husain, *Aspects of Drayton's Poetry*, Delhi: Doaba House, 1988
Newdigate, Bernard H., *Michael Drayton and His Circle*, Oxford: Blackwell/Shakespeare Head Press, 1941, revised 1961
Noyes, Russell, "Drayton's Literary Vogue since 1631", in *Indiana University Studies*, 22(107), 1935
Tannenbaum, Samuel A., *Michael Drayton (A Concise Bibliography)*, New York: Samuel A. Tannenbaum, 1941
Westling, Louise Hutchings, *The Evolution of Michael Drayton's "Idea"*, Salzburg: Institut für Englische Sprache und Literatur (Salzburg University), 1974

Despite the appearance of the acclaimed *Works* between 1931 and 1941, and constant critical attention, the popular status of Michael Drayton remains today much as it was a century ago: in Samuel Tannenbaum's words (1941), "his work will be of value to the historian, the geographer, the antiquarian, the folklorist, and the hiker, but the general reader will always shun him". His increasing importance in New-Historicist criticism may finally force Drayton before a more general readership.

TANNENBAUM's bibliographical study lists editions of, and books and articles on, Drayton to 1940, updated to 1965 by GUFFEY; although lacking annotation, these volumes are well indexed and should be used to support HARNER's immense achievement in providing a year-by-year guide to Drayton studies, with full descriptive annotation.

Placing itself in a "third revival" of interest in Drayton, following that of 1748 and Charles Lamb, ELTON claims that "nearly everything as yet known about this poet ought to be found in this brief volume". Beginning with a short biography, he discusses Drayton as a "representative" poet, and provides a rapid survey of his works and critical reputation, hoping that "the true rank of Drayton may be clearly discerned and admitted, and his whole works made accessible". Now superseded in most aspects, it remains useful for its 50-page bibliography of Drayton editions, and its appendix providing an index to the various incarnations of the sonnets. (The book is a major revision of *An Introduction to Michael Drayton*, Manchester: J.E. Cornish, 1895).

NOYES' brief monograph remains invaluable for its gathering of a huge range of critical verdicts on Michael Drayton from 1631 to 1855. Noyes traces a trajectory where "Drayton's popularity, already waning at the time of his death, sank almost, if not quite, into oblivion during the years of Dryden and Pope" before a Victorian re-evaluation, which has left Drayton standing "on his own merits a worthy member of the giant race". Stopping short at 1855, however, this alleged critical stature is not documented.

NEWDIGATE makes imaginative use of the biographical fragments that remain, many of them introduced here. While admitting that his comments on Drayton's schooling "rest chiefly, but not wholly, on conjecture", Newdigate attempts to trace "our poet's life-long devotion" to Anne Goodere (in whose family he served), in allusions to *Idea*; identifies Lucy Harington as "Selena" in the 1606 eighth eclogue; considers claims that Drayton might be the "Rival poet" of Shakespeare's sonnets, and that his patron Walter Aston might be the "lovely boy"; and reviews Drayton's supposed friendship with Ben Jonson in the conflicting light of Jonson's "conversations" with William Drummond of Hawthornden (the Drayton/Drummond correspondence is printed here). Laid out chronologically, with several illustrations, this work suffers from what Newdigate saw as its strength – its insistence on using Drayton's life as a "biographical commentary" on the poetry.

BERTHELOT structures his study around Drayton's literary development over 40 years: "from a relatively second-rate Petrarchist in his early years, he became a highly diversified and accomplished, if not great, poet in his later years". Taking Drayton as "the complete Renaissance poet", whose canon gives "a meaningful representation of most of the poetic material, modes, and styles popular from 1590 to 1630", Berthelot devotes chapters to Drayton's revisions through six editions of *Ideas Mirrour*; the pastoral and fairy poetry; the historical poetry; *Poly-Olbion* ("a poem best enjoyed by reading carefully chosen selections"); his religious poems, occasional poems, satires, odes, and elegies; surveys of his poetic theories and critical reputation; and general conclusions: although many have "considered him a poet who remained an Elizabethan throughout his entire poetic career", this, Berthelot argues, "is neither an adequate nor an accurate judgment". Berthelot also provides a brief annotated bibliography and a tabular analysis of the six major editions of *Ideas Mirrour*.

Despite HARDIN's claims that he "set out more to understand Drayton than to evaluate his poems", his study is primarily an attempt to bring literary and social history to bear on this "least fashionable of important Elizabethan poets". Hardin sees Drayton as "a public poet moved by an educated faith in English destiny", who evolved from an imitator like his peers into "a poet of essentially unique temperament and concerns". Most of the major works are discussed in a short section, also dealing with wider subjects such as history in verse, antiquarianism, the body politic, Drayton's perception of the moral and political decline of England and the concomitant fall of its literary output. The final chapter examines Drayton's prophetic vision of England's future ten years before the outbreak of the Civil War.

WESTLING focuses on the growth of Drayton's sonnet sequence from 1594 to 1619 "by investigating the clearly announced pose of the libertine, which obviously serves as the persona of the sequence from 1599". This is a full-length study, its chapters devoted to: Drayton's critical reputation and apprenticeship as a sonneteer; the remodelling of *Ideas Mirrour* (also rendered by a chart); the 1619 edition; and the sequence's place in the development of the English lyric. Westling argues that the evolution of Drayton's sonnet work "gives us firm evidence for understanding how Elizabethan poetics could absorb the major force of innovation which produced metaphysical poetry".

Noting that much Drayton criticism has neglected his satires, verse-romances, odes, and elegies, JAFRI asserts that "his poetry is fascinating for its variety, as a record of the patriotic aspiration and sentiments and as reflecting the literary tastes of its age", practising both popular genres and new classical forms. Each genre is discussed in its own chapter, as Jafri offers fresh insights through allegorical interpretations, and offers possible causes of Drayton's comparative oblivion during and after the Commonwealth.

BRINK offers a "deeply revisionary" analysis of Drayton's life and works, applying some of the lessons of New Historicism to a chronological account. Arguing that his "place in the canon needs revision; we have paid too much attention to his chorographical poem and too little to his satire", Brink sees previous critical approaches as "colored by a biography that ignores and misconstrues the realities of literary clientage, the relation of poets and patrons". He traces these themes in Drayton's early experiments with genre, and focuses on his laureate ambitions and early clientage connections. Later chapters provide similarly historicised readings of: *Englands Heroicall Epistles*, his "Jacobean work"; *Poly-Olbion* as a statement about the function of humane letters; the 1619 *Ideas Mirrour* and *Poems*, his two Caroline folio collections; and *The Muses Elizium*, as a final statement about future of public poetry. The study concludes with re-evaluation of Drayton's legacy as critic and poet.

ALAN STEWART

Dream-Vision Literature

Bridges, Margaret, "The Sense of an Ending: The Case of the Dream-Vision", in *Dutch Quarterly Review*, 14, 1984

Lynch, Kathryn L., *The High Medieval Dream Vision: Poetry, Philosophy, and Literary Form*, Stanford, California: Stanford University Press, 1988

Payne, Roberta, *The Influence of Dante on Medieval Dream Visions*, New York: Peter Lang, 1988

Piehler, Paul, *The Visionary Landscape: A Study in Medieval Allegory*, London: Edward Arnold, 1971
Spearing, A.C., *Medieval Dream-Poetry*, Cambridge and New York: Cambridge University Press, 1976
Weldon, James F.G., "The Structure of Dream Visions in *Piers Plowman*", in *Medieval Studies* (Pontifical Institute of Medieval Studies, Toronto), XLIX, 1987

Medieval dream-vision literature has, unfortunately, not received the amount of critical attention proportionate to, or indicative of, its diversity and complexity. Critical attention has focused mainly on either constructing a historical framework within which the medieval dream-vision tradition can be placed, or, alternatively, reading the genre as an expression of medieval thought on spirituality, psychology, and the processes involved in the creation of fictions.

PIEHLER's approach is influenced by psychoanalytic elements in general and a Jungian slant in particular. His study explores medieval dream-vision literature, or, as he terms it, medieval visionary allegory, as a genre that portrays the psychic journey and self-discovery of the dreamer. The dreamer finds himself in a state of spiritual crisis and turmoil through which he progresses with the help of a figure of authority, arriving at the recognition of the causes of his anguish, defeating them, and regaining spiritual equilibrium. Piehler identifies the problems dealt with as both personal and social, spiritual and secular. He states that the fusion of the particular and the general characterizes both content and form of medieval visionary allegory in that this genre offers the reader "spiritual participation" in the processes of recognition and healing. He looks in detail at the works of Boethius, Alain de Lille, Dante, Guillaume de Lorris, and Jean de Meun, as well as the anonymous *Pearl*-poet, portraying in each study further extensions and variations in the use of medieval visionary allegory for psychoanalytic purposes. Piehler's study will appear dated, in that it applies modern psychoanalytical terminology uncritically to medieval texts, seemingly without awareness of temporal and cultural differences. The impression that Piehler presupposes a universal human psyche, essentially unchanged by time, is built up throughout the text through his frequent generalizations, such as his belief in "the eternal dreams of the human spirit". However, his outline of a vocabulary to be used specifically in the analysis of medieval visionary allegory and his closing statement that "allegories still have direct potential relevance to contemporary predicaments" are valuable points, which should be borne in mind in any future study of medieval dream-vision literature.

SPEARING begins his highly influential study with the outline of classical and Christian traditions, which he sees as the predecessors of the medieval dream-vision genre, thus positing it within a historical and literary continuity. Like Piehler, he sees this continuity of themes and concepts as evidence of a "universal psychic archetype". For Spearing, the main function of the dream vision is to present the acquisition of knowledge by, and through, the dreamer. He examines the ways in which the intellectual or spiritual journey is presented in a very broad spectrum of texts encompassing numerous authors, from Chaucer to the poets of the Alliterative Tradition, and the use by Scottish poets of the "creative principles" set up by Chaucer in his four dream-poems. This study offers a general overview of the literary traditions and concepts that helped shape the medieval dream-vision genre as well as the structural and thematic changes and variations within the works of different authors. Although this general approach does not enable a detailed study of any one work, it offers the reader a coherent introduction to the genre as a whole.

BRIDGES' approach, in contrast, is more specific in that it focuses solely on the aspect of closure in medieval dream-vision literature. She opens her essay with a brief discussion of Frank Kermode's critical exploration of "books as fictive models of the temporal world". She argues that books allow us to escape a fixed scheme of time as well as simultaneously fulfilling our need for linear temporal plot development. She applies these concepts to medieval dream-vision literature because she states that the "dream framework constitutes an ideal playground for the tussle between the desire for form and the need to revolt against finality". Bridges explores both the manner in which medieval authors such as Chaucer and Langland, as well as the early-modern writer John Bunyan, introduce expectations of closure in their dream visions, and how these expectations are confounded or undermined throughout the texts, thus drawing the reader's attention to the self-conscious processes of the creation of fictions.

WELDON's essay focuses on one particular aspect in one particular medieval dream vision: the prologues to the dreams in the B-Text of Langland's *Piers Plowman*. He has chosen this text because of its unique employment of "connected multiple dreams, interspersed by significant observations and actions of the Dreamer in his waking moments", and emphasizes the prologues because of their function as "the form's modifying or interpretative element". Weldon examines Langland's experiments with this genre by dividing the eight dreams of the B-Text into three groups, each group connected within itself by a set of interrelated themes and motifs. The first group of three dreams begins with a dreamer set firmly in a secular world and frame of mind. Through the next two dreams the dreamer begins to comprehend the nature of spiritual progress, and by the time we reach the second group Weldon identifies a dreamer changed in outlook. Group three is distanced from the first two, which still share certain themes. Here the dreamer, although not free from his human nature, has reached increasingly higher levels of spirituality. Weldon's study is interesting because of its concentrated focus. Furthermore, his final assessment of *Piers Plowman* can be applied in studies of other dream-vision texts: "the repetition of key themes and motifs group the dreams into structural units, and deviation allows us to distinguish their differences and to follow the dreamer's evolution".

The importance of both philosophical and poetic theory as a framework to an examination of medieval dream-vision literature is stressed by LYNCH. She uses this approach with regard to five writers: Boethius, Alain de Lille, Jean de Meun, Dante, and John Gower. Lynch's study is dense and thorough. She outlines her aims clearly, the chapters concentrating consecutively on the close examination of the concepts that outlined a medieval world view, the dream-vision genre's specific suitability for presenting these concepts, the relation of form and content within the genre, historical reasons for specific developments within dream-vision literature, Dante and his incorporation of contemporary intellectual and social developments in his *Commedia*, and, finally, a discussion of Gower, whom she sees as a "transitional figure, both reaching back and pointing forward". These main units are subdivided under more detailed headings, thus enabling Lynch to present an argument that is both broad and specific. Additionally, she defines the terminology she employs, demonstrating an awareness of the difficulties encountered when dealing with the products of a different culture and age.

PAYNE's study of Dante's influence on medieval English dream visions concentrates initially on the concept of "literary borrowing" in its multiple possibilities (i.e., on the linguistic level or on a conceptual level). Generally, Payne sees the uses of Dante by medieval English poets as examples not of "slavish imitation" or "simplistic borrowing", but rather of "careful and appropriate manipulations of creatively chosen sections". She examines these in relation to *Pearl*, Chaucer's *The House of Fame* and *The Parliament of Fowls*, as well as to the less popular *The Temple of Glass* and King James' *Kingis Quair*. She defines the type of dream poetry she discusses along the lines of Macrobius's *visio*-category: "poetry . . . centred around a spiritual crisis in the life of an individual". Her view of Dante's influence on medieval English poets is put forward in discussions of such concepts as the use of language, the processes of creating poetry, the interrelation of dreaming and writing, as well as in a comparison of the treatment of courtly love in Dante and Chaucer. Her argument is constructed in a way that demonstrates the influence of Dante's *Divina Commedia* on the structure and form as well as on the thematic content of medieval English dream-vision literature.

ANKE BERNAU

Dreiser, Theodore 1871–1945

American novelist

Elias, Robert H, *Theodore Dreiser: Apostle of Nature*, New York: Knopf, 1949; revised edition, Ithaca, New York: Cornell University Press, 1970

Frohock, W.M., *Theodore Dreiser*, Minneapolis: University of Minnesota Press, 1972

Hussman, Lawrence E., Jr., *Dreiser and His Fiction: A Twentieth-Century Quest*, Philadelphia: University of Pennsylvania Press, 1983

Kazin, Alfred, and Charles Shapiro (eds.), *The Stature of Theodore Dreiser: A Critical Study of the Man and His Work*, Bloomington: Indiana University Press, 1955

Lehan, Richard, *Theodore Dreiser: His World and His Novels*, Carbondale: Southern Illinois University Press, 1969; London and Amsterdam: Feffer & Simons, 1969

Matthiessen, F.O., *Theodore Dreiser*, New York: William Sloane, 1951; London: Methuen, 1951

Moers, Ellen, *Two Dreisers: The Man and the Novelist*, New York: Viking Press, 1969; London: Thames & Hudson, 1970

Pizer, Donald, *The Novels of Theodore Dreiser: A Critical Study*, Minneapolis: University of Minnesota Press, 1976

Pizer, Donald (ed.), *New Essays on "Sister Carrie"*, Cambridge and New York: Cambridge University Press, 1991

Swanberg, W.A., *Dreiser*, New York: Charles Scribner's Sons, 1965

Zanine, Louis J., *Mechanism and Mysticism: The Influence of Science on the Thought and Work of Theodore Dreiser*, Philadelphia: University of Pennsylvania Press, 1993

Criticism of Theodore Dreiser has, understandably, tended to focus on his two major novels, *Sister Carrie* and *An American Tragedy*, and his seminal contribution to the realist and naturalist movements in American literature in the early years of the twentieth century. Recent criticism has, however, taken more account of the later novels (notably the posthumously published *The Bulwark* and *The Stoic*), the autobiographical writings, and the development of Dreiser's ideas in the last ten years or so of his life, in an effort to revise what have become established, and entrenched, critical positions. The publication of newly edited works and previously unpublished manuscripts under the auspices of the University of Pennsylvania Press has greatly expedited current research.

ELIAS's critical biography is a relatively early work of Dreiser scholarship but, in many respects, it has not been superseded. Elias aims to avoid evaluative consideration of Dreiser and biography proper: the interest, as stated in his 1948 Preface, "is primarily to investigate the apparent contradictions, trace their development, and interpret them in relation to Dreiser's career. How did the sensitive son of an ardently Catholic father come to be the Dreiser who wrote a novel that was labeled as lewd and profane?" In exploring these "contradictions" he touches on many aspects of Dreiser's career and the influences, both biographical and intellectual, which shaped his fiction, particularly those of Darwinian evolutionary theory and the writings of the English social Darwinist, Herbert Spencer, to whom he turned after his readings in T.H. Huxley and John Tyndall. "A Survey of Research and Criticism" prepared for the 1970 edition usefully summarizes significant critical and scholarly work on Dreiser.

MATTHIESSEN's is an important critical study by one of the major figures of contemporary American criticism. Matthiessen gives all the major novels their due, pointing to the considerable weaknesses of works such *The Titan* and *The "Genius"*, but the centrepiece of his book is the chapter on *An American Tragedy*, where he argues both for the novel's strength as a work of documentary fiction and for its weakness as tragedy: "he sees man so exclusively as the overwhelmed victim that we feel hardly any of the crisis of moral guilt that is also at the heart of the tragic experience".

KAZIN and SHAPIRO's collection remains an extremely valuable compilation of early reviews, reminiscences, and critical essays, arguably the best place to begin for anyone embarking on a study of Dreiser. Included here are Ford Madox Ford's "Portrait of Dreiser", selections from the correspondence of James T. Farrell and Dreiser, the influential early critical essays of Sherwood Anderson, Stuart P. Sherman, H.L. Mencken, and Randolph Bourne, Lionel Trilling's "Reality in America", Saul Bellow's "Dreiser and the Triumph of Art", and other intelligent commentaries from John Berryman, Alexander Kern, Eliseo Vivas, and Charles Child Walcutt.

FROHOCK's brief study in the "Pamphlets on American Writers" series offers a lucid overview of both the life and the work. The biographical details are brief, but generally accurate, and the critical commentary on the novels is valuable for its insistence on the differences between Dreiser's "American" naturalism and that of French progenitors, most notably that of Emile Zola, Frohock arguing that Dreiser's "theories", if they can be so designated, are best understood as metaphors. Frohock sees *An American Tragedy* as a work of "romantic realism" and seeks to defend the novel against those critics who found it shapeless and lacking fictional craft.

SWANBERG's remains the closest to a "definitive" life of Dreiser that we have. The work is indispensable as a source document, and while it offers very little in the way of literary criticism or interpretation, its value for those interested in the genesis of Dreiser's works, his habits and methods of composition, or his relationships with his contemporaries is enormous.

Both LEHAN's and MOERS's books are examples of life-and-works critical studies, and both suffer a little from the repetition of biographical detail and a somewhat mechanical sense of the "marriage" of biographical evidence to the fiction. Lehan stresses the impossibility of Dreiser's reconciling of "his own romantic aspirations with his belief in a world of physical limits" and the manner in which his fiction externalizes "his own sense of conflict"; Moers offers a not dissimilar critical and philosophical overview, but the emphasis in her book is on Dreiser's two "masterworks" and, in effect, she writes the "stories" behind these two stories, exploring with great assiduity the complex pattern of historical, intellectual, and sociological influences that helped shape the fiction. Both books contain intelligent criticism: Lehan's (which has 16 pages of photographs) is the more useful for an overview of the fiction, Moers's for anyone with particular interests in *Sister Carrie* and *An American Tragedy* or Dreiser's affinities with William Dean Howells, Stephen Crane, Alfred Stieglitz, and the "Ash-Can" school of painters.

PIZER's 1976 book is the most substantial critical study of Dreiser's work to date. Concentrating on the eight published novels, the book's aim, as Pizer writes in his Preface, is "to establish the facts of the sources and composition of each of Dreiser's novels and to study the themes and form of the completed work". Extensive use is made of the manuscript material and, though biography is largely eschewed, of relevant biographical evidence. Pizer argues that Dreiser criticism has suffered "from a tendency to sacrifice the distinctiveness of particular novels for a symmetrical interpretation of the career as a whole", and in seeking to redress this the chapters of his book, each given over to an individual novel, take the form of a series of discrete critical essays, which can be easily and conveniently read independently of one another. Pizer recognizes that, above all, Dreiser's achievement is in the medium of the novel, and his book is by far the best literary critical study available.

HUSSMAN, like a number of recent commentators, is eager to challenge the conventional wisdom that sees Dreiser as "a dour scientific determinist and a Social Darwinian" by examining, in detail, the political, philosophical, and spiritual ideas of his later years to encourage a greater appreciation of his writing. The approach is chronological, and an interesting first chapter explores the complex, and sometimes contradictory, fascination the young Dreiser had for philosophic naturalism, supernatural causation, and mystical religiosity. Later chapters are largely given over to individual novels, but one particular virtue of Hussman's book is the chapter on the short stories, notably those that treat "the mostly harmful effects of marriage on both husbands and wives".

PIZER's 1991 collection on *Sister Carrie* contains essays written in the light of the 1981 University of Pennsylvania Press edition of the novel. The editor writes informatively on the publishing history of the novel, Thomas P. Riggio analyses the characterization of Carrie, drawing on new evidence both from the Pennsylvania text and the handwritten first draft of the novel, while Barbara Hochman explores the issues of "representation", linking Dreiser as an "actor" in the process of writing with Carrie's experiences in the theatre. Other essays from Richard Lehan and Alan Trachtenberg complete a volume of valuable, new, critical approaches to Dreiser's novel.

ZANINE's recent book addresses a central topic in any discussion of late nineteenth-century naturalism – the influence of scientific thought and scientific method on both the theory and the practice of fictional mimesis. Zanine recognizes the important contributions of earlier Dreiser scholars (notably Elias and Moers), but he considerably extends the study of scientific influence by taking the debate beyond evolutionary and social-Darwinian thought into areas of "physio-chemical" theory and the more philosophical problems that arise when an accommodation between science and religion is sought. Like Lehan and Moers, he demonstrates a conflict between realist and Romantic aspirations in Dreiser's fiction and, like Hussman, he seeks to challenge the simplistic and conventional wisdom that categorizes Dreiser as a materialist and naturalist. Zanine's book explores Dreiser's brief period of research at Carnegie Biological Laboratory at Cold Spring Harbor in 1937, his spiritual awakening or "epiphany" while he was there, and the "shape" of his philosophical and religious thought over the last eight years of his life, drawing extensively throughout on posthumously published materials and editions. It could be argued that he attempts to give coherence to Dreiser's thinking where no coherence can be found; but among recent work on Dreiser this is the most distinguished.

HENRY CLARIDGE

Dryden, John 1631–1700

English poet, dramatist, and prose writer

Frost, William, *John Dryden: Dramatist, Satirist, Translator*, New York: AMS Press, 1988

Hammond, Paul, *John Dryden: A Literary Life*, London: Macmillan, 1991; New York: St Martin's Press, 1991

Harth, Phillip, *Contexts of Dryden's Thought*, Chicago: University of Chicago Press, 1968

Hopkins, David, *John Dryden*, Cambridge and New York: Cambridge University Press, 1986

Hughes, Derek, *Dryden's Heroic Plays*, London: Macmillan, 1981

Miner, Earl, *Dryden's Poetry*, Bloomington: Indiana University Press, 1967

Miner, Earl (ed.), *John Dryden*, London: G. Bell & Sons, 1972; Athens: Ohio University Press, 1972

Pechter, Edward, *Dryden's Classical Theory of Literature*, Cambridge and New York: Cambridge University Press, 1975

Winn, James A., *John Dryden and His World*, New Haven, Connecticut, and London: Yale University Press, 1987

Dryden has for some time stood in need of rehabilitation, and there are signs that it is now happening. Response to him has been generally lukewarm over much of the twentieth century, with the result that only a handful of his works are widely known – notably the satires *Mac Flecknoe* and *Absalom and Achitophel*. Recent criticism has tended to move in two new directions. First, Dryden's translations of classical (and some other) poetry have begun to receive more attention, a development altering our sense of the overall shape of his work. Second – and especially through the efforts of American critics – his complex and shifting position as a political writer is being reassessed.

MINER's 1967 monograph was for many years a standard general study on Dryden's poetry; it was one of the first full-scale modern accounts to move from discussion of Dryden's ideas to critical analysis of his poems. It also takes in one play, *All for Love*. Miner's stress on the satires goes together with his view that "most of [Dryden's] poetry is radically public and engaged"; but detailed readings of other kinds of poems, notably lyric, help to provide balance, as does the chapter-length treatment of Dryden's *Fables Ancient and Modern*. Miner's argument for the structural unity of this collection of translations has sponsored several further studies along these lines, most recently rejecting his thesis. Though Miner sees the best of Dryden's poetry as indubitably great, he discerns limitations – most seriously, "an over-intellectualized response to human experience".

HARTH's book remains in some ways the standard work on the poet's religious and philosophical thinking. His procedure is to start from Dryden's ideas as expressed in their literary contexts, then analyse them in terms of "individual historical movements of thought". Harth argues that Dryden is neither a Pyrrhonist nor a fideist; he is a conventional sceptic, which for his period implied investigation through "freedom of enquiry" and "modesty and diffidence". He is a moderate and orthodox Catholic in *The Hind and the Panther*: this poem and *Religio Laici* are the works on which Harth has most to say.

MINER's 1972 essay-collection aims to do justice to Dryden's diversity as a writer by assembling the work of diverse critics. However, the essays often return to a small group of texts (especially *Absalom and Achitophel*), suggesting, as the editor admits, that the contributors, like others, tend to see Dryden too narrowly. In partial compensation, there is an extensive selected bibliography of modern and some pre-twentieth-century editions, critical books, and articles on the full range of Dryden's work. Perhaps the most useful of the contributions are the introductory accounts of Dryden's classical translations (William Frost) and of "Dryden and Seventeenth-Century Prose Style" (K.G. Hamilton), and two essays on his plays. The collection includes one of the few general essays on Dryden's shorter poetry, "Dryden's Panegyrics and Lyrics" (Arthur Hoffman).

PECHTER's book is a standard work on Dryden's critical prose, though it makes reference also to some poems, notably *Mac Flecknoe*, by way of moving from Dryden's theory to his practice. Pechter seeks to show why Samuel Johnson thought of Dryden as "the father of English criticism". His criticism is articulated within the classical tradition of "the balance of the mean"; the classical quality of his outlook is documented through treatments of his views on, for example, French versus English drama, judgement versus fancy, metaphysical versus Augustan. His mixture of freedom and restraint reflects his openness to different ideas, and is part of what Johnson called his "variety".

HUGHES's study is standard for Dryden's drama, an area that has attracted comparatively little attention in recent years. It deals with the five "heroic" plays, written between 1664 and 1675. Taking issue with the view that these works are largely uncritical celebrations of an ideal, Hughes sees them as constituting "a serious, humane study of the disparity between divine aspiration and mortal reality". Hughes seeks to demonstrate that the heroic characters are psychologically explored, and that the "minutely integrated cohesion and sheer artistic intelligence" of the plays has been underrated. These lines of argument are more effective with the later than the earlier ones. An appendix discusses sources and analogues for Dryden's plays in seventeenth-century European drama.

HOPKINS's study is the best place to go for a general account of Dryden's poetry; it offers less on him as dramatist and prose writer. Hopkins challenges the received idea of Dryden as pre-eminently a satirical commentator on his times, stressing the importance of Dryden's translations from the classical poets, from Boccaccio, and from Chaucer. These works, Hopkins argues, force us to see him as above all a great philosophical poet. A useful introductory chapter explains the principles and possibilities of the heroic couplet as used by Dryden; the rest survey the poetry chronologically, blending biographical discussion with criticism to produce a powerful overall reading of Dryden's poetic career. Hopkins's emphases, within the writing which that career produced, are those of the pre-twentieth-century view of Dryden – a view, he argues, that should be taken seriously.

HAMMOND's "literary life" is an introductory work, in some ways complementary to Hopkins's. Hammond discusses Dryden's early satires, his plays, and his criticism at greater length, and the translations at less. He contextualizes and expounds, without providing full critical analysis. To Hammond, Dryden's works "enact a struggle for integrity in a world where violent change seemed to threaten every kind of stability which made life intelligible".

FROST's book collects together his many writings on Dryden to make up a volume which, while claiming no comprehensiveness, surveys a wide range of the poet's work. The introductory essay, "Dryden in Context", is one of the more stimulating short discussions of the literary and cultural world of Dryden's era. Chapters follow on *Aureng-Zebe* and on Dryden's theory and practice of satire, leaving the bulk of the book for Dryden as translator, in which Frost reprints from his pioneering study *Dryden and the Art of Translation* (1955) and elsewhere. Scholarly material arising from Frost's editorial work on Dryden is of more specialized interest than several lively, attractively written essays on the translations from the

Latin classics, especially Virgil. There is also an essay on verse translation in general, setting out general principles on which such poetry can be studied.

WINN's substantial biography of Dryden immediately became standard, and is unlikely to be improved on for many years. Winn sees himself as gaining Dryden "a fairer hearing": he rightly observes that Dryden's reputation still suffers from the work of "Victorian scholars whose own politics compelled them to label him a turncoat and timeserver". He unearths some new facts, airs some new speculations, and discovers many personal and political allusions in Dryden's poems and plays. The book takes account of all recent scholarship and is heavily documented.

STUART GILLESPIE

Du Bois, W.E.B. 1868–1963

American prose writer and novelist

Broderick, Francis, *W.E.B. Du Bois: Negro Leader in a Time of Crisis*, Stanford, California: Stanford University Press, 1959

Brodwin, Stanley, "The Veil Transcended: Form and Meaning in W.E.B. Du Bois's *The Souls of Black Folk*", in *Journal of Black Studies*, 2, March 1972

Horne, Gerald, *Black and Red: W.E.B. Du Bois and the Afro-American Response to the Cold War, 1944–1963*, Albany, New York: State University of New York Press, 1986

Kostelanetz Richard, *Politics in the African-American Novel: James Weldon Johnson, W.E.B. Du Bois, Richard Wright, and Ralph Ellison*, New York: Greenwood Press, 1991

Marable, Manning, *W.E.B. Du Bois: Black Radical Democrat*, Boston: Twayne, 1986

Munslow, Alan, "The Black Intellectual: W.E.B. Du Bois and the Black Divided Consciousness", in his *Discourse and Culture: The Creation of America, 1870–1920*, London and New York: Routledge, 1992

Although Du Bois left a vast body of written work, his literary fiction was limited to five novels, *The Quest of the Silver Fleece* (1911), *The Dark Princess* (1928), and *The Black Flame*, a trilogy incorporating *The Ordeal of Mansart* (1957), *Mansart Builds a School* (1959), and *Worlds of Color* (1961). Du Bois's traversing of generic boundaries in his writing, often within the same article, novel, or collection, has been responsible, in part, for a critical legacy that is strikingly diverse in its treatment of his work. Generally speaking, his fiction displays a pedagogical and political intent before it lays claim to any aesthetic design. At the same time, though, many critics point to a literary, sometimes poetic, orientation in certain of his academic essays and sketches, most particularly so in sections of what has become his most famous, and arguably his most influential, work, *The Souls of Black Folk* (1903).

BRODWIN tackles *The Souls of Black Folk* as an exercise in literary rhetoric, claiming that only from such an approach can the "true meaning" of the text be derived. To this end he chases the variety of literary techniques deployed by Du Bois, taking the use of allegory, personal confession, (auto)biography, musical motif, Greek myth, biblical allusion, and a range of rhetorical tropes as constituting a conscious attempt on Du Bois's part to create "an aesthetic commonality between himself and his white reader".

The argument fixes on the duality of Du Bois's famous "twoness" motif, and its eventual resolution through what Brodwin perceives to be a "neo-Hegelian" dialectic, whose search for "a meaningful synthesis between self-consciousness and culture" finally transports its writer to "a spiritual realm of historical understanding that does not merely rend, but transcends the veil of color". When considered in the contexts of recent literary theory, Brodwin's line is contentious and, arguably, deeply conservative; but his treatment of the identity issue throws a different light on the ways in which other critics have dealt with Du Bois's seemingly ambivalent stance regarding racial assimilation. Most interestingly, the "personal dialectic", which Brodwin finds in *The Souls of Black Folk*, eventually sounds more Jungian than Hegelian (an impression perhaps reinforced by the parallels he draws with Ralph Waldo Emerson and William James), giving the argument an intriguing angle on the moral dimension of Du Bois's political thought.

Grounding his analysis in Antonio Gramsci's theory of hegemony, and also drawing on Michel Foucault, MUNSLOW builds a rather less affirmative critique of *The Souls of Black Folk*. Focusing, as does Brodwin, on Du Bois's "divided consciousness", Munslow argues that Du Bois failed to imagine convincingly the theoretical terrain on which a viable oppositional black culture might be built. Between his demands for integration on the one hand, and the need for black cultural autonomy on the other, Du Bois "incorporated the potentially independent and oppositional black social formation by depriving it of effective intellectual leaders like himself", and, "by colonising its discourse at the tropic and narrative levels".

This latter contention produces the most challenging aspect of a tightly argued study, in which Munslow returns repeatedly to Du Bois's use of the "veil of race" trope, and its relation with what is read to be Du Bois's "annexation by the white academic social and political imagination". Munslow's negative assessment of the famous "Talented Tenth" theory is not in itself breaking new ground, but his linkage of the idea to Gramscian categories gives the discussion a theoretical underpinning that is lacking in other studies. Alongside his early analyses of class, self-improvement, and the primary importance of education in racial advancement, Du Bois's "re-signifying" of Darwinian positivism as "Reform Darwinism" is offered, here, as the endorsement of a dominant, white, corporatist republican ideology. Thus, where other critics have seen ambivalence in Du Bois, Munslow perceives what is "a highly conservative integrationist ideological message".

An altogether more "traditional" approach is taken by KOSTELANETZ, who reads Du Bois's novels, in a chronological account, as a straightforward, fictional embodiment of his political thought. Kostelanetz's appraisal of Du Bois as "a peculiarly opportunistic, second-rate political mind", whose thinking is underscored by "chronic" and "characteristic ambivalences", feeds naturally enough into his assessment that Du Bois was also "slow to adjust to the necessities of fiction": *The Quest of the Silver Fleece*, for example, is striking for the writer's "inability to weave all the strands of a multiple plot into a coherent whole". This critique of authorial control may, as Kostelanetz himself notes, seem slightly outmoded today, but the close ties which are identified between Du Bois's evolving ideological agenda(s) and his fictional writing provide a valuable illumination of the political role that Du Bois envisaged his novels might fill. Kostelanetz points to the surfacing of the "Talented Tenth" idea in *The Quest of the Silver Fleece*, and the emergence, in *The Dark Princess*, of "a kind of catholic colored internationalism", which gives fictional life to Du Bois's Pan-Africanist agenda. Concluding a lengthy chapter on Du Bois, Kostelanetz offers an extended reading of *The Black Flame* trilogy, a series of novels which, he suggests, "achieves a polemical effectiveness" that is missing in the earlier fiction.

What Munslow, Kostelanetz, and the majority of critics have perceived as ambiguous, conflicting, and even paradoxical strands in Du Bois's writing, MARABLE sees as "a basic coherence and unity" of thought, which he subsumes under the epithet "Radical Democrat". In his Preface, Marable says that he has attempted to present this radical democratic vision, so far as was possible, in Du Bois's own words, and the text contains citations of, and commentary on, more than 60 of Du Bois's writings, both published and unpublished, spanning the entirety of his public life and the wide generic spectrum across which he wrote.

Du Bois, it is suggested, "made no distinction between art and political engagement", a position to which Marable himself adheres throughout his own commentary. Accordingly, Du Bois's writing is placed within extensive historical, political, and biographical contexts: *The Black Flame* trilogy is read, in effect, as autobiography, "one of the most candid perspectives left by Du Bois about his own life and his views of other leaders". The "most lasting contributions" Du Bois made to black literature in the early years ("before 1910") are identified as the poem *The Song of the Smoke*, and the prose-poem *Credo*, the works in which Du Bois outlined "the central principles that motivate his political and cultural work". Commenting on *The Quest of the Silver Fleece*, Marable hints at parallels with the tradition of American naturalism, an observation made in passing, and one which, frustratingly, is never developed. Students of Du Bois might find Marable's "Bibliographic Essay", and his selected bibliography of secondary sources, particularly useful.

In Du Bois's lifetime, BRODERICK suggests (writing four years before Du Bois's death) that "Du Bois has become an almost mythical figure, and no one has contributed to this myth more sedulously that Du Bois himself. In one autobiographical essay after another, he has reconstructed the heroic figure of an austere man of principle fighting a universal battle for the right, against an ignorant or hostile world". In a notoriously disparaging survey of his extant life and work, Du Bois is accused of racism, arrogance, and vanity, and to a large degree his position as a pioneering figure, central to the development of black activism, is played down. Broderick, who had access to Du Bois's personal papers, finds little of value in either the fictional or the non-fictional writings. While granting that "the bulk of Du Bois's scholarly articles and books commands attention", he claims that: "no single work, except *The Philadelphia Negro* [1899], is first-class"; his novels and poetry are characterised by "set speeches" and metaphors, which are "labored" and "obtuse"; and "when he is being most consciously literary", Du Bois is at his "least successful". Broderick's, then, could hardly be considered an affirmative study of Du Bois, but neither is it the entirely polemical denunciation that Marable, for one, has suggested it is. Despite himself, Broderick expresses admiration for certain aspects of *The Souls of Black Folk*, and gives a generous, if grudging and somewhat brief, assessment of Du Bois's journalism ("his best work"): his monthly editorials, Broderick suggests, "with their brevity, luster and punch, are his lasting literary monument."

A commonplace assumption in much earlier criticism of Du Bois (Broderick included) points to his increasingly marginal role in the intellectual debate of the Cold-War period. Where Marable rejects this position implicitly, HORNE devotes a persuasive, full-length study to the repudiation of an argument which, he suggests, betrays a "crude obtuseness" in Du Bois's critics. For Horne, accounts of Du Bois's relative isolation after World War II reveal, at best, a misunderstanding of black politics and, at worst, an insidious white ethnocentrism, which identified Du Bois's defence of the Soviet Union with his involvement in black activism. During the Red Scare, Horne says, "an Afro-American community that often found it expedient to depart from the consensus on, for example, rope and faggot justice, of necessity was in the forefront in the fight to protect the right to dissent". Because of "the disproportionate southern racist influence in the anticommunist upsurge", it was unavoidable that attempts would be made to isolate Du Bois from the rising tide of civil rights struggle. Thus, "racism ineluctably accompanied anticommunism".

Horne, then, revises the context within which Du Bois's later novels might be read: *The Black Flame* trilogy "subtly attempted to link the fates of the Soviets and Afro-Americans, the early years of the NAACP [National Association for the Advancement of Colored People], Blacks and trade-unions, socialism and the communist party". Showing how the popularity of Du Bois's writing with the publishing houses "ebbed and flowed along with the vicissitudes of the Cold War", Horne comments widely on Du Bois's continuing centrality in the mainstream of black American thought and culture, during the frequently neglected but demonstrably "rich" period of his later years.

DAVID HOLLOWAY

Dunbar, William c.1460–c.1520

Scottish poet

Bawcutt, Priscilla, *Dunbar the Makar*, Oxford: Clarendon Press, 1992
Baxter, J.W., *William Dunbar: A Biographical Study*, Edinburgh: Oliver & Boyd, 1952
Reiss, Edmund, *William Dunbar*, Boston: Twayne, 1979
Ross, Ian Simpson, *William Dunbar*, Leiden, Netherlands: E.J. Brill, 1981
Scott, Tom, *Dunbar: A Critical Exposition of the Poems*, Edinburgh: Oliver & Boyd, 1966
Taylor, Rachel Annand, *Dunbar: The Poet and His Period*, London: Faber & Faber, 1931

Wood, H. Harvey, *Two Scots Chaucerians: Robert Henryson; William Dunbar*, London: Longmans Green, & Co., 1967

Along with Robert Henryson, William Dunbar is the finest poet of the late medieval period in Scotland, his work exhibiting the widest variety of forms and styles of any poet of the time.

Although supplemented by material in later critical texts on Dunbar (particularly Bawcutt), BAXTER still provides the standard biography of the poet. The work traces what is known or surmised of Dunbar's period as a student at Saint Andrews, and his later career as a cleric and relatively unsuccessful courtier in the service of James IV. As with all accounts of Dunbar's life, much of the comment is inferential, but the work provides an exhaustive account of the poet's contexts in the universities, court, and towns of the period, and thus provides a necessary background to the poems, particularly those set in the court or dealing with Dunbar's mixed feelings towards the religious establishment.

TAYLOR is a slight and vitriolically unsympathetic study, which fails to reflect any of the re-estimation of the poet introduced by the "Scottish Renaissance". While it does cover the range of his work with some degree of comprehensiveness, it is of significance mainly in that it is an early, if negative, recognition of Dunbar's importance, and primarily interesting in the way in which it represents the general attitude to Dunbar at a time before his poetry came to be seriously considered and carefully read.

SCOTT, in the first book-length account of the poet, provides a fresh and interesting approach, which emerged in the wake of the "Scottish Renaissance" revaluation of Dunbar, especially in the writing of Hugh MacDiarmid. Scott, himself a Lallans poet, presents a lively if somewhat impressionistic account, reading Dunbar very much in modern terms and presenting him as a bawdy and comic, rather than serious, poet. Scott covers what have come to be seen as the major areas of Dunbar's work – the religious poems, poems on women, poems on court life, the flyting with Walter Kennedy, and Dunbar's poems that reflect the social life of town and court. Scott is perhaps least sympathetic to Dunbar's religious poems, and this is an area which comes in for serious attention only later.

In a short but still useful study, WOOD deals with Dunbar, along with Robert Henryson, as a Scottish Chaucerian, giving particular attention to Dunbar's aureate poems, and to "The Tua Marrit Wemen and the Wedo". Although less fully documented than later studies, and less lively than Scott, it still provides the best initial introduction to the poet, being thoroughly reliable and presenting with a greater or lesser degree of completeness the whole range of Dunbar's work.

In the earliest of what can properly be considered to be contemporary studies of Dunbar's work, REISS specially emphasises the ironic element in Dunbar (an area which Bawcutt is sceptical about), and of all the texts under consideration is most concerned to see Dunbar as a profoundly moralistic poet. In his presentation of Dunbar in terms of this blend of morality and irony, Reiss thus provides the reader with a Dunbar who is at once rooted in the medieval scene, but equally, in the poet's ironic scepticism towards his subject, reflects more contemporary attitudes. Indeed, the nature of the irony that Reiss perceives in Dunbar is perhaps more modern, finally, than medieval.

ROSS provides a much more serious and academic account, seeing Dunbar very much as a poet of his time, and relating the work to the major intellectual movements of late medieval Scotland. He is particularly interesting on the aureate and moral poems. The work is divided into two parts, the first third providing an account of Dunbar's life and background, the remainder discussing the poems in the categories in which they are found in the Bannatyne manuscript. This approach reinforces what is becoming an increasing concern in Dunbar studies, to see the poet not in isolation but as inextricably rooted in the tradition, both social and manuscript, from which he emerges.

In the latest and much the most thorough study, BAWCUTT presents the most comprehensive critical account of the poet to date. This work is particularly rich in the way it relates Dunbar's poetry to a range of similar poems by less well-known medieval Scottish poets, and gives proper attention to poems that elsewhere receive little appreciation. This is particularly the case in her treatment of the flyting dialogue between Dunbar and Kennedy, and the background she provides to this. While Bawcutt's account fails, not unexpectedly, to illuminate all the obscurities of this difficult poem (or poems), it does make the text much more accessible than before. The work is particularly attractive in the way in which it presents a strong sense of the dramatic movement of Dunbar's poetry, and contains a detailed bibliography of both work on Dunbar and primary and secondary background material on his period. If Wood is perhaps the first critical text to be read on Dunbar, then Bawcutt is certainly, to date, the most useful and comprehensive.

ROBIN HAMILTON

Durrell, Lawrence 1912–1990

English novelist, poet, and travel writer

Begnal, Michael H. (ed.), *On Miracle Ground: Essays on the Fiction of Lawrence Durrell*, Lewisburg, Pennsylvania: Bucknell University Press, 1990
Fraser, G.S., *Lawrence Durrell: A Study*, London: Faber & Faber, 1968, revised 1973
Friedman, Alan Warren (ed.), *Critical Essays on Lawrence Durrell*, Boston: G. K. Hall, 1987
Kersnowski, Frank L. (ed.), *Into the Labyrinth: Essays on the Art of Lawrence Durrell*, Ann Arbor: UMI Research Press, 1989
Moore, Harry T. (ed.), *The World of Lawrence Durrell*, Carbondale: Southern Illinois University Press, 1962
Unterecker, John, *Lawrence Durrell*, New York: Columbia University Press, 1964
Weigel, John A., *Lawrence Durrell*, New York: Twayne, 1965; revised 1989

Durrell enjoyed a small but increasing reputation as a lyric poet for 20 years before the appearance of *The Alexandria Quartet*, a tetralogy of novels published successively (1957–60), brought him sudden if fairly shortlived fame and success. He continued to write poetry, and a further two sequences of novels followed the *Quartet* through the 1970s and 1980s, but critical and popular interest in his work (which is wide and varied, including also travel writing, plays, humorous sketches and journalism) has diminished sharply.

FRIEDMAN's useful volume of reviews and essays spanning 25 years, appearing after the completion of Durrell's final cycle of novels, the Avignon *Quintet*, records the writer's career, and includes excerpts from some of the major critics summarised below. His Introduction, esteeming Durrell as "prolific and protean", and more than just the author of the *Quartet*, reviews the history of Durrell criticism, especially its tendency to veer between excessive praise and denigration. A representative range of views, more and less appreciative, is included and Durrell's debatable status acknowledged.

MOORE's much earlier compilation of brief memoirs, reviews, and essays, with a few letters by Durrell appended, is obviously more limited in scope but also in critical range, since it appeared shortly after publication of the *Quartet*, at the height of Durrell's success, and is consequently almost entirely enthusiastic, even adulatory, in approach. It contains important material though (some reproduced in Friedman) and should not be neglected.

Among more comprehensive individual critiques, UNTERECKER's is the earliest, a 50-page monograph providing a survey of Durrell's career to date and sympathetic, insightful criticism, centring on the *Quartet*, and introducing principal themes and issues (relativity theory and multiple narrative, among others) in the writing. WEIGEL's more substantial study followed shortly after, a critical and partly biographical assessment, written five years after the *Quartet* was completed. Capable and informative, if chatty in tone, it is like much criticism of Durrell, amiable and indulgent. While the range of Durrell's work is covered, attention centres on the *Quartet*, whose multi-dimensional narrative and structure are summarised and respectfully, if slightly uncertainly, welcomed as experimental and representatively modern. Love, sex, and death are its central concerns, while truth is understood to be multiple and relative. These perceptions are repeated, with variations, throughout criticism of Durrell, and of the *Quartet* in particular.

FRASER, in the standard earlier critical study, amplifies and extends this assessment. His book, in its revised edition, is able to take account of the post-*Quartet* pair of novels *Tune* and *Nunquam* (known together as *The Revolt of Aphrodite*) but not the later *Quintet* (also known as the *Quincunx*). Valuably, it contains Alan G. Thomas's substantial bibliography of Durrell's writing (much of which, especially the poetry, is in rare and inaccessible editions). Like Weigel, Fraser deals extensively with the range of work to date, assessing the career, the man, and the reputation, mixing criticism and biography, enlivened also by personal acquaintance and reminiscence, and again providing friendly and sympathetic treatment, attending most fully to the *Quartet*. Widely read, perceptive, and concerned to relate Durrell to wider literary perspectives, Fraser takes a perhaps too-rosy view of Durrell as optimist and "comedian", but is nevertheless helpful and insightful.

A couple of more recent collections honour Durrell as a grand old man of letters, though with some regretful awareness that his star seems to have waned. KERSNOWSKI's compilation of 18 essays is a mix of criticism and personal reminiscence marking Durrell's 75th birthday, and the tone is appropriately celebratory and nostalgic. The important friendship with Henry Miller is recorded and assessed, and again the varied range of work (including Durrell's painting) is usefully covered, with efforts to elucidate Durrell's aesthetic of fiction. As well as the *Quartet* (a couple of useful if generalised treatments) the later fiction is examined, though with more enthusiasm than critical force.

BEGNAL's smaller collection, derived from a symposium honouring Durrell (with an attractively self-deprecating response from its subject), considers his "distinguished" achievement over 50 years, restricting its purview to the fiction. A range of critical perspectives, some more theoretical than others, treat Durrell as experimental, modernist, even playfully postmodernist, while his serious concern with Eastern religion and associated ideas and issues (gnosticism, Jungian theories, Georg Walther Groddeck, intuitive spirituality against Western rationalism) are given important consideration. There is also a more substantial consideration of the later post-*Quartet* fiction.

JEREMY LANE

E

Edgeworth, Maria 1768–1849

Anglo-Irish novelist and essayist

Butler, Marilyn, *Maria Edgeworth: A Literary Biography*, Oxford: Clarendon Press, 1972
Butler, Marilyn, "Maria Edgeworth", in her *Jane Austen and the War of Ideas*, Oxford: Clarendon Press, 1975; New York: Oxford University Press, 1987
Harden, Elizabeth, *Maria Edgeworth*, Boston: Twayne, 1984
Hurst, Michael, *Maria Edgeworth and the Public Scene: Intellect, Fine Feeling and Landlordism in the Age of Reform*, London: Macmillan, 1969; Coral Gables, Florida: University of Miami Press, 1969
Newcomer, James, *Maria Edgeworth the Novelist*, Fort Worth: Texas Christian University Press, 1967
Owens, Cóilín (ed.), *Family Chronicles: Maria Edgeworth's "Castle Rackrent"*, Dublin: Wolfhound Press, 1987; Totowa, New Jersey: Barnes & Noble, 1987

Although the reception of her earliest works has assured Maria Edgeworth of a place in English literary history, and despite the maintenance of her status by the regular appearance, after her death, of Edgeworth family letters and memoirs, it is only since the publication of Butler's biography that a comprehensive assessment of her artistic achievements and cultural significance has been possible. Both the biography and Butler's important 1975 essay bring together the disparate elements of her subject's long and complex career, in contrast to earlier studies, such as those of Hurst and Newcomer, which tend to focus on one of those elements.

The success of BUTLER's 1972 *Biography* as a work of synthesis derives in the first place from Butler's mastery both of a great deal of primary material and of the Edgeworth family's complex history. While sympathetically aware of Edgeworth's political outlook as a member of the Anglo-Irish landlord class, and of the ways in which this influenced her sense of mission as a writer, the work also deals at length with Edgeworth's endeavours as an educator and her intimate and wide-ranging familiarity with the main scientific, literary, and political currents and personalities of her time. The varied nature of Edgeworth's artistic output is also detailed, and her reputation as a novelist of manners, routinely noted by historians of the novel, is seen afresh in the light of the history of women's writing. This emphasis on the feminist, rather than the broadly social, dimension of such neglected Edgeworth novels as *Belinda* (1801) and *Patronage* (1814) introduces valuable new perspectives on Edgeworth's historical significance. In addition to being a most impressive feat of of scholarly exposition, the biography also contains an effective critical revaluation of its subject's works.

BUTLER further develops her critical assessment of Edgeworth in her 1975 essay. This work is the most judicious and intellectually searching account of Edgeworth's artistic achievements. The "War" in question is the ideological ferment created in English letters by the French Revolution. Ideological positions implicit in Edgeworth's fiction are discussed within the diverse context of contemporary fictional production. Edgeworth's liberalism and its influence on her fiction are analysed, the distinct character of her feminism is established, and her awareness of French thought and French conditions is outlined. A sense of the essentially public nature of Edgeworth's writing emerges from a revealing exposition of her early works, notably *Moral Tales* (1801). The essay concludes that "Maria Edgeworth is not Jane Austen, but she has a far sounder literary instinct than any other contemporary writer of prose fiction, until Scott".

HURST's monograph makes a somewhat similar case for Edgeworth's later career (1832–48): it is "an attempt through the life of one highly intelligent and observant woman to pinpoint many of the problems of those times, and not only from a particular United Kingdom angle, but from a general one relevant to a wider context then and now". Edgeworth added virtually nothing to her *oeuvre* in the years under review. But it was during that period that populist, democratic politics first made their presence felt in Ireland, under the leadership of Daniel O'Connell. Hurst's mention of the United-Kingdom angle is a reference to Edgeworth's aristocratic and Unionist politics. The changes in Irish social reality, which O'Connell threatened, concerned not only the political sphere but the economic system underlying it. The book carefully contextualises Edgeworth's comments on this period of marked uncertainty. In doing so, it charts not only the ideological interests and social destiny of the Edgeworth family, but provides a study of a class in crisis. Essentially historical rather than literary in approach, the work is a cogent account of Edgeworth's vigilant and level-headed analysis of social forces and political actuality. This analysis usefully supplements the sense of public-spiritedness and social harmony that underwrites most tellingly the plots of her Irish novels.

NEWCOMER's study, in contrast, is almost exclusively concerned with the theory and practice of Edgeworth's fiction. A brief biography is included, emphasising Edgeworth's literary origins. The novelist's fictional world is dealt with in detail, and the artistic strategies which typify her representation of it are also surveyed. This survey constitutes the theoretical element of the work, and draws on an essentially New-Critical approach. Edgeworth's contribution to the rise of the novel is interestingly clarified through an analysis of her fiction in the light of the adverse critical commentary that has been directed against it. The core of the study consists of a critical reading of key Edgeworth texts – *Patronage*, *Ormond*, and in particular *Castle Rackrent*, to which two chapters are devoted. Especially noteworthy in the treatment of *Castle Rackrent* is Newcomer's controversial view of its narrator, Thady Quirk. This reading of Thady makes this study one with which all subsequent critics must reckon.

OWENS' volume is a compilation of essays and extracts from a wide range of materials relevant to *Castle Rackrent*. The array of contributions underlines the achievement of Edgeworth's most celebrated work. Various approaches to the text are represented – linguistic, folkloric, historical, pedagogical, and moral. The editor's Introduction deals succinctly with relevant issues concerning the novel's sources, reception, and the "variety of perceptions to which *Castle Rackrent* has given rise". The work also contains a comprehensive annotated bibliography.

HARDEN's introductory study shows the influence of Butler's biography. Organised around the idea that education is central to all facets of Edgeworth's output, it provides a comprehensive overview of the complete *oeuvre*. A particular advantage of this approach is that usually overlooked works such as *Leonora* (1806) and *Manoeuvring* (1809) are dealt with, thereby facilitating a sense of the consistency of Edgeworth's fiction. This study's expository character, reliance on "traditional analysis", and substantial annotated bibliography make this work a useful starting place for students.

GEORGE O'BRIEN

Edwards, Jonathan 1703–1758

American prose writer

Cooey, Paula M., *Jonathan Edwards on Nature and Destiny: A Systematic Analysis*, Lewiston, New York, and Queenstown, Ontario: Edwin Mellen Press, 1985

Fiering, Norman, *Jonathan Edwards's Moral Thought and Its British Context*, Chapel Hill: University of North Carolina Press, 1981

Guelzo, Allen C., *Edwards on the Will: A Century of American Theological Debate*, Middletown, Connecticut: Wesleyan University Press, 1989

Holbrook, Clyde A., *The Ethics of Jonathan Edwards: Morality and Aesthetics*, Ann Arbor: University of Michigan Press, 1973

McDermott, Gerald R., *One Holy and Happy Society: The Public Theology of Jonathan Edwards*, University Park: Pennsylvania State University Press, 1992

Scheick, William J. (ed.), *Critical Essays on Jonathan Edwards*, Boston: G.K. Hall, 1980

The most studied of America's theologians, Jonathan Edwards has been discussed primarily in terms of intellectual and cultural history. Literary critics tended to approach him biographically, or as an influence on other writers, rather than as an author in his own right. This neglect slowly changed after 1949, when studies of Edwards's management of imagery, especially in his famous sermon "Sinners in the Hands of an Angry God", led to later considerations of his experiments in structure, especially in his contrived memoir known today as "Personal Narrative". Although Edwards is valued more for his theological thought than for his verbal management of this thought, there is today a better appreciation of the relationship between his beliefs and his literary strategies, including his editorial practices.

HOLBROOK reads Edwards as a theological objectivist – one who insists on the absolute primacy of God – rather than as a theological subjectivist – one who is concerned with security in the human sphere. Holbrook admits that his reading fails to explain every feature of Edwards's writings, including their "baffling" call for human effort. Holbrook's book is noteworthy for its attempt to systematize the ethical component of Edwardsean doctrine and for the emphasis it provided for McDermott's later study; but in its reductive, often dogmatic, approach it rhetorically dismisses anomalies in its argument and precariously sidesteps such important matters in Edwards's work as the nature of influence, of context, and of the self.

My own (SCHEICK's) anthology offers excerpts from a wide assortment of twentieth-century responses to Edwards. This book is divided into: sections on the factual and interpretive biographies of the theologian; discussions of Edwards's theological, philosophical, and historical thought; the influences on Edwards and his influence on others; and the nature of Edwardsean language and structure. The Introduction offers an overview of the directions in the commentary on the theologian as well as suggestions for future investigations.

FIERING provides a meticulous atomization of Edwards's sources, including Nicolas Malebranche, Samuel Clarke, and William Wallaston. He also revises the claim, evident in Holbrook's study, that Edwards restored the capricious *Deus absconditus* of early Calvinism, when in fact this understanding of the deity was not typical of Edwards, who rationally focused on the divine order and harmony inherent in creation. Fiering's findings result in a major revision, a systematization of Edwardsean thought, which, in contrast to Holbrook's approach, does not reduce or avoid the drifts and inconsistencies in the theologian's evolving ideas.

COOEY also tries to systematize Edwards's thought, unfortunately with less satisfying results than Fiering's effort. She finds that Edwards was less interested in sensible and sentient reality (nature) than in its creator, who is nonetheless manifested in the order and interelationships of the material world. For Edwards, Nature is the deity's act of self-communication aimed at fulfilling divine self-glorification. Cooey's interpretation of the theologian's view of nature is accurate, and so provides a good introduction to some basic Edwardsean concepts. However, she appears to be unaware that her interpretation cannot be advanced especially on Edwards's behalf, because the ideas she discloses are precisely those of Edwards's Puritan predecessors, who inherited them as part of the Augustinian tradition informing Reformed theology.

GUELZO presents a detailed intellectual history designed to refute the generally held notion, as seen in several entries in Scheick's volume, that Edwards's theology was highly influential in the subsequent development of American culture. Guelzo demonstrates not only how such followers as Timothy Dwight confiscated Edwards's authority but also how he and other New Divinity divines failed to carry on Edwards's heritage. Guelzo's study importantly challenges a common perception.

McDERMOTT, in response to Holbrook, explores Edwards's implicit social theory. McDermott specifically considers the role of America in the millennium, the place of patriotism, and the definition of proper citizenship in light of Edwards's advocacy of improvements in communal life. Edwards did not, however, anticipate America's Manifest Destiny policy, McDermott carefully observes; in fact, Edwards went against the grain of the emergent revolutionary consciousness of his time by pessimistically prophesying the probable failure of New England. McDermott has made the strongest possible case for Edwards's social views, although it remains a case necessarily dogged by the fact that the theologian's criticism of monarchical power and his interest in civil liberties were decidedly secondary in his thought.

WILLIAM J. SCHEICK

Elegy and Poetry of Death

Kay, Dennis, *Melodious Tears: The English Funeral Elegy from Spenser to Milton*, Oxford: Clarendon Press, 1990; New York: Oxford University Press, 1990

Pigman, G. W., III, *Grief and English Renaissance Elegy*, Cambridge and New York: Cambridge University Press, 1985

Ramazani, Jahan, *Yeats and the Poetry of Death: Elegy, Self-Elegy, and the Sublime*, New Haven, Connecticut, and London: Yale University Press, 1990

Ramazani, Jahan, *Poetry of Mourning: The Modern Elegy from Hardy to Heaney*, Chicago: University of Chicago Press, 1994

Sacks, Peter M., *The English Elegy: Studies in the Genre from Spenser to Yeats*, Baltimore: Johns Hopkins University Press, 1985

Smith, Eric, *By Mourning Tongues: Studies in English Elegy*, Ipswich, Suffolk: Boydell Press, 1977; Totowa, New Jersey: Rowman and Littlefield, 1977

The genre of elegy has received a good deal of critical attention in the last 20 years, in the form of a number of increasingly sophisticated studies.

PIGMAN's book offers an informed and lucid analysis of the shifts that characterise "attitudes towards mourning . . . during the English Renaissance". Drawing on a range of texts produced between the early sixteenth and seventeenth centuries – including "letter-writing treatises and moral-theological tracts" – Pigman shows how initial suppression of, and hostility toward, grief gradually yielded to an increasing emphasis on sympathy, toleration, and acknowledgement. Having established its broad cultural framework in the early chapters, the book goes on to develop a more literary and text-centred analysis of contemporary elegists from the Earl of Surrey and Edmund Spenser to Ben Jonson, Henry King, and John Milton. This is an accessible and useful study, which avoids the appearance of being programmatic through a willingness to challenge the critical and cultural narrative it constructs.

KAY's book is a hugely scholarly and illuminating account of the English funeral elegy in the Renaissance, with particular reference to examples of the genre from Spenser, Philip Sidney, John Donne, and Milton. Kay situates his analyses in the context of the cultural shifts produced by the Reformation, tracing the way in which the funeral elegy became an increasingly secularised mode defined by a variety of purposes which exceeded those related solely to questions of death and immortality. The genre is thus shown to function, for example, as a "laboratory in which [writers] learnt about composition" (and were able to display capacities for improvisation and innovation) or, again, as a medium of introspection. This is a wide-ranging and erudite study. Historically and critically informed, and copiously detailed, its arguments remain nonetheless both well-focused and engaging. The book also contains a still-valuable bibliography of studies in the field.

SMITH offers a "critical discussion of major English elegies" from those of Milton to Tennyson's. The emphasis of this ultimately somewhat pedestrian book is largely thematic and formalist. The opening chapter provides the terms of reference for the readings that follow, with expositions of "attitudes to time", "the role of nature", "the mourner and the mourned", and "patterns of consolation". Smith's main contention concerns the elegy as an "expressive monument" whose chief characteristic is its "duality": "the very process of ordering grief, whether real or imaginary, into a work of art may be the consolation", Smith writes, "the search for which is the ostensible subject of the poem". The critical shortcomings of the book are compounded – perhaps even produced – by its ahistorical approach, which turns historically and culturally specific texts into the bearers of messages about "the human condition".

A far more rewarding and sophisticated approach is taken by SACKS. While he acknowledges the force of poststructuralist arguments about "an essential lack . . . inscribed within language", he suggests that such arguments tend to diminish the lived pathos of "disjunction and loss" out of which the elegiac text is born. The book's first chapter offers a theoretically grounded interpretation, rather than description, of elegy's conventions. Sacks draws on psychoanalysis (in particular Freud's accounts of the Oedipus complex and "the work of mourning") in order to examine how "an elegist's language emerges from . . . an originating sense of loss" and the ways in which it struggles for forms of compensation. This important chapter is followed by close readings of individual texts from Spenser to W.B. Yeats. The book also includes a seemingly anomalous, but in fact pertinent, discussion of grief, revenge, and language in plays by Thomas Kyd and Shakespeare, and an Epilogue on the American elegy. This is an excellent and provocative study, which has proved influential in the field.

The central concern of RAMAZANI's 1990 book "lies", he tells us, "in interpreting the psychological, ontological, and rhetorical dimensions of Yeats's poetry of death and its informing genres". These genres – of elegy, "tragic joy and the sublime", and self-elegy – are insightfully discussed in the three long chapters on Yeats's major lyrics that form the book's core. Making use of contemporary critical theory, but devoted to "the difficulties of the poetry itself", Ramazani shows how that poetry can be construed in terms of a fundamental vacillation between "the repression of death and the avowal of its finality". As well as focusing on how Yeats responds to death (whether his own or that of others) as a "private experience" Ramazani makes the important point that any "thanatological" representation is always mediated by literary and cultural tradition. He also situates the poetry of Yeats's middle and late phases, equally importantly, in relation to the "dehumanizing" of death brought about by World War I and the increasing technological violence of twentieth-century history. This is one of the best studies of both the poetry of death and Yeats to have appeared in recent years.

RAMAZANI's brilliant 1994 study looks beyond Yeats to embrace a wide range of twentieth-century elegists located within a variety of culturally specific contexts – British, white American, and African-American. The book's most striking feature is the historicized nature of its argument. For Ramazani, the modern elegy – which includes poems by less obviously elegiac writers like Sylvia Plath and Langston Hughes – is defined, ironically, by its anti-elegiac tendencies. Sacks's model of the elegy as a consolatory genre, offering compensation for loss, is thus "inadequate for understanding twentieth-century elegies". These tend "not to achieve but to resist consolation, not to override but to sustain anger, not to heal but to reopen the wounds of loss". They are texts that remain, in large measure, violent, unresolved, and ambivalent. Yet as well as constructing such an opposition between "traditional" and "modern" elegy, Ramazani indicates how the former nonetheless persists, to various degrees, within the latter, exploring the work of Amy Clampitt and Seamus Heaney as examples of such a survival. In a brief but suggestive coda the book explores two contemporary non-literary elegiac forms – the Vietnam Veterans Memorial and the AIDS Memorial Quilt – as they "attest to the broad cultural need for active but nontranscendental sites of public mourning". This is, to date, the best analysis of twentieth-century elegy available and should be widely read.

CARL PLASA

Eliot, George 1819–1880

English novelist and essayist

Bennett, Joan, *George Eliot: Her Mind and Art*, Cambridge: Cambridge University Press, 1948

Cecil, David, *Early Victorian Novelists: Essays in Revaluation*, London: Constable & Co., 1934; Indianapolis, Indiana: Bobbs-Merrill, 1935

Dodd, Valerie A., *George Eliot: An Intellectual Life*, London: Macmillan, 1990; New York: St Martin's Press, 1990

Haight, Gordon (ed.), *A Century of George Eliot Criticism*, Boston: Houghton Mifflin, 1965; London: Methuen, 1966; New York: Oxford University Press, 1968

Haight, Gordon, *George Eliot: A Biography*, Oxford: Clarendon Press, 1968

Hardy, Barbara, *The Novels of George Eliot: A Study in Form*, London: Athlone Press, 1959, 2nd edition, 1963; New York: Oxford University Press, 1967

Harvey, W.J., *The Art of George Eliot*, London: Chatto & Windus, 1961; New York: Oxford University Press, 1962

Leavis, F.R., *The Great Tradition: George Eliot, Henry James, Joseph Conrad*, London: Chatto & Windus, 1948; New York: G.W. Stewart, 1948

Newton, K.M., *George Eliot*, London: Longman, 1991

Perkin, J. Russell, *A Reception History of George Eliot's Fiction*, Ann Arbor, Michigan: UMI Research Press, 1990

Shuttleworth, Sally, *George Eliot and Nineteenth-Century Science: The Make-Believe of a Beginning*, Cambridge and New York: Cambridge University Press, 1984

Welsh, Alexander, *George Eliot and Blackmail*, Cambridge, Massachusetts: Harvard University Press, 1985

The twentieth century was slow in coming to terms with the literary greatness of the Victorian period; envy, the snobbery of modernity, and sheer ignorance and stupidity all played a part. CECIL, in what later readers and critics might think a somewhat tepid defence of her, speaks of her standing as still comparatively low. Her reputation for intense seriousness, which for many incurious souls seemed to inhibit any appreciation of her earthy humour and deep knowledge of everyday life, delayed her rehabilitation longer than that of Charles Dickens and Anthony Trollope. Cecil's own stress on this moral seriousness was coupled with a certain impatience at her religious difficulties, and scepticism about her credulity in supposing that Ludwig Feuerbach could be a reliable guide to the separation of religion and morals. He was nevertheless impressed by the subtlety and many-sidedness of *Middlemarch*.

BENNETT's book was a cautious attempt at rehabilitation, by a tactful author anxious not to claim too much. She asserted, at a time when it was still fashionable to say that the early works were the best, the superiority of *Middlemarch* and *Daniel Deronda*; she admires them especially for their presentation of the long, unforeseen effects of time: in contrast to many novelists, Eliot studies long drawn-out consequences of forgotten or concealed actions.

George Eliot was one of five novelists in whom LEAVIS embodied his "Great Tradition". But although his critique of her consists of less than 100 pages, the book has a central importance both in the criticism of Eliot and in the general estimation of the novel form: in its lasting influence it may be compared to the prefaces of Henry James. Here, the apologetic, cautiously rehabilitating tone of Bennett gives way to a crusading affirmation of the moral and artistic value of the five novelists – Jane Austen, George Eliot, Henry James, Joseph Conrad, and D.H. Lawrence – proclaimed as embodying the "Tradition". Of these, only three – Eliot, James, and Conrad – are seriously discussed. But, writing on George Eliot, he conducts a weighty campaign against earlier valuations, especially those of David Cecil. Quoting his "she admired truthfulness, chastity and industry and self-restraint, she disapproved of loose living and recklessness and deceit and self-indulgence", he confesses to "sharing these beliefs, admirations and disapprovals . . . they seem to me favourable to the production of great literature". "There is nothing", he goes on, "restrictive or timid about her ethical habit". His admiration is not undiscriminating; he rejects sometimes what had previously been admired (for instance, the "soulful side" of Maggie Tulliver in *The Mill on the Floss*), and, much more questionably, the whole Jewish plot of *Daniel Deronda*, proposing a truncation of the novel into a study of Gwendolen Harleth. He is critical, with fair justice, of authorial self-indulgence in the treatment of Dorothea Brooke and Ladislaw in *Middlemarch*, but salutes the "magnificent achievement of the novel as a whole", while putting in a shrewd plea for the virtues of the neglected *Felix Holt*.

HARDY, writing in 1959 (second edition, 1963), saw the Jamesian theory of novel form, especially as celebrated in Percy Lubbock's influential *The Craft of Fiction* (1921), as the great obstacle to full recognition of Eliot's greatness. Her art is seen "as complex and as subtle as the composition of Henry James or Proust or Joyce, but very much less conspicuous". Endorsing Eliot's own idea of aesthetic teaching as resulting in an extension of sympathies, she enters a firm defence of the device of the omniscient author. Direct addresses to the reader, when cleverly handled – she concedes that in the early works they are not always so – lead to "thematic intensification", and enhance the value of dramatic scenes. She sees her artistic development as moving "from the ordinary man struggling with tragedy to the extraordinary man struggling with ordinary life". Her most valuable and original insights relate to patterns of imagery. She has detailed and illuminating accounts of, among others, the mirror image in *Adam Bede*, water images in *The Mill on the Floss* and *Middlemarch*, and animal images in *Daniel Deronda*. The book was significant, too, for what it did not need to say; here, as in most later studies, the greatness of Eliot could be taken for granted. She had been elevated once again to a status almost, though not quite, as high as she had been accorded by the late Victorian élite.

HARVEY's approach is in some ways similar to Hardy's. He is equally sceptical of Henry James's theorizing, and sharply critical of his account of George Eliot. His is the most balanced and discriminating account of her use of the omniscient author convention, though he can be fiercely dismissive of inept critics like George Steiner. On Chapter 17 of *Adam Bede*, a *locus classicus* of the omniscient author, he can almost, for a moment, sound like a Jamesian, when he says: "the reader is repelled by having his actions determined for him; he feels himself, and not the character, to be a puppet manipulated by the author". But he gives an able defence of the author's presence in *Middlemarch*, saying that the moral comments are "essential to George Eliot's purpose, both moral and aesthetic, and to that mode of contemplation which . . . is the right relationship of reader to novel". In *Felix Holt*, and especially in *Middlemarch*, he finds a fruitfully ironic use of the omniscient author convention itself, comparing it to Chaucer's self-mockery in *The Canterbury Tales*. His analysis of the author's treatment of time, her arousal and disappointment of expectations, and her use of coincidence, are all subtle, original, and valuable.

HAIGHT is one of the most assiduous and devoted of Eliot scholars, and the editor of her letters. His 1968 biography is not notably distinguished as a critical study, but is valuable for its accurate analysis of personal factors affecting the production of each work, including the influence and interaction of George Henry Lewes and of her publishers. He demonstrates that careful preparation and note-taking form part of her method in her early "spontaneous" work, just as much as in *Romola* and later works. By judicious use of both Eliot's own letters and those she received, he contrives to bring us as near as we can hope to be to the process of creation.

HAIGHT (1965) also selected shrewdly from a century of criticism. Of particular interest is the fierce controversy about the character of Stephen Guest in *The Mill on the Floss*. The judicious masculine distaste of Leslie Stephen, the sly, cautious innuendoes of Henry James, and the vitriolic rhetoric of A.C. Swinburne all gain added interest from their juxtaposition. The influence of the whirligig of time on reputation is well illustrated by a quotation, which asserted in 1934 that Eliot's reputation was lower than that of Charlotte Brontë (a barely credible judgement), while a too-short extract from John Holloway's *The Victorian Sage* links Eliot with the philosophical speculation of her time.

SHUTTLEWORTH's study is useful in showing the imaginative influence of wide scientific reading. Charles Lyell (perhaps the scientist most generally influential in the work of great Victorian writers), J.S. Mill, Auguste Comte, and Herbert Spencer all receive full treatment. An interesting unpublished Eliot essay is quoted as showing her reflections on Darwinian mutation: "fortunate irregularities are discoveries in art; they are stages in its development". However, Shuttleworth exaggerates her distance from fictional tradition in the writing of *Daniel Deronda*, saying that "it does not adhere to the convention of spatial or temporal continuity". This is to underrate the technical originality of her predecessors, especially Dickens.

WELSH's study is the most fascinating and original contribution to Eliot studies for many years, but also, in some ways, a perverse one. If blackmail seems a limiting subject for a long book, the reader of the whole is likely to be satisfied that by involving it in secrecy, guilt, shame, repentance, and amendment, the author has succeeded in finding material for a weighty book. Yet certain persistent obsessions, with Alfred Hitchcock's films, with Freudian psychoanalysis, mar the subtlety and strength of many interesting passages. To call Deronda "a lay analyst and a poor one" is to confuse categories; a much closer analogy to the relation of Deronda and Gwendolen would be that of confessor and penitent. Questionable, too, is Welsh's attempt to find a direct influence of personal guilt in her treatment of her characters' guilt. But an excellent feature of the book is the close study of the impact of strangers and interlopers (Marner, Bulstrode, Lydgate) on well-knit, traditional societies, where everyone knows who everyone's grandfather was.

DODD's study concentrates on the intellectual formation that Eliot experienced before commencing as a novelist in the late 1850s. This is of particular value in Eliot's case, because she was so learned and intellectual, because she was already well-known before she first appeared (with her identity at first concealed) as a novelist, and because there is often a hidden philosophical aspect in her narratives.

PERKIN's reception history is a useful handbook. NEWTON emphasises the influence of Thomas Carlyle in a careful study of philosophical structure. Personal memory is stressed, perhaps overstressed. Not everyone would agree that in *Silas*

Marner we see "alienation and lack of identity caused by the loss of formative memory". It may be noted that in the whole history of Eliot criticism, *Silas Marner* has presented critics with issues of peculiar difficulty, because different parts seem to demand different critical methods. Newton's summarizing phrase, that George Eliot was a "romantic humanist", though controversial is sensibly argued.

Compared with that of some great writers (Milton and Dickens, for instance), the critical history of George Eliot is curiously homogeneous. Her reputation has oscillated, certainly, but the best critical work has not needed to refute or undermine the conclusions of earlier workers; the broad outlines of critical judgement were settled long ago, and have not been challenged. But there has been a notable development in relevant information, and in subtlety and refinement.

A.O.J. COCKSHUT

Eliot, T.S. 1888–1965

American-born English poet, dramatist, critic, and editor

Ackroyd, Peter, *T.S. Eliot: A Life*, London: Hamish Hamilton, 1984; New York: Simon & Shuster, 1984
Bagchee, Shyamal (ed.), *T.S. Eliot: A Voice Descanting: Centenary Essays*, London: Macmillan, 1990
Bush, Ronald (ed.), *T.S. Eliot: The Modernist in History*, Cambridge and New York: Cambridge University Press, 1991
Clarke, Graham (ed.), *T.S. Eliot: Critical Assessments*, 4 vols., London: Christopher Helm, 1990
Crawford, Robert, *The Savage and the City in the Work of T.S. Eliot*, Oxford: Clarendon Press, 1987; New York: Oxford University Press, 1987
D'Ambrosio, Vinnie-Marie, *Eliot Possessed: T.S. Eliot and FitzGerald's "Rubáiyát"*, New York: New York University Press, 1989
Eliot, Valerie (ed.), *The Letters of T.S. Eliot: Volume 1, 1898–1922*, London: Faber & Faber, 1988; San Diego, California: Harcourt Brace Jovanovich, 1988
Ellmann, Maud, *The Poetics of Impersonality: T.S. Eliot and Ezra Pound*, Brighton, Sussex: Harvester Press, 1987; Cambridge, Massachusetts: Harvard University Press, 1987
Gordon, Lyndall, *Eliot's Early Years*, Oxford and New York: Oxford University Press, 1977
Gordon, Lyndall, *Eliot's New Life*, Oxford and New York: Oxford University Press, 1988
Lobb, Edward (ed.), *Words in Time: New Essays on Eliot's "Four Quartets"*, London: Athlone Press, 1993
Longenbach, James, *Modernist Poetics of History: Pound, Eliot and the Sense of the Past*, Princeton, New Jersey: Princeton University Press, 1987
Manganiello, Dominic, *T.S. Eliot and Dante*, London: Macmillan, 1989
Moody, A.D., *Thomas Stearns Eliot: Poet*, Cambridge: Cambridge University Press, 1979
Murray, Paul, *T.S. Eliot and Mysticism: The Secret History of "Four Quartets"*, London: Macmillan, 1991
Olney, James (ed.), *T.S. Eliot: Essays from "The Southern Review"*, Oxford: Clarendon Press, 1988; New York: Oxford University Press, 1988
Reeves, Gareth, *T.S. Eliot: A Virgilian Poet*, London: Macmillan, 1989
Ricks, Christopher, *T.S. Eliot and Prejudice*, London: Faber & Faber, 1988; Berkeley: University of California Press, 1988
Schwartz, Robert L., *"Broken Images": A Study of "The Waste Land"*, Lewisburg, Pennsylvania: Bucknell University Press, 1989
Shusterman, Richard, *T.S. Eliot and the Philosophy of Criticism*, London: Duckworth, 1988
Sigg, E.W., *The American T.S. Eliot: A Study of the Early Writings*, Cambridge and New York: Cambridge University Press, 1989
Southam, B.C., *A Student's Guide to the Selected Poetry of T.S. Eliot*, London and Boston: Faber & Faber, 1968, 6th edition, 1994
Stead, C.K., *Pound, Yeats, Eliot and the Modernist Movement*, London: Macmillan, 1986; New Brunswick, New Jersey: Rutgers University Press, 1986

Since the centenary of Eliot's birth (1988), the major issues in Eliot criticism have been redefined. There is currently an immense amount of secondary material, and still disagreement on vital matters, but recent studies have moved away from the New-Critical stance encouraged by Eliot's own poetics to assume a variety of perspectives.

ACKROYD's biography is a remarkable study, given that the Eliot estate withheld permission to quote from published work or unpublished correspondence. The tone is disinterested and judgements impartial, the book deriving its strength partly from the deftness of Ackroyd's literary insight but also from his dispassionate treatment of the major trauma of Eliot's life, the marriage to Vivien and its tragic breakdown. Ackroyd is good on such matters as the daily routine of Eliot's later life and editorial work. He understands Eliot's poetics and polemics, and has an eye for the devastating detail – for instance, a curious item in Vivien's *Notebook* (but in Eliot's hand) about the sterility and crudity of the relationship between man and woman as opposed to the subtlety of that between man and cat. Ackroyd's is not the last word on its subject, but should remain the standard account until an authorised version is commissioned.

The two studies by GORDON complement Ackroyd well. As she notes in her 1988 volume, the idea that Eliot's poetry is rooted in private aspects of his life is now more generally accepted than when her first book was written, and when Eliot's doctrine of impersonality prevailed. Unlike Ackroyd, she could quote from copyright materials, and although her intent is primarily biographical her readings are incisive and intelligent. Gordon largely achieves her declared goal of chronicling the growth of the poet's mind. Her sense, in the first study, of Eliot's early years as "an interrupted journey towards sainthood", while metaphorically extreme, may be yet the best way of relating the life to the literature; and her exegesis of the *vita nuova* in the second, with its account of Eliot's relationship with Emily Hale, is compelling and compassionate. She sees a pattern of spiritual autobiography beginning as early as 1910, shaped by "unattended moments" as recorded in the poetry; and her second volume deals movingly with the personal qualities of the later drama. Gordon's strength lies in her lucidity and scrupulous documentation, and her metaphor of Eliot's life as a spiritual journey disrupted by Ezra Pound and marriage(s) can be ignored only if her reliance on unpublished materials is discounted.

Valerie ELIOT, who earlier edited the manuscript of *The Waste Land* (1971), is also editor of Eliot's *Letters*. Her credentials are impeccable: an intimate knowledge of Eliot, an exacting standard of scholarship, and access to everything that matters. The result is an illuminating account of the years 1888–1922, and the promise of an equally compelling one to follow. The letters extend the understanding of Eliot into the private dimension, while the inclusion of several by, and about, Vivien supports Eliot's comment (cited in the Introduction) that the marriage brought her no happiness and him the state of mind out of which came *The Waste Land*. The letters have led not to a radical revaluation of the poetry but to an enriching of what is known. Fascinating in their own right, for the trivial as much as the profound, they are an indispensable part of the life. The only caveat might be that they are still but a selection, the editor's choice being absolute, with veils (some drawn by Eliot himself) over certain areas of the experience.

In a category of its own is CLARKE. This comprises some 1,900 pages and 254 articles, ranging from early reviews to recent critiques. Volume I contains memoirs, interviews, and responses by Eliot's contemporaries; Volume II concentrates on *The Waste Land* and early poems; Volume III, the religious poetry and drama; Volume IV, criticism and general studies. There are some significant omissions because of copyright complexities, but it is a remarkable compendium that brings together almost everything of lasting merit in the tradition of Eliot criticism.

SOUTHAM's *Guide*, currently in its sixth edition, does not go beyond *Ash-Wednesday*, but has helped countless students untangle the earlier poems. The notes are brief but lucid, intended for the reader responsive to the poetry but baffled by its difficulty. They claim not so much originality (many derive from the scholarship of others) as convenience of reference and common sense. The Introduction is sound, covering aspects of biography, textual history, and interpretation, yet cautioning restraint with source-hunting and allusion. There are minor omissions, but as a students' guide Southam will remain a reliable standard text.

MOODY combines intricate background and textual detail with an assertion of the primacy of the poetry and a defence of impersonality (he cites Eliot as saying that men of letters should emulate small marine creatures whose skeletons contribute to coral islands: "like these obscure little creatures, it is only what we leave behind that matters"). His is an excellent account of the formative years, and he shows how *The Waste Land* transmutes private agonies into something rich and strange. Moody isolates "the nuclei of direct experience" at the heart of the poem, and derives internal coherence from the relationship of other parts to these. His analysis of the Hyacinth garden passage forms the heart of his reading, for he sees that moment of pure feeling as compelling the poet's conscious analysis of his experience. He does justice to the intensity of Eliot's wit and feeling, as well as to the nightmare world of the poem; and he shows how an individual sensibility became the expression of a wider cultural crisis. Although sensitive to how Dante provides the forms for Eliot's feeling, and appreciative of the music of poetry, Moody is less at ease with the religious poetry. His discussion of Eliot's Christian society is critical of its theocratic absolutism, and he is not vitally concerned with the drama. Moody's strength is close reading backed by scrupulous detail, and his conviction that Eliot was indeed a Poet.

STEAD sees Eliot's development as a movement towards Imagism, in which Pound's maieutic role was crucial. He is unhappy with the old orthodoxy (Brooks, Williamson, Smith) who rely (he feels) too much on "meaning"; but he also attacks Gordon's sense of the "personal and confessional" poet. He sees *The Waste Land* as a balanced work, drawing ("no doubt") on the private life, but finding the right kind of objective correlative to achieve the impersonality Eliot's poetics required. Stead traces the affinities of Eliot's verse with symbolism, as the symbolist impulse became sharply focused in the single image or line. Like Moody, Stead is less appreciative of the later poetry (he dismisses *Four Quartets* as a kit-set poem, for academics to take apart), feeling Eliot's language to be increasingly atrophied here. He affirms his faith in modernism as the principal poetic movement of the century, but a faith under threat, as instanced in his image of Pound emerging as the lone ant from the broken anthill of Europe, holding on to those poetic principles which Eliot in his later writings had compromised. Good as he is, Stead may be fighting a rearguard battle for his own poetic, and the study is curiously dated, the kind that should have appeared a decade earlier when a modernist critic was required to swear primary allegiance to Pound.

CRAWFORD contends that the linking of the primitive and barbaric with the most sophisticatedly urban forms the fascinating, enduring, and potent aspect of Eliot's achievement, and he uses the metaphor of "primitive terror" to throw light (and darkness) upon the works between "Prufrock" and *The Waste Land*. A strength of his book is that its key points seem later so obvious – St Louis as the gateway to a Wild West; James Thomson as guide to the City of Dreadful Night; symbolist primitivism in King Bolo ("a savage in a bowler hat"); the lure of jazz and the jungle; Eliot's praise of Stravinsky. Crawford is excellent on the discredited anthropological climate of the age, and reinstates Jessie Weston, Sir James Frazer, and Jane Harrison as lasting influences upon Eliot. He discusses *Sweeney Agonistes*, asserting its continuities with earlier work and sensing how Eliot's anthropological impulse responded to personal pressures through ritual, combining the comedy of music-hall with the underlying cruelty of Greek drama. Crawford notes a conscious renunciation of the theme of savage and city after 1927, in that the later works deal with death and life but not copulation; even so, he detects in the auditory imagination an atavistic sense of primitive rhythms.

MURRAY's study of *Four Quartets* offers a thoroughly documented discussion of Eliot's mysticism. Murray is excellent on the Augustinian echoes, varieties of mystical experience, the "language of paradox" in St John of the Cross, and other doctrines of transcendence; he is sensitive to music, stillness, meditation, and art; and he confronts the technical problem of translating mystical insight into poetical form. His is an essential introduction to the *Quartets*, despite a dry style and tendency to over-intellectualise: one might (perhaps unfairly) desire less knowledge and more of the poetical experience.

The current debate over *Four Quartets* is summarised in LOBB's collection of essays. The recurrent theme is "the poetics of discourse" and the difficulties of devising procedures in response to Eliot's discursive mode. Some of the essays (Donoghue, Litz) do not avoid recycling the already known, and others (Lobb, Gordon, Kearns) essentially restate their authors' previous themes. Levenson's treatment of Eliot's spatialization of time, whatever its insights into tradition, curiously omits all reference to the Incarnation; and nowhere is there a sustained account of musical form. One essay stands out: Ronald Schuchard's "Eliot, Herbert and the Way to 'Little Gidding'", with its incisive analysis of the Devotional poets and their "personal quality", is a compelling introduction to the final poem.

Since the centenary, many other collections have appeared. Those edited by Bush, Bagchee, and Olney typify the trends. BUSH's theme of "The Modernist in History" loosely links selected papers from a Californian conference, and although there are some fine touches (Gordon on the American background of "The Dry Salvages") the overall quality is unimpressive. BAGCHEE is also erratic. He claims in his Editor's Note that the image of modernism prevailing in the postmodern consciousness is ominously spectral rather than benignly old-fashioned, there being something of the Bloomian slaying of precursors in its revaluation of the canon. The essays scrutinise Eliot in terms of a postmodern sensibility: some of them (Cuddy, Murphy) are in danger of evaporating into truisms; others (Shusterman, Altieri) refocus provocatively traditional problems of impersonality and objectivity; and yet others (Singh, Needham) catch disconcertingly the sense of being between two worlds. OLNEY's essays from *The Southern Review* represent the best insights of the 1980s. Olney states that recent work on Eliot has attempted to restore the proper sense of personality to the poetry, and the essays illustrate his point: Gross's "The Figure of Saint Sebastian" sees in *The Waste Land* a sado-masochistic outlook, which also finds expression in *The Cocktail Party*; Schuchard's "Eliot and the Horrific Moment" defines Eliot's "poetics of horror"; Brooker's "Substitutes for Christianity" traces the process by which Eliot came to Faith; and Perl's "The Significance of T.S. Eliot's Philosophical Notebooks" accounts for the deep vein of scepticism in Eliot's religious thought. This collection has become an important forum in the debate between traditional scholarship and the postmodern, and has made many scholars realise the latter simply will not go away.

Several specialist studies have appeared recently, some of dubious merit. SIGG reads the early poetry by the light of F.H. Bradley to find "a nineteenth century aestheticist American sensibility", but Sigg ignores the French connections and is insensitive to dramatic context or linguistic decorum. SCHWARTZ annotates *The Waste Land*, but is critically naive and uneven in his insights. ELLMANN's much-acclaimed study suggests that *The Waste Land* embodies a rhetoric of disembodiment and stages the ritual of its own destruction; but her sense of the poem as "a cacophony beyond control" might be applied (uncharitably) to her own reading, because excessive use of jargon and silly verbal play ("abject" and "object", "waste" as excremental catharsis, "Ezra" as an inversion of "arse") fundamentally obscures the commentary.

Yet there have been excellent specialist studies as well. D'AMBROSIO uses the indebtedness of "Gerontion" to A.C. Benson's Life of Edward FitzGerald to inquire into the image of the little old man and the way that figure grew into "an archetype linked to the myths of racial memory", as in Tiresias. Excellent on the juvenalia and minor poetry, notably "Animula", this study of the lasting influence of the *Rubáiyát of Omar Khayam* on Eliot's sensibility is a curiously compelling piece of criticism in a minor key. LONGENBACH approaches Eliot in the spirit of modern historicism, presenting the Bradleyan paradox that the past composes a simultaneous order because it exists only in the present, and exploring the problematical relationship between individual interpreter and the past. REEVES documents perhaps too fully Eliot's sense of Virgil, showing how Eliot's changing vision of religion and politics led to the emblematic conception of Virgil as adventist Christian in the later writings. And MANGANIELLO, though his study is a little dessicated, offers a satisfactory account of Eliot's chief literary mentor.

Two excellent traditional studies will conclude this essay. SHUSTERMAN places Eliot in his intellectual milieu, invoking the standards of Bertrand Russell and G.E. Moore against those of Bradley. He traces Eliot's theoretical development from the intitial attraction to, and analytical revolt against, Bradley towards a wider historicist view. Clear and compelling, professional in his philosophy, and sensitive in his reading, Shusterman accounts for the analytic and objective component of Eliot's early thought, the change towards subjectivity during the 1920s, and the pragmatic elements of Eliot's philosophy of criticism throughout his life. His is a sceptical inquiry, which affirms the importance of both traditional analysis and hermeneutics, yet argues by example that there will always be room for reinterpretation of Eliot in terms of contemporary perspectives.

RICKS's study of Eliot and prejudice is a great moral essay. Ricks confronts the paradox of the unpleasantness of much great poetry by examining the assumptions built into the "ordinary" use of language, and discerning in Eliot a self-scepticism, which distinguishes art from rhetoric. Anti-semitism is addressed in a compelling yet dispassionate way. Ricks analyses Eliot's "queasy, resentful feelings about Jews", as exemplified by such poems as "Gerontion" and the unpublished "Dirge" ("the ugliest touch of anti-semitism in Eliot's poetry"). He cites Eliot's infamous comment in *After Strange Gods* that "reasons of race and religion combine to make any large number of free-thinking Jews undesirable. . . . And a spirit of excessive tolerance is to be deprecated", noting that Eliot's later attempts to qualify it are not persuasive. The study is remarkable for the quality of rhetorical analysis through which Ricks analyses not only the nature of prejudice (in Eliot and others), but the role of punctuation, stress and accent ("assassination by intonation") in conveying subtleties of meaning. Ricks is not polemical, but acutely responsive to the way that language creates prejudicial effects. This may be old-fashioned criticism, the play of sensibility among words and nuances, but it is a book that fascinates, absorbs, and makes one appreciate how much an acute critical intelligence can add to the words of the poet.

CHRIS ACKERLEY

Elizabethan Literature *see* British Literature: Renaissance

Ellison, Ralph 1914–1994

American novelist and essayist

Benston, Kimberly W. (ed.), *Speaking for You: The Vision of Ralph Ellison*, Washington, D.C.: Howard University Press, 1987
Bloom, Harold (ed.), *Ralph Ellison*, New York: Chelsea House, 1986
Hersey, John (ed.), *Ralph Ellison: A Collection of Critical Essays*, Englewood Cliffs, New Jersey: Prentice-Hall, 1974
Lynch, Michael F., *Creative Revolt: A Study of Wright, Ellison and Dostoevsky*, New York: Peter Lang, 1990
Nadel, Alan, *Invisible Criticism: Ralph Ellison and the American Canon*, Iowa City: University of Iowa Press, 1988
O'Meally, Robert (ed.), *New Essays on "Invisible Man"*, Cambridge and New York: Cambridge University Press, 1988
Tanner, Tony, *City of Words: American Fiction 1950–1970*, London: Jonathan Cape, 1971; New York: Harper & Row, 1971

After the publication of *Invisible Man* in 1952, Ralph Ellison became one of the most conspicuous figures in the realm of American literary criticism. Early scholarship, which was dominated by dissertations, articles, and book chapters, established a foundation upon which a number of essay collections and single-author book-length studies have appeared. The publication of two volumes of essays by Ellison, *Shadow and Act* (1964) and *Going to the Territory* (1986), consolidated his position as a key figure in American letters and the cultural politics of race. In the Introduction to her collection, Kimberly Benston remarks on a schism that characterizes academic responses to Ellison's writing: it tends, she suggests, "to collect at either of two extremes: descriptive-aesthetic and prescriptive ideological". Another consideration is the universal enthusiasm with which Ellison's work is greeted. The most stimulating contributions to Ellison scholarship are often those that aim to bridge the artificial divide between formal and political questions, and to avoid the eclipse of critical analysis by critical appreciation.

The centrepiece to NADEL's fascinating study is the proposition that *Invisible Man* is "deeply framed and informed by the issue of 'canonicity', of how to speak to and through tradition without sacrificing the speaker's voice or denying the tradition it attempts to engage". Nadel argues convincingly that Ellison explores the institutionalization and suppression of voices through a radical use of literary allusion. In a critique that sustains a fruitful balance between close, textual scrutiny and large-scale cultural and theoretical concerns, Nadel investigates Ellison's intertextual references to Ralph Waldo Emerson, Herman Melville, Mark Twain, and Lewis Mumford, in relation to contemporary critical debates surrounding ethnocentrism and logocentrism, and marginality and decentring. The argument in this investigation is consistently inventive without being overly ingenious, and Nadel uses technical terminology to supplement his ideas rather than as a substitute for them. This volume is demanding and rewarding in roughly equal measures, and undoubtedly constitutes one of the most substantial contributions to Ellison scholarship produced to date.

In his influential survey of mainstream American fiction in the mid-twentieth century, TANNER devotes a chapter to Ellison's work, entitled "The Music of Invisibility". Tanner's fundamental proposal is that *Invisible Man*, "so far from being limited to an expression of anguish and injustice experienced peculiarly by Negroes, is quite simply the most profound novel about American identity written since the war". The fact that this essay has been reprinted in the collections edited by Hersey and Bloom is a testament to the value attributed to this contention by some critics. Here Tanner argues that prose fiction published between 1950 and 1970 was essentially preoccupied with the collision between the "individual" and various "systems". Within this context certain configurations are repeated: structural opposition between forms of "fixity" and "fluidity"; a quest for an "unpatterned, unconditioned life"; and a variety of stylistic subversions performed by the writers, which mirror the non-conformism of their primary characters. Tanner attempts to fix each individual novel he examines, including *Invisible Man*, into this thematic system. Consequently, the reading of Ellison's work in this volume privileges generalized "themes", particularly in the shape of "binary oppositions", over the social specificity favoured by some subsequent critics, such as Nadel. Tanner's lack of interest in determinants of individual identity such as race, class, and gender, as well as the associated systems of white hegemony, patriarchy, and capitalism, may be a product of his overall preoccupation with the work of white, male, middle-class writers.

LYNCH's study is based upon the contention that there is a fundamental synchronicity between the worldview expressed in canonical nineteenth-century Russian fiction and that in mid-twentieth-century black American fiction, especially in relation to the concepts of individual responsibility and "creative revolt". This contention is elucidated through detailed cross-textual analysis of *Invisible Man*, Richard Wright's *Native Son* and "The Man Who Lived Underground", and Dostoevsky's *Notes from Underground*, *The Devils*, and *The Brothers Karamazov*. Lynch draws particular attention to the "redemptive and even sacramental character of suffering", which he believes is central to these works. As in Tanner's essay, there is a drift in Lynch away from the subject of racial identity towards the question of identity *per se* and its associated philosophical, spiritual, and aesthetic concerns. Lynch defines Ellison's position in terms of an antagonism towards naturalism in the aesthetic sphere, materialism in the political sphere, and collectivism in the social sphere. At the core of this reading there is the assumption that such positions owe less to the material conditions confronted by Ellison as a black American writer than to the direct influence of Dostoevsky.

The four most noteworthy and stimulating collections of essays on Ellison have been edited by Hersey, Bloom, O'Meally, and Benston. HERSEY's collection contains a representative sample of critical responses to *Invisible Man* produced between the mid-1960s and the early 1970s. Many of the contributors echo the Tanner thesis (included in the volume) that "Ellison speaks for all men when he probes the questions of non-identified existence and the total human identity". An extract from Irving Howe's *A World More Attractive*, in which Howe criticizes Ellison for departing from the tradition of modern black protest fiction in the mould of Wright and James Baldwin, represents a rare and significant departure from the general tone of the volume.

BLOOM's collection offers a sound introduction to some of the most influential readings of the author's work. Most of the mainstays of Ellison scholarship are covered here – the use of intertextuality, jazz, and African-American folklore. There is only one original piece in the volume, but it does represent a discerning synthesis of articles dispersed through the field.

O'MEALLY's collection gravitates towards the aesthetic and philosophical wing of Ellison criticism. In his Introduction, O'Meally applauds the critical tradition of approaching *Invisible Man* "not as some sort of demonstration but as a work of art", without endeavouring to explain how the aesthetic and the political dimensions of a text can be disentangled. "*New Essays*", while not strictly a misnomer, does deflect from the fact that many of the subjects addressed in this volume are remarkably similar to those addressed during the previous 30 years of criticism of *Invisible Man*. However, this still represents an accessible and comprehensive introduction to the novel.

Initially the most impressive aspect to BENSTON's collection is the sheer breadth of critical materials gathered together in a single volume. Readings are offered by no less than 30 contributors, in the form of critical explication, biography, letters, poetic homages, and interviews. The collection is divided into six sections: biography; readings of *Shadow and Act*; myth, ideology and aesthetics; literary tradition; reinterpretations of *Invisible Man*; and a comprehensive bibliography. Given the sheer number, range, and generally high quality of the materials collected here, this is clearly the most extensive and useful collection on Ellison currently available.

BRIAN JARVIS

Emerson, Ralph Waldo 1803–1882

American prose writer and poet

Barish, Evelyn, *Emerson: The Roots of Prophecy*, Princeton, New Jersey: Princeton University Press, 1989
Buell, Lawrence (ed.), *Ralph Waldo Emerson: A Collection of Critical Essays*, Englewood Cliffs, New Jersey: Prentice-Hall, 1993
Cady, Edwin, and Louis J. Budd (eds.), *On Emerson*, Durham, North Carolina: Duke University Press, 1988
Cavell, Stanley, *Conditions Handsome and Unhandsome: The Constitution of Emersonian Perfectionism*, Chicago: University of Chicago Press, 1990
Cayton, Mary Kupiec, *Emerson's Emergence: Self and Society in the Transformation of New England, 1800–1845*, Chapel Hill: University of North Carolina Press, 1989
Gougeon, Len, *Virtue's Hero: Emerson, Antislavery, and Reform*, Athens: University of Georgia Press, 1989
Greenberg, Robert M., *Splintered Worlds: Fragmentation and the Ideal of Diversity in the Work of Emerson, Melville, Whitman, and Dickinson*, Boston: Northeastern University Press, 1993
Hodder, Alan D., *Emerson's Rhetoric of Revelation: Nature, the Reader, and the Apocalypse Within*, University Park: Pennsylvania State University Press, 1988
Michael, John, *Emerson and Skepticism: The Cipher of the World*, Baltimore: Johns Hopkins University Press, 1987
Mott, Wesley T., *"The Strains of Eloquence": Emerson and His Sermons*, University Park: Pennsylvania State University Press, 1989
Poirier, Richard, *The Renewal of Literature: Emersonian Reflections*, New York: Random House, 1987; London: Faber & Faber, 1988
Porte, Joel, *In Respect to Egotism: Studies in American Romantic Writing*, Cambridge and New York: Cambridge University Press, 1991
Richardson, Robert D., Jr., *Emerson: The Mind on Fire*, Berkeley: University of California Press, 1995
Robinson, David M., *Emerson and the Conduct of Life: Pragmatism and Ethical Purpose in the Later Work*, New York: Cambridge University Press, 1993
Sealts, Merton M., Jr., *Emerson on the Scholar*, Columbia: University of Missouri Press, 1992
Stack, George J., *Nietzsche and Emerson: An Elective Affinity*, Athens: Ohio University Press, 1992
Van Leer, David, *Emerson's Epistemology: The Argument of the Essays*, Cambridge and New York: Cambridge University Press, 1986

Emerson has been a central figure in the intellectual history of America since the mid-1830s, and studies of him are numerous; this discussion therefore concentrates on commentaries published recently. Of earlier biographical and critical interpretations, two in particular must be acknowledged – Stephen Whicher's *Freedom and Fate: The Inner Life of Ralph Waldo Emerson* (1953), the best version of the development of Emerson's ideas, and Jonathan Bishop's *Emerson on the Soul* (1964), which remains one of the finest explicatory studies of Emerson's thought.

Positive latter-day views of Emerson see him as the embodiment of the spiritual conscience of nineteenth-century America, whose message – as contained in his *Essays* and *Journals* – has profound implications for the quality of American life through to the present day. Adversarial views see him as a self-absorbed thinker, whose ideas promulgated the urge towards rampant individualism in the American psyche. Debates about him circulate around these competing views, and around the effort to relate the other-worldly philosophical nature of his writings to the work of his contemporaries in America and Europe. In the most commendatory view he is regarded as the father of nineteenth- and twentieth-century American thought, whose impact on his artistic and intellectual contemporaries and successors has been immense. Over the past few years the major impulse of Emerson commentary has been to show the depth of his commitment to the political and moral issues of his day, and to see his philosophy as more pragmatic and less esoteric than used to be the case.

BARISH has written the foremost intellectual biography of Emerson's early years, using family documents, correspondence, and Emerson's early journals and letters to uncover the foundations of his intellectual convictions, read against the background of his personal and cultural surroundings. She is particularly interesting on the role of certain women in Emerson's life, particularly his mother Ruth and his aunt Mary Moody, and she shows how the poverty of Emerson's early years bred in him the discipline and virtue of self-denial and a responsiveness to the charity of others, conditions which played their part in the development of his concept of "self-reliance". RICHARDSON is Emerson's most recent biographer, but this is less a life-and-times study than an account of Emerson's inner life, developed through a reading of the writers Emerson himself read and the records he kept of his studies in the *Journals*. Richardson shows the impact of ancient and modern European philosophers on Emerson, and reveals the extent of his familiarity with Asian religion and literature. Through these means Richardson brings to life the intellectual and spiritual intensity of Emerson's thought as it came to fruition in his writings.

ROBINSON is one of the most admired of present-day Emerson critics, and his earlier study of Emerson, *Apostle of Culture* (1982), is considered seminal. In this recent book (1993) Robinson concerns himself with interpreting Emerson's writings on "the moral texture of social life". He focuses on the later works – those called Emerson's "post-visionary" writings – and is interested in Emerson as a social and political moralist, and philosopher. Robinson's work is part of that current preoccupation with the political dimensions of Emerson's writings and the endeavour to rescue him from an earlier conventional view as an aloof, self-absorbed seer. Robinson investigates Emerson's response to the 1850 Fugitive Slave Act, which intensely politicised his thinking, and, in accounts of the essay "Experience" and the two works *The Conduct of Life* and *Society and Solitude*, sees Emerson's philosophic thought as embodying a form of proto-pragmatism, which brings him into sympathy with one of the most powerful strains of later American philosophy. Robinson's work is widely regarded as among the best of recent discussions of Emerson's history and achievement.

GOUGEON disputes the three most common views of Emerson – that he was conservative in his own character and in his philosophy; that his work indirectly validated *laissez-faire* American capitalism and the aggressive individualism that goes with it; and that he was by nature an aloof scholar, one who kept the tensions of the social fabric at arm's length. On the contrary, Gougeon shows that Emerson became increasingly involved with abolitionism from 1844, a political engagement deepened by his despair over the annexation of Texas, the Mexican War, and the passing of the Fugitive Slave Act. Gougeon argues that Emerson saw these events as indicative both of the failure of politics and politicians, but also of his own ideals of the prospective harmony of social and individual culture envisioned in his writings. He shows the intensity of Emerson's involvement with the anti-slavery crusades of the 1850s, and how these reformist impulses survived in Emerson through the Civil War and into the period of Reconstruction. This is a much-admired study, central to our present conceptions of Emerson and his response to the moral and political issues of his times. SEALTS, like Robinson and Gougeon, gives us a more "political" Emerson than has been customary, especially in relation to Emerson's increasingly public commitment to the abolitionist cause. For Sealts, one of the central questions for Emerson was whether the thinker should not also be a man of action, and the drive of this study is to answer that question in the affirmative. Sealts does this by paying particular attention to the essays that develop the ideal figure of the scholar in Emerson's writing, "The American Scholar", "The Divinity School Address", and *Representative Men*, as well as many journal entries and some rather obscure late speeches, and from these materials traces Emerson's thinking about the opposition between a life given to contemplation and one fully engaged with the public issues of the day.

Wider ranging selections of articles on Emerson are offered by Buell, and Cady and Budd. BUELL has edited a selection of essays by a group notable Emersonians and commentators on the nineteenth-century intellectual culture of America – Perry Miller, William L. Hedges, Buell himself, Stephen E. Whicher, Mary Kupiec Cayton, Sacvan Bercovitch, Richard Poirier, Jonathan Bishop, Harold Bloom, Julie Ellison, Glen M. Johnson, Stanley Cavell, and Merton M. Sealts, Jr. – in a collection that updates the 1962 "Twentieth Century Views" anthology on Emerson. It is invidious to choose from such company, but Stanley Cavell's belated response to the essay "Experience" is seminal, as is Jonathan's Bishop's essay on "Tone", the vocal register that conditions all communication, and Mary Kupiec Cayton's narrative of Emerson's journeyings in the role of public speaker. But this collection as a whole is wonderful value. CADY and BUDD have selected what they consider to be the best articles on Emerson published in one of the foremost journals of American literary scholarship, *American Literature*, between 1929 and 1987. This is an ideal collection from which to assess the development of Emerson's reputation over much of this century, though many of the earlier essays will now seem outdated in the light of work on Emerson over the past 20 years.

Cayton and Greenberg seek to place Emerson in his immediate cultural and social contexts. CAYTON gives a reading of Emerson as a figure within a social matrix, not apart from it, as she explores "some of the specific life circumstances that led Emerson to his peculiar philosophy of nature, invidiualism, and self-reliance". The focus of her work is Emerson's response to the developing capitalist ethos of Boston from the 1830s to the 1850s, set within its central role in the development of New England's religious, political, and cultural institutions. Cayton reads Emerson's "moral critique" of human and social potential against the particulars of this Bostonian foreground, a strategy that accords his writings a specificity of address not generally acknowledged. GREENBERG writes of the ways Emerson and his contemporaries responded to the cultural facts of social, religious, and political fragmentation in American nineteenth-century life, specifically in such phenomena as the increasingly crowded urban landscapes of the major towns, the rise and fall of competing religious denominations, and the political splinterings of the 1840s and 1850s, which were to lead to the Civil War. Greenberg works through a close analysis of the relationships between particular texts by each of his chosen writers (Herman Melville, Walt Whitman, and Emily Dickinson, as well as Emerson) to the contexts in which they were written, and shows how Emerson and his contemporaries manipulated ideals of Romantic diversity as a way of countering the contemporary threat of fragmentation, developing in the process a form of cultural and social relativism.

HODDER's book is especially useful for its study of Emerson's first important essay, *Nature* (1836), the starting-point for all students of Emerson's work, which Hodder sees as heavily influenced by the Scriptures, known intimately to Emerson through his brief career as a theology student and minister. He sees the Bible as providing the model for Emerson's conception of nature, and writes particularly of the importance of the Book of Revelation for him, and the idea of apocalypse as a form of revelation. He argues that Emerson's style not only tells of revelation but enacts the process, occasions, and circumstances of it. Hodder is especially rewarding in those chapters where these ideas of revelation and apocalypse are illustrated through close analysis of particular parts of Emerson's early essays and journal entries.

Also concerned with religion, MOTT has made a close study of Emerson's sermons from his time as a Unitarian minister, and wants to see Emerson's later literary career as one evolved from the New England Unitarian culture he was educated in, a culture which "nurtured while it confined". More contentiously, Mott claims that there are continuities of vision and technique between the sermons and Emerson's early essays, a view which breaks faith with the conventional understanding that Emerson's early essays are the product of a kind of Pauline awakening of the self to its own potential, an awakening quite antipathetic to his earlier role as a Unitarian minister. The value of this study lies in its attention to a neglected area of Emerson's work, rather than in its thesis of the connection between the sermons and the essays.

MICHAEL also challenges some common assumptions about the importance of Emerson, based on a view of his commitment to an aggressive individualism. The import of such a reading is to deny the essentialist concept of the self in Emerson, as though Michael is both at war with the centrally determining idea in Emerson's thought and yet sympathetic to the reaches of this thought, as it eventually issues in an idea of self much more problematic and sympathetic to our contemporary understanding of the contingency of selfhood. The value of this study is in its challenge to some orthodoxies about Emerson, and in the ways in which it makes us reconsider the implications of scepticism.

POIRIER takes Emerson's work as a bench-mark of seriousness in the intellectual culture of America from the 1830s to the present day, and sees a stoical grandeur and steeliness in Emerson he finds wholly admirable. In a way, this book offers a version of an Emersonian tradition, featuring such later writers as Robert Frost, Wallace Stevens, and others, who, for Poirier, lived up to Emersonian standards in their confrontation with life's potential and its costs. Some part of the animus of this book is against the specious impersonalism of much modernist writing, hence its validation of Emerson's personalism and his celebration of the "self".

PORTE centres his critique of nineteenth-century American writing on the figure of Emerson, reading the central exponents of this tradition as conditioned by Emerson's "age of the first person singular". Porte astutely argues that this tradition represents "the startling confrontation of the agonized Puritan conscience with both the real and imaginative possibilities of the American sublime". The value of this study is less for what it proposes about Emerson than for its incisive readings of his contemporaries.

Providing philosophical examinations of Emerson, and placing him in a philosophical context, are the aims of Cavell, Stack, and Van Leer. CAVELL's rather daunting philosophical study investigates what may be called the ideology of "Perfectionism" in Emerson, that moral impulse to spiritual and intellectual self-improvement he defined as "Self-Reliance", the title of one of his most famous essays. Cavell questions whether such moral perfectionism is inherently élitist, since it seems to privilege the self over all other considerations. He finds that Emersonian perfectionism is a condition of becoming rather than being, and "consents to democracy" because it both contributes to it and is dependent upon it. Thus, he sees perfectionism as the process of transfiguration enacted between the individual and society. In addition, Cavell situates these arguments within a framework provided by twentieth-century American and European philosophers and their work on language, ethics, and justice. STACK calls on Emerson as an agent in Nietzsche's enterprise, arguing that the German philosopher was deeply indebted to the American's ideas. He sees Nietzsche's "will to power" as implicit in Emerson's Over-Soul, and proposes that they shared an admiration for the idea of the "Superman" or genius, and a detestation of the common majority. More interestingly, Stack later turns his attention to the gendered language of both writers' discourse, and sees them as preoccupied with the representation of a world in which the masculine is dominant. Beyond this, Stack sees both Emerson and Nietzsche as anticipatory of twentieth-century ideas of language in their conceptualization of language as a system of arbitrary significations. VAN LEER examines the scope of Emerson's work in formal philosophical terms, addressing the origins and nature of his writings on theories of knowledge, the bed-rock of much philosophical discourse since Descartes. His challenge is to see beyond the seductive rhetoric of Emerson's style so as to assess the quality of the ideas, which inform that style. This is a particularly difficult task with a philosophical thinker who does not systematize in a conventional way, and who is more open than other philosophers to the charge of inconsistency, especially in relation to the modes of rigorous analytical thought commonly associated with studies in epistemology and metaphysics. This admirable study will seem daunting to those unfamiliar with the traditions of academic philosophy, but it has much to show us about the nature and quality of Emerson's ideas on a wide range of topics.

LIONEL KELLY

Encounter Literature *see* Exploration Literature, Travel Literature

Epistolary Novel

Altman, Janet Gurkin, *Epistolarity: Approaches to a Form*, Columbus: Ohio State University Press, 1982
Black, Frank Gees, *The Epistolary Novel in the Late Eighteenth Century: A Description and Bibliographical Study*, Eugene: University of Oregon Press, 1940
Day, Robert Adams, *Told in Letters: Epistolary Fiction Before Richardson*, Ann Arbor: University of Michigan Press, 1966
Favret, Mary A., *Romantic Correspondence: Women, Politics and the Fiction of Letters*, Cambridge and New York: Cambridge University Press, 1993
Goldsmith, Elizabeth, *Writing the Female Voice: Essays on Epistolary Literature*, Boston: Northeastern University Press, 1989; London: Pinter Press, 1989
Kauffman, Linda S., *Discourses of Desire: Gender, Genre, and Epistolary Fictions*, Ithaca, New York: Cornell University Press, 1986
MacArthur, Elizabeth J., *Extravagant Narratives: Closure and Dynamics in the Epistolary Form*, Princeton, New Jersey: Princeton University Press, 1990
Perry, Ruth, *Women, Letters, and the Novel*, New York: AMS Press, 1980
Singer, Godfrey Frank, *The Epistolary Novel: Its Origin, Development, Decline, and Residual Influence*, Philadelphia: University of Pennsylvania Press, 1933

Epistolary fiction, or the novel in letters, flourished in Britain between the time of Sir Roger L'Estrange's translation into English of Guilleragues' *Lettres portugaises* (*Five Love-Letters from a Nun to a Cavalier*, 1678) and the conspicuous abandonment of the form by Jane Austen, Sir Walter Scott, and others in the early nineteenth century. Leading examples of this important narrative sub-genre include Aphra Behn's *Love-Letters Between a Nobleman and His Sister* (1684–87), Samuel Richardson's *Pamela* (1740) and *Clarissa* (1747–48), Tobias Smollett's *Humphry Clinker* (1771), and Frances Burney's *Evelina* (1779). Some of the most useful analyses of epistolary fiction and its narrative characteristics are, in fact, to be found in critical studies of these individual writers (and of French writers like Choderlos de Laclos, author of *Les Liaisons dangereuses*), rather than in books devoted to a purely generic approach.

Readers must still turn to SINGER for a general historical introduction to epistolary fiction in English, and his book, though methodologically outdated, retains some usefulness as a broad-brush survey. BLACK confines himself to a shorter period (1740–1800), in which he estimates that as many as one-third of all novels published in English were solely or largely written in the form of letters. Like Singer's, Black's study is now of little critical interest, and it is not to be trusted in all points of detail (not least his erratic bibliography of primary sources). But neither of these books has yet been replaced by a good alternative written in the light of more recent developments in literary history and theory.

The period before Richardson is better served by DAY, whose book has been influential in bringing to light a wealth of material published before the *Pamela* controversy of 1740. While not denying the extraordinary innovative qualities of *Pamela* and *Clarissa*, Day lays to rest definitively any assumption that the form of the novel in letters sprang fully-grown from Richardson's head. Instead he demonstrates at length the surprising vigour and sophistication of the form in the Restoration and early eighteenth-century period, ably describing and classifying the variety of different types (and some outstanding individual examples) practised in these years.

The major theoretical study in English remains ALTMAN's *Epistolarity* (a term for which she gives as her "working definition: the use of the letter's formal properties to create meaning"). Drawing in particular on the French tradition from *Lettres portugaises* to *Les Liaisons dangereuses*, Altman focuses on the inescapable literariness of the form, persuasively refuting the still widespread assumption that epistolary fiction might be no more than some primitive precursor of the stream-of-consciousness novel. Instead she describes a narrative sub-genre with distinctive and complex properties of its own, which flourishes in particular "at those moments when novelists most openly reflect upon the relation between storytelling and intersubjective communication and begin to queston the way in which writing reflects, betrays, or constitutes the relations between self, other, and experience". A useful by-product of this study is its demonstration that epistolary fiction is far from being a phenomenon exclusive to the eighteenth century, and Altman makes good use of several recent experiments with the form.

Philosophical questions about narrative representation, and historical or social questions about the representation in particular of gender, are at the heart of studies by KAUFFMAN and MacARTHUR. Drawing on poststructuralist and feminist theory, both writers share a common interest in the capacity of the form to disrupt or subvert conventional mimetic expectations. Both are based in the field of French literary studies, however, and neither has a great deal to say about sources in English. Perhaps more useful is GOLDSMITH's collection of essays, though several of these have more to do with the related field of familiar-letter writing than with epistolary fiction itself. This collection as a whole explores themes in gender and narrative continuous with those of Kauffman and MacArthur, and it includes some powerful readings of individual texts: Patricia Meyer Spacks's essay on Austen's *Lady Susan* is a notable highlight.

A less theoretical and more historically rigorous strain of scholarship is represented by PERRY's pioneering study, which addresses questions of markets and readership in order to represent early novels in letters as establishing a bridge for their readers between romantic fantasy (represented in their plots) and the quotidian experience of domestic life (represented in their form).

FAVRET's subtle and witty book focuses in detail on the later part of the period (1789–1830) to argue that letter-fiction, as well as letters themselves, increasingly became media as much for political, as for merely sentimental, expression. Favret's book is ambitious in scope, dealing not only with fictional letters but also with political pamphlets in letter form, travel letters, and other epistolary productions available for public consumption. This range does not prevent her from providing, along the way, one of the most thorough and intelligent accounts to date of Jane Austen's complex relationship to a form of fiction with which she was never able, or willing, to break entirely.

TOM KEYMER

Equiano, Olaudah 1745–1797

African born autobiographer

Baker, Houston A., Jr., *Blues, Ideology, and Afro-American Literature: A Vernacular Theory*, Chicago: University of Chicago Press, 1984

Costanzo, Angelo, *Surprizing Narrative: Olaudah Equiano and the Beginnings of Black Autobiography*, New York: Greenwood Press, 1987

Fichtelberg, Joseph, "Word Between Worlds: The Economy of Equiano's *Narrative*", in *American Literary History*, 5(3), 1993

Marren, Susan M., "Between Slavery and Freedom: The Transgressive Self in Olaudah Equiano's Autobiography", in *PMLA* [*Publications of the Modern Language Association*], 108(1), 1993

Sandiford, Keith A., *Measuring the Moment: Strategies of Protest in Eighteenth-Century Afro-English Writing*, Selinsgrove, Pennsylvania: Susquehanna University Press, 1988

Equiano's autobiography has typically been claimed by two main groups of critics: those who wish to situate it within the Anglo-African tradition of writers, such as Ignatius Sancho and Ottabah Cugoano, and those who wish to position it within the African-American autobiographical tradition as the prototype of nineteenth-century slave narratives. As William Andrews argues, however, the fact that Equiano was a British citizen, whose autobiography was addressed to the English Parliament as part of the anti-slavery campaign, suggests that it is most appropriate to consider Equiano an Anglo-African writer. Most recently, critics have raised questions about Equiano's complicated relationship to both African and English culture, as that relationship is manifested in a text directed toward a predominantly white audience.

COSTANZO offers a valuable introduction to the genre of early black autobiography in general, and to Equiano's autobiography in particular. In addition to considering the impact of African culture on early writers, Costanzo usefully discusses the way in which popular eighteenth-century literary forms, such as sentimental fiction, primitivistic writings, orations, jeremiads, sermons, spiritual autobiographies, and picaresque tales informed early black autobiography. Costanzo's lengthy examination of Equiano's autobiography from varied perspectives, both thematic and structural, is most persuasive when it seeks to position the autobiography within its rhetorical context.

BAKER draws on Michel Foucault, Fredric Jameson, and Hayden White in his lead chapter, "Figurations for a New American Literary History: Archaeology, Ideology, and Afro-American Discourse", in order to develop a new approach to African-American literary history, one which situates African-American discourse within concrete, material situations. Baker's ideological analysis of the discursive structure of Equiano's *Narrative* serves as his paradigm for uncovering the basic subtext that, he contends, "necessarily informs any genuinely Afro-American narrative text". Baker asserts that:

> . . . all Afro-American creativity is conditioned by a historical discourse which privileges certain economic terms. The creative individual (the *black subject*) must, therefore, whether he self-consciously wills it or not, come to terms with "commercial deportation" and the "economics of slavery".

Thus, Equiano was able to free himself from his status as property by becoming a successful trader, by mastering "the rudiments of economics that condition his very life". Baker's essay has become an important starting place for critics interested in poststructuralist and historicist approaches to the autobiography.

SANDIFORD offers a valuable discussion of the intellectual milieu and the socio-historical context of the three most prominent African writers in eighteenth-century Britain – Ignatius Sancho, Ottobah Cugoano, and Olaudah Equiano. Sandiford provides the detailed information contemporary readers need in order to understand the varied and complex rhetorical strategies these writers used in order to reach a predominantly white audience. Particularly useful is the first chapter, which discusses the seventeenth- and eighteenth-century African intellectuals who established the written tradition that Sancho, Cugoano, and Equiano went on to develop. Sandiford positions Equiano's *Narrative* in the context of the British anti-slavery movement, arguing that Equiano united "religious and humanitarian sentiments with his personal experience of slavery to define the Black struggle in its clearest racial and political terms".

FICHTELBERG pursues one of the key critical issues of the *Narrative*: to what extent was it possible for Equiano to subvert the master discourse by turning that discourse against itself? Challenging Baker's argument, Fichtelberg contends that despite Equiano's attempts to emancipate himself by adopting bourgeois discourse, he remained entrapped within that discourse. Rather than recording Equiano's movement toward freedom, the text in fact demonstrates Equiano's failures to assert freedom. Equiano escaped slavery, "the enslaving commodity relation", only to inhabit a position in which the "isolated self is defined through things".

MARREN examines Equiano's response to the central paradox confronting eighteenth-century black authors: although race was inescapable, race had to be escaped if black writers were to speak at all. Thus Equiano had to "manipulate the terms of racial representation both to demonstrate a black man's capacity for reason and to elide any definitive, silencing racial categorization". He accomplished this by fashioning a "transgressive" narrative self, one which challenged the oppositional terms (male/female, black/white, freedom/slavery, and so on) that organized Western culture. As a black author inhabiting a position that was neither slave nor free-man, Equiano did not embrace an essentialist or stable identity, whether African or English, but instead adopted "a fluid positioning, a mode of articulation of newly imagined, radically nonbinary subjectivities".

AMY E. WINANS

Erdrich, Louise 1954 –

American poet and novelist

Bak, Hans, "Toward a Native American 'Realism': The Amphibious Fiction of Louise Erdrich", in *Neo-Realism in Contemporary Fiction*, edited by Kristiaan Versluys, Amsterdam: Rodopi, 1992

Chavkin, Allan, and Nancy Feyl Chavkin (eds.), *Conversations with Louise Erdrich and Michael Dorris*, Jackson: University Press of Mississippi, 1994

Holt, Debra C., "Transformation and Continuance: Native American Tradition in the Novels of Louise Erdrich", in *Entering the 90s: The North American Experience*, edited by Thomas E. Schirer, Sault Sainte Marie, Michigan: Lake Superior State University, 1991

Lee, A. Robert, "Ethnic Renaissance: Rudolfo Anaya, Louise Erdrich and Maxine Hong Kingston", in *The New American Writing: Essays on American Literature since 1970*, edited by Graham Clarke, London: Vision Press, 1990; New York: St Martin's Press, 1990

Rainwater, Catherine, "Reading Between Worlds: Narrativity in the Fiction of Louise Erdrich", in *American Literature*, 62(3), 1990

Silberman, Robert, "Opening the Text: *Love Medicine* and the Return of the Native American Woman", in *Narrative Chance: Postmodern Discourse on Native American Indian Literatures*, edited by Gerald Vizenor, Albuquerque: University of New Mexico Press, 1989

Since the publication of her first and best-selling novel, *Love Medicine* (1984), Louise Erdrich has received much popular and critical attention. Much of the criticism of Erdrich's work looks at her novels in the context of other Native American writers, as critics are just beginning to formulate theories of Native American literature. Critics are also interested in the ways in which Erdrich's novels incorporate elements of both Western society and Native American culture and tradition. So far, little critical attention has been given to Erdrich's poetry.

SILBERMAN analyzes *Love Medicine*, comparing it to the Native American literary tradition established in the writings of D'Arcy McNickle, N. Scott Momaday, Leslie Marmon Silko, and James Welch. Silberman maintains that Native American literature lends itself to recent developments in literary criticism and critical theory:

> The many shared elements in the works, as well as the equally telling differences, make them a perfect case study for the analysis of combinations, oppositions and inversions beloved in structuralist criticism. Though not engaged in a technical, philosophical debate, Native American writers reveal an obsessive concern with the relation between speech and writing that is worthy of the deconstructionist critics. Finally, this body of literature incorporates among its major social and political concerns a preoccupation with origins, marginality and otherness that would have delighted Foucault.

Silberman enumerates the ways in which Erdrich works within the boundaries of established conventions while simultaneously "recasting" the tradition.

LEE examines the work of Rudolfo Anaya (a Chicano), Maxine Hong Kingston (a Chinese American), and Erdrich as examples of writers who formulate their identities as writers and individuals based on their experiences as ethnic Americans. As someone with "mixed blood" (French-Chippewa on her mother's side, and German-American on her father's side), Erdrich writes what Lee describes as "an ethnic American story", re-imagining and remaking the American experience. Focusing his discussion of Erdrich on *Love Medicine*, *The Beet Queen*, and *Tracks*, Lee traces an "'Indian' pattern . . . in which the circle is all and life operates as a kind of mysterious or magic revolving wheel" through each of the novels. Each narrative defies linear logic and development, as it moves readers and characters through space and time, weaving together their lives and experiences. In each novel, Lee argues, Erdrich attempts to reconcile the experiences of the Chippewa and the mainstream American.

RAINWATER explores *Love Medicine*, *The Beet Queen*, and *Tracks*, concentrating on the themes of marginality and liminality as central concerns of each novel, and arguing that each novel contains conflicting codes, which produce "in the reader an experience of marginality". Rainwater divides these conflicting codes into two major categories: Western-European codes (Christianity, mechanical time, the nuclear family, privileged characters, and privileged narrative voices) and Native American codes (shamanic religion, ceremonial time, tribal kinship systems, characters of equal status, and dialogical or polyphonic narrative development). The "simultaneous presence" of these conflicting cultural codes "vexes the reader's effort to decide upon an unambiguous, epistemologically consistent interpretive framework", which leads to "the marginalization of the reader by the text".

HOLT's study analyzes the structure of Erdrich's novels *Tracks*, *Love Medicine*, and *The Beet Queen* in light of Native American rituals. Citing Paula Gunn Allen, Holt points out that women's rituals celebrate stability, while men's rituals promote change. In each novel, Erdrich reconciles the feminine idea of stability and the masculine idea of change in circular narratives, which "reflect the paradoxical notion that in a changing universe, everything moves toward wholeness". Holt compares Erdrich's vision to that of mainstream feminists, who call for men and women to "tap into the power of femininity, power that both stabilizes and energizes".

BAK examines Erdrich's *The Beet Queen*, the most traditionally "realistic" of Erdrich's novels, in order to illustrate the writer's commitment to a realism that accommodates both the oral tradition of tribal narrative and an awareness of postmodernism. While acknowledging that Erdrich's novels contain non-realistic (tribal and postmodern) elements, Bak maintains that ultimately such elements fail to undermine the "realistic texture" of Erdrich's fiction, as she remains aesthetically committed to "mimetic realism". Erdrich employs a "magic" realism, composed of various "tribal elements – shamanism, spirits, witchcraft, charms, love medicines" and "non-Western concepts of space and time".

CHAVKIN and CHAVKIN's book contains 23 interviews conducted with Erdrich and her husband, Native American writer and scholar Michael Dorris, since the publication of *Love Medicine*. More than half of the interviews are joint interviews, and the book contains two previously unpublished ones. The writers' collaboration began in 1981, shortly after their marriage; most of what each writer has written since then has been a product of this collaboration. The interviews contain details about their collaborative process and the influence of Native American heritage on their writing. The book also contains a useful "Chronology" of each writer's life and work.

KRISTA L. MAY

The Erotic in Literature

D'Arch Smith, Timothy, *Love in Earnest: Some Notes on the Lives and Writings of English "Uranian" Poets from 1889 to 1930*, London: Routledge & Kegan Paul, 1970

Keach, William, *Elizabethan Erotic Narratives: Irony and Pathos in the Ovidian Poetry of Shakespeare, Marlowe, and Their Contemporaries*, New Brunswick, New Jersey: Rutgers University Press, 1977; Hassocks, Sussex: Harvester Press, 1977

Polhemus, Robert M., *Erotic Faith: Being in Love from Jane Austen to D.H. Lawrence*, Chicago: University of Chicago Press, 1990

Spender, Stephen, "Foreword", in *Erotic Poetry: The Lyrics, Ballads, Idyls, and Epics of Love – Classical to Contemporary*, edited by William Cole, New York: Random House, 1963; London: Weidenfeld & Nicolson, 1964

Wagner, Peter, *Eros Revived: The Erotica of the Enlightenment in England and America*, London: Secker & Warburg, 1988

Young, Wayland, *Eros Denied: Sex in Western Society*, New York: Grove Press, 1964; London: Weidenfeld & Nicolson, 1965

A good general introduction to the theme of the erotic in literature, and to erotic poetry in particular, is SPENDER's Foreword to William Cole's *Erotic Poetry*. Spender concentrates on the distinction between what he terms the "sensuous" and the "sensual", within the context of the relaxation of censorship laws following the "Lady Chatterley" trial (1960). On the problem of definition, Spender associates the deliberately erotic with the idea of the religious, finding in both a "reverence for life" and a "sense of mystery", which lead him to conclude that truly erotic poems are "as rare as truly religious poems": in truly religious writing, the truly erotic dissolves "into trance". D.H. Lawrence, Spender suggests, insists on the anonymity of loving, which indicates a shift towards instinctual physical passion. William Blake's "The Moment of Desire" is considered in the context of the reader's auto-eroticism or pornographic interest: here Spender is at pains to stress that the erotic is not to be equated with the pornographic, though erotic writing may be *used* as pornography.

The problem of definition is mirrored in what YOUNG sees as the general confusion surrounding sex and love that permeates Anglo-Saxon culture. This book is largely concerned with ideas of freedom and "unfreedom"; as far as literature is concerned, the author uses texts to illustrate manifestations of these ideas in literature as products of the societies that engendered them. The general tone of this study is one of outrage at the (then) prevailing attitude towards sex and sexuality as excluded "from the realm of the normal". Such polemic may now seem outdated, but the book offers useful insight into the difficulties faced only a short time ago by scholars attempting to conduct serious research into the erotic in literature.

D'ARCH SMITH's book concentrates on the "Uranian" poets, 1889–1930, and explores the thematics and structures of homoerotic literature. Smith stresses that his work is not a polemic for homosexuality but an attempt to discuss the poetry in terms of a sublimation of homoeroticism. The book is particularly informative on the theme of the boy-lover; Rudyard Kipling's "love of fair English boys", for example, is seen as a form of patriotism – a reply to the Graeco-Roman domination of this kind of affection. Smith also has interesting things to say on the appropriation of Christian imagery and doctrines in homoerotic literature – for example, the martyrdom of boys, the comparison of homoerotic love with the friendship of Jesus, and especially the relationship of David and Jonathan in 2 Samuel ("Thy love to me was wonderful, passing the love of women"). Smith also discusses the pauper-into-prince theme, where, under the influence of an older man, a boy "supersedes his lower-class birthright" and "becomes a boy of great beauty and intellect".

In his study, KEACH sets out to "identify the expressive possibilities and the literary significance of a group of late Elizabethan poems which have not received the kind of attention they deserve". This literature, Keach suggests, characteristically embodies a "convergence of the beautiful and the disconcerting, the tender and the violent, the passionate and the comic, the seriousness of desire and the fun of titillation". Most importantly, the book takes issue with the neglect – except for Marlowe's "Hero and Leander" and Shakespeare's "Venus and Adonis" – of poems written during the vogue of Ovidian narrative; Keach does not challenge the canonical status of these two works, but seeks to widen the canon itself to include works such as Thomas Heywood's *Oenone and Paris*, and Thomas Edwards's "Cephalus and Procris" and "Narcissus". His study of thematics and structure discusses the comic "abruptly juxtaposed with or superimposed upon tragedy", the relationship between irony and pathos, conventional moral perspectives and piquant eroticism, and between dramatic colloquial speech and "elegant verbal artifice". Keach finds the erotic narrative characterised by an "ironic literary self-consciousness", which co-exists with an "urbane awareness" of human contradictions, and claims that it is this that qualifies the genre as Ovidian "in more than just a superficial sense". In Marlowe's treatment of Hero and Leander he finds a "disturbingly perceptive ambivalence", which represents a "fully coherent extension" of his views of the erotic experience. Keach also sees processes of suppression, restriction, or moral "placing" of Ovidian themes in Edmund Spenser, which lead him to conclude that Spenser's poetry, though it demonstrates what he terms "generous inclusiveness", does not completely satisfy the need for an artistic evaluation of the erotic.

WAGNER returns to the problems of definition, and in particular to the problem of distinction between the erotic and the pornographic. The book is chiefly concerned with eighteenth-century interpretations of each of these terms, and attempts to demonstrate that literature and the art of Eros "were by no means set apart from the rest of contemporary culture and history". The claim here is that the works discussed not only reflected the society that produced them, but also affected the economic and political thought of their time.

POLHEMUS discusses the work of Jane Austen (*Pride and Prejudice*) and Sir Walter Scott (*The Bride of Lamermoor*) in the context of "eroticizing history". This idea he connects with the "pastoral erotic" of Thomas Hardy in *Far From the Madding Crowd* and the "resurrection of the body" in Lawrence's *Lady Chatterley's Lover*. His claim here is that "the relationship of sexuality, letters and love" is central to "any inquiry into the European novel" and the history of the erotic, and he widens his approach to include love-letters, which he sees as means of both seduction and "displaced erotic gratification", as well as being a means of "sanctifying" erotic love and engendering the belief "that it is the most important thing in life" (though this approach ignores vital connections between Christianity and the appropriation of its imagery and vocabulary in erotic literature). Polhemus finds the nineteenth century and its fiction to be shaped by "the dynamic interaction of physical sex, writing and erotic longing"; reading and writing make love "both the discourse of two corresponding selves" and "the single self in touch with its own reflecting"; the erotic drama he sees as "internalized", an "erotic process of bourgeois individualism".

SIMON BRITTAN

The Essay

Boetcher Joeres, Ruth-Ellen, and Elizabeth Mittman (eds.), *The Politics of the Essay: Feminist Perspectives*, Bloomington: Indiana University Press, 1993

Butrym, Alexander J. (ed.), *Essays on the Essay: Redefining the Genre*, Athens: University of Georgia Press, 1989

Dobrée, Bonamy, *English Essayists*, London: Collins, 1946

Good, Graham, *The Observing Self: Rediscovering the Essay*, London and New York: Routledge, 1988

Lopate, Philip (ed.), *The Art of the Personal Essay: An Anthology from the Classical Era to the Present*, New York: Anchor Books, 1994

Lukács, Georg, "On the Nature and Form of the Essay", in his *Soul and Form*, translated by Anna Bostock, Cambridge, Massachusetts: MIT Press, 1974; London: Merlin Press, 1974

Snyder, John, *Prospects of Power: Tragedy, Satire, the Essay, and the Theory of Genre*, Lexington: University Press of Kentucky, 1991

In a brief but highly informative narrative, DOBRÉE provides a useful summary of the English essay from its origins in the sixteenth century through the first half of the twentieth. Limiting his review to a survey of major essayists, Dobrée sketches the outline of the development of the genre in England, quoting liberally from numerous authors to illustrate their personal styles and the changes in both tone and subject matter over four centuries. While the brevity of his work makes it difficult for readers to gain more than a cursory understanding of individual essayists, the volume is a helpful introductory study.

By contrast, in the opening chapter of his first collection of published writings, LUKÁCS offers a highminded justification for the essay as a legitimate form of art. Reviewing the aesthetic qualities that distinguish it from other modes of writing, he surveys a few of the great essayists to highlight their contributions to the development of the genre. More polemical than analytic, Lukács offers a strident defense of the critical essay, calling it "an art form, an autonomous and integral giving-of-form to an autonomous and complete life". Though of limited value for understanding the breadth of subjects with which the essayist deals, or for appreciating the importance of style, Lukács' brief examination of form and function is a useful reminder of the genre's elastic nature and a good introduction upon which to base more detailed study of individual practitioners.

The function and nature of the essay as genre is also the subject of SNYDER's highly theoretical analysis. His introductory chapter outlines the status of genre theory in the late twentieth century. Defining genre as "differential power", Snyder takes issue with many poststructuralist critics whose definitions of genre lack an appreciation for the historical dimension of most writing. The essay, however, is not as bound historically as other genres. The most fluid of all forms of writing, the essay is "definable neither by what it says" nor by "how it says what it says"; rather, it is the medium most dependent on the writer's urge simply to say something. Essayists such as Francis Bacon and Ralph Waldo Emerson are compared to major figures who have written in other languages (e.g., Cicero, Montaigne, Rousseau, Nietzsche) to illustrate the flexibility provided by the form.

GOOD is also interested in exploring the possibilities inherent in the form of the essay. Beginning with a chapter he calls a "historico-philosophical" introduction, Good examines the intellectual conditions that gave rise to the essay and spurred its continued development in England. Much of the theoretical framework for his discussion is borrowed from Lukács and Theodor Adorno; throughout, Good focuses his attention on the methods essayists use to construct the object of their investigation "in terms of ideas and general strategies". Good's selection of writers is limited to mainstream figures – he devotes a chapter each to Montaigne, Bacon, Samuel Johnson, William Hazlitt, Henry James, Virginia Woolf, T.S. Eliot, and George Orwell – but his extensive bibliographical notes provide readers with excellent guidance to other writers and additional critical works.

Combining the methods of theorists and practical critics, the 21 writers who contribute to the collection edited by BUTRYM explore the nature and complexity of the essay as a literary genre. Divided into five major sections, and eclectic in its approach, the collection includes highly theoretical analyses of form and function, as well as detailed examinations of individual essayists. In the central section several contributors sketch the historical development of the essay written in English; their work ranges from analyses of Johnson and Emerson to commentary on twentieth-century essayists, such as Woolf, Eliot, D.H. Lawrence, Loren Eiseley, and James Baldwin. The volume concludes with an enlightening commentary on the place of the essay in the modern curriculum.

Defining the term "essay" quite broadly, editors BOETCHER JOERES and MITTMAN have gathered work by numerous feminist writers whose individual chapters in this collection examine formal and informal non-fiction by women from many countries. Writers in English such as Woolf, Alice Walker, and Florence Nightingale are considered in a wider context, which includes commentary on feminists Flora Tristan, Christa Wolf, and Gabriela Mistral. The editors admit to a political bias, calling politics "the central issue" motivating their study. The volume is intended to fill a scholarly void: in their view "virtually no critical literature" exists to describe "the cultural implications" of the essay as it has been used by women writers. Boetcher Joeres and Mittman believe that both the essay and criticism of the essay have traditionally been patriarchal forms of writing; their collection aims to provide a feminist perspective on the genre.

LOPATE's Introduction to his anthology of personal essays is a useful and clear summary of the qualities that characterize so many exemplary compositions. Lopate makes careful distinctions between the personal essay and other forms of non-fiction, enumerating and defining its principal characteristics as intimacy with the reader, a conversational tone, a tendency toward disputation and self-deprecation, and a willingness to speak honestly (often controversially) on a range of subjects. Noting that "the essay is a notoriously flexible and adaptable form", Lopate reviews the ways personal essayists have employed formal techniques to gain control over their subjects. In both his introduction and in the selections he includes in the volume, Lopate is eclectic in choosing examples to support his claims for the diversity and complexity of the form. Selections by writers from many literary periods and from dozens of countries and cultures supplement the major sections on British and American essayists. The volume serves as a superb introduction to the genre.

LAURENCE W. MAZZENO

See also **Prose and Journalism**

Etherege, Sir George 1636–1692

English dramatist and poet

Dobrée, Bonamy, *Restoration Comedy 1660–1720*, Oxford: Clarendon Press, 1924; New York: Oxford University Press, 1958
Fujimura, Thomas H., *The Restoration Comedy of Wit*, Princeton, New Jersey: Princeton University Press, 1952; London: Methuen, 1952
Holland, Norman N., *The First Modern Comedies: The Significance of Etherege, Wycherley and Congreve*, Cambridge, Massachusetts: Harvard University Press, 1959
Huseboe, Arthur R., *Sir George Etherege*, Boston: Twayne, 1987
Markley, Robert, *Two-Edg'd Weapons: Style and Ideology in the Comedies of Etherege, Wycherley, and Congreve*, Oxford: Clarendon Press, 1988; New York: Oxford University Press, 1988
Palmer, John, *The Comedy of Manners*, London: Bell & Sons, 1913; reprinted, New York: Russell & Rusell, 1962
Underwood, Dale, *Etherege and the Seventeenth-Century Comedy of Manners*, New Haven, Connecticut: Yale University Press, 1957; London: Oxford University Press, 1957

Few critical studies have been devoted to Etherege alone; the most important discussions of his plays have been in more general studies. Each is driven by a thesis about the whole of Restoration comedy.

PALMER set the terms for much of the twentieth-century critical debate about late seventeenth-century comedy. Reacting against the moral censure of Restoration comedy by Thomas Babington Macaulay and the Victorians, Palmer argues that the plays offer a serious and accurate reflection of their society and should be appreciated as such, rather than condemned for failing to meet social or moral standards of another time. Didactic art, for Palmer, is an oxymoron. It was Etherege who "found a form for the spirit of his age": "*She Would If She Could* was the first finished example of the new comedy of manners"; and *The Man of Mode* realized the full potential of the new form.

DOBRÉE, too, attacks the moral arguments against Restoration comedy. It should not be seen as the expression of "licentiousness," but rather "the attempt to rationalize sexual relationships". He places the comedy of manners in the tradition of English and Continental stage comedy, a tradition consisting of three kinds of comedy: (1) critical: the vast bulk of social comedy; (2) "free": that is, value-free and amoral; (3) great: the comedy of disillusion, "perilously near tragedy". Most Restoration comedy is "critical"; but Etherege's is the exception. In many ways a minor writer, Dobrée's Etherege is nonetheless "a brilliant butterfly", with the rare ability to write comedy that is "realistic in semblance, and faithfully copies the outward aspects of the time", but "creates an illusion of life that is far removed from reality". Most critics, however, find Etherege's comedies more typical of their time.

FUJIMURA challenges the "manners" critics (including Palmer and Dobrée) for de-emphasizing the moral issues at the heart of Restoration comedy. The plays deal with moral issues naturalistically, and "wittily rather than soberly". Fujimura shares the traditional view that "wit is the very quintessence of Restoration comedy", but he insists – and demonstrates – that wit meant much more to the playwrights than verbal pyrotechnics. After examining the philosophical and intellectual background, Fujimura presents an "aesthetics of wit comedy" through which he reads Etherege (and Wycherley and Congreve):

> What we should look for in Etherege's comedies, then, is not interest in "manners," but such features of wit comedy as witty dialogue, naturalistic content, and realistic technique. We should also expect malicious laughter at fools, and the expression of a skeptical and libertine philosophy in witty form.

Fujimura finds exactly what he looks for in Etherege's plays.

UNDERWOOD sees Restoration comedy as a "thoughtful, carefully ordered and pervasively ironic form of drama", which deals with a "special society" and, through it, with "problems fundamental not only to the seventeenth century but to the nature of man". Like Fujimura's, his view of Etherege is grounded in his reading of the philosophical-intellectual background of the age. Underwood finds the plays informed by the tensions between opposing traditions, the one Christian and heroic, the other Machiavellian and Hobbesian. He explores this tension most fully in the figure of the *honnête homme* and (especially) the libertine. Etherege's comedies are read sequentially in order to reveal "the comic view", "the comic form", and "the comic values" of Restoration comedy. Underwood then analyzes the language of Etherege's plays, finding it substantive, abstract, schematic, and oppositional. Finally, he places Etherege's comedy in an English tradition that runs from John Lyly to Congreve.

HOLLAND also begins with an argument against "morals" critics. Since Restoration comedies "represent the truth", they are not immoral. The truth they capture centers on:

> ... the conflict between "manners" (i.e., social conventions) and anti-social "natural" desires. It is this dialectic between inner desires and outward appearance – not instincts alone or manners alone – that informs the comedies with masks, play-acting, disguise, intrigue, and perhaps most important, creates their language.

Since the same dialectical tensions are felt by twentieth-century readers and writers, they provide a renewed relevance for Restoration comedy. Holland devotes a chapter to each of Etherege's plays, exploring their varying uses of his central dialectical themes. His focus on the thematic use of the distinction between nature and appearance leads to considerable attention to a second theme, "the right way-wrong way simile", important both as a figure of speech and as "a basic frame in the entire action" of the plays.

HUSEBOE offers an introductory survey of Etherege's life and works to meet the specifications of the Twayne series. He discusses Etherege's poems and letters as well as his plays, making a case for Etherege as a letter-writer of great skill and interest. Huseboe provides the fullest narrative of Etherege's life to date. He then devotes a chapter to each of the plays, with detailed plot summaries and a focus on character and plot. He reads the plays through Etherege's life and times.

MARKLEY explores "the complex functions of dramatic language in the attempts of Etherege, Wycherley, and Congreve to register the ironies of fashionable existence in the late seventeenth century", especially "the ways in which stylistic structures describe, respond to, and suppress the trauma of historical change". Drawing on Mikhail Bakhtin's dialogical theory of discourse along with his concept of ideology as "an activity created by the contradictions and conflicts within and among social utterances", Markley examines late seventeenth-century theories of language, finding in them not the expected concern for developing a "theory of style", but rather a vehicle for the promotion of "the ideology of privilege". Etherege's characters use style with varying degrees of success to cope with "the tensions and ambiguities" of their culture. Their reliance on wit to uphold their social ideals ultimately fails because of the deconstructive nature of language: it questions and subverts their ideology so thoroughly that the language of wit could no longer be used with confidence for ideological purposes by Etherege's successors.

BRIAN CORMAN

Exploration Literature

Adams, Percy G., *Travel Literature and the Evolution of the Novel*, Lexington: University Press of Kentucky, 1983

Campbell, Mary B., *The Witness and the Other World: Exotic European Travel Writing, 400–1600*, Ithaca, New York: Cornell University Press, 1988

Carter, Paul, *The Road to Botany Bay: An Essay in Spatial History*, London: Faber & Faber, 1987; New York: Knopf, 1987

Franklin, Wayne, *Discoverers, Explorers, Settlers: The Diligent Writers of Early America*, Chicago: University of Chicago Press, 1979

Pratt, Mary Louise, *Imperial Eyes: Studies in Travel Writing and Transculturation*, London and New York: Routledge, 1992

Todorov, Tzvetan, *The Conquest of America*, translated by Richard Howard, New York: Harper & Row, 1984

There is little theory distinguishing between writing generated by the distinct motivations of discovery, exploration, settlement, and travel itself. Moreover, there is no comprehensive study of exploration accounts as a kind of writing, rather than simply records of experience, encompassing every global sector. There is, however, increasing recognition that this is a field wide open for study, though the number of useful studies is yet small.

CAMPBELL studies the prehistory of a genre now called "travel writing", a genre that begins to consolidate itself with the copious literature of discovery and exploration. She examines the earliest phase extending from fourth-century Christian pilgrimage to Walter Ralegh's discovery account of the Orinoco, Venezuela, and Guiana. Campbell tells two stories. In one, Europe conceptualizes its "Other" in changing modes and forms; in her other story, religious pilgrimage, crusade, and commercially-motivated excursions into exotic regions (such as Marco Polo's) culminate in the travels of discovery and exploration, and accounts of these rather different, historically situated, travels become formative aspects of contemporary travel literature. Campbell shows how the "Age of Discovery" (and Exploration) enabled travel accounts to be subject, for the first time, to verification, and shows the practical consequences of this, namely European conquest and domination: early travel texts are the "linguistic shadows of European imperialism". As a work that contextualizes early travel accounts within both literary/generic and historical boundaries, Campbell's study is noteworthy.

TODOROV seeks to narrate and theorize Christopher Columbus's discovery of America (actually, the Caribbean region) in 1492, and its conquest throughout the sixteenth century; for Todorov, these events constitute "the most astonishing encounter of [European] history". Using the prolific accounts of Columbus and his followers, Todorov shows how narratives of discovery were firmly held in a pre-modern grip, building as much on established "knowledges" – the Bible, the narratives of Marco Polo – as on empirical observation. Todorov's study views this decisive cultural encounter as a very dark one, noting that it instigated "the greatest genocide in human history", and he is concerned to untangle the several different threads of the history. Classic narratives of discovery, exploration, and conquest, beginning with those of Columbus and Hernando Cortés, not only form a body of imperialist discourse but also initiate a European obsession with "the Other", which ultimately becomes a psychological quest. Todorov thus offers a wider essay in cultural theory along with a carefully argued account of the first great voyage of discovery.

FRANKLIN provides a coherent account and theory of the travel writing of early America, treating discovery, exploration, and settlement texts as different phases of a unitary phenomenon, and choosing narratives from each phase for their exemplary rather than extraordinary nature. Franklin assumes that the American colonial experience is special, marked by an exceptionally close relation between language and event. Yet he also follows more recent theory in stressing how the various travel accounts of all three phases presented America as "a verbal construct, an artifact". Conversely, Europe exerts all the weight of its cultural and conceptual history to domesticate and recuperate the New World: "American travel books tell us . . . about the enormous Old World energies which went into the attempt at controlling the West by means of the symbolic system of language". Franklin's book argues a particular importance for the study of historical travel writing in its specific contexts as a different and significant *kind* of writing, responding to old cultural pressures and novel actualities.

PRATT's main subject is travel and exploration accounts in the context of European economic and political expansion since 1750. By that date, exploration writing was as much concerned with inland as with maritime exploration, a shift that coincided with the development of natural science as a discipline with connections to Eurocentric imperialism. Pratt's volume does not offer a chronologically or geographically oriented account, and she tends to conflate the different kinds of travel writing. Among the explorer accounts she analyses are those of John Barrow in southern Africa and Mungo Park in West Africa. Pratt's is a study of both genre and the ideology of imperialism. Travel writing, she believes, constructed the imperial subject. Several distinctive terms emerge to establish connections between imperial exploration and the work written accounts accomplished: "planetary consciousness" for a Eurocentric global view; "contact zone" for the literal and metaphoric space where colonial encounters occurred; and "anti-conquest" for the discursive rationalizations that enabled imperial projects to prosper under the guise of a neutral and benevolent search for knowledge.

CARTER, too, believes that historians have used the accounts of discoverers, explorers, and settlers in the service of imperial history. In the context of Australia, however, he draws liberally on such accounts, beginning with those of Sir Joseph Banks and Captain Cook, to suggest that they be reinterpreted as "spatial history", the process by which historical *space* became reformulated as historical stage and *place*. Carter argues that discoverers and their successors in exploration and settlement were engaged in making history, and his project is to study those processes, which we know as processes of language. By contrast, imperial history has overlooked process in order to subject actions located in space and time to a naturalizing imperial gaze. Carter pays attention to texts of discovery and exploration as producing an incomplete language of naming and travelling, a language that is specific and distinctive. His study is, to this date, one of very few sophisticated studies of exploration literature available, and carries discussion beyond the now fully acknowledged connection between imperial discourse and travel writing.

Although the title of ADAMS' study seems to subordinate travel literature to the history of the novel, his work is the most suggestive catalogue and preliminary survey of travel literature yet to have appeared. The chapter on "Travel Literature before 1800" is an encyclopedic list, which situates the literature of exploration within its historical and generic contexts. Adams notes the paucity of study of all kinds of travel literature as modes of discourse, and his own work remains indispensable to anyone seeking to investigate travel writing generally, and exploration literature specifically.

PATRICK HOLLAND

See also **Travel Literature**

F

Fantasy Literature

Apter, T.E., *Fantasy Literature: An Approach to Reality*, Bloomington: Indiana University Press, 1982; London: Macmillan, 1982

Attebery, Brian, *The Fantasy Tradition in American Literature from Irving to Le Guin*, Bloomington: Indiana University Press, 1980

Attebery, Brian, *Strategies of Fantasy*, Bloomington: Indiana University Press, 1992

Hume, Kathryn, *Fantasy and Mimesis: Responses to Reality in Western Literature*, London and New York: Methuen, 1984

Irwin, W.R., *The Game of the Impossible: A Rhetoric of Fantasy*, Urbana: University of Illinois Press, 1976

Jackson, Rosemary, *Fantasy: The Literature of Subversion*, London: Methuen, 1981

Manlove, Colin N., *The Impulse of Fantasy Literature*, Kent, Ohio: Kent State University Press, 1983; London: Macmillan, 1983

Manlove, Colin N., *Christian Fantasy: From 1200 to the Present*, Notre Dame, Indiana: University of Notre Dame Press, 1992

Rabkin, Eric S., *The Fantastic in Literature*, Princeton, New Jersey: Princeton University Press, 1976

Siebers, Tobin, *The Romantic Fantastic*, Ithaca, New York: Cornell University Press, 1984

Spivack, Charlotte, *Merlin's Daughters: Contemporary Women Writers of Fantasy*, Westport, Connecticut: Greenwood Press, 1987

Swinfen, Ann, *In Defence of Fantasy: A Study of the Genre in English and American Literature since 1945*, London and Boston: Routledge & Kegan Paul, 1984

Todorov, Tzvetan, *The Fantastic: A Structural Approach to a Literary Genre*, translated by Richard Howard, Cleveland, Ohio: Case Western Reserve University Press, 1973

TODOROV produced the earliest theoretical work dealing specifically with fantasy. His theory is suggestive but also narrow. He finds the effect of "the fantastic" in "the reader's hesitation". When the reader cannot decide whether a seemingly fantastic event in the narrative is simply metaphoric or actually happening, "the fantastic occupies the duration of this uncertainty". In the case of the former, the text is in the genre of what he calls the "marvellous"; in the latter, the genre becomes the "uncanny". In effect this theory limits fantasy to the ambiguous tale, so that many subsequent critics have found it confusing rather than helpful, although it is often cited as a pioneering look at the genre.

IRWIN's wide-ranging book offers an original perspective on fantasy, which he regards as intellectual play. He starts with a definition of fantasy as "a story based on and controlled by an overt violation in what is generally accepted as possibility". Fantasy fiction is therefore the "narrative result" of transforming this violation into seeming fact. The game involves both writer and reader. The author distinguishes fantasy from other forms of unrealistic fiction, such as science fiction, gothic romance, and the ghost story. He finds a great variety of intellectual play in numerous writers, both well-known, like C.S. Lewis and Franz Kafka, and relatively obscure, like W.H. Hudson and Kenneth Grahame. There is no extended analysis of single works but rather brief references to specific books as examples of specific kinds of intellectual play. The style is lively, and the content based on a vast knowledge of fantasy literature.

RABKIN asserts that the fantastic occurs when "the ground rules of a narrative world are suddenly made to turn about 180°". Since the fantastic involves this reversal of rules, a narrative world itself may reverse the rules of the extra-textual world. Although there is similar shift in so-called "escape" fiction, including adventure and mystery stories, only fantasy achieves this complete diametric reversal, which can serve as a meaningful psychological escape. Through a variety of examples, ranging from the brothers Grimm and E.T.A. Hoffmann to Agatha Christie and Arthur C. Clarke, the author demonstrates a spectrum of fantasy, concluding that it is a basic mode of human knowing. He draws on psychoanalysis to establish the connection between knowing and escape in this theoretical and thought-provoking approach.

ATTEBERY, in his 1980 study, notes the bias against fantasy in America, but traces the emerging tradition to its achievement of a distinctively American fairyland. He deals with fantasy in the context of folk tradition, legend, and romance, citing examples from Washington Irving, Edgar Allan Poe, Nathaniel Hawthorne, and Herman Melville. Especial importance is attached to L. Frank Baum's Oz stories, since *The Wizard of Oz* is "the first unquestionably American fantasy". In a chapter on fantasy and escape, the author deals with such writers as James Branch Cabell, H.P. Lovecraft, William Burroughs, and Edward Eager. A long concluding chapter considers the range of American fantasy after J.R.R. Tolkien, whose *Lord of the Rings* radically changed the nature of the genre. Although such writers as Peter S. Beagle, André Norton, and Anne McCaffrey are cited, the major example here is Ursula K. Le Guin, a writer who has had a "profound effect on our perception of the world we know". This convincing and important study defends the American fantasy as offering a uniquely valuable and positive experience.

JACKSON applies Marxist and Freudian theories to the texts of fantasy literature, rejecting what she calls "transcendental" criticism in favour of an approach grounded in social context. Furthermore, since fantasy expresses unconscious drives, she argues that psychoanalytic interpretation is not only relevant but necessary. Central to the Freudian readings is the psychologist's essay on the uncanny, and the Marxist readings interpret fantasy as beginning in cultural subversion and moving toward non-signification. The approach taken here is narrowly focused. The value of the fantasy genre is seen in its inherently subversive nature, the purpose of which is "the dissolution of an order experienced to be oppressive and insufficient". But the arbitrary limitations of the Marx-Freud emphasis reduces and distorts that purpose by eliminating the element of the transcendental and spiritual altogether.

A psychoanalytic study of fantasy literature is presented by APTER. The author sees fantasy "not as an escape from reality but an investigation of it". The examples chosen to illustrate this approach are not those based on an imaginary secondary world but rather on our own world. The fantasist's purpose is seen as parallel to the psychoanalyst's, for in therapy the divergence from perceived reality provides the means to discover that reality. He focuses on six literary themes: fantasy as morality, the uncanny, the double, fantastic objectivity, the fantasy of order, and logical fantasy. Each is illustrated by selected writers, including non-English authors such as Dostoevsky, Kafka, and Jorge Luis Borges. In spite of its single focus on psychoanalysis, this book is wide-ranging in its ideas and coverage.

MANLOVE (1983) locates the essential impulse of fantasy literature in one central theme, the celebration of the wondrous identity of created things. He focuses on six modern fantasists who celebrate this individual uniqueness in different ways. Charles Williams is a religious writer, with a theological view of the universe. Le Guin writes conservative fantasy, concentrating on the idea of balance in her Earthsea trilogy. Edith Nesbit combines two perspectives, the realistic and the supernatural. George MacDonald's dream fantasies exhibit a motif of circularity, an image of returning to the starting point. T.H. White, unlike most fantasists, must deal with loss and failure because of his Arthurian subject. Mervyn Peake's work is distinctive for its separation of body and mind. All create a sense of delight and wonder concerning "things". The commentaries are perceptive from this singular point of view.

HUME's thesis is that literature is the product of two impulses – mimesis, the desire to imitate reality, and fantasy, the desire to alter reality. Using a broad critical overview rather than detailed scholarship in any one area, she deals with the nature of fantasy through four basic literary responses to reality. First is escapism, the literature of illusion exemplified in most popular fiction; second is the literature of vision, which offers a new interpretation of reality; third is didacticism, the literature of revision, which reinterprets reality; fourth is the literature of disillusion, which rejects the possibility of knowing reality. The wide-ranging final section of the book deals with the functions of fantasy, delving into the human need for fantasy and focusing on reader response. Hume is eminently sensible in her study of these twin impulses.

SIEBERS is primarily concerned with the relations between literature and superstition, using the fantastic literature of the nineteenth century as an example. As he expresses it, "the Romantic fantastic reenacts the logic of superstition in aesthetic form". These nineteenth-century authors used the fantastic as a weapon against the rationalists. In a chapter on laughter and the fantastic, Siebers deals with Baudelaire, Hoffmann, and Gogol. All three of these writers associated supernaturalism and laughter, and regarded laughter as diabolical. He offers a more detailed analysis of Hawthorne, who discovered the parallels between the Romantic aestheticization of superstition and popular beliefs in witchcraft. In a concluding chapter on the Romantic self, he discusses the use of madness in fantasy, seeing both madness and superstition as "supremely mimetic". This work is useful to those interested in Romanticism rather than in fantasy in general.

English and American fantasy since 1945 is the subject of SWINFEN's book. She identifies the central ingredient in fantasy as "the marvellous", i.e., "anything outside the normal space-time continuum of the everyday world". Unlike some critics, who organize their studies in terms of authors, Swinfen's approach is thematic. She deals with animal fantasy, time fantasy, secondary worlds, philosophical and political idealisms, and symbolism. Numerous works of fiction are considered, including several of the most popular series, such as those of Tolkien, Lewis, Le Guin, and Lloyd Alexander. In conclusion, she summarizes her defence of fantasy fiction as a serious form of the modern novel, engendering "an enhanced perception of the nature of the primary world" and leading the reader into a "transcendent reality, embodied in imaginative and spiritual otherworlds". Far-ranging in coverage, this book is also perceptive and sensitive.

My own book (SPIVACK's) explores the relationship between fantasy and the feminine in women writers of the genre. I delve into ten contemporary women fantasists (André Norton, Katherine Kurtz, Mary Stewart, Patricia A. McKillip, Vera Chapman, Gillian Bradshaw, Susan Cooper, Le Guin, Evangeline Walton, and Marion Zimmer Bradley) and the subversive messages embodied in their fiction. Along with the obvious attention to strong female protagonists and the assumption of a feminine point of view on subject matter traditionally presented from the male perspective, these works exemplify three subversive themes – the renunciation of the power principle in politics, the vindication of morality, and the depolarization of values. These works also tend to exhibit a circular rather than a linear narrative structure, stressing continuity and renewal over the usual progression towards achievement. To date, this book is the only one to concentrate on women fantasy writers.

ATTEBERY's 1992 study approaches fantasy through recent literary theory. His prototypical example is *Lord of the Rings*, which he examines by looking at how several schools of critical thought treat the text. He finds that the most useful theoretical bases for understanding Tolkien's work are language theory, the Jungian psychology of inner inexperience, and the ecological treatment of humanity's place in the natural world. He also deals suggestively with fantasy set not in a secondary world but in our primary world, a genre which he labels "indigenous". More than merely defending fantasy, the author argues persuasively that fantasy-writers rather than realists are best able to "recapture the modern world for the imagination". Throughout the book he maintains a refreshingly rational attitude towards the subject of theory, the task of which is simply "to provide a framework capable of accounting for the story's success on its own terms".

Christian fantasy is "a fiction dealing with the Christian supernatural, often in an imagined world", according to MANLOVE (1992). He begins with medieval examples, including Dante's epic *Divine Comedy*. With Edmund Spenser we move from the otherworld into the landscape of the soul. From the Renaissance the author also deals with Christopher Marlowe's *Doctor Faustus*, selected poems of John Donne and George Herbert, and Milton's *Paradise Lost*. After a brief look at William Blake, John Bunyan, and Emanuel Swedenborg, and a more detailed look at George MacDonald and Charles Kingsley, he moves to a consideration of modern Christian fantasy, which became a distinct genre because of the historical de-supernaturalizing of Christianity. For the twentieth century, he focuses on the novels of Charles Williams and C.S. Lewis, but omits their fellow Inkling, Tolkien. Briefer consideration is given to several other recent writers, including Sarah Cooper, Madeleine L'Engle, and many more. Far-ranging in scope, and sophisticated in critical commentary, this is an excellent study of the subject of Christian fantasy.

CHARLOTTE SPIVACK

See also **Science Fiction, Utopian Literature**

Farquhar, George c.1677–1707

Irish dramatist

Anselment, Raymond A. (ed.), *Farquhar: "The Recruiting Officer" and "The Beaux' Stratagem": A Casebook*, London: Macmillan, 1977

Farmer, A.J., *George Farquhar*, London: Longmans, Green & Co., 1966

James, E. Nelson, *The Development of George Farquhar as a Comic Dramatist*, The Hague and Paris: Mouton, 1972

Kenny, Shirley Strum (ed.), *The Works of George Farquhar*, 2 vols., Oxford: Clarendon Press, 1988; New York: Oxford University Press, 1988

Rothstein, Eric, *George Farquhar*, New York: Twayne, 1967

Stafford-Clark, Max, *Letters to George: The Account of a Rehearsal*, London: Nick Hern Books, 1989

George Farquhar's last two plays, *The Recruiting Officer* and *The Beaux' Stratagem*, were the most original of his works (some of which were adaptations), and throughout the eighteenth century the most popular of his plays. Twentieth-century criticism has seen no reason to alter that judgement; for in those two plays Farquhar modulated the corrosive wit of his Restoration forebears, William Wycherley, Sir George Etherege, William Congreve, and Sir John Vanbrugh, while at the same time breaking away from the London scenes and people those playwrights had portrayed. Farquhar found instead fresh comic potential in the provincial enclaves of Shrewsbury and Lichfield.

KENNY's magisterial two-volume edition of Farquhar's complete works is the best starting point for students of Farquhar's reputation. She presents authoritative, old-spelling texts of Farquhar's works, complete with generous annotations. Most usefully, she provides long Introductions for each of Farquhar's works. Here she eschews formal or thematic analysis, offering instead the history of each play's composition, its known sources, its subsequent eighteenth-century performances, and the later history of the play's reputation. Taken together, these Introductions build up a composite picture of Farquhar's afterlife, from the opprobrium heaped upon his Irish head by English contemporaries envious of his success (Kenny records numerous such racist attacks) to the genial affection which, by the end of the eighteenth century, had attached itself to his last two plays, and which has dominated subsequent discussions of them.

ANSELMENT's *Casebook* complements Kenny's outline of Farquhar's reputation. His brief, lucid Introduction summarises the history of aesthetic evaluation of Farquhar's two most celebrated plays, while his anthology of critical extracts prints a generous sampling of pre-twentieth-century criticism, from John Oldmixon's emotional obituary through to William Hazlitt's and Leigh Hunt's celebrated remarks on Farquhar, which helped keep him in the public eye and which founded the current consensus that Farquhar provides a witty and humane transition from "high" (and acidic) Restoration comedy to the genialities of Oliver Goldsmith and Richard Brinsley Sheridan, both, like Farquhar, Irish comic playwrights for the English stage. Anselment also prints William Archer's commentary on *The Beaux' Stratagem*. Archer's commitment to Ibsenite social realism led him to appreciate the serious vein of Farquhar's treatment of divorce in that play. Explorations of Farquhar's use of Milton's *Doctrine and Discipline of Divorce* have become increasingly common in criticism since World War II. Anselment prints several key readings from that archive, among them Kenneth Muir's clear-sighted plotting of Farquhar's experiments with comic form, and Bill Gaskill's explanation of his (Brechtian) directorial approach in his ground-breaking, class-obsessed productions of *The Recruiting Officer* (1963) and *The Beaux' Stratagem* (1970).

FARMER's British Council pamphlet is a useful, though slight, contribution to Farquhar studies. He gives a sprightly account of the little that is known of Farquhar's biography, followed by thumbnail sketches of Farquhar's plays. His critical insights are solid, but the brevity of his monograph make his no more than a good orthodox beginning for Farquhar students, who will need more nourishment than Farmer provides.

ROTHSTEIN provides stouter fare. His biographical account is the more substantial of the two, and he persuasively links Farquhar's plays with his non-dramatic writings (poems and sequences of fictional letters). Unlike Farmer, Rothstein accounts for all of Farquhar's plays, though expending most of his critical energy on lengthy and solid descriptions of the famous two. Rothstein refutes claims for Farquhar as a realist. He shows how the early plays are little more than lively congeries of plots and characters frequently to be seen on late seventeenth-century stages, but somewhat less frequently to be encountered in the world outside London's theatres. Even in the last two plays, Rothstein maintains that "Farquhar's characters come directly from contemporary fiction". Farquhar's sources are thus the prior plays he draws from (rather than any shrewd observation taken directly from Farquhar's short and hapless life); and his success was in renovating the form of comic drama rather than introducing novel subject matter to the stage. Rothstein's approach is thus resolutely formalist.

JAMES endorses the utility of Rothstein's approach, conducting his inquiry into Farquhar's experiments with the forms of comic drama with the rigour of a committed structuralist. He prefaces this quest with an exhaustive summary of Farquhar's treatment at the hands of earlier critics. James quotes these critics extensively, only to condemn them for being obsessed with tracking Farquhar's life and times through his plays. Like Rothstein, James is keener on finding traces of Restoration drama throughout the works. Thus he discovers that "*Love and a Bottle* is a burlesque of Restoration comedy" and that "*The Recruiting Officer* really owes more to Farquhar's experiences in the theater than it does to his experiences in Shrewsbury". James supports his argument with a number of charts, plotting character and narrative in the plays; his is the most rigorous and sustained account of Farquhar available.

STAFFORD-CLARK's, on the other hand, is by far the most engaging modern account. He wrote his *Letters to George* while rehearsing a new production of *The Recruiting Officer* for London's innovative Royal Court Theatre. Hypothesising Farquhar as his correspondent, Stafford-Clark daily reports on problems his actors encounter both with Farquhar's language and with re-imagining early eighteenth-century Shrewsbury, where the play is set. They tackle the latter by daytripping to Shrewsbury, where they discover that little has changed in the town since Farquhar recruited there in 1704. The language they learn by breaking each scene into units, discovering the objective of every phrase in the play. Stafford-Clark gives a fascinating glimpse of a modern company at work on a canonical play-text; but his insights have much to offer students of these plays too. His rehearsals (like his final production) reveal how funny Farquhar can be (and how real), as well as showing how well-constructed and precise Farquhar's language and plots are. Stafford-Clark thus discovers validity in both sides of the Farquhar debate: Farquhar knew well enough how to make crowd-pleasing plays; but he did so by stocking them with the people, their language, and their landscapes, that he observed and cherished throughout his writing life.

MARK HOULAHAN

Faulkner, William 1897–1962

American novelist, short-story writer, poet, and screenwriter

Bleikasten, André, *The Ink of Melancholy*, Bloomington: Indiana University Press, 1990

Brodhead, Richard (ed.), *Faulkner: New Perspectives*, Englewood Cliffs, New Jersey: Prentice-Hall, 1983

Brooks, Cleanth, *William Faulkner: The Yoknapatawpha Country*, New Haven, Connecticut, and London: Yale University Press, 1963

Fowler, Doreen, and Ann Abadie (eds.), *Fifty Years of Yoknapatawpha: Faulkner and Yoknapatawpha*, Jackson: University Press of Mississippi, 1979

Irwin, John T., *Doubling and Incest/Repetition and Revenge*, Baltimore: Johns Hopkins University Press, 1975

Kinney, Arthur F., *Faulkner's Narrative Poetics: Style as Vision*, Amherst: University of Massachusetts Press, 1978

Matthews, John T., *The Play of Faulkner's Language*, Ithaca, New York: Cornell University Press, 1982

Minter, David, *William Faulkner: His Life and His Work*, Baltimore: Johns Hopkins University Press, 1980

Parker, Robert Dale, *Faulkner and the Novelistic Imagination*, Urbana: University of Illinois Press, 1985

Roberts, Diane, *Faulkner and Southern Womanhood*, Athens: University of Georgia Press, 1994

Sundquist, Eric J., *Faulkner: The House Divided*, Baltimore: Johns Hopkins University Press, 1983

Vickery, Olga, *The Novels of William Faulkner: A Critical Interpretation*, Baton Rouge: Louisiana State University Press, 1959

Watson, James G., *William Faulkner: Letters and Fictions*, Austin: University of Texas Press, 1987

Zender, Karl F., *The Crossing of the Ways: William Faulkner, the South, and the Modern World*, New Brunswick, New Jersey: Rutgers University Press, 1989

Since the 1960s William Faulkner has received more critical attention than any other American writer of the twentieth century. Early criticism tended toward explication and unification of the dense plots and narrative strategies. More recently, the burgeoning of sophisticated critical approaches has given new life to Faulkner studies. The language and characters of the novels are rich in possibilities for a wide array of readers, from psychoanalytic critics, to deconstructionists, to New Historicists. The result is a wealth of provocative readings, which only underscore Faulkner's compelling presence in American letters. Beginning with Vickery's 1959 study, the following discussion charts important and useful critical works chronologically up to Roberts' 1994 volume.

VICKERY's book is a standard among New-Critical texts on Faulkner. She provides a thorough, if perhaps overly unified, picture of the development of the canon. Her closing chapters on Faulkner's approaches to time and language, to myth and "truth" are among the best early forays into what have become the central issues for many critics.

BROOKS' study of Faulkner's Yoknapatawpha county focuses on the sense of place that yokes the characters to the themes in 14 novels. Clear, plot-driven analyses connect Faulkner's particular "postage stamp of soil" to broader themes in American literature. The study organizes and unifies the Yoknapatawpha canon in terms of its common locale and as an exploration of the idea of community, and many of Brooks' readings are still standard. *Light in August*, for example, is presented as a classic story of an individual's struggle within and against a community bound by racist traditions and rigid codes of behavior. Joe Christmas' story becomes the tragedy of the American isolated individual, interspersed with darkly comedic subplots, which Brooks takes as Faulkner's position on the futility of much human endeavor.

KINNEY reads Faulkner through his style, or narrative poetics, declaring that he "shapes his work to reveal the visions of his characters; their visions thus become his style". The long, winding sentences, shifts in time and perceptions, and fascination with apparent rather than actual fact are the hallmarks of Faulkner's fiction and his vision of what it means to be human in the modern world. Kinney first traces evidence that Faulkner was influenced by the great novelists of consciousness such as Joseph Conrad, Fedor Dostoevsky, Marcel Proust, and James Joyce. Arguing that Faulkner's style borrows from those novelists' recognition of the constitutive nature of human consciousness, Kinney then makes a case for the fiction as the account of Faulkner's exploration of the difficult but necessary task of articulating life.

IRWIN begins by acknowledging the interplay among several novels, particularly *The Sound and the Fury* and *Absalom, Absalom!* But the focus here is on the complex substructure of doubling, incest, repetition, and revenge that characterizes Faulkner's continual retelling of the effort to tell his story. Moving between psychoanalytic and structuralist modes, Irwin creates a fresh and provocative context in which to re-think the dilemmas of Quentin Compson, Joe Christmas, Thomas Sutpen, and other doomed Faulknerian obsessives.

FOWLER and ABADIE have edited the 1979 volume of the University of Mississippi series on the annual Faulkner and Yoknapatawpha Conference. This volume commemorates the 50th anniversary of the publication of *Sartoris*, the first Yoknapatawpha novel, with essays by biographer Joseph Blotner and critics such as Michael Millgate and Noel Polk. All of the essays contribute perspectives on the intricacies of the relation between Faulkner's fiction and his fictional county.

MINTER's study recounts Faulkner's life in relation to his writing and uncovers the complexity of the connections and contradictions in them. Drawing on interviews, letters, and essays, as well as Faulkner's poetry and fiction, Minter underscores the "reciprocities of Faulkner's great art and his flawed life". Accounts of his Hollywood years and his struggle with alcoholism offer a rich context in which to read both the triumphs such as *Absalom, Absalom!* and the tangled flaws of *A Fable*.

A lively Derridean reading of *The Sound and the Fury*, *Absalom, Absalom!*, *The Hamlet*, and *Go Down, Moses* is presented in MATTHEWS' book. In an introductory chapter, "How to Approach Language", Matthews argues that Faulkner's style and subject are comprehensible and integrated by their recognition that "language plays in its failure to present what it represents". The chapter on *Absalom*, for example, avoids deconstructing the text into meaninglessness by carefully presenting it as an investigation of the possibilities for meaning, which indeterminacy allows to both the writer and his readers.

BRODHEAD has gathered six essays, which present some of the best and most provocative strains of Faulkner criticism, as well as Faulkner's own two versions of the Introduction to *The Sound and the Fury*. The rationale for the new selections is that while Faulkner's reputation as a major American writer is now unassailable, the canon itself demands our continual rethinking. The essays provide a wide range of perspectives on Faulkner's style, the social and cultural contexts of the novels, and the process of re-imagining history and experience.

Six novels are examined by SUNDQUIST to detail how they reveal and complicate Faulkner's preoccupation with Southern history. Sundquist brings fresh insights to old thematic problems by tracing Faulkner's growing awareness of the South's troubled legacy of racial unrest. For example, the analysis of Joe Christmas' ambiguous and racialized relations to himself and others contextualizes *Light in August* in 1930s' Jim Crow culture, and thus provides a new perspective on the violence and turmoil characteristic of the narrative.

PARKER focuses on four central novels, but also develops a theory to illuminate other texts as well. Beginning with Faulkner's fascination with "tactical and epistemological" gaps, Parker traces the interaction between created expectation and violation of expectation in the plots and narrative strategies of *As I Lay Dying*, *Sanctuary*, *Light in August*, and *Absalom, Absalom!* The discovery of each novel's "hidden but discoverable shape" defines Faulkner's considerable contribution to the genre.

Connections among the published letters, the fictional letters, and the letter writers Faulkner creates are established by WATSON. In this approach, Watson demonstrates how Faulkner's acute awareness of the connection between epistolary strategies and fiction writing reveals the evolution of a world "from what he called his 'postage stamp of soil' into a cosmos of my own". The book traces the "law of letters" from the early poetry in *Mayday* to Gavin Stevens' letters to Linda Kohl in the Snopes trilogy.

ZENDER's title and thesis are taken from Allen Tate's assertion that the flowering of modern Southern writers and their particular historical moment is a "quite temporary . . . crossing of the ways". He analyzes Faulkner's art as having been profoundly influenced by the disappearance of the agrarian South into a modern, "deregionalized" America. Rather than focus on the socio-cultural context of the novels, however, Zender argues that Faulkner transforms his account of that difficult time into a comprehensive exploration of the experience of loss and uncertainty. The discussion of voice and dynamics of sound and silence in the novels, for example, reveals Faulkner's anxiety about art as a means to control perception and experience.

The focus of BLEIKASTEN is Faulkner's most prolific period, the late 1920s to the early 1940s, and particularly "the four children of this miracle", *The Sound and the Fury*, *As I Lay Dying*, *Sanctuary*, and *Light in August*. His purpose is to focus primarily on the texts themselves and to supplement close readings with discussions of their meanings in "biographical, sociocultural, and historical terms". The result is a rich and complex re-reading of the fiction, which both updates Bleikasten's earlier work on the novels and reinforces their dense intertextuality.

ROBERTS provides a comprehensive assessment of Faulkner's representations of women, specifically six versions of Southern womanhood. Whether the women in the novels are black or white, they are always some manifestation of the "Other". From that premise, Roberts delineates Faulkner's transformation of received images of women as one version of his struggle to negotiate the gap between fiction and experience. Finally, Faulkner's failed desire is, like Horace Benbow's, for the woman/fiction to be the "still unravished bride of quietness".

JUDITH LOCKYER

Feminist Literary Theory

Armstrong, Isobel (ed.), *New Feminist Discourses: Essays in Literature, Criticism, and Theory*, London and New York: Routledge, 1992
Betterton, Rosemary (ed.), *Looking On: Images of Femininity in the Visual Arts and Media*, London: Pandora, 1987; New York: Routledge, 1987
Butler, Judith, *Gender Trouble: Feminism and the Subversion of Identity*, London and New York: Routledge, 1990
Cameron, Deborah (ed.), *The Feminist Critique of Language: A Reader*, London and New York: Routledge, 1990
Crowley, H., and Susan Himmelweit (eds.), *Knowing Women: Feminism and Knowledge*, Cambridge: Polity Press/Open Univeristy Press, 1992
Donaldson, Laura, *Decolonizing Feminisms: Race, Gender and Empire-Building*, London: Routledge, 1992; Chapel Hill: University of North Carolina Press, 1992
Fuss, Diana, *Esssentially Speaking: Feminism, Nature and Difference*, London and New York: Routledge, 1989
Greene, Gayle, and Coppélia Kahn, *Making a Difference: Feminist Literary Criticism*, London and New York: Methuen, 1985
Gunew, Sneja (ed.), *Feminist Knowledge: Critique and Construct*, London and New York: Routledge, 1990
Gunew, Sneja (ed.), *A Reader in Feminist Knowledge*, London and New York: Routledge, 1990
Humm, Maggie (ed.), *Feminisms: A Reader*, Hemel Hempstead, Hertfordshire: Harvester Wheatsheaf, 1992
Jardine, Alice, and Paul Smith, *Men in Feminism*, London and New York: Methuen, 1987
Millett, Kate, *Sexual Politics*, London: Rupert Hart-Davis, 1970; Garden City, New York: Doubleday, 1970
Mills, Sara, Lynne Pearce, Sue Spaull, and Elaine Millard, *Feminist Readings/Feminists Reading*, Hemel Hempstead, Hertfordshire: Harvester Wheatsheaf, 1989; Charlottesville: University of Virginia Press, 1989
Moi, Toril, *Sexual/Textual Politics: Feminist Literary Theory*, London and New York: Methuen, 1985
Moi, Toril (ed.), *French Feminist Thought: A Reader*, Oxford: Blackwell, 1987
Showalter, Elaine, *A Literature of Their Own: British Women Novelists from Brontë to Lessing*, Princeton, New Jersey: Princeton University Press, 1977; London: Virago, 1978, revised 1982
Ware, Vron, *Beyond the Pale: White Women, Racism and History*, London: Verso, 1992

Feminist critical theory has always been an interdisciplinary subject; for those who are primarily engaged in literary criticism, it has always been necessary to look beyond the boundaries of purely textual analysis in order to explore both the factors that contribute to the discriminatory treatment of women and those factors that enable women to resist and counter discrimination. Feminist critical theory has never been a unified subject and it is common to refer to "feminisms" and "feminist theories" rather than assume that there is one single approach to analysis or theorising. In early feminist theorising it was thought that feminism could be divided into liberal, radical, and revolutionary phases; that is, into those who argued for equality with men, those who celebrated women's supposed difference from men, and those who wished to deconstruct the system of gender difference. However, it is clear that feminist theory has now become far more complex a field than these simple definitions can encompass.

Feminist critical theory can be said to have begun in the 1960s and 1970s with work that questioned the representation of female characters in male-authored texts and also questioned the exclusion of women authors from the canon. MILLETT documented the way that, in a large number of canonical male literary works, women are represented as sexual objects, whose needs are subservient to those of the central male protagonist. Her work led many readers to reconsider fundamentally their evaluations of certain male writers, such as D.H. Lawrence, and the term "sexual politics" became a very common focus of debate. SHOWALTER provided a survey of previously little-known literature by women from the eighteenth and nineteenth centuries. Her work caused many critics to ask questions about why these books by women were not included on literature courses and why they were often not in print. Showalter also sparked off a debate about the constituents of canon-building and argued that women's writing should be considered within a separate canon. MOI's 1985 overview of this early feminist criticism was a useful, yet critical, guide to possible problems in these two tendencies, of analysis of female characters, and of analysis of female literary traditions. Her work, more than that of any other, introduced many readers to the possibilities of incorporating critical theory into feminist work, since she surveyed the work of the French feminists Luce Irigaray, Hélène Cixous, and Julia Kristeva.

This opposition between what was termed "French feminism" and Anglo-American feminist criticism foregrounded a difference between those who were interested in incorporating overtly theoretical concerns into their work, and those who preferred to concentrate on the analysis of experience and issues – such as canonicity – that were seen to be more "real" and urgent. The opposition between French and Anglo-American feminisms gradually disintegrated, since it became clear that theoretical concerns were being articulated by both types of feminisms, yet in different ways. Yet the distinction did serve to provoke debate about how feminists could work within institutions, how theoretical work initially developed by males could be used, and how accessible to other women feminists' theoretical work should be. MOI's 1987 overview of French feminist theory was a useful addition to her earlier work in that it introduced many readers to the original texts by these theorists. MILLS, PEARCE, SPAULL, and MILLARD's collection of essays attempted to read well-known literary texts by male and female authors, using a range of different theories, both Anglo-American and French.

Interdisciplinary work has always been essential in feminist critical theories, and there have been a number of useful surveys of feminist thought from different disciplines. HUMM surveys a wide range of theoretical texts by French and Anglo-American critics, as well as texts by Asian, black, and lesbian women. Her reader covers such issues as sexuality and reproduction, history, language, psychoanalysis, and education, and as such serves as a thorough introduction to women's studies and feminist critical theory in general. GUNEW's two volumes provide a theoretical overview of feminist critical theory across a range of subject areas, and a selection of key theoretical texts and surveys of disciplinary studies. CROWLEY and HIMMELWEIT's edited collection similarly offers an overview of some of the key areas of feminist theory, while raising important questions about the very nature of knowledge and gender difference. BETTERTON's collection of essays on the relationship between gender and representation highlights debates about images of women within visual studies, but also has implications for literary analysis, especially in terms of the depiction of characters. CAMERON's edited collection of theoretical texts on language and gender deals with issues such as whether there is a separate women's language or style of speaking and writing, and whether women have been excluded from the processes of naming and representation in language. Language has always been a central issue in debates on women's writing, and this collection gathers together some of the most important theoretical texts.

There have been a number of edited collections that attempt to focus on feminist literary analysis. GREENE and KAHN's collection introduced many readers to the variety of feminist literary theory and its possible applications to the process of reading texts. ARMSTRONG's more recent collection focuses on readings of women's writing, and also makes interventions into feminist theoretical debates.

There are a number of debates currently raging in feminist critical theory. The first is over the issue of essentialism versus constructionism, that is, whether women and men are in essence different from one another or not. Within an essentialist point of view, all women share certain qualities with one another, while a constructionist viewpoint would suggest that cultures construct gender difference through systematic social conditioning of children and adults. BUTLER and FUSS have engaged in a rigorous theoretical debate about the nature of essentialism, and have caused many feminists to question the very nature of gender difference. This has far reaching implications for feminist theory in general, since feminist theory aims at changing the way gender difference is regulated within society, but is nevertheless premised on the basis of the existence of gender difference.

A further issue to engage feminist theory from the 1970s until the present is the involvement of men. Many feminists feel that men cannot be feminists, and suspect the motives of men who are involved with feminist work; others are more open to the possibility of men being pro-feminist. JARDINE and SMITH's edited collection of essays opens up this debate with heated exchanges between many of the female and male contributors.

There has been a realisation in recent feminist theory that its early forms reflected the concerns of those who primarily developed and popularised it for a wide audience – that is, Western, white, middle-class women. Much early feminist work made global assumptions based on the experience of a very narrow range of women. Black women have articulated their concerns about the racism of this type of theoretical work, and there has been a move to analyse feminisms from different groups of women. This concern has been most apparent in work on gender and colonialism and postcolonialism. WARE analyses British and American women's involvement in slavery and the anti-slavery movements, and also feminism's relation to imperialism. In this way she examines the racial aspects of the construction of white femininity, and points to new ways of analysing the relationship between race and gender. DONALDSON's complex intervention into the examination of gender and postcolonialism is a textual analysis, which foregrounds systematic rhetorical strategies within colonial and postcolonial texts. She also considers the ways in which Western feminism can move forward from its perceived narrow and potentially racist concerns.

SARA H. MILLS

See also **Gender and Literature**

Fiction: Theory

Bakhtin, Mikhail, *The Dialogic Imagination*, edited by Michael Holquist, translated by Caryl Emerson, Austin: University of Texas Press, 1981

Booth, Wayne C., *The Rhetoric of Fiction*, Chicago: University of Chicago Press, 1961

Lukács, Georg, *The Theory of the Novel: A Historico-Philosophical Essay on the Forms of Great Epic Literature*, translated by Anna Bostock, London: Merlin Press, 1978; Cambridge, Massachusetts: MIT Press, 1971

Mitchell, W.J.T. (ed.), *On Narrative*, Chicago: University of Chicago Press, 1981

Sacks, Sheldon, *Fiction and the Shape of Belief: A Study of Henry Fielding, with Glances at Swift, Johnson and Richardson*, Berkeley: University of California Press, 1964

Scholes, Robert, and Robert Kellogg, *The Nature of Narrative*, New York and Oxford: Oxford University Press, 1966

Stevick, Philip (ed.), *The Theory of the Novel*, London: Collier-Macmillan, 1967; New York: Free Press, 1967

Ideas about fiction are mostly constructed around two issues – the act of reading, how the reader and text create narrative spaces; and the notion of truthfulness or realism – the extent to which fiction is an honest or misleading evocation of something recognizably real. Thus, discussions of fiction actually become expositions of systems of belief, examinations of the epistemology of persuasion.

In that regard BOOTH's work is seminal. He moves the discussion of fiction away from simple formal realism and directly moral didacticism to the question of communication, how fiction manipulates language to persuade us of an author/reader compact. His emphasis on "control" in narrative and on the subtle communion between the writer and the audience challenges traditional ideas by demonstrating that the process of persuasion is similar in all fiction. Beginning with Boccaccio, Booth goes on to examine the rhetorical postures of the major eighteenth-, nineteenth-, and early twentieth-century writers. He is particularly good on Henry Fielding, Laurence Sterne, Henry James, and James Joyce. Booth is not at all interested in "what" fiction has to say but insists that literary criticism examine "how" fiction operates, recognizing that all strategies of authority are entirely issues of process.

SACKS is committed to a moral interpretation of the form and function of fiction. His primary examples are taken from eighteenth-century English literature, but his theoretical position, what he calls his grammar of fiction, is applicable across the canon. Sacks uses his "grammar" to identify three principal kinds of narrative fiction – satire, apologue, and direct action – each with its own rhetorical approach to representing the "moral norm" in society. Recognition of normative morality, socially conscious behaviour, and shared systems of belief makes Sacks a conservative critic. His study emphasizes the classical ideal of "character in action", a concept Sacks uses as the basis of his moral philosophy of literature; to Sacks, fiction matters because through it we can come to know the motives for performing social actions: fiction teaches us the importance of sympathy and the need for a recognizable set of values.

SCHOLES and KELLOGG remain the standard introduction to modern critical attitudes about fictional narrative. Their work begins with a discussion of the "oral heritage of written language" and goes on to establish a "classical heritage of modern narrative". These two chapters of their study are a highly readable and surprisingly thorough history of the development of fiction as a sophisticated literary form. Subsequent chapters look at meaning, character, plot, and point of view in an articulate but readily accessible style, which is free of jargon and unnecesary theorizing. They are particularly strong in exploring fictional characterization, setting their position in the context of Henry James' astute observations in "The Art of Fiction". This study regularly returns to classical examples as a foundation for its longer reaching speculations and is, accordingly, a useful starting point for readers just beginning to familiarize themselves with critical theories about fiction.

BAKHTIN represents a more philosophically sophisticated theoretical position. The four essays in his study emphasize the disruptive and subversive aspects of fiction, drawing distinctions between the teleological form of the epic and the open-ended inventiveness of the novel. Bakhtin is particularly adept in his discussion of comic fiction, especially the pivotal role of Sterne's *Tristram Shandy* in the development of the English novel. He appreciates the comedic sensibility in fiction for its historic role in undermining the "official function of the novel". In critiquing romantic fiction, he draws attention to the absence of any "necessary internal limits", an observation extended into an elaborate exploration of the temporal diversity and flexibility that typifies much prose fiction. Bakhtin writes extensively about time and narrative, arguing that any sense of reality in fiction comes about as a direct result of the reader's experience of the temporal in the text. This is a difficult study, highly original and influential, and very much worth the effort necessary to engage it.

LUKÁCS also focuses on the relationship between official and unofficial forms of fiction, beginning, like Bakhtin, by establishing a distinction between epic and novel. This is an explicitly Marxist theory of fiction and, although Lukács deals with a broadly European context, his work is crucial in establishing the discourse for the political and social analysis of fiction. Surprisingly, Lukács is one of the few theorists to emphasize the short story, which, he says "expresses the ultimate [mood] of the creative process . . .. It sees absurdity in all its undisguised and unadorned nakedness". For Lukács, fiction, especially the novel, is at its best as "immanent self-criticism", as the "self-destruction of reality", as "disharmony between the interiority of the individual and the substratum of his actions". Lukács' concept of the dialectic of idealism and disillusionment is the starting point for understanding the politics of modernism.

A comprehensive range of most of the theoretical perspectives on fiction is provided by Stevick and Mitchell. STEVICK's is the more traditional survey, embracing 53 essays and excerpts from novelists and theorists and ranging from Henry James and E.M. Forster through A.A. Mendilow and Northrop Frye. Mark Shorer's essay on the technique of discovery in fiction remains a crucial contribution to theory, and Mendilow's discussion of time in narrative is still the most lucid introduction to that vexed, yet central, notion. The collection is divided into traditional themes and topics: "Generic Identity", "Narrative Technique", "Point of View", "Plot", "Character", "Time", "Symbol", and "Life and Art". The examination of realism is particularly useful, because all of the points of view on the topic are derived from practising novelists. This combination of practice with commentary makes Stevick's volume a good choice for a concise and accessible introduction to ideas about narrative.

MITCHELL brings together exclusively theoretical essays on fiction, all of which originally appeared in the journal *Critical Theory* (1980–81). Jacques Derrida, Paul Ricoeur, Frank Kermode, Hayden White, and Barbara Herrnstein Smith are each represented here at their best. Derrida on genre, Ricouer on time, and Kermode on secrecy make crucial contributions to the theory of fiction, and Mitchell's text is a succinct and ready access to these often difficult critical positions. Of particular interest is the series of "Afterthoughts" and "Critical Responses" in the final two chapters of the collection. Here Mitchell sets various theorists in opposition to one another, demonstrating both the wide range of opinion about fiction and the deeply contradictory and conflicted nature of literary criticism in practice. Such candor about critical theory as an art form is both informative and reassuring.

STEPHEN W. BROWN

See also **Narrative Theory**

Fiction to 1700

Chandler, Frank W., *The Literature of Roguery*, 2 vols., London: Constable, 1907; Boston: Houghton Mifflin, 1907

Davis, Walter R., *Idea and Act in Elizabethan Fiction*, Princeton, New Jersey: Princeton University Press, 1969

McKeon, Michael, *The Origins of the English Novel, 1600–1740*, Baltimore: Johns Hopkins University Press, 1987; London: Century Hutchinson, 1988
Margolies, David, *Novel and Society in Elizabethan England*, London: Croom Helm, 1985
Nelson, William, *Fact or Fiction: The Dilemma of the Renaissance Storyteller*, Cambridge, Massachusetts: Harvard University Press, 1973
Pooley, Roger, *English Prose of the Seventeenth Century, 1590–1700*, London: Longman, 1992
Schlauch, Margaret, *Antecedents of the English Novel 1400–1600: From Chaucer to Deloney*, London: Oxford University Press/PWN (Warsaw), 1963
Spencer, Jane, *The Rise of the Woman Novelist: From Aphra Behn to Jane Austen*, Oxford and New York: Blackwell, 1986

Critical attention on fiction prior to 1700 is mainly in the form of broad introductory studies, with a concentration on its influence on the novel form. However, there have been more specific examinations of, for example, European influences, the picaresque, or Renaissance ideas about the relationship between fiction and truth. Overall, there is much material on individual writers, especially those of the latter part of the period, like Robert Greene or Aphra Behn.

In his work, DAVIS endeavours to separate an examination of Elizabethan fiction as an important genre in its own right from critical attempts to view it simply as an antecedent to the modern novel. He does not set out to provide a comprehensive survey of Elizabethan fiction, limiting his investigation instead to writings that are novelistic in length, thereby excluding, for example, novellas and jest books. His professed aim is to provide a "study of . . . the central endeavor of that fiction, that is, the testing of ideas of value by means of experience". In the extremely useful introductory chapter "On Reading Early Fiction", Davis employs classical paradigms in his negotiation of the somewhat knotty interrelations of novel, romance, allegory, and tale, and their relationships with realism and psychological identification. Positioning his study historically, he argues that the:

> . . . characteristic action of classical fiction began when the protagonist was driven off his intended course by a storm or some other nonhuman force, that of medieval fiction when the knight issued forth from his castle into some unknown realm of nature. The action of Renaissance fiction begins when the hero accepts a concept . . . we have a mode of fiction which submits ideas of value or order to the test of experience.

Davis applies his dynamic and cogent thesis to courtly fiction, pastoral romance, and the enduring influence of classical models on early fiction. Particularly illuminating is his chapter "Robert Greene and Greek Romance" where the pervading influence of Boccaccio is acknowledged. Davis's work in addition contains a serviceable chronology of the texts he considers.

A chapter of MARGOLIES' study is also devoted to an examination of Greene's fiction. As the title of Margolies' book indicates, he employs a rigorously historical technique for his analysis, which serves usefully to contextualise the writing under review. Margolies at once conveys a deeply human sense of Greene as a struggling writer – "not a gentleman reluctant to appear in print nor a man for whom writing was merely an honourable pastime, he wrote to earn his living" – and as a great and complex artist. His close readings of the texts he examines in the course of his study as a whole are illuminating, and he often acknowledges his debt to Davis (see above) while retaining a style quite his own. Of Thomas Deloney, for example, he writes that he "was English literature's first propagandist for a modern bourgeoisie" – a statement that both provides a practical insight into the writer and delights the reader with its audacity and immediacy. The book also includes two extremely useful and comprehensive bibliographies, the first containing the full titles of the primary fiction he investigates, the second supplying an extensive list of relevant secondary, critical works. Overall, Margolies presents a broad and valuable study.

POOLEY's work provides an overview of all varieties of seventeenth-century prose – from biography and autobiography to polemical, religious, or political works. His "Introduction: Reading Seventeenth-Century Prose" gives a clear, relevant historical and critical context for his research, and arguably places him in opposition to Davis (see above) in his central identification of the prose fiction as being important as direct precursor of the novel:

> . . . this is the period of the origins of the novel . . . but only by hindsight; it does not feel the same as the essay, where the writers are self-consciously producing and naming a new form. Prose fiction is as old as storytelling; though towards the end of the century it starts to acquire that fascination with novelty, or "the news", which is part of being a novel.

Pooley's first two chapters are most relevant for an introduction specifically to prose fiction in the period. With a Bakhtinian eye, in "Elizabethan Fiction – Sidney, Lyly, Nashe and Deloney", he looks at, for example, romance and pastoral. Apparently owing some debt to Margolies, his conclusion to the chapter is devoted entirely to Deloney, whose "paradoxical blend of the values of romance and realism, of the court and the progressive individual, retained its readability – and its saleability". His study of Restoration fiction, to be found in his second chapter, centres on John Bunyan, Behn, and William Congreve, and again provides a solid introduction rather than any ground-breaking analysis. The book has a detailed chronology appended, where prose and other works are clearly juxtaposed with important historical and cultural events.

One of the most influential and sophisticated studies of prose fiction before 1700 as antecedent of the novel is that by McKEON. In his Introduction, the author positions himself in relation to other critical interpretations of the topic, especially that expressed by Ian Watt in *The Rise of the Novel* (1957) where, according to McKeon, he "is concerned to argue a connection between the rise of the novel and the transformation of the social context of early eighteenth-century England". McKeon's concern is to apply a quasi-Bakhtinian construction of genre theory to the subject. He declares that the reader must be alert to seventeenth- and eighteenth-century usages of terms like "romance", "history", or "novel". Like Nelson (see below), McKeon also investigates the tensions and ambiguities that exist between categories like "history" and "story" in writing of the medieval and early-modern period. The book is intensively researched and well-constructed, with comprehensive notes and numerous relevant and intriguing illustrations provided in support of the central theses. What McKeon provides overall is a very specific, in-depth, and challenging theoretical approach to the subject.

A thorough and readable study is provided by SCHLAUCH, who examines prose-writing during 1400–1600, looking at, for example, medieval fiction and courtly romance. Her work emphasises the European influence, considering a wide range of primary texts, and her Introduction gives a brief but clear overview of the process by which they evolved into the novel form. The book is in part an attempt to answer a question relating to the first novelists – "did these innovators create in a vacuum when portraying people of their own sort, or did they operate within a tradition which was able to contribute something from an earlier time to their conceptions of realism?" Her overall search, then, is for "evidences of continuity in style and subject matter within such traditions as lead to the novel". At times her style is a little outdated – she tells the reader in her opening sentences, for example, that "medieval romance, as is well known, was extensively concerned with ladies" – but if this can be overlooked, then what she does provide is an intensive, general study, bringing as it did some neglected texts to light for the first time.

CHANDLER's Volume 1 is an important introduction to English picaresque writing, which he places in relation to foreign models of the genre, analysing it under headings like "The Anatomies of Roguery", "The Criminal Biographies", and "Rogues of Elizabethan and Restoration Fiction". Concentrating on the importance of the anti-hero in early-modern fiction, Chandler describes his work as:

> . . . a study of realism, for it investigates the role enacted in literary art by the observation of low-life. Specifically it traces in English letters a notable series of gradations from the first crude records of actuality to the complete reshaping of experience by the imagination, and in this process it points a constant tendency toward romanticism, counteracted at times by fresh returns to fact.

Again, there is mention of Robert Greene, but also considerable concentration on his contemporaries – Thomas Nashe, Henry Chettle, and Nicholas Breton. Chandler's research is at times so thorough and well-documented as to threaten to interrupt the flow of his argument, as he maps the relationship between the decline of the picaresque form and the rise of the romance. However, his synopses of original fictional plots are lively and entertaining to read. Each chapter of the work is ended with a useful, if partly out-of-date, bibliography, containing suggestions for further reading and recommendations for the best editions of primary texts.

NELSON too offers amusing and adept plot summaries of the works under analysis in his study, which not only looks at prose fiction, but also contains some insight into poetry, including Spenser's *Faerie Queene*. As the title of the work suggests, what is at issue is the relationship between fiction and falsity in the Renaissance, and how the writing of the period was influenced by the complex tensions that inhered between the two – fact and fiction. As Nelson writes in his Introduction, "travelers, fishermen, and politicians proverbially find truth for its own sake less valuable than other considerations". His first chapter, "From Fraud to Fiction", is an investigation of the slow historical process which, from classical times, gradually led to a separation of story from history. This process can be traced right through to the end of the study, where the phenomenon of seventeenth-century storytellers declaring that their tales were "not fiction but true as history is true" is investigated. Again, there is an emphasis on the romance form, but also examination of what Nelson terms the "pseudohistorical tale". Nelson's is a slim volume, but it deals thoroughly with the very specific literary-historical questions it sets out to answer.

Although only the first part of her study focuses on prose fiction before 1700, SPENCER's work deserves some mention because of the way in which it establishes parallels between the rise of the novel form and the rise of the woman writer. As Spencer avers in her introductory remarks, "the rise of the novel cannot be understood fully without considering how its conventions were shaped by the contributions of a large number of women". Of particular note here is her section on "Writers as Heroines: Foundations for Women's Literary Authority in the Seventeenth Century", where she looks briefly at the significant influence of writers like Katherine Philips, Margaret Cavendish, and Aphra Behn, and the relationship of their works to seventeenth-century notions of femininity.

EMMA L.E. REES

Fiction: 18th Century *see* Novel: 18th Century

Fiction: British – 19th Century *see* Novel: Romantic Era, Novel: Victorian

Fiction: British – 20th Century

1. General

Blamires, Harry, *Twentieth Century English Literature*, London: Macmillan, 1982, 2nd edition, 1986; New York: Schocken Books, 1982
Bradbury, Malcolm, *The Modern British Novel*, London: Secker & Warburg, 1993
Crosland, Margaret, *Beyond the Lighthouse: English Women Novelists in the Twentieth Century*, London: Constable, 1981
Green, Martin, *The English Novel in the Twentieth Century (The Doom of Empire)*, London: Routledge & Kegan Paul, 1984
Smith, David, *Socialist Propaganda in the Twentieth-Century British Novel*, London: Macmillan, 1978; Totowa, New Jersey: Rowman & Littlefield, 1979

Stevenson, Randall, *Reader's Guide to the Twentieth-Century Novel in Britain*, Hemel Hempstead, Hertfordshire: Harvester Wheatsheaf, 1993

Critical books on twentieth-century British fiction fall into two broad categories: those that serve as introductory studies to literary developments and movements (Blamires, Bradbury, Crosland, and Stevenson) and those that pursue a particular line of inquiry in order to construct a tradition of writing (Green and Smith).

Writing for the Macmillan "History of Literature" series, BLAMIRES seeks to contextualize developments in British fiction (and related literary forms) by examining the historical, political, and philosophical forces that act upon and inform cultural production. He follows a "loosely structured chronological sequence", paying particular attention to "the Modern Movement" of writing, which he sees to mark a break between the twentieth-century and a pre-modern past. The book interweaves a contextualized overview of major literary trends with commentaries on "individual writers' achievements".

In a more recent introductory survey, STEVENSON plots the development of the literary novel from Edwardian and modernist reactions to the concerns and form of the Victorian novel, through the anti-modernist and politically committed fiction of the 1930s, the loss of innocence dramatized in the postwar novel, and the renaissance of experimentation in 1960s' fiction. He concludes with a brief consideration of the contemporary novel, which he re-classifies as fiction written in English rather than "British". Now dominated by writers from the former colonies, he discerns a fragmentation of an Anglocentric hegemony in the 1980s and with it a growing "sense of cultural separateness" and plurality. In conclusion, he modifies David Lodge's metaphor of "The Novelist at the Crossroads" (1969), by suggesting a "spaghetti junction" is a more appropriate term for describing the state of 1990s' fiction.

BRADBURY links up with Stevenson's closing comments by stressing the importance of considering the twentieth-century "novel as it has developed in English", rather than as part of a parochial British tradition. In this lengthy book, Bradbury presents a critical overview of the novel from the 1870s to the 1990s and provides an extensive "List of Major Works" for the reader's reference. From the early twentieth-century modernists through to the postcolonialist writers of the 1980s, he outlines the novel's "varied but continuous evolution", returning perennially to the modern themes of "travel, exile, emigration and exterior influence". The question of the "narrative frontier" recurs throughout twentieth-century fiction – from the modernist fusion of lyricism, reportage, and autobiography with mimetic nineteenth-century forms, to the "interfused styles, mixed cultural layers, oddly merging traditions, multi-cultural pluralism" of postmodern writers. The concerns of modernism (for Bradbury, both a periodizing concept and an experimental kind of writing) inform the postwar preoccupation with the death of the novel and its increasingly marginal role in the modern world. Yet even in the last decade before the millennium, Bradbury sees that continual reinvention is coupled to the survival of the novel as "a major expression of artistic, cultural and intellectual curiosity".

GREEN's study focuses on fiction written under, and in reaction to, the British Empire. He begins from the premise that "in 1900 Englishmen ruled a great empire . . . now in the 1980s they have lost it", and traces the "confrontation between literature and imperialism" from Rudyard Kipling, D.H. Lawrence, and James Joyce, to Evelyn Waugh, Kingsley Amis, and Doris Lessing. Green upholds Kipling, rather than the modernist writers, as the primary influence on twentieth-century British fiction. Even among those later writers, who "grew up at a time when Kipling was a taboo" and who were explicitly hostile to his "jingoism and imperialism", Green discerns the "shadow of Kipling paralyzing" their imaginations. The author's central relationship to this late Victorian is ambivalent: he respects his literary legacy, but suggests that since the end of World War I the loss of "imaginative life" in British letters is more than partly bound up with "Kipling's shadow".

In a more explicitly politicized book, SMITH focuses on the representation of socialist propaganda in twentieth-century fiction. He examines the interface between politics and literature, concentrating on the period between 1906 and 1956, at which time he detects the voice of socialism in fiction to be at its most potent. Opening with a description of the revival of socialism in the early twentieth century (for him, signified by the election to Parliament of 30 candidates of the Labour Representation Committee in 1906), he traces its historical growth and demise as a viable political position through "a study of the works themselves, of what they say, and more importantly, how they say it". Smith studies a variety of "committed" writers (including H.G. Wells, Robert Tressell, Jack Lindsay, and Doris Lessing), many of whom he deems as finding the right balance in their novels between "art" and "propaganda".

CROSLAND documents the fictional output of British women in the twentieth century, sparing some of her observations for Commonwealth literature. Although there is a feminist subtext running through her book, in the respect that fiction is an expression of women's emancipation and their "will to create", she claims that she is more interested "in showing how women's writing is different from men than in trying to prove it must be better". Crosland is primarily a close reader of women's fiction, and the book is full of her personal responses. She begins with a commentary on late Victorian women's writing, and moves through the century, paying attention to the range of themes and styles, from a "preoccupation with the psychology of women" in the experimental novels of Dorothy Richardson and Virginia Woolf, through Elizabeth Bowen's and Rosamond Lehmann's novels of love, to the second wave of experimentation in the fiction of Anna Kavan and Lessing. Crosland considers the lives of the women writers as well as their novels in her effort to celebrate the scope and richness of twentieth-century women's writing.

MARTIN HALLIWELL

2. Before World War II

Bergonzi, Bernard, *Reading the Thirties: Texts and Contexts*, London, Macmillan, 1978; Pittsburgh: University of Pittsburgh Press, 1978

Bradbury, Malcolm, and James McFarlane (eds.), *Modernism: A Guide to European Literature, 1890–1930*, Harmondsworth, Middlesex: Penguin, 1976, 2nd edition, 1991; Atlantic Highlands, New Jersey: Humanities Press, 1976

Levenson, Michael H., *The Genealogy of Modernism: A Study of English Literary Doctrine, 1908–1922*, Cambridge and New York: Cambridge University Press, 1984

Stevenson, Randall, *Modernist Fiction: An Introduction*, Hemel Hempstead, Hertfordshire: Harvester Wheatsheaf, 1992; Lexington: University Press of Kentucky, 1992

Tindall, William, *Forces in Modern British Literature, 1885–1956*, New York: Knopf, 1947

Waugh, Patricia, *Practising Postmodernism, Reading Modernism*, London: Edward Arnold, 1992

Although some critics deal with the variety of British literature published during this time, either as a whole (Tindall) or within a narrower historical period (Bergonzi), most criticism is addressed to different aspects of literary modernism (Bradbury and McFarlane, Levenson, Stevenson, Waugh).

TINDALL's book indicates many of the important trends of writing in the first half of the twentieth century. Where the study lacks depth it compensates by positioning the various forms of British literature between interlinked cultural "forces" deriving from Europe and America. Tindall states his primary aim is to investigate the "meanings and values" of literature, through which he detects certain developments of previous literary modes. Thus, early-century writers attempted to broaden the project of realism by propelling it into "new areas of experience", whether in the naturalistic direction of George Gissing or toward the psychological novels of James Joyce and Virginia Woolf. To balance these aesthetic currents, Tindall traces the politics that inform the literary products, both from the Left (the Fabians through to "the Auden generation" of the 1930s) and from the Right (characterized by the imperialism of Rudyard Kipling and the nationalism of W.B.Yeats).

In the preface to the 1991 reprint of BRADBURY and McFARLANE's collection of essays on European modernism, the editors claim that "the Modern movement" should be seen as the "shaping art" of the twentieth century. The 40 years under scrutiny are described as "part of a disturbed transformational period of European history", providing the platform for a burgeoning of experimental aesthetic practices. Bradbury and McFarlane proceed to claim that modernist writers should be understood as the "true forerunners of our own multicultural, introspective, self-conscious and relativistic age". The book is divided into two sections: the first dealing with attempts to understand modernism from aesthetic and sociohistorical positions, and the second concentrating on representative trends in the three dominant literary forms (poetry, the novel, and drama). The collection is wide-ranging and illuminative, including also a chronology of events, a series of brief biographies of the major writers, and a useful bibliography of modernism.

STEVENSON opens his book on the modernist novel by suggesting that, as the twentieth century approaches its close, it is possible to gain a historical vantage point from where the critic can view and judge the achievement of modernist writers. Stevenson's emphasis is primarily on modernist "fiction written in English" (he concentrates on the work of Henry James, Ford Madox Ford, Joseph Conrad, Dorothy Richardson, D.H. Lawrence, Wyndham Lewis, Joyce, and Woolf), but he also stresses that the "complex conditions of national or cultural identity" experienced by many of these writers inform the trajectory and the ideology of modernism. He follows an opening chapter on the basics of modernist thought with a series of chapters on the dominant modern themes of "space", "time", and "art", and he concludes the book with a thoughtful evaluation of modernism from his "historical perspective".

In a lucid "study in literary transition", LEVENSON explores the "structure of English modernism", its concepts and its doctrines, in an attempt "to redeem certain lines of development which have been obscured or neglected". Following an opening section on the "Progenitors" of modernism – Matthew Arnold, Aldous Huxley, Walter Pater, and Conrad – who are positioned within "the context of late Victorian ideology", Levenson explores the complex web of associations and influences that formed the nucleus of modernism in England. He focuses on the years 1908–14 in which Ford, Lewis, Ezra Pound, T.E. Hulme, and T.S. Eliot wrote some of their most important critical and creative work, through to the founding of the journal *Criterion* by Eliot in 1922, which Levenson views as the coming of age of modernism and the "institutionalization of the movement". One of the most important genealogical concerns of the book is to trace the "tangled series of attempts to formulate a successful definition of modernity", through which Levenson tackles the complex nature of modernism.

WAUGH re-examines modernism by reading its literary products through the matrix of postmodernism and poststructuralist theory. She views modernism and its cultural progeny as belonging to a broad "tradition of specifically aestheticist modern thought", which derives from Romantic philosophy and art. Waugh asserts that postmodernism can be viewed "as a culmination of a gathering critique of Western cultural forms of representation". Modernism is thus understood as being both complicit with, and critical of, these "forms of representation". She claims previous readings of modernism remain uncritical of the aesthetic theory of autonomy, a position which she seeks to redress by re-reading a number of central modernist texts – Conrad's *Heart of Darkness* (1901), Woolf's *To the Lighthouse* (1927), Eliot's essay on "Tradition and the Individual Talent" (1919), and Joyce's *Ulysses* (1922). She also claims aesthetic autonomy is not an inherent property of modernism, but owes its existence primarily to the New Critics who exalted it "in the terms of formal self-sufficiency, impersonality, the autotelic art-object". Waugh argues that only by shifting the theoretical frame away from autonomy and toward postmodernist notions of the "situated" and "constructed" nature of art can this modernist illusion be dispelled.

BERGONZI states that his book is an attempt "to read the thirties as a collective subject, even a collective text", in which he subsumes readings of individual writers beneath a concern for the general "mythology" of the thirties as a literary period. The principal writers (among them W.H. Auden, Stephen Spender, Louis MacNeice, Graham Greene, and

Anthony Powell) actively resisted the experimentalism of modernism for a concern with the social function of literature. Many of these writers were the products of "minority culture" and upper-middle-class backgrounds, but, despite their different political motivations, they realized that the "closeness of literature to social questions" meant a rejection of the formal excesses of modernism. In tracing these points of transition, Bergonzi combines literary criticism, cultural history, and a "sociology of literature" in "a set of essays which consider . . . different cross-sections of the literature of the thirties".

MARTIN HALLIWELL

3. Postwar Period (to 1960s)

Gindin, James, *Postwar British Fiction: New Accents and Attitudes*, London: Cambridge University Press, 1962; Berkeley: University of California Press, 1962

Gorra, Michael, *The English Novel at Mid-Century: From the Leaning Tower*, London: Macmillan, 1990

Newby, P.H., *The Novel: 1945–1950*, London: Longmans, Green & Co., 1951

Paul, Ronald, *"Fire in Our Hearts": A Study of the Portrayal of Youth in a Selection of Post-War British Working Class Fiction*, Gothenburg, Sweden: Acta Universitatis Gothoburgensis [Gothenburg University Press], 1982

Rabinovitz, Rubin, *The Reaction Against Experiment in the English Novel, 1950–1960*, New York: Columbia University Press, 1967

Sinfield, Alan (ed.), *Society and Literature, 1945–1970*, London: Methuen, 1983

Many of the critical works on postwar British writers reconsider the representations of class and moral values as depicted in the fiction published during what is often interpreted as a culturally conservative age.

The novelist P.H. NEWBY considers many of the representative trends of literature written during and immediately after World War II. Newby's initial focus is on the theme of innocence, represented variously in the fiction of A.L. Barker, L.P. Hartley, and Elizabeth Bowen: a result of "the state of unbelief or bewilderment" caused by war and a symptom of "the growing disillusionment of the times". He claims that neither the value placed on Victorian commonsense nor a Romantic "belief in the importance of art" are tenable in this age: "the young writer must think as he has never thought before". He detects a "rejection of the immediate past" and a marked break with the formal and "technical virtuosity" of the modernists in a sustained attempt to recapture the art of "straightforward" storytelling. In his conclusion, Newby asserts that the renewed interest in the basics of fiction writing are the surest signs of commitment for the postwar writer.

GORRA concentrates on a rarefied group of middle-class writers, including Henry Green, Anthony Powell, Graham Greene, and Evelyn Waugh, as representing one of the dominant currents of postwar writing. He takes for his starting point Virginia Woolf's 1940 essay "The Leaning Tower", in which she describes a socially privileged and self-confident sector of the literati attempting to portray "the whole of life", "even in the aftermath of the Great War". The succeeding generation of writers, according to Gorra, mark a departure from this attempt in their renunciation of the freedom and expansiveness of such an ideal. Like Newby, he stresses the homogeneity of these writers in their return to the novel's traditional function, to represent "the relation between subjective experience and the objective world", after an experimental period of modernism. He discerns a closer link to less radical modernists, like E.M. Forster and Ford Madox Ford, in their re-assessment of the specifically *English* condition in contrast to the more cosmopolitan modernist impulse. The "dwindling toward twilight" of the British Empire, as Gorra calls it, inscribes the space for the mid-century novelist, and with it a sense of the novel's "limitations".

In addition to focusing on the anti-experimental impulses of the postwar generation of writers, RABINOVITZ stresses the growing importance of tradition and a renewed interest in the Victorian arts. The "concern for humanity", a common thread through much fiction of this period (particularly that written by Kingsley Amis, Angus Wilson, and C.P. Snow), constitutes a revival of a "realistic style" and a "concern with social and moral themes". As a representative strand of cultural production, the interest in traditional fictional forms is mirrored by the revival of Victorian plays in London in the 1950s and the boom in BBC adaptations of "classic" novels. Although Rabinovitz does not claim Victorian revivalism was ubiquitous (he comments that Amis and John Wain were influenced more by the picaresque tradition), he charts its popularity with reference to widespread social change after the War. Not only did these changes influence the concerns of middle-class fiction as described by Gorra, but also they influenced the re-emergence of the working-class novel with its stress on documentary realism. In conclusion, however, Rabinovitz admits that the 1950s was not a "fruitful" decade for the novel.

GINDIN begins his survey by characterizing John Kemp, the central character of Philip Larkin's novel *Jill* (1946), as a prototype for many of the postwar writers. Kemp is an "intelligent and irreverent young man" from working-class origins, "educated by scholarship but let loose in a society still permeated by class distinction and respect for breeding". Gindin understands this type of character (often labelled the "Angry Young Man", but not always angry) as a device by which authors like Amis, Wain, and Alan Sillitoe can interrogate values "of conduct and of class". He indicates that there is a long history of this type of fiction, but the various depictions of the existential hero, often viewed from a comic perspective, represent a series of attempts "to puncture [postwar] society's bloated self-estimation". Gindin's work focuses on a range of novelists, combining close reading with wider questions concerning the identity and experience of "contemporary man".

Following on from Rabinovitz's comments on the resurgence of working-class fiction, PAUL's book discusses a selection of postwar novels depicting and dealing with working-class youth. In the work of Jack Common, Brendan Behan, Sillitoe, and Barry Hines, Paul discerns a common commitment to rendering "artistically integrated and psychologically convincing portrayals of working-class anti-heroes". This argument counters what he cites as a common conception of the "magnified" and stereotyped male working-class hero, who is "uncritically" portrayed as possessing the ingenuity to overcome the ill-fortune of his upbringing and economic position. Paul substantiates this argument by tracing British working-class fiction back to Chartist literature of the 1840s and the revival of working-class militancy in the 1880s. He claims that many of the "fictional responses to the plight of the masses", although often undervalued for aesthetic reasons, represent concerted and committed attempts "to amalgamate literature and politics".

In SINFIELD's interdisciplinary book, literary and cultural products are considered from within a framework of social and political analysis. The two sections, "Society in Literature" and "Literature in Society", characterize Sinfield's intention to provide a materialist reading of the writer "as product and interpreter of society". The aim of the book is to assess the socio-cultural condition of the postwar years, in the hope that the collection "may contribute to the emergence of other, better places to stand" in relation to accepted views of this period. Many of the critics locate "lines of development", by which they understand the "formal choices" of postwar writers to develop both from the pressures of social change and "the demands of the particular forms of experience . . . which they are seeking to represent".

MARTIN HALLIWELL

4. Recent and Contemporary

Bradbury, Malcolm, *The Modern British Novel*, London: Secker & Warburg, 1993

Bradbury, Malcolm, and David Palmer (eds)., *The Contemporary English Novel* (Stratford-upon-Avon Studies series), London: Edward Arnold, 1979

Higdon, David Leon, *Shadows of the Past in Contemporary British Fiction*, London: Macmillan, 1984

Lee, Alison, *Realism and Power: Postmodern British Fiction*, London and New York: Routledge, 1990

McEwan, Neil, *The Survival of the Novel: British Fiction in the Later Twentieth Century*, London: Macmillan, 1981

Massie, Allan, *The Novel Today: A Critical Guide to the British Novel, 1970–1989*, London: Longman, 1990

Morris, Robert K. (ed.), *Old Lines, New Forces: Essays on the Contemporary British Novel, 1960–1970*, Rutherford, New Jersey: Fairleigh Dickinson University Press, 1976; London: Associated University Presses, 1976

Stevenson, Randall, "Postmodernism and Contemporary Fiction in Britain", in *Postmodernism and Contemporary Fiction*, edited by Edmund J. Smyth, London: Batsford, 1991

Criticism in this area takes issue with the supposed "death" of the postwar British novel, proclaimed most famously by Bernard Bergonzi in *The Situation of the Novel* (1970). Commentators demystify the widespread impression that British writers returned exclusively to an ossified social-realist mode after modernism, stubbornly isolating themselves from the international experimentalist movement. Many critics see contemporary and recent British fiction as achieving what David Lodge calls an "aesthetics of compromise" between tradition and innovation. With the advent of postmodern criticism, the anxiety over British inferiority largely disappears.

MORRIS has brought together essays on British novelists of the 1960s, including Anthony Burgess, John Fowles, and Angus Wilson. Morris's Introduction sets the tone: he argues that the seemingly retrograde postwar preference for social realism (typified by the work of the "Angry Young Men" in the 1950s) must be seen in the context of a *Zeitgeist* of disillusionment, and that 1960s' writers could embrace technical novelty only after the hard-earned realization of the value of culture and tradition in a fragmented world. The essays echo this "triumph through adversity" theme; Barbara Bellow Watson's piece on Doris Lessing's *The Golden Notebook* says of the novel's formal innovations that: "nothing could be more orderly, nothing could be more a response to chaos than this structure".

BRADBURY and PALMER (1979) have edited a collection of seminal essays by leading critics and authors. Both A.S. Byatt's piece on the "realism versus experimentalism" debate and Bergonzi's on the relationship of history and fiction in the light of contemporary theoretical advances are essential reading. Bradbury and Palmer's Preface usefully debunks the "folklore" of British isolationism, pointing out early experimental tendencies in works from the 1950s and 1960s. Though somewhat outdated now, this collection is of central importance to researchers in this field.

McEWAN sets out to characterize an intrinsically *British* form of contemporary fiction without defensively defining it against writing from other countries. He contends that, without rejecting influences such as the *nouveau roman*, "writers in Britain have achieved a creative relationship with the traditional novel" appropriate for the reading tastes of the English public, which maintains a love for nineteenth-century realism and Leavisite morality. McEwan identifies how this reconciliation of tradition and experiment manifests itself in works by Fowles, Iris Murdoch, and others, and investigates the role of the critical community in shaping contemporary trends.

HIGDON's study deals with the emphasis on the past, which is the distinctive feature of much contemporary British writing. Higdon relates this preoccupation to the English desire to retrieve a lost sense of cultural continuity after the modernist dread of history as "nightmare". The methods of "confronting" the past are divided into three broad rubrics: retrospective dialogue; imitation of earlier fiction; and the use of protagonists, such as geologists, who are metaphors for the act of recovery. Higdon's examples – comprising novels by Fowles, Jean Rhys, and others – illustrate his argument. Given the prominence of this *topos* in recent British fiction, Higdon's book is a necessary addition.

LEE provides a much-needed examination of how postmodernism, as a set of literary practices, has developed in contemporary English fiction. Following a cogent presentation of the theoretical premises needed to appreciate postmodern writing, Lee explains how what Linda Hutcheon calls "historiographic metafiction" arose to problematize the assumptions of realism. Lee concentrates on key authors, giving textually-detailed readings of texts such as Graham Swift's *Waterland*, Peter Ackroyd's *Hawksmoor*, and D.M. Thomas's *The White Hotel*, with special attention to how these novels topple the "master narratives" of history, rationalism, and psychoanalysis. The chapter on "performance" as a trope for the processes of representation and reception in postmodern fiction is particularly original and thought-provoking.

MASSIE's book is a survey of British fiction from the mid-1970s on. Although he discusses many authors in short order, Massie does not allot his space equally; he dismisses some major figures (Salman Rushdie) rather quickly, and lingers over others of questionable importance. Massie states his interest as being the welcome gravitation of the British novel back to mainstream accessibility after its flirtation with experimental "cleverness". He shows a marked preference for moralism and well-drawn characters in the humanist mode. Massie's survey is appealing in its brevity and inclusiveness, but should be used with an awareness of its biases.

STEVENSON's article outlines succinctly the fundamental ideas and texts for a study of postmodern British fiction. He begins by reviewing the extent to which such fiction carries on the legacy of modernism in terms of three of its principal "initiatives": 1) self-reflexivity, 2) innovations in narrative structure, and particularly in temporal ordering; 3) the internalization of narrative perspective. Stevenson, too, defends contemporary British writing against the charge that it retreated into the insularity of naive social realism after World War II; he highlights the history of British and Irish experimentalism, from Samuel Beckett and Flann O'Brien to B.S. Johnson and Christine Brooke-Rose, as well as the legitimate influence of international models. He usefully identifies some of the alternatives to realism, such as fantasy, being adopted by writers like Angela Carter. Finally, the article answers the detractors of postmodernism who see it as superficial; according to Stevenson, postmodern fiction challenges the reader to "rethink cultural codes and established patterns of thought".

BRADBURY's 1993 general survey is an indispensable reference guide by one of the leading authorities in the field. Although most authors are touched on only briefly, Bradbury's extensive bibliography can assist scholars wishing to pursue individual subjects. The two chapters covering recent and contemporary writing situate the fiction within specific (if perhaps somewhat over-simplified and deterministic) cultural and political milieux. Chapter 6 traces developments such as deconstructive theory as they pertain to changes in literary praxis. It wisely fastens on Lessing's *The Golden Notebook* and Fowles's *The French Lieutenant's Woman* as the two pivotal novels, which ushered in a new era of meta-fiction and what A.S. Byatt calls "greedy rewriting" – that is, the ransacking of the past and past forms. The growing interest in the fantastic and grotesque in the 1970s is mentioned in context of works by Carter, Martin Amis, and Ian McEwan. Chapter 7 focuses on postmodernist techniques of historiography, intertextual pastiche, and comedy, in works by authors such as Graham Swift and Salman Rushdie, as reactions to the bleak Lyotardian "condition" of contemporary reality under Thatcherism and nuclear threat. Bradbury's book is the perfect place to acquire a concise but thorough overview of this field.

LYNN S. WELLS

Fiction: American – General

Bercovitch, Sacvan, and Myra Jehlen (eds.), *Ideology and Classic American Literature*, Cambridge and New York: Cambridge University Press, 1986

Bradbury, Malcolm, and Sigmund Ro (eds.), *Contemporary American Fiction*, London and Baltimore: Edward Arnold, 1987

Chase, Richard, *The American Novel and its Tradition*, Garden City, New York: Doubleday, 1957; reprinted, Baltimore: Johns Hopkins University Press, 1990

Cooke, Michael G., *Afro-American Literature in the Twentieth Century: The Achievement of Intimacy*, New Haven, Connecticut, and London: Yale University Press, 1984

Fiedler, Leslie, *Love and Death in the American Novel*, New York: Criterion Books, 1960; revised edition, Stein & Day, 1966

Godden, Richard, *Fictions of Capital: The American Novel from James to Mailer*, Cambridge and New York: Cambridge University Press, 1990

Harris, Susan K., *Nineteenth Century American Women's Novels: Interpretive Strategies*, Cambridge and New York: Cambridge University Press, 1990

Messent, Peter, *New Readings of the American Novel: Narrative Theory and Its Application*, London: Macmillan, 1990

Michaels, Walter B., *The Gold Standard and the Logic of Naturalism: American Literature at the Turn of the Century*, Berkeley: University of California Press, 1987

Owens, Louis, *Other Destinies: Understanding the American Indian Novel*, Norman: University of Oklahoma Press, 1992

Petter, Henri, *The Early American Novel*, Columbus: Ohio State University Press, 1971

Rainwater, Catherine, and William J. Scheick (eds.), *Contemporary American Women Writers: Narrative Strategies*, Lexington: University Press of Kentucky, 1985

Ruland, Richard, and Malcolm Bradbury, *From Puritanism to Postmodernism: A History of American Literature*, London and New York: Routledge, 1991

Swann, Brian, and Arnold Krupat (eds.), *Recovering the Word: Essays on Native American Literature*, Berkeley: University of California Press, 1987

Tallack, Douglas, *The Nineteenth Century American Short Story: Language, Form and Ideology*, London and New York: Routledge, 1993

As the first postcolonial literature of the modern age, US fiction has characteristically displayed a particular awareness of itself *as* American. In consequence, American literary criticism too has tended to stress, in more or less explicit ways, its own peculiarly national character. Since the 1960s, developments in literary and critical theory have heightened further a fundamental tension between the diversity of the American experience and the search for a defining national identity. As a result, much recent criticism of American fiction has become overtly politicised, paying particular attention to the processes by which literary representation is included in, or excluded from, the American canon.

RULAND and BRADBURY offer a narrative history of American literature, which, while subdivided into four broad periods, effectively illuminates a number of the cross-currents and continuities, which mark the literature out as distinctively American. Their commentary is particularly expedient in illuminating tensions within a body of literature that has striven to become both independently and self-evidently "American" and yet, in certain instances simultaneously, has also sought to be the definitive, transnational literature of the modern age. In a sense then, this study is as much intellectual history as it is literary history, and will certainly provide useful material for readers who wish to ground the literature within a socio-historical context, spanning periods from pre-Republican writings in the seventeenth century to the present day. The breadth of historical focus does not permit lengthy discussion of individual writers, but alongside its qualities as an accessible narrative history, a lengthy index with extensive cross-referencing grants the text a functional role for reference purposes.

Readers seeking a presentation of applied literary theory might turn to MESSENT, who applies structuralist models, reader-response theory, and critical methodology developed by Mikhail Bakhtin and Roland Barthes to a collection of major American novels by Edith Wharton, F. Scott Fitzgerald, William Faulkner, Ernest Hemingway, Mark Twain, Willa Cather, and Zora Neale Hurston. Messent attaches no particular weight to any one theoretical position, and the text is a welcome one for the flexibility it offers the reader. What starts out "as a pedagogic exercise", Messent suggests, ends "as a political one", and his study is indeed useful both as a concise exposition of specific literary theory, and as a collection of politicized commentary upon writers who continue to occupy a privileged space within the American canon.

Towards the earlier end of the historical scale, PETTER provides a descriptive and critical survey of the American novel between (and in one or two cases before) the framing of the Constitution and 1820. While he suggests that it may be undesireable, "and indeed impossible", to conceal "the fact that most of the early American novels are failures", Petter nonetheless attempts to suspend the notion of value, instead considering the "clues to an understanding of Virginia interests and tastes" that these early writings might offer, in what was a crucial period in the history – if not the literary history – of the Republic. Petter's study thus affirms a critical position that looks to the later 1830s for the first stirrings of a more sophisticated native literary tradition, and accordingly gives an historical account of what he considers to be, at best, "pioneer efforts made to keep the novel alive". Of particular use to students of early American fiction will be the lengthy appendix, in which Petter offers around 80 plot synopses of novels written in the period discussed.

The bulk of BERCOVITCH and JEHLEN's collection examines writing from the American Literary Renaissance of the mid-nineteenth century, with substantial commentary on the writings of Herman Melville. The sustained focus of the collection, however, is less upon a particular period of American literature, than it is upon shifting patterns in the meaning of American literary criticism since World War II. These essays, Jehlen suggests, go some way to summarising a critical self-consciousness which stands as the "sober and skeptical heir" to the notionally apolitical readings of the New Critics in the 1950s. This overtly revisionist tone is lent a particular poignancy with the inclusion of Henry Nash Smith's own reassessment of his study *Virgin Land* (1950). The interest which the text sustains in the role of critical practice will not, however, diminish the reader's appreciation of the commentaries offered. Bercovitch and Jehlen have assembled an impressive battery of American cultural historians and literary critics, including, among others, Leo Marx, Jane Tompkins, Alan Trachtenberg, Richard Slotkin, and Donald Pease. Throughout, the writing is provocative and to the highest academic standard. Readers looking for socio-political critique of Poe, Hawthorne, Harriet Beecher Stowe, Henry David Thoreau, and Melville will find this edition stimulating, and as an introduction to revisionist strategy in American literary criticism the collection has few rivals.

TALLACK's is a challenging study of the nineteenth-century short-story form, which, in applying deconstructionist techniques by way of reclaiming the short story from the tenets of Romantic and modernist critique, also takes time to reflect upon the formal implications of deconstruction itself. Working, as Tallack is, from within a critical paradigm as self-consciously aware of itself as deconstruction, this is hardly less than appropriate, and a setting of deconstructionist principles against the heightened visibility, in short-story form, of beginnings and endings, of boundaries that mark "what is inside and outside" the text, opens up a range of critical possibilities generally neglected in short-story criticism. A number of threads – notably the relation between public and private realms – run throughout the text, in which Tallack initially considers the relationship between language and form, before moving on to a second section of "position-taking essays", which "argue for genre as a dynamic element in individual texts". So although Tallack also sustains an enquiry into form and genre, readers chasing sophisticated criticism of Poe, Hawthorne, Melville, Charlotte Perkins Gilman, and Henry James will be well rewarded.

Less theoretical, and less overtly revisionist in tone, though not necessarily less iconoclastic, is an earlier tradition of criticism which (as Gerald Graff puts it, in Bercovitch and Jehlen) "attempts to characterize the 'Americanness' of American literature in terms of some single and overriding theme or conflict". For CHASE, whose concern is with questions of genre, American fiction is marked out by its repeated reconfiguration of romance forms, alongside, and woven into, the rise of social realism. Romance forms, Chase contends, map organically onto a body of national fiction which tends to reject normative codes, proposing and accepting, in their place, a tendency toward contradiction, extremity, and radical disunity – "the profound poetry of disorder we find in the American novel". Following the genre from its early American groundings in Charles Brockden Brown's melodramas and what Twain would call James Fenimore Cooper's "literary offenses", Chase moves through fairly conventional territory in readings of Hawthorne and Melville, before pointing up, via discussion of William Dean Howells, Frank Norris, Faulkner, and Fitzgerald, the persisting significance of the Romantic imagination as American writers first lean toward, and then embrace, modernism. It is perhaps worth noting here that Chases's assumptions regarding anti-normative thinking in American fiction have been challenged by American feminists, notably by Jane Tompkins (again, in Bercovitch and Jehlen), who suggests that the tradition to which Chase belongs "has prevented even committed feminists from recognizing and asserting the *value* of a powerful and specifically female novelist tradition".

Similar concern has been expressed with regard to FIEDLER's famous (and for some, infamous) design, which, echoing Chase's trajectory, seeks "to define what is peculiarly American in *our* books". Written in a highly accessible style, and ranging across a wide spectrum of American fiction, Fiedler constructs a loose amalgam of Marxian, Jungian and Freudian categories, "syncretically", as he puts it, and "cavalierly . . . yoked together". The "pruned and condensed" second edition of the text is organised thematically, rather than by author or genre, and aims to provide a twin psychological/sociological account for the place of love and death as definitive issues in American fiction. Masculine fear of heterosexual relationships (i.e., of women), Fiedler claims, leads to an American fiction chronically underpinned by the novelistic suppression of sex, and a substitutive emphasis upon male bonding. In language that itself invites a gender-based reading, Fiedler contends that the imaginative "vacuum", which results from this suppression, is then "filled" with gothic images, through which are also projected "certain obsessive concerns of our national life", including "the ambiguity of our relationship with Indian and Negro, the ambiguity of our encounter with nature", and "the guilt of the revolutionist who feels himself a parricide".

Borrowing from structuralist, deconstructionist, reader-response, and reception theory, HARRIS's is an important study, which, in developing its own narrative thematic, is far more than the sum of its constituent theoretical strands. Although this is a commentary specifically interested in reading women's writing, it is not concerned with the explication of a particular literary theory. Identifying a tension between the overt authorial voice and more covert values in a range of novels, from Susanna Rowson's *Charlotte Temple* (1791) to Willa Cather's *O Pioneers!* (1913), Harris deploys the contested principle of authorial sovereignty in challenging ways, and discovers, in the space between rhetorical authorial intent and the less visible claims of the text itself, a subversive mode of writing more subtly engaged with its own institutional conventions than has generally been recognised. Harris also includes discussion of writings by Catharine Maria Sedgwick, Augusta Evans Wilson, Susan Warner, Fanny Fern, Elizabeth Drew Stoddard, E.D.E.N. Southworth, Elizabeth Stuart Phelps, Louisa May Alcott, Sarah Orne Jewett, and Kate Chopin.

Commenting on Gilman's *The Yellow Wallpaper*, MICHAELS says that it is for him an "exemplary text . . . not because it criticizes or endorses [a] culture of consumption but precisely because . . . it *exemplifies* that culture". This controversial study of naturalism, with its insistence that "the only relation literature as such has to culture as such is that it is part of it", continues to provoke a divergent, and sometimes polemical range of critical response. Michaels' New Historicism steps aside from conventional definitions of naturalism, and considers a particular kind of subjectivity, a "double-identity", which he perceives as intrinsic within this mode of writing – an argument he illustrates by reference to, among others, Theodore Dreiser, Hawthorne, and Norris.

The Marxist account of American literary representation offered by GODDEN is valuable reading in itself, irrespective of the texts it critiques. Given that a Puritan heritage in the American experience has led even a non-Marxist historian such as Carl Degler to suggest that capitalism came to the continent "in the first ships" (*Out of Our Past*, 1959), sustained economic readings of American literature have been scarce. Godden takes as his context the "extended social economy" of Fordist production and consumption from the 1920s to the 1960s, and examines the economic determinants, and shifting representations of selfhood, in writings by Hemingway – "an exponent of 'capitalist realism' . . . a style of writing unknowingly saturated in the logic of consumerism" – Fitzgerald, and Norman Mailer. In addition, chapters given over to Southern writing in the years of the Great Depression – Faulkner, John Crowe Ransom, and Allen Tate – and a contextual "interlude", in which Godden addresses himself directly to Fordist economic practise, help construct a provocative, persuasive, and unrelentingly historicist study, which plugs in some measure a significant gap in American literary criticism.

Harris's interest in the formal, or structural, properties of women's fiction is pursued further by RAINWATER and SCHEICK, who ask, in their introductory chapter, whether female authors can be said to:

> . . . participate in a literary tradition which has consistently disenfranchised and misrepresented women; or has this very disenfranchisement and misrepresentation brought about the total displacement of women artists from tradition to the extent that their works depart radically in form and content from those of their male counterparts?

A focus upon narrative structure, as deployed by ten contemporary writers, allows the contributors to demonstrate different ways in which women's texts have reshaped, and thus reclaimed, formal aspects of American literary tradition. Mary Robertson, for example, discusses Anne Tyler's disruption of reader expectation in the "family novel", and William Scheick examines the relation between "translucent surface detail" and a depth of concealed meaning in writings by Annie Dillard. Individual chapters are also assigned to discussions of work by Ann Beattie, Grace Paley, Anne Redmon, Cynthia Ozick, Alice Walker, Maxine Hong Kingston, Toni Morrison, and Marge Piercy, and the text gives bibliographies for each of the writers considered.

COOKE charts a development in African-American literary self-consciousness, away from the defensive nuances of what he calls "self-veiling", and toward the "intimacy" of his title. The terms of this movement reveal themselves gradually as his argument unfolds through several stages, leading to the exposition of a literary selfhood characterised, he suggests, by "freedom from compulsion", and "a condition in which the Afro-American protagonist . . . is depicted as realistically enjoying a sound and clear orientation toward the self and the world". Intimacy, in this definition, appears to mesh an ideal American commitment to self-evidence and authentic subjectivity with a body of literature that remains, nonetheless, immersed in the "difference" of the African-American experience. "In a sense", Cooke suggests, "this is a study of the gathering to greatness of Afro-American literature". Cooke has an impressively wide frame of reference here, but still finds space for substantial discussion of several major twentieth-century writers, including Jean Toomer, Zora Neale Hurston, Richard Wright, Ralph Ellison, James Baldwin, Robert Hayden, Alice Walker, James Weldon Johnson, Michael Harper, and Eldridge Cleaver. His closing chapter considers more recent writing "after intimacy", and examines the shifting position, significance and function of history in several works, prominent among which are John Edgar Wideman's *Damballah* (1981) and David Bradley's *The Chaneysville Incident* (1981).

SWANN and KRUPAT's collection of over 20 essays might be approached in a number of ways. As an introduction to the broad canvas of Native American studies, the text offers an extensive and genuinely interdisciplinary survey not only of the literature itself, but also of the theoretical positions that have been taken, and the various debates which have emerged, in its academic study. There are contributions here from linguistics (William Bright and M. Dale Kinkade) and anthropology (Donald Bahr and Joel Sherzer), from literary and critical theory (William Gingerich and Arnold Krupat), and also from poets and folklorists. The text, then, is not wholly a study in social science, nor is it wholly a study in literary history, practice, theory, or aesthetics. In the broadest fashion, as the editors suggest, "all the essays in this book may be considered as addressing the linked and overlapping issues of the presentation and interpretation of Native American literatures". Among the viewpoints offered, Duane Niatum resists the idea that there exists today any distinctive, culturally autonomous Native American aesethetic, and compares moments from Albert Camus and Faulkner with extracts from recent Native American fiction; William Bevis argues against this position, asserting that the fiction is "drenched in a tribalism most whites neither understand nor expect in the works of contemporary Indians"; and Paula Gunn Allen looks at the significance of tradition and continuity in the writing. OWENS focuses on Native American novels from John Rollin Ridge's *The Life and Adventures of Joaquin Murieta* in the nineteenth century to those of the present, adopting a dialogic approach, by way of Bakhtin, to account for the relationship between oral and written culture, and between the activities of speaker and listener in the creation of a story.

Finally, for an overview of issues in more contemporary fiction, readers might turn to BRADBURY and RO, the Preface to which identifies a recent tendency in American literature toward "multi-directionality and variety", over and against any concern for strong aesthetic definition – a trend which, it is suggested, implies the need for "a similar range of mapmakers", and a plurality of critical perspectives. This text serves just such a need. From within the writing of the eight contributors, each of which engages with different aspects of post-World-War-II fiction, what indeed emerges as a characteristic theme of the text is an attempt to "map" a way through the multiplicity of postmodernist American literatures. Ihab Hassan, for example, considers the contemporary role of the quest/adventure genre, while Keith Opdahl looks at John Updike and argues for the continuing importance of the American realist tradition. Other entries discuss "anti-characterisation and the problem of the subject in American postmodernist fiction", and recent developments in both Jewish-American and African-American writing. The explosion of postmodern theory, Bradbury suggests, "has perhaps been not so much the cause of or the explanation for contemporary American writing, but a visible and powerful intellectual context surrounding it". In effect, the separate chapters included here mediate nicely between the context and the fiction, and, in the light of Bradbury's comment, one particular strength of this study might be its general aversion to overt position-taking, on what has become the increasingly position-strewn issue of postmodernism itself.

DAVID HOLLOWAY

Fiction: American – 19th Century

Bell, Michael Davitt, *The Development of American Romance: The Sacrifice of Relation*, Chicago: University of Chicago Press, 1980

Brooks, Van Wyck, *The Flowering of New England 1815–1865*, Boston: Dutton & Co., 1936; London: Dent & Sons, 1936

Cowie, Alexander, *The Rise of the American Novel*, New York: American Book Company, 1948

Lee, A. Robert (ed.), *The Nineteenth-Century American Short Story*, Totowa, New Jersey: Barnes & Noble, 1986; London: Vision Press, 1986

Lewis, R.W.B., *The American Adam: Innocence, Tragedy and Tradition in the Nineteenth Century*, Chicago: University of Chicago Press, 1955

Miller, Perry, *The Golden Age of American Literature*, New York: George Braziller, 1959

Shulman, Robert, *Social Criticism and Nineteenth-Century American Fictions*, Columbia: University of Missouri Press, 1987

Much critical theory analyzes the evolution of a distinct and individualistic American literary culture. While the romance is examined as the most prominent genre of this period, other critical studies are devoted to short stories, characterization, poetry, and style.

BROOKS' narrative interweaves historical fact with speculative fiction as he brings to life via creative description several major authors and their times, as suggested by chapter titles like "Harvard College in 1815" and "The Autocrat". Brooks's charming, accessible style explores the terrain, settings, and personages which form the backdrop for evolving American fiction, depicting relationships and exploring streams of thought as they emerged in the lives of these writers. His theme, "the New England mind, as it has found expression in the lives and works of writers", takes a clear biographical approach.

LEWIS examines the confluence of past memory and future hope that defines a predominant theory of nineteenth-century American literature. In his review of several major authors, such as Nathaniel Hawthorne, Oliver Wendell Holmes, Walt Whitman, Henry James, George Bancroft, and Francis Parkman, between the years of 1820 and 1860 (primarily in the New England/Atlantic Seaboard region), Lewis attempts to "disentangle from the writings and pronouncements of the day the emergent American myth and the dialogue in which it was formed". In the literary context that compared America's development to a second Eden as a "divinely granted second chance", the Adam-figure summarizes these authors' experiences, ranging from Puritanical Calvinism to modern humanism. The nineteenth-century American hero, "bereft of ancestry . . . standing alone, becomes a self-reliant and self-propelling symbol of cultural individualism".

COWIE reflects on the development of the American novel from the beginning through the late nineteenth century. His desire to "indicate the evolution of the American novel by means of comparatively full treatments of representative writers" outlines a critical as well as historical review of several important works, including fiction by lesser-known but representative authors like Susanna H. Rowson, John Davis, Hugh Henry Brackenridge, Samuel Woodworth, Lydia Maria Child, William Gilmore Simms, and Edward Eggleston. Sentimental, didactic, and gothic genres and themes are explored, along with conventions such as satire and the historical romance. While his list of authors is not exhaustive, it is extensive.

MILLER's work focuses on six major writers of the nineteenth-century Romantic era as examples of the creative literary talents and expanding intellect that represented the budding nation's best minds: Edgar Allan Poe, Ralph Waldo Emerson, Henry David Thoreau, Hawthorne, Herman Melville, and Whitman. Miller's Introduction explains his perceptions of the shared dreams and distinctive talents of these authors as members of a newly-emerging culture of post-revolutionary culture. Cautioning that examining the sociology of literature is not his particular aim in his work, Miller expresses his view that these six authors expanded the boundaries of American literature in new, fruitful directions. Each of the sections on these authors provides portions of some of the writer's best-known work that reflects this premise: for example, Poe's "Fall of the House of Usher", Emerson's *The American Scholar*, and Whitman's *Song of Myself*.

BELL, in the role of cultural historian, briefly acknowledges the theoretical debate concerning the experimental tradition of romance in American fiction as a literary entity separate from the concept of the British novel, which had preceded it. But, more importantly, Bell explains that his book is an attempt to understand the major romancers' use of the term "romance" as it applied to their writing both individually and collectively. Specifically Bell argues that authors like Charles Brockden Brown, Washington Irving, Poe, and to an even greater extent Hawthorne and Melville, adapted their experimental styles of form and validity in fiction to the larger perspective of national culture.

SHULMAN analyzes "the ways American authors responded to the changing market society that increasingly dominated nineteenth century American life". His socio-economic perspective brings together, in unique relationships, the polarities of individual and society, and literature and the marketplace, as dominant forces of nineteenth-century America. Works like Melville's *Bartleby, the Scrivener*, Hawthorne's *The Scarlet Letter*, and Mark Twain's *The Adventures of Huckleberry Finn* provide focal studies for the concept of individualism as fostering growth as well as conflict in both marketplaces – that of ideas, and of products. Shulman argues that nineteenth-century authors "deal perceptively with the conflicts in and between classes and within and between the representative selves who embody the practices and values of their society".

LEE's collection of critical essays on the development of the American short story begins with Poe in the 1830s and stretches to Kate Chopin in the 1890s. Each essay provides a unique perspective about a particular writer's short-story style and its contribution to the evolving canon. While not exhaustive, the collection provides a compendium of views on the short-story genre as it developed in nineteenth-century America, and considers some of the styles and problems encountered by the featured authors.

DEBRA JOHANYAK

Fiction: American – 20th Century

1. General

Adams, Timothy Dow, *Telling Lies in Modern American Autobiography*, Chapel Hill: University of North Carolina Press, 1990

Bradbury, Malcolm, *The Modern American Novel*, New York and Oxford: Oxford University Press, 1983, revised 1992

Goldsmith, Arnold L., *The Modern American Urban Novel: Nature as "Interior Structure"*, Detroit: Wayne State University Press, 1990

Hilfer, Tony, *American Fiction since 1940*, London: Longman, 1992

Lee, Brian, *American Fiction, 1865–1940*, London: Longman, 1987

Long, Elizabeth, *The American Dream and the Popular Novel*, London and Boston: Routledge & Kegan Paul, 1985

Young, Thomas Daniel (ed.), *Modern American Fiction: Form and Function*, Baton Rouge: Louisiana State University Press, 1989

LEE's book covers American fiction written since the Civil War and before 1940. Consequently, it is most useful, for our purposes, for the material included in Part Two, "The American Century, 1900–1940". In six chapters Lee discusses a range of fictional practice: radical realism and urban writing; liberal realism and "the revolt from the village"; the epics produced by Thomas Wolfe and John Dos Passos; the range of fictional styles described as modernism; and a detailed study of William Faulkner. Lee's interest lies in the relationship between emerging literary interests and techniques, and the patterns of economic, social, and intellectual change that characterize the cultural context of modern writing. Technological innovation, the communications revolution, the growth of Hollywood, the impact of World War I, the Jazz Age, and the Depression – all these factors influenced the style of fiction produced by American writers, as did the emergence of a powerful expatriate literary community and the rise of international modernism. Lee's book is a valuable exploration of these important issues, written in an engaging and accessible style; but even more useful is the extensive bibliography provided. Information is given in clearly defined specialist bibliographies, which cover the social and cultural contexts, reference works, history and criticism, and special topics; bibliographical information is also given on individual authors, together with notes on biography and critical works.

HILFER's book complements Lee's perfectly; as part of the same series it includes all the same useful contextual apparatus of chronology and bibliography. Hilfer's range is perhaps the most impressive characteristic of this extremely helpful book. He describes the major social and cultural forces operating in the period – Cold War politics, the rise of feminism, the Civil Rights movement, the creation of a mass popular culture. Within this well-developed context, he then charts the major literary trends of the twentieth century: the shift from modernism to postmodernism, in all its variety; the rise of regional and ethnic literatures, such as Southern, Jewish-American, and African-American; the emergence of women's writing; the writing of social protest; and the reformulation of realist styles. These trends are exemplified in the detailed discussion of two representative writers, with whom the book conludes – Donald Barthelme and Toni Morrison.

BRADBURY also surveys the range of fiction produced in America this century, and provides a selective list (with no bibliographical detail) of American novels published since 1890. His bracketing years are 1890 and 1991; consequently, Bradbury is able to survey a wide fictional scene, placing special emphasis upon such movements as naturalism and impressionism, the growth of modernism, the move from social realism in the 1930s to liberal realism in the 1950s, postmodern fictional experimentation of the 1960s, and the work of quite recent contemporary writers working in the fields of women's fiction, minority writing, and the gay novel. In the course of this survey Bradbury continues his polemic in defence of realism against the threat posed by postmodernism, which is a distinct feature of his critical writing. In fact, in this account of late twentieth-century fiction, Bradbury attempts to give expression to "the end or fading of postmodernism"; to my mind it seems a little too hasty to proclaim just yet the death of postmodernism and the emergence of the "post-postmodern novel".

LONG's book addresses a relatively neglected aspect of twentieth-century fiction – the popular writing of the period, which forms the overwhelming bulk of fiction produced in the United States. Long does, however, place her exploration of popular forms within the resilient intellectual context of the American Dream. Long considers the ways in which modern fiction continues the tradition of celebrating the entrepreneurial spirit and individual enterprise begun with Benjamin Franklin's writings and exemplified by the work of Horatio Alger at the outset of the twentieth century. But the conflicts and contradictions of the Dream, which figure so prominently in postwar writing, are also given due consideration. This is an informative book, which helps to give a balanced impression of modern American fiction by acknowledging best-sellers and their relationships with highbrow fiction and the culture that has produced both.

The books by Adams, Young, and Goldsmith provide not surveys but critical explorations of themes and styles, which unify the works of twentieth-century fiction as a meaningful category. Each of these critics expresses a distinct view of the coherence of modern American fiction.

ADAMS discusses the collapse of the distinction between telling the truth and lying in a number of literary autobiographies where an unreliable narrator strives for a metaphorical truth rather than historical authenticity. This spiritual truth would describe the reconciliation of the lived life with subjective identity through the creation of a personal myth. Misrepresentatiuon is discussed as a substantive theme and a significant narrative strategy in the texts Adams examines: he discusses the personal narratives of Gertrude Stein, Sherwood Anderson, Richard Wright, Mary McCarthy, and Lillian Hellman. Telling the truth in the modern world is a complex and difficult matter, as Adams shows. His book provides a useful context for the evaluation of truth and authenticity in modern non-biographical fictions as well.

GOLDSMITH analyses the relationship between the urban environment and nature in seven exemplary modern texts: Dos Passos's *Manhattan Transfer*, James T. Farrell's *Studs Lonnigan*, Henry Roth's *Call It Sleep*, Harriette Simpson Arnow's *The Dollmaker*, Bernard Malamud's *The Assistant*, Edward Lewis Wallant's *The Pawnbroker*, and Saul Bellow's *Mr Sammler's Planet*. He challenges the assumption that Nature is absent from the modern American urban novel by showing the ways in which Nature functions as an important aspect of setting, language, symbolism, and, at times, characterization. His interest is in demonstrating how Nature binds physical description with narrative symbolism, themes with imagery, and patterns of metaphor with the development of individual characters. by focusing upon image patterns, Goldsmith is able to identify distinctively modern attitudes towards society and the natural world and relate these attitudes to their narrative representation in key texts.

The essays collected in YOUNG's volume present us with an impression of modern fiction as a mode where form is the function: modern fiction "shows" rather than "tells" a story: telling stories is seen to be the work of more conventional, pre-modern styles of writing. The volume covers the entire field of modern fiction, from Henry James to John Barth, and includes extensive discussion of Richard Wright, Eudora Welty, Flannery O'Connor, and Walker Percy. The writers represented here are predominantly from the South, and the recurring themes of the volume reflect this regional bias. The issue of belief, the influence of existentialist philosophy, and the power of nihilism to influence moral imperatives are of concern to many of the contributors. The emergence of a distinctively modern style of American writing, within the context of a twentieth-century crisis of belief, and the narrative techniques to support this modern style – a modern hero, modern narrative structure, and the like – are the foci of the essays.

DEBORAH L. MADSEN

2. Before World War II

Bradbury, Malcolm, *The Modern American Novel*, Oxford and New York: Oxford University Press, 1983, revised 1992

Elliott, Emory (ed.), *The Columbia History of the American Novel*, New York: Columbia Uinversity Press, 1991

Geismar, Maxwell, *Writers in Crisis: The American Novel*

Between Two Wars, Boston: Houghton Mifflin, 1942; London: Secker & Warburg, 1947
Geismar, Maxwell, *The Last of the Provincials: The American Novel, 1915–1925*, Boston: Houghton Mifflin, 1947; London: Secker & Warburg, 1947
Geismar, Maxwell, *Rebels and Ancestors: The American Novel, 1890–1915*, Boston: Houghton Mifflin, 1953
Kazin, Alfred, *On Native Grounds: An Interpretation of American Prose Literature*, New York: Harcourt, Brace & World, and Reynall & Hitchcock, both 1942; London: Jonathan Cape, 1943
Kenner, Hugh, *A Homemade World: The American Modernist Writers*, New York: Random House, 1974
Lee, Brian, *American Fiction, 1865–1940*, London: Longman, 1987
Litz, A. Walton (ed.), *Modern American Fiction: Essays in Criticism*, New York: Oxford University Press, 1963
Massa, Ann, *American Literature in Context, 1900–1930*, London: Methuen, 1982
Magny, Claude-Edmonde, *The Age of the American Novel: The Film Aesthetic of Fiction Between the Two Wars*, translated by Eleanor Hochman, New York: Frederick Ungar, 1972
Millgate, Michael, *American Social Fiction: James to Cozzens*, Edinburgh: Oliver & Boyd, 1964
Minter, David, *A Cultural History of the American Novel: Henry James to William Faulkner*, Cambridge and New York: Cambridge University Press, 1994
O'Connor, William Van (ed.), *Seven Modern American Novelists: An Introduction*, Minneapolis: University of Minnesota Press, 1964; London: Oxford University Press, 1964
Spindler, Michael, *American Literature and Social Change: William Dean Howells to Arthur Miller*, Bloomington: Indiana University Press, 1983; London: Macmillan, 1983
Walcutt, Charles Child, *Seven Novelists in the American Naturalist Tradition: An Introduction*, Minneapolis: University of Minnesota Press, 1974; London: Oxford University Press, 1974

Any account of the criticism and scholarship that deals with American fiction between 1900 and 1940 must, necessarily, be very selective. There is, of course, a profusion of critical materials on the major authors (particularly William Faulkner, F. Scott Fitzgerald, and Ernest Hemingway) and, indeed, on the significant literary movements of the period, such as modernism, naturalism, and proletarian realism, so the student is advised to cast his or her net widely when looking for relevant materials. The critical consensus that a high point in American fiction is realized in the years between 1920 and 1940 remains largely unchallenged, but there is an ongoing revision of earlier writers, such as Frank Norris and Theodore Dreiser, which seeks to afford realists and naturalists their proper places in any history of the period.

KAZIN's book remains one of the great works of modern American criticism. Though it was published in 1942 it is suprisingly "up-to-date", both for the range of its coverage of what Kazin calls "prose literature" in the first four decades of the twentieth century and for its frequently imaginative weaving together of literary criticism with historical narrative. Kazin's methodology is, at its roots, sociological ("modern literature in America is at bottom only the expression of our modern life in America"), but his readings are neither reductive nor simply historical, since he is interested at every turn in the *critical* case that can be made for those writers who merit our attention. There is hardly a prose writer from the period who doesn't get some mention here; the "minor" figures, such as James Branch Cabell, Joseph Hergesheimer, Robert Herrick, and Ludwig Lewisohn are deftly and economically dealt with, while the "major" figures, particularly Willa Cather, John Dos Passos, Dreiser, Faulkner, Hemingway, and Fitzgerald, are discussed at length. A number of chapters are given over to non-fictional prose, notably literary criticism and scholarship, philosophy, and political and social journalism. One significant feature of Kazin's work is that, for the time in which it appeared, it does not, on the whole, deal with "established" reputations, and this lends a vitality to his writing that comes, in effect, from a report from the "front lines". There are few better places to begin one's study of American fiction in this period than here.

GEISMAR's three volumes, in what was a projected five-volume study of "The Novel in America", offer an account of the American novel between 1890 and 1940, the discussion beginning with Frank Norris and ending with John Steinbeck. In chronological order of subject matter, the first volume, *Rebels and Ancestors*, deals with Norris, Stephen Crane, Jack London, Dreiser, and Ellen Glasgow; the second, *The Last of the Provincials*, covers H.L. Mencken, Sinclair Lewis, Cather, Sherwood Anderson, and Fitzgerald; and the third Ring Lardner, Hemingway, Dos Passos, Faulkner, Thomas Wolfe, and Steinbeck. Though there are two anomalous inclusions here (Mencken discussed for his journalism and his social and political commentary, Lardner as a short-story writer), Geismar's account is devoted exclusively to the American achievement in the novel form. His account is in part historical (each of "these writers is viewed in some, or large, detail against both the epoch of prosperity and that of depression") and in part formalist ("a writer's technique reveals his inner personality . . . just as it makes his tone, his central vision of life"), but both kinds of commentary are woven together with effortless ease, and while there are some lapses of scholarship and some unorthodoxies of judgement these volumes remain required reading.

MILLGATE's book is a study of the social novel in America from about 1880 to the early 1950s: he begins with Henry James, and particularly his treatment of the "business hero" (Christopher Newman in *The American* and Lambert Strether in *The Ambassadors*), and takes his argument through to the fiction of James Gould Cozzens. Many of the chapters are devoted to individual writers (Norris, Edith Wharton, Dreiser, Sherwood Anderson and Sinclair Lewis, Fitzgerald, Dos Passos and Cozzens himself), but there are also more general chapters on the treatment of institutions in American fiction (notably business, the military, and the academy) and on "American Novelists and American Society", which lend the book a sociological character. Millgate's thesis offers an important challenge to that "theory" of American literature which emphasises the pre-eminence of the Romantic and the anti-realist at the expense of "those American novelists who have been specifically concerned with the presentation of American society". Millgate points out in his Preface that he traces, in particular, "the development of the image of the businessman through both its 'epic' and its 'obscure' phases", watching the dramatization of "the individual in his relation to the ever-increasing institutionalisation of modern American society". This is an informed and intelligent account of many of the major American novelists of the period.

O'CONNOR's edition brings together seven of the essays on individual authors in the University of Minnesota "Pamphlets on American Writers" series. The authors covered are Wharton, Lewis, Fitzgerald, Faulkner, Hemingway, Wolfe, and Nathanael West, and there is also a general Introduction by the editor. These are brief but eminently serviceable introductory guides, and they are reprinted here with their selected bibliographies.

LITZ's collection brings together a body of valuable essays, by various hands, on American fiction from Stephen Crane to Robert Penn Warren. Predictably, Fitzgerald, Faulkner, and Hemingway are at the centre: three essays on Fitzgerald, and four each on Faulkner and Hemingway – but there are, additionally, essays on Gertrude Stein, Sherwood Anderson, Lewis, Dos Passos, Wolfe, and Steinbeck. The concluding essays, by Malcolm Cowley, Ihab Hassan, and Wright Morris, grouped together under the heading "Foreground", seek to take account of "the present and future of American fiction in terms of the new realities in American life". Four essays, two by Henry James (including "The Art of Fiction"), the others by William Dean Howells and Hamlin Garland, serve as a preface to the volume, and define for us, to some extent, the realistic limits of the American novel. Despite its being something over 30 years old, this remains an indispensable collection.

MAGNY's important study is translated from the 1948 French edition. Her thesis is that a young and largely undeveloped art form, the moving film, profoundly affected the techniques of literary expression in American fiction during the inter-war years, notably in the usage of cutting, collage, ellipsis, and close-ups. Two chapters, in particular, are entirely devoted to the close correspondence between "Ellipsis in the Movies and in the Novel" and "Cutting in the Movies and in the Novel". Other chapters look at major authors of the period, and those on Dos Passos and Faulkner were ground-breaking and influential accounts of the film aesthetic of their fiction. There are some inaccuracies here, and the occasional questionable judgement, but these flaws do not seriously mar what is a major contribution to an important stylistic and technical debate.

WALCUTT's collection complements that of O'Connor (see above). Again these essays reprint pamphlets in the University of Minnesota series, though here the emphasis is on the American naturalists – Stephen Crane, Norris, Dreiser, London, Sherwood Anderson, Steinbeck, and James T. Farrell. Walcutt's Introduction usefully maps out the intellectual and literary context, and the pamphlets are again reprinted with their selected bibliographies.

KENNER's book has liveliness, lucidity, wit, and, indeed, the polemic one associates with his best criticism. His account is guided by his belief that those writers who make up the modernist canon in America, despite their obvious dissimilarities, "hang together" because they "shared hidden resources of craftsmanship, hidden incentives to rewrite a page, which we can trace to a doctrine of perception – the word valued both in itself and in its power to denote". Kenner challenges a number of orthodoxies, notably the insistence on the American modernists' indebtedness to their European predecessors, particularly James Joyce, and he makes a strong case for an indigenous American modernism growing out of local circumstances and conditions. Not all of this book is devoted to fiction, but there are substantial chapters on Faulkner, Fitzgerald, and Hemingway, and briefer, but no less illuminating, discussions of Sherwood Anderson and Gertrude Stein. The whole book makes for very invigorating reading.

BRADBURY's study begins in the 1890s and extends as far as the late 1970s, but the heart of the book (some four chapters of seven) is devoted to the period between 1900 and 1940. In "Modernity and Modernism: 1900–1912", his second chapter, Bradbury describes what he sees as the "turn" from naturalism to expressionism in fiction at the beginning of the twentieth century. He argues that naturalism in the hands of writers such as London and Sinclair was both "populist and popular", but that its terms of reference were quickly exhausted and replaced by fictional forms that "drove attention inward to the psychology of awareness", notably in the early writings of Gertrude Stein, whose *The Making of Americans* Bradbury sees as "a crucial work of American innovation, a high modernist novel we are now coming to understand better". In the subsequent chapter, "Artists and Philistines: 1912–1920", Bradbury shows how developments in the plastic arts, particularly in the dramatic impact of the Armory Show of 1913, brought home to an American audience the "message of vitalism, abstraction, and modernism" and how these led to the "emergence in America of a new generation of writers who responded to and in varying degrees were influenced by the rising modernist spirit". This chapter contains extensive discussion of Sherwood Anderson's fiction, especially *Winesburg, Ohio*, and end with thoughts on Sinclair Lewis who, in his preoccupation with the details of social life, is seen as a writer at odds with the newer strategies of modernism: Bradbury concludes that "it was Anderson's path of consciousness and form that seemed to count the more". The next two chapters take Bradbury's "story" on through the 1920s and 1930s. "Art-Style and Life-Style: The 1920s" concerns itself with that distinctive achievement in American fiction we associate with the "high modernism" of Fitzgerald, Hemingway, Dos Passos, and Faulkner, and Bradbury's account of the decade is particularly alert to the "paradox" of an essentially "conservative" period setting in motion such radical innovation in fiction (and, indeed, in poetry). "Realism and Surrealism: The 1930s" outlines the reassertion of realist and naturalist fictional models in the work of Michael Gold, James T. Farrell, Erskine Caldwell, Steinbeck, and, though rather less obviously, Thomas Wolfe. The chapter ends with two "countervailing" voices, those of Henry Miller and Nathanael West, the former reminding us that the "novel of radical extremity took other than a directly social form in the Thirties", and the latter introducing the "surreal canvas" that became such a staple of American fiction in the 1960s. Some readers may find Bradbury's account conducted at too great a level of generality, and may be disappointed that there is little in the way of sustained meditation on the great writers of the period; but for an intelligent and informed outline of American fiction in the period this work has rarely been bettered. Bradbury's survey is not exhaustive, however, and there are some omissions, most strikingly no mention of Willa Cather or Ring Lardner.

MASSA's book is aimed very much at the undergraduate reader. Beyond a brief Introduction it is entirely structured around individual authors, and critical discussion of each is preceded by a short quotation (usually three to four pages long) from a representative work, which, as the general editor remarks, provides "a springboard for wider discussion and analysis". The writers covered here encompass virtually all the major figures one associates with the period (Wharton, Henry Adams, Henry James, Stein, Wallace Stevens, Ezra Pound, Sherwood Anderson, Lewis, Jean Toomer, H.L. Mencken, Fitzgerald, Hemingway, Eugene O'Neill, and Faulkner), but the distinctive achievement in American poetry in this period is somewhat under-represented (there are no essays, for example, on Hart Crane, Robert Frost, or William Carlos Williams). For a critical survey of the fiction, however, this is a serviceable work, though it should be noted that the essays on individual writers are quite brief.

SPINDLER's book shares some common ground with that of Millgate, and while it is not narrowly concerned with fiction much of the discussion is centred on the novel and the short story. Spindler's approach is interdisciplinary, and the book is offered as an attempt "to relate literary developments in America to economic and social change". The methodology is broadly Marxist: the "conceptual framework is supplied by that key element in Marxist cultural analysis – the proposition of a determining base and a determined superstructure". He seeks to show how "the ideological confusions and contradictions" in American social history have moulded its literature, and his account of the genesis of a literary work is, therefore, deterministic and occasionally reductive. The chapters are divided along topical and thematic lines, and not by individual author, but the table of contents (more so than the index) enables the book to be consulted selectively, though the reader needs to look carefully at the Introduction and the first two chapters to understand the controlling thesis.

LEE's one-volume critical history of American fiction from 1865–1940 has many virtues, chief among which is his intelligent grouping of writers under "topical" headings, which makes for easy reference. The first part of his study deals with the implications for American fiction of the unprecendented industrial and economic development of the United States in the years following the end of the Civil War. Part Two, however, which carries the sub-title "'The American Century' 1900–1940", is largely concerned with the reaction to what Lee calls the impact of "International Modernism", and here in some six chapters he takes us from early twentieth-century writings to the "high modernism" of Faulkner. The arrangement by topical and thematic headings enables Lee to draw together materials that may not be contemporaneous with one another but have common preoccupations: for example, his chapter on "Realists, Radicals and the City" reads early reformist writings, such as those of Upton Sinclair and Ernest Poole, alongside later, and more radical, accounts of urban life such as we find in Michael Gold and Richard Wright. Thus, Lee avoids some of the monotony and lack of critical focus that one often associates with more descriptive histories of American fiction. The book concludes with a useful chronology and good bibliographies for both individual authors and general topics.

ELLIOTT's collection of essays in his history of the American novel contains an important section devoted to "The Early Twentieth Century". Nine essays are gathered here: Valerie Smith provides a brief introduction to the period, reminding us that "culture and cultural production in the United States and around the world in the first half of the twentieth century were shaped by momentous political, technological, economic, and social developments". But the subsequent eight essays are topical and thematic in character, and deal with modernism, American proletarianism, popular fiction, ethnicity and the marketplace, race and region, the treatment of the west, technology and the novel, and society and identity. The quality of the essays is rather uneven, but the student will find much that is of interest and value here. Those looking for commentary on individual authors are advised to consult the index.

MINTER's "cultural history" of the modern American novel has echoes of those essays gathered in Elliott, and is informed by the new discourses of class, race, ethnicity, gender, family, and nationality, while at the same time keeping canonical figures at the forefront of the discussion. He sees the novel as an artistic product that arises from, but remains embedded in, culture, though culture, as Minter conceives it, is something more than the received wisdom of the great works of hight art and is, instead, more an arena in which "authors, texts, and nonliterary events enter into multivalent relationships with readers". In the United States particularly, he suggests, novels "have worked in countless ways to authorize what should or should not be honored as 'American'", and to this end his readings of major writers such as James, Cather, Hemingway, Fitzgerald, Dos Passos, and Faulkner is informed by complex notions of marginality, rejection, commitment, selfhood, and nation. Minter's chapters are thematic in character, but the brief synopses of each chapter in the table of contents facilitate a reader's ease of access. This said, however, the force of his argument is of course best understood by reading the book from beginning to end, and the study as a whole is one of the most significant of recent contributions to the debate over the shape of American fiction in the first half of this century.

HENRY CLARIDGE

3. Postwar and Contemporary

Adelman, Irving, and Rita Dworkin, *The Contemporary Novel: A Checklist of Critical Literature on the British and American Novel since 1945*, Metuchen, New Jersey: Scarecrow Press, 1972

Bradbury, Malcolm, and Sigmund Ro (eds.), *Contemporary American Fiction*, London and Baltimore: Edward Arnold, 1987

Clarke, Graham (ed.), *The New American Writing: Essays on American Literature since 1970*, New York: St Martin's Press, 1990; London: Vision Press, 1990

Hendin, Josephine, *Vulnerable People: A View of American Fiction since 1945*, Oxford and New York: Oxford University Press, 1978

Hornby, Nick, *Contemporary American Fiction*, New York: St Martin's Press, 1992; London: Vision Press, 1992

Klinkowitz, Jerome, *Structuring the Void: The Struggle for the Subject in Contemporary American Fiction*, Durham, North Carolina: Duke University Press, 1992

LeClair, Tom, *The Art of Excess: Mastery in Contemporary American Fiction*, Urbana: University of Illinois Press, 1991

Massa, Ann, *The American Novel since 1945: An Annotated Selection of 200 Works*, London: National Book League, 1975

O'Donnell, Patrick, and Robert Con Davis (eds.), *Intertextuality and Contemporary American Fiction*, Baltimore: Johns Hopkins University Press, 1989

Saltzman, Arthur M., *Designs of Darkness in Contemporary American Fiction*, Philadelphia: University of Pennsylvania Press, 1990

Swinfen, Ann, *In Defence of Fantasy: A Study of the Genre in English and American Fiction since 1945*, London and Boston: Routledge & Kegan Paul, 1984

Waldmeir, Joseph J., *American Novels of the Second World War*, The Hague: Mouton, 1969

Zavarzadeh, Mas'ud, *The Mythopoeic Reality: The Postwar American Non-Fiction Novel*, Urbana: University of Illinois Press, 1976

The term "postwar" enjoyed particular currency in the 25 years after 1945, as a designation for an era and for a significant body of writing seen as qualitatively different to pre-war fiction. Use of the term has diminished since then, while other designations, such as "postmodern", have become common. MASSA hints at this in her Preface, where she lists the emergent trends in postwar fiction: the growing eminence of Jewish-American fiction, black fiction, the non-fiction novel, multi-media novels, absurdism, and black humor. Her catalogue of primary works offers a very useful survey and a starting-point for readers who are unacquainted with the range of postwar fiction. She provides an annotated list of some 200 works, which describes briefly the plots and the characteristic themes, techniques, and concerns of their writers. The bibliography compiled by ADELMAN and DWORKIN provides a complementary guide to secondary critical literature on postwar fiction. They include journal articles and books, but only book reviews that are of exceptional interest. The novelists whose work is included are those who have been writing since 1945, those writing before this date but who published their major work after World War II, and those whose reputations emerged after 1945. For each author included, criticism of every novel (pre- and postwar) is surveyed. Authors are treated in alphabetical order, and secondary works are listed novel by novel; the listing is preceded by a section devoted to general works, and is followed by a listing of bibliographical guides.

Massa notes that in fiction after 1945, war is increasingly present both as a subject and as a metaphor. WALDMEIR takes this trend as his subject in a study that analyses the body of fiction, written by or about Americans, in which combat figures prominently, and which deals explicitly with the ideological issues of the War. As a consequence of his selection criteria, Waldmeir excludes a number of authors and texts one would expect to find here; but the compensation for these omissions is a coherent comparative study of the texts considered. The bibliography provides full details of a very large number of World-War-II novels for those who wish to pursue their primary reading.

HENDIN discusses two dozen writers. She argues for the social value of art, and for the understanding offered by fiction of the past half century of how personal lives are patterned and shaped by social influences. It is in this respect that recent fiction departs most clearly from the dominant modernist attitudes of the pre-war period. Where modernist writers saw the personal and the cultural as continuous, and therefore subject to the same kinds of crises, postwar writing represents individuals as freer from history and society, and therefore more able to explore their choices and possibilities. And the role of the writers Hendin discusses is represented as that of the informer – someone who returns the reader to the world better informed.

Where Hendin contrasts postwar fiction with pre-war fictional practice, many critics focus their attention on one of the several styles of fiction to have emerged in the postwar era. ZAVARZADEH discusses the emergence of the non-fiction novel. He begins with an account of the aesthetic ideas that motivate this style, and then goes on to consider its distinct modes. His is, then, a generic interest, one which draws on developments in structuralist theory and semiotics, but he is concerned to identify not only the generic features but also the intellectual and cultural contexts of this style of writing.

SWINFEN is also concerned with generic issues, this time in relation to postwar fantasy writing. Rather than emphasise the uniqueness of a new fictional style, as Zavarzadeh does, Swinfen is concerned to establish points of continuity between late twentieth-century fantasy and antecedants reaching back to nineteenth-century Romanticism. In particular, she is concerned with the relationship between fantasy and realism in fiction written in both Britain and America. The presiding genius here is J.R.R. Tolkien and his re-legitimation of the marvelous as a subject and style for literature. The nature and purpose of fantasy in the culture of the postwar world are engagingly discussed in this study where national differences are less important than generic continuities and postwar innovations.

The essays edited by CLARKE exemplify the trend towards opening up the contemporary canon to include greater numbers of women writers and writers from a diversity of ethnic traditions. The volume focuses upon writers who have come to prominence since 1970, and the essays deliberately avoid writers who self-consciously react against the principles of "high" modernism. Rather than deal exclusively with postmodernist writers and texts, the book seeks to explore the range of fictional practice within recent American culture. The writers who emerge as the dominant voices include E.L. Doctorow, Don DeLillo, Toni Morrison, Raymond Carver, Gordon Lish, Louise Erdrich, Maxine Hong Kingston, and Rudolfo Anaya, and among the dominant fictional genres that have received revisionary attention is crime fiction.

BRADBURY and RO also have edited a collection of essays, which surveys the variety of contemporary fiction in America.

Ethnic writing, women's writing, postmodern fiction, and the more conventional realistic fiction that makes up the bulk of fiction written in the United States are all accounted for here. Taken together, these essays propose an alternative to postmodernism as the motivating force behind contemporary fiction writing: realism and accompanying notions of voice, representational presence, and consensual reality are of common concern to all contributors. The image created by this book of the contemporary fiction scene is of a practice dependent upon inherited concepts of artistic realism at the expense of contemporary concepts of artifice and artistic play.

In contrast, the collection of essays edited by O'DONNELL and DAVIS stresses the importance of intertextuality and notions of rhetorical construction in contemporary fiction. Contributors examine aspects of the intertextual relationship: the book moves in turn from intertextuality and parody to revisionary intertextuality, then to intertextuality and the postmodern subject. Some essays approach these issues thematically, others deal with specific writers (Kathy Acker, John Barth, Norman Mailer) or specific relationships (such as the connections between Alice Walker and Zora Neale Hurston). The diverse ways in which contemporary fiction has made problematical the entire concept of the self-contained book – where does it begin or end? – are explored here with subtlety and insight.

HORNBY's book continues the trend toward rethinking the canon by introducing a new group of writers. His work focuses closely upon the group known as "dirty realists", named for the two Granta collections *Dirty Realism* and *More Dirt*, which brought to prominence such writers as Raymond Carver, Bobbie Ann Mason, Jayne Anne Phillips, Joy Williams, Richard Ford, and Tobias Wolff. Against this group, Nick Hornby contrasts those writers who are, in his account, the heirs of the *The New Yorker* style: Ann Beattie exemplifies the style, characterized by delicacy of language and theme; but elements of this style are also identified in the fiction of Anne Tyler, André Dubus, Elizabeth Tallent, and Lorrie Moore.

Jerome Klinkowitz, Tom LeClair, and Arthur Saltzman do not survey the range of contemporary American fiction, but instead argue for their own views of dominant themes and patterns of connection among the writers and texts that comprise the canon. KLINKOWITZ deals with those writers he sees as continuing the achievements in fictional innovation made in the 1960s by Kurt Vonnegut and Richard Brautigan: these include Max Apple, Gerald Rosen and Rob Swigart. The issue which these writers have received as their artistic inheritance is the problem of continuing to write when fictional "content" seems no longer to exist. The "void" that requires "structuring", then, is the absence left by the retreat of substance, and the common strategy adopted by contemporary writers is to transform their artistic struggle with this void into the subject for fiction. To structure the unrepresentable and to deal with powerful cultural constraints upon the facility for imaginative structuring (gender and the Vietnam War are discussed here) – this is the agenda set by Klinkowitz's exemplary contemporary writers.

LeCLAIR is also concerned with contemporary fictional achievement – specifically, the contribution made by the "big" novel to the nature of contemporary fiction. *Gravity's Rainbow* (Thomas Pynchon), *Something Happened* (Joseph Heller), *The Public Burning* (Coover), *Letters* (Barth), *Women and Men* (Joseph McElroy) and *Always Coming Home* (Ursula K. Le Guin) are his exemplifying texts, and LeClair is unashamed in his evaluation of these as "great" art. Their greatness resides, in large part, in their sheer length. "Nothing succeeds like excess. Nothing matters like mastery", LeClair writes. His case is founded on the conviction that only long books possess the power and stature to succeed in the necessary task of deconstructing the powerful traditions of the past and imagining powerful alternatives for the future. The subversive force of contemporary fictions such as these is shared by the reader who learns, in the process of reading, how to read and understand, and so master the complex cultural systems by which we are surrounded.

SALTZMAN also sees contemporary fiction as subversive, but in his account, this subversion is directed as much at the reader as at American cultural systems. Writers such as Walter Abish, Barth, Barthelme, Coover, DeLillo, Doctorow, John Hawkes, Jerzy Kosinski, and Gilbert Sorrentino are seen to be pursuing a common strategy in novels that promote a "goal oriented" style of reading, seeming to promise some final meaning, which they then subvert by frustrating the narrative quest for truth, certainty, and resolution. Where classic modernist texts culminated in epiphany, postmodernist texts promise, but are unable finally to represent, such an epiphanic revelation. Thus, Saltzman provides an incisive distinction between modernist and contemporary fictional works, while preserving a sense of the diversity of the contemporary novelistic achievement.

DEBORAH L. MADSEN

Fiction: African

Chinweizu, Onwuchekwa Jemie, and Ihechukwu Madubuike, *Toward the Decolonisation of African Literature: African Fiction and Poetry and Their Critics*, Enugu, Nigeria: Fourth Division, 1980; Washington, D.C., Howard University Press, 1983; London, KPI, 1985

Cook, David, *African Literature: A Critical View*, London: Longman, 1977

Larson, Charles, *The Emergence of African Fiction*, Bloomington: Indiana University Press, 1971; London: Macmillan, 1978

McEwan, Neil, *Africa and the Novel*, London: Macmillan, 1983; Atlantic Highlands, New Jersey: Humanities Press, 1983

Palmer, Eustace, *An Introduction to the African Novel: A Critical Study of Twelve Books*, London: Heinemann, 1972

Palmer, Eustace, *The Growth of the African Novel*, London: Heinemann, 1979

Stratton, Florence, *Contemporary African Literature and the Politics of Gender*, London and New York: Routledge, 1994

Taiwo, Oladele, *Female Novelists of Modern Africa*, London: Macmillan, 1984; New York: St Martin's Press, 1984

Critical perceptions of African fiction in European languages have been shifting since the 1950s when American and European anthropologists, missionaries, intelligence agents, and Peace Corps volunteers saw the novel as a gateway to the African mind.

LARSON was among the first Western critics to explain systematically "the reasons African writing is frequently different from Western writing". Though Larson carefully identifies the ethnocentric pitfalls of early European criticism, his own work is explicitly ethnocentric and heavily dependent on nineteenth-century theories of race. These flaws are particularly serious in Chapters 4, 5, and 6, which deal respectively with "time, space, and description", the "situational" novel, and "characters and modes of characterization", in Chinua Achebe, Ngugi wa Thiong'o, and Peter Abrahams. The study of representations of time is conditioned by his racial myth that "interest in time is peculiar to Western civilisations" while "lack of interest in time may often be more typical of non-Western cultures". Such anthropological preoccupations prevents his following up his critical insights into the interpenetrations of oral and written conventions in the novels.

PALMER's 1972 study of 12 novels by seven novelists, one of the first book-length studies of African novels by an African, owes much to mainstream Western practice of the period, characterised by a pronounced aversion to political themes, an unmotivated comparison with Western models, and an insistence on evaluating African novels by European aesthetic tastes and fashions. The rejection of Cyprian Ekwensi's and Wole Soyinka's works for not conforming to "well-made novel" conventions reveals the limitations of this approach. In his 1979 work, PALMER continues his historical survey through a broader choice of writers, including Ekwensi, Soyinka, several less-known or newer writers, and several works translated from the French. Like its predecessor, however, this book is really a series of essays in literary criticism, which are only by default concerned with developmental patterns.

COOK's work treats all three major genres as well as works on literary criticism, anthropology, and ideology, and it is organised according to definite thematic patterns. Of the three parts, Part I, "Broad Perspectives", comprises two chapters: Chapter 1 examines the respective social environments that nourish African and Western literary traditions, while Chapter 2 surveys the poetry; Part II comprises detailed studies of selected novels and plays; while Part III examines Okello Oculi's *Prostitute*, Jomo Kenyatta's *Facing Mount Kenya*, Frantz Fanon's *The Wretched of the Earth*, and Lewis Nkosi's *Home and Exile* as products of the same interplay of forces that engendered literary creativity.

The first genuine attempt to establish an African aesthetic for African literature is that of CHINWEIZU and his colleagues. The book probes the strategies and consequences of Western imperialism over African literature during the period 1950–75. In addressing such controversies as the definition of African literature, the distinction between the African and the European novel, Africa's oral antecedents to the novel genre, perceptions of time and space and their implications for literary plots, and principles of characterisation, the authors range through European and African literatures to expose many false assumptions, which have become entrenched as self-evident truths.

Evaluating Africa's contributions to the novel form in the last 30 years, McEWAN brings a necessary corrective to conventional perceptions of indigenous Africa as "past" and Europe-influenced Africa as "modern". The first three main chapters examine novelists' interpretations of different phases in Africa's encounter with Europe, while the fourth evaluates more recent themes. These are offset in Chapter 5 by examining the work of two white South African writers. McEwan displays a weak grasp of Soyinka's novels, but painstakingly explores Achebe's fiction to reveal the language strategies by which Achebe in his rural novels simulates African thought patterns or signals the increasing intrusion of the European world.

TAIWO's study of 12 African female novelists is one of an increasing number dedicated to female writers since the late 1970s, with particular chapters dealing with major writers like Flora Nwapa, Adaora Lily Ulasi, Buchi Emecheta, Grace Ogot, and Bessie Head. Taiwo characteristically balances detailed literary appreciation with a general "assessment" of the writers' literary development, though there is no sustained investigation of the gender distinctiveness of these works. STRATTON, though, is concerned with identifying such distinctively female dimensions, and relating them to the patriarchal ordering of much African literature and culture. Stratton's claims of rescuing Africa's female writers "rendered invisible in literary criticism" simply ignore similar extant scholarship, however, and they collapse under her surprising preoccupation with established rather than new or ignored female writers. She also tends towards an uncritical reliance on travellers' tales and questionable sources. Her gendered re-reading, in Section One, of male canonical texts typified by Achebe's *Things Fall Apart*, or of four established female novelists (Ogot, Nwapa, Emecheta, and Mariama Bâ), in Section Two, and her evaluation of recent developments in male authors' perceptions of gender issues in Section Three are important for contributing extra details rather than for fresh insights.

CHIDI OKONKWO

Fiction: Australian

Argyle, Barry, *An Introduction to the Australian Novel 1830–1930*, Oxford: Clarendon Press, 1972

Daniel, Helen, *Liars: Australian New Novelists*, Ringwood, Victoria, and New York: Penguin, 1988

Hamilton, K.G. (ed.), *Studies in the Recent Australian Novel*, St Lucia: University of Queensland Press, 1978

Hergenhan, Laurie, *et al.* (eds.), *The Penguin New Literary History of Australia*, Ringwood, Victoria, and New York: Penguin, 1988

Mitchell, Adrian, "Fiction", in *The Oxford History of Australian Literature*, edited by Leonie Kramer, Melbourne, Oxford, and New York: Oxford University Press, 1981

Shoemaker, Adam, *Black Words, White Page: Aboriginal Literature 1929–1988*, St Lucia, Queensland: University of Queensland Press, 1989
Spender, Dale, *Writing a New World: Two Centuries of Australian Women Writers*, London and New York: Pandora, 1988
Wilde, William H., Joy Hooton, and Barry Andrews (eds.), *The Oxford Companion to Australian Literature*, Melbourne, Oxford, and New York: Oxford University Press, 1985, with corrections, 1991, 2nd edition, 1994

Perception – the manner in which the individual demarcates the environment, and the methodology by which that individual in turn communicates a personal geography to someone else – has been the defining concern of Australian fiction from James Hardy Vaux down to Peter Carey and Elizabeth Jolley. Australian narrative has always tended to test reality and to press upon boundaries of all kinds.

MITCHELL accounts for those qualities, in part, by suggesting that the memoir is the essential narrative model for Australian experience. Beginning with the journals of eighteenth-century criminals, Mitchell argues that self-observation and personal accounting are chief points of historic continuity in Australian fiction. With the "transition from factual memoirs to fiction", the writer remains intent upon "observing himself" and stressing that "he is not of the common cut". Mitchell provides a detailed account of the history of fiction-writing in Australia, treating equally men and women writers, and identifying British influences without succumbing to a colonialist interpretation of the tradition. The survey concludes that most Australian fiction displays an "interest in the procedure by which narrative is presented" and a "concern with reality in its different guises".

HERGENHAN has edited a volume of essays designed to provide an intellectual context for Australian literature. Relevant to the genre of fiction are Dorothy Jones and Barry Andrews on humour, Elizabeth Webby on print history, and Ken Stewart on journalism. Susan Sheridan contributes an essay on women writers, and there are chapters on the novel and short fiction: Ken Gelder's discussion is too cursory to say much of value about the novel, but Kerryn Goldsworthy argues convincingly, albeit briefly, for the reclamation of the nineteenth-century short story. There is more intellectual history in this study than in Mitchell's, and by design it has a greater concern for broad cultural issues.

In WILDE, HOOTON, and ANDREWS, the reader has a compendium of information – biographical, literary, cultural, and historical. Among the 3,000 entries are comprehensive essays on thematic materials, brief lives of all the major – and most of the minor – fiction-writers, all accompanied by detailed reference sources. Information about all of Australia's literary journals is provided. Cross-references would make the material in the volume more accessible, as would a detailed subject index. Still, this is an important source of facts about Australian fiction and its authors.

ARGYLE's book is well designed to introduce salient critical arguments about the rise of the Australian novel through the nineteenth century and up to 1930. He begins in 1832, with the first true novel in Australia, and then examines in chronological order ten major works of fiction. The writers of these establish a tradition that exploits the Australian scene as a novelty for European audiences much as "Scott had exploited Scotland's". That peculiarly Australian flavour is diluted throughout the twentieth century, in Argyle's opinion, by the increasing familiarization with Australia, and by the developing cosmopolitanism of the novelists.

HAMILTON picks up where Argyle leaves off in the 1930s, and follows the Australian novel down to David Ireland and Frank Moorhouse. The eight essays in the collection are all from different hands, and deal with the work of 16 novelists; however, only one woman writer, Christina Stead, is discussed in any detail. Critical approaches vary, but the essays all tend toward close readings of specific works, exploring style and themes in conventional ways. The volume opens with Hamilton's own essay, tracing the history of Australian fiction from 1930 through 1976. The chapter includes some discussion of literary periodicals but is mostly a chronological listing of the major works of fiction, with only a slight attempt to set the novels within any theoretical framework.

SPENDER is the best source for the history of Australian women novelists. She begins by drawing on the letters and journals of Australia's early women settlers, defining notions about identity and authority in those voices. She identifies anxiety and reassurance as the dialectical forces in women's fiction, and indicates an attraction toward comic relief in these writers. Spender suggests that women have positioned themselves with the Aboriginal Australians by sharing and articulating the same issues. She emphasizes the "difference of view", which marks Australian women writers from the eighteenth century onwards, and identifies Anna Maria Bunn as the progenitor of that characteristic. Spender's book is filled with quotations from a wide selection of women authors, and from a significant number of little-known and unavailable texts. In Spender's words, her research has uncovered "a buried treasure" of women's fiction. Certainly this is a crucial study for any reader seeking an introduction to this aspect of Australian fiction.

SHOEMAKER's book is the first comprehensive examination of black literature in Australia. His is an historical survey, at times emotional, which stresses the socio-cultural opposition against which Aboriginal fiction has defined itself. Sex and violence are described as critical themes in black writing, and Shoemaker concludes by insisting upon the ultimately political nature of all black fiction, which has displayed "a growing realization that activism is often an essential – and inevitable – component of the Aboriginal writer's experience". This is an important work for anyone attempting to understand Aboriginal Australian fiction, as much so for its social history as for its literary criticism.

DANIEL's book is an imaginative and innovative look at eight contemporary Australian novelists. She stresses the fantastic and the absurd in current fiction, identifying deception and paradox as the salient characteristics in the authors she reads. At times the approach Daniel takes is too clever by half, and her own critical stance is both too derivative and too preoccupied with the trends of popular cultural criticism. Despite this, however, Daniel does provide sensitive readings of Peter Carey, David Ireland, and Elizabeth Jolley, writers whose tendencies toward the bizarre are well suited to the book's critical posture. If nothing else, Daniel proves a point that is continually asserted by critics: Australian fiction is characterized by an obsession for the unique and the peculiar in human experience.

STEPHEN W. BROWN

Fiction: Canadian

Davey, Frank, *Post-National Arguments: The Politics of the Anglophone-Canadian Novel since 1967*, Toronto and Buffalo, New York: University of Toronto Press, 1993

Jones, Joseph, and Johanna Jones, *Canadian Fiction*, Boston: Twayne, 1981

Kuester, Martin, *Framing Truths: Parodic Structures in Contemporary English-Canadian Historical Novels*, Toronto and Buffalo, New York: University of Toronto Press, 1992

MacLulich, T.D., *Between Europe and America: The Canadian Tradition in Fiction*, Toronto: ECW Press, 1988

Siemerling, Winfried, *Discoveries of the Other: Alterity in the Work of Leonard Cohen, Hubert Aquin, Michael Ondaatje, and Nicole Brossard*, Toronto and Buffalo, New York: University of Toronto Press, 1994

Söderlind, Sylvia, *Margin/Alias: Language and Colonization in Canadian and Québécois Fiction*, Toronto and Buffalo, New York: University of Toronto Press, 1991

Criticism of English-Canadian fiction has moved through phases of cataloguing, thematizing, and sociological study to the present phase, where there is a tendency to deal with aspects of both English-Canadian and Québécois fiction in the same volume, to theorize the material in terms of one or other of the poststructuralist paradigms, and to move far beyond the nationalist/identity concerns that so dominated criticism three decades ago, when Canadian literature was a burgeoning field in both writing and theory.

The JONES' brief study, a volume in the Twayne "World Authors" series, is an excellent primer on Canadian fiction up to 1975. Its first four chapters organize the material chronologically, from Frances Brooke to Hugh MacLennan. A second series of chapters, dealing with the explosion in fiction that occurred in postwar Canada, explores issues like regionalism, humour, diversity ("Indians and Eskimos" in literature, immigrant writing, Jewish fiction), and experimentation. The volume makes no attempt at critical rigour; its usefulness lies, rather, in its sense of history, its comprehensiveness, and the suggestive ways it organizes materials. A chronology, bibliography, and notes add to its usefulness as an initial research tool, which economically situates both major and minor writers and texts within the larger context of Canadian fiction.

MacLULICH presents a history of Canadian fiction from Frances Brooke's *The History of Emily Montague* (1769) to the generation of Margaret Laurence. He uses a literary-historical/sociological approach to argue that, in Canada, "a colonial literature that was overwhelmingly class-conscious . . . in spirit was transformed into a branch of the democratic North American mainstream". This approach proves useful in drawing a map of English-Canadian fictional writing, even when the map's adequacy is doubtful. For MacLulich, the Canadian tradition – distinct from, but related to, both the British and US traditions – arrived with the generation of Frederick Philip Grove, Morley Callaghan, Ernest Buckler, Hugh MacLennan, Robertson Davies, Ethel Wilson, Sinclair Ross, and W.O. Mitchell. Their works exhibit signs of Canadian relatedness (a "family resemblance"), and have been used by subsequent writers as a point of departure. Establishing this orienting site enables MacLulich to produce a comprehensive history of the Canadian novel, which situates minor as well as major figures, and provides broad interpretations of their work in literary/sociological rather than thematic terms. MacLulich insists that a Canadian tradition attained maturity by linking documentary realism with a limited modernism at the same time that it moved away from Europe and towards America. Unfortunately, because he idealizes this "bourgeois tradition" , MacLulich has very little to say about the exponential increase in fictional production from diverse sources since the 1960s.

It is precisely the diverse sources of fictional production that DAVEY attends to. Davey is one of several Canadian critics responsible for moving analysis of the nation's Anglophone novel away from nationalist, thematic, and aesthetic categories to an interrogation of political and ideological discourses as they necessarily inhabit every facet of textual construction. Davey discusses 16 Canadian Anglophone novels published since 1967. Some – novels by Margaret Laurence, Rudy Wiebe, Margaret Atwood, and Mordecai Richler – have gained recognition as "classics", while others – emanating from the so-called margins – have already called into question any centralizing approach to Canadian literature. Davey's interest, however, is not in developments *within* cultural production, like meta-fiction and postmodernism. Rather, he focuses on the issue of national discourse itself, and on the novel as one among several discourses for which the politics of the nation are at the front and centre. Resisting celebration or consolidation, Davey, through careful analysis, shows how contemporary novelists appear to conjure images of "Canada" while, in fact, they reveal the fragility of the nation's citizens, attempting negotiation with social and political formations, which are caught up in the flux of a "post-national" world. The nationalism that historians and critics saw mobilized in the decade of Canada's centenary enters the new fiction only in ironized forms.

KUESTER has produced a study of a special field, that of the historical novel, noting how central – in Canada and elsewhere – historical mediation has become in fiction. This is not an exhaustive study. It omits Rudy Wiebe and Michael Ondaatje, choosing Timothy Findley, George Bowering, and Atwood as exemplary for different problems and procedures. While Kuester's study is very readable, it also employs a sophisticated theorized framework in the shape of Russian formalism, Bakhtinian dialogics, Hayden White's new historiography, and Linda Hutcheon's extensive work on irony, parody, and the postmodern. If Canada is, as Kuester suggests, sceptical about its possession of a history, then its novelists' inclusion of prior forms of historical articulation as motivated parody serves to define "Canada" as a pre-eminent site for historic deformation and reformation. John Richardson's appropriation and revision of Sir Walter Scott provides the starting point for

Kuester's study. The major chapters focus on three contemporary works, which use intertextuality and parody with distinct motivations: Findley's *The Wars* becomes a "manifesto of pacificism", Bowering's affiliations are with an international postmodernism, and Atwood, in *The Handmaid's Tale*, parodies male historians.

SÖDERLIND's book is a significant contribution to the study of recent Canadian fiction, in both English and French, within the contexts of postcolonialism and postmodernism. Her key concepts are alienation, alterity, and marginality, and her theoretical basis comes from sources as different as Derridean deconstruction and Russian formalism and semiotics. There are substantial readings of novels by English-Canadian writers Leonard Cohen, Dave Godfrey, and Robert Kroetsch, and Québécois writers Hubert Aquin and André Langevin. Söderlind underscores the assumption that, in writing of this kind, *ideological* resistance in thematics almost inevitably goes along with *textual* resistance in style and strategy. Her study proceeds, however, to show that this is not always the case, and that the relationship between these two very influential contemporary discourses is by no means simple. Söderlind's study is characteristic of the kind of work currently underway on Canadian fiction.

So also is SIEMERLING's related study of alterity, which also draws on fictional materials from the two cultural and linguistic wings of Canadian writing. Increasingly, what used to be seen as an inclusive interest in variety or variation (in the Native figure, the immigrant, the homosexual figure, the outlaw) is now being recognized as a central concern in the postcolonial, postmodern world with exploring and problematizing the notion of stable, unified identity. Thoughtful encounters with "Otherness", often in fictional texts, choose not to domesticate or demonize the "Other", but rather to figure it as irreducible and, indeed, vital in the construction of identity. Siemerling's essays on Cohen and Ondaatje will prove indispensable for readers seeking to understand the tricky richness of these Canadian writers.

PATRICK HOLLAND

Fiction: Indian

Crane, Ralph J., *Inventing India: A History of India in English-Langauage Fiction*, London: Macmillan, 1992

Hemenway, Stephen, *The Novel of India*, 2 vols., Calcutta: Writer's Workshop, 1975

Naik, M.K. (ed.). *Perspectives on Indian Fiction in English*, New Delhi: Abhinav Publications, 1985

Ramamurti, K.S., *Rise of the Indian Novel in English*, New Delhi: Sterling, 1987

Sagar, Aparajita (ed.), "Fiction of the Indian Subcontinent", in *Modern Fiction Studies*, 39(1), Spring 1993

Shirwadker, Meena, *Image of Woman in the Indo-Anglian Novel*, New Delhi: Sterling, 1979

While early assessments of Indian fiction in English tend to locate it in a continuum with the English novel, more recent studies explore its postcolonial nature. Furthermore, a survey of critical works on this topic reveals that only the novel is perceived as a legitimate genre in fiction.

HEMENWAY's two-volume work is premised on the notion that the seminal text of this genre is E.M. Forster's *A Passage to India*. For Hemenway, all subsequent novels published on/in India have been a response to, and an extension of, the Indo-British encounter and the central theme of the incompatibility of Indians and English. Volume 1, subtitled "*The Indo-Anglian Novel*", deals with the significance of *A Passage to India*, its impact on the two traditions, and the Anglo-Indian novels after 1924 by George Orwell, John Masters, and Rumer Godden. Volume 2 furthers the theme of East-West conflict in the novels of Mulk Raj Anand, R.K. Narayan, Khushwant Singh, Bhabani Bhattacharya, and Raja Rao. Though dated, the premise of this remains interesting, as does the juxtaposed analysis of the Anglo-Indian and the Indo-Anglian novel.

SHIRWADKER's work is in the tradition of early feminist criticism of the second wave of feminism (1960s and 1970s), and acknowledges its debt to Susan Koppelman Cornillon's *Images of Women in Fiction* (1973). Shirwadker sets out her chapters chronologically, starting with images of women in Anglo-Indian fiction, and in contrast, Indo-Anglian fiction. In the chapter "Women in the Family," she discusses the perpetuation of the stereotype of the self-sacrificing Sati-Savithri in fiction by both male and female writers, listing as evidence characters from Narayan's, Anand's, Kamala Markandaya's, and Bhattacharya's novels. She concludes that more recent novelists, such as Anita Desai and Nayantara Sahgal, "have started depicting reality, yet they have generally limited themselves to the sophisticated urban surroundings as the novelists have dealt purely with problems of the urban family".

NAIK's collection, in contrast to Sagar's, has contributors who all reside in India and who teach at Indian universities. The preoccupations of these essays are different from Sagar's particularly. The writers in this volume reveal their disinterest in notions of subjectivity, or the nation, or the relationship between the First World and the Third World. These essays, instead, deal with the major themes of some of the well-known Indian writers – Anand, Narayan, Markandaya, and Desai.

RAMAMURTI's work, like most critical works on Indian fiction, agonizes over the legitimacy of Indian writing in English. Once past this stage, this work focuses on the legitimation of the genre in India between 1850 and 1920, and has chapters on early South Indian novelists and women novelists. Echoing the classic work *The Rise of the Novel* (1957), in which Ian Watt suggests that the genre is closely associated with the rise of the middle class, Ramamurti insists that in British India, too, the emergence of the middle class led to the rise of the Indian novel. The chapter on women novelists is interesting, because it deals with Toru Dutt, Cornelia Sorabji, and Krupabai Sathianathan, and links the genre to the emancipation of Indian women as well as the construction of India as nation.

CRANE starts from the premise that "India has captured the British imagination in a way that no other part of the Empire ever managed to do", before proceeding to deconstruct the traditional dichotomy between fiction (imaginative) and history (real) to study the history of English India and Independent India via fiction. Crane's work sets itself apart from Benita Parry's *Delusions and Discoveries: Studies on India in the British Imagination* (1972) and Allen Greenberger's *The British Image of India* (1969) because these works do not braid the lives of Indians and the British. Crane's work attempts to deal with both. For instance, his chapter on *swaraj* deals with Paul Scott's *Raj Quartet* as well as Narayan's *Waiting for the Mahatma*. This juxtaposition gives an all-around perspective of the British colonial encounter as well as the decolonization.

SAGAR's edited work is concerned with three different issues – the construction/production of the postcolonial subject; the embedding of discourses and narratives of the nation in literary/cultural texts; and the mutual interdependency of the First World and the Third World. Rajeswari Sunder Rajan's essay on Shashi Deshpande and Nina Sibal is noteworthy, as is D.C.R.A Goonetillake's essay on Sri Lankan literature. Also, the reviews of a variety of archival/theoretical works on South Asian literary criticism are very useful.

RADHIKA MOHANRAM

Fiction: New Zealand

Evans, Patrick, *The Penguin History of New Zealand Literature*, Auckland and New York: Penguin, 1990

Jones, Joseph, and Johanna Jones, *New Zealand Fiction*, Boston: Twayne, 1984

Jones, Lawrence, *Barbed Wire and Mirrors: Essays on New Zealand Prose*, Dunedin: University of Otago Press, 1987, revised 1990

Jones, Lawrence, "The Novel", in *The Oxford History of New Zealand Literature in English*, edited by Terry Sturm, Auckland, Oxford, and New York: Oxford University Press, 1991

New, William H., "New Zealand: Escape into Distance," in his *Among Worlds: An Introduction to Modern Commonwealth and South African Fiction*, Erin, Ontario: Porcepic Press, 1975

New, William H., *Dreams of Speech and Violence: The Art of the Short Story in Canada and New Zealand*, Toronto: University of Toronto Press, 1987

Rhodes, H. Winston, *New Zealand Novels: A Thematic Approach*, Wellington: Price Milburn/New Zealand University Press, 1969

Rhodes, H. Winston, *New Zealand Fiction since 1945*, Dunedin: John McIndoe, 1968

Roberts, Heather, *Where Did She Come From? New Zealand Women Novelists 1862–1987*, Wellington: Allen & Unwin/Port Nicholson Press, 1989

Smith, E.M., *A History of New Zealand Fiction from 1862 to the Present Time with Some Account of Its Relation to the National Life and Character*, Dunedin: A.H. & H.W. Reed, 1939

Stevens, Joan, *The New Zealand Novel 1860–1965*, 2nd, revised edition, Wellington: A.H. & H.W. Reed, 1966

Stevens, Joan, *The New Zealand Short Story*, Wellington: Price Milburn, 1969

Sturm, Terry, "Popular Fiction", in *The Oxford History of New Zealand Literature in English*, edited by Sturm, Auckland, Oxford, and New York: Oxford University Press, 1991

Wevers, Lydia, "The Short Story", in *The Oxford History of New Zealand Literature in English*, edited by Terry Sturm, Auckland, Oxford, and New York: Oxford University Press, 1991

Williams, Mark, *Leaving the Highway: Six Contemporary New Zealand Novelists*, Auckland: University of Auckland Press, 1990

There have been few comprehensive surveys of New Zealand fiction that include all periods and genres. Rather, most studies deal with specific genres and/or periods.

SMITH's was the first attempt at a general history. Her book, really a long essay divided into short chapters, is loose, impressionistic, descriptive rather than analytic, with little specific discussion of individual texts and authors. The approach is social-historical, an attempt to find the "enlightenment" offered by the fiction "upon the character of New Zealand people, their social and political background, their reaction to their surroundings, and their gradually changing habit of thought". The discussion is arranged in thematic chapters focusing on such issues as utopias and satires, history, the Maori people, women (as writers and as subjects of fiction), and local colour. There is no index, but there is a very full and useful bibliography of the early fiction, which remains the primary reason for consulting the book.

The only other attempt at a comprehensive history, that by Joseph and Johanna JONES, part of the Twayne "World Authors" series, is similar in its aims and arrangement, with a series of thematic chapters, although they do follow a roughly chronological pattern in their emphases. The approach is informal and descriptive, with many unanalysed excerpts from the novels and quotations from the critics. The result is a pleasant, superficial introductory book, a tourists' guide to the fiction written from outside the ongoing critical discourse. There is an index and a useful selective bibliography of the fiction and some of the critical materials.

NEW's brief 1975 essay is likewise thematic but is very different in method and, despite the book's subtitle, not at all introductory. New makes a sophisticated structuralist use of "recurrent structural patterns" to outline "underlying cultural sensibilities". His elliptical, condensed argument ranges freely through a variety of texts (both short fiction and novels) and is built on a series of related oppositions: New Zealand vs. England, reality vs. dream, childhood vs. adulthood, safety vs. danger, self vs. other. The result is not a discussion of individul texts and authors or a literary history, but rather a structuralist psychological portrait of a culture.

EVANS's four chapters on fiction (chapters 3, 6, 9, and 12) form something of a comprehensive history, but Evans is conducting a contentious argument, not trying to cover all of the texts and authors, and he skips rapidly over those authors who do not fit into his argument (however, the bibliographical notes at the end of each chapter fill most of the gaps). In relation to fiction, his aim is to deconstruct the dominant tradition of male critical realism, an aim he carries out with wit and verve.

RHODES's 1968 booklet concentrates on only one of the periods Evans deals with, 1945–67, and is a defense and explication of the realist tradition that Evans deconstructs.

Rhodes deals with all of the important short-story writers and novelists of the period in brief separate sections, prefaced by an overview of their postwar setting. My (JONES's) longer 1990 book likewise focuses mostly on the tradition of male realism, although it contrasts it more explicitly with a counter-tradition of female psychological impressionism. It is essentially a collection of detailed discussions of individual texts and authors, but these essays are placed within an historical framework so that they add up to a history of the novel and short fiction from 1935 to 1985, although not all of the important writers and texts are discussed.

Among the studies of the novel in general, RHODES's 1969 booklet was intended for use in high schools while STEVENS's 1966 book was written for adult education classes. Rhodes's is suggestive rather than comprehensive, useful in outlining the primary themes of New Zealand fiction and listing novels expressing them. It also has sample approaches to several individual novels and novelists. Stevens's is a comprehensive account of both serious and popular novels. It is necessarily brief in its discussions, but is compressed and authoritative and presents clearly a developing historical pattern. Its appendices contain study outlines of selected novels and topics for discussion. My (JONES's) 1991 essay is an account of all the novels before about 1890 and of the serious novels after that (see Sturm for the popular novels). The arrangement is historical, and the focus is "not on individual novels or novelists, but on the establishment of the form, and on the development of its themes and modes" through four distinct periods. The essay attempts to deal with all of the significant novels up to 1986, and can be viewed as the fullest single survey to date; and John Thomson's bibliography in the *Oxford History* is a valuable accompaniment, as it is to the essays by Sturm and Wevers (see below).

Several studies of the novel focus on particular periods or types. ROBERTS's book is restricted to novels by women but is relatively comprehensive in that it includes both popular and serious novels. Although there are a few significant omissions, it discusses most of the important novels and novelists. Roberts's aim is "to do something about bringing to life a large number of women novelists whose work has been forgotten and ignored", and her approach is that of a traditional historical-sociological feminism, focusing on the depiction of women's lives in the fiction. The result is a clear, well-organised, but relatively superficial, study. STURM's essays also deal primarily with women authors, as most of the popular novelists he discusses are women. He restricts himself to work since 1890. He does not attempt to discuss all of the popular novels of the period, but rather focuses on some representative writers of romance, detective fiction, and other modes. In his subtle analyses he reveals the development of the underlying patterns of the fiction and relates them to the "sustaining myths" of the changing societies that they depicted. WILLIAMS's book limits itself to the novels of the 1980s, focusing on six writers, but placing them in relation to their literary and social environment. Williams's concern is to relate his writers both to "the current formal directions of fiction" in New Zealand and to "a deep-seated unease about New Zealand's cultural situation". He shows his novelists shifting away from exclusive dependence on realism as they depict a society undergoing radical change.

The remaining studies focus on the short story alone. STEVENS's 1969 booklet was intended for use in high schools, and is intentionally introductory. It applies some general questions on structure, theme, and technique to specific stories selected from anthologies. NEW's 1987 book is more substantial and much more sophisticated in method, aimed at a very different audience. In this comparative study of Canadian and New Zealand short fiction, New opposes the kind of New-Critical theory that Stevens takes for granted, with its emphasis on unity and coherence, and shows instead how the writers from marginalised cultures have "sought ways of structuring stories so that they might break free from received conventions of speech and form, hence break formally free from the shaping social conventions that were lodged in their inherited language". The book starts with a deconstruction of short-story theory, moves through a brief history of the form in relation to the culture, and ends with close and subtle analyses of a few selected stories. This is not an introductory study, but rather is a contribution to an on-going critical discourse that presupposes prior knowledge of the subject.

WEVERS's contribution to the *Oxford History* is likewise sophisticated in its approach, drawing on poststructural techniques as New does, including postcolonial theory, but with a more feminist emphasis, and with the aim of a more general, less academic audience. Like New, she wishes to show how the forms and themes of short fiction develop in relation to the culture, but this is a more comprehensive history, making a judicious selection from the full range of texts from popular-magazine fiction to avant-garde stories in little magazines. The focus is on "the short story as a form of cultural history, the sign by which 'New Zealand' is produced", and on "the preoccupying narratives" of the most important writers. The result is a densely written but accessible narrative, subtle in its reasoning and suggestive in its analyses – the best available single account of New Zealand short fiction.

LAWRENCE JONES

Fielding, Henry 1707–1754

English novelist, dramatist, and journalist

Battestin, Martin C., *The Moral Basis of Fielding's Art: A Study of "Joseph Andrews"*, Middletown, Connecticut: Wesleyan University Press, 1959

Battestin, Martin C., with Ruthe R. Battestin, *Henry Fielding: A Life*, London and New York: Routledge, 1989

Compton, Neil (ed.), *Henry Fielding: "Tom Jones": A Casebook*, London: Macmillan, 1970

Hatfield, Glenn, W., *Henry Fielding and the Language of Irony*, Chicago: University of Chicago Press, 1968

Hume, Robert D., *Henry Fielding and the London Theatre 1728–1737*, Oxford: Clarendon Press, 1988; New York: Oxford University Press, 1988

Hunter, J. Paul, *Occasional Form: Henry Fielding and the Chain of Circumstance*, Baltimore: Johns Hopkins University Press, 1975

Rawson, Claude (ed.), *Henry Fielding and the Augustan Ideal under Stress: "Nature's Dance of Death" and Other Studies*, London and Boston: Routledge & Kegan Paul, 1972

Rawson, Claude (ed.), *Henry Fielding: A Critical Anthology*, Harmondsworth, Middlesex: Penguin, 1973

Smallwood, Angela J., *Fielding and the Woman Question: The Novels of Henry Fielding and Feminist Debate 1700–1750*, Hemel Hempstead, Hertfordshire: Harvester Wheatsheaf, 1989; New York: St Martin's Press, 1989

Early critical studies of Fielding took as their foundation the moral complexity of the fiction and its formal intricacy. For critics in the 1950s and 1960s Fielding's interest in freedom and licence appealed strongly. More recently, critics have reclaimed the importance of the dramatic works, while others have begun to investigate the fiction from feminist perspectives. For the contemporary student, a greater range of contextual information and biographical detail is available than ever before.

COMPTON provides an indispensable anthology of critical reactions to Fielding's work. Part One deals with critical reactions before 1920 (including Samuel Johnson, Samuel Taylor Coleridge, Sir Walter Scott, William Hazlitt, William Thackeray, and G.K. Chesterton). The second part includes magisterial studies such as Dorothy van Ghent's "On Tom Jones" and Middleton Murry's "In Defence of Fielding". Battestin's "Osborne's *Tom Jones*: Adapting a Classic" (1966) argues that the modern period is more open to satire, and may therefore "rediscover" Fielding's temperament. In another essay, Ronald Paulson uses Lucianic satire to demonstrate the mobility of character and commentator in Fielding's novels. Fielding emerges as a pioneer, a kind of conservative innovator. Robert Alter's "On the Critical Dismissal of Fielding" defends the author against the attacks of F.R. Leavis and Frank Kermode, who tend to prefer Richardson's moral seriousness. The range of critical strategies included make this a valuable collection.

RAWSON's *Critical Anthology* (1973) has a greater range of *earlier* critical material than Compton. Although the collection is larger, shorter extracts provide critical glimpses rather than extended and systematic interpretation. The book is divided into three parts: the first assembles critical opinion to 1755; the second part takes the reader to 1938; the third, covering modern critical opinion, is divided into smaller sections dealing with general estimates of Fielding's work, as well as essays on individual works. There is only one essay on *Joseph Andrews*, and the collection seems to be preoccupied with the novels as comic epics in prose. In common with much early criticism of Fielding, there is very little on the dramatic works.

HATFIELD evaluates a range of topics, such as language and society; writers, critics, and hacks; politics and politicians; polite society; and the professions. The study deals effectively with irony and action, and with the irony of dramatized authority. There is also a discussion of Fielding's drama, often unduly neglected. Just as Battestin sought to make a case for taking Fielding's morality seriously, so Hatfield seeks to demonstrate that Fielding's use of language is not simply festive but self-conscious and purposeful. As the book proceeds, tensions emerge between the close analysis of language and the desire to provide a historical or cultural foundation that precedes the use of irony. The study can be seen as emerging from the pressures of formalism and New Criticism at the time of its publication. In the course of the study there is sometimes a loss of direction in the argument. Given the development of theory since the 1960s, the modern reader may feel that that study's theoretical machinery is insufficienlty developed to deal with the complexity of Fielding's fiction. Nonetheless, Hatfield provides a useful analysis of Fielding's recognition of the nominalistic world, and his response to it in terms of language.

HUNTER argues that Fielding presents different "faces" because he is a product of the age of masquerades. At a literary level, this may be demonstrated by Fielding's obsession with the transformation of forms and his ability to renew tired traditions. Hunter carefully draws together rhetorical features of the texts and the social and cultural forces that went into their making. In this regard, he provides a range of models and contexts for Fielding's writing. He usefully locates Fielding's standing in relation to his contemporaries. The book has two excellent essays on the novels. Both "The Conquest of Space: Motion and Pause in *Joseph Andrews* and *Tom Jones*" and "Symmetry and the Limits of Symmetry in *Tom Jones*" demonstrate that Fielding was a flexible and compassionate figure. Turning to Fielding's dramatic works, Hunter argues that Fielding had difficulty forming objective correlatives or observable action in his drama. His fiction is marked by a "dialectic of perspectives". Hunter concludes that Fielding's theatrical experiments nonetheless anticipate aspects of his later innovative narrative method. This is an excellent introduction to the study of Fielding.

HUME's scholarly reassessment of the dramatic works has filled a large gap in Fielding studies. The book is divided into five sections: "The London World of the 1720s"; "The Young Playwright 1729–31"; "The Drury Lane Years 1732–33"; "The Years of Uncertainty 1734–35" and "Impresario at Little Haymarket 1736–37". Appendices deal with *Miss Lucy in Town* and *The Good Natur'd Man*. Hume's study provides a detailed contextual history of Fielding's theatrical career and critical criteria appropriate for a sympathetic understanding of the drama, showing that these pieces are much more than a literary apprenticeship for the later works. Hume explores the plays in the context of the theatre of the period, and he also discusses Fielding's contemporaries. The influence of economic and political factors is not neglected. Hume argues that the 1730s were comparable to the 1660s as a period of theatrical innovation. Fielding was at the centre of this dramatic revolution, and he made himself the most influential playwright in London since Dryden. Hume argues that Fielding's plays, taken as a whole, are complex works, clearly displaying a degree of maturity impressive in a young writer.

RAWSON's collection (1972) effectively compares Fielding with his contemporaries and with writers of the modern period. Rawson demonstrates that Fielding can hold his own against Alexander Pope, Jonathan Swift, Daniel Defoe, Tobias Smollett, and George Orwell, among others. In the first part of the study, called "Nature's Dance of Death", Rawson characteristically explores themes rather than pursuing any total vision of eighteenth-century culture. He identifies a notion of wholeness only in the context of its inevitable fragmentation, and he confesses that this procedure leads to overlapping and recurring motifs. Although Rawson asserts that our cultural climate is different from Fielding's, he deploys a range of modern writers to emphasize Fielding's relevance for our own period. The second part of Rawson's book, "Heroes, Clowns and Schoolboys: Mutations in Mock-Heroic", includes a fascinating study of the manner in which *Jonathan Wild* tends toward amoral or "black" humour. Rawson is at his best teasing out Fielding's inconsistent contrast between villainy and the ridiculous, and he emerges as a brilliantly idiosyncratic and innovative critic of Fielding's fiction.

BATTESTIN's rigorous 1959 account of the ethical foundations of Fielding's fiction prepared the way for his monumental biography, which appeared 30 years later. The earlier book deals with issues such as the "Good Man" as hero; vanity, Fortune and the classical ideal; and Fielding's ethics and his "defence" of the clergy. Although this is primarily a book concerned with *Joseph Andrews*, Battestin ranges widely over Fielding's fiction. He avoids the danger of generalization and rigid typology, noting, for instance, that Parson Adams has been too easily taken as the ethical model for Fielding's works as a whole. The continuous emphasis on Fielding's morality is, at points, rather overworked. As a result we lose sight of Fielding's comic genius, as well as his role as a satirist. Nonetheless, Battestin's study valuably contrasts the uncritical appreciation of Fielding's "sunshiny, breezy spirit" with a pressing sense of his fundamentally moral complexity and ethical subtlety.

BATTESTIN's biography (1989) deals in copious detail with Fielding's life, work, and times. This monumental volume (700 pages) is divided into four sections. Part One deals with Fielding's boyhood in the West Country, and his education at Eton (1707–26); the second section is primarily concerned with Fielding as a playwright and libertine in the period 1727–39; the third section discusses Fielding's involvement in politics, his novels, and the law (1739–49); and the final section, entitled "Magistrates and Reformers", deals with the years 1749–54, and shows Fielding's expanding interest in public affairs and social issues. The bibliography includes works probably and erroneously attributed to Fielding, as well as notes on letters and manuscripts. This scholarly volume is highly recommended to the general reader; for the student of Fielding it is an invaluable reference book.

SMALLWOOD's book contains stimulating sections dealing concisely with politics, law, sexual morality, education, and marriage. Other chapters deal with issues such as the tyranny of custom and patriarchal politics. *Jonathan Wild* emerges as an attack on primitive masculinity. *Joseph Andrews*, on the other hand, leads to an assessment of femininity and effeminacy. The final section shows the different ways in which *Amelia* transcends conventions. A useful bibliography lists documents debating issues relating to women during 1680–1760. Overall, the book demonstrates the groundlessness of Fielding's masculine ethos. Other contextual material is introduced as a means of analysing areas of inequality between the sexes. Smallwood provides a clear-sighted feminist overview of traditonal critical responses to Fielding. This is an excellent introduction to the new directions opened up by feminism in eighteenth-century studies.

I.D. McCormick

Film and Literature

Bluestone, George, *Novels into Film: The Metamorphosis of Fiction into Cinema*, Baltimore: Johns Hopkins Press, 1957; Berkeley: University of California Press, 1957

Chatman, Seymour, *Coming to Terms: The Rhetoric of Narrative in Fiction and Film*, Ithaca, New York: Cornell University Press, 1990

Cohen, Keith, *Film and Fiction: The Dynamics of Exchange*, New Haven, Connecticut, and London: Yale University Press, 1979

Davies, Anthony, and Stanley Wells, *Shakespeare and the Moving Image: The Plays on Film and Television*, Cambridge and New York: Cambridge University Press, 1994

Giddings, Robert, Keith Selby, and Chris Wensley, *Screening the Novel: The Theory and Practice of Literary Dramatization*, London: Macmillan, 1990

Manvell, Roger, *Theatre and Film: A Comparative Study of the Two Forms of Dramatic Art, and of the Problems of Adaptation of Stage Plays into Films*, Rutherford, New Jersey: Fairleigh Dickinson University Press, 1979; London: Associated University Presses, 1979

Ross, Harris, *Film as Literature, Literature as Film: An Introduction to and Bibliography of Film's Relationship to Literature*, New York: Greenwood Press, 1987

The interrelationship between literature and film is a complex one. As essentially *narrative* forms, fiction and film obviously have much in common, and their respective formal properties invite comparison. CHATMAN offers a sophisticated overview of theories of narratology, examines concepts and formulations which remain controversial, and investigates areas of disputed commonality in fiction and film, particularly differences between literary or cinematic narrators, and the concept of character "point of view".

Because cinema has often drawn on fiction for its source material – about one third of Hollywood productions have literary origins – there is extensive critical literature on issues relating to the adaptation of fiction and drama for the screen. The majority of these works are by literary scholars, who tend to be concerned with "fidelity" of film to its source. Where they claim to value cinema, it is usually because a particular film has managed to "illuminate" the written text in some way, rather than because of any appreciation/understanding of film as a qualitatively different medium. BLUESTONE, however, remains a seminal text, offering pioneer work which deals with general problems of adaptation and the strengths and limitations of both film and literature, accepting – as not all later theorists do – that the transfer of a narrative from one medium to another inevitably involves a qualitative change. For Bluestone, what is adapted is "the novel viewed as raw material" so that "the filmist becomes not a translator for an established author, but a new author in his own right". Six specimen adaptations are offered.

GIDDINGS, SELBY, and WENSLEY focus on the relationship between literature and contemporary means of production and distribution, exploring the mutual opportunities and restrictions in this relationship. Central to their discussion is the way in which "our class structure and the means for the distribution and consumption of culture seriously distort our perceptions of the past", conspiring to produce sanitised versions of, particularly, the nineteenth-century novel. Their introductory chapter provides a valuable overview of "The Literature/Screen Debate", and they take Charles Dickens's *Great Expectations* and William Makepeace Thackeray's *Vanity Fair* as sample case studies.

The fiction/film dynamic is not uni-directional. Many twentieth-century novelists acknowledge the influence of cinema on their writing. (Sergei Eisenstein – rearranging parts of Milton's *Paradise Lost* into a shooting script – even proposed that "the film sense" was apparent in writing long before the emergence of cinema.) The influence of film on literature is most fully explored in COHEN, who argues that the "film sensibility" has influenced all the arts in the twentieth century, the modern novel in particular manifesting cinematic influences in its distortions of time, its play of multi-perspectivism, and its use of montage. The works of Marcel Proust, James Joyce, and Virginia Woolf are offered as exemplification.

MANVELL remains the only general work to attempt a juxtaposition of theatre and film, offering a general introduction which remains useful. Stressing the differences between the two forms, Manvell discusses factors such as stage sets and studio sets/locations; dramatists/screenplay writers; the role of the director, acting styles, audiences/spectators; and the economics of production. The second section of the book offers ten examples of adaptations from stage to screen (including, for example, *Pygmalion*, *A Streetcar Named Desire*, and *The Marat-Sade*), together with a section on "Shakespeare on Film".

DAVIES and WELLS offer an excellent collection of essays on Shakespeare. Davies's introductory chapter provides an overview of critical writing on filmed Shakespeare and a useful discussion of the relationship of cinematic to television versions of the plays. Essays include a discussion of BBC Shakespeare productions, of films of the history plays and comedies, of versions by individual directors such as Akira Kurosawa, of the challenges offered by specific plays such as *King Lear*, and a filmography.

For an overview of scholarship on all the above areas, the bibliography by ROSS remains the most complete source. The introductory section offers an exploration of critical positions on a variety of key debates: the extent to which the camera is a film's narrator; whether film can be "narrated in the first person" and whether it can "describe"; what it means to speak of film as a "present tense" art, and prose fiction as a "past tense" art; whether there is anything in prose fiction comparable to the filmic shot; relationships between filmic space and dramatic space, and filmic and dramatic illusion.

The interrelationship of literature and film has not yet attracted much research adopting poststructuralist or psychoanalytical approaches. In particular, questions relating to the processes of reception – as reader and as spectator – await appropriate investigation.

CAROLINE M. COOPER

Findley, Timothy 1930 –

Canadian novelist and short-story writer

Dellamora, Richard, "Becoming-Homosexual/Becoming Canadian", *Double-Talking: Essays on Verbal and Visual Ironies in Contemporary Canadian Art and Literature*, edited by Linda Hutcheon, Toronto: ECW Press, 1992

Hutcheon, Linda, *The Canadian Postmodern: A Study of Contemporary English-Canadian Fiction*, Toronto, New York, and Oxford: Oxford University Press, 1988

Pennee, Donna Palmateer, *Moral Metafiction: Counter-Discourse in the Novels of Timothy Findley*, Toronto: ECW Press, 1991

Roberts, Carol, *Timothy Findley: Stories from a Life*, Toronto: ECW Press, 1994

Williams, David, *Confessional Fictions: A Portrait of the Artist in the Canadian Novel*, Toronto: University of Toronto Press, 1991

York, Lorraine M., *Front Lines: The Fiction of Timothy Findley*, Toronto: ECW Press, 1991

Critical interest in Timothy Findley's work began after *The Wars* (1977), although two novels – *The Last of the Crazy People* (1967) and *The Butterfly Plague* (1969) – had appeared earlier. Most discussion focuses on *The Wars*, *Famous Last Words* (1981), and *Not Wanted on the Voyage* (1985). Criticism of Findley's recent novel, *Headhunters* (1993), is at present confined to newspaper and journal reviews.

HUTCHEON has no separate chapter on Findley or any of his seven novels in her brief study of contemporary English-Canadian fiction. Throughout the book, however, Hutcheon shows how Findley – like Leonard Cohen, Rudy Wiebe, George Bowering, Margaret Atwood, and Michael Ondaatje – practises a distinctively Canadian form of postmodernism, which she calls "historiographic metafiction". Its features include foregrounding the problematic nature of narratives of history; the reader's participation as active agent in constructing such narratives; and the link between the novels' self-reflexivity and their "ground[ing] in historical, social, and political realities". Within this wider context of contemporary English-Canadian fiction, Hutcheon's study is particularly useful for the novels *The Wars, Famous Last Words*, and *Not Wanted on the Voyage*.

Writing about *Famous Last Words* as a Canadian "portrait of the artist," WILLIAMS explores the intertextual subtleties of the novel's relation to Ezra Pound, particularly his celebrated poem carrying as title the name of Findley's protagonist. He uses a reading of Pound to produce an interpretation that offers a critique of the character Mauberley from the outside. He adjudicates between positions also of concern to Hutcheon and Pennee – those of politics and aesthetics. Williams considers whether the motivation of Hugh Selwyn Mauberley, in inscribing his story on hotel walls, is confession or apology, and concludes that it is the latter; the novel, in fact, has the effect of *endorsing*, not *confessing* (and repenting), aestheticism. Williams disagrees with those critics who see Findley, through protagonist Mauberley, as utilizing postmodern and meta-fictional techniques to expose the lies of history.

PENNEE considers Findley's novels from *The Last of the Crazy People* (1967) through to *The Telling of Lies* (1986).

Pennee acknowledges Hutcheon's identification of the category "historiographic metafiction" and develops it. Using the more reference-oriented kinds of poststructuralist theory (feminism, postcolonialism), she examines Findley's meta-fictions in relation to moral issues and history. Critics have neglected the "political effect" of Findley's fictions for the reader, and so she explicitly prioritizes the political over the aesthetic. Consequently, Pennee produces careful readings, which foreground the way in which Findley challenges his readers to acknowledge their human and moral involvement as they read fictions that, through their meta-fictional effects, consistently draw attention to the inscription of history in the form of competing discourses. In recognizing this discursivity, readers also recognize their capacity to resist simplistic narratives which "naturalize" history.

The title of YORK's study refers to the "concept of warfare", which she finds central to an understanding of Findley's work. York, utilizing Hayden White's new historiographical insights and Jonathan Culler's theory of intertextuality, finds that documentary texts of war – written records and photographs – combine with Findley's reconstruction of personal lives and situations to produce a textual system. For York, war is inextricably involved with patriarchy, so that gender becomes her second theme. York, like Pennee, explores the degree to which Findley is a politically committed writer who actively seeks to involve readers in the recognition and critique of political values. Where Pennee finds a certain ambivalence in Findley's counter-positioning of politics and aesthetics, York asserts that "the notion of reading as ideological warfare" emerges, particularly in *Famous Last Words*. York's study incorporates many quotations from conversations with Findley, conducted by several interviewers.

DELLAMORA enters the debate about Findley and counter-discourse skeptically. He takes account of Findley's position as a Canadian and a homosexual figure in *Famous Last Words* as one of exclusion. However, Dellamora suggests, the Prince of Wales (Edward VIII) as character provides an invitation to read the novel with a special kind of ironic and liberating awareness, given his erotic appeal to men (from a gay standpoint) and his appeal to the Anglo-Canadian establishment. Thus, while Dellamora seems to endorse Williams' interpretation on the surface, he shows how Pennee's counter-discursive model can lead to a subversive, moral/political reading.

ROBERTS offers the first biography of Findley, which is brief and uncritical. For a number of reasons, however, it is worth consulting as a supplement to the published criticism. It provides an account of the process of composition and publication of the seven novels up to, and including, *Headhunters*. There is useful material also on Findley's other production, as actor, scriptwriter, dramatist, and writer of stories, along with generous excerpts from the many interviews Findley has given, and brief summaries of the reviews of his major works. The book concludes with a useful bibliography. The volume's occasional triviality is offset by insights into personal events and relationships, character-types, and motifs that recur throughout the fiction.

PATRICK HOLLAND

Fitzgerald, F. Scott 1896–1940

American novelist and short-story writer

Allen, Joan M., *Candles and Carnival Lights: The Catholic Sensibility of F. Scott Fitzgerald*, New York: New York University Press, 1978

Bryer, Jackson R. (ed.), *The Short Stories of F. Scott Fitzgerald: New Approaches to Criticism*, Madison: University of Wisconsin Press, 1982

Eble, Kenneth, *F. Scott Fitzgerald*, New York: Twayne, 1963, revised 1977

Fryer, Sarah Beebe, *Fitzgerald's New Women: Harbingers of Change*, Ann Arbor, Michigan: UMI Research Press, 1988

Miller, James E., Jr., *The Fictional Art of F. Scott Fitzgerald*, The Hague: Nijhoff, 1957; revised edition, as *F. Scott Fitzgerald: His Art and His Technique*, New York: New York University Press, 1964

Sklar, Robert, *F. Scott Fitzgerald: The Last Laocoön*, New York: Oxford University Press, 1967

Stern, Milton R., *The Golden Moment: The Novels of F. Scott Fitzgerald*, Urbana: University of Illinois Press, 1970

Way, Brian, *F. Scott Fitzgerald and the Art of Social Fiction*, London: Edward Arnold, 1980; New York: St Martin's Press, 1990

During his lifetime only a handful of serious critics conscientiously debated Fitzgerald's artistic development. Though they were quick to point out weaknesses as well as strengths, their assessments now have the eerie feeling of prophesy in predicting the status of Fitzgerald's posthumous literary reputation and the direction of the critical response that has established it during the five decades since his death. Among these were Edmund Wilson, H.L. Mencken, John Peale Bishop, Paul Rosenfeld, and T.S. Eliot, the latter of whom called *The Great Gatsby* "the first step that American fiction has taken since Henry James". As the poet laureate of the Jazz Age, the creator of the flapper in fiction, as author of more than 150 stories in slick magazines like the *Saturday Evening Post* and, with his wife Zelda, a highly visible public personality, Fitzgerald became an easy target for superficial evaluations of his work during his lifetime. However, the 50-odd years of careful scrutiny of the body of Fitzgerald's work have more than borne out the confidence of those few contemporary critics who, in his lifetime, saw for him a permanent place among the immortals of American literature. Since 1940 there have been hundreds of journal articles, a dozen biographical studies, and more than 30 critical volumes devoted to Fitzgerald and his work.

MILLER's was the first book-length critical study devoted exclusively to Fitzgerald's work. There are two versions of this book: the 1957 edition, which traces the development of Fitzgerald's fictional technique from *This Side of Paradise* (1920) through *The Great Gatsby* (1925), and the 1964 edition, which extends the thesis through to the end of Fitzgerald's life, including discussions of *Tender is the Night* and *The Last Tycoon*. Miller establishes a context for his theories about Fitzgerald's artistic development by first clarifying his definition of the term "technique", settling on Mark Shorer's comprehensive definition: "everything is technique which is not the lump of experience itself, and one cannot properly say that a writer has no technique or that he eschews technique, for, being a writer, he cannot do so". Miller, therefore, examines Fitzgerald's technique in broad terms of "the development of theme, point of view, and the manner of representing events". He convincingly argues that Fitzgerald moved steadily away from the novel of saturation, of which *This Side of Paradise* is a good example, toward the Jamesian and Conradian novel of selected incident. The pinnacle of Fitzgerald's achievement, according to Miller, is *The Great Gatsby*, in which "for the first time in his career [Fitzgerald] was able to disengage himself from his subject and treat his material from an artistic and impersonal perspective". In the 1964 edition, Miller shows that *Tender is the Night* and *The Last Tycoon* are magnificent failures of sorts, because Fitzgerald's artistic standards were too carefully considered during the time of composition of these works; he simply could not realize them as fully as he had done in *The Great Gatsby*. The earlier novel, *The Beautiful and Damned*, by contrast, failed because it grew out of a time of theoretical uncertainty and transition in Fitzgerald's life. Miller's discussion of the technique of Fitzgerald's first three novels, and the selected stories that cluster around them, is based on detailed, sensitive analysis of the works, almost scene by scene. He also includes pertinent sections of letters and reviews by Fitzgerald, which indicate beyond much doubt that Fitzgerald's shift from the novel of saturation to the novel of selected incident was conscious and carefully reasoned. Some will argue that Miller's choice for analysis of the Malcolm Cowley "author's-final-intention" edition of *Tender is the Night*, which re-establishes the novel's chronological sequence of events, is unfortunate in that this edition works against Miller's thesis. But the issue of which version of *Tender is the Night* is "best" has become one for critical examination in itself, and, with or without his chapters on this novel and *The Last Tycoon*, Miller's study is seminal, situating Fitzgerald as it does in the mainstream of the development of literary theory and practice.

EBLE's book does what few introductory works in a series such as the Twayne series are able to do: it provides a comprehensive overview of the canon; it breaks new ground, particularly in its stylistic analysis of major works; and it provided, as we can now see in retrospect, a blueprint for the direction of Fitzgerald studies in the three decades that followed it. Eble systematically examines the novels and the stories against the backdrop of Fitzgerald biography, finally drawing conclusions about the relative strengths of the works, particularly the novels, by New-Critical standards. He typically proceeds in chronological order, though in the case of groups of stories like the Basil Duke Lee series, written in the late 1920s, his analysis comes early since these retrospective autobiographical works cast light on Fitzgerald's life as an adolescent.

In the course of his analyses Eble makes observations, some of them original and some of them echoes of earlier appraisals, which are now the foundation of the conventional wisdom of Fitzgerald scholarship. Drawing heavily on Arthur Mizener's 1951 Fitzgerald biography *The Far Side of Paradise*, he demonstrates beyond any question that Fitzgerald's fictional works typically come directly from his personal experience. This is scarcely a startling proposition for anyone mildly acquainted with Fitzgerald's life and work; but what Eble manages to do with this observation is to demonstrate which kinds of life experiences and which kinds of narrative points of view seem to work best for Fitzgerald. Eble shows, for example, how much stronger dramatic episodes in the Basil stories are artistically than those based on similar episodes drawn from life in Fitzgerald's first novel, *This Side of Paradise*, a point which leads to the conclusion that Fitzgerald does better with experiences that have had time to cool. Eble also makes the point that Fitzgerald's seemingly magical leap in ability from his first two novels, which have glaring faults, to *The Great Gatsby*, his masterpiece, published only three years after *The Beautiful and Damned*, is less startling when one considers the brilliance of such early stories as "The Ice Palace" and "May Day", as well as isolated bursts of prose genius in even the weakest works.

Since the so-called "Fitzgerald Revival" was building momentum during the 20-odd years between Fitzgerald's death and Eble's book, his study draws heavily on the accumulated wisdom of scores of journal articles devoted to Fitzgerald during this time, as well as on Miller's study. Eble, however, breaks new ground, and the areas of his concern predict the directions of much of the scholarship that follows. He focuses on Fitzgerald's revisions in the galley proofs of *The Great Gatsby*, for example, to demonstrate not only what a careful craftsman Fitzgerald could be, but also to show how he was able, with subtle changes and simple brush strokes, to convey entire personalities and scenes. Textual scholars, most notably Matthew J. Bruccoli, have, since Eble, produced volumes of collations, textual editions, and commentary, which painstakingly document Eble's general point about Fitzgerald's methods of composition and revision. Eble also, in his final appraisal of Fitzgerald's work, clearly articulates the reasons why Fitzgerald's reputation has remained high, positioning him with other such great American writers as Herman Melville, Nathaniel Hawthorne, and Henry James: "the first is the hard core of morality. . .. Second, unlike a majority of modern American writers, he offers a fiction which is hard to imitate but from which much can be learned". Here again, scores of articles and several volumes (among them Allen's, discussed below) have pursued the point of Fitzgerald's "hard core of morality" as well as the qualities of his style that make it "hard to imitate". And finally, Eble pushes the limits of what had been considered work worthy of consideration by literary critics into the realm of lesser-known and previously uncollected stories, a foreshadowing of the direction of much current Fitzgerald scholarship, which is expanding the canon toward "the neglected works" (e.g., Jackson Bryer's forthcoming [at the time of writing] *The Neglected Stories of F. Scott Fitzgerald*, Columbia: University of Missouri Press).

Counting Eble's book and Miller's 1964 revised volume, the decade of the 1960s saw 15 books devoted exclusively to Fitzgerald's work published in the United States, more book-length critical studies on Fitzgerald than have been published in any other single decade. Two of these were introductory studies, seven (counting Eble, Miller, and a translation from Italian of an earlier study) were comprehensive studies of the Fitzgerald canon, one was a study of the composition of *Tender is the Night*, and five were collections of critical essays. The comprehensive studies were characteristically aimed at affirming Fitzgerald's position in the mainstream of American literary history and at deepening the reader's understanding of the precise nature of his achievement relative to the tradition of which he was a part.

SKLAR's study, the last of the 1960s' volumes, is built on the metaphor (first constructed in relation to Fitzgerald by Malcolm Lowry) of Apollo's priest, Laocoon, who, in Virgil's *Aeneid*, pierced the wooden horse with his spear to warn his countrymen against the trickery of the Greeks. His Trojan countrymen paid him no attention, and Athena called serpents from the sea to destroy Laocoon and his sons. Sklar, taking Lowry's cue, suggests that Fitzgerald warned the American people against the enemy that would destroy them – the loss of "chivalry and decency" – but he, like Laocoon, was ignored and finally destroyed for delivering his message.

Sklar does not dwell on the earlier interpretations of Fitzgerald's work, many of which he, no doubt, would see as missing the mark; but instead, he constructs a coherent theory, which takes into account virtually every Fitzgerald novel and story as well as the known facts about Fitzgerald's life. Sklar sees Fitzgerald, on the one hand, as taking seriously his legacy of the genteel tradition; on the other hand, he believes that Fitzgerald devoted his life artistically to the search for a way to modify this legacy to make it morally defensible in a modern world, which presented so many rational challenges to the genteel tradition, a world with "all Gods dead, all wars fought, and all faiths in man shaken". To Sklar, any study of Fitzgerald's work must take into account the seriousness with which Fitzgerald pursued his artistic goal of creating a believable modern hero who has retained whatever was salvageable from the genteel hero. As Sklar phrases it, "it is difficult to see how an uncritical portrait of the genteel hero could be possible in a serious work of fiction; and that makes it even more important to recognize how deeply the heroes of Fitzgerald's mature novels – Jay Gatsby . . . Dick Diver . . . and Monroe Stahr – have the roots of their characters implanted in the nature of the genteel hero, the creator of romantic dreams".

While Sklar does not discount the importance of examining the evolution of Fitzgerald's art and technique, he believes that it is of greatest importance to follow what might be seen as Fitzgerald's pursuit of a morally and intellectually tenable position in the modern world. And for this it is essential to follow the influences on Fitzgerald's thinking – of, among many others, Wells, Shane Leslie, and Monsignor Sigourney Fay (*This Side of Paradise*), to Mencken and Frank Norris (*The Beautiful and Damned*), to Joseph Conrad (*The Great Gatsby*), to Oswald Spengler and Carl Jung (*Tender is the Night*), to his own original vision (*The Last Tycoon*). Sklar's study is a step-by-step working-through of each major Fitzgerald hero, showing how each tries a new solution, informed by Fitzgerald's reading, reflection, and soul searching, which ultimately is not acceptable to Fitzgerald himself.

The decade of the 1970s was a transitional period in Fitzgerald studies, during which numerous primary documents such as scrapbooks, notebooks, and letter collections, with material previously unavailable except through special collections in various libraries and private collections, were made available in book form. Also, bibliographical studies and volumes containing previously uncollected Fitzgerald short stories published during this decade provided an Aladdin's cave of material for Fitzgerald scholars. There were fewer book-length critical studies in this period than in the 1960s, and those that were published typically, as one might expect, moved in one of two general directions: toward making mid-course corrections in what had become mainstream critical opinion on Fitzgerald, using the earlier studies as a platform; or toward filling what were perceived as gaps in the body of criticism.

Typical of this first group is STERN's account, in which the author suggests that many previous critical studies, like Miller's, had seemed to miss what he perceived to be the major point of Fitzgerald's work. What was missing, and what Stern's study attempts to provide, is a unified study "that would parallel Sklar's by talking about the national rather than the literary development of Fitzgerald's talent". Stern's book examines the four complete Fitzgerald novels, those best known to the general American reading public through what he characterizes as "Fitzgerald's personality".

Illustrative of the second group is ALLEN's study. While not challenging the validity of earlier appraisals, Allen believes that the influences of Fitzgerald's early Roman Catholic upbringing on his art have been neglected. Her study examines sections relevant to her thesis of Fitzgerald's major novels and stories, with the purpose of showing "that his Roman Catholic early education and family experiences, the complexities of Catholic upbringing in an atmosphere of inadequate paternity and oppressive maternity and ambivalence about money, formed his moral consciousness".

What might be characterized as a strong third wave in Fitzgerald criticism has been in progress since the early 1980s, a decade launched by Bruccoli's definitive biography, *Some Sort of Epic Grandeur: The Life of F. Scott Fitzgerald* (1981), and shows little sign of weakening in the 1990s. In the early part of the period were book-length reappraisals – and such studies will continue to appear from time to time – which, with rather traditional critical methods applied to a selected number of Fitzgerald works, attempt to alter or augment the record of existing scholarship. WAY's book, which contains an excellent chapter on the short stories, is such a study. Way grants that Fitzgerald has always been seen as a social historian who chronicled the Jazz Age and alerted readers to the failure of the American Dream, but he maintains that most earlier studies failed "to appreciate Fitzgerald's own complexity of attitude, his capacity to be fascinated with the collective adventure of Jazz Age America and at the same time highly critical of it".

The recent studies have, more characteristically, however, followed the lines of the changing face of literary criticism itself. Fitzgerald criticism has moved toward an explosion of the Fitzgerald canon, on the one hand, expanding more deeply into the 178 stories, the majority of which have received very little critical attention; on the other hand, it has also moved in the direction of gender-based and reader-response theory. Though seeds of this movement can be found in many of the studies of the 1960s and 1970s, perhaps the most influential volume in moving Fitzgerald studies in this direction is BRYER's. For this volume, Bryer commissioned 22 essays from outstanding Fitzgerald scholars as well as literary critics whose work had not hitherto been focused on Fitzgerald.

The book itself contains a valuable summary by Bryer of the areas of greatest neglect in Fitzgerald studies and, at the end, a comprehensive bibliography, which, aside from its usefulness, indicates how little in-depth criticism there has been of the short stories. The essays in the collection are divided into two sections "Overviews" and "Individual Stories"; in both, the most distinct qualities of the essays are their originality of approach and their movement into previously uncharted territory. In the first section, an essay by Eble, for example, addresses for the first time the subjects of alcoholism and mental illness strictly in terms of Fitzgerald's fictional treatment of them, not in terms of biographical connections to the Fitzgeralds' lives. Ruth Prigozy examines a cluster of seldom-discussed stories from the early 1930s to cast light on the connection between the crises of Fitzgerald's middle years and the evolution of what was to become, in the late 1930s, his "new" style. Joseph Mancini, Jr., provides a Jungian analysis of the Basil Duke Lee stories, using an approach that had rarely been applied to Fitzgerald's works – oddly so since Fitzgerald was influenced by Jung during the composition of *Tender is the Night*. Alan Margolies takes the often-noted fact that many of Fitzgerald's early *Post* stories suffered because they were written to satisfy biases of *Post* readers, and adds a fascinating new dimension: that the weaknesses of some of these stories were compounded by the fact that Fitzgerald wrote them with a Hollywood market also in mind.

The essays in the "Individual Stories" section particularly are characterized by close attention to the texts of stories that have previously received only passing comment – "The Bridal Party", "Financing Finnegan", "The Swimmers", "Rags Martin-Jones and the Pr-nce of W-les", and "The Adjuster", for example. One excellent illustration of the kinds of insights provided in these analyses is found in Christiane Johnson's study of "The Adjuster". Johnson takes the shadowy figure of Dr Moon in the story and challenges earlier suggestions – granted these are almost offhand suggestions – in the criticism that he is meant to be a psychoanalyst. By arguing that he is instead intended to represent Time, Johnson is able finally to identify the subject of passing time as a central theme, one tied clearly to the idea that time itself is "the adjuster" in this story. As Bryer notes in the Introduction, as of 1979 only 75 articles or book chapters had been devoted to Fitzgerald's stories, and only 22 of the 178 stories that Fitzgerald wrote had been dealt with in chapters or full essays. It is noteworthy that before Bryer's book, only one volume had been devoted exclusively to the short stories, whereas in the early 1990s three books, each devoted to the short fiction, have appeared.

Of the critical studies that draw on new approaches and multi-disciplinary perspectives, FRYER's, grounded solidly in Fitzgerald studies and feminist theory, is perhaps the finest example. Fryer draws on numerous historical studies to establish the plight of women and a definition of the "New Women" of the postwar decade in America, finally making this assertion in her Introduction:

> They are a curious blend of confidence and uncertainty, for they live on the threshold of a new era and still feel the influence of the old order, which stubbornly insists on subordinating them to men . . . they try very hard to accept themselves for who they are and to enjoy their lives to the fullest as they proudly – even defiantly – struggle to develop and preserve their integrity.

In Fryer's opinion Fitzgerald's women conform to this picture, but there has been little attempt to understand them except in terms established by critics and biographers, mostly male, of their character flaws: "poor housekeeping skills, vanity, material acquisitiveness, stubbornness, restlessness, purposelessness, boredom, [and] attention getting antics". Granted, however, that "Fitzgerald himself was confused in his expectations of women", Fryer sees him, first, as being accurate as a social historian in portraying women in the 1920s, and second, as demonstrating sensitivity toward the plight of women in his time. His novels, she maintains, "chart the progression of the social and sexual revolution of the 1920's". Fryer supports these assertions with careful analyses of the major Fitzgerald heroines – Rosalind Connage, Gloria Gilbert, Daisy Buchanan, Nicole Diver, Kathleen Moore – whom she sees finally, in varying degrees, as believable, three-dimensional characters. Countering the charge by some critics that Fitzgerald's women are superficial, Fryer notes that "Fitzgerald has drawn female characters who struggle with conflicts common to many twentieth-century women who are brought up to *marry*, not work". Again in varying degrees, these characters are victims, less of Fitzgerald's conception of them than they are of a patriarchal society, which has taught them that they are to be taken care of. Fryer sees Fitzgerald's women as often struggling valiantly to establish autonomy. In her analysis of Nicole Diver, for example, Fryer demonstrates, first, the obvious ways in which Nicole is exploited, and finally the subtle ways in which she asserts her freedom and establishes her dignity. "It is a tribute to the artistry of F. Scott Fitzgerald", she maintains, "that he could so accurately record these New Women's voices – and that he could listen to them so well in the first place".

Reviewing the general state of Fitzgerald criticism in the mid-1990s, a half century into the revival of critical interest in his work, one is inclined to agree with the appraisal of Fitzgerald's contemporary, Stephen Vincent Benét, writing in a review of *The Last Tycoon* during the year following Fitzgerald's death: "you can take off your hats now, gentlemen, and I think perhaps you had better. This is not a legend, this is a reputation – and, seen in perspective, it may well be one of the most secure reputations of our time".

BRYANT MANGUM

Fletcher, John 1579–1625

English dramatist

Appleton, William W., *Beaumont and Fletcher: A Critical Study*, London: Allen & Unwin, 1956

Bentley, G.E., *The Jacobean and Caroline Stage: Volume III*, Oxford: Clarendon Press, 1956

Cone, Mary, *Fletcher Without Beaumont: A Study of the Independent Plays of John Fletcher*, Salzburg: Institut für Englische Sprache und Literatur (Salzburg University), 1976

Finkelpearl, Philip J., *Court and Country Politics in the Plays of Beaumont and Fletcher*, Princeton, New Jersey: Princeton University Press, 1990

Leech, Clifford, *The John Fletcher Plays*, London: Chatto & Windus, 1962; Cambridge, Massachusetts: Harvard University Press, 1962

Pearse, Nancy Cotton, *John Fletcher's Chastity Plays: Mirrors of Modesty*, Lewisburg, Pennsylvania: Bucknell University Press, 1973

Waith, Eugene, *The Pattern of Tragicomedy in Beaumont and Fletcher*, New Haven, Connecticut: Yale University Press, 1952

John Fletcher was a prolific and popular playwright for London's Jacobean and Caroline stage, often in collaboration with Francis Beaumont and others (including Shakespeare and Philip Massinger). When a folio collection of Beaumont and Fletcher's plays was published in 1647, the pair became only the third and fourth dramatists, after Ben Jonson and Shakespeare, to be so honored. Whereas Fletcher's plays were revived with great success in the Restoration period and influenced that generation's playwrights (an expanded Beaumont and Fletcher Folio, with 52 plays, was issued in 1679), eighteenth- and nineteenth-century critics turned against what they regarded as his ambivalent morality, brittle wit, and formulaic plotting. In the twentieth century, Fletcher criticism has run the gamut from disdain to praise, while the plays are rarely performed.

WAITH discusses the rhetorical pattern of the plays, which derives from Seneca the Elder's *Controversiae* with an infusion of romance and satire; Fletcher therefore depended upon a knowledgeable and appreciative audience. Contrived confrontations, in the manner of law courts, between apparent moral opposites are standard occurrences in the tragicomedies, the best of which, says Waith, are six late ones Fletcher wrote by himself – *The Mad Lover*, *The Loyal Subject*, *The Humorous Lieutenant*, *Women Pleased*, *The Island Princess*, and *A Wife for a Month*.

APPLETON, like M.C. Bradbrook (in *Growth and Structure of Elizabethan Comedy*, 1955) and Robert Ornstein (in *The Moral View of Jacobean Tragedy*, 1960), offers an equivocal assessment, dismissing most of the tragedies (the collaborative *Maid's Tragedy* is an exception) and doubting whether the comedies are informed by a basic comic situation. He does praise *The Wild Goose Chase*, however, for capturing "the gaiety and ebullience of the period" and "demonstrating how Fletcher's mastery of tragi-comedy could be turned to effective use for comic purposes". While the tragicomedies are hybrid dramas reflecting the decadence of the age, they are also, he says, important forerunners of Restoration heroic drama, just as the comedies are influential predecessors of the later comedy of manners.

BENTLEY devotes 128 pages to Fletcher in this third of five far-ranging volumes on the early seventeenth-century drama. He provides a bibliography and then summarizes the basic biographical information (with sources), lists collected editions, and chronologically treats the entire canon (including those of questionable attribution), discussing for each play its sources, date, texts, early stage history, and influence on later drama. Because much of Fletcher's work was done in collaboration with others, Bentley also deals with authorship problems.

LEECH examines 12 plays that reveal different facets of Fletcher's craftsmanship in comedy, tragedy, and tragicomedy. He concludes that Fletcher, while writing in an informal and clear style, usually places stereotypical characters in atypical situations, which provide novelty for audiences. The tragicomedies, he says, are more complex than the tragedies, which lack "grand scale" and have relatively simple plot lines. Among the comedies, Leech thinks most highly of *The Humorous Lieutenant*, a successful mingling of humours comedy, irony, satire, and romance – qualities in Fletcher that often are overlooked. Of the tragicomedies, he notes the variety in *Philaster* and the careful structure of the more serious *A King and No King*, while praising the "sense of the actual" in the generally ignored *A Wife for a Month*. The tragedies, of which *The Maid's Tragedy* is the best known, are lesser than those of many of his contemporaries, because the characters "are not pitted against the universe and its darkness [but] exist only within a web of human intrigue".

PEARSE's study rebuts the view, commonplace since the Restoration, that Fletcher's plays were obscene (Richard Flecknoe), had "more bawdry in one play . . . than in all ours together" (John Dryden), were frequently "founded on rapes . . . incestuous passions [and] mere lunacies" (Samuel Taylor Coleridge), and offended "a refined delicacy" (G.C. Macaulay). Noting that authors of commendatory verses in the 1647 Folio praised the moral didactism of the plays, she considers two brief moralities (*The Triumph of Death* and *The Triumph of Time*, c.1608–13) by Fletcher, which glorify chastity, and says that almost half the plays in the canon have chastity as a major motif, are preoccupied with "marriage and constancy", and have a morality-play structure. She places the plays in their contemporary context by discussing Renaissance social and religious attitudes toward chastity as well as legendary, historical, and fictional examples of virtuous and unchaste women. The major chastity plays, according to Pearse, are *The Loyal Subject*, *The Custom of the Country*, *A Wife for a Month*, and *The Humorous Lieutenant*.

CONE picks up where, she says, others have left off. Acknowledging that critics have discussed satire (and the Jonson influence) in the collaborative plays, she looks at Fletcher's satiric techniques in those solely by him, his use of the play within the play device, the "characters that stand out as striking individuals", and his imagery. Primary among the objects of Fletcher's satire, according to Cone, are the concept of divine right of monarchs, duelling, Puritans, medical practitioners, and political corruption. In all but *The Faithful Shepherdess* Fletcher has interior plays, mostly masques, and *The Wild Goose Chase* alone has four. Although she accepts previous judgments that Fletcher's characters are familiar types, Cone believes that many are nevertheless lifelike and memorable. Her review of the imagery (following Caroline Spurgeon's pattern) concludes that though much of his comic imagery often is original, it usually is "conventional and sometimes monotonous and vague".

FINKELPEARL, proposing to restore some of the esteem Beaumont and Fletcher enjoyed in the seventeenth century, suggests they are not the decadents that many describe, but instead simply dramatized the "moral vacuum" and "hollow center" of their age, with "political criticism of court and king . . . a central urge" in the most significant plays. He thus partially echoes Cone's views. His analyses develop these themes; he shapes his biographical sections to show that, contrary to prevailing opinion, neither was close to the court or monarch; and he says that Jacobean stage censorship was less stringent than is generally thought. In accord with his general thesis, Finkelpearl groups *Philaster*, *The Maid's Tragedy*, and *A King and No King* (which he does not consider tragicomedies) as "a trilogy about the public and private consequences of princely intemperance". A useful assessment of *The Faithful Shepherdess* (the prototypical Fletcher tragicomedy) draws on James J. Yoch's important 1987 essay (in *Renaissance Tragicomedy: Explorations in Genre and Politics*, edited by Nancy Klein Maguire) in linking Clorin with Queen Elizabeth, and Pan with King James I.

GERALD H. STRAUSS

Ford, Ford Madox 1873–1939

English novelist, poet, essayist, and critic

Green, Robert, *Ford Madox Ford: Prose and Politics*, Cambridge and New York: Cambridge University Press, 1981

Hynes, Samuel, *Edwardian Occasions: Essays on English Writing in the Early Twentieth Century*, London: Routledge & Kegan Paul, 1972; New York: Oxford University Press, 1972

Judd, Alan, *Ford Madox Ford*, London: Collins, 1990; Cambridge, Massachusetts: Harvard University Press, 1991; revised edition, London: Flamingo, 1991

Mizener, Arthur, *The Saddest Story, A Biography of Ford Madox Ford*, London: Bodley Head, 1971; Cleveland, Ohio: World, 1971

Saunders, Max, "Ford/Pound", in *Agenda* (Ford Madox Ford double issue), 27(4) and 28(1), 1989–90

Snitow, Ann Barr, *Ford Madox Ford and the Voice of Uncertainty*, Baton Rouge: Louisiana State University Press, 1984

Ford Madox Ford (he changed his name from "Hueffer" in 1919) used many writerly *personae* in his efforts – with his early collaborator, Joseph Conrad – to evolve an "impressionist" form of writing, from which the writer's own self is excluded. The critical reaction to Ford's writing has varied in alternately resisting, and deliberately failing to resist, the temptation to go to Ford's colourful life to "find the originals for characters that are themselves autonomous upon the page" (as Gore Vidal wrote, on Ford, in the *Times Literary Supplement*, 22 June, 1990). There has been some consensus, however, about which of Ford's 32 novels (less than half his total *oeuvre*) deserve extensive treatment: these are *The Fifth Queen* (historical romance trilogy), *The Good Soldier* (novel), and *Parade's End* (novel tetralogy).

In his critical biography, MIZENER has been Ford's most conscientious critic by tracking down letters and documents from Ford's life that may help to illuminate Ford's fiction. He also stresses the view of Ezra Pound, one of Ford's younger protégés, that Ford "fabricated and celebrated his *life* as assiduously as he fabricated . . . his books". Mizener's own assiduity has some important consequences. His overview of a narrative is often to the point: "the essential subject of *Parade's End* is the inner process by which Christopher and Valentine are transformed from Edwardians to modern people, and *Parade's End* is designed to dramatise this process". In its detail, Mizener's argument is heavily absorbed in the ways in which fiction draws upon the "facts" of a life's experience: therefore in *The Good Soldier*, "there is nothing in Edward's nature that Ford did not believe part of his own". The process of tracing "the genesis of Ford's major characters" from his life runs two risks: first, that of seeing Ford as helpless victim of his own imagination; second, that it draws critical attention away from the writing itself.

HYNES's study defends Ford's own right to be unreliable in his use of historical evidence and fact. He stresses that the impressionist aesthetic, for Ford, is based on a radical move toward complete subjectivism: the writer's strength, as well as his weakness, is the degree to which he is true to his *sensations*, the degree to which he renders the *appearance* of reality. This leads Hynes to a reading of *The Good Soldier* as a first-person narrative, which, far from being weakened by the defects of its narrator, John Dowell, "raises uncertainty about the nature of reality to the level of a structural principle". Hynes argues that the fictional creation of a world simpler and less abrasive than our own, in Ford's various Edwardian romances, has become an integral element in the later Fordian hero and heroine. But this romancing habit is seen to collide, in *The Good Soldier* and *Parade's End*, with Ford's other great themes – the need for love, the need for money, and the need to behave well under pressure. These are objective realities, which bring into focus the *expense* of romance, in an England fraught with moral uncertainty, in which nostalgia for notions of honour can be a legitimate refuge.

GREEN borrows Ford's comment that "you cannot write about Euripides and ignore Athens" as an epigraph to his book: his is an historical and political reading which anticipates recent criticism both in its historicism and in its use of Ford's "lesser" works. Thus, *The Inheritors* (an early collaboration with Conrad) prefigures his political concerns in both a realist text like *The Fifth Queen* and the modernist experiments that allied him (in *The Good Soldier*) with Pound and Wyndham Lewis. Paradoxically, this radical side of Ford's aesthetics is inextricably yoked to his fear about the innovations of social reformers like the Fabians and early socialists. The latter are satirised, in *The Inheritors*, in a fantasy *roman-à-clef*. Green persuasively interprets these texts in relation to Edwardian politics and Ford's nostalgia for a kind of aristocratic feudalism.

SNITOW's approach to Ford's often contradictory politics (which she envisages as the dream of a sort of socialist feudalism) is via close analysis of the competing "voices" made available to him in Edwardian writing. Ford emerges as a kind of brilliant but inconsistent ventriloquist, taking his inspiration from the detailed and scrupulous irony of Henry James, the utopian comedy of G.K. Chesterton and H.G. Wells, and even the authoritarian satire of Wyndham Lewis. Although Snitow acknowledges that Ford paid a price for his pluralism as a "quintessentially Edwardian" writer of wandering tone, his finest work – both as an extraordinarily sensitive editor of *The English Review* (1908–10) and as writer of *The Good Soldier* – achieved a rare synthesis of these competing voices. Ford's John Dowell is, in her reading, the most sophisticated deployment of a voice composed from fluctuating, comic and ironic, tones: a fitting reverberation to come from the "Janus head, always inventive, always atavistic" of Ford himself.

JUDD's critical and biographical study traces Ford's avowed search for a "speaking voice" in both his poetry and fiction; he echoes Snitow (and indeed Ezra Pound) in arguing for the importance of Ford's "quiet, informal, conventional" modes and styles. His rediscovery of texts such as *The Spirit of the People* (from Ford's early trilogy on the English) partly confirms the view of Ford as impressionist: he looks in Ford's fiction "not [for] the known facts but the suggested life". Judd does not avoid the debate about Ford's personality intruding into his art (given that "opinions do not make art"), acknowledging that the artist's known views and beliefs "might be *why* he created and shaped something as he did". The entry of aspects of Ford's personality directly into John Dowell or *Parade's End*'s Christopher Tietjens is thoughtfully construed as neither artlessness nor naive didacticism. Rather, in acknowledging that Ford's "art is not, after all, simply a matter of impressions, but a recognition of the real", Judd works judiciously towards finding an appropriate synthesis of writing and biography.

SAUNDERS's collection of essays offers a stimulating variety of recent views on Ford, with Saunders's own essay on Pound and Ford demonstrating that it has often been writers rather than academic critics who have showed most enthusiasm for Ford's work. The collection's deft balancing of the impressionistic and the realistic in Ford's writing itself points to Ford's achievement in *Parade's End*, his novel sequence of World War I. The neglect of the latter "passes [to borrow the sentiments of W.H. Auden from 1961] my comprehension": to that situation, these essays offer a timely redress.

COLIN J. EDWARDS

Ford, John 1586–c.1640

English dramatist

Anderson, Donald K., Jr., *John Ford*, New York: Twayne, 1972

Anderson, Donald K., Jr. (ed.), *Concord in Discord: The Plays of John Ford, 1586–1986*, New York: AMS Press, 1986

Clark, Ira, *Professional Playwrights: Massinger, Ford, Shirley and Brome*, Lexington: University Press of Kentucky, 1992

Hopkins, Lisa, *John Ford's Political Theatre*, Manchester: Manchester University Press, 1994

Huebert, Ronald, *John Ford: Baroque English Dramatist*, Montreal: McGill-Queen's University Press, 1977

Neill, Michael (ed.), *John Ford: Critical Revisions*, Cambridge and New York: Cambridge University Press, 1988

Stavig, Mark, *John Ford and the Traditional Moral Order*, Madison: University of Wisconsin Press, 1968

The sole author of only seven extant plays, John Ford has generated a minor critical industry out of all proportion to the quantity of his dramatic writing, though that industry has yet to produce a comprehensive, annotated modern edition of his works. There are however several excellent texts of *'Tis Pity She's a Whore*, *The Broken Heart*, and *Perkin Warbeck*. Criticism has focused on these three plays, widely reckoned to be Ford's most sustained pieces of theatrical invention. Of the three, only *'Tis Pity* has been performed frequently enough for the claims of the study to be tested on the stage.

'Tis Pity's incestuous subject matter, together with the controlled hysteria of its violent final scenes, have proved irresistible for our own theatres of cruelty. Yet that same attraction gave rise to the suggestion that Ford's was a theatre of decadence, and that he prompted the Renaissance theatre's decline into decadence in the decade before the closing of the London playhouses in 1642. Modern criticism has sought to rescue Ford from these charges not by denying the extremity of that violence, but rather by establishing a wide range of theatrical purposes which seem to justify that violence.

STAVIG presents Ford as an ethical ironist. He establishes through close readings of the early writings that Ford "was a traditional and quite orthodox Christian who was deeply influenced by classical ethics. [He] believed that man, through reason, resolution, and perseverance, could steer between the extremes of passion and achieve the golden mean of a well-ordered life". Thus the baleful fate of Giovanni and Annabella in *'Tis Pity* arises out of "their abandonment of reason and virtue"; their spiritual decline accompanies "their continuing revolt against the moral order". We are encouraged to sympathise with the plight of Ford's characters to learn from their failings to act differently. Stavig provides a useful intellectual context for reading Ford, and shows how seriously Ford can be read; but he tends to underestimate the corrosive power of Ford's tragedies.

ANDERSON (1972) sees Ford as "more interested in theatrical effect than in characterization", and pays considerable attention to the "effective use of spectacle; gesture, posture, and grouping assume unusual significance, especially in the portrayal of love and death". He shows how theatrical power complicates Stavig's simplistic moral schemas: spectacle encourages an empathy that the thoughtful moralist would condemn. The resulting paradoxes mark all of Ford's plays, most notably *'Tis Pity*, which Anderson endorses as Ford's greatest achievement. Despite this preference he does comment in some detail on all of Ford's plays, briefly reviews Ford's life and times, and summarises the history of the criticism. In short, Anderson's is the ideal primer with which to begin reading Ford.

HUEBERT's study is much more ambitious. He proclaims Ford as an artist of the Baroque period, and attempts extended comparisons between effects in Ford's plays and the great monuments of European Baroque art, such as Bernini's yearning statue *The Ecstasy of St Teresa*. As in this statue so also in Ford's dramas, Huebert claims, "the erotic world and the religious world mingle, intertwine and become almost indistinguishable from one another . . . the baroque artist and the baroque dramatist transform illusions into visionary truth . . . a glimpse of the higher world beyond reason". Thus Ford fully empathises with the plights of Giovanni and Calantha:

he celebrates their flights beyond societal norms. Huebert's analogies are useful rather than persuasive; he presents an engaging context rather than demonstrating the final key to Ford's mysteries. The book's impact is hampered, though, by cheap black-and-white reproductions of the artworks referred to.

Two recent collections, both spurred by the quadricentenary of Ford's birth, attest to the growing interest in Ford's drama. ANDERSON's begins with four essays on general aspects of Ford's art; these are followed by essays on each of his seven plays. The general essays are the most useful, especially Thelma N. Greenfield's account of the "confrontation between private values and the impossibility of translating those values intact into action". This gives rise to the oxymoronic yet poignant "revulsion – compassion" which, it is currently assumed, is the appropriate reaction to Ford's more sensational scenes. Thus, Eugene Waith notes in his contribution, Ford's masque-like effects tend towards the exaltation, not the degradation, of love. NEILL's collection attempts equitable coverage also; like Anderson he offers readers at least one essay on each of Ford's plays, though the accounts of the "minor" plays are insufficient to shift attention away from *'Tis Pity*, *The Broken Heart,* and *Perkin Warbeck*. As with Anderson's collection, the general essays are the most useful. Neill provides an economical history of Ford criticism as a context for his revisionists. Roger Warren's evocation of recent Ford performances and Colin Gibson's close readings of Ford's "poetry of death" are the most helpful of the subsequent essays. The two contributions on *'Tis Pity* – Neill's own deciphering of Annabella's steaming heart on Giovanni's dagger and Verna Foster's description of the play as a hybrid "city tragedy" – are the most stimulating accounts of individual plays. Altogether Neill's seems the better of these two collections.

CLARK builds on the contextual studies Neill and Anderson provide. He constructs a detailed picture of Ford's place in the professional playwriting milieu of Caroline London. He refutes earlier moral and psychological depictions of Ford's characters, and claims instead that their importance is sociological. Ironically, that sociology involves Ford's characters responding to crisis by insisting on their personal integrity, won by living out specific social roles with a massive consistency that would elude weaker individuals. The result is what Clark calls "Ford's Tragedy of Ritual Suffering". He offers a worked example of his theory in a reading of *The Broken Heart* that highlights the play's exploitation of ritual forms and incantatory verse to create a kind of mesmeric empathy in the audience.

HOPKINS notes also the ritual quality of both Ford's emblematic staging and his limpid verse, and she attends in impressive detail to the patronage context within which Ford's plays were first printed and dedicated. In this she is allied with the detailed attention to historical, political, and aesthetic contexts that is a marked feature of Anderson and Neill's respective collections and Clark's monograph. That triple focus seems likely to remain orthodoxy in Ford scholarship for some time. Hopkins adds to this picture by depicting Ford as part of "a coterie with . . . markedly Catholic leanings", which he honours in his dedications and whose interests, more importantly, he attends to in his plays. Hopkins thus reads Ford as politically conservative, longing for a specifically Catholic polity, marked by ritual observance and aristocratic government. These values she traces throughout Ford's plays. At times Hopkins sounds like a conspiracy theorist let loose in a well-stocked library; yet her attention to Ford's verbal texture is exemplary. She may not be right, but her work is a sign of the seriousness with which Ford has been studied in the last generation.

MARK HOULAHAN

Forster, E.M. 1879–1970

English novelist, short-story writer, and critic

Colmer, John, *E.M. Forster: The Personal Voice*, London and Boston: Routledge & Kegan Paul, 1975

Das, G.K., and John Beer (eds.), *E.M. Forster: A Human Exploration: Centenary Essays*, London: Macmillan, 1979

Furbank, P.N., *E.M. Forster: A Life*, 2 vols., London, Secker & Warburg, 1977–78; New York: Harcourt Brace Jovanovich, 1978; one-volume edition, Oxford: Oxford University Press, 1979

Gardner, Philip (ed.), *E.M. Forster: The Critical Heritage*, London and Boston: Routledge & Kegan Paul, 1973

Gillie, Christopher, *A Preface to E.M. Forster*, London: Longman, 1983

Page, Norman, *E.M. Forster*, London, Macmillan, 1987; New York: St Martin's Press, 1988

Stape, J.H.(ed.), *E.M. Forster: Interviews and Recollections*, London: Macmillan, 1993; New York: St Martin's Press, 1993

Trilling, Lionel, *E.M. Forster: A Study*, Norfolk, Connecticut: New Directions, 1943; London: Hogarth Press, 1944, revised 1967

Wilde, Alan (ed.), *Critical Essays on E.M. Forster*, Boston: G.K. Hall, 1985

Lionel TRILLING's study, published during Forster's lifetime, made a major contribution to the establishment of Forster's status as a novelist, especially in America, and is still worth reading for its insights on Forster's moral vision and the relationship between ideas and technique in his novels. Trilling's Forster is a representative of the "liberal imagination" who both attacks the conventions of contemporary society and affirms a highly individual moral and ethical creed. His masterpiece is *Howards End* (not a widely fashionable view either at the time or among later critics), and *The Longest Journey*, despite technical shortcomings, is also a key text for anyone wishing to understand his moral stance. These are, significantly, the novels in which Forster offers most directly and explicitly a critique of the "condition of England". At the same time Trilling gives full weight to the importance of comedy in Forster's fiction. Two introductory chapters are followed by separate considerations of the five novels published in Forster's lifetime (*Maurice* had not, of course, appeared at this time), with additional chapters on the short stories and the literary criticism.

GARDNER's anthology of reviews contains nearly 200 items published between 1905 and 1971, and illustrates the reception of Forster's individual volumes from *Where Angels Fear to Tread* to *Maurice*. A long and very informative introductory essay traces the growth of Forster's critical reputation. Gardner notes "the gradual and steady rise in Forster's reputation from 1905 to 1924", and the "almost complete unanimity" with which *A Passage to India* was hailed as his finest novel when it appeared in the latter year. Gardner also points out how quickly Forster's highly individual voice and vision were recognized by early reviewers, and how often they applied to his work the words "original" and "originality". Apart from the reviews, which constitute the bulk of this volume, there are a number of interesting items revealing private responses and drawn from such sources as D.H. Lawrence's letters and Katherine Mansfield's journal.

COLMER's book is one of the earliest studies to take into account the posthumously published fiction and to draw on the fuller knowledge of his life and friendships that became available after Forster's death. It is also comprehensive in giving an account of the full range of Forster's writings, including the considerable amount of non-fictional prose from the years following his abandonment of the novel, and it makes effective and discriminating use of the large archive of Forster manuscripts and other unpublished materials. A chapter on Forster's life and times is followed by consideration of the short stories, the Italian novels, and the other novels published during his lifetime, with further chapters on "India and Alexandria", the posthumous fiction, and on Forster as literary critic, biographer, essayist, lecturer, and broadcaster. Colmer's aim is to provide a reassessment of Forster's achievement in the climate of greater frankness and explicitness that became possible after his death. Taking as his starting-point Forster's own remark that he belonged to "the fag-end of Victorian liberalism", Colmer also places Forster in the social and cultural context of his age and class.

FURBANK's long biography, though written only a few years after Forster's death, has still not been superseded and is essential background reading both for the factual information it contains (concerning, for instance, the friendships that were so important to him and the circumstances in which his books were written) and for its insights into Forster's mind and personality. The first volume covers the years to 1914, much less than half of Forster's life, but the period during which most of his creative work was produced. It gives a full account of Forster's family background, early life, and education, bringing out the importance of his time at Cambridge. The second volume provides particularly full coverage of the complex background to the composition of *A Passage to India*. Throughout, much use is made of unpublished material, including Forster's letters and diaries.

The collection of 24 essays specially written for the volume edited by DAS and BEER range from personal reminiscences to comparative studies of Forster and other writers. Of the individual novels, *A Passage to India* receives by far the largest share of attention, with four essays, by V.A. Shahane, John Colmer, Benita Parry and Michael Orange; of the other novels only *The Longest Journey* receives separate attention (from S.P. Rosenbaum), though there is also an essay by Judith Scherer Herz on the early short fiction. Comparative studies connect Forster with D.H. Lawrence (C.E. Baron), T.S. Eliot (G.K. Das), Virginia Woolf (H.K. Trivedi), and Anton Chekhov (James McConkey) and there is also an interesting contribution by P.N. Furbank on "Forster and 'Bloomsbury'".

The short but useful volume by GILLIE belongs to a series designed to provide the student with a concise account of a writer's life and work as well as essential background materials. Its division into short, clearly labelled sections makes it easy to use as a work of reference, but it is also lively and accessible enough to be read straight through. A biographical section deals with Forster's ancestry (with particular attention to his family connections with the Clapham Sect), childhood, education, and later life, and is followed by a summary of the intellectual and literary context of his work, including his relationship to both the liberal tradition of J.S. Mill, Matthew Arnold, and Edward Carpenter, and the practice of earlier novelists such as Jane Austen, Samuel Butler, and George Meredith. Further sections deal with the novels, and there is also a bibliography, a gazetteer, and a useful "Who's Who" of Forster's circle.

The collection of essays by WILDE conveniently assembles a range of previously published material. Furbank's fine essay "The Personality of E.M. Forster" is followed by earlier accounts by Virginia Woolf, Lionel Trilling, and others, but the bulk of the volume is devoted to sections on "Morality and Sexuality" and on the major novels. Somewhat eccentrically, perhaps, the latter section is restricted to discussions of only two texts (admittedly, the two most widely studied at present), *A Passage to India* being represented by four items and *Howards End* by two.

Like some others published since Forster's death, my volume (PAGE) in the "Modern Novelists" series seeks to give an account of his achievement as a writer of fiction in the context of what has become known concerning his personal life, in particular his homosexuality and the almost mystical significance he attached to the idea of friendship. In addition to a chapter outlining his life and literary career, there are separate discussions of the five major novels and a separate chapter devoted to *Maurice* and the short stories. A feature of the book is the comparison between earlier assessments of individual works and their reassessment in the light of later knowledge of Forster and later developments in critical approaches to fiction.

STAPE's volume provides a valuable supplement, or complement, to the published biographies of Forster by Furbank and others by bringing together 46 accounts of Forster (some previously unpublished) but those who knew or encountered him at various periods of his life. Unlike the biographies, these are first-hand accounts, sometimes coloured by the prejudices or previous convictions of the eye-witness and ear-witness, but often vivid and insightful. Those represented include not only some of Forster's friends but also by fellow-writers such as Virginia Woolf, Christopher Isherwood, Stephen Spender, and Siegfried Sassoon. As these examples indicate, not all the contributors are of Forster's own generation. As Stape points out, the coverage of Forster's life cannot be even, for there are few accounts of his early years or of his greatest creative period, from 1901 to 1914.

Inevitably, given the material available, the emphasis falls on the later years of great and international fame. However, the interest of the subject matter and the high calibre of most of the witnesses makes reading this volume a rewarding experience for anyone seeking further insight into Forster's mind and personality. There are useful biographical and explanatory notes on the extracts, and a chronology of Forster's life for easy reference.

NORMAN PAGE

Fowles, John 1926–

English novelist

Fawkner, Harald William, *The Timescapes of John Fowles*, Rutherford, New Jersey: Fairleigh Dickinson University Press, 1983
Huffaker, Robert, *John Fowles*, Boston: Twayne, 1980
Loveday, Simon, *The Romances of John Fowles*, London: Macmillan, 1985; New York: St Martin's Press, 1985
Olshen, Barry N., *John Fowles*, New York: Frederick Ungar, 1978
Onega, Susana, *Form and Meaning in the Novels of John Fowles*, Ann Arbor: UMI Research Press, 1989
Runyon, Randolph, *Fowles/Irving/Barthes: Canonical Variations on an Apocryphal Theme*, Columbus: Ohio State University Press, 1981
Woodcock, Bruce, *Male Mythologies: John Fowles and Masculinity*, Brighton, Sussex: Harvester Press, 1984; Totowa, New Jersey: Barnes & Noble, 1984

Criticism on John Fowles has developed along fairly standard lines: early accounts of his work, enthusiastic but somewhat critically naive, have gradually given way to analytic and theoretically informed readings.

OLSHEN's brief study looks at Fowles's works up to, and including, *Daniel Martin*, and starts from Fowles's own declared ambition "to write one book in every imaginable genre". The Introduction offers a thumbnail sketch of Fowles's career, biography, and personality, while each of the main chapters is essentially a straightforward introduction to the work it discusses, outlining plot, theme, and character in fairly summary form. This is a sometimes gushing survey, which nonetheless draws usefully on a range of interviews and personal writings, and provides a number of pertinent starting points for readers relatively unacquainted with Fowles's work.

HUFFAKER similarly devotes a chapter to each of (in this order) *Daniel Martin*, *The Magus*, *The Collector*, *The French Lieutenant's Woman*, and *The Ebony Tower*, and covers the same biographical terrain with an equally favourable disposition towards his subject. (It is no coincidence that Olshen and Huffaker both depend for some of their information on personal interviews with Fowles himself.) Each of the chapters is divided into rather short and sometimes arbitrarily organised sub-sections (for example, on *The French Lieutenant's Woman*: "The Novel's Genesis"; "The Plot"; "The Novel's Historic Quality"; "The Intrusive Author"; "The Novelist as Character"; "The Endings: Victorian and Modern"; "Biological and Social Evolution"). Huffaker sees Fowles as a "naturalist" whose reputation "will outlast the century". Like Olshen, he regularly tends to allow enthusiasm to supplant analysis.

RUNYON's enterprise is a much more adventurous and complex one. "Fowles, Irving and Barthes," he claims, "both illuminate and are illuminated by Tobit, as well as by each other. And it is not clear that what they wrote was influenced by that text from the Old Testament Apocrypha in the traditional sense. . . . It is their repetition of the story in Tobit that brings them together". Tobias reappears, for Runyon, in the characters of Charles Smithson and Daniel Martin. His opening chapter, "Fowles's Enigma Variations", makes much of Sarah Woodruff's celebrated Toby jug ("Could the Toby jug be an image of Charles – his stand-in, his *lieutenant*?") as a point of entry to "certain hidden themes" in *The French Lieutenant's Woman*, then explores *The Ebony Tower* stories in the light of these, and finally passes to a consideration of "the Apocryphal journey" in *Daniel Martin*.

Fowles himself contributes a substantial foreword to FAWKNER's book and confesses "though I am fortunate in the amount of study that has been devoted to my work, this is one of the few times it has been approached in a way that particularly interests me personally". Fawkner himself remarks that he has "deliberately avoided reading critical works on Fowles. . . . The present project is therefore disidentified from a handful of journalistic introductions to the Fowlesian landscape". Celebrating Fowles's "estrangement from modes of literary enquiry based on patriarchal models", Fawkner himself writes a curious and highly original "scientised" account of Fowles's work using "temporality" as his fundamental organising concept. The result is one of the most challenging and difficult critical books to be found in the field of contemporary literature.

By contrast with the studies already discussed, WOODCOCK's originates in a British academic milieu. Its refreshing self-consciousness about politics and questions of social power distinguishes it from its predecessors. Woodcock is interested in the "social construction of masculinity" and feels that "by looking at Fowles's writing about men, not only is an analysis of contemporary masculinity possible, but the very problems of undertaking such an analysis are laid bare". He goes on to discuss *The Collector*, *The Magus*, *The French Lieutenant's Woman*, *Daniel Martin*, and *Mantissa* with analytic trenchancy and considerable theoretical acumen. For instance, he brings recent theories of pornography to bear illuminatingly on *Mantissa*, and shows how the male fantasy of *The Collector* is essentially ambiguous, as one's reaction to it depends on whether one takes up a "male" or "female" reading position. On balance, this is probably the best single book yet to have emerged within Fowles criticism.

LOVEDAY finds Fowles's fiction up to *Daniel Martin* "built around four major themes: the Few and the Many; the domaine; the contrast between the masculine and the feminine mentality; and the difficult necessity of freedom". Although these ideas are constant, they "are by no means free from incoherence and contradiction in the form in which they are applied in the fiction". Loveday goes on to invoke Northrop Frye on the tendency for tragedy and comedy to "project" themselves into philosophy and, adapting this to the category of "romance", concludes that Fowles's "philosophy is the expression of his fiction, rather than (as he has always maintained) the other way round". This standing of Fowles on his head may appear questionable, but Loveday reaches his conclusion after a number of sensitive and insightful discussions of Fowles's *oeuvre*: the chapter on "the range of repetitions, patternings and connections between events" in *The French Lieutenant's Woman* is an impressive case in point.

ONEGA's book is the only one discussed here that includes a reading of *A Maggot*, which she sees as "another variation of *The Magus*, still another version of the hero's quest". Onega herself could also be said to return to the method of earlier studies, allowing Fowles to preside somewhat over the interpretation of his work. The volume concludes with the transcript of a public interview between Onega and Fowles, which is engagingly unrehearsed but rather weakened by the affability required as Fowles's due for agreeing to participate. Onega's express desire is to show how Fowles continually resolves the tension between realism and experimentalism by "one major metafictional device: parody or literary inversion". Nonetheless she holds that between *The Magus* and *A Maggot* is "a world of difference, the huge stretch that goes from his hesitant and unsatisfying first attempt to express his vision of the world, to the last, masterfully neat and accomplished expression of it".

MACDONALD DALY

Frame, Janet 1924–

New Zealand novelist, short-story writer, and poet

Alley, Elizabeth (ed.), *The Inward Sun: Celebrating the Life and Work of Janet Frame*, Wellington: Daphne Brasell Associates Press, 1994
Dalziel, Margaret, *Janet Frame*, Wellington: Oxford University Press, 1980
Delbaere, Jeanne (ed.), *Bird, Hawk, Bogie: Essays on Janet Frame*, Aarhus, Denmark: Dangaroo Press, 1978; revised as *Ring of Fire: Essays on Janet Frame*, Sydney: Dangaroo Press, 1992
Evans, Patrick, *An Inward Sun*, Wellington: Price Milburn, 1971
Evans, Patrick, *Janet Frame*, Boston: Twayne, 1977
Janet Frame issue of *Journal of New Zealand Literature*, 11, 1993
Mercer, Gina, *Janet Frame: Subversive Fictions*, Dunedin: University of Otago Press, 1994; St Lucia: University of Queensland Press, 1994
Panny, Judith Dell, *I Have What I Gave: The Fiction of Janet Frame*, Wellington: Daphne Brasell Associates Press, 1992
Williams, Mark, "Janet Frame's Suburban Gothic", in his *Leaving the Highway: Six Contemporary New Zealand Novelists*, Auckland: Auckland University Press, 1990

Discussions of Janet Frame's work fall into two groups, those written in the 1970s at the end of her most prolific period of writing fiction, and those written in the1990s after the publication and filming of the autobiographies.

EVANS's 1971 booklet was the earliest comprehensive study of the novels. Written for use in high schools, it consists of brief analyses of the first six novels (1957–67), each followed by questions for discussion and understanding, supplemented by two general chapters on imagery and narrative viewpoint. It is superseded by EVANS's much fuller 1977 book, in the Twayne "World Authors" series. The book follows the usual pattern of the series – a brief interpretive biography in the first two chapters, followed by analyses of individual novels and the collections of stories and the volume of poems taken in chronological order, with an evaluative epilogue. A feature of the book is Evans's consistent relating of Frame to her New Zealand social and literary environment. The approach is that of New-Critical close reading supplemented by historical understanding. Evans calls his book a "rope bridge" to serve until more permanent structures are built, but it remains the best introduction to Frame in general and to all of the works up to 1977, although of necessity it does not deal with the late novels and the autobiographies.

DALZIEL's shorter booklet, in the Oxford "New Zealand Writers and Their Work" series, is arranged differently and takes a somewhat different approach. The first chapter is a chronological run-through of the novels and stories, focusing on character and action, and tends to be too compressed; the valuable second chapter ranges through all the works to discuss Frame's special use of language; and the somewhat moralistic third chapter deals with the "progression of thought" through the novels. The booklet as a whole is a sound, commonsensical introduction to Frame's work, less full in its analyses than Evans's book, but covering one more novel (*Living in the Maniototo*) and dealing more explicitly with language and style.

The studies of Frame appearing in the 1990s tend to be less general and introductory, more specialised in their approach, often from psychoanalytic and/or poststructural perspectives. WILLIAMS's chapter focuses primarily on the late novels, and thus complements the discussions of Evans and Dalziel. At the same time Williams relates these novels to the earlier work and shows the development of Frame's vision within the context of the New Zealand fictional tradition of social criticism. A special feature of his discussion is his emphasis on "the sense of words and things steeped in the Christadelphian faith that Frame learned from her mother", which he sees as "the inspiration of her resistance as a writer to the values of her society".

PANNY's study is more substantial in coverage but narrower in critical approach. She discusses all of the novels and the novella *Snowman, Snowman*, but does not discuss the other short fiction and the poetry, and while she draws upon the autobiographies (as does Williams), she does not discuss them as texts in themselves. In her approach she focuses on what she calls "the allegorical component of Frame's work", although the term is somewhat misleading because her understanding of "allegory" is loose, and includes sustained allusion and structural metaphor and archetype as well as formal allegory. The approach is not equally successful with all of the novels, but it does yield many specific insights, especially concerning Frame's numerous implicit allusions to other literary works and her characteristic use of verbal puzzles. The book is more useful for such details than it is for a general approach to Frame.

MERCER's book deals with the early stories, all 11 novels, and the autobiographies, but omits the later short fiction and the poems. The approach is intentionally "partial . . . written from a particular, and subjective, point of view – that of a feminist with an Anglo-Australian background". The feminism involves a sophisticated use of the insights of the French feminists Hélène Cixous and Luce Irigaray concerning the "other" and the "feminine", but there is no single, linear argument; rather, the book "explores different texts from slightly different angles". The result is a dense but readable and illuminating book, which brings out some important aspects of Frame's work while necessarily ignoring others, especially its New Zealand context – for the Frame of this book is an international feminist, not a New Zealand writer. There is a very full and useful bibliography and an appendix on the typescripts of the novels.

The 1990s have seen several collections of essays about Frame. The one edited by ALLEY is a "celebration" – a tribute to Frame on her 70th birthday from her friends and readers. The contributors were asked to "leave aside critical analysis in favour of personal response", and their efforts include poems and fiction as well as accounts of experiences with Frame and/or her writings. In contrast, the Janet Frame issue of the *Journal of New Zealand Literature*, the proceedings of a conference held in 1992, is analytic and academic, and includes essays by Evans, Panny, and Mercer, among others. Several deal with general questions, others discuss the autobiographies; but the majority deal with individual novels, both early and late. Using a range of approaches, including post-structural and psychoanalytic ones, they vary in quality, but together form a useful collection of insights. This is not an introductory volume but is well worth consulting.

DELBAERE's 1992 collection incorporates her 1978 one, and thus contains essays written both before and after the appearance of the autobiographies. Contributed by critics from around the world, the essays include several general accounts as well as discussions of all of the individual novels (sometimes several discussions) and the autobiographies. There is one essay on a short story, but otherwise the short fiction is excluded, and there is nothing on the poetry. The essays vary greatly in quality, but the best are very good indeed. The comprehensiveness of the coverage and the indispensable annotated Bibliography by Alexander Hart and W.H. New, the most complete available, make this an essential volume for the study of Frame, although it should be supplemented by Evans in relation to the short fiction and poetry.

LAWRENCE JONES

Franklin, Benjamin 1706–1790

American prose writer and autobiographer

Aldridge, Alfred Owen, *Benjamin Franklin and Nature's God*, Durham, North Carolina: Duke University Press, 1967

Breitwieser, Mitchell Robert, *Cotton Mather and Benjamin Franklin: The Price of Representative Personality*, Cambridge and New York: Cambridge University Press, 1984

Buxbaum, Melvin H. (ed.), *Critical Essays on Benjamin Franklin*, Boston: G.K. Hall, 1987

Granger, Bruce Ingham, *Benjamin Franklin: An American Man of Letters*, Ithaca, New York: Cornell University Press, 1964

Lemay, J.A. Leo, *The Canon of Benjamin Franklin, 1722–1776: New Attributions and Considerations*, Philadelphia: University of Pennsylvania Press, 1986

Seavey, Ormond, *Becoming Benjamin Franklin: The Autobiography and the Life*, University Park: Pennsylvania State University Press, 1988

Van Doren, Carl, *Benjamin Franklin*, New York: Viking Press, 1938; London: Putnam, 1939; reprinted, Westport, Connecticut: Greenwood Press, 1973

Wright, Esmond, *Benjamin Franklin: His Life As He Wrote It*, Cambridge, Massachusetts: Belknap Press of Harvard University Press, 1990

Benjamin Franklin's position in popular culture continues to be maintained almost entirely by the *Autobiography*, which is, despite the popularity of self-exposure in this century, still one of the most prominent examples of that genre. Periodical writings, however, constitute the bulk of the Franklin canon, and a tendency among his critics to respond to his rhetoric in the act of criticism attests to his power in that art. Recognition of this tendency constitutes the bulk of the criticism in recent decades.

The *Autobiography* has been variously interpreted as a work of art, an adventure story, or a variation on the *Pilgrim's Progress* theme. Written late in life, it embodies all the important Franklin rhetorical positions: "profound skepticism concerning reason, his implied positions on eighteenth-century theological and psychological debates on voluntarism, and his pessimism concerning the vanity and selfishness of mankind" (Lemay). American readers do not need the guidance of the historian or literary critic to read Franklin, so accurately did he represent the type they are taught as children to recognize, however far from this type American culture may have evolved. Not surprisingly, Franklin criticism has historically centered on Franklin's text-oriented personality, and found its forum in biography. As a part of American popular culture, Franklin's own, carefully-crafted self-image of the balding bespectacled sage – parodied by D.H. Lawrence as "the snuff-coloured Doctor Franklin" – persists despite efforts by most twentieth-century biographers to dispel it.

In recent decades, interest in Franklin as representative of the eighteenth-century American political consciousness has generated some interest in rhetorical analysis of his work, dividing the critical canon into readings of the public over the private Franklin, rhetorical analysis sharply delineating itself from psycho-social biographical criticism. Franklin lived a highly public self-examined life, well into old age, so his biographies are substantial, on balance less thematically speculative than those of other colonials. The factual liberties taken by notorious hagiographers such as Weems, however, introduced to make Franklin's deism more palatable to nineteenth-century readers, inhibited the Franklin narrative for more than a century, and inhibited serious criticism until 1938, when VAN DOREN published the first complete scholarly biography.

Despite the numerous biographies published since Van Doren, Franklin scholars continue to speculate about the "real"

Franklin. The long introduction in BUXBAUM reviews the important biographies, mostly unfavorably, as a call for renewed interest in objective historical scrutiny of Franklin's role in early American political history. This concern about the quality of Franklin biography is of interest because of the inseparability of life-writing from literary criticism in Franklin's case. Buxbaum begins with D.H. Lawrence, whose essay-attack launched an era of Franklin-bashing dependent on reading Franklin as lesser philosophy to the exclusion of more broadly cultural considerations of his texts. Lawrence paints Franklin in shades of utilitarian grey, places him in opposition to the survival of the European, particularly English, cultural heritage, which he saw as a separate issue from the political differences Franklin, and cultureless Americans in general, privilege.

WRIGHT has mixed life-writing with criticism by compiling excerpts from all of Franklin's papers into a chronological "autobiography", which he calls a "psychohistory". Most, but not all of this work is taken from the *Autobiography*, mixing personal letters with the more polished original. Read in conjunction with the original, it yields a clearer appreciation of the art within Franklin's self-creation.

BREITWIESER's comparative study of Cotton Mather and Franklin departs from the model of the life to analyze the lives of the two men as literary/political self-creations, fabricated on their own highly idealized models. He explains that both Mather and Franklin saw themselves as exemplary, that differences between them are more attributable to their times than to the immediately apparent contrasts in personality, and that Franklin is a logical intellectual descendent of Mather. Like SEAVEY, and much of the biographical criticism of Franklin, Breitwieser examines Franklin's sensitivity to public image, but he expands on the narrowly personal to include an extensive psychosocial discussion of the influence that contemporary ideas and the Puritan past played in forming Franklin's character.

ALDRIDGE examines Franklin's moral development in a more conventional historical frame than other works devoted exclusively to the deism question. He holds the arguable view that Franklin was nominally an Anglican in his mature years. Aldridge, a distinguished Franklin scholar and biographer, attributes Franklin's life-long interest in organized religion in general to his admiration for order in social relations rather than to the influence of deism.

LEMAY, in sharp contrast to Aldridge's practical, psychological interpretation of Franklin's rhetoric, takes the position that Franklin deliberately embraces then discards philosophies, because of his characteristic literary multi-personality and delight in satire for its own sake. Lemay tends towards textual criticism as he re-examines contested Franklin essays, arguing against the genuineness of some pieces that have been included in the past, asserting the legitimacy of others. This work is particularly useful in recreating the context for political arguments which have long since lost their relevance, because his discussions depend upon both an extensive knowledge of historical context and long experience with the subtleties of Franklin's style.

Purely literary criticism of Franklin is rare, specialized, and strangely out of place among overwhelmingly social criticism. GRANGER divides Franklin's *oeuvre* into genres. Beginning with the generally held view of Franklin as an accomplished rhetorician, Granger applies his analysis not only to the *Autobiography*, but to his journalism, short works, and correspondence.

CLARA ELIZABETH SPEER

Frontier and Western Literature

Allmendinger, Blake, *The Cowboy: Representations of Labor in an American Work Culture*, New York and Oxford: Oxford University Press, 1992

Armitage, Susan, and Elizabeth Jameson (eds.), *The Women's West*, Norman: University of Oklahoma Press, 1987

Bredahl, A. Carl, Jr., *New Ground: Western American Narrative and the Literary Canon*, Chapel Hill: University of North Carolina Press, 1989

Fender, Stephen, *Plotting the Golden West: American Literature and the Rhetoric of the California Trail*, Cambridge and New York: Cambridge University Press, 1981

Folsom, James K. (ed.), *The Western: A Collection of Critical Essays*, Englewood Cliffs, New Jersey: Prentice-Hall, 1979

Fussell, Edwin S., *Frontier: American Literature and the American West*, Princeton, New Jersey: Princeton University Press, 1965

Haslam, Gerald H. (ed.), *Western Writing*, Albuquerque: University of New Mexico Press, 1974

Hazard, Lucy Lockwood, *The Frontier in American Literature*, New York: Thomas Y. Crowell, 1927; reprinted, New York: Barnes & Noble, 1941

Hitt, Jim, *The American West: From Fiction (1823–1976) into Film (1909–1986)*, Jefferson, North Carolina: McFarland, 1990

Pilkington, William T. (ed.), *Critical Essays on the Western American Novel*, Boston: G.K. Hall, 1980

Taylor, J. Golden, *et al.*, *A Literary History of the American West*, Fort Worth: Texas Christian University Press, 1987

Tompkins, Jane, *West of Everything: The Inner Life of Westerns*, New York and Oxford: Oxford University Press, 1992

Tuska, Jon, and Vicki Piekarski (eds.), *Encyclopaedia of Frontier and Western Fiction*, London and New York. McGraw-Hill, 1983

Wild, Peter (ed.), *The Desert Reader*, Salt Lake City: University of Utah Press, 1991

Frontier Literature, the West, and Regional Voices

TAYLOR'S 1,353 page encyclopedic sourcebook of western American literature is the most comprehensive compendium of "frontier" literary perspectives available to date (it is also in the process of being revised and updated at this writing). The essays are written by leading contemporary scholars, including Max Westbrook, James H. Maguire, Gerald Haslam, George F. Day, Helen Stauffer, Thomas J. Lyon, William T. Pilkington, and many others. Headings include "Part One: Encountering the West" – essays exploring the oral traditions of Native Americans, adventure narratives, the beginnings of genres in the West, and so on – and "Part Two: Settled In: Many Wests" – essays divided by literary regions and ethnicity: "The Far West", "The Southwest", "The Midwest", "The Rocky Mountains", "Ethnic Expression", and "Present Trends". This text effectively documents the development and shifting focus of American letters, as their authors emigrated from "Sea to Shining Sea". Celebration of the diversity of literature dominated by an initial "frontier" ethic which, since World War II, has begun to settle into its own is an underlying principle of this book. Also, Gerald Haslam, introducing the "Present Trends" section, notes how the Vietnam War was "central to re-visioning our national experience", leading to a "hard-edged maturity in western American letters".

HAZARD's book was originally published in 1927 during which time American literature in general was being evaluated in terms of the westward movement. American literary originality was viewed as paralleling historian Frederick Jackson Turner's infamous theory "that life in America has been conditioned by the perennial rebirth of the frontier". Hazard discusses how the body of American literature, from Benjamin Franklin, Ralph Waldo Emerson, and Henry David Thoreau to Frank Norris, Sinclair Lewis, and Sherwood Anderson either directly, or indirectly, incorporates and responds to this "frontier ethic". Characters are either triumphing in a land of "unlimited" fresh resources, or are victimized by an erroneous romanticized belief in paradise. Hazard concludes by claiming that mid-century Americans were reining in their attitudes of conquest of the continent in favor of the development of the inner person, or "spiritual pioneering".

A thin volume, which has become in a mere 20 years a "classic" text on western American literature, is HASLAM'S anthology, in which eminent western authors Wallace Stegner, George R. Stewart, J. Frank Dobie, Vardis Fisher, A.B. Guthrie, Jr., Bernard DeVoto, and David Lavender have their say about the character of frontier literature and how it is perceived in the literary world at large. Despite Hazard's apparent assumption 50 years before that there exists a serious "frontier literature", Haslam still feels it is necessary to respond to the western writer's inferiority complex by pointing out, somewhat comically, in his Introduction: "with *The Oxbow Incident* (1940), of course, Walter Van Tilburg Clark had laid forever to rest the serious doubts that great literature could come out of the West. This novel was so strong that many critics asserted that, although set in the West, it was not western literature". Haslam's authors disrupt the public's assumptions of the romantic "mythical" West in favor of a real place. The essays in this volume seriously attack "formula westerns" and what their proliferation has done to the critical acceptance of genuine and "serious" western American literature, a literature "with a complexity of vision alien to popular notions fostered by formula westerns".

PILKINGTON's anthology contains both general criticism on the western novel and critical essays on individual novelists. Top critics of western literature are represented here – John R. Milton, Max Westbrook, Richard Etulain, Don D. Walker, Delbert Wylder, Pilkington himself, and others. It is interesting to note that both Haslam's and Pilkington's volumes are collections of men writing about men – with the exception of Pilkington's essay on Jean Stafford's *The Mountain Lion* – attesting to the dominant patriarchal nature of frontier topics. The boundaries of this collection exclude short-story writers, such as Katherine Anne Porter, as well as early "eastern" American frontier-novelists, like James Fenimore Cooper, geographical setting being more important to this editor than chronology. Pilkington, like Haslam, also feels it is necessary to "apologize" for western American literature's place on the literary map by commenting, after Richard Etulain, that "'first-rate scholars' are now turning their attention to the literary West and producing provocative books and essays about the subject. Western literary studies are no longer in their adolescent stage".

Several of these essays address post-World-War-II writers Ed Abbey, Larry McMurtry, and William Eastlake, as well as ethnic American voices Rudolfo A. Anaya and N. Scott Momaday. These essays do not merely "celebrate" western/frontier literature, but approach it with honest eyes, so that, for example, Kerry Ahearn cuts critically into Larry McMurtry: "pleasing the audience has engendered a disappointing carelessness in his work, so much so that I wonder what community of writers he works in, and whether there is anyone to read and seriously criticize him as he writes".

"Nature writing" makes up a considerable force in frontier letters, and WILD's collection of classic selections accompanied by his critical remarks is an excellent introduction to this genre. The *Reader* includes essays by John Wesley Powell, Horace Greeley, John C. Van Dyke, Mary Austin, Aldo Leopold, Edward Abbey and others. Wild argues for the environmental benefits of this kind of writing, claiming, in his analysis of J. Frank Dobie, that "without the awareness drummed up by activists, regional writers among them, we would have no Yosemite, or any other park for that matter".

BREDAHL re-examines the American literary canon and, while acknowledging that new strides have been made by adding women and minority writers to the canon, laments that western American literature has yet to be given its critical due. In his essay on contemporary Montana author Ivan Doig, he contends that it is "especially appropriate to the imagination's effort to understand surface" when contemplating such western/frontier literary cornerstones as "place" and "space". Taking "space" as the central fact for the American imagination, he quotes poet Charles Olson in *Call Me Ishmael*. "'I take SPACE to be the central fact to man born in America . . . I spell it large because it comes large here. Large, and without mercy'".

PENELOPE REEDY

Frontier Literature, the Western Genre, and the Pioneer Experience

Early critical approaches to the "western" centred on the work of literary authors, but recently interest has grown in the analysis of the actual frontier dwellers, their lives and writings.

FUSSELL, who prefaces his work by acknowledging his debt to Henry Nash Smith's *Virgin Land: The American West as Symbol and Myth*, 1950, attempts to map out the western experience by considering the output of major writers (James Fenimore Cooper, Nathaniel Hawthorne, Edgar Allan Poe, Henry David Thoreau, Herman Melville, and Walt Whitman). Stating that the west and the frontier were not definable geographical areas, he forcibly excludes large sections of the western genre by fixing 1860 as the date when the frontier disappeared as either a vague locality or as a spur to the literary imagination. Working through the authors, Fussell considers the frontier to be a region in which conflicts between east and west, civilisation and wilderness, the past of European tradition and the bright future of American optimism and individuality were enacted.

TOMPKINS continues this approach of decoding the west through western fiction and films. She categorises the western genre as "a narrative of male violence", which marginalises women and Native Americans. Men, aiming to break free from the feminisation of nineteenth-century Eastern society, subdue the land, women, Indians, and enemies alike, using power and silence. She traces the female/male opposition through the writings of Owen Wister, Zane Grey, and Louis L'Amour, and highlights the manner in which the western not only became the vehicle by which American males could reclaim their identity, but also symbolised the turn-of-the-century shift from a dominant to a dominated female.

FOLSOM's collection includes both historical and literary accounts of the west, and questions the reliability of both. While identifying the west more as a symbolic place, "a landscape of the mind", a region open to interpretation by cultures other than those raised in it, the essayists discuss the significance and impact of western fiction-writers. Of particular note is Richard Etulain's analysis of the growth of western American literary scholarship, linking it to a new historiography capable of interpreting actual historical events as well as our means of understanding them. Etulain's study, which contains an excellent bibliography, provides greater depth than Fussell and, indeed, questions the conclusions of these earlier critics.

The exploitation of the west as either a proving-ground for eastern males, a necessary "rite of passage", or as a land promising wealth and freedom resulting from the seemingly endless opportunities stemming from the mid-century Gold Rush, is uncovered by FENDER in his examinations of pioneer diaries and journals. Female/male oppositions recur continually, with the women's writings concentrating on the difficulties of existence and the smaller details of family life in the wilderness, while the men, employing scientific language, attempt to authenticate and claim the undiscovered territories. Such evidence is later contrasted with the work of Twain, Cooper, and Hawthorne, among others, to show how writers used the stories emanating from the west to provide literature for the east.

ARMITAGE and JAMESON's collection of 21 essays redresses the gender balance by giving voice to the female within the western genre. Establishing that "women have been virtually absent from traditional western history", the contributors use previously overlooked female source material to stress how the traditional male view of western history is one of an adventure based on male individualism and violence. Kathryn Adam's examination of the literature of Laura Ingalls Wilder is particularly instructive in the reconstituting of the female identity, revealing Wilder's acceptance of, and adherence to, fundamentally white male social values. Melody Graulich similarly uses women's writings to reveal the dependent and subordinated position of the female in western society, and to expose the way in which patriarchal authority realised its ultimate potential in the violent abuse and domination of the female.

TUSKA and PIEKARSKI's reference work provides a comprehensive and wide-ranging index to the work of western fiction writers within chapters covering "Historical Personalities", "House Names", "Native Americans", "Pulp and Slick Western Stories", and "Women on the Frontier". The editors preface the author entries (which attempt to place each writer within the tradition) by stating that western literature is an altogether different genre than western film. The version of the west represented here is one centred on the lives of real people: "the story of the American West, truly, has nothing to do with heroes and romance; it is rather a question of human endurance in the face of tragedy and defeat".

ALLMENDINGER's study, detailing the oral and written traditions of cowboys since the mid-nineteenth century, is an excellent renegotiation of the western as a genre. Rejecting the previous critical works of Fussell and Tompkins because of their use of non-cowboy texts, which figure cowboys as metaphors rather than as actual historical people, he reproduces the songs and myths that cowboy groups created and circulated. With the encroachments of eastern civilisation, the invention of barbed-wire fencing, and the inevitable assimilation within non-cowboy society, individual cowboys chose to write down the previously invisible cowboy discourse. By providing a literate society with cowboy stories, these writers were both presenting the cowboy as metaphor and unconsciously reflecting "the fragmentation of a frontier culture", which turned to consider non-cowboy themes within its poetry and fictions.

HITT's work, which discusses the adaptation of western fiction into film, provides a concise – and therefore restricted – account of how western fiction written between 1823 and 1976 became films between 1909 and 1986. Devoting chapters to the themes of the early explorers, original western myths, conflicts between settlers and native tribes, the growth of the cowboy-gunslinger role, and the formula and revisionist westerns of the more recent past, Hitt provides brief summaries of both the written text and its subsequent film(s), and discusses the excisions or additions involved in the transfer. His study is completed by an invaluable appendix detailing both the western-authors' work and the various film productions of it, complete with publication and production dates, and details of film directors and producing companies.

PHILIP MCGOWAN

Frost, Robert 1874–1963

American poet

Bloom, Harold (ed.), *Robert Frost*, New York: Chelsea House, 1986
Brower, Reuben, *The Poetry of Robert Frost: Constellations of Intention*, New York: Oxford University Press, 1963

Cox, James (ed.), *Robert Frost: A Collection of Critical Essays*, Englewood Cliffs, New Jersey: Prentice-Hall, 1962
Kearns, Katherine, *Robert Frost and a Poetics of Appetite*, Cambridge and New York: Cambridge University Press, 1994
Lentricchia, Frank, *Robert Frost: Modern Poetics and the Landscapes of Self*, Durham, North Carolina: Duke University Press, 1975
Lynen, John, *The Pastoral Art of Robert Frost*, New Haven, Connecticut: Yale University Press, 1960
Marcus, Mordecai, *The Poems of Robert Frost: An Explication*, Boston: G.K. Hall, 1991
Oster, Judith, *Toward Robert Frost: The Reader and the Poet*, Athens: University of Georgia Press, 1991
Poirier, Richard, *Robert Frost: The Work of Knowing*, New York and Oxford: Oxford University Press, 1977
Rotella, Guy, *Reading and Writing Nature: The Poetry of Robert Frost, Wallace Stevens, Marianne Moore and Elizabeth Bishop*, Boston: Northeastern University Press, 1991

Robert Frost's poetic and public personae, rebarbative and performative, have frequently generated controversy. Characteristic is the hostility sustained over three volumes by his official biographer, Lawrance Thompson, which in turn provoked defensive reactions in the *Centennial Essays* edited by Jac Tharpe from 1974 to 1978. A more temperate biography is by William Pritchard, *Frost: A Literary Life Reconsidered*, 1984. Frost has always somehow had to be taken whole, unmanageable, dangerous, and unpredictable. In the 1960s and 1970s, his irony, scepticism, and their bearing on his modernity were live issues, and the best critics were stung by their urgency. Recent criticism, of the 1990s, is more theory-laden and less passionate.

LYNEN, in this seminal study, identifies Frost's pastoralism as an assertion of the value of individual perception against the fragmentation of a technology-driven world: the mythicizing of New England, the mastery of the colloquial register, the indirection and analogical mode of thought signify Frost as a modern rather than a regionalist. In this emphasis Lynen provides a directive for subsequent criticism.

COX has edited a remarkable collection of critical essays produced at the time when the poet's participation in the Kennedy Inaugural had made him a national institution. Cox's intelligent Introduction rescues him from the roles of cracker-barrel versifier or "smiling public man" and re-engages with the many-sidedness of the Frost myth. Other contributions include an extract from Lawrance Thompson's 1942 book, *Fire and Ice*, and also from Lynen (discussed above), but the great essays of this collection are those of Yvor Winters and Randall Jarrell: their combative voices have the passion of a no-holds-barred debate. Winters' magisterially dismissive subtitle, "The Spiritual Drifter as Poet", signals an ideological attack on Frost's appeal to readers' sentiment and nostalgia, a rejection of his language – "poetry is not conversation, and I see no reason why poetry should be called upon to imitate conversation" – and a contempt for the philosophy of a poet who "wilfully refrained from careful thinking". Such candour, even if wrongheaded, is refreshing. Jarrell's essay is a piece of fullblooded, headlong, extravagant admiration, citing "Design" and "Directive" as key poems. How much these titans cared about it all.

BROWER's attentive readings of the metrical subtleties of individual poems have never been surpassed; his book is a learning experience in this respect. It is complemented by a scholarly grasp of Frost's range and assurance within the poetic tradition. The range encompasses classicising in the Horatian and Virgilian vein, the composition of "eighteenth century essay-poems", an appraisal of, and independent ability to diverge from, William Wordsworth, an affinity with the sceptical side of Ralph Waldo Emerson, and a modern stance – with W.B. Yeats, Ezra Pound, and T.S. Eliot – as one of the renewers of the speaking voice. The comparison with Wordsworth is the most sustained and searching: Brower concludes that Frost differs from Wordsworth in that "he stands alone with the ironic attitude his only resource. With this reduction he is most surely of our time".

LENTRICCHIA rejects the view of Frost as an American farmer-poet lacking a coherent poetics, and positions him as a writer of philosophical seriousness in the context of international modernism: the central drama of his work is the encounter between the fiction-making imagination and the anti-fiction of the environment. Lentricchia recognises Frost's affinities with the pragmatism of William James and with Wallace Stevens, affinities which are American, yet not parochial. This is a thought-provoking study working in broad strokes, concerned with the poetry seen as a whole, as a series of "landscapes of the self", symbolic configurations of brook, house, and woods, which express a poetics. Lentricchia ranks Frost with Stevens as a luminary in the modernist firmament.

POIRIER, the critic most aware of the creative tensions in Frost, links him with Emerson, Henry David Thoreau, and William James in the "effort to hold the miraculous within the quotidian". He argues that Frost's ultimate subject is the interpretive process itself and shows how the insistently ordinary elements in his work *seem* to work against this, yet generate a productive paradox. Poirier also tackles the issue of Frost's reputation and public *persona*, the question of the "massively settled official portrait", which is more easily accommodated to the poet's formalism than to his sense of form as provocation. This is a wide-ranging study, claiming Frost as a great poet of sexuality and marriage, discussing his manipulation of chronology, and considering the political and American dimension of his writing as well as its relation to modernism; it also offers brilliant readings of individual poems, both famous and lesser-known, responsive to their distinctive modulations of voice. This remains the best book on Frost, and reveals him as a major poet.

BLOOM, linking Frost with the darker side of Emerson, introduces eight essays, which include extracts from Poirier and Lentricchia. In general, the tenor of the contributions is intertextual: Sidney Lea argues that Frost "de-mistified" (sic) Wordsworth; David Bromwich links Wordsworth, Frost, and Wallace Stevens in an analysis of "Two Tramps in Mud Time" and "The Old Cumberland Beggar"; Charles Berger invokes Frost as a mythologist of origins. These sophisticated critics, adroit in placing Frost's "house in earnest" in circulation with Stevens's "dwelling in the evening air", are less combative than their predecessors, yet concur in focusing on "Directive" as the central poem.

ROTELLA's book is not exclusively on Frost but is important in the connections it makes between Frost and his peers, and in the move in emphasis away from an exclusively modernist interpretation. The useful introductory chapter sets out the American tradition of writing about nature from its Puritan origins. The subsequent chapters situate the four poets considered – Stevens, Marianne Moore, Elizabeth Bishop, and Frost – in relation to that tradition. Rotella questions the too easy categorising of Frost as modernist or postmodernist, reminding us that the poet "still feels the tug towards moral interpretation exerted by a long New England habit in poems describing nature".

MARCUS, as his title suggests, provides an unpretentious handbook for undergraduates, with commentary on all 355 poems in Edward Connery Lathem's now standard edition, *The Poetry of Robert Frost*. Students will value the clarity and helpfulness of this book as a starting point, and the detailed bibliography provides further direction.

OSTER's reader-response study argues that Frost's readings of nature and relationships are an education in how to read. Her expression is at times too fulsome and histrionic: she is of the "reading as perilous adventure" variety of reader-response critic, envisaging herself as a Dante to Frost's Virgil leading her through "hell as part of my trial and education"; but there are also detailed readings of individual poems in which Oster suggests that their resistance to closure anticipates postmodernism.

KEARNS draws on feminism and deconstruction to propose that Frost's poetry enacts a contest between the feminine metamorphosing power of metaphor and the masculine "heautocratic" (Michel Foucault's term) control of form. The ambiguities and instabilities that ensue force a deconstructive reading of the poems. This is a very dense, at times laboured and congested, study, not for the beginning student; the method of circulating brief quotations from a large number of poems in a variegated theoretical orbit is directed to the knowing reader. There is little sense of the exhilaration of reading individual poems, and the sexuality of the poetry becomes rather dulled when it is so endlessly recycled and explicated; but the focus on the tension between the feminine and masculine aspects of Frost's sensibility is timely.

PAT RIGHELATO

Fugard, Athol 1932–

South African dramatist

Gray, Stephen (ed.), *Athol Fugard*, Johannesburg and New York: McGraw-Hill, 1982
Gray, Stephen (ed.), *File on Fugard*, London: Methuen, 1991
Seidenspinner, Margarete, *Exploring the Labyrinth: Athol Fugard's Approach to South African Drama*, Essen, Germany: Die Blaue Eule, 1986
Vandenbroucke, Russell, *Truths the Hand Can Touch: The Theatre of Athol Fugard*, New York: Theatre Communications Group, 1985; Craighall, South Africa: Ad Donker, 1986
Walder, Dennis, *Athol Fugard*, London: Macmillan, 1984

Although Athol Fugard is one of the most renowned of contemporary dramatists, there are relatively few studies covering the entire spectrum of his work. Critics tend to focus on individual plays, and when attempts are made at a more comprehensive analysis there is a strong tendency for the emphasis to become biographical or political, without a corresponding interest in the dramaturgical, aesthetic, or literary aspects of his work. This is partly because for many years Fugard seemed like a lone voice in South African theatre, closely identified with the struggle against apartheid. His influences derive from the work of Jean-Paul Sartre, Albert Camus, Samuel Beckett, Eugene O'Neill, and William Faulkner; he is not part of a rich South African literary or theatrical tradition, and critics have been slow to contextualise his work.

Two of the most informative books on Fugard are, in fact, no more than collections of reviews, interviews, and essays, both edited by Stephen Gray. The earlier of the two publications (GRAY, 1982) is the more substantial. Gray provides a chronology of Fugard's life, an introduction to his work, a section entitled "Literary Background", which contains material relating to the writing of the plays, including programme and introductory notes written by Fugard, and interviews with the playwright. The second section includes a series of reviews covering his productions from *The Blood Knot* to *Tsotsi*. A further series of interviews is followed by a section entitled "Symposium", a collection of ten critical essays. By far the most interesting of these essays is Don Maclennan's "The Palimpsest: Some Observations on Fugard's Plays", originally published in *The Bloody Horse* in 1981. Wide-ranging in reference, penetrating in critical insight, idiomatic in style, the article explores the existentialist aspects of Fugard's art. In contrast, a number of the other essays in the volume are more pedestrian, and a tradition seems to have developed in Fugard criticism of illustrating literary discourse through diagrams, which allegedly depict various conflicts in the plays or points more than adequately made in the essays. More illustrations from the productions would have been preferable.

GRAY's second volume (1991) is an accessible introduction to the playwright, valuable for its collation of reviews and background material. From the point of view of the reception of Fugard's work, this is a useful source of information.

With Fugard's work so heavily rooted in his South African experiences, it is remarkable to find that the first book-length studies of the playwright should have been written by WALDER and VANDENBROUCKE, both working from outside South Africa. But then South African critics at that time, slow to give Fugard the recognition he deserved, were less than fully engaged in the task of analysing his work. Vandenbroucke admits in his Introduction to not having visited South Africa before writing the book. This lack of actual experience of the country is reflected in a certain naivety regarding the political situation and a rather esoteric manner, suggested in the very title of the book. But Vandenbroucke is familiar with the plays in performance and the context of their international reception. Both Walder's and Vandenbroucke's books can be recommended as introductions to Fugard's drama, intended for the reader unfamiliar with the plays, although neither can be regarded as a penetrating critical study. Both books are in need of revising to reflect the developments in Fugard's writing during the last ten years.

For a scholarly, incisive, critical study of Fugard, the book by SEIDENSPINNER is the most recommendable. It is in effect a doctoral thesis, published apparently without any rearrangement of the original typescript. The book certainly needs editing and re-presenting in a more accessible style. That being said, Seidenspinner's approach is comprehensive, with individual chapters on the historical and cultural context of South African drama, Fugard's South African heritage, identity, and career, and Fugard's development as a writer. The most interesting chapter is entitled "From Universalism to Solitude: The Consolidation of Fugard's Regional identity", which includes discussion of the "Wasteland Setting" and the "Veld metaphor", while moving into the realm of psychoanalytic criticism. Until perhaps Maclennan is encouraged to write a book on Fugard, Seidenspinner's thesis remains the standard critical work.

BRIAN PEARCE

Fugitives and Agrarians

Burt, John, *Robert Penn Warren and American Idealism*, New Haven, Connecticut, and London: Yale University Press, 1988

Carrithers, Gale H., Jr., *Mumford, Tate, Eiseley: Watchers in the Night*, Baton Rouge: Louisiana State University Press, 1991

Conkin, Paul K., *The Southern Agrarians*, Knoxville:University of Tennessee Press, 1988

Doreski, William, *The Years of Our Friendship: Robert Lowell and Allen Tate*, Jackson: University Press of Mississippi, 1990

Gray, Richard, *American Poetry of the Twentieth Century*, London: Longman, 1990

Myers, Jack, and David Wojahn (eds.), *A Profile of Twentieth Century American Poetry*, Carbondale: Southern Illinois University Press, 1991

Parini, Jay, and Brett C. Millier (eds.), *The Columbia History of American Poetry*, New York: Columbia University Press, 1993

Sullivan, Walter, *Allen Tate: A Recollection*, Baton Rouge: Louisiana State University Press, 1988

Young, Thomas Daniel, and Elizabeth Sarcone (eds.), *The Lytle-Tate Letters: The Correspondence of Andrew Lytle and Allen Tate*, Jackson: University Press of Mississippi, 1987

"The Agrarians" is the name of a group of regional writers of the Southern United States in the 1920s and 1930s. Antagonistic to the homogenising pressures of economic uniformity imposed on the South by the industrialised capitalism of the Northern states, they celebrated the virtues of provincialism and the cultivation of modes of life historically grounded in the South. The dominant members of the group were Donald Davidson, Andrew Lytle, John Crowe Ransom, Allen Tate, and Robert Penn Warren. Born and bred in the South, most of them were originally teachers at Vanderbilt University in Nashville, Tennessee, where they published their little magazine, *The Fugitive* from 1922 to 1925 (hence their earlier appellation, "The Fugitives"), and three important symposia, *I'll Take My Stand* (1930), *Culture in the South* (1934), and *Who Owns America?* (1936). In these three collections they argued for a "natural" economic system, developing out of the ways in which people adapt to the geography of a region, and cultivating an organic relationship between people and place that is also moral and aesthetic. If their advocacy of the South and its agriculturally based economy now looks like a nostalgic agenda for economic, moral, and aesthetic renewal of the lives of the citizens it addressed, the Agrarian movement was significant in its time for its polemical value, and in due course Ransom, Tate, and Warren became important in the wider frame of mid-twentieth-century American culture for their work in poetry, fiction, and criticism.

Of the books discussed below, Conkin, Gray, Myers and Wojahn, and Parini contain general discussions of the Fugitive and Agrarian phenomenon, with an emphasis on its three leading figures – Ransom, Tate, and Warren.

CONKIN is the ablest recent historian of Agrarianism, and this short book is the best general history of the movement, informed, dependable, and full of detail about the individuals at the centre of the movement. Conkin gives an impressively balanced treatment of its cultural politics, and is particularly informative on the differences between the primarily aesthetic concerns of those who contributed to *The Fugitive*, which was essentially a magazine of new poetry, and the overt regionalist and political concerns of the Agrarians. Conkin argues for a comparison between the Agrarians and the nineteenth-century New England Transcendentalists, and sees both groups as loose circles of like-minded intellectuals "with vague outer boundaries and frequent shifts in membership". The value of this comparison, flattering as it is to the Agrarians, serves to emphasise their roles as latter-day advocates of a life centred in a set of moral pieties quite alien to the mercantilist spirit of mid-twentieth-century America, though the impact of the 1929 Wall Street Crash and the Great Depression on buoyant American capitalist ideals at this time must also play its part in an account of Agrarian ideology. Conkin surveys the individual histories of the leading members of the Agrarians through to the survival of their ideals in the work of Andrew Lytle, and in the epilogue to his book demonstrates the insuperable difficulty of the Agrarian scheme – how to transpose its vision of a more humane social order into a living reality.

GRAY's survey includes sections on the Fugitives and on "Traditionalism and the South", covering Ransom, Tate, and Warren. Gray, one of the ablest commentators on Southern culture and writing, sets up his account of the Fugitives by comparing them with their contemporaries, the Anglo-American, London-based group the Imagists, and this proves a useful way of defining the nature of Fugitive poetry. Noting the Fugitives' commitment to traditional forms, metre, and diction, their belief in regionalism, and their passionate attachment to the South, Gray sees the opposition between the Imagists' experimentalism and the Fugitives' conservatism as embodying the two modes that most later American poetry in this century would choose to follow. In his subsequent attention to those Fugitive poets who acquired national reputations through their later work, Gray's brief commentary on Ransom, Tate, and Warren provides succinct analyses of their development as poets and of their strengths and limitations.

MYERS and WOJAHN's anthology of criticism includes Edward Hirsch's coverage of the Fugitives and of Ransom, Tate, and Warren as the most accomplished poets of the group, in an account of the regional "modernism" of American poetry in the 1920s. Hirsch's summary account follows the customary identification of these writers with classicism, traditionalism, and regionalism, and he writes instructively on Ransom's "furious war against abstractionism" and his desire to unite reason and sensibility. Although he has space for no more than a few paragraphs on these writers, they are worth reading for their introductory value.

In PARINI's history, Patricia Wallace has a chapter on "Warren, with Ransom and Tate", an ordering that indicates her present-day sense of their posthumous reputations. Though she acknowledges that Ransom is a more "polished" poet than Warren, and that Tate "labored harder to write a perfect (and perfectly difficult) poem" – the "Ode to the Confederate Dead" – she also argues that Ransom and Tate "hold something back in their poetry", and thus lack what has been described elsewhere as Warren's particular quality, his poetry of "tragic joy". This is an excellent contribution to the *Columbia History* – lively, informative, judicious, and convincing about all three poets.

The concentration on Warren is extended in BURT's monograph study, which goes beyond the parameters of Warren's Agrarian interests and deals with his political and historical writings, three of his major novels, his elegies, and the narrative poems. This is an attempt to search out what Burt calls the "promise of meaning" he finds in all these areas of Warren's work, an investigation of Warren's restless creative search for absolutes, which he rejected the moment he settled on them. Burt shows a writer drawn in contrary directions, impelled by a late Romantic self-authenticating view of experience, who persistently undercuts his own certitudes by a withdrawal into a modernist irony. This is a thorough reading of Warren, intelligent and persuasive. (For other studies of Warren see the separate entry on this writer.)

The remaining books to be discussed all concentrate on the figure of Tate. CARRITHERS writes in praise of Tate along with the cultural critic Lewis Mumford, and the anthropologist and historian of science Loren Eiseley as latter-day prophets of American society and civilisation. He sees them as possessed by "a sort of Old Testament calling to unmask false gods and denounce earthly practice and doctrine, in the name of the true God of life", and traces each writer's development chronologically through their "prophetic" essays. This gives us a very conventional reading of Tate's intellectual progress through his association with the *The Fugitive* and the three Agrarian symposia, and his long career as a teacher, poet, and critic. Carrithers suggests that despite Tate's celebration of the economic and social virtues of traditional Southern life, it is proper to see him as "from" the South but not "of" it, a point of view designed to accommodate the increasing cosmopolitanism of Tate's role as a literary critic from the late 1930s onward, and his temperamental discomfort in relation to the demands of a practical agrarianism, underscored by his decision to use the cultivation of language as the form of labour most congenial to him.

SULLIVAN's memoir of Tate is honorific and affectionate, full of respect for Tate's intellectual and human generosity. He provides an insider's account of the life and times of this eminent man of Southern letters, yet at the same time portrays something of the unpalatable aspects of Tate's personality and conduct, specifically in the context of his treatment of women. Sullivan proposes that Tate suffered a kind of melancholy in relation to the contingencies of domestic and social life, and that to relieve his boredom he lived a life of sexual profligacy which caused great emotional hurt to the women who loved him. However, this revealing study is marked by Sullivan's devotion to Tate, and the account of Tate's working life and intellectual conflicts is engrossing.

Finally, Doreski's volume together with Young and Sarcone's edition provide very useful material for understanding Tate in his poetic and critical contexts. DORESKI's study of the relationship between Tate and Robert Lowell is valuable for its use of previously unpublished documents from the Tate archive at Princeton University and the Lowell archives at Harvard and Texas universities, especially in relation to the correspondence between them and the terms of their friendship in the years after the appearance of Lowell's *Life Studies* (1959). Tate, Lowell's mentor through the early years of his career, had been distressed by the degree of self-exposure of Lowell's psychoses in *Life Studies*, resulting in a temporary fracture in their friendship. Doreski documents the recovery of the friendship following Tate's welcoming response to Lowell's *For the Union Dead* (1964), though he makes rather less of the issue of influence and competition between them, given that one of Tate's most admired poems is his "Ode to the Confederate Dead". Despite this, Doreski's book is full of interest and has a wealth of material on both poets. YOUNG and SARCONE's edition of the correspondence between Tate and Lytle is an important contribution to the cultural history of the 1930s, when Tate and Lytle became friends. Lytle, a novelist, historian and essayist, followed Tate as editor of the *Sewanee Review*, and the two became close friends through their binding commitment to the Agrarian cause and their mutual concern with the fate of poetry and fiction in the modern world. This correspondence reveals their criticism of each other's work unconstrained by their friendship and mutual admiration, and gives ample evidence of their responses to the work of other writers submitted to the *Sewanee Review* and the other journals and books they were associated with. As these letters demonstrate, Tate was a brilliant correspondent, and widely respected for his epistolary skills.

LIONEL KELLY

Fuller, Margaret 1810–1850

American essayist, critic, translator, and poet

Allen, Margaret V., *The Achievement of Margaret Fuller*, University Park: Pennsylvania State University Press, 1979
Chevigny, Bell G. (ed), *The Woman and the Myth: Margaret Fuller's Life and Writings*, Old Westbury, New York: Feminist Press, 1976
Dickenson, Donna, *Margaret Fuller: Writing a Woman's Life*, London: Macmillan, 1993
Douglas, Ann, *The Feminization of American Culture*, New York: Knopf, 1977
Myerson, Joel (ed.), *Critical Essays on Margaret Fuller*, Boston: G.K. Hall, 1980
Urbanski, Marie M.O., *Margaret Fuller's "Woman in the Nineteenth Century": A Literary Study of Form and Content, of Sources and Influence*, Westport, Connecticut: Greenwood Press, 1980

Margaret Fuller's life and writings have always seemed inseparable from each other: her "galvanic" presence tested the narrow limits of Boston Transcendentalism; her journalism for the *New York Tribune* pioneered feminist social reform issues, and, as the first woman foreign-correspondent for the newspaper, she supported the revolutionary cause in Italy. Her struggle for self-definition had its rough passages, but Ralph Waldo Emerson and others, in editing her papers after her death (published as *Memoirs*, 1852), devalued the writing and distorted the life. The subsequent "Margaret-myth" damaged her reputation until Thomas Wentworth Higginson's admirable biography, *Margaret Fuller Ossoli* (1884) began to turn the tide. He claimed that she was "the best literary critic America has yet seen".

The twentieth century produced further biographies, but was slow to take up Higginson's revaluation. However since the 1970s there has been a steady Fuller industry disseminating the primary texts for critical assessment: selections of her work with a critical introduction have been edited by Bell Gale Chevigny (1976) and Jeffrey Steele (1992). *Woman in the Nineteenth Century*, now regarded as a seminal work of American feminism, came out in a new edition in 1994. The publication from 1983 to 1993 of Fuller's letters in a scholarly edition by Robert N. Hudspeth has further enhanced her literary reputation. The full range of her writing takes its place now in American letters.

CHEVIGNY's selected edition of Fuller's writings deserves inclusion here because of the fullness of its Introduction and commentary. All the selections – letters, essays, or criticism – are given dates and prefaced by explanatory material. The central issues and stages of Fuller's development are set out in five sections, with admirable clarity. Editorial problems are touched upon, and there are some textual cuts, for example in *Woman in the Nineteenth Century*, but these are identified. This is an excellent book which combines the function of a critical introduction and a basic textual resource.

DOUGLAS devotes a chapter to Fuller in this groundbreaking feminist study, but the book is valuable throughout in that the overall subject, the cultural construction of femininity in mid-century America, sheds light on her predicament: "in a culture which was beginning to identify femininity with male relaxation, Fuller found few takers". Douglas has a bracing, non-sentimental approach to Fuller's search for identity, and notes with approval that she refused to write for magazines typical of feminine sub-culture, such as *Godey's*. The argument of the chapter is that Fuller disavowed fiction for history, and that she was the only one of the Transcendentalists who had any talent for it; her final feat was to "translate Italy for Americans from the realm of 'literature' back into the realm of 'history', an active, participatory sense of history". This is an essential book for understanding the culture of which Fuller was inescapably a part, but inevitably contested as a writer.

ALLEN is the first critic in a book-length study to focus primarily on Fuller's intellectual achievements, examining her role as a commentator on, and her influence upon, American culture and claiming that she was the equal of Emerson and Henry David Thoreau, but that the conditions of her life were more difficult. The argument of this study is that Fuller's response to the worldly, tolerant humanism of Goethe fermented in a valuable creative tension with the Puritan-Transcendentalist aspect of her thinking. Allen's view is that Fuller "never found the best vehicle for her expression" but that she shared with Goethe a belief in evolution in spirit and writing, a desire, in Goethe's words, to "utter what lives and is active ... *no matter what form it takes*". This optative momentum anticipates many of the struggles of twentieth-century expression, and thus Fuller is now recognised as an "exile ... coming home". A balanced and astute appreciation of Fuller as a writer and thinker, more broadly based than feminist perspectives, this remains a valuable book.

MYERSON, as might be expected from a scholar who has compiled bibliographies of Fuller, provides a helpful and detailed introduction to this indispensable collection of critical essays, which range from contemporary reviews of the 1840s to those of the 1970s. Some of the contemporary reviewers, such as Orestes A. Brownson finding "Miss Fuller ... wholly deficient in a pure, correct taste, and especially in that tidiness we always look for in a woman", merely make it evident what an uphill task she had, but Edgar Allan Poe's essay is a genuine critical assessment of her style and, unusually, praises it as registering the cadences and transitions of the speaking voice. The controversy that Fuller's personality generated is evident in the responses to the posthumous publication of the *Memoirs*: Harriet Martineau attacks the "pedantry" of her American life; Nathaniel Hawthorne's spiteful comments confided to his journal, then published by his son, are refuted by her nephew, Frederick T. Fuller, who comments appositely that Mr Julian Hawthorne is "not one to spoil a sensation to save a friend". By 1903, Henry James's reference to "the unquestionably haunting Margaret-ghost" shows that the virulence has abated, but the negative repercussions of a damaging preoccupation with personality remain in his dismissive reference to "her written utterance being nought". The twentieth-century contributions in this collection, worthy and at times stolid, take her more seriously as a critic, interpreter of German literature, and essayist. The most notable is by Francis E. Kearns, contextualizing the uneasy relationship of Fuller's feminist commitment to the rather tardy sympathy she showed for the Abolition movement.

URBANSKI, confining her study (apart from a brief biographical Introduction) to the essay *Woman in the Nineteenth Century*, presents it as an example of Transcendental idealism, and argues that in this respect, and in its psychological complexity, the essay differs from other feminist writing of the period. Fuller's mode of address, the "sermon-oration form", and her soaring, circular, non-syllogistic style unfolding from the subconscious in spiralling thought patterns are also analyzed as representatively Transcendentalist. This book has a limited thesis, and so does not address the issue of stylistic development; but it is informative on the Transcendentalist and feminist movements, and their interactions in the period. Between the first version, entitled "The Great Lawsuit" and published in *The Dial*, and the final version of *Woman in the Nineteenth Century*, Fuller added the controversial feminist contemporary references. Urbanski's dispassionate account of this text and its sources is an antidote to the more heated debates on Fuller's status.

DICKENSON has written the most accessible book on Fuller and claims it is the first to be based completely on the authenticated edition of the letters by Hudspeth. The argument of this feminist study is that the New England phase was a "moratorium", a dormant phase in which her family responsibilities and the "frugal capacity for sympathy" of her Transcendentalist male peers held back her development. Only thereafter, in the New York and Italian periods, was her writing to come alive. Dickenson cites the "True Woman paradigm" as the cultural formation from which Fuller tried to escape in her efforts to construct a "Romantic feminism" of psychological and sexual insights based on "affirmative difference" of gender and on political activism. Although over-defensive of her at times, this book would make a good introduction to Fuller: the theory is not stifling, but informs a reading aware of the moving passages in a life and writing never in equilibrium, but always ardent.

PAT RIGHELATO

G

Gaddis, William 1922 –

American novelist

Green, Jack, *Fire The Bastards!*, Normal, Illinois: Dalkey Archive Press, 1992

Johnston, John, *Carnival of Repetition: Gaddis's "The Recognitions" and Postmodern Theory*, Philadelphia: University of Pennsylvania Press, 1990

Karl, Frederick R., *American Fictions: 1940–1980: A Comprehensive History and Critical Evaluation*, New York: Harper & Row, 1983

Kuehl, John, and Steven Moore (eds.), *In Recognition of William Gaddis*, Syracuse, New York: Syracuse University Press, 1984

Moore, Steven, *A Reader's Guide to William Gaddis's "The Recognitions"*, Lincoln: University of Nebraska Press, 1982

Safer, Elaine B., *The Contemporary American Comic Epic: The Novels of Barth, Pynchon, Gaddis, and Kesey*, Detroit: Wayne State University Press, 1988

Singer, Alan, "The Ventriloquism of History: Voice, Parody, Dialogue", in *Intertextuality and Contemporary American Fiction*, edited by Patrick O'Donnell and Robert Con Davis, Baltimore: Johns Hopkins University Press, 1989

Tanner, Tony, *City of Words: American Fiction 1950–1970*, New York: Harper & Row, 1971; London: Jonathan Cape, 1971

For much of his literary career William Gaddis has been burdened with the distinction of being famous for not being famous enough. As a general rule, academics have lavished attention on "big novels" written by American authors; encyclopaedic prose narratives such as Herman Melville's *Moby-Dick* or Thomas Pynchon's *Gravity's Rainbow* have generated entire critical industries within the scholastic community. The labyrinthine novels of William Gaddis are a puzzling exception to this rule. For 20 years after the publication of his first, there were considerably more words between the covers of *The Recognitions* (1955) than there were words written about it. Since his receipt of the National Book Award for *JR* (1975), however, there has been a gradual turn-around in Gaddis's critical fortunes. The second 20 years of his career have witnessed the emergence of a hardcore Gaddis following in a number of dissertations, articles, and essays, although there are still relatively few extended analyses of his work. Much of the criticism that currently exists is preoccupied with *The Recognitions* and to a lesser extent *JR*. To date, with the exception of short reviews, there have been no detailed commentaries on *A Frolic of His Own* (1994).

GREEN's diatribe was published by the Dalkey Archive Press in 1992, on the 30th anniversary of its original appearance in the countercultural journal *newspaper*. In his Introduction, Steven Moore explains the rationale behind this commemorative edition: "it is the first sustained commentary on one of the greatest novels of our time, and it raises disturbing questions about the book-review media that are as pertinent today as they were thirty years ago". While the stylistic and typographic experimentation in Green's polemic inevitably appear somewhat jaded, this vigorous assault on the critical establishment contains some quirky insights and detailed exegesis of the initial response to *The Recognitions*.

In his study of American fiction in the mid-twentieth century, TANNER provides one of the earliest and most accessible recognitions of Gaddis's literary merits. Tanner foregrounds the author's thematic preoccupations. He asserts that *The Recognitions* is concerned essentially with imitation – the theory and practice of forgery in a variety of aesthetic, religious, and socio-economic contexts. Tanner also seeks to position Gaddis within an American prose-narrative tradition of problematizing the relationship between "fiction" and "reality".

Following Tanner, KARL addresses Gaddis's work in the context of a survey of contemporary American fiction, and detects a quest for "a more intense truth . . . beyond the reach of all aspects of counterfeiting". Karl gestures towards an historical context for *The Recognitions* – "perhaps *the* novel of the fifties" – although his account of the "Counterfeit Decade" remains rather anecdotal. Similarly, his argument concerning a synchronicity between the stylistic design of *JR* and the existential textures of a capitalist information economy is promising but underdeveloped.

JOHNSTON's study begins with the proposal that *The Recognitions* occupies a pivotal position between European modernist and American postmodernist fiction. He proceeds to develop the thesis that Gaddis's work anticipates many of the critical debates that have arisen in the academic world since the 1960s around concepts such as intertextuality, subjectivity, and origin(al)s. In an intricate and stimulating interpretation, Johnston utilises Mikhail Bakhtin's work on the dialogic and the carnivalesque as well as the poststructuralist model of the simulacrum. The concluding chapter explores the relationship of *The Recognitions*, *JR*, and *Carpenter's*

Gothic (1985) to postmodernism. Although not as immediately accessible as earlier "theme-centred" approaches, Johnston's application of critical theory to Gaddis's work is ultimately more rewarding. *Carnival of Repetition* represents the most substantial extended analysis of *The Recognitions* published to date.

SINGER's essay is worth mentioning in conjunction with Johnston's critique, since it also makes extensive use of Bakhtin's theory of the dialogic, or polyphonic novel, in relation to *Carpenter's Gothic*. While Tanner and Karl share the belief that Gaddis's work destabilizes the relationship between reality and a realm of fictions, Singer and Johnston propose that it constitutes a far more radical deconstruction of the very notion of a "real world", a "true" history, and a centred subjectivity.

While many of the more recent contributions to Gaddis scholarship are clearly indebted to the poststructuralist challenge to traditional philosophical orthodoxies, SAFER's work appears sublimely disinterested in recent critical debates. This work aims to fix the generic identity of *The Recognitions* and relate it to expressions of a comic sensibility in postwar American fiction. Safer addresses an important element in Gaddis's work that is sometimes overlooked, but her argument is often hampered by a rather insouciant shuffling between discrete critical terms, such as "irony", "satire", "parody" and "absurd humour".

KUEHL and MOORE have compiled a valuable collection of Gaddis criticism. The essays can be divided into three main areas of interest – the composition and reception of Gaddis's novels, the use of intertextual reference, and "theme-centred" readings of *The Recognitions* and *JR*. John Seelye's "Dryad in a Dead Oak Tree: The Incognito in *The Recognitions*" is worthy of attention since it falls outside of the standard parameters of Gaddis scholarship, adopting a less than favourable stance towards the author's problematic representation of homosexual men and heterosexual women.

As well as editing *In Recognition of William Gaddis* and writing an introduction to *Fire The Bastards!*, MOORE has also produced a reference guide to *The Recognitions*. In the Preface, Moore confesses to a regrettable imbalance between erudition and interpretation. Nevertheless, his scholarly endeavours make this a serviceable tome for the Gaddis votary.

BRIAN JARVIS

Gaskell, Elizabeth

1810–1865

English novelist and short-story writer

Craik, W.B., *Elizabeth Gaskell and the Provincial Novel*, London: Methuen, 1975

Duthie, Enid L. *The Themes of Elizabeth Gaskell*, London: Macmillan, 1980; Totowa, New Jersey: Barnes & Noble, 1980

Easson, Angus (ed.), *Elizabeth Gaskell: The Critical Heritage, 1848–1910*, London and New York: Routledge, 1991

Fryckstedt, Monica Correa, *Elizabeth Gaskell's "Mary Barton" and "Ruth": A Challenge to Christian England*, Uppsala, Sweden: University of Upsala, 1982

Lansbury, Coral, *Elizabeth Gaskell: The Novel of Social Crisis*, London: Paul Elek, 1975; New York: Barnes & Noble, 1975

Selig, Robert L., *Elizabeth Gaskell: A Reference Guide*, Boston: G.K. Hall, 1977

Stoneman, Patsy, *Elizabeth Gaskell*, Brighton, Sussex: Harvester Press, 1987; Bloomington: Indiana University Press, 1987

Uglow, Jenny, *Elizabeth Gaskell: A Habit of Stories*, London: Faber & Faber, 1993; New York: Farrar Straus, 1993

Wright, Edgar, *Mrs Gaskell: The Basis for Reassessment*, London & New York: Oxford University Press, 1965

Until quite recently Gaskell's wide range of form, style, and subject matter has led, paradoxically, to a narrowing of critical approaches to her work. In her lifetime, *Mary Barton*, her first novel, *Ruth*, and *North and South* became associated with the purposive social-reform fiction of Charles Kingsley and Benjamin Disraeli. The strongly felt appeal of *Cranford*, *Cousin Phillis*, and *Wives and Daughters* in particular appeared less challenging, containing, in the words of one reviewer, "a delicate perception of character, a latent sense of true humour . . . and a power of conferring interest in the ordinary affairs of life" (review of *Wives and Daughters*, in *New York Times*, 26 February 1866). Critics remained divided as to their preferences, and dismissive where these were not answered. The division remains, but has more recently led to new approaches and findings, acting as a stimulus to wider critical activity rather than delimiting it.

UGLOW's excellent critical biography of Gaskell takes account of many of these recent developments, particularly in her discussion of Gaskell's feelings about her own sex and its special potential. She lays well-documented emphasis on Gaskell's own wide and liberal education, and its relation to the educational options and practice of the Unitarian movement over the period. Her critical examinations of Gaskell's writings are sensitive and illuminating; particularly valuable is her detailed contextualization of Gaskell's work, and her use of a generous range of contemporary reference. Her notes are copious and exact, but she does not provide a formal bibliography.

SELIG's *Reference Guide* is extremely comprehensive; books and shorter writings, on, or relating to, Gaskell and her work are listed under separate headings chronologically under each year from 1848 to 1974. Brief, pointed summaries accompany all the entries, which are also fully indexed. Particularly valuable are citations or quotations of reviews published in Gaskell's lifetime and shortly afterwards: these are often anonymous, and otherwise difficult of access. There is a short, useful Introduction indicating the main shifts of emphasis in Gaskell criticism over the period dealt with, and taking into account some key developments taking place while the book was in preparation.

EASSON's volume on Gaskell in the *Critical Heritage* series provides full materials for a critical perspective of Gaskell's work. He gives particular attention to the ambivalence of earlier approaches, and shows how, from the 1950s onward, more recent attempts to resolve these, from whatever direction, have approached her achievement with new seriousness and depth of scholarship.

WRIGHT's book does much to fulfil the promise of its subtitle. He searches for unity:

> There is no argument but that Mrs Gaskell does have impulses that pull in different directions; *Cranford* and *Ruth* were being written at the same time, while a powerful study of the supernatural, "The Old Nurse's Story", was also produced in the same period. Any serious consideration of her art will need to consider the pattern into which words so apparently different . . . can be fitted. We need to look for unity behind the dissimilarity.

Wright finds this unity largely in Gaskell's religious perceptions, and in her own artistic choices made as her experience broadened.

FRYCKSTEDT also finds Gaskell's religious standpoint of central importance, but takes its effects much further. In her study of *Mary Barton* and *Ruth* she argues that Gaskell has plan and purpose: to inform her readers of whole ranges of social injustice, of which many people were simply ignorant, and by doing so to direct compassion into public reform through the private re-evaluation of the prejudices and assumptions that she saw standing in the way of this. Fryckstedt sees Gaskell's aims as consistent with those of the Unitarian movement, and as directing her artistic energies towards the awakening of truly Christian awareness. This Gaskell saw Christianity as the only basis for any solution to the problems of social oppression and injustice, in particular as regarded "fallen" women.

CRAIK sees Gaskell as part of a group of novelists, which includes the Brontës, Anthony Trollope, George Eliot, and Thomas Hardy, who, "see the world from a standpoint which is not metropolitan". Gaskell's northern settings, like Trollope's Barset or Hardy's Wessex, provide a focus for the close examination of the interplay of character in a fully detailed social context, within which she is able to develop her readers' perception of human qualities, which are in themselves universal though activated by specific localised pressures. Craik lays emphasis on Gaskell's range, and on the lateral development of her art: "*Sylvia's Lovers* could never have been predicted from *North and South*, any more than *Ruth* could from *Mary Barton*". This standpoint gives particular illumination to Craik's analysis of Gaskell's style and narrative techniques.

LANSBURY is one among a number of recent critics who consider that Gaskell's reputation has been fundamentally undermined by the popularity of *Cranford*. Her deeply serious examination of Gaskell's art is based on a political reading of her works, from which she emerges as a "social historian of unusual prescience". Lansbury's discussion of *Wives and Daughters*, in particular, is finely perceptive.

DUTHIE's approach to the problem of the "scope and variety" of Gaskell's work allows her both balance and inclusiveness, since the themes she discusses in many ways intertwine across the range of Gaskell's writing. This is among the most valuable of recent studies, illuminating not only the major novels, but also many of the shorter and little-known works. Her chapter on "Mystery and the Macabre" is of special interest in this respect.

STONEMAN's book was contributed to the "Key Women Writers" series (general editor: Sue Roe). Her starting point is that Gaskell has been "misread . . . systematically" as either a "lady novelist" or a "social problem novelist". Her own feminist reading is sensitive and flexible, and throws genuinely fresh light on Gaskell's work, clearing ground rather than establishing new standpoints.

ELIZABETH PORGES WATSON

Gawain-Poet *fl.* 14th Century

Anonymous poet

Blanch, Robert J., Miriam Youngerman Miller, and Julian N. Wasserman (eds.), *Text and Matter: New Critical Perspectives of the Pearl-Poet*, Troy, New York: Whitston, 1991

Davenport, W.A., *The Art of the Gawain-Poet*, London: Athlone Press, 1978

Johnson, Lynn Staley, *The Voice of the Gawain-Poet*, Madison: University of Wisconsin Press, 1984

Nicholls, Jonathan, *The Matter of Courtesy: Medieval Courtesy Books and the Gawain-Poet*, Woodbridge, Suffolk: D.S. Brewer, 1985

Spearing, A.C., *The Gawain-Poet: A Critical Study*, Cambridge: Cambridge University Press, 1970

Stanbury, Sarah, *Seeing the Gawain-Poet: Description and the Act of Perception*, Philadelphia: University of Pennsylvania Press, 1991

The anonymous author of *Sir Gawain and the Green Knight*, *Pearl*, *Patience*, and *Cleanness* (or *Purity*) is most commonly referred to as "the Gawain-Poet" and, sometimes, as "the Pearl-Poet". Critical usage is here a rough guide to the relative volume of critical writing. The last 25 years have produced some 400 articles and books on *Gawain*. Next comes *Pearl*, whose critical tradition, while not quite so overwhelming, is nevertheless well-established. The other two poems have received, and continue to receive, much less attention, and there are very few treatments of the entire *oeuvre* of the Gawain-Poet. These last works are characterized by an attempt to find, in the chivalric ethos of *Gawain*, the richly suggestive symbolism of *Pearl*, and the scriptural focus of *Patience* and *Cleanness*, threads which bind the poems together.

A beginner could do worse than to turn to SPEARING's accessible 1970 study. It does suffer from the common critical practice of considering the four poems serially – there is a chapter for each work, each essentially a traditional close reading – but a useful introductory chapter places the poet and the poetry in their appropriate cultural contexts and outlines a common pattern, in the four works, of the confrontation between man and a supernatural power.

DAVENPORT notes that Spearing's approach tends to de-emphasize what the poems have in common, and in his own attempt to present "a full appreciation of [the poet's] skill as an artist" he includes introductory and concluding statements that argue for a poetic art based on the presentation of multiple levels of meaning. The poems are dramatic in their narrative approach, and the significant amount of dialogue offers the reader a variety of perspectives on important moments in the work. It is characteristic of the Gawain-Poet to focus on antithesis and conflict. Thus Davenport's analyses of the individual poems tend to emphasize tension – in *Pearl* between the emotion and form, in *Cleanness* between the poet's narrative and didactic impulses, and in *Gawain* between romance and realism. Despite his reservations about serial reading, Davenport's organization and emphasis on close reading makes this book similar in approach and effect to Spearing's work.

JOHNSON also insists on the need to study the four poems together, and finds the links in the spiritual context of the poems. We must "recognize the degree to which medieval thought was influenced by medieval Christianity". Like many critics, she compares the biblical poems to their sources. In the case of *Gawain*, she argues for a triple time-scheme – cyclic, degenerative, and regenerative – which intersects with Gawain's adventures and prepares the audience for his failure. The discussion of *Pearl* includes an interesting exploration of the implications of iconography and astrology for our understanding of the central Parable of the Vineyard. In all of the Gawain-Poet's works, the common thread is that of moral failures, choices, and transformations. Figures like Jonah and Gawain "suggest ideals larger than themselves while pointing up the weaknesses and struggles of man in general". Other critics have traced many of these patterns before, but there is valuable commentary here, particularly on the more neglected poems.

NICHOLLS turns from the familiar field of Scripture to explore instead the courtesy-book tradition. He begins by tracing the courtesy book from its origins, which he places in monastic rules, to later secular texts concentrating on good manners in courtly society. The moral subtext of many of these works is clear; these writers and, Nicholls argues, the Gawain-Poet, are concerned with "the harmonisation of inner virtue with outer gesture". In the second part of the book, Nicholls shows how the courtesy-book tradition may inform the works of the Gawain-Poet. Its relevance is most obvious in *Gawain* itself, and the importance of courtesy has been explored in many readings of the poem. Nicholls is nevertheless able to offer some new insights into the role of courtesy in *Gawain*. The courtesy-book framework also leads to an illuminating discussion of feasting in *Cleanness*. *Pearl* and *Patience* prove, as the author acknowledges, less amenable to this sort of analysis. While all the poems suggest an interest in courtesy, it would be wrong "to force upon them a convenient theory that would argue for their having been written to illustrate the poet's thesis of the efficacy of courtesy in human affairs". This book, then, offers new insights into individual works – no mean feat at this date – while eschewing any effort to provide a cohesive and conclusive analysis of the Gawain-Poet's work as a whole.

STANBURY does intend to present an analysis that will apply equally and persuasively to all the poems, and like Nicholls, offers a new paradigm through which to read the works. Her focus is on visual perception. All four poems simultaneously call on and reject sensory perception as a guide to knowledge. The Gawain-Poet's concentration on description allows him to explore the problematic relationship between sensory and spiritual perception: "in these poems description becomes a powerful narrative tool for dramatizing the limitations of human experience, an effect that is created in part by structuring descriptive passages according to the mechanics of perception". Stanbury's approach yields fruit in each of the four poems. In the discussion of *Pearl*, Stanbury uses the visual tradition of the illustrated Apocalypse to focus her emphasis on the relation between the visionary experience and the seer. In *Purity*, the failures by some of the characters in each parable allow the reader to witness the development of "mankind's ability to read visual signs". *Patience* uses the enclosed spaces in which Jonah appears to dramatize his limited vision, in contrast to God's omniscience and omnipresence. Finally, *Gawain* here appears as a drama of gaze and counter-gaze, of multiple perspectives which deprive the reader of the interpretive framework that might be offered by a single point of view. A concluding chapter explores the relation of the Gawain-Poet's "visual poetics" to the practices of Ricardian poetry and to the emphasis on the visual in English mysticism.

The recent anthology by BLANCH *et al.* reflects a renaissance in the study of the Gawain-Poet's more neglected works; three of the 15 essays are on *Patience*, and three on *Purity*. The renaissance has at least something to do with the extent to which the fields of *Pearl* and *Sir Gawain* have already been ploughed, a fact which is reflected in the repetition, by some of the *Gawain*-contributors, of material already substantially published elsewhere. Many of these essays look to aspects of the fourteenth-century context in order to explicate their subjects, sometimes with considerable ingenuity. There are contributors here who have made significant advances in the study of the Gawain-Poet, but the lack of organization or theme in this volume makes it inappropriate if one is seeking a first look at the entire *oeuvre*.

SIÂN ECHARD

Gay and Lesbian Literature

De Jongh, Nicholas, *Not in Front of the Audience: Homosexuality On Stage*, London and New York: Routledge, 1992

Dynes, Wayne R., and Stephen Donaldson (eds.), *Homosexual Themes in Literary Studies*, New York: Garland, 1992

Griffin, Gabriele (ed.), *Outwrite: Lesbianism and Popular Culture*, London and Boulder, Colorado: Pluto Press, 1993

Hobby, Elaine, and Chris White (eds.), *What Lesbians Do in Books*, London: Women's Press, 1991

Jay, Karla, and Joanne Glasgow (eds.), *Lesbian Texts and Contexts: Radical Revisions*, New York: New York University Press, 1990; London: Onlywomen Press, 1992

Lilly, Mark (ed.), *Lesbian and Gay Writing: An Anthology of Critical Essays*, London: Macmillan, 1990; Philadelphia: Temple University Press, 1990

Munt, Sally (ed.), *New Lesbian Criticism: Literary and Cultural Readings*, Hemel Hempstead, Hertforshire: Harvester Wheatsheaf, 1992; New York: Columbia University Press, 1992

Murphy, Timothy F., and Suzanne Poirier (eds.), *Writing AIDS: Gay Literature, Language, and Analysis*, New York: Columbia University Press, 1993

Summers, Claude J., *Gay Fictions, Wilde to Stonewall: Studies in a Male Homosexual Literary Tradition*, New York: Continuum, 1990

Woods, Gregory, *Articulate Flesh: Male Homo-Eroticism and Modern Poetry*, New Haven, Connecticut, and London: Yale University Press, 1987

Zimmerman, Bonnie, *The Safe Sea of Women: Lesbian Fiction 1969–1989*, Boston: Beacon Press, 1990; London: Onlywomen Press, 1992

The early key texts on lesbian and gay literature – by such writers as Barbara Greer, Jane Rule, James Lewin, Georges-Michel Sarotte, Robert K. Martin, and Stephen Adams – grew out of the same impetus that fuelled gay liberation politics in the 1960s and 1970s. Included under the rubric of lesbian and gay literature are (to quote Claude J. Summers, *Gay Fictions*):

> . . . the fictional representation of lesbians and gay men by gay male and lesbian writers; the evolution of conceptions about homosexual identity; and the construction, perpetuation, revision, and deconstruction of fictions (including stereotypes and defamations) about homosexuality and homosexuals.

Recent years have seen the emergence in the academy, alongside this tradition, of a wider-ranging and theoretically sophisticated lesbian and gay studies, and the new "queer studies".

In his inimitable style, WOODS explores male homoeroticism in poetry (predominantly from the period 1914–1984, but with an extraordinary range of reference), insisting on the centrality of the male body and seeing homoeroticism as "a major, self-referential part of male sexuality as a whole". In the first half, he suggests three main *topoi* of male homoeroticism: the dismantling and reconstructing of the male body; observing the male body in, and after, energetic action, such as war or sports; and considering it as an instrument of creativity, "the author, text, and subject of its own futures". The second half comprises readings of D.H. Lawrence, Hart Crane, W.H. Auden, Allen Ginsberg, and Thom Gunn. Woods also provides an excellent bibliography, and in his lively Introduction, a provocative discussion of what constitutes a "gay text": "a gay text is one which lends itself to the hypothesis of a gay reading, regardless of where the author's genitals were wont to keep house".

ZIMMERMAN offers an overview of predominantly US lesbian fiction published primarily by alternative feminist presses in the 1970s and 1980s. Eschewing the language of critical theory in favour of a more accessible language, and taking in 167 works, the study is valuable for its attempt to "read this fiction as the collective voice of what we loosely call 'the lesbian community'", using the fiction "to identify what lesbians of the past two decades believe to be the 'truth' about lesbian existence". Zimmerman reads lesbian fiction as the expression of a collective "myth of origins", taking four forms: the lesbian self, the lesbian couple, the lesbian community, and community and difference.

LILLY brings together ten contributions, wildly disparate in style and quality, focusing on topics as diverse as Ivy Compton-Burnett, Maureen Duffy, Ann Bannon, Sylvia Townsend Warner and Valentine Ackland, contemporary lesbian erotic poetry, alienation, Tennessee Williams, gay male pornography, paradox in gay men's poetry, and Ronald Firbank. While equal weight is given to lesbian and gay male contributions, the two are strictly divided, and Lilly's brief Introduction makes no attempt to provide an overview.

SUMMERS argues for a male homosexual literary tradition between 1895 and 1969 – here including Oscar Wilde, Willa Cather, E.M. Forster, Gore Vidal, Truman Capote, Tennessee Williams, James Baldwin, and Christopher Isherwood – not in order to establish a canon, "but to explore strong representative texts that both reflect and reflect on the status of gay men in these earlier crucial decades". Through clear, well-researched, and fluently written readings, he traces "a tradition of gay fiction that is roughly analogous to the development of homosexual consciousness" and puts the case that these gay fictions merit a place "in the broad range of the Anglo-American literary tradition".

In "the first British collection of explicitly lesbian essays of literature" HOBBY and WHITE offer 12 diverse pieces, under the headings "Lesbian Books", "Lesbian Reading", and "Lesbian Writing". Through lesbian readings of lesbian texts – including lesbian detective fiction and thrillers, contemporary lesbian poetry, and fiction by Sappho, Virginia Woolf, Radclyffe Hall, and Edith Ellis – the contributors struggle to find a language and frame of reference in which to talk about lesbian culture, desire and identity in diverse historical moments. Employing Gillian Hanscombe's notion of "lesbian specs", through which the lesbian reader can read cultural frameworks, languages, and encodings, there are readings of Katherine Mansfield, Rosemary Manning, and lesbian motifs in Sanskrit myth. The study concludes with discussions of the activities of various lesbian writers – the seventeenth-century poet Katherine Philips, the London-based Blacklesbian poetry, and Caeia March on her own work.

DE JONGH offers an enjoyable survey of the treatment of male homosexuality on stage (predominantly the London West End theatre) from the 1920s through to the mid 1980s, taking in McCarthyism, censorship, heterosexual prejudice, and the AIDS epidemic. While coverage of most plays and the lesser-known playwrights is necessarily cursory, de Jongh devotes more time to key figures such as Noel Coward, Terence Rattigan, Tennessee Williams, Joe Orton, John Osborne, Mart Crowley, Martin Sherman, and Larry Kramer. His speculations on history and sexuality away from the stage are less reliable.

DYNES and DONALDSON reprint 22 classic articles, many of them difficult to find elsewhere, covering a vast range of modern Western literature with a noticeable gay male bias. The sheer diversity renders their introductory overview inevitably sketchy. Articles include Catherine Stimpson's account of the lesbian novel in English, Eve Sedgwick on Henry James, and essays on everything from the "love of boys in medieval Hebrew poetry of Spain" to gay science fiction and fantasy by way of Horace Walpole, William Beckford, Alfred Lord Tennyson, Herman Melville, Wilde, Marcel Proust, Federico García Lorca, Woolf, Williams, Patricia Nell Warren, and John Rechy, with contributions by Chris Dunton on homosexuality in African literature, and Juan Brice-Novoa on the Chicano novel.

JAY and GLASGOW collect 22 essays "about reader-writer interaction, the question of audience for the lesbian writer, the question of audience for the nonlesbian writing about lesbians or researching women and/or developing characters who represented diverse classes, races, religions, or values". Subjects of critical readings include Emily Dickinson, Woolf, Cather, Radclyffe Hall, H.D., and Djuna Barnes, alongside Ann Allen Shockley, Monique Wittig, Nicole Brossard, Paula Gunn Allen, and recent lesbian plays and autobiographical writings. The collection is concluded by a useful bibliography of primary and critical reading, and a succinct afterword by Catherine Stimpson on lesbian studies in the 1990s.

MUNT's collection includes some thoughtful questionings of a lesbian theory "rife with its own insecurities": Bonnie Zimmerman analyses the potentialities and pitfalls in recent directions of lesbian studies; Reina Lewis pits structuralist theories of the author against the need for positive images of lesbians; Munt's Introduction interrogates the positioning of lesbian studies within the academy. Essays focus on: the 1950s as a key literary moment in the construction of a lesbian identity; the intersection of African-American and lesbian criticisms; the limitations of postmodernist parody and play in a lesbian agenda; lesbian utopian fiction; lesbian pornography; and lesbian culture's crossover with popular culture. Authors discussed include Sarah Schulman, Audre Lorde, Jane Rule, Sally Miller Gearhart, Joanna Russ, Jeanette Winterson, and Pat Califia.

GRIFFIN's collection attempts to counter the high-culture, canonical, white, middle-class bias of much lesbian criticism by exploring the intersection between popular and lesbian cultural production – lesbians as producers of, as represented in, and as consumers of, popular culture – and is appropriately couched in a fairly accessible style. Included are discussions of representations of lesbian sex, mid-century lesbian romances, different ways of telling lesbian *her*story, coming-out stories discussed as lesbian biblio-mythography, lesbian thrillers, lesbian/feminist science fiction, lesbian cinema, and the use of popular music in constructions of a lesbian identity.

MURPHY and POIRIER's collection is devoted to the impact of the HIV and AIDS epidemics on gay literature, on the understanding that "AIDS has irremediably changed the way that gay literature can be either written or read, whatever the reader's or writer's feelings about the epidemic or the homoerotic". Following Poirier's excellent introductory essay are 13 contributions, many from eminent academics, dealing with the rhetorics associated with the epidemic and AIDS activism, media coverage, the teaching of AIDS as an academic subject, and with writings by (among others) Edmund White, Andrew Holleran, Paul Monette, and Hervé Guibert. The collection concludes with a superb annotated bibliography demonstrating the explosion of fiction, poetry, drama, biography, autobiography, essays, criticism, and analysis inspired by AIDS.

ALAN STEWART

Gender and Literature

Butler, Judith, *Gender Trouble: Feminism and the Subversion of Identity*, New York and London: Routledge, 1990

Cranny-Francis, Anne, *Engendered Fictions: Analysing Gender in the Production and Reception of Texts*, Kensington: New South Wales University Press, 1991

Faderman, Lillian, *Surpassing the Love of Men: Romantic Friendship and Love Between Women from the Renaissance to the Present*, New York: William Morrow, 1981; London: Women's Press, 1985

Greene, Gayle, and Coppélia Kahn (eds.), *Making a Difference: Feminist Literary Criticism*, London and New York: Methuen, 1985

Millett, Kate, *Sexual Politics*, Garden City, New York: Doubleday, 1970; London: Rupert Hart-Davis, 1972

Millor, Nancy K. (ed.), *The Poetics of Gender*, New York: Columbia University Press, 1986

Moers, Ellen, *Literary Women*, Garden City, New York: Doubleday, 1976; London: W.H. Allen, 1977

Poovey, Mary, *Uneven Developments: The Ideological Work of Gender in Mid-Victorian England*, London: Virago, 1989; Chicago: University of Chicago Press, 1989

Sedgwick, Eve Kosofsky, *Between Men: English Literature and Male Homosocial Desire*, New York: Columbia University Press, 1985

Wall, Cheryl A. (ed.), *Changing Our Own Words: Essays on Criticism, Theory, and Writing by Black Women*, New Brunswick, New Jersey: Rutgers University Press, 1989; London: Routledge, 1990

Woolf, Viginia, *A Room of One's Own*, London: Hogarth Press, 1929; New York: Fountain Press, 1929; several subsequent reprints, including Harmondsworth, Middlesex: Penguin Books, 1993

Although discussion of gender seems to be a relatively new aspect of literary criticism emerging in the late 1980s, it has a much longer history, notably in feminist criticism. For practical and New Criticism, gender was outside the literary critic's field of vision, located in the (apparently) extra-textual realm of sociological study. These literary-critical modes institutionalised an approach to literature that claimed objectivity; invariably the critic's claim to neutrality and disinterestedness in matters of gender, as in sexuality, race, and class, was undermined by the distinctly exclusive and exclusionary canon and the system of values employed (and reproduced) in the literary-critical act. The concept of gender enables feminist critics to expose the critical sleight of hand that systematically marginalises women's writing and women's representations of women in literary criticism. Thus, the vast majority of books on this subject are concerned principally with femininity, though there is evidence of an increasing interest in masculinity.

As early as 1928 the masculine literary tradition and the gendered "difference of view" were identified as significant obstacles to women writers. WOOLF's invitation to speak to Cambridge undergraduates on the fraught relationship between "women and fiction" resulted in an influential, controversial, and ambiguous study in feminist literary criticism. Woolf established the different socio-historical conditions that have prevailed for the woman writer, and the need for equal opportunities: economic as well as psychological freedom determine any experiment with language, or attempt to represent desire between women. Most controversial is Woolf's view that androgyny is necessary for literary excellence. The possibility that a woman may write from a position undistinguished by gender difference is one to which feminist critics have more recently returned.

Feminist literary criticism established the inseparability of literature from gender, and identified the sexual division on which F.R. Leavis's "Great Tradition" was founded. The significance of a female literary tradition to the woman writer is explored in MOERS's study. Moers examines the socially determined and historically specific characteristics associated with sexual difference. She argues that women's writing (mainly in the novel genre) demonstrates recurring images and motifs, which are related to women's experience.

While Moers analyses literary women and their writing, MILLETT is concerned with a critique of literary representations of women, mainly in male-authored writing. Millett's study is well-known for its identification of disempowering representations of women by authors such as D.H. Lawrence, Norman Mailer, Henry Miller, and Jean Genet. Often overlooked is its wide-ranging, historicising analysis of the relationship between the subordination of women in literature and in society. In addition to the argument that sexual difference is a political issue, Millett persuasively argues that in the literary representation of gender sexuality is not only implicated but violently engendered. More problematic is the expressive realism adopted here, most obviously in the final section entitled "The Literary Reflection".

The interdependence of gender and sexuality is explored by FADERMAN, whose controversial study analyses literary representations of women in relation not to men, but to other women. Faderman establishes a literary tradition of women loving women. The concept of "romantic friendship" between women in the eighteenth and nineteenth centuries has been criticised for its emphasis on friendship at the expense of the erotic. However, Faderman argues that "romantic friendships" were widely condoned rather than condemned because they were constructed within the constraints of the conventionally feminine. But, when women's desire for other women was accompanied by a challenge to ideas of femininity, it was then condemned: "at the base it was not the sexual aspect of lesbianism as much as the attempted usurpation of male prerogative by women who behaved like men that many societies appeared to find most disturbing". Therefore, like Millett, Faderman explores gender in literary representations of women, establishing the inevitable and complex relationships between gender and sexuality that critics have more recently developed. Both critics' approaches to gender are, however, shaped by prevailing assumptions about women's experiences and the validity of "women" as a category which have since been challenged.

The shift in literary criticism that such a challenge initiated is represented here by two anthologies, which focus attention on differences among women and approaches other than expressive realism. GREENE and KAHN's anthology includes important essays by black and lesbian critics, essays which discuss French feminists' work on language and the acquisition of gender identity, and psychoanalytic approaches. This excellent survey of the diversity of feminist scholarship, which "employs gender as a fundamental organizing category of human experience", is made accessible by the synopses provided for each essay.

MILLOR's anthology draws together papers from the colloquium held at Columbia University (New York) in November 1984. It includes work on "textual strategies" as well as on the material conditions in which gender operates. Beginning with the contention that "feminist criticism generally and necessarily asks what it might mean to read and write through the prism of gender", the critics pursue topics such as "the social conditions of literary production; the politics of reception and the discourses of canon formation; female authorship and literary history; sexual difference and the languages of theory".

POOVEY's study of mid-Victorian British culture established the "ideological work of gender", identifying its attempts towards "coherence and authenticity", but stressing its "internal instability and artificiality", and the inevitably "uneven developments" of its work. Although not confined to literary representations, she demonstrates that dominant ideological constructions of gender are put under strain in texts such as Charles Dickens's *David Copperfield* and Charlotte Brontë's *Jane Eyre*. She contends that "representations of gender at mid-century were part of the system of interdependent images in which various ideologies became accessible to individual men and women". For Poovey, gender and ideology is constructed and contested in a variety of cultural representations.

Similarly, CRANNY-FRANCIS extends her analyses to popular fiction and fairy tales, examining the ways in which fiction reproduces, as well as produces, gender, relating this to patriarchy and the rigidly dualistic gender discourse on which this depends. This study is concerned with the "representational function of a text" and "the relationship between the text and its audiences". While the reader is foregrounded in this study, a discussion of the "signifying practices of masculinity" deliberately precedes those of femininity. Rather than "a capitulation to patriarchy" this is "an attempt to begin the deconstruction of patriarchy at a site which is often ignored".

In the same spirit, SEDGWICK's study examines the representations in literature of "male homosocial desire" using Gayle Rubin's argument about the "traffic in women". This exemplifies an increased interest in masculinity (which is regarded by some feminist critics as a problematic step).

In WALL's anthology black feminist critics discuss the rights and "risks of speaking" out, exchanging theoretical ideas about writings by black women. Many of the essays challenge the isolation of gender as an aspect of critical discourse, and address the universalising effects of the category of women. Although "women" has been used together with "gender" as categories to identify an oppressive social division in society, the former has tended to exclude black women. Moreover, as Valerie Smith says, the anxious response from white critics – "the move to include black women as historical presences and as speaking subjects in critical discourse", which is emphatically historicising – is problematic:

> This association of black women with reembodiment resembles rather closely the association, in classic

> Western philosophy and in nineteenth-century cultural constructions of womanhood, of women of colour with the body and therefore with animal passions and slave labor.

Black feminist literary theorists, perhaps uniquely, attend to "the conditions of the black women's oppression" which are "specific and complex" and therefore "seek particularized methodologies . . . which are necessarily flexible, holding in balance the three variables of race, gender, and class and destabilizing the centrality of any one".

BUTLER's influential and interdisciplinary study sustains and develops Millett's insistence that feminists address the relationship between gender and sexuality. Butler challenges many assumptions regarding identity, gender, and sexuality. Most remarkably, she argues that the sex/gender distinction is untenable: sex, like gender, proves to be discursive; and therefore an insistence on the pre-discursive place of sex/the body serves to maintain a dualism that reinforces heterosexuality. She explores other theorists' conceptualisations of gender as an attribute (a mark, a role, a factor, or dimension): to what extent is gender determined, to what extent a matter of choice? Butler rejects the Hegelian basis of many arguments about gender, proposing instead a performative theory of gender: "there is no gender identity behind the expressions of gender; that identity is performatively constituted by the very 'expressions' that are said to be its results". Butler's exemplifying texts are not confined to the literary; the writings of Monique Wittig are analysed, together with phenomena such as parody, drag, and transsexuality. The conjunction of literature and gender proves to be highly contested by feminists and poststructuralists alike.

KATHARINE MARY COCKIN

See also **Feminist Literary Theory**

Georgian Poetry

Day, Gary, "The Poets: Georgian, Imagists, and Others", in *Literature and Culture in Modern Britain*, edited by Clive Bloom, London: Longman, 1993

Reeves, James (ed.), *Georgian Poetry*, Harmondsworth, Middlesex: Penguin, 1962

Riding, Laura, and Robert Graves, *A Survey of Modernist Poetry*, London: Heinemann, 1927; Garden City, New York: Doubleday, Doran & Co., 1928

Rogers, Timothy (ed.), *Georgian Poetry, 1911–1922: The Critical Heritage*, London and Boston: Routledge, 1977

Ross, Robert H., *The Georgian Revolt: Rise and Fall of a Poetic Ideal 1910–1922*, Carbondale: Southern Illinois University Press, 1965; London: Faber & Faber, 1967

Stead, C.K., *The New Poetic: Yeats to Eliot*, London: Hutchinson, 1964; New York: Harper, 1966; revised edition, Philadelphia: University of Pennsylvania Press, 1987

The label "Georgian poetry" is given to the work of those poets who shared roughly similar views of poetry to those of Edward Marsh and whose works appeared in his five anthologies of poetry aptly entitled *Georgian Poetry* (1911–22), which were published by Harold Munro at the Poetry Bookshop. Paradoxically, a number of poets who appeared in Marsh's anthologies objected to his calling them Georgians; Edward Thomas, on the other hand, whose work is often cited as that most characteristic of the Georgians, never appeared in Marsh's books. The most immediate successes were Rupert Brooke and James Elroy Flecker.

A number of common characteristics define the nature of Georgian poetry, among them an emphasis on physical description. Indeed, the paucity and simplicity of ideas in Georgian poetry has often led to their works as being judged as bucolic and unphilosophical Romantic restatements. The Georgians' style was lyrical and their subject matter influenced by a delicacy of feeling and a nervous sensibility, often referring to the birds and flowers of rural England or to classical worlds with little relevance to modern sensibilities. The subject matter of many Georgian poets during World War I appeared to be divorced from the cataclysmic upheavals that were taking place on the Continent. The movement has often been judged to be the last flicker of the Romantic movement, and many modern critics have dealt harshly with the poetry produced under the aegis of Marsh. Among the most published Georgians were Robert Graves, Siegfried Sassoon, John Masefield, Ralph Hodgson, Robert Nichols, Francis Brett Young, Edmund Blunden, Lascelles Abercrombie, Walter de la Mare, and Vita Sackville-West.

The first sustained critical attack on Georgianism appeared five years after Marsh's final anthology appeared. RIDING and GRAVES characterised the movement primarily from a stylistic standpoint: Georgianism, for them, meant poetry which concentrated on the removal of archaic diction and pompous language from its text. Further, Georgians avoided religious, philosophical, and improving themes in their poetry as a reaction against the didactic nature of Victorian literary values. The poetry was pro-English, pantheistic, and easy to read. Eventually, Georgianism "became principally concerned with Nature and love and leisure and old age and childhood and animals and sleep and other uncontroversial subjects". World War I allowed the Georgians a second wind, for it offered an opportunity to contrast details of trench life with pastoral England. For Riding and Graves, Georgianism died because no one was "capable of writing a new poetry within these revised forms".

REEVES' main concern in the Introduction to his Penguin anthology of Georgian poetry is to identify exactly which poets should be accepted into the Georgian canon. In search of an adequate conclusion, Reeves examines what elements constituted Georgian subject matter and concludes that the true Georgians celebrated Englishness in all its manifestations; that is to say, that their poetry offered "natural simplicity, emotional warmth, and moral innocence. In many ways like the Romantics, the Georgian poets valued plain language and subject matter which reflected the mundane and pastoral in contrast to the more complex language and philosophical speculations of the modernists.

STEAD is of the opinion that the Georgian poets were in revolt against the political and public poetry of Alfred Austin and William Watson. Stead localised the impetus of the Georgian Movement in this rejection of the didactic and patriotic poetry written by the Edwardians. The Georgians desired to return to the pure poetry that they felt had been written by the Aesthetics. However, this hankering back to a purer poetic form was not escapistic, as is often claimed, but rather a literary and stylistic revolution attempting to reclaim lost ground taken by the Edwardians.

ROSS's study was the first to look exclusively at the Georgians and at their age, and it functions as a cultural and literary history of the period and the writers involved in the production of *Georgian Poetry*. Ross divides the Georgian movement into two phases: the systolic (1910–17), during which writers such as Lawrence, Brooke, and Masefield were seen to offer a sense of "spiritual euphoria, a sense of vitality, anti-Victorianism, realism, and a freedom of poetic diction"; and the diastolic, during which editors and poets such as Edward Shanks, W.J. Turner, and John Squire vitiated the energy from the movement. Ross discusses Edward Marsh's tactics to promote the Georgians, as well as the mercenary value judgments put on sales. Very little is said about the poetry itself, however, and Ross fails to explain why Georgian poetry fell out of favour and became stereotyped as pastoral "lark-loving" writing.

ROGERS admits early on in his study of the Georgians that he has concentrated on the writers who appeared in the five volumes of Marsh's *Georgian Poetry* for the reason that the larger, diverse groups of poets loosely called "Georgians" do not have uniform characteristics. In Rogers' view, Edward Marsh's intention was to serve English poetry by carefully selecting the best poetry for the anthologies; in order to demonstrate Marsh's criteria, Rogers reprints all the introductions to the volumes of *Georgian Poetry*. The collection shows the unevenness of talent: from the masterpieces of Lawrence (who appears in four volumes) and the wonderful fantasias of Walter de la Mare to the rather unreadable works of John Drinkwater and the relatively weak selections in the final volume. Rogers' selection of Georgian criticism, however, is all encompassing and affirms Marsh's perceptive taste in poetry along with his own breadth of learning and occasional dissatisfaction with critics who railed against his final anthology.

DAY gives an overview of the critical responses of Georgian poetry, prefacing it with Edith Sitwell's harshly critical description of the movement and its adherents as those "who only seemed to be able to write about sheep" as a starting point to examine the marginalisation of the movement. Day asks whether the fact that many of the writers of Georgian poetry did not travel the public-school/Oxbridge route may have contributed to the unfashionableness of the movement. Further, he suggests that the devaluing of Georgian simplicity and little-Englishness by the modernist critics was an attempt to legitimise their own work and to ensure that poetry remained an élitist preserve. Arguing from a Marxist perspective, Day claims that "Georgian poetry functions to prop up the ideology of individualism, and its demise has less to do with its aesthetic qualities than with the change from an individualist to a collectivist state". For Day, Georgian poetry represents the crisis of lost subjectivity of the individual in the emerging confusion of the modernist world.

PATRICK J. M. QUINN

Gibbon, Edward 1737–1794

English historian

Bond, Harold L., *The Literary Art of Edward Gibbon*, Oxford: Clarendon Press, 1960

Bowersock, Glen W., John Clive, and Stephen R. Graubard (eds.), *Edward Gibbon and "The Decline and Fall of the Roman Empire"*, Cambridge, Massachusetts: Harvard University Press, 1977

Braudy, Leo, *Narrative Form in History and Fiction: Hume, Fielding and Gibbon*, Princeton, New Jersey: Princeton University Press, 1970

Burrow, J.A., *Edward Gibbon*, Oxford and New York: Oxford University Press, 1985

Craddock, Patricia B., *Young Edward Gibbon, Gentleman of Letters*, Baltimore: Johns Hopkins University Press, 1982

Craddock, Patricia B., *Edward Gibbon, Luminous Historian, 1772–1794*, Baltimore: Johns Hopkins University Press, 1989

Low, David M., *Edward Gibbon, 1737–1794*, London: Chatto & Windus, 1937

Porter, Roy, *Edward Gibbon: Making History*, London: Weidenfeld & Nicolson, 1988

Womersley, David, *The Transformation of "The Decline and Fall of the Roman Empire"*, Cambridge and New York: Cambridge University Press, 1988

The past generation has witnessed dramatic changes in the quality, quantity, and nature of Gibbon scholarship. His *The Decline and Fall of the Roman Empire* still attracts most attention, but whereas it used to be acknowledged as a masterpiece of English prose, then largely left to the historians, it is now subjected to repeated close readings. Furthermore, the historians' former tendency to judge *The Decline and Fall* by the standards of their own day has been recognised as anachronistic. Alert response to linguistic detail and extensive research into Gibbon's intellectual background enable readers to measure Gibbon's true stature by his contribution to eighteenth-century historical thought, and to see how his style is intimately associated with his subject. LOW's classic biography remains an excellent starting-point. Many of the more recent critics acknowledge their debt to him.

BOND's examination of *The Decline and Fall* demonstrates the benefits to be derived from applying the techniques of literary criticism to a work that, being neither novel, poem, play nor essay, is often automatically excluded from the literary canon. Bond deals systematically with such topics as "The Argument", "Narrative", "Character", "Satire", and "Language". Every aspect is related to Bond's perception of the work as a unified, balanced, moving, and ultimately optimistic prose epic: "in Gibbon's understandings of the causes of the fall, we find affirmation of the values and justification of the bases of the new culture which phoenix-like sprang from the ashes of the old". Bond's greatest difficulties arise from the question of structure, which causes problems for many Gibbon scholars. Bond admits that, over the 20 years that elapsed during its composition and publication, Gibbon discovered that "the topic and scope of the undertaking were continually growing in his mind". The original outline, comprising only the fall of Rome, was "transcended" to include the subsequent recovery of Europe from the Dark Ages. Gibbon could not have foreseen the end of his history when he wrote the beginning. Nevertheless, Bond finds "a unity of form in the whole which is nothing less than astonishing".

BRAUDY's original and imaginative comparison of Gibbon with David Hume and Henry Fielding explores changing and overlapping concepts of history and fiction in the eighteenth century, setting valuable interdisciplinary precedents. Braudy sees *The Decline and Fall* as a dynamic work, in which Gibbon successfully attempts to find a suitable "narrative voice", which he then uses as an "interpretative tool". Braudy believes both Hume and Gibbon changed their own assumptions about the nature of the past and the historian's role as intermediary between past and present. Yet, like Bond, Braudy still maintains his faith in the structural integrity of *The Decline and Fall*.

BOWERSOCK, CLIVE, and GRAUBARD have amassed an impressive array of international scholarship. Distinguished contributors in many fields, from Islam to the history of art, have co-operated to enrich the cultural and biographical context for the study of *The Decline and Fall* and its author. Many chapters cover material inaccessible or uncongenial to Gibbon; others offer important reassessments of Gibbon's judgments on familiar issues. In every case, however, emphasis is laid on understanding Gibbon better, rather than on filling gaps in *The Decline and Fall*.

CRADDOCK's two volumes together form the best existing biography of Gibbon. Unlike previous biographers, who have all relied on the fifth draft of Gibbon's *Memoirs*, Craddock uses the sixth, written "on a new plan, one that had room for his human inconsistencies and irrelevancies". Gibbon's lesser-known works also receive due consideration. She offers both a "guide" through the "riches of Gibboniana" and an "interpretation" of her findings. Her first volume traces the emotional and intellectual struggles of a man who "both achieved Augustanism and had it thrust upon him". Her second covers Gibbon's later career, entwining the mundane contingencies of his life with the composition of his great work. Craddock also shows how Gibbon's attitude to history changed over this period, as he realised that "the historian must not only select and embellish, but, through his invention of the connecting tissues between facts and sources, discover". She has triumphantly succeeded in her aim to "portray the man as well as the historian".

BURROW's contribution to the "Past Masters" series is a lucid, sensibly balanced introduction to Gibbon's life and works. He presents Gibbon as the author of two masterpieces – the "vast canvas" of *The Decline and Fall* and the "exquisite miniature", the *Memoirs*. Although Burrows recommends Craddock (1982) for further reading, so must be aware of her reservations, he uses the fifth draft of the *Memoirs* as his text, pointing out that Gibbon's publication plans were "equivocal". He carefully defines Gibbon's role as philosophic historian – no mere theorist, but "first an antiquarian and a lover of history".

PORTER offers a "study of Gibbon as historian: a product of his own time, and an enduring voice in our own". Appropriately for inclusion in this series, entitled "Historians on Historians", the book is packed with information on Gibbon's historical methods and intellectual milieu. Porter claims that Gibbon was born in an age when "the past was almost too alive, too 'present' to permit great histories". Following the growing interdisciplinary trend, Porter supports historical argument with verbal analysis: "Gibbon weaves his own interpretation into the very texture of his words, tone and narrative".

Like Bond and Braudy, WOMERSLEY is primarily a literary critic. Nevertheless, his treatment of eighteenth-century historiography and Gibbon's sources displays broad knowledge, keen vision, and meticulous command of detail. His reading of Gibbon's text is remarkably sensitive, his own prose superb. Most significantly, he faces the implications of Gibbon's changing views on human nature and historical causation. For Womersley, *The Decline and Fall* is not "a flawless example of neo-classical expertise", but "a work which even much preparatory rough-hewing could not bring to balance and stability".

CAROLYN D. WILLIAMS

Gilman, Charlotte Perkins 1860–1935

American novelist, short-story writer, and essayist

Ceplair, Larry (ed.), *Charlotte Perkins Gilman: A Nonfiction Reader*, New York: Columbia University Press, 1991

Degler, Carl N., "Charlotte Perkins Gilman on the Theory and Practice of Feminism", in *American Quarterly*, 8, Spring 1956

Hill, Mary A., *Charlotte Perkins Gilman: The Making of a Radical Feminist 1860–1896*, Philadelphia: Temple University Press, 1980

Lane, Ann J., *To "Herland" and Beyond: The Life and Work of Charlotte Perkins Gilman*, New York: Pantheon, 1990

Meyering, Sheryl L. (ed.), *Charlotte Perkins Gilman: The Woman and Her Work*, Ann Arbor, Michigan: UMI Research Press, 1989

Scharnhorst, Gary, *Charlotte Perkins Gilman*, Boston: Twayne, 1985

In 1956 Professor Carl N. Degler wrote that Charlotte Perkins Gilman had "suffered a neglect in American intellectual history difficult to explain". Scholars responded slowly to Degler's call, and it required the subsequent emergence of feminist criticism to fuel the rediscovery of Gilman began by Degler. All Gilman's major works have now been reprinted, yet critical attention has until recently remained focused only on Gilman's most well-known works, namely "The Yellow Wallpaper" and *Herland*, neglecting the enormous range of her *oeuvre*. There are still few book-length critical analyses of her writing, although there are many articles in leading literary journals. Perhaps the single most indispensable contribution to the study of Gilman was Gary Scharnhorst's bibliography (*Charlotte Perkins Gilman: A Bibliography*, 1985). The pervasive and enduring critical tendency has been towards bio-criticism, while critical analysis of the formal and strategic properties of her work remains sparse.

DEGLER's work was the first critical assessment of Gilman published since her death in 1935, and as a result the long overdue rediscovery of Gilman as an important turn-of-the-century American writer was underway. His essay is an appreciative overview of Gilman's main ideas, providing a valuable introduction to her work. While keen to demonstrate the value of Gilman's contribution (Degler sees her as anticipating modern writers such as Simone de Beauvoir, Margaret Mead, and Ashley Montagu), Degler nevertheless notes some of the weaknesses in her thinking too. He cogently sums up some of the contradictions in the relation between theory and practice in her work:

> Her freedom from preconceptions and traditions allowed her to make fresh and often penetrating examinations of the human institutions around her. But that same attitude of mind also prevented her from appreciating the tenacious hold which prejudice, tradition, and sentiment had upon most of the men and women she was attempting to convince. Hence when she came to offer means to attain goals she set, her rationalism and radicalism, so incisive in analysis, merely served to vitiate her realism.

Unlike later critics, Degler focuses much more on Gilman's work than her life, paying attention to the latter only in footnotes.

HILL's book was the first full-scale, archival-based study to appear, and is the first volume of a projected two-volume study. In it Hill makes extensive use of documents from the Gilman collection at the Schlesinger Library, including letters from Gilman to her first and second husbands. She also focuses on Gilman's relationship with her parents, her female friends, and with other significant figures, and relates her life to her work. Hill sees the seeds of Gilman's radical feminism as being rooted in an early struggle for independence, self-assertion, and self-respect. Her analyses are detailed and thoughtful, choosing not to employ psychological categories.

SCHARNHORST's study is a welcome analysis of Gilman's written work, and is an indispensable contribution to Gilman scholarship. His view of Gilman's imaginative work is that "... her literary theory was, fundamentally, an unapologetic defense of didacticism". In doing so, Scharnhorst paved the way for later critics, by analysing Gilman's didacticism without condescension. Scharnhorst shows Gilman's writing as vital and relevant to the society in which it was written and to which it was addressed.

MEYERING's collection was the first edition of critical essays on Gilman, and her avowed claim is "to do justice to the enormous range and amount of imaginative work Gilman left us. Each article maps a way for readers to approach such a large body of fiction and poetry". Carl Degler's early article is reprinted, and Mary A. Hill provides an essay, which is a distillation of the central arguments of her earlier book. While "The Yellow Wallpaper" and *Herland* are amply covered, there are also articles on Gilman's verse, her novel *What Diantha Did*, and her connections with Walt Whitman. Particularly valuable is Christopher P. Wilson's analysis of *Herland*'s literary devices and its implicit commentary on art, gender, and property. Wilson shows how Gilman's effort to counter what she saw as a bourgeois and masculine aesthetic often had elusive and paradoxical consequences.

LANE follows in the dominant bio-critical tradition of Gilman scholarship, reading her work in the light of her life. Her focus is Gilman's inner life and its development, hence the book is structured around the central relationships in Gilman's life: it begins with her father and mother, includes three close and intimate women friends, two husbands, the neurologist who treated her, and concludes with her daughter. Embedded within these chapters is a two-part section on Gilman's work, giving an account of all her major writings and ideas. Lane's work is significant not only because of its comprehensive account of Gilman's life and work, but also because it exemplifies the still-dominant tendencies of Gilman scholarship – in its emphasis on the paramount significance of Gilman's heterosexual relationships (as opposed to her relationships with women); in its use of the public-private conflict as the paradigm for Gilman's life and work; and in its neglect of Gilman's formal and aesthetic concerns.

CEPLAIR's edition includes significant critical and analytic essays accompanying each section of Gilman's previously uncollected non-fiction works. His Introduction begins the process of rooting Gilman in her intellectual milieu, which continues throughout the volume, and includes a valuable overview of the critical response to Gilman's work. Each section of Gilman's essays (divided into "The Early Years 1860–1889", "The Club and Lecture Years 1889–1898", "The Book-Writing Years 1898–1909", "The Forerunner Years 1909–1916", and "The Last Years 1917–1935") is preceded by its own valuable introduction, outlining Gilman's intellectual influences and directions of thought. Ceplair says "there is no corpus of fin-de-siècle theorizing in the United States in which so many concepts intertwine", and he invaluably shows how Positive Darwinism, the social gospel, social welfare, feminism, socialism (Bellamy's Nationalism and Fabianism), populism, and progressivism all merge in Gilman's thinking.

VAL GOUGH

Ginsberg, Allen 1926–

American poet

Burns, Glen, *Great Poets Howl: A Study of Allen Ginsberg's Poetry, 1943–1955*, New York: Peter Lang, 1983
Hyde, Lewis (ed.), *On the Poetry of Allen Ginsberg*, Ann Arbor: University of Michigan Press, 1984
Merrill, Thomas F., *Allen Ginsberg*, New York: Twayne, 1969, revised (Boston) 1988
Miles, Barry, *Ginsberg: A Biography*, New York: Simon & Schuster, 1989; London: Viking, 1989
Schumacher, Michael, *Dharma Lion: A Critical Biography of Allen Ginsberg*, New York: St Martin's Press, 1992
Tytell, John, *Naked Angels: The Lives and Literature of the Beat Generation*, New York: McGraw-Hill, 1976

There are few full-length monograph studies of Ginsberg's poetry, although many smaller articles and essays have appeared in small-press journals and magazines. Of those full-length critical studies that do exist, BURNS produces a sophisticated and intricate reading of Ginsberg's poetry within the context of the poststructuralist ideas of writers like Jacques Derrida, Jean-François Lyotard, Jacques Lacan, Gilles Deleuze, and Félix Guattari, and the theorists of the Frankfurt School. This study construes "Howl" as a seminal postmodernist work, and a work in which Ginsberg achieves the finest articulation of his individual voice. In five chapters, Burns traces a biographical and cultural context for Ginsberg's poetry, and then moves through Ginsberg's early poetry written around the time of his Blake vision, the poetry of *Empty Mirror* inspired by William Carlos Williams, close attention to the poem "Siesta in Xbalba", and then a chapter devoted to "Howl". "Howl" is considered to be a significant break with traditional modes of poetry, and is treated as a key event in the contemporary struggle for artistic and political freedom.

Unlike Burns's closely argued approach, HYDE's book is a collection of critical perspectives on Ginsberg's writing, although it models itself on the trajectory of Ginsberg's early career. Beginning with various early letters between Marianne Moore, William Carlos Williams, and Ginsberg, the collection moves through responses to "Howl" in the 1950s by various critics, critical essays on *"Kaddish" and Other Poems*, and then onto responses to more recent poems in the 1960s, with a final retrospective conclusion. This is a large and substantial body of critical views, which includes even the FBI among its list of many respected critics, authors, poets, and other contributors. Reflections on biographical, political, cultural, and spiritual settings of the work by such people as Lawrence Ferlinghetti, Czesław Miłosz, Robert Bly, Ekbert Faas, Hayden Carruth, and John Tytell, are situated alongside documents as evidence for those settings, like *Time* articles, government files, and memoirs of specific occasions, such as the day Timothy Leary gave Ginsberg hallucinogenic mushrooms. The paucity of contemporaneous information concerning Ginsberg as political poet, practising Buddhist, and his activity in gay politics is acknowledged by Hyde as a limitation of the book, to be rectified by further future research.

MERRILL's study is a critical work on Ginsberg's poetry, which tends to suggest that it is more therapeutic than artistic. He begins with a biographical and socio-historical study of Ginsberg, arguing that the posture of disaffiliation and disengagement characterised the Beat ideology and movement, and considering how these personal and intellectual traits positioned Ginsberg and his associations with William Burroughs, Jack Kerouac, and Neal Cassady. There follows an account of the development of his life through experimentation with drugs, his gradual attraction to, and exploration of, Buddhism, and how these influenced Ginsberg's strategies of writing. Delineating the context of Charles Olson's and William Carlos Williams' poetics, Merrill shows how a text like "Howl" draws upon, and then pushes beyond, the limits of their poetic theories as Ginsberg and Kerouac gradually developed their ideas of "Spontaneous Prose", although Merrill oddly denies that "Howl" was a new departure from Ginsberg's earlier poetry. Although rather orthodox in his critical approach, Merrill does acknowledge that the poetry's open form cannot be adequately understood by "New Critics or any breed of absolutists". The book contains detailed readings of all of Ginsberg's major works, concluding that in Ginsberg's persistent reference to the holiness of the self, the *Collected Poems* "amounts to nothing less than an autohagiography".

Also focusing on his desire for saintliness, TYTELL's study tends to explore the difficulties and struggles that Ginsberg had in finding a new poetic form, as well as in coming to terms with his homosexuality. Yet it is the critical, rather than the biographical, interest that dominates this study of the Beat Generation and the trio Burroughs, Ginsberg, and Kerouac in particular. The book focuses on John Clellon Holmes's image of "a broken circuit to suggest the lack of connection to the immediate present felt by the members of his generation". Situated within this social and cultural alienation, the long chapter on "Allen Ginsberg and the Messianic Tradition" concentrates on the literary and conceptual affiliations of Ginsberg with William Blake, Walt Whitman, William Carlos Williams, and surrealism. It also discusses the way in which Ginsberg "used drugs as an aid to releasing blocked aspects of his consciousness which are expressed in his poetry, like the 'Moloch' vision in 'Howl'". Although Tytell perceives Ginsberg's poetry to be "a record of surprising conversions", he concludes that it exists as a "demonstration that poetry need not be disembodied, removed from a natural base in chant and song". Ginsberg's significant achievement lies partly in his ability to use "the rhythmic qualities of language to change ordinary conditioning so that new perceptions can occur".

The other type of book-length study is biographical. MILES's massive study is an intimate and highly detailed portrait of a life, which draws extensively on Ginsberg's journals and correspondence, as well as interviews. This study elaborates on several periods of significance in Ginsberg's life: his student life and the early association with Kerouac and Burroughs and his support for their work; the movement from visionary poet and *enfant terrible* of the Beat Generation to prize-winning elder statesman, without any compromising of the integrity of his radical politics; the enthusiasm for exploring the properties of hallucinogenic drugs, and his subsequent interest in spiritual enlightenment in Buddhism; the peace activist who sought to calm anti-war demonstrations in 1968 by chanting peace mantras; and the activist for gay rights and a tireless advocate of free expression in both his poetry and his private life. In addition, the book discusses his relationships with Neal Cassady and Gregory Corso, and the close on-and-off relationship with Peter Orlovsky. The encounters with such writers as William Carlos Williams, Ezra Pound, and W.H. Auden are charted, as are significant events in Ginsberg's association with the Beat Generation, such as the now famous Six Gallery reading of "Howl" in 1955, the emergence of the San Francisco Renaissance, and Ginsberg's associations with Bob Dylan and the Beatles.

SCHUMACHER's vast study is the other major biographical source, which combines critical readings of Ginsberg's major writings with a wide range of interesting photographs. It concludes in 1981 for a variety of reasons, although there is a Postscript summarizing Ginsberg's writing and political activities in subsequent years, which supplements Miles's biography as well. Schumacher's study is just as large as Miles's work, and as equally well documented; and the two together offer invaluable historical contexts for the Beat Generation's activities.

TIM S. WOODS

Gissing, George 1857–1903

English novelist, short-story writer, and essayist

Collie, Michael, *The Alien Art: A Critical Study of George Gissing's Novels*, Folkestone, Kent: Dawson, 1979; Hamden, Connecticut: Archon Books, 1979

Federico, Annette, *Masculine Identity in Hardy and Gissing*, Rutherford, New Jersey: Fairleigh Dickinson University Press, 1991; London: Associated University Presses, 1991

Goode, John, *George Gissing: Ideology and Fiction*, London: Vision Press, 1978; New York: Barnes & Noble, 1979

Korg, Jacob, *George Gissing: A Critical Biography*, Seattle: University of Washington Press, 1963; London: Methuen, 1965

Poole, Adrian, *Gissing in Context*, London: Methuen, 1975; Totowa, New Jersey: Rowman & Littlefield, 1975

Tindall, Gillian, *The Born Exile: George Gissing*, London: Temple Smith, 1974; New York: Harcourt Brace Jovanovich, 1974

Interest in the unusual facts of George Gissing's life rather than the merits of his work tended to dominate the early commentaries. Until the 1930s and even beyond, Gissing's novels were accepted as interesting failures, and his life and personality were used by friends and critics to explain what they perceived as his literary shortcomings. From the 1930s more discriminating voices begin to emerge. Virginia Woolf claimed that his novels had "life and completeness" ("The Novels of George Gissing", *Times Literary Supplement*, 11 January 1912), and in 1948 George Orwell wrote that "England has produced very few better novelists" ("George Gissing", in *London Magazine*, June 1960). His status as a writer has grown steadily since then, and several of his many novels, notably *The Nether World* (1889), *New Grub Street* (1891), *Born in Exile* (1892), and *The Odd Women* (1893), have received critical acclaim.

KORG's work marks the beginning of serious critical interest in Gissing. He takes what was by then the established biographical approach, but uses the information scrupulously to set Gissing's work in context and to explore the literary and social forces of the late nineteenth century. Further information about Gissing has come to light since Korg wrote his book, but it remains a valuable contribution to Gissing studies. His conclusion, that Gissing's dominant theme is "the destruction of human character in the crushing mill of social evils", and that "doubt and curiosity seemed to liberate" his literary talents, has provided a sound foundation for further critical examination.

TINDALL also makes Gissing's life the starting point of her analysis; but in an original and idiosyncratic book, she makes vigorous connections between biographical information, psychological analysis, and literary speculation. She brings a female – though not feminist – perspective to bear on his work by questioning the conditions of his life in relation to his literary production and develops her discussion of his powerful female characters through information about his wives and women friends. She prefers the shot in the dark to rigorous literary criticism, but her comment that "when you have said that Gissing's books are often flawed by behaviour on the part of the character which despite much exposition, the plot never quite manages to explain, you have named the peculiar quality in Gissing's own story" also articulates what other critics working from a biographical viewpoint have tried to say, before and since.

POOLE was a significant figure in the Gissing "revival" in the 1970s. He still follows a broadly chronological structure, but he is more concerned to place Gissing in the context of the late Victorian publishing world and the literary debates of that time. Poole uses Lacanian theory to foreground the role of "the city" in Gissing's work and its influence on him as a writer. His aim – to bring a theoretical unity to the study of Gissing's novels – is a worthwhile one and this book is full of useful information and textual insights. His most valuable contribution, however, is to advance Gissing studies by his recognition of approaches other than the biographical. His book is probably best read for its parts than for its elaborately constructed overall argument.

GOODE's criticism also lifts Gissing out of the biographical trap. In his Marxist analysis he uses Gissing's work to investigate the way fiction that draws on urban material is compelled to reproduce or confront the ideology embodied in urban structures. This is not an easy book to read, and Goode's prose, particularly in the earlier part of the book, can appear unnecessarily impenetrable. Even so, it is well worth the effort. Goode convincingly demonstrates the link between the writer's creativity and his historical context in his discussions of Gissing's treatment of the city. He is at his best in the analysis of individual novels. *The Nether World*, one of Gissing's most written-about novels, is brilliantly illuminated here as a "deterministic hell". Equally challenging is Goode's discussion of *The Odd Women*. This is not necessarily a book readers can expect to agree with, but it has not been bettered as a political analysis of the unique impact of Gissing's writing.

COLLIE expands on an important but neglected aspect of Gissing's work. Although references to his interest in European writers and philosophers occur frequently throughout Gissing criticism, the novels are usually considered to be in the British tradition. Collie argues that Gissing should be seen as a European, and that the tensions in his narrative art are evidence of an artistic struggle to bring together contemporary Victorian taste and European perceptions. This position enables Collie to range across a variety of issues, and his book is useful as one of the first to build constructively on earlier critical works. His consideration of Gissing's textual revisions are very welcome and useful, and his laudatory summary, when he claims that "he [Gissing] succeeded in perfecting a means by which his social and psychological interests could be integrated in convincing, but also enigmatic fictions", is a valid conclusion to his argument.

FEDERICO's is, to date, the most recent full-length study of Gissing, and one which Gissing shares most appropriately with his contemporary Thomas Hardy, although the argument as a whole could have made more of this potentially productive link. It is an interesting book for several reasons. Federico places her work within gender studies, and addresses the question of masculinity in Gissing's novels since, as she argues, "the male novelist of the 1880s and 1890s created male characters which are structured in ambivalence". This is a promising way into Gissing's work, although the book is not entirely satisfactory. Federico claims to do a "close reading of the text", but she does so through questionable cultural stereotypes – Nasty Boy, Pathological Gentleman, and so on. However, it is good news for future Gissing criticism that Federico breaks away from the survey approach to give a few novels – in this case *In Year of Jubilee* (1894), *The Odd Women*, and *The Whirlpool* (1897) – detailed treatment.

LYNNE HAPGOOD

Godwin, William 1756–1836

English novelist and prose writer

Clark, John P., *The Philosophical Anarchism of William Godwin*, Princeton, New Jersey: Princeton University Press, 1977

Clemit, Pamela, *The Godwinian Novel: The Rational Fictions of Godwin, Brockden Brown, Mary Shelley*, Oxford: Clarendon Press, 1993; New York: Oxford University Press, 1993

Locke, Don, *A Fantasy of Reason: The Life and Thought of William Godwin*, London and Boston: Routledge & Kegan Paul, 1980

Marshall, Peter H., *William Godwin*, New Haven, Connecticut: Yale University Press, 1984

Paul, C. Kegan, *William Godwin: His Friends and Contemporaries*, 2 vols., London: 1876; reprinted, New York: AMS Press, 2 vols., 1970

Smith, Elton Edward, and Esther Greenwell Smith, *William Godwin*, New York: Twayne, 1965

Critical interest in William Godwin, who was a wildly successful and influential political and social theorist in the1790s, faded within a decade to a controlled whisper as consumers of political theory turned away from radical texts such as his. *Political Justice* and his first novel, *Caleb Williams*, were read as companion pieces then, and generate the most critical interest still, although Godwin also produced plays, histories, essays, and children's books in his long career. His experiments with the novel form are widely considered to have been influential with early mystery writers, though modern readers will have difficulty discerning such an influence in Godwin's sometimes pompous approach to storytelling, so sharply does it contrast to the glibness of Charles Dickens, and the sleek, cerebral sparseness of the better modern mystery novelists. The family line is nevertheless detectable within plot elements, most notably in the long-distance pursuit and legal imbroglio, pioneered by Godwin, that have set many a mystery-novel stage since. Similar claims have been made for Godwin's influence upon early socialists and anarchists. The threat of government intrusion into the privacy of the politically unempowered individual, a major concern to Godwin, found an audience within proletarian movements throughout the century, as his works were translated first into French, then later into Spanish and Russian.

Much critical attention has centered in recent decades upon Godwin's persistent promotion of social theories which often lacked a strong base in public opinion, particularly within his novels and plays, an approach which was, of course, popular with the pamphleteers of the eighteenth century, and still familiar to late-century readers. His was a very different didacticism from that which had in the past been employed to foster normative morality in the middle and lower orders of British society. Biographers and critics alike make much of the psychological bridge from early Calvinism to late atheism in succeeding editions of Godwin's works, relying heavily upon correspondence, prefaces, and contemporary reviews of particular editions. Mary Wollstonecraft scholars perform similar psychological analysis upon his biography of Mary, his first wife, who is arguably a source of much of the current interest in Godwin.

His political theories and associations, however, were more important to nineteenth-century critics than his literary accomplishments in the melding of political discourse and fictional narrative. By the time PAUL published his biography of Godwin in 1876, the dust had settled upon the Jacobins, yet the delicacy with which he handles Godwin's radical associations is an indicator of the power of former instabilities to unsettle the critical and biographical narrative. This work is particularly useful in understanding the literary climate within which Godwin sought to use the novel as an instrument of social change, and is fascinating in itself for its rhetorical stance and near contemporary relationship to Godwin and his circle.

As late as 1965, the SMITHS noted a lack of interest in Godwin's texts among literary critics. *Political Justice* was still being read by philosophers and historians, but Godwin's distinctive style and radical re-invention of the novel's role in social relations was all but ignored by literary scholars. Only a few years later, the rediscovery of Mary Wollstonecraft would improve Godwin's stock as a spokesperson for individual rights, and renew interest in reaching beyond the canon to revive critical interest in the social novels, which proliferated in the late eighteenth and early nineteenth centuries, were immensely popular for a spell, then faded. The Smiths' work serves as a re-introduction of Godwin the novelist, including valuable summaries of his lesser-known works. Their well-documented anecdotes of Godwin's bohemian lifestyle, perhaps meant to give Godwin relevancy in the 1960s, provide valuable context and motivations for his least plausible characters.

LOCKE has combined biography with an in-depth appraisal of Godwin's philosophy. He reads Godwin's fiction from a political scientist's perspective, although Godwin's well-documented personal failings are here presented as well. He proposes an interesting reassessment of the "Mary Wollstonecraft" chapter in particular, casting it in practical rather than romantic or psychoanalytical terms. This chapter was first written in the years closely following her death, was appropriated by Wollstonecraft biographers during her induction into the canon in the late 1960s, and has never quite fully returned to the lesser significance it deserves in an examination of Godwin's contribution to English literature and thought. Godwin's fame after publication of *Political Justice* and his fiction by its very nature invited response, and Locke extensively examines the evolution of the Godwin dialectic and its influence upon his later works. The result is a narrative framed by succeeding editions of Godwin's work, which reveal the evolution of his thought, the gradual decline of his power.

MARSHALL's biography picks up on the traditional biographical narrative by a disciple a century after Paul, and with access to additional documentation. It is useful as a single source on Godwin, but troubled by a rehabilitating tone. Consulted in tandem with Locke's critical biography, a narratively complete Godwin emerges, necessary to any productive reading of Godwinian texts.

CLEMIT proposes a comparative grouping of Godwin, Mary Shelley, and Charles Brockden Brown's fiction into a sub-genre of social fiction, the "Godwinian novel", because each partakes of a "common pattern of literary, philosophical, and political interchange", the complexity of which had to have commenced a generation before Brown and Shelley with the completely articulated philosophy of Godwin. Her analysis includes extensive re-examination of the contemporary criticism, considerable examination of biographical and intellectual influences, parallel innovations in other narrative modes, and a final placement of the Godwinians in contrast to their successors in the novel form.

CLARK devotes himself entirely to Godwin's theories, avoids critical comment on specific texts, but is included here because he is an accessible source of theoretical explication, necessary when philosophers turn to fiction. Godwin's work has little life beyond the context and content of his theories. Godwin's style sometimes falters, making meaning difficult to access without help such as that provided here.

CLARA ELIZABETH SPEER

Golding, William 1911–1993

English novelist

Boyd, Stephen J., *The Novels of William Golding*, Brighton, Sussex: Harvester Press, 1988, revised 1990; New York: St Martin's Press, 1988

Crompton, Don, *A View from the Spire: William Golding's Later Novels*, Oxford: Blackwell, 1985

Johnston, Arnold, *Of Earth and Darkness: The Novels of William Golding*, completed and edited by Julia Briggs, Columbia: University of Missouri Press, 1980

Kinkead-Weekes, Mark, and Ian Gregor, *William Golding: A Critical Study*, London: Faber & Faber, 1967, revised (also Boston), 1984; New York: Harcourt Brace, 1968

Redpath, Philip, *William Golding: A Structural Reading of His Fiction*, London: Vision Press, 1986; Totowa, New Jersey: Barnes & Noble, 1986

Tiger, Virginia, *William Golding: The Dark Fields of Discovery*, London: Calder & Boyars, 1974; Atlantic Highlands, New Jersey: Humanities Press, 1974

Although William Golding is still best known for his first novel *Lord of the Flies* (1954) he was, at the time of his death, also the author of ten other novels, a play, two volumes of essays, a travel book, and a collection of short stories. Golding's later fiction and his work in genres other than the novel rarely receive the same degree of critical attention that is, even now, given to the early novels, while almost all of the considerable body of critical writing on Golding's early work dwells on his fascination with the concept of evil. Overall, the great majority of Golding's critics are preoccupied with the author's interest in moral and spiritual issues, although the moral perspective from which the novels are evaluated tends to be that of orthodox Christianity. Golding has tended to attract critics who enthusiastically admire his work, although some feminist scholars deplore what they see as his one-dimensional portrayal of women.

TIGER's book focuses upon Golding's first five novels, although a brief concluding chapter offers appraisals of *The Pyramid* and *The Scorpion God*. The book places a strong emphasis on the mythic dimension of Golding's work, and provides a convincing evaluation of its structural complexity. Tiger is also interested in the intertextual nature of Golding's writing, and devotes considerable space to assessing the "backgrounded" text which, in most cases, Golding is "rewriting". The chronological structure of Tiger's book allows her to chart the increasing sophistication of Golding's narrative technique while also offering the opportunity to note the constant preoccupations of his fiction.

JOHNSTON's study considers all of Golding's novels up to, and including, *Darkness Visible* (1979). He relates Golding's life to his work and gives very detailed and extremely close readings of all the texts he discusses. He is particularly interested in the developing power of Golding's technique and in the recurrence of what he sees as his principal themes – rationalism, evil, and the moral and spiritual dualism of humanity. The book contains useful biographical information, and has an impressively detailed bibliography of primary and secondary sources. Johnston has a keen eye throughout for both Golding's strengths and his weaknesses, noting, for example, that "Golding's use of other literary works as ironic parallels to his own, and his apparent requirement of a protagonist who is a foil to his own vision, is at once his most striking limitation and a major source of his unique power".

KINKEAD-WEEKES and GREGOR's book was first published in 1967, but revised in 1984, and the new edition contains evaluations of *Darkness Visible* and *Rites of Passage*. Their book is, however, emphatically concerned with Golding's early fiction. Like almost all of Golding's critics the authors offer close readings of all the novels, and devote considerable time to evaluations of the texts Golding is "rewriting"; but unlike many critics, they are particularly interested in the formal properties of his fiction, as opposed to the ideas the novels might contain, and they focus intently upon imagery, structure, and, especially Golding's experimentations with narrative perspective. The authors persistently stress the role of the reader, and preface the book by noting that "the critical reading of a contemporary is not merely a matter of sensing the evolution in the work, but of becoming aware of the evolution in our own responsiveness as readers".

CROMPTON's book is the first to look specifically at the later fiction, and he offers detailed readings of six of Golding's novels, from *The Spire* (1964) to *The Paper Men* (1984). Crompton's constant reference to other authors constitutes a persuasive attempt to place Golding's work within the larger context of English literature. The book is theoretically uninflected in a way that is, overall, characteristic of critical writing on Golding's work, and Crompton's primary concern throughout the book is with the moral vision he discerns in Golding's fiction. The chapter on *Rites of Passage* incorporates an evaluation of the anthropologist Arnold van Gennep's influential work *The Rites of Passage*.

REDPATH's book is the most uncharacteristic of all the full-length texts published so far on Golding. This is a highly theoretical study of all of Golding's fiction up to, and including, *The Paper Men*, which employs methods indebted to the ideas of, in particular, Roland Barthes, Jacques Derrida, and Jacques Lacan. Redpath, again uniquely for a critic of Golding's work, discards chronology in his assessment and groups the novels according to what he sees as shared characteristics. Above all, Redpath is interested in Golding's use of language, and prefaces his study with the comment that "Golding's art is an art of discovery, but not an art that seeks to explain. The discovery it makes is that the universe is inexplicable and cannot be wholly described in words, and yet words are all the novelist has with which to describe the universe".

Although BOYD discusses Golding's collections of essays and his short stories, his book is principally concerned with all of Golding's fiction – the revised edition contains evaluations of Golding's last two novels. Like Crompton, Boyd is particularly interested in the moral and spiritual aspects of the fiction, and he also pays considerable attention to Golding's use of backgrounded texts. Boyd's approach is unashamedly old-fashioned, and the names of other English novelists appear far more frequently in his book than do the names of French theorists. The textual cross-referencing is extensive and Boyd consistently argues that while Golding is a writer of powerful originality, his work is demonstrably part of an English literary tradition.

KEVIN MCCARRON

Goldsmith, Oliver 1730–1774

Irish poet, dramatist, novelist, and essayist

Ginger, John, *The Notable Man: The Life and Times of Oliver Goldsmith*, London: Hamish Hamilton, 1977

Hopkins, Robert H., *The True Genius of Oliver Goldsmith*, Baltimore: Johns Hopkins University Press, 1969

Kent, Elizabeth E., *Goldsmith and His Booksellers*, Ithaca, New York: Cornell University Press, 1933; London: Oxford University Press, 1933

Quintana, Ricardo, *Oliver Goldsmith: A Georgian Study*, New York: Macmillan, 1967; London: Weidenfeld & Nicolson, 1969

Sells, Arthur Lytton, *Goldsmith: His Life and Works*, London: Allen & Unwin, 1974

Swarbrick, Andrew (ed.), *The Art of Oliver Goldsmith*, Totowa, New Jersey: Barnes & Noble, 1984; London: Vision Press, 1984

Taylor, Richard C., *Goldsmith as Journalist*, Rutherford, New Jersey: Fairleigh Dickinson University Press, 1993; London: Associated University Presses, 1993

Wardle, Ralph W., *Oliver Goldsmith*, Lawrence: University of Kansas Press, 1957

Twentieth-century Goldsmith scholars, like his eighteenth-century friends, tend to regard him with affection, admiration, exasperation, and bewilderment. The man and his works are equally resistant to categorisation. Biographers have to contend with mysterious gaps in the information about his early life: a shortage of documentary evidence is exacerbated by his habitual disregard for truth. Where reliable reports of his speech and actions exist, they are hard to reconcile with any consistent interpretation of his character: he is often regarded as a psychological enigma. Critics face two main problems. Firstly, Goldsmith's characteristic evasiveness and frequent employment in anonymous journalism make it hard to settle the canon of his works. Secondly, the versatility of his talents, combined with his failure to assemble a substantial body of writing in the genres normally covered by conventional literary criticism, encourage a fragmentary approach rather than an overall perspective. His plays, for example, are often considered in conjunction with those of Richard Brinsley Sheridan. Nevertheless, there are some excellent surveys of his life and works, while some of the more selective studies offer fascinating insights into various facets of Goldsmith's career. The 1960s and 1970s saw controversy over Goldsmith's drama and *The Vicar of Wakefield*, his only acknowledged novel: was he a sentimentalist or a satirical master of covert irony? More recently, the diversity of his achievement has provoked a more innovative response, which has widened the boundaries of conventional literary criticism.

KENT's book provides a brief but trenchant account of Goldsmith's observations on the book trade, followed by a series of short biographies of the men who commissioned and published his works. They often had strained relations with Goldsmith, who wrote voluminously and received generous advances, but had chronic trouble with debt and deadlines. The book provides much information about the booksellers "who rose to prominence in the Age of Authors". It is an early but important example of a critical approach that has since become much more popular: a study of the connections between a writer's work and material conditions of production.

WARDLE produced the twentieth century's first attempt at a scholarly biography of Goldsmith: it is still a standard work. He portrays Goldsmith as a misunderstood figure, whose reputation for idiotic speech and actions, apparently inconsistent with his brilliance on paper, was created by literal-minded listeners who failed to recognise his humour. He was "a jigger fallen among goons". Yet his often outrageous behaviour was inspired by genuine insecurity, envy, and frustration. This anomalous nature affected his writings, which can be variously interpreted as ironic or sentimental.

QUINTANA is more interested in Goldsmith's greatness as a writer than his personal problems: he was "a genius and the greatest master of comedy to appear during the second half of the century". He claims the Age of Johnson is also the Age of Goldsmith. He examines the full range of Goldsmith's works, setting them in their Georgian context, depicting Goldsmith as a subtly ironic artist in full control of his faculties, "no more at the mercy of his private experience than of the material he found in books".

HOPKINS examines all aspects of Goldsmith's works except his drama, using close explication to illustrate the elegance, moral urgency, and persuasive power of his verse and prose. Determined to "place Goldsmith back on the pedestal where he properly belongs", he portrays him as a flawlessly accomplished ironic satirist. The narrative inconsistencies and improbabilities in *The Vicar of Wakefield* are interpreted as strategies to make the reader recognise the narrator's folly and "hypocrisy". He denies all charges of carelessness, haste, sentimentality, or wishful thinking.

SELLS draws on an extensive and detailed knowledge of eighteenth-century Britain and France: his chief contribution to Goldsmith scholarship is his examination of Goldsmith's unacknowledged debts to French literature. He defends the Vicar of Wakefield from Hopkins' extremism, arguing that "Goldsmith had put so much of himself into his character that he cannot have wholly disliked him". His other theories are more controversial: he believes *The Vicar of Wakefield* is a parody of Laurence Sterne's *Tristram Shandy*, and that *The Good-Natured Man* is a "farcical parody of a sentimental play". Yet his ideas always merit careful consideration.

GINGER's title alludes to two eighteenth-century meanings of the same word: "notable" could mean "famous" (which Goldsmith was), or "businesslike" (which he was not). His critical biography offers psychoanalytical readings of an author whose contradictory character is inextricably bound up with his work: "if Tony Lumpkin is Goldsmith's culminating self-portrait, it is clearly a portrait of the *id* and not the *ego-ideal*".

SWARBRICK's collection of essays, all but one of them commissioned specially for this volume, is a treasury of critical excellence. Every aspect of Goldsmith's work is covered, and a wide variety of analytical approaches employed, by writers equally distinguished for their keen interest in Goldsmith and their overall grasp of eighteenth-century affairs. This is the best general introduction to Goldsmith.

TAYLOR brings twentieth-century studies of Goldsmith full circle by concentrating on the literary marketplace. He also indicates new points of departure, considering material only recently restored to the canon, and adopting a contextual approach that includes political material of a kind normally handled by historians. Goldsmith's journalistic work emerges as "a career in itself". The conditions of eighteenth-century journalism not only made his career possible, "but they became the author's primary material, out of which he constructed a narrative of authorial survival".

CAROLYN D. WILLIAMS

Gordimer, Nadine 1923–

South African novelist and short-story writer

Bazin, Nancy Topping, and Marilyn Dallman Seymour (eds.), *Conversations with Nadine Gordimer*, Jackson: University Press of Mississippi, 1990

Clingman, Stephen, *The Novels of Nadine Gordimer: History from the Inside*, London and Boston: Allen & Unwin, 1986; revised edition, Amherst: University of Massachusetts Press, 1992

Cooke, John, *The Novels of Nadine Gordimer: Private Lives/Public Landscapes*, Baton Rouge: Louisiana State University Press, 1985

Ettin, Andrew Vogel, *Betrayals of the Body Politic: The Literary Commitments of Nadine Gordimer*, Charlottesville: University Press of Virginia, 1992

King, Bruce (ed.), *The Later Fiction of Nadine Gordimer*, London: Macmillan, 1993

Newman, Judie, *Nadine Gordimer*, London and New York: Routledge, 1988

Smith, Rowland (ed.), *Critical Essays on Nadine Gordimer*, Boston: G.K. Hall, 1990

While Nadine Gordimer's works display a steady politicisation, her literary reception has undergone shifts of focus. Heralded at first for her acute, almost lyrical sensitivity, and richness of style and detail, she also attracted adverse comment for her lack of narrative muscle, and the coolness of her tone. As detachment fell away, attention focused on Gordimer's ability to sustain a tense dialectic between the personal and the political.

CLINGMAN reads her life largely in terms of the conditioning force of South Africa, situating her novels in relation to social and ideological codes, and charting their response to the history of their society. The first edition of this volume was immediately identified as the major critical study of Gordimer's novels. Essentially Clingman's new material in the second edition amounts to a prologue of 34 pages, offering a discussion of *A Sport of Nature* (a more extensive version of which occurs in King's collection, see below) and *My Son's Story*. In the former, Clingman emphasises the role of physicality as fundamental to resistance against oppression. Since apartheid divided according to the body, only the whole body can function as a sign of reintegration, a whole body resurrected from a past state of fracture.

ETTIN's approach is quite the reverse of Clingman's, yet his largely ahistorical method shares some of Clingman's concerns. For Ettin, Gordimer has always been telling the same story, a tale full of betrayal and deception, revolving around the politics of the family, the ambivalent relation of the individual to home, sensuous experience, and issues of social self identity. The pursuit of patterns of imagery and theme initially appears old-fashioned, but does yield some valuable results. A major strength is the attention paid to the short stories, generally neglected in critical studies. For Ettin, too, Gordimer sings the body electric, sexuality as the way out from the white family into social freedom. Her general distaste for feminism is persuasively read as the product of her firm socio-economic grasp: in the context of South Africa she envisages feminism as élitist, arising from the bourgeois white intellectual's refusal to face up to her true position of power. Feminism becomes a surrogate protest; the racial situation is the real.

Narrative voice, not generally discussed by Clingman or Ettin, is a special emphasis of my (NEWMAN's) study, which argues that individual novels subvert Eurocentric conventions and pose the question "Whose story is it?" quite variously: by establishing a counterpoint between male and female protagonists, white and black interpreters; by employing double plots, which re-adjust the relation between social context, text, and subtext; by the reconstruction of the implied reader; and by interrogating the linguistics of the South African cultural voice. The relation between gender and genre is a particular focus here.

In a more "personal" reading, COOKE emphasises Gordimer's unusual childhood as a decisive influence, noting the recurrent motif of the possessive mother, and suggesting that

Gordimer has endowed her private history with public associations, notably in the proposition that liberation from familial restraints requires a challenge to the dominant political order. The theme of landscape is illuminatingly evaluated.

Three collections are worthy of note. SMITH offers (in the words of the reviewer for *Choice*) "a spectrum of the most useful scholarship by major critics". The essays cover the period from 1953 to 1986, with contributors from four continents and very different critical perspectives. The editor's Introduction is a first-rate account of Gordimer's historical and artistic development. KING has brought together 15 essays, usefully discussing the later fiction. Though the collection as a whole (and some of the essays) suffers from some lack of focus, it is worth singling out Michael Wade's evaluation of the place of Jewishness in Gordimer's writing, Karen Lazar's essay on the ambiguities of Gordimer's feminism, Graham Huggan on commitment, and Lars Engle on the "political uncanny". Finally, BAZIN and SEYMOUR have gathered together almost all of Gordimer's major literary interviews, from 1958 to 1989, arranged chronologically. Six of the interviews have never before appeared in print; two of them (with Bernard Sachs in 1961 and Claude Servan-Schreiber in 1979) make it clear that Gordimer is a radical, not a liberal, and focus closely on political events.

JUDIE NEWMAN

Gothic Fiction

Delamotte, Eugenia C., *Perils of the Night: A Feminist Study of Nineteenth-Century Gothic*, New York and Oxford: Oxford University Press, 1990

Massé, Michelle A., *In the Name of Love: Women, Masochism and the Gothic*, Ithaca, New York: Cornell University Press, 1992

Miles, Robert, *Gothic Writing 1750–1820: A Genealogy*, London and New York: Routledge, 1993

Punter, David, *The Literature of Terror: A History of Gothic Fictions from 1765 to the Present Day*, London: Longman, 1980

Sage, Victor, *Horror Fiction in the Protestant Tradition*, London: Macmillan, 1988; New York: St Martin's Press, 1988

Varma, Devendra P., *The Gothic Flame: Being a History of the Gothic Novel in England: Its Origins, Efflorescence, Disintegration and Residuary Influences*, London: Arthur Baker, 1957; reprinted, New York: Russell & Russell, 1966

VARMA's pioneering work has been an effective tinder-box to the latest gothic revival. By excavating neglected texts, like Jane Austen's "horrid" novels, and in rehabilitating the work of Horace Walpole and Ann Radcliffe, he demonstrates, in the words of J.M.S. Thompkins, that the gothic romance is "not a cul-de-sac but an important arterial development of the novel". In addition to exploring the origins and major trends within gothic novels, Varma has also considered the way in which they function as an index to the social and political concerns of their era.

PUNTER's survey, which encrypts Marxist and Freudian readings of texts, ranges from the mid-eighteenth century through to the Victorian period, from American gothic to the horror film, and from Romanticism to Mervyn Peake. The advances towards developing a theory of the gothic (towards the end of the book) remain some of the most enduring points of reference for scholars in this field. The gothic is seen as a mode of cultural self-analysis, which represents deep-rooted social and psychological anxieties. More specifically it has been deployed by the middle classes as a means of articulating their own paranoia. For example, it articulates the barbaric, and resolves the tensions involved in the nature of taboo. But the result can leave Punter's reader of gothic in a state of delirium, in being the recipient of "unassimilable impressions".

MILES insists that gothic should be relocated within the centrality of Romantic debate. This controversial study succeeds in building new bridges between texts and ideologies and effectively conveys their complexities as a tool for cultural criticism and as an expression for the fragmented subject. Miles employs Michel Foucault's notion of "genealogy" to show that gothic writing does not consist of a single "neat line of hegemonic descent" but of a multiplicity of genealogies from which to choose, which are able to accommodate genres other than the novel. Miles explains this methodology in terms of the "carnivalesque", which also accounts for the dialogic quality of gothic literature, to be found especially in female gothic writing. Among the most useful chapters are those that deal with the distinctions between male and female gothic (wisely he leaves Mary Wollstonecraft to unravel Rousseau's statement "but for her sex, a woman is a man") and the female sublime, primarily in relation to Ann Radcliffe.

SAGE traces the theological underpinnings of the nineteenth-century horror novel, harking back to the Reformation. Instead of seeing the horror novel as marginal, he regards it as a vehicle for affirming the cultural experience of its contemporary readership. Furthermore, he argues that horror fiction is a species of historical romance, which has a degree of greater rhetorical sophistication than has hitherto been appreciated by many. Organising the chapters around a number of key concepts, like the *Doppelgänger*, Sage looks at a variety of writers, including Charles Dickens, Wilkie Collins, Edgar Allan Poe, and Bram Stoker.

Gothic fiction has increasingly become a focus of feminist debate. DELAMOTTE, like critic Eve Kosofsky Sedgwick, enlists a spatial model as the basis of her argument that gothic is about an anxiety over boundaries. Unlike Sedgwick, she gives emphasis to the bifurcation between self and other, in regard to making oneself inaccessible to the outside world. Representations of various aspects of the self, she argues, are deployed through a symbolic language, which is expressed by the conventions employed within the gothic romance. The second part of her analysis deals with the gothic as a woman's genre, with particular reference to the Brontës. MASSÉ reappraises female masochism through her readings of several signal texts. She argues that the representation of the oppression of women through gothic can help towards a greater understanding of how the abused can replicate her own abuse. The way in which femininity as a culturally induced trauma colludes with male dominance is illustrated most graphically through sado-masochism. In chapters entitled

"Kissing the Rod: The Beaten and *Story of O*" and "This Hurts Me More than It Does You: The Beater and *Rebecca*", Massé explores the way in which literary texts dramatise the beating drama and draw attention to the dangers of gothic courtship.

MARIE MULVEY ROBERTS

Gower, John c.1330–1408

English poet

Echard, Siân, and Claire Fanger, *The Latin Verses in the "Confessio Amantis": An Annotated Translation*, East Lansing, Michigan: Colleagues Press, 1991
Fisher, John H., *John Gower: Moral Philosopher and Friend of Chaucer*, New York: New York University Press, 1964
Gallacher, Patrick J., *Love, the Word and Mercury: A Reading of John Gower's "Confessio Amantis"*, Albuquerque: University of New Mexico Press, 1975
Peck, Russell A., *Kingship and Common Profit in Gower's "Confessio Amantis"*, Carbondale: Southern Illinois University Press, 1978; London: Feffer & Simons, 1978
Minnis, Alastair J. (ed.), *Gower's "Confessio Amantis": Responses and Reassessments*, Woodbridge, Suffolk: D.S. Brewer, 1983
Olsson, Kurt, *John Gower and the Structures of Conversion: A Reading of the "Confessio Amantis"*, Cambridge: D.S. Brewer, 1992; Rochester, New York: Boydell & Brewer, 1992
Yeager, R. F. (ed.), *John Gower: Recent Readings*, Kalamazoo: Western Michigan University Press, 1989
Yeager, R.F., *John Gower's Poetic: The Search for a New Arion*, Woodbridge, Suffolk: Boydell & Brewer, 1990
Yeager, R.F. (ed.), *Chaucer and Gower: Difference, Mutuality, Exchange*, Victoria, British Columbia: University of Victoria Press, 1991

In his *Troilus and Criseyde*, Chaucer apostrophized his contemporary John Gower as "moral Gower". The epithet, with the various responses that it evokes, has been with Gower ever since. For several centuries after his death, Gower was considered the equal of Chaucer and John Lydgate, but changing literary tastes (and assumptions about "moral" poetry) then relegated him to the obscurity in which he has, until recently, remained. An enduring effect of this literary history may be seen in the tendency, even among modern Gower scholars, to all but apologize that their poet is not Chaucer.

FISHER's book, the first major study of Gower, takes a literary-historical approach. It focuses on Gower's life and his work, attempting to place the poet in his appropriate medieval context so that his moral and political philosophy can be appreciated fully. Other writers are of course a part of this context, and Fisher sets the tone of much later criticism by noting the large shadow that Chaucer has cast over Gower: "it has been the fate of John Gower to appear to succeeding ages almost constantly in the company of Geoffrey Chaucer". While critical approaches have changed, this book remains one of the few to examine the full range of Gower's work.

The comparison with Chaucer has continued to be the starting-point for other studies of Gower. YEAGER 1991 is a special collection of essays on the nature of that relationship, and several of the essays in Yeager 1989 (see below), another important collection of recent responses to renewed interest in Gower, also address similarities, differences, and debts between the two poets.

PECK's concentration on Gower's political and moral ideas in the *Confessio* notes their inextricable link to the art of the poem. The tales are an exemplification of sin and virtue which are intended to educate Amans and, by extension, to illustrate the essential relationship between kingship, as both personal and political governance, and common profit, the mutual benefit of all social beings: "the key to Gower's encyclopedic moral philosophy is 'comun profit,' by which he means the mutual enhancement, each by each, of all parts of a community for the general welfare of that community taken as a whole". Every part of the poem, Peck argues, is tied to the elucidation of this philosophy.

GALLACHER's focus is on the language of the *Confessio*; his work proceeds from the perspective of the medieval interest in the intersection of God's Word (Logos) with human words. He finds it inevitable that a poem patterned on confessional manuals "should show a recurring emphasis on the various aspects of human speech". He also notes the importance of words to both prayer and courtship: the *Confessio* traces Amans' progression from faulty human to divine speech. Mercury is identified as the medieval symbol of eloquence, but it may well be that the reader will be less convinced of his centrality to the *Confessio* than is Gallacher.

Two important collections of essays, MINNIS and YEAGER (1989), demonstrate the vitality of Gower studies in the 1980s. Many of these pieces address a current interest in ideas of authority in medieval literature. They examine Gower's relationship with his sources; his perception of himself as an *auctor*, an authoritative writer; and the various means by which he promoted and attempted to control that self-perception through the Latin apparatus of his poem. The contrast between the Latin and English voices render the work considerably more complex than it has often been thought to be; some readers see the Latin as an attempt to control the transgressions of the vernacular, and point as well to the intriguing failures of this effort. My (ECHARD) and FANGER's annotated translation of the Latin verses scattered throughout the *Confessio* allows modern readers who are not sufficiently familiar with Latin to follow Gower's quirky and difficult verse the opportunity to read the poem with some of this apparatus restored.

The 1990s have seen the full flowering in the resurgence in Gower studies through the publication of two major studies, by Olsson and Yeager. YEAGER's 1990 approach is comprehensive, considering Gower's poetic line, his (complex) relationship to his source materials, the overall structure of the *Confessio*, and its thematic centre, which Yeager finds in the offering of love as the antidote to the discord and division that pervades the human and political realms of the poem. The *Confessio* is seen as "an extended treatment of marriage, envisioned both as sacrament and as metaphor". While the *Confessio* is the focus here, Yeager's integration of Gower's French and Latin poetry into the commentary makes his book one of the fullest pictures to date of Gower's poetic practice.

OLSSON uses the notion of voice as the point of departure for his discussion of the *Confessio*. The *Confessio* is mediated through many voices, none of which speaks for the poet, but each of which offers some important insight into the central moral themes of the work. An advantage of Olsson's approach is that it allows the exploration of the entire range of stories in the *Confessio*, stories whose diversity has often defeated commentators on the poem. It is odd, then, that Olsson spends a good deal of the book arguing against that apparent diversity in favour of thematic unity, a unity which he finds in the focus on the moral correction of Amans.

SIÂN ECHARD

Graves, Robert 1895–1985

English poet, novelist, critic, and children's writer

Canary, Robert H., *Robert Graves*, Boston: Twayne, 1980
Carter, D.N.G., *Robert Graves: The Lasting Poetic Achievement*, Totowa, New Jersey: Barnes & Noble, 1989; London: Macmillan, 1989
Cohen, J.M., *Robert Graves*, Edinburgh: Oliver & Boyd, 1960; New York: Grove Press, 1961
Day, Douglas, *Swifter Than Reason: The Poetry and Criticism of Robert Graves*, Chapel Hill: University of North Carolina Press, 1963; Oxford: Oxford University Press, 1963
Hoffman, Daniel, *Barbarous Knowledge: Myth in the Poetry of Yeats, Graves, and Muir*, New York: Oxford University Press, 1967; London: Oxford University Press, 1970
Kirkham, Michael, *The Poetry of Robert Graves*, London: Athlone Press, 1969
Mehoke, James S., *Robert Graves: Peace Weaver*, The Hague: Mouton, 1974
Quinn, Patrick J., *The Great War and the Missing Muse: The Early Writings of Robert Graves and Siegfried Sassoon*, Selinsgrove, Pennsylvania: Susquehanna University Press, 1994; London: Associated University Presses, 1994
Seymour-Smith, Martin, *Robert Graves*, London: Longmans, Green & Co., 1956
Snipes, Katherine, *Robert Graves*, New York: Frederick Ungar, 1979

The critical reaction to Robert Graves has generally been uneven. Contemporary critics have never been sure what to make of his ever-changing attitude toward poetry or of his often unorthodox views of other writers. Graves passed through many phases as a poet, which took him from Georgian to modernist, from the flawless seeker of perfection under the strict aegis of Laura Riding to the acolyte of the White Goddess. On this journey, Graves also managed to write several well-received historical novels, some valuable literary criticism, as well as explorations into Greek and Hebrew mythology. Surprisingly, there has not been a book-length study dedicated to examining Graves' prose works. Perhaps Graves would not have minded so much, for as far as he was concerned, his poetry was the yardstick with which he hoped his writing to be measured by future generations.

SEYMOUR-SMITH's study was the first to attempt to put all of Graves' work into an organisational pattern and to establish that, in spite of Graves' remonstrances, the author's prose ought to be studied prior to any in-depth reading of his poetry. Seymour-Smith used Graves' autobiography, *Good-Bye to All That* to show how Graves' life had informed many of his novels, and then demonstrated how novels like *Antigua, Penny, Puce* illustrated the scope of Graves' imagination. Seymour-Smith's historical view of Graves' contribution to criticism is particularly useful as an overview of Graves' shifting approach to poetry, and his discussion of *The White Goddess* is very useful for its ability to summarize the main points of a complex study in one page of prose. On the question of the impulse for Graves' poetry, Seymour-Smith concludes that Graves was constantly searching for an authoritarian figure who would replace the lost cultural certainties of the Edwardian world, while at the same time freeing him from restrictions of sexuality that dominated his adolescent years. The creation of the White Goddess and her various female manifestations served that need well.

COHEN's decision to follow Graves' own suggestion, that is, that his poetry was at the heart of his work and that everything else was peripheral, was to become the benchmark for the critics of Graves' work who followed him. With his resolve to examine poems that Graves had eliminated from his *Collected Poems*, Cohen offers a coherent context within which the development of Graves' early material into the controlled emotional love lyrics of the late 1950s can be observed. The book's penetrating study of the autobiographical influences on Graves' early poetry helps also to illuminate the autobiographical elements of Graves' novels of the 1930s. Cohen's close analysis of Graves' poems of the 1930s and of the early 1940s, as well as his explanation of Graves' analeptic method (the intuitive recovery of forgotten events by a deliberate suspension of time), provides a particularly useful insight into Graves' methods of writing novels.

DAY's choice, in his study, to divide Graves' poetry up into four major periods is also useful, and indeed the majority of critics have since adhered roughly to Day's categorisation of Graves' poetry into his Georgian period, his philosophical period, his "Riding" period, and his "White Goddess" period. Day's decision to structure his book around Graves' eight books of criticism, as opposed to the autobiography, which other critics had used, is valuable: in his view, Graves' "criticism is perhaps most valuable as an indicator both of the progress of his ideas about the function of poetry and criticism and of the standards by which he composed the poems of each of his four periods". The strength of Day's book lies in the fact that Day manages to make incisive investigations into a number of poems using Graves' own criticism as an organisational tool.

HOFFMAN employs a Freudian psychological-biographical approach in his study of Graves' poetry. Hoffman surmises that Graves' poetry was a product of the severe psychological disturbances engendered in his early upbringing, disturbances which were further exacerbated by the neurasthenic traumas experienced on the battlefields of World War I. Hoffman concludes that "conditions of emotional stress, dream, paranoia, and delusion offer the materials of true poetry, if not the finality of poetic statement. Graves found his own poetic materials in such materials long before he recognised their universality in myths". For Hoffman, Graves' worship and obeisance of the White Goddess in his later poetry was the result of a natural development step from his earlier work.

Critics preceding KIRKHAM had tended to downplay the important influence of Laura Riding (Graves' American muse figure from 1926–39) on Graves' poetry, but Kirkham offers a detailed investigation into Riding's role in changing Graves' intellectual, moral, and religious outlook. Having established the nature of Riding's influences, Kirkham then was able to investigate the change in tone and technique of Graves' poetry during the Riding period. Further, Kirkham was the first critic to examine the Black Goddess phase of Graves' poetry, in which the poetic dominance of the White Goddess is replaced by the gentler Sufi-based muse. Kirkham's detailed reading of Graves' works follows a historical development and offers a comprehensive bibliography of Graves' poetic and critical works up to 1968.

The fascination with Graves' approach to mythology, especially with his obsession with the White Goddess, was the impetus behind MEHOKE's study of Graves' muse. In this idiosyncratic study, Mehoke argues that the trauma of war caused Graves to lose his faith in Christianity as well as to suffer disassociations from his culture. These war-engendered phenomena led Graves to search for a unifying mythos that would restore a sense of justice to his mind. The answer to the search was found in the myth of the White Goddess and his poetic service to her. The goddess poetry typifies the archetypal struggles facing modern man in the wasteland of the twentieth century. The book focuses largely on the later phases of Graves' poetry, but also offers insightful commentary on difficult prose works, such as *Hercules, My Shipmate* and *King Jesus*, where the White Goddess can be discovered in her various manifestations.

SNIPES's study of Graves is an amalgam of material, which attempts to give an overview of his career. The book serves largely as an introduction for new readers to Graves. The book's main use is to give a taste of nearly every important piece of prose Graves wrote. Samples provided, for example, of *Wife to Mr. Milton* or of the Sergeant Lamb novels offer useful insights into Graves' eclectic mind. The detailed "Chronology" and ample "Bibliography" update Graves scholarship.

CANARY's Twayne study of Graves' work is thorough and well written. Like most critics, the writer uses Graves' prose to elucidate Graves' poetry, and Canary's regard for *My Head! My Head!* and *Watch the North Wind Rise* offer important insights into Graves' religious and classical concerns. Canary echoes Kirkham's conclusion about the importance of Laura Riding in Graves' literary and emotional development, and concludes that "in submitting himself to the views of Laura Riding, Graves purchased a kind of freedom from oppressive memories of the past, particularly the war".

CARTER's particular service to Graves' criticism is his incisive observations about the poetry that Graves wrote late in his career. Carter aptly points out that Graves' muse-poetry failed to discern the essence of a flesh-and-blood love affair but seemed to be addressed to a distanced and disembodied representation of a woman: the concrete is sacrificed for the abstract. Carter has sifted through the muse-propaganda poems of the last 15 years of Graves' career and has turned up impressive works such as "Fact of the Act". Carter's demonstration of Graves' thematic consistency regarding the nature of eroticism in love in, for example, "The Nape of the Neck" and "To Sleep" support Carter's contention that Graves' poetry is most effective when it is addressing authentic love situations and concerns.

My (QUINN's) book on Graves examines in detail the poetry that he wrote during, and immediately after, World War I. The book describes the social, economic, and cultural pressures on Graves after the War and his attempts to exorcise the experience of war and its after-effects from his psyche by poetic means. My contention is that while Graves eventually moved to prose (writing *Good-Bye to All That*) in order to expiate the War from his consciousness, the resulting experimentations produced some of his most memorable poems. The book argues for a re-evaluation of Graves' early work, and attempts to demonstrate the quality and versatility of much of it.

PATRICK J. M. QUINN

Green, Henry 1905–1973

English novelist and short-story writer

Bassoff, Bruce, *Toward "Loving": The Poetics of the Novel and the Practice of Henry Green*, Columbia: University of South Carolina Press, 1975
Holmesland, Oddvar, *A Critical Introduction to Henry Green's Novels: The Living Vision*, London: Macmillan, 1986
Mengham, Rod, *The Idiom of the Time: The Writings of Henry Green*, Cambridge and New York: Cambridge University Press, 1982
Odom, Keith C., *Henry Green*, Boston: Twayne, 1978
Russell, John, *Henry Green: Nine Novels and an Unpacked Bag*, New Brunswick, New Jersey: Rutgers University Press, 1960
Ryf, Robert S., *Henry Green*, New York: Columbia University Press, 1967
Stokes, Edward, *The Novels of Henry Green*, London: Hogarth Press, 1959
Weatherhead, A.K., *A Reading of Henry Green*, Seattle: University of Washington Press, 1961

While appreciating the beauty and humanity of Green's writing, critics generally have had difficulty in finding the right approach for explaining and assessing it. The progress of Green criticism demonstrates how long it took to develop an aesthetic adequate for innovative poetic prose fiction such as his.

The first book on Green's major fiction was by STOKES, who clearly felt frustrated by the state of novel theory at the time; but what honest effort – and statistics – can do, is done. After discussing Green's characters "as though they were actual people", he reviews the deployment of scene, summary, description, characterisation, commentary, and point of view, noting

Green's "basically scenic method", before analysing the handling of time (especially usefully for *Caught*). "The basic theme of Green's art is that of love versus loneliness", in the context of social dissolution and alienation, he suggests, though he is generally tentative in proposing themes and meanings of specific novels. Symbols, colours, sentence-lengths and modifications of grammar, percentages of preterit verbs, and such like, are tabulated, sometimes quite usefully: an informative if baffled study.

RUSSELL provides a good example of traditional criticism, responsive to technique but more interested in assessment of the author's attitudes to life. Placing Green as part of the less extremist element of the modernist tradition (E.M. Forster is evoked), he discusses style and other formal features – the taste for symbolism, pattern, and symmetry – but is more concerned with character-discussion (done quite well in the pre-Freudian, humanist mode), Green's comedy as value and technique, and Green's moral values. Seeking connections and development in Green's writing career, he explores responses to class, war, and social change, seeing a developing pessimism and sense of human limitations, a turning from the heroic-tragic to a valuing of traditional compromises and social commitments. Similarities with Franz Kafka, in ambiguity, irony and yearning after "the blisses of the common-place", are suggested.

WEATHERHEAD's chronological study concentrates on the developing theme of self-creation, employing particularly Kierkegaard's theory of personality development, which seeks growth but also produces dread of anxiety. Archetypal patterns of descent into darkness are generally found; Freudian theories of "dream-work" are behind accounts of how the "realist" and "social" elements, including settings and secondary characters, figure aspects of the protagonists' psychological careers and concerns. Samuel Taylor Coleridge's distinctions between fancy and imagination, and John Crowe Ransom's between texture and structure underpin analyses of style, particularly of figurative writing, as Weatherhead attempts not only to analyse and evaluate style, but to relate it to Green's developing perceptions of reality.

RYF's introductory booklet outlines storylines adequately, concentrating on engaging with themes in a speculative manner, without much consideration of Green's stylistic experimentation. Ryf praises Green's psychological verisimilitude, the use of visual fragmentation, brief scenes, and montage; and the last novels' deployment of dialogue is seen as an extension of earlier methods. In 1960s' fashion, he offers "the problem of communication" as Green's central theme, and attempts to claim him for existentialism. He is perhaps most commendable for the emphasis on "the organic cohesiveness achieved by Green's technique" throughout his *oeuvre*, "the achievement of . . . connectedness of structure, or pervasiveness of central idea".

BASSOFF sets discussion of Green's writing in the context of early 1970s' literary theory, with notably more sympathy for the formalist-structuralist approach of such as Viktor Shklovsky and Alain Robbe-Grillet than the realist-moralist approach (e.g., Georg Lukács). The theoretical discussion might not get very far; however, Bassoff does provide some useful analyses of technique – verbal style and linguistic peculiarities (as in *Living*), and the use of compositional motifs, scene-juxtaposition, and patterns of imagery (*Concluding*, *Caught*, and *Party Going*). An attempted analysis of structural "enjambment" is not wholly persuasive. The final chapter concentrates on *Loving*, defending its comic mode, its balance of character and style, dialogue and narrative, and its overall "harmoniousness, its seamless quality".

ODOM's volume in the Twayne "English Authors" series, chronologically ordered, is a step backward. Each chapter is divided, rather mechanically, into separate sections on its novel's theme, narrative techniques, characterisation, style and symbolism, a method that is clear but hinders an integrated sense of the whole. Discussion is sensible but not perceptive. There is a brief account of Green's theory of fiction, and the "poetic richness" of the writing is praised but little analysed: "with his ear for everyday speech, Green virtually has his style created for him" (!). Conscientiously noting other critics' views, Odom offers as "the most striking of Green's themes . . . social and economic change", particularly the upper classes' marginalisation and loss of control.

The last two studies discussed here show the most critical sophistication, getting beyond realist narratology in the attempt to engage with fundamental concerns. MENGHAM's chronological analysis, the first to use Green's manuscripts (in the British Library), is informed by Freudian psychoanalytic theory (there's a suggestive Oedipal interpretation of *Blindness*). The main concern is with text, with writing as such, "the writing which takes place is *superfluous* to the novel", as it conceals meanings and evades and subverts established conventions of thought, communication, and narration (Green's "imagery . . . [is] . . . primed to present a maximum inconvenience to narrative exposition", his intention being "the gradual attrition of a hard surface formed by corporate doctrines"). Mengham usefully traces literary echoes and analogues, relates Green to the context of 1930s' and 1940s' writing and thinking, and provides close and subtle discussion of style and imagery. Unfortunately, despite some good insights and interesting passages, Mengham's own writing is frequently obscure and evasive of clarity, and so not always very helpful.

By contrast, HOLMESLAND writes clearly and effectively, acutely and sensitively analysing Green's technique and relating it to the author's moral preoccupations. The emphasis is on Green's dynamic juxtaposition of scene, imagery, and mode, related (with Green's early interest in film in mind) particularly to Sergei Eisenstein's theories of film montage ("only a montage-based approach can provide the key to understanding", as Holmesland repeatedly insists), and, to a lesser extent, Romantic poetic practice. Fragmentation and juxtaposition are presented as central to Green's re-creative power and development of tone (narrational stance or implicit evaluation), helping to provoke the reader's imaginative engagement with not merely a text, but with imagined life and "humanly sustaining values". The analyses are full, detailed, and illuminating, and the arguments persuasive, as Holmesland, perhaps surprisingly, reclaims Green for a realist, humanist tradition.

R.E. PRITCHARD

Greene, Graham 1904–1991

English novelist, dramatist, screenwriter, and essayist

Adamson, Judith, *Graham Greene: The Dangerous Edge: Where Art and Politics Meet*, London: Macmillan, 1990
Allain, Marie-Françoise, *The Other Man: Conversations with Graham Greene*, translated by Guido Waldman, New York: Simon & Schuster, 1983; London: Bodley Head, 1983
Cuoto, Maria, *Graham Greene: On the Frontier: Politics and Religion in the Novels*, London: Macmillan, 1988
Donaghy, Henry J. (ed.), *Conversations with Graham Greene*, Jackson: University Press of Mississippi, 1992
Duran, Lepoldo, *Graham Greene: Friend and Brother*, translated by Euan Cameron, London: Harper Collins, 1994
Kelly, Richard, *Graham Greene: A Study of the Short Fiction*, New York: Twayne, 1992
Meyers, Jeffrey (ed.), *Graham Greene: A Revaluation: New Essays*, London: Macmillan, 1990
O'Prey, Paul, *A Reader's Guide to Graham Greene*, London: Thames & Hudson, 1988
Parkinson, David (ed.), *The Graham Greene Film Reader: Mornings in the Dark*, Manchester: Carcanet, 1993
Shelden, Michael, *Graham Greene: The Man Within*, London: Heinemann, 1994
Sherry, Norman, *The Life of Graham Greene*, Volumes 1–2, London: Jonathan Cape, 1989–94; New York: Viking Press, 1989–94

The life of Graham Greene is as fascinating as his writing, but this has led to a critical emphasis on the biographical aspects of his work, and the exploration of "Greeneland", with the result that his books have not yet received adequate appraisal. Greene's place in literary history, though assured, remains enigmatic. Perhaps he would have preferred it that way.

Greene himself authorised SHERRY to write his biography, two volumes of which have now appeared. These have been criticised as too long and detailed, for being uncritical of Greene's less attractive aspects, and for Sherry's personal response to his subject. This seems unfair, as much was written while Greene was alive, and Greene's trust in Sherry's fairmindedness led to his divulging intimate personal material. Given Sherry's tenacious pursuit of his subject around the world (finding the Mestizo in Mexico was a particular coup), his reliable research, and lively style, it is unlikely that his will be displaced as the definitive biography.

Yet there are other accounts. SHELDEN implicitly challenges Sherry, and is more astringent in attending to Greene's depressive tendencies, his political and sexual complexities, his anti-semitism, and even the celebrated Russian roulette (Shelden is sceptical). He sees Greene's Catholicism as defined by hatred, and his friendships with various figures (Torrijos, Castro) as a complex case of arrested development, perhaps originating from his unhappy schooldays. Nevertheless, Shelden's is a serious study and many criticisms hit their mark, if sometimes sporadically. DURAN is also uneven, but more engagingly so. His book is based on a genuine friendship (he is the model for Monsignor Quixote) during the last years of Greene's life, and has a strange innocence and simplicity. His opinions often disagree with Greene's, but he offers insight into the personal side, the religious impulse, the changing nature of Greene's Catholicism, his failed marriage, and the restless sense of human fallibility that drove the writer.

Two records of conversations appeared a decade apart. The first is a fascinating curiosity: Greene, in 1979, revealed to ALLAIN his attraction to "the dangerous edge" and the intricate bonds between his life and fiction. Greene is open about his divided loyalties, his failures and contradictions, and the way he spies on his characters. Intriguing are his accounts of political horror, notably in Haiti, and of religion, with his sympathy for the "semilapsed". Allain lets Greene speak directly, and he reveals much about himself, in a lively manner. The second book lacks such freshness. DONAGHY assembles 50 years of interviews, but Greene's wariness of personal disclosure prevails. Yet there are valuable moments: these include a 1949 "table-talk" with Père Jouve and Marcel Moré, wherein Greene admits his pre-occupation with sin; a comment to V.S. Pritchard about "the Foreign Legion of the Church"; and two late interviews with Pierre Joannon, which reveal interesting aspects of Greene's politics.

O'PREY offers a useful handbook, saying the right things rather than any new things, but giving an overview of Greene's life and writing. He stresses the moral complexity of Greene's work, and invokes its richness and depth to defend Greene from the usual charges of being either "narrowly Catholic" or obsessively troubled by his own psyche. He appreciates the journalistic quality of Greene's writing, and his own has similar virtues, making it an excellent introductory study.

Greene's politics attract frequent attention, yet studies of them often lack literary insight. CUOTO is disappointing. She sees Greene's novels proceeding from an interpretation of Catholicism as a structure of signification in which the fiction mediates between different polarities; and this unhelpful beginning leads her to view Greene in a postcolonial context. Comments on individual works are not imperceptive, yet the total achievement is slight, and an interview with Greene reiterates ideas discussed elsewhere. ADAMSON is more comprehensive. She offers a coherent introduction to Greene's political writings from the early years until the end; yet her subtitle (*The Dangerous Edge*) refers to the interface between politics and art, rather than wavering faith; and that neglect of the religious dimension limits her theme.

The essays chosen by MEYERS suggest that the best criticism of Greene may be found in short articles rather than longer studies. Though some are garrulous (Donald Greene on Evelyn Waugh and Greene as "Catholic Novelists" in fact says little about Greene), others are perceptive – Eugene Goodheart on the religious underpinnings of Greene's occasional criticism, Roger Sharrock on his plays, and William Chace on espionage fiction, to select but three. Meyers omits a bibliography, but extensive footnotes suggest useful further reading.

Two specialist studies may intimate an imminent appraisal of Greene's stature. KELLY gives a full account of the short fiction, including most of Greene's relevant comments, an excellent summary of previous criticism, and a detailed bibliography of primary and secondary materials. His is a definitive treatment of this small but significant part of Greene's creative life. PARKINSON on film is also comprehensive. His is a major compendium of Greene's film reviews, essays, and articles, including interviews, lectures, letters, film scenarios and treatments. Parkinson's Introduction is superb, his notes and annotations informative, and he gives useful appendices and indices of films and names. He intimates indirectly the extent to which cinematic technique shaped the fiction. If the final evaluation of Greene is yet to be made, and the fiction still to receive the attention it deserves, these two studies, in company with Sherry's biography, have mapped the route that others must follow.

CHRIS ACKERLEY

Greene, Robert 1558–1592

English novelist, pamphleteer, and dramatist

Assarsson-Rizzi, Kerstin, *Friar Bacon and Friar Bungay: A Structural and Thematic Analysis of Robert Greene's Play*, Lund, Sweden: C.W.K. Gleerup, 1972

Crupi, Charles W., *Robert Greene*, Boston: Twayne, 1986

Helgerson, Richard, *The Elizabethan Prodigals*, Berkeley: University of California Press, 1976

Jordan, John Clark, *Robert Greene*, New York: Columbia University Press, 1915

Lucas, Caroline, *Writing for Women: The Example of Woman as Reader in Elizabethan Romance*, Milton Keynes, Buckinghamshire: Open University Press, 1989

Senn, Werner, *Studies in the Dramatic Construction of Robert Greene and George Peele*, Bern: Francke, 1973

Robert Greene was one of the most versatile of Elizabethan writers, making his living from his writing for a large part, if not all, of his life. With his complete works running to 15 volumes in Grosart's late Victorian edition, it is not surprising that critics have rarely attempted an overview of his work, concentrating instead on his plays, or aspects of his prose work.

JORDAN's study devotes three chapters to the prose works, and a chapter each to Greene's poetry and plays. It locates Greene's work as characterised by versatility and fertility of invention, and argues powerfully that to judge him as a "sober littérateur" is to employ unhelpful criteria for a writer whose work was principally borrowing and imitating. Jordan insists that Greene's "autobiographical" final prose works are inspired by literary sources rather than Greene's own life. Surprisingly, he argues that Greene's poetry, most of which is embedded in his prose romances, is surpassed only by that of Sir Philip Sidney among his contemporaries in the production of new forms and metrical effects. Though aspects of the work have dated, and much space is inevitably taken up with bibliographical matters, this is a readable and combative revaluation of Greene after centuries of neglect.

ASSARSSON-RIZZI's book focuses on Greene's most popular play, providing an exhaustive study of sources, plot, themes and values, style, and rhetoric and the nature of the play world. Some of this, for example the discussion of themes (love, chastity, magic, pride, friendship, humility, and patriotism), is clearly focused but unambitious. More interesting is the concentration on the question of genre (one that vexes scholars of the prose also), on the play's form, and on the characters' rhetoric. Assarsson-Rizzi concludes that *Friar Bungay* would have been recognisable to its original audience as a comedy, but that it combines elements of morality, romance, romantic comedy, and history (in its sense of "true story"). She concludes that the play is complex in its presentation of magic's morality, and that its formal sophistication, combining effectively three places of action and two major lines of action, has no precedent in pre-1590 popular English drama. Within the limits it sets itself, this is a useful study.

SENN also concentrates on form, investigating the construction of three plays each by George Peele and by Greene (*Alphonsus King of Aragon*, *Friar Bacon*, and *James IV*). After a methodological Introduction, he covers sources, arrangement of action, character, and action, considering under these headings causation, juxtaposition, climactic patterns, surprise, suspense, anticipation, delay, and acceleration, as well as character and plot. Senn's comparative method allows him to demonstrate that Greene was the more original and daring of the two writers, principally in his command of structure, which provokes a comparative and reflective approach to the events shown. Senn's work is even more narrowly taxonomic than Assarsson-Rizzi's, and its achievement is correspondingly limited to showing Greene's grasp of the craft of writing plays in the early years of playhouse theatre in London.

HELGERSON devotes a chapter of his book to the idea of Greene as a prodigal writer, whose prose career conformed to the pattern of the prodigal-son tales he began by imitating. For Helgerson, Greene's writing began as "the exploration of the romantic other", and became increasingly autobiographical as he came "home to the guilty self". The initially didactic humanism of his imitation of *Euphues* was soon reversed, the stoic woman celebrated, and action traced to passion or Fortune rather than rational moral thought. In this, Greene was following a larger trend, the return of the "repressed" romantic fictional impulse to the scene of the dominant mid-century humanism. The social stresses of the late 1580s, and changing literary priorities embodied in the works of such as Thomas Nashe, led to Greene's "repentance" and a partial repudiation of romantic fiction, and a didacticism (in the coney-catching pamphlets) that was ironically just as fiction-based as his earlier romances. Helgerson's account of Greene is a valuable overview of his prose career, approaching him via a theoretically aware historicising of the conventions within which Greene worked.

CRUPI's book covers the same territory as Jordan, though devoting much more space to the plays, and ignoring Greene's poetry. It includes a concise but comprehensive biographical summary, detailed analysis of six prose works (including *Pandosto*), an overview of the other prose works, detailed work on the five canonical plays, and a section on Greene's reputation. Crupi is most combative on the prose, as he sees Greene studies underplaying the didacticism of these pieces, partly because of Greene's use of the romance genre, and partly through an unproductive concentration on questions of authenticity, originality, and sincerity. Crupi approaches Greene's borrowing and imitations as providing crucial evidence of his didactic intent, and provides a convincing overview of Greene's career with this as the key. Crupi takes a similar tack on the plays, arguing that to read them as proto-Shakespearean romantic comedies is to undervalue their didactic and emblematic elements. This broad survey provides the most comprehensive coverage of Greene's life and work available, is sensitive to the many genres in which Greene worked, and contains a useful bibliography.

LUCAS's starting point is the increase in the number of books for women – practical and fictional – from the 1570s onwards. Building on recent feminist revaluations of contemporary romantic fiction, her chapter on Greene's prose focuses on his strong female characters, arguing that their independence and resourcefulness "are exercised to effect women's own subordination". The heroine's primary concern is her reputation, or role as a "mirror", and consequently she is judged by others and herself insofar as she is a more, or less, good example. This concern of the heroine is then replicated in the female reader; male readings, because less directly implicated, are characterised as voyeuristic. However, Lucas asserts that readers can resist this kind of reading, and instead enjoy the fiction because it shows women's lives taken seriously and their thoughts and feelings given significance. Lucas's feminist reader-response approach powerfully lays bare the ways in which even positive images of women are enmeshed in complex and oppressive narrative strategies.

STEPHEN LONGSTAFFE

The Grotesque

Bakhtin, Mikhail, *Rabelais and His World*, translated by Helene Iswolsky, Cambridge, Massachusetts: MIT Press, 1968
Clayborough, Arthur, *The Grotesque in English Literature*, Oxford: Clarendon Press, 1965
Kayser, Wolfgang, *The Grotesque in Art and Literature*, translated by Ulrich Weisstein, Bloomington: Indiana University Press, 1963
McElroy, Bernard, *Fiction of the Modern Grotesque*, London: Macmillan, 1989
Rhodes, Neil, *Elizabethan Grotesque*, London and Boston: Routledge & Kegan Paul, 1980
Thomson, Philip J., *The Grotesque*, London: Methuen, 1972

The term "grotesque" originates in sixteenth-century Rome, when it was used to describe a form of figurative ornamentation discovered in the chambers of newly excavated buildings from Ancient Rome; in early uses, "grotesque" evokes the rooms – *grotte* – -where these paintings were found, but soon came to be applied to the paintings themselves, which explore the margin between the animate and the inanimate, the human and the inhuman. The first literary use of the term seems to have been Montaigne's. He uses the term to describe his own misshapen, aberrant prose, and the rambling, associative style of his essay-writing. Modern scholarship on the grotesque in literature has focused firstly on framing a history of the term and its uses, and secondly on studying a variety of writers and periods where the grotesque is central to the affective intent of those works or artists.

KAYSER highlights the modern obsession with investigating the grotesque, for the "art of our own day shows a greater affinity to the grotesque than that of any other epoch". However, his standard study is rigorously historical in its scope. He reviews the history of the term, surveying its origin in Renaissance writings on art history, and usefully describes the painterly grotesques of the sixteenth and seventeenth centuries, especially those of Bosch and Velasquez. He then covers the grotesque in literature, beginning with Montaigne, but focusing most particularly on Romantic and nineteenth-century grotesques. He is most illuminating, for example, on the tales of E.T.A. Hoffmann, later made famous by Freud. He brings grotesque into the twentieth century, with surrealism in visual art, and the writings of Thomas Mann and Franz Kafka. For readers of literature in English, Kayser thus provides clear and succinct definitions, and places English grotesques in a much wider European context. Though his own focus is on the Germanic grotesque, he claims that the English have "an innate predisposition for the grotesque". That claim is invesitgated by CLAYBOROUGH, who attempts to do for English literature what Kayser achieved for the Germanic. Clayborough eschews discussion of visual art *per se*, but his is the most comprehensive survey of early uses in English of the term "grotesque", occurring first in English in 1640, and first used extensively as a literary term by Sir Walter Scott in his 1827 essay on Hoffmann. Clayborough's own main examples are the many grotesques of Charles Dickens; but these tend towards a listing rather than an explanation of their effect. He attempts also to account for the psychology of the grotesque, but these are much less successful than his semantic surveys of uses of the term. His psychology, in comparison, tends to be mechanistic and insufficiently flexible.

THOMSON's contribution to the Methuen "Critical Idiom" series, on the other hand, is most at home in exploring the affective dimensions of the grotesue, drawing on a wide range of extracts from Samuel Beckett, Kafka, and other modern writers to build up his definitions of the term. For modern grotesques he emphasises the importance of incompatible responses, horror, and disgust, with laughter: feelings which are the more powerful for being unresolved. He yokes the grotesque with terms that cover similar layers of feeling – the absurd, the bizarre, and the macabre – all of which can be used to describe texts where senses of ambivalence and alienation provoke horror as well as humour. Thomson gives a brief history of the grotesque, before discussing his generous range of modern examples; he never settles on a single definition of the grotesque, offering rather a potpourri for readers to select from. Nevertheless his book is clear and straightforward: for readers new to grotesque this is the best place to start.

More challenging, but far more important, is BAKHTIN's seminal study of Rabelais, written during the 1930s, but not known in the West until the 1960s. Since then Bakhtin has deservedly won a vast international audience. He studies Rabelais's *Gargantua and Pantagruel* in relation to the populist carnivals of Renaissance Europe, of which Rabelais presents a sophisticated, literary redaction. The carnivals celebrated the "material lower bodily stratum", immersing all individual human beings in the communal and earthly processes of eating and defecating, of birth and death, connecting human beings with the rest of creation. Bakhtin emphasises the carnality of these processes as well as their communality. Most importantly he has drawn attention to the joyousness of these carnivals, as human beings reconnect with their material selves. That joy, he says, was lost in later carnivals of the baroque and rococo periods, when communal festivities became private chamber soirées, and the grotesque retreated from the world rather than embraced it. Exuberant and exhaustive, Bakhtin's is the most joyful and the most influential book yet written on the grotesque.

RHODES tackles the Renaissance grotesque also, though his scope is considerably more modest than Bakhtin's. He places the scurrilous, grotesquely inventive pamphlets of Thomas Nashe, from the 1590s, in relation to the growth of comic drama in London in the 1590s and early 1600s. He shows how Nashe's prose and imagery influenced Thomas Dekker, Thomas Middleton, Shakespeare, and Ben Jonson. Most usefully, he analyses Shakespeare's Falstaff and Jonson's *Bartholomew Fair* as classically grotesque creations, celebrating the corporeal but showing its limitations as well. Jonson's great play "is the apotheosis of the Elizabethan grotesque", partly because it draws on the base materiality of Elizabethan London, and partly because it puts that materiality into a religious and moral context. The play brings together "sermon, saturnalia and satire". Rhodes's own study of these three modes is judicious, sensible, and safe.

For readers of modern literature, McELROY performs the same yeoman service. He builds on Thomson's brief survey, though he gives more extensive reading of his chosen grotesques, those by Beckett, Kafka, James Joyce, Vladimir Nabokov, Dostoevsky, and Gabriel García Márquez. McElroy's grotesque is existential. In all his writers he notes a fascination with the monstrous, which marks "the world as we fear it might be". That monstrosity is internal and psychological as much as external and material, fuelling the paranoid vision of Kafka as well as the human decay García Márquez depicts in *One Hundred Years of Solitude*. McElroy's readings of these writers are dark and adroit; his selections straddle the modern and the postmodern self struggling against a "hostile environment", enduring a "grotesque inner life". While that remains the case for many writers and readers, McElroy's readings will remain useful.

MARK HOULAHAN

Grub Street *see* Popular Literature in Britain

H

Hardy, Thomas 1840–1928

English novelist, poet, and short-story writer

Bayley, John, *An Essay on Hardy*, Cambridge and New York: Cambridge University Press, 1978
Brady, Kristin, *The Short Stories of Thomas Hardy*, London: Macmillan, 1982; New York: St Martin's Press, 1982
Brooks, Jean, *Thomas Hardy: The Poetic Structure*, London: Paul Elek, 1971
Brown, Douglas, *Thomas Hardy*, London: Longmans, Green & Co., 1954, revised 1961
Bullen, J.B., *The Expressive Eye: Fiction and Perception in the Work of Thomas Hardy*, Oxford: Clarendon Press, 1986
Cox, R.G. (ed.), *Thomas Hardy: The Critical Heritage*, London: Routledge & Kegan Paul, 1970
Draper, R.P. (ed.), *Hardy: The Tragic Novels: A Casebook*, London: Macmillan, 1975, revised 1991
Draper, R.P. (ed.), *Thomas Hardy: Three Pastoral Novels: A Casebook*, London: Macmillan, 1987
Garson, Marjorie, *Hardy's Fables of Integrity: Woman, Body, Text*, Oxford: Clarendon Press, 1991; New York: Oxford University Press, 1991
Gatrell, Simon, *Hardy the Creator: A Textual Biography*, Oxford: Clarendon Press; New York: Oxford University Press, 1988
Gibson, James, and Trevor Johnson (eds.), *Thomas Hardy: Poems: A Casebook*, London: Macmillan, 1979
Gittings, Robert, *Young Thomas Hardy*, London: Heinemann, 1975; Boston: Little Brown, 1975; revised edition, Harmondsworth, Middlesex, and New York: Penguin, 1978
Gittings, Robert, *The Older Hardy*, London: Heinemann, 1978
Kramer, Dale, *Thomas Hardy: The Forms of Tragedy*, Detroit: Wayne State University Press, 1975; London: Macmillan, 1975
Kramer, Dale (ed.), *Critical Approaches to the Fiction of Thomas Hardy*, London: Macmillan, 1979; Totowa, New Jersey: Barnes & Noble, 1979
Kramer, Dale (ed.) *Critical Essays on Thomas Hardy: The Novels*, Boston: G.K. Hall, 1990
Ingham, Patricia, *Thomas Hardy*, Hemel Hempstead, Hertfordshire: Harvester Wheatsheaf, 1989
Larkin, Philip, *Required Writing; Miscellaneous Pieces 1955–1982*, London: Faber & Faber, 1983; New York: Farrar, Straus, Giroux, 1984
Leavis, F.R., *New Bearings in English Poetry: A Study of the Contemporary Situation*, London: Chatto & Windus, 1932, revised 1950; Ann Arbor: University of Michigan Press, 1960
Lodge, David, *Language of Fiction: Essays in Criticism and Verbal Analysis of the English Novel*, London: Routledge & Kegan Paul, 1966; New York: Columbia University Press, 1966
Mallett, Phillip V., and R.P. Draper (eds.), *A Spacious Vision: Essays on Hardy*, Newmill, Cornwall: Patten Press, 1994
Miller, J. Hillis, *Thomas Hardy: Distance and Desire*, Cambridge, Massachusetts: Belknap Press of Harvard University Press, 1970; London: Oxford University Press, 1970
Millgate, Michael, *Thomas Hardy: A Biography*, Oxford: Oxford University Press, 1982; New York: Random House, 1982
Paulin, Tom, *Thomas Hardy: The Poetry of Perception*, London: Macmillan, 1975, 2nd edition 1986; Totowa, New Jersey: Rowman & Littlefield, 1975
Seymour-Smith, Martin, *Hardy*, London: Bloomsbury, 1994
Smart, Alastair, "Pictorial Imagery in the Novels of Thomas Hardy", in *Review of English Studies* (journal), 1961
Springer, Marlene, *Hardy's Use of Allusion*, Lawrence: University Press of Kansas, 1983
Taylor, Dennis, *Hardy's Poetry, 1860–1928*, London: Macmillan, 1981; New York: Columbia University Press, 1981
Taylor, Dennis, *Hardy's Metres and Victorian Prosody*, Oxford: Clarendon Press, 1988; New York: Oxford University Press, 1988
Widdowson, Peter, *Hardy in History: A Study in Literary Sociology*, London and New York: Routledge, 1989

Thomas Hardy's novels, though they have always been popular with the reading public, have often been attacked by the critics for being too much at the mercy of their plots, in which change and coincidence play an excessive part, and his prose style has been condemned as an ill-judged mixture of dialect speech with ponderously latinate diction and syntax. But, as BROWN points out, the techniques of the ballad rather than nineteenth-century standards of realism provide better criteria for the judgement of Hardy's narrative methods; and, as LODGE argues, the seemingly incompatible elements in Hardy's style are a means of achieving both "a quality of immediacy, of 'felt life'" and "a quality of distance, both of time and space, through which the characters can be seen in their cosmic, historical and social settings". The poetry – Hardy's first love, the genre in which he wrote before taking to the novel, and in which he continued to write long after his abandonment of fiction in 1897 – has until comparatively recently suffered undue neglect. Hardy himself complained that the studied irregularity of his versification (which he compared to the "Gothic" principle in architecture) went unnoticed by reviewers; and even as sympathetic a critic as LEAVIS considered that out of the nearly 1,000 poems in all only a dozen achieve greatness. On the other hand, LARKIN declared that he "would not wish Hardy's *Collected Poems* a single page shorter". Contemporary opinion agrees much more with Larkin than with Leavis, and for many Hardy's distinction as a poet equals, and possibly exceeds, his now unquestioned distinction as a novelist.

MILLGATE remains by far the best-informed, and most judicious, of Hardy's biographers. He leans neither to what one might call the "revisionist" view of Hardy's relationship with his first and second wives, Emma and Florence, which presents him as a selfish and emotionally null husband in stark contrast with the liberal humanist figure projected by the novels – the view expressed in GITTINGS's two volumes – nor to the overprotective view embodied in the most recent biography, that by SEYMOUR-SMITH. Like Seymour-Smith however (and unlike Gittings), Millgate is primarily interested in Hardy as a writer, and he uses his extensive knowledge of Hardy's life and times essentially to understand and interpret his literary achievement. This is properly a work of biographical criticism, covering the entire range of Hardy's output, but is especially strong on the novels.

MILLER's book, though published 25 years ago, remains a classic of structuralist criticism. He is ambitious enough, though aware of his own limitations, to attempt the identification of a single theme, or underlying structure, which will provide the key to "a comprehensive view" of the whole of Hardy's work, including the novels, short stories, poems, and *The Dynasts*. This unifying principle he labels "distance and desire", by which he means a recurrent dualism in Hardy's authorial stance between immediacy and emotional involvement (especially in sexual love) on the one hand, and coolness and critical detachment on the other. As with the linguistic distinction between "deep structure" and "surface structure" (from which this approach derives), there is a tendency to assume that the unifying, deeply buried, abstract principle is somehow more interesting and profound than the variations of expression at the surface, and the effect of such an approach can be reductive. Miller, however, is aware of this, and compensates with much illuminatingly detailed analysis. He is at his best with large-scale works, especially *The Dynasts*, which lends itself very well to this type of criticism. He is also revealing and stimulating in his detection of underlying relationships between the disparate elements of Hardy's total *oeuvre*. Comparisons with other authors, especially Marcel Proust, can also be surprising, but revealing. This is not the best introduction to Hardy, but an exciting book for the reader already well acquainted with Hardy's work.

BROOKS' study covers the whole range of Hardy's work, but, as her title suggests, she views even the prose fiction through the rainbow archway of his "emotionally charged poetic pattern". Accordingly, she begins with a detailed critical study of the philosophical poems, the shorter lyrics, the extraordinarily plangent and moving poems written in 1912–13 after the death of Hardy's first wife, Emma, and the dramatic and narrative lyrics – and only after having established the primacy of his imaginative vision and poetic methods does she move on, via the combination of poetry and narrative as illustrated in his shorter fiction, to criticism of the major novels from *Far from the Madding Crowd* to *Tess of the d'Urbervilles* and *Jude the Obscure*. She rounds off with *The Dynasts*, where, again, "the effects of form are poetic". This remains one of the best overall introductions to Hardy's work, and an excellent counterbalance to the more limited critical tradition based on nineteenth-century realism.

KRAMER's 1975 study focuses on six major novels, using them as examples of the varying structures employed by Hardy in the development of his sense of tragedy. *Far from the Madding Crowd* is a "non tragic predecessor"; *The Return of the Native* a treatment of two antithetical characters, Eustacia and Clym, linked ironically in different tragic fates by Egdon Heath; in *The Mayor of Casterbridge*, the fates of Henchard and Farfrae follow a more classical structure of rise and fall (though the fall of Farfrae is implicit rather than actual); in *The Woodlanders*, tragedy is diffused throughout tone and atmosphere, but in *Tess* and *Jude* it is based in, and derived from, the subjective consciousness of the protagonists.

A brilliant, but quirkish, critic, BAYLEY works by subjective impressionism and sensitive analysis in a way that demands a more than usual willingness on the part of the reader to trust his sometimes wayward perceptions. The core of the *Essay* is not easy to define, but is perhaps summed up in Bayley's observation that the "basic law" of Hardy's imagination is "the separation of one order of perception and comment from another". His style is one of "characteristic instability", with a disjunction "between the physical perceptions, which are always his own, and the opinions and ideas which seldom are". An unexpected consequence of this approach is that the earlier novels are preferred to the later ones as being more genuinely the produce of this divided sensibility. The passionate intensity of *Tess* on the other hand, is seen as almost a flaw – Hardy lets himself go too much. It is unlikely that many readers will find themselves in complete agreement with Bayley, but the *Essay* is an original and highly individual piece of criticism, which, if it sometimes makes one blink, also makes one look at Hardy again.

Following in the wake of SMART's seminal essay, "Pictorial Imagery in the Novels of Thomas Hardy", BULLEN's study is perhaps the most scholarly, and certainly the most discerning, of a number of books and essays devoted to the exploration of Hardy's very informed insight into the visual arts and, in particular, the strongly pictorial nature of his imagination. Concentrating mainly on the novels, it deals not only with the influence on Hardy of such artists as Joshua Reynolds, J.M.W. Turner, and the French Impressionists, but with the way Hardy develops his "seeing" of his characters and their settings from a descriptiveness that is comparatively static and external in the earlier work to something more active, psychologically internalised, and at the same time ideologically coloured in the later work. This is a fascinating, well-documented specialist study, which also becomes an illuminating critical commentary.

Sometimes accused of being an autodidact who uses his hard-won knowledge too self-consciously, Hardy is a writer whose allusiveness is scattered thickly on the surface of his writing. SPRINGER's study usefully surveys how this is done in the novels, and attempts to assess the contribution it makes to their overall effect. The best chapters are those on *The Return of the Native*, *Tess*, and *Jude*, where Hardy's interest in the Arnoldian conflict between Hellenistic and Hebraic values is reinforced by classical and biblical allusion.

Recent scholars have paid much attention to Hardy's texts, particularly focusing on the differences between serialised and book-printed versions of the novels. GATRELL is one of the foremost among such scholars. His "textual biography" traces the chameleon forms undergone by Hardy's text as he revised and re-revised for the different paintings of his work. It is a salutary reminder of the often-ignored fact that there is no Platonically ideal state of the text, and that critical judgement needs to take this properly into account.

INGHAM's brief study belongs to a "Feminist Readings" series and is directed by a perspective that owes much to the growing body of modern feminist criticism (though, it should be added, the author's approach is by no means that of a militant feminist). Her concern is to place Hardy within the context of those male-dominated, or "patriarchal", assumptions that are taken for granted in most early and mid-Victorian fiction, but which begin to come under hostile scrutiny towards the end of the nineteenth and beginning of the twentieth century. Hardy's early work reflects the conventions more or less uncritically, but he becomes increasingly uneasy with them in his later work, until in *Jude*, and especially in *The Well Beloved*, a "dialectical structure" is developed in which the "voice of patriarchy falters before the women that Hardy creates". The conventional "well beloved" becomes exposed for what it is – a creature of standard womanliness emanating from the consciousness of a self-deluded anti-hero. Largely free from the jargon that afflicts some avowedly feminist criticism, Ingham's study is at once readable and stimulating – an invaluable corrective to traditional view of Hardy.

Another challenge to received Hardy opinion – though on the whole a less successful one – is thrown out by WIDDOWSON. His argument is that a "naturalized edifice of established critical orthodoxy" has been built up around Hardy as the celebrator of a fictional version of the South-West of England called "Wessex", and as elegiac commentator on the tragically doomed individual. The culprit is liberal humanism and its meekly unquestioning academic followers, whose critical principles are based on "realism" and a false assumption that Hardy is "not for an age, but for all time". For Widdowson there is no objective Hardy as such, but only a series of Hardys as constructed by his readers; though, as with other such would-be iconoclastic views, the paradoxical implications seem to be that a more disturbingly "real" Hardy underlies the smooth façade that critics have manufactured. Widdowson is at his best in his two chapters on versions of Hardy presented by the media, and in his re-interpretation of the neglected novel, *The Hand of Ethelberta*.

GARSON similarly sets out to disrupt accepted versions of Hardy. Her approach, however, is in line with recent developments in feminist criticism – though more radically psychological than Ingham's. In particular, she derives much of the rationale for her approach from Lacanian psychology, with its emphasis on the longing for wholeness. Certain recurrent figures and images are interpreted as the indices to underlying anxieties, which give the six novels that Garson treats their peculiarly imaginative tensions. Where such tensions are lacking, Hardy's work is flat. Although Garson claims to be concerned with "the larger structures of plot and character", she states quite frankly:

> . . . in general I deal with Hardy's characters not as if they were real people, with an inner life which is amenable to analysis, but rather as nodes or pressure points in the mythic structure – as generated by Hardy to solve certain personal as well, in some cases, as fictional and professional problems.

The result is an intelligent and provocative study, but one which avowedly treats the fictional works in question as "fables" rather than novels.

Various collections of essays also contain valuable criticism of Hardy. COX's *Critical Heritage* volume is particularly useful for its extensive collection of early reviews, which throw interesting light on Hardy's relationship with his contemporary reading public and the difficulties caused by his growing frankness in sexual matters. My (DRAPER's) *Casebook* (1975) on the tragic novels includes some early comments, along with extracts from significant earlier critics such as Lionel Johnson, Virginia Woolf, and D.H. Lawrence (whose distinction between the inevitability of classical tragedy and the merely social nature of Hardy's tragedy still remains a challenging, if questionable, concept). Later critics include Robert C. Schweik and Tony Tanner; and (in the 1991 revised edition only) Peter J. Casagrande and three feminist critics – Elaine Showalter, Kristin Brady, and Rosemary Sumner. The *Casebook* on the pastoral novels (DRAPER, 1987), dealing with *Under the Greenwood Tree*, *Far from the Madding Crowd*, and *The Woodlanders*, includes earlier criticism (by Henry James, J.M. Barrie, and Virginia Woolf, among others) and more recent pieces considering the relationship of these novels to traditional pastoral, their sociological implications, and their narrative techniques.

KRAMER (1979 and 1990) is particularly sensitive to recent trends in "theory" and, without being exclusive, favours essays with a structuralist or deconstructionist (Marxist or otherwise) as well as feminist approach. His own prefaces discuss these categories, with reference to the examples included, and in so doing form a useful introduction both to modern developments in criticism generally, and to criticism of Hardy in particular. MALLET and my (DRAPER's) volume contains essays and poems by members of the Thomas Hardy Society (including Millgate, Morgan, Sumner and Bullen), focusing in the main on the modernity of Hardy.

PAULIN's book is arguably the best, and still the most readable, monograph devoted to Hardy's poetry. Paulin's emphasis is, appropriately, on the acute and accurate details of "perception" that anchor Hardy's poetry so firmly to reality; but he also demonstrates the visionary quality which, while remaining concrete, enables Hardy to transcend his own earthliness. The book is also rich in sensitive and judicious "practical criticism". TAYLOR's two books on the poetry between them constitute the most carefully documented treatise on Hardy's technical virtuosity and conscious awareness of the foundations of his art. *Hardy's Poetry* pays special attention to what Taylor calls the "meditative lyric"; *Hardy's Metres* is notable for its meticulous examination of the great variety of Hardy's verse forms. Together these are indispensable tools for the study of Hardy's poetry. The GIBSON and JOHNSON *Casebook* on the poems follows a similar pattern to the Casebooks on the novels. It includes early and more recent criticism, with important contributions by Edward Thomas, Cecil Day Lewis, Samuel Hanes, Thom Gunn, and Frank R. Giordano.

There is a limited amount of criticism devoted to Hardy's short stories. BRADY's study therefore fills a gap – and fills it competently. Each of the stories is discussed in terms of its publication history, plot, theme, and characterisation, and attention is also paid to the structural effects of grouping them in separate volumes. The analyses of "For Conscience' Sake", "On the Western Circuit", and "The Fiddler of the Reels" are particularly interesting.

R.P. DRAPER

Harlem Renaissance

Baker, Houston A., Jr., *Modernism and the Harlem Renaissance*, Chicago: Chicago University Press, 1987

Bone, Robert A., *The Negro Novel in America*, New Haven, Connecticut: Yale University Press, 1958

Douglas Ann, *Terrible Honesty: Mongrel Manhattan in the 1920s*, New York: Farrar, Straus, Giroux, 1995

Huggins, Nathan, *Harlem Renaissance*, New York and Oxford: Oxford University Press, 1971

Hull, Gloria, T., *Color, Sex and Poetry: Three Women Writers of the Harlem Renaissance*, Bloomington: Indiana University Press, 1987

Johnson, James Weldon, *Black Manhattan*, New York: Knopf, 1930

Kramer, Victor, *The Harlem Renaissance Re-Examined*, New York: AMS Press, 1987

Lewis, David Levering, *When Harlem Was in Vogue*, New York and Oxford: Oxford University Press, 1981

Singh, Amritjit, William S. Shiver, and Stanley Brodwin (eds.), *The Harlem Renaissance: Revaluations*, New York: Garland, 1989

Wall, Cheryl, "Poets and Versifiers, Singers and Signifiers, Women of the Harlem Renaissance," in *Women, the Arts, and the 1920s in Paris and New York*, edited by Kenneth W. Wheeler and Virginia Lee Lussier, New Brunswick, New Jersey: Transaction Books, 1982

Wintz, Cary D., *Black Culture and the Harlem Renaissance*, Houston, Texas: Rice University Press, 1988

So much critical energy has been devoted to debunking the Harlem Renaissance that it is hard to know how it ever became canonized as such. Strictly speaking, the term refers to the brief but powerful renaissance in African-American arts and letters centred in Harlem during the 1920s. But to define it thus obscures the contributions made by African-American writers in other parts of the country, even as it obscures the rich cultural tradition that both preceded and followed it. Similarly, to emphasize literature at the expense of the other arts – as many scholars have done – obscures the dynamic role of African-American theatre, music, dance, and song, which not only inspired many of the writers of the Harlem Renaissance, but, in the eyes of some, eclipsed their achievements as well. However one ultimately defines it, the Harlem Renaissance has elicited a fractious debate over its success or failure, the answer to which depends, in large part, on the degree of co-option attributed to its white audience. And it should come as no surprise that that debate began long before the Harlem Renaissance was over – more often than not among its chief partisans.

The opening salvo in what might be described as the critical retrospective of the Harlem Renaissance was initiated by JOHNSON, one of the towering intellectual figures of the movement. His book is as much a product *of* the Harlem Renaissance as it is *about* it. That is to say that Johnson was inspired by the optimistic faith of the movement he describes. Accordingly, his is a history of African-American accomplishment, beginning with the arrival of the Dutch in what was then New Amsterdam, and ending with the Harlem Renaissance itself. Johnson's primary interest is in the black theatrical tradition, which he sees as perhaps the most important black contribution to American culture. Indeed, Johnson argues that the song and dance found on the black stage – from "Under the Bamboo Tree" to the charleston – supplied a newly emergent popular culture with its distinctive repertoire. (He ought to know something about that – as the partner in a famous songwriting team he wrote many of those popular songs himself). When the Harlem Renaissance is viewed from a theatrical perspective (rather than a purely literary one), as is the case here, it is not only enriched, but its chronological boundaries are greatly expanded as well. Johnson makes a good argument for beginning the renaissance in black art with the theatrical productions of the 1890s, like the *Creole Show*, *The Octoroons*, and *Oriental America*, instead of beginning with, say, the publication of Jean Toomer's *Cane* in 1923. This is when African-American actors began to reclaim the roles they had been forced to surrender to white minstrels. He also examines shows like *A Trip to Coontown* and *Clorindy* at the turn of the century, when the racist conventions of minstrels were dramatically reworked by productions organized by African Americans. While Johnson's book is not terribly analytical, he has gathered and organized an immense amount of material into a capacious vision of black expression, which has set the standard against which all subsequent studies are measured.

For many years after Johnson's book, commentary on the Harlem Renaissance was limited to the fiction and memoirs of its participants. Wallace Thurman wrote a biting satire on the pretentiousness of the movement's most prominent figures in his *roman à clef* entitled *Infants of the Spring* (1932). And Langston Hughes displayed a profound ambivalence toward the primitivism that both enabled the Renaissance and finally limited it, in his autobiography *The Big Sea* (1940). The only scholarly study of any real significance before the 1970s is

BONE's, which argues for an opposition between two distinct, discursive traditions in the African-American novel – a radical cultural nationalism, which emphasizes racial difference, versus a middle-class, assimilationist stance, which seeks to efface that difference. Bone discovers this opposition in the Harlem Renaissance as played out between the advocates of the "Harlem School" (Langston Hughes, Claude McKay, Wallace Thurman, *et al.*) and their "Old Guard" critics (Benjamin Brawley, William Stanley Braithwaite, and in more qualified ways, Walter White and W.E.B. Du Bois). In Bone's argument, the former withdraw their allegiance from the values of the dominant culture and search for alternative values in the folk culture of the slaves and their African origins, while the latter write largely to educate a white audience about the injustices of black life and to justify their claims to equality based on their demonstrable capacities. Bone's study is balanced and judicious, but it is essentially a rehash of the old debate between naturalism and genteel culture. Moreover, it suffers from an overweening dualism that does not do justice to the complexities of the cultural moment.

The first critical study to bring those complexities into focus is HUGGINS's (the first book-length study devoted entirely to the movement itself). More than any other study published before or since, it has defined the period and set the terms for the critical debate over its significance. This is due in no small part to his provocative claim that the Harlem Renaissance was a failure, because of the inability of African-American writers to transcend a certain "provincialism", which had its roots not just in black experience, but in the history of the nation as a whole. Huggins argues that, from its inception, American society has been plagued by an anxiety over the status of its cultural achievements *vis à vis* those of Europe. That anxiety has led Americans to imitate the models of an exalted European tradition even as they exaggerate their own achievements. It is only with the astonishing burst of creativity in the first three decades of the twentieth century that some Americans were able to leave that pathology behind. According to Huggins, the African-American writers of the Harlem Renaissance were not among them. Tethered to a system of white patronage, uncertain of their audience, and most of all victims of a virulent racism, they remained "ethnic provincials". Their every act was scrutinized for evidence of the Negro's inherent potential or secret inadequacy. The burden was too much to bear. It made for a damning "self-consciousness that crippled [their] art". "Such deep doubt", Huggins insists, "makes conservatives and, sometimes, mimics". In the case of Countee Cullen, Nella Larsen, and Jessie Fauset, that meant a "slavish" devotion to the genteel conventions of the "late Victorians", i.e., "morality and uplift, a faith in progress . . . and the aspiration for a learned (not native) culture". (One hears echoes of Bone's thesis here.) In the case of Zora Neale Hurston, Claude McKay, and Rudolph Fisher, that self-consciousness meant a willingness to play the primitive for a white audience in search of exotica. Bound by these formidable limitations, Huggins argues that the writers of the Harlem Renaissance were unable to explore the richness and complexity of the modern black experience. To Huggins's mind, only Jean Toomer and, to a much more limited extent, Langston Hughes were able to achieve a virtuosity comparable to the leading blues and jazz artists of the day.

Like Huggins, LEWIS also takes up the failure of the Harlem Renaissance. For Lewis, this failure is attributable to the extravagant faith its authors maintained in the capacity of the arts to overcome racial division – a stance he dismisses as civil rights by copyright. Ultimately, however, the success or failure of the Harlem Renaissance is of less interest to Lewis than providing an exhaustively researched study of the movement as a whole. This book is probably the fullest elaboration of the Harlem Renaissance available, filling in the historical gaps left by Huggins's more tendentious approach. Among other things, Lewis examines in detail the careers of those patrons, critics, and publicists who made the Renaissance possible (Jessie Fauset, Charles S. Johnson, Caspar Holstein, Walter White, James Weldon Johnson, and Alain Locke) as well as its "stars" (McKay, Toomer, Hughes, and Cullen). Where Huggins places the Renaissance within the context of America's historical quest for identity as a provincial culture, Lewis situates the movement within its more immediate social and political milieux – i.e., northern migration, the Harlem real-estate market, Marcus Garvey's UNIA movement, a new sense of black entitlement after World War I, as well as the race riots and lynchings that followed.

Both literary histories are usefully supplemented by WINTZ. Wintz offers an extended commentary on the foundations of the "New Negro" philosophy in the work of Booker T. Washington and Du Bois, as well as investigation into the literary roots of the Harlem Renaissance in the art of Paul Laurence Dunbar and Charles W. Chesnutt. Wintz also contributes some illuminating material on the Renaissance's severest critics, like Braithwaite and Brawley (both of whom are overlooked in all but Bone's study), and of course Du Bois and Garvey. Wintz is particularly interested in their respective periodicals to counter (and occasionally to censor) the "Van Vechten school's" preoccupation with what Du Bois described as the "debauched tenth" – a phenomenon they all felt exposed black America's "worst elements" to a critical white audience.

DOUGLAS sees her book as an "effort to engage and debate" Lewis's (and Huggins's) construction of the Harlem Renaissance as a failure. Douglas argues that that judgement is "unduly harsh . . . demanding of Harlem's leaders powers of hindsight inevitably . . . inaccessible to them". In stark contrast to such judgements, she reads the Harlem Renaissance as an unqualified success, comparable to "a second Emancipation Proclamation". Arguing along the same lines as Johnson, she describes the emergence of a "mongrelized" urban, popular culture during the 1920s, which was made possible by "the conjunction of the black performance tradition and the white media". Unfortunately, in both Johnson's and Douglas's accounts, the terms of that conjunction remain relatively unexamined. Neither Johnson nor Douglas pay sufficient attention to the dynamics of power involved (each for very different reasons) leading them both to place too much faith in the success of their conflicted collaboration. Douglas is on firmer ground with her attempts to place the Harlem Renaissance within its white context. In particular, she explores white America's fascination with the primitive – derived from Freud, and figured in the image of black Harlem – as a means of criticizing a psychologically repressed and socially repressive civilization. This argument has been made before, but

Douglas's chief contribution lies in her capacity to contextualize white interest in Harlem within the overarching critical ethos of the 1920s.

All of the foregoing studies might be characterized as old-fashioned literary histories. They are rich in detail, thoroughly researched, and together they provide an indispensable overview. But none of them provide much in the way of a textual, thematic, or theoretical analysis of the period's major works. Most of the more sophisticated investigations in this regard are buried in collections of essays devoted to the period. SINGH *et al.* and WHEELER and LUSSIER have some of the best essays on specific texts and authors (a few of them more obscure than they should be) as well as essays that take up important related topics, like primitivism and therapeutic culture, the influence of the Harlem Renaissance on Afro-French négritude, and so on. KRAMER has also put together a collection of stimulating essays: in addition to pieces on Larsen, Thurman, and an especially good article on black women playwrights by Nellie McKay, there are a number of noteworthy essays devoted to the work of white writers like Eugene O'Neill, DuBose Heyward, and Carl Van Vechten, who were influenced by, and in turn influenced, the Harlem Renaissance.

With the exception of individual author-studies, very little has been written on the collective contributions that women made to the Harlem Renaissance. This omission surely has its roots in the misogyny of some of the movement's most prominent participants (such as Alain Locke), as well as in the masculinist bias of the New Negro philosophy itself. Scholars who are interested in radical politics or formal innovation have likewise dismissed the contributions of women because of their tendency to "succumb" to the middle-class, genteel conventions of the day. (Zora Neale Hurston has been the lone exception to this state of affairs, no doubt because of her preference for a more anthropological orientation.) HULL has gone a long way toward rectifying this bias. Her examination of three neglected poets – Alice Dunbar-Nelson, Angelina Weld Grimke, and Georgia Douglas Johnson – promises, as she puts it, to broaden the "temporal, geographical and critical boundaries" of the Harlem Renaissance "tyrannized by periodization, the hierarchy of canonical forms, critical rankings of major and minor". Through a series of careful readings Hull discovers these writers' own deep ambivalence toward the genteel conventions in which they wrote – an ambivalence that, she argues, is ultimately the source of their best poetry. Hull's thesis finds its antithesis in WALL's provocative essay, which argues for the inadequacy of the genteel aesthetic in representing the black experience. There is no news there; that argument follows a relatively standard line laid down by Huggins and Douglas. But Wall goes on to discover a far richer tradition of black female expression in the blues artistry of, among others, Bessie Smith: "free from the burdens of an alien tradition", she observes (and Huggins would agree), "Bessie Smith could establish the standard of her art; in the process she would compose a more honest poetry than any of her literary sisters". Although her discussion of the blues is rather cursory, Wall's essay adumbrates a rich line of inquiry that has been picked up by a variety of ethno-musicologists and cultural anthropologists too numerous to mention. (The best place to begin is probably with Jervis Anderson's *This Was Harlem* and Samuel Floyd's *Black Music in the Harlem Renaissance.*)

Like Douglas and Hull, BAKER rejects the thesis of failure (although on very different grounds). In fact, he finds it suspicious that black scholars should devote so much energy to proving the inadequacy of a moment in African-American cultural history of such obvious achievement. Baker attributes this misreading of the Harlem Renaissance to the application of standards of judgement derived from, and sanctioned by, an alien tradition of Anglo-American modernism. Rather than measuring the Harlem Renaissance against a tradition from which black experience has been largely excluded, it would be more appropriate, Baker argues, to generate a reading of the Renaissance and African-American modernity from a "problematic" that is grounded in the specific history and interests of African Americans themselves. Accordingly, Baker chooses to speak not so much about black literary achievement (with its implicit comparisons to white literary achievement), but more about the expansion of the discursive possibilities available to African Americans in a racist society. In particular, Baker focuses on two discursive strategies, which he describes as "the mastery of form and the deformation of mastery". Beginning with Booker T. Washington's Atlanta Exposition Speech in 1895, and moving forward through Du Bois's *Souls of Black Folk* and Locke's seminal Harlem Renaissance text *The New Negro*, Baker explores a complicated dialectic through which these writers alternately display a mastery of the dominant forms of Western culture (a strategy of concealment to allow for maximum self-protection and advancement) and a deformation of those forms (a strategy of resistance to the master's language and its damning consequences). In the process Baker chronicles the gradual expansion and enrichment of the discursive possibilities available to African Americans with which to understand their own circumstances. In that context, the Harlem Renaissance is not only *not* a failure, it represents a genuine advance in what Baker describes elsewhere as the "'spirit work' of a racial genius" (*Afro-American Poetics*, 5).

JONATHAN VEITCH

Harris, Wilson 1921 –

Guyanese-born British novelist and poet

Cribb, T.J., "Wilson Harris – Sworn Surveyor", in *Journal of Commonwealth Literature*, 29(1), 1993

Gilkes, Michael, *Wilson Harris and the Caribbean Novel*, Trinidad and London: Longman, 1975

Gilkes, Michael (ed.), *The Literate Imagination: Essays on the Novels of Wilson Harris*, London: Macmillan, 1989

James, C.L.R., "On Wilson Harris" and "Discovering Literature in Trinidad: The 1930s", in his *Spheres of Existence: Selected Writings*, London: Allison & Busby, 1980

Maes-Jelinek, Hena, *Wilson Harris*, Boston: Twayne, 1982

Maes-Jelinek, Hena (ed.), *Wilson Harris: The Uncompromising Imagination*, Aarhus, Denmark: Dangaroo Press, 1991

Critical recognition of Wilson Harris began soon after the publication of his first novel in 1960, and has grown steadily, particularly among academics concerned with postcolonial literatures. There is now a small industry of scholars dedicated to Harris's work. Yet he is usually considered a difficult writer, presenting problems for novel-readers more accustomed to recognisable narratives, easily comprehensible language, and definable characters and relationships. Harris's fiction offers a critique of what we have grown used to in novels, yet it is, perhaps surprisingly, immediately accessible in terms of its energy, colour, and emotional tone, and his vocabulary is not especially recondite or obscure in itself. His best critics have conveyed the excitement of his work as well as its seriousness.

The best introduction to his work as a whole is the collection of essays and tributes by various friends and critics, edited by MAES-JELINEK (1991) for Harris's 70th birthday. This includes interviews and "critical dialogues", which cover a variety of fundamental themes in Harris's writing (such as his use of myth, the role of language and the imagination, his comic vision, his association with Scotland, the kind of resistance to naturalism his novels set up), as well as readings of specific novels in his *oeuvre*. *Palace of the Peacock*, *Heartland*, *Tumatumari*, *Black Marsden*, *Carnival*, *The Infinite Rehearsal*, and *The Four Banks of the River of Space* all receive close readings. There is also a well-researched bibliography. The contributors range widely in age, critical approach, and personal background, so there is a multi-faceted quality to the book, which embodies a freshness and seriousness that is appropriate for its subject.

MAES-JELINEK's 1982 book in the Twayne series is somewhat dated now, but remains a valuable introduction to Harris's earlier work, with commentaries on all the earlier novels, explicating narrative procedures and giving a vivid impression of the visionary drive animating Harris's prose. A final chapter pursues the metaphor of "The Novel as Painting", which is particularly appropriate to Harris's multi-layered, densely textured work. There is a chronology giving the bare bones of Harris's life-story, but no biography.

Maes-Jelinek is also one of the contributors to the collection of essays edited by GILKES (1989), along with eight other academics and Harris himself. The essays are grouped in three titled clusters: the first, "Phenomenal Space", includes Mark McWatt's analysis of "whore/madonna" imagery and the significance of women in Harris's fiction; the second, "Language and Perception", includes an essay by Jean-Pierre Durix on the difficulties of translating Harris; the third, "The Dialectical Imagination", deals mainly with Harris's metaphysical engagement with time and narrative.

GILKES also produced the earliest book-length introduction to Harris (1975) in the literary context of Caribbean novelists such as Edgar Mittelholzer, George Lamming, V.S. Naipaul, and the poet Derek Walcott. His Introduction is a lucid assessment of Harris's place in the constellation of Caribbean literature, as seen in 1972. From *Palace of the Peacock* to *Black Marsden*, Gilkes's reading of Harris is friendly, accessible, and carefully judged, sensitive to the dangers of over-reading and the "aberrations of critical judgement" to which some critics of Harris are susceptible.

It is worth returning to one of the earliest appreciations of Harris, by the great Caribbean scholar and thinker JAMES. His essays link Harris to existentialism and phenomenology, referring to Heidegger, Kant, Jaspers, and Sartre. Yet James's enthusiasm, freshness, and immediacy are engaging and infectious. Harris, James observes, has arrived at crucial philosophical positions beginning at a different point to, and following other routes than via, the European philosophers. James is very clear about Harris's early orientations regarding literature in English and Western traditions, and Harris's tendency "to be writing English as if his native language were German"; yet he is in no doubt about Harris's "very vital reality", and he conveys it quickly.

CRIBB's essay is the best example of recent original research, unearthing biographical data that genuinely illuminates Harris's fiction. Cribb has studied documents in the archives of the Ministry of Public Works in Guyana relating to Harris's early expeditions, as an official Government Surveyor, into the interior of the rainforest, experiences that have informed his imagination ever since. He explicates in great detail Harris's understanding of the links between scientific discovery, imaginative apprehension, and literary commemoration, and establishes an important argument about Harris's moral imperative. He sees, first, that:

> The compelling coordinates of time and place that inform the realist novel are still there [in Harris's work] but the reader is forced to locate the same events simultaneously on quite different scales of perception and value. Hence the strenuousness of reading Harris, but hence too a sense of liberation that grows with every reading.

Moreover, Cribb is able to point out that Harris's writing is responsible to the experiences he shared with the men and women he worked and travelled with for 15 years before his writing career began: as Harris noted, "they were not interested in what they already knew about themselves, but in something more. So realism was not the answer . . . I have kept faith with those men and women". Cribb's essay is a necessary corrective to those commentaries on Harris's work that treat his work in a purely conceptual and intellectual way, and it is a possible point of entry for readers who suspect Harris to be merely esoteric and élitist.

ALAN RIACH

Hawkes, John 1925–

American novelist, short-story writer, and dramatist

Greiner, Donald J., *Comic Terror: The Novels of John Hawkes*, Memphis, Tennessee: Memphis State University Press, 1974, revised 1978

Greiner, Donald J., *Understanding John Hawkes*, Columbia: University of South Carolina Press, 1985

Kuehl, John, *John Hawkes and the Craft of Conflict*, New Brunswick, New Jersey: Rutgers University Press, 1975

O'Donnell, Patrick, *John Hawkes*, Boston: Twayne, 1982

Olderman, Raymond, *Beyond the Waste Land: The American Novel in the Nineteen-Sixties*, New Haven, Connecticut: Yale University Press, 1972

Scholes, Robert, *Fabulation and Metafiction*, Urbana: University of Illinois Press, 1980

Tanner, Tony, *City of Words: American Fiction 1950–1970*, London: Jonathan Cape, 1971; New York: Harper & Row, 1971

John Hawkes occupies an important position in postwar American fiction not simply because of his considerable achievement in the novel and short-story form (his plays are less successful), but also for his contributions to what has become a recognizably American version of fictional post-modernism. His novels are at once dislocations of those conventional routes by which the reader enters the fictional universe of an author and powerful reminders of the violence that frequently exists under the "normal" surfaces of everyday life. Given Hawkes's importance, it is surprising that there is so little in the way of intelligent, sustained criticism of his work, and beyond the titles considered here the student would do well to look for criticism of Hawkes among the many general studies of modern, particularly innovative, fiction of the United States.

TANNER's discussion of Hawkes in the chapter "Necessary Landscapes and Luminous Deteriorations", from his excellent book on American fiction between 1950 and 1970, addresses itself, in part, to Hawkes's fictional settings, Tanner noting "that his novels have settings as various as post-war Germany, post-war and Renaissance Italy, post-war England, the American West, and islands in the Atlantic and the South Seas". All these settings, however, are re-imagined, and each is, as Hawkes himself said in an interview, "a totally new and necessary fictional landscape". Tanner deals with most of Hawkes's early writings, notably *The Cannibal*, *The Beetle Leg*, the two short novels which make up *The Goose and the Grave*, *The Lime Twig*, and *Second Skin*, and his overarching thesis is that they are, in some way or another, related to war, and as a result often centre on "landscapes of desolation and decline which point to the progress of entropy quite as graphically as the lansdcapes of Burroughs and Pynchon". Moreover, Tanner argues, "Hawkes's private nightmares of violence and evil are at the same time probings of our common world". This remains one of the seminal essays on Hawkes.

OLDERMAN's consideration of *The Lime Twig* is contextualized by his account of what he sees as a modern version of the "Waste Land" myth in 1960s' American fiction. The various motifs that one associates with this myth are traced with assiduousness through a series of writers who came to prominence in the decade, notably John Barth, Joseph Heller, Ken Kesey, Thomas Pynchon, and Kurt Vonnegut. In *The Lime Twig*, he suggests, Hawkes "explores the individual's dream, and the violent terror – the lust for death – that haunts the heart of that dream". The novel is constructed from "memory and desire", and Hawkes, like T.S. Eliot, "works to show the ever-present contemporaneity of the past" while at the same time addressing the central question as to what could be the "role of the artist in the waste land world?".

KUEHL explores "the relationship between Hawkes's central theme and his craft" (what we might express, more simply, as the relationship between form and content), though his argument turns on a rather tentative distinction between the fiction before 1960 and that after 1960: the former, he says, is "death-oriented", while in the latter Eros exists alongside Thanatos. This distinction is not immediately perspicuous to the reader of Hawkes, and Kuehl pursues it somewhat relentlessly, though his book is important for showing how a Freudian vocabulary can, when intelligently applied, illuminate the fiction. A postscript links *Death, Sleep, and the Traveler* to *The Blood Oranges*, while an appendix prints a valuable, if at times rather confusing, interview with Hawkes.

GREINER, in his 1978 revised version of his 1974 original, treats Hawkes as a black humorist who, in both style and content, has affinities with satirists of the eighteenth century. The satire, he suggests, frequently encompasses parody, and where the early novels parody conventional fictional forms, such as the detective novel and the western genre, the later novels offer parodies of the fictional process itself – though, paradoxically, this later fiction is more "conventional" in respect of composition and thematic and structural arrangement. *The Owl*, Greiner suggests, with its patterns of language and recurring motifs, is the most successful of the early works, and while much can be made of the moral instability of the major fiction he argues that Hawkes maintains a faith in the "invulnerability of basic values: love, communication, sympathy". This remains, arguably, the best book-length study of Hawkes.

SCHOLES has two chapters on Hawkes, which address, respectively, his theory of fiction and what many would view as his most distinguished novel, *The Lime Twig*. Scholes argues that Hawkes works within a picaresque tradition, and that his admiration for writers such as Nathanael West, Flannery O'Connor, William Faulkner, and Vladimir Nabokov "suggests the kind of delight in formal and verbal dexterity that is the essence of fabulation". In what has become typical of the "anti-mimetic" novel, Hawkes reduces the "overt plottiness of his fiction" so much that "by driving his plot underground Hawkes has made it less visible but no less important". The "dislocations of time and space serve the same purpose that they do in Conrad, Ford, and Faulkner", that of involving the reader "in the constructive process". Of *The Lime Twig* Scholes says that here Hawkes "has gone well beyond easy satire . . . and by pruning his somewhat surrealistic exuberance, and coming to terms (even if somewhat ironic and parodic ones) with fiction's need for plot, he has achieved a controlled intensity of effect which bridges beautifully the gap between terror and tenderness". Scholes's discussion is conducted within a larger literary and theoretical context of modern "fabulation", and Hawkes's contributions to the development of anti-realist fiction are seen alongside those of writers such as Barth, Donald Barthelme, Robert Coover, William Gass, Gabriel García Márquez, Pynchon, Nathalie Sarraute, and Vonnegut, among others.

O'DONNELL's study (in the Twayne "United States Authors" series) is a very useful introductory guide to Hawkes. He shows how Hawkes's novels "encourage psychoanalytical, structural, mythic, even historically oriented readings, so that in any speculation on his work one must choose an approach perhaps to the detriment of others". Above all, he suggests, his work is "comprised of fictions about the makings of fictions, and it offers much to the contemporary assessment of the imaginative process as systematic, yet paranoid, generative, yet attracted to the death throes of our apocalyptic culture". His discussion centres on eight novels and three novellas, and considerations of space preclude any account of the short stories, the plays, and the poetry. The opening chapter offers a brief overview of Hawkes's career, and the concluding chapter, "Hawkes among His Contemporaries", intelligently assesses his writing alongside that of Faulkner, Nabokov, Pynchon, and West. In addition there is a chronology and a good selective bibliography.

GREINER's later (1985) book, in the "Understanding Contemporary American Literature" series, is more of an introductory guide than his earlier study. He examines each of the major novels up to 1985, stressing the extent to which *The Owl*, with its combination of the comic and the frightening, forms the ideal introduction to the fiction. He emphasizes the extent to which Hawkes extends the boundaries of fiction, particularly with respect to plot, character, setting, and theme. This later book is valuable for its consideration of the postmodernist features of the fiction, especially those that bear on what we might call "the wilful dislocation of the reader".

HENRY CLARIDGE

Hawthorne, Nathaniel 1804–1864

American novelist and short-story writer

Baym, Nina, *The Shape of Hawthorne's Career*, Ithaca, New York: Cornell University Press, 1976
Bloom, Harold (ed.), *Nathaniel Hawthorne*, New York: Chelsea House, 1986
Colacurcio, Michael J., *The Province of Piety: Moral History in Hawthorne's Early Tales*, Cambridge, Massachusetts: Harvard University Press, 1984
Colacurcio, Michael J. (ed.), *New Essays on "The Scarlet Letter"*, Cambridge and New York: Cambridge University Press, 1985
Crews, Frederick C., *The Sins of the Fathers: Hawthorne's Psychological Themes*, New York: Oxford University Press, 1966
Fogle, Richard Harter, *Hawthorne's Fiction: The Light and the Dark*, Norman: University of Oklahoma Press, 1952, revised 1964
Levine, Robert S., *Conspiracy and Romance: Studies in Brockden Brown, Cooper, Hawthorne and Melville*, Cambridge: Cambridge University Press, 1989
Miller, J. Hillis, *Hawthorne and History: Defacing It*, Oxford and Cambridge, Massachusetts: Blackwell, 1991
Millington, Richard H., *Practicing Romance: Narrative Form and Cultural Engagement in Hawthorne's Fiction*, Princeton, New Jersey: Princeton University Press, 1992
Pfister, Joel, *The Production of Personal Life: Class, Gender and the Psychology of Hawthorne's Fiction*, Stanford, California: Stanford University Press, 1991
Swann, Charles, *Nathaniel Hawthorne: Tradition and Revolution*, Cambridge and New York: Cambridge University Press, 1991

BLOOM's volume brings together essays originally published between 1954 and 1984, which represent many of the major points of focus in criticism of Hawthorne's work. Larzer Ziff discusses morality and Hawthorne's theory of romance in relation to "The Custom House"; Daniel G. Hoffman explores Hawthorne's personal nostalgia and the "folklore of love" in "The Maypole of Merry Mount". In this same symbolic or mythical vein, Clark Griffiths contrasts "substance words" and "shadow words" in *The House of the Seven Gables*, and R.W.B. Lewis analyzes "returns into time" in *The Marble Faun*. Bloom's Introduction traces Ralph Waldo Emerson's influence on *The Scarlet Letter*, and A.N. Kaul identifies continuities between Puritan tradition and New England Transcendentalism in *The Blithedale Romance*. Stylistic studies are represented by Frederick C. Crews, who uses psychoanalytic theory to describe the concept of compulsion in "Roger Malvin's Burial", John Caldwell Stubbs discusses the comic elements of *The House of the Seven Gables*, and Nina Baym considers the elegiac mode of *The Marble Faun*. The relationship between Hawthorne's work and literary or national tradition receives treatment from Richard H. Brodhead, Keith Carabine, and Michael J. Colacurcio. Attention is also paid to Hawthorne's stories: Leo B. Levy analyzes the problem of faith in "Young Goodman Brown", Sheldon W. Liebman discusses Hawthorne's Romanticism in "The Artist of the Beautiful", and "Rappaccini's Daughter" is analyzed by Richard Brenzo.

Many of the postwar monographs on Hawthorne deal with the unique characteristics of his fictional style. Of these, symbolism was seen as the most significant, in a period when formalist analysis was the dominant analytical model in literary studies. In the heyday of the New Criticism, Hawthorne's use of imagery was viewed as the crucial element of his work. FOGLE's study exemplifies this approach, and it established the groundwork for other critics. Realism provides the measure in terms of which Hawthorne's literary innovations are described. The accusations of fancifulness, irrelevance, and inauthenticity are answered by a detailed analysis of Hawthorne's use of imagery to convey his meanings. Hawthorne's ambiguity is represented rather as a paradoxical union of opposites, among which Fogle identifies "a unique and wonderful combination of light and darkness". The clarity of design, which characterizes his fiction, contrasts with the darkness of tragic complexity, so that the clarity is interfused with subtlety and ambiguity. And it is symbolism that carries this double freight – symbolism which Fogle interprets with sensitivity to a number of contexts: American Romanticism, Hawthorne's role as author, and the nuances of narrative design.

Hawthorne's craft is described not only by contrast with the demands of narrative realism but also in terms of his use of the romance form. Hawthorne's famous distinction between the novel and the romance has been explored by several critics both in relation to what the term tells us about Hawthorne's literary achievement, and his attitude towards the American literary context in which he was working, and in relation to Hawthorne's place among such contemporaries as Charles Brockden Brown, James Fenimore Cooper, Herman Melville, and others. MILLINGTON addresses the former issues and discusses in detail the four major romances – *The Scarlet Letter*, *The House of the Seven Gables*, *The Blithedale Romance*, and *The Marble Faun*. He relates the development of Hawthorne's distinctive romance structure to the artist's need to make his work relevant and valuable to the community in which he lived. Therefore, questions such as the authority of the writer and the justification of the imaginative life come to the fore in Millington's analysis of the relationship with the reader that Hawthorne tried to nurture. The complex interplay of private impulse and public consequences, or cultural impact, is shown to have a profound influence on the subjects and figures Hawthorne chose to represent, as well as on the tone of anxiety that intrudes into his fiction and its style. Millington's major contribution to the debate concerning Hawthorne's use of romance is his perception that its narrative form enabled the precise representation of Hawthorne's analysis of merican character and his understanding of antebellum culture. Thus, Millington skillfully interweaves the biographical, literary, and cultural contexts of Hawthorne's work with a penetrative formal analysis of the narratives.

LEVINE, whose work exemplifies the comparative approach to Hawthorne's romances, follows in the tradition of Joel Porte's *The Romance in America: Studies in Cooper, Poe, Hawthorne, Melville and James* (1969) and George Dekker's *The American Historical Romance* (1987). Studies such as these focus on points of unity among the early canonical writers, and consequently a basic assumption, often left unsaid, is that these similarities offer important clues to the "Americanness" of American literature. Levine enters this debate by offering a reading of Hawthorne's romance that shares an obsessive concern with the very issues that troubled the early Republic. These issues, according to Levine's persuasive account, relate to the threat posed by "subversives" – French revolutionaries, secret societies, Catholic immigrants, African slaves – to undermine the order and integrity of the new nation. Such threats are seen to be incorporated into the fabric of the American romance, as are the conflicts and ideals of the Republic. Literary history and national history converge, therefore, in this account of Hawthorne and his contemporaries.

The innovation of BAYM's work, when published in 1976, lay in her encouragement to go beyond a study of Hawthorne's major romances. She documents the development of Hawthorne's artistic sensibility by showing how his work changed as he grew older and as the circumstances surrounding his writing developed. So, the image of Hawthorne that emerges from her pages is quite different to the figure of the romancer whose ideas found their exemplary expression in only a handful of texts. By examining Hawthorne's writings from *Fanshawe* through to the unfinished romances, and by studying not only the "serious" fiction but also the sketches, children's stories, and non-fiction works as well, Baym shows that Hawthorne's career was marked by consecutive changes and a process of development. All the texts Hawthorne intended for publication, and on which he intended his reputation to rest, are analyzed, in chronological order and in the developing context these works provide for one another. One of the insights that emerges from such an approach is that Hawthorne's work is not necessarily opposed to the tenets of literary realism, but that realism, like Romanticism, characterised one of the many stages of his entire artistic career.

The relationship between Hawthorne's writing and the passing of time, "history", is tremendously complex, subtle, and difficult. But full justice is done to this relationship by SWANN's meticulously researched and painstaking account of the entire corpus of Hawthorne's work. Swann identifies a fundamental conflict between the demands of tradition and the excitement of revolutionary change and innovation. This ambivalence remained a characteristic element of Hawthorne throughout his career, as Swann's detailed discussion of the major works makes clear. But the argument does not depend solely on the reading of Hawthorne's best-known work, though it gains in persuasive power from these readings. The neglected and sorely underrated texts – the early "Alice Doane's Appeal" and the unfinished *The American Claimant Manuscripts* and *The Elixir of Life Manuscripts* – receive a welcome revisionary interpretation, which reveals the full extent of Hawthorne's achievement and the sheer variousness of his engagement with the concept of history in general, and the problematics of American history in particular. This impressive study demonstrates a keen sensitivity to the subtleties of Hawthorne's fiction in combination with an intelligent appreciation of the complexities of dealing with the past.

Swann distinguishes his project from COLACURCIO's landmark 1984 study, which argues for Hawthorne's importance as a moral historian, and which places Hawthorne's achievement firmly within the context of American religious history. Colacurcio discusses the early tales only, and his emphasis is on Hawthorne's representation of the Puritan past. In this way, the intellectual inheritance of the study – Perry Miller's work on colonial rhetoric and Puritan ideology, and Sacvan Bercovitch's development of that work in the direction of studying American national character and the evolution of a national mythology out of Puritan beginnings – becomes clear. But Colacurcio's achievement is to place this historical context clearly in relation to Hawthorne's fictional craft and to elucidate this relationship through the minute textual analysis of key tales. The sheer detail that Colacurcio presents is daunting, as is the breadth and depth of his historical knowledge and the scholarly precision of his argument, which make this a landmark study.

Hawthorne's perception of his national and family history is less important to Hillis MILLER, who is concerned to use Hawthorne's work as part of his own exploration of the abstract relationship between literature and history. "The Minister's Black Veil", together with Hawthorne's prefaces and Henry James's response to Hawthorne's work, is the occasion for a complex meditation on the nature of historical discourse. Hillis Miller's contention is that history is created by literature rather than represented by literary texts. He uses J.L. Austin's notion of performative speech acts to theorize literature, and the reading and criticism of literary works, as a way of "doing things with words", which is consequently possessed of important social and ethical functions.

There is a marked trend in recent approaches to Hawthorne to apply to his work developments in critical theory. In this respect, CREWS' controversial psychoanalytic treatment of Hawthorne's fiction marks a starting-point. Crews uses Freudian theory to elucidate Hawthorne's psychological themes and his formal departures from realism. The contentious aspect of Crews' study is the way in which he creates a direct correspondence between the fiction and Freudian theories. In a sense, Crews is guilty of the sin of allegorization, of which Hawthorne himself has been so frequently accused.

PFISTER also addresses Hawthorne's representation of psychological themes or "the personal life", as Pfister calls it, but with much greater theoretical sophistication. The cultural context that Pfister elaborates is the historical emergence of a distinctively middle-class domestic life in the mid-nineteenth century, and he restricts his discussion of Hawthorne's fictions to the texts produced during the same period. Critical discourses relating to the development of concepts of gender, the body, and sexuality inform the history that Pfister brings to bear in his interpretation of the psychological dimension of Hawthorne's writing. Thus, this study combines the strategies of cultural criticism with psychoanalysis and gender studies to illuminate the major works.

COLACURCIO's 1985 volume of essays on *The Scarlet Letter* brings together a number of readings of Hawthorne's narrative, which are representative of recent theoretically informed approaches, especially New Historicism. The editor's Introduction offers a highly informative account of the history of critical responses to *The Scarlet Letter*, from Hawthorne's contemporaries to our own contemporaries who use the insights of formalism, psychoanalysis, structuralism, and feminism in their analyses. In the essays that follow, Michael Davitt Bell reassesses the novel/romance debate by considering the conventions that govern the romance style; David Van Leer and Colacurcio consider the function of Puritan inheritances in relation to the text and Transcendentalism generally; and Carol Bensick views *The Scarlet Letter* in terms of "the novel of adultery", which she defines with careful historical specificity. Each of these essays, then, provides a contextual and broadly New-Historical reading of some aspect of Hawthorne's enterprise in his best-known work, and the volume as a whole exemplifies some of the best contemporary criticism on Hawthorne.

DEBORAH L. MADSEN

Hazlitt, William 1778–1830

English essayist and critic

Baker, Herschel, *William Hazlitt*, Cambridge, Massachusetts: Belknap Press of Harvard University Press, 1962

Bromwich, David, *Hazlitt: The Mind of a Critic*, New York and Oxford: Oxford University Press, 1983

Jones, Stanley, *Hazlitt: A Life: From Winterslow to Frith Street*, Oxford: Clarendon Press, 1989; New York: Oxford University Press, 1989

Kinnaird, John, *William Hazlitt: Critic of Power*, New York: Columbia University Press, 1978

Park, Roy, *Hazlitt and the Spirit of the Age: Abstraction and Critical Theory*, Oxford: Clarendon Press, 1971

Wardle, Ralph M., *Hazlitt*, Lincoln: University of Nebraska Press, 1971

Since Herschel Baker published his interpretive biography, interest in William Hazlitt has grown. Recent scholars have attended to the links between his criticism and his involvement in political discourse and cultural controversy, and have reassessed his significance for the English Romantic period. A new appreciation of Hazlitt as a mediating figure has accompanied better knowledge of his life and fuller analysis of his ideas.

WARDLE assumes that there is intrinsic value in trying to understand the writer as well as his works, through a sympathetic biographical approach. Beginning his study with Hazlitt's father, a radical Unitarian, migrating to America in search of a pulpit, Wardle follows the son William from birth to death, and ends with a chapter on Hazlitt's reputation. A useful aspect of this biography is the space it allots to quotation, not only from Hazlitt's writings but also from those of his family and contemporaries. Wardle sees Hazlitt as a complex character, a difficult person never quite at home in the world. Choosing to focus on Hazlitt's "development as man and as writer", he offers little analysis or assessment of the writings, and neglects historical and intellectual contexts.

For those contexts, and for a more thorough study of the works, the reader should consult BAKER, who presents Hazlitt as an uneven, powerful writer of integrity, who exemplified "gusto", his own most important critical invention. In this long and careful study, an analysis of Hazlitt's intellectual inheritance and contribution, Baker sets the writer firmly in his age and place, emphasizing the importance of the Dissenting tradition and Hazlitt's related passion about the French Revolution. He also deals fully with the writer's involvement in journalism, relating him to contemporaries like Wordsworth, Coleridge, and Keats, and demonstrating close connections between literature and social/political commentary. Baker ultimately disqualifies Hazlitt from serious consideration as social critic, underlining instead his stubborn and long-held convictions arising from feeling and experience rather than from reasoned argument. Baker's biography, though earlier than Wardle's narrative, provides an intellectual depth lacking in the latter, and contains important insights for readers seeking to understand Hazlitt's contribution to the literature of British Romanticism.

JONES's biography is unusual, in that it covers the life only from 1808, when Hazlitt left London to live in the Wiltshire village of Winterslow; necessary background, however, is dealt with in a long first chapter. Jones takes Hazlitt more seriously than either Wardle or Baker, both on his own terms, and in terms of social, political, and ideological affiliations; he seems closer to his subject and hence more sympathetic. He sees Hazlitt's work as marked by a polarity in the writer, represented by Jean-Jacques Rousseau and Edmund Burke; Hazlitt was "drawn first towards one of these two opposed symbolic figures and then towards the other". Unlike Baker, Jones salutes Hazlitt as master of the English Romantic prose-poem. Jones provides a significant supplement to the work of his two predecessors in biography.

In his long and useful study, KINNAIRD aims at intellectual biography, concentrating on works of criticism rather than on essays and writings with autobiographical inflection. Kinnaird identifies "power" as Hazlitt's major theme, whether we interpret power in the political or imaginative sense. Kinnaird proceeds by working through this theme in the fields of philosophy, then of politics, literature, and art, and finally in the realm of the personal and cultural. He sees Hazlitt as mediating between the world of the Enlightenment and emergent Romantic and post-Romantic worlds, but also as a figure absolutely central for English Romanticism, in that he dealt with all of that movement's major stress-points.

BROMWICH, too, in the most recent of major studies to date, acknowledges Hazlitt's centrality, arguing that a careful reading will locate a strong sense of history, rather than of apocalypse, and thus lead to some reconsideration of English Romanticism as a whole. Bromwich does not make inflated claims for the importance of reading Hazlitt, asserting that the close study of seminal figures from the past simply makes us "good citizens of our age". Moreover, he does not see Hazlitt as demonstrating significant intellectual development through his career, though he notes that in Hazlitt certain eighteenth-century concepts – "ideal" and "imitation" for example – change their meaning. The term "critic", according to Bromwich, is inadequate for Hazlitt, who crossed and re-crossed boundaries between metaphysics, politics, and poetry. Hazlitt, an "anti-professional" writer, is considered throughout in terms of the age he lived through and the writers he read. Bromwich's book is a full and eminently accessible exploration of Hazlitt, offering its reader a firm and interesting assessment.

Dealing with Hazlitt as "metaphysician, painter, critic", PARK intends something less expansive but more ambitious – establishing a consistent theoretical base for his subject's critical practice. For Park, Hazlitt was "the most outspoken and consistent English critic of abstraction in the early nineteenth century", one who has always been slighted because of the stardom that Coleridge's work has assumed. Park's densely-argued study sets Hazlitt beside the utilitarian Jeremy Bentham on the one hand, and the idealist Coleridge on the other, with Kantian philosophy not far in the background. For Park, Hazlitt's significance lies in his engagement with the gap between poetry and science, reformulated as a gap between poetry and abstraction. Hazlitt emerges as a determined fighter against abstraction in every form, who insists upon the *experiential* as a crucial category. Park's work is the first in the contemporary phase of Hazlitt scholarship to provide a theoretical grounding for an experiential critic, and to affirm Hazlitt's importance in the English critical tradition in those terms. In doing so, Park somehow produces an unlikely figure, an anti-theoretical theorist.

PATRICK HOLLAND

H.D. *see* Doolittle, Hilda

Heaney, Seamus 1939 –

Irish poet and critic

Andrews, Elmer (ed.), *Seamus Heaney: A Collection of Critical Essays*, London: Macmillan, 1992
Corcoran, Neil, *Seamus Heaney*, London and Boston: Faber & Faber, 1986
Curtis, Tony (ed.), *The Art of Seamus Heaney*, Bridgend, Glamorgan: Poetry Wales Press, 1982; Chester Springs, Pennsylvania: Dufour Editions, 1985; 3rd edition, Bridgend, Glamorgan: Severn Press, 1994
Foster, Thomas C., *Seamus Heaney*, Boston: Twayne, 1989
Hart, Henry, *Seamus Heaney: Poet of Contrary Progressions*, Syracuse, New York: Syracuse University Press, 1992
Parker, Michael, *Seamus Heaney: The Making of the Poet*, London: Macmillan, 1993; Iowa City: University of Iowa Press, 1993

Seamus Heaney is commonly considered one of the most important and accessible contemporary poets writing in English, and his work has attracted a substantial amount of critical attention. Much of this has been devoted to locating the poet's personal and cultural background in Northern Ireland, and on the emergence of his aesthetic commitments and artistic awareness in the context of the civil disorder in his native country. Analysis of his verse as such tends to be more effectively carried out in essays.

PARKER deals with all of Heaney's verse up to, and including, *Seeing Things*. The book's aim is "to identify and analyse the biographical, literary, historical and political influences and experiences that have shaped the poetry of Seamus Heaney". An extremely detailed account of the poet's origins and developments follows, supported by copious documentation. Such information helps solidify the reader's grasp of the poet's raw material. Emphasis on Heaney's background can, on occasion, overshadow critical engagement with the poetry itself; but the study may be relied on as a useful and comprehensive work of reference.

ANDREWS has compiled a collection of essays, which covers all the poet's verse up to, and including, *Seeing Things*. His play and two books of essays are used in a supplementary manner. The book's objective is "to offer close analysis and assessment of Heaney's work from a variety of standpoints, and to relate it to its social, political and artistic contexts". Among the perspectives included are ones examining the place of ritual in Heaney's verse, the manner in which the poetry addresses "the poetics of identity", Heaney's translations, and an adversarial evaluation of the poet, which finds that "his doors into the dark have not illuminated the Catholic Irish subconscious, and his doors into the light release a figure curiously masked and chained". A number of the other essays, all of which are by noted academic critics, see Heaney's work in terms of growth and development, which students will find particularly useful.

CORCORAN surveys Heaney's career from its beginnings to the publication of *Station Island*. Published as part of a "Student Guide" series, and intended "primarily as a commentary on Seamus Heaney's poems which may help the reader better to understand and appreciate them", the work opens with a biographical introduction, and goes on to examine each of Heaney's volumes of poetry in turn. Literary and political allusions in the verse are explained, and the initial critical reception of each volume is summarised. Changes in the poet's focus, and corresponding changes in the tone and texture of the various volumes, are carefully noted. The manner in which Heaney's early works consolidate "characteristic Heaney territory", and how the later works – from *Field Work* on – place more emphasis on personality is clearly delineated. This process is said to culminate in the "Sweeney Redivivus" section of *Station Island*, though the inevitable provisionality of all judgements concerning a poet in mid-career is acknowledged. This is a useful work for students, and it contains a helpful bibliography.

CURTIS's collection of essays has also been compiled with students in mind. The result is a comprehensive treatment of all the poet's major works, with the exception of *The Cure at Troy*. Included are noteworthy explorations by other British and Irish poets of Heaney's most recent collections of verse. There are also essays by a number of eminent contemporary critics. The editor's belief that "Seamus Heaney is best understood by cumulative analyses of his development" ensures that each of his books is dealt with in turn, including the rather unfamiliar *Stations* (1975) and both volumes of his prose. Of great interest is an essay on Heaney's revisions of his *Selected Poems 1965–1975* (1980) to make *New Selected Poems 1966–1987* (1990), and the reproduction of manuscript drafts of the poem *North*. The broad spectrum of critical response enables the poet's growth to emerge in all its instructive complexity.

FOSTER likewise adopts a chronological approach, dealing with Heaney's output from the beginning to *The Haw Lantern* (1987). A brief sketch of the poet's personal and cultural background is provided prior to a detailed reading of each of his successive volumes of poetry. The overall critical intention "seeks to trace the various threads of [the] poetry as they weave back and forth . . . for although the subjects and the treatments change from volume to volume, Heaney's themes, concerns, images, and practices crop up time and again". The craft of Heaney's early books, and particularly their artful language and rural subject matter, is emphasised. The poet's early phase is said to yield to a mythographic approach, particularly in *North* (1975). Metaphors of flight and occasions of reflection and renewal are shown to play a fundamental part in Heaney's later works. Careful critical attention is also paid to the poet's use of the lyric sequence – for example "Glanmore Sonnets" in *Field Work* (1979). This thorough, unassuming study contains a useful chronology and an annotated select bibliography.

HART also surveys Heaney's work up to, and including, *The Haw Lantern*. Rather than the largely expository approach of many other studies, this work argues for a particular point of view, based on the idea that Heaney's poetry "vacillates between antinomies": "at the root of his work is a multifaceted argument with himself, with others, with sectarian Northern Ireland, with his Anglo-Irish heritage, and with his Roman Catholic, nationalist upbringing". The study goes on to examine evidence of major contraries in Heaney's poetry. Among these are: pastoral and anti-pastoral tensions in the early volumes; the impact of coloniser on colonised in, for example, *North*; and the attempt to create a space where possession and loss might co-exist in *Field Work*. The study closes with an intriguing account of *The Haw Lantern* as a critique of deconstruction. Central to Heaney's response to these problems is the suppleness of his poetic language, and this study pays handsome tribute to the range and variety of the poet's verbal accomplishments. Heaney's awareness of the poet's vocation and of poetic tradition also plays an important part in the thesis of a work that is the most sophisticated treatment of this deceptively "elusive" poet.

GEORGE O'BRIEN

Hearn, Lafcadio 1850–1904

Greek-born American (later Japanese) novelist, essayist, and travel writer

Cott, Jonathan, *Wandering Ghost: The Odyssey of Lafcadio Hearn*, New York: Knopf, 1990; London: Kodansha International, 1990

Dawson, Carl, *Lafcadio Hearn and the Vision of Japan*, Baltimore: Johns Hopkins University Press, 1992

Kunst, Arthur E., *Lafcadio Hearn*, New York: Twayne, 1969

Rosenstone, Robert A., *Mirror in the Shrine: American Encounters with Meiji Japan*, Cambridge, Massachusetts: Harvard University Press, 1988

Webb, Kathleen M., *Lafcadio Hearn and His German Critics: An Examination of His Appeal*, New York: Peter Lang, 1984

Yu, Beongcheon, *An Ape of Gods: The Art and Thought of Lafcadio Hearn*, Detroit: Wayne State University Press, 1964

Most criticism of Hearn deals less with the literary characteristics of his work (journalism, commentary, folk-tales, and sketches) and more with his significance as cultural critic and theorist of cross-culturalism. In addition to the relative unavailability of Hearn's writing, both its fragmented nature and its resistance to conventional literary and national categories have inhibited extensive treatment. Recent developments such as interest in "world" literature, travel writing, and ethnography, are, however, finding Lafcadio Hearn relevant.

In his brief introductory survey, KUNST provides good coverage of the American, West-Indian, and Japanese periods, with a chapter devoted to Hearn's knowledge of French nineteenth-century writing and his several translations from the French. Noting that Hearn achieved no success in the major literary genres, Kunst shows how Hearn had to find alternatives to plot in attention to detail, and in incorporation of elements of dream and nightmare in his sketches and "tales". He shows how, in translating, Hearn added freely and made the translated work his own. Though his extensive Japanese output made Hearn a translator in a wider sense, Kunst emphasizes that he was both an American writer, particularly one in the gothic tradition of Edgar Allan Poe and William Faulkner, and an *immigrant* American writer, who introduced other cultures to America. The usefulness of Kunst's study is affirmed by a clear chronology and bibliography – though the latter needs to be updated.

YU takes the often marginalized Hearn very seriously, and his study of Hearn's creative writing, criticism, and philosophy is unlikely to be superseded for some time yet. Yu believes it possible to examine the several apparently inconsistent aspects of Hearn's literary production, and bring them into a synthesis by concentrating on his art and thought, particularly the latter, since Hearn's work is "the literature of philosophical voyage". Quoting extensively, and offering firm analyses, Yu underlines his subject's opposition to realism in literature, ethnological ambitions, evolutionist philosophy, Buddhist sympathies, idealism, and aspirations for a world literature and global perspective. Yu does justice to the whole range of Hearn's experience, from his American journalistic career, through his early travel writing and translations, to the voluminous production of the Japanese period, and he demonstrates Hearn's incredibly wide-ranging and informed knowledge. The full scholarly apparatus of Yu's volume makes it particularly useful to serious students of Hearn's life and work.

WEBB's monograph has a restricted focus, seeking to account for Hearn's popularity in Germany at different times, and for different reasons. Its significance lies in the emphasis it places on the culturally-situated reader of texts in the construction of meaning. Inevitably, Webb's study will be of value to a relatively narrow audience.

ROSENSTONE's book is an innovative biography of three nineteenth-century American Japanologists – Hearn, William Griffis (a teacher-missionary), and Edward Morse (scientist) – dealing especially with their Japan years. Rosenstone is concerned with how individuals live in, and attempt to understand, other cultures. His study enlists techniques from the "new historiography" associated with Hayden White's writings to produce a multi-layered, self-reflexive narrative, which stresses the provisionality of historical narrative and his own subjectivity in piecing together his particular narrative. This unusual approach is reflected in Rosenstone's format: its parts are entitled "Landing", "Searching", "Loving", "Learning", and "Remembering"; within each part, a section is devoted to each of Griffis, Hearn, and Morse. This approach enables Rosenstone to paint an intimate and sympathetic – and very informative – portrait of Hearn, built up with a generous use of quotation from Hearn's works. His study is relevant to readers interested in American nineteenth-century Japanology and Hearn's place within it.

DAWSON focuses on Hearn's last, significant years in Japan, 1890–1904. While his study is not a biography, he prefaces his analysis of Hearn's Japanese career with a helpful account of Hearn's life and background to 1890. More importantly, one chapter relates Hearn to other writers of the period who tried to satisfy an almost insatiable demand for Japanese images and experiences – Pierre Loti, Rudyard Kipling, and Ernest Fenollosa. Dawson argues that Hearn's "Japanbook" (as he calls Hearn's 15 or so separate Japanese texts) is the fullest, most sophisticated, and most complex vision of Japan available then or now. The core of Dawson's study is two chapters on Hearn's Japanese books, which he divides into two groups – those that reshape Japanese episodes, tales, and folklore, and those that are brief, impressionistic "glimpses". Dawson provides a comprehensive portrait of a man and writer whose genius was to "enter fully into a vital world and pass at will through walls of convention". Dawson's work is informed by recent theories of cross-cultural encounter by Edward Said (*Orientalism*) and James Clifford (*The Predicament of Culture*); and even though Hearn's Japan, like that of Roland Barthes, is less an actual country than an idealized, fictional system, it represents a "collective reality".

COTT has produced a biography, which is unabashedly admiring. He associates himself with modern American writers – Kenneth Rexroth and Henry Miller among them – who acquired a passion for Japan from Hearn. While Cott resists the several derogatory labels Hearn has acquired over the years, as Romantic, sensualist, or morbid wanderer, he himself romanticizes his subject as a modern nomad, with the nomad's gift of probing beyond cultural surfaces to essences. The most valuable feature of Cott's book is its generous use of quotation. In a situation where little of Hearn's work is available in print, the combination of accurate, readable chronicle of the life with running anthology is indeed valuable.

PATRICK HOLLAND

Heller, Joseph 1923 –

American novelist and dramatist

Merrill, Robert, *Joseph Heller*, Boston: Twayne, 1987
Nagel, James (ed.), *Critical Essays on Joseph Heller*, Boston: G.K.Hall, 1984
Pinsker, Sanford, *Understanding Joseph Heller*, Columbia: University of South Carolina Press, 1991
Ruderman, Judith, *Joseph Heller*, New York: Continuum, 1991
Seed, David, *The Fiction of Joseph Heller: Against the Grain*, London: Macmillan, 1989; New York: St Martin's Press, 1989

The essays collected by NAGEL offer a survey of the kinds of approach to Heller's work that were made in the years following the publication of *Catch-22*. The earliest criticism focused on the black humour, the relationship to literature of the absurd, satirical elements, and the structural innovations represented by *Catch-22*, and these approaches are exemplified in this volume by the articles of Robert Brustein, Julian Mitchell, Stephen L. Sniderman, Clinton S. Burhans, Jr., James Nagel, Gary W. Davis, and Leon F. Seltzer. Criticism of the later novels, *Something Happened* and *Good as Gold*, as well as Heller's plays, is also well represented and is evidence of the increasing theoretical sophistication with which Heller's work has been treated. Not only are previously published reviews and essays reprinted here, but original articles by Melvin J. Friedman, James M. Mellard, Joan DelFattore, and Linda McJ. Micheli complete the critical survey. Nagel has provided an extremely useful Introduction, which sets the context for the essays that follow by surveying the first two decades of Heller criticism.

Though Nagel devotes an entire section of his volume to Heller's drama, there is a tendency in general studies of Heller to treat him purely as a novelist and to ignore this dramatic work. However, Merrill, in the first book-length study of Heller's work, and Ruderman, in her more recent general treatment of Heller's writing, avoid this tendency, and both place discussion of the drama right in the centre of their critical studies. Seed's book, though it refers in the title only to the fiction, also gives prominence to the plays. Granted, MERRILL's discussion is entitled "The Novelist as Playwright", but still the plays are treated as independently significant works. Two chapters are devoted to *Catch-22*, testimony to the importance of that novel in all critical assessments of Heller's career. The first chapter treats the novel in relation to literary tradition and the second offers an analysis of the structure and meaning of the text. While *Something Happened* is discussed in the context of its mixed critical reception, *Good as Gold* and *God Knows* are discussed as "Jewish Novels".

Merrill offers useful information in the form of a chronology and an annotated selected bibliography.

SEED's study is distinguished by the scholarly care and detail of its presentation. This is most apparent in the bibliography, which is comprehensive and very informative. Seed situates Heller's work in what he describes as a "gap between political rhetoric and national reality" and he goes on to analyze each text with special attention to Heller's satirical gaze, which is focused closely on the public values of American life. The book is structured according to the chronology of Heller's career, from *Catch-22* to *Picture This*, and Seed includes a biographical account as well as discussion of Heller's stories and plays. As a result, this book provides an excellent complement to the earlier general studies.

RUDERMAN also provides a compelling account of Heller's literary career up to the publication of *Picture This*. Again, she begins with a biographical sketch before proceeding to discuss each text in chronological order of publication. While Ruderman offers very competent analyses of the texts in terms of structure, themes, influences, and the like, it is her penultimate chapter, where she considers Heller as a Jewish novelist, that holds the greatest interest. For Ruderman does not restrict her discussion to the most obviously Jewish novels – *Good as Gold* and *God Knows* – but instead she identifies the ethnic elements at work throughout Heller's writing. This book, then, provides both an accessible introduction for the less sophisticated reader, while offering some stimulating ideas for the more advanced of Heller's readers.

PINSKER has directed his study more clearly at the non-academic reader. This book considers only Heller's fiction – a restriction that is the consequence of the format of the series ("Understanding Contemporary American Fiction") to which this study belongs, and which also prescribes the pitch of the book. Despite these limitations, Pinsker's is an engaging and stimulating approach to Heller's work, with subtle and often insightful analyses of the novels, expressed through an easily accessible prose style. Although the account of Heller's work is not theoretically sophisticated, that is not to be expected in a study aimed at the general reader. In fact, despite the several excellent general accounts of Heller's writing, there is a decided absence of advanced theoretical approaches set out in book-length studies.

DEBORAH L. MADSEN

Hellman, Lillian 1905–1984

American dramatist and screenwriter

Adams, Timothy Dow, *Telling Lies in Modern American Autobiography*, Chapel Hill: University of North Carolina Press, 1990

Adler, Jacob H., "Modern Southern Drama", in *The History of Southern Literature*, edited by Louis D. Rubin, Jr., Baton Rouge: Louisiana State University Press, 1985

Dick, Bernard F., *Hellman in Hollywood*, Rutherford, New Jersey: Fairleigh Dickinson University Press, 1982

Falk, Doris V., *Lillian Hellman*, New York: Frederick Ungar, 1978

Goldstein, Malcolm, *The Political Stage: American Drama and Theater of the Great Depression*, New York: Oxford University Press, 1974

Lederer, Katherine, *Lillian Hellman*, Boston: Twayne, 1979

Miller, Jordan Y., and Winifred L. Frazer, *American Drama Between the Wars: A Critical History*, Boston: Twayne, 1991

Moody, Richard, *Lillian Hellman: Playwright*, New York: Bobbs-Merrill/Pegasus, 1972

Arguably America's best-known woman playwright, enjoying both controversy (her first play, *The Children's Hour*, 4was banned in Boston for its alleged treatment of lesbianism) and considerable commercial success (*The Children's Hour* ran for 691 performances, a figure exceeded by only a handful of productions in the history of modern American theatre), Lillian Hellman's critical reputation has, however, suffered from a paucity of intelligent commentary on her work. A good deal of the better writing about her has appeared in essays and books on American drama rather than in studies devoted entirely to her. Recent criticism has been more concerned with her autobiographical writings (especially *Pentimento: A Book of Portraits* and *Scoundrel Time*) than her plays.

MOODY's book, the first book-length study of her, treats the major plays fairly exhaustively, but his interpretation of them is doggedly pedestrian, and offers little that is not immediately obvious to anyone who has seen or read them.

GOLDSTEIN's excellent book on American theatre in the 1930s contains some brief commentary on *The Children's Hour*, *The Little Foxes*, and *Days to Come*. He argues that *The Children's Hour* is a play about "the plight of the open-minded individual when assaulted by a stubborn and powerful conservative force", and shows how in "tone, if not characterization, it was a world apart from the most celebrated Broadway works of the decade". The later plays he discusses in the context of what he calls the "non-institutional theater", Hellman being its "most respected author". *The Little Foxes* is read for its indictment of *laissez-faire* capitalism, while *Days to Come* is criticised for a failure to rise above "melodramatic intrigue" in its treatment of management-labour relations.

FALK's biography makes some attempt to see Hellman's writing in the contexts of American history, the development of American theatre, and, more generally, the arts in America. Falk draws extensively on Hellman's memoirs and interviews (arguably not the most reliable of sources), and there is little in the way of what one might call interpretation of the life. The plays are discussed in plot-summary fashion.

LEDERER's book (in the Twayne "United States Authors" series) offers both biography and dramatic criticism. Lederer argues that Hellman's work is "ironic and novelistic", and draws interesting connections between her work and that of other dramatists, notably Anton Chekhov and Tennessee Williams. The penultimate chapter on the non-fiction usefully summarizes Hellman's autobiographical writings, though largely uncritically. Brevity has meant that there is no discussion here of her film scripts, her adaptations of the work of others (such as Jean Anouilh's *The Lark*, or Voltaire's *Candide* for Leonard Bernstein's 1957 comic operetta), or cinematic versions of her plays; but this remains the best book-length study available.

DICK's short book is narrowly focused on Hellman's Hollywood career, exploring both her relationship to the film industry and her writing for the screen. The concluding chapters examine the autobiographical short story "Julia" (from *Pentimento*) and Fred Zinnemann's 1977 cinematic adaptation of it.

ADLER gives brief attention to Hellman in his chapter on modern Southern drama, arguing that her Southern background (she was born in New Orleans of Jewish parents, though little has ever been made of this aspect of her upbringing), which was exploited most obviously in *The Little Foxes*, has been a barrier to the success of her plays abroad, her world being "less comprehensible to foreigners, less universal, than that of [Tennessee] Williams" (though one might want to put the case more simply and say that Williams is a much superior dramatist). Most of this short chapter is devoted to Williams's plays.

ADAMS is exclusively concerned with Hellman's autobiographies, or what he calls "life-writing", and much of his long chapter on her is an attempt to sort out both the litigious and the literary implications of her four books of autobiography (*An Unfinished Woman*, *Pentimento*, *Scoundrel Time*, and *Maybe*). His reading turns on a number of theoretical issues, which arise in any discussion of the autobiographical record: the deconstruction and reconstruction of the autobiographical "I"; the duplicity of memory; the limitations inherent in any individual's capacity to understand, and represent, his or her self; and the ontological status of the "autobiographical lie". He defends Hellman against the merciless assaults on her veracity from Hilton Kramer and Mary McCarthy (among others), but he is insistent about her failure (like that of the other writers he discusses in this frequently fascinating book) to render the "unvarnished truth".

MILLER and FRAZER, like Goldstein, concentrate on Hellman's early plays, identifying them as examples of "the well-made play" written within broadly realistic conventions. Like other critics, they note her proclivity for melodramatic scenes and her strong "sense of dramatic construction", though they also share the conventional wisdom that *The Little Foxes* is poised, ambiguously, between melodrama and documentary social reform. The two important postwar plays *The Autumn Garden* and *Toys in the Attic* are not considered here.

HENRY CLARIDGE

Hemingway, Ernest 1899–1961

American novelist, short-story writer, and journalist

Benson, Jackson J. (ed.), *New Critical Approaches to the Short Stories Of Ernest Hemingway*, Durham, North Carolina: Duke University Press, 1990

Bloom, Harold (ed.), *Ernest Hemingway*, New York: Chelsea House, 1985

Comley, Nancy R., and Robert Scholes, *Hemingway's Genders: Rereading the Hemingway Text*, New Haven, Connecticut, and London: Yale University Press, 1994

Cooper, Stephen, *The Politics of Ernest Hemingway*, Ann Arbor, Michigan: UMI Research Press, 1987

Godden, Richard, *Fictions of Capital: The American Novel from James to Mailer*, Cambridge and New York: Cambridge University Press, 1990

Kenner, Hugh, *A Homemade World: The American Modernist Writers*, New York: Knopf, 1974; London: Marion Boyars, 1977

Kert, Bernice, *The Hemingway Women*, New York: Norton, 1983

Messent, Peter, *New Readings of the American Novel: Narrative Theory and Its Application*, London: Mamillan, 1990

Messent, Peter, *Ernest Hemingway*, London: Macmillan, 1992; New York: St Martin's Press, 1992

Raeburn, John, *Fame Became of Him: Hemingway as Public Writer*, Bloomington: Indiana University Press, 1984

Spilka, Mark, *Hemingway's Quarrel with Androgyny*, Lincoln: University of Nebraska Press, 1990

Tetlow, Wendolyn E., *Hemingway's "In Our Time": Lyrical Dimensions*, Lewisburg, Pennsylvania: Bucknell University Press, 1992; London: Associated University Presses, 1992

Wagner, Linda W. (ed.), *Ernest Hemingway: Six Decades of Criticism*, East Lansing: Michigan State University Press, 1986

Weber, Ronald, *Hemingway's Art of Non-Fiction*, London: Macmillan, 1989; New York: St Martin's Press, 1990

High quality book-length studies of Hemingway, a writer of international stature, have been surprisingly sparse until recent years. There are two reasons for this: first, a great deal of writing about Hemingway has been in the form of biographies and memoirs; second, the image of the tough experiential writer, who wrote his novels and stories out of the matrix of his own lived experience, made him an unfashionable topic for academic criticism. This second difficulty has now been largely removed since the Hemingway archives at the John F. Kennedy Library have become available to scholars, and over the past decade or so the critical commentary has become more searching, interesting, and challenging. Added to this, the posthumous publication of *The Garden of Eden* has generated an enormous amount of new interest in Hemingway, so that, as one of his best most recent critics has commented, it is now intellectually respectable to declare a serious interest in Hemingway. However, it remains true that the biographical and memoirist interest in him remains strong. Of the wealth of Hemingway biographies, the most respected are those by Kenneth Lynn (1987), and the ongoing definitive work in several volumes by Michael Reynolds.

General studies of Hemingway are provided in Bloom, Kenner, Messent, Raeburn, Wagner, and Godden.

BLOOM reprints some classic early commentary from the 1940s and 1950s by Lionel Trilling, Edmund Wilson, Harry Levin, and Malcolm Cowley, along with essays more recently published. Especially recommended are Steven K. Hoffman's study of the concept of *nada* as a unifying theme in the short fiction, and John Hollander's analysis of the enigmatic and symbolic dimensions of Hemingway's landscapes. Equally valuable is Paul Smith's study of the short stories Hemingway wrote between 1919 and 1921, where Smith, drawing on manuscript materials, shows the process of Hemingway's search for an appropriate style. There is a refreshing mix of orthodox and innovatory commentary in this useful collection.

KENNER, one of the most eminent critics of Anglo-American modernism, identifies Hemingway's aesthetics as late nineteenth-century in origin, deriving from Walter Pater's aesthetics of "appreciative intensities", and W.B. Yeats's belief in the relation between the perfection of a style and the perfection of a life. In Hemingway, as in Yeats, this leads to the search for absolute mastery of the techniques appropriate to any moment of crisis – what Hemingway called the need to "tell it how it is". For Kenner the spare yet sufficient language of the short stories provides Hemingway with the means to depict the reality of the lived moment in the most complete and persuasive way, while the constraints of the form and scale of the short story work to Hemingway's advantage against the prolixity endemic to the novel.

MESSENT's 1992 study comes in a series devoted to major modern novelists, and though it follows the formula of the series this is a lively and engrossing introductory study organized around a series of topics germane to Hemingway's work and to the contemporary arena of literary-critical debate. Thus, Messent has a chapter on Hemingway's "style", arguably the single most important aspect of his work, and goes on to consider what used to be called "themes" but is here described as "The Status of the Subject", that is to say what it is that Hemingway writes about. Messent then turns to issues of gender and sexuality, topics increasingly foregrounded in contemporary studies of Hemingway, and moves then to the fictional and non-fictional locations of the work in America, Spain, and Africa. Messent adds a coda on what may be read as Hemingway's own coda or late apologia for his work, *A Moveable Feast*, his memoirs of his life as a writer. MESSENT's earlier (1990) study of the application of narrative theory to a number of American novels includes a narratological account of character in *The Sun Also Rises*.

RAEBURN investigates the impact of early fame on Hemingway's cultivation of a public image, a process here seen as a continuous manipulation of shifting roles. Raeburn makes good use of Hemingway's non-fictional work as well as the novels and short-story collections to show how issues of self-promotion and self-protection reflect Hemingway's engagement with his own public image.

WAGNER's excellent collection of essays has commentary on all the major aspects of Hemingway's career, including three by his current biographer Michael Reynolds on various aspects of the writer's personal life. Notable critics in this collection include Larzer Ziff, who writes on aspects of Hemingway's style, James Nagel on the treatment of time in *A Farewell To Arms*, George Monteiro on the resonance of the 23rd Psalm in *A Farewell To Arms*, and "A Clean Well-Lighted Place", and Mark Spilka on the issue of lesbianism in *The Garden of Eden*. Other essays discuss the vexed topic of the representation of women, and Hemingway's attitude to the American West.

GODDEN's complex study of the relations between American capitalism and the American novel from Henry James to Norman Mailer includes one of the most adverse critiques of Hemingway to have been written. This is not a book for beginners, for Godden situates his arguments within a framework of economic, political, and literary-critical theories of considerable sophistication. However, the relationship he argues between what he calls "economic plots" and fictional forms is less intimidatintg than may first appear. Economic plots are the structures of American capitalism from the 1880s to the 1960s, which determined the facts of social relations throughout that period. In their turn social relations are the source of "what stories can or cannot be told", and these take "their significant impetus" from the economic plots Godden identifies. In this account of the modern American novel, Hemingway is indicted as the laureate of "capital realism". Few general readers of Hemingway will recognise him in the version Godden offers, but it must be said that this is one of the most impressive and sustained critiques there is of the relationship between the literary text and its social origins.

The subject of gender in Hemingway's works is the focus of the studies by Comley and Scholes, Kert, and Spilka.

COMLEY and SCHOLES's study of gender issues in Hemingway is a brilliant book, one of the best currently available because of the way it opens up the debate about the representations of men, women, and sexuality in Hemingway's work, and provokes debate about everything Hemingway wrote. The opening chapter is a rather playful exercise in what may be construed from the familiar term "Papa Hemingway", by which he was known to a wide range of intimate associates; but the following chapters on the kinds of presentation of women, the destabilising of sexual identity in *The Garden of Eden*, and the attitudes to the homosexual imperative in many of the stories and novels are stimulating readings bound to generate further commentary. A singular feature of this book is the authors' definition of what constitutes the Hemingway we read, for here this means not only the novels, stories, and non-fictional writings, but all the manuscript materials in the John F. Kennedy Library, a crucially important resource for their work. It is in this particular sense that the notion of the "Hemingway text" exists, one which includes all his published and unpublished work, as well as the biographical and bibliographical materials about him. The effect of this book, along with some other recent studies, is to radically undermine the long prevailing myth of Hemingway as the celebrant of the male world and its machismo values.

KERT challenges the customary view critics take of women in Hemingway, in which the stereotypes of the aggressive bitch and the idealised passive heroine have long predominated. Kert has researched the archival materials and draws on unpublished letters and interviews to give a different account of the status of women in Hemingway's life from the perspective of what she shows us about his wives and lovers, and his relations with his mother. This is one of the more exhaustively researched studies of recent years in the re-evaluation of the Hemingway woman.

SPILKA argues that if the cult of manliness in Hemingway was nurtured by his father's commitment to versions of pioneer adventurism, his mother provided a counter emphasis in cultivating the tenets of Christian manliness in her son, which instilled a capacity for tenderness in him he subordinated both in his adult life and his writings. Spilka writes from what he calls "neofeminist" perspectives, allied to his interest in the "taboo on tenderness in modern fiction". His thesis is that Hemingway's celebration of male bonding and physical courage in a world where men survive best without women represents a conflict between Hemingway's overt motives and his "secret muses", his mother, sisters, wives, lovers, and those fictional women who challenge his male-centred world. Spilka sees Hemingway's late work, the unfinished novella "The Last Good Country" and the posthumous *The Garden of Eden* as endeavours to resolve this central conflict and to face up to the creative implications of what Spilka calls Hemingway's androgynous nature. This is an important study motivated by an ardent desire to dismantle the Hemingway of popular mythology.

BENSON has gathered an indispensable collection of commentary on the short stories, the form in which Hemingway was most often at his best. It opens with a reprinting of Hemingway's "The Art of the Short Story", originally published in *The Paris Review* in 1971 but not otherwise in print. The critical articles that follow are organised in sections, of which the first has essays applying contemporary literary-critical theories of writing and reading to some famous stories: this gives us narratological, semiotic, psychoanalytic, structuralist, textual, reception-theory, feminist, and historical-biographical readings of individual stories, and among the best is Robert Scholes' semiotic commentary on "A Very Short Story" and Nina Baym's implicitly feminist commentary on "The Short Happy Life of Francis Macomber". Thereafter there are sections on short-story techniques and themes, interpretations of particular stories, an overview of the criticism of the short stories by Paul Smith, and a comprehensive checklist of criticism from 1975 to 1989. This is the best book currently available on Hemingway's work in this form.

COOPER's study is unusual in its focus on Hemingway's political convictions and the way these are embodied in his writing. He traces Hemingway's political scepticism about reform to his spell on the staff of the *Cooperative Commonwealth* in 1920, and suggests that this scepticism conditions the negative picture of social value systems in *The Sun Also Rises* and the other work of the 1920s and early 1930s. Cooper writes well of Hemingway's commitment to the Republican cause in the Spanish Civil War, and disputes the view that he supported the Cuban revolution. This is a useful study as far as it goes but it cannot be said to exhaust the major issue of the politics of Hemingway's writing.

TETLOW's subject is Hemingway's first commercial publication, the stories of *In Our Time*, which she reads as governed by the aesthetics and structural techniques of the modernist poetic sequence, as in Eliot's *The Waste Land* and Ezra Pound's *Hugh Selwyn Mauberley*. She argues that the stories of *In Our Time* are presented lyrically, rather than dramatically, and that Hemingway's concern is with atmosphere and feeling rather than action, his purpose less to do with the conflicts depicted within each story than with a pervasive realisation of sterility and failure of communication across the whole collection. This is a plausible account of the dominant lyrical tone and unity of preoccupation in this early work, though Tetlow's reading is somewhat forced and not always reliable on matters of narrative practice.

WEBER makes an important case for the value of the major non-fiction works as deserving equal attention with the fiction. He argues that the young Hemingway's journalism for *The Kansas City Star* allowed him to cultivate a personal voice which bore fruit particularly in the mix of factual observation and personal commentary in *Death in the Afternoon* and *The Green Hills of Africa*. Weber is critical of the editorial intervention in the manuscript materials posthumously published as *The Dangerous Summer*, and writes fascinatingly of the differences between the published version of *A Moveable Feast* and the manuscript, from which it departs significantly. This is a welcome and essential study for those interested in Hemingway's non-fictional writing.

LIONEL KELLY

Herbert, George 1593–1633

Welsh poet

Fish, Stanley E., *Self-Consuming Artefacts: The Experience of Seventeenth-Century Literature*, Berkeley: University of California Press, 1972

Fish, Stanley E., *The Living Temple: George Herbert and Catechizing*, Berkeley: University of California Press, 1978

Martz, Louis L., *The Poetry of Meditation: A Study in English Religious Literature of the Seventeenth Century*, New Haven, Connecticut: Yale University Press, 1954

Nuttall, A.D., *Overheard by God: Fiction and Prayer in Herbert, Milton, Dante and St. John*, London and New York: Methuen, 1980

Schoenfeldt, Michael C., *Prayer and Power: George Herbert and Renaissance Courtship*, Chicago: University of Chicago Press, 1991

Strier, Richard, *Love Known: Theology and Experience in George Herbert's Poetry*, Chicago: University of Chicago Press, 1983

Summers, Joseph H., *George Herbert: His Religion and Art*, Cambridge, Massachusetts: Harvard University Press, 1954; London, Chatto & Windus, 1954

Tuve, Rosemond, *A Reading of George Herbert*, Chicago: University of Chicago Press; London, Faber & Faber, 1952

Vendler, Helen, *The Poetry of George Herbert*, Cambridge, Massachusetts: Harvard University Press, 1975

George Herbert's poetry has attracted the attention of substantial scholars and excellent critics. The critical heritage since Tuve in 1952 is extraordinarily rich and varied. All commentators agree on the critical status of the author, and one tendency of the criticism is to establish the independence of Herbert's achievement from that of Donne. Some critics try to read the poetry apart from the theology, others insist it can only be read in the light of it. Herbert has been situated in every division of the English Church, from a Laudian High Anglicanism to radical Puritanism. In all these critical works, Herbert's highly self-conscious art elicits fine readings of particular poems. Vendler's book can be seen as a latterday zenith of the New-Critical approach to poetic texts, while Schoenfeldt is the first New-Historicist reader of *The Temple*.

TUVE offers in the first half of her book a reading of "The Sacrifice" conceived as a reply to William Empson's remarks upon the poem in his *Seven Types of Ambiguity* (1930).

Empson's basic revulsion at least made him take the idea of the atonement seriously, and his reaction is valuable, but Tuve insists that such poems cannot be self-sufficient in terms of providing the knowledge for their own interpretation, and her study stresses the importance to proper understanding of the liturgical and iconographic traditions the poems depend on.

MARTZ'S influential study places Herbert in the Catholic meditative tradition as modified by St François de Sales. Basic meditative structures are seen as accounting for the tripartite shape of *The Temple* (a "Sacramental Introduction", "Body of Conflicts", and "Plateau of Assurance") and of individual poems. A section examines Herbert's art of sacred parody, his use of the devices and situations of secular love poetry.

SUMMERS' general study anticipated many later areas of critical interest, and remains the essential introduction. There is a sound treatment of the life, especially in relation to Walton's hagiographic account, and of the religious background of both the man and his ideas of form and language, and a critical discussion of Herbert's plainness.

FISH's studies in Herbert began with an article entitled "Letting Go", expanded and incorporated in *Self-Consuming Artefacts*, in which the poems are seen as constituting a dialectic between an egocentric self and the self-annihilating insight "Thy word is all, if we could spell". Herbert asserts that God is everything, and so the claims for other entities to a separate existence (i.e., the speakers and readers of the poems) have to be given up. The reader's illusion of independence is destroyed, while the poet writes himself out of his poems, which are revealed as gifts from God, not to God. Then in 1977, Fish proclaimed "The Mystery of *The Temple* Finally Explained", ideas expounded at large in this 1978 study. He takes Chapter 21 of Herbert's *A Priest to the Temple* as the key. The chapter deals with how a quasi-Socratic catechist elicits answers and self-discovery from his catechumen. This activity parallels for Fish the roles of poet and reader, and incidentally reconciles the two prevailing views of Herbert as either tranquil, or prone to abrupt changes of heart (states corresponding to the roles of catechist and catechumen). Central to catechising lay the idea of the Temple, perfect in Christ, to be built constantly in the heart of man. Critics of Fish point out that there is a larger scheme within which the catechistic tradition lay, doctrines about the Fall of Man, which Fish fails to discuss. In more recent public pronouncements Fish seems willing to assail his author, via a view of "the dark side of the force": a built-in obsolence affects the restless criticism by this provocative critic.

"Imagine – if you can – God reading this poem", begins NUTTALL's study, a startling reminder to the twentieth-century student of the special audience envisaged by the seventeenth-century poet. In this highly individual, brief study, Nuttall asks basic questions in a Socratic way, probing our responses to the inconsistency of the self-humbling man who presumes in poem after poem to supply words, thoughts, and reactions for God. Lively and engaged, wearing its scholarship lightly, but giving a very intelligible account of doctrines the humanist author professes to find "unintelligible" (such as Calvin's position on Grace), this is very *literary* literary criticism, illuminating the account with passages of George Crabbe, Dostoevsky, T.S. Eliot – and, symptomatically, Laurence Sterne, Lewis Carroll, and P.G. Wodehouse. Describing himself as an "ill conditioned and rebellious reader", Nuttall explores the logical tensions in Herbert, and finds the poetry to be "riven by moral and theological contradiction", which Nuttall uses to suggest where Herbert departs from strict Calvinism.

"No new generalisations about Herbert are proposed in this book", VENDLER says in the Introduction to her collection of particular readings. The poetry is discussed in aesthetic terms, the author proposing as its primary subject the workings of Herbert's own mind and heart rather than the expression of certain religious beliefs. Vendler takes as a principle the view that Herbert's apparent simplicity is deceptive, and shows how poems repudiate, correct, rephrase, rethink, and re-invent facile first thoughts or responses. She analyses failures as well as successes, when Herbert's free play of ideas about traditional ideas or concepts fails, and the poems become versifications of socially acceptable sentiments and theology. Finding *The Temple* to be "one of the most beautiful and finished books in the language", and rating the poet above Donne, Vendler can sometimes be felt to be admiring new beauties *she* has made; but this is in general exceptionally fine criticism.

While making the apposite point that individuals can shape cultures, something particularly germane when the writer was as widely influential on his contemporaries as Herbert, SCHOENFELDT's study is New Historicist in tendency, and analyses Herbert's devotional modes as "entangled in and enriched by the manipulative tactics of supplication that he practised in the social world". This methodical decontruction or de-hagiographying of Herbert opens with a clear account of the author's position in relation to recent critical practices, while masking the extent to which this book opposes itself to less materialist readings. There may be a suggestion that the critic is himself too adroit a courtier, finding some agreement with all recent types of reading. The emphasis on "the insurgent energies of sexual passion" in Herbert may seem to some readers to follow more from the inveterate interests of post-Foucaultian scholarship than from real tensions in the poetry. Herbert's negotiations with his Lord and Master are deconstructed into courtship, in which a rhetoric of submission becomes self-construction; the poems about divinely afflicted pain are related to the gruesome extremes of the period's means of political coercion. Deliberately mould-breaking and consistently anti-hagiographic, this is nevertheless the challenging book it set out to be, and the readings re-activate unattended and uncomfortable meanings in the texts.

STRIER's book is arguably the best single study of Herbert, as the continuous argument with this work in Schoenfeldt witnesses. Strier's study could not be as pioneering, nor can be as seminal as the insights of Fish have been, but the combination of convincing theological location of the writer (as a strict Lutheran) and fine close readings of the poems makes this both reliable and rewarding. Strier maintains that agreement with Luther's denial that man can merit salvation was central to Herbert's beliefs. He examines Herbert's treatment of sin, and finds it habitually conceived of (as in the writings of Luther) in psychological and intellectual terms rather than as physical sensuality (compare Schoenfeldt's emphasis). Chapters on Herbert's assault on reason analyse the poems about the ways in which the operation of grace affronts the merely human reason. Strier goes beyond the common interest in the gloomier side of seventeenth-century religious psychology by expounding the full importance of the Lutheran doctrine of comfort in Herbert. The importance of the emotions in the poet's thought is asserted, seen in the poems that show God affected by human needs. The third chapter engages with the arguments put forward by Fish.

ROY J. BOOTH

Heroic Tragedy *see* Tragedy: Restoration

Historical Drama

Axton, Marie, *The Queen's Two Bodies: Drama and the Elizabethan Succession,* London: Royal Historical Society, 1977
Bevington, David, *Tudor Drama and Politics: A Critical Approach to Topical Meaning*, Cambridge, Massachusetts: Harvard University Press, 1968
Champion, Larry, *"The Noise of Threatening Drum": Dramatic Strategy and Political Ideology in Shakespeare and the English Chronicle Plays*, Newark: University of Delaware Press, 1990; London and Toronto: Associated University Presses, 1990
Harben, Niloufer, *Twentieth-Century English History Plays: From Shaw to Bond*, London: Macmillan, 1988
Peacock, D. Keith, *Radical Stages: Alternative History in Modern British Drama*, New York: Greenwood Press, 1991
Ribner, Irving, *The English History Play in the Age of Shakespeare*, Princeton, New Jersey: Princeton University Press, 1957; London: Methuen, 1957, revised 1965
Wikander, Matthew H., *The Play of Truth and State: Historical Drama from Shakespeare to Brecht*, Baltimore: Johns Hopkins University Press, 1986

Though many critics have attempted to define historical drama as a genre, what little agreement there has been is on its political nature, and that it has flourished when it has engaged critically with the public world rather than confined itself to biography.

RIBNER's extremely influential work surveys historical drama from the close of the medieval period to the closing of the theatres in 1642. It is primarily concerned with proposing a definition of the genre and demonstrating how plays conform to it. He defines the Renaissance history play as one seeking to accomplish the dominant purpose of history at the time: to teach rather than to present an "objective" picture of the past for its own sake. The genre grew through a dialectic between the modes of romance and morality play, with the eventual dominance of the latter in the theatre leading to the drama losing contact with the purposes of history after the accession of James I. The breadth of Ribner's coverage has not been equalled since, and has the advantage of not being confined to as narrow a reading of the plays as some: for example, he rejects E.M.W. Tillyard's thesis that the providentialism of Edward Hall's chronicle was the only basis for the serious history play. Ribner's definition of the genre as primarily didactic leads him to devalue comic history. He emphasises that Falstaff is a destructive element in Shakespeare's *Henry IV* plays, and that Hal must reject him. He also emphasises the plays' orthodoxy, which he sees as necessitated by censorship, rather than the oppositional elements or gaps in orthodoxy critics have more recently concentrated on. The plays are not imagined theatrically, within a social context, or as having an afterlife after their first performances. Given that its primary purpose is not critical, however, this is still an extremely useful guide to, and definition of, the genre.

BEVINGTON's book, which in covering the Tudor drama treats many of the same plays, is not concerned overly with questions of generic definition. It places historical plays as part of a prevalent "political dramaturgy", working via analogy, whereby biblical, classical, or historical stories were used to comment on current events or issues. He traces the rapid growth of the history play in the late 1580s to "war fever" and a demand for plays portraying historic victories. Like Ribner, he does not find a uniform outlook, and stresses the diversity of perspectives on even such a seemingly xenophobic and jingoistic subject. Like Ribner, he does distinguish between "romantic" histories (George Peele's *Edward I*, Robert Greene's *James IV*) and more factually based plays, finding the former much less restrained. Most other history plays are considered as "orthodox reply" to the issues raised by the social and political stresses of the 1590s in their portrayals of aristocratic rebellion or commons rising. As he is less concerned with a developmental narrative than Ribner, he is more sensitive to the plays' engagements with current affairs. As with Ribner, the book's scope precludes detailed critical discussion, but it is still a reliable guide to the plays' "topical meaning".

AXTON focuses more closely on drama's engagement with the issues raised by Elizabeth I's refusal to name a successor. Like Bevington she finds a continuity in political vocabulary and dramaturgy between histories and other plays – specifically between the public history plays of the 1590s and the coterie drama of the 1560s and 1580s. She historicises the significance of certain characters in the succession debates, and traces their appearance in public history plays. Analogical significance rather than generic identity is her index of serious political comment. In showing how plays used characters and events already significant through succession polemics, she shows how even "romantic" history (the anonymous *Locrine*, Greene's *Friar Bacon and Friar Bungay*) engages with politics, though her assumption that public theatre audiences were as well informed about such matters as coterie audiences needs more argument than it is given here.

CHAMPION posits a heterogeneous audience for histories, and suggests that the histories he studies are framed to permit (or even encourage) multiple interpretations, and that this sophistication extends to such denigrated plays as the anonymous *The Famous Victories* or *Thomas Lord Cromwell*. However, in his readings of several plays this multiplicity of perspective is not present, as he writes of spectators being forced to take up positions by texts. Though there is an interesting case made for Shakespeare's *King John* as a turning point in the genre's possibilities, the treatment of Shakespeare's plays generally is thin, and there is virtually no attempt to provide more than a New-Critical reading of the five non-Shakespearean histories. As a book on the history play, this is narrow in scope, but it does provide useful close readings of some little-discussed plays, and show that such marginal plays can frame coherent oppositional or demystificatory perspectives.

WIKANDER begins where Champion ends, with Shakespeare's "Henriad", and traces what happened to English historical drama after Shakespeare, especially in the half century after the Restoration. His study does not contextualise Shakespeare's plays as the above studies do, concerned as it is with the afterlife of the Shakespearean kind of history play, which he defines as challenging preconceptions about the act of understanding the past, and balancing the requirements of truth and poetry. Only Ben Jonson's *Sejanus* and George Chapman's *Byron* plays (neither on British history) attempted to follow this humanist agenda, and both fell foul of censorship. Shakespeare and John Fletcher's *Henry VIII* set the sceptical, spectacular, nostalgic, and pathetic agenda for the post-Shakespearean history. After the Restoration, the dominant concern became "the pathos of power", locating the public/private tension of Shakespeare's best histories solely in amorous intrigues. The true heirs of the Shakespearean history are rather European: Friedrich Schiller, Georg Büchner, Alfred de Musset, August Strindberg, and Bertolt Brecht. As a historical survey this is inadequate, especially on the twentieth century, and this vitiates its assertion of the distinctiveness of the Shakespearean history; but its readings of individual plays and the politics of history immediately after the Restoration are well argued and useful.

HARBEN's survey of twentieth-century British drama overlaps slightly with Wikander, but it concentrates on George Bernard Shaw, T.S. Eliot, and Edward Bond, none of whom feature in Wikander's dismissive account of modern drama. Harben attempts to define the history play as one "evincing a serious concern for historical truth or historical issues" in order to include Bond's *Early Morning*, which she sees as dealing with underlying historical processes via grotesque distortion of known history. She deals with minor dramatists of the 1930s and 1960s, but is concerned principally to show how the dominant conventions of nineteenth-century individualism are negotiated by major writers. Shaw is shown to have decisively broken with the primarily romantic spectacular and histrionic Victorian history in his use of comic irony and modern psychology. Eliot, though concerned with historical veracity, wrote outside realist conventions in his use of ritualistic theatricality and poetic language. The readings of Shaw's *St Joan*, Eliot's *Murder in the Cathedral*, and Bond's *Early Morning* are persuasive, and show the variety of modern British historical drama.

PEACOCK's book is as much about theatre as drama, tracing how different kinds of company and staging contributed to the vitality of the postwar historical drama. Peacock documents how social realism (Arnold Wesker), documentary history (The Theatre Workshop's *Oh What a Lovely War!*), and community-based documentary (at Stoke's Victoria Theatre) were all employed to present alternative historical perspectives to the dominant "great men" school of history. He documents 1960s' disillusionment with the postwar world, and 1970s' radical and protest theatre, concluding with the seeming death of the large-scale history play in the 1980s. Many plays are discussed and situated politically and theatrically. This acute survey, though heavily centred on England rather than Britain as a whole, is a comprehensive refutation of Wikander's pessimistic conclusions, and is a good guide to recent alternative historical theatre and drama, which is driven (as were the Elizabethans) by contemporary political engagements.

STEPHEN LONGSTAFFE

Historical Fiction

Fleishman, Avrom, *The English Historical Novel: Walter Scott to Virginia Woolf*, Baltimore: Johns Hopkins University Press, 1971

Jacobs, Naomi, *The Character of Truth: Historical Figures in Contemporary Fiction*, Carbondale: Southern Illinois University Press, 1990

Lukács, Georg, *The Historical Novel*, translated by Hanna and Stanley Mitchell, London: Merlin Press, 1962; Boston: Beacon Press, 1963

Rance, Nicholas, *The Historical Novel and Popular Politics in Nineteenth-Century England*, London: Vision Press, 1975; New York: Barnes & Noble, 1975

Sanders, Andrew Leonard, *The Victorian Historical Novel 1840–1880*, London: Macmillan, 1978; New York: St Martin's Press, 1979

Shaw, Harry E., *The Forms of Historical Fiction: Sir Walter Scott and His Successors*, Ithaca, New York: Cornell University Press, 1983

Simmons, James C., *The Novelist as Historian: Essays on the Victorian Historical Novel*, The Hague: Mouton, 1973

Since the publication of *Waverley* by Sir Walter Scott, the reading public has shown exceptional fascination with historical fiction. Critical analysis has been lively and widespread; much effort has been given to defining the genre and distinguishing it from other forms of realistic writing and from the romance.

Many would argue that serious study of the theory of historical fiction begins with LUKÁCS' work, originally published in Russian in 1936, but subsequently translated into English. A proponent of Marxist ideology, Lukács applies his considerable critical expertise to a "theoretical examination of the interaction between the historical spirit and the great genres of literature which portray the totality of history". Lukács is interested in the development of the historical consciousness that made possible the rise of Marxist doctrine. Liberally sprinkled with references to bourgeois attitudes and proletarian aspirations, the study nevertheless sets out the conceptual limits in which historical fiction operates. Beginning with an analysis of Scott's novels, Lukács ranges widely to include examinations of works by European and American authors as well as those of Britain. For him, events in Europe after 1848 led to the demise of true (i.e., Marxist) historical fiction, but he finds some glimmer of a revival in novels published after World War I.

In what is certainly one of the finest studies of the genre following Lukács, FLEISHMAN offers readers a critical survey of historical fiction. Bringing great scholarly expertise to his examination of representative works in the tradition, he aptly demonstrates the relationship of the novel to history and develops a sound theory of historical fiction: "the standard for genuine historical fiction is its governance by . . . the historical imagination", which is synthetic, "creating order from the vertiginous kaleidoscope of temporal experience". The historical novelist must see history as both "an object of study and a way of seeing". Fleishman's survey of historical novels from the early nineteenth to the mid-twentieth century demonstrates how the best practitioners exhibit that quality of imagination. His study offers readers a solid introduction to both individual works and the theory that unites them as a distinctive genre.

Although SHAW's book concentrates attention on the works of Scott, the author's purpose is wider than simple critical analysis of a single influential novelist. Convinced that historical fiction has been misunderstood, Shaw believes a careful examination of the genre's strengths and limitations can help readers develop a deeper aesthetic sensibility and also "clarify certain aspects of the nature of history itself, and of our situation as historical beings". Freely acknowledging his debt to Lukács, Shaw sets forth a definition of the historical novel, carefully analyzing previous criticism and providing a thorough examination of the problem writers have in presenting history in fiction. Shaw argues that, despite Lukács' insistence on the primacy of the representation of historical process as the criterion for evaluating historical fiction, novelists must also be judged on their "grasp of historical particularity".

SIMMONS' brief survey of Victorian historical fiction contrasts the followers of Scott with the originator of the genre, pointing out how quickly imitators repeated Scott's faults while failing to duplicate his strengths as a storyteller who based his work on historical record. Paradoxically, as historical novels became popular, readers turned to fiction more frequently than to standard works of history for information about the past, creating a special obligation for the novelist to represent historical events accurately. Simmons draws careful distinctions between the historical novelist and writers of historical romance, a genre immensely popular until mid-century. As the British public became more discriminating about historical fiction, Simmons believes lightweight productions gradually gave way to more serious attempts to integrate history into the novel. From mid-century on, historical novels were regarded as serious literature.

RANCE concentrates his attention on historical novels written before the Second Reform Act of 1867, believing that in them readers can see how authors of the period dealt with the "popular protest and revolution" prevalent at the time. In an introductory chapter he reviews the problems of urbanization, and the growing historical consciousness among the reading public which made possible the production of historical works. A separate chapter outlines the turbulent events of the 1840s and 1850s, which gave rise to the great historical fiction of Charles Dickens, George Eliot, Elizabeth Gaskell, and George Meredith. Novels by each of these writers are examined in detail.

SANDERS concentrates his critical gaze on representative novels written during the four decades after Scott's death. In an introductory chapter he explains the significance of Scott's achievement in freeing the novel from "the limitations of a picaresque or a domestic tradition" and making it possible for his successors to use fiction as a vehicle for portraying "man as a diverse, noble, historic animal, more aware of himself by reference to the historic forces that had moulded him". According to Sanders, Scott's successors perceived history as "contemporary, synchronic, and developing". To illustrate his thesis, Sanders goes to several texts considered standard fare for criticism of the genre. In addition to reviewing such works, however, he also provides insightful commentary on less well-respected novels of the period, devoting separate chapters to works by William Harrison Ainsworth, Edward Bulwer-Lytton, and Charles Kingsley.

In her provocative and illuminating study, JACOBS examines the use of historical figures in fiction. Devoting a chapter to an exploration of earlier works (from the Renaissance through the nineteenth century) in which historical figures play a significant role, she concentrates her attention on a number of twentieth-century writers who make use of real-life figures in a variety of ways in their works. Unlike their predecessors, these novelists feel no compulsion to present past events with strict historical accuracy. Instead, they "see facts as dead until transformed by imagination". Freed from the bonds of realism, writers have returned to the tradition prevalent in the Renaissance of using historical figures for larger literary and philosophical purposes. Jacobs's study also illustrates the practical problems of dealing with living figures, who may sue for libel. Her bibliography is extensive and her speculations about the future of historical fiction intriguing.

LAURENCE W. MAZZENO

Hobbes, Thomas 1588–1679

English philosopher and prose writer

Brown, K.G. (ed.), *Hobbes: Studies*, Oxford: Blackwell, 1965; Cambridge, Massachusetts: Harvard University Press, 1965

Cantalupo, Charles, *A Literary "Leviathan": Thomas Hobbes' Masterpiece of Language*, Lewisburg, Pennsylvania: Bucknell University Press, 1991; London: Associated University Presses, 1991

Johnston, David, *The Rhetoric of "Leviathan": Thomas Hobbes and the Politics of Cultural Transformation*, Princeton, New Jersey: Princeton University Press, 1986

Shapin, Steven, and Simon Schaffer, *"Leviathan" and the Air-Pump: Hobbes, Boyle, and the Experimental Life*, Princeton, New Jersey: Princeton University Press, 1985

Sorell, Tom, *Thomas Hobbes*, London and New York: Routledge, 1986

Tuck, Richard, *Hobbes*, Oxford and New York: Oxford University Press, 1989

Thomas Hobbes is the first undoubtedly great philosopher to write in the English language; and the quality of his writing, as well as his ideas, is worth attending to. While his main contribution, especially in *Leviathan* (1651), is in political philosophy, he was also very interested in the philosophy of language, in new developments in science, and in mathematics, particularly geometry. Philosophical discussion of his work has been particularly focused on his idea of the social contract and his apparent support for absolute monarchy; scholars concerned with the historical context have seen his work as a complex response to the English Civil War, or have concentrated on the influence of his French contacts; and recently, attention on Hobbes' philosophy of language has turned to consider the role of rhetoric in *Leviathan*, and how that book, in particular, demonstrates his ambivalence about his own powers of persuasion.

TUCK has written the best short introduction to Hobbes. There is a reliable account of his life, which takes full account of the varying contexts in which Hobbes worked. He gives equal weight to Hobbes' thinking on ethics, science, politics, and religion – this last one being one of the most neglected areas of study, considering the space devoted to it in *Leviathan*, and the furore caused by his alleged atheism. The accounts of Hobbes' thought are lucid without being routine. The final section deals with modern versions of Hobbes, as a natural-law theorist (Tuck's own interest), as a demon of modernity, as a social scientist, and as a moralist. Tuck's own position is that Hobbes is best seen as a sceptic.

Many of the arguments about Hobbes among contemporary philosophers and political scientists can be traced in the essays in BROWN's collection. There are statements and refutations of the "Taylor thesis" about Hobbes and morality. This is also the most convenient place to read C.B. Macpherson's controversial essay on Hobbes as a bourgeois political theorist (a thesis extended in his *The Political Theory of Possessive Individualism*, 1962). There is a subtle rejoinder by Keith Thomas, who identifies elements of a reformed aristocracy, and attention to the needs of the poor, as well as the middle classes, in Hobbes' prescriptions for civil society. Other competent and combative essays make this an important starting-point for students of Hobbes' thought even now.

SORELL's book is part of a series on "The Arguments of the Great Philosophers" and takes its emphasis from that approach. The book begins with a discussion of how Hobbes' conception of "civil science" fits in with other sciences of the day, particularly logic-book science, and what it meant for Hobbes to work from first principles. Hobbes is often linked with the Empiricists, and there is a good account of sense and the passions in his philosophy. The final chapters, illuminatingly called "The Pursuit of Felicity and the Good of Survival" and "Absolute Submission, Individual Sovereignty", deal with the central problems of morality and civil society in Hobbes' thinking. Sorell is concerned to stress the links with subsequent discussion – of contract theory, liberty, and moral psychology – but he does not strain the connections, and remains historically sensitive.

SHAPIN and SCHAFFER set Hobbes in the context of seventeenth-century scientific debate, and in particular contrast Robert Boyle's practice of experimental science, symbolized by the air-pump, with Hobbes' suspicion of experimentalism as not being proper philosophy. The book is an important counter to the way Hobbes has been written out of the history and philosophy of science; and in doing so, it also raises questions of how ideas come to be proved, or assented to, in the thought of both Hobbes and Boyle. For good measure, a translation of Hobbes' *Dialogus Physicus* is included.

One of the great oppositions in Hobbes' thought is between reason and rhetoric. JOHNSTON's study tackles this head-on. He analyses the differences between the barer, more "scientific" *Elements of Law* (1640) and the similar ideas expressed in more expansive, polemic, and rhetorical terms in *Leviathan*. He argues that *Leviathan* does not represent a change in Hobbes' ideas so much as a changed perception of what is needed for them to be put into practice. Hence, for example, the amount of biblical material in the later work – Hobbes is pressing for a cultural transformation, an abandonment of magic and superstition for logical assent. The fear of death, and what happens after death, is another attitude that Hobbes wanted to revise. In tackling the logic versus rhetoric distinction, Johnston goes well beyond that issue into a portrait of Hobbes as a social visionary.

CANTALUPO organises his study of the literary qualities of *Leviathan* along the lines of a commentary. This has the virtue of attending to what Hobbes wrote in the order that he wrote it, and of not downplaying the third and fourth parts, "Of a Christian Commonwealth", and "Of the Kingdom of Darkness", which get little attention in philosophical discussion. The disadvantage is that it rarely brings together the various discussions of language in the way that Johnston, for example, does. There is a certain repetitiveness about it, too, though he does respond well to the high points in the text, for example on the famous Chapter 13, "Of the Natural Condition of Mankind".

ROGER POOLEY

Hopkins, Gerard Manley 1844–1889

English poet

Allsopp, Michael E., and David Anthony Downes (eds.), *Saving Beauty: Further Studies in Hopkins*, New York: Garland, 1994

Bender, Todd, *Gerard Manley Hopkins: The Classical Background and Critical Reception of His Work*, Baltimore: Johns Hopkins University Press, 1966

Bump, Jerome, *Gerard Manley Hopkins*, Boston: Twayne, 1982

Downes, David Anthony, *Gerard Manley Hopkins: A Study of His Ignatian Spirit*, New York: Bookman, 1959; revised edition, as *The Ignatian Personality of Gerard Manley Hopkins*, Lanham, Maryland: University Press of America, 1990

Ellis, Virginia Ridley, *Gerard Manley Hopkins and the Language of Mystery*, Columbia: University of Missouri Press, 1991

Lichtmann, Maria R., *The Contemplative Poetry of Gerard Manley Hopkins*, Princeton, New Jersey: Princeton University Press, 1989

MacKenzie, Norman H., *A Reader's Guide to Gerard Manley Hopkins*, Ithaca, New York: Cornell University Press, 1981; London: Thames & Hudson, 1981

Mariani, Paul, *A Commentary on the Complete Poems of Hopkins*, Ithaca, New York: Cornell University Press, 1970
Milroy, James, *The Language of Gerard Manley Hopkins*, London: André Deutsch, 1977
Motto, Marylou, *"Mined with a Motion": The Poetry of Gerard Manley Hopkins*, New Brunswick, New Jersey: Rutgers University Press, 1984
Plotkin, Cary H., *The Tenth Muse: Victorian Philology and the Genesis of the Poetic Language of Gerard Manley Hopkins*, Carbondale: Southern Illinois University Press, 1989
Roberts, Gerald, *Gerard Manley Hopkins: A Literary Life*, London: Macmillan, 1994; New York: St Martin's Press, 1994
Sprinker, Michael, *"A Counterpoint of Dissonance": The Aesthetics and Poetry of Gerard Manley Hopkins*, Baltimore: Johns Hopkins University Press, 1980
Storey, Graham, *A Preface to Hopkins*, London: Longman, 1981, 2nd edition, 1992
Sulloway, Alison, *Gerard Manley Hopkins and the Victorian Temper*, New York: Columbia University Press, 1972; London: Routledge & Kegan Paul, 1972

Although Hopkins was a Victorian, his poetry did not become known until its publication by his friend Robert Bridges in 1918, and it did not become well known until two decades or more later. So in one sense it is possible to say that all criticism on Hopkins is recent criticism. But even the last half-century has seen changes, from an early emphasis on Hopkins as a proto-modernist born out of his due time, through periods that assessed elements in his background contributing to his innovative techniques, or which attempted to isolate his aesthetic qualities, to the most recent criticism, which subjects him or his work to various reigning critical methodologies. Hopkins has proved endlessly fascinating to his readers: few poets – especially poets with as small an output of finished verse as Hopkins – have provoked such a large volume of criticism, and criticism of very high quality. Perhaps the major limitations of this criticism are its occasional reductiveness and its occasional lapses into what Matthew Arnold would call the historical or the personal fallacy.

Two books provide good overviews for someone reading Hopkins for the first time. STOREY's introduction is divided into three sections: the biographical background, including religious and literary influences on Hopkins and studies of such important topics as sprung rhythm and the poet's use of transitive verbs; a critical analysis of each of 11 poems; and a reference section, which includes information on Hopkins' friends, and a useful gazetteer. The 11 poems in the middle section were chosen because they are in the author's judgment the most difficult ones, as well as the author's favorites. Fortunate is the student who finds his or her assigned poem among the 11, and frustrated is his or her counterpart who wishes information on poems, including better-known works such as "Spring and Fall" or most of the dark sonnets, which are not among those few. BUMP gives an excellent summary of some of the influences at work on the youthful Hopkins: the Pre-Raphaelites, for example, or the Ruskin-abetted Victorian enthusiasm for things medieval, or the renewed interest in the sublime as a source for nature poetry. He is also very good on Hopkins' understanding and use of typology as he learned it from the Tractarians. Perhaps the chief limitation of the book comes from the fact that almost two-thirds of it concentrates on the period before Hopkins wrote "The Wreck of the Deutschland" and his other major poems.

Similarly, two books offer excellent commentaries on all of Hopkins' poems. MARIANI proposes to offer for the general reader a chronological discussion of all of the complete poems and most of the fragments. In each case he places the poem within its context in the poet's life and thought, then explicates and paraphrases it and judges its relative success. In the poetry taken as a whole Mariani sees the poet engaging in a "dialogue with God about the things of God". He places special emphasis on Hopkins' puns and on his cultivation of ambiguity. MacKENZIE clearly aims at the general reader also. One problem such a reader will face is that the author arranges his guide to correspond to a now-outmoded edition of the poetry, so the early poems both precede and follow the major poems. But the large second section covering these major poems provides a mine of information on each work – the circumstances of its composition, the poet's comments on it, the sources of its imagery and allusions, its metrical and stanzaic forms, and a summary of different interpretive possibilities, including a line-by-line analysis of some of the more difficult parts. A useful reference section at the end covers such important topics as inscape, instress, and sprung rhythm.

For the beginning reader of Hopkins, who does not have time to read the excellent scholarly biographies but who wants a brief overview of the poet's life as it relates to the poetry, the slim volume by ROBERTS is a good choice. The author chronicles Hopkins' life from its beginnings in suburban London to its conclusion with the poet's death in Dublin from typhoid fever. Always the goal is "to evaluate Hopkins' poetry within the context of his own life", a task in keeping with the purpose of the "Literary Lives" series, which proposes "to trace the professional, publishing, and social contexts" that have shaped "the most widely read British and Irish authors".

Many readers of Hopkins will want to explore his complex poetry in greater depth than these general introductions can offer. Much good scholarship has been done on a wide variety of topics relating to the background for Hopkins' poetry, and there is room here only to discuss representative books on its literary, religious, and cultural aspects.

BENDER describes the many ways Hopkins drew upon his deep familiarity with the classical literatures of Rome and Greece. After all, the poet graduated from Oxford with a Double First in "Greats", taught classics at several Jesuit schools, and ended his career as Professor of Greek at University College, Dublin, and Fellow in Classics at the Royal University of Ireland. Bender carefully demonstrates the close connection between Hopkins' seemingly idiosyncratic techniques as a poet and his knowledge of, and theories about, the practice of the classical poets. Thus "The Wreck of the Deutschland", for example, shows marked affinities to the Pindaric ode as Hopkins understood it. Similarly his syntax and his imagery evolve from reading and reflecting upon authors such as Pseudo-Longinus and Martial.

Hopkins saw himself first and foremost as a priest and only secondarily as a poet. DOWNES traces the effect upon the poet's work of his training as a priest, especially his training as a member of the Society of Jesus. The formation of a Jesuit required long and careful attention to the *Spiritual Exercises* of Ignatius of Loyola, an attention reinforced by annual retreats and other customs. This Ignatian spirituality shaped Hopkins' aesthetic, philosophical, and theological views. More importantly, Downes argues, it also gave him certain habits of mind, which shaped his poetic practice. Some of the major poems follow the devotional pattern of an Ignatian meditation, for example, while others reflect Ignatian spirituality in their emphasis on the central role of Christ, including the need for tireless activity on Christ's behalf no matter what the personal cost.

While the poet's works clearly evidenced his literary and religious training, both of which drew upon earlier periods, he was also inevitably a man of his time, and his time was mid-Victorian England. SULLOWAY locates the poet squarely in his age. She demonstrates his debt to John Ruskin as the master who taught him how to "see". From the Tractarians Hopkins acquired his missionary zeal and the notion of the "gentleman prophet", both of which affected the substance and tone of the poetry. The final chapter of the book connects "The Wreck of the Deutschland" with contemporary Victorian theories about, and representations of, the Apocalypse.

Perhaps no feature of Hopkins' poetry is as striking as his highly distinctive poetic language. Two books are particularly helpful in explaining the nature and origins of that language. In the first section of his book MILROY synthesizes Hopkins' theories about language, and then in the second, and even more valuable, section he goes on to demonstrate what those theories meant when applied to the specifically poetic task of "heightening" language. Milroy relates Hopkins' ideas about heightening to his belief that poetry connected with the spoken, rather than the written, word and to his study of other languages, such as Welsh. The effects of theory upon practice, especially in the areas of syntax, diction, and sound patterning, are shown to be profound. Meanwhile PLOTKIN locates the origin of some of these ideas in the "new science" of language becoming prominent at mid-Victorian Oxford during Hopkins' student days. Language theoreticians like Max Müller promoted ideas that corresponded closely to Hopkins' own interests, especially on the relationship between sound and meaning. This book is especially helpful in understanding the direction of Hopkins' early poems, while Milroy offers more help on the later ones; also it is fair to say that Plotkin emphasizes Hopkins' indebtedness while Milroy emphasizes his originality.

Critical assessments of Hopkins' poetry abound. SPRINKER approaches the poems from a deconstructionist perspective, hoping "to liberate those texts from the weight of a critical tradition that has rendered them more or less innocuous". He desires to read them "in the most extreme terms possible" and therefore sets out to be iconoclastic. The result sometimes is a new, sharp, invigorating reading of a poem. At other times the book becomes a predictable member of its species: when the opening paragraphs quote Jacques Derrida, Julia Kristeva, and Harold Bloom, for example, and when every poem seems to become a poem about writing a poem, and when the author's strategy involves juxtaposing Hopkins' poetry with Mallarmé, the Russian formalists, Derrida's attacks on logocentrism, and Nietzsche's doctrine of "the prison house of language", we know where we are. Special attention is given to "The Wreck of the Deutschland", "The Windhover", and the late sonnets.

MOTTO traces what she calls "motions of assent" and "motions of recurrence" in Hopkins' poetry. Hopkins' celebrations of the natural, revealed world around him constitute his "motions of assent", while his constant probing for significance by seeing meaningful connections between seemingly discrete events make up his "motions of recurrence". She sees in the poet a struggle between his Romantic heritage as a poet and the Christocentric convictions that focused his life as a priest. The motions of assent and recurrence become his poetic means for asserting the dominance of the latter over the former, although this struggle to assert dominance is never easy – doubt and fear permeate the works, especially the later ones – and never wholly successful. The most valuable chapter may be the third, which identifies four characteristic syntactic structures in the poetry and relates them to Hopkins' ideas about "calling". Only two poems receive extended treatment – "Spelt from Sibyl's Leaves" and "The Wreck of the Deutschland".

LICHTMANN identifies parallelism as the most significant characteristic of Hopkins' poetic technique. Each poem, she believes, strives to find unity in "many-ness" and relies on a multiplicity of often subtle parallelisms to accomplish this end. The poet's metaphysical beliefs rest upon the centrality of the principle of contraries: the world evidences differences, changes, dissolutions, and the goal is to reconcile them by finding the underlying unity which these contraries presuppose. The poem becomes, for Hopkins, a means to this end because it embodies and gives language to the contemplative moment when all contraries are acknowledged and yet dissolved. Perhaps the most interesting aspect of Lichtmann's argument is her contention that the later, darker sonnets reflect the gradual breakdown of this metaphysics.

Not all critics accept the notion of Hopkins' poetic career demonstrating a loss of faith and consequently of direction and meaning. The most recent of these critical monographs is also in some ways one of the most old-fashioned, at least in terms of both the questions it poses and the answers it gives. What are the sources, ELLIS asks, of the power which so many readers find in Hopkins' poetry? What must such a reader know, what resources must he or she bring to that reading? She wants to interpret the works, believing, in direct opposition to Sprinker and others, that a work "cannot mean less or wholly other than what is consciously intended". Like Motto, she accepts the importance of recurrence, but for her recurrence is not so much a willed gesture as it is a reflection of Hopkins' concept of mystery. The author lays out this theory of mystery in the opening chapter and then devotes subsequent chapters to "The Wreck of the Deutschland", the nature poems, and the dark sonnets respectively. She argues, again in opposition to Sprinker, that Hopkins refuses to accept the prison-house of language, because God is behind and beyond it; mystery does not need to mean uncertainty.

Finally, the volume edited by ALLSOPP and DOWNES represents the most recent addition to the many fine collections of essays on Hopkins that have been published over the years. Over a dozen such collections have appeared, an unusually high number for a poet who has only been well known for half a century. This particular collection is strong on essays connecting Hopkins' ideas and practice to his reading and his life experiences: to his reading, for example, of Augustine and Duns Scotus, or of Rossetti, Tennyson, and Walt Whitman among his contemporaries; to his life experiences, encountering the doctrinal controversies at 1860s' Oxford, for example, or adjusting to the people and principles which formed his life as a Jesuit, or to meeting the youthful Yeats in Dublin.

The reaction to Hopkins by his readers has much resembled the typical response to a strikingly original composer such as Beethoven in the nineteenth century or Schönberg in the twentieth: at first horror, then grudging acceptance, then approval and admiration. Hopkins will never be an "easy" poet for someone who reads his work for the first time. But his themes and his stylistic features, however much they have to be explained by the critics who have written about him, will never prove to be more than a temporary barrier to a fuller appreciation of his poems. The books which have just been surveyed all serve to demonstrate that F.R. Leavis's proclamation of Hopkins as the greatest poet of the Victorian age was, while perhaps an exaggeration, at least not an unconscionable one.

FRANCIS L. FENNELL

Horror Literature

Bloom, Clive (ed.), *Creepers: British Horror and Fantasy in the Twentieth Century*, London: Pluto Press, 1993

Carroll, Noël, *The Philosophy of Horror, or, Paradoxes of the Heart*, New York and London: Routledge, 1990

Grixti, Joseph, *Terrors of Uncertainty: The Cultural Contexts of Horror Fiction*, London and New York: Routledge, 1989

Jancovich, Mark, *Horror*, London: Batsford, 1992

Twitchell, James B., *Dreadful Pleasures: An Anatomy of Modern Horror*, New York and Oxford: Oxford University Press, 1985

As late as the end of the 1960s horror fiction was less a "popular" genre than a focus of the enthusiasms of specialist groups of *aficionados*. By the 1980s this had changed. Horror was (and remains) highly visible culturally, and "in 1987 it was rumoured in the publishing world that one out of every four books printed had Stephen King's name on the cover" (Carroll). This transformation owes much to cinema – notably the 1973 film *The Exorcist* and its aftermath; of the considerable critical literature on horror a sizeable proportion is interested mainly in film. This essay's concern, though, is with books addressing primarily (though seldom exclusively) prose fiction.

TWITCHELL's book is lively and provocative, and his approach – which he describes as "ethnological" – is powerfully influenced by structuralist approaches to narrative. The author admits to being "not much interested in specific . . . texts" but rather in the underlying patterns and systems of horror fiction. "You search for what is stable and repeated; you neglect what is 'artistic' and 'original'". The search yields three central myths of horror which, Twitchell argues, form the foundation of three narrative formulas at the heart of the genre – "the vampire, the hulk-with-no-name, and the transformation monster" (Dracula, Frankenstein, Jekyll and Hyde). The strength of the book is in the boldness and scope of the enquiry: William Hogarth's engravings, Milton's Satan, and prehistoric cave paintings all figure here. With problems of the definition of horror and its relation to adjacent genres and experiences Twitchell offers little assistance however.

Of all the work under consideration here, GRIXTI's offers the most substantial literary analysis, with major chapters on James Herbert and Stephen King. There is sharp analysis of language, especially in relation to King, where linguistic ambiguity is shown to contribute importantly to the reader's "terrified uncertainty" as to the significance of the unfolding events of the plot. Grixti convincingly presents King's world as one in which "frequent unreliability of perception" is instrumental in the generating of horror. The interest is not exclusively formal. There is a useful (if conventional) overview of the development of the genre, and a consideration of the appeal of horror, which engages critically with theories of the cathartic function of horror in "discharging" the "beast" within all human beings and human societies. In Chapter 5 Grixti is rightly critical of studies of the "effects" of horror and media violence, which omit to locate the reading of horror against broader patterns of cultural consumption; and in a final chapter we are given a useful survey of some of the ways in which readers use horror fiction in making sense of their social experience.

CARROLL makes a significant contribution to the exploration of the aesthetics of popular culture. A philosopher by training, Carroll is seeking general propositions – initially a definition of the experience of horror (he offers "fear and repulsion at the thought of monsters") and later for the "characteristic horror plot" and for the reason why, paradoxically, readers enjoy what must by its nature be terrifying or perverse. Along the way there are correctives to some of the uncritical taken-for-granteds of the genre – notably the processes of reader identification with the victim. Carroll demonstrates convincingly in Chapter 2 that *identification* is not a *sine qua non* of *sympathy*. There is some consideration of the boom in the popularity of horror, especially in America since the 1970s. The explanations focusing on social instability and cultural anxiety are familiar enough, but Carroll goes on to make broadly based connections with the tendencies of postmodernism. Tucked away in the final chapter, this appears more an afterthought than a systematic historicising of taste, but it is interesting nonetheless.

JANCOVICH's book is compact, lucid, and accessible. The approach is that of cultural studies, and the emphasis throughout is on the mutations of horror in the context of shifting historical locations. There is no pretension to any original re-appraisal of the genre, but as an introductory survey for students the book is excellent. The coverage achieved in so short a book is remarkable, particularly since the survey embraces critical perspectives on the genre alongside its literary history. The approach is one that encourages in students critical engagement as part of the process of absorbing the insights of psychoanalytic, cultural, and gendered readings of horror.

BLOOM's collection considers British texts only, and ranges widely from the 1890s to the present, from the "civilised" ghost stories of M.R. James to the nastiness and perversity of horror of the 1980s. There are particularly interesting essays on popular-magazine stories of the early twentieth century (by Victor Sage) and on Dennis Wheatley, who is characterised (by Gina Whisker) as "very much a middle class Englishman's man". The essays cohere as a collection particularly in their success in conveying the evolution of horror through the century away from the fringes of the canon towards its massive contemporary popularity and notoriety. The success with which individual contributors seek to explain this growth varies greatly. Alasdair Spark provides an interesting and thorough analysis of the early writing of James Herbert in the context of the working classes' experience of Britain during the 1970s. John Nicholson's essay, entitled "Scared Shitless: The Sex of Horror", concludes with an attempt to link fictional perversity with the real-life horrors surrounding killers Frank Beck, Dennis Nielsen, and others. The context here, explicitly and perhaps predictably, is "Thatcherdom": but such connections need to be explored. As undertones or footnotes, they are bound to appear facile.

BOB ASHLEY

Housman, A.E. 1859–1936

English poet

Bayley, John, *Housman's Poems*, Oxford: Clarendon Press, 1992
Graves, Richard Perceval, *A.E. Housman, the Scholar-Poet*, London: Routledge & Kegan Paul, 1979
Leggett, B.J., *Housman's Land of Lost Content: A Critical Study of "A Shropshire Lad"*, Knoxville: University of Tennessee Press, 1970
Leggett, B.J., *The Poetic Art of A.E. Housman: Theory and Practice*, Lincoln: University of Nebraska Press, 1978
Marlow, Arnold Norman, *A.E. Housman, Scholar and Poet*, London: Routledge & Kegan Paul, 1958
Page, Norman, *A.E. Housman: A Critical Biography*, London: Macmillan, 1983
Ricks, Christopher (ed.), *A.E. Housman: A Collection of Critical Essays*, Englewood Cliffs, New Jersey: Prentice-Hall, 1968

A.E. Housman was a distinguished textual scholar, whose main professional work was on Latin poets such as Manilius and Juvenal; but he is best known for his small body of lyric poetry, especially the collection *A Shropshire Lad*. Though immensely popular with the common reader, his poems were dismissed as old-fashioned and sentimental by the New Critics and adherents of the Cambridge journal *Scrutiny* (edited by F.R. Leavis). There are signs, though, that his poetry is now returning to critical favour.

MARLOW's book includes a biographical sketch, a chapter on Housman's juvenilia, and one on his nonsense verse. It is mainly useful, however, for its exhaustive treatment of influences on Housman's poetry. RICKS's collection usefully brings together poems by W.H. Auden, Ezra Pound, and Kingsley Amis, and essays and comments by Edmund Wilson, Cyril Connolly, and some of the New Critics. His Introduction discusses the current (i.e., 1968) state of Housman's critical reputation, and his own essay on "The Nature of Housman's Poetry" argues that "his poems are remarkable for the ways in which rhythm and style temper or mitigate or criticise what in bald paraphrase the poem would be saying". LEGGETT, in his two works, defends Housman against the New Critics, basing his case on the psychoanalytic theory of poetry, which he finds implicit in Housman's work. He argues that Housman's poetry has a "mithridatic function", which "requires that we experience a controlled amount of pain as defence against the much greater pain inherent in the nature of the world outside the poem".

GRAVES's book is a very readable and sympathetic account of Housman's life and work. As biography it is excellent; as criticism rather too bland. PAGE's study is a very informative biography, which brings out the paradoxes of Housman's life – "the poet-don, the emotional over-reactions of scholarly controversy coexisting with the seemingly passionless nature, worldly success of a highly conventional and approved kind masking crude unsatisfied appetites". It also includes a chapter on Housman's professional work as a Latin scholar, and one on his poetry which is valuable as a clear, succinct, and well-balanced introduction to a proper critical consideration of Housman's poetic achievement. Page also has some useful comments to make in praise of Housman as a prose writer.

BAYLEY examines the poetry sensitively and in considerable detail, making many shrewd points concerning, for example, its "vibration", Housman's peculiar use of *personae* and near-parody effects, "that small internal voice of irony rarely absent in his poetry", and the nature of Housman's Shropshire as a "mythical alternative" to the real world. Bayley also ranges widely over other poets whose work he wishes to compare or contrast with that of Housman. This book is the fullest and, on balance, the best strictly critical examination of the poetry as yet available.

R.P. DRAPER

Howells, William Dean 1837–1920

American novelist, dramatist, critic, and journalist

Bennett, George N., *William Dean Howells: The Development of a Novelist*, Norman: University of Oklahoma Press, 1959
Bennett, George N., *The Realism of William Dean Howells, 1889–1920*, Nashville, Tennessee: Vanderbilt University Press, 1973
Cady, Edwin H., *The Road to Realism: The Early Years, 1837–1885, of William Dean Howells*, Syracuse, New York: Syracuse University Press, 1956
Cady, Edwin H., *The Realist at War: The Mature Years, 1885–1920, of William Dean Howells*, Syracuse, New York: Syracuse University Press, 1958
Carrington, George C., *The Immense Complex Drama: The World and Art of the Howells Novel*, Columbus: Ohio State University Press, 1966
Carter, Everett, *Howells and the Age of Realism*, Philadelphia: J.B. Lippincott, 1954

Crowley, John W., *The Black Heart's Truth: The Early Career of William Dean Howells*, Chapel Hill: University of North Carolina Press, 1985

Gibson, William M., *William Dean Howells*, Minneapolis: University of Minnesota Press, 1967

Lynn, Kenneth S., *William Dean Howells: An American Life*, New York: Harcourt Brace Jovanovich, 1971

McMurray, William, *The Literary Realism of William Dean Howells*, Carbondale: Southern Illinois University Press, 1967

Nettels, Elsa, *Language, Race, and Social Class in Howells's America*, Lexington: University Press of Kentucky, 1988

Prioleau, Elizabeth, *The Circle of Eros: Sexuality in the Work of William Dean Howells*, Durham, North Carolina: Duke University Press, 1983

Criticism of Howells has, understandably, focused on his contribution to the American novel and, more particularly, to the development of American realism, though it should be remembered that during his own lifetime he was an extremely influential critic and journalist, and a prolific playwright. What might be called his "relationship with his age" has also been the subject of serious scrutiny, whether it be with his artistic contemporaries (the correspondence with Henry James and Mark Twain, for example) or his political contemporaries (notably his editorial work on the speeches of Abraham Lincoln and his place as a political journalist).

CARTER's study remains by far the best contextual study of Howells and the emerging philosophy of literary realism in the America of the 1880s and 1890s. He sees Howells as "the dominant and representative sensibility of his age", and this age is, he argues, co-extensive with the emergence of modern America, so much so that Howells does not merely contribute to a major American literary movement, but also, perhaps unwittingly, gives definition to what America will become in the new century. The context Carter establishes is, however, not narrowly American: he considers Howells's writings and ideas in the broader context of European realism, and his affinities with writers such as Henrik Ibsen, Leo Tolstoy, and Émile Zola are intelligently documented. Theoretical questions of literary realism, literary naturalism, and critical realism are also addressed here.

BENNETT's two books on Howells, separated by 14 years, remain among the best of the critical studies devoted to his fiction. In the earlier work (1959) he challenges the conventional view that Howells's novels are simply novels of manners, and argues instead that they offer frequently profound commentaries on the human condition; at the same time he explores the breadth of Howells's interests and his literary friendships, notably with Henry James and Mark Twain. The later work examines the novels of the last part of Howells's career, in essence his twentieth-century novels, such as *The Son of Royal Langbrith* and *The Vacation of the Kelwyns*, and here he emphasises the psychological realism of the late fiction.

CARRINGTON's study, which was thought somewhat sensationalist in character by its early reviewers, constructs a Howells who seems a more late twentieth-century than late nineteenth-century novelist. Anticipating later studies (such as those of Crowley and Prioleau) Carrington sees Howells as a "neurotic" artist, "a writer harmed but not wholly controlled by defects in his psychic economy". He marginalises Howells's realism and emphasises, instead, what he calls a preoccupation with alienation and terror in the major fiction, adopting a critical language that is at times psychoanalytic, at times existentialist, in order to throw light on the relationship between the works and the man. This book is frequently illuminating and perceptive, despite Carrington's occasional temptation to overstate his case.

McMURRAY discusses 12 of Howells's best novels, from *A Foregone Conclusion* (1875) to *The Vacation of the Kelwyns* (1920), the latter published in the year of the novelist's death. McMurray argues that Howells's realism closely resembles the pragmatism of the philosopher William James, suggesting that Howells, like James, posited a world where freedom is impossible and illusory and, as a consequence, man is unable to reconcile his intentions and actions. Beyond this, McMurray seeks to assess Howells's place in the broader tradition of American literature, pointing to his affinities with Nathaniel Hawthorne and Henry James.

GIBSON's University of Minnesota pamphlet remains a good, general guide: the biographical account is lucid and informed, the critical consideration of the novels is brief but perceptive, and the concluding pages offer an intelligent overview of Howells's critical theory.

CROWLEY's study is, in part, biographical, but it brings to both the life and the work a markedly Freudian and psychoanalytic approach, in which *A Modern Instance* (1882) is given a central place in the Howells canon. Crowley reads the novel in the light of what he calls Howells's "youthful neuroticism", drawing, in part, on an earlier essay by Edwin H. Cady (see below); his interest is in how the novel illuminates the life, and it is read as a document of "psychic stress", though this is not to suggest that the critical insights Crowley offers are insubstantial. PRIOLEAU, like Crowley, offers a markedly (some might say stridently) Freudian view of Howells, identifying five psycho-sexual stages in his development as a novelist, ranging from what she sees as "youthful neurosis" to a "mature adult love ethic". She sees Howells's preoccupations with sex and gender in essentially late twentieth-century terms, but she is sensitive to the ways in which his major fiction explores questions that transcend what we might call his essentially Victorian understanding of these topics, making this book a valuable complement to Crowley's study as well as a concerted plea for Howells's "relevance" for a modern readership.

NETTELS's book is an attempt to provide a kind of sociolinguistic basis for the study of Howells and, at the same time, to read his work in the light of modern critical preoccupations with matters of race and class. Her book offers an overview of the state of American English as it appeared to many nineteenth-century commentators, and goes on to show how Howells's concern with language, particularly the colloquialisms and syntax of speech, comes from a belief that the accurate reporting of these is important in maintaining the realistic surface of his novels. Occasionally, and rather regrettably, the critical discussion of the novels amounts to little more than annotation of the differing styles of spoken English they employ.

CADY's two-volume study is essentially a work of biography, but it remains invaluable for its informed and exhaustive account of Howells's growth and development as a writer;

the first volume establishes the familial, historical and cultural context, taking the reader through to 1885, while the second concentrates on "his mature achievement and its significance". The latter is the more important of the two volumes for its account of Howells's contribution to literary realism.

LYNN's biography, like Cady's two-volume biographical study, is a significant work of historical scholarship, and while much time is taken up with contextual matters (Howells's relationships with other writers, his political and philosophical views, the growth of his interest in the theatre, etc.) Lynn offers a good deal of intelligent close criticism of his imaginative writings, particularly the major novels. The chapter on Howells's admiration of Tolstoy ("The Example of Tolstoy") remains the best published discussion of what Lynn calls "his surging Tolstoyism", and the brief consideration of *Annie Kilburn* (1888) as a "rebuttal" of *Anna Karenina* is especially perceptive.

HENRY CLARIDGE

Hughes, Langston 1902–1967

American writer of poetry, fiction, plays, children's books, and prose

Barksdale, Richard K., *Langston Hughes: The Poet and His Critics*, Chicago: American Library Association, 1977

Emanuel, James A., *Langston Hughes*, Boston: Twayne, 1967

Gates, Henry Louis, Jr., and K.A. Appiah (eds.), *Langston Hughes: Critical Perspectives Past and Present*, New York: Amistad Press, 1993

Jemie, Onwuchekwa, *Langston Hughes: An Introduction to the Poetry*, New York: Columbia University Press, 1976

Mikolyzk, Thomas A. (ed.), *Langston Hughes: A Bio-Bibliography*, New York: Greenwood Press, 1990

Miller, R. Baxter, *Langston Hughes and Gwendolyn Brooks: A Reference Guide*, Boston: G.K. Hall, 1978

Rampersad, Arnold, *The Life of Langston Hughes*, 2 vols., New York and Oxford: Oxford University Press, 1986–88

Investigation of Langston Hughes should begin with perusal of two important reference guides by Miller and Mikolyzk. MILLER offers a valuable introductory essay, which outlines major trends in Hughes criticism from the 1920s through the 1970s, and highlights several important articles from each decade. According to Miller, Hughes scholarship in the 1920s fell under three primary rubrics: studies that compared the artist to his contemporaries in the Harlem Renaissance, studies that considered his use of musical forms in poetry, and studies that evaluated his presentation of black dialect. The historical context of the 1930s, Miller argues, influenced a shift toward Marxist interpretations of Hughes's work, while the 1940s ushered in a period of expanding attention in which Hughes's creative output was examined from a variety of perspectives ranging from biographical considerations to stylistic critiques. The 1950s marked the period of Hughes's highest productivity with his publication of over 20 major works; thus, Miller states, most material written about Hughes during this decade consisted of popular and scholarly commentaries on these works, in particular. Hughes's death on May 22, 1967, led to an explosion of interest, both national and international in scope, which Miller traces through the 1978 publication of his guide. Following this overview of criticism, Miller identifies and summarizes both full-length books and shorter writings about Hughes, which were produced each year between 1924 and 1977.

MIKOLYZK's 1990 study importantly updates and revises the material found in Miller's guide. Although titled a "bio-bibliography", Mikolyzk examines Hughes's life only briefly, intending instead to provide a detailed resource on "all collectable published work by the author, as well as virtually every critical piece published throughout the world". Mikolyzk read each item listed in an effort to insure the relevance of the piece to Hughes scholars, the accuracy of the citation, and the availability of the source, thus making this book an invaluable tool for students and researchers who must rely primarily on systems of inter-library loan to obtain material. The bio-bibliography consists of an annotated list of books by Hughes, which is categorized according to genre (e.g., autobiographies, books for children, edited books, novels, plays, etc.), including: translations by, and of, the author; shorter works by Hughes, including essays, interviews, letters, plays, poetry, and short stories; secondary books and articles, which are either wholly or partly devoted to Hughes; an alphabetical listing of Hughes's works; descriptions of primary source locations; and information about *The Langston Hughes Review*, the semi-annual "Official Publication of the Langston Hughes Society". Mikolyzk's work offers the most comprehensive bibliography of Hughes material to date.

As these bibliographies confirm, Hughes has received extensive critical attention over the years. EMANUEL's work, completed the year before Hughes's death, however, is the first book-length study of the author, and as such stands as a ground-breaking contribution to Hughes scholarship. A poet himself, Emanuel attempts, through close analysis of Hughes's creative productions, "a literary examination of the writer's whole works, rather than a sociological glance at them". According to Emanuel, "at a time when 'the Negro condition' is fast becoming the American condition morally, it is vital that students – whose standard anthologies are significantly devoid of literature by Negroes – be offered an esthetic approach to the very substance which they will be required to transform by their future ethics and actions" (Preface). Emanuel therefore, in thematically arranged chapters, weaves together contextual biographical information with rather formalist readings of the artist's poems and short stories. Also included in this study are a chronology of Hughes's life and works as well as a selected bibliography of primary and secondary sources.

Two important critical studies serve as valuable starting points for the genre for which Hughes received highest critical acclaim – his poetry. JEMIE's study is "intended as an introduction" to Hughes's work, and addresses only the author's collected poems in an effort to "delineate Hughes's major themes and techniques, especially as they relate to Afro-American oral tradition". In six chapters, organized according to theme, Jemie examines Hughes's poetry from the "dual perspective of the oral tradition and the tradition of struggle and protest", which, Jemie argues, Hughes articulated in his

1962 essay "The Negro Artist and the Racial Mountain". BARKSDALE's study builds on Jemie's work by reconsidering Hughes's poetic contributions, as well as assessing critical responses to that poetry over the course of Hughes's career. Each chapter contains a critical introduction to the poetry and a discussion of the reactions of critics to these poems. The chronological organization of the text allows for an understanding of how scholarly appreciation and critique of Hughes's work has evolved.

The most thorough and influential biography thus far of Hughes has been produced by RAMPERSAD. Although Faith Berry published an illuminating study in 1983 (*Langston Hughes: Before and Beyond Harlem*), restrictions on important sources limited her work. Based on full access to the Hughes papers, extensive archival research, and interviews with Hughes's friends and colleagues, Rampersad's investigation aims to correct "much misinformation concerning Langston Hughes" that "has passed into print – some, perhaps most, from his own pen, and especially in his two volumes of autobiography". Rampersad does so in carefully researched and eminently readable chapters, which are organized chronologically, according to the main events and circumstances that shaped Hughes's life. The first volume of Rampersad's biography spans the years between 1902 and 1941; the second covers 1941 to 1967. Employing traditional biographical methods, cultural history, and literary analysis, Rampersad's text provides the definitive resource on Hughes for serious scholars of the writer.

Finally, the collection of essays edited by GATES and APPIAH offers a valuable combination of historical reviews of Hughes's works and more recent critical articles assessing the artist's literary significance. "The sequence of reviews that open this volume", according to editor Gates, "chronicle the development of Hughes's oeuvre, from his discovery of dialect to his forays into fiction and autobiography". Penned by such notable figures in American literary history as Countee Cullen, Jessie Fauset, Sterling A. Brown, Sherwood Anderson, Richard Wright, J. Saunders Redding, Carl Van Vechten, and James Baldwin, these reviews provide important insight into both Hughes's work and his relationship to his literary peers. The remainder of the collection is devoted to critical essays by the most noted scholars of Hughes, including Miller, Emanuel, Barksdale, Jemie, and Rampersad, as well as Steven Tracy, Raymond Smith, Leslie Catherine Sanders, Susan L. Blake, and Maryemma Graham. The topics addressed range from Hughes's use of folklore and the blues to his humanistic techniques and his "practice of social art". This is an immensely valuable collection of past and present visions of the poet and his work.

HEATHER A. HATHAWAY

Hughes, Ted 1930–

English poet and dramatist

Faas, Ekbert, *Ted Hughes: The Unaccommodated Universe, with Selected Writings by Ted Hughes and Two Interviews*, Santa Barbara, California: Black Sparrow Press, 1980
Gifford, Terry, and Neil Roberts, *Ted Hughes: A Critical Study*, London: Faber & Faber, 1981
Robinson, Craig, *Ted Hughes as Shepherd of Being*, London: Macmillan, 1989
Sagar, Keith, *The Art of Ted Hughes*, Cambridge: Cambridge University Press, 1975, revised 1978
Sagar, Keith (ed.), *The Challenge of Ted Hughes*, London: Macmillan, 1994; New York: St Martin's Press, 1994
Scigaj, Leonard M., *The Poetry of Ted Hughes: Form and Imagination*, Iowa City: University of Iowa Press, 1986
Walder, Dennis, *Ted Hughes*, Milton Keynes, Buckinghamshire: Open University Press, 1987
West, Thomas, *Ted Hughes*, London: Methuen, 1985

Ted Hughes burst into public acclaim as an "animal poet", with poems such as "The Thought-Fox", "The Jaguar", and "Hawk Roosting", from his early volumes *The Hawk in the Rain* (1957) and *Lupercal* (1960). However, critics soon recognised him as having much wider concerns, and with volumes such as *Crow* (1970–72) and *Gaudete* (1977) he acquired the reputation of being an uncompromisingly visionary poet with an urgent message for the late twentieth century. Critical controversy has focused particularly on his treatment of violence, which some see as a necessary counterbalance to the abstraction and denial of natural energies typical of a technological age, and others as a symptom of male-macho aggressiveness. His marriage to Sylvia Plath, and his subsequent relationship with Assia Gutsmann – both partners committed suicide – have attracted some dubious biographical controversy; but since his appointment as Poet Laureate in 1984, and the publication of more recent poems such as "That Morning" (from *River*, 1983) and "Little Whale Song" (from *Wolfwatching*, 1989), he has been seen in a more optimistic light as an "ecological poet".

The first full-length study treating Hughes as a major poet, SAGAR's 1975 volume (revised 1978) is a patient work of exposition and still a valuable source for the student of the earlier volumes up to, and including, *Gaudete*. The seriousness with which Sagar treats Hughes's achievement is impressive, though rather more discrimination is called for in assessing its poetic quality. More recent work is treated in the essays by various hands that make up SAGAR's 1994 collection. Particularly interesting contributions to this volume are Leonard M. Scigaj's "Ted Hughes and Ecology: A Biocentric Vision" and Nathalie Anderson's "Ted Hughes and the Challenge of Gender". FAAS makes extensive use of Hughes's prose, and includes valuable interview material. He provides an especially helpful assessment of Hughes's use of Trickster legends in *Crow*.

GIFFORD and ROBERTS pay much attention to the originality of Hughes's language, especially its intensely physical and metaphorical quality; but their main focus is on the anthropological/religious dimension of his work, in particular his debt to Robert Graves's *The White Goddess* and his use of shamanism. They are especially good on the factitious nature of the "myth" developed in Hughes's work, and on his rejection of the possibility of replacing "a provisional or false myth with a permanent and true one". Crow, for example, is a creature "exploring the universe without preconceptions, discovering from direct experience what is needed for survival".

Gaudete is analysed in detail, but found to be an interesting failure. Hughes's greatest success to date (1981) is judged to be *Cave Birds*, where (as to a lesser extent in *Remains of Elmet* and *Moortown*), he manages to fuse the animal and the distinctively human in a satisfying whole. This remains a valuable study by virtue of its thoughtful combination of exegesis with critical judgement.

WEST's book is a 121-page essay on the techniques of literary exorcism by means of which Hughes seeks to heal the split he sees in the modern psyche. His poetry "is a variation on the Dr Jekyll and Mr Hyde theme, with this twist: Hyde, the body and repulsive toad, is the real possessor of knowledge, and Jekyll, the enlightened or sophisticated mind, is the guilt-ridden, accused party".

Hughes's debt to Jungian psychology and oriental philosophy is widely recognised, but SCIGAJ is the most informative commentator on these aspects of his work. Scigaj discerns three stages in Hughes's development (up to 1986): (1) the New-Critical formalist, whose emphasis is on the dense, compact craft of poetry; (2) the 1960s' poet of mythic surrealism; and (3) the more recent creator of a mystic landscape, who belongs to a "more purely visionary conception of the artist as seer". This is a valuable sourcebook for the understanding of Hughes's work.

WALDER's short study is an introduction to Hughes's poetry written for Open University students in Britain. It concentrates on discussion of particular poems representative of the different stages of Hughes's poetic development; but it also encompasses general themes such as the ambiguously potent natural energies evoked by the poetry (and the controversy over violence), Hughes as a "war poet", and Hughes in relation to both the Romantic tradition and contemporary feminism. There is a recurrent emphasis on "the inner reality of primitive, instinctual energies which, he [Hughes] feels, are warped and obscured by our rational, social selves".

ROBINSON argues that Hughes's work aims to heal the breach between reason and feeling that bedevils the modern world: it is in this sense that Hughes is a "shepherd" of Heideggerian wholeness of "Being". His methods for achieving this end are a readjustment in the processes of thinking, an original use of highly physical metaphor, and a special kind of verbal music favouring "heavy stresses, monosyllables that make us pause and large vowel sounds", the effect of which is to make "each word bear its full weight of world". Robinson finds Hughes's most important work in *Gaudete*, *Cave Birds*, and *Moortown*, works which, he claims, "form the core of an achievement as substantial as that of any English-born poet since Wordsworth".

R.P. DRAPER

Hurston, Zora Neale c.1901–1960

American novelist, dramatist, and prose writer

Awkward, Michael (ed.), *New Essays on "Their Eyes Were Watching God"*, Cambridge and New York: Cambridge Univesity Press, 1990

Bloom, Harold (ed.), *Zora Neale Hurston's "Their Eyes Were Watching God"*, New York: Chelsea House, 1987

Gates, Henry Louis, Jr., and K.A. Appiah (eds.), *Zora Neale Hurston: Critical Perspectives Past and Present*, New York: Amistad Press, 1993

Hemenway, Robert E., *Zora Neale Hurston: A Literary Biography*, Urbana: University of Illinois Press, 1977

Turner, Darwin, *In a Minor Chord: Three Afro-American Writers and Their Search for Identities*, Carbondale: Southern Illinois University Press, 1971

American novelist Alice Walker is generally credited with rediscovering the importance of Zora Neale Hurston's work in the 1970s. At that time, Hurston's novels were long out of print, and in college/univeristy courses and writing on the literature of the Harlem Renaissance her name was often relegated to an appended list of "minor" writers. Other African-American writers began to acknowledge Hurston's literary influence, and her work then found new popularity. Hurston's writing, which reflected both her artistic talents and her copious academic fieldwork, are now considered significant in the field of American literature.

HEMENWAY's book is generally recognized as the major critical book-length study of Hurston's life and work. Hemenway views Hurston's work as an example of how the promise of the Harlem Renaissance had sadly deteriorated after World War II, as well as how black artists in America have been neglected. He accomplishes this through his groundbreaking work in situating Hurston's work in the social, political, and historical context of the 1920s–40s in America. Hemenway painstakingly reconstructs details of Hurston's travels from her native Southern origins in Florida, to Howard University, New York, and Columbia University to pursue her writing and folklore studies, and back to the South on folklore-collecting expeditions. He also details her brief forays into other literary and academic activities, such as performance drama and script-writing, journalism, university teaching, and lecturing. Hurston is depicted as a dynamic and flamboyantly witty, ambitious, and determined writer who, although dependent on the fickle generosity of wealthy white patronage to support her work, managed to maintain an absolute conviction in unearthing and writing the authentic African-American folklore of the South. Virtually all of Hurston's published work is discussed, including her political essays as a journalist during World War II. Her texts are mainly presented in the context of circumstances surrounding their production and publication; Hemenway does not shirk from details of Hurston's life and their effects on her literary career, including such low points as political conflicts with other Harlem Renaissance writers, who disparaged her anti-Communism and accused her of caricaturing Negro life, and her ill health and descent into poverty. Hemenway is most critical of Hurston's autobiography *Dust Tracks* (1942), depicting it as a contradictory text, which tries to mask the obstacles of racial prejudice and disparity she faced as a writer while simultaneously celebrating her all-black upbringing and heritage. However, he ultimately defends it on the basis that it was apparently self-consciously written and manipulated for a white editor and audience.

TURNER's book is also a work of recovery. Turner looks specifically at the work of three African-American writers (Jean Toomer, Countee Cullen, and Zora Neale Hurston) as examples of Harlem Renaissance writers who struck a "melancholy minor chord" in their writings, in contrast to their more popular contemporaries. Like Hemenway, Turner expresses criticism of Hurston's autobiography as myopic in its affability and denial of the racial politics of her relations with white patronage. However, Turner uses her newspaper essays to show that, in fact, she supported political, social, and cultural autonomy of black communities. Using the autobiography as a starting point from which to discuss Hurston's complexity in her writing, Turner recovers her novels as possessing insightful and authentic representations of Southern black vernacular, folklore, and feminine psychology. He identifies self-realization as the quest that is a common thread in novels such as *Jonah's Gourd Vine* (1934) and *Their Eyes Were Watching God* (1937). He also identifies the latter as the artistically superior of the two, because of its more powerfully constructed protagonist, Janie, as well as the restraint in "adornment" of the plot with literary devices such as metaphor and exaggeration. In addition, Turner recovers Hurston's talent for satire and irony in *Moses, Man of the Mountain* (1939), which satirizes the Negro plight using the narrative of Moses and the enslavement of the Hebrews. Turner identifies Hurston's most ambitious and artistically competent novel as *Seraph on the Swanee* (1948), noting that its somberness in comparison to her earlier work may contribute to its relative obscurity. Ultimately, Turner emphasizes that the strength of Hurston's writing lies in her careful attention to both aesthetics and authenticity in her presentation of folklore and vernacular.

AWKWARD's slim, accessible volume brings together essays on Hurston's most popular work, *Their Eyes Were Watching God*, by established scholars Hemenway, Nellie McKay, Hazel V. Carby, and Rachel Blau DuPlessis. Awkward, in an informative Introduction, acknowledges the work that black and feminist scholars have done since the 1970s to propel Hurston's novels into their widely recognized present positions as forerunners of African-American women's fiction. The essays here look at why *Their Eyes Were Watching God* was marginalized for so long in American literary history, the autobiography genre and the novel, and the novel's romanticization of black Southern rural life. The collection concludes with DuPlessis's feminist interpretation of the novel, which takes into account not only plot and other narrative choices, but also its title and the circumstances surrounding the writing of the text.

BLOOM's collection of essays on *Their Eyes Were Watching God* turns away from social factors and attempts to investigate closely the rhetoric in Hurston's writing. Essays by critical luminaries such as Houston A. Baker, Barbara Johnson, and Henry Louis Gates, Jr., focus on ideology and narrative form in the novel, indirect discourse, as well as metaphor, metonymy, and voice. Other essays focus on Hurston's role in a black female literary tradition and the rhetoric of intimacy in the novel.

GATES and APPIAH's book of essays is a timely volume, which brings together old and new critical interpretations of Hurston's work. The Preface by Gates and Appiah is quite brief, and notes the previous absence of such a critical work. The first section is a series of reprinted reviews of Hurston's novels, by critics who were her contemporaries. The second section is a series of new essays on Hurston's works, which look at them not only from a literary perspective, but also as texts of auto-ethnography and as important documents of an authentic black woman's voice. Houston A. Baker makes an unusual investigation of the figure of the "conjure woman" and conjuring itself, with its associations with tricksterism, conspiracy, and the occult, as constituting a trope enabling a space for black women's creativity, exemplified in Hurston's *Mules and Men* (1935).

KAREN HAR-YEN CHOW

Huxley, Aldous 1894–1963

English novelist, short-story writer, essayist, poet, and dramatist

Adorno, Theodor W., "Aldous Huxley and Utopia", in his *Prisms*, translated by Samuel Weber and Shierry Weber, London: Neville Spearman, 1967; Cambridge, Massachusetts: MIT Press, 1981

Baker, Robert S., *The Dark Historic Page: Social Satire and Historicism in the Novels of Aldous Huxley, 1921–1939*, Madison: University of Wisconsin Press, 1982

Bowering, Peter, *Aldous Huxley: A Study of the Major Novels*, London: Athlone Press, 1968

Ferns, C.S., *Aldous Huxley: Novelist*, London: Athlone Press, 1980

Firchow, Peter, *Aldous Huxley: Satirist and Novelist*, Minneapolis: University of Minnesota Press, 1972

Nance, Guinevera A., *Aldous Huxley*, New York: Continuum, 1988

Although theory has yet to have much impact upon them, Huxley studies have always occurred within ongoing debates over "élitist" and "populist" conceptions of literary culture. His uneasy place in the canon shows few signs of resolution. Perhaps as a result there is often a kind of diffidence about Huxley's supporters, as if they feel somehow obliged to acknowledge the lingering shadow of academic disapproval over his writings, and to concede in advance the idea that any case for him has to be a special one.

BOWERING for example is clearly attracted by the moral and spiritual ideas in Huxley which many critics pass over or dismiss as derivative, and he provides much useful information about them, while still employing Leavisite terminology in his judgements: for example, *Eyeless in Gaza* is Huxley's "most interesting work" because it has "the quality of felt experience from beginning to end". Bowering's is a solid, perhaps over-trustful survey, according much the same amount of attention to each novel. He prizes Huxley's irony rather than his comic inventiveness. He makes scant use of biographical material: at the time of his writing less was available, and it was less fashionable to involve it.

FIRCHOW organises groups of works together, giving only *Point Counter Point* a chapter to itself. He makes interesting use of the early poems, where Huxley's concern with "the imbalance of matter and spirit" is established from the outset; he stresses the importance of the young Huxley's stint as a reviewer for the *Athenaeum* in honing his professional writing skills; and he places Huxley firmly in the tradition of empiricism, for all his mystical leanings. In comparing Huxley with Jonathan Swift, Firchow sketches a resemblance between what he calls the "four stages" of Huxley's development, and the four voyages of Gulliver, before rather self-protectingly erasing it as too "limiting". He illuminates the satirical techniques of both the fiction and the non-fiction, although his attempt to distinguish "constructive" from "destructive" satire seems over-schematic.

FERNS champions the "populist" against the "élitist": "the flaws typical of a Huxley novel are more than usually offensive to the critic's notion of what fiction ought to be", but "the ordinary reader . . . would appear to be far less troubled by such things". The straightforward appeal of fantasy, in *Brave New World* and *After Many a Summer*, has been ignored or patronised by critics who prefer the complexity and sophistication elsewhere in the novels. Ferns gains much of his momentum from attacking other critics, the bulk of whom are "conspicuously mediocre", "narrow-minded", "stupid", and "dishonest". In between his hectic and self-recommending tirades, he makes an effective case for the "popular" elements and the sheer brilliance of Huxley's satirical imagination. He also offers a more dubious argument, that the success of the fantasies derives in part from the greater control they allow their author over the deployment and reception of his messages – which rather begs the question of Huxley's implication in the totalitarianism he exposes.

BAKER confines himself to the interwar novels and concentrates on Huxley's attitudes to history. Huxley "insisted upon . . . the arbitrary randomness of events", and devoted much of his satire to characters who think otherwise, the historians, antiquaries, romanticisers, and autobiographers who populate his novels. Baker's analysis of individual works emphasises how imagery of houses, towers, burrows, etc., helps construct the link between aspiration and enclosure, which he sees as characteristic of Huxley's vision. He has many interesting things to say about Huxley's attack on de Sade as the apostle of a "false" detachment, and of the prefiguring, especially in *Point Counter Point*, of concerns normally associated with the 1930s' generation. The arguments often slither, however, in a morass of detail, and for all Baker's efforts to define "historicism", the reader may ultimately be as confused as enlightened.

NANCE's book follows the late 1980s' trend towards student-friendly introductory monographs. It breaks little new ground, but offers a judicious, undemanding, readable summary of Huxley's career, taking him very much on his own terms, and emphasising his professed desire to "build bridges" between disciplines.

Ever since the *Herald Tribune* remarked in 1928 that Huxley himself "was the most perfect representative of the mood he describes", his supporters have had to confront the problem that his work could as well be seen as a symptom of its period as a challenge to it. For ADORNO, this belongs with other contradictions enmeshing the bourgeois intellectual, which Huxley, with his recurrent utopian designs, acutely exemplifies. It is panic at his impotence before mass production that gives rise to the contrast between "eternal philosophical truths" and the worthless ephemera of history; he lends his weight to oppositions, between mind and matter, or the individual and the collective, which evade deeper connections. Hence in Adorno's analysis of *Brave New World*, "the very construction that . . . denounces the totalitarian world-state . . . glorifies retrospectively the individualism that brought it about". There is no room for an altogether different concept of mankind, which would see it neither absorbed into the coercion of the system, nor reduced to the status of "contingent individuals". Huxley in later life acknowledged the lack of a third option in *Brave New World*, although his proposal for it would scarcely have satisfied Adorno; the latter, however, unlike many Anglo-Saxon critics, regarded Huxley as a sufficiently important writer to argue with.

N.H. Reeve

I

Imagism

Coffman, Stanley K., Jr., *Imagism: A Chapter for the History of Modern Poetry*, Norman: University of Oklahoma Press, 1951
Gage, John T., *In the Arresting Eye: The Rhetoric of Imagism*, Baton Rouge: Louisiana State University Press, 1981
Harmer, J.B., *Victory in Limbo: Imagism, 1908–1917*, London: Secker & Warburg, 1975; New York: St Martin's Press, 1975
Hughes, Glen, *Imagism and the Imagists: A Study in Modern Poetry*, Stanford, California: Stanford University Press, 1931; Oxford: Oxford University Press, 1931; reprinted, London: Bowes & Bowes, 1960
Wees, William C., *Vorticism and the English Avant-Garde*, Manchester: Manchester University Press, 1972; Toronto: University of Toronto Press, 1972

Written on the back of a resurgent interest in Imagism in the 1930s, one of the first important literary studies of Imagism was HUGHES's book, which is now better read for historical interest rather than its critical or analytical insight. Beginning with the origins of Imagism in French symbolism and the gradual coalescence of writers around the philosopher and aesthetic theorist T.E. Hulme, the book proceeds to record and discuss the controversial critical reception of the Imagists' work as it appeared. The furore created at the time was partly due to the controversy over the distinction between poetry and prose, which is givern some attention by the book. There then follows literary pen-portraits of the key figures associated with the Imagist movement, such as Richard Aldington, H.D., John Gould Fletcher, F.S. Flint, D.H. Lawrence, Amy Lowell, and Ezra Pound. Occasionally somewhat anecdotal in style, it is rather tentative and cautious about judging a group of writers many of whom were still active on the literary scene.

Much the same territory is covered by COFFMAN's book. However, this book is more analytical and recognises the variety of practices contained within the term "Imagist Movement". In the introductory chapters, charting the rise of the movement in two stages (roughly dividing into the periods before and after Pound fell out with the Amy Lowell in 1914), the book gives a fairly comprehensive account of the principal events, publications, and theories of the aesthetic tendencies grouped around Imagism. These chapters form the general background for the remaining ones, which analyse in greater detail the parts played by key theorists and writers, such as Hulme and Pound, and movements such as symbolism, Lowell's "Amygism", Vorticism, and other lesser subjects. The book concludes with a brief assessment of the limitations and strengths of the movement, and a cursory glance at its legacy. The book is now rather dated in its methodology, but nevertheless contains some interesting information in unpublished extracts from correspondence and private interviews.

HARMER's book continues this wide-ranging analysis of Imagist and associated poets. It begins by analyzing the Edwardians and their "tired" poetics, against whom Hulme and the Imagists directed their poetic criticisms, and out of which they developed the imagist aesthetic. Principally chronicling the rise of Imagism from Hulme through Pound to Lowell's version, attention is also paid to some of the lesser yet nonetheless significant writers – Aldington, Lawrence, H.D., Flint, and Ford Madox Ford. The cultural and aesthetic context of Imagism is also explored, especially the significance of the French symbolist poets and the aesthetic influence of *vers libre*, Impressionism, the Chinese ideogram, and the development of Imagism into Vorticism. Finally, the book concludes with another somewhat cursory glance at the legacy of Imagism for American poetry in the 1950s, as well as the Beat lyrics of some popular music. The book's predominant argument is that the Imagists sought to rescue poetry from the doldrums of the late Victorian period, and that their success is still unclear, despite the great significance of the image in contemporary mass culture. It is a somewhat old-fashioned assessment, which tends to adopt the terms, concepts, and judgements of the Imagists themselves a little too uncritically.

GAGE, on the other hand, has produced one of the best critical discussions of Imagist poetics, centring on the gap between Imagist theory and Imagist practice, and arguing that "imagist theory is inadequate to account for the reader's actual experience of the imagist poem". Focusing on the *rhetoric* of Imagism, the book concludes that the Imagists' theories of the author-reader relationship are highly problematic, as are their concepts of language and the degree of control that the poet has over the reception of meaning. Considering the use of the image as a rhetorical device, the book examines the techniques espoused by Imagists like Hulme and Pound. Analysing a selection of Imagist poems, the book explores the epistemological and cognitive theories that underpin the poetry, and demonstrates the varieties of Imagist poetic results, which sit unconvincingly with the theoretical premises. With a chapter on the paradox of the long Imagist poem, the book concludes with the conflicting attitudes of various Imagists towards language and communication. Untrammelled by difficult theoretical jargon, this book is nevertheless informed by contemporary theoretical concepts of language, and utilizes them to great effect in its dissection of Imagist poetic theories.

When Imagism splintered into various groups in the mid-1910s, one significant development was Vorticism, often associated with Imagist principles, owing to one of its central exponents being Ezra Pound. Although arguably more influential as a style of visual art rather than writing, Vorticism, WEES's book makes clear, was an intersection for a variety of artists and writers – like Wyndham Lewis, Pound, and Ford – which created a symbiotic interest in the two media. After initially placing the movement within its socio-historical, cultural, and aesthetic environment, chapters take up the specific accomplishments as they appeared in painting and sculpture, as well as in the important journal *Blast;* a variety of illustrations of Vorticist art and extracts from *Blast* are included. This is an invaluable sourcebook for students of the avant garde and modernist art, and the literary scene.

TIM S. WOODS

See also **Modernism: Poetry**

Indian Literature

Dwivedi, A.N. *Indian Writing in English*, 2 vols., Delhi: Amar Prakashan Press, 1991

Kalinnikova, Elena J., *Indian-English Literature: A Perspective*, edited by K.K. Sharma, translated by V.P. Sharma, Ghaziabad: Vimal Prakashan, 1982

Naik, M.K., *A History of Indian English Literature*, Delhi: Sahitya Akademi Press, 1982

Narasimhaiah, C.D., *The Swan and the Eagle*, Shimla: Indian Institute of Advanced Study, 1968, 2nd edition, 1987

Nelson, Emmanuel S. (ed.), *Reworlding: The Literature of the Indian Diaspora*, Westport, Connecticut: Greenwood Press, 1992

Tharu, Susie, and K. Lalita (eds.), *Women Writing in India: 600 B.C. to the Early Twentieth Century*, New York: Feminist Press of the City University, 1991; London: Pandora, 1991

Tharu, Susie, and K. Lalita (eds.), *Women Writing in India: The Twentieth Century*, New York: Feminist Press of the City University, 1993; Delhi: Oxford University Press, 1993; London: Pandora, 1993

Viswanathan, Gauri, *Masks of Conquest: Literary Study and British Rule in India,* New York: Columbia University Press, 1989

In evaluations of Indian literature in English, both the time of writing and the continent in which they were written and published are important in determining approaches.

VISWANATHAN's work contextualizes discussion of Indian literature in English as containing the marks of colonialism within it. Her theoretical premise is from Antonio Gramsci's dictum that cultural domination works more by persuasion and consent rather than force. According to Viswanathan, the hegemony of Britain was deployed and maintained by, among other things, English literary studies. She attempts to locate "the relationship between the institutionalization of English in India and the exercise of colonial power". Only by enframing Indian literature in English within such a theoretical model can its postcolonial nature be traced.

NARASIMHAIAH's work suggests that instead of examining Indian literature as representing British colonization in India, it must be read as a syncretic literature, which could have begun only in the colonies. Narasimaiah's title indicates the braiding of the Apollonian and the Dionysian (the swan and the eagle) to produce Indian English literature. There are chapters on Toru Dutt, Aurobindo, Nehru, Mulk Raj Anand, R.K. Narayan, and Raja Rao, all of which extend this theme.

KALINNIKOVA's work is interesting for its attempt to place Indian literature in English not within British literary traditions, but within Indian writing in indigenous languages. She admits to the centrality of British colonialism, but maintains that "Indian-English writers are the custodians of their national traditions and customs". Furthermore, she delineates differences between North and South Indian writing in English, suggesting that the former is characterized by a certain degree of syncreticism, in that Northern writers were more influenced by the Mughal and British cultures than those in the South.

NAIK's work contextualizes Indian literature in English within a social, political, and historical context. Accordingly, Naik's first chapter locates his subject within British colonialism before it attempts to decolonize this area of study from British literature since "it is legitimately a part of Indian literature [as] its differentia is the expression of an Indian ethos". Naik chronologizes the first manifestation of early Indian-English literature within the establishment of the East India Company, followed by the production of literature in the Empire, in the Independence movement, and in the post-Independence era. He covers all genres – prose, poetry, drama, and fiction.

DWIVEDI's work is in two volumes. For a critical work published in 1991, these two volumes display very traditional scholarship in that there is no discussion of postcoloniality or any of the major writers of the 1980s and 1990s. Volume 1 deals with Indian poetry, and the second volume with all the other genres. There is also an odd inclusion of a gloomy essay on the need to restructure higher education in India.

NELSON's edited collection is useful not only as an introduction to diasporic Indian writers, but also as an examination of the exilic sensibility itself. The Introduction complicates the concept of India by pointing out that "the post-1947 India, the political unit, is an artificial colonial construction, carved out of a larger subcontinental collective in order to meet political exigencies". Such foregrounding permits the inclusion of authors who are not technically Indian, such as V.S. Naipaul, Salman Rushdie, Sara Suleri, and Michael Ondaatje, as well as discussions of Indo-Fijian, Indo-Trinidadian, Indo-Caribbean, and Indian writers in Singapore and South Africa.

THARU and LALITA's work is an edited anthology of writings, which indicates an alternative tradition of writing (albeit now translated) to the postcolonial wave of writers such as Kamala Markandaya, Anita Desai, and Bharati Mukherjee. The Introduction to Volume 1 deals with gender as difference, its continuum with American feminist criticism, and the application of Western feminist theory to women's writing in India; the Introduction to Volume 2 deals with the construction of India as nation in the literary works of postcolonial Indian women writers. Both Introductions are required reading.

RADHIKA MOHANRAM

Irish Literature: General

Brown, Malcolm, *The Politics of Irish Literature: From Thomas Davis to W.B. Yeats*, London: Allen & Unwin, 1972; Seattle: University of Washington Press, 1973
Brown, Terence, *Ireland's Literature: Selected Essays*, Dublin: Lilliput, 1988; Totowa, New Jersey: Barnes & Noble, 1988
Deane, Seamus, *A Short History of Irish Literature*, London: Hutchinson, 1986; Notre Dame, Indiana: Notre Dame University Press, 1986
Harmon, Maurice, and Roger McHugh, *A Short History of Anglo-Irish Literature*, Dublin: Wolfhound, 1982; Totowa, New Jersey: Barnes & Noble, 1982
McCormack, W.J., *Ascendancy and Tradition in Anglo-Irish Literary History from 1789 to 1939*, Oxford: Clarendon Press, 1985; New York: Oxford University Press, 1985
Mercier, Vivian, *Modern Irish Literature: Sources and Founders*, edited by Eilís Dillon, Oxford: Clarendon Press, 1994; New York: Oxford University Press, 1994

The complexities of Irish literary history are only beginning to be appreciated, and much work still needs to be done in such areas as defining the canon of Irish writing in English, genre, and periodisation.

Malcolm BROWN indicates some of the preliminary difficulties associated with the field in his original and astute reading of formative issues in the origins of Irish modern literature. The articulation of these issues – which include the relationship between literature and politics, the connection between imaginative work and ideology, and the link between literary form and national identity – by different authors during the 50 years from the middle of the nineteenth century to the beginning of the Irish Revival constitutes the core of the study. The effect of such movements as Young Ireland, Fenianism, and Home Rule on the concept of literature is economically charted. Extensive use is made of nineteenth-century newspapers and other popular sources of "felt history". This study lives up fully to its claim that "to assemble the history . . . and set it against the poetic version is a productive and enlightening exercise".

DEANE is the best-known Irish literary intellectual of his generation, and his work represents a daring attempt to present "[a] story about a literary tradition which has undergone a series of revivals and collapses, all of them centred on an idea of Ireland". Such an approach provides the work with not merely a literary agenda but also with a cultural and political one. Thus, the reader is not presented with a mere chronology of events and titles, but with a vivid sense of some of the worldly purposes, influences, and consequences of various modes of literary production and cultural representation. Irish and European literary connections are also illuminatingly stressed. The book opens with a sketch of the Gaelic penumbra, out of which Anglo-Irish literature emerged. The social and political conditions of its emergence in the early eighteenth century are then dealt with, followed by an intriguing analysis of the Celticism of the late eighteenth century. The study then examines the novel and the drama in the period before the Literary Revival, while the account of the Revival itself is provocatively bracketed under the term "Irish Modernism". A survey of Irish literature from 1940 to 1980 concludes the study. There is a brief bibliography and a very useful chronology of cultural and historical events. The work is inevitably condensed, yet the author's ideological overview, his emphasis on text and context, and his incisive, aphoristic style ensures that there is much provocative and insightful analysis of what is "in many ways, a specifically modern literature bred out of the most dishevelled and improbable circumstances".

HARMON and McHUGH provide a somewhat broader coverage of the cultural territory demarcated by Deane, described here as "a bifurcated literary heritage". Gaelic Ireland is surveyed in an opening section, and the work proceeds in a straightforward chronology thereafter. The Irish Literary Revival is singled out as a distinctive period in its own right, and the extent to which the Revival overshadows subsequent developments in Irish literature is assessed. Coverage is conceived of essentially in terms of genre, and the critical approach evaluates works and tends to focus on their aesthetic effects rather than on their cultural significance: the discussion of W.B. Yeats's poetic output in terms of "its organic growth, an aspect which is vital to literary criticism" is typical of the authors' traditional method. A very comprehensive bibliography is included, and there is an appendix on the language of J.M. Synge's plays which new readers of them will find helpful.

McCORMACK's work is at the opposite end of the critical spectrum in terms of its sense of the problematic nature of Irish literary production and Irish literary history, its blend of archival scholarship with extreme critical acuteness, and its conceptual sophistication. The work's twin ambitions are to investigate "the sociological formation of 'Protestant Ascendancy'" and to challenge "the Yeatsian elaboration of an Irish literary 'tradition'". Rather than providing an exhaustive survey of materials pertinent to these interconnected tasks, the work deals with texts and literary careers that possess unexpected ideological nuances and cultural complexities. Among texts analysed are two by Maria Edgeworth and James Joyce's short story "Eveline"; while among the exemplifying careers are those of a number of Irish Victorian authors. This work occupies a unique place in the current critical reconstruction of Irish literary culture.

Terence BROWN's collection of essays – "a series of soundings in Irish literary and cultural history" – covers virtually all of the ground between the invention of Anglo-Irish literature in the eighteenth century to the work of the contemporary novelist Brian Moore and poets from Northern Ireland. Major authors such as Yeats, Joyce, and Samuel Beckett are dealt with, but the work valuably includes essays on lesser-known authors, who are shown to exemplify significant cultural strains and tendencies. The emphasis on the significance of Irish nineteenth-century literary culture is an important instance of the progressive revisionism currently making its presence felt in Ireland. More broadly-based essays on such topics as contemporary poetry from Northern Ireland, and history and contemporary Irish literature, help to sharpen further the focus of this revisionism. The author's scholarly resources and accessible style make this book an extremely useful interim report on problems and possibilities in Irish literary history.

MERCIER's work is a collection of essays dealing with various facets of Anglo-Irish literature and culture, published posthumously, rather than the comprehensive overview suggested by its title. Of particular value are the studies of Protestant Evangelicalism in nineteenth-century Ireland, Beckett and the Bible, and "European-Irish Literary Connections in the Twentieth Century". Essays on the major figures of the Irish Literary Revival are also included. Lucid, erudite, wide-ranging and accessible, they make a valuable addition to the canon of Irish literary criticism by emphasising the diversity of its fields of inquiry.

GEORGE O'BRIEN

Women Writers

Boland, Evan, *A Kind of Scar: The Woman Poet in a National Tradition*, Dublin: Attic Press, 1989

Donovan, Katie, *Irish Women Writers: Marginalised by Whom?*, Dublin: Raven Arts Press, 1988

Donovan, Katie, A. Norman Jeffares, and Brendan Kennelly, *Ireland's Women: Writings Past and Present*, London: Kyle Cathie, 1994

Innes, C.L., *Woman and Nation in Irish Literature and Society 1880–1935*, Hemel Hempstead, Hertfordshire: Harvester Wheatsheaf, 1993; Athens: University of Georgia Press, 1993

Johnson, Toni O'Brien, and David Cairns, *Gender in Irish Writing*, Milton Keynes, Buckinghamshire: Open University Press, 1991

Weekes, Ann Owens, *Irish Women Writers: An Uncharted Tradition*, Lexington: University Press of Kentucky, 1990

The researcher into Irish women writers will uncover few volumes of general criticism. Although this situation is being rectified, one of the problems facing those interested in this field of study is the fact that Irish women writers have fallen between the literary and nationalist debates. On the one hand their works are seen by the critical establishment as having been checked by the brilliance and domination of the Irish male writer's articulation of national intensity. On the other hand the growth of comparative gender studies in literature has happened before a comprehensive recognition of a tradition of Irish women's writing has fully entered the critical arena.

BOLAND's small pamphlet offers an excellent starting point for any investigation of the literature of Irish women in that it raises the questions central to an understanding of its achievement and its marginalisation. Her central premise is that "over a relatively short time . . . certainly no more than a generation or so . . . women have moved from being the subjects and objects of Irish poems to being the authors of them. It is a momentous transit. It is also a disruptive one". Boland clearly analyses the problems encountered in such a move: the virulence and necessity of the idea of nation in Irish writing; the poetic ethic, which springs from the tensions between writer and nation; and the need for women to combat "the association of the feminine and the national . . . and the consequent simplification of both". She seeks to repossess the idea of nation and language through the subjectivity of her own "darkness as an Irish poet" and in doing so has produced a critical text that is not local, personal, or parochial, but broadens out across Irish women's writing and has further implications for Irish literature generally.

DONOVAN's argument in this small, but substantial, pamphlet centres on the contemporary debate as to the direction studies of Irish women writers should take. Articulating the arguments for and against an "isolationist spotlight", she asserts a critical perspective that allows for a comparative place within the Irish literary tradition for the woman writer:

> If Irish women writers are to be recalled and examined with more credit and understanding than they currently receive, they must be taken from the outhouse and ushered into the centre of the Irish literary tradition . . . Only then can we begin to see where the differences and similarities between our major writers are determined by sexual identity or other factors.

In the subsequent discussion, she not only examines the significant contribution of several women writers to Irish fiction, but also isolates certain trends in the tradition, and in the marginalisation of Irish women writers.

DONOVAN, JEFFARES, and KENNELLY's title is deceptive; this work is not strictly an anthology of writing by Irish women, nor is it strictly about Irish women; it is more a "kaleidoscope, presenting the experience of Irish women as seen by many or all depending on how you read it". Its greatest contribution in terms of Irish women's writing is the wide range of poetry by Irish women included in the volume. It is also useful in that it touches on works that would otherwise have no outlet and gives an overall view of the contributions of and responses to Irish women's artistic talents across a wide range of disciplines. The "Notes on the Writers" is also useful.

INNES' work is essential to an understanding of the complex relationship between gender and nationality within the cultural and literary context. Ascribing to the need for comparative criticism, this work succeeds in illuminating the contributions of women activists and writers in the nationalist debate and in providing fresh readings of selected works of male Irish writers. The comparative and analytical approach allows the women discussed a place within the tradition of Irish culture and literature by analysing the writings of both men and women involved in the nationalist movement in their historical, economic, and political contexts and especially in the context of the "discourses and icons which marked the cultural nationalism of their time".

JOHNSON and CAIRNS's essay collection addresses many of the most relevant and contemporary issues in the context of Irish women's studies today. Across the selection of essays, purism and compartmentalism of gender issues are abandoned and replaced with a critical approach that combines historicism and cultural materialism, together with deconstructive, linguistic, and psychoanalytical analysis. The selection and focus of these essays exemplifies the critical trend in feminist discourse in the 1990s. Christine St Peter's contribution to this text, "Jennifer Johnston's Irish Troubles: A Materialist-Feminist Reading", points out some of the problems associated with the study of writing by contemporary Irish women in terms of Irishness and womanhood.

WEEKES's acknowledges that her study of Irish women writers is only a "blueprint" for further study. The work is however the most comprehensive available and is only limited by the necessity for selection. This critical study, even allowing for limits of selection, offers the student and scholar an excellent range of critical analysis across a broad time span and selection of writers. The chapter entitled "Seeking a Tradition" establishes a complex and comprehensive theoretical approach and contextualises the theoretical work to date.

MARGARET E. ROBERTS

Irish Literature: Literary Revival to the Present

Cairns, David, and Shaun Richards, *Writing Ireland: Colonialism, Nationalism and Culture*, Manchester: Manchester University Press, 1988

Deane, Seamus, *Celtic Revivals: Essays in Modern Irish Literature 1880–1980*, London and Boston: Faber & Faber, 1985

Fallis, Richard, *The Irish Renaissance*, Syracuse, New York: Syracuse University Press, 1977

Foster, John Wilson, *Colonial Consequences: Essays in Irish Literature and Culture*, Dublin: Lilliput, 1991

Howarth, Herbert, *The Irish Writers: Literature and Nationalism 1880–1940*, London: Rockliff, 1958; New York: Hill & Wang, 1959

Longley, Edna, *The Living Stream: Literature and Revisionism in Ireland*, Newcastle-upon-Tyne: Bloodaxe Books, 1994

Because of the absence of a comprehensive critical history of the Irish Literary Revival, it remains a phenomenon difficult to define. There is no scholarly consensus as to its causes, character, duration, significance, and legacy. Current trends continue to be seen in the light of the Revival.

HOWARTH's study – "meant primarily for the general reader" – is exclusively concerned with the canonical figures of the Revival, with George Moore, Lady Gregory, W.B. Yeats, George William Russell (AE), J.M. Synge, and James Joyce receiving a chapter each. An introductory chapter deals with the main political, cultural, and intellectual influences on the Revival. The most pronounced of these is that of the Irish political leader Parnell, the exemplary force of whose career is implicated in the allegedly messianic tendencies in Revival literature.

DEANE is the most noted Irish critic of his generation, and has been in the forefront of many of the current controversies in Irish cultural debate. One of his main areas of interest has been Yeats's ideological role in the Revival. The provocative and incisive essays collected here deal not only with this issue, but with the leading figures of both the Revival and of Irish literature since 1960. No explicit attempt is made to compare the two periods, though given both periods' historical turbulence and nationalist contexts the comparison may be readily made. Doing so is rendered all the more plausible by the author's statement that "ultimately, Irish writers were obliged to find some way of dealing with history, a category which includes language, landscape, and the various ideologies of the rediscovered past which grew out of them". The author claims this as his theme, which is introduced by an essay entitled "Arnold, Burke and the Celts", which assesses some of the Revival's ideological preconditions. This essay is followed by the influential "The Literary Myths of the Revival". The Revival's major figures are dealt with, and the revisionist case made for Joyce being one of them is particularly intriguing. Among the post-1960s' writers to be considered are the crucial, though critically neglected, poets Thomas Kinsella and Derek Mahon.

FALLIS writes essentially for an American audience, and relies on narrative more than on interpretation. His account is a useful starting-place for the student. Fallis divides the Revival into three distinct historical phases covering the years 1885–1940, though the year 1885 has admittedly been chosen "rather arbitrarily". These phases coincide with the origins and development of Yeats's poetic career. The approach deals at length with the historical context of literary events. Chapters devoted to each of the major genres are included in the section dealing with the crucial 1900–23 period. The third of the study's three sections addresses some of the anxieties of influence and originality that beset Irish literature in the wake of the Revival. A sketch of post-1960 developments is also included. There is a comprehensive bibliography.

FOSTER's collection of essays, which may be usefully compared and contrasted to Deane's, dwells for the most part on issues in contemporary Irish literature and culture. The author writes from the rather unfamiliar perspective of Northern Irish Unionism, and a number of the most important items in the work – notably "The Critical Condition of Ulster" – are valuable and original instances of the author's "regionalist" approach. The significance of this approach is stated as follows:

> Regionality expresses continuity in time; but I see it as no mere contraction in figurative space: rather should it be a progressive critique of modernism as it accepts the benefits of modernity. Meanwhile, for pressing local reasons, the realistic acknowledgment of Ulster's regionality is a necessary posture in our present difficulties.

Northern Ireland also provides a focus for the volume's more literary essays, among which are studies of the poetry of Patrick Kavanagh, W.R. Rodgers, John Hewitt, and Seamus Heaney. The perspective is not exclusively regionalist, however: the volume contains wide-ranging discussions of the topographical dimension of Irish fiction and verse, as well as of the literature of the Revival, particularly the contributions of Joyce and Yeats.

LONGLEY's volume of essays is something of a companion piece to Foster's. Here, however, the literary and cultural distinctiveness of a "region" is linked to a tradition of cultural dissidence in Ireland as a whole. The role of Protestant poets and thinkers in the creation of this tradition is argued: Yeats, Louis MacNeice, John Hewitt, and the essayist Hubert Butler are among the cases in point. A number of these unabashedly revisionist essays – "From Cathleen to Anorexia: The Breakdown of Ireland", and "Poetic Forms and Social Malformations" in particular – are central to contemporary Irish debate about literature's ideological implications and social value.

CAIRNS and RICHARDS use the two opening chapters of their comprehensive and challenging work to analyse the cultural components of British colonialism in its Elizabethan and Victorian manifestations and their effects on the nature of Irish cultural identity. Mostly, however, their study deals with the problems connected with the emergence of Irish literature in English during the twentieth century. Key figures and episodes in the Irish Literary Revival are evaluated. The problem of continuity in Irish literary history is implicitly addressed in the authors' treatment of the interwar period, with particular emphasis on the careers of Kavanagh and Sean O Faolain. The study concludes by focusing mainly on the contributions to Irish literature and culture of such Northern Irish writers as Brian Friel and Seamus Heaney. The critical method used is that of cultural materialism, relying heavily on the theories of Antonio Gramsci. Such an approach emphasises that the public work of culture has an inevitable political dimension. There is a very useful bibliography, and a glossary of Irish terms.

George O'Brien

Irony

Booth, Wayne, *A Rhetoric of Irony*, Chicago: University of Chicago Press, 1974

Brooks, Cleanth, *The Well Wrought Urn: Studies in the Structure of Poetry*, New York: Reynal & Hitchcock, 1947; London: Dennis Dobson, 1949, revised 1968

Green, D.H., *Irony in the Medieval Romance*, Cambridge and New York: Cambridge University Press, 1979

Handwerk, Gary J., *Irony and Ethics in Narrative: From Schlegel to Lacan*, New Haven, Connecticut, and London: Yale University Press, 1985

Mellor, Anne K., *English Romantic Irony*, Cambridge, Massachusetts: Harvard University Press, 1980

Muecke, D.C., *The Compass of Irony*, London and New York: Methuen, 1969

Muecke, D.C., *Irony*, London and New York: Methuen, 1970

Perhaps the most useful introduction to the term is provided by MUECKE's (1970) account of irony for the Methuen "Critical Idiom" series, which sets out to classify the properties and functions of irony, and offers a brief historical survey of the range of phenomena the term has referred to. Although his account is seen as somewhat limited by later theorists, it pre-empts a number of issues they raise. Muecke points out the crucial distinctions between the term "irony", the concept of irony, and the phenomena which have at various historical moments been perceived as "ironic". For example, Muecke describes an incident from Homer's *Odyssey*: "Odysseus returns to Ithica and, sitting disguised as a beggar in his own palace, hears one of the suitors scouting the idea that he (Odysseus) could ever come home again". Muecke claims that although we would now classify this as situational irony it would not have been recognized as irony at all until the late eighteenth century. Prior to that date, although the term "irony" existed in English, it referred only to those phenomena that would today be classified as verbal irony. As Muecke points out however, this is not to say that the effects of such devices were not, and have not always been, recognized and appreciated.

The process of categorisation adopted by Muecke in the above account, and his earlier work *The Compass of Irony* (1969), addressed below, is in part a reaction to the perceived over-generalisation of the term at the hands of the New Critics, and particularly at those of BROOKS, who addresses the concept of irony as the defining feature of all literature. Brooks' argument is that, to the extent that a poem such as Tennyson's "Tears Idle Tears" consists of mutually modifying and qualifying elements which form a unity, the effect can be described as ironic: "irony is our most general term for indicating that recognition of incongruities – which . . . pervades all poetry to a degree far beyond what our conventional criticism has been heretofore willing to allow". For Brooks, then, through its particular usage of language, poetry is inevitably ironic.

MUECKE (1969) argues that Brooks "has done his best to finesse the word 'irony' out of useful existence", and suggests that this has led to a need for the concept to be clarified. Muecke therefore offers an account of the forms and functions of irony as a rhetorical device, distinguishing between different grades of irony and the modes within which they might be realised, and categorising elements characteristic of each. He also gives an account of irony as a mode of consciousness that arises out of a particular set of historical conditions, and in doing so distinguishes between specific and general irony. He suggests that specific irony is characteristically found in societies that have established values and beliefs. Typically, this form of irony is corrective or normative in the sense that it is a rhetorical device employed with the aim of criticising perceived aberrations. Its effects are therefore localized and are not perceived as intended to destabilise established norms. General irony is typical of the modern period, which Muecke describes as having lost these earlier certainties. From around the late seventeenth century irony developed from a rhetorical device into a mode of consciousness, which Muecke identifies as having arisen out a growing awareness of the "fundamental contradictions" in life. Romantic irony arose in turn out of general irony, and is a strategy for "coming to terms with a world that seems to be fundamentally at odds with mankind".

BOOTH addresses irony primarily as a rhetorical device whose effects require that a writer's conscious intention to be ironic is recognized as such by the reader. He argues that this occurs because most uses of irony are "stable", and that "the whole thing cannot work unless both parties to the exchange have confidence that they are moving together in identical patterns". Booth is concerned to account for how authors achieve ironic effects through textual signalling and how readers draw appropriate inferences based on these cues. He focuses on what Muecke would classify as specific irony, in that he suggests that the effects of "stable" irony are local: this form of irony provides a "kind of context telling us when to stop". Addressing a range of literary texts, Booth argues that the search for ironic effects needs to be limited, since if carried too far some authors' works (he mentions Henry Fielding and E.M Forster, for example) can be diminished. Questions of ironic effect are also therefore seen to be questions of literary value.

GREEN's account of irony in the medieval romance would also fall within Muecke's category of specific irony. Green's aim is to show that the romance, as a genre, was particularly receptive to irony for both aesthetic and sociological reasons. Green suggests that the romance poets, who usually had a clerical background, were generally trained in rhetoric, and that their texts contain cues signalling a dual perspective, particularly in relation to the presentation of chivalry and love. He suggests that this arises out of perceived discrepancies between the values of the court and those of the Church, and discrepancies between ideal and actual behaviour within each ethos. The critique offered by such irony is normative and localised in that "it is not so much the courtly ideal as some aberration from it which is the true target of the poet's irony". It is only in comparison to the Church that the courtly ideal itself is ever ironised, in that the poet "sees it as subordinate to something more embracing and doubts the justification of making an absolute value out of it".

MELLOR focuses on Romantic irony, developing Muecke's account of its origins in general irony, to claim that it arises out of "philosophical skepticism and the social tùrbulence of the French Revolution and the American War of Independence; it posits a universe founded on chaos and incomprehensibility rather than in a divinely ordained teleology". She draws on Schlegel's theory of Romantic irony, which she interprets as a "way of thinking about the world that embraces change and process for their own sake" in order to address a range of texts. Mellor contrasts works of Byron, John Keats, and Thomas Carlyle with those of Samuel Taylor Coleridge and Lewis Carroll to argue that while the former are "authentic romantic ironists," in that their works embrace "with enthusiasm and hope a vision of the universe as dynamic becoming", the writings of the latter mark a point where Romantic irony alters: while Coleridge "shared Schlegel's view of ontological reality", he responded with a sense of guilt. Carroll's response is defined as anxiety.

HANDWERK's account also addresses the effects of general irony, but takes issue with both Mellor and Booth, arguing that the former misinterprets Schlegel, while the latter offers an account of irony which is too static. Handwerk's argument is that Schlegel's account of Romantic irony has an ethical strand in that "the literary irony so central for Schlegel is profoundly concerned with the capacity of discourse to generate and regenerate reflective community". Handwerk's account draws on Lacanian psychoanalysis to address the construction of the human subject through the effects of what he terms "ethical irony".

CHRISTINE CHRISTIE

Irving, Washington 1783–1859

American writer of short stories, sketches, and prose

Aderman, Ralph M., *Critical Essays on Washington Irving*, Boston: G.K. Hall, 1990

Antelyes, Peter, *Tales of Adventurous Enterprise: Washington Irving and the Poetics of Western Expansion*, New York: Columbia University Press, 1990

Bowden, Mary Weatherspoon, *Washington Irving*, Boston: Twayne, 1981

Hedges, William L., *Washington Irving: An American Study, 1802–1832*, Baltimore: Johns Hopkins University Press, 1965

Rubin-Dorsky, Jeffrey, *Adrift in the Old World: The Psychological Pilgrimage of Washington Irving*, Chicago: University of Chicago Press, 1988

Von Frank, Albert J., "Geoffrey Crayon and the Gigantic Race", in his *The Sacred Game: Provincialism and Frontier Consciousness in American Literature, 1630–1860*, Cambridge and New York: Cambridge University Press, 1985

Williams, Stanley T., *The Life of Washington Irving*, 2 vols., New York: Oxford University Press, 1935

Critics often associate the terms "Anglophile" and "expatriate" with Washington Irving, whose obvious affinity for England in his earlier writings is sometimes viewed as tantamount to a betrayal of his budding homeland's quest for aesthetic independence. Even today in the classroom, the persistence of the stereotype of Irving as Anglophile suggests the difficulty of seeing him as both an admirer of English culture and a Republican idealist. Contemporary scholarship, however, has begun to reassess this pigeonholing of "America's first man of letters".

WILLIAMS' two-volume biography, though formidable, is still the standard work on Irving's life. By emphasizing Irving's contemporary reality (rather than a critical methodology), Williams manages to avoid many of the pitfalls of other, more recent critics in attempting a portrait of an author in his times. While today we can often easily differentiate between art, politics, and literature, Williams' understanding of the intertwining of these at the turn into the nineteenth century is his greatest strength. Irving's reputation, his self-image, his love-hate relationship with his literary contemporaries: all these Williams paints on a dynamic background of a young America coming to terms with itself as an autonomous nation. Though Williams acknowledges that Irving the man is far less interesting than Irving the American in the early nineteenth century, he believes that a thorough portrait of Irving (who was himself so thorough in keeping an accurate record of his times) will provide us with a firm foundation for understanding the evolution of American culture.

ADERMAN's collection of essays and reviews is an essential starting point for any modern critical evaluation of Irving's work. It combines a select list of contemporary reviews of Irving's works with selected twentieth-century essays on the most fundamental avenues of study into Irving himself. These latter include essays on Irving's reputation as a writer, Irving and politics, Irving and the gothic mode, and Irving as the creator of the sketch. Besides being an excellent primary source in its own right, this collection includes an extensive Introduction by the editor detailing the history of criticism on Irving.

HEDGES recognizes the question of "allegiance" in his study of Irving, arguing that such "basic misconceptions" of Irving's motivations derive from the "overly enthusiastic reception originally given *The Sketch Book* (1819–20) in England". Hedges touches on Irving as an uncertain symbol of American culture in its infancy: while idol-smashing abounds, there is nevertheless an omnipresent quest for order, a reverence for tradition. Perhaps the most limiting aspect of this study is Hedges' own penchant for qualifying himself. He is not trying to "start an Irving revival", but rather is straightening a portrait already hung on the wall. Hedges nestles Irving in a broader picture of America in the nineteenth century and, as a result, Irving the man takes a backseat to Irving the American. Despite this shortcoming, Hedges' work represents the critical center on which the debate over Irving's political sensitivities turns.

RUBIN-DORSKY examines each of Irving's major works from 1815 to 1832. He asserts that Irving's affinity for England is *not* pure Anglophilia (linked with all its political ramifications in post-War-of-1812 America), but represents a need for "home" naturally fulfilled by that motherland from which America was born. Grappling with the notion of "Americanness", Rubin-Dorsky vindicates Irving of betraying his homeland's quest for cultural independence by clarifying the artistic and socio-political environment in which Irving wrote. Though Rubin-Dorsky's reductive methodology sometimes forces him to oversimplify his conclusions, this study provides valuable considerations of Irving's motivations for writing during the period.

VON FRANK also argues that Irving, patriotic but practical, recognized young America's need for a cultural "mother". Irving's constant references to America's "youth" are, according to von Frank, his recognition of this fact. "Irving sees that . . . America was not born young, but evolved slowly into something like adolescence as British colonial culture lost the integrity of its style and thereby its capacity to connect Americans with Europe". Irving, being "among the first to consider this issue seriously", is caught by the paradox of "public boasting and private misgiving". Von Frank asserts that Irving, in seeking the best for America's future, holds up English culture as a model to be emulated, and it is this practical position that led to Irving being vilified by his contemporaries for being an Anglophile.

ANTELYES' study proposes that, through the emergence of a narrative, which reflected the very "ideals and . . . tensions" of American economic expansion in the nineteenth century, adventure writers, particularly Irving, sought to reconcile the goals of literary art with the demands of Manifest Destiny capitalism. As Antelyes himself notes, too many critics try to brush aside Irving's later works because they seem to dim in significance when compared to *The Sketch Book* or *Bracebridge Hall*. Yet – and again we return to Irving's "Americanness" here – Antelyes demonstrates Irving's concerns with the development of America's culture side-by-side with its economic philosophy. After tracing the history of the tale of adventurous enterprise, Antelyes places Irving in a tradition of adventure writers without limiting him to that tradition. Indeed, Antelyes demonstrates Irving's innovative adaptation of the adventure tale as a singular voice of American western expansionism.

BOWDEN's study is, as with most in the Twayne series, a good place to start for the serious scholar. Helpful are the short biographical sketches that preface each chapter, which set Irving the man in the context of his times. For Bowden, Irving is a true soldier of liberty and freedom, if sometimes troubled and often obscure in his presentation of these notions in his writings. Most provocative in this study are the fundamental assumptions of Irving that Bowden ignores in favor of some of her own: Irving was not a short-story writer, but a "composer of books"; he was not the social élitist or political conservative, but a "staunch Jeffersonian" (Preface). This study's approach to Irving counterbalances nicely the conservative portrait of him we often receive in the lecture hall.

Until recently, Irving's claim to fame was twofold: he invented the sketch, and he was America's first bestselling author both abroad and at home. Yet, criticism of the last 30 years or so has firmly established his "Americanness", whether as a politically sensitive sketch writer or as an adventure writer adept at capturing the flavor of the nation's economic philosophy in its literature. Few today can claim that America's first man of letters was merely a poor imitator of his English idols.

CHRIS POURTEAU

Isherwood, Christopher 1904–1986

English, later American, novelist, dramatist, screenwriter, and prose writer

Finney, Brian, *Christopher Isherwood: A Critical Biography*, London: Faber & Faber, 1979; New York: Oxford University Press, 1979

Fryer, Jonathan, *Isherwood*, London: New English Library, 1977; revised edition, as *Eye of the Camera: A Life of Christopher Isherwood*, London: Allison & Busby, 1993

Piazza, Paul, *Christopher Isherwood: Myth and Anti-Myth*, New York: Columbia University Press, 1978

Schwerdt, Lisa M., *Isherwood's Fiction: The Self and Technique*, London: Macmillan, 1989

Summers, Claude J., *Christopher Isherwood*, New York: Frederick Ungar, 1980

Wade, Stephen, *Christopher Isherwood*, London: Macmillan, 1991

Initial responses to Christopher Isherwood came as part of the general reception of the 1930s' generation of British writers. Isherwood was, in particular, bracketed with his close friend and writing collaborator, W.H. Auden. After the World War II, with Isherwood now living on the west coast of America, critics felt that the early promise of *All the Conspirators* and *Goodbye to Berlin* had not been fulfilled – an impression, many argued, that the 1954 novel *The World in the Evening* confirmed. However, with Isherwood's later American novels, and in particular autobiographical works like *Kathleen and Frank* and *Christopher and His Kind*, there was a resurgence of interest in him. Isherwood was seen as a writer who challenged the understanding of the boundaries between fiction and autobiography. Perhaps, though, a rising interest in the 1930s lay behind some of this increase in attention, rather than a universal enthusiasm for Isherwood's own latter day interests and concerns.

WADE contributes a short and clear introductory monograph on the author, covering the main areas. It begins with an account of Isherwood's life, identifying the key themes and preoccupations of his writing – for example, his interest in reportage and observation, his homosexuality, and his philosophical and religious interests. As well as surveying the fiction in the subsequent chapters of the book, Wade also has sections on the Vedanta and on the relation between autobiography and fiction. However the book, perhaps because of its place within a series on modern novelists, fails to grapple fully with the autobiographical works or with Isherwood's collaborative ventures. The final section, "Some Critical Perspectives", is weak in its attempts to place Isherwood in a broader frame. This is a book that serves as a basic introduction, but misses the opportunity to be an incisive study in its own right. SUMMERS' criticism in his general survey is often more penetrating. That said, the structure he chooses – working through the main texts in chronological order – constrains his argument, though there is a useful section on the collaborations with Auden. The tone of enthusiasm and admiration is energizing if, finally, this leads to somewhat uncritical praise of Isherwood and his writing.

FRYER has now revised his 1977 biography of Isherwood. Where much of the writing is autobiographical, and with much of the criticism closely relating the fiction to the life, a biography can be an important resource. Fryer is economical and his text writerly, but the biography is overly dependent on an unquestioning use of Isherwood's own accounts. A full scholarly biography is awaited – Fryer's text cites no secondary sources at all – but this book provides an urbane stopgap. Biographically inclined, FINNEY's carefully researched study proceeds from the premise that there are "few other writers whose work invites biographically informed criticism to the extent that Isherwood does". After a 50-page account of Isherwood's early life to the end of his troubled education, Finney introduces chapters of criticism interspersed by further instalments of biography. This allows him to discuss the work in its own right while being able to draw on a base of biographical knowledge that he has already built up. He reaches the conclusion that, paradoxically, Isherwood's increasing cultivation of a direct autobiographical mode provided the greatest space for insightful, subtle, and creative writing.

PIAZZA's book attempts to mount an argument that accounts for the trajectory of Isherwood's life and career. He sees Isherwood's mother, Kathleen, as establishing a myth of what her son's life should be: particularly she held that Christopher should take the same path through life as her late husband. Isherwood's response – the literature that we read, the life he led – forms the anti-myth, a rejection of her attitudes and values. Piazza's book provides a valid, if somewhat predictable, account of Isherwood-as-rebel. When read against SCHWERDT's text, though, Piazza's book gains a new interest, because Schwerdt presents a strikingly opposed view. Using a model of development that grounds itself in (some might say adopts unquestioningly) American ego psychology, Schwerdt seeks to graft Erik Erikson's model of human identity formation onto the author. With very retarded development – he is 40 when Schwerdt sees him passing out of "adolescence" – Isherwood's course is seen as being one of slow maturation and adaptation to the world outside him. As a criticism of this approach – and this may be a limitation not only of the book but also of the theoretical model – one might point out that there is a tendency to view society around the individual as somehow "right", the individual and their accommodation with that society being seen as the problem, his difficulties placing him in the "wrong". Isherwood was concerned with the self, but he engaged passionately with the society in which he lived, vigorously excoriating it for what he believed to be its faults. Not surprisingly Schwerdt has little time for Piazza's book: it is "finally limiting in itself and vexing in its incompleteness".

Efforts at a psychological explanation of Isherwood's life and writing such as those mounted by Schwerdt and Piazza will always be tempting, but there is much work still to be done investigating Isherwood's deceptively simple and straightforward writing practise, and on contextualizing the author.

HOWARD J. BOOTH

J

Jacobean Literature *see* British Literature: Renaissance

Jacobs, Harriet 1813–1897

American autobiographer

Braxton, Joanne M., *Black Women Writing Autobiography: A Tradition Within a Tradition*, Philadelphia: Temple University Press, 1989

Carby, Hazel V., *Reconstructing Womanhood: The Emergence of the Afro-American Woman Novelist*, New York and Oxford: Oxford University Press, 1987

Garfield, Deborah M., "Speech, Listening, and Female Sexuality in *Incidents in the Life of a Slave Girl*," in *Arizona Quarterly*, 50(2), 1994

Kaplan, Carla, "Narrative Contracts and Emancipatory Readers: *Incidents in the Life of a Slave Girl*", in *Yale Journal of Criticism*, 6(1), 1993

Nudelman, Franny, "Harriet Jacobs and the Sentimental Politics of Female Suffering", in *English Literary History*, 59(4), 1992

Yellin, Jean Fagin, *Women and Sisters: The Anti-Slavery Feminists in American Culture*, New Haven, Connecticut: Yale University Press, 1989

Early critics of African-American literature dismissed Jacobs' autobiography *Incidents* as the work of her editor, white abolitionist Lydia Maria Child, because it did not seem to fit the conventions of the slave narrative, and appeared to resemble a sensationalized sentimental novel. After Jean Fagin Yellin established the authorship of *Incidents* in 1981, however, critics quickly realized that the text uncovered and challenged the masculine assumptions that had heretofore shaped our understanding of the slave narrative as a genre. Many critics have since explored the ways in which Jacobs refashioned and critiqued literary conventions, particularly those of the sentimental novel, in order to reach her white, middle-class female audience. Most recently, critics have begun to question the extent to which Jacobs's agency and resistance have been valorized, and have pointed to ways in which Jacobs herself was inscribed within the dominant culture.

CARBY's important examination of the ways in which Jacobs negotiated the complex relationship between black and white women's roles in nineteenth-century America laid the foundation for much future scholarship. Approaching *Incidents* from a feminist, materialist perspective, Carby argues that Jacobs demystifies the literary conventions and ideology of true womanhood by illustrating how these conventions conflicted with her life experience. Jacobs demonstrates the racialized nature of the ideology of true womanhood as she defines an "alternative discourse of black womanhood".

BRAXTON, in her lead chapter "Outraged Mother and Articulate Heroine: Linda Brent and the Slave Narrative Genre", argues for a reconsideration of the criteria traditionally used to define the slave narrative, because those criteria have typically excluded works by women. Arguing that Jacobs's text is exemplary of the autobiography of slave women, Braxton proposes constructing a paradigm for female-authored slave narratives. Such a paradigm might rely in part on "the archetype of the outraged mother" and on the outraged mother's use of "sass", or talking back. Unlike the individualist hero of the male slave narrative, the outraged mother celebrates collective efforts, especially those among generations of black women. Sass, "a word of West African derivation that is associated with the female aspect of the trickster", unsettles social hierarchies and functions as a means of psychological and, in some cases, physical resistance for slave women.

YELLIN provides valuable background for *Incidents* by exploring nineteenth-century women's political activism as well as the complicated relationship between abolitionism and feminism. When white women re-gendered the famous abolitionist emblem of the enchained African male supplicant, they used the new emblem for both abolitionist and feminist ends. By identifying themselves with their enslaved "sisters", they used the emblem not only to represent their own victimization under patriarchy, but also to subordinate their slave "sisters" to passive positions. Yet Jacobs, like Sojourner Truth, subverted these subtly racist reconfigurations of true womanhood by positing an active role for black women. Yellin's work is most useful in describing the conflicted background of feminism and abolitionism against which Jacobs's text was written.

GARFIELD focuses on the roles of oral agency and sexuality within nineteenth-century abolitionist discourse in order to uncover a unique dimension of Jacobs's relationship with her audience. Because many abolitionists believed that speech not only converted the intellect and soul but also ravished the senses, female abolitionists found themselves in narrowly circumscribed positions. Even more troubling than the potentially sexual dimension of oral communication was the sexual context of many abolitionist speeches. Ironically, in *Incidents* sexual abuse is displaced into language: sexual threats are coded as verbal rather than physical threats. Yet Jacobs did not simply accept the sexual mores of the dominant culture; rather, she manipulated the sign-systems of abolitionist discourse to "reverse the roles of master and slave in her text, as well as the corresponding hierarchy of coddled reader and writer victim". In so doing she demonstrated the link beween white women's decorum and white men's sexual aggression.

NUDELMAN challenges an assumption that has become a critical commonplace in Jacobs scholarship – that *Incidents* is unique in its rejection of the conventions of the dominant discourse of sentimentality. Nudelman contends instead that in fact "sentimental conventions and values generate and determine Jacobs's critique". Jacobs neither entirely accepts nor entirely rejects dominant codes; rather:

> Caught between a domestic ideology that relies on female sexual purity and an abolitionist discourse that insistently publicizes the sexual victimization of slave women, Jacobs is peculiarly able to elaborate on their interrelatedness, the ways they concur and conflict, and their particular limitations for the narration of black female experience.

Particularly useful in Nudelman's essay is its carefully nuanced discussion of the history and politics of sentimentality and its demonstration of sentimentality's inherent contradictions.

KAPLAN addresses one of the key critical issues of *Incidents*: how does Jacobs make her readers rethink freedom and agency, as Jacobs puts it, "not in the usual way"? Typically, critics who examined Jacobs's resistance unwittingly "fostered a sentimentalization of the marginal, the oppositional, and the subversive". Understanding resistance in *Incidents*, contends Kaplan, entails examining Jacobs's negotiation of contracts, both social (within the text itself) and narrative (between the writer and readers). Although Jacobs does value the notion of individuality, which the idea of social contract embodies, she rejects narrative contract because it is something which gives others power over her. By avoiding the conventional relationship between reader and writer, she "seeks to create a new black narrative position, one founded in a rejection of both the attestory position of slave narrators and the seductive one typical of white women's romances". Kaplan's work is particularly useful for its critique of current scholarship and for its provocative approach to the subject of readership.

This is a time of rapidly increasing interest in Jacobs. Forthcoming (at the time of writing) are two book-length collections of criticism devoted to *Incidents* – a volume in Cambridge University Press's American literature series, edited by Deborah Garfield and Rafia Zafar (*Harriet Jacobs: "Incidents in the Life of a Slave Girl": New Critical Essays*), and a volume edited by Henry Louis Gates and K. Anthony Appiah (*Harriet Jacobs: Critical Perspectives Past and Present*). Both promise to be of great interest.

AMY E. WINANS

James, Henry 1843–1916

American novelist, short-story writer, and critic

Anesko, Michael, *"Friction with the Market": Henry James and the Profession of Authorship*, New York and Oxford: Oxford University Press, 1986
Bell, Ian F.A., *Henry James and the Past: Readings into Time*, Basingstoke: Macmillan, 1991
Bell, Millicent, *Meaning in Henry James*, Cambridge, Massachusetts: Harvard University Press, 1991
Davis, Lloyd, *Sexuality and Textuality in Henry James: Reading Through the Virginal*, New York: Peter Lang, 1988
Fogel, Daniel Mark, *Covert Relations: James Joyce, Virginia Woolf and Henry James*, Charlottesville: University Press of Virginia, 1990
Fogel, Daniel Mark (ed.), *A Companion to Henry James Studies*, Westport, Connecticut: Greenwood Press, 1993
Freedman, Jonathan, *Professsions of Taste: Henry James, British Aestheticism, and Commodity Culture*, Stanford, California: Stanford University Press, 1990
Fussell, Edwin S., *The Catholic Side of Henry James*, Cambridge and New York: Cambridge University Press, 1993
Griffin, Susan M., *The Historical Eye: The Texture of the Visual in Late James*, Boston: Northeastern University Press, 1991
Habegger, Alfred, *Henry James and the "Woman Business"*, Cambridge and New York: Cambridge University Press, 1989
Horne, Philip, *Henry James and Revision: The New York Edition*, Oxford: Clarendon Press, 1990; New York: Oxford University Press, 1990
Jolly, Roslyn, *Henry James, History, Narrative, Fiction*, Oxford: Clarendon Press, 1992; New York: Oxford University Press, 1992
Poole, Adrian, *Henry James*, Hemel Hempstead, Hertfordshire: Harvester Wheatsheaf, 1991
Posnock, Ross, *The Trial of Curiosity: Henry James, William James and the Challenge of Modernity*, New York and Oxford: Oxford University Press, 1991
Tintner, Adeline R., *The Museum World of Henry James*, Ann Arbor, Michigan: UMI Research Press, 1986
Walton, Priscilla L., *The Disruption of the Feminine in Henry James*, Toronto and Buffalo, New York: University of Toronto Press, 1992
Williams, Mefle, A., *Henry James and the Philosophical Novel: Being and Seeing*, Cambridge and New York: Cambridge University Press, 1993
Woolf, Judith, *Henry James: The Major Novels*, Cambridge and New York: Cambridge University Press, 1991

James criticism has always been polarized between tendencies variously labelled "aesthetic" and "American", or "formalist" and "historicist", including issues of technique, treatment, and influence as well as subject-matter. Recent work has also articulated the axis of sexuality and gender, and perhaps shifted the focus of enquiry away from earlier interest in "early" and "late" James novels towards the problematic "middle period", the tales, and the non-fiction, especially *The American Scene*. The following discussion will attempt to chart the variety and development of the main currents of thought in James criticism in successive years since the mid-1980s.

TINTNER's detailed authoritative work, though "old fashioned", is more than a visual-art compendium or reference guide. She covers James's entire *oeuvre* and a corresponding range of art from classical sculpture to the cinematograph. Prolonged attention to James's preoccupation with visual art leads beyond source-spotting to assessments related to current critical concerns with influence, interpretation, and revision.

ANESKO, in contrast, uses James's phrase "friction with the market" to approach a strikingly contemporary issue: the uncomfortable but stimulating relationship between artist and publisher in book production, and the sense of an audience, registered through sales, shaping the voice of the author, in mutual exemption from "mere personal dreams". This is a lively account of the novels of the middle years in terms of fictional investment, emotional exploitation, and "games of power and knowledge" also played out in business terms by author and publisher. Anesko gives chapter and verse, totals and vulgar fractions, contracts and negotiations, for a "master" who is also a dealer.

DAVIS gives an early example of reading James through Freud and post-Freudians such as Jacques Lacan and Julia Kristeva, shifting emphasis from sexuality to textuality. The "virginal" is presented as a site of dramatization and inscription where "the traditional Jamesian narrative of the passage from innocence is reformulated as both the characterized virgin's and the text's entrance into the complexities of the sociosexual order", thus re-integrating intimate concerns with a public field of discourse.

HABEGGER addresses questions of gender in a stronger historical, biographical, and intertextual context, challenging the received idea of James as implicitly "feminist" in sensibility by exploring the importance of his father's belated antifeminist rigidity. The death of his father while James worked on *The Bostonians* evidently affected his handling of gender issues in this vexed text. Anesko also contextualizes *The Portrait of a Lady* as James's "answer" to popular romances by rival female authors. This is an important if contentious study.

FOGEL's 1990 study approaches James's intertextuality in a very different temper. He attempts "critically to modify [Harold] Bloom's theory of the anxiety of influence, and to respond to feminist revisions of the Oedipal model of incestuous ambitions amongst writers", giving "a gentler pattern of transmissions and departures". Particularly exciting on James and Virginia Woolf, whose penultimate diary entry movingly quotes the Master's sentence "Observe perpetually".

FREEDMAN brilliantly articulates questions of literary context and sexual orientation with wider issues of historical and economic concern in a revisionary investigation, which is both critical and cultural. Starting from the Victorian inheritance, John Ruskin, and the Pre-Raphaelites, then analysing James's reactions to Walter Pater and Oscar Wilde, Freedman shows that "James's various, subtle and shifting responses to aestheticism not only shaped his own art but . . . remodelled the expectations and understanding of the Anglo-American cultural elite". James and the Aesthetes consciously opposed the commodification of art in the despised market economy; yet their own developing "aesthetic professionalism" contributed to the process they criticized. Freedman's thesis provides a "richer genealogy of modernism, and indeed, postmodernism" in a study that is densely informative, closely theorized, and well presented.

HORNE's investigation touches on the marketplace and on intertextuality, but holds the focus securely on James's own work. The central tenet of his persistently revelatory reading is that all expression displays a revisionary aspect, establishing a complex relationship between perception and the text. James is fascinated by relations between experience and expression, and among writer, text, character, and reader – a nexus he explores repeatedly through looping recurrences in his fiction, revisions, and critical prefaces. He jokingly labelled the New York Edition "a Monument"; but Horne shows that it is part of an unending process of exploration. Where Anesko reveals the business talents in James, Horne's tactful, lively scholarship reasserts his uncompromising insistence on artistic judgement "and hang the expense".

Millicent BELL also displays patient flexibility and discrimination as she ranges unusually widely over James's *oeuvre* to show how the reading process permits us to entertain plots and possibilities the novels themselves foreclose and forego, heuristically generating readerly sympathies with contradictory elements in character, which defy logical analysis and challenge lazy generalization. As she notes, "James himself was always fascinated by the paradoxical combination, in particular, of refinement and intelligence with moral callousness".

Ian BELL concentrates on *Washington Square*, *The Bostonians*, and *The Europeans* to "recover issues of history, economics and social change as specifically determinant of James's works of the 1870s and 1880s". Informed by theories of the Frankfurt School and Jean Baudrillard, this densely argued study relates the romance genre, which James inherited from Nathaniel Hawthorne, to market-place pressures in the onset of consumer culture, exploring "the Romance of display, surface and performance".

POSNOCK also holds that James should be seen "in the company of American social thinkers" like Thorstein Veblen, and "among such European theorists of urban modernity as [Georg] Simmel and [Max] Weber, as well as their successors in and around the Frankfurt school". *The Ambassadors*, *The American Scene*, the prefaces, and autobiographies can be read as "an interconnected unit" revealing "James's aesthetic, cultural, and psychological responses to modernity and their challenging, even radical, political implications". Posnock explores *The American Scene* and the *Autobiography* as "culturally exemplary" texts. Recognising the centrality of the novelist's relationship with his brother William James, Posnock interestingly brings Henry's novel *The Ambassadors* together with William's *Varieties of Religious Experience* (1901), in the light of Baudrillard's assertion that ambivalence, "suppressed by a culture of consumption, incessantly producing a chaotic multiplicity of needs, values and desires" resurges in failure, which alone "preserves the subject's questioning concerning his own desire". Failure is thus freedom in a "mysterious economy of lost opportunity", and Posnock argues that it is effectively revolutionary.

GRIFFIN also seeks to rehistoricize the reading of James by examining "the stock figure of the Jamesian perceived" in the context of "the perceptual stream wherein James constructs – and reconstructs – his own historical self [and which] displays his ambivalent participation in the political and economic conditions that surround him". Griffin uses William James's *Principles of Psychology* (1890) to place the observer figure in a psychological rather than philosophical context, correcting the passive model of associationist perception that had informed Romantic writers with a more active functionalism: "just as the functional self is simultaneously creator and creature of its environment, so it is also producer and product of its own history". This is a lucid, combative, and revisionary reading of *The Ambassadors*, *The Golden Bowl*, and *The American Scene*.

WOOLF addresses the non-specialist reader in a clear introduction to "the excitement rather than the difficulty of reading James". An intriguing feature of this clear work on nine novels is Woolf's grounding of James in the English novel tradition, citing Henry Fielding, Samuel Richardson, Charles Dickens, and George Eliot.

POOLE's work is also lively and free of visible obstructions from secondary material, though effectively informed by the same historical, economic, and cultural ideas preoccupying several studies in this year. He explicates "the restlessness Henry James found in the particular cultures he knew, and the forms in which he represented it", linked with analysis of "the comfort and discomfort of writing and reading prose fiction". Six chapters cover a great range, working from the "resources" of money, health, cities, other writers, and language, with which James began in the 1870s, through novels from *The American* to *The Ambassadors*, and the "pivotal" *Princess Casamassima* and *The Tragic Muse*, to *The Bostonians*, *The Spoils of Poynton*, *What Maisie Knew*, and *The Awkward Age*, where sexual politics expose modern forms of power and property, and to the late novels and a shifting focus of power through international plutocracy. *The Turn of the Screw* is the climactic tale of "revenge and reparation", for Poole finds an "element of discreet retaliation in all Henry James's writing".

In an important contribution to the gender-studies critique of James, WALTON aligns the "masculine" with literary realism as "two functions of dominant ideology", but argues that James's texts display a "feminine polyvalency". Working from *Roderick Hudson* to *The Golden Bowl*, with one eye on the critical essays and prefaces, the other on the fissures of the fiction, she shows that "while the earlier stories hold *implicit* critiques of their Realist/humanist ideology, the language of the later works effects a more general . . . subversion of the Realist concept of knowability".

FUSSELL steps outside previous boundaries of James criticism in exploring the Roman Catholic element of his work. Yet this innovatory study relates persuasively to other commentaries on cultural and ideological context. Noticing the "profound Catholic imagery" in James, Fussell discusses the tensions between his friendship with John La Farge and other Catholics and the heritage of James Fenimore Cooper, Nathaniel Hawthorne, and Ralph Waldo Emerson, besides the contemporary ambivalence of Mark Twain and William Dean Howells. Examining an unusual range of work, from the early reviews to *Guy Domville*, as well as *The Golden Bowl*, Fussell suggests that "the religious mix in the [American] literary scene provided James with a commercial opportunity to explore his penchant for the Protestant-Catholic theme".

JOLLY reads James's novels in the light of nineteenth-century debates about the morality of authorship and politics of reading. James wrote anxiously about history as challenging or authenticating the novelist's enterprise, so that fiction "moves from being history's censured 'other' in the early works to . . . a valued mode of problem-solving". Jolly explores James's engagement with "the reading practices of groups marginalized by high Victorian culture", such as women, alien cultures, and the avant garde. In his own work, the "anti-romance enterprise of novel-as-history" is challenged by characters arrogating powers of authorship to themselves and rebutting "the power of history to define their world".

WILLIAMS sees James's fictional practice, where "processes of moral choice and development become dynamic, dramatic, and constantly absorbing for his characters and his inevitably implicated readers alike," in terms of a storytelling model of philosophical enquiry. Maurice Merleau-Ponty and Jacques Derrida are invoked in the philosophical development of this process, which forges conceptual discriminations through fictional trial. Thus James is a proto-phenomenologist, a novelist who anticipates these theorists' epistemological, moral, and linguistic concerns.

FOGEL (1993) compiles a considerable volume of substantial essays by 20 distinguished Jamesians on all aspects of his writing, "intended to provide both advanced students and scholars with a reference guide to Henry James studies". Most helpful is the keynote introductory essay by Richard Hocks, "From Literary Analysis to Postmodern Theory: A Historical Narrative of James Criticism", which gives a lucid and penetrating account of movements and landmarks in this field.

NICOLA BRADBURY

James, William 1842–1910

American philosopher and psychologist

Cotkin, George, *William James: Public Philosopher*, Baltimore: Johns Hopkins University Press, 1990
Edie, James M., *William James and Phenomenology*, Bloomington: Indiana University Press, 1987
Feinstein, Howard M., *Becoming William James*, Ithaca, New York: Cornell University Press, 1984
Myers, Gerald E., *William James: His Life and Thought*, New Haven, Connecticut: Yale University Press, 1986
Posnock, Ross, *The Trial of Curiosity: Henry James, William James, and the Challenge of Modernity*, New York and Oxford: Oxford University Press, 1991
Seigfried, Charlene Haddock, *William James's Radical Reconstruction of Philosophy*, Albany: State University of New York Press, 1990

William James has been the object of renewed attention in recent years, as philosophers and literary theorists, led by Richard Rorty, have advocated a "new pragmatism" – a method of assessing truths by consequences, designed to break the epistemological impasse posed by poststructuralism. While the "neo-pragmatists" have claimed James as a predecessor, many James scholars have rejected the identification of old and new pragmatisms, arguing that the former was more cognizant of empirical "facts", and more socially progressive, than the latter. Continuing debates over the meaning and efficacy of pragmatism in contemporary philosophy and literary theory should make critical studies of James interesting to a wide audience.

MYERS's study supersedes Ralph Barton Perry's *The Thought and Character of William James* (1935) as the standard survey of James's life and work. Its first chapter outlines James's career, first in physiology, then in psychology, and finally in philosophy, and discusses influences on his thought. Subsequent chapters investigate James's views on a series of issues: the nature of consciousness; perception; space and time; memory; attention and will; emotion; thought; knowledge; reality; self; and morality and religion. The chapter on "Knowledge" is the most important, explaining in detail what James meant by a pragmatic approach to truth, and providing detailed information about the opposition his pragmatism encountered in its time – opposition proleptic of the reception of neo-pragmatism. Myers's own view of James's pragmatism is laudatory, leading some critics to charge that he fails to engage seriously with its internal contradictions, and others to maintain that he ignores questions about its ideology. This lucid and wide-ranging book remains, nonetheless, the necessary starting-point for any serious study of James's work.

FEINSTEIN adopts a Freudian approach to James's life and philosophy. He argues that James's advocacy of positive thinking (and ultimately his pragmatism) resulted from his early battles with depression – in particular those induced by his father's insistence that he abandon his artistic vocation for a career in science. If Feinstein's causal claims are not always convincing, he performs a valuable service in emphasizing the therapeutic purpose of Jamesian philosophy. The book will also be useful to readers interested in the implications of Jamesian pragmatism for aesthetics; it details James's early education in visual art, reproduces several of his drawings, and traces the references to art woven into the fabric of his psychological and philosophical writings.

COTKIN's impressive study situates James's personal problems and writings within a broad cultural, social, and political milieu. Part One explores the historical factors contributing to James's formative depression, particularly the social stigma attached to his failure to participate in the Civil War. But it is Part Two, which examines James's subsequent role as a "public philosopher" in the tradition of Ralph Waldo Emerson, that is most illuminating. It explains the social needs that James's popular lectures and essays on heroism were meant to address – a despair induced by determinism and a decline in religious belief, and a *tedium vitae* owing both to the widespread acceptance of Spencerian evolutionism and to excessive material comfort. These, Cotkin points out, were the needs of an upper-class audience; James's inspiring words were of limited value to the poor, in discouraging the collectivism necessary for genuine social change. The study concludes with a perceptive analysis of how thinkers like Bertrand Russell misread both James's "discourse of heroism" and his pragmatism as justifications for imperialist suppression. Such a reading, it argues, ignores several aspects of James's philosophy developed precisely to *counter* imperialism – its insistence on pluralism, on the role of dialogue in truth-making, and on the importance of respecting the inner subjectivity of others.

POSNOCK has written a difficult but rewarding comparison of the work of William and his brother Henry. In explaining how Henry's narrative style – particularly in works like *The American Scene* – realizes William's specifications for pragmatic truth-making, he suggests that pragmatism may be usefully employed as a paradigm for literary modernism. He also points out key differences between the two brothers, particularly in their conceptions of self and society; William's commitment to the concept of an autonomous self, and his hidden rationalist assumptions, make him the less radical of the two.

EDIE is unusual among James scholars in emphasizing the philosopher's role not as pragmatist, but as phenomenologist. He argues that James anticipated (and influenced) the descriptive technique usually attributed to Edmund Husserl. After discussing the sections in *Principles of Psychology* outlining this technique, he shows how James applied it, first in early essays like "The Sentiment of Rationality", and finally in *Varieties of Religious Experience* ("the only phenomenology of religious experience", Edie says, "to have been written up to now"). Edie's study will be useful to scholars of American modernism in demonstrating that it is not necessary to turn to Europe for a model for the phenomenological poetry of Robert Frost, Gertrude Stein, and Wallace Stevens.

SEIGFRIED's book may be the most important of recent studies, engaging seriously and sympathetically with apparent contradictions in James's work. Critics have seen inconsistencies in James's claim to be repudiating metaphysics while asserting several metaphysical positions, and in his insistence on both the self-interest involved in perception and the necessity of checking truth-claims against "the facts". Seigfried argues that these contradictions are explicable in the approach to reality James called "radical empiricism" – a method incorporating both pragmatism and phenomenology. She also explains that James's essays must be viewed as exercises in rhetoric, rather than logic. Seigfried's ultimate goal is the same as Rorty's – to demonstrate the value of James's "radical reconstruction of philosophy" in the wake of poststructuralism – but she suggests that Rorty's characterization of James is fatally flawed in ignoring his commitment to verification procedures. Her revisionary view of James, which has important implications for his politics, is certain to play a central role in continuing discussions about the place of pragmatism in contemporary thought.

PATRICIA RAE

Jeffers, Robinson 1887–1962

American poet

Brophy, Robert (ed.), *Robinson Jeffers: Dimensions of a Poet*, New York: Fordham University Press, 1995

Everson, William, *The Excesses of God: Robinson Jeffers as a Religious Figure*, Stanford, California: Stanford University Press, 1988

Falck, Colin (ed.), *Robinson Jeffers: Selected Poems*, Manchester: Carcanet, 1987
Hunt, Tim, *The Collected Poetry of Robinson Jeffers*, 4 vols., Stanford, California: Stanford University Press, 1988 – (3 vols. to 1991)
Hunt, Tim, and Hugh Witemeyer (eds.), *American Poetry* (special Jeffers issue), 5(1), 1987
Karman, James, *Robinson Jeffers: Poet of California*, San Fancisco: Chronicle Books, 1987
Karman, James (ed.), *Critical Essays on Robinson Jeffers*, Boston: G.K. Hall, 1990
Wyatt, David, *The Fall into Eden: Landscape and Imagination in California*, Cambridge and New York: Cambridge University Press, 1986
Zaller, Robert, *The Cliffs of Solitude: A Reading of Robinson Jeffers*, Cambridge and New York: Cambridge University Press, 1983
Zaller, Robert (ed.), *Centennial Essays on Robinson Jeffers*, Newark: University of Delaware Press, 1991; London: Associated University Presses, 1991

Robinson Jeffers published 18 books of poems in his lifetime, and further volumes of poems, letters, and essays appeared posthumously. Despite the durability of his status as a significant poet, his work has rarely achieved wide acceptance in the mainstream of criticism, and although there is a sustained revival of interest in him currently, he remains something of a special case in modern American poetry. There are two reasons for this. First, though he was always an accomplished lyric poet, much of his mature work was in long narrative poems written when this mode seemed hopelessly outdated by comparison with the formal experimentalism of his modernist contemporaries. Second, while he shared T.S. Eliot and Ezra Pound's interest in ancient classical literature, his narrative poems transpose the violent incidents of classical tragedy and myth to the backwoods families of California, and the human scene he depicts in these poems frequently involves incest, rape, and murder: in his poetry he expressed almost total disdain for the achievements of human culture, and developed a theory he called "Inhumanism", which celebrated the abiding strength and beauty of the physical world of nature against the impoverished and self-destructive human world. For much of this century such ideas were regarded as politically and morally disreputable, so that at the end of his life his reputation was at a very low ebb. Our present ecological and environmental anxieties have done something to redeem Jeffers' ideas, and there is a sense in which his work is now more acceptable than it has ever been before. The present-day interest in Jeffers is the result of the work of a small group of writers whose names appear repeatedly in the following discussion, whose biographical and critical studies have rescued Jeffers from critical hostility and consequent neglect.

EVERSON has been a passionate advocate for Jeffers in a series of books, essays, and special editions of the poet, culminating in this recent study, in which he insists that Jeffers is a mystic with a "sacred vision", a view deliberately at odds with the prevailing representation of him as a philosophical poet. Everson sees Jeffers as a poet of what is called the "numinous" and the revelatory, and calls on the work of the German theologian Rudolf Otto, whose 1923 book *The Idea of the Holy* provides the particular vocabulary that informs this reading. This is especially evident in the long concluding chapter, a meditation on sex and religion, in which Everson explores Jeffers' poems through Otto's specifications of the numinous in such terms as "longing, solemnity, and fascination". Everson is very persuasive on these matters, and this book has had a deep influence on other commentators, so that the idea of Jeffers as a mystic is becoming part of the current critical orthodoxy.

BROPHY is the author of *Robinson Jeffers: Myth, Ritual, and Symbol in His Narrative Poems* (1973), numerous essays, editions of the poems, and editor of the *Robinson Jeffers Newsletter* since 1968. This 1995 collection of new essays by those mostly responsible for the revaluation of Jeffers over the past 20 years opens with Brophy's own assessment of the ambivalences at the heart of Jeffers, caught as he is between the contradictory impulses of the "mystic and the prophet". Alex Vardamis surveys the fluctuations in Jeffers' critical reputation throughout his life, and Robert Zaller investigates Jeffers' theory of Inhumanism and its relation to human history as expressive of the conflict between Hegelian and Nietzschean ideas of history. Terry Beers looks at "Thurso's Landing" to argue for the unity of the narrative point of view between the authorial voice of the poem and its characters as a way of articulating Jeffers' commitment to a communal expression of values. There is a certain congruity between Beers' conclusions and the following essay by Tim Hunt, an account of narrative voices and consciousness in "Roan Stallion". David J. Rothman makes a passionate defence of Jeffers' "versecraft", his handling of prosody, which he sees as neither traditional nor "free", but carefully "inscribed" as though worked in stone, and he argues persuasively that we shall hardly make sense of the content of the poems if we remain indifferent to the techniques by which they are realised. The remaining parts of this collection include a panel debate on the "Female Archetype" in Jeffers, an essay excerpted from Everson's book (discussed above), and an assessment of the "dialogue" between Jeffers and the Polish poet Czesław Miłosz in relation to their opposed value systems.

HUNT and WITEMEYER have edited a special issue of *American Poetry* devoted to Jeffers, and though this journal has now ceased publication it can be found in major libraries. This issue includes a useful overview by Terry Beers of the academic neglect and widespread critical rejection of Jeffers until the last two decades, and the notable German scholar Eva Hesse writes instructively on what she takes to be the true meaning of Jeffers' concept of Inhumanism and his idea of man's unpaid debt to Nature. One of the most interesting essays is Harold Schweizer's account of the tragic mode in some of Jeffers' longer poems and shorter lyrics, with particular reference to "Roan Stallion", "Cawdor", and "Thurso's Landing". Schweizer takes his perspective from Matthew Arnold's comparison of the introspective anxieties of much nineteenth-century poetry set against the sense of intellectual deliverance offered by classical tragedy, and implicitly argues for Jeffers' classicism in this context. Jeffers is seen to reject the urban and psychologically *Angst*-ridden questionings of his modernist contemporaries in the way he situates the tragic sense of the contemporary within our conflictual relationship to the natural world, setting its permanence against our mutability. This collection includes a "Forum" section, in which a number of poets and critics debate their responses to Jeffers, and the whole concludes with a résumé (by Tim Hunt) of Jeffers studies up to the centenary year of 1987.

HUNT is also the editor of a fine new edition of Jeffers, planned in four volumes, of which three have appeared so far. In the Introduction to the first volume Hunt provides an excellent account of the crucial events in Jeffers' life and the way these affected the choices he made as to the form and content of his work, and his refusal of the kinds of technical experimentalism of his modernist contemporaries, such as William Carlos Williams, Pound, and Eliot. Hunt writes well on Jeffers' formal mastery of the unrhymed accentual line and the direction of his work in the 1920s. While it is true that Jeffers has suffered considerable critical neglect until recently, it is also true that few other twentieth-century American poets have been honoured by a collected edition of their work as handsome and usable as this one (even if it is very expensive).

The material gathered in KARMAN's collection includes contemporary reviews of Jeffers' books from *Flagons and Apples* (1912) to *"The Beginning and the End" and Other Poems* (1963), and there is no better way to follow the arc of this poet's reputation than by reading through these reviews, which make up more than half of this book. These are followed by 13 critical essays of more recent times, mostly appreciative of Jeffers, including Everson's introduction to the 1970 edition of *Cawdor and Medea*, Brophy's "*Cawdor* and the Hippolytus Story", and Hunt's account of Jeffers as an "antimodernist". A notable exception to this enthusiasm for Jeffers comes in Kenneth Rexroth's curiously named essay of 1957, "In Defense of Jeffers", a brief but wholesale repudiation of every aspect of Jeffers' work, which can be summarised by this statement: "in my opinion Jeffers's verse is shoddy and pretentious and the philosophizing is nothing but posturing". Against this, Hunt's cogent account of the poet's choice of narrative forms, and his placing of Jeffers within a Wordsworthian tradition provides a secure opening to a way of reading Jeffers. Karman's Introduction to this volume gives a thorough and unflinching account of the history of the poet's reception, and one which properly reflects the adverse view of him by many of the leading critics of the middle years of this century. This is an indispensable collection, both for its historical perspective and for the representation of recent critical work on Jeffers. KARMAN's 1987 study builds on the interest in Jeffers developed through the late 1960s and 1970s in this general biographical and critical overview, a reliable and informative guide to Jeffers' life and work.

ZALLER's 1983 book is important for its Freudian contextual approach to Jeffers' preoccupation with incest, castration, and parricide, particularly in the narrative and dramatic poems, a necessary study of that element of Jeffers imagination that offended so many critics across the spectrum of American intellectual life and contributed significantly to his eventual isolation. Zaller relates these matters to Jeffers' own psychological difficulties, especially in his relationships with women, and to his doctrine of Inhumanism. This is an indispensable account by one of Jeffers' foremost commentators. ZALLER's 1991 anthology of essays bears witness to the strength of recent commentary on Jeffers, with nine essays specially commissioned for this volume. The longest contribution is again by William Everson – three linked essays on Jeffers' second book *California* (1916) and on two subsequent early collections unpublished in their complete form until after Jeffers' death, *"The Alpine Christ" and Other Poems* (1973), and *"Brides of the South Wind": Poems, 1917–1922*, (1974). In these three essays Everson gives an illuminating account of the emergence of Jeffers from his apprentice work to the first flowering of his creative maturity. Tim Hunt discusses the problematic representation of nature in *"Tamar" and Other Poems* (1924), and reads these poems for what they show us of Jeffers' ideas about history, culture, and human agency – a reading deliberately set against the assumptions of modernist orthodoxy. This good collection includes a sympathetic reading of "The Loving Shepherdess" by the British critic R.W. (Herbie) Butterfield, while other essays deal with Jeffers' symbolism, his metrics, and his relation to modernism.

While it would be too limiting to see Jeffers merely as a regional poet, there is no doubt that the rugged landscapes around Carmel, California, where he settled with his wife in 1914 and lived throughout the rest of his life, inspired his celebration of the natural against the human. This aspect of Jeffers is discussed in WYATT's book as part of his survey of the literary response to California by a number of writers. This very readable and intelligent study gives an assured assessment of the instigatory power of the Californian mountains and forests, which provide the setting for Jeffers' narrative poems.

FALCK's centenary edition of a selection of the poems prints 60 of the lyrics, three short narrative poems, and an excerpt from Jeffers' adaptation of Euripides' *Medea*. In an appreciative Introduction characterising Jeffers as an "American Romantic", Falck writes well on the language of these poems and the risks Jeffers took in working in a "neutral but heightened conversational idiom adequate to his cosmic concerns", and notes the consequent dangers of tonal monotony and the 'hollowly oracular' effects which sometimes follow. Falck raises the question of the psychological origins of Jeffers' interest in human and familial violence in the narrative poems; but since those poems are not represented in this selection, that aspect of Jeffers' work is dealt with rather inadequately. Indeed, there is a certain apologetic tone about much of this Introduction, at odds with Falck's evident enthusiasm for his subject; but this is a useful selection of Jeffers' lyric poems and a good book to go to for a sampling of the poet.

LIONEL KELLY

Jefferson, Thomas 1743–1826

American prose writer; US President 1801–09

Becker, Carl L., *The "Declaration of Independence": A Study in the History of Political Ideas*, New York: Harcourt Brace, 1922

Boorstin, Daniel J., *The Lost World of Thomas Jefferson*, Boston: Beacon Press, 1948

Fliegelman, Jay, *Declaring Independence: Jefferson, Natural Language, and the Culture of Performance*, Stanford, California: Stanford University Press, 1993

Malone, Dumas, *Jefferson and His Time*, 6 vols., Boston: Little Brown, 1948–81; London: Eyre & Spottiswoode, 1949–81

Mayer, David N., *The Constitutional Thought of Thomas Jefferson*, Charlottesville: University Press of Virginia, 1994

Onuf, Peter S. (ed.), *Jeffersonian Legacies*, Charlottesville: University Press of Virginia, 1993

Wills, Gary, *Inventing America: Jefferson's "Declaration of Independence"*, Garden City, New York: Doubleday, 1978

There is a long tradition of excellent twentieth-century scholarship on Jefferson, much of it historical. Jefferson's writings on race have received special attention lately, and the issue continues to divide scholars, sometimes sharply. Of late, Jefferson has been discussed in terms of "liberalism" and its legacy, a legacy around which certain critical camps have developed. Jefferson's "doubleness" (i.e., he was a slave owner who decried the institution of slavery) continues to make him a source of interest to scholars.

BECKER focuses exclusively on the Declaration of Independence, especially in terms of how it was informed by natural-rights philosophy. Becker's book explores several drafts of the Declaration, thus situating it as a document reflective of human agency rather than an "eternal" document of transcendent truth. Additionally, Becker's chapter "The Literary Qualities of the Declaration" is insightful, and one of the better extended treatments of the Declaration as literature, despite the fact that currently distinctions between "literature" and "history" are questioned.

BOORSTIN's important book has influenced generations of scholars seeking to "recover" Jefferson's era in an effort to better understand Jefferson himself. "My purpose", wrote Boorstin, "has been to get inside the Jeffersonian world of ideas – to see the relation among their conceptions of God, nature, equality, toleration, education and government". Especially strong are Boorstin's chapters on physiology and natural history, where Boorstin places Jefferson in the context of other thinkers and writers.

MALONE's massive and comprehensive six-volume study of Jefferson remains a landmark in Jefferson scholarship, its standing partially attested to by the fact that nearly every book on Jefferson published in the last 20 years mentions Malone. While sometimes faulted for being too much of an apologist for Jefferson, Malone remains an invaluable source of information on him.

Early in his book, WILLS announces that "I thus distinguish the Declaration of *Congress* (which is mainly political) from the Declaration of *Jefferson* (which is philosophical in the eighteenth-century sense, that is, scientific), and from *our* Declaration (the thing we have reshaped even as it was shaping us)". While there might be room to quarrel with Wills's assumption that "politics" can so easily be made into a separate category, his study of the Declaration nonetheless remains one of the best. Particularly original is Wills's chapter on the Declaration as a "scientific paper", where he recovers the scientific meaning in Jefferson's day of some of its key words.

FLIEGELMAN's bold and innovative book is written, in the author's own words, "as a single continuous essay, divided into titled sections but not broken into chapters" in an effort to reflect an eighteenth-century "interactive culture" in which the "political" and the "non-political" were mixed. Beginning with the premise that Jefferson wrote the Declaration of Independence to be "read aloud", Fliegelman explores the significance of "the elocutionary movement in America that helped destabilize the distinction between the natural and the theatrical". Fliegelman's ambitious archival work and engaging writing style, as well as his inclusion of many useful illustrations, make this a truly valuable interdisciplinary book.

ONUF's collection of 15 essays is one of the most important and tantalizing books to appear on Jefferson in the last decade. With contributions by scholars ranging from Joyce Appleby to Jack P. Greene and Gordon S. Wood, this collection offers sophisticated reassessments of Jefferson's legacy. Of particular interest are two essays on Jefferson and race: Lucia C. Stanton explores Jefferson's conflicted and sometimes disturbing stances on slavery and race, while Scot A. French and Edward L. Ayers explore the historiography of the public image of Jefferson and race from 1943 to 1993, and nicely capture the perils and strengths of "revisionist" readings of Jefferson.

MAYER seeks to fill a gap in Jeffersonian scholarship by providing a "thorough study of his constitutional thought". At the same time, Mayer rejects the "liberalism"-versus-"civic republicanism" paradigm so often used to categorize Jeffersonian thinking. Although Mayer's attempt to examine Jefferson's consitutional thought "on its own terms" is admirable, it does leave his book without a guiding methodology. In this sense, his book is more explication than argument, though explication of very high order.

NICHOLAS ROMBES

Jewish-American Writers

Bilik, Dorothy Seidman, *Immigrant Survivors: Post-Holocaust Consciousness in Recent Jewish-American Fiction*, Middletown, Connecticut: Wesleyan University Press, 1981

Fried, Lewis (general ed.), *Handbook of American-Jewish Literature: An Analytical Guide to Topics, Themes and Sources*, Westport, Connecticut: Greenwood Press, 1988

Girgus, Sam B., *The New Covenant: Jewish Writers and the American Idea*, Chapel Hill: University of North Carolina Press, 1984

Guttmann, Allen, *The Jewish Writer in America: Assimilation and the Crisis of Identity*, New York: Oxford University Press, 1971

Harap, Louis, *Creative Awakening: The Jewish Presence in Twentieth-Century American Literature, 1990–1940s*, Westport, Connecticut: Greenwood Press, 1987

Harap, Louis, *In the Mainstream: The Jewish Presence in Twentieth Century American Literature, 1950s–1980s*, Westport, Connecticut: Greenwood Press, 1987

Harap, Louis, *Dramatic Encounters: The Jewish Presence in Twentieth Century American Drama, Poetry and Humor and the Black-Jewish Literary Relationship*, Westport, Connecticut: Greenwood Press, 1987

Pinsker, Sanford, *Jewish-American Fiction, 1917–1987*, New York: Twayne, 1992
Sherman, Bernard, *The Invention of the Jew: Jewish-American Education Novels, 1916–1964*, New York: Thomas Yoseloff, 1969
Walden, Daniel (ed.), "Jewish Women Writers and Women in Jewish Literature" issue of *Studies in American Jewish Literature*, 3, 1983

Jewish-American literature is a major form of twentieth-century writing, which reached its highest achievement in the fictional form after World War II. Although many of its best-known practitioners are not entirely happy with the label "Jewish-American writer", thinking it reductive, the term does describe a particular kind of writing with notable concerns and themes. Two prominent authors associated with the genre were awarded the Nobel Prize for Literature – Saul Bellow (1976), and Isaac Bashevis Singer (1978).

SHERMAN's monograph is particularly good in its analysis of Jewish-American writing from World War II to the mid-1960s. He sees the central type of Jewish-American novel as the *Bildungsroman*, the novel of education – in particular that of a "youth's initiation into the adult world and, second as a rhetorical device to carry out an examination of social conditions". This "initiation" mirrors the experience of American Jewry, with its movement from the isolated *shtelt* (East European Jewish village) to America.

Though becoming somewhat dated, GUTTMANN's study remains one of the best introductions to Jewish-American writing. Taking what are two of the most important themes in this literature – assimilation and identity crises – the author discusses their appearance and development from the literature's beginnings with Emma Lazarus, Mary Antin, and Abraham Cahan to Saul Bellow. Brief but useful discussions on all the important writers within the genre, as well as discussions of historical and cultural issues, make this still a useful text.

In her study, BILIK attempts to distinguish between Jewish-American fiction written in the 1950s and 1960s, and what she refers to as the "new immigrant novel", which is concerned with the "post-Holocaust sensibility". This concern is not with an assimilator, but with an immigrant shaped by the events of 1939–45, whether or not he is a survivor. This figure, thought by some critics to have disappeared from Jewish-American fiction, is usually a saintly man, who acts as a "teacher and moral example to others". He preserves traditions and can be seen in the works of Edward Lewis Wallant, Singer, Bellow, and Bernard Malamud, among others. This is an interesting perspective on some more recent characters in Jewish-American fiction.

WALDEN has collected 20 essays in this issue of the periodical *Studies in American Jewish Literature*. Writing both by, and about, Jewish women has existed for more than a century, and in these essays a wide range of topics and authors is discussed and analysed. The general perspective revealed is of the restrictions experienced by women from European and immigrant Orthodoxy, followed by their easing in terms of lifestyle and literary expression.

GIRGUS develops the idea that the Jewish experience of persecution, and the value placed upon justice in Judaism, has caused Jewish writers to be very attracted by American values – to make them their own, to propagate and defend them, to try to "interpret America to herself". Like the Puritans before them, Jewish writers and intellectuals have used the jeremiad, "preaching to the people to understand the meaning of America". Thus, Jewish-American writers have taken on a prophetic role in America. This is an interesting thesis, cleverly developed.

HARAP's three volumes comprise a most impressive survey of both Jewish-American literature and of the treatment of Jews in the writings of non-Jewish authors. Historical and cultural, as well as literary, issues are discussed, with each volume treating its period or topic in a similar manner, thus creating a continuity between the three. There are critical discussions of the texts and biographical details of the authors. The writing is placed within literary and historical contexts, with literature being viewed as both an artistic and social phenomenon, an approach particularly appropriate to the treatment of Jews in literature.

FRIED has collected 18 essays on various aspects of Jewish writing in America. In addition to the expected pieces on fiction, drama, and poetry, there are discussions of Yiddish literature and criticism, as well as of the effects of the Holocaust and Zionism on American Jewish writers. The relationship of American Jewish literature to other cultures and literatures is discussed, with the collection as a whole covering virtually all areas and issues relevant to the field.

PINSKER, aware of Harap's attempt at comprehensiveness, does not pretend to be writing a *magnum opus*. He has selected certain authors and works, which, he feels, are representative, and through judicious analysis of works and social/cultural movements attempts to show the development of Jewish-American literature from its beginnings to "international importance". The task is somewhat too large for the book's brief format, but the writing is lively, and many of the major issues raised in this literature are discussed.

EDWARD A. ABRAMSON

Jhabvala, Ruth Prawer 1927–

German-born American novelist, short-story writer, and screenwriter

Cronin, Richard, *Imagining India*, London: Macmillan, 1989; New York: St Martin's Press, 1989
Gooneratne, Yasmine, *Silence, Exile and Cunning: The Fiction of Ruth Prawer Jhabvala*, New Delhi: Orient Longman, 1983; London: Sangam Books, 1983
Jha, Rekha, *The Novels of Kamala Markandaya and Ruth Prawer Jhabvala: A Study in East-West Encounter*, New Delhi: Prestige, 1990
Long, Robert Emmet, *The Films of Merchant Ivory*, London: Viking, 1992; New York: Abrams, 1991
Rubin, David, *After the Raj: British Novels of India since 1947*, Hanover, New Hampshire: University Press of New England, 1986
Sucher, Laurie, *The Fiction of Ruth Prawer Jhabvala: The Politics of Passion*, London: Macmillan, 1989; New York: St Martin's Press, 1989

As a Polish-German-Jewish refugee, with British citizenship (from 1948), an Indian (Parsi) husband, residence in New York, and now American citizenship, Ruth Prawer Jhabvala exemplifies in her life the trans-nationality of many postcolonial writers. As a result she has been approached from a variety of perspectives.

GOONERATNE's volume, the first substantial study, is the best starting-point for any critical appreciation of Jhabvala's work. Essentially a general and comprehensive overview, the book has not dated appreciably in more than ten years and remains essential reading. Gooneratne proceeds on a novel-by-novel basis, with chapters also treating the short fiction and the film-scripts. The study benefits from interviews, personal correspondence, and a wide knowledge of Jhabvala's early reception.

In a more narrowly focused, but penetrating, feminist study, SUCHER takes her cue from John Updike's description of Jhabvala as an "initiated outsider" in her account of sexual politics in her fiction. Politics in the more general sense is therefore somewhat lacking, with more attention paid to Jhabvala's Jewish background and her themes of exile and disinheritance, than to the postcolonial – or even the Indian – context. After a brief survey of the early work, Sucher opts for close study of four novels (*A New Dominion*, *Heat and Dust*, *In Search of Love and Beauty*, and *Three Continents*) with some related short stories (a particularly fine reading of "Desecration"). The major thrust of her argument concerns Jhabvala's transmutation of the hothouse atmosphere of sexuality into its comic opposite and then back again, as gothic deflates into – and out of – comedy. Sucher establishes Jhabvala's major concern as "right interpretation" of deceiving circumstances, with her techniques of understatement and telling omission compelling the reader to interpret the clues.

Several critics concern themselves with the vexed relationship between Jhabvala and European traditions. As her subtitle suggests, JHA examines the encounter between East and West – whether political, religious, socio-economic, or philosophical – in a comparative study of the novels of Jhabvala and Kamala Markandaya. Although essentially descriptive and thematic, the volume includes a particularly useful chapter on the two novelists' handling of the English language. Jhabvala emerges as more successful than Markandaya in the treatment of her Indian characters' expression. RUBIN, however, is less sympathetic, arguing that far from being an Indian novelist, Jhabvala merely continues the traditions of the colonial British novelists of the half-century preceding Indian independence, particularly in her participation in the myth of India as sexual destroyer. Rubin discusses all the major works up to *In Search of Love and Beauty*, offering a fairly harsh reading, but one which later critics will have to take into account.

CRONIN's is an important study, also elucidating links between Jhabvala and her predecessors, in this case E.M. Forster, whose liberal-humanist creed of the primacy of personal relations is thoroughly revised in *Heat and Dust*. Cronin's detailed and scholarly account of the parallels between Forster's *The Hill of Devi* and Jhabvala's best-known novel is indispensable to any later readings.

No understanding of Jhabvala's work could be complete without an awareness of her other creative career as screenwriter, in partnership with James Ivory and Ismail Merchant. LONG provides a fascinating account of the films made by the trio, lavishly illustrated with stills, and drawing on interviews with all concerned. After a biographical sketch of each of the threesome, Long proceeds chronologically, film by film, covering such topics as finance, differences in opinion over the scripts, and practical difficulties on location. The discussion of the influence of film on Jhabvala's fictional technique is illuminating, particularly in relation to the progression from the film of *Autobiography of a Princess* to *Heat and Dust* (novel), and thence to *Heat and Dust* (film).

JUDIE NEWMAN

Johnson, Samuel 1709–1784

English lexicographer, essayist, critic, and poet

Alkon, Paul, *Samuel Jonson and Moral Discipline*, Evanston, Illinois: Northwestern University Press, 1967

Bate, Walter Jackson, *The Achievement of Samuel Johnson*, London and New York: Oxford University Press, 1955

Bate, Walter Jackson, *Samuel Johnson*, New York: Harcourt Brace Jovanovich, 1977; London: Chatto & Windus, 1978

Bronson, Bertrand, "The Double Tradition of Dr Johnson", in *English Literary History*, 18, June 1951; reprinted in his *"Johnson Agonistes" and Other Essays*, Berkeley: University of California Press, 1965

DeMaria, Robert, Jr., *The Life of Samuel Johnson: A Critical Biography*, Oxford and Cambridge, Massachusetts: Blackwell, 1993

Fussell, Paul, *Samuel Johnson and the Life of Writing*, New York: Harcourt Brace Jovanovich, 1971; London: Chatto & Windus, 1972

Greene, Donald, *The Politics of Samuel Johnson*, New Haven, Connecticut: Yale University Press, 1960; 2nd edition, Athens: University of Georgia Press, 1989

Greene, Donald, *Samuel Johnson*, New York: Twayne, 1970, revised 1989

Hagstrum, Jean H., *Samuel Johnson's Literary Criticism*, Minneapolis: University of Minnesota Press, 1952; 2nd edition, Chicago: University of Chicago Press, 1967

Kernan, Alvin, *Printing Technology: Letters and Samuel Johnson*, Princeton, New Jersey: Princeton University Press, 1987, reprinted as *Samuel Johnson and the Impact of Print*, 1989

Woodman, Thomas, *A Preface to Samuel Johnson*, London and New York: Longman, 1993

It was his writings, of course, that made Johnson famous in his own lifetime – his *Rambler* essays, his *Dictionary*, and his literary criticism and scholarship. Ironically, after Johnson's death, James Boswell's great biography had the effect of concentrating so much attention on Johnson the man that his works were neglected in comparison. Later Johnson came to be thought of as no more than a great English eccentric or misinterpreted as a reactionary dogmatist. A great deal of criticism and scholarship has been devoted to Johnson this century, and he has been recognised again as a great writer as well as a great man. T.S. Eliot and F.R. Leavis were among those who praised the criticism and the poetry (especially the *Vanity of Human Wishes*), and W.K. Wimsatt's careful studies showed that Johnson's prose style was highly precise rather than long-winded and over-elaborate. The 1950s marked the real beginning of a modern understanding of Johnson's thought, a radical reinterpretation based on the recognition that, contrary to the popular misconception, *experience* rather than abstraction and theory was at its heart.

The discrepancy between the popular and the scholarly view of Johnson is the subject of BRONSON's fine essay, which also serves as a brief introduction for those still under the influence of the old ideas. Bronson shows that the main source of the popular stereotype is Thomas Babington Macaulay's Victorian vulgarisation of Boswell. Even the academic tradition down-played Johnson the writer for many years, but by the time Bronson was writing that had changed considerably. Johnson's conservatism had come to be seen in relation to the violent, even radical, side of his temperament, so that we gain the impression of "energy . . . controlled only by determined and unremitting effort". Johnson's literary criticism had also been rediscovered at a time when it was "romantic" values that were more likely to be questioned. None of these academic labours had much effect, however, as Bronson wryly notes, on the popular view, and even to this day very few of those, for example, who visit Johnson's houses in London and Lichfield have ever read any of the works.

HAGSTRUM's book is one of the first full-length products of the revisionist view of Johnson. As he says, Johnson's forceful expression has made him seem dogmatic and he has been presented as the last voice of an outmoded neoclassical criticism. Yet his real intellectual affinities lie with a distinctively English scientific and philosophic tradition associated with Francis Bacon and John Locke, which emphasises experiment and experience. This clearly has implications, which go far beyond literary criticism, and Hagstrum's first chapter, a survey of Johnson's attitude to reason and experience, is one of the best introductions to Johnson's thought. Obviously the book also makes a major contribution to the revival of interest in Johnson's literary criticism as such, and Hagstrum demonstrates that the literary theories and rules that Johnson espoused themselves arise from concrete experience, not authority. The positive criterion of "Nature", for example, is not an abstract, but a norm based on the broad stream of human behaviour. Equally the idea of morality in literature, which many readers feel Johnson over-emphasises, can never be completely divorced from its corollary, pleasure.

BATE is another critic who takes Johnson's ideas with complete seriousness and shows why they still *matter*. Though Johnson has always been understood to be a moralist, this was usually interpreted in a didactic and dogmatic way. Bate's great contribution (1955) is to show that Johnson does not write prescriptively but analytically, probing the roots of human motivation with subtle psychology. He traces three central themes in Johnson – the "hunger of the imagination", the "treachery of the human heart", and the "stability of truth". The first is the perception that nothing we grasp in the present moment is ever sufficient to satisfy us: this is why we seek novelty, and it also lies behind the whole "vanity of human wishes", the fact that even when our wishes come true they fail to bring us fulfilment. The "treachery of the human heart" is Johnson's rich analysis of all our mechanisms of self-deception and self-defence, an account which strikingly anticipates Freud's, but which is also both comic in its own way and highly compassionate. The next chapter shows that, despite his awareness of all our baser motives and our inevitable disappointments, Johnson still believes we must turn outwards to activity and reality. In the final chapter Bate, like Hagstrum, shows that Johnson's literary criticism transcends technicalities and relates to the empirical thrust of his thought as a whole.

BATE's 1975 study expands on these earlier insights, and has been recognised as one of the greatest literary biographies of the twentieth century. It is both an extremely comprehensive account of Johnson's life and times and a detailed critical analysis of all his works, but it is especially remarkable for Bate's psychological grasp of its complex subject. He is able to strike the difficult balance of empathising with Johnson's sufferings and struggles while at the same time recognising that he *transcends* his subjective difficulties to become of central moral significance both in his life and his work. Johnson, says Bate eloquently, gives us "the precious gift of hope", proving, against great obstacles, that it is "possible to get through this strange adventure of life and to do it in a way that it is a tribute to human nature".

GREENE's work on Johnson's politics (1960, revised 1989) is one of the most important revisionist studies, since the idea of Johnson's "bigoted and unbending Toryism" has been one of the most tenacious obstacles to appreciation. Green shows that the simple Whig/Tory antithesis is a product of oversimplified historiography. Eighteenth-century "Toryism" covers a variety of different ideologies and groupings, and Johnson's version was an oppositionist, anti-establishment creed for much of his life. These points are substantiated in a detailed chronological analysis, which pays particular attention to Johnson's neglected political journalism, where his humanitarian, anti-militarist, and anti-colonialist stance is readily apparent. Even his support for George III's governments, Green argues, is far from "subservient and uncritical". There are elements of special pleading in this section as elsewhere, and the book has recently been attacked by J.C.D. Clark; but there is no doubt that Greene dealt the death-blow to the old oversimplifications.

GREENE's 1970 general study remains one of the best introductions to the whole range of Johnson and his achievements, and it is constantly enlivened by Greene's own special concerns. He reasserts firmly in his Preface, for example, that Boswell must not be taken as the final authority on Johnson, and this has become a commonplace of modern scholarship. Greene provides an excellent guide to Johnson's poetry, his moral writings, including *Rasselas*, his achievements as a biographer and as a critic and writer on language, and he also devotes a whole chapter to the wide variety of journalism and occasional writing, arguing that "no student of Johnson should remain satisfied with a knowledge merely of his major works". The whole book illustrates Greene's passionate conviction of what he terms, in his conclusion, the "modernity of Samuel Johnson".

ALKON greatly deepens understanding of Johnson's moral teaching by situating it in its intellectual context and analysing the combination of old and new in his work. He begins with a systematic analysis of Johnson's views on human nature and its various faculties. He goes on to demonstrate that although

Johnson is very influenced by more naturalist and empirical thought he uses the new ideas in the service of traditional moral values. He has an especially sharp sense of our tendency towards self-delusion, and the attempt to remove the obstacles this produces is at the heart of the moral discipline he seeks to encourage. Ultimately, it is clear, Johnson's aims are Christian ones; but there is a great deal of commonsense temporal concern as well. It is time, Alkon argues, for Johnson to be taken seriously as a "moral philosopher", who creates an "imposing intellectual edifice that combines a tough-minded theory of human nature with a clear sense of moral imperatives".

FUSSELL's exciting survey treats Johnson's life and writings in the light of his conception of literature. After a short, lively, and sympathetic account of Johnson's life, Fussell goes on to analyse his double-sided, and in some respects, contradictory attitude to literature – rhetorical, with a strong sense of the impersonality of art on the one hand, and on the other hand "sacramental", with a sincere religious dedication. Fussell then surveys some of the chief categories of Johnson's writing – the *Rambler*, for example (which is often neglected by students), and the relationship between its mode of composition and its themes; the *Dictionary*, a fascinating project, the importance and excitement of which Fussell conveys; and the *Lives of the Poets*. These latter, a fitting climax to Johnson's "life of writing", are seen finely here as illustrating the fundamental "irony of literary careers", the way that all the greatest achievements of the human mind are menaced by our simultaneous "impulse to delusion, triviality, incompetence, vanity, sloth and plain stupidity". This is a readable and humane introduction to Johnson, constantly illuminated by apt modern parallels without any pretence that his preconceptions are the same as ours.

KERNAN presents a striking case for Johnson's modernity in one particular but crucial context – his relationship to the print revolution. The new technology made a vast impact on the literary and intellectual world, but this took a long time to establish itself, and it was not until the eighteenth century that the effects were widely disseminated. Johnson, in Kernan's view, "stands out as perhaps the only writer of stature" in the period "who fully understood, acknowledged, and consciously acted upon an awareness that print was now inescapably the primary fact of letters". He proudly accepts his role as a professional writer and dismisses the old system of aristocratic patronage. He plays a major role in the age of print with his edition of Shakespeare, his *Dictionary*, and his history of poetry in the *Lives of the Poets*. Above all, he becomes a very powerful example of the new figure of the "Author as Hero", who makes meaning in the face of scepticism and emptiness.

My own book (WOODMAN's) is intended as an introduction to Johnson and his works for students and the general reader. Following the usual format of the "Preface" series, I begin with a short biography of Johnson and then describe his intellectual background: his attitudes to philosophy, morality, and religion, and how the ways in which the traditional ideas he continued to espouse were influenced by the new science and psychology of the time, which – broadly speaking – he welcomed. The book goes on to examine Johnson's politics and his surprisingly positive attitude to one of the most important social developments of his period, the rise of a commercial society. The next sections survey Johnson's literary background, his relationship to neo-classicism, his attitudes to contemporary writing, and his views and work on language. Part II consists of a detailed examination and explication of a series of extracts intended to illustrate the wide range of Johnson's achievement. The study concludes with a reference section, which is made up of brief notes on people who were important to Johnson and some suggestions for further reading in the wide realms of Johnson criticism and scholarship.

DeMARIA gives us an ambitious attempt at a new synthesis. This is primarily an intellectual history rather than a biography as such (like Bate's), and its central argument in a sense goes against the grain of much of what has been said of Johnson's modernity, presenting him as essentially a late-European Renaissance writer, who was forced to accept the new conditions of his time and found great difficulty in doing so. The book overstates this central thesis, but it is packed with interesting ideas and references to recent work. Contemporary literary theory as such has made very little impact on Johnson criticism as yet, but De Maria's book shows the continuing value of more traditional approaches and the great vitality of modern Johnson studies.

THOMAS WOODMAN

Jolley, Elizabeth 1923 –

Australian novelist, short-story writer, and radio dramatist

Bird, Delys, and Brenda Walker (eds.), *Elizabeth Jolley: New Critical Essays*, North Ryde, New South Wales: Angus & Robertson, 1991

Jones, Dorothy, "The Goddess, the Artist and the Spinster", in *Westerly*, 29(4), 1984

Kirkby, Joan, "The Call of the Mother in the Fiction of Elizabeth Jolley", in *Span*, 26, 1988

Riemer, Andrew, "Between Two Worlds: An Approach to Elizabeth Jolley's Fiction", in *Southerly*, 43(3), 1983

Salzman, Paul, *Helplessly Tangled in Female Arms and Legs: Elizabeth Jolley's Fictions*, St Lucia: University of Queensland Press, 1993

Although Elizabeth Jolley's work gained immediate critical attention when it was published after years of rejection – her first book, a collection of short fiction, "*Five Acre Virgin*" *and Other Stories*, appeared in 1976 – and she quickly achieved a national, then an international, critical reputation, to date only one book-length critical study and one edited collection of critical essays on her has been published, although at least two further critical monographs are being written at present (1995). Journal articles and interviews with Jolley still comprise the most significant body of criticism about her work, and those cited here represent important areas of interpretation, and have themselves been influential. Jolley's writing is notable for its resistance to any single critical paradigm and for its simultaneous awareness and parody of contemporary literary hermeneutics. Indeed, Salzman opens his study of Jolley's fiction by noting that "Elizabeth Jolley often subjects the whole process of literary interpretation to satirical scrutiny". Jolley has a high public presence in Australia's cultural life, attested to, or perhaps generated by, the unusual number of published interviews and personal profiles. Not surprisingly a persistent tendency in much Jolley criticism is to read the fiction in terms of the known facts of her life and her published opinions, an irony in relation to writing that deliberately evades critical definitions.

RIEMER wrote the earliest academic criticism of Jolley's fiction, and has remained a significant presence in the field, having published a series of articles and statements on her work. The article cited here was his first, taking up the important theme of migration and exile which he and other critics continue to focus on in different ways. Riemer argues that most of Jolley's major characters are "displaced persons", "to a greater or lesser extent isolated, perplexed, trapped within a society or an institution which seems a temporary residence or imprisonment". Such displacement is not necessarily treated negatively. Riemer's criticism exemplifies traditional readings of Jolley as a cultural icon, writing within a history of Western humanist values. The crucial question of why Jolley's work was ignored by publishers for so long, then so rapidly accepted, preoccupies many critics. Riemer contends "that we were not ready . . . to acknowledge a voice as individual as hers, or literary preoccupations emerging from a quite remarkable mixture or crossing of cultural allegiances".

JONES and KIRKBY have each published articles on Jolley from a feminist perspective, an approach that has been particularly significant in relation to Jolley's work, with its interest in the possibilities of female sexuality and creativity as well as with the inscription of the feminine within discourse. However, Jolley's work is also resistant to criticism that claims it as "feminist". Kirkby uses a Kristevan psychoanalytical framework to interpret the constructions of woman she perceives in the text, dealing, for example, with the representation of motherhood using Kristeva's notion of the abject. While rewarding, this critical mode disallows any conceptualisation of the feminine except as repressed. Jones's work is representative of a less rigidly schematised feminist critical enterprise, part of an interpretive practice that is more alert to the possibilities of a celebratory, if unconventional, presentation of women's lives in Jolley's writing. Jolley's use of land as a metaphor of belonging has drawn much critical comment, and it is feminised in Jones's article.

The 17 critical essays edited in my (BIRD) and WALKER's collection aim to demonstrate both the strength and variety of responses to Jolley's fiction. From Australian, American, British, and Continental-European critics, who use a range of theoretical paradigms, the essays refer to many of the dominant preoccupations of Jolley criticism, including: scrutiny of the formal qualities of Jolley's work; its conscious fictivity; the yoking of humanist sentiment with parody and irony; the theme of exile, with its accompanying expressions of location and dislocation; the traditional Western cultural inheritance on which Jolley draws in her use of biblical sources, music, and classical, German, and English literature; and a concern with women's lives and sexuality, including sometimes an interest in the representation of lesbian experience, as well as in the problematics of mother/daughter and father/daughter relationships. The collection presents a diversity of critical opinion and approach, and includes a bibliography of all Jolley's writings, including articles, reviews and selected interviews, to that time. The short introduction to the bibliography refers to the impossibility of "dating" Jolley's work, or of seeing it in terms of a progression: its effect is described as "kaleidoscopic", and it is noted, for instance, that "drafts of *My Father's Moon* and *Cabin Fever* were actually the first novels she wrote".

In a short, but dense and very comprehensive, study, SALZMAN begins with an exploration of critical opinion of Jolley's work, which has been divided between traditional humanist readings, which praise the work for its validation of compassion, love, and universalising value systems, and newer, postmodernist approaches, which seek out its parodic playfulness, its transgressive and meta-fictional qualities. Salzman advocates neither of these totalising interpretative practices. Instead, his solution is to develop a criticism that is as flexible and multifaceted as its subject is: "to offer a series of different critical perspectives on aspects of Jolley's work, without demanding a final view of Jolley as either the disruptive postmodernist or the life-enhancing creator of characters in search of selves". Salzman's insightful criticism, broadly poststructuralist, is often directed through an exploration of the theme of desire in all its possibilities in the works. He proceeds not by readings of individual fictions, but through topics, using illustrations from many of Jolley's writings and from much of the criticism that accompanies it.

DELYS BIRD

Jonson, Ben 1572–1637

English dramatist, poet, and prose writer

Barton, Anne, *Ben Jonson: Dramatist*, Cambridge and New York: Cambridge University Press, 1984

Cave, Richard Allen, *Ben Jonson*, London: Macmillan, 1991

Duncan, Douglas, *Ben Jonson and the Lucianic Tradition*, Cambridge and New York: Cambridge University Press, 1979

Helgerson, Richard, *Self-Crowned Laureates: Spenser, Jonson, Milton and the Literary System*, Berkeley: University of California Press, 1983

Knights, L.C., *Drama and Society in the Age of Jonson*, London: Chatto & Windus, 1937; New York: G.W. Stewart, 1937

Norbrook, David, *Poetry and Politics in the English Renaissance*, London and Boston: Routledge, 1984

Orgel, Stephen, *The Jonsonian Masque*, New York: Columbia University Press, 1981

Parfitt, George, *Ben Jonson: Public Poet and Private Man*, London: Dent, 1976; New York: Barnes & Noble, 1977

Riggs, David, *Ben Jonson: A Life*, Cambridge, Massachusetts: Harvard University Press, 1989

Womack, Peter, *Ben Jonson*, Oxford: Blackwell, 1986

Ben Jonson has suffered relative neglect, partly because of his proximity to Shakespeare in the chronological canon of English Literature, and partly because of his self-styling as a learned poet whose work looks back to classical literary models. As Barton has pointed out, Jonson was damned with faint praise by John Dryden, who wrote that he admired Jonson but loved Shakespeare, and, to a large extent, this evaluation has been shared generally.

RIGGS argues in his highly readable and scholarly biography that Jonson had two distinct and opposite sides to his character: the reckless and excessive personality of "a drunken, swaggering, murderous sponge who gained his livelihood by writing libellous plays and flattering poems" has to be set against the "modest" individual whose sole aim was to curb such extravagance and promote the qualities of "plainness, moderation, and sober rationality" in his life and literature. Riggs' book is a mixture of social and intellectual history (an attempt to fit Jonson's public art into his period) and psychological biography (an attempt to gain an insight into the writer's private creative process). Jonson's life, according to Riggs, was dominated by his social and literary ambition: in his satirical comedies, "Jonson simultaneously released his pent-up aggressions and reconstituted himself as a man of letters, a leading figure in the literary avant-garde of Renaissance England". Overall, "Jonson's writings reveal the malcontent troublemaker, astute careerist, and literary artist to be one and the same person".

Riggs' book owes a great deal to the pioneering work of HELGERSON, who argues that Jonson reinvented the conception of an English poetic laureateship, modelling his career on Horace (rather than Virgil, as Edmund Spenser, the only previous poet with similar ambition to Jonson, had done). According to Helgerson, Jonson tried to fashion himself as a good man able to criticise the ills of society in his literary works, a satirical stance that clashed with his designs of grandness by positioning him too close to the world of vice he was trying to correct. As a result, in plays such as *Cynthia's Revels* and *Poetaster*, Jonson showed more concern for his own virtue than a desire to correct the vices of others. Similarly, in his poetry, Jonson constructed an image of himself – the poet – as a figure of constancy in contrast to the vicissitudes of the world. In choosing to write masques for the court, he had to convince his contemporaries that the form could carry the *gravitas* of the epic and would not consist of simple flattery, an enterprise that was not always successful.

BARTON perceives the same conflict of interests as Riggs. Her study emphasises the importance of the central Jacobean comedies, but also provides important re-evaluations of the neglected Caroline comedies *The New Inn* and *A Tale of the Tub*. Barton suggests that Jonson's plays can best be read as a developing sequence, and she emphasises the playfulness of Jonson's work, arguing that in *Volpone*, while the central character "cannot be forgiven . . . our indulgence sets Volpone free". Barton also has a useful chapter on Jacobean and Caroline nostalgia for the reign of Elizabeth.

Less scholarly and more student-orientated is CAVE, who concentrates upon the theatricality of Jonson's work, commenting that "Jonson's initial tactic is frequently to remind an audience precisely where it is and why". According to Cave a relaxed audience was anathema for Jonson, who sought to challenge the beliefs of playgoers through his dramatic technique and force them to make judgements about performance beyond the duration of the play itself. Cave asserts that, despite his reputation for pedantry, "Jonson is the most flamboyantly theatrical of Renaissance dramatists", while employing a wider range of styles than Shakespeare because he responded to changing fashions and wrote for a number of different playing spaces, audiences, and theatrical companies. Cave tries to restore the reputation of *Sejanus, His Fall* as a major tragedy, arguing that at its conclusion the audience is tempted to laugh as the evil Tiberius destroys his unlovely enemies, but feels uncomfortable because to do so would be to be complicit with his underhand strategies.

KNIGHTS has largely been superseded by more recent research and so should be used with caution. Nevertheless, this is still a useful study of Jonson's plays in their historical context, providing useful information on enclosure and the transfer of land ownership from aristocratic to merchant hands, and the development of capitalist finance. Knights situates Jonson in terms of "the anti-acquisitive tradition inherited from the Middle Ages", claiming that his English style is not "polite", but rather "sprang from the wisdom of the common people", so that Jonson remains "one of the main channels of communication with an almost vanished tradition". Knights provides stimulating readings of *Volpone*, *The Devil is an Ass*, and *The Staple of News*, and his book also serves as a useful corrective to those who see Jonson simply as a learned, aristocratic writer.

DUNCAN is a scholarly yet highly readable analysis of Jonson's debt to a vitally important classical tradition. Lucian's legacy was the *joco-serium*, the art of being serious in play, and a crucial influence on the work of Erasmus and Sir Thomas More, as well as on sixteenth-century dramatic forerunners of Jonson such as Henry Medwall and Christopher Marlowe. Duncan reads Jonson's most critically acclaimed comedies – *Volpone*, *The Alchemist*, *Epicoene*, and *Bartholomew Fair* – in terms of this tradition of writing, concluding that Jonson sought to transform the role of the theatre into a humanist literary practice, "by making it a proving-ground of virtue", where the audience was asked uncomfortable moral questions and forced to make difficult judgements.

ORGEL is a crucial work, both in terms of Jonson scholarship and in terms of recent critical interest in the masque. He shows how Jonson adapted the masque form in order to incorporate the monarch, James I, into the spectacle, and also made the structure of the performance more sophisticated by developing the role of the anti-masque, which "set up a problem for which the masque was a solution". Both advances in technique reflected Jonson's absolutism and belief in James' conception of the divine rights of kings: Jonson frequently contrasted the anti-masque world of "particularity and mutability" with the masque world of "ideal abstractions and eternal verities". Orgel concludes that the masque enabled Jonson to perfect his idea of theatre as "unmediated confrontation of actor and spectator", something not possible in the playhouse. In *The Vision of Delight*, James himself became the centre of the masque: "it was of course about him, but also, in a purely physical sense, he was the chief viewer: only from his chair did the perspective of the stage achieve its proper effect".

NORBROOK is the most significant study of the literature and politics in the sixteenth and seventeenth centuries to be published in recent years. Norbrook emphasises Jonson's anti-republican politics and growing hatred of the marketplace of the popular stage. Jonson, according to Norbrook, conceived of the state as a work of art and the duty of a work of art to serve the state. His collection of verse, *The Forest*, significantly referred to the area in which the King could hunt, so that the published collection of poetry and the process of enclosure were equated. Jonson hoped for a new age of moral poetry, valued hierarchy and stability, and vigorously opposed radical Protestant literature.

PARFITT is a useful and straightforward study of the drama (plays and masques), prose, and criticism, and provides a comprehensive overview. Parfitt writes well about the relationship between knowledge and virtue in Jonson's thought, showing how he tempered a desire to be prescriptive with a tough realism, notably in the portrait of the good but insipid Celia and Bonario in *Volpone*, who survive simply because the more attractive bad figures destroy themselves. There is a good analysis of *Discoveries* and William Drummond's *Conversations*.

WOMACK is a far more radical and provocative study, which adopts a sophisticated, theoretically informed approach. Womack discusses questions of language games, carnival and misrule, oral and literate culture, and questions of audience and authority, using ideas propounded by Mikhail Bakhtin, Walter Ong, Antonin Artaud, Marx, and others. Womack divides his book up into topical headings – "Speaking", "Characters", "Languages", "Theatre" – in order to show how certain themes and socio-literary practices occur throughout Jonson's writing. Womack argues that Jonson is a far more disruptive writer than Shakespeare: whereas in the latter's comedies "marital resolution makes a harmony of language and nature through the healing fusion of institutional and creatural categories, Jonson's coercive unmaskings fix a sceptical space between words and things". Womack's analysis of literary characterisation in early-modern England should be essential reading for any student of Jonson.

ANDREW HADFIELD

Journalism and Literature in Britain

Adburgham, Alison, *Women in Print: Writing Women and Women's Magazines from the Restoration to the Accession of Victoria*, London: Allen & Unwin, 1972

Boyce, George, James Curran, and Pauline Wingate (eds.), *Newspaper History: From the Seventeenth Century to the Present Day*, London: Constable, 1978; Beverly Hills, California: Sage, 1978

Brake, Laurel, *Subjugated Knowledges: Journalism, Gender and Literature in the Nineteenth Century*, London: Macmillan, 1994; New York: New York University Press, 1994

Curran, James, and Jean Seaton, *Power Without Responsibility: The Press and Broadcasting in Britain*, London: Fontana, 1981; 4th edition, London and New York: Fontana, 1991

Escott, T.H.S., *Masters of English Journalism: A Study of Personal Forces*, London: T. Fisher Unwin, 1911; reprinted, Westport, Connecticut: Greenwood Press, 1970

Gross, John, *The Rise and Fall of the Man of Letters: Aspects of English Literary Life since 1800*, London: Weidenfeld & Nicolson, 1969; New York: Macmillan, 1969; with new Introduction and Afterword, Harmondsworth, Middlesex: Penguin, 1991

Hartley, John, *Understanding News*, London and New York: Methuen, 1982

McNair, Brian, *News and Journalism in the UK: A Textbook*, London and New York: Routledge, 1994

Williams, Raymond, *The Long Revolution*, London: Chatto & Windus, 1961; New York: Columbia University Press, 1961

The subject of journalism alone is an enormous one, and the serious scholar will need to draw on works dealing with the history of the press, memoirs, and biographies, as well as the periodicals themselves. The emphasis of this article is on the interplay between literature and newspaper- and magazine-journalism. As an area of scholarly debate it has become more widespread recently, but is still outside the mainstream of English criticism. Much scholarly work on the press has been historical in slant, though more recently semiotic, content-analysis, and other critical approaches have been used to investigate the language of the media, in particular news reporting.

BOYCE, CURRAN, and WINGATE's study provides less an overarching "history" of British newspapers than a collection of essays by 20 writers on aspects of the press. It was however the first major work since H.R. Fox Bourne's 1887 history to attempt a comprehensive historical survey. Introductory articles challenge "certain hallowed themes" seen as common to most early historical accounts, and raise questions about the organisation and control of the press, and its relationship to British political, social, and cultural change. Such issues are further explored in case studies of institutions (e.g. Reuters), topics such as political caricature or the socialist press, and more general articles such as Anthony Smith's examination of factors which, over the centuries, influenced the practice of journalism, in particular the strength of its attachment to objectivity. One section gives chronologically arranged accounts of the "structure, ownership and control of the press" from 1620 to 1976. The bibliography is usefully divided into general histories, accounts of individual journals, and studies relating to particular historical periods.

ESCOTT was a journalist rather than a scholar, but the focus of his book, upon the history of the journalist rather than the journal, distinguishes it from early accounts of the newspaper press. For the modern reader his inclusion of material from his own experience and information supplied by many colleagues makes his lively account of early modern journalism still valuable. Escott saw the antecedents of the modern journalist as existing in classical Greece and Rome, and his respect for the Fourth Estate encouraged him to explore the development of journalism in Britain as much through its exponents who were also eminent writers (e.g., Daniel Defoe, Joseph Addison, Jonathan Swift, William Cobbett, John and Leigh Hunt, Charles Dickens) as through the work of those more shadowy newspapermen he sought to reclaim for posterity. For Escott, "the makers of the English newspaper were also the makers and the masters of English prose" and "the much-talked of antagonism between journalism and literature" did not exist. There are brief references to such women as Harriet Martineau and Eliza Linton. References to sources are sporadic. There is a useful index, but no bibliography.

GROSS uses the term "Men of Letters" in the sense it carried during the latter decades of the nineteenth century – "a critic, someone who aimed higher than journalism but made no pretence of being primarily an artist". He traces the changing role of the "middlemen of literature", the commentators, interpreters, and reviewers, from the founding of the *Edinburgh* to the 1980s, when he notes the functional division of the critic into "academic expert" and "mass media pundit". The lively, vivid account of English literary culture is told largely through a substantial gallery of figures, such as Francis Jeffrey, Matthew Arnold, Thomas Carlyle, Richard Hutton, Leslie Stephen, Edmund Gosse, and John Middleton Murry, through to Raymond Williams, F.R. Leavis, Cyril Connolly, and Geoffrey Grigson. The personalities, however, are always located within a broader discussion of developments within publishing, journalism, and political debate. There is a useful bibliography. It is a pity that in such an otherwise excellent account the masculine emphasis of the title (as with Escott) so fully reflects the emphasis of the text. Despite the considerable output of women reviewers and commentators during the period in question, only George Eliot receives serious consideration.

ADBURGHAM's readable and ground-breaking account aimed to rescue "from the limbo of forgotten publications" the magazines for women largely ignored by press historians, and foregrounds the early female journalists, especially those of the eighteenth century. Journals are viewed within their broader social and cultural contexts, and the women discussed range from businesswomen like Mrs Johnson, founder of the first Sunday newspaper, the journalists Mary Manley and Lady Blessington, to Aphra Behn the dramatist, and Mary Wells the actress. Adburgham's own background and her knowledge of fashion makes the chapters dealing with domestic features and women's clothing especially valuable. Periodicals mentioned in the text are listed in a chronological table.

Planned originally as a continuation of his earlier *Culture and Society*, WILLIAMS' now classic text is as much an expression of his own political and intellectual stance on the long cultural revolution he felt a part of, as it is a wide-ranging account of changes in English society since the late eighteenth century. His work was influential in drawing the attention of literary critics to the value of the study of popular literature and journalism, and his chapters on the reading public and the press offer a mass of factual information in small compass, as well as contributing to his thesis. References to sources are meagre, but Williams remains readable and challenging.

BRAKE's work addresses directly the way in which the "English literature" of academia became detached from "an alternative kind of writing for the common reader" called "journalism". The study of a range of individual periodicals is located within a continuing debate about the ways in which journalism has been "subjugated" by critics, and its interconnections with "literature" severed. She challenges what she regards as mistaken assumptions about the nature of Victorian literature by much modernist criticism – "that modes of production and circulation have little to do with textuality"; "that fiction is overwhelmingly the dominant genre of the time"; and that the text is isolated from its cultural context, with "the relegation of textuality to the high ground of aesthetics". The second part of the book centres on a different kind of "subjugation" – the gendered discourses of the Victorian press. Her theoretical stance gives the book a wider relevance than a period study implies.

While professional texts for journalism students are outside the scope of this essay, sociological and semiotic analyses, like historical surveys, often offer useful perspectives to the literary student. Such studies may be as much concerned with broadcasting as with the press. CURRAN's classic study and HARTLEY's textual analysis of form and content of British journalism are both accessible for students. McNAIR's overview of the frameworks within which British journalism currently operates is interesting for its well-referenced contemporary evidence from interviews with media professionals, and from journals and government publications.

BARBARA M. ONSLOW

See also **The Essay, Prose and Journalism**

Joyce, James 1882–1941

Irish novelist, short-story writer, and poet

Attridge, Derek (ed.), *The Cambridge Companion to James Joyce*, Cambridge and New York: Cambridge University Press, 1990

Bloom, Harold (ed.), *James Joyce*, New York: Chelsea House, 1986

Deming, Robert H. (ed.), *James Joyce: The Critical Heritage*, 2 vols., London: Routledge & Kegan Paul, 1970

Ellmann, Richard, *James Joyce*, Oxford and New York: Oxford University Press, 1959, revised 1982

French, Marilyn, *The Book as World: James Joyce's "Ulysses"*, Cambridge, Massachusetts: Harvard University Press, 1976

Hart, Clive, and David Hayman (eds.), *James Joyce's "Ulysses": Critical Essays*, Berkeley: University of California Press, 1974

Kenner, Hugh, *Ulysses*, London: Allen & Unwin, 1980; revised edition, Baltimore: Johns Hopkins University Press, 1987

Litz, A. Walton, *The Art of James Joyce: Method and Design in "Ulysses" and "Finnegans Wake"*, London and New York: Oxford University Press, 1961, revised 1964

Peake, Charles, *James Joyce: The Citizen and the Artist*, London: Edward Arnold, 1977; Stanford, California: Stanford University Press, 1977

Pierce, David, *James Joyce's Ireland*, New Haven, Connecticut: Yale University Press, 1992

Roughley, Alan, *James Joyce and Critical Theory: An Introduction*, London: Harvester Wheatsheaf, 1991

Senn, Fritz, *Joyce's Dislocutions: Essays on Reading as Translation*, edited by John Paul Riquelme, Baltimore: Johns Hopkins University Press, 1984

The aesthetic range, allusive density, formal novelty, and ethical complexity of James Joyce's fiction have brought into being a vast quantity of critical commentary and scholarly exegesis, the most important site of inquiry being *Ulysses*.

ELLMANN's biography is one of the most widely admired landmarks in postwar literary scholarship. Not only does it provide an exhaustive account of Joyce's complicated career and labyrinthine personality, it also contains much shrewd criticism. The manner in which the life is implicated in the work is a critical issue in coming to terms with Joyce's art, and this volume is intriguingly alert to the implication's numerous forensic and imaginative subtleties. This alertness is most clearly visible in the author's reading of Joyce's story "The Dead", where primary research data of an intimate and fugitive nature is married to cultural context and artistic strategy to form a sensitive and influential explication of an important text. Another aspect of the biography that has had important critical consequences, is the author's familiarity with Joyce's intellectual interests. The result has been a keener appreciation of Joyce's writings as tapestries of ideas and the consolidation of his internationalism. The biography's second – "new and revised" – edition contains "many corrections" and a "considerable amount of new information".

DEMING has provided an invaluable contribution to literary and cultural history in his compendium of early responses to Joyce's work. These responses not only chart in comprehensive detail the problematic reception of all of Joyce's fiction, but are also fascinating appendices to the long and challenging revolution in aesthetic sensibility and cultural values known as "modernism". The influence of Joyce's writings on the sociology and ideology of taste is an important aspect of that revolution. The volumes are arranged chronologically: the first covers the years 1902–27, the second 1928–41. The first volume opens with a small selection of biographical material by Joyce's Irish contemporaries, and goes on to reprint reviews of, and commentary on, all of Joyce's publications. Major English and American periodicals are the main sources for the material, although European publications are also cited, where relevant. Contributors include all the influential men of letters of the day. The supplementary commentary is provided by artists and scholars, and this material is not necessarily contemporaneous with the reviews. The editor notes that "the criticism and commentary and opinions presented in this volume are concerned, by and large, with Joyce's 'machinery' and only rarely with Joyce's vision". Essentially the same format and approach is used in the second volume: the contents do not reflect the burgeoning of academic interest in Joyce's work. Commentary from the years following Joyce's death focus on biographical records of the author. In all, this is an invaluable research tool.

ATTRIDGE has compiled a set of essays that "is offered as a first resort for those who wish to deepen and extend their enjoyment and understanding of Joyce's writing". The volume contains sophisticated readings of Joyce's works by recognised authorities. There are also a number of essays on the critical context. From the biographical standpoint, Joyce's status as virtually *the* definitive international author is underlined by three essays dealing with his Irish origins, his life in Paris, and his fundamental identification with European, rather than English, literature. The critical context is represented by essays that draw on such contemporary discourses as feminism and postmodernism. A useful chronology of Joyce's life and an extensive bibliography is also provided. By way of introduction, the editor has contributed an essay entitled "Reading Joyce", which makes an important case not only for the open, multi-layered nature of Joyce's fictional universe but also for the reader's readiness to encounter that universe in a dynamic, interactive, unpreconditioned manner.

BLOOM's collection of essays is a mixture of extracts from standard works in the canon of Joyce criticism and articles by emerging Joyce critics. In a sense, this volume may be regarded as a synopsis of academic Joyce criticism, the various tendencies in which are noted in the editor's Preface. Among the standard works excerpted are those by Ellmann (see above) and Kenner (see below). Younger critics invoke various aspects of poststructuralist methodology. All of Joyce's writings are covered, including his poetry and *Exiles;* there are also studies on the manuscript of *Ulysses*, and a number of different commentaries on Joyce's linguistic dimension. In a typically wide-ranging and provocative Introduction, the editor focuses on the significance of the Jewishness of Leopold Bloom. The volume contains a substantial bibliography and a chronology of Joyce's life.

PEAKE's study is aimed at the non-specialist reader, but Joyceans at every level have singled it out as one of the most accessible and balanced overviews of its subject. Drawing on earlier critics' identification of the "dialectical pattern" resulting from the interrelationship in Joyce's *oeuvre* between the artist and the citizen, the author enlarges the pattern's "complexities and ramifications". The critical discussion is anchored in a scrupulous use of Joyce's own statements about his artistic intentions and objectives, with a particularly sensitive and revealing use of Joyce's letters. Much of the work is devoted to *Ulysses*, and the claim that its "moral vision . . . is penetrating, substantial and coherent" is argued at length in an account of not only its "form and subordinate structures" but also in each individual chapter. Prior to the three chapters on *Ulysses*, there are equally attentive and level-headed treatments of *Dubliners* and *A Portrait of the Artist as a Young Man*. The study concludes with a brief chapter on *Finnegans Wake*, so that the author's aim of underlining "the developing continuity of Joyce's methods as well as of his vision" is realised.

ROUGHLEY describes his work as "an introduction and selective guide". Nevertheless, its range is formidable. While acknowledging that by no means all critical tendencies are covered, the most significant recent theoretical departures – structuralism, semiotics, feminism, Marxism, psychoanalysis, deconstruction – are discussed in the light of their impact on Joyce studies. Joyce's writings are particularly apt candidates for such a study, since "the history of Joyce studies can in some ways be seen as a microcosm of the historical development of critical theory and its application to literary texts". The concept of "historical development" is elaborated within the chapters examining each of the selected critical discourses. Thus, the chapter devoted to structuralist criticism examines the critical work of what are called "pre-structuralism structuralists", while, throughout, the works of specific critics within a given discourse are singled out for commentary. Among those critics are Umberto Eco, Terry Eagleton, Hélène

Cixous, and Jacques Derrida. The fundamental attraction between the theorists and Joyce's work is that the latter's formal, stylistic, and aesthetic properties represent what is considered to be its essentially subversive nature. Joyce's work calls into question so many of the conventions of literary art as to require theoretical intervention. By intervening, theory makes explicit some of the social, political, sexual, and cultural aspects of Joyce's work, thereby rendering unmistakable its worldly, post-lapsarian nature. Such an emphasis highlights the work's cunning, rather than the silence and exile in which it was executed, and which earlier critics thought indispensable to interpreting it.

PIERCE addresses an aspect of Joyce's life and art that critics frequently take for granted, in a work that is part biography, part illustrated guidebook to Joyce's Dublin, and part critical analysis. Of these, the second aspect is the most illuminating. The author's extensive researches have brought to light much documentary material, and this work is a handsome showcase for it. In view of the substantial amount of this material present in various forms throughout Joyce's fiction, it is valuable to have such an elaborately annotated album of them. The author's use of photographs, maps, and other pictorial items provide fascinating glimpses of the young Joyce's personal, social, and cultural milieux. But these items also silently underpin the work's other two elements. They add colour and novelty to the biographical data, and they provide a basis for the author's critical approach. The implicit emphasis is that of cultural materialism, and this is to a certain extent borne out by the author's treatment of such unfamiliar topics as Joyce and Victorian Ireland, Joyce as "a profoundly class-conscious writer", and Jewish culture in *Finnegans Wake*. A thorough chronology is provided, and there is an appendix containing thumbnail sketches of Joyce's Irish contemporaries and European associates.

The remainder of the books discussed here concentrate largely on *Ulysses*. FRENCH, herself a well-known novelist, has produced one of the more consistent and instructive of the large number of critical approaches to that work. Asserting that "only by focusing on style can the basic structuring principles of *Ulysses* be revealed", the study goes on to provide "a close, chapter-by-chapter reading of the text" in order to determine how the virtuosity of Joyce's verbal manoeuvres are in themselves a primary source of the epic novel's meaning. By "style", the author has more in mind than felicitous vocabulary: tone and point of view are also intrinsic to her conception of verbal fabric. This approach designates the reader as the proper Odysseus of *Ulysses*, and argues that the novel's epic qualities are exemplified by the reader's stylistic adventures. The experience of epic is constituted by two complementary journeys: one takes the reader into the external world of Dublin; the other takes the reader into the internal world of character. The interplay between these two journeys relativises the significance of each of them. It is this relativity that frames the fundamentally human scale of the novel. And it is in the novel's verbal sophistication that the experience of this relativity is primarily encoded.

HART and HAYMAN approach "the unified diversity" of *Ulysses* by asking 18 different critics to write on the novel's 18 different chapters. This focus on the novel's "multivalence" naturally results in a wide range of critical approaches and insights. All the major figures in American Joyce studies are represented. The editors point out that the contributions take a "novelistic" approach to *Ulysses*, by which they mean a concentration on such formal conventions as character and narrative development. Treatment of such matters as symbolic resonances and thematic richness is less to the fore ("much of *Ulysses* can be explained on the naturalistic level"). However, this work appeared at an important time in Joyce studies, when an essentially Anglo-American model of empirical inquiry was about to be challenged by criticism of a more frankly theoretical nature. Nevertheless, students encountering *Ulysses* for the first time will readily appreciate the resources of this volume's approach, particularly in its readings of the "Telemachus", "Wandering Rocks", "Nausicaa", "Oxen of the Sun", "Circe", and "Ithaca" chapters.

KENNER has also written a book that, with its deft weave of learning and wit, students will find helpful, all the more so since it may be regarded as the distillation of the thoughts of not only the author of numerous influential books and articles on Joyce, but also one of the foremost pioneers of the academic study of modernism. One of the author's particular areas of fascination is *Ulysses*' encyclopedic character. Despite the admission that "the book's quantity of interlocked detail is beyond reckoning", much ingenuity and originality is displayed in assessing the various ways in which Joyce deploys the data of everyday Dublin. This activity of assessment takes the form of locating a balance of probability on which critical judgment may rest. In this sense, the work is a comprehensive corrective to the tendency towards flightiness that has marked some Joyce criticism. Other important areas that engage the author's down-to-earth appreciation of *Ulysses*' unique but undeniable realism are those dealing with Joyce's use of Homer and the nature of the phenomenon known as "The Arranger". The manner in which the novel's Homeric parallels both particularise and universalise its characters – supplying them, by virtue of their literary antecedents, with what is tantamount to human nature – is detailed. The complicated critical construct known as "The Arranger" (a name which neither Joyce nor the author invented) refers to the tendency of the prose in the later section of the novel to radicalise its ostensible aims: here its presence is further complicated by the claim that it has a "latent" existence throughout. A bibliographical essay is included. The revised edition's citations are aligned with the pagination of the Gabler edition of *Ulysses*.

LITZ, also a pioneer of the teaching and study of modernism, has produced a study of the growth of Joyce's perception of his artistic task in both *Ulysses* and *Finnegans Wake*. The overall aim is to arrive at a sense of "Joyce's lifelong search for a form in which expression and substance are uniquely joined". Described as a "biography" of the two texts in question, this book is an original and influential excursion into Joyce's manuscripts. The conception of Joyce's methods of composition that emerges is one of a "mosaic", in which various manuscript sources – including drafts, notes, and letters – are shown to contribute to the final text. The revised edition contains a particularly illuminating addendum, in which raw materials are set alongside finished product, graphically supporting the author's claim that "no writer ever revised more carefully or used his rough notes and sketches more economically than Joyce". A valuable chronology of Joyce's works in progress, 1914–39, is included.

SENN's volume of essays collects a number of his more important writings on Joyce. Many of these explicate verbal and contextual conundrums in *Ulysses*, a procedure at which the author is an acknowledged master. The volume also contains more general considerations of problems raised by various Joyce texts. As a polygot Swiss, the author is particularly suited to hear Joyce's range of verbal and linguistic registers. Moreover, he is fully aware of approaching Joyce as a foreigner, and turns this cultural circumstance to his advantage. The nature of this advantage is suggested in the volume's subtitle, and the author develops it with impressive flexibility and resourcefulness:

> As a rule, foreign readers will deviate to that substitute for the original text that replaces each of its single items and turns the whole into quite a different arrangement of letters and sounds while pretending to retain somehow its soul or spirit ... In a much larger sense, everything Joyce wrote has to do with translation, is transferential.

Such a view emphasises two crucial and interrelated aspects of Joyce's language, its dynamism and its instability – "a restless Joycean strain that works against premature interpretation". The eternally provisional status of language in the Joyce text – present throughout his writings but unavoidably evident in *Ulysses* and *Finnegans Wake* – keeps the texts open and resistant to reductionist interpretation. As the words of the essay, "Dislocution" put it: "a prime characteristic of *Ulysses* is its lofty reluctance to conform, its resistance to any of our categories, to any kind of methodization". This author's insistence on the value of that characteristic, and his cogent, conscientious exemplification of it, form the sophisticated contents of this book.

GEORGE O'BRIEN

Julian of Norwich 1342/43–After 1416

English mystic and theologian

Baker, Denise Nowakowski, *Julian of Norwich's "Showing" from Vision to Book*, Princeton, New Jersey: Princeton University Press, 1994

Jantzen, Grace, *Julian of Norwich: Mystic and Theologian*, London: SPCK, 1987

Llewellyn, Robert, *With Pity Not with Blame: Reflections on the Writings of Julian of Norwich and on the "Cloud of Unknowing" for Today*, London: Darton, Longman, and Todd, 1982, 2nd edition, 1989

Molinari, Paul S.J., *Julian of Norwich: The Teaching of a 14th Century English Mystic*, London: Longmans, Green, & Co., 1958

Nuth, Joan M., *Wisdom's Daughter: The Theology of Julian of Norwich*, New York: Crossroad Publishing, 1991

Vinje, Patricia Mary, *An Understanding of Love According to the Anchoress Julian of Norwich*, Salzburg: Istitut für Anglistik und Amerikanistik (University of Salzburg), 1983

The articulation of Christian theology over the centuries has been almost entirely male. The religious writings by women have been mainly relegated to the discipline of "spirituality", usually residing in a position subordinate to the kind of doctrinal theology studied in both the religious communities and the academy. It is only in the twentieth century, more specifically the past 20 years, that the *Book of Showings* by Julian of Norwich has provoked a considerable volume of critical scholarship. Julian's *Showings* was a result of her 16 visions of the crucified Jesus accompanied by revelations about the love of God, in May 1373. She recorded her experiences first in what is now known as the short text of her *Showings*. Although there is much speculation about the authenticity and authorship of the two versions, contemporary scholars agree with the standard explanation presented by Edmund Colledge and James Walsh (in the Introduction of their Middle English edition of the *Showings*), that Julian herself composed both versions and that the short text preceded the long text by 20 or more years. A woman remarkable for both her substantial learning and her unorthodox position as a female visionary, Julian of Norwich has recently become a favorite subject of theologians, historians, and feminists, who attempt to situate her within the cultural spaces of her own milieu and the social schema of the modern-day curriculum.

JANTZEN's study integrates "the findings of scholarship with the interests of contemporary spirituality", urging the readers to contextualize Julian's writing within her intellectual and social backgrounds before transposing her theology to modern times. She examines philosophical questions about mysticism – "questions about language, epistemology, and certainty, about selfishness, evil and freedom, about context and interpretation and whether there could be a mystical core of religion". Jantzen compares Julian's adaptations of metaphors of motherhood to various spiritual writers and theological records as she pursues her investigation of Julian's expression of "love" – her language of sin and suffering, spiritual growth and healing, her teaching on human nature and asceticism. VINJE's reading of Julian's *Book of Showings* also focuses primarily on images and metaphors within Julian's theological framework, especially on her notion of love. This work aims at demonstrating Julian's use of the popular exegesis of her time, which exemplifies a mode of medieval thinking as well as a spiritual philosophy. Vinje's close reading of Julian's image of love is not only useful for illustrating the typical medieval penchant for using the mystery of love to describe, metaphorically, the nature of God, but also foregrounds a poetic tradition that makes its presence felt among the writings of patriarchs, poets, prophets, scholars, and saints.

MOLINARI approaches Julian's text, as Vinje claims, as a "treatise on prayer", intending to study objectively Julian's doctrine on prayer and contemplation. Molinari juxtaposes various stages of Julian's religious experience and her fundamental attitude to God with those of other great spiritual figures of traditional Christian mysticism. He reconstructs the different phases of Julian's soul's ascent to God and systematizes the various types of prayer and contemplation ("longing, unitive prayer, beholding which is not *shewing*, beholding which is *shewing*") in the stages of her revelation. He claims that his synthesis of Julian's revelations helps him to understand objectively both Julian's personal exposition and her artistry as a doctrinal writer. LLEWELLYN, a priest, also explores and interprets Julian's prayer and her personal exposition, but here in the light of the *Cloud of Unknowing*, another medieval religious doctrine by an anonymous author. Llewelyn adapts Julian's prayers as a petitionary doctrine of faith and love for God. In other words, he draws his inspiration from several quotations from Julian's writing while he reincorporates and redefines them into his own preaching. It becomes even more thought-provoking when he compares his reading of Julian's spiritual insights to the teachings of Carl Jung and Zen Buddhism. His reading of Julian's confessions within contemporary, sometimes cross-religious, frameworks successfully argues for the timelessness and versatility of Julian's doctrines.

NUTH presents Julian as a paradigm for (re)articulating the relationship between theology and women. While Nuth cautions against reading Julian as a feminist, she argues that Julian's spiritual text is nevertheless gendered and politicized. Nuth's analysis of Julian's works aims to place her religious experience within economic, social, and sexual diversity, as well as within the mystical tradition of Christianity. Her book points out that Julian's theology reflects a level of philosophical sophistication that may be described by the term "systematic theology", whereby the development of her conversion experience may be traced. Like Llewelyn and Molinari, Nuth emphasizes the significance of Julian's writings on love in her close readings of the *Showings*.

BAKER's book delineates Julian's maturation from a visionary into a theologian through the process of composing the two versions of her *Showings*. This scholarship evokes provocative questions about "her motivation and preparation for authorship". Baker wishes to provide the cultural frames of reference for the texts of *Showings* by investigating the affinity of Julian's writings with various traditions of medieval spirituality and theology. By examining the spiritual language that Julian incorporates into her own account of the revelation, Baker aims to locate a medieval religious culture through her writings. The final chapters trace Julian's intellectual transformation from a visionary into a theologian by studying her strategy of revisions and her development as a doctrinal writer despite all the prohibitions against women's education during her time.

EILEEN CHIA-CHING FUNG

K

Keats, John 1795–1821

English poet

Babbitt, Irving, *Rousseau and Romanticism*, Boston: Houghton Mifflin, 1919

Bate, Walter Jackson, *John Keats*, Cambridge, Massachusetts: Harvard University Press, 1963; Oxford: Oxford University Press, 1963

Bayley, John, "Keats and Reality", in *Proceedings of the British Academy*, XLVII, 1962

Bennett, Andrew, *Keats, Narrative and Audience: The Posthumous Life of Writing*, Cambridge: Cambridge University Press, 1994

Gittings, Robert, *John Keats*, Boston: Little Brown, 1968; London: Heinemann, 1968

Heinzelman, Kurt, "Self-Interest and the Politics of Composition in Keats's *Isabella*", in *English Literary History*, 55, 1988

Homans, Margaret, "Keats Reading Women, Women Reading Keats", in *Studies in Romanticism*, 29, 1990

Keach, William, "Cockney Couplets: Keats and the Politics of Style", in *Studies in Romanticism*, 25, 1986

Lau, Beth, *Keats's Reading of the Romantic Poets*, Ann Arbor: University of Michigan Press, 1991

Levinson, Marjorie, *Keats's Life of Allegory: The Origins of a Style*, Oxford and New York: Blackwell, 1988

McGann, Jerome J., "Keats and the Historical Method in Literary Criticism", in *Modern Language Notes*, 94, 1979

Ricks, Christopher, *Keats and Embarrassment*, Oxford: Clarendon Press, 1974; New York: Oxford University Press, 1974

Trilling, Lionel, "The Poet as Hero: Keats in His Letters", in his *The Opposing Self: Nine Essays in Criticism*, New York: Viking Press, 1955; London: Secker & Warburg, 1955

Van Ghent, Dorothy, *Keats: The Myth of the Hero*, revised and edited by Jeffrey C. Robinson, Princeton, New Jersey: Princeton University Press, 1983

Vendler, Helen, *The Odes of John Keats*, Cambridge, Massachusetts: Harvard University Press, 1983

Ward, Aileen, *John Keats: The Making of a Poet*, New York: Viking, 1963; London: Secker & Warburg, 1963

Wasserman, Earl, *The Finer Tone: Keats' Major Poems*, Baltimore: Johns Hopkins University Press, 1953

Watkins, Daniel P., *Keats's Poetry and the Politics of the Imagination*, Rutherford, New Jersey: Fairleigh Dickinson University Press, 1989

Since his death in 1821 until, perhaps, the last 20 years, Keats has been considered the quintessential lyric poet in English, the one for whom poetry has fully transcended the realms of history, politics, passion, and sexuality, for the "realms of gold". This is true of the extraordinary outpouring of poems to, or about, Keats throughout the first 150 years of his posthumous existence and of most of the considerable mass of criticism. When his love-letters to Fanny Brawne were first published in the 1870s, there was a cry of protest that the publication (for commercial benefit) of his immersion in a completely uncontrolled passion sullied the eternal purity of his poetry and even of his being, which often was more important to his eulogists. Matthew Arnold's adverse criticism of a Keats whom he otherwise admired was based on the view that his untoward passion reduced permanently the maturity – and the capacity for maturity – of Keats as a poet.

While the influential Arnold found not only Keats but the other major Romantic poets wanting in maturity and education; and while early twentieth-century critics like BABBITT castigated the Romantics as escapist, the academic tradition until the 1970s has tended to praise them precisely for being "mature" and, more importantly, has located in their poems a program for maturity and self-realization. With the instance of Keats, this program reaches its pinnacle in his Odes, the *Hyperion* poems, and above all in his letters. In his brilliant essay, TRILLING praises Keats for his "mature masculinity", his capacity to experience the world as pleasure and yet see the world as tragic, a heroism produced by his "hard core of self". This tradition, supported by many studies of his poems, including that of WASSERMAN, sustained the earlier notion of Keats as quintessential poet, buttressed now by the belief in the strength, resilience, and good humor of the poet himself, a view that has encouraged and been reinforced by the many biographies of Keats, the best and most recent of which were all written in the 1960s. Drawing on Hyder Rollins's then recent collections of Keats materials (*Letters* and *The Keats Circle*), many of which are located at Harvard University's Houghton Library, the biographies by BATE, WARD, and GITTINGS concretized the sense of Keats's personal heroism and poetic genius, concentrated in 25 years, with amazingly detailed reconstructions of monthly, weekly, and even daily life. The most recent study of the poetry that brings together these traditions surrounding Keats is by VENDLER, who attends closely to each of the six odes. Her painstaking readings exist to confirm the belief in Keats's maturity, figured here as brilliance in poetic craft entwined in "pure" poetic attention and philosophical wisdom.

The best of the more recent criticism, however, moves the discussion of Keats in a different direction, starting from different principles. Beginning with the part of Trilling's essay featuring Keats's sensuousness and with BAYLEY, attention has been focused less on the poem as an embodiment of successful struggles with identity and self-realization. Bayley, in particular, finds identity, and Keats's own preoccupation with it (e.g., in his "vale of soul-making" letter of Spring 1819) as nearly neurotic. Instead he finds Keats's interest in the "vulgar" and the sensuous – what Bayley calls "Das Gemeine" – to be the poet's greatest strength and contribution: *The Eve of St. Agnes*, and not the Odes, is Keats's best work, with its visual and tactile intensities.

RICKS – following Bayley and other British critics such as Bernard Blackstone and John Jones – elaborated sensuousness as a primary Keatsian absorption. While readers and poets (like Tennyson and the Pre-Raphaelites) have always characterized Keats as employing a sensuous vocabulary and celebrating the senses, this study sets the stage for the efforts of recent Keatsians to demonstrate the poet's *social* awareness, declared thankfully absent by the tradition. "Embarrassment" occurs when one acknowledges the dissonance between one's delight in the senses and in sexuality and society's presumed disapproval of it: Ricks notes the "blush" in Keats's poetry, even in his most "perfect" ode, "To Autumn".

As an important variant on this approach, VAN GHENT sees sensuousness played out in Keats's interests in myth, in particular, the monomyth of the hero (there are references to James Frazer, C.G. Jung, Jane Harrison, and Joseph Campbell). For Van Ghent, Keats's uniqueness lies in his immersion in (often) erotic mythic experience, and his strength is in his poetry's immersion in the collective imagery of the Western tradition. This book is one of the first specifically to value both the role of female characters in Keats's poetry and the place of erotic love.

Feminist criticism of Keats has considered the curious phenomenon, among the Romantics, of Keats's appeal to women readers as well as his ambivalence towards women in general. This issue is beginning to emerge as significant in the discussion of his poems and images, as can be seen in essays by, among others, Susan Wolfson and Margaret HOMANS. In this last, Keats's position with regard to his female readers is seen as involving a defensive reaction to their implicit power over his poetry. Keats "needs women to want him and his books, yet he resents women's power in the literary marketplace as much as he resents their sexual power over him".

History and politics have entered recent Keats studies in terms of the poet's sense of vocation, the role of the editing and publishing of his work, the response of reviewers to his volumes, and the place of audience. HEINZELMAN describes *Isabella* as a poem "about a poet pondering whether his success or failure as a modern poet can be determined solely in aesthetic terms". McGANN, in a highly influential essay, has shown that certain versions of Keats's poems, when the version authorized by the poet has not been clear, have been preferred over others according to the politics of the book's or journal's editor – in particular the "Ode on a Grecian Urn" and "La Belle Dame sans Merci". Similarly, KEACH studies the violence of the reviewers of Keats's first-published (1817) volume, resulting from the political implications of Keats's loose couplets in such poems as "Sleep and Poetry" or "I stood tiptoe upon a little hill". The obviously deliberate transgression in these poems of the securely closed couplets of Alexander Pope and his politically conservative followers enraged the reviewing establishment: Keats's loose (heavily enjambed) couplets correspond to his loose ("Cockney") politics as follower of the liberal Leigh Hunt.

Both Keach's and McGann's essays make clear the political resonances in Keats's poetry and, like much recent criticism, show how the Victorian and early-modern eras suppressed much of the political energies released by it at the beginning of the nineteenth century. (The issue of *Studies in Romanticism* in which Keach's essay appears is devoted to "Keats and Politics".) The same is true of WATKINS, who studies the poetry as a function of its appearance just after the fall of Napoleon and the full flowering of bourgeois capitalism – an age, he says, of "historical anxiety". BENNETT focuses on questions of narrative and audience as a means to offer new readings of the major poems; "narrative" is an implicitly social poetic function – telling a story to someone else. The book explores the way in which Romantic writing figures reception as necessarily deferred to a time after the poet's death: reading as the "posthumous life" of writing.

Part of the effort to contextualize Keats, to locate him beyond the "pure serene" of poetry, involves studies of sources and allusions. LAU is a very useful guide to allusions in Keats to the other Romantic poets (Wordsworth, Coleridge, Byron, Shelley). It is at once a fascinating cross-referencing of sources and echoes, and a prose discussion of Keats's reading among his most famous contemporaries. (A valuable addition to Lau's work would now include the place of the contemporary *women* poets in Keats's imagination.)

LEVINSON is required reading for any current student of Keats if for no other reason than it synthesizes and assesses, in highly suggestive and provocative ways, the entire tradition of Keats scholarship, criticism, and biography just summarized. She argues – against the tradition – that Keats was not a pure poet, an original, but rather one who, conscious of his lower-middle-class position, tried to gain access "through the back door" to the aristocracies of literature that Wordsworth, Byron, and Shelley, for example, had given to them free. Thus Keats's work teems with quotation and allusion in a kind of patchwork; he is a "second-hand" poet, who, as he becomes more expert in his craft, can use this marginal position to mock or "hoodwink" the tradition. Drawing on Byron's and others' sneers about Keats as an infantile and autoerotic sexual person, she reads his poems in order to confirm the charges, if not the implications, of their badness. Criticism has been beleaguered by the power of the eulogized Keats; Levinson's is the first major study to give a genuinely new reading of some of the poems (particularly the romances) in a long time.

There have been many other book-length studies of Keats, some of which are very good from the perspective outlined at the beginning of this survey. (See, for example, those by Sperry and Dickstein and Waldoff.) But the new and most powerful directions since the mid-1970s include the mix of articles and books noted here. To date, the subject that has received less discussion than it deserves is a revisionist account of Keats's poetics.

JEFFREY C. ROBINSON

Kempe, Margery ?1373–?1438

English mystic and autobiographer

Atkinson, Clarissa W., *Mystic and Pilgrim: The Book and the World of Margery Kempe*, Ithaca, New York: Cornell University Press 1983

Beckwith, Sarah, "A Very Material Mysticism: The Medieval Mysticism of Margery Kempe", in *Medieval Literature: Criticism, Ideology and History*, edited by David Aers, Brighton, Sussex: Harvester Press, 1986; New York: St Martin's Press, 1986

Glasscoe, Marion, *English Medieval Mystics: Games of Faith*, London: Longman, 1993

Knowles, David, *The English Mystical Tradition*, London: Burns & Oates, 1960; New York: Harper, 1961

Lochrie, Karma, *Margery Kempe and Translations of the Flesh*, Philadelphia: University of Pennsylvania Press, 1991

McEntire, Sandra J. (ed.), *Margery Kempe: A Book of Essays*, New York: Garland, 1992

Wallace, David, "Mystics and Followers in Siena and East Anglia: A Study in Taxonomy, Class, and Cultural Mediation", in *The Medieval Mystical Tradition in England: Papers Read at Dartington Hall, July 1984*, edited by Marion Glasscoe, Cambridge: D.S. Brewer, 1984

Margery Kempe has never had a secure place in the canon of so-called "Middle English mystics". Her text's refusal to distance mystical experiences from their human and social dimensions was initially a source of embarrassment to the chiefly theological chroniclers of the English mystics scene. Early critical judgements were condescending and reductive, condemning the author as "hysterical". More recent studies have championed Kempe and her work in the name of gender politics, but have tended towards a rather naive and uncritical admiration. Much of the criticism, negative and positive, has been unable to separate discussion of the woman from critical appraisal of the text. More greatly theoretical and historical approaches have, however, avoided the biographical trap.

The brief chapter by KNOWLES has been the most influential negative assessment. Though finding Kempe sincere and devout, he derides her for her exhibitionism and for the "large hysterical element" in her personality, in contrast to the "sobriety" of other female mystics. This estimation allows him to dismiss Kempe as not really part of a tradition of mysticism at all: her communications with God are "a series of banal conversations in an otherwise well-written novel of adventure", the result of a "vivid imagination and retentive memory". His judgements rest on an implicit appeal to the notion that mysticism is a negative theology, which bypasses its human mediators.

ATKINSON's book, the first full-length study, marked a turning point in Kempe criticism by taking the author seriously as a mystic, and in being free of derogatory judgements. A woman-centred, rather than feminist, study, it seeks to rescue Kempe from freakish marginality by presenting her text and experience as a complex but wholly explicable response to Continental mystical and vernacular traditions of popular piety, urging on the reader a better understanding of Kempe rather than interrogating the categories within which the *Book* has traditionally been read. The volume is informative, scholarly yet accessible, and aware of the need for some psychological and anthropological frames to understand the mystical phenomena that are not represented in wholly theological terms in Kempe's *Book*. It does, however, take a fairly naive view of the relationship of writer, life, and work.

WALLACE's important article confronts the problem of how Kempe's text eludes the categories in which it has habitually been placed, turning to the cultural practices surrounding the Continental mystic Catherine of Siena, in an attempt to break out of the critical impasse that had condemned the *Book* and its author within an insular understanding of mysticism. Wallace's recontextualising of Kempe is not presented as a defence of the author, but takes the form of a detailed consideration of the cultural and iconographic materials to which her life and text were a direct response. Chief among these is the *Meditationes Vitae Christi*, composed originally in Siena, and diffused through Europe via Franciscan channels. Wallace probes the extent of Kempe's reaction to the tradition of imaginative involvement enjoined by its brand of popular spirituality, showing how her whole life became a living picture-book of dutiful responses to the *Meditationes'* religious imperatives, and a testimony to the dramatic power of visual images and their role in devotion to the humanity of Christ. However, while arguing that Kempe's text exceeds clerical demands in aspiring to be "self-directing", and that she was able to challenge her clerical opponents by "mirroring back the truths the clergy has supplied her with", he concludes that these challenges do not amount to "a triumph over clerical discourse".

BECKWITH is also sceptical, but from a feminist perspective, about treating the *Book* as evidence for the subversive potential of mysticism for women. Informed by post-structuralist and Marxist theory, her article views Kempe's text as a site for the exploration of what is at stake in the representation of mysticism. Drawing on an examination of mirror imagery in medieval mystical writings and on Jacques Lacan's analysis of the mirror phase, Beckwith argues that the *Book* offers a series of identifications with Christ that re-enact female objectification and debasement. Beckwith's analysis thus tends to read Kempe as caught in ideology, insofar as she views mysticism's ideological work as offering an outlet for dissatisfaction while also redirecting it in a way that upheld the social order. Yet her argument that the text's insistence on the social dimension of Kempe's piety radically embarrasses the myth of God's transcendence points towards the possibility of the release of other meanings in Kempe's text.

Like Beckwith, LOCHRIE is interested in the power-relations at work in mysticism; but she also wants to claim the *Book* for feminist readers. Central to her argument is a revision of medieval theories of the body. She challenges the traditional identification of women with the passive and corruptible body, demonstrating rather their association with the rebellious flesh. Kempe's text exploits this gendered physiological association, actively violating language through her "laughter" and "crying". Lochrie also offers a valuable reappraisal of Kempe's "illiteracy", and of the reception history of the *Book*. This ambitious and theoretically informed study covers important ground. Yet, despite its avowed commitment to shifting discussion of Kempe away from the theological and towards the literary, its conception of the literary remains firmly theological. Rather than a rigorous exploration of the possible meanings (including feminist meanings) that lurk in the material surfaces of texts, Lochrie's study is still bound to the idea that meaning lies *beyond* the text.

McENTIRE's anthology is divided into three broad sections – the woman, her work, and her world. The Introduction largely sets the tone of the collection by offering Kempe as an unproblematic feminist role-model ("a vibrant, resilient, intelligent, resourceful, insubordinate, mystical, energetic, sexual woman"). Two essays compare Kempe with Chaucer's Wife of Bath; one reads her in relation to Protestant charismatic and revivalist religion, and another to shamanism. Szell interestingly discusses the structure of the *Book* in the light of Freud's "fort-da" model. Many of the essays add profitably to the available information that readers can bring to bear on the writer, her text, and her brand of piety (the *Revelations* of Elizabeth of Hungary; the "pilgrimage" influence of Bridget), but few succeed in adding significantly new insights to received critical readings of Kempe.

Written by a scholar steeped in the English mystical tradition, GLASSCOE's book offers a reader's guide to the text in the light of its spiritual intentions. A general overview of the *Book* is followed by sections that deal with blocks of chapters, arranged thematically ("Spiritual Awakening"; "Persecution for the Faith"). Glasscoe quotes liberally in the original Middle English, offering close readings of selected passages that are controlled by some larger frames – pilgrimages, signs, and her governing thesis that "faith is a game wherein the wisdom of God is born in man". Kempe's spirituality is presented, somewhat simplistically, as a therapeutic reaction to depression and guilt to which the reader should respond humanely. One effect of the chapter's theological emphasis is to smooth out contradictions, so that the *Book* and Kempe emerge as rather bland, shorn of their excitement and dissident possibilities.

RUTH EVANS

Kerouac, Jack 1922–1969

American novelist and poet

Cassady, Carolyn, *Off the Road: My Years with Cassady, Kerouac, and Ginsberg*, New York: William Morrow, 1990

Clark, Tom, *Jack Kerouac: A Biography*, San Diego, California: Harcourt Brace Jovanovich, 1984

Gifford, Barry, and Lawrence Lee (eds.), *Jack's Book: Jack Kerouac in the Lives and Words of His Friends: An Oral Biography of Jack Kerouac*, New York: St Martin's Press, 1978; London: Hamish Hamilton, 1979

McNally, Dennis, *Desolate Angel: Jack Kerouac, the Beat Generation, and America*, New York: Random House, 1979

Nicosia, Gerald, *Memory Babe: A Critical Biography of Jack Kerouac*, New York: Grove Press, 1983; Harmondsworth, Middlesex: Viking Press, 1985

Stephenson, Gregory, "Circular Journey: Jack Kerouac's *Duluoz Legend*" in his *The Daybreak Boys: Essays on the Literature of the Beat Generation*, Carbondale: Southern Illinois University Press, 1990

Tytell, John, *Naked Angels: The Lives and Literature of the Beat Generation*, New York: McGraw-Hill, 1976

Weinreich, Regina, *The Spontaneous Poetics of Jack Kerouac: A Study of the Fiction*, Carbondale: Southern Illinois University Press, 1990

Monographs about Jack Kerouac's writing tend to have been dominated by memoirs, reminiscences, biographies, and other articles, whereby various friends and writers have paid homage to, and presented their intimate accounts of, the writer's life. Other than as the celebration of a bohemian lifestyle, Kerouac's writing has been largely scorned and marginalised by the orthodox academic critical machinery, and where there has been critical engagement with the writing, this has frequently occurred in small-press magazines, journals, and newspapers. However, recently new attention has been focused on Kerouac, and critical analyses are now emerging. This review will pay attention to these two halves of Kerouac analysis.

In the biographical approach, GIFFORD and LEE present a series of firsthand accounts of Kerouac from friends and acquaintances, as the result of a series of interviews with them. The editors desired to present "a big, transcontinental conversation, complete with interruptions, contradictions, old grudges, and bright memories". The results of these personal intimacies is that "you will read again and again, in many voices, that Kerouac's novels were fiction, not reportage". Kerouac utilised people, situations, events, as the stuff of altering reality, memory being the key instrument, as Kerouac's various nicknames – "Memory Babe" and "the great rememberer" – indicate.

McNALLY's biography tends to the historical, and traces Kerouac's frenzied, complex, and intense life from his childhood to his years at Columbia University, where he met Allen Ginsberg and Neal Cassady. The book recounts the frantic cross-country journeys and experiments with drugs and sex. In an easy-going, accessible style, the book captures Kerouac's pace, energy, and total commitment to all his actions. Its focus on the historical environment contextualises Kerouac's life within the jazz scene in the 1940s, the emergence of the Beat Generation in the 1950s, and the San Francisco poetry "renaissance".

By contrast, CLARK's biography tends to be rather introductory, spare and minimal in its detail, although it has a useful accompanying bibliography. It is also liberally illustrated with photographs of Kerouac's various friends and writing acquaintances over the years. Less densely written than some biographies, this book is nevertheless more straightforwardly and undeviatingly concerned with Kerouac's life rather than with positioning him within a social history.

Another memoir, of interest more for its woman's perspective on the goings-on of the male Beat crowd than its critical engagement with Kerouac's writing, is CASSADY's personal history. Framed by her meeting with Neal Cassady and his death, this book gives some detailed information, but tends to indulge her tortured attraction to Cassady, Kerouac, and the Beat Generation's bohemian representation.

The text that begins to bridge the biographical and the critical approaches to Kerouac is NICOSIA's substantial and authoritative critical biography. Somewhat idolising in its perspective, the book nevertheless seeks to integrate critical analysis of Kerouac's texts with a life of the man. For instance, there is a description of the way Kerouac wrote the non-stop 120 foot manuscript roll of *On the Road*, followed by an account of its themes and the influences of Walt Whitman and Thomas Wolfe on the novel. This biography is easily accessible and informative, although one ought to balance the book's veneration with a more rigorous critical engagement with Kerouac's life and writings.

Critical, rather than the biographical, interest dominates TYTELL's study of the Beat Generation and of the trio William Burroughs, Ginsberg, and Kerouac in particular. The book focuses on John Clellon Holmes's image of "a broken circuit to suggest the lack of connection to the immediate present felt by the members of his generation". Situated within this social and cultural alienation, the long chapter on Kerouac entitled "Eulogist of Spontaneity" considers how Kerouac's notion that writers should "sketch the flow that already exists in the mind" informs the novels. Tytell treats Kerouac as a serious artist who had the artistic goal of representing the "bared power of the actual and the ordinary", rather than merely chronicling the activities of the Beats, and argues that "paradoxically, he lived primarily for words and the rhythms of his work, and not for the bohemian adventures associated with his books".

STEPHENSON's analytical chapter-study of Kerouac's writing occurs within the framework of a study of the Beat Generation as "daybreak boys", because of their "journey through darkness to light". The Kerouac essay focuses on the motifs of the road and journey in the 12-novel sequence, "The Legend of Duluoz", and its quests for identity, community, and spiritual knowledge. The sequence is described as a "bildungsreise", a narrative of development and education-into-life achieved by means of a journey. However, Jack Duluoz is finally dehistoricised and mythologised in this essay, as he is finally described as "not merely the alter ego of the author, he is a generic, representative man, a contemporary Everyman".

The principal single critical assessment of Kerouac's writings is WEINREICH's monograph, which argues that Kerouac wrote his fiction with a "grand design" in mind, conceiving of his books as "one vast book", a "Divine Comedy of Buddha" called "The Legend of Duluoz". Furthermore, the book analyses how Kerouac's "spontaneous prose" and language experiments are associated with jazz rhythms and techniques. Finally the book focuses on how successive groups of novels seek to answer and address the aesthetic and structural problems thrown up by the former works. Consequently, the fiction is regarded as having a unified aesthetic project propelling it forwards. This book comes with a useful recent bibliography, which updates Clark's.

TIM S. WOODS

Kingsley, Charles 1819–1875

English novelist and prose writer

Chitty, Susan, *The Beast and the Monk: A Life of Charles Kingsley*, London: Hodder & Stoughton, 1974

Colloms, Brenda, *Charles Kingsley, The Lion of Eversley*, London: Constable, 1975; New York: Barnes & Noble, 1975

Kendall, Guy, *Charles Kingsley and His Ideas*, London: Hutchinson, 1947; reprinted, New York: Haskell House, 1973

Martin, Robert B., *The Dust of Combat: A Life of Charles Kingsley*, London: Faber & Faber, 1959; New York: Norton, 1960

Thorp, Margaret Farrand, *Charles Kingsley, 1819–75*, Princeton, New Jersey: Princeton University Press, 1937, reprinted 1969

Uffelman, Larry K., *Charles Kingsley*, Boston: Twayne, 1979

Charles Kingsley was a popular Victorian novelist, as well as a controversial writer and speaker on social and religious issues. Inevitably his reputation waned in the twentieth century, when the battles he had fought had been either won or lost and thus seemed strangely irrelevant. At one stage it looked as if he would only be remembered for that part of *The Water-Babies* that is a charming story for children and that part of *Westward Ho* that is a thrilling historical novel; the philosophy behind both stories and the novels of social protest seemed doomed to be forgotten. But, in the second half of this century, Kingsley began to be recognized as an important figure, not just for the historical insights he provided into the temper of the Victorian age, but also for his surprisingly un-Victorian political and sexual views.

THORP's study, deservedly reprinted in 1969, is a monument to careful scholarship, drawing upon much unpublished material. Its emphasis is religious, as can be seen by the title headings of individual chapters like "Esau Has a Birthright" and "I Am a Church of England Parson – and a Chartist". Even the novels of social protest are seen more as religious than political tracts. Kingsley's increasing conservatism and adoption by the British establishment are recorded, but not lamented. Difficulties and tensions between Kingsley and his family are only hinted at tactfully in this pioneer work, which clearly was intended to restore a Victorian hero to his pedestal.

KENDALL's book has a very different flavour from Thorp's. Written during World War II, and published in the austere period after it, this work lacks its predecessor's generosity. Kingsley the man is seen as more important than Kingsley the novelist, and indeed the novels are only really discussed in one short chapter where they are dismissed as boring because of an excess of authorial moralizing. Politics and education are seen as more important than religion in Kingsley's preaching, although there is a good discussion of nineteenth-century views on Eternal Damnation and the quarrel with John Henry Newman. Biographical information is scant, but there is an illuminating appreciation of the contrast between Kingsley's public optimism and his private despair.

MARTIN's biography is a balanced appreciation of "the impetuous workings of a fitful heart and quick chaotic mind". The background against which Kingsley wrote is deftly sketched in, and there are excellent portraits of Kingsley's friends like Mansfield, Maurice, and Ludlow. Sexual tensions among Kingsley's friends, family, and even Kingsley himself are mentioned more frankly than in previous biographies, but not as openly as our own permissive age would expect. Kingsley's quarrelsome nature and his love of controversy are seen as faults, but his kindness towards his family and his parishioners is stressed. Martin does not leave much room for discussion of the novels, seen perhaps rightly as only one of Kingsley's interests, and not one in which he achieved the first rank.

CHITTY's somewhat sensationally entitled work draws upon unpublished letters between Kingsley and his wife, and diaries of Mrs Kingsley, to which the author had been allowed privileged access (although previous biographers had known about them). Kingsley's combination of strong sexual feelings and Christian asceticism appear to have been shared by his wife, and Chitty is probably right to treat them sympathetically, although most students of Kingsley in the century after his death would have seen something sinister and sadomasochistic in such practices as flagellation. Where this book fails is in enabling these new discoveries to shed much light on many aspects of Kingsley's varied work, and it would be unfortunate if he were only known as a pioneer in unusual sexual practices.

COLLOMS's full biography appeared in the centenary of Kingsley's death and is an appropriate synthesis of previous work. There are long but carefully chosen selections from Kingsley's writings. Family troubles are frankly but tactfully acknowledged. Kingsley's passion for his wife and his hatred of homosexuality, perhaps feared in his brother Henry, are mentioned but not exaggerated. His novels receive due recognition for their frankness in discussing sexual as well as political and religious issues. Kingsley's obvious public charm eventually wins over most biographers, as it won over Queen Victoria, Cambridge University, and Chester Cathedral, and this particular biographer is perhaps too kind to Kingsley in his later years. The discussion of the novels is excellent, and Colloms is particularly helpful in trying to rescue *Westward Ho* and *Hereward the Wake* from the oblivion that overtakes most Victorian historical novels.

UFFELMAN's modest work is more critical than biographical. It contains a summary of Kingsley's life, a more detailed account of his novels, and a chapter on his poetry. There are separate chapters for "Novels of Social Purpose" and "Historical Novels". Oddly, *The Saint's Tragedy* and *The Water-Babies* have an individual chapter to themselves, allowing Uffelman to explore Kingsley's views on sexuality and on science. Other novels are discussed by concise plot summaries leading to careful, if hardly original, insights into Kingsley's views on religious and social issues. An excellent bibliography gives a brief account of most previous work on this author.

T.J. WINNIFRITH

Kipling, Rudyard 1865–1936

English writer of poetry, novels, short stories, children's stories, and essays

Gilbert, Elliot L. (ed.), *Kipling and the Critics*, London: Peter Owen, 1966; New York: New York University Press, 1966

Mallett, Philip (ed.), *Kipling Considered*, London: Macmillan, 1989

Moore-Gilbert, B.J., *Kipling and Orientalism*, London: Croom Helm, 1986

Parry, Anne, *The Poetry of Rudyard Kipling: Rousing the Nation*, Milton Keynes, Buckinghamshire; Open University Press, 1992

Sullivan, Zoreh T., *Narratives of Empire: The Fictions of Rudyard Kipling*, Cambridge and New York: Cambridge University Press, 1993

Tompkins, J.M.S., *The Art of Rudyard Kipling*, London: Methuen, 1959, 2nd edition, 1965; Lincoln: University of Nebraska Press, 1965

Following Rudyard Kipling's rapid rise to fame in the early 1890s, critics became increasingly wary of his right-wing politics and conservative literary style. At the time of his death in 1936, his writings received little serious critical attention. In 1941, T.S. Eliot's introductory essay to his selection of Kipling's verse prompted a renewal of interest and further appraisals by writers such as George Orwell and Lionel Trilling. A welcome aspect of recent critical study has been its attempt to recover the historical background to Kipling's writing and imperial politics.

TOMPKINS begins by explaining that her study will be principally thematic, avoiding contentious political topics and focusing instead upon the "permanent human and moral themes that run through all the tales". She explains how, in the later stories, the theme of healing begins to predominate over themes of hatred and revenge, establishing a "halcyon" period in Kipling's art. In her chapters entitled "Laughter" and "Hatred and Revenge" Tompkins stresses the importance of humour and ritual in Kipling's work, suggesting that both enable the expression of "primitive" feelings in a "civilised" context. Despite the neglect of the social and political background, Tompkins' readings of the stories remain sensitive and stimulating.

GILBERT's collection includes important essays and addresses by, among others, George Orwell, Lionel Trilling, and C.S. Lewis. In its rejection of the "shallow and familiar charge that Kipling is a 'fascist'", Orwell's defence nevertheless relegates Kipling to the status of "good bad poet", whose verse expresses the sentiment and emotion of a public normally averse to poetry. Trilling is similarly cautious about Kipling's literary standing, and even more damning about his Tory politics. C.S. Lewis considers Kipling a "very great artist", who reclaims for literature the lost territory of work. Nevertheless, he suspects that Kipling champions professional discipline primarily for its promise of exclusive fraternity and professional brotherhood, echoing the ambivalent note sounded in many of the other essays. The volume also features good examples of earlier criticism, in the pieces by Andrew Lang and Henry James. Robert Buchanan's important "The Voice of the

Hooligan" is also included, as is the interesting curiosity "P.C., X, 36" – a satire on Kipling by Max Beerbohm.

MOORE-GILBERT aims to explore the relationship between Kipling's work and the characteristic literary and political discourses of Anglo-Indian culture. This provides the groundwork for a challenge to Edward Said's writings on "Orientalism" – a term used to denote the stereotypical depiction of the Orient as "less a place than a *topos*, a set of references, a congerie of characteristics". Moore-Gilbert argues for the existence of a distinctly Anglo-Indian "Orientalism" distinguishable from its English "metropolitan" counterpart. The book includes detailed reference to a range of works by lesser-known Anglo-Indian authors, exploring Kipling's indebtedness to a specifically Anglo-Indian tradition. There is also extensive quotation from the two main newspapers for which Kipling wrote, the *Pioneer* and *Civil and Military Gazette*. Although the dual aim of the book and the sheer range of reference sometimes limit the overall attention to Kipling's writing, the close analysis of the literary and political context makes it essential reading.

MALLETT has brought together a group of essays that reflects the wide range of approaches to Kipling in modern criticism. Clare Hanson uses psychoanalytical theories derived from readings of Freud and Jean-François Lyotard in her assessment of the "adversarial relation" between image and narrative in Kipling's late stories. Patrick Williams invokes Said's interpretation of "Orientalism" in order to challenge the "traditional" view of Kipling's *Kim* as a repudiation of racist attitudes. David Lodge's account of the notoriously obscure "Mrs Bathurst" draws upon a wide range of modern narratological theories to explain how "indeterminacy of meaning leads to an *increase* of meaning". Other essays by Danny Karlin and Robin Gilmour focus upon Kipling's changing conception of the Anglo-Indian community, and his subversion of the genre of the Victorian school-story. The diversity and adventurousness of the essays make Mallett's book a useful introduction to contemporary Kipling criticism.

PARRY offers a comprehensive account of the critical response to Kipling's poems at the time of their publication. By coupling this reception-orientated approach with analysis of the political climate, she assesses the relation of the poems to the principle versions of imperial policy contested in administrative circles. This enables her to define the specific character of Kipling's own politics. Kipling emerges as the bard of the "visionary" imperialists, intent upon a federated and socially inclusive Empire, which acknowledges the role of the working class and the importance of co-operation between ruling nations. The vision of social unity essential to Kipling's imperialism proves a constant challenge to both the literary and administrative establishments:

> It is not surprising, therefore, that verse with such a potential should be considered a literary anomaly and outlawed as vulgar. Whether it comes from the left or the right it bears with it the possibility of influencing significantly the areas of exchange between classes where hegemonic leadership is won.

Parry emphasises the importance of Kipling's own arrangement of the poems in each published volume, maintaining that their sequence is an essential aspect of their meaning. This rediscovery of historical context, original form of publication, and critical reaction makes Parry's an excellent and compelling book.

SULLIVAN argues that Kipling perceives India in terms of a "strained familial model", whereby metaphors of the inner circle of home and club are projected onto the outer circle of nation and Empire. The book draws upon Lacanian psychoanalytical theory to explain how this enforcement of the familial trope causes a suppression of desire (an absence or lack), which subsequently manifests itself in images of bodily mutilation and the dialectic of blindness and sightedness in the stories. In Kipling's autobiographical fragment, *Something of Myself*, this "suppression" gives rise to an ellipsis and self-censorship that becomes a paradigm of colonisation, reorganising the "territory" of the writer's past. Although some readers might question the exclusive commitment to a psychoanalytical approach, Sullivan makes refreshing use of unpublished material, and the close-readings of Kipling's letters are frequently illuminating.

ANDREW HAGIIOANNU

L

Lamb, Charles 1775–1834

English essayist, critic, poet, and children's writer

Aaron, Jane, *A Double Singleness: Gender and the Writings of Charles and Mary Lamb*, Oxford: Clarendon Press, 1991; New York: Oxford University Press, 1991

Barnett, George L., *Charles Lamb*, Boston: Twayne, 1976

Courtney, Winifred F., *Young Charles Lamb 1775–1802*, London: Macmillan, 1982; New York: New York University Press, 1982

McFarland, Thomas, "Charles Lamb and the Politics of Survival", in his *Romantic Cruxes: The English Essayists and the Spirit of the Age*, Oxford: Clarendon Press, 1987; New York: Oxford University Press, 1987

Monsman, Gerald, *Confessions of a Prosaic Dreamer: Charles Lamb's Art of Autobiography*, Durham, North Carolina: Duke University Press, 1984

Randel, Fred V., *The World of Elia: Charles Lamb's Essayistic Romanticism*, Port Washington, New York, and London: Kennikat Press, 1975

Riehl, Joseph E., *Charles Lamb's Children's Literature*, Salzburg: Institut für Anglistik und Amerikanistik (Salzburg University), 1980

It is appropriate that much perceptive criticism of Lamb's work is in essay form. Although this review deals only with books, the *Charles Lamb Bulletin* (published by the Charles Lamb Society in London) offers an excellent index to the developments in Lamb studies. Early critical work on Lamb was often marked by an apologetic or defensive note, but work on trends of reception and the gendering of reputation has allowed recent scholars to explore the cultural register of Lamb's voices without the need to categorise him as a scaled-down Romantic poet.

RANDEL's study takes bearings from M.H. Abrams's definition of Romanticism, and makes early use of literary history with psychology and Bloomian influence theory to present Lamb's Elian essays as a coherent whole. Disagreeing with critics (including Barnett) who regard an infusion of personality as Lamb's main innovation, Randel shows Lamb to be sceptical about the ideas of his predecessors and contemporaries. The chapters on gastronomic detail and ludic consciousness in Elia argue that "Lamb's humour, while it assimilates man's appetites and his illogicality, punctures his more imposing formulations about time and space". Randel's well-balanced attention to genre allows the reader to see Elia as a cultural as well as a personal configuration.

BARNETT has produced a general survey of Lamb's writing with reference to scholarship "beyond the disparagement of the New Criticism". Six short chapters provide an overview of the circumstances of Lamb's life, his experimentation with different kinds of writing in the pre-Elia period, and the reception of Lamb's work, with individual chapters on Elia and Lamb's criticism. Particularly valuable is Barnett's chapter on the texture of Lamb's letters and their proximity to the essay genre. Alert to Randel's psychoanalytic approach to the dream literature, Barnett chooses to emphasise Lamb's "realism and empiricism". Well-indexed, and with full notes and references, this is a useful introductory study.

RIEHL's deftly contextualised work shows how Charles and Mary Lamb's stories and poems for children opposed the sentimental moralising of contemporary children's literature. After brief consideration of Lamb's early failures in the novel, poetry, and drama, attention centres on *Tales from Shakespeare* and *The Adventures of Ulysses*, to reveal Lamb's association with – but ultimate independence from – William Godwin, Wordsworth, and Coleridge. Riehl detects "a movement from the practical concerns of writing for children . . . toward a more general and philosophical attempt to understand the basis of the childish imagination, to educate the public taste, and to argue for freedom from repressive educational theories". Riehl's comprehensive study of one aspect of Lamb's writing illuminates the rest of his work.

COURTNEY provides a detailed account of Lamb's life up to the age of 27. Although it does not supersede E.V. Lucas's biography, Courtney's work is valuable for the focus it places on Lamb's radicalism. Refuting early standard assumptions about Lamb's indifference to politics, Courtney documents Lamb's brief involvement with Unitarianism and the longer-term association with English Jacobins, which made him a target of the *AntiJacobin* magazine in 1798. In short chapters, quoting generously from Lamb's lesser-known journalism for the radical newspaper *The Albion*, Courtney examines Lamb's poetic collaboration with Coleridge and Charles Lloyd, *Rosamund Gray*, and *John Woodvil*. Lamb's first known published essay (on Jacobinism) is included as an appendix.

MONSMAN concentrates on a dozen essays to explore the ways in which Lamb's "personal defects (madness, celibacy, stammer, limp) become the metaphors of his art". Based on psychoanalytical readings of absence, together with etymological clues, Monsman traces recurring symbols and the tissue woven by Elia over the figure of Lamb's dead mother. Providing detailed readings of Elia's verbal games – anagrams, puns, epistolary deceptions, and pseudonymous disguise – this is an accessible and stimulating study.

McFARLAND distils copious learning to locate Lamb in a European context as an important cultural figure and exemplar of the Romantic movement (brilliantly defined *contra* Abrams in the course of the essay). Reading Lamb's politeness and whimsy as an intricate defence system against suicidal madness, McFarland illustrates the complex displacements and "subtexts of desperation" through writing by and about Lamb. Coleridge emerges as an *alter ego* sanctioning Lamb's "retreat into smallness and prose", and the 28 essays of Elia become "the record of Lamb's psychic odyssey", the Romantic epic Coleridge never wrote. This large claim is convincingly argued in McFarland's passionately humane interpretation.

AARON's monograph begins with historical research into Charles and Mary's ambiguous social status as children of domestic servants, and their alienating experience of being "marked" by madness. Using feminist and psychoanalytic literary theory she examines Lamb's resistance to the cult of manliness in his criticism, novel, and dramatic writing. Aaron advances Randel's discussion of the ludic function in Lamb's writing, arguing that the Elian essays invite the reader to share in the "sanity of play" enabled by feminine qualities of empathy, "in which the multiplicity of the subject in its many guises can be accepted without projection" and the urge to power by any one facet of the self is checked and balanced. Aaron suggests that the intense sibling bond (not unusual among Romantic writers) between Charles and Mary fostered an atypical merging of gender roles, ultimately allowing Charles to deconstruct the masculinist stance commonly identified with Romanticism. Aaron has assimilated the diverse contributions of feminist theory, from Virginia Woolf to Julia Kristeva, to produce a landmark in Lamb scholarship.

JANE STABLER

Landscape and Literature in 18th- and 19th-Century Britain

Brownell, Morris R., *Alexander Pope and the Arts of Georgian England*, Oxford: Clarendon Press, 1978

Copley, Stephen, and Peter Garside (eds.), *The Politics of the Picturesque: Literature, Landscape and Aesthetics since 1770*, Cambridge and New York: Cambridge University Press, 1994

Hunt, John Dixon, *The Figure in the Landscape: Poetry, Painting, and Gardening During the Eighteenth Century*, Baltimore: Johns Hopkins University Press, 1976

Hunt, John Dixon, *Gardens and the Picturesque: Studies in the History of Landscape Architecture*, Cambridge, Massachusetts: MIT Press, 1992

Janowitz, Anne, *England's Ruins: Poetic Purpose and the National Landscape*, Oxford and Cambridge, Massachusetts: Blackwell, 1990

Kelsall, Malcolm, *The Great Good Place: The Country House and English Literature*, Hemel Hempstead, Hertfordshire: Harvester Wheatsheaf, 1993

Malins, Edward, *English Landscape and Literature, 1660–1840*, London and New York: Oxford University Press, 1966

Paulson, Ronald, *Emblem and Expression: Meaning in English Art of the Eighteenth Century*, London: Thames & Hudson, 1975; Cambridge, Massachusetts: Harvard University Press, 1975

Roston, Murray, *Changing Perspectives in Literature and the Visual Arts, 1650–1820*, Princeton, New Jersey: Princeton University Press, 1990

Early works on the relationship between landscape and literature may now seem somewhat dated in many of their assumptions, but still provide an enormous amount of valuable material: notably, E.W. Manwaring's *Italian Landscape in Eighteenth-Century England* (New York, 1925) and R.A. Aubin's *Topographical Poetry in Eighteenth-Century England* (New York, 1936) are still invaluable in their sheer breadth of scope. Since the 1970s there has been an increased interest in the garden as a nexus of verbal/visual relations. In these terms the garden has become not simply a discrete aesthetic object set apart from culture, but also a means of understanding that broader culture of which it is a part. As an area of critical investigation, landscape studies is inevitably interdisciplinary, and therefore critical discussion is scattered across a range of journals and books in such fields as historical geography and social history, sociology, and literary, architectural, and art history. The *Journal of Garden History*, established in 1981, has been some help in this regard as a focus for scholarly activity across a large number of different fields.

MALINS' aim is to "trace the direct influence of contemporary writers and artists on the formation of [the landscape garden]". His study remains a valuable, if at times pedestrian, introduction to the major trends of the period. However, many of his judgements have been superseded by more recent work, not least from those critics who have increasingly questioned the ideological self-justifications of the landscape garden. Equally, garden historians have in the last ten years begun to question also the neatness and uniformity of that chronological movement from formality to a more "natural" design upon which Malins' narrative is based.

The 1992 collection of HUNT's essays includes some of the most astute contributions to the study of the relationship between literature and landscape in this period. Notably in his essay "Emblem and Expressionism", written in the 1970s, Hunt introduces a distinction between the emblematic and expressive that continues to have much currency. In these terms, changes in the design of the landscape garden can be understood in terms of the movement from iconographical unravelling, based on a shared education, to the creation of a space in which the visitor is not hampered by coercive structures and is left free to experience emotions in a relatively untrammelled manner. In his important study of 1976 HUNT elaborates upon this theme and seeks to explain the difference between the complex gardens at Stowe or Alexander Pope's at Twickenham and those created later in the century by "Capability" Brown. He stresses the importance of literary structures and allusion in the contemporary design and interpretation of the garden, and like a number of writers since, attempts to trace the alignment of eighteenth-century gardens with a patrician culture of self-consciously literary production. PAULSON's work elaborates upon the emblem/expression divide in a book-length study, which argues that in the eighteenth century British art as a whole can be understood in terms of this same movement. It is a study that has proved influential for many later works.

BROWNELL's study of Pope and the arts provides an enormous amount of information for the earlier part of this period, with substantial sections on landscape gardening and architecture. For Brownell, Pope embodies the virtuoso ideals that the Earl of Shaftesbury had attempted to inculcate, and the study seeks to rebut the charge that both the poet and the age were insensible to the arts. In particular, Brownell finds Pope a useful point of focus for the interrelation of the arts, and employs the country house, the landscape garden, and Pope's own literary production as means of defending eighteenth-century culture as a whole.

As part of a broader study of the relationship between the arts from the late seventeenth to the early nineteenth century, ROSTON sets himself the task of explaining some of the "subliminal impulses" behind the sudden English concern for creating landscape in the period. And one element of such a drive, he suggests, is to be found in the "displacement of certain suppressed religious impulses" and their reappearance in other more secular and aesthetic forms. While much of the ground Roston covers seems in many ways familiar, his study also suggests some intriguing new possibilities, and makes a good case for further exploration of the interconnections between religious beliefs and aesthetic forms.

JANOWITZ's takes as her subject the paradox that in eighteenth-century ruins "the figure of decay was at the same time the image used to authorize England's autonomy as a world power". Exploring the sense in which "country" came to mean both the physical landscape and the nation – with the ruin as a crucial image of that merger – she presents a series of acute essays in which ruins, physical and poetic, emerge as means of binding culture to nature, of asserting permanence even in the act of creation. This study of such writers as John Dyer, William Blake, William Wordsworth, and Byron is one of a number that have revitalized interest in the picturesque.

Indeed, in recent years the picturesque has become a focus of substantial attention, and one of the most recent and indeed most interesting contributions to its study has been the collection of essays edited by COPLEY and GARSIDE. The term itself has been increasingly problematized in the last decade, and a great deal of emphasis has fallen upon its often contradictory ideological functions and assumptions in late eighteenth- and nineteenth-century popular and patrician culture. The subjects of essays in the collection range from William Gilpin and black-lead mining to the politics of the picturesque in women's fiction, from gypsies in Sir Walter Scott's landscapes to the Chartist revolts of the 1830s. According to the editors, "the cultural importance of the Picturesque stands in direct proportion to the theoretical imprecision of its vocabulary".

KELSALL concentrates on the English country house, beginning with Ben Jonson's Penshurst early in the seventeenth century, but dwelling for much of the time on the eighteenth and nineteenth centuries. In a series of brief but elegant and illuminating essays, Kelsall explores the continuing life of the Roman-villa ideal in literary and architectural form, tracing the tradition from Pope, Samuel Richardson, and Henry Fielding, to Jane Austen, Benjamin Disraeli, William Morris, and H.G. Wells. He suggests that as a literature written by outsiders (i.e., not owners) it is a tradition of both upward mobility and inevitable scepticism, but also one seeking to establish a sense of place, and with it a sense of Englishness.

STEPHEN BENDING

See also **Topographical Poetry**

Langland, William c.1332–c.1390

English poet

Alford, John A. (ed.), *A Companion to "Piers Plowman"*, Berkeley: University of California Press, 1988

Colaianne, A.J., *Piers Plowman: An Annotated Bibliography of Editions and Criticism 1550–1977*, New York: Garland, 1978

Di Marco, Vincent, *Piers Plowman: A Reference Guide*, Boston: G.K. Hall, 1982

Du Boulay, F.R.H., *The England of "Piers Plowman": William Langland and His Vision of the Fourteenth Century*, Cambridge and Rochester, New York: D.S. Brewer, 1991

Frank, Robert Worth, Jr., *"Piers Plowman" and the Scheme of Salvation: An Interpretation of Dowel, Dobet, and Dobest*, New Haven, Connecticut: Yale University Press, 1957

Godden, Malcolm, *The Making of "Piers Plowman"*, London: Longman, 1900

Simpson, James, *Piers Plowman: An Introduction to the B-Text*, London: Longman, 1990

Yearbook of Langland Studies, (journal), East Lansing, Michigan: Colleagues Press, 1987 –

Extant in numerous manuscripts, and found in three versions completed at different moments in the poet's life, William Langland's *Piers Plowman* is the greatest representative of the Middle English alliterative tradition and, despite certain flaws, is an unquestioned masterpiece of English and world literature, on a par with a work such as Dante's *Divine Comedy*. The poem is the spiritual biography of the main character Will (seen by many scholars as at least in part the poet's alter ego). In a number of dream visions and shorter waking episodes, Will describes and reflects on his own spiritual development as he attempts to resolve for himself a number of political, social, educational, and religious questions, of the kind that preoccupied late fourteenth-century thinkers. A brief summary of this vast exploration of the human intellect and plumbing of the human heart cannot do the poem justice, but beginners will appreciate the extended summaries in most of the works discussed below.

COLAIANNE provides a selective annotated list of 672 scholarly works dealing with *Piers* produced between 1875 and

1979. She divides her work into four chapters dealing respectively with authorship; problems related to establishing the text; interpretative studies; and language, style and metre. A fifth chapter suggests directions for future studies. Beginners will find the introductory essays to each chapter useful guides to the development of *Piers Plowman* scholarship.

DI MARCO's work is a more comprehensive annotated list of most scholarship to 1979, including doctoral dissertations and selected reviews of most books. The entries are arranged alphabetically by author within each year. Readers will appreciate the lists of scholarly references to *Piers* from the very earliest in 1395, permitting them to trace the literary and scholarly fortunes of Langland's masterpiece in the first few centuries after its creation. Di Marco also provides an index of authors, titles, and selected subjects. For scholarship since 1985, readers will wish to consult the annotated bibliographies appearing annually in *The Yearbook of Langland Studies*.

The *Companion* edited by ALFORD provides "essential information on every major aspect of the [poem]", as well as "an overview of modern critical approaches". Following an introductory chapter, which offers an overview of the poem's critical heritage (Anne Middleton), a section on the late medieval context of the poem contains discussions of the poem's design (Alford), historical context (Anna Baldwin), and Langland's theology (Robert Adams). A second section concerning generic influences deals with Langland's practice of allegory (Stephen Barney), his use of satire (John Yunk), and his debt to medieval sermons (Siegfried Wenzel). A third section on the text and language of the poem contains chapters on the physical text and its manuscript tradition (George Kane), its dialect and grammar (M.L. Samuels), and its alliterative style (David Lawton). The volume's epilogue on the legacy of *Piers Plowman* (Anne Hudson) traces critical and literary reactions to the poem in the 250 years after its creation. The essays, models of conciseness, are both illuminating and stimulating, although the chapters in the third section may prove daunting for beginners; the bibliographies following each chapter constitute excellent guides to the major scholarship in a given area.

Beginners will find DU BOULAY's work a thoughtful reflection on *Piers Plowman* from the point of view of the historian rather than that of the literary critic. Du Boulay's reading seeks to uncover not only the historical Langland and his place in the chronological events of his time, but more importantly Langland the man, the poet, and the visionary, fully immersed in the great debates of the period. He begins with a cautious, but at times refreshing, search of all three texts for the creator of *Piers*. Chapters 2 and 3 present a solid and occasionally detailed overview of English society and the societal problems that plagued the later fourteenth century, as well as a picture of the English Church and the practical, theological, and spiritual questions with which churchmen grappled and with which Langland himself struggled throughout his life. Less satisfying – perhaps because Du Boulay spends considerably less time on them and must be content with more general critical statements or with summaries of the action of the poem – are the last three chapters on the poem's main themes (of being true and doing well), on the identity of Piers, and on the meaning of the poem's last vision.

Few books provide a more cogent analysis of the poem's themes and structure than FRANK's. In the tradition of *explication de texte*, he provides a detailed analysis of key passages in their immediate context, or in the light of relevant passages elsewhere in the poem when the immediate context is insufficient for a clear explication of the literal text. Where additional help is required, he places the passage in the larger historical context of relevant current ideas and attitudes, as reflected in the more easily available compendia of general knowledge and of biblical and moral commentaries. Frank believes that the structural key to the poem is found in viewing each of the ten dream visions of the B-text as thematic units, with the intervening waking episodes at times marking the movement from one vision to another, or at other times introducing or pointing up a theme to be developed in the following vision. The two dreams-within-dreams allow the poet to interrupt the development of one theme for a time while he attempts to resolve a different but related problem, returning to the main dream vision when that has been accomplished. Frank's analysis of the poem's structure and his many fine critical insights into individual sections of *Piers* have remained of lasting value to both the beginner and the seasoned scholar over the last 30 years.

GODDEN attempts to describe the development of Langland's imaginative process by analyzing the poet's creation from the earliest stages through the final revisions of the C-version. He sees in the Z-version (rejected by many editors and critics as a scribal compilation only) a simple two-vision poem in support of a largely secular ideal, which is transformed in the A-version, through the addition of a third vision – concerning the theme of the good life and its relation to salvation, and raising a number of issues related to learning and authority – into a work where religious and spiritual ideals dominate. Returning to his work, this time in the B-version, Langland then moved from solutions based on learning and work to an emphasis on simplicity and poverty, reaching the high point of his poem in the fifth and sixth visions, which celebrate a Messianic king dispensing a justice sublimated by mercy and Grace. In the concluding visions of B, Langland returns to the actual world in an effort to show how the fruits of redemption applies to contemporary society, with a continued hope in some authority figure (Conscience calls out to Piers, the narrator to Grace) who will reorganize the Church and triumph over the forces of the World and Antichrist. In his final revision, the C-version, Langland thus comes to grips with certain problems that still plague him, but overall he demonstrates here a more balanced, less passionate view than that of his earlier texts. Throughout his analysis, Godden highlights a number of themes and conflicts which he sees as dominating Langland's thinking, such as the opposition of justice and mercy, but locates the essence of Langland's literary personality in "the inner conflict between his yearning for a kind of oneness and simplicity and his intense and often excited awareness of plurality and complexity". There has been some scholarly objection to Godden's seeming easy readiness to blur the distinction between the real Langland, author of the work, and Will, his literary creation.

SIMPSON finds the relations of justice and love to be the controlling theme of the poem. The "unremitting justice" of the earlier visions gives way in the later to the understanding that charity "can supervene justice without violating the demands of justice", the sacrament of penance in the charge of the Church being the instrument of merciful God through which His justice is satisfied. Langland achieves a dynamic, not static or declaratory, statement of his theme through an exploration of the deepest recesses of the soul, moving from its rational part in vision three, through the will, as guided by patience and conscience in vision four, to the whole Anima, comprising not only rational and affective powers but also certain religious aspects of the soul, including conscience and charity in the later visions. But Simpson sees also an intimate relationship between the exploration of self and that of social and religious institutions, especially the Church, with Langland moving away from an allegiance to authoritarian and hierarchical institutions and towards more non-hierarchical models, where charity is the dominant quality. Reading the work in the light of modern literary theory, Simpson also finds that throughout his narrative Langland subverts those authoritative genres of his age that he comes to view as inadequate in favor of forms of discourse that are more "affective and synthetic".

RAYMOND ST-JACQUES

Larkin, Philip 1922–1985

English poet and novelist

Booth, James, *Philip Larkin: Writer*, Hemel Hempstead, Hertfordshire: Harvester Wheatsheaf, 1992

Cookson, Linda, and Brian Loughrey, *Critical Essays on Philip Larkin: The Poems*, London: Longman, 1989

Day, Roger, *Larkin*, Milton Keynes, Buckinghamshire: Open University Press, 1987

Everett, Barbara, "Philip Larkin: After Symbolism", in *Essays in Criticism*, 30(3), July 1980

Motion, Andrew, *Philip Larkin*, London and New York: Methuen, 1982

Motion, Andrew, *Philip Larkin: A Writer's Life*, Faber & Faber, 1993; New York: Farrar, Straus, Giroux, 1993

Rossen, Janice, *Philip Larkin: His Life's Work*, London: Harvester Wheatsheaf, 1989

Thwaite, Anthony (ed.), *Selected Letters of Philip Larkin, 1940–1985*, Faber & Faber, 1992; New York: Farrar, Straus, Giroux, 1993

Timms, David, *Philip Larkin*, Edinburgh: Oliver & Boyd, 1973; New York: Barnes & Noble, 1973

Tolley, A.T., *My Proper Ground: A Study of the Work of Philip Larkin and Its Development*, Ottawa: Carleton University Press, 1991; Edinburgh: Edinburgh University Press, 1991

Whalen, Terry, *Philip Larkin and English Poetry*, London: Macmillan, 1986, revised 1990

Philip Larkin did not receive much critical notice until after the publication of *The Less Deceived* in 1955, after which his reputation grew rapidly until he became one of the best-known and most widely read of twentieth-century English poets. In part this was due to his becoming associated (though he denied any formal connection) with the down-to-earth, ironic, anti-modernist stance of the so-called "Movement"; but, more plausibly, his readability and his markedly contemporary subject-matter, coupled with scrupulous control of form, spoke directly to a disenchanted postwar generation. Subsequently, criticism has expanded on these features of his work, but has also sought to offset them by attention to neglected aspects, including his supposedly submerged romantic/symbolist tendencies. The main debate, however – which still rages – is between those who see him as a narrow personality and a negative writer, and those who admire both his formal restraint and his positive responses, albeit to a world stripped of illusions.

TIMMS' 1973 book is a pioneering study of Larkin's work, but since it was published before the appearance of *High Windows* it is necessarily incomplete. It still, however, serves a useful purpose as an introduction to Larkin, and especially his relationship to the Movement. MOTION's brief 1982 study is both sympathetic and judicious – though arguably a little over-concerned to rescue the romantic/symbolic elements in the poetry. (In this respect it should be coupled with EVERETT's 1980 essay, which gives special attention to the indebtedness of Larkin's "Sympathy in White Major" to Theophile Gautier's "Symphonie en blanc majeur" and Mallarmé's "Salut".) But, undoubtedly, MOTION's major contribution is his full, detailed, and very well-written Life (1993), which deals not only with Larkin's private affairs and their relationship to the composition of his work, but also with literary influences, the vicissitudes of publication, and the development of Larkin's reputation. In conjunction with THWAITE's selection of the *Letters*, it provides a mass of information around which both favourable and unfavourable accounts of Larkin's personality have been built, and is indispensable to any reader interested in the biographical approach to his work.

Opposed to the way critics and readers have been ready to assume that the extravagances and vulgarities of some of Larkin's poems voice his own views, WHALEN puts the emphasis on the non-confessional element in Larkin's work: "Larkin is a dramatic poet in the sense that he creates centres of consciousness which are not necessarily expressive of his entire view, but are created, rather, as personae which liberate the poet to explore the multiple concerns of his art". Larkin is situated in the tradition of English poetry, and is shown to have affinities not only with Thomas Hardy, Thom Gunn, and R.S. Thomas, but, rather more surprisingly, with Samuel Johnson and D.H. Lawrence. Whalen also argues for him to be seen as a poet of "solitary wonder" and as possessing a "hunger of the imagination" – balanced, however, by a close "empirical" attention to the known, familiar world, which reveals a "specifically Imagist aesthetic . . . at the core of his own poetic practice". These themes are illustrated by a close examination of Larkin's poems, which is valuable as both explication and criticism. The book provides a good general introduction to Larkin, as well as being a useful corrective to a too-personal and pessimistic view of him.

DAY's short study is an introduction to Larkin's work for students relatively unfamiliar with it. He does not make judgements so much as suggest varieties of approach. Nevertheless, he does characterise Larkin as an accessible poet of circumstantial detail, who is traditional and clear, though not always uncomplicated in meaning. Day puts the chief emphasis on Larkin's treatment of such great commonplaces as death and time.

The collection of essays edited by COOKSON and LOUGHREY is deliberately various, intending to show that there is no permanently agreed "line" to be taken on Larkin's poetry. Each essay is written by a different author, expressing his/her own attitude to Larkin and his/her critical method (though jargon and excessive technicality are scrupulously avoided). Besides being an interesting book for the general reader, this is particularly useful for teaching purposes.

ROSSEN's study includes Larkin's novels and critical writings as well as his poetry. Though not a biography as such, it is based on a biographical approach, and is more concerned with subject matter and attitudes than form. Its themes include the half-suppressed "romantic" and "symbolist" elements in Larkin's poetry, and near-misogyny involved in his "difficulties with girls", his sardonic treatment of his own reputation, and his fear of death. Early on, Larkin struggled with his own sense of failure as a novelist, but learnt how "to write poetry about rejection and failure". He had a deep sense of isolation and enclosure, and great anger seethed under his often ironic surface; but the poetry gave paradoxically vital expression to these negative feelings. This is an interesting and well-written book, which proves to be quite sympathetic to Larkin in its slightly back-handed way.

TOLLEY argues the comparatively rare thesis that there is substantial change in Larkin's career – from the early imitator of, first, W.H. Auden, then W.B. Yeats, through Larkin as the prime exhibit of the so-called Movement, who gained "the right to be colloquial . . . funny or flippant" (a quotation taken from Larkin himself), to the mature Larkin of *The Whitsun Weddings*, and finally the later Larkin of "a hardening conservatism". Though sometimes a little pedestrian, this is the most substantial and thoroughgoing of the books on Larkin so far. Work from each phase of his development is analysed in detail, and there is a particularly interesting chapter on "The Making of the Poems", which makes extensive use of Larkin's notebooks.

BOOTH is concerned to protect Larkin's poetry from the distortions of critics who try to read specific commitments into it: "the meaning of each poem is a unique, provisional embodiment of emotions and attitudes, not a didactic statement or an ideologically motivated mystification". An interesting chapter devoted to the novels suggest that their form owes much to the poetic method of Virginia Woolf, and that Larkin had to work this influence through before he could write his best verse. On the poems themselves Booth is a sensitive and well-informed commentator, particularly expert in revealing the commendable "artifice" beneath what "sounds natural and unforced". He questions the more recent critical tendency to explain many of the first-person poems as expressing the views of ironically presented *personae* rather than Larkin's own, arguing that it is preferable to see them as "utterances of the same speaker in different, more or less ironic or self-doubting moods". There is much excellent analysis of individual poems; but perhaps the most thoughtful, and provocative, chapter is that which deals with the poems on sex and love.

R.P. DRAPER

Latino Writers

Bruce-Novoa, Juan, *Chicano Authors: Inquiry by Interview*, Austin: University of Texas Press, 1980
Bruce-Novoa, Juan, *Chicano Poetry: A Response to Chaos*, Austin: University of Texas Press, 1982
Bruce-Novoa, Juan, *Retrospace: Collected Essays on Chicano Literature: Theory and History*, Houston, Texas: Arte Público Press, 1990
Candelaria, Cordelia, *Chicano Poetry: A Critical Introduction*, Westport, Connecticut: Greenwood Press, 1986
Hernández, Guillermo, *Chicano Satire: A Study in Literary Culture*, Austin: University of Texas Press, 1991
Horno-Delgado, Asunción, Eliana Ortega, Nina M. Scott, and Nancy Saporta Sternbach (eds.), *Breaking Boundaries: Latina Writing and Critical Readings*, Amherst: University of Massachusetts Press, 1989
Huerta, Jorge A., *Chicano Theater: Themes and Forms*, Ypsilanti, Michigan: Bilingual Press/Editorial Bilingüe, 1982
Kanellos, Nicolás, *Biographical Dictionary of Hispanic Literature in the United States: Puerto Ricans, Cuban Americans and Other Hispanic Writers*, Westport, Connecticut: Greenwood Press, 1989
Lattin, Vernon E., *Contemporary Chicano Fiction: A Critical Survey*, Binghamton, New York: Bilingual Press/Editorial Bilingüe, 1986
Lee, A. Robert, "*Chicanismo* as Memory: The Fictions of Rudolfo Anaya, Nash Candelaria, Sandra Cisneros and Ron Arias", in *Memory and Cultural Politics: New Approaches to Ethnic American Literatures*, edited by Amritjit Singh, Joseph A. Skerrett, and Robert E. Hogan, Boston: Northeastern University Press, 1995
Lomelí, Francisco A. (ed.), *Handbook of Hispanic Cultures in the United States 4: Literature and Art*, Houston, Texas: Arte Público Press, 1993
Mártinez, Julio A., and Francisco A. Lomelí (eds.), *Chicano Literature: A Reference Guide*, Westport, Connecticut: Greenwood Press, 1985
Mohr, Eugene V., *The Nuyorican Experience: Literature of the Puerto Rican Minority*, Westport, Connecticut: Greenwood Press, 1983
Padilla, Genaro M., *My History, Not Yours: The Formation of Mexican American Autobiography*, Madison: University of Wisconsin Press, 1993
Saldivar, Ramón, *Chicano Narrative: The Dialectics of Difference*, Madison: University of Wisconsin Press, 1990
Sánchez, Marta Ester, *Contemporary Chicana Poetry: A Critical Approach to an Emerging Literature*, Berkeley: University of California Press, 1985

Latino/a writing in North America covers a broad front – the literature and art of an American literature whose history lies in Spanish-speaking and *mestizo* beginnings. But three historic traditions of *hispanidad* are of particular prominence: Chicano (sometimes, though not uncontroversially, termed Mexican-American), *riqueño* (Puertorican-American, with *nuyorriqueño* as its best-known manifestation), and *cubana-americano*

(Cuban-American as centred in Florida though increasingly more diverse). Each tradition exists alongside and syncretically interplied with, Anglophone American literature, an (at least) two-language heritage, whose Native American and African shapings equally make their contribution.

LOMELÍ's *Handbook* offers one of the best overviews to date of all three major Latino traditions with emphases on the double-language tradition, cinema, music, and the press, as well as each literary genre. MÁRTINEZ and LOMELÍ set out in detail the Chicano gallery, a meticulously researched and articulated encyclopedia of authors, dates, titles, summaries, and bibliographies, together with coverage of *literature chianesca* (literature about *chicanos* by non-*chicanos*). This is now the standard work of reference in its field. Its companion volume is KANELLOS, the non-Chicano Latino tradition given exactly the same kind of scholarly annotation – the "double" Puertorican record (spanning Island to "Spanish Harlem" and Manhattan), the post-exile Cuban-American record (especially its best-known name and work, Oscar Hijuelos and his *The Mambo Kings Play Songs of Love* [1989]), and the eclectic wider literary *hispanidad*, whether of *dominicano*, *chileno*, *guatemalteco*, *peruano*, or other Latin-American or Caribbean origin. All three reference-works make for essential reading.

BRUCE-NOVOA, a leading theorist-critic of Chicano writing, made his debut in the early 1970s with the proposition that "Chicano literary space" was a domain of immense long-standing and variety still to be fully mapped. His *Retrospace* – 15 essays covering topics such as "Hispanic Literatures in the United States", "Pluralism v. Nationalism", "Spanish-Language Loyalty and Literature", and "Canonical and Non-Canonical Texts" – gives a good measure of own contribution to putting that to rights. The intelligence and edge are unmistakable; they speak to, and from, almost all the main debates about literary *chicanismo*. His *Chicano Authors*, working interviews with leading Chicano authors, supplies a valuable sense of individual aspiration and context.

LATTIN's collection contains no less than 25 essays, from "Towards a Dialectic of the Chicano Novel" to case-studies of primary names: José Antonio Villarreal, Oscar Acosta, and Raymond Barrio from the 1960s; Tomás Rivera, Rolando Hinojosa, Rudolfo A. Anaya, Ron Arias, Estela Portillo Trambley, and Nash Candelaria from the great modern generation of Chicano authorship; and virtuosi of Spanish-language fiction like, Miguel Méndez, Aristeo Brito, Alejandro Morales, and Lin Romero. So comprehensive a critique does genuine good service. In smaller compass, my (LEE's) article addresses the force of Chicano memory as a collective dynamic, specifically in the fiction of Anaya, Candelaria, Sandra Cisneros, and Arias.

SALDIVAR addresses these and other names more as a cultural-studies exercise. His close, diagnostic readings are given over to the *corrido* tradition (especially Américo Paredes's *With His Pistol in His Hand* [1958]), to figures like Tomás Rivera, Oscar Zeta Acosta, and Richard Rodriguez, as well as Anaya and Arias, and to a Chicana generation of Isabella Ríos, Sandra Cisneros, and Cherrié Moraga. These he situates within the "dialectics" of American literary canon-formation and the nature of ideology in Chicano writing and its analysis. The aim, as he insists, is to help "reconstruct" American literary history and to close the "boundaries" whereby Chicano narrative has been marginalized. PADILLA pursues a more historical, excavatory line, in examining the Mexican-American antecedent names (axially the generation of Juan Seguín, Cleofas Jaramillo, and Mariano Vallejo) who paved the way for contemporaries like Acosta, Moraga, Rodriguez, and Gloria Anzaldúa. Likewise, the feminist/Chicana record has had its proponents and theorists. SÁNCHEZ scrutinizes in detail, and with considerable acumen, the quartet of Alma Villanueva, Lorna Dee Cervantes, Lucha Corpi and Bernice Zamora. HORNO-DELGADO spans all the main Latina traditions, *chicanas* like Moraga and Cisneros, *puertorriqueñas* like Rosario Ferre and Aurora Levins Morales, and *cubana-americanas* like Dolores Prida.

Chicano poetry and theatre has been more specifically served in: BRUCE-NOVOA's *Chicano Poetry*, key accounts of a line that includes José Montoya, "Corky" Gonzalez, Alurista, Bernice Zamora, and Gary Soto; CANDELARIA's, who offers at one and the same time a sense of context, an attempt at a "chicano poetics", and detailed analyses of the principal individuals; and HUERTA's informed monograph, which especially highlights the work of Luis Valdez's Teatro Campesino. These are complemented by HERNÁNDEZ, who takes the writings of Luis Valdez, José Montoya, and Rolando Hinojosa as confirmation of a longstanding tradition of Chicano literary irony and subversion.

MOHR does a first-class synoptic job in setting out the literary terrain of *riqeño* writing. He begins from the early exile and immigrant *barrio* writers, examines autobiographies like Elana Padilla's *Up from Puerto Rico* (1958), takes on the central achievement of Piri Thomas's *Down These Mean Streets* (1967), which almost singlehandedly won wider attention for the tradition, offers a chapter-length analysis of the fiction of Nicholasa Mohr, and rounds out with an overview of the code-switching, English/Spanish poetry of Victor Hernandez Cruz, Tato Laviera, and Pedro Pietri. An epilogue looks to *riqueño* writing beyond *El Barrio*, whether in the plays of Miguel Piñero or Jaime Carrero, the fiction of Pedro Juan Soto, or the autobiography of Ester Comas.

A. ROBERT LEE

Laurence, Margaret 1926–1987

Canadian novelist and short-story writer

Buss, Helen M., *Mother and Daughter Relationships in the Manawaka Works of Margaret Laurence*, Victoria, British Columbia: University of Victoria, 1985

Kertzer, J.M., *Margaret Laurence and Her Works*, Toronto: ECW Press, 1988

Morley, Patricia A., *Margaret Laurence*, Boston: Twayne, 1981; revised as *Margaret Laurence: The Long Journey Home*, Montreal and Kingston, Ontario: McGill-Queen's University Press, 1991

Sparrow, Fiona, *Into Africa with Margaret Laurence*, Toronto: ECW Press, 1992

Thomas, Clara, *The Manawaka World of Margaret Laurence*, Toronto: McClelland & Stewart, 1976

Woodcock, George (ed.), *A Place to Stand On: Essays by and about Margaret Laurence*, Edmonton, Alberta: NeWest Press, 1983

Margaret Laurence is generally recognized as a transitional figure in English-Canadian fictional writing, looking back to such modernists as Morley Callaghan and Hugh MacLennan, and forward to writers like Margaret Atwood and Alice Munro. Criticism has mirrored what many readers respond to in Laurence herself, her sympathy with characters searching for connection, wholeness, and reconciliation. It has also stressed the ways in which Laurence's vision coincided with a general English-Canadian preoccupation with national and cultural identity during the 1960s and 1970s.

KERTZER's introduction to Laurence – a brief study in the "Canadian Writers and Their Work" series – will prove a good starting-point for both students and general readers. The biographical section emphasizes her prairie Scots-Presbyterian heritage, and the significance of her years in Africa (1950–57), which inspired almost half of her major works. For Kertzer, Laurence's strong sense of social justice, her commentary on colonialism, and her feminist sympathies are important. These features link her African writing with stories and novels set on the Canadian prairies, in Manawaka, the fictional town modeled on Neepawa, Manitoba, where Laurence was born and spent her childhood. Kertzer sees Laurence as inheriting much from such classic prairie realists as Sinclair Ross and W.O. Mitchell; other aspects of her fictional practice come from the modernist tradition as exemplified by Joseph Conrad, Henry James, and others. A selected bibliography enhances the value of this introductory study.

SPARROW explicates the five volumes that originated in Laurence's African experience. Laurence lived in both Somalia and Ghana, and the written production that resulted comprises a volume of translations of Somali oral literature, a book of travel, a collection of stories, a novel, and a critical study of some West African writers. Sparrow underlines the importance of this writing to an understanding of Laurence's Canadian fiction. Some important characteristics of her work were discovered and first employed in the African books – journey as metaphor; water as image and symbol; and rich biblical allusion. Sparrow argues that Laurence's engagement with Africa was serious and sympathetic, even if the commitment was not permanent. Her primary inclination to go beyond observation *of* character to sympathy *with* character made her a supportive outsider during the period when African colonies were struggling for, and achieving, independence. Sparrow argues that Laurence's youthful optimism – about individual people, about the decolonization process and issues of achieving social and cultural harmony – gave way to disillusionment, so that, while her African writing is about the nature of freedom, her Canadian fiction concerns the more basic potential for survival. Since Canadian critics have tended to pay only lip-service to Laurence's African work, Sparrow's book is useful indeed.

THOMAS, among the first to make a serious study of Laurence's work, devotes considerable space to the African books, placing them alongside the writing of Nigerians Chinua Achebe and Wole Soyinka and West Indians George Lamming, Edward Kamau Brathwaite, and Derek Walcott. The connection, according to Thomas, is that these writers were all engaged with problems of identity and culture formation common, from the 1950s through the 1970s, to Commonwealth countries emerging from colonial status. Thomas, however, views the African work as an apprenticeship, and sees Laurence's major fictional accomplishment as the realization, through five works, of the life of the Canadian small town. Manawaka, her fictional town, is paradigmatic of the lived experience of Canadians from pioneer days to the recent past. Thomas argues that the tribe is the relevant model for the social structures of such towns, and that, although they were autocratically run and restrictive, they were formative also of sympathetic artists like Laurence who, after leaving their towns behind, would both record them in their specificity and give them a universality by imaginatively portraying them as place, people, history, and crucible. The value of Thomas's work is limited by its celebratory tone and lack of critical depth, but it is nevertheless useful as coherent chronicle, and because it shows how – and how highly – Laurence was esteemed during the latter part of her writing career, just prior to the emergence of new kinds of fiction.

BUSS wishes to move beyond the theme-and-technique kind of criticism which she sees as having prevailed in Canada, and has produced a monograph that advocates an archetypal approach, which she uses to explore mother-daughter patterns in Laurence's work. Buss notes that Laurence was a pioneer in the modern Canadian field of women writing about women (including such later writers as Audrey Thomas, Alice Munro, and Margaret Atwood), and therefore her writing invites explication in these particular feminist and archetypal terms. The theoretical base comes from the work of Carl Jung, as elaborated by Erich Neumann's study of *The Great Mother*, and the relevant deep myth is that of Demeter/Persephone, culminating in an "iconographic moment" when mother and daughter reunite. In Laurence's fiction, this moment occurs only in *The Diviners* (1974), but the search for a concept of the feminine in which the personal mother image coincides with the archetype runs through all the Canadian fiction, beginning with Hagar in *The Stone Angel* (1964). While Buss illuminates this particular aspect of Laurence's work, it is noteworthy that feminist studies of other contemporary women writers tend to use more materialist and historicized theoretical bases (Freud, Lacan, Gallop), so that Buss's application of theory might be considered to be out of fashion.

WOODCOCK's unusual anthology brings together some of Laurence's own essays with interviews and articles on aspects of her work. Woodcock endorses the view that Laurence was a pivotal writer, contributing to a new sense of Canadian identity by constructing "necessary myths" in fiction. During the 1960s a key element in such myths was that of survival, and the potential of survival and endurance for creativity. Woodcock's anthology is organized in sections. A selection on Laurence, her writerly views and techniques, and her world, is followed by sections on the African work and on the Manawaka fiction. Contributions come from several well-known writers and critics, like Atwood, Robert Kroetsch, W.H. New, and Woodcock himself. A selective bibliography supplements this useful and varied anthology, which is a good introduction to Margaret Laurence's writing and critical responses to it.

MORLEY's revision of her 1981 Twayne survey offers the fullest biographical narrative to date. It contains a useful chronology, a biographical chapter, chapters on the African work and on the Manawaka cycle, and an epilogue, which covers the last 13 years of Laurence's life. In the epilogue, Morley addresses the question of why no significant (adult) fiction followed *The Diviners* (1974). The epilogue demonstrates the degree to which Laurence had become a public figure in Ontario by 1974, and how much time she devoted to public debates about peace, women's issues, and the role of literature in culture, throwing new light on Laurence's life and career as a whole. The book's earlier sections do not differ significantly from patterns of criticism that had been established during the 1970s.

PATRICK HOLLAND

Lawrence, D.H. 1885–1930

English novelist, short-story writer, poet, essayist and travel writer

Black, Michael, *D.H. Lawrence: The Early Fiction: A Commentary*, London: Macmillan, 1986

Black, Michael, *D.H. Lawrence: The Early Philosophical Works: A Commentary*, London: Macmillan, 1991

Brown, Keith (ed.), *Rethinking Lawrence*, Milton Keynes, Buckinghamshire: Open University Press, 1990

Clark, L.D., *The Minoan Distance: The Symbolism of Travel in D.H. Lawrence*, Tucson: University of Arizona Press, 1980

Daleski, H.M., *The Forked Flame: A Study of D.H. Lawrence*, London: Faber & Faber, 1965; Evanston, Illinois: Northwestern University Press, 1965

Draper, R.P. (ed.), *D.H. Lawrence: The Critical Heritage*, London and Boston: Routledge & Kegan Paul, 1970, revised 1979

Gilbert, Sandra M., *Acts of Attention: The Poems of D.H. Lawrence*, Ithaca, New York: Cornell University Press, 1972; 2nd edition, Carbondale: Southern Illinois University Press, 1990

Hobsbaum, Philip, *A Reader's Guide to D.H. Lawrence*, London: Thames & Hudson, 1981

Hough, Graham, *The Dark Sun: A Study of D.H. Lawrence*, London: Duckworth, 1956: New York: Macmillan, 1957

Leavis, F.R., *D.H. Lawrence: Novelist*, London: Chatto & Windus, 1955; New York: Knopf, 1956

Leavis, F.R., *Thought, Words and Creativity: Art and Thought in D.H. Lawrence*, London: Chatto & Windus, 1976; New York: Oxford University Press, 1976

Lockwood, M.J., *A Study of the Poems of D.H. Lawrence: Thinking in Poetry*, London: Macmillan, 1987

Pinion, F.B., *A D.H. Lawrence Companion: Life, Thought and Works*, London: Macmillan, 1978; New York: Barnes & Noble, 1979

Sagar, Keith, *The Art of D.H. Lawrence*, Cambridge: Cambridge University Press, 1966

Spilka, Mark (ed.), *D.H. Lawrence: A Collection of Critical Essays*, Englewood Cliffs, New Jersey: Prentice-Hall, 1963

Widdowson, Peter (ed.), *D.H. Lawrence*, London: Longman, 1992

The earliest of the works listed above, LEAVIS's seminal 1955 study of Lawrence's novels and (despite the title) shorter fiction, remains what could be called the primary work of secondary criticism of Lawrence, because it is the one work to which all subsequent writing about the fiction inevitably refers back. As such, it is essential reading. Often the reference back is for the purpose of attacking Leavis, or at least recording differences of opinion, emphasis, or interpretation. This began very respectfully with Hough; since Leavis's death his reputation has been challenged with increasing virulence. On the whole, this has been beneficial to Lawrence studies, in that so many other critics have been spurred by Leavis into refining and sharpening their own readings, and led by him away from biographically-based generalising vagueness towards close analysis of the texts themselves. At the same time, the canon-obsessed Leavis's aggressive, accusatory, dismissive absolutist personal style has perhaps contributed almost as much as Lawrence's own strong personality to the tendency of critics (like other readers) to adopt extreme positions as they argue which aspects of Lawrence are good or bad and wrangle over which of his writings are best or worst. Leavis's high moral tone, judgemental and all-or-nothing in its *obiter dicta*, has particularly got up the noses of later commentators; but his related insistence on Lawrence's religious passion and reverence for life has been extremely influential, as has the insistence that Lawrence was both highly intelligent and far from being an uneducated, unthinking genius. In this, Leavis is contradicting T.S. Eliot's view of Lawrence, and, from his first page to his last, Leavis wages war on this particular enemy, as in this characteristic passage:

> In the same place as that in which he imputes cruelty to Lawrence, T.S. Eliot also speaks of an absence "in all of the relations of Lawrence's men and women" of "any moral or social sense" . . . One could fail to see it, I think, only if one approached ["Daughters of the Vicar"] with a "moral sense" that approximated to the "moral sense" with the aid of which Miss Mary enables herself to accept Mr Massy. One might in that case feel that the tale tended somehow to bring the moral sense into discredit. But what the tale brings into discredit is the spirituality of *The Cocktail Party*. It is preoccupied (being in this profoundly representative of Lawrence) with defining the nature of a true moral sense – one that shall minister to life".

In his 1976 book, LEAVIS returned to this mode, reaffirming Lawrence's superiority ("a far greater genius than Eliot") in the same large terms like "life" and with a particular defence of Lawrence as an artist of "delicate perfection" and a thinker both profound and original – again taking on Eliot's notorious allegation of Lawrence's "incapacity for what we ordinarily call thinking". By now, though, Leavis seems to be fighting battles that had largely been won, and mainly through his own immense influence, so the maintenance of his hyperbolic and challenging assertiveness preserves him in a mood either querulous or hysterical. Once again, however, his criticism is distinguished by powerful argument backed by careful readings, especially in the two novels *The Rainbow* and *Women in Love*, to which Leavis, pre-eminently, has secured wide pre-eminence.

HOUGH's is another "classic" account, hot on Leavis's heels, and admitting that there is little to add to the discussion of the two chosen major novels. But Hough has nothing of the narrow exclusivity of Leavis, and what he adds is a much greater range of Lawrence's works: not just other novels and stories, but the poems and what Lawrence called his "philosophicalish" writings. The critical but appreciative response to the poetry as a continuity, and the still very useful account of Lawrence's "doctrine", combine with excellent analyses of nine novels and a range of shorter fictions in what is one of the best general studies of Lawrence. Hough's balance can be seen in his bowing to Leavis's rankings while leaving room – to take one example – for the view that *Sons and Lovers* remains Lawrence's masterpiece "to those who abide by the central tradition of the novel".

One aspect of the doctrine – duality – is taken up by DALESKI in his study of six "representative" novels, with an appendix on an aspect of a seventh. The war between the male and female principles is taken as the chief polarity, seen as being established in the early works, attempting reconciliation in the major phase, taking the masculine line in the leadership novels, and vindicating the female principle in the last phase. Duality has since been seen as more complex in Lawrence, especially in the "third thing" that springs out of the relationship between the opposites, and extends to more than the male-female duality (as Hough had recognised), but Daleski did much clearing of the ground, and his readings are thoughtful and detailed throughout. Relating everything to his topic, moreover, has not resulted in simplifying or distortion, the usual outcome when a schematic reading is imposed; Daleski's approach is too subtle and sophisticated for that, as when he qualifies other single-minded readings:

> The opening pages of *The Rainbow* are not only an impassioned prose poem designed to evoke the traditional way of life at the Marsh Farm, nor do they only point to the rhythmic principle underlying the organisation of the novel: they are a concentrated, introductory statement of theme. The description of the seasons, for instance, is couched in terms which make it clear that the activity of nature is both a reflection and an affirmation of the fundamental desires of men and women . . .

Taking Lawrence's career in the same four stages as Daleski – this time described as discovery, maturity, uncertainty, and regeneration – is the much more general study by SAGAR, with attention to an even greater range than Hough, and for many years this has been the nearest to a "standard" text, Leavis being too limiting and eccentric to bear such a label. Sagar does not have Leavis's brilliance, being very sober and solid, even stolid at times, but he does not lack humour and is a very sensitive as well as sensible critic, and much more scholarly than Leavis. He pays particular attention to the last phase of Lawrence's life, with its new vision and new arts, not only in fiction, but also in poetry, painting, and non-fictional prose:

> The Lawrence of these years is usually presented to us as a tortured, embittered outcast, circling wildly round Europe and throwing things at Frieda. We need only look at the rhythms of the ending of *The Man Who Died* to see the complete falsity of this picture. As he nears death, Lawrence seems to live more fully, with an almost preternatural awareness of the quality of life in the instant moment, and with a joy, an insouciance which glows through the later prose.

Sagar's judicious and carefully articulated response to Lawrence's art in the context of his life, especially in tracing the development of different forms in the different phases of that life, with extensive documentation and citation throughout, has been, and will continue to be, relied on by students.

Less reliable are some of the critics assembled by DRAPER, but his astute and sizeable selection of early critical responses, 1909–32, is indispensable in showing how reviewers reacted to Lawrence and, in turn, how Lawrence reacted to his critics. Some of the more hostile critiques are omitted, as are most of the more bizarre, but the evidence of the first reception of each of Lawrence's books will remain valuable, as will the editor's lucidly informative introductory survey of Lawrence's early critical reputation.

GILBERT's remains the most substantial of the increasing number of monographs on the poetry, and its close examinations of a large number of poems make up some of the most detailed and penetrating "acts of attention" ever paid to this vital part of Lawrence's *oeuvre*. She is especially adept at identifying what is characteristic of the poetry of different periods of Lawrence's life, how this developed, and how it can be related to the work of other poets as well as to Lawrence's other writings, as in this characteristically thought-provoking passage:

> It is, however, when he treats his own specific life-crises – the death of desire, a problem just for some men, rather than death, a problem for all men; his own special anger rather than archetypal oceanic anger – that Lawrence at this point writes what must be considered truly confessional verse – poetry which, though it doesn't name names as Lowell's or Plath's or even Yeats' does, deliberately uses the personal as a model for the universal.

In the new edition, this leading feminist critic also questions her admiration for Lawrence, the notorious feminist hate-object, in a Preface, and in an Afterword explores her subject's subversion of orthodoxy. LOCKWOOD also focuses on Lawrence's thought in his poetry, but takes it further in relation to his philosophy, and in particular to his religious concerns: this makes for a coherent and also rather moving account of Lawrence's poetic development, valuably complemented by some discussion of earlier manuscript and other versions of particular poems.

PINION's handbook covers as great a range of Lawrence's works as any, and is packed with factual information, maps, lists of people and places, and so on. But what distinguished it from many such "companions" is that it is also critical: Pinion is not afraid to offer opinions on everything from the poems to the plays, the travel essays to the "thought-adventures". He pays special attention to symbolic imagery in the fiction, showing how it functions in a variety of objects, scenes, and characterisations.

A particular pattern of symbolic imagery is also the focus of CLARK's magnificent book. This grew out of retracing Lawrence's travels around the world to assess his evocation of "the spirit of place" and explore the resulting patterns of "geographical symbolism" in the works; but it is far from being limited to Lawrence's travel writing: indeed, almost every genre receives lovingly detailed attention, and the book as a whole genuinely illuminates. More than one commentator considers this the best book ever written on Lawrence, and it is certainly one of the most coherent, lucidly exploring its subject's bewildering multiplicity without resorting to any misleading oversimplification. The links between different aspects of Lawrence's artistic and personal "pilgrimage" are notably revelatory yet unstrained, as in the following easy yet thoughtful transition from Australia to America:

> . . . the prominent geographical symbol for the surging passional forces in *Kangaroo* is the sea, which rolls just below the steep bank where the cottage stood in which Lawrence wrote the book and watched himself and Frieda come and go as Somers and Harriet. In this element of the novel Harriet eventually becomes almost as implicated as her husband, when she emerges as a precursor to the women in search who predominate in the fiction of Lawrence's American period.

HOBSBAUM's is one of the briefest possible guides to the whole range of Lawrence's writings, and his barely 150 pages could not claim to do justice to that range; but he does have a sharp eye for what is essential and a concise way of making this clear. His critical opinions are stimulating and keep the book lively, though he is not above distorting, as when he suppresses crucial words in the poem "Piano" in a mistaken attempt to show it is more sentimental than the manuscript draft, which flies in the face of other commentators and the evidence. In a text widely used by students, this sort of thing is unfortunate, as is, say, the renaming of Lawrence's Miss Frost as Miss Snow to help a suggested identification with Charlotte Brontë's Lucy Snowe of *Villette*. But Hobsbaum is not always as unreliable as this, and when he relies on more scholarly research of his own or others he can be very helpful, as in his detailed demonstration of how the characterisation of Clifford Chatterley changed in the three successive versions of Lawrence's last novel.

In the 1980s the great Cambridge edition of Lawrence's works got under way, and studies began to use the much more reliable new texts and information that became available. One of the first in the field was BLACK's first commentary (1986), on the early fiction. The splendid index, with its full detailing of topics, indicates the wonderfully detailed way in which Black has analysed these works: once again, as with so many of the best studies of Lawrence, the special focus is on imagery, and Black's account of it in the early novels and stories is unlikely to be bettered. Here is a typical example:

> The word "gripped", used of Miriam several times, may remind us of gestures of the hands, especially of Siegmund's hands clenched over his thumbs. It also links back with the phrase "gripped into incandescence" used of Mrs Morel, so that there is a carrying-forward of the basic light-image used of both women. It is the pressure-lamp again, as "overcharged" suggests . . . The implicit contrast is with Walter Morel . . . One striking element in the description of his "light" was that it had "a dusky golden softness". This in him which is soft and golden and ruddy is contrasted with something hard and white in them: something warm with something cold, something sun-like with something moon-like.

It is much to be hoped that he will in future extend his method to the later Lawrence; meanwhile, BLACK has also used the Cambridge edition very profitably in his second commentary (1991), on the early philosophical works, again with a close linguistic attention to the texts, and this time exploring writings that have hitherto not been subjected to this kind of meticulous scrutiny. In both books, a fresh reading brings about a fresh understanding of Lawrence's method and message.

Finally, three of the many collections of essays on Lawrence have been singled out. SPILKA's, as one of the first and most widely circulated, has had tremendous influence, for ill (such as the undervaluation of the plays) as well as for good (such as the recognition of Lawrence's darker sides as the necessary corollary of what Leavis sees as his normative positives). More recent developments are represented in WIDDOWSON's anthology, with sections on postmodernism, class, history, ideology, psychoanalysis, gender, sexuality, feminism and "Post-Structuralist Turns". There is a shortage of structural and other types of formal analysis, however, which gives the book an imbalance, as such recent typical studies are unrepresented; readers will find the balance righted in BROWN's excellent collection, with attention paid to such neglected areas as Lawrence's comedy, textual genesis and verse technique, as well as recent formal approaches, including two essays on Lawrence and Mikhail Bakhtin. In addition, there is a recognition that Lawrence cannot be confined in an "academic gaol", and several of the essayists do what Lawrence himself is seen as doing, "continually goading his audience to a comparable liveliness of response".

MICHAEL HERBERT

Leavis, F.R. 1895–1978

English critic and editor

Bell, Michael, *F.R. Leavis*, London and New York: Routledge, 1988

Bilan, R.P., *The Literary Criticism of F.R. Leavis*, Cambridge and New York: Cambridge University Press, 1979

Boyers, Robert, *F.R. Leavis: Judgment and the Discipline of Thought*, Columbia: University of Missouri Press, 1978

Buckley, Vincent, *Poetry and Morality: Studies on the Criticism of Matthew Arnold, T.S. Eliot and F.R. Leavis*, London: Chatto & Windus, 1959

Casey, John, *The Language of Criticism*, London: Methuen, 1966

French, Philip (ed.), *Three Honest Men: Edmund Wilson, F.R. Leavis, Lionel Trilling: A Critical Mosaic*, Manchester: Carcanet New Press, 1980

Greenwood, E.B., *F.R. Leavis*, London: Longman, 1978

Gross, John, *The Rise and Fall of the Man of Letters: English Literary Life since 1800*, London: Weidenfeld & Nicolson, 1969; New York: Macmillan, 1969

Hayman, Ronald, *Leavis*, London: Heinemann, 1976; Totowa, New Jersey: Rowman & Littlefield, 1976

Hobsbaum, Philip, *Essentials of Literary Criticism*, London: Thames & Hudson, 1983

Inglis, Fred, *Radical Earnestness: English Social Theory 1880–1980*, Oxford: Martin Robertson, 1982

Kinch, M.B., William Baker, and John Kimber (eds.), *F.R. Leavis and Q.D. Leavis: An Annotated Bibliography*, New York: Garland, 1989

McCallum, Pamela, *Literature and Method: Towards a Critique of I.A. Richards, T.S. Eliot and F.R. Leavis*, Dublin: Gill & Macmillan, 1983; Atlantic Highlands, New Jersey: Humanities Press, 1983

Mulhern, Francis, *The Moment of "Scrutiny"*, London: NLB, 1979

Robertson, P.J.M., *The Leavises on Fiction: An Historic Partnership*, New York: St Martin's Press, 1981; London: Macmillan, 1981

Samson, Anne, *F.R. Leavis*, London: Harvester Wheatsheaf, 1992; Toronto and Buffalo, New York: University of Toronto Press, 1992

Steiner, George, *Language and Silence: Essays on Language, Literature and the Inhuman*, New York: Atheneum, 1970; as *Language and Silence: Essays 1958–1966*, London: Faber & Faber, 1970

Thompson, Denys (ed.), *The Leavises: Recollections and Impressions*, Cambridge and New York: Cambridge University Press, 1984

Walsh, William, *F.R. Leavis*, London: Chatto & Windus, 1980; Bloomington: Indiana University Press, 1980

Watson, Garry, *The Leavises, the "Social" and the Left*, Swansea: Brynmill, 1977

From early in his career, F.R. Leavis was able to attract an extent of contumely unusual in the English critical tradition. By the time he became an assistant lecturer, at an age when other academics of his generation were being considered for chairs, the discussion had become frenetic. George Gordon, Merton Professor of English Literature at Oxford *and*, in his time, also Professor of Poetry, stated that "Dr Leavis of Cambridge ... I am credibly informed, has recently declared his inability to perceive any poetry worth speaking of (with the exception of Donne and a few odds and ends) between Shakespeare and Gerard Hopkins. Hysteria, plainly, if this be true". The 1934 lecture where this comment was made was reprinted, without apology or qualification, in Gordon's collection of *causeries*, *The Discipline of Letters* (1946), even though by that time Leavis had published *Revaluation*, with appreciative essays on Alexander Pope, William Wordsworth, and John Keats, among others, in what amounted to an informal history of the English verse tradition.

Gordon's comment, nevertheless, was to set the tone of much controversy thereafter. No wonder, as HAYMAN detailed in his biography of Leavis, his protagonist was passed over for a full-time lectureship while such luminaries as T.R. Henn, L.J. Potts, and Joan Bennett were promoted ahead of him. But much that is related by Hayman derives from hearsay proffered by a number of witnesses who either did not know Leavis very well or else were not sufficiently interested to convey with any degree of specificity the knowledge that they had. THOMPSON is preferable. There is a superior degree of acquaintance among those contributing to his biographical volume – among them, M.C. Bradbrook, L.C. Knights, D.W. Harding, and Raymond Williams. But their acquaintance with the subject is attenuated by the fragmentary nature of their comments. WATSON is far more useful when it comes to documentation. His is a careful study of the largely hostile reception Leavis had from the reviewers. He points to Frank Kermode, an admirer of Clive James, joining with James in a community of discourse regarding Leavis's late book, *Nor Shall My Sword*. Watson further points to Martin Amis – an intimate of a metropolitan literary scene compulsively hostile to Leavis – describing another late book, *The Living Principle*, as "totalitarian", fitting in with denunciations by Oxbridge professors such as John Carey, who claimed that Leavis was "encouraging youths scarcely out of short trousers to deliver judgement on the masterpieces of the past". All these figures wrote for journals almost permanently antagonistic to Leavis: the *Times Literary Supplement*, *The Observer*, the *New Statesman*, *The Spectator*. (Indeed, Peter Ackroyd, the then literary editor of the last-named magazine, is to be found 20 years later, in the *Times* of 26 January 1995, declaring that Leavis's "'great tradition' corrupted more readers than a thousand television book programmes".)

Clearly, there must be something adverse in Leavis to elicit so extreme an extent of hostility. One salient characteristic has been defined by GREENWOOD, in a British Council pamphlet, as "an animus ... closely linked to an animation which is inseparable from the intensity of conviction with which he tries to communicate his insights". Another is outlined in an edition of a broadcast concerning Leavis. Here, FRENCH speaks of the brutal dismissals suffered by Leavis on account of his prose style. Another contributor to the discussion suggests that only the most "fanatical" followers could have taken any pleasure in it.

Of course Leavis has had his defenders, but some of them are not much more discerning than the assailants already instanced. WALSH, in what is little more than a volume of hagiography, suggests that Leavis was "Johnsonian in temperament, Arnoldian in the practice of criticism, and Coleridgean in his conclusions". This is a proposition that appears no more meaningful now than in 1980, when it was made. STEINER has a study of language in relation to politics, which comments on Leavis that "in his achievement the centrality is manifest; the humanity has often been tragically absent". This is a statement that seems debatable, if not self-contradictory.

Leavis's advocacy of D.H. Lawrence, in particular, has proved unpopular. BUCKLEY, in a study that includes Matthew Arnold and T.S. Eliot, puts Leavis on their level, but disagrees with him as regards Lawrence's "spiritual and emotional health". BOYERS, in a series commenting on contemporary figures and trends, terms Leavis "the most influential English critic of his generation". But he also speaks of "the shrill and improbable hysteria that characterises the worst passages of his book on Lawrence".

Something of Leavis's peculiar quality was put across by MULHERN, the strength of whose account is that it sees Leavis in the context of his long-running periodical. "The *Scrutiny* group quickly came to believe that if the *endoxa* of `mass civilization' was inimical to `standards', England's reigning `minority' was scarcely less so". So far from being mindless disciples, the *Scrutiny* circle were "major exponents of the new poetry and criticism and trenchant commentators on cultural and social problems". What appeared genuinely new was Leavis's "projection". Artistic achievement was "inexplicable" apart from the community that "shaped" and "sustained" it. Mulhern admits he is a Marxist sympathiser, though, and it may be felt that he consequently takes "artistic expression" for granted.

BILAN, in the most valuable study so far, points out that for Leavis and his colleagues on *Scrutiny* the twentieth century was "a time of dissolution and disintegration". This is to suggest that the *Times Literary Supplement* and similar organs were part of the malaise that Leavis saw around him. It is no wonder, then, that they answered back. Bilan believes that Leavis's "positive" inheres in his sense of the effective presence of a literary tradition, and his sense makes it possible to engage in literary criticism. "Leavis insists that the poetic-creative use of language is found in major novelists as well as major poets" says Bilan, and concludes that "in any attempt to analyse Leavis's work, the novel criticism should be given separate treatment". Therefore it would seem that ROBERTSON is helped by his specific focus on the novel, which also brings to centre stage Q.D. Leavis's contribution to her husband's achievement. The Leavises both recognise "energy" and "poetry" as factors of a novel's success. Unlike certain other critics, Robertson has no especial difficulty with the Leavises' terminology, finding it grounded in, and supported by, the specific approach of comparison and analysis that they undertake. He recognises that there is an ethical imperative behind their verbal analysis. This is discussed more centrally by BELL in a contribution to the series "Critics of the Twentieth Century". He compares Leavis's approach with that of the German philosopher, Martin Heidegger. Leavis "gives us not so much a `model' of language as a sharply focused awareness of it in the light of particular questions and demands".

SAMSON, writing for a series called "Modern Cultural Theorists", adds Oswald Spengler, Michael Polanyi, and Marjorie Grene to a possible list of analogues. It cannot be too much emphasised, however, that Leavis himself refused to be classified as a philosopher or to be drawn into debates concerning literary theory. In a book attempting to reconcile philosophy with criticism, CASEY finds the grounds of Leavis's exposition obscure: "Intelligence, self-knowledge, maturity, reality stand together against immaturity, self-dramatization, sentimentality, day-dream, self-indulgence. It is obvious that there is a large set of terms in Leavis's criticism which are closely interrelated, and sometimes even equated".

Seeking to identify a "method" in modern criticism, McCALLUM sees in Leavis's work "a circularity of justificatory argument". This may be because she tends to extrapolate conclusions from Leavis's discussion of specific works. Perhaps McCallum would not perceive as self-referential Leavis's ethical positives, such as "life" and "community", if she related them back to the analysis that occasioned them. She appears, like Casey, to be reading Leavis as something other than a critic.

Read as a philosopher, Leavis can sound at times like Thomas Carlyle and John Ruskin, and seem cloudy as to his foundations. But these are, so to speak, critics without texts, and, in contrast, Leavis has to be assessed in relation to the texts he discussed. A text, moreover, is only what a consensus of readers can agree it to be. INGLIS, in a sociological study which places John Maynard Keynes and R.G. Collingwood alongside Leavis, reminds us of the latter's reiterated formula, "this is so, is it not?". So far from being dogmatic, Leavis belongs to a critical forum.

KINCH, BAKER, and KIMBER quote the present writer (HOBSBAUM) as saying that "no one did more to educate a literate minority than Leavis". No critic is perfect, but none developed so influential a critical technique or founded so genuine a critical school. The man who had L.C. Knights, D.W. Harding, James Smith, and D.J. Enright among his associates can hardly be said (*pace* GROSS) to brainwash his disciples.

PHILIP HOBSBAUM

le Carré, John 1931–

English novelist

Barley, Tony, *Taking Sides: The Fiction of John le Carré*, Milton Keynes, Buckinghamshire: Open University Press, 1986

Beene, LynnDianne, *John le Carré*, New York: Twayne, 1992; Oxford: Maxwell Macmillan, 1992

Bold, Alan (ed.), *The Quest for John le Carré*, London: Vision Press, 1988; New York: St Martin's Press, 1988

Homberger, Eric, *John le Carré*, London and New York: Methuen, 1986

Monaghan, David, *The Novels of John le Carré: The Art of Survival*, Oxford and New York: Blackwell, 1985

Monaghan, David, *Smiley's Circus: A Guide to the Secret World of John le Carré*, London: Orbis, 1986

Wolfe, Peter, *Corridors of Deceit: The World of John le Carré*, Bowling Green, Ohio: Bowling Green State University Popular Press, 1987

Book-length studies of John le Carré have begun to appear since the mid-1980s after the publication of his *Quest for Karla* trilogy, a set of novels regarded as a major phase in le Carré's development, and which have made his relegation to the status of genre-writer an increasingly difficult task. Two marked tendencies in le Carré criticism have emerged over the last decade. The first sees him as a sophisticated literary practitioner and apologist for liberal humanism, whose novels harken back to F.R. Leavis's "Great Tradition". It is concerned with defending le Carré against the frequently levelled criticism that he is merely a spy novelist with literary pretensions, and with acknowledging his rare success in bridging the gap between popular and "serious" audiences. The second tendency brings to bear on his work the powerful critical methodologies of Marxism, structuralism, and popular-culture studies, which emerged in the 1970s. This type of criticism attends to the ideological forces and narratological techniques that contend in, and structure, le Carré's fiction, thus offering a useful balance to the first type which tends to participate in the same liberal humanism which it sees the novels as exemplifying. If there is a weakness in le Carré criticism it is its sometimes repetitive insistence on him as a writer worthy of study.

BARLEY's excellent book takes its approach from Marxism, without holding with what it sees as Marxism's more reductive aspects. It thus rejects the simplistic view that the meaning of le Carré's novels can be exhausted by their ideological content, arguing instead that it is precisely the individual experience of ideology that the novels dramatize. Le Carré is seen as demonstrating the inevitable interpenetration of personal and political subject matter. Barley chooses to focus on him as political novelist and psychologist, placing most of his emphasis on the "'mature' thrillers" from *The Spy Who Came in from the Cold* to *The Little Drummer Girl*. The book locates le Carré's relationship to the spy thriller in his inversion of material considered central to the traditional formula – his making of the narrative suspense secondary to character development and his displacement of the climax in favour of dispersive narrative information. It also notes le Carré's collapsing of oppositions as structuring the thriller, most importantly that of a safe, conflict-free "us" and a foreign, conspiratorial threat. There are insightful analyses of class – Barley observes an absence of class-consciousness in le Carré's depiction of the espionage establishment – and gender, in particular le Carré's subversion of female stereotypes and his construction of a quasi-homosexual, compensatory world of male spies.

BEENE's book, an introductory survey in the Twayne "English Authors" series, covers the fiction from *Call for the Dead* to *The Secret Pilgrim*, as well as containing a useful chronology and extensive bibliography of primary and secondary material. It is notable for its discussions of le Carré's short stories and of *The Naive and Sentimental Lover*, both of which are usually given short shrift. The latter, despite its being panned by critics, is seen as a significant phase in le Carré's development, an excursion outside of the thriller genre, which embodies the Schillerian themes that are elaborated in the novels of the 1970s. Beene notes the disturbing effect of le Carré's eschewal of thriller formulae, seeing his precursors in Joseph Conrad and Graham Greene. She addresses commonly noted themes in his fiction while adding her own observations, such as on the significance of betrayal as a strategy in le Carré's plots. An extensive discussion of the Smiley character's ambivalence toward his work points to the larger hypocrisy, dramatized in the novels, in the West's espousal of a Christian, humanist ethic when, at the same time, individualism, far from being prized, is regularly crushed by a collectivism represented in microcosm by the espionage establishment. There are frequent biographical and historical contextualizations of le Carré's fiction.

BOLD's book is a collection of essays offering a range of critical approaches to le Carré's work up to *A Perfect Spy*. Space limitations prohibit a comprehensive summary of its contents, although a number of essays should be mentioned. Owen Dudley Edwards identifies another tradition for le Carré by examining him in the context of Arthur Conan Doyle and P.G. Wodehouse; Glenn W. Most considers him more generally in the detective-novel context, suggesting that *A Small Town in Germany* "may well anticipate the end of the genre"; Robert Giddings provides a narratological analysis of *The Spy Who Came in from the Cold*; Stewart Crehan sees the fiction as operating an "assimilation strategy" by which cultural and ideological "otherness" is made consistent with a Western, liberal-humanist imperialism. Margaret Moan Rowe's essay is an important feminist account of the fiction, which notes the evolving complexity of le Carré's female characters up to his choice of a woman protagonist in *The Little Drummer Girl*, while maintaining that his fictional world remains essentially a masculine place, in which women's secondary role is to assist in the development of male plots and characters. The volume also contains an interview between le Carré and Melvyn Bragg about *The Little Drummer Girl*.

HOMBERGER's book, published in the Methuen "Contemporary Writers" series, is a useful introduction, which surveys the novels chronologically up to *A Perfect Spy*. It notes the evolution of different thematic preoccupations throughout le Carré's career: the moral corruption attendant on the pursuit of abstract ideals in the novels of the 1960s; the nature of closed intelligence communities in the trilogy; and the family as central metaphor for espionage in the later novels. Homberger addresses the literary/popular debate directly by reference to Leavis's "Mass Civilization and Minority Culture" essay, and places the trilogy in the tradition of postwar novel sequences by Anthony Powell, Lawrence Durrell, and Doris Lessing. He observes in le Carré a formal and political nostalgia and a moral seriousness preoccupied with betrayal, seeing him as a writer for whom morality is inseparable from politics. There is an extensive bibliography of primary and secondary works.

MONAGHAN's 1985 study covers the novels of the 1960s and 1970s, with a final chapter on *The Little Drummer Girl*, which he examines in the context of the earlier fiction. Of the four central chapters on formal and thematic aspects, the first sees le Carré's fiction as exemplifying a "unifying vision", in which the central Schillerian duality of the naive versus the sentimental is unsuccessfully reconciled by his characters. Chapter 2 looks at le Carré's use of symbolic landscapes and his mapping of a spiritual geography in which only the Chinese Hong Kong of *The Honourable Schoolboy* encourages the achievement of "complete humanity". Chapter 3 examines the influence on le Carré's fiction of Conrad, Greene, and of the popular spy-thriller, of which Monaghan provides a structural analysis. Chapter 4 offers a history of the George Smiley character who, despite his varied career, remains essentially the same throughout the novels. This conclusion is carried into the final chapter, which argues that *The Little Drummer Girl*'s moral outlook, despite the novel's expansion into new locales and a different set of characters, remains essentially the same as in the earlier fiction. Le Carré's novels are thus seen as variations on the same basic moral themes.

MONAGHAN's second book (1986), a dictionary of the characters, geography, bureaucracies, and jargon of the novels up to *Smiley's People*, is based on the premise that le Carré's fictional world is a consistent, self-enclosed entity comparable to William Faulkner's Yoknapatawpha. It is useful mainly as a guidebook, since beyond some brief comments on the development and elaboration of the Circus in the novels of the 1960s and 1970s, there is no extensive critical discussion of le Carré's use of the fictional-world technique.

WOLFE's book is a chronological survey, which, after four introductory chapters, covers all the novels up to *The Little Drummer Girl*. It is a somewhat superficial study, much of which is devoted to plot summary, which tends toward reductive and unhelpful generalizations – for example, that George Smiley mixes "one part derring-do to ten parts intellectual endeavour". The book summarizes central themes, arguing that for le Carré espionage has strayed from "living values" into bureaucracy and technique. It does make occasional interesting observations, specifically about le Carré's use of gallows humour and his penchant for androgynous character-names, though these are often marred by incomprehensibly argued conclusions – in the case of androgynous naming, that "espionage attack[s] the basic component of the dialectic".

NOEL PEACOCK

Lesbian Literature *see* Gay and Lesbian Literature

Lessing, Doris 1919–

British novelist and short-story writer

Green, Gayle, *Doris Lessing: The Poetics of Change*, Ann Arbor: University of Michigan Press, 1994
Kaplan, Carey, and Ellen Cronan Rose, *Approaches to Teaching Lessing's "The Golden Notebook"*, New York: Modern Language Association of America, 1989
King, Jeannette, *Doris Lessing*, London: Edward Arnold, 1989
Maslen, Elizabeth, *Doris Lessing*, Plymouth, Devon: Northcote House, 1994
Moan Rowe, Margaret, *Doris Lessing*, London: Macmillan, 1994; New York: St Martin's Press, 1994
Rubenstein, Roberta, *The Novelistic Vision of Doris Lessing: Breaking the Forms of Consciousness*, Urbana: University of Illinois Press, 1979
Sage, Lorna, *Doris Lessing*, London: Methuen, 1983
Sprague, Claire, *Rereading Doris Lessing: Narrative Patterns of Doubling and Repetition*, Chapel Hill, North Carolina: University of North Carolina Press, 1987
Taylor, Jenny (ed.), *Notebooks/Memoirs/Archives: Reading and Re-Reading Doris Lessing*, London and Boston: Routledge & Kegan Paul, 1982
Thorpe, Michael, *Doris Lessing's Africa*, London: Evans, 1978, New York: Holmes & Meier, 1979

Early critical reaction to Doris Lessing tended towards pigeonholing: Lessing was a writer about "race relations in Africa" (review of *Five*, in *New Statesman*, 11 July 1953), or a woman writer writing for, and about, women. Wide popularity and a more serious critical appraisal came with the publication of *The Golden Notebook* in 1962. As the scope of her novels has extended to embrace a variety of genres, so the quantity and range of Lessing criticism has grown, particularly in the United States. Lessing is unapologetically more interested in ideas than in style, and has acquired something of the status of prophet or seer; this has tended to divide critics between admirers, often indifferent to her stylistic lapses, and detractors, often dismissive of her ideas as naive. If the body of works about Lessing has a characteristic weakness, however, it is a certain uncritical enthusiasm.

THORPE's study focuses on the African novels and stories, placing them in their social, political, and historical contexts. Through his detailed discussion of *The Grass is Singing*, the African stories, and the Children of Violence novel sequence, Thorpe invites the reader to recognise the actual and potential breadth of Lessing's vision, commenting:

> . . . her African writing is not limited by the word "African"; because she never yielded to the temptation to treat the "colour problem" simplistically, but kept instead a clear compassionate eye upon the humanity of all she portrayed, her work transcends the relatively brief episode of white settlement and places it in firm perspective as one of the seemingly tragic histories of universal distrust and hostility between races, creeds and classes.

The book also contains a still-useful bibliography of further reading relevant to the African background of the early work.

RUBENSTEIN adopts a Jungian approach to the major novels up to 1979, interpreting them as explorations of consciousness, and positing Hegel, Marx, and Jung respectively as Lessing's philosophical, political, and psychological mentors. The book contains some revealing quotations from Lessing on the subject of Jungian and Freudian psychoanalysis, which seem to adumbrate Lessing's growing sympathy with Sufi mysticism. Rubenstein's emphasis on Lessing's multiplicity has laid the basis for many subsequent readings (including Sprague's), and her thesis that "while the focus of a particular novel may appear to be political, social, psychological, feminist or mythic . . . the common denominator in Lessing's fictional world is the mind: the mind discovering, interpreting and ultimately shaping its own reality" makes the book an interesting early example of the psychoanalytical approach taken up by a number of subsequent critics.

TAYLOR has brought together a disparate group of women writers from a number of disciplines, resulting in a substantial book of criticism whose variety and multiplicity reflect those of Lessing's own *oeuvre*. Taylor herself wrote the very useful Introduction, "Situating Reading", which places Lessing in broad historical, political, and literary contexts. Other essays deal with specific themes and texts, including an unusual analysis (by Nicole Ward Jouve) of the Children of Violence novels as an ultimate statement of anti-realism. The range and quality of writing make this a valuable collection.

SAGE has written a short, accessible survey of the major works up to *The Making of the Representative for Planet 8*, with a particularly interesting chapter on the African fiction, a rather broad chapter on the English stories and novels, and a third chapter on "New Worlds" (*The Memoirs of a Survivor* and the Canopus novels). The brevity of her book precludes very detailed analysis of individual texts, and Sage's view of Lessing as a writer about marginality offers no surprises. Nevertheless, this is a an excellent short introduction to Lessing's major themes and methods.

SPRAGUE's book is a substantial and detailed analysis of 18 of Lessing's novels, taking a broadly feminist, psychoanalytical approach, and focusing on Lessing's use of "doubling" and repetition throughout her *oeuvre*. Taking as her starting-point a phrase of Rubenstein's, in which she refers to Lessing's "profoundly dialectical consciousness", Sprague makes a very thorough investigation of what she considers to be Lessing's dialectical discourse, and extrapolates a convincing theory of multiplicity as the underlying trope of all Lessing's writing. Sprague calls upon some disciplines, such as numerology and art history, which are unfamiliar in the field of Lessing criticism, and she includes, unusually, a chapter on *Retreat to Innocence*, a work that Lessing more or less suppressed as a failure. There is also an extensive (mostly American) bibliography.

KING has written another broad survey of Lessing from *The Grass is Singing* to *The Good Terrorist*, more detailed than Sage's yet more selective – it makes no reference to Lessing's short stories, for example. The author makes use of modern literary theory, incorporating Lacanian psychoanalytical theory, feminism, and structuralism into her stimulating and intelligent interpretation of Lessing's development. King reads Lessing as a predominantly realist writer, who seeks constantly to challenge and redefine the limits of realism from her position at the margins of the dominant (Western European, patriarchal) culture. Accessible, but never simplistic, this book is an ideal introduction to Lessing criticism.

Of the most recent studies, several are worth examining. KAPLAN and ROSE's self-explanatory teaching guide, part of a series on prominent writers and works, includes such luminaries of Lessing criticism as Dee Seligman, Eve Bertelsen, Sprague, and Rubenstein. MASLEN's brief but scholarly account of the major works encompasses a range of theoretical perspectives, with specific reference to the ideas of Mikhail Bakhtin and Michel Foucault. Rigorous and wide-ranging, but not beyond the grasp of the non-specialist, it also contains a useful bibliography. MOAN ROWE's study, in the "Women Writers" series, offers a sound general survey of the fiction up to *The Fifth Child*. Her approach is broadly feminist without espousing any strictly theoretical analysis, and will be useful for serious student and general reader alike. More substantial than Maslen or Moan Rowe is GREEN, who offers what its publisher describes as an "eclectic and essentially feminist" approach to the major novels up to *The Good Terrorist*, which explores in a detailed manner the notion of Lessing as prophet – in her fiction – of changing social structures. Lessing's "essential feminism" is here seen as residing in the subversive potential of the novels' ideas and forms.

PENELOPE JOWITT

Lewis, C.S. 1898–1963

English critic, essayist, and writer of novels, short stories, and children's books

Green, Roger Lancelyn, and Walter Hooper, *C.S. Lewis: A Biography*, London: Collins, 1974; New York: Harcourt Brace Jovanovich, 1974

Hooper, Walter, *Past Watchful Dragons: The Narnian Chronicles of C.S. Lewis*, London: Collins, 1979; New York: Collier Books, 1979

Manlove, C.N., *C.S. Lewis: His Literary Achievement*, London: Macmillan, 1987

Schakel, Peter J., *Reading with the Heart: The Way into Narnia*, Grand Rapids, Michigan: W.B. Eerdmans, 1979

Schakel, Peter J., and Charles A. Huttar (eds.), *Word and Story in C.S. Lewis*, Columbia: University of Missouri Press, 1991

Walker, Jeanne Murray, "*The Lion, the Witch and the Wardrobe* as Rite of Passage", in *Children's Literature in Education* (Exeter, Devon), 16(3), 1985

Walsh, Chad, *The Literary Legacy of C.S. Lewis*, New York: Harcourt Brace Jovanovich, 1979; London: Sheldon Press, 1979

Wilson, A.N., *C.S. Lewis: A Biography*, London: Collins, 1990; New York: Norton, 1990

Because C.S. Lewis's writings were so many and various, and particularly because of the extent of his work as a Christian apologist, much of what has been written about him subsequent to his death has emphasised extra-literary aspects, such as his marriage and the closing years of his life. The unashamedly hagiographical tone of some of this material would probably have surprised its subject. Nevertheless, there has also been an increasing willingness to scrutinise his fictional writing and to apply some of the approaches of modern literary theory to it.

GREEN and HOOPER, although not quite the earliest in the field, may be said to have provided a biographical foundation for the C.S. Lewis industry. As might be expected from Lewis's personal friends, their approach is almost inevitably uncritical of either the man or his work, but the contextualisation of different areas of his writing, such as the literary history and criticism, the Ransom trilogy, the apologetics, and the *Narnia* books, was something that later writers, concentrating on a more limited section of his *oeuvre*, needed as a preliminary. The later, less adulatory, biography by WILSON has the advantage of using more recently available material, and of being more detached from a personal bias in favour of its subject. It has, however, relatively little to add to the critical debate.

HOOPER's 1979 book grew from his essay on Lewis in a more general collection (*Imagination and the Spirit*, edited by Charles Huttar, Grand Rapids, Michigan: W.B. Eerdmans, 1971). The book has the merit of treating the *Narnia* books seriously, and is of some historical significance, frequently being referred to by later critics. His title is derived from an essay by Lewis in *From Other Worlds* (edited by Hooper himself, 1966), and the book imagines Lewis's strategy:

> Supposing that by casting all these things [God and the sufferings of Christ] into an imaginary world, stripping them of their stained-glass and Sunday-School associations one could make them for the first time appear in their real potency? Could one not thus steal past those watchful dragons?

Usefully too, Hooper resurrects some of Lewis's juvenilia and earlier versions of the *Narnia* stories, but the scholarly value of the book is somewhat diminished by the amount of personal anecdote.

The thesis of SCHAKEL's book, which concentrates on the *Narnia* series while occasionally also relating it to other works, especially *Mere Christianity*, is that:

> . . . the Chronicles are to be read as stories, responded to with the heart, before they are reflected upon with the head . . . Because of the archetypal nature of the stories, because their roots reach down to basic human instincts and emotions, out of that enjoyment "meaning" will come at its own time and in its own way.

He makes considerable use of the work of Northrop Frye, both in tracing patterns related to the seasons, and in examining the movement within the series between the genres of romance, tragedy, and comedy. This important book is a landmark in the process of seeing the *Narnia* books as important literary artefacts rather than purely as allegories of the Christian religion with an explicitly didactic purpose.

WALSH takes the brief of considering the whole of Lewis's output, including his poetry, with the inevitable danger of superficiality in the discussion of each area. He makes much of the well-stocked mind which the author brought to his fictional writing, and presents a useful study of some of the influences that can be detected from other sources, concluding that the roots of Lewis's vision are to be found in his unconscious mind.

MANLOVE, while omitting poetry and non-fictional works, makes a study of the whole range of Lewis's fiction, from the perspective of a critic who has himself written a good deal on fantasy. The links he makes between Lewis and his literary antecedents, particularly George MacDonald, are well supported, and his treatment of symbolism is interesting. Themes, motifs, and patterns are traced extensively, so that "what often seemed to be 'mere' stories have shown themselves to be patterned in ways we could not have supposed, with formal structures far beyond those of simply linear narrative".

A number of shorter essays are also worth attention. One of these is by WALKER, who shows how *The Lion, the Witch and the Wardrobe* "bears all the salient features of the rite of passage, as formulated by Arnold Van Gennup". This means, she claims, that the book "explicitly articulates the bifurcated experience of the reader . . . [who] both is (by empathy) and is not the hero, both is and is not the initiate, both does and does not attain a status change". The topics covered in the wide range of stimulating essays collected by SCHAKEL and HUTTAR include most of Lewis's fictional works. The editors' thesis is that "an awareness of Lewis's ideas about language and narrative is essential to a full understanding and appreciation of his thought". Michael Murrin illustrates his contention that the ways of transit into Narnia (door, picture, railway station and the wood between the worlds) can be related to "two interpretive possibilities" – the dialogues of Plato and the tradition of the art fairytale. Murrin claims that Lewis both draws attention to the nature of his art and, "by the juxtaposition of worlds . . . creates a narrative equivalent of a Platonic dialectic". Thus he sees Lewis as establishing a moral hierarchy: England and Narnia are places of testing on the way to true reality, Aslan's country. Stephen Medcalf argues that changes in Lewis's style can be related to developments in the ways he saw and presented himself throughout his life. Among the other articles in this book are Piehler's tracing of the eighteenth-century ancestry of the Ransom stories, and Manlove's broader study of images and narrative structures. This collection, the perusal of which should probably be postponed until after some of the other books mentioned above have been read, gives an indication of how much fertile ground Lewis's work provides for theoretical consideration.

PAT PINSENT

Lewis, Sinclair 1885–1951

American novelist, short-story writer, and essayist

Dooley, D.J., *The Art of Sinclair Lewis*, Lincoln: University of Nebraska Press, 1967

Light, Martin (ed.), "Sinclair Lewis" issue of *Modern Fiction Studies*, 31(3), Autumn 1985

Lundquist, James, *Sinclair Lewis*, New York: Frederick Ungar, 1973

Schorer, Mark, *Sinclair Lewis: An American Life*, New York: McGraw-Hill, 1961; London: Heinemann, 1961

Schorer, Mark (ed.), *Sinclair Lewis: A Collection of Critical Essays*, Englewood Cliffs, New Jersey: Prentice-Hall, 1962

Wilson, Christopher P., *White Collar Fictions: Class and Social Representation in American Literature 1885–1925*, Athens: University of Georgia Press, 1992

Critical appraisal of the first American to have won the Nobel Prize for Literature (1930) has been thin on the ground in recent years. One reason for this might be found in a critical heritage that has consistently debated the literary value of Lewis's writing, and tends to agree that his best work was limited to the 1920s.

If DOOLEY's engagement with Lewis's more renowned work is perhaps less substantial than other accounts, his narrative treatment of the writing – in which critical commentary is juxtaposed with biographical detail and broader historical contextualisation – is valuable in other respects. Sections dedicated to the early works, and a reading of Lewis's fiction in the 1930s as an idiosyncratic shift from satire to a coded defence of republican virtue, provide effective insights into periods of Lewis's writing that have received less critical, and less curricular, attention than the major novels of the 1920s. Dooley assigns a closing chapter to discussion of Lewis's critical heritage, and includes a selected, but extensive, bibliography.

SCHORER's editorial to the collection of critical essays in the "Twentieth Century Views" series begins on a note as richly paradoxical as any of Lewis's fiction itself. Observing that Lewis's work has hardly ever been the subject of substantial literary critique, he then introduces a collection that includes commentary by H.L. Mencken, Sherwood Anderson, Walter Lippmann, E.M. Forster, Ford Madox Ford, Lewis Mumford, Alfred Kazin, and Malcolm Cowley. (The irony is not lost on Martin Light – see below – in his own editorial to the *Modern Fiction Studies* collection, though it should be noted that, taken as a whole, the volume edited by Schorer is less consistently affirmative of Lewis's work than that edited by Light.) Schorer collects 24 short essays on diverse aspects of Lewis's writing, including Mumford's much quoted piece from *Current History* (1931), in which he suggests that the previous year's Nobel Prize for Literature should more deservedly have been awarded to Robert Frost.

LIGHT's editorial Introduction to the *Modern Fiction Studies* collection celebrates the 100th anniversary of Lewis's birth, and ponders the waning critical fortunes of its subject. This collection of ten short essays is better suited either to readers well acquainted with the main body of Lewis criticism or those seeking critical perspectives on particular aspects of his work. Of most interest is Roger Forseth's discussion of Lewis's alcoholism and the effects it had on his life and work. As Light notes in his introductory comments, this is an area which has generated minimal debate, and even less sympathy, elsewhere in Lewis criticism. Among the articles included are accounts of Lewis's friendship with Kathleen and Charles Norris, the influence of Edith Wharton on *Main Street*, Lewis's literary treatment of marriage, the importance of *Main Street* to Nella Larsen's *Quicksand*, and a summary of positions taken in recent Lewis research.

Although the issue is never explicitly addressed in any substantive terms, the central chapter of LUNDQUIST's commentary is concerned with Lewis's positioning on the less experimental periphery of American modernism. Lundquist traces the major novels of the 1920s as a developing engagement with cultural shifts in American life, which marked the transition from an economy of scarcity to an economy of abundance, and implies that Lewis's roots in pre-war liberal progressivism have been significant in the critical neglect accorded him, relative to younger contemporaries such as F. Scott Fitzgerald and Ernest Hemingway. In this regard though, Lundquist's commentary on Lewis's erratic prose-style is perhaps more convincing. Lundquist, nevertheless, defends Lewis against received critical opinion, and argues a case for him as an "essayist of considerable power and skill", an area of Lewis's work which, it is suggested, has been ignored to the detriment of both his literary reputation and a fuller understanding of the man himself.

WILSON builds a number of commentaries on individual writers into a study that works well, either as a series of s elf-contained essays, or as a specific site of inquiry frequently disregarded by American literary historians. It is in the latter context that this book will be of interest to readers of Lewis, who will gain a rare and well-researched socio-economic perspective in which to situate his writings. Wilson considers literary treatments of, and by, an emergent American middle class, foregrounding "the determinants of white collar experience and ideology" in a turn-of-the-century writing "that often denied their presence", and his commentary throughout constitutes a major study of cultural representation mediated by shifting patterns in commercial practice and political authority. The readings of class and social representation that emerge contextualise a lengthy chapter devoted to Lewis, in which Wilson discusses the writer's engagement with Fabian socialist thought, and demonstrates how an understanding of his writing in the early and middle periods is indivisible from an appreciation of the commercial and class milieu in which Lewis wrote and, as a journalist and publicist, worked.

Returning to an earlier stage of the Lewis debate, SCHORER's monumental biography (1961) still remains the major study of Lewis's life. Exhaustively detailed, the text is quoted at some stage by almost every critic to have considered Lewis at any length, and is most famous for the observation that Lewis was perhaps the worst literary writer that America had ever produced. Schorer's treatment of Lewis's writing punctuates and enlivens his biographical accounts, with less emphasis than Wilson on the writing's socio-cultural positioning, and little of the direct textual engagement that may be found in Dooley or Lundquist. As a study that grounds Lewis's work in the shifting fortunes of a particularly "American life", however, Schorer's text remains an invaluable companion to the literature itself. If his assessment of Lewis's work is finally less sympathetic than might be anticipated from the writer of an 800-page biography, then the study may nonetheless be seen to distil much of the criticism that has seemed attracted to, and yet simultaneously repulsed by, Lewis's writing. For perhaps more than anything else, it is to Lewis's relatively uncultured literariness that so many critics have been drawn, when considering the unselfconsciously American qualities of Lewis's prose.

DAVID HOLLOWAY

Lewis, Wyndham 1882–1957

English novelist, critic, and essayist

Ayers, David, *Wyndham Lewis and Western Man*, London: Macmillan, 1992

Bridson, D.G., *The Filibuster: A Study of the Ideas of Wyndham Lewis*, London: Cassell, 1972

Foshay, Roby Arard, *Wyndham Lewis and the Avant-Garde: The Politics of the Intellect* Montreal and Buffalo, New York: McGill-Queen's University Press, 1992

Jameson, Fredric, *Fables of Aggression: Wyndham Lewis: The Modernist as Fascist*, Berkeley: University of California Press, 1979

Kenner, Hugh, *Wyndham Lewis*, London: Methuen, 1954; Norfolk, Connecticut: New Directions, 1954

Schenker, Daniel, *Wyndham Lewis, Religion and Modernism*, Tuscaloosa: University of Alabama Press, 1992

Wagner, Geoffrey, *Wyndham Lewis: A Portrait of the Artist as the Enemy*, London: Routledge & Kegan Paul, 1957; New Haven, Connecticut: Yale University Press, 1957

Wyndham Lewis himself was convinced that his work had been met by a "conspiracy of silence", and in comparison with the other modernists he was indeed late to receive critical recognition. One complicating factor was the spectre of Lewis's support for fascism, which, as we shall see, has continued to haunt Lewis criticism.

KENNER's early pioneering study was an attempt to situate Lewis among the formative artists of the early twentieth century, and his importance is underlined by the fact that he wrote so extensively on the *Zeitgeist*. Kenner identifies a series of Lewis surrogates running through his fiction who are engaged in an ongoing struggle against time, and he labels as "Vorticist prose" a kind of sentence Lewis devised in the 1910s. This prose minimizes the function of verbs to represent action and relocates dynamism in combinations and sequences of words. Kenner argues that in Lewis the self is defined by function and that the latter's polemics tend to be rhetorical and not the result of deep thought. The brevity of his study, however, does not really enable him to demonstrate this characteristic in any detail. Finally, Kenner sees *The Vulgar Streak* as marking the high point in Lewis's late period for its investigation of phoneyness.

WAGNER, by contrast with Kenner, presents a densely detailed and erudite account of the intellectual context for Lewis's writings. Pursuing the line that Lewis remained a neoclassicist throughout his career, Wagner identifies a number of debts to Continental theorists, like Julien Benda and Charles Maurras, which helped to sharpen up Lewis's opposition to Henri Bergson, communism, etc. Wagner compares Lewis's use of *personae* with that of modernist contemporaries like W.B. Yeats, noting its importance for Lewis's ideal of the detached observer; he gives a tactful discussion of Lewis's attitude to the Jews; and he documents the changes in political stance from the problematic *Hitler* to subsequent pieces of political commentary like *The Hitler Cult* and *Anglosaxony*. Wagner argues plausibly that Lewis has been excessively stigmatized for supposed right-wing allegiances that were common to most of the early modernists, and also that his attitudes were anyway always more complex than a simple label like "fascist" could recognize. Wagner's study remains an essential one within Lewis criticism because, apart from the sheer quantity of relevant information it assembles, the analysis never attempts to evade weaknesses in Lewis's writings. Thus his preoccupation with the "time-philosophy" leads him to mount an "inexplicable" attack on James Joyce in *Time and Western Man*. And again, Lewis was so keen to present Romanticism as unreality that he never bothered to investigate German neoclassicism. Given Wagner's general emphasis on intellectual history it is predictable that the thinnest part of his study should be literary technique. He comments shrewdly that the vortex represented for Lewis the "principle of unity in the maelstrom of our life's diversity", but does not develop this point at any length. And, although he declares that *The Apes of God* is "probably his greatest book", beyond noting Lewis's use of references to automatism he says little about the methods of that complex novel. For detailed stylistic analysis the reader must look elsewhere.

BRIDSON places an emphasis very similar to Wagner's on Lewis's intellectual development, and sets out to rescue the writer from ignorant condemnation. He opens his discussion with an examination of Lewis's study of Shakespeare, *The Lion and the Fox*, which is seen to demonstrate a lively originality of ideas and at the same time a tendency to use characters' sentiments as evidence for arbitrary assumptions about Shakespeare's beliefs. Even more importantly, Lewis's study demonstrates his suspicion of despotism. Bridson is judicious to a fault and often punctuates his argument with statements of the pattern: "whatever we may think of the idea, it does have a historical validity". Nevertheless he has many valuable insights to offer. Like Wagner, he too notes debts to Maurras and Benda, and he shrewdly suggests that *Paleface* is as much about "*White* emancipation" as racism. He argues indeed that Lewis was well aware of cultural imperialism, and repeatedly attacked the West's ignorance of Far-Eastern art. Confronting the issue of Lewis's supposed fascism, Bridson stresses that *Hitler* should be read within the context of Lewis's heterodox notion of socialism as a national reorganization. *The Filibuster* offers useful commentary on a number of subjects central to Lewis's career – the youth cult, his attacks on John Bull, and his respect for American social attitudes. One section where Bridson begins to develop the implications of his title is that where he discusses Lewis's egocentric persona "Ned", who, in writings of the 1930s, is played off against his foil "Nidwit". Bridson, like many Lewis critics, has his own special choice from Lewis's last phase, and he proposes that *Rotting Hill* marks a new departure by its inclusion of Lewis within the process of political change.

JAMESON's study represents another, this time rather ambiguous, attempt to deal with Lewis's writings from a political viewpoint. Taking his lead from Gilles Deleuze and Félix Guattari's *Anti-Oedipus*, Jameson approaches the fiction in order to extrapolate Lewis's sentence production considered as a symbolic act, an approach Jameson was to develop in *The Narrative Unconscious*. Taking *Tarr* as a radically innovative work, Jameson argues that Lewis removes metaphor from its traditionally privileged position and reinstates metonymy in his early fiction. Second, he places Lewis in a dialogical tradition where heterogeneous discourses inhabit even the same sentence. Jameson makes a number of local arguments about the prominence of rooms and houses in Lewis's fiction, the composition of collages out of capitalist detritus, and the illusory nature of the "personal". His study is particularly challenging as a piece of Marxist stylistic analysis offering original insights on Lewis's use of cliché, for instance. As political analysis it is disabled by the virtual absence of any consideration of the non-fiction, and the study has been taken to task by reviewers like Alan Munton for misreadings, for the use of later revised texts to make points about the original works, and for a number of other faults. Despite these serious weaknesses, *Fables of Aggression* remains a stimulating and provocative account of Lewis's fictional methods.

AYERS pursues the "concept of the self" through Lewis's *oeuvre*. Where previous critics have positioned Bergson as an oppositional figure, Ayers argues for a direct influence in the separation of the mind from the world and in the self's intuitive self-perception. These notions are then related to Lewis's anti-semitism, which was reinforced by Lewis's association of femininity with passivity. Part II of Ayers' study focuses on a series of specific works, starting with the 1914 play *Enemy of the Stars*, which is highlighted as revealing the opposition between real and social selves. An analysis of *Time and Western Man* demonstrates that the concept of the self is now built around a "vacant space", and Ayers then argues that the depiction of the afterlife in *The Childermass* is consistent with Lewis's historical and anti-materialist view of the self. In summary, Ayers suggestively locates a pair of opposing impulses in Lewis's work, which "remains remarkable for the vigour with which it pursues the chimerical self while simultaneously questioning its existence".

FOSHAY confirms an implicit tribute that critics pay to Lewis's variety by latching on to different works as seminal to his *oeuvre*. This time the choice goes to *The Caliph's Design*, which Foshay sees as a blueprint for getting away from the academy and from studio art. Following Peter Bürger, Foshay sees the avant garde as characterized by self-consciousness, and he counters Jameson by declaring that "Lewis opposed all egalitarianism and collectivism, whether democratic or socialist". He too finds *Enemy of the Stars* to be a pivotal work, but crucial for showing the conflict between mind and body. The figure of Nietzsche shadows Foshay's study, which argues consistently that Lewis's "crisis of modernity" should not be seen as just a question of style but also of developing philosophical ideas. This is a particularly welcome point to make since it corrects an impression given by some critics that Lewis essentially kept his beliefs unchanged. Later chapters in Foshay's study deal with *Tarr* (showing an ambivalence over control of the self), *The Revenge for Love*, and *Self-Condemned* respectively. In the last of these Foshay suggests that Lewis finally abandoned transcendental value.

SCHENKER concentrates initially, despite his title, on identifying phases in Lewis's career and the nature of his satire. After considering Zagreus as a mock-priest in *The Apes of God* and Lewis's performance of a "priestly function" in *Snooty Baronet*, Schenker concludes that Lewis possessed a dualistic sensibility, which combined a Protestant temperament with a quasi-Catholic "ideology of the old". The prime values of Schenker's study lie in his critical discussion of the *Human Age* series and his demonstration that the subject of this trilogy had antecedents in Lewis's interest in Eastern and Western religions. Schenker reads the Bailiff of *The Childermass* as a surrogate of Lewis caught between scepticism and the desire for a transcendental truth. Lewis returned to this series in the 1950s to develop what Schenker terms a "theology of imperfection", helped partly by Albert Camus's impact on Lewis. Schenker significantly adds to our awareness of these late works and of Lewis's career as a whole by tracing out the latter's developing attitude towards the absolute.

No commentary on Lewis criticism can afford not to comment on the gradual reprinting of his works, which has been undertaken by the Black Sparrow Press. These reprints are being edited by international scholars and establish reliable texts for the first time. Each work comes with a detailed Introduction, annotations, and a table of textual variants.

DAVID SEED

Life Writing *see* Autobiography, Biography

Literary Aesthetics: Renaissance

Attridge, Derek, *Well-Weighed Syllables: Elizabethan Verse in Classical Metres*, Cambridge: Cambridge University Press, 1974

Gilman, Ernest B., *Iconoclasm and Poetry in the English Reformation: Down Went Dagon*, Chicago: University of Chicago Press, 1986

Hadfield, Andrew, *Literature, Politics and National Identity: Reformation to Renaissance*, Cambridge and New York: Cambridge University Press, 1994

Kinney, Arthur F. (ed.), *Markets of Bawdrie: The Dramatic Criticism of Stephen Gosson*, Salzburg: Institut für Englische Literatur und Sprache (Salzburg University), 1974

Lewalski, Barbara Kiefer (ed.), *Renaissance Genres: Essays on Theory, History, and Interpretation*, Cambridge, Massachusetts: Harvard University Press, 1986

Shepherd, Geoffrey (ed.), *An Apology for Poetry; or, The Defence of Poesy* by Sir Philip Sidney, London: Thomas Nelson, 1965; New York: Barnes & Noble, 1973

Smith, George Gregory (ed.), *Elizabethan Critical Essays*, 2 Vols., Oxford: Clarendon Press, 1904; reprinted, London and New York: Oxford University Press, 1964

Spingarn, Joel E., *A History of Literary Criticism in the Renaissance*, New York: Columbia University Press, 1899; reprinted, New York: Harbinger, 1963

Thompson, John, *The Founding of English Metre*, London: Routledge & Kegan Paul, 1961

SMITH is the indispensable guide to this subject, being a comprehensive collection of the main treatises of literary criticism of the era: it includes Sir Philip Sidney's *Apology for Poetry*, George Puttenham's *Art of English Poetry*, Samuel Daniel's *Defence of Rhyme*, plus works by Thomas Campion, Roger Ascham, Sir John Harington, and Gabriel Harvey. There is also a useful and substantial Introduction, which deals with Puritan attacks on poetry, sources of debates and opinions (classical, medieval, contemporary European), and prosody, diction, and decorum as dominant conceptions of literary composition of the time. The edition, excellent as it is, is badly in need of updating and should be supplemented by KINNEY, who collects the important writings of Stephen Gosson together with useful commentary and notes. Gosson was the writer whose attacks on the theatre in *The School of Abuse* (1579) led to Sidney's famous reply in defence of literary composition partly because, strangely enough, Gosson had dedicated his treatise to Sidney. Gosson attacked drama and literature on the grounds that they effeminised men and made the nation dissolute: Kinney discusses his work in terms of Protestant ideology.

Sidney defended poetry on the grounds that it inspired its readers to virtuous action. The best modern edition is SHEPHERD's, which provides comprehensive notes and Introduction, discussing the text in terms of Sidney's life, times, and sources. There are also important essays of wider relevance on theories of imitation, the uses of rhetoric, the relationship between literature and history, and humanism.

SPINGARN is still useful, being a survey of European literary criticism, principally in France, Italy, and England.

Spingarn's basic argument is that "a unified body of poetic rules and theories had been developed in Italy, and then passed into France, England, Spain, Germany, Portugal, and Holland, and through Holland into Scandinavia, so that by the beginning of the seventeenth century there was a common body of Renaissance doctrine throughout Western Europe". He also points out how indebted most English theorists were to earlier Italian writers as well as to classical models, suggesting that the crucial influence was Horace.

Spingarn has some comments on English metre, but this subject is dealt with more thoroughly in ATTRIDGE. Attridge is concerend with the attempts by Gabriel Harvey, Edmund Spenser, Sidney, and others, to introduce Latinate quantitive metres into English verse, a series of experiments eventually attacked successfully by defenders of rhyme like Samuel Daniel. Attridge deals with Elizabethan teaching of Latin and the general existence of a Latinate culture, explaining that the "Elizabethan admiration for quantitive verse was part of their admiration for intricately-worked artifice". Although the adoption of a more idiomatic English dictated that such experiments were doomed to failure, there remains a substantial collection of quantitive verse which deserves reconsideration and re-reading. Readers should supplement Attridge's account with the more orthodox literary history of THOMPSON.

Much recent criticism dealing with literary aesthetics has concentrated on the relationship between Protestantism and literature. GILMAN is a useful contribution to such study, examining the works of Spenser, Francis Quarles, John Donne, and Milton in terms of post-Reformation debates concerning the question of pictoralism. Gilman argues that Reformation iconoclasm posed a crucial dilemma for the literary imagination of the period: "how to employ poetic language in the service of the spirit if the very imagining power of the mind is tainted". He suggests that Spenser became a divided artist in order to "accommodate the adversary postures of the age" and that Quarles' *Emblemes* became "less a 'readable text' and more an 'unreadable' rebus – like a dream, dissociated, compressed, and deceptive in ways that jeopardize discursive interpretation".

My own (HADFIELD's) volume contains discussion of Sidney, George Puttenham, Gosson, and Sir Thomas Wilson, author of *The Arte of Rhetorique* (1553), perhaps the most influential treatise on rhetoric in the early English Renaissance. I argue that literary criticism needs to be read in terms of debates concerning the form an English national identity should take, so that they cannot be perceived purely as literary historical texts, and contrast Gosson's militaristic conception of a nation and its literature with Puttenham's praise for "courtly makers" as the most significant writers of a national literature, a view of the English Renaissance that has held sway ever since. The book proposes that "*The Arte of English Poesie* ... represents the transformation of a potentially critical literary medium and poetics into the art of a 'cunning princepleaser'" and that Sidney was "trying to establish literature as a series of national forms, which are both noble and masculine, with the goals of providing models for others to copy".

LEWALSKI deserves mention as a recent and very full discussion of an important aspect of Renaissance literary aesthetics, genre theory, in terms of modern literary theories. The volume contains a number of useful and distinguished essays, which analyse the complex nature of generic classification, notably the problem of mixing or transforming various forms and styles. There are essays dealing with the English georgic, city comedy, the elegy, pastoral, satire, epic, the sonnet, the complaint, the letter, and the epigram, in terms of audience, political context, literary history, as well as genre theory itself.

ANDREW HADFIELD

Literary Aesthetics: Romantic

Ashton, Rosemary, *The German Idea: Four English Writers and the Reception of German Thought 1800–1860*, Cambridge and New York: Cambridge University Press, 1980

Copley, Stephen, and Peter Garside (eds.), *The Politics of the Picturesque: Literature, Landscape and Aesthetics since 1770*, Cambridge and New York: Cambridge University Press, 1994

De Bolla, Peter, *The Discourse of the Sublime: Readings in History, Aesthetics and the Subject*, Oxford and New York: Blackwell, 1989

Eagleton, Terry, *The Ideology of the Aesthetic*, Oxford and Cambridge, Massachusetts: Blackwell, 1990

Ferguson, Frances, *Solitude and the Sublime: Romanticism and the Aesthetics of Individuation*, London and New York: Routledge, 1992

Kipperman, Mark, *Beyond Enchantment: German Idealism and English Romantic Poetry*, Philadelphia: Pennsylvania University Press, 1986

McGann, Jerome, *The Romantic Ideology: A Critical Investigation*, Chicago: University of Chicago Press, 1983

Weiskel, Thomas, *The Romantic Sublime: Studies in the Structure and Psychology of Transcendence*, Baltimore: Johns Hopkins University Press, 1976

Romantic aesthetics, and Romantic aesthetic ideology, have been significantly reappraised in the final quarter of the twentieth century. The reasons for this are manifold and complex, and reflect the interests of critics from a wide political spectrum. Historicist critics, for instance, have sought to expose and correct the perpetuation of Romantic values in supposedly critical studies. At the same time, a renewed interest in Kantian aesthetics has been at the heart of key postmodern philosophies, most notably Jean-François Lyotard's *The Postmodern Condition*. EAGLETON's historical survey of aesthetic philosophies has suggested the immense influence of German Romanticisms on subsequent art theories and practices. Indeed the link between Kant, Johann Fichte, and Hegel and contemporary British writers has been well documented. KIPPERMAN and ASHTON have persuasively argued for a significant German influence in Britain in their recent studies. However, the following discussion concentrates on more localised readings of specifically British Romantic aesthetic modes. The picturesque and particularly the sublime are the preferred modes in which British Romantic artists tended to express the *Naturphilosophie* inherited from the Continent.

The sublime has a long history. Longinus' classical model set out the sublime as a public rhetorical device, which enables a speaker to distract, elevate, and ultimately "transport" the minds of listeners. In the modern era, it has functioned as a mechanism for determining the extent, and representing the effect, of the power-relationship between natural forms and human subjects. For Edmund Burke, the sublime is a quality of objects that one cannot experience control of. For Kant, however, the sublime can reside in the very *potential* of nature to resist human control and exert power over social being, but also in the exhilarating knowledge that it is our reason that attributes such qualities to nature. At the turn of the eighteenth century, the sublime was the preferred mode of those who wished to document the changing relationship of man and the natural cosmos in the light of Newtonian physics, agrarian capitalism, and industrial urbanisation.

DE BOLLA's work reads the sublime not as the aesthetic experience of a sentient subject, or an inherent or potential quality of material objects. Rather, a Foucauldian model of how experience and knowledge are discursively produced is deployed. De Bolla demonstrates that the only way ideas of the sublime can be reconstructed by the twentieth-century historian is by viewing it as a linguistic discourse, a rhetorical choice that intersects with other discourses, from religion and alpine touring to cookery and political economy. For instance, in the 1750s and 1760s economists represented Britain's credit economy, teetering on the brink of bankruptcy, in the discourse of the sublime, just as a poet or painter might describe the experience of an actual mountain precipice. De Bolla's key distinction is between the discourse *of*, and the discourse *on*, the sublime. The former is a rhetoric employed by the subject experiencing sublimity, the latter is that of a detached observer or commentator on it. De Bolla demonstrates, in a number of astute and controlled close readings, the effect gleaned by discourses *on* the sublime using the discourse *of* sublimity. Coleridge's essay on the sublimity of gothic cathedrals is a fine example of this perhaps inevitable effect. De Bolla shows how Coleridge's reflection begins coolly, and with detachment, but is gradually brought to near-frenzy by his sense of insignificance in the cathedral's vast and all encompassing space. The writer can only conclude, in the face of the sublime, that "I am nothing!"

The two other most significant readings of the sublime by literary critics in recent years have also seen the aesthetic as a linguistic figure, but in radically different ways. As its subtitle suggests, WEISKEL's 1976 study combines Freudian psychoanalysis and structuralist linguistics in viewing the sublime as an "economy" with similar dynamics to both language and psychic development. The sublime is for Weiskel a classically Romantic experience, in which the subject walks a sort of tightrope of linguistic meaning. The subject can be thrown into vertiginous sublimity by either a profound over- or under-determination of signification: a mountain range is too vast to be comprehended, perhaps, or a scene too dark to be made meaningful. Even a single word read on a page can be beyond comprehension or be too loaded with significance. In either case, psychic health and commonplace perception must be restored. The normality that was so profoundly disrupted by the sublime moment/movement is quickly recouped, yet the experiencing or reading subject is left with a sense of the transcendent. Like the Freudian subject, whose oedipal development is a necessary but residual rite of passage, the subject returns to normality but is forever changed. Weiskel detects just such a twin process occurring in the work of Blake, Shelley, Wordsworth, and in later poets of Romantic temperament, notably W.B. Yeats and Wallace Stevens. Weiskel's best chapters deal with perhaps the two most anachronistic users of the Romantic sublime. For Blake, the sublime moment introduces not transcendent heights but the profound depths to be experienced in the material cosmos. The Wordsworthian sublime deals not with excesses of signification (too much sensory or linguistic information) but excessive under-determinations of meaning. In expressing the blank terror of fading memory or when undervaluing the "wealth" of daffodils, Wordsworth evidences what Weiskel calls his bathetic "gentling [of] the daemonic".

FERGUSON also sees the sublime as a linguistic economy, in a reading substantially informed by the deconstruction theories of Jacques Derrida and Paul de Man. In this wide-ranging and rigorously argued study, Ferguson suggests that because the sublime is like language, in that its users are unable to control the excess of representation which is produced in aestheticising a material object, it is a mode that "defeat[s] the notion of intention". The sublime's excess of signs over signified matter suggests the artist's or subject's "inability to control all the elements involved in producing a word or a sentence, much less an artistic object". The sublime becomes the ongoing and often unconscious experience of powerlessness in the face of one's experience, sensory perception, or language. The sublime, as Lyotard claims and Derrida seems to imply, is at the heart of the postmodern condition. By contrast, Ferguson detects in the two most influential eighteenth-century models of the sublime – Edmund Burke's "empiricist psychology" and Kant's "formalist idealism" – the emergence of a modern subjectivity in which language and experience are the authoritative issue of a sentient subject. More specifically, these models are shown to be a significant motive force for contemporary artist and thinkers interested in those breaches of normal experience that lead to overspill and excess: Romantic poetry, gothic novels, Thomas Malthus's population theory, and picturesque tour guides all deploy discourses of, or on, sublime excess. For Ferguson, the picturesque is in part a peculiar subset of the sublime. Most often expressed in tour guides, which stress the importance of viewing "correctly", this aesthetic resembles one half of Kant's sublime, that which suggests that nature's power resides in our framing and describing it as such, rather than as an inherent quality. Ferguson suggests that in such a gesture, the subject supposes nature to be proof of its own individuation. The picturesque tour guide requires and thus constructs a "place in which the [individuated] viewer stands . . . the experience of pleasure in a nature that is indifferent to your reactions, produces self-consciousness as a version of imagining where any kind of meaning might originate".

The importance of the picturesque as a key British Romantic aesthetic is demonstrated by a number of powerful reassessments in the collection of essays edited by COPLEY and GARSIDE. The picturesque interest in landscapes of property renders it an especially significant political discourse in the social and economic reconstruction of Britain during the late eighteenth and early nineteenth centuries. Vivien Jones's reading of "Politics and the Picturesque in Women's Fiction" includes a succinct commentary on the nuances of picturesque politics and its tendency to objectify woman as though she were a spatial property. Jones follows Ferguson in seeing the picturesque mobilised alongside the sublime in waging war against the tyranny of the feminised aesthetic of the beautiful, which "becomes the site of predictable bourgeois taste and moralised femininity". Other articles deal with the picturesque's fascination with, and aesthetic appropriation of, actual marginalised figures in the landscape. Garside's essay discusses Sir Walter Scott's use of the picturesque to establish a representational space for the controlled and therefore "safe" viewing of gypsies, such as Meg Merrilies in the novel *Guy Mannering*. According to Gilpin, an early picturesque theorist, such figures should only feature in art when used "to mark a road – to break a piece of foreground – to point out the horizon in a sea-view". As the editors suggest in their introductory essay, the picturesque rests on a productive tension in which the socio-economic place, and use, of objects and people such as gypsies are pitted against their aesthetic uses and effects. As they point out, there is increasingly a suggestion that the picturesque is a more complex political aesthetic than previously supposed, and that it seems to be "an unstable and mutating aesthetic, even in the Romantic period".

McGANN's groundbreaking book is not strictly a work on aesthetics, but rather a critique of the perpetuation of Romantic aesthetic ideology in supposedly critical studies of Romanticism. It is perhaps the most influential text on the direction of studies in British Romantic aesthetics in recent years. According to McGann, nineteenth-century readers, New Critics, and the "Yale School" led by Geoffrey Hartman have, not always unwittingly, continued the transcendentalising tendencies of Romantic thinkers in their failure to account for the historically specific material conditions of Romantic aesthetic production. As Marjorie Levinson has suggested elsewhere, such "critics" have not read texts incorrectly so much as too sympathetically. McGann's project is a call for readers of Romanticism to undertake a politicisation of the aesthetic, to look beyond the precinct of Romantic values and uncover the historical and material and discursive conditions in which Romanticism flourished. Many studies of importance have resulted from this commitment. McGann's book includes readings of Wordsworth and Byron, which put this materialist theory into practice. Wordsworth's famous "Tintern Abbey" poem is claimed to be not merely the sublime musing of a nature worshipper, but the gesture of a political poet for whom the natural-spiritual realm functions as a substitute for a now-excised sympathy for revolutionary France. It is however McGann's theoretical commitments that emerge as the lasting influence from this book, which has proved a crucial intervention in the study of British Romantic aesthetics.

TIM BURKE

Literary Theory: General

Belsey, Catherine, *Critical Practice*, London and New York: Methuen, 1980

Berman, Art, *From the New Criticism to Deconstruction: The Reception of Structuralism and Post-Structuralism*, Urbana: University of Illinois Press, 1988

Daiches, David, *Critical Approaches to Literature*, London: Longman, 1956; Englewood Cliffs, New Jersey: Prentice-Hall, 1956

Eagleton, Terry, *Literary Theory: An Introduction*, London: Blackwell, 1983; Minneapolis: University of Minnesota Press, 1983

Eagleton, Terry, *The Significance of Theory*, Oxford: Blackwell, 1990

Foulkes, A.P. (ed.), *Uses of Criticism*, Bern: Herbert Lang, 1976

Hobsbaum, Philip, *Theory of Criticism*, Bloomington: Indiana University Press, 1970

Krieger, Murray, *Theory of Criticism: A Tradition and Its System*, Baltimore: Johns Hopkins University Press, 1976

Newton, K.M., *Interpreting the Text: A Critical Introduction to the Theory and Practice of Literary Interpretation*, London: Harvester Wheatsheaf, 1990

Singh, Charu Sheel, *Contemporary Literary Theory: Linear Configurations*, Delhi: B.R. Publishing, 1990

Wellek, René, *A History of Modern Criticism 1750–1950*, 8 vols., New Haven, Connecticut, and (Volumes 7–8) London: Yale University Press, 1955–92; Volumes 1–2 and 5–6, London: Jonathan Cape, 1955 and 1986 respectively; Volumes 1–4, Cambridge: Cambridge University Press, 1981–83

Wellek, René, *Concepts of Criticism*, edited by Stephen G. Nichols, New Haven, Connecticut, and London: Yale University Press, 1963

Wimsatt, W.K., Jr., and Cleanth Brooks, *Literary Criticism: A Short History*, New York: Knopf, 1957; London: Routledge & Kegan Paul, 1970

In searching through general surveys of critical theory the first obstacle one is faced with is the inevitable effect a particular critic's theoretical affiliations will have on his or her framing of what a general survey will look like. The questions asked, and especially the answers provided, will change drastically depending on the orientation of the writer (who never can create a neutral, purely objective, space to write in). Thus, Wellek's and Wimsatt's approaches are very different from the Marxist-influenced work of Eagleton or the poststructuralist work of Belsey. What these various approaches do share is a desire to summarize different forms of literary theory over defined historical time periods. To differing degrees, these surveys examine individual theorists and changing theoretical trends. Some works provide a more focused, self-conscious, look at the notion of theory itself.

DAICHES' text is presented in three parts:

> Part One considers how various critics have answered the question "What is the nature of imaginative literature; what is its use and value?" Part Two deals with

> the practical critic, and the different ways in which specific works of literary art have been and can be evaluated. Part Three takes up those fields of inquiry in which the literary critic touches other kinds of investigation, such as the psychological and the sociological; it inquires into the relationship between literary criticism and these other disciplines.

Though not as detailed as Wimsatt and Brooks' history, Daiches provides helpful introductions to the various positions held by Plato, Aristotle, Philip Sidney, John Dryden, Samuel Johnson, William Wordsworth, Samuel Taylor Coleridge, Percy Bysshe Shelley, and I.A. Richards. In Part Two, Daiches makes a plea for readers to examine the "practical critic" since "while we may take our general view of the nature of literature from some philosopher or aesthetician who has impressed and convinced us, we are regularly called upon to make our own evaluation of particular works". The practical critics Daiches provides for our instruction include Ben Jonson, Dryden, Samuel Johnson, and T.S. Eliot. In Part Three, Daiches investigates the relationship between literary theory and psychology and sociology. Clearly, a case for aesthetics is put forth: "if we believe in literary criticism at all – as distinct from literary history and from mere explanation and description – we must believe that there are criteria of literary excellence derived from the nature of literature itself". Daiches' text provides an entrance into discussing the parameters of literary theory and the objects of its study. At several moments in his text he asks rather open ended questions which his text does not try to answer. The book concludes with the inclusive statement that "every effective literary critic sees some facet of literary art and develops our awareness with respect to it; but the total vision, or something approximating it, comes only to those who learn how to blend the insights yielded by many critical approaches".

WIMSATT and BROOKS provide a sweeping history of literary criticism; their history traces how Plato and Aristotle's debates regarding mimesis, poetic inspiration, and poetic responsibility have been replayed over the centuries. Their history is presented in four parts. Part I provides an explication of the main arguments presented by Plato, Aristotle, Horace, and Longinus; Part II examines the debates that were carried on on the stage of sixteenth-, seventeenth-, and eighteenth-century Europe; Part III chronicles the developments from Romanticism to Aestheticism and the rise of Matthew Arnold; Part IV does not provide an inclusive history of twentieth-century theory, but rather focuses heavily on New Criticism and the importance of I.A. Richards and T.S. Eliot, while acknowledging the rise of myth criticism and the importance of Sigmund Freud. While Part IV demonstrates Wimsatt and Brooks' bias against Marxist criticism and their commitment to New Criticism, there are several merits in their work which make it valuable. They create a persuasive narrative – the grand pendulum of debate between the Ancients and the Moderns, between the mimetic poet and the expressive poet, between the moralistic and the purely pleasurable.

WELLEK's eight-volume history examines the time period 1750–1950, and covers most of Europe, Russia, and the United States in the attempt to "trace the history of literary theory, i.e. poetics of all imaginative writing whether in verse or prose". The method of tracing this history is through presenting portraits of individual writers. Thus, Wellek's text is different in texture from Wimsatt and Brooks'. Wellek begins with the decline of neoclassicism in the eighteenth century and the rise of Romanticism, and he discusses theories of mimesis, genre, and morality. A thorough explication of German Romanticism is provided, along with useful introductions to the Schlegels, Schleiermacher, Schopenhauer, and Hegel are provided. Similarly, the main figures in American and French criticism are presented. Volume 5 demonstrates most clearly Wellek's personal preference for New-Critical theory. While Wellek "refuses to be lumped together with the New Critics", he does express his conviction "that New Criticism has stated or reaffirmed many basic truths to which future ages will have to return". The figures of T.S. Eliot, I.A. Richards, and F.R. Leavis loom positively in his work, as well as the American New Critics. Volume 7 examines twentieth-century German, Russian, and Eastern-European criticism, and the influence of Freud, Jung, and Heidegger is discussed. Also, Russian formalism, Marxism, and Mikhail Bakhtin are discussed. Volume 6 was published in 1986, with the striking nostalgic Postscript Wellek attaches to his text. Feminist criticism is given a passing line of recognition, and Marxist critics, such as Eagleton, are decried as "younger propagandists" who ignore the aesthetic function of art. Eliot and Leavis are again heralded, and their dominance of the "critical scene in 1950" is obviously yearned for: the "importation of French structuralism" changed the theoretical landscape. Wellek's rejection of Jacques Derrida and poststructuralism emphasises his goal of preserving a distinct space for art and an aesthetic, a goal which permeates his whole project. Contra Derrida, Wellek states: "literature is not simply language: it is an art like painting, sculpture, and music, and thus a theme of aesthetics".

WELLEK's 1963 text examines several concepts useful for literary criticism – the Baroque, Romanticism, realism, and form. Wellek also explores the concept of literary criticism: after providing a history of the term, Wellek calls for the following program in which he delineates theory as incorporating concrete criticism and literary history: "we must return to the task of building a literary theory, a system of principles, a theory of values which will necessarily draw on the criticism of concrete works of art and will constantly evoke the assistance of literary history". Wellek's work is interesting for historical reasons, as a document which both critiques and upholds several New-Critical positions, and as a sign of where "literary theory" stood before the "importation of French structuralism" and poststructuralism. His detailed portrayals of individual theorists are still informative.

HOBSBAUM's text is not a general survey of critical theory, but rather an example of New-Critical theory in practice. Hobsbaum's total acceptance of New Criticism leads to some entangled and vague discussions regarding critical disagreements over interpreting texts. For example, he blames the work of art if it is not capable of allowing critics to agree:

> Some poems are misread; but there are many poems which cannot be read at all. They communicate nothing with any degree of precision, and so fail to impose a similar reading on different readers. Interpretation gives

> place to endless misreading – endless, because the text is incapable of providing any check against them.

While his text provides an example of New Criticism in action, it presents its position as doctrine, having none of the self-reflective questioning one finds in Krieger's work. Thus, as either a survey of broad historical changes or as a wide ranging dialogue on the nature of literary theory, Hobsbaum's work is not helpful. KRIEGER's text, while sympathetic to New Criticism, is far more cautious of accepting New-Critical attitudes. One of Krieger's strengths is that he takes contrary positions into account, and thus provides a wider space for discussion. For example, he acknowledges that his stance may be questioned: "we can, of course, deny the possibility and/or the desirability of aesthetic or poetic experience as I have defined it, and, consequently, we can deny the self-enclosure of literary objects". Krieger succeeds in studying a range of historical critics (Plato, Sidney, Alexander Pope, Johnson, Coleridge, and Arnold), and he succeeds in raising several wide-ranging questions about the role of theory, without imposing a singular answer on these questions. Krieger's opening words "literary theory is a vain discipline" set a fundamentally different tone from that found in Hobsbaum's work.

FOULKES has collected several essays which deal with various theoretical concerns. Jerold Wikoff's essay examines the work of Wellek and Wimsatt, and analyses some of the debates regarding how theory should be used in the classroom. Kuna describes some of the battles between New Criticism and Marxist theory. Lillian S. Robinson describes the blurring between literary theory and cultural criticism in her article "Criticism: Who Needs It?". What Foulkes' collection enacts is the struggle between those critics who uphold New-Critical positions and those who help undermine New Criticism.

BELSEY's text is more than a history of several schools of twentieth-century theory; she presents a history with a purpose of exposing the inadequacy of liberal humanist suppositions underpinning much of late nineteenth- and early twentieth-century theory. While Belsey's theoretical allegiance to poststructuralism is evident, this does not interfere with her clear and balanced introductions to New Criticism, the work of Northrop Frye, reader-response criticism, and Saussurean linguistics. The latter half of her text explicates the various poststructural positions of Roland Barthes, Jacques Lacan, Louis Althusser, and Derrida. For Belsey "there is no practice without theory, however much that theory is suppressed", and thus discussions regarding literary theory can never be bracketed off as a purely academic and aesthetic enterprise. Here lies one of Belsey's virtues, for she persuasively shows through her survey that the theoretical stance we adopt will have noteworthy affects on our daily practice. Even those discussions involving "common sense" regarding literature or "reality" will be affected by the theoretical arguments of poststructuralism:

> . . . the notion of a text which tells a (or the) truth, as perceived by an individual subject (the author), whose insights are the source of the text's single and authoritative meaning, is not only untenable but literarily unthinkable, because the framework which supported it, a framework of assumptions and discourses, ways of thinking and talking, no longer stands.

Belsey's slim, but potent, volume is an important survey of twentieth-century theory, where she elucidates the larger issues at stake in the debates waged.

EAGLETON's 1983 introduction to twentieth-century literary theory is one of the best introductions to several schools of theory, even though it does not explicitly deal with feminist or Marxist criticism. He describes in a detailed, accessible manner phenomenology, hermeneutics, reception theory, structuralism, and semiotics, the work of the New Critics and Northrop Frye, poststructuralism, and psychoanalysis. Eagleton's work, like Belsey's, would be anathema to Hobsbaum and Wellek, or any other critic who emphasizes a separate space for an aesthetic object and a literary theory dealing solely with it. For Eagleton, "the history of modern literary theory is part of the political and ideological history of our epoch". Eagleton asks:

> . . . whether it is possible to speak of "literary theory" without perpetuating the illusion that literature exists as a distinct, bounded object of knowledge, or whether it is not preferable to draw the practical consequences of the fact that literary theory can handle Bob Dylan just as well as John Milton.

In EAGLETON's 1990 text he continues to problematize the category of "theory". He insists that "just as all social life is theoretical so all theory is a real social practice". Any distinction between "'theory' and 'life' is misleading". While his chapter "Art after Auschwitz" is too specifically focused on the work of Theodor Adorno to be of value for those interested in general surveys of theory, Eagleton's chapter "The Significance of Theory", where he thoughtfully and wittily "theorizes about theory", is a useful read. He expands on his claim that "the question of the uses of theory is, then, in the first place a political matter rather than an intellectual one".

BERMAN's main purpose is to examine "the reception of structuralism and poststructuralism within the environment of American literary criticism". He examines the empiricist underpinnings of New Criticism and its influence on American academia. Before examining structuralism and poststructuralism a variety of movements are discussed, including the work of psychologists, existentialists, the linguistics of Noam Chomsky, and the myth criticism of Frye. Berman provides excellent introductions to understanding the work of Ferdinand de Saussure, Claude Lévi-Strauss, Michel Foucault, Lacan, Althusser, and Derrida. While not as broad in its scope as Eagleton's work, Berman's text successfully traces the changes from New Criticism to poststructuralism.

SINGH provides a "critical and analytical study of contemporary literary theory . . . as it grows, develops, and manifests itself in New Criticism, Structuralism, and Post-Structuralism". He describes the rise of New Criticism and introduces the work of Saussure, Émile Durkheim, Lévi-Strauss, Barthes, and Derrida. A chapter is devoted to Frye, where Singh delineates the differences between Frye and New Criticism. Singh largely succeeds in "presenting three major twentieth century literary-critical and theoretical movements . . . in their historical outgrowth, along with their drawbacks and points of strength".

NEWTON has written an excellent survey, which describes "the developments of literary interpretation, in terms of both theory and practice, from its emergence in the 1930s in the work of the New Critics up to the interpretative practice of several of the most influential contemporary critical schools". Newton's main focus is on interpretation, which has gained importance over the century: "what has changed in the modern period is that critics have regarded interpretation as much more central to literary criticism . . . that had rarely been attempted before the twentieth century". Through surveying several schools of theory, Newton supplies helpful introductions to New Criticism, hermeneutics, poststructuralism, Marxist criticism, New Historicism, and reception theory. His chapter "Feminist Interpretation" supports his contention that "the emergence of feminist interpretation as a major force in literary criticism has been the most dramatic happening in literary studies since the war". For both its scope and clarity of presentation, Newton's text should be included in any study of critical theory.

BRUCE R.A. LORD

Literary Theory: Postwar Approaches

Atkins, G. Douglas, and Laura Morrow (eds.), *Contemporary Literary Theory*, London: Macmillan, 1989; Amherst: University of Massachusetts Press, 1989

Bradford, Richard (ed.), *The State of Theory*, London and New York: Routledge, 1993

Cohen, Ralph (ed.), *The Future of Literary Theory*, New York and London: Routledge, 1989

Eagleton, Terry, *Literary Theory: An Introduction*, Oxford: Blackwell, 1983; Minneapolis: University of Minnesota Press, 1983

Ellis, John M., *The Theory of Literary Criticism: A Logical Analysis*, Berkeley: University of California Press, 1974

Fokkema, D. W., and E. Kunne-Ibsch, *Theories of Literature in the Twentieth-Century: Structuralism, Marxism, Aesthetics of Reception, Semiotics*, London: Hurst & Co., 1977, corrected 1979; New York: St Martin's Press, 1978 (corrected edition)

Hawthorn, Jeremy, *Unlocking the Text: Fundamental Issues in Literary Theory*, London: Edward Arnold, 1987

Jefferson, Ann, and David Robey (eds.), *Modern Literary Theory: A Comparative Introduction*, London: Batsford, 1982, revised 1986; New York: Barnes & Noble, 1984

Lentricchia, Frank, and Thomas McLaughlin (eds.), *Critical Terms for Literary Study*, Chicago: University of Chicago Press, 1990

Murfin, Ross C., *Joseph Conrad: "Heart of Darkness": A Case Study in Contemporary Criticism*, New York: St Martin's Press, 1989

Payne, Michael, *Reading Theory: An Introduction to Lacan, Derrida, and Kristeva*, Oxford: Blackwell, 1993

Selden, Raman, *A Reader's Guide to Contemporary Literary Theory*, Brighton, Sussex: Harvester Press, 1985; Lexington: University Press of Kentucky, 1985; 2nd edition, Hemel Hempstead, Hertfordshire: Harvester Wheatsheaf, 1989; 3rd edition, with Peter Widdowson, Lexington: University Press of Kentucky, 1993

Selden, Raman, *Practising Theory and Reading Literature: An Introduction*, Hemel Hempstead, Hertfordshire: Harvester Wheatsheaf, 1989

Webster, Roger, *Studying Literary Theory: An Introduction*, London: Edward Arnold, 1990

Wellek, René, and Austin Warren, *Theory of Literature*, New York: Harcourt Brace, 1949; London: Jonathan Cape, 1949

What is immediately striking when one looks at studies of literary theory in the English language in the twentieth century is that the great majority of these studies were published fairly recently. Though a more analytic approach to literature emerged in the first quarter of the century with the Russian formalists and I A. Richards, it is doubtful whether they would have regarded themselves as theorists of literature in the modern sense. It is more likely that they would have seen themselves as establishing critical principles. It is only in the last 25 years or so that theory has become a major force in literary studies.

WELLEK and WARREN's study is one of the few books on critical theory published more than 40 years ago. Wellek's role is the dominant one. He came to the United States from Europe and had been associated with the Prague structuralist school. He brought this background into contact with American New Criticism, and the outcome of that meeting is *Theory of Literature*. Warren was a more orthodox New Critic. After discussing questions such as the nature of literature, they split literary criticism into the "extrinsic" and the "intrinsic" approach, the former dealing with literature's relation to such things as biography and society, and the latter concentrating on the formal aspect of literature. Wellek and Warren attempt to justify in theoretical terms the New Criticism's emphasis on form and internal coherence, though there is an awareness of the semiotic – the work of art as "a structure of signs" – that looks forward to structuralist approaches.

ELLIS is a theorist who fundamentally supports the main tenets of the New Criticism and his book is a defence of those on principles derived to some degree from the later philosophy of Ludwig Wittgenstein. He believes that literature cannot be defined constitutively so as to distinguish it absolutely from non-literature. Its distinctiveness derives from its use by society; certain texts are selected for a special kind of study that involves separating them off from their authorial and historical origins and placing them in a context divorced from their original context. For him, historical contextualisation undermines the very concept of literature since a literary text, by definition, is one that does not depend on its original context for its meaning. He thus defends central New-Critical concepts such as the primacy of the text and anti-intentionalism.

FOKKEMA and KUNNE-IBSCH's book gives a useful account of such areas as Russian formalism, French structuralism, Marxism, reception theory, and semiotics. The focus is almost entirely on Continental theorists. The authors aim "to present the outlines of current theories of literature, and to arrange them in such a way that their underlying assumptions and implied value judgements become explicit". Also Continental in emphasis is Payne, who concentrates on the major works of Jacques Lacan, Jacques Derrida, and Julia Kristeva, namely *Ecrits*, *Of Grammatology*, and *Revolution in Poetic Language*. The book is a very useful introduction and interpretation of these central but difficult texts, and concludes with an intriguing discussion of these theorists' readings of paintings.

JEFFERSON and ROBEY's book has essays on most of the main twentieth-century critical and theoretical approaches, starting with Russian formalism and ending with feminist criticism. It has eight chapters written by different hands, most of the contributors being scholars in modern languages rather than English studies. All of the chapters are interesting and accessible, and it is a book that can be safely recommended to students.

EAGLETON's introduction has been something of a best-seller in the realm of literary theory. It is written in a very lively style and unlike most guides to literary theory it does not adopt a neutral and descriptive tone. He claims in the Preface that he has aimed to "popularize" rather than to "vulgarize", and that as there is "no 'neutral', value-free way of presenting [literary theory], I have argued throughout a particular *case*". Ideally readers should have read a more conventional introduction before reading Eagleton, as this would put them in a better position to respond critically to Eagleton's account; otherwise there is a danger of uninitiated readers being carried away by Eagleton's rhetoric. The book is also less thorough in its coverage than most of the other theory introductions. The book's great merit, however, is to make literary theory an exciting subject.

A different approach is adopted by HAWTHORN. Instead of looking at the various critical schools, he tackles issues and problems. He covers such matters as the definition of literature and criticism, whether an "intrinsic" criticism is possible, the question of language, the genesis of literary works, realism, and the role of the reader, all in an interesting manner. Also dealing with issues and concepts rather than particular critical schools, WEBSTER's study is an introduction directed mainly at a student readership, and has chapters on such topics as "Language and Narrative", "'Society' and the 'Individual'", and "Textual Relations".

SELDEN and WIDDOWSON's reader's guide, the third edition published in 1993, has a very wide coverage. It starts with the New Criticism and the "moral formalism" of F.R. Leavis, goes on to Russian formalism, and in its final chapters discusses postmodernism, postcolonialism, and a wide variety of feminist theories. Many topics are discussed rather briefly, and perhaps such brevity runs the risk of superficiality of treatment of some extremely complex subjects; but in general this is an impressive overview of twentieth-century theory.

SELDEN's *Practising Theory* (1989) is an attempt to show how various theories work in practice by giving sample demonstrations of particular theoretical approaches in relation to different literary texts. In objection it could be argued that this is a form of pastiche rather than criticism. Clearly, Selden is more sympathetic to some critical approaches than to others, and readers will therefore not be seeing theory being applied in its most powerful form in many instances. On the other hand, Selden's readings have the benefit of being clear and will be of help to readers who would struggle with much of the criticism by the major exponents of particular theoretical approaches.

ATKINS and MORROW's book resembles Jefferson and Robey's in that it contains essays by several hands on the major twentieth-century critical schools and theories. It does, however, cover some areas which Jefferson and Robey omit, such as archetypal criticism. Also, almost all of the contributors are American critics who have published previously in the areas they are writing about. In particular, Michael Ryan (on political criticism) and Joel Weinsheimer (on hermeneutics) are well known in their fields. One especially valuable feature of this book is that each chapter includes an extensive annotated bibliography.

MURFIN's book is representative of a series designed to show critical theory in practice. In this example, on Joseph Conrad, after the text of *Heart of Darkness* the rest of the volume is devoted to a series of essays on the text from a number of theoretical standpoints. Each of these essays has, first of all, a ten-page (or so) discussion of the particular theoretical perspective – such as feminism, deconstruction, or New Historicism – followed by an essay using that perspective in relation to *Heart of Darkness*. The volumes in the series also contain glossaries of critical terms.

Twenty-five essays by leading theorists, who discuss the prospects for theory in the 1990s, appear in COHEN. Virtually all of the essays are worth reading, with Elaine Showalter and Gerald Graff contributing particularly interesting pieces; but there is no debate *within* the volume, as each contributor is writing without knowledge of the other contributors' standpoints. The principal interest of the volume lies in major theorists reflecting on the future for their particular perspectives.

LENTRICCHIA and McLAUGHLIN contains chapters on 22 key critical terms – for example, representation, structure, discourse, rhetoric, canon – by major critics and theorists, such as J. Hillis Miller, Stanley Fish, and Stephen Greenblatt. Given the high reputations of contributors, these terms are reinterpreted appropriately in the light of recent critical and theoretical developments, but at the same time the essays are designed to be accessible to a general audience.

Similar to Cohen is BRADFORD, but on a much smaller scale. It contains ten chapters by British theorists – for example, Antony Easthope, Thomas Docherty, and Steven Connor – reflecting on the current state of critical theory. Several of the essays focus on the problem of teaching theory: Antony Easthope believes that the "theory wars" of the 1970s are over and that a new paradigm has now replaced the old, while Patrick Parrinder, after reviewing the considerable number of theory guides in print, argues that these guides unwittingly demonstrate the need for a return to criticism in the sense of the study of specific texts.

K.M. NEWTON

Literary Theory: Contemporary Approaches

Bhabha, Homi, *The Location of Culture*, London and New York: Routledge, 1994
Docherty, Thomas (ed.), *Postmodernism: A Reader*, Hemel Hempstead, Hertfordshire: Harvester Wheatsheaf, 1993; New York: Columbia University Press, 1993
Dollimore, Jonathan, *Sexual Dissidence: Augustine to Wilde, Freud to Foucault*, Oxford: Clarendon Press 1993; New York: Oxford University Press, 1993
Humm, Maggie (ed.), *Feminisms: A Reader*, Hemel Hempstead, Hertfordshire: Harvester Wheatsheaf, 1992
Jackson, Leonard, *The Poverty of Structuralism: Literature and Structuralist Theory*, London: Longman, 1991
Nelson, Cary, and Lawrence Grossberg (eds.), *Marxism and the Interpretation of Culture*, Urbana: University of Illinois Press, 1988; London: Macmillan, 1988
Veeser, H. Aram (ed.), *The New Historicism*, London and New York: Routledge, 1989

With the vast and ever increasing literature on critical theory, this entry will focus on a small selection of texts which represent some of the diversity and new developments of recent critical thinking on Marxist, New-Historicist, feminist, gender, postmodernist, and postcolonial theory.

Among the recent work on Marxist cultural theory, NELSON and GROSSBERG's anthology covers many of the salient areas of debate in interesting and provocative ways. Including many of the leading writers and scholars working on the applications of Marxist thought, the volume presents Marxism as a vital field of debate and cultural analysis. Covering areas like the crisis in Marxism, the politics of modernity and postmodernity, hegemonic culture and countercultures, the politics of science, technology, and ethics, these perspectives testify to Marxism's continuing centrality in literary theory and its ability to suggest alternative horizons for interpretative activity.

Emerging out of Marxism, albeit frequently displaying a suspicion of some of its contentions, New Historicism has been one of the most talked-about developments in contemporary criticism. A key text, VEESER's anthology of essays demonstrates how New Historicism seeks alternatives to critical orthodoxies ranging from New Criticism to recent Franco-American literary theory, by bringing a reconsideration of history to the centre-stage. With essays by the principal figures of this critical tendency, the book addresses questions such as the "Third World" as signifier, the relationship between feminism and New Historicism, the issue of "class" as a category, and the current efficacy of cultural materialism. The multiplicity of approaches in these essays is indicative of the way New Historicism challenges the assumptions that help to compartmentalise the disciplines.

HUMM's anthology also demonstrates how one of feminism's strengths is its cross-disciplinary approach to the issues of gender politics. One of the better of the recent clutch of feminist "readers", this book "aims to encapsulate the diversity of feminist views – about race, sexuality, language and creativity, politics and class – and the many challenging feminist questions about the continued subordination of women". From Virginia Woolf to Adrienne Rich, the anthology includes key feminist ideas and perspectives on the family, sexuality, work, education, patriarchy, race, language, culture, and representation. With assessments of the first and second waves of feminism in Britain, Europe, and the United States, the book provides a perspective on the variety of modern feminisms that have emerged in the twentieth century, with good section-introductions, a glossary of key terms, and a chronology of the principal events and texts from 1900 to the 1990s.

DOLLIMORE's book also treats sexuality and gender theory, although in this case the aspect of how sexual and gender dissidence prove illuminating for current debates in literary theory, psychoanalysis, and cultural materialism. It is concerned with the way in which homosexuality has been so strangely integral to the very societies that obsessively denounce it, and how history has produced this paradoxical situation. In a book which focuses on the early modern period, Dollimore links the literature of writers as diverse as Shakespeare, André Gide, Oscar Wilde, Jean Genet, and critics like Michel Foucault, Frantz Fanon, and St Augustine, to question, extend, and probe the issues of postmodernity. It includes chapters on transgression and its containment, contemporary theories of sexual difference, gay sensibility, and transvestite literature in the theatre of Renaissance England.

The persistent complexity of the "map of postmodernism" is also usefully described and contextualised in DOCHERTY's extensive anthology of the principal texts and thinkers, among them Jürgen Habermas, Jean-François Lyotard, Richard Rorty, Jean Baudrillard, Charles Jencks, and Fredric Jameson. The Introduction provides an excellent overview of the postmodernism debate, and there are good section-introductions which place the essays within their social, cultural, and political contexts. In addition to the extensive bibliography, the book covers postmodernism and its impact upon the areas of architecture and urbanicity, politics, feminism, postcolonialism, the avant-garde, and aesthetic and cultural practices. The gathering of sympathetic and antipathetic material on postmodernism over such a diverse range reveals the manner in which there is a substantial overlap of ideas and debate across disciplines.

The development of poststructuralism out of structuralism is the focus of JACKSON's book. After outlining Saussure's original claims, he charts the ways in which the structuralism of Saussure was transformed and adapted by French literary theorists in the 1950s and 1960s. This analysis illuminates the parallel and quite separate adaptations of Ferdinand de Saussure via Claude Lévi-Strauss, in the work of theorists like Roland Barthes and Jacques Derrida. Arguing that the result of this process was the creation of an idealistic Saussure that bore little relation to the original, Jackson offers a realist theory of language as a new agenda for contemporary literary theory. Conceived and written in "plain English" in order to reach undergraduate and general readers, this book provides a useful account of the developments of structuralist thought, as well as offering critiques and other models of language to set against it. The book concludes with a very useful up-to-date bibliography, and should prove an accessible introduction to structuralism and poststructuralism.

Constantly divulging incisive thought, provocative ideas, and exciting illumination on every page, BHABHA's book must rate as one of the principal texts of recent postcolonial theory. He brings together seminal essays in skilful and effortless explorations of a diverse variety of writers and issues. He provides interesting analyses of writers like Toni Morrison, Nadine Gordimer, Derek Walcott, Salman Rushdie, and Joseph Conrad, as well as analyses of documents and archives from the Indian Mutiny, discussions of nineteenth-century colonial history, Third-World cinema, national identity, social agency, and postmodern space – all the while demonstrating an uncanny ease with the mobilization of a vast intellectual array of ideas, and of theorists like Jameson, Fanon, Derrida, and Jacques Lacan. Bhabha's central preoccupation is the manner in which the European practice of cultural analysis hitherto has glossed over the *ambivalence* about the location of culture. His efforts are aimed at exploring how to articulate (indeed, whether one can articulate) this liminal space of marginality in cultural production. Bhabha wishes to escape the polarities of East and West, Self and Other, Master and Slave, and arrive at a position "which overcomes the given grounds of opposition and opens up a space of translation: a place of hybridity, figuratively speaking, where the construction of a political object that is new, *neither the one nor the other*, properly alienates our political expectations, and changes, as it must, the very forms of our recognition of the moment of politics". Bhabha demonstrates the cultural and social necessity of striving for a discursive difference in politics – a *negotiation* not a *negation* – which opens up the possibility of articulating the antagonistic and contradictory elements of hybrid sites, rather than having them destroyed by "practical-political reason".

TIM S. WOODS

Locke, John 1632–1704

English philosopher and prose writer

Caruth, Cathy, *Empirical Truths and Critical Fictions: Locke, Wordsworth, Kant, Freud*, Baltimore: Johns Hopkins University Press, 1991

Fox, Christopher, *Locke and the Scriblerians: Identity and Consciousness in Early Eighteenth-Century Britain*, Berkeley: University of California Press, 1988

Mabbott, J.D., *John Locke*, London: Macmillan, 1973

MacLean, Kenneth, *John Locke and English Literature of the Eighteenth Century*, New York: Russell & Russell, 1936; reprinted, New Haven, Connecticut, and London: Yale University Press, 1962

O'Connor, D.J., *John Locke*, London: Penguin, 1952; New York: Dover, 1967

Quintana, Ricardo, *Two Augustans: John Locke, Jonathan Swift*, Madison: University of Wisconsin Press, 1978

Schouls, Peter A., *Reasoned Freedom: John Locke and Enlightenment*, Ithaca, New York: Cornell University Press, 1992

Tuveson, Ernest Lee, *The Imagination as a Means of Grace: Locke and the Aesthetics of Romanticism*, Berkeley: University of California Press, 1960

Walker, William, *Locke, Literary Criticism, and Philosophy*, Cambridge and New York: Cambridge University Press, 1994

Yolton, John W., *A Locke Dictionary*, Oxford and Cambridge, Massachusetts: Blackwell, 1993

The twentieth century has seen an explosion in Locke studies. Earlier works tended to be defensive as they confronted the rigours of Ludwig Wittgenstein's philosophy. Recent studies have negotiated the demands of postructuralism and mainstream European philosophy. One radical extension of this approach has been the notion that philosophy is itself a kind of text in which we may uncover hidden narratives and the play of metaphor. Other critics have taken Locke's influence on literary texts as their starting point, in some cases showing the impact of Locke's thinking on the political and social issues of his day.

QUINTANA admits modestly that his book is designed for the general reader rather than the professional philosopher or academic critic. Nonetheless, he takes account of modern scholarship. His approach is not generally biographical. Instead, he uses Locke and Jonathan Swift in order to illustrate the attitudes, tensions, and the contradictions of the period. He avoids the temptation to assimilate the philosophy of the period to its literature, demonstrated in Tuveson and MacLean's work. Quintana argues convincingly that Locke was largely hostile to poetry, and that it was subsequent literary critics, such as Joseph Addison, who adopted and adapted ideas from Locke's *Essay Concerning Human Understanding*. This volume is an excellent introduction to the complex and subtle thought of Locke and Swift.

MABBOTT's study quotes exetensively from works published in Locke's lifetime. Nonetheless, the authority of these texts is supplemented by a sense of the inconsistencies and ambiguities that they contain. Manuscript sources are therefore used as a means of filling some of the gaps. As the study proceeds, it emerges that the central problem in understanding Locke is less a matter of scholarly reconstruction, and more an awkwardness of approaching his philosophy from a modern perspective. Locke acknowledged that many problems were the product of confusions in language, but Locke does not pursue the kind of linguistic exactitude that his philosophy seemed to propose. Clearly, the kind of modern benchmark for assessing Locke is Wittgenstein. In terms of this standard, Locke fails to identify and resolve some basic linguistic confusions. Mabbott also has difficulty with Locke's epistemology, which in large part appears to be undermined by the modern discipline of psychology. Locke does emerge, however, as a shrewd commentator on the political, social, and historical issues of his time. Despite reservations concerning Locke's verbosity, Mabbott concludes that it would be difficult to deny the claim that Locke was the founder of philosophy in English.

O'CONNOR justifies the relevance of Locke by drawing a distinction between philosophy and science. He notes that the progress of philosophy is of a different kind from the progress of science. O'Connor also notes that Locke tends to deal with matters that would be proper to psychology in our own period. Like Mabbott, he is less concerned with intellectual influences on Locke, than with a trenchant critique of Locke. The *Essay*, he notes, is a poorly constructed, repetitious work. Locke is side-tracked by minor problems, but gives inadequate space to more important issues. As a result, Locke's *Essay* is a difficult text for beginners. Although O'Connor tends to be dismissive, he acknowledges that Locke's distinction between real and nominal essences in his theory of language is original and valuable. Despite the influence of the philosopher A.J. Ayer, this study benefits from returning to a moderate empiricism rather close to Locke's own position. It was originally published in 1952, so some of the problems with which the text deals are now obsolete.

MacLEAN's book is an excellent starting point for understanding how Locke's philosophy evolved in the hands of a range of eighteenth-century writers. These include Addison, Richard Blackmore, Lord Shaftesbury, Voltaire, Samuel Johnson, Henry Fielding, Oliver Goldsmith, William Wordsworth, Isaac Watts, and Matthew Prior. The book is arranged loosely in terms of the division of Locke's *Essay*. Sections are therefore entitled "Neither Principles nor Ideas are Innate"; "Of Ideas"; "Of Words"; and "Of Knowledge and Probability". This policy generally works well, although writers for whom Locke was important tend to be scattered across the text. Noting Laurence Sterne's statement that the principal influences on his life were the Bible and Locke, it is rather unfortunate that MacLean does not have a section devoted in detail to him. A longer section on the Scriblerus Club would have been useful, and more could cerainly have been said about Alexander Pope and Swift. Nonetheless, this book demonstrates that the frequent re-publication of Locke's *Essay* attests to its influence in the period 1725–65. Without supplying any overall theory of influence, this is an excellent description of the range and variety of Locke's impact on the eighteenth century; and MacLean clearly shows the revolutionary ramifications of Locke's denial of innate ideas of God and morality and the limitations of human knowledge.

TUVESON explores how Locke's concept of the mind was to have a revolutionary impact on the Romantic imagination. After Locke, it is argued, art is no longer an objective form of knowledge but a subjective impression. At times the argument makes up in neatness for what it lacks in discrimination. The analogies between the philosophy and the literature are sometimes insufficiently worked through. The book readily assimilates introspection, for instance to a form of poetic "reverie". Tuveson argues that Francis Hutcheson took Locke's ideas to a logical extreme to produce a naive aesthetic of Romanticism. The final chapter, "The Imagination: Beginnings of Symbolism", dealing with Edmund Burke and W.B. Yeats, can only be read as the introduction to a new work, rather than the conclusion of what came before.

WALKER notes that readings of Locke have enabled literary critics to postulate generic and literary categories such as the sublime, the novel, and Romanticism. Yet these have often simplified Locke's text as though it were the source of a consistent doctrine. Walker demonstrates, for instance, that the mirror is not the only figure of mind in Locke's *Essay*. He shows that many of Locke's terms are gendered, and that critics have neglected the tactile in favour of the ocular. Walker suggests that literal and figurative statements compete. Arguing against Paul de Man (who reads Locke against his explicit statements) he shows that metaphor does not inevitably rule philosophy. Walker disputes R.F. Jones's vision of the Restoration as the rejection of rhetoric and the adoption of a plain style. In Locke's case he demonstrates that the rhetorical tradition is contested and repressed. This convincing study brilliantly negotiates contemporary literary theory, and Locke emerges as a major philosopher within that framework. This refreshing study energetically attacks the general sense that British empiricism must be excluded from the Continental philosophical tradition and contemporary literary theory.

Seeking to displace the notion that self-understanding is purely a product of observation, CARUTH's study argues that thought may in fact turn uncannily upon itself. In this reading, Locke's empiricism is explored as though it were a kind of narrative. Caruth proceeds to argue that the associationist tradition is a Romantic narrative, and that its single derivation from Locke is a fiction. One of the values of this study is its recognition that Locke's initial concern in his *Essay* is part of the wider Enlightenment programme to understand the extent and the limits of the understanding. Within this framework, reason finds its own territory where it establishes a degree of certainty for itself. In Caruth's poststructuralist reading of Locke, the literal constantly mutates into the figurative; language loses its referentiality; hidden narratives are rooted out and pursued through Wordsworth, Kant, and Freud.

SCHOULS is primarily concerned with Locke's attitude to the role of education. He focuses on rationality, learning, freedom, and the nature of the passions. Locke emerges as a radical philosopher who shows that human beings may fulfil themselves, and their birthright, with the benefit of education. Schouls lucidly places Locke's thinking within the broader tradition of Enlightenment thought. Locke develops a Cartesian methodology, in which the right method leads to mastery of nature. Although Schouls rarely cites literary texts, this provocative study enlarges our sense of the range, and the complexity, of Locke's thought.

As the author of a number of distinguished studies of Locke, YOLTON is well-equipped to demonstrate the subtlety and precision of Locke's use of specific philosophical terms across a range of texts, and over a period of time. The *Dictionary* is therefore particularly useful in clarifying the different philosophical usages of a particular term in the seventeenth and early eighteenth century. Yolton recommends browsing through the *Dictionary*'s 130 items, and this may be a productive strategy for introducing oneself to the complexity of Locke as a philosopher. Specific topics also provide enough information to direct one back to the original works. The *Dictionary*, everywhere informed by Yolton's lifelong work on Locke, his erudition, and his scholarship, is indispensable for the beginner, and a valuable resource for the advanced student.

I.D. McCormick

London, Jack 1876–1916

American novelist, short-story writer, and essayist

Barltrop, Robert, *Jack London: The Man, the Writer, the Rebel*, London: Pluto Press, 1976

Geismar, Maxwell, "Jack London", in his *Rebels and*

Ancestors: The American Novel, 1890–1915, Boston: Houghton Mifflin, 1953
Johnston, Carolyn, *Jack London: An American Radical?*, Westport, Connecticut: Greenwood Press, 1984
Kingman, Russ, *Jack London: A Definitive Chronology*, Middletown, California: Jack London Research Center, 1992
Labor, Earle, *Jack London*, New York: Twayne, 1974, revised, with Jeanne Campbell Reesman, 1994
London, Joan, *Jack London and His Times: An Unconventional Biography*, New York: Doubleday, Doran & Co., 1939; reprinted, Seattle: University of Washington Press, 1969
Lundquist, James, *Jack London: Adventures, Ideas, and Fiction*, New York: Frederick Ungar, 1987
Martin, Stoddard, *California Writers: Jack London, John Steinbeck, The Tough Guys*, London: Macmillan, 1983; New York: St Martin's Press, 1983
Sinclair, Andrew, *Jack: A Biography of Jack London*, New York: Harper & Row, 1977; London: Weidenfeld & Nicolson, 1978
Tavernier-Courbin, Jacqueline (ed.), *Critical Essays on Jack London*, Boston: G.K. Hall, 1983
Walcutt, Charles Child, *Jack London*, Minneapolis: University of Minnesota Press, 1966
Watson, Charles N., Jr., *The Novels of Jack London: A Reappraisal*, Madison: University of Wisconsin Press, 1983

Jack London's popularity and the fascination that, understandably, attends on his adventurous life have, to some extent, got in the way of intelligent commentary on his contribution to American literature. There is, quite simply, no outstanding critical study of his fiction, and there is an overabundance of biographical writings; but there are numerous guides to him, which frequently weave, albeit with varying degrees of success, the life and the work together. Most studies of London emphasise the intellectual influences that bear on his fiction, especially those associated with Social Darwinism and other variations of evolutionary thought, his "primitivism", and his articulation of a kind of individualistic socialism

GEISMAR affords London a longish chapter in his study of the major American novelists at the turn of the century. London's work, he suggests, "brought to a climax the Darwinian cosmos of monsters and horrors in which man became 'the noblest game of all,' and the thunder-borne edicts of Jehovah echoed the law of the pack". His essay is general in nature, but it touches on many central features of London's work: his social Darwinism and its relations to his notions of the "superman"; his somewhat un-American preoccupation with the politics of class, notably in the socialist writings and *The Iron Heel*; his glorification of physical prowess and virility; and, perhaps above all, the essentially Romantic character of his worldview. Geismar brings the life and the writing effortlessly together, and his essay, despite being nearly half a century old, remains one of the best account's of London's work.

WALCUTT has written intelligently about American literary naturalism (particularly in *American Literary Naturalism: A Divided Stream*, 1974), and his short study of London (in the University of Minnesota "Pamphlets on American Writers" series) emphasises the Darwinian and evolutionary aspects of his fiction, seeing him as a writer simultaneously drawn to Social Darwinism and social justice, individualism and socialism. A short biographical overview precedes a somewhat longer, but still necessarily very abbreviated, chronological discussion of the major fiction, notably *The Call of the Wild*, *White Fang*, *The Sea-Wolf*, and *Martin Eden*. Walcutt concludes by suggesting that London contributed "greatly to one myth of the American writer", that of sacrificing art to a life of excess. He notes that London wrote no novels of manners nor anything that we might conventionally call "social fiction", and he contends that his strengths as a writer appear in "his command of detail and pace", and his gift for producing realism and suspense.

LONDON's biography of her father is very much a life-and-times account, and is recommended for its treatment of London's politics and his political writings, notably the impact (in the United States and beyond) of *The Iron Heel*. This biography draws extensively on Charmian London's *The Book of Jack London* (1921), but it is better organized and written with greater disinterestedness.

LABOR has written extensively on London, and his short study (in Twayne's "United States Authors" series) is a useful introduction. A biographical overview, in which London is seen as "a rugged individualist who preached Socialism" and a type of the American "Adamic" hero, is followed by a series of critical readings, largely devoted to the major fiction. Labor's book is valuable for its account of what has been called "the Mauve Decade" of American writing – one eager to suppress impropriety and reward gentility and sentimentality – and he shows how London (along with other "realists") challenged these conventions without taking on a messianic role. London's "ultimate greatness", he suggests, "derives from his 'primordial vision' – the mythopoeic force which animates his finest creations".

BARLTROP writes on London from a socialist perspective, and his book is largely an account of London's literary radicalism, especially what Barltrop calls his dramatisatation of "some of the theories of the young socialist movement". His book is part biography, part criticism, but its value resides largely in the chapters that discuss London's socialism: Barltrop is one of the few commentators on this important aspect of London's writing to insist that the social and political essays reveal, despite "their impressive language", ideas that "verge on absurdity or are meaningless". The strengths of London's propagandist writings, he suggests, are to be found in his attacks "on the evils of society in *The People of the Abyss*, in the early chapters of *The Iron Heel*, and in some essays and parts of autobiographical books". Though he is critical of the consistency of London's thinking, Barltrop makes large claims for London's importance, arguing that what is "remarkable" about the work on which "his popularity rests is the extent to which it was ahead of the taste or the mood of his time", and the simple "vigour and simplicity" of his prose. Though there are some manifest weaknesses in this book it remains one of the best studies of the totality of London's contributions to imaginative literature and social thought.

MARTIN's book contains a long essay on London, relating him to a "California tradition" in fiction, which began to take shape at the end of the nineteenth century. He sees Wolf Larsen, the hero of *The Sea-Wolf*, as a "classic literary embodiment of the Nietzschean *Ubermensch*", and a preoccupation with London's thinking about moral and physical superiority, and the attendant issues of race and class, runs through his essay. Martin suggests that London's place in Californian fiction is somewhat paradoxical, for "his fellow-Californians ... were content to use his name for commercial purposes and construct a great inegalitarian civilisation that had little in common in spirit with the utopian pastoral society of the strong of which he had most consistently dreamed".

SINCLAIR's biography is aimed very much at the general reader. London's writings are largely used to amplify and supplement the biographical portrait of him, and there is little in the way of extended discussion of any of the major fiction. Sinclair has benefited from access to most of the extant London materials, and while his biography aims to offer a lively and readable life story it is also accurate, balanced, and reliable.

WATSON seeks to "reappraise" London, and his book is written from the "conviction that London is a serious and compelling writer whose reputation has suffered at the hands of critics interested more in advancing a larger thesis than in doing justice to individual writers and works". In an effort to challenge the "conventional wisdom that London was a good short story writer but a poor novelist", Watson devotes his study to, essentially, eight novels – *The Call of the Wild*, *Martin Eden*, *The Sea-Wolf*, *White Fang*, *The Iron Heel*, *Burning Daylight*, *The Valley of the Moon*, and *The Little Lady of the Big House*. The only deviation from this pattern is an early chapter on *A Daughter of the Snows*, a novel which, he argues, sheds some light on the development of London's major themes. Watson is particularly good at showing how major art can grow out of popular materials: he notes that in works such as *Before Adam* and *The Scarlet Plague* "though London was exploiting the contemporary vogue of primitive fantasy, he was also improving on the popular formula, probing the loneliness and insecurity of his protagonist and tracing the evolution of a rudimentary cooperative society out of an earlier anarchic individualism". He is alert to London's weaknesses (his longer novels "tend to founder somewhere in the middle, perhaps because his initial enthusiasm for an idea was prone to diminish"), but he persuasive in his account of those aspects of the fiction that ensure London's popularity – his interest in the elemental and primordial, the "richness" of experience from which he drew his fictional materials, and, finally, the mythic dimension of his achievement. Among recent studies Watson's is one of the best.

TAVERNIER-COURBIN's anthology is arguably the best collection of critical essays on London so far compiled. A number of the pieces here are reprintings of earlier essays, but among the new ones worth noting are: Earl J. Wilcox's "Overtures of Literary Naturalism in *The Son of the Wolf* and *The God of the Fathers*", which seeks to establish the naturalist credentials of these early stories, pointing, particularly, to the intellectual influences of Adam Smith, Charles Darwin, Karl Marx, and Herbert Spencer; Earle Labor's account of London's writings about Polynesia, which, he suggests, were "brought to life" by London's reading of Jung's *Psychology of the Unconscious*; and Susan Ward's "Ideology for the Masses: Jack London's *The Iron Heel*", where she intelligently relates London's parable of a totalitarian state to the influence of Edward Bellamy's *Looking Backward* and London's readings in popular fiction.

JOHNSTON's book is narrowly concerned with London's politics, her overarching argument being that his politics should be construed as those of a "rebel" rather than a "radical". She sees London as a contradictory thinker, someone corrupted by the bourgeois life against which, in both his life and his writing, he rebelled, and she convincingly shows how London's views of the proletariat were simultaneously sympathetic and disdainful. Johnston's book both supplements and amplifies Barltrop's (see above), and it offers a valuable overview of London's political thought.

LUNDQUIST's study is a critical biography written by someone suspicious of London's account of himself, and both the biography and the criticism here have the virtues that come from disinterestedness. Lundquist deliberately downplays the importance of London's "adventures" to his fiction, and suggests instead that much of what is of interest in his writings is a consequence of his reading and other kinds of intellectual influences. This book adds little, though, to what we already know about London's life and times, and the criticism offered here is informed but unadventurous. Nevertheless, it is a good general book on its subject.

KINGMAN's is one of the most valuable of the biographical guides. It provides a day-by-day account of London's life, combined with admirably thorough bibliographical data up to 1992. There is no editorial "intrusion" on the chronology of events, and nothing in the way of commentary; but it is an indispensable addition to the biographical record.

HENRY CLARIDGE

Lovecraft, H.P. 1890–1937

American novelist and short-story writer

Burleson, Donald R., *H.P. Lovecraft: A Critical Study*, Westport, Connecticut: Greenwood Press, 1983
Burleson, Donald R., *Lovecraft: Disturbing the Universe*, Lexington: University Press of Kentucky, 1990
Cannon, Peter, *H.P. Lovecraft*, Boston: Twayne, 1989
Joshi, S.T. (ed.), *H.P. Lovecraft: Four Decades of Criticism*, Athens: Ohio University Press, 1980
Joshi, S.T., *H.P. Lovecraft*, Mercer Island, Washington: Starmont House, 1982
Lévy, Maurice, *Lovecraft: A Study in the Fantastic*, translated by S.T. Joshi, Detroit: Wayne State University Press, 1988
Schultz, David E., and S.T. Joshi (eds.), *An Epicure in the Terrible: A Centennial Anthology of Essays in Honor of H.P. Lovecraft*, Rutherford, New Jersey: Fairleigh Dickinson University Press, 1991; London: Associated University Presses, 1991
Schweitzer, Darrell, *The Dream Quest of H.P. Lovecraft*, San Bernardino, California: Borgo Press, 1978

With the exception of Edmund Wilson's succinct dismissal of H.P. Lovecraft as "not a good writer" and a stylist both "verbose and undistinguished" in a 1945 review for *The New Yorker*, Lovecraft criticism has been launched by a small but devoted coterie of fellow horror writers and fans generally outside of academic and literary circles. As with Lovecraft's short fiction, the first wave of critical response appeared in "fanzines", periodicals with often limited resources and circulation. Somewhat justifiably, because of the history of academic disdain for Lovecraft, most of this body of early criticism finds itself concerned with proving that Lovecraft is worthy of serious attention.

Grown in critical sophistication, the second wave of Lovecraft criticism begins around 1980; since that time, two important journals – *Lovecraft Studies* and *Studies in Weird Fiction* – have appeared, along with two compilations of critical articles and three major, book-length studies. The consensus of both waves holds that works written by Lovecraft after 1926 are generally superior to the earlier work, with "The Colour Out of Space" (1927) regarded as the best work of his career. The poems are awarded some merit, while material from Lovecraft's extensive output of letters to friends and other writers are often drawn on as keys to the man's philosophy, lifestyle, and artistry. Lovecraft's own study of the horror genre, *Supernatural Horror in Literature* (revised edition, 1935), is typically valued as one of the landmark works in this field.

JOSHI's 1980 collection brings together 19 important articles written between 1945 and 1978. A fair representation of the first wave, this book includes Wilson's *New Yorker* article and Fritz Leiber's indispensable general overview of the Lovecraftian *oeuvre*. Leiber's 1949 article establishes the parameters of both waves of criticism, focusing on genre position and structural matters, the symbolism of Lovecraft's self-styled pantheon of extra-terrestrial and primordial entities (the Cthulhu or Lovecraft mythos), and Lovecraft's historical and geographical revisions. Joshi's collection itself is divided into five major categories: general studies, the Lovecraft mythos, literary influences, analyses from philosophical, psychological, and historical perspectives, and a brief last section on Lovecraft's poetry. Joshi writes a useful introductory biography (with Kenneth W. Faig, Jr.), an overview of the critical field, and a chronology of Lovecraft's fiction, while an appendix provides concise précis of the collected works of Lovecraft, as well as the essential biographical, critical, and bibliographical texts.

SCHULTZ and JOSHI's 1991 editorial collaboration updates Joshi's earlier collection. The more recent work represents the second wave of Lovecraft scholarship. The three sections of this work focus on biographical, thematic, and comparative genre studies respectively. In the first case, the book sheds new and vital light on the influences of Lovecraft's parents, geographical heritage, and the pulp-magazine tradition; each of these articles is firmly grounded in Lovecraft's astounding personal letters. Of particular interest in the final category is an exploration of images and techniques shared by Lovecraft and Jorge Luis Borges.

SCHWEITZER's simplified introduction to Lovecraft typifies the state of book-length criticism from the first wave. Schweitzer introduces Lovecraft's background, then works through the tales in chronological order, exploring literary influences such as Lord Dunsany and Edgar Allan Poe as he goes. However, Schweitzer's work is often so brief as to be pointless, with treatments of individual texts rarely going beyond plot summary, many of which are not even accurate. Thus, Schweitzer's text is most useful as an introduction to the problems and pitfalls of the first wave.

JOSHI's 1982 study resembles Schweitzer's in its brevity, and again typifies the small-press approach to Lovecraft scholarship. Joshi's approach is less problematic than Schweitzer's own, however, which reflects nothing so much as the central role that Joshi has played in insuring Lovecraft's critical attention in America: he edits *Lovecraft Studies*, he has compiled a 12-volume edition of Lovecraft's collected works with extensive notes and commentary, he has assembled the first annotated bibliography devoted to Lovecraft (*H.P. Lovecraft and Lovecraft Criticism: An Annotated Bibliography*, 1981) and he has been involved in editing the first major collections of contemporary criticism. While more accurate than Schweitzer's work, most of Joshi's solo effort still offers the reader little more than an overview of Lovecraft's life and works. The concluding chapter is most important, introducing some of the major themes and stylistic issues. Joshi formulates his notion of a philosophical unity underlying Lovecraft's aesthetic of weird fiction (that horror's exploration of humankind's greatest emotion, fear, must go hand-in-hand with scientific rationalism) and his "cosmicism" (or, "cosmic attitude – the realization that mankind is a negligible atom lost in the vast vortices of space and time").

LÉVY wrote the first book-length study of Lovecraft, which was originally published in France in 1972, and translated by Joshi in 1988. Lévy limits his analysis to establishing Lovecraft's place within the genre of weird fiction. The book concludes that Lovecraft's emphasis on dreams constitutes his most vital contribution to this genre. For Lévy, dream-images reveal "the universality of the structures of the imagination", and he finds in Lovecraft's orienting devices – the consistent, imaginary New England coastline and the mythos of extraterrestrials – an ultimately *therapeutic* function. The tradition of American Puritanism and the archetypal foundations of human experience, Lévy argues, are part of a search for a "cure" for the ills of modernity; by this account, Lovecraft's racism, anti-semitism, and fascism are part of the totalizing tendencies of myths of origin and subsequent corruption, of lost, primordial purity and ancient evil.

CANNON presents a study similar in format to the earlier, brief works by Schweitzer and Joshi and yet, having the resources of the growing field of Lovecraft scholarship to draw on, comes up with a much more solid and useful analysis. Like those earlier works, his begins with a biographical sketch, followed by a brief look at Lovecraft's literary production outside of the weird-tale format – the letters, travel writing, ghost writing, and poetry. The book next provides a detailed look at the earliest stories written by Lovecraft. Cannon establishes Lovecraft's thematic and stylistic development through close readings of the stories and brief asides regarding the influences of Dunsany, Poe, the editors of the pulp magazines who first encouraged Lovecraft, and the French Decadents. The remainder of the book is organized around geographical locales, imaginary or real, and moves in roughly chronological fashion through close readings of individual stories and novels. Though often tending toward plot summary, Cannon traces the development of Lovecraft's imagery, settings, the pantheon, narrative strategies, and, to a lesser extent, the major themes with more sophistication than most of the critics before him. Of the shorter overviews of Lovecraft's career, Cannon's book is, finally, the most useful.

In addition to the collection edited by Schultz and Joshi, BURLESON's 1990 publication also attempts to critically update Lovecraftian scholarship. Rather than the psychoanalytical, biographical, myth-oriented, and formalist approaches that have dominated the Lovecraftian field, Burleson proposes a poststructuralist, or deconstructive, criticism. After an overview of this approach, the book launches into a chapter-by-chapter analysis of 13 tales. Burleson is a bit too anxious to indicate the fact that Lovecraft's texts stand up to deconstructionist analysis rather than to pursue the content suggested *by* this approach; nevertheless, the overriding claim that Lovecraft's own stories deconstruct texts and minds opens up Lovecraft's work to new readings and, perhaps, new readers. Burleson's claims stem from his earlier text, (BURLESON, 1983). In this important work, he explores the "cosmicism" at the core of Lovecraft's aesthetic theory, and proposes the notion of "ironic impressionism", the central tenet being that humans are just intelligent enough to realize their increasing insignificance in the face of an ultimately chaotic cosmos. Burleson is at the forefront of authors committed to doing more than proving that Lovecraft is worth studying and getting on with the task itself.

TRACE REDDELL

Lowell, Robert 1917–1977

American poet

Axelrod, Steven Gould, and Helen Deese (eds.), *Robert Lowell: Essays on the Poetry*, Cambridge and New York: Cambridge University Press, 1986

Bell, Vereen, *Robert Lowell: Nihilist as Hero*, Cambridge, Massachusetts: Harvard University Press, 1983

Cosgrave, Patrick, *The Public Poetry of Robert Lowell*, London: Victor Gollancz, 1970

Doreski, William, *The Years of Our Friendship: Robert Lowell and Allen Tate*, Jackson: University Press of Mississippi, 1990

Giroux, Robert (ed.), *Robert Lowell: Collected Prose*, New York: Farrar, Straus, Giroux, 1987; London: Faber & Faber, 1987

Hobsbaum, Philip, *A Reader's Guide to Robert Lowell*, London: Thames & Hudson, 1988

Matterson, Stephen, *Berryman and Lowell: The Art of Losing*, London: Macmillan, 1988

Rudman, Mark, *Robert Lowell: An Introduction to the Poetry*, New York: Columbia University Press, 1984

Simpson, Louis, *A Revolution in Taste: Studies of Dylan Thomas, Allen Ginsberg, Sylvia Plath and Robert Lowell*, London and New York: Macmillan, 1979

Wallingford, Katharine, *Robert Lowell's Language of the Self*, Chapel Hill: University of North Carolina Press, 1987

Williamson, Alan, *Pity the Monsters: The Political Vision of Robert Lowell*, New Haven, Connecticut, and London: Yale University Press, 1974

From the mid-1950s for a decade or more, Robert Lowell was widely admired in America and Europe as probably the greatest poet then writing in English. This estimation was based partly on the achievement of his early publications, written in tightly controlled verse forms in that his common subject was the desolation of the present without the consolations of faith. In the early 1950s Lowell effected a personal revolution both in the formal style of his poems, and in their subject matter, a change of direction that had an immense public impact. While never entirely abandoning his technical expertise in verse forms, his "baroque" style was jettisoned in favour of a looser self-expressive style, in which his subject was himself, his social and psychological anxieties, and his family history, as in the aptly titled *Life Studies*. This was followed by the more politically conscious verse of *For the Union Dead*, where self-expressiveness was framed within a consciousness more eloquently articulate about the poet's social responsibilities. These two volumes marked the high watershed of his achievement, and though the later work is full of interest, he was never again to match his public image as a poet with the intense appropriateness of subject and form met in these two books. His troubled life was a history of crises, about which he wrote with great power and lacerating self-scrutiny, but this material nurtured an obsessive interest in the man himself, and for many years the primary focus on Lowell has been the relationship between the life portrayed in his poems and that lived in experience.

In the two decades since his death his reputation has declined considerably, and though his work still generates some excellent commentary, it is largely true to say that he has become a case study for biographers, literary historians, and those who are more interested in the figure of the poet as a social type than in the accomplishment of his poetry. There is a fascinating view of Lowell operating as the public spokesperson for poetry and the high seriousness which goes with it in Norman Mailer's book about the Civil Rights movement, *Armies of the Night*. The dominant biographical studies of recent years are those by Ian Hamilton (1982) and Paul Mariani (1994).

COSGRAVE's book has a singular virtue for its time – the effort to take Lowell seriously as a writer with something important to say about his times, rather than his own life. Thus, he reads Lowell as writing in the tradition of the later W.B. Yeats, where the conflict between the private tensions and pressures, which is reflected in the poems, is set within a frame of public and social preoccupations and responsibilities. He reads *Life Studies* as a programmatic ritual of self-scrutiny, which served to reclaim Lowell from the welter of his personal psychoses and render him a fitter agent of social engagement and political awareness. This programme was extended in *For the Union Dead*, which Cosgrave regards as a real advance, a volume celebrating Lowell's understanding of his public role. Cosgrave's study makes a serious claim for Lowell's resolution of the problem endemic to all writing in this century: how can the writer escape the solipsistic obsession with self in a way that makes his or her critique of society both valid and instructive?

WILLIAMSON has similar concerns to those of Cosgrave. Williamson pays more attention than was then customary to the late books, especially *Near the Ocean*, and *Notebook*, in both versions, because he believes these books unite the poet's public and private preoccupations in ways that allow them to marry the socially prophetic function of the poet. This is an accomplished critique for its time.

SIMPSON writes as a poet-critic, and this account of Lowell and others is marked by the tact the writer brings to critical commentary on the work of his contemporaries. This is a good general view of Lowell's whole creative career, though on a brief scale, and therefore synoptic in the relatively summary accounts of the various volumes of poems. Late in the Lowell chapter Simpson cites Lowell's expression that writing had been his "indissoluble bride" for 30 years, a citation Simpson uses to underscore both the intensity of Lowell's commitment to poetry and the life-threatening dangers of such an absolute commitment. Simpson sees an understanding of Lowell as central to an understanding of a whole generation of American poets from World War II to the end of the 1970s.

BELL has written one of the best general studies of Lowell, covering the whole corpus, though like other such overviews of the work Bell regards the early volumes as modest in kind, primarily interesting for what they suggest about the work to follow. However, his acute commentary on "The Quaker Graveyard in Nantucket" properly registers the high achievement of this poem, widely regarded as one of the best verse elegies in American writing since Walt Whitman's "When Lilac's Last in the Dooryard Bloom'd". The unarguable achievement of Lowell in his middle years puts the work of Bell and other commentators at a disadvantage in celebrating what is already celebrated; thus he is more interesting in those areas where he has a more difficult task to accomplish, as in the account he offers of the late work, where he argues with considerable conviction for the consolations he finds to redeem the bleak vision of this last phase.

RUDMAN's introductory study has the merit of attempting a wide-span view of all Lowell's poetry, guided by the impulse to show how Lowell "could weave his words out of the fibers of the world". This is an account in which the private resources of Lowell's art are more in focus than is usual, for the "fibers" and "weaving" of Rudman's approach are read through an account of the way in which relations among childhood, landscape, language, and the imagination provide the materials of Lowell's art. This book is marked by Rudman's enthusiasm for Lowell and its accessibility as a general guide to the poems.

AXELROD and DEESE provide one of the best collections of essays on Lowell, in which the primary focus is on the poems rather than the life. Albert Gelpi claims that the lasting achievement of Lowell may be measured by the accomplishment of his early work, especially *Lord Weary's Castle*, and A. Kingsley Weatherhead contrasts the style of the late *Day by Day* with the earlier books to argue that Lowell's late style recognizes an impoverishment of the "glorious fallen powers he has lost through infirmity". A group of these essays naturally centre on Lowell's most famous book of poems, *Life Studies*. Lawrence Kramer's psychoanalytic reading sees Lowell's practice of self-inquisition in this book as his way of inquiring into the nature and possibility of selfhood, and the question of the self's relation to language and culture; Sandra M. Gilbert pays special attention to "Skunk Hour" as a poem replete with both modernist and postmodern anxieties; and Marjorie Perloff looks at *Life Studies* and *For the Union Dead* as works that mark the end of what she calls "the Genteel Tradition" in mid-twentieth-century American poetry. With regard to Lowell's late work, Calvin Bedient writes interestingly on the obsessive revisions of the late books from *Notebook 1967–1968*. *Day by Day* is read by Alan Holder as evidence of Lowell's concern with powerlessness, while Helen Deese finds in it forms of release through the energies Lowell found in the visual arts, and George McFadden finds the book's humour sufficient to compete with its dominant mood of despair.

WALLINGFORD examines the conjunction of two intellectual strains in Lowell – the moral demands of self-scrutiny entailed in the tradition of New England Puritanism, and the practice of self-examination through psychoanalysis. This ambitious enterprise, though secure and interesting in intention, is overburdened by Wallingford's nervous relationship to the body of critical writing on Lowell. In the end it achieves less than it promises in what it tells us of either Lowell's poetry or the psychoses that tormented him for much of his life.

HOBSBAUM is packed with information on the literary, social, and personal sources of the poems, and he also gives a useful guide to the various developments in Lowell's reputation over the years. Hobsbaum's serious interest in Lowell predates the 1960s, when Lowell became one of the most fashionable poets writing in English, so that Hobsbaum's perspective on the work is long and deeply sympathetic. His account of the earliest books of poems is especially valuable for the way he reports on the poet's creative relationship with his American mentors Allen Tate and John Crowe Ransom, and for the way he situates Lowell's earliest attempts to write obliquely about his family in response to the pressures of belonging to one of the social and cultural aristocracies of the white Protestant ascendancy.

MATTERSON's dual focus on Lowell and Berryman is helpful as a way of showing the creative interplay between them, though Matterson properly attends to their differences. He argues that Lowell abandoned the "poetics of recovery" learned from Tate and Ransom for the "rhetoric of destitution" that marks *Life Studies* and the later work, which in this view is determined by a "poetics of loss". He sees Lowell's early conversion to Catholicism as a necessity born of his fear of disorder and parental, personal, and cultural loss. However, this emphasis on kinds of loss has to be seen in relation to what Matterson regards as the emergence of Lowell's unique voice and the development of formal techniques and idioms of writing that would become the sign and triumph of his creative identity. This is an excellent study, which suffers only from its extreme brevity.

DORESKI gives the fullest account of the Lowell-Allen Tate relationship, which survived for 40 years. The strength of this book is in Doreski's use of unpublished documents from the Lowell archives at Harvard and Texas universities, and the Tate archive at Princeton. As one of the major influences on Lowell's first books of poems, Tate was horrified at the revelations of family intimacies in the confessional poems of *Life Studies*, as is well known; on the other hand, Doreski's account of Tate's approval of the next collection, *For the Union Dead*, is less familiar, and deserves more attention than is given here, for the documents he has worked on show the durability of their friendship and the importance of issues of creative influence and competition between them. However, this remains a fascinating account of an important part of Lowell's creative life, and is very accessible.

GIROUX has collected Lowell's prose writings on poetry and poets – an important collection, which enlarges our understanding of Lowell. Lowell claimed to reject the formality of the critic's public role because he preferred to be "much sloppier and more intuitive" in what he wrote about others; but this claim cannot disguise the sustained power of high critical intelligence he brought to the art of the review and the occasional essay. He was a brilliant commentator on the work of his contemporaries – passionate, responsive, and perceptive to a remarkable degree. This is an indispensable book for anyone seriously interested in Lowell.

LIONEL KELLY

Lowry, Malcolm 1909–1957

English novelist

Ackerley, Chris, and Lawrence J. Clipper, *A Companion to "Under the Volcano"*, Vancouver: University of British Columbia Press, 1984

Bareham, Tony, *Malcolm Lowry*, London: Macmillan, 1989; New York: St Martin's Press, 1989

Bowker, Gordon, *Pursued by Furies: A Life of Malcolm Lowry*, London: Harper Collins, 1993; Toronto: Random House, 1993

Grace, Sherrill (ed.), *Swinging the Maelstrom: New Perspectives on Malcolm Lowry*, Montreal and Kingston: McGill-Queen's University Press, 1992

McCarthy, Patrick, *Forests of Symbols: World, Text, and Self in Malcolm Lowry's Fiction*, Athens: University of Georgia Press, 1994

Mota, Miguel, and Paul Tiessen (eds.), *The Cinema of Malcolm Lowry: A Scholarly Edition of Lowry's "Tender is the Night"*, Vancouver: University of British Columbia Press, 1990

Salloum, Sheryl, *Malcolm Lowry: Vancouver Days*, Madeira Park, British Columbia: Harbour Publishing, 1987

Scherf, Kathleen (ed.), *The Collected Poetry of Malcolm Lowry*, Vancouver: University of British Columbia Press, 1992

Tiessen, Paul, and Gordon Bowker, *Apparently Incongruous Parts: The Worlds of Malcolm Lowry*, Metuchen, New Jersey: Scarecrow Press, 1990

Vice, Sue (ed.), *Malcolm Lowry Eighty Years On*, London: Macmillan, 1989

Recent criticism of Malcolm Lowry has been largely re-evaluative, with new editions of his life, letters, and filmscripts either published or forthcoming, and other studies consolidating past work. Several previously unpublished manuscripts (the poetry, the 1940 *Under the Volcano*, *La Mordida*) have also been edited. While the primacy of *Under the Volcano* in Lowry's achievement has not been challenged, recent criticism accentuates the variety of his writing and qualifies the common perception of him as a one-novel author.

BOWKER's biography is a detailed and accurate account of his life. Bowker has separated facts from the myths accumulating about Lowry, and thereby corrected many errors in earlier accounts. He has elucidated such mysterious episodes as the 1931 visit to Norway, the suicide of Paul Fitte, and the probable circumstances of Lowry's death; and he has accounted dispassionately for the failure to finish much in the final years: the sordid record of Lowry's drinking and violence does not form a romantic image. Bowker's chief weaknesses are a lack of generosity in some acknowledgements, an over-reliance upon the opinions of Jan Gabrial, and his limitations as a literary scholar. Little insight into the work is given, and an irony thereby arises, for the discredited (and barely mentioned) biography by Douglas Day, for all its factual errors, may convey a better impression of the total achievement. SALLOUM's tidy account of Lowry's Vancouver days gives a more intimate record than Bowker. Hers is a labour of love, which includes photographs, maps, and personal recollections. Although eclectic, it is reliable, readable, and rewarding.

For the student unfamiliar with Lowry, BAREHAM offers a sensible start: he offers a summary of the life, an account of *Ultramarine*, a survey of *Under the Volcano*, and an overview of the short stories and posthumous novels. Bareham is not particularly incisive, and is sometimes in error (he assumes that the short-story version of *Volcano* predates the novel); but as a general introduction his study is satisfactory.

The standard guide to *Under the Volcano* is the *Companion* edited by me (ACKERLEY) and CLIPPER. This offers a concise annotation, in note form, of the many difficulties the novel presents – literary allusions, historical references, cabbalistic curiosities, geographical and biographical details. The approach is factual, but establishes Lowry's text as more densely allusive than *Ulysses*, and Lowry's working habits as compulsively recyclical.

That tendency is also reflected in the filmscript of *Tender is the Night*, edited by MOTA and TIESSEN. They reveal how Lowry re-explored problems and themes from the *Volcano* period to recreate a text quite distinct from F. Scott Fitzgerald's original. The excellent Introduction and notes demonstrate the nature of Lowry's life-long commitment to the cinema, and to the nature of Lowry's cinematic imagination.

In her comprehensive, definitive edition of the poetry, SCHERF suggests that Lowry's approach to his writing was at all times poetical. Her approach is bibliographical, and the study includes all the known poetry, lists significant manuscript variants, and contains useful essays upon such diverse matters as dates, papers, typefaces, marginalia, and working habits. The poems are also extensively annotated. Because Lowry's poetry was written throughout his life, Scherf's edition affords unexpected insight into his overall achievement, and a considered reading of the verse reveals a talent more various than hitherto imagined.

Three volumes of essays also honour Lowry's diversity. That edited by VICE is the least impressive. Although it offers a couple of interesting rambles (Binns on the filming of *Under the Volcano*, Bradbrook on Lowry's Cambridge), some essays are of an undergraduate quality, and the Introduction is perfunctory. TIESSEN and BOWKER provide an unbalanced but interesting selection, including an interview with Julian

Trevelyan, Paul Tiessen's discovery of Gerald Noxon, a curious essay by Duncan Hadfield, a fascinating account of Lowry's "Strange Profession" by Ronald Binns, and a postmodernist excursion "Through the Panama" with Sherrill Grace. The most important edition is that of GRACE, who organised the 1987 Vancouver Symposium at which most of her selections were given. There are curiosities: papers on poetry that seem unaware of Scherf, and some chosen for eminence of author rather than quality of content. Nevertheless, Grace's editing is excellent, her Introduction assured, and the variety of papers impressive. Particularly significant are the textual studies by Frederick Asals (*Under the Volcano*) and Victor Doyen (*October Ferry*): these may not attract general readers, but the few to whom they matter will be truly appreciative. The edition is a fine record of a superb conference.

A summary of Lowry's achievement is expressed by McCARTHY. Exploring Lowry's tendency to see himself as part of a cosmic web of correspondence, McCarthy discusses the patterns of synchronicity Lowry perceived in the macrocosm. He is excellent on the neglected theme of Lowry's occultism and attraction to the Law of Series, yet notes Lowry's curious ability in *Under the Volcano* to detach himself from such matters, so that the Consul's obsessive private readings of his world become a major cause of his destruction. Lowry's later work, McCarthy argues, is less detached and more entangled in webs of subjectivity, as Lowry attempted to assimilate all his writing into the unfinishable cyclic vision of *The Voyage That Never Ends*. Lowry could rarely be objective about a life in which he too was written, and that paradox forms a satisfactory conclusion (read: an unsatisfactory inconclusion) to a literary life that is compelling as much for its failures as for its success.

CHRIS ACKERLEY

Lyly, John c.1554–1606

English prose writer and dramatist

Barish, Jonas A., "The Prose Style of John Lyly", in *English Literary History*, 23, 1956

Bond, R. Warwick (ed.), *The Complete Works of John Lyly*, 3 vols., Oxford: Clarendon Press, 1902, reprinted 1967

Croll, Morris W., and Harry Clemons (eds.), *Euphues, The Anatomy of Wit; Euphues, His England*, by Lyly, London: Routledge & Kegan Paul, 1916; New York: Dutton, 1916; reprinted, New York: Russell & Russell, 1964

Feuillerat, Albert, *John Lyly: Contribution à l'histoire de la Renaissance en Angleterre*, Cambridge: Cambridge University Press, 1910

Houppert, Joseph W., *John Lyly*, Boston: Twayne, 1975

Hunter, G.K., *John Lyly: The Humanist As Courtier*, London: Routledge & Kegan Paul, 1962; Cambridge, Massachusetts: Harvard University Press, 1962

Saccio, Peter, *The Court Comedies of John Lyly: A Study in Allegorical Dramaturgy*, Princeton, New Jersey: Princeton University Press, 1969

Scragg, Leah, *The Metamorphosis of "Gallathea": A Study in Creative Adaptation*, Washington, D.C.: University Press of America, 1982

Wilson, John Dover, *John Lyly*, Cambridge: Macmillan & Bowes, 1905; reprinted, New York: Haskell House, 1970

Twentieth-century Lylian studies may be divided into two stages. The early years of the century produced major work in both the editorial and biographical fields, while critical studies remained rooted in the concept of Lyly as a precursor of later, and more significant, writers. The second half of the century, by contrast, has seen relatively few major editorial advances, but has witnessed a total reassessment of Lyly's dramatic achievement and the subtlety of his style. For the modern scholar, Lyly is no longer a marginal figure in Renaissance studies, of interest solely for the influence he exerted, but a highly innovative writer with a wholly distinctive vision.

BOND's old spelling edition of the complete works laid the foundations of twentieth-century Lylian studies and remains the definitive version of the majority of the plays. A full collation of editions is supplied together with substantial and highly informative notes. The introductory material, however, is no longer reliable, while the critical judgements are typical of their era in the emphasis laid on Lyly's influence on Shakespeare.

FEUILLERAT's study, published only eight years after the appearance of Bond's *Complete Works*, occupies the same niche in terms of biography that Bond holds in the editorial sphere. All the materials pertinent to Lyly's life are drawn together and Bond's misapprehensions over the dramatist's parentage are corrected. The work as a whole has yet to be superseded.

CROLL and CLEMONS, working in the same period as Bond and Feuillerat, are responsible for what remains the standard modern-spelling editions of the two parts of *Euphues*. The text is provided with substantial notes and a full Introduction offering a detailed history and analysis of the euphuistic style. The study remains invaluable, but its conclusions should be read in conjunction with those of Barish (see below).

WILSON's study is typical of its period in its location of the work within an evolutionary process, and its assessment of the plays by inappropriate criteria. The importance placed on complex character, for example, frustrates the appreciation of a drama rooted in verbal wit and the exploration of ideas, while a concern with plot as an interlocking sequence of events works against understanding (and enjoyment) of the conceptual relationships set up between scenes.

BARISH initiates the remarkable reassessment of Lyly that has taken place in the latter half of the twentieth century through a fresh consideration of the euphuistic mode. Distinguishing three types of antithetical structure underpinning Lyly's prose, he argues for an essential relationship between style and vision, suggesting that "the notion that things contain within them their own contraries, or the power to work contrary effects occurs so often . . . that by sheer frequency of repetition it comes to be felt as a major insight". It is this insistent location of "doubleness" that for Barish is the principal characteristic distinguishing Lyly from previous exponents of the euphuistic style, and which, for later commentators, is the distinctive feature of both Lyly's prose and dramatic work.

HUNTER's book is generally regarded as the cornerstone of modern Lylian studies. The work locates the writer's career within the context of the humanist movement, and includes a fresh appraisal of the life, as well as detailed chapters on the prose and dramatic works and a useful comparison with Shakespeare. The gallimaufry nature of *Euphues* is emphasized, while particular stress is laid on complexity of the construction of the plays. The categories imposed on the comedies are unhelpful, but the recognition that "Lyly's success as a dramatist lies in his power to organize his materials" constitutes a significant advance in the understanding of his work.

SACCIO's study is focused on five of the comedies, and constitutes the most detailed and perceptive analysis of a substantial proportion of the corpus that has yet appeared. The work concentrates on the dramatist's choice of materials, dramaturgical techniques, and evolving "allegorical" modes, exposing the insistent ambiguity of the worlds held up for observation. Where Barish describes Lyly's vision in terms of "doubleness", and Hunter likens *Euphues* to a "piece of shot silk", Saccio sees the court comedies in terms of "a central reality slowly turning like a prism for us to inspect its various facets".

HOUPPERT's monograph is a disappointing one in a number of respects. Although it offers a detailed account of the history of Lylian scholarship, and includes a useful biography, it fails to incorporate the advances of other scholars in its concept of the work, or to relate the euphuistic mode to other aspects of the plays. The introductory "overview" and concluding chapter on "The Plays and the Critics" remain helpful, however, for those embarking on study of the work.

My (SCRAGG's) book is devoted to *Gallathea* (widely regarded as Lyly's best play) and its influence on the Shakespearean corpus. The play itself is discussed in a lengthy chapter, while subsequent sections explore the adaptations that the drama undergoes in a succession of comedies from *Love's Labour's Lost* to *Cymbeline*. Particular emphasis is placed on Lyly's vision of a world in process of flux and on the protean character of the work.

LEAH SCRAGG

Lyric in Medieval Literature

Diehl, Patrick S., *The Medieval European Religious Lyric: An Ars Poetica*, Berkeley: University of California Press, 1985
Dronke, Peter, *The Medieval Lyric*, London: Hutchinson, 1968, revised 1978; New York: Perennial Library, 1969
Gray, Douglas, *Themes and Images in the Medieval English Religious Lyric*, London and Boston: Routledge & Kegan Paul, 1972, revised 1978
Moore, Arthur K., *The Secular Lyric in Middle English*, Lexington: University Press of Kentucky, 1970; reprinted, Westport, Connecticut: Greenwood Press, 1970
Oliver, Raymond, *Poems Without Names: The English Lyric 1200–1500*, Berkeley: University of California Press, 1970
Reiss, Edmund, *The Art of the Middle English Lyric: Essays in Criticism*, Athens: University of Georgia Press, 1972
Woolf, Rosemary, *English Religious Lyric in the Middle Ages*, Oxford: Clarendon Press, 1968

"Lyric" is a manufactured term used to describe medieval short verses, conventionally divided into the religious and the secular. Themes, images, and verse forms migrated across Europe, so the chosen scope of many critical works is European, including Latin, rather than any single-language tradition.

DRONKE's is a seminal study of the European repertoire from 850 to 1300. It opens with the early Latin and Germanic song traditions, attending to performance contexts. In the second editon, Dronke commends newer sociological studies which have increased discrimination in this area, particularly in relation to the *trouvères*. The development of a set of stylised sensibilities relating to the subject of refined love is traced from the end of the eleventh century, and ideas derived from Franciscan and Cistercian spirituality provide for a major departure in the thirteenth and fourteenth centuries. The Middle English corpus is seen as distinctive for its verbal dexterity, anticipating seventeenth-century metaphysical poetry. Considerations of unrefined dancing songs and of the minority of unconventional verses of real personal expression complete the book.

WOOLF's specialised study of the English religious lyric appeared in the same year as Dronke's work. It begins by arguing that the term "lyric", suggesting light-hearted song, is profoundly misleading when applied to the serious short-verse prayers, meditations, and treatises of the English tradition, distinctive because it had no strong native courtly tradition by which to be influenced. The book attempts to impose chronological order on the tradition. The early Harley, and later Vernon, manuscript collections are singled out as providing striking examples of particular developmental moments, as are the forms of expression which characterised the writers of the mystical school. A more exuberant narrative style is seen to have emerged in the fifteenth century, influenced by developments in the painted and plastic arts.

GRAY's book, which is also focused on English religious verse, is singled out for commendation by Dronke. The author warns against treating late gothic culture as self-consistent. Notwithstanding, he convincingly presents a distinctive English devotional lyric emerging from a Latin, French, Anglo-Norman, polyglot culture, and drawing ultimately on the "imaginary museum" of 12 centuries of Christianity. The sources for its imagery, principally the liturgy and the Psalms, are supplemented by Anselmian and Franciscan piety until they reach a climax in the sentimental devotion of the fifteenth century. Although the tradition is not personal, it draws inspiration from prayer, carolling, and even from the erotic love song. Individual chapters explore dominant preoccupations – Christ and the Virgin, the Annunciation and Nativity, the Passion, the Resurrection and Assumption, and the passage of the Christian life.

MOORE's work on secular lyric from the same period has endured less well: its evaluative approach may seem particularly discordant to the present-day reader. The author highlights the very diffuse nature of the corpus of available verse, particularly the interplay of indigenous popular song with the extremely artificial imported forms of the *ballade*, *roundel*, and *virelay*. He is unimpressed by densities of cliché and by unsophisticated humour, and is happier reviewing the art lyric, which drew on the traditions of Continental style books, the *Romance of the Rose*, allegory, and synthesised syllabic and accentual metrical conventions, although the art lyric, too, soon slipped into the decadence of fifteenth-century aureation. Nevertheless, the Scot William Dunbar is singled out from the "debris of transition" in the fifteenth century as a lyricist of some merit.

OLIVER's work is equally unsympathetic for different reasons. As a principally stylistic study, it is extremely reductive. All medieval lyrics, because they are anonymous, practical, and public, are said to have more formal unity as a body than the complete works of a single modern poet. All verse in question is then mustered under ten categories, some dictated by content, others by occasion, in an attempt to write a poetic sub-language. The ensuing lexical analysis finds a want of connotative language and a sparseness of figures. Some "gross structuring principles", many of them borrowed schemae, like the ten commandments, are propped up by devices of local organisation. The book concludes that because of the strictly denotative properties of the genre which it has identified, anyone having once identified the rules can write a medieval lyric.

REISS is altogether more prepared to find the poetically remarkable among the lyrics that he singles out for study. Where others have found naivety, he sees the economy of simplicity, quoting St Augustine's definition of *eloquentia* – to teach in order to instruct; to please in order to hold; and also, assuredly, to move in order to convince – as a definition of the artistic achievement of medieval lyric verse. The remainder of the book is a very useful close study of 25 English lyrics, printed in their entirety. It may not be as fully culturally theorised as more recent critical tastes might wish, but the collection severally and conjointly serves to demonstrate elaborate handling of metres, refrains, points of view, and images which, moreover, cross the artificial divide between the religious and the secular. "I syng of a myden" is inevitably here, its uncluttered yet universally suggestive artifice laid bare, alongside the hellish cacophony of "Swarte-smekyd smethes" with which the collection ends.

DIEHL's study returns to the European context to construct a retrospective *ars poetica* for medieval non-narrative poetry. His central thesis is that all texts are glosses and translations, migrating from language to language, stylistic level to stylistic level. In the book's general chapters, seven functions of the lyric are identified. Means by which lyric unity is achieved are analysed, and the commoner elements of formal rhetoric described. In the chapters on specific languages, the unsuitability of the long alliterative line is blamed for the late beginning of the English tradition. It began to flourish when religious lyric passed to the friars and was directed at a popular audience. The author sees the Black Death as a convenient division between this and the development of the art lyric. The book also offers a powerful critique of the failure of many preceding studies to acknowledge cultural difference, particularly when they flatter present-day senses of individuality, history, and society.

PAMELA M. KING

M

Macaulay, Thomas Babington 1800–1859

English historian, essayist, and poet

Clive, John, *Macaulay: The Shaping of the Historian*, New York: Knopf, 1973; London: Secker & Warburg, 1973

Clive, John, and Thomas Pinney, "Macaulay", in *Victorian Prose: A Guide to Research*, edited by David J. DeLaura, New York: Modern Language Association of America, 1973

Edwards, Owen Dudley, *Macaulay*, London: Weidenfeld & Nicolson, 1988; New York: St Martin's Press, 1989

Geyl, Pieter, *Debates with Historians*, London: Batsford, 1955; revised edition, London: Fontana, 1974

Hamburger, Joseph, *Macaulay and the Whig Tradition*, Chicago: University of Chicago Press, 1976

Levine, George, *The Boundaries of Fiction: Carlyle, Macaulay, Newman*, Princeton, New Jersey: Princeton University Press, 1968

Millgate, Jane, *Macaulay*, London and Boston: Routledge & Kegan Paul, 1973

Pinney, Thomas (ed.), *The Letters of Thomas Babington Macaulay*, 6 vols., Cambridge: Cambridge University Press, 1974–81

Thomas Babington Macaulay's skills as narrator, wit, and writer of clear and invigorating prose have been recognized since his first *Edinburgh Review* article appeared, when he was 24. He wanted to write in his *History of England* a history to satisfy readers of novels. Macaulay's distinctive style, which has tended to either enthrall or infuriate, has received mixed responses: his nineteenth-century critics – Leslie Stephen, John Morley, and Matthew Arnold – saw it as philistine, while it was well received by the general public. His critics have also always debated whether he was too constrained by his assumptions, beliefs, and certainties, for he spoke for both a class and a political party.

The outline of Macaulay's critical fortunes can be followed in CLIVE and PINNEY's survey of the scholarly studies up until 1971. This survey may be supplemented by the annual "Bibliography of Victorian Studies" in the journal *Victorian Studies*, and the volume *Bibliographies of Victorian Studies, 1974–1985* (edited by Richard Tobias, New York: AMS Press, 1991). Useful contextual information is included in the comprehensively annotated six-volume edition of the letters, edited by PINNEY, which provides both a window on Macaulay's era and insights into his prose style.

The earliest of the studies discussed here, GEYL's, sees Macaulay as wrongly interpreting history on account of the limitations of his nineteenth-century perspective. Macaulay's devotion to the idea of progress is seen as leading him into viewing the past with self-righteous condescension and impatience, becoming "in the deepest sense unhistoric". His style Geyl regards as that of an orator, full of contempt and scorn for those whose thought differed from his ideal. However, despite Geyl's dim view of Macaulay's sense of history, he says little about Macaulay's work.

CLIVE is nearly as witty and clear in narrative as Macaulay himself, and he has the advantage of a broad perspective on Macaulay and his age. Although he narrates the life only to Macaulay's return from India in 1838, he is informative about both the origin of *The Lays of Ancient Rome* and the *History*. He aims to trace "some of the forces – familial, intellectual, political, and personal – which helped to shape the man and the historian", outlining Macaulay's struggle for success by "sheer talent and energy".

LEVINE contrasts Macaulay with John Henry Newman and Thomas Carlyle, who used their versions of history to shape and direct their societies. In Levine's view, Carlyle and Newman sought to reform, while Macaulay celebrated Victorian culture with its, and his, ideas of compromise, expedience, property, free trade, and progress. Levine notes "the pleasant superficiality" of Macaulay's writing, but sees him as an imaginative writer who possessed clarity, common sense, and decorum. Levine finds clues to a "buried life" in the sub-texts of the works, in which Macaulay emerges as a "romantic who clung with his feelings to things his intellect ought to have taught him to despise". Macaulay's attitude to literature is not regarded by Levine as that of a literary critic, since his motivation for reading was escapist rather than analytical or evaluative, while the *History* is admired for its architectural sense, its vividness, its almost epic method, its heroic juxtapositions, and its astonishing reconciliation of a childlike imagination with scientific knowledge. Since he "had the rare good fortune of being endowed with gifts of genius and the commitments of the majority", Macaulay turned history into romance for his readers, and the contradictions and avoidance of complexity in his style are interpreted as paradoxes typical of the man. Levine's study, in short, is the best analysis of Macaulay as a writer.

MILLGATE defends Macaulay as an artist with an acute sense of his audience and a gift for narrative. In her close analyis of the literary methods of the *History*, she admires the work's structure and unity, and shows how Macaulay's journals from his visit to Ireland informed his treatment of Irish events of 1689, drawing attention to his insistence on the relevance of his seventeenth-century subject to his nineteenth-century audience.

HAMBURGER vigorously questions definitions of Macaulay's politics as simple Whiggism. Noting Macaulay's concept of "noiseless revolutions" and his passion to avoid both anarchy and tyranny, his thought is seen here to be pre-eminently political, and he should thus be judged, Hamburger proposes, on those grounds rather than as a historian or literary figure. Hamburger attends more to Macaulay's religious beliefs, or lack of them, than do other commentators; his Macaulay is also more dialectical in his thinking than others'.

EDWARDS's book appeared in the series "Historians on Historians", and it covers a range of Macaulay's work, with chapters on his life, poetry, criticism, and the *History*. Edwards emphasizes the Scottish background, but he also notes Macaulay's efforts to unite various elements of British society. Edwards is generous in his praise of Macaulay as historian (in contrast to Geyl's comments) and prose writer, and clear in presenting Macaulay's motivations. He portrays a brave, humane, yet sometimes uncontrolled man who nevertheless strove to present to the world a veneer of perfect composure.

RICHARD C. TOBIAS

McCullers, Carson 1917–1967

American novelist and short-story writer

Bloom, Harold (ed.), *Carson McCullers*, New York: Chelsea House, 1986
Carr, Virginia Spencer, *The Lonely Hunter: A Biography of Carson McCullers*, Garden City, New York: Doubleday, 1975; London: Peter Owen, 1975
Carr, Virginia Spencer, *Understanding Carson McCullers*, Columbia: University of South Carolina Press, 1990
Cook, Richard M., *Carson McCullers*, New York: Frederick Ungar, 1975
Evans, Oliver, *Carson McCullers: Her Life and Work*, London: Peter Owen, 1965; as *The Ballad of Carson McCullers*, New York: Coward-McCann, 1966
Westling, Louise Hutchings, *Sacred Groves and Ravaged Gardens: The Fiction of Eudora Welty, Carson McCullers and Flannery O'Connor*, Athens: University of Georgia Press, 1985

The initial critical response to Carson McCullers' work, which was marked by an unease at what was perceived as its gothic sensationalism, shifted with the publication of a collected edition of her longer fiction under the title of *The Ballad of the Sad Cafe*, in 1951. Criticism henceforth tended to focus on McCullers' treatment of the "universal" concerns of spiritual isolation, loneliness, and love, frequently making reference to McCullers' statement in her essay "The Flowering Dream: Notes on writing" that:

> Spiritual isolation is the basis of most of my themes. My first book was concerned with this, almost entirely, and all of my books since, in one way or another. Love, and especially love of a person who is incapable of returning it or receiving it, is at the heart of my selection of grotesque figures to write about – people whose physical incapacity is a symbol of their spiritual incapacity to love or receive love – their spiritual isolation.

This predominantly thematic approach to McCullers' work has also been accompanied by an attention to the figure of the grotesque in her fiction, particularly insofar as this forms part of a genre of Southern literature, and by analysis of the putatively religious or metaphysical aspects of her work, as they are articulated through the form of allegory. Critical readings of McCullers' works have continued to be notably informed by biographical detail. The application of Freudian theory to her work became popular in the 1960s, and more recently feminist theorists have made a significant contribution. In general, however, commentators on McCullers' work have tended to avoid the spectrum of modern critical theory, preferring to deploy a more traditional literary criticism.

EVANS's study provides an analysis of the themes and symbols of McCullers' fiction, and is predominantly biographical in its structure and focus. This material is presented with a circumspection arising from an apparent moral conservatism. CARR's 1975 biography of McCullers is informed by a close knowledge of the preoccupations of her fiction and essays, which she frequently cites. It foregrounds the issue of sexual ambivalence, which was subsequently to be recognised as a central concern of McCullers' work. It provides some useful information about her literary friendships and influences and about the publication and critical reception of her work.

COOK offers a lucid, liberal-humanist analysis of McCullers' major works. Although attentive to social, particularly racial and sexual, determinants of narrative, character, and symbolism, where this appears to be invited by the fiction, he argues that "McCullers has consistently subordinated moral outrage and social and political commentary to her overriding concern with the mysteries of individual human nature . . . we are asked to look inward to the heart rather than outward to political and economic structures in society for any final answers to human problems". The book concludes with a useful evaluation of the trajectory of McCullers' literary career and concerns.

WESTLING's three-author study demonstrates the increased influence of feminist theory on McCullers criticism in the 1980s. Westling acknowledges her debt to Virginia Woolf and Ellen Moers in her identification of an historical tradition among Southern women writers. In her opening chapters, Westling argues convincingly that common to the works of each of her selected writers is the negotiation of both an inherited Southern ideal of womanhood, which was used to deflect attention from problems of slavery and racism, and of the cultural anxiety and guilt that was produced by the latter. In her chapter about McCullers' novels, "Tomboys and Revolting Femininity", she analyzes the crisis produced in McCullers' female protagonists, as they are forced "to abandon masculine independence and accept feminine identity", concluding that

McCullers' narratives ultimately fail to envision a positive adult femininity.

BLOOM presents a succinct but stimulating Freudian interpretation of McCullers' themes of alienation and love in his Introduction to this edition of critical essays. Several of these essays offer formalist analyses of the plots and symbols of the fiction. Of note, however, are: an influential early analysis by Marguerite Young, which focuses on the metaphysical dimension of McCullers' work; an essay by Richard Gray, which connects the transitional point which McCullers occupies on the trajectory of Southern literature to the occlusion of "history" within her work; and the concluding feminist essays by Westling and Barbara A. White, which set out to redress what they see as the sexism inherent in the "universalist" criticism of McCullers by attending to the sexual specificity of her fiction.

CARR's 1990 study provides a useful introduction to McCullers' work. Presented according to the format of the "Understanding Contemporary American Literature" series, it offers a work-by-work thematic and stylistic analysis of each of McCullers' works, including her plays and short stories. A substantial amount of biographical material is mobilized to interpret the texts, including a commentary on the influence of McCullers' musical background on the structure of her fiction. The book includes a still-useful annotated bibliography.

JOANNA PRICE

MacDiarmid, Hugh 1892–1978

Scottish poet and essayist

Buthlay, Kenneth, *Hugh MacDiarmid (C.M. Grieve)*, Edinburgh and London: Oliver & Boyd, 1964; revised edition, Edinburgh: Scottish Academic Press, 1982

Cribb, T.J., "'The Cheka's Horrors' and *On a Raised Beach*", in *Studies in Scottish Literature*, 20, 1985

Gish, Nancy K., *Hugh MacDiarmid: The Man and His Work*, London: Macmillan, 1984

Gish, Nancy K. (ed.), *Hugh MacDiarmid: Man and Poet*, Orono, Maine: National Poetry Foundation, 1992; Edinburgh: Edinburgh University Press, 1992

Glen, Duncan, *Hugh MacDiarmid and the Scottish Renaissance*, Edinburgh: Chambers, 1964

Kerrigan, Catherine, *Whaur Extremes Meet: The Poetry of Hugh MacDiarmid, 1920–1934*, Edinburgh: James Thin, 1983

McCarey, Peter, *Hugh MacDiarmid and the Russians*, Edinburgh: Scottish Academic Press, 1987

Morgan, Edwin, *Hugh MacDiarmid*, London: Longman, 1976

Morgan, Edwin, *Crossing the Border: Essays on Scottish Literature*, Manchester: Carcanet, 1990

Riach, Alan, *Hugh MacDiarmid's Epic Poetry*, Edinburgh: Edinburgh University Press, 1991

Critical response to Hugh MacDiarmid began with the furore caused by his early essays in *The Scottish Educational Journal*, collected as *Contemporary Scottish Studies* (1926), in which he attacked Scotland's literary and cultural establishment, savaging its sentimentalism and parochialism. In Scotland, hostility to MacDiarmid grew from that point. Simultaneously, his poetry began to attract a small international readership. In the words of David Daiches, his 1926 masterpiece, *A Drunk Man Looks at the Thistle*, broke "on a startled and incredulous Scotland with all the shock of a childbirth in a church". But for decades he was ignored by the English, and then the Anglo-American, critical establishment, often dismissed for his political extremism and linguistic obscurity, or simply for being Scottish (read: minor). He is conspicuously absent from some influential accounts of modernism and poetry of the 1930s. After the 1962 publication of his *Collected Poems* (in America), however, critical appraisal began to accumulate. Today, critics who are familiar with his work as well as that of W.B. Yeats, Ezra Pound, and T.S. Eliot, see him as their peer. Following republication of his work in the 1990s, recent commentators are beginning to understand the significance of his political and social criticism, while his poetry is becoming more widely recognised as one of modern literature's key texts.

BUTHLAY's ability to condense information about MacDiarmid's sources and influences, and ideas about poetry, nationalism, and society, makes his brief and reader-friendly book an excellent introduction. Ground-breaking when first published, the later version is extensively revised, but nevertheless fails to deal adequately with MacDiarmid's epic poetry. There are close readings of individual poems, and Buthlay's discussion of MacDiarmid's use of the Scots language does dissolve most of the difficulties new readers might have with such rebarbative diction.

Another kind of introduction is provided by GLEN, locating MacDiarmid in a broad historical context of Scottish literature, summarizing Scotland's literary traditions, and representing MacDiarmid's role in the Scottish (literary) Renaissance of the 1920s, with reference to his contemporaries in poetry, the novel, and drama. There is an extensive bibliography, including selected references for MacDiarmid's journalism.

KERRIGAN sticks to work written up to 1934, so has little to say about the later poetry. However, her book is meticulous in its accumulation of detail about the varied backgrounds of MacDiarmid's early intellectual life, ranging through literary, linguistic, philosophical, aesthetic, economic, scientific, biological, and biographical fields. Especially valuable is Kerrigan's account of MacDiarmid's involvement with the influential London-based journal edited by A.R. Orage, *The New Age*, in the 1920s.

CRIBB's carefully written essay focuses on the central poem of MacDiarmid's career, the profound, philosophical "On a Raised Beach", developing a brave argument connecting MacDiarmid's ruthless materialism with his equally ruthless social and political beliefs. This remains a challenging and rewarding essay on the most difficult aspects of an intractable poem.

Taken together, MORGAN's British Council booklet (1976) and the essays on MacDiarmid in his 1990 collection offer a succinct, eloquent, and sweeping introduction to the phenomenon of MacDiarmid. Morgan provides detailed analyses of aspects of MacDiarmid's later poetry, including *The Battle Continues* (which he links to the Scottish tradition of "flyting", or polemical hate-poetry), and comparative studies of *In Memoriam James Joyce* and *The Kind of Poetry I Want*.

GISH offers a more comprehensive introduction to MacDiarmid's work as a whole, with illuminating use of biography in her opening chapter, and a clear sympathy for his later work, linking it to post-1945 American literature. In her collection of essays she brings together a range of different approaches, including reminiscences by friends and relations, interviews with fellow poets such as Seamus Heaney, comparative contextual essays, and close textual analyses by academics. Particularly valuable is Stephen P. Smith's reading of MacDiarmid's 1943 autobiography *Lucky Poet*. There is also an extensive bibliography by W.R. Aitken.

Recent MacDiarmid criticism focuses on particular areas of his work: many discoveries are yet to be made. McCAREY's is a comparative study of MacDiarmid and five Russian writers – Dostoevsky, V.S.Solovyov, Alexander Blok, Vladimir Mayakovsky, and Leo Shestov. A well-informed Introduction gives a refreshingly broad overview of the post-Romantic European context of all these writers, showing how Scotland was a seminal point of reference in the Romantic period, and how the legacy of Sir Walter Scott, Byron, and "Ossian" (James Macpherson) in Russia in the nineteenth century was matched by the influence twentieth-century Russia had on MacDiarmid.

My own study (RIACH) focuses intensively on MacDiarmid's later poetry, particularly *In Memoriam James Joyce*, and offers historical and theoretical literary contexts, while linking MacDiarmid's achievement with that of other writers of modern "epics" – Pound, William Carlos Williams, Charles Olson, Berltolt Brecht, and James Joyce himself. An introductory chapter locates the Scottish national movement in its historical context with other national and socialist movements arising in the wake of the nineteenth century. The last chapter deals with MacDiarmid's alleged "plagiarism" of other texts and argues a theoretical and pragmatic justification of MacDiarmid's deliberate transgressions.

ALAN RIACH

MacLennan, Hugh 1907–1990

Canadian novelist and essayist

Cameron, Elspeth, *Hugh MacLennan: A Writer's Life*, Toronto and Buffalo, New York: University of Toronto Press, 1981

Cameron, Elspeth (ed.), *Hugh MacLennan: 1982* (Proceedings of the MacLennan Conference at University College, Toronto), Toronto: University of Toronto Press, 1982

Cockburn, Robert H., *The Novels of Hugh MacLennan*, Montreal: Harvest House, 1970

Goetsch, Paul (ed.), *Hugh MacLennan*, Toronto, Montreal, and New York: McGraw-Hill Ryerson, 1973

Lucas, Alec, *Hugh MacLennan*, Toronto: McClelland & Stewart, 1970

MacLulich, T.D., *Hugh MacLennan*, Boston: Twayne, 1983

Morley, Patricia A., *The Immoral Moralists: Hugh MacLennan and Leonard Cohen*, Toronto: Clarke, Irwin & Co., 1972

Tierney, Frank M. (ed.), *Hugh MacLennan*, Ottawa: University of Ottawa Press, 1994

Woodcock, George, *Hugh MacLennan*, Toronto: Copp Clark, 1969

Hugh MacLennan has been described as Canada's nearest approach to the artist-as-statesman. From the 1940s to the 1960s he was regarded as the country's premier novelist, and the first to articulate consciously a Canadian tradition in fictional terms. Critical reception of MacLennan, however, has often been ambivalent about the relationship between his storytelling and his didacticism. His generally recognized skills as social historian have not necessarily resulted in undisputed artistic excellence.

WOODCOCK's monograph is the first full-length study in English of MacLennan's work, predated only by Paul Goetsch's 1960 dissertation in German on MacLennan's "literary nationalism". As a social historian, Woodcock maintains, MacLennan approaches in his novels the writing of a Canadian *Comédie humaine*. But Woodcock's central thesis is that MacLennan makes unconscious use of the Odysseus myth as a guiding and unifying structure for the recurring character-types and patterns of event in his novels, as he composes "the fictional delineation of a nation's odyssey". He suggests that MacLennan has thus assumed a "largeness", which is "not necessarily the same as greatness" – in fact he is ambivalent about MacLennan's achievement, criticizing especially his substitution of rhetoric for feeling at moments of emotional intensity and his philosophic fatalism, which in Woodcock's view results in mechanistic fiction. Nevertheless, he compares MacLennan to the great Russian novelists in his concern with "the sense of space and history, and of man in relation to both", and to Charles Dickens and Honoré de Balzac in being "the kind of novelist who interprets a rapidly expanding society to its own people".

The earliest book on MacLennan to be thoroughly critical is the one by COCKBURN, who argues that MacLennan's "appetite for ideas interferes with his obligations as a novelist" – even with those that MacLennan himself articulated. In particular, Cockburn criticizes MacLennan for "using techniques which properly belong to non-fiction" and for "what must be called poverty of imagination" evident in stereotypical romance plots, sentimental distortions, and characters who are "walking ideologies" – often, indeed, being "a different body with MacLennan's brain and thoughts", and thus all speaking alike. MacLennan's skill with minor characters shows up the dullness of the main ones, and his excellence with scenes of action shows up the weakness of much of his didactic prose. Though Cockburn sees MacLennan's novels as ultimately unsuccessful, he declares: "the all-important thing is that MacLennan made this voyage into the previously uncharted waters of a nation's spirit and being".

MORLEY is less interested in MacLennan's mythic archetypes and writing techniques than in defining him as a modern-day puritan mystic. In the three-quarters of her book that concern MacLennan, she shows how his condemnation of puritanism as negative and pernicious contrasts with his own espousal of historically Puritan values such as hard work, moral seriousness, self-discipline, and rationality. Morley sees the connection between what MacLennan condemns and what he affirms as being responsible for an ambivalence in his attitudes to sex, beauty, and pleasure, and to certain life-affirming, but morally unconventional, characters such as Kathleen in *Two Solitudes* and Marielle in *The Return of the Sphinx*.

The discerning in MacLennan's novels of an Oedipal pattern, pointed out at the end of Woodcock's study in relation to *The Return of the Sphinx* and elaborated in Buitenhuis's book, is linked in subsequent criticism with the name of Alec LUCAS. Primarily concerned with myth, symbol, archetype, traditional plot taxonomies, and formal symmetry, Lucas's brief book in fact spends only a few pages arguing that the Oedipus myth, because it stresses a son frustrated by a domineering father as well as a search for national identity, is more consonant than the Odysseus myth with MacLennan's central interests. Lucas's argument that MacLennan is "essentially a religious novelist", whose novels are "parables centred on religious humanism", receives fuller attention in MacLULICH's 1983 volume. MacLulich maintains that MacLennan's fiction has made "a significant contribution to the study of the culture of guilt" in criticizing the excesses of his Calvinist background, even while growing to affirm a spiritual dimension as the way through the impasse of materialist determinism. MacLulich also develops the Oedipal theme: he focuses on MacLennan's use of fiction to define and eventually resolve conflicts that arise from "the divided feelings of a dutiful but independent-minded son toward a demanding and undemonstrative father". Arguing that MacLennan typically portrays national and international politics as "family dynamics writ large", MacLulich suggests that "the social and religious dimensions of MacLennan's fiction are often simply enlarged versions of his recurrent subject, the patriarchal family". He concludes that, by the time the last novel is written, "in emotional, artistic, religious, and philosophical terms, MacLennan has learned to live in his father's house".

MacLulich's close readings of the novels as covert autobiography is a conscious extension of CAMERON's thesis. Her biography, a thorough (over 400 pages) and well-documented if sometimes repetitive study of MacLennan's life, includes valuable references to MacLennan's essays and private correspondence as well as to his novels, and covers in some detail both his pre-publication struggles and the reception of his work by contemporary critics in Canada and the United States. Cameron's central tenet is that the "characteristic patterns of action in [MacLennan's] novels . . . bear a profound relationship to the course of his life"; in fact, she argues that his aesthetic theories in general are formed out of intense personal struggles, such as coming to terms with both an autocratic father and, later, the terminal illness of his first wife. The link between MacLennan's development as a thinker, and the form, as well as the content of his novels, is persuasively presented. Against the popular view that MacLennan's seven novels signal developing stages in the Canadian national consciousness, Cameron argues, in equally sweeping terms, that "the evolution of his own life and his inherent nature symbolize that process and the nature of the majority of people living here".

The earliest collection of essays on MacLennan is that edited by GOETSCH. His book includes 20 papers and reviews, and aims "to document the major trends in MacLennan criticism" in Canada between 1950 and 1970, particularly the growing recognition of the symbolic power of MacLennan's plots rather than the criticism of them as unconvincing social realism. The papers are of uneven quality, but include an early essay by Woodcock, and stimulating papers by Hugo McPherson on problems of form and structure, Robert D. Chambers on MacLennan's view of history, William H. New on imagery of weather and nature, Dorothy Farmiloe on MacLennan's development of the myth of the voyageur, and Keiichi Hirano on the parallels between Jerome Martell and Norman Bethune.

The papers of the 1982 MacLennan Conference edited by CAMERON provide useful reflections on the earlier material. Particularly valuable are the three papers by Stanley B. Ryerson, A.B. McKillop, and Robin Mathews on issues of social class and political quietism in MacLennan, and the subsequent rebuttal by Patricia Morley, who identifies MacLennan as a "materialist idealist". Important too is the paper by Eli Mandel on MacLennan's place in the tradition of Canadian fiction, which offers a Freudian reading of his use of recurrence and repetition, in particular of his "obsessive return to the primal scene as a pivotal moment in individual and social history". A personal reminiscence by his former student Robert Kroetsch declares that "Hugh MacLennan, more than any other writer, made it possible for me to write".

The most recent collection of essays to date, edited in 1994 by TIERNEY, offers a reappraisal of MacLennan in light of contemporary interrogations of the Canadian literary tradition and MacLennan's status in it. The range is wide, and includes: unstinting praise from MacLennan's former editor at Macmillan, Douglas Gibson; an assessment by Elspeth Cameron of the cost that MacLennan paid in submitting to "national duty" as a writer; a description by Christl Verduyn of MacLennan's correspondence with Marian Engel; an examination by Barbara Pell of the effect on MacLennan's fiction of his movement towards a "theology of mediation"; and a re-reading by James Steele of the novels as instances of the struggle between the forces of civilization and barbarism that MacLennan had first identified in his doctoral dissertation on the Roman colony of Oxyrhynchus. Camille La Bossiere reappraises MacLennan's moderation as typical of Augustan "wise passiveness"; Francis Zichy reappraises MacLennan's countermodernism and finds him inadequately engaged with the modern condition. Two papers concern themselves with issues of gender: Donna Smyth's feminist reading of MacLennan's vision of the city as a centre of power and desire; and David Leahy's discussion of MacLennan's strong female figures who mirror patriarchal anxieties about women's emerging economic and sexual freedom.

DEBORAH C. BOWEN

MacNeice, Louis 1907–1963

British poet and dramatist

Brown, Terence, *Louis MacNeice: Sceptical Vision*, Dublin: Gill & Macmillan, 1975; New York: Barnes & Noble, 1975

Coulton, Barbara, *Louis MacNeice in the BBC*, London and Boston: Faber & Faber, 1980

McDonald, Peter, *Louis MacNeice: The Poet in His Contexts*, Oxford: Clarendon Press, 1991; New York: Oxford University Press, 1991

McKinnon, William T., *Apollo's Blended Dream: A Study of the Poetry of Louis MacNeice*, London and New York: Oxford University Press, 1971

Marsack, Robyn, *The Cave of Making: The Poetry of Louis MacNeice*, Oxford: Clarendon Press, 1982; New York: Oxford University Press, 1982

Smith, Elton Edward, *Louis MacNeice*, New York: Twayne, 1970

Louis MacNeice's poetry has always been treated as secondary to the "greater" work of W.H. Auden, and has been generally subsumed into the work of the "Thirties' poets". It consequently failed to receive significant attention in its own right for almost a decade after his death. The criticism of Louis MacNeice's poetry that then emerged was largely dominated by the tendency to relate biographical information to an interpretation of the poetry. With a few notable exceptions, this has resulted in a series of comparably similar humanist treatments of MacNeice's work, no doubt taken from MacNeice's own lead. However, recent reassessments have opened up MacNeice's philosophical, ideological, and aesthetic interests.

SMITH's study was the first major work dedicated to MacNeice, and attempts to project his originality and significance into the light after years in Auden's shadow. Structured by a biographical trip through the poet's life, the book develops three themes: "MacNeice as representative man of his time; a poet who ended as he began; one who fulfilled his early literary promise". In close analyses of many poems, the book somewhat pedantically lists and then traces the themes evident in the early poetry through their repetitive exploration in later works. Smith concludes that MacNeice's later poetry displays the classical humanist position to which he was always moving, and construes MacNeice's life as archetypal of the middle of the twentieth century, "strongly representative in microcosm of all the macrocosmic trauma of European man through those same years".

McKINNON's work is far a more interesting study of a poet torn between the conflicting impulses of Apollonian and Dionysian aesthetics. Exploring what McKinnon conceives of as the two dominant aspects of MacNeice's poetry – the abiding consciousness of the poet's need for belief and an expressive form appropriate to that belief – the book is structured as a study of MacNeice the metaphysician and the maker. However, despite the innovative approach of this study, it concludes with the rather tired and trite formulation that "in resolving his personal paradoxes", MacNeice "achieved the status of Everyman – a very rare and particular Everyman".

Continuing this philosophical focus, BROWN seeks to "defend MacNeice from the charge of superficiality, to take him seriously". Instead of perceiving a "decent liberal, but rather commonplace agnosticism" lying at the heart of MacNeice's work, he argues that it is characterised by a thoroughgoing and rigorous "philosophical scepticism". This sceptical vision is embodied in a matrix of complex ideas about the falsity of a transcendent reality, as well as in the technical aspects of the verse, all of which argue firmly against the view of MacNeice as a light, entertaining poet.

MacNeice's significant career with the British Broadcasting Corporation is the focus of COULTON's book, which chronicles his prominent involvement with the developments of the Features Department between 1941 and 1963, from the war propaganda for America to the more stimulating dramas and features, which took him to different parts of the world. Coulton's history of the BBC and its association with writers during the postwar years is interesting in itself; but her principal concern with MacNeice's outstanding dramatic achievements for radio illustrates his extraordinary sense of what radio could convey that the written word could not. With his increasing interest in sound experiments, MacNeice's radio drama frequently displays an innovative conjunction of words and music, and Coulton points out how his poetic writing influenced (and was influenced by) his dramatic interests.

MARSACK's study is in many respects an unadventurous restatement and reinforcement of some of the dominant ideas about MacNeice, once again taking a biographical approach. Rooting MacNeice's poetry in the "grim period of incubation" of his Ulster childhood, Marsack treats the poems as doorways into his alienated, isolated life, and his "suspicion of existing in parenthesis". The chapters progress through the inevitable chronological "pattern of life", with assessments of his involvement with the Spanish Civil War and anti-fascist politics, his slough of despondency after the War, and the eventual renewed success in the late 1950s before his death. Marsack's claim is that the poems constantly repeat and rework the themes of his early writings, and that his best poems are those that are rooted in immediate personal experience. MacNeice emerges from this dull book as a poet who was technically impressive but who recognised his limitations.

The recent study of MacNeice by McDONALD is by far the most interesting to date. Concerned with examining the contexts of the two principal canons in which MacNeice has been usually interpreted – the "Auden group" and that of Anglo-Irish literature – the book aims to allow "contextual analysis to complicate the workings of the 'literary' canons which tend to condition our approaches to modern poetry in general". McDonald demonstrates how MacNeice's *Poems* (1935) was keenly aware of its own contexts, as it consciously evaluates and questions the terms of the aesthetic and political ideologies of the day, such as individualism, private and public realities, and history and temporality. Despite following the by now *de-rigeur* chronological structure, McDonald does open up new debates about MacNeice's use of parable and his engagement with 1930s' politics. He reassesses the apparent poetic failure of the postwar years as a necessary period of literary and formal experimentation. And, in the final chapter, he offers a revaluation of MacNeice the Irish poet. This is certainly the most stimulating work on MacNeice.

TIM S. WOODS

Macpherson, James 1736–1796

Scottish poet and historian

Bysveen, Joseph, *Epic Tradition and Innovation in James Macpherson's Fingal*, Uppsala, Sweden: University of Stockholm, 1982; Atlantic Highlands, New Jersey: Humanities Press, 1982

DeGategno, Paul J., *James Macpherson*, Boston: Twayne, 1989
Gaskill, Howard (ed.), *Ossian Revisited*, Edinburgh: Edinburgh University Press, 1991
Haywood, Ian, *The Making of History: A Study of the Literary Forgeries of James Macpherson and Thomas Chatterton in Relation to Eighteenth-Century Ideas of History and Fiction*, Rutherford, New Jersey: Fairleigh Dickinson University Press, 1986; London: Associated University Presses, 1986
Stafford, Fiona J., *The Sublime Savage: A Study of James Macpherson and the Poems of Ossian*, Edinburgh: Edinburgh University Press, 1988
Thomson, Derick S., *The Gaelic Sources of Macpherson's Ossian*, Edinburgh: Oliver & Boyd, 1952
Weinbrot, Howard D., *Britannia's Issue: The Rise of British Literature from Dryden to Ossian*, Cambridge and New York: Cambridge University Press, 1993

Tobias Smollett greeted Macpherson's *Fingal* in 1762 by claiming that "this admirable piece will, even according to Aristotle's definition, be found a truly epic poem and . . . in many places superior even to Homer and Virgil"; the work was subsequently to prove a key agent in the definition and development of European Romanticism. Macpherson produced three Ossianic publications, each of them winning immense early popularity throughout Britain and across Europe: *Fragments of Ancient Poetry, Collected in the Highlands of Scotland, and Translated from the Galic or Erse Language* (1760); *Fingal. An Ancient Epic Poem . . . Composed by Ossian, the Son of Fingal. Translated from the Galic Language* (1762); *Temora, an Ancient Epic Poem . . . Composed by Ossian, the Son of Fingal. Translated from the Galic Language* (1763). The reputation of these works has been dogged ever since, however, by allegations of spuriousness, most noisily levelled in the first place by Samuel Johnson. It is regrettable that the issue of forgery in Macpherson continues to distract attention from the qualities, implications, and sheer strangeness of the writing itself.

THOMSON, a Gaelic scholar, builds on the evidence collected by Henry Mackenzie and others in the celebrated *Report of the Committee of the Highland Society of Scotland, Appointed To Enquire into the Nature and Authenticity of the Poems of Ossian* (1805). His study definitively establishes the presence of material drawn from a range of traditional sources, including popular Highland ballads and passages from Gaelic manuscripts, while at the same time recognising that much in Macpherson's writing is alien to the oral traditions from which it presents itself as deriving. In this light it becomes possible to see Macpherson not in some simple category of original poet, or cynical forger, or mere translator, but as something of all these things – as the orchestrator of compelling mixtures of original and ancient, of palimpsests in which eighteenth-century sensibility clashes intriguingly with the ancient values of epic; as a writer who attempts to re-animate the poetry of the present through stylistic appropriations from the past, and so finds his English counterparts in the contemporaneous experiments with ancient styles of Thomas Chatterton and Christopher Smart.

The analogy with Chatterton in particular is usefully explored by HAYWOOD, while BYSVEEN turns back to the influence of Macpherson's classical studies at the University of Aberdeen to "investigate the ways in which the traditions of the epic in its classical form and, to some extent, in its conjectural ancient Scottish form, influenced *Fingal*". GASKILL rightly appeals for a stylistic study of Macpherson's English idiom to be carried out by a scholar with a background in Gaelic, with a view to establishing "how far Macpherson's English, and the peculiar effects which it is able to achieve, might have been shaped by his mother tongue and his knowledge of its literary traditions".

Gaskill's own collection brings together scholars from a range of disciplines to compile the most up-to-date account available of Macpherson's sources and early reception. The editor surveys the current state of the "authenticity" debate; Donald E. Meeks makes a persuasive argument for Macpherson's importance as both disseminator and creative employer of the Gaelic ballad tradition; and John Valdimir Price reads Ossian in the larger context of canon formation in the Scottish Enlightenment. There are further essays on the reception of the Ossianic texts at the hands of early readers as different as Hugh Blair, David Hume, Thomas Jefferson, William Wordsworth, and the first audience in Germany.

Two of Gaskill's contributors are also authors of critical monographs on Macpherson. STAFFORD's is the best general study to date of the Ossian poems, locating them, to illuminating effect, in the social, political, and intellectual contexts of Macpherson's experience. Framing her readings with biographical accounts of Macpherson's Speyside childhood during the bloodshed of the 1740s, and his prosperous middle age in London as Member of Parliament for Camelford in Cornwall, Stafford explores telling contradictions in both the life and the works, finding in each "a constant struggle to reconcile conflicting loyalties to North and South". DeGATEGNO's book is a briefer, but still useful, introductory study, reading Macpherson above all as a pre-Romantic whose work heralds or intensifies "the return to nature, melancholy, primitivism, sentimentalism, individualism, and exoticism".

Increasingly, the Ossian poems are now recognised again as central and necessary points of reference in wider discussions of eighteenth-century culture and national identities. WEINBROT's book gives an eminent example of this trend. By calling the Ossianic cycle "a poem of Scotland after Culloden" he briefly opens the promising and under-explored question of Jacobite innuendo in Macpherson; but his main emphasis falls on "the poem's competing desires to be part of British national literature while also celebrating the distinguishing marks of a Celtic past". For Weinbrot, Ossian represents an irresistible fusion of traditions, which sealed the eighteenth-century construction of a newly flexible and inclusive Britishness, "affirming Scottish genius, history and identity while helping Macpherson and Scotland move toward the south, as Scottish culture already long had been doing". Much remains to be said on the ways in which the reception of these influential texts also helped England move toward the north, as English culture had been significantly behindhand in doing; but Weinbrot is surely justified in writing here, as he puts it, of "Britannia's issue and Scotia's issue . . . blended in cacophonous harmony".

TOM KEYMER

Madness and Literature

Feder, Lillian, *Madness in Literature*, Princeton, New Jersey: Princeton University Press, 1980
Felman, Shoshana, *Writing and Madness*, translated by Martha Noel Evans and Felman, with Brian Massumi, Ithaca, New York: Cornell University Press, 1985
MacLennan, George, *Lucid Interval: Subjective Writing and Madness in History*, Leicester: Leicester University Press, 1992
Rieger, Branimir M. (ed.), *Dionysus in Literature: Essays on Literary Madness*, Bowling Green, Ohio: Bowling Green State University Popular Press, 1994
Sass, Louis A., *Madness and Modernism: Insanity in the Light of Modern Art, Literature and Thought*, New York: Basic Books, 1992

Since the publication of Michel Foucault's *Madness and Civilization*, a veritable industry of madness in discourse has sprung to life. Books relating to specific periods – especially the eighteenth, nineteenth, and twentieth centuries – are numerous. The classical period also remains a focus of interest, continuing the tradition of inquiry into the representation of ritual madness, often Dionysian. In the interest of preserving focus, I list here only works concerned with a broad range of literature, representing a range of theoretical and methodological approaches. These are also fairly recent works; readers who wish to delve deeper may use these books and their bibliographies as a guide to earlier studies.

FEDER's book is highly recommended as a solid overview of literary treatments of madness from Euripides to Wole Soyinka. The organization is chronological: Feder gives historically contextualized readings of literary against non-literary texts dealing with madness. Feder is not simply interested in the representation of madness, but in the logic of madness itself. Her theoretical orientation is psychoanalytical, and readers may be put off by the apparent conflation with literary representation of real human pathologies. Feder addresses this concern in her Introduction, taking essentially a Jungian view of the role of the artist as representative of group, as well as individual anxieties.

RIEGER's book is valuable as a collection of essays from a variety of perspectives, including the pedagogical, the theoretical, and the psychological. De Beaugrande provides an overview of different literary theories' treatment of the concept of madness; Lindauer examines the classic connections between creativity and madness from "an empirical perspective"; other essays cover topics ranging from madness in film, to Dostoevsky, William Blake, Virginia Woolf, William Faulkner, Kurt Vonnegut, and Stephen King. The collection finishes with an essay on teaching "Madness in Literature" as an undergraduate course. Although somewhat uneven in tone, the essays are generally accessible to the undergraduate or non-specialist, and show a diversity of approaches rarely seen in the Freudian, Jungian and most recently Foucauldian-dominated treatments of the topic.

FELMAN works through Foucault, Jacques Derrida, and Jacques Lacan to produce a book about writing about madness. In pointing out that language is itself "a difference by which madness is deferred", Felman locates the difficulty in writing insanity, a task with which literature has been historically entrusted. Felman works primarily with authors who write directly about madness: Gérard de Nerval, Gustave Flaubert, Honoré de Balzac, Lacan, and extensively with Henry James. Although only the chapter on James falls directly within our purview here, Felman's methods and theoretical insights are exemplary of the period in which the book was written and are foundational for much of the work that has succeeded it. Its style is, unfortunately, also exemplary of its historical moment and theoretical lineage.

MacLENNAN covers specific authors from the seventeenth through the nineteenth centuries who were, with one exception (John Bunyan) diagnosed and treated as mad. MacLennan is interested in the relationship historically attributed to madness and inspiration, and examines how Torquato Tasso, Thomas Hoccleve, James Carkesse, Bunyan, George Trosse, William Cowper, John Clare, and de Nerval construct the experience of madness – or mad subjectivity – within their poetic and/or autobiographical works. MacLennan traces a gradual "interiorisation" of madness – and experience generally – culminating in the Romantic ideal of creative madness. His approach is self-identified as Foucauldian, although he criticizes Foucault for an essentialist romanticizing of madness as truth – a common (and justifiable) observation.

SASS's massive volume is an essential read for those who wish to go beyond the history of representations of madness and look for objective connections. Sass provides readings of modern literature and art, within the context of current psychological and biological knowledge about schizophrenia. Sass reads schizophrenia itself as phenomenologically analogical to the modernist aesthetic, exploring connections between modern and schizophrenic subjectivity. The analysis is subtle and escapes the reductionism that such an argument might suggest. This book will be far more technical and less focused on literature than the casual reader or student will require – or desire – as literature and art are tertiary topics within it. For those with a serious interest, however, in the history of madness or the construction of subjectivity within modernism, Sass's book will be richly rewarding.

PAMELA K. GILBERT

Mailer, Norman 1923–

American novelist, political journalist and film director

Bailey, Jennifer, *Norman Mailer, Quick-Change Artist*, London: Macmillan, 1979; New York: Barnes & Noble, 1979
Braudy, Leo (ed.), *Norman Mailer: A Collection of Critical Essays*, Englewood Cliffs, New Jersey: Prentice-Hall, 1972
Leigh, Nigel, *Radical Fictions and the Novels of Norman Mailer*, London: Macmillan, 1989; New York. St Martin's Press, 1990
Manso, Peter (ed.), *Mailer: His Life and Times*, New York: Simon & Schuster, 1985; Harmondsworth, Middlesex, Viking Press, 1985
Middlebrook, Jonathan, *Mailer and the Times of His Time*, San Francisco: Bay Books, 1976

Mills, Hilary, *Mailer: A Biography*, New York: Empire, 1982; Sevenoaks, Kent: New English Library, 1983

Poirier, Richard, *Mailer*, London: Fontana, 1972; New York: Viking Press, 1972

Radford, Jean, *Norman Mailer: A Critical Study*, London: Macmillan, 1975; New York: Barnes & Noble, 1975

Rollyson, Carl, *The Lives of Norman Mailer: A Biography*, New York: Paragon House, 1991

Wenke, Joseph, *Mailer's America*, Hanover, New Hampshire: University Press of New England, 1987

Criticism of Mailer's fiction has been bedevilled by a tendency to read autobiographical significance into his novels and by critics' evident unease at Mailer's wilfully provocative stance in most of his writings. He has been concerned throughout his career to identify and examine the different styles of power in American life, whether through his non-fictional writings on political leaders or through his fictional depiction of figures from the Mafia, and the military or intelligence community.

BRAUDY's collection is admittedly a preliminary assessment of Mailer in mid-career, but it contains essays that still retain value. Braudy identifies personal reference and ideological polemic as the two main obstacles to a balanced critical assessment. Diana Trilling explores the paradoxes within Mailer's stance, arguing that his adversarial posture is a sign of engagement. George Alfred Schrader, one of many early critics to consider the existential dimension to Mailer's work, locates a "primeval vitality of romantic passion" similar to positions outlined in Kirkegaard. Stanley Edgar Hyman comments on the extraordinary energy of Mailer's similes, but leaves these comments in a vacuum, whereas Leo Bersani's essay on *An American Dream* explores the imagery of private myth. Mailer, Bersani insists, is not a realist and should not be measured against anachronistic criteria.

POIRIER picks up and elaborates this last proposition in the volume he contributed to the Fontana "Modern Masters" series. For all its apparent presumption, this study remains one of the most incisive analyses of Mailer's writings to date. Poirier breaks new ground in demonstrating the technical means Mailer adopts to project himself as an "embattled cultural hero", and he argues that a Faustian energy is at work in Mailer's drive to pursue the contradictions in American life. Poirier also demonstrates that the projected shape of Mailer's career has remained one of his most persistent fictions, one always larger than any individual work. The influence of figures like Freud, Marx, and Wilhelm Reich is clearly shown, but Poirier ties their presence in with Mailer's chosen structures and methods. He emerges from this account as an accomplished "ventriloquist of styles" and a radical commentator on both the technological and sexual revolutions.

RADFORD, like Poirier, seeks to do justice to Mailer's intellectual reach, but does so by devoting her first chapters to themes. Concentrating mainly on the period 1948–68, she sees an extended philosophical debate on man taking place in the novels of the period, whose index is the shifts in the figure of the hero from novel to novel. She then considers the political themes, before demonstrating the emergence of Mailer's literary styles. Echoing Poirier she, too, sees *Advertisements for Myself* as marking a turning point, but her comments on voice lead her to understate Mailer's complex self-fictionalizing here. In her last main chapter Radford begins a discussion of Mailer's treatment of gender, which unfortunately stays on a fairly prosaic level in pointing out that female characters are "secondary human beings" in his fiction. By the early 1970s Mailer, for her, has reached a point of crisis in his work, mired in the contradictions of his culture.

MIDDLEBROOK's principal insight into Mailer is the manner in which he uses American materials. Indeed, Middlebrook's account repeatedly draws comparisons between Mailer and Ralph Waldo Emerson to bring out a transcendental dimension to the former's fiction. *The Naked and the Dead* is interpreted as an appropriation of 1930s' styles for Mailer's own use in starting his career. Next comes a powerful exploitation of the mundane in *Barbary Shore*. For all Middlebrook's local insights (the distinction between Mailer and his protagonists cannot be insisted on too much) his main argument does not seem strong enough to carry his critical points, especially when, for instance, his discussion of *An American Dream* is interrupted by comparisons with William Langland, John Keats and Robert Browning.

BAILEY's very title signals her new and productive approach to Mailer. She see his best works (for her, those of the 1960s) as centring on a "series of rapidly shifting voices". Through his use of these voices, and therefore of different *personae*, Mailer at once manipulates his audiences and bridges the gap between individual and public concerns. Bailey's study sheds particularly helpful light on the sheer theatrical rapidity of Mailer's works – fictional and non-fictional. Her approach discusses both categories in very similar terms, and by so doing she demonstrates the unity of Mailer's *oeuvre*. Once again the notion of opposing forces crops up, through certain key metaphors, which articulate the act of writing as a combative action. Bailey sees a turning point for the worse in *Of a Fire on the Moon* (1969), which ushers in a decade where Mailer's imagination can no longer get a firm purchase on public events, like the American moonshot.

MILLS does for Mailer's life what Bailey had done for his fiction. Her Mailer is always, in some sense, on stage, performing before a public. Thus she does ample justice to the disparate self-images that Mailer projects of himself – the "nice Jewish boy from Brooklyn", the fighter, the provocateur, and so on. Mailer criticism has repeatedly struggled with the complex issue of how his writings relate to his biography, and Mills injects a much-needed sophistication into her discussion of the latter. Looming over Mailer stands the macho figure of Ernest Hemingway, against whom he has been struggling, in and out of print, for years. This biography offers a mine of information on Mailer's writings, and shows how he repeatedly courts controversy in, for instance, proposing a conspiracy theory of Marilyn Monroe's death.

MANSO makes a startling contrast with Bailey. Rather than a linear biography, it is a compilation of comments on Mailer, arranged chronologically, by his friends and associates. In that respect it represents selections from scores of interviews, which normally make up the raw data for a bibliography. What we lose in analysis we gain in a unique source of information, which testifies to Mailer's chameleon-like versatility. On the subject of his dealings with women he is described as a feminist, a male chauvinist, *and* as an incurable romantic! Manso's collage method juxtaposes different views of controversial events like the 1949 Waldorf Conference, and also assembles many suggestive reactions to Mailer by fellow writers. For Kurt Vonnegut he behaved "like an English gentleman"; for William Phillips of the *Partisan Review* he compulsively identified with anti-establishment movements; while Diana Trilling discusses his interest in the "Theatre of Ideas". Manso then provides a mass of material that nicely complements Mailer's own writings.

For WENKE "America" signifies the mythic and millennial images of the country as well as its actual political landscape. He argues that Mailer has pursued a remarkably consistent vision of his country as being under constant threat from totalitarianism. In his discussion, Wenke tends to rely heavily on character-analysis and he has little to say about Mailer's theatricality. For him, too, "The White Negro" marks a shift towards the darker vision of works like *Why Are We in Vietnam?* Wenke first presents a view of Mailer as an engaged writer, always dealing in issues. Second, he sees him as returning constantly to existentialism and transcendentalism throughout an essentially unified career, whether he is writing fiction or political reports.

LEIGH fleshes out a subject that few critics have examined in any detail – Mailer's interest in politics, specifically political power. He pursues this throughout Mailer's fiction with the one exception of *Tough Guys Don't Dance*. Thus, *The Naked and the Dead* is glossed as an oblique examination of the rise of fascism in America, *The Deer Park* as a drama of opposition between ideology and a politics of sensibility, and so on. Leigh demonstrates that Mailer's engagement with history is complex and ambivalent, but he tends to set limits on his own study by concentrating on characters as personifications of political viewpoints. This approach does not work too badly for Mailer's early fiction, but falters rather when considering the complexities of voice in *An American Dream* and *Why Are We in Vietnam?* The least susceptible work to Leigh's approach is *Ancient Evenings*, which he appears to regard as an exercise in escapism. For the rest, Leigh's work remains valuable for its reading of Mailer's fiction against the background of contemporary US politics.

ROLLYSON builds his biography primarily around Mailer's ambition to become a writer and includes much new information on material from his early Harvard days, when, for instance, *The Naked and the Dead* first appeared as a play. Rollyson has much to say on the planning that went into Mailer's fiction: he notes the original intent of *Barbary Shore* to be a parody of Christopher Isherwood, and compares the *Esquire* and book versions of *An American Dream.* A complex story emerges of Mailer's search for appropriate methods and of his ongoing love-hate relationship with reviewers. It is a welcome new emphasis in Mailer criticism for Rollyson not to read Mailer's career as peaking in the 1960s; on the contrary, he praises the succinct style of *The Fight*, the unusually self-effaced voice of *The Executioner's Song*, and the new stylistic means of expressing consciousness in *Ancient Evenings*. His account breaks off on the eve of the publication of *Harlot's Ghost*, but his study combines sensitive accounts of Mailer's composition, a recognition of the variety of his post-1960s works, and sheds valuable light on Mailer's status as a dignitary on the literary scene when he served as president of PEN.

DAVID SEED

Malamud, Bernard 1914–1986

American novelist and short-story writer

Abramson, Edward A., *Bernard Malamud Revisited*, New York: Twayne, 1993
Alter, Iska, *The Good Man's Dilemma: Social Criticism in the Fiction of Bernard Malamud*, New York: AMS Press, 1981
Cohen, Sandy, *Bernard Malamud and the Trial by Love*, Amsterdam: Rodopi, 1974
Ducharme, Robert, *Art and Idea in the Novels of Bernard Malamud: Toward "The Fixer"*, The Hague and Paris: Mouton, 1974
Field, Leslie A., and Joyce W. Field (eds.), *Bernard Malamud: A Collection of Critical Essays*, Englewood Cliffs, New Jersey: Prentice-Hall, 1975
Helterman, Jeffrey, *Understanding Bernard Malamud*, Columbia: University of South Carolina Press, 1985
Hershinow, Sheldon J., *Bernard Malamud*, New York: Frederick Ungar, 1980
Salzberg, Joel, *Critical Essays on Bernard Malamud*, Boston: G.K. Hall, 1987
Walden, Daniel (ed), "Bernard Malamud: In Memoriam", special issue of *Studies in American Jewish Literature*, 7(2), Fall 1988

Having been awarded two National Book awards and a Pulitzer Prize, Bernard Malamud is an important American author whose primary concern is with the growth of the individual through humanity, selflessness, and love. Although he disliked being labelled a "Jewish-American" writer, he was nonetheless seen as one of the foremost representatives of the genre.

COHEN is primarily concerned with an explication of "self-transcendence", which he feels is Malamud's central theme. Many of Malamud's characters are seen as selfish and insecure people who, in order to attain both happiness and human insight, move from *eros* to *caritas*, from a sense of self to one that subsumes the self in a love for another human being; this movement comprises the "trial by love" of the title. He also notes the mythical basis of a good deal of Malamud's writing and the irony that accrues when myth conflicts with realism.

DUCHARME has written a very competent study, which focuses on Malamud's use of myth, irony, and the theme of the father-son relationship, with its tensions and conflicts created by the protagonists' need for various spiritual fathers. Also, he notes that with *The Fixer* a new note enters Malamud's work: Yakov Bok rejects suffering, whereas previous novelistic protagonists were resigned to it. This shift is an important one, as it shows an increase in pessimism in Malamud's writing. This is a sophisticated and closely argued study. It is a pity that the author was not able to consider *The Tenants* and *God's Grace*, later novels which further support his ideas.

This second essay collection edited by FIELD and FIELD (their first was limited to work from the 1960s) contains a useful list of Malamud's short stories, with place and date of original publication, a good bibliography of articles covering the earlier work, and an interview with Malamud. There is also an essay by Cynthia Ozick. In all, there are five pieces never published before, with the choice of essays being impressive.

HERSHINOW has produced a short book, which takes as its starting point Malamud's concern with morality and the importance of putting into practice. The author depicts Malamud's view of humanity as rooted in ethical struggle. There are plot summaries, with the study providing a beginner's introduction not dissimilar from HELTERMAN's. The latter's guide appears in a series designed for students of contemporary literature. Malamud's mythological structures comprise an important concern here, in an approach that is clear and easily accessible.

ALTER's study defines "social criticism" rather broadly, and she is forced to admit that Malamud is not a social critic in the usual sense of the term. Her discussions of Edenic mythology in *A New Life* and of Malamud's treatment of blacks and Jews, however, are useful, as are her observations of the importance he places on Jewish history. Her use of feminist ideology is somewhat too heavy-handed, particularly in her analyses of *A New Life* and *The Assistant*.

SALZBERG's essay collection contains 12 reviews and 12 essays. The editor has written a very useful Introduction, in which he discusses Malamud's career and the history of criticism of Malamud's works. The selection is astute, with the reviews adding a good deal of insight, complementing the essays well, which in their turn are of a very high calibre and cover a wide range of material. All in all this is a very useful collection.

In my (ABRAMSON's) study, I stress the importance he placed on a developing sense of suffering as the cause of moral growth, compassion, and sympathy for others. Its recent publication date allows coverage of all Malamud's work, including the posthumously published *"The People" and Uncollected Stories*.

Finally, WALDEN's second number of *Studies in American Jewish Literature* to be devoted to Malamud (the first was Spring 1978) is subtitled "Bernard Malamud: In Memoriam", and is a recognition of the loss suffered by American letters through his death in 1986. There are 11 articles, with three essays on the often under-represented *Dubin's Lives*. There is a piece entitled "Malamud's Last Interview? A Memoir", in which Joel Salzberg relates a 45-minute telephone conversation with Malamud on 27 January 1986; Malamud died two months later. The final piece is a useful bibliographical essay, in which Richard O'Keefe presents both primary and secondary sources.

EDWARD A. ABRAMSON

Malory, Sir Thomas *fl.* 15th Century

English author of *Le Morte Darthur*

Bennett, J.A.W. (ed.), *Essays on Malory*, Oxford: Clarendon Press, 1963
Field, P.J.C., *Romance and Chronicle: A Study of Malory's Prose Style*, London: Barrie & Jenkins, 1971; Bloomington: Indiana University Press, 1971
Field, P.J.C., *The Life and Times of Sir Thomas Malory*, Cambridge: D.S. Brewer, 1993; Rochester, New York: Boydell & Brewer, 1993
Kennedy, Beverly, *Knighthood in the "Morte Darthur"*, Woodbridge, Suffolk: D.S. Brewer, 1985, 2nd edition, 1992
Lambert, Mark, *Malory: Style and Vision in "Le Morte Darthur"*, New Haven, Connecticut: Yale University Press, 1975
Lumiansky, R. (ed.), *Malory's Originality: A Critical Study of "Le Morte Darthur"*, Baltimore: Johns Hopkins University Press, 1964
McCarthy, Terence, *Reading the "Morte Darthur"*, Cambridge: D.S. Brewer, 1988
Matthews, William, *The Ill-Framed Knight: A Skeptical Inquiry into the Identity of Malory*, Berkeley: University of California Press, 1966
Moorman, Charles, *The Book of Kyng Arthur: The Unity of Malory's "Morte Darthur"*, Lexington: University Press of Kentucky, 1965
Parins, Marylyn Jackson (ed.), *Malory: The Critical Heritage*, London and New York: Routledge, 1988
Spisak, James W. (ed.), *Studies in Malory*, Kalamazoo: (Medieval Institute of) Western Michigan University Press, 1985

A discussion of "Thomas Malory" must begin by acknowledging that there is some doubt as to who Thomas Malory actually was. There are five Thomas Malorys known to have been alive at about the time that the author of the *Morte Darthur* tells us he was writing (as noted by Field, 1993), and at least two have had their serious defenders. The consequent interest in matters biographical has perhaps been enhanced by the rather racy life of the leading contender, the frequently imprisoned Sir Thomas Malory of Newbold Revel in Warwickshire. MATTHEWS, in what he characterizes as a "skeptical inquiry" into the authorship question, runs counter to received opinion in promoting a candidate from Yorkshire instead of the Warwickshire Malory. He points to what he sees as Northern aspects of Malory's language, as well as to Malory's use of Northern sources, to support his candidate. This man was not, so far as we can tell, either a knight or a prisoner, but Matthews dismisses this objection by taking "knight-prisoner" to mean "prisoner of war". He questions whether the Warwickshire Malory could have had the necessary sources to hand in Newgate prison, and argues that the library of nearby Greyfriars lacked many of these texts. Matthews makes certain assumptions, among them, that an old man, as the Warwickshire Malory would have been, could not have written such a work, given the conditions of a fifteenth-century prison; or that an immoral man, as the Warwickshire Malory certainly appears to have been, would not have written a work with so strong a moral centre. The relevance of what Matthews called the "moral gap" between the Warwickshire Malory and the *Morte* has in particular been doubted. FIELD (1993) revisits Matthews' evidence and adds some more of his own in a densely-written biography, which methodically and convincingly supports the case for the Warwickshire Malory. The Yorkshire Malory, he makes clear, was never a knight, and this fact alone means that he cannot have been the author of the *Morte*. The linguistic evidence should be understood as a reflection of Malory's sense of what suited his stories. This impeccably documented book, in the absence of any new evidence, must stand as the last word on the subject.

Since the discovery of the Winchester Manuscript in 1934, a second major concern for Malory scholars has been whether Malory intended to write a "hoole book", as in William Caxton's 1485 edition, or eight separate tales. The latter position was advanced in Eugène Vinaver's magisterial 1947 edition of the Winchester MS. Many of the works discussed below include arguments or assumptions about the unity of the *Morte*. McCARTHY's book, intended to be a guide for the educated first-time reader of Malory, outlines both the authorship and structure issues, as well as many central themes of the work, in a succinct and useful way, and can be recommended as a point of entry into both Malory's work and the equally interlaced world of Malory scholarship.

There are many anthologies of Malory criticism: Bennett's and Lumiansky's remain standard. BENNETT's collection is a series of "replies" to Vinaver's edition. Oakeshott's account of the momentous discovery of the Winchester MS documents a vital moment in Malory studies, and the "conversation" between C.S. Lewis, Vinaver himself, and D.S. Brewer over the question of unity remains of interest today. LUMIANSKY's affiliations in this discussion are clear from the organization of his collection: each essay considers a single "tale" in relation to its sources and to the rest of the work, here conceived as a "hoole book". One of the contributors to this volume is Charles MOORMAN, who later reprised and expanded several of his earlier articles in *The Book of Kyng Arthur*. He argues that Malory's work has both a "critical unity", by which he means that the work "had unity thrust upon it" in the process of completion, and "historical unity", by which he addresses the notion of Malory's intention to produce "a comprehensive and unified statement of the Arthurian legend".

Among the more recent anthologies, the collection edited by SPISAK ranges among Malory's use of sources, his treatment of key characters, his narrative method. A minor "theme" emerges in the group of three essays which deal with editions of Malory. More interesting, perhaps, is PARINS' collection, which offers the history of critical reaction to Malory, from Caxton's preface up to the early twentieth century. Most of the material is from the nineteenth century, but there is a wide enough range that the modern reader can appreciate the varying reactions of readers from the past.

There have been many book-length studies of Malory. FIELD (1971) stands as the first book devoted to Malory's prose style, and as one of many contributions by this prolific Malory scholar. Field finds Malory's roots in the language of chronicles, of *Mandeville's Travels*, of the Paston letters, rather than in the rhetorical tradition of the learned writer. He connects this colloquial "non-tradition" to Malory's purpose by arguing that it leads to an emphasis on action and to a narrative presence that appears factual. Nothing interferes with Malory's "guileless vision" of the Arthurian past, or with his "enthusiasm for knightliness". LAMBERT revisits the stylistic question, and compares Malory to his sources to find both the common and the distinctive aspects of his style. In Malory's use of formal speech, qualitative description, catalogues, and conventional details, he sees the attitude of the historian. He notes that Malory frequently stylizes description, characters, and action. The last half of the book considers Malory's last tales and the effect of "Malorian style" in these tales.

Malory's treatment of chivalry has long been a focus for his readers. KENNEDY argues that Malory explores three kinds of knighthood, all current in fifteenth-century England. Gawain embodies the earliest form of Heroic knighthood: he is a warrior and a fatalist. The Grail knights represent True Christian knighthood. They are "radical Christians", guided by a sense of providential purpose. Arthur is representative of Worshipful knighthood. The Worshipful knight is a "rational pragmatist" whose character looks forward to the Renaissance to come. These three kinds of knighthood then become the structural focus of the work, rigorously organized in Kennedy's view around the conflicts between these typologies. Malory's deployment of these typologies allows the reader to understand the end of Arthurian civilization in either human or spiritual terms, within the framework of providential history.

SIÂN ECHARD

Malouf, David 1934–

Australian novelist, poet, and short-story writer

Hansson, Karin, *Sheer Edge: Aspects of Identity in David Malouf's Writing*, Lund, Sweden: Lund University Press, 1991

Heseltine, Harry, "An Imaginary Life – The Dimensions of Self", in *Australian Literary Studies*, 14, 1989–90

Indyk, Ivor, *David Malouf*, Melbourne: Oxford University Press, 1993

Mansfield, Nick, "Body Talk: The Prose of David Malouf", in *Southerly*, 49(2), 1989

Neilson, Philip, *Imagined Lives: A Study of David Malouf*, St Lucia: University of Queensland Press, 1990

Pierce, Peter, "David Malouf's Fiction", in *Meanjin*, 41(4), 1982

If there is a common starting-point for much of the critical debate that surrounds David Malouf's work over the past 20 years, then that impetus comes from the author himself, from his "imaginary life". Malouf's particular blend of the romantic and the historical with what is often an intense lyricism is fertile ground for those searching for a successor to Patrick White as the next great Australian novelist. If Malouf has shown an early preference for poetry, the short story, and the novella, he has also shown a preference for the larger issues of the day, most notably the influence of place and history on personal and national identity. His continual questioning of received myths and ideas surrounding Australia's historical experience, from white settlement to World War I and the Anzac legacy, is secondary only to his analysis of the relationships between men – as fathers, brothers, sons, and lovers.

PIERCE, in the relatively early article, concentrates on Malouf's use of the novel form, in particular his use of the short novel or novella. As elsewhere, comparisons are drawn between Malouf and Patrick White. The focus in this essay moves from an examination of the narrative reflexivity of

Malouf as author and autobiographer, as evident in *Johnno*, to the themes of provenance and exile, which occupy *An Imaginary Life*. Pierce also makes interesting use of Howard Nemerov's essay "Composition and Fate in the Short Novel" to explain Malouf's early preference for the novella. His conclusion forms an effective summary of Malouf's richness:

> The uncomplicated disclosure of himself is nowhere to be found in Malouf's work. What he has expounded "by fantasies" (by his variations on a single plot) is his intuition of the poignant fallacy of any belief that independence from time, place or other people is possible, together with his yearning that this might not be so.

HANSSON's study is an important introduction to Malouf's work from the perspective of someone outside the Australian literary academy. She begins her analysis with an examination of Malouf's literary heritage, the cultural construction of Australian identity, and the quest for a national canon. In this context Patrick White emerges as the most obvious literary progenitor of Malouf's studies of the "mystery of failure" in men's relationships with one another and with the land they inhabit. If there is a sense of failure, there is also a recognition of the celebratory strain that pervades Malouf's analysis of the male-male dynamic. Hansson incorporates both Malouf's poetry and prose in her examination of the function of time, place, language, and metaphysics in the creation of identity, while stressing that the "most important recurrent ideas are organically integrated by means of unifying elements of imagery and symbolism".

The dilemma of the author as exile is prominent in HESELTINE's examination of Malouf's watershed work – *An Imaginary Life*. The epic nature of Malouf's project is compared with that undertaken by A.D. Hope, Randolph Stow, and White in their work. He argues that Malouf's adoption of Ovid, a key figure in European cultural development, should not be seen "as a flight from philistine Australia nor an uncritical acceptance of Europe" but as a point of departure for a commentary on the way in which we reconstruct the past, adapting and shaping it to provide us with a way of understanding the present. In this he sees Malouf linking historical data "not just with contemporary Australian issues but with some of the prevailing themes of twentieth century literary culture: dreamwork, myth, the unconscious, and consciousness at the extremes of human behaviour".

The temptation of epic also occupies INDYK's work. This is a detailed and well-argued examination of masculinity and sexuality in Malouf's work, and includes a reading of the drama as well as the prose and poetry. Of particular interest is his commentary on Malouf's use of the pastoral mode, primitivism, and an underlying homoeroticism in *An Imaginary Life*. This primitivism is also understood as a search for links with the past, as an "acting to repair breaks in social continuity of the kind that stem from migration". The use of the masculine double and the desire to create a form of masculine succession separate from the female realm are central in this examination, in that they draw attention to the genetic fantasy that pervades the relationship between father and son in a novel like *Harland's Half Acre*.

NEILSEN's study concentrates on Malouf's exploration of what it is to be Australian and his provision of a set of mythologies of Australian-ness. Drawing on the work of Roland Barthes and Claude Lévi-Strauss, Neilsen pursues a structuralist interpretation of Malouf's work, concentrating in particular on the mythologising function of the early fiction and poetry. Of interest also is the attention paid to Malouf's interpretation of Paul Carter's ideas on spatial history, with regard to the individual construction of place in a novel like *The Great World*.

MANSFIELD's article assesses Malouf's concern with the role and function of the artist when faced with a physical environment that overwhelms. In this, he suggests the similarities of Malouf's concerns to those of the Romantic writers, in particular where the issues of language and expression are concerned. He traces the role and function of "body-talk", the attempt to bring the body and language together, and highlights the instability of both: linguistic breakdown, in this analysis, is most often accompanied by comparable bodily metamorphosis. He concludes that "the body is an unstable site for language which approaches an unknown there", and in his view it is this element of the unknown, of the "other", that marks Malouf's challenge to European ethnocentrism.

JULIE MULLANEY

Mamet, David 1947–

American dramatist, screenwriter, and essayist

Bigsby, C.W.E., *David Mamet*, London and New York: Methuen, 1985

Brewer, Gay, *David Mamet and Film: Illusion/Disillusion in a Wounded Land*, Jefferson, North Carolina: McFarland Press, 1993

Carroll, Dennis, *David Mamet*, London: Macmillan, 1987; New York: St Martin's Press, 1987

Cohn, Ruby, *New American Dramatists 1960–1980*, London: Macmillan, 1982, revised as *New American Dramatists 1960–1990*, 1991

Dean, Anne, *David Mamet: Language as Dramatic Action*, Rutherford, New Jersey: Fairleigh Dickinson University Press, 1990; London: Associated University Presses, 1990

Harriott, Esther, *American Voices: Five Contemporary Playwrights in Essays and Interviews*, Jefferson, North Carolina: McFarland Press, 1988

Kane, Leslie (ed.), *David Mamet: A Casebook*, New York: Garland, 1992

Kolin, Philip C. (ed.), *American Playwrights since 1945: A Guide to Scholarship, Criticism, and Performance*, Westport, Connecticut: Greenwood Press, 1989

Malkin, Jeanette R., *Verbal Violence in Contemporary Drama: From Handke to Shepard*, Cambridge and New York: Cambridge University Press, 1992

The author of more than 20 plays, Mamet came to prominence with *Sexual Perversity in Chicago* (1974), in which the coarse, street-wise language of sexual confrontation between his characters revealed an absence of emotional engagement, hence the "perversity" of the title. This was followed by

American Buffalo (1975), hailed as a classic, and the play that brilliantly foregrounded Mamet's use of demotic language as the medium for articulating his central concerns. All serious commentary on Mamet confronts this violent demotic speech in his work, read as the crucial realisation of Mamet's response to the varieties of social, cultural, and mythic experience, which constitutes, for his characters, contemporary America.

KOLIN's wide-ranging survey of the work of 40 American playwrights who have come to critical acclaim since 1945 includes an entry on Mamet, written by Joycelyn Trigg. This is a very useful research tool since the format of this book provides an account of each playwright's achievement and reputation, a primary bibliography, a production history of each of the plays, a survey of critical commentary, an outline of future research opportunities, and an alphabetical checklist of secondary sources. Though now slightly out of date as far as Mamet is concerned, this remains a useful place to start for the serious student and would-be writer on Mamet.

BIGSBY is one of the best critics of twentieth-century American drama, as this short study of Mamet exemplifies. His commentary provides a subtle yet accessible account of the major preoccupations of the plays in a way that has yet to be equalled, and much subsequent writing on Mamet feeds off Bigsby's work. Central to Bigsby's reading is his analysis of Mamet's concern with character as a product of language and social myths, against which his protagonists perform their rudimentary yet verbally violent struggles of self-realisation. Bigsby sees this drama as expressing Mamet's belief in the capacity of the imagination to reinvent itself, despite the constraints of language and society, and it is this interplay between that which constrains and the impulse towards liberation that is the centre of the human drama in Mamet's work.

CARROLL groups the plays in four thematic categories – business, sex, learning, and communion – and while these are helpful categorisations, most readers and audiences of Mamet will recognise these concerns as the interrelated field of all his work. This is an introductory study, which goes in for plot summaries and the elucidation of thematic motifs as well as commentary on the critical reception of the plays in production. Carroll situates his own critique of Mamet in an argument about the collective moral dismay that informs Mamet's vision of the world, and while this is a secure perspective, it hardly equates with the excitement generated by these plays in the theatre. This, though, is a thorough overview, recommended for beginners.

DEAN responds sympathetically to what she perceives as Mamet's ambition to write poetic drama, and thus concentrates not only on his realization of language as gesture and meaning, but on language as the very substance of the conflicts expressed in the theatre and in his screenplays. In this reading, validated in part by Mamet's own insistence on the primacy of language as the expressive centre of our verbal rhythms, which "prescribe our actions", Dean attends to the technical problems posed by Mamet's work, especially as these are revealed in the screenplays of *The Postman Always Rings Twice* and *The Verdict*, where problems of exposition and narrative voice become central. Dean's analysis of the resolution of these problems in the screenplays is followed by a sustained reading of the five major plays to that date. This is a sound study, intelligently alert to the reaches of Mamet's work in the theatre.

KANE's *Casebook* gathers together a variety of commentaries on Mamet's work in theatre and film, and some of the essays herein offer the best current examples of writing on Mamet. For example, Matthew Roudané's overview of the plays discovers a thematic undercurrent of nostalgia for an idealised American past steeped in a myth of organic unity, which survives in the plays as a silent referent against which the verbal and physical violence of the present is acted out, especially in the environments of consumerist capitalism where Mamet frequently sets his dramas. Ruby Cohn writes instructively of the language of Mamet's plays, and Dennis Carroll comments on Mamet's most recent work in film. Kane (with Gay Brewer) provides a useful, selective annotated bibliography of critical commentary on Mamet. In common with others in this series, this is a helpful book to go to for a reliable version of the terms in which the whole range of Mamet's work is discussed.

COHN is one of the most notable critics of twentieth-century American drama, and this short study of the American theatre through three decades (in the revised edition) is full of original insights. Cohn ends this short book with a chapter on Mamet and Sam Shepard, which she coyly titles "Eloquent Energies: Mamet, Shepard", for eloquence is probably the last word that most critics would think of in relation to these two playwrights. But, as Cohn ably demonstrates, the scatalogical and abrasive language of Mamet in his central corpus of work constitutes a form of eloquence that is captivating in the theatre, however alienating we might find it on reflection. Like Bigsby, Cohn is a seminal critic in this field, and this is a very accomplished study despite the relative brevity of treatment its space allows for all the writers considered.

HARRIOTT's study includes Mamet along with Sam Shepard, Lanford Wilson, Charles Fuller, and Marsha Norman, and consists of summary essays on their work followed by interviews with each writer (except Shepard, who generally refuses interviews). The interview with Mamet dates from 1984, and thus is now of less value, given the range of Mamet's work since that time. Harriot's critical essays are of an introductory kind, briefly summarising Mamet's career in the theatre, and offering a consensus view of his essential preoccupations.

MALKIN isolates a small group of plays by American and European postwar dramatists, including Mamet, which she claims are distinctive in "their elevation of language to the central action, and actor" and in which the human agents become prisoners of their speech. Malkin's study is freighted with a variety of philosophical and linguistic theories of language in support of her central thesis that the verbal aggression of these plays follows from our common loss of the securities of social speech and the resources of language as a means of self-identification and expression. In the event, Malkin's discussion of individual plays is less theoretically sophisticated than this account suggests, and her reading of the verbal violence in Mamet's plays is conventional. Nonetheless, it is useful to see his work debated within a frame of reference that includes some of his American contemporaries.

BREWER's user-friendly study is the first book-length account of Mamet's film work, both as screenwriter and director, and provides a cogent discussion of the dominant themes and images Mamet calls on in this medium. In elucidating patterns of imagery and theme Brewer makes useful reference to the plays, and he has researched through drafts of the film scripts to show how these concerns become manifest in the finished products. This is a valuable if uncontroversial study of an important dimension of Mamet's work, and certainly the fullest account of it to date.

LIONEL KELLY

Mansfield, Katherine 1888–1923

New Zealand short-story writer

Alpers, Antony, *The Life of Katherine Mansfield*, London: Jonathan Cape, 1980; New York: Viking Press, 1980
Berkman, Sylvia, *Katherine Mansfield: A Critical Study*, New Haven, Connecticut: Yale University Press, 1951; London: Oxford University Press, 1952
Meyers, Jeffrey, *Katherine Mansfield: A Biography*, London: Hamish Hamilton, 1978; New York: New Directions, 1980
Pilditch, Jan, *A Critical Response to Katherine Mansfield*, Westport Connecticut: Greenwood Press, forthcoming (1996)
Robinson, Roger (ed.), *Katherine Mansfield: In from the Margin*, Baton Rouge: Louisiana State University Press, 1994
Tomalin, Claire, *Katherine Mansfield: A Secret Life*, London: Viking Press, 1987; New York: Knopf, 1988

Early Mansfield criticism was testimony to her promise as a writer, but her varied life and her tragically early death from tuberculosis ensured not the growth of a reputation, but the growth of a legend. French criticism in particular tended to concentrate on Mansfield as an ethereal creature with a mind too fragile for this world. There were numerous articles written by those who had known, or thought they had known, some portion of the Mansfield story, while her husband John Middleton Murry's own editing and subsequent publication of her letters and journals made public a large body of intimate detail about Mansfield, which distracted critics from Mansfield's work for some 30 years after her death. Some four-fifths of Mansfield's output is in the form of letters and journals, ensuring her continuing interest to biographers. Changes in critical practice, however, saw Mansfield's work take precedence over her life. Her work responded well to feminist critical practice, and, while some critics have concentrated on these aspects of her work, others have sought to define her place as an innovator of modernism. Of recent times she has gained a place in the eyes of critics as a writer of major stature who transformed the nature of the short story.

BERKMAN's balanced appraisals were among the first not to be wholly dependent on the *Journal* and *Letters* for their impressions of Mansfield. Berkman comments with some unease about Murry's justifiable, but indiscriminate, publication of Mansfield material, and its effects. The Mansfield of the *Journal* was, to say the least, an unreliable entity, and Berkman takes advantage of New Zealand sources for a work that continues to be one of the best full-length studies of the woman and her work.

Several biographical studies give essential background to Mansfield the writer. Alpers' 1953 biography (*Katherine Mansfield*) was replaced, rather than revised, by his great 1980 work. The latter remains the most valuable, complete, and authoritative of all Mansfield biographies. Alpers is a skilful narrator and, a New Zealander himself, he is well equipped to assess the childhood material. He provides a balanced and thorough interpretation of Mansfield's life, dealing, among other topics, with Mansfield's marriage to Middleton Murry, their friends and acquaintances (which, of course, included many of the major literary figures of the day), and the lifelong devotion of Ida Baker. MEYERS' biography presents a Mansfield self-destructively in revolt against respectability. He examines in detail her rebellion against the parochialism of colonial New Zealand, her lesbian friendships, her erratic emotional relationships, and he links the extraordinary events of Mansfield's life to her development as an artist. TOMALIN's book offers a different, but also valuable, interpretation of Mansfield's life, and at times functions as a good corrective for Alpers' interpretations of events. It argues that the links between Mansfield and D.H. Lawrence were more important than hitherto had been supposed, and examines the life in terms of the myths that have surrounded it, with a view to separating fact from fiction.

ROBINSON's edited collection of essays was the result of a Mansfield Centennial Conference in 1988, and contains recent assessments of her work by major scholars in the field. O'Sullivan's essay "Finding the Pattern, Solving the Problem" is an acute and central assessment of Mansfield's place as a twentieth-century voice in relation to history, World War I, and the philosophies of her day. Other essays examine her relation with women artists, offer revealing readings of individual stories, assess the French connection, and include in their number Motelier's essay on Mansfield's relationship with Francis Carco. Methodology varies, but overall, as the title suggests, the collection situates Mansfield as a central figure of twentieth-century culture.

My (PILDITCH's) edited collection traces, via a documentary section, the variety of response to Mansfield's work from early reviews to recent critical assessments. The book reproduces essays from the major critics and authors who have commented on Mansfield's work and her place in twentieth-century literature. Mansfield was always a writers' writer and her critical history includes comments from Virginia Woolf, Elizabeth Bowen, and Conrad Aiken among others. The work follows the critical history through the period of Mansfield as "cult", and the New Criticism of the early 1960s, to the advent of feminist criticism and the innovative methodology of the 1970s and 1980s. A full bibliography is included.

JAN PILDITCH

Marlowe, Christopher 1564–1593

English dramatist and poet

Bakeless, John, *The Tragical History of Christopher Marlowe*, 2 vols., Cambridge, Massachusetts: Harvard University Press, 1942

Friedenreich, Kenneth, Roma Gill, and Constance B. Kuriyama (eds.), *"A Poet and a Filthy Play-maker": New Essays on Christopher Marlowe*, New York: AMS Press, 1988
Healy, Thomas, *Christopher Marlowe*, Plymouth, Devon: Northcote House, 1994
Kuriyama, Constance Brown, *Hammer or Anvil: Psychological Patterns in Christopher Marlowe's Plays*, New Brunswick, New Jersey: Rutgers University Press, 1980
Sales, Roger, *Christopher Marlowe*, London: Macmillan, 1991; New York: St Martin's Press, 1991
Shepherd, Simon, *Marlowe and the Politics of Elizabethan Theatre*, Brighton, Sussex: Harvester Press, 1986
Steane, J.B., *Marlowe: A Critical Study*, Cambridge: Cambridge University Press, 1964
Urry, William, *Christopher Marlowe and Canterbury*, edited by Andrew Butcher, London: Faber & Faber, 1988
Zunder, William, *Elizabethan Marlowe: Writing and Culture in the English Renaissance*, Hull, Humberside: Unity Press, 1994

Christopher Marlowe's work has been traditionally linked to his life. And it is important to be clear about what information, most of it derived from official documents, we have about his career. The best guide to this is still BAKELESS, whose first volume contains practically all the documentation. But it needs to be supplemented by URRY, who has written a fascinating account of Marlowe's social origins and ideological – that is to say, specifically Protestant – context in Canterbury, and produced one of the few reliable narratives of his death; and also by an essay on Richard Baines, a fellow agent of Marlowe's in Elizabeth's secret service, by Constance Brown Kuriyama in FRIEDENREICH.

STEANE, for example, does not question the liberal-humanist assumption that there is a direct, unmediated relation between a writer's experience and his/her writing, or the characteristically Leavisite assumption that the writer is morally responsible for his/her text. What is seen as the typical instability of Marlowe's writing – the sudden shifts of attitude or emotion – is thus seen as emanating in an unproblematic way from some kind of emotional imbalance, even immaturity, in the author. Nevertheless, the book proposes readings of the plays that were widely influential: *Tamburlaine* was constructed as a debate about its hero, in which his ambition was finally endorsed; the attitude in the *Jew of Malta* to Barabas was fundamentally ambivalent; *Edward II* represented a reductive narrowing of vision; and *Doctor Faustus* amounted to a personal psychomachia of the author's. The reading of *Hero and Leander* as both comic and tragic also has had its influence.

The first substantial challenge to this kind of reading came with KURIYAMA who, in a psychoanalytical study, proposed that, while emanating from a single personality, Marlowe's work evinced the characteristic patterns of a male homosexual subjectivity. Thus the aggression of *Tamburlaine*, especially *Part I*, stemmed from fear of the father; the egocentrism of Barabas amounted to a partial identification of Marlowe with his protagonist; the latent meaning of *Edward II* is Marlowe's negative identification with the passivity of the King; and in *Doctor Faustus* the rivalry between son and father is projected as the irreconcilable conflict between Faustus and God. Kuriyama also has interesting insights into the historical context of the writing – her suggestion, for instance, that the homosexual Edward II was at least partly modelled on the future James I and his early affair with Lennox.

A more radical and self-conscious challenge has come from SHEPHERD, who deploys the new insights of post-structuralism in relation not only to Marlowe, but more widely to late sixteenth-century drama other than Shakespeare's. This drama is seen as essentially deconstructing the dominant ideology of hierarchy and monarchy, not openly, because this would have been too dangerous in an age of censorship and increasing state power, but covertly and implicitly. The disparity between assertion and spectacle in *Tamburlaine* reveals the barbarity of Tamburlaine's heroic enterprise. The audience's pleasure in Barabas undermines his status as a stage villain and unsettles the ostensible morality of the drama. In *Edward II* the pathos generated for the deposed king is subverted by his illegitimate homosexual passion. And in *Doctor Faustus* scopic pleasure renders the morality framework of the play uncertain, indeed ironical. Generally – in a final Foucauldian turn – the plays reveal current certainties to be no more than discourses sustained by oppressive power relations: ultimately, by state power. This is accomplished less by the working of a settled, individual consciousness than by the functioning of the texts themselves.

Less polemically, SALES develops and reapplies Shepherd's proposals. His book is in two parts. The first sees late sixteenth-century English society as one essentially dramatised. The Babington Plot of 1586, for example, is seen as a kind of drama; public executions are seen as a sort of street theatre; and, again following Michel Foucault, the function of the drama is to reinforce state power. The spectacle, however, was unstable, and open to more than one interpretation. This can be seen within Marlovian drama itself, which is discussed in *Part II*: Tamburlaine, no more than a shepherd, is unsettlingly given the accoutrements and rhetoric of rule; the theatrical pleasure provided by Barabas questions the play's anti-semitism – just as the play's representation of the Machiavellian Ferneze challenges the integrity of state authority; the apparent neutrality of *Edward II* is a way of initiating a forbidden debate on questions of deposition, homosexuality, and punishment – yet the play is remarkably, even traditionally, limited in scope; and in *Doctor Faustus* the voices of orthodoxy are in an unresolved dialogue with voices of doubt and revolt: in a Bakhtinian sense, the text is dialogic. The great weakness of this book – and it is one shared to a lesser extent by Shepherd – is its inability to see the plays as doing more than challenging orthodoxy: it cannot propose any positions for the plays themselves.

My own (ZUNDER's) book, written from a broadly historicist standpoint, draws on poststructuralist notions of textuality, but is fundamentally informed by a Marxist humanism. *Tamburlaine* is seen as assertive of contemporary English imperialism, but also of a radical individualism that challenges the dominant discourse of hierarchy. This individualism is tempered in *Part II* by a traditional sense of natural limit into a no-less radical stoicism. Economic individualism is rejected in the *Jew of Malta*, ridiculed even, in the figure of the Jew –

part traditional usurer, part new Machiavel – in the interest of the current social order embodied in Ferneze, possibly a representation of Walsingham, head of the secret service and a cousin of Marlowe's patron. In *Edward II* the disorderliness of the feudal nobility, the political individualism of Mortimer, and the ineffectiveness of Edward as a ruler are rejected in favour of the royal absolutism developing at the end of the sixteenth century, and embodied proleptically in the figure of the young Edward III. At the same time, the play radically endorses the homosexual relationships in the drama as humanly valid – an endorsement taken further in *Hero and Leander*, which ultimately denies the legitimacy of any gender difference in sexual relations. And in *Doctor Faustus* the new science of the sixteenth century, seen historically in a figure like Copernicus, is rejected as presumptuous and absurd under the prompting not only of a desire to preserve the current order but also of an insistent, Calvinist sense that Free Will is both real and illusory. The ideological contradictions of Marlowe's work, especially the dialectic between individualism and hierarchy, are proposed as stemming from his contradictory social position – of the rising middle class, yet committed to the monarchical interest.

HEALY's book draws together several poststructuralist and historicist strands. It is resolutely anti-humanist. Healy describes what he calls the "Marlowe effect" – moments of extravagance, like Tamburlaine's speech about "aspiring minds" in *Part I*, which challenge accepted norms and invite the audience to imagine new worlds of possibility. He questions the romanticised, intellectually dangerous Marlowe, and sees him rather as a writer trying out roles. The texts, nevertheless, are best seen not as the product of one individual author, but as participating in a complex, increasingly commercial contemporary culture. They are discontinuous, moving from one moment of wonder or spectacle to another, with no settled position or alternative set of values. In particular – drawing on postcolonialist theory – the presence of the exotic among the familiar creates a hybridity in the text, which unsettles the familiar without absorbing the strange. Nevertheless, Healy does propose specific readings. In *Dido Queen of Carthage*, which Steane saw as a celebration of romantic love and epic heroism, there is an Ovidian perspective centring on the female Dido, which interrogates the play's Virgilian perspective centring on the male Aeneas: thus the play also interrogates contemporary notions of masculinity. *Tamburlaine* enacts the successful rise of its protagonist, and so challenges current social orthodoxy; but the spectacle of possibilities is at once present and remote. All the characters in the *Jew of Malta* are Machiavellian; the play proposes no alternative to its anti-semitism; and the providential close is not endorsed. *Edward II* confirms Calvin's notion of the world as a deceptive theatre, though the play's homosexual relations are less radical than they might seem: Elizabethan categories were different, wider than our own. The theatricality of *Doctor Faustus* suggests that the world outside the play – the world of truth and falsehood, good and bad, criminality and justice – may also be a theatre of illusion. Healy, moreover, stresses the Protestant perspective of the plays, their notion of England as God's chosen nation, especially in the *Massacre at Paris*, though, typically, it is claimed there is uncertainty in the text about Henry III's deathbed address to Elizabeth, an uncertainty that possibly undermines the play's advocacy of an Anglo-French Protestant crusade. (My own study proposes this reading). Healy's final stress is on the unresolved quality of the plays: settled positions, or settled interpretations, are seen as reductive. This unresolvedness, which for Steane was a sign of personal, indeed moral, disorder, is here material for celebration.

William Zunder

Marston, John 1576–1634

English dramatist and satirist

Allen, Morse S., *The Satire of John Marston*, Columbus, Ohio: F.J. Heer, 1920

Caputi, Anthony, *John Marston, Satirist*, Ithaca, New York: Cornell University Press, 1961

Colley, John Scott, *John Marston's Theatrical Drama*, Salzburg: Institut für Englische Sprache und Literatur (Salzburg University), 1974

Finkelpearl, Philip J., *John Marston of the Middle Temple: An Elizabethan Dramatist in His Social Setting*, Cambridge, Massachusetts: Harvard University Press, 1969

Foakes, R.A., *Marston and Tourneur*, London: Longman, 1978

Geckle, George L., *John Marston's Drama: Themes, Images, Sources*, Rutherford, New Jersey: Fairleigh Dickinson University Press, 1980; London: Associated University Preses, 1980

Ingram, R.W., *John Marston*, Boston: Twayne, 1978

Scott, Michael, *John Marston's Plays: Theme, Structure and Performance*, London: Macmillan, 1978

After centuries of relative neglect, John Marston returned to the forefront of critical attention in the early part of this century, with all the elements that polarised contemporary opinion about him still intact. Alfred Harbage considered him "a five-act lapse in good taste", and while Robert Ornstein thought him "one of the more stable personalities", Samuel Schoenbaum wrote of his "precarious balance". As T.S. Eliot wrote, "about Marston a wide divergency of opinion is still possible. His greater defects are such as anyone can see; his merits are still a matter for controversy". More recent debate has centred on the sincerity, or otherwise, of Marston's work – is his work serious but poor, or is it successfully parodic?

ALLEN's study falls into two sections – a detailed account of Marston's alleged quarrels with Joseph Hall and Ben Jonson, and an analysis of his formal satires and the satiric elements of his plays. Casting Marston and Jonson as the most important players in the "War of the Theatres", Allen speculates as to the meaning of certain Marston characters in the context of the debate. Considering Marston's satire to be part of a literary fashion, Allen reads the dramatic *oeuvre* as comprising two consistent elements, lust and satire, the latter divided into categories of general satire, morals, humours, fashions, classes, and literature. Appendices deal with doubtful attributions and sources.

CAPUTI examines Marston's "remarkably unified canon" not through his unifying beliefs but through his artistic development, analysing his literary persona and the historical development that conditioned it, laying particular emphasis on Marston's neo-Stoicism: "Marston the dramatist was in some profound way a Marston who had assimilated the orphan poet, the sharp-fanged satirist, the Neo-Stoic, and the private playwright". Arguing for Marston's serio-comic view of the Renaissance world, Caputi provides a formal study of his works as a continuous experiment in satirical-comic forms. Appendices deal with problems of dates and authorship in the plays, and provide a survey of Marston's occasional pieces.

FINKELPEARL produces his detailed and influential examination of Marston from a study of Marston's milieu, the Middle Temple: "a consideration of the interaction between his sensibility and the particular environment of the Inns provides a valuable way of assessing Marston's purposes and of defining his achievements". The first section of his book is devoted to a fascinating account of life at the Inns of Court, and in particular to their dramatic activities. The second section, focusing on Marston, is perhaps inevitably less satisfying, as Finkelpearl attempts to tie down the meaning of each play to specific political and cultural events and personalities, often centring on the Middle Temple, producing some rather narrow readings. Against Caputi's neo-Stoic argument, Finkelpearl asserts Marston's Calvinism.

COLLEY presents a detailed appreciation of Marston's plays, which he sees as "'theatrical' in every sense", in many cases "'replies' to the moral concerns and artistic strategies of the great classics of the Elizabethan stage". His readings (which ignore the verse satires) therefore focus on the theatrical aspects of Marston's work. Colley argues, however, that Marston, for whom aesthetics and ethics were irrevocably entwined, was ultimately unable to find harmony in his writings because of a "'doubleness' of vision", which arose from the unwieldy combination of his satiric nature and his Calvinism.

INGRAM sees the key to Marston as the theatricality of his work, a consistent and ongoing concern with genre, language, music, disguise, stock characters, and the possibilities of stage conventions of the day, such as boy-players. Tracing a direct line from his verse satires into his theatrical work, Ingram argues that the plays provided a much-needed structure for his satirical material, with Marston's comic craft developing to the pinnacle of his career in *The Malcontent*, his firm control maintained less fruitfully in his final works. Speculating on links with fellow dramatists, Ingram portrays Marston as "a theatrical man", "the playwright's playwright" rather than "the dramatist's dramatist".

In a brief introductory study, FOAKES presents Marston as an important but disputed talent, arguing that Marston is "better to be understood as a kind of gentleman amateur poet and dramatist". Sections are devoted to Marston's world, his satires (seeing his verse as limited in both style and content), his drama ("his talents seem to have been exactly suited to the possibilities for drama that could be developed in the private theatres"), and to *The Malcontent* ("he came near to discovering a drama of the absurd long before the twentieth century"), with a useful bibliography of relevant critical writings.

SCOTT attempts to reconcile recent arguments about the aims and tones of Marston's plays through an examination of the relationship of the plays' themes to their structures, focusing on the effect of the drama in production and using the theatrical approaches of Konstantin Stanislavsky and Jean Genet. Through this test, "an attempt to see 'life' in Marston's drama rather than regarding it as mere historical documentation", he argues, that we can define how individual works should be approached. He goes on to consider the theatricality of the plays, and concludes with a discussion of their major productions and adaptations since Marston's day.

Rejecting Caputi's neo-Stoic Marston and Finkelpearl's Middle-Temple Marston, GECKLE offers historical criticism, providing new interpretations of the nine plays ascribed solely to Marston, approaching each play on its own terms. Against the trend to see Marston as a theatrical experimenter, Geckle believes Marston is best understood as a moralist, a playwright of his times, but more self-conscious and cynical than his contemporaries. His opening chapter provides a brief biographical sketch and a useful survey of early and contemporary Marston studies. Each chapter is devoted to a detailed, convincing reading of a single play, and Geckle includes a lengthy bibliography.

ALAN STEWART

Martineau, Harriet 1802–1876

English novelist and prose writer

Bosanquet, Theodora, *Harriet Martineau: An Essay in Comprehension*, London: Frederick Etchels & Hugh Macdonald, 1927

David, Deirdre, *Intellectual Women and Victorian Patriarchy: Harriet Martineau, Elizabeth Barrett Browning, George Eliot*, Ithaca, New York: Cornell University Press, 1987; London: Macmillan, 1987

Hoecker-Drysdale, Susan, *Harriet Martineau: First Woman Sociologist*, Oxford and New York: Berg, 1992

Sanders, Valerie, *Reason over Passion: Martineau and the Victorian Novel*, Brighton, Sussex: Harvester Press, 1986; New York: St Martin's Press, 1986

Walters, Margaret, "The Rights and Wrongs of Women: Mary Wollstonecraft, Harriet Martineau, Simone de Beauvoir", in *The Rights and Wrongs of Women*, edited by Juliet Mitchell and Ann Oakley, Harmondsworth, Middlesex: Penguin, 1976

Webb, Robert K., *Harriet Martineau: A Radical Victorian*, New York: Columbia University Press, 1960; London: Heinemann, 1960

In her lifetime, Harriet Martineau was both influential and controversial. In the twentieth century early interest in Martineau focused on her extraordinary personality. The feminist movement of the 1970s created renewed scholarly interest in her ideas and writings, though, as both Walters and David indicate, Martineau remains a problematic figure for feminist critics.

BOSANQUET's modest aim is "to relate Miss Martineau's life and opinions, and her continual, if sometimes eccentric, progress towards the final phase of her remarkable career, to the personal influences which so clearly and powerfully affected her". Basing her work on both Martineau's own *Autobiography* and other records by her contemporaries, she quotes liberally from these sources, though references are virtually non-existent. Despite this weakness, Bosanquet's range of material makes for a rounded and insightful portrait of her subject, corrects some of the impressions in Mrs Florence Fenwick Miller's 1884 biography, and as Webb notes, her style is "sprightly". James Martineau's lengthy letter to the *Daily News* following the Fenwick Miller biography is included in the Appendix.

WEBB offers a scholarly biography, drawing on a most impressive range of manuscript sources, and the journals and newspapers for which Martineau wrote. In particular he was able to use Martineau's own *Daily News* cuttings collection. A historian by background, he approaches his subject in order to discover the forces which formed her opinions. These opinions themselves are characterised as ranging from "penetrating judgements and superb common sense to almost unbelievable dogmatism and just plain silliness". The result is both a fascinating well-documented account of Martineau's extraordinary personality, her work and ideas, and a study of Victorian radicalism. Webb remains essential reading for those interested in Martineau.

WALTERS' essay locates Martineau within a "bourgeois feminist tradition" in which each of the three women discussed "fought alone", working as individuals rather than contributing to a feminist movement. Martineau's widely-scattered writings on feminist issues are viewed as a whole. She is seen as a pungent, often audacious, journalist, and, if not an original thinker, an exceptionally effective populariser of ideas . The sympathetic commentary on the *Autobiography* and the remarks on *Deerbrook* highlight the personal conflicts Martineau faced in her approach to the position of women, a theme which Sanders later develops more extensively. This is a brief but very useful starting-point for students interested in this aspect of Martineau's life and work.

HOECKER-DRYSDALE is a sociologist rather than a historian or literary critic, and her subtitle indicates the emphasis of this account of Martineau's life and work. She presents her subject "as a significant figure in the tradition of British social science and of nineteenth century sociological thought". She argues that Martineau's sociological proclivities are evident in virtually all that she wrote from her very earliest work for the *Monthly Repository,* and including her travel writing, fiction, and treatment of such varied subjects as illness and practical advice to intending servants. The slant of the book thus highlights some of those writings that both historical and literary critical approaches may marginalise.

SANDERS' book is valuable in offering a detailed study of Martineau's fiction. Admitting that all her subject's substantial fiction was written between 1827 and 1846, while the decades that followed were filled with her prolific journalistic and polemical writings, Sanders argues that by her contemporary critics Martineau's fiction was highly valued. She points out that her "important and innovatory" work appeared before Elizabeth Gaskell, Charlotte Brontë, and George Eliot embarked on novel-writing, and pre-dated the major works of Charles Dickens and Charles Kingsley on working-class life and social problems. It is within this historical and cultural context that Sanders offers her study of *The Illustrations of Political Economy, Deerbrook,* and the *Autobiography*, as well as many of the short tales, and the travel writings. Martineau is seen as an important precursor of later writers, both in the themes she introduces and in her concern that fiction should reflect all social groups, and that it should reveal the heroism of the struggles of ordinary men. Detailed analyses of particular works support Sanders' theory. Thus *Deerbrook*, in offering "the outwardly-controlled single woman with the powerful 'inner life' . . . pilots the core plots of *Jane Eyre* and other Brontë novels", and her treatment and use of the doctor-hero foreshadow later work by other novelists. Despite its acknowledged weaknesses, that novel is of permanent interest because it poses central questions taken up by Martineau's successors. Sanders' title indicates what she sees as a continuing conflict in Martineau's art as a writer, that between her rationality and her imagination.

DAVID's approach is avowedly feminist. Three remarkable Victorian women – Martineau, Eliot, and Elizabeth Barrett Browning – all of formidable intelligence, all successful and, within their own time, prominent professional writers, are seen as constantly battling against, and yet accommodating themselves to, the patriarchal cultural hegemony: "an insistence that we see these writers as both saboteurs and collaborators is essentially what this book is all about". Martineau is selected not simply because she was so powerful as a political journalist, but because of the variety of genres and modes in which she wrote. Martineau's career is defined by what David calls her "auxiliary usefulness to a male-dominated culture". However convinced and courageous her feminism, the real function of her prodigious literary output was by way of "textual services" to the English middle class and its radical political and economic ideas, which she endorsed. Within this framework David considers Martineau's *Autobiography*, her fiction, history, and political and travel writings. While Martineau's feminism is thus seen as always ambivalent, David treats her subject with sympathy and admires her for her energy, achievements, and tough-mindedness. Within the limits of such an approach the book is stimulating and perceptive.

BARBARA M. ONSLOW

Marvell, Andrew 1621–1678

English poet

Carey, John (ed.), *Andrew Marvell*, Harmondsworth, Middlesex: Penguin, 1969

Chernaik, Warren L., *The Poet's Time: Politics and Religion in the Work of Andrew Marvell*, Cambridge and New York: Cambridge University Press, 1982

Colie, Rosalie L., *"My Ecchoing Song": Andrew Marvell's Poetry of Criticism,* Princeton, New Jersey: Princeton University Press, 1970

Leishman, J.B., *The Art of Marvell's Poetry*, completed by John Butt, London: Hutchinson, 1966, 2nd edition, 1968

Patterson, Annabel M., *Andrew Marvell*, Plymouth, Devon: Northcote House, 1994

Critical perspectives on Andrew Marvell have been considerably altered since the 1970s by the attention paid by New-Historicist critics to the mid-seventeenth century. In Marvell's case the effect has been to distance him from the metaphysical poets with whom he had been traditionally grouped, deflecting attention from his lyric poems, which had been central to critical accounts of him since T.S. Eliot's influential 1932 essay (reprinted by Carey), and giving a new priority to his political poems and his prose writing. Something of this change of emphasis can be seen in the fact that the "Horatian Ode upon Cromwell's Return from Ireland", which has become the most frequently discussed and contended of Marvell's poems, is given only two pages by Leishman, where he proposes that Marvell's admiration for Cromwell is "quite disinterested and ... aesthetic".

CAREY's anthology provides generous reprintings of writing about Marvell from his own time up to the time of its publication in 1969. In the light of the developments in Marvell criticism since then, it can be instructive to see in Carey's selection essays such as the one written in 1946 by Christopher Hill – which have become influential in the work of New Historicism – contended by other critics of the time, such as F.W. Bateson. Equally, Cleanth Brooks's reading of the "Horatian Ode" from the perspective of the New Criticism of the 1940s makes interesting reading in the light of the poem's more recent critical history. Carey frequently places essays in stimulating juxtaposition – an enjoyable example sees William Empson, Frank Kermode, and Pierre Legouis contending over the poem "The Garden" – in such a way as to highlight critical debate and to caution implicitly against taking persuasive critical readings at their own valuation. These debates are tartly elaborated and commented on in Carey's own introductory sections.

LEISHMAN's study was left unfinished at his death in 1963 and completed from his notes by John Butt. Leishman quite overtly considers Marvell's political and satirical poems (with the exception of "Horatian Ode") as being "of small intrinsic importance", but he offers detailed accounts of Marvell's other poetry. His is a valuable examination of Marvell's writing in terms of its stylistic inflections, its intellectual parameters, and its indebtedness to literary traditions and *topoi*. Characteristically he seeks to clarify Marvell's poetic practice by discussing analogous poems by other writers, and he brings to the task formidable scholarly range and careful, detailed critical analysis. The resulting accounts afford valuable insights, but can equally seem over-laboured, difficult to contend with or respond to in their own terms, and their own terms too exclusively "literary". COLIE, too, is concerned with literary traditions rather than ideological contexts, and her work is in part indebted to what she calls "Leishman's painstaking examination of Marvell's poetical habits". Her work is no less scholarly than his, but her critical touch is lighter, and her accounts of the poems can seem fresher, more alert to the verve and to "the arch novelty", as she puts it, of Marvell's use of traditional materials. She identifies in the poems a subtle critical self-consciousness, an awareness of the relationship between tradition and experiment, and a level of implicit critical commentary on the materials of literary tradition.

If these two books are representative of predominantly "literary" characterisations of Marvell's work, that of CHERNAIK gives the reader access to that strain in more recent criticism that has re-emphasised the political, although much of this work is to found not in book-length studies but in journal essays and in individual chapters of more general books about the period. Chernaik goes out to relocate in the centre of his account of Marvell precisely those of his works that critics like Leishman and Colie had sidelined or ignored. By re-examining the relationship between earlier and later writings, and between lyric and polemical writing, he constructs an important and influential re-reading of the poet's moral and ideological positions and of the nature and direction of his literary output.

PATTERSON's short study for the "Writers and Their Work" series condenses in part her earlier and longer book on Marvell (*Marvell and the Civic Crown*, Princeton University Press, 1978). In the four main chapters she covers what is known of Marvell's life and career, and constructs overviews of his religious writing, his poetry about public events, and his satirical work. She carefully negotiates the intellectual and political tensions in Marvell's work, and in so doing shows Marvell negotiating, but not always resolving, the intellectual and political tensions of his time. In prioritising religious and political poems Patterson constructs an account of Marvell that is very decidedly the product of the more recent critical trends, and indeed she often alludes to these critical developments. It is therefore not surprising to find that her discussion of the lyric poems, which from Eliot to Leishman and beyond had come to be regarded as the Marvell "canon", is relegated to a brief "epilogue". Patterson regards them as "marvellous" poems, concedes that they have been the most anthologised and the most taught of his poems, but shares with much recent criticism the view that they are not the part of Marvell's output that is most interesting and valuable.

DAVID BLAIR

Marxist Literary Theory

Caudwell, Christopher, *Illusion and Reality: A Study of the Sources of Poetry*, London: Macmillan, 1937

Eagleton, Terry, *Criticism and Ideology: A Study in Marxist Literary Theory*, London: NLB, 1976; Atlantic Highlands, New Jersey: Humanities Press, 1976

Eagleton, Terry, *Marxism and Literary Criticism*, London: Methuen, 1976; Berkeley: University of California Press, 1976

Jameson, Fredric, *Marxism and Form: Twentieth-Century Dialectical Theories of Literature*, Princeton, New Jersey: Princeton University Press, 1971

Jameson, Fredric, *The Political Unconscious: Narrative as a Socially Symbolic Act*, London: Methuen, 1981; Ithaca, New York: Cornell University Press, 1981

Lukács, Georg, *The Meaning of Contemporary Realism*, translated by John and Necke Mander, London: Merlin Press, 1963

Macherey, Pierre, *A Theory of Literary Production*, translated by Geoffrey Wall, London and Boston: Routledge & Kegan Paul, 1978

Williams, Raymond, *Marxism and Literature*, Oxford: Oxford University Press, 1977

Marxist Criticism, until fairly recently, was associated with critics who were committed in ideological and political terms to Marxism as a system, and for that reason it tended to occupy a marginal role in literary criticism and theory. Contemporary critical theory, however, recognises that Marxism is central to current debates. One reason for this is that Marxism itself has changed. For many contemporary thinkers it is no longer regarded as a monolithic belief system, but as a developing theory in its own right, one which can enter into fruitful relationships with other theories, such as psychoanalytic theory or Foucauldian cultural theory.

CAUDWELL applies traditional Marxian ideas to literature. He interprets literary works in reflective terms, that is, he sees them as being directly determined by socio-economic forces. This approach is often described as "vulgar Marxism". Of Tennyson's *In Memoriam* he writes: "the unconscious ruthlessness of Tennyson's 'Nature' in fact only reflects the ruthlessness of a society in which capitalist is continually hurling down fellow capitalist into the proletarian abyss". Though most contemporary Marxists would see this approach as over-simplified, its directness still has considerable appeal.

LUKÁCS' book can certainly not be dismissed as the work of a "vulgar Marxist". Lukács was a critic in the Hegelian Marxist tradition. One of the main worries contemporary critics have with his work is that he was unsympathetic to modernism and supported the Soviet aesthetic of socialist realism. However, in this book his position is one of considerable subtlety. He argues that the major nineteenth-century realist novelists did not merely reproduce reality in terms of bourgeois ideology but also used the form of the novel to reveal the contradictions within that ideology. Thus, bourgeois literary forms such as the realist novel are not merely reflective, and can incorporate an implicitly Marxist critique.

MACHEREY's book was published in French in 1966 and was very much influenced by Althusser's anti-Hegelian form of Marxism. The book clearly has affinities with structuralist and poststructuralist thinking, though Macherey still aspires to create a science of criticism. He modifies reflectionist theory by arguing that literary texts only reflect partially and selectively, and that the selection "is symptomatic; it can tell us about the nature of the mirror". Literary texts have a relation to history, but history is like the unconscious: one cannot gain direct access to it. Gaps and contradictions in the text offer indirect access to the shaping of historical reality.

JAMESON's 1971 book is a defence of Hegelian Marxism. He does, however, take account of criticism of the Hegelian Marxist tradition from within Marxism itself, in particular from the Frankfurt school. Theodor Adorno has a long chapter devoted to him, and Walter Benjamin is also discussed. Lukács's work is defended, and the book ends with a chapter entitled "Towards Dialectical Criticism". Jameson attacks conventional formalism, arguing that form is historically determined by socio-economic content. Thus though content in this sense precedes artistic form, the two are always in dialectical relationship with each other.

EAGLETON's *Marxism and Literary Criticism* is a short history of Marxist criticism. It discusses its origins in the writings of Marx and Engels, goes on to deal with the relation between form and content, considers the question of commitment, and ends with looking at art as production, with Benjamin and Bertolt Brecht being discussed. His conclusion is that "Marxist criticism is not just an alternative technique for interpreting *Paradise Lost* or *Middlemarch*. It is part of our liberation from oppression". EAGLETON's *Criticism and Ideology* is a more ambitious undertaking. It responds to attacks on reflectionist theory by Louis Althusser and Pierre Macherey. He goes part of the way with their critique of reflection, but does not want to go all the way with it. He recognises that a series of complex mediations operates in the relation between history and the literary text, but there is a relation nonetheless. He argues that Marxist criticism should strive to be a scientific criticism on the basis of a "science of ideological formations". In his treatment of individual writers he attempts to avoid discussing their consciousnesses in ideological terms, as "vulgar Marxists" had tended to do. He focuses rather on ideological contradictions within the text itself.

WILLIAMS's book is both an introduction to Marxist criticism and an attempt to create a revisionist form of it, which takes account of reflectionist theory, Althusser and Macherey, and Marxist thinkers like Antonio Gramsci. A key chapter is one in which he modifies reflectionist thinking by arguing that there are always oppositional elements in any social formation, which resist the dominant ideology, and that these are not static. They may be "residual" cultural forces – the product of a previous cultural formation – or they may be "emergent", representing "new meanings and values, new practices, new relationships and kinds of relationships". The relationship between the residual, the dominant, and the emergent is a continually shifting one.

JAMESON's second study of Marxist criticism (1981) is a very densely written work, which will present difficulties to those not thoroughly familiar with Marxist theory and contemporary criticism. It is an attempt to reconcile Althusserian Marxism with the Hegelian Marxist critical tradition. More ambitiously it is an attempt to create a totalising Marxist criticism, which can subsume not only Althusser but also virtually all non-Marxist critical schools, such as formalism, structuralism and poststructuralism, and archetypal criticism. He argues that "all literature must be read as a symbolic meditation on the destiny of community". Works of art reflect ideologies, which he sees as "strategies of containment", which repress historical contradictions. The literary critic's role is to restore "to the surface of the text the repressed and buried reality" of a history characterised by class struggle and the attempt to "wrest a realm of freedom from a realm of Necessity".

K.M. NEWTON

The Masque

Butler, Martin, "Ben Jonson and the Limits of Courtly Panegyric", in *Culture and Politics in Early Stuart England*, edited by Kevin Sharpe and Peter Lake, Stanford, California: Stanford University Press, 1993; London: Macmillan, 1994

Butler, Martin, "Reform or Reverence? The Politics of the Caroline Masque", in *Theatre and Government under the Early Stuarts*, edited by J.R. Mulryne and Margaret Shewring, Cambridge and New York: Cambridge University Press, 1993

Campbell, Lily Bess, *Scenes and Machines on the English Stage During the Renaissance: A Classical Revival*, Cambridge: Cambridge University Press, 1923; New York: Barnes & Noble, 1960

Chan, Mary, *Music in the Theatre of Ben Jonson*, Oxford: Clarendon Press, 1980; New York: Oxford University Press, 1980

Gordon, D.J., *The Renaissance Imagination*, edited by Stephen Orgel, Berkeley: University of California Press, 1975

Limon, Jerzy, *The Masque of Stuart Culture*, Newark: University of Delaware Press, 1990; London: Associated University Presses, 1990

Lindley, David (ed.), *The Court Masque*, Manchester: Manchester University Press, 1984

Marcus, Leah Sinanoglou, "Masquing Occasions and Masque Structure", in *Research Opportunities in Renaissance Drama*, 24, 1981

Nicoll, Allardyce, *Stuart Masques and the Renaissance Stage*, London: Harrap, 1937; New York: Harcourt Brace, 1938

Orgel, Stephen, *The Jonsonian Masque*, Cambridge, Massachusetts: Harvard University Press, 1965

Orgel, Stephen, *The Illusion of Power: Political Theater in the English Renaissance*, Berkeley: University of California Press, 1975

Orgel, Stephen, and Roy Strong, *Inigo Jones: The Theatre of the Stuart Court*, 2 vols., London, Sotheby Parke Bernet, 1973; Berkeley: University of California Press, 1973

Peacock, John, "Inigo Jones's Stage Architecture and Its Sources", in *Art Bulletin*, 64, 1982

Sharpe, Kevin, *Criticism and Compliment: The Politics of Literature in the England of Charles I*, Cambridge and New York: Cambridge University Press, 1987

Veevers, Erica, *Images of Love and Religion: Queen Henrietta Maria and Court Entertainments*, Cambridge and New York: Cambridge University Press, 1989

Welsford, Enid, *The Court Masque: A Study in the Relationship Between Poetry and the Revels*, Cambridge: Cambridge University Press, 1927

Recent years have seen an explosion of writing on the court masque. Whereas earlier studies of the masque concentrated upon the origins of the form (particularly its relation to Elizabethan entertainments and Continental analogues) or the iconographical significance of its elements and its literary and formal properties, recent criticism has emphasised the occasionality of the form and its interconnections with the politics of the Jacobean and Caroline court. Influenced by the contextualisations of New Historicism and the micro-histories favoured by historical revisionism, recent masque scholarship has completely re-assessed the previously denigrated Caroline masque, accompanied by an increased consideration of the diversity of the masque tradition, both within the court, through non-Jonsonian exemplars, and outside the court, through aristocratic entertainments – a consideration spurred by the steady recovery of lost texts and documentation. Masque criticism has moved a long way from the early defences against accusations of sycophancy and ephemerality, and most scholars now share the perception of masque as a central early-modern cultural form closely allied to the traditions of educative panegyric (*laudando praecipere*) espoused by humanism. Awareness of compliment has been replaced by sensitivity to criticism, and now the debate centres on the limits of the form, its success and failure as a vehicle of communication between monarch, court, and nation.

The earliest studies of the masque, as such, Welsford and Orgel, explore the formal properties of the masque. WELSFORD takes an evolutionary approach, examining the interplay of mummery, disguising, and sacred and folk rituals to show how they contribute to the Renaissance genre. Welsford places considerable emphasis on the interaction between Italian, French, and English forms, while her final chapter considers the broader questions of the function of art in Renaissance culture. Although many elements of this study (notably the anthropological and evolutionary approach) appear dated, the book marshals a vast body of theatrical evidence, much of it still the basis of masque-criticism. Although ORGEL, in his *Jonsonian Masque*, specifically rejects many of Welsford's premises, he also focuses on the formal dimensions of the masque. Orgel examines the dual position of the texts as both art and theatre, stressing how the form should be defined by its purpose. The main purpose of the book is to evaluate Jonson's central contribution to the form, which Orgel locates in the achievement of independence of the text from its initial production and occasion, and in Jonson's ability to unify the diverse elements of an earlier tradition, creating a coherent and powerful whole but with an additional emphasis on the rhetorical and literary elements. The late 1980s saw a brief return to this approach by LIMON, who stresses how the masque in performance and the masque in textual form belong to different semiotic systems, whose meanings operate in different ways. He argues that masque criticism needs to recognise the essentially journalistic nature of many masque descriptions, the interaction of elements within the masque, and the interconnection of masques with each other and with other forms of courtly entertainment, celebration, and display.

A dominant strain in early masque studies extended the iconographical approach to Renaissance art pioneered by Aby Warburg, Erwin Panofsky, and Edgar Wind, and embodied in England by the Warburg Institute (London). For instance, GORDON's essays (edited by Orgel) study the interaction of verbal and visual elements, and the collaboration between Jonson and Inigo Jones. ORGEL and STRONG (1973) is a monument to this interpretative strategy, providing complete texts and copies of Jones's designs for the majority of the court masques and some of the Caroline court dramas, along with contemporary responses and documents. The near book-length

Introduction covers many artistic issues, and provides a clear statement of the Orgel-Strong thesis, which envisages masques as a "liturgy of state". Although many of the interpretations of art-historical sources and some of the attributions are now being questioned (especially by John Peacock), this volume remains an essential sourcebook.

ORGEL's *Illusion of Power* provides the best example of the earlier masque criticism, bringing a new sophistication to the interaction between formal, iconographic, and political elements. In a brief compass Orgel shows how masques "were expressions of the age's most profound assumptions about monarchy", a literal embodiment of the governing ideas and ideals of Renaissance society, which sought to inculcate virtue through emulation in the spectators and participants, giving "higher meaning to the realities of politics and power", and whose "fictions created heroic roles for the leaders of society". For Orgel, the masque is both Platonic and Machiavellian, an aestheticisation of power, which expresses the ideals of rule while justifying, perhaps even disguising, its realities. The approach integrates the arts of design and poetry to illuminate the central philosophical and intellectual tenets of masquing, while relating political meanings to changing formal elements, such as the use of pastoral imagery or the introduction of increasingly elaborate anti-masques based on the "realities of Whitehall".

The new political criticism that came to dominate masque scholarship in the 1980s moved away from Orgel's broad sweep and concentrated on the micro-politics of particular masques and their relation to specific moments of production or identifiable political issues and factions. MARCUS argues that the occasions of performance are central to their meaning, while BUTLER (in "Ben Jonson and the Limits of Courtly Panegyric") embraces a more sophisticated approach to this occasionality, examining the "complex political transactions" of masque as panegyric, and paying particular attention to the limitations of the form. These studies belong to the period of exponential growth in masque criticism, with its numerous essays exploring the potential meanings or contexts for particular texts, and which fostered greater awareness of the diversity of the form. Norbrook in "The Reformation of the Masque" (in LINDLEY) encapsulates the issue of diversity in his exploration of Protestant attitudes to the masque. To parallel the new complexity seen in readings of panegyric, Norbrook traces a Protestant masque tradition, which articulates a critique of both the content and form of the court masque. He cites Samuel Daniel as standing in opposition to the Jonsonian masque (later critics add George Chapman and Thomas Middleton too), and connects neglected masques, such as the *Cole-Orton Masque*, with other potentially oppositional texts, such as Milton's *Masque at Ludlow*.

The greatest shift in attitudes is the prominence now given to the Caroline masque. SHARPE trenchantly argues against the traditional view, which sees the Caroline masque as a degenerate form reflecting the narrowing of court culture associated with Charles I's nascent absolutism. Instead Sharpe argues that Caroline masques were an effective form of communication within the court, allowing sections of the governmental community to raise issues with the monarch, while formal changes are traced less to the Jones-Jonson rivalry (and the former's triumph) than the different tastes and attitudes of the new monarchs. The taste of Queen Henrietta Maria lies at the heart of VEEVERS, which considers the influence of a modified strand of French *preciosité* upon the English court, envisaging the King and Queen engaged in a political dialogue through their masques and other cultural activities. The book is particularly interesting in its careful delineation of the philosophical and spiritual forces that shaped Henrietta Maria's Catholicism, and on the interaction between religious ceremony and masque. A more sceptical corrective to the Sharpe thesis is offered by BUTLER (in "Reform or Reverence?"), who detects a tension between criticism within the masque and the formal rules of compliment by which it was bound. Rather than a successful means of communication both within the court, and between the court and the wider nation, a failure in monarchical propaganda is depicted by Butler, a failure that severely restricted the King's options when he faced the crisis of 1640.

Despite the explosion in criticism, the mechanics of staging and the importance of design and music remain neglected. The standard books, CAMPBELL and NICOLL, date from the 1920s and 1930s, and have not been revised, despite considerable new work available in Orgel and Strong's book, or in other studies (notably John Orrell's *The Theatre of Inigo Jones and John Webb* and *The Human Stage: English Theatre Design, 1567–1640* [Cambridge University Press, 1985 and 1988 respectively], which re-assess the nature of court stagings). Design has fared better, extensively treated in Orgel and Strong (now supplemented by John Harris and Gordon Higgott, *Inigo Jones: Complete Architectural Drawings* [London: Zwemmer, 1989]). PEACOCK has provided significant new information and a radically different interpretation, with much greater historical evidence and attention to questions of transmission and dissemination (also in his chapter in Lindley). His *The Stage Designs of Inigo Jones: The European Context* (forthcoming, at the time of writing) will be a major addition to the literature. Music is covered by CHAN.

JAMES D. KNOWLES

Massinger, Philip 1583–1640

English dramatist

Adler, Doris Ray, *Philip Massinger*, Boston: Twayne, 1987

Clark, Ira, *Professional Playwrights: Massinger, Ford, Shirley and Brome*, Lexington: University Press of Kentucky, 1992

Clark, Ira, *The Moral Art of Philip Massinger*, Lewisburg, Pennsylvania: Bucknell University Press, 1993; London: Associated University Presses, 1993

Cruickshank, Alfred, *Philip Massinger*, Oxford: Blackwell, 1920; New York: Frederic A. Stokes, 1920

Dunn, T.A., *Philip Massinger: The Man and the Playwright*, London: Thomas Nelson, 1952

Garrett, Martin (ed.), *Massinger: The Critical Heritage*, London and New York: Routledge, 1991

Howard, Douglas (ed.), *Philip Massinger: A Critical Reassessment*, Cambridge: Cambridge University Press, 1985

Since 1920 modern Massinger critics have had to lay the ghost of T.S.Eliot, whose notorious dismissal of Massinger's verse as anaemic, and the playwright himself as the initiator of the dissociation of sensibility, has cast such a long shadow. Recent commentators have mounted a stout challenge to Eliot's hegemony, presenting a Massinger who is politically astute, whose stagecraft is adroit, and whose stage poetry is effective and, at times, moving. Despite these innovations, Massinger's plays (like those of most of Shakespeare's contemporaries) are more frequently read than performed; and those readings cluster around a small number of the plays. The comedies *A New Way to Pay Old Debts* and *The City Madam* still attract most critical commentary and remain the Massinger texts most frequently anthologised and studied in undergraduate classrooms.

GARRETT's anthology in the *Critical Heritage* series traces the development of Massinger's reputation during his playwriting career, and from his death in 1640 up to the end of the nineteenth century. Garrett notes that "there has been a broad consensus that Massinger is an eloquent, rarely obscure, politically aware playwright rather than an impassioned or lyrical poet". Garrett's lucid Introduction traces the shifts of taste within this consensus, and offers a representative (though not exhaustive) sampling of pre-twentieth-century Massinger criticism. The selection allows readers to observe the decline in Massinger's reputation during the Restoration and early eighteenth century, followed by its spectacular rise in the Romantic period, sparked by Gifford's monumental 1805 edition of Massinger's plays, William Hazlitt's, Samuel Taylor Coleridge's, and Charles Lamb's dextrous and appreciative commentaries, and Edmund Kean's excoriating performance as Sir Giles Overreach. Kean's famous depiction of Overreach's descent into lunacy and defeat induced in many – as it did for Byron – "the agony of reluctant tears . . . the choking shudder". With the generation of Edmund Gosse and Leslie Stephens, Massinger's reputation sank under the accusations of decadence, which prepared the way for Eliot's diagnosis of pernicious theatrical anaemia.

CRUICKSHANK attempted the first book-length examination of Massinger's plays. He endorses previous charges that Massinger's Caroline age "lacked moral fibre . . . without being exactly corrupt". Against this background he depicts Massinger as politically aware. Had he lived, Cruickshank speculates, "we can imagine that he would have been one of those who eventually fought under protest for the King". Notwithstanding the charm of such historical fantasies, Cruickshank's major emphasis is formalist; he highlights the beauty, grace, and musicality of Massinger's verse. He comments on the general features of Massinger's stagecraft and gives useful thumbnail sketches of many of Massinger's plays. He accepts the orthodox position that *A New Way to Pay Old Debts* is Massinger's best play; and in general he provides a platform from which the considered close reading of Massinger's works can proceed.

DUNN's life of Massinger, which forms the first chapter of his study, remains the best biography in print. Dunn reports all the documents recording Massinger's early life, his subsequent career as collaborator with Francis Beaumont and John Fletcher, and his final incarnation as independent playwright. Dunn sets Massinger's life to one side, however, in his subsequent chapters, which consider the plays in depth, covering usefully – though seldom excitingly – plotting, stagecraft, characterisation, and style. On all these matters Dunn writes with more attention to detail than Cruickshank, though without really advancing the argument much further. His most useful chapter, "Criticism of Life", surveys Massinger's ideals, especially the high value placed on ethical conduct between men and women and between monarch and subject.

ADLER abandons the aesthetic consideration of Massinger, advancing instead a rigorously historical approach advocating "reading the plays in the context of their particular moment rather than with the hindsight of history". Read this way, Massinger's plays prove to be riddled with coded political criticism, allegories of, and analogies to, the politics of the 1620s and 1630s, and Massinger emerges as a strong, independent critic of Stuart governance. Adler covers a lot of ground briefly, and makes a vigorous case for her point of view. Not everyone will endorse the specific political spin she puts on Massinger; but her book is perhaps the best first text for newcomers to Massinger criticism.

Equally useful, though more scholarly, is HOWARD's collection of recent critical essays on Massinger. His Introduction summarises the decline in Massinger's reputation and explains how each of his contributors refutes the charges made against Massinger, as chronicled in Garrett's anthology. The collection attends to aspects of Massinger's language, stagecraft, and politics, and offers new readings of key plays. Especially useful are Nancy Leonard's account of *A New Way to Pay Old Debts* and Michael Neill's excavation of religious imagery in *The City Madam*. The collection concludes with Anne Barton's review essay about Philip Edward's and Colin Gibson's five-volume edition of Massinger's plays (1976), which has considerably advanced the contemporary reconsideration of Massinger's reputation. She challenges the scholastic and theatrical community to conceive of a Massinger who is politically, theatrically, and poetically adroit, and whose plays, especially the neglected and powerful *Roman Actor*, deserve more revivals than they have received. Barton elegantly summarises the position of Howard's contributors, who work out in scholarly yet readable detail what Barton merely sketches. As a whole, the collection demonstrates what a vigorous art Massinger criticism has become; with the publication of this volume, Massinger criticism may be said to have purged itself of Eliot's anaemia.

Clark's two recent volumes are solid evidence of this. CLARK (1992) places Massinger in the context of the three other major Caroline playwights, James Shirley, John Ford, and Richard Brome. Clark focuses on the manipulation of inherited convention not for its own sake but for the sociopolitical goal of "maintaining and reforming the self, the family, and the community". He emphasises Massinger's conservatism, his gratitude for the succour of his patronage networks and, despite his criticisms of absolutist politics, his confidence that traditional forms of English society could yet accommodate necessary reforms. He supports these views with a close reading of *The Picture,* which he sees as a characteristic "tragicomedy of reformation". CLARK's 1993 monograph, devoted entirely to Massinger, extends these positions by way of close readings of the major Massinger plays, *The Roman Actor*, *A New Way to Pay Old Debts*, and *The City Madam*, which attest to Massinger's moral and aesthetic purposefulness. Like many Massinger scholars, Clark argues for the serious consideration of "a number of his many collaborations with Fletcher" together with "several of his far undervalued solo plays". Modern criticism has shared Clark's zeal, though not necessarily all his views; the realities of publishing suggest that students will continue to read with enthusiasm those Massinger plays already in the anthologies. The rest of the canon seems likely to remain the preserve of the research scholar.

MARK HOULAHAN

Medicine and Literature

Ceccio, Joseph, *Medicine in Literature*, London: Longman, 1978

Clarke, Bruce, and Wendell Aycock (eds.), *The Body and the Text: Comparative Essays in Literature and Medicine*, Lubbock: Texas Tech University Press, 1990

Gordon, Richard (ed.), *The Literary Companion to Medicine: An Anthology of Prose and Poetry*, London: Sinclair-Stevenson, 1993

Literature and Medicine (journal), currently edited by Anne Hudson Jones, Baltimore: Johns Hopkins University Press, 1981 –

Ober, William B., *Boswell's Clap and Other Essays: Medical Analyses of Literary Men's Afflictions*, Carbondale: Southern Illinois University Press, 1979; London: Harper & Row, 1979

Roberts, Marie Mulvey, and Roy Porter (eds.), *Literature and Medicine During the Eighteenth Century*, London: Routledge, 1993

Trautmann, Joanne (ed.), *Healing Arts in Dialogue: Medicine and Literature*, Carbondale: Southern Illinois University Press, 1981

The journal *Literature and Medicine* is published twice a year, and edited by Anne Hudson Jones. It effectively serves the purpose for which it was founded – to encourage dialogue between medical practitioners and literary scholars. Having helped to consolidate research in this burgeoning field, it has also proved influential in both signalling and shaping future trends. Individual volumes have been devoted to special issues such as "Literature and Bioethics", "The Cultures of Medicine", "The Physician as Writer", "Use and Abuse of Literary Concepts in Medicine", and "Fictive Ills: Literary Perspectives on Wounds and Diseases".

CECCIO's anthology, arranged thematically, deals with the relationship of medicine to a number of topics, including the limitations of medicine, interpersonal relationships, humour, mental health, the scientific impulse, and the nurse. These areas were selected because of the literary activity they generated between the seventeenth and twentieth centuries in authors such as Thomas Nashe, John Donne, Anton Chekhov, George Bernard Shaw, and Anne Sexton. Topics for writing and discussion have been appended to each section with undergraduate students of both literature and medicine, and premedical students, in mind. However admirable and useful this critical anthology is, it cannot fail, however, to live up to its claim of encompassing the breadth of this interdisciplinary field.

CLARKE and AYCOCK have picked 14 essays originally presented as papers at a conference in 1989 on "Literature and Medicine". Arranged thematically, these fall into three sub-divisions: 1) history, theory, and pedagogy; 2) comparative literature and medicine; 3) the broader context of society, religion, and politics. The key note is sounded by Anne Hudson Jones, whose informative essay lays the groundwork for the areas where literature and medicine converge. In addition to the more familiar territories concerning themes of disease, the image of the healer, and the writer-physician, she also looks at the therapeutic dimensions of literature. The range of the volume is quite astonishing in that it explores attitudes towards the body and text in Ancient Greece, the exposure of quackery in a medieval play, an analysis of the disease-ridden characters in Émile Zola's fiction, and William Styron's Nazi doctors. Almost unexpectedly, out of such an eclectic assemblage of papers, there emerges an overarching theme, which is the susceptibility of our corporeality to the healing text.

GORDON's reluctant inclusion of an extract from his own *Doctor in the House* is in keeping with this anthology's focus on the doctor in literature. Apart from the section quaintly entitled "Three Victorian Lady Doctor-Novelists", which contains a few meagre passages from the novels of Charlotte M. Yonge, Mary Braddon, and Arabella Kenealy, women writers are generally under-represented. Another bias is towards prose since, in spite of the subtitle, there is scarcely any poetry, notwithstanding, a smattering of Alfred Lord Tennyson and Robert Bridges. Aside from the preference given to doctors, male writers, and prose, what remains is a fairly random selection of writings. What can be perplexing for the reader is to determine why some passages have been included to the exclusion of others, especially those that would have exhibited a more relevant medical context. There are exceptions to this, as when Gordon isolates some celebrated passages from his largely canonical choices, which lie at the juncture between literature and medicine.

OBER is a pathologist whose racy selection of topics includes discussions of James Boswell's gonorrhea, A.C. Swinburne's masochism, and the Earl of Rochester's impotence. Sexual diseases and perversions account for the most sensational chapters in the book like "Lady Chatterley's *What?*" On a slightly more subdued note, Ober dismisses any suggestion that the poetry of three eighteenth-century poets is symptomatic of madness, and that Keats had written "Ode to a Nightingale" under the influence of opium. While setting out to dispel the stereotypes surrounding a number of famous case-histories associating sickness and addiction with creativity, Ober mischievously makes full use of them in order to produce a highly readable and eye-catching book.

My own (ROBERTS) and PORTER's collection aims to show that before medicine and literature became divided between the "two cultures", they had enjoyed a close partnership during the period of the Enlightenment. Advances made in this field by scholars like George S. Rousseau (whose essay "Medicine and the Muses: An Approach to Literature and Medicine" is included) are discussed in the Introduction. Other contributors include Pat Rogers, who writes on "Fat is a Fictional Issue", and Gloria Sybil Gross, who examines the expediency of falling ill for some of Jane Austen's characters. Other novels that are the focus for specific essays are Laurence Sterne's *Tristram*

Shandy and Jonathan Swift's *Gulliver's Travels*. Satires of the emerging professional doctor, the feuds between Grub Street and the medical colleges, and the treatment of women by both doctors and writers are also covered.

TRAUTMANN's edition confronts the modern dilemma of the fissure between literature and medicine, which can no longer be accommodated within a holistic world-or cosmic view. She does not attempt to provide definitive answers, but to bring instead into sharp relief the ongoing dialogue between the two disciplines. The book has grown out of a series of meetings organised by the American Institute on Human Values in Medicine. Contributors include Denise Levertov, a nurse turned poet and Nancy C. Andreasen, an English professor turned psychiatrist. By arranging the content so that dialogist's essays, poems, stories, and correspondence between meetings are interjected with editorial commentary, Trautmann has ensured that the exploratory nature of the original dialogues has been retained.

MARIE MULVEY ROBERTS

Medieval Literature *see* British Literature: Medieval

Melodrama

Gerould, Daniel C. (ed.), *American Melodrama*, New York: PAJ Publications, 1983
Herr, Cheryl (ed.), *For the Land They Loved: Irish Political Melodramas, 1890–1925*, Syracuse, New York: Syracuse University Press, 1991
Kilgariff, Michael (ed.), *The Golden Age of Melodrama: Twelve 19th-Century Melodramas*, London: Wolfe, 1974
Krause, David (ed.), *The Dolmen Boucicault*, Dublin: Dolmen Press, 1965; Chester Springs, Pennsylvania: Dufour Editions, 1965
Rahill, Frank, *The World of Melodrama*, University Park: Pennsylvania State University Press, 1967
Redmond, James (ed.), *Melodrama* ("Themes in Drama" series), Cambridge and New York: Cambridge University Press, 1992
Smith, James L., *Melodrama*, London: Methuen, 1973

Melodrama as a specific theatrical form experienced its zenith from the nineteenth to the early twentieth century. With its direct appeal to the emotions, melodrama has been accused of being overly sentimental and lacking in intellectual content. However, melodrama is currently experiencing a revaluation by critics, who note aspects of social rebellion in the rise of the oppressed individual and who appreciate the technical advances created for the demanded *tour-de-force* spectacles.

RAHILL surveys the history of melodrama as it evolved in France, England, and the United States, identifying how artists in each country borrowed from one another with regard to source material, themes, character types, and production devices. The study is divided into three sections corresponding to the focus countries. The chapters within each section are rich with specific details about productions; the bibliographic notes provide information about where play texts may be found, choice of extracts, and translations. Rahill gives much attention to René de Pixérécourt as the "king of melodrama", who set the standard for other melodramatists, and to Dion Boucicault for bringing the form to "something like maturity". Rahill also gives colorful glimpses of other important figures such as Charles Fechter, Charles Keane, and David Belasco. In the final chapter, Rahill analyzes how stage melodramas crossed into film, serving as models for films like *Ben Hur* and *High Noon*.

KILGARIFF insists that his book "is intended for the casual enquirer" rather than for scholars. Kilgariff's brief biographies of various playwrights, as well as use of press notices and advertisements, help set the tone for the golden age of melodrama, but his conclusions and choices of "representative" texts must be questioned. When he terms melodrama "that debased form of theatre" and claims that no artist of merit or work of lasting impact emerged from it, his admitted ambivalence sounds like disdain. Kilgariff insists that melodrama pacifies the oppressed and serves the status quo "by showing us all our prejudices and persuasions satisfyingly confirmed". The book ends with two important appendices, one on breaking the Patent Houses' charter and the other apologizing for plagiarism.

SMITH discusses melodrama on a grand scale, recognizing Pixérécourt as the originator of the pattern, yet connecting the melodramatic nature to plays from Greek classics to contemporary drama. Decrying the denigration of melodrama by some critics, Smith appeals: "any art form deserves to be judged by its highest, not by its lowest achievements", citing Shakespeare's *Henry V*, Bertolt Brecht's *Mother Courage*, and Euripides' *Trojan Women* as "the peaks of melodramatic triumph". Smith calls triumph, despair, and protest "the basic emotions of melodrama", and he divides his analysis of melodramas accordingly. In his introductory chapter, Smith argues that the difference between tragedy and melodrama lies in the difference between fragmentation of the tragic character versus the singular wholeness of the melodramatic character (whether villain, hero, or clown, etc.). Smith's greatest contribution to the discussion is in his breadth of vision regarding melodrama, a vision which does reclaim for serious attention the art form.

REDMOND's collection of essays read at the Themes in Drama International Conference in 1990 provides wide-ranging discussion of the history, value, and theory of melodrama. This series intends specialized considerations of drama in a way that can be "readily appreciated by non-specialists". For the most part these essays live up to that intention, with one notable exception: Morse's "Desire and the Limits of Melodrama" distances the general reader because of the author's theoretical and stylistic flourishes. Morse claims that melodrama is "counterproductive exactly because it is popular" – it fails to to indict high culture because it is inscribed by that culture. Ironically his own language does exactly what he accuses melodrama of doing, in supporting high culture. The problem here is that Morse's argument is based on a theoretical presupposition about cultural discourse rather than on careful analysis of either texts or cultural contexts. Marcoux's essay, "Guilbert de Pixérécourt: The People's Conscience", might be read as a counter to Morse. Clearly analyzing the origins of French melodrama, using both historical-cultural and biographical approaches, Marcoux convincingly demonstrates "that French melodrama as a dramatic genre was a product of revolution . . . a form hurtling toward democracy" with a morality "no longer imposed from above" in a high-culture hierarchy, but with "a kind of grass-roots imperative". Other essays, tracing the elements of melodrama in Euripides and Shakespeare, up through nineteenth-century gothic writers, to modern writers like John Arden and Margaretta D'Arcy, contribute to making this volume an excellent choice for those who want to rethink the value of melodrama.

GEROULD introduces "The Americanization of Melodrama" in a stimulating essay that explores "the way in which melodrama has shaped the American popular imagination, molding our perceptions of self and country". Gerould convincingly points out the strong relationship between melodrama and the American psyche – a desire for novelty, admiration for innovation, obsession with sensation, a preference for action over contemplation, a belief in democratic ideals. Gerould also provides background information on the four plays contained in this volume: Dion Boucicault's *The Poor of New York*, George Aiken and Harriet Beecher Stowe's *Uncle Tom's Cabin*, Augustin Daly's *Under the Gaslight*, and David Belasco's *The Girl of the Golden West*.

HERR clarifies the literary lineage of Irish melodrama from Boucicault to his increasingly political heirs, J.W. Whitbread and P.J. Bourke. Herr argues that these Irish melodramatists were colonists writing against the British Empire, attempting to "promote social change" by focusing on historical moments of great significance to Irish independence and identity, such as the Irish rebellion of 1798. Herr establishes the context of Whitbread's and Bourke's melodramas on a scale that encompasses history and politics, but most of all personalities – the personalities of such men as Fitzgerald and Wolfe Tone, who loom larger than life and are well suited to melodrama. Following Herr's essay, the texts of four melodramas are provided: Whitbread's *Lord Edward, Or, '98* and *Wolfe Tone*; and Bourke's *When Wexford Rose* and *For the Land She Loved*, the latter a victim of censorship on the grounds of its supposed sedition. The volume ends with a small but helpful glossary of Irish terms and further notes on the specific play texts and their productions.

KRAUSE's editing of Dion Boucicault's three most important Irish melodramas provides a worthy introduction to the works of the premier melodramatist writing in English during the Victorian era. Krause's introductory essay includes biographical information and summarizes the significant contributions of this Irish master of melodrama. Krause credits Boucicault with mastery of not only the melodramatic form but also the technical aspects: the creation of cliffs, raging waves for watery graves, tenements burning on stage, etc. Krause also makes it clear that Boucicault's power was immense, reaching from London to New York, with ongoing influence over the works of such as George Bernard Shaw and Sean O'Casey. Krause's essay chiefly praises Boucicault's contributions, defusing negative critiques about Boucicault's direct exploitation of current affairs (uprisings in India, slavery in the United States), and leaving the impression that melodrama, perhaps even drama in its varied aspects, would be weaker overall without his pleasurable works. Following the Krause essay and the texts of *The Colleen Bawn*, *Arrah-na-Pogue*, and *The Shaughraun*, a glossary of Irish terms used in the plays is provided as well as music to the songs.

DAWN E. DUNCAN

Melville, Herman 1819–1891

American novelist, short-story writer, and poet

Bryant, John (ed.), *A Companion to Melville Studies*, Westport, Connecticut: Greenwood Press, 1986

Chase, Richard, *Herman Melville: A Critical Study*, New York: Macmillan, 1949

Chase, Richard (ed.), *Herman Melville: A Collection of Critical Essays*, Englewood Cliffs, New Jersey: Prentice-Hall, 1962

James, C.L.R., *Mariners, Renegades and Castaways: The Story of Herman Melville and the World We Live In*, New York: n.p., 1953; reprinted, Detroit: Bewick, 1978; also reprinted, London and New York: Allison & Busby, 1985

Lawrence, D.H., "Herman Melville's *Typee* and *Omoo*" and "Herman Melville's *Moby-Dick*", in *Studies in Classic American Literature*, New York: Seltzer, 1923; London: Secker, 1924

McSweeney, Kerry, *Moby-Dick: Ishmael's Mighty Book*, Boston: Twayne, 1986

Milder, Robert (ed.), *Critical Essays on Melville's "Billy Budd, Sailor"*, Boston: G.K. Hall, 1989

Olson, Charles, *Call Me Ishmael: A Study of Melville*, San Francisco: City Lights, 1947; London: Jonathan Cape, 1967

Pullin, Faith (ed.), *New Perspectives on Melville*, Edinburgh: Edinburgh University Press, 1978; Kent, Ohio: Kent State University Press, 1978

Rogin, Michael Paul, *Subversive Genealogy: The Politics and Art of Herman Melville*, New York: Knopf, 1983

Samson, John, *White Lies: Melville's Narratives of Facts*, Ithaca, New York: Cornell University Press, 1989

Shurr, William H., *The Mystery of Iniquity: Melville as Poet, 1857–1891*, Lexington: University Press of Kentucky, 1972

Thompson, Lawrance, *Melville's Quarrel with God*, Princeton, New Jersey: Princeton University Press, 1952

During his lifetime, Melville was known as "the man who had lived among the cannibals", the author of "romances" of the South Seas. *Moby-Dick* received mixed reviews, and *Pierre* saw the eclipse of his popularity completely. His later work was generally neglected, and when he died in obscurity he was still known mainly for his early novels. By 1907, however, *Moby-Dick* was considered a classic by some, though others (notably Joseph Conrad) disagreed. A widespread revival of interest only began when Raymond Weaver produced the first critical biography of Melville in 1921. This was enormously influential, and major reassessments followed, both critical and biographical, through the 1920s and 1930s. By the time of F.O. Matthiessen's monumental *American Renaissance*

(1941), there was no doubt about Melville's canonical status and the significance of *Moby-Dick* as a literary classic. Jay Leyda's *The Melville Log* (1951), a sourcebook of biographical information, prompted subsequent biographical studies, deepening and sharpening critical understanding of the works. Critical studies have multiplied since the 1950s, and Melville is now an academic industry. Yet it may be advisable to avoid the armada of recent critics and go first to three early writers from beyond the academies, whose response remains intensely illuminating.

OLSON's little book is an indispensable meditation on *Moby-Dick*, but it also opens the door to Melville's entire imagination, his understanding of American society and economics, the relation between the New World and the Old, and the place of Melville's work in Western culture. Olson grounds Melville in economics (whaling as industry), but also explores the distinctively American mythopoeic dimension of "space" in Melville's writing. His oracular style is enormously suggestive about psycho-religious aspects of Melville's thinking. For Olson, Melville "comprehended man as mythological in an archaelogical present". Raised among fishermen, Olson had spent years working on Melville, and had succeeded in tracking down Melville's library, discovering and revealing the extent and profundity of his reading of Shakespeare. Olson charts a movement in Western literature, from Homer through Dante to Melville, as man's consciousness of the world expanded from the Mediterranean, through to the Atlantic, and finally into the Pacific. With Melville, the world is circled. "Ahab is full stop". Olson's study is a masterpiece of rhetorical organization, building dramatically to climactic revelation.

Partly behind, yet also to one side of, Olson stands LAWRENCE, whose essays on Melville present an apocalyptic vision of "the greatest seer and poet of the sea". In Lawrence's reading, Melville denies the social world, sees corruption inherent in exotic places, and understands how readily the road to hell is paved with good intentions. Ultimately, Lawrence rejects what he sees as Melville's nostalgia and idealism, but the flashing rhetoric of Lawrence's essays still startles and annoys, in equal proportions, as he presents the case for the *Pequod* as a doomed ship "of the white American soul". The essays should be read in context, for Lawrence's book is infectiously and infuriatingly engaged, and what he says about Melville is balanced by what he says about the larger world of predominantly "sane" America from which Melville sought to escape.

The full title of JAMES's book suggests the approach he takes, reading Melville for a sustained critique of the industrialized world of the mid-twentieth century. Writing mainly while he was interned on Ellis Island before being expelled from the USA, James is shrewd but passionate in his application of social understanding to Melville's greatest work. He is admirably direct, jargon-free, and imaginatively committed to literature as a social force. His relation of Ahab to the modern monsters of totalitarian monomania is a wonderful testament to his own clarity of judgement and balanced, humanitarian sensibility. For James, the "outstanding fact" of the nineteenth century was that "Melville [understood] . . . what the future of capitalism was going to be".

For a more academic reading of *Moby-Dick*, McSWEENEY's conversational, readily accessible book comprises a series of interrelated essays on the main themes and aspects of the book – its historical context, composition, and reception, Ishmael as narrator, the character of Ahab, and the formal characteristics of the novel as epic and as tragedy. McSweeney is discursive, patient, and even-tempered, providing a useful counter-balance to the soaringly passionate responses Melville sometimes provokes, and demonstrating how possible it is to write lucidly on extremely intractable matters.

Perhaps the single most helpful volume of Melville criticism is the comprehensive work edited by BRYANT. Twenty-five essays by different experts cover the range of approaches to Melville's life, his world, his reputation, his works, his thinking, his art, his legacy in the twentieth century, and his international influence in translation. This is scholarship at its best, with excellent readings of individual texts, general surveys of the shape of Melville's literary and personal career, the character of the *oeuvre*, and, in M. Thomas Inge's essay, "Melville in Popular Culture", a refreshing appraisal of the paradoxical reversal of fortune that has overtaken Ahab and the White Whale between the 1880s and the 1980s. Each chapter has a valuable list of "Works Cited" for further reference.

The 1949 study by CHASE, one of the most influential postwar Melville critics, is somewhat dated, yet still valuable. His description of "the development of Melville's mind" in his writings, through recurring and developing images, symbols, ideas and moral attitudes, is an attempt to understand Melville as "a great man in a great culture". Unfashionable as such terminology has become, Chase is nevertheless an invigorating and conscientious reader. He considers Melville's symbols – of space, tower, cave, phallus, stone, the Fall, and the Quest – offering a neo-Freudian reading of Melville's sexual and familial identity. For Chase, Melville is not an obscure failure but a politically vital thinker for modern, liberal, and progressive humanism.

The collection of essays CHASE edited in 1962 collects various chapters from books and essays from journals, including some of the best Melville criticism of the 1950s. Among the most valuable are Robert Penn Warren's introduction to Melville's poetry, Henry A. Murray's outdated yet magniloquent attempt to overcome what he calls his own "trained disability" to praise Melville adequately, Newton Arvin's chapter on the South Seas fiction, and readings of the later novellas and stories.

Another classic study of Melville from the immediate postwar era is THOMPSON's. Essentially, the argument here is that all his life, Melville was "harping on the notion that the world was put together wrong and that God was to blame and that only the self-promoting authoritarians pretend otherwise, in order to victimize the stupid". Thompson recognizes, moreover, that Melville took "wry and sly pleasure in the irony of disguising his riddle-answers behind the self-protective riddle-masks of his ingenious art". The book is a magisterial survey of Melville's major works of fiction, including *Mardi* and *Pierre*. It is a dark reading, adumbrating a thesis with dense, pondered argument.

More recent book-length studies develop particular kinds of reading or deepen certain channels of approach, relating *Moby-Dick* to Melville's other novels, and locating his work in its full historical and political context. SAMSON focuses on *Typee*, *Omoo*, *Redburn*, *White-Jacket*, *Israel Potter* (one of

Melville's most unjustly neglected novels), and *Billy Budd*. These novels belong to the popular nineteenth-century genre of factual narratives (the literature of exploration is the best example of the genre). Samson is informed, but not shackled, by recent literary theory, and discusses Melville's determined exposition of the contradictions within the narrators of his novels. For Samson, the racism, religious bigotry, and economic determinism of nineteenth-century America was endorsed by white patriarchal narratives, and Melville opened these to questioning.

ROGIN traces connections between Melville's work and his prominent patrician family, illuminating the ways in which members of that family were involved in political events, and how these in turn became part of Melville's fiction. This is a necessary reminder that however remote from social life and American political culture Melville's books appear to be, they are steeped in them. The crisis in Melville's writing career reflected the crisis in national politics, involving the expansionist policies leading to the Mexican War of 1848, and the contradictions of democracy, racism, slavery, and the onset of the Civil War. "Melville rendered American history symbolically", Rogin writes, and his study brings out the symbolic resonance of American history in Melville's work.

Most of Melville's writing after 1857 was poetry; but *Billy Budd* and his later stories are more frequently read with his earlier fiction. Yet it is only by understanding his later poetry that a full sense of his literary career can be established. SHURR's study gives both a new illumination of the shape of a great career, and lucid, sustained readings of individual books of poems and the stories and sketches Melville wrote concurrently with them. Much of the book is a critical analysis of the enormous poem *Clarel*, which elucidates complexities and carefully judges the poem's "static elements" as against the "dynamics of the symbol". Rich with contextual details, this study shows Shurr is an eloquent and judicious writer, and this is a pioneering work, which should be more widely known.

Recent essay collections have gathered a wide variety of readings from academics and critics of different persuasions. PULLIN's collection is especially valuable for the contributions by Hayford and Parker, editors of the definitive Northwestern-Newberry *Complete Works* of Melville, who focus on doubleness in *Moby-Dick* and the "flawed grandeur" of *Pierre*. While other novels and short stories are discussed, revealing essays also explore the themes of "Shakespeare and Melville's America" and "Melville's England". The contributors are literary critics and academics from both America and Britain, and the book is designed to reflect an internationalist approach.

MILDER's collection of work on *Billy Budd* begins with an Introduction helpfully summarizing that book's critical reception. There follows a commentary on the text by the editors of the Northwestern-Newberry edition, and some early critical responses. The bulk of the book is taken up with scholarly essays, which not only provide insightful readings of *Billy Budd* itself, but also offer sidelights on Melville's work as a whole. Joyce Sparer Adler, for example, quoting Melville and Wilson Harris, strikes through to a general truth when she writes: "Melville's imagination, as it makes itself known in all his works, even the most bitter, does not see civilization's forms as static, complete, devoid of all potentiality for 'promoted life'. It is incapable of 'that unfeeling acceptance of destiny which is promulgated in the name of service or tradition' ".

ALAN RIACH

Meredith, George 1828–1909

English novelist, poet, and essayist

Beer, Gillian, *Meredith: A Change of Masks: A Study of the Novels*, London: Athlone Press, 1970

Bernstein, Carol L., *Precarious Enchantment: A Reading of Meredith's Poetry*, Washington, D.C.: Catholic University of America Press, 1979

Fletcher, Ian (ed.), *Meredith Now: Some Critical Essays*, London: Routledge & Kegan Paul, 1971; New York: Barnes & Noble, 1971

Lindsay, Jack, *Meredith: His Life and Work*, London: Bodley Head, 1956

Muendel, Renate, *George Meredith*, Boston: Twayne, 1986

Stevenson, Lionel, *The Ordeal of George Meredith*, New York: Scribner, 1953; London: Peter Owen, 1954

Wilt, Judith, *The Readable People of George Meredith*, Princeton, New Jersey: Princeton University Press, 1975

At his death in 1909, Meredith was regarded as the "Grand Old Man" of English letters, but the estimation in which he was held did not last far into the twentieth century. While F.R. Leavis's influential *The Great Tradition* (1948) had no place for Meredith, in recent years his stock has risen again, for reasons similar to those which underpinned his reputation in the late nineteenth century – admiration of his challenges to Victorian intellectual, political, and discursive orthodoxies.

STEVENSON's traditional critical biography is useful for context and background. Its title, alluding to Meredith's novel *The Ordeal of Richard Feverel*, signals that the biography interprets his life as a series of tests of character and endurance. In its evenhanded way, it provides a sounding-board for subsequent critics. LINDSAY is unreliable in some factual details, but challenging in his contentions. He brings a Marxist perspective to Meredith's work, arguing that Meredith is to be read as a political novelist, not because "he habitually deals with the externals of politics, parliamentary elections and the like", but because "the central focus of each of his works implies a considered judgment, based in political economy, of the fundamental forces determining the general movement of society. The personal struggles of his characters are always seen within this general movement".

Around 1970 Meredith appeared set for a revival. Cline's edition of the letters (1970) and Williams's *Critical Heritage* volume on Meredith's reception (1971) came out, as well as Beer and Fletcher, still the most comprehensive and stimulating critical works. BEER, in her suggestive study, argues that Meredith was a consciously experimental writer, whose work is "crucial to an understanding of the way the English novel developed towards the end of the nineteenth century". She also asserts that he is "a novelist whose ambitious imperfection suggests more about the potentialities and limits of the novel-form than a fully achieved artist would do". She concentrates on six novels in order to discuss such issues as: Meredith's use of autobiographical material; his relationship with the realist tradition, and especially the self-reflexiveness of his fiction; and language and style. Beer draws on unpublished material, subsequently edited by Beer and Harris as *The Notebooks of George Meredith* (1983).

The volume of 16 essays edited by FLETCHER opens with a discussion of Meredith's reputation, followed by a chapter on the poetry, and treatments of all the novels. The editor emphasises – justifiably – that the volume not only presents a comprehensive coverage, but also illuminates the variety of Meredith's work. Some of the essays (Jan B. Gordon's structuralist account of *Diana of the Crossways*, and John Goode's address to *The Egoist*, which maintains "that it is not finally very helpful to demonstrate its internal efficiency; what is needed is a means of assessing the novel's terms of reference") are innovative in their critical method; others work in more traditional methods (Ian Fletcher's dazzling display of learning in "*The Shaving of Shagpat*: Meredith's Comic Apocalypse", and Leonée Ormond's "*The Tragic Comedians:* Meredith's Use of Image Patterns").

WILT focuses on the construction of the reader in, and by, Meredith's texts, in her original and occasionally idiosyncratic consideration of Meredith's enactment of his philosophy in his writing. Her selection of novels includes the best-known (*Richard Feverel* and *The Egoist*), but gives valuable prominence also to the dense, late *One of Our Conquerors* and *The Amazing Marriage*.

Meredith's poetry, with the exception of *Modern Love*, has been neglected by comparison with the fiction, although at times Meredith, like Thomas Hardy, chose to represent himself as principally a poet. BERNSTEIN is notable as the first major study of the poems since Trevelyan's *The Poetry and Philosophy of George Meredith* (1906), and its value in part derives from the attention she gives to the range of his poetic production and not only *Modern Love*. She has the advantage of Bartlett's 1978 critical edition of the poems on which to base her demonstration of the extent and significance of Meredith's poetic experiments. From her acute analysis of the artifice of Meredith's style, she develops an argument based on the proposition that "the relation of the perceiver to the natural world is crucial in Meredith's poetry and informs even those poems where 'Nature' is not the main subject". Isobel Armstrong's important *Victorian Poetry* (1993) acknowledges and illuminates Meredith's experimentalism.

MUENDEL provides the most accessible and topical introduction to this difficult writer. She eschews the terms Meredith himself offers as relevant for discussion of his work (the "Comic Spirit", "Blood and Brain"), and builds on the work of previous critics in tracing succinctly the recurrent concerns of his "experimental and problematic art". Her account balances attention to formal aspects of Meredith's writing with an awareness of its engagement with social and political concerns, notably issues to do with women.

MARGARET HARRIS

Metaphysical Poetry

Keast, William R, (ed.), *Seventeenth Century English Poetry: Modern Essays in Criticism*, New York and Oxford: Oxford University Press, 1962, revised 1971
Mackenzie, Donald, *The Metaphysical Poets*, London: Macmillan, 1990
Martz, Louis L, *The Poetry of Meditation: A Study in English Religious Literature of the Seventeenth Century*, New Haven, Connecticut: Yale University Press, 1954, revised 1962
Parry, Graham, *Seventeenth-Century Poetry: The Social Context*, London: Hutchinson, 1985
Roberts, John R. (ed.), *New Perspectives on the Seventeenth Century Religious Lyric*, Columbia: University of Missouri Press, 1994
Smith, A.J., *Metaphysical Wit*, Cambridge and New York: Cambridge University Press, 1991

MARTZ proposes that there was a meditative tradition in English poetry, descending from the Jesuit martyr and poet Robert Southwell, not from John Donne, with the poets drawn into resemblance through the common influence of certain methods of religious meditation derived from St Ignatius Loyola and St François de Sales. The meditative structures, methods of self-examination, the "practice of the presence of God", and meditations on death and upon Mary Magdalene's tears are seen as fundamental to the practices of the Metaphysical poets, who therefore might be subsumed into this larger category, "poetry of meditation". Donne is seen as particularly influenced by the techniques of Loyola, and the heated fusion of thought and feeling his discipline required, while George Herbert is viewed as falling in more with the less extreme methods suggested by de Sales. Donne's secular poems are accordingly characterised by the poet's "search for the one", which underlies and explains his erotic discontents. Martz's main focus is on the Anniversaries, read as products of a single year and of the spiritual crisis Donne faced when deciding whether to enter the Church. Critics of the book have pointed out that Martz's readings tend to make the Holy Sonnets over-deliberate, calmly planned and executed exercises in dismissing despair, and that the poems as experienced suggest less assurance in repelling despair. Martz himself, reviewing the evolution of his book in Roberts (see below), admits that there were aspects of Protestant devotional practice that came too late to his notice, but defends the relevance of the structures of these Catholic techniques of meditation.

KEAST edits a useful collection of essays. It aims to represent the developing twentieth-century debate about Metaphysical poetry, and starts with classic essays: Grierson, and Helen Gardner, whose introductions to selections from the Metaphysical poets are both still considered to be among the best general discussions, with, inevitably, T.S. Eliot's review-essay of Grierson. Donne, Herbert, and Andrew Marvell are central authors, with essays on specific poems (Williamson on Donne's "The Ecstasy", Kermode on Marvell's "The Garden") and others of a more general nature (Leishmann on Donne's influence, Earl Miner on wit, the latter concerned largely to differentiate from imagery ideas about the operations of Metaphysical wit by stressing definition and logical argument).

Mazzeo on "Modern Theories of Metaphysical Poetry" addresses the theories of Mario Praz, Benedetto Croce, J.L. Austin, and Robert Penn Warren about how the conceited manner came into existence. The selection is representative rather than polemic; Keast is not concerned to align his anthology with a particular critical movement, and several non-Metaphysical poets are also discussed.

PARRY's book is ostensibly a poet-by-poet survey under one "social context". Among the Metaphysicals, chapters are given to Donne, Herbert, Henry Vaughan, and Marvell. Parry is concerned with the experience of the seventeenth-century reader on first encountering some of the most important collections of poetry published in the period, the manner of their presentation to the reader, and their designs upon their audience. In the case of Donne, poetry is seen as his means of access to the circles of power. Parry emphasizes the social function of the poems. As the book goes on, the "*Social Context*" of the subtitle becomes "contexts". A particularly successful discussion of devotional context examines Herbert and Anglicanism; Marvell is seen in the context of English millenarianism, the feeling that the end of the world was near. Parry has published a notable study of the 1630s as a Stuart "Golden Age Restored", and this elegantly written account is particularly assured on the seventeenth-century poetry of retreat – gardens, paradises, and states of innocence.

ROBERTS' is a collection of specially commissioned essays, which discuss seventeenth-century religious poetry in the light of new critical interests, particularly in the cultural contexts (political, social, theological) that shaped the poems – and their writers. Literary contexts are not forgotten, and how far the religious lyric is a distinct genre of poetry is examined (by Helen Wilcox). Essays on Metaphysical poets include Anthony Low on Donne's religious/erotic metaphors, Christopher Hodgkins on Herbert's awareness of the seductive power of language and rhetoric, and Claude Summers on the poetry of Anglican survivalism in Vaughan (how the experience of persecution affected the writings). In the most important contribution to the volume, Michael Schoenfeldt suggests a cultural poetics for the religious lyric as a "poetry of supplication", looking at the ways such poems in the hands of the socially dependent Donne drew upon socially deferential conversation as a model for discourse with the divine, a fusion of social and religious experience Donne passed on to Herbert, but which Schoenfeldt notes is absent in Vaughan, Thomas Traherne, and Richard Crashaw. The editor opens the volume with an introductory discussion of its rationale and of the arguments his contributors present, and closes it with a year-by-year bibliography on the subject, 1952–1990.

SMITH's study is the last part of an undeclared trilogy of linked studies, coming after *Literary Love* (1983) and *The Metaphysics of Love* (1985). On individual poems, it is possibly less incisive than the earlier studies, but presents a wide survey of conceited and metaphysical wits, and of the Renaissance theorists of witty writing. The critical position is rather old-fashioned: essentially Smith stands for a Donne who presents a union of thought and feeling, an undissociated sensibility, despite the subsequent critical history of Eliot's suggestion of 1921. Donne, very much the hero of the book, appears after chapters on Continental metaphysical poets, and is presented as a poet of mutual love valued above denaturing obsessions with wealth, honour, and place. A much less heartfelt Donne could easily be advanced. The book, very much a labour of love, follows its own course without engagement with other critical voices. But it commands attention for its referential range within the period, and as a latter-day example of humanist/essentialist criticism.

MACKENZIE's slim (117-page) volume looks first at the classic accounts of Metaphysical poetry by Samuel Johnson, Samuel Taylor Coleridge, and T.S. Eliot, with the author offering a useful critique of the "disassociation of sensibility" myth based on Frank Kermode's dismantling. A useful survey of criticism leads to Mackenzie's own summary, which is always apt if necessarily on standard topics. Contexts for the poets are suggested (Donne and the poetry of the 1590s, Herbert and the New Testament, Marvell and the political upheavals of the 1640s), comment is made on metre, and the book ends with a reminder of the strangeness of the Metaphysical mode at its best. This is a lively and economically written introduction, offering help in dealing with the array of critical opinions.

ROY J. BOOTH

Middle English Literature *see* British Literature: Medieval

Middleton, Thomas 1580–1627

English dramatist

Brittin, Norman A., *Thomas Middleton*, New York: Twayne, 1972
Covatta, Anthony, *Thomas Middleton's City Comedies*, Lewisburg, Pennsylvania: Bucknell University Press, 1973
Farr, Dorothy, *Thomas Middleton and the Drama of Realism: A Study of Some Representative Plays*, Edinburgh: Oliver & Boyd, 1973
Friedenreich, Kenneth (ed.), *"Accompanyinge the Players": Essays Celebrating Thomas Middleton 1580–1980*, New York: AMS Press, 1983
Heinemann, Margot, *Puritanism and the Theatre: Opposition Drama under the Early Stuarts*, Cambridge and New York: Cambridge University Press, 1980
Holmes, David N., *The Art of Thomas Middleton: A Critical Study*, Oxford: Clarendon Press, 1970
Kistner, A.L., and M.K. Kistner, *Thomas Middleton's Tragic Themes*, New York: Peter Lang, 1984
Rowe, George E., *Thomas Middleton and the New Comedy Tradition*, Lincoln: University of Nebraska Press, 1979
Schoenbaum, Samuel, *Middleton's Tragedies: A Critical Study*, New York: Columbia University Press, 1955

Thomas Middleton's reputation has been a steadily rising one among twentieth-century critics.

SCHOENBAUM, one of the first scholars to defend Middleton's authorship of *The Revenger's Tragedy*, devotes a section of the book to this and other authorship problems in the canon. On the basis of five tragedies, three of which he regards as masterpieces, he assigns Middleton "the foremost place after Shakespeare in the hierarchy of Jacobean writers of tragedy". Along with *The Revenger's Tragedy*, both *Women Beware Women* and *The Changeling* are seen as poetic and dramatic masterpieces. The author also appreciates the art of two traditionally underrated plays, *Hengist* and *The Second Maiden's Tragedy*. Schoenbaum's study is an important and influential one.

HOLMES differs from most critics in seeing Middleton as an essentially didactic writer, concerned to protect the virtuous from the "insidious inroads of the vicious". Themes seen as being of especial importance to the playwright are justice, and filial and marital obligation. In his characterization, Middleton tends to let an individual's virtues compensate for his shortcomings. The heroines of the two best known tragedies, *Women Beware Women* and *The Changeling*, suffer from ignorance both of the world and of themselves, along with notable moral incompetence. Holmes thus finds a prevailing moral seriousness in the works of this playwright, whose moral design is simple but whose characters are complex, often sympathetic, but never sentimentalized.

BRITTIN's survey of Middleton's career follows the Twayne "English Authors" series format of biography followed by brief analysis of literary works. After a review of the playwright's early poetry and prose writings, the author deals in turn with the comedies, tragicomedies, and tragedies, noting *A Chaste Maid in Cheapside* as his supreme achievement in comedy. Among the tragicomedies *A Fair Quarrel* is singled out for praise, especially for its "remarkable psychological penetration". The two tragedies *Women Beware Women* and *The Changeling* are his highest achievements. In a final chapter on assessments, the author reviews the opinions of critics as well as affirming his own high estimate of Middleton. The approach to the plays is brief and synoptic, but lucidly written and helpful simply as an overview of this prolific writer.

COVATTA is concerned with the comedies primarily as forms of comedy, studying the plays not as social or moral documents but as fictions, with high praise for the "skillfully wrought chaos" of his comic structures. He finds a primarily ironic mode to be characteristic of the early comedies. Individual chapters are devoted to the major comic works: the most genial of the city comedies is *A Mad World, My Masters*, and the most accomplished is *A Chaste Maid in Cheapside*, Middleton's masterpiece and his "fullest statement of life's ability to overcome all obstacles". Essentially the author argues that Middleton's plays offer a positive vision of a society, with characters drawn from all age groups and all walks of life, who embody "the essentially valuable tendencies of the human spirit".

FARR has selected seven plays for consideration in this study of the playwright as realist. In Farr's view, early in his career Middleton explores comic situations in such plays as *A Trick to Catch the Old One*, *A Chaste Maid in Cheapside*, and *The Widow*; *A Fair Quarrel* is seen as a transitional play between the comedies and the later tragedies; in *The Changeling* and *Women Beware Women* the playwright penetrates the experience of ordinary people in circumstances beyond their control. Finally Middleton turns to the political scene for his *A Game at Chess*. The author concludes that the playwright's work is an "unfinished achievement". A short book (124 pages), this offers a sensitive reading of selected plays from the viewpoint of realism.

ROWE's work is a study of Middleton's relationship with the highly conventional classical tradition of New Comedy, with a focus on nine plays. First Rowe deals with the apprentice works, *The Phoenix* and *The Family of Love;* as he matured, Middleton turned away from the strict classical model to explore other, often potentially terrifying aspects of comedy, in such works as *A Mad World, My Masters* and *A Chaste Maid in Cheapside*; and by the time of *The Old Law*, the comic has become "a horrifying nightmare". Similarly the tragicomedies reveal "the terror beneath the surface". In these plays the conflict is harsh and discordant, and there is no harmonious resolution at the end. In a final chapter Rowe considers comic elements in the tragedies. This work is original in dealing with the close relationship between the comedies and tragedies in Middleton's mature works.

HEINEMANN studies the political context of Middleton's late plays, with emphasis on what she calls "opposition drama". In this period of rapidly growing commercial drama, Heinemann considers the influence of Parliamentary Puritans on such matters as censorship, which was much tighter in the Jacobean period than it had been in the Elizabethan. Heinemann rejects the idea that Middleton's satire was simply anti-citizen, arguing that it was much more universal. The last section of the book is devoted to drama and opposition in the final 20 years before the closing of the theatres. What was notable about Middleton in respect of this complex and troubled period was his close connection with both the citizens and Parliament. Heinemann's work is very valuable for its knowledgable consideration of the playwright in the troubled political milieu of his time.

FRIEDENREICH's essay collection celebrates Middleton's quatracentenary year. The editor's Introduction deals with "how to read Middleton", and essays by Roma Gill and Norman Brittin are general studies of the playwright's world and style. The remainder of the essays deal with either specific plays or points of view. Comedies dealt with in individual essays include *Michaelmas Term*, *A Trick to Catch the Old One*, *A Chaste Maid in Cheapside*, *More Dissemblers Besides Women*, *No Wit to Help Like a Woman's*, and *The Witch*. There are also three essays on the two major tragedies. Ranging from moral design to the relationship of adjectives and authorship, the essays touch on a wide range of topics, constituting a fitting tribute to the playwright on his anniversary.

The KISTNERs' primary purpose is to examine the close relationship between themes and structures in Middleton's plays. They deal with six basic themes – loss of identity, abuse of authority, conflict (or reason and passion), deceptive appearances, fortune, and moral degradation. The basic structures through which these themes interact are parallels of plot and character and use of key words which echo and mirror the meaning through repetition. The authors include comedies, tragedies, and tragicomedies, for they find that Middleton makes no distinction in choice of themes and structures for the different genres. The playwrights' concern is with the "eternal verities on the condition of mankind". This book offers close readings of several plays, following their formula of thematic structures.

CHARLOTTE SPIVACK

Millay, Edna St Vincent 1892–1950

American poet and dramatist

Brittin, Norman A., *Edna St Vincent Millay*, New York: Twayne, 1967, revised 1982
Cheney, Anne, *Millay in Greenwich Village*, University: University of Alabama Press, 1975
Clarke, Suzanne, *Sentimental Modernism: Women Writers and the Revolution of the Word*, Bloomington: Indiana University Press, 1991
Thesing, William B. (ed.), *Critical Essays on Edna St Vincent Millay*, Boston: G.K. Hall, 1993
Walker, Cheryl, *Masks Outrageous and Austere: Culture, Psyche, and Persona in Modern Women Poets*, Bloomington: Indiana University Press, 1991

Edna St Vincent Millay's eventful life has inspired a great many biographies, her letters have been published, and her poems have been widely read; but up until very recently her poetry was dismissed by the academy as "popular" and "sentimental". However, recent interest in revising the modernist canon and re-examining the constructed opposition between popular forms and the avant garde has led to a renewed interest in Millay and her verse. Though still in its infancy, the study of what Suzanne Clarke refers to as "sentimental modernism" looks as if it will redefine our conception of literary modernism.

BRITTIN's revised (1982) critical discussion of Millay moves chronologically through Millay's life and poetry in a predictable fashion. This is a useful introduction to the poet and her life, but for any kind of in-depth analysis one must look elsewhere.

CHENEY's study is a lively reconstruction of Millay's cultural milieu in the 1910s and 1920s, though discussions of modernist aesthetics are limited, and there is little textual analysis. Cheney recognizes the symbolic function the poet served as a representative of "the freedom and hedonism of the Village", and provides an insight into the life of one of America's most famous bohemians.

CLARKE reconsiders the way in which "sentimental" writers such as Millay have been constructed in gendered terms as frivolous and irrelevant, and the manner in which modernism "is caught in and stabilized by a system of gendered binaries: male/female, serious/sentimental, critical/popular". Not only is Clarke's study useful as an historical revision of modernist literary discourses, but it also offers a series of perceptive re-readings of Millay's poetry.

THESING's collection of critical essays is an invaluable contribution to studies of Millay. It contains a selection of the best of recent essays on her, such as Gilbert's study of the fetishization of the female poet, and Gilbert Allen's "Millay and Modernism", which compares "high" modernism with popular modernism. It also includes an extensive range of reviews and essays on the poet from 1918 onwards, which shows how the poet and her work were viewed in the modernist context.

WALKER's collection of essays on modern women writers includes a provocative account of the way in which the commodification of the female body is reflected in the textual "body" of Millay's verse. Walker considers Millay's poetry in terms of a "literary spectacle" and Millay as "a poet of the body who presented the text and her own flesh as mirroring one another". Millay's work is worth attention for the ways in which it operates as an "index of cultural strains", and Walker suggests that women's poetry need not be read simply as a subversion of patriarchal discourses.

VICTORIA BAZIN

Miller, Arthur 1915–

American dramatist

Bigsby, C.W.E. (ed.), *Arthur Miller and Company*, London: Methuen, 1990
Carson, Neil, *Arthur Miller*, London: Macmillan, 1982; New York: St Martin's Press, 1982
Hayman, Ronald, *Arthur Miller*, London: Heinemann, 1970; New York: Frederick Ungar, 1972
Huftel, Sheila, *Arthur Miller: The Burning Glass*, New York: Citadel Press, 1965; London: W.H. Allen, 1965
Miller, Arthur, *Timebends: A Life*, New York: Grove Press, 1987; London: Methuen, 1988
Nelson, Benjamin, *Arthur Miller: Portrait of a Playwright*, New York: McKay, 1970; London: Peter Owen, 1970
Roudané, Matthew C. (ed.), *Conversations with Arthur Miller*, Jackson: University Press of Mississippi, 1987
Welland, Dennis, *Miller: A Study of His Plays*, London and New York: Methuen, 1979; 3rd, revised edition, as *Miller the Playwright*, 1985

Arthur Miller's voluminous writings on his own work, added to his suggestion that all of his plays are autobiographical, has tempted many critics to be over-biographical in their approach. Attention must be paid to Miller the man, but not at the risk of reading the plays as "secret histories". Together with the inclination to conflate life and work goes the tendency to imply that Miller is old-fashioned, irredeemably rooted in realism.

HUFTEL's early study is a good example of the biographical approach. While she provides a lucid and accessible summary of Miller's impact on postwar American theatre, she insists that: "the uniqueness, the split balance in the plays that is also their wholeness, probably comes from a division in Miller himself". Huftel contrasts Miller's work productively with that of the "victim drama" of Tennessee Williams: "where Williams sympathises, Miller more restlessly looks for a cure". At the same time, Miller avoids the didacticism of Bertolt Brecht. For Huftel, Miller expertly negotiates the two extremes of public platform and cloistered confessional.

NELSON sets out to evaluate Miller's "strengths and weaknesses", and this is indeed a judicious and balanced account of the *oeuvre*. Nelson draws his chapter-titles from Miller's life and work, but the final and finest section takes E.M. Forster's famous advice, "Only Connect", as its heading. Nelson claims that "all of Miller's writing is invisibly prefaced" by these words: "it is precisely this lack of connection, followed by the realisation of its importance, and the ultimate commitment to its achievement, which forms the underlying thematic pattern of Miller's plays". Nelson believes Miller to be "one of the most rebellious writers in the modern drama". Nelson is excellent on the plays, but less convincing on Miller's politics, or on their cultural and historical context. He has some perceptive comments on Miller's adaptation of *An Enemy of the People*, stating that he "misread Ibsen's play", and maintaining that "in its thematic leadenness Miller's adaptation seems far more academic and ponderous than the original".

HAYMAN's study opens with an interview that elicits some sharp observations on the plays in performance. The main text is taken up with Hayman's own analyses of the plays, from *All My Sons* to *The Price*. The final chapter, "Arthur Miller, Sartre and Society", claims a "strong case could be made for calling Miller the most Sartrean of living dramatists", but goes on to present Miller as Sartre's intellectual inferior, and to praise *Death of a Salesman* as the only play to depart successfully from the chronological sequence and the causality of the Sartrean social vision. Miller is at his best, according to Hayman, when he blends past and present and becomes more theatrical than social, that is, as a playwright rather than a political thinker.

CARSON sees Miller as a "religious writer", hence Miller's overriding concern with the fate of the individual. Carson is keen on the question of language, and celebrates "Miller's contribution to the development of a distinctively American stage rhetoric", arguing that his "best dialogue is that based on the slangy, wise-cracking speech of ill-educated or bilingual New York immigrants, mainly Jewish and Italian", within which he achieves "a remarkable range of feeling". Carson contends that Miller is less a "social" dramatist, nor even a "family" dramatist, than a dramatist of "men", and is critical of his representation of women. He concludes that critics drawn to Miller's work "see in the drama one of man's most powerful means of exploring his own destiny".

WELLAND places Miller firmly in context, contesting the notion that his work is outdated. He reflects on Miller's conventional dramatic forms and his canonical status, yet insists on his contemporary relevance. He regards Miller as "a concerned dramatist rather than a committed one; a thinking writer rather than the intellectual that he has often been called". Welland sees the plays as dealing primarily with family tensions, but unlike Edward Albee, Eugene O'Neill, Thornton Wilder, or Tennessee Williams, Miller "relates the frictions of family life to those of the macrocosm outside: his families live in a recognisably real world". Welland comments on Miller's Jewishness, and the apparent gap in his treatment of it between *Focus* and the post-1960s plays. Welland records a shift in the reception of Miller, from a playwright whose language was felt to be insufficiently heightened to one whose quotidian economy was praised.

BIGSBY collects the views of actors, designers, directors, reviewers, and writers in a volume marking Miller's 75th birthday. Contributors include Dustin Hoffman, Václav Havel, David Mamet, Doris Lessing, Joseph Heller and Harold Pinter. Mixed in with the soundbites and trivia are some beautifully observed portraits, and these are supplemented by an interview with the playwright, in which Miller offers some intriguing insights into productions of his work.

Finally, two volumes of primary material are of relevance to Miller's drama and its context. ROUDANÉ collects 39 interviews conducted between 1949 and 1986, arranged chronologically, including a fascinating exchange with Studs Terkel. Roudané's purpose is "to present what to my mind stand as the best Miller interviews since his emergence as a dramatist in the late 1940s". This is a compelling collection, especially enlightening on Miller's attitude to his contemporaries and his view of American theatre. And MILLER's autobiography is a crucial text, because of the biographical nature of his work and much of the criticism on it. Miller shows himself to be astonishingly knowledgeable about the workings of modern American theatre, and its distance from his own dramatic vision: "it seems to me now that I have always been caught between two theatres, the one that exists and the one that does not". Too often "invisible" at home, while enjoying a continuing international esteem, Miller reflects dispassionately, with much wit and good sense, on the place of theatre in American culture. Miller's obsession with memory is a constant refrain, and one which works to undermine the charge that his drama is time-bound.

WILLY MALEY

Milton, John 1608–1674

English poet and prose writer

General

Danielson, Dennis Richard (ed.), *The Cambridge Companion to Milton*, Cambridge and New York: Cambridge University Press, 1989

Freeman, James A., *Milton and the Martial Muse: "Paradise Lost" and European Traditions of War*, Princeton, New Jersey: Princeton University Press, 1981

Hill, Christopher, *Milton and the English Revolution*, London: Faber & Faber, 1977; New York: Viking Press, 1978

Hunter, William B., Jr. (general ed.), *A Milton Encyclopedia*, 9 vols., Lewisburg, Pennsylvania: Bucknell University Press, 1978–83; London: Associated University Presses, 1978–83

Kerrigan, William, *The Prophetic Milton*, Charlottesville: University Press of Virginia, 1974

Martz, Louis L., *Poet of Exile: A Study of Milton's Poetry*, New Haven and London: Yale University Press, 1980, revised as *Milton: Poet of Exile*, 1986

Nyquist, Mary, and Margaret W. Ferguson, *Re-Membering Milton: Essays on the Texts and the Traditions*, New York and London: Methuen, 1987

Patrides, C.A., (ed.), *Milton's Epic Poetry: Essays on "Paradise Lost and "Paradise Regained"*, Harmondsworth, Middlesex: Penguin, 1967

Walker, Julia M. (ed.), *Milton and the Idea of Woman*, Urbana: University of Illinois Press, 1988

The middle third of this century saw a powerful attempt, led by T. S. Eliot, F.R. Leavis, and others, to evict Milton from the canon. His diction and syntax were declared un-English and ritualistic, lacking sensitivity. Controversy about his theology and about the structure of his *Paradise Lost*, harking back to John Dryden, William Blake, and Percy Bysshe Shelley, suggested that consciously or not he was hostile to the God of Christianity and was of Satan's party. Now the "Miltonolaters" have won, and reinstated Milton as a great English poet, presenting him as a visionary prophet, an undefeated revolutionary, or a radical Christian humanist. Controversy nowadays centres on whether the poet is an egalitarian feminist or a stubborn, misogynistic bogey. There is also disagreement over the hero of *Samson Agonistes*: whether he is a saintly champion of God or a brutal, satanic destroyer.

HUNTER and his associate editors have assembled a company of more than 150 Milton scholars and critics to produce this excellent guide. The clear, readable essays range from critical and bibliographical introductions to the works, through studies of theological, literary, social, and intellectual interest, to comments on relevant persons, places and things. There are articles on such topics as "Style and Levels of Style", on "Metaphysics", on "Wrath", on "Mannerism", and on obscure figures like Lieuwe van Aitzema, a diplomat the poet met when he was Secretary of Foreign Tongues. This is an invaluable guide for junior students as well as specialists.

The volume of essays selected by PATRIDES (1967) on the epics is one of the best of its kind. Some of these are central to the mid-century controversy, such as the one by Leavis, who suggests that Milton's verse is inescapably monotonous, ritualistic, and alien, lacking Shakespearean "subtle and delicate life". Leavis constructs a writer defective in intelligence and imagination. Waldock argues that Milton set himself an impossible task in trying to represent an omniscient God who is just, as well as merciful. For Waldock, the strains are intolerable: "rifts begin to open . . . presently there is a chasm". The piece by Lovejoy on the Fortunate Fall became a cliché of scholarship, but is now questioned.

KERRIGAN sees Milton as more than a teacher who claims to be gifted and inspired by God: he argues that Milton believed he was a prophet and secretary of God. To call the poet merely a "Christian humanist" is to minimise the charismatic, mystic role of *propheta* he assumed, associating himself with Moses and Isaiah. Kerrigan is to be associated with a group of scholars who, like Wittreich and Lieb, stress the vatic, the sacerdotal element in the poet. Another group includes Burden, Bennett, and Radzinowicz, who emphasise "rationalism" and "humanism" in the poet. From their point of view, Kerrigan misrepresents a movement in the later work away from a passive role as transcriber of received truths to one that stresses "the light of reason" and the tempering of passions.

HILL, a Marxist historian, sets the poet in a richly detailed historical context and presents him as a radical social revolutionary, muzzled but unbowed by the Restoration. Hill shows that the censored, underground, "lower-class heretical culture" of Familists, Mortalists, Anti-Trinitarians, Ranters, Muggletonians, Levellers, and Hermeticists nourished the poet's radicalism and the political thrust of all his poetry. *Samson* is thus the defiant manifesto of an ever-optimistic revolutionary. Hill's reading of Milton the man, as someone who was courageous, "sweet and affable", kindly, "delightful company," and anything but a misogynist, corrects and enriches even standard biographies.

MARTZ ranges over Milton's three great volumes of poetry, with valuable reconsiderations of the poet's relationship with Ovid, Virgil, and Luis de Camões. He sees the books as a triptych ranging from the "green, youthful, chiefly joyous" early work of pastoral creation to the "austere, ascetic, reasoned, rigorous work of age". In *Paradise Lost*, "the sombre tones of a wise and suffering maturity enfold that vision within scenes that reveal the possibilities of tragic failure and redemptive hope". As he wrote it, Milton felt himself expatriated and exiled in his own country and doubly exiled from human community by his blindness. In *Paradise Regained*, through a process of renunciation and withdrawal, truth is given a voice while, in *Samson Agonistes*, an ancient literary form is developed to show "the workings of free will and grace".

FREEMAN shows that in proclaiming "that battle actualizes the most odious elements of human potential" and that there is no such thing as a "desirable conflict", Milton stood almost alone in Western thought, even in Christian tradition. Milton uses his knowledge of military manuals and literary *topoi* subtly, showing Satan and the demons to be ideal soldiers in theory and practice. "*Paradise Lost* speaks against war with such learning, complexity, and humaneness that it still towers over other statements in our long Western tradition". This study of "Milton the civilian" is especially relevant to the current controversy over the poet's attitude to violence in his *Samson*.

NYQUIST and FERGUSON come armed with instruments from Marx, Max Weber, Louis Althusser, and Michel Foucault to analyse Miltonic economy, production and authority; from Freud, Carl Jung, and Jacques Lacan to track sub-textual sexuality; from Ferdinand de Saussure, Roland Barthes, and Jacques Derrida to illuminate signs and signification. It was time for Milton to be submitted to such postmodern critical scrutiny. The Milton academy is dismissed in the Preface for its "theoretical innocence", and there are other flickers of smugness. This book is sometimes irritating; but it seldom fails to stimulate. Carolivia Herron's fine essay on African-American literature shows how the white "British Homer" can touch the marginalised consciousness in sad and sometimes bitter ways. There are interesting feminist readings by Nyquist and Cook, elegant new studies of Milton's language by Bradford and Marks, and other well-reasoned essays by Eagleton and Fish. The underlying dialogue about the role of the academy will remain a monument to a nervous contemporary *crise de conscience* even when Milton studies have moved on to fresh theories and issues new.

WALKER's collection drops the reader into the contemporary feminist controversy over Milton and the "idea of woman". The bias here favours those who, like Virginia Woolf, see Milton as a bogey whose misogyny intimidates women. For the editor, Milton "was ill-equipped to come to terms with woman as an idea". Since he could know woman only "as an intellectual text", woman emerges in his work "only as an idea not as an intellectual truth". For Halley, Milton strives for poetic transcendence as a "strategy for evading dangers imposed by the female figure". Woods finds "no evidence he has given woman's nature any real thought at all". Although there is a very sensitive reading by Ulreich of the poet's positive presentation of Dalila, on the whole a much more balanced case could be made for a feminist Milton.

DANIELSON's *Companion* followed Nyquist's collection, but the Milton academy, from whose ranks the distinguished contributors were drawn, did not choose to strike back. As it makes its "Authorised Version" of the writer, it averts its gaze from the whole postmodern enterprise, apart from a whisper or two from Mikhail Bakhtin and the occasional flicker of a signifier. The essays are uniformly lucid. They are personal responses to Milton's works, with occasional useful reactions to opposed critical positions. This collection is balanced and coherent. There is a particularly interesting survey of Milton's influence by Dustin Griffin, and, in a stylish article, Kerrigan speculates about Milton's place in intellectual history. The essays by Johnson, Corns, Christopher, and Radzinowicz deserve special notice. There is also a selective bibliographical commentary, guiding the student through the overwhelming lists of readings that precede it.

Paradise Lost

Danielson, Dennis Richard, *Milton's Good God: A Study in Literary Theodicy*, Cambridge and New York: Cambridge University Press, 1982

Empson, William, *Milton's God*, London: Chatto & Windus, 1961, revised 1965: Norfolk, Connecticut: New Directions, 1962; augmented edition, Cambridge and New York: Cambridge University Press, 1981

Lewalski, Barbara Kiefer, *"Paradise Lost" and the Rhetoric of Literary Forms*, Princeton, New Jersey: Princeton University Press, 1985

Lewis, C.S., *A Preface to "Paradise Lost"*, London: Oxford University Press, 1942, revised (also New York), 1960

Patrides, C.A., *Milton and the Christian Tradition*, Oxford: Clarendon Press, 1966; Hamden, Connecticut: Archon Books, 1979

Ricks, Christopher, *Milton's Grand Style*, Oxford: Clarendon Press, 1963

Summers, Joseph H., *The Muse's Method: An Introduction to "Paradise Lost"*, Cambridge, Massachusetts: Harvard University Press, 1962; London: Chatto & Windus, 1962

C.S. LEWIS attempted to answer the then new attacks on the poet, but he is not entirely convincing. He effectively concedes the case to Leavis: "he sees and hates the very same [stylistic practices] that I see and love". He distinguishes between primary epic and secondary epic. Style, in the latter, must provide solemnity and so is ritualistic. He finds fault with Milton's anthropomorphic God, and with the last two books, which are "untransmuted" into poetry. Although Lewis often preaches on his own account about God and man, good and evil, this remains a useful introductory work and is full of valuable literary-historical information about early epic form and diction, Augustinian theology, and Christian traditions.

EMPSON sees Milton's theodicy as a struggle "to make his God appear less wicked" and "less morally disgusting". His "poem is not good in spite of but because of its moral confusions". The legalistic Father, who schemes and cheats, is appalling. Adam and Eve fall because of Raphael. Empson writes splendidly in defence of Dalila. However, he strains bits and pieces of evidence and his readings are often arbitrary. This argument is brilliant, compelling, and worth encountering; but it is quite perverse.

SUMMERS eschews the specialist's apparatus of footnotes and bibliography in his elegant and urbane introduction. He aligns himself within the Milton controversy, but avoids polemic. Milton's style is not all "organ voice" or somehow automated, but is constantly varied with subject, and requires an alert reader: "burlesque, parody, and comedy were as essential as the heroic, the divine, and the tragic" and can work to show the latent absurdity in the "heroism" and "reality" of Hell and Satan, and also to reflect and imitate the major actions and emotions of human life. Satan has the trappings of the conventional military hero – precisely what Milton despises. The structural shift from the ten- to the twelve-book version was important, emphasising "the divine image of God's ways at their most providential". In his careful examination of the last two books, Summers shows how Adam, and the reader, learns of God's power, providence, methods, and of the ultimate good of man. "We must weep and we must dry our tears": the way is lonely but it is shared . . . and there is love.

RICKS attacks the attackers of the poet's style on their own ground: Milton's style is not grand and orotund, it is grand and powerful, but also subtle, precise, delicate, and expressive. He creates effects by other means than metaphor. His incongruities are often meaningful. His Latinate diction and syntax often emphasise or refine meaning. His style commands "nervous energy, subtle involutions, tentacular imagery and linguistic daring". It is rich with "innumerable tiny, significant, internal movements". And he is often memorably simple, laconic, and colloquial. Ricks's defence was not initially considered effective, but now this work is seen as seminal and persuasive.

PATRIDES (1966) shows that *Paradise Lost* is an emphatically Protestant rather than Christian epic. Claiming to reject traditions for the primacy of the Word in the Bible, nonetheless, Milton did invoke the Fathers if they supported his interpretation of Scripture. His poem is by no means a versification of the subordinationist theology of *Christian Doctrine*. He is often close to the Christian tradition of Paul and Augustine as in his view of grace and of the unity of the Godhead. He accepts mortalism following tradition. Patrides shows that the poet "used traditional ideas in such a way that they were transformed into seeming novelties", as he examines Milton's treatment of Creation, the Fall, Nature, Love, the linear Christian view of history, and the *Eschata*. This historical study is a work of immense erudition and critical sensitivity.

DANIELSON begins with a simplified outline to the complex philosophical issues he will explore, then gradually moves on to the inevitable complexities involved in writing of Creation, chaos, pre- and post-lapsarian life, divine foreknowledge, Free Will, and determinism. His main concern is with theodicy, the justification of providence, given the problem of evil. He demonstrates the theological traps set by the doctrine of the "Fortunate Fall", so long a cliché of Milton scholarship. Milton's God is material, and Creation is *ex deo*. The poet is an Arminian in his views on Grace, predestination, and Free Will, a moderate between the extremes of Calvinism and Pelagianism. As a declared Christian, the author believes there "is a God who is omnipotent and wholly good" and that "the theological problem of evil can be solved". His book deals with these difficult issues in a style that is lucid and highly readable.

LEWALSKI (1985) brings her great scholarly knowledge of genre to show "the range and comprehensiveness of the forms" sensitively adapted by Milton within the epic framework. She shows how he "makes constant, complex, and highly conscious use of the Renaissance genre system, and the cultural significances and moral values associated with the different kinds, as a means of imagining his unimaginable subject". Heroic tragedy, romance quest, Ovid, and the Book of Exodus serve to shape Satan's epic narrative, while pastoral, georgic, and lyric hymns present the angels. An even greater generic multiplicity helped Milton to imagine and suggest his literary God and Son. A dignified pastoral mode presents prelapsarian Edenic life, while genres of complaint, elegy, and lament are more appropriate after the Fall.

Other Poetry and The Prose

Barker, Arthur E., *Milton and the Puritan Dilemma, 1641–1660*, Toronto and Buffalo, New York: University of Toronto Press, 1942

Leishman, J.B., *Milton's Minor Poems*, edited by Geoffrey Tillotson, London: Hutchinson, 1969

Lewalski, Barbara Kiefer, *Milton's Brief Epic: The Genre, Meaning and Art of "Paradise Regained"*, Providence, Rhode Island: Brown University Press, 1966; London: Methuen, 1966

Lieb, Michael, and John T. Shawcross (eds.), *Achievements of the Left Hand: Essays on the Prose of John Milton*, Amherst: University of Massachusetts Press, 1974

Radzinowicz, Mary Ann, *Toward "Samson Agonistes": The Growth of Milton's Mind*, Princeton, New Jersey: Princeton University Press, 1978

BARKER'S classic study traces the transformation of the Horton poet into the "immeasurably greater poet of the last poems". The prose is a sincere and "painful attempt ... to achieve coherence of thought in the midst of social disintegration". Milton was not a logical thinker, sometimes grasping at convenient ideas in the heat of polemic. His thought moved steadily from the Puritan Right to an independent position on the extreme Left. He also moved from stressing the depravity of reason in the early pamphlets to emphasising reason's potentialities in *Areopagitica* and later. When Milton defined liberty, he distinguished between fallen nature and nature rectified: true natural liberty, since the Fall, is the liberty of Grace. It is for those who act in accordance with the perfect law, cleared in their hearts by the Spirit. It is this that justifies resistance to unjust magistrates. He did not accept the harsh, orthodox theory of regeneration, but he did believe in an aristocracy of Grace, since not everyone would achieve regeneration, without which they could not claim Christian liberty. Discipline must come from within, and heavenly privileges depended on the exercise of that discipline according to absolute divine truth.

LEISHMAN, with his vast knowledge of European literature, is close to being Milton's "fit" or ideal reader. He shows how, even when young, Milton was one of our greatest artists of language, never abandoning his vocation as a moral or religious teacher. Although he was like Ben Jonson in his respect for the craft of poetry, and in "l'Allegro" and "Il Penseroso" he had something of John Donne's wit and dialectic, he was primarily the disciple of Edmund Spenser. *Comus* has affinities with pastoral drama and court masque, but is really *sui generis*. Milton is a master of spiritual architecture, and writes poetry more like Shakespeare's than any other writer does. *Lycidas* is a more original, unprecedented kind of poem than those who classify it as pastoral elegy realise. Milton's originality is built on an indebtedness to his predecessors to an extent we can barely understand today.

Some critics have argued that *Paradise Regained* is not an epic but a moral allegory or a psychological drama. Although no classical epics exist as models for Milton's brief epic, LEWALSKI (1966) establishes the validity of the genre, demonstrating the authority of the Bible and Hebrew poetry, and pointing out its formal epic elements. A long tradition of exegesis held that the Book of Job was a heroic poem, equal to the classics in poetic sublimity and narrative technique. Christ combats Satan in a great duel, an epic martial combat of temptations overcome. He learns his own nature and mission; his mediatorial role as prophet is defined and tested; he learns kingship over self, and about his public office as priest and king. Milton produced a poem that was unique, but set in a tradition of which it was the crowning achievement in decorum, epic dimension, and style.

RADZINOWICZ's densely textured study places *Samson Agonistes* "in Milton's intellectual development". She analyses the tragedy in the context of the other works, with special focus on: his logic or dialectic; his conception of history "as a pattern which can be interpreted as a tragic design"; his politics; his ethics, with particular reference to the influences of the Book of Job and the Psalms; his theology, with cautious reference to his *Christian Doctrine* and his biblical proof-texts; and his poetics in their Aristotelian and Renaissance contexts. The play is "a drama of the English Revolution" and also the personal drama of a sinner's rise from sickness to spiritual health. Samson delivers himself as well as his nation. He learns through patience and faith how to renew and rediscover his relationship with God. In an appendix, there is a convincing argument for dating the play late, still a disputed question. This impressive work of scholarship is the definitive defence of Samson as a Christian hero and champion of God. However, the author discounts or fails to notice the gathering controversy over Samson's status and Milton's intentions, and the growing tendency to see Samson as a brutal destroyer, unforgiving and ignorant of Christian charity.

The collection of essays by LIEB and SHAWCROSS on Milton's prose is very useful. Their emphasis is on content rather than on style, and they help the reader to understand Milton the intellectual, the revolutionary, and also the poet. Hunter shows that *Christian Doctrine*, with its subordinationist positions and its Arminian Christology, is addressed to European branches of the Reformed or Calvinistic churches. Huntley traces the changes in Milton's conception of the function of the poet and poetry as this changes from 1642 to 1659. For Shawcross, the writer of *The Tenure of Kings and Magistrates* was an idealistic radical, rejecting compromise. Wittreich shows that the pamphleteer's fit audience was not yet the "few" he addressed in his last poems but the spiritual élite of Europe; he develops an ideal image of a true, wise orator drawn from Cicero and Quintilian, but modified by Christ and St Paul. In a valuable bibliographical appendix, John Shawcross surveys all the prose works in detail.

DEREK N.C. WOOD

Modernism: Fiction

Auerbach, Erich, *Mimesis: The Representation of Reality in Western Literature*, translated by Willard R. Trask, Princeton, New Jersey: Princeton University Press, 1953

Beach, J.W., *The Twentieth Century Novel: Studies in Technique*, New York and London: Century, 1932

Eysteinssonn, Astradur, *The Concept of Modernism*, Ithaca, New York: Cornell University Press, 1990

Friedman, Alan, *The Turn of the Novel: The Transition to Modern Fiction*, New York and London: Oxford University Press, 1966

Gilbert, Sandra M., and Susan Gubar, *No Man's Land: The Place of the Woman Writer in the Twentieth Century*, 3 vols. (*The War of the Words*, *Sexchanges*, *Letters from the Front*), New Haven, Connecticut, and London: Yale University Press, 1988–94

Isaak, Jo Anna, *The Ruin of Representation in Modernist Art and Texts*, Ann Arbor, Michigan: UMI Research Press, 1986

Kermode, Frank, *The Sense of an Ending: Studies in the Theory of Fiction*, London and New York: Oxford University Press, 1966

Levenson, Michael, *Modernism and the Fate of Individuality: Character and Novelistic Form from Conrad to Woolf*, Cambridge and New York: Cambridge University Press, 1991

Lukács, Georg, *The Meaning of Contemporary Realism*, translated by John and Necke Mander, London: Merlin Press, 1963

Malamud, Randy, *The Language of Modernism*, Ann Arbor, Michigan: UMI Research Press, 1989

Meisel, Perry, *The Myth of the Modern: A Study in British Literature and Criticism after 1850*, New Haven, Connecticut, and London: Yale University Press, 1987

Pecora, Vincent P., *Self and Form in Modern Narrative*, Baltimore: Johns Hopkins University Press, 1989

Scott, Bonnie Kime (ed.), *The Gender of Modernism: A Critical Anthology*, Bloomington: Indiana University Press, 1990

Stevenson, Randall, *Modernist Fiction: An Introduction*, Lexington: University Press of Kentucky, 1992; Hemel Hempstead, Hertfordshire: Harvester Wheatsheaf, 1992

In the first major study of literary modernism, *Axel's Castle* (1931), Edmund Wilson did not distinguish between fiction, poetry, and drama. Marcel Proust, James Joyce, and Gertrude Stein were placed alongside Arthur Rimbaud, Paul Valéry, and W.B. Yeats. Modernism, he argued, was a second wave of symbolism, which, in turn, was a second wave of Romanticism. In the first major study of modernist fiction, BEACH took a similarly long view, placing the work of the modernists he discussed in relationship to naturalist and realist writers in the nineteenth century. But while Wilson did this to describe what he considered to be the common limitations of the modernists, who, he claimed, rejected the rational aims and the commitment to everyday life of the naturalist and realist traditions for the aestheticism and irrationalism of the symbolists, Beach found the techniques of the modernists – the use of symbol and the stream of consciousness – to be authentic responses to the relativist and post-Freudian sensibility of the period. He placed Joseph Conrad and D.H. Lawrence under the heading of "Impressionism", Joyce under "Post-Impressionism", and Virginia Woolf under "Expressionism".

It is remarkable how persistent these initial judgements have been: not only reproduced, albeit with ever-increasing sophistication, in the criticism of the postwar period, but also in ways that reflect the political disposition of the critic and the political climate of the day. In "The Brown Stocking", the last and most subtle chapter of his magisterial study of the history of Western representation in literature, AUERBACH echoed Wilson's judgement by finding in the modernism of Joyce and Woolf (who was the focus of his discussion) a weakening of traditional modes of representation as both writers shifted from the unity of form to the unity of symbolisation.

This was a position reflected even more forcibly by Marxist critics. In the most influential Marxist analysis of modernist fiction from Franz Kafka, Joyce, and Robert Musil to William Faulkner and Samuel Beckett, LUKÁCS criticised modernism for its subjectivism, its "static" view of the human condition, its destruction of character, its obsession with extreme and pathological states, and, above all, its lack of a belief in history. Lukacs' s views are now often discounted as crude and simplistic, but they still warrant attention because they pose substantial objections to the practices of modernist fiction.

FRIEDMAN's wide-ranging study was the first major postwar study to examine modernist novelists – principally Conrad, E.M. Forster, and Lawrence – through a contrast with their nineteenth-century precursors. Like Beach, he found that the contrast worked very much in favour of the modernists: for modernist novels were not only an authentic moral expression of the contemporary situation but were formally open and unresolved in ways in which many nineteenth-century novels were not. Thomas Hardy, he argued, was an important intermediate figure in the development of modernist fiction.

KERMODE made use of the same distinctions, but he differed by finding that modernist novelists (Lawrence and Wyndham Lewis) and modernist poets (Yeats and T.S. Eliot) tended, in spite of their own scepticism, towards closed fictions – in this case, apocalyptic fictions of the end derived from the millennial anxiety out of which early modernism had been born. In a study that has influenced the writing of fiction as well as criticism, Kermode effected an important revision, not only making distinctions between open and closed modernist fictions, but also placing Joyce as the central, liberal figure within the modernist canon.

From the outset, critics of modernist fiction have been as much concerned with the fragmented nature of modernity as with the fiction it has inspired. From the 1970s onwards, as they marked the end of modernity and the birth of a new, postmodern age, critics have examined very explicitly the relationships between the texts of modernism and the contexts of modernity. PECORA, drawing upon Theodor Adorno, Walter Benjamin, and Lukács, related modernist fiction to the contradictions of modern technological society in the capitalist era of imperialism. In a series of immensely subtle analyses of Henry James, Conrad, and Joyce, he described the problematic loss of social agency he found present in the texts of the modernist canon:

> There is absolutely nothing straightforward about imperialism in Conrad's narratives; they are above all the formal representation of the paralysis of the bourgeois subject in the face of a rationalized socio-political reality that fully accepts, indeed agrees with, that subject's opposition to unjust practices while reducing opposition to the aporetic ramblings of a damaged storyteller.

This is a complex but important reading because it relates the crisis of modernist fiction to the crisis of bourgeois society in ways that are infinitely less reductive than those of Lukács.

The most substantial revisionist view, however, has been offered by feminist critics. In their three-volume study, GILBERT and GUBAR have not only related the specific styles and content of male modernist writers to the emergence of women into the literary market, both as consumers and as producers, but have also found in the writing of the female modernists a subversive celebration (and enactment) of female language. These readings are accomplished within richly observed and widely researched social and cultural histories of the period, which place the writing of male and female modernists in an illuminatingly new context. Gilbert and Gubar, in one of the most important contributions to the history of modernism, have shown convincingly the breadth, variety, and complexity of the contribution of women's writing to literary modernism. In her anthology, SCOTT follows suit. This includes brief extracts from the writings of over 20 American and British female modernists (mostly novelists), each one prefaced by a brief critical essay written by a leading feminist critic, with an extensive bibliography of primary and secondary material. This is an indispensable guide, both for the general reader and for the advanced student. The anthology, which includes the work of a few well-known writers, and many neglected ones, contains an important account of the complicated networks through which many of the authors in the anthology were linked and sustained.

One of the consequences of the feminist emphasis both upon sexual difference and the subversive effect of the fiction of female modernists in relation to patriarchy has been a reconsideration of the relation of the fiction of male modernists to the patriarchal law. ISAAK's interdisciplinary account of modernist practice in painting (cubism, constructivism) and modernist fictional practice (Joyce, Lewis, and Stein) persuasively places the disordering of syntax in the work of male modernists alongside the work of female modernists within a common anti-patriarchal endeavour. MALAMUD's analysis of the fragmented and fragmentary language of male and female modernists (Woolf, Eliot, and Joyce) similarly finds in their radical departure from conventional language the bases not only of their greater truthfulness but also of their critique of what is untruthful in conventional language. These are demanding but lucidly written and rewarding studies.

MEISEL's study, which acknowledges its debt to the deconstructionists, reflects their distrust of literary history, with its dependence not only upon the clear-cut concept of the cultural period but also upon the idea of novelty, which sustains it – the myth of the modern. To counteract these tendencies, he distinguishes between those modernists (Matthew Arnold, Lawrence, and Eliot) whose sense of belatedness he believes resulted in defensiveness and assertiveness, and those (Forster, Joyce, and Woolf) who seized upon the opportunity of belatedness as an opportunity for textual (and intertextual) extravagance and play. The importance of Meisel's treatment lies in the richness of its descriptions of modernist textuality and intertextuality. It is, nevertheless, possible to see here the repetition in more sophisticated guise of earlier distinctions between closed and open form.

Most recent critics, however, have not turned away from literary history or from the concept of the period. In his invaluable introduction to modernist fiction, STEVENSON relates changes in form, subjectivity, the representation of consciousness, and the uses of language (in James, Conrad, Ford Madox Ford, Lawrence, Dorothy Richardson, May Sinclair, Joyce, Lewis, and Woolf) to new concepts and new experiences of time and space both at the beginning of the century and after World War I. Written for a more advanced readership, EYSTEINSSONN's comprehensive account explicates the work of the most significant European and American theorists of modernism from the 1930s to the present day, relates the impact of their ideas upon the practice of literary study in the twentieth century, and examines the radical and conservative appropriations of modernist ideas and practices in the post-modern(ist) period. This work also contains an excellent bibliography. LEVENSON, whose *A Genealogy of Modernism* (1984) proved one of the most widely admired of recent accounts of British literary modernism because it drew a distinction between the relativism of the literary practices of the modernists and the absolutism of their critical judgements, shows an equal finesse in his 1991 study of the different ways in which British modernist novelists (Conrad, Ford, Lawrence, Joyce, Lewis, Woolf) constructed their central characters. The transformation of form in modernist fiction, he argued, had a necessary impact upon the drawing of character. Reversing Pecora's emphases, he relates the problem of characterisation in modernist fiction, succinctly and subtly, as much to inner (formal) developments as to external (social, historical, and philosophical) ones.

ALISTAIR DAVIES

Modernism: Poetry

Baker, Houston A., Jr., *Modernism and the Harlem Renaissance*, Chicago: University of Chicago Press, 1987

Ellmann, Maud, *The Poetics of Impersonality: T.S. Eliot and Ezra Pound*, Brighton, Sussex: Harvester Press, 1987; Cambridge, Massachusetts: Harvard University Press, 1987

North, Michael, *The Political Aesthetic of Yeats, Eliot, and Pound*, Cambridge and New York: Cambridge University Press, 1991

Perkins, David, *A History of Modern Poetry: From the 1890s to the High Modernist Mode*, Cambridge, Massachusetts: Belknap Press of Harvard University Press, 1976
Perkins, David, *A History of Modern Poetry: Modernism and After*, Cambridge, Massachusetts: Belknap Press of Harvard University Press, 1987
Ross, Andrew, *The Failure of Modernism: Symptoms of American Poetry*, New York: Columbia University Press, 1986
Schwartz, Sanford, *The Matrix of Modernism: Pound, Eliot, and Early Twentieth-Century Thought*, Princeton, New Jersey: Princeton University Press, 1985
Scott, Bonnie Kime, *The Gender of Modernism: A Critical Anthology*, Bloomington: Indiana University Press, 1990
Smith, Stan, *The Origins of Modernism: Eliot, Pound, Yeats and the Rhetoric of Renewal*, Hemel Hempstead, Hertfordshire: Harvester Wheatsheaf, 1994
Stead, C.K., *Pound, Yeats, Eliot, and the Modernist Movement*, London: Macmillan, 1986; New Brunswick, New Jersey: Rutgers University Press, 1986

Modernism in poetry is a vast subject, and there has been a constant state of literary and ideological struggle over the boundaries and demarcation lines. Many of the established orthodoxies concerning poetic modernism derived from the polemics of the poets themselves, like Ezra Pound, T.S. Eliot, and W.B. Yeats. However, in recent times, these hegemonic versions of modernism perpetuated by a masculine, conservative, and middle-class ideology have begun to be eroded by versions of modernism that perceive a far wider and more diverse activity than has previously been represented. This survey of the critical material seeks to draw upon the variety of positions taken with regard to these debates.

PERKINS' study is a monumental survey, which traces the development of "high-modernist" poetry from the 1890s to the 1970s, in two volumes. The first volume outlines the manner in which the Romantic, popular style of poetry was abandoned or altered in three phases – the aesthetic-impressionist-symbolist poetry of the 1890s; the conservative reaction of "popular modernism" during 1910–18 in Yeats, William Carlos Williams, and Pound; and the "high modernism" evident in Eliot's *Poems* (1919) and Pound's *Hugh Selwyn Mauberley* (1920). The volume closes with a chapter on Yeats, who is seen as a major figure throughout these different phases. The second volume charts the continuing effort of poets since the 1920s to modify or break away from the high-modernist style, and studies such writers and movements as the 1930s' generation, Dylan Thomas, Philip Larkin, the Movement, and the 1950s' and 1960s' reaction against the genteel codification of high-modernist values associated with New Criticism. The two volumes constitute a useful guide to the chronological development of modernism in poetry, as they seek to broaden the canon of modernist poets, and to place their careers within an historical, social, and political context.

More specific in its focus, STEAD charts in three stages the rise of modernism from 1900 to 1925, the politics of modernism during 1925–50, and a postscript to modernism since 1950, focusing on Donald Davie's definition of modernism. An extension of an earlier book, this study is particularly interested in the rise of modernism in the early work of Eliot and Pound, and there is a detailed reading of the drafting of *The Waste Land* and Pound's involvement in it. In attempting to define modernist poetic practice according to what it is not, the author uses Yeats and Thomas Hardy as points of comparison and contrast, arguing that they were "two moderns who were not Modernists". In a book that is overtly sympathetic to the modernist poetry of Eliot and Pound, Stead perceives 1925–50 as a period when modernists were under increasing pressure to respond to public issues directly, particularly politics and economics. In the cases of W.H. Auden, Eliot and Pound, he describes all three making retreats and shifts of belief and position with regard to modernist discourse. Despite its limitations and somewhat orthodox approach, the book nevertheless makes an informative contribution.

NORTH's monograph is far more challenging and incisive in its interrogation of the scandalous and embarrassing politics of the high-modernist poets, and it considers the desperate attempts by critics to "save" the poetry of Yeats, Eliot, and Pound from contamination. Informed by Marxist thought, North focuses on the function of history for these poets, demonstrating how it formed part of their attack on liberalism and capitalism. These poets looked to the aesthetic sphere for a reconciliation of their political problematics, and North argues that their political failure rested upon their inability to join, in their aesthetics, the political antitheses of authoritarian structures and isolated individuals. Their ultimate value for North rests in the way that they struggled to keep their problems in view. An excellent study of the politics of modernist aesthetics, this is a carefully documented, closely argued, scholarly monograph, which presents three incisive studies of the key English-speaking high-modernist poets.

On the subject of the "failure of modernism", ROSS's principal argument is that it results from a confusion of subjectivism with subjectivity: "modernism ... equates a philosophical (or theoretical) attack on the epistemological and metaphysical tradition of subjectivism with a literary (or practical) attempt to dispossess or to purge poetic discourse of subjectivity *tout court*". Consequently, the book focuses on the successive attempts by modernist writers to eradicate subjectivity from poetic form and language, in order to "establish a discourse that is assumed to be more authentic or 'true' to our experience of the natural world". How and why the experience of failure is inscribed within modernist writing becomes the central focus of studies of Eliot, Charles Olson, and John Ashbery. That modernism perceived subjectivity to be a problem that could be solved by reforming language itself proves to be a provocative and stimulating thesis, in a book that opens up a number of significant philosophical preoccupations of modernist poetics.

The philosophical foundations of Eliot's and Pound's modernist poetry forms the basis of SCHWARTZ's study. The affiliations between modernist poetics and the contemporaneous developments in philosophy by people like Henri Bergson, William James, F.H. Bradley, and Nietzsche are indisputable, but rather than looking at the single influence of one philosopher on one author, this book looks at how a poet participates in developments that may be difficult to define but are nevertheless "in the air". Hence, a matrix is outlined, which seeks to demonstrate that the principal stylistic and conceptual characteristics of modernist poetry are not mere accidents or isolated arbitrary phenomena, but emerge within significant changes within a whole range of fields. The study focuses principally on the tension between abstraction and experience evident in modernist thought, and produces an interesting and informative new perspective on how modernist ideas, such as authorial impersonality, the poetic image, and the autonomy of the literary text, emerged from an engagement with philosophical and aesthetic ideas from other disciplines.

In contrast to the orthodox critical approach of Schwartz, ELLMANN interrogates the theory of impersonality evident in Eliot's and Pound's poetry from a self-consciously poststructuralist and psychoanalytic stance. In this way the book has two foci – the "vicissitudes of impersonality in the *theories* of Eliot and Pound" and "how their poems 'murder and create' their fictive selves". Attending to the processes by which these poets' texts *construct* forms of subjectivity, rather than merely *reflecting* personalities already constituted, Ellmann perceives poetry as "the workshop of the self" for Eliot and Pound, "where personal identity is both constructed and dismantled". After considering Eliot's relation to Bergson, the book explores Eliot's early poems, *The Waste Land*, and the *Four Quartets*. It then turns to Pound's *Personae*, but particularly to *Mauberley* and the *Cantos*. A major critical text on these poets, it is strikingly innovative, suggestive, and stylish.

Although not openly affiliated to Ellmann's poststructuralist approach, SMITH's study clearly owes methodological debts to such ideas in his attempt to uncover the "origins" of modernism. He argues that "modernism as an ideological operation refuses its origins in the national, class and gender politics of its day, promising through the 'mythical method' egress from the nightmare of history . . . situating itself both before and after but never *in* the realm of historical Event". In a lively, informative, and clearly written book, Smith examines the modernists' compulsion to date themselves as part of their preoccupation with memory, history, and ordering, so crucial to the modernist sense of poetry. Focusing on Eliot, Pound, and Yeats, Smith argues that whereas modernism is a recuperation of origins to explain the present, postmodernism treats the past as suppositional and as a figment to preserve illusions. Modernism, therefore, Smith concludes, "is a retrospective artefact, a movement constituted backwards". As do North and Ellmann, Smith analyses how modernism has been constructed retrospectively to preserve certain contemporary hegemonic aesthetic and political ideologies.

A similar interrogation of how modernism in poetry has been ideologically constituted occurs in SCOTT's analysis of how modernism has been unconsciously gendered as masculine. The intention of this anthology "is to demonstrate that modernism was inflected, in ways we can only now begin to appreciate, by gender". The text demonstrates a different "matrix of modernism" in poetry, as it establishes the tangled web of interrelationships and influences between male and female modernist writers. In contradistinction to the "men of 1914" (Pound, Eliot, Yeats), this text necessitates a reassessment of the canon of modernism, a reconsideration of who, why, and what is defined as modernist in poetry, as the previously suppressed imperatives of gender and race are reintegrated into critical analysis.

Whereas Scott focuses on gender, BAKER focuses on race. The Harlem Renaissance has often been disparaged for its supposed failure to produce "modern" art of the order of Anglo-American modernist literature. Focusing on the work of writers like Booker T. Washington, W.E.B. Du Bois, and Alain Locke and his 1920s' anthology *The New Negro*, Baker demonstrates that the traditional assumptions and critical approaches to modernism are inappropriate for an assessment of African-American cultural achievements. Baker elaborates how a distinctively African-American modernism heralded such phenomena as sure signs of progress, an escape from feudal slavery, and an occasion for their entry onto the stage of conscious modern history.

TIM S. WOODS

See also **Imagism**

Moore, George 1852–1933

Anglo-Irish novelist, short-story writer, and art critic

Brown, Malcolm, *George Moore: A Reconsideration*, Seattle: University of Washington Press, 1955
Cave, Richard Allen, *A Study of the Novels of George Moore*, Gerrards Cross, Buckinghamshire: Colin Smythe, 1978; New York: Barnes & Noble, 1978
Dunleavy, Janet Egleson (ed.), *George Moore in Perspective*, Naas, County Kildare: Malton, 1983; Totowa, New Jersey: Barnes & Noble, 1983
Grubgeld, Elizabeth, *George Moore and the Autogenous Self: The Autobiography and Fiction*, Syracuse, New York: Syracuse University Press, 1994
Hone, Joseph, *The Life of George Moore*, London: Victor Gollancz, 1936; New York: Macmillan, 1936; reprinted, Westport, Connecticut: Greenwood Press, 1973
Hughes, Douglas (ed.), *The Man of Wax: Critical Essays on George Moore*, New York: New York University Press, 1971

Best known as a novelist, George Moore was also prominently and often controversially involved in a number of the key artistic movements of his time – French Impressionism, English naturalistic fiction, and the Irish Literary Revival. The scope of his activities, the size and range of his *oeuvre*, and his compulsive revising of his works have perhaps militated against his having received his full critical due.

BROWN's study remains the most comprehensive and most satisfactory overall view of the relationship between Moore's life and art. Beginning with a judicious biographical account of Moore's Anglo-Irish lineage and heritage, and of his formative Paris period, the work goes on to chart the successive influences of Émile Zola and Walter Pater on the novelist's development. Moore's participation in the Irish Literary Revival is then chronicled, and the manner in which "the mood of the Celtic twilight profoundly affected Moore's imagination" are detailed. The ultimate expression of Moore's aesthetic principles are revealed in the "last novels . . . built on pure motion, pure pageant". An assessment of Moore's criticism completes the study. Much is made throughout of Moore's genius for making enemies, not only in a biographical sense, but also from a critical standpoint, since Moore's outspokenness is also credited with having had a salutary effect on – particularly English, as opposed to Irish – conceptions of fictional form and Victorian conventions of literary decorum.

CAVE divides his far-reaching treatment of Moore's novels into three sections, reflecting the three different phases of Moore's career as a novelist. The first of these phases is the best-known, and the commentary on such works as *A Mummer's Wife* and *Esther Waters* establishes the controversial novelty of Moore's early artistic aims. The study's second section evaluates Moore's development as a novelist, with particular emphasis on refinements in his sense of form and style. Richard Wagner's influence on Moore is shown to be crucial to his artistic growth. The claim that "it was his deepening understanding of the literary possibilities of Wagner's ideas and method which saved Moore from the imaginative poverty into which he had sunk" is elaborately substantiated. The culmination of this phase is *The Lake*, an extensive analysis of which opens the study's third section. Wagner is also credited with Moore's choice of historical subject for his last three novels, a discussion of which concludes this section. Moore's status in the minds of younger novelists such as James Joyce and Virginia Woolf is mentioned. The latter's comment that Moore's fiction constitutes a revolution in feeling is cited as a fitting judgment on his achievement.

DUNLEAVY's collection of essays, published to mark the 50th anniversary of Moore's death, is an attempt to trace his "aesthetic journey." It contains useful information concerning Moore's family and social history, and his Paris and Dublin periods. Articles on those subjects are followed by a number of critical appraisals of various aspects of Moore's literary significance. Of particular interest are articles linking Moore with various other important Irish writers, especially James Joyce and Samuel Beckett. There is also an article analysing the novels of Moore's last years. From a strictly scholarly point of view, the most important item in the collection is an appendix dealing with the almost incurably vexed state of Moore's bibliography.

GRUBGELD has produced an important study of a hitherto surprisingly neglected aspect of Moore's output. As well as being the author of numerous works of autobiography, Moore also made use of the concept of the *persona* – beloved of writers of his period – in ways that are artistically intriguing and theoretically significant. This study takes a broad view of the autobiographical dimension of Moore's work, finding the self-fashioning, or autogenous self, in his fiction as well as in the autobiographical texts as such. The approach distinguishes different aspects of autogeny, and analyses their complexity and development across a range of texts. A full spectrum of how "his work incorporates within itself both a profound recognition of the historical world and a declaration of his own self-determination" is thereby revealed. This study is a sophisticated and illuminating study of not just the autobiographical Moore but of the portrait of the artist that all his works project.

HONE's remains the standard biography. Drawing on deep familiarity with Moore's family and social circle, and also on the author's own experience of the Dublin of Moore's day, the work is a comprehensive record of the subject's life and times. The familiar chronological trajectory of Moore's career is traced with particular authority, given the author's complete access to Moore's papers and to the memories of his friends and acquaintances. Among the latter is Moore's housekeeper, whose recollections of her employer during his last years constitutes one of the biography's two closing chapters; the other is a critical assessment of Moore's artistic achievement by Desmond Shawe-Taylor, which provides a narrative account of Moore's development and concludes that his works are ultimately "eccentric" to the English literary tradition. The volume concludes with a brief but convenient bibliography.

HUGHES's comprehensive collection of essays to some extent supplements Hone's biography, by containing various accounts of personal encounters with Moore. This largely anecdotal material is followed by some notable critical essays, which do a good deal to provide the student with an initial grasp of such fundamental issues in Moore criticism as the influence of French naturalism, literary Wagnerism, and the landmark status in English literary culture of *Esther Waters*. Other essays cover Moore's short stories, autobiographies, and late fiction. There is a useful chronology of Moore's life and career.

GEORGE O'BRIEN

Moore, Marianne 1887–1972

American poet

Bloom, Harold (ed.), *Marianne Moore*, New York: Chelsea House, 1987
Costello, Bonnie, *Marianne Moore: Imaginary Possessions*, Cambridge, Massachusetts: Harvard University Press, 1981
Goodridge, Celeste, *Hints and Disguises: Marianne Moore and Her Contemporaries*, Iowa City: University of Iowa Press, 1989
Heuving, Jeanne, *Omissions Are Not Accidents: Gender in the Art of Marianne Moore*, Detroit: Wayne State University Press, 1992
Holley, Margaret, *The Poetry of Marianne Moore: A Study in Voice and Value*, Cambridge and New York: Cambridge University Press, 1987
Martin, Taffy, *Marianne Moore: Subversive Modernist*, Austin: University of Texas Press, 1986
Parisi, Joseph (ed.), *Marianne Moore: The Art of a Modernist*, Ann Arbor: UMI Research Press, 1986
Slatin, John, *"The Savage's Romance": The Poetry of Marianne Moore*, University Park: Pennsylvania State University Press, 1986
Tomlinson, Charles (ed.), *Marianne Moore: A Collection of Critical Essays*, Englewood Cliffs, New Jersey: Prentice-Hall, 1969
Willis, Patricia (ed.), *Marianne Moore: Woman and Poet*, Orono: National Poetry Foundation, University of Maine, 1990

Marianne Moore rarely occupies a central position in critical reconstructions of modernism, and up until fairly recently she had also been excluded from feminist revisions of the modernist canon. Early feminist criticism of Moore, based as it was on a reflectionist model of reading, tended to characterize Moore's impersonal poetics as a betrayal of feminine identity. Thus in Suzanne Juhasz's *Naked and Fiery Forms*, Moore's poetry is interpreted as a retreat and denial of female experience. Adrienne Rich finds little comfort in Moore as a literary precursor, characterizing the older poet as "maidenly, elegant, intellectual, discreet". However, in recent years, a number of critical assessments of the poet confirm her as, in Wallace Steven's words, "a poet that matters" and her reputation as a conformist is being challenged quite convincingly.

A wide-ranging set of views on Moore is provided in four essay collections, edited by Tomlinson, Bloom, Parisi, and Willis, respectively.

TOMLINSON's collection includes responses by Pound, Stevens, and Williams to Moore's work, as well as many of the most important New-Critical responses from critics such as John Crowe Ransom, Kenneth Burke, and Randall Jarrell. It is worth consulting Tomlinson for a sense of how the poet was received by her contemporaries and by those engaged in constructing modernism in America in the 1930s and 1940s.

BLOOM's collection reprints a number of essays by critics well versed in modernism and Moore's poeticism, such as Hugh Kenner, John Slatin, and Bonnie Costello. Bloom's own Introduction is notable for its estimation of Moore as "not quite of the eminence of Frost, Stevens, Crane", and also for his dismissal of certain kinds of feminist critical practice.

PARISI's collection of critical essays is, in many ways, an antidote to Bloom's more pedestrian collection. Here a number of critics who are relatively new to Moore criticism offer fresh insights into the poet and her work. Particularly successful is Richard Howard's "The Monkey Business of Modernism" and Susan Gilbert's discussion of the critical construction of Moore and Edna St Vincent Millay.

WILLIS has gathered together an enormous range of essays in the volume she has edited. A great deal of original research appears in this collection, and perhaps most valuable of all is the comprehensive bibliography at the end of the volume. This is an excellent resource for any Moore scholar.

COSTELLO's book-length study of Moore's poetry reinvents her as a poet of "gusto" from whom language is self-referential, playful, and excessive. Costello's Moore is far from the modest and "maidenly" spinster of the earlier criticism. She is radically experimental, inventive, and above all modern. Costello describes Moore's poetics in modernist terms: "for Moore, a poem is not a functional utterance; rather, it is an ordering of language". The detailed textual analyses of individual poems are excellent in being both meticulous and inventive.

GOODRIDGE focuses on Moore's reviews and essays on Ezra Pound, T.S. Eliot, Wallace Stevens, and William Carlos Williams. This is the first book-length study of Moore's prose, and is helpful as a companion to Moore's *Complete Prose*. Unfortunately, Goodridge only focuses on Moore's literary relations with male poets; Moore's reviews of H.D. and Bryher are ignored, as are the essays on other women writers such as Gertrude Stein and Elizabeth Bishop. This study tends to reconstruct modernism as a boy's club and Moore as an honourary member of that club.

MARTIN finds good reason to suggest that Moore was in fact a "subversive Modernist" as her poetry refuses to conform to the modernist ideals of unity and coherence, preferring instead a postmodern instability and playfulness. However, Martin's thesis assumes that "modernism" and "postmodernism" are terms that represent distinct and easily identifiable sets of discursive practices. The opposition between the two should surely be treated with a degree of scepticism.

SLATIN deals with Moore's poems up to, and including, 1936. Also seeing Moore as distinctive, Slatin represents her as an isolated figure on the modernist landscape, he develops readings of the poetry that refer back to the poet's own search for an independent poetic voice. Slatin refers to the texts of the poems as they were published in the magazines where they originally appeared, and he also includes discussions of "Black Earth" and "Roses Only", two poems not included in the inaccurately titled *Complete Poems*. This is a valuable discussion of Moore, as it is careful to consider the poet within a distinct historical frame, and thus provides an insight into the particular difficulties confronting a woman writer during this period.

HOLLEY's discussion "is prompted by the question of what it could possibly mean to be a moralist in the midst of the twentieth century". Moore's poems explore, in aesthetic terms, the qualities that provide the grounds for judgement. Holley manages to find a theoretical framework that accounts for Moore in both moral and modernist terms. She also includes a very useful chronology at the end of the book, which lists the dates of publication for each poem.

HEUVING appropriates Luce Irigaray's theory of language as a "specular economy", which positions women as "other" within language. She argues that Moore "attempts to subvert the specular propensities of lyric poetry to establish a poetry of her own 'self-affection'". However, she also concedes that modern literary practices in general may be read as a subversion of a specular poetics, so it remains unclear as to how Moore as a *woman* poet writes her "radical otherness" into her work. Heuving's close textual analysis is acute and penetrative, though her discussion of Irigaray is limited.

VICTORIA BAZIN

More, Sir Thomas 1478–1535

English prose writer and poet

Chambers, R.W., *Thomas More*, London: Jonathan Cape, 1935

Grace, Damian, and Brian Byron (eds.), *Thomas More: Essays on the Icon*, Melbourne: Dove, 1980

Greenblatt, Stephen J., *Renaissance Self-Fashioning: From More to Shakespeare*, Chicago: University of Chicago Press, 1980

Marin, Louis, *Utopics: Spatial Play*, translated by Robert A. Vollrath, Atlantic Highlands, New Jersey: Humanities Press, 1984; London: Macmillan, 1984

Marius, Richard, *Thomas More: A Biography*, New York: Knopf, 1984; London: Dent, 1985

Martz, Louis L., *Thomas More: The Search for the Inner Man*, New Haven, Connecticut, and London: Yale University Press, 1990
Sylvester, R.S., and G.P. Marc'hadour (eds.), *Essential Articles for the Study of Thomas More*, Hamden, Connecticut: Archon Books, 1977

Critical approaches to the writings of Thomas More have been dominated by two concerns: his biography and *Utopia*. More's status – as Lord Chancellor of England, as the foremost English humanist, and as a Catholic martyr – has inevitably cast a long shadow across the reception of his literary works. Much of this criticism has been polarized by More's religious reputation, producing concerted attacks upon the saint-like image and equally vigorous defences. *Utopia*, as More's most accessible and famous work, is central to consideration of More as a writer, although even here biographical criticism remains the dominant mode. Consequently, discussions of the range of texts produced by More – including his *History of Richard III*, epigrams and translations, engagement with religious controversies, letters, and openly devotional works – are often to be found in biographies rather than literary-critical works. The most useful resource remains the Yale *Complete Works* and its accompanying editorial material.

CHAMBERS' biography devotes space to a consideration of all aspects of More's writing, giving particular attention to letters. These texts are treated as "sources" for a portrait of More, but Chambers provides a great deal of useful information about the preservation and transmission of More's work. Chambers asserts that "a man may be known by his fantasies as well as by his more solemn utterances", and gives a useful, if brief, summary of the difficulties resulting from the sheer volume of works produced by More. His suggestion that a commentator may be judged by the selection of quotations from More is extremely valuable, and should be applied to any reading of Chambers' own work.

The collection edited by SYLVESTER and MARC'HADOUR offers no less than 47 articles on More's life and literary works, and is divided into four sections – "Biographical Studies", "*Utopia*", "Other Works", and "General Views". Included are pieces by major historians of the period, such as G.R. Elton, Chambers, and Derrett, and literary figures such as C.S. Lewis, Robert Bolt, and G.K. Chesterton. Essays by McCutcheon on the use of *litotes* in *Utopia*, and Anderegg on early More biographies are particularly illuminating. Most of those scholars renowned in More studies (such as Surtz, Marius, Schoeck, and of course the editors) make a contribution, and there is a predominantly biographical and historicist tone. Although a more recent collection would no doubt look very different, many of the essays included here are indeed "essential".

The most interesting essay in GRACE and BYRON's work is Condren's consideration of the political motivations behind invocation of the examples of More and Socrates. Warning against the dangers of anachronism and partiality, Condren tackles the historical specificity of concepts such as conscience, state, and right, and recognizes the need to maintain awareness of such specificity in any comparison of the two men. Also included are pieces in which Marc'hadour discusses More's dialogues and his love of conversation; A.C. Cousins argues for a positive reappraisal of More's English lyrics; Byron addresses himself to More's reconciliation of faith with wealth; Minns looks at the use of scriptures in anti-heretical polemics; and Purcell suggests that the *Dialogue of Comfort* is intended for More's own use, rather than for the comfort of his family. All the articles included give a positive image of More.

GREENBLATT's influential work is the founding text of New Historicism, the chapter devoted to More being the first, and perhaps most important, in the book. Greenblatt's task is to describe "the complex interplay in More's life and writings of self-fashioning and self-cancellation, the crafting of a public role and the profound desire to escape from the identity so crafted". Central to this piece is a complex and careful reading of *Utopia* which, Greenblatt suggests, "is at once the perfect expression of his self-conscious role-playing and an intense meditation upon its limitations". More's other works, including his letters, are also drawn upon in this analysis of individual and cultural power. Greenblatt's "cultural poetics" has been criticized from many angles, perhaps attesting to its significance, and whatever its limitations Greenblatt's persuasive prose has provided a new vocabulary for critical approaches to early-modern studies.

If Chambers' biography is the summit of attempts to represent More as a saint in this century, then MARIUS's work is the clearest demonstration of an urge to humanize that portrait, even if this results in a somewhat tarnished image of the martyr. Marius begins with a polemical and entertaining survey of previous biographies, including that by Chambers, and sets the parameters of his own study. More's choice of marriage rather than priesthood is emphasized, as is his fury at heretics, and a combination of sexuality and violence characterizes Marius's depiction of More. There are specific chapters on More's *Richard III*, "Four Last Things", and three on *Utopia*, but More's various works are liberally drawn upon in Marius's attempt to reveal the man rather than the martyr.

Beginning with an analysis of the neutral in the "no-place" that is Utopia, a place or space that is precisely *between* two contraries, MARIN attempts a structural and historical examination of *Utopia* and of the nature of utopic discourses. Marin locates his historical interests in the work in his assertion that "More's *Utopia* is neither England nor America, neither the Old nor the New World; it is the in-between of the contradiction at the beginning of the sixteenth century of the Old and New Worlds". The book's descriptions of the play of text and space are complex and philosophically based in Kant and Husserl, and as one of the few attempts to treat *Utopia* as a text rather than as an index to More's biography it offers a stimulating discussion.

MARTZ's book may be seen as a riposte to the revision of More's reputation carried out in recent years, most notably by Richard Marius. Eager to counter Marius's emphasis on More's sexuality, ambition, and religious zeal, Martz uses More's late works – in particular the Last Letters, *Dialogue of Comfort*, and *De Tristitia* – to produce an image of the "inner man". Stressing More's Augustinian style of argumentation, Martz interprets these works as a progressive meditation upon Christ's passion and More's own impending tribulations. Such readings are valuable, even if Martz's broader arguments about More's character are ultimately unconvincing.

MARK ROBSON

Morris, William 1834–1896

English poet, novelist, and essayist

Calhoun, Blue, *The Pastoral Vision of William Morris: The Earthly Paradise*, Athens: University of Georgia Press, 1975
Hodgson, Amanda, *The Romances of William Morris*, Cambridge and New York: Cambridge University Press, 1987
Kirchhoff, Frederick, *William Morris: The Construction of a Male Self, 1856–1872*, Athens: Ohio University Press, 1990
MacCarthy, Fiona, *William Morris: A Life for Our Time*, London: Faber & Faber, 1994; New York: Knopf, 1995
Silver, Carole G., *The Romance of William Morris*, Athens, Ohio: Ohio University Press, 1982
Thompson, E.P., *William Morris: Romantic to Revolutionary*, London: Lawrence & Wishart, 1955; New York: Monthly Review Press, 1961; revised edition, London: Merlin, 1976; New York: Pantheon, 1976

Early critical readings of William Morris cultivate, to varying degrees, the myth of Morris "the idle singer of an empty day", interpreting his poetry, prose romances, and social commentary as consolatory and escapist, and his Marxism as the temporary aberration of a "dreamer of dreams". More recent analyses focus on the continuities and interrelatedness of Morris's political, literary, and other artistic activities, placing Morris's medievalism in psychological, social, political, and historical contexts.

THOMPSON places Morris in the Romantic tradition, and Romanticism in a revolutionary tradition. Although this reading undervalues Morris's Pre-Raphaelitism and demonstrates a suspicion of romance – a genre Thompson views as Romanticism shorn of revolutionary hope in Morris's Pre-Raphaelite years, and as a "self-indulgence" in Morris's later non-political romances – Thompson nevertheless succinctly analyses the strengths and limitations of Morris's theory of art, and rescues Morris's medievalism from the charge of escapism, arguing that in his mature work it represents an historical perception of an "organic pre-capitalist community" rather than a "faery world". Just as Thompson's influential first edition stands at the beginning of modern Morris scholarship, a touchstone for much subsequent criticism, his revision, particularly the "Postscript: 1976", opens new avenues, particularly in its discussion of the relationship of Morris's utopianism to his Marxism.

CALHOUN's study of *The Earthly Paradise* places Morris in the pastoral tradition, a tradition in which the idleness of Morris's "idle singer" is "less escape than creation of a compensatory image, a kind of aesthetic activity with social significance". This significance seeks a classical detachment rather than an escape, which allows for a "double awareness" – of past and present, nature and civilization, idleness and energy. Calhoun views the pastoral as both an evaluative critique and a dialectical process, which constructs classical antitheses that resist Romantic synthesis. Calhoun sees Morris's *Earthly Paradise* not as a vision of a paradisal ideal but as a detached pastoral warning against the alienating nature of the Romantic quest. Although this book fails to place Morris's use of pastoral and romance in an historical context, it is particularly interesting for its construction of an anti-romantic Morris.

SILVER explores Morris's "preoccupation with the thematic trinity" of love, fate, and death in a thorough study covering all the major works and many minor ones too. Broadly psychological in its treatment, this book shows Morris confronting and transforming his "latter-day romantic" anxieties about love and death to create in his later works a humanized vision of history as "psychological and sociological myth" – at once Marxist, utopian, and Romantic – in which individual and communal concerns harmonize with nature's cycles. Despite its uneasy tension between historical and mythopoeic concerns, in what Silver calls the "realm of pure imagination" of Morris's late romances, the book is a good introduction to the man and his work, covering a wide range of Morris's non-political writings.

HODGSON's study of Morris's development as a writer in the romance tradition avoids restrictive definitions of genre; it examines how "his views and beliefs found natural and potent expression in this antiquated form". Hodgson's Morris is never completely without doubts about the escapism of his art and medievalism; instead, these doubts become the driving force behind his urge to form "organic links – between species, races, historical periods". Although Hodgson's apparent association of mythopoeic "eternal truths" with the "essence of Socialism" is open to question, this book is noteworthy for its balanced evaluation of Morris's idiosyncratic prose style, its concise synopses of Morris's frequently labyrinthine romances, and its insightful readings of works from all periods of his career.

KIRCHHOFF takes a psycho-biographical approach to Morris, adapting Heinz Kohut's object-relations psychology and Eve Sedgwick's model of the triangulated sexual economy to construct "a narrative of Morris's psychological development". "Narrative" is the key term. For Kirchhoff, Morris's early prose and poetry constitute "his chief mode of confirming the self". Through narrative storytelling, Morris simultaneously confronts, escapes, and compensates for the anxieties of relationships – sexual, familial, with other men, and with women – relationships that construct the image of male selfhood. The evolution of this constructed male selfhood may be measured by the Otherness of Morris's female characters, whose struggle within the continuum of male homosocial relations Kirchhoff sees as corresponding to Morris's own liberation from High Romanticism's identification of libido and self. This book is a valuable study of the early Morris and his work to 1872.

MacCARTHY's biography sets out to give us a William Morris "*For Our Time*": "a passionate social reformer, an early environmentalist, an educationalist and would-be feminist". MacCarthy's approach to Morris as writer reflects both her own and her subject's eye for design: "There is no real way of understanding Morris until you can see, almost with his eyes, the particular pattern of a landscape, the relationship of buildings, the precise lie of the land". MacCarthy's Morris is a sensual observer of the material world, a lover of crafted objects and humanized landscapes: her 20 chapter-headings name houses and geographic locations to emphasize Morris's acute sense of place, a point reflected in her discussion of Morris's writings. Her treatment of Morris's cautious sympathy for intellectual anarchism – important to an understanding of his libertarian utopianism in *News from Nowhere* – challenges Thompson's more orthodox reading of Morris's Marxism. An admiring but fair biography, this book succeeds in placing Morris in his artistic and political context.

BRIAN J. DAY

Morrison, Toni 1931–

American novelist and essayist

Bloom, Harold (ed.), *Toni Morrison*, New York: Chelsea House, 1990
Carmean, Karen, *Toni Morrison's World of Fiction*, Troy, New York: Whitston, 1993
Harris, Trudier, *Fiction and Folklore: The Novels of Toni Morrison*, Knoxville: University of Tennessee Press, 1991
Heinze, Denise, *The Dilemma of "Double Consciousness": Toni Morrison's Novels*, Athens: University of Georgia Press, 1993
Mbalia, Dorothea D., *Toni Morrison's Developing Class Consciousness*, Selinsgrove, Pennsylvania: Susquehanna University Press, 1991; London: Associated University Presses, 1991
Otten, Terry, *The Crime of Innocence in the Fiction of Toni Morrison*, Columbia: University of Missouri Press, 1989
Rigney, Barbara Hill, *The Voices of Toni Morrison*, Columbus: Ohio State University Press, 1991
Toni Morrison issue of *Callaloo*, 13(3), Summer 1990

Terry OTTEN's was the first-published book-length study of Morrison's novels, but rather than provide a basic introduction to the unique features of her writing, Otten analyzes the recurrent motif of the biblical Fall, and moves from the identification of such mythic patterns to a discussion of the social, political, and cultural concerns of Morrison's writing up to *Beloved*. The contention of this book is that in a world dominated by racism, where moral values have been turned upside down, and to be black is necessarily to be evil, innocence is debilitating; it is, perhaps, the greatest sin. A fall from "grace" is, then, essential as the only potentially redemptive act if Morrison's characters are to live authentic lives, though the consequences of such a fall may be destructive, painful, and ironic.

The collection of essays edited by BLOOM reflects critical responses to Morrison's work throughout the 1980s. Some of the essays were commissioned, but most are reprinted from journals. The essays cover formal, thematic, and contextual issues: Cynthia A. Davis discusses Morrison's use of myth in relation to the psychic violence of racism and the possibility of freedom; the use of symbolism to respond to alienating white value systems is discussed by Melvin Dixon and by Theodore O. Mason in his consideration of Morrison as storyteller; to this theme is added a feminist perspective in Deborah E. McDowell's analysis of *Sula* and the black female text. Hortense J. Spillers attends to black female characterization in *Sula*; Keith E. Byerman deals with the irrational and fantastic elements of Morrison's fiction, as does Margaret Atwood in her appraisal of *Beloved*. Roger Sale celebrates the greatness of *Beloved*,and Marilyn Sanders Mobley places that text within the tradition of slave narratives. Madonne M. Miner writes on rape, madness, and silence in *The Bluest Eye*; Terry Otten's discussion of the "crime of innocence" in *Tar Baby* is essentially a version of that included in his own book (see above); and the volume concludes with an essay by Morrison herself, which considers in miniature the issue she has since explored at length in *Playing in the Dark*: that is, the repressed African-American presence in American literature.

In the same year as Bloom's collection was published, *Callaloo* published a special section devoted to Toni Morrison. These essays also reflect the prevailing interest in Morrison's formal innovations, examples being: Shelley Wong's discussion of transgression as poesis in *The Bluest Eye*; Morrison's aesthetic responses to the ideology of racism, as in Michael Awkward's analysis of myth, ideology, and gender in *Song of Solomon*; and Morrison's place within African-American literary tradition, in Sandra Pouchet Paquet's comparison between *Tar Baby* and *Their Eyes Were Watching God* and in Karla Holloway's discussion of *Beloved* and the spiritual.

MBALIA extends the exploration of Morrison's work within the context of African-American culture to embrace the struggle of all African people. Mbalia perceives a strong pattern of progressive continuity or evolution, which links all of Morrison's novels in sequence. This unity is based on the development of Morrison's commitment to share the struggle for a solution to the problems facing African people. According to Mbalia's view, the novels document Morrison's increasing understanding of the role of historical materialism in discovering the source of, and the solution to, the oppression of African people. Both racial and gender oppression are seen to be the consequences of class exploitation. The weakness of this approach lies in the tendency to interpret the novels selectively and to focus on the extent to which they exemplify an extrinsic political position; the strength of such an approach is that it provides a valuable context for any consideration of Morrison's representation of black consciousness, culture, and history.

HARRIS explores the importance of the black oral tradition both in shaping Morrison's distinct style of writing and in placing Morrison's work firmly within the African-American literary tradition. In an informative introductory chapter, Harris sets out clearly the folkloric inheritance with which Morrison works, from early slave narratives to a range of twentieth-century writers. In the discussion of the novels that follows, Harris makes a well-documented and articulately argued case for the status of Morrison's novels as "speakerly texts" or "talking books", which fuse form and content through the skillful use of traditional story-telling materials.

Where the studies by Harris and Mbalia explore in detail many of the issues identified by Morrison's early critics, RIGNEY's study brings to bear on these issues an explicitly feminist theoretical approach, which illuminates the texts in new ways. She identifies a black feminine/feminist aesthetic operating in Morrison's fiction, and it is the perception of this feminist element that motivates her discussion of Morrison's radical use of language, her reformulations of self and identity, her reinterpretations of history as both fact and mythology, and her representations of both magic realism and historical witness. Thus, Rigney documents the many ways in which Morrison's voices are political expressions. The theorizing of Morrison's work, such as Rigney achieves, is an area awaiting future expansion.

HEINZE contributes to the work of bringing together considerations of theoretical perspectives and attention to Morrison's literary practice. She considers Morrison's paradoxical role as a black and female "minority" writer, who has been enthusiastically embraced by mainstream white America in terms of W.E.B. Du Bois's concept of "double consciousness". Morrison is thus an "outsider within" the mainstream. Accepted by the established value system, she is also what Heinze calls a "mythbasher", who discredits the myths that underlie the American way of thinking. Heinze uses theoretical perspectives developed by Mikhail Bakhtin and African-American critics such as Henry Louis Gates to describe the dialogic quality of Morrison's work, the indirection and delicate balance that enable her simultaneously to subvert and sustain Western values.

An extremely useful study, which sets itself the task of accounting for Morrison's "total" achievement, is that by CARMEAN. In this, Morrison's work is viewed not within the potentially restrictive categories of black writing or women's writing but as a unified canon, expressing Morrison's own development as a writer, as well as her distinctive stylistic traits and her special thematic concerns. Each text, from *The Bluest Eye* to *Jazz*, is treated comprehensively in terms of critical reception and the authorial experiences and pressures that inspired it, as well as the thematic and formal characteristics of the narrative. Two introductory chapters provide, first, an overview of Morrison's literary career and the issues that recur in her work – self-discovery, personal freedom, history and myth – and, second, the relevant biographical background, suggesting ways in which Morrison's developing artistic interests are informed by personal experience. Perhaps most useful of all is the annotated bibliography included here, which provides a valuable guide to all the critical work published on Morrison to 1993.

DEBORAH L. MADSEN

The Movement

Alvarez, A., *The New Poetry*, Harmondsworth, Middlesex: Penguin, 1962, revised 1966

Morrison, Blake, *The Movement: English Poetry and Fiction of the 1950s*, Oxford and New York: Oxford University Press, 1980

O'Connor, William Van, *The New University Wits and the End of Modernism*, Carbondale: Southern Illinois University Press, 1963

Thwaite, Anthony, *Contemporary English Poetry: An Introduction*, London: Heinemann, 1959; Philadelphia: Dufour Editions, 1961

Tomlinson, Charles, "The Middlebrow Muse", in *Essays in Criticism*, 7(2), April 1957

Early critical reactions to the Movement – which includes poets and novelists as diverse as Philip Larkin and Thom Gunn – range from Tomlinson's dismissal in "The Middlebrow Muse" to Thwaite's cautious praise in *Contemporary English Poetry*. There have not been many worthwhile studies of the Movement written since O'Connor's, apart from the "classic" Morrison study of 1980, which remains the best introduction to the subject.

TOMLINSON's analyses of the writers are questionable (especially the pompous paragraph on Larkin), and he makes no direct reference to "the Movement"; but his essay is important because it is one of the earliest critical responses to the grouping of these writers. He reviews Robert Conquest's seminal anthology *New Lines*, which contains Movement writers such as D.J. Enright and Elizabeth Jennings, and immediately disparages it in the opening quotation gleaned from Schopenhauer's "On Reading and Books," in which the latter distinguishes "classic" literature from the ephemeral. He attacks Conquest's manifesto – which champions a new, non-Romantic school of poetry – as a myth, refers to the Movement as a journalistic invention in the opening paragraphs, and demeans John Wain's writing as "a sentimentally ingrained habit of mind that knows what the customer wants". The consumerist nature of the poetry results in Tomlinson's critical label for it as "middle-brow". Gunn is conceived as promising, but as yet "no poem of his . . . seems completely and maturely achieved". Enright is chided for self-congratulation and philistinism. Donald Davie is the only poet who is congratulated for producing decent poetry, whereas Larkin is derided as not taking note of Laforgue's self-deprecating texts, and ignoring T.S. Eliot's essay "Tradition and the Individual Talent". All of the writers in Conquest's anthology are derided for not being tuned to reality in the way that Tomlinson thinks he is: "they show a singular want of vital awareness of the continuum outside themselves, of the mystery bodied over against them in the created universe, which they fail to experience with any degree of sharpness or to embody with any instress or sensuous depth".

THWAITE's response to the Movement is contained in Chapter 11 of his study, "Poetry since 1950", and forms a good general, if critically unsophisticated, introduction to the subject. Whereas Tomlinson declines to make many links between the poets, Thwaite locates them in a group dedicated to empiricism and "common sense": "[they] scrupulously refuse to say what they don't mean, and are sometimes almost painfully concerned to record the exact shades of their responses. Their honesty very often expresses itself in terms of bluff common sense, in easy and colloquial language". Thwaite praises this "honesty" rather than attacking the writers for a lack of mysticism. And whereas Tomlinson reads the Movement as philistine, he vilifies it for being too academic, which, he argues, results in a "frigid decorum and a studious impersonality". He then evaluates each writer in turn: for example, Wain is too moralistic, Kingsley Amis has a satisfying "roughness", and Davie manages to fuse the intellectual and poetic, but is sometimes patronising. Larkin is recognised early as the most sophisticated writer in the group because he shifts from the concrete to the general. He is also praised in terms of being a universal "ordinary, decent man", which is ironic in the context of the furore surrounding Larkin's letters, edited by Thwaite over 30 years later. Despite using the term "the Movement", Thwaite warns against "the tying on of superficial critical labels".

ALVAREZ's reaction to the Movement takes another line of attack in the Introduction to his poetry anthology. He argues that it forms the third stage in the development of poetry since Eliot, after the political commitment of Auden's generation and the anti-intellectualism of 1940s romanticism. Like Tomlinson, he finds little to praise in Conquest's anthology: the Movement is regarded as a system that works as a series of negatives, such as "anti-emotion" and "anti-mystical". Unlike Tomlinson, he begins to make comparisons between the individual members of the group, and argues that they have "a kind of unity of flatness". Larkin is reproached for writing poetry that preserves the idea that "life in Middle England goes on much as it always has, give or take a few minor changes in the class system". Against this parochialism, Alvarez offers a new set of poets, including Ted Hughes, who react to historical events such as the Holocaust with a "new seriousness".

O'CONNOR's full-length study begins to make more connections between the writers: he locates the Movement in the historical context of the decline of the British Empire and the Welfare state, and follows Tomlinson in his preface by evaluating the writing as "little", "limited", and precluding "the entrance of a larger vision". In Chapter 1 ("A New Literary Generation"), he states that he prefers the term "University Wits" for the group because it does not carry the connotation of "bandwagon" or "mutual admiration society", as "the Movement" does. A comprehensive history (despite the lack of rigour in the annotation) of the group follows, with individual chapters on Larkin, Wain, Iris Murdoch, and Amis. Larkin's work is "narrow", lacking energy and excitement, Wain's is "thin", Murdoch's is suitably playful, and Amis is championed as the "voice of the 1950s". The criticism is, at times, appallingly simplistic: for example, he summarises plots for much of the analysis of Larkin, and offers poor evaluations, such as "the tone is ironic and the language is his own".

MORRISON's comprehensive study fills the previous gap in the market for a complex engagement with the subject, and forms the definitive introduction to the Movement. His is the most ambitious attempt to "identify certain beliefs, attitudes, tones, forms and techniques which are common to [the writers'] work". He is sceptical of the common conception of the Movement as a journalistic invention, and prefers to show that "it often stands . . . for what is central and enriching" in the literary texts. His section on "The Origins of the Movement" is more detailed than O'Connor's, and includes an analysis of the friendships between the different members, for example, at Oxford during 1940–51. The incisiveness of Morrison's criticism compared to O'Connor's is demonstrated in the section on "Class and Culture", where he uncovers the Movement's desire to minimise social differences as an embarrassed class-consciousness.

ANTONY ROWLAND

Muir, Edwin 1887–1959

Scottish poet, literary critic, novelist, and translator

Aitchison, James, *The Golden Harvester: The Vision of Edwin Muir*, Aberdeen: Aberdeen University Press, 1988

Butter, P.H., *Edwin Muir: Man and Poet*, Edinburgh: Oliver & Boyd, 1966

Knight, Roger, *Edwin Muir: An Introduction to His Work*, London and New York: Longman, 1980

McCulloch, Margery, *Edwin Muir: Poet Critic and Novelist*, Edinburgh: Edinburgh University Press, 1993

Marshall, George, *In a Distant Isle: The Orkney Background of Edwin Muir*, Edinburgh: Scottish Academic Press, 1987

Phillips, Michael, *Edwin Muir: A Master of Modern Poetry*, Indianapolis, Indiana: Hackett, 1978

Wiseman, Christopher, *Beyond the Labyrinth: A Study of Edwin Muir's Poetry*, Victoria, British Columbia: Sono Nis Press, 1978

Until two decades ago, the critical attention given to the work of Edwin Muir was at best, modest, and even after a surge of popularity in the 1970s the study of Muir's works was often limited by a concentration on the ways in which the events of Muir's life (particularly his early childhood) manifested themselves in his poetry and prose. Although many of these texts give excellent accounts of Muir's traumatic emigration from the solitude of the Orkney Islands to the slums of Glasgow, they generally do not explore the thematic and philosophical underpinnings of his work, nor are there many critical texts that examine Muir in the light of developments in contemporary literary theory. Only in the last few years has Muir criticism overcome its biographical narrowness, and finally a number of new books have begun to re-evaluate Muir's work through the lenses of politics, psychology, and historical contextualization.

BUTTER's early study of Muir is worthwhile examining if only for the extraordinary intimacy with which he recounts the details of the Muirs' everyday lives. Butter was Muir's confidante for many years, and his book represents the foundation on which most of the biographically oriented studies of Muir were constructed. The book's bibliography is also filled with excellent source material, which any student of Muir's work will find indispensable. The analytical sections of Butter's book provide some fine close readings of Muir's poetry. His religious interpretations of the poems in the collection *Variations on a Time Theme* are particularly well done. Although Willa Muir once commented that she thought Butter overestimated the extent to which Muir was influenced by the iconography of Christianity, most of Butter's observations are well-grounded in solid textual analysis.

MARSHALL provides one of the most thoughtful biographical studies of Muir's poetry and novels. One of his main goals is to clarify some of the episodes that Muir describes in the two versions of his autobiography, *An Autobiography* and *The Story and the Fable*. Marshall takes a Jungian approach to a number of recurrent images in Muir's work, and argues that Muir creates many of his heroes out of the Orcadian collective consciousness. Marshall also suggests a number of ways in which Muir's early life in the islands may have formed the basis for some of the images of isolation, which run through his verse and may provide a symbolic corollary for the sense of existential alienation that Muir detected in the modern age. Marshall's work distinguishes itself from the great mass of biographical studies on Muir by giving an excellent account of Orkney history and folklore.

KNIGHT also moves beyond simple biographical reductionalism by revealing the ways in which the nature of Muir's early life made him acutely aware of the upheaval of values that necessarily accompanied the development of industrialized Scotland. Knight sees Muir's work as unique because of its unaffected approach to themes of cultural dislocation: "plenty of second-rate writers are ready to peddle warm and hazy versions of vanished pastoral ease . . . Muir's credentials being so impeccable, his descriptions have a quite unusually strong claim upon our attention". Knight argues that Muir's attitude toward industrialization places him squarely in the vein of writers like D.H. Lawrence and George Sturt who criticized the anaesthetizing aspects of contemporary civilization. Knight's book also gives an excellent account of Muir's furtive and generally unsuccessful experimentation with composing poetry in Lowlands Scots dialect, and offers one of the most extensive surveys of Muir's critical writings yet available. Knight is also one of the few critics to recognize properly the deep activist strains in Muir's critical work, seeing it as "part of a critique of contemporary values" and argues that Muir's political views were often sharply at odds with those of the British literati. The book also includes some revealing remarks by Muir about the realities of communism in Eastern Europe and the sufferings of the Czech people.

PHILLIPS' study charts simultaneously Muir's development as a poet and his career as a translator of works by German-language writers. The book reveals some remarkably tight correlations between the thematic and structural aspects of the works Edwin and Willa Muir introduced to English-speaking audiences and developments in Muir's own verse. Phillips argues that a kind of dialogue developed between Muir and the writers he translated, and that much of Muir's poetry took the form of a philosophical reaction to the dark, nihilistic tendencies he detected in the works of writers like Kafka. Phillips sees Muir as a profoundly conventional poet, whose work champions established values and commonplace joys, and stands in direct opposition to the bleak, mechanistic visions of central-European and German writers:

> . . . Edwin Muir . . . filled in the religious void created by Kafka with poetic structures reasserting the value and worth of traditional human experiences – experiences such as appreciation of other people, love, contribution to the general and individual happiness, salvation, spiritual richness, emotional plenty and economic wealth.

One of Phillips central claims is that Muir's exposure to German-language writers served to set him apart from his British contemporaries; that it shaped the unique character of his poetry, and may help to explain the relatively slow pace at which Muir's work finally found critical appreciation. Phillips' book will be an essential source for those interested in issues of intertextuality in Muir's work.

AITCHISON traces the development of Muir's approach to myth from his days as a young Nietzschean in 1920s' Glasgow to his flirtation with Jungian allegories, and then to his eventual use of Christian images of Fall and Redemption. Aitchison's book also includes some interesting readings of a number of Muir's more complex poems and an excellent Jungian interpretation of the "Ballad of the Soul". Aitchison argues that the sometimes indifferent critical response to Muir's work is the fault of critics who "note the difficulty and then shy away from it". Aitchison's work is important because it does much to illuminate the often elaborate mythic structures within Muir's poetry and prose, though it does not extensively explore the cultural and historical forces which may have determined the character of Muir's work.

McCULLOCH's recent study of Muir's works breaks a significant amount of new, critical ground by studying the literary environment in which Muir first emerged, and by comparing Muir's works with those of the writers of the Scottish Literary Renaissance, such as Hugh MacDiarmid and Thom Gunn. In doing so, she creates an interesting analysis of Muir's views of Scottish politics, nationalism, and literary identity. McCulloch is one of the only critics who does not set Muir apart as an isolated Orkneyman (more Nordic than Celtic) and instead sees him as "deeply influenced by his Scottish background, not least by the deterministic philosophy of Calvinism against which he fought in poetry and prose". McCulloch's work is also unique in its focus on Muir's prose and later poetry, which she sees as less biographically rooted than his earlier work. She explains that "while an autobiographical element may still be present in the inspiration of a poem, knowledge of this is not essential for understanding". McCulloch's refusal to foreground biographical elements makes it possible for her to devote time to exploring Muir's literary identity, which she characterizes as strikingly anti-modern and more like the work of Matthew Arnold and Arthur Hugh Clough than his modernist contemporaries.

WISEMAN's book calls into question much of the conventional wisdom concerning the technical complexity of Muir's poetry. He writes that even Muir's most sympathetic critics have branded his work "strange and even quaint, and their typical reaction has been to treat him as some sort of exception to the rule". Although most of the scholarship on Muir emphasizes his anachronistic reliance on the forms and practices of earlier generations of poets, Wiseman argues that Muir's work is technically innovative and has much in common with the post-symbolist movement. Wiseman claims that "concepts [such] as time and eternity are not incorporated rationally and logically in Muir's poetry, but explored and released into meaning through symbol". Although Wiseman's arguments are sometimes weakened by his redemptionist zeal, he does provide a sound technical analysis of Muir's poetry.

KEVIN P. BRADY

Munro, Alice 1931–

Canadian short-story writer

Carrington, Ildikó de Papp, *Controlling the Uncontrollable: The Fiction of Alice Munro*, Dekalb: Northern Illinois University Press, 1989
Carscallen, James, *The Other Country: Patterns in the Writing of Alice Munro*, Toronto: ECW Press, 1993
Dahlie, Hallvard, *Alice Munro and Her Works*, Toronto: ECW Press, 1985

Heble, Ajay, *The Tumble of Reason: Alice Munro's Discourse of Absence,* Toronto and Buffalo, New York: University of Toronto Press, 1994
Redekop, Magdalene, *Mothers and Other Clowns: The Stories of Alice Munro*, London and New York: Routledge, 1992
Smythe, Karen E., *Figuring Grief: Gallant, Munro, and the Poetics of Elegy*, Montreal and Kingston, Ontario: McGill-Queen's University Press, 1992

Alice Munro's eight volumes of short fiction, from *Dance of the Happy Shades* (1968) to *Open Secrets* (1994), have gained her an international standing among practitioners and readers of contemporary fiction. The ever-increasing subtlety and complexity of her stories have been accompanied by increasing sophistication in critical response, so that those who read her work closely no longer see her simply as a "Canadian realist". In the most recent critical responses, she earns examination and analysis within the diverse contexts of contemporary literary and cultural theory.

DAHLIE's brief monograph is still a useful introduction to Munro, even though it deals with only one half of her writing to date, the half up to and including *Who Do You Think You Are?* (1978). A brief biographical Introduction includes passages from interviews with Munro, and locates her formative years in the rural and small-town world of southern Ontario in the 1930s. Dahlie relates Munro to her predecessors, who practised documentary realism as their major mode. Although Munro remains a kind of realist, she departs from realism to the extent that she is sensitive to a metaphysical dimension, exploring "beyond bounds of empirical reality". Dahlie notes also Munro's place in a dominant tradition of short-story writing, and pays some attention to her affiliations, in the early work, with the gothicism of the American South. Some stories from the first four volumes receive careful readings. Dahlie's book is limited by its relatively early date in the chronology of Munro criticism, but remains a sound introduction for the beginning student and general reader.

CARRINGTON, examining Munro's published work from 1950 to 1988, has produced a critical study that argues for her coherence and consistency. She acknowledges the surface realism of her stories, but considers Munro to be something very different from a realist; and she admits the fragmentation of Munro's vision, but insists that the stories ultimately express pattern and unity. The unity of the work, considered as a whole, derives from the fusing of significant theme with narrative techniques containing allusions, metaphors, and split point of view. Her narratives register the shame and humiliation felt by characters inhabiting a universe of uncontrollable forces, and expresses impulses to control both those forces and the humiliations they impose. Carrington's study is systematic, and devotes considerable space to each of the volumes up to *The Progress of Love* (1986). The enclosing chapters, however, discuss the themes and techniques, all of them related to the issues of control and the uncontrollable. This remains a solid and useful study, though subsequent critique has not found it so important to insist on unity of theme or style, and has invoked theoretical perspectives that make greater allowance for disconnection, gaps, and anarchy, elements that situate Munro within a modernist-postmodern continuum.

CARSCALLEN has written a very long study (more than 500 pages) for the general reader as well as for the academic specialist. His aim is interpretation, engendered by a model that seeks to free Munro's own structures from the texts, up to *Friend of My Youth*. The author has chosen not to follow a chronological pattern. Instead in Part One he lays out an interpretative model, which locates a structure of "great human myths" beneath surface ordinariness while finding a host of "associative connections" between the stories, canonical myths, and works of literature. Ultimately, Carscallen's interpretative approach seems to derive from the mythopoeia of Northrop Frye, so commonly met in Canadian criticism of an earlier generation. He finds that Munro's stories move between polarities, of reality and truth, of home and an "Other" place, and these polarities reflect a larger structure bounded by sense on the one side, and sensibility on the other. Carscallen thus repeats a familiar response to Munro's work, in which surface realism is haunted by uncanny epiphanies. Munro's admirers will find in Carscallen's work an amazing grasp of the volumes' details, an intertextual subtlety, and a limited yet flexible model to enable comprehensive interpretation.

HEBLE offers a helpful reading of Munro in a theoretical context defined by the structuralism of Ferdinand de Saussure and Roman Jakobson, and the more developed textual theory of Roland Barthes. Heble calls Munro's practice "paradigmatic discourse". According to this, getting at meaning – a prime activity of both narrators and characters in a Munro story – involves acknowledging how what "happened" is haunted always by absent potentialities. Munro is interested in how we come by knowledge of a "real" world, and points readers to the manner in which any such world is always, inevitably, a fictional construct. Heble resituates Munro within critical discussion of realism rather than removing her from it, eschewing alignment of her writing with that of experimentalists like Jorge Luis Borges, Robert Kroetsch, and Michael Ondaatje. Instead, through a close reading of the major fiction collections, he shows how Munro uses narrative gestures to problematize common-sense assumptions about reality. Heble's study thus mediates between earlier criticism, which placed Munro firmly within a tradition of realism, and later criticism, which has located her within such terms as "magic realism", "meta-fiction", and "postmodernism". For Heble, Munro probes the conventions she works in, exploring the space between surface reality on the one hand, and the "limits of representation" on the other.

REDEKOP's study addresses itself to readers who feel that Munro, neither a theorist nor a feminist herself, opens up a feminine aesthetic – a view that can make sense of the fiction collections and throw light on the way in which Munro's female figures go about making sense of the world. Munro writes stories rather than novels because her narrative is not a "progress" (patriarchal, authoritative) but a circus parade. Her narratives circle around concerns, destabilizing traditional and powerful myths and symbols. Like Heble, Redekop sees Munro "repeatedly undermin[ing] her own fiction". Munro's aesthetic is concerned with mother-figures whose clowning enables the simultaneous compassion and irony such figures need to survive, to act in the world, and to celebrate the role of motherhood. Redekop's accessible and useful book is divided into two sections, the first of which lays out the carnivalesque theory in narrative form, while the second offers readings of Munro's texts up to *Friend of My Youth* (1990). Both Heble's and Redekop's studies characterize Canadian criticism in its current sophisticated, theory-inflected phase; however, neither study is reductive, both critics write clearly, and both offer helpful, perceptive readings of Munro's *oeuvre*.

SMYTHE's more closely focused study places Munro alongside Mavis Gallant in a project to theorize a genre Smythe calls "fiction-elegy". In this genre, elegy is not simply theme, but also form; the genre, therefore, calls for a poetics. Smythe views Gallant and Munro as writers who found their elegiac texts on modernist precursors Virginia Woolf and James Joyce, like them concerned with time, loss, and death as implicated in larger public and private issues. In Munro's work, responses to loss, particularly to loss of the mother, involve the production of personal histories. Moments of special insight – of epiphany – mark self-reflexive crystallizations of these histories, and the epiphanies bring story into a paradoxical relation to silence. Smythe sees Munro as evolving an increasingly complex style as she engages with the problem of translating life into story. This study, like those by Heble and Redekop, assumes both that Munro's stature is international, and that there is the potential in Munro's fiction to induce reflection on literary, theoretical, and cultural issues exceeding the apparent thematic and stylistic shapes of the stories themselves.

PATRICK HOLLAND

Murdoch, Iris 1919–

English novelist, dramatist, and philosopher

Bloom, Harold (ed.), *Iris Murdoch*, New York: Chelsea House, 1986

Byatt, A.S., *Degrees of Freedom: The Early Novels of Iris Murdoch*, London: Chatto & Windus, 1965; revised edition, London: Vintage, 1994

Conradi, Peter J., *Iris Murdoch: The Saint and the Artist*, London: Macmillan, 1986, 2nd edition, 1989

Dipple, Elizabeth, *Iris Murdoch: Work for the Spirit*, London: Methuen, 1982; Chicago: University of Chicago Press, 1982

Hague, Angela, *Iris Murdoch's Comic Vision*, Selinsgrove, Pennsylvania: Susquehanna University Press, 1984; London: Associated University Presses, 1984

Johnson, Deborah, *Iris Murdoch*, Brighton, Sussex: Harvester Press, 1987

There are relatively few full-length critical studies on Iris Murdoch's fiction. This may be due to the fact that Murdoch firmly eschews the wilder reaches of postmodernist style in favour of an unorthodox realism, which looks back to the nineteenth-century novel and the Anglo-Russian tradition. Her work is therefore of limited interest for postmodern theorists. There nevertheless exists a body of criticism that defends Murdoch's achievements against early hostility and later neglect.

Part One of BYATT's study was first published in 1965 and is unrevised. Byatt here relates the themes of freedom and enslavement in Murdoch's first eight novels to an increasing anti-existentialism, and notes the introduction of the theme of "goodness" in *An Unofficial Rose*. New to the second edition is a collection of lectures, pamphlets, and reviews of the novels up to *The Book and the Brotherhood*. This section lacks a sustained thematic focus, but includes a longer essay on "The Writer and Her Work". Throughout, Byatt makes connections between Murdoch's moral philosophy, literary theory, and fiction, and traces allusions to Plato, Kant, Wittgenstein, Freud, Sartre, and Simone Weil. Byatt's writing style is sometimes rebarbative, but her generally straightforward approach and extended plot summaries make the book an accessible introduction to Murdoch's work.

HAGUE manages to categorise many of Murdoch's novels as comic by dint of a wide-ranging definition of comedy (after Northrop Frye), which incorporates irony, fantasy, tragedy, and realism. Following a chapter on Murdoch's theory and practice of comic fiction, she focuses on the three novels that best represent this theory in practice – *An Accidental Man* ("Murdoch's fictional depiction of the relationship between comedy and contingency"), *The Black Prince* ("the novel that contains Murdoch's clearest statements about irony"), and *The Sea, The Sea* ("uses the relationship of art to life . . . as its comic premise"). Hague sees the trajectory of Murdoch's work departing from the dark comedy of her first two novels and returning to this perspective after *The Nice and the Good*. This recovery is interpreted as the mature recognition that "the comic mode is the most appropriate vehicle for the novel". There is some truth in the assertion that "most Murdoch critics tend to de-emphasize the comic dimension of her work", but in the attempt to redress this imbalance Hague has produced a study noticeably skewed in the opposite direction.

DIPPLE promotes Murdoch's moral seriousness as an antidote to postmodernist frivolity. She writes long, detailed essays on theme, plot, characterisation, and form in the novels up to *Nuns and Soldiers*. Against earlier studies, which emphasise the influence of Sartre, Dipple stresses Murdoch's Platonism. Her moral and religious focus makes for a sober-minded study, but one justified by extensive reference to the fiction, literary theory, and moral philosophy. While BLOOM also upholds Murdoch's stature as a religious writer, he regards her rejection of postmodernism as a failing. He evinces a marked disdain for her "formulaic procedures" and "anachronistic style and outmoded narrative devices". He declares that she fails in her goals of characterisation, states that he finds her spiritual stance "repellant", and, like Byatt, criticises a narrative tendency towards telling rather than showing (itself an old-fashioned criticism). The contributors to this volume are less grudging, although Frank Kermode manages to damn with faint praise, asserting that "each novel contains somewhere the ghost of a major novel". Louis L. Martz, in an essay on "The London Novels", examines Murdoch's detailed depiction of location and identifies her as the heir to Charles Dickens. He asserts that realistic description indicates Murdoch's perennial concern with the ethical implications of other subjects, and also functions to describe character. Lorna Sage identifies Murdoch's as an "aesthetic of imperfection", which may result in "casual signs of haste". She identifies the technique, exemplified in *Henry and Cato*, of allowing minor characters a time on centre stage, but notes that such figures may remain "emblematic". This collection also includes essays by Byatt, Dipple, Richard Todd, and Murdoch's own essay "Against Dryness", so that Bloom's claim to present a "selection of the best criticism available" (at the time) is substantiated.

JOHNSON turns a feminist eye on the misogynistic male narrators and female characters of Murdoch's fiction. She identifies a tension between female author and fictional character, and asserts that gender identity is called into question. A correlation is made between the open plot-structures of the later texts and the liberation of women characters; but Johnson concentrates on sexual stereotype at the expense of Murdoch's wider interest in issues of free will and determinism, and ignores the fact that the early novels predate second-wave feminism. Furthermore, her references to French theories of sexual difference are often awkward: for example, of Dora's overbearing husband in *The Bell* she notes: "Paul's desire for offspring says everything about his position as a representative and agent of patriarchy (he is the very embodiment of Lacan's 'symbolic order'!)". Although, as Johnson admits, Murdoch "cannot ultimately be claimed as a feminist writer", this does not invalidate feminist critiques of her work. However, the attempt here to cover both Anglo-American and Continental feminist approaches does justice to neither.

CONRADI traces Murdoch's literary rather than philosophical antecedents, bringing an expertise in Russian literature to bear. He provides the reader with an illuminating biography of Murdoch and substantial critical accounts of the novels up to *The Book and the Brotherhood*. Conradi pays particular attention to the binaries in Murdoch's work – the artist and saint of the title, the nice and the good – suggesting that fictional characters and themes always occupy an intermediate position. He concludes that after various oscillations between the open and closed structure, realism and fantasy, Murdoch attains a happy medium. He frequently clarifies and revises the readings of Sage, Byatt, Dipple, and Todd, and although he misrepresents Bloom as Murdoch's "champion", he more cogently argues that the meta-fictive and playful elements in her work are peripheral rather than central. Conradi, in fact, says little new, but says it with critical acuity. This book marks the maturation of Murdoch criticism.

CATHERINE BURGASS

Music and Literature

Barricelli, Jean Pierre, *Melopoiesis: Approaches to the Study of Literature and Music*, New York: New York University Press, 1988

Brown, Calvin S., *Music and Literature: A Comparison of the Two Arts*, Athens: University of Georgia Press, 1948

Cluck, Nancy Anne (ed.), *Literature and Music: Essays on Form*, Provo, Utah: Brigham Young University Press, 1981

Donnington, Robert, *Opera and Its Symbols: The Unity of Words, Music and Staging*, New Haven, Connecticut, and London: Yale University Press, 1990

Orrey, Leslie, *Programme Music: A Brief Survey from the Sixteenth Century to the Present*, London: Davis-Poynter, 1975

Schmidgall, Gary, *Literature as Opera*, New York: Oxford University Press, 1977

Winn, James Anderson, *Unsuspected Eloquence: A History of the Relations Between Poetry and Music*, New Haven, Connecticut, and London: Yale University Press, 1981

In the field of literature and music there are a variety of critical approaches. These include biographical and psychoanalytical studies; comparisons of individual works; discussions of terms and formal techniques common to both arts; analyses of aesthetic movements and their influences; and technical musical and harmonic analyses. The earliest study (Brown's) still defines the general areas of comparative inquiry. Much of the work following Brown's book has departed from his methods to focus on the meaning of music and its effect on the listener. Most recently scholars have called for precise comparisons between the two arts which rely on professional competence in both fields.

BARRICELLI offers a collection of his essays, which appeared previously in various periodicals. Using Brown's book as his foundation, he advocates a critical approach that acknowledges the difference between musico-poetic comparisons that rely on inference, and those that rely on more precise analysis. Thus he exposes the weaknesses in much of the writing about T.S. Eliot's *Four Quartets* and Tchaikovsky's *Francesca da Rimini*. Because both of these works suggest only vague links between music and literature, precise connections cannot be made. The essay on Liszt's *Dante Symphony* exemplifies the more accurate analogies possible in works that intricately combine the two arts.

BROWN's book, as the first full-length survey of the field, strongly influences current approaches. The first two sections establish rhythm, pitch, timbre, and imitation as the formal elements that music and literature have in common. A third section explores some differences between the two arts. Extended examples of literary attempts to replicate the fugue, the sonata, and the rondo demonstrate that the indispensable musical elements of variation, balance, and contrast are not easily reproduced in verse and prose. The fourth section exemplifies the more successful syntheses of the two arts in Conrad Aiken's poetry and in Thomas Mann's literary leitmotifs.

CLUCK has assembled a collection of 20 essays, which address the larger questions of form in literature and music as they were first laid out in Calvin Brown's book. Her book indicates the major developments in the field since Brown's survey appeared. Most significant is the section devoted to T.S. Eliot. This features a variety of perspectives on Eliot's allusions to music, particularly in the *Four Quartets*.

DONNINGTON moves chronologically from Monteverdi to Michael Tippett to explore the way that words, music, and staging combine to communicate the archetypal symbols and characters central to opera. He advocates a consistent (albeit conservative) approach to staging, designed to enhance, but not to interpret, symbols and themes. His psychoanalytical analyses elucidate Wagner's treatment of redemptive heroines. But a long account of Bizet's relationship with his mother detracts from the high-spiritedness of *Carmen*.

ORREY's book is a useful account of the major developments in program music, with a more extensive look at the twentieth century than has been offered previously. Because his predecessor (Niecks) has provided an extensive treatment of the genre through the nineteenth century, he limits his survey to instrumental music, for which there is a written program sanctioned by the composer. He provides very few musical examples, but there is a useful appendix which lists standard and lesser-known works.

SCHMIDGALL moves chronologically through 12 operas, focusing on specific aesthetic trends that either attract writers and composers to each other or complicate their collaboration. He shows how musical and literary developments fit into the intellectual climate of each century he covers. For example, against an Augustan backdrop, he discusses the affinities between Beaumarchais's use of natural speech and Mozart's flexible musical syntax. Most controversial is his defense of Tchaikovsky's *Eugene Onegin*. Rather than attacking the composer's disregard for Pushkin's irony (as in Barricelli), Schmidgall explains the "aesthetic bias" that accounts for Tchaikovsky's treatment of the poem. Given the graciousness and flexibility of this reading, Schmidgall's Afterword is surprising in its description of how postwar drama "discourages operatic translation". A closing "Symposium" offers a collection of famous quotations about opera.

WINN provides a general account of the relationship between music and poetry, beginning in Classical Greece and extending to the present day. He focuses on "the many occasions on which a development in the theory or practice of one of these arts has decisively altered the course of the other". For example, he shows that the attempts of some extreme Renaissance music theorists to make song more like speech ultimately could not subvert formal musical patterns. Similar efforts to introduce quantitative verses and eliminate rhyme also failed. Skillful metrical and harmonic analyses elucidate the aesthetic trends discussed, and there is an extensive bibliography.

ELIZABETH GARDNER

Mystery Plays *see* **Drama: Medieval**

Mystical Literature

Beer, Frances, *Women and Mystical Experience in the Middle Ages*, Woodbridge, Suffolk, and Rochester, New York: Boydell Press, 1992

Glasscoe, Marion, *English Medieval Mystics: Games of Faith*, London: Longman, 1993

Hughes, Jonathan, *Pastors and Visionaries: Religion and Secular Life in Late Medieval Yorkshire*, Woodbridge, Suffolk: Boydell Press, 1988

Lagorio, Valerie M. (ed.), *Mysticism, Medieval and Modern*, Salzburg: Institut für Anglistik und Amerikanistik (Salzburg University), 1986

Petroff, Elizabeth Alvilda, *Body and Soul: Essays on Medieval Women and Mysticism*, Oxford and New York: Oxford University Press, 1994

Riehle, Wolfgang, *The Middle English Mystics*, translated by Bernard Standring, London and Boston: Routledge & Kegan Paul, 1981

Sells, Michael A., *Mystical Languages of Unsaying*, Chicago: University of Chicago Press, 1994

Watson, Nicholas, *Richard Rolle and the Invention of Authority*, Cambridge and New York: Cambridge University Press, 1991

Watson, Nicholas, "The Composition of Julian of Norwich's *Revelation of Love*", in *Speculum*, 68, 1993

Study of the mystical writers of the thirteenth and fourteenth centuries has changed radically over the last three decades. Until the 1970s the subject was commandeered by clerics and those of strong religious affiliation, especially men. Typical of works by such scholars is Edmund Colledge's *The Mediaeval Mystics of England* (1962), an anthology with useful introductory survey, written from a Catholic standpoint, on the historical and cultural milieux of the mystics; the extract from Walter Hilton is ten times longer than that from Richard Rolle, and four times longer than those from Julian of Norwich's and Margery Kempe's texts. Assertively Catholic are David Knowles's *The English Mystical Tradition* (1961), originally a series of lectures, with sparse footnotes and lacking a bibliography, and his *What is Mysticism?* (1966, reprinted 1988); the tone of each is doctrinaire and partial: Rolle is inferior to Hilton, the *Cloud* author is treated most fully, and ahistorical comparisons with Teresa and John of the Cross are unhelpful. T.W. Coleman attempts a "free churchman's" view of mysticism in *The English Mystics of the Fourteenth Century* (1938, reprinted 1971), which is essentially descriptive rather than evaluative, while Gerald Bullett in *The English Mystics* (1950), alone among earlier critics, extends discussion of mysticism to the whole area of English literature , especially the metaphysical and Romantic poets and Cambridge Platonists. Today the subject has broadened considerably: now writers on mystics are predominantly women, who deal with body matters, and the cultural aspects and psychology of mysticism; "transcultural" study of mysticism sets English mystics in the context of writers from all faiths, especially Judaism and Islam (see Sells, below); and one controversial but objective general study of mysticism, Richard Kirby's *The Mission of Mysticism* (1979), even includes science fiction. It is now the practice to identify a continuity of English mystical tradition from Old English poetry and the *Ancrene Riwle* to the later Middle Ages, and to relate English mystics to their Continental counterparts. Critical commentary (for example, in *Mystics Quarterly*) is currently focused on Hildegard of Bingen, the beguines, and Rhineland mystics. Richard Rolle is being reconsidered, especially as his Latin works are translated and critiqued (see Watson, below). Walter Hilton's Latin *oeuvre* has largely been identified, and translated, and the *Cloud* author has continued to receive attention since the publication of Hodgson's Early English Texts Society's editions of his works. Much is being written on Julian of Norwich and Margery Kempe. Barry Windeatt's (ed.) *Medieval English Mystics* (1993) and Karen

Armstrong's *The English Mystics of the Fourteenth Century* (1991) provide recent anthologies of the English mystics in translation.

RIEHLE's study was the first to apply consistently a comparative method of analysis over the whole spectrum of mystical writing in English. His work, which has generated much writing on mystics in the 1980s and 1990s, is a close study of the imagery and diction of the mystics. He discusses the primary source of mystical imagery, *The Song of Songs*, and considers the mystical metaphors for God and spiritual union. His study is still both useful and inspiring because it considers the English mystics in relation to Continental mystics from Bernard of Clairvaux on. Riehle was the first to demonstrate that Rolle was not wilfully eccentric in his Latin works, but deploying imagery which had long been traditional in Latin mysticism. Mystical theology is analysed in terms of its linguistic expression, and the interplay between mystical theology and experience is helpfully explored as a search for terms of expression for the inexpressible – for example, as "spiritual" sense perception, like "tasting God", and terms for mystic rapture ("excessus mentis") and the presence of God within the reformed soul. The book is linguistically demanding, in that neither Latin terms and quotations are translated, nor are Middle English ones. The notes, bibliography, and index, though, are full and helpful.

BEER's study attempts, not entirely successfully, to place writings about women, and by women, in a historical frame which alters with shifts in cultural emphasis, from woman as leader in the martial imagery of Abbess Hildegard of Bingen, through the growth in courtly sentiments shown in the nobly-born Mechtild of Magdeburg's use of the diction of sentimental and sexual love, to the self effacing modesty of Julian of Norwich, who writes of Christ's intimacy and maternal tenderness: he is "a kindly teacher, and she his student", who in turn becomes "a teacher for us all". In this progression, the works of the so-called *Katherine*-Group are pivotal, demonstrating the cultural moment in which woman is demoted from active to passive agent in spiritual as well as social behaviour. Unfortunately, texts are sometimes forced into this simplified mould, and there are inaccuracies, such as the consistent translation of *Ancrene Riwle* as *Nuns' Rule*: the recipients of *Ancrene Riwle* were anchoresses, not nuns, as a correct translation of the title indicates.

Much surer in its historical basis, GLASSCOE's book provides an introduction to the five main medieval English mystics – Rolle, the *Cloud* author, Hilton, Julian, and Margery Kempe – by analyzing the content of their major writings in English and explaining their methodology in terms of contemporary liturgical and devotional practice. The focus is on readership, both then and now. The title is based on Hilton's *Scale of Perfection* (a different quotation on "play" is supplied on the frontispiece) but does not fit all the medieval writers' approaches to mystical love treated here, which may initially confuse some readers. For the beginner who knows little of medieval religion, this is an excellent starting-text, with glossed illustrative quotations in Middle English and full translation of Latin terms and quotations in both text and notes.

PETROFF discusses, in the form of essays on medieval religious women, some of which have been previously published, Continental women of religion who influenced the medieval English mystics such as Margery Kempe, who knew of their lives and writings, and used them. It is also instructive to contrast these mystics with Julian of Norwich. Four of the chapters here focus on mystics: the first identifies the cultural setting which devout medieval women, to some extent, transcended (there is a brief section here on Julian of Norwich). The last two chapters examine Dutch and Italian mystics respectively, while Chapter 3 focuses on the beguines of Northern Europe, especially Hadewijch and Beatris of Nazareth. Other medieval women (who were mystics as well as leaders) treated here include Clare of Assisi and Hildegard of Bingen. Petroff follows the modern critical focus on "body", but identifies in mystical writings a "boundaryless sexuality in which desire and satisfaction cannot be distinguished", just as masculine and feminine cannot be distinguished'. This is paradoxical since the mystics, especially female mystics, used the language of passionate sexual love (*minne*) to express the total union of the soul with its Creator. Petroff translates all her quotations, and provides an essential contextualizing topic for studying the English mystics.

Other works worth consulting are: LAGORIO, which includes four essays on English writers from Anglo-Saxon times to the late fourteenth century; HUGHES, which offers evidence of the readership for mystical writings in fifteenth-century Yorkshire; SELLS, which is a scholarly survey of apophatic mysticism from Plotinus to Johannes Eckhard, including Arabic and Jewish traditions; and WATSON's 1991 study of Richard Rolle. Finally, WATSON's 1993 article contains an up-to-date bibliography of books and articles on medieval mystical writers, and an excellent overview of the current state of critical opinion on mystical writings.

ROSAMUND S. ALLEN

N

Nabokov, Vladimir 1899–1977

Russian-born American novelist, short-story writer, poet, dramatist, and critic

Alexandrov, Vladimir E., *Nabokov's Otherworld*, Princeton, New Jersey: Princeton University Press, 1991

Bader, Julia, *Crystal Land: Artifice in Nabokov's English Novels*, Berkeley: University of California Press, 1972

Grayson, Jane, *Nabokov Translated: A Comparison of Nabokov's Russian and English Prose*, Oxford: Oxford University Press, 1977

Hyde, G.M., *Vladimir Nabokov: America's Russian Novelist*, London: Marion Boyars, 1977

Rampton, David, *Vladimir Nabokov*, London: Macmillan, 1993; New York: St Martin's Press, 1993

Rowe, William Woodin, *Nabokov's Deceptive World*, New York: New York University Press, 1971

Sharpe, Tony, *Vladimir Nabokov*, London: Edward Arnold, 1991

Stegner, Page, *Escape into Aesthetics: The Art of Vladimir Nabokov*, New York: Dial Press, 1966; London: Eyre & Spottiswoode, 1967

Wood, Michael, *The Magician's Doubts: Nabokov and the Risks of Fiction*, London: Chatto & Windus, 1994; Princeton, New Jersey: Princeton University Press, 1995

Many readings of Vladimir Nabokov's work have been diagnosed, by HYDE at least, as emitting "a nervous exegetical jangle": "his work seems often to have been over-read by critics whose whole delight has been to work out the intricacies that Nabokov has carefully worked in. There seems to have been a tendency to have the meaning (lots of meaning, all at one go) and miss the experience". This fundamental debate about the business of criticism has divided Nabokov's audience for far too long. Hyde is in no doubt that aesthetics, for Nabokov, are fundamentally subsidiary to his real concern, which is morality. Critics like BADER, by contrast, see art as:

> . . . inevitably a rendering of emotion, observation, and philosophical speculation in aesthetic terms . . .. In Nabokov it is not that the action or characters of a novel "stand for" or "represent" the writing of a novel or the figure of the artist, but that certain descriptions of experience, character, or emotion illuminate and approximate artistic creation.

Thus, the aesthetic is seen as Nabokov's ultimate concern, and one can call on a multitude of Nabokovian renunciations of social, moral, political or philosophical purposes to justify it.

STEGNER's study (which Hyde rightly terms "misleadingly entitled") sets out to undermine a view like Bader's. His point "in discussing the games and deceptions, the parodies and distortions, the allusions and illusions is . . . that they, in fact, suggest a whole vision of reality and life". This endeavour comes up against some solid barriers, however: Stegner feels, for example, that *Pale Fire* reaches the "danger point at which preoccupation with form and style begins to leave content a little thin, character a little flat, and author and reader find themselves playing the game simply for its own sake". But he has no such problem with, for instance, *Lolita*, which, he avers, moves us to "a compassionate understanding of the suffering produced by an idealistic obsession with the never-to-be-had". Quite how this is to be squared with a document as typical as Nabokov's 1963 Introduction to *Bend Sinister* ("I am neither a didacticist nor an allegorizer") is hard to see.

WOOD's book is another that aims to come to terms with the moral rather than cerebral qualities of Nabokov's fiction (although, like all other Nabokov critics, Wood hardly sees these two features as unrelated). This is clear enough from the one or two emotional excesses Wood allows himself: for instance, Nabokov's Sebastian Knight, he tells us, "was born in language in Paris in 1938, and moves me close to tears now, in Devon, in 1994" – proof, for Wood, that Knight's "merely textual" existence is far from negligible. The enormous affective power of the "merely textual" is offered here as testimony against its detractors, who shun textual self-enclosure on the grounds that it bears little relation to "reality". The problem, however, is that Wood cannot explain to us precisely what it is about Sebastian Knight that provokes his incipient lachrymosity. His conclusions are much firmer when he is dealing with poststructuralist literary theories or applying an unfashionably New-Critical words-on-the-page approach to Nabokov's prose.

SHARPE, in the conclusion to his study, tries to iron out some of the dilemmas of the "aesthete or moralist" debate. He suggests that "any assessment of Nabokov's artistic achievement must start with his undoubted brilliance as a prose stylist". If we accept that he is indubitably this, we may legitimately go on to ask if we can "deduce an ethics from the aesthetics of Nabokov's highly-wrought fictions". Sharpe wants to answer in the affirmative, but, in fact, in trying to do so, he merely collapses back into a Nabokov-endorsed aestheticism: the novel "is moral, in Nabokov's view, to the degree that it is uninhibited by considerations from outside the realm of fiction". But isn't morality outside the realm of fiction? If it were not, doubt as to the relation between literature and ethics would be entirely inappropriate, and Sharpe's own response to the male protagonist of *Lolita* ("we find ourselves compelled by Humbert's fancy prose-style even as we deplore his morals") rather difficult to sustain.

RAMPTON's discussion of Humbert's "sense of horror" at his behaviour (a guilt that persists despite all his self-justificatory contortions) demonstrates just how difficult it is to pin Nabokov to the ethical wall in this way: "such pronouncements need have no special status, and one can easily imagine a critique that reveals them to be simply elaborate parodies of an ideology that requires moralistic tags to conclude its stories". He consequently makes the point that, although obvious, has been a long time coming in Nabokov criticism: "an appeal to internal evidence cannot by itself resolve such questions". Whether or not Nabokov's fictions can be shown to be *intrinsically* ethical is not the issue: what matters is criticism's wish or reluctance to construct an ethical discourse around them.

The style/ethics axis is, of course, only one of the concerns of the studies already mentioned. Each also takes up at length the familiar Nabokovian obsession with language. The preoccupation is perhaps pushed to imitative extremes in ROWE's study, which is replete with animadversions on semantic and other linguistic minutiae, including appendices providing "A Selection of Passages Wherein Sound Instrumentation, Especially Assonance, Contributes to Meaning in Nabokov's Works" and reflections on Nabokov's apparently sexual intent in various deployments of the "suggestive shapes" of the letters "l" and "v". Most commentators are concerned with somewhat broader issues, and particularly with the consequences of Nabokov's imposed "exile", for fictional purposes, in the English language. But, surprisingly, few really do justice to the complex relationship between Nabokov's work in Russian and that in English. Hyde admirably emphasises that the novels "reveal Nabokov's continuity with classic Russian literature" ("with its unshakeable moral concern", he adds in a tendentious parenthesis), but, with an oddity that is inexplicable (for Hyde is skilled in Russian) he treats the Russian works "as if they were first written in English: an unscholarly procedure, of course".

Neither Grayson nor Alexandrov, who have produced perhaps the most scholarly monographs on Nabokov to date, is content with such a policy. GRAYSON's book is, indeed, specifically concerned with the relationships between Nabokov's Russian and English prose and, as well as individual chapters on what she terms the "major reworkings" (*Laughter in the Dark*, *Despair*, *The Eye*, and *King, Queen, Knave*) and a chapter on "minor reworkings" (such as *Lolita* and *Mary*), includes an extensive discussion of Nabokov's theory and technique of translation, and an impressive comparative examination of his style. Grayson's approach is clearly of considerable value to the comparative linguist and (because of the greater or lesser changes he usually made when translating) the critic interested in Nabokov's development. She is convinced that the most striking tendency in the *oeuvre* is "towards increasing stylisation, increasing deployment of artifice. The controlling hand of the author is more openly revealed, the reader is continually reminded that the action and the characters are but products of the artistic imagination".

ALEXANDROV announces that the aim of his book "is to dismantle the widespread critical view" that Nabokov "is first and foremost a meta-literary writer". But he does not wish to reinvoke the now familiar "writer's obligation to address existing, 'real' problems". Instead, he wishes us to re-orient ourselves in a direction that differs from both of these extremes. This direction is indicated by the "central theme" of Nabokov's work, which he variously labels "the otherworld", "the hereafter", and "the beyond". The cue here is taken from Nabokov's wife, Vera, who laid claim to this "central theme" in her Foreword to a posthumous (1979) collection of Nabokov's Russian poems. Although Alexandrov's subsequent discussions of Nabokov are trenchant and sophisticated, this is a very weak first link in his chain, and the addition of a second, in the form of Nabokov's posthumously published lecture "The Art of Literature and Common Sense", does not necessarily strengthen his position. What matters is not so much the insecure platform on which Alexandrov erects his interpretation of Nabokov, but his willingness to seek a way out of that moral/aesthetic impasse in which Nabokov criticism has often trapped itself. More – better – escape routes need to be established.

MACDONALD DALY

Naipaul, V.S. 1932–

Trinidadian novelist, short-story writer, and travel writer

Cudjoe, Selwyn R., *V.S. Naipaul: A Materialist Reading*, Amherst: University of Massachusetts Press, 1988
Hassan, Dolly Zulakha, *V.S. Naipaul and the West Indies*, New York: Peter Lang, 1989
Hughes, Peter, *V.S. Naipaul*, London: Routledge, 1988
Kamra, Shashi, *The Novels of V.S. Naipaul: A Study in Theme and Form*, New Delhi: Prestige, 1990
King, Bruce, *V.S. Naipaul*, London: Macmillan, 1993; New York: St Martin's Press, 1993
Neill, Michael, "Guerrillas and Gangs: Frantz Fanon and V.S. Naipaul", in *Ariel*, 13, 1982
Nixon, Rob, *London Calling: V.S. Naipaul: Postcolonial Mandarin*, Oxford: Oxford University Press, 1992
Thieme, John, *The Web of Tradition: Uses of Allusion in V.S. Naipaul's Fiction*, London: Hansib, 1987

In 1960 George Lamming attacked Naipaul's "castrated satire", initiating a stream of criticism of Naipaul from Third World critics ever since, usually consisting of accusations of defeatism, racism, and generally of being a lackey of neocolonialism. Rarely can so many critics have written books about a writer whom they appear to detest. None the less, Naipaul remains one of the most challenging of contemporary novelists, his writing firmly focused on the realities of postcolonial societies and the legacy of Empire.

Always an intensely allusive writer, Naipaul frequently launches an intertextual challenge to Eurocentric scripts in his fiction. THIEME's outstanding study, a major contribution to the understanding of both Naipaul's work and the nature of intertextuality, establishes that Naipaul uses allusion in a highly original way, extending the Western literary tradition to accommodate other fictive worlds (e.g., calypso culture, the Spanish picaresque, Hindu fable, Arthurian legend). The discussion of Naipaul's relation to Joseph Conrad is illuminating, and the modesty of the book's tone should not obscure its standing as the one essential work on Naipaul.

In a substantial essay, NEILL examines Naipaul's literary career in terms of a gradually unfolding argument with a very different writer, his fellow West Indian Frantz Fanon, exploring their common exploration of the themes of psychological dependence and individual freedom, the politics of neocolonialism, revolution, and apocalypse, and the novelist as historian. Neill concedes that Naipaul's Fanonian indignation at the destructive legacy of imperialism is matched by a deepening despair, but he elucidates the sources, literary and political, of that despair in a scholarly and sophisticated fashion.

Sophistication is not the major virtue of CUDJOE's study, which sets out to account for the complex relation between Naipaul's mastery of narrative forms and his problematic ideological relationship with the Third World. In his view, the high points of Naipaul's career are *A House for Mr Biswas* (charting the transition from feudalism to capitalism) and *The Mimic Men* (formal independence and its consequences). Thereafter it is downhill all the way as Naipaul supposedly identifies with imperialist ideology and fails to deliver socially useful and morally uplifting fiction. Cudjoe fails to consider that Naipaul may have Swiftian virtues, rather than a desire to purvey Arnoldian sweetness and light, and his continual identification of the views of characters or narrators as Naipaul's own does not create confidence. There are many minor factual errors, and the psychoanalytic readings are unconvincing.

HASSAN's is the second study by a Caribbean critic, and is more sympathetic, envisaging Naipaul as an honest commentator on a tenuously rooted colonial society. The book begins with two highly informative chapters on the history and politics of Trinidad, drawing often on hard-to-obtain primary materials from West Indian newspapers and journals. Although the remainder of the book devotes too much space to plot summary and to discussion of other critics, Hassan's emphasis on Naipaul as satirist and the highlighting of issuses of ethnicity, race, and religion in Naipaul criticism make interesting reading.

KAMRA also reads Naipaul as a Third-World writer, offering an analysis of the function of the polarized narrator- and protagonist-positions as an index of his commitment. By emphasising subjective truth, Naipaul deconstructs social authoritarianism. A particular strength of the volume is Kamra's discussion of the failures of individualism: "Naipaul shows that in a democratic world which stresses respect for the individual, survival is possible only in power groups".

Naipaul often calls metropolitan cultural norms into question by a blurring of the lines between literary forms, and by a conscious trespassing across the boundaries of novel, history, essay, cultural critique, travelogue, and autobiography. NIXON concentrates on the non-fiction, now arguably greater in volume and significance than the novels. As his ironic, censorious title suggests, Nixon sees Naipaul's true affiliation as being to metropolitan values, and finds him dismissive of the Third World. The more useful (indeed, outstanding) part of the volume locates Naipaul in relation to British traditions of travel writing, in that liminal area where travelogue, autobiography, and ethnography meet. Conrad is also, predictably, a major focus. In his vigorous contestation of Naipaul's role as expert on the Third World, however, it does not appear to have struck Nixon that a writer is not responsible for his readers. This dimension of the volume is less a study of Naipaul than of the crudities and misrepresentations inherent in his reception.

Two general introductions can be recommended, each of which reflects one of the dominant trends in Naipaul criticism. HUGHES writes elegantly and provides one of the best accounts of the later work, particularly highlighting the allusions to non-fictional writers, including William Hazlitt, William Cobbett, and Thomas De Quincey, although there are points where the weakness of his awareness of the social context shows. KING amply compensates for this lack with a firm sense of the specificities of political history and two useful appendices on Naipaul's family background and on the racial politics of Trinidad.

JUDIE NEWMAN

Narayan, R.K. 1906–

Indian novelist and short-story writer

Beatina, Mary, *Narayan: A Study in Transcendence*, New York: Peter Lang, 1993

Harrex, S.C., "Celebrating Malgudi's Golden Jubilee", in *CRNLE Reviews Journal* (Adelaide), 1–2, 1988

Holmstrom, Lakshmi, *The Novels of R.K. Narayan*, Calcutta: Writers Workshop, 1973, revised 1992

McLeod, A.L. (ed.), *R.K. Narayan: Critical Perspectives*, New Delhi: Sterling, 1994

Naik, M.K., *The Ironic Vision: A Study of the Fiction of R.K. Narayan*, New Delhi: Sterling, 1983

Walsh, William, *R.K. Narayan: A Critical Appreciation*, London: Heinemann, 1982; Chicago: University of Chicago Press, 1982

R.K. Narayan, who published his first novel, *Swami and Friends* in 1935 is one of India's foremost English-language novelists and short-story writers, and arguably the best known. Although his work has by now been the subject of considerable critical attention, it has not perhaps attracted as much as one might expect of a writer who has published over two dozen novels and collections of short stories. This may be in part because of his continued preference for pre-modernist fictional techniques, which are anathema to some critics and reviewers. While some critics see his work as naive, much of the published criticism has enthusiastically celebrated Narayan's comedy, his irony, and his creation of the fictional world of Malgudi, seen by many as a microcosm of India. Only recently – and rarely – have more theoretical critical perspectives been applied to Narayan's work.

HOLMSTROM has written a brief survey of Narayan's fiction up to *The Sweet-Vendor* (1967). The over-generalised introductory history of the English language in India, and the somewhat idiosyncratic concluding chapter on the tradition of Indian fiction in English and Narayan's place in it, tend to detract from her analysis of Narayan's art. However, the two central chapters – on the development of themes in the novels and on Narayan's techniques of fiction – constitute a useful introduction to the early fiction. In particular she offers a useful discussion of the cyclical pattern in Narayan's fiction.

WALSH offers what is essentially a Western humanist reading of Narayan's fiction, which is especially useful for the way it treats Narayan in relation to some Western practitioners of the novel – such as Henry James, E.M. Forster, D.H. Lawrence – while also emphasising the characteristics that distinguish his fiction from Western forms. Treating the work as serious comedy he charts the maturation of Narayan's fiction up to *The Painter of Signs* (1976), through what he sees as a series of well-defined progressive stages, which communicate the increasingly complex life of Malgudi. While it is difficult to agree with some of Walsh's assertions – for example, that Narayan is not a political novelist, or that there is no colonial indignation in his work – this is nevertheless a significant study.

NAIK has written a detailed, thoughtful, and substantial study of Narayan's fiction, which presents him as a major novelist (and lesser short-story writer) whose work deals with "the quintessential irony of what man can make of himself and of the entire business of living". He challenges those critics who have dismissed Narayan as an amusing social ironist, and argues that rather than offering the reader superficial irony, Narayan has developed his irony into a vision. The book, which treats the novels to *The Painter of Signs* and the short stories to *Old and New* (1981), also contains some interesting and useful appendices: a graph of the narrative technique in *The Guide*; a map of Malgudi and its environs and a plan of the street layout of Malgudi itself; and a (mainly Indian) bibliography.

HARREX's piece, ostensibly a review of *Talkative Man* and *Under the Banyan Tree*, is actually a lively and engaging retrospective of the first 50 years of Narayan's fiction, which provides an excellent, succinct introduction to his work. Harrex discusses, in particular, the narrative stategies Narayan uses in his fiction, including "the metamorphosis of facts from personal life into fictive form", which he illustrates with an extract from an interview with a real-life Sampath, the man behind Narayan's character of the same name in the novel *Mr Sampath*.

BEATINA argues that rather than presenting the human condition *per se*, Narayan's fiction presents the human condition through spiritual experience – which may, on a naive level, take the shape of encounters with the gods, but is more often and thoroughly explored through realistic events, which nevertheless take a character into a radically different world. The book does not attempt to offer a comprehensive study of Narayan's *oeuvre*, but rather provides a detailed analysis of the four novels which best fit her thesis – *Swami and Friends*, *The Bachelor of Arts*, *The English Teacher*, and *The Guide*.

McLEOD presents 18 papers (originally delivered at a Narayan conference in Mysore, 1992) which approach Narayan's work from a variety of theoretical (feminist, Marxist, dialogic) and comparative (with Patrick White, Margaret Laurence, Chaman Nahal) perspectives. The majority of essays, like the opening homage by M.M. Mahood, are celebratory without being uncritically enthusiastic. Some others, however, such as those by Britta Olinder and D.A. Shankar, are considerably more qualified in their praise. Taking as a starting point Michel Foucault's view that power is everywhere, Olinder examines the nature of the power or powerlessness of Narayan's female characters. Shankar, in turn, criticises what he sees as a damning lack of social realism in Narayan's fiction, caused by his ignoring of the role of caste in Indian life. He argues that by presenting caste only in its broadest (*varna*) sense and ignoring the complex but essential sub-caste (*jati*) system altogether, Narayan cannot portray an authentic picture of the Indian social scene. The range of opinions and critical approaches represented here, and the generally high quality of the contributions, make this a welcome and valuable addition to Narayan scholarship.

RALPH J. CRANE

Narrative Theory

Bonheim, Helmut, *The Narrative Modes: Techniques of the Short Story*, Cambridge: D.S. Brewer, 1982
Chatman, Seymour, *Story and Discourse: Narrative Structure in Fiction and Film*, Ithaca, New York: Cornell University Press, 1978
Lanser, Susan S., *The Narrative Act: Point of View in Prose Fiction*, Princeton, New Jersey: Princeton University Press, 1981
Martin, Wallace, *Recent Theories of Narrative*, Ithaca, New York: Cornell University Press, 1986
Rimmon-Kenan, Shlomith, *Narrative Fiction: Contemporary Poetics*, London and New York: Methuen, 1983
Sturgess, Philip J.M., *Narrativity: Theory and Practice*, Oxford: Clarendon Press, 1992
Toolan, Michael J., *Narrative: A Critical Linguistic Introduction*, London and New York: Routledge, 1988

CHATMAN's text has become a classic of narratological theory and still constitutes an indispensable introduction for the undergraduate. His premises derive from French theory – notably his elaboration of Barthes's concept of *noyau* and *catalyse* – to provide a very useful and more user-friendly schema of "kernels" and "satellites" as an underpinning for the analysis of narrative events. Chatman's eclectic mind, however, also draws on American film theory, cartoon strips, post-Chomsky linguistics, and speech-act theory to garner into one elegantly written volume his views on such crucial elements as plot, time, suspense, style, point of view, and implied narrators/narratees. The novitiate to narratology will find especially useful his exposition of temporal modes in terms of "summary", "ellipses", "scene", "stretch", and "pause". Unusually for a structuralist, he believes the idea of "character" is still important, and his paradigm of traits will delight any follower of A.C. Bradley. The book throughout is fully furnished with literary (rather than philosophical) examples, has extremely helpful explanatory diagrams, no bibliography, but comprehensive footnotes and two good indexes.

RIMMON-KENAN's study has become the standard handbook on all aspects and basic elements of narrative theory. Despite many refinements effected in the field in recent years, it remains an indispensable starting-point and guide for all students of the subject. Rimmon-Kenan commences by exploring the question of what constitutes a story: using A.-J. Greimas, Vladimir Propp, and Claude Bremond, she problematises issues such as time and causality, narrative grammars, and deep versus surface structure. A fine chapter on characterisation (much indebted to Chatman and Barthes) leads on to a discussion of the handling of time and focalisation in narrative – the former providing a thorough and practical reading of Gérard Genette, the latter anticipating Lanser in its use of Boris Uspensky to distinguish focalisation from mode of narration.

Rimmon-Kenan then moves from the "what" of a narrative to the "how", furnishing the reader with detailed and uncontroversial analyses of levels of narration (taking issue with Chatman here on the vexed question of the implied author), a typology of narrators and their reliability, and finally a brief but extremely helpful account of mimesis, diagesis, and free indirect speech.

Rimmon-Kenan's clarity of style and presentation, together with her extensive coverage of the topic and appropriate use of literary examples, makes this introductory textbook a must for all beginners in the field; the bibliography, though dated, is still useful and the index is excellent.

LANSER's text, unlike Chatman's or Rimmon-Kenan's, is not intended as a general introduction to all aspects of narrative theory, but is a study of one particular central aspect, the "fictionalisation of point of view". To this end, Lanser employs not only traditional formalist/structuralist material, but also the speech-act theories of J.L. Austin and John Searle. Moreover, the *literary* act, Lancer claims, can never avoid being ideological, since point of view is what mediates between fictional presentation and the way we perceive social reality. After an introductory survey of the relationships obtained between authorial voice, narrator, characters, and audience (and the ways in which these have been presented by twentieth-century theorists from formalist/structuralist critics to Uspensky, Yuri Lotman, R. Weiman, and Roger Fowler), she proceeds to develop a highly sophisticated theory of point of view. This involves problematising "the ontological status of the narrative voice" by means of an examination of such features as extra-fictional devices, the implied author, levels of narration, focalisers, and narrative authority. Finally, using Genette's narrative categories, she works out a remarkably complex chart of the authoritative status of the narrator (omniscient, reliable, etc.), his/her mode of contact with the narratee (direct, contemptuous, etc.), and his/her stance (diegetic/mimetic, spatial-temporal, psychological, and ideological). The book concludes with illuminating studies of Kate Chopin's "The Story of an Hour" and Ernest Hemingway's "The Killers"!

Although this is not an easy study, it is rewarding for its insights on many aspects of point of view: some may find the speech-act material rather extraneous and of little practical use in the analysis of long narratives, and one could certainly complain that not enough literary examples are provided throughout the theoretical parts of the text; but the excellent diagrams and the applicability of the methodology demonstrated in Chapter 6 make this book a welcome addition to the mighty corpus of works on narrative theory.

The slant of TOOLAN's book in the Routledge "Interface" series is indicated by its subtitle, "*A Critical Linguistic Introduction*". The first three chapters cover much the same ground as Rimmon-Kenan (*fabula/sjuzet*, Barthes's functions, Propp's actants, Genette's theories of narrative time), though with much greater attention to aspects of language; but Chapter 5 deals in much more extensive detail with the topic of free indirect discourse. The examples are extremely illuminating and the critique of Ann Banfield's "unspeakable sentences" is incisive and well-judged. The remaining three chapters cover new ground by examining Labov's six-part model of oral narrative as "socially-situated" discourse, surveying, with cogent examples, the rapidly-expanding field of interest in children's narratives and deconstructing the language of political and ethnic expression.

Each chapter is accompanied by copious notes, suggestions for further reading, and stimulating exercises. Toolan's style is highly readable, terminology is clearly explained, his examples are almost invariably apt, and the stress on linguistic elements (especially in the section on children's narrative) is particularly welcome and provides a good introduction to the literary stylistics of scholars such as Roger Fowler, Geoffrey Leech, Mick Short, Paul Simpson, and Willie Van Peer. The glossary is too brief and rather random in its selection of items; but the bibliography is full and up to date. This is very much a book for the neophyte, but in no way does it oversimplify its subject, and it will stimulate a desire to explore this area further.

BONHEIM's is a more specialised study, since it is concerned primarily with short stories, stresses the importance of beginnings and endings, and uses a highly statistical method of analysis based on a reading of 600 short stories and 300 novels. It would be wrong to conclude from this, however, that Professor Bonheim is too dryly Teutonic in his approach, since the rather daunting figures (Anteriority, 67.66% ... Epanalepsis . . . 9%, etc.) are mercifully confined to two appendices. Prior to this, we have had a highly readable account of what Bonheim regards as the four quintessential narrative modes: report, speech, description, and comment. These are applied to a very wide range of fiction from the sixteenth century onwards, often with surprising and revealing results – twentieth-century short stories tend to open with speech, nineteenth-century ones prefer description: Canadian, American, and English texts differ very considerably in this respect. Especially helpful are Chapters 4 and 5 on "Sub-Modes of Speech" and "Inquits" respectively: this is an area few other narratological theorists have explored so fully. Bonheim's enormous range of quotations also has the pleasing effect of making you want actually to read the stories from which they have been excerpted.

Finally, Bonheim's critique of French and American structuralist methodology and his use of German models to provide a simpler, yet flexible, narratological schema offers a welcome antidote to some of the complexities other theorists have indulged in, and should appeal to students and general readers alike.

Perhaps the most wide-ranging study in the 1980s has been MARTIN's. This is a useful complement to the other books reviewed here, since not only does Martin deal with such issues as the semiotics of narrative, the structural analysis of sequences, meta-fiction, language and ideology, and the composition of character, but he also provides an incisive critique of the handling of these issues by other theorists from 1945 onwards. Moreover, in Chapter 3, he discusses how narrative theory applies not only to fictions but also to other disciplines, such as history, autobiography, and psychoanalysis. Particularly welcome too (and this is largely neglected by the other writers reviewed here) is his scrupulous attention in Chapter 7 to the act of reading, where the work of Wolfgang Iser and Roland Barthes (in *S/Z*) receive their due share of analysis.

Another unique feature of this study is that, instead of applying the various critical theories to a collection of literary texts at the end of the book (as Lanser does), Martin uses three works of fiction, by Katherine Mansfield, Hemingway, and Mark Twain, as threads running throughout the entire book to demonstrate the theoretical ideas under debate. For its clarity of exposition, range of coverage, and helpful charts and diagrams, this book should be on every undergraduate's required reading list. Each chapter is furnished with a brief but well-selected bibliography.

Even more interesting, however, is STURGESS's innovative attempt to define narrativity. This could be described roughly as the enabling force that generates narrative, a set of necessary principles, which motivate the production of stories; this is not unlike the structuralists' view of structure as the prior enabling mechanisms that allow individual texts to come into being. Narrativity thus is always syntagmatic and "determines not only the chronology of a novel's story, but equally every interruption of that chronology, and every variation in the mode of representation of that story". To demonstrate this, Sturgess elaborates six key principles, which provide a logic of narrativity, including causal correspondence, auto-coherence, and non-contradictoriness. Having surveyed other approaches, for example those of Paul de Man, Jonathan Culler, Jean Piaget, Bremond, Paul Ricoeur and Barthes, he concludes that *post hoc, ergo propter hoc* is the guiding motto for the analysis of narrativity. The second part of his study consists of subtle, intricate, and provocative analyses of four vastly different novels (by Joseph Conrad, James Joyce, Edna O'Brien, and Arthur Koestler) to test to the utmost the theory of narrativity worked out in Part One.

This is a richly complex, sometimes irritatingly opinionated, but always fascinating exploration of a hitherto little-studied aspect of narratology, and a review such as this cannot possibly convey the depth and incisiveness of Sturgess's thought: it is not easy reading – the style can be highly abstract at times – but it should certainly pay rich dividends to those who persevere.

A.W. LYLE

See also **Fiction: Theory**

Native American Literature

Allen, Paula Gunn, *The Sacred Hoop: Recovering the Feminine in American Indian Traditions*, Boston: Beacon Press, 1986

Coltelli, Laura, *Winged Words: American Indian Writers Speak*, Lincoln: University of Nebraska Press, 1990

Krupat, Arnold, *The Voice in the Margin: Native American Literature and the Canon*, Berkeley: University of California Press, 1989

Lincoln, Kenneth, *Native American Renaissance*, Berkeley: University of California Press, 1983

Owens, Louis, *Other Destinies: Understanding the American Indian Novel*, Norman: University of Oklahoma Press, 1992

Ruoff, A. LaVonne Brown, *American Indian Literatures: An Introduction, Bibliographic Review, and Selected Bibliography*, New York: Modern Language Association of America, 1990

Vizenor, Gerald (ed.), *Narrative Chance: Postmodern Discourse on Native American Indian Literatures*, Albuquerque: University of New Mexico Press, 1989

Wiget, Andrew, *Native American Literature*, Boston: Twayne, 1985

Since the publication of N. Scott Momaday's Pulitzer Prize-winning *House Made of Dawn*, Native American literature has been undergoing what critics have come to refer to as a "Native American Renaissance". During the last two decades, readers have witnessed an amazing outpouring not only of contemporary American Indian literature but of studies devoted to that literature. Native American literature encompasses an ancient, yet ongoing oral tradition, as well as a written literature that began to develop after contact with European invaders, so many studies discuss the oral tradition, the written work, and the relationship between the two.

The title of LINCOLN's book reflects the recent powerful surge in Native American work. Lincoln stresses the importance of the tribal sense of interconnectedness in Native American literature: "the bonds of the Indian world turn on a tribal sense of relation to all being". Because of this bond "to all being", the ancient oral tradition has a profound impact on even the most recent written work; thus, Lincoln attempts to trace "the connective threads between the cultural past and its expression in the present". This is complicated by the fact that most work on the oral tradition has been anthropological instead of literary-critical, so Lincoln claims that his book is "neither anthropology nor literary criticism, strictly speaking, but a hybrid". Taking a rather experimental approach, the book progresses by way of surprising juxtapositions, "collating literature, folklore, history, religion, handcraft, and the expressive arts". For example, Lincoln uses a Blackfeet creation parable to shed light on the "Blackfeet epistemology" found in James Welch's novels: "This Blackfeet myth [about Old Man and Old Woman] illustrates the dialectic nature of a world where men and women are fated as counterfools. Reason meets its limitations, wedded to folly. Reality teeters on a fulcrum of absurdity".

WIGET's work provides an excellent general introduction to Native American literature, giving thorough treatment to both the oral tradition and the written work. Wiget does an especially good job of discussing the former. He provides a fine overview of the various types of oral literature, including the narratives, oratory, lyric poetry, and ritual poetry. His discussion of aspects of creation myths, such as the Earth-Diver stories and trickster figures, incorporates many compelling examples of these as they occur in various tribal narratives. Starting with Chapter 3, Wiget turns to the written work and treats the various genres (the "as-told-to" autobiographies, and those composed in English by Native Americans, the non-fictional religious and political writings, the histories, fiction, and poetry) chronologically up through the 1970s. Wiget provides excellent summaries of works, much good biographical information on authors, and important historical contexts for the works examined, which include those of William Apes through the contemporary fiction and poetry of Momaday, Leslie Silko, Welch, Wendy Rose, Simon Ortiz, and others.

ALLEN's book is a broad-ranging study of not only Native American literature but also American Indian tribal culture and the importance of that culture in the work of authors from Mourning Dove and D'Arcy McNickle to contemporaries such as Momaday, Welch, Silko, Gerald Vizenor, and Linda Hogan. Allen divides her book into three major sections. "The Ways of Our Grandmothers" discusses the gynocratic, or woman-centered, structures of tribes such as the Cherokee, Iroquois, Keres, and Hopi, and how that gynocratic structure slowly eroded after contact with European colonizers. "The Word Warriors" discusses both "traditional and contemporary American Indian literature", and incorporates much interesting commentary on the interaction between oral and written culture, and on how the former has had such an important impact on the latter. Throughout this section (and indeed throughout the book) Allen emphasizes the need to understand how profoundly cultural presuppositions color our understanding of literatures, and that Native American literature differs vastly in its presuppositions from Western ways of perceiving the world. Allen's explanations about such tribal concepts as ceremony and myth help the non-Native American reader see how such values are integral to both traditional and contemporary works. If one is to understand even minimally works by American Indians, it is necessary to understand and work through this difference: "the basic reality experienced by tribal peoples and by Western peoples are not the same, even at the level of folklore". Allen's final section, "Pushing up the Sky", speculates more daringly about the gynecentric structure of American Indian tribal culture, allowing full sway to her major premise that Anglo-European colonization caused "a progressive shift from gynecentric, egalitarian, ritual-based social systems to secularized structures closely imitative of the European patriarchal system". This shift may have, according to Allen, masked the important role played by lesbians and gays in tribal culture. At the very least, patriarchal acculturation and assimilation have distorted and disguised tribal attitudes concerning the acceptance of homosexuality.

VIZENOR has gathered an excellent collection of post-modern essays on contemporary Native American literature. He suggests that postmodern criticism (from Bakhtinian dialogism to deconstruction, to reader-response theory) can help shed a healthy light on Native American works. Indeed, his introductory essay ("A Postmodern Introduction") is a defence of postmodernism, which he says "liberates imagination and widens the audiences for tribal literatures; this new criticism rouses a comic world view, narrative discourse and language games on the past". Here are a few of the book's engaging approaches: Kimberly Blaeser ("*The Way to Rainy Mountain*: Momaday's Work in Motion") uses Wolfgang Iser's reader-response theories to discuss the tripartite structure of Momaday's book; Alan Velie ("The Trickster Novel") relies on Bakhtin's idea of the "chronotope" to focus mainly on Vizenor's *Darkness in Saint Louis Bearheart*; and Louis Owens ("'Ecstatic Strategies': Gerald Vizenor's *Darkness in Saint Louis Bearheart*") waxes eclectic with his borrowings from Michel Foucault, Roland Barthes, Jacques Lacan, and others to illuminate Vizenor's trickster novel.

KRUPAT wrestles with the idea of the canon in his study, devoting much of it to theorizing about canon formation. Ultimately he favors founding the canon on historicist and experiential, rather than formalist (New-Critical and deconstructionist), criteria. Such criteria dictate that we must include both Native American and African-American literature in the canon: "any proposed canon of American literature that does not include more than merely occasional examples of the literature produced by red and black people as well as white people ... is suspect on the very face of it". Krupat relies on Bakhtin's ideas of dialogism and "heteroglossia" both to counter contemporary formalists (Jacques Derrida, Paul de Man, J. Hillis Miller, and others) and to read Native American autobiographies as examples of the many-voicedness found in Native American literature. The autobiographies reflect a "difference within a normative context", a "secular heterodoxy" that "can be a social, not only a textual, principle, one authorizing a cosmopolitan world order".

COLTELLI has collected an important set of interviews with contemporary Native American authors Paula Gunn Allen, Louise Erdrich, Michael Anthony Dorris, Joy Harjo, Hogan, Momaday, Ortiz, Rose, Silko, Vizenor, and Welch. Each interview begins with a brief sketch of the author's life and work, and then Coltelli asks a set of questions, some of which are similar, of each of her interviewees. Her most helpful and interesting questions ask the authors to relate their work to what has gone before either in the oral tradition or in early written work; for example, Coltelli asks Allen "is there a difference in the use of humor in the old Indian stories and in the contemporary ones?", or asks Ortiz "would you talk about the storytelling tradition and its importance to you as a writer?" The answers to such questions provide valuable insights for readers of these authors' works.

RUOFF's book offers much as a research tool. Ruoff begins with a short, 70-page Introduction to Native American literature, which discusses the oral tradition and the written work through the 1980s. He follows this with a helpful bibliographic essay on both primary and secondary sources; his remarks on anthologies and collections of oral literature provide a much-needed guide for students and teachers interested in, but unfamiliar with, these works. Finally, he ends with a bibliography of Native American writing. Such categories as "Films and Videotapes", which lists videos of storytellers' and singers' performances, make Ruoff's work useful.

OWENS focuses solely on the Native American novel and its development from John Rollin Ridge's nineteenth-century novel (*The Life and Adventures of Joaquin Murieta*) to Vizenor's contemporary trickster novels. Owens relies on Bakhtinian dialogism in his approach to the novels, partly because the Native American novel grows out of an oral tradition in which "speaker and listener are coparticipants in the telling of a story". This critical perspective leads to interesting and compelling readings of the novels. In his examination of Silko's *Ceremony*, for example, he points out that "ultimately, Tayo must comprehend the web of meaning in his world through what Bakhtin calls 'internally persuasive' discourse, that which is 'affirmed through assimilation, tightly interwoven with one's own word'". Along with excellent explication of the novels, Owens offers helpful biographical, cultural, and historical information to contextualize his discussions.

MICHAEL HOBBS

New Criticism

Brooks, Cleanth, *The Well Wrought Urn: Studies in the Structure of Poetry*, New York: Reynal & Hitchcock, 1947; London: Dennis Dobson, 1949, revised 1968

Eagleton, Terry, *Literary Theory: An Introduction*, Oxford: Blackwell, 1983; Minneapolis: University of Minnesota Press, 1983

Richards, I.A., *Principles of Literary Criticism*, London: Kegan Paul, 1925; New York: Harcourt Brace, 1925

Richards, I.A., *Practical Criticism: A Study of Literary Judgement*, London: Kegan Paul, 1929; New York: Harcourt Brace, 1929

Robey, David, "Anglo-American New Criticism", in *Modern Literary Theory: A Comparative Introduction*, edited by Ann Jefferson and David Robey, London: Batsford, 1982, revised 1986; New York: Barnes & Noble, 1984

Wimsatt, W.K., Jr., with Monroe C. Beardsley, *The Verbal Icon: Studies in the Meaning of Poetry*, Lexington: University Press of Kentucky, 1954; London: Methuen, 1970

It is difficult to discuss American New Criticism without reference to earlier developments in a British context. Probably the most significant influence on the critical practices articulated by the New Critics was the work of I.A. Richards. RICHARDS (1925) argues that criticism needs to be a science of close reading, analysing the words on the page. Literature is to be read as a pseudo-statement rather than a referential use of language, an organising of emotions that communicates an experience of significant value. The critic should be a highly sophisticated reader whose job is to help other readers reach a comparable level of competence, "for the critic is as closely occupied with the health of the mind as the doctor with the health of the body". RICHARDS (1929) is an analysis of a sample of Cambridge English undergraduates reading a group of poems. Richards provides a series of recommendations for the study of poetry, suggesting that all works need to be read in terms of four aspects: sense, feeling, tone, and intention. He argues that "all respectable poetry invites close reading" and that the reader must "refrain from applying his own external standards" and, rather, be open to new perceptions.

BROOKS is one of the first American New-Critical studies of poetry, acknowledging its debt to Richards. Brooks argues that the language of poetry is the language of paradox, and provides a series of readings of individual poems from John Donne (the Metaphysical poets, especially Donne, were to be staple favourites of the New Critics) to W.B. Yeats to illustrate this. The poems are analysed principally in terms of their formal qualities and not their historical contexts. Brooks concludes with a central New-Critical idea, "The Heresy of Paraphrase", arguing that a poem has a formal identity and cannot be discussed as if it had a content independent of this form. Brooks' study is lucid and often engaging, and remains one of the best examples of New-Critical theory in action.

WIMSATT and BEARDSLEY give perhaps the most sophisticated theoretical argument for the value of New Criticism. The arguments of Richards are qualified considerably, the poem now being conceived of as "an object in the public domain, not the private creation of an individual", and to consider the thoughts of the author in question is to fall prey to the "intentional fallacy". All that matters is whether the individual text succeeds or fails as poetry. The authors also coined the term "affective fallacy" to deal with Richards' view that poetry was an expression of emotive language: Wimsatt and Beardsley maintain that a poem needs to be studied as an independent object and a vocabulary needs to be developed for practising this. Poetry is concerned with the reconciliation of opposites, something which occurs in the text itself, not the mind of the author or reader. Like Richards and Brooks, Wimsatt and Beardsley value metaphor as the principle vehicle of poetry because it is an attempt to achieve this reconciliation. Poetry should be "iconic", all features – metrical structure, figures of speech, syntactical arrangement – serving to reinforce one and other.

ROBEY provides a useful overview of the achievements of the New Critics, pointing out how influential their ideas still are in terms of institutional, if not theoretical, practice, and the crucial role of Richards. Robey argues that Richards' aesthetic principles are severely limited because he saw language as a transparent medium for communicating the emotional state of the author (a problem partly dealt with by later New Critics), and because of his limiting of the problem of interpretation to a simple question of closer reading. His influence has been the greater in America than Britain because of his insistence on the need for a theoretical defence of literary study. Robey points out that much New Criticism reaches conclusions similar to those reached by the Russian formalists and the structuralists of the Prague School, although they were far less interested in literary innovation and had a far narrower notion of structure. Robey doubts whether the "reconciliation of opposites is really a sound principle for defining poetry", suggests that the New Critics dealt poorly with avant-garde writing and relied too heavily on intuition as a critical principle, having faith in a consensus of literary judgement among experienced readers, "a consensus which, the recent history of criticism seems to suggest, is not all that often achieved".

Robey criticises the New Critics' rather limited view of the relationship between literature and history, pointing out that, according to most New Critics, "the only history that the critic must master is the history of words", so that the public meaning of a particular poem can be grasped. This criticism is developed in EAGLETON, who argues that the New Critics effectively dematerialised the text, cutting it off from any historical or social reality, and imbued it "with an absolute mystical authority which brooked no rational argument". Eagleton accuses New Criticism of being a "full-blooded irrationalism" which privileged the lyric poem over all other literary genres, converting it into a "fetish". He argues that the critical principles developed were unable to deal adequately with more discursive literary forms such as the novel, which cannot be analysed simply as "tightly organized structures of symbolic ambivalence", and that the disinterested and ironic stance recommended was "a recipe for political inertia, and thus submission to the political status quo". Eagleton's polemical attack simplifies the intellectual subtly displayed by thinkers such as Wimsatt and Beardsley and homogenises a group of often diverse individuals, but his comments expose many of the weaknesses of the New-Critical position.

ANDREW HADFIELD

New England Literature

Astro, Richard, and James Nagel (eds.), *American Literature: The New England Heritage*, New York: Garland, 1981

Buell, Lawrence, *New England Literary Culture from Revolution Through Renaissance*, Cambridge and New York: Cambridge University Press, 1986

Cohen, Daniel A., *Pillars of Salt, Monuments of Grace: New England Crime Literature and the Origins of American Popular Culture, 1674–1860*, New York and Oxford: Oxford University Press, 1993

Donovan, Josephine, *New England Local Color Literature: A Women's Tradition*, New York: Frederick Ungar, 1983

Dowling, William C., *Poetry and Ideology in Revolutionary Connecticut*, Athens: University of Georgia Press, 1990

Lowance, Mason I., Jr., *The Language of Canaan: Metaphor and Symbol in New England from the Puritans to the Transcendentalists*, Cambridge, Massachusetts: Harvard University Press, 1980

The study of New England literature is problematic because New England literary culture was, as Buell writes, "neither wholly generated nor unique", which makes "clear-cut demarcation of the territory impossible". And yet some account is obviously necessary when we consider that the New England literary tradition – from the early colonial writings of Anne Bradstreet, Cotton Mather, and William Bradford to the works of twentieth-century New England immigrants like Bernard Malamud and Norman Mailer – has had enormous impact on both American literature and American culture. Recent scholarship generally attempts to understand New England literature in terms of a broad range of cultural, social, historical, political, and ideological factors, which determine the production and perception of literary texts.

LOWANCE examines the impact of medieval and Reformation scriptural exegesis on seventeenth-century New England Puritans, and then shows how the Puritans' metaphorical modes of expression influenced the symbolic writings of the American Renaissance, especially those of Transcendentalist writers like Ralph Waldo Emerson and Henry David Thoreau. Lowance sees the "language of Canaan", the phrase Puritans used to describe "the language the saints will use when [God's] kingdom has been established", as profoundly affecting even mid-twentieth-century writers like Robert Frost. In fact, Lowance concludes that "America's deepest rhetorical impulse has always been the expression of future promise, an articulation of imminent fulfillment that will no doubt characterize the literature throughout the centuries to come".

ASTRO and NAGEL bring together ten distinguished American literary scholars in this volume, which offers a diverse range of critical approaches to New England literature, from Joel Myerson's look at the literary outgrowth of Puritan culture, to Leslie Fiedler's exploration of Harriet Beecher Stowe's *Uncle Tom's Cabin* in relation to the antebellum South, to William Robinson's overview of the shaping influence of New England black literature written prior to the 1920s' Harlem Renaissance. Linda Wagner, the sole female essayist presented, analyzes the contributions of Emily Dickinson, Anne Sexton, and Sylvia Plath to a non-traditional, distinctly female articulation of alienation, loss of place, and the search for a sense of self.

DONOVAN discusses the New England school of women local colorists – Beecher Stowe, Rose Terry Cooke, Elizabeth Stuart Phelps, Sarah Orne Jewett, and Mary E. Wilkins Freeman – to show that these writers forged a strong tradition of literary realism to counteract the "inauthentic female characters" of the sentimental romance, which dominated American women's writing well into the nineteenth century. Moreover, the local colorists, she suggests, shaped the first American women's literary tradition to transcend a negative critique of male-dominated attitudes and customs: "the New England women created a counter world of their own, a rural realm that existed on the margins of patriarchal society, a world that nourished strong, free women". Readers may object to Donovan's selection of only the most canonical of this "uncanonical" group of writers, and they may find too neat her somewhat totalizing view of these writers, who often held quite disparate notions concerning literature; nonetheless, Donovan addresses what had previously been a relative void in studies of New England literature, and she also points out the influence of these local colorists on twentieth-century writers like Edith Wharton, Willa Cather, Flannery O'Connor, and Eudora Welty.

BUELL stresses the ideology of provincialism, particularly the New England strain, by focusing on canonical and marginal writers between 1770 and 1865. Establishing the "Theoretical Premises" of his work, Buell surveys the practical limitations of various theoretical approaches to New England literature – New Criticism, semiotics, and deconstruction among them – and locates a Jamesonian kind of Marxist literary historiography through which "we may venture to approach the truth of history, whatever that truth may be". Buell's Appendix analyzes the career patterns of some 276 "major" and "minor" writers, according to period, ethnicity, gender, and class. Though, as Buell admits, such aggregate study tells us little about the individual aesthetics of literary production, it does facilitate some understanding of the "phenomenon of literary emergence" by illuminating the social, political, and economic factors shaping New England literary history and, by extension, the history of American literature in general. Although the study is rather pretentious in its handling of theoretical material, readers may still find it an intriguing and rewarding book.

DOWLING limits his study to the poetry of the small group of late eighteenth-century writers known as the "Connecticut Wits" – John Trumbull, David Humphreys, Timothy Dwight, and Joel Barlow. He sees these poets as "literary Augustans of the Revolution and early republic", continuing on their side of the Atlantic the struggle of English writers like Alexander Pope, Jonathan Swift, and James Thomson against the outmoded order symbolized by Robert Walpole's Whig government. Borrowing from twentieth-century early-republican historians like J.G.A. Pocock, Dowling identifies the country ideology of the Connecticut Wits, the negative or unmasking quality of their poems prompted largely by the literary opposition in England. Though some may feel that he too often privileges an Anglocentric worldview in his examination of American poetry, Dowling successfully illustrates how an understanding of historical context both informs and demystifies the role that poetry plays in the construction of the world.

COHEN traces colonial and early national readers' fascination for a variety of New England crime literatures written between 1674 and 1860. He surveys contemporary "popular" genres, including execution sermons, conversion narratives, crime ballads, trial reports, crime novels, and newspaper stories to show how, during the first half of the nineteenth century, "the print culture of crime evolved into a competitive industry, dominated by lawyers, journalists, professional authors, and cheap publishers, that saturated a mass consumer market with narratives of sex and violence". Cohen also shows how both technological advances in the printing industry and the rise of literacy helped shape New England crime publications. Although frequently repetitive, and while his claims concerning the audience of many of the genres discussed appear at times quite speculative, this study is certainly worthwhile reading for those interested in the development of American popular culture's insatiable curiosity for sensational, quasi-journalistic treatments of sex and violent crime.

PAUL W. DEPASQUALE

New Historicism

Fisher, Philip (ed.), *The New American Studies: Essays from "Representations"*, Berkeley: University of California Press, 1991

Greenblatt, Stephen J., *Renaissance Self-Fashioning: From More to Shakespeare*, Chicago: Chicago University Press, 1980

Greenblatt, Stephen J. (ed.), *Representing the English Renaissance*, Berkeley: University of California Press, 1988

Howard, Jean E., and Marion F. O'Connor (eds.), *Shakespeare Reproduced: The Text in History and Ideology*, New York and London: Methuen, 1987

Veeser, H. Aram (ed.), *The New Historicism*, New York and London: Routledge, 1989

Veeser, H. Aram (ed.), *The New Historicism Reader*, New York and London: Routledge, 1994

Wilson, Richard, and Richard Dutton (eds.), *New Historicism and Renaissance Drama*, London: Longman, 1992

New Historicism was the most potent sign of the "return to history" in English and American literary criticism of the 1980s. Derridean deconstruction had come to seem a formalist dead-end, an arch and empty form of New Criticism. New Historicism offered ways of considering the historical status of texts while not neglecting their formal attributes, which made literary texts so powerful for their readers. The most enthralling New-Historicist readings blend the tactic of "thick description" of a specific culture (a term borrowed from Clifford Geertz's anthropology) with Michel Foucault's claims as to the power of the state to compel obedience from its subjects as well as to control their subjective identity. They then demonstrate how literary texts are implicated in this process.

GREENBLATT's ground-breaking 1980 study, the first major New-Historicist monograph, demonstrates the power of the method. He studies a series of major male figures from the English Renaissance – Thomas More, Thomas Wyatt, William Tyndale, Edmund Spenser, Christopher Marlowe, and Shakespeare – and examines the conditions under which either their own subjectivity was formed, or under which it was possible for them to imagine characters with the illusion of autonomy and free will. He finds them fettered on all sides by the ubiquitous ideological and physical controls exerted by the manifold baleful powers of Tudor monarchs. Greenblatt's book is essential for any student of New Historicism, for the brilliance of his readings (especially of *Othello* and *The Faerie Queene*), the power of his writing, and the starkness of his Foucauldian account of the powers of the early-modern state.

HOWARD's anthology is eloquent witness that New Historicism quickly became a phenomenon more talked about than practised. Howard and O'Connor's introductory essay re-emphasises the centrality of Shakespeare in New-Historical accounts of Renaissance literature, and demonstrates the links between New Historicism and the emerging field of Cultural Studies, for "historicizing the text thus comes to mean, not only locating it within the coordinates of Renaissance culture, but mapping its uses at subsequent moments of reception and reproduction". For the creating of such a genealogy, the first two essays in the book, Walter Cohen's "Political Criticism of Shakespeare" and Don E. Wayne's "Power, Politics, and the Shakespearean Text: Recent Criticism in England and the United States", are very useful. They track New Historicism through its own historical moment, during the Reagan-Thatcher years of the 1980s, as critics who had trained during the 1960s achieved the institutional power with which they could critique those same institutions. They demonstrate as well both the similarities and the differences between New Historicism in North America and its feistier British cousin, usually called "cultural materialism".

GREENBLATT's 1988 anthology returns the scene of instruction to America, through a collection of essays by Greenblatt and other key New Historicists – Louis Montrose,

Joel Fineman, Stephen Orgel – all of which were first published in *Representations*, the journal co-edited by Greenblatt, effectively the flagship of New Historicism, and still the place where many critics of this persuasion enunciate their newest readings. The anthology thus maps both the continuing power of New-Historicist methodologies, and its seminal, darkened vision of the English Renaissance as the source of modern subjectivity in the West and – not coincidentally – the source also of the ideological powers of the modern state. Greenblatt attempts a brief account of those methods in his Introduction, but he has always been more comfortable with practising his theories than with theorising his own (and his associates') practice. VEESER's first New-Historicist anthology (1989) is much more useful in this latter regard. Veeser himself takes the position not of the practitioner but of the enthusiastic exegete. His Introduction is one of the most useful surveys of the field. He emphasises: New Historicism's hybrid bracketing of "literature, ethnography, anthropology, art history" to combat the rituals of formalist studies devoid of historical inflection; its insistence that art not be separated from the other symbol systems of any given culture; that scholars be implicated in the works (and ideologies) they describe, and, moreover, that they recognise the relationship between their own endeavours and the giddy circulations of the capitalist economies that support their research. Greenblatt himself acknowledges such matters, in a key essay reprinted by Veeser, where he shifts his terms from "New Historicism" to "cultural poetics" or the even looser metaphors of negotiations and exchange that mark Greenblatt's work thoughout the late 1980s. Veeser prints also a crucial essay by Louis Montrose, who enunciates the elegantly phrased principle of "the historicity of texts and the textuality of history", a mantra frequently cited by New Historicists, and closes his book with a nicely sceptical Postscript by Stanley Fish, who applauds the skills and successes of New Historicists but casts doubt on most of their claims.

Veeser includes material on Romantic and nineteenth-century texts, dispelling the illusion that New Historicism peters out some time around 1642. Rather, its methods have been adopted throughout the chronological range of English and American literary scholarship. FISHER's anthology is ample proof of this. Like Greenblatt, he collects a series of essays first printed in *Representations*. In turn these represent, as it were, the new orthodoxy in American studies. Ranging from readings of Benjamin Franklin to *The Birth of a Nation*, Fisher's selection effectively sketches a new cultural history of the United States: "a culture in its full institutional and individual variety is here in play". Fisher characterises the change in American studies as a shift from the study of founding myths – the shining city, the new frontier – to the study of rhetorics, "the place where language is engaged in cultural work". That shift implies an ongoing contest for meaning and power in the republic, and a consequent decline in the power of the East-Coast "Brahmins", whether priests or intellectuals, who had previously shaped America's cultural image of itself. For those not curious about America, Fisher's Introduction alone would bear reading, as a concise definition of the current ambitions of New Historicists.

WILSON and DUTTON's anthology returns again to the primal scene of New Historicism, the theatre of the English Renaissance. Theirs is the most useful guide for beginners. They reprint key New-Historicist essays, with a headnote elucidating the context in which that essay first appeared, and explaining its use of crucial New-Historicist terms; these are keyed to a user-friendly glossary where those terms are given basic but accurate definitions. Their own punchy Introduction sets out to "historicize New Historicism", which they see as the product of Reaganite capitalism, produced between a "political New Right" and "a demoralised Left". Their scathing comments signal the much stronger political commitments of British New Historicists (or cultural materialists), in their self-identified task, as "oppositional critics", to "amplify the voices of the ruled, exploited, oppressed and excluded".

VEESER's most recent anthology (1994) is the best one-volume introduction to New Historicism available to date. He prints, in full, crucial essays by Greenblatt, Montrose, and others, thus allowing readers to savour the pleasure as well as the power of New-Historicist texts. His Introduction expands on his earlier anthology, giving a more comprehensive account of New-Historicist origins and antecedents, emphasising not just the debt to Geertzian anthropology but also to the work on Renaissance culture pioneered at the Warburg and Courtauld Institutes in London. In particular Fances Yates's work on Renaissance iconography can now be seen as a crucial determinant of Greenblatt's, Montrose's, Orgel's, and Fineman's poetic readings of power. In the final section of his *Reader*, Veeser attempts to sketch a future for New Historicism, where its methodologies are invoked in readings of genders, sexualities, and postcolonial societies. Veeser is relentlessly upbeat about New Historicism's future. If he is right, it will continue to fertilise the voices of dissent, opposition, and change.

MARK HOULAHAN

New Literatures: General

Ashcroft, Bill, Gareth Griffiths, and Helen Tiffin, *The Empire Writes Back: Theory and Practice in Post-Colonial Literatures*, London and New York: Routledge, 1989

Barfoot, C.C., and Theo D'haen (eds.), *Shades of Empire in Colonial and Post-Colonial Literatures*, Amsterdam: Rodopi, 1993

Boehmer, Elleke, *Colonial and Postcolonial Literature: Migrant Metaphors*, Oxford and New York: Oxford University Press, 1995

De Weever, Jacqueline, *Mythmaking and Metaphor in Black Women's Fiction*, London: Macmillan, 1992; New York: St Martin's Press, 1992

King, Bruce (ed.), *Literatures of the World in English*, London and Boston: Routledge & Kegan Paul, 1974

King, Bruce (ed.), *The Commonwealth Novel since 1960*, London: Macmillan, 1991

Larson, Charles, *The Novel in the Third World*, Washington, D.C.: Inscape, 1976

Maes-Jelinek, Hena, Kirsten Holst Petersen, and Anna Rutherford (eds.), *A Shaping of Connections: Commonwealth Literature Studies – Then and Now: Essays in Honour of A.N. Jeffares*, Sydney: Dangaroo Press, 1989

Myrsiades, Kostas (ed.), "Teaching Postcolonial and Commonwealth Literatures", double isssue of *College Literature*, 19(3) & 20(1), 1992–93

Tiffin, Chris, and Alan Lawson (eds.), *De-Scribing Empire: Post-Colonialism and Textuality*, London and New York: Routledge, 1994

Walsh, William, *A Manifold Voice: Studies in Commonwealth Literature*, London: Chatto & Windus, 1970; New York: Barnes & Noble, 1970

Walsh, William, *Commonwealth Literature*, London and New York: Oxford University Press, 1973

The surge of nationalism in the colonies of European powers after World War II was both a political and a literary phenomenon, as people agitating for decolonisation recognised, from imperial examples, the role of literature in the management of reality. Within the former British Empire, these new literatures were first studied as "Commonwealth literature". With increasing translation of works from other languages into English, the term "New Literatures in English" (or "New English Literatures") came into use. The current trend is to study them within the wider context of postcolonial studies.

WALSH's 1970 work maintains that the Commonwealth embodies not just a political label but certain shared values. Walsh emphasises the bonds between literary creation and language as cultural products, and applies that principle in comparative studies of: native English speakers like the Australians Patrick White and A.D. Hope and the Canadian Morley Callaghan; second-language users, who also have a classical heritage of indigenous writing, like the Indian writers R.K. Narayan and Nirad C. Chaudhuri; and second-language users whose cultural heritage is oral, like the Nigerian Chinua Achebe. Katherine Mansfield and V.S. Naipaul receive attention as writers who, despite living in England, have written from a consciousness largely shaped by a different world.

WALSH continues his study of Commonwealth literature in his more concise 1973 book. The material is organised differently, in six chapters focused on India, Africa, the West Indies, Canada, New Zealand, and Australia. This arrangement enables a more intensive treatment of materials within each tradition, with greater attention to questions of historical roots and continuity, and embracing a greater number of writers. Some material from the earlier book is re-used, as in Walsh's discussion of Achebe.

KING (1974) brings together a group of essays on developments in creativity and criticism in Australia, Canada, England, India, Ireland, Kenya, Nigeria, South Africa, the USA, and the West Indies. Of these, A. Norman Jeffares examines the grey zone when English-language literature written by Irish people shifts from being Anglo-Irish to Irish literature – a discussion that also applies to Anglo-Indian literature. The dilemma of Third-World writers in European languages is confronted by B. Rajan and D.S. Izevbaye, writing on Indian and Nigerian literatures. In some of these essays, one sees the emergence of attempts to define new canons.

LARSON's pretentiously titled work undertakes, from a meagre sample of ten novels from four continents, to account for Third-World literatures through nineteenth-century anthropological theories of race. Larson offers a model of Third-World writing based on what he considers to be "common traits", which reflect a peculiarly Third-World ontology, namely: "the situational plot, involving a group of people instead of an individual; the lack of a developing character; the cyclical use of time; the extensive use of the oral tradition for establishing milieu and character; and the use of anthropological materials for recording the death of a culture". Larson generally avoids in-depth exploration in favour of superficial scanning of texts for features that, wrenched from their contexts, seem to confirm his preconceptions. Thus, he interprets René Maran's *Batouala* as reinforcing the myth of Africans as a slothful race with no sense of time: "the Africans had always lived in the present. Work for the white man, the Africans were learning [under colonial slavery] was related to objectives in the future". Similarly, his examination of history, time schemes, and characterisation in Chapter 2, based on African Yambo Ouologuem's *Bound to Violence* and Vincent Eri's *The Crocodile*, serves his argument about black people's lack of the sense of history, time, and causation, and he reminds his readers that although Eri's novel pits a Third-World people "against the Australians instead of the Europeans . . . this is still black against white, the emotional versus the analytical". Such arguments are endlessly reiterated in different contexts throughout the book, leaving little energy or time for genuine literary criticism.

KING's 1991 anthology combines a survey of major developments in Commonwealth literature since the 1960s with explorations of global developments in literary and cultural studies. The 11 chapters of Part One ("National and Regional Literatures") examine trends in Australia, Canada, East Africa, India, New Zealand, West Africa, the West Indies, and the lesser-known traditions of Malaysia and Singapore, Oceania, and Sri Lanka. Part Two ("Movements and Directions: Comparative Essays") engages directly the new interests in globalism and multiculturalism. Among the most significant is Nan Bowman Albinski's study of aboriginal writing from Australia and New Zealand to argue that, despite national, individual, and formal differences, "the mutual experiences of nearly 200 years of white colonisation and displacement is a unifying circumstance". Craig Tapping argues that a common trend in West Indian, West African, and North American novels since the 1960s is their nationalistic assertion of "otherness" and "rootedness in specific locales". Comparing women's texts from Ghana, Jamaica, Australia, and Canada, Diana Brydon's "Contracts with the World: Redefining Home, Identity and the Community in Four Women Novelists" argues against critical and theoretical models that would use gender, ethnicity, or race as sole analytic categories.

BARFOOT and D'HAEN bring together 21 articles, most originating in papers delivered at the Fourth Leiden October Conference, 1990, on problems of criticism and definition. The possibilities of evaluation across ethnic, racial, ideological, religious, and gender frontiers are examined in August Fry's "Coming to Judgment: On Evaluating Literatures in English".

Fry identifies a major problem in cultural theorists' current fascination with "indeterminacy", a principle borrowed from the study of electrons. Theo D'Haen's "Shades of Empire in Colonial and Post-Colonial Literatures" foregrounds the crisis in the study of colonial encounter literatures, given complex gradations between literatures created by colonisers and literature created by the colonised, or between colonial and postcolonial literatures. The ideological operations of literary discourse, particularly the exploitation of formulaic elements in narrative, incident, and character to rationalise imperial hegemony, are explored in Robert Druce's "Ideologies of the Anglo-Indian Novel from 1859 to 1957".

The essays in TIFFIN and LAWSON's work focus the problems of postcolonial discourse conducted within the legacy of assimilationist imperial discourse. These are organised in four parts: "Post-Colonial Theory", "Race and Representation", "Reading Empire", and "Re-Writing and Re-Reading Empire". The Introduction strikes the theme with the illustrative incident of the British establishment press's appropriation of the climbing of Mount Everest for the imperial symbolism of the 1953 coronation. Stephen Slemon's "The Scramble for Post-Colonialism" argues, in view of the current Babel of terminology and theories, that postcolonial studies may lose their relevance to the "politics of anti-colonialism", and become a specialisation within the Western humanities, a view given cogency by the tendency towards self-dramatising mystification in some of the theoretical essays. Chris Prentice's "Some Problems of Response to Empire in Settler Post-Colonial Societies" considers the complications posed for postcolonial studies by the ambiguous positions of European settler populations.

ASHCROFT, GRIFFITHS, and TIFFIN's book frequently reflects the anxieties of such populations, poised between identification with their Western heritage and embarrassment with the West's history of imperialism. Though offering a viable definition of postcolonial literatures, the authors' conceptualisation of postcoloniality is broad to the point of meaninglessness, embracing the entire world outside Western Europe. The United States thus becomes a postcolonial society on the grounds that "[despite] its current position of power, and ... neo-colonizing role ... its relationship with the metropolitan centre as it evolved over the last two centuries has been paradigmatic for post-colonial literatures everywhere". Their use of crucial terms like "metropolis", "centre", and "margin" accordingly becomes idiosyncratic. Far more successful are their construction of critical models, readings of particular texts, and examination of intersections between postcolonial discourse and contemporary European movements like postmodernism and poststructuralism.

MAES-JELINEK, PETERSEN, and RUTHERFORD have edited a *Festschrift* to honour Derry Jeffares, combining tributary essays with papers on criticism and critical theory. Together, these chart the history of Commonwealth literature studies since the early 1960s. Recurrent themes and concerns include questions about the appropriateness of the "Commonwealth" label, the challenges of defining the discipline's scope and underlying philosophy, and the dangers of reading the New English Literatures as offshoots of the literature of the British Isles. Representative essays are Diana Brydon's "New Approaches to the New Literatures in English: Are We in Danger of Incorporating Disparity?" and Stephen Slemon's "Reading for Resistance in the Post-Colonial Literatures". Kirsten Holst Petersen's "An Elaborate Dead End: A Feminist Reading of Coetzee's *Foe*" reads J.M. Coetzee's novel through Daniel Defoe's *Roxana*, and concludes that these works have affinities beyond thematic echoes and parallel scenes to hypocritical attitudes to women.

MYRSIADES' work is a collection of eight full-length essays and over one-and-a-half dozen shorter pieces, which foreground the pedagogical challenges of postcolonial, Commonwealth, and Third-World literatures in the face of totalizing discourses like Derridean postmodernism and its Third-World derivative, "Minority Discourse". Particularly notable are Rajeswari Mohan's "Dodging the Crossfire: Questions for Postcolonial Pedagogy" and Abiola Irele's "Dimensions of African Discourse". Some of the shorter pieces are accounts of personal teaching experiences, and there are a dozen book reviews.

A strictly feminist reading is adopted in DE WEEVER's study of 17 novels by seven black American women reworking European, African, African-American, and Native American myths in exploring America's multicultural realities. In analysing the writers' use of mythography as a vehicle for social commentary (Chapter 1), explorations of psychic fracture (Chapters 2 and 3, "Metaphors of Transformation" and "Metaphors of Alienation" respectively), and revisions of traditional mother archetypes (Chapter 4: "Mothers: Devouring and Nurturing"), De Weever repeatedly demonstrates that the female authorship of these novels is central to their full appreciation. Nevertheless, the study exposes the limitations of Western-defined gender discourse. Reformulating Marxist theories of class struggle in gender terms, De Weever denies the importance of historical, economic, and political factors in Third-World women's predicaments, and proceeds from unexamined assumptions that women's experiences in European cultures are paradigmatic of those of women in all cultures. Her discussion of the mother trope adopts the baffling premise that "power relations between mother and child are often simply a reflection of power relations in patriarchal society", and she side-steps the implications of matriarchal households in America and matrilineal cultures in Africa by invoking standard rhetoric about women's sexual subordination. (Even the Spanish extermination of Native American populations is insensitively explained metaphysically, rather than historically, as a "transformation and rebirth" archetype in which the Native Americans' bones fertilise the soil.) These failings notwithstanding, the study illuminates both the social fragmentation, the neuroses, and the rich texture of multicultural life, which the writers portray from perspectives that are simultaneously American and black.

BOEHMER's chronological approach explores the patterns of representation in English-language literatures from Victorian times to the 1990s. Boehmer's salutary contribution to this chaotic field begins with useful distinctions between concepts like "imperial", "colonial", "colonialist", and "post-colonial/postcolonial". The first two chapters ("Imperialism and Textuality" and "Colonialist Concerns") explore the ideological exploitation of symbolic systems in colonial and colonialist writing. Chapter 3 ("The Stirrings of New Nationalism") analyses the beginnings of actual postcolonial writing:

writing that "critically scrutinises the colonial relationship". The equivocal attitude of early twentieth-century Western modernism towards empire is discussed in Chapter 4, "Metropolitans and Mimics". Boehmer further contends that disestablishment of Western literary canons does not imply "a recognition of reciprocal affinities" with Third-World peoples, but masks enlistment of "the foreign and the 'primitive' as instruments of [the West's] own internal renewal". For illustration, she cites undercurrents of imperialist attitudes among "critics" of colonialism, ranging from Leonard and Virginia Woolf to D.H. Lawrence, E.M. Forster, and Evelyn Waugh. This chapter further examines the crisis of writers in colonised cultures, themselves "creations of a colonial world", while the last two chapters discuss the post-World-War-II nationalist literatures and the growing crop of women and aboriginal writers. A concluding bonus is a "Chronology of Key Events and Publications" between 1719 and 1993.

CHIDI OKONKWO

See also **Postcolonial Theory**

New Zealand and South Pacific Literatures

New Zealand Literature

Evans, Patrick, *The Penguin History of New Zealand Literature*, Auckland and New York: Penguin, 1990
Jones, Lawrence, "Versions of the Dream: Literature and the Search for Identity," in *Culture and Identity in New Zealand*, edited by David Novitz and Bill Willmott, Wellington: GP Books, 1989
McCormick, E.H., *Letters and Art in New Zealand*, Wellington: Department of Internal Affairs, 1940
McCormick, E.H., *New Zealand Literature: A Survey*, Wellington: Oxford University Press, 1959
Reid, J.C., *Creative Writing in New Zealand: A Brief Critical History*, Auckland: Whitcombe & Tombs, 1946
Reid, J.C., "The Literature of New Zealand", in *The Commonwealth Pen: An Introduction to the Literature of the British Commonwealth*, edited by A.L. McLeod, Ithaca, New York: Cornell University Press, 1961
Reid, J.C., "Literature", in *The Pattern of New Zealand Culture*, edited by A.L. McLeod, Ithaca, New York: Cornell University Press, 1968
Reid, J.C., "New Zealand Literature", in *The Literatures of the British Commonwealth: Australia and New Zealand*, edited by Gerald A. Wilkes and Reid, University Park: Pennsylvania State University Press, 1970
Sturm, Terry (ed.), *The Oxford History of New Zealand Literature in English*, Auckland, Oxford, and New York: Oxford University Press, 1991
Walsh, William, "New Zealand", in his *Commonwealth Literature*, London and New York: Oxford University Press, 1973

Until about 1940 there was almost no written New Zealand literary history. After that time, the 1930s' writers (the *Phoenix* group) began to formulate a view of themselves as the founders of a genuine national literature. This view was not fully stated in any one place but appeared piecemeal – in Allen Curnow's essays and Introductions to his poetry anthologies, in M.H. Holcroft's essays, in Frank Sargeson's essays and talks, and in Charles Brasch's editorials in *Landfall* – and it was incorporated into E.H. McCormick's literary histories. The writers, critics, and anthologists of the next generation modified this view somewhat to make room for the new work of the 1950s and 1960s, but they did not question its broad outlines, and it is implicit in most of their critical discussions of individual authors. A new generation in the 1980s questioned the consensus view more radically, and the major literary histories of the 1990s are written from a revisionist position.

McCORMICK's 1940 work, one of the Centennial Surveys commissioned by the government to mark 100 years of European settlement, helped to form that consensus view. Written near the beginning of the richest period of New Zealand literary history, it has been overtaken by events, but it remains an important document, still useful for its excellent selection of the most interesting texts and movements in pre-1930 New Zealand literature, including fiction, non-fiction, and poetry (but not drama). The final chapter, dealing with the writers of the 1930s, is shrewd in its judgements, almost unerringly fixing on the figures who have come to be seen as the most important. McCORMICK's 1959 survey builds on and expands that first book, and is the definitive literary history of its generation. The chapter on the 1930s develops more fully the insights from the 1940 account, and is the last word on the consensus view that "in a few agitated years a handful of men and women produced a body of work which, in an intimately organic sense, belonged to the country as none of its previous writings had done, a body of work which created the nucleus of a literature". The final chapter on the 1940s and 1950s is necessarily more diffuse, but is impressively even-handed in its treatment of diverse schools and tendencies. Throughout both books McCormick expresses the literary nationalism of his generation of writers in Leavisite metaphors of growth and development, as in his noting in 1940 the "signs, few but positive, of adult nationhood", or his conclusion in 1959 that "a new accent is becoming audible, the native accent of New Zealand".

REID's 1946 booklet is thinner and less authoritative than McCormick's books. While it acknowledges that the 1930s saw "a considerable body of talented writers giving expression to something like an indigenous literary spirit", it criticises the consensus view from a more conservative religious and moral position, arguing that most New Zealand writers have been severely handicapped by the materialistic and secular nature of their country's culture. Where McCormick saw promise in "the emergence of a distinctive outlook, humanistic, compassionate, somewhat sceptical", Reid bemoaned that New Zealand has been "cut off from her spiritual heritage", so that "the dynamic cultural force of Christianity has been replaced by political humanitarianism and social dilettanteism". This difference in outlook is most marked in his discussion of the writings of the 1930s, where he focuses not on nascent cultural nationalism but on the deficiencies of "secular humanitarianism".

In his later essays REID modifies that position considerably and moves closer to the consensus position. His 1961 essay is a brief, informal tourist's guide to the literature to 1960. The fuller 1968 essay is more thoughtful and assured, if somewhat superficial, and deals not only with fiction, poetry, and non-fiction, but also with drama and literary criticism. His 1970 essay is his fullest account, an updating and expansion of his previous essay, with a brief chronological overview followed by separate sections on poetry, the novel, the short story, drama, and general prose. By this time his view is very much in accord with McCormick's.

Nothing as full as Reid's account appeared in the 1970s and 1980s. WALSH's essay is a quick, assured survey from the outside. Walsh lingers only on Katherine Mansfield's New Zealand stories, but has some shrewd brief comments on other writers, although the account after 1960 degenerates into a mere listing. My essay (JONES's) is a periodised chronological account of the ways in which the literature has variously defined a changing New Zealand cultural identity in its increasingly critical handling of the national dreams of the Just City and the Pastoral Paradise. The essay is paradigmatic rather than detailed, with a wide range of brief quotations and references.

While various essays in the 1980s questioned the consensus view of New Zealand literary history, EVANS's book became the first comprehensive revisionist history. Evans has described the book as: "a linear account of the series of annunciations that have been made over the last hundred years of the birth of a New Zealand literature, a description of the successive appearances of groups and, after the *Phoenix* interruption, of generations whose aim it has been to write themselves into our cultural history". From a self-declared position of "soft-structuralism" (an amalgam of feminist, postcolonial, and neo-Marxist approaches), Evans describes the previous consensus view as "a story told by a particular group of people who had placed themselves at the beginning of things in order to enhance their own importance". A lively, provocative, contentious book, Evans's is not one to which to turn for academically safe generalisations, but rather is one to see as part of a disputed discourse. It does not attempt to be "definitive" or scholarly, and there are no footnotes, but Evans does list his sources in the very useful bibliographical essays that follow each chapter. The book reads as a coherent argument and gives a strong sense of historical period, for it is arranged in triadic groups of chapters, the first in each group looking at "the infrastructures by which literature organised itself in the period under discussion, the second at the poetry, the third at the fiction". As that description shows, the coherence is gained at the cost of comprehensiveness, for the book omits drama, non-fiction (except for literary criticism, history, and theory), popular literature, and children's literature.

STURM's history is revisionist in the sense that it takes a fresh look at the entire corpus of New Zealand literature and does not simply accept the previous consensus view. But it is quite different from Evans's book, though complementary to it. It is much longer, is the work of 11 different authors, does not have any single thesis or approach, is quite scholarly, aims at being definitive for its time, and is arranged by genres rather than by periods. It is more inclusive, both historically, with much fuller accounts of the nineteenth century, and generically, with sections on not only poetry (by MacD.P. Jackson and Elizabeth Caffin), the novel (by Lawrence Jones), the short story (by Lydia Wevers), and the "literary infrastructure" ("Publishing, Patronage, Literary Magazines" by Dennis McEldowney), but also on non-fiction (by Peter Gibbons), the drama (by Howard McNaughton), children's literature (by Betty Gilderdale), popular fiction (by Terry Sturm), and Maori literature (a survey of materials by Jane McRae). The approaches vary, from the relatively theorised ones of Wevers and Gibbons to the more traditional ones of Jackson, Caffin, myself (Jones), and Gilderdale, and the range of focus within sections varies from the extremely broad discussions of drama and the novel to highly selective ones of the short story and popular fiction. The generic arrangement means that there is much less of a sense of literary periods than in Evans's account, much more of a sense of the development of specific forms. More a reference work than a single argument, the book is the logical place to start in investigating any aspect of New Zealand literature. John Thomson's bibliography, "a discursive guide to the various kinds of material available, and to the literature about individual authors", is indispensable for pointing the reader to further, more specialised studies.

LAWRENCE JONES

South Pacific Literature

Arvidson, Ken, "The Emergence of a Polynesian Literature", in *Mana*, 1, 1976 (reprinted in Sharrad)

Daws, Gavan, *A Dream of Islands: Voyages of Self-Discovery in the South Seas*, New York: Norton, 1980

Mishra, Vijay, "Indo-Fijian Fiction: Towards an Interpretation", in *World Literature Written in English*, 16(2), 1977 (reprinted in Sharrad)

Sharrad, Paul (ed.), *Readings in Pacific Literature*, Wollongong, New South Wales: New Literatures Research Centre, 1993

Subramani, *South Pacific Literature: From Myth to Fabulation*, Suva, Fiji: University of the South Pacific Press, 1985, revised 1990

Wendt, Albert, "Towards a New Oceania", in *Mana*, 1, 1976 (reprinted in Sharrad)

South Pacific literature is one of the newest of the "New" literatures in English, with a burgeoning critical tradition that is still mainly confined to articles rather than book-length studies. Most of these articles can be found in the journals *Mana*, *Pacific Moana Quarterly*, *World Literature Written in English*, *Landfall*, and *Span*, and in an exhaustive annotated bibliography of critical writings of Nicolas J. Goetzfridt's *Indigenous Literature of Oceania* (Westport, Connecticut: Greenwood Press, 1995). Opinions differ on what constitutes the South Pacific in terms of a literary region, but the definition adopted for our purposes is Subramani's, which is of the 11 English-speaking Commonwealth countries served by the University of the South Pacific: the Cook Islands, Fiji, Kiribati, Nauru, Niue, the Solomon Islands, Tokelau, Tonga, Tuvaulu, Western Samoa, and Vanuatu.

DAWS' study is of influential nineteenth-century European figures associated with the Pacific; it has chapters on the missionary John Williams, whaler-turned novelist Herman Melville, politician Walter Murray Gibson, Robert Louis Stevenson, and Paul Gauguin. In the context of literature on the South Pacific, Daws thus discusses missionary and travel writing, the adventure novel, and the island romance – all of which had an important effect on the way in which the Pacific was seen by Europe, and forming the body of literature against which indigenous Pacific writers are writing. The colonisation of the Pacific was in many ways different to that of other areas, and Daws shows the diversity of European interests in the area, and the different types of representation.

ARVIDSON primarily discusses the works of the Maori writers Witi Ihimaera, Hone Tuwhare, and the Samoan Albert Wendt. He identifies some of the problems for an emerging Polynesian literature: first that "the use of literature as a creative outlet is a relatively new phenomenon in the islands of Polynesia", and second that the "writing [is] being done in virtual isolation in the Pacific", and with no local publishing houses, writers have practical difficulties in getting their work published.

The Samoan novelist, poet, and academic, WENDT calls for a regional identity for the indigenous writing from the South Pacific, which began appearing in the late 1960s, but which "came of age" with the publication of Wendt's *Sons for the Return Home* (1973). His foundational article addresses the debilitating European romanticisation of the Pacific in the literature of W. Somerset Maugham, James Michener, *et al.*, and argues that colonisation has suppressed indigenous Pacific cultures on the basis of their supposed inferiority to European culture. He calls for the "creation of new cultures which are free of the taint of colonialism and based firmly upon our own pasts", arguing that an emerging South Pacific literature should play an important role in celebrating the cultural diversity of the area.

SUBRAMANI traces the beginnings of a written tradition in the South Pacific, exploring the reasons why indigenous writings in English took so long to get established. Chapters include: an examination of the relationship between social position and the emerging literature; a discussion of the many oral forms of Pacific literature – tall tales, myths, legends, epics – and their influence on the new writing; a consideration of the negative influences of European writing, and particularly of the missionary writing that demonised traditional Polynesian cultures, and was dismissive of European fiction; the evolution of short stories, with particular reference to the tall tales of the Tongan writer, Epeli Hau'ofa; and an important consideration of Albert Wendt's fiction. Subramani focuses his analysis on "the general shift from a mythic conception of the world to a historical and problematic view of life", arguing that the multitudinous influences on the Pacific have created the potential for an extraordinarily rich literature. His book has been criticised for an uncertain methodology and a clumsy style, but it has recently (1990) been updated, and still provides the only developed consideration of Pacific literature.

MISHRA approaches Indo-Fijian writing through the work of Satendra Nandan, Subramani, and Raymond Pillai. Indians began to arrive in Fiji in 1879 as indentured labourers on, as Mishra describes it, "a failed millenia quest": ironically, like the Europeans to whom they were indentured, the Indian labourers shared a paradisal expectation of the Pacific. He argues that Nandan and Subramani are interested in exploring the themes of displacement, and the inability of the Indo-Fijian community to come to terms with changing historical circumstances, through the spiritual experience of the indentured individual. Against this, Mishra shows Pillai's work to be a "conscious departure from such 'reflective' treatment of ideology to a much more 'transformed' treatment of indenture consciousness". Pillai seeks to avoid evoking a spiritual past, and concentrates instead on the racial and social problems faced by the Indo-Fijian community today.

SHARRAD reprints many of the most important articles defining Pacific literature and its problems, but confines himself to articles written by 1985, and his definition of South Pacific literature includes indigenous writing from New Zealand and Papua New Guinea. The collection has a balance between articles that address general problems, and provide overviews of the region and its literature, and articles that give close readings of individual authors such as Wendt and Hau'ofa. Sharrad's book provides a good introduction to the region's literature, its main themes, and problems, and gives a useful bibliography for those who wish to follow up an author or a region.

NIGEL RIGBY

Newman, John Henry 1801–1890

English theologian, prose writer, and poet

DeLaura, David J., *Hebrew and Hellene in Victorian England: Newman, Arnold, and Pater*, Austin: University of Texas Press, 1969

Dessain, Charles Stephen, *John Henry Newman*, London: Thomas Nelson, 1966; 3rd edition, Oxford: Oxford University Press, 1980

Ker, Ian, *John Henry Newman: A Biography*, Oxford: Clarendon Press, 1988; New York: Oxford University Press, 1988

Newsome, David: *The Convert Cardinals: John Henry Newman and Henry Edward Manning*, London: John Murray, 1993

O'Faolain, Sean, *Newman's Way*, London: Longmans, Green & Co., 1952

Strange, Roderick, *Newman and the Gospel of Christ*, Oxford and New York: Oxford University Press, 1981

Trevor, Meriol, *Newman: The Pillar of the Cloud* and *Newman: Light in Winter*, London: Macmillan, 1962; Garden City, New York: Doubleday, 1962–63

Ward, Wilfrid, *The Life of John Henry, Cardinal Newman, Based on His Private Journals and Correspondence*, 2 vols., London & New York: Longmans, 1912

Though he was unquestionably one of the greatest writers of the nineteenth century, criticism of John Henry Newman has never taken a purely literary form; it has always been closely entwined both with biographical and theological material. This has been inevitable because of the intensely personal character of everything, and the occasional character of almost everything, that he wrote, and because so much of it formed part of continuing religious controversy.

WARD was excellently placed to write, by his connection (through his father, W.V. Ward) with Newman's early Oxford years, by his philosophical and theological training, and by long years of careful research. His book is deliberately unbalanced in one way, because it concentrates almost exclusively on Newman's life after 1845, so that some important writings are hardly discussed. But he shows a deep understanding of the developing mind, of the continuity of Newman's thought, and of what was often neglected by later writers – his brilliant gifts of irony, sarcasm, and satire. Though a strong admirer, Ward is candid in pointing to facets of the work that might show intemperate judgement or special pleading. The chapters devoted to major works are notable for keen literary judgement and fine understanding of historical context.

O'FAOLAIN set out to redress the balance by concentrating more on the early years, and on the continuing power of early family associations in later life. His general view is well conveyed by his phrase "brave, kind, solitary, tormented angel". The word "tormented" may have been meant to question the greater serenity and consistency of Newman as portrayed by Ward. He stresses throughout the interplay of intellect and emotion in Newman's thought, saying of his adolescent Calvinist conversion that he "always transformed emotion into intellect". He stresses by telling quotation Newman's sense of the divine symbolism in ordinary events, and sees the late "Grammar of Assent" as a theoretical justification of Newman's close linking of logic, temperament, and feeling.

TREVOR's work had the advantage of the special assistance of the Fathers of the Birmingham Oratory, and of a long personal familiarity with its archives. Its limitation is that its devoted centring on Newman's own feelings tends to blur the importance of friends, enemies, opponents, and the general character of the England in which he lived. The content and argument of Newman's controversial works is sketchily treated, and when, for instance, she describes the Achilli trial as a "dreadful social disgrace", she does not appear to know that *The Times* – the arch-bastion of middle-class Protestant patriotism – severely castigated the jury that found against Newman for its anti-Catholic prejudice.

DeLAURA's excellent contribution places Newman among the great Victorian thinkers and sages, using Matthew Arnold, and to a lesser extent Walter Pater, as litmus papers to test the quality of Newman's thought and the power of his influence. He well describes Newman and Arnold as "bound together in an almost unique (though long-distance) master-disciple relationship compounded of affection, respect, flattering mutual interest, and a kind of awed and wary incomprehension", and says "they display a similarly motivated reluctance to commit the highly organized intelligence to the clamorous demands of practical life". He does full justice, too, to ways in which they were unlike because they worked on different principles: "by Newman's standards, Arnold's paragon is a kind of fraudulent copy of St Paul's 'saint'". He rightly shows Pater as more strongly imbued with Newman's spirit, quoting testimony that he thought at the end of his life that "we are all" tending towards the Catholic Church.

DESSAIN's book is a simple handbook, based on a unique knowledge of all Newman's writings, especially letters and journals. He stresses the virulence of his early Protestantism and the development in steady progression of his thought and literary personality, emphasizing the boldness of his educational views in *The Idea of a University*.

STRANGE skilfully links Newman the historian of theology with his inner religious history. He sees him as notably consistent in his deep meanings and principles, and finds that his changes, so startling and complete to the world, were themselves the outcome of this consistency. A particularly interesting and original section on Atonement theology masterfully summarizes arguments for and against the view that Newman was a Scotist, believing that God's plan would have included incarnation independently of the need to redeem man from sin. He deals neatly with the charge of "Judaizing" levelled against Newman and his colleagues in the Oxford Movement by Thomas Arnold.

KER gives throughout a careful analysis of arguments in Newman's prose, and links them skilfully with his use of imagery. He is concerned to show both the man and the writer as stronger, rougher, and more masculine than he appears in some previous versions. He particularly emphasizes satire and humour. In the *Apologia* he finds, beside the more familiar personal narrative, much that was topical and relevant to the Ultramontane controversy within the Catholic Church in the 1860s. The weakness, as with Trevor's volumes, lies in a too-complete absorption in Newman's own personality, so that the importance of outside influences, of the people and things to which Newman reacted, is sometimes missed.

By placing Newman side by side with Henry Edward Manning, showing well-known contrasts in a new and subtle light, NEWSOME has written a book of great originality and abiding value. Feeling that Newman has sometimes been unjustly exalted at Manning's expense, he shows them as perfectly complementary, and presents their joint contribution to English Catholicism as much greater than that which either could have made separately. In a fine exposition of *The Dream of Gerontius*, he shows Newman as moving closer to Manning, and away from his fellow-Oratorian Frederick William Faber, in his purgatorial imagery, and praises his historical and topical writings for their "inspired provocative generalization". He is shrewdly analytical of Newman's imagery and of his power of rhetoric, especially in the *Apologia*.

A.O.J. COCKSHUT

Nigerian Literature *see* African Literature: West

Ngugi wa Thiong'o 1938 –

Kenyan novelist, dramatist, and essayist

Cook, David, and Michael Okenimpke, *Ngugi wa Thiong'o: An Exploration of His Writings*, London: Heinemann, 1983

Killam, G.D., *An Introduction to the Writings of Ngugi*, London: Heinmann, 1980

Robson, Clifford B., *Ngugi wa Thiong'o*, London: Macmillan, 1979

Sicherman, Carol, *Ngugi: The Making of a Rebel: A Source Book in Kenyan Literature and Resistance*, London and New York: Hans Zell, 1990

Ngugi wa Thiong'o is undoubtedly the best-known and most influential of the East African writers. There is extensive critical writing about his work in many journals concerned with African Literature (see especially *African Literature Today*, London: James Currey). However, book-length critical works are still limited. A paucity of critical discourse is a problem for all but a tiny minority of the "giants" of African literature, largely because of the lack of publishing outlets throughout the continent, but also because African literature is a growing but still minority area of international literary concern.

There are two strands to Ngugi criticism, which in turn reflect the development of his work. Earlier and more traditional critics tend to admire the humanist novels culminating in *A Grain of Wheat*, whereas more radical commentators have appreciated the experimentations in form consequent to Ngugi's increasingly revolutionary political convictions.

ROBSON's book has chapters on each of the novels up to *Petals of Blood*, and includes a fairly damning summary-chapter on the plays. He looks at Ngugi's work from the point of view of how well the writer operates within the Western conventions of the well-made play or novel. Robson therefore applauds the earlier work for such merits as in-depth characterisation and skilful interweaving of plot elements. However, he refuses to deal with the increasingly overt politicisation of Ngugi's work, and simply writes-off later experimentation with form and content in the *ouevre* after *A Grain of Wheat* as comparative failure according to rather rigid notions of what constitutes a "good" piece of fictional writing.

KILLAM looks at Ngugi's novels from *The River Between* to *Petals of Blood*, and at the play *The Trial of Dedan Kimathi*, with a separate chapter for each work. He uses extensive quotations throughout to give a clear liberal-humanist oriented interpretation of the writings. The main emphasis of the text is to concentrate on how the development of individuals is handled, although Ngugi's political progress is also taken into account. Killam gives more detailed consideration to Ngugi's best-known play, *The Trial of Dedan Kimathi*, than any other book discussed here, and is more sympathetic to Ngugi as a playwright than are many commentators. This book is particularly strong on Ngugi's literary influences, emphasising a stylistic debt to Joseph Conrad and the political importance of the writing of Frantz Fanon.

COOK and OKENIMPKE have produced an incisive work, which covers the entire canon of Ngugi's novels, short stories, and plays. They also, most helpfully, contextualise his work, looking not only at Ngugi's career, but also taking on board Kenyan political history. They analyse the writer's crucial political evolution from Christian-humanist to Marxist-influenced revolutionary, as mirrored in both the fictional and polemic texts. There is an air of excitement about this book as it plots Ngugi's move away from psychological realism towards ever more extreme stylistic experiment, as he finds the traditional novel form cannot encompass a need to convey passionately held convictions about the oppression of the Kenyan people. Cook and Okenimpke are not afraid to point out problems in the evolution of Ngugi's style and his occasional awkwardness as a playwright. However, Ngugi's daring in breaking new literary ground and his stunning use of satire in *Devil on the Cross* are analysed with great sensitivity. This is an excellent book, clearly written, and essential to anyone who wants help in penetrating beyond the surface of Ngugi's world.

SICHERMAN has produced a comprehensive international bibliography of writing by and about Ngugi, from his juvenilia through to 1989. She has gone to considerable lengths to track down journal entries not only from Africa and the West, but also from Japan, Eastern Europe, and the former Soviet Union. (It is intriguing to find, for example, that Ngugi has been translated not only into the world's major languages, but also into Uzbek, Finnish, and Korean.) This is an essential handbook for the serious Ngugi scholar.

JANE PLASTOW

Norris, Frank 1870–1902

American novelist

Bell, Michael Davitt, *The Problem of American Realism: Studies in the Cultural History of a Literary Idea*, Chicago: University of Chicago Press, 1993
Borus, Daniel H., *Writing Realism: Howells, James, and Norris in the Mass Market*, Chapel Hill: University of North Carolina Press, 1989
French, Warren, *Frank Norris*, New York: Twayne, 1962
Frohock W.M., *Frank Norris*, Minneapolis: University of Minnesota Press, 1968
Geismar, Maxwell, *Rebels and Ancestors: The American Novel 1890–1915*, Boston: Houghton Mifflin, 1953
Graham, Don, *The Fiction of Frank Norris: The Aesthetic Context*, Columbia: University of Missouri Press, 1978
Kazin, Alfred, *On Native Grounds: An Interpretation of Modern American Prose Literature*, New York: Harcourt Brace, and Reynal & Hitchcock, 1942; London Jonathan Cape, 1943
Marchand, Ernest, *Frank Norris: A Study*, Stanford, California: Stanford University Press, 1942
Pizer, Donald, *The Novels of Frank Norris*, Bloomington: Indiana University Press, 1966
Pizer, Donald, *Realism and Naturalism in Nineteenth-Century American Literature*, Carbondale: Southern Illinois University Press, 1966, revised 1984

The early critical and scholarly writings on Frank Norris focus on his centrality in any historical account of the emergence of literary realism and naturalism in the United States at the turn of the century, his indebtedness to the writings of the French novelist Émile Zola, his treatment of the Californian landscape (both rural and urban), and the sources of his ideas in late nineteenth-century evolutionary and social thought. More recent studies have taken greater account of his Romantic proclivities, particularly those evident in the minor novels, and his place in an Emersonian tradition of transcendentalist thinking.

MARCHAND's is one of the earliest critical studies of Norris, and while in many areas it has been superseded by subsequent research and scholarship it still has many virtues. He gives an intelligent, if incomplete, account of the "resemblances" between the fiction of Norris and Émile Zola, and in the discussion of individual novels he frequently provides a valuable summary of the early reviews (notably the 1899 reviews of *McTeague*). Marchand stresses Norris's gift for the depiction of sensory experience (especially that of smell), his moralism, his reforming zeal, and his moral courage, all of them traits which, he argues, Norris shares with Zola.

KAZIN devotes only a few pages to Norris in his pioneering study of modern American literature, but his accounts of the "struggle for realism" at the turn of the century and of the relationship between progressive movements in American politics and the emergence of the naturalist novel are still of considerable value. He stresses Norris's "toughness" as a novelist and his "peculiarly indiscriminate" gifts, seeing him finally as a figure who straddles, on the one hand, a declining "genteel tradition", and on the other an embryonic modernism.

GEISMAR devotes his first chapter to Norris, seeing him as the product of an odd blend of "literary radicalism and the smart set in California". His approach weaves biography and criticism a little uneasily together, but the commentary is frequently lively and challenging. This should be seen as an interesting general essay on Norris rather than one promoting a particular thesis or interpretation of his work.

FRENCH argues in his short book (in Twayne's "United States Authors" series) that Norris is best understood as a Romantic moralist, writing out of a Transcendentalist, Emersonian tradition: "far from being an exotic whose affinitities are principally with French naturalists, Norris is a Far West answer to the call from Concord – a writer who hoped to break New World dependence upon the Old". This line of reasoning is pursued fairly vigorously through the major fiction, and French sees the two most distinguished novels, *McTeague* and *The Octopus*, as experimental efforts in which Norris tries to clarify the terms of his thinking. French holds that the lack of artistic integrity in Norris "is not the result of hypocrisy, but of inadequate self-analysis". His book opens with a serviceable biographical chapter, and the subsequent chapters are entirely devoted to critical commentary, which is often trenchant and perceptive.

PIZER's critical study, *The Novels of Frank Norris*, remains the best single-author exposition of Norris's novels; the chapter on "*Vandover and the Brute* and *McTeague*" alone contains some of the best criticism of the two works. Pizer argues that Norris's novels are written in response to some of the important intellectual dilemmas of his time, notably "the conflict between traditional concepts of God, man, and nature and a growing body of scientific knowledge impinging on those concepts". Pizer shows how important Norris's reading of Zola's *L'Assommoir* and *La Bête humaine* was to the composition of *McTeague*, and he is particularly alert to the ways in which late nineteenth-century scientific and social-anthropological ideas of the criminal personality govern both the portrait of McTeague and the unfolding drama of the novel. He has a higher estimation of *Vandover and the Brute* than many critics. His reading of the novel centres on its treatment of what he calls "an evolutionary ethical dualism", and he then shows how this theme is rendered more concretely and with greater maturity in *McTeague*. The subsequent chapter discusses the minor novels *Moran of the Lady Letty*, *Blix*, and *A Man's Woman*, while the final chapter is devoted to analyses of *The Octopus* and *The Pit*, the two completed novels from the incomplete trilogy that was to be known as "The Epic of the Wheat". A valuable bibliography covering critical works up to the date of publication is appended.

PIZER's general study of realism and naturalism in late nineteenth-century American fiction devotes three chapters to Norris – one to his defintion of naturalism, another to his literary criticism, and the third to *The Octopus*. There is some repetition here of the ideas and arguments developed in the critical study of Norris (see above), but the discussion of *The Octopus* is largely written as a reply to ideas put forward by Leo Marx in his influential essay "Two Kingdoms of Force" from *The Machine in the Garden*, where Marx argues that American literature is characterized by the opposition between "two cardinal images of value" – one rural, the other technological. For those interested in the more general intellectual and critical context of Norris and his theories of fiction, this book is indispensable reading.

FROHOCK's brief guide to Norris (in the "Pamphlets on American Authors" series) provides a short biographical overview with a general essay on the fiction. He sees Norris as a writer for whom literature was a serious matter, and while he is aware that most readers are more sensitive to Norris's weaknesses than his strengths, he argues that "in spite of his penchant for melodrama, Norris's better novels played their part in substituting flesh and blood people for the myth-figures . . . in the literature of the American West".

GRAHAM explores Norris's fiction from a new perspective, that of his involvement in what Graham calls "the aesthetic atmosphere of the nineties" and his youthful fascination with the fine arts. He sees *Vandover and the Brute* as a novel that combines sensational naturalism with "aesthetic documentation", *McTeague* as "a guidebook to plebeian taste, a kind of manual of kitsch art", and *The Octopus* as a novel suffused with "aesthetic commentary", the central character of Presley being, he suggests, an "amalgam of aesthetic images: Mallarmean faun, San Francisco aesthete, socialist poet in the Markham tradition, and would-be natural poet". Graham's readings are not always totally convincing, and *The Pit* especially seems somewhat resistant to his terms of reference; but this remains a valuable study, which forces us to rethink and enlarge our sense of the literary and cultural environment informing the major novels.

BORUS's book is a major contribution to our understanding of the socio-economic context in which the "struggle for realism" in the United States took place. There is, unfortunately, very little in the way of extended discussion of the three novelists who lend their names to the subtitle. But the detailed account Borus offers of issues such as the American reading public's dissatisfaction with romance, the implementation of new copyright laws, technological advances in publishing, book marketing, and the emergence of the professional literary agent, and the ways in which these shaped fictional realism, is invaluable for anyone interested in Norris as a *professional* writer.

BELL's recent book is of considerable relevance to any student of Norris, though only one, relatively short, chapter is devoted entirely to his fiction. In "The Revolt Against Style: Frank Norris" Bell argues that the "confusions and fallacies rampant in Norris's writings about naturalism" are self-evident, but that we should recognize that "the ultimate significance of naturalism for Norris . . . was far more centrally personal than literary". This has some echoes of French's thesis, but Bell is eager to pursue Norris's "theories" of naturalism rather than stress his affinities with Emersonian Transcendentalism. Bell's discussion offers many perceptive points about the major novels, particularly *McTeague*, *The Octopus*, and *The Pit*, and he is especially attentive to the use of "concrete detail" in the novels. He concludes that "Norris's theory of naturalism would seem to have destroyed his power as a writer". The whole book is a valuable addition to our understanding of the intellectual and literary contexts in which Norris worked.

HENRY CLARIDGE

Novel: General

Allen, Walter, *The English Novel: A Short Critical History*, New York: Dutton, 1954; London: Phoenix House, 1954
Allen, Walter, *The Modern Novel in Britain and the United States*, New York: Dutton, 1964; as *Tradition and Dream: The English and American Novel from the Twenties to Our Times*, London: Phoenix House, 1964
Alter, Robert, *Partial Magic: The Novel as Self Conscious Genre*, Berkeley: University of California Press, 1975
Chase, Richard, *The American Novel and Its Tradition*, New York: Doubleday, 1957; London: Bell & Sons, 1958
Hollahan, Eugene, *Crisis-Consciousness and the Novel*, Newark: University of Delaware Press, 1992; London: Associated University Presses, 1992
Kawin, Bruce F., *The Mind of the Novel: Reflexive Fiction and the Ineffable*, Princeton, New Jersey: Princeton University Press, 1982
Kettle, Arnold, *An Introduction to the English Novel*, 2 vols., London: Hutchinson, 1951, revised 1967; New York: Harper & Row, 1968
McCarthy, Mary, *Ideas and the Novel*, New York: Harcourt Brace Jovanovich, 1980; London: Weidenfeld & Nicolson, 1981
Schwarz, Daniel R., *The Humanistic Heritage: Critical Theories of the English Novel from James to Hillis Miller*, Philadelphia: University of Pennsylvania Press, 1986; London: Macmillan, 1986
Smith, Grahame, *The Novel and Society: Defoe to Eliot*, Totowa, New Jersey: Barnes & Noble, 1984; London: Batsford, 1984
Stevenson, Lionel, *The English Novel: A Panorama*, London: Constable, 1960; Boston: Houghton, Mifflin 1960
Van Ghent, Dorothy, *The English Novel: Form and Function*, New York: Rinehart, 1953, revised 1967
Weinstein, Arnold, *Fictions of the Self: 1550–1800*, Princeton, New Jersey: Princeton University Press, 1981

Though published separately and under different titles, ALLEN's two volumes are best considered as a single unit. Long considered standard texts in criticism of the novel, this survey is best at offering readers breadth of coverage rather than depth of analysis. In highly organized chapters, which compartmentalize works of fiction by historical period, Allen relates the accomplishments of major novelists to those of many lesser luminaries. While the first study deals almost exclusively with British fiction, the second expands to include a number of American writers. The limitations of space force Allen to be quite sweeping in his review of novelists before the twentieth century; four centuries of literature are reviewed in a single volume. Because he is able to devote an entire book to a study of the modern novel, Allen is able to be more detailed in his analysis of works from the 1920s to the 1950s. Stressing the differences between the novelists on either side of the Atlantic, Allen gives a decade-by-decade comparison of these writers; he also devotes a chapter to authors of the American South, who seem to be somewhat out of the mainstream of American fiction. A fiction writer himself, Allen is interested in explaining to fellow novelists as well as to scholars why certain works have achieved greatness. With the exception of early American writings, the major works of long fiction written in English here receive a reasonably comprehensive, sensitive review.

Like Allen's work, KETTLE's provides wide coverage; however, though he too organizes his study historically, Kettle is less interested in the historical context than he is in aesthetic accomplishment. After briefly reviewing the concerns and contributions of eighteenth-century masters of the form, he turns his attention to two dozen novels which he considers among the best written in English. Each receives careful scrutiny, and while the critical commentary lacks the rigor of later scholarly treatises, Kettle's examinations are thorough and level-headed; hence, his survey offers an excellent starting point for those who wish to study any of these novels in depth.

The subtitle of STEVENSON's book is particularly appropriate, for the author provides the general reader with a panoramic survey of the English novel from its beginnings in the Renaissance to the post-World-War-II fiction of writers such as C.P. Snow and John Wain. Taking as his starting point a broad definition of the novel as a long work of fiction intent on creating an illusion of reality, Stevenson conducts a historical review of significant contributions in each of the 17 periods he considers distinct in the development of the form. His work, like Allen's, is a good introduction for those wishing to understand something of the growth of the novel as a distinct genre, and who wish to familiarize themselves with themes constant over five centuries or peculiar to a particular period.

Though VAN GHENT has organized her study along historical lines, she is really most interested in exploring the formal properties of novels. Influenced by psychological critics, she investigates the ways in which 18 novelists give life to characters and provide insight into the human condition. Written as a textbook to supplement the study of these important and influential works, Van Ghent's book contains separate analytical essays on each novel and a section listing specific critical issues for discussion. Perhaps the best testament to her enduring influence is the strong reaction she has evoked among later critics, who often feel compelled to take her to task for her judgments.

CHASE purports to write a genre study, seeking to define the American novel and distinguish its principal characteristics. His focus lies in sorting out the qualities of romance that are present in so many of the best works of American long fiction. Concentrating on approximately 20 novels by

11 important figures in the American tradition, he explains how "the American romance-novel", a more "daring, more brilliant fiction", contrasts with "the solid moral inclusiveness and massive equitability of the English novel". The roots of these novels lie principally in America's Puritan background and in the mood of nostalgia for a simpler life which disappeared as the country underwent a transformation from an agrarian nation to an industrial one. Chases's analysis of individual works by Herman Melville and Frank Norris, and his sound appreciation of figures such as William Faulkner, remain particularly enlightening for readers.

ALTER is interested in the ways novelists have conducted "purposeful experiments with form" in order to draw readers' attention "to fictional form as a consciously articulated entity rather than a transparent container of 'real' events". He sees in the tradition of the novel a number of works which he classifies as self-conscious, wherein the author deliberately points out the artificiality of the work being read. Far from being a casual anomaly, the tradition of the self-conscious novel begins with Cervantes' *Don Quixote* and includes important works by Henry Fielding, Laurence Sterne, and James Joyce in England; Denis Diderot and Alain Robbe-Grillet in France; John Barth and Robert Coover in America; Jorge Luis Borges and Julio Cortázar in Latin America; and Vladimir Nabokov, the foremost practitioner of self-conscious fiction in the twentieth century. Alter offers a sensible explanation of the qualities of the genre, selecting examples from authors of many cultures. His study reveals how, from its beginnings, but especially in the twentieth century, the novel has become an international genre in which technique transcends national and cultural boundaries.

HOLLAHAN presents a history of the novel from an unusual scholarly perspective. Influenced by poststructuralist literary theory, his work focuses on what he calls the "crisis-trope"; the presence of crisis in the novel offers him a way of studying the development of fiction which reveals something about the nature of writers and readers in various decades and countries for the past three centuries. His viewpoint forces a somewhat skewed view of the novel's heritage, as one might expect; emphasis is placed on works which exhibit most clearly both the use of the word "crisis" in the text and the development of scenes that give rise to the phenomenon he calls "crisis consciousness", which he identifies as "a radical form of self-consciousness" and "a historically verifiable element in the formation of modern consciousness". Roughly 50 novels are reviewed, though the emphasis on English novels (fewer than half-a-dozen Americans are included) may cause one to wonder if the phenomenon is culturally based rather than, as Hollahan claims, universal.

Poststructuralist theory provides KAWIN, too, with a methodology for bringing the tools of semiotics and philosophical analysis to bear on the study of modern literature. Concerned with examining "the novel, the self, and the knowable", Kawin looks at a number of novels from Melville's *Moby-Dick* to Faulkner's *Absalom, Absalom*, as well as works by experimentalists such as Samuel Beckett, which exhibit a "peculiar inward turning of the narrative, a gaze into the cosmos that doubles back to produce an image of the gazing self". The book is really about ways of knowing and of expressing knowledge about the world. Kawin is interested in showing how certain novelists have explored humankind's epistemological limits, displaying in their works the futility of attempts to describe that which is ultimately beyond the power of language to explain. Though highly technical, the work is provocative and illuminating for those determined enough to read it through. Like most of his contemporary critics, WEINSTEIN also relies heavily on poststructuralist theory to construct highly formalist and atemporal readings of numerous sixteenth-, seventeenth-, and eighteenth-century works by English and Continental authors. His bias, he asserts boldly, is that "the work of art, especially fiction, depicts strategies for living which may be shaped by a specific age but which are rich in meaning for all ages". His analysis of early novelists' attempts to create concepts of self is illuminating, and his readings of disparate texts reveal how authors' attempts to address problems of aesthetics transcend cultural and temporal boundaries.

At the opposite end of the critical spectrum from Weinstein and his poststructuralist colleagues, SMITH is interested in exploring the relationship of novels to the social milieu that gave rise to their production. Arguing that "great novels characteristically raise difficult questions about their relation to a social context because they subject it to a demanding scrutiny", Smith concentrates on a handful of books traditionally considered significant works by major novelists. Much of the argument set forth in what he calls a "theoretical" first chapter and carried through his discussion of individual works is aimed at refuting claims of New Critics and their poststructuralist successors that hermetic readings of literary texts should be given primacy of place in criticism. Smith's careful examination of "the connection between even the details of artistic techniques and elements wider than those of literature considered in isolation" is a welcome reminder that novelists often wrote not only to create art but also to communicate meaning – and to change their readers' minds about important social and political issues.

McCARTHY's lengthy essay on the fate of the novel of ideas delivers more than it promises. Ostensibly an argument against the tendency of modern novelists and critics to divorce the intellectual from the stylistic components of fiction, her work is also an excellent brief survey of fiction from the nineteenth to the mid-twentieth century. She includes commentary on novels by Continental as well as British and American writers; further, she writes without the heavy hand of the academic, passing judgments which will seem reasonable to the well-schooled reader. There is no doubt she favors a reconciliation between ideas and style, and she makes the case for intellectual fiction with knowledge of the literature and command of her own argument.

The question of which novels are read and studied, and why, is the subject of SCHWARZ's analysis of the important literary critics of the twentieth century. Identifying an "ideology of reading", which he calls the "humanistic heritage", Schwartz traces the history of Anglo-American criticism as it has been applied to the English novel over 70 years. Selecting texts he considers to have been most influential in shaping the reading habits and teaching preferences in English-speaking countries, Schwartz contrasts the humanistic approach which dominated critical sensibility until the 1960s with the more radical poststructuralist approaches that have risen to prominence in the latter half of the twentieth century. Understanding how these critics selected novels for analysis gives readers a better sense of how the canon of English literature has developed and why individual novels continue to attract wide readership.

LAURENCE W. MAZZENO

Novel: 20th Century

Bock, Hedwig, and Albert Wertheim (eds.), *Essays on Contemporary Post-Colonial Fiction*, Munich: Max Hueber, 1986
Bradbury, Malcolm, *The Modern American Novel*, Oxford and New York: Oxford University Press, 1983, revised 1992
Bradbury, Malcolm, *The Modern British Novel*, London: Secker & Warburg, 1993
Breen, Jennifer, *In Her Own Write: Twentieth-Century Women's Fiction*, London: Macmillan, 1990; New York: St Martin's Press, 1990
Elliott, Emory, with Cathy N. Davidson *et al.*, *The Columbia History of the American Novel*, New York: Columbia University Press, 1991
Henderson, Lesley (ed.), *Contemporary Novelists*, London and Chicago: St James Press, 1991 (5th revised edition)
McHale, Brian, *Postmodernist Fiction*, London and New York: Methuen, 1987

There has been no attempt as yet to produce a book that will cover the twentieth-century novel in one fell swoop, at least not since the 1960s. As Adrian Page noted in 1990, "it seems that very few books nowadays attempt to characterize the novel *per se* as was once the case": the twentieth-century novel in English is such a many-headed creature. What we do have are books that confine themselves to narrower limits.

Taking into account the kind of books readily available, any hypothetical study of the twentieth-century novel as a whole would probably need to have sections on the following: the modern American novel; the modern British novel; and the so called "New Literatures in English" (what used to be called "Commonwealth Literature", and notwithstanding the problem of national demarcations). Genre fiction – such as science-fiction, horror, fantasy, detective fiction, spy fiction, romance, and gay literature – is often omitted from considerations of the novel, even though much of this literature is incredibly popular. The reason for such exclusion probably lies with the fact that a majority of definitions of the novel depend upon some notion of "realism", allied with a sense of formal innovation: generic fiction, by its very nature, tends to be formulaic. Our hypothetical book's Introduction would probably reflect the widely discussed debate over the "death of the novel", draw attention to the fact that the vast numbers of novels that continue to be written and read is evidence that the novel remains vital to culture (notwithstanding the paradox that this plethora consists largely of the genre fiction), and point out that the appearance of the novels in the New Literatures in English has given the novel form an important boost.

BOCK and WERTHEIM's edited collection of essays on precisely this latter topic is a gentle introduction to an area that is becoming increasingly theorised. Each essay focuses on an individual writer, and takes a fairly standard critical approach, giving biographical details along with plot outlines and the major thematics. Thus the book does lack an overview of postcolonial writing, for which readers will need to turn to more recent work where the initial concern is postcolonial theory rather than the fiction itself. However, with 22 novelists included, ranging from Chinua Achebe to Janet Frame, anyone new to this area would do well to seek this book out.

BRADBURY's 1993 book covers the twentieth-century British novel. The following quotation is fairly typical of Bradbury's view of the health of the novel: "the present book takes it for granted that the novel . . . has survived and is surviving, serving as a major expression of artistic, cultural and intellectual curiosity, exploring the nature of our contemporary narratives". Bradbury wisely notes the difficulty in talking about a national literature and tradition "in our international, global-village age". There continues to be a certain amount of irony in tracing the lineage of the modern British novel, since its fathers (the novel's descent is still seen, quite incorrectly, as patrilineal) are Irish, American, and Polish – James Joyce, Henry James, and Joseph Conrad. Bradbury eschews the likes of Patrick White, Nadine Gordimer, and Chinua Achebe as belonging to some other lineage (these are all included in the Bock and Wertheim). The narrative scheme used by Bradbury is to supplement the usual story of twentieth-century fiction as the movement from modernism to postmodernism, with another narrative strand, which finds a tradition that adheres to the tenets of realism. Given the acknowledged limitations, the book deals with its subject-matter quite capably. There is the usual tendency of surveys merely to cite names rather than to analyse, something that is especially noticeable as the fiction of the immediate present looms ever larger and the benefits of hindsight ever smaller.

BRADBURY also provides his version of the modern American novel (1983, revised 1992). His narrative here is definitively from modernity and modernism to postmodernism. The book is (incredibly) much shorter than the one on the British novel, and consequently often simply reels off the titles of novels. It does have the advantage of giving a strong sense of a direction and pattern to the century's literature, however, and so provides a helpful framework in which to view more specialised or more expansive works. The form of genre fiction that surely should have been mentioned here is the western.

BREEN's stated aim is not to be comprehensive in her survey of women's twentieth-century fiction, but to draw on examples from this literature that lend support to a particular analysis of the "world-view" of women's fiction. It is a mixture of the theoretical, thematic, and political. Although at times verging on the simplistic and theoretically retrograde ("any technique for creating a character's voice depends not on resurrecting material which stems from the author's own life, but on imagining a fictional human being who is believable"), it is a useful way into modern women's fiction, and helps to complement and focus material that will naturally be found in other volumes covered here.

The twentieth-century sections (edited by Valerie Smith and Patrick O'Donnell) of ELLIOTT's *The Columbia History of the American Novel* are highly recommended. It is a comprehensive history of the American novel from the beginnings, in the form of a series of essays from different contributors. Its great strength is the variety of contexts it uses and the fact that it does not keep solely to the "classic" line. There are entries on "American Proletarianism", "Popular Forms", "Ethnicity and the Marketplace", as well as writings on Canadian and Caribbean literature. Our hypothetical history of the twentieth-century novel in English could usefully adopt such a breadth of organisation.

McHALE's book might be considered too specialist for a general survey, but is included here because it has had a considerable influence on thinking about fiction, and because it deals with the type of fiction that represents the most innovative kind in the second half of the twentieth century. He uses a broad distinction, which many have found useful elsewhere: according to McHale, modernist literature is primarily concerned with epistemology (questions of knowledge) and postmodernist literature with ontology (questions of being/world), and he makes much of postmodernist writers creating "worlds". Some of the literature analysed, especially that more usually known as "magical realist", is not English-language, but nevertheless this book is excellent for those interested in this aspect of twentieth-century fiction.

The one book that is perhaps the nearest to a general survey of living authors is HENDERSON's, which is the fifth, revised edition of a title first published in 1972. Although essentially a reference book, with information on a vast array of authors, this is a reasonable way into the contemporary area. The entries provide publication details, general descriptions of the authors' lives, and analytical essays on the novels. The contrast between Walter Allen's preface to the first edition and Jerome Klinkowitz's to the fifth (Allen's introduction is helpfully reprinted) is illuminating. Both tackle the issue of whether there is life left in the novel. Allen concedes that the novel is no longer culturally central, thanks to journalism, films, documentary, and the kind of non-fiction that "deals with people". Definitions of what constitutes the novel are always problematic. Allen states: "for me, although I recognise variants such as the novels of Melville, the novel is a broadly realistic representation of man's life in society which is also a criticism of life and society". With some considerable foresight he notes "the sudden and unexpected appearance of the novel within the past three decades or so in the new countries where English is spoken, the Caribbean islands, India, the countries of Africa". Klinkowitz, writing 20-odd years later, and demonstrating his own bias, ignores these latter novelists in his preface and emphasises the arrival of the postmodern writers (John Barth, Thomas Pynchon, John Hawkes, Donald Barthelme). The case of Salman Rushdie illustrates, for him, the continuing importance of the novel, and he sees that women writers have benefitted most from the novel's form (should this not, perhaps, be the other way around?).

STEVEN EARNSHAW

Novel: Recent and Contemporary

Anderson, Linda, *Plotting Change: Contemporary Women's Fiction*, London: Edward Arnold, 1990
Ashcroft, Bill, Gareth Griffiths, and Helen Tiffin, *The Empire Writes Back: Theory and Practice in Post-Colonial Literatures*, London and New York: Routledge, 1989
Bradbury, Malcolm, *The Modern American Novel*, Oxford and New York: Oxford University Press, 1983, revised 1992
Gasiorek, Andrzej, *Post-War British Fiction: Realism and After*, London: Edward Arnold, 1995
Henderson, Lesley (ed.), *Contemporary Novelists*, London and Chicago: St James Press, 1991 (5th revised edition)
McHale, Brian, *Constructing Postmodernism*, London and New York: Routledge, 1993
Palmer, Paulina, *Contemporary Women's Fiction: Narrative Practice and Feminist Theory*, London: Harvester Wheatsheaf, 1989; Jackson: University Press of Mississippi, 1989
Smyth, Edmund J. (ed.), *Postmodernism and Contemporary Fiction*, London: Batsford, 1991

This entry considers the novels and fictional movements and preoccupations of roughly the last 30 years. HENDERSON (reviewed more fully in the "Novel: 20th Century" entry), the fifth edition of a title originally published in 1972, provides a reference source for the period, offering thumbnail biographies, lists of works, and brief critical profiles of living writers in English.

The American context of this broad scope is perhaps most clearly introduced through BRADBURY's survey of the American novel in the twentieth century, which spends three chapters considering "contemporary" fiction. Bradbury refers to most of the principal novelists, making extended comments on a selected few, and places them within a general socio-historical and cultural climate. Moving from the "clear return to politics and history" and "the spirit of avant-garde revival" in the 1960s, through postmodernism experiments and into the "late postmodern" interest in a new realism, Bradbury emphasises particularly the multiplicity of the contemporary American novel.

The British context of these decades has been recently treated by GASIOREK in a book which argues that for postwar fiction realism has not been a spent force superseded by various postmodernisms. This study challenges the conventional notion of realism as outdated and untenable, and perceives it as a heterogeneous phenomenon, as contemporary British fiction produces a variety of different reworkings of it. Concentrating on novelists like Ivy Compton-Burnett, V.S. Naipaul, John Fowles, Angela Carter, Sara Maitland, Graham Swift, Julian Barnes, and Salman Rushdie, this book claims to be a modest act of retrieving fictional strategies and aesthetic practices which have been homogenised by the invocation of postmodernism as the cultural dominant. Even those writers associated with postmodernism who subject realism to a searching critique emphasise the dangers of rejecting realist aesthetics and epistemology altogether. In an interesting and provocative manner, this book explores not only some of the major recent developments in

British fiction, but also how and why realism has been challenged during the past 40 years.

The fiction of postmodernism has received innumerable treatments in recent years. One of the most accessible and interesting discussions has been that of McHALE. He argues that postmodernism is "not a found object, but a manufactured artifact". From this premise, he develops a series of readings of contemporary novels by Umberto Eco, Thomas Pynchon, Joseph McElroy, Christine Brooke-Rose, and various cyberpunk science-fiction writers, although the range of reference is much wider. McHale's characterisation of postmodernism has been criticised for being too formalist, yet he nevertheless provides interesting discussions of postmodern fiction and its relation to such cultural phenomena as television, cinema, paranoia and nuclear anxiety, angelology, and the cybernetic interface. SMYTH's collection of essays tends to be more theoretical in its orientation, although the essays include critical evaluations of contemporary fiction. After examining the evolution of postmodernism within contemporary literary history, the book seeks to answer the question "what is postmodernism?" by discussing those features that distinguish it from modernism. The first section examines writers from around the world who are associated with postmodernism, like Alasdair Gray, Fowles, Rushdie, John Barth, Pynchon, Ronald Sukenick, Alain Robbe-Grillet, Eco, Italo Calvino, Gabriel García Márquez, and Julio Cortázar. Part Two considers more general questions, such as the cultures and politics associated with postmodernism and feminism. This is a useful guide to the trends in recent fiction, as well as a series of good essays concerning the critical debate about postmodernism.

The past 30 years have seen significant developments in the conscious exploration of the exclusions, limitations, and horizons of women's writing. ANDERSON's collection of essays explores diverse writers and topics – Doris Lessing, Angela Carter, Alice Walker, Grace Paley, Alison Lurie, women's science-fiction, contemporary lesbian feminist fiction, the reconceptualisation of history in contemporary women's fiction – aimed at "how women find out ways of contesting their own silence, asking different questions related to difference, and powerfully striving against boundaries". Self-confessedly less a set of conclusions than a set of questions, these essays consider how contemporary women's fiction questions inherited literary traditions in its desire to find a new and different territory. The variety of strategies of subverting the dominant modes of thought are analysed in the way these writers push their styles beyond realism, using fantasy, humour, utopia, and fairytale as techniques to re-imagine women's relationship to history, and to their racial and sexual identities.

PALMER's book is an exploration of women's writing since the 1960s, investigating the extent to which narrative practice and feminist theory are integral aspects of much of the creative writing currently being produced by women. It discusses a wide range of women writers who are usually excluded from academic debate, including British and American radical-feminist and lesbian writers like Emma Tennant, Fay Weldon, Marge Piercy, Alice Walker, Kate Millett, Aileen La Tourette, Anna Wilson, Jan Clausen, May Sarton, and Toni Cade Bambara. In examining these writers, Palmer highlights the variety of feminisms of the 1970s and 1980s, such as radical feminism, socialist feminism, and psychoanalytic feminism, and includes a useful glossary of these and other terms. The scope of the investigation includes questions about the construction of women's writing, topics of femininity, collectivity, sisterhood, and experiences of motherhood, as well as providing a useful overview of major areas of feminist thought.

Alertness to differences in cultural production has also extended to examining the issue of race in contemporary fiction. ASHCROFT *et al.* examine the new writing that experiences of colonisation and the challenge of the postcolonial world in India, Australia, Africa, Canada, and the Caribbean have produced. Opening debates about the interrelationships of these literatures, the book shows how these texts effect a radical critique of the assumptions underlying Eurocentric notions of literature and language. It looks at writers like Lewis Nkosi, Naipaul, Michael Anthony, Janet Frame, and R.K. Narayan. In its two-fold structure of identifying the range and nature of these postcolonial texts, and describing the various theories which have emerged so far to account for them, the book considers issues of hegemony, language, place, displacement, hybridity, and various theories of national literatures. This is a very useful introductory guide to the debates concerning the contemporary postcolonial novel, and how postcolonial theory interacts with, and dismantles, some of the assumptions of European theory.

TIM S. WOODS

Novel: British – General

Allen, Walter, *The English Novel: A Short Critical History*, London: Phoenix House, 1954; New York: Dutton, 1954

Baker, Ernest A., *The History of the English Novel*, 10 vols., London: Witherby, 1924–39

Forster, E. M., *Aspects of the Novel*, London: Edward Arnold, 1927; New York: Harcourt Brace, 1928; edited by Oliver Stallybrass, as *"Aspects of the Novel" and Related Writings*, London: Edward Arnold, 1974

Hardy, Barbara, *The Appropriate Form: An Essay on the Novel*, London: Athlone Press, 1964

Kettle, Arnold, *An Introduction to the English Novel*, 2 vols., London: Hutchinson, 1951–53, 2nd edition, 1967

Leavis, F.R., *The Great Tradition: George Eliot, Henry James, Joseph Conrad*, London: Chatto & Windus, 1948; New York: G.W. Stewart, 1948

Pritchett, V.S., *The Living Novel*, London: Chatto & Windus, 1946; revised edition, New York: Random House, 1964

Saintsbury, George, *The English Novel*, London: Dent & Sons, 1913; New York: Dutton, 1913

Showalter, Elaine, *A Literature of Their Own: British Women Writers from Brontë to Lessing*, Princeton, New Jersey: Princeton University Press, 1977; London: Virago, 1978, revised 1982

Spender, Dale, *Mothers of the Novel: 100 Good Women Writers Before Jane Austen*, London: Pandora,1986; New York: Routledge & Kegan Paul, 1986

Watt, Ian, *The Rise of The Novel: Studies in Defoe, Richardson and Fielding,* London: Chatto & Windus, 1957; Berkeley: University of California Press, 1957
Wheeler, Michael, *English Fiction of the Victorian Period 1830–1890*, London: Longman, 1985

The term "English novel", in contradistinction to the European, and occasionally American, tradition was that commonly used until relatively recently, and Irish, Scottish, and Welsh novelists writing in English figure under this title. The earlier critical surveys of the novel tend to be chronological accounts of the historical development of the genre. Saintsbury's, which claimed to be the first to undertake such an overview, and Baker's monumental ten-volume study are of this type. By the mid-twentieth century criticism focused more attention on structural and aesthetic issues, and the debate between liberal humanist and early Marxist theorists had major implications for the literary canon itself. In recent decades feminist critics have been particularly influential in this regard, not merely arguing for an extended canon with greater representation of women writers, but offering radical re-interpretations of both individual novelists and the development of the genre. There have also been a number of critical studies focusing on subgenres, such as science fiction, historical novels, or crime fiction, or on issues such as politics and gender.

SAINTSBURY, arguing against distinctions between genres, traces the English novel from the romances of the middle ages to the end of the nineteenth century. The "Four Masters" of the novel are for him Henry Fielding, Walter Scott, William Makepeace Thackeray, and Jane Austen. His views on individual writers seem often idiosyncratic; he can be wittily savage, and modern feminists are likely to take issue with his overall placing of women writers. Yet his scope is broad and his comments on individual works, for instance on Anne Caldwell's "forgotten but remarkable" *Emilia Wyndham*, are often an encouragement to rediscovery. It is typical that though he credits Fielding, Samuel Richardson, Tobias Smollett, and Laurence Sterne, with the establishment of the modern novel, the subsequent chapter argues that the minor work of a time is of great importance in studying literary developments. There is an index but no bibliography.

BAKER's work, which aimed "to trace the origins and growth of English prose fiction" from its beginnings, is now primarily of value as a reference book. Its coverage is extensive and detailed. Volume I begins with Greek romance and Volume X ends with D.H. Lawrence. The criticism is uneven. Some of the views expressed, particularly when dealing with women novelists, seem absurdly dated (e.g., on the "distinctively feminine" resemblances of any randomly chosen women novelists, and the absurdity of trying to "do the like with Dickens and Thackeray, Meredith and Hardy"). Yet the same chapter offers a workmanlike if modest introduction to Katherine Mansfield's peculiar skills. Its bibliographies, though unfortunately omitting the publishers, have a value for students of nineteenth- and early twentieth-century criticism.

In the nineteenth century, the reviewing of fiction was as much the province of novelists as of professional scholars. Critical essays in the serious quarterlies and monthlies were as able to debate the state of contemporary fiction, aspects of the art of the novel, or the *oeuvre* of writers both living and dead, as to assess the latest issues from the presses. Two twentieth-century novelists whose criticism still merits attention are E.M. Forster and V.S. Pritchett.

FORSTER's book is based on the annual Clark lectures he gave under the aegis of Trinity College, Cambridge, in 1926–27. He was the first novelist to be offered the lectureship, and had, indeed, little time for academic criticism. He does not attempt to offer here any sustained theory of fiction, and the choice of the word "Aspects" in his title is significant. What he gives is a series of commentaries from a practising novelist on narrative structure and character, and what he called "fantasy and prophecy". The main emphasis of the lectures is on the English novel, though Forster notes its limitations when compared with great Russian and French works. Although some of his judgements are contentious, Forster's incidental remarks on novelists as diverse as Jane Austen, Max Beerbohm, and D.H. Lawrence are often wittily illuminating and sharply perceptive. Oliver Stallybrass's Introduction to the 1974 edition, and its appendices, notes, and index, usefully contextualise Forster's work within its contemporary critical debates.

PRITCHETT's collection of "short journeys of rediscovery" of some of the standard novelists he had re-read as "expectant novelist" rather than as critic, derived from his wartime reading, a circumstance which must have affected its composition. The British section is by far the largest, and despite his claim to revisit the canon, the selection is eclectic. It begins with Fielding and ends with "Two Writers and Modern War", the war being the American Civil War, and the writers being Walt Whitman (because of his war reports) and Stephen Crane. While neither Jane Austen nor Thomas Hardy appear, Thomas Day's *Sandford and Merton*, Arthur Morrison's *The Hole in the Wall*, and Somerville and Ross's *The Real Charlotte* are given a reading sufficiently sympathetic to send one back to the originals. Irish and Scottish writers are well represented, and include Scott, Sheridan Le Fanu, and John Galt. Original and still highly readable, it remains engaging and stimulating.

ALLEN was a novelist, a critic, and broadcaster, but his book derives, even when it diverges, from the chronological histories. The publishers claimed such a work was "badly needed, for no general survey of the English novel from the beginnings to the eve of the Second World War has recently appeared"(jacket blurb). Sadly he did not follow his original plan to bring it up to his own day, when he might have assessed his own contemporaries. Elizabeth Bowen, Evelyn Waugh, and James Hanley among others do not receive the detailed treatment he intended. The survey ends with Lawrence and James Joyce. Though tracing the development of the novel for the general reader, Allen is aware of contemporary scholarly views, and is not afraid to take issue with them (for example, "if Fanny Burney has been overrated, Mrs Charlotte Smith has been persistently underrated"). His opinions on such writers as James Hogg, or his judgement of George Eliot's "essential modernity" as lying in her "very thoroughness and intensity of her analysis" of character, still strike the 1990s' reader as modern, and his perceptive comments in "1914 and After" on the dilemmas facing his own contemporaries are now of considerable historical interest. This is a book deservedly still on reading lists.

LEAVIS's work was powerfully influential on an entire academic generation. Although its opening sentence announces categorically that the great English novelists are Austen, George Eliot, Henry James, and Joseph Conrad, the study confines itself almost entirely to the last three, and attaches a sharply argued Appendix acclaiming, most unusually for its time, *Hard Times* as Dickens's unacknowledged masterpiece. (Within his narrow definition of the "Great Tradition" Leavis included Lawrence, to whom he subsequently devoted a book.) As the 1962 paperback edition advertises, his criticism "has always been notable for its uncompromising association of literature and morality" and it is indeed this fundamental aspect of Leavis's critical creed that has disturbed many later critics, who otherwise admire his discussion of the individual novels. Notwithstanding, this book remains a stimulating and incisive contribution to the criticism of fiction.

HARDY's main concern in her lucid discussion of a group of novelists is with narrative form; but structural considerations are never divorced from her reading of their moral arguments and representation of what she terms "truthfulness" in preference to "realism". It is within this framework that Henry James's economy and concentration of narrative is contrasted with the more expansive structures of George Eliot and Dickens, and it enables her to make fruitful comparisons between Daniel Defoe, Charlotte Brontë, Hardy, and Forster, whose novels are seen as restricted by the pressure of their ideologies. Other chapters, each illustrating a different structural pattern, are devoted to novels by Meredith, George Eliot, Lawrence, and Leo Tolstoy.

Though ostensibly dealing with only three novelists, all of them eighteenth-century writers – Defoe, Richardson, and Fielding – WATT's study has had much wider critical influence than this focus might suggest. In presenting them as the founding fathers of the new literary form, the novel, Watt argues for the importance of the social and economic trends and the new philosophical arguments of the eighteenth century in favouring the kinds of innovation that these writers introduced. Thus, for Watt, the rise of capitalism and individualism is not only reflected in Defoe's themes and characterisations – "motives such as economic egoism and social alienation" – but impelled Defoe towards his characteristic, almost exclusive, concentration on hero or heroine and his or her ideas about their world. His illuminating discussion of these writers ensured the book's place in its day as essential secondary reading. More recently feminists have attacked his view that the influence of women readers and women novelists, including even Jane Austen – whose technical excellence receives much praise – led to the restriction of social horizon and human situation that affected the later development of the English novel.

KETTLE's approach, though in no way offering a history of the genre, is also historical, since for him historical circumstances crucially affect literary production. His method is to concentrate on a selection of novels, interspersed with brief introductions to the period in question. The first volume starts with John Bunyan and Defoe, and ends with George Eliot. The second includes some 16 works, beginning with Henry James and ending with Henry Green. Kettle's Marxist critique is evident in his treatment of Hardy's *Tess of the d'Urbervilles* and of Austen's *Emma*; it is evident too in his attitude to John Galsworthy's or Ivy Compton-Burnett's subject-matter. Yet it is a measure of his stature as a critic that his opinions are rarely dogmatic. His critical judgement remains acute, whether analysing the weakness of Galsworthy's treatment of the central conflict of *The Man of Property*, or the strengths of Compton-Burnett's construction of dialogue. The annotations to the reading-lists offer helpful guidance to earlier critical works.

SHOWALTER's ground-breaking study argues for a specific female tradition of the nineteenth- and twentieth-century novel. Like her nineteenth-century predecessors (discussed by Dale Spender, see below) who surveyed women's achievements in the genre, she is as much concerned with the personal and social conditions in which women wrote and were published as with their innovative genius and technical skills as writers. The book remains a valuable resource, particularly for those interested in minor and little-documented writers, and contains useful listings and a bibliography.

SPENDER's study attacks both Watt's assessment of the role of women writers in developing the genre and the contemporary orthodox scholarly view of Defoe, Fielding, Richardson, Smollett, and Sterne as its founding fathers. In surveying women's fiction from the end of the seventeenth century to the emergence of Jane Austen she argues that women made the major contribution to the development of the novel, and that Jane Austen was their inheritor, rather than an isolated female writer perfecting the models provided by men. Spender provides a number of case studies of "lost" women writers. Particularly interesting is the basis of her choice of a dozen eighteenth- and early nineteenth-century novelists – including Charlotte Lennox, Charlotte Smith, and Mary Brunton, as well as the more expected Fanny Burney and Maria Edgeworth – for detailed examination. It is informed by the consensus of views of female critics.

WHEELER's book is included as an example of one of a series of student guides to English fiction in its historical and cultural context. Others in the series cover the eighteenth century, and the Romantic and early modern (1890–1940) periods. The volume's aim is to provide a critical introduction to its subject, including some account of methods of publication, development and conventions of the form and its subgenres, and recurrent themes. Though inevitably the treatment of individual writers is relatively brief, the book provides a useful overview of its subject, taking account of recent criticism, and is a good starting-point for college and university students. Generous space is devoted to information valuable for its intended readership: it includes a chronological table placing fiction against other publications and contemporary events, a series of annotated bibliographies on the topics treated in the text, and brief biographical and bibliographical notes on over 50 writers.

BARBARA M. ONSLOW

Novel: 18th Century

Armstrong, Nancy, *Desire and Domestic Fiction: A Political History of the Novel*, New York and Oxford: Oxford University Press, 1987

Castle, Terry, *Masquerade and Civilization: The Carnivalesque in Eighteenth-Century English Culture and Fiction*, London: Methuen, 1986; Stanford, California: Stanford University Press, 1986
Davis, Lennard J., *Factual Fictions: The Origins of the English Novel*, New York: Columbia University Press, 1983
Hunter, James Paul, *Before Novels: The Cultural Contexts of Eighteenth-Century English Fiction*, New York: Norton, 1990
McKeon, Michael, *The Origins of the English Novel 1600–1740*, Baltimore: Johns Hopkins University Press, 1987; London: Raduis, 1988
Richetti, John, *Popular Fiction Before Richardson: Narrative Patterns 1700–1739*, Oxford: Clarendon Press, 1969
Spacks, Patricia Meyer, *Imagining a Self: Autobiography and Novel in Eighteenth-Century England*, Cambridge, Massachusetts: Harvard University Press, 1976
Watt, Ian, *The Rise of the Novel: Studies in Defoe, Richardson and Fielding*, London: Chatto & Windus, 1957; Berkeley: University of California Press, 1957

The emergence of the novel in a recognisably modern form is usually identified with the eighteenth century. Fiction in this period has always, therefore, been the subject of considerable critical debate, particularly as regards its "origins".

Studies of the eighteenth-century novel continue to reflect the influence of WATT, even if his account has inspired as many opponents as disciples. Watt took as the origins of the English novel the moment when it acquired the features of "formal realism" – fidelity to the everyday and to human individuality – and he examined the novels of Daniel Defoe, Samuel Richardson, and Henry Fielding in the light of this definition. For Watt, the rise of the novel paralleled the rise of the middle class, an uncontroversial thesis which he elaborated by studying the novel's readership as well as its characteristic preoccupations. Though Watt has subsequently been taken to task for his dismissal of non-canonical texts, and for his inattention to questions of gender, his book was pioneering in its materialism and in its emphasis on epistemology.

By his own admission, Watt paid no attention to the precursors of the best-known eighteenth-century novels, and RICHETTI was one of the first to rectify this omission. Though his study is confined to the first four decades of the century, it is a valuable survey of the large number of narratives preceding those of Defoe, Richardson, and Fielding, and challenged the assumption that the novel emerged with Defoe's *Robinson Crusoe*, Aphra Behn's *Oroonoko*, or any other single work. Richetti identified various sub-genres into which early novels fell – whore and criminal biographies, travel narratives, scandal chronicles, and amatory and pious novels. He thus mapped out a number of territories that have since been explored in greater detail by critics who have not felt his discomfort in dealing with popular literature.

To SPACKS, the novel and the related genre of autobiography reflected eighteenth-century preoccupations with the instability of human identity. By affirming the continuity and coherence of an individual's experience, novelists such as Defoe, Richardson, and Fanny Burney assuaged their readers' fears that neither memory nor imagination were sufficient evidence of selfhood. Spacks was among the first critics to address the question of sexual difference with regard to the eighteenth-century novel, and she afforded a separate chapter to the particular ways in which female identity was constructed in fiction.

According to DAVIS, the early-modern English novel did not develop in reaction to romance, but instead grew from what might be termed a "news/novel discourse". The novel, unlike the seventeenth-century ballad and other early forms of journalism, was marked by fictionality but also, like news, by claims to historicity or verisimilitude. The relationship between news and the novel, illustrated by the preponderance of novelists who were also journalists, weakened in the first quarter of the eighteenth century as a consequence of new legislation, which rendered overly factual narratives open to legal action, and made it necessary to underline a novel's inventedness. Nonetheless, in contrast to the romances of the seventeenth-century, novels retained a characteristic emphasis on factuality and probability.

CASTLE draws on the theories of Mikhail Bakhtin concerning the functions of the carnivalesque in early modern culture to support her thesis that the masquerade epitomised the eighteenth century's fascination with transgression and subversion. Castle uses the methodologies of the psychoanalyst and the anthropologist to analyse fictional representations of the masquerade. The novel was especially drawn to this theme, she argues, by virtue of the masquerade's conspicuous presence in contemporary society and, more importantly, by its potential for unsettling conventional generic categories. Focusing on Richardson's *Pamela, Part II*, Fielding's *Amelia*, Burney's *Cecilia*, and Elizabeth Inchbald's *A Simple Story*, Castle demonstrates the importance of the masquerade as a plot device in importing utopian, fantastic elements into didactic, mimetic texts. He is innovative in his juxtaposition of the novel with other cultural phenomena, and in his energetic assault on the view of the eighteenth century as a period of Augustan order and rationalism.

ARMSTRONG argues that the bourgeois subject, which emerged in the course of the eighteenth century, was female, and that this represented a triumph of middle-class femininity over aristocratic masculinity in a sphere not normally recognised as political – the household. Reflecting Foucauldian ideas about the ideological function of literature, Armstrong suggests that the novel was crucial in this triumph. Enlightenment philosophy had appeared to render human identity apolitical, and the novel reinforced this by turning from the social contract to sexual relationships, and from the public to the private sphere. Although her book follows the novel into the nineteenth century, Armstrong provides a lengthy analysis of *Pamela* as an example of the novel form's instrumentality in the domestication of the political: Richardson's middle-class heroine redeems her upper-class would-be seducer. She also demonstrates that the human subject is formed by language: Mr B comes to see that he can only know Pamela through her writings. Richardson's novel therefore dramatises the assumption which informs all eighteenth-century fiction, that novels determine the conduct of their readers. For Armstrong, as for Watt, the rise of the novel was intimately related to the rise of the middle classes; but Armstrong's radical departure from Watt (and from conventional feminist criticism) is to see the relationship in terms of women's political ascendancy.

McKEON's magisterial treatment of the origins of the novel is both a reaction to, and a recapitulation of, Watt's thesis. McKeon applies Marxist dialectics to literary history, arguing that Western narrative has traditionally followed a progression from romance, to realism, to self-conscious "skepticism". In the eighteenth century, novelists such as Defoe and Richardson became increasingly historicist and empiricist in opposition to the improbabilities of the earlier romance-writers; realist novels, however, gradually succeeded to becoming knowing anti-romances, such as Fielding's.

HUNTER's wide-ranging and ambitious study describes the social and literary contexts of the eighteenth-century novel, in particular its readership and literary predecessors ("pre-texts"). He identifies these as: journalism (particularly that associated with the publisher John Dunton); narratives designed to arouse wonder; and didactic texts. Hunter shows how all these genres shared features with the novel, in particular their concern with observation and interpretation. He also draws attention to the importance of modern ideas of selfhood and subjectivity for the novel, and for other forms such as the diary and the autobiography. In stressing both the intellectual background to the novel and the nature of its readership, Hunter attempts to synthesize divergent approaches to the subject while also offering insights of his own into the nature of early-modern novels.

KATHERINE A. ARMSTRONG

Novel: Romantic Era

Baker, Ernest A., *The History of the English Novel*, Volumes 5 (*The Novel of Sentimental and the Gothic Romance*) and 6 (*Edgeworth; Austen; Scott*); 10-volume series, London: Witherby, 1924–39; New York: Barnes & Noble, 1950

Butler, Marilyn, *Jane Austen and the War of Ideas*, Oxford: Clarendon Press, 1975; New York: Oxford University Press, 1987

Kelly, Gary, *The English Jacobin Novel 1790–1805*, Oxford: Clarendon Press, 1976; New York: Oxford University Press, 1976

Kelly, Gary, *English Fiction of the Romantic Period 1789–1830*, London: Longman, 1989

Kiely, Robert, *The Romantic Novel in England*, Cambridge, Massachusetts: Harvard University Press, 1972

Poovey, Mary, *The Proper Lady and the Woman Writer: Ideology as Style in the Works of Mary Wollstonecraft, Mary Shelley, and Jane Austen*, Chicago: University of Chicago Press, 1984

Criticism of fiction in the Romantic period has tended to fragment and compartmentalise the material. There have been numerous studies of Jane Austen and Sir Walter Scott, and a growing interest in the gothic novel; but is has been much rarer for critics to attempt to study the topic as a whole. The 1790s have often been annexed to studies of the eighteenth-century novel, while studies of the nineteenth-century novel have been dominated by the Victorians and have therefore often given only fleeting attention to the early 1800s.

BAKER's massive history can still be useful, even if stylistically and critically it seems very much a product of its time. His view of the period after the great eighteenth-century novelists is that it is marked by dramatic decline, redeemed only by Maria Edgeworth, Austen, and Scott, whom he presents as providing a redemptive bridge to the Victorians. More contemporary criticism has been less exercised by ideas of "greatness" and "decline" and so has rewritten literary history. While Baker's work, therefore, needs to be handled with some circumspection, it is exhaustive, detailed, and informative about often obscure texts.

KIELY brings a keen critical intelligence to bear on the material without being over-exercised by a thesis or by a theoretical agenda. He offers 11 readings of individual novels from Horace Walpole's *The Castle of Otranto* to Emily Brontë's *Wuthering Heights*, in which he examines the potential for disjunction when Romanticism's interest in "private vision and extreme emotion" tries to accommodate itself to a genre, the novel, that had grown up with ideas of social order and the objective stability of middle-class institutions. Kiely's view of Romantic fiction is not exhaustive and does not purport to be. The great value of the book lies in his stimulating and lucid readings of his chosen novels.

One of the important aspects of BUTLER's book when it appeared was its preparedness to locate Austen in the ideological and intellectual turmoils of the period, and further to relate her fictional practice to other strands in the fiction of the time. The second part of her book focuses on Austen, but in the first part Butler provides illuminating discussions of the sentimental novel, the political novel, and Edgeworth. The effect is not just to counteract criticism's tendency to keep Austen aloof from some of the more robust intellectual aspects of her time, but to suggest a more integrated approach to the literary history of the period, which has subsequently been taken up by other literary critics and historians.

KELLY's 1976 book offers more exhaustive discussions of some of the novels and novelists considered by Butler in her second and third chapters. His study is confined to writers using the novel as a vehicle for radical social and political views – Thomas Holcroft, William Godwin, Robert Bage, Elizabeth Inchbald; but the radical strand in the intellectual and literary life of the period has come to feature much more prominently in our understanding of it, and Kelly's detailed study of some neglected texts and writers clarifies the places which they occupy on the literary and intellectual map of the 1790s and early 1800s. It is a specialist book, but constitutes an energetic and definitive account of a kind of novel-writing which is a significant part of the development of fiction in the period.

POOVEY's book too is, in its way, specialist, and addresses only a small clutch of writers. However, like Butler's it constructs a framework within which Austen can be discussed alongside contemporary novelists from whom older criticism would have tended to dissociate her. Poovey's accounts of the novelists are driven by an examination of the way in which women's images and roles were determined within the male-dominated culture of the late eighteenth century, such that "the cultural pressure to conform to the image of proper (or innate) femininity directly contradicted the demands of professional authorship". She discusses extensively the tensions and "strategies" that she finds in women writers as they variously accommodate themselves to this image. The result is an important and stimulating book, which is much more versatile than might be suggested by labelling it as "feminist criticism". It is especially interesting where Poovey offers re-readings of familiar texts such as Mary Shelley's *Frankenstein* and Austen's *oeuvre*.

KELLY's 1992 book is the first attempt since Baker's to construct an extensive overview of the topic; but unlike Baker he accommodates the material more to a history of the period than to a history of the genre, and so his accounts of literary texts are vigorously intercut with accounts of broader social and intellectual issues. From his vantage point he sees the "central thematic and formal issues" of fiction in this period as being:

> . . . the gentrification of the professional classes and the professionalization of the gentry, the place of women in a professionalized culture that denies them any significant role in public or professional life, the establishment of a "national" culture of distinction and discrimination in the face of fashion and commercialized culture, the re-siting of the authentic self in an inward moral and intellectual being so cultivated as to be able to negotiate successfully the varieties of social experience and cultural discriminations, the establishment of standard speech based on writing, and resolution of the relationship of authoritative narration and detailed representation of subjective experience.

It is a formidable list; and Kelly exercises an equally formidable knowledge of the period in pursuing it. Scott and Austen get separate chapters, but in the others Kelly moves stimulatingly from major novels to minor, and from the novel to magazine fiction and children's fiction. Throughout he subtly uses the tools of cultural materialism to produce a rewritten and re-argued history of the role of fiction in the complex imaginative, social, and ideological negotiations of the period.

DAVID BLAIR

Novel: Victorian

Beer, Gillian, *Darwin's Plots: Evolutionary Narrative in Darwin, George Eliot and Nineteenth-Century Fiction*, London and Boston: Routledge & Kegan Paul, 1983

Bivona, Daniel, *Desire and Contradiction: Imperial Visions and Domestic Debates in Victorian Literature*, Manchester: Manchester University Press, 1990

Crosby, Christina, *The Ends of History: Victorians and "The Woman Question"*, New York and London: Routledge, 1991

Litvak, Joseph, *Caught in the Act: Theatricality in the Nineteenth-Century English Novel*, Berkeley: University of California Press, 1992

Miller, D. A., *The Novel and the Police*, Berkeley: University of California Press, 1988

Perera, Suvendrini, *Reaches of Empire: The English Novel from Edgeworth to Dickens*, New York: Columbia University Press, 1991

Pykett, Lyn, *The Sensation Novel from "The Woman in White" to "The Moonstone"*, Plymouth, Devon: Northcote House, 1994

Yeazell, Ruth Bernard (ed.), *Sex, Politics, and Science in the Nineteenth-Century Novel*, Baltimore: Johns Hopkins University Press, 1986

Criticism of the Victorian novel has in recent years been dramatically transformed by developments in critical theory – especially feminism, deconstruction, postcolonialism, and New Historicism. As a consequence it is at present a particularly exciting area of critical debate as once-familiar texts are opened to new ways of reading.

YEAZELL's book draws together six theoretically informed essays on Victorian fiction – mainly British but also American – from Anthony Trollope to Henry James. The collection is striking both for the consistently high quality of its contributions and for its methodological refusal to "isolate the writing of fiction from other forms of representation". In this way the volume provides an exploration not only of the Victorian novel but also of the culture in which it participated and helped, indeed, to shape. Contributors give particular attention to the "concealments and evasions" surrounding a set of "cultural anxieties" relating to questions of science, writing, sexuality, and gender. Topics include the relations of writing, prostitution, and usury in George Eliot; "the Victorians' intensified sense of evanescence [and] their efforts to counter oblivion" through a search for origins by means of fiction and science alike; syphilis at the *fin de siècle* and its inscriptions as literary fantasy in Robert Louis Stevenson, Thomas Hardy, and Bram Stoker; and the writing of "homosexual panic" in James. This is an important and provocative book which deserves a wide readership.

BEER's study also concerns itself with science and the novel in the Victorian period, and provides a subtle and fascinating account of their interplay. In its first two parts the book carries out a detailed reading of Charles Darwin's *Origin of Species*, drawing particular attention to what might be called its "literary dimensions" – its "metaphors, myths, and narrative patterns". The book's third and longest part deals with fictional responses to Darwin, focusing on George Eliot and Hardy. Beer elaborates, as she puts it, "the ways in which evolutionary theory has been assimilated and resisted" by the Victorian novel and usefully discusses that theory's effects at the levels of language, theme, and narrative form.

For CROSBY, the Victorian period is defined in terms of a simultaneous obsession – with "history", on the one hand, and "the ceaseless posing of 'the woman question'" on the other. The logic of the relation between these two obsessions is traced through analyses of several major Victorian novels (George Eliot's *Daniel Deronda*, Thackeray's *Henry Esmond*, Dickens's *Little Dorritt*, and Charlotte Brontë's *Villette*), which are read alongside a range of "non-literary" texts, from Hegel's *Philosophy of History* to works by Thomas Babington Macaulay, Henry Mayhew, Andrew Fairbairn, and John Ruskin. Even in writers overtly sympathetic to women (Eliot and Charlotte Brontë, for example) history is irrevocably gendered, in the end, Crosby argues, as "masculine": it is the medium in which, and through which, the middle-class Victorian male defined himself as universal subject in a process that necessarily consigned women to the spaces of the "intrinsically unhistorical". This is an original, challenging, and complex study, which illustrates the possibilities opened up by feminism and critical theory for cultural analysis in the Victorian period.

PYKETT's book is part of the critical reassessment of the sensation novel that has taken place over the last 20 years or so. The opening chapter of this brief but unreductive study defines "The Sensation Phenomenon" in the 1860s and includes a stimulating analysis of the cultural meanings of sensation fiction. These consist primarily in the genre's ability to bring into focus a number of "interrelated social tensions and anxieties" concerning the family, instabilities of gender and class, and issues of law and property. The second and third chapters respectively discuss "questions of identity" in Wilkie Collins and women's sensation fiction, with particular reference to Mary Elizabeth Braddon, Ellen Wood, and Rhoda Broughton. The book concludes with a survey of the ways in which elements of sensationalism become diffused into other kinds of fiction in the mid- to-late Victorian period. Pykett provides a clear introduction to a genre that is receiving growing critical attention.

PERERA is strongly influenced by Edward Said's work (in the field of colonial discourse theory) on the complicitous relations of culture and imperialism. This she uses (together with the insights of feminist criticism) as the framework for analysis of works by Dickens, Elizabeth Gaskell, Charlotte Brontë, and Thackeray (as well as earlier texts by Maria Edgeworth and Jane Austen). Perera's readings – or re-readings – are striking for their demonstration of the extent to which the seemingly private worlds of domesticity and the "feminine" are articulated, in nineteenth-century fiction, with questions of race, empire, and nation. Her study is also notable for a particularly subtle handling of rhetorical and narrative elements in the novel, combined with sharp historical awareness and theoretical sophistication. This book is an incisive and engaging work, persuasively resituating a number of "canonical" Western texts within an historically and culturally informed context.

BIVONA's study explores the "cultural imprint" of the "imperial experience" as it appears in Victorian (and early twentieth-century) literature usually taken to have little to do with such things. Texts "that have always been associated with the discourse on empire" (from Benjamin Disraeli's *Tancred* to Rudyard Kipling's *Kim*) are juxtaposed with works that have not been viewed from an "imperial" perspective but nonetheless can be read as allegories or parables of empire (Disraeli's *Coningsby* and *Sybil*, Lewis Carroll's *Alice's Adventures in Wonderland*, and Hardy's *Jude the Obscure*). Together with thus suggesting the pervasiveness of the "imperialist mentality", Bivona is concerned, equally, to elucidate some of the ways in which such a mentality is contested. *Alice's Adventures* offers for example, Bivona contends, "the century's most dramatic critique of cultural imperialism". Works by Rider Haggard, Hardy, and the early Joseph Conrad raise questions, similarly, about the hierarchies that Victorian England sought to maintain between its own "civilized" self and a "primitive" "other".

Despite the ostentation of its title, the central focus of MILLER's self-styled "book of essays" is not on the police in the literal sense of an institution formed during the course of the nineteenth century. The concern, rather, is with the "ramification" within Victorian culture of "less visible, less visibly violent modes of 'social control'". Self-consciously indebted to the work of Michel Foucault, Miller's study is a compelling demonstration of how the novel itself functions as an agent of a disciplinary culture: it is, he argues, "the primary spiritual exercise of an entire age", whose point was "to confirm the novel-reader in his identity as 'liberal subject'". Miller supports his case through extended discussions of five major Victorian novels – Dickens's *David Copperfield* and *Bleak House*, Trollope's *Barchester Towers*, and Collins's *The Woman in White* and *The Moonstone* – in a work that offers a sophisticated perspective on the collusions of culture and power.

In contrast, drawing on feminist and gay theory, LITVAK's study forms an interesting and subtle challenge to Miller's reading of the Victorian novel as a disciplinary apparatus. Concentrating on a variety of Victorian novels from Charlotte Brontë's *Jane Eyre* to Henry James's *The Tragic Muse* (together with Austen's pre-Victorian *Mansfield Park*), Litvak shows how inscriptions of theatricality provide "transgressive openings" within these texts in which culturally subversive energies are to be located. Such energies, Litvak argues, cannot always be fully recuperated by a culture's regimes of power. Theatricality thus destabilizes the regulated "liberal subject" of Miller's Foucaldian reading, together with the patriarchal/heterosexual narratives by which that subject is incarcerated. In addition to giving us a searching counter-statement to Miller, Litvak raises some important general questions about the performativity of literary criticism itself.

CARL PLASA

Victorian Novel of Social Conscience

Cazamian, Louis, *The Social Novel in England, 1830–1850: Dickens, Disraeli, Mrs Gaskell, Kingsley*, translated by Martin Fido, London and Boston: Routledge & Kegan Paul, 1973 (original French edition, 1903)

Eagleton, Mary, and David Pierce, *Attitudes to Class in the English Novel: From Walter Scott to David Storey*, London: Thames & Hudson, 1979

James, Louis, *Fiction for the Working Man, 1830–1850: A Study of the Literature Produced for the Working Classes in Early Victorian England*, London and New York: Oxford University Press, 1963

Keating, P.J., *The Working Classes in Victorian Fiction*, London: Routledge & Kegan Paul, 1971

Klaus, H. Gustav (ed.), *The Socialist Novel in Britain: Towards the Recovery of a Tradition*, Brighton, Sussex: Harvester Press, 1982

Klaus, H. Gustav, *The Rise of Socialist Fiction, 1880–1914*, Brighton, Sussex: Harvester Press, 1987; New York: St Martin's Press, 1987

Smith, Sheila, M., *The Other Nation: The Poor in English Novels of the 1840s and 1850s*, Oxford: Clarendon Press, 1980; New York: Oxford University Press, 1980

The reign of Queen Victoria, 1837–1901, is mistakenly seen by many to be one of uniform complacency in spite of the many changes that occurred in it and the many forms of protest for, and against, these changes. The novels of Charles Dickens are clearly a corrective against this simplistic view, although Dickens wrote only in the first half of Victoria's reign, and his brilliant insights into the various ills of society run counter to those of many other writers. With the exception of Keating, no critic has been able to encompass all the novelists of protest in the Victorian age, and Keating's view is, of necessity, a hurried one. Other works cited below, when not concerned with writers before and after Victoria's reign, tend to concentrate on the two great periods of protest at the beginning and end of this reign. Some are more interested in books *about* the working classes, others in books *for* the working classes. Oddly, and rather embarrassingly, much of the interest in this contentious subject comes from outside Britain.

CAZAMIAN's work, admirably translated, and with a useful foreword by the translator, still remains a standard text for this subject, although its optimism about human progress and its French origin give it a detached and outdated air. Dickens is correctly shown as moving away from attacks on specific abuses in the early novels to denouncements of general malaise as reflected in the later greater works, and, again correctly, this move is shown to be against the trend set by other novelists like Benjamin Disraeli, Charles Kingsley, and Elizabeth Gaskell. The importance given to Kingsley as artist and social reformer may seem surprising since, apart from a few rather lurid biographies, he has received little critical attention recently. On the other hand Cazamian's theoretical approach and his apparently effortless comprehension of historical and philosophical trends gives this work a surprisingly modern air.

JAMES, in spite of his title, does not have a great deal to say about novels that tried to do something about the condition of British workers. Instead, he focuses attention on the kind of cheap literature that the working class actually read, covering an enormous range of penny dreadfuls, plagiarisms of Dickens, religious tracts, and imports from France. The low literary level of all these works is not disguised; indeed, it is reinforced by some lurid illustrations. In discussing the anti-aristocratic and anti-clerical works of G.W.M. Reynolds, James performs a valuable service in providing a contrast to the less crude, but perhaps less sincere, work of established novelists writing for a middle-class audience.

KEATING aims to expand the study of the working class in English fiction from the rather narrow focus of Cazamian on novels dealing with the industrial conflicts of the middle of the century. Dickens and Kingsley are mentioned, the latter's pessimism being contrasted with Dickens's exuberance about the vitality of working-class life. But the main concentration of this book is on the last two decades of the century and on writers who described the urban and industrial working class realistically. There is a long chapter on George Gissing, written before the recent rise of critical interest in this author, and an affectionate chapter on Rudyard Kipling. Walter Besant and Arthur Morrison are two less famous figures who receive extended treatment, although Keating is honest about Besant's narrowness and Morrison's pessimism. The three concluding chapters on the Cockney School, industrialism, urbanism and the class conflict, and the phonetic representation of Cockney cover a lot of ground, but like the rest of this book they are more interesting for the social historian than the student of literature.

EAGLETON and PIERCE cover a wide period in a short book, with only three chapters dealing with the Victorian period. The novels of the 1840s and 1850s are dealt with briskly under the title "The Ungovernable" and tend to be regarded as if they were social tracts rather than novels, getting high or low marks for their degree of revolutionary fervour. Thus Charlotte Brontë's *Shirley* is condemned for its lack of enthusiasm for the workers' cause. There is a useful discussion of George Eliot's thoughtful handling of social issues and her treatment of sexuality. A chapter entitled "Oppositional Fiction" takes us to the end of the century and beyond it: George Moore and Thomas Hardy, two other writers to link sex and class, are considered here, although there is some mention of socialist novels.

SMITH's study began life as a doctoral thesis, and retains traces of its origin. On the other hand one cannot but be grateful for the wealth of documentation that supports her investigation of novelists like Dickens, Gaskell, Disraeli, Kingsley, and, rather surprisingly, Charles Reade. There are also some useful discussions of minor novelists like Elizabeth Stone, who wrote the same story as Mary Barton from the employer's point of view, and Augustus Mayhew, brother of the author of *London Labour and the London Poor*. Dickens is praised for the realism of his descriptions, Kingsley and Disraeli for their insights into the life of the rural poor, Reade for his attack on prison conditions, and Gaskell for her genial sympathy; but Smith sees all these novelists as members of the middle class writing for the middle class. She regards the evidence of poets, popular ballads, blue books, and artists, all of whom she usefully cites, as better indications of the reality that stirred the novelist's imagination.

Klaus has edited two volumes of essays on the socialist novel. Many of his contributors are, like himself, German. The earlier book (KLAUS, 1982) covers novels from 1850–1960, the latter (KLAUS, 1987) has a more restricted time range. Both volumes contain discussions of a wealth of lesser-known writers with socialist aims, and make out a case for why these writers should be better known. J.W. Overton, Margaret Harkness, Charles Allen Clarke, William Edwards Tirebuck, and Grant Allen all receive extended treatment. Inevitably, as these writers are virtually unknown, their novels' plots need to be summarised, and since they are being discussed for their ideas there is little room for literary criticism or for discussion of major authors, although William Morris is sensibly treated. But this book does deserve commendation for the way in which it looks at nineteenth-century fiction in a new light.

T.J. Winnifrith

O

Oates, Joyce Carol 1938–

American novelist, short-story writer, dramatist, poet, and essayist

Bastian, Katherine, *Joyce Carol Oates's Short Stories: Between Tradition and Innovation*, New York: Peter Lang, 1983

Grant, Mary K., *The Tragic Vision of Joyce Carol Oates*, Durham, North Carolina: Duke University Press, 1978

Johnson, Greg, *Understanding Joyce Carol Oates*, Columbia: University of South Carolina Press, 1987

Norman, Torborg, *Isolation and Contact: A Study of Character Relationships in Joyce Carol Oates's Short Stories, 1963–1980*, Gothenburg, Sweden: Acta Universitatis Gothoburgensis, 1984

Wagner, Linda W. (ed.), *Critical Essays on Joyce Carol Oates*, Boston: G.K. Hall, 1979

Wesley, Marilyn C., *Refusal and Transgression in Joyce Carol Oates' Fiction*, Westport, Connecticut: Greenwood Press, 1993

Since her appearance on the literary scene in 1963, Joyce Carol Oates has published more than 60 books, which include novels, short-story collections, poetry, and essays. Her notable productivity and her use of almost every mode to analyse the personal and social turmoil that characterize modern American life have attracted the interest of many critics who have tried to define her place on the American literary scene.

GRANT's study was one of the first book-length analyses of Oates's fiction. Focusing mainly on the first six novels (from *With Shuddering Fall* [1964] to *Do With Me What You Will* [1973]), Grant places Oates's work within the genre of tragedy, and her main argument is that "tragedy, for Joyce Carol Oates, is . . . an expression of the failure to answer the inexplorable need to create community". Grant attempts to situate Oates within the wider context of twentieth-century fiction by establishing comparisons with, among others, D.H. Lawrence on the possibility of tragedy and of "an affirming celebration of life", and with Flannery O'Connor on their differing uses and ultimate consequences of violence. Grant explores Oates's belief in the necessity of words to recreate the world and in the need to move the reader toward a new consciousness through the uses of violence and spiritual poverty in her fiction. Thus, for Grant, beneath the grimness, violence, and grotesque that characterize her fiction, Oates's intention is educative, and she is ultimately affirmative in her celebration of a "sense of life". Even though this didactic reading can posit problems, Grant's volume is a helpful and balanced analysis of Oates's early work.

The excellent collection of essays edited by WAGNER offers a good overview of Oatesian criticism and is a telling example of the divided response to Oates's body of work. Wagner's introductory essay surveys the breadth and variety of Oates's work and major concerns, as well as the varied critical reactions to her writing. The collection is divided into two sections: the first includes 17 reviews, which are reprinted here as a valuable sample of the critical reaction contemporary with the novels and short-story collection that are the subject of the critical essays in the second part of the book. Among the latter, particularly valuable are: Walter Sullivan's "The Artificial Demon: Joyce Carol Oates and the Dimensions of the Real", which analyzes both short stories and novels in an attempt to point out the ideas that inform Oates's vast literary production and the formal problems that arise from them; Joyce Weg's "'Don't You Know Who I Am?' The Grotesque in Oates's 'Where are You Going, Where Have You Been?'", a detailed analysis of one of Oates's most frequently anthologized short stories, which sees the use of the grotesque as allowing Oates to "achieve a highly skillful integration of the multiple levels of the story" and to "suggest a transcendent reality which reaches beyond surface realism to evoke the simultaneous mystery and reality of the contradictions of the human heart"; and, finally, Eileen T. Bender's "'Paedomorphic' Art: Joyce Carol Oates' *Childworld*", written specifically for this collection, which focuses on that novel in its relationship with Vladimir Nabokov's *Lolita*, and as an example of Oates's relationship with literary tradition ("Oates sees the literary tradition not as a trap to be skirted but as a realm of reality open to infinite revision and counter-statement, a realm of play and illusion. Her imitations are thus not the parodic acts of a fabulator; they are serious and even passionate responses to other fictive worlds"). As the first published collection of essays on Oates, this book is still a fundamental tool for the student of her work.

BASTIAN's important study explores Oates's short stories as an index of the author's "unique position as one straddling the realms of a passé literary tradition and of modern innovation". The book begins with an examination of Oates's "re-imaginings" of five classic works (Henry James's "The Turn of the Screw", Franz Kafka's "The Metamorphosis", Henry David Thoreau's "Walden", James Joyce's "The Dead", and Anton Chekhov's "The Lady with the Dog") in order to show

how she contemporizes, both formally and thematically, her models. Bastian then moves on to consider Oates's production in the context of the short-story genre: she divides the stories into three sub-genres – of the extraordinary, of recognition, and of initiation – and ascertains the interdependence of the new and the old in Oates's writing ("Oates strives not to revolutionize the short story but to create a literary vehicle adequate of expressing contemporary experience through the traditional means available to her").

NORMAN's study is a dissertation, which applies speech-act theory to the short fiction Oates wrote between 1963 and 1980 in order to examine how character and context are revealed through the verbal interaction of the characters. Norman is trying to demonstrate that "Oates's characters in their opposition to isolation and in their striving towards affirmative contact are on the move from a traditionally prevalent individual outlook towards a dynamic community of inter-relationships". The close readings that Norman offers of some of the short stories, even though they do not offer a new perspective on Oates's fiction, are a good starting point for future analysis.

JOHNSON's study of Oates's fiction has been conceived as an introduction, which provides the novice reader with a preliminary overview of the themes, fictional concerns, and characteristic style defining her work. The book includes a detailed reading of six of Oates's novels (*A Garden of Earthly Delights*, *Expensive People*, *Them*, *Wonderland*, *Son of the Morning*, and *Angel of Light*) and of two collections of short stories (*The Wheel of Love* and *Last Days*), and attempts to trace a progression in her career between 1967 and 1984. Though useful as a quick reference guide, and containing a fairly good and full bibliography, the limited scope of this text does not provide the reader with an extensive overview of all Oates's major fiction and her work in other genres.

WESLEY offers a much-waited-for feminist analysis of Oates's work, which uses the most recent theoretical developments in poststructuralism, Marxism, and psychology "to discover in Joyce Carol Oates's fiction of the American family systematic strategies of resistance". Wesley individuates the family in Oates's fiction as the locus in which power relationships and struggles are played out. She focuses her analysis mainly on the young protagonists, who struggle against the traditional definition of the patriarchal family and of the society that endorses it through "marked patterns of resistance which I define as refusal and transgression". Wesley's book is a valuable tool for a new and alternative reading of Oates's prose.

DAVIDA GAVIOLI

O'Casey, Sean 1880–1964

Irish dramatist

Ayling, Ronald (ed.), *O'Casey: The Dublin Trilogy: A Casebook*, London: Macmillan, 1985
Jones, Nesta (ed.), *File on O'Casey*, London and New York: Methuen, 1986
Jones, Nesta, *O'Casey & Expressionism* (book and slide set), London: Chadwyck-Healey, 1988
Kenneally, Michael, *Portraying the Self: Sean O'Casey and the Art of Autobiography*, Gerrards Cross, Buckinghamshire: Colin Smythe, 1988; Totowa, New Jersey: Barnes & Noble, 1988
Kilroy, Thomas (ed.), *Sean O'Casey: A Collection of Critical Essays*, Englewood Cliffs, New Jersey: Prentice-Hall, 1975
Kleiman, Carol, *O'Casey's Bridge of Vision: Four Essays on Structure and Perspective*, Toronto: University of Toronto Press, 1981
Krause, David, *Sean O'Casey and His World*, New York: Scribner, 1976; London: Thames & Hudson, 1976
Mitchell, Jack, *The Essential O'Casey: A Study of the Twelve Major Plays*, Berlin: Seven Seas, 1980; New York: International Publishers, 1980
O'Connor, Garry, *Sean O'Casey*, London: Hodder & Stoughton, 1988; New York: Atheneum, 1988
O'hAodha, Michéal, *The O'Casey Enigma*, Dublin: Mercier Press, 1980
Simmons, James, *Sean O'Casey*, London: Macmillan, 1983

From the moment when his plays were first presented on the stage of the Abbey Theatre in Dublin, O'Casey has been the subject of critical disagreement. From first to last there has been a tendency to conflate the quality of the work with the personal history of the man in a way that makes objective judgement difficult, as evident in some assessments below. Much criticism centres on the best-known plays, especially the apparently naturalistic Dublin Trilogy, and while the controversial *The Silver Tassie* also gets some attention, the later, more experimental work, created in England without the close contact with rehearsal process that the Abbey had provided, tends to receive less. Apart from Kenneally's complex analysis of the Autobiography, and Kleiman's critique of the organic development of the dramatist's expressionist and absurdist techniques, there is little evidence that contemporary critical theory has embraced O'Casey. Further, despite the availability of archive photographs and despite more recent performances, there is often a tendency towards a literary, rather than a theatrical, perspective, which is disappointing in view of O'Casey's mastery of stagecraft and the visual detail embedded in his texts.

Both an earlier and a recent biography best illustrate the tendency towards personalised assessment of the writer. KRAUSE, who has long had especial contact with family records, emphasises the notion that O'Casey felt that he had a double responsibility, to his art and his class. Enriched by many contemporary pictures and other source material, the book is also not immune from the kind of lapses into purple phraseology that Krause accuses his "noblest proletarian of them all" of sometimes using. Within a biographical frame, he discusses the major plays' theatrical forms and techniques, although O'Casey's political concerns are perhaps underplayed as an "ecumenical communism", subordinate to artistic concerns. Ex-Royal Shakespeare Company director and Laurence Olivier biographer O'CONNOR's more recent work, also rich in sources and photographs, attempts to show how the paradoxical O'Casey created himself out of the real John Casey. Aware of these tensions, O'Connor gives accounts of the reception of performances rather than developed textual analysis, but there are interesting references to different drafts made after productions – and this approach counterbalances over-literary criticism. His view that O'Casey considers politics more important than aesthetics opposes Krause. KENNEALLY's critique of the six-volume Autobiography, written over 20 years, provides a complex analysis of the principles of selection, arrangement, representation, and narrative strategy through which O'Casey, as contemporary self, objectifies himself as the "Other" historical self "to clarify for himself and demonstrate the forces that had moulded his unique character". This insight illuminates the different processes through which O'Casey transformed his experiences into plays or autobiography, the slippages and shifting perspectives accounting to some extent for differing critical attitudes which others adopt towards both work and man.

JONES (1986) follows the house format of this series, with a detailed chronology, play summaries with source material, followed by – in this case a disappointingly short – section of "the writer on his work". The range of reviews of both contemporary and recent productions usefully reveals the controversial aspects of audience reception, including differences grounded in nationality or ideology. For example, where *The Daily Worker* saw *Cock-a-Doodle-Dandy* as "strange wise and wonderful", the *Irish Times* felt it was "blind and bitterly destructive".

Essay collections edited across a period of ten years by Kilroy, O'hAodha, and Ayling all show similarly conflicting perspectives. AYLING focuses on the Dublin Trilogy: contrasting essays by Krause and Raymond Williams frame sections of comment and review, as well as detailed analysis of the plays, including clear exposition of the historical context and dispute about the degrees of naturalism and expressionism manifest even in these earlier works. As O'hAODHA's book contains nine centenary lectures first broadcast by Radio Telefis Eireann, the agenda is more celebratory then critical of O'Casey's enigmatic qualities. Contributions vary from the professional – the director Tomas MacAnna and the actor Cyril Cusack – to the political – James Plunkett on representations of class trade-unionism – and the personal – Robert Hogan and Brendan Kennelly on biographical aspects. KILROY contextualises O'Casey within qualified assessments of the three main figures of the Irish dramatic movement. However, his response to O'Casey's symbolism as unambiguous seems limited, and his accusation of "false poeticism" seems unaware that where writing "has to be completed on stage" rather than seem contained on the page, it may be seen as a virtue rather than a vice. Among the essays, John Arden's "Ecce Hobo Sapiens" gives a spirited, detailed reading of O'Casey's staging, especially his use of colour, linking his techniques to medieval morality plays, Shakespeare, and Victorian toy theatre, pointing out that the ideology of the later plays is in tension with the commercial theatre which generally produces them. Including extracts from Lady Gregory's diary, essays which cover the full play range in detail, and discussion of the complexities of O'Casey's form and language, as well as staging techniques and political issues, this book gives a comprehensive overview of the field, although its publication date precludes more recent critical methodologies.

Productive comparisons can be drawn between the scholarly, if clearly left-wing, readings of Mitchell and what can only be described as an injudiciously biased assessment by SIMMONS, then a lecturer at the University of Ulster. The latter is guilty of the "ungenerous ill-tempered and empty" attitude that he ascribes to O'Casey's journalism. Although he highlights many of the weaknesses which other more objective critics have appropriately detected, he undermines the validity of his observations by loading them with crude value-judgements, such as "the author is trying to show off a literary flair that he does not possess". MITCHELL's approach, valorising the former East Germany's frequent productions of the later plays, tends to be reductive in emphasising the relationship between their post-Brechtian aesthetic and potential mass revolutionary struggle, as well as the self-alienation produced by capitalism. Nevertheless, detailed discussion of 12 major plays attempts to deal positively with implicit contradictions, both aesthetic and ideological. He groups the plays conceptually, according to aspects of national and class struggle, and while there is detailed investigation of the dialectical relationship between themes and dramatic style and structure, the discussion is based more on text than performance.

JONES's 1988 monograph and accompanying colour slides illuminate O'Casey's problematic relationship with expressionism, and the text is perceptive and informative in a way that exceeds the merely descriptive. KLEIMAN's excellent exploration of *The Silver Tassie* and *Red Roses for Me* as a focus for evaluating O'Casey's increasing use of potentially expressionist and absurdist elements finds fascinating structural and signifying parallels in these plays, as well as such traces in earlier texts. Shrewd distinctions between O'Casey's work and European theatre practice are drawn – for example, his use of comedy is contrasted with Ernst Toller's heavier didacticism. Where European movements are seen as evocative of the disintegrating modern world, Kleiman feels O'Casey's exuberant language and transformations harmonise discordant elements, like the grotesque and sublime, the real and abstract, through his integrated stagecraft. Although semiotic terms are not used, detailed readings expose the symbolic potential of O'Casey's theatre, including its mixture of proletarian melodrama and poetic mysticism. Kleiman's imaginative yet well-grounded readings, while not ignoring just criticisms of O'Casey's flaws, nevertheless convey the strength of his dramatic and ideological vision.

MARGARET L. LLEWELLYN-JONES

O'Connor, Flannery 1925–1964

American short-story writer and novelist

Asals, Frederick, *Flannery O'Connor: The Imagination of Extremity*, Athens: University of Georgia Press, 1982

Bleikasten, André, "The Heresy of Flannery O'Connor" in *Critical Essays on Flannery O'Connor*, edited by Melvin J. Friedman and Beverly Lyon Clark, Boston: G.K. Hall, 1985

Browning, Preston M., *Flannery O'Connor*, Carbondale: Southern Illinois University Press, 1974

Feeley, Sister Kathleen, *Flannery O'Connor: The Voice of the Peacock*, New Brunswick, New Jersey: Rutgers University Press, 1972

Friedman, Melvin J., "Flannery O'Connor's Sacred Objects", in *The Added Dimension: The Art and Mind of Flannery O'Connor*, edited by Melvin J. Friedman and Lewis A. Lawson, New York: Fordham University Press, 1966
Gentry, Marshall Bruce, *Flannery O'Connor's Religion of the Grotesque*, Jackson: University Press of Mississippi, 1986
Hawkes, John, "Flannery O'Connor's Devil", in *Sewanee Review*, 1962; reprinted in *Critical Essays on Flannery O'Connor*, edited by Melvin J. Friedman and Beverly Lyon Clark, Boston: G.K. Hall, 1985
Martin, Carter W., *The True Country: Themes in the Fiction of Flannery O'Connor*, Nashville, Tennesse: Vanderbilt University Press, 1968
Muller, Gilbert H., *Nightmares and Visions: Flannery O'Connor and the Catholic Grotesque*, Athens: University of Georgia Press, 1972
Orvell, Miles, *Invisible Parade: The Fiction of Flannery O'Connor*, Philadelphia: Temple University Press, 1972; as *Flannery O'Connor: An Introduction*, Jackson: University Press of Mississippi, 1991
Shloss, Carol, *Flannery O'Connor's Dark Comedies: The Limits of Inference*, Baton Rouge: Louisiana State University Press, 1980

Despite the slim range of her *oeuvre* (two novels, 31 short stories, and one book of essays), there has been extensive critical attention devoted to Flannery O'Connor's fiction. O'Connor was a devout Roman Catholic, who insisted that her writing reflected her spiritual beliefs. The major issue regarding her work is, as Robert E. Golden argues, "the relation between O'Connor's stated religious intent and the realization of that intent within the fiction".

HAWKES' seminal – and controversial – article sees the fiction as an unrelenting disparagement of human rationality, and so asserts that O'Connor's satiric voice belongs on the side of the demonic, rather than the divine. O'Connor herself had misgivings about Hawkes' assessment, writing to Robert Fitzgerald: "I have argued for years with him [Hawkes] about his Devil, which he don't [sic] know is an unfallen spirit of some purely literary kind". While Hawkes' critique entails a polemic against the "constraining realism" of the 1950s (he maintains that O'Connor's work goes "to the core of what we may call the contemporary 'anti-realist' impulse"), the essay is not simply a prescriptive description of his own poetics as a writer. Offering a truly perspicacious reading of the finely nuanced paradoxes and incongruities of O'Connor's work, Hawkes' essay is a fundamental contribution to the commentary.

FRIEDMAN's essay elucidates the tension that exists between the realistic and the symbolic in O'Connor's writing by linking her narrative style to those (often French) literary experiments that accentuate a "literature of Things". Friedman usefully draws on Mircea Eliade's concept of the *hierophany* – an ordinary object endowed with a numinous quality – to explicate the hermeneutic difficulties involved in reading the fiction. In their tendency to lavish an almost quirky attention to physical objects, O'Connor's narrators and characters resemble those of Samuel Beckett, though in her work, the depiction of such objects pointedly, but enigmatically, conjoins the sacred with the profane.

MARTIN's acclaimed study offers a particularly Christian reading of the fiction. Frequently citing O'Connor's lectures and essays, Martin views the stories from a "sacramental" vantage point, a method that illuminates the religious questions posed by the author, but which often obscures the inherent ambiguity of the texts. Arguing that the stories "attest to a belief that God writes straight with crooked lines", Martin helpfully clarifies the texts' allegorical complexity for the secular reader (much as Dante's often confusing ethical judgments need to be contextualized within the framework of medieval theology). This being said, Martin's thematic analysis will seem too narrowly schematic for those who find troublesome the belief that O'Connor's fiction directly – and solely – corresponds to a Christian ethos.

FEELEY offers a detailed interpretation of the fiction from a Roman-Catholic viewpoint. In many ways a homage to O'Connor, this study has the particular virtue that its author had access to O'Connor's personal book-collection and to people who knew her. Since her analysis of specific stories proceeds side by side with an account of what O'Connor was reading during composition and the accompanying marginalia she made, Feeley's study is indispensable to those scholars interested in producing a critique of O'Connor as reader/author, as well as to those who are unable to undertake original archival research. Feeley's doctrinal reading usefully engages O'Connor's theological concerns; however, as with many of the other specifically Christian studies, this study verges on being reductive or chooses to ignore textual evidence that complicates a Christian interpretation. A noteworthy feature of the book is its bibliography of O'Connor's library.

MULLER's study is one of the first to examine O'Connor's reliance on the "grotesque" as a literary strategy for revealing metaphysical problems. Providing a thoughtful treatment of the philosophical and aesthetic issues involved in the generic attributes of the grotesque, Muller places O'Connor's work within the tradition of Hieronymus Bosch, Rabelais, Edgar Allan Poe, and the existentialists. (A brief discussion differentiating O'Connor's writing from surrealism signals a useful direction not yet taken by scholars.) To Muller, O'Connor's grotesquely animated landscapes mirror the "cultural grotesque" of a Southern society cut adrift from its past and theological traditions. Alienation, then, whether spiritual, historic, or existential, forms the basis of the various odysseys undertaken by O'Connor characters. According to Muller, O'Connor's "greatest literary gift" comes from her "fusion of grotesque vision and theological vision . . . her ability to shape reality convincingly to orthodox Christianity".

ORVELL begins his treatment of O'Connor's writing by usefully placing it within the American tradition of satiric romance. Like Herman Melville, Nathaniel Hawthorne, and Poe, O'Connor creates a fiction of surfaces, which concommitantly reflect the aspects of the psyche's traumatic investigation of "reality". Using Wayne C. Booth's theories regarding the "implied author" to contest interpretations based primarily on Catholic doctrine, Orvell's work also initiates a (still largely unexplored) reader-response critique of the fiction's dynamics. (A perhaps unwitting, but substantial virtue, of Orvell's book is its considerable worth to the contemporary scholar interested in a hermeneutic or meta-critical approach to O'Connor studies.) Integrating his analysis with references that range from

Heideggerian "care" to W.C. Fields' comic strategies and 1960s' cinema, Orvell has an intimately eclectic familiarity with the cultural milieu in which O'Connor herself wrote.

BROWNING provides a fine introduction to O'Connor's fiction. Including a biographical summary, the book is sagacious regarding the Christian/secular debate. Arguing that O'Connor countered "the 'ontological void' posited by Ionesco and other modern writers" more from the perspective of theistic existentialism than that of orthodox Christianity, Browning also contends that O'Connor's satire was expressly directed against the "positivism" of American culture in the 1950s. While Browning's discussion covers the novels, the book's greatest value lies in its extended analyses of the short stories. More than most scholars, Browning recognizes that O'Connor's characters "elude easy classification", but more importantly, he offers lucid and original interpretations of their enigmatic, contradictory psyches to support his claims.

BLEIKASTEN follows Hawkes in the attempt to distinguish between O'Connor's public descriptions of her religious beliefs and the visionary directions explored in the fiction by what he calls "the writing self". The essay's focus concerns the two novels' protagonists and their struggle against a schizophrenic "mirror world of doubles, where the self is always experienced as other, and the other apprehended as a reflection of self". The strength of Bleikasten's argument lies in its ability to attend carefully to the fiction's psychological and oneiric dimensions while not losing sight of how thoroughly O'Connor's work is circumscribed by Christian thought; indeed, for him, the fiction particularly evidences "Christian truths gone mad" in their confrontation with the Absurd.

SHLOSS bravely confronts the Christian/secular debate by attempting to delineate the dimensions of O'Connor's "model reader". Noting O'Connor's persistent use of the third-person, Shloss argues that only rarely is this narrative technique used to guide the reader into the particular understanding of the numinous that the author frequently espoused in her personal life. O'Connor knew that her religious views did not coincide with those of her audience, but she resisted forcing her beliefs on readers explicitly. Shloss sees O'Connor's fiction as trying to reside "in the precarious territory where one neither offended nor obscured by excessive indirection". Different from the subjectively based modernist epiphany, epiphanic moments in O'Connor's fiction, Shloss maintains, are thrust upon her characters by an external presence. Aware that our historical moment provides "no communal values [which] can guide the assignment of anagogical meaning", Shloss believes that O'Connor's most successful fiction, such as "The Artificial Nigger", openly depicts Christian revelation, deliberately leaving "nothing . . . to inference". Shloss' careful readings will be problematic, however, for readers who prefer to interpret O'Connor from an ironic vantage point.

ASALS, for many, has written one of the strongest studies of O'Connor. Because he sees the fiction as manifesting the existential tensions created by an "ineluctable human dualism", Asals meticulously examines O'Connor's penchant for conjoining the seemingly incommensurate without, however, confining her vision to that of the demonic or divine. O'Connor's "aesthetics of incongruity" moves toward an inclusive bifurcation – images contain the "hylic" and "numinous" perspectives equally, narratives are shaped through the intersections of various antithetical *Doppelgänger* figures, and "comic perception" strains against "melodramatic plotting". Attentive to O'Connor's non-fiction and marginalia, Asals' erudite analysis probes further than most other scholars, especially in its consideration of O'Connor's complex response to existentialist thought. To Asals, O'Connor conducted a lifelong debate with herself, and her fiction exhibits the openness of that dialogue.

GENTRY's often brilliant reassessment of the "grotesque" in the fiction combines Mikhail Bakhtin's distinction between the "positive and negative grotesque" with recent discoveries in narrative theory. For Gentry, O'Connor's fiction (similar to Bakhtin's dialogic novel), maintains a struggle between "rebellious characters" and the narrators' "authoritarianism". This conflict engages a dialectic progression between oppositional elements: the grotesque and the ideal, the individual and communal, the consciously understood and the unconsciously desired. In his consideration of the major stories and the novels, Gentry presents highly original insights, while remaining close to the spirit of O'Connor's attempts to understand the processes of human "redemption".

MICHAEL TRUSSLER

Old English Literature *see* Beowulf, Poetry: Old English, Prose: Old English

Olson, Charles 1910–1970

American poet and essayist

Bernstein, Michael, *The Tale of the Tribe: Ezra Pound and the Modern Verse Epic*, Princeton, New Jersey: Princeton University Press, 1980

Butterick, George F., *A Guide to "The Maximus Poems" of Charles Olson*, Berkeley: University of California Press, 1978

Byrd, Don, *Charles Olson's "Maximus"*, Urbana: University of Illinois Press, 1980

Christensen, Paul, *Charles Olson: Call Him Ishmael*, Austin: University of Texas Press, 1979

Davenport, Guy, "Olson", in his *The Geography of the Imagination: Forty Essays*, San Francisco: Northpoint Press, 1981; London: Pan Books, 1984

Dorn, Edward, "What I See in *The Maximus Poems*" (1960 article), in *Views*, edited by Donald Allen, San Francisco: Four Seasons Foundation, 1980

von Hallberg, Robert, *Charles Olson: The Scholar's Art*, Cambridge, Massachusetts: Harvard University Press, 1978

Early critical reaction to Olson was usually either hostile or over-enthusiastic. Through the 1960s, he attracted flatterers and acolytes, but was also dismissed by academic critics as a mere follower of Ezra Pound, unoriginal and overblown. His poetic theories were opposed to "closed" verse forms and were therefore unappealing to critics who had been trained to deal with such forms. His own verse ran all over a large page, often abandoning the right-hand margin: this was equally unattractive to traditionalists. Since the late 1970s, however, a body of critical work has established Olson's seminal position in a distinct tradition of American poetry – that of the long, "epic" poem.

DORN's early essay on Olson's epic *The Maximus Poems*, (written when only the first poems of the sequence were available) remains a beautifully poised and honest response to the challenge of the work. Anti-academic (as its title warns), the essay focuses on the importance of "place" for Olson's project, alert to the way Olson's chosen place (Gloucester, New England) gives rise to a specific ethos. Yet Dorn is dismissive of mere evocation: the buildings, streets and images of place are unimportant, he argues, compared to Olson's refutation of egocentric lyricism, and his engagement with the common "oceanic" sense all men have "of their predicament". For Dorn, "*Maximus* returns to a pre-Christian ordering of the ego, or however, comes forward to a non-Christian ordering". He indicates "the best single poem to go to to test his own statements about verse is 'On first Looking out Through Juan de la Cosa's Eyes'". Dorn's essay is both tentative and authoritative – a crucial point of reference.

Diametrically opposed in method is BUTTERICK's gargantuan reference work, a compendium of scholarly notes and glosses, ten years in the making. Comprising thousands of annotations to *The Maximus Poems*, the *Guide* is an indispensable accompaniment to a close reading of Olson's epic. Butterick undertakes to explain as fully as possible in 800 pages the vast range of personal, public, local, and literary references with which *Maximus* abounds. Inevitably, there are references that remain unexplained, some probably inexplicable; but this is an essential exegetical tool.

CHRISTENSEN's book is a lucid general introduction to Olson, including a balanced consideration of his shorter poems, prose essays, and influential poetic theories. Christensen is perhaps too literal in his application of Olson's ideas of "projective verse", offering diagrammatic expositions of Olson's poetic method; but there are valuable complementary reproductions of Olson's hand-corrected typescripts. A final chapter assesses some of the poets Olson influenced – Robert Creeley, Paul Blackburn, Edward Dorn, and others.

BYRD contrasts Pound's career ("built on remembering") with Olson's, where the key-term "projective" is singularly apposite. Olson "knew the past Pound longed for was irretrievably and not unhappily lost". Byrd gives a close explicatory reading of *The Maximus Poems* and is sensitive to the democratic politics and volatile energies animating and charging them throughout.

A different emphasis is placed by VON HALLBURG on Olson's pedagogical intentions. He explicates Olson's poetic style and links it to political events subsequent to World War II and the Washington administration from which Olson resigned, and to the reclamation of forms of discourse more frequently excluded from poetry: "Olson's best poetry is offered as explanation and understanding, not as expression". For von Hallberg, Olson's poems deserve close attention because they do not conform to expectations of the poetic, and they open possibilities for forms of engaged political poetry, which are more frequently suppressed. The book gives accounts of Olson's involvement in politics, his place in the tradition of the American long poem, his world of ideas, his shorter poems as well as the *Maximus* sequence, and pushes forward into a comprehensive statement about the context of late twentieth-century poetry in which it was Olson's fate to reside, the function and value of his "anti-poetic strategies", and their beneficent influence on younger poets such as Amiri Baraka, Dorn, J.H. Prynne, and John Ashbery.

DAVENPORT's brief, busy, often startling essay on Olson is a succinct account of Olson's entire dynamic, and a close but speculative and highly suggestive reading of his most important short poem, "The Kingfishers" (which, Davenport says, "divides decisively modern from postmodern poetry"). For Davenport, Olson is "a prophet crying bad weather ahead, and [he] has the instruments to prove it".

BERNSTEIN devotes a third of his book to Olson, but his argument – that the modern verse epic represents an attempt to reclaim for poetry the popular provenance of the novel and to harmonize innumerable discourses, which conventional wisdom leaves to specialists – is closely applied, and Olson's work benefits enormously from being considered in relation to his older contemporaries Pound and William Carlos Williams. Bernstein appreciates the flaws in Olson's work – its slips into sentimental nostalgia, its occasionally bullying masculinity, its vaguely populist regionalism, the recourse to egocentrism in the last years of Olson's life – but he is equally sensitive to Olson's desire to show forth "an actual earth of value", and his book as a whole courageously presents the defence for a "quality of seriousness" that it is the business of poetry to maintain.

ALAN RIACH

Ondaatje, Michael 1943–

Canadian poet, novelist, and critic

Barbour, Douglas, *Michael Ondaatje*, New York: Twayne, 1993

Mundweiler, Leslie, *Michael Ondaatje: Word, Image, Imagination*, Vancouver: Talonbooks, 1984

Siemerling, Winfried, *Discoveries of the Other: Alterity in the Work of Leonard Cohen, Hubert Aquin, Michael Ondaatje, and Nicole Brossard*, Toronto: University of Toronto Press, 1994

Solecki, Sam (ed.), *Spider Blues: Essays on Michael Ondaatje*, Montreal: Véhicule Press, 1985

Waldman, Nell Kozak, *Michael Ondaatje and His Work*, Toronto: ECW Press, 1990

From his first books of poetry to his recent widely acclaimed novel, *The English Patient* (1992) Michael Ondaatje has received serious and very favorable critical reception. The early confidence of the Canadian critical establishment, which to some appeared rather indiscriminate praise, has been justified by his subsequent artistic achievement: Ondaatje's work has been warmly promoted and praised by academies and reviewers since the mid-1960s, and he is the subject of numerous articles, several book chapters, and a few critical volumes.

MUNDWEILER, in one of the earliest book-length studies, discusses Ondaatje's poetry and autobiographical prose in terms of its imaginative vitality. He pointedly eschews discussing biographical, cultural, and literary influences. Instead, Mundweiler's primary concern is to show how Ondaatje's work forces upon the reader "the necessity of imagination", and to examine the nature of the imaginative process of both the artist and the readers. Although he does give useful specific analyses of some of the early poems, too often these are overshadowed by lengthy discussions of "the history of imagination from Bruno to Schiller". In a book of only 146 pages, repeated references to Collingwood, Heidegger, Merleau-Ponty, Sartre, and Schiller do not so much enlighten our view of Ondaatje's work as to keep us from closely examining more of it.

SOLECKI's 269-page collection offers a substantial sampling of Ondaatje criticism through 1985. The 29 selections, most by Canadian academics, range from three-page contemporary reviews to 25-page essays on Ondaatje's postmodern poetics, his relationship to other contemporary writers, his use of myth, and his exploration of extremist art. They are framed by interviews which the editor had with the writer in 1975 and 1984. The essays, one-third of which was commissioned for this volume, are generally insightful and largely favorable, both about Ondaatje's work and his comparative ranking with other writers, such as Margaret Atwood. Solecki divides the essays under two major headings, "The Poetry" and "The Longer Works", the latter comprising two-thirds of the total. Some of the longer essays provide detailed analyses, which will be useful for later critics. Overall, both sections reflect the early – and consistent – high praise and underscore a comment in the Introduction lamenting "the inevitably missing engagement between Ondaatje's work and the strong critic who, in his own field, is Ondaatje's equal in stature".

WALDMAN's brief book, 52 pages inclusive of notes and bibliography, is the clearest, most balanced essay on Ondaatje's life, work, and critical reception through 1990. After beginning with a brief biographical sketch drawn largely from Ondaatje's autobiographical *Running in the Family*, Waldman highlights the artistic milieu of Ondaatje's adoptive Canada in the early stages of his career in the 1970s. She discusses the "collective reflex action of praise" the Canadian critical establishment heaped rather indiscriminately on each new Ondaatje work. Her own assessment of Ondaatje's poetry and prose draws on the earlier studies, but is more even-handed and measured. She has no theoretical axe to grind. Consequently, she is able to justify seeing *The Collected Works of Billy the Kid* (1940) as both "startling and powerful" and "dated in its experimental quality and hyperbolic in its intent". Her refusal to gloss over the weaknesses in the works and her sharp eye for detail and nuance make her generally favorable assessment of Ondaatje's achievement, especially of the later works, more convincing than much earlier criticism.

BARBOUR's study is the first, and thus far the only, book-length study to examine Ondaatje's longer works in detail and to attempt to place the writer in the modernist/postmodernist tradition. Barbour provides intelligent, sympathetic readings of all of Ondaatje's major works. His close, careful analyses illuminate the imaginative achievement of the early and the later poetry, the mixed-genre works, the autobiographical works, as well as Ondaatje's movement from lyric poetry to lyrical novels. Barbour convincingly demonstrates Ondaatje's skilled balancing of "authority" and "artifice". In a world in which "flux and ambiguity rules over all", Barbour suggests that Ondaatje's "indeterminate" texts, in which "nothing, not even the documentation on which they are based, escapes the rough if loving hands of change and force", best reflect our modern reality. He effectively shows how Ondaatje "creates characters who behave with such velocity of feeling that they seem transparently familiar, yet in fact remain opaque to any rational understanding". The later prose, as well as the early poetry, is "deceptively anecdotal, casual in tone, and seemingly artless in narration". Barbour draws on earlier critics of Ondaatje's work and modern critical theory in order to explicate individual works and place the entire *oeuvre* in the context of postmodernism. Barbour terms Ondaatje's indeterminate texts, which blur the distinctions between genre, "deeply dialogic": a memoir such as *Running in the Family*, for example, "simultaneously allows and denies conventional readings". The critical jargon is a little turgid in places. The only other weakness in this informative and well-informed book is Barbour's insistence on discussing only the positive aspects of the works, occasionally ignoring or dismissing views that are not completely laudatory. But Barbour's study must be considered the most detailed, most interesting, and most important critical work on Ondaatje to date.

SIEMERLING's book explores "the relationship between self and other as textual figures of the unknown". About one-third of the book is devoted to Ondaatje's three long prose works before *The English Patient*, in a chapter entitled "'Scared by the Mirror': Temptations of Identity and Limits of Control in the Work of Michael Ondaatje". Some of the issues and terminology will be familiar to readers of Barbour's book. The richly ambiguous qualities of Ondaatje's prose allows him to use common literary conventions and undermine them at the same time. Ondaatje is able both to suggest and to avoid, meaning, autobiographical and historical accuracy, and definitive characterization. Of *Coming Through Slaughter* Siemerling suggests that "writing appears as a tracing web that closes in on Bollen, but is ultimately both, created and eluded by his movement". Similarly, she writes:

> Ondaatje reduces the contrast between inside and outside, and between self and other in a way . . . that is typical of metaphor – before shattering the resulting sameness. At the moment of identity, self and other meet in a simultaneous mutual deviation from their respective "proper" course, a strange heterology in which writing produces "the shape of an unknown thing".

Siemerling concludes that "Ondaatje thus has and has not written" about the central characters in his fiction and himself in his autobiographical work. The "ambiguous equations between fictive characters and narrators" is echoed by those between narrators and author. As Barbour also proposes, Siemerling suggests that Ondaatje's linguistic ambiguity reveals an artistic achievement in which meaning has been replaced by multiple perspectives and historical fact is only one manifestation of an often elusive truth.

DANNY L. ROBINSON

O'Neill, Eugene 1888–1953

American dramatist

Barlow, Judith, *Final Acts: The Creation of Three Late O'Neill Plays*, Athens: University of Georgia Press, 1985

Bogard, Travis, *Contour in Time: The Plays of Eugene O'Neill*, New York: Oxford University Press, 1972, revised 1988

Cargill, Oscar, N. Bryllion Fagin, and William J. Fisher (eds.), *Eugene O'Neill and His Plays: Four Decades of Criticism*, New York: New York University Press, 1961; London: Peter Owen, 1962

Chothia, Jean, *Forging a Language: A Study of the Plays of Eugene O'Neill*, Cambridge and New York: Cambridge University Press, 1979

Engel, Edwin A., *The Haunted Heroes of O'Neill*, Cambridge, Massachusetts: Harvard University Press, 1953

Falk, Doris, *Eugene O'Neill and the Tragic Tension: An Interpretive Study of the Plays*, New Brunswick, New Jersey: Rutgers University Press, 1958

Floyd, Virginia, *The Plays of Eugene O'Neill: A New Assessment*, New York: Frederick Ungar, 1984

Gelb, Barbara, and Arthur Gelb, *O'Neill*, New York: Harper & Row, 1962, revised 1974; London: Jonathan Cape, 1962

Liu, Haiping, and Lowell Swortzell, *Eugene O'Neill in China: An International Centenary Celebration*, New York: Greenwood Press, 1992

Miller, Jordan Y., *Eugene O'Neill and the American Critic: A Summary and Bibliographic Checklist*, Hamden, Connecticut: Archon Books, 1962, revised 1973

Raleigh, John Henry, *The Plays of Eugene O'Neill*, Carbondale: Southern Illinois University Press, 1965

Ranald, Margaret Loftus, *The Eugene O'Neill Companion*, Westport, Connecticut: Greenwood Press, 1984

Robinson, James A., *Eugene O'Neill and Oriental Thought: A Divided Vision*, Carbondale: Southern Illinois University Press, 1982

Sheaffer, Louis, *O'Neill, Son and Playwright*, Boston: Little Brown, 1968

Sheaffer, Louis, *O'Neill, Son and Artist*, Boston: Little Brown, 1973

Tornqvist, Egil, *A Drama of Souls: Studies in O'Neill's Super-Naturalistic Technique*, New Haven, Connecticut, and London: Yale University Press, 1969

Wainscott, Ronald H., *Staging O'Neill: The Experimental Years, 1920–1934*, New Haven, Connecticut, and London: Yale University Press, 1988

As "father" of the American drama, O'Neill is singular in the autobiographical nature of his plays, a tradition observed in varying degrees by later American dramatists. Thus there is an abundance of biographical material in O'Neillian criticism, beginning with a thin, 108-page monograph by Barrett Clark in 1926, when O'Neill was only 38. To analyze or judge O'Neill's plays is to base that discussion in his personal life and that of his family and of the Irish emigration to America. His own unfinished cycle of autobiographical plays is witness to this phenomenon, as is his generally regarded major play, *Long Day's Journey into Night*. The autobiographical theme, in turn, has fostered a series of bibliographical works which, in the most recent scholarship leading to his centenary in 1988, have drawn attention to many unfinished and/or previously unknown plays. In addition, scholars have approached O'Neill's drama in terms of source, influence, writing habits, psychoanalysis, archetype, mysticism, genre, language, and comparison with European writers. With so stylistically and thematically varied a dramatist, any one approach usually involves a rich mixture, for in the end O'Neill's work, like his life, denies scholars easy compartmentalization.

The development of scholarship and criticism of O'Neill's plays over the years has not changed direction radically so much as it has widened and deepened. As the archival depository for O'Neill's papers, Yale University has played a major role in making the papers available to scholars after the death of O'Neill's wife, Carlotta Monterey, who exercised tight restrictions during her lifetime. (Yale has, as well, been entangled in legal controversy with surviving members of O'Neill's family on financial matters of the O'Neill estate.) The following discussion considers biographical and bibliographical scholarship, before looking at a selection of critical approaches since the 1950s.

Among the few granted access to her husband's papers by Monterey, and with help provided by two of O'Neill's previous wives, Kathleen Pitt-Smith and Agnes Boulton Kaufmann, Barbara and Arthur GELB (the latter a writer for the *New York Times*) have tracked O'Neill's life "with the ingenuity and perseverance of police reporters", interviewing more than 400 people "who knew one aspect or another of O'Neill's elusive life". Prolific quotations from interviewees and letter-writers, together with the many family portraits and photographs, create an intimate and vivid picture of the world of O'Neill. Published ten years after his death, when so many of those who knew O'Neill were still alive, this 990-page work comes very much to life, its 25-page index providing scholars with easy access to those names that populated O'Neill's world. The Gelbs' reportorial style has an immediacy and freshness undiluted by time.

The first (1968) of SHEAFFER's two biographical volumes ends in 1920 with the first Broadway production of *Beyond the Horizon*. The events of his life during this period are woven in with the characters in his plays and with his increasing correspondence with authors and critics. Basing his work almost entirely on primary sources and hitherto untapped material – such as two rounds of letters to 180 surviving members of O'Neill's Princeton class and his (Sheaffer's) reading of every issue of two newspapers printed in New London, Connecticut, from the mid-1880s to late 1919 – Sheaffer uncovers errors of earlier chroniclers, and questions the conclusions drawn from those mistakes. He also covers hitherto undealt-with aspects of O'Neill's life, such as his knowledge of, and interest in, farm life in plays such as *Beyond the Horizon* and *Desire under the Elms*. In the second volume, published five years after the first, SHEAFFER (1973) begins the biography of son as artist with the year in which two conspicuous events occurred: the death of O'Neill's father and O'Neill's Broadway premiere. Interviews with O'Neill's last two wives and with a huge number of those who knew O'Neill enrich the volume.

A form of biography different from that of the Gelbs and Sheaffer, BOGARD details "the course of his [O'Neill's] life in art". Biography and criticism are successfully blended into a genre of its own. The book's 491 pages deal chronologically with all of O'Neill's plays (62 completed drafts and remnants of many others). Bogard views the plays as O'Neill's attempts at a quest for identity, the stage as O'Neill's mirror, and the sum of the play as autobiography. The book is, as well, a history of the American theatre and the story of O'Neill's influence in the shaping of that theatre. A valuable appendix of cast lists of first productions and important revivals, along with an index, concludes this major work, in which Bogard illuminates the Gelbs's and Sheaffer's biographies, to complete, as it were, a trilogy of requisite reading for the student of O'Neill.

To the works of the Gelbs, Sheaffer, and Bogard should be added that of MILLER, who provides the scholar with the most varied bibliographical tools in O'Neilliana. These tools consist of a completely recast chronology of O'Neill's life; a chronology of composition, copyright, and publication (including a descriptive bibliography); a catalogue of major productions; and bibliographies of primary (including non-dramatic) writings, secondary books, articles, reviews, and graduate research. A well-designed format makes all aspects of bibliographical information invitingly accessible.

Floyd, Barlow, Ranald, and Wainscott combine textual/historical scholarship and literary-critical discussion in their approaches.

FLOYD's intent in her "new assessment" is to bring to contemporary students and general audiences an O'Neill who heretofore "had seemed to be the exclusive domain of a coterie of scholars". She reinterprets O'Neill's 50 completed plays, drawing on her own intensive editing and annotating of O'Neill's notebooks written during his last creative years (1939–45) and published in the volume *O'Neill at Work* (1981). The plays are divided into four chronological periods and are numbered 1–50, each section concluding with a list of notebook sources containing ideas that parallel those of the plays of that period. Beginning with *A Wife for a Life* and concluding with *A Moon for the Misbegotten*, Floyd's use of previously untranscribed materials expands and enriches previous studies. Her 1988 centenary publication entitled *O'Neill's Unfinished Plays* completes, as it were, her own trilogy of books about O'Neill.

BARLOW traces each of O'Neill's three major plays – *The Iceman Cometh*, *Long Day's Journey into Night*, and *A Moon for the Misbegotten* – from "early notes to finished text", using his work diary, letters, manuscripts, typescripts, and Carlotta Monterey's diary. Helpful to the student are the insights she provides, such as O'Neill's having worked on "outlines" – a Baker Workshop term for scenario – for *Iceman* and *Journey* within the same four-week period. The connections among the three plays grow in Barlow's treatment of the changing nature of O'Neill's characters as he revised the plays, for example, in Jamie and Jim in *Journey* and *Moon* respectively. Of a piece, the three plays indeed form a trilogy, their characters and themes focused and illuminated in Barlow's combined approach of scholarship and interpretation.

RANALD compiles a traditional "companion" volume, in which plays are arranged alphabetically along with names of persons involved in O'Neill's life and writing, and the names of characters in the plays. A synopsis of each play is followed by a "comment" and production data – date, place, text used, etc. Appendices include a chronology of completed plays by date of completion; film, musical, operatic and balletic adaptations of O'Neill's plays and their casts; and assessments of his experiments in realism, expressionism, myth and mask.

WAINSCOTT brings to life 14 early years of the staging of O'Neill's plays (1920–34), a time during which 23 O'Neill plays were produced in a "virtually unbroken line of professional productions", followed by a 12-year drought. One of the many centenary books on O'Neill, the volume is an important addition to the biographical, critical, and historical approaches, and deserves sequels dealing with the productions that resumed in the 1940s. Wainscott's is an absorbing narrative of production details, including O'Neill's active participation in those productions, as evidenced in, for example, his views on the use of masks. Successful direction by George Cram Cook, Arthur Hopkins, Robert Jones, James Light, Rouben Mamoulian, and Philip Moeller looms importantly during this period, preparing the way for the next generation of theatrical directors and designers of O'Neill's plays.

Published in the year of O'Neill's death, ENGEL's archetypal study considers the haunted O'Neillian hero in the context of a father-son conflict modelled after the God-man struggle. At first part of Freud's primal horde, he is provoked to rebellion against his father, who blocks his sexual demands and desire for power. The struggle is traced through its four stages: the Darwinian brute, whom O'Neill abandons after *The Hairy Ape*; the apocalyptic stage, which he forsakes after *Lazarus Laughed*; Nina as Everywoman in *Strange Interlude* and Mannon as Everyman in *Mourning Becomes Electra*; finally, in *The Iceman Cometh*, the hero moves from the House of Laughter to the House of Death, where his fear of death is purged.

FALK argues Jungian tensions between conscious and unconscious states in their progress to a "gradual realization of the inner, complete personality through constant change, struggle, and process". The tension in O'Neill's plays culminates in *Long Day's Journey into Night*, a tragedy in which the four heroes, portrayed as part god-like in their responsibilities and part victims of family fate, all discover that they succumbed to their deeply rooted character flaws. The Aristotelian pattern of Greek tragedy as the genre of ultimate human reality is the basis for her approach to O'Neill's plays.

CARGILL, FAGIN, and FISHER have collected an unequalled array of critics, scholars, literary historians, actors, and even O'Neill himself as writer of letters and articles. O'Neill's stature as a playwright is dealt with by noted critics: there is Francis Fergusson's view of O'Neill as melodramatist, George Nathan's pronouncement of O'Neill as "our premiere dramatist", Lionel Trilling's account of O'Neill's genius, Bernard De Voto's minority report, John Gassner's homage, and Eric Bentley's instructions on how to like O'Neill. In full flower, the controversies about language and repetitious style that have dogged O'Neill, even among his admirers, are aired. Even T.S. Eliot and Sean O'Casey grace the collection. One section is devoted to letters and articles by O'Neill, another to international critics, and one to O'Neill's language. The appendices include an alphabetical list of plays, a chronology of play productions, the requisite bibliographies of primary (including non-dramatic works) and secondary sources, and an index. As a representative of its genre (collected criticism) the volume belongs in O'Neilliana with the monumental biographies by the Gelbs and Sheaffer and the bibliography by Miller (see above).

RALEIGH, to whose work succeeding scholars make frequent reference, places O'Neill's plays in traditional contexts of cosmology, geography, and history, expanding these in a section entitled "Mankind", and concluding with two chapters devoted to form (structure and style) and to O'Neill's uniqueness as an American writer. Thematic and stylistic qualities emerge in such motifs as O'Neill's use of day/night and land/sea. He sees O'Neill as the least articulate among American writers such as Edgar Allan Poe, Nathaniel Hawthorne, and Herman Melville, yet the most inexhaustible. Extended end notes and index are included.

TORNQVIST considers every dramatic device – characterization, stage business, scenery, lighting, sound effects, dialogue, among others – in his interpretation of O'Neill as a dramatist who disguises irrational inner phenomena by a layer of realism and who breaks with illusionism at the same time. Using formal rather than thematic criteria as his approach, Tornqvist draws on John Northam's study of Ibsen's plays, Una Ellis-Fermor's investigation of dramatists' attempts to transcend the limitations of the dramatic form, and the studies of Shakespearean imagery by Robert Heilman and Wolfgang Clemen. O'Neill's special use of laughter, music and songs, and silence (even such naturalistic detail as smoking and drinking), patterned language, parallel characters and situations – these are only some of the experimental means by which O'Neill creates a *Gesamtkunstwerk*, in which "correspondences among different play elements . . . express those spiritual values that concern him". Tornqvist illustrates his theories liberally with passages from the plays. Appendices include his own bibliography of the plays – with regard to dates of composition – and a bibliography of secondary sources.

CHOTHIA approaches O'Neill's plays from that aspect of his plays – language – around which controversy about O'Neill's stature as a playwright has swirled. Explaining and illustrating, rather than engaging in controversy, she combines critics' comments with her own analysis of O'Neill's development – from the American vernacular in the early years, through the failure of language in the middle years, to its "significant form" in *Long Day's Journey into Night*. She concludes her study by placing O'Neill in a historical context from W.B. Yeats to Samuel Beckett and Harold Pinter. Appendices include a literary biography of O'Neill, a note on the Irish dialect in the last plays, and one on the cycle of his American history plays.

ROBINSON's study of Eastern-versus-Western values in O'Neill's plays builds on Frederic Carpenter's description of O'Neill's orientalism as the most important aspect of his work, but at the same time the most difficult to define. Readings in Ralph Waldo Emerson, Buddhism, and Taoism began O'Neill's journey, which took him through "northwest passages", such as Schopenhauer, and then back to the East in his plays after *Anna Christie*. Robinson concludes that in the lifelong struggle that was O'Neill's own life, the divided self, the *yin* prevails over the *yang* in his last play, *A Moon for the Misbegotten* – his last journey home.

LIU and SWORTZELL have collected papers presented at the international conference entitled "Eugene O'Neill: World Playwright" held at the University of Nanjing, China, in 1988 in honour of O'Neill's centenary year. The essays are presented under five broad groupings: "O'Neill's Philosophical and Religious Motifs", "O'Neill in Comparison", "O'Neill as Playwright", "O'Neill on Stage", and "O'Neill Abroad". With Virginia Floyd as keynote speaker, paper presenter, and book dedicatee, her aim in an earlier work to open O'Neill to others than the early coterie of scholars is realized here in the wide-range of participants – American, Asian, and European. The contributors and their topics (e.g., comparisons with August Strindberg and Leo Tolstoy, oriental mysticism and Nietzschean influence) reflect celebration and internationalism rather than break new ground. The volume is an interesting companion to the earlier Cargill-Fagin-Fisher collection.

SUSAN RUSINKO

Orwell, George 1903–1950

English novelist and essayist

Crick, Bernard, *George Orwell: A Life*, London: Secker & Warburg, 1980, revised 1981; Boston: Little Brown, 1980

Hollis, Christopher, *A Study of George Orwell: The Man and His Works*, London: Hollis & Carter, 1956

Ingle, Stephen, *George Orwell: A Political Life*, Manchester: Manchester University Press, 1993

Lee, Robert, *Orwell's Fiction*, Notre Dame, Indiana: University of Notre Dame Press, 1969

Rodden, John, *The Politics of Literary Reputation: The Making and Claiming of "St George" Orwell*, New York and Oxford: Oxford University Press, 1989

Shelden, Michael, *Orwell: The Authorised Biography*, London: Heinemann, 1991; New York: Harper Collins, 1991

Stansky, Peter, and William Abrahams, *The Unknown Orwell*, London: Constable, 1972; New York: Knopf, 1972

Stansky, Peter, and William Abrahams, *Orwell: The Transformation*, London: Constable, 1979; New York: Knopf, 1979

Williams, Raymond, *Orwell*, London: Fontana, 1971

Woodcock, George, *The Crystal Spirit: A Study of George Orwell*, London: Jonathan Cape, 1966; Boston: Little Brown, 1966

George Orwell is an author whom most people want to be on their side. Jane Austen is another such author, peculiarly English, peculiarly embedded in the English class system, peculiarly difficult to tie down in literary criticism or biographical studies. But Austen wrote only novels. Orwell, like Austen tragically cut down in the middle of a creative career, was an interesting journalist, whose major works can be seen as vehicles of political propaganda rather than novels. Orwell did not want his biography to be written, although his fiction is strongly autobiographical. His work has been seized upon by politicians of all complexions and intellectuals of various persuasions, most of whom he would have despised. The mass of contradictions surrounding Orwell – an international author, yet so strongly English, the old Etonian, yet so strongly interested in the working class – are not really dealt with in a totally satisfactory fashion by any of the following biographical or critical works.

HOLLIS's genial biographical study owes little to literary criticism, although there are conscientious plot summaries of Orwell's major works. As a fellow scholar of Orwell at Eton, Hollis has some valuable insights into this esoteric coterie, denied to many biographers and critics. As a Catholic and Conservative Member of Parliament, albeit a liberal in his Catholicism and Conservatism, Hollis was clearly opposed to Orwell's gritty brand of socialism and agnosticism. This combination of sympathy and antipathy makes the commentary on Orwell's life and works curiously bland, although admirably free from the partial and partisan approaches of later biographers and critics, who tend unjustly to dismiss Hollis as a right-wing critic trying to label Orwell as a fellow conservative.

WOODCOCK's title is taken from a poem by Orwell. His book is a generous tribute to a man whom the author came to know well in the last years of his life. The appreciation of Orwell in the 1940s sums up the man much better than later biographers whose careful recordings of minutiae fail to capture Orwell's essential spirit. There then follows a careful analysis of the novels, perhaps marred by too much plot summary, and hostility to *Keep the Aspidistra Flying* and *A Clergyman's Daughter* quite out of keeping with the praise for *Burmese Days* and *Coming Up for Air*. Orwell's writing for periodicals is discussed in the third chapter, entitled not unfairly "The Spirit of Conservatism". This chapter does not spare Orwell's quirkiness, his tendency to exaggerate, or his contradictory attitudes, summed up in the biographical chapter as those of a man who could not decide whether he was Don Quixote or Sancho Panza. On the other hand Woodcock is at pains to stress Orwell's honesty, decency, and love of ordinary life. The final chapter on Orwell's style emphasises his command of the English language, a vehicle he used to condemn the newspeak which still threatens us more than a decade after 1984.

LEE's rather badly written book attempts to look at Orwell as a novelist, paying no attention to biography and little attention to Orwell as a journalist or political commentator. Political commentary is however introduced when the first three novels are dismissed as naively conservative. *Homage to Catalonia* is seen as a watershed, turning Orwell into a radical, although there is seen to be hostility to communism in this book, *Animal Farm*, and *1984*. Lee's elaborately literary constructions, such as the discussions of symbiology, and the misconstructions of English social life, such as the viewing of Miss Creevey's school as a public school, are plainly misleading. Nevertheless the author deserves gratitude for his genuine attempt to discuss Orwell as a novelist rather than as a political commentator.

WILLIAMS's short book is interesting not only for what it says about Orwell, but for what it says about Williams who, like Orwell, straddled the barrier between literary, cultural, and political criticism. The poor Welsh boy who went to Cambridge naturally had a different perspective from the old Etonian who became a tramp, and they also wrote at different times. Williams's study in 1971 reflected an increasing disillusion with Orwell on the part of left-wing thinkers, who were particularly incensed with the pessimism of *Animal Farm* and *1984*. After the Russian invasion of Hungary, the denouncement of Stalin by Kruschev, and the dismemberment of the British Empire, Orwell was seen as out of date and defeatist, although there was still admiration for his early rebellious writings and his journalism. As left-wing thinkers sought a new philosophy, Orwell did not seem to offer them much help, although this premature dismissal now seems out of date itself, as we are faced by new forms of totalitarianism.

STANSKY and ABRAHAMS began their interest in Orwell as a writer involved in the Spanish Civil War. Their first volume takes the story of Eric Blair to the point where his first work under the name of Orwell was published, and the second volume continues the story until the writing of *Homage to Catalonia*. True to its title, *The Unknown Orwell* contains many new insights into the author's early life. He is shown as slightly more successful than in previous biographies, the long chapter on Eton being particularly revealing in this respect. Orwell's preparatory school, St Cyprians, is examined objectively, but there is a bad mistake about the schools at which Orwell taught: these were in no way comparable to St Cyprians. On the whole the authors are remarkably adept in tracing the intricacies of the English class system, revealing Orwell's aristocratic forebears and the pattern of friendships he enjoyed at Eton. Although helped by Orwell's sister, Stansky and Abrahams did not enjoy the confidence of Sonia Orwell, and their work is handicapped because they could not refer in detail to Orwell's writings.

CRICK's biography is full of interesting information, and provides some useful insights into Orwell as a thinker. He wrote it with the support of Orwell's second wife, although she came to disapprove of it. Unlike previous biographers, Crick had unlimited access to Orwell's papers and was able to quote extensively from his works. This book is likely to remain the standard biography, although it is full of misprints and does not present Orwell as a particularly attractive figure. Candid details of Orwell's sexual behaviour, though suitable for the candid present day, seem a little offensive. In addition Crick might seem too ready to fit Orwell's quirky mixture of radicalism and conservatism into the mould of mainstream right-wing socialism, although he himself insisted on his neutrality, modestly describing his work as an annotated bibliography.

RODDEN's long study provides some extremely valuable criticism of other writers on Orwell, notably Crick and Williams. It attempts to explain how Orwell has been seized upon by both left-wing and right-wing thinkers as prophet, patron saint, and occasionally public enemy. Although the structure of the book is confusing, and the style somewhat verbose, it succeeds in its aims. It does not attempt to explain, however, why Orwell has been acclaimed and derided in so many different camps. Rodden tends to concentrate on *Animal Farm* and *1984*, and he tends to write for an American audience. There is, for instance, a fascinating study of Orwell in the curriculum, largely based on American education, although quite correct in what it says about English education. *Animal Farm* and *1984* are of course international books, but they are set in the English farm and English city; it is

Orwell's peculiar brand of patriotism that this admirable book just misses.

SHELDEN's biography arose from dissatisfaction with Crick's work by some of Orwell's family and friends. Inevitably the two biographers cover much the same ground in much the same way, although Shelden is more personal and less political. He was able to draw upon letters to and from Orwell's first wife, who takes a more prominent role in this book, where she appears as a remarkably sympathetic figure. There are also new facts gleaned from correspondence between Orwell and his literary agent, Louis Moore, another unsung hero. Orwell's preparatory school, which exercised such a bizarre fascination on Orwell and his biographers, receives extended treatment. Shelden is kinder than most to the proprietors of this school. With this exception, it cannot really be said that this book adds any new insights into Orwell's life or the way Orwell used his life in his fiction. Nor is this biography much help in trying to assess Orwell's contributions to journalism, literary criticism, or political thought.

INGLE's work is the latest on Orwell, but has a curiously old-fashioned air. There is a biographical framework, but no new biographical information, and some curious mistakes (e.g., the Eton wall game is not a kind of mass rugby). What distinguishes this book is its attempt to make Orwell an orthodox socialist thinker, it being part of a series devoted to major figures in the Labour movement. The attempt, though laborious, and phrased in a stilted and repetitive English, of which Orwell would have been critical, is not, though, entirely unsuccessful.

T.J. Winnifrith

Osborne, John 1929–1995

English dramatist and screenwriter

Brown, John Russell, "John Osborne: Theatrical Belief", in his *Theatre Language: A Study of Arden, Osborne, Pinter and Wesker*, London: Allan Lane, 1972; New York: Taplinger, 1972

Carter, Alan, *John Osborne*, Edinburgh: Oliver & Boyd, 1969, revised 1973; New York: Barnes & Noble, 1973

Egan, Robert G., "*Anger* and the Actor: Another Look Back", in *Modern Drama*, 32, 1989

Hayman, Ronald, *John Osborne*, London: Heinemann, 1968, revised 1970; New York: Frederick Ungar, 1972

Hinchliffe, Arnold P., *John Osborne*, Boston: Twayne, 1984

Taylor, John Russell, *John Osborne: "Look Back in Anger": A Casebook*, London: Macmillan, 1968

Trussler, Simon, *The Plays of John Osborne: An Assessment*, London: Victor Gollancz, 1969

Osborne criticism has been limited by three stumbling-blocks: the "Angry Young Man" mythology; the biographical fallacy, or tendency to confuse the dramatist with his characters; and a reluctance to bestow on him the kind of detailed analysis that has been provided for contemporaries such as Harold Pinter and Tom Stoppard. There are also relatively few books on Osborne, and most of these were written in the 1960s and early 1970s. However, while it is hard to trace a distinct development in the available commentary on his plays, it is possible to isolate certain studies, Brown's and Egan's for example, which have something innovative, as well as just useful, to say. Most commentators point to the histrionic nature of such characters as Jimmy Porter, Archie Rice, or Pamela in *Time Present*, but it is only those that go beyond a simple "protagonist = actor" formula who help to establish this writer as a major force in late twentieth-century drama.

BROWN's discussion of Osborne's theatre language examines gesture and silence as well as the spoken word. For this critic, the dramatist's view of character is "essentially theatrical". He shows how Jimmy Porter (*Look Back in Anger*), Archie Rice (*The Entertainer*), Martin Luther (*Luther*), and Bill Maitland (*Inadmissible Evidence*) are all performers who fear, and yet do their best to reach, that moment when the show stops and they must suffer a defeat out of which "some personal affirmation" may emerge. When this happens the audience, too, is led "to understand 'ordinary despair', and the level of living beneath, or beyond, that of 'rhetoric'". This perceptive combination of metadramatic and redemptive theory remains one of the most rewarding appraisals of the major plays.

CARTER divides Osborne's dramatic output through *West of Suez* into plays of the public and the private voice. In the first category he places such major works as *Look Back in Anger*, *Luther*, and *Inadmissible Evidence*, in which the dramatist succeeds in "catching and interpreting the moods of a given time". The second consists of satirical plays such as *The World of Paul Slickey* and *The Blood of the Bambergs*, whose effect is undermined by authorial subjectivity. The critic is at his best responding to the loneliness of the protagonists and the impassioned rhetoric of their monologues; but, though he rests his case on "how well these plays work in the theatre", he does not in the end progress much further than a rather repetitive discussion of character, theme, and language.

EGAN approaches *Look Back in Anger* as a play about performance. Unlike Brown, he argues that such is the "proximity of medium to message" that there is no reality for the protagonist outside his apartment/stage. Jimmy Porter is "incapable of action in any sphere other than the histrionic", and Alison's return after a miscarriage signals entrapment in her husband's "fictive world". This postmodernist reading should lead to a fruitful reappraisal of both *Look Back in Anger* and the later plays.

HAYMAN believes that Osborne's plays are more or less failed attempts at integrating the conventions of realism with varieties of stylization, such as monologue, music-hall routine, or Brechtian distancing. In *Time Present*, *Hotel in Amsterdam*, and *West of Suez*, Osborne's art "seems to be aspiring towards the conditions of an interview" as Pamela, Laurie and Wyatt Gillman answer the inexhaustible question: "what does Osborne dislike?" These negative points are strongly, at times sarcastically, made, and suggest reasons for the dramatist's failure to produce any significant plays after the early 1970s; however, one wonders if a popular series on world dramatists is the right context for so unsympathetic a critique. As regards its presentation, the book is valuable for its production photographs, but there is too much lengthy and undigested quotation from the texts.

HINCHLIFFE discusses the plays through *Watch It Come Down* in terms of language, the theatrical presence of the protagonists, and critical response. This approach leads to some valuable commentary on, for example, the audience discomfort created by Archie Rice's unfunny routines, the interdependency of character and form in *Inadmissible Evidence*, and the relationship between language and betrayal in *West of Suez* and *Hotel in Amsterdam*. The author also pays attention, albeit unsystematically, to Osborne's affinities with Pinter, Tennessee Williams, Anton Chekhov, and George Bernard Shaw. This book suffers from the fragmentation of other monographs in Twayne's "English Authors" series, but Hinchliffe's dialogue with other critics is a stimulating one.

TAYLOR's *Casebook* on Osborne's best-known play contains a comprehensive collection of reviews, five occasional pieces by the dramatist – including the notorious "Letter to My Fellow Countrymen" of 1961 – some substantial critical studies by Katharine J. Worth, George E. Wellwarth, Mary McCarthy, and others, and shorter comments on the play. While the book provides a useful background to the later plays as well as *Look Back in Anger*, the commentary drifts too often towards sociology and away from dramatic analysis. Exceptions are Wellwarth's debunking of the angry young man mythology and McCarthy's valuable note on *mise-en-scène*. There are a number of indexed allusions to August Strindberg, Shaw, and Williams – including an *en passant* comparison of Jimmy Porter with Williams's Stanley Kowalski (*A Streetcar Named Desire*) – which warrant further exploration.

TRUSSLER has written the most balanced and objective book on Osborne's plays. While recognizing their emotional content and instinctive craftsmanship, he avoids the biographical and mythological pitfalls. His study is distinguished by its expert analysis of dialogue, and a number of insights: that, for example, *Look Back in Anger* is "a play about a particular kind of sexual relationship"; that Bill Maitland's tragedy consists of "a complete self-awareness"; or that in *Hotel in Amsterdam* the dramatist succeeds for the first time in creating a balanced group of characters with individual voices. There is also a chapter on Osborne's journalism and a summary of his achievement. Writing in 1969, Trussler saw his subject as "a potentially great dramatist", a view which time has, it is sad to say, not established.

JOHN LINGARD

Owen, Wilfred 1893–1918

English poet

Bäckman, Sven, *Tradition Transformed: Studies in the Poetry of Wilfred Owen*, Lund, Sweden: C.W.K. Gleerup, 1979

Hibberd, Dominic, *Wilfred Owen*, London: Longman, 1975

Hibberd, Dominic, *Owen the Poet*, London: Macmillan, 1986; Athens: University of Georgia Press, 1986

Hibberd, Dominic, *Wilfred Owen: The Last Year 1917–1918*, London: Constable, 1992

Kerr, Douglas, *Wilfred Owen's Voices: Language and Community*, Oxford: Clarendon Press, 1993; New York: Oxford University Press, 1993

Lane, Arthur E., *An Adequate Response: The War Poetry of Wilfred Owen and Siegfried Sassoon*, Detroit: Wayne State University Press, 1972

Owen, Harold, *Journey from Obscurity: Wilfred Owen 1893–1918*, 3 vols., London and New York: Oxford University Press, 1963–65

Welland, D.S.R., *Wilfred Owen: A Critical Study*, London: Chatto & Windus, 1960, revised 1978

White, Gertrude M., *Wilfred Owen*, New York: Twayne, 1969

There have been two major poles in Owen criticism – the one focusing on his technical innovations, the other on the social aspect of his poetry. Yet, there is no clear dichotomy: most criticism deals with both issues but with differing degrees of emphasis. One recurring question is how Owen's importance is to be derived: from his technical innovation of developing "pararhyme", or from the power of his social conscience? Most critics position Owen as the greatest World-War-I poet, but his significance to the history of modernism is a matter for debate. What all Owen scholars seem to agree on is that W.B. Yeats was in error to exclude Owen from his edition of the *Oxford Book of Modern Verse* (1936). Most critics elucidate how Owen had long studied the poetic tradition and had not simply started writing in reaction to the War. Some point to his poetry as continuing an elegiac tradition. In the sense that his poetry may be seen to be written for future fallen soldiers and bystanders, one may even call his work pre-elegiac. Though critics' strategies differ, most present his poetry in terms that will help it emerge from the shadows of T.S. Eliot and Ezra Pound, and Leavis' influence on poetic preference.

WELLAND's study was written before Harold Owen published his work, and before C.D. Lewis published his *Collected Poems of Wilfred Owen* in 1963. While his study is useful in setting the historic context for Owen's poetry, it is no longer the best introduction to Owen's work: it is better read in tandem with later critics, especially those who have the advantage of reading Owen's letters and the definitive collection of his poetry, Jon Stallworthy's 1983 two-volume *Wilfred Owen: The Complete Poems and Fragments*. Welland states that we should not "over-emphasize his impassioned protest against the war" but focus on "the quality of that poetry". Welland's chapter on half-rhyme is useful in pointing out the significance of Owen's technical innovations; however, his proposal that Owen's use of half-rhyme ("pararhyme") can be traced to French poet Jules Romains has been contested. Although critics debate the specifics of Welland's study (for example, Bäckman disagrees with Welland's assumption that "Owen deliberately chooses his vowels so that there is almost invariably a fall from a high-pitched to a low-pitched one"), many agree with his appraisal of Owen's merit.

Harold OWEN's biography of his brother has been seen by some critics as a tool for studying Wilfred Owen's poetry. Unfortunately, despite its subtitle, this work is an autobiography of Harold Owen rather than a sustained investigation of his brother's work or life – Wilfred disappears for several chapters at a time. While Stallworthy and Hibberd provide more useful biographies, Owen's discussions regarding his brother are interesting for those with adequate time to search out the few relevant passages.

WHITE traces Owen's poetic development through the authors he was known to have admired and those writers he met. She speculates that although French symbolist poet M. Laurent Tailhade "had no direct influence on Owen's poetry", his pacifist views could have influenced his attitude towards war. White agrees with Welland that Owen was unlikely to find suggestions for using half-rhyme from the Welsh language, and recommends Tailhade as the conduit to Romains. White's most helpful chapter details the growth of Owen's reputation. She discusses how initial acceptance and praise for Owen was eclipsed in the 1920s by attention given to Pound, Eliot, Yeats, and the Imagists. Though the influence on W.H. Auden, Stephen Spender, Cecil Day Lewis, and Louis MacNeice of Owen's "experiments with assonance and half-rhyme is clear and unquestionable", White cautions us that "the content of Owen's poetry had not influenced these poets; only his use of half-rhyme". Thus it may be a mistake to overstate Owen's influence on the 1930s' poets. The range of subjects covered in this text make it a significant advancement over Welland's ground-breaking study.

LANE begins his comparison of Owen's poetry to the poetry of Siegfried Sassoon and Rupert Brooke with a productive analysis of how the genre of war poetry has traditionally been situated on the epic side of the epic-lyric spectrum. One of the problems that the World-War-I poets had to solve was finding "a mode of expression adequate to their subject". The title of Lane's work implies that the lyric poetry of Owen and Sassoon was an adequate response, for "it was the First World War, not the artists, which lacked Homeric grandeur". Lane's strength lies in how convincingly he paints the milieu of Owen's poetry. Placed among patriotic propaganda, and the nationally sanctioned poetry of Rupert Brooke, Owen's poetry begins to take on a significance that is often lost when the poems appear in anthologies.

BÄCKMAN's study investigates how critical opinion regarding Owen's work changed during 1920–79. An important addition to Owen scholarship, Bäckman clearly delineates how Owen's image "has suffered from the dominance of the Leavisite perspective". In part, his study corrects some of the damage, arguing he was "a formative influence on later poets such as Stephen Spender, Cecil Day Lewis, Dylan Thomas, and Ted Hughes". Bäckman acknowledges re-writings of British literary history in which Owen's achievements "make him one of the forerunners of British poetic modernism". One of the most clarifying chapters sorts through critical debate regarding Owen's use of pararhyme, where a "systematic and consistent account of Owen's actual use of approximate rhymes" is given. Welland's hypothesis of Jules Romains as Owen's source is scrutinized, and Welsh, though doubted, is not fully discounted as a source. Scholarly, though at times overly complex for an introduction, Bäckman's text is a must for serious explorations of how Owen has been received by the literary community.

HIBBERD has produced some of the best introductions to Owen's poetry. His 1975 text is brief, but has a wealth of information for those requiring a concise overview. Hibberd provides a short biography, describes the social milieu of Owen's times, examines several poems, details Owen's stay at Craiglockhart, and concisely states why pararhymes are of note: "one of the principal themes in Owen's poems is that war prevents young soldiers from fulfilling their lives. Pararhymes are themselves unfulfilled; the reader expects a full rhyme and gets instead only an incomplete one". HIBBERD's 1986 work is a vastly expanded and revised continuation of the 1975 introduction. Here, Owen's poetic growth is examined chronologically, through the shaping forces of "Romantic dedication, Victorian energy, Evangelical fervour, the French and English Decadence, and Georgian innovation". Hibberd argues a case for Owen's importance as a transitional poet between the nineteenth century and modernism, "inheriting the aspirations and moral urgency of the Romantics and Victorians but seeing the need for Modernist 'insensibility'".

HIBBERD's 1992 work details Owen's relation with Sassoon at Craiglockhart, and stresses the importance of Dr Brock, whose "programme of ergotherapy" led Owen to editing the hospital magazine *The Hydra*. Hibberd deals with issues of poetic inspiration: "his debt to Keats has often been exaggerated; he thought Shelley a greater genius and was influenced by many other nineteenth-century writers". The several facsimiles of Owen's handwritten changes and Hibberd's analysis shows the difficulty editors have in dating and copying text. Hibberd also demonstrates how Owen's image was manipulated by his family. For example, Hibberd documents the forgery of Owen's award for the Military Cross where the phrase "inflicted considerable losses on the enemy" was changed to "took a number of prisoners". The forged document was "found among the family papers and quoted as correct in the *Collected Letters*". Hibberd also rejects Harold Owen's presentation of Wilfrid as being without sexual inclinations. The three works by Hibberd provide a thorough introduction to interconnections between Owen's poetry, his times, and his own life.

KERR introduces Bakhtinian theory into the discussion of Owen's work, and examines his poetry "in terms of its relationship with the communities, and their discourses, which helped to shape it". He looks at Owen's poetry in terms of the four "strata of heteroglossia" that had the most influence: "Family, Church, army, and poetry were his schools of language". Kerr closes his work by examining Owen's relationship to English elegies and other poets writing about war. This perceptive discussion makes Kerr's work an asset for Owen scholarship.

BRUCE R.A. LORD

P

Paine, Thomas 1737–1809

English prose writer

Aldridge, Alfred Owen, *Man of Reason: The Life of Thomas Paine*, Philadelphia: J.B. Lippincott, 1959; London: Cresset Press, 1960

Butler, Marilyn (ed.), *Burke, Paine, Godwin and the Revolution Controversy*, Cambridge and New York: Cambridge University Press, 1984

Conway, Moncure Daniel, *The Life of Thomas Paine*, New York and London: London: G.P. Putnam's Sons, 1892

Dyck, Ian, *Citizen of the World: Essays on Thomas Paine*, London: Christopher Helm, 1987

Fennessy, R.R., *Burke, Paine, and the Rights of Man: A Differance of Political Opinion*, The Hague: Martinus Nijhoff, 1963

Foner, Eric, *Tom Paine and Revolutionary America*, New York: Oxford University Press, 1976; Oxford: Oxford University Press, 1977

Powell, David, *Tom Paine, the Greatest Exile*, London: Croom Helm, 1985

Wilson, Jerome D., and William F. Ricketson, *Thomas Paine*, Boston: Twayne, 1978

Every American schoolchild knows of Thomas Paine, the patriot who inspired a revolution with *Common Sense*, then followed George Washington's army into battle as the first modern war correspondent. Although in life he had not been the man of action implied by the textbook myth, he was dramatic in his rhetoric, and the *Crisis Papers* could have been penned by the light of a campfire, a drum for a desk. Older children also learn that Paine ended his republican career in a French prison after barely escaping the guillotine, through an error in designation of the daily doomed, worthy of the least plausible Hollywood plot. This "historical" Thomas Paine provides an oddly heroic contrast to the damaged soul that continues to haunt the Paine biographical narrative.

Tom Paine is arguably the best example in Western literature of symbolic reinvention through biography, especially when the dearth of documentary evidence about him is balanced against the dozens of biographies that have been written, many of them lengthy and, narratively speaking, complete. Nearly all of his biographers after Conway have detailed the tug of war with Paine's reputation begun when the Pitt administration commissioned George Chalmers to write the first biography. Valuable now as the only available source of information about Paine's early life, it was aimed at undermining confidence in Paine and his writings at a time when the British government feared revolutionists in their midst. Other attacks followed publication of *Age of Reason*, and were met by a proliferation of equally unreliable vindicatory biographies, the most notable of which played an important role in the early nineteenth-century struggle for freedom of the press in Britain.

DYCK details the part Paine's ideas played in this and other reform movements in the several decades after his death, and includes valuable information about the publishing history of Paine's work. Numbers matter in a study of Paine's writings, because they had no other life beyond rhetorical persuasion: much of his publishing was in cheap, and therefore ephemeral, pamphlet form, meant for an immediate audience so that though demand is guessed at on a first printing, subsequent printings demonstrate confidence on the part of printers in getting a return for their labors. Dyck's main interest is in the uses to which Paine's texts were put after his death, after revolutionary focus had shifted away from kings and aristocrats to other villains. Paine's works were recycled many times in the next century, mostly in Britain, by political organizations rather than mainstream publishers for distribution to a select, radical audience. The real-world workers who inspired the rabble of Benjamin Disraeli's *Sybil* and Elizabeth Gaskell's *North and South* knew Paine from such sources. It is notable that Paine plays a uniformly dim role in English industrial fiction, even in Charles Dickens, where his portrait or a frayed, cheap edition of *Rights of Man* (or worse yet, *Age of Reason*) symbolizes secret, sinister trade-union thuggery.

BUTLER has collected Paine, his contemporary pamphleteers, mainstream political philosophers, and other political activists into one volume, with representative texts from each, and an introductory critical essay to establish context. Since Paine is unreadable without historical context, but often appears to students in anthology form, this is a useful introduction to late Enlightenment political rhetoric.

Unitarian, abolitionist, and socialist, CONWAY's landmark biography continues to be my favorite resource on Paine, not only for the author's skill as a scholarly biographer, but also for his florid, Carlylean style, which imbues his work with a literary flavor few biographies possess. His personal association with radical politics and reform religion make him an important part of the history of Paineite rhetoric, as well as a probable inspiration to fictionalized biographies, which continue to appear every decade or so in this century. All Paine biography is influenced to some extent by the first century of practitioners, and none escape the tint of political bias Paine can still release on his readers.

POWELL is a valuable source of current Paine myth as it lives in the British consciousness, proof that William Pitt was justified in his fear of Paine. He calls his work biography, while excluding all other biographies of Paine from his select bibliography, creating a "newborn" Paine who is free of a long and important biographical past. Others have done the same for the American Paine myth, which is less complex, less politically polar than the British version.

The ALDRIDGE biography is a more accessible history than Conway's. Like Conway, Aldridge researched original documents, frames his narrative with political events, and acknowledges the impossibility of "reading" Paine's life except through his published works. Aldridge believes strongly in Paine's historical importance, and this assumption underlies his interpretation of the role Paine played, especially in the American Revolution.

FONER (and many others too numerous to list here) analyzes Paine's politics from the American point of view, FENNESSY from the British. WILSON's aim is to illumine historical context for political arguments that have long lost currency, trace philosophical influence, and argue for the originality of Paine's political views, yet he does so within a biographical frame, and devotes a chapter to updating Conway's history of the biographies, including an extensive discussion of minor and fictional biographies.

Cheap print enabled Paine to reach a broad audience from the early days of the American Revolution and well into the nineteenth century, long after his death in obscurity 1809. His was a distinctive, populist political rhetoric, plain in style, modern-sounding to the late twentieth-century ear. His greatest skill was in identifying, then targeting an idealistic core audience with a plain, emotionally charged, voice of reason, the echo of which is nearly always present in the discourse of those who have interpreted his texts for subsequent generations of readers.

CLARA ELIZABETH SPEER

Parker, Dorothy 1893–1967

American poet, short-story writer, screenwriter, and drama critic

Frewin, Leslie, *The Late Mrs Dorothy Parker*, New York: Macmillan, 1986

Hellman, Lillian, *An Unfinished Woman: A Memoir*, Boston: Little Brown, 1969; London: Macmillan, 1970

Keats, John, *You Might As Well Live: The Life and Times of Dorothy Parker*, New York: Simon & Schuster, 1970; London: Secker & Warburg, 1971

Kinney, Arthur F., *Dorothy Parker*, Boston: Twayne, 1978

Meade, Marion, *Dorothy Parker: What Fresh Hell is This?*, New York: Villard Books, 1988; London: Heinemann, 1988

Miller, Nina, "Making Love Modern: Dorothy Parker and Her Public", in *American Literature*, 64(4), 1992

Dorothy Parker's reputation as a writer rests largely on the publication of several collections of poetry and a collection of short stories, which met with popular enthusiasm and considerable critical acclaim. "Big Blonde" won the O. Henry Award for the year's best short story in 1929. At the same time, Parker is possibly as famous for being the woman with a ready wit who was part of the round-table literati lunch-crowd at New York's Algonquin Hotel in the 1920s. Critical response to the published corpus of work has been somewhat "dogged" by what might be described as the vexed relationship between Parker's writing and Parker's *persona* as a modern woman emblematic of her time. All too often the writing has been read as if it were an unproblematic reflection of the life, and vice versa.

HELLMAN's book includes one chapter on Dorothy Parker, which Kinney describes as "an incisive but affectionate personal memoir". Hellman is somewhat reticent about making critical judgements of Parker's writing, but she does give a brief overview of the work. For Hellman, Parker's writing falls into three categories: "sentimental short stories about the little dressmaker or the servant", good short stories such as "Big Blonde", which are "imaginative projections", and "light verse" and other stories, which serve as a record of their time.

KEATS has written the "standard, popular biography" of Parker. As Kinney rightly suggests, the literary analysis is sparse. Unlike other biographers, however, Keats does attempt to situate Parker's writing within a broader literary tradition, noting the influence of Thomas Hood, A.E. Housman, and Edna St Vincent Millay, for example, in much of the poetry. Although Keats tends to read the fiction as a reflection of Parker's life, he also seeks to place the best of her short stories alongside other contemporary writing by John O'Hara and Ernest Hemingway. Keats has included a useful bibliography of the periodicals in which Parker's dramatic criticism and book reviews can be found.

KINNEY has written a detailed and systematic analysis of the whole range of Parker's writing, from "Her Apprenticeship: Essays, Light Verse, Drama" to "Her Accomplishment: Poetry, Fiction, Criticism". The book is a sustained attempt to shift the study of Parker's work away from overly biographical readings. It is, therefore, a sound academic introduction to Parker criticism. While suggesting that Parker's "mature" work (and here he cites her play *The Ladies of the Corridor* as an example) comes to embody much more of her life, Kinney also emphasises the imaginative transformation of experience that has taken place to produce a personal aesthetic. Kinney argues, with some plausibility, that insufficient attention has been paid to the influence on Parker's later poetry of the classical traditions of Horace and Catullus, which reached her through the work of Millay, Elinor Wylie, and Housman. For Kinney, Parker's significance as a poet is ultimately vested in the way in which she comes to develop the epigrammatical style inherited from the early twentieth-century revival of interest in Roman poetry. Kinney includes a useful bibliography, in which he gives a brief summary of each of the secondary sources.

FREWIN has written a biography, which focuses predominantly on Parker's witty *persona* and her social milieu. Although the book includes copious quotations from other critics, it does not engage in a serious critical dialogue. Little, if anything, is added to Parker criticism, other than the suggestion that many of the famous witticisms and epigrams are derivative. The book might well be described as disingenuous in its persistant use of rhetorical questions such as "Easy without being slipshod? Cultivated without affectation?". Frewin pathologises Parker – along with other poets both before and after her, such as John Donne, William Cowper, and Sylvia Plath – by arguing that the writing is symptomatic of what he refers to as her manic-depressive psychosis.

MEADE has written a biography of Parker, which scrupulously avoids the patronising tone of Frewin's book. Meade does not attempt any literary criticism and reads Parker's fiction and poetry as a seamless transposition of her life. For example, Meade suggests that "Big Blonde" recounts the ending of Parker's first marriage. The merit of Meade's biography is to be found in its thorough documentation of Parker's life as a professional woman writer.

MILLER's impressive achievement is to develop the relationship between Parker's poetry and the public persona far beyond the usual model of art reflecting life. Drawing on semiotic theory, and informed by a practice of feminist poetics, Miller reads Parker's love poetry in the particular cultural context in which it was produced – a "sophisticated" woman writing about "modern love". For Miller, the Parker persona becomes the very means by which Parker, the woman poet, gives a public voice to the "conventionally" private business of love. Although this article is concerned specifically with the poetry rather than the fiction, it is an ideal introduction to a more theoretical and less biographical approach to Parker criticism. The footnotes are excellent.

CHRISTINE BLAKE

Parody

Bennett, David, "Parody, Postmodernism, and the Politics of Reading", in *Critical Quarterly*, 27(4), Winter 1985

Hanoosh, Michelle, "The Reflexive Function of Parody", in *Comparative Literature*, 41, 1985

Hutcheon, Linda, *A Theory of Parody: The Teachings of Twentieth-Century Art Forms*, London and New York: Methuen, 1985

Rose, Margaret, *Parody/Metafiction: An Analysis of Parody as a Critical Mirror to the Writing and Reception of Fiction*, London: Croom Helm, 1979

Rose, Margaret, *Parody: Ancient, Modern, and Post-Modern*, Cambridge and New York: Cambridge University Press, 1993

ROSES's first book (1979) is a pioneering study of parody, which she regards as the prime generating force of metafiction. Her study is in two parts – an extensive attempt to define parody, followed by an examination of the uses of parody (and related theories) in art, architecture, and literature. In the first section, Chapter 1 ranges from the etymology, intertextuality, and ways of "signalling" parody to its effects on the reader and the attitude of the parodist. Chapter 2 usefully distinguishes parody from related forms, such as burlesque and pastiche, along with a suggestive diagram differentiating parody from satire and irony.

Section Two provides an extensive analysis of parody and self-parody as metafiction, with literary examples from Cervantes, Laurence Sterne, and James Joyce, backed up by a sophisticated exploitation of Gilbert Ryle and Michel Foucault, and underpinned with a subtle analysis of the Cretan liar paradox. A further section employs illustrations like Jastrow's duck/rabbit and Magritte's *Ceci n'est pas une pipe* to look at ways in which parody "raises our awareness of how we receive literary texts", "complicating the normal processes of reception". The ensuing parallels with psychoanalysis are perhaps less convincing, but the treatment of self-parody makes suggestive use of Chaucer and Jorge Luis Borges, though the style is rather elliptical and "self" seems often really to mean "reflexive".

The final lengthy section analyses what Rose calls the "parodistic episteme". By this she means primarily the relationship between the parodist as decoder of text A and encoder of text B, and the reader's response to both A and B. After using the work of John Searle as theoretical basis for examining the idea of verification in metafiction and political parody, she provides a detailed examination of the concept of the implied reader and the reader's expectations, based largely on the work of Wolfgang Iser. She then contrasts her theory of parody as reworking with the "iterability" theories of Jacques Derrida – much to the latter's disadvantage! A detailed critique of Foucault's use of parody texts in *Les Mots et les choses* as discursive dialogue with the prevailing episteme leads onto an analysis of Velasquez's *Las Meninas* and of modernist meta-painters, such as Magritte. Rose demonstrates here how parodistic meta-narrative undermines theories of reflection and representation, and formulates a dialectical theory based on Hegel, Theodor Adorno, Hans-Robert Jauss, and Mikhail Bakhtin.

This is an important book and should not be regarded as superseded by Rose's later study. The use of illustrations and examples drawn from German literature are admirable; the lack of translations of large blocks of complex German is regrettable.

Unlike Rose, HUTCHEON chooses to concentrate on twentieth-century manifestations of parody. This narrower focus enables her to formulate a more rigorously theoretical basis and to analyse in depth a more homogeneous body of texts (though her examples are, nevertheless, very wide-ranging and testify to the great variety of modern and postmodern parody). She also supplements Rose by utilising fruitfully elements from intertextual theory. Since the scope of parody is so wide, Hutcheon refuses to provide a systematic schema of common techniques on the grounds that this would be reductive; instead, she concentrates on "the pragmatic functions of parody as we know it today".

In Chapter 2 we get a broad definition of parody based on the claim that there can be no trans-historical prescriptions, and that the modern variety by no means always ridicules its target text: parody can be reverential as well as ironically mocking. Hutcheon also emphasises that parody can be seen as an extreme (circumscribed) form of intertextuality. After distinguishing parody from pastiche, plagiarism, burlesque, travesty, quotation, and satire, she launches (in Chapter 3) into a complex analysis of the pragmatics of parody, arguing for a much wider range of application, stressing how modern writers often prefer to exploit creatively parody's potential for ironic ambivalence rather than mere ridicule. She uses fascinating examples from contemporary art, literature, and music to demonstrate the parodic line from scornful satire to respectful recontextualisation.

Hutcheon then provides a Bakhtinian analysis of parody's paradoxically dual nature – both textually authoritative and aesthetically or ideologically transgressive: what she terms "the legitimized quality of parodic multivalence". This leads into a discussion of parody's intentions (reverential, didactic, ridiculing, etc.) and its relationship to contemporary metafiction. Hutcheon finally turns to the role of the writer (encoder) and reader (decoder) of parody, showing how metafiction forces us to re-examine both the function of the inferred enunciator and the degree of literary competence required of the reader. Her examples – from Henry Fielding to Italo Calvino and John Fowles – are apt and convincing.

In conclusion, Hutcheon offers a theory of (modern) parody as a consciousness-raising device, a form of *Ideologiekritik*, which relates parody to "the world" – not just to the author (Romanticism), to the text (formalism), or to the the reader (response theory) – and also, Oedipally, to its historic past. The strengths of this book lie in its broad range of reference, its clarity of style and inclusion of analogies in the fields of architecture and music. The bibliography (to 1984) is exemplary.

ROSE's most recent study (1993) is much more rigorously theoretical than her earlier contribution. The stress is still largely on modern and contemporary views of parody, but she does not now confine her examples to metafiction, and can include observations on the works of theorists Jean Baudrillard, Fredric Jameson, Ihab Hassan, Charles Jencks, and Umberto Eco. She begins by outlining six ways of defining parody: the first analyses its etymology, using mainly ancient Greek examples; the second concentrates on the relationship between parody and comedy (*to geloion*), emphasising that it is mainly the structural use of comic incongruity that distinguishes parody from allusion or imitation; a section on reader-response theory clarifies and expands her earlier treatment by furnishing 15 "signals" for the expectation and detection of parody; the attitudes espoused by the parodist are then arranged on a spectrum ranging from respect for the hypotext to criticism of it; and her final section demonstrates the characteristics of both specific and general parody to arrive at a definition: "the comic refunctioning of preformed linguistic or aesthetic material". Many would disagree with the normative inclusion of the term "comic", but in other respects this first chapter, despite its daunting 151 footnotes, constitutes an admirably full and clear attempt to formulate a flexible working definition.

The next chapter distinguishes (mainly on a historical basis) parody from related forms such as travesty, persiflage, *pekoral*, pastiche, satire, and irony. This repeats much of her earlier work, and one might feel that her treatment of burlesque is rather vague and imprecise, but the treatment of parodic use of both form and content is admirable, as is the discussion of pastiche. Having thus cleared the definitional decks, Rose then turns her attention to more specific modern and late-modern uses of parody. An extremely extensive treatment of Victor Shklovsky and other Russian formalists precedes a well-focused study of Bakhtin and his dialogic concept of parody as "varidimensional, double-voiced discourse". Rose is particularly good here on Bakhtin's emphasis on the contribution of parody to the evolution of the novel, though one might feel that her lengthy treatments of *The Dialogic Imagination* and of the "carnivalesque" somewhat outstay their welcome. A section on the contributions of Hans-Robert Jauss and Wolfgang Iser to parodic theory, based on their formula of evocation and subversion of the reader's expectations, is followed by a cogent description of the work of structuralist and poststructuralist theorists (Kristeva, Lachmann, Foucault), concentrating especially on the idea of intertextuality.

Finally, Rose turns her attention to postmodern theories of parody, and supplies an extremely helpful survey based on whether the writers adopt a positive or negative approach towards their subject. Too extensive to summarise here, this represents the most up-to-date account of contemporary parodic theory available in English. After a critical resumé of Fredric Jameson and Charles Jencks, Rose brings her study to a close with a lively glance at different types of parody in Umberto Eco's *The Name of the Rose* and the novels of David Lodge.

The only major reservation about this book concerns Rose's repeated and rather irritating insistence that parody is necessarily "comic". As Hutcheon has well demonstrated, this is simply not true, and some of Rose's own examples would appear to undermine her position. Nevertheless, this is a major study, and is particularly useful in directing our attention to the works of major Continental theorists such as Alfred Leide and Theodor Werveyen. There is a useful glossary, a state-of-the-art bibliography (1993), and a comprehensive index.

The article by HANOOSH takes its starting point from the writings of Rose but goes much further in discussing parody's "capacity to reflect critically back on itself, not merely upon its target". She goes on to demonstrate that this aspect results in parody's ability to challenge the notion of fixed works (the canon) altogether. In analysing the way in which parody calls itself into question, she relies heavily on the work of Richard Poirier ("The Politics of Self-Parody", *Partisan Review*, 35, 1968). In talking about the idea of parody as endlessly self-referential, she floats two interesting possibilities: 1) the analogy with the Lacanian concept of the eternally deferred signifier, and 2) the formalist function of regenerating tradition and "furthering the development of literary forms".

Parody, she goes on to claim, may also suggest elements of other potential parodies and provide hints for alternative versions of the original parodied. Her examples are highly persuasive: a detailed analysis of *Northanger Abbey* shows how Jane Austen's gothic parody not only reveals the absurdities of the genre and its readers, but helps to perpetuate the original and even open up the possibilities of related stories. Some of this may sound a trifle contrived, but her subsequent examples from Richard Brinsley Sheridan's *The Critic* and from Cervantes' *Don Quixote* convincingly illustrate how parodies-within-parodies and alternative versions may conjure up visions of endless parodic variations. Some may feel that the idea of parody engaged in eternal, vertiginous self-reflexivity is stretching the boundaries of the term too far. There is a short bibliography.

BENNETT's study is also dependent on Rose, but he extends the reader-response element to demonstrate that any text, if read contextually, can be seen parodically as an "intertextual strategy of reading". In analysing the "constitutive role of the reader", he (like Hanoosh) develops the theories of Poirier to project a theory of parody that actually makes fun of itself "as it goes along". Discussing the writings of authors such as John Barth, Vladimir Nabokov, and Thomas Pynchon, he elaborates a specifically postmodern view of parody, which takes issue with Jameson's contention that in this age, with no linguistic norms to guide us, parody has given way to pastiche.

After some cogent remarks on the incongruous mixture of genres that characterises postmodernist fiction, Bennett engages in a detailed critique of Pynchon's *The Crying of Lot 49* to illustrate his claim that this text not only parodies the assertions of causality typical of the realistic novel, but also makes ambiguous the status of Oedipa Maas as both heroine of the script and object of satirical irony. In an anti-positivist coda, Bennett propounds a theory of parody as facilitating a "hermeneutics of indeterminacy", which of course is what postmodernism is all about. This is a useful supplement to the studies discussed above, but one might justifiably wish for more detailed literary analysis.

A.W. LYLE

Pastoral Literature

Chaudhuri, Sukanta, *Renaissance Pastoral and Its English Developments*, Oxford: Clarendon Press, 1989; New York: Oxford University Press, 1989

Cooper, Helen, *Pastoral: Medieval into Renaissance*, Ipswich, Sussex: D.S. Brewer, 1977; Totowa, New Jersey: Rowman & Littlefield, 1977

Empson, William, *Some Versions of Pastoral: A Study in the Pastoral Form in Literature*, London: Chatto & Windus, 1935; reprinted, Norfolk, Connecticut: New Directions, 1968

Greg, Walter W., *Pastoral Poetry and Pastoral Drama: A Literary Enquiry with Special Reference to the Pre-Restoration Stage in England*, London: A. H. Bullen, 1906; reprinted, New York: Russell & Russell, 1959

Loughrey, Brian (ed.), *The Pastoral Mode: A Casebook*, London: Macmillan, 1984

Marinelli, P. V., *Pastoral*, London: Methuen, 1971

Patterson, Annabel, *Pastoral and Ideology: Virgil to Valéry*, Berkeley: University of California Press, 1987; Oxford: Clarendon Press, 1988

Williams, Raymond, *The Country and the City*, London: Chatto & Windus, 1973; New York: Oxford University Press, 1973

There is an enormous critical literature on the subject of the pastoral in English, and what is presented here is a highly selective introduction of general titles.

MARINELLI is the most succinct and accessible introduction, which provides a series of perspectives and a historical overview from Ovid and Theocritus to modern fiction like William Golding's *Lord of the Flies*. Marinelli argues that "the dominant idea in pastoral is a search for simplicity away from a complexity represented either by a specific location . . . or from a specific period of human existence". Pastoral is always in search of an "original splendour", a golden age, but exactly how this is to be achieved, or what form it takes, varies considerably. On the one hand there are myths of the recovery of a prelapsarian state in the Garden of Eden; on the other, visions of an Arcadian retreat, which is always painfully aware of the military threat from its neighbour, Sparta, and so "represents a midway point between perfection and imperfection".

GREG is a scholarly survey which retains its importance. Greg regards the desire for the pastoral as "deep-rooted in the nature of humanity" and points out the irony of its flourishing most "amid the artificiality of a decadent court" during the Renaissance. Pastoral takes on various forms in its long literary history, but always contains "the recognition of a contrast . . . between pastoral life and some more complex type of civilization". Greg provides a historical account of the development of the genre from Ancient Greece to pre-Restoration England, concluding with a series of influential essays on some examples of English pastoral – John Fletcher's *Faithful Shepherdess*, Ben Jonson's *Sad Shepherd*, and Thomas Randolph's *Amyntas* – as well as masques and their development up to Milton.

EMPSON is a similarly influential, albeit more idiosyncratic, work, which consists of a series of interrelated essays rather than the demonstration of a coherent thesis. Empson writes on proletarian literature, childhood in Lewis Carroll's *Alice in Wonderland*, mock-pastoral in John Gay's *The Beggar's Opera*, as well as more obvious subjects such as Andrew Marvell's representations of gardens, Milton's conceptions of innocence, and Shakespeare's pastoral plots, in order to demonstrate the range of pastoral forms and subjects. Empson is particularly incisive on Lewis Carroll's playful parodies of William Wordsworth's sombre pastoral verse in order to discuss the problem of growing up and to cast the child as threatened swain, the assumptions of the pastoral mode ("you can say everything about complex people by a complete consideration of simple people"), and the question of double plots.

COOPER's argument is that "it was only in England that the full potential of the European pastoral poetry of the Middle Ages was worked out with the new brilliance of the Renaissance". In contrast to Empson, her study involves a very specific definition of pastoral as "the traditional image of the shepherd world" because other notions of the simple life had their own literary histories and genres. Cooper considers works from the Latin and vernacular eclogues of the Middle Ages to the works of Philip Sidney, Edmund Spenser, Michael Drayton, and Shakespeare, concluding with an essay on the representation of Elizabeth I as the shepherds' queen. Cooper's work can be supplemented by CHAUDHURI, which is a thorough survey of English Renaissance pastoral and its related literary contexts.

WILLIAMS is an important Marxist-inspired study, which seeks to expose the material conditions of urban and rural production, which are mystified in the variety of pastoral forms. Williams' overview of English literature extends from the Renaissance to the present day and he provides many readings of literary works that must either be accepted or refuted, but which cannot be ignored. He points out that "it is not easy to forget that Sidney's *Arcadia*, which gives a continuing title to English neo-pastoral, was written in a park which had been made by enclosing a whole village and evicting the tenants". Was Sidney aware of the irony, or simply blind to the problem? Similarly, Williams argues, in the country-house poem of the early seventeenth century, the "magical extraction of the curse of labour is in fact achieved by a simple extraction of the existence of labourers". Our conceptions of the relationship between the country and the city, Williams suggests, stem from a capitalist mode of production which needs to be resisted. PATTERSON has a certain amount in common with Williams, being an extensive study of reading Virgil's *Eclogues*, from Varus and Octavian to Paul Valéry and Samuel Palmer, exploring "what we can learn from the curves in its reception history about the larger history of which it is the shadow". It contains illuminating discussions of Spenser, Alexander Pope, George Crabbe, Oliver Goldsmith, and Wordsworth.

LOUGHREY is a useful and easily obtained collection of essays on pastoral, containing brief extracts from pre-Victorian theorists – Sidney, George Puttenham, Thomas Hobbes, Wordsworth, William Hazlitt – and more substantial pieces from recent studies – Greg, Frank Kermode, Renato Poggioli, Harry Levin, Northrop Frye, James Turner, and others. Loughrey suggests in his Introduction that "from Vergil onwards, pastoral poetry has been pre-occupied with ... tensions between the world of reality and the world of the imagination", accommodating both Christian and classical mythologies. There are useful general articles as well as individual discussions of Shakespeare's *As You Like It*, the poetry of Katherine Philips, Milton's *Lycidas*, Leo Tolstoy, Robert Frost, Thomas Hardy, Wordsworth, and others.

ANDREW HADFIELD

Pater, Walter 1839–1894

English prose writer and novelist

Bloom, Harold (ed.), *Walter Pater*, New York: Chelsea House, 1985

Brake, Laurel, and Ian Small (eds.), *Pater in the 1990s*, Greensboro, North Carolina: ELT Press, 1991

Donoghue, Denis, *Walter Pater: Lover of Strange Souls*, New York: Knopf, 1995

Fletcher, Ian, *Walter Pater*, London: Longman, 1959, revised 1971

Iser, Wolfgang, *Walter Pater: The Aesthetic Moment*, translated by David Henry Wilson, Cambridge and New York: Cambridge University Press, 1987

McGrath, F.C., *The Sensible Spirit: Walter Pater and the Modernist Paradigm*, Tampa: University of South Florida Press, 1986

Ward, Anthony, *Walter Pater: The Idea in Nature*, London: MacGibbon & Kee, 1966

Williams, Carolyn, *Transfigured World: Walter Pater's Aesthetic Historicism*, Ithaca, New York: Cornell University Press, 1989

Modern evaluation of Pater's work may be said to have begun with the contrary judgements of T.S. Eliot and W.B. Yeats. Eliot's essay on "Arnold and Pater" (1930) damns with faint praise in remarking that, contrary to his own best imperatives, "Pater is always primarily the moralist" – this notwithstanding Eliot's earlier and different rebuke in his essay on *Hamlet* (dubbed, in clear insinuation of Pater's impressionism, "the 'Mona Lisa' of literature"). As if to invert these observations, Yeats later refashioned Pater's reading of the Mona Lisa as the first poem in his *Oxford Book of Modern Verse* (1936), proposing that it foreshadows "a poetry, a philosophy, where the individual is nothing" and "flux", temporal and experiential, is all.

FLETCHER's short monograph, first published in 1959, is informed by the assessments of Eliot and Yeats alike, and offers a synopsis of Pater's major fascinations for subsequent commentators. Thus Pater is claimed, in corrective if cautionary fashion, as the moralist of his own critical dilemma, his professed "quarrel with himself" implicating Yeats' dictum on poetry as the product of such a quarrel. Inhabiting "a twilight of categories between criticism and creation", Pater's modernity is identified at once with his embrace of the "relative" over the "absolute", and with his attempt to posit value *in* rather than *against* that relativism. In this respect, more is made of the early than the late work; the injunction to "the love of art for art's sake" with which *The Renaissance*, in its first version, concludes, is considered unsustainable beyond its own moment. Pater's "aesthetic" project, which conceives sense-experience as a condition of critical reflection, and art as the order in which life is realised at its maximum, is acknowledged as under stress in both its practice and idea.

In revising his essay for its second edition, Fletcher takes special note of the intervening work of WARD, whose book was the first English study substantively to address Pater's relationship to Charles Darwin and Hegel. By historicising his subject, Ward recovers the intellectual drama of Pater's own historicism, central to which is the latter's vision of the Mona Lisa as "symbol of the modern idea". According to this account, Leonardo's portrait absorbs a Darwinist view of organic mutation within an Hegelian history of "world-spirit", calling forth and incorporating both the dialectic of historical longing, which contributes to the portrait's genesis (the Renaissance "return of the Pagan world"), and the successive interpretations, which give the picture its patina. In the artwork, spirit becomes matter, and flux the path of Logos. Ward suggests that, in this "synoptic" approach to criticism, Pater seeks escape from the "determinist nightmare", which s o preoccupied his generation. Thereafter, however, Ward describes the impasse of this very historicism, condemned, in the words of Pater's "Conclusion", to keep "as a solitary prisoner its own dream of a world".

If we are reminded here of Eliot's "Thinking of the key, each confirms a prison", it is to engage, by association, ISER's conclusion that Pater marks "a moment when Late Romanticism was about to give way to Modernism". Iser's study, a long-overdue translation of his *Die Autonomie des Ästhetischen* (1960), describes Pater's ambiguous paternity of modernist poetics in terms of an unfinished revolution. For Pater, aesthetic value is posited "in contradiction to reality", yet open conflict with that reality is avoided because it would risk a correlative loss of the aesthetic ideal. Iser focuses on Pater's bid "to legitimise autonomous art" by what is designated, in *Plato and Platonism*, the "historical method". Pater's criticism has, in this reading, a vitally mythopoeic function, valorising the very "transitoriness and the in-between state of aesthetic existence" as a nexus of empathic connection with past worlds. Central for Iser is Pater's myth of the "House Beautiful" of art, in which no achievement is ever lost to recollection. Iser's analysis is, in turn, most compelling when revealing the *limits* of legitimation in this Platonising of critical activity.

The same concerns are taken up by WILLIAMS, whose book considers Pater's attempt to reconcile, in aesthetic criticism, the (for Plato) dichotomous realms of ideas and phenomena. Williams observes that, like other self-appointed "moderns", Pater is drawn to a particular aspect or interpretation of Platonic doctrine, "the practice or method of a tentative, hesitant, never-concluding aspiration toward 'ideals'" – an aspiration at once analysed and exemplified by Pater's historical fictions *Marius the Epicurean* and *Gaston de Latour*. The strength of Williams' book is its attention to the reflexive narrative and rhetorical strategies shared by Pater's criticism and fiction. In both, certain historical figures represent, in phenomenal form, turning-points in history's pursuit of its "idea" (for example, Marius the Epicurean becomes Marius the Early Christian). For Williams, "a 'figure' is first a rhetorical figure", and thus by extension an historical trope. Figuration is held to constitute the essentially recreative act of this criticism, which looks through the particular artwork and artist toward their general historical function and significance.

Paterian transfiguration renders the material world curiously spectral, and makes for the haunted and haunting qualities of his prose. But such writing is itself summoned in response to a world of physical and epiphenomenal process where, as Pater's translation of Heraclitus has it, "all things give way: nothing remaineth". For McGRATH, Pater's critical "fusion of empiricism and idealism" seeks to bestow a wider valency on his otherwise singular apprehensions. In this endeavour – distinguished by an "epistemological skepticism" toward its own project – lies what McGrath terms the "modernist paradigm" of Pater's work. McGrath places Pater in open dialogue with British and German philosophical traditions, as well as with a wide range of modernist literature; his final chapter demonstrates his thesis through a close reading of Paterian presences in Joyce's *A Portrait of the Artist As a Young Man*. The dynamic of Pater's writing is akin to Joyce's presentation of Stephen; both describe a tension, or dialectic, between absorbtion in the object-world and creative or critical reflection; both write a prose that turns, in Pater's phrase, upon the "clauses of experience".

BLOOM's collection of "Modern Critical Views" dwells, in its editor's Introduction, upon Pater's appropriately etherial influence on later writers, through whose work we view his achievement in, as it were, refined form. Bloom's essay sets a seal on the revaluation of Pater in its rejection of Eliot's legacy; indeed, within his agonistic model of literary history, Eliot is placed in a "neo-orthodox" line of poets, who paradoxically affirm Pater's influence while vainly seeking to translate it to "the religious sphere". This historiography shadows Pater's own in "The School of Giorgione", where the artist lives on (and only) in the painterly effect of the "Giorgionesque" bestowed upon his successors. Bloom's revisionist perspective informs both McGrath's "paradigmatic" study and Williams' analysis of Pater's language – a language generated, according to J. Hillis Miller's "Walter Pater: A Partial Portrait" (originally 1976), by the "problematic trope of personification" in which perceived historical meaning always exceeds its "sensuous embodiment". In Bloom's Introduction (originally 1974) and Miller's essay we may locate the formulation of an avowedly "deconstructive" turn in Pater criticism.

Different concerns are prominent by the time of BRAKE and SMALL's collection. They open it by noting that "formalist" interpretation of Pater has been supplemented by a "new" historicism for which history is a "field of significations" and the text a "discursive web rather than a unified and self-enclosed artifact". This proposition is heuristically conceived in embrace of Pater's "Conclusion", where even the unitary self is but "a design in a web, the actual threads of which pass out beyond it". In consequence, Pater's "archive" is not only recharted, bestowing new prominence upon unpublished or uncollected work, but Pater is discovered in other people's archives; in, for example, Lesley Higgins' study of the essays prepared for him by Gerard Manley Hopkins, or in Billie Inman's narrative of the sexual scandal that stifled Pater's career in the mid-1870s. Richard Dellamora's attention to the sexual politics of Pater's "Critical Impressionism" typifies – not least in its critique of Bloom and Miller – a collective endeavour to describe the convergence of textual and ideological design in his work. Pater is made more tangible even as his writing is exorcised of its animating ghosts.

Taking full measure of this recent research, DONOGHUE offers the best general account of his subject since Ian Fletcher. In its reading of Pater's life and work, this many-sided volume stands as an essay in equivocation toward the vital principle of Paterian criticism, its necessary bracketing of aesthetic experience (the "moment" of apprehension) from the claims of any greater continuum. Not for the first time, Pater offers an occasion for argument as to the proper conduct of criticism. Donoghue extends the genealogy of debate both backward and forward from the judgements of Eliot and Yeats. The Pater who emerges from this richly textured excursus is an "antinomian" figure, "independent of the law rather than against it", who practises criticism as, at best, "an opportunity for the exercise of self-consciousness". The provocation and principal bequest of Pater's writing is deemed the "disjunction of sensation from judgement" enacted in its syntax and valued by Donoghue in full recognition of its equal tendency to solipsism and imaginative release. It follows that if, for Yeats, Pater foreshadows "the flux of *The Cantos* of Ezra Pound", this is perhaps most profoundly so in the sense confessed by Canto 116: "I cannot make it cohere".

IAN FAIRLEY

Peacock, Thomas Love 1785–1866

English novelist and poet

Butler, Marilyn, *Peacock Displayed: A Satirist in His Context*, London and Boston: Routledge & Kegan Paul, 1979
Campbell, Olwen Ward, *Thomas Love Peacock*, London: Arthur Baker, 1953
Dawson, Carl, *His Fine Wit: A Study of Thomas Love Peacock*, Berkeley: University of California Press, 1970; London: Routledge & Kegan Paul, 1970
Kjellin, Håkan, *Talkative Banquets: A Study in the Peacockian Novels of Talk*, Stockholm: Almqvist & Wiksell, 1974
Mills, Howard, *Peacock: His Circle and His Age*, Cambridge: Cambridge University Press, 1969
Priestley, J.B., *Thomas Love Peacock*, London: Macmillan, 1927; reprinted, New York: St Martin's Press, 1966

Critical books on Peacock tend to focus on his five satirical novels, commenting on their originality and innovation. Many critics acclaim him for his engagement with, and satirical treatment of, the social and cultural issues of Regency England, but they are more ambivalent about the depth of his fictional worlds and his one-dimensional characters. Recent studies of his poetry and essays cast light on Peacock as a complex literary figure, especially in his relation to Romanticism.

Writing for the "English Men of Letters" series, PRIESTLEY's study of Peacock combines biographical material with commentaries on his novels and lyrical poems and an appraisal of his reputation as a writer. The biographical section traces Peacock's life from early age, through his meeting and complex friendship with Percy Bysshe Shelley in the 1810s, to his time working for the East India Company, as well as his life as a writer. Priestley comments upon the differences between his "novels of talk" (considering his two romances separately), but, when compared with other literary forms of the time,"their common likeness and their originality" are stressed. His work is seen to combine elements of the French satirical tradition with a comic strain of literature (found in the work of Henry Fielding), which blend to make Peacock "one of the clear voices of English prose". However, it is the "baffled idealist", rather than the assured political satirist, that presents Priestley with his lasting impression of this "prose humourist".

CAMPBELL, in a short but informative study, begins from the premise that in Peacock's satirical works "he is mocking opinions, not human beings". Thus, the characters in his fiction are means for embodying "ideas equally peculiar or exaggerated". To illustrate this, Peacock's caricatures and burlesques are interestingly contrasted with Jane Austen's complex fictional characters, although Campbell notes "minor points of similarity in style and sentiment". He meditates upon the difficulty of classifying Peacock's fiction, but suggests that his conversational pieces constitute a "mixture of farce, scholarship and fantasy, satire and romance". A study of Peacock's life is interspersed with critical commentaries on all his major works, in which the author returns to the "romance and charm" of the fiction. As do many of the other critics, Campbell lauds *Nightmare Abbey* (1818) for its "brilliant" interfusion of satire and farce, a combination which he deems to be marred by the "semi-serious arguments of the other novels".

Like Campbell, BUTLER begins her detailed consideration of Peacock by comparing his fiction with Austen's novels. Although she claims they both possess the "ability to create a fictional world of unusual clarity and charm", it is Peacock's awareness of, and engagement with, the spirit of his times that constitutes the major difference between them. Butler appreciates what she calls a "degree of seriousness and intelligence" in his novels, despite the fact that Peacock has "never persuaded the world of his seriousness". She writes at length on each of his major novels and concludes with an interesting appraisal of Peacock as a social critic. Here she discerns that his "aim to intervene in affairs" is apparent in his satire, through which he injects a variety of comic elements into the neoclassical agenda of a committed "liberal, intellectual and humourist".

KJELLIN takes the title of this study from Priestley's description of Peacock's six conversational novels. Peacock is characterized as a neoclassical writer, who attempts to synthesize the instructive and pleasurable dimensions of literature through the vehicle of his satire. Despite Peacock's apparent hostility to the spirit of Romanticism, as expressed in *The Four Ages of Poetry* (1820), Kjellin detects that his intellectual framework did not "blind [him] to the merits of individual poems", whether written by Byron or Shelley. The focus of the book is upon Peacock's development of the novel of ideas (represented in the work of Voltaire, William Godwin, and Robert Bage), from an emphasis on active characters towards a virtually exclusive concern for what they say and what they represent. His formal innovation is stressed over and above the content of the novels (which is often slight), a development by which Peacock was able to "satirize contemporary cultural and political opinions without taking sides".

The assumption that Peacock has a significant role in the literature of the Regency era is one that is central to DAWSON's book. He focuses on Peacock's versatility as a writer, an "outspoken enemy of industrial might, a feminist, [and] a student of mythology". Although Peacock's satire is sharp when detached from his comedy, Dawson suggests that he was not an anti-intellectual, but set himself against "dangerous cultural trends", fads, bombast and intellectual arrogance. Dawson speculates that his transition from poetry (in which he detects similarities with that of Thomas Gray and William Collins) to fiction may have coincided with a realization that he could not compete with the growth of Romantic poetry. The book charts Peacock's transition from writing poetry to his development of a "brilliantly eclectic fictional form". Dawson claims his dialogic form encourages the reader to work through a series of competing points of view, in order to engage with the central debates of the age.

In an impressive book Howard MILLS positions Peacock, the personality and the writer, within his Regency setting. For Mills, Peacock personifies a curious blend of Augustan and Romantic traits, which combine to equip him with a unique perspective upon "the currents of his age". Peacock has often been seen as "a harmless eccentric" in an age of lyrical Romanticism; however, Mills views him within a wider circle of Regency literary figures, including Coleridge, Byron, and

Shelley, in an attempt to "re-open" Peacock's case as an important satirist and essay-writer. The central argument asserts that his friendship with Shelley "*made* Peacock" and was "the central condition of his quality" as a writer, not only in the 1810s, but throughout his career. Mills examines rare material (for example, Peacock's "Essay on Fashionable Literature" of 1818 and his articles on music) alongside the conversational novels, which, together with a valuable bibliography, distinguishes this volume as a fine piece of scholarship.

MARTIN HALLIWELL

Pearl-Poet *see* Gawain-Poet

Pepys, Samuel 1633–1703

English diarist

Barker, Francis, *The Tremulous Private Body: Essays in Subjection*, London and New York: Methuen, 1984

Brome, Vincent, *The Other Pepys*, London: Weidenfeld & Nicolson, 1992

Bryant, Arthur, *Samuel Pepys,* 3 vols. (*The Man in the Making*, *The Saviour of the Navy*, *The Years of Peril*), London: Collins, 1933–39; New York: Macmillan, 1933–39

Latham, Robert, and Matthews, William (eds.), *The Diary of Samuel Pepys*, 11 vols., London: Bell & Sons, 1970–83; Berkeley: University of California Press, 1970–83

Ollard, Richard, *Pepys: A Biography*, London: Hodder & Stoughton, 1974; New York: Holt, Rinehart, & Winston, 1975

Spender, Dale (ed.), *The Diary of Elizabeth Pepys*, London: Grafton, 1991

Taylor, Ivan E., *Samuel Pepys*, New York: Twayne, 1967

As a man, Pepys played his many allotted parts – civil servant, virtuoso, book collector, historian – with unrivalled vigour and panache. As a writer, his fame rests on his vast *Diary*, recorded from 1660 to 1669, which he bequeathed in bound volumes, along with the rest of his library, to Magdalene College, Oxford. Since its shorthand code was broken in the 1820s, the *Diary* has been one of the most celebrated and best-loved of all English books; and, as a consequence, Pepys's private life is now the most public of any seventeenth-century writer. Commenting on the *Diary* of necessity has involved commenting on Pepys himself; a further stroke of luck has ensured that such an attractive figure has attracted skilled biographers.

BRYANT's three volumes remain the most spirited of these Lives. Written at the height of the British Empire, their central focus is the celebration of quintessential Englishness, and Pepys's influential role in forming the modern navy, which made that Empire possible. Bryant sets the *Diary* within a ripe evocation of Pepys's life, times, and landscapes. He sees Pepys as a great – because entirely unconscious – artist, gifted nevertheless with "the artist's two gifts of selection and sincerity. . . . It is this catholic inclusiveness in material and this unerring artistry in selection that places this clerk's journal among the unperishable books of the world". Bryant practises the Pepysian all-inclusiveness he preaches, for his three volumes are the longest life available, as well as the most empathetically uncritical of modern accounts.

TAYLOR opts instead for the characteristic brevity of the Twayne "English Authors" series. He begins with a useful chronology of Pepys's life, but the bulk of his text is taken up with evoking the many facets of Pepys's daily life which the *Diary* reveals: Pepys at the Coronation of Charles II; at his music; at the theatre; with his ladies (as well as his wife); and Pepys at the office. He emphasises the teeming variousness of the *Diary*, Pepys's skill as a narrator, his pleasure in the poetry of the quotidian commonplace, and the infectious gusto with which Pepys recounts the zestful day he has already lived.

LATHAM and MATTHEWS's magisterial 11-volume edition of the *Diary* is essential reading for all students of Pepys. Theirs is the first complete transcription of everything Pepys wrote for posterity, including the many descriptions of his sexual indiscretions, and which all previous editions of the *Diary* had censored. Since the completion of the *Diary* itself, Latham has published *The Illustrated Pepys* and *The Shorter Pepys*. These offer a taste of the *Diary*'s variety, with extended extracts from Pepys's unforgettable accounts of the Plague of 1665 and the Great Fire of 1666. Volume 10 of the complete *Diary* is a companion, with entries on Pepys's life, associates, his times and its customs. An extensive introduction to the first volume surveys Pepys's life, describes in exhaustive detail the physical nature of the original *Diary*, and gives the standard account of its importance as an historical, as well as a literary, text. Latham and Matthews emphasise the fullness of Pepys's evocation of his life, myriad details recorded in a style that approximates Restoration speech. Most importantly they highlight the *deliberate* nature of Pepys's achievement; entries were frequently worked up from rough notes, a cunning artistic simulation of improvised recollection. Moreover, the *Diary* was preserved for the benefit of future readers, consciously created thus as confidantes for the prurient and industrious Pepys. The *Diary* stands then as a great, but far-from-accidental, work of art.

OLLARD's is the best one-volume biography available, less fulsome than Bryant's, but with a sharp epigrammatic wit of its own. A second edition (1990) is sumptuously illustrated with resonant Restoration portraits and scene paintings. Ollard exploits the resources of the complete Latham and Matthews *Diary*; he also abandons the modesty of previous biographers. He sees Pepys's life as a whole as a work of art, as having the shapeliness we have learnt to call self-fashioning. The *Diary* in his eyes becomes a synoptic version of this crafted life: "the Diary is a great work, as literature, as history, as a psychological document and as a key to what has been known as the English character in an age of national cultures perhaps soon to become extinct". Ollard's is the most attractive introduction to the man as well as his text.

Deconstructors have followed in Ollard's wake. BARKER furiously attacks Pepys as an archetypal bourgeois subject – "a typical man. A bourgeois man. Riven by guilt, silence, and textuality" – repressing even in his hidden *Diary* his baser urges. Beneath Pepys's vivacity, in Barker's post-Freudian "outing", can be seen a timid puritan soul, its loneliness proof that the "scene of writing and of reading is, like the grave, a private place". Deliberately outrageous and insulting, Barker's is the most provocative piece of modern Pepys criticism. Less adroit is BROME's character assassination, presenting Pepys as coward, wife beater, hypocrite, toady, and corrupt official. Surprisingly the *Diary* survives this onslaught; the silent receiver of obsessive confessions, it combines "skill normally attributed to a novelist with a concern for factual truth-telling". Brome usefully summarises Latham and Matthews, but has nothing much beyond this to offer. Equally spirited, SPENDER's pastiche is more original. She highlights Pepys's callous treatment of his wife, his meanness, and his pathological jealousy. More importantly, she imagines Elizabeth Pepys diarising before her husband did. Her scribbling thus provokes his. One of the great (and most original) masculine texts of the seventeenth century turns out to be feminist. Spender popularises recent feminist archaeology of seventeenth-century woman writers, on whom she has based her fictional entries; and her dialogue with the *Diary* itself provides a spirited, questioning voice to put beside Pepys's endless but admittedly self-regarding flow.

MARK HOULAHAN

Performance Theory *see* Drama: Theory

Philips, Katherine 1632–1664

English poet and translator

Andreadis, Harriette, "The Sapphic-Platonics of Katherine Philips, 1632–1664", in *Signs*, 15(1), 1989
Hageman, Elizabeth, "The Matchless Orinda", in *Women Writers of the Renaissance and Reformation*, edited by Katherine Wilson, Athens: University of Georgia Press, 1987
Hobby, Elaine, *Virtue of Necessity: English Women's Writing 1649–88*, London: Virago, 1988; Ann Arbor: University of Michigan Press, 1988
Hobby, Elaine, "Katherine Philips: Seventeenth Century Lesbian Poet", in *What Lesbians Do in Books*, edited by Hobby and Chris White, London: Womens Press, 1991
Souers, Philip, *The Matchless Orinda*, Cambridge, Massachusetts: Harvard University Press, 1931
Thomas, Patrick, *Katherine Philips ("Orinda")*, Cardiff: University of Wales Press, 1988

Katherine Philips – often referred to by her *persona*, "Orinda" – has only recently begun to attract serious critical attention. Most of the useful critical material on her work is to be found in journals and extended essays; as with many early-modern women writers, there is no recent full-length critical study.

SOUERS' 1931 book is a full-length, biographically-based work, valuing Philips' poetry for "the vivid and agreeable picture which she has drawn of herself, a picture of an interesting personality who lived in an interesting and romantic age". Souers is more concerned with Philips' life, her family and literary connections, and her post-Restoration public poems than her earlier, "friendship" poems. He takes the idea of a society of friendship literally, condemning it as "an extravagance which was excusable only on the score of youth". Souers is often lukewarm, or worse, about Philips' work; her great success, *Pompey*, "is lacking in poetical quality" but "not contemptible". She is of interest chiefly for her keeping the courtly mode alive during the Cromwellian period. While Souers is an informative guide to Philips' life (and so much of her poetry is occasional that this knowledge is indispensable), his evident contempt for much of her poetry, and his insensitivity to Philips' position as a woman writer often isolated both politically and geographically, make this book too simplistic in its judgements to be much use as a work of criticism.

HAGEMAN's essay and selection of Philips' poems places her writing much more firmly in the context of the various genres she used – pastoral, elegy, epitaph, epithalamion, poems of wooing and parting – than of the occasions giving rise to individual works. Following a point made by Souers, she examines Philips' use of John Donne's poetry, and her application of its conventions to female friendship. In re-emphasising the stimulus given Philips' writing by other writers, Hageman presents her as an original and intelligent poet, whose work, when it was publicised, was commercially successful. This introductory overview revalues Philips as a poet, while also drawing attention to her original use of existing modes.

THOMAS's short book follows Souers' strategy in narrating Philips' life and treating the poetry in chronological order. It is strongest when detailing reactions to Philips' poetry, both before and after her death, but restricts itself to an overview of Philips' main characteristics as a writer rather than commenting in depth on her work. Thomas traces Philips' creation of a Platonic world of friendship as a reaction to the "chaotic Interregnum years", and her adoption of the heroic public mode on the Restoration as a reaction to her husband's precarious position as a former Cromwellian. While Thomas succeeds in showing how her poetry could be part of complex negotiations of political and social dangers, his approach does tend to reproduce Souers' view of Philips as primarily a Royalist poet, and gives little space to the equally complex negotiations faced by a woman engaged in writing. The book's narrative focus (it is part of a series on Welsh writers) enables a clear picture to emerge of Philips' poetic development; but this is at the cost of a serious critical engagement with the critical issues her poetry raises.

HOBBY's section on Philips in her 1988 book seeks to show how the "Orinda" persona of modern critical accounts – unconcerned with publication, "dabbling with versification in a rural Welsh backwater" – ignores the typical courtly preference for circulating poems in manuscript, and Philips' position as the Royalist wife of a leading Parliamentarian. She seeks to show her as a serious, and well-known, poet in her chosen Royalist literary circle. Philips' letters, a primary source of this image, are shown to be both contradicted by her actions, and bound by conventions of what a woman could assert. Philips' use of the courtly-lover *persona* (previously almost entirely a male preserve) marks an attempt to find a free space amid the double disempowerment of being a Royalist among Parliamentarians, and a woman subject legally to a husband.

Hobby's feminist approach to Philips' attempt to construct in her writings a "space of autonomy for herself and her female friends" registers both Philips' achievement as a poet, and the response in her work to the gendered limitations of women's lives and writing.

ANDREADIS's article traces Philips' contemporary reputation to her "unique manipulation of the conventions of male poetic discourse", particularly the work of Donne and the Cavalier poets of platonic heterosexual love, but states that this originality was driven by "important personal needs" rather than a desire to court success. Philips' passionate attachments to her female friends are both expressed and masked by her use of these poetic conventions. Andreadis reads Philips' letters as giving direct access to her feelings, and as confirming her love for Lucasia and Rosania. She then proposes Philips' poetry as lesbian texts "insofar as they convey an experience of passion or eroticism that expresses 'libidinous energy', whether or not it includes verifiable experience of genital activity". Philips' use of poetic conventions to give shape to these passions is necessary to make them acceptable to herself and others. Andreadis' article engages closely with Philips' poetry in its appropriation of Donne's passionate-lover *persona*, assuming that this *persona* reflects a real passion; that this point is not argued through is a weakness in an otherwise valuable contribution to the location of lesbians in relation to early-modern culture.

HOBBY's 1991 chapter expands her passing reference to lesbian love in her earlier work on Philips. In it she demonstrates that "women's desire for women was thinkable" in seventeenth-century England, before reading Philips' "'closetedness' about sexuality" as consistent with the coded Royalism of her poetry. Just as, in *Orinda to Lucasia*, pastoral hid politics, so too the Platonic or courtly-love conventions could encode lesbian desire, while leaving it possible for readers to miss both the politics and the desire. Philips' concern with "what it means to form relationships within threatening and powerful constraints" is also consistent with lesbian identity. Hobby clearly locates this identity as involving sexual desire rather than an asexual "passion", through a reading of Philips' puns on "death", and through her rewriting of the heterosexual desire of poetic tradition into images of mirroring and mutuality. Her chapter is more accessible and closely argued than Andreadis' article, and is a clear introduction to this aspect of Philips' poetry.

STEPHEN LONGSTAFFE

The Picturesque *see* Landscape and Literature, Literary Aesthetics: Romantic

Pinter, Harold 1930–

English dramatist, screenwriter, and poet

Almansi, Guido, and Simon Henderson, *Harold Pinter*, London and New York: Methuen, 1983

Baker, William, and Stephen Ely Tabachnick, *Harold Pinter*, Edinburgh: Oliver & Boyd, 1973

Burkman, Katherine H., *The Dramatic World of Harold Pinter: Its Basis in Ritual*, Columbus: Ohio State University Press, 1971

Burkman, Katherine H., and John L. Kundert-Gibbs (eds.), *Pinter at Sixty*, Bloomington: Indiana University Press, 1993

Burton, Deirdre, *Dialogue and Discourse: A Sociolinguistic Approach to Modern Drama Dialogue and Naturally Occurring Conversation*, London: Routledge & Kegan Paul, 1980

Diamond, Elin, *Pinter's Comic Play*, Lewisburg, Pennsylvania: Bucknell University Press, 1985; London: Associated University Presses, 1985

Esslin, Martin, *The Peopled Wound: The Plays of Harold Pinter*, London: Methuen, 1970; New York: Doubleday, 1970; 2nd, revised edition, as *Pinter: A Study of His Plays*, London (Methuen) and New York (Norton), 1973; 3rd and 4th revised editions, both as *Pinter the Playwright*, London: Methuen, 1982, 1984

Gabbard, Lucina Paquet, *The Dream Structure of Pinter's Plays: A Psychoanalytic Approach*, Rutherford, New Jersey: Fairleigh Dickinson University Press, 1976; London: Associated University Presses, 1976

Gordon, Lois G., *Stratagems to Uncover Nakedness: The Dramas of Harold Pinter*, Columbia: University of Missouri Press, 1969

Merritt, Susan Hollis, *Pinter in Play: Critical Strategies and the Plays of Harold Pinter*, Durham, North Carolina: Duke University Press, 1990

Page, Malcolm (ed.), *File on Pinter*, London: Methuen, 1993

Quigley, Austin E., *The Pinter Problem*, Princeton, New Jersey: Princeton University Press, 1975

Sakellaridou, Elizabeth, *Pinter's Female Portraits: A Portrait of Female Characters in the Plays of Harold Pinter*, London: Macmillan, 1988; Totowa, New Jersey: Barnes & Noble, 1988

Thompson, David T., *Pinter: The Player's Playwright*, London: Macmillan, 1985

Harold Pinter is the subject of an ever-increasing critical industry, deploying a very wide range of critical stances in order to try to understand the plays. One of the key issues of Pinter criticism has always been the sense that, as Pinter himself put it in a 1962 speech, "below the word spoken is the thing known and unspoken". As Merritt shows, many critics have attempted to find a single key to explain the underlying mystery and to make explicit the unspoken, using whatever tools have seemed the most appropriate. The works chosen here have been selected not only for their intrinsic worth, but also with the aim of conveying some idea of the diversity of that body of material and indicating some of the main lines of inquiry.

Page and Merritt offer very useful maps of the territory. Although it is very brief, PAGE is the best guide to the facts of Pinter's career. It includes a chronology of Pinter's career and a short compilation of details of first and subsequent major productions, together with brief critical extracts on the plays, film scripts, and other writings, rounded off with a section on "The Writer on His Work". MERRITT offers a much more complex account of Pinter criticism, divided into sections on critics who have approached Pinter through, respectively, "themes and techniques, rituals and games, and fantasies and dreams (mostly psychological or psychoanalytic figures)"; "language, structure, and comedy"; and "social and sexual relations". Her lengthy accounts of the strategies and rhetorical positions of critics constitute not only a very useful guide to the variety of approaches, but a sustained meditation on the nature of the critical project in its various manifestations. It is a sophisticated and illuminating reading of the strengths and weaknesses of a great range of critical positions, that pays due attention to the importance of journalistic critics in creating Pinter's reputation.

Early studies of Pinter laid down lines of inquiry that are still being pursued. ESSLIN, who had initially treated Pinter in *The Theatre of the Absurd* (1961) as one of its "Parallels and Proselytes", offers plot summaries, followed by interpretations based on a slightly reductive, loosely Freudian, psychological reading of the characters and plays, but his study remains, in its various versions, an important influence on Pinter criticism. GORDON anticipated Esslin with the first full-length Freudian analysis of Pinter's works, and her use of Eric Berne's transactional analysis was also significant, since it paved the way for later work directly influenced by formal linguistics. GABBARD developed the psychoanalytical approach to Pinter with a comprehensive reading of the plays up to *No Man's Land*. She is particularly concerned with reading them as Freudian psychoanalysis reads dreams. It is a useful pioneering study, but needs to be read carefully in view of recent developments in post-Lacanian Freudian criticism.

Other broadly psychological readings concentrate on specific aspects of Pinter's output. BAKER and TABACHNICK concentrate on the Jewish elements in Pinter's work. Their argument is that he "achieves universality through a ruthless application of the particular and the personal", but their exhaustive search for Jewish nuances can sometimes be reductive rather than illuminating. SAKELLARIDOU offers the first full-length study of Pinter's dramatic presentation of women, following archetypal critical lines; although she notes the absence of women as protagonists, or even as characters, in many of Pinter's plays, Sakellaridou argues, not entirely convincingly, that he has moved away from an initial sexism towards a much more androgynous approach. BURKMAN's key, as her title suggests, is the discovery of ritual patterns in Pinter's work, particularly seasonal and fertility rituals involving scapegoats, and the death of the old king. She is heavily influenced by James Frazer's *The Golden Bough* and by Gilbert Murray. The problem with all such readings is their tendency to insist on their exclusive claims to explain every aspect of Pinter's work.

Another important line of critical development stems from Irving Wardle's 1958 description of *The Birthday Party* as a "Comedy of Menace". Although Wardle soon repudiated the term, its apparent aptness has resulted in it being applied and developed by other critics concerned with the formal and generic aspects of Pinter's achievement. DIAMOND examines the ways in which Pinter draws, often parodically, on a wide range of existing forms and styles, both traditional and contemporary, in an analysis of his comedic strategies which shows how he uses a "manipulation of traditional comedy as a means of positioning and ultimately destabilizing his audience". THOMPSON uses his knowledge of Pinter's early acting career and the plays he appeared in to demonstrate some of the ways in which he used and developed some of his characteristic stylistic and plot elements from the thrillers and other repertory staples of his early years as an actor.

Many critics have drawn attention to Pinter's characteristic use of language, but QUIGLEY's important study takes many of the looser critical formulations and reformulates them in stricter terms, applying insights from linguistics derived from M.A.K. Halliday, among others. This has proved a fruitful line of inquiry, mainly in essays and in BURTON, which takes Pinter as an exemplary case study.

ALMANSI and HENDERSON offer a broadly postmodernist reading of Pinter as a games player whose plays are designed to resist explanation: earlier critics searched for an underlying structure that would explain the apparently incomprehensible, but for Almansi and Henderson the plays are precisely vehicles for the creation of "bafflement, irritation, fear, a general sense of impotence, feelings of helplessness, a seething resentment, an acrid hostility".

Pinter has tended to be seen as a non-political writer, particularly by those who have wished to use him as a stick with which to beat other more overtly committed writers. So the politically concerned plays of the 1980s pose a challenge to settled critical debates by introducing a new frame of reference. One of the key elements here is Pinter's interview with Nick Hern in an edition of the playwright's *One for the Road* (London: Methuen, 1985). Most recent books give this new development some consideration, but it has clearly upset some well-established critical assumptions about Pinter, to the point that a whole section of BURKMAN and KUNDERT-GIBBS is devoted to "Political Pinter".

TREVOR R. GRIFFITHS

Plath, Sylvia 1932–1963

American poet and novelist

Axelrod, Steven Gould, *Sylvia Plath: The Wound and the Cure of Words*, Baltimore: Johns Hopkins University Press, 1990
Bassnett, Susan, *Sylvia Plath*, London: Macmillan, 1987
Butscher, Edward, *Sylvia Plath: Method and Madness*, New York: Seabury Press, 1976
Macpherson, Pat, *Reflecting on "The Bell Jar"*, London and New York: Routledge, 1991
Markey, Janice, *A Journey into the Red Eye: The Poetry of Sylvia Plath – A Critique*, London: Women's Press, 1993
Rose, Jacqueline, *The Haunting of Sylvia Plath*, London: Virago, 1991; Cambridge, Massachusetts: Harvard University Press, 1992
Wagner-Martin, Linda, *"The Bell Jar": A Novel of the Fifties*, New York: Twayne, 1992

Sylvia Plath provides a particularly vivid example of the ways in which literary texts have tended to be interpreted in the light of the biography of their author. The voyeuristic speculation surrounding her failed marriage to Ted Hughes, her intermittently unstable mental state, and the final period of feverish and brilliant artistic productivity, which ended in her suicide at the age of 30 have prompted many readers to approach her work with the grim smile of dramatic irony. From the apparently elevated position of hindsight, many critics have judged her work to be "about" anguish and despair, offering documentary evidence of the author's tragic trajectory towards suicide. This type of approach places a highly restrictive frame on Plath's work, limiting its appeal and eliding its wit, energy, subtlety, and stylistic inventiveness. However, the late 1980s and early 1990s have seen the emergence of a number of critical studies that offer positive and creative departures from these traditional critical techniques and emphases.

BUTSCHER's 1976 study introduces itself as a "critical biography", and seems to epitomize many of the problems associated with author-centred readings of literary texts. Butscher reads Plath's work in conjunction with her life, conflating the aims and strategies of literary criticism and literary biography. The speakers of Plath's poetry and prose are almost invariably identified as Plath herself. Reading a poem is assumed to provide a "window" onto the writer's experience, while studying biography is supposed to provide "insight" into the writer's work. Viewed in this light, the project of the critical biography may be seen as somewhat circular, self-generating, and self-justifying.

If Butscher reads Plath's work as the relatively narrow expression of the pathology of its author, then MARKEY provides a stark contrast to this approach. She argues that Plath is aggressively and confidently defiant of the conventions and hypocrisies of British and American culture in the 1950s and 1960s, and that she offers "a vision of compassion and sanity" in the face of an increasingly technological, bureaucratic, and consumerist society. Plath's work is thus located within "a great moralist tradition". Gender stereotypes, romantic love, and Christianity are all identified as targets of its satire. Markey presents controversial readings of several of the well-known poems, effectively cutting through many of the accumulated clichés of traditional Plath criticism.

MACPHERSON's study of Plath's novel, *The Bell Jar*, also offers an analysis that situates Plath's writing within its specific cultural and historical context. Macpherson provides an extremely readable and informative account of an American postwar society dominated by figures such as Senator Joseph McCarthy and J. Edgar Hoover, and a regime of "social hygiene". Restrictive norms of mental "health", gender alignment, and political and sexual conformity were generated and enforced. As Macpherson points out, the opening pages of *The Bell Jar* are haunted by the execution of the Rosenbergs: in this way the novel immediately confronts the reader with the specific events and anxieties of its contemporary political climate. Macpherson analyses Plath's response to issues such as the "us and them" mentality of Cold-War paranoia, the widely accepted misogyny of the time, the confinement of women to the roles of housewife and mother, and the stifling morality, which vilified homosexuality and lesbianism and condemned any expression of sexuality outside the marriage bed.

WAGNER-MARTIN's "reader's companion" also opens with an interesting and accessible analysis of *The Bell Jar* as both product and critique of 1950s' America. Furthermore, it provides a useful account of the novel's critical reception, and a detailed exploration of how it might be classified and interpreted in terms of genre. *The Bell Jar*, Wagner-Martin argues, is a feminine adaptation of various traditionally masculine literary forms, such as the *Bildungsroman* and the quest novel – but also draws on, and subverts, the traditionally feminine domestic or marriage novel with its romantic love plot. In these ways Wagner-Martin's book explores both formal and thematic issues, drawing out both the literary and the socio-political references of the text.

AXELROD offers the reader "a biography of the imagination" – a study which might be seen as a theoretically sophisticated version of Butscher's critical biography. Rather than seeking to "know" Plath "through" her texts, Axelrod sets out to read Plath's psyche *as* a text. Working within a Freudian idiom, he (psycho)analyses the relationships between Plath, her mother, her father, and her husband – as represented in the various available texts. Axelrod also explores Plath's problematic relationship to her *literary* fathers, such as Chaucer, Shakespeare, and William Blake, and her attempts, as a woman writer, to "think back" through literary mothers such as Emily Dickinson and Virginia Woolf.

BASSNETT's book is published in the Macmillan "Women Writers" series. In response to the demands of this format, it is a relatively brief and very accessible analysis, providing a lucid and innovative introduction to the study of Plath's work. Rather than focusing on this work as simply an expression of the author's suffering, she concentrates on its enabling aspects, reading it as a multifaceted exploration of struggle and survival. She examines, for example, Plath's representations of motherhood, the family, love, God, Nature, and writing – and ends with a fascinating investigation of the ways in that Plath has functioned as a muse for other women and other writers.

ROSE's study of Plath offers a theoretically challenging and intriguing analysis of the various critical positions which have been taken up in relation to Plath. Rose focuses with great insight and rigour on the ways in which the figure of "Sylvia Plath" has been constructed and contested by literary criticism. She sets out to analyse the violent and polarized reactions generated by Plath's life and work, and what these reactions might reveal about the implicit assumptions and investments of various critical approaches. She also makes a strong case for the radical potential of Plath's work, reading it in the light of (post)Freudian psychoanalysis. Rose provides fascinating discussions of the editing and censorship of Plath's work, her "shameless" relationship with popular culture, and her controversial use of Holocaust imagery.

ANNA TRIPP

Poe, Edgar Allan 1809–1849

American short-story writer, poet, and essayist

Bloom, Harold (ed.), *Edgar Allan Poe*, New York: Chelsea House, 1985

Bloom, Harold (ed.), *The Tales of Poe*, New York: Chelsea House, 1987

Bonaparte, Marie, *The Life and Works of Edgar Allan Poe: A Psycho-Analytic Interpretation*, translated by John Rodker, London: Imago, 1949; New York: Humanities Press, 1971

Hoffman, Daniel, *Poe Poe Poe Poe Poe Poe Poe*, Garden City, New York: Doubleday, 1972; London: Robson Books, 1973

Lawrence, D.H., *Studies in Classic American Literature*, New York: Thomas Seltzer, 1923, and subsequent reprints; London: Martin Secker, 1924, and subsequent reprints

Lee, Robert A. (ed.), *Edgar Allan Poe: The Design of Order*, London: Vision Press, 1987; Totowa, New Jersey: Barnes & Noble, 1987

Muller, John P., and William J. Richardson, *The Purloined Poe: Lacan, Derrida and Psychoanalytic Reading*, Baltimore: Johns Hopkins University Press, 1988

Silverman, Kenneth, *Edgar A. Poe: Mournful and Never-Ending Remembrance*, New York: Harper Collins, 1991; London: Weidenfeld & Nicolson, 1992

Silverman, Kenneth (ed.), *New Essays on Poe's Major Tales*, Cambridge and New York: Cambridge University Press, 1993

Williams, Michael J.S., *A World of Words: Language and Displacement in the Fiction of Edgar Allan Poe*, Durham, North Carolina: Duke University Press, 1988

Few writers in American literary history have inspired such wildly antithetical critical responses as Edgar Allan Poe. While it would be a generalisation to suggest that these opinions divide exclusively upon geographical lines, it is noticeable that Poe's writing has been met with considerably more enthusiasm outside his homeland than within it. Many of Poe's most ardent detractors have been American writers and academics. Henry James once famously declared that "an enthusiasm for Poe is the mark of a decidedly primitive stage of reflection". In a similar vein, T.S. Eliot's judgement on Poe was that he possessed "the intellect of a highly gifted young person before puberty". Influential voices within the American academic establishment have often concurred with these negative appraisals. In his *American Renaissance* (1941), F.O. Matthiessen excluded Poe from his canon of nineteenth-century American writing on the grounds that his writing was "factitious" and "hostile to democracy". More recently, Harold Bloom has been unable to stifle his aversion to Poe's stylistic deficiencies and intellectual under-development, even while editing two major collections of essays on his work.

Outside America reactions to Poe have generally been more favourable. The locus of appreciation in this respect has been, and continues to be, France. Initially the banner was carried by distinguished Gallic poets, including Charles Baudelaire, Stéphane Mallarmé, and Paul Valéry, who championed "Edgarpoe" as an estranged cousin and *poète maudit*. Subsequently Poe's work has been thrown into the limelight by the attentions of French scholars, including Marie Bonaparte, Jacques Lacan, and Jacques Derrida. Notwithstanding Aldous Huxley's mischievous suggestion that Poe's popularity was restricted to those for whom English was not a first language, the first important point to recognize about Poe criticism is that it gravitates towards excesses reminiscent of the writer's *oeuvre*. The impressive range of materials within the Poe canon (short stories, a novel, poetry, philosophy, and criticism) has spawned an equally vast range of academic responses. Not surprisingly, given the nature of his thematic preoccupations, a large number of these responses have been heavily indebted to psychoanalytical theory. Critics have often responded to Poe's work as explorations and/or expressions of various pathologies. The texts listed below are offered as a representative sample of "classic" surveys and well thought-of recent contributions to Poe scholarship.

LAWRENCE's reading of Poe's work reveals as much about the Nottinghamshire writer's own idiosyncratic worldview as it does about the subject under consideration. Lawrence condemns Poe for his "pride of human conceit in KNOWLEDGE", and translates his *oeuvre* into a manifesto for figurative vampirism. At the same time he concedes that Poe's work has an intense power and fascination. Given that this piece has become a touchstone for a number of subsequent critics, it is well worth exploring.

Between late nineteenth-century poets and twentieth-century poststructuralists, the figure who did most to maintain Poe's high profile in French academia is BONAPARTE. Her mammoth 700-page study has all of the strengths and weaknesses of classical Freudian literary analysis. Bonaparte founds her reading of Poe's life and work upon the contention that the writer experienced incestuous desires as a child on seeing his mother's corpse. Without attempting to substantiate this claim (a forlorn task since there is no tangible evidence to support it) Bonaparte proceeds to analyse each aspect of Poe's career in relation to this determining moment in his psychological development. Despite, or perhaps because of, the reductive simplicities of Bonaparte's thesis, this line of interpretation has become a commonplace of Poe criticism. In the process of her filtering of the Poe canon through Freudian orthodoxy, however, she frequently minimises the significance of contemporary historical and literary influences, and of Poe's consciousness as a writer, and she marginalizes any textual details that threaten her central thesis. Regardless of one's opinion of its efficacy, and given its impact and centrality in the field, Bonaparte's work ought to be taken seriously by all readers who wish to take Poe seriously.

HOFFMAN's volume, as the title intimates, is an eccentric and inventive addition to the field. As a poet himself, Hoffman employs a flamboyant and unconventional style, which is stimulating and excessively ingenious in approximately equal measures. He adopts a broadly psychoanalytical approach, in conjunction with personal anecdote and stylistic ornamentation. He offers an extended commentary on Poe's verse, its practice and its theory, his philosophy as expounded in *Eureka*, and the tales, including some of those less frequently commented on. Almost certainly there is a much here that readers will find exaggerated, obscure, and indulgent. But Hoffman's readings frequently produce the kind of productive disagreement that more conventional offerings rarely inspire. What comes across most of all in this study, and threatens to redeem it, is the sheer intensity of Hoffman's passion for Poe's writing. Overall, this book is as extravagant as it is suggestive, and constitutes an excellent starting-point for the reader new to Poe scholarship.

The collection of essays compiled by SILVERMAN represents an accessible introduction to Poe's major tales. Most of the essays are confined to the mainstays of Poe scholarship. There are readings of: "emotional dynamics" in "The Tell-Tale Heart" and "The Black Cat"; "symbolism" and "morality" in

"The Fall of the House of Usher"; "truth" in the Dupin tales; and "misogyny" in "Ligeia" and the "Dark Lady" tales. One significant and stimulating exception to this general trend is David Reynolds' reading of "The Cask of Amontillado". From a New-Historicist perspective, Reynolds takes the unusual step of not translating the text into a psychological or philosophical case study, but instead relates its details to cultural context. Reynolds argues convincingly that in writing for a mass audience Poe fed off contemporary cultural anxieties associated with alcoholism, Masonry, and Catholicism. Silverman's collection offers a sound starting-point for anyone unfamiliar with criticism of Poe's gothic tales.

Bloom has edited two collections of essays on Poe. BLOOM 1985 brings together, in the chronological sequence of their original publication between 1927 and 1984, a number of influential readings of *Eureka*, *The Narrative of Arthur Gordon Pym of Nantucket*, and the tales. Shoshana Felman's contribution is worth particular mention for its spirited defence of Poe's standing as a poet, alongside its assessment of the "limits and possibilities" of psychoanalytical approaches to his writing (specifically in relation to works by Krutch, Bonaparte, and Lacan). BLOOM 1987 is a collection of more recently published materials, which offers close readings of the "major" tales. The analysis in this volume tends to focus on the same texts as those covered in Silverman's collection (with especial concentration on "The Fall of the House of Usher" and "Ligeia"), but with a marginally higher degree of theoretical sophistication and self-consciousness.

LEE has compiled a stimulating collection of original essays, which explores a range of materials from the Poe canon with considerable verve. Intricate close readings of specific tales and *Pym* are complemented by more wide-ranging investigations of Poe's humour, the significance of his relation to the South, and his mythologisation in France. Eric Mottram makes a convincing case for reading Poe as a writer who both reflected and deepened the cracks in the American Republic that others were attempting to paper over with codes of civil and political law.

MULLER and RICHARDSON's volume represents a comprehensive guide to the encounter between Poe and post-structuralism. This encounter was initiated by the French psychoanalyst Jacques Lacan when, in 1956, he proposed a radically new model of psychoanalysis that was based on a reading of Poe's detective story "The Purloined Letter". In his reading Lacan focused on relationships between characters, the nature of the letter, and the significance of "lost objects" in the tale. In the process he advanced a number of extremely sophisticated and innovative ideas about inter-subjectivity, signification, and the relationship between loss, memory, repetition, and what Freud termed the "death instinct". Lacan also offered definitions of language and truth that contradicted the orthodoxies of contemporary literary theory. Almost two decades later, in 1975, the gauntlet thrown down by Lacan was picked up by his compatriot Jacques Derrida. In an article entitled "Le Facteur de la vérité", Derrida developed a detailed and equally sophisticated critique of the Lacanian thesis. Subsequently, this article itself spawned a series of critical essays, and Poe's tale found itself at the heart of a maelstrom of theoretical debates concerning subjectivity and signification. Muller and Richardson's study brings together the key texts in this debate, including the "The Purloined Letter" itself, the readings of it offered by Lacan and Derrida, a selection of essays that both refer to and supplement these readings, and some useful commentary by the editors. For those readers hostile to poststructuralist and psychoanalytical theory, the title of this volume will appear entirely apt and unintentionally ironic: the manner in which the third story in the Dupin collection has been lifted from the realm of traditional Poe criticism and "lost" in the midst of current critical debates may strike some as reminiscent of the crime on which "The Purloined Letter" is based! For those with the pre-requisite knowledge of, and inclination towards, poststructuralism and psychoanalytic approaches, this is, however, an indispensable volume.

WILLIAMS offers his study as an exploration of the ways in which Poe's texts "examine and reflect on the nature of their own signifying practices – that is, with the degree to which language itself is a topic of those texts". In the opening sections, Williams argues that Poe's poetics anticipate twentieth-century accounts of semiotics and subjectivity; in particular he suggests that Poe's writing prefigures the notion of the arbitrary nature of the sign and the contemporary challenge to the idea of a stable and unified self at the centre of experience. Williams reads Poe's tales in the light of his thesis, and emphasises their challenge to worldviews established on the assumption of centred selves and logocentrism: "[Poe] exposes the futility and necessary failure of idealist attempts to evade the radical displacements inherent in the use of language". This study represents one of the more accessible applications of poststructuralist theory to Poe's writing. Williams largely resists the temptation to indulge in arcane verbal confectionery and excessive displays of interpretative ingenuity, though, like much of the criticism in this field, the "radicalism" of poststructuralism's own orthodoxies is rather taken for granted. However, Williams is more concerned than some poststructuralists to ground his propositions in textual detail.

Given the frequency with which Poe critics use biographical information to interpret his texts (and vice versa), a detailed knowledge of Poe's personal history can be extremely useful. SILVERMAN's relatively recent biography (1991) offers a thoroughly researched and sensibly organized account of the major phases and figures in the author's life. This comprehensive and scholarly survey largely resists lapsing into an excessive Poe "mystique", while at the same time confirming the cliché that the writer's life, in certain respects, resembled one of his own bizarre tales.

BRIAN JARVIS

Poetry: Theory

Barfield, Owen, *Poetic Diction: A Study in Meaning*, London: Faber & Faber, 1928, 2nd edition, 1953; Middletown, Connecticut: Wesleyan University Press, 1973

Davie, Donald, *Purity of Diction in English Verse*, London: Chatto & Windus, 1952; New York: Oxford University Press, 1953; new edition, London: Routledge & Kegan Paul, 1967

Easthope, Antony, *Poetry as Discourse*, London and New York: Methuen, 1983

Empson, William, *The Structure of Complex Words*, London: Chatto & Windus, 1951, 2nd edition, 1952; New York: New Directions, 1951; reprinted, Cambridge, Massachusetts: Harvard University Press, 1989

Frye, Northrop (ed.), *Sound and Poetry: English Institute Essays, 1956*, New York: Columbia University Press, 1957

Fussell, Paul, *Poetic Meter and Poetic Form*, New York: Random House, 1965, revised 1979

McAuley, James, *Versification: A Short Introduction*, East Lansing: Michigan State University Press, 1966

Wesling, Donald, *The Chances of Rhyme: Device and Modernity*, Berkeley: University of California Press, 1980

The attempt to differentiate form from content, aesthetics from epistemology, has dominated twentieth-century textual and stylistic criticism and the prosodic study of poetic language. The question of word meaning – or the semantics of poetic diction – alongside rhetorical and formal structure has been prominent in recent critical studies, and is therefore the main focus of the works to be considered below.

BARFIELD's influential study of poetic diction, first appearing in 1928, presents an historical, philological overview of poetic language from the earliest European societies to modernity. This book charts a shift from concrete to abstract thinking in the evolution of European consciousness, with poetic diction registering this shift in the change from a figurative, mythopoeic "origin" via metaphor to a logical, abstract prosaic diction. Archaic words, according to Barfield, possessed a total, integral meaning that was unconscious and prior to the transference of metaphor and logical abstraction. Barfield's semantic theory is thus intimately linked to a primitivist psychology of the poetic imagination.

DAVIE's reading of late eighteenth-century poetic diction offers an empiricist critique of "impure" or ambiguous poetic language from rationalist and moralistic premises. "Purity" of diction is equated with moral sympathy, and discrete inner scruple narrowed down to social adaptability, responsibility, and taste. In the same way, a "chaste" diction derives from restraint and propriety in the use of metaphor; strength of poetic statement derives from a civilised urbanity and discriminate taste; and decadence in poetic diction derives from aestheticism, intellectual ingenuity, and individualistic expressionism. Davie's theorisations of poetic diction in terms of moral and psychological common sense thus links avant-garde innovation with a decadent aestheticism.

EASTHOPE's discourse-analysis of English poetry since the Renaissance defines poetry as a metric "foregrounding" of the materiality of language over and against the expressive elements of language. As such, the position adopted is formalistic rather than psychological or philological, with an emphasis being placed on linguistic concepts of signification and the ideological and aesthetic aspects of poetic representation. Easthope's primary historical argument is that English poetry since the Renaissance is co-terminous with bourgeois capitalism and thus represents a bourgeois poetic discourse. As such, the "poetic" is translated into hermeneutic categories derived from psychoanalysis, linguistics, and literary theory, which are, in turn, applied historically to discursive forms.

EMPSON's semantic interrogation of word meaning is more properly a collection of psychological and thematic insights into the emotive aspects of poetic diction. It also attempts to trace the exact difference between emotive and cognitive aspects of poetic language, and thereby to differentiate questions of aesthetic value from questions of poetic knowledge. Empson examines – using a variety of linguistic symbols – the combinations and habitual uses of words in a wide range of literary authors, including Shakespeare and William Wordsworth. What is not clear in this line of reasoning is whether the complex semantic structure of words in literary texts is the result of thematic ambiguity – and hence an example of aesthetic artifice and/or psychological insight – or whether they point to a more radical ambiguity between grammatical and figurative structure in language as a whole.

FRYE's collection involves close textual analyses of the chief characteristics of "musical poetry" – continuity and stress accent rather than assonance or metrical prosody. The scansion techniques employed in readings of works by Edmund Spenser, Milton, Shakespeare, and James Joyce, among others, are thus accentual, based on stress and rhythm, rather than on metrical divisions. The question of sound-patterns in poetry rather than complex meaning or ambiguity raises interesting possibilities for the study of rhythmic stress and orientates the collection as a whole.

FUSSELL's prosodic analysis of metrical structure refuses the rhetorical and linguistic in favour of forms of a more stylistic inquiry into the influence of poetic metre on meaning. The "metrical contract" between reader and poem should thus be understood using expressive metrical criteria such as variation, counterpoint, and substitution in so far as they contribute to the overall meaning-effect of the poem. Historically these criteria have been differentially weighted, with "freer" metrical forms coming into prominence in the twentieth-century. The formal implications of such metrical analysis are examined with reference to generic examples – sonnets and stanzaic forms – alongside an historical overview of the use of poetic devices in English poetry.

McAULEY's introduction to versification is, simultaneously, a formal and historical overview of accentual-syllabic verse in English poetry, and a study of the metrical variations and patterns that occur within accentual-syllabic form. Comparisons between metrical accent and speech stress as indicated by differing scansion techniques, and between speech sounds and versification, provide examples of historical shifts in poetic practice and critical understanding. A short glossary of technical terms also provides terminological clarification.

WESLING's discussion of Romantic and post-Romantic notions of rhyme presents a particular view of poetic history and aesthetic theories of poetic form in relation to the "intention" of poetry. This repeats the idea of an historicity of style, though a rather different history of rhyme from the above prosodic-versification accounts emerges. The wariness with rhyme in avant-garde texts of modernity is taken to denote a greater historical awareness of poetic convention in the context of other stylistic devices – an awareness that derives from an organicist poetics of the poem as object. This intriguing idea is discussed in relation to the break-up of formal rhetoric in

1795 and the rise of modernism (1919–45). However, this historical opposition inevitably raises questions of simplism, which the examples chosen do not answer.

D.S. MARRIOTT

Poetry: General

Attridge, Derek, *The Rhythms of English Poetry*, London: Longman, 1982
Bloom, Harold, *Poetry and Repression: Revisionism from Blake to Stevens*, New Haven, Connecticut, and London: Yale University Press, 1976
Brooks, Cleanth, *The Well Wrought Urn*, New York: Regnal & Hitchcock, 1947; London: Dennis Dobson, 1949, revised 1968
Easthope, Antony, *Poetry as Discourse*, London and New York: Methuen, 1983
Eliot, T.S., *On Poetry and Poets*, London: Faber & Faber, 1957; New York: Farrar, Straus, & Cudahy, 1957
Hollander, John, *Rhyme's Reason*, New Haven, Connecticut, and London: Yale University Press, 1981, revised 1989
Leavis, F.R., *Revaluation: Tradition and Development in English Poetry*, London: Chatto & Windus, 1936
Paulin, Tom, *Minotaur: Poetry and the Nation State*, London: Faber & Faber, 1992; Cambridge, Massachusetts: Harvard University Press, 1992
Ricks, Christopher, *The Force of Poetry*, Oxford: Clarendon Press, 1984; New York: Oxford University Press, 1984
Smith, Barbara Herrnstein, *Poetic Closure: A Study of How Poems End*, Chicago: University of Chicago Press, 1968

The books discussed here are considered on their own merits as introductions to various aspects of poetry in English, in general, rather than as constituting a thematic development (a development precluded by the very scope and diversity of poetry in English).

LEAVIS's study is ambitious in its scope: it spans three centuries, with chapters on "The Line of Wit" (Thomas Carew, Abraham Cowley, and Robert Herrick), "Milton's Verse", "Pope", "The Augustan Tradition" (Thomas Gray, James Thomson, Edmund Spenser etc.), "Wordsworth", "Shelley", and "Keats". His aim is stated clearly in the useful Introduction to the book: he wishes to focus on the structurality of poetry and "give as clearly as can be given without misleading simplification the main lines of development in the English tradition". This focus on historical figures takes its cue from Eliot's infamous 1919 essay "Tradition and the Individual Talent". Leavis paraphrases it in the introduction: "in dealing with individual poets the critic, whether explicitly or not, is dealing with tradition, for they live in it. And it is in them that tradition lives". Even though Leavis assures the reader in the Introduction that the book was conceived before the essays that compose the individual chapters, the study is a series of separate critical evaluations rather than a coherent thematic survey. Although Leavis's premises of "originality", "transcendence", and "genius", have been lambasted by recent theorists such as Roland Barthes, the book remains a good introduction to poetry because of the (albeit misguided) critical seriousness and sheer enthusiasm that he unleashes on the texts. The chapter on Milton is particularly interesting in the context of his "revaluation" in Paulin's study (see below): the poet is in Leavis denounced as "magniloquent", full of "impressive pomp", "callousness", and intolerable "booming swell".

BROOKS's study is a useful introduction because it is rigorous as well as entertaining: his playfulness is indicated in the titles of chapters, such as "The Motivation of Tennyson's Weeper", "Yeats's Great Rooted Blossomer", and "The Heresy of Paraphrase". He mirrors Leavis's introduction in the Preface by arguing that his book is not "a miscellaneous collection, but . . . a book with a defined objective and a deliberate plan". His premise is more accountable than Leavis's: Chapter 1 ("The Language of Paradox") sets up the methodology of the text: poetry is a genre heavily influenced by the linguistic phenomenon of paradox. The infamous close reading of John Donne's "The Canonisation" as a vacillation between profane and divine love is one of the most incisive accounts of the poem in Donne criticism, and Wordsworth's poetry is evaluated as that of paradoxical situations. The New-Critical symbol of the text as a "well wrought urn" able to transcend the limitations of contemporaneity seems, however, hopelessly outdated since the advent of poststructuralism. In Chapter 11, poems are (laughably) sacred bodies: "if we allow ourselves to be misled by the heresy of paraphrase, we run the risk of doing even more violence to the internal order of the poem itself".

ELIOT's book combines "classic" general essays, such as "The Social Function of Poetry" and "The Three Voices of Poetry", with studies on individual poets, such as "Virgil and the Christian World" and "Johnson as Critic and Poet". Eliot does not pretend that the individual chapters have an overall coherence: as he states in the Preface, all the essays are subsequent to his *Selected Essays*, and over half were written to be public addresses. The chapter entitled "The Function of Criticism" is especially interesting, as it attacks New Criticism as focusing on explication rather than "feeling" and understanding poems, and pre-empts Roland Barthes's "The Death of the Author" by judging the author to be virtually irrelevant to the appreciation of poetry.

SMITH's text, as the title suggests, is about how poems end. As the preface states, this is one of the first studies in this field of poetics. In the Introduction, she argues that closure must be analysed in the context of the poem as a whole: "the sense of conclusiveness . . . like the finality of the last chords of a sonata, seems to confirm retrospectively, as if with a final stamp of approval, the valued qualities of the entire experience we have just sustained". The third section of Chapter 5 ("Closure and Anti-Closure in Modern Poetry") is both illustrative of her methodology and prophetic if readers apply it to Hélène Cixous's concept of "loose" poetics in "The Laugh of the Medusa", and the Language poetry of the last two decades (see, for example, the work of the Canadian poet Daphne Marlatt).

BLOOM's "classic" text is learned, idiosyncratic, and theoretically unoriginal, despite the impressive-looking opening diagram, which proposes a "dialectic of revisionism". The key, but difficult, first chapter ("Poetry, Revisionism, Repression") offers an "original" way to look at poetry via Vico and Freud, but the concept of poems repressing language but retaining other things is gleaned from Saussurean linguistics. Indeed, Bloom is a structuralist: "we are studying a kind of labor that has its own latent principles, principles that can be uncovered and then taught systematically". He retains the idea of "genius" with his "Oedipal" model of poets writing against their predecessors (in which women writers, therefore, have no room for manoeuvre), but this is essentially a Freudian re-hash of Eliot's "Tradition and the Individual Talent". Bloom also echoes Brooks in his notion of readings as reductionism. He would have us believe the absurdity of a "poetic" text as a psychic battlefield rather than a collection of signs, and that "trope" is linked intrinsically to "entropy", when there is no etymological evidence to support his case. If readers wish to progress, there are chapters on "Blake and Revisionism", "Shelley and His Precursors", and "Keats: Romance Revised", among others.

HOLLANDER's brief but packed study is one of the best introductions to the formal aspects of poetry. Chapters include "Accentual Meters", "Pure Syllabic Verse", and "Aberrant Forms"; the titles are more daunting than the actual examples. Metre is a notoriously difficult subject to explain simply, and yet Hollander manages it with ease in the section on "Accentual-Syllabic Verse". He uses explanation to illustrate the technique, as in the lines below:

> Iámbic méter rúns alóng like thís
> Pentameters will have five syllables
> More strongly stressed than the others nearby –
> Ten syllables all told, perhaps eleven.

For readers who know their iambs from their anapaests, the section on different types of free verse is particularly illuminating. However, Hollander cannot resist the temptation to attack this type of poetry: ". . . such verse often tends/ To fall very flat". He also has interesting sections on the more rare poetic forms, such as the "skewed quatrain" and "double dactyl", and an informative "Suggestions for Further Reading" section.

ATTRIDGE's in-depth study of rhythm and metre is the definitive introduction to the subject for the more advanced reader. The first two chapters provide a general historical overview of traditional and linguistic approaches, and argues that these are inadequate. In Part Two, he discusses the rhythms of English speech, and the difference between four- and five-beat rhythm. In Part Three, he inserts rhythm into the rules of metre, and demonstrates how this works in the final section. The book's argument is too complex to summarise in a few lines, but Attridge provides refreshing alternatives to the classical approach to metre, for example, with his concept of tension rather than substitution, and his use of various symbols to provide a more sensitive close reading of poetry, such as "ô" for an implied offbeat (these are all listed in the Appendix). EASTHOPE's book is in many ways a response to Attridge's. He praises Attridge, but also disparages him for giving "theoretical priority to syllable and stress, to units within the line rather than the line itself", and puts forward an alternative appreciation of poetry via discourse theory. His discussion is always entertaining, with examples from Shakespeare as well as football chants, and rigorous, such as Part One's analysis of discourse as language, ideology, and subjectivity. However, his argument hinges on the tenuous formalist notion of poetry as distinct from prose because it makes a "special use . . . of the signifier in patterns of repetition and condensation". His analysis of the pentameter as a bourgeois form is interesting but erroneous: a glance at the tradition of dialect poetry in English would confirm this. Despite the extended close reading of the anonymous "Three Ravens", Easthope displays the lack of sensitivity in metrical analysis that Attridge deplores, as in his comment that four-stress lines are "not concerned with unstressed syllables".

RICKS's collection of essays cohere because "each attends to an aspect, feature, or resource of the language manifested in poetry". For example, there are essays on Gower and diction, Milton, sound, and sense, line-endings in Wordsworth, bathos (in Stevie Smith) and punctuation, brackets and hyphens in Geoffrey Hill's poetry. Tom Paulin attacks the latter (see below) as a formalist obsession, "the nadir of traditionalist close textual analysis. To read Ricks on the hyphen is to taste that abject world of trivialising critical duncery which filled Pope with such savage despair". To be fair to Ricks, there is nothing innately wrong with this mode of criticism: his dismissal of theoretical approaches to literature is irritating and simplistic, but if readers are patient and enjoy finding out details such as the significance of the dates in Hill's "September Song", the extensive (447-page) study is worth reading. The discussion is sometimes illuminating in its rigour, as in the analysis of the final line of Philip Larkin's "An Arundel Tomb" as shifting between the classical and Romantic.

PAULIN's study is, as the blurb on the front cover announces, "an energetic, pungent and highly readable volume". It takes its cue from Hegel's discussion of "the state", and argues in the introduction that it is "only by identifying the shadow those nets ['nationality, language, religion' (Joyce)] cast upon texts whose formal joys we return to again and again can we begin to go beyond the power-relations they embody". Poetry and the state are discussed across authors as diverse as Christina Rossetti, D.H. Lawrence, Zbigniew Herbert, and Peter Reading. The chapter entitled "Pure Primitive Divinity: The Republican Epic of John Milton" is fuelled by a passionate defence of Milton's poetics, which responds to Leavis's dismissal of the poet. Paulin compares Milton to Walt Whitman, and invites American readers who are "congealed in the royalist kitsch of present-day Britain to remember and admire this great servant of human liberty". The chapter "John Clare in Babylon" is "energetic" in its linguistic love for the neglected "Romantic" poet. The language he employs to praise him is sparked by the inventiveness of Clare's phrases, such as "moozing" and "crumping". The only flaw in this study is the occasionally over-bearing "state" reading of the poetry, as in the chapter on Philip Larkin ("She Did Not Change"). Here he argues that the falling leaves in the opening lines of "Afternoons" are "like colonies dropping out of the empire". As James Booth recognises in a recent paper on Larkin, the reading is insistent.

ANTONY ROWLAND

Poetry: 20th Century

Corcoran, Neil, *English Poetry since 1940*, London: Longman, 1993
Garratt, Robert F., *Modern Irish Poetry: Tradition and Continuity from Yeats to Heaney*, Berkeley: University of California Press, 1986
Gray, Richard, *American Poetry of the Twentieth Century*, Cambridge and New York: Cambridge University Press, 1976
Hamilton, Ian (ed.), *The Oxford Companion to Twentieth Century Poetry in English*, Oxford and New York: Oxford University Press, 1994
Martin, Graham, and P.N. Furbank (eds.), *Twentieth Century Poetry: Critical Essays and Documents*, Milton Keynes, Buckinghamshire: Open University Press, 1975
Stead, C.K., *Pound, Yeats, Eliot and the Modernist Movement*, London: Macmillan, 1986; New Brunswick, New Jersey: Rutgers University Press, 1986

CORCORAN's insightful study of the more recent English poetry views it in the light of "the history of reaction to the high Modernist moment of writing in English" from 1900 to the 1930s. The book therefore opens with a chapter on Eliot and Auden before moving on to discuss the work of the first generation of British modernists, Louis MacNeice, Edwin Muir, Basil Bunting, and David Jones, and so on through the Movement poets, the "Neo-Modernists", down to "Martian" poetry. Throughout, Corcoran also has some helpful chapters on poets from the North of Ireland. Each chapter offers a discussion of two or three poets, and through some telling juxtapositions Corcoran is able to offer sharp criticisms of the individual poets. There are also some handy general introductions to the poetry produced in each decade. One potential, but perhaps inevitable, problem with the book is that by having as a catch-all last section "Since 1970", Corcoran is in danger of not fully accounting for more recent trends, and the foregrounding which he gives to the Martian school might come to seem increasingly contentious as some of the less publicity-conscious trends in the period work themselves through.

GARRATT's book offers a similarly-structured history of Irish poetry. It reviews the influence of the modernist poetics of Yeats, and, in a separate chapter, discusses the crucial importance of James Joyce's notions of tradition and aesthetic impersonality or distance upon subsequent work. Garratt then offers broad discussions of the work of key poets in the Yeatsian tradition of Irish poetry: Austin Clarke, Patrick Kavanagh, Thomas Kinsella, John Montague, and Seamus Heaney. By limiting his discussion of other more recent poets in the tradition to a brief final chapter, however, Garratt's history might seem to some blinkered and canonical – a history based perhaps exclusively on the notions of "strong" poetry as described by Harold Bloom, on poets who are extremely sensitive to the burdens of influence imposed upon them by a major earlier figure.

GRAY's survey of American poetry groups the poets according to the movements to which they had nominally signed up. There are sections on the Modernists, Formalists, Confessionals, Beats, Fugitives, and on those poets who followed in the Whitman tradition. There is a useful final chapter, which worries through the whole problem of literary nationality in modern poetry, by examining the symptomatic case of T.S. Eliot. The book contains shrewd close readings of representative poems by each poet in the process of outlining the general course of his or her career against the background of poetic movements. This can lead to a slight feeling that the individuality of each poet is muffled by the ideas they hold in common with others; but Gray's is still a lively and challenging approach.

HAMILTON's *Oxford Companion* provides a handy reference guide to poetry in English from all nations. It is divided into short articles devoted to authors, and each entry includes full biographical and publication information as well as being in itself a short critical essay on its subject. The *Companion* is remarkable in that many of its contributors are among the most prominent contemporary poets, and so it provides a rare opportunity to read one poet on another who is important to him or her (although this involves a bit of a hunt through the whole volume, as contributors are identified only by their initials). The articles by Seamus Heaney on Robert Lowell and by Tom Paulin on Ted Hughes are particularly bold and insightful.

MARTIN and FURBANK's book is a collection of brief documents relating to twentieth-century poetry. It includes pieces on their poetic ideas by all of the major modernist poets. It is subdivided into sections on "The Language of Literary Criticism", "Versification and Verse-Speaking", "Poetry and Belief", "The Poet and Society", and "Modernism". The second part of the book contains major essays on a range of major poets in the century, including Thomas Hardy, Ezra Pound, Eliot, W.B. Yeats, W.H. Auden, Philip Larkin, Lowell, Hughes, and Sylvia Plath, by critics including Hugh Kenner, Donald Davie, William Empson, and Denis Donoghue. The book is therefore an extremely useful and handy guide to poetic ideas, and provides some telling readings of the poetry of some major figures.

STEAD's book charts the "Rise of Modernism" from its inheritance in the French symbolist poets of the late nineteenth century. Stead gives close readings of key modernist works by Yeats and Pound, as well as an important discussion of *The Waste Land* as a work of collaboration between the two. In the second part of the book, Stead traces the impact of modernist poetics upon the poetry of Auden and the revolutionary Left, before considering the relation between the poetic experimentalism of the modernists and their later-espoused, rightward-leaning political views. In a Postscript, Stead considers the work of Donald Davie, in which he emerges as a representative case for the inheritance of early-century ideas. Stead's concern throughout is to develop a committed sense of modernist practice and of its political impact across the century, and the book presents a cogent, informed, and illuminating argument.

STEVEN MATTHEWS

Poetry: Recent and Contemporary

Bloom, Harold (ed.), *Contemporary Poets*, New York: Chelsea House, 1986
Chevalier, Tracy (ed.), *Contemporary Poets*, 5th edition, Chicago and London: St James Press, 1991
Corcoran, Neil, *English Poetry since 1940*, London: Longman, 1993
Davie, Donald, *Under Briggflatts; A History of Poetry in Great Britain 1960–1988*, Manchester: Carcanet, 1989; Chicago: University of Chicago Press, 1989
Easthope, Anthony, and John O. Thompson (eds.), *Contemporary Poetry Meets Modern Theory*, Hemel Hempstead, Hertfordshire: Harvester Wheatsheaf, 1991
Gray, Richard, *American Poetry of the Twentieth Century*, London: Longman, 1990
Markham, E.A. (ed.), *Hinterland: Caribbean Poetry from the West Indies and Britain*, Newcastle-upon-Tyne: Bloodaxe Books, 1989

General surveys of contemporary poetry in the English-speaking world tend to present a poetry of consolidation and contraction rather than one of radical experiment or innovation; a poetry of recovery, formalism, and subjectivity, rather than one of avant gardes, ideology, and public or epic statement. Relatively few books approach the whole range of poetry in English (the exceptions discussed here are Easthope and Thompson, and Chevalier), and the selection here therefore includes studies of British, American, and Caribbean poetry respectively.

CHEVALIER's reference book, the fifth revised edition of a title first published in 1970, has entries on over 700 living poets across the English-speaking world. Each entry includes a biographical outline, lists of primary and critical works, and a short critical essay by a contributor. It serves as an introduction to, and reference source for, both the well-known contemporary poets as well as many who have received relatively little commentary thus far.

EASTHOPE and THOMPSON'S book brings together essays on American poets Gertrude Stein, Adrienne Rich, John Ashbery, Charles Bernstein, and Susan Howe, and essays on British poets J.H. Prynne, Seamus Heaney, Tony Harrison, and Tom Raworth. The essays included are strictly interpretative, drawing on an impressive range of recent critical theory to discuss problems of social reception, meaning, and textuality in contemporary Anglo-American poetry. However, the predominance in the essays of a certain poststructuralist account of language and signification occludes the equally crucial questions of deictics, intentional or motivated utterance, metrical structure, and formal constitution of meaning in the poems discussed. The book should be considered an interesting attempt to bring contemporary poetry and theory together, rather than a rigorous hermeneutic or poetics of poetic form.

CORCORAN's critical overview of British poetry since 1940 sees the development of a poetry of regionalism – especially by Northern English and Irish poets – as testifying to both the dissolution of a cultural consensus in contemporary Britain and the failure of the Arnoldian-Leavisite notion of an "organic" poetic culture, which could unify the British poetry scene as a whole. Corcoran's attempt to provide a genealogy of such regionalism argues that most poetry written during this period has been a direct response to the poetic legacy of modernism. This genealogy is traced through successive generations of British poets with especial attention being paid to the shift in poetic diction and questions of gender and voice in works of individual authors, as well as in British poetic culture as a whole. Contemporary poets discussed include Keith Douglas, Douglas Dunn, Paul Muldoon, Craig Raine, Carol Rumens, and James Fenton.

DAVIE's idiosyncratic history of British poetry 1960–88 – engaging with such issues as language and national identity, the legacy of modernism in British poetry, and the importance of cosmopolitan translation as against cultural insularity – presents the cultural history of British postwar poetry as one of regionalism, public philistinism, and retrenchment. Davie's ongoing complaint against contemporary British poetry is that it, at times, threatens to forget the modernist conviction that poetry is an art with international, multi-ethnic, and multilingual significance. The cultural parochialism and civic narrowness of much contemporary British poetry is thus, for Davie, a sign that modernist principles have either been assimilated or forgotten, as well as a sign of how much the continuing international modernism of poets such as Charles Tomlinson, J.H. Prynne, and F.T. Prince, goes against the grain.

BLOOM's edited collection of essays essentially identifies two strains, those of the English Romantic and Emersonian bardic, in contemporary American poetry. The emergence of transcendentalism and confessionalism as two dominant modes of poetic representation goes hand in hand, according to Bloom, with a reaction to modernist experiment, which sees a particular version of American Romanticism emerging in the 1970s and 1980s. This Romanticism expresses an anxiety concerning the relation of poetic form to the world of fact. The ongoing experiments of American poets with open and closed forms, with spiritual stances and ideological stances, is thus taken to represent a continued fascination with the question of shaping fact into significant form. This Romantic revivalism could be cited as evidence of a diminished poetic scope; however, the sheer diversity of American poets represented in this volume defers such summary judgement. Biographical notes and individual author bibliographies also ensure a detailed coverage of each author's work.

GRAY's overview of twentieth-century American poetry shows a continued postwar concern with, on the one hand, subjectivity and the language of personal experience and, on the other hand, a commitment to expressive authenticity – the precise application of word or event without ornament, both of which are neither strictly regional, nor modernist, but national. Both trends evince a disillusionment with formalism and ideology as signalled by the many experiments with free and organic verse forms and the insistent preoccupation with a poetry of objectivism and truthfulness to nature. Both trends also suggest the extent to which contemporary American poetic practice remains narrowly nationalistic in its hopes and aims. Excellent bibliographies and notes make this a comprehensive survey of modern American poetry and aesthetics – a valuable reference work.

MARKHAM's selection of Anglophone Caribbean poets is regionalist in intent and strictly commemorative, attempting to introduce to a wider audience West Indian poetry currently being written in English. While avoiding a reduction of this poetry to sociological sources, Markham does provide a cultural and historical context in which contemporary Caribbean poetry can be read. The unique positioning of the Caribbean as a multi-lingual, multi-ethnic, and multi-national culture, Markham argues, is reflected in the multiple poetic experiments with dialect in the departure of this poetry from standard English usage, and in the stress on performance and the commitment to orality as against undue emphasis being placed on the silent printed page. The marriage of an oral and scribal tradition in many West Indian poets is thus an important aspect of this poetry as it is currently being written, and goes some way to explaining its ongoing commitment to folk culture. Markham's Introduction is full of useful source information on the different styles and thematic pursuits of individual poets. The interviews with several poets and detailed author bibliographical notes also provide useful additional information.

D.S. MARRIOTT

Poetry: British – General

Armstrong, Isobel, *Victorian Poetry: Poetry, Poetics and Politics*, London and New York: Routledge, 1993

Bradford, Richard, *A Linguistic History of English Poetry*, London and New York: Routledge, 1993

Burrow, John, *Ricardian Poetry: Chaucer, Gower, Langland and the "Gawain" Poet*, London: Routledge & Kegan Paul, 1971; New Haven, Connecticut: Yale University Press, 1971

Corcoran, Neil, *English Poetry since 1940*, London: Longman, 1993

Corns, Thomas N. (ed.), *The Cambridge Companion to English Poetry: Donne to Marvell*, Cambridge and New York: Cambridge University Press, 1993

Easthope, Antony, *Poetry as Discourse*, London and New York: Methuen, 1983

Hampson, Robert, and Peter Barry (eds.), *New British Poetries, 1970–1990: The Scope of the Possible*, Manchester: Manchester University Press, 1993

Hobsbaum, Philip, *Tradition and Experiment in English Poetry*, London: Macmillan, 1979

Hopkins, David (ed.), *The Routledge Anthology of Poets on Poets: Poetic Responses to English Poetry from Chaucer to Yeats*, London and New York: Routledge, 1994

Machin, Richard, and Christopher Norris (eds.), *Post-Structuralist Readings of English Poetry*, Cambridge and New York: Cambridge University Press, 1987

Norbrook, David, *Poetry and Politics in the English Renaissance*, London and Boston: Routledge & Kegan Paul, 1984

Ward, John Powell, *The English Line: Poetry of the Unpoetic from Wordsworth to Larkin*, London: Macmillan, 1991

Watson, J.R., *English Poetry of the Romantic Period, 1789–1830*, London, 1985, revised 1992

Two sorts of general surveys of British poetry are represented here: surveys which tend to be organised by period, and surveys which are guided by a particular methodology or line of argument. This is not to say, however, that the former do not have methodologies or particular lines of argument, merely that their inclusion here is for their emphasis on a particular literary period. Of the hundreds of books which fall into the first type of survey, the entry has tried to discuss recent representative works accessible to sudents and to discuss critical surveys of many of the significant periods of British poetry from the medieval age to the present day.

HOBSBAUM's study offers itself as an informal history of poetry in English, trying to steer a path between scant literary reference and selection to the point of ceasing to be a history at all. It begins with the medieval *Piers Plowman*, and moves through the traditional major poets like Chaucer, Shakespeare, and Wordsworth, to some of the significant figures of the twentieth century. Its opening claim, that "the concept of tradition in this book is the key theme that links its several chapters together", announces its ideological and methodological preoccupations, and its limitations. Against this "tradition" is measured the "experiment", which is regarded as the damage done to the "tradition" by too much imitation of foreign modes. This is a study that is now very dated, absorbing as it does many assumptions into its analysis which are now regarded as *passé* – if not also politically suspect – after the introduction of greater theoretical self-consciousness in the past decade. With hindsight, its ideological prejudices are so clearly portrayed on its sleeve that this book best demonstrates how all "history" can in turn be historicised.

On a similar tack, WARD's survey centres upon what has been defined as "the English line", the strand of major English poets that is seen to include William Wordsworth, John Clare, Tennyson, Arnold, A.E. Housman, Edward Thomas, Wilfred Owen, Robert Frost, Louis MacNeice, and Philip Larkin, and who are associated with "Englishness". Characterising their qualities as a certain matter-of-factness, the use of everyday language, a melancholy both musical and haunting, and a craving for a secure and familiar landscape, this study – although not unaware of recent critical developments – tends to analyse these poets' work in an approach marked by practical criticism. There are brief gestures towards women poets' contributions, but this study is dominated by the male "line". Despite raising questions about such potentially interesting issues as canon-formation, nationhood, subjectivity, and language, this book promises more than it finally gives, unable to free itself from the very discourses it seeks to interrogate.

As part of a series that seeks to provide an "interface" between language and literature, BRADFORD's book acts as a guide to the language of poetry from both an historical and a linguistic perspective. Working with attention to the innovative theory of double articulation, the study contains detailed stylistic analysis of syntax, vocabulary, rhythm and metrics, while seeking to contextualise each poem in terms of the major historical and aesthetic categories of literary studies. After a chapter outlining theories of poetics much influenced by Roman Jakobson, the book makes use of these analytical tools on a range of texts from Elizabethan drama to modernist poetry by E.E. Cummings. Conceived of as a possible course textbook, it also includes a range of exercises and questions for further study.

Unlike the other texts considered here, HOPKINS's survey anthology is a source book rather than a critical work. Containing a collection of poetic responses by English poets to one another's work, the book is divided into two sections. Part One contains poets' writing on the nature, qualities, and purpose of poetry, covering such subjects as the formal properties of the poetic craft, the poet as creator, and the poet and nature. Part Two is a chronological collection of poets' writings – usually quoting extracts from poems written about other poets – on their peers, with an individual entry for each poet. The general notion is that all poets are influenced by, or owe an unspoken debt to, their poetic forebears. Although useful for its documentary information, this book appears to be born out of a somewhat conservative concept of poetic development as producing an organic "truth". As the Preface states, "all members of the community of poets are united in their common pursuit of a species of truth which is unique and irreplaceable". The book is also limited by its concluding with Yeats, thereby suggesting its rather limited concept of the British "poetic tradition".

A different type of survey occurs in EASTHOPE's book, since it makes no claims for being a history. This analysis of the development of British poetry becomes the vehicle for demonstrating what he appears to regard as the more important theoretical arguments about discourse. After a series of preliminary chapters, which self-consciously outline his theoretical tools and approaches concerning discourse, subjectivity, and representation, the study seeks to "describe English poetry as a discourse defined in the way it foregrounds and promotes a position for the reader as subject of the enounced while aiming to disavow the reader's position as subject of the enunciation". This literary legerdemain is analysed in the poetry from the Renaissance down to modernism, analysing examples of various forms like the iambic pentameter, the feudal ballad, and the heroic couplet, and touching on poets like Shakespeare, Alexander Pope, Wordsworth, T.S. Eliot, and Ezra Pound. Although selective and sometimes too general, there is much that is useful in this book, especially in its persistent focus on how the subject has been formed and reformed in English poetry.

Amid the plethora of books in the past two decades dealing with theoretical developments in highly abstract terms, MACHIN and NORRIS have edited a collection of essays that seeks to show how the possible application of deconstruction and poststructuralist ideas can take place in concrete ways. The essays cover the periods of the Renaissance, the Augustan, Romanticism, and modernism, and with the editors' contemporary theoretical motivation, offer innovative and alternative ways of conceiving of British literary history. Reading such familiar texts as *Macbeth* and *The Rime of the Ancient Mariner*, these essays form an unusual survey of British poetry, opening up the numerous issues and processes still to be considered as we attempt to understand the formation of canons and the construction of literary history.

Almost in defiance of the attempt to organise part of this survey by period, BURROW's book acknowledges that the four poets to whom he attends "do not belong together, in the established history of English poetry, as representatives of a single period. . . . Despite its fertility, indeed, the age of Chaucer and Langland has failed to achieve the full status of a literary 'period'". For this reason, he invents "Ricardian" for the writers under review, and although it is recognised that this is a contentious periodisation, which throws up as many problems as it solves, and that the book was published 20 years ago, this survey still remains one of the most authoritative and accessible to students. Discerning the features of "Ricardian" style, narrative, and its "image of man", the study looks at the principal poems of these four writers, and seeks to establish in these poems the characteristics which make "in something like the full literary sense, a period".

Surveys of Elizabethan poetry abound, although many also focus on the drama. NORBROOK's focus is almost exclusively on English poetry from 1578 to 1637, and on the impingement of European politics, humanism, and the Reformation on the poets. Moving from Sir Thomas More's *Utopia* through Philip Sidney, Edmund Spenser, Ben Jonson, and the Spenserians to the early Milton, the book analyses the extent to which aesthetic and political ideologies have played their part in establishing or marginalising poets from critical attention. Arguing that Renaissance poetry was always involved in politics, it looks at the way in which the aestheticisation of politics and the politicisation of aesthetics are strategies at work in the poetry itself, and strategies at stake in the more recent critical appraisals of that poetry. Cautiously aware of the way "recent critical theory has opened up new ways of analysing the relationships between texts and power which go beyond simply lining up poets according to their explicit political views", Norbrook seeks to demonstrate that for the poets "the act of writing became for them a means of moving away from received ideas and experimenting with new political values, of 'feigning commonwealths'". Lucidly written and clearly annotated, this book remains one of the most authoritative books on the subject. Supplementing this book is CORNS's collection of essays by eminent scholars, which focuses on many of the poets omitted from, or skimmed, over in Norbrook's study. Individual studies of John Donne, Jonson, Robert Herrick, George Herbert, Thomas Carew, Sir John Suckling, Richard Lovelace, Richard Crashaw, Henry Vaughan, Andrew Marvell, and Milton are complemented by more general essays, which attend to the political and religious contexts of the poetry, explore its gender politics, explain the material circumstances of its production and circulation, and consider the issues of rhetoric and genre. As a volume in the "Cambridge Companion to English Poetry" series, this book is part of a good collection of introductory books for students, which together act as a comprehensive survey of English poetry.

From the many surveys of Romantic poetry that have been written, WATSON's literary-critical history of Romanticism is a solid introduction, which alerts students of the period to most of the current critical debates, although it is limited in its discussions of gender politics. A volume in the Longman introductory survey series "Literature in English", it commences with a discussion of what many regard as the principal preoccupations of Romantic poetry, such as prophecy, imagination, nature, and dreams, and also discusses aspects of the historical and socio-cultural context of the period. The book then turns to study the six Romantic poets traditionally regarded as the principal ones – William Blake, Wordsworth, Samuel Taylor Coleridge, Byron, Percy Bysshe Shelley, and John Keats. The book does insert a chapter on the poetry of Walter Scott, George Crabbe, and John Clare, but this does little more than act as something of a side-glance from the principal focus. As with all the books in this Longman series, this one includes a series of useful appendices – a chronology of events and publications, a good general bibliography, and a series of biographical notes on the salient writers.

Post-Romantic British poetry is given an authoritative scrutiny and exploration in ARMSTRONG's massive volume, which studies how Victorian poetics and poetry were intertwined with theology, science, philosophy, and theories of language and politics. Focusing on two movements in the development of British poetry – "one exploring various strategies for democratic, radical writing, the other developing, in different forms, a conservative poetry" – this book explores the demanding and revolutionary questions posed by this poetry and the experiments with forms to find a poetic language equal to its cultural interrogations. The chapters investigate the work of poets like Tennyson, Robert Browning, Arthur Hugh Clough, Matthew Arnold, L.E.L. (Letitia Landon), Christina Rossetti, Algernon Charles Swinburne, Gerard Manley Hopkins, and George Meredith, as well as investigating the way these poets reacted to domestic and colonial upheaval and pressures. In all respects this is a monumental study, and no scholars of nineteenth-century poetry can afford to ignore it.

CORCORAN's book is a more up-to-date critical introduction and survey of British poetry since 1940. Divided into five main parts, it commences with an exploration of the late modernism and T.S. Eliot, W.H. Auden, Louis MacNeice, David Jones, and Basil Bunting. Proceeding then with a breakdown of each subsequent decade from the 1940s, the study covers most of the significant poets and poetic movements and brings the history right up to the current, questionably "post-modern", experiments of people like Denise Riley and J.H. Prynne, as well as the "renaissance" of the poetry of Northern Ireland. Combining energetic readings of individual poems with discussions of the influences on these poets, as well as the transformation of what constitutes an "English" poetic tradition, as far as surveys of modern and contemporary British poetry are concerned this is a very useful book which ought to be invaluable to students of the period.

If there is a weakness in Corcoran's book, it is the inadequate treatment of the "alternative" British poetries since World War II. HAMPSON and BARRY collect an excellent set of essays, which try to map out the field of the so-called "British Poetry Revival" since the 1960s. Often written by practising poets themselves, these essays attend to the politics of small-press poetry, the impact of black poetry and its politics, the problems of subjectivity, language, and gender (which are widely explored in these "alternative" poetries), as well as providing some "case studies" of a few of the principal writers.

TIM S. WOODS

Poetry: Old English

Alexander, M.J., *Old English Literature*, London: Macmillan, 1983; New York: Schocken Books, 1983

Damico, Helen, and Alexandra Hennessy Olsen (eds.), *New Readings of Women in Old English Literature*, Bloomington: Indiana University Press, 1990

Godden, Malcolm, and Michael Lapidge (eds.), *The Cambridge Companion to Old English Literature*, Cambridge and New York: Cambridge University Press, 1991

Pearsall, Derek, *Old English and Middle English Poetry* (Volume 1, Routledge History of English Poetry series), London and Boston: Routledge & Kegan Paul, 1977

Shippey, T.A., *Old English Verse*, London: Hutchinson, 1972

Swanton, Michael, *English Literature Before Chaucer*, London and New York: Longman, 1987

In the later twentieth century, Old English scholarship has moved away from its previous bias towards the study of the language. The last two decades have witnessed the publication of a large number of literary histories, many of which challenge the idea that Old and Middle English literature are incomparable. While the view of Old English scholarship as the last bastion of "traditional" criticism unsullied by modern literary theories still prevails in many quarters, recent interest in subjects such as the history of women has had its impact on this area of learning as on many others.

SHIPPEY's classic study covers a wide range of verse, including saints' lives and poetry from the *Junius Manuscript*, one of the most important Old English codices, which contains mainly Old Testament translations and paraphrases. There is a section explaining language and style, and all quotations are accompanied by translations. In the opening "Apology for Verse" Shippey defends the study of a "dead" language and literature on the grounds that it both "presents a challenge to any theory of literature based on our modern tradition" and "can remind us of the differences, affecting literature, in society and in human behaviour", and he warns the reader against bringing twentieth-century assumptions to their reading of the literature of this period. However, his avowed intention to "avoid the urge to make the unfamiliar conform to the accepted, to label genres and mark transitions" is undermined rather by the inclusion of chapters on heroic poetry, the elegies, and the decline of verse in the later Anglo-Saxon era.

PEARSALL's book surveys English poetry from the alliterative verse of the Anglo-Saxon period to the court poetry of the fourteenth and fifteenth centuries, and in addition to chapters on *Beowulf* and heroic writing, and religious verse, it considers "transitional" Middle English works descended from the Old English tradition. Pearsall argues that in order to understand early poetry both its function and the conditions of its production have to be studied, and he concludes that the principal difference between poetry of the medieval and Renaissance periods "is a shift in the role of poetry from a social form to an art form". He emphasises the necessity, firstly, of locating medieval poetry in its European context, and, secondly, of seeing it as the product of a manuscript culture.

ALEXANDER's book, which looks at poetry and prose together, views Anglo-Saxon literature as very different to that of the later Middle Ages, and consequently confines itself to the period leading up to the Norman Conquest. In order to make the material accessible to the general reader as well as to the scholar, Alexander quotes in translation either entire texts or substantial extracts, and includes a chapter on Anglo-Saxon culture and the historical and religious background. Particularly enlightening are the closing sections of the book in which the account of *The Battle of Maldon* comes after that of three less well-known later Old English poems, *The Phoenix*, *Judith*, and *Brunanburh*. As a starting point, this book has the advantages of being concise, readable, and informative.

Like Pearsall, SWANTON crosses the traditional divide between Old and Middle English poetry. Without either abandoning a basically chronological approach or opposing the notions that history progresses and literature evolves, he dismisses traditional periodisation on the grounds that it distorts our thinking by over-emphasising the changes at the expense of the continuities. Swanton's central argument is that certain themes and sentiments can be traced throughout the literature in this study, from the seventh-century "lay" *Widsith* to the lyrics and romances of the thirteenth century. In his introduction, for example, he asserts that "From Migration to Crusade there was a restlessness in the age", and goes on to suggest that the anxiety attendant to this restlessness was shared by warrior exile and knight errant alike. Particularly useful is the annotated list of writers and writings, which appears at the end of the volume.

The volume edited by GODDEN and LAPIDGE is organised thematically, and as a result poetry and prose are not separated artificially from one another. While an entire chapter is, once again, devoted to *Beowulf*, others deal with broader topics such as "Pagan Survivals and Popular Belief", "Fatalism and the Millennium", "Perceptions of Transience", and "Perceptions of Eternity". In line with Alexander's book, the first essay deals with the relationship between Old English literature and the society that produced it. However, going against the trend in recent scholarship, and despite the fact that translations are provided of all quotations in Old English, the first essay is followed by fairly detailed introduction to the language itself. Such a shift in emphasis reflects the book's rather more scholarly approach.

While Godden and Lapidge pay some attention to the roles of women in Anglo-Saxon history and literature, this subject is the principal focus of the volume edited by DAMICO and OLSEN. The essays are grouped under four headings – "The Historical Record", "Sexuality and Folklore", "Language and Difference in Characterisation", and "The 'Deconstructed' Stereotype" – and among the poems discussed are riddles and gnomic poems, *Elene*, *Juliana*, *Judith*, *Wulf and Eadwacer*, *The Wife's Lament*, and, of course, *Beowulf*. The introduction provides an overview of both feminist literary criticism and research on women in the field of Old English. Damico and Olsen claim that their aim is to "address, correct, and begin fresh exploration of a neglected area of study in Old English literature", and without doubt their excellent collection fulfils this objective.

Dianne Watt

Poetry: Middle English

Allen, Judson Boyce, *The Ethical Poetic of the Later Middle Ages: A Decorum of Convenient Distinction*, Toronto: University of Toronto Press, 1982

Boitani, Piero, and Anna Torti (eds.), *Poetics: Theory and Practice in Medieval English Literature*, Cambridge: D.S. Brewer, 1991; Rochester, New York: Boydell & Brewer, 1991

Camargo, Martin, *The Middle English Verse Love Epistle*, Tübingen: M. Niemeyer, 1991

Lynch, Kathryn L., *The High Medieval Dream Vision: Poetry, Philosophy, and Literary Form*, Stanford, California: Stanford University Press, 1988

Reed, Thomas L., Jr. (ed.), *Middle English Debate Poetry and the Aesthetics of Irresolution*, Columbia: University of Missouri Press, 1990

Spearing, A.C., *Readings in Medieval Poetry*, Cambridge and New York: Cambridge University Press, 1987

Vance, Eugene, *Mervelous Signals: Poetics and Sign Theory in the Middle Ages*, Lincoln: University of Nebraska Press, 1986

Current writing on medieval poetry tends to take one of two approaches. On the one hand are the single genre studies, works here represented by Camargo, Lynch and Reed. On the other are the theoretical attempts to describe a medieval poetic; Allen's book, Vance's essays, and the collection edited by Boitani all represent this method. While all of these works have something important to contribute to the study of Middle English verse, many of them range across linguistic and national boundaries.

SPEARING's book is unusual, then, in that it confines itself to Middle English poetry while ranging widely through the genres of that poetry. In a collection of elegantly written essays, Spearing addresses the difficulties faced by modern readers encountering medieval texts. Spearing's theoretical eclecticism allows him to range through his chosen texts, simultaneously demonstrating both the insights to be found through various modern approaches and the ways in which the medieval texts resist conforming to any single one of those approaches. Along the way, he rehabilitates some less-than-popular works, like *King Horn*, and provides new readings of canonical works like Chaucer's *Troilus and Criseyde* and William Langland's *Piers Plowman*. Spearing's own preference is for works that appear to frustrate literary closure, a preference which may be seen in, for example, his exploration of deep-seated doubt in works like *The Alliterative Morte Arthure*. Spearing's argument that such doubts are embedded in the text because they are also "embedded . . . within the text of the culture that produced it" moves his collection beyond individual close readings to participate in the larger project of the construction of a medieval poetic.

A revolutionary effort to construct that poetic is to be found in ALLEN's discussion of what he calls the "ethical poetic" of the Middle Ages. Medieval commentators perceived classical and medieval literature as belonging to the branch of philosophy called ethics. Thus, Allen argues, to define ethics is to define poetry, and the reverse is also true. Ethics thus becomes fundamentally rhetorical, "a body of truth within which the strategies and decorums empirically characteristic of poetry have some intrinsic place". These strategies and decorums are to be recovered from medieval commentary: every medieval poet would have learned his Latin through receiving introductory lectures to the set texts of the Western literary tradition, and the categories of these lectures would have become his own mental categories for the understanding and creation of poetry. To understand this poetry, we must replace modern literary terms with a set of terms drawn from medieval Latin commentaries. This much of Allen's argument has been taken up by later writers; Alastair Minnis's work on medieval authorship and the tradition of medieval Latin commentary has gone a long way towards providing and making more precise the vocabulary Allen seeks. In addition, Allen reminds us of the role of the audience, arguing that literary thinking is no different from normal thought: "the true poem fully exists as its textuality is supplemented by audience and commentary, in a relationship of assimilation". Throughout, Allen calls upon modern critics to ask not what a medieval poem means, but how it means, to its own medieval audience.

While Allen seeks to replace modern theoretical vocabulary with terminology drawn from medieval traditions, VANCE demonstrates the ways in which a dominant strain of modern criticism, semiotics, is not only congenial, but in fact central, to medieval literary theory. He argues that the "major thread of coherence in medieval culture was its sustained reflection . . . upon language as a semiotic system – more broadly, upon the nature, the functions and the limitations of the verbal sign as a mediator of human understanding". In a collection of essays, which surveys Latin, French, Italian, and English texts, Vance traces the ways in which medieval poetic texts "reflect upon the processes of language, including those of poetic language itself". The two essays on Augustine with which the volume begins have now become a standard point of departure for modern readers seeking to understand the medieval exploration of language, an exploration which, Vance argues, built into the poetry that resulted a critical consciousness, which would become, in the Renaissance, "the autonomous discourse that we now call 'criticism'".

The collection edited by BOITANI and TORTI offers ample evidence of the continuing efforts to identify and apply a medieval poetics. Many of the essays concern themselves with issues of readership and authority. Jill Mann examines Chaucer's depictions of (flawed) readers and the authority of the audience; Alastair Minnis explores the fifteenth-century "querelle de la *rose*", a controversy over the authority of the *Roman de la rose*; and Helen Cooper explores the "collocations" of secular authority, philosophic or moral authority, and the authority of the poet. The interest in language is manifested in pieces dealing with Platonic language and concepts by Eugene Vance and Paul Taylor, in discussions of *Pearl* and Chaucer's *The Legend of Good Women* respectively. The essays in this volume vary in their theoretical purchase, but there are many demonstrations here of poetics in practice.

The other books dealt with here begin from the point of a particular genre. While they are often informed by the critical discussions outlined above, their primary purpose is to outline the characteristics of one particular poetic form.

LYNCH sets out to examine the "philosophical vision", a sub-genre of that ubiquitous medieval form, the dream vision. She discusses Boethius's *Consolation of Philosophy*, Alain de Lille's *De planctu naturae*, Jean de Meun's section of the *Roman de la rose*, Dante's *Purgatorio*, and John Gower's *Confessio Amantis*. There is also a theoretical program here; Lynch argues that the current critical tendency to prefer works that subvert their conventions limits our ability to recognize that "adherence to convention – the recreation of past models – is a far from disinterested literary activity . . . poems can have an equally significant effect by their profound compliance with accepted patterns, by their position in a carefully worked-out harmony of ideas". Some of Lynch's analyses seem nevertheless to gloss over the difficulties and contradictions that many readers are convinced do exist in her chosen texts.

CAMARGO and REED seek both to define and to analyze the genres of medieval poetry that have not hitherto been discussed systematically. Camargo explores medieval epistolary conventions as the background to his discussion of verse love letters. He locates the decisive moment in the history of the genre in Chaucer's *Troilus and Criseyde*, and then traces the influence of the model in fifteenth-century examples. Reed surveys examples of debate poetry, concentrating on England from 1200 to 1450. The works discussed include *The Owl and the Nightingale*, *Wynnere and Wastoure*, and Chaucer's *Parlement of Foules*; Reed also assesses the debate-like qualities of works such as *Gawain and the Green Knight* and Marie de France's *Lanval*. Reed argues that the sociological and ideological unrest of the later Middle Ages manifests itself in these poems in the apparently unreconcilable conflict between experience and authority. While one might expect disputation to produce resolution, it leads instead, Reed argues, to a carnivalesque conclusion, whose ludic subversion provides recreation without seriously challenging prevailing orthodoxies.

SIÂN ECHARD

See also **Alliterative Tradition**

Poetry: Renaissance

Braden, Gordon, *The Classics and English Renaissance Poetry: Three Case Studies*, New Haven, Connecticut, and London: Yale University Press, 1978

Fowler, Alastair, *Triumphal Forms: Structural Patterns in Elizabethan Poetry*, Cambridge: Cambridge University Press, 1970

Helgerson, Richard, *Self-Crowned Laureates: Spenser, Jonson, Milton and the Literary System*, Berkeley: University of California Press, 1983

Hulse, Clark, *Metamorphic Verse, The Elizabethan Minor Epic*, Princeton, New Jersey: Princeton University Press, 1981

Lewis, C.S., *Oxford History of English Literature: English Literature in the Sixteenth Century, Excluding Drama*, Oxford: Clarendon Press, 1954

Low, Anthony, *The Re-Invention of Love: Poetry, Politics and Culture from Sidney to Milton*, Cambridge and New York: Cambridge University Press, 1993

Norbrook, David, *Poetry and Politics in the English Renaissance*, London and Boston: Routledge & Kegan Paul, 1984
Waller, Gary, *English Poetry of the Sixteenth Century*, London: Longman, 1986, revised 1993

LEWIS contributed this volume to the "Oxford History of English Literature" series. He touches upon most poets and prose writers of the period. Divided into three sections ("Late Medieval", "Drab", and "Golden"), with a chronological table and (now inevitably outdated) bibliography, Lewis's encyclopaedic study casts a wide and fine net, and, right or wrong, Lewis's opinions, being his, are always quotable. The book sets off with a bracing onslaught on the humanists ("New Learning and New Ignorance"), "Drab" is Lewis's professedly non-invidious term for the Tudor court poets, while "Golden" brings us to Sidney, Edmund Spenser, and the sonneteers. Lewis is innocent of the heavily politicising readings of more recent criticism, and on any erotic poetry uneasy and embarrassed, but even Waller (see below), re-reading this volume for his own survey, and despite his different perspectives, discovers himself agreeing with many of Lewis's judgements.

FOWLER is the leading figure in numerological readings of English Renaissance poetry, the "triumphal" (significant central points and symmetries) and "temporal"' (especially in Epithalamic verse, poetic re-creations of particular days) patterns "visible to God and the Angels" he and his followers discern in some poetry of the period. His study challenges attention, sometimes disbelief, but retrieves an important element for understanding and analysis, without asserting the priority of such meanings over explicit content.

BRADEN's book, subtitled "*Three Case Studies*" examines Arthur Golding's translation of Ovid, Christopher Marlowe's "Hero and Leander" as imitation of Musaeus, and the effects Robert Herrick gains by quotation from classical lyric poetry. These examples span the period, and their various verbal interfaces with classical texts exemplify larger tendencies in English Renaissance poetry. Despite this apperently narrow focus, many other poets are mentioned – Ben Jonson and his classical forebears, Ovidian influences on Edmund Spenser, George Chapman, and Shakespeare. Braden looks closely at verbal details, and shows how new kinds of poetry came to be made. This is the best book on a crucial aspect of English Renaissance verse.

HULSE's book on minor epics claims for the genre a central place in the Elizabethan literary system. He examines the genre's fluidity, the contribution of lyric, prophetic, iconic, historical, and epic forms to its nature, and sees the experiments of its practitioners as carrying them far from their contemporary theory of literature, their "metamorphic" verse of mutability and flux implicitly challenging the tendency of the age to read poetry moralistically. He also examines the place of minor epic in relation to ideas about the shape of a poet's career, as a genre for "young poets ceasing to be young". Marlowe, Shakespeare, and Spenser are the main subjects of discussion which, starting with the minor epic, aims towards a definition of the Elizabethan literary system.

NORBROOK looks at the relation between politics and literature in the period, in the case of both conservative (Sidney, Spenser, and Fulke Greville) and radical poets. In this factual and sober survey, the topicality of the poetry – how the writers spoke to their time – is the centre of attention. Norbrook is excellent at filling in the gaps: the literature of Queen Mary's reign, the historical events, and biographical circumstances and allegiances that affected what poets said or chose not to say are all discussed. Politically situating the literature of the period with massive assurance, the book, though shabbily produced by its publishers, is an authoritative foundation for further study.

HELGERSON studies three poets who consciously set out to achieve moral authority within their culture, rather than adopting the available pose of literary amateurism: Spenser as the New Poet, the English Virgil; Jonson as the English Horace; and Milton, read opposite the mob of Gentlemen who "wrote with ease". The costs of this sense of cultural mission are examined: when the poet becomes both the conscious prosecutor and (because his art shares in the seductive energies he condemns) unconscious defendant. Spenser and the destruction of the Bower of Bliss, Jonson and Volpone, Milton and Satan locate conflicts which lead to loss of belief in the mission, Spenser withdrawing from the public world to meditate on mutability, Milton turning repeatedly to the uncertainties of greatness in history. The book complements, via the generic choices of its authors, Hulse's study (see below) of the literary system and the constraints certain generic choices placed upon authors.

LOW's ambitious and wide-ranging study, with chapters on Sidney, John Donne, Thomas Carew, Milton, and others relates the changes in the modes of love poetry to changes in cultural, political, and economic circumstance, from Sidney's "nostalgically feudal" model for a lover's behaviour to Donne's poetry of union as shelter and defence against a disillusioning world, as poets struggled to replace the Petrarchan tradition with forms of love poetry more attuned to their changing world. Milton, read in the context provided by his divorce pamphlets, is presented as the poet of marital compatibility and incompatibility. Despite the elusive nature of the subject, this readable and graceful study, with its well chosen illustrative texts, points to genuinely symptomatic developments.

WALLER's book is a general history, stressing the ideological struggles and private anxieties that disrupt or dislocate various texts. Lively, challenging, and wide-ranging, this successful revision of previous general accounts which, in Waller's view, tended to advance ideas of unity, order, and hierarchy as central to how modern readers should understand the poetry, takes in the court poets, three Sidneys, Spenser, Shakespeare, and Donne, and does not neglect women writers of the period. The second edition extends this latter aspect of the book, and has a note on gay voices in the poetry of the period. Waller includes a chronology, general and individual bibliographies, and is throughout concerned to make the poetry interesting and accessible to the modern student.

ROY J. BOOTH

Poetry: 18th Century

Bate, Walter Jackson, *The Burden of the Past and the English Poet*, Cambridge, Massachusetts: Belknap Press of Harvard University Press, 1970; London: Chatto & Windus, 1971

Doody, Margaret Anne, *The Daring Muse: Augustan Poetry Reconsidered*, Cambridge and New York: Cambridge University Press, 1985

Rothstein, Eric, *Restoration and Eighteenth-Century Poetry 1660–1780* (Volume 3, Routledge History of English Poetry series), London and Boston: Routledge & Kegan Paul, 1981

Trickett, Rachel, *The Honest Muse: A Study in Augustan Verse*, Oxford: Clarendon Press, 1967

Weinbrot, Howard D., *The Formal Strain: Studies in Augustan Imitation and Satire*, Chicago: University of Chicago Press, 1969

Weinbrot, Howard D., *Britannia's Issue: The Rise of British Literature from Dryden to Ossian*, Cambridge and New York: Cambridge University Press, 1993

Eighteenth-century poetry suffered long and seriously from Matthew Arnold's condescending late nineteenth-century label for the period, an "age of prose and reason". Some of the power and complexity of the poetry has since been rediscovered, yet it is still too common to view it as characteristically decorous, polite, safe, and unsubtle. This is why several of the studies listed below stress opposite qualities, such as its verve, generic instability, and overall diversity. Newer labels for the period also need questioning: terms such as "neoclassical", "Augustan", "Augustan humanism", and "Age of Sensibility" have provided all-too-handy formulae with which to simplify a complex continuum.

TRICKETT's respected book is a study of "attitudes" in eighteenth- and some seventeenth- century poetry. She focuses on the "Augustan ideal of honesty" – honesty both in the sense of truth to fact, and in the sense of "integrity", hence applying both to the subjects of poetry and to the poet's stance. She has most to say on the satires of John Dryden, Jonathan Swift, John Oldham, the Earl of Rochester, Alexander Pope, and Samuel Johnson, and the book is most useful in conveying a sense of the broad development of some poetic genres over time. Johnson, who for Trickett "seems to epitomize the principles, the experience, and the genius of the Honest Muse", is the poet with whom she is most in tune.

WEINBROT's 1969 book explores the background and conventions of Augustan imitation and formal verse satire, thence developing readings of the most important later examples. More specifically, work in these genres by major eighteenth-century poets – Pope, Johnson, and Edward Young – is viewed in the context of earlier work by Abraham Cowley, Rochester, Oldham, and others. Though not an introductory book, it is still a standard treatment of several major eighteenth-century poems – Young's *Love of Fame*, Pope's *Imitations of Horace*, and Johnson's *London* and *The Vanity of Human Wishes*.

BATE's readable and provocative book has been very influential, but its thesis has been increasingly called into question in recent years. For Bate, the eighteenth century is crucial in making the transition from Renaissance to modern ways of writing poetry and thinking about poetry, in that this period shows in acute forms "the remorseless deepening of self-consciousness, before the rich and intimidating legacy of the past". Dryden, Pope, and others, Bate contends, felt themselves to be "late-comers", unable to compete with the achievement of the "Ancients" and of English classics such as Milton. One problem is that this thesis is based almost entirely on the discursive remarks of the writers discussed, together with those of contemporary aestheticians such as David Hume. There is much evidence in the poetry of the eighteenth century itself that, for major writers at least, knowledge of the literary past was not a burden but an inspiration.

ROTHSTEIN's study is well-conceived if not eminently readable. Though a work of literary history, it aims to go beyond the mere "survey": Rothstein hopes to assist in dispelling old myths (as he sees them) about the period's poetry – the "fissure" between classicism and Romanticism, the "age of prose and reason". The book consists of four long chapters, on the use of the genres before and after 1720, on poetic style, and on the adaptations of classical, national, biblical, and Ossianic poetic traditions. Here he anticipates Weinbrot (1993, see below). Rothstein's reading of eighteenth-century poetry is conspicuously thoughtful and often persuasive, but probably requires to be approched *en bloc*, and by experienced students. A very extensive appendix consists of a useful listing of the major poems and poetry-collections published over the whole period.

DOODY's book is an overtly revisionist account of English poetry from the Civil War to George Crabbe. Its emphasis is on "the excitement of the works, and on their strangeness"; the image of "dull correctness" for the period is exploded. This is an enjoyable and provocative survey, not least provocative in its questioning of the assumptions often implied in the use of the term "Augustan" for the period. For Doody, eighteenth-century poetry is most notable for such features as its innovative mingling of genres, modes, and styles, and its self-consciousness. Her strengths as a critic lie in catholicity of taste, an engaging enthusiasm, and an ability to say interesting things about individual works without wishing to have the last word on them. The volume also includes a batch of well-chosen illustrations from early printings of the poetry, useful for acquiring a sense of the way it was presented and read.

WEINBROT's 1993 volume is a bulky and demanding study of the creation of a British literary consciousness through a complex set of negotiations with classical norms, especially in poetry. It has polemical aims: Weinbrot questions the usefulness of concepts such as Augustanism, neoclassicism, and Harold Bloom's "anxiety of influence". He delves into several of the less well-charted waters of eighteenth-century verse, such as responses to Hebrew literature (especially in Christopher Smart), Scottish writing, and the phenomenon of Ossian, the Gaelic bard "translated" by James Macpherson. But he also surveys the development of better-known territory, such as the ode and Homeric imitation. Weinbrot shows the emergent canon of British poetry mixing native and foreign elements, and the eighteenth century appropriating the power and prestige of the traditional literary models in the service of a modern commercial empire.

STUART GILLESPIE

Poetry: Romantic

Abrams, M. H., *Natural Supernaturalism: Tradition and Revolution in Romantic Literature*, New York: Norton 1971; London: Oxford University Press, 1971

Bloom, Harold, *The Visionary Company: A Reading of English Romantic Poetry*, Ithaca, New York: Cornell University Press, 1961, revised 1971; London: Faber & Faber, 1962

Bloom, Harold, *The Anxiety of Influence: A Theory of Poetry*, New York and London: Oxford University Press, 1973

Hoeveler, Diane L., *Romantic Androgyny: The Women Within*, University Park: Pennsylvania State University Press, 1990

Jordan, Frank (ed.), *The English Romantic Poets: A Review of Research and Criticism*, 4th edition, New York: Modern Language Association of America, 1985

Kroeber, Karl, and Gene W. Ruoff (eds.), *Romantic Poetry: Recent Revisionary Criticism*, New Brunswick, New Jersey: Rutgers University Press, 1993

Mellor, Anne K., *Romanticism and Gender*, New York and London: Routledge, 1993

Raimond, Jean, and J.R. Watson (eds.), *A Handbook to English Romanticism*, London: Macmillan, 1992; New York: St Martin's Press, 1992

Watson, J. R., *English Poetry of the Romantic Period, 1789–1830*, London and New York: 1985, revised 1992

The vast amount of published criticism that might be categorised as concerning Romantic subjects that appears each year is, for the most part, devoted to individual authors or carefully delimited subjects. Unsurprisingly, few critics try to encapsulate something that is both as varied and as wide-ranging as Romantic poetry; but several studies do recommend themselves.

JORDAN constitutes the best place from which to start research on any of the six major Romantic poets (Blake, Wordsworth, Coleridge, Byron, Shelley, Keats). There is a chapter on each of these writers, and a seventh introductory chapter on "The Romantic Movement in England". Each of the seven chapter-authors have done a magisterial job of summarising and evaluating a huge body of criticism on the subject. The work is also an index to changing attitudes to the Romantic poetic canon – Blake was introduced only in this fourth edition (1985). Perhaps later editions of the work will include some women writers.

RAIMOND and WATSON is an encyclopedia, with entries (usually a couple of pages long) on all the major writers of poetry and prose from the period, as well as a great number of contextual entries (e.g., "The Abolition of the Slave Trade", "German Philosophy and Criticism", "Dreams", "The Sublime", and so on). The whole is very handy, although the standard of individual entries varies, depending on which of the 30 contributors has written it; and the lack of a bibliography makes it difficult to follow up points it raises. Also good, as a straightforward and unpretentious guide to the major poets of the period, is WATSON.

Two older critics have shaped responses to Romantic poetry to a greater degree than any other. ABRAMS' classic study complements his earlier work on Romantic critical theory (*The Mirror and the Lamp*, 1953) by ranging widely over Romantic poetry (defined widely – D.H. Lawrence gets a look in, for instance). Abrams sees traditional (Judaeo-Christian) theological ideas as central to Romantic themes and concepts. Romantic poets (Wordsworth gets a great deal of attention, Byron hardly any) are seen as involved in a process of secularising religious ideas in order to express their own spiritual sense of the "supernatural".

Harold Bloom's two studies of Romantic poetry have also been extremely influential, both on studies of the Romantics and also on general criticism of poetry. BLOOM (1961), written before he developed his famous theory of poetic "influence", studies what he terms "the dialectic of nature and imagination in Romantic poetry". Each of the main Romantic poets is looked at in turn, and the tension between, on the one hand, the internal world of their poetic imagination, and, on the other, the outer natural world is seen as informing their writing. Blake, unusually for so early a study, is taken as in some degree paradigmatic, and the critique of (for instance) Wordsworth as, in a radical sense, "not a poet of nature" is arresting and thought-provoking. More widely known is BLOOM's 1973 study, a brief manifesto of critical technique, which explores the conception of the strong Romantic poet, who misreads his influential forebears in order to create a poetic space for his own writing. A typical poet is likely to have been inspired to write poetry by the work of some past figure (Milton often finds himself in this role); but to avoid the danger of merely producing derivative work, and in order to discover his own "voice", this typical poet needs to misread creatively the forebear. Many critics have explored Bloom's theories of poetry in greater detail, and they have a wide currency to this day.

HOEVELER takes the six famous male Romantic poets and examines their representations of women, and in particular their treatment of androgyny, which earlier critics have seen as something of a Romantic ideal, inasmuch as it represents the union of male and female. Hoeveler, however, demonstrates that such union is always seen as problematic, and that the major poets' "appropriation of women" is never a positive one. MELLOR's excellent study examines the whole question of gender in Romantic poetry, providing as it goes along interesting critiques of most of the major female figures from the period, many of them (as Mellor points out) almost entirely overlooked by criticism. Although she starts out by clearly distinguishing between "male" and "female" Romanticism, she concludes by admitting that "the binary opposition of masculine and feminine Romanticism becomes far more complexly interwoven when we scrutinize individual authors and specific works". In the process, Mellor not only provides fruitful readings of those more famous women writers from the period (Jane Austen, Dorothy Wordsworth), but also treats in detail writers such as Felicia Hemans and L.E.L. (Letitia Landon), who have hardly been touched.

Interestingly for a collection that explicitly sets out to map the ways recent literary criticism and theory has revised our understanding of Romantic poetry, KROEBER and RUOFF arranges its essays under the six headings of the traditional male Romantic canon: Blake, Wordsworth, Coleridge, Byron, Shelley, Keats. The essays collected here (all previously published elsewhere) are not necessarily the most influential or famous in the field, but they do effectively demonstrate the ways radical literary theory, and feminist and other approaches, are changing attitudes to the work of the Romantic poets.

ADAM ROBERTS

Poetry: Victorian

Armstrong, Isobel, *Language as Living Form in Nineteenth-Century Poetry*, Brighton, Sussex: Harvester Press, 1982; Totowa, New Jersey: Barnes & Noble, 1982

Edmond, Rod, *Affairs of the Hearth: Victorian Poetry and Domestic Narrative: Victorian Narrative Poetry and the Ideology of the Domestic*, London and New York: Routledge & Kegan Paul, 1988

Faas, Ekbert, *Retreat into the Mind: Victorian Poetry and the Rise of Psychiatry*, Princeton, New Jersey: Princeton University Press, 1988

Fletcher, Pauline, *Gardens and Grim Ravines: The Language of Landscape in Victorian Poetry*, Princeton, New Jersey: Princeton University Press, 1983

Richards, Bernard, *English Poetry of the Victorian Period, 1830–1890*, London and New York: Longman, 1988

Shaw, W. David, *The Lucid Veil: Poetic Truth in the Victorian Age*, Madison: University of Wisconsin Press, 1987; London: Athlone Press, 1987

Slinn, E. Warwick, *The Discourse of the Self in Victorian Poetry*, London: Macmillan, 1990; Charlottesville: University Press of Virginia, 1991

RICHARDS provides readers a good introduction to the study of Victorian poetry. Organized thematically, his work addresses both the technique and content of important poets of the period. A key chapter offers an analysis of the image of the poet and the function of poetry as it was practiced by the Victorians. Two chapters are devoted to a review of poetic diction and versification. Richards also discusses the Victorians' fascination with the past, the importance of domesticity, the threat new discoveries in science posed to received theological doctrine, and the war between culture and the growth of popular literature. His detailed bibliography offers readers a ready source for discovering additional information about general topics and individual authors.

ARMSTRONG's main interest is in examining the ways in which nineteenth-century poets used language to create a distinctive impression of the world. She argues forcefully against the critical commonplace that Victorian poetry is simply self-expressive. Relying on the prosodic theory of Gerard Manley Hopkins and the philosophical writings of Hegel and Marx, Armstrong explores ways poets created what she calls "idealist language". Her careful readings of works by William Wordsworth, Percy Bysshe Shelley, Robert Browning, and Tennyson, as well as her analysis of poems by Hopkins and W.B. Yeats, explain "the connections between epistemology and the structure of poetic language" as it evolved from the late eighteenth to the early twentieth century.

Taking her cue from several previous studies of the Victorian poets' use of landscape, FLETCHER examines the works of dozens of these writers to see what can be learned about their political and social values from the use of manmade and natural settings in their works. She provides detailed analysis of poems by Tennyson, Matthew Arnold, Robert Browning, Christina Rossetti, William Morris, A.C. Swinburne, and Thomas Hardy to show how landscape functions in individual works; but she also discusses how, in the course of the century, the concept of landscape and its function in literature was gradually transformed so that it was considered more "democratic" (in contrast to eighteenth-century views) and less anti-social (in reaction to the Romantic notion of using landscape as a form of escapism).

EDMOND challenges received notions about the idyllic family life of the Victorians through his study of representative narrative poems by major authors of the period. Pointing out "the ubiquity of family narratives" in nineteenth-century English literature, he offers a careful analysis of works by Tennyson, Arthur Hugh Clough, Elizabeth Barrett Browning, Christina Rossetti, and George Meredith, placing them "within a larger discussion on the family and domestic ideology which had become of central importance by the middle of the nineteenth century". Relying on theoretical studies by Michel Foucault, Raymond Williams, and Terry Eagleton, he exposes the Victorians' preoccupations with sexuality, gender, and parent-child relationships. His discussion ranges widely, touching on poetry, fiction, and non-fiction; he selects examples which support his claim that, contrary to popular belief, there are "very few durable happy families in Victorian literature". Edmond's study offers readers not only a deeper appreciation of Victorian narrative poetry, but also a more sensible understanding of Victorian middle-class life.

In a fashion similar to that used by Armstrong, SHAW makes an ambitious attempt to examine "the connection which exists between Victorian poetics and changing theories of language and knowledge". His examination of metaphors used by Victorian poets, scientists, and writers of *belles lettres* demonstrates how authors of the period grappled with the representation of truth and developing notions of self-consciousness. Of special interest to Shaw is the influence of Hegelian thought on the development of the historical consciousness as a controlling idea for the production of poetry. He is especially good at identifying examples from both major and minor poets to illustrate his thesis.

Highly theoretical in his approach to his subject, SLINN uses contemporary theory of discourse as the principal touchstone for his examination of selected Victorian poetic texts. Readers will need to be familiar with the work of Hegel and Jacques Derrida to appreciate fully Slinn's argument. Throughout he stresses the shift in the attitude of writers from a belief in the possibility of transcendence to the more sobering position that such a philosophical position is impossible, because of the fluid and insubstantial nature of language. The work is particularly valuable for its commentary on long narrative poems (works by Tennyson, Robert Browning, and Arnold are the chief focus of his analysis), but the technical vocabulary makes Slinn's study less accessible to students than other critical commentaries.

In his carefully documented and well researched study, FAAS explores the "new psychological poetry" of nineteenth-century Britain and its relationship to the growing interest in mental science. Predictably, the major focus is on poems now classified as dramatic monologues; consequently, Robert Browning and Tennyson receive significant attention. Faas goes much farther in his study, however, examining the works of nearly 400 Romantic and Victorian poets, and reviewing the reaction of contemporaries to their works as evidenced by reviews in nineteenth-century journals. In the course of his investigation, Faas explores the representation in poetry of topics of great interest to proponents of the new science of the mind – alienation, murder, suicide, self-analysis, morality, insanity, and revolution. His extensive bibliography provides readers with a sound resource for initiating further study of this intriguing topic, which Faas claims has received relatively little attention from either literary critics or historians of psychiatry.

LAURENCE W. MAZZENO

Poetry: British – 20th Century

1. General

Bergonzi, Bernard, *The Myth of Modernism and Twentieth-Century Literature*, Brighton: Harvester Press, 1986

Fraser, G.S., *The Modern Writer and His World*, London: Derek Verschoyle, 1953; revised edition, London: André Deutsch, 1964

Fraser, G.S., *Vision and Rhetoric: Studies in Modern Poetry*, London: Faber & Faber, 1959

Fraser, G.S., *Essays on Twentieth-Century Poets*, Leicester: Leicester University Press, 1977

Hamilton, Ian (ed.), *The Oxford Companion to Twentieth-Century Poetry in English*, Oxford and New York: Oxford University Press, 1994

Hoffpauir, Richard, *The Art of Restraint: English Poetry from Hardy to Larkin*, Newark, Delaware: University of Delaware Press, 1991; London: Associated University Presses, 1991

Smith, Stan, *The Origins of Modernism: Eliot, Pound, Yeats and the Rhetorics of Renewal*, Hemel Hempstead, Hertfordshire: Harvester Wheatsheaf, 1994

Thwaite, Anthony, *Twentieth-Century English Poetry: An Introduction*, London: Heinemann, 1978; New York: Barnes & Noble, 1978

Vinson, James, and Kirkpatrick, D.L. (eds.), *Great Writers of the English Language: Poets*, London: Macmillan, 1979; revised as part of *Reference Guide to English Literature* (2nd edition), 3 vols., edited by Kirkpatrick, London and Chicago: St James Press, 1991

Ward, John Powell, *The English Line: Poetry of the Unpoetic from Wordsworth to Larkin*, London: Macmillan, 1991

There is a certain amount of overlap between FRASER's three volumes. Perhaps the most useful (though limited now by the earliness of its date) is *The Modern Writer and His World* (1953), which is full and judicious in its coverage up to 1950, and places writers in their social context. The later volumes (FRASER, 1959, and FRASER, 1977) are more in the nature of collected essays and reviews, often anecdotal in manner, though always reinforced by sensitive and incisive "practical criticism". Fraser is catholic in taste, equally responsive to experimental and more conventional writers, and disinclined to take sides in the modernist/anti-modernist debate.

As a clear, informative, sensible, though not too exacting, introductory survey of twentieth-century English poetry, THWAITE's short book remains a useful guide. He begins with Gerard Manley Hopkins (here, as elsewhere, co-opted as an honorary modern) and has separate chapters on W.B. Yeats, T.S. Eliot, W.H. Auden, and Dylan Thomas. These provide the cardinal points of reference. Other poets – from Wilfred Owen and D.H. Lawrence to Philip Larkin, Ted Hughes, and Seamus Heaney – are clustered together and given less extensive treatment.

BERGONZI reflects the reaction against modernist standards of difficulty, learned allusion, and formal experiment, which is detectable in the increasingly "postmodern" 1960s and 1970s. Although his book includes essays on novelists such as Lawrence and Virginia Woolf, it is predominantly concerned with poets, from Eliot to Donald Davie and Larkin. The thesis underlying otherwise seemingly disparate essays is that "Modern" has now become established paradoxically as "a historical category", and should not be allowed to blot out other worthwhile writers in the modern period.

In similar vein, WARD's "English line" seeks to define a context of development linking poets such as Hardy, Edward Thomas, A.E. Housman, Owen, Louis MacNeice, and Larkin with their twentieth-century forebears: and HOFFPAUIR enters rather more combatively into the critical debate between "modernist" and "traditional", upholding, as his title suggests, the sensible, restrained (but not unemotional) qualities to be found in the poetry of Hardy and his successors against the extravagance and rhetoric of Yeats. Unusually for a modern critic Hoffpauir also argues for the importance of the didactic element in poetry and the need for defensible moral values: "the traditional plain style also is the moral style. When the presentation is plain, inadequate thought is readily exposed; there are no aesthetic contrivances to hide behind".

SMITH is more emphatically pro-modernist. He argues that originality is always in reality a reworking of, or reaction against, influences that are usually hidden, but which modernists self-consciously display what they have done with their sources: "Modernism's originality . . . lies in making the transformative act of translation, adaptation, repetition its real content". The disintegrated voices of modernist poetry are seen as potentially liberating "polyphony" – in the Bakhtinian "dialogical" and "carnivalesque" implications of that word. But the yearning for "coherence" is "the epic delusion" that frustrates the realisation of this potential, with the result that modernism becomes an essentially reactionary movement. Though focused on the three dominant modernist poets – Yeats, Pound, and Eliot – this book provides a provocative discussion of the phenomenon that underlies so much of modern British poetry in general.

Though designed as works of reference, VINSON and KIRKPATRICK's 1976 volume (whose entries reappear, in a revised form, in Kirkpatrick's 1991 volumes) and HAMILTON's

Oxford Companion are much more than typical "companions". Vinson and Kirkpatrick cover the entire range of English poetry, from Chaucer on, but the fullness of their treatment of the twentieth century makes them worthy of inclusion here. In both volumes entries are written by a wide variety of experts, and some of them are quite lengthy essays in their own right, covering not only all the major, and great many of the minor, twentieth-century poets, but also, in Hamilton's volume, a number of poetry periodicals and such general topics as "Lallans", "Concrete Poetry", and "Feminist Criticism". Both also provide useful bibliographical information relating to primary and secondary texts. In the *Oxford Companion* poets themselves are frequent contributors, and often write particularly interesting pieces. Given its more recent date, this is probably the most comprehensive and most generally useful guide to the twentieth-century poetry scene currently available.

R.P. DRAPER

2. Before World War II

Caesar, Adrian, *Dividing Lines: Poetry, Class and Ideology in the 1930s*, Manchester: Manchester University Press, 1991

Christ, Carol T., *Victorian and Modern Poetics*, Chicago: University of Chicago Press, 1984

Koestenbaum, Wayne, "*The Waste Land*: T.S. Eliot's and Ezra Pound's Collaboration on Hysteria", in *Twentieth Century Literature*, 34(2), 1988

McDiarmid, Lucy, *Saving Civilization: Yeats, Eliot, and Auden Between the Wars*, Cambridge and New York: Cambridge University Press, 1984

Ross, Robert H., *The Georgian Revolt: Rise and Fall of a Poetic Ideal 1910–22*, Carbondale: Southern Illinois University Press, 1965; London: Faber & Faber, 1967

Scott, Bonnie Kime (ed.), *The Gender of Modernism: A Critical Anthology*, Bloomington: Indiana University Press, 1990

Simon, Myron, *The Georgian Poetic*, Berkeley: University of California Press, 1975

Smith, Stan, *The Origins of Modernism: Eliot, Pound, Yeats and the Rhetorics of Renewal*, Hemel Hempstead, Hertfordshire: Harvester Wheatsheaf, 1994

Stead, C. K., *Pound, Yeats, Eliot and the Modernist Movement*, London: Macmillan, 1986; New Brunswick, New Jersey: Rutgers University Press, 1986

Walter, George, "Loose Women and Lonely Lambs: The Rise and Fall of Georgian Poetry", in *British Poetry, 1900–50: Aspects of Tradition*, edited by Gary Day and Brian Docherty, London: Macmillan, 1995

Ezra Pound's modernist injunction to "make it new" might be said to define the project of much recent criticism with regard to the poetry of this period, modernist or otherwise. In broad terms, critics have sought to go "beyond formalism" in order to explore relations between the poetic and the political, raising, in particular, new and exciting questions about gender, race, class and the institutions and procedures of critical reading itself. This essay concerns itself principally with the British poets associated with modernism, with some attention to W.H. Auden and the 1930s' generation, and to the Georgian poets. (The War Poets are treated in a separate entry).

STEAD's book examines "the phenomenon of Modernism as a way of defining both the poets who were Modernists and the poets who were not" and is divided into two main parts. The first (chapters 1 to 4) concentrates on the poetic output of W.B. Yeats, T.S. Eliot, and Ezra Pound between 1900 and 1925, adopting an approach that is largely "aesthetic" in emphasis. Here Stead usefully delineates Pound's central role – as poet, critic, theorist, and impresario – in the "Rise of Modernism". Following a less persuasive "interludic" chapter on Yeats and Thomas Hardy as "Moderns", whose shared concern with "fixed forms" debars them from a truly "Modernist" credential, the book's second part (chapters 6 to 9) considers the poetry written between 1925 and 1950. In this section the critical perspective is much more overtly political, in response to what Stead sees as the "increasing pressure" on poets during these years to confront the social, economic, and political crises of their own historical moment. The book concludes with a brief reflection – via the example of Donald Davie – on the implications for British poetry written after 1950 of its characteristic retreat from the more radical possibilities opened up by the modernist experiment. Despite an occasionally personalized tone and some intrusive value-judgements, this is a substantial, lucid, and wide-ranging work.

Among "[those] who were not" modernists in this period are the Georgian poets, to whom, in fact, Stead gives no great space. Such an emphasis is symptomatic of a larger marginalization of the Georgians within criticism dealing with the poetry of these decades as a whole. Of the existing full-length studies of Georgian poetry perhaps those by ROSS and SIMON are the most notable. Ross's book seeks to overturn the "oversimplified stereotypes and critical half-truths" by which, he argues, this poetic group is characteristically beset. In so doing it provides a detailed and informative literary-historical perspective. Simon's study takes Ross's in a more overtly critical direction, including helpful chapters on the "intellectual background" to Georgian poetry and the aesthetic principles that inform it. Evidently, however, the efforts made by these critics at bringing Georgian poetry out from the modernist shadow remain fairly isolated. Recent criticism on the Georgians is scarce and relatively lacking in innovation. Thus, for example, while WALTER's essay rehearses and to some extent updates the work of Ross and Simon with useful concision, it ultimately breaks little new ground.

The concern of CHRIST's study, by contrast with Stead's view of modernism as a radical break with the past, is to illustrate the continuities between modernist poets (Yeats, Eliot, and Pound once again) and the influences which they explicitly rejected – those of Victorian poetry (principally Matthew Arnold, Tennyson, and Robert Browning). Linking Victorian and modernist poets in terms of a shared distrust of Romantic subjectivity, Christ argues that both groups "strive to establish a more objective context for poetic discourse than they felt was available to them in the Romantic tradition". The use of mask and persona in modernism thus emerges as an extension of techniques associated with the dramatic monologues of Browning and Tennyson; modernist theories of the image are shown to have precedents in Arthur Hallam's formulation of "the picturesque"; and modernist constructions of myth and history are related to the Victorian need to locate the self in patterns and contexts outside itself. Pursuing the argument to its logical end, the book's final chapter discusses "Modernism and Anti-Victorianism" and questions the value of periodization both with regard to the poets Christ studies and literary history as a whole. This is a stimulating, forceful, elegant, sophisticated, and rewarding work.

The emphasis in both these books on the exclusively male constituency of modernist poets is powerfully challenged in SCOTT's critical anthology – a work whose significance is not misrepresented by its size (over 700 pages). Dedicated to "the forgotten and silenced makers of modernism", this book puts the insights of feminist criticism and theory into practice in order to recover a sense not only of the importance of women writers within modernism but also of modernism's own implication in the discourses of gender, which much earlier criticism tends either to ignore or repress. Together with a comprehensive and sophisticated Introduction by Scott herself, the book contains some 26 chapters, each of which prefaces extracts from a particular writer with a brief, but frequently trenchant and informative, critical discussion from one of the book's various contributors. The anthology moves freely between genres, and contains material on, and by, a number of writers usually excluded or marginalized in the construction of the canon of modernist poetry – H.D., Mina Loy, Charlotte Mew, Marianne Moore, May Sinclair, and Gertrude Stein, among others. The book is essential reading for anyone seriously concerned with revising conventional definitions of the modernist movement.

The productiveness of a gendered account of modernist poetry is illustrated in KOESTENBAUM's fascinating reading of Eliot's *The Waste Land*. Noting the *fin-de-siècle* co-temporality of the beginnings of psychoanalysis with those of modernism, Koestenbaum draws an ingenious but fruitful parallel between the intellectual partnership of Sigmund Freud and Josef Breuer, which produced *Studies on Hysteria* (1895), and the collaboration between Eliot and Pound, resulting in *The Waste Land* (1922). In its manuscript version, Eliot's poem is read by Koestenbaum as an "hysterical" text, marked by that "deep-going functional disorganization of speech" which characterizes, for Freud and Breuer, the discourse of the (female) hysteric. In working with Eliot to edit and revise *The Waste Land* into publishable form, Pound effectively conferred a "masculine" order on an initially hysterical/"feminized" text, converting a disrupted series of poems into what Pound at least took to be a single unity. Koestenbaum's is an important essay, which casts new and provocative light on a text generally agreed to constitute the modernist poem *par excellence*.

Like Christ, SMITH adopts a sceptical and revisionary stance toward modernist claims to a radical newness. Focusing in detail on the period in which the modernism of Eliot, Pound, and Yeats first established itself (1910–22), Smith shows how "the great Modernist texts return repeatedly to remotest origins . . . seeking in Homer, Virgil, Propertius, Li Po, Dante, etc., the authorising pre-text of their discourse". Modernism's "originality" is gained, in Smith's view, not so much through suppression of the texts it reworks as by "making the transformative act of translation, adaptation, repetition its real content". In this way modernist texts "appear to turn their backs on Eliot's 'immense panorama of futility and anarchy which is contemporary history'". Yet that which they seek to repress – the contemporary discourses of "class, race, nation and gender" – constantly breaks back in on them. Modernist poetry's inescapable entanglement in the history and politics it seems to evade becomes glaringly evident, as Smith notes, from the retrospect afforded by the "crisis years" of the 1930s. This is an admirable work, both historically and theoretically informed, if at times somewhat verbally overwrought.

The concern of McDIARMID's study is with the "various answers" sought by Yeats, Eliot, and Auden to the question of poetry's intricate relation to the changing social and political realities of the interwar period. Unlike many critics, she contests the identification of Yeats and Eliot as wholly "reactionary" writers, and of Auden and his followers as wholly "revolutionary". Arguing that these poets are "less doctrinaire" than usually thought, McDiarmid goes on to demonstrate some important links between them. "All three", she writes, "sought to save civilization through some form of communal identity based on inherited myths, legends, and religious truths". Equally, however, the project of cultural redemption moves through an arc – in Yeats, Eliot, and Auden alike – from "enthusiasm and involvement" to ultimate "rejection of the whole idea". The collective recognition, consequently, is that, in Auden's phrase, "the [only] field in which the poet is a man of action [is] the field of language". McDiarmid's arguments are elegant and persuasive.

CAESAR's book offers an intelligent, meticulous, and well-written "critique of the matrix of ideas, words and images" that constitute what he calls the "myth of the 1930s". Such a myth, he argues, is propagated by a literary history and criticism at once "partial and ideologically freighted". Its most pernicious element takes the form, for Caesar, of the promotion of "Auden and the Audenesque" as representative not only of 1930s' poetry as a whole but of a left-wing politics also. By decentring Auden and critiquing the politics of his poetry, Caesar brings out a sense of "the horizontal panorama of the world of poetry in the 1930s". Examining the complex interplay among style, class, and ideology, he demonstrates both the formal heterogeneity and the political range of the poetry of the decade. This study constitutes one of the most sophisticated and clear-sighted accounts of an important literary and cultural moment too often reduced to the level of cliché and distortion.

CARL PLASA

3. Postwar Period (to 1960s)

Bedient, Calvin, *Eight Contemporary Poets*, London and New York: Oxford University Press, 1974

Corcoran, Neil, *English Poetry since 1940*, London: Longman, 1993

Davie, Donald, *Under Briggflatts: A History of Poetry in Great Britain 1960–1980*, Manchester: Carcanet, 1989

King, P.R., *Nine Contemporary Poets: A Critical Introduction*, London and New York: Methuen, 1979

Longley, Edna, "Poetry in Ireland, Scotland and Wales, 1920–1990", in *The Columbia History of British Poetry*, edited by Carl Woodring and James Shapiro, New York: Columbia University Press, 1994

Sherry, Vincent, "Poetry in England, 1945–1990", in *The Columbia History of British Poetry*, edited by Carl Woodring and James Shapiro, New York: Columbia University Press, 1994

Thwaite, Anthony, *Poetry Today, 1960–1973*, London: Longman, 1974, revised as *Poetry Today: A Critical Guide to British Poetry 1960–1984*, 1985

The poets selected by BEDIENT are Charles Tomlinson, Donald Davie, R.S. Thomas, Philip Larkin, Ted Hughes, Thomas Kinsella, Stevie Smith, and W.S. Graham. Written as a series of discrete essays loosely connected by the theme that postwar British poets display a characteristically "*sceptical* energy", this is an impressionistic and somewhat rhetorically high-toned book, which betrays its date in its choice of leading figures, but conveys nevertheless an interesting picture of poetry in the three decades from 1945 to 1974.

THWAITE's first edition gives a brief, useful survey of poetry in the 1960s and early 1970s, commenting on the continuing work of already established writers such as W.H. Auden, Roy Fuller, and R.S. Thomas, and on the then newer work of Ted Hughes, Sylvia Plath, Geoffrey Hill, *et al.* He is especially interesting (though maintaining an attitude of cool scepticism) on the experimental elements of the 1960s, including concrete and performance poetry, and the development of regional and national poetry in the British Isles. His revised edition extends his coverage to include the early 1980s.

KING's nine poets are Larkin, Tomlinson, Thom Gunn, Hughes, Plath, Seamus Heaney, Douglas Dunn, Tom Paulin and Paul Mills. His book reflects the limitations of its date – for example, in dealing with what would now be thought of as early Hughes and Heaney, and restricting women poets to Sylvia Plath. But as an avowed "introduction" to varieties of style and purpose among more recent poets, it is still very readable, and especially useful for students.

DAVIE, a distinguished poet-critic, writes from a conservative standpoint, a little curiously modified by his ambiguous interest in Ezra Pound and Pound's English follower Basil Bunting (author of *Briggflatts*). His book is a collection of free-standing essays rather than a "history".

CORCORAN's survey, though not exhaustive, is probably the most helpful currently available. His method is to group poets together in pairs, or three or four at a time, sometimes as revealing antitheses (for example, the later Eliot versus the later Auden), but more often on the basis of shared concerns (for example, David Jones and Basil Bunting as poets since 1940 "who most radically pursued the technical experiments of high Modernism", Stevie Smith and R.S. Thomas as "two solitudes", Heaney, David Longley, and Derek Mahon as Northern Ireland poets). Historical background, modern "theory", and illustrative "practical criticism" are all used to give the flavour of the poets and to relate their poetry to the changing movements and critical standards (including, notably, feminism) characteristic of the later twentieth century. Corcoran seeks to avoid labelling his chosen poets, and is scrupulous in his attention to their individual qualities; but if there is a unifying theme throughout the book it is the process that leads one group of poets to react against the influence of an earlier group.

The contributions by LONGLEY and SHERRY to *The Columbia History* are lively, well-informed, original essays. Both are sensitive to the wide, and to some extent confusing, diversity of recent poetry in English; and Longley in particular, viewing the scene from a Northern Ireland perspective, is acutely aware of the melting-pot situation created by the fact that currently "the English lyric no longer belongs to England".

R.P. DRAPER

4. Recent and Contemporary

Booth, Martin, *British Poetry 1964 to 1984: Driving Through the Barricades*, London and Boston: Routledge & Kegan Paul, 1985

Corcoran, Neil, *English Poetry since 1940*, London: Longman, 1993

Davie, Donald, *Under Briggflatts; A History of Poetry in Great Britain 1960–1988*, Manchester: Carcanet, 1989; Chicago: University of Chicago Press, 1989

Easthope, Anthony, and John O. Thompson (eds.), *Contemporary Poetry Meets Modern Theory*, Hemel Hempstead, Hertfordshire: Harvester Wheatsheaf, 1991; Toronto and Buffalo, New York: University of Toronto Press, 1991

Hampson, Robert, and Peter Barry (eds.), *New British Poetries: The Scope of the Possible*, Manchester: Manchester University Press, 1993

Riley, Denise (ed.), *Poets on Writing: Britain, 1970–1991*, London: Macmillan, 1992

Schmidt, Michael, and Grevel Lindop (eds.), *British Poetry since 1960: A Critical Survey*, Oxford: Carcanet, 1972

General surveys of contemporary English poetry tend to be either descriptive or polemical accounts of general trends, rather than analytically investigative and comprehensive accounts of poetic language and representation drawing on recent advances in critical theory. Recent publications have sought to change this.

SCHMIDT and LINDOP's influential critical anthology, in its assumption that empirical lyricism is the dominant trend in postwar British poetry, circumnavigates the extent to which the Pound-Olson-Williams tradition of objective percipience is also an important factor. The poetry of Geoffrey Hill, Jon Silkin, and Charles Tomlinson is singled out for its literal exactitude about phenomenal experience, rather than for its reduction of perceptible qualities to intellectual content: this misreads the extent to which such poetry says more about the act of knowing than its engagement with natural knowledge. This thesis, although influential, represents a singularly skewed view of the range of recent English lyric poetry currently being written.

BOOTH's study is a personal polemic ranging over many small press and mainstream poets. His opening chapter offers an historical overview of poetry's public life during the decade 1964–74, and illustrates well Booth's main thesis that a dissociation of sensibility occurred between contemporary poetry and its potential mass audience in the following decade, 1974–84. This dissociation is attributed to two things – academicism and aestheticism – both of which have conjoined to alienate existing and potential poetry readers. Booth's response is to argue for a return to an emotional theory of poetic language and a referential grounding of poetic imagery in empirical lyricism – an account of poetry and language, and poetry and culture, that is now critically dated.

DAVIE's collection of review articles is not a literary history as such, but a series of notices of the poetry of Basil Bunting, Hugh MacDiarmid, Geoffrey Hill, Philip Larkin, Ted Hughes, and C.H. Sisson. Questions concerning poetry, language and national identity; the interrelationship between rationalism and syntax in postwar British poetry; the legacy of modernist poetic tradition; the importance of cosmopolitan translation as against cultural insularity – all persist throughout Davie's varied commentaries. The evaluative conviction that British poetry in the 1950s underwent a contracting process of anti-intellectual philistinism and civic narrowness which was essentially anti-modernist, and that an alternative resuscitation of modernist tradition is to be found in the poetry of Bunting and Tomlinson persists throughout the collection. Some commentators would disagree with Davie's emphasis on the over-orchestrated perceptual and imagistic poetry of Tomlinson – in contrast to the fierce rhetorical scholasticism and intellectual precision of J.H. Prynne – as *the* most important inheritor of modernist poetics. In fact, Davie's study remains valuable precisely for its scattered insights rather than its overall approach.

EASTHOPE and THOMPSON's book brings together essays on American poets Gertrude Stein, Adrienne Rich, John Ashbery, Charles Bernstein, and Susan Howe with essays on British poets Prynne, Seamus Heaney, Tony Harrison, and Tom Raworth. The essays included are strictly interpretative, drawing on an impressive range of recent critical theory to discuss problems of social reception, meaning, and textuality in contemporary Anglo-American poetry. However, the predominance in the essays of a certain poststructuralist account of language and signification occludes the equally crucial questions of deictics, intentional or motivated utterance, metric structure, and formal constitution of meaning in the poems discussed. The book should be considered an interesting attempt to bring contemporary poetry and theory together, rather than a rigorous hermeneutic or poetics of poetic form.

CORCORAN's overview is a rigorous reading of how succeeding generations of British poets from the 1940s to the 1970s have attempted to define various attitudes towards modernism. Poets discussed include R.S. Thomas, Donald Davie, David Jones, Keith Douglas, Douglas Dunn, Paul Muldoon, Craig Raine, Carol Rumens, and James Fenton. The development of a poetry of regionalism by Northern English and Irish poets, and feminist and black British poets since the 1960s is intriguingly analysed in terms of a dissolution of cultural consensus and the Arnoldian-Leavisite notion of an "organic" poetic tradition. Corcoran sees the central issues of such poetry as the interrelationship of lexis and factionalism, and the shifting balances of poetic language and cultural and historical memory, gender and voice. Providing accessible introductions to each decade and extensive general and individual author bibliographies, Corcoran's study is an incisive and wide-ranging overview of contemporary British poetry.

HAMPSON and BARRY's book covers what the editors deem to be a marginalised or repressed body of contemporary poetry outside of mainstream public life. The book is divided up into a series of general theoretical essays on women's poetry, "open work" poetry, the politics of lyric subjectivity, and language and ideology. The attempt by the contributors to move away from dominant forms of representation and theoretical paradigms is refreshing, while the inclusion of an interesting essay by Fred D'Aguiar on contemporary black poetry in Britain widens the scope of the otherwise fugitive and contradictory pronouncements by Eric Mottram and Peter Middleton, who esteem "difficult" contemporary poetry for its resistance to received norms of expectation, while bemoaning its exclusion from these selfsame norms – the latter read as a problem of contemporary British culture. The lack of an achieved or sustained poetics or theory of poetic "difficulty" in this book means that too often the poems discussed are characterised in terms of a reductive generality that fails to illumine either them or the cultural politics of experimental British poetry in which they are placed.

Also moving away somewhat from the poetic mainstream, RILEY's collection of an important though neglected body of small press writers working within the lineage of late high modernism, provides a "promotional" opportunity for these writers – such as Allen Fisher, Tom Lowenstein, Anthony Barnett, Mary Oliver, and John Wilkinson – to talk about their work and their writing processes. While the editorial Introduction reneges on either contextual criticism or historical overview, the division of the book – into definitions and conditions of writing, ways of working, readings and particular studies – offers an interesting glimpse into the contexts of reception and recognition with which these contemporary poets are engaged.

D.S. MARRIOTT

Poetry: American – General

Bercovitch, Sacvan (ed.), *The Cambridge History of American Literature, Volume 1: 1590–1820*, Cambridge and New York: Cambridge University Press, 1994

Dowling, William C., *Poetry and Ideology in Revolutionary Connecticut*, Athens: University of Georgia Press, 1990

Fender, Stephen, *American Literature in Context, Volume 1: 1620–1830* , London and New York: Methuen, 1983

Gelpi, Albert, *The Tenth Muse: The Psyche of the American Poet*, Cambridge, Massachusetts: Harvard University Press, 1975; Cambridge: Cambridge University Press, 1991

Hammond, Jeffrey A., *Sinful Self, Saintly Self: The Puritan Experience of Poetry*, Athens: University of Georgia Press, 1993

Harding, Brian, *American Literature in Context, Volume II: 1830–1865*, London and New York: Methuen, 1982

Lee, A. Robert, *Nineteenth-Century American Poetry*, London: Vision Press, 1985; Totowa, New Jersey: Barnes & Noble, 1985

Matthiessen, F.O., *American Renaissance: Art and Expression in the Age of Emerson and Whitman*, London and New York: Oxford University Press, 1941

Parini, Jay (ed.), *The Columbia History of American Poetry*, New York: Columbia University Press, 1993

Schweitzer, Ivy, *The Work of Self-Representation: Lyric Poetry in Colonial New England*, Chapel Hill: University of North Carolina Press, 1991

It has long been a commonplace of American cultural history to see the work of its nineteenth-century writers as giving original literary expression to the sense of an emergent national identity following the War of Independence and the founding of the new Republic. It follows from this that nineteenth-century poetry receives much more attention in literary histories than does the poetry that preceded it, except for specialist studies of the Puritan literary imagination. In this context the work of MATTHIESSEN is central, for his book exercised a dominant influence on the course of cultural and literary-critical history in America for several decades. Matthiessen wrote before the publication of Thomas H. Johnson's edition of Emily Dickinson's poems (1955), and Dickinson therefore occupies a minor role in his version of literary development. Over the past three decades that situation has changed dramatically, so that Walt Whitman and Dickinson, and to a lesser extent Edgar Allan Poe, receive far more attention than any other nineteenth-century poets. The effect of this has been the general neglect of such figures as William Cullen Bryant, Henry Wadsworth Longfellow, and John Greenleaf Whittier, to name merely three of the nineteenth-century poets who were both popular and considered important in their time. In the twentieth century the poets of North America are many in number and of infinite variety: taken as a whole they provide work of unrivalled quality in the English-speaking world.

Whitman, Dickinson, Poe, and the major movements and figures of twentieth-century American poetry are given substantial treatment elsewhere in the present volume. The discussion here therefore aims to be somewhat compensatory in emphasis, with a concentration on the Colonial and early Republican periods, and on some of the more "minor" poetic figures of the nineteenth century.

The early history of American verse begins with the metaphysical and devotional poetry of the Puritan period, characterised especially by the work of Anne Bradstreet and Edward Taylor. The best-known eighteenth-century poets are Philip Freneau, once called the "Father of American poetry", and Phillis Wheatley, the black woman poet who had been taken as a child from Africa and sold into slavery. (The Boston family that bought her had her educated according to the conventions of the day: in due course she became the first published black American woman writer, in 1773). Some of the most recent publications to deal with the long history of American verse now acknowledge the contribution to that history of the oral tradition of the Native American tribal communities as well as focusing on the African-American tradition.

PARINI's monumental history is less thorough than might be expected from its 800 pages, for it privileges twentieth-century poetry to a marked degree, with commentaries on the work of this century occupying three-quarters of the book's length. In consequence American poetry from the early seventeenth to the end of the nineteenth century is condensed in the first eight chapters, and since three of these deal with Whitman, Dickinson, and Poe, what we are given is a selective history in which there is no room for Freneau, while Bryant, James Russell Lowell, and Whittier receive minimal attention. No doubt this organisation reflects the present unfashionable status of these poets, but it underlines the extent to which the *History* is selective, a charge that must also be made of its coverage of some twentieth-century poets. Despite this criticism, Parini's anthology is a welcome survey, and includes many fine individual contributions. Francis Murphy gives a brief but assured discussion of Bradstreet and Edward Taylor in relation to the traditions of metaphysical devotional poetry common both to Britain and America for much of the seventeenth century. Carolivia Herron provides an overview of the earliest expressions of African-American poetry from the middle of the eighteenth century to the early 1920s, and thus sets Wheatley's work in a tradition of African-American writing. John McWilliams gives a very instructive account of the varieties of nineteenth-century epic, a form he shows to have flourished in the work of a great many nineteenth-century writers ambitious to write the epical narrative of the "New World" in one guise or another: McWilliams's account ranges from Timothy Dwight's *The Conquest of Canaan* (1785) to Stephen Vincent Benét's epic poem about the Civil War, *John Brown's Body* (1928). Dana Gioia's timely rereading of Longfellow works through an anatomy of the aesthetics of modernism and the literary-critical practices it nourished to show how Longfellow's virtues as a narrative poet became occluded from view in the twentieth century. This is an innovative essay, and should encourage a renewed interest in the author of *Hiawatha*. Lawrence Buell's reading of the Transcendentalist poets is revisionary in his insistence that we read the poetry of Emerson, Thoreau, William Ellery Channing the younger, Christopher Pearse Cranch, and Jones Very within a transatlantic Anglophone community of poetry, in which its virtues can be seen for what they are, rather than as an impoverished conservative deflection away from the dramatic centre of nineteenth-century American poetry in Whitman. Buell is a powerful and persuasive advocate of this revisionary view, as his analysis of the negotiation between the ego and the expression of an impersonal self in this poetry makes abundantly clear. Finally, I refer to just one of the many chapters on twentieth-century poetry in this collection because it attends to women poets, who are generally neglected in critical commentary: Jeanne Larsen looks at some popular poets of the early years of the century, such as Sara Teasdale, Elinor Wylie, and Edna St Vincent Millay, and situates their work in relation to women poets more frequently discussed in academic criticism – Amy Lowell and Louise Bogan.

GELPI writes in a distinguished tradition established by Perry Miller's *The Life of the Mind in America* (1953), Roy Harvey Pearce's *The Continuity of American Poetry* (1961), and Hyatt H. Waggoner's *American Poets from the Puritans to the Present* (1968). For Pearce's use of the concept of "mind" as central to the consciousness of American writers, Gelpi substitutes the word "psyche", and this has come to be a quite widely accepted way of dealing with that complex fusion of inner self and social self as it features in the American poetic tradition: hence Gelpi's sub-title, which acknowledges the psyche as the indigenous American "muse", as his main title acknowledges the primacy of Bradstreet. Gelpi opens this account with an essay on Taylor, and there is something providential for Gelpi in Taylor's secretive practice of poetry and his wish that his poems should not be published after his death. Gelpi reads Taylor's case as a paradigm of the difficult negotiations American poets would have to make throughout the next three centuries in speaking both for the private self and for the social world of which they were a part. Gelpi sees Taylor's poetic and psychic enterprise as dramatised by what he calls "typological" and "tropological" imperatives, exploiting the symbolic representation of scriptural types within the structures of formal verse patterns through an intensely figurative poetic idiom. Thus, he sees in Taylor a native American cast of mind that is quite distinct from the creative mind-set of his British seventeenth-century forebears and contemporaries. Gelpi's subsequent reading of Emerson, Poe, Whitman, and Dickinson investigates the relationship between self, poetic form, and the world beyond the self, as the complexities of social and national life weigh upon the poet.

Three of the volumes (forthcoming at the time of writing) in the *Cambridge History of American Literature* will prove to be essential in studying the history of American poetry: Volume 4 will deal with poetry from 1790 to 1920, Volume 5 with poetry and criticism from 1910 to 1950, and Volume 8 with poetry and criticism from 1940 to 1990. In the meantime, Volume 1 (BERCOVITCH), which covers the extensive period from 1590 to 1820, has two sections to note here, Emory Elliott's account of the poetry of "New England Puritan Literature", and Michael T. Gilmore's commentary on the poetry of "The Literature of the Revolutionary and Early National Periods". Elliott confronts an apparent enigma: poetry, like all the other arts, was understood to be anathema to the strict world of Puritan doctrine, where the use of figurative language was forbidden except for religious instruction. Yet Puritan poetry is a concrete fact, as the work of Bradstreet, Taylor, Michael Wigglesworth, and others testifies. Elliott resolves this paradox through the story he traces of the leavening of this harsh doctrine from the 1650s onwards, and shows how the Puritans came to admit the value of an expressive and often sensuous eloquence in public as well as private discourse, and in the written word. Elliott pursues this process through an account of all those Puritan writers who have contributed in some measure to poetry, and if the conventional view of Bradstreet and Taylor as the primary exponents of this poetry remains unchallenged in Elliott's narrative, our understanding of the varieties and reach of the Puritan poetic imagination is extended by this absorbing account. Gilmore's range extends from the imitative neoclassical poetry of the second half of the eighteenth century through the native strains of an emergent Romanticism in the work of Bryant. Gilmore takes us through the early Republican years, when poetry "enjoyed an intimate relation to national consciousness" without producing any poets or poems of the first rank, concentrating here on the group of writers known as the "Connecticut Wits", tutors and students at Yale University who were bound to the common cause of literary independence through celebration of America's revolutionary history. Thereafter, Gilmore deals principally with Wheatley, Freneau – whom he sees as embodying the contradictory compulsions of patriotism and individualism both in his life and poetry – and Bryant, whose best work appeared in his first collection of poems (1821). Gilmore's account of the idea of the poet as a public spokesperson, and the way in which this idea increasingly competed with the expressive individualism more characteristic of the nineteenth century, is thorough and authoritative.

The remaining studies to be discussed tackle rather narrower ranges in the field of American poetry. Schweitzer and Hammond deal with the pre-revolutionary period. SCHWEITZER's iconoclastic study of Puritan poetry is driven by feminist and psychoanalytic imperatives. Her Introduction addresses the Puritan understanding of the idea of a "spiritual marriage" between man and God, and reads this ambition for union as a way of achieving what she calls a "redeemed subjectivity" figured as "an obliteration of the original self through adopting the feminized position of Bride". Schweitzer thus examines the ways in which universal human experience becomes gendered in this poetry, to the disadvantage of women: if the feminized position of the Bride is one of submission and subordination, the carnal nature of this condition is read by Schweitzer as reflecting on the way women's experience is appropriated as emblematic of man's relation to God, but in a way that devalues the uniqueness of women's experience. From this it is but a short step to the idea that Taylor's poetry searches for a "redeemed subjectivity" through the role of spouse, a role that for Schweitzer embodies the culmination and "dead end" of Puritan ideology. Nor is it surprising to find Schweitzer arguing that Bradstreet becomes a "cultural figure ... constructed and used by masculinist Puritan culture". The detailed exposition of these arguments is developed through Schweitzer's analyses of the tension in the speaking voice of the Puritan lyric, a tension that serves to dramatize the "conception and articulation of voice and identity" in Puritan poetry.

HAMMOND's title relates to his understanding of the "holy war" engaged in between the "natural" self and the "gracious" self in the Puritan world, a conflict of base and spirit assumed to rage in every soul according to the poets Hammond deals with – Bradstreet, Taylor, and Wigglesworth. There are two principal directions in Hammond's thinking, the one dwelling on the inter-connectedness of idea and expression in these three poets, the other concerned with their typical understanding of their audiences, which then conditioned the terms of their rhetorical address. Thus Hammond uncovers significant similarities between Bradstreet's "Elegies", Taylor's "Preparatory Meditations", and Wigglesworth's "Riddles Unriddled", and shows how these poets argued their readers towards a full understanding of the necessities laid upon the self to achieve a fully Christian life.

Moving forward to the revolutionary era, DOWLING's book on the Connecticut Wits concentrates on John Trumbull, David Humphreys, Timothy Dwight, and Joel Barlow. He argues that the Wits saw themselves as the American counterparts of the earlier eighteenth-century British Augustans, particularly Alexander Pope, Jonathan Swift, John Gay, and James Thomson, whose satiric attacks on the social and economic corruptions of the Hanoverian dynasty and Prime Minister Sir Robert Walpole were echoed by the Wits' attacks on George III and his ministers of state. Dowling investigates the ideological complications of the writings of the Wits, as their political and religious conservatism conflicted with the burgeoning egalitarianism of the post-Revolutionary phase of American history, and as the orthodoxy of Calvinism began to surrender to a more tolerant religious spirit and practice. This very valuable study is the first book-length account of its subject for many years.

FENDER's volume in the "American Literature in Context" series has a useful section on two eighteenth-century poets, Freneau and Joel Barlow, focused on their use of the figure of Columbus in (Freneau's) "The Pictures of Columbus" (1788) and (Barlow's) *The Vision of Columbus* (1787), the latter revised and expanded as *The Columbiad* (1807). As Fender shows, both poets chose Columbus as a figure of appropriate historical significance for the founding of the new Republic, around whom a national epic of emergence into nationhood might be composed, based on the classical models of epic. Fender sees in Freneau's poem an implied picturing of Columbus as the "type of alienated, romantic artist" equally aware of the dark consequences of the European settlement of America as well as the bright prospects of a new beginning for European society; by contrast, Barlow's inflated epic has not survived its ambitious synthesis of a proleptic history of the founding of the Republic with a vision of a future "union of all mankind in a single world government". In the second volume in this series, covering 1830–65, HARDING has a section on Longfellow, examining a wide range of his poems and prose to explore the poet's advocacy of the ideal of domestic love as the model for public unity and concord – an ideal persistently threatened by the aggressive materialism of his times, "whose ultimate expression was war".

LEE's collection of essays pays customary attention to Whitman, Dickinson, and Poe, but it is included here principally for its attention to poets now less frequently discussed within the frame of nineteenth-century verse – Emerson, Herman Melville, the "Fireside Poets" (Bryant, James Russell Lowell, Longfellow, Whittier, and Oliver Wendell Holmes), Jones Very, and Frederick Goddard Tuckerman. In addition there is a fascinating essay by Graham Clarke on the relationship between paintings and the poetics of nineteenth-century American landscape, a nice adaptation to the American scene of the classical belief in the sisterly relations between poetry and fine art. Brian Harding examines the paradoxical fusion of architectural and musical form in Emerson's poetry, through attention to Emerson's famous "The Snow Storm", related poems in his *Poems* (1847), and the posthumously published "Music". In such poems Harding traces Emerson's attempts to write of the unity of process and change, through analogies with musical expression, and ideas of permanence and durability through architectural imagery. Lee argues the case for Melville's poetry, in a scrupulous account of the long verse-narrative of literal and spiritual pilgrimage, *Clarel*, and makes a good case for its value as the poetic counterpart to *Moby-Dick*. James H. Justus investigates the Fireside Poets, who collectively made poetry into what Justus calls "a public treasure". The question Justus asks is, if these poets became "institutionalized as national poets because they articulated the values of their culture", how then did they formulate these values? In ways peculiar to the individual range of each of these poets Justus finds them all celebrating an ideal correspondence between the virtues of domestic harmony and public or civil well-being precisely because such ideas of harmony were repeatedly threatened throughout much of the nineteenth century. David Seed's comparative study of Very and Tuckerman is an ideal introduction to both poets. He lucidly charts the vexed issue of Very's relationship to the Transcendentalists, and argues for the importance of the concept of "voice" in Very as an index to the poet's sense of himself as a vessel for God's voice. Seed distinguishes between these poets by defining Very as one who engages his readers "in the drama of salvation", whereas the imperative of Tuckerman's work is one of "quiet self-examination", a poet of "anxious introspection" with a more natural appeal to the twentieth century reader.

LIONEL KELLY

Poetry: American – 19th Century

Donoghue, Denis, *Connoisseurs of Chaos: Ideas of Order in Modern American Poetry*, New York: Macmillan, 1965; London: Faber & Faber, 1966

Gelpi, Albert, *The Tenth Muse: The Psyche of the American Poet*, Cambridge, Massachusetts: Harvard University Press, 1975; Cambridge: Cambridge University Press, 1991

Kramer, Aaron, *The Prophetic Tradition in American Poetry, 1835–1900*, Rutherford, New Jersey: Fairleigh Dickinson University Press, 1968

Lee, A. Robert (ed.), *Nineteenth-Century American Poetry*, London: Vision Press, 1985

Parini, Jay (ed.), *The Columbia History of American Poetry*, New York: Columbia University Press, 1993

Pearce, Roy Harvey, *The Continuity of American Poetry*, Princeton, New Jersey: Princeton University Press, 1961, revised 1965

Shucard, Alan R., *American Poetry: The Puritans Through Walt Whitman*, Amherst: University of Massachusetts Press, 1988

Waggoner, Hyatt H., *American Poets from the Puritans to the Present*, Boston: Houghton Mifflin, 1968; revised edition, Baton Rouge: Louisiana State University Press, 1984

Wells, Henry W., *The American Way of Poetry*, New York: Columbia University Press, 1943

Winters, Yvor, *In Defense of Reason: Primitivism and Decadence: A Study of Experimental American Poetry*, Denver, Colorado: University of Denver Press, 1947; London: Routledge & Kegan Paul, 1960

There is now an extensive body of critical and scholarly writing on individual poets of the nineteenth century, particularly major figures such as Emily Dickinson, Edgar Allan Poe, and Walt Whitman. There is, however, rather less devoted to the shape of nineteenth century American verse in general, and it remains the case that among the best critical resources are those that treat American verse as a whole.

WELLS's early study attempts an account of what is "truly indigenous and unique in the American tradition itself", the "tradition" here being that of American poetry which Wells considers, perhaps somewhat controversially, the "chief . . . of the arts in America". Wells's approach is by topical and thematic routes rather than chapters on individual poets: thus "Matter and Spirit", a chapter that deals, primarily, with Whitman, is about Transcendental self-knowledge, "Cambridge Culture and Folk Poetry" organizes the discussion of Henry Wadsworth Longfellow, James Russell Lowell, and John Greenleaf Whittier, while Herman Melville's *Clarel* is read as "A Religious Quest". Wells's book takes the history of American poetry through to figures such as T.S. Eliot, Robert Frost, and Hart Crane, but the first half of the book is substantively concerned with the nineteenth century, and the lucid, direct style of writing makes the book very accessible, if not always authoritative.

WINTERS's essays on nineteenth-century poetry remain hard to ignore. This influential volume brings together most of his major writings on the verse of the period, notably those essays that made up *Maule's Curse* (1938). Jones Very and Ralph Waldo Emerson are considered together in a controversial essay, which challenged the prevailing orthodoxy of judgment by arguing Very's superiority over most of his contemporaries, Melville and Dickinson excepted. The essay on Dickinson puts a forceful case for her as one of the greatest lyric poets of all time and remains valuable, also, for its detailed account of her use of metre. Whitman and what Winters rather contemptuously called "the Emersonian doctrine" surface in the famous essay on Hart Crane, "The Significance of *The Bridge* by Hart Crane, or What Are We to Think of Professor X?"

PEARCE's book, one of the most distinguished on the subject, is "an account of the development of American poetry from the seventeenth century to the recent past". Its thesis is that American poetry is unified by a preoccupation with the relation between the self and the external world; this is, in part, a philosophical matter, and Pearce sees the American poet as insistently engaged with the idea of poetry as an act of creation, not merely invention. Pearce's book remains notable for its analysis of the place of the long poem in American poetry – both the early attempts at epic in such works as Joel Barlow's *The Columbiad* or Whitman's "Song of Myself" and the reflective and philosophical long poem of a poet such as Wallace Stevens. This remains indispensable reading.

DONOGHUE's volume of essays (first delivered as lectures at the University of Cincinnati) is, like Pearce's book, concerned with continuities between nineteenth- and twentieth-century American verse. The eight essays are evenly divided between nineteenth- and twentieth-century poets and the four poets, under discussion in the first half of the volume are Whitman, Frederick Goddard Tuckerman, Melville, and Dickinson. These essays can be read quite independently of one another, but they lose something of their force since Donoghue's readings turn on the connecting theme of the American poet's treatment of the contrary states of order and chaos.

KRAMER's is a kind of social history of American poetry in the latter half of the nineteenth century, seeing individual poets in the light of the major historical and social concerns of the age, such as the Mexican-American War, the debate over the abolition of slavery, the growth of mass, or "mob", culture and the attendant problems for a democratic nation, the treatment of the American Indian, and, finally, the Spanish-American War. The readings of individual poems are occasionally rather leaden and pedestrian, but many poets, particularly minor ones, are illuminatingly discussed against the relevant historical background. A useful bibliography, if now a little outdated, is appended.

GELPI's book is one of the most highly regarded of recent critical studies of the American poet. His point of departure is what he calls "the separation of American poetry from its British parent" and the attendant issues of "imagination, voice, form, and technique", which give a distinctively national character to American achievements in verse. He argues that American culture has forced on the American poet a debate between intellect and passion, and that many of the thematic and formal features of poetry are to be understood in the light of this debate. The argument necessitates a psychological approach, since the poet's mind is part of his "psyche", and the readings of individual poets are informed by a critical language that owes much to Carl Jung and neo-Freudians such as Erik Erikson and Norman O. Brown. The opening chapter is general in character, the second discusses the Puritan poet Edward Taylor (and is arguably the best chapter in the book), and subsequent chapters deal with Emerson, Poe, Whitman, and Dickinson. This is a challenging book, and is not always easy reading, but the effort is well repaid by Gelpi's insights.

WAGGONER's revised edition of his 1968 volume brings his historical survey up to date with material on poets who came to the reading public's attention in the late 1960s and 1970s. This is one of the most ambitious, and readable overviews of the whole history of American poetry, and because it is not constrained by any thesis it can be easily used as a kind of critical reference tool. Waggoner writes at some length on major poets of the nineteenth century (William Cullen Bryant, Dickinson, Longfellow, Poe, and Whitman) as well as giving due consideration to most of the minor figures of the period (Oliver Wendell Holmes, Sidney Lanier, James Russell Lowell, William Vaughn Moody, Whittier, etc.) and to those better known as novelists who also wrote verse, particularly Melville. The bibliography, covering both primary and secondary works, provides a very good point of departure for further reading.

LEE's collection of newly commissioned essays concentrates on "canonical" figures from the latter half of the nineteenth-century, though David Seed writes intelligently about the "minor" New England poets Tuckerman and Very (Winters, of course, sees Very as a major figure). The editor's Introduction speaks of "the double tension in American poetry, its inward and outward inclination", and many of the essays in his collection sensitively illuminate the paradox of meditation and confession at the heart of American poetry. Mark Kinkead-Weekes, dismissing Whitman's ideas as "sadly flabby", looks at the language and syntax of two of Whitman's more elegiac and contemplative poems, "When Lilacs Last in the Dooryard Bloom'd" and "Out of the Cradle Endlessly Rocking"; Lee himself makes a bold case for the modernist "difficulty" of Melville's poetry, mainly by pointing to its kinship with his *Moby-Dick* and the major prose works; Eric Mottram reads Whitman as a prophet of political and sexual health; Robert von Hallberg writes on Poe's poetry and its relationship to his criticism; and Jim Philip and Brian Harding offer challenging new views of, respectively, "mind" in Dickinson and "architecture" as an image of the imagination in Emerson. In the two remaining essays, James H. Justus analyses the "fireside poets" (Bryant, Longfellow, Whittier, Holmes, and James Russell Lowell), and Graham Clarke examines the pictorialism in American landscape poetry from Bryant to Whitman and beyond.

SHUCARD's study traces the development of American poetry from the seventeenth century to the late nineteenth century and, like Kramer's book, charts this development against a background of cultural, political, and social change. Much of the book is concerned with the achievements of the nineteenth century, and in addition to chapters on Poe, Emerson, and Whitman there is a valuable overview of American Romanticism, though considerations of space have resulted in rather abbreviated accounts of individual poets.

PARINI's recent volume is a collection of newly commissioned essays on American poetry, among which are several on nineteenth century poets. John McWilliams writes perceptively about "The Epic in the Nineteenth Century" in ways that will be familiar to anyone who knows his study *The American Epic: Transforming a Genre, 1770–1860* (1989); Dana Gioia considers Longfellow in the light of what might be called the historical poetics of modernism; Lawrence Buell discusses the Transcendentalist poets, notably Emerson, Thoreau, and Very; and Dickinson, Whitman, and Poe are covered in essays, respectively, by Cynthia Griffin Wolff, Donald Pease, and Jeffrey Meyers.

HENRY CLARIDGE

Poetry: American – 20th Century

1. General

Blackmur, R.P., *The Double Agent: Essays in Craft and Elucidation*, New York: Arrow, 1935; reprinted, Gloucester, Massachusetts: Peter Smith, 1962
Candelaria, Cordelia, *Chicano Poetry: A Critical Introduction*, Westport, Connecticut: Greenwood Press, 1986
Ehrenpreis, Irvin, *Poetries of America: Essays on the Relation of Character to Style*, edited by Daniel Albright, Charlottesville: University Press of Virginia, 1989
Gibson, Donald B. (ed.), *Modern Black Poets: A Collection of Critical Essays*, Englewood Cliffs, New Jersey: Prentice-Hall, 1973
Limón, José E., *Mexican Ballads, Chicano Poems: History and Influence in Mexican-American Social Poetry*, Berkeley: University of California Press, 1992
Parini, Jay (ed.), *The Columbia History of American Poetry*, New York: Columbia University Press, 1993
Vendler, Helen, *Part of Nature, Part of Us: Modern American Poets*, Cambridge, Massachusetts: Harvard University Press, 1980

In the twentieth century, American writing has provided many of the innovations in literature in English. This is most evident in poetry where – from Robert Frost's realist repudiation of Georgian pastoralism, through the work of T.S. Eliot and Ezra Pound with its modernist zenith in Wallace Stevens, to the Harlem Renaissance and Langston Hughes, the Black Mountain School and Robert Creeley, the Beats and Allen Ginsberg, the new Romanticism of E.E. Cummings, Theodore Roethke, and John Berryman, the Confessional School and Sylvia Plath, the aestheticism of John Ashbery, and the more recent writing of black and Chicano poets – immigration, ethnic diversity, jazz, and the radical linguistic influence of urban dialects have produced in the United States a poetics so various as to be nearly without a common denominator. The disintegration since the 1960s of any universal notion of an American identity in poetry is the predictable outcome of the one dominant trait of American writing since the 1920s: intense individualism marked by innovative technical virtuosity.

PARINI brings together 31 essays in a comprehensive volume, which covers the traditions of American poetry from the seventeenth to the late twentieth century, with nearly 600 pages devoted to modern and contemporary poets. Margaret Dickie's examination of "women poets and the emergence of modernism" is particularly valuable, as is John Elder's piece on nature and the tradition of environmentalism in American poetry. While the contributors here are all academics, many are also practising poets, a qualification which informs W.S. Di Piero's writing on Pound and George Oppen. Some, but not all, of the essays are accompanied by short bibliographies suggesting further reading. Comprehensiveness is this volume's chief virtue, including as it does discussions of Hopi oral tradition, the standard canon, and the recent controversies surrounding issues of race, gender, dialect, and sexuality. John Shoptaw's essay on James Merrill and John Ashbery provides one of the better summations of the current state of American poetry in its continuing obsession with "transitory presences". This volume's 84-page index is no small part of its usefulness.

BLACKMUR's book brings together essays written in the 1930s, several as reviews, four of which respond to the immediate impact of the poetry of E.E. Cummings, Marianne Moore, Wallace Stevens, and Hart Crane on their contemporary readers. These are seminal pieces, in which a great theoretical mind engages with the most challenging of the American poetry written in the 1930s, giving us insight into the stylistic originality of Cummings in particular: Blackmur says of Cummings' work, in the process of summing up modernism, that in such poetry "no feeling is ever defined. No emotion betrays a structure . . . . In the end we have only the thrill of substance". The obscurity of much modern American poetry becomes something religious, even mystical, in Blackmur's essays.

VENDLER's collection, like Blackmur's, includes book-reviews with essays. The volume discusses nearly 50 books of poetry written by 34 poets, both men and women, whites and blacks. Vendler is, perhaps, the best commentator on the work of Stevens and Robert Lowell; her discussion of Ginsberg is less enlightening. She is particularly adept at rendering clear and accessible some of the most perplexing of modern American poetry. Among women poets, Moore and Adrienne Rich find in Vendler a thoughtful and sensitive reader. The final two chapters of the book are long review-essays examining respectively eight and ten volumes by some of the more innovative new voices in poetry in the late 1970s. Of special interest is the examination of A.R. Ammons in two essays, the one dealing comparatively with Ammons, Berryman, and Cummings.

EHRENPREIS brings a scholar's preoccupation with biography and influence to his essays on Stevens, Pound, Eliot, Robert Penn Warren, Elizabeth Bishop, Berryman, Lowell, James Merrill, and Ashbery. Again, many of the pieces appeared first in literary reviews, especially the *New York Review of Books* and the *Times Literary Supplement*. Ehrenpreis is good on the effects of religion on Merrill and Berryman, and on the lines of influence that connect poets like Crane, Eliot, and Lowell. He describes the ways in which "games with form and technique become poignant" in much modern American poetry, where "doctrines do not collaborate to give poems direction". This is a book that deals with the male mainstream of modern American poetry; it is very much an intellectual appreciation, long on analysis, short on passion.

GIBSON's volume is the best single collection of essays on black poets. The book begins with the "New Negro" of the 1920s, and finishes with pieces on the "poetry of Black Hate" and the "humanistic protest" of African-American poetry in the 1970s. Black women poets are well represented, particularly in R. Roderick Palmer's study of Sonia Sanchez and Nikki Giovanni. Gibson's own introductory chapter is a reliable, concise, and informative brief history of black poetry in America, emphasizing four major influences: the Harlem Renaissance; the protest writing of the 1930s; the Beat movement and jazz; and the life and work of Amiri Baraka (LeRoi Jones). The book includes a general bibliography of work about African-American poetry and shorter bibliographies for studies of Gwendolyn Brooks, Countee Cullen, Robert Hayden, Langston Hughes, Baraka, Claude McKay, Melvin Tolson, and Jean Toomer.

As Spanish quickly assumes an equal status with English in a bilingual United States, Chicano poetry, new as it is, is becoming a very influential voice. CANDELARIA's book identifies 1967 as the critical year for legitimising the Chicano poetic voice. Hers is an attempt to establish a new poetics for postcolonial Hispanic writing in the United States, and she emphasizes the importance of parody and parable, tracing those traditions back to Cervantes and the secular resistance to the sexual repressiveness of the Spanish Catholic Church. Candelaria is persuasive in her arguments distinguishing Chicano writing from both white and black American poetry through the continuing influences of Catholic and Mexican traditions. The book includes a brief bibliography and a crucial glossary of Hispanic words that have become part of Chicano poetic diction. LIMÓN locates the birth of Chicano poetry in the years between 1965 and 1972, when Chicano vernacular met "critical populist modernism". This is a more scholarly and political study than Candelaria's, and provides the important insight that the virile appearance of Hispanic writing in the 1970s suggests the extent to which the racial complexity of twentieth-century American culture has made possible a national poetry that is heterogeneous to the point of near incomprehensibility. But finally, the emergence of Chicano poetry is, in the words Irving Howe used to describe the literature of immigration, a testimony to the ways in which transplanted cultures "survive [in America] long after their more self-conscious members suppose them to have vanished". Modern American poetry is not about cultural change but cultural reclamation.

STEPHEN W. BROWN

2. Before World War II

Baker, Houston A., Jr., *Modernism and the Harlem Renaissance*, Chicago: University of Chicago Press, 1987
Bloom, Harold (ed.), *American Poetry 1915–1945*, New York: Chelsea House, 1987
Gelpi, Albert, *A Coherent Splendor: The American Poetic Renaissance, 1910–1950*, Cambridge and New York: Cambridge University Press, 1987
Gilbert, Sandra M., and Susan Gubar, *No Man's Land: The Place of the Woman Writer in the Twentieth Century: Letters From the Front* (Volume 3 of three-volume series), New Haven, Connecticut, and London: Yale University Press, 1994
Nelson, Cary, *Repression and Recovery: Modern American Poetry and the Politics of Cultural Memory, 1910–1945*, Madison: University of Wisconsin Press, 1989
Walker, Cheryl, *Masks Outrageous and Austere: Culture, Psyche, and Persona in Modern Women Poets*, Bloomington: Indiana University Press, 1991
Walker, Jeffrey, *Bardic Ethos and the American Epic Poem*, Baton Rouge: Louisiana State University Press, 1989

Although landmark analyses of the American poetic tradition (among them Roy Harvey Pearce's 1961 *The Continuity of American Poetry* and Hyatt Waggonner's 1968 *American Poets: From the Puritans to the Present*) include generous readings of the early twentieth-century material, only recently have critical studies been limited to the period itself. Nonetheless, the available criticism is vast and various, and offers both predominantly formal readings by scholars interested in aesthetic and textual theory and, concurrently, more politically engaged readings by scholars working from the theoretical vantage points of cultural criticism, feminism, and Marxism. The latter have brought to the forefront the contentious issue of canonical membership. Although the half-dozen or so traditionally central figures of the period continue to draw considerable attention, the boundaries of the canon have been radically reconfigured. As a result, both the material at hand and the vantage points from which we engage that material have multiplied, and the study of modern American poetry is all the richer for it.

BLOOM's edited volume of selected criticism from 1939 to 1986 offers a measure of such critical pluralism. His Introduction, sketches of eight of the 25 poets treated in the collection, consists of both close readings and critical polemic, which can be as illuminating as it is obfuscating. Although

Bloom's own canonical program is at work here – Ralph Waldo Emerson and Wallace Stevens are central to his cultural genealogy – his critical selections are impressive. Along with essays on more predictable figures, Bloom includes work on Paul Laurence Dunbar, H.D., and the Harlem Renaissance. Varied theoretical approaches are also given space: juxtaposed with traditional evaluative scholarship are deconstructive readings and landmark feminist studies. Although not chronologically arranged, the collection charts some of the recent developments in the study of modern American poetry, while locating several critical highpoints.

GELPI, a lively voice in the otherwise tired practice of defining modern American poetry, treats the period as "the linear but sometimes parricidal offspring of Romanticism". That he does so comes as no surprise; his study is actually the counterpart to his earlier and influential work on nineteenth-century American poets, *The Tenth Muse: The Psyche of the American Poet* (1975), an area of expertise that brings a larger sense of the poetic tradition to this more narrowly bound study. Although modernism and its enthusiasts tend to define the movement in opposition to Romanticism, Gelpi argues for a subtle continuity between the two, which lies in modernism's reconstitution of the aesthetic and epistemological questions that troubled its predecessors. Gelpi frames a series of monographs on Stevens, T.S. Eliot, Ezra Pound, H.D., William Carlos Williams, Allen Tate, and Hart Crane with a look at what he calls the pre-modernist poetry of Robert Frost and John Crowe Ransom, and the anti-modernist poetry of Yvor Winters and Robinson Jeffers.

Jeffrey WALKER, who draws from the critical mainstream of the modernist long poem, does so with a compelling grasp of rhetorical theory. Marking Whitman's epic as the prototype for like-minded ventures on the American scene (Pound, Crane, Williams, and Charles Olson) Walker outlines the limitations of the modernist inheritance of "a Jeffersonian historico-political vision, as revised according to vitalistic premises; and a belletristic theory of bardic utterance, as filtered through Emersonian and subsequently modernist orphism". The result is a troubling mythology of the poet's suasory mission – to which each of these writers is fatally committed – that is out of sync with the rhetorical strategies typically employed in the "bardic poem". Walker's careful analysis not only provides a unique reading of the long poem, but also offers a strong introduction to that particular tradition.

GILBERT and GUBAR set their own work against the decidedly masculine readings of Bloom, Gelpi, and Walker with their three-volume study of twentieth-century women writers. The final instalment, which gives preference to, but is not confined by, the early decades of this century and the borders of the United States should be central to the study of modern American poetry. Volume 1 sets out the authors' reconstruction of twentieth-century "sex wars" and "sexchanges", and chronicles the formulation and interrogation of sexual politics across a broad spectrum of writers. With this socio-historic and literary framework in mind, Volume 3 offers the trilogy's most intensive poetic readings, including those of Edna St Vincent Millay, Marianne Moore, and H.D., along with analyses of their subsequent impact on writers such as Elizabeth Bishop, Sylvia Plath, Anne Sexton, and Adrienne Rich. In this third volume, Gilbert and Gubar focus on the impersonations and masks that women employ as complicit but subversive strategies of writing. Maintaining that "there is a distinction between the projects of male and female modernists", the authors focus on women writers whose "differently engendered way" grants them access to a cultural unconscious sensitive to social change. The result is a critical *tour de force*, which not only redefines the modernist map, but also offers substantial readings on a number of key poets from a perspective sure of its place among the many critical feminisms.

Cheryl WALKER also offers a feminist reading of the work of modern American women poets, in this case at the intersection of psycho-biography, cultural critique, and poetics. The study is written in the wake of her earlier examination of the nineteenth century in *The Nightingale's Burden* – which traces the dramatic appearance of women poets on the American literary scene – but unlike its predecessor focuses more carefully on individuals and on what Walker calls "persona poems". Arguing that each poet creates her own textual *persona* mediated by the dominant patriarchal culture, Walker reads the work of Amy Lowell, Sara Teasdale, Elinor Wylie, H.D., Millay, and Louise Bogan with a sensitivity to the writers' complicity with, and resistance to, that culture.

BAKER, noting that the dominant definitions of modernism are set up as ideals against which the achievements of black American writers are measured, challenges the prevailing notion that poets such as Claude McKay and Countee Cullen failed to achieve the standards of the period. Given that such judgements are distorted by a powerful ethnocentrism, Baker sets out to describe – in this first book of a critical trilogy – the interpretive codes proper to the writers of the Harlem Renaissance. African-American modernism is characterized by a tension between the "mastery of forms" and the "deformation of mastery", which merge successfully in the work of Sterling A. Brown. These dichotomous strategies of cultural resistance (one employs an elusive masking, the other guerilla tactics) find their earliest modern expression in, respectively, the prose works of Booker T. Washington and W.E.B. Du Bois. Baker's criteria, and the resulting enshrinement of Alain Locke's anthology *The New Negro* as black America's "first national book", challenges the cultural myopia that prevails in definitions of modern American poetry.

NELSON provides an equally powerful redefinition of the modern American poetic canon in a study that brings astute theoretical awareness to the practice of literary historiography. Arguing that literary history remains a safe haven for supposedly disinterested methodologies, wilfully blind to their own presuppositions, Nelson calls for the recognition that critics tell a selective story, which excludes vast amounts of relevant material through a process of ideological filtering. By reintroducing the suppressed work of blacks, women, and leftist writers (such as Sterling A. Brown, Else von Freytag-Loringhoven, and Ralph Chaplin), Nelson attempts to recover the diversity of American modernism, with the proviso that history cannot be reconstituted as an unmediated and self-present entity. Nelson argues that poetic discourse has become culturally irrelevant under the auspices of a conservative critical industry that has silenced any voice that does not reinforce the dominant ideology.

MICHAEL J. O'DRISCOLL

3. Postwar Period (to 1960s)

Breslin, Paul, *The Psycho-Political Muse: American Poetry since the Fifties*, Chicago: University of Chicago Press, 1987
Davidson, Michael, *The San Francisco Renaissance: Poetics and Community at Mid-Century*, Cambridge and New York: Cambridge University Press, 1989
Diehl, Joanne Feit, *Women Poets and the American Sublime*, Bloomington: Indiana University Press, 1990
Donoghue, Denis, *Reading America: Essays on American Literature*, New York: Knopf, 1987
Gardner, Thomas, *Discovering Ourselves in Whitman: The Contemporary American Long Poem*, Urbana: University of Illinois Press, 1989
Gray, Richard, *American Poetry of the Twentieth Century*, London: Longman, 1990
Jackson, Richard, *The Dismantling of Time in Contemporary Poetry*, Tuscaloosa: University of Alabama Press, 1988
Keller, Lynn, *Re-Making It New: Contemporary American Poetry and the Modernist Tradition*, Cambridge and New York: Cambridge University Press, 1987
Libby, Anthony, *Mythologies of Nothing: Mystical Death in American Poetry 1940–70*, Urbana: University of Illinois Press, 1985
McClatchy, J.D., *White Paper: On Contemporary American Poetry*, New York: Columbia University Press, 1989
Myers, Jack, and David Wojahn (eds.), *A Profile of Twentieth Century American Poetry*, Carbondale: Southern Illinois University Press, 1991
Parini, Jay (ed.), *The Columbia History of American Poetry*, New York: Columbia University Press, 1993
Pope, Deborah, *A Separate Vision: Isolation in Contemporary Women's Poetry*, Baton Rouge: Louisiana University Press, 1984
Schweik, Susan, *A Gulf So Deeply Cut: American Women Poets and the Second World War*, Madison: University of Wisconsin Press, 1992
Stephenson, Gregory, *The Daybreak Boys: Essays on the Literature of the Beat Generation*, Carbondale: Southern Illinois University Press, 1990
Stitt, Peter, *The World's Hieroglyphic Beauty: Five American Poets*, Athens: University of Georgia Press, 1985
Vendler, Helen, *The Music of What Happens: Poems, Poets, Critics*, Cambridge: Massachusetts: Harvard University Press, 1988

American poets prominent in the postwar period include the Black Mountain poets, the Beat poets, the San Francisco Renaissance poets, the "Confessional" poets (such as Robert Lowell, John Berryman, Anne Sexton, Sylvia Plath, and W.D. Snodgrass, none of whom ever subscribed to this term), the so-called "Deep Image" poets (such as Robert Bly, and James Wright in his early work), and the New York School of John Ashbery, Frank O'Hara, and Kenneth Koch. Two other "schools" also feature prominently, one generally grouped under the description of "Formalists" (such as Richard Wilbur, Robert Penn Warren, and Elizabeth Bishop), who kept to the use of conventional verse forms, and the other known as the "open form" school (Charles Olson, Robert Duncan, Ed Dorn, and many others), which followed the example of Walt Whitman, Ezra Pound, and William Carlos Williams. The studies considered here focus on recent books from the 1980s and 1990s, and the discussion moves from general studies to examinations of particular poetic groups, forms, and themes.

PARINI's history of American poetry is a massive compilation of essays by 32 critics, an 800-page volume of which the last 600 pages cover poetry of this century. In general these essays are either general surveys of a specific group or movement, or revisionary arguments which offer a fresh view of familiar work, and these are the most interesting. Of the essays relevant to this entry I recommend: W.S. Di Piero's brilliant account of George Oppen, alongside Pound, in the piece called "Public Music", one of the two best essays in the entire volume; Lea Baechler's study of the elegy in the work of Berryman and Theodore Roethke; and Diane Wood Middlebrook's scrupulous questioning in "What Was Confessional Poetry?" Good examples of the survey manner include Ann Charters' history of the Beat poets and the San Francisco Renaissance, and Lynn Keller's overview of "The Twentieth-Century Long Poem", useful in its range of coverage (though she has little space to say anything of substance about the works mentioned).

The last two chapters of GRAY's excellent survey deals with American poetry since World War II, one devoted to "Formalists and Confessionals", the other to "Beats, Prophets, and Aesthetes", a rather loose catch-all set of categories which brings Ashbery and James Merrill into view towards the end of this book. Gray organizes these chapters into sections that address indicative aesthetic practices, as in "From the Mythological Eye to the lonely 'I'" and "Varieties of the Personal: The Self as Dream, Landscape, or Confession", and these very helpful sections allow him wide scope in dealing with poets who belong to the same generation, and share some concerns, but write very differently. Thus we rightly find Elizabeth Bishop keeping close company with Lowell, but from a different poetic practice. Her formalist techniques and convictions are juxtaposed with varieties of confessionalism as found in Roethke's primitivism, Lowell's use of personal and public history, Berryman's strategic use of the self as martyr, and Sylvia Plath as a prophetess of doom. Gray is a fine reader of poetry, responsive to the intricacies of language, idea, and movement in any given poem, as well as to the social and cultural contexts in which poems have their origins and being. The only problem with his account of these poets is one endemic to the survey book – insufficient space is available for a substantial reading of any one poet. One particular virtue of his chapter on the "Beats, Prophets, and Aesthetes", though, is his inclusion of black American poets under the rubric of American rebelliousness (in general these survey books rarely cover the writings of various ethnic communities in America, though this pattern is changing). Another virtue is in the bibliographical material Gray provides on all the poets he discusses, along with lists of anthologies and works of criticism.

DONOGHUE's first book on American poetry was *Connoisseurs of Chaos* (1956), a study of "Ideas of Order in Modern America Poetry", reissued in an expanded form in 1985 with the inclusion of an essay on Bishop. This most recent collection of his essays has a final 100 pages on modern poets from Conrad Aiken to Ashbery, and though many of these pieces first appeared as reviews, and therefore lack the organizing thesis-driven command of his earlier work, Donoghue is always worth reading on this subject.

McCLATCHY's collection of essays is organised in three sections, and opens with an adversarial view of much postwar poetry, which he sees as guilty of "that deep American fear of 'artifice'". What he wants is not simply the "beneficence of craft" as in the idea of the well-made poem, but the attempts at "myth-making", where poets summon up the courage to attend to "the grit of first things and to the magnitude of the last". He writes of Robert Penn Warren, the Confessionals, Merrill, Richard Howard, Ashbery, and others, and in the section "Reading" provides exemplary commentaries on Charles Wright's "The Southern Cross", Ashbery's "Soonest Mended", and Bishop's "The End of March" to demonstrate his belief that what is crucial in poetry, for the poet and the reader, is "voice", where this word is used not as a synonym for "style", but as the aural and vocal centre of a poet's being, what speaks to us as readers. Wright is seen as an example of Schiller's naive poet, a self-effacing voice of "calm and natural order", and Ashbery as Schiller's sentimentalist, "ironic, self-interrogating, delighting in irregular forms". (In fact he hears two voices in Ashbery – the citizen-ironist, and the quintessential Ashbery whose voice is all "*luster*", registering "the deep call of memory, desire, impulse, art".) Bishop's reticent voice is shown to be an impacted dialogue with her chosen precursors and contemporaries, expressed by McClatchy in his version of Bishop's active reading of Wallace Stevens in her own work. This is a fine study, and highly recommended.

One of the merits of MYERS and WOJAHN's profile is that it is specifically organised in terms of decades, and while this leads to some rather arbitrary decisions about who belongs where, it does give a semblance of narrative coherence to this very readable critical survey. The problem of definition is nicely demonstrated in Mark Doty's account of the 1950s, where he writes that "any division into firmly defined 'schools' is finally a historian's artifice", and goes on to say "that any boundaries tend to blur and finally disappear". Doty then skilfully comments on the Beats, the Confessionals, the "open form" poets, and the traditional formalists within the cautionary terms established at the start of his essay. The problem of boundaries and affiliations is exemplified by the case of Bishop, who is included in the section called "Possibilities of the Self", which is substantially concerned with Berryman and Lowell in their confessional mode, despite the fact that Bishop intensely disliked the soul-baring of Lowell's *Life Studies*, much as she admired some individual poems in it. Leslie Ullman's history of the 1960s opens with a brief re-telling of the "war of the anthologies" between Donald Hall's *New Poets of England and America* (1958) and Donald Allen's *The New American Poetry 1945–1960* (1960): Hall and his co-editors presented poets under 40 who worked in the New-Critical tradition of formal, detached, and ironic poetry, while Allen favoured work developed out of the experimental practices of Pound, Williams, Kenneth Rexroth, and Louis Zukofsky. Ullman locates in these avant-garde practices the impact of a battery of technological and social phenomena, which had the effect of making the world seem smaller, and yet more complex, and the individual's sense of relation to it much more problematic. From this she leads into a discussion of the Confessional poets, adding W.D. Snodgrass, Plath, and Anne Sexton to the familiar pairing of Lowell and Berryman. Taking her cue from Marshall McLuhan's dictum that "the medium is the message", Ullman organizes this history of the 1960s in relation to the concept of the "Medium", so that the Confessionals express "Personal History" as medium, the Projectivists (Olson, Creeley, Denise Levertov, Robert Duncan, Gary Snyder, Paul Blackburn) express "Body as Medium", the New York Poets offer "Experience as Medium", the Deep Imagists (Bly, James Wright, and others) give "The Subconscious as Medium", and so on through this decade. She also covers work by Galway Kinnell and W.S. Merwin under the captivating notion of "Soft Surrealism", varieties of formalist poetry, and the poetry of protest engendered by Ginsberg and his San Francisco Renaissance companions. That Doty and Ullman write broadly of the same dozen or so poets further indicates the radical difficulty of demarcating the development of American poetry decade by decade; but both these essays give highly intelligent readings of the cultural conditions that partially determined the routes taken by the poets they deal with. If these essays seem to be dominated by the presence of male poets, this bias is corrected in Kate Daniels' chapter on women's poetry in twentieth-century America.

BRESLIN gives an acerbic analysis of the accomplishment of three decades of American poetry from Ginsberg to Ashbery by way of commentary on Confessional, Deep Image, Projective, and other poetries, and finds them all lacking an adequate political vision. He sees Ginsberg and the Confessionals as empowered by their revolt from American capitalist materialism and the state's cultural and military imperialism, and thus forced into a language of vatic protest, which rarely succeeds: Ginsberg is said to fail a genuinely Blakeian "prophetic madness", Lowell's poems are inadequately sustained, Plath is "indefensibly presumptuous" in her appropriation of Holocaust imagery, and thus a poet of "outrageous moral confusion". James Wright is the only respectable Deep Image poet, and Ashbery, included here because of his high contemporary reputation, is largely dismissed for his self-centred aestheticising of the practice of poetry. There is a refreshingly impious quality to this caustic overview, though too many of his arguments begin from untenable positions. However, Breslin is a good close reader, and this is a passionately argued book.

VENDLER is one of the most eminent critics of twentieth-century American poetry, whose work on Stevens has long been widely admired. This collection of her writings from the mid-1970s onwards includes a section on the generation of poets who mostly came to prominence in the years after World War II – Bishop, Ashbery, Louise Glück, Ginsberg, Plath, Sexton, and A.R. Ammons – while a later section deals with more recent writing. Vendler is concerned with aesthetic power, aesthetic success, and aesthetic response, and cites Theodor Adorno's *Aesthetic Theory* in support of her practice. She offers a particularly telling figure of the critic as being like a musical interpreter, the "pianist or conductor", who holds up the work before us "in a new and coherent manifestation, revealing it in one of its many possibilities". Vendler is an austere and demanding critic, a highly intelligent reader of poems who writes responsibly and often memorably of the pleasures and the difficulties of poetry.

Women poets are the subject of Diehl, Pope, and Schweik. DIEHL writes of the way five women poets respond to the transcendental sublime as identified with Emerson (as its theorist) and Whitman (as its major expositor). She sees Whitman as a positive model, in the way he unites the imagination with gender, but at the same time sees his insistent maleness as a limitation, and proposes that Emily Dickinson, Marianne Moore, Bishop, Plath, and Adrienne Rich answer the example of Whitman by creating a "Counter Sublime" poetics, which empowers the feminine voice. The chapters here on Dickinson, Moore, Bishop, and Plath are especially good, though the section on Rich curiously lacks the energy of her analysis of the others, just at the point where the feminine voice in this reading becomes most insistently assertive of its power.

The multiplicity of women's voices in the field of twentieth-century American poetry provokes POPE to a re-examination of the conventional language of aesthetic criticism. She addresses what she calls the discourses of isolation to "determine the ways in which contemporary American women's poetry qualifies or extends our understanding of the alienated sensibility as it has been described by men". In the following account of the poetry of Louise Bogan, Maxine Kumin, Levertov, and Rich, she sees the situation of women artists as representative of the marginalization of all women, and reads the expression of isolation in their work as the determinants of culture and gender, not as the condition of solitude or loneliness.

SCHWEIK's brilliant study of the way women poets negotiated writing about war is partly concerned with the ways they assumed the right to address these issues from the perspective of involved non-combatants. Thus the "Gulf" of Schweik's title (with its source in Virginia Woolf's *Three Guineas*) is that between the man and woman, soldier and woman, and home-front and front-line. Schweik writes as a "social historian of ideologies", and investigates that terrain in which good poems were created out of their need to address terrible circumstances, as in the case of Ada Jackson's poem "Behold the Jew", which was reviewed by Marianne Moore and which compelled her to write her famous World-War-II poem "In Distrust of Merits", a poem whose ideology and authority was notoriously questioned by Randall Jarrell in a conflict Schweik reads as indicative of the gender problems faced by male and female poets in their responses to war. Later sections of this book deal with the work of the "nisei", US-born children of Japanese immigrants, and the "oblique" approach to the topic of war exemplified in the poetry of H.D. and Bishop, in which we are reminded of Emily Dickinson's famous American Civil War comment: "war seems to me such an oblique place".

Two studies here centre on the San Francisco and Beat poets. DAVIDSON focuses on the literary scene in San Francisco from 1955 to 1965 in this account of the emergence of a revolutionary poetry and aesthetics within a given historical perspective, including the history of its own self-mythologizing. He writes of what he calls the "enabling fictions of community", as manifest in work by Rexroth, Duncan, Jack Kerouac, Philip Whalen, and others, including some women poets (though they are minimally treated). This is an intelligently partisan study of the San Francisco Renaissance, especially in Davidson's attention to the communal spirit of much of this work. STEPHENSON writes on Kerouac, Ginsberg, William Burroughs, Gregory Corso, Lawrence Ferlinghetti, and others in the period from 1944 to 1962. This is an informative study of the Beat writers, though Stephenson has an enthusiasm for this work that frequently leads him into critical naivety. He writes of the Beats as visionary artists in the traditions variously established by William Blake, W.B. Yeats, the Gnostics, Henry David Thoreau, and Whitman, and while these are appropriate creative connections, Stephenson's rather uncritical assessment of the Beats claims more for the power of their social and moral radicalism than is now commonly accepted.

Study of a particular form is GARDNER's concern. With examples from Pound's *Cantos* to Merrill's *The Changing Light at Sandover* (1980), the American "long poem" in this century is a subject on its own, and a difficult one. In this book, Gardner discusses a line of inheritance from Whitman through Berryman, Galway Kinnell, Roethke, Duncan, Ashbery, and Merrill. The problem Gardner locates in Whitman and his successors is the way to negotiate the inherent conflict between the lyric and the epic, for the long poem in this reading has its psychic origins in selfhood, while it persistently seeks an expansive cultural engagement with the world it speaks of, and for, as in the self-portraiture of Whitman's "Song of Myself", where he seeks to express and speak for the totality of American selfhood. Gardner reads Whitman's followers as responding to their view of how Whitman resolved the dual imperatives of this difficult enterprise, and centres his argument on their responses to Whitman's equivocal notion of "embrace". Thus Berryman and Kinnell read embrace as a substantive gesture always deferred by Whitman through "a fear of sex and death"; and Duncan and Roethke rewrite the problematic embrace in aesthetic rather than psychological terms, while Ashbery and Merrill make it an issue of language. This is a powerful reading of a difficult subject, and one of the best available.

The ways in which later twentieth-century American poets deal with other precursors – their modernist ones – is the subject of KELLER's study. She works with a sequence of pairings, reading Ashbery with Stevens, Bishop with Moore, Creeley with Williams, and Merrill with W.H. Auden. Keller marks out the terms of a paradoxical imitation of, and rebellion from, their precursors in the work of the younger poets, noting their impulse towards continuity and discontinuity in relation to the mainstream of modernism, and their common use of the unheroic language of daily life to explore the satisfactions of marginality in a poetry deliberately subjective in voice and provisional in statement. Most of these pairings are conventional, but Keller's reading of them is very adroit and instructive.

Thematic issues are tackled by Jackson, Stitt, and Libby. JACKSON's learned study is of the difficult topic of "time" in the poetry of Warren, John Hollander, James Wright, Ashbery, Levertov, and Charles Simic, chosen because their work has "time as a central and directly treated theme". The theoretical directives of Jackson's study are taken from the writings of Martin Heidegger and Jacques Derrida. Despite acknowledging the differences among them, Jackson sees Warren, Hollander, and Wright as working within a concept of the stable self and a conventionally referential world, unlike Ashbery, whose world is Derridean, so deconstructed that "even his own language cannot compass it, symbolize it, or transcend it". It is extraordinary how often Ashbery's work seems to bring out the best in the critics who write on him, as in Jackson's case, where his chapter on what he calls "Nomadic Time" in Ashbery performs a compelling analysis of the poet's "flirtation with narrative" idioms. Jackson sees Levertov and Simic searching for structures to circumvent the time of their poems to "invent an extra-textual time".

STITT is concerned to find a thematic preoccupation with varieties of transcendence in the work of five poets – Richard Wilbur, William Stafford, Louis Simpson, James Wright, and Warren. In this context, transcendence is understood as a unified conception of the world, one that unites "the subjective and the objective, the physical and the metaphysical, the material and the spiritual in a seamless whole". For Stitt, these five poets express a visionary unity, while their Confessional contemporaries fail to achieve this unity between "their inner vision of the ideal and their outer vision of the real". This study is a good example of the kinds of opposition generated by some aspects of Lowell's and Berryman's work and of the turn to valorize their less self-declamatory formalist contemporaries. The argument about transcendence and unity is, however, not very convincing, and to argue against the Confessional writers in these terms is to charge them with failure on grounds where they did not compete.

The nature of "nothingness", or "hymns to negativity", informs LIBBY's study of the mid-twentieth-century preoccupation with death "as metaphor and as actuality" in poetry. After an early section on the meditative poetry of some major American modernists, Libby looks at the work of Lowell and Roethke, and goes on to consider Plath, the precocious celebrant of suicide, Bly, and Merwin. These poets are seen as sharing a preoccupation with death and apocalypse, with "figural or literal death as the ground of revelation" within the idea of the "dark night of the soul" as the necessary condition of the suffering that must precede revelation. Death as a topic is central to the history of American poetry, as in the work of Whitman and Dickinson, and this valuable study illuminates the continuity in this century of the tradition of revelation through negation.

LIONEL KELLY

4. Recent and Contemporary

Altieri, Charles, *Self and Sensibility in Contemporary American Poetry*, Cambridge and New York: Cambridge University Press, 1984
Andrews, Bruce, and Charles Bernstein (eds.), *The L=A=N=G=U=A=G=E Book*, Carbondale: Southern Illinois University Press, 1985
Bernstein, Charles, *A Poetics*, Cambridge, Massachusetts: Harvard University Press, 1992
Conte, Joseph M., *Unending Design: The Forms of Postmodern Poetry*, Ithaca, New York: Cornell University Press, 1991
Frank, Robert, and Henry Sayre (eds.), *The Line in Postmodern Poetry*, Urbana: University of Illinois Press, 1988
Fredman, Stephen, *Poet's Prose: The Crisis in American Verse*, Cambridge and New York: Cambridge University Press, 1983, revised 1990
Hallberg, Robert von (ed.), *Politics and Poetic Value*, Chicago: University of Chicago Press, 1988
Hartley, George, *Textual Politics and the Language Poets*, Bloomington: Indiana University Press, 1989
Holden, Jonathan, *Style and Authenticity in Postmodern Poetry*, Columbia: University of Missouri Press, 1986
Holden, Jonathan, *The Fate of American Poetry*, Athens: University of Georgia Press, 1992
Ingersoll, Earl G., Judith Kitchen, and Stan Sanvel Rubin (eds.), *The Post-Confessionals: Conversations with American Poets of the Eighties*, Rutherford, New Jersey: Fairleigh Dickinson University Press, 1989
Kalaidjian, Walter, *Languages of Liberation: The Social Text in Contemporary American Poetry*, New York: Columbia University Press, 1990
Lerner, Andrea (ed.), *Dancing on the Rim of the World: An Anthology of Northwest Native American Writing*, Tucson: University of Arizona Press, 1990
McCorkle, James, *The Still Performance: Writing, Self, and Interconnection in Five Postmodern American Poets*, Charlottesville: University Press of Virginia Press, 1989
McCorkle, James (ed.), *Conversant Essays: Contemporary Poets on Poetry*, Detroit: Wayne State University Press, 1990
Melhem, D.H., *Heroism in the New Black Poetry: Introductions and Interviews*, Lexington: University Press of Kentucky, 1990
Perloff, Marjorie, *Poetic License: Essays on Modernist and Postmodernist Lyric*, Evanston, Illinois: Northwestern University Press, 1990
Quartermain, Peter, *Disjunctive Poetics: From Gertrude Stein and Louis Zukofsky to Susan Howe*, Cambridge and New York: Cambridge University Press, 1992
Reinfeld, Linda, *Language Poetry: Writing as Rescue*, Baton Rouge: Louisiana University Press, 1992
Spiegelman, Willard, *The Didactic Muse: Scenes of Instruction in Contemporary American Poetry*, Princeton, New Jersey: Princeton University Press, 1990
Steele, Timothy, *Missing Measures: Modern Poetry and the Revolt Against Meter*, Fayetteville: University of Arkansas Press, 1990
Tatum, Charles M. (ed.), *New Chicana/Chicano Writings*, Tucson: University of Arizona Press, 1992

The word "postmodern" is frequently used to describe contemporary American poetry, though the usefulness of this term is not always evident in some of the books discussed below, where it is often no more than a term defining the period after modernism. The central debates in these books often turn on the familiar problems of the traditions of formal verse against those of "free verse" or "open verse", and the persistent commentaries on the social function of poetry and the way this function is served by the poets discussed. The Language poets have received considerable attention, and more recently contemporary writers from ethnic minorities have had their voices heard.

ALTIERI is one of the most prominent critics of American modern and postmodern poetry, a reputation established through a series of books which rehearse Altieri's anxieties about the place of poetry in society. In this book he writes about a number of contemporary poets whose work charts some of the difficulties of this social relationship. In the case of Adrienne Rich, for example, the address of her poetry and essays envisages a specific audience, primarily of women, and while this focus partially endears her to Altieri, her exclusiveness does not. Other poets considered in some detail here include Robert Creeley and John Ashbery, and Altieri writes well on the enigmatic practice of Ashbery in his late work. A good part of this book deals with the academic institutionalization of the figure of the poet in creative writing schools in the American universities, a practice of "professionalism" in the arts which Altieri sees as damaging to the public function of poetry. Altieri is eloquent on this subject, and in general this book is freer of the complexities of abstract language that makes some of his work intolerably difficult to read.

CONTE's important book offers a typology of postmodern poetry in this account of the dominant kinds of poetic form used by the successors of modernism, and he defines these typologies as those of "serial" form and "procedural" form. "Serial" form – a concept derived from Roland Barthes and others – involves a combination of elements, which are neither mechanistic nor organic in structure but develop from "a set of mobile and discontinuous objects" in which "each new combination produces a new meaning, reorients itself as a new aesthetic object". Furthermore, serial works are characterized by "the discontinuity of their elements and the centrifugal force identitied with an 'open' aesthetic". He gives examples of this form in the work of Robert Duncan, Paul Blackburn, Creeley, Jack Spicer, George Oppen, Louis Zukofsky, and Lorine Niedecker. "Procedural" works are "typified by the recurrence of elements and a centripetal force that promises a self-sustaining momentum" in which "lexical and semantic" recurrence predominates, and he gives examples from Ashbery, Creeley and Zukofsky again, Weldon Kees, and others. This is a very intelligent anatomy of some formal practices in American poetry of this century, and is especially useful for Conte's attention to poets like Oppen and Zukofsky. It remains to be seen whether his designation of "serial" and "procedural" forms will become widely accepted terms in critical debate.

HOLDEN's well-received study of 1986 opens by asking what we want from poetry; he is answered by his own appeal to notions of sincerity (a notoriously difficult criterion of aesthetic judgement), and to work that is morally serious and worthwhile in intentions and ideally leading to revelation. For Holden there is always something unassailably "mysterious" about good poems, as well as great poems, whatever the criteria of value. These requirements are developed through his analysis of the prevailing poetic conventions of the present time, citing the "conversation poem" as a particularly dominant idiom. He is especially fond of that strain of poetry that is quiet in mood, such as he finds, curiously, in Walt Whitman, and more convincingly in William Wordsworth, and in their twentieth-century American inheritors, Robert Frost, William Stafford, Richard Hugo, and Denise Levertov, who all share the virtues of a "low mimetic mode" in a "vernacular poetry of personal ethos". A good many features of the contemporary poetry scene are a matter for discontent in HOLDEN's later book (1992), and it is noticeable that if he earlier had some time for Ashbery's "ludic" and whimsical discourse, he now seems wholly alienated from him, disapproving of Ashbery's discursive practices of prose within the later longer poems. He wants poetry to broaden its subject matter and seek a wider audience and to escape the stiflingly long reach of American modernism, which has imposed a cultural élitism on the practice of poetry. He would like poets to go for "moral wisdom", and in the enlarging of the "estate of our poetry" wants didactic poetry and narrative to be reclaimed, though not apparently in the narrative idiom of Ashbery's late work. There is something admirable about Holden's anti-modernist, anti-élitist desire for a poetics of simple moral grandeur; but these demands in his work look increasingly like a factional discontentment with what is elsewhere admired and celebrated.

McCORKLE (1989) examines five postmodern poets whose work exemplifies the problematic relationship between self and society, where the grounds of fertile communion seem to have been eroded. Ashbery, Elizabeth Bishop, W.S. Merwin, Adrienne Rich, and Charles Wright are invoked in McCorkle's argument that what binds them is the refusal of a unitary theory of personal vision: thus they represent the destruction of the personal in contemporary life through deconstructed visions of the self, where the provisionality of selfhood enables the questioning and re-envisioning of all forms of interconnection with that which is beyond the self. It does seem that the concept of "interconnection" is what is most crucial here, where McCorkle refers to all the active relations stirred into being when we encounter texts, addressing not only a poem's knowledge of itself – if that is meaningful – but our ways, as readers, of knowing that knowledge. I do not find much of this debate relevant to Bishop or Merwin, though the sense of a provisional self is clearly adumbrated in many poems by Ashbery. McCorkle's best work here is on Rich, perhaps because in her poems the programme of self-revisioning is so foregrounded.

McCORKLE's 1990 assemblage of 53 essays by contemporary poets and poet-critics on the art of poetry is a rich repository of material. These essays are bound together by two topics – the poet's relation to society and conversely the social view of poetry and its uses – and these concerns provide an essential unity of preoccupation in a collection that includes a wide sampling of American and European poets. In addition, McCorkle has arranged these contributions under a set of practical headings – the sufficiency of language, questions of form, readings, tracing the personal, histories, and speculations. One of the special virtues of this collection is the substantial representation of women poets, including Judy Grahn, Levertov, Alice Fulton, Amy Clampitt, and Alicia Ostriker. All these essays are reprinted from their original publications, and many of them are very well known: to have them gathered together in this way is the singular virtue of this book.

PERLOFF's collection of essays, which were originally published between 1985 and 1990, includes accounts of Gertrude Stein, Sylvia Plath, Merwin, Allen Ginsberg, Blackburn, Ashbery, Steve McCaffery, and Susan Howe. Perloff's long dispute with Helen Vendler and others over their privileging of the tradition of Wallace Stevens, against that of Ezra Pound, is re-animated by Perloff's essay here on the publication of contemporary American poetry in French journals, which are hospitable to a poetry that has its theoretical base in French poststructuralist theory and interested in "performance poetics" and the work of the Language poets.

Aspects of poetic form and genre are tackled by Frank and Sayre, Fredman, Kalaidjian, and Steele.

FRANK and SAYRE have collected a set of essays on the technical, conceptual, and aesthetic considerations of the prosody of contemporary poetry, bound together by a unified interest in the notion of the line of verse, the basic unit of measure in composition. There are essays here by notable critics and poets, including Jonathan Holden, Marjorie Perloff, Sandra M. Gilbert, Mary Ann Caws, James Scully, and a consortium of Language poets. If this address to the concept of the "line" as a primary aesthetic consideration is dominated by interpretations of work in "free verse" forms, Sandra M. Gilbert does useful service in reminding us of Plath's compulsion to work in formal units of composition where the sense of implicit – and often explicit – fracturing of the rhythms of blank verse is indicative of the condition of fracture in the psychology of the poems. On the whole these essays seem most interesting when they deal with poets who manipulate the tensions inherent between "open" and "closed" forms, free verse, and formal verse. The concluding section of this study, "Language Lines", is a very good place to go for an experience of what constitutes the compositional line of measure in this avant-garde idiom: it is full of fun, interest, and instruction.

FREDMAN's subject is the composition of poetry in sentences rather than verse, a deflection from the more normative description of the "prose poem". The word "crisis" in his title relates to certain kinds of poetry of the last three decades, as in the work of "performative" poets such as David Antin and the Language poets, though this crisis is seen as originating in the earlier examples of William Carlos Williams's *Kora In Hell*, Creeley's *Presences*, and Ashbery's *Three Poems*. Fredman's attention to the performative and Language poets is especially welcome in the ways he accounts for the philosophical, linguistic, and sociological determinants of their work. If the argument about the political and communal reach of this poetry has now become familiar in the commentaries on it, Fredman's largely pioneering study remains an exemplary account.

KALAIDJIAN is one of several writers who address what they see as the failures of the post-Romantic lyric voice in contemporary American poetry, and in this study Kalaidjian takes James Wright and Robert Bly to task for their perceived limitations. He argues that the self-expressive lyric poem in this century seems unwilling to acknowledge that its language is socially constituted, and without this acknowledgement such poetry cannot play its part as an agency of social consciousness. Furthermore, he sees the lyric mode as displaced by the epics of postmodernism, as in Charles Olson's *Maximus Poems* and James Merrill's *The Changing Light at Sandover*. The communal imperative is met for Kalaidjian in these poems and in the work of Adrienne Rich and Gwendolyn Brooks in the way they offer an alternative feminist and African-American poetics engaged with the communal and social. This is a vigorously polemical study, even if Kalaidjian's arguments sometimes seem partial to a degree.

STEELE is a powerful apologist for what is called the "New Formalism", that revolt against the idioms of "open form" and a return to the use of strict forms in the work of many younger contemporary American poets. Steele here provides a detailed history of the emergence of "free verse" in the early years of this century in poetry in English, and its dominance thereafter where the examples of Pound and Eliot are primary. Steele develops his study in five sections, opening with an account of what was perceived as the fatigued styles and language of late Victorian poetry, which instigated the search for alternative modes: the turn to prose fiction as an alternative model of excellence for poetry; the evaluative distinctions between "verse" and "poetry"; the aesthetic argument used to support the idea of the autonomy of "inner unity" against the "outer unity" of structure imposed by formal verse kinds; and the relationship posited between new expressive verse idioms and developments in modern science. Steele's knowledge of ancient and modern theories of poetics and rhetoric is very impressive and used to good effect in this valuable study.

QUARTERMAIN's study deals with a line of experimental American poetry in this century, working from a prefatory chapter on Gertrude Stein and thence to the British poet Basil Bunting and the Americans Charles Reznikoff, Robert Creeley, Robert Duncan, Guy Davenport, and Susan Howe: however, Quartermain's essential focus is on Louis Zukofsky, the subject of five of the 13 chapters of this book and the most important point of reference throughout, sharing a centrality in this experimental tradition with William Carlos Williams. This focus on Zukofsky is especially welcome, for this difficult poet is often cursorily honoured but rarely discussed in close detail, a situation this book ably corrects. Quartermain does a brilliant service in his close explicatory readings of all these poets, and his work on Zukofsky in this mode is particularly illuminating. In this critical practice he is concerned to show us how these very difficult poets demand to be read, rather than telling us what their poems mean. The "disjunctive poetics" of his title both refers to this experimental tradition and to the idea that this poetry is written out of opposition to the mainstream of American modernism. Quartermain's great achievement is to show us how to make sense of these poets and their works.

Sites of instruction in contemporary American poetry are to be found in a line that runs from W.H. Auden through to James Merrill, according to SPIEGELMAN, taking in Howard Nemerov, Anthony Hecht, Allen Ginsberg, Robert Pinsky, A.R. Ammons, and Adrienne Rich. By instruction, Spiegelman means a "style of teaching" in the sense we should understand from an ancient belief: that the purpose of writing is to instruct by pleasing, a classical and neoclassical precept, which Spiegelman turns to good advantage. If the end of all art is didactic, as it must be from these premises, then it must come in forms acceptable to its audience, and in these poets Spiegelman reads the pedagogic impulse as:

> . . . inflected with irony, wit, self-deprecation, and skepticism, all of them modernist stances as well as the legacy of an ingrained American common sense. In other words, it combines direct preaching with the "indirection" associated with modernism in early Eliot and Auden, as well as in their novelistic contemporaries.

It must be said at once that this is an odd collection of poets to put together: for example, Hecht and Ginsberg will seem quite radically different from each other in their mode of address to their audience, and the manner in which they voice the instructional imperative in their work. Here, differences of this kind seem to matter less than each poet's willingness to take on the admonitory role of the truth-teller, however deeply ironised that role may be. Spiegelman is at his best in his chapters on Ammons and Merrill, and his claims for Merrill are substantial: "he is the first poet since Yeats to have seriously defined a universe or created a system, and to have recreated, in *The Changing Light at Sandover*, not only a scene of instruction and revelation but also a textbook for a spiritual and physical understanding of the universe".

The Language poets have received significant attention from critics, in Fredman (see above), Andrews, Bernstein, Reinfeld, Hallberg, and Hartley.

ANDREWS and BERNSTEIN here collect material from the first three volumes of the journal *L=A=N=G=U=A=G=E*, the primary medium of publication for the Language poets since its inception in 1978. In introducing this work, the editors state that "it is our sense that the project of poetry does not involve turning language into a commodity for consumption; instead, it involves repossessing the sign through close attention to, and active participation in, its production". This anthology is organised in three sections under the headings "Poetics and Language", "Writing and Politics", and "Readings", dealing with the aesthetics of Language poetry, its address to its social and political imperatives, and critical readings of particular texts. This is an excellent anthology, a document of singular importance for anyone interested in Language poetry.

BERNSTEIN has become one of the most public witnesses to the nature and ambitions of the Language poets, a position of some discomfort to him given the egalitarian ethos of this "school" of writing, which is antagonistic by definition to all notions of hierarchical discourse, including discourses of this kind. However, Bernstein is an eloquent explicator of his own work and that of his companion Language poets, and one could not do much better than go to this collection of disparate essays for a clear view of what Language poetry is. There are moments in these essays when the compelling desire to pay honour to his companions leads to a kind of risible earnestness, but on the whole Bernstein is endlessly interesting and instructive in the confrontational stance and breadth of preoccupation with the state-of-the-art poetry scene in contemporary America.

REINFELD's account of Language poetry concentrates on Charles Bernstein, Michael Palmer, and Susan Howe, in this patient consideration. The cultural politics of the Language poets is antagonistic to the conventional use of the poem as a vessel that contains meaning, and indeed seeks to replace notions such as "subject, theme, and meaning" in poetry by foregrounding language itself as the common concern of writer and reader. Reinfeld usefully cites Bernstein in this account of the programme of the Language poets: "if, as Bernstein contends, the self exists not as an isolated and singular entity but rather as a socially determined function of a shared language, then poetry serves as an articulation of self only so far as the community of reader and writer is realized in the body of the poem". There is a radical political agenda in Language poetry to alert us to the social orthodoxy of language use in the mainstream culture, especially where it is seen as an instrument of cultural domination and oppression. Reinfeld's account of how the Language poets enact this "replacement" of the social function of poetry is intelligent and painstaking, though the aesthetic, philosophical, and political differences between this poetry and other kinds remains somewhat obscure.

HARTLEY's discussion of the Language poets is an intellectually demanding guide to their work, which asks some pertinent questions of its practitioners from within their own theoretical boundaries. He focuses on those poets who see their work "as a socialist critique of the ideology of capitalism" – Ron Silliman, Bob Perelman, Barrett Watten, Charles Bernstein, Bruce Andrews, and Steve McCaffery. His most compelling work comes in the final chapter where he considers the possibilities of poetry beyond the "hegemony of realism" as the dominant literary mode of capitalist society, where he proposes the syntagmatic axis of language as the model for much Language poetry. He provides a useful line of poetic origins in his opening chapter, traced from Emily Dickinson's parataxis and indeterminancy to Olson's projectivist poetics, and Ashbery's opaque word-play; the philosophical and political lineage of the Language poets is read in Marxist theories through Georg Lukács, the Frankfurt School, Louis Althusser, and Fredric Jameson. The difficulties of this book for the ordinary reader are commensurate with the work it confronts.

HALLBERG'S anthology of essays on the relationship between politics and poetic value first appeared as a special issue of *Critical Inquiry*, and comes in this format with five additional contributions, including a useful piece by Jed Rasula, responding to Jerome J. McGann's essay in the journal issue. The burden of Rasula's argument is in his account of the persistent marginalization of poetry as a mode of potential political discourse in this century. He argues that the Language poets are insistently political in their theory and practice in that their writing is "a politics of poetry", constituted in their attempt to "sustain an alternative system of production and distribution within a capitalist society", addressing "a more authentic community-audience" than is usually generated by the marketing practices of publishers in the orthodox business community. The liberal politics of the Language poets is well defined in this cogent essay.

Poetry written by the various ethnic minorities of the United States has traditionally been all but ignored in the mainstream culture, with the exception of some forms of black American writing, as in the Harlem Renaissance. This situation is now changing, though whether we can continue to use the questionable designation "ethnic" for this work is open to debate. Though extended criticism is rare, the work of, for example, Native American and Chicano poets in English is now being published, often in wide-ranging anthologies with useful introductions: TATUM and LERNER can be recommended as good examples.

Finally, two selections of interviews provide useful contextual material for considering American poetry of the present. MELHEM's collection of interviews with six black American poets does something to modify the large-scale neglect of these writers (with the exception of Gwendolyn Brooks) in the critical discourse on contemporary American poetry. Melhem's interviews are with Amiri Baraka (LeRoi Jones), Brooks,

Dudley Randall, Haki R. Madhubuti (Don L. Lee), Sonia Sanchez, and Jayne Cortez, and in these Melhem works with the rather faded idea of the poet as a legislator, an extension of the concept of leadership she sees as implicit in the lives and works of these poets. It is notable that Brooks withdraws from ideas of this kind in favour of the idea of "Familyhood" or communality as that which binds the work of these poets to their audience, for whom they speak. Despite the governing tone of piety Melhem uses in her commentary, this book does valuable service in bringing these interview materials to light.

INGERSOLL's collection of 19 interviews with poets who have mostly come to prominence in the 1980s includes Charles Wright, Michael S. Harper, Gregory Orr, Nancy Willard, Rita Dove, and Jonathan Holden. Ingersoll's co-editor itemizes the common preoccupation of these poets with three particular issues. First there is the question of sincerity, an issue said to devolve from the "crisis of authenticity" in contemporary poetry as a consequence of the "failed prophetic ambitions" of the 1960s. Thus, these poets are said to share "a modesty about the position of the self" as a source of ultimate discovery, and even at their most personal seek a synthesis between the private and the communal. Their two other common interests are those of "audience and history", and "language and form", but both these are clearly entailed in the first. In any case, these are the psychological, cultural, and aesthetic problems faced by poets throughout history, and I do not see much advantage in itemizing them here. What remains is the quality of what each of these poets reveals through the procedure of interview; it is worth noting, however, that ethnic American writers are served by only two black American poets, Michael S. Harper and Rita Dove, and women are generally under-represented.

LIONEL KELLY

Poetry: Australian

Brooks, David, and Brenda Walker (eds.), *Poetry and Gender: Statements and Essays in Australian Women's Poetry and Poetics*, St Lucia: University of Queensland Press, 1989

Elliott, Brian, *The Landscape of Australian Poetry*, Melbourne: Cheshire, 1967

Kane, Paul, *Australian Poetry: Romanticism and Negativity*, Cambridge: Cambridge University Press, 1995

Kirkby, Joan (ed.), *The American Model: Influence and Independence in Australian Poetry*, Sydney: Hale & Iremonger, 1982

Paige, Geoff, *A Reader's Guide to Contemporary Australian Poetry*, St Lucia: University of Queensland Press, 1995

Taylor, Andrew, *Reading Australian Poetry*, St Lucia: University of Queensland Press, 1987

In Australia numerous poetry anthologies and collections by individuals have appeared over the years, along with journal articles and books on specific poets. Australian critics, however, have not devoted many general, full-length studies to poetry. Making less impact overseas, Australian poetry does not receive the attention accorded to fiction in international studies.

One of the first important books in this field is ELLIOTT's examination of how the Australian landscape affected Australian poets from the colonial period through the mid-twentieth century. Elliott points out that at first the strange landscape, so different from the English countryside celebrated in the poetry the colonial poets took as their model, hindered expression and produced an imitative poetry. By the early twentieth century, however, the poets considered the peculiarly Australian landscape as a source of emancipation and freedom from the Old World. Examining scores of poets from the colonial period through the 1950s, the book not only provides a concise history of Australian poetic development but also insight into the way the landscape hindered, then encouraged that development.

Many critics contend that Australian poetry came into its own only after World War II, and did so through the discovery of American poetry. KIRKBY's collection of essays documents how "the impact of American poetry on Australian poetry was seen as primarily a liberating one – less a matter of influence than of example", as Kirkby notes in her excellent Introduction. Most of the essays are written by Australian poets, including such figures as John Tranter, Bruce Dawe, and Faye Zwicky, who reveal how they discovered American poets and how those discoveries affected them and their work. Adding dimension to the collection are two essays by American poets – Galway Kinnell and Louis Simpson. Because Australian critics shy away from comparative study, the book remains especially valuable, and breaks ground for more detailed work in this field.

Poet-critic TAYLOR relies on poststructuralist theory to examine the Australian poetic tradition, and focuses in particular on major figures such as Kenneth Slessor, A.D. Hope, Judith Wright, and Les Murray. The opening chapter, "A Book on Australian Poetry", provides an overview of the genre and proposes some intriguing questions on a poetry that Taylor says "is always being overtaken and supplanted by its own definitions". In the chapter on "Romantic Disinheritance", Taylor examines the ever-present landscape in Australian poetry, and concludes that it is "unlikely that Nature will emerge within Australian writing as the vital and nourishing force she once was". Following the individual studies, the final chapter takes up the poetry of World War I, which Taylor sees as a process of mythmaking. An intelligent and at times heavily theoretical approach to Australian poetry, the study is rewarding but demanding.

The collection edited by BROOKS and WALKER is subtitled "Statements and Essays in Australian Women's Poetry and Poetics". It includes "Statements" from 27 contemporary women poets concerning such matters as their reactions to being labeled "women poets" and the way this label affects their work. The 13 essays by prominent Australian critics, male and female, take up general subjects, such as poetry by Aboriginal women, and the work of individual writers, such as Judith Wright and Dorothy Hewett. Even-handed in its approach, the book proves that the editors, as they admit, were "wary of . . . a disproportionate emphasis on gender".

KANE argues that Australia lacked a Romantic literary movement, and this absence brought about the need for poets to invent a new tradition that would embrace their obsession with origins and identity. Calling the lack of Romanticism "negativity", Kane relies on contemporary critics of Romanticism and on philosophers of negativity to trace the development of Australian poetry from the colonial period to the present. Although focusing in part on earlier writers, the book is devoted mainly to writers in the contemporary period, including Hope, Slessor, and Murray. Through the careful analyses of these major writers, the work sustains the argument of negativity throughout to establish historical relationships and to trace overall development. This theoretical and detailed reading of Australian poetry is intended for informed readers.

PAIGE provides a helpful introduction to Australian poetry from the 1940s to the mid-1990s. Intended for a non-specialized audience, the book opens with a concise and accessible survey of the way contemporary Australian poetry has developed, including commentary on publishing, public readings, factional disputes, outside influences, and general trends. The main part of the book contains brief biographical sketches and two- to three-page "commentaries [that] at least suggest congenial starting places and/or possible routes of exploration" for 100 poets, including a broad range of figures who represent all aspects of the lively poetry scene. Paige concludes with a discussion of poetry anthologies since the late 1960s, and lists the major anthologies. He also provides a bibliography for "Further Reading" in the work of 100 more poets. Paige's book offers the general reader a way into contemporary Australian poetry, and serves as a convenient reference tool.

ROBERT L. ROSS

Poetry: Canadian

Bowering, George, *A Way with Words*, Toronto: Oberon Press, 1982

Dudek, Louis, and Michael Gnarowski (eds.), *The Making of Modern Poetry in Canada: Essential Articles on Contemporary Canadian Poetry in English*, Toronto: Ryerson Press, 1967

Jones, Douglas G., *Butterfly on Rock: A Study of Themes and Images in Canadian Literature*, Toronto: University of Toronto Press, 1970

Kamboureli, Smaro, *On the Edge of Genre: The Contemporary Canadian Long Poem*, Toronto and Buffalo, New York: University of Toronto Press, 1991

Mandel, Eli, *The Family Romance*, Winnipeg, Manitoba: Turnstone Press, 1986

Woodcock, George, *George Woodcock's Introduction to Canadian Poetry*, Toronto: ECW Press, 1993

Although poems have been written in Canada since earliest European settlement, recognizable "schools" emerged only during the 1950s, and criticism did not generally begin to find consolidating patterns until the 1960s. Consequently, only during the past two decades has it become possible to talk about a tradition of Canadian poetry in English, and to recognize developing critical approaches.

DUDEK and GNAROWSKI's critical anthology, subtitled "*Essential Articles on Contemporary Canadian Poetry in English*", has considerable historical importance, given its publication date. The volume includes prefaces and introductions to significant anthologies, manifestos, reviews, and documentary newspaper and magazine articles. Given the dearth of analytic and critical work before this volume was published, their collection is extremely useful for uncovering the origins of a conceptual tradition for Canadian poetry. Besides the contributions of Dudek – an influential figure for Canadian modernism – there are items going back to Arthur Stringer early in the twentieth century, and extending to writers like George Bowering, Eli Mandel, and Al Purdy, all relatively unknown when the volume appeared. Lack of an index and the presence of an apparatus that makes locating the items' sources and dates difficult somewhat detract from this anthology's usefulness.

JONES discusses both poetry and fiction. He studies themes and images within the context of the creation of Canadian culture in experiential and literary terms. Jones follows Northrop Frye's model of Canada as a "garrison" culture, formed by the need to secure human cultural endeavour against the wilderness. He shows how Canadian writing has reflected the nation's developing imaginative drives, from the confederation poets to the postmodern experiments of Bowering, Leonard Cohen, Gwendolyn MacEwen, and Mandel in the late 1960s. Jones considers the writing of pioneers Bliss Carman, Archibald Lampman, and D.C. Scott, but the focus is on the mythopoeic thematics of modernists (Dudek, A.M. Klein, Irving Layton, A.J.M. Smith) and late modernists (Margaret Avison, Earle Birney, Jay Macpherson, John Newlove, and Al Purdy). This book usefully demonstrates how Canadian literary culture was formulating a significance for its poetic tradition as the 1970s began.

BOWERING, ten eventful years later, collects his essays on Canadian poets from several journals. Writing about such figures as Avison, James Reaney, D.G. Jones, Newlove, and Atwood, Bowering locates contemporary Canadian poetry within "the same river-system as the chief American one", that of William Carlos Williams and Ezra Pound. He rejects the critical stances of Northrop Frye, who saw Canadian poetry in mythopoeic and regional terms, in favour of the projectivism of the Black Mountain school (Charles Olson, Robert Duncan, and Robert Creeley). Significantly, Bowering was involved with the innovative journal *Tish*, founded in Vancouver in the 1960s, which promoted Black Mountain open form and projectivism in Canada.

MANDEL's book, too, is a collection of occasional papers. Mandel, however, structures these into a coherent volume, which provides a clear sense of the development of (English) Canadian poetry, and the critical issues surrounding it. He mentions or discusses most major figures at some point, from modernists like Layton and P.K. Page to very contemporary postmodernists like Christopher Dewdney. Mandel skillfully mediates between the older conceptual models of Frye and Jones, the language-based approach of Bowering, and a post-structuralist band of discourse, which is ultimately concerned with ways in which writing is implicated in wider cultural issues. Insofar as Mandel affiliates with a distinctive critical approach, it is with that of Harold Bloom and the "anxiety of influence", for Mandel "proposes an account of tradition in Canadian writing" that "seeks primal scenes,

scenes of nomination, identification, origins". Readers who do not find the alignment with Bloom's theory helpful will nevertheless gain a good sense of contemporary Canadian poetry and its criticism.

WOODCOCK provides the most comprehensive historical and analytical survey of Canadian poets and poetry to date. A revised compilation of his Introductions to volumes in ECW Press's major project of mapping the territory of Canadian poetry through a series of volumes on groups of writers, it provides a chronological narrative. Beginning with early writers like Charles Mair and Isabella Valancy Crawford, it proceeds through the modernist period of consolidation (Smith, Birney, Raymond Souster, Avison, and others), and culminates in the postmodernist movement (Bowering, bp Nichol, bill bissett, Dewdney). Woodcock does not identify himself with any particular critical movement. He relates Canadian poetry to larger, international movements, while being fully aware of specific national traditions like the mythopoeic impulse and regionalism. An index would have added to his volume's usefulness.

KAMBOURELI pays sophisticated theoretical and critical attention to the Canadian long poem, a form and practice which criticism neglected until recently, because it requires discussion in quite different terms from the lyric. Kamboureli considers it as a major twentieth-century Canadian form, registering significant "aesthetic and ideological shifts"; but it was also prominent in Canada in the early nineteenth century. Kamboureli positions the long poem as a form that has engaged with major issues in Canadian writing – regionalism, identity construction, and recently the narrative/perspectival challenges of postmodernism. Kamboureli concludes that long poems in effect define themselves by resisting formal definition. Given the form's centrality in Canada, from Crawford through to Michael Ondaatje, Kamboureli finds that it calls for special consideration.

PATRICK HOLLAND

Politics and Literature

Bhabha, Homi K. (ed.), *Nation and Narration*, London and New York: Routledge, 1990

Humm, Peter, Paul Stigant, and Peter Widdowson (eds.), *Popular Fictions: Essays in Literature and History*, London and New York: Methuen, 1986

Patterson, Mark R., *Authority, Autonomy, and Representation in American Literature, 1776–1865*, Princeton, New Jersey: Princeton University Press, 1988

Said, Edward, *Orientalism*, New York: Pantheon, 1978; London: Routledge & Kegan Paul, 1979

Said, Edward, *Culture and Imperialism*, New York: Knopf, 1993

Tennenhouse, Leonard, *Power on Display: The Politics of Shakespeare's Genres*, New York and London: Methuen, 1986

Trilling, Lionel, *The Liberal Imagination: Essays on Literature and Society*, New York: Viking Press, 1950; London: Secker & Warburg, 1951

Von Hallberg, Robert (ed.), *Politics and Poetic Value*, Chicago: University of Chicago Press, 1987

Wilding, Michael, *Political Fictions*, London and Boston: Routledge & Kegan Paul, 1980

"Politics and Literature" may refer to various aspects of the relations between these two categories: political ideas more or less explicit in a text; the political role of literature as an institution; or the political nature of particular interpretive strategies on the part of reader or critic, to name a few. The works considered here vary in approach, but all tackle the interrelationship between literature and politics, and suggest that our understanding of either may be enhanced by studying the two together.

Critics of the 1940s and 1950s are often accused of having been formalists, uninterested in politics. The work of TRILLING demonstrates that at least some of these critics cared passionately and wrote thoughtfully about the relationship between literature and politics (although their conclusions may differ considerably from those of more recent critics). Perhaps the most important essay in this collection is "Reality in America", in which Trilling reveals the limits of liberal approaches to literature by comparing the work and critical reception of Henry James and Theodore Dreiser in terms of contrasting standards of political and aesthetic value. Other essays treat the political and social implications of specific writers and works, including Sherwood Anderson, Rudyard Kipling, Mark Twain's *Huckleberry Finn*, and James's *The Princess Casamassima*, as well as cultural phenomena like the Kinsey Report. This collection is interesting both for its approach to the issues at hand as well as for the light it sheds on the history of the study of literature and society.

SAID's 1978 work examines a broad area of discourse, both imaginative and academic, regarding "the Oriental" to reveal the close ties between this discourse and the socio-economic and political circumstances of Western imperialism. Literature and politics here are tightly interconnected, in "a dynamic exchange between individual authors and the large political concerns, shaped by the three great empires – British, French, American – in whose intellectual and imaginative territory the writing was produced". Said argues that the study of this discourse is essential to an understanding of the history and politics of which it was a part: "without examining Orientalism as a discourse one cannot possibly understand the enormously systematic discipline by which European culture was able to manage – and even produce – the Orient politically, sociologically, militarily, ideologically, scientifically, and imaginatively". Said's choice of texts and method of analysis in this now classic work have influenced many subsequent considerations of the relations between literature and politics.

WILDING notes that many earlier critics addressing "political fictions" restricted their studies to realism. In contrast, Wilding argues that a strong trend in twentieth-century political fiction has sought alternatives to realism in "vernacular picaresque, dream vision, imaginary book, found manuscript, collage, utopian projection, dystopian fable, neo-neoclassicism, and through various mixed forms". In searching for alternative forms, writers were attempting to suit the form to the political content of the works. Wilding analyzes the political significance of both form and content of a number of such works – *Huckleberry Finn*, William Morris's *News from Nowhere*, Jack London's *The Iron Heel*, D.H. Lawrence's *The Rainbow* and *Kangaroo*, and George Orwell's *Nineteen Eighty-Four*. Wilding's analyses of the political content and significance of these works are clear and accessible, and in some cases (notably Lawrence) present a significant challenge to previous scholarship, which has neglected the political dimensions of such works or the political implications of literary form.

The collection edited by HUMM, STIGANT, and WIDDOWSON brings together essays on popular literature which were originally published in the early 1980s in the journal *Literature and History*. Emphasizing the social role of popular literature, these essays all address the relationship between "writing, history, and ideology". The essays treat both "canonical" but popular works (Charles Dickens's *Pickwick Papers*, Mary Shelley's *Frankenstein*) as well as works popular in their time but not widely read or studied today. Issues addressed include the production of text as commodity, the appropriateness of traditional aesthetic standards of evaluation for noncanonical texts, and the cultural and political significance of the reproduction of a text in various forms, including the move from one medium to another (especially from print to film). This collection is useful in clarifying the relations among the canon debates, the political content or political significance of literature, and the politics of literary criticism.

TENNENHOUSE provocatively analyzes what has traditionally been considered a formalist concern – genre – in terms of specific historical and political circumstances. This analysis of Shakespeare's genres attempts to demonstrate the effects of politics and to show how different genres, at a given point in time, share political interests. Thus, Tennenhouse ascribes Shakespeare's generic shifts not to the writer's psychology but to changing cultural forces during the Elizabethan and Jacobean periods. One important result of this approach is a refreshing emphasis on the political significance of Shakespeare's comedies. Some readers may feel that Tennenhouse forces some of his readings to fit a neat Elizabethan/Jacobean division. However, the overall method and thesis are intriguing. Showing that in the Renaissance "political imperatives were also aesthetic imperatives", Tennenhouse illustrates one way in which critics may seek to analyze the connection between literature and politics.

Studies of literature and politics often focus on narrative forms, especially fiction. However, the volume edited by VON HALLBERG focuses on poetry and politics, collecting 17 essays, most of which appeared in a 1987 special issue of *Critical Inquiry*. A unifying concern of the essays is the evaluation of political poetry. The essays, written by poets and critics, discuss a wide range of poetry, from classical to contemporary. Specific poets covered include John Milton, Oliver Goldsmith, John Clare, Kipling, and Marianne Moore. Several essays address movements, including feminist poetry, and black South African poetry. An exchange between Jerome McGann and Charles Altieri debates the political claims of experimental poetry, especially Language writing.

PATTERSON analyzes "the relationships between the origin of the United States' political identity as a representative democracy and the simultaneous rise of its self-conscious literary tradition". Focusing on what he calls "representative figures" (Benjamin Franklin, Hugh Henry Brackenridge, Charles Brockden Brown, James Fenimore Cooper, Ralph Waldo Emerson, and Herman Melville), Patterson delineates these writers' often uneasy attitudes toward American society and the ways in which these political attitudes were enacted in specific texts. His focus is on the tension between the individual's desire for autonomy and society's need for authority. Patterson sees Franklin, Brackenridge, and Brown as linked by a fear of demagogues. The later writers had more diverse responses to these political tensions. Although Patterson's choice of "representative" writers from the mainstream literary tradition seems limited, overall this is an interesting example of an analysis that focuses on specific texts in terms of a very specific political issue.

The collection edited by BHABA explores the relation between narrative and the modern nation. Although the essays as a group are largely informed by poststructuralist theory and cultural-studies methods, the strength of the collection lies in its diversity. Some of the essays work primarily on a broad theoretical level. Notable examples are Bhaba's own contribution, "DissemiNation: Time, Narrative, and the Margins of the Modern Nation", and Simon During's essay, which draws attention to ways in which literature has sometimes "operated in different social spaces than nationalism" – challenging the conventional notion that literature almost inevitably serves nationalist ends. Other essays focus on specific national literatures – Latin American, Australian, English, African American, American. Still other essays focus more narrowly on specific writers or works. Among other articles, Rachel Bowlby challenges previous criticism of Harriet Beecher Stowe's *Uncle Tom's Cabin*, basing her view on a reinterpretation of the novel's conception of the state, and Bruce Robbins considers carefully the political implications of Dickens's attitudes toward the professions and philanthropy in *Bleak House*. The diversity of topic, focus, and approach make this collection useful for surveying current thinking on the relation of literature and politics in a broad sense.

In his 1993 work, SAID explores the relations between imperialism and culture, with special emphasis on narrative literature. Said examines the relationship between narrative fiction and imperialism in analyses of works like Dickens's *Great Expectations*, Jane Austen's *Mansfield Park*, and Kipling's *Kim*. Then, the long third chapter analyzes works of Third-World intellectuals whose writings contributed to a cultural resistance to imperialism. The final section focuses on American ascendancy. Encompassing literature of imperialist nations, as well as the literature of resistance, all tied to the history and politics of English, French, and American imperialism in various parts of the world, the scope of this book is broad. This wide focus means that the discussion of a given work or topic is often less than exhaustive. However, Said's incisive commentary, ranging over this expanse of material, also illustrates the potential of serious scholarship to account for literature as a part of political struggles in a world where "all cultures are involved in one another" and in which it is now possible to explore "the overlapping experience of Westerners and Orientals, the interdependence of cultural terrains in which colonizer and colonized co-existed and battled each other".

ANGELA VIETTO

Pope, Alexander 1688–1744

English poet, prose writer, and translator

Brower, Reuben, *Alexander Pope: The Poetry of Allusion*, Oxford: Clarendon Press, 1959

Dixon, Peter, *The World of Pope's Satires: An Introduction to the "Epistles" and "Imitations" of Horace*, London: Methuen, 1968

Edwards, Thomas, *This Dark Estate: A Reading of Pope*, Berkeley; University of California Press, 1963

Fairer, David (ed.), *Pope: New Contexts*, Hemel Hempstead, Hertfordshire: Harvester Wheatsheaf, 1990

Gordon, Ian, *A Preface to Pope*, London: Longman, 1976, revised 1993

Hammond, Brean, *Pope*, Brighton, Sussex: Harvester Press, 1986

Leavis, F.R., *Revaluation: Tradition and Development in English Poetry*, London: Chatto & Windus, 1936; New York: G.W. Stewart, 1947

Mack, Maynard, "'Wit and Poetry and Pope': Some Observations on his Imagery", in *Pope and His Contemporaries: Essays Presented to George Sherburn*, edited by James L. Clifford and Louis Landa, Oxford: Clarendon Press, 1949

Mack, Maynard (ed.), *Essential Articles for the Study of Alexander Pope*, Hamden, Connecticut: Archon Press, 1964, revised 1968; London: Frank Cass & Co., 1964

Mack, Maynard, *The Garden and the City: Retirement and Politics in the Later Poetry of Pope 1731–1743*, Toronto and Buffalo, New York: University of Toronto Press, 1969; London: Oxford University Press, 1969

Mack, Maynard, *Alexander Pope: A Life*, New Haven, Connecticut, and London: Yale University Press/Norton, 1985

Morris, David, *Alexander Pope, Genius of Sense*, Cambridge, Massachusetts: Harvard University Press, 1984

Despite his many enemies, Alexander Pope was recognised during his lifetime as uncontestably the greatest poet of his age. With Joseph Warton's famous *Essay on the Genius and Writings of Pope* the view that his poetry was not of the greatest kind began to establish a foothold, although Samuel Johnson countered this eloquently with the rhetorical question: "if Pope be not a poet, where is poetry to be found?" Even in the nineteenth century Pope had significant admirers, such as Byron; but Romantic and Victorian preconceptions about poetry called his whole status into question, and this found its most notorious formulation in Matthew Arnold's claim that Pope was "a classic of our prose" but not of our poetry. It was not until the 1920s and 1930s that a major critical rehabilitation began. This was influenced indirectly by T.S. Eliot's reaction against Romantic ideas, but it was largely a product of the work of the New Critics, who defined themselves as paying close attention to the verbal texture of poetry. Although this approach had its most striking effect on the reputation of the Metaphysical poets, such as John Donne, it paradoxically improved the stock of Pope as well since it became apparent that he had more in common with them than might at first appear.

LEAVIS argued this case eloquently and cogently in an essay that still makes a useful brief introduction to Pope. Far from being merely a classic of our prose, Pope has the same qualities of serious wit and complexity of tone as the finest seventeenth-century poets, and his verbal effects, imagery, and use of rhythm always repay the closest attention. What differentiates Leavis from most of the New Critics was the way he succeeded in linking the "poise and subtle variety" he found in Pope's work to the poet's imaginative ethical response to the age in which he lived. It may be noted at this point that this combination of close reading with an informed sense of Pope's context and his relationship with his own contemporary society is present in all the best writers on Pope, and an essential precondition for fruitful study of his work.

MACK also obviously has the New-Critical criteria in mind in his influential essay of 1949, but he is concerned to show that Pope's verse has its own special qualities as well as those which it shares with the Metaphysicals and the Romantics. He is prepared to be more respectful to Matthew Arnold than most of Pope's champions are. He agrees that Pope's work has all the merits of the best prose – clarity and concision and so on – and even goes some way to conceding that it often seems to lack the richness of imagery that the New Critics required from major poetry. But his real point is that such prose qualities in Pope are not gained at the cost of specifically poetic ones. Pope's poetry *is* rich in imagery at times, as Leavis says, but he also uses allusion, puns, irony, and mock-heroic to achieve an effect *analogous* to metaphor, and he is thus able to fuse together the best qualities of prose and verse.

BROWER's indispensable book takes up what might seem the narrowly technical point of Pope's classical allusions and his allusions to other poetry, and turns it into a key to his whole career and value system. He combines sensitive close reading of Pope's work *as poetry* with expert knowledge of the classical background, his main concern being to show how he "uses the poetry of the past for his own poetic purposes". He demonstrates in detail how literary allusion, both in positive and ironic contexts, functions as "a resource equivalent to symbolic metaphor and elaborate imagery in other poets". Pope's original audience shared a knowledge of this background, whereas most modern readers are unfamiliar with the classical aspects of it at least, and they find this a major difficulty in responding fully to Pope's work. Brower's book sketches in that background with such sensitivity that the reader is able to grasp something of what the classics *meant imaginatively* for Pope. In so doing Brower also provides what is still in many ways the best overview of Pope's whole work and development.

EDWARDS also surveys the whole career, and insightfully charts Pope's development from what he terms as "Augustan" mode of synthesis to a "grotesque" mode of anger and alienation. But this is a brief, suggestive book rather than a comprehensive study like Brower's. Edwards largely eschews background and context to let the poetry speak for itself. This is a fascinating and sympathetic study of Pope by a modern reader convinced of his relevance and power, and eager to compare him with, for example, William Blake or such twentieth-century poets as W.B. Yeats and Robert Frost.

An enormous amount of academic criticism and scholarship on Pope was by now being produced. MACK's extensive 1964 selection is an invaluable guide through the thickets, though the editor himself in his Preface reveals embarrassment about the "*Essential*" of the title. Some of these articles could certainly have been omitted as being too specialized to meet the needs of the primary readers of such a collection. A more genuinely "essential" core is present within this volume, however, and it provides a helpful series of detailed readings of all of Pope's main poems: for example, Rebecca Parkin on "Epistle to a Lady", Paul Alpers on "Epistle to Bathurst", and Elias Mengel on "Epistle to Dr Arbuthnot" (patterns of imagery, significantly). An especially useful group of essays by George Sherburn, Howard Erskine-Hill, and others help with the explication of the *Dunciad*, one of Pope's most difficult poems, but for some time now also thought of as his greatest.

DIXON greatly assists the contextualization of Pope by his study of Pope's satire in its relationship to contemporary social ideals and realities. Early on he provides a definitive account of the complex question of Pope's "persona" in these poems, which feeds upon "a range of values drawn from literary tradition" but also incorporates an "idealized version of Pope's own personality". He goes on to show the importance of ideals of conversation, gentlemanliness, and rural virtue in Pope's value system. For Pope these traditional values clash with the symbolic associations and the realities of court corruption and urban capitalism. Dixon concludes with a highly perceptive analysis of Pope's simultaneous attraction to, and yet transcendence of, traditional ideas of Stoicism and moderation.

MACK's 1969 volume in many ways covers similar ground to Dixon, but in a more speculative and inventive fashion, so that it constitutes the most original of all of this author's manifold contributions to Pope studies. This is a brilliant study of the symbolic, indeed mythic, dimensions of Pope's whole career, which, in Mack's view, involves a highly self-conscious fusion of life and art on the poet's part. Instead of being a private hobby, Pope's gardening, for example, and even his famous grotto symbolically enacted a commitment to retirement, philosophical wisdom, and harmony of soul. As the book goes on to show, Pope's work became much more politicized from the early 1730s on, and he developed his life at the villa at Twickenham into the symbolic antithesis to the values of a corrupt court and the influence of the Whig Prime Minister, Sir Robert Walpole. Mack ends by eloquently affirming that the vision of an ideal, civilized community, a perfect city set against the corruptions of London, is always at the heart of Pope's greatest poetry.

MACK later incorporates these insights and his other work on Pope into his 1985 biography, the first "completed attempt since 1900" to give "a comprehensive account of the man in his times". Mack surveys all that is known of Pope's personal life and circumstances, and sets him brilliantly in the whole context of his period. He also provides a detailed critical account of most of Pope's poems. This is a book that is valuable for consultation as an encyclopedia of knowledge about Pope or for a magisterial reading of a particular poem; but it is also one to read as a whole – a considerable, imaginative re-creation.

GORDON's, on the other hand, is the best *short* introduction for students and the general reader. It begins with a brief but sensitive account of Pope's life and literary career and then proceeds to sketch in various important contexts, such as Pope's attitude to the social developments in his period – the clash between city and the country values in particular –, his literary and aesthetic preconceptions, and his religious and philosophical ideas. The next section provides close analyses and explications of well-chosen extracts from Pope's poems, and these will be of special value to students. The book is well illustrated and highly readable and it also has a useful reference section, which includes details of Pope's friends and enemies, who are so often mentioned in his poetry and can cause puzzlement to begin with.

MORRIS's is the best attempt in recent years at a comprehensive survey of the poetry as such, aiming, in its author's words, to "encompass [Pope's] entire career, treating specific poems at considerable length". "Sense" in Morris's terminology is intelligence as it reveals itself in social and moral life; but this is a very broad survey, and Morris attempts to "recover the visions" that originally inspired Pope through focusing on a series of central themes, which the poet worked and reworked throughout his career. There are excellent analyses of, in particular, *Eloisa to Abelard*, the *Essay on Criticism*, and the *Essay on Man* (once regarded as Pope's most important poem, but often neglected in recent years). The treatment of the *Epistles to Several Persons* (*Moral Essays*) in terms of the themes of property, character, and money can also be recommended as a helpful demonstration of the unifying concerns behind these apparently disparate poems.

HAMMOND obviously begins instead with the desire for modern relevance uppermost in his mind. This is one of the best attempts to bring some of the insights of contemporary literary theory – Marxism and feminism in particular – to Pope. Whatever attitude the reader is inclined to take to these theories, there can be no doubt of the importance of ideology – class interest as reflected in general cultural considerations – in Pope's work. The great strength of Hammond's book is that he explains this is a very lively way, with a strongly humane and sympathetic sense of Pope's personality and his personal and social difficulties, and that he avoids the jargon that mars so many similar studies. The discussion of Pope's "misogyny" in the *Rape of the Lock* and the *Epistle to a Lady* is one of the most balanced there has been, for example.

FAIRER's well-edited selection is a good sample of essays incorporating these and other recent critical approaches. As Fairer explains, Pope is not seen here as "a representative spokesman for any set of ideas" but on the contrary as a poet in whose work "a fascination and fruitful crisis is evident, and the full Popeian context is one of tension, contradiction and engagement". The collection begins with essays on Pope's problematic relationship with the political movements of his time. There follow discussions of his ideologies of the feminine and his conceptions of the body and its relationship to the idea of the text. Other essays tease out some of the complexities of situating Pope's work in the context of the values we traditionally associate with Romanticism. A final major theme which emerges is Pope's ambivalence towards the polite and popular cultures of his time. These essays are not easy reading, and unlike Hammond's book they do not avoid the jargon so often associated with recent critical approaches. The book can be recommended, however, as a stimulating, state-of-the-art illustration of some of these new approaches and as an index of the way things have changed from the time when it was Pope's cultural authority and centrality that were celebrated, not his subversiveness and contradictoriness.

THOMAS WOODMAN

Popular Fiction: General

Ashley, Bob, *The Study of Popular Fiction: A Source Book*, London: Pinter, 1989; Philadelphia: University of Pennsylvania Press, 1989

Berger, Arthur Asa, *Popular Culture Genres: Theories and Texts*, Newbury Park, California, and London: Sage, 1992

Hawkins, Harriett, *Classics and Trash: Traditions and Taboos in High Literature and Popular Modern Genres*, Hemel Hempstead, Hertfordshire: Harvester Wheatsheaf, 1990; Toronto: University of Toronto Press, 1990

Leavis, Q.D., *Fiction and the Reading Public*, London: Chatto & Windus, 1932; reprinted, Norwood, Pennsylvania: Norwood, 1978; Harmondsworth, Middlesex: Penguin, 1979

Palmer Jerry, *Potboilers: Methods, Concepts and Case Studies in Popular Fiction,* London and New York: Routledge, 1991

The literary category "popular literature", with overwhelmingly the largest readership, and arguably (though not transparently) the greatest cultural influence, has been for the most part despised or ignored. Since Q.D. Leavis first took note of popular fiction in Cambridge (England) during the 1930s, progress towards recognition or acceptance of the category has been slow and at some remove from the main streams of developments in literary criticism. Possibly the most significant advances have occurred since 1970 in the academic field of cultural studies. Methodology and theory have invariably been foregrounded, drawing extensively on writings in structuralism, poststructuralism, feminism, psychoanalysis, and postmodernism. Most of the work is genre-based. There are relatively few wider surveys of the field, though it is with such surveys that this essay concerns itself.

Q.D. LEAVIS's book was the first and most influential. It is easy to be dismissive of Leavis's attitude to the "reading public". They are the "herd", whose increasing cultural visibility and undiminished incapacity to excercise "taste" constitutes a threat to everything that is of lasting value in the arts, and ultimately in society itself. And so, for many, the archaic Leavis's "élitism" is vilified and little else remains to be said. And yet the book has much to offer. Part 2 presents a detailed and intelligent analysis of the development of popular fiction in the context of the processes of industrialisation and urbanisation in Britain, and its endorsement of an historicised approach is its principal legacy to subsequent enquiry. Uncritical "Queenie-bashing" is inclined to be decidedly *un*historical.

BERGER's study locates itself exclusively within a structuralist perspective, and begins with a useful survey of most of the influential work on genre. He then follows with case studies, applying theory to such prominent popular texts as Mary Shelley's *Frankenstein*, Raymond Chandler's *The Maltese Falcon*, and Ian Fleming's *Dr. No*. It would be easy to point to the simplifications and omissions in this book (he surveys structuralist narratology without a mention of Roland Barthes), but Berger is attempting an introductory survey for students, and much in the book is student-friendly in that territory where simplification and accessibility merge. His fondness for the diagrammatic presentation of plots and formulae is a useful dimension in highlighting the tensions between "convention" and "invention", which Berger, following John Cawelti, regards as central to popular texts. This is an author who is not reluctant to state the obvious (not necessarily a bad thing), and the book as a whole is a useful starting point, whose incompletenesses may usefully remind students that the published critic is not the ultimate authority. The book leaves lots of space for expansion and some for objection.

PALMER's book offers a critical survey of the full spectrum of substantive approaches to popular narratives, followed by case studies of several of the most popular contemporary genres (crime novels and film, soap operas and romance, and situation comedy). His discussion ranges widely over televisual and cinematic, as well as prose, narratives, and his Introduction contains a useful defence of this breadth, recognising differences between written and visual forms at the semiotic level, but arguing that "narrative is an entity whose structures do not depend entirely on the signs out of which it is built up and therefore it is legitimate to investigate it across a range of media". The strength of the book is its first part – a succinct survey of the most influential theoretical approaches – and though there are few surprises in the ground covered, the author is concerned throughout to explore the interrelations between "formal/structuralist" and "ideological" analysis.

My own (ASHLEY's) sourcebook has modest aims. Very much a teaching aid, it is designed to introduce students to a range of the most important and influential perspectives on popular narrative. Arrangement is by theoretical perspective, and each section begins by reprinting extracts from the "classic" interventions themselves (Leavis, Vladimir Propp, Theodor Adorno, Raymond Williams, Walter Benjamin, Louis Althusser, Barthes, etc.) and then continues with readings (many also "classic" in their own right) applying theory to particular textual material. The book seeks to point to the questions that need to be addressed (identified in brief introductory essays to each section) and then to provide some of the most useful, and frequently competing, published attempts at engaging with them.

HAWKINS, from a feminist perspective, provides a lively and wide-ranging exploration of the high/low cultural divide. The "*Classics*" of her title amounts principally to Shakespeare, the "*Trash*" to popular culture. She provides fascinating evidence of the common ground between them (especially good on such formulaic figures as the double or the benign alien/monster), and her thesis that the divide is more illusory than real is welcome given the weight of the commonsense assumption to the contrary. And yet the "trash" Hawkins discusses is of a somewhat superior quality. She writes on *King Kong* and on *The Red Shoes* (the classics of trash?), but on contemporary blockbusters – Jackie Collins or the soap opera *Dynasty* – she has little to offer. Part of her argument is that popular culture offers powerful stereotypes of gender roles –

especially to young American females – a familiar enough argument, of course, endorsing the assumption that popular culture is dangerous terrain. Having successfully problematised the high/low divide, Hawkins appears to operate within hierarchies of trashiness which effectively distance her from the worst of the "junk".

I began with Leavis and end with Hawkins. It is important to recognise that in the 60 years separating them, and especially since 1990, many scholars have succeeded in both engaging with the "junk" and addressing questions of meaning, production, and reception. It is probably more important still, however, to recognise that the obstacles to such engagement are still very powerfully with us.

BOB ASHLEY

Popular Fiction for Women

Baym, Nina, *Woman's Fiction: A Guide to Novels by and about Women in America, 1820–1870*, Ithaca, New York: Cornell University Press, 1978

Christian-Smith, Linda K., *Becoming a Woman Through Romance: Adolescent Novels and the Ideology of Femininity*, New York and London: Routledge, 1990

Cranny-Francis, Anne, *Feminist Fiction: Feminist Uses of Generic Fiction*, New York: St Martin's Press, 1990; London: Polity Press, 1990

Douglas, Ann, *The Feminization of American Culture*, New York: Knopf, 1977

Dudovitz, Resa L., *The Myth of Superwoman: Women's Bestsellers in France and the United States*, London and New York: Routledge, 1990

Fowler, Bridget, *The Alienated Reader: Women and Romantic Literature in the Twentieth Century*, Hemel Hempstead, Hertfordshire: Harvester Wheatsheaf, 1991

Harris, Susan K., *19th-Century American Women's Novels: Interpretive Strategies*, Cambridge and New York: Cambridge University Press, 1990

Jensen, Margaret Ann, *Love's $weet Return: The Harlequin Story*, Bowling Green, Ohio: Bowling Green State University Popular Press, 1984

Miner, Madonne M., *Insatiable Appetites: Twentieth Century American Women's Bestsellers*, Westport, Connecticut: Greenwood Press, 1984

Modleski, Tania, *Loving with a Vengeance: Mass-Produced Fantasies for Women*, Hamden, Connecticut: Archon Books, 1982; London: Methuen, 1984

Papashvily, Helene Waite, *All the Happy Endings: A Study of the Domestic Novel in America, the Women Who Wrote It, the Women Who Read It, in the Nineteenth Century*, New York: Harper, 1956

Payant, Katherine B., *Becoming and Bonding: Contemporary Feminism and Popular Fiction by American Women Writers*, Westport, Connecticut: Greenwood Press, 1993

Radway, Janice A., *Reading the Romance: Women, Patriarchy and Popular Literature*, Chapel Hill: University of North Carolina Press, 1984; London: Verso, 1987

Raub, Patricia, *Yesterday's Stories: Popular Women's Novels of the Twenties and Thirties*, Westport, Connecticut: Greenwood Press, 1994

Showalter, Elaine, *A Literature of Their Own: British Women Novelists from Brontë to Lessing*, Princeton, New Jersey: Princeton University Press, 1977; London: Virago, 1978, revised 1982

The following represents a selective survey of the range of work written about women's popular fiction. Popular novels came into their own in the nineteenth century, when mass literacy and cheap printing made a distinction between "popular" and "high" literature possible. Research has tended to focus on the following areas: the British and American nineteenth centuries; the twentieth century in general, often in cross-cultural perspectives; the twentieth-century romance; and specifically feminist uses of popular fiction. Although discussed below is fiction both *by* women and intended *for* women, often the two categories overlap. There appears, as yet, to be no study focusing exclusively on male authors writing for women consumers.

SHOWALTER's ground-breaking book is essential reading for the understanding of British women's literary history. The book charts a specifically female literary tradition of influence, concentrating on the aesthetics and thematics of the novel in this period, seen as evolving toward a more self-aware, "female" consciousness, as distinguished from earlier "feminine" and "feminist" stages. Showalter is generally less concerned with popular than canonical authors, yet her work brought many writers to notice who had been almost forgotten. In addition, her biographical appendix, filled with short entries on a range of authors, is an excellent place to start work on nineteenth-century popular writers in Britain. FOWLER also concentrates on Britain, with a special emphasis on Scotland, tracing the romance novel in detail from the 1930s onward. Fowler's work shows a more sophisticated use of theory than many of the other texts on romance discussed here; her approach is post-Marxist. Using Bloch's work on utopia, she finds that the romance exhibits a regressive tendency to collude with patriarchy and capitalism, and "distorts the structure of social reality".

In contrast to Showalter, the emphases of Douglas, Baym, Papashvily, Harris, Raub, Miner, and Payant are on American popular forms and traditions.

DOUGLAS's work is still considered foundational. It is written as a history, with literature, both canonical and popular, woven into a general consideration of American culture. She deals primarily with American Victorian culture, tracing it back to its roots in late eighteenth-century religious thought, and focuses on the role of religion in "sentimental" humanistic culture. Her approach is feminist and class conscious; her prose is clear and readable. This is not primarily a book about literature, but it is solid and readable, and well worth the time needed to work through it.

BAYM's excellent work on American popular novels of the nineteenth century does what Showalter did for the British women's novel. Baym's chronological bibliography of popular novelists provides essential background for anyone with an interest in the field; her lucid prose and clear historical treatment of women's fiction is a pleasure to read. She notes that "trials and triumph" have always been the staple of the women's novel; it is the form that the formula takes in any given period that embodies specific historical issues. Baym is sympathetic to popular literature, both aesthetically and politically, seeing it as often emancipatory in intent and sometimes in effect. PAPASHVILY is somewhat outdated, but is still cited as the original germ of the study of the nineteenth-century American women's novel. Although the casual or beginning student should simply read Baym, the scholar interested in the development of the field will wish to read Papashvily also.

HARRIS provides a thoroughly up-to-date overview of both the literary history of American nineteenth-century popular women's literature, and of the literature itself. Intelligently and clearly written, this book offers a more historically and theoretically nuanced reading than was possible in the late 1970s and early 1980s. In addition to a richly detailed attention to literary culture generally in this period, Harris includes fairly detailed readings of 13 novels, and also gives considerable emphasis to issues of reception.

RAUB offers an excellent in-depth analysis of women's novels in the 1920s and 1930s in the United States. The emphasis is feminist, and the argument uses textual analysis to posit the literature's effect on readers. Direct study of readers, however, is not entered into. The book is most valuable for its fairly broad survey of a number of bestsellers, which have since vanished from critical view; those interested in the period will find this survey, even at the bibliographic level, helpful. Bestsellers are also the subject of MINER and Dudovitz (see below). Miner escapes the narrow emphasis on romance or other sub-genres that has characterized women's twentieth-century popular-culture studies since Modleski and Radway. She also brings in a wider time span, beginning with Margaret Mitchell's *Gone with the Wind* (1936) and taking us through Judith Krantz's *Scruples* (1978). A chapter each is also given to Kathleen Winsor's *Forever Amber*, Grace Metalious's *Peyton Place*, and Jacqueline Susann's *Valley of the Dolls*. Her focus is psychoanalytic; each of these enormously popular texts, read and loved by a mostly female audience, revolves around conflict between an emotionally and sometimes physically "starved" daughter and an absent or inadequate mother-figure. The readings are detailed and convincing.

PAYANT writes about American women writers from the 1970s onward. Although not strictly discussing popular literature *per se*, she covers enough works that may be considered as falling into that category (e.g., Lisa Alther's *Kinflicks* and Erica Jong's *Fear of Flying*) to include her here. Like Cranny-Francis's (see below), Payant's interest is in specifically feminist works. Although her Introduction seems rather anti-theoretical, the book is not anti-intellectual, dealing with feminist theory when appropriate. However, in keeping with the survey nature of the work, it consumes a fair amount of space in summaries; this is a good book for a student beginning work on the topic of late twentieth-century feminist fiction. Those familiar with the topic already, however, will find it less revealing.

Less concerned with national traditions are the general studies by Cranny-Francis, Dudovitz, and Modleski, and the analyses of romance fiction by Radway, Jensen, and Christian Smith.

Pithy, readable, and theoretically aware, CRANNY-FRANCIS's book is a good survey of various types of genre fiction. Her focus is on deliberately feminist uses of these genres, and she explores genres that can all trace their roots to the nineteenth century and the emergence of a popular readership, though the majority of texts she deals with are twentieth-century ones. Topics include feminist science fiction, fantasy, utopian fiction, detective fiction, and romance. Her bibliography will be especially helpful to the reader who wishes to delve further into a particular genre.

MODLESKI's slender and readable volume was a landmark in popular culture and women's studies in 1982, and is still widely referred to today. Focusing on late twentieth-century popular culture that is consumed largely by women, including Harlequin romances, gothic novels, and soap operas, Modleski examines the texts themselves and the market conditions under which they are produced and consumed in order to examine the complexities of popular culture's capacity to both serve and subvert patriarchal values.

DUDOVITZ does a good job of surveying women's bestsellers in the nineteenth and twentieth centuries, across a range of sub-genres (romances, society novels, historical novels, family sagas) in America and France, leading up to the late-1980s' "superwomen" stories. Like other critics in this area, she pays close attention to market conditions, somewhat less to reader responses. Readers must be patient with this book – Dudovitz's good work is obscured by poor editing and appalling production (lines mysteriously disappear, typographical errors are frequent, lexical problems frequently obscure meaning).

RADWAY produced the earliest definitive analysis of romances and their readers. Working with a particular community of readers, through interviews and questionnaires, Radway began a tradition in popular culture studies of not only examining popular texts through traditional literary analysis and feminist readings, but also of carefully situating those texts in the "institutional matrix" of production and consumption, and in a context of real readers, their responses, and their uses of the texts. Harlequin romances are the exclusive focus of JENSEN. Her observed distinction between mimetic and formula fiction is oversimplified, but that does not affect her well-researched and lively presentation of the Harlequin industry. It provides a good supplement to some of the other books here (see especially Fowler, discussed above) for its excellent market information and analysis of plot structures in the Harlequin products. CHRISTIAN-SMITH's book, focusing on late twentieth-century American teen romances, like the Kate William *Sweet Valley High* series, works in the tradition of Radway and Modleski. Christian-Smith provides considerable analysis of plot, theme, and character in a range of the novels. Additionally, as an educator of adolescents, the author also uses detailed tracking of readers' responses to examine the ways in which adolescent girls both embrace and resist the stereotyped plots and characters offered to them by such books, often through school reading programs. The theoretical perspective is perhaps overly simplified; however, the book is very readable and its real value is in its fine empirical reader-response research.

PAMELA K. GILBERT

See also **Romance Fiction**

Popular Literature in Britain

Bennett, Tony (ed.), *Popular Fiction: Technology, Ideology, Production, Reading*, London and New York: Routledge, 1990

Bromley, Roger, *Lost Narratives: Popular Fictions, Politics, and Recent History*, London and New York: Routledge, 1988

Modleski, Tania, *Loving with a Vengeance: Mass-Produced Fantasies for Women*, London and New York: Methuen, 1984; Hamden, Connecticut: Archon Books, 1982

Neuburg, Victor, *Popular Literature: A History and Guide: From the Beginning of Printing to the Year 1897*, Totowa, New Jersey: Woburn Press, 1977; Harmondsworth, Middlesex: Penguin, 1977

Shiach, Morag, *Discourses on Popular Culture: Class, Gender and History in Cultural Analysis, 1730 to the Present*, Oxford: Polity Press/Blackwell, 1989; Stanford, California: Stanford University Press, 1989

Williams, Raymond, *Culture and Society 1780–1950*, London: Chatto & Windus, 1958; New York: Columbia University Press, 1958

Popular literary forms have engaged readers and critics of English literature since at least its nineteenth-century emergence as a discrete academic discipline. However, rigorous scrutiny of the terms "popular" and "culture" did not begin until the 1950s, with the publication of Richard Hoggart's *The Uses of Literacy* (1957) and Raymond Williams's massively influential 1958 study of the interaction of economic formulations and aesthetic forms and practices. It is difficult to overestimate the influence of Williams on the postwar study of British popular literature; each of the books discussed here is in some way indebted to his pioneering work.

WILLIAMS's study does not so much examine popular forms as make their examination possible. In fact, the book's most substantial chapters deal with the notion of "the Romantic Artist", whose "feeling of dissatisfaction with the 'public' . . . became acute", and the work of Jeremy Bentham and Samuel Taylor Coleridge, neither of whom sold widely or possessed a populist, "common" touch. Rather, Williams demonstrates that each culture, and that which popularly thrives within it, is historically relative, and its aesthetic choices are more or less determined by economic and political practices. A range of High Romanticisms, for instance, are deemed to be more or less a reaction to commercialisation and privatisation. For this reason, Williams, unlike many later historicists, is able to exonerate the anti-populist tendencies of "high" art forms; but this view also hinders a full recognition of the creative agency of individual cultural participants: "the idea of culture rests on a metaphor: the tending of natural growth. . . . But the emphasis of the idea of culture is right when it reminds us that a culture, essentially, is unplannable".

The individual artist is depicted as similarly determined by the politico-economic sphere in SHIACH's study. The most interesting chapter in this book examines the work of British "peasant poets" in the years 1730–1848. The publication of Stephen Duck, Mary Collier, Mary Leapor, Ann Yearsley, and John Clare rested on the economic and social system of patronage; all of these poets depended upon the intervention of wealthy patrons, who cajoled their social circle into paying advance subscriptions. Shiach argues that the peasant poets were doubly determined. First, a fashion for philanthropic patronage followed Stephen Duck's elevation from corn thresher to poet at Queen Anne's court in the 1730s. In addition, the philosophy of "natural genius" – that uneducated writers, unlike those of the polite and court classes, somehow retained a spontaneity and inspiration occasioned by proximity to raw nature – also influenced the "over-promotion" of subsequent peasant poets beyond their talents. Interest in plebeian poetry, concludes Shiach, depended on its ability to strengthen certain accounts of nature, and legitimate particular theories of writing. The poets are represented as a synecdoche of modern British culture, which originates in the struggle of the natural and the industrial, what Raymond Williams in 1958 called "the organic versus the organised". Later chapters on workers' theatre and popular song follow the terms of this Marxian dialectic, and the book closes with the triumph of the "un-natural" in a discussion of television's role in Western cultural decline. Shiach, like Williams, paradoxically tends to romanticise popular practices while arguing for their determination by political and economic forces.

MODLESKI's study is interested in the psychodynamics, rather than the political economies, of how popular literature is produced and how it produces narrative pleasure. It is concerned with texts that are popularly consumed rather than produced by members of the "common people". Modleski detects a number of narrative strands, which have particularly addressed the social and psychic demands of women readers. The gothic and the sentimental novel forms of the late eighteenth century, the "domestic" fictions of the nineteenth, and the Harlequin romances and soap operas of the twentieth century are connected in important ways. These texts appear to be complicit with male expectations of both female art and behaviour, but conceal subversive subtexts and historically sensitive expressions of resistance. Modleski argues that the romance form "reflects and contributes to" Freud's diagnosis of the hysteric woman, who daydreams and fictionalises herself to escape monotonous family life. Romances, with their endlessly replicated plots, "involve the reader in regressive fantasies" which conform to, but render the reader self-conscious of, the processes by which female subjects are normalised by patriarchal society. Romance is a resistant and creative "hysterical text". The gothic, for instance, is set in a spatially remote and temporally distant past, and functions as a cultural site for the "*female* oedipal complex". It has "the contradictory function of showing women that while there is some basis for their paranoid fears, they must also struggle against succumbing to them . . . Gothics provide one way for women to come . . . to terms with their ambivalent attitudes towards the significant people in their lives". The "domestic" novel, in which the "evil" woman lurks behind the veneer of "good" feminine domesticity, is an extension of the gothic, and, Modleski argues, the precursor of modern televised soap operas, which radically decentre the "domestic" woman into a further ambiguous position. She is invited to be at once surrogate mother to all of the characters, while identifying most strongly with the "bitch" type who strategically disrupts the nuclear family ideal. If one accepts Modleski's premise that historically specific texts can be read subtly via the universal denominations of psychoanalysis, then this is a convincing and revealing study.

Modleski's chapter on soap opera is among the many keynote contributions to the collection of essays edited by BENNETT. The editor, like Raymond Williams or Terry Eagleton a leading exponent of postwar Marxist cultural analysis in Britain, adopts a pluralistic editorial policy in offering studies of a variety of cultural genres and media from the range of theoretical approaches. Each of the six sections – on "Cultural Technologies", "Fictioning the Nation", "Pleasure and Gender", "Detective Fiction", "Production", and "Reading" – contains four essays, each with a different theoretical angle. Highlights include Catherine Belsey's deconstructionist approach to Arthur Conan Doyle's Sherlock Holmes stories, whose project, Belsey argues, "is to dispel magic and mystery, to make everything explicit, accountable, subject to scientific analysis . . . echo[ing] precisely the structure of the classic realist text". Only one figure can elude this will-to-truth, namely the "mysterious" woman, whose resistance to categorisation reveals a fissure in the realist project. The reader is offered "a form of knowledge" not about sexuality or "the world", "but about the nature of fiction itself". Another key text contained here is Laura Mulvey's reappraisal of her classic, and much anthologised, article on "Visual Pleasure and Narrative Cinema". As she concedes, the original study's exclusive use of the male third person to nominate the spectator of narrative cinema tended to "close off avenues of inquiry that should be followed up". Rejecting Freud's thesis that scopophilia is a solely active/masculine practice, which the female spectator must provisionally and disablingly adopt, Mulvey now suggests that *all* gendered subject positions are temporary, and that spectatorship's defining feature is "oscillation". A number of similarly ground-breaking studies make Bennett's collection an invaluable guide to the reading of popular fictions.

BROMLEY's study is rather more specific than a general survey of British popular fiction, but is nevertheless significant for its examination of the ways in which nostalgia for, and sentimentalisation of, the past are significant aspects of many popular forms. Bromley examines representations of the interwar years in the popular narratives, documentaries, and political rhetorics of postwar Britain. His critique is based on Roland Barthes's notion that "history slips into myth by a process of elision, omission and simplification", and Marx's notion of the "forgetting" which occurs when the past is "naturalised". Bromley's argument is especially compelling in his discussion of popular fictions, in which the central figure is female. In recent reappraisals of the inter-war years as a time of social bonding and coherence rather than, as previously thought, instability and division, textual instability is displaced onto the "heroine", in her "psychic, familial, sexual" relations. Bromley suggests that these purportedly documentary fictions tend to reveal much more about the postmodern era in which they emerge. The *eventual* triumph of such heroines is thus a merely token process in which they are "reconstructed into redeemers of the patriarchy". Bromley's is the least general of the texts referred to here, but merits inclusion as a sophisticated reading of a highly popular subgenre.

NEUBURG's study is an invaluable tool for readers interested in pre-twentieth-century popular literature. The book is neatly divided into five chronological chapters, covering the years to 1600, the seventeenth and eighteenth centuries, and the years 1800–97, with a concluding chapter on the survival of oral popular forms. The author also provides a comprehensive bibliography. This is a scrupulously researched guide, but Neuburg has by no means overlooked his commitment to provide a passionately and polemically argued history of the popular. Particular care is taken in detailing the historical tensions that condition the rise of literacy and the subsequent demand for popular forms of literary entertainment and education. In a commercialising and industrialising society, the powerful have a complex, and alternating, interest in both the literacy and the ignorance of the labouring classes. Neuburg deals with the thorny issue of the "conspiracy theory" of popular culture sensitively and astutely. While recognising that sedition legislators and entrepreneurial printers had various stakes in the material production and regulation of these cultures, Neuburg does not read cultural forms as hegemonic tools of repression or false consciousness. In fact, he argues for the creative and subtle reading skills of newly literate groups, pointing out also that many publishers abandoned political for capital interests, profitably producing satirical ballads, chapbooks, and polemics, which railed against their narrow class interests.

TIM BURKE

Grub Street and Popular Publishing

Altick, Richard, *The English Common Reader: A Social History of the Mass Reading Public 1800–1900*, Chicago: University of Chicago Press, 1957

Brake, Laurel, Aled Jones, and Lionel Madden (eds.), *Investigating Victorian Journalism*, London: Macmillan, 1990

Cross, Nigel, *The Common Writer: Life in Nineteenth-Century Grub Street*, Cambridge and New York: Cambridge University Press, 1985

Dalziel, Margaret, *Popular Fiction 100 Years Ago: An Unexplored Tract of Literary History*, London: Cohen & West, 1957

James, Louis, *Fiction for the Working Man, 1830–1850: A Study of the Literature Produced for the Working Classes in Early Victorian Urban England*, London and New York: Oxford University Press, 1963

Pinkus, P., *Grub St. Stripped Bare: The Scandalous Lives and Pornographic Works of the Original Grub St. Writers*, London: Constable, 1968

Rogers, Pat, *Grub Street: Studies in a Subculture*, London and New York: Methuen, 1972, abridged as *Hacks and Dunces: Pope, Swift and Grub Street*, 1980

The original Grub Street was once home to struggling writers. The term has been current since the seventeenth century, and in its most usual meaning refers to publishers and hack writers of cheap, ephemeral, and often scurrilous material, as Samuel Johnson's *Dictionary* definition implies. In the present century the name has lost some of its opprobium, and has even been used as an affectionate term for writers generally. The works discussed here are all concerned with the popular press, and what may be termed "low" and "middlebrow" literature.

The Grub Street of PINKUS is that of late seventeenth- and early eighteenth-century London; but it is also "a metaphor, evoking the eternal spirit of the hack writer". Much of the material he discusses had not been in print since the eighteenth century, and the generous space devoted to the hacks' writing makes for a book "substantially more Grub Street than commentary". These selections, however, are usefully contextualised and the broad divisions – into "Publishers" (including Abel Roper, Edmund Curll, and John Dunton), "Authors" (Tom Brown, Ned Ward), "Political Pamphleteers" (focusing on the controversies surrounding Defoe), "Broadsheets", and "Trivia" – make for a lively account of authorship and publishing. It also has a good bibliography.

The metaphor of Grub Street, as it is imaginatively exploited by Augustan satirists, especially Alexander Pope and Jonathan Swift, is the mainspring of ROGERS' vivid and authoritative study. In the course of his exploration of "the genesis of the metaphor, the interaction of tenor and vehicle" he considers the history and character of Grub Street proper, the social and literary characteristics, and the psychology of the hack writer. The topography and the conditions of eighteenth-century life, including disease and its causes, rioting and the mob, are discussed not just as occurrences in literature but as resonating motifs in satire. The range of professional writers dealt with by Rogers is extensive, but Defoe's career, seen as both typical and aberrant, is accorded special attention. The abridged version, centring on the satirists' treatment of the Dunces, while a useful student edition, lacks the breadth of scope of the original.

CROSS's study benefits from his knowledge of, and access to, the archive of the Royal Literary Fund, of which he was cataloguer. Though the fund was originally set up in the late eighteenth century to support "Men of Genius and Learning in Distress", during the following 130 years it assisted some 2,500 men and women authors of varying literary talents. It is the breadth of this sample, when added to usual sources such as the *Cambridge Bibliography of English Literature* and the *Dictionary of National Biography*, memoirs, letters, etc., that distinguishes Cross's account of the professional lives of nineteenth-century book writers. Though authors of street literature are excluded, those of fictional books "however dreadful" are discussed. Cross charts the varying fortunes of the book trade affected by social and technological change, and of those who struggled to make a living writing for it. Chapters are also devoted to journalism, "The Female Drudge", and George Gissing's novel *New Grub Street*.

ALTICK's influential and ground-breaking study of the growth of the mass reading public in England remains an important classic text in its field. Writing from a historian's point of view he argues that the "history of the mass reading audience is, in fact, the history of English democracy seen from a new angle". His scope of interest is commendably wide and he is equally concerned with the "incalculable" influence of the impact of the "common reader" on modern English literature. Introductory chapters outline the growth of literacy from Caxton onwards, but the main emphasis of the book is on the nineteenth century. The influence of educational initiatives, including public libraries, and of developments within the book trade and periodical publishing on popular reading is discussed in some depth. The bibliography is still valuable to scholars because of its emphasis on contemporary sources.

DALZIEL's survey of popular cheap fiction focuses on a particular point in the development of the mass reading public, the mid-nineteenth century. In some ways it sets out to refute the argument, articulated by Q.D. Leavis, among others, that twentieth-century popular literature has represented a cultural decline from the standards of the previous age. Dalziel's examination of cheap periodical fiction indicated to her little difference in aesthetic standards. On moral grounds – e.g. accounts of violence – however, she considers "bad literature" of the late 1950s showed a serious level of deterioriation. Her wide-ranging study covers "penny dreadfuls", the "family" and Christian periodicals, and railway fiction, and considers the stereotypical treatment of hero and heroine, attitudes to class, work and money, and religion and morals. The book offers a good overview of the publishing context of cheap fiction, and its continuum with the publication of novelists such as Charles Dickens, and Edward Bulwer-Lytton. It remains a readable and useful account.

JAMES' detailed coverage of an earlier period charts developments in fiction during two decades when technological improvements and the increase in the literate urban population encouraged the production of literature for this emergent market. Where Altick is concerned with the readership, James concentrates on the literature, assessing its interaction with canonical fiction, including the plagiarism of Dickens' work, and the influence of the Romantics. For James this study of "low" literature has its value for the literary student. As he says, "by revealing the extent and nature of the field, it throws new light on the lower levels of literature that inevitably shifts the perspective of the total scene". He considers such topics as the domestic and gothic sub-genres, didacticism, and the importance of American and French literature in the fiction of the time. The appendices, which include listings of penny-issue novels and a substantial bibliography of both primary and secondary sources, are still a valuable resource.

BRAKE and her co-editors foreground scholarly practice in the study of journalism to exploit the possibilities for interdisciplinary approaches, drawing on bibliographical, literary-critical, and historical methodologies. The impressive range of specialisms of the contributors makes for authoritative individual essays and a collective willingness to move beyond subject boundaries in order to focus on the periodical press (using the term in its widest sense) as a subject worthy of study in its own right. The interrelationship between the popular press and its contemporary society is explored in topics as varied as nineteenth-century Welsh periodicals, modern printing technology, and popular narrative in *Reynolds's Weekly Newspaper*. The theoretical approach makes this a book for the serious student rather than the general reader, and it includes an extremely useful annotated bibliography.

BARBARA M. ONSLOW

Porter, Katherine Anne 1890–1980

American short-story writer, novelist, and essayist

Bloom, Harold (ed.), *Katherine Anne Porter*, New York: Chelsea House, 1986

Brinkmeyer, Robert H., *Katherine Anne Porter's Artistic Development*, Baton Rouge: Louisiana State University Press, 1993

Demouy, Jane Krause, *Katherine Anne Porter's Women: The Eye of Her Fiction*, Austin: University of Texas Press, 1983

Givner, Joan, *Katherine Anne Porter: A Life*, New York: Simon & Schuster, 1982; London: Jonathan Cape, 1983; revised edition, Athens: University of Georgia Press, 1991

Machann, Clinton, and William Bedford Clark (eds.), *Katherine Anne Porter and Texas: An Uneasy Relationship*, College Station: Texas A & M University Press, 1990

Unrue, Darlene Harbour, *Understanding Katherine Anne Porter*, Columbia: University of South Carolina Press, 1988

Walsh, Thomas F., *Katherine Anne Porter and Mexico: The Illusion of Eden*, Austin: University of Texas Press, 1992

An overview of the critical reception of Katherine Anne Porter's work shows that in spite of its universal appeal and the status Robert Penn Warren accorded her – as a member of a group of writers, including James Joyce and Ernest Hemingway, "who have done serious, consistent, original, and vital work in the form of short fiction" ("Irony with a Center", in Bloom) – she is always identified with the Southern United States, her Texas roots, and her affinity with Mexico. Critics turn repeatedly to these regional influences in discussions of her fiction. Regionalism aside, critics praise her sharp, evocative phrasing, and describe her style as direct, unpretentious, and candid. Clearly, Porter's place in American letters is undisputed. Critical dissent arises, however, concerning theories of thematic unity or a comprehensive interpretation of her canon. Demouy suggests that her "stories do not mirror each other pattern for pattern, but are rather like the spokes of a wheel", and that they call for mythic interpretation. Others apply feminist readings to find a unifying structure. However, the richness of her texts stands up to scrutiny by critics of many persuasions, and their popularity continues to attract new generations of scholars.

GIVNER's biography provides a lengthy but insightful account of Porter's life. She gives copious family background and delves into personal relationships, correspondence, and the development of Porter's fiction. As Givner points out, Porter grew up amid vivid memories of the Civil War and lived through two subsequent world wars, frequently managing to be in the right place at the right time to see history in the making. She describes Porter's world travels, her professional and personal struggles and triumphs, along with her political affinities. Ultimately, Givner suggests that Porter's life "was a variation on that theme so persistent in the history and literature of her country – the American Dream". The book also contains a collection of photographs of Porter, family, and friends.

DEMOUY explores the woman-centered world of Porter's fiction. She argues that Porter's stories chronicle "how women were affected psychologically by attitudes in their society and by the other women they encountered". Demouy categorizes the stories chronologically, interweaving biographical and critical discussion. First, she discusses portrayals of virgins and mothers in the works spanning the years 1922–34, explaining that in her early stories Porter "examines [this] archetypal duality of womanhood". Next, she explores the Miranda motif in stories from 1935 to 1936, and finally, concerning the years 1942–62, Demouy discusses Porter's only novel, *Ship of Fools*, suggesting that in this work Porter "brings to a climax" a long career of examining women's issues concerning independence, selfhood, and love. Demouy's study emphasizes the importance of analysis of Porter's central female characters.

BLOOM's collection of essays brings together critical commentary on Porter's works by such distinguished writers and critics as Robert Penn Warren, Robert B. Heilman, Eudora Welty, and others. The diversity of examples of critical approaches presented by these writers is one of the great values of this collection. It may be seen as a resource for analytical tools to use in approaching Porter's fiction. The essays include discussions of "Flowering Judas", contrasting views of *Ship of Fools*, an interpretative reading of "The Grave", an analysis of "Pale Horse, Pale Rider", oppositional views of "He", and a feminist reading of "Old Mortality".

UNRUE's book is an easily accessible text, which discusses Porter's works according to regional influence. Mexico, the Old South, the rural southwest, New England, and Greenwich Village are all linked with the stories they have inspired. In addition to her own commentary, Unrue includes critical discussion from a variety of other Porter scholars. She also gives special attention to Porter's wartime works and to *Ship of Fools*.

BRINKMEYER analyzes the positions and identities embraced by Porter, which illustrate her "intellectual and artistic evolution". He focuses especially on the developments that he considers the crucial shaping influences on her writing, such as her interest in Mexico in the 1920s, her rediscovery of her Texas heritage, and her embracing of a Southern identity in the late 1920s and 1930s, and her rebellion against totalitarianism in the 1930s. Brinkmeyer's approach to Porter's works is greatly influenced by scholars of the "Southern Renascence", such as Louis D. Rubin, Jr., Fred Hobson, and Anne Goodwyn Jones, and by the literary theorist Mikhail Bakhtin, whose ideas on the monologic and dialogic imagination Brinkmeyer applies to Porter's engagement of memory in her stories.

WALSH provides a comprehensive look at the influence Porter's experiences in Mexico had upon her fiction. The book is both a biography and a literary critique, in which Walsh "explores imagistic and thematic links between Porter's notes, letters, essays, and fiction, Mexican *and* non-Mexican". He explains that "knowing the autobiographical sources of her fiction, one may determine how their emotional and intellectual content survives in the text and deepens the understanding of it". Walsh's work synthesizes Porter's life and writings in detail, creating a thoroughly researched study based on his friendship with Porter and his years of contemplating her works.

MACHANN and CLARK have compiled an interdisciplinary collection of essays on Porter by Cleanth Brooks, Paul Porter, Joan Givner, Thomas F. Walsh, and Darlene Harbour Unrue, to name only a few. The common thread linking the essays is that of Porter's sometimes troubled relationship with the literary and academic circles in her home state of Texas. Folklorist Sylvia Ann Grider colorfully points out that "Porter's emotional attachment to her home state fell victim to the cowboy mentality that has traditionally proclaimed Texas a fine place for men and horses, but hell on women and oxen". The essays are categorized in three sections: "Personal Recollections", including memoir accounts of the writer by Brooks and Paul Porter; "Katherine Anne Porter and the Transfiguring Imagination", covering critical accounts of Porter's development as a writer, and commentary on her major works by Givner, Walsh, Unrue, and others; and, finally, "'The Homeless One Home Again': A Texas Bibliography of Katherine Anne Porter", which contains a substantial overview of Porter's critical reception, and includes a select bibliography covering the years 1905–84, which encompasses Porter's primary works, articles and books about Porter, and much of her correspondence. The "insider" quality of the information about Porter and her works in these essays makes this collection a valuable resource.

JULIE D. CAMPBELL

Postcolonial Theory

Ashcroft, Bill, Gareth Griffiths, and Helen Tiffin, *The Empire Writes Back: Theory and Practice in Post-Colonial Literatures*, London and New York: Routledge, 1989

Bhabha, Homi K. (ed.), *Nation and Narration*, London and New York: Routledge, 1990

Bhabha, Homi K., *The Location of Culture*, London and New York: Routledge, 1994

Fanon, Frantz, *Black Skin White Masks*, translated by Charles Lam Markmann, New York: Grove Press, 1967; London: MacGibbon & Kee, 1968

Guha, Ranajit, and Gayatri Chakravorty Spivak (eds.), *Selected Subaltern Studies*, Oxford and New York: Oxford University Press, 1888

Said, Edward, *Orientalism*, New York: Pantheon, 1978; London: Routledge, 1978

Said, Edward, *Culture and Imperialism*, New York: Knopf, 1993

Spivak, Gayatri Chakravorty, *In Other Worlds: Essays in Cultural Politics*, London and New York: Methuen, 1988

Young, Robert, *White Mythologies: Writing History and the West*, London: Routledge, 1990

Young, Robert, *Colonial Desire: Hybridity in Theory, Culture, and Race*, London and New York: Routledge, 1995

Postcolonial literatures are concerned with economies of power in acts of colonial occupation. The "post" in "postcolonial" refers not to the "past", but rather to the implication of imperialism as a continuous effect within the present. Perhaps the first influential work for postcolonial studies was FANON's, which explored intersections among subjectivity, economics, and politics, and which highlighted the complex contradictions of colonialism. It examined the way colonialism infiltrates native conceptions of resistance and nationalism. Fanon was also concerned with the forms of subjectivity colonialism imposes on all involved in it but which are psychically and materially disabling for "subaltern" (i.e., pertaining to those subject to coercive and ideological domination) identities. Fanon undertook a "sociodiagnostic" examination of the problems confronting indigenous peoples living in postcolonial states and metropolitan centres. The influence of 1950s' theory was strong, with recurring references to existentialism, phenomenology, psychoanalysis, and Marxism. None of these disciplines is used abstractly in Fanon's tracing of colonialism's material and ideological impacts on selfhood.

SAID's 1978 study also emphasises a materialist approach to Western colonial, diplomatic, and academic conceptions of the Orient. He traces the links between power and knowledge, which build and naturalise these conceptions. Said concludes that orientalism eventually transforms into a racial and political dogma that not only degrades its subject matter but also blinds its practitioners. Despite a focus on cultural politics, a kind of structural rigidity limits Said's text. Like the orientalist movement it critiques, it accepts a series of oppositions between "us" and "them", the familiar and the strange. In this light Said reproduces the dominant discourse and does not move beyond it, though he acknowledges that an alternative understanding of East-West relations is possible. However, he does not suggest how this alternative has been historically articulated or has challenged imperialism.

ASHCROFT, GRIFFITHS, and TIFFIN provide an account of such discourses of resistance and challenge. Though beginning with the opposition between imperial centre and postcolonial margins, they progressively undermine it, examining the various discursive strategies that question and subvert imperial cultural formations. Four models of postcolonial textuality – national or regional, race-based, comparative, and hybrid – are analysed in terms of two key strategies: one that repudiates imperialist discourse, and one that appropriates it, contesting its Eurocentric premises and producing discourses of "cultural and racial hybridization". Where repudiation may essentialise native and national identities, even mirroring racial and class divisions imposed by imperialism, Ashcroft *et al.* maintain that strategic transformations and re-readings decolonise literary forms and radically dismantle European codes, while both subverting and appropriating dominant European discourses.

SAID's recent book (1993) responds to the emphasis on strategies that decentre and subvert imperialist power. He delineates resistance through a critical method that re-reads the cultural archive contrapuntally rather than univocally. Again, Said analyzes the complicity between intellectual and aesthetic culture and imperialistic power, but goes on to examine a "culture of resistance" as both reacting to imperialism and conceiving of human history in an alternative way. He emphasises, firstly, the location of interdependent histories, and secondly the exercise of intellectual and political choices. The choices, Said stresses, must not be between nationalist, ethnic, or religious essences; rather, they must emphasise liberation as an intellectual mission that resists and opposes imperialist strategies.

In a series of widely influential articles, Bhabha has also explored the dynamics of power in colonial discourse. Bhabha began by responding to the tenets of Said's *Orientalism*: in Bhabha's view, when Said analyzes the West's delineation of "Eastern" stereotypes, he insufficiently acknowledges the capacity of Eastern peoples to assert their own influence within colonial relationships. In his 1990 study, BHABHA argues that while the West may assert its power over the East, its own authority is disrupted in the act of occupation. Contesting the notion that metropolitan cultures are simply imprinted on local cultures, Bhabha suggests that cultural meanings are negotiated, subjected to the pressures of other knowledges and, in the process, changed or "hybridized". In Bhabha's view, colonial "transparencies", which authoritatively regulate spaces and places, are unsettled by the inscrutability of native signs. These signs disrupt the demand of colonial authority to unify its message. Because local "knowledges" can disarticulate colonial "knowledges", the colonial stereotype is more than an effect of domination: it is an ambiguous, contradictory mode of representation.

One reason for the widespread acceptance of Bhabha's theory of hybridity is that it has the potential to turn narratives of domination into narratives of resistance and liberation. Hybridity, however, eventually begs the question "do literary evocations of resistance to colonial power exist as liberatory texts in themselves, or is their potency retrospectively inscribed upon them by acts of postcolonial projection?". In response to Bhabha's theory, YOUNG has argued in his 1990 book that, particularly because of his use of psychoanalytic models, Bhabha's theory itself universalises postcolonial relations, thus failing adequately to recognise the material conditions of specific colonial encounters that cannot be contained within the parameters of a clever close reading. Young's is a study that problematises "the history of history", and explores the efforts of Said, Spivak, and Bhabha to decolonise Western notions of history as articulated by traditional Marxist formulations.

In his 1994 collection of essays, BHABHA maintains that his writings to date *do* engage with "subaltern" attempts to "unpick" imperial narratives in the process of hybridization. However, this study does attempt to address (and perhaps to redress) criticisms of his universalising tendencies by struggling not to assimilate material relations within a liberatory paradigm or within organic notions of cultural value. Bhabha specifically engages with the question of "how culture signifies, or what is signified by culture", as he describes it. Here he is more attuned to the specificities of cultural difference.

In writing of the "subaltern", SPIVAK (1988) is concerned with the representations of colonial subjectivity that inevitably inscribe the "Other" in the act of defining a self. She suggests in her 1988 book that in many postcolonial essays the presence of the subaltern is no more than "a theoretical fiction to entitle the project of reading". Here she locates this awareness within a broad-ranging study of contemporary methodologies. In GUHA and SPIVAK the essays engage with the difficulty of defining subaltern history, and with the "gaps", "absences", and "ellipses" that represent the absence of a subaltern narrative history of India. Yet they are also aware that simply to locate subaltern consciousness as an "absence" is to polarise it in opposition to imperial "presence", and in so doing to replicate imperial modes of knowledge, and the essays thus seek to overcome this polarisation.

In his latest book (1995), YOUNG theorises the material relations that pertain to the historical formation of "the hybrid". Arguing that "culture" is a way of giving meaning and value to sameness and difference, Young explores racist notions of "cultivation" and evolution as a way of asserting cultural definitions of self and other. The stylistic simplicity of this study departs radically from the rather tortuous writing of Bhabha, Spivak, and many other postcolonial theorists: it thus seems intended as a multi-disciplinary study rather than one aimed exclusively at literary theorists.

LLOYD DAVIS AND PHILIPPA KELLY

See also **New Literatures**

Postmodern Literature

Hutcheon, Linda, *A Poetics of Postmodernism: History, Theory, Fiction*, London and New York: Routledge 1988
Hutcheon, Linda, *The Politics of Postmodernism*, London and New York: Routledge, 1989
McCaffery, Larry (ed.), *Postmodern Fiction: A Bio-Bibliographical Guide*, New York: Greenwood Press, 1986
McHale, Brian, *Postmodernist Fiction*, London and New York: Methuen, 1987
Nash, Cristopher, *World Games: The Tradition of the Anti-Realist Revolt*, London: Methuen, 1987; as *World Postmodern Fiction: A Guide*, London: Longman, 1993
Smyth, Edmund J. (ed.), *Postmodernism and Contemporary Fiction*, London: Batsford, 1991

The danger of saying anything about the contemporary is that the definition of "contemporary" changes so fast that obsolescence of statement is virtually automatic. McCAFFERY's bibliography of postmodern fiction, while an admirable enterprise, was radically out-of-date even at the moment of its publication, although, with its many valuable overview articles and biographical dictionary (which runs postmodern fictionists alongside commentators on postmodernism), it will remain a key resource. It is probable that the present attempt to summarise current critical ventures is also likely to be overtaken by events. Things are rendered even more provisional by the lack of consensus about postmodernism in general, and the fact that the term itself has almost become a sign without signification.

The retitling of NASH's book in 1993, indeed, demonstrates that "postmodernism", even in academic texts, can be a marketing term rather than a scholarly one. The book was first published as *World Games: The Tradition of Anti-Realist Revolt*, a title which describes its content much more accurately than that of its reincarnation. Nash offers "not the chronicle of a movement towards one kind of fiction, but the display of the products of a movement *away* from (what its proponents have tended to regard as) one sort of fiction, namely Realism, and *toward* several *different alternative sorts*". A single term like "postmodernist literature" is one that on this ground alone ought to be eschewed. This said, Nash's study, even if half of it has a foot in what would more properly be called modernism, is one of the richest, most complex and enthralling studies of what other commentators are quite happy to call "postmodernist" literature. Nash himself considers the book "a 'topology', with whose heuristic companionship (citing conceivable routes, landmarks, asking questions as it goes) the reader might find his or her *own* way through the literature's terrain". For once, such self-descriptions are reasonably accurate.

McHALE is more concerned to distinguish than to conflate modernism and postmodernism. He does so by claiming that modernist texts tend to be grounded in questions of *epistemology*, whereas postmodernist texts demonstrate largely *ontological* concerns. The distinction makes good sense when McHale applies it to specific texts, which he does continually. The first chapter, for instance, offers a history of the transition from modernism to postmodernism in thumbnail accounts of Samuel Beckett, Alain Robbe-Grillet, Carlos Fuentes, Vladimir Nabokov, Robert Coover, and Thomas Pynchon. This insistent internationalism of reference is a salient feature of most writing on literary postmodernism. It may turn out, at a more advanced stage of the canon-formation in which the critics here discussed are involved, that attempts will be made to recoup postmodernism along the traditional nationalist lines that modernism now finds itself channelled into. The main limitation of McHale's work is its tendency towards formalism. He refuses to offer an explanation as to *why*, historically, modernism should have mutated into postmodernism.

HUTCHEON (1988) makes an attempt to historicize postmodernism, but not in a way that would obviate the criticism just made. She is interested in "the paradoxes set up when modernist aesthetic autonomy and self-reflexivity come up against a counterforce in the form of a grounding in the historical, social, and political world" and thus sees what she calls "historiographic metafiction" as characteristic of postmodernist fiction. Her chapter on "Historicizing the Postmodern: The Problematizing of History" is therefore concerned not with an historical explanation of how postmodernism came about, but with how postmodernist texts themselves conceive of the representation of historical processes. Her conclusion is that they "problematize" our conventional ways of conceptualising history (that is, they reveal the questionable positivism that underpins most of them). The fact that they do so may, by extension, be the reason why Hutcheon, like so many commentators on postmodernism, finds it difficult to offer historical explanations of the more traditional kind.

HUTCHEON (1989) turns to the politics of postmodernism, which she memorably describes as "double-coded", in the sense that parody (a staple of most postmodernist forms) both subverts *and* legitimises what it parodies. Postmodernism is thus a politically contradictory phenomenon in which "authorised transgressions" abound. Again, the way in which history is problematised in postmodernist literature is highlighted, but all too briefly, since a number of other representational forms – particularly photography and film – have to be covered. The main problem for any reader of Hutcheon is not the progress of the argument (which is satisfactory), but the crowd of examples adduced in illustration of it. Reference to an individual text seldom extends to more than two or three pages, and is often a mere paragraph or even a sentence. This brevity at times comes to seem a matter of convenience rather than a striving for comprehensiveness. Michael Ondaatje's *Running in the Family* is, for example, merely mentioned in passing. To adjudge it "a very postmodern autobiography", without supporting argument, is to risk claims of exaggeration from many Ondaatje readers. More sustained exploration may have gone some way towards pre-empting such responses.

SMYTH's collection of articles persists in the summarising, synoptic mode of the books already discussed, foregoing in-depth analysis of particular texts for surveys conducted along various "national" lines. The first half of the book, for instance, consists of five chapters which examine Britain, the United States, France, Italy, and "Spanish America" respectively as "Centres of Postmodernism". The second half turns to "The Critical Agenda" in a now familiar linkage with critical theory. The volume thus epitomises the kind of work currently being conducted around postmodernism by emphasising approaches originating in comparative literature, by constantly reading in the light of theory, and by reflecting that peculiar moment in the canon-formation process in which inventory-style mapping of the field is the dominant practical activity of critics.

MACDONALD DALY

Postmodernist Literary Theory

Connor, Steven, *Postmodernist Culture: An Introduction to Theories of the Contemporary*, Oxford: Blackwell, 1989
Cunningham, Valentine, *In the Reading Gaol: Postmodernity, Texts, and History*, Oxford and Cambridge, Massachusetts: Blackwell, 1994
Fekete, John (ed.), *Life after Postmodernism: Essays on Value and Culture*, New York: St Martin's Press, 1987; London: Macmillan, 1988
Harvey, David, *The Condition of Postmodernity: An Enquiry into the Origins of Cultural Change*, Oxford and Cambridge, Massachusetts: Blackwell, 1989
McRobbie, Angela, *Postmodernism and Popular Culture*, London and New York: Routledge, 1994
Nicholson, Linda J. (ed.), *Feminism/Postmodernism*, London and New York: Routledge, 1990
Norris, Christopher, *The Truth about Postmodernism*, Oxford and Cambridge, Massachusetts: Blackwell, 1993
Perryman, Mark (ed.), *Altered States: Postmodernism, Politics, Culture*, London: Lawrence & Wishart, in association with *Signs of the Times*, 1994

A distinction is commonly made between "postmodernity", defined as an historical period, and "postmodernism", defined as the aesthetic and cultural forms associated with this period. Postmodernism has been hailed as a liberating reaction against the political and aesthetic strictures of modernism, and has been adopted by feminist and postcolonial theorists. However, the political consequences of radical scepticism have been decried. Critical response remains divided, and although the death of postmodernism has been announced the debate is very much alive.

FEKETE's collection is at the vanguard of a movement that attempts to reintroduce questions of value to the postmodern agenda. Fekete argues in his Introduction that value is an inescapable condition of existence; the pragmatic stance taken by the majority of contributors means that postmodern scepticism is seen as a positive force leading not to the loss of value but to the rigorous examination of any value judgement. Barbara H. Smith therefore argues for "Value Without Truth-Value". Essays by Fekete, Jay M. Bernstein, and Arkady Plotnitsky concentrate on the functioning of literary and aesthetic value, and draw on the convergence of philosophy and literary theory which forms the backbone of postmodern critical theory. This is an interdisciplinary study, and for the non-specialist some of the essays may be somewhat obscure: for example, Charles Levin's essay is an extremely dense and complex investigation into psychoanalysis, aesthetics, and sociology. In contrast, Susan Stewart's analysis of the social function of graffiti and Arthur Kroker's account of the art of Francis Bacon and Alex Colville are positively entertaining.

HARVEY analyses the socio-economic conditions of postmodernity. He maintains the continuing relevance of the Marxist meta-narrative, identifying postmodernism as a particularly marked crisis within capitalism, and provides a detailed account of the socio-economic and political structures that produce postmodern cultural forms. His thesis – that the shift from production-related capital to speculative or theoretical capital is both mirrored by, and commented on by, postmodern art forms – is convincing. The study falters at precisely the point where Marxism is adulterated. Harvey argues that twentieth-century developments in information technology and communications have produced a space-time compression. In spite of his insistence on social context, the space-time model threatens abstraction and over-determination of the analysis.

CONNOR focuses on postmodernist cultural forms which, he argues, include theories of postmodernism. Connor surveys and arbitrates between these theories; in addition to a section on Jean-François Lyotard, Fredric Jameson, and Jean Baudrillard, he expounds and critiques the arguments of less exalted theorists. There are also sections on architecture and the visual arts, literature, the performance arts, and popular culture. The discussion of cultural forms is sandwiched between a consideration of the function of postmodernist theory in the academic institution and a meditation on its political and ethical consequences. Connor argues that postmodern theory, while potentially liberating, can also constrain by perpetuating the power structures it sets out to critique; he concludes with an agenda for a future postmodernism. This study is an accessible and clear-headed account of the diverse strands of postmodernist culture.

NICHOLSON's book occupies the theoretically productive ground where feminism and postmodernism meet, but suffers from serious limitations. While there is critique of postmodern theorists (most coherently of Michel Foucault by Nancy Hartsock), French theorists of the feminine are unaccountably marginalised. Several of the essays would certainly baffle the undergraduate reader, and Judith Butler's "Gender Trouble, Feminist Theory, and Psychoanalytic Discourse" is a particularly egregious example of obscurantist psycho-babble. By comparison, essays by Seyla Benhabib and Andreas Huyssen (both reprinted from *New German Critique*) are models of clarity, but focus on postmodernism at the expense of feminism. This collection is most useful as an indication of the state of US feminist theory in the late 1980s.

Although his analysis is politically motivated, NORRIS counters what he sees as the wrong-headed incursion of nihilistic postmodernism into politics by addressing its source – misreadings of Enlightenment philosophy. He corrects Foucault's and J. Hillis Miller's misreading of Kant, and critiques Lyotard, Richard Rorty, and other postmodern notables. The positive argument is for the ethical and political need to re-arm Enlightenment concepts of truth and critical reason against postmodern scepticism and relativism. Norris protests a little too much the philosophical connections of William Empson's argument for reason against the critical mysticism of Leavis *et al.*: "Empson mentions Hegel only in passing ... but the book [*Some Versions of Pastoral*] has numerous passages that suggest at least some measure of familiarity with his thought". Nevertheless, an appreciation of postmodernism's philosophical inheritance such as Norris provides is as important as an understanding of its socio-economic context.

McROBBIE considers the approaches of sociology and cultural studies to postmodernism, while considering how postmodernism in turn influences and informs these models. She asserts that while traditional sociological approaches rely on an overly rigid Marxist model, a cultural-studies approach tends to ignore conditions of material production in favour of textual signification. Analysis of youth and popular culture, she argues, requires a combination of the textual and the sociological approaches. Against depictions of postmodernism as nihilistic and apolitical, which she attributes to an "older generation", McRobbie suggests that the accelerated cycle of production and consumption of cultural forms associated with postmodernism frequently unites both positive pleasure and agency for the consumer. Her model of "interactive cultural sociology" both recognises and accounts for this fact. Only two of the essays are published here for the first time, so at times the structure of the book suffers. The middle section comprises a discussion of Susan Sontag and Walter Benjamin, and an interview with Gayatri Spivak, but lacks the insights into the relations betwen cultural studies, postmodernism, and popular culture of the first and last sections.

The first three essays in PERRYMAN's collection barely pay lip service to postmodernism, simply bemoaning the sorry state of Labour politics in post-Thatcherite Britain. It would be logical to turn first to Kevin Davey's essay, which describes the context and genesis of the theoretically sophisticated post-Marxist Left, with which most of the contributors align themselves. A common criticism is that the Left has failed to modernise, while Conservatism has successfully mobilised the forces of postmodernism. Wendy Wheeler considers the Conservative exploitation of postmodern nostalgia for a mythical lost community and argues that responding to such cultural myths is tactically essential for the Labour party. David Morley is critical of the cultural imperialism of postmodernism, and

Adam Lent highlights the conflict between postmodern relativism and political action; but both maintain the necessity of working with postmodernism in all its forms. Marc-Henri Glendening represents the token right-winger, pointing out the dangers to a Conservative government of the New Left's purchase on postmodernism. With this exception, the book comprises a coherent left-wing intellectual critique of Labour party-politics in postmodernist culture.

CUNNINGHAM denounces the ahistoricism and textualism of much contemporary theory, arguing that there is a connection between word and world which postmodernism does its best to ignore. New Historicism is criticised for its tendency to gloss over historical fact, while poststructuralist theorists come under constant attack. Imaginative writing is explicitly prioritised over mere theory, which Cunningham asserts should be strictly limited to the service of practical criticism. Throughout, Cunningham undertakes a close reading of various texts, particularly classic realist works, which foreground the tension between text and context. He actually makes extensive use of the textual strategies of deconstruction, resulting in a sometimes laboured punning. This is a "performative" text, but one which shackles itself to historical fact. Although Cunningham here levels a sustained assault on postmodernist theories, he actually modifies certain of these theories for his own use; his book therefore represents a stage in the progressive assimilation of postmodernism.

CATHERINE BURGASS

Poststructuralism *see* Deconstruction, Semiotics

Pound, Ezra 1885–1972

American poet and essayist

Ackroyd, Peter, *Ezra Pound and His World*, London: Thames & Hudson, 1980; New York: Scribner, 1980

Brooker, Peter, *A Student's Guide to the Selected Poems of Ezra Pound*, London: Faber, 1979

Carpenter, Humphrey, *A Serious Character: The Life of Ezra Pound*, London: Faber, 1988; Boston: Houghton Mifflin, 1988

Davenport, Guy, *Cities on Hills: A Study of I–XXX of Ezra Pound's Cantos*, Ann Arbor: UMI Research Press, 1983

Gibson, Andrew (ed.), *Pound in Multiple Perspective: A Collection of Critical Essays*, London: Macmillan, 1993

Hamilton, Scott, *Ezra Pound and the Symbolist Inheritance*, Princeton, New Jersey: Princeton University Press, 1992

Kaye, Jacqueline (ed.), *Ezra Pound and America*, London: Macmillan, 1992; New York: St Martin's Press, 1992

Kenner, Hugh, *The Pound Era*, Berkeley: University of California Press, 1971; London: Faber & Faber, 1972

Longenbach, James, *Stone Cottage: Pound, Yeats, and Modernism*, New York: Oxford University Press, 1988

Makin, Peter, *Provence and Pound*, Berkeley: University of California Press, 1978

Makin, Peter, *Pound's Cantos*, London: Allen & Unwin, 1985; Baltimore: John Hopkins University Press, 1992

Rabaté, Jean-Michel, *Language, Sexuality and Ideology in Ezra Pound's Cantos*, London: Macmillan, 1986; Albany: State University of New York Press, 1986

Ruthven, K.K., *Ezra Pound as Literary Critic*, London and New York: Routledge, 1990

Sherry, Vincent, *Ezra Pound, Wyndham Lewis, and Radical Modernism*, New York and Oxford: Oxford University Press, 1993

Singh, G., *Ezra Pound as Critic*, London: Macmillan; New York: St Martin's Press, 1994

Sullivan, J.P., *Ezra Pound: A Critical Anthology*, Harmondsworth, Middlesex: Penguin, 1970

Terrell, Carroll F., *A Companion to "The Cantos" of Ezra Pound*, 2 vols., Berkeley: University of California Press, 1980–84

Thomas, Ron, *The Latin Masks of Ezra Pound*, Epping, Essex: Bowker, 1977; Ann Arbor: UMI Research Press, 1983

Woodward, Anthony, *Ezra Pound and "The Pisan Cantos"*, London and Boston: Routledge & Kegan Paul, 1980

That difficult individual Ezra Pound remains a figure of controversy. The only certainties are that his influence has been considerable and his life and poetry will remain problematic. Much of the critical endeavour involves the attempt to "make sense" of Pound. One of his more passionate advocates is Hugh KENNER, whose monumental study of *The Pound Era* (1972) has largely defined the subsequent debate. Kenner has an uncanny ability to hear *le refrain joyeux*, even amid the more strident writings. Profiting from direct contact with Pound, his intimate sense of detail and intricate, allusive style illuminate the writings. Kenner can be stimulating even when wrong, and although his study is often uncritical of its subject, insights into such matters as the "method of the ideogram" and the "subject-rhyme" are invaluable. While his assertion of Pound as *the* central figure of the modernist era meets with resistance, notably from feminist critics, Kenner has defended a tradition whose central tenets derive directly from its most vocal practitioners. *The Pound Era*, for better and worse, is to recent criticism what *The Cantos* are to modern poetry.

The contradictions of Pound's life and writings are demonstrated in CARPENTER's excellent biography, which has rendered less necessary earlier good efforts by Noel Stock and Norman Douglas. Carpenter does not share Kenner's adulation of Pound, but seems aware of the foibles and irritabilities of his subject as well as the unexpected generosities and multiple talents. The biography is detailed, lucid, and dispassionate, with a fine balance between the facts of the life and the poetic use made thereof. Its only weakness is a partial failure to appreciate sufficiently the intense poetic moments which offset the many aberrations. Pound's was a fascinating life, rich and cantankerous, and in his depiction of these complementary aspects Carpenter provides a fascinating portrayal of perhaps the most interesting literary figure of his times.

ACKROYD's small study also offers excellent portraits of Pound, chiefly the 111 magniloquent photographs that accompany a succinct but readable text. There are small errors in the commentary, deriving from Ackroyd's sometimes uncritical absorption of previous accounts; but the pictures and reproductions form powerful and moving ideograms of a life that expressed itself with eloquence before retreating into silence.

Two familiar commentaries make a good introduction to Pound. SULLIVAN's anthology is a handy compendium in two parts – the first, early criticism to 1945, including much by Pound himself; the second, criticism from 1945 until the 1960s, with judicious selections from leading poets and critics. Pound's achievement is placed in context, with contemporary accounts of, and reactions to, such important movements as Imagism, and controversies such as the treason trial and the Bollingen Prize. BROOKER's guide is a good complement. His emphasis is on the direct treatment of the poems themselves: information is clear and precise, annotation illuminating and useful. Students of *Hugh Selwyn Mauberley*, for example, will find exactly what they need to excavate a difficult poem. The major drawback to Brooker's guide is its dependence on the (dreadful) Faber *Selected Poems*, which means that much of Pound is ignored, and that those teaching or studying his poetry need to buy two books rather than one.

There are many specialist studies of particular aspects of Pound's *oeuvre*. MAKIN on Provence (1978) explores the territory Pound proclaimed his own. He details Pound's intimate knowledge of troubadour song, showing how it not only directed Pound's early themes but represented a standard of technical excellence to which he might aspire. He clarifies Pound's thesis of the "Tradition", with its origins in the Eleusinian mysteries and a heritage passed from Provence through Tuscany to Chaucer and the Elizabethan songwriters. Makin's study is useful for its sensitive readings of the Provençal poems (notably his account of "Near Perigord"), and for indicating how Provençal history is mirrored in Pound's own life – his poetry finding an early lyric voice, which disappeared, to emerge again at the *tour abolie* of Pisa.

LONGENBACH's *Stone Cottage* details the relationship between Pound and W.B. Yeats during the three winters of 1913–16, when Pound acted as Yeats's secretary. He traces the literary influence of each upon the other, noting Pound's growing interest in the occult and the development of "unfortunate excesses" from the dream of an artistic enclave and its realisation in political terms. In tracing the effects of that collaboration Longenbach argues a significant revision of modernist history.

HAMILTON engages in a different kind of revision. Citing Pound's well-known rejection of symbolism ("slither"), he demonstrates that Pound nevertheless sustained a lasting dialogue with his English and French predecessors, and by invoking the ironic mode of Théophile Gautier and Jules Laforgue was able to find his distinctive modern voice. Hamilton challenges the accepted view of Pound's youthful infatuation – then rejection – of an obsolescent literary past, arguing *au contraire* that the symbolist influence was enduring, formed a subtle part of his modernist vision, and returned powerfully in the Pisan Cantos.

SHERRY continues the argument. Accepting some elements of Longenbach's revisionist history, he nevertheless dissents from the notion of its occult roots, and argues instead a subtle relationship between aesthetics and politics, arising from the ideologies of Continental philosophers such as Julien Benda, Georges Sorel, and Henri Bergson. Sherry traces the change in Pound's poetics from an aesthetic based on rhythm towards the intaglio method for entering visual precision into verbal texture. He explores the paradox of a radical modernism and experimental art rooted in tradition, and shows how this led Pound and Wyndham Lewis to the language of a new political discourse. While Sherry's conclusions are not themselves radical, his sense of how Pound's visual intelligence entered into the composition of *The Cantos* is profound.

THOMAS is concerned not simply with classical influence nor translation, but rather with Pound's use of Latin masks and metamorphoses as the link between his self and those of the past. He roots Pound's anti-Romanticism in classical Latin times; redefines it in terms of the *fin-de-siècle* opposition of Hellenism and Hebraism; and considers Pound's career as a heroic struggle to discover meaning in a meaningless age, classical masks assumed to scrutinise the present. Thomas identifies Pound's determination to write a non-Virgilian epic by reconstituting Catullus (lyric), Propertius (dramatic), and Ovid (epic) as his great triumvirate of Latin masks. He is learned, but never pedantic; and his apparently narrow focus forms an excellent means of evaluating both classical particulars and the wider cultural issues.

Two collections of essays, edited by KAYE and GIBSON, exemplify some recent concerns. Of the two, Kaye's is the stronger, being more tightly linked to one theme (Pound and America), and including two fine essays – A.D. Moody's contention that the structure and composition of the Adams Cantos is more intricate than previously suspected, and Richard Taylor's report on the much-needed Variorum edition of *The Cantos*. Gibson's contributors reconcile their various perspectives by emphasising the relationship between Pound and other authors (Robert Browning, Wyndham Lewis, James Joyce, Eliot, Yeats, Ford Madox Ford, and Walt Whitman), which provokes a lively debate, albeit in a minor key.

Two studies with similar titles but opposite perspectives consider Pound's criticism. SINGH is the more orthodox. He considers Pound, as might Kenner, a master of maieutics whose criticism induced the birth of modern poetry; and his aim is to generate from that the elements that constitute Pound's poetics. This produces an uncomplicated study of Pound's credo, with sensible statements of the theory of Imagism, translation, the craft of poetry, Pound's influence on Eliot, and his thoughts on the state of contemporary letters. Singh can be recommended to those who need such basics, but he offers little that is new or provocative. RUTHVEN *is* provocative. Four years earlier than Singh (though, curiously, unmentioned by the latter), he challenges every assumption Singh uncritically assumes. He dismisses any need to see Pound's criticism as constituting a dispersed poetics of his collected poems, preferring instead to evaluate it against the assumptions, academic and social, of its time – but that "time" scrutinised with the insights of recent critical theory. He examines Imagism as Pound's need to dominate the discourse of his age; the sexual politics involved in that movement and the little magazines of the 1920s; and the politics of power (masculine and fascist) underlying Pound's judgements. That Ruthven can make such postmodernist revaluations without losing the immediacy of his subject is a tribute to the clarity of his persuasion.

RABATÉ is more complex. Despite the political correctness of his title (*Language, Sexuality and Ideology*) and the invocation of every fashionable name from Heidegger to Jacques Lacan, he delineates clearly a strategy of reading, which focuses on Pound's achievements and references in terms of various and vertiginous experiences of the limits of language. Rabaté is stimulating and thoughtful, appreciative of the complexities of Pound, yet modest in his enunciation of them. His is a challenging account, not always easy, and often indirect; but it enriches the poems by relating them to a plurality of discourses, past and present.

The Cantos constitute the core of Pound's achievement. They have attracted considerable exegesis, which the following texts can only hint at. DAVENPORT offers close readings of the first 30 cantos, but these are less valuable than his broader argument that the poem reflects the emergence of the civilised state in various cultures; and that its tragic statement concerns the ruin of cultures, from within and without. He defines clearly the "ideogrammatic method" and stresses the reading of *The Cantos* as an imaginative act; and if his own readings are sometimes too imaginative (and often uncritical), he nevertheless guides others on an adventurous *periplum*. WOODWARD is less exciting, but a better guide for the uninitiated. He admits the equivocal standing of even the Pisan Cantos, but accepting their central theme as "the ruin of history"; he delineates simply the central paradigms and (three) major climaxes; and he recovers from the fragmented presentation and the dimensions of the elegiac voice of the timebound poet.

Much of MAKIN's 1985 study of *The Cantos* consists of commentary, concise, informative, and helpful, each group of poems given separate consideration in order of composition. Yet the most useful part of his study may be his early chapters, shaping and defining the matrix from which the longer poem was born. Makin considers the unfortunate Ur-Cantos and their translation into final form as Pound found (then lost) control of structure and theme, musical form and quantitative rhythm, image and ideogram. Complex issues are condensed into clear statement, and Makin's critique realises admirably the intention of his general editor. This is a reliable and stimulating work of reference in a conveniently accessible form.

TERRELL provides *the* truly indispensable companion to *The Cantos*. His annotations were designed for the beginning reader, to answer immediate questions, to suggest where to go next for further exegesis and comment, and to indicate Pound's sources. Notes are given line by line, with clear citations and generous cross-references. There is an excellent bibliography, a simple index, and glossaries of foreign phrases (including Chinese characters). The *Companion* is the product of dozens of scholars over a long period. It does not pretend to be a complete compendium of knowledge about the poem, and since its publication certain errors and omissions have become apparent; but these are usually minor, and Terrell's monumental work of scholarship is a fitting tribute to its "cryselephantine" original.

Pound always claimed that the best criticism comes from the creative artist who does the next job. The last word, accordingly, goes to Basil Bunting's poem "On the Flyleaf of Pound's Cantos":

There are the Alps. What is there to say about them?
They don't make sense. Fatal glaciers, crags cranks
    climb,
jumbled boulder and weed, pasture and boulder, scree,
et l'on entend, maybe, *le refrain joyeux et leger*
Who knows what the ice will have scraped on the
    rock it is smoothing?

There they are, you will have to go a long way round
if you want to avoid them.
It takes some getting used to. There are the Alps,
fools! Sit down and wait for them to crumble!

CHRIS ACKERLEY

Powys, John Cowper 1872–1963

British novelist, poet, essayist, and critic

Cavaliero, Glen, *John Cowper Powys: Novelist*, Oxford: Clarendon Press, 1973
Coates, C.A., *John Cowper Powys in Search of a Landscape*, London: Macmillan, 1982
Fawkner, H.W., *The Ecstatic World of John Cowper Powys*, Rutherford, New Jersey: Fairleigh Dickinson University Press, 1986; London and Toronto: Associated University Presses, 1986
Graves, Richard Perceval, *The Brothers Powys*, London: Routledge & Kegan Paul, 1983
Hooker, Jeremy, *John Cowper Powys*, Cardiff: University of Wales Press, 1973
Krissdottir, Morine, *John Cowper Powys and the Magical Quest*, London and Sydney: Macdonald & Janes, 1980

Despite being in some ways a traditionalist, inheriting the English Romantic celebration of landscape and the Victorian concern with the social life of a region, Powys was at the same time a central figure of 1920s' modernism. He shared and developed all its concerns with the fluid inner life and the problematic nature of personality. His novels explore the "epiphany" or "moment of being" that was a feature of the work of James Joyce and Virginia Woolf. His novels demonstrate a breakdown of the binary moral and metaphysical assumptions of dualism, propounding instead the concept of a "multiverse" of infinitely varied visions and phenomena. Powys's work is unique in its creation of extraordinary landscapes of the mind, subtle combinations of sense, memory, and myth – an under-explored but instantly recognisable private world.

In spite of an achievement praised by Angus Wilson, George Steiner, and P.J. Kavanagh, Powys is still neglected by academic critics. One problem is the fact that he has been subjected to a number of esoteric interpretations focusing on so-called "mystical " elements in his work. He has too often been seen as an isolated eccentric. This is why GRAVES's study of the Powys brothers is particularly helpful. He provides a useful context for the novelist, not only within his family, but within a group of writers that includes Sylvia Townsend Warner,

Theodore Dreiser, and Dorothy Richardson. (Powys's study of his friend and fellow innovator, *Dorothy M. Richardson*, is still to be found in bibliographies of her work.) Graves's careful research makes this work a necessary companion to Powys's *Autobiography*, which does not include women.

CAVALIERO offers a lucid and systematic account of Powys's novels, placing them in their literary context and in relation to the development of the English novel. He establishes the groupings of the novels: first, the early three as prentice pieces in the tradition of late nineteenth-century Romanticism; then the great Wessex quartet of *Wolf Solent* (1929), *A Glastonbury Romance* (1932), *Weymouth Sands* (1934), and *Maiden Castle* (1936) as important explorations of "the nature and limitation of romantic experience"; third, the vast historical epics of *Owen Glendower* (1940) and *Porius* (1942); and, last, the fantasies of his old age, of which perhaps only *Atlantis* (1954) has much merit. Discriminating close reading and apt quotation provide an excellent introduction to Powys's work and a reasoned case for recognition of the novelist's stature.

HOOKER's all-too-short essay combines a distinguished style with a capacity for succinct generalisations, which provide clues to many problems readers have had with Powys. He is particularly illuminating on Powys as the "novelist of margins", as "explorer of the border between the human and non-human constituents of human nature", as well as on Powys's use of the concept of "life-illusion", or self creation, seeing the question "what is reality in a cosmos that runs to personality?" as at the heart of Powys's writing. Hooker sees *Porius* as Powys's greatest novel, and comments interestingly on Nature and sexuality, both invoking and denying a Freudian reading of the text. He comments on the necessary isolation of Powys's characters and how that isolation differs from the stereotypical *Angst* of much modern literature

KRISSDOTTIR's study is a balanced investigation of the occult side of Powys and his concern with the demonic and grotesque. It is a scholarly exploration of Powys's interest in the Grail Quest, Welsh legends, and the traditions of alchemy, and a convincing demonstration of how these influenced the form of his novels. This study avoids the excesses sometimes committed when writing of Powys and the occult.

My (COATES's) book examines the fusing in Powys's texts of private fantasy, myths, taboos, and daydreams with the physical landscape through which the central characters move. Close attention is given to Powys's minute and subtle renderings of changing consciousness in particular instances, notably in *Wolf Solent*. My argument is that this rendering is central to his achievement and forms his distinctive contribution to the twentieth-century English novel.

FAWKNER's study reflects several of the concerns of current literary theory. He perceives in Powys's work the refusal found in Nietzsche and Jacques Derrida to take for granted the "self-unity of a thing, the primordial self-sameness of any given entity that we innocently believe has some autonomous stability, as a fixed given in a world of fixed givens". He suggests that Powys's thought questions the tacit assumptions of the entire post-Cartesian era. He stresses the philosophical importance of Powys's obsession with difference, displacement, and contingency and argues that Powys's tortuous, self-complicating writing shows the "characteristic desire to escape from the conventional conceptualizations and (linguistic-imagistic) compartmentalizations of traditional thought". This is a closely argued, highly theorised reading of Powys.

CAROLE COATES

Pratt, E.J. 1882–1964

Canadian poet

Brown, E.K., *On Canadian Poetry*, Toronto: Ryerson Press, 1943, revised 1944; reprinted, Ottawa: Tecumseh Press, 1977
Buitenhuis, Peter (ed.), *Selected Poems of E.J. Pratt*, Toronto: Macmillan, 1968
Clever, Glenn (ed.), *The E.J. Pratt Symposium*, Ottawa: University of Ottawa Press, 1977
Clever, Glenn, *On E.J. Pratt*, Ottawa: Borealis Press, 1977
Collin, W.E., *The White Savannahs*, Toronto: Macmillan, 1936
Davey, Frank, "E.J. Pratt, Apostle of Corporate Man," in *Poets and Critics*, edited by George Woodcock, Toronto: Oxford University Press, 1974
Pitt, David G., *E.J. Pratt: The Truant Years 1882–1927*, Toronto: University of Toronto Press, 1984
Pitt, David G., *E.J. Pratt: The Master Years 1927–1964*, Toronto: University of Toronto Press, 1987
Sutherland, John, *The Poetry of E.J. Pratt: A New Interpretation*, Toronto: Ryerson Press, 1956
Wells, Henry W., and Carl F. Klinck, *Edwin J. Pratt: The Man and His Poetry*, Toronto: Ryerson Press, 1947
Wilson, Milton, *E.J. Pratt*, Toronto: McClelland & Stewart, 1969

Pratt's early poems – *Rachel* (1917) and "Clay" (1923) – gave little promise of the mature poet's achievements. Recognition came with the narrative poems *The Witches' Brew* (1925), *Titans* (1926), and *The Roosevelt and the Antinoe* (1930), and though he published a substantial body of lyric verse, it is as a narrative poet that Pratt is remembered. *The Titanic* (1935), and especially *Brébeuf and His Brethern* (1940) and *Towards the Last Spike* (1952), assured his reputation as the poet of the Canadian national epic. Despite Pratt's fame – in 1937 he received the first Governor General's Award for Poetry – critical response was sparse until after his death, and critics have found him difficult to place in a specific tradition. He is usually situated as a bridge between worn-out nineteenth-century Romanticism and twentieth-century modernism (see Brown, below).

Although written when Pratt was still in mid-career, COLLIN's study laid the groundwork for most subsequent Pratt criticism. Including Pratt in a study of the first Canadian modernists, Collin credits him with having rejuvenated and reformed Canadian poetry "by turning it away from wilted, sentimental flower-gardens, by overcoming its soft femininity, by restoring its pulse with tonic realism and inebriating fun".

For Collin, Pratt's poetry is essentially heroic, and concerned with the actions of groups rather than of individuals. It is realist, meticulously researched, and often Rabelaisian in its extravagance, irreverent caricature, and "heroic merriment". Collin also notes the importance of science for Pratt, and his exploration of humankind's tragic relation with technology. The *hubris* that sinks the *Titanic*, for example, is that of an entire culture, which ignores the warnings of the very instruments it has invented to aid in the unequal struggle with nature.

BROWN's chapter gives a brief biographical sketch, and notes that paradoxically – for Pratt is first of all a poet of Newfoundland and the sea – Pratt's maturation coincided with his move to Toronto. Like Collin, Brown notes the absence of individuality in Pratt's characters. He writes that "the closest Pratt has ever come to animating a character with genuine life is in the latest of his major works, *Brébeuf and His Brethern*", but concedes that individuality is unnecessary in Pratt's narratives. The poet's concern is with force, size, and physical and spiritual strength that transcend ordinary limits. The fifth section of Brown's chapter is dedicated to Pratt's shorter poems, which, he suggests, show a poet ill at ease in a more-limited space, a view that has been echoed in later criticism.

KLINCK's contribution to his and WELLS's study is a biography, which situates Pratt and the writing of his more important poems in the context of contemporaneous literary developments in Canada. Wells provides a series of readings of Pratt's poems through texts from the classical and English canons. With the exception of Herman Melville's *Moby-Dick*, the English texts are limited "to works before the rise of the aristocratic school of Dryden and Pope" because "Pratt's heart is closer to the world before its new sophistication under the influence of modern French culture". Wells argues that Pratt followed Matthew Arnold's advice by turning for his sources and models to the Elizabethans and the poets of the Middle Ages and Antiquity, from Aeschylus to Aesop, and Dante to Shakespeare. Pratt's inspiration, however, is unlike that of T.S. Eliot, for example; it is heroic and robust, and free of sentimentality and nostalgia. Wells considers Pratt wholeheartedly a poet of his century, one who embraces technology as an essential part of life; indeed, it is a crucial element in his tragic and epic narratives. Yet Pratt's central concern is death, which, like his great predecessors, he sees as the ultimate test of human worth.

In his introduction to Pratt's *Selected Poems*, BUITENHUIS argues against SUTHERLAND's and Northrop Frye's view that Pratt was a Christian humanist. He considers the central metaphor of Pratt's poetry to be the evolutionary process, which continued informing his work long after it had ceased to trouble most poets and thinkers in this century. Buitenhuis sees Pratt as, stylistically, the contemporary of Tennyson and Thomas Hardy, and philosophically far more American than English, his vision most akin to those of the novelists Jack London and Frank Norris, and the poet Robinson Jeffers. He proposes that Pratt's literary isolation allowed him, in a time when the un-heroic and the ambiguous and obscure were the norm in literature, to develop a vision of collective heroism and a linguistic clarity that carry the narrative and drama of his long poems.

WILSON divides his book into three parts: "The Shorter Poems", "Extravaganzas", and "The Sea, the Railway and Brébeuf", in which he treats, respectively, Pratt's lyrics, his Rabelaisian narratives, and his epics. Concurring with earlier critics, Wilson judges Pratt's shorter works inferior to his narratives, and considers *Brébeuf* the poet's masterpiece, quoting Pelham Edgar who "once said of *Brébeuf*: 'a Protestant poet writes the greatest Catholic poem of our day'". For Wilson, the central theme of Pratt's work is the problem of communication, of bridging the void that separates communities. This void is as material as it is metaphorical, hence Pratt's fascination with, and recurrent use of, modern technologies – such as radio and the railroad – used to communicate over great distances. This book includes a short but still useful bibliography.

CLEVER's *On E.J. Pratt* provides a brief review of earlier criticism, and argues against both Sutherland's Christian reading and DAVEY's thesis that for Pratt man is essentially a corporate animal. For him, "in Pratt the essential myth is achievement, to moral purpose". Clever's main contribution is his discussion of Pratt in light of late nineteenth-century Canadian literature. CLEVER's *Symposium* is a collection of essays by writers and critics at the 1976 Pratt Symposium. The essays are written from a variety of perspectives, and the book provides a good introduction to the range of critical approaches employed by Pratt scholars. Included also is a comprehensive bibliographic checklist, of criticism as well as of the poet's own writing.

PITT's two-volume biography focuses on the poet's life and poetic development. Although by its very length it addresses itself more to the Pratt specialist than to the student or general reader, the book is nevertheless accessible to non-specialists. Pitt's detailed account of Pratt's life is combined with discussions of his poems in their historical and social contexts, providing much new critical material, especially useful for the study of Pratt's lesser-known poems.

NICOLA VULPE

Pre-Raphaelitism

Hönnighausen, Lothar, *The Symbolist Tradition in English Literature: A Study of Pre-Raphaelitism and "Fin de Siècle"*, Cambridge and New York: Cambridge University Press, 1988

Hunt, John Dixon, *The Pre-Raphaelite Imagination 1848–1900*, London: Routledge & Kegan Paul, 1968; Lincoln: University of Nebraska Press, 1969

Journal of Pre-Raphaelite Studies: 1992–

Pearce, Lynne, *Woman/Image/Text: Readings in Pre-Raphaelite Art and Literature*, Toronto and Buffalo, New York: University of Toronto Press, 1991; London: Harvester Wheatsheaf, 1991

Pointon, Marcia (ed.), *Pre-Raphaelites Reviewed*, Manchester: Manchester University Press, 1989

Sambrook, James (ed.), *Pre-Raphaelitism: A Collection of Critical Essays*, Chicago: University of Chicago Press, 1974

Stevenson, Lionel, *The Pre-Raphaelite Poets*, Chapel Hill: University of North Carolina Press, 1972

Warner, Michael, *et al.*, *The Pre-Raphaelites in Context*, San Marino, California: Huntington Library and Art Gallery, 1992

Woodring, Carl, *Nature into Art: Cultural Transformations in Nineteenth-Century Britain*, Cambridge, Massachusetts: Harvard University Press, 1989

Despite their brief existence as a self-styled "Brotherhood", the artists and writers associated with Pre-Raphaelitism (among them, the Rossettis, John Everett Millais, and Holman Hunt) exerted a profound but diffuse influence over the aesthetics (primarily British, but also French and North American) of the latter half of the nineteenth century. Certainly the movement created a rich corpus of poems, texts, and paintings, wherein some of the distinctive concerns of Victorian culture find their most remarkable expression, notably: the interplay between visual and verbal art; the exploration of a combined religious and erotic imagery; the richly confusing conflation of appeals to medievalism and naturalism; and the worship of beautiful women, in so many ways the expression (as Pre-Raphaelite history made scandalously apparent) of a morbid attachment to the iconographic femininity of a patriarchal social imagination. While the actual period of bravado and intimate camaraderie among the original members of the Brotherhood was brief, only truly thriving for a few years, their popular and controversial appeal was inherited by other and later artistic figures, most importantly William Morris and Algernon Charles Swinburne, whose quite different philosophies of art belied a Pre-Raphaelite affiliation. Likewise, Christina Rossetti, although never properly a "Brother", produced a corpus of poems that extends the range and depth of the Pre-Raphaelite tradition.

Readers interested to know more about the Pre-Raphaelites will find that important criticism is dispersed across two disciplines (literature and art history) and several methodological approaches (literary history, biography, formalist studies, feminism, and cultural studies). Moreover they will find little consensus – but several provocative discrepancies – in the scholarship that addresses the nature, history, distinguishing features, and dominant figures of Pre-Raphaelitism. A good place to begin, though, is SAMBROOK's collection of essays. Because they consist of critical writings both by and about the Pre-Raphaelites, the chronologically arranged articles offer a reliable overall sketch of the movement's discursive evolution and gradual consolidation as an object of twentieth-century criticism. WOODRING's remarkably learned and broad-ranging chapter on the Pre-Raphaelites is also a useful introduction. Contextualized within an analysis of Victorian attitudes towards art and nature, his discussion traces the affinities and encounters between the Pre-Raphaelites and other major artists of the period, including Tennyson, Robert Browning, John Ruskin, and George Meredith. More thorough, although occasionally unreliable, are STEVENSON's and HUNT's books, both of which devote themselves exclusively to Pre-Raphaelitism, primarily in its literary expressions. Although aware of the importance of symbolism in Pre-Raphaelite methods, neither Hunt nor Stevenson pays full attention to the movement's use of allegory and typology. HÖNNIGHAUSEN fills in this gap admirably, offering a detailed and scholarly account of symbolism in Pre-Raphaelite art. The approach here is comparative, diagnosing the uses of symbolism by major and minor Pre-Raphaelites as part of a larger nineteenth-century current, which also includes French symbolist poets and British poets of the *fin de siècle*.

The changing critical perspectives of the 1980s and 1990s have generated some provocative studies of the ideological and economic underpinnings of Pre-Raphaelitism. PEARCE's controversial study draws on the critical paradigms of Pierre Macheray and feminist film theory in order to assess Pre-Raphaelite representations of women. In a series of essays that link eight paintings to eight poems, Pearce attempts to reclaim the works for feminist viewers by interpreting them in a creative and iconoclastic fashion, an approach she describes as reading "against the grain" of the texts' surface ideology. The essays collected by POINTON fall under the rubric of contemporary cultural criticism, as do the arguably more successful ones in WARNER *et al.*, which includes a compelling discussion by Jerome McGann (one of his many on Pre-Raphaelite subjects) of Morris's response to the Victorian print industry. Finally, readers wishing to know more on any specific topic pertaining to the Pre-Raphaelites may wish to consult the *Journal of Pre-Raphaelite Studies* (published in Kutztown, Pennsylvania), which has been in publication since 1992.

SUE ZEMKA

Proletarian Literature in America

Aaron, Daniel, *Writers on the Left: Episodes in American Literary Communism*, New York: Harcourt, Brace & World, 1961; Oxford: Oxford University Press, 1977; reprinted, New York: Columbia University Press, 1992

Coiner, Constance, *Better Red: The Writing and Resistance of Tillie Olsen and Meridel Le Sueur*, New York and Oxford: Oxford University Press, 1995

Foley, Barbara, *Radical Representations: Politics and Form in U.S. Proletarian Fiction, 1929–1941*, Durham, North Carolina: Duke University Press, 1993

Gilbert, James, *Writers and Partisans: A History of Literary Radicalism in America*, New York: Wiley, 1968; reprinted, New York: Columbia University Press, 1992

Murphy, James F., *The Proletarian Moment: The Controversy over Leftism in Literature*, Urbana: University of Illinois Press, 1991

Nelson, Cary, *Repression and Recovery: Modern American Poetry and the Politics of Cultural Memory, 1910–1945*, Madison: University of Wisconsin Press, 1989

Rabinowitz, Paula, *Labor and Desire: Women's Revolutionary Fiction in Depression America*, Chapel Hill: University of North Carolina Press, 1991

Rideout, Walter B., *The Radical Novel in the United States 1900–1954: Some Interrelations of Literature and Society*, Cambridge, Massachusetts: Harvard University Press, 1956; reprinted, New York: Columbia University Press, 1992

"Proletarian literature" in the United States has come to refer to the body of literature – poetry, fiction, drama, and essays – produced in the context of the cultural and political debates, often inspired by the Communist Party, during the Great Depression of the 1930s. The temporal dimension of the term could be expanded on either side of the decade, but it was during the 1930s that many writers identified themselves as conscious participants in a "proletarian" literary movement, and sought to arouse or shape class consciousness through their writing.

The pioneering studies by Rideout and Aaron, both written during a historical moment when the Cold War held sway in American life, and both reprinted in 1992, continue to shape scholarship and debate about the subject. RIDEOUT's study is primarily concerned with analyzing the radical novel of the 1930s, but he locates this generation of writers in the context of their historical antecedents: the sizeable body of literature produced by those writers who responded affirmatively to socialism early in the century. And he traces the influence of these writers into post-World-War-II American life. Rideout's discussion of both well-known and neglected novels make his work an authoritative and definitive study of the fiction of the period. AARON's book was pivotal in establishing US literary radicalism as a distinct field of scholarly and popular inquiry. A chronicle of the involvement of American writers in progressive and radical movements, from the bohemian exuberance of the early twentieth century to the disillusionment of the 1940s, it recounts the controversies and careers of major and minor writers of the period – Max Eastman, Floyd Dell, Randolph Bourne, John Reed, Joseph Freeman, and Michael Gold, among others. It also examines the key journals, organizations, conferences, and debates of the era, and remains an indispensable sourcebook.

GILBERT's study, first published in 1968, follows some of the same literary-historical terrain as Rideout and Aaron; but Gilbert is specifically concerned with charting the trajectory of the modernist, anti-Stalinist communists who were associated with *Partisan Review* after it broke officially with the Communist Party during 1936–37. Through a careful analysis of the evolving views of *Partisan Review* editors Philip Rahv and William Phillips, Gilbert effectively captures the ideological ferment, tensions, and debate that characterized the outlook of the anti-Stalinist Left during the period.

NELSON signals an attempt to recuperate the neglected tradition of left-wing poetry in the United States. By challenging received views of literary modernism, as well as deeply entrenched notions of the literary canon, he opens up new space for the consideration of marginalized American poets. His arguments on behalf of socially and politically engaged poetry, particularly the poetry of the 1930s, are persuasive; and his readings of specific poets and traditions, ranging from those associated with the Harlem Renaissance to those who appeared in the pages of *New Masses*, are compelling. Nelson's study defines a new and important direction for scholarship in the field.

MURPHY's volume focuses on the critical discussions about leftism and proletarian literature that flourished during the 1920s and 1930s, locating them within their national and international contexts. Arguing that the dominant view of 1930s' literary debates has been shaped by those figures most deeply implicated in them – the writers associated with *Partisan Review* – Murphy demonstrates that these exchanges of view were much more wide-ranging and complicated than their critics have acknowledged. His work is an important and necessary corrective to much of the writing about this period. Also revisionist is the appraisal of proletarian fiction offered by FOLEY. Directly challenging the anti-communist paradigms that have shaped the dominant discourse about American literary radicalism, Foley re-interprets this moment of American cultural history, insisting on a degree of complexity and richness in the cultural debates of the era often overlooked in traditional accounts. At the same time, she articulates a model for examining the interplay between political beliefs and literary conventions and genres.

RABINOWITZ's work is a reconception of the prevailing scholarship, and an attempt to "engender" the histories of 1930s' literary radicalism. She argues that a rich body of writing was produced by women during this period, and that their gendered narratives of class struggle require a rethinking of not only class and gender as conceptual categories, but also the 1930s themselves. Her discussions of novels by Clara Weatherwax, Meridel Le Sueur, and Tillie Olsen, among others, establishes the foundation for her call for a "materialist-feminist literary history". COINER's study signals one response to Rabinowitz's call for attention to the intersection of American feminism and the Left, being the the first full-length study to examine Olsen and Le Sueur – two key figures of the 1930s – and their relationship to the American Communist Party and the literary Left.

JAMES A. MILLER

Prose: Old English

Bately, Janet M., *The Literary Prose of King Alfred's Reign: Translation or Transformation?* (lecture), London: University of London, 1980; reprinted in *Old English Newsletter*, Subsidia 10, edited by Paul Szarmach, Binghamton, New York: Center for Medieval and Early Renaissance Studies, 1984

Frantzen, Allen J., *King Alfred*, Boston: Twayne, 1986

Frantzen, Allen J., *Desire for Origins: New Language, Old English, and Teaching the Tradition*, Brunswick, New Jersey: Rutgers University Press, 1990

Greenfield, Stanley B., and Daniel G. Calder, *A New Critical History of Old English Literature*, New York: New York University Press, 1986

Lees, Clare A., "Working with Patristic Sources: Language and Context in Old English Homilies", in *Speaking Two Languages: Traditional Disciplines and Contemporary Theory in Medieval Studies*, edited by Allen J. Frantzen, Albany: State University of New York Press, 1991

Szarmach, Paul (ed.), *Studies in Earlier Old English Prose: Sixteen Original Contributions*, Albany: State University of New York Press, 1986

Szarmach, Paul, and Bernard F. Huppé (eds.), *The Old English Homily and Its Backgrounds*, Albany: State University of New York Press, 1978

Belonging to a period now marginal to the discipline of English Literature, and neglected in comparison with the poetry, Old English prose is the Cinderella of literary history. Despite the challenges of recent work by Frantzen and Lees, among others, criticism of the prose is still firmly rooted in the philological traditions of the nineteenth century, with source analysis the favoured methodology of study. "Literary" readings are still broadly New Critical and author-based; interestingly, the prose has never been subjected to the allegorical interpretations so common in criticism of Old English poetry.

SZARMACH and HUPPÉ's rather uneven collection covers the later Anglo-Saxon period, focusing on its dominant textual productions, the homilies. Many of the essays use comparative analyses of Latin sources and vernacular writers to argue for Ælfric's pre-eminent place in Anglo-Saxon and European literary history, as populariser, stylist, and developer of the scholarly intellectual project initiated by Alfred. There are also contributions on the forms, themes, and rhetorical devices of Wulfstan's *Sermo Lupi*, and the Blickling and Vercelli homilaries. One interesting essay in the collection (by Keith Tandy) deploys the category of "verbal aspect" from modern (as opposed to historical) linguistics to investigate Ælfric's prose style. The collection's emphasis on literary and stylistic readings was ground-breaking, highlighting the status of vernacular prose rather than seeing it as the poor relation of its supposedly more illustrious Latin sources. However, Pauline Stafford's opening essay on monastic and political interrelations in the Benedictine Revival argues for the cultural and social rather than purely literary meanings of the late tenth-century prose texts.

BATELY's lecture, both populist and scholarly, argues for the remarkable exploitation of the vernacular in ninth-century "Alfredian" prose. Analysing three translations from the earlier part of the Anglo-Saxon period (Alfred's *Boethius*, Orosius, and the psalms), Bately demonstrates how Alfred's twin objectives – educational reform and the cultivation of divine wisdom – inform the handling of the Latin sources, resulting in a "transformation" of the material. Two aspects of her argument are noteworthy: that Alfred's educational programme had social as well as the spiritual aims, and that an historically-informed knowledge of the purposes of translators can avoid simplistic judgements of their achievements.

GREENFIELD and CALDER's book, an updating of Greenfield's earlier and standard *Critical History*, has several points in its favour: a new section (by Michael Lapidge) on the Anglo-Latin background; triple the amount of space given to prose as compared to the earlier volume; and substantial discussion of some unfamiliar areas (the anonymous homilaries; legal and scientific prose) beside the familiar ones (Alfred and the ninth century; Ælfric and Wulfstan). The volume is nevertheless a survey, and while it offers a sense of the range of Anglo-Saxon vernacular prose material, discussion is necessarily telescoped. Occasionally effusive, the commentary proceeds by way of biography, source comparisons, literary evaluations, and syntheses of scholarly opinion. There are some valuable observations, particularly about Ælfric's style and translation practices, but aesthetic judgements tend to be normative, and to adhere to a traditional progressive model, whereby (for example) the poetic style of some early prose "finds its most refined use in the works of Ælfric and Wulfstan". More seriously, there is no sense whatsoever that there might be anything at stake in this material or the study of it.

The essays in SZARMACH's important 1986 collection on the early prose represent the best of traditional scholarship. Szarmach's very useful introduction identifies three representative positions among the writers of the first group of essays (on Alfred): the so-called traditionalist view (of an agreed Alfredian canon, refined by scholarship); the revisionist view (that Alfred didn't compose any of the works attributed to him); and a third position, that declines to consider the issue of authorship, but is only concerned with the texts' "literary" qualities. The remaining essays deal with anonymous early material (*Laws*, *Chronicle*, Orosius, *Martyrology*, translations of Gregory's *Dialogues*, Bede's *History*, *Life of St Guthlac*), largely from a New-Critical perspective. Berkhout's Appendix, "Research on Early Old English Literary Prose, 1973–82", supplements the standard field bibliography, Greenfield-Robinson. Mary Richards's interesting essay, though lacking a theoretical frame, goes beyond its positivist mode to ask different questions about the function of the Old English Laws, arguing that they "did not remain records of the past, fixed in form, but were used as resources for the present", functioning not only as legal records but as "living vernacular documents" of instruction and Christian belief.

FRANTZEN (1986) confines his discussion to the five works confidently attributed to Alfred: translations of Augustine and Boethius, Gregory's *Pastoral Care*, the psalms, and the laws. He deliberately avoids traditional critical biography, reading the texts as products of the pressing social concerns of the ninth century, which shaped Alfred's political and educational project: Alfred's translation of *Pastoral Care* is not just determined by spiritual reasons but is a text of political theory, concerned with power, dealing with "rulers and subjects, sexuality, and sorrow for sin". The adventurous critical approach is still rather muffled, but there are valuable gestures towards non-traditional frameworks for understanding Alfred's project, such as that of authorial self-fashioning: "his confidence in rewriting Scripture seems to have been inspired not only by devotion, but also by his awareness of a Davidic identity as a teacher and a leader, a king and a man of prayer".

Frantzen's recent work and Lees's essay mark a significant break with previous work on the prose. Both writers are concerned about the current isolated and isolationist status of Old English. FRANTZEN's polemical study (1990) should be taken as a rigorous questioning, not refutation, of the premises of source study, and its primary aim is not to generate new readings but to argue a case about the institutional fortunes of Anglo-Saxon studies. Thus the Caedmon episode in the late ninth-century Old English version of Bede's *Ecclesiastical History* is used as a focal point for investigating the ideological functions of traditional textual criticism, especially its function in erasing the role of present constructions in the evocation of a meaningful past. By focusing on Caedmon's resistance to the role ascribed to him, Frantzen shows how the episode's accepted "meaning" as an origin story, as a great national and Christian myth of harmonious conversion, involves the admission of incompatible narratives.

LEES offers an important critique of the positivist premises of the scholarly sources enterprises, premises that make difficult the assessment of "the broader sociohistorical significance" of the Old English homiletic corpus. She aims to bridge the gap between traditional philology and postmodern theory by drawing on socio-linguistics and the social uses of language advanced in the work of Hans Robert Jauss and Michel Foucault, thus enabling different models of history, analysis of the relationship between language and power, and insight into what texts reveal about the effects of the Benedictine Reform.

RUTH EVANS

Prose: Renaissance

Fish, Stanley (ed.), *Seventeenth Century Prose: Modern Essays in Criticism*, New York: Oxford University Press, 1971

Hall, Anne Drury, *Ceremony and Civility in English Renaissance Prose*, University Park: Pennsylvania State University Press, 1991

Mueller, Janel M., *The Native Tongue and the Word: Developments in English Prose Style 1380–1580*, Chicago: University of Chicago Press, 1984

Pooley, Roger, *English Prose of the Seventeenth Century, 1590–1700*, London: Longman, 1992

Webber, Joan, *The Eloquent "I": Style and Self in Seventeenth-Century Prose*, Madison: University of Wisconsin Press, 1968

Williamson, George, *The Senecan Amble: Prose Form from Bacon to Collier*, London: Faber & Faber, 1951; Chicago: University of Chicago Press, 1966

At the beginning of the twentieth century, the understanding of Renaissance prose was dominated by an awareness of the Latin and Greek models of style most highly regarded by Renaissance humanist scholars: particularly influential was the work of Morris Croll, modified and in some ways superseded by the work of R.F. Jones (representative essays by both are in Fish). The theories and taxonomies of style that they produced have been questioned, but alternative models are only just beginning to emerge from scholarship on the period after 1640, linked with neoclassicism and the rise of science. Recent critics on the earlier period have tended to do something different: rather than generalise about style, they have homed in on the construction of the self, on political and religious ideas, and on genre. The prose canon has become markedly different, too: gone are the anthologies of prose extracts from essayists and preachers.

WILLIAMSON is still in the Croll line; his book is an account of the Senecan pattern of style in the seventeenth century, seen as beginning in anti-Ciceronianism, and then developing in different ways – the pointed style, the particular varieties of word-play, particularly in antithesis, and the general ambition to write as if one were simply transcribing thought. He has a key advantage over Croll in spending much more time on close analysis, rather than on prescriptions for writing, which are notoriously unreliable. He undoubtedly has a point; for any seventeenth-century prose writer or his/her critic, the identification with Seneca was an important stylistic, political, and philosophical consideration. The difficulty with it is that so many features of witty prose count as "Senecan" that it is difficult to credit it as an analytic tool. However, Williamson's book is still valuable as a resource, particularly as the gap between Renaissance Latinity and our own lack of it, even at the scholarly level, increases.

As noted, FISH's collection is an important resource for earlier theories of seventeenth-century style – Croll, Jones, Williamson, and others fill the first 200 pages, before an extensive collection on individual authors, including Francis Bacon, John Donne, Ben Jonson, Lancelot Andrewes, Robert Burton, Thomas Browne, Milton, John Bunyan, and John Dryden. In most of these essays, style is the key to what these writers do (the subtitle is "Individual Styles"). However, there is space for Fish's own particular practice of analysing the experience of reading (here, on Bacon's essays), and for generic work as well, like Rosalie Colie on Burton and Leonard Nathanson on Browne.

MUELLER'S book ends where Williamson begins, with John Lyly. It is an outstanding example of a thesis convincingly pursued over a wide and unusual chronological range. Her main contention is that a particular sentence form, which comes to be common over the late medieval and early-modern period, owes its existence to the translation of Scripture into English. While the key role is reserved for William Tyndale, there is an important discussion of John Wycliffe and other pre-Reformation attempts to bring Scripture into the vernacular. Her book is valuable for stressing the native rather than Latin influences on the development of the vernacular, while also stressing that the main source of neologism, at a profound structural, syntactic rather than vocabulary, level, is down to the Bible rather than the classics.

WEBBER sustains the tradition of seeing prose style as revealing ideology, but refocuses it by concentrating on the construction of the self in the seventeenth century. The book opens with a virtuoso chapter contrasting Donne's *Devotions* and Bunyan's *Grace Abounding* as revealing the styles of two faiths, Anglican and Puritan. The remaining chapters concentrate on single authors, Burton, Richard Baxter, Browne, John Lilburne, Milton, and Thomas Traherne, but develop the method in interesting ways. While notions of the early-modern "self" have changed markedly since 1968, most notably through Francis Barker's influential, Foucauldian *The Tremulous Private Body*, Webber's work remains stimulating and revealing, and more than just a position worth arguing against.

HALL's study similarly advocates a general position from a study of a carefully selected range of texts and authors – Bacon's *History of Richard III*, Sir Philip Sidney, Richard Hooker, and Browne. The method is interesting; though she has been influenced by some of the strategies of New Historicism on the way that literature often bolsters authority, she also wishes to hang on to Enlightenment categories of the aesthetic and imaginative inwardness. Her book, like so many on the prose of this period, is a study in the rise of modernity. Her version is that the "pathos and exaltation of an erotic-pastoral-spiritual discourse are re-inflected with the circumspections, hesitations, and ironic deflections of modern civil prose".

My own (POOLEY's) book ranges widely over the period, attempting a generic classification across narrative prose (fictional and non-fictional), religious prose (including the Bible), essays, the cornucopian texts like those of Burton,

Thomas Nashe, and Browne, concluding with the new, modern discourses of politics and science. It is the closest to a survey currently available, aside from the big Oxford histories. Though the book revises and extends the prose canon to some extent, it is also a plea for attention to these major texts, which have been sidelined in undergraduate studies as the prose anthology has (for understandable reasons) gone out of print and out of favour.

ROGER POOLEY

Prose and Journalism: 18th Century

Black, Jeremy, *The English Press in the Eighteenth Century*, London and Sydney: Croom Helm, 1987
Irving, William Henry, *The Providence of Wit in the English Letter Writers*, Durham, North Carolina: Duke University Press, 1955; reprinted, New York: Octagon Books, 1975
Marr, George S., *Periodical Essayists of the Eighteenth Century* , London: J. Clarke, 1923; reprinted, New York: Phaeton Press, 1970
Rivers, Isabel, *Reason, Grace and Sentiment: A Study of the Language of Religion and Ethics in England, 1660–1780: Volume I*, Cambridge and New York: Cambridge University Press, 1991
Spector, Robert D., *Political Controversy: A Study in Eighteenth-Century Propaganda*, Westport, Connecticut: Greenwood Press, 1992
Stauffer, Donald A., *The Art of Biography in Eighteenth-Century England*, Princeton, New Jersey: Princeton University Press, 1941
Sullivan, Alvin (ed.), *British Literary Magazines: The Augustan Age and the Age of Johnson, 1698–1788*, Westport, Connecticut: Greenwood Press, 1983

English prose writing in the eighteenth century developed along several different avenues. Journalism – periodical essays, literary journals, newspapers – was the most prolific of these avenues, and has received the most attention from scholars. Other eighteenth-century prose forms previously regarded as primarily of historical interest, such as letter writing, biography, and religious prose writing, are increasingly treated as literary art forms.

MARR's study traces the eighteenth-century periodical essay through its various formal manifestations – the moral essay, the little didactic tale, the Eastern allegory, the imaginary characters, etc. Essays from approximately 150 periodicals are surveyed in chronological order, from Daniel Defoe's *A Review* to *The Comic Magazine* of 1796. The essays of Joseph Addison and Richard Steele, Henry Fielding, Samuel Johnson, and Oliver Goldsmith are treated in separate chapters. The essays of Addison and Steele provide the standards against which Marr evaluates the other essayists. Despite this bias, the book is valuable for providing a detailed and lengthy survey of the essay, which remains definitive for the greater names, and which brings lesser names to light.

BLACK's book, while a useful, general introduction to eighteenth-century newspapers, refuses to simplify historical complexities for the sake of a tidy argument. Black can discuss, for example, newspapers whose political party sponsors differed fundamentally on socio-economic issues, while arguing that the eighteenth-century press made political consensus a goal. The book challenges traditional arguments concerning the eighteenth-century press more than it presents new ones. The result is an informative historical overview, covering early development of the press, content of newspapers, efforts to acquire a readership, sources and distribution of news, relationship between the press and politics, censorship, foreign news, and the press as an instrument of instruction. The book is well documented, with a detailed biography, making it a good guide to more specialized works, in addition to its own merits as an excellent introduction to the field.

SULLIVAN's book, one of a four-volume reference project, profiles 87 literary magazines published during 1698–1788. Each profile contains a concise historical essay about the magazine, its publication details, locations of original copies and of reprints, and a list of relevant secondary works. The book limits its scope to: periodicals of literary significance; periodicals with literary material, or material written by literary figures; and periodicals which contributed to the development of genres, or to the literary canon, or performed literary functions. The volume's Introduction, though brief, provides a concise history of the development of the literary periodical, and summarizes the important scholarly work done in the field. This book is valuable as a reference source for a number of literary periodicals, and as a guide to other areas in the field of eighteenth-century literary periodicals.

SPECTOR focuses on five political essay-sheets published at the end of the Seven Years War (1763). By identifying and studying literary devices used by earlier eighteenth-century political propagandists to influence the growing reading public, however, Spector covers more of the eighteenth century than is suggested by this narrow scope. From the work of Defoe, Jonathan Swift, Alexander Pope, Henry Bolingbroke, and Fielding, among others, Spector delineates a literary tradition in political writing. He then shows that the readers' letters, editorial annotations, and marginal comments in essay-sheets, which reprinted essays from other essay-sheets, constitute a genre worthy of academic study. In addition to a trenchant and interesting argument, this book offers the reader a notable literary treatment of a prose form hitherto studied primarily for its historical significance.

IRVING argues that the great age of letter writing began and ended in the eighteenth century. The greatest of that century's letters managed to "hit the right balance" between the personal and the literary. Irving portrays the evolution of letter writing in the eighteenth century as "a groping toward an art [whose] principles and theories never got quite clearly articulated". Irving gives those principles and theories firm definition. While using classical forms as a standard, Irving nevertheless evaluates letters on the grounds of their own particular virtues. Highest praise is accorded to the letters of Pope, Johnson, William Cowper, and Horace Walpole. But in addition to lengthy discussions of these writers, chapters such as "Grub Street Activity", "The Blue Stockings", and "The Scotch Letter Writers" demonstrate the book's value in also covering eighteenth-century letter writing of less renown.

RIVERS's book studies the kinds of language that various religious and secular writers used to express how they perceived changes in the relationship between religion and ethics. Rivers demonstrates how resistance from orthodox Reformation thought influenced the rise of a new Anglican orthodoxy, promoting the conception of free-will and human reason as complements to divine Grace. The book's five chapters move from covering the background of the dispute, to the Anglicans responsible for defining and popularizing the new orthodoxy during 1660–1700, to the Nonconformist movement of 1660–90, to the development of Dissent in the first half of the eighteenth century, and finally to John Wesley's efforts to reform the Church through a synthesis of competing elements from earlier traditions. Rivers's exploration of religious and ethical thought in the eighteenth century provides not only a cogent historical analysis, but, in its explication of the cultural milieu surrounding each movement or writer, the book also provides a clear and detailed introduction to the field of eighteenth-century religious prose writing.

STAUFFER's book focuses on how, as an art form, eighteenth-century biography was influenced by, and had an influence on, other literary art forms of that century. Biographies are classified in terms of their relationship to the drama, the novel, the romantic spirit, lives of social eccentrics (i.e., criminals' lives), and the "life within" – early psychological portraits. A separate chapter is reserved for discussing those whom Stauffer terms the "great" biographers: Sir Thomas North, Edward Gibbon, William Mason, Goldsmith, Johnson, and James Boswell. The concluding chapter discusses historical patterns in the development of eighteenth-century biography and the regard in which biography as an art form was held by writers of that age. As an evaluative criterion, Stauffer uses the degree to which a biography succeeds "in conveying the sense of a life being led". The egregious biographies of George III thus receive less discussion than does the biography of John Ewles, an obscure parliamentarian. Furthermore, Stauffer treats only briefly biographies, such as Johnson's *Richard Savage*, that have received ample discussion in earlier studies. Nevertheless, this study, along with its supplementary annotated bibliography of primary sources, provides a highly detailed and surprisingly engaging introduction to eighteenth-century biography.

CRAIG G. PETERSON

Prose and Journalism: Romantic – Historical and Political

Boulton, James T., *The Language of Politics in the Age of Wilkes and Burke*, London: Routledge & Kegan Paul, 1963; Toronto: University of Toronto Press, 1963; reprinted, Westport, Connecticut: Greenwood Press, 1975

Butler, Marilyn (ed.), *Burke, Paine, Godwin and the Revolution Controversy*, Cambridge and New York: Cambridge University Press, 1984

Everest, Kelvin (ed.), *Revolution in Writing: British Literary Responses to the French Revolution*, Milton Keynes, Buckinghamshire: Open University Press, 1991

Klancher, Jon P., *The Making of English Reading Audiences 1790–1832*, Madison: University of Wisconsin Press, 1987

Smith, Olivia, *The Politics of Language 1791–1819*, Oxford: Clarendon Press, 1984; New York: Oxford University Press, 1984

Worrall, David, *Radical Culture: Discourse, Resistance and Surveillance, 1790–1820*, Hemel Hempstead, Hertfordshire: Harvester Wheatsheaf, 1992; Detroit: Wayne State University Press, 1992

BOULTON introduces his monograph with the claim that his work constitutes the first sustained literary analysis of the political prose of the late eighteenth century. Focusing on the John Wilkes crisis of 1769–71 and the French Revolution debate of the 1790s, his intention is to illuminate the meaning and assumptions of the texts he studies through analysis of their imagistic usages, and to evaluate their success as literary texts in order to account for their degree of contemporary influence and subsequent fame. To this end, Boulton is particularly interested in the texts' degree of permanent interest, political wisdom, and engagement with universal issues. This now-dated methodology makes Boulton's work seem to underestimate the ideological constraints within which texts operate; but his work constitutes a useful and comprehensive introduction to the Revolution debate in particular, and in its close analysis of texts is accessible, compelling, and often brilliant.

Boulton's declared aim of recovering political prose for literary analysis is shared by BUTLER in her edition of texts from the Revolution debate. In her illuminating critical Introduction and notes introductory to each writer, Butler also seeks stylistic reasons for the contemporary influence of particular texts; but her emphasis is more rhetorical and political. She examines the class associations of the various literary forms employed by political writers of the period, and explores the ways in which these are deployed in order to persuade their readers of their proper political attitudes and social roles.

SMITH's work has been, as Butler acknowledges, an influence here. Smith's study goes beyond recuperation to theorize the political debate of the period and to broaden our understanding of what constitutes a "political" text. Concentrating by turns on the political theories of Edmund Burke and Thomas Paine, popular pamphlets by radicals like Thomas Spence, accounts of the trials of William Hone, a variety of grammar books, and the literary criticism of Wordsworth and Coleridge, Smith constructs a compelling account of the class assumptions that underlie every use of language in the period – assumptions which commit a large part of radical activity to undermining the linguistic hegemony that sees "refined" language use as the only one suitable to the discussion of politics and as an infallible index of intellectual and moral capability.

Like Smith's, KLANCHER's is a theorized discussion of Romantic prose, which draws on Mikhail Bakhtin in order to explore four kinds of reading audience in the period – middle-class, mass, radical, and intellectual – and to argue that the creation of each is an ideological response to the political exigencies of an "inchoate cultural moment", where, instead of addressing the stable society of the eighteenth century, writers were obliged to *create* the reading publics they wished to address.

Klancher's discussion ranges widely, but he sees the political debates of the 1790s and post-Waterloo period as defining contexts. Invoking Arthur Young, Daniel Isaac Eaton, and Coleridge, he shows how in the 1790s "truth" became a contested issue, the idea of healthy "circulation" was opposed in conservative discourse to subversive "dissemination", and groups of readers in this conflictual period defined themselves in relation to what they were not. Detailed examination of Burke, Paine, Young, and the later Radical writings of the post-Waterloo period shows that while Burke and Paine make their arguments by the structural deployment of reconciliatory or antithetical tropes, Young's politically ambiguous writings reflect their content in their anti-rhetorical exploratory style. In Thomas J. Wooler's *Black Dwarf* writings he identifies a "symbolic textual violence", which presents the radical body as written on by class and power and mutilated at Peterloo, while in William Cobbett he identifies a style that in its breadth of discursive appropriation crosses barriers within the working class to "speak" it in a literalist way, thus resisting attempts to transform it into a "sign".

This interest in popular radicalism is shared by WORRALL, whose chosen area of study is the ultra-radical Spencean underworld. Worrall's study is self-confessedly recuperative, reintroducing obscure political figures in a way he claims is analogous to feminist literary archaeology, and emphasising historical narrative over critical analysis or theoretical positioning. Worrall's study introduces an entirely new perspective on political prose of the period since his elusive subjects work less through written media and more through the speech, the symbol (coins, pictures, etc.), and the trial report. By redefining our sense of what constitutes political discourse in this way, Worrall's work indirectly emphasises the various bravery, limitations, or self-censorship of that radical political prose which did find its way into print, as well as alerting the reader to the possibility of a subterranean seam of Spencean imagery underlying more mainstream political debate.

The construction of discursive context undertaken by all these texts is a problematic yet crucial issue for the collection of essays edited by EVEREST. In an introductory essay Philip W. Martin charts the New-Historicist concern to see historical context as constituted by the recovering critic and in turn to see that critic's concerns as constituted by the past. In this context he questions the historical methods of critics like Butler and Smith, who are in danger of creating "an objectified past against which signification is transfixed", and which, at its most extreme, can present the "unregarded provisionality of historical knowledge" as "finite and beyond disruption". Everest argues that a more critically self-conscious approach can enable conclusions which "surprise and confound our expectations ... [and] tell us what we do not perhaps necessarily wish to hear". Thus Kathryn Sutherland explores the discursive and political strengths of Hannah More's conservative Christian feminism, John Whale analyses the now problematic literalism of Paine's attack on Burke, Harriet Devine Jump explores the tensions within Mary Wollstonecraft's support for revolutionary France, and Tom Furniss identifies the expression of Wollstonecraft's feminist radicalism as in some ways adjacent to Burke's aesthetic and political imagery.

LEONORA NATTRASS

Prose and Journalism: Victorian

DeLaura, David J. (ed.), *Victorian Prose: A Guide to Research*, New York: Modern Language Association of America, 1973

Donn Vann, J., and Rosemary T. Van Arsdel, *Victorian Periodicals: A Guide to Research*, 2 vols., New York: Modern Language Association of America, 1978–89

Holloway, John, *The Victorian Sage: Studies in Argument*, London: Macmillan, 1953; New York: St Martin's Press, 1953

Loesberg, Jonathan, *Fictions of Consciousness: Mill, Newman, and the Reading of Victorian Prose*, New Brunswick, New Jersey: Rutgers University Press, 1986

Parrinder, Patrick, *Authors and Authority: A Study of English Literary Criticism and Its Relation to Culture, 1750–1900*, London and Boston: Routledge & Kegan Paul, 1977, revised, as *Authors and Authority: English and American Criticism 1750–1990*, 1991

Shattock, Joanne, and Michael Wolff (eds.) *The Victorian Periodical Press: Samplings and Soundings*, Leicester: Leicester University Press, 1982; Toronto and Buffalo, New York: University of Toronto Press, 1982

Stokes, John, *In the Nineties*, Hemel Hempstead, Hertfordshire: Harvester Wheatsheaf, 1989

Victorian Periodicals Review (quarterly journal), published by the University of Colorado Press for the Research Society for Victorian Periodicals, and, from 1979, by the University of Toronto

Willey, Basil, *Nineteenth Century Studies*, London: Chatto & Windus, 1949

Willey, Basil, *More Nineteenth-Century Studies: A Group of Honest Doubters*, London: Chatto & Windus, 1956; New York: Columbia University Press, 1956

Much scholarly criticism in this field concentrates on particular writers or periodicals, though in recent years attention has increasingly been drawn to various genres, such as criticism and autobiography.

DeLAURA covers quite well the critical field to the late 1860s, and may be useful to graduate students making forays into this area, in tracing scholarship to that date. Inevitably the selection of writers covered now seems limited. The only woman to merit attention is Jane Welsh Carlyle.

WILLEY's 1949 collection of essays on prominent writers claimed to be merely "a preliminary inquiry into the history of religious and moral ideas in the nineteenth century". In dealing with Samuel Taylor Coleridge, Matthew Arnold, John Henry Newman, Thomas Carlyle, J.S. Mill, Auguste Comte, and George Eliot, however, he brings his considerable erudition to bear on some of the greatest prose writers of that century, and lucidly illuminates their contexts and explains their philosophies. In beginning with Coleridge, Willey indicates the importance of his influence on the later writers rather than seeking to establish essential differences between "Victorian" and "Romantic" thinking. The book remains a useful, accessible introduction to nineteenth-century philosophical writing. His sequel (WILLEY, 1956) focuses on the theme of "loss of faith" and "honest doubters". Among the writers here considered in some detail are Francis Newman, J.A. Froude, and John Morley.

HOLLOWAY's study focuses on a group of Victorian writers who were concerned with moral and philosophical attitudes "to express notions about the world, man's situation in it, and how he should live". These writers, for whom he uses the term "the sage", include novelists such as George Eliot, Benjamin Disraeli, and Thomas Hardy. Though the mix is unusual it is particularly appropriate, for Holloway argues that since the sage's main task is to quicken his reader's perceptiveness, rather than attempt to convince by logical argument, "he draws upon resources cognate . . . with those of the artist in words". Thus, in his treatment of the works of Carlyle, Newman, and Arnold, he is as concerned with the rhetoric of their writing as with its "content", interested as much to help the reader appreciate its artifice as to understand its meaning. Indeed, meaning and artifice are so interrelated that the methods of literary criticism are harnessed to examine what, in each case, Holloway sees as the "essentially individualistic methods of the artist". This study is perceptive and free of critical jargon, though perhaps not a book for the beginner.

PARRINDER's discussion of Victorian literary critics is located within a broader study of the role of the literary critic and the basis and force of his authority throughout a period of 250 years. Like Holloway he positions the early Victorian critics as "sages". Moving away from the individualism of Romantic beliefs about genius, they were concerned to "pronounce upon the totality of social life in the prophetic manner". Writing for a mass audience "they combined an appeal to traditional sanctities or absolute value with an expression of the new historical awareness that came in with the romantics". Arnold receives extended treatment. Carlyle, Tennyson, Mill, John Ruskin, William Morris, and from the later period Walter Pater, C.A. Swinburne, Frederic Harrison, George Saintsbury, Henry James, Leslie Stephen, A.C. Bradley, and W.B. Yeats are discussed. Apart from brief reference to George Eliot, however, the "Men of Letters" emphasis means that the Victorian women reviewers who interpreted literature for the middle-class readership are ignored.

The impact of structuralist and poststructuralist critical theory within literary criticism generally has encouraged new ways of reading Victorian prose. LOESBERG's study is an example of such an approach. Drawing on the place of the autobiographies of Newman and Mill within their *oeuvres* as a whole, Loesberg sees autobiography as a genre that "transforms philosophy into narrative". The nineteenth-century philosophic debate on consciousness is seen as closely linked to narrative structures in the contemporary literature, and the autobiographical genre as offering writers a mediating position between opposing philosophical stances. Through his analysis of the writings Loesberg develops a methodology for reading Victorian philosophical prose as a literary form with a narrative structure. This is a fascinating but difficult text.

Once the student moves beyond prose published in book form to periodicals – those most fruitful areas in which so many of the century's finest prose writers were published – the sheer scale of the material available is daunting. DONN VANN provides a most valuable starting-point, guiding the reader to available bibliography, listings, background material, and through the complexities of identification of authorship.

STOKES' stimulating and informative collection of essays concentrates on the *fin de siècle*. "Topicality" is seen as a central element in the literature and culture of the period. The starting-point for each essay is a topic as it was presented in the contemporary press. The discussion then moves outwards to other "texts", taking the word in a broad sense to include the pictorial as well as the fictional and critical. "Fact is compared with fiction, journalism with literature, in the certain knowledge that the papers were omnivorous and omnipresent". Crucial issues in the journalisitic developments of the period, in particular "The New Journalism", are also addressed. Stokes wears his scholarship lightly. The book's style is accessible, and both the chapter notes and the suggestions for further reading make it eminently suitable for the beginning student, as well as of interest to the established scholar.

SHATTOCK's collection of essays takes as its starting-point the view that despite the frequent references in scholarship and popular biography alike to the Victorian periodical press, "the systematic and general study of that press has hardly begun". The essays by scholars from various disciplines offer an interesting range of approaches, which aim to stimulate further research. Three broad areas are covered: the involvement of major literary and intellectual figures with journalism; proprietorial, financial, and editorial control of the press; and the interrelationship of journalist, journal, and reader. Walter Houghton's essay, which opens the book and argues that periodicals both displaced books and created them, gives an excellent, wide-ranging, yet concise overview of the importance to the cultured class of Victorian periodical literature.

No researcher in the field ought to be unaware of the existence of *Victorian Periodicals Review*, but it is not nearly as well disseminated as its progenitor *Victorian Studies*. *VPR* continually keeps in play the interrelationship between literature and journalism, contains scholarly articles on both periodicals and writers, and most importantly provides, on a regular basis, bibliographies of recent scholarship, and updates the *Wellesley Index*.

BARBARA M. ONSLOW

Prose in America: Historical and Political

Baym, Nina, *American Women Writers and the Work of History, 1790–1860*, New Brunswick, New Jersey: Rutgers University Press, 1995

Fliegelman, Jay, *Declaring Independence: Jefferson, Natural Language, and the Culture of Performance*, Stanford, California: Stanford University Press, 1993

Greene, Jack P., *The Intellectual Construction of America: Exceptionalism and Identity from 1492 to 1800*, Chapel Hill: University of North Carolina Press, 1993

Kraus, Michael, and Davis D. Joyce, *The Writing of American History* (revision of Kraus's 1937 edition), Norman: University of Oklahoma Press, 1985

Levin, David, *History as Romantic Art: Bancroft, Prescott, Motley, and Parkman*, Stanford, California: Stanford University Press, 1959

Parrington, Vernon Louis, *Main Currents in American Thought: An Interpretation of American Literature from the Beginnings to 1920*, 2 vols., New York: Harcourt, Brace & World, 1927, additional volume, 1931, and the 3 vols. reprinted, 1958; original 2 vols., London: Rupert Hart-Davis, 1963
Warner, Michael, *The Letters of the Republic: Publication and the Public Sphere in Eighteenth-Century America*, Cambridge, Massachusetts: Harvard University Press, 1990

Most studies of US historical and political prose focus on specific time periods and groups of writers; however, several works provide a broad overview and general introduction to the field. PARRINGTON traces the main trends of American political and economic ideas through a wide variety of theological, political, and philosophical writings, as well as fiction and poetry. The work is divided into three volumes: the first, *The Colonial Mind*, covers 1620–1800; the second, *The Romantic Revolution*, covers 1800–60; the final volume, *The Beginnings of Critical Realism*, although never completed, covers 1860–1920. This division of the work follows from Parrington's conception of the shape of US intellectual history, which he sees as falling into three broad phases of "Calvinistic pessimism, romantic optimism, and mechanistic pessimism". Given its date of publication the work is inevitably now dated; however, it provides a broad overview of the political ideas it traces, covering the works of numerous writers, and delineating the influences of economic trends and European philosophy on US political ideas.

KRAUS and JOYCE survey American historical writing from the European origins through the twentieth century. Although the treatment of some individual writers is brief, especially in the early chapters, this volume covers a broad range of historical writers. Joyce's revision of Kraus's book (originally published 1937) has brought the volume up to date, with new chapters on historical writing since World War II. Despite the lack of in-depth analysis of individual authors, this volume provides a useful survey of the entire range of American historical writing, and therefore serves as a useful introduction.

Focusing more narrowly on one thread of political ideology, GREENE surveys three centuries of writings concerning American exceptionalism, reviewing a large number of commentators on the economic, political, and social potential of America (referring here to the 13 British colonies). Greene argues that the conception of America as different and better was not a nineteenth-century invention, as some have claimed. "Virtually all contemporary analysts who systematically addressed themselves to the task of defining America during the late colonial and revolutionary eras contrasted it with the Old World in terms of its unusual social elasticity and its abundant life chances for individuals". Greene admits that exploitation and social inequities existed in early-modern America, but argues that the basic claims of American promoters were empirically true: New England was a land of greater opportunity and social equality than the Old World. As Greene admits, however, the "intellectual constructs" based on the idea of America's distinctiveness "ignored the darker side of American life" – that is, the treatment of Native Americans and African slaves.

LEVIN examines four nineteenth-century American historians, arguing that their works were "not a curious by-product but a central expression of romantic thought in America". Levin begins by outlining the basic philosophical premises of these historians and the connections between those assumptions and the literary techniques used in the histories. Delineating the conventional characters in the work of this group of historians, Levin illuminates the connection between the Romantic model of history and specific conventions for depicting both individual types and whole races. His detailed analyses of three specific histories illustrate his points well. This work is important for its detailed attention to George Bancroft, William Hickling Prescott, John Lothrop Motley, and Francis Parkman, for its contention that those writers should be located within the central tradition of nineteenth-century American literature, and for its sustained argument about the importance of literary technique in historical writing.

WARNER analyzes the bourgeois public sphere in colonial America, delineating "large-scale changes in the relation between print and political culture". Warner's analysis of the transformation of the public sphere in the early eighteenth-century colonies argues that although seventeenth-century colonial printing was relatively inactive, by 1765 "print had come to be seen as indispensable to political life". Because print culture was identified with a public sphere separate from the sphere of the state, it enabled criticism of the state. Among other specific analyses, Warner explores the significance of textuality in interpreting the US Constitution. This is an important study of the relationship of print culture and political discourse in early US writings.

In contrast to Warner, FLIEGELMAN stresses the performative and oratorical aspects of early US political writing, focusing on the Declaration of Independence. By examining the textual nature of the Declaration, Fliegelman argues, critics have missed the importance of mid-eighteenth-century assumptions about rhetoric and public speaking. The Declaration was written with the intention of being read, both to the Congress and to the public throughout the colonies. This "made the Declaration an event rather than a document . . . Read out loud, the document that denounced a false community would galvanize the bond of a true one". With this concept of the essentially oratorical nature of the Declaration, Fliegelman goes on to analyze the eighteenth-century "elocutionary revolution", with its stress on expression of personal emotion and sincerity, and a performative understanding of selfhood. Contextualizing the Declaration within this analysis of rhetorical theory and practice, Fliegelman provides both an important complement and challenge to readings that stress the importance of print culture.

BAYM has uncovered a large body of historical writing by women, most of which has been neglected by previous scholarship on historical writing. Baym discusses over 350 works by over 150 American women writers published between 1790 and 1860, covering a variety of genres, including histories and chronicles, textbooks, historical plays, poems and novels, travel narratives. In the early national period, as Baym shows, history was considered an important part of women's education, and this was one reason that women became writers of history. Substantial chapters cover each of the primary genres presented, and a section of biographical notes on American women writers of history, compiled by Eric Gardner, along with the bibliography of historical writings by women, provide valuable resources for further research. This essential work of scholarship and criticism will almost certainly have a drastic impact on the future direction of scholarship on American historical writing.

ANGELA VIETTO

Prose in America: 19th Century

Bercovitch, Sacvan, *The American Jeremiad*, Madison: University of Wisconsin Press, 1978
Berlin, James A., *Writing Instruction in Nineteenth-Century American Colleges*, Carbondale: Southern Illinois University Press, 1984
Curti, Merle Eugene, *The Growth of American Thought*, 3rd edition, New York and London: Harper, 1964
Hansen, Olaf, *Aesthetic Individualism and Practical Intellect: American Allegory in Emerson, Thoreau, Adams and James*, Princeton, New Jersey: Princeton University Press, 1990
Matthiessen, F.O., *American Renaissance: Art and Expression in the Age of Emerson and Whitman*, London and New York: Oxford University Press, 1941
Samuels, Shirley (ed.), *The Culture of Sentiment: Race, Gender and Sentimentality in Nineteenth-Century America*, Oxford and New York: Oxford University Press, 1992
Walker, Peter F., *Moral Choices: Memory, Desire, and Imagination in Nineteenth-Century American Abolition*, Baton Rouge: Louisiana State University Press, 1978
Woodress, James L., *et al.* (eds.), *Eight American Authors: A Review of Research and Criticism*, revised edition, New York: Norton, 1971

American non-fictional prose of the nineteenth century addressed many of the same concerns that occupied novelists – the eloquence of Nature, the beginnings of a national identity, the suffering of women, the evils of slavery, etc. Style took a particularly American path from the beginning, away from the literary models favoured in Europe toward an imitation of American speech patterns, especially those practiced upon the soap-box and in the pulpit. The passionate voices, particularly those raised against slavery and for women's rights, were also *read*, but not without establishing a following in public lecture-halls first, and it is within the oral tradition that much of this published work belongs.

By mid-century the airy voice of Ralph Waldo Emerson exerted considerable influence upon prose style. He was temperamentally more philosophical, more secular, more creatively literate in his use of language than his predecessors in prose had been. Abolitionist rhetoric, the best of which is contemporary with Emerson, continued to follow pulpit models, as much of the published works of these authors were lectures and speeches. Ironically, because many abolitionists credited Emerson as an influence, if he did not exactly *shun* immediate problems he kept just above them by addressing his primarily male, middle- and upper-class audiences through a film of abstraction marked by the invention and reinvention of philosophical vocabulary, even as his syntax tended toward the plainness of well-formed written argument. At his lectures, listeners sat spellbound. That his message actually *reached* few of them was beside the point. By the 1890s, successful social rhetoric was calm, measured, logical, if occasionally academic, as writers less inspired than Emerson followed the trend away from pulpit prose. Placement of typical early-century non-fictional works alongside late ones yields sharp Aristotelian extremes of emotional appeal. Rhetorical excess happens in any generation, but in the 1890s florid prose was, as a rule, less popular, and those who did favor it borrowed from the secular Romantics popularized by Emerson, and not from religion.

After decades of Emersonian domination of public discourse devoted to developing an American philosophy and language, American non-fictional prose all but forgot its early associations with revolutionary rabble-rousing and tent meetings, except among feminists and Negro separatists. Prose writers continued to take up discussions of religion, race, and gender, but expanded the definition of "social" to include America's place in world politics as well – in cool, plain language, especially after the Civil War had removed the most divisive topic, slavery, from public debate. The rise of the American public university system in the second half of the century greatly changed the character and sophistication of the reading public, who were more easily moved by appeals to public responsibility than by exhortations to moral obligation. Liberal political writing, the great generator of cheap reading and spirited controversy, concentrated its influence among educated Eastern and, to a lesser extent, Southern, men, who sought to influence each other as a means of effecting public policy change. The young upper-middle-class male read Thomas Carlyle, then he read Emerson, and if converted he took up the pen to address wrongs not generally suffered personally to address an audience of his peers. Few women, for a variety of reasons, flourished in this masculine community as Mary Wollstonecraft had briefly done in England a century earlier.

CURTI remains a useful overview of American thought during its nineteenth-century adolescence, although his scope is much broader. An understanding of nineteenth-century rhetorical training in the universities depends upon an understanding of the religious roots of the private universities, and Curti gives considerable space to reviewing the work of literary scholars such as Perry Miller, who, while their interests centered almost exclusively on colonial prose, have had considerable influence upon how we now read the nineteenth-century writers who followed the colonial clerics. His is a "history of ideas" approach, overwhelmingly broad in many respects; but specific information about minor authors and intellectual movements is still readily accessible. Prose-writing before Emerson was an eclectic mix, inclined to land-use law arguments still approached with eighteenth-century Rights-of-Man rhetoric, alongside religious tractarianism in the style of Hannah More, argued with equally high-minded zeal.

BERLIN concerns himself only with treatises on rhetorical theory and the movements in rhetoric that influenced how writers were trained. He provides the best summary of the major theorists necessary for an understanding of the views shared by members of the community of writers led by

Emerson and the teachers who influenced them. (Successful prose writers of the century were generally university trained: men of colour and women, of course, were home- or self-educated with few exceptions.) He provides a good bibliography of similar studies as well.

BERCOVITCH has theorized that the unique character of American rhetoric, the voice he calls the "American Jeremiad", which is at the same time optimistic and critical, began in the European Puritan pulpit, but developed over time into a uniquely American joining of religious symbol, shared myth, and an impulse towards public service, which is never quite free of the language of predestination. It is a self-analyzing historical narrative, an actively molded ongoing part of public and individual life, which must be continuously scrutinized and improved upon. According to this model, American rhetoric rarely allows for a "last word" on any subject, because it does not give itself permission to arrive at solutions. While "American Jeremiad" is an original label, Bercovitch's theories about connections between the Judaeo-Christian heritage and the use of symbol in non-fiction prose is also popular in life-writing theory, which postulates similar connections between religious symbol and the plotting of lives in biography and autobiography. His long middle chapter, "Rituals of Consensus", addresses in detail the use of typology in war rhetoric at mid-century, which assumes a uniquely American interpretation of revolution in apocalyptic terms (i.e, destructive, with a regenerative purpose). Bercovitch's "American Jeremiad" certainly helps explain why Americans continue to be moved by "The Battle Hymn of the Republic".

MATTHIESSEN was the first to describe the literary period preceding the Civil War as the "American Renaissance". He chose this title to reflect the creative richness of this period, owing perhaps to a fondness among these authors for the Elizabethans. Elizabethan language exerted no particular influence, but Elizabethan method did. This is arguably the most important of the works cited here for beginning students of the period, not just because much of the subsequent research on non-fiction writers of the period makes reference to this text, but because Matthiessen condenses and explains Emerson lucidly, no mean feat, and connects his views on language to the developing styles of Henry David Thoreau and others who followed his lead.

WOODRESS provides a useful overview of trends in Emerson, Edgar Allan Poe, Mark Twain, and Henry James criticism, including the non-fictional works of each, by major scholars, most of them editors of editions. He also offers comprehensive surveys of the biographies, and bibliographies. The compressed style of this study makes it a good quick-reference volume, a ready source of encapsulated Transcendentalism.

HANSEN limits his analysis to Emerson, Thoreau, Henry Adams, and William James. This is philosophy of history densely written, but his insights into rhetorical and linguistic innovations reflective of the times, crystallized within the prose, integrates much that has been written in recent decades into a fresh discussion. His inclusion of James and Adams broadens the traditional scope of discussion. By eliminating the category of contemporary fiction writers who dabbled in prose criticism, and sticking to history and philosophy, he eliminates much of what is overwhelming to students interested in understanding the intellectual currents of the nineteenth century. His final chapter, in which he examines allegory as a central literary device in the nineteenth century, is particularly worth careful reading.

WALKER and SAMUELS are included here as representative of critical works, most of which are historical and biographical, on the largely oral tradition that fuelled the anti-slavery and women's suffrage movements. Walker provides an excellent overview of representative abolitionists, their rhetorical strategies, and the milieux that produced them. Samuels has collected essays on the language of the body in the anti-slavery movement, women's suffrage literature, and lectures produced by women. Of particular interest in this collection, for the purpose of understanding women's contribution to America's nineteenth-century rhetorical tradition, is an essay by Karen Sanchez-Epler, "Bodily Bonds: The Intersecting Rhetorics of Feminism and Abolition". Both works include useful bibliographies.

CLARA ELIZABETH SPEER

Psychoanalytic Literary Theory

Brooks, Peter, *Reading for the Plot: Design and Intention in Narrative*, Oxford: Clarendon Press, 1984; New York: Knopf, 1984

Davis, Robert Con (ed.), *Lacan and Narration*, Baltimore: Johns Hopkins University Press, 1984

Feldstein, Richard, and Judith Roof (eds.), *Feminism and Psychoanalysis*, Ithaca, New York: Cornell University Press, 1989

Feldstein, Richard, and Henry Sussman (eds.), *Psychoanalysis and . . .*, New York and London: Routledge, 1990

Felman, Shoshana, "Turning the Screw of Interpretation", in *Yale French Studies* 55–56, 1977

Silverman, Kaja, *The Subject of Semiotics*, New York and Oxford: Oxford University Press, 1983

The field of psychoanalytic criticism is vast and prolific. Basic Freudian texts such as *The Interpretation of Dreams*, especially chapters VI on "The Dream Work" and VII on "The Psychology of the Dream-Processes," *Jokes and Their Relation to the Unconscious*, and articles such as "The Unconscious" and "On Repression" need to be read before sense can be made of psychoanalytic criticism. Since the 1960s and 1970s, when Freudian psychoanalytic criticism was popular, this field has seen the practise of Lacanian psychoanalytic criticism, feminism and psychoanalysis, psychoanalysis and deconstruction, psychoanalysis and Marxism, and semiotic psychoanalysis, to name just a few of the permutations it has gone through.

FELMAN's essay, written in the 1970s, is a classic, often designated as required reading in introductory (post)graduate seminars on psychoanalysis and literature. Felman gives a Freudian reading of Henry James's *The Turn of the Screw* which is longer than the Jamesian text she interprets. In this substantial essay, she examines through psychoanalysis the relationship of the reader to the text and event and its implications for psychoanalytic interpretation itself. She produces a symptomatic reading of James, where the structure of the novella, its deceptions, its textual feints are reproduced in her analysis of it. This is an extremely seductive article.

SILVERMAN's work is particularly useful at the undergraduate level because it methodically follows a formula of laying out the theoretical framework with an application of it to literary and cinematic texts. This work insists on the centrality of psychoanalysis to semiotics, in that both the subject and its signification are seen as effects of discourse. Silverman's initial chapters on Ferdinand de Saussure's and Charles Peirce's work lays the groundwork for the comprehension of the rest of the material. She shows the links between their works and Freud and Jacques Lacan to teach the student how to read and interpret the signifying process.

BROOKS's text is required reading for the advanced undergraduate/graduate student of literary criticism. In this work, the basic element of plot, glossed over by its sheer obviousness, is theorized by Brooks. He uses the works of Freud as the blueprint of psychic processes as well as the dynamics of narration. Readings of Stendhal's, Charles Dickens's, and William Faulkner's texts among others are provided. Of particular value are the chapters "Narrative Desire" and "Freud's Masterplots: A Model for Narrative." The former chapter deals with desire as the dynamic of signification and the latter provides a meta-theoretical reading of Freud's *Beyond the Pleasure Principle*.

DAVIS's collection includes a variety of essays by critics of English, American, and French literary texts. Of particular use are Davis's two essays "Lacan and Narration" and "Lacan, Poe, and Narrative Repression". In the first, Davis locates the link between Freud and Lacan, and psychoanalysis and linguistics. In the second essay, he shows the centrality of the concepts of repression and unconscious (within psychoanalysis) to narration itself. Davis demonstrates this link by providing an analysis of Edgar Allan Poe's "The Tell-Tale Heart". These two accessible essays are part of a collection which includes the work of important psychoanalytic critics such as Juliet Flower MacCannell, Shoshana Felman, Jeffrey Mehlman, and Jerry Aline Flieger.

FELDSTEIN and ROOF go beyond the early premise of psychoanalytic feminist criticism, which posits the familial triangulated relationship of father, mother, and child, and through which configuration feminism (daughter) perceives itself in a relationship with psychoanalysis (father). This work extend this feminist-psychoanalytic alliance by positing an irreducible third term, which is that "'other' alien force, that which founds, mediates, or affects discourses, ideologies, categories, [language] . . . recognized as distinct from either feminism or psychoanalysis, but which affects feminism and psychoanalysis". The essays are divided into two sections – "Theoretical Texts" and "Literary Texts". Noteworthy among the essays in the first section are those by Jane Gallop, Jacqueline Rose, and Ellie Ragland-Sullivan, all of which analyze the materiality of language and its implication for feminist practice.

FELDSTEIN and SUSSMAN's work belongs to the second-generation of psychoanalytic criticism, which is characterized by post-structuralism, post-Lacanian Freudianism, and post-Derridean notions of *différance*. Unlike psychoanalytic criticism of the 1950s and 1960s, which dealt primarily with the decoding of text, this collection deals with the larger philosophical, political, social, and epistemological questions within culture. Among others, Flieger's and Kahane's essays deal with feminist issues of subjectivity and agency, and Ross studies classed and gendered subjects in historically specific cultures. All the essays are located in the intersections of feminism, Marxism, semiotics, film theory, and deconstruction, as well as psychoanalysis.

RADHIKA MOHANRAM

Puritan Literature: British

Berry, Boyd M., *Process of Speech: Puritan Religious Writing and "Paradise Lost"*, Baltimore: Johns Hopkins University Press, 1976

Haller, William, *The Rise of Puritanism*, New York: Columbia University Press, 1938

Heinemann, Margot, *Puritanism and Theatre: Thomas Middleton and Opposition Drama under the Early Stuarts*, Cambridge and New York: Cambridge University Press, 1980

Hill, Christopher, *Writing and Revolution in Seventeenth-Century England* (Volume 1, *Collected Essays*), Brighton, Sussex: Harvester Press, 1985; Amherst: University of Massachusetts Press, 1985

Keeble, N.H., *The Literary Culture of Nonconformity in later Seventeeth-Century England*, Leicester: Leicester University Press, 1987

Sasek, Lawrence A., *The Literary Temper of the English Puritans*, Baton Rouge: Louisiana State University Press, 1961

Smith, Nigel, *Perfection Proclaimed: Language and Literature in English Radical Religion, 1640–1660*, Oxford: Clarendon Press, 1989; New York: Oxford University Press, 1989

Stachniewski, John, *The Persecutory Imagination: English Puritanism and the Literature of Religious Despair*, Oxford: Clarendon Press, 1991; New York: Oxford University Press, 1991

Watkins, Owen C., *The Puritan Experience*, London: Routledge & Kegan Paul, 1972; New York: Schocken Books, 1972

Puritanism is best understood as a radical movement for "a more godly thorough Reformation", largely within the Church of England until 1649, then increasingly separatist; after 1662 it is better described as Nonconformity. It is theologically identified with Calvinism, though the Church of England was more widely Calvinist for much of this period. In literature, Puritanism flowered only late, with Milton and John Bunyan, probably Andrew Marvell, and minor figures such as George Wither. Before then, Puritans in literature were largely targets, particularly for the comedies of Ben Jonson. "Puritan" has a more general meaning, of a certain rectitude; D.H. Lawrence was famously described as "puritanical" in his approach to sex, though this is overstretching an already loose term.

HALLER began by trying to understand Milton's *Areopagitica* (1644) in context, and ended up by producing a cultural, theological, and rhetorical portrait of Puritan faith and practice, which remains convincing, though it needs supplementing and questioning in the light of more recent studies. Like many American scholars of the period, he is aware of the origins of American society, particularly as regards the debates about liberty, in English Puritanism. His chapter "The Rhetoric of the Saints" is still a useful starting-point for the ambivalence of Puritan thought about language, and his account of the paradigms of conversion and the attacks on Arminian bishops retain the virtues of clarity and full documentation. The story is continued in his *Liberty and Reformation in the Puritan Revolution*.

SASEK's book is not much referred to, but it is valuable as an investigation of the supposed Puritan hostility to art, and literary art in particular. (As long ago as 1930, Percy Stubbs had convincingly refuted the "Philistine" accusation levelled at Puritans in his *The Puritans and Music*.) He sketches what might be a Puritan poetics, in the chapter on "Brevity, Perspicuity, Spirituality"; mostly he is concerned with the negative features, and the way figures like Milton were held to sacrifice their art for the single-minded revolutionary spirit.

WATKINS is a study of the Puritan spiritual autobiography. After opening chapters on the importance of personal experience in Puritan spirituality, there is a mixture of chapters on important individuals (Bunyan, Baxter, Robert Norwood) and more general categories (Quaker journals, for example). The material is drawn from a wide area, and is modestly and carefully discussed.

BERRY's book concludes with a reading of *Paradise Lost*, but for more than half its length is concerned to build up a picture of Puritan culture that would account for Milton's approach to writing. Stylistically and doctrinally Milton is not a representative Puritan, but Berry lays out some of the important congruences and differences.

HEINEMANN's book is mainly a study of Thomas Middleton, but it needs to be seen as an essay in this more general category, too. Firstly, it shows how many Puritan figures in the 1620s and 1630s were by no means as hostile to the drama as the stereotype would suggest: it builds up the picture of an oppositional use of drama located in the city of London rather than the court. Secondly, it contains an important concluding chapter on the influence of the drama on Leveller style, especially in the writings of Richard Overton.

For many years, the work of Christopher HILL has built into a library on revolutionary Puritanism. He is unusual among historians in giving so much attention to literature as a source of history (he has written monographs on Milton and Bunyan). The first volume of his collected essays contains a number of his key pieces on literary Puritanism, not just Milton, Marvell, and George Wither, but the radical prose of the Levellers, Diggers, and Ranters. There is also an important piece on censorship. Throughout, the book is informed by Hill's straightforward approach to literature, and his sense of the revolutionary, innovative nature of Puritanism. The collection, though, is not exclusively about Puritan writing.

KEEBLE concentrates on the major period of Puritan writing, the Restoration. Although there is substantial discussion of Milton, Bunyan, and George Fox, the range of reference is enormous and the organisation according to topics rather than authors. So there are chapters on the Nonconformist response to persecution, the press and censorship, learning and creativity, introspection and individualism, heroism, style, and story. The study gives the fullest picture of Nonconformist literature in the period; it brings together a number of topics and authors who are normally discussed separately; and it argues against the view that Milton and Bunyan are anomalous figures in a movement largely hostile to art.

SMITH's book, which can usefully be read alongside his more general study, *Literature and Revolution in England, 1640–1660*, deals with the language of the religious radicals who went far beyond the Lutheran/Calvinist synthesis. The focus is on the prophets, visionaries, and mystics rather than the canonical literary figures. Smith negotiates his way around the proliferation of sects and theological influences with great aplomb to bring out the features of a remarkable religious sub-culture. A list of some of the main writers discussed – Anna Trapnel, Sara Wight, Gerard Winstanley, Abiezer Coppe, Robert Everard, and John Saltmarsh will give only half the picture. On the new sense of the self, on the influence of Jakob Böhme, and on the relationship between spiritual power and rhetoric in religious radicalism, Smith has important new things to say.

Though STACHNIEWSKI subtitles his book "*English Puritanism*", his remit is the literary reaction to Calvinism. In the second section, he discusses the Calvinist edge to despair in Robert Burton, John Donne, and Christopher Marlowe, as well as in Milton. He identifies the Calvinist God as constructing a "persecutory imagination" in his adherents, and links the psychic, the social, and the literary in his reading of Bunyan, which is substantial and revealing. Stachniewski is unusual in dealing with the darker side of the doctrines of Reformation Christianity, and his analysis of the effects of Calvinism on subjectivity is unusual and innovative. Questions might be asked about the peculiar unchronological order of his chapters, but this is not a study to be easily dismissed.

ROGER POOLEY

Puritan Literature: American

Caldwell, Patricia, *The Puritan Conversion Narrative: The Beginnings of American Expression*, Cambridge and New York: Cambridge University Press, 1983

Hammond, Jeffrey A., *Sinful Self, Saintly Self: The Puritan Experience of Poetry*, Athens: University of Georgia Press, 1993

Leverenz, David, *The Language of Puritan Feeling: An Exploration in Literature, Psychology, and Social History*, New Brunswick, New Jersey: Rutgers University Press, 1980

Lowance, Mason I., Jr., *The Language of Canaan: Metaphor and Symbol in New England from the Puritans to the Transcendentalists*, Cambridge, Massachusetts: Harvard University Press, 1980

Scheick, William J., *Design in Puritan American Literature*, Lexington: University Press of Kentucky, 1992

Schweitzer, Ivy, *The Work of Self Representation: Lyric Poetry in Colonial New England*, Chapel Hill: University of North Carolina Press, 1991

Early studies of Puritan writings suspected that the Calvinistic heritage informing them accounted for their alleged failure as *belles-lettres*. During the 1940s and 1950s, several studies noted the ways in which the Puritan criterion of a plain style could accommodate certain kinds of verbal artifice, principally simile and structure. Subsequent studies, of which there are very many, have been far more venturesome, whether defining Puritan art from within its authors' intentions and its readers' contexts, or defining it from without, in terms of current psychoanalytic, feminist, or cultural theories.

CALDWELL finds that English conversion narratives present reassuring conclusions, which anticipate heavenly hope, provide an image of England as a place of fixed identity, rely on clear similes based on Scripture, and offer a conventional morphology of the conversion experience. The American versions of this genre, in contrast, are characterized by irresolute and somewhat discontent conclusions, an image of New England as disappointingly lacking in identity, similes with blurred biblical contexts, and an asymmetrical and incomplete morphology of the conversion experience. Caldwell's investigation is a landmark contribution to comparative studies of Puritan literature.

LOWANCE explores the increasing tendency in Puritan writings to demarcate divine providences throughout nature and history. This tendency rivaled the conservative tradition of typological exegesis and also encouraged individuals to see their personal rational capacities as endowed with legitimate powers of interpretation. This ascendancy of regard for personal authority eventually relegated institutional authority to a secondary position. Especially good is Lowance's discussion of Jonathan Edwards's extension of the jeremiad tradition; especially debatable is his discussion of Edward Taylor's recapitulation of prophetic biblical types.

LEVERENZ's psychoanalytical approach discloses the unconscious ambivalence of leading Puritan ministers when responding to paternal authority. This ambivalence, derived in part from the simultaneous Puritan stress on radical voluntarism and on complete submission, resulted in fantasies of nursing and obsessive literary styles. The Puritans' vision of the perfect father and their fear of female contamination informed their child-rearing practices and their condemnation of stage performances. Leverenz's study of the disruptive nature of Puritan male identity suffers from the absence of comparative English examples (so successful in Caldwell's book), a tendency toward exaggeration when applying psychoanalytic categories, and a failure to address the possibility that the patterns he sees are more universal than his report suggests. Nevertheless, the intelligence and insight his approach offers outweigh such reservations.

My own study (SCHEICK's), considering another feature of the dichotomy noted by Leverenz, selects various examples of seventeenth- and eighteenth-century poetry and prose to discern special literary sites ("logogic cruxes" defined by Renaissance and Reformed traditions) where Puritan authors and readers would likely have hesitated. Such pauses were designed to encourage the contemplation of a central paradox in the Puritan understanding of language – its dual capacity to conceal self-idolatry and reveal deific design. This Christ-like verbal intersection of the material and the divine collapses in Jonathan Edwards's early sermons, which convey only a skepticism toward language and an iconoclastic impulse.

SCHWEITZER takes another angle on the voluntarism/submission dichotomy discussed by Leverenz, and she presents a feminist reading of the paradigm of conversion studied by Caldwell. Puritan culture, Schweitzer contends, represented redeemed subjects as essentially male, yet at the same time problematically applied metaphors drawn from female subjugation to these redeemed male figures. This manner of appropriation empowered male Puritan authors to theatricalize themselves as both potentially empowered assertive saints (males) and disempowered passive recipients of divine Grace (females). In this way, males confiscated the actual identity of female passivity to legitimate their authority over both women and the creative process. Schweitzer's thoughtful book is worth careful reading.

HAMMOND (like Scheick) is interested in the ways Puritan authors wrote with their readers in mind. He finds that the verse of Edward Taylor, Anne Bradstreet, and Michael Wigglesworth required compositional completion through its readers' closure with the biblical origins of the verse. A meta-self is projected in this poetry, a paradigmatic self, which struggles beyond sin to gain an imagined assurance in spiritual redemption. Taylor's later poems, in particular, dramatize this loss of earthly self for a nearly achieved neo-biblical identity similar to the Canticles Bride of Christ. Hammond offers here a substantial study.

WILLIAM J. SCHEICK

See also **American Literature: Early Period**

Pynchon, Thomas 1937–

American novelist and short-story writer

Berressem, Hanjo, *Pynchon's Poetics: Interfacing Theory and Text*, Urbana: University of Illinois Press, 1993
Berube, Michael, *Marginal Forces/Cultural Centres: Tolson, Pynchon, and the Politics of the Canon*, Ithaca, New York: Cornell University Press, 1992
Dugdale, John, *Thomas Pynchon: Allusive Parables of Power*, London: Macmillan, 1990
Eddins, Dwight, *The Gnostic Pynchon*, Bloomington: Indiana University Press, 1990
Kharpertian, Theodore D., *A Hand to Turn the Time: The Menippean Satires of Thomas Pynchon*, Rutherford, New Jersey: Fairleigh Dickinson University Press, 1990; London: Associated University Presses, 1990
McHoul, Alec, and David Wills, *Writing Pynchon: Strategies in Fictional Analysis*, Urbana: University of Illinois Press, 1990; London: Macmillan, 1990
Madsen, Deborah L., *The Postmodernist Allegories of Thomas Pynchon*, Leicester: Leicester University Press, 1991
Maltby, Paul, *Dissident Postmodernists: Barthelme, Coover, Pynchon*, Philadelphia: University of Pennsylvania Press, 1991

O'Donnell, Patrick (ed.), *New Essays on"The Crying of Lot 49"*, Cambridge and New York: Cambridge University Press, 1991

Slade, Joseph W., *Thomas Pynchon*, New York: n.p., 1974; revised edition, New York: Peter Lang, 1990

Pynchon criticism began to gather pace after the publication of *Gravity's Rainbow* in 1973. The majority of comment has focused upon this work, and it has proved the standard by which his other work has come to be judged. With respect to this, *V.*'s reputation in particular has suffered, and the short-stories written early in Pynchon's career, collected together in *Slow Learner* (1984), are regarded as blueprints for the thematic and stylistic concerns of the novels. In more recent years *The Crying of Lot 49* has gained in critical stature, attracting a book of collected essays and an extended study devoted solely to what was once considered a fairly slight work. The publication of *Vineland* in 1990 was met by a lukewarm response, the general reaction being that it represented a retrograde step after the achievement of *Gravity's Rainbow*.

Pynchon's fictional works have generated what one critic has dubbed a "Pyndustry", and this shows no sign of abating. The amount of critical material on "the greatest living writer in the English-speaking world" (Edward Mendelson) is staggering, already gaining the honour of an extensive bibliography (*Thomas Pynchon: A Bibliography of Primary and Secondary* Materials, edited by Clifford Mead, 1989). Not surprisingly, the amount of criticism that can be called "appreciative" far outweighs readings "against the grain". It is noticeable that many writers on Pynchon are anxious to avoid the "reader trap", that is, anxious to avoid repeating the same hermeneutic strategies that the novels and central characters adopt (more properly, perhaps, it should be called the "critic-trap"). This has lead to critics prefacing their arguments with illustrations of where other critics have "fallen" and how they will in turn succeed. Nevertheless, Pynchon has attracted some of the most interesting literary criticism, and his work continues to be valuable wherever discourses on, among other subjects, postmodernism, narrative, character, science and literature, metaphor, and genre are debated. The following discussion deals with the various approaches in order of publication.

SLADE's book is a second edition of his 1974 publication. It was the first book to attempt a full account of Pynchon, and Slade has, wisely, not "tinkered" with it in the light of later criticism. The only new material is a discussion of *The Small Rain* and an Afterword, which puts contemporary Pynchon criticism into perspective. Slade's work set the agenda for the critical commentaries that followed, and it remains an excellent introduction to Pynchon, which manages to identify many of the thematic concerns and influences connected with his work. Another edition to include commentary on *Vineland* would be most welcome.

DUGDALE gives a straightforward close reading of Pynchon's work pre-*Gravity's Rainbow*, in order to take this material "on its own terms". The book's title is misleading in that, unfortunately, only the "allusive" aspect has any dominance: the parables of power are confined to the section on *The Crying of Lot 49*. Dugdale describes in detail the artistic, and to a lesser extent, the political subtexts of this novel, the short stories, and *V*. Allusions are assiduously tracked down, and their significances and resonances are analysed. As for the political subtext, it is up to the critic "to discern and decode, to find internal and external to read between and behind the words on the page". For other Pynchon critics, this would amount to falling into the "reader trap". Dugdale's lack of theoretical guile, however, makes this one of the more immediately accessible appreciations of Pynchon.

EDDINS believes the aim of his book goes against contemporary literary theory. This is certainly true, since he tries to find a deep structure, "a sort of 'unified field theory'" that will account for *all* of Pynchon's work. Eddins finds this continuity in a religious response he identifies as "gnosticism", and which he proceeds to split into "cabbalistic gnosticism" and "existential gnosticism". He looks at gnosticism's modern expansion in the work of Hans Jonas and Eric Voegelin, although doesn't claim any direct influence of these writers upon Pynchon. Eddins's book is one of the more fascinating commentaries on Pynchon, even as it goes against current taste for non-totalising schemes. If there is a falling-off of argument, it is in the chapter, on *Gravity's Rainbow*, the one novel which would appear to fit most neatly in Eddins's central thesis.

KHARPERTIAN's book aims to redress what it regards as a significant omission in Pynchon criticism – the attention to form. To this end he identifies Menippean satire as uniting the first three novels. In explaining the project's rationale Kharpertian writes: "assuming as a primary heuristic premise that a reader's conception of a text's genre makes possible and coherent the production of its significance, I identify two formal conventions, attack and variety, and two functional conventions, fertility and delight". Kharpertian also effectively positions Pynchon within two other discourses – postmodernism and American fiction – "to provide the most effective matrices in which to develop a productive reading of Pynchon's fiction". At least a third of the book is devoted to developing these matrices, and so provides a very useful contextualisation. The results of the analysis in the remainder of the book tend to be disappointing though, in that a rather obvious criticism accompanies each identification of the satirical impulse.

McHOUL and WILLS's book begins aggressively by berating virtually every other Pynchon critic for adhering to conservative modes of analysis and ignoring contemporary literary theory: "what surprises us is that such a theoretically 'advanced' figure as Pynchon should be treated, by and large, in such a theoretically retarded fashion". They see all criticism as having been concerned with Pynchon's writing as a logocentric event – *spoken* by Pynchon about a real world. Instead, they want to consider "Pynchon" (and believe everybody else should consider "Pynchon") as Writing. Theory, for them, means Jacques Derrida, whose work is read alongside Pynchon's – what they call "bookmatching". As they admit, the reader needs to be very conversant with Derrida before beginning to engage with their book. It is a typical post-structuralist critical performance, with the reader most likely to emerge knowing everything about deconstruction and nothing about Pynchon. Their most (only?) illuminating section concerns Pynchon's differing treatment of binarity in the first three novels (Berube – see below – makes good use of this).

MADSEN's approach provides a sophisticated account of Pynchon's novels using a generic framework. By using allegory – which she classifies as genre, in opposition to the modal form that constitutes satire (cf. Kharpertian) – she claims to avoid repeating the quests for ultimate meaning (the pretext or transcendental signified) that occur in the novels, and which other critics, as already stated, fall into (the "reader-trap"). "The motivating force of allegory" is defined as "the attempt to isolate the sacred from the profane", but in the postmodern quest "the force is frustrated by a sustained deferral of the promised revelation". That allegory is a politically determined structure is made clear when Madsen notes that *Vineland* is non-allegorical because the "allegorical strategy is no longer appropriate in the 1980s when state control of reality is not only explicit, it has become its own justification". This comparison of genre helps make more understandable the switch from the narrative technique of *Gravity's Rainbow* and before to that of *Vineland*.

O'DONNELL's edited collection of essays on *The Crying of Lot 49* are new only in the sense of recent, since the type of issues they write about can easily be found elsewhere. They do provide a useful introduction to many of these issues however: the value and function of Oedipa Maas's "character"; poetics and narrative strategies; and Pynchon's use of entropy, especially as it relates to information and communication (Hayles is particularly useful here). The last essay, "A Re-Cognition of Her Errand into the Wilderness" by Pierre-Yves Petillon, is very good as it puts the novel into a number of different contexts – historical "mood", literary affinities, linguistic texture and its allusiveness.

MALTBY uses Pynchon, Donald Barthelme, and Robert Coover as "case studies", reading them as "pursuing the political implications of language, with special reference to their heightened perception of the integrative powers of language in its prevailing late-capitalist forms". It seeks to contest the idea, as argued by Fredric Jameson and Terry Eagleton, that postmodern art is non-adversarial. Maltby is a good communicator of traditional concerns, such as entropy and excluded middles, as well as with newer concepts (via postmodernism) like "the erosion of the public sphere". The chapters on Barthelme and Coover hold little interest for readers concerned mainly with Pynchon, and the work on *Vineland* is weaker than the rest of the book.

BERUBE seeks to examine how Pynchon, a determinedly marginal figure through the themes in his work and his public reclusiveness, gains the cultural centre stage while Melvin Tolson, a neglected African-American modernist poet who wanted to be culturally central, continues to be marginalised. Pynchon and Tolson allow Berube to make "a comparative analysis of how canonization works, or fails to work, for writers in the age of institutional criticism". The choice and positioning of Tolson by Berube is arguable, but nevertheless the chapters that focus on Pynchon are insightful, and his work is noteworthy for including the first major attempt to scrutinise Pynchon's "pornography" along with the other "p-words" of "postmodernism, poststructuralism, preterition, and paranoia". This scrutiny is truly belated, and Berube has probably opened up a whole new field for Pynchon critics. The larger argument about the transmission of "cultural texts" and reception history are very highly informed and make fascinating reading, but may be of less interest to those whose specific focus is Pynchon.

BERRESSEM's Introduction begins: "the creation of a 'poststructuralist Pynchon' is long overdue". Thus Pynchon is discussed in the light of Jacques Lacan, Derrida, and Jean Baudrillard. There is surely a certain redundancy to this, in that Pynchon can be construed as already having been there (which would account for the feeling of belatedness), although from Berressem's writing you might think the theory came first: "In *V.*, Pynchon fictionalizes Baudrillard's vision of a fully simulated subject". This book translates Pynchon's work into the official jargon of contemporary literary theory, unfortunately, without much gain.

STEVEN EARNSHAW

R

Radcliffe, Ann 1764–1823

English novelist

Berglund, Birgitta, *Woman's Whole Existence: The House as an Image in the Novels of Ann Radcliffe, Mary Wollstonecraft and Jane Austen*, Lund, Sweden: Lund University Press, 1993

McIntyre, Clara Frances, *Ann Radcliffe in Relation to Her Time*, New Haven, Connecticut: Yale University Press, 1920

Murray, Eugene B., *Ann Radcliffe*, New York: Twayne, 1972

Stoler, John A., *Ann Radcliffe: The Novel of Suspense and Terror*, New York: Arno Press, 1980

Todd, Janet, "'The Great Enchantress': Ann Radcliffe", in her *The Sign of Angellica: Women, Writing and Fiction, 1660–1800*, London: Virago, 1989; New York: Columbia University Press, 1989

Ware, Malcolm, *Sublimity in the Novels of Ann Radcliffe: A Study of the Influence upon Her Craft of Edmund Burke's "Enquiry into the Origin of Our Ideas of the Sublime and Beautiful"*, Uppsala and Copenhagen: Lund University Press/Ejnar Munksgaard, 1963

The same year that Horace Walpole ushered in the gothic genre, the writer who would be credited with bringing the genre to its peak, Ann Radcliffe, was born. Considered the "Shakespeare of romance writers", Ann Radcliffe was as mysterious as the novels she wrote. She left behind no great volume of letters or record of her life other than her novels and an obituary written by her husband. The critical view of Radcliffe has changed since her own time, when she was viewed as one of the most critically successful writers of her day, to the current view of her as one of the most important mediocre writers of the eighteenth century.

McINTYRE reconstructs Radcliffe's life from reviews of her work, the 1824 obituary written by her husband, and from her travel journals. While attempting to put the few facts available about Radcliffe into accessible, albeit somewhat sentimental, form, and consider the sources that Radcliffe may have drawn on for her own writing, McIntyre also re-evaluates the contemporary literary opinion on Radcliffe. Beginning with the faint praise meted out for *The Castles of Athlin and Dunbayne*, and ending with the debate over which of the later novels was actually superior, McIntyre traces the changing critical opinions of Radcliffe's works and examines her importance and influence in the literary world. McIntyre also puts forth new literary sources for Radcliffe's travel descriptions, pointing out that her own travels in Europe took place after her five major novels had been published, and conducting detailed analyses of passages to demonstrate similarities between Radcliffe and these sources.

MURRAY's study examines Radcliffe's use of the sentimental conventions through the five novels published in her lifetime, and attempts a "real analysis" of what actually takes place in those novels. According to Murray, the primary virtue of the Radcliffean heroine is her "disinterestedness", juxtaposed with the calculated self-interest of the villain. He goes on to trace the use of the sentimental, sublime, supernatural, and picturesque through the novels that might have inspired her work. While ignoring *Gaston de Blondeville* and dismissing her poetry as "mediocre, unimportant and irrelevant", he devotes a chapter to each of her individual novels, focusing on the contributions each made to the development of Radcliffean gothic. Murray ends with a general evaluation of her works and her influence on later writers and the novel itself, concluding that she "both aided and restrained the explosion into Romanticism which characterized the 1790's".

WARE's study does not examine in detail sublimity in the eighteenth-century British aesthetics (such studies already exist), but instead shows that the terror generated in Ann Radcliffe's works is deeply rooted in the sublime as defined by Edmund Burke. To prove that Burke's influence on Radcliffe is undeniable, Ware discusses the seven visual concepts (obscurity, power, privation, vastness, infinity, difficulty, and magnificence) that Burke argued produced the sublime experience, and applies them to the gothic genre to discover how they operate in Radcliffe's and other authors' works. Ware's discussion of the difference between gothic terror and gothic horror makes this an important work for anyone studying the gothic novel and the concepts of Radcliffean and Lewisite gothic.

According to BERGLUND, changes in the eighteenth-century workplace and the increasing number of men working outside of family businesses forced a change in the view of the home, making it into an idealized place of physical and mental safety from the world, with the wife as the "Angel of the House" securing this refuge. For women, the home became both a refuge and a prison. Berglund focuses on the differences in male and female interaction with the home, surveying the works of Jane Austen, Mary Wollstonecraft, and Radcliffe for images of the house. She analyses how they describe houses and rooms and what those descriptions tell us about the lives of middle-class women. For Radcliffe, interested more in helping her women survive in a male-dominated system than in the victimization of women, the house becomes a reflection of its owner, with signs that can be read and interpreted. Berglund concludes that Radcliffe's main contribution to the novel and its view of the house was her use of description and the way those descriptions "are related to and integrated" into the themes of her novels to form a close relationship between character and environment.

STOLER's study focuses on the techniques used by Radcliffe to arouse and maintain terror and suspense within her novels. Looking at the five novels published in her lifetime, Stoler defends Radcliffe's use of the explained supernatural as a skillful method of revealing to her reader the degree of fear being experienced by the heroine. By revealing the terrors and torments the heroine is experiencing as mere figments of her imagination, she impresses on her reader the terror of the heroine. According to Stoler, this use of psychological terror links Radcliffe with the development of the psychological novel. In his attempt to place Radcliffe's work in its proper historical context and trace the reasons for her popularity, Stoler includes a detailed discussion of the changing social and literary philosophies of the eighteenth century.

TODD's study looks at the differences between Radcliffe's work and the extremes of sentimental fiction practiced by Wollstonecraft and Mary Hays. According to Todd, in her desire to "harness the sentimental novel ... for serious purpose" and "return it to the moral ethical aim of the earlier novel of sentiment", Radcliffe empowered her heroines and protected them from their male-imposed vulnerability with the firmness of her narrative. While noting the appeal of obscure gothic interiors and veiled terrors in her works, Todd also comments on the appropriateness of fear as a response on the part of women to their male-dominated society.

LESLIE K. POURTEAU

Ralegh, Sir Walter ?1552–1618

English poet and prose writer

Greenblatt, Stephen J., *Sir Walter Ralegh: The Renaissance Man and His Roles*, New Haven, Connecticut, and London: Yale University Press, 1973

Latham, Agnes (ed.), *The Poems of Sir Walter Ralegh*, London: Constable & Co., 1929; Boston: Houghton Mifflin, 1929; reprinted, London: Routledge & Kegan Paul, 1951 and 1962

May, Steven W., *Sir Walter Ralegh*, Boston: Twayne, 1989

Mills, Jerry Leath, *Sir Walter Ralegh: A Reference Guide*, Boston: G.K. Hall, 1986

Montrose, Louis, "The Work of Gender in the Discourse of Discovery," in *Representations*, 33, 1991, reprinted in *New World Encounters*, edited by Stephen Greenblatt, Berkeley: University of California Press, 1993

Oakeshott, Walter, *The Queen and the Poet*, London: Faber & Faber, 1960; New York: Barnes & Noble, 1961

Until the past several decades, discussions of Sir Walter Ralegh's works generally tended toward one of two critical schools – those espousing a romantic view of Ralegh (patriot, lover, adventurer), and those considering him little more than a talented amateur who sought through his writings a Machiavellian-like gratification of his own political and material ambitions. While problems of chronology, canon, and authorship persist, recent criticism seems to agree that – whatever our view of the man – Ralegh was indeed an important figure, who exerted a significant degree of political and literary influence during the reign of Elizabeth I.

LATHAM's edition of the courtier's poems, which were not previously available in easily accessible form, marks an important contribution to Ralegh scholarship. To Latham, Ralegh's poetry "was no part of his public character, but something essentially intimate and private", a comment which Greenblatt would later argue. But Latham may not be as naive as Greenblatt thinks, for she recognizes that the courtier could be as artificial as anyone and, further, that his poetry – no matter that he did not care to make it public – was indeed designed to win the Queen's favor, and her patronage. As such, Latham perhaps anticipates the work of critics like Oakeshott and even Greenblatt himself, who demonstrate the inseparability of Ralegh from his art. While her chronology and canon have since been debated, Latham's edition, which includes a good biographical sketch of Ralegh, as well as explanatory and textual notes to the poems, still remains useful.

OAKESHOTT argues against the Victorian notion that Ralegh wrote for pleasure, a hobby in which he indulged periodically. He examines Ralegh's poetry, correspondence, and related court documents in the context of the courtier's life from 1580 to 1597 to show that Ralegh's life and his writings are inextricably linked: Ralegh's poems were generally written for a specific occasion, "the occasion most often being to please, or to pacify, the Queen". He analyzes the evidence of Edmund Spenser's *Colin Clout's Come Home Again* and the *Faerie Queene*, bearing on the relationship between Elizabeth and Ralegh, and identifies several interesting parallels between Ralegh and the *Faerie Queene*'s Timias. Oakeshott also reopens the issue of Shakespeare's *Love's Labour's Lost* as a possible satire of Ralegh and his association with the "Academy", a group of friends – Thomas Hariot, Christopher Marlowe, and John Dee among them – with whom Ralegh discussed alchemy and astronomy. (Because of such associations Ralegh was often criticized as an atheist. See M.C. Bradbrook's *School of Night*, 1936, reprinted 1965.) Readers will find valuable Oakeshott's detailed commentary on *The Ocean to Cynthia*, as well as his inclusion of several works not previously considered part of the Ralegh canon.

GREENBLATT pursues even further the connectedness of Ralegh's life and art in this examination of what he terms Ralegh's "histrionic sensibility", his sense of self-dramatization where, at crucial moments in the courtier's career, "the boundaries between life and art completely break down, and to understand such moments, the conventional distinction between reality and the imagination must give way to a sense of their interplay". Greenblatt discusses (although selectively, he admits) the central moments in Ralegh's life – the Queen's displeasure at learning of his secret marriage to Elizabeth Throckmorton; his explorations of Guiana in 1595 and 1616; the charges of treason brought against him by James I in 1603; and the courtier's composure moments before his execution – in the context of Ralegh's court poetry, letters, speeches, and major prose works *The Discoverie of Guiana* and *The History of the World*. Greenblatt also analyzes such influential works as Giovanni, Comte Pico's *Oration on the Dignity of Man*, Juan Luis Vives's *Fable about Man*, Baldassare Castiglione's *Book of the Courtier*, and Machiavelli's *The Prince* to show the two contradictory traditions underlying Ralegh's dramatic sense of life: "one that likened life to a play to express the emptiness and unreality of man's earth-bound existence, the other that saw in playing an image of man's power to fashion the self".

MILLS surveys the major Ralegh criticism appearing in book- or article-form between 1901 and 1984. This helpful research guide provides a good sense of the important critical shifts in evaluations of Ralegh's works, but some may feel that Mills is often vague in his estimations of the scholarship he discusses. He includes a useful introduction to the significant trends in Ralegh criticism, which emphasizes the need for a definitive edition of the courtier's works.

MAY makes extensive use of biographical details in order to inform his reading of Ralegh's verse and prose works. Like Oakeshott, he believes that Ralegh wrote for specific occasions, and he thus discusses the courtier's early verse commendations for George Gascoigne and Edmund Spenser as well as the poems written between 1587 and 1591 that allude to Ralegh's "bitter struggle with the earl of Essex for the queen's affections". By the time of his 1592 disgrace, Ralegh's poetic skills had matured commensurate with "the new styles that created the golden age of Elizabethan lyric and dramatic poetry", and the courtier had now prepared himself for his most technically and aesthetically sophisticated poetry, reflected, according to May, in the "Ocean to Cynthia" poems. May also examines Ralegh's prose works, including several rarely discussed political tracts. Some may be frustrated by this work's rather romantic view of Ralegh's biography and its lack of a clear thesis, but May's analyses are frequently insightful, especially in the final chapter where he looks at Ralegh's contribution to English literature.

MONTROSE's essay views Ralegh's *Discoverie of Guiana* as an example of an early colonialist discourse of discovery that projected Western European notions of gender into its representations of the New World and its inhabitants. He looks at the *Discoverie* in the context of Ralegh's preoccupation with the prospect of tremendous personal wealth and political power, for which he had as his models the Spanish conquistadors Cortés and Pizarro. Informative, but never simplistic, Montrose's essay is a valuable analysis of the work that has been viewed in many recent colonial and postcolonial studies as Ralegh's most significant and controversial.

PAUL W. DEPASQUALE

Rao, Raja 1908–

Indian novelist and short-story writer

Dey, Esha, *The Novels of Raja Rao: The Theme of Quest*, New Delhi: Prestige, 1992

Ivask, Ivor (ed.), "Raja Rao: Our 1988 Neustadt Prize Laureate", in *World Literature Today*, 62(4), 1988

Naik, M.K., *Raja Rao*, New York: Twayne, 1972

Narasimhaiah, C.D., *Raja Rao*, New Delhi: Arnold-Heinemann, n.d. (c.1970)

Narayan, Shyamala A., *Raja Rao: Man and His Works*, New Delhi: Sterling, 1988

Sharrad, Paul, *Raja Rao and Cultural Tradition*, New Delhi, Sterling, 1987

Raja Rao's work has been the subject of considerable critical attention both in and out of India. Together with Mulk Raj Anand and R.K. Narayan, who all published their first novels in the 1930s, he is widely regarded as one of the pioneering writers of Indian fiction in English. His first novel, *Kanthapura*, was considered by E.M. Forster to be the best novel written in English by an Indian, while his second, unashamedly metaphysical, novel, *The Serpent and the Rope* (the title points to the Vedantic concept of illusion and reality), confirmed him as a major international writer. Critical opinion about Rao's work is healthily divided between those who prefer his earlier novels and stories and those who prefer the expansive, philosophical later works.

NAIK's book, the first full-length study of Rao's fiction, is an excellent early introduction to the novelist's work. Naik argues that Rao has brought to Indian fiction in English "an epic breadth of vision, a metaphysical rigor and depth of thought, a symbolic richness, a lyrical fervor, and an essential 'Indianness' of style". Beginning with a useful biographical chapter, which is standard in the Twayne series, Naik goes on to analyse each of the books up to *The Cat and Shakespeare* (1965).

NARASIMHAIAH's study is another good introduction to the work up to *The Cat and Shakespeare*, although somewhat conservative in its insistence, shared with Naik, on the "Indianness" of Rao's fiction. Of particular interest is the chapter on *Kanthapura*, which, Narasimhaiah argues, is not only the most authentic account of Indian village life in any novel in the English language, but also the novel which best captures the spirit of Gandhi's politics and the fight for Indian freedom. His engaging discussion considers the novel in its political, religious, and historical contexts, and treats the style and language of the novel in some depth.

SHARRAD's book, one of the few full-length studies of Rao written by a non-Indian, opens with a useful and trenchant survey of critical responses to Rao's novels, and goes on to provide a comprehensive text-centred analysis of what was then, and perhaps still is, Rao's most complex work, *The Serpent and the Rope*. Unlike the majority of critics, who have chosen to emphasise the Indianness of Rao's fiction, Sharrad sets out to show the reader the variety in *The Serpent and the Rope* in relation to culture in a more universal sense. His instructive appendix – which lists the literary names that appear in the novel – reveals at a glance the international cultural framework within which *The Serpent and the Rope* is written. The chronology for the novel and the bibliography which conclude the study are both helpful.

NARAYAN's very accessible study, which usefully builds on the earlier studies by Naik and Narasimhaiah, is another general introduction to the themes and techniques in Rao's works, up to *Comrade Kirillov* (1976), with a rather adversely critical appendix on *The Chessmaster and His Moves* (1976), which she believes fails to live up to the high standard of his earlier works. While the study offers few surprises, one of its strengths lies in its extensive comparative references to other Indian novels and novelists.

IVASK has edited a special issue of *World Literature Today*, which includes a 100-page symposium entitled "Raja Rao: 1988 Neustadt Laureate". The symposium includes 14 critical essays as well as Ivask's Introduction, the texts of the presentation of the Neustadt prize, some primary material, three poems in homage, a chronology of Rao's life, a selected bibliography, and a small collection of photographs of Rao. Edwin Thumboo's "Enconium for Raja Rao" is a succinct introduction to the themes, style, structure, and language of Rao's fiction. In other essays both R. Parthasarathy and Thumboo argue that *The Chessmaster and His Moves* is Rao's major achievement to date: Thumboo eloquently suggests that while Rao's work is uniquely Indian in spirit, *The Chessmaster and His Moves* "offers perhaps the broadest, deepest internationalism we have in fiction". Also of particular interest are Wilson Harris's essay on *The Serpent and the Rope* and S.C. Harrex's piece on Rao's experiments with the short story. The high quality of the material gathered here makes this a significant collection.

DEY's book, written largely in the 1970s, applies a loosely structuralist-formalist approach to Rao's first four novels, from *Kanthapura* to *Comrade Kirillov*, interpreting them as explorations of the displacement in space and time experienced by many Indians, particularly those who grew up in the shadow of the nationalist struggle for independence, and their subsequent quest for identity. In his interesting linguistic analyses of the four novels, Dey demonstrates how the sense of alienation is encapsulated in even Rao's use of language. At the same time his linguistic analyses dispute "Indianist" readings of Rao's novels. There are also two postscripts – on *The Chessmaster and His Moves*, which he sees as Rao's magnum opus, and on *"On the Ganga Ghat" and Other Stories*, which he describes as "a classic of fabulation". The inclusion of this final chapter in a study which is otherwise devoted to the novels is justified on the grounds that prior to *On the Ganga Ghat* "his stories were regarded largely as by-products of the novels".

RALPH J. CRANE

Reader-Response Theory

Freund, Elizabeth, *The Return of the Reader: Reader-Response Criticism*, London and New York: Methuen, 1987

Holub, Robert C., *Reception Theory: A Critical Introduction*, London and New York: Methuen, 1984

Many, Joyce, and Carole Cox (eds.), *Reader Stance and Literary Understanding: Exploring the Theories, Research, and Practice*, Norwood, New Jersey: Ablex, 1992

Slatoff, Walter, J., *With Respect to Readers: Dimensions of Literary Response*, Ithaca, New York: Cornell University Press, 1970

Suleiman, S.R., and I. Crossman (eds.), *The Reader in the Text: Essays on Audience and Interpretation*, Princeton, New Jersey: Princeton University Press, 1980

Tompkins, Jane P., *Reader-Response Criticism: From Formalism to Post-Structuralism*, Baltimore: Johns Hopkins University Press, 1980

SLATOFF's pioneering work aims to supplement the apparent scientific precision of the New Criticism with an examination of "literary works in relation to readers". Anticipating Wolfgang Iser, he stresses the way we "flesh out" scenes and characters in novels that would otherwise remain mere verbal constructs. While acknowledging that eventually we may come to regard the text as a spatial entity, Slatoff insists on the initially temporal nature of reading and the fact that a rereading will of necessity actualise a different work. He proceeds to look at the question of involvement, pointing out that a fusion of objective knowledge and subjective emotional response is essential – the reader is both active participant in the text and detached spectator of it.

After dealing with the issues of identification, sympathy, and empathy, Slatoff discusses how neither author nor text can fully control the reader's actualization and the divergences of response that this entails, involving, as it does, important problems of belief and resistance. These points are well illustrated with analyses of Mark Twain's *Huckleberry Finn* and Shakespeare's *The Merchant of Venice*. A rather impressionistic chapter on the presence of the narrator in the text is less satisfying, having been largely superseded by more recent theoretical work in the field of narratology. In Chapter 5 Slatoff anticipates many of the issues raised by deconstruction, arguing that art frequently does *not* provide an experience of harmony, unity, and equilibrium, but rather an "essentially uncomfortable and disruptive" one. This stance enables him to analyse the way in which literary texts can disturb the reader's equanimity through discord, ambivalence, and unresolvedness.

The book ends with an eloquent plea for reader involvement rather than detachment or distance from the text. The virtues of this study lie in its pioneering championship of the reader's enjoyment of literary texts; its shortcomings result largely from the inevitable (for 1970) lack of any theoretical rigour or critical vocabulary. One might also complain that the author is almost entirely concerned with prose fiction.

SULEIMAN and CROSSMAN's anthology is prefaced by a useful Introduction, in which Suleiman outlines various approaches to reader-oriented criticism. These include analysis of: the act of communication between the implied author and the implied reader; the codes and conventions readers bring to the text to make it readable; the phenomenologically-based approach of Iser and the unresolved tensions between readerly freedom and textual control; the psychoanalytical subjectivism of David Bleich and Norman Holland; and the social and collective nature of reading as expounded by Lucien Goldmann and Hans-Robert Jauss. The subsequent 16 original essays explain all aspects of these different positions, ranging from a rather generalised prolegomenon from Jonathan Culler (though the examination of different readings of William Blake's "London" is illuminating) to a highly sophisticated reading of Nicolas Poussin's *Arcadian Shepherds* by Louis Marin.

Particularly notable are the contributions by Christine Brooke-Rose – a witty study of over-, under-, and non-determined encoded readers, using *Rip van Winkle*, Flann O'Brien's *At Swim-Two-Birds*, and Edgar Allan Poe's "The Black Cat" to illustrate her claims – and by Gerald Prince (a sensible review of textual control over the reading activity). Peter Rabinowitz offers a fascinating essay on authorial and narrative audiences and the degree of intertextual competence needed to interpret such texts as Alain Robbe-Grillet's *Les Gommes* and Tom Stoppard's *Rosencrantz and Guildenstern Are Dead*. Other articles worth reading cover Montaigne and Renaissance rhetoric, and Norman Holland's "transactive criticism" of Poe's "The Purloined Letter". To be avoided are the arid, abstract, and opaque effusions of Steirle, Maranda, and Leenhardt.

The great merit of this collection is that it extends the bounds of reader-response theory to embrace phenomenology, sociology, psychoanalysis, and close reading. The annotated bibliography, though somewhat dated, is still helpful.

The anthology edited by TOMPKINS provides an extremely useful complement to Suleiman's, there being no overlap in the choice of essays. Her Introduction is not nearly so theoretical and extended, but the selection of studies it prefaces is invaluable. While notations of readers, mock readers, and arch readers have become generally accepted, very little attention had been paid to the concept of the narratee: it is therefore gratifying to find here the pioneering study by Gerald Prince. Equally to be welcomed are Michael Riffaterre's classic analysis of approaches to Charles Baudelaire's "Les Chats" (though this is as much structuralist as readerly), Iser's seminal introduction to "The Reading Process", Stanley Fish's early essay on affectivist stylistics, and a stimulating piece by Norman Holland.

The anthology concludes with a contextualisation of the role of the reader throughout history by Tompkins herself. As can be seen, this is a collection of well-known rather than avant-garde articles, but it is useful to have them all in one volume. Particularly notable is the meticulously annotated bibliography, though, of course, this only includes work up to 1980.

FREUND's book is the first general survey in English to trace the new emphasis on the activity of reading as opposed to the cognitive, impersonal interpretative methods of the New Critics; but, as she points out, the sheer proliferation of constructed readers makes it impossible to extrapolate any one general theory of the reading process and how it generates meaning, let alone cope with the wider issue of the "reception" of a work by its audience.

Her emphasis is on the work of Anglo-American theorists, so she documents first of all the attempt to resolve the dualism of object (text) and subject (reader) in the writings of I.A. Richards, while acknowledging the inadequacy of his neuro-physical view of response, and lamenting the fact that his appropriation by the formalists meant that his psychological theories of metaphor and "transference" remained embryonic. After a detailed survey of the New Critics and their "avoidance of reading", Freund proceeds to outline the shift from the formalist view of the text as a static, timeless, piece of language to the epistemological stress on the dynamic, temporal, and subjective stance of the responding reader as he/she actualises that text.

The impact of this shift is demonstrated in four detailed essays on Culler, Fish, Holland, and Iser. These incisive studies give a clear picture of the main tenets of reader-response theory: the intertextualised reader and the associated concept of literary competence; "affectivist stylistics" and the problematics of the dialectical text and interpretative communities; the ego-psychology centred work of Holland; and the phenomenologically-based theories of indeterminacy, virtuality, and wandering viewpoint that we associate with Iser's *Act of Reading*. This book is an excellent introduction to the principal strands of specifically-reader-response theory. It does not cover *Rezeptionsästhetik* or offer exemplary readings of literary texts, but its cogent critical assessments and extensive lists of references should make it indispensable for the neophyte.

HOLUB's book expands the range of readerly criticism by studying the collective responses of audiences (or *Rezeptionsästhetik*). As distinct from the exploration of the actual reading process, reception theory emphasises the need for a diachronic and cultural definition of the repertoire that audiences bring to an actualization of the text. In stressing the cohesive group nature of reception theory, Holub pays particular attention to the German theorists, notably Jauss and Hans-Georg Gadamer.

After surveying the precursory influences of Russian formalism, Prague structuralism, the phenomenologically-based work of Roman Ingarden and the hermeneutics of Gadamer, Holub presents us with a fully-elaborated exploration of the major writings of Jauss and Iser, stressing the difference between the former's historical focus on the collective "horizon of expectation" and the latter's attention to the reading processes of the individual. His explication of *aesthesis*, *poesis*, and *catharsis* is exemplarily lucid, including a very useful chart of modalities of identification. A final section looks at the shortcomings of a purely empirical approach such as that practised by the theorists of the former East German state. The value of Holub's study lies largely (though by no means exclusively) in its comprehensive introduction for English-speaking readers to an exciting area of response theory hitherto available only in German.

A different approach to the way people read is adopted in the essays edited by MANY and COX. Most of these are concerned with empirical analysis of the reading process and, since the writers are mainly professional educationalists, the results can be fascinating and a welcome antidote to purely theoretical discussion. After an introductory survey of reader-response theory up to Mikhail Bakhtin by Cox, Michael Benton provides a suggestive model of the "secondary worlds" that dialogic reading evokes, using the openings of works by a selection of authors. Even more thought-provoking is the ensuing paradigm of six modes of reader stance offered by Bill Corcoran, together with his use of Umberto Eco to define readings that "follow, resist, or redefine the grain".

Part II of this collection gathers together various students' perspectives when reading and responding. Particularly interesting is the study of efferent and aesthetic responses by the editors themselves, though the more pragmatic essays by Galda and Smith should not be neglected. Richard Beach and Kerry Freedman focus on the cultural aspects of response, an element sometimes ignored in theories of the ideal reader or super-reader. The third section is likely to be of less interest to scholars of literature, since it is largely concerned with classroom teaching. This is a refreshingly different set of studies, involving as it does responses of real readers rather than hypothetical constructs. Each chapter is accompanied by a very full and comprehensive bibliography. It should prove useful to students and practising teachers alike.

A.W. Lyle

Realism: General

Auerbach, Erich, *Mimesis: The Representation of Reality in Western Literature*, translated by Willard R. Trask, Princeton, New Jersey: Princeton University Press, 1953

Becker, George J. (ed.), *Documents of Modern Literary Realism*, Princeton, New Jersey: Princeton University Press, 1963

Boyle, Nicholas, and Martin Swales (eds.), *Realism in European Literature: Essays in Honour of J.P. Stern*, Cambridge and New York: Cambridge University Press, 1986

Davis, Lennard J., *Factual Fictions: The Origins of the English Novel*, New York: Columbia University Press, 1983

Furst, Lilian R. (ed.), *Realism*, London: Longman, 1992

Grant, Damian, *Realism*, London and New York: Methuen, 1970

Halperin, John (ed.), *The Theory of the Novel: New Essays*, New York and London: Oxford University Press, 1974

Levin, Harry, *The Gates of Horn: A Study of Five French Realists*, New York: Oxford University Press, 1963

Levine, George, *The Realistic Imagination: English Fiction from Frankenstein to Lady Chatterley*, Chicago: University of Chicago Press, 1981

Lucente, Gregory L., *The Narrative of Realism and Myth: Verga, Lawrence, Faulkner, Pavese*, Baltimore: Johns Hopkins University Press, 1981

Nochlin, Linda, *Realism*, Harmondsworth, Middlesex: Penguin, 1971

Stern, J.P., *On Realism*, London and Boston: Routledge & Kegan Paul, 1973

Watt, Ian, *The Rise of the Novel: Studies in Defoe, Richardson and Fielding*, London: Chatto & Windus, 1957; Berkeley: University of California Press, 1957

Realism can be seen both as a specific historical mode and as a far broader technique that plays a role of some kind in most narratives. As an artistic *movement*, Realism refers to a body of texts in the latter half of the nineteenth century which expressed the dominant mimetic fashion of the time, informed by a rationalist epistemology in reaction against the fantasies of Romanticism, and responsive both to political and social changes and to the scientific and industrial advances of the day. In earlier and subsequent texts, realism takes different forms and has been given a wide variety of interpretations, dependent upon various understandings of the real; concern about the consequent elasticity of the term "realism" is more or less ubiqitous in the critical literature.

No study of realism would be complete without the inclusion of AUERBACH's *Mimesis*, that celebration of three thousand years' worth of European literature, which Watt calls "a brilliant panorama of realistic representation in literature from Homer to Virginia Woolf", and Furst cites as the spark that lit a twentieth-century revival of interest in realism as a serious genre. Auerbach's intention is not to theorize realism so much as to explore how everyday subjects have been treated "seriously, problematically, or tragically", given that everyday subject-matter had traditionally been understood as appropriate only for comedy or, perhaps, idyll. Some critics (such as Lucente) regret Auerbach's pragmatism and emphasis on textual exegesis at the expense of theory; others (such as Stern) celebrate the richness of his portrayal of a literary-historical continuity and his "practical criticism in the service of an historical design". In fact Auerbach does, inevitably, work deductively as well as inductively. He distinguishes as the foundations of modern realism five factors which underlie his exegesis from the beginning: a serious treatment of everyday reality, figured paradigmatically in the Christian Gospels; a consequent flexibility in mixing the classical stylistic levels of representation; the problematic, rather than stereotypical, presentation of socially inferior people as central subject-matter; the embedding of people and events into a definite period of contemporary history; and a fluid, rather than a static, historical background. Auerbach, writing from exile in Istanbul during World War II, explains the method of modern literature "which dissolves reality into multiple and multivalent reflections of consciousness" as "a mirror of the decline of our world", and expresses the hope that his book may "contribute to bringing together again those whose love for our western history has serenely persevered".

Insofar as realism is understood as primarily a fictional mode, WATT's more circumscribed book has also become a classic text. However, Watt too extends the definition of realism beyond the nineteenth century. Making overt links with philosophical realism, he in fact locates the first significant works of literary realism in the eighteenth century: once truth was understood (after René Descartes and John Locke) to be discoverable by the individual through the senses, independent of the legacies of past thought, the novel became a logical literary development in its reaction against the traditionalism of universal human types in a conventionalized background. Watt points out that "*réalisme*" was first used as an aesthetic description in 1835 to denote the "*vérité humaine*" of Rembrandt as distinct from the "*idéalité poétique*" of neoclassical painting, though Watt himself abjures the simplistic use of realism as an antonym for idealism; its specifically literary use was made official by the founding in 1856 of the short-lived French journal *Réalisme*. Developing Auerbach's ideas, Watt sees the novel's formal realism as consisting in the attempt of its narrative method to embody "a full and authentic report of human experience" through particularization of time, place, and person; a natural and lifelike sequence of action; and "the creation of a literary style which gives the most exact verbal and rhythmical equivalent possible of the object described".

Watt points out, however, that these are just as much conventions as their predecessors, even though the formal demands they make upon the reader are comparatively small. Watt's belief that formal realism is an ethically neutral mode of presentation leads him to privilege the novel, in which there is both a coherent plot and a controlling moral intention – that harmonious, humanist unity of "realism of presentation" with what he calls "realism of assessment". He also points out that in these eighteenth-century fictions there is no absolute dichotomy between an internal and an external approach to character, and thus shows how the later tendency to equate novelistic realism with an emphasis on society rather than the individual is a misconstruing of the realist tradition as he understands it.

BECKER takes a much narrower view of literary realism, equating it quite precisely with the naturalism of the nineteenth century, and then chiefly in France; he argues that, though realistic elements have always been present in most works, "realism rarely, if ever, dominated and controlled a whole work before the mid-nineteenth century". His collection of "documents influential in the development of the movement" provides easy access to a variety of primary materials from the nineteenth and early twentieth centuries, a number of them in translation (from Russian, Spanish, Portuguese, and Italian, as well as French); included are Zola's famous treatise on "The Experimental Novel" and pieces by Gustave Flaubert, George Eliot, Theodore Dreiser, Henry James, Edmund Gosse, Leo Tolstoy, August Strindberg, Friedrich Engels, and Maxim Gorky, to name just a few. At the same time, reviews and commentaries by less well-known figures give historical insights into the public reception of realism in Europe and, later, the United States. Becker's Introduction is engaging in its discussions of the tendency of realistic subject-matter to "drift downward" in the social or cultural scale, and of the inevitable presence of symbolic and mythical structures in the work of even the most ardent naturalist. His troubled ruminations over the impossibility of objectivity have dated somewhat, the authorial commentary itself (which overtly declares an intention to avoid bias) bearing eloquent witness to this problematic.

Though NOCHLIN's study is ostensibly even more strictly limited, in considering Realism as a historical movement, which "attained its most coherent and consistent formulation" in nineteenth-century European painting, the book also offers a wider social and aesthetic context. Continental Realism developed in a period of political upheaval and in what the Hungarian Marxist critic Georg Lukács called "epistemological agnosticism". A concern for democracy in the arts opened up a new range of subjects previously considered unworthy of representation, and all idealization in art and literature was rejected in favour of depictions of tangible contemporary reality. Realist work was determined by scientific attitudes, which confined the artist to accurate observation and notation of empirical phenomena and a description of how, rather than why, things happen. Unlike Watt, Nochlin understands the truthful depiction of unidealized lower-class subjects to be inevitably a moral stance: "the personal contribution was, by definition, a social one". Moreover, the common notion of Realism as "styleless, or transparent style, a mere simulacrum or mirror image of visual reality" is a gross simplification because it is based on "the belief that perception can be 'pure' and unconditioned by time or place" or aesthetic convention. After a helpful introductory chapter on "The Nature of Realism", Nochlin considers the Realist treatment of death, work, and contemporaneity, making frequent allusion to literary texts of the period. Nochlin's contention that "the image of the random, the changing, the impermanent and unstable seemed closer to the experienced qualities of present-day reality than the imagery of the stable, the balanced, the harmonious" suggests interesting parallels with post-modernism.

A short introduction to realism from a modernist perspective (with Wallace Stevens and Henry James as the authorities) is provided by GRANT. Arguing that realism is a critical term only by adoption from philosophy, he explains the origins of the contrasting uses of the word to connote, on the one hand, the materialist-particular and, on the other, the idealist-universal. In charting realism's history of "unmanageable elasticity" and "chronic instability", Grant distinguishes two almost contradictory nineteenth-century phases of meaning, which correlate broadly with these two philosophical connotations. The correspondence theory of conscientious, or naive, realism espouses a positivist belief in the reality of the external world, and understands its descriptions of that reality to be objective reflections according to scientific principles. The coherence theory of conscious, or informed, realism recognizes the place of creativity and language in the achievement, or making, of the real, and expresses the interest in psychology and in dreams – the invisible real – at the end of the nineteenth century. Grant clearly favours the coherence theory and a redefinition of realism that not only rejects naturalist determinism but also sounds remarkably like symbolism. He concludes with a brief dismissal of socialist realism because the idealist dogmatism of its presuppositions renders it programmatic.

In his study of nineteenth-century French literary realism, LEVIN echoes Lukács in contending that "realistic fiction has been a characteristic expression of bourgeois society" – "bourgeois" understood primarily as connoting the culture of cities, and realism asserting "the predominance of citizen over courtier". The realist novel had its beginnings in a breaking away from the convention-dominated romance, and its method has continued to be an undermining of preconceptions: "realism presupposes an idealism to be corrected, a convention to be superseded, or an orthodoxy to be criticised". Through detailed readings of Stendhal, Honoré de Balzac, Flaubert, Zola, and Marcel Proust, Levin sets out to demonstrate what he sees as the inherently critical stance of realism, which thrives in "the mobile institutions of an open society". However, realism can never completely dispense with convention, "a necessary difference between art and life". Since realism is actually indebted to romance for basic themes, symbols, and gestures, it may be understood as "a synthesis: the imposition of reality upon romance, the transposition of reality into romance". Literature is a social institution in reciprocal relationship with life: "epic, romance, and novel are the representatives of three successive estates and styles of life: military, courtly, and mercantile". But Levin allows the widest connotation to realism when he argues that, whatever the genre, "all great writers, in so far as they are committed to a searching and scrupulous critique of life as they know it, may be reckoned among the realists".

Such generosity of definition also characterizes STERN's book, where he offers "variations on the kind of undertaking we find in Auerbach", which Stern finds exemplary. Stern applies Wittgenstein's theory of family resemblances to the concept of realism, thus expecting to find likenesses between members but not necessarily a common property. He investigates the doubleness of the word "realism" as part both of a literary vocabulary and of everyday life, and concludes that realism is not just a period term for the mid-nineteenth century novelists' synthesis of description and assessment, but "a perennial mode of representing the world and coming to terms with it", a mode of writing which describes "a delicate meeting-place between imagination and knowledge", and differs from age to age. He defines realism not as a philosophical issue but as an historical one, a mode that places individuals and their institutions in a single working perspective, and imposes a balance between private and public meanings. Insisting on referential meaning, Stern stresses realism's "creative attention to the visible rather than the invisible", and sets it against symbolism, doctrinaire social realism, and the recent "literature of language-consciousness" as a mode whose theme is "the reach of common indication" and whose concern is "the system that works – this, and nothing but this, is reality for the realist".

Thirteen years later, on Stern's retirement from the Chair of German at University College, London, BOYLE and SWALES published a collection of essays giving further consideration, in light of subsequent developments in critical discourse, to problems touched on by Stern. Graham Hough's paper on "Language and Reality in *Bleak House*" counters the criticism of realism as naive positivism by arguing that language in realistic literature as elsewhere is "not merely reflective, but is itself constitutive of reality"; the signifier as much as the signified is the object of realist concern, particularly as the language is that of specific characters through whose experience reality is mediated. Hough contends that the realism of Charles Dickens shows how individual human freedom can effect real change in the confusions of the system. Also concerned to expand the role of realism beyond the determinism to which naturalism had confined it is Stephen Heath's important neo-Marxist essay on "Realism, Modernism, and 'Language-Consciousness'". Heath counters Stern's fear that realism is in decline by pointing out that "the production, recognition, and definition of realism are themselves historical through and through"; traditional realism itself is not neutral but a "politics of reality", a particular representation of reality as intelligibly making sense, rather than contradictory and heterogeneous, as Heath believes it to be. Heath argues that "language-consciousness" effects an important shift in realism by recasting the understanding of relations between text, self, and world, and by presenting reality as a transformable human production: "to turn realism into its writing is to attend to its representation".

HALPERIN argues that formal realism sees every detail of personal experience as morally important, and that it intends to alert readers to the moral implications of what they do; in both Augustan and mid-nineteenth-century novel theory, the emphasis on mimetic adequacy is really emphasis on the effect on the reader – the more "realistic", the greater the effect. The symbiotic relationship between formal realism and mimesis only begins to break down as writers become increasingly interested in mental processes; by the first half of the twentieth century, novel theory is concerned less with the relationship between reader and text than with relationships among structural elements in the fiction itself. The most pertinent essay in Halperin's collection is George Levine's "Realism Reconsidered". Levine suggests that realism as a literary method implies that ordinariness is more real, that is, truthful and representative, than heroism; that people are morally mixed rather than simply good or bad; and that the firmest realities are objects rather than ideas. Identifying romance as the source of all impositions of form on experience, Levine argues that realistic fiction is paradoxically romantic, "an essentially comic form" which resolves difficulties by imposing shape and meaning upon reality in palpably unrealistic ways. Thus realism can never be understood as an unmediated record of reality: "the predominating energy in most fiction . . . is not the representation of reality but the shaping of the rendered experience". Consequently, Levine suggests, "there is a Frankenstein in every great realistic fiction struggling to get out" – a notion he develops in *The Realistic Imagination*.

Describing realism here as a historical phenomenon in need of reappraisal, LEVINE sets out to show that nineteenth-century realists were never naive about the nature of their medium and its relationship to the real world; that realism is a process, responsive to the changing nature of reality as culturally understood; and that there is a direct continuum between realism and modernism. In a move not unlike Auerbach's, Levine declares himself less concerned with a definition of realism than with "a study of its elusiveness". He argues that realism "was not a solidly self-satisfied vision based in a misguided objectivity and faith in representation, but a highly self-conscious attempt to explore or create a new reality", by writers aware of "a world deconstructing all around them" as the result of radically new formulations in philosophy, theology, and science. Realist rejection of the literary is seen in the coincidence of realism and parody; in the desire to make the ordinary significant; in the exploratory nature of realist literary method; in the "apparently digressive preoccupation" with surfaces and particularities; and in an anti-generic freedom with literary structures. In exegesis of texts from Jane Austen to D.H. Lawrence, Levine explores changing manifestations of the central realist concern to "use language to get beyond language, to discover some non-verbal truth out there", and charts the relationship between realism's desire that the world be meaningful and good, and realism's fear that it turn out to be monstrous and uncontrollable. Using Frankenstein's monster as an image for this uncontrollable disorder, Levine shows how excess is inevitably figured in those realistic domestic fictions intended to deny and exclude it, and how, over the course of the century, there is a turn to recognize civilization as a veneer, objectivity as an impossibility, reality itself as "monstrous", and, finally, irrationality as intense and potentially life-giving energy.

LUCENTE embraces this synthesis. His book is a sophisticated attempt "to outline ways in which the signs of myth interact with those of realism to create meaning in narrative fiction". He sees realism and myth as "finally inseparable", arguing that realist narrative depends upon aesthetic convention and illusion, and develops only through a combination of the basic components of mythic idealism and realist materialism in interaction at all levels of narration, plotting, and character configuration. His book offers, first, a historical overview of the development of realism and of myth from classical beginnings; next, an argument for the inevitability of relations between these two concepts; and, third, readings of texts by the four writers (two Italian, one British, one American) of his title. Lucente explores the changing locus of meaning, from the transcendent to the worldly, and then from the exterior to the interior of the individual subject, which pushes realism toward modernism. He suggests that, exactly because of its imbrication with myth, realist literature is able to maintain a stance "at once conservative and visionary, grounded in the fictionalized life of its present yet mindful of both the past and the future".

DAVIS responds to a similar awareness of the doubleness of realism in a quite different way: he investigates the cultural nature of the early modern novel as a uniquely "factual fiction". In contrast to Watt, Davis traces the development of the novel from its material origins in what he calls the "news/novels discourse" of sixteenth-century journalism, where fact and fiction were not clearly differentiated, to the eighteenth, where the move to legal definitions of fact and fiction necessitated parallel literary ones (news was taxable, fiction not!). Davis charts both the reasons why, and the ways in which the metaphysically or morally real (the ideal) and the experientially real (the particular) have been constantly in ambiguous relationship in literary history. His readings of Daniel Defoe, Samuel Richardson, and Henry Fielding argue for a more ideologically and historically sensitive approach to issues of the real in fiction. He asserts that the discourse of the novel continues to be constitutively ambivalent in its exploitation of the disjunction between reportage and invention, but that this contradictory realism has become "so self-evident as to be commonplace, hence invisible".

For a catholic introduction to a number of the issues mentioned here, FURST's compilation of critical essays may well constitute the most helpful starting-point. Furst's Introduction offers a somewhat oversimplified reading: she traces the movement from:

> . . . earlier notions of realism as a direct and uncomplicated reporting of the truth of everyday life to a more differentiated understanding of the writer's partial relationship to his or her world, to the complexities, constraints and artifices involved in trying to depict it, including the role of literary form in determining a writer's options, and the dynamics of readers' responses to those strategies.

This evolutionary approach hardly seems to do justice to the sophistication of earlier writers. However, Part One of the book brings together theories of nineteenth-century realism by writers such as Balzac, Flaubert, Henry James, and Guy de Maupassant; Parts Two and Three pair twentieth-century readings of realism – humanist (Auerbach, Watt), Marxist (Lukács, Macherey), structuralist (Barthes, Lodge), rhetorical (Hamon, Lodge), reader-oriented (Iser, Walton), psychoanalytic (Bersani, Brooks), and postmodern (Hillis Miller, Boumelha – a feminist critique). Emphasizing the "sheer variety of meanings encompassed by the very term realism" and "the fluidity of the term as a historical category", Furst reasonably suggests that in the future we may "pay less attention to realism than to realisms".

DEBORAH C. BOWEN

Realism in American Literature

Becker, George. J. (ed.), *Documents of Modern Literary Realism*, Princeton, New Jersey: Princeton University Press, 1963

Berthoff, Warner, *The Ferment of Realism: American Literature 1884–1919*, New York: Free Press, 1965; London: Collier-Macmillan, 1965

Berthoff, Warner, *Fictions and Events: Essays in Criticism and Literary History*, New York: Dutton, 1971

Budick, Emily Miller, *Engendering Romance: Women Writers and the Hawthorne Tradition 1850–1900*, New Haven, Connecticut, and London: Yale University Press, 1994

Carter, Everett, *Howells and the Age of Realism*, Philadelphia: J.B. Lippincott, 1954

Fisher, Philip, *Hard Facts: Setting and Form in the American Novel*, Oxford and New York: Oxford University Press, 1985

Holman, C. Hugh, *Windows on the World: Essays on American Social Fiction*, Knoxville: University of Tennessee Press, 1979

Porter, Carolyn, *Seeing and Being: The Plight of the Participant Observer in Emerson, James, Adams, and Faulkner*, Middletown, Connecticut: Wesleyan University Press, 1981

Quirk, Tom, and Gary Scharnhorst (eds.), *American Realism and the Canon*, Newark: University of Delaware Press, 1994; London: Associated University Presses, 1994

Stein, Allen F., *After the Vows Were Spoken: Marriage in American Literary Realism*, Columbus: Ohio State University Press, 1984

Stowe, William W., *Balzac, James and the Realistic Novel*, Princeton, New Jersey: Princeton University Press, 1983

Sundquist, Eric J. (ed.), *American Realism: New Essays*, Baltimore: Johns Hopkins University Press, 1982

Vernon, John, *The Garden and the Map: Schizophrenia in Twentieth-Century Literature and Culture*, Urbana: University of Illinois Press, 1973

An increasing reaction against literature that concerned itself with "muck-raking", with the sordid and aberrant, a desire to create new forms of writing and ways of theorising social change, and the censorship imposed during World War I, effectively killed off "Realism" as a major literary form, although writers have carried on using realist modes to the present.

BECKER's volume of American, European, and English statements about, and manifestos of, realism is an indispensable starting-point for a study of this field, especially as it makes no attempt to differentiate naturalism from realism or to impose any definition upon the movement, which was as disparate as those writers who used one of its banners to proclaim their divergence from the past and their adherence to the project of exposing the previously concealed.

BERTHOFF's 1965 book set the tone for a renewed interest in the genre, with its dedication "to Liberalism and Democracy", and its programme of defending literature with a "fundamentally moral cause" from both the aestheticism of the modernists and the "crudely deterministic psychology" of naturalists such as Frank Norris, Stephen Crane, and Theodore Dreiser, whom he sees as lost in impressionism and alienation. Henry James, William Dean Howells, Edith Wharton, and Willa Cather he defends because he believes them to be fighting "the acquisitive merchandising society of modern times". The characteristics he ascribes to realism are not only its morality but its accuracy, its local colour, and its "objective knowledge of regional and local history", as in Cather. He deplores the movement in middle to late Henry James, away from the faithful reporting of social manners and towards formal experiment.

CARTER develops these distinctions, between realism as the portrayal of what is "essentially true about men in general – man in essence" and the romanticism of naturalism, which puts facts in the service of theories. Such beliefs that "man is a microcosm" and that such universal truths can best be expressed by letting "a story speak for itself", without overt moralising, are astonishingly naive by today's standards; but Carter's comments about giving the reader a "discursive symbolism" to which they can respond as if it were their real environment is much less so. Roland Barthes's *Writing Degree Zero* was to render such simplistic mimeticism untenable. On the other hand, Carter makes a good case for Howells and the other realists as social satirists who expressed the "ideological tumult" and "bewilderment" of Americans in a time of very rapid social change to industrialisation and urbanisation.

BERTHOFF's 1971 collection of essays responds to the increasing awareness of the instability of realism as a concept, and in "Literature and the Measure of Reality" he tries to distinguish three levels of reality – the political or pragmatic, the semiotic or informational, and the collective or social – but these distinctions soon collapse back into the liberal view that realism's task is to awake us to an insight into the lives of others so as to incite "us to recognition of the reality of other beings", and to acknowledge our common humanity.

VERNON's book attacks these certainties from a sophisticated Bergsonian stance, from which perspective realism's characters are locked into representing portions of the social "map". Their self-consciousness and stability give the impression that their knowledge "mirrors" or reflects the real, and that their actions map our common world. The consequence of such objectifying and fixed knowledge is to see ourselves also as objects in the field of knowledge. The suppression of our unknowing, exploratory, active emotional life produces what Vernon calls "schizophrenia", an imprisonment in the false and timeless world of "common-sense". The inevitable end-product of this perspective is the determinism of naturalism, which is, therefore not an opposed mode but a extension of some of the realist's assumptions.

HOLMAN defends realism, not in the earlier universalist terms but in James's language of an "absolute projection". Instead of giving us the typical, and hence the intelligible, because generalisable, "facts", he argues that William James was intent upon giving us the obdurate and resistant, which awakens us to the limits of our knowledge, and to the "power of blackness" in the world, and which in turn leads us to adopt a pragmatic attitude of "making do" rather than an attitude of mastery or control. such a definition of realism enables it to be extended to include Cather's *My Ántonia*, and to be brought forward to include Southern writers such as Flannery O'Connor.

SUNDQUIST's collection represents the most impressive and useful arguments to date, and makes any easy distinction between realism and naturalism redundant. His own contribution is an argument that is indispensable for any discussion of the subject. His starting point is that the "real" is that which resists containment by the imagination, and so "realism", especially at a time when the literal itself is under threat, is an impossible genre. Like Hawthorne's idea of the romance, the imagination can only create a neutral territory where conflicting demands and needs can be made visible and negotiated, in fantasy at least. It follows that realism, far from being opposed to the romance tradition against which it defined itself, is its natural inheritor, and the psychological realism of Stephen Crane and Henry James represents the use of romance traditions to express the "growing absorption of the self into the facade of the material world" and the "increasingly visible construction of social reality", which are the consequences of the extension of the market in fully developed capitalism. The self becomes a "virtual product of its . . . products", while the biological becomes "mechanised and exteriorised". Far from being a form of transparent writing, the best realist writing foregrounds technique as a way of showing how "mind and the material shrink away from each other even as they become wholly dependent upon one another, and both come more explicitly to inhabit the constructed world of language". Realism, he argues, is a transitional form between the romance and the modernism it anticipates.

Other essays in this volume include Howard Horowitz's on Norris's *The Pit* and theories of market value, Walter Benn Michaels' on Dreiser's *The Financier*, and Philip Fisher's on *Sister Carrie* where, he argues, Dreiser makes a decisive break with Enlightenment values by refusing to "contrast acting with sincerity" or "to oppose the representation of what one is not to authentic self-representation".

STOWE picks up the European critique of realism as represented by Barthes, and argues that Henry James had more in common with Honoré de Balzac than has been conceded, and that both were "highly self-conscious about the literary conventions they employ". Far from being a more primitive and naive forebear, Balzac gives self-reflexive abilities to his characters and demands the same qualities of his readers as does James. Neither writer reduces his characters to moralising object lessons in failure, but instead both "develop visions of experience as drama", as a "series of more or less consciously enacted scenes".

PORTER, in sharp contrast, sees a gulf between the American and European traditions, for the latter allowed for the "possibility of active dissent" and for a withdrawal from failure into personal interiority, whereas the highly integrated and conformist middle-class American strata allowed only for an aloof detachment into being a "participant observer", an alienated vantage point from which the world appears meaningless because seen across a "cognitive abyss", and observers are helpless because they are merely "see-ers".This peculiarly American disjunction between lived, sensuous experience and a reified and rationalised social world is traced by Porter from Ralph Waldo Emerson, through Henry James and Henry Adams, to William Faulkner.

STEIN's work on a much more prosaic, but nevertheless salutary, level, traces the continuing pessimism concerning matrimony as a recipe for personal growth of either men or women in the major works of Henry James, Howells, Kate Chopin, Edith Wharton, and Robert Herrick. In this respect realism continues the older tradition of romantic fiction, but updates it into a portrayal of the problematics of the modern companionate marriage.

FISHER argues that the apparent artlessness and simplicity of realism is a result of its capacity to make the economic laws governing our lives so clear and visible that they become "common-sense", unlike the creations of high culture, which remain extraordinary and hence un-incorporated. Thus realism's strength is also its apparent weakness, in that it reduces to the commonplace those "radically new terrains which it colonises". Dreiser, especially, seen in this light, becomes a major writer for the ways in which his version of the city becomes "the metonymy for the total system of desires", while for "a man inside the city his self is not inside his body but around him, outside his body".

BUDICK perceives a radical difference between the male and female writers of realism, because of the different ways in which they picked up the romance tradition. Re-introducing universals of human nature, she argues that, because women's activities of home building, reproduction, and child-rearing are universal and biological social customs for them, they reflect duties that are essentialist and natural, rather than "formalistic and legalistic" as they are for men, who keep them at arm's length by subverting them. The Hawthornian romance, with its exploration of the tensions between custom and consensus, conformity and community, is one which has proved eminently usable by women writers such as Wharton and Cather, who use it to re-locate self-reliant individuals back into the human community in which they all should reside. This is a living tradition, which continues in women' writing to the present day.

QUIRK and SCHARNHORST similarly extend the definitions of realism, their contributors surveying nineteenth-century women poets, Native American autobiographies, and the tensions between romance and realism in Jewish stories of assimilation, as well as reviving interest in the western stories of Bret Harte and in Mark Twain's ability to tell "people things they don't want to hear but that they know are true". Ultimately all that is left of realism as a literary genre here is this desire to point out patterns of oppression and habit concealed in the familiar.

D.T. CORKER

See also **American Literary Naturalism**

Reaney, James 1926–

Canadian poet and dramatist

Atwood, Margaret, "Reaney Collected", in *Canadian Literature*, 57, 1973

Bowering, George, "Why James Reaney is a Better Poet", in his *A Way with Words*, Ottawa: Oberon Press, 1982

Bowering, George, "Reaney's Region", in his *A Way with Words*, Ottawa: Oberon Press, 1982

Dragland, Stan (ed.), James Reaney issue of *Essays in Canadian Writing*, 24–25, 1982–83; issued separately as *Approaches to the Work of James Reaney*, Toronto: ECW Press, 1983

Jones, Manina, "'The collage in motion': Staging the Document in Reaney's *Sticks and Stones*", in *That Art of Difference: "Documentary-Collage" and English Canadian Writing*, Toronto: University of Toronto Press, 1993

Lee, Alvin A., *James Reaney*, New York: Twayne, 1968

Reaney, J. Stewart, *James Reaney*, Toronto: Gage Educational, 1977

Woodman, Ross, *James Reaney*, Toronto: McClelland & Stewart, 1971

The playfulness, wit, curiosity, passion, and depth of James Reaney's works, to say nothing of the range of genres in which he has contributed to Canada's literature, have complicated and clouded many critical approaches to his *oeuvre*. Some critics, such as Lee (see below), have sought to read Reaney's work through a structuralist system, where everything can be explained, almost iconographically, in terms of good and evil in their varying degrees – an approach that is supported historically by Reaney's association (as a student) with Northrop Frye's symbolic and structuralist readings of literature, ideas which helped to shape Reaney's iconographic perspectives as expressed in his literary periodical, *Alphabet* (1960–71). Others, such as BOWERING in "Why James Reaney is a Better Poet", have sought to reduce the Frye connection by examining Reaney's work as a poet dependent on his particular locality for his individual vision.

Most of the debate over the debt owed by Reaney to Frye has stemmed from LEE's impressive and comprehensive study, which applies a structuralist reading to the works. In what Lee termed an "interim report", he sought to trace the development of Reaney's works through "an antithetical symbolism composed of two distinctive but closely interrelated poetic visions: one of an idealized pastoral order of reality; the other of a macabre, nightmarish world of human experience". However encompassing Lee's reading is, it could not have anticipated the broadening of Reaney's vision, ushered in by *The Donnellys*.

WOODMAN points out that Reaney's sense of binary oppositions is a trademark of his works from the earliest days, again an observation that carries Frye-biased connotations. Woodman strives to examine the lengths to which Reaney has gone to bridge the worlds of the documentary and the mythic.

In the case of ATWOOD's brief examination of Reaney's poetic work up to 1972, there is an attempt to dismiss the Frye connection altogether, and to see Reaney as a poet of natural responses to his somewhat gothic environment. His particular love of southwestern Ontario's past and place, which might appear merely local and parochial, is ultimately universal in its scope, according to BOWERING in "Reaney's Region". By extending Charles Olson's definition of *polis* (a very Black Mountain slant on the matter), Bowering traces Reaney's concept of locality, a view enlarged by Diane Bessai in her essay "Documentary into Drama: Reaney's *Donnelly* Trilogy" in Dragland (see below). This line of thought has been pursued recently by JONES in her reading of Reaney's plays, particularly the *Donnelly* trilogy, which are seen as "found poems" – local legends, bordering on the mythic, that combine fact and folk history. Jones here is moving against the tide of Reaney criticism by pointing out that Reaney may be attempting to break away from the Frye dictum of the separateness of literary and non-literary writing by forging a link between history and poetry.

The issue of the Frye influence continues in DRAGLAND's collection, where he concludes this compendium of nine essays and two interviews with his observations on the theoretical stances adopted by Frye and Reaney. For Dragland, Reaney's structuralism represents a pedagogical need to create a system whereby the world and its chaotic elements can be viewed within the context of order and comprehension, the pursuit (in Frye's words) of "unity, not uniformity".

J. Stewart REANEY (James Reaney's son) exceeds Lee's study in that he uses his familial insight in his discussion of the dramatic works with illuminating historical detail. He makes observations on the sources of his father's creativity – the Peking Opera, the elements of childhood play and fantasy – as well as the means by which the plays themselves test the limits and limitations of drama for both the author and the audience, and the underlying eschatological dialectic between good and evil in the works.

The matter of the two contrasting views of Reaney, as either systematizer and universal orderer or local historian and chronicler of an environment, may not be resolved until Reaney's works are seen as artistic entities which stand apart from preconceived theoretical systems.

BRUCE MEYER

Reception Theory *see* Reader Response Theory

Religion and Literature

Cheyette, Bryan, *Constructions of "The Jew" in English Literature and Society: Racial Representations, 1875–1945*, Cambridge: Cambridge University Press, 1993

Levi, Peter (ed.), *The Penguin Book of English Christian Verse*, Harmondsworth, Middlesex: Penguin, 1984

Lewalski, Barbara Kiefer, *Protestant Poetics and the Seventeenth-Century Religious Lyric*, Princeton, New Jersey: Princeton University Press, 1979

New, Elisa, *The Regenerate Lyric: Theology and Innovation in American Poetry*, Cambridge and New York: Cambridge University Press, 1993

Phillips, D.Z., *From Fantasy to Faith: The Philosophy of Religion and Twentieth-Century Literature*, London: Macmillan, 1991; New York: St Martin's Press, 1991

Rozett, Martha Tuck, *The Doctrine of Election and the Emergence of Elizabethan Tragedy*, Princeton, New Jersey: Princeton University Press, 1984

Smith, Nigel, *Perfection Proclaimed: Language and Literature in English Radical Religion, 1640–1660*, Oxford: Oxford University Press, 1989

Aimed at the non-academic reader, LEVI's Introduction to *The Penguin Book of English Christian Verse* contains a useful discussion of the problems of definition: on the one hand, Christian poetry might be "any verse written by a Christian": on the other the genre might be restricted to "whatever poem purely and deliberately expressed Christianity". Levi claims that the reader should not demand a "narrow dogmatic rectitude" as a matter of definition, and stresses the point that, if we narrow our definition to poetic expressions of Christian dogma we are left with very little good Christian verse at all. What Levi pinpoints in his Introduction is a continuing problem: anyone wishing to discuss the religious in literature is faced with such questions of definition. Is religious poetry, for example, the same thing as devotional poetry? And what of those poems that begin by praising physical beauty, but go on to transcend it and discuss it in terms of the divine – are these religious poems or "purely" love-sonnets? The selection of books discussed below has been chosen to cover a range of definitions of what "religion" in literature means.

LEWALSKI discusses the idea that the "spectacular flowering" of religious lyric poetry in the seventeenth century occurred in response to the Protestant emphasis on the Bible as a book, as such "requiring philological and literary analysis". Using contemporary Protestant texts, Lewalski finds a "substantial and complex poetics of the religious lyric", and discusses its figurative language, its symbolism, and the self-analysis of the genre. Her main argument is that the major religious lyricists of the seventeenth century "owe more to contemporary, English, and Protestant influences than to Counter Reformation, continental, and medieval Catholic resources". This revisionist approach is also apparent in her suggestion that the poets on which her study is based shared a "broad Protestant consensus in regard to doctrine and the spiritual life", which she finds is based on a firm belief in the "absolute priority and centrality" of scripture. The book contains useful discussions of the poetry of the major "Metaphysicals" – a term whose imprecision the author is careful to point out – as well as poets now rather less widely read, such as Thomas Traherne and Henry Vaughan.

The main focus of ROZETT's study is the extent to which conventions of characterization in Elizabethan tragedy depended "upon attitudes about the nature of man's relationship with God or the concepts of good and evil as manifested in human behaviour". Rozett examines how far playwrights reacted to the audience's expectations, and how far those expectations were formed by a familiarity with morality plays and sermons, arguing that "the defining tensions in Elizabethan England were . . . above all religious".

The placement of religious literature in its historical context is continued in SMITH, who identifies the "extraordinary qualities of expression and conception in the writing of the Civil War and Interregnum religious radicalism". The main premise, here successfully argued, is that it is pointless to attempt a division between those critical approaches we term "literary" and those we term "historical". Against this background, Smith offers close textual analyses of the prophetic writings associated with the Ranters and the Quakers, pointing to their concern with what he calls the "sense of self". He goes on to consider the allegorical language of the literature of dreams and visions, finding parallels to Milton's Eve in *Paradise Lost*, Book V; and he discusses the development of the religious writings of the period in terms of a movement from rhetoric to style. The flourishing of early Dissent produced, Smith argues, "its own culture, literature, and language-uses", which were as diverse as the sects themselves, and this literature and usage are seen as central to an understanding of their own historical world not only because of the use of devotional literature in radical worship, but also because "notions of the acts of speaking and writing were at the heart of radical theology".

PHILLIPS's book is a collection of short essays, whose expressed aim is to consider "central issues concerning religion" within the context of twentieth-century literature. The book addresses both the question of what is to replace religion, the premise being that religion plays a continually decreasing role in modern life, and the possible problems inherent in moral constructs seen as independent of religion – for example, the possibility that morality "like religion may degenerate into a vulgar prudence". Phillips touches upon works by a selection of authors, and raises some interesting points on T.S. Eliot; but the general tone is rather simplistic, and the book tends towards a too-easy categorizing of authors' attitudes.

A much more serious work is CHEYETTE's, which conducts close readings of works by Matthew Arnold, Anthony Trollope, George Eliot, John Buchan, Rudyard Kipling, George Bernard Shaw, H.G. Wells, Hilaire Belloc, G.K. Chesterton, T.S. Eliot, and James Joyce. Cheyette argues convincingly that the idea of literary anti-semitism as an unacknowledged commonplace has become entrenched by past studies of the "Jew in English literature", which have "defined Jewish literary representations as fixed stereotypes, myths or images"; whereas in fact, so Cheyette tells us, writers do not "passively draw on eternal myths of 'the Jew' but actively construct them" within the context of their own literary and political concerns. The book finds that all of the writers it discusses demonstrate a desire to incorporate "the Jew" within a "transcendent discourse", but that the issue is always blurred by the "supposedly all-pervasive nature" of "semitic confusion".

NEW discusses the religious theme in American poetry, from Edward Taylor and Ralph Waldo Emerson, through Walt Whitman, Emily Dickinson, and Hart Crane, to Wallace Stevens, Robert Lowell, and Robert Frost. The author takes as her starting-point the idea of American poetry as "prospective speech whose chief object is a recovery of the newness that the Fall occluded", and deals with the poetry she discusses as the religious centre of an "already religiocentric literature", with the aim of refuting Emerson's pre-eminence in the American canon. She does this by taking into account the movement in American poetry that existed alongside the Emersonian tradition, but which Emerson "did not fit us to recognize", and which the author of this well-written study identifies as "theological in character – at times nearly scholastic; at others, self-consciously heretical". The author's approach makes this a very useful volume for anyone interested in the religious in nineteenth and twentieth-century American literature.

SIMON BRITTAN

Renaissance Literature *see* British Literature: Renaissance

Restoration Literature *see* British Literature: Restoration

Rhys, Jean 1894–1979

Dominican-born English novelist and short-story writer

Angier, Carole, *Jean Rhys*, Harmondsworth, Middlesex: Penguin, 1985; New York: Viking Press, 1985

Frickey, Pierrette (ed.), *Critical Perspectives on Jean Rhys*, Washington, D.C.: Three Continents Press, 1990

Harrison, Nancy R., *Jean Rhys and the Novel as Women's Text*, Chapel Hill: University of North Carolina Press, 1988

Howells, Coral Ann, *Jean Rhys*, London: Harvester Wheatsheaf, 1991; New York: St Martin's Press, 1991

James, Louis, *Jean Rhys*, London: Longman, 1978

Kloepfer, Deborah Kelly, *The Unspeakable Mother: Forbidden Discourse in Jean Rhys and H.D.*, Ithaca, New York: Cornell University Press, 1989

Le Gallez, Paula, *The Rhys Woman*, London: Macmillan, 1990; New York: St Martin's Press, 1990

O'Connor, Teresa F., *Jean Rhys: The West Indian Novels*, New York: New York University Press, 1986

The critical reception of Jean Rhys's work has an interesting history. Despite a good reception for her early stories and first four novels in the 1920s and 1930s, her work subsequently went out of print, and she herself disappeared from public attention. It was not until the BBC's adaptation of *Good Morning Midnight* in 1957 that she began to resurface as a writer. The publication of her fifth and last novel *Wide Sargasso Sea* (1966) led to acknowledgement of her as a West Indian writer by her Caribbean compatriots, and her earlier work resurfaced to command attention after more than 20 years of obscurity. Critical interest has varied, from Caribbean critics who draw attention to the uniquely West Indian character of her work, to American and European critics' interrogation of the Rhys heroine, alienation, and modernism in her texts. Feminist criticism has alternatively claimed her and denied her. Often the criticism has included a speculative biographical reading of her novels at the expense of her skills as a creative writer. (Her own unfinished autobiography *Smile Please* [1979] and her correspondence in *Jean Rhys Letters 1931–1966*, edited by Francis Wyndham [1984], are useful for an accurate account of her life.)

JAMES's early (1978) work on Rhys is important because it unambiguously places her within the developing genre of Caribbean writing. The biographical section, written with "unfailing and most generous help" from Rhys, draws attention to her as colonial exile. The subsequent analysis of her work remains true to these foundations, and assesses what Ford Madox Ford called Rhys's "singular instinct for form", not in the sense of theoretical constructs of art, but within a "structure of mood and psychological meaning". The bibliography of early Rhys criticism is extremely useful.

ANGIER's study focuses on the novels and the life, and makes an argument for the close relationship between life and art. Discussion of the novels is meticulous, intricate, and persuasive in its view that Rhys's authority as an artist was unique for "distilling truth out of evasion and art out of pain". The work is by far the most comprehensive yet written, sources are impressive, and research exhaustive. The short stories are not covered (for reasons of space only), and this work (together with the two autobiographical works mentioned above) is a good basis for investigation of Rhys.

O'CONNOR's study focuses on the West Indian elements in Rhys's novels *Voyage in the Dark* and *Wide Sargasso Sea*, which both illuminate the Dominican experience. Her insistent concentration on Rhys as an autobiographical writer subdues the individual narrative voices of the female characters in the texts, though O'Connor's exploration of themes of colonial alienation and the personal mythology of Rhys are useful.

HARRISON begins her study of Rhys's work with the assumption that "women's novels in this century seemed to be more directly autobiographical than are men's novels". From this overly generalised (as she acknowledges) perspective, she then proceeds to investigate Rhys's work as "political and ([auto]biographical) in terms of author, woman and reader". Her use and definition of "[auto]biographical" illustrates the complexity of her argument: "By [auto]biography, I mean the principle of women's fiction in which the 'author' steps, not down, but away from the centrist position of authority, effectively bracketing out her 'self,' the autobiographical 'I,' to share the writing of her text with her readers". Her interest in the rhetorical situation of the woman writer in the twentieth century leads her through a complex and detailed intellectual and critical investigation of Rhys's writing practice, with a focus on what she terms the "emphatic subjectivity" of the texts. She emphasises Rhys's ability to offer a "woman's text" and a possible "way out of the bounds of an oppositional cultural text that attempts to maintain itself by adoption and imposition of the 'unifying' tool of a dominant idiom".

KLOEPFER offers a feminist reading of Rhys, investigating the feminist poetics with little concentration on the Caribbean elements. She argues convincingly for the "absent mother", and offers an interesting analysis, which places the difficulties women face within the context of suppressed female languages, particularly in mother-daughter relationships, instead of locating the problem purely within patriarchal discourse. Rhys's stories of pain and silence take on a wider psychological meaning within a female modernist aesthetic in the hands of this intriguing critic.

FRICKEY's collection offers many varied and superb critical perspectives on Rhys's work, addresses issues important to the understanding of her fiction, and includes autobiographical information on Rhys through "what she herself chose to reveal rather than from speculation". The contributions cover West Indian and European/American criticism. Contributions in the first part, "Perspectives", are impressive, particularly V.S. Naipaul's "Without a Dog's Chance" and Lucy Wilson's "'Women Must Have Spunks': Jean Rhys's West Indian Outcast"; and the following essays on "The Works" offer a balanced analysis of content, style, and structure in the short stories and novels.

LE GALLEZ's structural analysis of Rhys, influenced by Gérard Genette's analytical approach, opposes the biographical and limiting "over-simplification" of "Rhys woman" as passive victim and ubiquitous character in the novels. Le Gallez concentrates on each main character as an individual personality, the complexities of language, and the struggle for authority. Le Gallez attempts and succeeds in arguing that her "Rhys Woman" has the power to formulate her own narrative.

HOWELLS's approach to Rhys is multidimensional and covers the three main foci of interest in the works – gender, colonialism, and modernism. The scrupulously written Introduction outlines the feminist concerns within a framework of questions to be addressed: "at the centre of our attention is the alienated Rhys heroine, but how do we 'read' this condition of alienation as Rhys describes it, and how do we identify Rhys's distinctive version of the feminine constructed in fiction that stretches – with a gap – over forty years?" To answer the questions posed, Howells uses not just textual analysis but also the different and varied perspectives within the field of critical responses to Rhys's work. She argues that Rhys ultimately presents the "literary" question of "the survival of the fragmented woman as text", thus producing a fiction that is secretive, but therefore at the mercy of the interpreters. The breadth of investigation here offers the student a good framework with which to approach the complexities of Rhys's work and reactions to it.

MARGARET E. ROBERTS

Rich, Adrienne 1929–

American poet and essayist

Altieri, Charles, *Self and Sensibility in Contemporary American Poetry*, Cambridge and New York: Cambridge University Press, 1984

Bennett, Paula, *My Life a Loaded Gun: Female Creativity and Feminist Poetics*, Boston: Beacon Press, 1986

Cooper, Jane Roberta (ed.), *Reading Adrienne Rich: Reviews and Revisions, 1951–81*, Ann Arbor: University of Michigan Press, 1984

Diaz-Diocaretz, Myriam, *Translating Poetic Discourse: Questions on Feminist Strategies in Adrienne Rich*, Amsterdam, Philadelphia: John Benjamins, 1985

Gelpi, Albert, and Barbara Charlesworth Gelpi (eds.), *Adrienne Rich's Poetry: A Norton Critical Edition: Texts of the Poems: The Poet on Her Work: Reviews and Criticism*, New York: Norton, 1975, revised as *Adrienne Rich's Poetry and Prose: Poems, Prose, Reviews, and Criticism*, 1993

Keyes, Claire, *The Aesthetics of Power: The Poetry of Adrienne Rich*, Athens: University of Georgia Press, 1986

McCorkle, James, *The Still Performance: Writing Self and Interconnection in Five Postmodern American Poets*, Charlottesville: University Press of Virginia, 1989

Martin, Wendy, *An American Triptych: Anne Bradstreet, Emily Dickinson, Adrienne Rich*, Chapel Hill: University of North Carolina Press, 1984

Yorke, Liz, *Impertinent Voices: Subversive Strategies in Contemporary Women's Poetry*, London and New York: Routledge, 1991

While Adrienne Rich clearly occupies a central position in contemporary American poetry, there are surprisingly few book-length studies of her work. Her work has been viewed through various critical lenses, but the field is primarily dominated by Anglo-American feminist criticism. Thus, much has been made of Rich's personal exploration of self and sexuality, her descriptions of patriarchal oppression, and her interrogation of masculine versions of history and literature. However, aware of the complex and often contradictory nature of aesthetic and political representation, Rich's recent work has begun to problematize her own position as a woman writing for, and about, other women. Some of the most recent criticism on Rich constructs the poetry in postmodernist terms, thereby disrupting the notion of a stable and unified poetic identity. Feminist revisions of psychoanalysis have also informed readings of Rich, and an emphasis on the structures of language and subjectivity has replaced notions of the poetry as an unmediated expression of female experience.

GELPI and GELPI include a selection of Rich's poetry and prose as well as a number of very useful critical essays. Particularly worth noting is W.H. Auden's early celebration of Rich as a poet who respects her elders, and also Albert Gelpi's own discussion, which uses Jungian theories of psychology to decode the poems. Helen Vendler's elegant response to Rich is both personally and critically astute.

COOPER's collection of critical essays on Rich gathers together a comprehensive range of Anglo-American feminist and New-Critical responses to the poet. Rich's poetry is contextualized in terms of the American poetic tradition in all its various guises, so that Rich is not only considered in relation to Walt Whitman and Ralph Waldo Emerson, but also H.D. Particularly useful is Adrian Oktenberg's discussion of *Twenty-One Love Poems*.

BENNETT's study is useful in its attempt to recover a female poetic tradition, though it tends to valorize contemporary women's writing over and above earlier writing by women, so Emily Dickinson and Sylvia Plath remain "dutiful daughters", while the later Rich achieves the status of "woman poet". However, Bennett does offer some useful readings of individual poems. MARTIN also considers Rich as part of a female poetic tradition, which includes Anne Bradstreet and Dickinson. However, like Bennett, she presumes there to be a progression from Bradstreet's "acceptance of traditional patriarchal values" to Rich's "vision of a new society", and thereby constructs a progressive model of poetry, which privileges contemporary verse over its antecedents. Though Martin claims that her study "attempts to create a full portrait of each poet as she lived or is living in her own time", she does little to provide the reader with a sense of the historical and social contexts out of which Rich has been writing.

ALTIERI's discussion of Rich comes at the end of what he calls an investigation into the "representative" contemporary American poet. Rich is understood as a poet who struggles with representation as something that is a political and aesthetic imperative, but which also tends to limit or confine the poetry. Altieri's reading of "Transcendental Etude" is very convincing, and while he takes Rich's feminist politics into account he also identifies the difficulties inherent in writing the personal as the political.

KEYES's book-length study of Rich's poetry considers all the poet's major collections up to *A Wild Patience Has Taken Me This Far* (1981). Refreshingly, Keyes doesn't simply dismiss Rich's early poetry as a denial of her feminine self, but considers it, in Elaine Showalter's terms, as "a double-voiced discourse", containing a "dominant" and a "muted" story. Several neglected early poems are recovered through this critical strategy. Though there are many thorough and penetrating discussions of certain key texts, Keyes is too often reliant on other feminist critics for direction.

DIAZ-DIOCARETZ considers the problem of translating feminist poetic discourse, and therefore discussions of the poems only appear after a considerable amount of theoretical preparation. However, despite using structuralist linguistics as well as work in reception aesthetics, the analyses of individual poems remain limited.

McCORKLE's collection of essays offers postmodernist reflections on Rich as well as on a number of other contemporary poets. His reading of Rich's poetry as a means of connecting self and ethos is convincing because it accounts for both the visionary and the political dimensions of Rich's work.

French feminist theories of language and subjectivity are used by YORKE as an interpretative tool in reading contemporary women's poetry. Though not exclusively devoted to Rich, there is an excellent chapter focusing on "Transcendental Etude". Yorke's description of a "female mythic model" of poetry reminds the reader of Alicia Ostriker's earlier survey of women's poetry, which also considers myth as a feminist structuring principle. However, Yorke constructs Rich as being somehow outside "the lofty egocentric transcendental formulations of Romanticism" when it might be more useful to consider the poet as struggling with those very terms herself.

VICTORIA BAZIN

Richards, I.A. 1893–1979

English critic and literary theorist

Brower, R., H. Vendler, and J. Hollander (eds.), *I.A. Richards: Essays in His Honour*, New York: Oxford University Press, 1973

Hotopf, W.H.N., *Language, Thought and Comprehension: A Case Study of the Writings of I.A. Richards*, London: Routledge & Kegan Paul, 1965; Bloomington: Indiana University Press, 1965

McCallum, Pamela, *Literature and Method: Towards a Critique of I.A. Richards, T.S. Eliot and F.R. Leavis*, Dublin: Gill & Macmillan, 1983; Atlantic Highlands, New Jersey: Humanities Press, 1983

Needham, John, *The Completest Mode: I.A. Richards and the Continuity of English Literary Criticism*, Edinburgh: Edinburgh University Press, 1982

Russo, John Paul, *I.A. Richards: His Life and Work*, Baltimore: Johns Hopkins University Press, 1989; London: Routledge, 1989

Schiller, Jerome P., *I.A. Richards' Theory of Literature*, New Haven, Connecticut, and London: Yale University Press, 1969

Commentaries on Richards' work generally stress his unconventional intellectual background and the impact this had on his career, in that it resulted in a remarkably diversity in the ideas and interests he developed both within and between the projects he undertook. Depending on the aim of the commentator, this diversity is celebrated, criticized, or else played down in the interests of coherence. Because of the breadth of Richards' interests, none of the published commentaries, apart from that of Russo's, attempt to address the full range of his writings, aiming instead to explain and critique specific aspects of his theories for specific ends.

HOTOPF's study, although published in 1965, primarily addresses Richards' pre-1942 writings. His aims are to clarify Richards' views on communication and the relationship between language and thought in order to construct a theory of meaning and value. As part of this process Hotopf sets out to correct misreadings of Richards' early works by philosophers and literary critics – particularly those by the New Critics, whose accounts Hotopf addresses in depth. He also applies Richards' theory of error to address fundamental errors in Richards' own works. Although Hotopf has latterly been criticised for himself misreading many of Richards' claims, his account offers a useful commentary on the early works, such as *The Meaning of Meaning*.

SCHILLER's aim is also to set out and take issue with earlier critiques of Richards' work and to show that, in spite of their claims to the contrary, a coherent theory of literature can be traced through Richards' full range of writings. Schiller achieves this coherence through a re-reading of Richards' earlier works on poetry in the light of his writings as a whole. As with all such attempts the result is somewhat reductive, in that Schiller often does not do justice to the complexity of Richards' theories.

BROWER *et al.* bring together a diverse set of commentaries, which addresses a broad range of Richards' works, and assesses his influence in fields such as English-language teaching, Coleridge studies, the classics, and the analysis of literary texts. Essays include: an account by Joan Bennet, one of the students who took part in the *Practical Criticism* protocols in the 1920s, on Richards' impact on contemporary Cambridge; an account of the ill-fated Basic English project by William Empson; and commentaries on various aspects of Richards' writings by literary critics such as Cleanth Brooks and W.K. Wimsatt, and by the behavioural psychologist Burrhus Frederic Skinner. The collection offers a good introduction to the diversity of Richards' writings and their impact, and includes a critical bibliography.

McCALLUM's aims are to expose the contradictory axioms of the liberal philosophies she uncovers in the writings of Richards, T.S. Eliot, and F.R. Leavis. Her argument is that what these writers have in common is a shared concern to displace the amoral ethos of *l'art pour l'art,* and goes on to comment that: "if they reasserted the ethical dimension in literature or culture, their theories floundered on the inability to explain satisfactorily the intellectual and moral efficacy of this value in society". McCallum traces the development of liberal thought from Thomas Hobbes to F.H. Bradley in order to explain the tensions she finds in Richards' writings, and to argue for their similarity to those found in the writings of Eliot and Leavis.

NEEDHAM's account also traces connections between the concerns of Richards, Eliot, and Leavis, but with the aim of developing a theory of continuity and change within English literary criticism. He focuses primarily on Richards' work, and then traces similarities in the theoretical concepts they develop backwards in time to the critical practice of Samuel Johnson and Samuel Taylor Coleridge, and forwards to that of Eliot and Leavis. Needham argues that Richards' concept of *interinanimation* is his most useful contribution to the analysis of poetic language, and that the work that comes before and after the development of this concept is "less satisfactory".

RUSSO takes issue with Needham's claims, among those of others others, in what must be seen as the definitive text on Richards. In a remarkable piece of work, which strenuously tries to avoid becoming a hagiography, Russo offers a biographical account of Richards career, a description and analysis of his writings, and a critical account of the most pertinent commentaries on Richards over a period of some 60 years. He traces Richards' earliest intellectual influences, and describes and comments on the development of his ideas and theories at length, situating them within the context of their inception and commenting on their reception. For example, Russo teases out Richards' development of concepts such as "sense" and "reference", "metaphor" and "complementarity". He then goes on to give an account of how these concepts are applied in the analysis of literary texts at various points in Richards' career, and shows how different critics have interpreted and used these concepts. Also to be found in Russo's work are discussions of relatively recent critiques of Richards' writing, including a useful account of the various Marxist responses. Russo also provides an updated critical bibliography, which includes works not covered in Brower *et al.*.

CHRISTINE CHRISTIE

Richardson, Dorothy 1873–1957

English novelist

Barrett, Michèle, and Jean Radford, "Modernism in the 1930's: Dorothy Richardson and Virginia Woolf", in *1936: The Sociology of Literature: Proceedings of the Essex Conference on the Sociology of Literature*, Volume 1, edited by Francis Barker *et al.*, Colchester: University of Essex, 1979

DuPlessis, Rachel Blau, "Beyond the Hard Visible Horizon", in her *Writing Beyond the Ending: Narrative Strategies of Twentieth-Century Women Writers*, Bloomington: Indiana University Press, 1985

Fromm, Gloria G., *Dorothy Richardson: A Biography*, Urbana: University of Illinois Press, 1977

Hanscombe, Gillian, *The Art of Life: Dorothy Richardson and the Development of Feminist Consciousness*, London: Peter Owen, 1982; Athens: Ohio University Press, 1983

Powys, John Cowper, *Dorothy Richardson*, London: Joiner & Steele, 1931

Radford, Jean, *Dorothy Richardson*, Hemel Hempstead, Hertfordshire: Harvester Wheatsheaf, 1991; Bloomington: Indiana University Press, 1991

Staley, Thomas, *Dorothy Richardson*, Boston: Twayne, 1976

In a review of Volume 7 of Dorothy Richardson's *Pilgrimage*, Virginia Woolf wrote that "there is no one word, such as romance or realism, to cover, even roughly, the works of Miss Dorothy Richardson" (*Contemporary Writers*, 1976). Woolf's statement continues to be pertinent. Can *Pilgrimage* be described as a novel, an autobiography, or both? The critical inability to fix and position this work, which once served as the reason for neglecting it, is now precisely the quality that attracts critical reappraisals. *Pilgrimage* has hovered on the edge of fame, never quite achieving it. The attempt to portray and project the consciousness of one main female character has been the cause of both *Pilgrimage*'s critical reputation and its rejection. Criticism has also tended to read the life of Richardson as inseparable from the literature, and biographical readings have tended to predominate. However, *Pilgrimage*'s apparently uncategorisable status, whether as novel, autobiography, technical experiment, historical document, or all four, provides the basis in the late twentieth-century for poststructuralist readings, especially by feminist critics, which move away from analysing the rewriting of a life to consider the historical and social significance of such a project.

POWYS's short text was one of the first critical studies of Richardson not only to be published but also to be taken seriously. It is very much a defence of Richardson's use of a single narrative perspective and her style, both of which had been criticised by reviewers. Indeed, the concentration on Miriam Henderson is necessary, he argues, since this is the "biography of a solitary human soul", which succeeds in presenting a female character who is "more living, more real" than "any woman in fiction". Her style's "obscurity" is integral, not indefensible, due to its "distinct affinity with poetry". Written when only nine volumes of *Pilgrimage* had appeared, the pamphlet's argument continues to be pertinent to the whole of Richardson's work.

STALEY's study provides a thorough overview of the production, position, and pertinence of *Pilgrimage*. He considers Richardson's literary influences, the cultural and social history of the period in which she was writing, and her technique. The single perspective of Miriam Henderson is described as Richardson's debt to Henry James. Examining each volume individually, Staley analyses its place in the development of the whole of *Pilgrimage* and of Miriam. The argument appraises *Pilgrimage*, but also attempts to account for its neglect. It is an ideal and balanced introduction.

"It would seem", argues FROMM at the beginning of her biography, that "in Dorothy Richardson's case at least, the critic and the biographer must truly join forces". The biography considers Richardson's life and her writing and examines how her struggles to get published affected her work. Fromm's text, recently reprinted with a new Foreword and index, is highly relevant for any student interested in considering the links between the writing and the writer.

BARRETT and RADFORD'S article provides an interesting counterpoint to the recent critical repositioning of *Pilgrimage* as a historical document. Reading Woolf's and Richardson's writing in the light of Georg Lukács' critique of modernism and Julia Kristeva's celebration of it, the argument provides a rare example of a cogently theorised questioning of Richardson's project, rather than an unsubstantiated rejection. If literature is, as they suggest, a "'lived relation' to historical process", then *Pilgrimage*'s "exclusion of third person narrative ('*histoire*') in favour of '*discours*' operates . . . as a *closure* rather than a revolutionary rupture". *Pilgrimage* is thus considered as a refusal of history, locked within a personal system, whereas Woolf's novels in contrast "explore social/historical realities as they impinge on the consciousness of her individual characters". Barrett and Radford's historical and sociological approach provides a concise and useful critique of theories of modernism applied to one of its founders.

HANSCOMBE's argument considers *Pilgrimage* as "a unique and definitive example of autobiographical fiction". Her book suggests that *Pilgrimage* represents the "distinctiveness of feminine consciousness", a project that is "continuous, not contiguous" with the "evolution of an experimental technique of fiction". The main contribution of this novel is, therefore, to enable the reader of fiction to understand "the demands of art and of the processes inherent to its generation". The traditionally defined divisions between art and life are challenged and questioned in *Pilgrimage*. This is an incisive feminist analysis, which provides many cogent and lucid readings of the text.

DuPLESSIS's essay provides a productive reading of *Pilgrimage*. She argues that the length and inconclusiveness of this novel sequence is a deliberate, feminist evasion of marriage, an institution that has represented the expected sexual and textual resolution for a young woman, both in life and literature. Its non-closure is thus a political triumph not a technical failure. Although brief, this article is essential for any reader of *Pilgrimage* who wishes to consider the political and historical significance of its technique.

RADFORD's book adopts a poststructuralist approach, using recent French feminist theory and psychoanalysis. The first three chapters consider the relationship between physical and textual space for a woman in *Pilgrimage*, and the importance of the novel's title. The last three examine the connections between feminism and modernism, and *Pilgrimage*'s links to both, in the context of Kristevan theories of subjectivity and language. The study employs difficult theory to open up and elucidate an often inaccessible text. It is, however, an excellent, illuminating and well-written book, which would be useful at both introductory and advanced levels.

LOUISE TUCKER

Richardson, Henry Handel 1870–1946

Australian novelist and short-story writer

Arkin, Marian, "A More Fortunate Reading Strategy", in *International Literature in English: Essays on the Major Writers*, edited by Robert L. Ross, New York: Garland, 1991; London: St James Press, 1991

Buckley, Vincent, *Henry Handel Richardson*, Melbourne: Lansdowne Press, 1961; 2nd edition, Melbourne: Oxford University Press, 1970

Clark, Axel, *Henry Handel Richardson: Fiction in the Making*, Brookvale, New South Wales: Simon & Schuster Australia, 1990; St Peters, New South Wales: New Endeavour Press, 1990

Elliott, William D., *Henry Handel Richardson*, Boston: Twayne, 1975

Green, Dorothy, *Ulysses Bound: Henry Handel Richardson and Her Fiction*, Canberra: Australian National University Press, 1973; revised edition, as *Henry Handel Richardson and Her Fiction*, Sydney: Allen & Unwin, 1986

Palmer, Nettie, *Henry Handel Richardson: A Study*, Sydney: Angus & Robertson, 1950

Although Henry Handel Richardson's fiction gained some popular attention in the 1930s, serious critical appraisal did not come until much later. And then the assessments strongly diverged over whether the work was naturalistic or psychological in character, and whether it bore the mark of genius or was second-rate.

PALMER was one of the first to recognize the work of an Australian-born writer who had spent all of her adult life in Europe, and the first critic to treat in a book-length study what she considered a significant achievement in Australian literature. Based on interviews with Richardson in England, Palmer constructs a lively personal account of the reclusive author, then analyzes each of the novels in subsequent chapters. The close readings develop the idea that Richardson relied on the "general method of holding to literal facts", a process Palmer explains fully in the chapter titled "Methods of Work". The autobiographical approach that this book takes continues to influence Richardson criticism.

The Australian poet and critic BUCKLEY was less generous when he published his short study in 1961, which appeared again in 1970 in a second edition. He called the trilogy *The Fortunes of Richard Mahony* an "impressive failure" and *The Getting of Wisdom* a "minor masterpiece". Contending that Richardson deserves more praise for her contribution to the development of Australian literature than for her fiction, Buckley criticized the work as being literal-minded, melodramatic, and inflexible in its naturalistic method. This judgment set the stage for the ensuing debate on the validity of Richardson's "genius".

GREEN's study challenges Buckley and other Australian critics who discounted Richardson as an unfashionable practitioner of naturalism and a chronicler who lacked imaginative powers. Green argues that Richardson consistently adds a metaphysical and psychological dimension to the factual material and autobiographical elements she employs. This approach underlines Green's extended discussions of the fiction. Republished in 1986, with its main text unaltered, the new edition incorporates in an Afterword materials from some of Richardson's personal papers, which had just become available. Although interesting, these excerpts from diaries and letters fail to shed much light on the fiction, because Green tends to present them as proof that her interpretation of Richardson's life and work continues to be the only accurate one. While Green's lengthy book remains the most thorough, original, and influential, the tone sometimes annoys by this assumption of its assessment's correctness.

A typical product of the Twayne series, ELLIOTT's book provides a detailed chronology, a biographical sketch, and chapters on each of the major works, along with a comprehensive, if now dated, annotated bibliography. In the Preface to this helpful introductory study, Elliott explains that his approach is "to reveal Henry Handel Richardson as the first Australian realistic novelist to develop a multi-dimensional single characer in an extended work of fiction". By underpinning his discussion in this manner, Elliott avoids the Australian-centered critical debate that dominates the earlier studies of Richardson.

The first volume of CLARK's proposed two-volume work on Richardson sets out "to describe the circumstances in which she developed into a woman exceptionally gifted and well-practiced in the art of making fiction". Following Richardson until 1897, the year of her mother's death, the book contains abundant "stories of her youth and of her parents' marriage, which provided the historical basis for her three major novels". More anecdotal than critical, the study covers familiar territory and stresses once more the autobiographical element in Richardson's fiction.

ARKIN opens her essay by surveying what she calls the "curiously divided" critical reception afforded Richardson's writing, which has set out "to prove that she was or was not: imaginative, self-centered, a realist, a naturalist, a writer in the Australian tradition, literal minded, a genius, second-rate". Calling for "a thoroughgoing reappraisal" of Richardson, Arkin believes that because of the fiction's "radical social vision" this "reappraisal will occur within a feminist framework". Arkin examines the Mahony trilogy, *Maurice Guest*, and *The Getting of Wisdom* through "a feminist lens", which brings into focus Richardson's radical elements and subversive qualities "so long obscured" by the more traditional and ongoing critical debate. Although this essay is hampered by its necessary brief treatment of the fiction, it introduces a decidedly original and valuable reassessment. An extensive annotated bibliography is included.

In 1996 all of Richardson's manuscripts and papers – including letters and diaries – become available to scholars. Held by the National Library in Canberra, Australia, most of these materials were previously sealed. (Richardson was a private person and made few public statements: she even retained this aloofness in her unfinished autobiography, *Myself When Young*.) Therefore, access to such personal records will undoubtedly lead to a renewed interest in the fiction and most likely to critical reassessments and reinterpretations.

ROBERT L. ROSS

Richardson, Samuel 1689–1761

English novelist

Bueler, Lois E., *Clarissa's Plots*, Newark: University of Delaware Press, 1994; London: Associated University Presses, 1994

Castle, Terry, *Clarissa's Ciphers: Meaning and Disruption in Richardson's "Clarissa"*, Ithaca, New York: Cornell University Press, 1982

Doody, Margaret Anne, *A Natural Passion: A Study of the Novels of Samuel Richardson*, Oxford: Clarendon Press, 1974

Doody, Margaret Anne, and Peter Sabor (eds.), *Samuel Richardson: Tercentenary Essays*, Cambridge and New York: Cambridge University Press, 1989

Eagleton, Terry, *The Rape of Clarissa: Writing, Sexuality and Class Struggle in Samuel Richardson*, Oxford: Blackwell, 1982; Minneapolis: University of Minnesota Press, 1982

Goldberg, Rita, *Sex and Enlightenment: Women in Richardson and Diderot*, Cambridge and New York: Cambridge University Press, 1986

Gwilliam, Tassie, *Samuel Richardson's Fictions of Gender*, Stanford, California: Stanford University Press, 1993

Harris, Jocelyn, *Samuel Richardson*, Cambridge and New York: Cambridge University Press, 1987

Keymer, Tom, *Richardson's "Clarissa" and the Eighteenth-Century Reader*, Cambridge and New York: Cambridge University Press, 1992

Kinkead-Weekes, Mark, *Samuel Richardson: Dramatic Novelist*, London: Methuen, 1973; Ithaca, New York: Cornell University Press, 1973

Warner, William Beatty, *Reading "Clarissa": The Struggles of Interpretation*, New Haven, Connecticut, and London: Yale University Press, 1979

There was no room for Samuel Richardson in the "Great Tradition" of F.R. Leavis, who proclaimed (with his usual blend of myopia and dogmatism) that "it's no use pretending that Richardson can ever be made a current classic again" (*The Great Tradition*, 1948). Fifty years later, Richardson certainly has become a "current classic again". If he has been made one, it is not least because new critical interests, agendas, and methodologies have found in his masterpiece *Clarissa* a text very much answerable to their varied concerns. With their intensity of focus on questions about literariness and meaning, gender and sexuality, writing and reading, power and struggle, the novels have proved unusually hospitable to the full range of modern theoretical approaches – often seeming, indeed, to anticipate these approaches in their structures.

Two books predating the rise of theory in Anglo-American literary studies remain valuable. Arguing that Richardson's technique of "writing to the moment" (epistolary narration by the protagonists, as the action proceeds) demands a corresponding critical method of "reading to the moment", KINKEAD-WEEKES offers detailed, phase-by-phase commentaries on the novels. A particular strength is the subtle attentiveness with which he traces the dramatic and psychological unfoldings of "an art that encourages reading between the lines". This emphasis on dramatic scene at the expense of epistolary report is sometimes too great, however. When Kinkead-Weekes writes that in Richardson "the experience of living from moment to moment . . . is more important than the letter convention", he underplays what for later critics has been the most interesting locus of struggle in Richardson's fiction – the letters themselves.

DOODY (1974) shares Kinkead-Weekes's concern with the rehabilitation of Richardson as a controlled and self-conscious artist. She takes a scholarly and historical approach, carefully locating the novels in a range of literary contexts: courtship novels by women writers of the early eighteenth century; Restoration heroic tragedy; and the literature of holy dying. A particularly valuable chapter reads *Pamela* in the traditions of pastoral and romance, and Doody is attentive throughout to the iconographic sources of Richardson's imagery. Her work in recovering such contexts and elucidating the deliberateness with which Richardson draws on or invokes them is further developed in HARRIS's introductory study (see also Harris's essay on "Richardson: Original or Learned Genius?" in Doody and Sabor, below.) Focusing with wonderful alertness on the intertextual allusiveness of Richardson's writing, Harris proves beyond question her underlying contention that Richardson's allusions "are rarely casual, but call up entire works to explain and express his meaning. They accumulate significance by expanding meaning, they 'reverberate' . . . throughout the whole, they create patterns that are almost metaphorical".

Deconstruction entered Richardson studies with all its early energy in WARNER's combative book of 1979. Citing Nietzsche and Jacques Derrida as his masters, Warner insists "that the textual field of *Clarissa*, with its intricate history, is like a vast plain where Clarissa and Lovelace, and their respective allies, and the two ways of interpreting the world they embody, collide and contend". Warner's argument is not helped by its methodological crudeness and its inaccurate evidence about the novel's textual history, and it is perhaps inevitable that a study of this kind would date quickly. Warner's book remains useful for its capacity to energize debate, however, and it fixes in clear view the contested nature of all meanings, both within the text and around it.

More sophisticated applications of theory to Richardson (again with particular reference to *Clarissa*) emerge in the work of Castle and Eagleton. Like Warner's, CASTLE's book belongs to a phase of the poststructuralist enterprise now long superseded, but her opening and closing chapters remain superb statements of the capacity of Richardson's narrative form to devolve final responsibility for the construction of meaning to the reader alone. Castle's weakness is her failure to recognize

Richardson's own alertness to this central characteristic of his narrative method, and she is as wrong about the author as she is right about the text when she writes:

> Though committed ostensibly to "Instruction" – an ideal transfer of meaning from author to reader – Richardson chose in *Clarissa* the form least suited to didactic ultimatum. Authorial "Instruction" cannot coexist happily with readerly "construction" – yet it is this last operation that the multiple-correspondent epistolary novel requires.

EAGLETON's witty and eloquent book is frustratingly undeveloped, but its brief chapters throw brilliant light on the obsessive literariness of all the novels, while also heralding a salutary return to historical and political contextualization. "Richardson was no Henry James, bland in the midst of ambiguities", as Eagleton insists: "he was a courageous spokesman for middle-class ideology, a properly didactic, propagandist writer". Eagleton shares with Castle a keenness to probe gaps between the semantic instability of Richardson's novels and the assumed intentions behind them, but he sets the two in a more complex and plausible relationship. Ever alert to the capacity of the novels to articulate (if not always to resolve) competing ideological positions, he describes an author engaged in heroic struggle with the awkward capacity of writing and meaning to proliferate beyond his control.

The best subsequent studies have combined a theoretical interest in the open, readerly nature of Richardson's texts with a progressively surer grasp of the cultural and historical contexts in which they were written and first read. Several follow Eagleton's lead in turning away from the dismissive attitude taken by many earlier critics towards the relevance and efficacy of Richardson's own commitments, activities, and intentions.

Feminist scholarship has been to the fore here. GOLDBERG is concerned in particular with *Clarissa*'s impact in Enlightenment France; but the early chapters of her book combine astute close reading with thorough analysis of the novel's relationship to the literature of female conduct. Within and beyond Richardson's circle, Goldberg argues, *Clarissa* could stand as a powerful myth about both religion and sexuality, variously interpretable "on the one hand as a model for docile behaviour in young women, and on the other as a frightening relocation of the notion of Christian trial in the sexual combat of the modern world".

GWILLIAM lacks Goldberg's historical rigour, but fully shares her interest in gender and myth. The psychoanalytical vigilance with which she approaches Richardson allows her to illuminate with some persuasiveness what she calls "the Tiresian roots of his imagination – his equivocal and by no means always egalitarian ability to identify with women". Finding in the novels an elaborate rehearsal of conflicting discourses about men and women in which the contradictions of gender construction are uniquely on show, Gwilliam describes a writer who combines rigorous inspection of these contradictions with fascinated absorption in the complex patterns of anxiety and desire that play across his work.

Criticism in the 1990s has been animated by DOODY and SABOR's collection of essays (published on the tercentenary of Richardson's birth), which represents a wide range of critical approaches, and combines strong readings of individual novels with several, more general pieces. A particular strength of the volume is its extension of prevailing debates about Richardson beyond the usual areas of *Pamela* and *Clarissa*. Gillian Beer's analysis of Richardson's reworking of Sir Philip Sidney's *Arcadia* in *Pamela II* is one highlight, while Carol Houlihan Flynn and Doody herself supply illuminating essays on *Sir Charles Grandison*. The volume also includes the first significant essays on Richardson's *Meditations* and *Collection of Sentiments*. Siobhán Kilfeather's account of "The Rise of Richardson Criticism" gives a useful overview of the entire field, and her call for a turn towards the New-Historical investigations and textual recoveries of current eighteenth-century studies continues to be answered in the most recent studies.

My own book (KEYMER) draws on the documented responses of *Clarissa*'s first readership to define the ethical, political, and ideological contexts of eighteenth-century debate, arguing that the novel;s vexedness of meaning is central to Richardson's project of entangling his readers in interpretative difficulty and making them (as Richardson puts it himself) "if not Authors, Carvers" of the text. BUELER draws on a range of scriptual, emblematic, and dramatic traditions to describe the novel's juxtaposition of competing plots, and her study lays similar emphasis on the active and strenuous role in which Richardson's reader is typically cast.

TOM KEYMER

Robinson, Edwin Arlington 1869–1935

American poet

Anderson, Wallace L., *Edwin Arlington Robinson: A Critical Introduction*, Boston: Houghton Mifflin, 1967

Barnard, Ellsworth, *Edwin Arlington Robinson: A Critical Study*, New York: Macmillan, 1952; reprinted, New York: Octagon Books, 1977

Barnard, Ellsworth (ed.), *Edwin Arlington Robinson: Centenary Essays*, Athens: University of Georgia Press, 1969

Coxe, Louis O., *Edwin Arlington Robinson: The Life of Poetry*, New York: Pegasus, 1969

Fussell, Edwin S., *Edwin Arlington Robinson: The Literary Background of a Traditional Poet*, Berkeley: University of California Press, 1954

Gray, Richard, *American Poetry of the Twentieth Century*, London: Longman, 1990

Murphy, Francis (ed.), *Edwin Arlington Robinson: A Collection of Critical Essays*, Englewood Cliffs, New Jersey: Prentice-Hall, 1970

Winters, Yvor, *Edwin Arlington Robinson*, Norfolk, Connecticut: New Directions, 1946, revised 1971

Edwin Arlington Robinson published 20 books of poetry in his 40-year career, and through his use of conventional verse forms and the colloquial language of everyday speech achieved considerable popularity in the first half of the twentieth century. Though he deliberately stood apart from the experimentalism of his modernist contemporaries, and was inclined to be modest in his claims for his work, it has been argued recently that his interest in narrative poetry, and his varied use of point of view, owes something to the practice of late nineteenth-century European novelists, especially Émile Zola and Joseph Conrad. And if his poetry is technically unadventurous, his native temperament is modern in its sceptical view of human potential, a disposition that makes for comparisons with both Robert Frost, his younger contemporary, and Thomas Hardy.

Robinson published his first book of poems, *The Torrent and the Night Before*, in 1896, including portraits of the characters of "Tilbury Town", the fictional equivalent of his hometown of Gardiner, in Maine. These Tilbury portraits became a recurrent feature of his subsequent collections, and include many of the poems for which he was best known, such as "Miniver Cheevy", "Flammonde", "Richard Cory", and "Luke Havergal" in which the characters conflict with the prevailing values of small-town New England life. (His use of the dramatic monologue in such poems resembles that of Robert Browning, though this was an influence Robinson always disputed.) His reputation was established by *The Town Down the River* (1910), *The Man Against the Sky* (1916), and *The Three Taverns* (1920). He maintained a prolific output during the second half of his career in a series of long poems, including some on the Arthurian legends such as *Merlin* (1917) and *Lancelot* (1920), and *Tristram* (1927), for which he won his third Pulitzer prize. Although Robinson has always had his advocates, his reputation has declined since the 1970s. The best writing on him by his mid-century critics is reprinted in the collections listed below. The recommended biography is Chard Powers Smith's *Where the Light Falls: A Portrait of Edwin Arlington Robinson* (1965).

WINTERS' work established the bench-mark for commentary on Robinson, as is clear from the frequent reprinting of his 1922 essay "A Cool Master" (see Murphy, below). In his later book, Winters gives a brief biographical account, places Robinson in the context of his New England heritage, assesses the influences on his style, and devotes chapters to the shorter poems, the Arthurian poems, and the long narrative verse. Winters is a cool, discriminating critic, who admires the shorter poems above all: in the best of these he finds Robinson's practical morality and passionate curiosity about individual dramas guided by the moral and spiritual values of the Christian tradition (this section is also reprinted in Murphy).

BARNARD's early (1952) study is a thorough chronological reading of all the work, and is valuable in its comprehensiveness. Barnard contributed substantially to the critical interest in Robinson for three decades, and later edited the collection of centenary essays (BARNARD 1969), most of which were original contributions. In the collection, Barnard contributes a history of the poet's reputation, and William J. Free analyses the narrative and verbal strategies of "Flammonde" to argue that Robinson was trying to re-invigorate the clichéd vocabulary of his day without, however, completely abandoning everyday language. David H. Hirsch assesses conflicting readings of "The Man Against the Sky", which leave its meaning unresolved, and provides a counter argument based on an analysis of its figurative and allusive devices. Robert Davis Stevick writes on Robinson's metre and diction to suggest the inadequacy of the label "traditional" as applied to his subjects, verse forms, and language. Wallace L. Anderson culls material from Robinson's comments on his practice to show his belief in the idea of poetry as a timeless continuum, to which individual poets bring their unique gifts. This article is followed by three essays on Robinson's Arthurian poems, by Charles T. Davis, Nathan Comfort Starr, and Christopher Brookhouse, and by Jay Martin's discussion of the aims of the late narrative poems. J.C. Levenson's essay on "Robinson's Modernity" argues for Robinson's continuing appeal through his handling of doubt, disbelief, and despair – states of being that are read as the primary facts of twentieth-century life. Finally, Radcliffe Squires writes on the Tilbury Town poems in relation to notions of tradition and modernity, seeing in the poems "temperate ironies, cool understatements and a language calculated to heal".

FUSSELL's study is one of the best mid-century readings: he argues for Robinson as a belated Romantic, who turned from Nature to the human scene as the fit subject for poetry. In doing so, Robinson revoked one of the strongest conventions of the Romantic tradition, and in its place brought wit, irony, and a stern intellectual discipline back into poetry, with an argumentative and colloquial language that is robust and resilient.

ANDERSON's sound introductory study is addressed to the general reader, and provides a critical and biographical overview of Robinson's life and work, dealing with his early infuences, his "philosophy" – though Robinson denied that he had one – and his poetics. Anderson writes well on the Tilbury poems, and does a competent job of situating Robinson's work in relation to the mainstream of early twentieth-century American poetry.

COXE gives an all-embracing view of Robinson's career, driven by a feeling for the intellectual sophistication of the poet's use of symbolism in the shorter poems and longer narratives. He acknowledges a relative sense of decline in the later work, but insists that Robinson's best work was the product of a fine sensibility, in which his mastery of form and colloquial speech found expression in a visionary clarity.

Much of the best critical commentary on Robinson is contained in the "Twentieth Century Views" volume edited by MURPHY. It includes one original piece, by Josephine Miles. The book opens with Winters' canonical "A Cool Master" essay of 1922, which celebrates Robinson not for the common humanity of his characters but for the technical accomplishment of his traditional forms and language, which are seen to yield portraits of "infallible precision" and balance. Murphy also reprints a chapter from Winters' book, "The Shorter Poems", where Winters privileges these poems for their analytical method and distinguished verbal style as against the more philosophic poems, which Winters finds careless in content and style. Murphy then gives three of Conrad Aikens's reviews of individual collections – *Avon's Harvest* (1921), *Collected Poems* (1922), and *Tristram* (1927): Aiken dwells mostly on the Arthurian poems, in which he discerns a compositional method halfway between the medieval "tapestries" of William Morris and the melodrama of Richard Wagner, and acknowledges the "tragic force" of these versions of the Arthur myth. In a brief assessment, Morton Zabel praises Robinson's mastery of form and toughness of language, while Robert Frost's reprinted Introduction from a posthumous edition of *King Jasper* (1935) honours the indivisible relationship between

Robinson's personality and literary style, where an overtly humorous idiom reveals inner seriousness. Louis Coxe debates the reasons for the decline in Robinson's reputation, which he attributes to mistaken assumptions about traditional forms and language, and finds instead a volatile energy beneath a calm surface in the best poems. The poet and novelist James Dickey writes enthusiastically of Robinson's power to expand poetic horizons: a similar view is argued by Fussell in an essay reprinted from his 1954 book. Josephine Miles' original contribution concerns the paradox of Robinson's combination of the visionary tradition of Romantic poetry with his plain idiom of poetic understatement, and argues that if his subject continued to be that of Romantic natural beauty, his treatment of it was sceptical. Warner Berthoff compares Robinson and Frost's common forging of a verbal realism in the early years of the century, a realism that Robinson found only in the novels of Nathaniel Hawthorne and Hardy. W.R. Robinson writes on versions of the alienated self in the poems, and argues that this is a remediable condition, whereas Hyatt Waggoner's "Cosmic Chill" sees a failure of unified sensibility, especially in the didactic poems where the disjunction between thought and feeling leads to what he calls "an impasse of the soul". Finally, Murphy reprints Levenson's essay on Robinson's modernity (also in the Barnard collection).

The best recent discussion of Robinson is in GRAY, which is sympathetic to the longer poems as well as to the dramatic monologues and the other shorter poems. Gray gives a clear account of Robinson's concern with human isolation and despair in a godless world, and of Robinson's temporising sense that the language we have to use is never quite adequate for the requirements we have of it. He sees the longer poems and the Arthurian versions as moving towards a mode of affirmation that might redeem man's spiritual poverty, and towards an implied sense of order in an otherwise meaningless universe.

LIONEL KELLY

Rochester, John Wilmot, Earl of

1647–1680

English poet

Farley-Hills, David (ed.), *Rochester: The Critical Heritage*, London: Routledge & Kegan Paul, 1978

Farley-Hills, David, *Rochester's Poetry: A Study of Rochester's Poetry*, Totowa, New Jersey: Rowman & Littlefield; London: Bell & Hyman, 1978

Griffin, Dustin H., *Satires Against Man: The Poems of Rochester*, Berkeley: University of California Press, 1973

Thormählen, Marianne, *Rochester: The Poems in Context*, Cambridge and New York: Cambridge University Press, 1993

Vieth, David M., *Attribution in Restoration Poetry: A Study of Rochester's "Poems" of 1680*, New Haven, Connecticut, and London: Yale University Press, 1963

Vieth, David M. (ed.), *John Wilmot, Earl of Rochester: Critical Essays*, New York: Garland, 1988

Rochester's notoriety – as (among other things) a rake, a sensualist, an atheist, and a shockingly obscene poet – began during his lifetime, and until very recent times his writings in whole or in part have been censored, suppressed, or passed over in silence. It has not even been possible to read his complete works in popular editions until the last few decades. Serious critical and scholarly concern with Rochester began in the second quarter of the twentieth century. Today, the old emphasis on biographical stories of vice and dissipation has given way to vigorous debate as to the kind of writer Rochester is and the kind of poetic stature he attains. Within his *oeuvre*, it has been the satires that have attracted most attention.

VIETH's 1963 volume was the first full-scale attempt to establish a canon for Rochester. It is a textual rather than a critical study, but in this case the former kind of work was a prerequisite for the latter. It formed a basis for, and did much to inspire, all subsequent writing on the poet. Vieth's findings on the canon and on the authenticity of the various versions of the texts have required only limited amendment by subsequent scholars.

GRIFFIN's study was the first modern critical monograph on Rochester; as his title indicates, its emphasis falls on Rochester as a satirist. Griffin introduces the poet in a chapter called "The Mind of a Sceptic", but sees Rochester as "a perplexed rather than a dogmatic doubter". The underlying dilemmas in the satires, he suggests, explain Rochester's wide appeal: his anxieties are those of civilized man at large. Griffin also raises issues still to the fore in Rochester criticism concerning the relationship between the poet and the speakers in the poems: he considers the speakers to be partly dramatic voices, exaggerated versions of the poet's own, though not fully distanced *personae*. The poem given most prominence is the *Satyr Against Mankind*, which, Griffin argues, is like all Rochester's best work in being effective not through its thought or formal poise but because of its energy and intensity.

FARLEY-HILLS's monograph (*Rochester's Poetry*) finds Rochester's best work in his satires, but he takes time to divide up the rest into lyrics, burlesques, and lampoons, and brings out the ways in which Rochester modifies the conventions of each genre. "The central preoccupation of Rochester's poetry" is "how to achieve order in a world that is essentially disorderly", and Rochester does so partly, Farley-Hills argues, through the way he handles conventional poetic forms as well as conventional attitudes. The poet's wit can create order out of the inanity of the world around him, and this is how Farley-Hills characterizes the satires. He is stimulating on the lyrics, which he finds "remarkably original", but his categorizations of them – "platonic", "anti-platonic", "libertine" – are unstable, and have not been widely adopted by subsequent critics.

FARLEY-HILLS's *Critical Heritage* volume appeared in the same year. It assembles responses to Rochester from the seventeenth century up to 1903. Much of the material is of only historical interest, but it clearly documents the tide of disapproval from the mid-eighteenth century down to the twentieth – even though the responses from 1850 to 1903 are headed "The Beginnings of Reassessment". It is evident how much Rochester's reputation as a poet suffered in consequence of his personal notoriety. There are some sidelights on Rochester's reputation abroad in the contributions from Pierre Bayle, Voltaire, and Goethe.

VIETH's 1988 collection assembles 17 standard articles from 1958 onwards; most date from the 1970s and early 1980s. Of these, six are general and seven are on the satires (of which five deal with *A Satyr Against Mankind*). Vieth notes that these kinds of study have been disproportionately common, and includes two essays each on the "obscene poems" and the lyrics in a partial attempt to redress the balance. The volume brings together a representative range of British and American critical essays on Rochester, and the opening section of "General Criticism" is a good place to go for a diversity of accounts of his work as a whole.

THORMÄHLEN offers her extensive recent study as an investigation of Rochester's work in relation to its cultural milieux – political, religious, intellectual, and social. She is also helpful on the literary background to the poems. This book is the first monograph on Rochester since those by Griffin and Farley-Hills in the 1970s, and it usefully gathers up some of the scattered strands of Rochester criticism and scholarship produced since those appeared. Like many other critics, Thormählen has trouble finding terms in which to discuss the scabrous and obscene parts of the Rochester *oeuvre*: are they funny, or tasteless, or childish? She concludes that the love lyrics are paradoxical, in that "erotic pleasure is important, but no reasons for its importance are ever advanced". And she is most at ease with the more "philosophical" satires, though here her explanations of the background tend to interfere with full attention to the works as poetry. This book is certainly now the place to begin serious study of Rochester; but Thormählen's work confirms that he stands in an awkward relation to some of the principles of academic literary criticism.

STUART GILLESPIE

Roethke, Theodore 1908–1963

American poet

Balakian, Peter, *Theodore Roethke's Far Fields: The Evolution of His Poetry*, Baton Rouge: Louisiana State University Press, 1989

Blessing, Richard Allen, *Theodore Roethke's Dynamic Vision*, Bloomington: Indiana University Press, 1974

Burke, Kenneth, "The Vegetal Radicalism of Theodore Roethke", in *Sewanee Review*, 58, 1950

La Belle, Jenijoy, *The Echoing Wood of Theodore Roethke*, Princeton, New Jersey: Princeton University Press, 1976

Parini, Jay, *Theodore Roethke: An American Romantic*, Amherst: University of Massachusetts Press, 1979

Sullivan, Rosemary, *Theodore Roethke: The Garden Master*, Seattle: University of Washington Press, 1975

Commentators on Roethke's poetry have typically considered him as part of a group of so-called "Confessional" poets because of the highly personal and idiosyncratic nature of his poetry. Because Roethke used metric forms and other formal devices more often than some other poets labeled "Confessional", criticism on Roethke has tended to focus slightly more on technique (although thematic readings are also important).

Perhaps the best technical study of Roethke's celebrated Greenhouse poems is still BURKE's essay. He carefully analyzes the diction and structure of these poems, its logical form, vocabulary and connotation, grammatical patterns, and lexical sense. Indeed, Burke's reading could be considered a model for analyzing Roethke's poems. Much of the later criticism of the Greenhouse poems is indebted to this essay.

BLESSING provides another excellent study of Roethke's technique. Blessing begins with the proposition, well supported by Roethke's teaching and notebooks, that for Roethke poetry was essentially kinetic, that poems were excess energy, capturing the motion which Roethke saw as the essence of life. The central problem of Roethke's poetry then becomes this question: "given that the poetic eye sees things in motion, given that energy is all, *by what techniques* does one transfer that motion and that energy to the page or to another's ear?" Blessing shows Roethke as growing more versatile in his technique and increasingly competent in using traditional metric forms to contain the energy that was so vital to his art. Blessing's attention to Roethke's earliest work and his use of unpublished notes and manuscripts enhances the usefulness of this excellent technical study.

SULLIVAN provides a sound chronological reading of the major sequence poems (the Greenhouse poems, "The Lost Son", "North American Sequence", "Meditations of an Old Woman"). Sullivan's approach to the poetry and the life is psychological, and relies heavily on Roethke's biography. Unlike many critics who emphasize the formal diversity of Roethke's individual books, Sullivan stresses the thematic continuity of Roethke's poems, providing coherent and contextualized readings of the various sequences. Sullivan finds the unity of Roethke's work in the pattern of rebirth: "the poems regard a perpetual 'journey to the interior,' most often a regression to the foundations of the psyche and a subsequent re-emergence of the self reconstituted and participant in new forms of unity". Like other critics, Sullivan takes the view that Roethke's mental disorders increased his poetic sensitivity.

Roethke showed great evidence of influence from a large group of poets throughout his work, and consequently, there are a great number of studies of such influences. The most important is LA BELLE's. La Belle proves the breadth of Roethke's indebtedness, but argues that his use of other poets was creative, not slavish imitation as some have charged. Her correlations are detailed and heavily documented, as she demonstrates specific sources, including such diverse poets as Dante, John Donne, William Wordsworth, Walt Whitman, T.S. Eliot, and W.B. Yeats, for specific poems. In addition, La Belle traces Roethke's use of other poets through several stages, arguing that "the growth of this poet's mind as he moves from his early lyrics to his final sequences is concomitant with his evolving relationship with his tradition, from his rage against the past to 'the pure serene of memory'". Because it is so thorough and well documented, La Belle's work is essential for any consideration of Roethke's poetic context.

PARINI emphasizes the specifically American nature of Roethke's Romanticism, examining his relationship to American poets from Ralph Waldo Emerson and Walt

Whitman to Wallace Stevens and Eliot. Parini's delineation of Roethke's relationship with his mentors Rolfe Humphries, Louise Bogan, and Stanley Kunitz is especially useful. Parini makes a strong case for Roethke's originality despite the poet's heavy reliance on tradition, and argues for "The Lost Son" sequence as Roethke's central work. Parini claims that the greatness of this sequence "derives from the tension between these two poles . . . the poet's subjective history . . . and the larger arena of shared experience represented by myth and archetypes".

BALAKIAN's readings of the poems identify both evolution and continuity in their themes and techniques, in a well-considered analysis of Roethke's poetic development. Balakian traces an overall shift from self-absorbtion to a concern with union with other human beings. He also provides an interesting discussion of Roethke's relationship with William Carlos Williams. This book is a readable and concise survey of Roethke's career, and could serve well as an introduction to the study of his poetry.

ANGELA VIETTO

Romance

Barron, W.R.J, *English Medieval Romance*, London and New York: Longman, 1987

Brewer, Derek (ed.), *Studies in Medieval English Romances: Some New Approaches*, Cambridge: D.S. Brewer, 1988

Crane, Susan, *Insular Romance: Politics, Faith, and Culture in Anglo-Norman and Middle English Literature*, Berkeley: University of California Press, 1986

Fewster, Carol, *Traditionality and Genre in Middle English Romance*, Cambridge: D.S. Brewer, 1987

Hopkins, Andrea, *The Sinful Knights: A Study of Middle English Penitential Romance*, Oxford: Clarendon Press, 1990; New York: Oxford University Press, 1990

Mehl, Dieter, *The Middle English Romances of the Thirteenth and Fourteenth Centuries*, London: Routledge & Kegan Paul, 1968

Mills, Maldwyn, Jennifer Fellows, and Carol M. Meale (eds.), *Romance in Medieval England*, Cambridge: D.S. Brewer, 1991; Rochester, New York: Boydell & Brewer, 1991

Ramsey, Lee C., *Chivalric Romances: Popular Literature in Medieval England*, Bloomington: Indiana University Press, 1983

From its roots in twelfth-century France, romance rapidly evolved to take centre stage in the European literary tradition. Indeed, so ubiquitous was the form and its associated "matters", that it has long been the critical practice to consider romance across national and linguistic boundaries. Early efforts to distinguish romance from epic and heroic traditions focused on French and Germanic works. In the first half of this century, criticism on sources, analogues, and folk motifs ranged widely through the romance corpus. Specialized studies on particular traditions, most notably the Arthurian, were also comparative in nature. And for a long time, the concentration on comparative analysis in romance criticism tended to slight Middle English romances: because they were later developments than their Continental counterparts, they were often read as epigones, shadowy and disjointed reflections of their more sophisticated originals. Happily, the last quarter of this century has seen a number of studies which read Middle English romance on its own terms, seeking thus to appreciate its own significant contribution to the development of the European romance tradition.

MEHL's 1967 German book was translated into English in 1968. It offers descriptions in varying lengths of almost 40 thirteenth- and fourteenth-century Middle English romances. It omits works by Chaucer and Gower, and it likewise omits most of the Charlemagne and Troy romances. The works considered are grouped according to length, with the exception of a chapter on what the author calls "didactic romances". These groupings reveal one of the most intractable problems in dealing with Middle English romance: that is, how one is to discuss together texts of such disparate form and matter. Mehl provides few solutions to these larger problems, but his book remains a useful guide to those romances with which it deals. The extensive primary bibliography is now somewhat out of date, because many of these romances have been re-edited in recent years, but it can still function as a checklist for basic reading.

BARRON is a more recent survey of the Middle English romance tradition. Like Mehl, Barron faces the problem of classification as his first task. Unlike Mehl, he chooses to follow Jean Bodel's famous grouping according to "matters", with chapters on the Matters of England, France, Rome, and Britain. A further chapter on the "Matter of Romance" explores the question of generic definition, while chapters on the "Nature of Romance" and the "Evolution of European Romance" provide the background necessary for such a discussion. Barron's work is thus more comprehensive than is Mehl's, although individual romances receive less attention than do those that are included in Mehl's study. Barron ably defends English romance against inappropriate expectations raised by readers approaching this corpus from a background of the *roman courtois*, arguing instead that the makers of the tradition "showed their independence in selection of source material, in the radical nature of their redactions, and the freedom with which they intermixed them with native folklore".

Brewer and Mills are both essay collections which, in their variety, offer ample evidence of the richness of the tradition described by Barron. The "*New*" approaches in BREWER are actually not very new; this collection reprints some (very important) older essays, and many of the items in the collection employ traditional approaches, most notably those of folktale criticism, to individual works. The volume is a useful collection of these pieces; of particular importance is the reprint of Derek Pearsall's 1965 article "The Development of Middle English Romance". The MILLS collection exemplifies some of the current preoccupations of romance criticism. Almost half of the papers deal with editorial issues and the larger, cultural problems of manuscript production and contexts. Other cultural factors are represented in essays on audience and on attitudes towards women. Three papers take up the genre problem, exploring the points of continuity between romance, epic, and history.

It remains to examine a few books which are neither surveys nor collections, but rather interpretive works on specific aspects of Middle English romance. RAMSEY's book eschews stylistic and structural analysis in favour of thematic exposition of his body of texts according to thematic patterns; in chapters on topics such as childhood, heroes and heroines, enemies, adventures, family and friends, magic and marvels, he reads Middle English romances as the bestsellers of their age. The effort is somewhat hampered by a failure to define fully the "popular" of his title, or to come to grips with the formal aspects of his texts. FEWSTER, on the other hand, concentrates on formal features in a work that argues that the hallmark of the Middle English romance is self-referentiality, which at times approaches the ironic subversion of the genre itself. CRANE, too, addresses the question of the "Britishness" of her texts, in this case Anglo-Norman romances and their Middle English counterparts. She argues that what she calls "insular" romances are the product of a particular cultural and political situation, which is reflected in the texts, and which thus distinguishes them from their Continental counterparts. The audience for these works was the barony, a group defined by landed power, whose literature represents their self-justification in the face of worsening political and economic conditions between 1066 and 1400. It is the concerns of this group that produce the characteristically "insular" focus on land and family rights in the romances of *Bevis of Hampton* and *Guy of Warwick*. The tastes of this group are also reflected in the didactic, exemplary romances concerning Guy, Amis and Amiloun, and Ysumbras. HOPKINS picks up this thread in a book which explores four Middle English romances – *Guy of Warwick*, *Sir Ysumbras*, *Sir Gowther*, and *Roberd of Cisyle* – as "penitential romance". Her definition of romance notes the range of texts usually encompassed in the term, and argues for a subgenre, one in which the religious and didactic concerns discernible in many Middle English (and other) romances become paramount. Her own focus on the pattern of sin, conversion, and expiation leads to a narrow focus on the four works named; other "religious" romances could certainly have been considered, but the works discussed here are given full and sympathetic treatment.

SIÂN ECHARD

Romance Fiction

Cranny-Francis, Anne, *Feminist Fiction: Feminist Uses of Generic Fiction*, New York: St Martin's Press, 1990; London: Polity Press, 1990

Fowler, Bridget, *The Alienated Reader: Women and Popular Romantic Literature in the Twentieth Century*, Hemel Hempstead, Hertfordshire: Harvester Wheatsheaf, 1991

Modleski, Tania, *Loving with a Vengeance: Mass-Produced Fantasies for Women*, Hamden, Connecticut: Archon Books, 1982; London: Methuen, 1984

Radford, Jean (ed.), *The Progress of Romance: The Politics of Popular Fiction*, London and New York: Routledge & Kegan Paul, 1986

Radway, Janice A., *Reading the Romance: Women, Patriarchy and Popular Culture*, Chapel Hill: University of North Carolina Press, 1984; London: Verso, 1987

Taylor, Helen, "Romantic Readers", in *From "My Guy" to Sci-Fi: Women's Writing in the Post-Modern World*, edited by Helen Carr, London: Pandora, 1989

Thurston, Carol, *The Romance Revolution: Erotic Novels for Women and the Quest for a New Sexual Identity*, Urbana: University of Illinois Press, 1987

Until comparatively recently romance fiction, perhaps because it is seen as a predominantly female genre, attracted less critical interest than other popular forms such as detective fiction or science fiction. Even feminist critics tended to be embarrassed by its apparent acquiescence in the practices and institutions of patriarchy: it was, in Germaine Greer's phrase, "dope for dopes". There is now a willingness from feminist and other critics to read romance fiction for signs of resistance to the dominant culture; an awareness that the genre encompasses the family saga, lesbian romance, and historical romance as well as formula fiction; and an interest in how meaning is shaped in the process of reading.

In her very useful brief introduction to the current state of criticism, TAYLOR outlines the problems involved in understanding romance fiction's enormous appeal for women readers. She argues that feminist criticism must acknowledge the complexity of both genre and readership, citing the "sexy-greedy" novels of Barbara Taylor Bradford as indicative of how the genre responded to the Thatcherite 1980s in Britain. Where the formula romance focuses on private experience, Taylor looks to the family saga for a historically determined sense of change and development, using her own work on Margaret Mitchell's *Gone with the Wind* to indicate the need for more research into readership. Like other critics of the genre, Taylor is very aware of questions not yet answered.

MODLESKI's book was one of the first to apply critical seriousness to the study of female popular fiction. Although she finds omissions and distortions in all of the three popular forms she discusses, Modleski rejects the distinction between "high" and "mass" art that would relegate them to obscurity. She argues instead that Harlequin romances, gothic novels, and soap operas speak to the real tensions, problems, and contradictions in successive stages of women's lives – courtship, marriage, and mothering respectively. Her analyses of all three depend on the idea of the female self as insufficient; thus, while Harlequin romances do register female anger and resistance, the heroine is denied full consciousness of her own motives and desires. Similarly, contemporary gothic novels allow safe expression of female paranoia, while the diffuse and unresolved form of soap operas effectively "disperses" the female spectator. Modleski's incidental readings are persuasive and interesting.

RADFORD's introductory essay justifies the wide range of topics in her collection by arguing for a "historically specific understanding of popular forms and their uses". Instead of seeing popular fiction as merely reproducing dominant ideology, essays such as Alison Light's "Writing Fictions: Femininity and the 1950s" examine the possibilities for transformation. Ann Rosalind Jones's "Mills and Boon Meets Feminism" is sharply specific in its treatment of the language of love scenes, and argues for a more flexible reading experience than the formulaic nature of the genre might suggest.

Its homogeneity of approach gives the book a sense of overall coherence sustained across a stimulatingly wide historical range.

In common with Modleski, RADWAY attempts to rescue popular romance from the charge of merely "recapitulating and recommending" patriarchy. What is distinctive is her investigation of a group of women romance readers, from which she concludes that formula fiction offers women "momentary" refusal of their limiting social roles and, in effect, opportunities to resist their situation as women. She also finds that the romantic hero is seen as nurturing, as well as courting, the heroine. Radway draws quite limited conclusions from these positive readings, finding that romance is radical only within the sphere of the imaginary. It may increasingly allow greater sexual freedom for the heroine, but this remains within limits. Radway concludes that romance articulates a protest that is "minimal but legitimate".

THURSTON makes larger claims than Radway for the radical potential of popular romance, and like the latter she is concerned with the political implications of the genre. Her approach is sociological as much as literary, using content analysis of a wide range of historical and formula romances alongside reader assessments and mail surveys. Her central argument, that the increasingly erotic nature of this fiction functions as a powerful agent of social change, is asserted rather than proved, although she also provides a wealth of detail on the production and consumption of these novels.

Also taking a primarily sociological approach, FOWLER extends the textual range of Thurston and Radway to consider the "non-formulaic but uncanonised" field of the blockbuster: she analyses, among others, Catherine Cookson, Judith Krantz, and Barbara Taylor Bradford, paying particular attention to the historical development of the form. Her critique abandons the "narrow psychoanalytic focus" which foregrounds gender at the expense of class, power, and ethnicity. Typically, she finds in Cookson both a realistic portrayal of working-class experience and a conciliatory, conservative resolution. Fowler sets up a very detailed analysis of women's reading patterns, cultural expectations, and social class: ultimately, however, she concludes that traditional romance colludes with patriarchy to "anaesthetise" lower-class women readers.

CRANNY-FRANCIS examines explicitly feminist reworkings of popular genres such as fantasy, detective fiction, utopian and science fiction, as well as romance. The intention of such revisions is to expose the workings of the essentially conservative genre-text without rendering it unrecognisable as a member of its generic "family". Cranny-Francis acknowledges that of all of her chosen genres feminist romance comes closest to being a contradiction in terms: it subsumes all narrative into the narrative of desire, whose patterns are overwhelmingly male. Feminist writers have yet to establish ways of expressing their own marginalised desires and experience, she argues. This leaves her very little to say on what feminist romance might look like, although Margaret Atwood's *Lady Oracle* and Fay Weldon's *Life and Loves of a She-Devil* are cited as (problematic) possibilities.

CATHERINE WELLS COLE

See also **Popular Fiction for Women**

Romanticism: British

Abrams, M.H., *The Mirror and the Lamp: Romantic Theory and Critical Tradition*, New York: Oxford University Press, 1953
Barfield, Owen, *Romanticism Comes of Age*, London: Anthroposophical Publishing, 1944; revised edition, London: Rudolph Steiner Press, 1965; Middletown, Connecticut: Wesleyan University Press, 1967
Bate, Jonathan, *Romantic Ecology: Wordsworth and the Environmental Tradition*, London and New York: Routledge, 1991
Christiansen, Rupert, *Romantic Affinities: Portraits of an Age, 1780–1830*, London: Bodley Head, 1988
Curran, Stuart (ed.), *Cambridge Companion to British Romanticism*, Cambridge and New York: Cambridge University Press, 1993
Engell, James, *The Creative Imagination: Enlightenment to Romanticism*, Cambridge, Massachusetts: Harvard University Press, 1981
Heller, Erich, *"The Artist's Journey into the Interior" and Other Essays*, New York: Random House, 1965; London: Secker & Warburg, 1966
Hoeveler, Diane L., *Romantic Androgyny: The Women Within*, University Park: Pennsylvania State University Press, 1990
Leask, Nigel, *British Romantic Writers and the East: Anxieties of Empire*, Cambridge: Cambridge University Press, 1992
McFarland, Thomas, *Romanticism and the Forms of Ruin: Wordsworth, Coleridge, and Modalities of Fragmentation*, Princeton, New Jersey: Princeton University Press, 1981
Riasanovsky, Nicholas, *The Emergence of Romanticism*, New York and Oxford: Oxford University Press, 1992

The outstandingly penetrating discussion of the central issues in Romanticism contained in HELLER's provocative book makes it essential background. All the major issues are discussed, and Heller goes deep into discriminating between reason and imagination, realism and idealism, and suggests that these traditional opposites are ultimately not to be seen as enemies but as brokered by a kind of marriage. Prolonged and interesting reflection is also given to the difference between the classical and the Romantic, especially as seen in the Romantics' own day by the highly influential Hegel. Other writers invoked in this book include Nietzsche, Goethe, and Schiller, along with non-literary creative work from painters, sculptors, and architects; for example, the essay entitled "The Romantic Expectation" revolves around the iconically Romantic canvas *Wanderer in the Mists* by Kaspar David Friedrich, relating it to the philosophical, literary, and political context of its time. A wide-rangingly reflective study, with a long sweep into the past and into the modern period (Heller ends by comparing Wittgenstein and Nietzsche) gives this work great value for contextualising, as well as characterising, Romanticism, and entertainingly demonstrates great power of synthesis and enquiry.

Ostensibly about a number of poets, McFARLAND's work is so broad in its range of reference as to be one of the best surveys of the subject available, always excepting ABRAMS' seminal and still indispensable volume. McFarland treats the major Romantic themes in music, the visual arts, and philosophy, as well as in literature and poetry, in England and Europe. "A Complex Dialogue" offers an excellent discussion of the Romantic's treatment of the topos of the Contraries and Polarity. The author's core idea, that Romanticism is diasporactive in character, the Romantic impulse arising in the fragmented or lost particle seeking its origin from the context of the ruin of that original state, brings the Romantic and the modernist aesthetics into meaningful proximity. It offers a more contemporary, and no less intriguing, discussion of the meanings of duality, which are raised in BARFIELD's unusual survey of some key issues.

As penetrating in its individual insights as it is wide in its range of survey, RIASANOVSKY's is an exceptional work, comprising, among other things, a conspectus of nearly all important Romantic criticism, focused closely on the English and Western-European Romantics, although written by a Russianist, and offering a refreshingly bold view of the movement. Its high-minded content is belied by readability and great brevity of expression from one of the intellectual heirs to Isaiah Berlin. Among this survey's many strengths is a careful distinction between pantheism and panentheism, which invites more precise and useful study of the Romantics' interest in the relation between the immanent and the transcendent.

James ENGELL's masterly book is notable for seeing Romanticism as the transformation of the Enlightenment rather than as the result of resistance to it. "The idea of the imagination forms a hinge between the Enlightenment and Romanticism". The book bears out this proposition with studies of many major figures of English and European Romanticism, including Keats, William Hazlitt, Wordsworth, Blake, Shelley, Johann Herder, Johann Fichte, Schiller, Friedrich Schelling, Goethe, Kant, Johann Nicolaus Tetens, Spinoza, Leibniz, David Hume, and Edmund Burke. Engell's special emphasis in the early sections is to treat the role of empiricism with sympathy; for example, Chapter 2 argues that the popularised tabula rasa theory of John Locke is an oversimplification. Engell's is not a Romanticism of casting off, but rather of inheritances and continuities. Broad sweep, detail, and depth characterise this book as much as the sketching of the bare bones characterises Riasanovsky's. Being reserved for the last chapter, Coleridge on imagination is the physical and intellectual apogee of Engell's study, Coleridge himself having imbibed virtually all the sources and traditions previously described.

CHRISTIANSEN explains that the intention to write his book grew "out of the feeling that the wealth of existing textbooks were – well, just not romantic enough, so I here try to portray the temper of an age through the medium of the lives and work of some of its most sensitive consciousnesses". Essays range over the entire period, concentrating in turn on betrayed visions, despondency and madness, the role of the female, European Romanticism, "Shakespearomania", and questions of canonicity. Notable again is an appreciation of the English in relation to the French and German Romantics.

"One of the most obvious facts that confront a reader of Romantic poetry is the profound unreality and amorphousness of the female character . . . at every stage the woman is the projection of the hero's split and ambivalent feminine aspect". HOEVELER's study suggests an explanation of why women in Romantic poetry were both idealised and feared, connected as this was with why the androgynous was both sought and fled. Men need women but they do not want real women, so runs Hoeveler's thesis; they want idealised sexual fantasies, so they create the ideal within themselves and then try to impose it on reality. The fantasy is of course doomed to explode from its own inherent contradictions and unreality. A less forceful case is presented by Meena Alexander in *Women In Romanticism* (London: Macmillan, 1990).

Nigel LEASK sets out to study the work of Byron, Shelley, and Thomas De Quincey, together with a number of other major and minor Romantic writers in relation to Britain's imperial designs on the Orient. It examines the anxieties and instabilities of Romantic representations of the Ottoman Empire, India, China, and the Far East, and argues that these anxieties were not marginal but central to the concerns of British Romantic writers. Substantial chapters on Shelley, Byron, and Coleridge, exemplify, with mention of other writers, the general spirit of Leask's case:

> The subject of this book is the complicities between enlightenment and Empire. . . . History is once again on the agenda, and the political and ideological concerns of poets like Wordsworth, Byron, Shelley and even Keats are now read as being constitutive of their poetry rather than merely background material . . . In mitigation of the dark picture which I am painting of the unbreakable spell of the Other for our constitutional imperial culture and those people subjugated in its name, I am aware of moments, such as environ Shelley's *Prometheus Unbound*, when the relations of power and desire are actively and creatively re-thought against the grain of history.

So the study as a whole is an erudite example of the repoliticisation of Romantic Studies. To those who have a taste for it, it is irreproachable.

BATE's main argument is that attacks on Romanticism fall in with a Left/Right model of politics which is no longer useful. He adds that "in a development parallel to the so-called new historicism in Renaissance Studies, the buzzwords among Romanticists are now history and politics. Terms like vision and imagination so central to the previous generation of critics are now treated with scepticism and often outright hostility". But, another view is on offer here. Wordsworth, for Bate, "articulates a powerful and enduring vision of human integration with nature which exercised a formidable influence on later conservation movements and is of immediate relevance to our current environmental crisis". Challenging the orthodoxies of New-Historicist criticism, Bate sets a new agenda for the study of Romanticism in the 1990s. His book claims to be a "preliminary sketch towards an eco-criticism" and has quickly proved influential. One chapter examines Wordsworth's version of pastoral, while another historicises the notion of ecology and finds important sources for it in Romantic attitudes to the environment. Besides Wordsworth, authors whom this study involves include Coleridge, Keats, John Stuart Mill, Hazlitt, William Morris, and John Clare.

As with most guides, understanding the range of references in CURRAN's depends on having already a considerable knowledge of Romanticism, simply because the contributors' standpoints differ so much. This collection offers valuable material on Blake and the visual; Peter Thorsley's chapter on German Romantic idealism is useful; William Keach's chapter on "Romanticism and Language" highlights contemporary linguistic theory; and there is a due amount of attention – rewardingly given by at least four of the essays – to the perennial wrangle over deciding what Romanticism is, or even whether the term has any useful application. Other matters not left behind are: fiction; women readers and women writers; and the *belle-lettrist* tradition and the role of the review, treated in Marilyn Butler's essay. The survey takes account of the "intersection of competing philosophical traditions, of political and class divisions, of gender distinctions, of high and low, sacred and profane cultures, of battles of the books, and of contested claims among the arts". Quite a lot of emphasis on the contingent, rather than the absolute, exemplifies a characteristically contemporary search "not for truth but for a pertinent place from which to have an effect". In addition, several claims emerge from this book to suggest that Thomas Carlyle is among the Romantics.

PAUL DAVIES

Romanticism and Transcendentalism in America

Buell, Lawrence, *Literary Transcendentalism: Style and Vision in the American Renaissance*, Ithaca, New York: Cornell University Press, 1973

Buell, Lawrence, *New England Literary Culture: From Revolution Through Renaissance*, Cambridge and New York: Cambridge University Press, 1986

Gilmore, Michael, *American Romanticism and the Marketplace*, Chicago: University of Chicago Press, 1985

Irwin, John T., *American Hieroglyphics: The Symbol of the Egyptian Hieroglyphics in the American Renaissance*, New Haven, Connecticut: Yale University Press, 1980

Leverenz, David, *Manhood and the American Renaissance*, Ithaca, New York: Cornell University Press, 1989

Lowance, Mason I., Jr., *The Language of Canaan: Metaphor and Symbol in New England from the Puritans to the Transcendentalists*, Cambridge, Massachusetts: Harvard University Press, 1980

Matthiessen, F.O., *American Renaissance: Art and Expression in the Age of Emerson and Whitman*, London and New York: Oxford University Press, 1941

Miller, Perry (ed.), *The Transcendentalists: An Anthology*, Cambridge, Massachusetts: Harvard University Press, 1950

Myerson, Joel (ed.), *The American Renaissance in New England* (*Dictionary of Literary Biography* series, Volume 1), Detroit: Gale Research, 1978

Porte, Joel, *The Romance in America: Studies in Cooper, Poe, Hawthorne, Melville, and James*, Middletown, Connecticut: Wesleyan University Press, 1969

Porte, Joel, *In Respect to Egotism: Studies in American Romantic Writing*, Cambridge and New York: Cambridge University Press, 1991

Reynolds, David S., *Beneath the American Renaissance: The Subversive Imagination in the Age of Emerson and Melville*, New York: Knopf, 1988

Shulman, Robert, *Social Criticism and Nineteenth-Century American Fictions*, Columbia: University of Missouri Press, 1987

Simon, Myron, and Thornton H. Parsons (eds.), *Transcendentalism and Its Legacy*, Ann Arbor: University of Michigan Press, 1966

Transcendentalism, as both a philosophic and literary movement, which flourished in New England from 1836 to 1860, has attracted numerous scholars and critics, and is generally considered as being, to an extent, part of the nineteenth-century Romantic movement that swept both Europe and America. Despite the usual inclusion of Transcendentalism in the umbrella term of "American Romanticism" – and the necessity for the reader to be aware of areas of overlap – there is a distinctiveness in the groups of writers usually linked with the two terms. "American Romanticism" is conventionally used to refer to a group of writers active during the period from roughly 1815 to 1865, who composed their works under the influence of European Romantics while generally at a distance from Transcendentalism: thus, Charles Brockden Brown, Washington Irving and the Knickerbocker group, William Cullen Bryant, James Fenimore Cooper and the frontier writers, Edgar Allan Poe, William Gilmore Simms, Nathaniel Hawthorne, Herman Melville, the domestic sentimental novelists, and numerous "minor" writers are normally included within the concept of American Romanticism, as are the so-called "fireside poets" – Henry Wadsworth Longfellow, Oliver Wendell Holmes, John Greenleaf Whittier, James Russell Lowell, and others. Important literary texts associated with the Transcendentalist Movement are Henry David Thoreau's *Walden*, Ralph Waldo Emerson's *Essays*, and various works by Bronson Alcott, Margaret Fuller, Jones Very, Theodore Parker, Elizabeth Peabody, and – in some respects – works by Emily Dickinson, Walt Whitman, and Herman Melville. Closely associated with New England Transcendentalism is the Unitarian movement in early American culture.

The following essay discusses those titles about American Romanticism in general before going on to look at some titles concerning the Transcendentalists more specifically.

MATTHIESSEN's monumental study of America's golden age of literature has continued to be perhaps the most influential treatment of American Romanticism, including Transcendentalism. American literature of the period is placed in a cultural setting wherein painters, sculptors, musicians, politicians, and popular artists of the period all aimed to re-create American culture. This work remains one of the best means of getting to know American culture – as well as the aesthetic background for American literature – during the period from 1840 to 1860. Although superseded in some ways, no one interested in American Romanticism or Transcendentalism can afford to ignore this study.

PORTE's 1969 collection is a collection of his essays dealing with Cooper, Poe, Hawthorne, Melville, and James. All the essays are insightful, clearly written, and accessible to both scholars and initiates. Although most of the essays are designed to clarify individual literary works, they are also useful in understanding the entire corpus of the authors' output. Porte observes in his Preface that he has "attempted to show that all these writers created, partially or completely, according to a theory of stylized art – heavily dependent on the use of conventional, or archetypal figures and on symbol, parable, dream, and fantasy – in order to explore large questions . . . about race, history, nature, human motivation, and art". Interestingly Porte apologizes for not including an essay on Melville's *Moby-Dick* in this book dealing with American romance, his defense being that there is a large "amount of expert commentary already available on *Moby-Dick*" that is "impressive and somewhat intimidating."

GILMORE's analysis of market conditions during the Romantic period should be considered alongside Shulman's study. Gilmore deals specifically with the way that conditions in the literary marketplace affected the composition, publication, and reception of Emerson's *Essays*, Thoreau's *Walden*, Hawthorne's *The Scarlet Letter* and *The House of the Seven Gables*, and Melville's *Moby-Dick* and *Bartleby, the Scrivener*. It was the commercialization of culture and society between 1832 and 1860 that helped shape the themes and forms of the American Romantics, according to Gilmore. SHULMAN's study is especially well-informed about the socio-economic changes that occurred in nineteenth-century America, and which subtly influenced the literary artists of that period. It is an exciting look at the ways American authors like Melville, Hawthorne, Whitman, William Dean Howells, and many others responded to the changing market society that increasingly dominated nineteenth-century American life. This is a book designed for those who desire to set important literary texts in their full historical context.

REYNOLDS' study is particularly useful for investigations into the literature that was popular at the time of Hawthorne's *The Scarlet Letter*, Melville's *Moby-Dick*, and Whitman's *Leaves of Grass*. Reynolds traces in detail how popular writing in pre-Civil-War America was both incorporated into literary works and sometimes sublimated by major American writers. Genres such as adventure stories, police gazettes, temperance tracts, pornographic tales, penny newspapers, popular songs, pseudo-scientific speculations – all these and more went into the literature of the American Renaissance, both canonical and popular. Reynolds makes quite clear the fact that a knowledge of nineteenth-century popular culture can enrich our reading of the literary masterpieces of the period. Seminal essays are "Transcendentalism – Transcendentalists, Whitman, and Popular Reform", "The Erotic Imagination", "Transcendental Wild Oats", "Whitman's Poetic Humor", and "The Sensational Press and the Rise of Subversive Literature".

PORTE's 1991 work is a study prepared by a leading scholar and critic of the Romantic Movement, who continues the tradition established by Quentin Anderson in *The Imperial Self* (1971) – a work that attempted to isolate a significant group of major American cultural figures who sought, within the confines of their own individual imaginations, all the riches of the universe, along with all authority and substance, that previously had been found in religious and philosophical values. This study is a reassessment of nineteenth-century American literature, focusing on the general question of the Romantic ego and its varying modalities of self-creation, self-display, self-projection, and self-concealment. Individual chapters deal with Brockden Brown, Irving, Francis Parkman, Cooper, Poe, Emerson, Hawthorne, Thoreau, Melville, Frederick Douglass, Harriet Beecher Stowe, Whitman, and Dickinson. The self as "divinity" is the subject of the investigation. A major disappointment for most readers of this book is that there is no close analysis of Whitman's "Song of Myself", which would seem to be the central text for a study of this type.

MILLER's anthology remains a standard source in the study of American Transcendentalism. Miller sought "to present the atmosphere of the Transcendental period rather than a systematic ordering of the ideas". Included in the anthology (supplemented with Miller's incisive and cogent commentary) are approximately 50 essays, articles, and letters, which reflect the history and doctrines, the religious radicalism, the literary aspirations, and the social and political visions of the American Transcendentalists. Included are selections from Thoreau's journal, excerpts from his poetry and that of Emerson, Bronson Alcott, and Margaret Fuller. Also included are Emerson's thoughts on aristocracy, Thoreau's on a "life without principle," and Fuller's on women in the nineteenth century. Minor Transcendentalists included are Charles Ellis, William Henry Channing, Orestes Brownson, Theodore Parker, and others. Miller presents the Transcendental Movement as "an excitement, an exhilaration, in the course of which a few bold American spirits made a gallant effort to introduce this mercantile and pragmatic nation to some of the deeper currents in the intellectual life of the West – and of the East".

SIMON and PARSONS have edited an important collection of essays on two general topics: "Revaluation" and "The Current". The reader who finishes the entire book will have gained a thorough background in American Transcendentalism. The lasting influence of Transcendentalism on subsequent American authors is made clear. Seminal essays in this collection are Kenneth Burke's "I, Eye, Ay – Emerson's Early Essay *Nature*", Glauco Cambon's "Emily Dickinson and the Crisis of Self-Reliance", and Joe Lee Davis's "Santayana as a Critic of Transcendentalism".

BUELL's 1973 volume is clearly one of the most significant on Thoreau, Emerson, and their circle to appear since Matthiessen's study (discussed above). In his Introduction, Buell states that it is his purpose, "through a combination of intellectual history, critical explication, and genre study . . . to outline the nature and evolution of the Transcendentalists' characteristic literary aims and approaches, and the ways in which these express the authors' underlying principles or vision". Although Emerson and Thoreau are the major concerns of the book, William Ellery Channing is fully discussed, and Buell concludes his study with an important essay on "Transcendental Egoism in [Jones] Very and Whitman".

MYERSON's work, as he observes in the Editor's Note, "contains biographical sketches of ninety-eight authors who participated in the American Renaissance. Represented are writers of short stories, juvenile literature, sermons, and popular literature, as well as novelists, poets, essayists, editors, humorists, translators, compilers, journalists, reformers, abolitionists, scientists, and lexicographers". Special attention is given to Emerson and Thoreau. The essays, all composed by well-qualified scholars, are of high quality. Considerable attention is paid to specific literary texts. An appendix titled "Books for Further Reading" will prove useful to both scholars and general students. Overall, this collection is an excellent introduction to the American Renaissance of 1830–60.

IRWIN's analysis, as he states in his Preface, "begins by examining the impact of the decipherment of the Egyptian hieroglyphics on nineteenth-century American literature", and then, ranging back and forth over literary history, practical criticism of individual works, and speculative criticism, it relates the image of the hieroglyphics to the large reciprocal questions of the origin and limits of symbolization and the symbolization, of origins and ends. Irwin pays most attention to the literary works of Emerson, Thoreau, Whitman, Poe, Hawthorne, and Melville.

LOWANCE's study deals with biblical linguistic usages associated with eschatology and millenialism. The book is especially concerned with the connections between Puritanism and Transcendentalism. Especially important for students of Transcendentalism is the final essay, "From Edwards to Emerson and Thoreau: A Revaluation". Students of the esoteric field of typology will find this study of major importance.

BUELL's 1986 study is regarded as the first truly comprehensive study of the development of New England literary culture and its institutions during the period from the American Revolution through the late 1800s. Buell explores the foundations, the development, and the results of the professionalization of the writing vocation. He pays special attention to the major figures (Emerson, Thoreau, Hawthorne, Beecher Stowe, and Dickinson), who are compared to minor figures, and to the common conventions, values, and institutions that helped shape their writing. It goes without saying that Unitarianism and Transcendentalism are dealt with in extravagant detail.

LEVERENZ's analysis of such nineteenth-century American male writers as Emerson, Hawthorne, Melville, Thoreau, and Whitman demonstrates that they were influenced much more profoundly by the popular model of the entrepreneurial "man of force" than they were by their literary precursors and contemporaries. Leverenz makes skilful use of the insights he has gained from feminist theory, gender studies, psychoanalysis, and social history. He is especially interested in showing that gender pressures and class conflicts played as critical a role in literary creation for the male writers of nineteenth-century America as they did for women writers. Numerous close readings of specific literary texts show how class and gender are inseparable. The treatment of Thoreau's *Walden* is especially acute, while Emersonian Transcendentalism pervades the entire discussion.

JAMES T.F. TANNER

Ross, Sinclair 1908–

Canadian novelist and short-story writer

Chambers, Robert D., *Sinclair Ross and Ernest Buckler*, Vancouver: Copp Clark, 1975

McMullen, Lorraine, *Sinclair Ross*, Boston: Twayne, 1979; revised edition, Ottawa: Tecumsah Press, 1991

Mitchell, Ken, *Sinclair Ross: A Reader's Guide*, Moose Jaw, Saskatchewan: Coteau Books, 1981

Moss, John, *Patterns of Isolation in English Canadian Fiction*, Toronto: McClelland & Stewart, 1974

Moss, John (ed.), *From the Heart of the Heartland: The Fiction of Sinclair Ross*, Ottawa: University of Toronto Press, 1992

Ricou, Laurence, *Vertical Man/Horizontal World: Man and Landscape in Canadian Prairie Fiction*, Vancouver: University of British Columbia Press, 1973

Although he published four novels and a number of short stories, Sinclair Ross's reputation has rested on his novel *As for Me and My House* (1946), which is firmly installed as a Canadian classic. Until very recently, critics considered Ross a prairie realist, generating universal insights through the local and particular. Only recently have readers begun to see more complex and diverse aspects to his work.

RICOU's analysis of the fiction up to *Whir of Gold* (1970) is part of a wider study of Canadian prairie fiction. It is interested in geography less in a regional sense, and more in a metaphysical sense. Ricou invents something he calls "prairie man", a figure experiencing simultaneously a feeling of his/her own importance, upright on a horizontal world, and utter insignificance and vulnerability. Since the prairie is such a challenge to the human imagination, Ricou accords his selected writers a key role in *imagining* the prairie; he is concerned with "subjective landscape". Ross's work, particularly *As for Me and My House*, represents the moment at which the "metaphorical possibilities" of the landscape become fully realized in Canadian fiction. Ricou's discussion is conventional in methodology but, in relating landscape description to theme, character, and moral issues, it demonstrates the reasons why this major novel has become the most celebrated literary work about the Canadian prairie.

MOSS (1974), like Ricou, incorporates discussion of *As for Me and My House* into a wider thematic study of Canadian writing. Emphasizing the classic status of the novel, he is at pains (like Ricou) to see Ross's setting, his characters, and their situations, in broader metaphorical terms, so that he credits Ross with a "geophysical imagination". Moss subjects Mrs Bentley, as character and mediating consciousness, to a rigorous critique, though the irony and ambiguity in narrative tone mitigates the harsher outlines of Moss's criticism. He universalizes the novel, which is "a compelling vision of the human condition", and his own metaphors tend towards the romantic, particularly in the links he draws between the novel and André Gide's *La Symphonie pastorale*, and his repeated figuring of Ross's text in terms of music.

CHAMBERS, writing for a literary guide series, pairs Ross with another Canadian writer, Ernest Buckler, known mainly for a single major novel (*The Mountain and the Valley*, 1952). This is an apt pairing, for Ross and Buckler were born in the same year, both grew up in rural Canada, both began their careers by writing short stories; and for both, belatedly-praised first novels were followed by ones that have failed to gain wide readership and commentary. Chambers makes these similarities critically significant. He says much less about prairie regionalism than he does about character and technique. He notes the thematic potential of the situation of a sensitive young man exposed to rural Canadian experience, and emphasizes the complexity of Ross's vision, his ambiguity of tone, and painstaking psychological analysis of alienated characters. Chambers also relates the literary careers of both Ross and Buckler to the publishing and critical environment in Canada between 1935 and the 1960s.

McMULLEN's book, a volume in the Twayne "World Authors" series, remains the fullest, most comprehensive treatment of Sinclair Ross, and is the first to integrate the late novel *Sawbones Memorial* (1978) into critical discussion. McMullen provides a brief biography/background section, and sets Ross firmly in the context of Canadian fiction writers. Although she follows earlier critics in privileging the short stories published as *"The Lamp at Noon" and Other Stories* (1968) and the novel *As for Me and My House*, she offers full commentary also on *The Well* (1958), *Whir of Gold* (1970), and *Sawbones Memorial*. She considers the last-named work "innovative" in the way it extends technique beyond simple realism. This study combines close reading with contextual density, and confirms that, despite his relatively slight output, Ross continues to deserve attention as a significant novelist working within the regionalist tradition.

Referring those who seek scholarly analysis to McMullen's study, MITCHELL offers a guide for the general reader, concentrating on exposition and thematic underlining. For Mitchell, the strength of Ross's writing is in its emphasis on the universal and "elemental". He also, however, sees the novelist's uncompromising realism and frankness as having inhibited wide acceptance by Canadian readers. Mitchell sees Ross as exemplifying the general condition of Canadian writers in the pre-World-War-II period, noting Ross's belated recognition, his struggle to produce in a period prior to federal subsidies for writers and publishers, his employment in a bank, expatriation, and initial publication outside Canada. For Mitchell, Ross is a writer who has "come into his own". His study devotes a chapter each to the stories, *As for Me and My House*, and *Sawbones Memorial*, treating *The Well* and *Whir of Gold* together in a single chapter. A useful aspect of this book is its reprinting of Ross's first, uncollected story, "Spike".

MOSS's 1992 collection of new essays by various hands represents the first attempt to evaluate Ross in the light of recent theoretical developments. Angela Esterhammer finds Ross's "realism" problematic; Frank Davey discovers complexity in the semiotic signs of the major novel; Helen Buss subjects it to feminist revision, while Wilfred Cude recognizes the book's "dark laughter". The nine contributors, individually and collectively, throw very different and refreshing lights over Ross and his production. The volume is an attempt to locate Ross anew, as someone who writes "from the heart of the Canadian heartland" yet who is not the "quintessential Canadian novelist".

PATRICK HOLLAND

Rossetti, Christina 1830–1894

English poet

Harrison, Antony H., *Christina Rossetti in Context*, Chapel Hill: University of North Carolina Press, 1988; Brighton, Sussex: Harvester Press, 1988

Kent, David A. (ed.), *The Achievement of Christina Rossetti*, Ithaca, New York: Cornell University Press, 1987

Marsh, Jan, *Christina Rossetti*, London: Jonathan Cape, 1994; New York: Viking, 1995

Mayberry, Katherine J., *Christina Rossetti and the Poetry of Discovery*, Baton Rouge: Louisiana State University Press, 1989

Rosenblum, Dolores, *Christina Rossetti: The Poetry of Endurance*, Carbondale: Southern Illinois University Press, 1986

After a long period characterized by a dearth of critical study and an overabundance of biography, scholarly interest in Christina Rossetti has been given new impetus by R.W. Crump's variorum edition of *The Complete Poems of Christina Rossetti* (1979–90).

ROSENBLUM's book-length feminist study considers Rossetti specifically as a female poet, and suggests that Rossetti mythologizes the female consciousness of being seen, creating the figure of the enduring stone-woman who is both spectacle and witness, the watcher watched. Rosenblum links Rossetti with the "sentimental" tradition of Felicia Hemans and L.E.L. (Letitia Landon), and with the "aesthetic of renunciation", which embraces denial and "self-canceling states of being", arguing that Rossetti evolved her own "poetry of endurance" out of this tradition. Rossetti, says Rosenblum, engages the male artistic tradition in a deliberately parodic fashion, intentionally adopting and critiquing its reification of women. Rosenblum examines Rossetti's female figures (mothers, daughters, sisters, brides, nuns, corpses, ghosts), and dedicates a full chapter to the pattern of desire, loss, and renunciation, and the figure of the nun who turns renunciation into valediction. Considerable attention is given to *Goblin Market*, reading it in the context of recurring motifs in Rossetti's other poems – gardens and anti-gardens, appetite and sufficiency, the self as ungerminating kernel-stone and fruit-bearing tree. Rosenblum cogently argues a thesis that serves to unify Rossetti's *oeuvre*; the drawback is that her study tends at times to be narrow.

KENT's collection consists of 13 essays, an Introduction, and Afterword, and the variety of critical approaches represented here enables a broader view of the poet than is offered in any other single book. Kent offers good coverage of Rossetti's writing, including essays devoted to her less-studied devotional prose and writing for children, as well as important studies of Rossetti's major works: of particular interest are D.M.R. Bentley's reading of *Goblin Market*, suggesting the relevance of Rossetti's work with "fallen" women, and William Whitla's groundbreaking examination of "Monna Innominata" and its questioning of sonnet conventions. In his "Afterword", G.B. Tennyson states the need to recognize the centrality of religion in Rossetti's art, and in this collection Rossetti's devotional writing in poetry and prose is given sustained critical attention in five essays. Furthermore, feminist concerns are evident in many of these essays and are central to contributions by Betty S. Flowers, Diane D'Amico, and Rosenblum. An important element in Kent is the desire to place Rossetti's work within the literary tradition, that is, in the context of predecessors (George Herbert, the Romantics, Dante, Petrarch) and contemporaries (the Tractarians, the Pre-Raphaelite Brotherhood).

HARRISON's ambitious study, informed by the methodologies of the New Historicism, reception theory, and feminist criticism, analyzes a range of major intellectual and aesthetic influences on Rossetti. Seeing Rossetti as a sophisticated and original artist, Harrison argues that Rossetti's writing is often deliberately self-reflexive and parodic, and boldly suggests that she is a key figure in the transition between Victorian and modern modes. Harrison begins by asserting that Rossetti was a "determined and careful artist", showing how her letters demonstrate her commitment to her poetic vocation, and citing the revisions documented in Crump's variorum edition as evidence that Rossetti was not the artless, spontaneous writer her brother described. He places Rossetti in the context of Pre-Raphaelitism, explores the influence on her of both Tractarian and Ruskinian aesthetics, and pays special attention to Rossetti's navigation of the opposing currents of renunciation and aestheticism. In an important reading of "Monna Innominata", Harrison interprets that "sonnet of sonnets" as a critique of Rossetti's own Victorian culture and also as a continuation and a revision of the amatory tradition exemplified by Dante and Petrarch.

Commenting on the lack of New-Critical treatment of Rossetti's poetry, MAYBERRY sets out to fill this gap in Rossetti scholarship; however, she states at the outset that she will not limit herself to close reading, but will also consider important biographical and historical contexts. Mayberry is particularly interested in Rossetti's commitment to her art in the context of a society in which such a choice was unconventional, and hypothesizes that Rossetti's poetry enacted a transformation of the pain and confusion of the raw material of life into the beauty and order of art. Mayberry devotes a chapter to reading *Goblin Market* as Rossetti's "detailed definition of her own poetics", and the final chapter's succinct summary of Tractarian influences on Rossetti's art is most helpful. While not as sophisticated as Harrison's or Kent's study, Mayberry's provides a clear and engaging introduction to Rossetti's work.

MARSH's sensitive and insightful study supersedes the long line of previous biographies through original research and a feminist sensitivity to the specific limitations placed on Victorian women. The most controversial element here is Marsh's speculative hypothesis that sexual trauma was the cause of Rossetti's adolescent breakdown and the periods of depression of her adult life. This conjecture is judiciously handled: it is persuasively presented but not forced on the reader; most importantly, the study's many other original insights do not depend on the reader's acceptance of this theory: Marsh does not read every poem in terms of an hypothesis that is, by its nature, practically unprovable. In limiting her application of this conjecture Marsh avoids the blunder at the heart of Lona Mosk Packer's otherwise original and useful biography (1963). There are readings of all the major poems here, and Marsh also offers close and revealing readings of works that have been less studied – the fiction, the writing for children, and the devotional prose. There is much original research here, which serves to set Rossetti in the context of a women-writers' literary scene and tradition. The focus is on Rossetti not as repining lover or reclusive saint, but as a professional writer, and the detailed backdrop of Victorian politics and sensibilities helps the reader situate Rossetti properly in her age.

MARY ARSENEAU

Rossetti, Dante Gabriel 1828–1882

English poet

Boos, Florence Saunders, *The Poetry of Dante Gabriel Rossetti: A Critical Reading and Source Study*, The Hague: Mouton, 1976

Cooper, Robert M., *Lost on Both Sides:Dante Gabriel Rossetti: Critic and Poet*, Athens: Ohio University Press, 1970

Howard, Ronnalie Roper, *The Dark Glass: Vision and Technique in the Poetry of Dante Gabriel Rossetti*, Athens: Ohio University Press, 1972

Johnston, Robert D., *Dante Gabriel Rossetti*, New York: Twayne, 1969

Rees, Joan, *The Poetry of Dante Gabriel Rossetti: Modes of Self-Expression*, Cambridge and New York: Cambridge University Press, 1981

Riede, David G., *Dante Gabriel Rossetti and the Limits of Victorian Vision*, Ithaca, New York: Cornell University Press, 1983

Riede, David G., *Dante Gabriel Rossetti Revisited*, New York: Twayne, 1992; Oxford: Macmillan International, 1992

Vogel, Joseph F., *Dante Gabriel Rossetti's Versecraft*, Gainesville: University of Florida Press, 1971

The critical reputation of the Victorian poet-painter Dante Gabriel Rossetti has risen and fallen a number of times. His early fame in his own time was as a painter, one of the founding members of the Pre-Raphaelite Brotherhood. Then came a period later in the century when his poetry was in the ascendency, so that someone like the laureate John Masefield could proclaim "Oh, but when I was a young poet we all looked upon Rossetti as the life force of poetry". After a fallow period, during which the only interest seemed to be in the more lurid details of his private life, Rossetti has re-emerged in the second half of the twentieth century as a more complex figure, the poet-painter whose achievement in one art is inseparable from his achievement in the other. But even here the critical tides have risen, especially in the two decades from the mid-1960s to the mid-1980s, and then fallen. And always – fortunately for our purposes here – the scholarly analyses of the poetry have been more numerous than those of the visual artistry. The tendency in more recent times has been to put aside the biographical obsessions that drove earlier generations in favor of more careful investigations of Rossetti the poetic craftsman.

Two books, both parts of the same "English Authors" series, serve as general introductions to Rossetti's work as a poet.

JOHNSTON's work, the earlier of the two, posits a tension between the flesh and the spirit as the key to a successful reading of the poetry, and as the inspiration for Rossetti's best work. However it manifests itself – the figures of Beatrice, Mary, and Love representing the spirit, for example, or the figures of Helen and Lilith representing the flesh – this tension gives a consistency to all of Rossetti's work, despite the darkening tone and the narrowing range, which characterize the later poems. Johnston, after a biographical overview, arranges his book into an approximately chronological survey, starting with the Italian background and then moving through the sonnets of *The House of Life* (two chapters), the narrative poems, and the final works. Rossetti, he argues, lacked objectivity and the ability to believe and commit; thus he failed to achieve transcendence, so that his greatest gift came to be his ability to inspire later poets such as the Aesthetes and, most particularly, W.B. Yeats.

RIEDE (1992) goes over much of the same ground as Johnston, and according to a similar organizational plan, but he offers more information about the paintings, and he advances a different thesis: that Rossetti tried to become the apotheosis of the Romantic legend of the artistic genius, one whose devotion to the idea of the artist's vocation led to the cult of the absolute autonomy of art. Riede counter-argues, from a characteristically modern perspective, that Rossetti's art should be understood in the context of "the material conditions of [its] history". Rossetti wished to remove art from the "mundane, vulgar world of commodity production", but ironically created an environment in which the artist himself became a commodity, so that he obscured his greatest skill, namely his superb craftsmanship. Riede accepts the current diminished role of Rossetti as poet.

A focus on Rossetti as poetic craftsman can link six books of criticism, all of which concentrate on the poetry and treat it in a serious way.

COOPER, agreeing with Johnston that Rossetti's poetry evidences few changes as time goes by, disagrees about the value of its animating tensions. Where for Johnston such tensions lead to Rossetti's greatest achievements, for Cooper the poet's attempt to "embrace both sides of every conflict" leads to imprecision and loss of direction. The book's major strength is the survey it gives of Rossetti's critical opinions and ideas about poetry. The author shows that Rossetti valued "fundamental brainwork" and the mastery of technique but contends that the poet failed many of his own standards.

VOGEL, writing on Rossetti's versification, proceeds on the quite contrary assumption that he was an excellent prosodist. The book offers sections on meter, on stanzaic forms, and on rhymes and other sound echoings, and concludes with a lengthy appreciation of the prosody of "The Blessed Damozel". While Vogel's analysis will be too technical for some readers, and while his dependency on statistics may smack of Gradgrindism, he always asks, of the traits he identifies, what differences they make in our interpretation of the poems themselves.

A concern with "the poems as art" also governs HOWARD's book. She traces the poet's themes and techniques chronologically from the late 1840s to the early 1880s, seeing a wider range of both than had been allowed previously. The poems need not be read autobiographically: the reader must recognize their many *personae*, forms, and meters, and also their characteristic themes such as the destructiveness of the libido, regret for the past, and "isolation, betrayal, [and] fate". All of these form parts of a larger vision according to which life is inherently mysterious, at times beautiful but always disappointing. Howard argues that the poems can be read as attempts to see through the "dark glass" of which St Paul speaks. Sometimes, as in moments of love, one can achieve this transcendence, but the glimpse beyond will be – must be – a momentary thing.

Part of any appreciation of Rossetti's technique must include a recognition of his indebtedness to other poets. BOOS, organizing her book around the *House of Life* sonnets, the narrative ballads, and the reflective and lyrical poetry, shows Rossetti's progressive adjustments to contemporary poetic taste, his relationships with other contemporary poets, his sources in earlier poetry, and his poetic preferences and prejudices; she also gives critical readings of many of the poems. Methodologically she uses a "linguistic" approach. She also places Rossetti's "woman-motif" and use of nature in their historical and sociological contexts – in short, she makes him a man of the Victorian age rather than some medieval dreamer born out of his due time.

REES also sees the poet as a true Victorian. By investigating Rossetti's "patterns of thought and imagination" she hopes to discover and define the modes of self-expression that were both his glory and his chief limitation. Rees sees the poet as more intelligent, especially about psychological processes, than has often been believed. His vocabulary of images, often grounded in this psychology, and his partiality for Dante and for the form of the sonnet all became modes of self-expression. Like Johnston and Cooper, Rees sees little evolution in Rossetti's career as a poet, since all of these modes of self-expression were present in his work at least incipiently when he began his career at the age of 19.

But RIEDE (1983) takes issue with Johnston, Cooper, and Rees: Rossetti *did* evolve as a poet, he *did* change and grow until he reached a creative peak at about age 40. Riede's most important contribution is his careful study of Rossetti's revisions. He tries to show that those revisions had specific directions, for example toward a "darker, more skeptical view of Christianity", wherein the poet expunged references to Christ and replaced them with the vaguer figure of "Love". Riede also wishes to rebut any notion of an animating tension coming from Rossetti's dual roles as painter and as poet. Rossetti did try to synthesize them, but failed, and thus widened the gap between the sister arts. Riede divides Rossetti's poetic career into three major phases, of which the second represents the best work. Rossetti's strengths, the author contends, are his careful observation of particulars and his widening of the subject matter for poetry. But these strengths must be placed against his deadly fondness for abstractions and his failed attempts to escape the narrow chamber of the individual mind. Rossetti's achievement – and this seems to be the current consensus about him – is real, but limited.

FRANCIS L. FENNELL

Roth, Philip 1933–

American novelist and short-story writer

Baumgarten, Murray, and Barbara Gottfried, *Understanding Philip Roth*, Columbia: University of South Carolina Press, 1990
Bloom, Harold (ed.), *Philip Roth*, New York: Chelsea House, 1986
Halio, Jay L., *Philip Roth Revisited*, New York: Twayne, 1992
Jones, Judith P., and Guinevera A. Nance, *Philip Roth*, New York: Frederick Ungar, 1981
Lee, Hermione, *Philip Roth*, London and New York: Methuen, 1982
McDaniel, John N., *The Fiction of Philip Roth*, Haddonfield, New Jersey: Haddonfield House, 1974
Milbauer, Asher Z., and Donald G. Watson (eds.), *Reading Philip Roth*, New York: St Martin's Press, 1988; London: Macmillan, 1988
Pinsker, Sanford, *The Comedy That "Hoits": An Essay on the Fiction of Philip Roth*, Columbia: University of Missouri Press, 1975
Pinsker, Sanford (ed.), *Critical Essays on Philip Roth*, Boston: G.K. Hall, 1982
Rodgers, Bernard F., Jr., *Philip Roth*, Boston: Twayne, 1978
Searles, George J., *The Fiction of Philip Roth and John Updike*, Carbondale: Southern Illinois University Press, 1985
Searles, George J. (ed.), *Conversations with Philip Roth*, Jackson: University Press of Mississippi, 1992

One of the most highly praised and consistently inventive writers of his generation, Philip Roth has also been one of the most controversial. The Jewish response to his first book, *Goodbye, Columbus* (1959), and to his fourth, his breakthrough novel *Portnoy's Complaint* (1969), was often critical, and occasionally hostile. Rather than accede to his critics' view of the proper role of the Jewish-American writer, Roth found in their response the stimulus for his less narrowly realist and more playfully intricate later work, in which he examines the relation between art and life, the writer and his work, within the context of his earlier interest in the difficulty faced by the American writer as he tries "to understand, describe, and then make credible" an already fantastic reality that easily outstrips his imaginative resources.

For McDANIEL the important struggle in Roth's fiction is artistic rather than religious. Following a preliminary chapter on Roth's "Artistic Stance", he discusses the "activist hero" of the early fiction, the "victim hero" of the later work, and the combination of types after *Portnoy's Complaint*, reaching "the tentative conclusion" that "Roth may best be assessed, in broad terms, as a writer whose artistic intentions are 'moral,' whose artistic method is 'realistic,' and whose central artistic concern is with man *in* society".

Briefer, more insightful, and more engagingly written, PINSKER's 1975 study emphasizes the Jewish sources of Roth's humor and the ways in which Roth plays public against private and "scathing satire" against "self-abasement" in his search for a technique of confession and concealment, which will enable him both to express and to transcend the "'hoit'". Clearly an admirer, Pinsker nonetheless feels that this immensely talented writer "has not yet been tested by a subject big enough to demand as much from his heart as we have come to expect from his mouth". The parts of this study that deal with *Goodbye, Columbus* and *Portnoy's Complaint* reappear in Pinsker's *Jewish-American Fiction, 1917–1987* (1992), along with discussion of the later novels *The Ghost Writer* and *Zuckerman Bound*.

Contending that the emphasis on Roth as a Jewish-American writer has caused other, equally important aspects of the fiction to be "consistently ignored or obscured", RODGERS reads Roth in the context of his non-Jewish contemporaries. His Roth is an experimental realist devoted to "finding subjects and techniques which will reveal the effect of the interpenetration of reality and fantasy in the lives of his representative Americans". Rodgers discusses Roth's literary sources at length and, unlike Pinsker, stresses the "developmental logic" of Roth's "otherwise diverse fictions". Thorough and intelligent, Rodger's book represents Twayne's "United States Authors" series at its very best. The same cannot be said of HALIO's follow-up volume. Halio's thesis – that Roth is essentially a comic, rather than specifically a Jewish-American writer – is sound enough, but his discussions of all the fiction and nonfiction (through *Patrimony*) amount to little more than summaries of the works themselves. The book's chief virtues are its comprehensiveness and annotated bibliography.

JONES and NANCE offer a more incisive critical assessment. Noting Roth's tendency to discuss his own work in a detached, almost academic way, and his ability to make his fiction both pleasurable and moral, they concentrate on the evolution of his art in relation to his thematic interest in the normal process of maturation, i.e., the struggle between conformity and personal identity, a struggle that "assumes many guises in Roth's fiction".

Page for page, LEE's brief study is arguably the best book, introductory or otherwise, yet written on Roth. Contending that for Roth "the registering of contemporary subject-matter involved the radical reworking of fictional forms", Lee identifies three thematic aspects of Roth's development: from "Jewish cultural ghetto to wider, if alien, spaces", from 1950s' innocence to 1980s' skepticism, and from "anecdotal realism" to various kinds of literary play. More specifically, Lee takes up the issue of "Jewish sons, adults, and novelists", before moving on to Roth's depiction of "vertiginous" postwar American reality, and finally the part "mentors, doubles and literary influences [play] in the search for self". Even as she praises Roth – especially his panache and his "welding" of inner voice to external reality – Lee is mindful of the limitations of his art.

The strength of SEARLES's book is the way in which he uses two seemingly very different writers (John Updike and Roth), in terms of background, temperament, and style, to highlight each other's achievement and, more especially, a shared concern for "the state of society" and the alienation of characters deprived of "the traditional pieties and received wisdom that sustained earlier generations". Searles provides a good overview of various aspects of Roth's style, but his view of Roth as "essentially a social realist, a novelist of manners" proves somewhat limiting, particularly as it leads him to undervalue Roth's "experimental phase".

Part of a series aimed at students and general readers, BAUMGARTEN and GOTTFRIED's book provides a solid introduction to Roth's career and major themes. Seeing him as "a writer who focuses on contradictions" and who subverts the "central ideal of American culture" – i.e., character – they emphasize Roth's "thick descriptions" of the modern world (the phrase is Clifford Geertz's) and his portrayal of characters who can neither change their world nor "embrace suffering as their destiny". In addition to discussing the fiction, the authors devote a separate chapter to Roth's critical and autobiographical writings, and append a very useful annotated bibliography.

The three collections of essays on Roth differ in approach, complementing, rather than competing with, each other. In addition to his survey of the critical response to Roth, PINSKER (1982) offers a judicious selection of 14 reviews (through *The Ghost Writer*) and 14 essays (three published here for the first time). Most of the essays focus on Roth's problematic Jewishness (see especially Kazin, Shechner, and Isaac), while others concern such topics as male-female relations and the Americanness of Roth's humor. Although there is some overlap (Hyman, Tractenberg, Guttman, Solotaroff's "personal view," and Irving Howe's important – albeit remarkably obtuse – downward "reassessment" of Roth's achievement), BLOOM's collection includes fewer reviews and five discussions drawn from books (McDaniel, Pinsker, Lee, Mary Allen on Roth's female characters, and Tony Tanner from his influential study of postwar American fiction, *City of Words*). Inclusion of Bruno Bettelheim's "Portnoy Psychoanalyzed" and Roth's essay-story "'I Always Wanted You to Admire My Fasting'; or, Looking Into Kafka" add to the collection's overall usefulness and importance.

MILBAUER and WATSON's collection comprises 13 items (12 of them new, the other, by Milan Kundera, translated here for the first time). The focus, according to the editors, is on reading Roth's fiction anew, paying greater attention to the works and less to Roth and the controversy that has surrounded him from the beginning of his career. Topics covered include Roth's fascination with asceticism, the quest motif, the drama of incomplete transformation, incorporation of show business material, repression, and the social/literary construction of the self. Especially noteworthy are Hana Wirth-Nesher's excellent discussion of "Roth's Place in American-Jewish Literary Tradition", Jonathan Brent's essay on *Zuckerman Bound*, and the editors' interview with Roth. This last also appears in SEARLES's 1992 volume, which reprints 38 of the 50 or so interviews that appeared between 1960 and 1991, and which includes the editor's brief but useful analysis of the Roth who emerges from the conversations.

ROBERT A. MORACE

Rushdie, Salman 1947 –

Indian-born English novelist

Afzal-Khan, Fawzia, *Cultural Imperialism and the Indo-English Novel: Genre and Ideology in R.K. Narayan, Anita Desai, Kamala Markandaya and Salman Rushdie*, University Park: Pennsylvania State University Press, 1993

Brennan, Timothy, *Salman Rushdie and the Third World: Myths of the Nation*, London: Macmillan, 1989; New York: St Martin's Press, 1989

Harrison, James, *Salman Rushdie*, New York: Twayne, 1992

Parameswaran, Uma, *The Perforated Sheet: Essays on Salman Rushdie's Art*, New Delhi: Affiliated East-West Press, 1988

Rao, M. Madhusudhana, *Salman Rushdie's Fiction: A Study ("Satanic Verses" Excluded)*, New Delhi: Sterling, 1992

Ruthven, Malise, *A Satanic Affair: Salman Rushdie and the Wrath of Islam*, London: Chatto & Windus, 1990; revised edition, London: Hogarth Press, 1991

Sardar, Ziauddin, and Merryl Wyn Davies, *Distorted Imagination: Lessons from the Rushdie Affair*, London: Grey Seal, 1990

Taneja, G.R., and R.K. Dhawan (eds.), *The Novels of Salman Rushdie*, New Delhi: Indian Society for Commonwealth Studies, 1992

Commentary about Salman Rushdie is divided into two distinct strains: criticism of his fiction, which discusses his political notoriety only as it relates to a literary context; and polemics on the controversy surrounding *The Satanic Verses*. With few exceptions, all post-1989 critical works address the issue of the controversy at least peripherally. The criticism involves a wide range of approaches, from thematically-oriented humanist arguments to readings drawing on current postcolonial and postmodern theories.

PARAMESWARAN has collected her own essays covering *Grimus*, *Shame*, and *Midnight's Children*, with the last receiving the most attention. There is considerable verbatim repetition among the essays, and the author acknowledges that they are "simplistic" in approach: that is, they do not engage contemporary theory. While Parameswaran's focus on "universal" themes, recurrent metaphors (the "sheet" of the title), and leitmotifs may initially seem outmoded, her insights are occasionally striking; for example, she describes Rushdie's style as making "the history of India read[s] like a family album".

BRENNAN treats Rushdie not as an individual artist *per se*, but rather as the representative *par excellence* of a group of international writers whom he dubs the "cosmopolitans". Working out of Edward Said, Fredric Jameson, and Antonio Gramsci, Brennan critiques the cosmopolitans (among whom number Gabriel García Márquez, Carlos Fuentes and Bharati Mukherjee) for their collusive role as Third-World authors who, as intellectual élitists, serve up palatable "pop" images of their nations for the First World to consume. In particular, Rushdie is attacked as an "Orientalist" who callously parodies holy texts and ridicules immigrants through stereotyping. Although it is startling to come upon a critic who so openly reviles his subject, Brennan's study is provocative and essential reading for all Rushdie scholars.

RUTHVEN has written a defence of Rushdie and *The Satanic Verses* in the wake of the controversy. As a non-Muslim British commentator on Islam, Ruthven is an informed source who nonetheless is predisposed to exonerate Rushdie. Ruthven's quarrel with the handling of the "affair" has to do with what he sees as the overly rigid, improper, and politically expedient application of Islamic law in this case, and with the wilful disregard of context, the failure to respect the "fictionality of fiction". Despite its clear bias, his book is especially valuable for its review of Islamic history and for its in-depth look at the response of the Muslim community in Britain.

SARDAR and DAVIES, conversely, justify the condemnation of *The Satanic Verses*, though they stop short of supporting the *fatwa*. Their argument centres on the fact that the "insult" of Rushdie's text came at a time when Western anti-Islamic sentiment was on the increase, and Islamic oppression under this "distorted" orientalist image had become unbearable. Through an "alternative" reading of Western history from an Islamic perspective, Sardar and Davies set out to prove that secularism is the privileged religion of the postmodern world, and, further, that Rushdie deliberately and maliciously seeks, through his novel, to impose this nihilistic theology on the faithful. The authors claim the purpose of their book to be the opening of dialogue and mutual understanding, but their tone often becomes shrilly offensive, such as when they call the *literati* who defend Rushdie's freedom of literary expression "a group of omnipotent/helpless children with weak egos and socially distorted super-egos".

HARRISON's study is the finest general survey of Rushdie's work and life. While cognizant of the contentious nature of Rushdie's work, Harrison approaches his subject fairly and respectfully, concentrating on literary achievement instead of politics. After a brief biography and general background of Indian history, Harrison devotes a chapter to each of Rushdie's novels, examining narrative point of view, social satire, and postmodern technique. For *The Satanic Verses*, Harrison usefully explicates and interrelates the dream sequences, which can be difficult to follow without guidance. Those dealing with Rushdie's work for the first time will find Harrison's book particularly helpful.

RAO's short critical study (which purposely excludes *The Satanic Verses*) begins with a prolix and rather confusing "preamble", but continues relatively clearly thereafter. Rao's key idea is that Rushdie's writing is only superficially political, and that it is really concerned with the abstract universal theme of "timelessness". Rao identifies timelessness in each of *Grimus*, *Midnight's Children*, and *Shame* as a "superstructure" overlaying the "real" events represented; the individual in Rushdie's work transcends chronological time, he contends, through the spiritual quest for identity, which takes the form of imagination, fantasy, dreaming and memory. This somewhat murky thesis is repeated in several different ways, often with reference to the manifestation of Rushdie's "dreaming self" in his writing. As an exclusively humanistic treatment of Rushdie's novels, Rao's book stands as a counterbalance, though an under-theorized one, to the politicized accounts.

TANEJA and DHAWAN have collected 24 articles, mostly by Indian scholars, on Rushdie's books, including the children's tale *Haroun and the Sea of Stories*, the non-fictional political memoir *The Jaguar Smile*, and the essay collection *Imaginary Homelands*. *The Satanic Verses* is not mentioned at all except in the context of Haroun. Since it has no Preface or Introduction, Taneja and Dhawan's study does not account for this almost complete omission; it also lacks an articulated thesis linking the articles. On the whole, the articles are thematic in nature, dealing with time, history, India, etc. Ron Shepherd's article "*Midnight's Children* as Fantasy" is a central piece of Rushdie criticism, and more easily accessible here than in its original journal publicaton.

AFZAL-KHAN's chapter on Rushdie situates him as a post-colonial writer relative to his Indian contemporaries. The chapter is best read in context of Afzal-Khan's Introduction, in which she explains how post-colonial writers use genre as what Fredric Jameson calls a "strategy of liberation" to resist the "containment" of orientalism. Rushdie's hybrid mixture of fantasy and realism is seen as an effective strategy to deconstruct ideological binaries; *The Satanic Verses* is praised as a response to inflexible thinking. Among postcolonial critics, Afzal-Khan's attitude toward Rushdie's work is refreshingly broad-minded.

LYNN S. WELLS

Ruskin, John 1819–1900

English prose writer and essayist

Anthony, P. D., *John Ruskin's Labour: A Study of Ruskin's Social Theory*, Cambridge and New York: Cambridge University Press, 1983

Landow, George P., *The Aesthetic and Critical Theories of John Ruskin*, Princeton, New Jersey: Princeton University Press, 1971

Miller, J. Hillis, "Catachresis, Prosopopoeia, and the Pathetic Fallacy: The Rhetoric of Ruskin", in *Poetry and Epistemology: Turning Points in the History of Poetic Knowledge*, edited by Roland Hagenbüchle and Laura Skandera, Regensburg, Germany: Friedrich Pustet, 1986

Miller, J. Hillis, "*Praeterita* and the Pathetic Fallacy", in *Victorian Connections*, edited by Jerome J. McGann, Charlottesville: University Press of Virginia, 1989

Millett, Kate, "The Debate over Women: Ruskin versus Mill", in *Victorian Studies*, 4, 1970

Rosenberg, John D., *The Darkening Glass: A Portrait of Ruskin's Genius*, New York: Columbia University Press, 1961; London: Routledge & Kegan Paul, 1963

Sawyer, Paul L., *Ruskin's Poetic Argument: The Design of the Major Works*, Ithaca, New York: Cornell University Press, 1985

Spear, Jeffrey L., *Dreams of an English Eden: Ruskin and His Tradition in Social Criticism*, New York: Columbia University Press, 1984

Wheeler, Michael (ed.), John Ruskin issue of *Nineteenth-Century Contexts*, 18(2), 1994

Wihl, Gary, *Ruskin and the Rhetoric of Infallibility*, New Haven, Connecticut, and London: Yale University Press, 1985

Victorian scholars in the 1960s and 1970s successfully established Ruskin as a Victorian "sage" writer – a master of non-fiction, whose highly nuanced prose style conveyed trenchant social criticism, ethical sensitivity, aesthetic education, and cultural guidance to a growing middle-class reading public. Criticism in this period focused on questions of intellectual history, rhetorical strategy, and biographical development. Such scholarship begins with ROSENBERG's study. This book treats the growth and development of Ruskin's ideas as a narrative, incorporating primarily the literary evidence, but also biographical and historical detail, in order to tell a story of the changes in his beliefs. Rosenberg approaches Ruskin as a "genius", a term that is seldom invoked uncritically in contemporary scholarship, but despite the sense of anomaly that accompanies this term, his work survives as a perceptive and convincing description of the main concerns in Ruskin's intellectual life.

LANDOW's approach combines insights into Ruskin's aesthetic and religious ideas. Landow takes the contrast between Ruskin's definitions of "typical" and "vital" beauty as emblematic of the pervasive tensions in his corpus, tensions that are, in Landow's opinion, a generative source of Ruskin's ideas and of the unique prose style in which he expressed them. He articulates these tensions as two-fold: on the one hand, they are rooted in the "bifurcated" aesthetics of the neoclassical and emotionalist traditions, and, on the other hand, they are representative of Ruskin's conflictual attraction to both Evangelical moralism and a subjective, emotionally-based response to beauty. In building his case, Landow brings a considerable knowledge of both Victorian aesthetics and biblical typology to bear upon his subject, and the resulting study is widely considered to be a standard commentary on Ruskin.

1985 saw the publication of two important studies – Sawyer's and Wihl's. SAWYER's work is more in the tradition of Rosenberg and Landow; like them, he discusses Ruskin in the context of Victorian intellectual and literary history, and relays a more or less linear narrative of one man's youth, crises, and resolutions. Each of the major works receives a careful and elegant treatment; of special value are the chapters on *Stones of Venice*, *Modern Painters III* and *IV*, and *Unto This Last*. WIHL's book departs from the tradition of appreciative criticism, focusing instead on the difficulties and contradictions in Ruskin's work. Initiating his study with the claim that Ruskin's prose is highly fragmentary in nature, Wihl proceeds to account for this fragmentary style by analyzing the discrepancies between Ruskin's theories and his practice, between his epistemological attack on deceptions, such as the pathetic fallacy, and his frequent rhetorical indulgences in the very deceptions he condemned.

The preceding books focus primarily on the aesthetic writings of the 1840s and 1850s – on *Modern Painters*, *The Seven Lamps of Architecture*, and *Stones of Venice*. Students interested in Ruskin's social thought may wish to consult ANTHONY, which brackets off Ruskin's aesthetic theories so as to focus on the later economic and political writings. Anthony advances the argument that, for modernity, Ruskin's political radicalism is at once impossible and, from a rhetorical perspective, better suited than other forms of political radicalism to contemporary concerns. His discussion foregrounds the famous chapter in *Stones of Venice* on the gothic style; the treatment that Ruskin here offers of "work" is, he suggests, historically and theoretically defensible, in spite of recent attacks which argue the contrary. Anthony places Ruskin in a tradition of Romantic or non-Utilitarian British radicalism; also in this camp are Thomas Carlyle and William Morris, two Victorian social commentators whose relevance to Ruskin is similarly analyzed by SPEAR. Spear's work is a unique foray into the social and political aspects of Ruskin's corpus. Eschewing the linear, biographical format of many of his predecessors, Spear pursues discrete topics in Ruskin's life (e.g., Evangelicalism, science, and the influence of Carlyle) in a non-chronological order. His study combines a careful research of biographical details with a good overall conception of nineteenth-century economic theory. The rationale for this approach is to understand Ruskin's social and political thought through his personal relationships.

The two essays by MILLER (1986 and 1989) develop further the deconstructivist approach to Ruskin initiated by Wihl. By focusing on Ruskin's definitions of the pathetic fallacy, a concept that he relates to *prosopopoeia*, Miller strategically reads the autobiographical techniques of *Praeterita* as instances of the simultaneous necessity and illogic of Ruskin's complex religious faith. Ruskin's condemnation of the pathetic fallacy, by Miller's account, ceases to have meaning once his religious faith is stripped away. Therefore his renunciation of this trope paradoxically survives the loss of faith that fueled the renunciation. Taken together, these two essays are compact and sophisticated contributions to Ruskin criticism.

MILLETT's essay represents an early feminist study of Ruskin's perceptions of women, which, she observes, were representative of the pervasive Victorian stereotype of women's nature. As an essay that juxtaposes Ruskin and J.S. Mill on "the woman question", this article is a clear introduction to Ruskin's place within the Victorian rhetoric of an essentialized femininity. The essays in the special edition of *Nineteenth-Century Contexts* (edited by WHEELER) devoted to Ruskin include a more recent feminist study and some interesting new historical essays. Among the topics discussed here are Ruskin's attitudes towards women artists, Ruskin's treatment of nationalism, and Ruskin's relationship with his father, John James Ruskin.

SUE ZEMKA

S

Salinger, J.D. 1919–

American novelist and short-story writer

Alsen, Eberhard, *Salinger's Glass Stories as a Composite Novel*, Troy, New York: Whitston, 1983
Bloom, Harold (ed.), *J.D. Salinger*, New York: Chelsea House, 1987
French, Warren, *J.D. Salinger*, New York: Twayne, 1963, revised (Boston) 1976
Grunwald, H.A. (ed.), *Salinger: A Critical and Personal Portrait*, New York: Harper, 1962; London: Peter Owen, 1964
Hamilton, Ian, *In Search of J.D. Salinger*, London: Heinemann, 1988; New York: Random House, 1988
Salzman, Jack (ed.), *New Essays on "The Catcher in the Rye"*, New York: Cambridge University Press, 1991; Cambridge: Cambridge University Press, 1992

Early criticism of Salinger in the USA was bedevilled by the now out-dated issue of the supposed crudeness of the language in *The Catcher in the Rye*. The novel caused an uproar in a number of high schools for this reason, right into the 1960s. The controversy also set a trend for subsequent Salinger criticism by its overwhelming concentration of attention on *The Catcher* at the expense of Salinger's shorter fiction. The second, slightly less marked tendency has been a confusion between Salinger's fiction and his life, ironically so in view of the novelist's continuing obsessive regard for his own privacy.

GRUNWALD's anthology gives the reader a flavour of the early debates about Salinger, misleadingly promising a composite or homogeneous account in the "portrait" of its title. Grunwald himself argues for the accuracy of Holden Caulfield's insights and uses Salinger's fiction to assemble a composite biography of "Sonny". The pieces in this volume range from accounts of the Salinger cult to rather skewed comparisons with the Beats. The better essays, however, have survived well. Ihab Hassan, for instance, argues convincingly that Salinger uses the notions of a retreat into childhood polemically to question the American Dream. Leslie Fiedler on the other hand uses *The Catcher* as a cultural symptom to challenge what he calls the "eye of innocence", i.e., the hegemony of the child's perspective in American literature.

FRENCH follows the standard format of the Twayne "United States Authors" series by opening his study with a summary of the known facts of Salinger's career, a summary that has not been bettered by subsequent writing. French gives a broad discussion of Salinger's *oeuvre*, which is greatly helped by detailed analysis of three key short stories. "Uncle Wiggily in Connecticut" exemplifies for him a clash between Salinger's "nice" and "phony" worlds; "The Inverted Forest" is glossed as an imperfectly realized allegory; and "A Perfect Day for a Bananafish" demonstrates the use of extended metaphor. One of French's main emphases is to show in *The Catcher* how Holden's criticisms of society apply equally well to himself.

ALSEN's monograph on the Glass stories makes a welcome break from the consensus focus on *The Catcher*, and sensibly discusses the recurrence of family members, which invites the reader to consider the stories as a whole sequence. Alsen considers each story in order of publication, and then shows that around the mid-1950s Salinger devised a plan for this series. In the event this plan was not realized. Nevertheless, in the course of his discussion Alsen presents new information on Salinger's interest in oriental religions, and constructs a helpful biography of Seymour, the key figure in the Glass family.

BLOOM's collection of critical essays assembles nine pieces published between 1958 and 1984, thereby enabling the reader to trace some of the shifts in Salinger criticism. William Weigand's opening essay diagnoses a collective dis-ease in Salinger's protagonists, whose hypersensitive awareness prevents them from participating in society. Alfred Kazin offers dated comments on how "cute" Salinger's protagonists are, and Max Schulz gives a shrewd and sustained discussion of the novellas, which demonstrates an identification by Salinger with Buddy, a "thorough romantic". Schulz's analysis is very well supported by a close attention to the verbal details of the novellas that is all too rare in Salinger criticism. Helen Weinberg rejects Freudian readings of Salinger in order to bring out the meta-fictional dimension of "Seymour", which she sees as a "story dealing with the narrator's conflict with his material"; and Bernice and Sanford Goldstein examine Salinger's use of Zen as a means of unifying his stories.

HAMILTON's volume has an unusually and ironically appropriate title. His initial intention was to write a biography of the novelist, and during his researches he unearthed a considerable number of unpublished letters. When his book had reached the galley stage Salinger objected, and objected again even to a rewritten version. There next followed a court case, which totally blocked publication of the biography. Hamilton then salvaged what he could from his project and told the story of his researches rather than their result. Despite all the obstacles Salinger, to his discredit, erected against Hamilton's study, it still manages to convey a considerable amount of useful information about the novelist. It is helpful to have on record the latter's admiration for F. Scott Fitzgerald and William Saroyan, as it is to hear about Salinger's meeting with Ernest Hemingway towards the end of World War II. And it at least starts a compositional study of *The Catcher* when Hamilton points out that Salinger commenced work on that novel a good ten years before publication.

SALZMAN's collection is a rather uneven one; but it does contain some excellent new readings of *The Catcher*, characterized by a formal rigour of analysis. Thus Michael Cowan demonstrates that the act of speaking is far more important to Holden Caulfield than verbal meaning. He identifies Holden's ideal addressee as a single individual, and disposes of the "wise child" cliché by showing that Holden's insights do not increase as the novel progresses. In another outstanding essay Christopher Brookemen sets *The Catcher* within a historical context by demonstrating that it is dominated by the code of the prep school. With reference to contemporary sociological works like David Riesman's *The Lonely Crowd*, he shows that Holden is simultaneously "insider and outsider", performing prescribed roles and commenting ironically on them. Joyce Rowe proposes that Holden is a potential rebel whose nonconformity is limited by diminished ideals, and Peter Shaw discusses how Holden's verbal mannerisms enable him to, as it were, "catch" experience and cope with loss. This collection as a whole is informed by a close and productive attention to language.

DAVID SEED

Sandburg, Carl 1878–1967

American poet, biographer, and children's writer

Allen, Gay Wilson, *Carl Sandburg*, Minneapolis: University of Minnesota Press, 1972
Callahan, North, *Carl Sandburg: Lincoln of Our Literature: A Biography*, New York: New York University Press, 1970; revised edition, as *Carl Sandburg: His Life and Works*, University Park: Pennsylvania State University Press, 1987
Crowder, Richard, *Carl Sandburg*, New York: Twayne, 1964
Duffey, Bernard, *The Chicago Renaissance in American Letters: A Critical History*, East Lansing: Michigan State College Press, 1954
Van Doren, Mark, *Carl Sandburg – with a Bibliography of Sandburg Materials in the Collection of the Library of Congress*, Washington, D.C.: Library of Congress, 1969
Van Wienen, Mark, "Taming the Socialist: Carl Sandburg's *Chicago Poems* and Its Critics", in *American Literature*, 63(1), 1991
Yatron, Michael, *America's Literary Revolt*, New York: Philosophical Library, 1959

Much remains to be said about the work of Carl Sandburg. His enthusiasts have, by and large, chosen to focus on his life story rather than his sizable and intriguing corpus of poetry, biography, history, children's stories, and journalism. As a result, there are numerous biographical studies (most of which have been superseded by Penelope Niven's monumental *Carl Sandburg: A Biography*, 1991) and relatively little commentary. In part, the standard critical estimations of Sandburg's literary output may be a factor here. The judgements of his own contemporaries – William Carlos Williams found the work "formless" and void of "motivating spirit", Robert Frost called him an "artificial and studied ruffian", and Amy Lowell dubbed him too much the "propagandist" – continue to hold sway. Such judgements, of course, leave open to question the aesthetic and ideological presuppositions that have barred Sandburg from the canonical mainstream.

DUFFEY's study, which includes a sub-chapter on Sandburg's achievements, is fairly typical of the early criticism in several respects: in Duffey's history of the Chicago renaissance between 1890 and 1920, Sandburg is only a dim star within a constellation of writers; the "mixed achievement" of his poetry is subordinate to his multi-volume biography of Abraham Lincoln; and his poetry is rendered distinct from his "non-literary labors as Socialist, reporter, and researcher". Duffey, however, also displays an unusual awareness of the socio-economic issues, historical context, and ideological motivations that helped to shape Sandburg's work, and argues that he wrote in a climate of the "newer spirit" and the "joyous iconoclasm" of socialism, suffragism, and agnosticism. Duffey regards Sandburg's early imagistic experiments as a foreign aberration in the context of the late Chicago renaissance, itself a reaction against genteel aestheticism in favour of a subjective and stark realism – qualities, Duffey contends, that characterize Sandburg's better, and consistently Romantic, work.

YATRON includes a lengthy chapter on Sandburg alongside criticism of Edgar Lee Masters and Vachel Lindsay – the two poets with whom he is typically juxtaposed. Yatron figures all three as the literary inheritors of late nineteenth-century agrarian populism – an eclectic blend of socialist, liberal, and democratic ideals characterized by revolutionary naivety and reactionary nostalgia. Despite Sandburg's reputation as an urban poet, and his lack of direct comment on the populist movement, Yatron argues that his early poem "Chicago" "has served to give him a false reputation as the bard of the city, of industrialism, and of twentieth century commerce. Such lines . . . have disguised Sandburg's Populistic antagonism toward these very same things and concealed his agrarian outlook". Despite this rather unique and enlightening perspective, Yatron's study is fairly conventional in its estimation of Sandburg's poetry as insufficiently universal and objective.

CROWDER, author of one of the earliest extended studies of Sandburg's corpus, focuses on what are considered the more literary texts – the verse, the Lincoln biography, Sandburg's early autobiography, and his only novel – and excludes journalistic material, children's stories, minor histories, and Sandburg's collections of American folk songs. The text includes a three-page chronology of Sandburg's life to the date of publication, which suggests the import of biography to Crowder's methodology. Indeed, Crowder mixes the writer's life story with samples and criticism of his work while determining Sandburg's critical reception and "his permanent position in American letters". Although Duffey's readings can be illuminating, the book concludes ambiguously on the subject of Sandburg's literary merit by offering a pointless list of his supposedly best work rather than a statement on how Sandburg can teach us more about his historical moment, his artistic medium, or the relationship between the two.

VAN DOREN's essay – actually the Introduction to a bibliography of the Sandburg holdings at the Library of Congress – was written as a lecture two years after Sandburg's death, and maintains a eulogistic tone throughout. Despite its high rhetoric and sentimentality, Van Doren's unqualified celebration of Sandburg's Lincoln biography and shorter poems offers a varied sampling of his work and a sensitivity to its themes and tone. The bibliography has been superseded by Dale Salwak's 1988 *Carl Sandburg: A Reference Guide*, which annotates the complete writings of both the author and his critics.

ALLEN's study, one in a series of "Pamphlets on American Writers", begins with a brief biographical sketch, followed by a chronological accounting of Sandburg's published works. Her readings are predominantly thematic, although she does turn to formal analysis in a spirited defence of Sandburg's *Complete Poems*. Allen, to her credit, is sensitive to Sandburg's literary reception and the reasons behind it, suggesting that his poems gave critics "few subtleties or ambiguities to challenge their ingenuity" and that his popularity and irreverence is out of step with the élitism of the Ezra Pound/T.S. Eliot tradition. Allen concludes by arguing for the superiority of the poet's final volume, *Honey and Salt*, a collection that has been given far too little attention.

CALLAHAN's reprinted and updated version of his 1970 survey is, with the exclusion of the Niven biography, the most recent extended treatment of the poet. Chronologically arranged, Callahan's study draws on a variety of primary and secondary materials, offering lengthy commentaries on Sandburg's verse, novel, and biography of Lincoln. Of particular interest is the central chapter on the poetry, which includes a review of its critical reception from the early work, through the long poem *The People, Yes* (1936), and onto the posthumously published *Breathing Tokens* (1978). Although Callahan acknowledges the debates over the status of Sandburg's writing, he neither takes a stand nor comments on a critical industry so desperate to maintain a distinction between the popular and the poetic.

VAN WIENEN's overview of the early critical treatment of Sandburg does address the poet and socialist radical's canonical status. Demonstrating "the power of literary and publishing establishments to suppress or reinterpret writing that questions their received values", Van Wienen argues that the political nature of Sandburg's early poetry has been suppressed in favour of its imagistic tendencies and lyrical impulse toward universal truths. He establishes through analysis of *Chicago Poems* not only the overriding ideological thrust of that volume, but also, through reference to contemporary letters and reviews, the modernist (and later New-Critical) unease with literature overtly situated within a socio-historic moment. Van Wienen suggests not only how Sandburg has been misread, but also why his vast corpus has been distilled down to a few harmless – but certainly not representative – imagistic niceties.

MICHAEL J. O'DRISCOLL

Satire: General

Elliott, Robert C., *The Power of Satire: Magic, Ritual, Art*, Princeton, New Jersey: Princeton University Press, 1960
Guilhamet, Leon, *Satire and the Transformation of Genre*, Philadelphia: University of Pennsylvania Press, 1987
Highet, Gilbert, *The Anatomy of Satire*, Princeton, New Jersey: Princeton University Press, 1962
Kernan, Alvin B., *The Cankered Muse: Satire of the English Renaissance*, New Haven, Connecticut: Yale University Press, 1959
Pollard, Arthur, *Satire*, London: Methuen, 1970
Rawson, Claude (ed.), *English Satire and the Satiric Tradition*, Oxford and New York: Blackwell, 1984
Sutherland, James, *English Satire*, Cambridge: Cambridge University Press, 1959

SUTHERLAND's early, and rather elementary, introduction to English satire commences with a useful distinction between comedy and satire and a discussable claim for the latter as "a department of rhetoric". Some irrelevant comparisons with William Wordsworth lead on to an analysis of the satiric spectrum from sheer invective to didactic irony. The former is explored in a discussion of scurrilous diatribe and flyting in the works of William Dunbar and John Skelton, and, subsequently, in the Elizabethan verse satirists and the Marprelate tracts. Succinct treatments of John Cleveland, the Earl of Rochester, Andrew Marvell, and Samuel Butler follow (with some useful remarks on burlesque), before Sutherland turns his attention (Chapter 3) to the stylistic characteristics of verse satire, based on the typical Juvenal/Horace distinction, and embracing a comprehensive analysis of satires by John Dryden and the mock-epic writings of Alexander Pope.

Chapter 4 is a fairly predictable examination of prose satire, ranging from Thomas More to George Orwell, but concentrating mainly on Swift. Short succeeding essays on satirical novels (Fielding and Thackeray) and on satire in drama (Ben Jonson, William Wycherley, George Bernard Shaw) are little more than bland summaries. Despite the flaws already indicated, this little introduction is still a worthwhile gateway to the world of English satire, inevitably dated, never provocative, but common-sensical, clearly-written, and guaranteed not to intimidate the novitiate.

HIGHET's magisterial work is an encyclopedic survey covering at least 100 writers, and ranging from Bion to Marcel Proust, from Petronius to Eric Linklater. He is very concerned to stress the realistic and philosophical aspects of satire, so the emphasis is here largely thematic, rather than formal or structural. Satires are primarily divided into monologues, parodies, and dramatic fictions. A chapter on diatribe traces forms of monologic satire from Bion and Menippus through the Renaissance to Robert Browning and Shelley Berman. Highet then provides a lengthy and wide-ranging analysis of the uses of parody in satiric writing: parodies of epic, prose romance, drama, and hoaxes are all dealt with in a style that is delightfully readable (even anecdotal), and which embraces such diverse writers as Prosper Mérimée and W.S. Gilbert, not to mention musical examples such as Ernst von Dohnányi's *Variations* or Alfredo Casella's *A la Manière ...*

The cogent distinction between mock-epic and burlesque is especially helpful. A useful chapter examines at some length the "distorting mirror" of satire, making clear definitions of lampoon, invective, and flyting, before engaging in the uses of other worlds, visions of the future, and animal fables. Among the texts analysed are Jonathan Swift's *Gulliver's Travels*, Samuel Butler's *Erewhon*, Seneca's *Apocolocyntosis*, George Orwell's *1984*, and the fables of *Reynard the Fox*. Final chapters glance at some typical structures of satire, history, biography, and caricature. Although this study may seem somewhat dated to some scholars, it is still valuable for its enormous coverage, its jargon-free stylistic felicity, and, above all, an infectious geniality, which should stimulate readers to engage with, and enjoy, as wide a range of satire as they can obtain.

POLLARD's little "Critical Idiom" introduction is clearly designed to put the initiate in touch with the fundamental features of satire in terms of its aims, topics, methods, tones, and effects. Covering verse and prose from Juvenal to Siegfried Sassoon in 75 pages, it is of necessity somewhat superficial, but Pollard does manage to make his points clearly and succinctly, and providing withal a wealth of illuminating quotations. After presenting the satirist as someone who, aware of the discrepancies between what is and what should be, is determined to castigate hypocrisy and other related vices, Pollard proceeds to examine the astonishingly wide range of satirical subject-matter, reminding us at the same time that satire is always a social, never a transcendental, mode of discourse. Religion, sex, and women are among the topics treated here, with good illustrations from Chaucer, Alexander Pope, Swift, and Rabelais. Pollard's lengthy third chapter on modes and means of creating satire is the most valuable, ranging from satirical infusion in the novel through allegories, beast fables, journeys, to forms of burlesque, in authors such as Chaucer, Henry Fielding, Swift, and William Makepeace Thackeray. (It is either a *tour de force* or a mistake to treat James Joyce's *Ulysses* in 27 lines!). The text concludes with some suggestive discussion of typical figures of speech. Some final brief remarks on irony, sarcasm, and their effects on the reader wind up this still-handy survey. A short, annotated bibliography (up to 1970) is provided.

As its title suggests, ELLIOTT's study adopts a very different approach, stressing satire's origins in the magical invectives of Greek phallic songs and in ritual cursing. This enables him to dwell on the effects of satire, emphasising the almost literal ability of satirical diatribes to "kill" their victims. His first chapter traces this history from Archilochus through Greek Old Comedy to Arabian *hijas* and (at rather excessive length) Irish *filids*. Elliott then proceeds to analyse the magical element in satire's primordial precursors, using the theories of Freud and Jane Harrrison: to those who have now fully assimilated their Claude Lévi-Strauss, some of this material might appear a trifle dated; but there remain many suggestive insights – especially in the discussion of the aetiology and history of ridicule and caricature.

In an extensive chapter dealing with the great misanthropes of literature (notably railers like Thersites, Apemantus, Timon, and of course Gulliver), Elliott advances the tantalising proposition that these characters, "hurling curses and invective", are in turn being satirised by their creators. The radical changes in character that such protagonists undergo (a fault, or course, in terms of realism) is well explained on the grounds of satirical necessity. The ensuing chapters on Wyndham Lewis and Roy Campbell are likely to be of less interest to the reader of today. Elliott concludes with some suggestive remarks on the uneasy relationship between the satirist and society. This is still a seminal work and, despite its lack of attention to structure and close verbal analysis, must be compulsory on any reading list dealing with satire.

Different from all the above texts is RAWSON's collection of essays in honour of Elliott. These, in chronological order, range from articles on Aristophanes to Jorge Luis Borges, and each explores a particular aspect of the satirist concerned. We have not sufficient space in this review to discuss in detail each of these scholarly monographs, but particularly useful contributions can be briefly summarised. Stephen Halliwell argues convincingly that artistic originality in Aristophanes outweighs any serious moral purpose; a very learned and entertaining essay on flyting in early popular poetry and in Dunbar and Skelton (by Douglas Gray) is succeeded by studies of creative anger in Jonson (Donaldson), the alienated *persona* in John Donne (Stein), and satiric cruelty and violence in Rochester (Robinson). An extremely interesting essay by Raman Selden contextualises the poetry of John Oldham in the traditions of "rough satire", the neoclassical line, heroic drama, and the Restoration court wits; Selden then convincingly demonstrates the influence of Oldham on Pope. Other essays include a highly sophisticated treatment of Gulliver as "living doll" (Traugott), varieties of irony in *Gulliver's Travels* (Anderson), a running commentary on Pope's use of Horace's "Epistle II" by Niall Rudd, and a stimulating discussion of the political satire in William Hogarth's *A Country Inn Yard at Election Time: The Stage-Coach* from Ronald Paulson.

Marilyn Butler contributes a decisive piece on William Hazlitt's *Liber Amoris*, Martin Price is suggestive on the relationship between fiction and satire, and Barbara Everett makes some cogent observations on the Americanness of T.S. Eliot's style in *Sweeney Agonistes*. Slightly quirky essays by Hugh Kenner on Wyndham Lewis and by John Sturrock on Borges conclude this excellent *Festschrift*, all in all a comprehensive collection of studies, which certainly does no shame to the memory of their "onlie begetter".

The most recent and rigorously theoretical of the works to be surveyed is GUILHAMET's. In an introductory section he makes an important claim for satire as a genre rather than a mode, and declares that his approach therefore (despite covering 2,000 years of satire) will be primarily synchronic. He distinguishes Mennipean from formal verse satire, simple from complex satire, and all of them from comedy and parody, while acknowledging that the latter can be a useful means to convey satirical import. A more detailed analysis follows, relating satirical forms to epideictic oratory (usually direct abuse), deliberative oratory (public examples of social deviance), and judicial (or forensic) oratory, where, as in Byron's *The Vision of Judgement*, wrongdoers are hauled before the satirist's tribunal for punishment.

The second part of Guilhamet's text is occupied with putting this theoretical framework into practice through detailed close analyses of works by Dryden, Swift, and Pope. Particularly notable are the explications of *Mac Flecknoe* as a mock-epic sessions poem, *Absalom and Achitophel* as Miltonic generic mixture, *The Rape of the Lock* in relation to the *carpe diem* theme, and *The Dunciad* in terms of generic metamorphosis. He concludes with a sophisticated treatment of *persona* and genre in *Gulliver's Travels*. By stressing the normal rather than thematic features of satire, Guilhamet has enlarged considerably our understanding of this mixed genre. It is perhaps a pity that his specific examples had to be drawn from such a restricted period of history, but I feel that the theoretical principles he so appealingly lays out can be usefully applied to satire of any age. The bibliography is excellent.

It would be inexcusable to leave this survey of works on satire without a mention, however brief, of KERNAN. Though devoted entirely to Renaissance satire, his masterly sketching of the satirical scene ("the faces peering out at us . . . seldom have normal features but are grotesquely distorted by the vices they mirror"), his presentation of the satiric *persona*, and his remarks on the plot of satire remain indispensable, as do the brilliantly written analyses on Cyril Tourneur, Jonson, and Shakespeare that follow. The treatment of language in "Comicall Satyre" is definitive, and I cannot see it ever being surpassed.

A.W. LYLE

Satire: 18th Century

Bloom, Edward A., and Lillian D. Bloom, *Satire's Persuasive Voice*, Ithaca, New York: Cornell University Press, 1979

Browning, J.D. (ed.), *Satire in the Eighteenth Century*, New York: Garland, 1983

Nokes, David, *Raillery and Rage: A Study of Eighteenth Century Satire*, Brighton, Sussex: Harvester Press, 1987

Nussbaum, Felicity A., *The Brink of All We Hate: English Satires on Women 1660–1750*, Lexington: University Press of Kentucky, 1984

Paulson, Ronald, *The Fictions of Satire*, Baltimore: Johns Hopkins University Press, 1967

Purvis, C.J., *The Offensive Art: The Liberation of Poetic Imagination in Augustan Satire*, Doncaster, Yorkshire: Brynmill Press, 1991

Rawson, Claude, *Satire and Sentiment 1660–1830*, Cambridge and New York: Cambridge University Press, 1994

Seidel, Michael, *Satiric Inheritance: Rabelais to Sterne*, Princeton, New Jersey: Princeton University Press, 1979

Weinbrot, Howard D., *Eighteenth-Century Satire: Essays on Text and Context from Dryden to Peter Pindar*, Cambridge and New York: Cambridge University Press, 1988

There has been an explosion of critical interest in eighteenth-century satire in the last 30 years. The period has seen some excellent articles, as well as a number of book-length studies. Some critics have analyzed the form of satire, its rhetorical strategies, and its literary models. Others have explored its social and historical context, sometimes drawing conclusions about the moral function and the ideological implications of satire. The studies selected below demonstrate a critical awareness of how satire functions, as well as explore the work of some exemplary exponents from the period.

The BLOOM's study is less a history of satire than an examination of technical and thematic problems. Importantly, the book deals with satire in relation to rhetoric. More specifically, the authors are preoccupied with satire as the pursuit of an innate quality, which they call *humanitas*. They warn that this is not to be confused with sentiment or gentility, but rather with Horatian satire and its "persuasive verbal pitch". Like Purvis's study, the argument tends to oscillate between rhetoric and morality. The historical range of the volume usefully includes Samuel ('Hudibras') Butler at one end of the period, and Samuel Johnson at the other. On another level, the Blooms' study works both from classical and modernist perspectives. The study excavates the important influences of writers as varied as Juvenal, Cicero, Quintilian, Erasmus, Boileau and Cervantes. Running through these authors, the Blooms focus on the view that satiric intention is the product of an impulse that is at once moral and didactic. As the discussion proceeds it emerges that satire is not merely a personal or vindictive activity. Satire is not confined to a particular occasion but expresses shared truths about our moral awareness. The study insists that satire has a capacity to effect reform. Satire involves moral reawakening and reaffirmation. This is rhetoric thoroughly informed by moral awareness.

BROWNING's collection of essays serves to demonstrate how much excellent work on satire has been done in the shorter, essay-length study. Richard Morton's Introduction to the collection emphasizes the aesthetic impact of satire. It is acknowledged that satire aims to reform, but that there are few victories. Morris Brownell's "English Verse Satire of the Country House, 1700–50" shows the move away from degenerate panegyric in estate poetry to Alexander Pope's rehabilitation of the country-house ideal. The essay concludes that Jonathan Swift, in turn, finally subverts the ideal. Michael DePorte's "Swift and the Licence of Satire" shows Swift's adoption of a primitive killer instinct in his satire. Examining both the poetry and the prose, DePorte demonstrates that Swift's ambivalence consists of a dual capacity to disturb and to delight. Charles Pullen's "The Greatest Art is to Hide Art" explores how Swift used personae to produce characters who finally satirize themselves. Michael Seidel's "Satire and the Metaphoric Collapse: The Bottom of the Sublime" argues that satire portrays a perpetually shifting and chaotic world. He proposes that the satiric process is a combination of the desire to destroy and the imperviousness to reformation of those attacked. William S. Anderson's "The Mock-Heroic Mode in Roman Satire and Alexander Pope" provides some useful background on the development of the mock-heroic in Roman satire, from Ennius to Juvenal. K.J.H Berland's "Satire and the *Via Media*: Anglican Dialogue in *Joseph Andrews*" explores how Fielding adapted the Aristotelian ethical system to the Anglican tradition. Martin Price's "Swift in the Interpreter's House" considers satire as a species of interpretive free-play. Satirical rhetoric, in Swift's handling descends brilliantly into madness rather than seeking to establish spiritual truths. Irvin Ehrenpreis's "Swiftian Dilemmas" examines the play of body against mind, dealing intuitively with the reader's response to the complexity, contradiction, and incoherencies of satirical masterpieces such as *Gulliver's Travels*. Moving beyond the purely literary, George Knox's essay considers Punchinello drawings; Ronald Paulson explores James Gillray's ambivalence as a political cartoonist. The critical breadth of this collection is also demonstrated in Robert Van Dusen's "Freedom and Constraint in Zachariae's Satire *The Braggart*", which considers the satiric combination of coarse language and refined irony. This is an excellent volume, which demonstrates a range of critical approaches to the study of satire in a wide range of texts.

PURVIS's study argues that Augustan satire is constructed by the poetic sensibility from conflicting thoughts, feelings, and experiences. As the book proceeds, Purvis shows that the terminology used to analyze satire is often reductive. He asserts, for instance, that invective does not do justice to the degree of expressiveness involved in satire; repudiation has its own kinds of richness. He proceeds to argue that satire serves more to enrich than to impoverish its world: it is a poetic affirmation. Dryden and Pope shared the conventions of their time, but satire was also a safe form of escape from the commonplace world. In this sense, Augustan satire was much more than the didactic promotion of the period's values. Purvis argues that satire can be a special form of understanding, but it is one in which imagination works with a sense of incomprehension. The satirist is a creator obsessed with the need to destroy his productions. Although at times the sense of unifying imagination, which supports a falling world, is overworked, much of Purvis's thesis is cogently argued.

PAULSON argues that the origin of satire, in its primitive form, was a kind of curse drawn from fertility rituals, and that satire frequently returns to its incantatory roots. Although satire imitates vice, it exaggerates in order to exorcise. Moving on from these primitive foundations, Paulson distinguishes between Horatian and Juvenilian satire, but he also shows the influence of Rabelais and Cervantes on eighteenth-century satire. He proceeds to illustrate the importance of Lucian, particularly in the construction of the pseudo-persona, or the self-condemning speaker. Paulson notes that the usual Augustan position was to remove the satirist from the fiction; the satirist in this sense is a detached observer, with a sustained rather than merely local point of view. Paulson also considers Milton's *Paradise Lost* as an influential satiric model according to its juxtaposition of Paradise with the impurity of the present. This is a thought-provoking and clearly written volume.

SEIDEL moves beyond the confines of purely rhetorical analysis. For him, satiric action should be considered as part of a wider representational context. He links satire suggestively with primitive aggression, and to magic. He also notes that satire is a species of linguistic violence, a kind of defence mechanism, and in its incantatory form a species of magic. Satire is also a kind of monstrous birth, exemplified in the false etymologies of the word itself as a kind of mixed dish, and as the satyr, a mythic beast. Seidel proceeds to argue that the satirist, having taken monstrosity as his subject matter, makes something of a monster of himself. As a result, satirists remove themselves from their productions. Examining Pope's depiction of an England overrun by dullness, Seidel notes that satiric action is a kind of bad seed: inheritance is a kind of descent, a falling away, often from some previous heroic condition. In common with other studies, Seidel carves out a literary tradition that is as much one of inheritance as revision. Rabelais and Cervantes emerge as giant figures in the practice of generic subversion. Seidel argues that scatology is a kind of threat to the social order; satire possibly cleanses and renews. There are here excellent chapters dealing with Swift's *A Tale of a Tub* and *Gulliver's Travels*, Pope's *The Rape of the Lock* and *The Dunciad*, and Sterne's *Tristram Shandy*.

RAWSON announces that his intention is to examine stress points, rather than to provide a rigidly progressive narrative. He focuses on particular issues in order to fragment the neatness of an evolving satiric tradition, finally exposed and expelled by Romantic priorities at the end of the eighteenth-century. In particular, Rawson provides a detailed examination of the role of war in the epic, which the mock-heroic tended to shun. The epic genre appeared to embody Augustan values, but it was also a repository of nightmares; it unavoidably imported the memory of past carnage, cruelty, and barbarity. Rawson dexterously uncovers moments of ideological doubleness, teasing out the full play of ambiguity in metaphor and allusion. His study also serves to compare the different priorities of satire and sentiment in Jane Austen's novels. In sections dealing with Swift and Pope, and with Percy Bysshe Shelley and Byron, Rawson carefully avoids slipping into mundane dualities; his study calls for a careful re-description of the satirical tradition, paying closer attention to overlapping tendencies, potentialities, and exposures. Rawson's display of erudition and his attention to detail militates finally against the sense of historical instability and cultural incoherence.

WEINBROT organizes his collection of essays into two sections. The first deals with contexts and contains his three influential studies – "The Pattern of Formal Verse Satire in the Restoration and the Eighteenth Century", "History, Horace, and Augustus Caesar: Some Implications for Eighteenth Century Satire", and "Masked Men and Satire and Pope: Towards an Historical Basis for the Eighteenth-Century Persona." Weinbrot makes a convincing case for a notion of satiric "persona", which avoids the necessity to read texts as expression of the author's real responses. Weinbrot eruditely marshals a range of classical authors in order to demonstrate that Horace, Cicero, and Quintilian equate speaker and writer. Ovid, Martial, Apuleius, and Ausonius, on the other hand insist on a distinction between their works and their lives. The second section of the book deals with texts, and includes essays on the Earl of Rochester, Dryden, Samuel Johnson, and Pope. In most cases, Weinbrot is at his best in unmasking the logic of influence, imitation, and improvement. While refining English verse, Weinbrot argues that Pope had a variety of classical models, which he mixed and mingled. Weinbrot concludes that the later eighteenth century was less competent in its imitation of models and its synthesis of tones and approaches. The first section of this study is less a theory of satire than an exploration of specific issues in the study of satire. As a result, some of the essays in the second section are autonomous items of criticism and scholarship, rather than tests of models proposed at the outset. Nonetheless, this is a magisterial volume, and essential reading for the student of satire.

NOKES's study is concerned with the ideology of satire. He argues that satire tends to be conservative, but that it may also be radical and subversive. The novel sustains an autonomous fictional world, but satire is directed at, and validated by, external reality. Nokes asserts that satire is necessarily critical of the society in which it is produced. He proceeds to outline the relationship between different kinds of eighteenth-century satire and the Augustan mentality, which he links to an imperial ethic. His study nonetheless moves beyond its materialist foundations to examine how the sense of reality is lost in the metamorphosing imagination of a satirist such as Pope. Nokes refuses a rigid categorisation of satire: his analysis shifts from distinctions between "snarling" and "smiling" satire to the familiar preoccupation with irony, parody, mock-heroic, and burlesque. Throughout the study, twentieth-century analogies are used to outline general themes. As a result, the critical terminology is shown to be less esoteric than it first appears, and to have a modern relevance which in turn serves to open up the earlier period. The study deals with Pope, Gay, Fielding, and Swift, but there are also sections dealing with non-canonical writers, pamphlet literature, and farce.

NUSSBAUM explores a wide range of anti-feminist poetic portrayal, arguing that such texts constitute a tradition that may be traced back to Juvenal's *Sixth Satire*. Examining these satiric *topoi*, Nussbaum shows how satirists negotiated the disturbing and ambivalent features of the female by means of conventions and myths. These satiric "fictions" represent women as rebels against the patriarchal order. Nussbaum reveals that the female victim was a constructed target, "produced" as a means of validating her savage depiction. She becomes an excuse for the entire scatological tradition. Nonetheless, satire also manufactured the ideal woman, such as the angelic wife, who was represented as dutifully devoted to domestic life. Nussbaum notes that the anti-feminist tradition in the later eighteenth-century tradition increasingly relied on the belief that women's capacity to reason was inferior to that of men. Satire operated effectively to reinforce gender boundaries and oppositions, while acting as a kind of framing device, constantly turning anxiety into a species of comedy. Nussbaum's study deals primarily with major authors, such as Swift and Pope. It is a sensitive exploration of misogyny, and is essential reading for any study of the relationship between gender and satire in this period.

I.D. McCormick

Schreiner, Olive 1855–1920

South African novelist, essayist, and short-story writer

Berkman, Joyce Avrech, *Olive Schreiner: Feminism on the Frontier*, St Albans, Vermont: Eden Press, 1979

Berkman, Joyce Avrech, *The Healing Imagination of Olive Schreiner: Beyond South African Colonialism*, Amherst: University of Massachusetts Press, 1989

Friedmann, Marion V., *Olive Schreiner: A Study in Latent Meanings*, Johannesburg: Witwatersrand University Press, 1954

Monsman, Gerald, *Olive Schreiner's Fiction: Landscape and Power*, New Brunswick, New Jersey: Rutgers University Press, 1991

Parkin-Gounelas, Ruth, *Fictions of the Female Self: Charlotte Brontë, Olive Schreiner and Katherine Mansfield*, London: Macmillan, 1991

Van Wyk Smith, Malvern, and Don Maclennan, *Olive Schreiner and After: Essays on South African Literature*, Cape Town: David Philip, 1983

Vivan, Itala (ed.), *The Flawed Diamond: Essays on Olive Schreiner*, Sydney: Dangaroo Press, 1991

Olive Schreiner's active political life and outspoken feminist and anti-imperialist views invite biographical criticism, the more so since her fiction was intended to illustrate her political ideals. Despite the enthusiastic reception accorded to the initial publication of *Story of an African Farm*, early critics tended to find her work aesthetically wanting, particularly in terms of structure. Schreiner uses digressions, sermons, and extended and very beautiful allegories (which were also collected separately), which seemed out of place to readers reared on the realist tradition. Even early critics, however, paid tribute to her matchless sense of landscape and region.

FRIEDMANN's brief book is an example of an unsophisticated psychoanalytic reading of Schreiner's life and works. However, her insights into Schreiner's use of oral imagery, Schreiner's interest in sadomasochistic situations, and her anger at the maternal figure are plausible. Although it is a very incomplete view of Schreiner and her work, and accounts for none of Schreiner's political and social work, it may be considered to add a useful dimension to other biographical criticism.

BERKMAN, of all her more recent critics, has understood Schreiner's thought best. Grounding her criticism of the novels and political writings in a rich understanding of Schreiner's life and environment, her 1979 work examines the fiction in the context of Schreiner's place in the intellectual culture of turn-of-the-century European thought. Berkman treats both the fiction and the non-fiction, especially *Women and Labour*, as explication of Schreiner's feminist and anti-imperialist ideas, tracing specifically Schreiner's critiques of Darwinism and Victorian scientific justifications of ethnocentrism.

BERKMAN's 1989 book is much more heavily biographical. However, it contains enough criticism to make it a worthwhile critical source. Taking her cue from Schreiner's early ambition to become a doctor, Berkman treats Schreiner's public life and writings as a sustained effort to "heal" the rift of binarism in Victorian thought, and indeed in Western thought generally. Again tracing the intellectual roots of Schreiner's philosophy, Berkman argues that Schreiner saw the time-honored dualities, like male-female, civilized-savage, and the like as "intellectual and social maladies", so that her "passion to cure [them] . . . was her preeminent intellectual contribution to posterity as well as her key weakness". A strength of this book is its grounding in current feminist theory.

PARKIN-GOUNELAS devotes slightly more than a third of her book to Schreiner, and places her in a tradition of women writers of female subjectivity, forerunners for today's women's writings. This is the only long treatment of Schreiner that situates her primarily in an international and literary (rather than national, political, or philosophical) context, and the only one that deals with Schreiner's ambivalent focus on the female self. The structure of Schreiner's works is explained as "organic" and appropriate to the portrayal of feminine subjectivity, for which models like the traditional *Bildungsroman*, and even William Wordsworth's *Prelude*, posed especial problems, particularly in the light of the period's aesthetic rejection of the personal.

VAN WYK SMITH and MACLENNAN divide their collection of essays into two parts – one on Schreiner, and the other on later South African writers. In the first section, many significant Schreiner critics are represented (including Clayton, Beeton, and Heywood). The principal scholars represented are British and Euro-African, and the essays focus principally on Schreiner in politics, history, and literary history. This work has the advantage of describing her impact on South Africa specifically, rather than emphasizing British reception.

VIVAN's more recent collection of brilliant essays offers a wide-ranging series of perspectives on Schreiner's work, defining it as foundational for the South African tradition. The first half of the collection treats Schreiner's work in historical and aesthetic terms, whereas the second traces Schreiner's influence on subsequent authors' work. Of particular value are essays by Vivan, Gentilli, and Ngcobo, because of their analyses of the fictional role of native Africans in Schreiner's tales, and the relation of that role to a historical reality not previously addressed. These essays demonstrate the overwhelmingly positive response of Italian critics to Schreiner's work, which has only recently been available in translation. (The essays represent the selected proceedings of a conference at the University of Verona.)

MONSMAN differs substantially from many of Schreiner's other critics in that he concerns himself principally with the novels rather than the political writings. Power and gender, according to Monsman, are the primary themes that Schreiner's fiction addresses, and the aesthetic structure of the novels is responsive and appropriate to those themes. Thus Monsman defends Schreiner's aesthetics from the persistent disparagement of critics as recent as Elaine Showalter. This book is most valuable for its close readings of the novels, especially its excellent comparison of the neglected *Trooper Peter Halket of Mashonaland* with H.G. Wells' *War of the Worlds*.

PAMELA K. GILBERT

Science and Literature

Amrine, Frederick (ed.), *Literature and Science as Modes of Expression*, Dordrecht, Netherlands, and Boston: Kluwer Academic, 1989

Benjamin, Marina (ed.), *A Question of Identity: Women, Science, and Literature*, New Brunswick, New Jersey: Rutgers University Press, 1993

Hayles, N. Katherine, *Chaos Bound: Orderly Disorder in Contemporary Literature and Science*, Ithaca, New York: Cornell University Press, 1990

Levine, George, and Alan Rouch (eds.), *One Culture: Essays in Science and Literature*, Madison: University of Wisconsin Press, 1987

Paulson, William R., *The Noise of Culture: Literary Texts in a World of Information*, Ithaca, New York: Cornell University Press, 1988

Peterfreund, Stuart (ed.), *Literature and Science: Theory and Practice*, Boston: Northeastern University Press, 1990

Porush, David, *The Soft Machine: Cybernetic Fiction*, London and New York: Methuen, 1985

Traditional disciplinary distinctions between the arts and the sciences have been challenged in recent years by a large volume of literary criticism, which studies science as a force that is as culturally significant as literature. Essays in Amrine's, Peterfreund's, and Levine's volumes respond to these challenges in a wide range of ways, and include contributions from notable figures in the field like Gillian Beer, Sally Shuttleworth, and Eric White.

Stephen Weininger's introduction to AMRINE's volume of essays is a concise general introduction to the evolution of literature-and-science criticism. After the nineteenth century it was only possible to trace a one-way influence from science to literature, because science was perceived to be freed from the vicissitudes of historical and cultural change by its commitment to rationalism and objectivity. Weininger convincingly argues that more complex formulations of the interactions between literature and science have been made possible since the 1960s by twin developments in the history and philosophy of science, and in literary theory. Now, science is not seen to be separate from other cultural activity, but to operate as a potent discourse within the culture. Particularly enlightening is Weininger's reading of Aldous Huxley's *Literature and Science* (1963) as a text that stands between the old and the new methodologies of literature and science criticism.

PETERFREUND's Introduction also stresses that literature-and-science criticism has moved from finding scientific ideas "in" literature to a position where both forms are seen as discourses operating within the culture. Eric White's "Contemporary Cosmology and Narrative Theory" demonstrates how such a standpoint can provide a rewarding reading of scientific texts, illuminating our understanding of issues pertinent to literary study. He uses cosmological theories about the history of the universe as a case-study to mediate the dispute about the legitimacy of narrative history – whether narrativity "provides an indispensable point of reference orienting our progress through the world", or whether the "totalizing finality of narrative history can only lead the mind into delusion". By suggesting that different versions of cosmology conform to the different archetypes of plot identified by Northrop Frye – tragedy, comedy, romance, and farce – he is able to show how scientific texts (or, at least, popular versions of scientific texts) are dependent on narrative forms, which help to dictate their meanings.

LEVINE's introductory chapter is a thoughtful summary of, and response to, the issues raised by this sort of scholarship, suggesting that there are two senses in which it is productive to think of literature and science as part of a single culture: "first, in that what happens in science inevitably matters to what happens everywhere else . . . second, in that it is possible and fruitful to understand how literature and science are mutually shaped by their participation in the culture at large". While suggesting that literary and scientific discourses derive from common cultural sources, Levine also emphasises the differences between them, warning against indulging in an intellectual free-for-all that makes literary and scientific "fictions" equivalent.

The focus of BENJAMIN's volume is more specific than that of the other collections of essays – the ways in which literature and science produce gendered identities. The values most associated with science, Benjamin argues in her introductory essay, are also those associated with masculinity – "objectivity, rationality, truth, progress, exploration, and power" – while those associated with nature, the object of scientific inquiry, are female. Benjamin rejects the feminist programmes that search for an essential female identity, arguing that a more flexible theoretical formulation is to think of female agency in terms of "*positionality* . . . the specific ontological position occupied by individual women in society", because "where *woman* is objectively placed with respect to the existing social order determines the parameters within which or outside of which *women* speak".

PORUSH's book-length study is an important analysis of the influence of cybernetics on postmodern culture, and is sometimes cited as a potent text in debates about the "cyberpunk" phenomenon in science fiction. He suggests that the metaphor of human as machine, which dates back at least as far as the seventeenth century, has been given a dramatic new twist with the arrival of cybernetics – the modelling of physical, biological, and other systems, in terms of information flow – as the paradigmatic twentieth-century science. The body, language, and the mind can now be understood as cybernetic systems, but, Porush argues, an important branch of postmodernist literature challenges this metaphor. By presenting themselves as cybernetic systems (sites where information is exchanged and processed) which do not, ultimately, work, "cybernetic fictions" parody the reduction of human to machine, and reassert the authority of the human by illustrating the inadequacy of the machine metaphor: "a cybernetic age has invoked a cybernetic fiction capable of reinventing the human remnant left after the machine has done its grinding".

In her book, HAYLES also focuses on a specific aspect of science, chaos theory, which, she argues, is analogous to other aspects of postmodern culture because it destabilises the rigid binary oppositions between order and disorder, and global and local. Like many scholars in the field, she does not suggest a direct mutual influence between science and literature, but makes the working assumption that seemingly isolated areas of the culture draw on the same metaphors and discourses, while using them in different ways. The metaphor she invokes to describe this, an "archipelago of chaos", is a useful one for understanding much of the work done on literature and science, because it suggests that seemingly isolated disciplinary "islands" may be linked beneath the surface of the culture by the same substrata. She goes on to imply that the dynamics of culture act like chaotic systems.

PAULSON offers a challenging, if controversial, blend of ideas from contemporary literary theory and information theory, drawing particularly on the notion of "self-organisation from noise" expounded by Henri Atlan. Taking this as evidence that noise (in terms of distortion and uncertainty) is fundamental to the production of new meaning and knowledge, he suggests that we reappraise literature's role in culture. Removed from its position at the centre of culture by the electronic media, literature is now positioned at the margins of the culture, functioning as a "noisy" transmission channel, disturbing the cultural norm. Rather than resisting this, Paulson suggests that literary studies should respond to this new cultural environment by embracing interdisciplinarity and challenging the idea "that criticism and interpretation are the only legitimate functions of literary studies". The issues raised by such considerations are, he claims, political, and to fail to address them is to fail to understand fully the role of literature within contemporary culture.

DANIEL CORDLE

See also **Medicine and Literature; Victorian Literature, Science, and Evolutionary Theory**

Science Fiction

Aldiss, Brian W., *Trillion Year Spree: The History of Science Fiction*, London: Victor Gollancz, 1986; New York: Atheneum, 1986

Barron, Neil (ed.), *Anatomy of Wonder: A Critical Guide to Science Fiction*, New York: Bowker, 1976; 4th edition, New Providence, New York: Bowker, 1995

Clute, John, and Peter Nicholls (eds.), *The Encyclopedia of Science Fiction*, London and New York: Granada, 1979; revised edition, London: Orbit, 1993; New York: St Martin's Press, 1993

Delany, Samuel R., *The Jewel-Hinged Jaw: Notes on the Language of Science Fiction*, Elizabethtown, New York: Dragon Press, 1977

Hassler, Donald M., *Comic Tones in Science Fiction: The Art of Compromise with Nature*, Westport, Connecticut: Greenwood Press, 1982

Magill, Frank N. (ed.), *Survey of Science Fiction Literature*, 5 vols., Englewood Cliffs, New Jersey: Salem Press, 1979; Epping, Essex: Bowker, 1979

Russ, Joanna, *To Write Like a Woman: Essays in Feminism and Science Fiction*, Bloomington: Indiana University Press, 1995

Suvin, Darko, *Metamorphoses of Science Fiction: On the Poetics and History of a Literary Genre*, New Haven, Connecticut: Yale University Press, 1979

Wolfe, Gary K., *The Known and the Unknown: The Iconography of Science Fiction*, Kent, Ohio: Kent State University Press, 1979

Wollheim, Donald A., *The Universe Makers: Science Fiction Today*, New York: Harper & Row, 1971; London: Victor Gollancz, 1972

The critical and historical works useful for the study of science fiction have proliferated and matured in the past quarter century far beyond their modest beginnings in the few academic and journalistic commentaries that had appeared in the 25 years before that, the sum of both periods dating back to the explosion of the first atomic bomb.

WOLLHEIM's book, in fact, opens with an acknowledgement of the influence that the first nuclear event had on the minds of science-fiction writers and fans. Further, he is squarely in the midst of a long tradition of fan writers who are "engrossed" by the wonder and possibility imaged in science and technology and in the fiction extrapolated from the two.

Thus, despite the bomb, and despite the comments of literary journalists such as Kingsley Amis, whom Wollheim attacks, and despite the pessimism of high art at the time, Wollheim, who quotes himself writing enthusiastically in fanzines from 1935 on, refuses to give up his optimism for the sheer social benefits that he believes will develop from the writing and reading of science fiction.

DELANY is also a fan commentator, because the bases for his critical writings grow out of his involvement as a writer and participant in the small science-fiction community – the same is true of Aldiss, Barron, Clute, and Russ (discussed below). But Delany provides a penetrating analysis of ways in which the thinking and the use of language seem to have developed differently in the fictions based on modern science when compared to other fiction. His methods are structural, linguistic, and often cleverly ironic, as in his title for his opening essay on method, "About Five Thousand Seven Hundred and Fifty Words". The brilliant analysis in this collection did much to stimulate the proliferation of science-fiction criticism.

MAGILL's massive reference- and survey-work collects the ideas of the growing body of academic critics who have been drawn to science fiction. A large number of critics have contributed interpretive essays on the major works (both novels and short-story collections) up to the end of the 1970s. The short essays include plot summaries, but also useful interpretive readings on theme and narrative strategy, so that an even quality of insight runs through the whole set. Now an updated edition of the work is in preparation for publication by Salem Press in 1997.

WOLFE's book is one of the early, comprehensive, academic studies of the genre. His approach is rather like the close reading of texts that grew from the New Criticism of poetry, and he does develop convincing arguments for the importance of certain repeating images or "icons" in science fiction. Replacing the wit and playfulness of Delany with workmanlike academic seriousness, Wolfe was one of the first to demonstrate that this literature could be analyzed not only for its new rhetoric, but also for internally consistent patterns of image; he treats science fiction as a mature literary genre.

SUVIN is by far the most ambitious theorist and academic critic of the genre to date. His book combines vast detail from literary history with a "socialist" theory of art that is at least as optimistic as Wollheim, if a lot more dense. Further, Suvin advances epistemological claims for the "newness" of thought in science fiction which go beyond Delany's language interest to suggest genuine changes in ideas – what he calls the "novum" of the genre. Suvin is genuinely revolutionary and optimistic both for the Wollheim-like social benefits of science fiction and for this new form of narrative, which depends so much on philosophy and science.

By the early 1980s the level and intensity of commentary on the genre, especially by academics, had risen to match the pitch of excitement in the writers themselves, such as Isaac Asimov, Arthur C. Clarke, Robert A. Heinlein, Frederik Pohl, and Philip K. Dick. My own book (HASSLER's) from this period traces the uses of comic irony as a defense strategy against the world's horrors, from the nervousness of late eighteenth-century writers who influenced Mary Shelley, such as Erasmus Darwin, to the very political Pohl among contemporary science-fiction writers.

The expanded history by ALDISS (he had called it *Billion Year Spree* in his 1973 version) is idiosyncratic but nicely comprehensive. He does highlight, also, the scientific enlightenment and the work of Erasmus Darwin and Mary Shelley as precursors of modern science fiction. Further, his historical narrative continually makes useful connections between writers who have produced primarily science fiction and more wide-ranging science writers, so that it is the most complete general history, to date, of science fiction and its importance in the history of ideas.

CLUTE and NICHOLLS also produced the original version of their magnificent reference work at that highpoint of commentary on the genre in 1979. Now, *The Encyclopedia* is widely acclaimed as an even more valuable tool and survey of science fiction. The large volume includes comprehensive entries on criticism and critics, on film and other media, on major themes such as "robotics", as well as on a vast array of fiction writers; an updated edition, with illustrations from the lively artwork associated with this field, is due in the near future.

The first edition of the book edited by BARRON appeared in 1976. Now in its fourth and, the editor claims, final edition, Barron's work collects important historical essays on the field and annotated bibliographic lists of both the fiction and commentary on the fiction. One of his consistently accurate collaborators and contributors, who has written the various historical sections on earlier science fiction, is the late Thomas D. Clareson, who was the founding editor of the first scholarly journal devoted to science fiction, *Extrapolation* (which published some early critical writings by Delany, Russ, Suvin, Wolfe, and myself).

For a genre that is "engrossed," as Wollheim says, with the future possibilities in society, the question of greater opportunities for women must be a major topic, and indeed some feminist criticism has flourished around science fiction lately. The recent collection by RUSS may be the most representative and useful because it collects a range of her essays on the topic since the 1970s. In some instances she elaborates on the new rhetoric, not only for women, but for science fiction in general, such as the "subjunctivity" of the genre, which is an adroit spin-off from a term derived from Delany. Russ is also a gifted fiction writer, as well as an academic and a "revolutionary" for future causes, so is an apt representative of the diverse strains that have been woven into the general commentary on science fiction.

DONALD M. HASSLER

See also **Fantasy Literature, Utopian Literature**

Scott, Sir Walter 1771–1832

Scottish novelist and poet

Brown, Douglas, *Walter Scott and the Historical Imagination*, London and Boston: Routledge, 1979
Devlin, D.D. (ed.), *Walter Scott*, London: Macmillan, 1968
Ferris, Ina, *The Achievement of Literary Authority: Gender, History, and the Waverley Novels*, Ithaca, New York: Cornell University Press, 1991

Lukács, Georg, *The Historical Novel*, translated by Hannah and Stanley Mitchell, London: Merlin Press, 1962; Boston: Beacon Press, 1963

Millgate, Jane, *Walter Scott: The Making of the Novelist*, Edinburgh: Edinburgh University Press, 1984; Toronto: University of Toronto Press, 1984

Welsh, Alexander, *The Hero of the Waverley Novels*, New Haven, Connecticut: Yale University Press, 1963; revised edition, Princeton, New Jersey: Princeton University Press, 1992

By the beginning of the twentieth-century the extraordinary esteem in which Scott had been held in his own time had all but dissipated. His often laboured narrative style and his contrived, slack plots were not to the taste of early twentieth-century readers at a time when "taste" was still a significant counter in literary criticism; nor were they equipped to withstand the kind of scrutiny directed at the novel by F.R. Leavis and his followers. It follows that almost all significant critical evaluations of Scott date from the second half of the century.

Thus the earliest essay required in DEVLIN's 1969 anthology for Macmillan's "Modern Judgements" series is by Edwin Muir, dating from 1945, which, characteristically for evaluations of Scott from that period, begins on the defensive, admitting, even apologising for, the novelist's considerable shortcomings. In his Introduction, Devlin remarked on how little critical work on Scott there had been even in the intervening 25 years. His anthology brings together representative, sometimes interesting, but sometimes rather stolid, old-fashioned writing on Scott. The most influential of the pieces, and still one of the most stimulating, is David Daiches's "Scott's Achievement as a Novelist" dating from 1951, in which he seeks to define the ambivalence in Scott's depiction of historical change between his regret for the loss of the feudal past and his rational acceptance of social and historical progress. Various other essays, for example by Robert E. Gordon and Joseph E. Duncan, can be seen responding to, and developing, Daiches's views.

More influential, however, has been the study by LUKÁCS, which was written first in 1937, but which did not appear in English translation until 1962. Lukács and Daiches both see the Waverley novels as being fundamentally concerned with large historical conflicts and changes, but Lukács's version of this argument has a distinctively Marxist inflection and locates Scott's practice within a broader thesis about the function of historical fiction in the historically and ideologically fraught worlds of nineteenth-century Europe. In this thesis, the emergence of the historical novel through Scott's work is the product of a particular moment in history – the French Revolution and the 25 years of European war that ensued. This era, Lukács argues, by engaging the common people more directly in the processes of historical change created for the first time what he calls a "mass experience of history". This modern consciousness of history lays the foundation for Scott's novels, with their detailed, realistic engagement with the past, their foregrounding of the ordinary individual's experience of historical crisis, and, most distinctively, their construction of "characters who, in their psychology and destiny, always represent social trends and historical forces". This places Scott at the head of an alternative tradition of the novel to that identified, for example, by Leavis, in which Scott had, and could have had, no part, and Lukács makes Scott the key figure in a radical reinterrogation of the novel as a literary form.

WELSH studies in detail the phenomenon of the "passive hero" in Scott's novels, pursuing a broad cultural and literary investigation which he focuses in three novels – *The Heart of Midlothian*, *Rob Roy*, and *Old Mortality*. He does not have a thesis as insistent or as bracing as Lukács's, allowing himself rather to consider carefully literary debate and literary change in the immediately preceding period, particularly the debate about "novel" and "romance", which he uses as a means of locating Scott's own fictional practice. He does, however, give some attention to the historical moment of Scott's work, as seen in his chapter on "Property". His work (extended in the 1992 edition, containing additional essays) has properly come to be regarded as a landmark in its attempts to understand Scott's work rather than appraise it or apologise for it, and to understand some of the cultural relations between the novel and the age.

Welsh had had access to Lukács only in German and mentions his work only twice in passing: but BROWN, in contrast, is able to engage in detail with Lukács's analysis (which he discusses judiciously in relation to that of Daiches) and with the reappraisals of Scott that followed its publication in English. Brown therefore consciously locates his work in the context of increased debate about Scott and esteem for his work. Brown gives detailed attention to Scott's ways of imagining the historical past as well as the processes of historical change, trying to balance overarching, theoretical considerations with the finer discriminations which emerge from close attention to individual novels. On the one hand, Brown offers stimulating readings of the major novels as he tracks Scott's development as a historical novelist. On the other, more broadly, the Scott who emerges from his analysis is more "Scottish" and less "European" than Lukács's version, and Brown argues for the influence on Scott of the Scottish "philosophical" historians of the late eighteenth century and for his historical vision being distinctively shaped by the specifics of Scottish history.

MILLGATE's interesting and lively critical account of Scott's career uniquely traces the development of Scott's art as a novelist back to the narrative poetry for which he was internationally celebrated, before he turned to novel-writing at the turn of the nineteenth century. Millgate is unique among the critics discussed here in treating Scott's poems, which she does carefully and penetratingly, finding there key and innovative elements in Scott's art, such as the integration of oral and written history. Nonetheless, her accounts of the major novels stand in their own right as intelligent and illuminating critical analyses, with a particular interest in narrative form and patterning.

FERRIS's book represents a new generation of studies of Scott. On the one hand, the scholarly enterprise at the core of Ferris's study – a close examination of the critical reception accorded to Scott's earlier novels – might be thought of as old-fashioned; but on the other, her work is informed throughout by the growth of literary theory, which has influenced all kinds of recent critical writing. She is particularly influenced by the work of Mikhail Bakhtin and by social theoreticians of literature such as Pierre Bourdieu. So, for example, she returns to the issue of "novel" versus "romance", which Welsh explored, but for her it is a gender issue not just a generic one, the novel being an emergent "male" discourse, the romance a "female" genre. Ferris's central thesis is that Scott's work and its reception mark the key point in the legitimation of the novel at the centre of literary culture. She argues that thesis through detailed reconstruction of, and reinterpretation of, the literary and cultural debates that centred upon Scott's novels – debates about gender, genre, the social location of literature, and authority. Her book shows how the issue of Scott's literary quality, and the kinds of debate initiated by Lukács, can be re-illuminated by contemporary theoretical concerns.

DAVID BLAIR

Scottish Literature: Medieval and Renaissance

Henderson, T.F., *Scottish Vernacular Literature: A Succinct History*, London: D. Nutt, 1898; 3rd revised edition, Edinburgh: J. Grant, 1910; reprinted, Folcroft, Pennsylvania: Folcroft Library Editions, 1974

Jack, R.D.S. (ed.), *Scottish Prose 1550–1700*, London: Calder & Boyars, 1971

Jack, R.D.S. (ed.), *Origins to 1660* (Volume 1 of *The History of Scottish Literature*, general ed. Cairns Craig), Aberdeen: Aberdeen University Press, 1988

Lindsay, Maurice, *History of Scottish Literature*, London: Robert Hale, 1977, revised 1992

McClure, J. Derrick, and Michael R.G. Spiller (eds.), *Bryght Lanternis: Essays on the Language and Literature of Medieval and Renaissance Scotland*, Aberdeen: Aberdeen University Press, 1989

Mackenzie, Agnes Mure, *An Historical Survey of Scottish Literature to 1714*, London: Alexander Maclehose, 1933

Shire, Helena Mennie, *Song, Dance and Poetry of the Court of Scotland under King James VI: Musical Illustrations of Court Song*, Cambridge: Cambridge University Press, 1969

Watson, Roderick, *The Literature of Scotland*, London: Macmillan, 1984

The Scottish medieval and Renaissance periods cover the early fourteenth century to the Union with England of 1707.

After a brief introduction to the development and decline of the Scottish vernacular, HENDERSON examines chronologically first poetry and then prose and traditional ballads and songs. He notes the negative influence of the Reformation and the Union of the Crowns on the vernacular (he goes on to discuss the revival of the vernacular in the eighteenth and nineteenth centuries). For each section Henderson supplies, when possible, quite detailed descriptions of the form and subject of both major and minor works, historical circumstances surrounding the writing and the subject matter, a brief history of the works' publication, the sources and influences, and biographical information. While Henderson's history is of worth as a source book, his opinions on the authors' skills are outdated and too idiosyncratic to be of much use as literary criticism.

MACKENZIE's history covers the literature in English and Scots (though not Gaelic) first chronologically, and then by genre. The early literature up to that of the Reformation is dealt with in some detail, but the literature of the last half of the sixteenth century and of the seventeenth century is not so thoroughly examined. This is perhaps as a result of Mackenzie's stated view that the Reformation thwarted the development of Scottish literature, and because of her clear dislike of the kings James VI and Charles I.

The first three chapters of LINDSAY's history are devoted to Scottish literature from its origins through the seventeenth century. Lindsay divides his text chronologically by century, noting the influences of politics, religion, and other literatures on the development of subject matter and style. Each chapter is further divided by genre (poetry, prose, oral ballad). Works written in both vernacular Scots and English are included, from established Scottish Makars and minor authors. For those writers whose works have "literary value", which he defines as "technically disciplined genuine feeling", Lindsay provides lengthy descriptions of their lives and works; others he briefly mentions and cursorily dismisses.

Chapters 1 through 4 of WATSON's history cover the beginning of Scottish literature through to the Union of 1707. As well as examinations of literatures in Scots and English, Watson incorporates substantial information on the development of Gaelic literatures. He also includes a detailed discussion of ballads. Political and religious events which influenced or were influenced by the literature are briefly summarised; as Watson outlines in his Introduction, emphasis is given to Scotland's "Presbyterian intellectual inheritance", an inheritance usually seen negatively rather than positively. A concise list for further reading is provided, as is a chronological table of authors and events.

JACK's history (1988) – the first of four volumes under the general editorship of Cairns Craig – attempts to cover almost 1,000 years of Scottish literature, from its origins to 1660. "Maximum coverage" is achieved through a "triple" approach: chapters cover a period chronologically, or focus on literary movements and forms, or deal primarily with one author. Each chapter is written by a specialist, and comprises careful scholarship, with detailed and diverse analyses and some reassessment of earlier criticisms. Jack includes essays on the medieval and Renaissance periods of vernacular prose, verse and drama, the oral tradition, and writers in Gaelic, Latin, and English. Each chapter contains a section of useful "Further Readings". If it lacks the continuum of single-author histories, the format of this essay collection allows for a more detailed study of periods, movements, and writers.

The collection of 36 essays edited by McCLURE and SPILLAR comprises a variety of essays on individual authors and works, and on diverse themes and movements in the medieval and Renaissance periods. Four essays on linguistics are included, as well as two on the relationship of Shakespeare to the Scots. While there is some overlap among essays (there are five essays on William Dunbar, for example), the different critical and thematic approaches manage, for the most part, to avoid repetition. Most essays include detailed notes or bibliographies, which provide useful information for further reading.

SHIRE's text examines Scottish court poetry and song of the sixteenth and seventeenth centuries, with specific interest in the poets and musicians of the Castalian Band in the court of James VI. Poetry is placed in the larger context of public celebration; thus, information includes not only details of the poets' lives and works, but also of the historical (political and religious) circumstances of the occasions of their writings, and of musicians and the influence of song on the poems. Among the poets Shire examines are Alexander Scott, James VI, Alexander Montgomerie, John Stewart of Baldynneis, Alexander Hume, William Fowler, and Sir Robert Aytoun. Special emphasis is placed on Montgomerie, especially his "The Cherrie and the Slae": Shire reviews past criticism of this poem and develops a religio-political reading. Shire also provides a fairly extensive bibliography, but often gives only sketchy documentation within the text.

JACK's anthology of prose works (1971) consists of a lengthy Introduction (by Jack) and selections from the works of John Knox, Thomas Maitland, George Buchanan, William Fowler, James VI, William Drummond, and Thomas Urquhart, among others. Each selection is introduced by a short commentary, which includes a biography and general comment on critical acclaim. A diversity of genres is represented: national and religious histories, sermons, romances, essays, poetic and political treatises, letters, and diaries. Jack argues in his Introduction that the events of these years may have curtailed the production of poetry, but that they provided a period of substantial development for prose. While a good introduction to prose of the period, this anthology is necessarily limited in its selections and critical commentary.

SANDRA J. BELL

Scottish Literature: 18th and 19th Centuries

Campbell, Ian (ed.), *Nineteenth-Century Scottish Fiction: Critical Essays*, Manchester: Carcanet, 1979; New York: Barnes & Noble, 1979

Craig, David, *Scottish Literature and the Scottish People 1680–1830*, London: Chatto & Windus, 1961

Crawford, Thomas, *Society and the Lyric: A Study of the Song Culture of Eighteenth-Century Scotland*, Edinburgh: Scottish Academic Press, 1979

Dwyer, John, *Virtuous Discourse: Sensibility and Community in Late Eighteenth-Century Scotland*, Edinburgh: John Donald, 1987

Gifford, Douglas (ed.), *Nineteenth Century* (Volume 3 of *The History of Scottish Literature*, general ed. Cairns Craig), Aberdeen: Aberdeen University Press, 1988

Hart, Francis Russell, *The Scottish Novel: A Critical Survey*, London: John Murray, 1978; as *The Scottish Novel: From Smollett to Spark*, Cambridge, Massachusetts: Harvard University Press, 1978

Hook, Andrew (ed.), *1660–1800* (Volume 2 of *The History of Scottish Literature*, general ed. Cairns Craig), Aberdeen: Aberdeen University Press, 1987

Lindsay, Maurice, *History of Scottish Literature*, London: Robert Hale, 1977, revised 1992

The Scottish Enlightenment saw in Edinburgh an intellectual activity arguably unparalleled in any contemporary European city. With the spread of the ideas of Francis Hutcheson, the activities of the Foulis Press, and the maturation of the University of Edinburgh during the generation of Adam Smith, David Hume, and Adam Ferguson, Scottish literature revived itself after the long dormant period imposed by Presbyterianism.

The Aberdeen University Press four-volume *History of Scottish Literature* is the definitive starting point for any study of the literary culture. Hook and Gifford, in Volumes 2 and 3, have brought together scholarly essays by the leading commentators on eighteenth- and nineteenth-century writing in Scotland. For HOOK, literature is an inclusive term, and he represents history, politics, and theology alongside philosophy, drama, poetry, and fiction. Hugh Ouston, Iain G. Brown, Richard B. Sher, and John R.R. Christie provide essays on cultural life, the politics of the Union, the Church of Scotland, and science. Especially useful is Alasdair Cameron's rare examination of the history of the restored theatre in Scotland between 1660 and 1800.

GIFFORD's volume is similarly organized. Essays by Christopher Harvie, David Withrington, and Mary Ellen Brown provide intellectual contexts for industrialism, religion, and social change. Gifford is justifiably liberal in the space given over to the survey of non-fictional prose, especially magazines and reviews. Andrew Noble's essay on John Wilson is seminal and Jenni Calder contributes a piece about women in nineteenth-century Scottish fiction. There are individual essays on Sir Walter Scott and Robert Louis Stevenson, but Gifford strives to be widely representative, including another essay by Alasdair Cameron who appears in Hook's volume, extending his survey of the theatre up to the end of the nineteenth century.

LINDSAY's history is more populist in its style and approach. Two long chapters are devoted to the eighteenth and nineteenth centuries, with the emphasis in the survey placed upon literature itself. Biography is stressed more than cultural history, and where Gifford includes Gaelic literature, Lindsay's focus is exclusively on the Lowlands. Primary texts are profusely quoted, and Lindsay practises a good deal of effective criticism in combination with his comprehensive literary history. Lindsay has a better critical appreciation for poetry than for prose. This is a reasonable survey with which to begin, but, unlike the volumes edited by Hook and Gifford, Lindsay's work requires definite enrichment from more thorough and scholarly studies.

CRAIG probes the cultural origins of the literary establishment of Enlightenment Scotland by examining the conflicted relationship between polite and vernacular sensibilities in the eighteenth century. He stresses the communal nature of Scots and finds that quality much in evidence in Scottish poetry. Craig's study has three strengths in its treatment of nineteenth-century literature: its identification of the reading public for fiction; its discussion of the impact of emigration on literary production and the national imagination; and its examination of Scottish publishing houses and periodicals. Craig's chapter on "Literature and the Native Tongue" remains a key study of the Scots language as a literary medium.

CRAWFORD's study of the song culture of eighteenth-century Scotland sets Robert Burns in the best possible populist contexts. The book argues convincingly that Scots puritanism denigrated oral culture and lauded the literary because the oral could not be confined effectively to the printed page. Crawford notes the marginalization of the lyric in David Craig's work and traces this tendency back to Robert Louis Stevenson's observations about Burns. Much of Crawford's primary material is taken from manuscript collections, making his book doubly useful: he recontextualizes the Scottish poetry of the period within popular culture; and, perhaps more importantly, he makes accessible a great number of lyrics not otherwise available in print.

DWYER looks above the popular culture to the philosophic republic of letters to establish the moral contexts for Scottish literature in the late eighteenth century. Drawing from Adam Smith on moral sentiments and tracing the role of periodicals, Dwyer identifies a discourse of sensibility that pervades and characterizes literature in Scotland. The development of the novel, Dwyer argues, provides a sort of literary "moral preceptor", with roots in the ideals of human sympathy set out in Hugh Blair's sermons. For Dwyer, it was Scottish moralists who made a great national literary culture possible and who gave to the novel in Scotland its enduringly characteristic "nostalgia for lost societies".

CAMPBELL puts together a collection of essays that picks up the story of the novel where Dwyer leaves off. Contributors include David Daiches on Scott, Colin Manlove on George MacDonald, and Alastair Fowler on Stevenson. One of the more useful studies looks at Mrs Oliphant's Scotland, and evaluates her "campaign . . . to break down what she regarded as naive stereotypes retained by English readers about Scotland". By and large this volume provides an accessible introduction to the critical issues surrounding the Scottish novel of the nineteenth century, but is neither comprehensive nor inclusive, nor claims to be.

HART offers a theory of Scottish fiction that is comprehensive and contrary to Dwyer's. Remarking on the late appearance of the novel in Scotland, he argues that a "neurotic" combination of "blasting irony" and "obsessive romanticism", "hostile cynic[ism]", and "condescending affection" characterizes Scottish uncomfortableness with fiction. Hart rightfully emphasizes the role of Blackwood's Publishers in shaping the aesthetic impulses of the "first identifiable generation of Scottish novelists". Thus John Galt assumes a place equal to Scott and surpassing Tobias Smollett as a primary influence on nineteenth-century Scottish fiction. Hart goes on in the second half of his study to connect the nineteenth- and twentieth-century sensibilities of Scottish novelists, an exercise that provides important contexts for future study of the literature of the 1800s.

STEPHEN W. BROWN

Scottish Literature: 20th Century

Aitken, William Russell, *Scottish Literature in English and Scots: A Guide to Information Sources*, Detroit: Gale Research, 1982
Craig, Cairns (ed.), *The Twentieth Century* (Volume 4 of *The History of Scottish Literature*, general ed. Craig), Aberdeen: Aberdeen University Press, 1987
Hart, Francis Russell, *The Scottish Novel: A Critical Survey*, London: John Murray, 1978; as *The Scottish Novel: From Smollett to Spark*, Cambridge, Massachusetts: Harvard University Press, 1978
Lindsay, Maurice, *History of Scottish Literature*, London: Robert Hale, 1977, revised 1992
Murray, Isobel, and Bob Tait, *Ten Modern Scottish Novels*, Aberdeen: Aberdeen University Press, 1984
Wittig, Kurt H., *The Scottish Tradition in Literature*, Edinburgh: Oliver & Boyd, 1958

As with criticism of many minority literatures, work on modern Scottish writing has been compromised by the small size and limited knowledge of the criticism's envisaged audience. Half of AITKEN's excellent bibliography deals with Scottish literature from 1900 to 1980, but reveals, among other things, that the plethora of literary works produced in this period has not been accompanied by a corresponding richness of critical endeavour: the section on "Literary History and Criticism" is a mere two-and-a-half pages long. On the one hand, a restricted market tends to make in-depth studies of individual authors economically non-viable, which explains why most of the work in this field is synoptic, often covering a large number of authors (and sometimes genres) in a fairly wide historical period. Most commentators seem to vacillate, too, between assuming knowledge of the literature and assuming ignorance, the resultant discourse usually hovering somewhere between literary analysis and literary introduction.

WITTIG's book is an example of synopsis *par excellence*. In 350 pages it purports to offer an account of Scottish literature between the end of the fourteenth century and the middle of the twentieth. A good quarter of the book is, however, consumed by two concluding chapters on the twentieth century. Wittig's intention is to bring to attention the main features in poetry, drama, and fiction. His recommendations (for example, of George Douglas Brown and Marion Angus) do not have the force of critical analysis behind them. Wittig's judgments are made before he writes, and he simply offers them in a style that will strike most readers as authoritarian; but such is the general mode of canon-forming enterprises. The fact that there is nothing very surprising *now* about the names Wittig offers as the major Scottish poets and novelists of the first half of the twentieth century – Hugh MacDiarmid, Edwin Muir, Lewis Grassic Gibbon, Thom Gunn – shows how influential his particular enterprise has been.

HART's later survey of fiction from Tobias Smollett to George Mackay Brown looks, paradoxically, more dated now. Partly, this is because it appeared in the decade before the explosion of Scottish fiction in the 1980s, which so dramatically altered the landscape Hart is attempting to describe. LINDSAY has circumvented this problem by updating his widely read 1977 volume with an additional chapter. The difficulty is that recent developments in Scottish writing cannot adequately be accounted for in a 15-page supplement. The decade-and-a-half in question would require at least a volume to itself, and clearly exhausts the survey mode in which criticism in this field has found itself trapped.

MURRAY and TAIT do attempt to combine construction of a rough and ready line for the modern Scottish novel with detailed reading of individual texts. If the decimal roundedness of the number of novels they choose seems somewhat arbitrary (and one reflects that Lewis Grassic Gibbon's *A Scots Quair* is not one novel at all, but three), so too does their critical approach, which is eclectic and unfocused. The novels scrutinised are *A Scots Quair*, Neil Gunn's *The Silver Darlings*, Fionn MacColla's *And the Cock Crew*, James Kennaway's *Tunes of Glory*, Muriel Spark's *The Prime of Miss Jean Brodie*, Gordon Williams' *From Scenes Like These*, George Mackay Brown's *Greenvoe*, William McIlvanney's *Docherty*, Robin Jenkins' *Fergus Lamont*, and Alasdair Gray's *Lanark*. Murray and Tait admit to having no clear criteria for selection. They discount the claim that these are the best novels of the 50-year period explored, but do not explain the logic of a 50-year period in the first place. The result is a set of readings of a rag bag of texts with no clear relationship to one another. The authors, indeed, expressly wish to give "the impression of a degree of cultural diversity and fragmentation astonishing in so small a country". They abandon the unifying notion of a "tradition", when they invoke it, by redefining the common experience which "tradition" signifies as one of *dis*unity: "our fractured national culture and communal divisions preoccupy and move all our novelists to some extent".

CRAIG's collection, which will probably be the definitve starting point for future work, also emphasises variety in refusing to conform to a "Scottish Renaissance" template. It covers writing before MacDiarmid in four ample opening chapters, and focuses on genres generally occluded by previous studies in chapters on literary criticism, the popular novel, and women's writing. MacDiarmid and the Scottish Renaissance are, of course, centrally *there*, but they are not allowed to overwhelm what is seen as a highly multifarious literary development. There are three chapters, for example, on an otherwise much marginalised Gaelic literature (one on poetry, one on prose, and one on Sorley Maclean). The only novelists to whom entire chapters are devoted, meanwhile, are Neil Gunn and Muriel Spark. The volume as a whole, then, offers a somewhat different inflection to the writing of Scottish literary history, and goes perhaps as far in coverage and pluralism as the survey-approach can. It may be that criticism of the rich body of twentieth-century Scottish writing can now break free of the historiographical straitjacket that has hitherto constrained it.

MACDONALD DALY

Semiotics

Culler, Jonathan, *The Pursuit of Signs: Semiotics, Literature, Deconstruction*, London: Routledge, 1981; Ithaca, New York: Cornell University Press, 1981

Eco, Umberto, *The Role of the Reader: Explorations in the Semiotics of Texts*, Bloomington: Indiana University Press, 1979; London: Hutchinson, 1981

Hawkes, Terence, *Structuralism and Semiotics*, London: Methuen, 1977; Berkeley: University of California Press, 1977

Innis, Robert E. (ed.), *Semiotics: An Introductory Anthology*, Bloomington: Indiana University Press, 1985; London: Hutchinson, 1986

Riffaterre, Michael, *Semiotics of Poetry*, Bloomington: Indiana University Press, 1978; London: Methuen, 1980

Scholes, Robert, *Semiotics and Interpretation*, New Haven, Connecticut, and London: Yale University Press, 1982

Out of the enormous range of texts on semiotics published in the last 25 years, I have selected two seminal contributions to the theory, three explanatory works, and one comprehensive anthology.

By far the most compelling attempt to refine semiotic theory and apply it scrupulously and meticulously to a wide range of literary texts is the study by RIFFATERRE. Starting from the basic premises that "the language of poetry differs from that of common usage" and that "a poem says one thing and means another", he develops a highly sophisticated programme of reading and interpretation, the main features of which can be summarised briefly: there are two stages of reading a text – a heuristic level, when we attend only to the mimetic or referential aspects of the poem, and a second retroactive or hermeneutic reading, wherein the non-realistic deviances (Riffaterre calls these "ungrammaticalities") spotted in the first encounter are integrated into a cohesive interpretation of the whole text. This process is effected by identifying a matrix word, which generates the poem through a series of "hypograms", which in turn produce the specific lexical choices that determine the final text. For instance, in Shakespeare's Sonnet 73 the structural matrix would be the word "ageing"(though this doesn't appear in the poem itself) and the hypogram some such cliché as "I'm in the autumn of my life", a phrase that energises all the autumnal metaphors that perfuse and organise the text.

The rest of this fascinating book is largely taken up with refining and expanding these basic concepts. Most importantly, Riffaterre demonstrates how hypograms entail an enormous freightage of intertextual reference, and it is this that gives resonance and richness of association to the sign system(s) of the poetic text. Highly detailed analyses of expansion, conversion, syllepsis, and intertextual punning lead to a discussion of the decoding activity of the reader and the importance of generic competence. All this is cogently documented with minute attention to the language of poems by Francis Ponge, Gérard de Nerval, Paul Claudel, Charles Baudelaire, and many others. Despite the fact that Riffaterre deals almost entirely with French poetry, his semiotic method is seductively easy to apply to English works; and, Culler's charges of reductivism notwithstanding (*The Pursuit of Signs*, Chapter 4), it has the overwhelming virtue of wedding the close-reading techniques of formalist criticism with a rigorous and complex theoretical basis.

Some of the most vital work on semiotic theory has come from the fertile pen of ECO. His *A Theory of Semiotics* (1976) and *Semiotics and the Philosophy of Language* (1984) are now acknowledged classics, but, since they deal mainly with the linguistic and philosophic aspects of semiosis, I have reviewed here his no-less significant collection of essays with a more literary bent, *The Role of the Reader*. Eco here provides a comprehensive theory of semiotic decoding, stressing the active part played by the reader in deciphering texts. It is impossible to summarise all the topics covered, but perhaps the most important contribution lies in Eco's use of C.S. Peirce to create a communication model of the reading process in which the "Model Reader"is actually postulated by the text and assumed to share the same intertextual competence as the "sender". After providing a highly sophisticated model of the act of reading, Eco demonstrates this in action through close analyses of fictive texts, including the comic strip *Superman*, James Joyce's *Finnegans Wake*, Eugène Sue's *The Mysteries of Paris*, and the novels of Ian Fleming.

Central to this discussion is Eco's distinction between the "open" text, which gives the reader considerable autonomy in actualising an interpretation, and the "closed" text, which attempts to control and prescribe the reader's response: in the former "the author offers the interpreter, the performer, the addressee a work *to be completed*". Chapters on metaphor, the "interpretant", and Edenic language further enrich this semiotic programme. Finally, Eco demonstrates his theories in action by offering a detailed and entertaining reading of Alphonse Alais's short story "Un drame bien parisien". Eco's is an indispensable seminal text. Based more on the logical schemes of Peirce than on the linguistic model of Saussure, it offers an invaluable methodology for the decoding of a wide range of literary texts.

HAWKES's introductory survey commences with an analysis of Saussure, stressing the semiotic elements in his work. A very full and detailed commentary on Claude Lévi-Strauss follows. Hawkes then provides a useful résumé of the works of the Russian formalists, Vladimir Propp, Roman Jakobson, and Tzvetan Todorov. The student will find his discussion of the culture-bound nature of genre particularly clear and helpful. All this, plus a glance at "signification" in the writings of Barthes, lays the foundations for a lucid, jargon-free analysis of the semiotic activity. Hawkes emphasises several important points: (1) that semiotics embraces all areas where sign-systems operate (zoosemiotics, proxemics, road signs, the codes of dress, perfume, gesture . . . and so on); (2) the crucial difference between iconic signs (which are images of things they represent), indexical signs (which point to their meaning – e.g., a weather cock), and symbolic signs (in which the relation of signifier to signified is arbitrary, as in language itself); (3) that the signifier remains empty until weighted with a definite signified, when it becomes a sign: this is evidenced in Barthes's famous examples of the bunch of roses and the black pebble in *Mythologies*. Hawkes's short volume is an introductory text for students. As such, it is a model of clarity and incisiveness: it isolates the key elements in structuralist-semiotic theory without oversimplifying, and the literary examples are always well-chosen.

CULLER basically regards semiotics as a system of literary signification, which embraces both the ways that signs operate in texts and the competence of the reader to decode them. After attacking the obsession with interpretation inherited from the New Critics, but still present in Northrop Frye, Stanley Fish, and even in American deconstruction, Culler surveys the origins of semiotics in Ferdinand de Saussure and Peirce and presents a cogent theory of the sign as being culturally determined, thus decentring the subject as the originator or meaning. The sign is not a token of some pre-existent object, but part of an ultimately logocentric system which *enables* meaning (literal and metaphorical) to be decoded on the basis of "*aliquid stat pro aliquo*". It is thus crucial that the reader has the competence to respond to those codes.

In a lengthy central chapter, Culler explores various theories of reading and reception, including those of Norman Holland, Hans-Robert Jauss, and Todorov, and gives an exemplary semiotic "reading" of William Blake's "London". A detailed exposition (and critique) of Riffaterre follows, and this in turn leads naturally to a highly stimulating account of intertextuality, presupposition, and generic awareness, drawing on the work of Laurent Jenny and Julia Kristeva. Culler next reproves Fish for not attempting to answer the question "how does the reader create meaning?"

The third part of the book is less interesting, being a ragbag of essays, including studies of metaphor and apostrophe. A chapter on "Story and Discourse" belongs more properly in a volume on narratology. But this remains a very helpful, wide-ranging book; the first two sections should be indispensable reading for anyone wishing to study the relation between linguistics and sign-systems in general. It admirably complements Hawkes's little introduction.

SCHOLES's book is an attempt to "show what happens when a practising semiotician enters the traditional domain of literary interpretation". To further this aim he employs a practical adaptation of Jakobson's six-fold schema of communication models to establish a system of codes that is both functional and related to human experience. Subsequent chapters develop this method, treating such types as the generic code of "elegy", the "ungrammaticalities" of the poetic text (cf. Riffaterre, *passim*), and narrative codes in film and fiction – this latter incorporating a stimulating account of narrativity, which, however, seems somewhat removed from semiotics, a charge which might equally be levelled at his approach to irony.

Three concluding chapters deal with short stories by Joyce and Ernest Hemingway, and with myths of the female body. Scholes's use of Barthes's five codes in analysing Joyce's "Eveline" is particularly convincing. This is a refreshing book, wide-ranging, jargon-free, and above all practical. Pointedly eschewing endless discussion of semiotic or pragmatic theories, Scholes provides the student with an eminently usable introduction to the subject.

INNIS edits an extremely useful collection of essays, bringing together many of the most essential semiotic explorations, including key extracts from the founding fathers, Peirce and Saussure. It is good to have Buhler's reflections on how *aliquid stat pro aliquo* and his trichotomy of signals, indices, and symbols – not least because it is on the latter that Jakobson formulated his famous six-fold communication model (also included in this anthology). There are useful extracts from the work of Susanne Langer, Charles Morris, and Meyer Shapiro, as well as Barthes's explanation of the polysemous nature of the image, Eco's study of metaphor, and Émile Benveniste's influential attempt to refine Saussure by separating the semantic from the semiotic realms within a language system. While many of the essays in this reader do not focus specifically on literature, they provide a handy compendium of the major theoretical statements upon which literary semiotics must be based. There is no general bibliography, but there is a useful subject index.

A.W. LYLE

Sentimentalism

Bernbaum, Ernest, *The Drama of Sensibility: A Sketch of the History of English Sentimental Comedy and Domestic Tragedy 1696–1780*, London and Boston: Ginn, 1915; reprinted, Gloucester, Massachusetts: Peter Smith, 1958
Brissenden, Richard F., *Virtue in Distress: Studies in the Novel of Sentiment from Richardson to Sade*, London: Macmillan, 1974
Conger, Syndy McMillen (ed.), *Sensibility in Transformation: Creative Resistance to Sentiment from the Augustans to the Romantics: Essays in Honor of Jean H. Hagstrum*, Rutherford, New Jersey: Fairleigh Dickinson University Press, 1990; London: Associated University Presses, 1990
Ellis, Frank H., *Sentimental Comedy: Theory and Practice*, Cambridge and New York: Cambridge University Press, 1991
Hagstrum, Jean H., *Sex and Sensibility: Ideal and Erotic Love from Milton to Mozart*, Chicago: Unversity of Chicago Press, 1980
Hilles, Frederick W., and Harold Bloom (eds.), *From Sensibility to Romanticism: Essays Presented to Frederick A. Pottle*, New York: Oxford University Press, 1965
Jones, Chris, *Radical Sensibility: Literature and Ideas in the 1790s*, London and New York: Routledge, 1993
Mullan, John, *Sentiment and Sociability: The Language of Feeling in the Eighteenth Century*, Oxford: Clarendon Press, 1988
Todd, Janet, *Sensibility: An Introduction*, London and New York: Methuen, 1986
Van Sant, Ann Jessie, *Eighteenth-Century Sensibility and the Novel: The Senses in Social Context*, Cambridge and New York: Cambridge University Press, 1993

Sentimentalism is generally treated as part of a constellation of related terms, including "sensibility", "sentiment", "sentimental", and "sympathy". These denoted concepts and qualities often detected in literature ancient and modern, but which enjoyed their fashionable, if controversial, heyday in the second half of the eighteenth century. When applied to literature,"sentimentalism" and "sentimental" are often used pejoratively, associated with vulgarity, naivety, and self-indulgent appeals to emotion for its own sake. The later twentieth century has witnessed steadily increasing interest in sensibility as a subject in its own right, particularly among scholars concerned with the relationship between literature and society.

BERNBAUM's study displays the scholarly strengths and conceptual weaknesses typical of his period. Less interested in social and economic causes than in literary effects, he traces the fortunes of sensibility throughout French and English drama from 1540 to 1760. He believes sentimentalism is a timeless, universal human characteristic: "the desire to think well of mankind is too constant and powerful a yearning of the human heart not to find occasional expression in the literature of any nation and any age".

HILLES and BLOOM have assembled 26 essays, covering poetry and poets from Alexander Pope to Byron, Percy Bysshe Shelley, and John Keats. Sensibility, in many guises, emerges as the crucial link. There is one caveat: "sensibility" is an unexamined term in this volume. Nevertheless, the excellence of the individual contributions and their thorough coverage of the period make this an indispensable guide for anyone who wishes to understand the relationship between Augustanism and Romanticism.

A structural precedent for later critics is set by BRISSENDEN: he begins by examining the intellectual and ideological implications of sensibility, before discussing selected novels. He provides illuminating accounts of the relationships among Samuel Richardson, Henry Fielding, Laurence Sterne, Henry Mackenzie, Ann Radcliffe, Courtney Melmoth, Goethe, Denis Diderot, Choderlos de Laclos, Jane Austen, and the Marquis de Sade. He pays close attention to philosophy and science, noting that Richardson's *Clarissa* is a "programmed experiment" designed to "test to destruction certain notions – such as man's innate humanity – which are basic to sentimental morality".

HAGSTRUM's study of "sex and sensibility at their intersection" was hailed as an instant classic on publication; subsequent assessments have done nothing to diminish its status. He examines literature, fine art, and music: he is one of the pioneers who showed what could be learned by taking opera librettos seriously. He traces the stormy emotional history of Europe over 150 years, deciding that "the deepest if not the most attractive legacy of the Age of Reason is the *coeur sensible*".

TODD has produced the most useful general introduction. She combines an impressively wide range of reading with an unerring eye for linguistic detail. She sets the eighteenth century in far wider contexts, tracing the sentimental tradition from Euripides' tragedies to the novels of D.H. Lawrence and Alice Walker. Todd exposes the paradoxical nature of sentimentality and its opponents: many of those who denounced it used sentimental techniques. The cult of female sensibility, glamorizing physical and intellectual weakness, emerges in this study as an effective means of limiting female power.

MULLAN explores further paradoxes. Sensibility, often considered the source of all the emotional sympathies and moral sanctions that make society possible, depends on a strength of individual response, which leads either to antisocial self-centredness or excesses of compassion, which can in turn drive the sufferer to withdrawal from society, even to death. Eighteenth-century medical theory reveals sensibility as the sign of a "privileged susceptibility", connected with social and intellectual superiority, physical weakness, and a tendency to mental illness.

CONGER has edited a collection of essays whose sophistication and scholarship are worthy of their dedicatee, Jean Hagstrum. The most original essay, "The Conscious Speakers" by Leland E. Warren, links sensibility with "the tradition of conversation books going back to the Renaissance". Mark S. Madoff's reading of Sterne's *Journal to Eliza* is a useful reminder of the part played by tuberculosis in creating the myth of the hypersensitive sentimental physique and psychology. In "The Poetics of Schiller and Wordsworth", Lore Metzger detects language that "displays the ideological tension between their commitment to revolutionizing the individual sensibility and to maintaining the social equilibrium that their arguments reinforce". The book concludes with a bibliography of secondary sources, covering English, French, and German scholarship.

ELLIS approaches sentimental comedy with a zest for quantification and definition which leaves few assumptions unexamined. He asks: "how much sentimentality is required to make a comedy sentimental?", and presents the reader with 15 indicators of sentimentality. These methods are not always convincing. More effective is the sensitive reading, which enables him to show that the supposedly serious main characters in Sir Richard Steele's *The Conscious Lovers* speak some very comical dialogue. Gender is a weak spot: if Ellis had paid more attention to Todd, he might have refrained from describing belief in women's superior sensibility as a "freak of eighteenth-century thought that has become a political movement in the twentieth century". Still, even those who disagree with Ellis's conclusions will find his questions worth considering. He also appends two important texts – William Whitehead's *The School for Lovers* and Elizabeth Inchbald's *Every One Has His Fault*.

JONES covers the 1790s in detail, revealing the ways in which sentimentality was exploited and contested in the course of bitter political conflict. Those staunch radicals William Godwin and Mary Wollstonecraft can be found in the thick of things. Jones discusses such relatively neglected writers as Robert Bage, Helen Maria Williams, and Charlotte Smith, as well as well-established canonical figures like Wordsworth and Coleridge: the former provide provocatively new perspectives from which to view the latter.

VAN SANT, following physiological and scientific routes mapped by Brissenden and Mullan, has discovered exciting new territory. Her totally compelling study covers sight and touch. "The first deals with a conflation of pathetic and scientific observation"; the second "focuses primarily on sensibility's physicalizing of psychological response". Richardson, Sterne, and Mackenzie are set firmly into context. Her choice of charities as a means to illustrate the overlap between "rhetorical and scientific methods of presentation" is inspired, but the inclusion of the Royal Humane Society, which operated on scientific principles, would have made her point even more effectively.

CAROLYN D. WILLIAMS

Shakespeare, William 1564–1616

English dramatist and poet

1. History of Criticism

Bristol, Michael D., *Shakespeare's America, America's Shakespeare*, London and New York: Routledge, 1990
Eastman, Arthur M., *A Short History of Shakespearean Criticism*, New York: Random House, 1968
Grady, Hugh, *The Modernist Shakespeare: Critical Texts in a Material World*, Oxford: Clarendon Press, 1991; New York: Oxford University Press, 1991
Harbage, Alfred, *Conceptions of Shakespeare*, Cambridge, Massachusetts: Harvard University Press, 1966
Holland, Norman N., *Psychoanalysis and Shakespeare*, New York: McGraw-Hill, 1966
Ralli, Augustus, *A History of Shakespearian Criticism*, 2 vols., London: Oxford University Press/Humphrey Milford, 1932
Siegel, Paul N., *Shakespeare in His Time and Ours*, Notre Dame, Indiana: University of Notre Dame Press, 1968
Stavisky, Aron Y., *Shakespeare and the Victorians: Roots of Modern Criticism*, Norman: University of Oklahoma Press, 1969
Thompson, Ann, "'The Warrant of Womanhood': Shakespeare and Feminist Criticism", in *The Shakespeare Myth*, edited by Graham Holderness, Manchester: Manchester University Press, 1988
Vickers, Brian, *Appropriating Shakespeare: Contemporary Critical Quarrels*, New Haven, Connecticut, and London: Yale University Press, 1993

This discussion treats not only changing interpretations of the plays but of Shakespeare as a cultural monument, gradually constructed and consciously appropriated. With Shakespeare as an icon, shifting from Right to Left and perhaps back again, the hitherto covert process by which literature is inevitably politicized becomes a visible object of study.

RALLI's somewhat unwieldy tome of over 1,100 pages traces Shakespeare's critical fortunes for over 300 years (the seventeenth century through 1925), not only in England, but in Germany and France as well. Critics are divided into 42 categories, arranged chronologically within nationality groupings. The Introduction to each category describes and evaluates the work of its individual members and their approaches. These are followed by detailed, often play-by-play, summaries of the writings of each critic. Ralli concludes the discussion of each group by indicating its most important trends. This is an old-fashioned but still very useful book.

HARBAGE's collection of essays is concerned with "The Shakespearean After-Image", with how Shakespeare has been seen by his biographers and critics, by theater people, and by those who dispute his authorship. Disturbed by the "myth of perfection", which has led to the staunch defense of Shakespeare's weakest work, Harbage nevertheless believes that even warped views of Shakespeare have contributed to his mythic quality. Among actors and directors, Shakespeare has been imaged as an entertainer. For over a century his plays were produced (or mis-produced) as spectacle (e.g., actor-manager Thomas Betterton, one of the most famous Hamlets, introduced six monkeys and 14 Chinese dancers into *A Midsummer Night's Dream*). Modern directors, dedicated to "making it new", are often just as guilty of desecrating Shakespeare texts. *King Lear*'s often unhappy critical fortunes from the seventeenth century to the present are the subject of one essay. In another, on "Shakespeare as Culture Hero", Harbage invokes Raglan, Rank, and Freud to analyze anti-Stratfordianism. Harbage's warm and appealing tone is one of the pleasures of this work.

HOLLAND's definitive and encyclopaedic work first expounds Freud's psychoanalytic theory of creativity as it relates to the artist and the work. (Interestingly, Freud was an anti-Stratfordian.) Part Two discusses the entire corpus of psychoanalytic Shakespeare criticism from the beginnings in 1897, when Freud attributed an Oedipus complex to Hamlet, to the mid-1960s. About 400 essays are discussed, some of them, concerning Desdemona's penis envy or Cordelia's incestuous desire for her 80-year-old father, apt to surprise the reader. Small wonder that Holland cautions against irresponsibly manufacturing an interpretation out of one or two words in the text, of treating protagonists as real people and psychoanalyzing them, or of identifying a protagonist with the playwright, and ascribing a psychological history to both. Influenced by New Criticism, Holland asserts that the hero is constructed out of images, and asks that we analyze not the single character but the entire play as the result of unconscious impulses and defenses against them. This important book includes an extensive bibliography.

EASTMAN discusses the evolution of Shakespeare criticism through analysis and appropriate quotation from writers chosen for their dissimilar views; Chapter 1 takes us from Shakespeare's contemporaries to Samuel Johnson. Ensuing chapters trace the responses of established critics through Northrop Frye and Arthur Sewell. English, American, German, and Canadian (Frye) critics are included. This work might be viewed as a condensed version of Ralli's monumental study, but, unlike his predecessor, Eastman is more concerned with the critics' general statements than with their commentary on individual plays. Eastman's evaluations are sensible and persuasive.

SIEGEL attempts to strike a balance between seeing Shakespeare's work solely through modern eyes and being aware of Elizabethan views. The fullest understanding draws on both. Siegel discusses Elizabethan takes on theological issues, on honor, and on the theatrical representation of Jews; for example, for Siegel the tragedies are providential, grounded in archetypes from the Bible, and Shylock is more Puritan than Jew. This revised edition includes essays on *Much Ado about Nothing* and *King Lear,* and on Shakespearean comedy and tragedy. Siegel explains the shift from romantic comedy to satire by looking to his earlier work on the Elizabethan Compromise, which held in equipoise the interests of the bourgeoisie and the nobility; with the collapse of the Compromise, and the triumph of the aristocracy, the old paradigm of order was disrupted. Siegel concludes that the romances, infused with a sense of wonder, imply a glorious future for the nation.

STAVISKY, in his contribution to the University of Oklahoma's "Roots of Modern Criticism" series, uncovers the ways in which twentieth-century criticism developed out of Victorian traditions. He analyzes both major and minor Victorian critics, such as E.A. Abbott, F.G. Fleay, J. Kirkman, Edward Dowden, and A.C. Bradley. Above all, he dwells on the bitter conflict between F.J. Furnivall and A.C. Swinburne, in which scientism, or order, and an intuitive moral aestheticism contended. Those favoring the former principles of criticism brought out new Shakespearean editions and grammars, listed dramatic elements, founded societies, and created authorship tests. For Stavisky, the sins of these critics were various – their quantifying methods, neglect of the play's poetry, and disintegration of the Shakespeare canon (ascribing to other authors whatever they found unworthy of a playwright they regarded as sublime). Notwithstanding, we are deeply indebted to them, not least for the historical scholarship so attractive to recent critics. Modern critics tend to seek to unite the two strands of Coleridgean imagination and historicism that divided the Victorians.

THOMPSON sets out to demystify the Shakespeare myth with regard to gender, that is, to the way the plays have been constructed by the patriarchal Right. Her 14-page essay adumbrates the major directions feminist Shakespeare criticism has taken and some of its most important practitioners, from its birth, in 1975 with the publication of Juliet Dusinberre's *Shakespeare and the Nature of Women*, through the late 1980s. Thompson focuses on the debate between those who see canonical figures such as Shakespeare as legitimate and important subjects for feminist criticism and those who urge working exclusively on women writers. She fears the latter approach will lead to the ghettoization of feminist criticism. Thompson observes that the plays are less misogynist than their male critics and directors. Shakespeare's feminist apologists may stress female community, rescue female characters, and suggest their equality with men in practice, albeit not in theory. Feminist critics of a less optimistic bent may prefer to read the plays in the context of social history, investigate the representation of female characters over the past four centuries, or consider the plays psychoanalytically – these last approaches concerning themselves with the larger subject of gender relations. Thompson concludes by calling for more attention to the comedies and histories, more close study of the plays' language, more women editors of Shakespeare, and more concern with including a feminist perspective in the teaching of Shakespeare to high-school students and undergraduates. Her review-essay, the token feminist contribution to the Holderness anthology, is nevertheless one of its best chapters.

GRADY's concern is with the political, aesthetic, and academic pressures informing Shakespeare criticism of the late nineteenth century and the twentieth century. Grady begins by acknowledging the insights theorists have been asserting since the 1980s if not earlier: critics cannot escape their time in the interests of "truth"; and critical developments are not sequential but discontinuous. He explains "modernist" Shakespeare criticism as produced by the convergence of two paths. One is the professionalizing of literary study: in England, professionalization goes back to Furnivall and Fleay, who, in 1873, founded the New Shakespeare Society; in America professionalization begins with the twentieth-century critic Elmer Edgar Stoll, who served as a spiritual father to Lily Bess Campbell and E.M.W. Tillyard. Opposed to what some saw as a technological or scientific approach is the moral, organic view that Grady finds in Matthew Arnold, the Newbolt Report, and F.R. Leavis's *Scrutiny*. Both these tendencies inform the work of British critics G. Wilson Knight ("spatial hermeneutics") and Tillyard, whose "old" historicism, as expounded in *The Elizabethan World Picture* and *Shakespeare's History Plays*, won wide acceptance. These predilections are discussed in detail, as are American 1940s' contributions: Brooksian New Criticism as applied to *Macbeth* in *The Well-Wrought Urn* and to *Henry IV, Part One* in Brooks and Heilman's *Understanding Drama*. Postmodernist Shakespeare, the subject of the last chapter, is an umbrella term under which one finds deconstruction, New Historicism, cultural materialism, Marxism, and feminism, the last being the most promising development. Grady's survey, while not the first of its kind, remains an important summary of the fashions in Shakespeare criticism.

BRISTOL proposes that "Shakespeare is an American institution" and that consequently "the interpretation of

Shakespeare and the interpretation of American political culture are mutually determining practices". Writing from a socialist perspective, Bristol critiques the American bourgeoisie's appropriation of Shakespeare. In Part One, "Shakespearizing America: The Institutional Infrastructure", he analyzes Shakespeare as a "tutelary deity or cult-object", tells the stories behind the great American Shakespeare research collections at the Folger and Huntington libraries, and at the University of Pennsylvania, and the editing of Shakespeare's plays, first by Americans working in the tradition of "scientific bibliography", and currently by American revisionists who, abandoning the idea of an "ideal text" or "lost original", are attempting to establish a sequence of revised performance versions. Part Two, "Americanizing Shakespeare: Critical Discourse and Ideology", studies Ralph Waldo Emerson's notion of Shakespeare as Representative Man, G.L. Kittredge's character-centered view that Shakespeare's genius lay in his rendering of private subjectivity, and Charles Mills Gayley's hegemonic view of American society. Similarly, "old" historicists A.O. Lovejoy, Theodore Spencer, and Hardin Craig attribute to Shakespeare their own conservative dedication to hierarchy, tradition, and religion, emphasizing the intellectual continuity of Renaissance thought with the dominant world-view of the Middle Ages. In "The Institutional Autonomy of Literature", Bristol surveys prominent post-World-War-II critics, notably Harry Levin, Northrop Frye, C.L. Barber, and Maynard Mack. The final chapter, "Subversion and Its Containment", looks to critics writing today – Stanley Cavell, Richard Levin, and Stephen Greenblatt, all of whom reveal a profound uneasiness with the older construction of an autopoetic Shakespeare. Bristol implies that it is time to study Shakespeare in his real historical context. This is a significant politically oriented study of the history of Shakespeare criticism.

VICKERS' sometimes curmudgeonly view of Shakespeare criticism since 1968 takes issue with Marxist, feminist, deconstructionist, psychoanalytic, and Christian critics who "distort the text as experience in the theatre or in private reading to make it fit their critical theories or ideologies". For Vickers, as for Samuel Johnson and Matthew Arnold from whom liberal humanism derives, there is a common reader whose experience can be generalized to "human nature". Vickers overlooks the fact that such a reader probably enjoys a privileged position by virtue of his or her race, religion, class, gender, and sexual orientation. Vickers calls for an "innocent" reader who brings no pre-conceived beliefs to the plays but instead exercises a kind of negative capability. While some – Bristol and Grady, for example – might regard this demand as an injunction to leave their brains in the cloakroom and to ignore the unhappy effects of unconscious conservative ideology, we can profit, nevertheless, from these 500 pages of critical summaries. Many of Vickers' evaluations do indeed probe the critics' weak points; particularly telling is the chapter "New Historicism: Disaffected Subjects". Vickers is often insightful and witty, challenging his opponents to greater accuracy, clearer thinking, and increased attention to the text.

DOROTHEA KEHLER

2. Recent and Contemporary Approaches

Dollimore, Jonathan, and Alan Sinfield (eds.), *Political Shakespeare: New Essays in Cultural Materialism*, Manchester: Manchester University Press, 1985; Ithaca, New York: Cornell University Press, 1985, 2nd edition (as *Political Shakespeare: Essays in Cultural Materialism*), 1994

Drakakis, John (ed.), *Alternative Shakespeares*, London and New York: Routledge, 1985

Dutton, Richard, *William Shakespeare: A Literary Life*, London: Macmillan, 1989

Eagleton, Terry, *William Shakespeare*, Oxford and New York: Blackwell, 1986

French, Marilyn, *Shakespeare's Division of Experience*, New York: Summit Books, 1981; London: Jonathan Cape, 1982

Greenblatt, Stephen, *Shakespearean Negotiations: The Circulation of Social Energy in Renaissance England*, Oxford: Clarendon Press, 1988; Berkeley: University of California Press, 1988

Hawkes, Terence, *That Shakespeherian Rag: Essays on a Critical Process*, London and New York: Methuen, 1986

Holderness, Graham (ed.), *The Shakespeare Myth*, Manchester: Manchester University Press, 1988

Howard, Jean E., and Marion F. O'Connor, *Shakespeare Reproduced: The Text in History and Ideology*, New York and London: Methuen, 1987

Hughes, Ted, *Shakespeare and the Goddess of Complete Being*, London: Faber & Faber, 1992, revised 1993

Jardine, Lisa, *Still Harping on Daughters: Women and Drama in the Age of Shakespeare*, Brighton, Sussex: Harvester Press, 1983; New York: Columbia University Press, 1989

Kahn, Coppélia, *Man's Estate: Masculine Identity in Shakespeare*, Berkeley: University of California Press, 1981

Kott, Jan, *Shakespeare Our Contemporary*, translated by Boleslaw Taborski, London: Methuen, 1964; Garden City, New York: Doubleday, 1964

Mahood, M.M., *Shakespeare's Wordplay*, London: Methuen, 1957; New York: Routledge, 1988

Partridge, Eric, *Shakespeare's Bawdy: A Literary and Psychological Essay and a Comprehensive Glossary*, London: Routledge, 1947, revised 1955 and 1968; New York: Dutton, 1948

Patterson, Annabel, *Shakespeare and the Popular Voice*, Oxford and Cambridge, Massachusetts: Blackwell, 1989

Ryan, Kiernan, *Shakespeare*, London: Harvester Wheatsheaf, 1989, revised, 1995; Atlantic Highlands, New Jersey: Humanities Press, 1989

Taylor, Gary, *Reinventing Shakespeare: A Cultural History from the Restoration to the Present*, New York: Weidenfeld & Nicolson, 1989; London: Hogarth Press, 1990

Vickers, Brian, *Appropriating Shakespeare: Contemporary Critical Quarrels*, New Haven, Connecticut, and London: Yale University Press, 1993

Shakespeare remains the single most contested site of literary and theoretical skirmish in the English-speaking world. Each new theoretical movement turns at some point to Shakespeare to prove its case; each produces its own backlash committed to proving Shakespeare's worth from an allegedly non-partisan perspective. Some of the most useful recent criticism has refrained from playing in this game directly, and has instead started more fruitfully to analyse the ways in which the notion of "Shakespeare" is implicated in contemporary notions of education, literature, Englishness, and morality.

"Superstar" editor TAYLOR provides a massive, well-researched, eclectic, and witty tome, "a product and a chronicle" of the current crisis in Shakespeare studies, explaining how, from the Restoration to the present day, Shakespeare has moved from being one star among many to his modern status as an overpowering "black hole". Taking in performances, editions, adaptations, and interpretations, Taylor goes beyond his ostensible subject: "a history of Shakesperotics becomes, inevitably, a history of four centuries of our culture".

PARTRIDGE's glossary to the lost sexual connotations of Shakespeare's language remains an indispensable tool for understanding the *double entendre* of the plays. By contrast, his prefatory essay, "The Sexual; The Homosexual; and Non-Sexual Bawdy in Shakespeare", is now clearly outdated by his refusal to distinguish between Shakespeare's possible use of homosexual references and the playwright's own sexuality. In her classic and accessible study of wordplay, MAHOOD asserts that, contrary to the prejudices of influential later critics from Johnson onwards, "wordplay was a game the Elizabethans played seriously". Rather than merely identifying the parts of this wordplay – "naming the parts does not show us what makes the gun go off" – Mahood insists on showing how "the study of Shakespeare's wordplay can take us to the central experience of each play", with convincing studies of the role played by wordplay in *Romeo and Juliet*, *Richard II*, the sonnets, *Hamlet*, *Macbeth*, and *The Winter's Tale*.

Gender has become a prominent topic in recent studies. KAHN draws on psychoanalysis, feminism, and literary criticism for her study of the psychological and social dimensions of Shakespearean manhood, claiming that Shakespeare was a "psychologist" who "possessed extraordinary and sophisticated insight into [the unconscious], insight that cannot be explained by humors psychology or the lore of melancholy". Drawing on a range of post-Freudian ego psychologists, Kahn argues that masculine identity in Shakespeare's work "centers on [the] adult struggle to achieve a second birth into manhood" in a patriarchal Elizabethan society: "his male characters are engaged in a continuous struggle, first to form a masculine identity, then to be secure and productive in it". FRENCH undertakes a substantial, iconoclastic study of "the gender principles" – the socially-constructed "masculine and feminine principles", which provide the basic distinction in the human social order – in the Shakespeare *oeuvre*. Detecting in the plays "a lifelong effort to harmonize moral qualities he . . . associate[d] with the two genders", she traces the playwright's career from an early "profound respect for 'masculine' qualities and profound suspicion of 'feminine' ones" through to the final romances, by which time "he had come to fear and deplore the power and capriciousness of the masculine principle, and to idealize certain aspects of the feminine", although "he never abandoned belief in male legitimacy or horror at female sexuality". JARDINE provides a response to previous "fragmentary, confusing and contradictory" feminist studies preoccupied with female characters and chauvinistic attitudes, either praising or damning Shakespeare's "inspired insights or warped fantasies of womanhood". In contrast, Jardine examines how the drama negotiates a series of specific cultural issues of the period – boy-players, education, inheritance laws, charges of shrewishness, sumptuary law, stereotypes of female heroism – and argues that the drama's strong interest in women is related to patriarchy's unexpressed anxiety about major social changes, with each chapter suggesting "a way in which 'femaleness' was significant in a network of possibilities for categorising and discriminating experience".

Many of these discussions examine Shakespeare in twentieth-century contexts. KOTT's study, particularly influential with theatre directors since its publication in the 1960s, argues that "by discovering in Shakespeare's plays problems that are relevant to our own time, modern audiences often, unexpectedly, find themselves near to the Elizabethans; or at least are in the position to understand them well". Having lived through both the Nazi terror and Stalinist repression, Kott, a Pole, believed "The violent deaths of the principal characters are now regarded rather as an historical necessity, or as something altogether natural".

DOLLIMORE and SINFIELD's collection has become a milestone of 1980s criticism (although its contents reach beyond that definition). Dollimore's opening chapter succinctly adumbrates the field of (British) cultural materialism and its relationship to the North American New Historicism, and introduces the key terms of the debate: consolidation, subversion, and containment. The essays include discussions of Shakespeare and colonialism, authority and subversion, misrule, feminist criticism, education, the theatre, film and television, and Bertolt Brecht's reading of Shakespeare. A revised edition in 1994 added Dollimore's analysis of the role played by feminist, lesbian, and gay critiques since 1985.

EAGLETON's short and readable book, described as "an exercise in political semiotics", detects "a deeply embarrassing dilemma" throughout Shakespeare's work: "his belief in social stability is jeopardized by the very language in which it is articulated". Drawing on Marxist, feminist, and semiotic ideas to interrogate language, desire, law, money, and the body in 17 plays, Eagleton demonstrates how "much of Shakespeare's drama is devoted to figuring out strategies for resolving" this dilemma.

DRAKAKIS asserts that while Shakespeare studies have remained "largely untouched" by the critical and theoretical concerns implicated in the "crisis of English studies", new critical approaches (including his ten "'alternative' Shakespeares") are forcing a "break with established canons of Shakespeare criticism". The essays include discussions of: poststructuralist Shakespeare; deconstructing the comedies; a semiotics of Shakespearean drama; "the discursive con-texts of *The Tempest*"; and history and ideology in *Henry V*. Outstanding are Jacqueline Rose's feminist psychoanalytic reading of *Hamlet* and *Measure for Measure*, and Catherine Belsey's influential account of sexual difference in the comedies. Somewhat similar in orientation, HOWARD and O'CONNOR collect 12 state-of-the-art essays from the 1986 International Shakespeare

Congress in West Berlin, from highly-regarded scholars, including Walter Cohen, Thomas Cartelli, Karen Newman, Michael Bristol, Jonathan Goldberg, and Robert Weimann. The editors' Introduction provides a lucid and thoughtful account of the place of Shakespeare within the US and British academies, pointing to the intellectual formation of the majority of contributors as students in 1960s' North America. With a focus on an earlier era, HAWKES' collection of imaginative, entertaining and provocative essays examines how and why English society "processes" Shakespeare. His particular focus is on the production of classic works of literary criticism at the turn of the century – including those of A.C. Bradley, Sir Walter (Alexander) Raleigh, T.S. Eliot, W.W. Greg, John Dover Wilson – to examine the involvement of Shakespeare and Shakespeare studies in our conception of English (the discipline) and Englishness.

Working within an explicitly cultural-materialist frame, HOLDERNESS presents an anthology of essays and interviews that explores the myriad ways in which Shakespeare permeates modern English life – from television commercials to British school examinations and banknotes. Included are interviews with Shakespeare practitioners in the theatre, education, and broadcasting, as well as eclectic and entertaining essays on Shakespeare and homosexuality, ideology ("Shakespeare and the Roadsweepers"), recent British plays using Shakespeare, and "Bardolatry". Terry Eagleton provides an Afterword.

Considerable discussion remains devoted to analysing Shakespeare in his contemporary contexts. DUTTON provides a straightforward and eminently readable account of Shakespeare's life and times, eschewing both overly creative reconstruction and dry archival material. He also provides a useful list of suggestions for further reading, giving particular credit to the mammoth achievements of Samuel Schoenbaum (*Shakespeare's Lives*, Oxford 1970, and *William Shakespeare: A Documentary Life*, Oxford 1975).

GREENBLATT brings together five outstanding essays, which remain among the most talked-about and controversial recent work on Shakespeare, and on the Renaissance more generally. Beginning, infamously, with his "desire to speak with the dead", Greenblatt attempts a "study of the collective making of distinct cultural practices and inquiry into the relations among these practices", a study which he terms "a poetics of culture". His concern is to interrogate "how cultural objects, expressions, and practices . . . acquired compelling force", a force which he describes as "social energy". After the theory is sketched in "The Circulation of Social Energy", Greenblatt's "distinct cultural practices" include the *Henry* plays and Thomas Hariot, *Twelfth Night* and hermaphroditism, *King Lear* and Samuel Harsnett, and *The Tempest* and the Virginia Company.

RYAN's concise and polemical book offers readings "designed to activate the revolutionary imaginative vision which invites discovery in his plays today". Taking issue with the new breed of historicists, who merely confirm the supposition of critics such as Tillyard – that Shakespeare was a conservative – Ryan proposes a new committed methodology, which seeks to ask: "how far, and in what specific ways, does the text succeed in challenging the principles of social and sexual relationship governing Shakespeare's world and our own?". Similarly, PATTERSON challenges the critical consensus (traced to Coleridge) that Shakespeare was a conservative supporter of Elizabethan social hierarchy, and argues that "a popular dramatist, himself the son of a country glover, and whose livelihood depended on the huge and socially diverse audience for the London public theater, was unlikely to have unquestioningly adopted an anti-popular myth as his own". Framing this question within modern thought about popular culture and popular protest, and writing within an explicitly humanist tradition, Patterson demonstrates, in a reading of seven plays, that Shakespeare engaged throughout his career in a structural critique which reached its apex in *Coriolanus*.

In a massive, detailed and original piece of creative criticism, HUGHES detects a "basic structural pattern, a fundamental dramatic idea" recurring in 14 of Shakespeare's mature plays, from *All's Well That Ends Well* to *The Tempest*, which he dubs "Shakespeare's myth". Identifying two of the most significant religious myths of the archaic world in *Venus and Adonis* and *The Rape of Lucrece* – "the Great Goddess behind Venus and the god behind Adonis" – Hughes argues that these myths gave Shakespeare a template for the construction of these 14 plays, rendering the *Complete Works* in effect, a "single, tightly integrated cyclic work".

Finally, setting itself against many of the approaches discussed above, VICKERS' massive tome is a forceful, and at times impatient, response to the theoretical movements of the last 20 years and to what the author sees as their partial and biased appropriation of Shakespeare. Outlining the derivation of current literary theory, or "anti-theories", from the thinkers of 1960s' Paris, Vickers attacks prevailing critical notions about language and the author, and harks back to an age when criticism was "essentially literary, concerned with the plays' structure, language, moral values, theatrical history". Each of the recent theoretical movements – deconstructionism, New Historicism, cultural materialism, psychoanalysis, Marxism, Christian theory – are surveyed in detail, with feminism – "the most aggressive development in recent times" – a particular target.

ALAN STEWART

3. Performance History

Bartholomeusz, D., *"The Winter's Tale" in Performance in England and America 1611–1976*, Cambridge and New York: Cambridge University Press, 1982

Foulkes, Richard, *Shakespeare and the Victorian Stage*, Cambridge and New York: Cambridge University Press, 1986

Gurr, Andrew, *The Shakespearean Stage: 1574–1642*, Cambridge: Cambridge University Press, 1970; 3rd, revised edition, Cambridge and New York: Cambridge University Press, 1992

Jackson, Russell "Shakespeare on the Stage from 1660–1900", in *The Cambridge Companion to Shakespeare Studies*, edited by Stanley Wells, Cambridge and New York: Cambridge University Press, 1986

Manvell, Roger, *Shakespeare and the Film*, London: Dent, 1971; New York: Praeger, 1971; revised edition, South Brunswick, New Jersey: A.S. Barnes, 1979

Mazer, Cary M., *Shakespeare Refashioned: Elizabethan Plays on Edwardian Stages*, Ann Arbor, Michigan: UMI Research Press, 1981
Salgādo, Gāmini, *Eyewitnesses of Shakespeare: First Hand Accounts of Performances 1590–1890*, London: Chatto & Windus, 1975; New York: Barnes & Noble, 1975
Speaight, Robert, *Shakespeare on the Stage: An Illustrated History of Shakespearian Performance*, London: Collins, 1973
Sprague, A.C., "Shakespeare's Plays on the English Stage", in *A New Companion to Shakespeare Studies*, edited by Kenneth Muir and Samuel S. Schoenbaum, London: Cambridge University Press, 1971
Styan, J.L., *The Shakespeare Revolution: Criticism and Performance in the Twentieth Century*, Cambridge and New York: Cambridge University Press, 1977
Thomson, Peter, *Shakespeare's Theatre*, London and Boston: Routledge & Kegan Paul, 1983
Wilson Knight, G., *Principles of Shakespearian Production*, Harmondsworth, Middlesex: Penguin, 1949; 3rd edition, as *Shakespearian Production*, London: Faber & Faber, 1964; Washington, D.C.: University Press of America, 1981
Winter, William, *Shakespeare on the Stage*, London: T. Fisher, 1913; reprinted, New York: Benjamin Blom, 1969

Studies of the performance history of Shakespeare's plays cover a wealth and variety of material, ranging from accounts of individual actors, directors, theatres, or companies, to studies of performance in a single period, or within a specific country, to studies of the performance history of individual plays. It should be noted, too, that there are a number of catalogues, records, and indexes, detailing casts, dates of productions, location of promptbooks, which are of interest to the scholar, but which fall outside the scope of this guide.

The two articles selected, by Sprague and Jackson, both of which attempt a concise survey of Shakespeare performance history, are useful and accessible starting points for the reader. SPRAGUE's article on Shakespeare performance in England from the Restoration to the time of writing (1971) is inevitably somewhat outdated now. Edward Gordon Craig, one of the foremost revolutionaries in twentieth century stage production, is not so much as mentioned, although he clearly influenced directors from Harley Granville Barker to Peter Brook. In Sprague's account, William Poel takes centre-stage as the foremost influence on the rise of the modern director. There is also a certain insularity in Sprague's thinking: for instance, no attention is paid to the influence of the Duke of Saxe-Meiningen's company on Henry Irving, although the influence of Charles Fechter is mentioned. Similarly, the influence of Continental directors, like that of Max Reinhardt on Granville Barker, falls outside the scope of Sprague's account, as if English Shakespeare performance occurred in a vacuum. Furthermore, the transition from the age of the actor-manager to that of the modern director is dealt with in a perfunctory way, and the important work of Herbert Beerbohm Tree is underrated. Hence, Sprague's account, although it is admirably concise, leaves out enough information to give a distorted and misleading impression.

JACKSON's article covers less ground than Sprague's, his account conveniently ending in 1900, and so he is able to avoid dealing with the problematic period of transition between the demise of the actor-manager system and the emergence of the modern director. The same book in which the article appears contains a supplementary piece by Roger Warren entitled "Shakespeare on the Twentieth-Century Stage", which effectively deals with the modern period. Jackson's article is stylish and scholarly, but once again a certain prejudice appears against the actor-managers who allegedly distorted Shakespeare's texts. Jackson writes:

> The history of Shakespearean production between 1660 and 1900 can be seen to be an account of 240 years of lost labours, in which a succession of actors and managers wrenched the plays into a shape basically unsuited to their meaning – or to most of the meanings we might wish to release from them.

To write off the art of David Garrick, Edmund Kean, Charles Macready, Irving, and the others, as "lost labours" is an extraordinary view for a theatre historian to adopt, especially when considering the kind of cuts, transpositions, and even re-writings common to modern Shakespeare on stage and film; the actor-managers arranged the plays to suit the theatrical conventions of the day and to release meanings that were relevant to their audiences.

SPEAIGHT's book is probably the most comprehensive and wide-ranging study of Shakespeare performance history to have appeared, encompassing stage production from Shakespeare's day to the time of writing (1973), and performance traditions in England, America, France, Italy, Germany, and Russia. Beautifully illustrated, and written in a lively and accessible style, this book does not contain much in the way of original thought or argument, but is an effective summary of popular opinion on performance history. Speaight, greatly influenced by his mentor William Poel, tends to undervalue the work of the late Victorian and Edwardian actor-managers, and his view of Beerbohm Tree could not be more sharply juxtaposed to that of Wilson Knight.

SALGĀDO's book is a collection of critical reviews and comments on stage performances of the plays, including the least famous, from 1590 to 1890. The selection of material shows discernment and the original reviews are effectively shortened and edited. Many of these reviews would be difficult to locate today and so this is a useful supplement to the other studies of Shakespearean performance.

GURR's study is an account of the original conditions of performance during the period 1574–1642, focusing on the companies of players, the playhouses, the audiences, and the staging conventions of the time. Attention is paid to styles of acting, the repertory system, the social status of players, as well as to famous clowns and tragedians. He discusses the different kinds of theatres available during the period, while in the chapter on staging he gives close attention to properties and costumes, realism, and the variety of staging techniques appropriate to the different theatres. The chapter on the players is particularly valuable in relation to the performance history of Shakespeare's plays. However, it should be noted that this study is wide-ranging in its scope, and includes detail relevant to the performance history of plays by most dramatists of the period.

THOMSON's book covers similar ground to Gurr's, except that it is more clearly focused on Shakespeare's plays, the Lord

Chamberlain's Servants, and the Globe Theatre, and includes important chapters on *Twelfth Night*, *Hamlet*, and *Macbeth*, from the point of view of reconstructing the original conditions of performance. This is a scholarly and well-written account, and is a valuable, although by no means comprehensive, analysis of Shakespeare performance during the period.

WINTER's book is of historical importance, and contains a wealth of information about performances during the eighteenth and nineteenth centuries, including those by Garrick, John Philip Kemble, Edmund Kean, Macready, Edwin Forrest, Edwin Booth, and Irving. Winter was a rather conservative dramatic critic, a great champion of Irving, but something of a reactionary in his assessment of European performers, including Sarah Bernhardt. The book contains chapters on *Richard III*, *The Merchant of Venice*, *Othello*, *Hamlet*, *Macbeth*, and *Henry VIII*, and it is a much better organised, informative, and selective account than George C.D. Odell's *Shakespeare from Betterton to Irving* (reprinted New York: Dover Publications, 1966), written during the same period.

FOULKES's book is a collection of essays on Shakespeare performance during the Victorian age, written by some of the leading theatre historians of today, including Peter Thomson, Cary Mazer, Michael R. Booth, and Foulkes himself. The articles range from studies of stage design, costume, and stage conventions to the analysis of particular productions, imitations of – and variations on – the plays, to accounts of Shakespeare production in Germany, France, and in the English provinces. There is a section devoted to the Lyceum dynasty, which includes a fine essay by Michael Booth on Ellen Terry, and a penetrating analysis of Irving by Peter Thomson, exploring the darker undertones and psychological complexity of the actor's identity.

MAZER's study focuses on Shakespeare production during the Edwardian period. The approach is highly conceptual, emphasis being given to understanding the conventions and theories of stage performance that developed during the period. Mazer presents a convincing argument that Edwardian stage reforms were brought about as much by the reactionaries as by the radicals, and that the traditionalists (i.e., the traditional actor-managers), as well as the Elizabethanists, shared the aesthetic prejudices of the day, in spite of their apparent antipathy towards each other. Individual chapters are devoted to the "Traditional Stagecraft", the "Elizabethan Revival", the "New Stage Craft", and Granville Barker. This is one of the most well-argued and well-researched studies of Shakespeare performance to have appeared in recent years.

STYAN's book concerns the revolution in Shakespeare production during the twentieth century after the advent of the modern director, and is particularly valuable in discussing the importance of Poel, Granville Barker, Nigel Playfair, Barry Jackson, Tyrone Guthrie, and Peter Brook. Styan appears completely unsympathetic to the Victorian spectacular productions of Irving and Tree against which the work of Poel and Barker reacted. However, the book is stimulating to read, and Styan convincingly argues for the impact of modern directors on the criticism of Shakespeare during the twentieth century.

WILSON KNIGHT's book is mainly concerned with theories of production in relation to the tragedies and his own stagings of Shakespeare. The book gives a fascinating insight into the way in which one of this century's most influential Shakespeare critics approached the problems of stage interpretation. Although there is little in the way of historical detail about other stage productions, there are some fascinating critical observations about the many productions the author had seen. The book includes a chapter on the respective merits of the staging conventions of Beerbohm Tree, Craig, Poel, and Harley Granville Barker, which reveals Wilson Knight to have been a great admirer of the art and interpretative approach of Tree (a producer who has been unfairly maligned by others, including Jackson and Speaight).

There is a sense in which Shakespeare performance history is contained within the stage history of a single play; that is, that by focusing on the interpretative history of a single work, we are given direct insight into the changing conditions of performance from the early seventeenth century to the present. BARTHOLOMEUSZ's scholarly and comprehensive account of the stage history of *The Winter's Tale* is a noteworthy example of this approach. The writer achieves a fine balance between a literary-critical understanding of the text and a historically based account of the play's theatrical transformations, exploring the interrelationship between critical and theatrical interpretation during the periods. Other good examples of the analysis of the performance history of individual plays include Bartholomeusz's *"Macbeth" and the Players* (Cambridge: Cambridge University Press, 1969) and John Ripley's *"Julius Caesar" on Stage in England and America 1599–1973* (Cambridge: Cambridge University Press, 1980). Giving much briefer coverage, and aimed at a student readership, is the "Text and Performance" series (London: Macmillan, 1983 –), which has short studies of selected, individual Shakespeare plays (along with some titles devoted to other dramatists). In addition there are some studies that look at the performance aspects of groups of Shakespeare plays, such as Roger Warren's *Staging Shakespeare's Late Plays* (Oxford and New York: Oxford University Press, 1990).

No study of the performance history of Shakespeare's plays would be complete without some reference to Shakespeare on film, particularly in view of the fact that many of the most famous stage performances in this century have been captured on film, or at least adapted for the screen. MANVELL's book is an admirable starting point. He discusses some of the important Shakespeare films of the century, including those by Laurence Olivier, Orson Welles, and Franco Zeffirelli, as well as the Peter Brook *King Lear* and the outstanding Russian *Hamlet* by Grigori Kozintsev. Individual chapters are devoted to silent film, the problems of adapting the plays for film, and stage productions that have found their way into film. For the reader interested in pursuing Shakespeare on film during the early years of the century, Robin Hamilton Ball's *Shakespeare on Silent Film* (London: Allen & Unwin, 1968) can also be recommended.

In conclusion, if one were to suggest one title for the reader wanting a broad introduction to Shakespearean production, the most comprehensive book to date has to be that of Speaight, which, for all its limitations, gives an overview of the subject such as no other modern theatre historian has attempted.

BRIAN PEARCE

4. Tragedies

Bayley, John, *Shakespeare and Tragedy*, London and Boston: Routledge & Kegan Paul, 1981

Bradley, A. C., *Shakespearean Tragedy: Lectures on "Hamlet", "Othello", "King Lear", "Macbeth"*, London: Macmillan, 1904, and subsequent reprints.

Campbell, Lilly Bess, *Shakespeare's Tragic Heroes: Slaves of Passion*, Cambridge: Cambridge University Press, 1930; reprinted, New York: Barnes & Noble, 1961

Charney, Maurice, *Shakespeare's Roman Plays: The Function of Imagery in the Drama*, Cambridge, Massachusetts: Harvard University Press, 1961

Danson, Lawrence, *Tragic Alphabet: Shakespeare's Drama of Language*, New Haven, Connecticut: Yale University Press, 1974

Dollimore, Jonathan, *Radical Tragedy: Religion, Ideology and Power in the Drama of Shakespeare and His Contemporaries*, Brighton, Sussex: Harvester Press, 1984, 2n edition, 1989; Chicago: University of Chicago Press, 1984

Everett, Barbara, *Young Hamlet: Essays on Shakespeare's Tragedies*, Oxford: Clarendon Press, 1989; New York: Oxford University Press, 1989

Holloway, John, *The Story of the Night: Studies in Shakespeare's Major Tragedies*, Lincoln: University of Nebraska Press, 1961; London: Routledge & Kegan Paul, 1961

Mehl, Dieter, *Shakespeare's Tragedies: An Introduction*, Cambridge and New York: Cambridge University Press, 1986

Nevo, Ruth, *Tragic Form in Shakespeare*, Princeton, New Jersey: Princeton University Press, 1972

Rackin, Phyllis, *Shakespeare's Tragedies*, New York: Frederick Ungar, 1978

Snyder, Susan, *The Comic Matrix of Shakespeare's Tragedies: "Romeo and Juliet", "Hamlet", "Othello" and "King Lear"*, Princeton, New Jersey: Princeton University Press, 1979

Spivack, Bernard, *Shakespeare and the Allegory of Evil: The History of a Metaphor in Relation to His Major Villains*, New York: Columbia University Press, 1958

Wilson Knight, G., *The Wheel of Fire*, London: Oxford University Press, 1930; 4th revised edition, London: Methuen, 1954; New York: Barnes & Noble, 1966

Thanks to nineteenth-century Romanticism, for most critics the tragedies are the apex of Shakespeare's achievement; similarly, criticism of the tragedies has been held in the highest regard. Character, structure, language, theme, genre, sources and influences, theories of tragedy, the play in performance – these are among the chief emphases of the various approaches. More recently, students of ideology have opened up fascinating, new critical possibilities.

BRADLEY's work is the best-known study of character in the critical canon. Although Bradley wrote out of a nineteenth-century Victorian tradition, no critic's work has been more influential in the twentieth century. While Bradley treated structure and imagery, they are secondary concerns. The basic axioms of *Shakespearean Tragedy* are first, that there is an inextricable relationship between character and action, and second, that the tragic flaw which destroys the hero also exalts him. Bradley focuses on the "great" tragedies: *Hamlet*, *Othello*, *King Lear*, and *Macbeth*. The character of Hamlet is distinguished by his suffering from melancholy because of his horror at his mother's remarriage; eventually he comes to believe in providence. Claudius, too, engages Bradley. Othello is uncomplicated, innocent, fervent – an idealist who proves easy prey for Iago, a brilliant, self-absorbed rationalist, driven to dominate. The play itself affords matchless suspense and horror.

King Lear strikes Bradley as superb but flawed by the blinding of Gloucester and, more broadly, by the Gloucester subplot. Bradley questions the play's unremitting grimnesss, arguing for a Lear whose heart, like Gloucester's, bursts smilingly. *Macbeth* has a special intensity due to its compactness; no other Shakespearean character changes as rapidly as Macbeth. Ambition mars the Macbeths, but because of their bravery and determination these tortured beings never entirely repel the audience. Bradley defines the tragic experience as an encounter with transitory but cruelly wasteful evil, destructive of great promise. Ultimately, these tragedies inspire us with a sense of human potential.

CAMPBELL's well-researched study also focuses on the great tragedies, but is more historically oriented than Bradley's. The book first dilates on the Renaissance view of tragedy, then on philosophical and scientific thought ("Moral Philosophy") in Elizabethan and Jacobean England, before devoting a chapter to each of the four plays. Tragedy, for Campbell, inheres not in action but in passion. According to Elizabethan psychology, when passion exceeds reason, undue heat dominates moisture, producing the melancholy characteristic of Shakespeare's tragic heroes. Perhaps too schematically, Campbell argues that each tragedy's hero is a slave to a particular passion, be it grief, jealousy, wrath, or fear; and that each play has its special concern: *Hamlet* deals with emotional response to misfortune, *Othello* with a racially differentiated response to jealousy, *King Lear* to ageing, and *Macbeth* to the limits of courage. Campbell's work is important in the development of historical criticism.

WILSON KNIGHT's volume, a collection of the critic's own essays, is significant for an approach to the tragedies anticipated in Bradley's discussion of *Macbeth*. Knight is concerned with the way Shakespeare uses language, particularly imagery and symbolism, to create thematic atmosphere. In Chapter 1, "On the Principles of Shakespearean Interpretation", he argues that the function of criticism should not be fault-finding but rather understanding the work's totality, its melding of the unique and the universal, the temporal and the spatial; this is Wilson Knight's "spatial hermeneutic". In *Hamlet*, a sense of imminent death accompanies the Prince, himself a courier of death, who suffers a loss of will, a death in life. In *Othello* the atmosphere is constricted by a more objective, less metaphysical style. The metamorphosis of the language Othello uses, as he struggles between the divine and the demonic, charts the progress of the tragedy. *Lear* merits two essays. The first is devoted to the "comedy of the grotesque", mirroring both the comic and tragic strains within the play, developed by the Fool and represented in Gloucester's attempted suicide and the indignities suffered by all the characters. The second essay is concerned with *Lear*'s atmosphere, which remains "inscrutable [and] enigmatic", but serves the theme of suffering which renews virtue and destroys evil. Wilson Knight also writes on the physically and ethically murky atmosphere of *Macbeth*, the negotiation between terror and evil, and the recurring symbolism of blood, storm, and non-human life. Wilson Knight's work, while marred by a labored visionary style, remains pivotal for its attempt to unify all the aspects of each play considered under a broad dramatic concept or theme.

SPIVACK, like Campbell, is historically oriented. He proposes that Shakespeare was familiar with the medieval dramatic conventions persisting into the Renaissance. Among the cruellest villains in Shakespeare's tragedies are Aaron the Moor and Iago, like Richard III and Don John more easily explained theologically than psychologically, being Renaissance versions of the medieval Vice figure. Spivack's scholarship is notable: much of the book traces the development of the Vice from the *psychomachia* (battle in the mind) through its incarnation in various morality plays, interludes, and the works of Shakespeare's contemporaries. Spivack begins and ends with Iago, whose immediate antipathy to virtuous characters marks both him and the Vice, connoting their affinity and allegorical function. Spivack's careful analysis of Iago's supposed motives – motives which the character himself appears to deprecate – points to Iago's main grounding in the Vice convention rather than in naturalistic psychology. Nevertheless, Spivack maintains that Shakespeare uses the convention sensitively, not schematically, in order to achieve a moral and aesthetic purpose. Spivack's blending of meticulous research and critical insight is exemplary.

CHARNEY treats *Julius Caesar*, *Antony and Cleopatra*, and *Coriolanus*, concentrating on their style, especially their verbal and non-verbal imagery (the latter also termed presentational or stage imagery) as these interface with each other. Charney's emphasis on non-verbal imagery reminds us that Shakespeare wrote for presentation and that props, actions, gestures, and the like deserve critical attention. To ignore the performance aspects of the plays is to diminish the totality of their achievement. For example, Cleopatra's asp-engendered death is the culmination of a strand of serpentine imagery threading its way through the entire play. Following two chapters of general introduction, "The Function of Imagery", and "Style in the Roman Plays", Charney considers each of the three tragedies in turn. In *Julius Caesar* iterative imagery (repeated references to an important subject of the play) is centered on disruptions of nature and other such prescient signs as fire and blood. *Julius Caesar*'s severe style is also found in the Rome of *Antony and Cleopatra*, but is contrasted with Egypt's lush, sometimes decadent imagery and exaggerated language. *Coriolanus* depicts a largely literalist society in which Menenius alone delights in figurative language. To delineate the play's class conflict, iterative animal imagery and allusions to sickness and food predominate. Charney capably develops suggestions made by Bradley and Wilson Knight regarding verbal and presentational imagery, constructing a convincing case for the "poetry of the theater".

HOLLOWAY, reacting against a moral view of Shakespeare as an asserter of "values", introduced an anthropological approach to the "great" tragedies and to *Antony and Cleopatra*, *Coriolanus*, and *Timon of Athens*. His innovation was to see the tragic hero as a scapegoat, playing the role of ritual victim, progressively alienated from his society and from the audience as the plays spiral downwards towards dissolution. In Holloway's words, the tragedies are "a momentous and energizing experience" showing us "the ordeal of the great and alienated who are pursued by life until they are sacrificed". As pre-inscribed victim, the hero's role supersedes his character. Another key idea Holloway advances is that during the course of his ordeal, the hero is metamorphosed into a monster, rejecting his brotherhood with humanity. Thus, Coriolanus and Timon, the last of Shakespeare's tragic protagonists, are finally isolated, men without a country. A useful appendix on myth and ritual concludes the work. While this book has been criticized for carelessness and insufficient documentation, and the working-out of its thesis has been disputed, Holloway's contribution is both original and thought-provoking.

NEVO counters emphasis on the play as poem or "expanded metaphor" – the approach suggested by Wilson Knight – or as the embodiment of the critics' moral notions. She is concerned, rather, with the dynamism of *drama*, with plot structure as a means of discovering each play's unique tragic idea. Examining *Romeo and Juliet*, *Richard II*, *Julius Caesar*, *Antony and Cleopatra*, *Coriolanus*, and the "great" tragedies from an Aristotelian standpoint, Nevo finds a five-phased structure common to all of Shakespeare's tragedies, deriving from their own five-act structures: the predicament, *psychomachia*, *peripeteia* (reversal), ironic and pathetic perspectives, and catastrophe. The hero first confronts an insoluble dilemma or predicament; its terms or conditions being further delineated, he undergoes a *psychomachia*, commits a fatal error that invites the *peripeteia*, abandons the dehumanizing values external to him, and comes to know himself. By dying, he ensures the continuance of a humane ethic. Nevo's book has been most commended for its chapters on *Othello* and *Antony and Cleopatra*. Though the approach may sound formulaic and mechanistic, Nevo is in fact remarkably sensitive, albeit not least when she seems to lose sight of her structural thesis.

DANSON urges the importance of Shakespeare's language, not only for its variety but for the problems of communication it poses. The hero faces the "self-expressive task and its tragic precariousness" in the world of the drama, a world of role-playing. He needs not only a verbal language but also a non-verbal one for his role. In Danson's view, Iago is an artist *manqué*; invaded by Iago's language, Othello loses his purchase on reality and falls prey to delusion. Each of the tragedies (with the exception of *Timon of Athens*, but including *Troilus and Cressida*) has an "expressive form" consisting of the problems of expression Danson ascribes to the characters, and their resolution by means of the tragedy's "shape". Since even non-verbal elements, such as costuming, set, props, and physical action, qualify as problems of expression, Danson's analysis is more thoroughgoing than his thesis would imply. This is a rewarding book for the reader who is willing to grant that Shakespeare's tragedies are "not only . . . dramas written *in* words but *about* words as well".

RACKIN's work, a component volume of Ungar's "World Dramatists" series, addresses "amateurs" who want to understand the tragedies' "human significance". Rackin devotes a chapter of criticism to each of the tragedies and a final chapter to staging. She employs a different focus for interpreting each play, sometimes calling attention to language, sometimes to plot, sometimes to character. In the *Titus* chapter, for example, she introduces the reader to historical and generic sources – the stage Machiavel, classical revenge tragedy, and medieval *de casibus* tragedy. She favors close reading of imagery, and dwells on its thematic and symbolic functions in *Romeo and Juliet*, *Hamlet*, *Othello*, and *Macbeth*. Her chapters on *Julius Caesar* and *Coriolanus* invoke the concept of the tragic flaw, whereas in analyzing *Hamlet* she discusses *peripeteia* and *anagnoresis* (recognition). Rackin has wisely avoided the temptation to impose a constricting overview on these very different plays. Such syntheses have their rewards in academe, but rarely do justice to the individual drama. A chronology and brief bibliography are included. This little volume can stand as a summary of standard but discerning views of the tragedies.

SNYDER focuses on comedy and tragedy as generic conventions. Positing that comedy was the first genre Shakespeare mastered, and hence the base from which he approached tragedy, she considers the comedic components of tragedy and the ways in which tragedy interrogates and eventually undermines the happy promise of comedy. *Romeo and Juliet* at first seems like a romantic comedy. *Othello* reverses the comic order, and uncovers that which comedy submerges; its tragic movement is initiated by a marriage destroyed by the obstacles comedy conquers. Offering plural views of truth, *Hamlet* makes tragic use of the discrepancy between appearance and reality on which Shakespearean comedy so often turns. *King Lear*'s tragic tone is produced by the discordant coupling of comic order and disorder. Snyder also observes developmental stages: *Romeo and Juliet* opposes comedy to tragedy, *Hamlet* treats them as mirror images of each other, and *Lear* implies that they are both parts of a single entity. Tragic inevitability is established, argues Snyder, when the expectations aroused by comedy are unfulfilled.

BAYLEY claims that Shakespeare's tragedies bypass a conventional fit between the protagonists and their situations. Instead, *Hamlet*, a revenge tragedy, lacks a willing avenger; *Othello* poses as romance; and *Lear*'s Cordelia rejects the response tradition has scripted for her, thus initiating a tragedy in which the deepest emotions experienced are gratuitous rather than inherent in the tragic form. Another distinction Bayley makes is that in the "great" tragedies, we are privy to the inner life of the protagonists, whereas in the Roman plays, we are distanced so that we can learn from them.

DOLLIMORE's discussion, while not limited to Shakespeare, is of major significance to Shakespearean criticism. Dollimore proposes that the tragic hero is the site on which the period's conflicting views are contested. Jacobean playwrights bent on subverting ideological prescriptions in early-modern England employed subtextual devices ("sub-literal encoding") accessible in performance though not in the reading, thus circumventing censorship. Ironic endings are a primary means of defeating organic or providential views. Others are parody, dislocation, and structural disjunction. Thus, in *Lear*, concerned with wealth and power, suffering does *not* bring salvation; similarly, *Antony and Cleopatra* and *Coriolanus*, rather than glamorizing warfare, interrogate it and reveal issues of greater importance for society. Dollimore was one of the first influential cultural-materialist interpreters of Shakespeare.

MEHL's work is similar to Rackin's with regard to the undergraduate audience it best serves and the clarity of its presentation, although Mehl originally wrote for German students. Eschewing innovative approaches in favor of scholarly conservative readings, Mehl analyzes *Troilus and Cressida* as well as the tragedies, reviews Shakespeare's sources, and notes major perspectives on each of the plays. He shows how Shakespeare depicts felt evil, represents human responses as unforeseeable, and poignantly expresses man's powerlessness before a malevolent or at best unconcerned fate. Perhaps because of his interest in performance, Mehl leans heavily on Bradleyan character criticism, while resisting modern psychological interpretations. Feminist critics may feel that Mehl's unselfconsciously male-centered outlook renders his interpretations of various important female characters simplistic. On the other hand, his extensive familiarity with Elizabethan stage conventions provides some enlightening insights. Mehl is at his best when treating Shakespeare's manipulation of audience response. The book also includes excellent bibliographic aids.

EVERETT's well-received collection of her own previously published essays emphasizes character while producing fruitful new ways of reading by attending to "basic, even elemental aspects of human experience". An excellent contribution is the title essay, calling attention to "Young Hamlet's deliberate challenge to his elders and his kinship with the child actors who "Exclaim against their own succession"; succeeding to maturity in Act V, Hamlet finds "young Osric" banal. Having grown up, Hamlet soon dies. Essays on the "great tragedies" in Part One ("Purchasing Experience") are followed in Part Two ("Approaches to the Tragedies") by further attention to these plays and others – *Romeo and Juliet*, *Troilus and Cressida*, and *Twelfth Night*. Everett investigates such varied topics as textual problems in the plays, minor characters (Juliet's Nurse), and Spanish influences on *Othello*. Despite occasional oversights – e.g., the unconscious racial slur in Desdemona's "I saw Othello's visage in his mind" – Everett's essays are acute and accessible contributions to Shakespeare study.

DOROTHEA KEHLER

5. Hamlet

Bradley, A.C., *Shakespearean Tragedy: Lectures on "Hamlet", "Othello", "King Lear", "Macbeth"*, London: Macmillan, 1904, and subsequent reprints

Davison, Peter, *Hamlet: Text and Performance*, London: Macmillan, 1983

Foakes, R.A., *Hamlet versus Lear: Cultural Politics and Shakespeare's Art*, Cambridge and New York: Cambridge University Press, 1993

Jones, Ernest, *Hamlet and Oedipus*, London: Victor Gollancz, 1949; Garden City, New York: Doubleday, 1954

Kerrigan, William, *Hamlet's Perfection*, Baltimore: Johns Hopkins University Press, 1994

States, Bert O., *Hamlet and the Concept of Character*, Baltimore: Johns Hopkins University Press, 1992

Writing in the aftermath of the Romantic period, and heavily influenced by the emergent discipline of psychoanalysis, BRADLEY's classic study takes as its main focus the plays' central characters. In the case of *Hamlet* there is only one worth major consideration: "all the persons in *Hamlet* except the hero are minor characters, who fail to rise to the tragic level". Bradley proceeds via a pseudo-biography, according to which Hamlet is predisposed to melancholy caused "not [by] his father's death. . . . Still less . . . the loss of the crown [but by] the sudden ghastly disclosure of his mother's true nature, falling on him when his heart was aching with love, and his body weakened by sorrow". Bradley's poetic analysis is evocative though inconclusive: "the sense has rather to be discerned beyond the words than found in them". Though dated, Bradley's meditation on *Hamlet* as "the symbol of a tragic mystery inherent in human nature" remains influential.

JONES's examination of the Prince is clearly indebted to Bradley: "no dramatic criticism of the personae in a play is possible except under the pretence that they are living people". Jones notes that prior to the Oedipal solution given by Freud "all the explanations of the mystery [of Hamlet's delay] end in blind alleys". He points out that Hamlet is distressed *before* he discovers the identity of his father's murderer and that it is "his mother's incest that dominates his emotions". Claudius now occupies the position that Hamlet desires and is thus an alter-ego of the Prince; this is the reason for his failure to act. Jones's account of *Hamlet* is compelling but when he goes on "to consider the relation of this particular imaginative creation to the personality of Shakespeare himself", it becomes increasingly hypothetical. Notwithstanding this tendentious psychobiographising, Jones's account is notable not only as a response to "the Sphinx of modern Literature" but as an *exemplum* of the problems and strategies of psychoanalytic literary criticism.

DAVISON's study is one of a series of short monographs on dramatic texts designed to wrench the play away from purely literary study: "it is usual, especially in England, for those of the theatre to despise academics". This concise study (80 pages) deals with textual issues and specific performances including David Garrick's 1772 production, Laurence Olivier's 1948 film version, and Charles Marowitz's iconoclastic adaptation, *Collage Hamlet*. Davison rightly acknowledges the flexibility of the dramatic text depending on medium and playing space, yet this elasticity has unexplained and intransigent limits. While he is prepared to justify modern rewrites, he is dismissive of the 1603 Quarto – of one of Hamlet's soliloquies he declaims that "said with spurious conviction on the stage it passes muster; but whatever else it is, it is not Shakespeare".

Bradley's treatment of *dramatis personae* as real people has often resulted in an embarrassment towards accounts that focus on characterisation. STATES notes, however, that *Hamlet* is "the quintessential drama of character" and he aims to recoup character and justify it as a critical tool. He suggests that it is immanent not in any single figure but in the interaction between different *personae* and the "world character" of the play itself. Hamlet is thus the "axial figure" whose position is illuminated by minor roles. There follows a sensitive chapter which explores how Horatio provides an audience perspective ("Our man in Elsinore") but there is also an untenable psychoanalytic reading of Ophelia, which States pursues despite his own doubts about the method. Of Ophelia's grave as "a gaping castrating vagina swallowing . . . two grown men", he notes ironically that it is "an image that would have made Ophelia blush all the way to her id". Occasionally, the analysis is marred by eccentric formulations: "given a choice, man . . . would rather be in Philadelphia than in a world plagued by death and mutability"; a character trait may be overlooked and "slip past us [like] a thoughtful grandmother at a picnic".

In the course of tracing the critical and theatrical reception of *King Lear* and *Hamlet* from the seventeenth century to the present day, FOAKES makes some stimulating comparisons. He argues that *Hamlet*'s intimacy compels us to empathise with the protagonist, while the mythic weight and historically vague setting of *King Lear* result in a greater distance from its characters. For Foakes, the abiding significance of *Hamlet* is its propensity "to focus various forms of disenchantment with the self or society". Foakes is scrupulous in his attentions to textual variants, but insists that these were calculated rather than careless – so the deliberate omission of several of Quarto 2's key speeches from the Folio "enhances the sense of mystery". Foakes is theoretically lightweight as he asserts that theatre evades academic study: "it is possible to learn how to interpret . . . without ever really living through the play, or yielding to that inward illusion that enables us to half-create and share in the emotions and anxieties of the characters". His description of theoretical approaches that "seem to enjoy trashing Shakespeare, like schoolboys suddenly released from subservience to a formidable headmaster" is churlish and inaccurate.

KERRIGAN describes his as "an idiosyncratic and unfashionable book". He is vehemently opposed to "the bland modern pride known as 'political correctness'" and contemptuous of recent theoretical criticism (Hawkes, Patterson, Garber, etc.): "they paw at it, make gestures at it, and mount mischievous little runs on its margins to catch at least a bit of the crumbling old classic in their nets of intertextuality". Despite this irascibility, Kerrigan provides a concise and accurate summary of the play's critical fortunes, and shows how its reception emphasises the distinctions between neoclassical attitudes, which stressed the importance of a well-fashioned plot, and the Romantic investment in a drama of character. Later chapters explore the motif of night in the play and the virgin/whore dichotomy in Hamlet's treatment of Ophelia. As with a number of the above studies, Kerrigan illustrates the enduring dominance of Bradlean criticism: "I would be reluctant to give up the primacy of character in Shakespeare studies, for that seems tantamount to giving up individualism".

PETER J. SMITH

6. King Lear

Bradley, A.C., *Shakespearean Tragedy: Lectures on "Hamlet", "Othello", "King Lear", "Macbeth"*, London: Macmillan, 1904, and subsequent reprints

Danby, John F., *Shakespeare's Doctrine of Nature: A Study of "King Lear"*, London: Faber & Faber, 1949

Dollimore, Jonathan, *Radical Tragedy: Religion, Ideology and Power in the Drama of Shakespeare and His Contemporaries*, Brighton, Sussex: Harvester Press, 1984, 2nd edition, 1989; Chicago: University of Chicago Press, 1984

Everett, Barbara, "The New *King Lear*" (originally 1960), in *Shakespeare: "King Lear": A Casebook*, edited by Frank Kermode, London: Macmillan, 1969, revised 1992

Kott, Jan, *Shakespeare Our Contemporary*, translated by Boleslaw Taborski, London: Methuen, 1964; Garden City, New York: Doubleday, 1964

Ryan, Kiernan, "'King Lear': The Subversive Imagination" (1989), in *New Casebooks: "King Lear": William Shakespeare*, edited by Ryan, London: Macmillan, 1993

Wilson Knight, G., *The Wheel of Fire*, London: Oxford University Press, 1930; 4th, revised edition, London: Methuen, 1954; New York: Barnes & Noble, 1966

The criticism of *King Lear* in the twentieth century has been dominated by BRADLEY. He saw the play as representing a world radically divided between the selfless and the selfish, between the characters centred on Lear and those centred on Edmund. And he saw it as interrogating, and prompting the audience to interrogate, the nature of this world. He confronts squarely the possible pessimism of the play in which the selfish prosper, at least temporarily, and the good are ultimately destroyed; yet he asserts that the play's outlook is finally optimistic. He does this by stressing Lear's culpability for the action, so the play's outcome is not simply unjust. But, more importantly, he sees in the play an immanent Christian structure. Bradley's own position was that of an idealist humanist. But he sees Lear's suffering as redemptive, death liberating (even that of Cordelia), the world worthless, and the soul everything. The play reveals "greatness in pain" and "solemnity in the mystery we cannot fathom"; and it advocates patience as the response to adversity, however terrible.

WILSON KNIGHT built on this interpretation. He too saw the play as radically divided. It presents a vision of humanity in which universal justice is questioned. In particular, it represents a world gone mad, in which suffering is not only grotesque but also comic. And yet suffering is purgatorial, and the play advocates a fine stoicism. And in the figure of Cordelia the play offers a vision of life able to transcend suffering and transform all the characters of the play, even the evil, self-destroying ones.

DANBY carried the interpretation further, but gave it a significantly historicised form. The divided society of the play is in fact a representation of the society of Shakespeare's time. Lear and the figures grouped around him represent the feudal past; Edmund and those around him represent the new, capitalist order. The "nature" invoked by Lear is that of Richard Hooker; that invoked by Edmund is the "nature" of Thomas Hobbes: traditional communality as opposed to new individualism. There is, however, a third nature envisioned in the play, represented by Cordelia – the utopian vision of a new, egalitarian community, one found in the Anabaptists in the sixteenth century, in Gerard Winstanley in the English Revolution, and in a later writer like William Blake. Danby sees this vision as an expression of "the very finest spirit of Elizabethan Christianity".

With EVERETT this whole tradition, in both its universalist and historicised forms, was presented with a severe challenge. She questioned the Christian and displaced Christian readings of the play, and offered instead a reading that was consciously humanist and secular. Lear on the heath is the most purely tragic image in Shakespeare – a man hopelessly facing a hostile universe and withstanding it only by his rage, endurance, and questioning. The play is about loss, suffering, and death, but also about the potential fullness of life that makes that loss tragic. It denies the Christian renunciation of life, and sees man as tragically poised, in Pascal's words, between nothing and everything. It is this last sense that informs the ending of the play, rather than a division between world and spirit.

This challenge was followed by a more radical re-reading of the drama. KOTT saw the play as representing a disintegration of both feudal and Renaissance values, a play making a mockery of all eschatologies. The play has a fundamental division of characters, like a morality play; yet both bad and good are destroyed. Like the world represented by Samuel Beckett, the world of *King Lear* is absurd: tragedy has given way to the grotesque, and the tragic hero has given way to the clown; as in Beckett's *Endgame*, Lear on the heath is a clown in a universe without meaning, and Gloucester's "suicide" is a grotesque pantomime.

DOLLIMORE, drawing on poststructuralist insights, especially the post-Marxism of Michel Foucault, gave the radical re-reading of the play a further turn. Rejecting all humanist readings, he constructed a cultural-materialist interpretation of the play. Material conditions precede and inform (but not determine) human values. In this play, power, property, and inheritance have priority, and constitute the play's primary concern; love and kinship are informed by ownership relations, and man is decentred, not through misanthropy, but in order to reveal social process and its ideological misrecognition. The play denies any innate or essential human nature, which always follows, never precedes, material reality. The twin deaths of Lear and Cordelia at the play's end sabotage any closure of the text or any recuperation of an ideology of divine, retributive justice.

Writing near the end of the twentieth century, and able to review the whole development of modern *Lear* criticism from its origins in Bradley, RYAN is concerned to reassert a humanist reading of the play from a Marxist and utopian perspective. He rejects the older view of mysterious, destructive forces at work in the play, which simply have to be borne, and asserts a sense in the play of human alternatives, historically realisable, though denied by history. The text carefully shows that all the suffering in the play is caused by individual people: it has a human origin. And it reveals the play as structured by two opposed ideologies – the social domination of Lear and his group, and the acquisitive individualism of Edmund and his. The play rejects both, while acknowledging strengths in each, and advocates an alternative position, one centring on equality, mutuality, and co-operation. The heath scene constitutes a space outside class society in which social difference is seen to have no legitimacy. The play aligns itself with the oppressed, but sees no place for them in a divided society, then as now. The Fool's prophecy points to the tragic contradiction between utopia and history at the heart of the drama. And the play ends with no affirmation of a scheme of justice or redemption.

WILLIAM ZUNDER

7. Histories

Campbell, Lily, *Shakespeare's "Histories": Mirrors of Elizabethan Policy*, San Marino, California: Huntington Library Publications, 1947

Hodgdon, Barbara, *The End Crowns All: Closure and Contradiction in Shakespeare's History*, Princeton, New Jersey: Princeton University Press, 1991
Holderness, Graham, *Shakespeare Recycled: The Making of Historical Drama*, London: Harvester Wheatsheaf, 1992
Jones, Emrys, *The Origins of Shakespeare*, Oxford: Clarendon Press, 1977
Kelly, Henry, *Divine Providence in the England of Shakespeare's Histories,* Cambridge, Massachusetts: Harvard University Press, 1970
Manheim, Michael, *The Weak King Dilemma in the Shakespearian History Play,* Syracuse, New York: Syracuse University Press, 1973
Ornstein, Robert, *A Kingdom for a Stage: The Achievement of Shakespeare's History Plays*, Cambridge, Massachusetts: Harvard University Press, 1972
Rackin, Phyllis, *Stages of History: Shakespeare's English Chronicles*, London: Routledge, 1990; Ithaca, New York: Cornell University Press, 1990
Riggs, David, *Shakespeare's Heroical Histories: "Henry VI" and Its Literary Tradition*, Cambridge, Massachusetts: Harvard University Press, 1971
Tillyard, E.M.W., *Shakespeare's History Plays*, London: Chatto & Windus, 1944; New York: Macmillan, 1947

Critical debates on the histories have centred especially upon questions of generic identity and of Shakespeare's relationship to other history plays, Renaissance historiography, and Tudor orthodoxy.

TILLYARD's World-War-II work powerfully revalued the histories (except *Henry VIII,* which he does not treat) by historicising them, and in doing so set the tone for much subsequent criticism. He spends nearly as much time on "the background" (historical, philosophical, and literary) as on the histories. Tillyard sees the key to the politics of the histories in two ideas. The first is a medieval Christian "doctrine of order", already expounded in his *The Elizabethan World Picture*, which was the frame for the disorders of the histories. The second is the "Tudor myth" that the accession of Henry VII providentially ended the Wars of the Roses, in which the hand of God could be traced, and that as a Welshman Henry was reviving the glory days of King Arthur. Tillyard identifies the Tudor myth operating most strongly in the chronicle of Edward Hall, which he sees as "the working out of a long chain of nemesis to its happy expiation". Shakespeare, for Tillyard, adopted Hall wholesale, and his eight plays covering Hall's period are a single unit. Even at the most chaotic points Shakespeare is aware of the "greater and permanent pattern". The *Henry VI* plays and *Richard III* are dominated by the Tudor myth and the idea of Respublica ("England" as protagonist): the *Richard II–Henry V* sequence adds the "epic idea" of an England at once recognisably medieval and contemporary. In stressing the intellectual background to the plays Tillyard attempts to counter the image of the histories as a simple manifestation of post-Armada euphoria; but in his attempt to recuperate the plays as political he often simply appropriates them for political orthodoxy.

CAMPBELL also does not subscribe to the "Armada" interpretation of the histories' politics, devoting substantial space to history, politics, and historiography before discussing the histories (though not *Henry VIII* or the *Henry VI* plays). She attempts to define Shakespeare's histories against the tragedies, as concerned with politics rather than ethics. She agrees with Tillyard that the histories show a Christian cyclic history patterned on the sins of the fathers being visited on the children, but her main focus is on the way in which particular monarchs or reigns had been used polemically to illustrate the Elizabethan present, and on how Shakespeare's histories participate in this process. Thus, *King John* mirrors Elizabeth's problems with the papacy and Mary, with Shakespeare's use of his sources seen to intensify contemporary parallels; through the figure of Richard II Shakespeare discusses the problems of deposing a king; and the main issue in the *Henry IV* plays is rebellion (Falstaff is a commentary on Elizabethan warfare). Campbell produces much polemical material to support her identifications of issues with reigns (though her discussion of *Richard III* falls rather flat when she cannot find a contemporary application for the play). Her work situates Shakespeare's histories firmly within the polemics of their time. Her political Shakespeare is, like Tillyard's, orthodox.

KELLY analyses the supernatural references in historical treatments of the period 1398–1485 up to, and including, Shakespeare's histories, beginning with chronicles contemporary with the events they relate, and dividing them into categories not only of "Tudor myth", but of "Yorkist" and "Lancastrian" myths also. He finds that supernatural causes were alleged to be behind specific events according to the inclinations of the writers. Opposing Tillyard, he shows that Hall's chronicle, as edited by Fleming, modified Hall's providential account of the rise of Henry VII. Shakespeare's histories sort these layers of partisanship reproduced in Hall and Holinshed and give the appropriate providential sentiments to the appropriate speakers. He concludes that "it would seem that the providential aspect of the Tudor myth as described by Mr Tillyard is an ex post facto Platonic Form, made up of many fragments that were never fitted together into a mental pattern until they felt the force of his own synthesising energy".

RIGGS' book deals with Shakespeare's relationship to the theatrical tradition of the heroic history in the *Henry VI* plays, *Richard III*, and *Henry IV, Part One*. He begins from the premise that Shakespeare's influences in his early histories were primarily his own rhetorical education and the histories on the London stage when he was beginning to write. Riggs identifies the early history play as primarily concerned with noble deeds and their fame, though these were subject to evaluation in their presentation, and denies that there was a coherent "morality of state" play tradition prior to the history play. The development of the history play, and of Shakespeare's histories, is towards an accommodation between the potentially subversive Marlovian heroic drive to excel and the official ethical position of Tudor "obedience". Shakespeare's achievement in the *Henry VI* plays was to place the hero within an ethical and political framework. Riggs traces this through a focus on the plays' presentations of personal or family honour, and the oratorical forms used to articulate this, downplaying the more choric speeches Tillyard's providential interpretation builds on. With Richard III, the consummate impersonator, and Prince Hal, who chooses rather than inherits honour, Shakespeare abandons the heroic view of history.

This study is well documented, and goes some way towards restating the importance of the literary context in understanding Shakespeare's work.

ORNSTEIN goes further in his study of all the histories, reacting strongly against historicising critics' views of them as conventional politically and therefore artistically. He sees the emphasis on didactic intention as playing down the plays' aesthetic achievements, and historicism as biased towards the conventional in its exploration of a society's norms. He questions whether either the histories, or Hall, embodies a "Tudor myth". The book's guiding principle is that historicism is often deterministic, and Ornstein rather provides ahistorical close readings, focusing closely on form. On this basis, he criticises *King John*, and proposes that the medieval world evoked in *Richard II* produces "artistic pleasure" rather than "political nostalgia". He stresses the individuality of situation and character, and proposes that the enemies of order are individualists rather than ideologists in a world where the family, rather than the cosmos, is the guarantor of order. The book is accessible and well written, though it does extract the plays too forcefully from contemporary political or artistic engagement.

MANHEIM, like Ornstein and Riggs, takes issue with Tillyard, arguing that most kings in the histories "seem to reflect a spirit more of national confusion and uncertainty than of national purpose and determination". He identifies Shakespeare's histories alongside others as registering the impact of Machiavellian thought about politics, and as showing how Machiavellianism can in some measure mitigate the problems of a weak monarch, whether that weakness is traceable to meekness or wantonness. What emerges in *Henry V* is a compromise between the "Christian" and "Machiavellian" codes of leadership. Manheim focuses on the manipulation of sympathy for the monarch, working chronologically to chart the tensions each play sets up around the weak king, which he sees as in some measure abated by gradual acceptance of manipulative politics. *King John*'s Falconbridge, *Richard II*'s Bolingbroke, and Hal are the "image makers" who triumph where the weak kings Richard II and John fail, after the anger at political realities displayed in the *Henry VI* plays. Manheim's thesis emphasises the continuity of theme through the histories and their engagement with contemporary images of the monarchy, though his readings of individual plays are sometimes overly impressionistic, and his virtual omission of the *Henry IV* plays weakens his discussion of the Machiavellian monarch.

JONES begins by taking issue with the idea of Shakespeare as a "comparatively bookless natural genius", showing how much of a literary education he received in grammar school. He goes on to argue that the example of a local mystery cycle may have informed the structuring of Humphrey's fall in *Henry VI, Part Two* or York's taunting in *Henry VI, Part Three*. He places the *Henry VI* plays, *King John*, and *Richard III* in "the critical period of Elizabeth's reign", the years following the 1586 Babington plot when fears of a civil war were strong, and several other civil-war plays were printed or reprinted. This civil-war theme accounts for Shakespeare beginning his histories in the middle chronologically. *Henry VI, Part One*, centres upon the contradictions of fame and presence, reputation and actuality, via its portrayal of Talbot. The prime concern of *Henry VI, Part Two* ("A Commonwealth Tragedy") is government, while *Henry VI, Part Three* stages the formlessness and disorder of England without a king. Throughout, Jones combines awareness of the plays' scenic and formal patterns with reminders of the Tudor literary context. He reads these histories as a culmination of sixteenth-century literature (not just drama), sensitively analysing formal and tonal continuities between them and other political literature. *King John* is read as reproducing the morality encounter between innocence and experience in the world. Most powerfully, *Richard III* is placed as a Tudor drama, a play of Fortune, courtiers, conspiracy, lament, and the ways of the tyrant. Jones's focus allows him to sidestep the common critical denigration of the earlier histories as stages towards greater achievements, and his work historicises Shakespeare's artistic continuity with earlier writings while also being sensitive to the plays' formal or stylistic innovations.

RACKIN's work has dual focus: to examine questions of dramatising the past through a discussion of historical causation, anachronism, and nostalgia, and to consider the representation of women and commoners in the histories. Her thematic approach means that not all the plays get equal coverage: *Henry VIII* and *Henry VI, Part Three* are sparsely treated. The book points out the tension between the debased stage and its exalted subject matter, and proposes that the plays inevitably disrupt any idealisation of history or of particular monarchs or period. Rackin points out that Renaissance historiography was both patriarchal and aristocratic, and that women in the histories often work to subvert patriarchal authority, just as commoners playing kings could question the naturalness of the aristocratic order they were portraying. Rackin's work tends to overestimate Renaissance history's commitments to uniformity, and consequently to overvalue the subversive possibilities of deviation from this. The first section makes some reasonable points, but relies too much on generalisations about practices and books that Rigg's and Kelly's work (not to mention others) have shown to be complex in their particulars. The second section on subversive voices is more based on sustained readings of the plays, and provides an excellent feminist reading of the histories. Rackin does not really engage with other critics' readings of the plays, preferring to cite them when they support her own points. This book's strength is in its particulars rather than its generalisations about Renaissance historiography, and it is most useful on the challenges to Renaissance historiography from those it excludes rather than on its internal contradictions.

HODGDON's title clearly indicates her theme of closure and contradiction in the histories. She includes accounts of modern performances, and is sensitive to the differences between Quarto and Folio versions of the plays. She investigates "closure" in the sense of endings, and in the sense of plays being able to close up or contain the issues or questions they raise. She analyses the history play's generic identity as allowing it the freedom to deploy comic or tragic endings, or substitute continuity or indeterminacy for such closures. Plays can also self-consciously stylise, displace, or truncate elements of conventional closures. So, *King John* offers a "complex . . . mirror for subjects" through a negotiation with its simpler precursors, just as recent productions of the play aim to disperse an orthodox view of the play as patriotic. This is a dense theoretically and theatrically informed exploration, primarily of formal aspects of the plays, though it historicises the plays' texts and their strategies of representing the monarch.

HOLDERNESS identifies the *Richard II–Henry V* sequence as embodying a "conscious understanding of feudal society as a peculiar historical formation", and posits an intellectual Shakespeare demystifying the past as anachronistic in its politics. In this reading, "knowledge through difference" is the key to understanding the plays. Holderness posits a tension between "tragic history" (exemplified in *Richard II*) and "comic history", free from the dominance of the literate tradition, providing a popular, egalitarian, oppositional energy (with Falstaff a key figure). This tension allows both orthodox and radical appropriations of the plays, as they themselves deploy oppositional discourse. He analyses Kenneth Branagh's and Laurence Olivier's films of *Henry V*, relocating Olivier's film as revealing the construction of patriotism in its framing devices, with Henry as much actor as monarch, and comments on how Branagh's construction as an "icon of Thatcherite initiative" is built on his repression of his Northern Irish roots. For Holderness, Branagh's *Henry V* must be read through Northern Ireland rather than the Falklands. Holderness is strongest on the afterlife of the plays in criticism and performance, but the whole book is a convincing cultural-materialist historicisation of the plays at the time of writing and through their subsequent performances.

STEPHEN LONGSTAFFE

8. Problem Plays

Bradshaw, Graham, *Shakespeare's Scepticism*, Brighton, Sussex: Harvester Press, 1987; New York: St Martin's Press, 1987

Campbell, Oscar James, *Shakespeare's Satire*, New York and London: Oxford University Press, 1943; reprinted, Hamden, Connecticut: Archon Books, 1963

Edwards, Philip, *Shakespeare and the Confines of Art*, London: Methuen, 1968, 2nd edition (also New York), 1981

Foakes, R.A., *Shakespeare: The Dark Comedies to the Last Plays: From Satire to Celebration*, London: Routledge & Kegan Paul, 1971; Charlottesville: University Press of Virginia, 1971

Frye, Northrop, *The Myth of Deliverance: Reflections on Shakespeare's Problem Comedies*, Toronto and Buffalo, New York: University of Toronto Press, 1983

Lawrence, William W., *Shakespeare's Problem Comedies*, New York: Macmillan, 1931

Schanzer, Ernest, *The Problem Plays of Shakespeare: A Study of "Julius Caesar," "Measure for Measure," "Antony and Cleopatra"*, New York: Schocken Books, 1963; London: Routledge & Kegan Paul, 1963

Thomas, Vivian, *The Moral Universe of Shakespeare's Problem Plays*, London: Croom Helm, 1987

Toole, William B., *Shakespeare's Problem Plays: Studies in Form and Meaning*, The Hague: Mouton, 1966

Wheeler, Richard P., *Shakespeare's Development and the Problem Comedies: Turn and Counter-Turn*, Berkeley: University of California Press, 1981

In his *Shakespere and His Predecessors* (1896) Frederick S. Boas coined the term "problem plays" to describe *All's Well That Ends Well*, *Measure for Measure*, *Troilus and Cressida*, and *Hamlet* – plays located within "highly artificial societies, whose civilization is ripe unto rottenness", presenting "intricate cases of conscience" and "issues [that] preclude a completely satisfactory outcome". Since Boas, critics have questioned and redefined the problem-play category while differing over which plays it should include, the most frequently chosen candidates being the first three.

LAWRENCE, a medievalist, was nevertheless first to devote an entire book to the problem plays *All's Well That Ends Well*, *Measure for Measure*, and *Troilus and Cressida*, with a glance at the romances, particularly *Cymbeline*. Resisting the earlier view of Edward Dowden and John Dover Wilson, which saw the problem plays as mirroring a crisis in the life of the playwright, souring his comedies, Lawrence posited a new purpose for Shakespeare: "to probe the complicated interrelations of character and action, in a situation admitting of different ethical interpretations". Lawrence defines these plays as sharing "the serious and realistic treatment of a distressing complication in human life, but without a tragic outcome". He explains the plays' serious issues and mood by examining not only their literary conventions, sources, and departures, but the folkloric, social, and political traditions behind them. Thus, Shakespeare revives such traditions as "healing the King" in *All's Well*, the chaste heroine of the medieval Virtue Stories in *Measure*, and the "wager" in *Cymbeline*. One of the book's strongest chapters is on *Troilus and Cressida*, notable for its review of the criticism and its persuasive thesis; Lawrence argues that both the play's cerebral discourse and impropriety were constrained by Shakespeare's Renaissance audience, with its changed attitudes towards the source characters, that *Troilus*'s dramatic deficiencies are compensated for by its psychological realism, and that the play is above all concerned with failure. Lawrence concludes by wisely cautioning critics against the dangers of periodizing the Shakespeare canon.

CAMPBELL locates *Troilus and Cressida*, *Measure for Measure*, *Coriolanus*, and *Timon of Athens* in their turn-of-the-century literary context, stressing the importance of the fashion for satire as practiced by Shakespeare's contemporaries Ben Jonson and John Marston. Campbell further asserts that while in every phase of Shakespeare's career we can find satire, we also find a movement from gentleness to severity. Witness Mercutio's high-spirited satire, followed by the grimmer treatment of Malvolio, and the ascerbic quality of the plays partaking of the 1598–1608 fashion, *Troilus and Cressida* and *Measure for Measure*, for Campbell the distinctive satires. Whereas *Hamlet* and *King Lear* develop the malcontent into the tragic hero, *Coriolanus* and *Timon of Athens* are "tragical satires", refusing to make explicit the moral values that prevail in other Shakespeare plays, and featuring questionable heroes scorned by other characters. Campbell also perceptively treats the satires' comic characters and malcontents. His work has special resonances for directors of these plays.

SCHANZER, much like Lawrence, defines problem plays as concerned with "a moral problem which is central to it, presented in such a manner that we are unsure of our moral bearings, so that uncertain and divided responses to it in the minds of the audience are possible or even probable". However,

Schanzer takes issue with Lawrence over *which* plays should be considered problem plays. According to Schanzer, *Julius Caesar* elicits the spectators' sympathy for Brutus until they see that Caesar's murder is neither just nor beneficial. *Measure for Measure* pits the heroine's chastity against her brother's death. In *Antony and Cleopatra*, the ultimate problem play, not only must Antony choose between desire and rule, but the audience must reconcile Cleopatra's morally questionable acts with a transcendant death. Schanzer considers *King Lear* and *Timon of Athens* as no less problematic than *Troilus and Cressida*, *All's Well That Ends Well,* and *Measure for Measure*. In consequence, he makes the important suggestion that we cease to categorize separately these last three plays.

TOOLE offers a Christian reading of *Hamlet*, *Troilus and Cressida*, *All's Well That Ends Well*, and *Measure for Measure*. After surveying the criticism, he discusses these plays' similarities while objecting to the problem-play category. All four share components deriving from medieval morality plays – "temptation, sin, remorse, repentance, penance, and pardon". Toole links Shakespeare with Dante, specifically with *The Divine Comedy*, arguing that for both "comedy" entails the Christian doctrine of salvation through Grace. *Hamlet*'s subject is Original Sin, with Claudius connoting "both the serpent and Cain, and the problems of Denmark the problems of postlapsarian man". Toole's allegorizing of *Measure* is less persuasive: Angelo is both Everyman and the Devil and, therefore, through the bed-trick "Angelo-Everyman is saved because Angelo-Lucifer has been deceived". *All's Well* and *Measure* adapt morality-play form insofar as their central characters suffer spiritually but ultimately find redemption, a possibility lacking in *Troilus*, a tragedy rather than a problem play. The Christian paradigm is not untenable, but Toole's application of it has been questioned.

EDWARDS illuminates *All's Well That Ends Well*, *Measure for Measure*, and *Troilus and Cressida* by taking as his governing axiom an irreconcilable conflict between art and nature. Edwards claims that the playwright's "restless changes in his forms of drama" are caused by "scepticism about the value of his art as a model of human experience". Shakespeare, nevertheless, attempts to resolve this conflict. Whereas the early comedies interrogate their ability to present convincingly experience, being modelled on a paradigm of separation, confusion, and integration, the more complex and ironic plays, *All's Well* and *Measure for Measure*, attempt to defeat disorder by codifying experience: but they fail. The conflict between an ethical man and an anarchic world is the subject of *Hamlet*, and *Troilus* is forthright in its insistence on anti-idealism. Reversing this pattern, the creation of Desdemona is Shakespeare's act of affirmation. In *The Winter's Tale* Shakespeare is more successful in finding a redemptive vision of humanity; he is even more so in *The Tempest*.

FOAKES approaches these plays as playscripts, an important development in modern Shakespeare criticism. Foakes concerns himself with the plays' structure and notes the ways in which they reflect productions by the children's companies. Psychologically, the characters of Shakespeare's problem plays are deliberately inconsistent and unappealing, inhabitants of a random world which, even if providential, remains unfathomable. Nevertheless, like the characters in satires by Jonson and Marston, they are interesting to analyze. The detachment they evoke in the audience is a significant and calculated effect. Moreover, the dark comedies are dramatic, sexual, and vital. A connection between the problem plays and the romances can be seen in the late tragedies. In these forms, Shakespeare again rejects naturalistic psychology and employs distancing. However, in the romances, with which Foakes concludes, the goal is to create a life-affirming tone. This is a short, competently written work covering a broad subject.

WHEELER's psychoanalytic approach is an important contribution to the critical canon. Wheeler treats the problem comedies *All's Well* and *Measure for Measure* as marking a transition between Shakespeare's earlier comedies and histories and the tragedies. In the former but not the latter, sexuality is unimpeded by family entanglements. The ways the individual and society deal with sexuality are primary subjects of the problem plays. The psychological charge of *All's Well* – especially the assertive characterization of Helena, too threatening to elicit an unmixed response – exceeds what the comedic form can contain. Bertram's bid for freedom, however psychologically understandable, must also be denied. By the same token, *Measure for Measure*'s implied closure is unconvincing, following upon the unsavory behavior of the male characters and what Wheeler sees as Isabella's frigidity. In the problem plays, as in the tragedies, desire cannot fit smoothly into the social formation. Only in the late romances, most notably in *The Tempest*, does Wheeler feel these sexual problems are resolved. Although this last point is certainly debatable, Wheeler's work is essential reading.

FRYE's initial concern is to distinguish the marks of the problem-play genre, but an inquiry into *Measure for Measure*, *All's Well That Ends Well*, and *Troilus and Cressida* leads Frye to oppose received opinion and deny the status of problem play to *All's Well* and *Measure for Measure*. Because they end in marriage and restore order, with the bed-trick serving in lieu of twins or the green world, they are not essentially different from other romantic comedies by Shakespeare. The quest for deliverance "or expanded energy or freedom" is portrayed through a plot that uses reversal and recognition, teleologically anticipating its end in its beginning. Again, since this, for Frye, is what comedy does, he can reclaim *All's Well That Ends Well* and *Measure for Measure*, harmoniously integrating them into his poetics of comedy. *Troilus and Cressida*, on the contrary, foreshadows the romances' concern with appearance and reality. Here "the ironic emphasis is too strong for the drive toward deliverance". Deferring to the resistance of *Troilus*, Frye succeeds in releasing two of the three plays from their historically constrained meanings by seeing them as part of a strictly literary formation. While outside the mainstream, this work is intriguing and provocative.

BRADSHAW stresses that, rather than presenting a monolithic moral view, Shakespeare's interest lay in a multiplicity of ethical stances, represented by various characters within each play. This, he refers to as "Shakespeare's interrogative perspectivism". Critics, both traditional and materialist, should resist identifying a particular speech or character with Shakespeare's (or the play's) view. We must also be alert to the ways meaning is created in poetic drama: which characters express themselves in prose, which in verse? What situations are the characters facing as they speak? Are their speeches "in character"? Although Bradshaw examines a wide range of plays – early and romantic comedies, histories, and tragedies – he privileges *Hamlet*, *Troilus and Cressida*, *Measure for Measure*, and *Macbeth*. *Troilus* takes its tone from the protagonist's query, "What's aught, but as 'tis valued?". Here Shakespeare deals with "the non-objectivity of values while [*Measure for Measure*] explores the incompatibility of different *absolute* values" and of different kinds of justice – "legal, ethical and divine". Bradshaw's philosophical approach is supported by detailed analysis of the plays' prosodic and other stylistic elements, which create their complementary, self-opposing tempers. His philosophical acumen is itself complemented by sympathetic and humane insightfulness.

THOMAS brings problem-play criticism full circle, looking back to William Lawrence in his understanding of *Troilus and Cressida*, *All's Well That Ends Well*, and *Measure for Measure*. After reviewing the criticism, he analyzes the three plays with exacting care, noting their similar "themes, atmosphere, tone and style" and the ways in which they defeat inclusion in the standard genre-categories. Other qualities they share are their likelihood of bemusing spectators, their challenging of traditional views, and their focusing on submerged problematic issues, all of which produce analytical, rather than emotional, audience responses. In *Troilus and Cressida*, which Thomas views as Shakespeare's triumph, Thersites (who has his counterparts in *All's Well* and *Measure*) is more a truth-speaker than a scold, more a denigrator than a clown, the product of a corrupt world. *Troilus and Cressida* is concerned with sexuality, honor, and other questions to which it provides no answers. Thomas's book provides an excellent introduction to recent criticism of the problem plays.

DOROTHEA KEHLER

9. Early Comedies

Berry, Edward, *Shakespeare's Comic Rites*, Cambridge and New York: Cambridge University Press, 1984

Bonazza, Blaze Odell, *Shakespeare's Early Comedies: A Structural Analysis*, The Hague: Mouton, 1966

Elam, Keir, *Shakespeare's Universe of Discourse: Language-Games in the Comedies*, Cambridge and New York: Cambridge University Press, 1984

Tillyard, E.M.W., *Shakespeare's Early Comedies*, edited by Stephen Tillyard, London: Chatto & Windus, 1965; New York: Barnes & Noble, 1965

Traversi, Derek, *Shakespeare: The Early Comedies: "The Comedy of Errors"; "The Taming of the Shrew"; "The Two Gentlemen of Verona"; "Love's Labour's Lost"*, London: Longmans Green & Co., 1960, revised 1964

Waller, Gary (ed.), *Shakespeare's Comedies*, London: Longman, 1991

Despite the mid-century surge of interest in Shakespearean comedy, the early comedies somehow escaped major critical attention, possibly because of their "conventionality" and their reliance on long-forgotten models. Over the past few years, however, there has been a tentative move towards retrieving these plays on their own terms, in particular using the tools of social anthropology, semiotics, and linguistic analysis.

In his opening chapters, TILLYARD draws on a theory of literary kinds ("the notion that there are permanently recurrent propensities or patterns of the human mind and that the literary kinds embody these"), arguing that comedy "assumes that society must be made to work, that creatures must somehow learn to live together. . . . What makes Shakespearean comedy different from other great comedy is the admixture of the status of mind proper to romance". He then devotes full chapters – not wholly linked to his theoretical approaches – to *The Comedy of Errors* ("the play has not been rated a major success only because it is Shakespeare's"), *The Taming of the Shrew* ("conspicuous more for richness than for homogeneity"), *The Two Gentlemen of Verona* ("it may be that Shakespeare himself was more satisfied . . . than the critics who have failed to take its technical side much into account"), *Love's Labour's Lost*, and *The Merchant of Venice*, with an appendix on "The Fairytale Element in *The Taming of the Shrew*".

TRAVERSI provides a brief survey, with chapters on *The Comedy of Errors*, *The Taming of the Shrew*, *Two Gentlemen of Verona* ("Shakespeare's most tedious play"), and *Love's Labour's Lost*, none of them "by any standards a complete masterpiece". He notes "the presence in them of an important element of convention, which has to be mastered before the human content of the plays, their relation to normal experience, can begin to make itself felt". Traversi deals with sources, plot, use of verse and prose forms, and the plays' "mature presentation of human relationships".

In order "to determine the stages in Shakespeare's progress as a comic dramatist from early experimentation to a finished pattern of execution in the fashioning of romantic comedy", BONAZZA employs a rather rigid four-part plot formula to analyse the early comedies – the framework plot, the romantic love story, the parodying subplot, and the atmosphere-providing plot. Schematically showing how Shakespeare explores Plautine comedy (*Comedy of Errors*), the language games of John Lyly (*Love's Labour's Lost*), and the complex romance of Robert Greene and Philip Sidney (*Two Gentlemen of Verona*), Bonazza arrives at Shakespeare's solution in *A Midsummer Night's Dream*.

ELAM's starting point is the common critical verdict that the early comedies are flawed by the too-prominent role played in them by language. Following Ernst Cassirer's identification of the "game of the pure self-activity of the word" as the main motive force, and arguing that linguistic forms were cultivated obsessively in the Renaissance, Elam draws on J.L. Austin's speech-act theory and Ludwig Wittgenstein's notion of the language-game to demonstrate the active role of language within Shakespearean comedy, "this active and self-advertising presence of language in use". In a detailed and brilliant "study of the self-consciousness of Shakespeare's language", he takes as his key text *Love's Labour's Lost*, perhaps the most maligned of all Shakespeare's plays for its "wordiness".

BERRY investigates the remarkable affinity between the structure of Shakespeare's romantic comedies and the rites of passage theorised by Arnold van Gennep through the stages of separation, transition, and incorporation. Noting that the romantic comedies form "an unusually tight-knit genre based on specific ritual structures – those of initiation, courtship, and marriage", Berry follows eight comedies (including the early comedies) as "they chart the tortuous course of pairs of lovers through courtship to marriage". He concludes that these plays:

> . . . do not merely reflect the structure of an Elizabethan rite or set of social customs. These may have suggested such a structure to Shakespeare, in shadowy and fragmentary outline, but it is he who created it, giving shadows substance and fragments dramatic form. . . . This dynamic structure makes Shakespeare's romantic comedies at once unique, Elizabethan, and universal.

WALLER's collection draws on recent theoretical approaches "to encourage different ways to produce 'our' Shakespeare", and argues that "we draw on both our most primitive and our most deeply encultured memories when we respond to and reproduce Shakespeare's comedies in our own histories". Focusing on *The Comedy of Errors*, W. Thomas MacCary roots out the experience of Shakespearean comedy in a psychoanalytic model of the family. Karen Newman argues that *The Taming of the Shrew* both produces social facts of patriarchal ideology and gives us a perspective on it, "clinging to Elizabethan patriarchal ideology and at the same time tearing it away by foregrounding or italicizing its constructed character". Louis Montrose draws on a social anthropological model of culture to explore *Love's Labour's Lost* as an "acute comic study of the uses to which humans at play . . . put the cultural forms that they create", while Norman N. Holland and Helen Golding provide psychoanalytic readings of *A Midsummer Night's Dream*. Waller's Introduction provides a useful history of the comedies' reception.

ALAN STEWART

10. Middle Comedies

Bamber, Linda, *Comic Women, Tragic Men: A Study of Genre and Gender in Shakespeare*, Stanford, California: Stanford University Press, 1982

Belsey, Catherine, "Disrupting Sexual Difference: Meaning and Gender in the Comedies", in *Alternative Shakespeares*, edited by John Drakakis, London: Methuen, 1985

Berry, Edward, *Shakespeare's Comic Rites*, Cambridge and New York: Cambridge University Press, 1984

Bristol, Michael D., *Carnival and Theatre: Plebeian Culture and the Structure of Authority in Renaissance England*, London and New York: Methuen, 1985

Brown, Steve, "The Boyhood of Shakespeare's Heroines: Notes on Gender Ambiguity in the Sixteenth Century", in *Studies in English Literature*, 30, 1990

Elam, Keir, *Shakespeare's Universe of Discourse: Language Games in the Comedies*, Cambridge and New York: Cambridge University Press, 1984

Erickson, Peter, *Patriarchal Structures in Shakespearean Drama*, Berkeley: University of California Press, 1985

Evans, Malcolm, "Deconstructing Shakespeare's Comedies", in *Alternative Shakespeares*, edited by John Drakakis, London: Methuen, 1985

Garber, Marjorie, *Vested Interests: Cross-Dressing and Cultural Anxiety*, London: Routledge, 1991; New York: Routledge, 1992

Howard, Jean E., "Cross-Dressing, the Theatre and Gender Struggle in Early Modern England", *Shakespeare Quarterly*, 39, 1988

Hunter, G.K., "Comedy, Farce, Romance", in *Comedy from Shakespeare to Sheridan: Change and Continuity in the English and European Dramatic Tradition*, edited by A.R. Braunmuller and J.C. Bulman, Newark: University of Delaware Press, 1986; London: Associated University Presses, 1986

Jardine, Lisa, *Still Harping on Daughters: Women and Drama in the Age of Shakespeare*, Brighton, Sussex: Harvester Press, 1983; Totowa, New Jersey: Barnes & Noble, 1983

Jardine, Lisa, "Twins and Travesties: Gender, Dependency and Sexual Availability in *Twelfth Night*", in *Erotic Politics: Desire on the Renaissance Stage*, edited by Susan Zimmerman, London and New York: Routledge, 1992

Krieger, Elliot, *A Marxist Study of Shakespeare's Comedies*, London: Macmillan, 1979; New York: Barnes & Noble, 1979

Laroque, François, *Shakespeare's Festive World: Elizabethan Seasonal Entertainment and the Professional Stage*, translated by Janet Lloyd, Cambridge and New York: Cambridge University Press, 1991

McLuskie, Kathleen, "The Act, the Role, and the Actor: Boy Actresses on the Elizabethan Stage", in *New Theatre Quarterly*, 3, 1987

Mahood, M., "Shakespeare's Middle Comedies: A Generation of Criticism", in *Shakespeare Survey*, 32, 1979

Neely, Carol Thomas, *Broken Nuptials in Shakespeare's Plays*, New Haven, Connecticut: Yale University Press, 1985

Nevo, Ruth, *Comic Transformations in Shakespeare*, London: Methuen, 1980

Orgel, Stephen, "Nobody's Perfect: Or Why Did the English Stage Take Boys for Women?", in *Displacing Homophobia: Gay Male Perspectives in Literature and Culture*, edited by Ronald R. Butters, John M. Clum, and Michael Moon, Durham, North Carolina: Duke University Press, 1989

Patterson, Annabel, *Shakespeare and the Popular Voice*, Oxford: Blackwell, 1989

Rackin, Phyllis, "Androgyny, Mimesis, and the Marriage of the Boy Heroine on the English Renaissance Stage", in *PMLA* [*Publications of the Modern Language Association*], 102, 1987

Rebhorn, Wayne A., "After Frye: A Review Article on the Interpretation of Shakespearean Comedy and Romance", in *Texas Studies in Literature and Language*, 21, 1979

Salingar, Leo, *Shakespeare and the Traditions of Comedy*, Cambridge and New York: Cambridge University Press, 1974

Smallwood, R.L., "The Middle Comedies", in *Shakespeare: A Bibliographical Guide*, revised edition, edited Stanley Wells, Oxford: Clarendon Press, 1990; New York: Oxford University Press, 1990

Smith, Bruce R., *Homosexual Desire in Shakespeare's England: A Cultural Poetics*, Chicago: University of Chicago Press, 1991, with new Preface, 1994

Stallybrass, Peter, "Transvestism and the 'Body Beneath': Speculating on the Boy Actor", in *Erotic Politics: Desire on the Renaissance Stage*, edited by Susan Zimmerman, London and New York: Routledge, 1992

Traub, Valerie, *Desire and Anxiety: Circulations of Sexuality in Shakespearean Drama*, London and New York: Routledge, 1992

Wiles, David, *Shakespeare's Clown: Actor and Text in the Elizabethan Playhouse*, Cambridge and New York: Cambridge University Press, 1987

Wilson, R., "The Quality of Mercy: Discipline and Punishment in Shakespearean Comedy", in *Seventeenth Century*, 5, 1990

In the early years of Shakespeare criticism the comedies were somewhat neglected in comparison to the tragedies, and what little commentary existed tended to make generalised contrasts between Shakespearean benignity and Jonsonian acerbity, or to concentrate on the characters of the plays. Analysis of Shakespearean comedy underwent a major revolution with the publication of Northrop Frye's *The Natural Perspective* (1948) and C.L. Barber's *Shakespeare's Festive Comedy* (1959). These two monographs provide the starting point for many contemporary discussions. The heart of Frye's work lies in a formal analysis of the structure of comedy, whereas Barber places more emphasis upon tone, mood, and social function. Modern criticism has extended these approaches, offered some correctives, and more recently has focused on gender and its representation, and the related issue of the politics of comedy. Useful surveys of past criticism, with discussions of work on individual plays, are provided by MAHOOD, SMALLWOOD, and REBHORN.

Many critics have struggled with the hybridity of Shakespearean comedy and its relation to other contemporary comic idioms. Renaissance comedy is far more various than any simple division into Shakespearean or Jonsonian modes would suggest, best described by HUNTER as a "spectrum . . . running from the dynamic to the static", encompassing all tones from farce to romance, the latter itself a diverse mode covering everything from the fantastic and exotic through to the historical. Formalist approaches are dominated by SALINGAR, although his book is also an erudite synthesis of the best elements in Barber's and Frye's work, paying attention to plot, dramatic antecedents, tone and function, as well as to the theatrical experience of the plays. This approach to the multi-faceted nature of Shakespearean comedy, drawing upon classical, Italian, and medieval antecedents, with an emphasis upon the celebratory nature of the form and a refutation of Frye's view of comedy as wish-fulfilment, provides the best introduction available. Formal and structural elements, in slightly different senses, lie at the heart of two other books. NEVO also considers Shakespeare's classical heritage, but focuses upon the transformations that the characters undergo as the plays work through confusion towards clarification. In contrast, ELAM provides a detailed study of the language games engaged in throughout the comedies, from a structuralist viewpoint. These views are reviewed by EVANS with an interesting polemical edge, which points up new directions in research.

Festive approaches to the comedies develop Barber's vision of the green world, a space in which mankind returns to a balanced interaction with Nature. The pervasiveness of Barber's model is illustrated by its obvious influence upon Salingar's tripartite division of Shakespearean comedy, and in more recent attempts to develop and historicise the earlier study. BERRY deftly mixes social history and anthropology to explore the ritual elements in the plays and their relation to Elizabethan ritualism. Like both Barber and Nevo he sees the transformative aspects of the plays as part of a wider pattern of rites of passage (initiation, courtship, marriage). LAROQUE provides an even more historicist approach, with a judicious and well-informed survey of popular, seasonal, and calendrical cultures in early-modern England, with particular emphasis upon Shakespeare's utilisation of popular forms and the potential for political subversion innate in such traditions. Although not solely concerned with the comedies, BRISTOL extends the political analysis of the popular elements in Shakespeare through his argument that the carnivalesque has a political valency, both as a negative critique of official culture and as a positive affirmation of collective traditions. Popular culture and Shakespearean comic appropriations of these elements become a way of resisting penetration by, and integration of, the growing power of the state. Whereas Bristol draws heavily on Mikhail Bakhtin and other theorists of the popular, WILES also considers the importance of popular traditions through a detailed and finely nuanced study of clowns and fools, drawing upon historical sources, and a judicious survey of folk traditions, such as the morris dance. Wiles sees the play as "comic ritual" through which the clown helps dissolve social boundaries and create a sense of community.

The most significant new directions in comedy criticism to emerge in the last decade have been the feminist and gender-oriented approaches. BAMBER voices the key issue when she contrasts the apparently pro-feminist comedies with the malevolent women of the tragedies, linking gender and genre. She explains this contradiction by seeing the tragedies as a conflict between the masculine self and the feminine "Other", an *agon* that the comedies subsume in their benign world. The comedies are the world of "psycho-sexual confidence" and present a "both/and" rather than an "either/or" structure. Whereas in the tragedies women are forced to choose, in the comedies this compulsion is absent, although this absence has ambiguous effects, in that it creates a positive world in which women can operate successfully, while it also renders women unthreatening. Other feminists have extended this approach, in the study of both the social relations of the sexes through wooing, wedding, and marriage (NEELY) and the dominant force of patriarchy that runs throughout the plays (ERICKSON). Both studies envisage Shakespeare's heroines within a highly conflicted territory, for Neely caught between idealisation and misogyny, for Erickson trapped in a battle between male homosocial bonds and marital ties. Erickson's work in particular emphasises the darker side of Shakespearean comedy, so that plays like *As You Like It* depict a "male utopia", rendering Rosalind ultimately as the powerless woman desired by patriarchy. BELSEY's essay provides a neat summary of these approaches, placing the plays against contemporary social history to provide the key to understanding gender and marriage in the comedies.

The interest in gender relations has been increased by a furious debate over the nature of the boy actors who performed these women's roles. Studies by JARDINE (1983), McLUSKIE, HOWARD, ORGEL, GARBER, BROWN, and STALLYBRASS (among others) have debated the precise impact of boys playing women, with a bewildering variety of conclusions, often in response to Lisa Jardine's earlier (and rather crude assertion) that the action of the audience was predominantly homoerotic (a conclusion updated and enriched in JARDINE 1992). Among the more interesting responses to these issues, directly relevant to the comedies, are Rackin and Traub. RACKIN considers the double figure of the hermaphrodite (both monstrosity and neo-Platonic perfection), and traces a parallel androgyny in comedy, creating a "necessary ambivalence" that allows for multi-valent sexual and representational possibilities. Comedy marries representation and escapism, eroticism and monstrosity, and the problem lies in the maintenance of these unions. TRAUB, on the other hand, presents an interesting challenge to the Foucauldian assumptions that underlie much work in this area, and argues for a much more responsive approach to "the material possibility" of the boy actor, where the erotic is activated in the special space of sixteenth-century theatre (standing outside limiting twentieth-century conceptions that sexuality must be either/or), depending on the specific actor, writer, play, and audience. Traub's complex and theoretically demanding book culminates with a fine and subtle discussion of the "homoerotics" of Shakespearean comedy. Supplemental to this approach is SMITH's judicious study of homoeroticism in Shakespearean England.

With the advent of New Historicism and the gender-based interpretations, attention has also returned to the issue of the politics of the comedies. KRIEGER's Marxist study, although interesting historically, reads the conflicts of the plays in class terms, a reductiveness that is avoided in Bristol and others (such as PATTERSON). The best of these approaches, and one of the most stimulating essays on Shakespeare in recent years, is WILSON's, which uses Michel Foucault's paradigm of the movement from punitive to carceral society, but locates this change in the late sixteenth century (rather than in the eighteenth century, as in Foucault), and so argues that mercy in the comedies is a method of extending power. Wilson provides a subtle reading of the connection between theatre and juridical arenas, but he also renders the comedies hugely threatening, so bringing out their darker side.

JAMES D. KNOWLES

11. Late Comedies (Romances)

Edwards, P., "Shakespeare's Romances: 1900–1957", in *Shakespeare Survey 11*, edited by Allardyce Nicoll, Cambridge: Cambridge University Press, 1958

Felperin, Howard *Shakespearean Romance*, Princeton, New Jersey: Princeton University Press, 1972

Granville Barker, Harley, *Prefaces to Shakespeare: "Cymbeline"; "The Winter's Tale"*, London: Batsford, 1930; Princeton, New Jersey: Princeton University Press, 1946

Mowat, Barbara A., *The Dramaturgy of Shakespeare's Romances*, Athens: University of Georgia Press, 1976

Pettet, E.C., *Shakespeare and the Romance Tradition*, London and New York: Staples Press, 1949

Strachey, Lytton, "Shakespeare's Final Period", in his *Books and Characters*, London: Chatto & Windus, 1922; New York: Harcourt Brace, 1922

Tillyard, E.M.W., *Shakespeare's Last Plays*, London: Chatto & Windus, 1938; Chester Springs, Pennsylvania: Dufour Editions, 1958

Traversi, Derek, *Shakespeare: The Last Phase*, New York: Harcourt Brace, 1953; London: Hollis & Carter, 1954

Warren, Roger, *Staging Shakespeare's Late Plays*, Oxford: Clarendon Press, 1990; New York: Oxford University Press, 1990

Wilson Knight, G., *The Crown of Life: Essays in Interpretation of Shakespeare's Last Plays*, London: Oxford University Press, 1947

Yates, Frances A., *Shakespeare's Last Plays: A New Approach*, London: Routledge & Kegan Paul, 1975

Lytton STRACHEY exposed one of the myths of the late nineteenth-century critical tradition – the view that the late plays are serene expressions of the playwright's old age. Strachey associates this doctrine with the major critics of the time – F.J. Furnivall, Edward Dowden, Ten Brink, Israel Gollancz, Georg Brandes, and Sir Sidney Lee – and he refutes it by drawing attention to Shakespeare's frequent "violence of expression" and to those aspects of the late plays that do not fit into the "scheme of roses and maidens". Rarely can such consensus of opinion have existed in relation to a group of Shakespeare's plays, and Strachey's criticisms were, therefore, undoubtedly revolutionary. However, Strachey's conclusion that Shakespeare was "bored with people, bored with real life, bored with drama, bored, in fact, with everything except poetry and poetical dreams" is the least original aspect of his essay, and, as a development of the then conventional notion that the late plays exhibit Shakespeare in "retirement", threatens the view he has himself just advanced.

GRANVILLE BARKER's *Prefaces* to *Cymbeline* and *The Winter's Tale* were of profound importance in the critical re-evaluation of the late plays as a group, for Barker was the first critic to discern the particular style of the late plays, noting the "artless artifice" of Cymbeline. Where Strachey's approach to the plays might be described as realistic, reacting against the biographical criticism of the late nineteenth century, attempting to debunk the plays by showing their remoteness from real life, Granville Barker's approach might be described as formalist, concentrating on style and dramaturgical structure, recognising that the plays are highly sophisticated, crafted works of art.

TILLYARD's book is a fine work of criticism, and the first book-length study of the late plays, though it should be noted that he considers only three of them – *Cymbeline*, *The Winter's Tale*, and *The Tempest*. Tillyard's approach is historicist in its emphasis, examining the relationships between the plays and the romance tradition, court masque conventions, the plays of Francis Beaumont and John Fletcher, revenge drama and Jacobean historical and political events. Tillyard is responsive to the plays' metatheatrical elements, writing about the theme of "re-enactment" in *The Tempest*. He is also perceptive in dealing with the masque, remarking on similarities between *The Tempest* and the plays of Luigi Pirandello. For all his historicism, Tillyard is able to relate the plays to the modern period. Outstanding in its day, this book is still a lively and stimulating study.

WILSON KNIGHT's book might be described as a primary example of the symbolic tradition of criticism, which, like the formalist and historicist traditions, gained ascendency during the twentieth century. Wilson Knight's study contains the essay "Myth and Miracle", first published in 1929, which more than any other work of criticism established the view that the late plays do not represent a falling off in Shakespeare's achievement (as Strachey claimed), but an actual advance, a development of the concerns and preoccupations of his earlier plays. Wilson Knight is concerned with exploring the visionary quality implicit in the imagery, paying close attention to the supernatural elements and the visions, which had been dismissed by the realistic tradition of criticism. Unlike Tillyard, Wilson Knight extends his analysis to cover both *Pericles* and *Henry VIII*. Indeed, Wilson Knight particularly values *Pericles*, a play which Tillyard is quick to dismiss.

While acknowledging the influence of the tradition of Seneca, Plautus, and Terence on the Elizabethan drama, as well as that of the miracle play, morality play, and interlude, PETTET argues that the primary influence on the drama of the age was that of romance literature. Pettet discusses the romance tradition, relating the comedies of John Lyly and Robert Greene to those of Shakespeare. His book includes chapters on Shakespeare's "Romantic" comedies and the "Dark" comedies ("problem plays"), and concludes with a chapter on the romances.

TRAVERSI's book is, one suspects, influenced by Wilson Knight, although Traversi is reluctant to acknowledge the influence of earlier critics. His Introduction begins with a refutation of Strachey, and he asserts that modern criticism regards Shakespeare in the late plays as not "falling back on convention, or lapsing from the tremendous achievement of the great tragedies", but rather, "reaching out in conscious experiment towards new dramatic forms, a natural response to fresh needs and emotions". Traversi analyses the plays in the light of the Christian ethic, which influenced Shakespeare and his audience, focusing particularly on the theme of reconciliation.

EDWARDS's article is valuable for its analysis of the critical literature on the late plays during the first half of the twentieth century. Many of the articles discussed focus on individual plays, which are related by the writer to studies of the plays as a group. Edwards isolates themes in the critical literature, noticing influences, trends, and developments that took place between 1900 and 1957 (when the article was written).

FELPERIN extends Pettet's and Tillyard's interest in the late plays from the point of view of the romance tradition. He begins by noting the extent to which the late plays have gained popularity among critics during the twentieth century: "more has been written on them in the past three and a half decades than over the previous three and a half centuries". He acknowledges, too, that this change in fortune is closely linked to changes in theatrical conventions and styles of performance: "now that the naturalism of Ibsen and Stanislavsky has faded from the scene, the contemporary theatre can approximate more closely than ever before the condition of the unlocalized stage within which the romances were first successfully mounted". The book places the late plays in the context of romance literature generally, and discusses the development in Shakespeare's art from comedy to romance. In the third part of the book, Felperin moves into an analysis of each of the late plays, including *Henry VIII*, which, in terms of its "Tragical-Comical-Historical-Pastoral" synthesis, he sees as being closely linked to *Cymbeline*. Finally, the book includes a useful appendix, entitled "The Fortunes of Romance", in which the reception of the Romances is discussed. He is somewhat critical of Wilson Knight for his "spirit of Nietzschean transvaluation", his apparent inability to distinguish between the literary mode of romance and religious experience, yet notes his historical importance:

> . . . his work on the Romances is very much a thing of time and history, a reaction against the explicit or implicit condescension to romantic modes of Strachey on the one hand and of Eliot and the New Humanists on the other, an attempt to champion the cause of romance when it was down.

In fairness it should be noted that T.S. Eliot was one of the first critics to recognise the value of Wilson Knight's work, while poems like "The Waste Land" (1922) and "Marina" (1930) hardly reveal any condescension on his part towards romance literature. The theme of "recognition", so important in Shakespeare's Romances, is central to Eliot's own poetry and drama. Eliot can in fact be seen as directly contributing towards the re-evaluation of the late plays.

MOWAT discusses the interrelationship between tragedy and comedy and such topics as "Dramatic Tactics" and "Dramatic Strategy" in the late plays. In Chapter 4, "The Romances as Open Form Drama", the form of the plays is analysed and contrasted to that of Aristotelian drama. Mowat is also concerned with how the form of the plays is related to their meaning, a topic which she explores in her final chapter. Essentially, Mowat's approach might be described as formalist, extending a tradition of critical interest in the late plays that can be traced back to Granville Barker's study of *Cymbeline*.

YATES discusses Shakespeare's late plays in the light of the Rosicrucian Enlightenment and the revival of Elizabethan ideals during the Jacobean age. Bringing a wealth of historical insight to the drama of the period, Yates analyses the relationship between Ben Jonson's and Shakespeare's views of the magician, as expressed in *The Alchemist* and *The Tempest*, Shakespeare presenting, through Prospero, a highly positive interpretation of the John Dee figure, while Jonson, in his characterisation of Subtle, suggesting that the alchemist is no more than a crafty trickster and that the ideals of the alchemists should not be taken too seriously. Yates's book, based on public lectures at University College, London, justifiably claims to present "a new approach", including fine chapters on *Cymbeline*, *Henry VIII*, and *The Tempest*, and well captures her enthusiasm for her subject.

WARREN's book focuses on the recent performance history of the late plays, as directly experienced by the author through attending the rehearsals of Sir Peter Hall, when he directed *Cymbeline*, *The Winter's Tale*, and *The Tempest* at London's (Royal) National Theatre in 1988. Warren also attended the rehearsals of director David Thacker's 1989 production of *Pericles* and the rehearsals for a series of productions at the Canadian Shakespeare Festival in Stratford, Ontario, in 1986. Warren is able to make comparisons between the different production approaches, while his book is informed by a thorough knowledge of the performance history – to which he significantly adds through his detailed documentation and commentary.

Finally, as a shortlist of essential reading from the items discussed, I would recommend Wilson Knight for his insight into the symbolic structure of the late plays, Felperin for a modern account of the plays in relation to the romance tradition, Mowat for an analysis of the dramaturgical structure, and Yates for her provocative interpretation of the plays from the point of view of their political, intellectual, and social history.

BRIAN PEARCE

12. Poetry

Booth, Stephen (ed.), *Shakespeare's Sonnets* (facsimile edition), New Haven, Connecticut, and London: Yale University Press, 1977

Hubler, Edward, *The Sense of Shakespeare's Sonnets*, Princeton, New Jersey: Princeton University Press, 1952

Ingram, W.G., and Theodore Redpath (eds.), *Shakespeare's Sonnets*, London: University of London Press, 1964

Keach, William, *Elizabethan Erotic Narratives: Irony and Pathos in Ovidian Poetry of Shakespeare, Marlowe and Their Contemporaries*, New Brunswick, New Jersey: Rutgers University Press, 1977

Leishman, J.B., *Themes and Variations in Shakespeare's Sonnets*, New York: Hillary House, 1961; 2nd edition, London: Hutchinson, 1963

Lever, J. W., *The Elizabethan Love Sonnet*, London: Methuen, 1956, 2nd edition, 1966

Muir, Kenneth, *Shakespeare's Sonnets*, London and Boston: Allen & Unwin, 1979

Nicoll, Allardyce (ed.), *Shakespeare Survey 15*, Cambridge: Cambridge University Press, 1962

Pequigney, Joseph, *"Such is My Love": A Study of Shakespeare's Sonnets*, Chicago: University of Chicago Press, 1985

Prince, F.T. (ed.), *Shakespeare: The Poems* (Arden Shakespeare series), London: Methuen, 1960; Cambridge, Massachusetts: Harvard University Press, 1960

Wells, Stanley (ed.), *The Cambridge Companion to Shakespeare Studies*, Cambridge and New York: Cambridge University Press, 1986

Winny, James, *The Master-Mistress: A Study of Shakespeare's Sonnets*, London: Chatto & Windus, 1968; New York: Barnes & Noble, 1968

After four centuries, the mysteries of Shakespeare's sonnets remain unsolved. The identities of the young man, the Dark Lady, the Rival Poet, the date and order of composition, events obscurely referred to, the very nature of the experiences distilled into poetry – all continue to be studied with fascination, but without agreement. There is increasing insistence that the relationship with the anonymous man was physical and that the poet was bisexual, but this is unresolved. Valuable work has been done on the poems in the Ovidian tradition.

There are several usefully annotated editions of the poems. PRINCE provides a helpful introduction to the verse and a detailed commentary on them. He counters attacks on the improper sensuality of *Venus and Adonis* and on its artistic clumsiness. He relates the poem to the romantic comedies with "their delight in human energies and emotions, their keen savour of everyday life mixed with abundant poetry, and their undertones of deeper seriousness". Sexuality is treated with sensuous enjoyment as comedy. *Lucrece* is a failure, although it throbs with "unfailing rhythmic power" and is rich with "ingenious fancies" and "vividly felt emotions and actions and images". The attractive edition by INGRAM and REDPATH, with its helpful glossary and key to the wordplay, is the best in which to read the sonnets. The identities of W.H., the Dark Lady, the Fair Youth and so on, are not dealt with by the editors, but learning and fine judgment are brought to bear on the interpretation of the poems. BOOTH prints the 1609 text in facsimile with his modernised edition on facing pages. More than 400 pages of dense commentary follow. It is sometimes inspired, but often follows random associations (especially sexual ones) at considerable length. He delights in finding "potentially dizzying complexity" where the writer appears to be simple and clear. He aims to reveal "a Renaissance reader's understanding of Shakespeare's idiom but also to answer academic questions about how the sonnets work".

There is no better survey of the early criticism nor better introduction to modern scholarship than NICOLL's collection of essays. Lever surveys the trends in criticism of the poems, showing the rise of interest in *Venus and Adonis*, once dismissed as lifeless or tasteless but "rehabilitated as a highly moral, even highly didactic poem, once Renaissance conventions were understood". The progress of *Lucrece* has been "sober, unspectacular". Its merits have been noted but it has "neither won enthusiastic support nor been heatedly condemned". The complexity of *The Phoenix and the Turtle* has excited much interest and perhaps the "undertones of triumph" rather than the note of tragedy indicate its true significance. Nejgebauer's survey of the sonnets – editions, text, date, sources, criticism – is also comprehensive. In the criticism, the trends are to see the sonnets as: autobiographical, sincere records of events in the poet's life; fictitious, either because of distaste for the morality implied in the poems or because of increasing knowledge of the conventions they elaborate; or esoteric, e.g., the sequence is an allegory of alcoholism. These surveys are followed by well-informed essays on several aspects of the poems.

HUBLER rejects the possibility that the love for the young man was sexual. He writes well on the unglamorous relationship with the Dark Lady and on the "economy of the closed heart", tracing the connections between sonnets and ideas expressed in the plays, notably the parable of the talents and the belief that virtue cannot be said to exist until it is expressed in action. Perhaps trying to avoid idolatrous over-praise, Hubler exaggerates the weaknesses of the poetry, complaining about the inferiority of the concluding couplets, the quibbles, and the obscurity and frigidity of some of the poems. He writes best on his declared topic – the *sense* of the sonnets.

About half of LEVER's book is on Shakespeare. He places the sonnets in their European context, illustrating how they were "adapted and transformed by distinctively English attitudes". He examines Sir Thomas Wyatt, the Earl of Surrey, Sir Philip Sidney, and Edmund Spenser, showing how the principles of imitation and invention functioned to establish thematic continuity within which individuality of style and poetic personality could be expressed. He points out how Shakespeare transmutes Erasmus, the *Arcadia*, and Ovid. In his "negation of conventional values", the sonneteer "defied tradition" in the poems to the man and similarly those to the woman. Yet, in Shakespeare's sonnets, with their "unprecedented scope, diversity and power", Lever concludes that "the Renaissance poetic tradition found its true English consummation".

Although LEISHMAN does briefly touch on the perennial topics of interest – the identity of W.H., the order of the sonnets, etc. – his main concern is to locate what is most individual, memorable, and unique – about Shakespeare's poetry. With considerable learning and equal critical delicacy, he compares Shakespeare with the great classical and European writers on similar themes. Only Horace has written with comparable resonance about poetry as the defier of *tempus edax rerum*. The publicness of the Roman poet contrasts with the privateness of Shakespeare, who avoids the condescension typical of Torquato Tasso and the arrogant self-glorification of Pierre Ronsard. There is a religiousness and spirituality about his adoring love, which is felt intensely, even intransigently, as an irreplaceable good: nothing could compensate for its loss. Love mitigates the strange mutations of this "vile world".

WINNY's introduction retraces readings of the sonnets as either autobiography or fiction, then argues that the inconsistencies within them, the lack of hard biographical evidence, and their failure to refer unambiguously to what we do know of the writer's life suggest Shakespeare's sequence is an exclusively imaginative creation, "a half-private adjunct of his main creative activity, in which some of the ideas which most preoccupy him are worked over intensively". The poet varies persona and viewpoint. The exploration of identity is pervasive, and is assisted by the fluid format of the intricate, shadowy relationship. Dualism is a conspicuous feature of the complex experience: the poet is frustrated in his desire for union with both friend and mistress; she is repellent and also fascinating; the friend is a shadowy phantom-like being. The sonnets are about a "self-destructive struggle within a body too deeply divided against itself to achieve unity of being".

KEACH's study of Ovid and the Ovidian romance, or *epyllion*, shows how the Elizabethans imitated the Roman poet but learned to give voice to their own human insights in so doing. They were fascinated by Ovid's ironic, playful inventiveness, his ambivalence, especially in treating eroticism, his "enigmatic conjunction of the witty and the painful". The theme of *Venus and Adonis* is "the opposition between sexual love so intense and aggressive that it becomes self-frustrating and beauty so selfish and inaccessible that it becomes self-destructive". A fine chapter on *Hero and Leander* enriches our understanding of Shakespeare's poems.

In his laconic, brisk, and authoritative overview of the issues and the problems, MUIR considers the state of scholarship on W.H., the Dark Lady, the Rival Poet, and the date, text, and order of the sonnets. There is a selective bibliography and a short history of worthwhile critical works. He glances at the vogue of the sonnet, and at analogues and themes in the tradition that are transformed by the poet's individual talent. There is a perceptive commentary on the shadowy narrative and a chapter on the blend of complexity with apparent naturalness in the style, and the variety of structure achieved within the Shakespearean form. Muir avoids affirming that the sonnets are fiction or autobiography, hinting that they are somehow drawn from actual experience which is reshaped to create "imaginative truth". The friend may be "an amalgam of more than one man" but "it is the very untidiness that helps to give the illusion of truth to life".

PEQUIGNEY's study is almost a manifesto, affirming emphatically the homoerotic nature of Shakespeare's love for the young man who, like the poet-persona, is called Will. He reconstructs the critical history of the sonnets as a conspiracy to repress or deny this homoeroticism. The Renaissance cult of idealised male friendship, so often affirmed, did not sanction much that is intrinsic to this relationship. He analyses the carnality of the sexual address to the male lover, pointing out erotic and bawdy allusions that have been generally overlooked or suppressed. The sonnets to the man record the growth, maturity, and decline of their love. The remaining poems explore the action of lust with the mistress. Pequigney uses Freudian and Lacanian psychoanalytic theory to reveal the "bisexual soul" of the poet, who, he is convinced, wrote autobiographically here.

WELLS's collection of lucidly written essays by distinguished Shakespearean scholars is helpful to inexperienced students as well as to specialists. It enables all such readers to see the nondramatic verse in the context of the other works. It ends with a helpful survey of reference works. An essay by Terence Hawkes outlines postmodern approaches to the poetry and drama. The compact, thoughtful reading of the sonnets and poems here by Ellrodt appears 25 years after his contribution to the *Shakespeare Survey* referred to above.

DEREK N.C. WOOD

Shaw, George Bernard 1856–1950

Irish dramatist, essayist, novelist, screenwriter, and critic

Bertolini, John A., *The Playwriting Self of Bernard Shaw*, Carbondale: Southern Illinois University Press, 1991
Dietrich, R.F., *Portrait of the Artist as a Young Superman: A Study of Shaw's Novels*, Gainesville: University of Florida Press, 1969
Ervine, St John, *Bernard Shaw: His Life, Work and Friends*, London: Constable & Co., 1956; New York: William Morrow & Co., 1956
Harris, Frank, *Frank Harris on Bernard Shaw: An Unauthorized Biography*, London: Victor Gollancz, 1931; New York: Book League of America, 1931
Hill, Eldon C., *George Bernard Shaw*, Boston: Twayne, 1978
Holroyd, Michael (ed.), *The Genius of Shaw: A Symposium*, London: Hodder & Stoughton, 1979; New York: Holt, Rinehart and Winston, 1979
Holroyd, Michael, *Bernard Shaw*, 4 vols., London: Chatto & Windus, 1988–92; New York: Random House, 1988–1992
Kaufmann, R.J. (ed.), *G.B. Shaw: A Collection of Critical Essays*, Englewood Cliffs, New Jersey: Prentice-Hall, 1965

Peters, Margot, *Bernard Shaw and the Actresses*, New York: Doubleday, 1980
Weintraub, Rodelle (ed.), *Fabian Feminist: Bernard Shaw and Woman*, University Park: Pennsylvania State University Press, 1977
Weintraub, Stanley, *The Unexpected Shaw: Biographical Approaches to G.B.S. and His Work*, New York: Frederick Ungar, 1982
Wilson, Colin, *Bernard Shaw: A Reassessment*, London: Hutchinson, 1969; New York: Atheneum, 1969

Bernard Shaw – playwright, philosopher, novelist, and critic – stands out among early twentieth-century writers both for his ideas and for the literary form they took. Shaw is perhaps second only to Shakespeare as a revered British playwright, quite a feat for an Irishman. His 60 plays, characterised by the brilliance of their discussion, remain his masterpieces; second to his dramatic material in respect comes his wealth of essays, some critiques of other artistic works, some critiques of politics and society, and some socialist treatises. Despite Shaw's prolific output (or perhaps because of it) many studies of him tend to be biographically oriented.

HARRIS subtitles his work *An Unauthorized Biography Based on First Hand Information*, a somewhat honest account of this intimate portrait by a friend and fellow Irishman. Shaw did not agree to authorize the book. However, Shaw well knew Harris's intent, provided anecdotal material previously unknown to Harris during their 20-year friendship, and proofed the book after Harris's death, so the designation "unauthorized" must clearly be suspect. The biography reads like intellectual gossip, full of name dropping and minutiae only available to participants; indeed, Harris seems almost as much a subject of the volume as Shaw, because of his tendency to refer much of his commentary to his own life and views. The first nine chapters focus on Shaw's birth, family, and early life up through his success as a music and theatrical critic in London. In Chapter 10 Harris begins to focus more on Shaw's socialism-communism. A subject that continues to crop up is Harris's fascination with Shaw's sex life. Only three of the 25 chapters place Shaw's playwriting at the center of the discussion, and then reflection and anecdote take the place of analysis.

ERVINE, like Harris, knew Shaw well. The closeness of the Ervines and Shaws – Ervine counted this friendship among the greatest happinesses of his life – gives the author access to Shaw's life beyond that enjoyed by Harris, whom Charlotte Shaw did not welcome. Despite Ervine's obvious bias – he seems to share Shaw's opinions about many subjects and people, such as a disdain for W.B. Yeats – the biography is neither a hagiography nor a chatty gossip-filled work. Written in a third-person, objective viewpoint, the information is well supported by multitudinous excerpts from documents such as letters, news clippings, diary extracts, and primary Shavian literary works. Rather than attempting chapter topics, Ervine writes about Shaw's life, work, and friends (whose histories are also given) chronologically, with page headings helpful to one skimming for particulars. The index also helps the interested reader or scholar find pertinent information. Pictures of Shaw and his friends appear in the middle of the volume.

WILSON attempts to place Shaw in perspective 18 years after Shaw's death. He begins by stipulating two points: Shaw must be viewed as a romantic but devoid of sentimentalism; Shaw's greatness arises from his "extremely high degree of objectivity", which he combined with his romanticism. Because Shaw has frequently been termed a social realist, these claims – especially the first – require careful support and in-depth discussion if the second is not to be seen as merely a loophole out of the first. Unfortunately Wilson betrays a less-than-objective bias when he allows the second point to stand on the basis that it is "self-evident". Following these introductory presuppositions, Wilson launches into a solid biographical study, raising questions about parts of Shaw's history that have been too readily accepted as truth based upon the telling of Shaw himself. While the questions are tantalizing, the answers are not often forthcoming, or the insinuations are as questionable as the standard story. While Wilson insists that Shaw's teen years as well as twenties have been "badly documented" by other biographers, he passes over the first 20 years of the writer's life in one chapter. However Wilson provides what he promises in the three chapters "The Long Apprenticeship", "The Economic Basis", and "The Unfair Critic" – a long, deep look into the "crucial" decade during which the young Shaw was in the process of becoming both artist and socialist, the mature Shaw.

HILL provides a solid overview of Shaw's life and works for the general reader. The book begins with a chronology of the important events in Shaw's life. After a sketch of Shaw's early years, Hill takes the reader chronologically through Shaw's creative life, focusing especially on productions of his major canonical plays. Thematically, he plays up Shaw's concern for social justice and his pacifism, "living ideas" that keep Shaw's dramas alive for contemporary audiences. The endnotes and select bibliography contain important references.

PETERS gives center stage to the actresses with whom Shaw was professionally and personally related. Refusing to allow Shaw to overshadow, Peters illuminates the contributions these artistic women made not only to Shaw but to modern drama and the cause of women. Specifically concentrating on "the actresses important during the crucial years of 1892–1907 when Shaw was striving for recognition as a dramatist", Peters brings to life Florence Farr, Janet Achurch, Elizabeth Robins, Ellen Terry, Mrs Patrick Campbell (to name a few) and Shaw's relationship with each. In this well-documented and richly anecdotal biographical look at Shaw and these actresses, Peters does not shy from the larger complicated issue of Shaw's overall attitude toward women, though she also does not turn to any facile answer that would deny the complexities.

HOLROYD provides the most extensive biography of Shaw to date, requiring four volumes, each of which is devoted to a particular period in Shaw's life – with the last (in the US edition as *The Last Laugh – An Epilogue, 1950–1991*, in the UK edition as *The Shaw Companion*) covering the postmortem (the status of the Shaw wills, house, royalties, and Shaw's effect on literature and theatre, as well as socio-political institutions, including the British Parliament). Included in the final volume are the notes and index for all four portions of the complete work. Twenty years in the making, Holroyd's chronological biographies and intriguing investigation into the after-effects of the Shavian inheritance have been rightfully termed masterpieces. These are essential reading for the curious and the scholarly. Able to extend through and beyond his scholarly predecessors, they present the fullest portrait yet of the complex enigma of the man who contained multiple selves yet maintained a unified whole as artist and philosopher. Here is the human Shaw, the personal and public images combined even as they are carefully analyzed, the motivation at the heart of the man revealed with care. The first volume (*The Search for Love, 1856–1898*) covers from birth to marriage, the 42 years Shaw spent moving toward maturity in his art and relationships; the second (*The Pursuit of Power, 1898–1918*) focuses on the public Shaw at the height of his social power, showing the circles in which he moved both as socialist and man of the theatre, and concluding with the stance that cost Shaw his public esteem – his pacifist and nationalist leanings during World War I; and the third volume (*The Lure of Fantasy, 1918–1951*) sheds light on the honorable elder Shaw, who manages to get back in the public graces with *Saint Joan*, as well as garner the Nobel Prize for Literature and an Oscar. Here is the Shaw unafraid to take on the Hollywood system, to go on a promotion tour for communism, and to face the death of friends, wife, and ultimately his own; yet this is a Shaw whose bite seems to have lost its teeth with his contemporaries. However, Holroyd's discussion of Shaw's plays helps to remind readers that Shaw's work still has power. Significantly, given Shaw's campaign for literacy and phonetic spelling, Holroyd's American editions of these volumes maintain British spellings in excerpts from such sources and keep Shaw's own spellings in order to make Shaw's points about the problematics and confusion in British spellings that the Irishman felt compelled to address.

BERTOLINI turns an astute critical eye on the artistry of Shaw's dramatic craft, too long given short shrift because of the interest in the life. Bertolini provides close critical analysis of *Caesar and Cleopatra*, *Man and Superman*, *Major Barbara*, *The Doctor's Dilemma*, *Pygmalion*, and *Saint Joan*, as well as Shaw's one-act plays. He demonstrates how the first five plays act as allegories on the act of writing, while *Saint Joan* provides the imaginative heroic image, which is the source for creation, and the one-acts illustrate Shaw's belief that comedy is the genre that can eradicate evil in a non-malevolent manner. Bertolini's knowledge of, and insight into, the conscious and unconscious crafting of the plays is impressive. Stressing the significance of word choice, Bertolini clarifies why Shaw insisted to his German translator that each and every word must be properly translated, not revised into a synonymous version. Noting that Shaw saw the play's life as both a production and a reading along the lines of a novel, Bertolini gives special attention to the detailed and poetic nature of Shaw's stage directions, directions which sometimes provide alternative readings to characters who might be interpreted differently if only dialogue and action were considered – case in point, Shaw's Caesar. Bertolini's analysis does justice to the care and consideration that Shaw insists comes with genius, turning the "trivial" into the necessary and natural.

Stanley WEINTRAUB assembles his exploration of the paradoxical in Shaw and his works in this culmination of research and revision of earlier essays and ideas. Though he opens the study with a portrait of Shaw as "everybody" seems to see him – "the familiar cocky Irishman", who styled himself as superior to Shakespeare, Weintraub then turns to lesser-known images of the playwright – amateur pugilist, actor, and art critic – and how these aspects directly or indirectly permeate his plays. Specifically, Weintraub provides insight into the creation of characters and plays such as *Saint Joan* and *Major Barbara*. Mingling the paradoxical impulses of the professional, public, and private Shaw, Weintraub writes telling chapters on his subject's relationships with Frank Harris and Sean O'Casey – the former giving a glimpse of the negative and the latter the positive in Shaw. Weintraub concludes with a chapter that argues that Shaw was creating "avant-garde" theatre long before the term had been coined, bringing to the stage techniques that "would revolutionize the staging of plays", techniques that included not only technical innovations but also transformed notions of character and dialogue.

DIETRICH demonstrates how Shaw's novels reveal the artistic working-out of his sense of the self as an artist, thus serving as the creative documentation of "the greater art of personality" that Shaw set out to fashion in his work and life. Realizing that many readers will be unfamiliar with the novels, Dietrich introduces his analysis with an explanation of the history and basic artistry of them. In the second section, Dietrich draws parallels between Shaw's creation of his artistic public persona and the creation of his novels' protagonists – both of which rely on Nietzsche's superman model. The lengthiest discussion is given to the books themselves, seen as a chronological development of the superman character. While Shaw's novels may be immature works, Dietrich clarifies their importance as evidence of the emerging artistic construction of the Shaw *persona*.

KAUFMANN gathers highly respected thinkers together to write essays intended "to set Shaw free from the bonds of misunderstanding", the popular consensus of the mid-century deeming Shaw a great personality rather than a great philosopher or playwright. In his introductory essay, Kaufmann compares Shaw to both Socrates and Shakespeare, to the former for his uncompromising views of society, and to the latter for his ability to give shape to social messages through the powerful medium of drama. While some of the essays seem a bit outdated, they provide a history lesson on scholarly views of Shaw. A few of the essays continue to stand out, some for who wrote them and some for both writer and content. Psychiatrist Erik H. Erikson's essay "Biographic: G.B.S. (70) on George Bernard Shaw (20)" is notable because of Erikson's status; unfortunately the bulk of the essay relies on quoting Shaw and then labeling the personality manifestation without further explanation or discussion. Bertolt Brecht provides an "Ovation for Shaw" as one playwriting revolutionary to another: calling Shaw a "terrorist" who "employs an unusual weapon – that of humor", Brecht argues that Shaw's plays change lives – "upsetting our habitual prejudices" and calling on all people to "act decently . . . even in the face of opposition". In "The Making of a Dramatist", Eric Bentley succinctly supports Shaw's artistic ability on the grounds of both content and form. Not content to call Shaw's plays merely idea-dramas, Bentley focuses on character and the plot that naturally flows from the characters, a notion that G. Wilson Knight also supports in "Shaw's Integral Theatre". Perhaps the most interesting and well-developed essay is Richard H. Ohmann's "Born to Set It Right: The Roots of Shaw's Style". Ohmann identifies Shaw's stance as the outsider, "the role of the opposer", in society. He traces this creed of opposition to Shaw's early biography, then illustrates how the stance takes form in Shaw's essays, plays, and novels through the syntactical use of negation.

Rodelle WEINTRAUB gathers 18 impressive essays analyzing Shaw's feminism, as expressed in his female characters, includes two interviews with significant women in Shaw's life – Clare Booth Luce and Megan Terry – and provides five of Shaw's own broadsides on feminism. The result is an important contribution to Shaw studies, providing insight relevant to an overall appreciation of the female in Shaw's *oeuvre* and to assist in understanding the role of women in Shaw's own life. Weintraub's Introduction deftly weaves anecdotal evidence of Shaw's relationships with women with historically documented episodes and quotations from Shaw's letters, essays, and plays to support her claim that Shaw should be regarded as an early feminist, who maintained his sensitivity to women and their plight throughout his life and work, proselytizing on behalf of women's emancipation through female characters that do not adhere to stereotypes. The essays are divided into three categories – "Literary and Mythic Influences", "Political and Economic Influences", and "Shaw's Liberated Women". The first two categories deal with the development of Shaw's feminist philosophy, the final grouping focuses more specifically on the demonstration of the developed ideas through specific characters. Among the influences connected to Shaw's feminist portraits are Shakespeare, Rudyard Kipling, Nietzsche, and Marx – both directly and indirectly, as influences to counteract or to emulate. Mythical influences include the Sphinx and the Transformation Myth. The Suffragette Movement, the legal climate, and Shaw's own experience with his mother are also explored as influences. Vivie Warren (*Mrs Warren's Profession*), Ann Whitefield (*Man and Superman*), and Eliza Doolittle (*Pygmalion*) receive attention as particularly significant female characters: Lisa Pedersen argues that Shaw's *Pygmalion* acts as a corrective for Shakespeare's *Taming of the Shrew*. In "Ann and Superman: Type and Archetype", Sally Peters Vogt attempts to make sense out of the disparate interpretations of the character of Ann Whitefield by analyzing the structure of the play and the surface Ann, then delving deep into the substructure for the mythical component that rounds out the character and makes of this woman the composite of Shaw's feminist ideas. Marlie Parker Wasserman provides an interesting psychological profile of Vivie Warren, arguing that though Shaw could not have been familiar with Freud at the time he created this character, Shaw had a depth of psychological understanding in keeping with Freud's work on institutional effects on children, an understanding based on Shaw's keen observation and analytical skills.

HOLROYD (1979) edits a collection of essays written by some of the foremost Shaw critics (authors of some of the other books surveyed here). These essays shed light on the multi-faceted genius of Shaw – as Irishman, critic of the various arts, Shellyan atheist, Fabian socialist, playwright, feminist, comedian, philosopher, playwright, and artist extraordinaire. The numerous illustrations (some produced here for the first time) that accompany the text support the prismatic perceptions of Shaw, and make this study not only scholarly but highly entertaining. Rather than to a narrow academic audience, this fine collection, which is full of Shaw's own words and witticisms, appeals purposely to "the general readers whom Shaw looked on as his natural audience", though scholars would do well to benefit from the pleasure of reading this volume. Holroyd acknowledges that some essays will seem to contradict others, as each writer was asked to focus on some accepted image of Shaw and to explore and explode it when necessary – for example, Barbara Smoker, John O'Donovan, and Irving Wardle each identify a different individual as the model for Higgins in *Pygmalion*. Indeed, one of the most interesting aspects of this volume is the intention of the editor to create a study in which the reader is encouraged to actively question and ponder, as Shaw would have advocated.

DAWN E. DUNCAN

Shelley, Mary 1797–1851

English novelist and short-story writer

Bennett, Betty T., and Charles E. Robinson (eds.), *The Mary Shelley Reader*, Oxford and New York: Oxford University Press, 1990

Botting, Fred, *Making Monstrous: "Frankenstein", Criticism, Theory*, Manchester: Manchester University Press, 1991

Dunn, Jane, *Moon in Eclipse: A Life of Mary Shelley*, London: Weidenfeld & Nicolson, 1978; New York: St Martin's Press, 1978

Fisch, Audrey A., Anne K. Mellor, and Esther H. Schor (eds.), *The Other Mary Shelley: Beyond "Frankenstein"*, New York and Oxford: Oxford University Press, 1993

Mellor, Anne K., *Mary Shelley: Her Life, Her Fiction, Her Monsters*, London: Methuen, 1988

Spark, Muriel, *Child of Light: A Reassessment of Mary Wollstonecraft Shelley*, London: Tower Bridge, 1951; revised edition, as *Mary Shelley*, London: Constable, 1988

Sunstein, Emily W., *Mary Shelley: Romance and Reality*, Boston: Little Brown, 1989; 2nd edition, Baltimore: Johns Hopkins University Press, 1991

Veeder, William, *Mary Shelley and "Frankenstein": The Fate of Androgyny*, Chicago: University of Chicago Press, 1986

SPARK's revision of her seminal study *Child of Light* (1951) is a good place to begin a discussion of modern approaches to Mary Shelley. Spark takes account of the work of more recent scholars like Betty T. Bennett, who has drawn attention to Mary Shelley's friendship with Isabel Robinson and her transvestite "husband". The book's division between biography and criticism can be seen to represent the conflict between the work and the life, which Spark sees as fundamental to the creative impulse, particularly in regard to Shelley herself. That Spark's prose style echoes that of its biographical subject is an indication of how her sensitivity has enabled her to get under the skin of Shelley. It is this empathy that renders Spark's portrait of a fellow novelist convincing.

DUNN's avowed aim is to rescue Mary Shelley from the brilliance of her husband's orb. Her critical biography is a valuable contribution to the pioneering work that has reclaimed

Shelley from obscurity. Making use of neglected and unpublished parts of her journal, Dunn throws new light on her fiction to show how it dramatised her life which, itself, was "a tale romantic beyond romance". SUNSTEIN's biography has been hailed as a ground-breaking addition to recent reassessments of Shelley's life and work. Her revisionary work has included reclaiming for the public domain Shelley's previously unknown writings, and rehabilitating her reputation, which suffered posthumously. The construction of Shelley as a passive figure is broken down to reveal a far more dynamic thinker, who engaged actively with the themes and issues arising out of the Romantic movement.

MELLOR's landmark study is characterised by the way in which she has successfully combined biography and literary criticism. Of particular interest is her exploration of the paradox contained within Shelley's advocacy of the egalitarian, bourgeois family in her fiction and the way in which her critiquing of masculine Romanticism and Romantic science contributed to the emergence of a feminine Romantic ideology. This is all the more important to note when considering the way in which Shelley has been regarded as her husband's appendage. The appendix demystifies the influences of Percy Shelley on his wife's work by identifying the precise nature of his editorial changes. Drawing on feminist cultural theory, New Historicism, and Marxism, Mellor substantially re-evaluates the way in which Mary Shelley has been traditionally construed by literary historians.

BENNETT and ROBINSON's anthology makes available the 1818 edition of *Frankenstein* along with *Mathilda*, tales and stories, letters, essays, and reviews, some which are reprinted here for the first time. There are, for example, letters documenting her impressions of Italy and Germany and essays on "The English in Italy" and "On Ghosts", where Samuel Taylor Coleridge is cited as not believing in ghosts because he had seen too many to put any trust in their reality. One could say that ghosts are the subtext of the *Reader*. These hauntings range from the Preface, describing the ghost-story competition at Villa Diodati, to the ghostly presences of Mary Wollstonecraft, William Godwin, and Percy Shelley.

BOTTING looks at the metaphor of monstrosity and the multiplicity of monsters in *Frankenstein*. His reading is informed by poststructuralism and draws on the work of Michel Foucault, Jacques Derrida, Freud, and Jacques Lacan. He engages with the problem of trying to supply a principle of unification before resolving this problem in favour of a plurality of approaches. It becomes apparent that the text is not only appropriated by the critic, but also conforms to the expectations of the reader. Botting's discussion of the relationship of the novel to the French Revolution and science effectively helps to ground the theoretical framework he has constructed within a historical context.

VEEDER's psychoanalytical approach to *Frankenstein* focuses on the way in which the novel can be carved up into various dualities, particularly those that reflect her interest in androgyny and bifurcation. In regard to the contextualisation of the novel, Veeder's concern to be fair to Percy Shelley prompts him to consider Mary Shelley and her work largely in relation to her husband's ideas.

FISCH, MELLOR, and SCHOR go beyond the reputation that Mary Shelley acquired as the author of *Frankenstein* to show that, she excelled in other areas, as an accomplished writer generally, and as a formidable intellectual. To this end, Alan Richardson resurrects her neglected verse dramas, *Proserpine* and *Midas*, Mary Favret and Susan Wolfson look at her editions of her husband's poetry, while Esther Schor explores her travel writing. Two "other" novels, considered to be her best after *Frankenstein*, are *The Last Man* and *Valpergis*, which are given more prominence here than are others, such as *Matilda*. The incestuous theme of the latter short novel has provoked speculation in connection with Shelley's relationship with her father, William Godwin. From within another context, Kate Ellis explores the impact of Godwin on his daughter, by suggesting that his daughter had adopted much of his radicalism. This departure from the emphasis on her mother, Wollstonecraft, is a dissenting voice to the generally feminist bias towards "otherness" that is expressed in this volume.

MARIE MULVEY ROBERTS

Shelley, Percy Bysshe 1792–1822

English poet

Bloom, Harold, *Shelley's Mythmaking*, New Haven, Connecticut, and London: Yale University Press, 1959

Cameron, Kenneth N., *The Young Shelley: Genesis of a Radical*, London: Victor Gollancz, 1950; New York: Macmillan, 1950

Cameron, Kenneth N., *Shelley: The Golden Years*, Cambridge, Massachusetts: Harvard University Press, 1974

Cherniak, Judith, *The Lyrics of Shelley*, Cleveland, Ohio: Case Western Reserve University Press, 1972

Cronin, Richard, *Shelley's Poetic Thoughts*, London: Macmillan, 1981; New York: St Martin's Press, 1981

Dawson, P.M.S., *The Unacknowledged Legislator: Shelley and Politics*, Oxford: Clarendon Press, 1980; New York: Oxford University Press, 1980

de Man, Paul, "Shelley Disfigured", in *Deconstruction and Criticism*, edited Harold Bloom *et al.*, New York: Seabury Press, 1979; London: Routledge & Kegan Paul, 1979

Everest, Kelvin (ed.), *Shelley Revalued: Essays from the Gregynog Conference*, Leicester: Leicester University Press, 1983

Foot, Paul, *Red Shelley*, London: Sidgwick & Jackson/Michael Dempsey, 1980

Gelpi, Barbara C., *Shelley's Goddess: Maternity, Language, Subjectivity*, New York: Oxford University Press, 1992

Hogle, Jerrold E., *Shelley's Process: Radical Transference and the Development of His Major Poems*, New York and Oxford: Oxford University Press, 1988

Keach, William, *Shelley's Style*, New York and London: Methuen, 1984

Scrivener, Michael Henry, *Radical Shelley: The Philosophical Anarchism and Utopian Thought of Percy Bysshe Shelley*, Princeton, New Jersey: Princeton University Press, 1982

Ulmer, William A., *Shelleyan Eros: The Rhetoric of Romantic Love*, Princeton, New Jersey: Princeton University Press, 1990

Wasserman, Earl R., *Shelley: A Critical Reading*, Baltimore: Johns Hopkins University Press, 1971

Shelley's reputation languished in neglect for much of the first half of the twentieth century. New Criticism, speaking broadly, saw little merit in Shelley's work; and F.R. Leavis famously dismissed him as second rate. For Leavis, Shelley was a lyric poet of occasional beauty but one lacking intellectual rigour. In particular, his use of language was attacked as being vague and indeterminate, failing to "apprehend" its subject (*Revaluation*, 1936).

BLOOM's 1959 study represented a significant contribution towards a positive reappraisal of Shelley's reputation, and it remains an influential and useful work. Bloom treats Shelley as a mythopoeic, or mythmaking, poet. Starting from Martin Buber's distinction between two primary words, "I-Thou" (the imaginative connection between human observer and reality) and "I-It" (the more scientific relation of experience and separation), Bloom moves on to see Shelley as articulating a visionary drama, inventing his own myths as means of entering into relation with reality. Bloom's study is limited (it ignores *Alastor* for instance), but by focusing on the evolving attempts Shelley made to interpret the world, and his correlative experimentation with language, it sets the tone for the bulk of Shelley criticism that has followed. Indeed, in a later preface Bloom averred that "the subject of this book is Shelley's internalized quest to reach the limits of desire".

WASSERMAN's large book has the virtues of a detailed commitment to the "hermeneutic mode" – the process of interpretation, ours and Shelley's. Wasserman sees the "hermeneutic circle" as open and unending, and reads Shelley's work sensitively and in context, arguing that the poetry mediates between scepticism and idealism, pessimism and optimism. He is particularly useful on Shelley's theories of "Power" and the doctrine of Necessity. There is, perhaps, a tendency to see him as more philosopher than poet, but the work contains a great deal of sensitive close reading. Moreover, the sheer comprehensiveness of Wasserman's makes it an ideal place from which to begin examining Shelley's *oeuvre*.

Many modern studies of Shelley have continued along the sorts of avenues suggested by Wasserman's approach. CHERNIAK reads Shelley's shorter lyrics in a straightforward and useful way, seeing the poet as interrogating an "epistemological puzzle", most obviously set out in "Mont Blanc". In other words, she sees Shelley as examining questions of knowledge, and in particular the question of *how* we know, and she traces Shelley's indebtedness to other Romantic lyricists, especially Wordsworth. EVEREST constitutes an excellent and varied collection of essays on a variety of themes, from studies of Shelley's publishers, and an examination of Shelley's early letters, to Marilyn Butler's wider ranging look at "Myth and Mythmaking in the Shelley Circle".

Many of these "traditional" studies of Shelley have explored directions more recently taken up enthusiastically by deconstruction. CRONIN, for instance, suggests that Shelley's main poetic endeavour was with language, or that (to quote *Prometheus Unbound*) "speech created thought,/Which is the measure of the universe". Cronin sees Shelley struggling with language, not so much on the level of vocabulary, but more in terms of syntax and structure, a struggle that led into various vigorous experiments with genre.

DE MAN's influential essay on "The Triumph of Life" initiated the deconstructive fascination with Shelley's poetry. De Man analyses those moments in Shelley's last work where the text seems to fold in on itself, and sees the "erasure" or "defacement" of the poem (something made explicit by the text's unfinished status) as typical of the way texts necessarily work. Indeed, it is remarkable that of all the Romantic poets Shelley is the one to which deconstructivists most often return; it is almost as if the *aporia* of Shelleyan language, the same gap between word and thing that Leavis earlier found so debilitating, has come under a new spotlight as a point of particular celebration.

Several studies from a deconstructivist perspective are excellent, if often complex and difficult. ULMER takes Shelley's notion of the pure love between self and "antitype", from the essay "On Love", and argues that this figure acts as "a paradigm for rhetorical and social relations throughout Shelley". The approach is primarily Lacanian/deconstructive, but takes account of psychoanalytical and historicist theories to explore "eros" (sexuality, love, sentiment) as an organising aesthetic for Shelley. Ulmer's conclusions see Shelley as implicated in patriarchal structures. The work is dense and hard going, but rewardingly sophisticated. HOGLE's study sees "Transference", a sort of Derridean resistence to closure, or *différence*, as being at the heart of Shelley's development.

Also complex but rewarding is GELPI's Lacanian study of Shelley's attitudes to mothering. Gelpi deploys "two intersecting ideologies" to read Shelley. On the one hand there is "the ideology of the maternal", which involves a great deal of contextual information about late eighteenth- and early nineteenth-century theories of mothering, as well as a Lacanian theoretical framework on infant development. On the other hand there is "the ideology of the aesthetic, as it has been defined by Terry Eagleton". Her study concentrates at length on *Prometheus Unbound*, and her readings are so fertile that it is something of a shame that she does not deal with a wider range of Shelleyan texts.

Deconstruction has by no means monopolised Shelley. KEACH, for instance, expresses his concern that deconstructivists "have been too little concerned with distinguishing the elusive activity peculiar to Shelley's writing from the problematic condition of language generally". His admirable study deals subtly yet lucidly with Shelley's use of language, arguing that his style develops from "a divided, often agitated understanding of language". The concern is less to describe Shelley's style (especially since his style is an evolving quantity), and more to explore the ways his style reflects the underlying concerns of Shelley's philosophical fascinations.

It is only comparatively recently that Shelley's political thought (so important in his life, as his poetics) have been given due attention. CAMERON's first volume (1950), biographical as it is, remained for many years the only serious study of Shelley's radicalism. FOOT's more recent work has received short shrift from many academics, often dismissed as souped-up journalism rather than serious scholarship, but such snobbery is misplaced. It is a fresh and enthusiastic reappraisal of Shelley's political sympathies, reads well, and makes many good points. More sophisticated is DAWSON, who provides a detailed and scholarly sense of Shelley's political background, his indebtedness to William Godwin, Thomas Paine, and his family's longstanding Whig sympathies. He interprets Shelley's famous dictum that poets are "the unacknowledged legislators of the world" in terms of "teachers" or "helpers" rather than governors:

> In the English political tradition a "legislator" is thought of as being a representative or even a delegate of the governed, rather than a ruler or the aide of a ruler . . . it would seem reasonable to associate his definition of poets as "unacknowledged legislators" with the democratic constitutional theories of the Reformers, rather than with the classic notion of the Lawgiver.

SCRIVENER also places Shelley in the context of the contemporary climate of radical thought, but his version of Shelley's politics sees them as far more radical, and far less reformist, than Dawson. The major texts are read as studies of alienation from (imperfect) society, and Shelley's "philosophical anarchism" is seen as the precursor to nineteenth-century anarchists such as Pierre Proudhon and Mikhail Bakunin. Scrivener brings to bear not only (in the early chapters) a detailed sense of historical determinants, but also (in the later ones) a psychological analysis of what he calls "the Oedipal configurations of Shelley's – and the reform movement's – political idealism".

ADAM ROBERTS

Shepard, Sam 1943–

American dramatist and screenwriter

Auerbach, Doris, *Sam Shepard, Arthur Kopit, and the Off Broadway Theater*, Boston: Twayne, 1982
DeRose, David J., *Sam Shepard*, New York: Twayne, 1992
Kleb, William, "Sam Shepard", in *American Playwrights since 1945: A Guide to Scholarship, Criticism, and Performance*, edited by Philip C. Kolin, Westport, Connecticut: Greenwood Press, 1989
Marranca, Bonnie, *American Dreams: The Imagination of Sam Shepard*, New York: PAJ Publications, 1981
Mottram, Ron, *Inner Landscapes: The Theater of Sam Shepard*, Columbia: University of Missouri Press, 1984
Orr, John, *Tragicomedy and Contemporary Culture: Play and Performance from Beckett to Shepard*, London: Macmillan, 1991; Ann Arbor: University of Michigan Press, 1991
Oumano, Ellen, *Sam Shepard: The Life and Work of an American Dreamer*, New York: St Martin's Press, 1987; London: Virgin, 1987
Shewey, Don, *Sam Shepard*, New York: Dell, 1985
Tucker, Martin, *Sam Shepard*, New York: Continuum, 1992
Wilcox, Leonard, *Rereading Shepard: Contemporary Critical Essays on the Plays of Sam Shepard*, New York: St Martin's Press, 1993; London: Macmillan, 1993

Most critics on Shepard cannot get past comparisons between the life and the work. The typical book or article will indulge in hagiography, treating Shepard as a handsome American (or western) hero, lucky in life and love, who has lived the American (or western) Dream. Thus, there has been much biographical, historical, and even psychological criticism, but very little in the way of feminist or poststructural perspectives, for instance, until the most recent works.

MARRANCA collects some primary documents of use to the Shepard researcher (interviews with Shepard, those who have directed his plays, and those who have acted in them). In addition, she includes various secondary sources, such as reviews of the plays, introductions written for published plays, and articles about Shepard and/or his works. With the exception of *True West*, the "family plays" are not discussed. Marranca's own essay contains a touch of feminist criticism. There are neither footnotes nor bibliographies, so the book is definitely for a popular rather than scholarly readership.

AUERBACH's scholarly study of Shepard concentrates on the early plays. She posits that because of the economics of commercial staging, Shepard would have been unable to develop as a playwright (and thus produce the more mature plays of his later period),were it not for the Off-Broadway theatre. Much of her work covers familiar territory, putting Shepard in the context of American and western myth, but her discussion of his unique theatrical contribution as the "love of logos" is intriguing. She notes that the hero's downfall can often be effected by words alone: "a hero is defeated by an opponent whose language has greater power to overcome passivity and initiate action".

MOTTRAM's book is important as the first full-length study of Shepard's plays, ending with *Fool for Love*. It also incorporates the playwright's non-fiction writings and essays, but not his film career. It is still one of the only sources to concentrate on semantic dimensions of the plays. Mottram denies the generally accepted notion that Shepard "appeals essentially to the senses rather than to the mind", arguing that Shepard the dramatist should be considered in the context of Samuel Beckett and Bertolt Brecht.

SHEWEY's and OUMANO's books are both highly readable biographies, but the former includes more critical analysis. Unfortunately, Shewey ignores previous critical works, relying solely on the plays and autobiographical writings to venture critical opinions. Still, Shewey is a theater critic, and thus his opinions have some weight. Both books continue the "artist as hero" theme and draw on the interplay between Shepard's life and his works. Oumano's book is slightly less concerned with criticism than Shewey's, and what criticism it does contain is abstract and general, with little specific evidence from the plays themselves to back it up. The informal writing style makes this book very readable, however, and its unique contribution is its recording of anecdotes about Shepard's New York days as remembered by friends and family.

KLEB's thorough bibliography supersedes previous Shepard bibliographies (by Dugdale and King). It covers both primary and secondary sources, although it combines the latter with reviews rather than keeping them separate. It includes short essays on Shepard's critical reputation, the production history of specific plays, and an overview of major critical studies.

ORR argues for a historical development from the tragicomedy in Pirandello, moving through Beckett and Jean Genet to Harold Pinter and Shepard. His discussion of production difficulties encountered in producing Shepard's plays will be of interest to drama and theater scholars. The bibliography is not particularly useful to the Shepard scholar, as it concentrates on the broader subjects of modernism and tragicomedy.

Like most volumes in the Twayne "United States Authors" series, DeROSE's volume is both well-researched and highly readable. In addition, its annotated bibliography is extremely useful: it contains both primary and secondary sources, the latter divided into types of sources, including play-by-play production reviews. DeRose's complaint is that Shepard has been treated "more as a social and literary phenomenon than a theater artist", and he sets out to rectify that situation with close readings of production reviews, stage directions, physical staging, and visual imagery. The book contains an important discussion of Shepard's "lost" plays, along with directions of where to find typescript copies of them.

TUCKER's book prefaces each chapter of interpretation and analysis with a brief biographical sketch covering the time period dealt with in the chapter. He pays particular attention to recurrences of imagery, and the overall thrust of his argument is psychological. He makes much, for example, of the fact that there are so many brothers in Shepard's plays but none in his real life. Comparing Shepard to D.H. Lawrence, Tucker feels that the two authors are comparable both in their treatment of parents and in their "mystical view of love as a polarized force allowing for distinctiveness as well as union". The bibliography is very useful, as it is equally divided between primary and secondary sources; the appendix contains an analysis of Shepard's recent play *States of Shock*.

WILCOX has collected essays mainly from drama/theater scholars in his attempt to address the "central questions of modernism, and postmodernism". Most of them treat just one or two plays, but some – like Gerald Weales' and Sherill Grace's – trace thematic ideas from the whole of Shepard's *oeuvre*. This is a good volume with which to introduce the reader to Shepard studies, as it covers everything from traditional approaches to semiotic readings; from myth criticism to autobiographical material, and from psychological insight to feminist criticism. Although it is a 1993 publication, *States of Shock* is not discussed. There is no comprehensive bibliography, but the notes to the individual essays are reasonably extensive.

CHARLOTTE M. WRIGHT

Sheridan, Richard Brinsley 1751–1816

Irish dramatist and poet

Auburn, Mark S., *Sheridan's Comedies: Their Contexts and Achievements*, Lincoln: University of Nebraska Press, 1977

Bingham, Madeleine, *Sheridan: The Track of a Comet*, London: Allen & Unwin, 1972

Davison, Peter (ed.), *Sheridan: Comedies: "The Rivals", "A Trip to Scarborough", "The School for Scandal", "The Critic": A Casebook*, London: Macmillan, 1986

Gibbs, Lewis, *Sheridan*, London: Dent, 1947

Loftis, John, *Sheridan and the Drama of Georgian England*, Oxford: Blackwell, 1976; Cambridge, Massachusetts: Harvard University Press, 1976

Sichel, Walter, *Sheridan*, 2 vols., London: Constable, 1909; Boston: Houghton Mifflin, 1909

Worth, Katharine, *Sheridan and Goldsmith*, London: Macmillan, 1992

Sheridan's critical reputation is beset by ironies. In the first place, he wished to be remembered by historians as a statesman, rather than by critics as a dramatist and theatre manager. *The Speeches of the Right Honourable Richard Brinsley Sheridan*, a far more voluminous publication than his plays, are the product of the most ardent enthusiasm and consistent hard work of his adult life. Furthermore, they are excellent of their kind. Nevertheless, he is regarded primarily as a dramatist: when his speeches are mentioned, it is generally to illustrate some point about the theatricality of their composition or delivery. The second irony concerns the nature of Sheridan's twentieth-century reputation. *The Rivals* and *The School for Scandal* share with *She Stoops to Conquer* (by Oliver Goldsmith) the distinction of being the most frequently performed eighteenth-century plays in the English repertoire. Yet Sheridan's plays, like Goldsmith's, have received far less critical attention than their theatrical stature seems to warrant. This neglect can be accounted for, in part at least, by the qualities that ensure their popularity: a cheerful mood, a favourable view of human nature, successful comic effects, and strict observance of sexual propriety can be dismissed as bland, sentimental, superficial, and prudish, especially in comparison with Restoration comedy. (In the eyes of posterity, the early reviewer who hailed Sheridan as a new Congreve did a disservice to both dramatists.) The 1970s, however, marked a turning point: the Georgian theatrical conventions within which Sheridan operated are increasingly regarded as distinctive and valuable on their own account, while critics and (equally significantly) theatre directors find greater subtlety in his plays.

SICHEL's massive critical biography is a mine of information about Sheridan, his family, friends, and associates, complete with social and political background. It remains essential for scholars intending serious study of Sheridan. Sichel relates the plays to Sheridan's life and character, and to their Restoration ancestry, but pays comparatively little attention to their contemporary theatrical context – the most important omission from a work which otherwise combines encyclopaedic breadth with scrupulous documentation. Sichel has great respect for Sheridan's political aspirations, depicting him as an essentially modern democratic reformer. Historians today may find this attitude anachronistic, but there is still credibility in Sheridan's claim that a nation that can be saved only by one man does not deserve to be saved. Like the other biographies mentioned, Sichel's is handsomely illustrated: to do justice to such fascinating, glamorous, and sensational material, Sheridan's biographers must convey an experience, rather than just tell a story.

GIBBS compresses his material into a more economical format. Less inclined than Sichel to invite readers to participate in an interrogation of conflicting contemporary accounts, he often describes events with a direct simplicity, which carries instant conviction. Unfortunately, he provides no annotation, only a "Selection of Authorities", which restricts his readership to seekers after general background information, and to scholars who already possess sophisticated research techniques.

Another sacrifice to brevity is a tendency to make unexplained historical and literary allusions.

BINGHAM follows Gibbs's example in the matter of annotations, but not where allusions are concerned: all people and events mentioned are set in context, making her book more accessible to the non-specialist reader. She writes with wit and understanding. A sympathetic imagination worthy of a novelist is brought to bear on data researched with the precision of a social historian. The result is a vivid recreation of Sheridan's life and times, which incidentally makes valuable contributions to literary criticism: it is much easier to understand the problems confronting eighteenth-century dramatists when we appreciate the dangers, discomforts, and claustrophobia suffered by eighteenth-century audiences.

LOFTIS makes a crucial breakthrough. His study of Sheridan's plays utilises much twentieth-century research, including his own, into eighteenth-century drama. He fills the gap left by Sichel and his followers, showing Sheridan as a man of his time, neither a Restoration throwback nor a maudlin sentimentalist, but a Georgian dramatist, expressing a "firmly conventional moral union of good sense and compassion" in "didactic comedy that evokes laughter and satirical perception".

AUBURN, working independently of Loftis but along parallel lines, has produced an excellent introduction to Sheridan's comedies. He displays an equally close acquaintance with eighteenth-century drama, but assumes less prior knowledge in the reader. He uses his expertise, on theatre in general, and eighteenth-century theatre in particular, to show how Sheridan's plays are designed to produce specific effects, and how the original casting can reveal the dramatist's intentions. Auburn also considers ways in which a scene can give rise to different, but equally valid, stage interpretations: a valuable lesson for students unfamiliar with drama criticism.

DAVISON's *Casebook* exceeds its brief by including an extract from Sheridan's tragedy *Pizarro,* and its source in a speech Sheridan made during the trial of Warren Hastings. The complex interplay between politics and drama provides a constantly recurring theme in this book. Davison pays due attention to other aspects of Sheridan's drama, selecting from a wide range of contemporary and later writers, and providing incisive comments on his selection. The result is a well-balanced survey of critical responses to Sheridan's theatrical and literary legacy.

WORTH argues that "Sheridan and Goldsmith are utterly distinct and distinctive as playwrights, let alone as men. Yet they do have a great deal in common, more than enough to justify their being discussed at least partly in tandem". She deals authoritatively with their lives in relation to their plays, eighteenth-century productions, and the controversy over sentimental comedy, before proceeding to cover individual plays in detail, with specific reference to recent professional productions: Sheridan and Goldsmith are credited with the ability to generate theatrical excitement still.

CAROLYN D. WILLIAMS

Short Fiction: General

Allen, Walter, *The Short Story in English*, Oxford: Clarendon Press, 1981; New York: Oxford University Press, 1981

Aycock, Wendell M. (ed.), *The Teller and the Tale: Aspects of the Short Story*, Lubbock: Texas Tech Press, 1982

Bates, H.E.,*The Modern Short Story: A Critical Survey*, London: Thomas Nelson, 1941

Bayley, John, *The Short Story: Henry James to Elizabeth Bowen*, Brighton, Sussex: Harvester Press, 1988; New York: St Martin's Press, 1988

Bonheim, Helmut, *The Narrative Modes: Techniques of the Short Story*, Cambridge: D.S. Brewer, 1982

Canby, H.S.,*The Short Story in English*, New York: Henry Holt, 1909

Chambers, Ross, *Story and Situation: Narrative Seduction and the Power of Fiction*, Manchester: Manchester University Press, 1984; Minneapolis: University of Minnesota Press, 1984

Current-Garcia, Eugene, and Walton R. Patrick (eds.), *What is the Short Story?: Case Studies in the Development of a Literary Form*, Chicago: Scott Foresman, 1961, revised, 1974

Hanson, Clare, *Short Stories and Short Fictions, 1880–1980*, London: Macmillan, 1985

Hanson, Clare (ed.), *Re-Reading the Short Story*, London: Macmillan, 1989

Head, Dominic, *The Modernist Short Story: A Study in Theory and Practice*, Cambridge and New York: Cambridge University Press, 1992

Lohafer, Susan, and Jo Ellen Clarey (eds.), *Short Story Theory at a Crossroads*, Baton Rouge: Louisiana State University Press, 1989

May, Charles E. (ed.), *Short Story Theories*, Athens: Ohio University Press, 1976

O'Connor, Frank, *The Lonely Voice: A Study of the Short Story*, London: Macmillan, 1963; Cleveland, Ohio: World, 1963

O'Faolain, Sean, *The Short Story*, London: Collins, 1948; New York: Adair, 1951

Prince, Gerald, *A Grammar of Stories*, The Hague: Mouton, 1973

Reid, Ian, *The Short Story*, London: Methuen, 1977; New York: Barnes & Noble, 1977

Shaw, Valerie, *The Short Story: A Critical Introduction*, London: Longman, 1983

Defining the short story has always been problematic, as most critics have acknowledged. In its widest sense, the term may cover any kind of shorter narrative, in prose or verse, but it remains obstinately relative (how short is short?). In practice, definition is usually more limited, restricted formally and generically to prose fiction, and chronologically to writing since the early nineteenth century. Modernity and the short story are often seen as intrinsically related. Most criticism, especially the frequently encountered anthologising kind, faced with the wealth of material encompassed even by the more limited conception of the modern short story, selects on some explicit basis (whether provenance or period, or by author, or subject matter, or theme). The criticism summarised here is usually more wide-ranging and general in scope, but there is variation in the ambit of its concern (and the genre is seldom contained exclusively within the bounds of literature in English).

CANBY deserves consideration as author of the first substantial critical and historical survey, extending from medieval times to the start of the twentieth century. He acknowledges the problem of definition, but claims a general identity for shorter fiction that accommodates the various and historically changing sub-categories he treats, from medieval hagiography to the modern sensation story. He describes and catalogues, rather doggedly perhaps, a considerable variety of earlier forms, but devotes nearly half his study to developments since the late eighteenth century, principally the establishment of the modern genre, drawing on the seminal figures of Edgar Allan Poe and Nathaniel Hawthorne while covering a range of American and British writers. His comparison of the modern story with journalism as "a manifestation of a nervous, curious, introspective age; it is as often superficial and sensational; as often vivid and interesting" is acute and influential.

BATES's well-known study (usefully indexed), by a professional practitioner of the genre, critical of the amateur, liberal-minded, and even mildly subversive for his day, presents an account of the short story from Poe and Nikolai Gogol to the 1930s, though deliberately excluding his own work. Straightforward and accessible, it is a competent, wide-ranging, chronologically-based survey, with some bias towards Bates's own kind of writing.

Distinguished from the tale, immeasurable in its antiquity, the short story as purposed artefact is modern, appearing as an achieved form only since the late nineteenth century. Central is its plasticity, its refusal to be rule-bound or constrained by subject despite efforts to define and contain it, for the writer's method is ultimately his own self. Bates pursues analogies with cinema, common in the period, and adduces a more sophisticated readership, responsive to narrative subtlety, to account for the story's growth as a serious literary form. Its brief history records an increasing range and profundity, developing from Russian to French, and forming a vital American tradition, but largely bypassing the moralising heavyweight prose of the Victorian British. Growing popularity encourages facility and superficiality, but in the best writers its essential modernity, its power of implication through compression and simplicity, wihout moralising bias, are evident. Its great virtues are directness, honesty, clarity of vision, epitomised variously in the best exponents, Anton Chekhov, Guy de Maupassant, Leo Tolstoy, James Joyce, and Ernest Hemingway. British writing is largely disdained (and Rudyard Kipling particularly pathologised as proto-fascist) until the emancipated modern story appears in the aftermath of World War I. The future, though unpredictable (Bates is writing in wartime), may be bright, though optimism is qualified. Bates covers the ground well, if rapidly: by no means deeply analytic, he's perceptive and discriminating on a basis of broad sympathy and interest. He concludes that the mark of good short fiction is balance, formally and intuitively realised.

O'FAOLAIN's book, a briskly sensible, plain-spoken critical introduction by another practitioner, with appended anthology, still has value. Partly descriptive and analytic, and partly, if cautiously, prescriptive, it bluffly emphasises the importance of the writer's creative personality and originality, for short fiction is seen primarily as intimate self-projection, expressing a unique sensibility. The creative personality is more important than technique, a priority acknowledged to be unfashionably against the emphasis of New Criticism (we are some way off the death of the author in this early postwar study). The focus is on modern short fiction (the later nineteenth century onward) viewed as giving increasingly "a sensation of communicated personality" and, consonant with this personalising approach, there are chapters on individual writers prefacing a selection of stories from Robert Louis Stevenson to Hemingway. Beforehand, four brief chapters attend to form and technique. Notwithstanding the emphasis on personality, the need for narrative conventions is affirmed as especially marked in short fiction, which strives for imaginative effect through compression. Suggestive power is paramount (hostility to realism is explicit), and the imaginatively fruitful idea or situation richer than the anecdote. Echoing Bates, O'Faolain claims that the successful story's subject is essentially the writer's self, refracted through significant incident, itself given appropriate and characteristic construction and focus, with an intensifying narrative economy in the modern tale, and an accompanying attentiveness to precise craft and suggestive language.

O'CONNOR (Michael O'Donovan) is the third in this mid-century trio of practitioner-critics, providing a slightly quirky and partial, but often sensitive and insightful, survey. His brief but suggestive Introduction echoes Bates in distinguishing the modern story as artefact, dedicated to the individual critical reader, from the tale, public and casual, and from the novel. He too acknowledges its origins in Gogol, defining the short story as, appropriately if perhaps restrictively, fiction of the "Little Man", of the defeated, outlawed, or isolated, of a "submerged population", excluded, marginal, and essentially, as his title indicates, lonely. Demanding greater artistry and dramatic sense than the novel, the form is constituted by three elements – exposition, development, and drama. Length should be self-determining: shortness is not an externally measurable qualification. Not miniature but pure (contrasted with the applied storytelling of the novel, the public telling of the tale), the form invites the danger of impersonality, loss of body and voice, intrinsic to its modernity. Generous, discriminating, and largely informal and expository appreciations of individual Europeans are followed by sharp diagnostic readings of a range of writers in English, with a brief but incisive epilogue on craft.

Since much useful commentary on the short story is itself in the brief format of essay or preface, collections of such criticism are helpful. CURRENT-GARCIA and PATRICK provide a substantial anthology of both criticism and exemplary stories, from Washington Irving to Joyce Carol Oates, arranged chronologically, with substantial critical input from practitioners. A stimulatingly eclectic body of often seminal and illuminating commentary by artists and critics results. The material is largely but not exclusively American, divided into three chronological divisions, reflecting the variety and conflicting nature of critical views and theories over the period of the short story's development, with a prefatory critical and historical introduction to each section by the editors. The first section contains a useful range of nineteenth-century commentary, mainly by creative writers, from Irving to Chekhov; the second focuses on earlier twentieth-century criticism, recording, analysing, and mainly reproving the growth of the commercial, popular, formulaic story, encouraged by magazine publication and technical handbooks, which is contrasted with Chekhovian truth to life and resistance to stereotype; the third section registers further developments in variety, force, and interest in the genre from the 1940s, with a growing critical awareness expressed by writers. Within this variety, four major ideas are discriminated: "inwardness", stressing subjective awareness and interiority; "individuality" – the artist's sincerity, personality, and refusal of formula; "method", stressing economy; and "responsibility or integrity" – the writer's seriousness, commitment, and industry. A substantial critical bibliography is appended.

MAY's selection of criticism, more limited but in some respects more salient, also has a predominantly American perspective. His Introduction regrets the current lack of both popular and serious readerly interest in the short-story form, and the paucity of substantial criticism, despite the commitment of practitioners. There is no full-length theoretical study, no achieved poetics of short fiction. Early twentieth-century studies proposed formulas and served as technical-commercial handbooks for the popular, anecdotal, O. Henry model of the story, while later criticism, recoiling, aligned the form with the lyric, rendering the genre esoteric, precious, or academic. Now (in the 1970s) the story is self-subverting, undermining classic attributes of narrative itself – mimesis, characterisation, discursive meaning. Various formalist studies have appeared but no unified theory, while writers themselves provide more passionate but partial accounts. Reflecting the incipient American devotion to theory of the early 1970s, May calls for the short story to be theorised on the basis of its generic "vision" rather than its form or content. A helpful critical bibliography is supplied.

AYCOCK's selection, briefer still, drawn from a 1980 American symposium of writers and critics, nonetheless raises important issues, such as the scope of the defining term "short story", the importance of narrative silences and gaps in the genre, the split between realist and anti-realist tendencies, and problems with translation, given the genre's international diffusion. Lively, if partisan, contributions from writer-academics (that largely American hybrid form) conclude the book.

HANSON's selection of ten contributions to a British symposium (plus her Introduction), mostly written, refreshingly, by women, seeks to introduce the short story into "contemporary critical debate". The story's marginal, "ex-centric" position, its "squint vision", its appeal to the exiled and dispossessed (cf. O'Connor), and not least to women (recent feminist anthologies are noted), are emphasised. No single theory accounts for the genre, but its modernity is acknowledged, and (again) also its affinity with cinema, as anti-discursive, disjunctive, oblique, favouring fantasy. Various contemporary critical approaches are exploited – reader-response theory, psychoanalytic ideas, poststructuralist positions – while relations and contrasts with the novel form a critical leitmotif. These perceptions of the story's challenge to the "tyranny of the whole book" are frequently acute and interesting.

The larger compilation, edited by LOHAFER and CLAREY, again symposium-based, claims to "map out the field conceptually", with a strongly academic and theoretical emphasis, and is divided into five sections, each introduced by Lohafer. Earlier essays treat questions of definition, surveying the critical field from practitioners to theorists, paying particular attention to the academic history of the genre. Definition must be attempted but should not be categorical: inductive accounts, which recognise the variability and historicity of the form, are preferred. Critical theories may be helpful, but the eclecticism of short-story criticism is itself valuable, though formalist approaches tend to dominate here, dealing with generic as well as formal aspects, especially narrative endings and story interrelations. Some attention is paid also to historical developments and contexts, especially relations with the novel tradition. Finally, more technical theoretical approaches, involving discourse analysis and deconstruction, are introduced, emphasising theories of reading and reception.

More theoretical and formalist book-length studies include PRINCE's highly abstract analysis of narrative forms. Its sources in Russian formalism, structuralism, and particularly earlier Chomskian linguistics are evident. The attempt to construct a grammar of basic narratives, while introducing some useful generalisations, has the limitations of the structuralist approach.

BONHEIM's highly systematic, confessedly "Teutonic", but very cogent study, analysing critically and statistically narrative modes and devices, and based on a "representative sample" of several hundred narratives, also raises fundamental questions of narratology in broadly structuralist ways. Four chief narrative modes are discerned – description, report, speech, and comment – with meta-narrative as an occasional fifth, and the story is viewed as a variable amalgam of these. Bonheim claims that this model, suitably refined, provides an adequately detailed and exact analysis of short fictions, diachronically as well as formally responsive, enabling critical definition without being simplistic, though realising tendencies rather than rigid laws.

CHAMBERS seeks to extend and complicate analysis beyond the structuralist model by stressing the force of story as discourse, as storytelling, always *related* (in a double sense, both told, connected with a teller and listener/reader, and concerned with a situation, having a context and point). The nature of the story's authority and seductive power is therefore of prime interest and is pursued through analysis of selected stories (by Poe, Henry James, and Joyce, among others) which themselves articulate an awareness of the relational force of narrative fiction, best concentrated in the short tale.

First of a trio of more general and descriptive studies, REID's pithy contribution to the "Critical Idiom" series is wide-ranging and attractively undogmatic. In his view, most of the interesting criticism comes from practitioners, though the theoretical perspectives of Russian formalism and its structuralist derivatives are valuable. The genre's sheer diversity prevents any summary definition, but working descriptions are possible and useful, while much of the problem with definition is simply terminological. A cursory but lively account of the short story's long history is given, then a straightforward assessment of the nature and importance of the modern short story, concurring largely with those of Bates and O'Connor, followed by a brief taxonomy of various elementary or "tributary forms", such as fable, fairytale, sketch, or parable, and their variable contribution to, or amalgamation in, developed short fiction. The novella and the story collection or sequence are also discussed. The modern emphasis on singleness of effect, derived from Poe, is criticised as too constricting, while Aristotelian prescription, though often descriptively helpful, is equally questionable, as the increasing and welcome tendency towards open forms shows.

SHAW, in her more extended study, also eschews any prescription, registering diversity through discussion of a wide range of examples, some fairly cursory, some more extended. A perhaps deliberate looseness or relaxedness characterises her approach: aspects of technique, form, and subject-matter are considered intelligently but fairly unsystematically. Writers rather than critics are cited, but an extensive critical bibliography is supplied. Shaw relates the short story back to the more primitive tale as well as across to other art forms, and she acknowledges and reflects the international scope of the genre. She surveys, swiftly but judiciously, the critical history, tracing the genre's increasing self-consciousness and sophistication and its claim to be representatively modern. An attractively generous breadth of critical response informs Shaw's study, which remains one of the fullest by an individual critic.

ALLEN's substantial book has become (with Shaw's, which it preceded slightly) the standard academic survey of the modern short story. Its focus is less international than Shaw's, limited to work in English, but fuller, moving in broad chronological sequence through a very wide range of individual writers. Definition of the genre is more historical than theoretical, but Allen agrees with the majority opinion, which identifies the modern story with the single and significant moment, incident, or perception. His approach is inductive not prescriptive, concerned with description and exposition of the work of the large body of writers (over 80) he includes. He deliberately eschews any conclusive judgment of a genre so various and still evolving. His study's virtue consists in its wealth of sober, balanced appraisals of a usefully representative range of storywriting.

HANSON's more limited and more systematic study treats the modern story from its late nineteenth-century efflorescence to the present, discerning, as a feature of literary modernism, a general movement towards more questioning, open narrative and a basic dichotomy between more traditional plot-based tale and lyrical, impressionistic fiction, both kinds deriving ultimately from Poe. The former she terms the "short story" proper, the latter "short prose fiction" . Her six chapters record chronologically developments over the period within this critical framework: thus, "Impressionists" are set against "Imperialists" in the late Victorian and Edwardian decades; then follows the shift into modernism and development of the psychological sketch, with emphasis on the momentary and epiphanic and an accompanying gain in artistic prestige; then subsequent reversion in the mid-century towards the more traditional story, followed by the further swing back to freer and more fluid short fiction, ending in the postmodernist problematising and fragmentation of narrative, with its associated ontological questioning. A substantial range of writers in English is covered.

BAYLEY covers some of the same material, less programmatically, with his customarily idiosyncratic and subtle critical approach. Characteristically oblique, he begins by discussing poetry, seeking to determine the imaginative quality of the short story as both autonomously poetic and, paradoxically, fully related to the real, overcoming the barren dualisms of formalism and theory. The modern short story "effect", identified romantically as the significance of the moment, is produced by the intensest artistry but also produces the fullest awareness of life and reality. Too great a sophistication, too determined an artistry, may tend, however, to divorce story from life, and for critic as for creator experience should counter the logic of theory. Bayley's strongly humanist stance is evident throughout his study, which moves, easily if unsystematically, and always through deft and discerning close readings, among the various major exponents he discusses.

HEAD's more narrowly focused study is thoughtful and well detailed, theoretically informed (by Althusserian and Bakhtinian concepts) but not drily abstract. It affirms the importance of dissonance and disruptiveness in the genre, its "*disunifying* devices", its capacity and desire for opening and pluralising narrative, and its intrinsic and generic relatedness to modernity and modernism. He reproves the tendency of short-story criticism, deficient and undeveloped, to determine formal unity or teleology and to secure and homogenise this narrative instability and fragmentariness. Five important twentieth-century writers are discussed in these terms, and given individual chapters, with a general theorising conclusion placing emphasis on socio-cultural context. Thus theory is informed by readings and vice-versa, while the individual writers are carefully and helpfully discriminated.

JEREMY LANE

Short Fiction: British

Allen, Walter, *The Short Story in English*, Oxford: Clarendon Press, 1981; New York: Oxford University Press, 1981

Bates, H.E., *The Modern Short Story: A Critical Survey*, London: Thomas Nelson, 1941

Bayley, John, *The Short Story: Henry James to Elizabeth Bowen*, Brighton, Sussex: Harvester Press, 1988; New York: St Martin's Press, 1988

Beachcroft, T. O., *The Modest Art: A Survey of the Short Story in English*, London: Longman, 1968

Hanson, Clare, *Short Stories and Short Fictions, 1880–1980*, London: Macmillan, 1985

Hanson, Clare (ed.), *Re-Reading the Short Story*, London: Macmillan, 1989

Head, Dominic, *The Modernist Short Story: A Study in Theory and Practice*, Cambridge and New York: Cambridge University Press, 1992

O'Connor, Frank, *The Lonely Voice: A Study of the Short Story*, London: Macmillan, 1963; Cleveland, Ohio: World, 1963

Reid, Ian, *The Short Story*, London: Methuen, 1977; New York: Barnes & Noble, 1977

Shaw, Valerie, *The Short Story: A Critical Introduction*, London: Longman, 1983

Most of the important statements on the genre have, until recently, been made by practising short-story writers, such as V.S. Pritchett, Sean O'Faolain, W. Somerset Maugham, Beachcroft, H.E. Bates and Frank O'Connor. The result has been a stress on the "who" and "how" rather than the "why". By virtue of repetition, a single aesthetic has emerged, a consensus by default, in effect. This consensus revolves around Edgar Allan Poe's focus on "unity of impression", "a single preconceived effect", and "symmetry of design". Only Bates and O'Connor have adapted these ideas to any significant degree, leaving more recent academic commentators to challenge Poe's long-term pre-eminence in the field of short-story theory.

BATES wrote the first notable survey of the modern story, emphasising the importance of Anton Chekhov and Guy de Maupassant, and tracing their influence through various writers including Katherine Mansfield, James Joyce, and D.H. Lawrence. He attempts to distinguish between two main types of story, which he defines as those of "action-and-character" and "atmosphere", a distinction that becomes increasingly difficult to maintain. As his thesis begins to break down, he changes emphasis to make a plea for stories in which life is "truly observed and painted, not conventionally analysed". This advances the argument to include many of the female writers largely ignored at that time, and a perceptive few pages are devoted to the Welsh story. It would be all too easy to dismiss the cliché-ridden language of Bates's study (he defines the "essentially feminine" story as "fluttering, gossipy, breathless"), but this would miss the breadth and frequent perceptiveness of this ground-breaking work.

O'CONNOR's immensely readable study has exerted probably more influence than any other book on the short story. He defines the genre as being "romantic, individualistic, and intransigent", where the most recurrent pattern is of "outlawed figures wandering about the fringes of society", exiled, ostracised, or alienated. His notion of the "submerged population" lends itself to an argument that the story has succeeded chiefly in unstable or developing cultures. Socially alienated and fragmentary, he finds the stories of Chekhov and Joyce, in particular, the perfect vehicle for the literary vision of the early twentieth century. The individual chapters provide a plethora of incisive commentary (especially on the Irish story), marred occasionally by a very narrow conception of the reader, and a desire to analyse everything on a symbolic level.

BEACHCROFT's title is actually a misnomer, as he concentrates almost entirely on the short story in England, particularly as practised by Thomas Hardy, Maugham, A.E. Coppard, and William Sansom. He has little time for questions of definition or form, and the interest of the book is confined to his presentation, *in précis* and with substantial quotation, of at least as many stories as he judges to be of particular account.

REID's book is the first scholarly attempt at examining the assertion that the modern short story is *the* Romantic prose form. He compares the story to contributory modes, such as the sketch, yarn, parable, and folk-tale, and then develops an elaborately detailed comparison between stories and novels, including discussion of the novella, story cycle, and framed miscellany. He summarises the uniqueness of the form as lying in its distinctive formal qualities: "it makes a single impression on the reader; it does so by concentrating on a crisis; and it makes the crisis pivotal to the plot". Thus for all its shrewd analysis and economical exposition, Reid's thesis finally falters on an over-simplified prescription. The idea that the response of readers, or the emotions of characters, can be anticipated or represented via formal shape and design, has proved pervasively misleading.

ALLEN's undergraduate handbook lists 83 practitioners on its Contents page, a masterpiece of critical brevity. The theorising is fairly perfunctory, suggesting associations with the joke, oral tale, and romance, before emphasising its affinities with lyric poetry by virtue of its "uncommon insight" and "single revealing incident". The strength of the book is Allen's usually reliable critique of a vast number of underrated and overlooked writers (i.e. Morley Callaghan, Frank Sargeson, Leslie Halward, Rhys Davies), and its weakness is the unavoidable but irritating compression of his analyses.

SHAW's discursive and wide-ranging survey of origins, stylistic techniques, characterisation, and sense of place is one of the best introductory guides to the genre. It includes a wealth of quotations from writers and academics, and makes particularly good use of Henry James and Eudora Welty. Shaw's principle advance is to discuss the relationship between the modern short story and Impressionist art, genres bound together by their "shared consciousness of form". Despite its suggestiveness, literature remains a temporal medium, and painting a spatial one. Her analogy risks obscuring the basic distinction between the metaphorical story "picture" and the literal, spatial image on the painter's canvas.

HANSON's 1985 theoretical study is a wide-ranging scholarly discussion that attempts both to define the concepts of the modern short story and to set it in its historical context. She distinguishes between short "stories" – the conventional plot-based type – and short "fictions", in which plot is subordinate to internal psychological drama. Although she runs into the same problems as Bates did 45 years earlier, Hanson's is a much more sophisticated approach than the initial sharp distinction will allow. She is particularly acute on problematic narrators, especially in the stories of Mansfield and Virginia Woolf.

HANSON has also edited a collection of articles (1989) on short-story theory. Most of the arguments raise more questions than they answer (which is probably the point), but all maintain a high standard of thoughtful analysis. Of particular note are Mial's reader-response theories, Mary Eagleton's feminism and women's stories, Hanson's own psychoanalytical discussion, and Sprague on Doris Lessing. The introductory essay recasts O'Connor's case for story-writing as the natural genre for the oppressed, ostracised, and marginalised, seeking to identify such groups as women, blacks, and gays as the most likely productive storytellers in the near future.

BAYLEY's long-awaited exploration of the short story centres on his belief that "dissonance" is the informing generic factor. This "unexpressed paradox", between the precision of its art and the imprecision of its mystery, gives the impression "that there is always something more to come". Instead of talking about "closure", Bayley suggests that critics use a word like "fulfilment", a notion that embodies inconclusiveness and provides its own commentary on itself. He proceeds to demonstrate this thesis by looking at a series of writers from the modernist era. Whether or not the argument would withstand scrutiny when applied to postmodern stories is a moot point, but his problematising of formal structure is certainly persuasive and important.

HEAD's argument takes Bayley's ideas one step further. If epiphany is not the moment of revelatory enlightenment leading to closure, then it must be the expression of a paradox fundamental to modernist poetics. Head sees the disruptive literary gesture as an instance of "relative autonomy". This Althusserian notion means something that is conditioned by, yet critical of, its ideological content. Formal rupture is conceived of as a locus for the story's justification – its ability to question and transform. This complicated theory is examined by reference to a variety of writers, some of whom (Woolf, Mansfield) it suits very well, others (Joyce, Malcolm Lowry) it doesn't. What is certain is that the critical commonplaces modelled on Poe's basic definition of the story cannot be restated with such consummate ease in the light of searching analyses by Bayley and Head.

SIMON BAKER

Short Fiction: American

Ford, Richard (ed.), *The Granta Book of the American Short Story*, London and New York: Granta/Viking Press, 1992

Gerlach, John, *Toward the End: Closure and Structure in the American Short Story*, University: University of Alabama Press, 1985

Leitch, Thomas, M., "The Debunking Rhythm of the American Short Story", in *Short Story Theory at a Crossroads*, edited by Susan Lohafer and Jo Ellyn Clarey, Baton Rouge: Louisiana State University Press, 1989

Peden, William, *The American Short Story: Continuity and Change 1940–1975*, Boston: Houghton Mifflin, 1964, 2nd edition, 1975

Poe, Edgar Allan, "Review of *Twice-Told Tales*", in *Graham's Magazine*, May 1842 (reprinted in subsequent essay collections)

Rohrberger, Mary, *Hawthorne and the Modern Short Story: A Study in Genre*, The Hague: Mouton, 1966

Stevick, Philip (ed.), *The American Short Story 1900–1945: A Critical History*, Boston: Twayne, 1984

Weaver, Gordon, *The American Short Story 1945–1980: A Critical History*, Boston: Twayne, 1983

Analysts of American short fiction are divided between those who, following Edgar Allan Poe, believe that a discussion of short fiction implicitly has the corollary of establishing a corresponding poetics, and those who concentrate on mapping historical patterns.

POE's review of Nathaniel Hawthorne's collection *Twice-Told Tales* commands singular stature in short-story theory; while numerous scholars have disputed his contention that a short story should move towards "a single *effect*", these same critics have not repudiated Poe's recognition of the importance of textual brevity to the reading experience. Indeed, Poe's emphasis on "the unity of effect or impression" created by a short work has subsequently led reader-response theorists – such as Suzanne Hunter Brown – to expand greatly our understanding of the mechanics of the short story as a genre.

ROHRBERGER's study, expanding from Hawthorne's belief that "romance" serves well to probe the secret "truths of the human heart", elucidates the genre's overall predilection for structures based on "classical archetypal . . . journeys, patterns of withdrawal and return". Alternating Freudian analyses of specific stories – from those of Hawthorne to Eudora Welty's – with discussions of modernist literary theory, Rohrberger shows how American short fiction organizes itself around a symbolic reading of exterior events. Reality lies "beyond the ordinary world of appearances" so that "meaning lies beneath the surface of the narrative". Though necessarily outdated in terms of recent literary theory, her study is especially useful in its pairing of basic Freudian thought with a formalist approach to genre, and the readings of individual stories are incisive.

PEDEN's critical history is written for scholars who wish to broaden their scope of research. Peden's extensive analysis, the work of an *aficionado*, is usefully preservative; that is, while engaging familiar authors, it also recalls those – such as William Goyen – who are often absent from canonical reading lists. Locating the fiction within the contexts of this century's intellectual trends and American political events, Peden's thematic procedure summarizes the major developments of the twentieth-century American short story – urban writing, the black and Jewish movements, and experimental fiction. A virtue of this study is Peden's ability to synthesize his analysis with an unusually informed discussion of literatures other than American.

WEAVER's collection of three essays traces chronologically how immediate postwar short stories, with their Jamesian examination of social manners, developed into the clash between experimental "fictions" and more traditional modes of narration characteristic of recent writing. In his Introduction, Weaver visualizes "the contemporary American short story as an index of national consciousness" – a sociological outlook, which extends to the essays that follow. Scrutinizing how short fiction details the ways in which abrupt social change has combined with the existential confrontation of the "absurd" to create the alienated individual, the essays tend toward character study. While this perspective is helpful in terms of mid-century writers such as John O'Hara, it does not sufficiently engage the complex theoretical issues involved with meta-fiction.

STEVICK's collection of essays, also a Twayne critical survey, is more attentive to the nuances of the period than is Weaver's, because the essays entail considerably more diverse methodologies. Stevick's splendid Introduction historicizes modernist short fiction by situating it not only within the non-literary discourses of still photography and film, but also through the theoretical observations of writers such as Sherwood Anderson and Raymond Chandler. While such critical surveys must, by necessity, be somewhat scanty in textual analysis, Stevick's book does well to elucidate the importance of Anderson as a pivotal transitional figure and to explore the interrelationship between William Faulkner's short fiction and his novels. Encapsulating a valuable history of the vagaries of early twentieth-century short-story publishing, the study also includes a fine critique of "the question of regionalism", a discussion which is especially useful owing to its treatment of Jean Toomer's multi-generic writing.

GERLACH's investigation of nineteenth- and twentieth-century American short fiction astutely combines theoretical insights with historical analysis. Using structuralist innovations regarding the study of narrative (but without relying on obtuse terminology), Gerlach furthers Poe's concerns about the short story's singleness of effect by arguing that the form "is that genre in which anticipation of the ending is always present". The sweep of Gerlach's inquiry is broad. Ranging from the work of Joseph Neal and Herman Melville in the nineteenth century to that of Katherine Anne Porter, Bernard Malamud, and William H. Gass in the twentieth, Gerlach undertakes a close examination of the development of closure in American short fiction. To clarify his theoretical observations, Gerlach performs a sensitive reading of one of John Cheever's short stories. Both analytic and mindful of historical change, this study is the best introduction to the field.

LEITCH's article inquires into the epistemological dimensions of American short fiction. Responding to Poe, Matthews, and Gerlach, he maintains that "short stories constitute not a form of knowledge but a challenge to knowledge". The primary focus of the piece concerns the ways that American short fiction renders problematic the notion of a unified self. Elucidating how the short fiction of Poe, Stephen Crane, and Flannery O'Connor involves a fundamental critique of identity, Leitch elaborates the surprising thesis that short fiction has provided a crucial contribution to the development of the modern novel.

FORD's essay, the observations of a practitioner, follows in the tradition of Poe, Welty, and Cheever. While he addresses such generic issues as the role of brevity and endings to the form, what is of greater interest to the scholar is Ford's lack of hesitation in engaging those crucial – though nebulous – questions that academics are trained to avoid. How do short stories reflect historicity but resist the constraints of milieu? Different from those who would reductively deduce the nature of the American character through an analysis of its literature, Ford contrasts short fiction's attempt to bring to light the almost inaccessible ambiguities of experience to journalism's portrayal of what the political columnist, Walt Lippman, calls "a picture of reality on which the citizen can act". The fecundity of Ford's essay is such that scholars of various interests will be able to draw insight from it.

MICHAEL TRUSSLER

Sidney, Sir Philip 1554–1586

English poet and romance writer

Greenfield, Thelma, N., *The Eye of Judgement: Reading the "New Arcadia"*, Lewisburg, Pennsylvania: Bucknell University Press, 1982; London: Associated University Presses, 1982

Hager, Dennis, *Dazzling Images: The Masks of Sir Philip Sidney*, Newark: University of Delaware Press, 1991; London: Associated University Presses, 1991

Hannay, Margaret P., *Philip's Phoenix: Mary Sidney, Countess of Pembroke*, New York and Oxford: Oxford University Press, 1990

Kay, Dennis (ed.), *Sir Philip Sidney: An Anthology of Modern Criticism*, Oxford and New York: Oxford University Press, 1987

Lindheim, Nancy, *The Structures of Sidney's "Arcadia"*, Toronto: University of Toronto Press, 1982

McCanless, Michael, *The Text of Sidney's Arcadian World*, Durham, North Carolina: Duke University Press, 1989

McCoy, Richard C., *Sir Philip Sidney: Rebellion in "Arcadia"*, New Brunswick, New Jersey: Rutgers University Press, 1979; Brighton, Sussex: Harvester Press, 1979

Rees, Joan, *Sir Philip Sidney and "Arcadia"*, Rutherford, New Jersey: Fairleigh Dickinson University Press, 1991; London, Associated University Presses, 1991

Rudenstine, Neil L., *Sidney's Poetic Development*, Cambridge, Massachusetts: Harvard University Press, 1967

Spiller, Michael, R.G., *The Development of the Sonnet: An Introduction*, London and New York: Routledge, 1992

Stillman, Robert E., *Sidney's Poetic Justice: The "Old Arcadia", Its Eclogues, and Renaissance Pastoral Traditions*, Lewisburg, Pennsylvania: Bucknell University Press, 1986; London: Associated University Presses, 1986

The admiration of Philip Sidney's own contemporaries, and in particular of his lifelong friend and biographer Fulke Greville, has fixed a halo over Sidney in almost every assessment of his life and work up until the last 50 years or so. John Buxton's *Sir Philip Sidney and the English Renaissance* (London: Macmillan, 1954) exemplifies this tradition at its sensitive and perceptive best, while highlighting its limitations.

The unearthing of new bibliographical material, and in particular Dobell's discovery of the *New Arcadia* in 1907, have led to modern critical editions of Sidney's work, from William Ringler's *The Poems of Sir Philip Sidney* (Oxford University Press, 1962) onwards. Their introductions, notes, commentaries, and apparatus have in turn contributed vital impetus to the shift of Sidneian studies into the mainstream of contemporary critical discourse, and their subsequent rapid expansion into all its specialist ranges. The innovative strengths of Sidney's writing, his artistic dedication and subtlety, are now receiving minute attention and full recognition.

The critical activity at present being concentrated on *Arcadia* in particular, in both its earlier and revised versions, is of special significance in this regard. The enormous popularity of Sidney's romance in the generations following his death was only initially accompanied by corresponding critical respect. Later, as the novel developed, the form and style of *Arcadia* became generally inaccessible even as entertainment, though it continued to be admired by discerning readers, Samuel Richardson and William Cowper among them. Then, for well over a century, it suffered from almost dismissive neglect. It is now being read with analytical seriousness hardly matched since Fulke Greville's close discussion of his friend's intentions and achievement in the biographical *Dedication to Sir Philip Sidney*, first published in 1652, but almost certainly written some 40 years earlier. In his great critical edition, Ringler drew attention to the range and quality of Sidney's adventurous experiments in the *Eclogues*, dividing the "Acts" of the early version of *Arcadia* (The "*Old Arcadia*"), and so opened new approaches to Sidney's aims and critical opinions through the *Defense* as well as the poems themselves. Full and well-annotated bibliographies are given in *Sidney in Retrospect*, edited by A. Kinney (Amherst: University of Massachusetts Press, 1988).

Developments in these fields, however, are at present running well in advance of existing publications. Sidney's use of allegory and other figurative techniques; his handling of gender roles and problems; the political text and sub-text of his prose and verse; the interaction of his life and work with the activities of his own circle and that of his sister, Mary Countess of Pembroke – all are among the areas at present being investigated in most detail. *The Sidney Newsletter and Journal*, published annually by the English Department of Guelph University (Guelph, Ontario) gives up-to-date reviews and announcements of work in progress. The titles cited below have been selected to give some indication of the range of criticism now available, as well as being valuable in themselves.

RUDENSTINE argues strongly for a coherent view of Sidney's work as laterally expansive from consistent critical principles, rather than as exhibiting progressive shifts in standpoint and aim. He takes full account of Sidney's contacts with European scholarship, both in his reading and through personal friendships. Development in his writing is seen in terms of increasing technical mastery, and in particular as activated by Sidney's "growing interest in the sonnet as a potentially dramatic form, and his desire to reinvigorate the Petrarchan language of love". Rudenstine's discussion of *Astrophil and Stella* is especially illuminating: he finds centrally influential the attention paid by Scaliger and other scholars to the Aristotelian concept of *energia*. This Rudenstine equates with Sidney's own term "forcibleness" and its synonyms, as cited throughout Sidney's *Defense* and put into increasing practice in his own writing.

McCOY's pioneering and provocative study concentrates chiefly on the political undertones of Sidney's work and their relation to the difficulties Sidney experienced in his own public career: "Sidney's life reveals the tensions within the Elizabethan world-order". He is particularly interested in Sidney's portrayal of the variously troubled relations between his fictional heroes and authority, as illustrated especially, though not exclusively, by the character of Amphialus in the *New Arcadia*. His perceptions are in many ways exciting, but he inclines sometimes to overplay his focus on biographical parallelism. Political irony tends, from his viewpoint, to override other considerations, critical and aesthetic, especially in his discussion of *Astrophil and Stella*.

GREENFIELD's approach is very different. She sees the flexibility of Sidney's narrative and descriptive techniques as developing from the *Old Arcadia* to the later version to engage the reader's judgement and perceptions with increasing subtlety, often at a number of levels simultaneously. While this process is given its richest scope in the *New Arcadia*, it functions in different ways throughout Sidney's work. Her presentation of Sidney's sources for *Arcadia*, recognition of which she takes as an important part of Sidney's expectations, is full and detailed, as is her citation of visual concepts and conventions that would have been familiarly available at the time. Her discussion of Pyrocles/Zelmane's Amazon disguise, and its ambiguous moral implications, is of great interest, and well exemplifies her central thesis that judgement, here and elsewhere, is carefully informed, but left finally as the reader's responsibility.

LINDHEIM's central thesis is that the *New Arcadia* is no mere expansion of the earlier version but a "re-vision", involving a shift to epic ground. She sees the *Aeneid* as a probable model here – thematic and tonal rather than narrative. She takes the enrichment of characterisation apparent throughout the episode of the imprisonment of the Princesses and Pyrocles/Zelmane by Cecropia in the *New Arcadia*, and the problems confronting the exercise of justice in the climactic trial scene of the original version, as offering specific keys to Sidney's formulation of his incomplete "re-vision". In general, "there remains a need to work with whatever parts of the original Books III–V still suit the new plan because the *New Arcadia*'s two oracles show that Sidney intended the same dénouement for his revised work".

McCANLESS reaches a similar conclusion, though for him it is something of a side-issue. His main concern is with the expanding techniques by which the "purely verbal world of his own Arcadian fiction" is realised and made relevant to Sidney's readers. This abstract approach is perhaps most effective in Part I of his book, where he analyses selected descriptive and narrative passages in close and often extremely rewarding detail.

KAY's collection of essays is deliberately representative, with a useful retrospective Introduction on the critical heritage of Sidney's work. Included is Thomas P. Roche's important essay "*Astrophil and Stella*: A Radical Reading" (slightly condensed), taking the sequence as "a journey from hope to despair as a fictional device for the analysis of human desire in Christian terms", and giving close attention to the importance of biblical and theological correlation in Sidney's work as a whole.

REES's is a very positive study, laying emphasis on Sidney's scope and originality, his "adventurous probing". She sees his interest in the capacity of women developing through *Astrophil and Stella*, arriving at an imaginative empathy, expressed in *Arcadia* most particularly through characters whose natures and situations are both difficult and ambivalent. Gynecia is her prime example, but her analyses are detailed and perceptive throughout.

HAGER's main thesis is that Sidney's capacity for the manipulation of irony – both objective and self-reflexive – informs not only his writing, but his whole career, and even his posthumous reputation. The book is an expansion, undertaken in depth and at leisure, of a seminal article, "The Exemplary Mirage: Fabrication of Sir Philip Sidney's Biographical Image and the Sidney Reader" (in the journal *English Literary History*, 1980). This is a valuable and erratically stimulating work.

STILLMAN sees justice as constituting Sidney's principal theme, outlined in his early work and brought to full coherence in *Arcadia*: "the pastoral entertainments . . . are simplified fictions in which the complex issues raised by the romance's main action can be evaluated and understood". This interdependence of justice with contentment is taken by Stillman as fundamental to English Renaissance pastoral, and as being related to wider questions of generic definition.

SPILLER's richly detailed book sets *Astrophil and Stella* (Chapter 7) in its full context of tradition, sources, and development. His approach to his enormous subject is concentrated on the potential of the sonnet form as a vehicle for self-projection and self-identification. *Astrophil and Stella*, in which Spiller very refreshingly finds humour as well as irony, is examined in relation to other English (and Scottish) sequences and in the light of a full range of recent scholarship.

HANNAY's book is among the very best of several recent studies centred on Sidney's sister, Mary, Countess of Pembroke. Any discussion of the siblings' relationship must go beyond Sidney's lifetime: Mary edited her brother's works, and was famous as a patron of letters, besides doing notable work of her own. Hannay sees Mary's own literary achievements as complementing those of her brother, especially in her fine and innovative completion of his last, unfinished, work, the translation of the Psalms.

ELIZABETH PORGES WATSON

Simms, William Gilmore 1806–1870

American novelist, poet, dramatist, and prose writer

Guilds, John Caldwell (ed.), *Long Years of Neglect: The Work and Reputation of William Gilmore Simms*, Fayetteville: University of Arkansas Press, 1988

Guilds, John Caldwell, *Simms: A Literary Life*, Fayetteville: University of Arkansas Press, 1992

Ridgely, J.V., *William Gilmore Simms*, New York: Twayne, 1962

Wakelyn, Jon L., *The Politics of a Literary Man: William Gilmore Simms*, Westport, Connecticut: Greenwood Press, 1973

Watson, Charles S., *From Nationalism to Secessionism: The Changing Fiction of William Gilmore Simms*, Westport, Connecticut: Greenwood Press, 1993

Wimsatt, Mary Ann, *The Major Fiction of William Gilmore Simms: Cultural Tradition and Literary Form*, Baton Rouge: Louisiana State University Press, 1989

After Edgar Allan Poe, William Gilmore Simms was the antebellum South's most eminent man of letters. Today, however, even scholars of nineteenth-century American literature have read few, if any, of his works. The reasons for this neglect are numerous. Simms was a prodigious writer, producing over 80 volumes, and leaving at least another 20 volumes of uncollected material scattered throughout magazines and newspapers. Added to this problem is the difficulty that Simms was prone to writing in haste, and the quality of his work is uneven. His reputation has also suffered from William Peterfield Trent's unsympathetic and deprecatory 1892 biography, the only full-length study of the author that was available for close to a century. Further, Simms's vehement pro-slavery stance tends to alienate modern readers. During the 1980s and 1990s, however, there has been a resurgence of interest. Several book-length studies of his major fiction, two new biographies, and reprints of his best romance novels are now available.

RIDGELY was one of the first critics to challenge Trent's judgement that Simms was a failed realist who was creatively stultified by his allegiance to the Old South. Instead, Ridgely believes that what "raises his romances above the dusty heap of the period's second-rate fiction is the theme of the South". Examining a dozen long romance fictions, he argues that Simms was attempting to create an image of the ideal Southern society, one founded on a carefully regulated class system.

WIMSATT provides perhaps the most comprehensive and accessible overview of Simms's fictional writings. Wimsatt, while frank in her assessment of his literary faults, argues that Simms was a sophisticated innovator within the romance tradition. In each chapter she briefly describes the literary, historical, and biographical background, and then examines Simms's literary strategies. Her readings of his Revolutionary-period romances, border fictions, comedies of manners, and frontier humour pieces are relatively straightforward, but they do explore with some insight how he uses various Southern locales, the American oral tradition, and a wide variety of source materials to modify traditional romance conventions. She also convincingly demonstrates the influence of British writers such as Sir Walter Scott, Byron, and William Makepeace Thackeray on Simms's writings.

WATSON, like Wimsatt, examines Simms's major fiction chronologically, tracing his evolution from Union supporter to polemical Southern sectional and slavery advocate. Drawing on a rich variety of historical documents, as well as Simms's non-fiction writings, Watson documents this political shift against a backdrop of intellectual and social movements in America. Unfortunately, Simms's fiction is reduced to little more than a repository of ideologically charged character types in Watson's political analysis.

GUILDS's biography is an obvious attempt to displace Trent's early work and reclaim some of the distinction due "a gifted and compelling author". Believing that the basis of Simms's claim to literary permanence lies in his novels, Guilds interweaves suggestive, and occasionally innovative, critiques of his fiction with his biographical material. For example, he suggests *The Yemassee* portrays the American Indian in more complex, realistic terms than the more well-known James Fenimore Cooper's *The Last of the Mohicans*. In his attempt to rescue Simms's reputation, Guilds avoids all discussion of slavery, despite the centrality of this theme in the author's work.

WAKELYN sees Simms as a central figure in South Carolina politics, and argues that he marshalled his talents to shape the antebellum South. Concentrating on his political journalism, Wakelyn asserts that Simms was diverted from his literary career to "defend his homeland". Given Simms's continuing and prolific production of fiction throughout his life, his reluctance to enter office, and his strong commitment to developing a unique American literature, one questions such an assertion. Certainly, his writings became more partisan as tensions grew between North and South, but they are hardly the propagandist tracts that Wakelyn suggests.

GUILDS's 1988 volume is the only collection of essays on Simms's work. The essays cover a range of topics, from in-depth studies of the novels *Woodcraft*, *Cassique of Kiawah*, and *Paddy McGann*, to broader genre and historical studies. Given Simms's voluminous output, the book necessarily ignores much of his work. Nevertheless, James E. Kebler, Jr.'s essay is the most substantial evaluation of Simms's poetry yet produced, and Louis D. Rubin, Jr. gives a provocative reading of why a reassessment of the writer has been so difficult.

SHANNON L. NICHOLS

Sinclair, Upton 1878–1968

American novelist, essayist, and dramatist

Bloodworth, William, *Upton Sinclair*, Boston: Twayne, 1977
Dell, Floyd, *Upton Sinclair: A Study in Social Protest*, New York: Doran, 1927; reprinted, New York: AMS Press, 1970
Smith, Carl S., *Chicago and the American Literary Imagination 1880–1920*, Chicago: University of Chicago Press, 1984
Upton Sinclair: Biographical and Critical Opinions, Darby, Pennsylvania: Folcroft Library Editions, 1972
Welland, Dennis, *Upton Sinclair: The Centenary of an American Writer*, Manchester: John Rylands Library (University of Manchester), 1979
Yoder, John, *Upton Sinclair*, New York: Frederick Ungar, 1975

One of American literature's most idiosyncratic talents, Upton Sinclair wrote prolifically throughout his life. Between 1901 and 1940 alone, more than 100 works were published in his name, in 47 different translations. Best known as the radical socialist pamphleteer and "muckraking" author of the novel *The Jungle*, Sinclair never enjoyed at home the acclaim that he found in Europe, an issue dwelt on in some degree by the majority of Sinclair critics. An eclectic range – including writings on diet, venereal disease, temperance, and extra-sensory perception – and a persistent scepticism regarding his literary merit have diminished academic interest in his work, and although recent literary theory has placed less emphasis on *literary value* as such, at the end of the twentieth century critical interest in Sinclair is small.

Written when the discrepancy between Sinclair's reputation at home and abroad was at its highest, DELL's early study (1927) is of interest precisely because of its own historical location, three decades before a waning of radical commitment in Sinclair's work would be confirmed by his defence of McCarthyism in the 1950s. Dell positions Sinclair within a Puritan tradition "just now very unpopular among the American intelligentsia", and cites the class-conscious dimension to his writing as a further brake on wider acceptance with an American readership. Nevertheless, Dell points to the "emotionally and objectively convincing" manner in which Sinclair had catalogued a significant epoch in American life and, with these as his criteria, suggests that as early as 1927 Sinclair had produced a body of work the equal of James Fenimore Cooper, Mark Twain, or Walt Whitman.

Separate chapters are given over to Sinclair's childhood in Baltimore and New York, and Dell charts the transition from joke-writer and dime-novel "hack", to muckraking socialist in *The Jungle*, and beyond to the novels *Love's Pilgrimage*, *King Coal*, *Jimmie Higgins*, and *Oil!*. A chapter dedicated to Sinclair's political pamphleteering – "ideological maps of the [American] landscape" – will be of particular interest to readers of Sinclair today. Occasionally the text tends toward hagiography, but in reading his work biographically, more as extension of the individual than engagement with a moment in history, Dell's is a very American "study in social protest", as enthusiastically imbued with the heritage of progressivism as Sinclair's own writing.

BLOODWORTH considers Sinclair's writing in a narrative line from "its juvenile origins to its last expressions", embedding the writer's work, as Sinclair himself would doubtless have insisted, in the social and political concerns that gave it life. Interweaving a biographical focus with substantial discussion of the more highly acclaimed novels – *The Jungle*, *King Coal*, *Oil!*, and *Boston* – Bloodworth's critique develops a commentary on a dialectic thread spun in Sinclair's writing, between a high idealism and the socio-political forces with which it was engaged. At its most complex, Bloodworth suggests, this conflict revealed a writer "not only opposed to an unjust society but also at odds with his . . . own social responsibilities, family loyalties, or deeply engrained cultural responses". Thus, Bloodworth suggests, emerges the deeply paradoxical figure of Upton Sinclair, "a genteel radical sensibility", and "a nineteenth century moral idealist somewhat ill at ease in the twentieth century".

The text includes a selected bibliography of both primary and secondary materials, and though Bloodworth suggests that more specific, more sympathetic and more critical interpretations of Sinclair have been written, this study sustains an effective, critically detached, and yet simultaneously affectionate stance toward its subject.

Upton Sinclair: Biographical and Critical Opinions forms a brief, rather odd, but quite fascinating collection garnered principally from short clippings of reviews and features in the world's press, and letters written to Sinclair. Of the entries that are given specific datings, the earliest is fixed at 1903, and the latest 1923. The excerpts offered include Jack London's citation of "Comrade Sinclair's" *The Jungle* as "The *Uncle Tom's Cabin* of Wage Slavery", and contributions from Henri Barbusse, Sinclair Lewis, H.L. Mencken, Bertrand Russell, and H.G. Wells.

"Those who consider Sinclair insignificant", YODER suggests, "base their rejection on aesthetic criteria, whereas Sinclair was concerned with the effect of his writings on his audience – a very different matter". Yoder goes to considerable and convincing lengths to assess the work on what he perceives to be Sinclair's own terms, and suggests that Sinclair's greatest crime, "in an age of specialization", was to be "the Renaissance Man who had discovered socialism". Importantly, he reads Sinclair's politics with less of the European inflection that some critics have brought to bear on the early work. Sinclair, he suggests, "called himself a socialist because he saw socialists as ideologists who embraced the implications of American liberalism more completely than do most Americans who call themselves liberals", and Yoder pursues this strain of American idealism to particular effect in discussing the later *Lanny Budd* series of novels.

Published in pamphlet form, WELLAND's discussion overtly claims a continuing literary significance for Sinclair, and though short, this study is valuable, and in itself significant, for the intriguing lines of enquiry which it opens up in Sinclair's work.

Commenting on "the speed and sensitivity with which Sinclair's antennae picked up what was in the air at any given time", Welland considers the importance of a Methodist upbringing to his political vision, and relates the writing variously to George Bernard Shaw, Nietzsche, F. Scott Fitzgerald, and Wagner. Discussing the lesser-known works *The Overman* and *Prince Hagen: A Phantasy* – a piece developed by Sinclair, in various forms, throughout 12 years either side of *The Jungle* – Welland identifies a range of derivation, influence, and cultural entanglement not usually deployed by Sinclair critics, and in the process reveals a more experimental writer, if not the more literary one which he seeks.

Though Welland reads Sinclair in revealing ways, neither he, nor Bloodworth, Floyd, or Yoder – notwithstanding their socio-political orientation – take much time to ground Sinclair within the urban-industrial milieu of Chicago, from which his most enduring literary success, *The Jungle*, was derived. "The challenge which Chicago raised to the literary imagination", SMITH suggests, "was to find modes of artistic control that would make it possible to write about the city in a way that revealed its essential nature". Critical debate surrounding *The Jungle* has tended to focus precisely on Sinclair's technical use of literary form – or modes of artistic control – and although Smith's discussion of Sinclair is brief, readers who wish to contextualise the early work more fully will find in this study a wide-ranging survey of literary response to a city, the rise of which became – and not just for Sinclair – "one of the emblematic events of the age".

DAVID HOLLOWAY

Singer, Isaac Bashevis 1904–1991

Polish-born American novelist, short-story writer, and children's writer

Alexander, Edward, *Isaac Bashevis Singer*, Boston: Twayne, 1980
Allentuck, Marcia (ed.), *The Achievement of Isaac Bashevis Singer*, Carbondale: Southern Illinois University Press, 1969; London: Feffer & Simons, 1969
Buchen, Irving H., *Isaac Bashevis Singer and the Eternal Past*, New York: New York University Press, 1968
Burgin, Richard (ed.), *Conversations with Isaac Bashevis Singer*, New York: Farrar, Straus, Giroux, 1985
Friedman, Lawrence S., *Understanding Isaac Bashevis Singer*, Columbia: University of South Carolina Press, 1988
Malin, Irving (ed.), *Critical Views of Isaac Bashevis Singer*, New York: New York University Press, 1969
Malin, Irving, *Isaac Bashevis Singer*, New York: Frederick Ungar, 1972
Walden, Daniel (ed.), "Isaac Bashevis Singer: A Reconsideration", special issue of *Studies in American Jewish Literature*, 1981

Isaac Bashevis Singer was awarded the Nobel Prize for Literature in 1978, a choice that was welcomed by many a reader and critic. His writings are set largely in the Jewish world of Eastern Europe that Hitler turned to ashes. Having an eternal quality about them, with their frequent undertones of the Hebrew Bible, folklore, and Jewish ritual and belief, they stress the human struggle to make sense of a capricious world, even when there is a belief in God. He once stated that "literature must have an address". This "address", the basis for his writing, is not parochial but speaks to all humanity.

BUCHEN has produced a useful work, which contains information about Singer's early life and its influence on his writing. There is a discussion of his attitude toward translation, and the importance he placed on being actively involved in translation of his work. The analyses of Singer's work stress the importance of the past and of "eternal values", with Singer seen as concerned with creating a sense of how the past and traditional values are essential to effective story-telling.

ALLENTUCK has collected and introduced 11 essays dealing with various aspects of Singer's work. Singer's relation to the Yiddish tradition receives interesting treatment, as does his use of the grotesque. The individual novels discussed include: *Satan in Goray*, *The Family Moskat*, *The Magician of Lublin*, *The Slave*, and *The Manor*. There is also attention paid to his children's stories and to *In My Father's Court*.

MALIN's 1969 essay collection is superior to Allentuck's in that it is more comprehensive. It contains 14 essays, plus a useful bibliography of primary and secondary sources. There are two good interviews with Singer, as well as a short piece by one of his translators, relating the method used in her translations with Singer at her side. There are useful essays on his demonology and ideas of good and evil. Also of note are the essays on his use of history and his interest in Spinoza's philosophy. This is a particularly good collection.

MALIN's 1972 critical study of Singer divides his fiction into three types. "Open Novels", which he describes as "broadly conceived", have a wide scope in terms of time and space: the family chronicles – *The Family Moskat*, *The Manor*, *The Estate* – fit into this category. "Closed Novels" are tight and concentrated, dealing with faith in an "obsessive way" through one centre of consciousness; such novels as *Satan in Goray*, *The Magician of Lublin*, and *The Slave* appear in this category. The short stories comprise the third section, wherein Singer is at his most powerful because of their extreme intensity. This is a workable division, which has here produced an effective, short study.

ALEXANDER points out Singer's multifarious nature as a writer – Yiddish, English, folkloric, etc. His emphasis is on the novels that have been translated into English. The study includes a useful chronology of the important events in Singer's life and a "Selected Bibliography". It is a good general study, in which all of Singer's major works, including the short stories, are discussed. The author views him as both a chronicler of a destroyed Jewish world and language, and as an author who may have created a new Jewish literature.

WALDEN has devoted to Singer an entire issue of the periodical he edits. This number is subtitled "Isaac Bashevis Singer: A Reconsideration", and contains 17 articles and five interviews. There are some good essays on particular novels, and a very useful section headed "Retrospectives/In Retrospect", which places Singer in a wider context of American literature, and looks back over his life's work. The interviews are illuminating, and often iconoclastically humorous, in Singer's own particular way.

BURGIN and Singer have produced a volume that is indispensable reading for anyone interested in Singer's work. Containing a series of interviews, which took place between 1976 and 1983, and presented thematically in chapters, Burgin manages to elicit from Singer his ideas on a wide range of topics from God to sex, Free Will to literature, modern society to vegetarianism. Singer's candour is such that his fiction becomes even more alive and meaningful after reading this fascinating work.

FRIEDMAN's study of Singer is meant for the beginning reader who wishes to have a simple and accessible guide. Part of a series designed to introduce readers to great authors, all of Singer's major works are discussed, and the author places him within his Jewish and American traditions. This is a useful, if basic, study.

EDWARD A. ABRAMSON

The Sitwells

Edith Sitwell 1887–1964

English poet and essayist

Osbert Sitwell 1892–1969

English poet, short-story writer, and essayist

Sacheverell Sitwell 1897–1988

English essayist, poet, and art critic

Cevasco, G.A., *The Sitwells: Edith, Osbert, and Sacheverell*, Boston: Twayne, 1987

Fifoot, Richard, *A Bibliography of Edith, Osbert, and Sacheverell Sitwell*, London: Rupert Hart-Davis, 1963, revised 1971

Lehmann, John, *A Nest of Tigers: The Sitwells in Their Time*, Boston: Little Brown, 1968; London: Macmillan, 1968

Mégroz, R.L., *The Three Sitwells: A Biographical and Critical Study*, London: Grant Richards Press, 1927; New York: George H. Doran, 1927

Pearson, John, *Facades: Edith, Osbert and Sacheverell Sitwell*, London: Macmillan, 1978

Wykes-Joyce, Max, *Triad of Genius*, London: Peter Owen, 1953

As writers and personalities, the Sitwells were widely admired and narrowly detested. Adverse criticism of them is generally hyperbolic and *ad hominem*; favourable remarks are often just as exaggerated and personal. Those who dislike them took every opportunity to discredit them publicly. F.R. Leavis, for one, dismissed Edith and her brothers as belonging "more to the history of publicity than poetry". Malcolm Muggeridge, for another, openly complained that "the Sitwells, individually and collectively, were among the major bores of the age". Evelyn Waugh, on the other hand, adulated the Sitwells, and summed them up nicely when he quipped: "they took the dullness out of literature". Partisanship aside, few can deny that Edith, Osbert, and Sacheverell established reputations that rest securely on a plateau far above mid-point in the hierarchy of twentieth-century literary figures.

MÉGROZ, who completed the first critical study of the Sitwells, wrote his book to stress the importance of their work; for the vagaries of various critics subjected Edith, Osbert, and Sacheverell to peculiar accusations. Those mainly of a personal nature Megroz dismissed as unworthy of consideration. Perplexed as to why the Sitwells should be denigrated as having "nihilist designs upon form and tradition", he goes to their defence, though he admits that he cannot ignore their shortcomings or partiality for eccentricity posing at times as originality. In trying to get at the meaning of "Sitwellism", Megroz delves into what he labels "tradition married to futurism". As writers, the Sitwells, Megroz concludes, were subjective interpreters of experience. Their poetry, fiction, biographies, and essays are worthy of all the praise received.

WYKES-JOYCE's biography focuses on the public and private lives and literary accomplishments of Edith and Osbert. His chief purpose is to fathom the Sitwell genius. (Though, as his title indicates, he planned to include Sacheverell in conjunction with his sister and elder brother, he decided to publish a complementary volume devoted entirely to the youngest Sitwell – but failed to do so). Wykes-Joyce stresses the range and significance of Edith's poetry, and Osbert's fiction and autobiographical volumes. As for Edith, he concludes that the number of major women poets cannot be more than four or five, but she is undoubtedly of that few. He judges *Miracle on Sinai* Osbert's best novel for "its prophecy of atomic warfare, its philosophical and theological arguments, its consummate characterisations, all composed in elegant prose". Osbert's five autobiographical volumes form "as complete a study of an artist as has ever been composed".

FIFOOT's descriptive bibliography is useful for all the obvious reasons, as well as for showing the amazing creativity of the three Sitwells. They were hardly pleased when their many individually written works were considered as "a mass production", when, as Edith once complained, they were reviewed as "an aggregate Indian god, with three sets of legs and arms, but otherwise indivisible". Early in their careers they did collaborate, but later, as this volume makes clear, they followed their own aesthetic inclinations. For each, Fifoot supplies full details of the first editions of their books, and some account of the many works they edited or to which they contributed. In addition, he supplies information on their numerous articles, reviews, musical setting, and public readings. Edith has some 400 listings, Osbert 600, and Sacheverell 340.

LEHMANN undertook his study with the full approval of the Sitwells themselves. His facts are accurate, though certain judgements may be somewhat skewed. What he attempted was no less than a description and interim assessment of their impact on the literary, artistic, and musical history of Britain at the time. Lehmann's provocative title is taken from a remark made by Edith herself and her brothers: "we are as cozy as a nest of tigers on the Ganges". Highly appreciative of their creativity, Lehmann discusses the most important or characteristic works of poetry, fiction, travel writing, and autobiography produced by each of the Sitwells. Since they had active and controversial intelligences, he gives interesting accounts of their lively engagements and disputes. Evaluating them as leading exponents of modern taste, he discusses how they often encouraged and aided many aspiring writers and artists. (Dylan Thomas, for one, serves as a good example.)

PEARSON claims in his Introduction that he was moved to write about the Sitwells because to him they were a mystery: and having written *The Autobiography of James Bond*, he was prone to dealing with mysteries. To the extent that their eccentricity, notoriety, complications, and contradictions could be understood, Pearson produced an admirable, sympathetic, and laudatory study of the Sitwells, the vastness of their literary output, the range of their friends and foes, and certain matters "slightly touchy". The Sitwells offered him bits of advice and allowed him to examine some of their manuscripts, letters, and unpublished materials. The result is an impressive, exploratory, and even-handed biography. The only weakness, which Pearson himself acknowledged, is a lack of attention paid to Sacheverell.

My own study (CEVASCO) is labeled "bio-critical". The lives of the Sitwells are considered briefly, but beyond the first chapter biography plays at best a supportive role, and in the ten chapters that follow the focus is analytical. No attempt is made to be all-inclusive, though virtually all the Sitwells' major works are considered. Special consideration is given to: Edith's *Facade* (one chapter); Osbert's five-fold autobiographical sequence, especially *Left Hand, Right Hand*; and Sacheverell's cultural studies, in particular *Mozart* and *Narrative Pictures*. My aim is to account for the trajectories of the Sitwells' individual careers, and I argue that as a literary family they accomplished far more than the Lambs (Charles and Mary), the Rossettis (Dante, Michael, and Christina), the Brontës, or "Michael Fields" (Katherine Bradley and her niece Edith Cooper).

G.A. Cevasco

Skelton, John c.1460–1529

English poet and dramatist

Edwards, Anthony S.G. (ed.), *Skelton: The Critical Heritage*, London and Boston: Routledge & Kegan Paul, 1981

Fish, Stanley E., *John Skelton's Poetry*, New Haven, Connecticut: Yale University Press, 1965

Kinsman, R., *John Skelton: Early Tudor Laureate: An Annotated Bibliography c.1488–1977*, Boston: G.K. Hall, 1979; London: George Prior, 1979

Kinsman, R., and T. Yonge, *John Skelton: Canon and Consensus*, Renaissance Society of America (Bibliographies and Indices, no.4), 1967

Walker, Greg, *John Skelton and the Politics of the 1520s*, Cambridge and New York: Cambridge University Press, 1988

John Skelton's work has not received full serious critical attention until this century, when his work has contributed strongly to developments in the handling of metre and poetic language. W.H. Auden, Edith Sitwell, and above all Robert Graves found him an important influence on their own poetry. The generation immediately following Skelton's own, however, brought in literary innovations associated particularly with Sir Thomas Wyatt and the Earl of Surrey: the resulting expansive shift in critical standards and expectations left Skelton's work behind. It was seen at best as being of little more than historical interest or curiosity, and such influence as may be found in satirical writing up to the Jacobean period is tangential. Even now it is difficult to obtain a balanced view of his surviving work: of the scholarly works on which his international reputation rested, and which qualified him for appointment as tutor to the future Henry VIII, only his translation of the *Bibleiotheca Historica* of Diodorus Siculus has survived (edited by F.M. Salter and H.L.R. Edwards, Early English Text Society, OS 233, 239, 1956–57). Little of his poetry was printed in his lifetime, and it is clear from his own retrospective listing of his works in the *Gerlande of Laurell*, issued in 1532, that much has been lost: the canon has been further abbreviated by the rigours of modern investigation. KINSMAN and YONGE (1963) stands as a milestone in this respect. In his 1979 study, KINSMAN has also supplied a full and exactly annotated bibliography, indispensable to Skelton studies.

EDWARDS, in the Skelton volume of the *Critical Heritage* series, has assembled a wide and salutary range of critical comment – from Erasmus, writing to Skelton's royal pupil, "that incomparable light and ornament of British letters" ("unum Brittanicarum litterarum lumen ed decus"), through Alexander Pope ("Skelton's poems are all low and bad; there's nothing in them that's worth reading") and Elizabeth Barrett Browning's excited praise of his "savageness", to the more moderately considered view of C.S. Lewis in 1954 ("the only poet of that age who is still read for pleasure").

FISH's book draws particular conclusions from a wide range of Skeltonic scholarship appearing in the 1960s, much of it devoted to establishing the poet's place in European as well as English literary traditions. Fish's book takes advantage of the work done in these fields in order to concentrate on the "psychological (spiritual) history of its protagonist" at the centre, as he analyses it, of each poem.

WALKER's study of Skelton's life and work in its public context lays emphasis on his use of, and reliance on, literary and satiric convention, especially in the anti-Wolsey polemics. "Because Skelton wished to satirise [Cardinal] Wolsey, and because Wolsey was a leading churchman, convention determined many of the charges which the poet was to use against him". His thesis is perhaps over-played, but is nevertheless corrective and stimulating.

Elizabeth Porges Watson

Slave Narrative *see* Douglass, Frederick; Equiano, Olaudah; Jacobs, Harriet

Smart, Christopher 1722–1771

English poet

Blaydes, Sophia B., *Christopher Smart as a Poet of His Time: A Re-Appraisal*, The Hague: Mouton, 1966
Davie, Donald, *The Eighteenth-Century Hymn in England*, Cambridge: Cambridge University Press, 1993
Dearnley, Moira, *The Poetry of Christopher Smart*, London: Routledge & Kegan Paul, 1968
Grigson, Geoffrey, *Christopher Smart*, London: Longmans, Green & Co., 1961
Guest, Harriet, *A Form of Sound Words: The Religious Poetry of Christopher Smart*, Oxford: Clarendon Press, 1989; New York: Oxford University Press, 1989
Sherbo, Arthur, *Christopher Smart: Scholar of the University*, East Lansing: Michigan State University Press, 1967
Spacks, Patricia Meyer, *The Poetry of Vision: Five Eighteenth-Century Poets*, Cambridge, Massachusetts: Harvard University Press, 1967

"I have seen his Song to David & from thence conclude him as mad as ever", wrote William Mason to Thomas Gray in 1763. Critical response to Smart's poetry, even when less stupid than Mason's, has consistently been dominated by the question of insanity. Smart's own nephew Christopher Hunter omitted much of his uncle's unconventional later work from the collected *Poems* of 1791, lamenting that it bore "for the most part melancholy proofs of the recent estrangement of his mind". A century later the *Athenaeum* for 19 February 1887 made lurid speculations about poetry "scratched . . . on the wall of a madhouse by a madman during a lucid interval", and in 1939 William Force Stead did little to dispel romantic myths of this kind when publishing his otherwise scholarly edition of Smart's masterpiece, *Jubilate Agno*, under the sensationalist (and inaccurate) title *Rejoice in the Lamb: A Song from Bedlam*.

It is only in relatively recent years that serious efforts have been made to define the critical debate in less narrow and debilitating terms. Stimulated perhaps by the eminent poet and critic Donald Davie's much-quoted suggestion (in his anthology of 1958, *The Late Augustans*) that Smart might well be thought "the greatest English poet between Pope and Wordsworth", a clutch of important studies appeared in the 1960s.

GRIGSON's pamphlet in the "Writers and Their Work" series elegantly combines the business of biographical and critical introduction, and his study is distinguished throughout by a poet's sensitivity to the nuances of Smart's imagery and verse. For Grigson, Smart is emphatically a poet of nature and local environment, whose terse writing works with unrivalled precision "to combine and condense a lifetime of sensory impact".

SHERBO's book remains the standard biography of Smart, and its painstaking reconstruction of the literary and intellectual contexts in which Smart lived and wrote has done much to prepare the ground for critics prepared to read the poems as more than some mere matter of divinely inspired derangement.

BLAYDES and DEARNLEY set themselves broadly comparable tasks, each being concerned to survey the main phases of Smart's poetic activity and to relate his work to the generic conditions and expectations of the period in which it was written. Dearnley's is the more ambitious, substantial and scholarly work, and the limited space her book allows to *Jubilate Agno* leaves room for some worthwhile close readings of lesser-known texts, as well as a wealth of contextual information. Blaydes has a much narrower range of reference, but her opening chapter remains a useful survey of Smart's critical reputation in the eighteenth and nineteenth centuries.

By far the liveliest criticism of the period is to be found in the two chapters devoted to Smart by SPACKS. Concerned above all with the play of imagery, and with the relationship in imagery between the visual and the visionary, Spacks is a brilliant illuminator of detail. She credits Smart with:

> . . . a special mode of "seeing," a unique form of perception which depends heavily on the establishment of such intricate connects and contrasts as those in the line touched on above ["For in my nature I quested for beauty, but God, God hath sent me to sea for pearls", *Jubilate Agno*]. Directed simultaneously outward and inward, it evaluates all perception and knowledge of the outside world against the poet's personal intuitions, and validates those intuitions by reference to their universality of implication.

A more recent stimulus has been provided by Karina Williamson's and Marcus Walsh's five-volume Oxford edition of Smart's poetry, and it is to be hoped that Smart will now receive the full and close attention he deserves. Criticism of his work was largely confined to articles in books and journals throughout the 1970s and 1980s, but GUEST's important study of 1989 is a welcome exception. Approaching Smart above all as a religious poet, Guest devotes three substantial chapters to *Jubilate Agno*, illuminating this enigmatic work with convincing reference to the theological, linguistic, and scientific speculations of its author. "*Jubilate Agno* is so unlike anything else written in the eighteenth century", she writes, that "critics, baffled by the strangeness of the text, have frequently tried to make sense of it by treating it as though it were part of the literature of the seventeenth century, or of the Romantic period, or, more simply, by treating it as an aberration occasioned by Smart's mental ill-health". No doubt her own reading of Smart will fail to prevent further evasions of this kind, but she constructs a formidable obstacle in their way.

Guest is also unusual in paying serious attention to Smart's Seatonian Prize poems of the 1750s, and she reanimates what had threatened to become a tired cliché of Smart studies – his reworking of techniques and conventions from Old Testament verse under the influence of Robert Lowth's *Lectures on the Sacred Poetry of the Hebrews* (1753). DAVIE too continues to emphasise Smart's character as a religious poet, and his chapters on "Christopher Smart and English Rococo" and "Smart's Elegance" make an eloquent case (with tactfully handled reference to niceties of theology and prosody) for Smart's virtuosity as a hymnodist.

TOM KEYMER

Smollett, Tobias 1721–1771

Scottish novelist and essayis

Bold, Alan (ed.), *Smollett: Author of the First Distinction*, Totowa: Barnes & Noble, 1982; London: Vision Press, 1982

Boucé, Paul-Gabriel, *The Novels of Tobias Smollett*, translated by Antonia White, London: Longman, 1976

Grant, Damian, *Tobias Smollett: A Study in Style*, Manchester: Manchester University Press, 1977; Totowa, New Jersey: Rowman & Littlefield, 1977

Kelly, Lionel, *Tobias Smollett: The Critical Heritage*, London: Routledge & Kegan Paul, 1987

Martz, Louis L., *The Later Career of Tobias Smollett*, New Haven, Connecticut: Yale University Press, 1942

Rousseau, G.S., *Tobias Smollett: Essays of Two Decades*, Edinburgh: T. & T. Clark, 1982

Rousseau, G.S., and P.G. Boucé (eds.), *Tobias Smollett: Bicentennial Essays Presented to Lewis M. Knapp*, New York: Oxford University Press, 1971

Sekora, John, *Luxury: The Concept in Western Thought, Eden to Smollett*, Baltimore: Johns Hopkins University Press, 1977

Spector, Robert D., *Tobias George Smollett*, Boston: Twayne, 1968, revised 1989

Discussing *Roderick Random* and *Humphry Clinker* in his study *Devolving English Literature* (Oxford: Clarendon Press, 1992), Robert Crawford finds the major English novels of the eighteenth century reluctant to pursue "any profound confrontation with the issue of being British as opposed to English", and credits Smollett by contrast as pioneer of "the British novel". If Daniel Defoe or Samuel Richardson confronted such issues, certainly, they did so more as author (or in Richardson's case, reviser) of *A Tour thro' the Whole Island of Great Britain* (1724–26) than in their capacities as novelists, while Smollett's intertwined allegiances as Scot, Londoner, and Briton impelled him to develop a kind of fiction uniquely attuned to the varieties and development of Britishness in the decades that followed the political Union of 1707.

Yet Smollett's Scottishness is all too often neglected in criticism, and it is for this reason that MARTZ remains an instructive source. Particularly useful is his reading of *Humphry Clinker*'s celebrations of national heterogeneity and national union in relation to Smollett's political journalism in *The Briton* (1762–63), and his remarkable but widely overlooked accounts of Scotland and England in *The Present State of All Nations* (1768–69). SEKORA uses some of these same sources to read *Humphry Clinker* as a warning, in the monitory traditions of Tory satire, about degeneration and enfeeblement arising (as Smollett's narrator Matthew Bramble puts it) "from the general tide of luxury, which hath overspread the nation, and swept away all, even the very dregs of the people".

The standard work of general criticism on Smollett remains BOUCÉ's compendious 1976 study, which abridges his earlier *Les Romans de Smollett* (Paris: Didier, 1971). Boucé begins with a useful biographical sketch and a chapter on disguised autobiography in the novels; then follow detailed and accomplished close readings of the novels, and a survey of literary devices. Aiming above all to rescue Smollett from the shadow of Henry Fielding, and from "his (largely undeserved) reputation as a careless, slapdash and even somewhat coarsely licentious novelist", Boucé does the job thoroughly and for the most part convincingly (though Smollett's brilliant coarseness is perhaps better relished than explained away). Necessarily the emphasis here is on formal analysis, but Boucé remains alert to thematic patterns as well, and like Sekora he describes a novelist "situated, on the historical and literary planes, at the crossroads of two cultures: that of a still rural society which is dying and that of a preindustrial society which is in the process of being born".

Missing from the English version of Boucé's book is his original chapter on "Aspects stylistiques", but readers may turn for such aspects to GRANT's elegant study. Taking issue with the moral and formal approaches predominant in earlier readings, Grant acts skilfully on his conviction that "only that criticism which is founded in criticism of style will ever be able to perceive the real value of Smollett as a writer". His attention to the playfulness, energy, and indeed licentiousness of Smollett's prose does much (as Grant proposes):

> ... to replace the conventional idea of Smollett as narrator, journalist, or whatever other inferior category, with a truer idea which will represent him as sharing in the same linguistic element with Jonson and Shakespeare, with Swift and Sterne, with Dickens and Joyce; with all those writers who have been glad guests at the "feast of languages", all those who have lived long, and luxuriously, on the "alms-basket of words".

What remains to be written is a study combining this alertness to the creative havoc of Smollett's language with attention to the pressing questions of social, national, and political order that animated his writing, and in light of which his most ingenious and disruptive linguistic practices will come to seem a matter of so much more than merely play.

More recent work has moved in the direction of historical contextualisation (a process likely to be assisted further as the standard Georgia Edition of the Works of Smollett continues to appear). Here SPECTOR usefully updates his original Twayne study of 1968 with expanded reference to Smollett's political, historical, and journalistic writing; the book as a whole represents the most extended and persuasive account available of Smollett as a consistently picaresque writer. The "essays of two decades" collected in ROUSSEAU's 1982 book trace a wealth of connections between the novels and various phenomena in eighteenth-century culture and society, and even the most inauspicious of these turns out to be illuminating. KELLY provides an invaluable collection of early responses to Smollett, from the earliest reception of *Roderick Random* to the reflections of his two great nineteenth-century heirs, Sir Walter Scott and Charles Dickens.

Two collections of essays are worth mentioning. ROUSSEAU and BOUCÉ's *Festschrift* for Smollett's biographer Lewis M. Knapp has useful readings of individual novels, as well as broader essays on caricature, travel, picaresque, and narrative structure. BOLD's more recent collection is a similar mixture of the general and the particular, with lively and accessible readings by Damian Grant of *Roderick Random*, Ian Campbell Ross of *Peregrine Pickle*, John Valdimir Price of *Sir Launcelot Greaves*, and R.D.S. Jack of *Humphry Clinker*.

TOM KEYMER

The Sonnet

Cruttwell, Patrick, *The English Sonnet*, London: Longman, 1966
Fuller, John, *The Sonnet*, London: Methuen, 1972
Fussell, Paul, *Poetic Meter and Poetic Form*, New York: Random House, 1965, revised 1979
Kallich, Martin, Jack C. Gray, and Robert M. Rodney (eds.), *A Book of the Sonnet: Poems and Criticism*, New York: Twayne, 1973
Lever, J.W., *The Elizabethan Love Sonnet*, London: Methuen, 1956, 2nd edition, 1966
Spiller, Michael R.G., *The Development of the Sonnet: An Introduction*, London and New York: Routledge, 1992

"Literary forms are often queerly enduring", Cruttwell writes at the end of his brief account of the sonnet in English; and the durability of this form in English poetry has been remarkable. Nonetheless, most criticism concerned with the sonnet tends to confine itself to the period from Sir Thomas Wyatt, who introduced the form into English verse at the time of Henry VIII, to John Milton. Accounts of the post-Milton sonnet are fragmentary and less then exhaustive.

Chapter 7 of FUSSELL's book provides a good technical account of the two basic forms of the sonnet – Italian/ Petrarchan and English/Shakespearean. He demonstrates unfussily the options that the form affords to, and the demands that it makes on, the writer, and his examples are interestingly chosen and illuminatingly discussed.

LEVER wrote his book in a climate where he felt that "the late-romantic antipathy to form and convention" had militated against full critical appreciation of the sonnet, with its values of technical constraint and observation of tradition. He aimed to track the integration of individuality and tradition in the work of the Tudor sonneteers, suggesting how poets adapted the form to their individual temperaments and to the sensibility of sixteenth-century England. His work is scholarly and closely argued, often involving detailed critical comparisons of English sonnets and their Italian and French models, and at its best it recovers the qualities of voice, wit, and allusiveness in individual poems and poets, vindicating the sonnet as a vehicle for individuality and even idiosyncracy. Specialists in the period may be less comfortable with his more generalising tendencies in respect of "the age" and "the English imagination" which beg too many questions. It remains, nonetheless, and not undeservedly, the standard book on the subject.

Of the two short surveys by Cruttwell and Fuller, Fuller's is the better and more thorough. CRUTTWELL spends half of his 50 pages going over the ground covered by Lever. His tendency to quote poems whole limits what he is able to say about them, but he may therein provide the non-specialist with a flavour of the Elizabethan sonneteers in a form more accessible than that provided by Lever. His account of later sonnet writing is inevitably extremely selective, but incorporates mention of the principal sonnet writers of the Romantic and Victorian periods, including a separate section on Gerard Manley Hopkins, which quotes admiringly but does little else. His account of twentieth-century sonnet writing lugubriously and misguidedly presumes that the sonnet is a "doomed" form (for which he appears to blame, in part, Rupert Brooke and in part modernism) and singles out W.H. Auden as the "only ... distinguished living poet who has made anything of the form". FULLER's deft study for the "Critical Idiom" series, on the contrary, ends by asserting that "the sonnet is alive and possible", and his account therefore discusses the sonnet as a vigorous, living form and is less in the nature of a memorial to past glories. Although historically aware, it is not just a historical narrative, but in its four chapters – on the Italian form of the sonnet, on the English form, on "Variants and Curiosities", and on "Sequences" – ranges broadly and stimulatingly across 450 years of sonnet writing, showing a good awareness of, and a partiality for, twentieth-century sonnets.

The compilation by KALLICH, GRAY, and RODNEY is useful on two counts: as an anthology of sonnets from Wyatt to the present (or at least to 1973) – although as such it is not as extensive as that provided, for example, by Robert Nye's *The Book of Sonnets* published by Faber – and as an extensive anthology of sonnet criticism from the Elizabethan period to about 1960. It also has an extensive bibliography. The anthology of poems is particularly interesting for its fourth section, "The Sonnet in America". The book does not itself contribute to debates about, or our understanding of, the sonnet, but can be recommended as providing broad and rapid access to the traditions of sonnet writing and writing about the sonnet.

SPILLER's account of the development of the sonnet ends at Milton, which can be thought of as the cessation of its development only if one takes a purist view of the matter and regards everything subsequent as being either bastardised or retrograde. On the other hand, he provides the most interesting and exhaustive account of how the sonnet as a form and idiom was transmitted and modified from its earliest origins to its arrival in England. There are careful and informative accounts of the pre-Petrarchan sonnet as well as of Dante and Petrarch, before chapters on Wyatt and the Earl of Surrey, on Philip Sidney, Edmund Spenser, Shakespeare, and on William Drummond and Milton. Spiller is extremely alert to technical detail, to the choices poets make about rhyme-scheme and rhetorical division and the consequences of those choices. There *is* a kind of purism at work in his account: he argues that Milton's formalism, and his re-voicing of eloquence and desire, which he sees as being "the essentials" of the European sonnet, mark simultaneously the end of a great tradition and a reassertion of its earliest imperatives. The book is illuminated by some fine close reading and by an impressive breadth of scholarship, but we still lack any account of the development of the English sonnet from the mid-seventeenth century to the present day.

DAVID BLAIR

South African Literature: General

Adey, David, Ridley Beeton, Michael Chapman, and Ernest Pereira, *Companion to South African English Literature*, Craighall: Ad Donker, 1986

Barnett, Ursula, *A Vision of Order: A Study of Black South African Literature in English (1914–1980)*, London: Sinclair Browne, 1983; Amherst: University of Massachusetts Press, 1983; Cape Town: Maskew Miller/Longman, 1983

Chapman, Michael, *Southern African Literatures*, London: Longman, forthcoming (1996)

Gray, Stephen, *Southern African Literature: An Introduction*, Cape Town: David Philip, 1979; London: Rex Collings, 1979; New York: Barnes & Noble, 1979

Miller, G.M., and Howard Sergeant, *Critical Survey of South African Poetry in English*, Cape Town: Balkema, 1957; Norwood, Pennsylvania: Norwood Editions, 1977

Nathan, Manfred, *South African Literature: A General Survey*, Cape Town: Juta, 1925

National English Literary Museum, *A Bibliography of South African Literature in English* [*ABSALE*], Grahamstown: forthcoming

Snyman, J.P.L., *Achievement of the South African Novel in English (1880–1930): A Critical Study*, Potchefstroom: Potchefstroom University of Christian Higher Education, 1952

Van Wyk Smith, Malvern, *Grounds of Contest: A Survey of South African English Literature*, Kenwyn: Juta, 1990

South African Library, *A South African Bibliography to the Year 1925*, 5 vols., London: Mansell, 1979–91 (revision and continuation of *South African Bibliography*, by Sidney Mendelssohn, 1910)

The world reputation of South African writing since World War II rests largely on the achievements of a handful of white novelists – Alan Paton, Nadine Gordimer, Wilbur Smith, André Brink, and J.M. Coetzee. Within South Africa there is a growing consciousness of the early roots and long continuities of the country's literature, but the popular and the academic versions (not necessarily coterminous with ethnic or linguistic categories) of tradition and practice are not identical.

Recent social and political history has changed both South Africans' own and the world's view of their history and culture, and the result has been lively debate at many levels of public life. Not much of the knowledge thus produced, however, has entered the kind of publication which can help the common international reader: polemic tends to generate opinion rather than information. In terms of the cartographical metaphor which many handbooks deploy, most South African guides offer route maps rather than overall charts and gazeteers, although there are some recent signs of progress.

NATHAN's survey covers all kinds of writing, including early travel journals (and the beginnings of Afrikaans literature), and is a guide to otherwise forgotten writers, particularly the early novelists. Some measure of his book's achievement is suggested by the fact that nothing comparable was attempted for over 50 years. By the time SNYMAN undertook his work, Peter Abrahams, Gordimer, Paton, and Daphne Rooke had all begun their writing careers. His critical study's account of only the first 50 years of the South African novel in English (Olive Schreiner's *The Story of an African Farm* was first published in 1883) offers an extensive bibliography, and within the limits of a New-Critical approach, a judicious guide. Nothing else covers the South African colonial novel in English so fully. Roy Campbell (1903–57) remains the most widely known South African poet (until, perhaps, Breyten Breytenbach), but South African literature in English is said to have begun with the work of a poet (Thomas Pringle, 1789–1834). MILLER and SERGEANT's critical survey was a belated acknowledgement of that continuity, and is still useful as survey, rather more than for its critical insight.

GRAY's introduction is based on the metaphor of Southern African literature as an archipelago, the islands representing so many separate cultural and linguistic enclaves, driven apart by the continental drift of race and history. Gray deals with the subject under the headings of various "myths" and *topoi*, such as "The White Man's Creation Myth of Africa" and "The Frontier Myth and the Hottentot Eve", isolating such typical figures as the traveller (real and imaginary) and the colonial hunter. The last two chapters focus on the novel tradition (initiated by Olive Schreiner) and the topic that has radically changed the substance and perception of South African literature, "The Emergence of Black English". The book includes very useful "Notes on Some Authors" and a well organized bibliography.

The 1970s in South Africa were the decade of "Soweto", a historical moment which found voice in the work of poets like Oswald Mtshali, Sipho Sepamla, and Mongane Serote. BARNETT's book is partly an acknowledgement of the cultural energy of black consciousness, which both generated new writing and led readers to discover a tradition of South African black writing that goes back into the early twentieth century. Among the writers dealt with here, who have probably not yet reached the international readership they deserve, are Sol Plaatje (1875–1932) and H.I.E. Dhlomo (1903–56). The study is organized into chapters covering poetry, novels, short stories, autobiography, drama, and critical writing. The bibliography (arranged in the same way) is particularly useful and deals in addition with secondary works of interpretation and history.

The maturing of both South African English literature and its readership is acknowledged in ADEY *et al.*'s alphabetically organized encyclopaedia of the subject. Although naturally subject to limitations of space and selection, the coverage is wide, and the editors have clearly attempted to offer information rather than interpretation. Most entries are devoted to individual authors, but there are substantial entries on topics such as "African-Language and Afrikaans Literatures", "Anthologies", "Bibliographies", and "Children's Literature". The *Companion* is notable for its coverage of poetry, giving a South African perspective on such contemporaries as Mazisi Kunene (1930 –) and Douglas Livingstone (1932–).

A particularly South African perspective is developed in the historical thesis of VAN WYK SMITH's survey, which takes "the dialectics of appropriation and renunciation of the land itself as both the ruling theme and metaphor" of the country's literature in English. The five chapters – "Origins and Frontiers", "Coming of Age: the Early Twentieth Century", "A World Apart: 1948 and After", "The Legacy of Sharpeville:

Writing Black Resistance", and "Possibilities Now" – move from the colonial period to the late 1980s. The bibliography is sensibly and sensitively directed towards the general reader, concentrating on anthologies and critical studies "still readily available" at the time of publication.

CHAPMAN's should prove to be the most ambitious work yet in this field, attempting a regional history of the national literatures of Southern Africa, including African vernacular languages and the Portuguese writing of Angola and Mozambique. It will incorporate some of the new perspectives that have been possible since February 1990.

Several useful bibliographical and reference sources are important for the student of South African literature. The South African Library *Bibliography* covers all kinds of writings about, and from, the region, but the individual reader will need to have some knowledge of the field to use it most profitably. The National English Literary Museum [NELM] bibliography, while concerned only with "literature", will nonetheless be extensive, perhaps beyond the knowledge of any individual reader. *The Journal of Commonwealth Literature* has included South Africa in its annual bibliographies and continues to do so. Since 1989, the journal *Current Writing* (University of Natal, Durban) has reviewed South African publications comprehensively. The National English Literary Museum has, since 1991, published an annual *Select Index to South African Literature*, the most recent issue, covering 1993, having appeared in 1994. This excellent work of reference is carefully organized, covering both books and items in periodicals, under generic headings, and including children's literature.

TONY VOSS

South African Literature: Black Writers

Alvarez-Pereyre, Jacques, *The Poetry of Commitment in South Africa*, translated by Clive Wake, London: Heinemann, 1984

Barnett, Ursula A., *A Vision of Order: A Study of Black South African Literature in English (1914–1980)*, London: Sinclair Browne, 1983; Amherst: University of Massachusetts Press, 1983; Cape Town: Maskew Miller/Longman, 1983

Christie, Sarah, Geoffrey Hutchings, and Don Maclennan, *Perspectives on South African Literature*, Johannesburg: Ad Donker, 1980

Horn, Peter, *Writing My Reading: Essays on Literary Politics in South Africa*, Amsterdam: Rodopi, 1994

Parker, Kenneth (ed.), *The South African Novel in English: Essays in Criticism and Society*, London: Macmillan, 1978; New York: Africana, 1978

Shava, Piniel Viriri, *A People's Voice: Black South African Writing in the Twentieth Century*, London: Zed Books, 1989; Athens: Ohio University Press, 1989

Watts, Jane, *Black Writers from South Africa: Towards a Discourse of Liberation*, London: Macmillan/St Anthony's College, Oxford, 1989; New York: St Martin's Press, 1989

White, Landeg, and Tim Couzens (eds.), *Literature and Society in South Africa*, London: Longman, 1984

Black South African literature started receiving dedicated critical attention only in the last two decades. Early critical works tended to include a sprinkling of black writers, usually selected from the famous quartet of Sol T. Plaatje, Ezekiel Mphahlele, Peter Abrahams, and Alex La Guma, in anthologies of European writing. In book-length studies, much attention has been paid to historical and thematic studies, reflecting various ideological convictions.

PARKER's anthology of nine essays includes three on black writers: Tim Couzens's "Sol Plaatje's *Mhudi*", which reassesses Plaatje's novel against early European ethnocentric perceptions; an extract from Michael Wade's 1972 book on Peter Abrahams, and an adaptation of a section from Wade's doctoral thesis. Similarly, CHRISTIE, HUTCHINGS, and MACLENNAN include the work of Plaatje and Mphahlele in their study of 14 white writers. These essays, designed for a student readership, offer brief thematic summaries supported with ample excerpts and brief comments on technique. The discussion of Mphahlele's *Down Second Avenue* particularly suffers from being approached through James Olney's poor anthropological work, *Tell Me Africa* (1973).

WHITE and COUZENS have edited a selection of essays originating in papers presented at a 1981 conference on literature and society in southern Africa. Besides the excellent Introduction, which offers a penetrating assessment of the contexts, problems, and development of South African literatures, eight of the 12 essays are primarily concerned with various aspects of black South African literature. Some of these are surveys of specific patterns or developments, like Tim Couzens's study of the beginnings of black written literature in "Widening Horizons of African Literature, 1870–1900", Ian Steadman's survey of the emergence of protest theatre in "Alternative Theatre: Fifty Years of Performance in Johannesburg", and Michael Vaughan's "*Staffrider* [journal] and Directions within Contemporary South African Literature". Other contributors are Leroy Vail and Landeg White, Jeff Opland, Janet Hodgson, and Mbulelo Vizikhungo Mzamane, the only black contributor to the anthology. Brian Willan's essay highlights Plaatje's lifelong struggle to promote his people's literature, even by translating great foreign works, notably Shakespeare's plays, into Tswana.

BARNETT's work is a ground-breaking study of over half a century of black South African writing, with a chapter dedicated to each of the major genres as well as to autobiographical writing and criticism. Barnett's focus is on the different genres that have developed within the peculiar circumstances of South Africa, and the authors and texts that have played pivotal roles. All these factors are insightfully analysed and evaluated. In dealing with poetry, the novel, the short story, autobiography, drama, and critical writing, Barnett regularly asks why each form began (or failed) to flourish at a particular time.

The 1980s saw the adoption of increasingly ideological approaches. SHAVA explores the varieties of ideological commitment in the literature created between 1916 and the 1980s. The first of Shava's seven chapters discusses literary responses to such developments as Boer expansion, industrialisation, urbanisation, and the emergence of a black proletariat. Subsequent chapters explore: the significance of exile and autobiographical writing in mid-century; the relationship between prison literature and the politics of non-violence; the significance of the failure of liberal politics; and the effects of the Sharpeville Massacre of 1960 and the Soweto Massacre of 1976, with the emergence and transformative effect of the Black Consciousness Movement. In exploring these familiar issues, Shava exposes several unfamiliar dimensions. The exploration of popular theatre in the particularly volatile 1970s (Chapter 6) is one of the few original reassessments of the activities of the famous Ipi Tombi dance troupe, which toured Africa during that decade.

ALVAREZ-PEREYRE's book is an important reminder that "white" does not necessarily mean "racist", as the post-Sharpeville activities of certain white liberals show. Alvarez-Pereyre persuasively argues that many showed such will, hence in black South African committed poetry's efforts to inform, accuse, and exhort, "it has enjoyed the by no means fortuitous support of committed white poetry". The study of the emergence and forms of commitment is organised in three parts, of which Part One examines the sociological context of the literature, while Part Two examines the works of liberal white writers. Part Three, "The Black Poets and the Struggle for Power", occupies roughly half of the book and explores the development of black poetry in the context of the radicalisation of the black majority.

WATT examines the process by which black South African writers have constructed an appropriate language, style, form, and ideology through which ordinary people can understand their history and "recognise the mechanical structures of their oppression". She identifies a movement from protest literature addressing an essentially European audience to *engagé* literature generated by an activist consciousness. This is traced across the careers of individual writers like Mphahlele and Mongane Serote, and literary tendencies like autobiographical writings and the "Literature of Combat". A careful balance of theory and criticism lends much cogency to Watt's argument and conclusions.

HORN's book comprises essays written over a 20-year period, comprising his own "interventions in various debates on South African Literature" in the 1970s and 1980s. In a startling metaphor of the cage that seeks out the bird, Horn's opening essay, "Privacy, Fantasy and Politics", sets out his dominant concern with how writers could "insert themselves into a political process" and align their work with the masses' struggle to bend the bars of the cage. Direct discussion of literature by black South Africans begins in Chapter 6, with an examination of poetry in a racist society, while Chapter 7 demonstrates how the oral tradition of praise poetry, *izibongo*, has been reactivated to serve the cause of liberation. Whether Horn is discussing the poetry of Serote, Mzwakhe Mbuli, or Jeremy Cronin, or discoursing on the necessity of a people's culture, his arguments and analyses offer strong challenges to the more stagnant ways of responding to the South African situation.

CHIDI OKONKWO

Southern United States Literature: General

Bain, Robert, Joseph M. Flora, and Louis D. Rubin, Jr. (eds), *Southern Writers: A Biographical Dictionary*, Baton Rouge: Louisiana State University Press, 1979
Bain, Robert, and Joseph M. Flora (eds.), *Fifty Southern Writers Before 1900: A Bio-Bibliographical Sourcebook*, Westport, Connecticut: Greenwood Press, 1987
Bain, Robert, and Joseph M. Flora (eds), *Contemporary Poets, Dramatists, Essayists, and Novelists of the South: A Bio-Bibliographical Sourcebook*, Westport, Connecticut: Greenwood Press, 1994
Flora, Joseph M., and Robert Bain (eds.), *Fifty Southern Writers after 1900: A Bio-Bibliographical Sourcebook*, Westport, Connecticut: Greenwood Press, 1987
Flora, Joseph M., and Robert Bain (eds.), *Contemporary Fiction Writers of the South: A Bio-Bibliographical Sourcebook*, Westport, Connecticut: Greenwood Press, 1993
Gray, Richard, *Writing the South: Ideas of an American Region*, Cambridge and New York: Cambridge University Press, 1986
Hobson, Fred, *The Southern Writer in the Postmodern World*, Athens: University of Georgia Press, 1991
Ketchin, Susan, *The Christ-Haunted Landscape*, Jackson: University Press of Mississippi, 1994
Rubin, Louis D., Jr. (general ed.), *History of Southern Literature*, Baton Rouge: Louisiana State University Press, 1985

Southern literature has received more scholarly criticism since the mid-twentieth century, and thus has a broad corpus of readily available biographical, bibliographical, and thematic reference material. Though there now are other more recent biographical studies, which also include bibliographical material, BAIN, FLORA, and RUBIN's 1979 *Biographical Dictionary* is still a convenient source for a brief review of biographical material on 379 Southern authors by 172 scholars.

RUBIN, the general editor, along with four senior editors, divides his 1985 *History of Southern Literature* into four periods. Part I, 1607–1860, examines the writings of this early period, when the idea of the separateness of Southern literature from American literature first emerged. Part II, 1861–1920, includes discussions of the diverse group of local-color writers, as well as others such as Kate Chopin and Mark Twain. Part III, 1920–50, the period labeled the "Southern Renascence", discusses the prolific, critically acclaimed time when writers such as William Faulkner, Eudora Welty, Robert Penn Warren, and Thomas Wolfe emerged from their native South to become some of America's most prominent writers. The final period, 1951–82, examines the work of such authors as William Styron, Carson McCullers, Flannery O'Connor, and Ernest J. Gaines, who were writing in an integrated, radically different South. Yet, as Rubin notes in his Introduction to this period, these and others writers "continued to draw on the life of their native region in ways that, however informed by the individual imagination, involved pervasive elements of continuity in form, theme, and language". There is no bibliography of available scholarship in this volume, though such was planned. However, Thomas Inge's essay on the study of Southern literature, offered as Appendix A, is a helpful guide for nineteenth- and twentieth-century criticism up to the early 1980s.

Bain and Flora's four volumes are bio-bibliographical sourcebooks, which are invaluable library holdings for Southern literature scholars.

In selecting *Fifty Southern Writers Before 1900* BAIN and FLORA (1987) state that they focused mainly on nineteenth-century writers whose works "give a sense of the long background behind the Southern Renascence". Diverse, often less well-known, writers such as Mary Boykin Chesnut, Sidney Lanier, Robert Mumford, as well as major authors such as Edgar Allan Poe, Twain, Chopin, and Frederick Douglass are discussed in essays by a variety of scholars. These essays each contain a biographical sketch, a discussion of themes, an assessment of scholarship, a chronological list of the author's works, and a bibliography of selected criticism. This survey and the companion volume reviewing writers after 1900 are helpful complements to Rubin's 1985 history. The overview of FLORA and BAIN's *Fifty Southern Writers after 1900* (1987) follows the same model of five-part essays by different scholars on the selected writers. Renascence writers, as well as those of the post-Faulkner generation, continued to write literature with what Bain and Flora call "Southern regional peculiarities", but with "universal bones".

Two more sourcebooks – *Contemporary Fiction Writers of the South* (FLORA and BAIN, 1993) and *Contemporary Poets, Dramatists . . . of the South* (BAIN and FLORA, 1994) – broaden the coverage of contemporary writers, especially of those born in the 1930s and later, who were not included in their earlier selections. Flora and Bain noted in 1987 the difficulty of restricting their selection of new writers, since there continues to be a growing list of Southerners with regional and national reputations. These two recent volumes focus on 49 fiction writers in one (1993), and 50 poets, dramatists, essayists, and novelists in the other (1994). These writers represent a more diverse range in class, gender, and race than the Renascence authors, who were mainly upper- and upper-middle-class white males. In both volumes, Flora and Bain have used their five-part essay model, which includes useful bibliographies of selected criticism. Only Anne Tyler is included in both the earlier volume of *Writers after 1900* and in *Fiction Writers*. Material on others, such as Doris Betts, Harry Crews, and Reynolds Price, is updated in Appendix A. Some of the writers in *Contemporary Poets, Dramatists . . .* have not received much national attention, yet are establishing significant positions in contemporary Southern literature.

GRAY's study of Southern literature responds to the academic developments that, he says, call into question the identity of the South. There are historians who point out that the South is not significantly different from the rest of the country and sociologists who theorize that the area is so diverse that there is no one region of the South. Gray surmises that the South is "primarily a concept, a matter of knowing even more than being, and as such part of the currency of our language and perception". By examining the work of some Southerners, Gray establishes his theory that Southern writers have not been *writing about* the South so much as *writing* the South; that is, they have been "reimagining and remaking" the South as they see, describe, and experience it. Gray begins with the colonial period in Virginia, citing the works of the early pamphleteers and the writings of statesmen such as Thomas Jefferson. He then sustains his argument through the periods of the Old South, New South, and the South between the wars. Chapter 5 is on Faulkner, and the final chapter examines the region since World War II, particularly as evoked in the works of Eudora Welty and Walker Percy.

A number of recent studies examine the works of contemporary Southern writers from the point of view that the South is now radically different in many ways, but especially different from the racially segregated, agrarian world that Faulkner characters inhabit. HOBSON's study of the writer in the "postmodern" South mainly looks at the writings of Southerners born during or after World War II. Hobson examines how these new voices since the 1970s still, in his view, share those thematic "concerns with place, family, community, religion, and the past which have been central in the most notable southern fiction of the first three-quarters of this century". KETCHIN'S study, named after Flannery O'Connor's observation that the South is not so much Christ-centered as Christ-haunted, examines the work of 12 contemporary Southern writers through the themes of faith and doubt. Each writer is introduced and interviewed by Ketchin, and an excerpt of his or her work is included. Ketchin finds that religious faith and questions about religion remain viable issues in Southern literature in the latter part of the twentieth century.

GWEN MCNEILL ASHBURN

Southern United States Literature: 19th Century

Gaines, Francis Pendleton, *The Southern Plantation: A Study in the Development and the Accuracy of a Tradition*, New York: Columbia University Press, 1924

Gray, Richard, *Writing the South: Ideas of an American Region*, Cambridge and New York: Cambridge University Press, 1986

Gwin, Minrose C., *Black and White Women of the Old South: The Peculiar Sisterhood in American Literature*, Knoxville: University of Tennessee Press, 1985

Hubbell, Jay B., *The South in American Literature 1607–1900*, Durham, North Carolina: Duke University Press, 1954

Mixon, Wayne, *Southern Literature and the New South Movement, 1865–1913*, Chapel Hill: University of North Carolina Press, 1980

Moss, Elizabeth, *Domestic Novelists in the Old South: Defenders of Southern Culture*, Baton Rouge: Louisiana State University Press, 1992

Ridgely, J.V., *Nineteenth Century Southern Literature*, Lexington: University Press of Kentucky, 1980

Rubin, Louis D., Jr. (general ed.), *History of Southern Literature*, Baton Rouge: Louisiana State University Press, 1985

Most critics of Southern literature write off the nineteenth century as generally mediocre, and its brightest lights as Southern only by birth, not in sentiment or style. HUBBELL argues that the "Abolitionist conception of a semi-barbarous South" made for a neglect of Southern literature in the mid-nineteenth century, which in turn led to its overrating by Southern apologists. He himself lists only Edgar Allan Poe, Mark Twain, and Sidney Lanier as evidencing "genius". His study is nonetheless both monumental and comprehensive. He provides detail on large numbers of fairly obscure figures and on the context necessary for any literary scene, discussing education, libraries and literary magazines. His work has been echoed and elaborated on, both in the essays in the RUBIN collection, and by RIDGELY. These generally agree that it was Southern readers' reluctance to support their regional literature, either in magazine- or book-form, together with a conservative preference for neoclassical forms that stifled the chance of a truly vital Southern voice in this period. Gray, however, argues that the greatest achievements of Twain stem directly from his tackling of Southern issues, and his reworking of his Missouri childhood. Craig Werner's essay in the Rubin book also concedes that some of Poe's darkest fiction can be read as allegories of the guilt and fear that stem from slavery, and Gaines places a character in Poe's "The Gold Bug" within the conventions of Southern defences of slavery.

The literature of the Old South is generally taken to mean specifically writing from the region produced in the antebellum period, but it can sometimes refer to a particular literary construction of that era, which was often written later, and not necessarily in the South. GAINES identifies the literary idea of the Old South as preoccupied with a leisurely plantation-based aristocracy and perennially happy slaves. He unexpectedly attributes some of the origins of the myth to Northern abolitionist literature as well as to Southern patriots and slavery's apologists, as well as acknowledging the intensely romantic haze Southern writers applied to the period from the 1870s.

GRAY, too, attempts to trace an idea, or ideas, of the South in writing, but he is specifically concerned with Southerners, who were, he argues, "reimagining and remaking their place in the act of seeing and describing it". He argues that as well as the aristocratic ideal typified by the Virginia planter, the Old South was also imagined in terms of the earthy "Kentucky farmer", both ideas dating back to the early visions of colonial settlement, which saw either a transplanted feudal structure or else a "white democracy" of self-reliant yeomen. He traces these respectively in the Arcadian images of Southern life purveyed by plantation novelists like William Gilmore Simms, and in the work of the southwestern humorists, and even finds a curious amalgam of the competing myths in the Congressional speeches of John Calhoun.

GWIN stretches her definition of the Old South to include both such later writers as William Faulkner and Margaret Walker, and Northern fictionalisations of the South in the 1850s. Her book argues that slavery's troubled knot of race and gender relations fascinated not just those with direct experience, but also writers who lived far from it, or long after emancipation. She asserts that for all these writers the relationship of slavewoman and mistress offers a compelling dialectic of sisterhood and oppression, "a quivering tension of connection and rejection". MOSS also provides a feminist perspective, but her book deals with five antebellum Southern authors who, she argues, had a wide female readership in their own day and also influenced later, more radical, Southern women like Ellen Glasgow. Her book contends that Southern domestic fiction differed significantly from the Northern variety, in that it was especially concerned with the state of North-South relations. Whether they were conciliatory appeals for harmony or fiercely sectionalist attacks on things Northern, she argues that these novels, in their variety, "illuminate the elusive mind of the South". Gwin's and Moss's studies provide a useful balance to some earlier criticism, which was relatively inattentive both to women writers, and to the large body of writing by freed slaves – which could perhaps be called a Southern genre in its own right.

MIXON writes about the end of the century, but finds later writers still preoccupied with the concerns of their forerunners. He deals with the literary response to the New South Movement, in its combination of sectional reconciliation, racial conservatism, and the advocation of an industrialized economy. In his account, older writers like John Esten Cooke met the industrial ethic ambivalently, wrapped in a nostalgia for a Cavalier tradition. Others, like Thomas Dixon, did manage to incorporate a bourgeois ethic into their plantation myth, translating in the process the racial paternalism of an earlier age into virulent "negrophobia". Meanwhile, writers like Charles W. Chesnutt and George Washington Cable attacked the racial politics of the New South, as did Mark Twain, who yet hankered after "an idyll innocent of cotton mills and blast furnaces".

SARAH MEER

Southern United States Literature: 20th Century

Berry, J. Bill, (ed.), *Home Ground: Southern Autobiography*, Columbia: University of Missouri Press, 1991
Cowan, Louise, *The Fugitive Group: A Literary History*, Baton Rouge: Louisiana State University Press, 1959
Gosset, Louise Y., *Violence in Recent Southern Fiction*, Durham, North Carolina: Duke University Press, 1965
Gray, Richard, *The Literature of Memory: Modern Writers of the American South*, Baltimore: Johns Hopkins University Press, 1977; London: Edward Arnold, 1977
Harrison, Elizabeth Jane, *Female Pastoral: Women Writers Re-Visioning the American South*, Knoxville: University of Tennessee Press, 1991
Humphries, Jefferson (ed.), *Southern Literature and Literary Theory*, Athens: University of Georgia Press, 1990
MacKethan, Lucinda H., *Daughters of Time: Creating Woman's Voice in Southern Story*, Athens: University of Georgia Press, 1990

Rubin, Louis D., and Robert D. Jacobs (eds), *Southern Renascence: The Literature of the Modern South*, Baltimore: Johns Hopkins University Press, 1953

Rubin, Louis D., *A Gallery of Southerners*, Baton Rouge: Louisiana State University Press, 1982

Rubin, Louis D. (general ed.), *The History of Southern Literature*, Baton Rouge: Louisiana State University Press, 1985

Simpson, Lewis P., *The Fable of the Southern Writer*, Baton Rouge: Louisiana State University Press, 1994

Tate, Linda, *A Southern Weave of Women: Fiction of the Contemporary South*, Athens: University of Georgia Press, 1994

The American South has produced the largest collection of notable writers in twentieth-century American literature. Criticism of this literature often is an attempt to explain and/or define this phenomenon, particularly the writers of the "Southern Renaissance", or the period from 1920 to 1950. Until the last 20 years or so, the term "Southern writer" usually referred to the most renowned white authors of this period, such as William Faulkner, Robert Penn Warren, Allen Tate, and John Crowe Ransom. The idea of a definable Southern literature has become a more complex and more complete as the work of black men and white and black women has been included for study. The region's history and its cultural ties to storytelling figure prominently in much of the critical work on this literature.

RUBIN and JACOBS' 1953 book is the early, standard collection of essays, which defined and analyzed the Southern Renaissance. It exemplifies the New-Critical stance of the Agrarians, and is organized as a comprehensive attempt to define the term "Southern writer" and to discuss the works of those authors whose work reveals the theme of "The Mind of the South". Contributors include Andrew Lytle, C. Vann Woodward, and Donald Davidson. The book offers clear analyses of the elements thought to comprise Southern literature: involvement with the past, particularly the Civil War; struggles against industrialism; obsession with family and hierarchy; and belief in the value of community.

COWAN gives a thorough account of one of the South's most important contributions to twentieth-century literature. Because she had full access to the writers of the Fugitive Group, as well as to their papers, her book is a meticulous critical narrative of the formation of *The Fugitive*, and the beginnings of New-Critical theory and Agrarianism. In particular, the portraits of Warren, Tate, Davidson, and Ransom offer details that connect both their poetry and their ideas about poetry to their experiences as members of the New South's intelligentsia.

GOSSET takes up a standard element in Southern literature – physical and psychological violence – and reads it as a central rhetorical strategy in much of the mid-century literature. The book offers a broad, New-Critical assessment of violence as the preoccupation and impetus for a range of writers, including Faulkner, Flannery O'Connor, Thomas Wolfe, and Erskine Caldwell. For each writer, Gosset contends, violence is an inescapable cultural fact through which characters and authors search for "normal" lives.

GRAY offers a thorough critical account of the literature of the major writers of the Southern Renaissance. His premise, that these writers share a common history and social context, provides a rich and complicated backdrop for his narrative of the flowering of literary talent from the Nashville Agrarians to post-World-War-II writers such as William Styron and Carson McCullers. Chapter titles such as "The Good Farmer" and "Back to the Old Plantation" define and categorize the period and its writers. While helpful to readers of that literature, the organization of the book also serves to highlight the exclusion of any writer who does not share the dominant heritage, including all Southern African-Americans.

RUBIN (1982) revisits the work of Faulkner, Welty, Wolfe, and Tate, as well as that of McCullers and Shelby Foote, to reconsider the qualities that make each indisputably Southern. The book is a collection of occasional pieces, which reinscribe the values of community and place as defining forces in the fiction. Although Rubin laments the passing of the life commemorated in the above writers' works, he reiterates the potency of the South as an enduring, definable region of the United States.

RUBIN has also edited the standard and comprehensive history of Southern literature in his 1985 volume. Well over half of the book focuses on literature written from the turn of the century through writers of the early 1980s. In addition to the standard entries, articles on writers such as Ernest J. Gaines, James Agee, Gayl Jones, and A.R. Ammons give a fuller analysis of the wealth of fiction and poetry that continues to be produced in the South. The book is particularly useful in that it takes up many lesser-known writers, and places all of them in the social-historical contexts in which they wrote.

HUMPHRIES has compiled 20 essays by members of the "post-Rubin generation of southernists", who offer a range of readings that apply literary and cultural theory to many standard twentieth-century texts. Among them are a Marxist reading of Warren's *All the King's Men*, deconstructionist readings of African-American writers Zora Neale Hurston and Charles Chesnutt, and several Bakhtinian studies of Faulkner novels. Humphries accurately characterizes his volume as a representation of rich, new readings made possible by the various critical tools available to readers in the late twentieth century. Inclusion of criticism of African-American writers' contributions to the literature of the South gives significant depth to this study.

MacKETHAN gives a feminist reading of the traditional claim that storytelling is a cultural norm in the South. Her thesis, that Southern women write to establish their own voices against the pervasive patriarchal structure of Southern life, is developed using the works of Ellen Glasgow, Hurston, Alice Walker, and Eudora Welty. Some attention is also given to Harriet Jacobs and Catherine Hammond. The stated focus of the book is on those women "who have turned the father's house of fiction into mother's gardens of lifegiving, freedom-singing story".

HARRISON looks at the characteristic Southern sense of place as it is re-viewed by six women authors. In each case, Harrison finds that the women have abandoned the traditional female romance plot to fashion active female heroes involved first-hand with Nature and the land. In doing so, she contends, they revise the traditional male pastoral tradition and take their place among those male writers whom critics define as definitively Southern. Writers as diverse as Ellen Glasgow, Harriette Arnow, and Sherley Williams subvert prevailing literary models, the plantation romance, and local-color fiction to create strong women characters who are active, rather than passive, subjects.

BERRY's book illustrates the complexities of the claim that it is Southern writers' personal experiences with family and with the past that gives resonance to their work. He has compiled a series of essays that explore the ways in which the "artist-autobiography" defines what it means to be a Southerner, and a writer of fiction and of one's own life. The first section of the book offers three examples of autobiographical criticism, in essays about the fiction and poetry of Faulkner, Richard Wright, and Warren. The second section offers five essays on a wide range of autobiographies, including those of Maya Angelou, Russell Baker, Welty, and Caroline Gordon and Tate. Five personal narratives comprise the final section.

SIMPSON begins his analysis by connecting the sense of history in Tate, Faulkner, Warren, and Walker Percy to the legacy left to them by Thomas Jefferson and John Randolph, who justified the support of slavery in the South via the ideology of States' Rights. The book is an analysis of the tension between guilt over slavery and the desire of self-determination in selected works by the white male writers who continue to represent the apex of Southern writing. Expanding on previous work, Simpson contemplates the drama of the literary self in search of its historical identity. That drama is self-consciously white because, Simpson argues convincingly, the theoretical work on southern African-American literature must first be presented by African-American critics; his challenge is that the two bodies of writing then be looked at intertextually.

TATE exhibits little hesitation in placing the work of black and white women authors together. Early on, she places herself as the granddaughter of poor white women who challenged traditional notions of white Southern womanhood. She also establishes that it is her intention "to make room for difference" that explains her attention to "concerns, issues, and priorities that cut across racial, class, and subregional lines". In chapters entitled "Family, Home, and Healing in the Changing South", "Black and White Sisters", "New Views on Southern History", and "Voices on the Margins", Tate weaves a lively and innovative tapestry of diverse women writers who foreground "talk" as a central method of making connections between their own lives and their work, and between the characters they create and the history they live in. Among the writers discussed are Alice Walker, Bobbie Ann Mason, Paule Marshall, and Ellen Douglas.

JUDITH LOCKYER

Southey, Robert 1774–1843

English poet, novelist, essayist, and biographer

Carnall, Geoffrey, *Southey and His Age: The Development of a Conservative Mind*, Oxford: Clarendon Press, 1960
Curry, Kenneth, *Southey*, London: Routledge & Kegan Paul, 1975
Haller, William, *The Early Life of Robert Southey, 1774–1803*, New York: Columbia University Press, 1917; reprinted, New York: Octagon Books, 1966
Madden, Lionel (ed.), *Southey: The Critical Heritage*, London and Boston: Routledge & Kegan Paul, 1972
Simmons, Jack, *Southey*, London: Collins, 1945; New Haven, Connecticut: Yale University Press, 1948

Southey, the close friend of Wordsworth and Coleridge (with whom he is classified as a "Lake Poet"), is also one of the great letter-writers of the nineteenth century. Not surprisingly, then, most of the critical literature on him is largely biographical. In modern criticism his poetry is usually derided as emotionless and pedantic. Critics however grant him a high place in the development of English prose style and acknowledge his influence as a social and moral critic. Some of Southey's prose writings – especially his biography of Admiral Nelson, certain of his articles in the *Quarterly Review*, and the nursery tale "Goldilocks and the Three Bears" (which first saw light in Southey's *The Doctor*) – are classics. Early critics emphasize his strength in prose narrative and his lucid plain style. A number of recent scholars trace the influence of Southey's social criticism on later writers, such as Thomas Carlyle, John Ruskin, and William Morris.

HALLER provides a detailed biography of Southey's early years as a radical, enamoured of the French Revolution, and important information about his friendship with Coleridge. The book also contains a critical overview of his first successes as a periodical-writer and poet, plot summaries for *Joan of Arc* and *Thalaba*, and a description of early critical reaction. Haller's biographical conclusions, narrowly motivational and essentially pre-Freudian, are based on published sources that are sometimes unreliable, in particular two nineteenth-century selections of Southey's correspondence, edited by Cuthbert Southey and John Warter.

SIMMONS's standard biography bows in the direction of Haller by focusing only briefly on Southey's childhood and early friendships in favour of the middle and later years. The generation of each of the major poems and their narrative content are discussed in passing. The reception of Southey's major works in poetry and prose is dealt with in some detail. In an influential final chapter, Simmons argues for the pre-eminence of Southey's prose over his poetry. The poetry is said to lack imagination and intensity, defects Simmons explains as the result of two factors – the poet's distractedness in the face of pressing financial engagements, and an unwillingness, born of hypersensitivity, to give himself up fully to the muse. As for the prose, Simmons points out the modernity of Southey's plain style, his skill with narrative description, his dry humour, and his ability to draw character. Simmons makes use of fresh biographical material and his grasp of the contemporary cultural milieu is especially sound.

CARNALL's authoritative study of Southey's ideas concentrates on his prose. The essential unity of Southey's thought is demonstrated through unpublished primary material and a rhetorical analysis of Southey's periodical contributions, many of which are here identified as Southey's for the first time. In an appendix, Southey's religious opinions – hitherto ignored or at best misunderstood by scholars – are shown to have been central in the information of his social and political philosophy. Carnall accurately concludes that Southey's Romantic Conservative philosophy of social reform anticipated the great Victorian Tory reformist politicians Michael Sadler, Richard Oastler, and the Earl of Shaftesbury, and directly influenced their literary counterparts, Thomas Carlyle, Charles Dickens, and John Ruskin.

MADDEN's contribution to the well-known *Critical Heritage* series illustrates the reception of Southey's poetry and major prose through excerpts from contemporary reviews and the correspondence of prominent writers. In a valuable, lengthy Introduction, in headnotes to the excerpts, and through the selections themselves, Madden balances an interest in aesthetic and humanist dimensions of Southey's work with historicist and material ones.

CURRY's biography, one of the Routledge "Author Guides", is intended for "non-specialist readers, whether students or the interested general public". Simple and clear, it is also a significant contribution to Southey scholarship. The biographical first half of the book makes judicious use of wholly new materials gleaned from an exhaustive survey of Southey correspondence and that of his many close friends and professional associates. In his *New Letters of Robert Southey* (2 vols., 1965), in a series of bibliographical articles, which expand the canon of Southey's writings, and in this book, Curry argues for Southey's greatness as a letter-writer and essayist. He makes that argument here in two sections devoted to a comprehensive analysis of Southey's writings divided by genre. The first section deals with non-fictional prose and *The Doctor*, the second with poetry. Curry's analysis is necessarily sweeping – no more than a page or two is devoted to each of the major poems and works in prose. Context is emphasized, conditions of composition and publication are described, and reception is attended to. Analysis of the prose concentrates on content and argument. The relevance of contemporary issues that motivated Southey's occasional pieces is also explored. In his analysis of the poetry, Curry draws some attention to genre issues. Otherwise his discussion is qualitative, biographical, and structural. Consequently, in the light of modern literary theory, readers may find some of the book's conclusions simplistic and limiting.

JONATHAN CUTMORE

Soyinka, Wole 1934–

Nigerian dramatist, poet, novelist, and essayist

Adejare, Oluwole. *Language and Style in Soyinka: A Systemic Textlinguistic Study of a Literary Idiolect*, Ibadan: Heinemann, 1992

Adelugba, Dapo (ed.), *Before Our Very Eyes: Tribute to Wole Soyinka*, Ibadan: Spectrum Books, 1987

Gibbs, James, *Wole Soyinka*, London: Macmillan, 1986

Jones, Eldred D., *The Writing of Wole Soyinka*, London: Heinemann, 1973; revised 1983 and 1989

Katrak, Ketu H., *Wole Soyinka and Modern Tragedy: A Study of Dramatic Theory and Practice*, Westport, Connecticut: Greenwood Press, 1986

Maja-Pearce, Adewale (ed.), *Wole Soyinka: An Appraisal*, Oxford: Heinemann, 1994

Ogunba, Oyin, *The Movement of Transition: A Study of the Plays of Wole Soyinka*, Ibadan: Ibadan University Press, 1975

Ojaide, Tanure, *The Poetry of Wole Soyinka*, Lagos: Malthouse Press, 1994

Peters, Jonathan, *A Dance of Masks: Senghor, Achebe, Soyinka*, Washington, D.C.: Three Continents Press: 1978

A distinguished playwright, poet, novelist, essayist, social activist, and Nobel Laureate (1986), Wole Soyinka has generated enormous critical attention and ideological controversy since the 1960s. Early responses, like JONES's, were mainly thematic surveys of his work in various literary genres. With OGUNBA's work began critical concentration on particular genres. Ogunba's chronological approach, combining sensitive analyses of themes, stagecraft, and literary techniques in eight plays, identifies an unfolding pattern, which he terms "the movement of transition" (conceived as a society's progression "from the state of colonialism to a new age of political and cultural awareness"), through which he plausibly accounts for the recurrent symbolism of "the road" in Soyinka's work.

PETERS' comparative study of Soyinka with Léopold Senghor and Chinua Achebe provides rewarding insights into the theoretical and practical aspects of their exploitation of mask and dance metaphors to interpret socio-historical experience. Based on a study of four plays altogether, the Soyinka section discusses the centrality of such metaphors, and their relationship with the mystery of Ogun and the "symmetrically contoured self-devouring snake", in Soyinka's treatment of cycles of creation and destruction in human history.

Taking full account of Soyinka's "rootedness in Yoruba culture, cosmology, and world-view", KATRAK appropriately begins by scrutinising the Yoruba roots and Western derivations of Soyinka's tragic theory, particularly as enunciated in "The Fourth Stage" ("Yoruba Myth and 'The Fourth Stage': Soyinka, Nietzsche, and Brecht – A Paradigm for Yoruba Tragedy"). From theoretical frames established here, subsequent chapters explore the metaphysical, historical, and sociological dimensions of Soyinka's tragic vision under such themes as "Death and the Living Community", "Individual Will and Tragic Destiny", and "The Repetitiousness of History". Katrak's integration of these dimensions offers brilliant insights into the "communicant" function of individual heroism in Soyinkan tragedy.

GIBBS examines Soyinka's plays against the background of influences ranging from personal circumstances and Nigeria's violent political history to Yoruba cultural practices and Graeco-Asiatic myth and dramatic culture. The study classifies Soyinka's plays from his years in Leeds to the present, and gains considerably from Gibbs' practice of relating the plays to other aspects of Soyinka's work in theatre and academia, and to the main currents of Western drama.

The question of Soyinka's "obscurity" is engaged with ADEJARE's systemic textlinguistic study of the novels (Chapters 2 and 3), augmented with samples from Soyinka's drama in Chapter 4. By inconsistently applying his own three selection criteria, however, Adejare excludes Soyinka's poetry, which seriously needs this kind of study, while devoting a chapter to the linguistically uncomplicated novel *Season of Anomy*, which does not even meet the criteria. Despite occasional specialist terminology, the study falls within conventional evaluation of language in literary criticism; but the total achievement is uneven.

OJAIDE confronts the difficulty of Soyinka's poetry in six chronological main chapters of critical commentary. His analyses of morpho-syntactic features, like parallelism, are sometimes unsatisfactory, and he often substitutes vague generalisations for probing analysis, as in: "such words as 'mercuric', 'exacerbation', 'fluorescence', 'incessant', 'suffusion', and 'dappled' are difficult to comprehend. . . . But they are evocative – they suggest the beauty of the night". However, the work will be useful college students, and indeed reads like teaching notes expanded to book length.

Soyinka has attracted two *Festschrifts* in the past decade, edited by Dapo Adelugba and Adewale Maja-Pearce respectively. ADELUGBA's compilation originated in articles intended to honour Soyinka's 50th birthday in 1984, but was delayed in publication until after Soyinka won the Nobel Prize in 1986. It comprises 11 personal tributes and personality profiles in Part One, and eight critical appraisals in Part Two. The tributes in Part One furnish, from multiple perspectives, a composite portrait of Soyinka from his youth onwards. Of the critical essays, many are concerned, directly or indirectly, with the controversy over the social relevance of Soyinka's art. David Cook's "The Potentially Popular Playwright", Brian Crow's "Soyinka and the Romantic Tradition", D.S. Izevbaye's "Assets and Liabilities: Unlimited Liability Company as an Artist's Investment in the Popular Cause", and Dapo Adelugba's "'Yapping': A Form of Patriotism" all revisit this controversy, among other concerns, with the last two relating Soyinka's 1983 populist musical album "Unlimited Liability Company" to the totality of his art. Joel Adedeji's "Aesthetics of Soyinka's Theatre" traces the crucial influence of Yoruba dramatic culture on Soyinka's construction of dramatic action, themes, characters, and language. In "Down from the Abyss of Transition: Oral Tradition and the Creative Writer", Olabimpe Aboyade suggests that *Death and the King's Horseman* is effectively a dramatisation of Yoruba metaphysics, as Soyinka's Author's Note insists, and only indirectly concerned with cultural clash.

The *Festschrift* edited by MAJA-PEARCE opens with a reprint of Soyinka's 1986 Nobel Lecture, "This Past Must Address Its Present" (dedicated to Nelson Mandela), and concludes with the text of a wide-ranging 1993 interview between Soyinka and 'Biyi Bandele-Thomas. Of the nine main articles, Wilson Harris's "The Complexity of Freedom" reviews the significance of Soyinka's *The Road* "within the paradoxes of this late twentieth-century age", while Kwame Anthony Appiah challenges Soyinka's concept of a distinctively African cosmos in *Myth, Literature and the African World*. The perennial controversy over the relevance of Soyinka's art to Africa's neocolonial predicament reverberates even in this second *Festschrift*, in Nadine Gordimer's insightful "Soyinka the Tiger," Femi Osofisan's "Wole Soyinka and a Living Dramatist", Martin Banham's "On Being Squelched in the Spittle of an Alien Race", and Adewale Maja-Pearce's "Against Ideology: Soyinka vs. Hunt". Abdulrazak Gurnah's "The Fiction of Wole Soyinka" is a straightforward thematic explication of Soyinka's novels but suffers from lack of coherence and central focus, while the dialectic of creation and destruction underlying Soyinka's revolutionary ideal is perceptively explored through reference to Yoruba cosmogony in Niyi Osundare's "Wole Soyinka and the Atunda Ideal". However, Gabriel Gbadamosi's "*Madmen and Specialists* – New Nigerian States and the Importance of a Tragic Art" is essentially an anecdotal, informal chat, which offers far less than the title promises, despite Gbadamosi's adventitious mention of "the present nationalist disintegration in Bosnia" and occasional references to various plays, including Soyinka's.

CHIDI OKONKWO

Spark, Muriel 1918–

Scottish novelist, poet, and biographer

Bold, Alan, *Muriel Spark*, London and New York: Methuen, 1986

Hynes, Joseph (ed.), *Critical Essays on Muriel Spark*, New York: Maxwell Macmillan, 1992; Boston: G.K. Hall, 1992

Kemp, Peter, *Muriel Spark*, London: Paul Elek, 1974

Page, Norman, *Muriel Spark*, London: Macmillan, 1990

Richmond, Velma Bourgeois, *Muriel Spark*, New York: Frederick Ungar, 1984

Stanford, Derek, *Muriel Spark: A Biographical and Critical Study*, Fontwell, Sussex: Centaur Press, 1963

Whittaker, Ruth, *The Faith and Fiction of Muriel Spark*, London: Macmillan, 1982

Two interlinked themes dominate critiques of Muriel Spark: her Catholicism and the formal self-consciousness of her fiction. Although of Scottish-Jewish descent, Spark has said that it was her conversion to Catholicism that enabled her to write fiction, because Catholicism provides "a norm from which one can depart" ("My Conversion", in *Twentieth Century*, Autumn 1961). Early reviewers criticise her detachment and her lack of realism. More recent studies, however, stress the complex relationship between her satiric view of human absurdity and her formal experimentation. Her work is often seen as a "transfiguration of the commonplace" after a book published by a character in *The Prime of Miss Jean Brodie*. Although critics differ in their assessments of her work, the ever-increasing amount of critical interest testifies to her importance as a writer.

STANFORD's highly personal study was an early attempt to assess Spark by a former friend and collaborator, and has been the main source for biographical information on Spark. It contains interesting material on her early career and on her poetry, criticism, and radio plays. However, readers may like to bear in mind Spark's comment that "all Derek Stanford's writings on me range from distorted to sheer invention" (Bold, 1986).

KEMP balances Spark's detailed presentation of the material world against her search for absolute truth – the "transfiguration of the commonplace". He charts her development from early explorations of the isolation of the individual, through her concern with semi-closed London communities, to the harsher satiric novellas. The final chapter is a reading of *The Hothouse by the East River* (then Spark's most recent novel) as concerned with the impossibility of finally knowing another person. Although Kemp does not regard this as Spark's most successful novel, he argues that it was the most comprehensive of her novels in its coverage of her most insistent themes and literary techniques.

WHITTAKER's influential account of the tension between Spark's faith and her sense of form laid the basis for much subsequent criticism. Situating Spark in the context of 1950s' social realism, the French *nouveau roman*, and postmodern experimentalism, and drawing useful comparisons with Evelyn Waugh and Graham Greene, Whittaker emphasizes Spark's independence as a writer. She discusses the Catholic converts of the early novels; the secular interests, including wealth and ownership, of the middle period; and the fascination with plots and plotters in the later novellas. Her final chapter focuses on Spark's concern with structure, her economical style with its shifts into lyricism, and the connection "between God's unifying purpose and that of the novelist". Whittaker argues that Spark's satiric view of human absurdity and her assertions of fictionality both spring from her faith in divine order. Ultimately, however, Whittaker remains disturbed by Spark's lack of emotional expression.

RICHMOND takes *The Prime of Miss Jean Brodie*, which she regards as Spark's most effective and distinctive work, as the starting point for her survey of the novels up to *The Only Problem*. An unusual chapter on the poetry and dramatic texts highlights Spark's emphasis on community, a theme in both her play *Doctors of Philosophy* and her children's story *The Very Fine Clock*. The final chapter, on Spark's "Comic Vision", explores Spark's belief in the dual purpose of art – to entertain and to inform. Richmond believes that Spark's "most distinctive quality is a detachment that reflects both deep concern for truth and relentless humour".

BOLD reads Spark as a "Poet and Dreamer", presenting her as a consummate stylist who brings a poetic vision and linguistic cunning to her exploration of fictional truth. He draws out literary influences on her work – particularly modernism and Metaphysical poetry. Stressing her "satirical scepticism" and her use of paradox to express complex truths, Bold explores Spark's vision of life as divine comedy, collapsing into farce. Although later critics dispute some of Bold's interpretations, his focus on Spark as poet makes this a valuable contribution.

PAGE has written a brief yet comprehensive survey of Spark's work up to *A Far Cry from Kensington*. He shows how Spark rewrites herself in the later novels and reminds readers that a Spark novel is often better understood in the light of subsequent work. Tracing her concern with the truth-telling possibilities of fiction, and with the connections between theology and aesthetics, he argues that "Muriel Spark is less interested in 'pure' realism or pure fantasy . . . than in the intersection or blending of the two". This brief, accessible book includes informed readings of the novels and offers a good introduction to Spark's work.

HYNES has collected a wide range of useful material, beginning with autobiographical essays and interviews, including comments by detractors, and then providing a survey of the "best criticism available". Valuable essays by Frank Kermode (regarded as Spark's most influential critic), Malcolm Bradbury, David Lodge, and John Updike are included, together with extracts from books on Spark by Alan Bold, Allan Massie, Ruth Whittaker, Peter Kemp, and Velma Bourgeois Richmond. Hynes, in his Introduction and the extract from his own book, insists that Spark must be evaluated according to her own aims and not berated because she is not a realist. The material is arranged in order of the publication of Spark's work, showing both her development and that of the critics charting her progress. An excellent introduction to Spark's critics, this collection also contains a useful bibliography.

DIANA WALLACE

Spenser, Edmund c.1552–1599

English poet

Berger, Harry, Jr., *Revisionary Play: Studies in the Spenserian Dynamics*, Berkeley: University of California Press, 1988

Bernard, John D., *Ceremonies of Innocence: Pastoralism in the Poetry of Edmund Spenser*, Cambridge and New York: Cambridge University Press, 1989

Coughlan, Patricia (ed.), *Spenser and Ireland: An Interdisciplinary Perspective*, Cork, Ireland: Cork University Press, 1989

Goldberg, Jonathan, *Endlesse Worke: Spenser and the Structures of Discourse*, Baltimore: Johns Hopkins University Press, 1981

Greenblatt, Stephen J., "To Fashion a Gentleman: Spenser and the Destruction of the Bower of Bliss", in his *Renaissance Self-Fashioning: From More to Shakespeare*, Chicago: Chicago University Press, 1980

Hamilton, A.C., *et al.* (eds.), *The Spenser Encyclopedia*, London, Toronto, and Buffalo, New York: Routledge/University of Toronto Press, 1990

Helgerson, Richard, *Self-Crowned Laureates: Spenser, Jonson, Milton and the Literary System*, Berkeley: California University Press, 1983

King, John, *Spenser's Poetry and the Reformation Tradition*, Princeton, New Jersey: Princeton University Press, 1990

Maley, Willy, *A Spenser Chronology*, London: Macmillan, 1994

Miller, David Lee, *The Poem's Two Bodies: The Poetics of the 1590 "Faerie Queene"*, Princeton, New Jersey: Princeton University Press, 1988

Montrose, Louie Adrian, "The Elizabethan Subject and the Spenserian Text", in *Literary Theory/Renaissance Texts*, edited by Patricia Parker and David Quint, Baltimore: Johns Hopkins University Press, 1986

Nohrnberg, James, *The Analogy of the "Faerie Queene"*, Princeton, New Jersey: Princeton University Press, 1976

Rambuss, Richard, *Spenser's Secret Career*, Cambridge and New York: Cambridge University Press, 1993

There is no reliable modern biography of Spenser, although Alexander Judson's *The Life of Edmund Spenser* (1945) is still worth consulting. MALEY quotes Conyers Read to point out that "outside of what Edmund Spenser himself wrote all that is positively known about his life could probably be written in a few short paragraphs. The rest is inference, surmise, and conjecture". Maley provides all the known details and a considerable amount of contextual information, placing special emphasis on Spenser's residence and official employment in Ireland and the complex web of his associations. The brief biographies of "The Spenser Circle" and transcriptions of all the known letters in Spenser's hand are most useful.

HAMILTON's massive reference work is essential reading for anyone working in the field. Hamilton has assembled a formidable team of scholars from various disciplines to provide virtually all the basic knowledge any reader could want. As well as entries dealing with Spenser's poetry, life, the main figures, contemporaries, influences, ancestors, and descendants, there are informative essays on such subjects as number symbolism (especially relevant for the study of the *Amoretti and Epithalamion*), romance, Renaissance theories of topography, justice (relevant to *The Faerie Queene*, V), biblical exegesis, dance, allegory, etc.. The only danger is that at times the sixteenth century becomes merely a backdrop for illuminating the writings of one author, and categories are established that do not possess the explanatory force they claim – the entry on "etymology", for example, assumes that Spenser believed implicitly in the value of etymological explanations rather than simply using them within his narratives, and the entry on "sex" is written without reference to what might be termed "sexual politics". The *Encyclopedia* will nevertheless remain the starting point for all Spenser scholars, at all levels, for years to come.

HELGERSON is an important re-evaluation of Spenser's career as a writer. He argues that Spenser was the only poet of his generation who had the desire and the talent to pursue a career as a professional poet laureate, who could presume to speak for the nation – an ambition that had only become realistic in the literary culture of the 1590s. According to Helgerson, Spenser modelled his career on the works of Ariosto and, more particularly, Virgil, starting with more humble pastorals like *The Shepheardes Calender*, and working up to the grand epic of *The Faerie Queene*. Spenser's problem was that he was uncertain of his new status in the political world and, although he cast off the distractions of love poetry successfully, he ended up representing the poet as a private figure at the end of *The Faerie Queene*, VI, at odds with the political world.

RAMBUSS challenges such a reading, arguing that Spenser wrote poetry to further his career as a secretary rather than to exalt himself as a great poet, and that throughout his writings Spenser demonstrates that he can keep secrets in order to advertise his virtues as a confidant of the great and powerful. Rambuss makes the important point that the publication of the *Complaints* in 1590 rather disrupts the Virgilian chronology assumed by Helgerson. Rambuss undoubtedly overstates his case, but he provides a particularly stimulating reading of that text and also the *Epithalamion*, which casts Elizabeth as an unwelcome intruder into her subjects' lives, as well as providing a corrective to more orthodox interpretations.

NOHRNBERG is probably the most comprehensive study of the allegory of *The Faerie Queene*, relating the poem to its classical and Christian sources, analogues, genres, and forebears. Nohrnberg reads the poem in terms of two equal and opposite forces – a principle of unification centred upon the figure of Pan and a principle of diversity and fragmentation, the epic duplex.

BERGER is a collection of previously published articles written over a period of 15 years. As such, there is no presiding theme outside a characterisation of Spenser's poetry as centred upon the literary motif, *discordia concors*. Berger provides numerous stimulating readings of poems and passages from longer poems, notably his well-known essay on the *Mutabilitie Cantos*, and his extensive commentary on *The Shepheardes Calendar*. Berger argues that the poem is based upon a "paradise principle" (a means of escaping from the cares of the world), which it simultaneously deconstructs, thus going beyond the normal limits of the pastoral literary genre(s) to which it formally belongs. There is also a series of useful essays on the sexual politics of Books II and III of *The Faerie Queene*.

GREENBLATT's reading of Guyon's destruction of Acrasia's Bower of Bliss (*The Faerie Queene*, II, xii) has legitimate claim to have been the single most influential piece of Spenser criticism of the last 20 years. Greenblatt's book helped inaugurate New Historicism, and placed both the Renaissance and Spenser's poetry at the forefront of contemporary literary debate. Greenblatt situates *The Faerie Queene* within three related sixteenth-century concerns – the discovery of the New World, the conquest of Ireland and Spenser's residence there, and the destruction of images in the wake of the Reformation. He argues that Spenser was questioning the status and purpose of art and affirming the need to obey a powerful ideological authority, in this case, the Queen. MONTROSE explores this problem further, qualifying Greenblatt's argument significantly. Montrose suggests that the poem is forced to represent the Queen in praising her and so, paradoxically, affirms its own power to authorize her existence. While not denying "that there exists an authority 'beyond the poem'", Montrose argues that *The Faerie Queene* unfixes "that authority, to put into question its absolute claims upon the subjects who produce the forms in which it authorizes itself".

GOLDBERG deserves attention as the first deconstructionist reading of *The Faerie Queene*, concentrating principally on Book IV. Using terms coined by Roland Barthes, Goldberg describes the poem as a "writerly text", "open, endless and reversible . . . demand[ing] the 'endlesses worke' of play, the discovery of and the dissolving of differences into deferred identity and unity". In short, the text refuses to come to a stable conclusion, being an allegorical fragment without a final key. Goldberg's book is both a stimulating reading of a usually neglected part of *The Faerie Queene* and a lucid introduction to a difficult area of literary theory. Goldberg provides a fascinating account of Spenser's text in the light of its rewriting of Chaucer's "The Squire's Tale", and his analysis of the roles of reader and narrator should be read alongside more factual accounts of Renaissance uses of allegory, like Rosemond Tuve's.

Goldberg's book can be criticised for its avoidance of the political significance of Spenser's allegory, something he has attended to in his later work, as has MILLER. Miller reads *The Faerie Queene* in psychoanalytic terms, as a futile quest for the whole body of the Queen. Using the insights of such political scientists as Ernst Kantorowicz, who pointed out that in medieval and Renaissance political theory the monarch was deemed to exist simultaneously as a private person and a public ruler, Miller argues that Spenser glorifies literature as an "autonomous domain with its own history and permanence: a reflection of the national state", and explores the paradox that the fiction of the poem has to differ from itself in order to realise its ideal form, which exists "only as a sublimated negative image of itself". Miller's Lacanian psychoanalytical criticism can be difficult to follow in places, but his reading of the relationship between Arthur and Gloriana, and their relationship to an extra-textual history, is without comparison. Chapters 4 and 5 provide similarly stimulating readings of the poem's sexual politics.

BERNARD conceives Spenser's poetic project as an attempt to escape from the tyranny of court politics, where the *vita activa* is essential, into the anti-courtly retirement of pastoral, with its concomitant emphasis on the truly poetic creativity of the *vita contemplativa* (Bernard's reading is set in opposition to those of Greenblatt, Miller, and Goldberg). Spenser exists at the head of a long line of poets who have dramatised such a struggle, from Theocritus, through Virgil and Horace, to the Florentine Renaissance, and, according to Bernard, *The Shepheardes Calender* presents itself as the site of a contest between two pastoral authorities – a political one, to which the humble would-be courtier appeals for patronage, and a potic one, where the arrogant young writer "insist[s] on his essential filiation to the line of poets, deriving from Virgil". Bernard reads *The Faerie Queene* in a similar way, suggesting that the first three books show that "the contemplative life is the indispensable foundation, if not the end, of the active", while the latter half goes further in rejecting the lures of politics in favour of pastoral retirement, a message also sent out by the *Amoretti and Epithalamion* and the *Fowre Hymnes*. Bernard's reading is provocative and scholarly (especially the first two chapters which trace the literary tradition in question), but he perhaps places too heavy a burden on the word "pastoral", which seems to encompass everything outside the life of the court.

KING argues that Spenser has too often been read simply in terms of sophisticated European and classical models of poetic achievement, and that the native Protestant heritage has been forgotten. He argues that Spenser practised an "inclusionist strategy", modifying genres as diverse as "ecclesiastical eclogues", "continental pastoral", and "protestant religious allegory" and was as keen to rewrite *Piers Plowman* as the *Aeniad* and *Orlando Furioso*. King provides illuminating readings of *The Shepheardes Calender* as an English Protestant text, marking Spenser out as a specifically Chaucerian poet setting himself against the "new" poetic of Elizabethan courtiers and against iconoclasm in *The Faerie Queene*, with King arguing that Spenser's attitude was dialectical rather than ambivalent (as critics like Greenblatt have maintained) and that he regarded the imagination itself as an ambiguous faculty, not a delusive one. King also maintains that in Spenser's view of married love, Britomart and Gloriana stand as counter-narratives for Elizabeth, depicting what might have been. There are also cogent analyses of Spenser's use of Protestant genres and royal iconography. King's work is essential reading on Spenser, but is perhaps too keen to overstate its case and homogenise a diverse tradition as "Protestant".

COUGHLAN is a collection of essays by literary scholars and historians, who debate the value and function of Spenser's poetry and prose as literary texts and as historical evidence in the light of his Irish experience. All the essays are perceptive and illuminating: Nicholas Canny's introduction summarises the state of the debate among historians and considers whether Spenser's work helped foster the development of an Anglo-Irish identity, and whether the *View of the Present State of Ireland* needs to be read as a "hard-line" Protestant statement; Ciaran Brady writes of the *View* as the dead end of a reform tradition developed since the reign of Henry VIII; Anne Fogarty explores "the colonisation of language" in the *View* and *The Faerie Queene*, VI; Richard McCabe argues that Spenser deliberately distorts the allegory of *The Faerie Queene*, V, to defend his erstwhile patron, Arthur Lord Grey De Wilton; and Patricia Coughlan surveys contemporary representations of the Irish and considers the dialogic form of the *View*. Perhaps not as careful in its consideration of the problem of genres as some of the other books discussed above, Coughlan's volume nevertheless highlights a whole area of hitherto under-explored areas of Spenser criticism, and is an ideal starting point for further study.

ANDREW HADFIELD

Stead, Christina 1902–1983

Australian novelist

Brydon, Diana, *Christina Stead*, London: Macmillan, 1987; Totowa, New Jersey: Barnes & Noble, 1987
Christina Stead issue of *Southerly*, 53(4), December 1993
Gardiner, Judith Kegan, *Rhys, Stead, Lessing and the Politics of Empathy*, Bloomington: Indiana University Press, 1989
Geering, R.G., *Christina Stead: A Critical Study*, New York: Twayne, 1969; revised edition, Sydney: Angus & Robertson, 1979
Gribble, Jennifer, *Christina Stead*, Melbourne, Oxford, and New York: Oxford University Press, 1994
Lidoff, Joan, *Christina Stead*, New York: Frederick Ungar, 1982
Rowley, Hazel, *Christina Stead: A Biography*, Melbourne: Heinemann Australia, 1993; New York: Holt, 1994; London: Secker & Warburg, 1995
Sheridan, Susan, *Christina Stead*, Brighton, Sussex: Harvester Press, 1988; Bloomington: Indiana University Press, 1988

Substantial critical discussion of Christina Stead's writing developed only after republication in 1965 of *The Man Who Loved Children*, a novel originally published in 1940. By the middle 1960s, the new feminism and the recognition of Australian literature as an appropriate subject for academic study provided a critical climate that stimulated attention to her sprawling, difficult fictions. When Stead's first works, *The Salzburg Tales* and *Seven Poor Men of Sydney*, were published in London in 1934, six years after she had set sail from her native Australia, they occasioned a division of critical opinion, which has continued in subsequent discussion: her flamboyant style and fascination with the exotic, whether in Australian or

European settings, were praised by some and damned by others. None the less, within a decade she had achieved distinct reputations in England, America, and Australia, which, however, declined in the postwar years.

An Australian, GEERING, produced the first book-length study of Stead's work, drawing in part on letters and other documents made available to him by the author (as her literary trustee, he prepared two posthumous volumes for publication, and edited a selection of letters). Its critical judgements have now been developed by others and contested, but its claim to serve as a general introduction to her work still holds. Geering's analysis supports Stead's own claim that "I'm a psychological writer, and my drama is the drama of the person".

While Geering included brief biographical details, the major biography, by ROWLEY, did not appear until 1993. This work, though widely acclaimed, was controversial particularly because of its unsparing depiction of the author in her later years. It is significant not only for the detail it provides about the writing and publication of Stead's work, but for the analogies it discerns between particular life experiences and the fiction, and for the perceptive readings of aspects of Stead's fiction.

LIDOFF stresses that Stead was a political novelist, defining "political" as "having an interest in power and its operations". (Stead was an avowed Marxist, though resistant to party-political labels.) Lidoff's study concentrates on an analysis of the domestic gothic of *The Man Who Loved Children* and *For Love Alone*, and includes the transcript of a long interview with the author. SHERIDAN also concentrates on these two novels in her feminist study, which refines much earlier discussion in its concern with language: "Stead's texts offer an especially vivid demonstration of the work of ideology in language, in discourses". In a lucid and illuminating work, Sheridan articulates central issues of feminist criticism in relation to Stead's fiction, and does not shirk the vexed question of Stead's own dismissal of feminism.

Both Brydon and Gribble are short books in series ("Women Writers" and "Australian Writers" respectively), which traverse Stead's entire career (Brydon did not have access to the posthumously published *Ocean of Story* and *I'm Dying Laughing*). They both focus on themes of love and creativity in Stead's work, and on issues of narrative technique. BRYDON writes from a materialist-feminist position, arguing that Stead's novels stress culture over nature, presenting both women and men challenging the interlocking forms of oppressive domination in patriarchal capitalism. Her cogent analyses bring out the penetration and complexity of Stead's fiction: "Stead's subject is power; Stead's style is dialectical. It is built on the acceptance of contradiction, of conflict and of struggle".

The humanist GRIBBLE takes her distance from feminist and Marxist appropriations of Stead, and claims that "the structures of her own narratives increasingly express the view that ideologies of every kind tend to suppress or ignore the ethical questions (and the life stories) they claim to address". The strength of her study is precisely in its exploration of the structures of Stead's narratives, though her essentialist position is open to debate.

GARDINER centres her argument on the concept of empathy in contemporary American feminist psychoanalysis (Nancy Chodorow, Dorothy Dinnerstein, Carol Gilligan), but draws also on English materialism and French poststructuralism. She is particularly concerned with female identity formation in the writing of three expatriate novelists from former British colonies, and offers an acute overview of Stead's work through to *I'm Dying Laughing*, and a searching extended discussion of *The Man Who Loved Children*.

Stead has always been well served by the Sydney-based journal *Southerly*, which published her writings during the 1950s and 1960s when she was not being published anywhere else: in addition the journal has carried many of the most important critical discussions of her work, sometimes in special issues, the most recent of which includes a number of papers originally presented at a symposium held to celebrate the tenth anniversary of Stead's death. Notable here are Virginia Blain's essay "*A Little Tea, A Little Chat*: Decadent Pleasures and the Pleasure of Decadence" and Kate Lilley's "The New Curiosity Shop: Marketing Genre and Femininity in Stead's *Miss Herbert (The Suburban Wife)*". These papers, like others in the volume, mark a new stage in criticism of Stead, distinguished by increased attention to previously neglected works, especially to those of her texts not set in Australia, and by the application of contemporary critical approaches to her fiction.

MARGARET HARRIS

Steele, Sir Richard 1672–1729

Irish dramatist, journalist, and editor

Aitken, George A., *The Life of Richard Steele*, 2 vols., London: William Isbister, 1889; Boston: Houghton Mifflin, 1889

Bloom, Edward A., and Lillian D. Bloom (eds.), *Addison and Steele: The Critical Heritage*, London and Boston: Routledge & Kegan Paul, 1980

Bond, Richmond P., *The Tatler: The Making of a Literary Journal*, Cambridge, Massachusetts: Harvard University Press, 1971; London: Oxford University Press, 1971

Connely, Willard, *Sir Richard Steele*, London: Jonathan Cape, 1934; New York: Scribner, 1934

Loftis, John, *Steele at Drury Lane*, Berkeley: University of California Press, 1952

Winton, Calhoun, *Captain Steele: The Early Career of Richard Steele*, Baltimore: Johns Hopkins University Press, 1964

Winton, Calhoun, *Sir Richard Steele, M.P.: The Later Career*, Baltimore: Johns Hopkins University Press, 1970

Richard Steele's flamboyant personality has constantly provoked unusually intense personal reactions from readers and critics. In this respect, he forms a distinct contrast with his friend and collaborator Joseph Addison (*q.v.*). There is a larger body of work on Steele as an individual than on Addison: this essay, therefore, concentrates on biographies of Steele, and criticism of works where he was known to have been the sole or main author.

Many important discoveries about Steele and his world have been made in the century since AITKEN's *Life* was published. Much perceptive criticism has been written. But Aitken has not been superseded, and scholars involved in research or publication on Steele ignore him at their peril. His monumental volumes embody the best of Victorian critical biography. Meticulously researched findings are enlivened by personal responses, as in the case of Steele's involvement with an invention to make hoop petticoats more convenient: "who likes him the worse for his regard to women?" This is a self-confessed work of "love", designed to show that "Steele's character is more attractive and essentially nobler than, perhaps, that of any of the greatest of his contemporaries in the world of letters". Yet he avoids his predecessors' excessive subjectivity, including William Thackeray's "loving pity" and "the avowed disdain of Macaulay".

CONNELY justified his "impertinence" in invading "the realms of Aitken" on the grounds that "the half-century since his work took shape yielded many new documents which in the lump seemed too supplemental of Steele, too appealing or too amusing to neglect". He has also been able "to amplify, to juxtapose, and especially to query" many of Aitken's references. Furthermore, he regards Aitken as "less a readable writer than an embalmer of records". Connely is irresistibly readable, combining infectious emotional involvement with fascinating background detail. Not only Steele, but post-Restoration Dublin, Oxford, and London spring to life. Although readers without prior knowledge of the period might be alienated by Connely's oblique allusions to historical events, acquisition of a few basic facts will enable them to appreciate his concretely personal presentation of events like the Glorious Revolution: "Oxford talked blood, bounce, and bombardiers as two kings, son-in-law and father-in-law, whetted swords in the isle of Steele's birth". Connely frequently lets Steele speak for himself, as in the transcription of his first known letter (not in Aitken), its mis-spelt postscript laced with Irish brogue: "Pray, madam, give my duty to my unkle and my good Ant, and my love to me Ingenious Cousin". Inevitably, allowances must be made for period. Historians today know more about eighteenth-century upper-class reproductive practices; they would hesitate to say, even in jest, that Lady Steele made a "decision" to embark on the pregnancy that eventually killed her. Readers sensitized by hindsight of the Holocaust and other genocidal atrocities might find distasteful the racist assumptions underlying Connely's picture of the half-English Steele begging the pugnacious Captain Kelly "to be less Irish". Nevertheless, the book is an enthralling account of Steele the man.

LOFTIS, too, begins by identifying his additions to Aitken's findings. Loftis has "examined Steele's theatrical career in the context of early eighteenth-century stage and dramatic history – especially in the context of the dramatic reform movement in which Steele played such a prominent part – as it was impossible for Aitken to do in a general biography". He tells the story of Steele's turbulent career as Governor of the Royal Company of Comedians, acting in Drury Lane, from 1715 to his death in 1729. Loftis's detailed account of political and legal controversies might be most valuable to specialists, but his survey of theatrical issues is of broad general interest, particularly the moral and critical controversy surrounding Steele's intentionally edifying sentimental comedy, *The Conscious Lovers*.

WINTON's volumes provide the best introduction to Steele for readers starting from scratch. His books, combining to form a complete biography, are lucid, informative, unfailingly interesting, and accessible: everything necesssary for comprehension of Steele's successive predicaments is fully yet concisely explained. His habit of modernising, and automatically correcting, source material can make everything appear rather too tidy. For example, his transcription of Steele's first letter, omitting the postscript completely, turns it into a model of correctness. The effect is less colourful than Connely's. Fortunately, where Steele is involved, there is always colour to spare.

BOND's study is an acclaimed masterpiece, a worthy forerunner to his definitive editions of *The Tatler* and *The Spectator*. He considers every aspect of Steele's journal, from the style and structure of the articles to the quality of the newsprint. Bond's interpretation of broader social issues is beginning to look rather unsophisticated. Marxist-feminists have encouraged readers to interrogate the liberal assumptions behind Bond's statement that only "conservative" writers in Steele's day preached the doctrine that women should practise "submission to masculine authority". Many readers today would detect profoundly misogynistic implications in the portrayal of woman as alternatively "destroying Fiend" or "Guardian Angel", which Bond praises as "just and pleasing dualism". But nothing cancels the debt which all critics, whatever their affiliations, owe to the scholarship that provides such abundant material with which to support their theories.

BLOOM and BLOOM begin their *Critical Heritage* volume with sections on Steele as "Man", "Pamphleteer", and "Dramatist", before proceeding to *The Tatler* and *The Spectator*. In the two concluding sections, devoted to Addison, Steele makes further appearances, as a commentator on Addison's play *The Drummer*, and as the subject of character studies by Macaulay and Thackeray. Most of the passages included are by Steele's contemporaries, making this collection a necessity for readers who wish to understand the close and complex relationship between the writer and his world. The nineteenth century is also judiciously represented, while later reactions are discussed in the Preface. A significant omission is Sarah Fielding's novel *The Governess* (1749), in which *The Funeral*, another of Steele's attempts at edifying comedy, is recommended for schoolgirls because of its impeccable morality. Steele would have been delighted.

CAROLYN D. WILLIAMS

Stein, Gertrude 1874–1946

American poet, novelist, essayist, short-story writer, and dramatist

Berry, Ellen E., *Curved Thought and Textual Wandering: Gertrude Stein's Postmodernism*, Ann Arbor: University of Michigan Press, 1992

Copeland, Carolyn Faunce, *Language and Time and Gertrude Stein*, Iowa City: University of Iowa Press, 1975

DeKoven, Marianne, *A Different Language: Gertrude Stein's Experimental Writing*, Madison: University of Wisconsin Press, 1983

Ruddick, Lisa, *Reading Gertrude Stein: Body, Text, Gnosis*, Ithaca, New York: Cornell University Press, 1990

Toklas, Alice B., *What is Remembered*, New York: Holt, Rinehart & Winston, 1963; London: Michael Joseph, 1963

Walker, Jayne L., *The Making of a Modernist: Gertrude Stein from "Three Lives" to "Tender Buttons"*, Amherst: University of Massachusetts Press, 1984

Early critical reaction to Stein centered on her as a public personality: She was well known for her Paris salon in the home she shared with Alice B. Toklas, her companion and lover for almost 40 years, and her American lecture tour (1934–35) was widely reported in major US newspapers, which were as interested in her unconventional appearance and mannerisms as they were in her ideas. Many critics have examined Stein as an experimental writer, focusing on her unconventional syntax and grammar. More recently, psychoanalytic and feminist critics have become interested in Stein's treatment of gender and lesbian sexuality.

TOKLAS reflects on her life with Stein, describing many of the artists and writers who visited the couple at their salon, including Pablo Picasso, Ernest Hemingway, Henri Matisse, and Sherwood Anderson. The book also offers interesting anecdotes concerning Stein's American lecture tour, providing insights into the reception of Stein's works in America and useful information about Stein's working methods.

COPELAND examines the narrator in Stein's works, as she charts Stein's experimentation with language in her attempts "to wrest from the English language new realities". Copeland divides Stein's *oeuvre* into three periods – the early years (1903–12), the middle years (1913–32), and the late years (1932–44) – analyzing the progression of the narrative voice from an objective third-person narrator in *Q.E.D.* to the self-generative language in *Tender Buttons*, and finally to "the narrative form which reflects a sense of liquid time".

DeKOVEN concentrates on what she terms Stein's "experimental writing", the work after *Three Lives* (1906) and before *The Autobiography of Alice B. Toklas* (1932), which represents a violation of grammatical convention and inhibits "normal reading". Between 1906 and 1932, Stein developed a "different language", which:

> . . . both disrupts conventional modes of signification and provides alternatives to them. The modes Stein disrupts are linear, orderly, closed, hierarchical, sensible, coherent, referential, and heavily focused on the signified. The modes she substitutes are incoherent, open-ended, anarchic, irreducibly multiple, often focused on what Roland Barthes calls "the magic of the signifier".

In DeKoven's view, these years were pivotal, because they found Stein developing and refining an anti-patriarchal language, which anticipated many current feminist theories of female language, most notably those of Luce Irigaray and Hélène Cixous.

WALKER focuses her study on Stein's works between the composition of *Three Lives* (1905–06) and *Tender Buttons* (1912). During these years, Stein's style changed rapidly and radically, and she was most concerned with the problem of representation, which, according to Walker, is the central issue of modernist art. By *Tender Buttons*, Stein "had already embraced the major premises that would shape most of her subsequent work: the epistemological model of present-tense vision, unmediated by memory or habitual associations, and the literary strategy of subverting, defying, or simply denying the normal discursive order of language". Instead of turning to modernist painting and Jamesian psychology for clues to Stein's intentions, Walker turns her attention to the theoretical concerns and working methods related in Stein's previously unpublished notebooks and manuscript notations, and argues that Cézanne, rather than Picasso, played the most crucial role in the development of Stein's aesthetics. "Unlike Picasso, Stein wholeheartedly embraced Cézanne's legendary ideal of 'realizing' his sensations in terms of the material resources of the medium", as she "struggled desperately to retain her faith that language could be manipulated to embody the structures and rhythms of reality". In *Tender Buttons*, however, Stein accepted that language can never realize such an ideal.

RUDDICK takes a psychoanalytic approach to Stein, as she investigates the influences of William James and Sigmund Freud on Stein's earlier work and traces the development of Stein's gnostic feminism. Ruddick examines Stein's movement away from James (whose influence is most clearly seen in "Melanctha") and toward Freud in *The Making of Americans*, which allowed Stein to begin exploring more fully her sexuality and her anger at patriarchal power, as her style became more experimental. Stein's later work, most notably *Tender Buttons*, found her moving in a feminist direction, anticipating theorists like Cixous, Irigaray, and Julia Kristeva, as she "comes to see woman or mother as an axis within language". Taking issue with those critics who view *Tender Buttons* as stylistically significant but devoid of any coherent or unifying theme, Ruddick argues that *Tender Buttons* constructs a feminist spirituality and positions Stein within the gnostic tradition.

BERRY discusses *A Long Gay Book*, *A Novel of Thank You*, *Lady Church Amiably*, *Mrs Reynolds*, and *Ida*, as she attempts to elucidate Stein's self-conscious employment of what critics now label as "postmodernist" strategies, and to historicize Stein's texts and the development of postmodernism. Quoting Andreas Huyssen's *After the Great Divide* (Bloomington: Indiana University Press, 1986), Berry defines postmodernism as "a slowly emerging cultural transformation . . . which distinguishes a . . . set of assumptions, experiences and propositions from those of a preceding period", and in this context focuses particularly on gender in Stein's texts.

KRISTA L. MAY

Steinbeck, John 1902–1968

American novelist, short-story writer, and screenwriter

Benson, Jackson (ed.), *The Short Novels of John Steinbeck: Critical Essays with a Checklist of Steinbeck Criticism*, Durham, North Carolina: Duke University Press, 1990

Hayashi, Tetsumaro, *A New Study Guide to Steinbeck's Major Works, with Critical Explications*, Metuchen, New Jersey: Scarecrow Press, 1993

Lisca, Peter, *John Steinbeck, Nature and Myth*, New York: Thomas Crowell, 1978

Noble, Donald R. (ed.), *The Steinbeck Question: New Essays in Criticism*, Troy, New York: Whitston, 1993
Owens, Louis, *John Steinbeck's Re-Vision of America*, Athens: University of Georgia Press, 1985
Owens, Louis, *The Grapes of Wrath: Trouble in the Promised Land*, Boston: Twayne, 1989
Timmerman, John, *The Dramatic Landscape of Steinbeck's Short Stories*, Norman: University of Oklahoma Press, 1990

John Steinbeck has been more often ignored than vilified by critics, but the early reviewers who did seek to bury him did so with great vigor. In the polarized worlds of magazine and academic criticism, he was too Left for the Right, too Right for the Left. Neither camp could be dissuaded in the 1930s and 1940s by the fact that his plots and symbolic choices lacked the strong sense of historical purpose and context favored by writers with political agendas to serve. The "flawed excellencies" of Steinbeck's work, which continue to occupy the critics, owe much of their substance to the specter of misreading initiated by early unfavorable criticism, and perpetuated by his thinner, less popular later work.

As critical speculation about Steinbeck's politics has declined, the field has been evenly divided among those interested in his commitment to verisimilitude and those interested in the complex symbolism that has shaped his fiction from the beginning. Biographical speculation abounds as to the state of Steinbeck's mind when he approached the portrayal of women and minorities, since his fictional world permits only white men to communicate or prosper successfully. His women are one-dimensional, constrained, and all but silent, his few non-whites equally flat and isolated, even with adjustment in perception for the times in which he lived.

The Steinbeck critical field is not a crowded one, compared to the interest Ernest Hemingway and William Faulkner still generate among scholars, and he has been all but ignored by the American east-coast critical establishment. He is popular, though, in the midwest and west, primarily with scholars in smaller universities, and, oddly enough, also in Japan, where cultural differences must surely have produced an entirely new reading of Steinbeck's America. (His widow inquired in a Japanese bookstore for works by her husband and was presented with "Angry Raisins".)

LISCA belongs to the vanguard of Steinbeck scholars. The spare clarity of critics like Owens owes a debt to early champions like Lisca, whose rambling narrative defense tends to delay the point but covers ground that has to be traversed once a critical subject's motives or talent has been impugned. Scholars who have founded their work in biography, as Lisca has done, tend to make defensive critics anyway, from over identification with the subject. Nevertheless, Lisca is a major source for, and influence on, the younger group, and a complete understanding of the current criticism is not possible without reference to Lisca's long association with Steinbeck.

OWENS has written in depth on Steinbeck's imagery and borrowings from myth in both works cited here. There are several good critical studies of *Grapes of Wrath* in addition to Owens' (1989). Despite the promise of wordplay in his titles, his approach is straightforward explication with little critical jargon. Steinbeck wrote extensively about craft, and Owens uses him as an authority as well as a standard against which to discuss specific imperfections in his works wherever they appear. Most critics agree that Steinbeck's powers declined toward the end of his life while disagreeing about the reasons. The intricate skill with which Steinbeck wove conventional literary threads into his fiction interests all Steinbeck scholars eventually, but is concentrated within Owens' work, even in the shorter essays contributed to collections.

NOBLE has brought together scholars from all over North America who raise a variety of new questions about Steinbeck's complex symbolism, but also about his women, his involvement in motion pictures, and background influences on his writing. This collection is dominated by questions about Steinbeck's approach to his craft and his checkered critical reception, making it a good source of supplemental background information, but somewhat less valuable as a source of literary criticism. It includes an extensive Introduction by Noble, plus an introductory essay by Jackson Benson, author of the standard biography.

HAYASHI's collection closely resembles an anthology of Steinbeck study notes for examinations. Although startling at first for its simplicity, but because Steinbeck was very prolific, a scholar surveying his entire career would find this collection very helpful. Each chapter is followed by a short annotated bibliography. Undergraduates and students from other disciplines will find it useful as well, in its format of plot summary followed by critical explication (some authors even obliging the student by revealing their critical approaches). Hayashi is founder of the *Steinbeck Quarterly* and an important force in international Steinbeck studies.

BENSON has put together an anthology of what he believes to be the best criticism of the short novels. Critical reception, as already noted here, was marked early on by reaction to the author's social and artistic sensitivity/lack of it, and Benson has organized this collection to present the most productive approaches to "the true strengths and weaknesses of the works". Benson has in his own work expressed a fascination with Steinbeck's personal quirks, and this collection builds on that interest. He has limited his choices to criticism devoted to individual texts, so that point and counterpoint among them is more readily apparent. Most of the essays in this collection have been previously published, but a few have been contributed by well-known Steinbeck scholars who before had not written about Steinbeck from a point of view consistent with the aims of this collection.

TIMMERMAN has selected all of Steinbeck's short fiction for this work of textual criticism, and arranged them in strict chronological order to demonstrate changes within his method over time. Like many other studies, this one includes considerable reference to Steinbeck's own examination of his craft in letters and articles. He makes a sensitive, detailed case for his conclusions about Steinbeck's growth as a literary artist.

CLARA ELIZABETH SPEER

Sterne, Laurence 1713–1768

English novelist

Cash, Arthur H., *Laurence Sterne: The Early and Middle Years*, London: Methuen, 1975

Cash, Arthur H., *Laurence Sterne: The Later Years*, London and New York: Methuen, 1986

Cash, Arthur H., and John M. Stedmond (eds.), *The Winged Skull: Bicentenary Conference Papers on Laurence Sterne*, Kent, Ohio: Kent State University Press, 1971

Conrad, Peter, *Shandyism: The Character of Romantic Irony*, Oxford: Blackwell, 1978

Freedman, William, *Laurence Sterne and the Origins of the Musical Novel*, Athens: University of Georgia Press, 1978

Iser, Wolfgang, *Laurence Sterne: Tristram Shandy*, translated by David Henry Wilson, Cambridge and New York: Cambridge University Press, 1988

Myer, Valerie Grosvenor (ed.), *Laurence Sterne: Riddles and Mysteries*, London: Vision Press, 1984; Totowa, New Jersey: Barnes & Noble, 1984

Stedmond, John M., *The Comic Art of Laurence Sterne*, Toronto: University of Toronto Press, 1967

Work, James A., "Introduction", in Sterne's *The Life and Opinions of Tristram Shandy, Gentleman*, New York: Odyssey Press, 1940

An Anglican clergyman from Yorkshire, Laurence Sterne published his first work at the age of 46, becoming for nine years the literary rage of Europe. His fame, however, was more sensational than sustained. Only in the second half of the twentieth century has Sterne's narrative reflexivity, his moral irony, and his fragmentary, anti-teleological style been fully appreciated. Sterne, who was dismissed as a cultural fad by his contemporary Dr Samuel Johnson, and relegated to a sarcastic footnote by F.R. Leavis in *The Great Tradition*, is now recognized as the most innovative eighteenth-century novelist.

WORK's edition of *Tristram Shandy* began the rehabilitation of the novelist by offering a well annotated and readily available text. The 65-page "Introduction" to that edition still provides an effective starting point for contextualizing the novel and characterizing its intellectual milieu. Work gives a succinct publication history and sets out clearly the notions of psychology and benevolence that Sterne draws from John Locke, the Earl of Shaftesbury, and Francis Hutcheson. Work's is a convincing and uncomplicated framework for the intellectual traditions on which Sterne drew, and which he manipulated to his own original purposes in *Tristram Shandy*.

STEDMOND's book was the most influential of several published on Sterne in the 1960s. He deals with both *Tristram Shandy* and *A Sentimental Journey*, doing much to rehabilitate the latter as a work of philosophical integrity equal to, if very different from, *Shandy*. Stedmond is particularly adept at explaining how Sterne used his many sources, and gives what is still one of the most lucid justifications for Sterne's direct borrowings, his apparent plagiarisms, of other authors. Stedmond is a sensitive close reader, and his analyses of Sterne's writing style are both astute and remarkable for their common sense. The chapter "Tristram as Clown" is useful for its genealogical exploration of Sterne's comic heritage, setting Sterne's ironic sensibility in a line of descent that includes Erasmus, Rabelais, Robert Burton, and Jonathan Swift.

CASH edited with STEDMOND the papers presented at the Bicentenary Conference at York, which marked the anniversary of Sterne's death with the reinterment of the author's bones. The collection is divided into six parts, but it is the four essays in the section entitled "Style and Composition" that provide the general reader with still-relevant insights. William Holtz's study, "Typography, *Tristram Shandy*, the Aposiopesis, etc.", is a brief but stimulating introduction to the clever games Sterne plays with the printed page and the conventions of the book trade. Also of interest in this collection is Marcia Allentuck's defense of *Tristram Shandy* as *non-finito*, applying the language of art history to explore Sterne's use of narrative space.

CASH is Sterne's best biographer. His two-volume study of the life and works is thorough and highly readable, chronological in form and sensible in its empirical psychology. Cash provides much detail about Sterne's life as a cleric before the publication of the first two volumes of his notorious novel in 1759, but is at his best exploring Sterne's relationships with women. The failure of Sterne's marriage, his flirtatious nature, and his ultimate and uneasy obsession with Eliza Draper, when fully developed in Cash's narrative, explain the anxiety about intimacy and the complex experience of the masculine in Sterne'e writing. Cash portrays Sterne as comfortably uncomfortable with the conventions of male behaviour, someone for whom the awkward and the embarrassing are the moments in life and fiction most fit for laughter. Cash eschews the psychoanalytic approach, emphasizing instead what happened in Sterne's life through a wealth of research and documentation. Fittingly, considering the sensibility of its subject, this is a wryly sceptical biography, a narrative without an argument.

FREEDMAN's is a thesis-driven work, but nonetheless insightful. Beginning with the biographical evidence for Sterne's lifelong love and practice of music, Freedman goes on to develop an intricate and convincing argument that *Tristram Shandy* is a "musical novel", in which time is a function not of plot but of formal rhythms. Emphasizing the centrality of improvisation in eighteenth-century musical performance and the formula of "statement, development and return" in baroque composition, Freedman analyzes the concentricity of Sterne's narrative, its avoidance of conventional telelogical patterns. Freeman draws his analogies from the chorale prelude and the Baroque fantasy in particular. Most useful are the connections Freedman makes between musical notation and typography, as Sterne adapts it in *Tristram Shandy*.

CONRAD sees Sterne as the father of Romanticism: "*Tristram Shandy*'s metamorphoses in German criticism demonstrate its transformation into a sacred text of romanticism". Sterne's almost constitutional sense of ambiguity becomes for Conrad the basis of an aesthetic practice that is distinctly Romantic in its anti-classical obsession with anxiety and the unpredictable. Conrad suggests something darker in Sterne than what most critics have experienced, especially in his references to the artist Henry Fuseli and his discussions of libertinism. The study is most useful for its exposition of the German criticism of Sterne and for Sterne's influence on European Romanticism: there is no better source than Conrad for those subjects, and this is one of the most original and best-written studies of Sterne.

MYER brings together 11 essays touching on literary sources, biography, literary influence, and interpretation. Of special interest are the contributions by Jacques Berthoud on "Shandeism and Sexuality", Roy Porter's "Against the Spleen", and Bruce Stovel on "Tristram Shandy and the Art of Gossip". Park Honan explores Sterne as an influence on Jane Austen, establishing in subtle and suggestive ways the Romanticism of *Tristram Shandy*'s sensibility. This is a short essay, heavy with quotations, but one that manages to suggest far more than its states. Honan claims that Austen adapted from Sterne a "narrator's voice [of] intimacy, authority and likeability".

ISER's book is an excellent single source of critical information about *Tristram Shandy*. It has a solid bibliography, a useful chronology, a history of publications of the novel from 1759 down to 1975, and a wide-ranging and intelligent critical study. Iser's own predisposition towards reader-response criticism is apparent, but does not become excluding: Iser discusses *Tristram Shandy* using both the terminology of semiotics and the materials of intellectual history, setting the novel comfortably within a number of critical traditions and theoretical approaches. This book is one of the volumes in the Cambridge University Press series "Landmarks of World Literature", and is a good starting point for the reader uninitiated with Sterne's works.

STEPHEN W. BROWN

Stevens, Wallace 1879–1955

American poet

Bates, Milton J., *Wallace Stevens: A Mythology of Self*, Berkeley: University of California Press, 1985

Berger, Charles, *Forms of Farewell: The Late Poetry of Wallace Stevens*, Madison: University of Wisconsin Press, 1985

Bloom, Harold, *Wallace Stevens: The Poems of Our Climate*, Ithaca, New York: Cornell University Press, 1976

Cook, Eleanor, *Poetry, Word-Play, and Word-War in Wallace Stevens*, Princeton, New Jersey: Princeton University Press, 1988

Fisher, Barbara, *Wallace Stevens: The Intensest Rendezvous*, Charlottesville: University Press of Virginia, 1990

Gelpi, Albert (ed.), *Wallace Stevens: The Poetics of Modernism*, Cambridge and New York: Cambridge University Press, 1985

Halliday, Mark, *Stevens and the Interpersonal*, Princeton, New Jersey: Princeton University Press, 1991

Leggett, B.J., *Wallace Stevens and Poetic Theory: Conceiving the Supreme Fiction*, Chapel Hill: University of North Carolina Press, 1987

Longenbach, James, *Wallace Stevens: The Plain Sense of Things*, New York and Oxford: Oxford University Press, 1991

Richardson, Joan, *Wallace Stevens*, 2 vols., New York: Beech Tree Books, 1986–88

Riddel, Joseph N., *The Clairvoyant Eye: The Poetry and Poetics of Wallace Stevens*, Baton Rouge: Louisiana State University Press, 1965

Vendler, Helen, *On Extended Wings: Wallace Stevens' Longer Poems*, Cambridge, Massachusetts: Harvard University Press, 1969

Early, seminal studies by Riddel and Vendler, plus the work done by Bloom in the 1970s, set the pace for the important work done on Stevens in the 1980s and early 1990s.

RIDDEL provides close readings of most of the work in the *Collected Poems*, and bases his explication on "a tentative account of [Stevens'] theory of imagination and how it relates to the changes in and development of his style". After establishing the idea that Stevens was "a good realist of the imagination" who "wrote only of what he experienced", and thought of "poetry as a normative, and central, human activity", Riddel proceeds to examine the poems in more or less chronological order. Riddel was one of the first critics to point out that "Stevens' work reaches its heights in the long poem"; thus, each of Riddel's chapters culminates in the discussion of a long poem. In order to establish the groundwork for his examination of the long poems, Riddel comments on many of the shorter pieces. This arrangement reflects Riddel's idea that "the movement of [Stevens'] *Collected Poems* is always toward the long poem, about which the separate, minor pieces cluster, providing the landscape of a mind rich in particulars but nonetheless composed or moving toward composure". Ultimately, for Riddel, this gathering of work into "the landscape of the mind" results in "Stevens' Grand Poem".

VENDLER devotes her study to comment on Stevens' long poems, relying on a careful, New-Critical examination of the poems, not so much as they reflect Stevens' ideas – "if I seem to neglect the poet as philosopher, it is because I believe he has often been badly served in being considered one" – but instead as they reveal the "experiments in style [that] Stevens undertook – experiments in diction, in rhetoric, in syntax, in genre, in imagery, in voice, and in meter". In uncovering Stevens' "experiments in style", Vendler suggests that "if [Stevens] has a dogma, it is the dogma of the shadowy, the ephemeral, the barely perceived, the iridescent", and it is this shadowy and ephemeral quality of the poetry that Vendler brings to our attention.

Coming more or less a decade after Riddel and Vendler, BLOOM's work on Stevens represents the culmination of the first generation of critics who grappled with the "anti-master-man". Bloom's book grew out of his early theories of influence developed in *The Anxiety of Influence* and *A Map of Misreading*. In an exhaustive reading of the poet's canon, Bloom tries to demonstrate how Stevens' poetry emerges from his "unacknowledged precursors: Wordsworth, Shelley, Keats, Emerson, and, most crucially, Whitman". Because he situates Stevens so convincingly and squarely in the canonical tradition of American and British Romanticism, Bloom's book is a central document in Stevens criticism, and whether one agrees or disagrees with his theories of influence, Bloom's book is unavoidable for Stevens scholars. Motivated by an anxiety-ridden desire for originality, Bloom's Stevens writes a poetry best described as a belated form of Romanticism, which attempts "the reimagination of the First Idea" by swerving away from or scorning not only nineteenth-century British and American Romantics but eventually even his own early poetry: "*The Auroras of Autumn* is packed with allusion to Stevens' own poetry, as if the poet's lifelong anxieties had flooded upon him again all at once". By passing Stevens through the prism of Emerson or Whitman or Wordsworth, Bloom refracts his readings into the "frigid brilliances" of Stevens' landscape. For example, in explicating *The Auroras of Autumn*, he points out that "The scene of canto I, as of the more overt canto II, is the beach-world, established by Whitman as the proper American *topos*, the place where the Poetical Character is incarnated and also where the poetic self is emptied out, voided".

LEGGETT's study of Stevens attempts to counter Bloom's approach by examining closely the intellectual and philosophical influences on the poet. Against Bloom's literary history based on an anxiety-driven urge to misread one's precursors, Leggett maintains that:

> In Stevens' version the possible poet instructs himself in his precursors; their huge imaginations induce neither envy nor despair, however, because their reality is remote and their men and women the living dead. The poet will not fear that they have filled all imaginative space, because the progression of mental states is incessantly creating new imaginative space.

Leggett's main point is that Stevens' poetry, taken by itself, "seems to guarantee that any formulation of a systematic or comprehensive theory" will prove contradictory and insufficient, so by examining thinkers such as Samuel Taylor Coleridge, Giovanni Vico, Charles Mauron, and Henri Focillon, Leggett attempts to establish a larger philosophical context within which to locate Stevens' poetry.

BERGER's book takes a very focused look at "the major poems, long and short, of Wallace Stevens' last decade", with emphasis on *Esthétique du Mal*, *The Auroras of Autumn*, "An Ordinary Evening in New Haven", and the late poetry of *The Rock*. He contextualizes this late work within the framework of World War II and the postwar world, with its awakening to the reality of the atomic bomb. Berger asserts that *Esthétique* and *Auroras* are poems of apocalypse written in the shadow of the World War and an impending sense of doom. "An Ordinary Evening" and the last poems that Stevens wrote are attempts at "counterapocalypse" or "eucalyptic" poems (a reference to Professor Eucalyptus): "if we call 'Auroras' an apocalyptic poem, then the revision which follows it [in 'An Ordinary Evening'] must be called eucalyptic".

As BATES asserts in his Preface, his study is not a biography of Stevens but instead a critical discussion of the poetry derived in part from the poet's impulse to create his life in his poetry: "I suggest how [Stevens] transcended biography by transforming it into fables of identity – what he called 'mythology of self'". Bates' work is a biography of Stevens' poetry and the various types of Stevensian selves we encounter in that poetry. Beginning with the poet's earliest works, Bates guides us through Stevens' myths of the self until we encounter the poet's "mythology of modern death" in his final works, and the self who, "abjuring the naked and solitary 'I' . . . adopts a 'we' that reflects his sense of communion with the spirit of poetry".

COOK provides a broad reading of Stevens' poetry with a particular emphasis on the sophisticated types of word-play found in his poems. Far more than clever punning, Stevens' use of word-play, according to Cook, encompasses "the play of rhetoric and dialectic against each other. . . . This is word-play that is essential, not ornamental, for Stevens' poetry". Cook devotes attention to the allusiveness and multilingual puzzles that lie disguised in Stevens' word games, as well as to the more overt comic effects of puns and jokes.

The poetics of eroticism in Stevens are FISHER's subject: "I am proposing that erotic energy is the key to the dynamics of Stevens' work and, further, that it is precisely these dynamics . . . that determine the vital structures and the configuration of the entire canon". Fisher makes use of Angus Fletcher's theories of liminality to illuminate the manifestations of "erotic energy", manifestations which Fisher variously locates in sublimation, parody, violence, or the mysterious.

LONGENBACH adopts a New-Historical approach in his work on Stevens: "appreciated in the context of American political and intellectual history, Stevens emerges not only as a poet aware of events taking place around him but as a poet whose work was often inspired by them". For the most part, critics have viewed Stevens' work as disassociated from public affairs and have instead located the poems in the private world of a powerful imagination. But Longenbach's book shows just how profoundly Stevens' world – both large events (the Great Depression) and small figures (Victor Serge, "a member of the Left Opposition to the Leninist regime") – shaped the poet's writing. According to Longenbach, works such as *Notes Toward a Supreme Fiction* "achieve their power not by avoiding the confrontation of public and private, retreating to one extreme or the other, but by dramatizing their tension and complicating their opposition".

GELPI's book is an interesting collection of essays, which attempts to define Stevens' relationship to modernism as well as postmodernism, to locate "Stevens' place in the evolution of Modernist poetics in English". Gerald Bruns ("Stevens Without Epistemology") and Marjorie Perloff ("Revolving in Crystal: The Supreme Fiction and the Impasse of Modernist Lyric") attempt to show that Stevens' poetry is intent on shutting out other voices and maintaining a monological control over its imaginary world. Michael Davidson ("Notes beyond the *Notes*: Wallace Stevens and Contemporary Poetics"), however, suggests that Stevens is a transitional figure in the shift from monological to dialogical poetry, as far as the shift from modernism toward postmodernism represents such a turn. There are also essays by Gelpi, Bonnie Costello, Charles Altieri, and Alan Golding.

HALLIDAY examines the relationship between Stevens and the reader of his poetry, and in general the study aligns itself with the approach to Stevens taken by Bruns and Perloff in Gelpi's collection. Halliday asserts that Stevens' poetry is, for the most part, thoroughly monological: "in Stevens there is a campaign to wipe out the fact that the self's isolation is a removal from visible other persons – a campaign whereby they either become utterly ignorable or can somehow be shown to be not truly other". Stevens' impulse is either to ignore or absorb the "truly other" voices of the world. Though Halliday does try to rescue Stevens from himself by demonstrating that Stevens has genuine concern for his reader, nonetheless, since he is so much a poet of solitude, Stevens falls short of producing "meditations on the failures and successes and mysteries of interpersonal relations".

RICHARDSON's two-volume biography of Stevens deals as much with the poetry as with Stevens' life, and offers readings of the poetry in light of biographical information, and vice versa. An important theme throughout Richardson's study is Stevens' contradictory impulse to guard his privacy intensely yet also to break out of the isolation which his need for privacy forced upon him. Richardson suggests that Stevens countered this dilemma through his poetry: "Stevens wanted to consummate a 'mystic marriage' between his spirit and that of his imagined ideal reader. Unlike Eliot's voice crying in the desert of twentieth-century civilization for the finding of another way, Stevens' voice cried for the recognition of his essential loneliness as much as it did for the recognition that there could be another way". Richardson's discussions about Stevens' imagined reader, and the relationship implied in his poetry between himself and his reader, shed useful light on Stevens' sense of the contemporary audience for his poetry.

MICHAEL HOBBS

Stevenson, Robert Louis 1850–1894

Scottish novelist, short-story writer, and travel writer

Calder, Jenni (ed.), *Stevenson and Victorian Scotland*, Edinburgh: Edinburgh University Press, 1981

Chesterton, G.K., *Robert Louis Stevenson*, London: Hodder & Stoughton, 1927

Eigner, Edwin M., *Robert Louis Stevenson and Romantic Tradition*, Princeton, New Jersey: Princeton University Press, 1966

Hammond, J. R., *A Robert Louis Stevenson Companion: A Guide to the Novels, Essays and Short Stories*, London and New York: Macmillan, 1984

Kiely, Robert, *Robert Louis Stevenson and the Fiction of Adventure*, Cambridge, Massachusetts: Harvard University Press, 1965

Maixner, Paul (ed.), *Robert Louis Stevenson: The Critical Heritage*, London: Routledge & Kegan Paul, 1981

Noble, Andrew (ed.), *Robert Louis Stevenson*, London: Vision Press, 1983; New York: Barnes & Noble, 1983

Saposnik, Irving S., *Robert Louis Stevenson*, New York: Twayne, 1974

Throughout most of the twentieth century, Robert Louis Stevenson has been the subject of less critical scholarship than his literary success during his lifetime would seem to warrant. This lack of scholarship has several causes – Stevenson's extraordinary character and public life, his reputation as a "children's writer", and the lasting perception that his work belonged firmly in the realm of the "popular" and was not, therefore, worthy of serious critical attention. The critical work on Stevenson can be divided into three main categories: early reviews and comments written at the time his works were published; biographical/critical studies popular primarily in the early twentieth century; and the more recent book-length critical studies, some devoted to specific aspects of his work, and others treating the entire Stevenson *oeuvre*.

MAIXNER provides a useful collection of reviews and letters, written by Stevenson's contemporaries from the time his work was originally published up until 1914. Maixner presents a section of early criticism on each of Stevenson's major works; he also includes, in most cases, Stevenson's comments on each work before publication, as well as his response to the critical reception of the work. The collection draws together a wide range of positive and negative responses by his contemporaries, and Maixner's Introduction helps the reader make sense of the changes Stevenson's reputation underwent throughout his career and during the two decades after his death.

CHESTERTON's book is the best example of the many biographically oriented critical works on Stevenson popular in the early 1900s. The raft of sentimental biographies and remembrances of Stevenson published by his family and friends – even a book by his former nurse – fed the public mania over his character in the decades after his death. In his book, Chesterton tries to turn the discourse on Stevenson toward his works; his stated purpose is to "review his books with illustrations from his life; rather than to write his life with illustrations from his books". Chesterton's attempt to recover Stevenson's work as a subject for serious inquiry is, however, based primarily on a personal appreciation for Stevenson, which he communicates clearly throughout the book. This book illustrates the extent of the concern that even serious critics had with Stevenson's life.

KIELY, in one of the earliest book-length studies of a major theme in Stevenson's work, examines his interest in adventure, and argues that it was an idea integral to the development of his aesthetic theory. Kiely discusses Stevenson's concept of art as exploration – "a bracing and healthful activity, stimulating to the body and purifying for the mind". He argues that adventure served as a developing metaphor throughout Stevenson's career, representing a progress through life: adventure begins for Stevenson as a simple expression of childish daydreams of escape, and becomes a "symbolic chart of the formidable risks in which life involves all men". A secondary purpose of Kiely's book is to reclaim and legitimize Stevenson as a subject of criticism; he argues that the books are neither merely popular nor meant to be read only by children.

EIGNER's book delineates the Romantic tradition of the nineteenth century and establishes Stevenson's place in it. He defines a genre of "nineteenth century prose romance" – represented by such works as Mary Shelley's *Frankenstein* and Emily Brontë's *Wuthering Heights* – which he differentiates from the "bad tradition" begun by Walter Scott. Specifically, Eigner examines the idea of the *Doppelgänger* in relation to the "prose romance" in general, and to Stevenson's work in particular. In discussing this idea, Eigner goes on to trace not only the influence of other nineteenth-century writers on Stevenson, but also his influence on twentieth-century writers such as James Joyce and Joseph Conrad.

The short collection of essays edited by CALDER places Stevenson's work in its Scottish context. Calder argues that "he was a man irrevocably shaped by his Scottish Calvinist background, but also by the wider social and cultural environment of the second half of the century". The essays in this collection historicize Stevenson's work, discussing the influence of the Scottish tradition; also addressed is the effect on his work of Stevenson's repudiation of the Victorian artistic ideals of realism and naturalism. This work includes essays by two influential Stevenson scholars, David Daiches and J.C. Furnas.

SAPOSNIK's book is the first of the more recent critical studies to survey all of Stevenson's works, rather than to focus on only one issue or theme in his writing. This guide includes a brief biography, followed by critical commentary on all of Stevenson's literary efforts; commentary is divided into chapters on essays, plays, poems, short stories, and novels, with a separate chapter providing a psychological reading of *Dr Jekyll and Mr Hyde*. Saposnik characterizes Stevenson's works as exploring "man's ability to meet brute circumstance with little more than his natural instincts". This book is one of the few that systematically examines Stevenson's poetry and drama; it also contains a still-useful bibliography.

HAMMOND's more recent study also considers most of Stevenson's works, but focuses on the prose. Hammond wishes to "attempt a balanced appraisal of his achievement – freed from both uncritical adulation and insensitive disparagement – which seeks to place his works in their literary context and assess his significance for the twentieth century". He focuses on Stevenson's interest in the "problems of duality and moral ambiguity". Like Calder, he also finds significant Stevenson's connection to Scotland: "a profound sense of its past, an emotional awareness of its history . . . coloured all his work". The book is divided into sections addressing essays, short stories, and novels; because it treats only the works in prose, it tends to go into more depth than Saposnik's study.

NOBLE's collection of essays on Stevenson differs from most of the recent Stevenson scholarship in that it "does *not* suggest it is time for a radical revaluation in his reputation". Rather, this is a collection of close readings, which examine issues of narrative, cultural influences, and "Stevenson's ambivalent relationship to his audience and to money". This collection contains essays by eight scholars and an introduction by Noble, in which he critiques the popular psychoanalytic and hermeneutic approaches applied to Stevenson, which "aspire to the revelation of hidden, latent inner meanings". Noble asks: "can the academic teaching of literature, in general, or Stevenson, in particular, withstand such a perverse compulsion for meaning?". Although in some ways Noble may go too far in decrying critical scholarship on the Stevenson *oeuvre*, the essays in this book are useful for their careful emphasis on the texts and their contexts.

SUSANNAH MILNER

Stoppard, Tom 1937–

English dramatist and screenwriter

Bigsby, C.W.E., *Tom Stoppard*, London: Longman, 1976, revised 1979

Billington, Michael, *Stoppard the Playwright*, London and New York: Methuen, 1987

Bloom, Harold (ed.), *Tom Stoppard*, New York: Chelsea House, 1986

Brassell, Tim, *Tom Stoppard: An Assessment*, London: Macmillan, 1985; New York: St Martin's Press, 1985

Corballis, Richard, *Stoppard: The Mystery and the Clockwork*, Oxford: Amber Lane Press, 1984; New York: Methuen, 1984

Dean, Joan Fitzpatrick, *Tom Stoppard: Comedy as Moral Matrix*, Columbia: University of Missouri Press, 1981

Delaney, Paul (ed.), *Tom Stoppard in Conversation*, Ann Arbor: University of Michigan Press, 1994

Hayman, Ronald, *Tom Stoppard*, London: Heinemann, 1977, 4th edition, 1982; Totowa, New Jersey: Rowman & Littlefield, 1977, 3rd edition, 1979

Hunter, Jim, *Tom Stoppard's Plays*, London: Faber & Faber, 1982; New York: Grove Press, 1982

Jenkins, Anthony, *The Theatre of Tom Stoppard*, Cambridge and New York: University of Cambridge, 1987, revised 1989

Kelly, Katherine E., *Tom Stoppard and the Craft of Comedy: Medium and Genre at Play*, Ann Arbor: University of Michigan, 1991

Page, Malcolm (ed.), *File on Stoppard*, London: Methuen, 1986

Rusinko, Susan, *Tom Stoppard*, Boston: Twayne, 1986

Sammells, Neil, *Stoppard: The Artist as Critic*, London: Macmillan, 1988; New York: St Martin's Press, 1988

Whitaker, Thomas R., *Tom Stoppard*, New York: Grove Press, 1983; London: Macmillan, 1983

Since catapulting to fame in 1967 with the production of *Rosencrantz and Guildenstern Are Dead*, Tom Stoppard has enjoyed a reputation as a dazzling pyrotechnician of stage language. With names like Oscar Wilde, James Joyce, and George Bernard Shaw occurring in the many stylistic comparisons with earlier writers, the praise has been mixed with reservations about the superficiality of the ideas – philosophy (*Rosencrantz and Guildenstern Are Dead*), morality (*Jumpers*), art (*Travesties*), physics (*Hapgood*), science and gardening (*Arcadia*). More interested in the artist as stylist (witness the main character of his only novel, *Lord Malquist and Mr Moon*) than as social commentator, Stoppard willingly acknowledges his superficial knowledge of subjects with which he has become familiar by voluminous reading, e.g. having "got interested in physics and all that while working on the plays on a popular level" (New York *Hapgood* programme, 1991). Additional critical reservations about Stoppard's plays have included his conservative politics and the absence of emotionally credible female characters. Stoppard's apologists, however, find explanation of the former in the main character of his very first play, *Enter a Free Man*, and attempts to rectify the latter in Annie of *The Real Thing* and in the heroines in *Hapgood* and *Arcadia*. Stoppard's place in contemporary drama continues to grow, as witnessed in the steadily increasing number of book-length studies of his plays during his own lifetime – over 20 at the last count.

BIGSBY's 44-page essay, with its general treatment of the themes that run through much of Stoppardian criticism, complements Hayman's more detailed play-summary approach, taking into consideration contextual matters such as the influences present in Stoppard's writing – Wilde, Luigi Pirandello, Samuel Beckett, Ludwig Wittgenstein. Bigsby sees a gradual progression from the absurdist world of *Rosencrantz and Guildenstern Are Dead* to that of *Night and Day*, one in which there is a "liberal resistance to a modern spirit of bogus rationalism and private and public pragmatism". Bigsby's use of the term "liberal" would seem to coincide with Jenkins' use of "conservatism with a small 'c'" in the advocacy of the necessity for a space in which conscience can operate. The wit with which Stoppard conducts his debates, Bigsby concludes, is "part of the guarantee" that that space exists.

Without academic apparatus of front- and back-matter, DEAN's five-part discussion continues Bigsby's, but in a more detailed fashion. Her contextual approach evokes not only other dramatists of the times whose influence can be discerned in Stoppard's plays, but painters and meta-fictionalist novelists Robert Coover, John Barth, and John Fowles. Her title is drawn from Stoppard's comment in his interview "Ambushes for the Audience" about art as a moral matrix, "the moral sensibility from which we make our judgements about the world". For example, Archie in *Jumpers* succeeds, if he does so, only in a worldly and materialistic sense, and George fails, if he does so, because he cannot live out the philosophy he enunciates. Stoppard is the moralist in providing ironic choices for the audience. Dean's contextual approach invokes past as well as present history to support her thesis that the comic genre leaves little room for narrowly political commitment, thus Stoppard's inevitable choice of that genre. What there is of failure in George is without despair, as comedic tradition posits. Finally, Dean's argument is consistently carried through in her relating of characters in one play to their predecessors in another – all within the cultural texture of the times.

HAYMAN works his way through each original play (stage, radio, and television), story, and the novel, as well as Stoppard's adaptations of other writer's plays. Unhampered by chapter divisions, thematic or stylistic approaches, or contextual matters, Hayman's book remains a seminal source for Stoppardian critics and scholars. It is especially valuable for the opening and concluding interviews with Stoppard (from 1974 and 1976) and for Stoppard's "reading through the whole [of the original] text and correcting some errors".

HUNTER's chapter titles – "Playing", "Staging", "Laughing", "Talking", "Travestying", "Thinking", and "Caring" – indicate the readership to whom the author addresses his book: performers, directors, audiences, and students. A concluding Study-Guide serves the combined function of bibliography, synopsis, annotation, and index. The organizational pattern allows Hunter to engage in lively commentary on stylistic and thematic matters, as well as on responses of audiences, such as the possible unnerving of some spectators by the appearance of intellectual complexity on matters philosophical, ethical, linguistic, and scientific.

WHITAKER celebrates the centres of levity around which Stoppard's writing revolves, much as Stoppard's subjects are celebrations of verbal celebrations of life. These involve the dazzle of verbal game-playing arising from anxieties, absences, logical absurdities, ethical ambushes, aesthetic prisms, and the *chiaroscuro* that is the nature of the plays between *Travesties* (1974) and *On the Razzle* (1981). Informal in his chronological approach, Whitaker invites the reader to join the audience ("we are at the Old Vic on an evening in April 1967"). He incorporates unobtrusively matters of production, play summary, and reviewers' reactions within his designations of Stoppard's style, and thus transcends the mechanical quality that characterizes standard chronological format. He concludes that levity centres are gravity enough, and they invite us to "rediscover the human balance and freedom that constitute Stoppard's open secret of play", which is unlike "Wilde's delightfully brittle world of masks" or Beckett's "exhilaratingly austere world of fragmentation and deprivation".

CORBALLIS defines the "mystery" as the uncertainty that is the real world, and the "clockwork" as the abstraction and the artifice of the dream world, the latter, according to Stoppard, to be avoided. The constant collision between the two is central to his plays, and its consequence is a style whose "complex and brilliant façade [is] supported by architecture which [is] masque-like in its simplicity". Corballis acknowledges his own posing of bold generalizations for readers to kick against until their own subtle interpretations emerge. His arguments weave convincingly through Stoppard's plays. An appendix contains discussions of Stoppard's minor works.

BRASSELL makes an "interim assessment" of Stoppard's plays within three broad issues: theatrical form as substitute for current naturalistic or realistic trends; the ostentatiousness of that theatricality; and a comic seriousness, which questions the idea of drama as a force for social change. Even the later so-called political plays set in Poland, Czechoslovakia, and Africa, seen by some as veering to social commitment, are evidence of the continuous source of his inventive style – his conservatism. With five chapters devoted to minor plays, and whole chapters devoted to each of four major plays – *Rosencrantz and Guildenstern Are Dead*, *Jumpers*, *Travesties*, and *Night and Day* – Brassell gives *The Real Thing* short shrift, contrasting it unfavourably with *The Dog It Was That Died* as part of the "Conclusions" chapter. Brassell's blend of new and old criticism provides both depth and scope for his assessment of Stoppard's distinctiveness. The appendices include first-performance information (in both London and New York) as well as the original ending of *Rosencrantz and Guildenstern Are Dead*.

BLOOM's erudite sensibilities are immediately evident in his introductory invocation of a Roman stage trope – "*contaminatio*" – a term he defines as the interlacing of the new and the old, and exemplified in Stoppard's contaminating *Hamlet* with *Waiting for Godot*. With his healthy scepticism of critical claims made for Stoppard, Bloom sees *Travesties* as a play whose notion, though splendid, is "not properly worked through". Yet he weighs into Stoppardian scholarship with an enviable collection of Stoppard-studies heavyweights, such as Hayman, Hunter, Whitaker, and Corballis. No less illuminating are: Allan Rodway, who echoes Bloom's scepticism in his essay on comic philosophy in *Jumpers*; Brian Crossley, whose investigation of *The Real Inspector Hound* concludes with a comment applicable to most of Stoppard's plays – that their questions are not answered, but merely "confounded and nullified"; G.B. Crump's experience of *Jumpers* as our "having listened to several inconclusive speculations" without having "discovered the identity of the murderer or the nature of his motive"; Howard Pearce's analysis of *Travesties* as a mirror of a stage that "puts us in play in a complex of referential structures"; June Schlueter's admiration of the supreme art in the characters of Moon and Birdboot, and Rosencrantz and

Guildenstern; John William Cooke's explication of perception and form in *Travesties*; William Gruber's conclusion that the artistic design in the characters of Rosencrantz and Guildenstern may be regrettable but so consoling, for "what, in the end, could be more like classical tragedy than that [i.e., the characters getting what they deserve]"; Hersh Zeifman's focus on the ambushes Stoppard employs in *The Real Thing*, ambushes in the endless circling of realities (mostly love relationships) back on themselves; and, finally, Keir Elam's demonstration of Stoppard's out-Wittgensteining of Wittgenstein in *After Magritte*. The essays, academic but lively, do justice to the scholarly tradition for which Bloom is widely respected, and to the intellectual cartwheels that characterize Stoppard's style.

PAGE provides instant accessibility to Stoppard's writing in a series format that contains maximum information in a concise, abbreviated, tightly organized pattern. Each work is described according to type and date staged, transmitted, and/or published. A brief plot summary of each piece, including adaptations, is followed by a medley of excerpts from reviews, selected to provide a balance of opinion. The front matter includes an essay by Simon Trussler, general editor of the series, regarding Stoppard's corrective comments about critics who take his work too seriously. There is also a section of excerpts from Stoppard's own comments about his writing, followed by a bibliography of primary and secondary sources. The book is useful as a reference source for factual matters, for refresher reading, and for a beginner's quick introduction to Stoppard; however, the slim volume has no interpretive comment by its compiler.

My own study (RUSINKO) provides chronological access to Stoppard's work in the traditional Twayne format, which includes chronology, biography, bibliography, index, and a work-by-work analysis of Stoppard's genres: novel, short stories, original stage-plays, adaptations, screenplays, radio and television plays. I trace two Stoppardian character types introduced in *Lord Malquist and Mr Moon*, throughout his work – the Moons, idealists who disappear into their contexts, and the Boots, stylists who survive the disasters of their lives and times. The survey includes a brief comparison/contrast between Stoppard and that other major stylist of the English stage revolution – Harold Pinter.

BILLINGTON's career as drama critic enlivens his chronologically organized impressions of the plays, productions, and comments from other reviewers. He addresses along the way two main charges brought against Stoppard: the absence of social commitment and avoidance of human emotions. Confessing to being pleasurably bewildered from the start, he remains so but with the pleasure so outweighing the bewilderment that "a new Stoppard" sends "a quiver of anticipation down my back". With Stoppard's later work set in Eastern Europe, he sees Stoppard still as an entertainer, but one with an ideal. And with *The Real Thing*, Billington asserts, Stoppard has begun to portray credible human emotion on the stage.

SAMMELLS argues for Stoppard's early writing as an aesthetics of engagement and his later work as a politics of disengagement, concluding that "by adopting tactics he had previously condemned" he "has put his work at the service of a political thesis which is at best self-contradictory and banal and, at worst, cynical and dishonest". He introduces his argument with a chapter on the Russian formalists, French naturalists, Czech structuralists, and on theorists Roman Jakobson and David Lodge. Literary change comes about not as new content but as new forms to replace old ones that have lost their credibility, according to formalist Viktor Shklovsky. Stoppard, like Beckett and Joyce, is an artist as critic, except in those cases where his spiritual loners become political dissenters. Sammells's concluding chapter, drawing largely on Stoppard's review of Paul Johnson's book *Enemies of Society*, demonstrates the dramatist's veering away from the aesthetics of disengagement at the heart of his earlier plays. Sammells's controversial argument is always cogent and engaging.

JENKINS posits a centre within Stoppard from which all his writing stems. That centre, conservatism with a small "c", is present even in his early work, Jenkins asserts. Consequently the later so-called "political" plays do not represent a change but rather a stronger insistence on the humanism of the earlier plays. The early Rosencrantz and Guildenstern, like the later Polish workers, are characters who share in the desire to be free, only to be entrapped within an unyielding system. Similarly, credible female characters exist as early as Dotty in *Jumpers*, so that Annie in *The Real Thing* is not a change of direction for him. As actor, director, and teacher of drama, Jenkins provides interesting sidelines, such as variants in the first pre-performance edition of *Jumpers* (1972). He includes no index or bibliography.

KELLY defines Stoppard's comic craft in terms of his aversion to the declamatory and the didactic, thus his use of open-ended debates and parody, beginning with *Enter a Free Man*, a play that reworks Arthur Miller's *Death of a Salesman*, John Osborne's *Look Back in Anger*, and Robert Bolt's *Flowering Cherry*. The parody in the early radio-, television-, and stage-plays turns to satire in his Eastern European plays and to postmodern polyphony in *The Real Thing* and *Hapgood*. Kelly, effectively demonstrates some of the theories argued in Sammells's formalistic approach. Her inclusion of Stoppard's early theatre criticism for *Scene* magazine is welcome, and her omission of his adaptations is not a major loss.

DELANEY's volume is a collection of 39 previously published, delivered, or aired pieces from newspapers, magazines, and books. Criticism, as well as varying amounts of question-and-answer style information, appears in these articles, 12 of which are traditional interviews with Stoppard. The compilation serves as a valuable decade-by-decade guide to Stoppard's work and an exhaustive year-by-year (1967–93) chronology of his works, articles, lectures, and interviews. Valuable as well, in the career of a writer still in his prime, is the updating of Stoppardian criticism on his recent play *Arcadia* (1993).

SUSAN RUSINKO

Stowe, Harriet Beecher 1811–1896

American novelist and prose writer

Ammons, Elizabeth (ed.), *Critical Essays on Harriet Beecher Stowe*, Boston: G.K. Hall, 1980

Brown, Gillian, *Domestic Individualism: Imagining Self in Nineteenth-Century America*, Berkeley: University of California Press, 1990
Crozier, Alice, *The Novels of Harriet Beecher Stowe*, New York: Oxford University Press, 1969
Donovan, Josephine, *Uncle Tom's Cabin: Evil, Affliction, and Redemptive Love*, Boston: Twayne, 1991
Fisher, Philip, *Hard Facts: Setting and Form in the American Novel*, New York and Oxford: Oxford University Press, 1985
Gossett, Thomas F., *"Uncle Tom's Cabin" and American Culture*, Dallas: Southern Methodist University Press, 1985
Roberts, Diane, *The Myth of Aunt Jemima: Representations of Race and Region*, London: Routledge, 1994
Sundquist, Eric J. (ed.), *New Essays on "Uncle Tom's Cabin"*, Cambridge and New York: Cambridge University Press, 1986
Tompkins, Jane, "Sentimental Power: *Uncle Tom's Cabin* and the Politics of Literary History", in *The New Feminist Criticism: Essays on Women, Literature, and Theory*, edited by Elaine Showalter, New York: Pantheon, 1985; London: Virago, 1986

Both in her own time and since, Harriet Beecher Stowe has provoked some furious controversy. Her novel *Uncle Tom's Cabin* is probably the most famous anti-slavery polemic of all time, but it has also been bitterly attacked as racist and patronising. Many critics have called her insipid and oppressive to women, but her contemporaries were scandalised by her exposé of Byron's incestuous history, and some late twentieth-century feminists have hailed her as a pioneer.

AMMONS' collection of essays conveys the range of these responses, incorporating both nineteenth- and twentieth-century commentary, extracts from reminiscences by those who knew Stowe, and criticism of her writing. There is discussion of the New England novels and the novels of manners, as well as the Byron furore and the slavery novels. There are attacks from J.C. Furnas (for being racist), from the London *Times* (for being politically incendiary), from Ann Douglas (for being sentimental and conservative), and passionate defences of Stowe (as feminist and writer) from Ellen Moers and from Ammons herself.

The SUNDQUIST collection is a less dramatic but equally invaluable addition to Stowe scholarship. Its essays place Stowe variously in relation to nineteenth-century African-American writing, the discourses of Woman's Rights and social reform, and a later generation of women writers. Although it deals mainly with *Uncle Tom's Cabin*, most of the essays have ramifications for the whole of Stowe's work. GOSSETT's book is similarly informative about much more than Stowe's most famous novel. Though oddly structured, being partly a biography, partly a critique, and partly a contextualisation of the novel, it offers detailed accounts of contemporary responses to the novel and the many commercial spin-offs it produced. Its commentary is perhaps more informative than incisive, but as a sourcebook for Stowe's impact on her culture it is fascinating.

Despite the passion Stowe provokes, CROZIER argues with some justification that she was long neglected as a writer. Her own thorough study is an attempt to rectify this. Arguing that Stowe was, like many of her contemporaries, deeply influenced by Byron and Sir Walter Scott, Crozier examines the New England novels, the journalism, and the Byron affair, as well as the slavery novels on which other critics tend to concentrate. She credits Stowe with originating the New England local-colour tradition, but maintains that Stowe's version differs from the bleaker work of later writers like Sarah Orne Jewett, in creating a confident, active world, projected into the past, which is nevertheless still optimistic about industrial progress. The relationship with Byron she draws as a struggle between literary passion and a genteel repugnance consequent on her friendship with, and sympathy for, his widow. Two chapters are devoted to close readings of *Uncle Tom's Cabin* and *Dred*, while another, following Stowe's own suggestion that her novels should be considered first as moral arguments, deals separately with "the merely artistic point of view".

The argument that Stowe's stylistic shortcomings are worth overlooking because of her cultural and political impact on her contemporaries has been enthusiastically taken up by subsequent critics. FISHER argues that though modern readers squirm at the emotional effusions of *Uncle Tom's Cabin*, in the nineteenth century the novel's power lay in its solicitations of feeling and empathy with the slave. TOMPKINS' article similarly aims to restore this novel to its contextual pre-eminence, and to champion it against the "modernist" aesthetic, which she believes has dealt particularly unjustly with the women's writing of the period. In her account, Stowe's novel cloaks an attack on patriarchy in a paean to domesticity as woman's rightful preserve. BROWN suggests that the novel's critique was more far-reaching still, in attempting to reform the domestic ethos that bound contemporary women, and in blaming of the sin of slavery on a masculine national economy. Her reading points to more complex (and less heroic) political impulses in the novel, though, as she observes that "Stowe's sentimentalism forwards both abolitionism and racism".

Recent readings of *Uncle Tom's Cabin* have reintegrated assessments of the political impact of the novel with a closer attention to its formal constituents. DONOVAN's claims that the novel is "realist" and exhibits fully developed characters and a consistent tone are unusual even among Stowe's champions. She also argues that the novel has a powerful contemporary relevance, since it can be read as a treatise on the "universal" problem of evil, of which slavery is just one manifestation. ROBERTS, by contrast, is interested in the novel's place in a historical discourse on race in the South, and discusses both its anti-slavery precursors, and Southern responses to it in the 1850s. She demonstrates that Stowe attacks slavery by representing its Southern home as an alien landscape, orientalising her picture of New Orleans to associate it with her reader's perceptions of heathen bondage in the East. She also argues that the novel played a part in the development of the Southern gothic, which later became a staple of Southern writing, although Stowe employed it to make the region seem strange and foreign.

SARAH MEER

Structuralism

Culler, Jonathan, *Structuralist Poetics: Structuralism, Linguistics, and the Study of Literature*, London: Routledge & Kegan Paul, 1975; Ithaca, New York: Cornell University Press, 1975

Jackson, Leonard, *The Poverty of Structuralism: Literature and Structuralist Theory*, London: Longman, 1991

Lodge, David, *Working with Structuralism: Essays and Reviews on Nineteenth- and Twentieth-Century Literature*, London and Boston: Routledge & Kegan Paul, 1981

Robey, David (ed.), *Structuralism: An Introduction*, Oxford: Clarendon Press, 1973

Scholes, Robert, *Structuralism in Literature: An Introduction*, New Haven, Connecticut, and London: Yale University Press, 1974

Sturrock, John, *Structuralism*, London: Paladin, 1986; revised edition, London: Fontana, 1993

Jonathan CULLER's book still remains one of the best and clearest introductions on the subject. In Part One he demonstrates the origins of structuralism in the work of Ferdinand de Saussure, paying particular attention to binary oppositions and to the famous *langue/parole* distinction on which structuralist theories rest. Structuralism is an enabling system, a set of prior rules and conventions without which individual utterances cannot be generated. Culler is highly illuminating in his discussion of Roland Barthes's view that structuralism is distinguished from previous theories in attempting to construct a science of literature, while admitting that this can be reductive, denying literary works that unique autonomy that the New Critics had awarded them.

In Part Two Culler takes up the question of literary competence in the reader, and examines such aspects as parody, irony, and genre. These conventions work to enable the reader to project meaning and coherence *into* a text rather than to extract them from it. The chapter on the poetics of the novel is perhaps the most theoretically challenging. Drawing on the work of Roland Barthes, Claude Bremond, Julia Kristeva, and A.-J. Greimas, Culler analyses the movement in reading from the mimetic "reality effect" to higher levels of integration. The book concludes with a richly suggestive discussion of character. Culler's is a remarkably wide-ranging study, employing the writings of all the major structuralists and applying it to an exciting spectrum of literary specimens. It is highly readable, and this aspect, along with its own structural clarity and logical order, makes it one of the most enjoyable introductions to the subject.

SCHOLES's introduction to structuralism employs the same basic definitions as Culler, but, unlike his, is more systematic, discusses individual writers in greater detail, and pays more attention to the historical background, placing structuralism in diametrical opposition to Marxism, which is an ideology concerned with the idea of progress. Structuralism, on the other hand, is a methodology and is synchronic. Scholes devotes much more space to the famous debate between Roman Jackobson and Michael Riffaterre on the meaning of Charles Baudelaire's "Les Chats", and, unlike Culler, analyses at length the work of Vladimir Propp, the Russian formalists, and Northrop Frye, whom he regards as a kind of proto-structuralist. On these bases, Scholes provides his own highly attractive modal schema as an aid to the structural analysis of fiction. The value of this method is attested in his cogent readings of Romantic poetry and James Joyce's *Ulysses*. Like almost all structuralist critics, he has little time for drama, though he does include a brief discussion of Etienne Souriau. This book is an excellent, comprehensive introduction for those who know little about structuralism. Obviously intended as a textbook for students, it is mercifully jargon-free, and, while lacking the interpretative sophistication and subtlety of Culler, is attractively written and should be regarded as a useful complement to Culler.

The book edited by ROBEY is rather different in being a collection of essays based on the Wolfson College (Oxford) lectures of 1972. It commences with a fairly predictable introduction to Saussurian linguistics by John Lyons, followed by a short piece from Culler, in which he stresses the inseparability of structuralism and semiotics, paying especial attention to N. Trubetzkoy. He illustrates helpfully the systematic nature of structuralism by scrutinising the work of Mary Douglas in anthropology, Michel Foucault's concept of the *episteme* in history and science, and aspects of popular culture and literary criticism. One might enquire as to why only four categories are selected, but it is useful to be directed to the debunking essays of Barthes in his *Mythologies* and to the theories of William Empson, whom Culler appropriates to demonstrate that the true task of the critic is not the interpretation of individual texts, but their "intelligibility" – *how* they can be understood.

Umberto Eco's highly entertaining essay has the virtue of linking structuralism to semiotics by invoking the work of C.S. Peirce and his tripartite division of signs into iconic, indexical, and symbolic codes – an aspect very much underplayed by Culler and Scholes. Tzvetan Todorov provides a "hard-line" structural analysis of the *Tales* of Henry James: taking the "figure in the carpet" as what Michael Riffaterre would call the structural "matrix", he engages in an illuminating quest for unifying features in stories such as "In the Cage" and "Sir Edmond Orme"; he also has interesting things to say on the nature of the fantastic, especially in *The Turn of the Screw*. Other essays in the collection cover science, philosophy, and mathematics. This book should be regarded as helpfully complementary to Culler and Robey, reminding us that structuralism is by no means a purely literary phenomenon, and indeed had its roots in the anthropology of Claude Lévi-Strauss long before it was applied to written texts.

In his volume, though, LODGE makes such an application, providing 15 interpretative essays, of which the first sets the scene by placing structuralism in a context of Russian formalism, modernism, and postmodern fiction (by John Fowles, Samuel Beckett, Kurt Vonnegut, John Barth, *et al.*), while the ensuing three deal with narratology, an area in which structuralism has achieved its most spectacular successes. Lodge's analysis of "Cat in the Rain" has become something of a classic, and is notable not only for the clarity of its exposition of narrative modes, but also for the elegance and cogency with which Lodge applies the methodologies of Barthes and Greimas to elicit a thoroughly convincing interpretation of Hemingway's story. A short essay on Henry James similarly employs the theories of Gérard Genette to explore the concepts of time and point of view in the novel. Lodge then proffers us a rather tongue-in-cheek utilisation of the archetypal Oedipus myth to produce a structuralist analysis of one of his own short stories – a welcome touch, humour being in short supply among many structuralists.

Three essays on Thomas Hardy demonstrate how structuralist readings can benefit from generic, formalist, and cinematographic theories. (The essays on Evelyn Waugh, on the other hand, seem to have nothing structuralist about them, being concerned with journalism and biography, and it is a mystery as to why they were included.) An illuminating study of narrative closure is succeeded by a final section on contemporary culture, among which we find an interesting reading of Ted Hughes's *Crow* in the light of mythic intertextuality. Lodge's kaleidoscopic collection is never dull or jargon-ridden; though inevitably a trifle dated now, it still stands as a model of how structuralism can be fruitfully applied to the close reading of literary texts.

STURROCK's is an extremely handy volume, offering a brief, succinct account of all the major branches of structuralist theory. A chapter on language does full justice both to the European tradition emanating from Saussure and to the Americans, such as Morton Bloomfield and Noam Chomsky (with their stress on syntax and innate mental structures). The following section provides a clear exposition of the seminal work of Lévi-Strauss in cultural anthropology and myth, together with a short discussion of the historiography of Fernand Braudel and Foucault. Chapter 3 is useful for its emphasis on the semiotic theories of Peirce, Louis Hjelmslev, and Barthes, while the ensuing section traces the development of literary structuralism, from its roots in Russian formalism, through the work of Propp on folk-tales, to Greimas's dense grammatical and semantic "actantial" theories and the codification of Barthes in *S/Z*. A final chapter takes us beyond mainstream structuralism to a lucid consideration of Jacques Derrida's attempts to de-originate the text and eliminate the "metaphysics of presence". The bibliography lists books only, but they are well chosen.

It has become a commonplace that structuralism as a dominant force was moribund by the mid-1970s, overtaken by poststructuralism, superstructuralism, and the emergent forces of postmodernism. JACKSON's study shows how the inherent flaws and weaknesses in the whole structuralist project led to this. A dense, very learned book, it offers a sustained attack on the structuralism of the 1960s, which, Jackson argues, so modified the work of Saussure as to bear little resemblance to its linguistic origins. Like R. Tallis (in *Not Saussure*), he feels that the result is a theory that is inadequate to investigate either language or literature. After a useful preface charting the main historical movements from Kant to Kristeva, he provides a contextual "placement" of Saussure, and points out that French and British structuralists latched on to the very feature of Saussure's work that was least satisfactory – the signifier/signified opposition – completely ignoring the much more scientific and up-to-date theories of Chomsky or Bloomfield.

A sophisticated examination of the concept of structure and an analysis of the "real Saussure" is followed by chapters focusing on the work of Jakobson, the Prague School, and the Geneva School, noting that the first phase of structuralism actually began in 1928. Jackson proceeds to examine the second phase – French structural anthropology and the philosophical theories of Derrida and Jacques Lacan – before launching an extended attack on what he calls "textual mysticism" (the discursive idealism that denies there is a reality outside the text), the concepts of phonocentrism, arch-writing, *différance*, and Husserlian phenomenology. After a detailed assault on linguistic idealism and a brief critique of Tony Bennet, Kristeva, and others, Jackson presents his own scientific theory of interpretation, condemning relativism, subjectivism, and metaphysics, and espousing instead the testable hypotheses of cognitive psychology and material realism. This is an invigoratingly acerbic reaction to poststructuralism, though many will find his assertion that *Hamlet* has "the same kind of reality as a computer programme" hard to swallow.

This final chapter is perhaps the least convincing part of Jackson's study, but in all other respects it is a very important book, casting as it does a cold eye on the easy assumptions, distortions, and irrationalities of the whole original structuralist enterprise. His scathing denunciations of Lacan and Derrida will no doubt antagonise many, but the arguments must be taken on board. As Jackson himself admits, the book is mainly "destructive", but for that very reason, stimulating, abrasive, and a welcome antidote to the hyper-laudatory attitude of some other writers on the subject.

A.W. LYLE

Styron, William 1925–

American novelist and essayist

Casciato, Arthur D., and James L.W. West III (eds.), *Critical Essays on William Styron*, Boston: G.K. Hall, 1982

Coale, Samuel, *William Styron Revisited*, Boston: Twayne, 1991

Crane, John K., *The Root of All Evil: The Thematic Unity of William Styron's Fiction*, Columbia: University of South Carolina Press, 1984

Morris, Robert K., and Irving Malin (eds.), *The Achievement of William Styron*, Athens: University of Georgia Press, 1975, revised 1981

Ratner, Marc L., *William Styron*, New York: Twayne, 1972

Ruderman, Judith, *William Styron*, New York: Frederick Ungar, 1987

RATNER's book, although not a definitive study by any stretch, remains a very useful introduction to Styron's work through *Confessions of Nat Turner*. Citing a "paucity of information", Ratner avoids bio-critical analysis, concentrating instead on Styron's "strong prose style and the moral issues with which he is absorbed". He devotes a chapter to each of Styron's first three novels and an early novella, in addition to chapters on social criticism, psychology, and Southern literature. Throughout his discussions of Styron's development and achievement, Ratner repeatedly returns to several central concerns of the writer and his works: the fragmented nature of a society pulled between Puritan and Romantic values; the price of individual self-discovery, responsibility, and rebellion in such a society; the conflicting pull between the past and present; the power and importance of "passion and imagination". To convey a sense of Styron's universal concerns and his individuality, Ratner cites comparisons with a wide range of classic and contemporary authors, from Euripides to Theodore Roethke. Styron is indebted in particular to apocalyptic writings of the Bible and those of secular writers for his "poetic imagination" and the "poetic structure" of his works. Ratner's own style, happily free of academic jargon, is generally clear and direct, and his account of Styron is balanced and informative.

MORRIS and MALIN's revision of their 1975 essay collection is a strong example of the value of such volumes. The 11 essays, about half of which are reprinted from academic journals, provide thought-provoking analyses of individual works, yet also keep our attention on Styron's overall achievement, his "vision and value". Styron's growth as an artist, his literary techniques, his passion for fusing the past and present, the mundane and the symbolic, are explored throughout. Essays on *Sophie's Choice*, *The Confessions of Nat Turner*, and on Styron's general themes and narrative techniques have been added to this revised edition. One third of the 385-page book is devoted to interviews with Styron (40 pages) and a still-useful bibliography (84 pages).

CASCIATO's anthology, one in a series titled "Critical Essays on American Literature", is a collection of 40 articles on Styron's work through *Sophie's Choice*. They are divided evenly among the major works, with a couple of essays each on *In the Clap Shack*, "The Long March", and Styron's reception in France. Five of the pieces are by Styron himself; the rest, reprinted from a variety of books, academic journals, and newspapers, are penned by writers ranging from established critics of American literature and culture to anonymous book-reviewers. The essays, which range from two to 25 pages in length, vary widely in quality, depth of analysis, relevance, and perspective. The editors note that the essays do not "necessarily represent a cross-section of [a] novel's reception". Rather, they strive for "a good sampling of opinion", based on "reviews and articles that have not been republished in other collections on Styron". Although uneven, the collection is a useful one for the Styron scholar.

CRANE's approach to realizing thematic unity in Styron's work is to re-read the early work in light of the revelations of *Sophie's Choice*. He notes that Styron's work has "clearly matured" and "because he demonstrates in *Sophie's Choice* exactly how the maturation took place, he has allowed us to return to his first three works and to see them, even though they themselves are not changed, in a different way". Beginning with the themes and techniques of *Sophie's Choice*, Crane analyzes each of Styron's major works in reverse chronological order, finding that "the thematic thrust of them emerges as remarkably the same". Working backwards allows Crane to examine the unrealized potential of Styron's early work against the fully realized achievement of *Sophie's Choice*. For Crane, "the root of all evil in Styron's universe is the inability to feel guilt for one's actions". Armed with this insight and an array of psychological terms, such as transfer, solitary, guilt, etc., he proceeds rather methodically to review and compare the works in order to assert his thesis. He ends with a lengthy chapter on the narrative structure of Styron's works.

RUDERMAN provides a brief general overview of Styron's life and work. She devotes a short chapter to each of the major works through *Sophie's Choice*, plus one on his writings on the military. The remaining three chapters discuss biographical details, Styron's relationship to the South and Southern writers, and his preoccupation with the "struggles for power and dominance" in human communities, violence, and alienation. The book is a useful introduction to Styron, although it lacks an in-depth analysis of his technique or his place in the twentieth-century literary canon.

COALE's study is a balanced, insightful, well-written analysis of both Styron's work and his critics through 1991. Coale does an excellent job of moving from Styron's typical literary creations, concerns, and obsessions, to larger creative/critical traditions in American literature. He focuses on Styron's fascination with "the encapsulated self . . . essentially asocial, narcissistic", which struggles within and against the established social order. In order to better delineate the moral and metaphysical quests of both Styron and his protagonists, quests to understand the nature of the self, guilt, evil, change, and redemption, Coale provides a succinct discussion of American gothic Romanticism, existentialism, and the Southern literary imagination. Included throughout are numerous quotations from a variety of literary critics over the years, which reveal a wide range of critical opinion on Styron's style, form, vision, and overall achievement. This compact study raises many points about the artist's need and ability to examine the individual in conflict with society; and Coale's refusal to gloss over Styron's artistic weaknesses makes his high praise for *Sophie's Choice* especially convincing.

DANNY L. ROBINSON

The Sublime *see* Literary Aesthetics: Romantic

Swift, Jonathan 1667–1745

English poet, essayist, and writer of prose satires

Bloom, Harold (ed.), *Jonathan Swift*, New York: Chelsea House, 1986
Downie, James Alan, *Jonathan Swift, Political Writer*, London and Boston: Routledge & Kegan Paul, 1984
Ehrenpreis, Irvin, *Swift: The Man, His Works, and the Age*, 3 vols., London: Methuen, 1962–83; Cambridge, Massachusetts: Harvard University Press, 1962–1983
Hunting, Robert, *Jonathan Swift*, New York: Twayne, 1967, revised (Boston), 1989
Nokes, David, *Jonathan Swift: A Hypocrite Reversed: A Critical Biography*, Oxford: Oxford University Press, 1985
Quintana, Ricardo, *The Mind and Art of Jonathan Swift*, London & New York: Oxford University Press, 1936; revised edition, London: Methuen, 1965; Gloucester, Massachusetts: Peter Smith, 1965
Quintana, Ricardo, *Swift: An Introduction*, London: Oxford University Press, 1955

Vieth, David M. (ed.), *Essential Articles for the Study of Jonathan Swift's Poetry*, Hamden, Connecticut: Archon Books, 1984

Zimmerman, Everett, *Swift's Narrative Satires: Author and Authority*, Ithaca, New York: Cornell University Press, 1983

Even before his death, Swift's reputation started to wane as rumors of his insanity began to color interpretations of his writings. Commentary during much of the nineteenth century bordered on the vitriolic, and only in the twentieth century has a systematic attempt been made to give a more balanced portrait of the man and his work.

During the early years of the twentieth century, academic criticism of Swift completed a restoration of both character and artistic reputation, begun by sympathetic biographers of the late Victorian age. QUINTANA's 1936 study is representative of that critical movement. Setting out to write an intellectual and literary biography, Quintana makes use of a host of primary source materials and the findings of political, intellectual, literary, and social historians, whose work offers explanations for much of the content and techniques of Swift's satires. Convinced that Swift is "the most compelling" of Augustan writers, Quintana offers a sensitive, detailed assessment of the author's major and minor works, identifying his greatness in "the moral realism through which all of Swift's terrific intellectual intensity found expression".

Readers looking for a good introduction to the character and accomplishments of Swift will do well to begin with QUINTANA's 1955 monograph. Written specifically for a general audience, the work is less detailed than Quintana's earlier scholarly examination of the satirist. Chapters are organized thematically, so one may get a sense of Swift's life and character; his adoption of the satirist's mask; his affiliation with politics, Church matters, and the citizens of Ireland whose champion he became; and his final years, when disillusionment, even despair, seemed to characterize his outlook. As he does also in his more extensive study, Quintana is careful in this work to debunk the many myths about Swift, which grew up in the centuries after his death, and which often obscure an honest appreciation of his work.

Another excellent starting point for those wishing to gain a general understanding of Swift's life and works is HUNTING's brief monograph. Like most books in the Twayne series, Hunting's study is intended specifically to be introductory rather than exhaustive; if he skims the surface of works that clearly require greater analysis, he does so intentionally, assuming readers interested in studying these writings will go to other criticism for more extensive commentary. Free of highly technical jargon, and eclectic in its approach to individual compositions, Hunting's work is most helpful in explaining "the eternal contemporaneousness" of Swift's writings.

Any serious student of Swift must take note of the comprehensive critical biography compiled by EHRENPREIS. In the tradition of scholars such as Edgar Johnson (biographer of Charles Dickens and Walter Scott) and Joseph Blotner (biographer of William Faulkner), Ehrenpreis includes in his study the results of a lifetime of research, painstakingly cataloging and interpreting the mass of biographical and critical information available to twentieth-century scholars. Though some may find the work tedious and pedantic, its significance to Swift scholarship is unquestioned.

Among non-specialized studies of Swift's writings, VIETH's collection is particularly valuable for two reasons. First, by contrast with his prose satire, Swift's verse has received relatively brief critical treatment. Second, much of what has been written has appeared in scholarly journals, many of which are not readily available. Vieth brings together 20 articles, which are frequently cited in subsequent commentaries, thus saving scholars much time in assembling materials for study and allowing for easy comparison of interpretations and critical approaches to the verse. At least one entry is included for each of Swift's major poems or collections. Several essays provide comparisons of Swift with his contemporaries, or with later poets such as Wallace Stevens. A handful of selections examine the poet's techniques of versification and the elements of biography that inspired some of his poems.

ZIMMERMAN's study is also limited in scope, focusing on two of Swift's long satires, *Tale of a Tub* and *Travels into Several Remote Nations of the World*. He examines both in light of the epistemological revolution that occurred in the seventeenth century and profoundly influenced the production of literature in that century and the next. Aiming to "explore the strategic position of Swift's satire in relation to major developments in intellectual history and narrative", Zimmerman analyzes the status and function of the narrator in these two works, which share many similarities. He discusses "the author's authority" in the contexts of Protestant biblical hermeneutics, the "new" science of Swift's day, and seventeenth-century politics. He is particularly adept at integrating scholarship from several fields into his analysis of Swift's writings, and at synthesizing clearly the critical positions of his predecessors.

As he does in other volumes in the "Modern Critical Views" series he has edited, BLOOM assembles in his anthology of secondary source materials essays by distinguished twentieth-century scholars to present "a representative selection of the best criticism" devoted to Swift. The claim may be somewhat hyperbolic, for the volume contains fewer than a dozen entries, and half of these focus almost exclusively on Swift's two major works, *Tale of a Tub* and *Gulliver's Travels*. In his introduction, Bloom provides a rationale for the process of selection, suggesting that *Tale of a Tub* is really Swift's greatest satiric accomplishment, despite the popularity of *Gulliver's Travels*. Fortunately, the second half of the volume contains more general assessments of Swift's method and philosophy. While these do not always substitute for longer works on the same subject, a number appeared only in journals, which may not be readily available to readers; for that reason, the collection is a most helpful introduction to twentieth-century critical perspectives.

Among several comprehensive studies completed in the latter decades of the twentieth century, DOWNIE's is particularly well researched and well written, though more specialized than a number of similar works. Taking a decidedly political slant, Downie ignores most of the myths surrounding the writer's life, and attempts to "offer an account of [Swift's] political ideas which is neither anachronistic nor unduly influenced by the (clearly) distorted views of his enemies". The effort leads to some interesting readings of the major works, especially since Downie insists Swift was never a Tory. Instead, he believes the satirist was more interested in attacking the excesses of both political parties, measuring them against his vision of the ideal society. This "pristine" state or "Golden Age", "in which human nature and human institutions" are in harmony, is the standard against which Swift judges the world around him – and finds it falling short of the ideal in almost every instance. Downie's commentary is provocative, if limited, and warrants careful attention.

NOKES has written what should be considered the standard one-volume biography of Swift for the late twentieth century. Meticulously researched and demonstrating careful, sensitive analysis of the satirist, the volume provides "a new, comprehensive view of the man and his works, based on the accumulated wealth of evidence which is now available". That body of information is extensive, and Nokes is conscientious in distinguishing fact from fiction. He is also courageous enough to restore to the story of Swift's life several anecdotes of questionable authenticity, because "they have played such an important part in the transmission of Swift's reputation through the ages". That he can do so should be seen as encouraging; it suggests that critics may have finally gone beyond the need to salvage the writer's reputation (a task that has taken nearly a century) and are ready to concentrate on interpreting his works. Nokes does a decent job of interpretation himself, understandably paying special attention to the biographical background of both the poetry and prose. If one were to choose a single work as a source for developing a sophisticated understanding of Swift's life and work, this would be it.

LAURENCE W. MAZZENO

Swinburne, Algernon Charles

1837–1909

English poet, essayist, critic, and dramatist

Harrison, Antony H., *Swinburne's Medievalism: A Study in Victorian Love Poetry*, Baton Rouge: Louisiana State University Press, 1988

Lafourcade, Georges, *Swinburne: A Literary Biography*, London: G. Bell & Sons, 1932; New York: William Morrow, 1932

Louis, Margot K., *Swinburne and His Gods: The Roots and Growth of an Agnostic Poetry*, Montreal: McGill-Queen's University Press, 1990

McGann, Jerome J., *Swinburne: An Experiment in Criticism*, Chicago: University of Chicago Press, 1972

Peters, Robert L., *The Crowns of Apollo: Swinburne's Principles of Literature and Art: A Study in Victorian Criticism and Aesthetics*, Detroit: Wayne State University Press, 1965

Praz, Mario, *The Romantic Agony*, translated by Angus Davidson, London: Oxford University Press, 1933, 2nd edition, 1951; Cleveland, Ohio: World, 1965

Riede, David G., *Swinburne: A Study of Romantic Mythmaking*, Charlottesville: University Press of Virginia, 1978

Rooksby, Rikky, and Nicholas Shrimpton (eds.), *The Whole Music of Passion: New Essays on Swinburne*, Aldershot, Hampshire: Scolar Press, 1993

The dip in Swinburne's reputation earlier this century, occasioned chiefly by modernist hostility to the sort of poetry that he was thought of as representing, has shown intermittent signs of reversing itself in recent years. Nonetheless, good criticism is rather thin on the ground, and a great many aspects of Swinburne's work remain unexplored.

LAFOURCADE constitutes a classic statement of traditional attitudes to the poet. Here, as in his earlier, more extensive biography (*La Jeunesse de Swinburne*, only in French, 1928) is articulated what was for many years the "standard" view of Swinburne, concentrating on the early work (*Poems and Ballads*, *Atalanta in Calydon*), giving a great deal of space to the political poetry, and mostly ignoring the plays, the criticism, and the bulk of the later work. Lafourcade's portrait is of two Swinburnes, the younger living furiously, embarked on drinking himself to death, and writing brilliantly; and the older, rescued by Watts-Dunton and living in Putney, living a slow and measured life, and writing nothing of interest. PRAZ, to instance a critic who subscribes to this view, concentrates almost entirely on the poetry of *Poems and Ballads*, although his reading of Swinburne as a crucial figure in the Decadent continuation of Romantic literature remains useful today. Praz is particularly interested in Swinburne's fascination with the archetype of the beautiful, deadly woman – "La Belle Dame Sans Merci" as his (lengthy) chapter styles it. To focus only on the (literally) sadistic aspects of Swinburne is necessarily to misrepresent the whole of Swinburne's output, but despite its limitations this is an influential and impressive study.

Swinburne's stock fell furthest during the 1940s and 1950s, and indeed it is only fairly recently that he has begun to be taken seriously again as a major figure of nineteenth-century literature. This resurrection of interest was marked partly by the publication of his astonishing letters (*The Swinburne Letters*, edited by C.Y. Lang, Yale University Press, 1959–62), and partly by works that examined Swinburne's aesthetics and theories of art. PETERS remains among the best of these, an examination of Swinburne's extensive and idiosyncratic critical writing, which places them in the context of contemporary debates concerning "Art For Art's Sake" and aestheticist developments in France. Chapter 1 surveys the criticism, and deals with the initial obstacles it presents to a reader, while pointing up its overlooked merits. The remainder of the book expounds Swinburne's wide-ranging critical ideas under various headings ("Morality and Art", "Form", and so on). Peters insists that Swinburne "belongs among the few truly vital critics of literature and art".

McGANN's experimental study remains one of the most useful and wide-ranging critiques of Swinburne we have. By casting his discussion as a dialogue between characters from Swinburne's circle, McGann is able to argue from many angles at once, and if this sometimes gives the study a rather slippery feel it does avoid narrow pigeonholing of its subject's enormous range. McGann deals with Swinburne's prose writing, and goes on to examine questions of Swinburne as a Romantic lyricist, and his relationship with the classics. The question of stylistic "impressionism", the alleged "vagueness and unintelligibility" of both his poetry and prose, is addressed but dismissed; and the study closes with a look at his sado-masochist poetry. This is criticism at its most engaging, which achieves both a certain comprehensiveness and also contains a great many detailed and sensitive close readings of the verse.

RIEDE's study is a little more pedestrian. Swinburne is read as a mythopoeic (myth-creating) poet, one trying to recreate Romanticism in the late-ninteenth century. The study opens with a detailed examination of Swinburne's book on William Blake, showing how he "retained Blake's respect for the holiness of man while rejecting his Christian mysticism". It then examines Swinburne's notion of poetry as "the perpetuation by individual singers of the eternal Apollonian song".

HARRISON's is a specialist study of Swinburne's many poems on medieval and chivalric themes, seeing them, and particularly his Arthurian epic *Tristram of Lyonesse*, as more than just recreations of a past age: "his medieval subjects enabled him to correct his own era's unwarranted and contagious idealisation" of the past to "express his relentlessly fatalistic world view". Since it is as an Arthurian author that Swinburne is being read by many, Harrison's work is especially useful.

LOUIS examines the evolution of Swinburne's rebellious attitudes towards Christianity. She evinces a four-stage development from Swinburne's poetry. An initial phase of bleak pessimism, such as informs *Poems and Ballads* and *Atalanta in Calydon*, is the nihilistic repudiation of conventional faith for which Swinburne was notorious. But this, Louis says, soon metamorphoses into a second phase of revolutionary fervour, in which Swinburne demonstrates a powerful faith in the human power to make a political reality of "Love, the beloved republic". The third stage involves a literary re-enactment and celebration of artistic triumphs over time. Louis's argument is perhaps weakest with respect to what she claims is the fourth and final stage – an acceptance of the ultimately uncertainty and ambiguity of the world; but the book as a whole is an intelligent piece of criticism.

ROOKSBY and SHRIMPTON have brought together an excellent series of original essays on Swinburne, the first such undertaking to date. Of particular merit are two essays by Rooksby himself, "A Century of Swinburne", which polemically surveys the poet's twentieth-century reputation, and "Thirteen Ways of Looking at *Tristram of Lyonesse*", a multi-perspective approach, or series of approaches, to the text many see as Swinburne's masterpiece. The standard of all the essays in this collection is high, and the volume also prints three unpublished poems by Swinburne.

ADAM ROBERTS

Synge, John Millington 1871–1909

Irish dramatist

Ayling, Ronald (ed.), *John Millington Synge: Four Plays: A Casebook*, London: Macmillan, 1992

Bickley, Francis, *J.M. Synge and The Irish Dramatic Movement*, London: Constable, 1912; New York: Houghton Mifflin, 1912

Corkery, Daniel, *Synge and Anglo-Irish Literature: A Study*, Cork, Ireland: Cork University Press, 1931; reprinted, New York: Russell & Russell, 1965

David, Pratap Chandra, *The Tragic View in the Plays of J.M. Synge*, Bareilly: Uttar Pradesh, India: Prakash, 1988

Frazier, Adrian, *Behind The Scenes: Yeats, Horniman and the Struggle for the Abbey Theatre*, Berkeley: University of California Press, 1990

Greene, David H., and Edward M. Stephens, *J.M. Synge, 1871–1909*, New York: New York University Press, 1959, revised 1989

Grene, Nicholas, *Synge: A Critical Study of the Plays*, London: Macmillan, 1975

Jones, Nesta (ed.), *File on Synge*, London: Methuen, 1994

Keily, David M., *John Millington Synge: A Biography*, Dublin: Gill & MacMillan, 1994

Kiberd, Declan, *Synge and the Irish Language*, London: Macmillan, 1979, 2nd edition, 1993; Totowa, New Jersey: Rowman & Littlefield, 1979

King, Mary C., *The Drama of J.M. Synge*, London: Fourth Estate, 1985

Kopper, Edward A., (ed.), *J.M. Synge: A Literary Companion*, Westport, Connecticut: Greenwood Press, 1988

Kopper, Edward A., *John Millington Synge: A Reference Guide*, Boston: G.K. Hall, 1979; London: George Prior, 1979

Maxwell, D.E.S., *A Critical History of Modern Irish Drama*, Cambridge: Cambridge University Press, 1984

O'Brien Johnson, Toni, *Synge: The Medieval and the Grotesque*, Gerrards Cross, Buckinghamshire: Colin Smythe, 1982; New York: Barnes & Noble, 1982

Price, Alan, *J.M.Synge and Anglo-Irish Drama*, London: Methuen, 1961

Saddlemyer, Ann, *J. M. Synge and Modern Comedy*, Dublin: Dolmen Press, 1968

Skelton, Robin, *J.M. Synge*, Lewisburg, Pennsylvania: Bucknell University Press, 1972

Thornton, Weldon, *J.M. Synge and the Western Mind*, Gerrards Cross, Buckinghamshire: Colin Smythe, 1979; New York: Barnes & Noble, 1979

Watson, G.J., *Irish Identity and The Literary Revival: Synge, Joyce and O'Casey*, London: Croom Helm, 1979; New York: Barnes & Noble, 1979

The controversy surrounding Synge's plays during his lifetime echoes through critical approaches written since. Assessments of his relationship with other key Abbey Theatre figures, and of the extent to which Dublin audience reaction misread his representation of Irish life, are inevitably coloured by the critic's degree of involvement with the cultural context, particularly in terms of religion and nationalism. This emotive strain in critical writing perhaps explains the predominant tendency towards biographical format, while there is relatively little trace of contemporary developments in critical theory. Such approaches are more evident in journals, but bibliographies in a few later works cited here include some of these more up-to-date critical approaches.

KOPPER's *Reference Guide* (1979) points out that "plays are cultural events as well as literary ones" and aims to "peel away the layers of prejudice – both derogatory and laudatory – that have blurred Synge's contribution". After an Introduction, which indicates some major reasons for controversy, a helpful annotated bibliography follows, although sometimes brevity and key words indicative of the tone and approach of certain critics may not do full justice to them. As a concise introduction to Synge, the most useful book is JONES. Following the series format, it includes a brief but densely packed chronology, play summaries with extracts from contemporary and more recent comment, some non-dramatic writing, and "the writer on his work", and a select bibliography, which includes audio and video recordings, although it omits Kiberd's significant work. The use of often contradictory extracts allows the reader to form personal judgements about critical responses and performances – including some from the 1980s. Similarly, AYLING's collection covers 1901–86, and while neither illustrating extreme critical responses cited in his Introduction nor recent innovative theoretical readings, it does include a good range of criticism from inside and outside Ireland, as well as by Kiberd, Maxwell, and O'Brien Johnson. Claiming "Synge possessed an instinctive understanding then, for what we now call Chekhovian features of Irish life as it was", Ayling suggests that he relegated social and political concerns to the dramatic background without marginalising them, leaving prose as a medium for advocating reform.

The qualitative differences among biographical studies is evident in a comparison of those by KEILY, and GREENE and STEPHENS. The former is an evocative rather than an academic work, although there is a select bibliography and end-notes with page references rather than precise numbering. Written in a journalistic and somewhat rhetorical style it makes assumptions about Synge's thought processes ("See Synge lying in the grass near Killeany . . . [he] is not interested in the antiquities of Inishmore; he has shed this passion as he has shed so many others"). Keily cites a range of sources, but his main concern is to celebrate Synge's life – suggesting that "audiences are now nostalgic seekers", that the plays' significance has passed "their satiric bite gone . . . the social issues are no longer relevant". Green and Stephens' revised biography (1989) includes hitherto unpublished writings and letters, and was written with the full co-operation of the Synge estate under the proviso that material previously collected by Stephens, Synge's nephew and custodian of his papers, would be appropriately acknowledged. In spite of this connection, Greene manages to keep a more objective academic perspective, with useful end-notes, bibliography, and index. Although the focus here is the man and his personal context, including the decay of the Ascendancy class, there is some discussion of the plays – for example of the changes made in the drafts of *Playboy of the Western World* and transformations wrought from the Aran material. Greene is convinced that despite the vicissitudes of Synge's career, his work assimilated the Gaelic past and interpreted the traditional life of Ireland with more insight than any other Irish writer.

"Irishness" – like questions of mixed genre, the role of European ideas, the relationship to modernism, and the authenticity of Synge's language – has been among critical preoccupations from the first. BICKLEY, for example, dismisses the hostility to Synge, putting it down to the limitations of Irishmen for whom "politics has blinded its victims to psychology as well as Art". Concerned with Synge's poetic ability in "borrowing from actual life, improving the embellishing", while apparently eschewing the symbolic, he praises *Riders to the Sea*: "tiny as is its scale, it is as plainly stamped with greatness as *Hamlet* or the *Agamemnon*". Rather than appreciate the Irish context, Bickley is concerned to credit Synge with Elizabethan qualities, returning English literature "back into the path it had left three hundred years ago and hence lost its drama". This kind of English canonical approach makes understandable CORKERY's notorious counterblast, which denies the validity of Anglo-Irish writing by the Ascendancy class, condemning the pernicious effect of the "overwhelming prestige of English culture". Corkery warms towards Synge for his attempt at living with the people, claiming that once "Europe . . . purged his eyes of the Ascendancy prejudice . . . it was Nationalism that lit the flame within them". However, he considers that while Synge was capable of absorbing the physical environment, he was incapable of understanding the spirituality of the people. In *Playboy*, Corkery considers that this weakness caused Synge to exchange the spiritual for the spirited. While regretting this, Corkery does admit that despite its offensive qualities, this play is not so much a satire but a tribute to the people. Thus he overvalues *Riders to the Sea*, and thinks that the Aran prose might well outlive the rest of Synge's work.

Later works like WATSON also problematise Synge's relationship with notions of Irish identity; as Watson notes, "one qualified only on grounds of descent, religion or politics, and usually one needed the combination of all three for native acceptance". Watson explores the ways in which Synge's primitivism and class attitudes reinforced each other, suggesting that his "idealisation of the peasant was in a large measure a creative act of the imagination". Watson defends audience hostility as a valid reaction of a colonised people to both the dominant culture and Synge's creative "misrepresentation of Irish life". He suggests that ultimately Synge obliquely asserts the separateness of the Anglo-Irish through the perspective of outsider figures. Watson, based significantly in Aberdeen, values Synge's work more highly than that of Sean O'Casey, whom he castigates for sentimentality and a nationalist politics blind to the complexities of the situation in Northern Ireland.

Linked with such differences of religious and political perspective is dissension about the extent of the debt owed by Synge to European, as opposed to Irish, culture. Earlier critics like Maurice Bourgeois emphasise the latter, often in association with considerations of naturalism and authenticity. PRICE praises Synge's observation of actualities, and the linguistic freedom derived from Anglo-Irish, but emphasises his selection from peasant language as more "compact and beautiful than the actual utterance of anyone". His critical approach tends towards narrative thickened with analysis, though highlighting the plays' tensions between dream and actuality, man and nature. Considering that despite poetic qualities, Synge's work lacks metaphysical and religious implications, Price feels that he is not quite in the first rank of great writers. As a structuring strategy, both SKELTON and GRENE link phases of Synge's life to particular locations and plays. Grene feels that Synge's nationalism was aesthetic rather than political, and that, having been distanced from his Ascendancy roots partly through intellectual and European experiences, "he settled interest in (Irish) rural areas – thus turning away from areas of social conflict where class and creed were not so urgent". The liberating effect of Aran is discussed not only in the context of the peasant's lives as "a primary contact with reality" but also of revisions made by Synge to his notes as he improved his skill in recording dialect. Claiming that "though his language is drawn from a virtually illiterate society, his effects are aimed at the educated", Grene's grammatical analysis of Synge's language anticipates the more detailed work of Kiberd. Grene also considers the dramatic impact of some images in performance, insisting that *Playboy* is rooted in the real, while noting the effect of the tension between mock murder and real violence in what might be seen to be an "unhappy comedy". He finds Samuel Beckett's tramps "more pretentious" than Synge's characters, feeling that Synge's ironies are less destructive. Grene stresses the importance of the Irish element in assessing Synge's work, which he claims can be compared with the best twentieth-century drama, since narrow dimensions do not preclude profundity. THORNTON claims his critique is not biographical, while insisting that despite the shock of Darwinism, Synge retained an interest in religion and philosophy. Feeling that European influences were small compared with the impact of Aran, Thornton suggests that archaic elements of Irish culture had a pagan quality, which had more in common with Indian than Western, Aristotelian perspectives. Thus, a more Eastern, holistic response to the relationship between mind and body, and a belief in the power of language to affect reality is claimed to have appealed to Synge, allowing him to embrace lived contradictions such as the islanders' mix of the Catholic and the pagan.

Questions of genre are also associated with such paradoxes. SADDLEMYER reminds the reader that Synge saw himself as an Irish European, living in the furthermost corner of Western Europe, and considers that Yeats' attitudes have been given too much credence. She states that the plays' themes are contrapuntally structured in their exploration of conflict and contradiction, where nature is "the one dependable reality in a world which restlessly hovers between the ecstasy of fulfilment and the tragedy of oblivion". Linking Synge with the development of contemporary black comedy and the European Absurd, she notes Rabelaisian incorporation of brutality within the comic, but stresses the great importance of irony. In contrast, DAVID sets Synge aside from what he considers to be the nihilism and pessimism of the Absurd, and, through rather old-fashioned analysis, praises universal, Stoic, and noble human qualities in the plays. He is at pains to establish a Greek tragic pedigree, and speculates too much on Synge's psyche, paying very little attention to either the Irish cultural context or the function of naturalism/realism.

Critics who emphasise European influences tend towards more philosophical or linguistic readings – using some more contemporary critical practices. KING stresses the role of European thinkers on Synge's theme of language, seen in relation to "the mediating, symbolic role of language and art . . . mediating between subject and object, self and society". In exploring Synge's linguistic and cultural conflict, she draws on the slipperiness of the sign as discussed by Voloshinov in order to suggest that the playwright uses a multivocal "transfigured realism", linked to juxtaposition of images in a related "pre-occupation with the nature of language and the nature of play". Her detailed critique of Synge's meta-dramatic and meta-textual strategies is provocative and well-informed, with a particularly interesting comparison of a range of potential draft endings for *Playboy*. Another more-sophisticated critique is O'BRIEN JOHNSON's exploration of the medieval and grotesque in Synge's plays. Through scholarly reference to the work of academics with whom Synge studied in France, she traces source material including *moralités*, and *fabliaux*, and comments on Synge's adaptation. O'Brien Johnson also defines the nature of the grotesque, with reference to Rabelais and Mikhail Bakhtin's theories of the function of carnival and the body, assessing both their roles within Synge's dramatic vision and their connections, through folk tradition, with incongruity, ugliness, and folly. She claims that there is a conceptual relationship between tragicomedy and the grotesque, which is linked to unresolved incompatibilities in Synge's work, but that the realistic embodiment of the grotesque prevents his plays from falling into romanticised medievalism. KIBERD's detailed work on Synge's language is equally impressive, and is claimed even by Ayling to be a turning point in Synge criticism. Kiberd's scholarly but fluent analysis of Synge's study of Irish in relation to the plays and to the Gaelic League is rooted in research. Further, in the new edition's Preface he relates the tripartite structure of *Playboy* to Frantz Fanon's "dialectic of decolonisation, from occupation, through nationalism to liberation". He also evaluates the "radical implications of the manly woman of Gaelic tradition" in Synge's dramatic representation of gender. Apart from brief Preface references, the Bibliography has not been updated to include newer theoretical approaches.

Most contributions to KOPPER's 1988 *Companion* are American, and they incorporate some newer methodologies, including Kopper's own references to Rabelais. For example, Richard Fallis writes in the light of Julia Kristeva's theories about intertextuality, and with reference to scholastic methods Synge encountered in France. He suggests that Synge sought "marginalised positions" and that his work shows a "modernist emphasis on dislocation – physical, historical, personal, and a modern sense of alienation". Although Bonnie Kime Scott claims to examine the language of Synge's women characters through the methodology of French feminist criticism, she does not produce a densely theoretical argument about differences between male and female discourses, apart from allusions to Kristeva's semiotics of desire. Her position needs further development and more textual illustration – at times it is very close to essentialism, indicating patriarchal elements in certain plays while lamenting the destruction of "natural love".

FRAZIER and MAXWELL provide sound historical contexts for Synge and his contemporaries. Maxwell's illustrated book covers a wide period and includes a number of writers and venues. Describing Synge's influences as both "Romantic and Jonsonian comedy, classic French and realist theatre", he nevertheless considers that his work "was the finest achievement of the aims and principles of the Irish movement". Frazier, working from a New-Historicist perspective, shows how Annie Horniman's influence on the Abbey extended beyond economics. Most reference to Synge occurs in the chapter on "Author and Audience", around the question of the representation of the national character. Reading both books helps to provide a balanced framework for the ongoing critical controversy.

MARGARET L. LLEWELLYN-JONES

T

Tagore, Rabindranath 1861–1941

Indian poet, short-story writer, novelist, dramatist, and essayist

Chatterjee, Bhabatosh, *Rabindranath Tagore and Modern Sensibility*, New Delhi: Oxford University Press, (forthcoming)

Dutta, Krishna, and Andrew Robinson, *Rabindranath Tagore: The Myriad-Minded Man*, London: Bloomsbury, 1995

Dyson, Ketaki Kushari, *In Your Blossoming Flower-Garden: Rabindranath Tagore and Victoria Ocampo*, New Delhi: Sahitya Akademi, 1988

Dyson, Ketaki Kushari (trans.), *I Won't Let You Go – Selected Poems*, by Tagore, Newcastle-upon-Tyne: Bloodaxe Books, 1991

Henn, Katherine, *Rabindranath Tagore: A Bibliography*, Metuchen, New Jersey: American Theological Library Association/Scarecrow Press, 1985

Kämpchen, Martin, *Rabindranath Tagore and Germany: A Documentation*, edited by Jeanne Openshaw, Calcutta: Max Müller Bhavan, 1991

Kripalani, Krishna, *Rabindranath Tagore: A Biography*, London: Oxford University Press, 1962; New York: Grove Press, 1962; revised edition, Calcutta: Visva-Bharati, 1980

Lago, Mary, and Ronald Warwick (eds.), *Rabindranath Tagore: Perspectives in Time*, London: Macmillan, 1989

Lal, Ananda (trans. and ed.), *Rabindranath Tagore: Three Plays*, by Tagore, Calcutta: M.P. Birla Foundation, 1987

Radice, William (trans. and ed.), *Rabindranath Tagore: Selected Poems*, by Tagore, Harmondsworth, Middlesex: Penguin, 1985, 3rd, revised edition, 1995

Radice, William (trans. and ed.), *Rabindranath Tagore: Selected Short Stories*, Harmondsworth, Middlesex: Penguin, 1991, revised 1994

Ray, Niharranjan, *An Artist in Life: A Commentary on the Life and Works of Rabindranath Tagore*, Trivandrum: University of Kerala, 1967

Robinson, Andrew, *The Art of Rabindranath Tagore*, London: André Deutsch, 1989

Thompson, Edward, *Rabindranath Tagore, Poet and Dramatist*, Oxford and New York: Oxford University Press, 1948; with an Introduction by Harish Trivedi, New Delhi: Oxford University Press, 1989

Thompson, E.P., *Alien Homage: Edward Thompson and Rabindranath Tagore* ,New Delhi: Oxford University Press, 1993

Much of the older writing and criticism on Rabindranath Tagore has to be discarded now, because it was based on inadequate or non-existent knowledge of the Bengali originals. The fame that Tagore won through his own English translations, and their many secondary translations into other languages, was a cultural and literary phenomenon in itself, and continues to merit some attention; but no one should suppose that the English *Collected Poems and Plays* (London: Macmillan, 1936) offers any real access to Tagore's range and vitality as a Bengali writer. For that, the English reader must approach Tagore's wider work through the translations and summaries of others.

My own (RADICE's) edition of *Selected Poems* of Tagore seems to have been the initiator of a new wave of Tagore translations. It sets out to capture, through 48 poems, the range and variety of Tagore's poetic output, and to supply the non-Bengali reader with background information through 22 pages of Introduction and 52 pages of notes. DYSON, whose selection of 140 poems and songs overlaps with mine by one poem, adopts a similar procedure, her Introduction and notes being very informative and lively. Her rapport with the feminine and feminist aspects of Tagore is also evident in her intricate study of his friendship with Victoria Ocampo. My (RADICE's) edition of Tagore's stories had a more difficult birth than the edition of the poems, but in its revised and corrected form gives, with its Introduction and appendices, as full an impression of Tagore's most fertile period as a short-story writer (the 1890s, which he spent managing his father's estates in East Bengal) as has so far been offered in English. It overlaps to some extent with Krishna Dutta and Mary Lago's smaller selection of short stories (London: Macmillan, 1991).

On Tagore's plays, accurate translation and 123 pages of detailed background information can be found in LAL, while on Tagore's paintings, ROBINSON has assembled 175 colour plates – though the Introduction is merely a compilation of English-language reviews and reactions, many of them half-baked.

A detailed bibliography on Tagore in English has been compiled by HENN; the Foreword to this volume, however, by Reverend Frank R. Podgorski, is embarrassingly determined to look to Tagore for a "Gospel" rather than for literary pleasure.

KRIPALANI still provides the best general biographical and critical introduction to Tagore. Kripalani worked with Tagore at Santiniketan in the 1930s, and married his granddaughter Nandini. His closeness to the poet prevents him from being entirely candid about Tagore the man, but he is deeply sensitive to his creative work. Through subtle description and summary, he conveys the power and fascination of Tagore's writings for Bengali readers, and the pantheistic and humanistic values that inform them.

RAY's study can be read with profit as an extension of Kripalani's work. He travels *con amore* through virtually all of Tagore's books, describing them vividly and fluently. His is the first study to turn to if one wants a synopsis of a novel or a play, or a sense of what a particular volume of verse contains. His chronological list of Tagore's works at the end is also useful.

Edward THOMPSON (1948), now that *père* has been followed by *fils*, is interesting to read not so much for his criticism on Tagore as for the object lesson his brave but unsuccessful study provides on the difficulties and dangers of inter-cultural interpretation. Both from Harish Trivedi's Introduction, and from E.P. THOMPSON's penetrating account (1993), we learn of what a bumpy ride the poet gave his first serious foreign critic and translator.

LAGO, both in her contribution ("Restoring Rabindranath Tagore") to her collection edited with WARWICK, and in *Imperfect Encounter: Letters of William Rothenstein and Rabindranath Tagore* (Cambridge, Massachusetts: Harvard University Press, 1972), writes with authority about the sequence of accidents that led to the award of the Nobel Prize to Tagore. Other useful contributions to Lago and Warwick are France Bhattacharya's essay on the supernatural in Tagore's stories, and Raymond Head's survey of settings of Tagore by Western composers.

For research into Tagore's international career, nothing in the English-speaking world has been done yet to match KÄMPCHEN, who achieves lucid completeness in his documentation of Tagore's visits to Germany and his subsequent *Rezeptionsgeschichte* there. This book greatly expands, but does not completely supplant, Alex Aronson's pioneering study *Rabindranath Tagore Through Western Eyes* (2nd edition, Calcutta: 1991). (Kämpchen's beautiful German translations of Tagore can be read in *Rabindranath Tagore: Wo Freude ihre Feste feiert – Gedichte und Lieder*, Freiburg: Herder Taschenbuch, 1990.) For the British side of the story, the compilation *Rabindranath Tagore and the British Press, 1911–1941*, edited by Kalyan Kundu *et al.*, and published in 1989 by the UK Tagore Centre, is a useful resource.

DUTTA and ROBINSON tell the dramatic story of Tagore's public career in India and abroad more candidly and in more detail than Kripalani, but their book will disappoint those looking for insight into Tagore's creative achievements. Their bibliography and notes, however, are a useful source of information.

Finally, new possibilities in the criticism and interpretation of Tagore are adumbrated in CHATTERJEE, whose collection of essays reflecting a lifetime of reading and thinking about Tagore delves for the first time in English into the complexities and contradictions that lie beneath the humanistic surface of Tagore's writing. And for an exciting entrée into that complexity, Kaiser Haq's translation of Tagore's novella *Quartet* (London: Heinemann [Asian Writers Series], 1994) is warmly recommended.

WILLIAM RADICE

Taylor, Edward c.1642–1729

English-born American poet and sermon writer

Davis, Thomas M., *A Reading of Edward Taylor*, Newark: University of Delaware Press, 1992; London: Associated University Presses, 1992

Gatta, John, *The Meditative Wit of Edward Taylor*, Columbia: University of Missouri Press, 1989

Hammond, Jeffrey A., *Edward Taylor: Fifty Years of Scholarship and Criticism*, Columbia, South Carolina: Camden House, 1993

Grabo, Norman S., *Edward Taylor*, New York: Twayne, 1961, revised 1988

Keller, Karl, *The Example of Edward Taylor*, Amherst: University of Massachusetts Press, 1975

Rowe, Karen E., *Saint and Singer: Edward Taylor's Typology and the Poetics of Meditation*, Cambridge and New York: Cambridge University Press, 1986

Scheick, William J., *The Will and the Word: The Poetry of Edward Taylor*, Athens: University of Georgia Press, 1974

Edward Taylor wrote many sermons, but is primarily regarded for his poetry, especially *Preparatory Meditations*. Written principally in relation to his ministerial participation in the sacrament of the Lord's Supper, these manuscript verse meditations, many revised and recast over time, reflect the traits of seventeenth-century Metaphysical poetry and, as well, such idiosyncratic features as a decorum of imperfection. These features interested Taylor's early critics, several of whom were disturbed by his seemingly free-associative manner and his putative Anglican and Roman Catholic disposition. Although somewhat more attention has been given to Taylor's aesthetics, including consistency in his use of imagery and transitions, recent responses still predominantly emphasize theme, theology, typology, context, and influence.

My own (SCHEICK's) book explores the Augustinian tradition informing Taylor's verse in order to explain the poet's fascination with language. In this tradition language reveals the state of the will and is a medium for imitating Christ's integration of the material and the spiritual. Taylor, accordingly, does not repudiate the physical world, which, even after the Fall of Adam and Eve, participates in the divine order.

KELLER's book, in contrast to my interest in Taylor's conscious artistic strategies, emphasizes the poet's primitivistic traits, especially his unconscious preoccupation with process. Rather than express meaning, Keller claims Taylor's poetry merely dramatizes a self in various roles, none of which are actual. The poet is most interesting when he is unintentionally humorous and fails at the conventions he tries to imitate. Keller's attention to voice and persona instructively alerts us to a major dynamic feature of Taylor's verse. His book, however, should be used cautiously, because Keller frequently ignores crucial contextual matters, misrepresents Taylor's actual words, and overlooks the depth and range of play evident in the poet's language.

ROWE responds to Keller, in part, by reaffirming the importance of the meanings and contexts of Taylor's verse meditations. Rowe meticulously discloses the sources of Taylor's typology. She traces a progression in his poems from an avoidance of applying ceremonial types to history, through a fashioning of provocative conceits and a preference of sacramental typological themes, to a use of typological reasoning as a medium to express a transcendent unitary meaning. While Rowe's book explicitly denigrates Taylor's poetry as the product of limited skill, her book is an excellent resource on the background, pattern, and significance of Taylor's typological imagery.

GRABO, too, is ambivalent about Taylor's artistic capability. In his revised study (1988) of Taylor's use of contemplation to intensify his religious experience, Grabo contends that the logic of a devotional idea is more important to the poet than is the development of poetic imagery. These poems incorporate mystical elements, but they are not expressions of the poet's attainment of mystical rapture. Grabo's revision evidences a little slippage in the consistency of its argument, but his small book still provides a useful introduction to Taylor.

GATTA focuses more than Grabo on Taylor's management of language. Through wit, modeled on the "comic incongruity" of Christ's union of the mundane and the sublime, the poet searches for salvation. For Gatta, a profound sense of joy and affirmation underlies Taylor's explicit expressions of self-deprecation. Although Gatta misses opportunities, uses analytical terms too loosely, and evades rather than attends to the subtleties of Taylor's intricate language, his book usefully insists on the place of humor in Puritan aesthetics.

DAVIS, who scrutinizes Taylor's manuscripts, reads the poet's meditative verse as essentially occasional, biographical, and developmental. These poems evidence a change from the poet's concern with the quality of his verse to his obsession with the condition of his soul. This development results in a diminishment of artistry. Noting significant alterations in Taylor's thought and poetic aims, Davis reveals as much as we presently know about the personal circumstances informing the poet's verse.

HAMMOND interrelates the preceding works and countless others in his review of the studies of Taylor published from the 1950s to the 1990s. His approach is chronological and thematic. Anyone interested in the state of scholarship on Taylor must begin with his stunningly thorough and even-handed book.

WILLIAM J. SCHEICK

Tennyson, Alfred, Lord 1809–1892

English poet

Collins, Philip (ed.), *Tennyson: Seven Essays*, London: Macmillan, 1992; New York: St Martin's Press, 1992

Jordan, Elaine, *Alfred Tennyson*, Cambridge and New York: Cambridge University Press, 1988

Joseph, Gerard, *Tennyson and the Text: The Weaver's Shuttle*, Cambridge and New York: Cambridge University Press, 1992

Joseph, Gerard (ed.), *Victorian Poetry*, 30(3–4), Autumn–Winter 1992

Ricks, Christopher, *Tennyson*, London and New York: Macmillan, 1972

Rowlinson, Matthew, *Tennyson's Fixations: Psychoanalysis and the Topics of the Early Poetry*, Charlottesville: University Press of Virginia, 1994

Shaw, Marion, *Alfred Lord Tennyson*, Brighton, Sussex: Harvester Press, 1988

Sinfield, Alan, *Alfred Tennyson*, Oxford and New York: Blackwell, 1986

Tennyson's critical fortunes have fluctuated dramatically in the twentieth century. Responses up to 1945 tended to construct Tennyson as a poet of emotion and technique, rather than one of intellectual depth, scope, or rigour, thus denying him serious critical attention. Stephen Dedalus in James Joyce's *Ulysses* patronisingly refers to, for example, the figure of "Lawn Tennyson, gentleman poet", while W.H. Auden regarded him as "the stupidest" of English poets. These initial dismissals had a considerable impact on subsequent critics, and it was not until the 1970s that Tennyson's poetry began properly to undergo significant re-evaluation. Since the 1980s much of the best criticism of Tennyson has been theoretically informed, addressing, in particular, questions of gender, empire, language, and subjectivity. It has also, importantly, sought to locate Tennyson within the broader cultural context of his own time, relating the poetry to contemporary discourses ranging from mythography and evolution to aesthetics, psychiatry, and sexual politics.

RICKS's study is a lucid example of the traditional liberal-humanist approach to Tennyson. In terms that now seem critically both naive and narrow, Ricks defines the three aims of his reading: to establish a "sense of what Tennyson in his private life underwent and became; to make an independent exploration of his poetry . . . and to suggest some of the relationships between the life and the work". Throughout this book Ricks shows himself to be a subtle and sensitive critic of particular textual details and passages, but the overall method is both theoretically problematic and, ultimately, reductive (as Ann Wordsworth has shown in a forceful critique of Ricks's position, in *Untying the Text: A Post-Structuralist Reader*, edited by Robert Young, 1981).

SINFIELD's reading – or re-reading – of Tennyson takes as its point of departure a critique and rejection of what he calls the "essentialist humanism" characteristic of the "established modes of criticism" practised by Ricks and others. Such a perspective is problematic, Sinfield argues, because it turns literary texts into "Literature", the purveyor of supposedly "universal" truths, thus effacing the "historical conditions which govern the activities of writing and reading". Attention to such conditions leads Sinfield "to locate the text in its ideological field" in a way that simultaneously involves a "positive engagement with the world". Using the insights of Marxism, feminism, and deconstruction, this study contains close readings of texts from *Poems, Chiefly Lyrical* to *Idylls of the King*. The Tennyson "produced" by Sinfield's cultural-materialist approach is one whose work disrupts comfortable notions of "sagacious coherence" or "acceptability", posing difficult and unsettling questions about language, ideology, and sexuality in their wake.

Like Sinfield, JORDAN's book seeks to "re-read [Tennyson's] poems" from a vantage point that acknowledges both her own position in "the England of the 1980s" and the historical and cultural shifts those poems negotiate between the 1830s and 1860s. Viewing poetry as "a special discourse, but not a restricted one", this engaging study draws on "work which crosses the boundaries of the literary" in order to situate Tennyson's writing amid a network of concerns, ranging from Victorian aesthetics to the "political and legal changes in the status of the middle classes and of women". Tennyson emerges as a "writer of the middle-class ascendancy", whose texts are marked by a set of ambivalences with regard to "manliness, war, and nineteenth-century scientific rationality". This book effectively combines close textual analysis with broad historical understanding and critical acuity, and provides some valuable insights.

Arguing that feminist literary criticism should address texts produced by men as well as by women, SHAW's study of Tennyson describes itself as "a woman's reading of a man's writing". The aim of the project is not, however, to unmask the misogynist content of Tennyson's poetry – though this is far from being a minor issue – but rather "to put the sex back into the text, to show the engendered and engendering nature of writing". What makes Tennyson's poems "desirable" for the "hetero-critical" feminist reader is the vulnerability of the gender-distinctions inscribed within them. Through the use of psychoanalytic theory, Shaw goes on to situate questions of gender in the broader context of a Tennysonian search for "the lost female body of earliest infancy", which is at once "sought and mourned, and often loathed". She traces this search through a number of key texts, from "Mariana" to "Lucretius", arguing that it is only by means of the "secondary loss – the death of Arthur Hallam" in *In Memoriam* that "the primary and irreparable losses of childhood can be forgiven and accommodated". This is a rewarding and provocative book.

JOSEPH deploys a variety of critical methods, from deconstruction to psychoanalysis and feminism, in his ambitious monograph study *Tennyson and the Text*. The book is divided into two parts dealing, respectively, with questions of perception (chapters 1 to 5) and gender (chapters 6 to 10). These two sections are linked by an interchapter on "The Lady of Shalott" which, with its figure of the weaving artist, constitutes the book's "theoretical and literal center". It is through this text that Joseph articulates and explores what he sees as the main question raised by Tennyson's poetry: "is the literary text woven by a historically definable, intending and 'choosing' Tennyson or by the 'unseen hand' . . . of an all-pervasive textuality that occludes personal intention . . .?" While this study refreshingly eschews the pose of "disinterestedness" characteristically assumed by much traditional criticism, it often seems overly self-conscious and certainly overwritten, caught up in its own self-generating metaphorical webs. Nonetheless it offers a number of interesting and original insights.

The collection of critical essays in *Victorian Poetry* edited by JOSEPH for the centenary of Tennyson's death is an extremely useful and evenly impressive indication of the variety and sophistication of current criticism on Tennyson's poetry. Phenomenological, deconstructionist, feminist, and cultural-materialist perspectives are used to good effect by the contributors, and result in some intriguing and significant new analyses of familiar texts, drawing out, for example, the relations between "Ulysses" and the ideology of colonialism. A particular strength of the collection is the group of seven essays on *Idylls of the King*. Focusing in particular on issues of empire, sexuality, nationality, genre, and language, these essays make a highly convincing case for the importance and continuing relevance of a text whose critical reputation has always been somewhat mixed. The attention given – albeit deliberately – to *Idylls* means that other texts are not discussed, the most striking and curious absence being that of *Maud*.

This omission is powerfully redressed, however, in another centenary collection edited by COLLINS, in the shape of an essay by Isobel Armstrong (reprinted in her *Victorian Poetry: Poetry, Poetics and Politics*, 1993). In a large and imposing analysis Armstrong links *Maud* to *In Memoriam* as a poem of "loss and mourning", but emphasizes the "radically different historical circumstances" in which they were written, tracing out between the texts a movement, as she puts it, "from geology to pathology". The essay is of particular interest for its unusual but persuasive contention that *In Memoriam* rather than *Maud* is the "aberrant" work within the Tennysonian *oeuvre*. This is certainly the outstanding piece in a volume that often seems disappointingly outmoded in terms of the approaches adopted by a number of other contributors.

Taking a deconstructive approach, ROWLINSON's study sets out to read "the major poems of Tennyson's early canon" as texts that "refer to their own conditions of existence". In five densely written and sometimes jargonistic chapters, he shows how Tennyson's early poetry figures or allegorizes its own material status through "the insistent topics of gender and topography". Rowlinson's additional claim is that the self-allegorizing tendency of Tennyson's early works is also operative within the textual field of the (mainly Freudian) psychoanalytic theory he brings to bear upon them. This is, to date, the most sophisticated analysis of Tennyson, going a long way to overturn the early twentieth-century stereotype of Tennyson's poetry as intellectually unrewarding or inconsequential. At the same time, however, the book's remorselessly abstract and somewhat mannered style makes the important issues it raises seem more complicated than is perhaps necessary.

CARL PLASA

Thackeray, William Makepeace

1811–1863

English novelist and essayist

Bloom, Harold (ed.), *William Makepeace Thackeray's "Vanity Fair"*, New York: Chelsea House, 1987

Colby, Robert A., *Thackeray's Canvass of Humanity: An Author and His Public*, Columbus: Ohio State University Press, 1979

Gilmour, Robin, *The Idea of the Gentleman in the Victorian Novel*, London: Allen & Unwin, 1981
Hardy, Barbara, *The Exposure of Luxury: Radical Themes in Thackeray*, London: Peter Owen, 1972; Pittsburgh: University of Pittsburgh Press, 1972
Lund, Michael, *Reading Thackeray*, Detroit: Wayne State University Press, 1988
McMaster, R.D., *Thackeray's Cultural Frame of Reference: Allusion in "The Newcomes"*, London: Macmillan, 1991
Miller, J. Hillis, *Fiction and Repetition: Seven English Novels*, Cambridge, Massachusetts: Harvard University Press, 1982; Oxford: Blackwell, 1982
Shillingsburg, Peter L., *Pegasus in Harness: Victorian Publishing and W.M. Thackeray*, Charlottesville: University Press of Virginia, 1992
Thomas, Deborah A., *Thackeray and Slavery*, Athens: Ohio University Press, 1993
Tillotson, Geoffrey, *Thackeray the Novelist*, Cambridge: Cambridge University Press, 1954

It seems appropriate to start with TILLOTSON's rather old-fashioned critical book about Thackeray, who is, in various respects, an old-fashioned novelist who has continued to attract old-fashioned criticism. Charles Dickens and most other leading Victorian novelists have been comprehensively re-read in recent years, but there have been far fewer interesting books and articles about Thackeray. This relative critical neglect is matched by a seeming reluctance on the part of publishers to take a chance on Thackeray: several of his major novels, including *The Virginians* and *Philip*, are not currently available. There are signs, however, of a reviving critical interest.

Tillotson's kind of approach reflects a long tradition in thinking about Thackeray. In an appreciative tone, which has much in common with George Saintsbury's Introductions to the Oxford Edition (1908), Tillotson comments on the timeless view that is encountered in Thackeray – "a novelist deals in old truth". The central emphasis of Tillotson is on Thackeray's commentary: "what we honour in Thackeray is our own mind at a finer pitch, working on our own experience widened and deepened". It is a view that many of Thackeray's Victorian readers shared, that Thackeray might be a lesser genius than Dickens but was by far the wiser moral commentator.

HARDY, contesting this "gentleman-talking-to-gentlemen" view, makes the case for a socially aware and radical Thackeray, a writer dealing with such issues as rank, class, trade, commerce, and money in novels that amount to "a shaped exposure of a cruel, cold, mad world". If there is a criticism that can be levelled against Hardy's book – which remains, nonetheless, just about the most illuminating overall account of Thackeray's major works – it is that she tends to reduce complex works to moral statements; but in this respect the book is simply consistent with the kind of moral approach that dominated British criticism at the time of its publication.

COLBY, in contrast to Hardy, sees Thackeray as "the 'Gentle Censor' of his age". The main attraction of Colby's book, however, is that it serves as an indispensable source of reference for anyone interested in Thackeray, as Colby consistently sets the novels in a fully documented nineteenth-century context. It is a massive and absorbing book, with a torrent of detail both in the main text and in the footnotes. If, as a whole, it lacks something in terms of critical sharpness, this is more than compensated for by its scholarly fullness.

GILMOUR's broad study of the gentleman in Victorian fiction, specifically in the chapter "Thackeray and the Regency", combines critical sharpness with a historian's sense of the contemporary context. The way in which Thackeray redefined the idea of the gentleman for a middle-class age has been much discussed over the years, but the distinctive quality of Gilmour's account is his awareness of the problematic and ambiguous nature of the concept of gentlemanliness in Thackeray and, indeed, in nineteenth-century society generally. Gilmour's account of what we encounter in Thackeray is an exemplary illustration of how close attention to textual evidence can be fused with attention to the period of a text's production.

MILLER's chapter on *Henry Esmond* in his work on fiction and repetition can be regarded as initiating a new era in Thackeray criticism. Writing as a deconstructive critic, Miller draws attention to two traditional approaches to Thackeray: on the one hand, there are those who see his works as "based on absolute standards by means of which English bourgeois society is judged as lacking", and, on the other hand, there are those who, making more of Thackeray's irony, see his works as cynical. Both approaches, however, pin Thackeray down; Miller suggests, by contrast, that "the reader remains lost in a work which is undecidable in meaning". There are many who have taken issue with Miller and what they see as deconstruction's relentless emphasis on negation, but it has to be recognised that his *Henry Esmond* chapter is just one strand in a very broad shift in critical emphasis that occurred in the late 1970s and early 1980s: a shift away from identifying the controlling view of the author, and a movement towards greater attention to the confusing evidence of the text itself.

BLOOM's collection of essays provides a number of examples of this shift in critical assumptions. Two essays in the volume, both of which pre-date Miller, are of outstanding interest. Robert E. Lougy, in "Vision and Satire: The Warped Looking Glass in *Vanity Fair*" (first published 1975), focuses on images of death and madness in the novel. *Vanity Fair*'s early chapters might be shaped by a belief in society and in man as a social animal, but as the novel continues, Lougy suggests, we are confronted with a world that is frightening and in which there are no answers. Maria DiBattista, in "The Triumph of Clytemnestra: The Charades in *Vanity Fair*" (first published 1980), suggests that in the figure of Clytemnestra we have a vision of classical disorder, which the idea of Christian order, implicit in the novel's title, can no longer control. Both essays illustrate the tendency of a great deal of recent criticism to turn away from the stance of the author and to make more of the moral and ideological ambivalence evident in the world presented.

LUND's book pursues this question of how an audience reads Thackeray, focusing in particular on the response of Thackeray's contemporary audience. This is not just a matter of noting the views expressed at the time, but of probing the deeper patterns of thought that informed the judgements of his first audience. For example, Lund deals with the fact that the audience was often reading a Thackeray novel in instalments and, as such, responding over a considerable period of time; this affected in significant ways the nature of their involvement in a text.

The general trend of recent Thackeray criticism has, therefore, been a movement away from the idea of the presence and authority of the author, and a consequent new interest in the intricate ways in which his novels express, and often unconsciously reveal, complex tensions and issues within Victorian society. It is inevitable that such criticism, moving on from structuralism and deconstruction, should display a renewed interest in history, for there has to be a foundation of historical knowledge to support a discussion of how a novel functions in the period of its production. The last three books discussed here reflect this renewed enthusiasm for criticism with a historical dimension. (If we were to probe a little further, it would become apparent that Thackeray's works – dominated as they are by manly narrators and an atmosphere of the gentleman's club, yet at the same time featuring a series of strong women characters and a number of heroes who almost worship their mothers – also have a great deal to offer those working in the fields of gender criticism and psychoanalytic criticism.)

McMASTER's book, focusing on the allusions and frame of reference in *The Newcomes*, might seem rather narrowly specialised; but the wealth of detail McMaster investigates in the novel is used to suggest the work's interest in process, its sense of the complicated nature of the social changes taking place in Thackeray's time. The details in the novel make us aware of the difficulty of "trying to formulate what we like to call reality".

THOMAS, rather than focusing on the range of references in one novel, focuses on a single image, the image of slavery, as used throughout Thackeray's fiction. As Thomas states, by the end of his life Thackeray "saw the human condition as one of bondage", but she is equally interested in the broader cultural and political implications of his incorporation of slavery imagery. Indeed, her description of her project in the work as a whole stands as an illuminating comment on the thinking that informs a great deal of historically based criticism: "my aim has been to open a window on an important aspect of Victorian culture and show how the light from that window enhances our understanding of Thackeray's work".

SHILLINGSBURG's book on Victorian publishing and Thackeray – covering such matters as Thackeray's attitude to writing, his dealings with publishers, and the various printings of his works – may be said to operate in the same area. The subject matter of the book might initially seem not only specialised but also rather dry, yet the reader soon becomes aware of how knowledge of this particular cultural context both illuminates and adjusts our sense of a number of Thackeray's novels. It is books such as these, by McMaster, Thomas, and Shillingsburg – which both acknowledge and explore the complexity of Thackeray's relationship to a challenging period in history, and, as such, enable us to see just how complicated his novels are – that are doing so much to create a renewed critical, and, one hopes, more general interest in Thackeray.

JOHN PECK

The Thirties Generation

Bergonzi, Bernard, *Reading the Thirties: Texts and Contexts*, London: Macmillan, 1978; Pittsburgh: University of Pittsburgh Press, 1978

Caesar, Adrian, *Dividing Lines: Poetry, Class and Ideology in the 1930s*, Manchester: Manchester University Press, 1991

Croft, Andy, *Red Letter Days: British Fiction in the 1930s*, London: Lawrence & Wishart, 1990

Cunningham, Valentine, *British Writers of the Thirties*, Oxford and New York: Oxford University Press, 1988

Hynes, Samuel, *The Auden Generation: Literature and Politics in England in the 1930s*, London: Bodley Head, 1976

Johnstone, Richard, *The Will to Believe: Novelists of the Nineteen-Thirties*, Oxford and New York: Oxford University Press, 1982

Tolley, A.T., *The Poetry of the Thirties*, London: Victor Gollancz, 1975

Poetry has been the major concern for critics of British literature published in the 1930s, specifically that of the "Auden group" (W.H. Auden, Stephen Spender, Cecil Day Lewis, and Louis MacNeice). Poets representing other generations – W.B. Yeats and T.S. Eliot for example – are not usually classified as 1930s' poets. Fiction has not aroused the same enthusiasm, and there has also been scant regard for women's writing, whether poetry or prose. The tendency in all cases is to approach the material in a socio-historical manner, looking for themes in the writing that correspond to the 1930s' *Zeitgeist* of social and political uncertainties and extremes, with issues of value and aesthetics usually secondary. Influential for the field has been Robin Skelton's anthology *Poetry of the 1930s* (1964), which published the work of poets born between 1904 and 1916, emphasising a coherence stemming from a shared social background.

CUNNINGHAM's book is by far the most comprehensive and thorough of the books on British literature of the 1930s. He points out that the 1930s comprised at least three literary generations, and he includes here those World War I poets still writing, Siegfried Sassoon and Edmund Blunden, as well as Robert Graves. Nor is Cunningham unaware of the importance of fiction for the decade. He begins with some heavy literary theory, yet ultimately this is simply the most widely researched book on the topic with a framework that still regards the Auden Group as canonical.

One of the earliest books devoted solely to poetry of the 1930s, TOLLEY's study is exemplary in that it takes a literary-historical approach – "chosen out of a sense of its appropriateness to a subject so intimately involved with the events of its time". Despite its attachment to this particular reading of the 1930s, Tolley's work is a useful overview, without the leisurely comprehensiveness of Cunningham.

The title of HYNES's book is the signal that the material within places Auden centre-stage. It takes the decade year-by-year, an indication of the topic's general tendency to invite socio-historical readings. The book appears unaware of Tolley's, published a year earlier, with which it might be said to overlap. Its main difference is its emphasis on the politics, with a look at some of the prose of the period through the work of Christopher Isherwood and George Orwell.

BERGONZI openly confesses to being "fascinated" by the mythology surrounding the Auden group, and his book is solely concerned with a rendering of this mythos. He cites Lucien Goldmann and Raymond Williams as his theoretical viewfinders for "reading" what he regards as a "collective text" in itself. Thus we look at themes such as "the frontier", social influences such as the cinema, as well as the aesthetic concerns of the group. The book lacks the comprehensiveness of Cunningham's and leaves the Auden group myth intact.

CROFT locates a golden literary age for the Left in the 1930s, and regards his book as "a study of one brief period when the left came to understand the value of a good read in the battle for the hearts and minds of our neighbours on this island, and recognised the transforming power of well-written and well-read political fiction". In this light he contests that the 1930s was not a decade of unmitigated failure, as it has often been represented, and that the fiction of the Left (over 300 novels) had a "small but significant" effect on the novel genre. This is another corrective to the Auden-centred mythos, but the question of literary worth remains unresolved, as with so many critiques of the 1930s.

Ostensibly also about 1930s' fiction, JOHNSTONE take his cue firmly from the framework that supports the critical writing on 1930s' poetry. He looks at six authors – Edward Upward, Rex Warner, Graham Greene, Evelyn Waugh, Isherwood, and Orwell – so grouped not because they are the most worthy of study, but because Johnstone notes a common context in education, date of birth, class, and "a crisis of belief" leading to either communism or Catholicism. Johnstone's continuous reference point is the Auden group, and it is as if he is creating a parallel canon for 1930s' fiction. It gives a fairly standard account, mainly thematic, of the decade's fiction, relating it to the broader social context.

CAESAR's intervention in the debate provides a perspective on the 1930s that is long overdue. It wants to "de-centre Auden's place in the 1930s" by showing that the literary world was divided by class, style, and ideology, and that the writers themselves were very aware of these divisions. He quite consciously does not attempt to assert some other central grouping (as Lucas does in *The 1930s: A Challenge to the Orthodoxy*). Caesar is clear throughout and moves easily between close reading and the social influences, without, as he puts it, collapsing text into context. His assessment of the politics of poetic form – the debate between the Georgians and the modernists – is interesting and acute. Understandably, he is not concerned with the vexed issue of the literary value of 1930s' poetry, although this is a pity.

STEVEN EARNSHAW

Thomas, Dylan 1914–1953

Welsh poet, dramatist and prose writer

Ackerman, John, *A Dylan Thomas Companion: Life, Poetry and Prose*, London: Macmillan, 1991

Brinnin, John Malcolm, *Dylan Thomas in America: An Intimate Journal*, Boston: Little Brown, 1955; London: Dent, 1956

Davies, Aneurin Talfan, *Dylan Thomas: Druid of the Broken Body*, London: Dent, 1964; new edition, Swansea: Christopher Davies, 1977

Davies, James A., *Dylan Thomas's Places: A Biographical and Literary Guide*, Swansea: Christopher Davies, 1987

Davies, Walford, *Dylan Thomas*, Cardiff: University of Wales Press, 1972

Peach, Linden, *The Prose Writing of Dylan Thomas*, London: Macmillan, 1988

Tindall, William York, *A Reader's Guide to Dylan Thomas*, New York: Farrar, Straus, & Cudahy, 1962; London: Thames & Hudson, 1962

On the death of Dylan Thomas, a veritable plethora of reminiscences, tributes, anecdotes, and eulogies were published. Such sensational notoriety became so powerful that in the end it had a distorting influence on the appreciation of him as a creative artist. The books discussed here are not all necessarily the most perceptive written about Thomas, but they do represent a fair cross-section of the kinds of criticism posthumously bestowed on him, for good or ill. Most of the discussion, when not biographical, has tended to fall into four categories: childhood, craft, religion, and Welshness.

BRINNIN's controversial book is a sincere but humourless account (and to put up with Thomas, one surely needed a sense of humour), dwelling on tales of "bohemianism and irresponsibility". It presents a tragic "Jekyll and Hyde figure", an endearing drunk traumatised by the diminution of his poetic talent. With little knowledge of Thomas's family or background, and virtually no critical exegesis, Brinnin has been principally responsible for the creation of the "Thomas-as-tortured genius" mythology. That such a dissolute character could have produced poetry of such metrical and linguistic complexity doesn't appear to be a question Brinnin bothered to ask himself.

If Brinnin is the Scylla of Thomas criticism, then TINDALL is the Charybdis. He methodically explicates the *Collected Poems* in sequence, stanza by stanza, at times line by line. The thematic and aesthetic analysis of the early "womb and tomb" poetry, through to the "brighter poems of childhood and Laugharne", is often perceptive and always interesting, but remains a useful critical tool rather than a coherent argument. Especially bemusing is the frequency of mythological or occult explanations, when a basic grasp of Welsh Methodism would have sufficed – but then it is always easier to criticise such an undertaking than it is to praise its undeniable value.

Aneurin Talfan DAVIES traces the influence of Welsh versification on Thomas's poetry, expanding the argument to include William Barnes and Gerard Manley Hopkins. As his title implies, he is particularly interested in Thomas's marrying of Celtic mysticism with more orthodox Christian metaphors. He identifies the unifying theme of all the poetry as "man's place in the economy of God's creation", without ever quite managing to convince the reader that Thomas ever possessed quite so coherent a vision.

Walford DAVIES is one of the most consistent and engaging critics of Thomas, through a handful of slim studies and numerous articles and reviews. His approach is invariably phenomenological, seeing the poems as an "attempt to merge and submerge personal elegy in a more general awareness of mortality whose pattern is not annihilation but change". Despite a tendency towards fulsome praise, Davies manages to convey the imminent danger of most of Thomas's poems, which is that "too much verbal glamour" frequently overwhelms both structure and any discernible meaning.

James A. DAVIES's biographical and topographical guide to Thomas's writing is intended for the general reader, tourist, and Thomas *aficionado*. It uses a wealth of photographic material and exhaustively detailed cross-references, which chart Thomas's meanderings through Swansea, London, the Continent, New York, and beyond. More than merely a gazetteer, it is a mine of instruction, information, and entertainment.

PEACH's rigorously theoretical analysis of Thomas's prose writing far exceeds the earlier, better-known, book by Annis Pratt, both in scope and in critical acumen. Peach delineates the sexual violence of the early stories, shrouded as they are in religious imagery, and relates it to the solipsistic, repressive Methodism of Thomas's upbringing. The dreamscapes are seen gradually to merge with more naturalistic observation in the later stories, where innocence and naivety are perceived as subverting the social tensions that bind the individual to the community. It must be said that for such a carefully structured analysis, the final chapter on "R.S. Thomas: Dylan's Successor?" is curiously out of place.

ACKERMAN has built his career on a series of books, which establish the fact that to understand why Thomas lived and wrote as he did one has to refer to his Welsh background. This study, subtitled "*Life, Poetry, Prose*" aptly demonstrates his thesis, principally by reference to Nonconformity, the idea of the bard, and the influence of Thomas's Anglo-Welsh peers. It is comprehensive and unremittingly informative, and a good deal more flexible than Tindall's similar explication three decades earlier. What is missing is any sense that literary criticism has advanced at all in those three decades. Neither Freud nor feminism are permitted to cloud Ackerman's judgement, and his discussion suffers from all the strengths and weaknesses that such a fact implies.

Critics have seen Thomas variously as a supreme craftsman, a paranoid schizophrenic, a verbal contortionist, a wounded genius, or a metaphysician. It is a tribute to either his genius, or his wilful obscurity, that no-one has yet succeeded in fully elucidating his writing, over half a century after his death.

SIMON BAKER

Thomas, R.S. 1913–

Welsh poet

Anstey, Sandra (ed.), *Critical Writings on R.S. Thomas*, Bridgend, Glamorgan: Poetry Wales Press, 1982, revised 1992

Dyson, A.E., *Yeats, Eliot and R.S. Thomas: Riding the Echo*, London: Macmillan, 1981; Atlantic Highlands, New Jersey: Humanities Press, 1981

Merchant, W. Moelwyn, *R.S. Thomas*, Cardiff: University of Wales Press, 1979, with new preface, 1989; Fayetteville: University of Arkansas Press, 1990

Phillips, D.Z., *R.S. Thomas: Poet of the Hidden God: Meaning and Meditation in the Poetry of R.S. Thomas*, London: Macmillan, 1986; Allison Park, Pennsylvania: Pickwick, 1986

Thomas, M. Wynn (ed.), *The Pages Drift: R.S. Thomas at Eighty*, Bridgend, Glamorgan: Seren, 1993

Ward, J.P., *The Poetry of R.S. Thomas*, Bridgend, Glamorgan: Poetry Wales Press, 1987

As one of the leading poets of this century, and the outstanding postwar Welsh poet in English, R.S. Thomas has received surprisingly little critical attention. Doubtless the reasons for this are the continuing preconceptions of him as being either an overtly political writer (of narrowly nationalistic sympathies) or a religious mystic, out of step with our postmodern, secular age.

MERCHANT's short study, the first of its kind, tends to reproduce both of the above standpoints. The reasons are twofold: firstly, it was sponsored by the Welsh Arts Council, for Welsh readers, by a Welsh critic; and secondly, Merchant's main interest as a scholar lies in the field of literature and theology. The latter half of its ten brief chapters, in which the focus is on "searching for Godhead in the spaces between the stars", has been hugely influential in its emphasis on Crucifixion imagery and the "waiting on a silent or absent God". Despite being reprinted in 1989 with a new preface, Merchant declined the opportunity to extend the scope of his study beyond 1979, arguing that the "new tranquillity" which Thomas discovered had made him less interesting.

DYSON pays Thomas a long overdue compliment by discussing him alongside W.B.Yeats and T.S. Eliot, company in which he is not found wanting, at least in his "spiritual explorations". Apart from some patronising comments about "Welsh tone", Dyson concentrates on some close readings of a number of key poems – "Pieta", "The Dark Well", "Here", and "The Kingdom". The critical exposition is rigorous and perceptive, identifying the crucial elements in the poetry of the 1970s as being: the limitations of language; the positive absence of God; the flaws in the very nature of creation and salvation; and the indissoluble union of God and Christ. Although Dyson has a fondness for multiple question-marks, which becomes rather irritating, his stress on *H'm* (1972) as a volume that significantly advances the metaphorical complexity of Thomas's poetry is only one of his many valuable insights.

ANSTEY's selection of essays was published a year later than Dyson's study, but unfortunately suffers heavily from the Merchant dichotomy of Thomas as either disillusioned nationalist or forlorn mystic. Welsh critics tend to sympathise with the politics and remain awestruck by the spirituality, while English critics are smugly patronising of both. Three gems, though, are Morris's discussion of the poems' topographies, Price's review of the earliest poetry, and Allchin's attempt to place the religious work in a wider context. The collection was reprinted in 1992 with seven of the same essays and seven new pieces, but the staggering originality of Thomas's poetry in the 1980s receives almost no attention. It should be noted that Anstey's edition of Thomas's *Selected Prose* (1986) is an invaluable gathering of the poet's few written statements.

WARD, a fine poet himself, has written the best general introduction to Thomas's poetry. He groups the work into four divisions, each marked by three substantial poetry collections: the Welsh landscape and its inhabitants; a period of indecision and self-questioning; a turning towards and search for God; and the relation of language to faith, to painting, and to silence. Ward's lack of interest in contextual matters of politics and religion is more than made up for by his subtle probing of Thomas's obsession with form and diction. The unravelling of often bizarre syntax, and the stress on disconcerting imperatives, is threaded through numerous insights into the circular nuances and cadences of Thomas's increasingly elaborate patterns. Ward's conclusion that the crux of the poetry is about "learning to wait, and waiting to learn" is as succinct as it is penetrating, and the Nietzschean epigraph is a fitting tribute to his subject: "I love the great despisers because they are the great adorers, arrows of longing for the further shore".

PHILLIPS's aim is to explore the philosophical and theological implications of the concept of a *deus absconditus* (a hidden God) in the poetry, and to relate this to contemporary developments in the philosophy of religion. As such, it is a philosophical rather than a literary-critical evaluation, which is both its strength and its weakness. Drawing heavily on Kierkegaard (one of Thomas's great heroes) and Simone Weil, Phillips argues that the poetry is crafted against received notions about God, and that "any religious affirmations are made or rather struck out of doubts, uncertainties, and tensions of faith". Put another way, it is the struggle to find an appropriate language for the silence of God. The literary reader will need to know something about Negative Theology to follow the argument, and might be perplexed by the number of misquotations. Nevertheless, Phillips deserves praise for shifting the serious discussion of Thomas's poetry into the area where his lasting reputation is most likely to rest.

Wynn THOMAS's collection of essays, to celebrate the poet's 80th birthday, spans a wide variety of responses and disciplines, from aesthetics to poetics, and politics to theology. Thomas's erudite and comprehensive Introduction, the fruit of over 30 years' reviewing and interviewing the poet himself, sets the parameters and the balance for the essays that follow. Of particular note are: Vendler's discussion of the painting poems as an escape from the Welsh landscape into "the interior landscapes of the mind"; Brown's biographical investigation into the sea and self-definition, revealing that the *deus absconditus* may owe something to the functional *pater absconditus*; and Ned Thomas's provocative displacement of the poet as someone working on the contentious boundaries of language, territory, and audience.

The high standard of recent criticism of R.S. Thomas, from both sides of the Atlantic, gives cause for optimism that he will no longer be categorised as a poet of "spit, phlegm and despair". Only time will tell if the critical reception of his work can match the scope and originality that the poet has shown in the last two decades.

SIMON BAKER

Thoreau, Henry David 1817–1862

American essayist, naturalist, and poet

Canby, Henry Seidel, *Thoreau*, Boston: Houghton Mifflin, 1939

Cavell, Stanley, *The Senses of "Walden"*, New York: Viking Press, 1972; revised edition, San Francisco: Northpoint Press, 1981; further revised edition, Chicago: University of Chicago Press, 1992

Garber, Frederick, *Thoreau's Redemptive Imagination*, New York: New York University Prees, 1977

Glick, Wendell, *The Recognition of Henry David Thoreau: Selected Criticism since 1848*, Ann Arbor: University of Michigan Press, 1969

Golemba, Henry, *Thoreau's Wild Rhetoric*, New York: New York University Press, 1990

Harding, Walter, *A Thoreau Handbook*, New York: New York University Press, 1959

Krutch, Joseph Wood, *Henry David Thoreau*, New York: William Sloane, 1948; London: Methuen, 1949

Matthiessen, F.O., *American Renaissance: Art and Expression in the Age of Emerson and Whitman*, New York and London: Oxford University Press, 1941

Metzger, Charles R., *Thoreau and Whitman: A Study of Their Esthetics*, Seattle: University of Washington Press, 1961

Meyer, Michael, *Several More Lives to Live: Thoreau's Political Reputation in America*, Westport, Connecticut: Greenwood Press, 1977

Miller, Perry (ed.), *Consciousness in Concord: The Text of Thoreau's Hitherto Lost Journal, 1840–1841*, Boston: Houghton Mifflin, 1958

Neufeldt, Leonard N., *The Economist: Henry Thoreau and Enterprise*, New York and Oxford: Oxford University Press, 1989

Paul, Sherman, *The Shores of America: Thoreau's Inward Exploration*, Urbana: University of Illinois Press, 1958

Richardson, Robert D., Jr., *Henry Thoreau: A Life of the Mind*, Berkeley: University of California Press, 1986

Rose, Anne C., *Transcendentalism as a Social Movement, 1830–1850*, New Haven, Connecticut, and London: Yale University Press, 1981

Van Doren, Mark, *Henry David Thoreau: A Critical Study*, Boston: Houghton Mifflin, 1916; reprinted, New York: Russell & Russell, 1961

There is now a profuse amount of critical and scholarly material on Thoreau, and a student embarking on a study of his writings can choose from a variety of perspectives from which to examine his work: Thoreau as transcendental philosopher, Thoreau as social critic and commentator, Thoreau as mystic, Thoreau as political anarchist, Thoreau as "modernist", etc. Recent commentary has sought to extend discussion into areas of ethnicity, gender, and race, but some of the earlier critical studies remain among the best accounts of Thoreau's life and work.

VAN DOREN's short book, which first appeared in 1916, is grounded largely in a study of Thoreau's *Journal*, and examines his theories and personality in the light of both immediate influences and the broader map of intellectual and religious life in the nineteenth-century, emphasising such things as his place in the long "tradition of Puritan and Quaker inward awe", his reading, his ideas about friendship and nature, and his position in any general history of American letters. Van Doren's book will look somewhat outdated to the modern reader, and it lacks both critical and philosophical methodology, but it is written for the general reader and, as introductory guide, is of considerable value.

CANBY's is a biographical study, which adds new material to the earlier biography by F.B. Sanborn, and offers a considerably fuller account than that contained in Van Doren. It is written very much with the general reader in mind, but it is a generally sympathetic and accurate account, supplemented by an extremely useful bibliography of early criticism and scholarship. The weaknesses arise largely from Canby's attempt to apply a rather muddled Freudian analysis to Thoreau's life; but the attempt to correct confusions about Thoreau's love life and, in particular, to enlarge our understanding of his relationship with Ellen Sewall remain of value.

MATTHIESSEN's opening section contains what is still some of the most sophisticated and intelligent commentary on the philosophical and literary relationship between Thoreau and Ralph Waldo Emerson. In keeping with Matthiessen's tendencies to see all the major figures of the American Renaissance in the light of his liberal and democratic proclivities, Thoreau is discussed as a "left-wing individualist" and his radicalism is given an almost Marxist slant. Matthiessen is eager to appropriate Thoreau to the cause of the literary arts in America and to protect him from those who see him only as a scientist who was wanting in method and accuracy, and, to this end, *American Renaissance* contains some of the first extended criticism of Thoreau's literary artistry. Matthiessen emphasises Thoreau's indebtedness to Coleridgean notions of organic form, particularly in his reading of *Walden*, in ways which help us to understand a great deal of both his writing and that of his contemporaries. While other commentators have extended our biographical and critical picture of Thoreau, Matthiessen's book is still indispensable reading for the serious student.

KRUTCH's book is a biographical and critical study. As biography it offers little that enlarges on the picture drawn by Canby, but the biographical material is effortlessly incorporated into a study that emphasises Thoreau as, on the one hand, a social critic and, on the other, a mystical naturalist. Krutch makes extensive use of the *Journal* and provides detailed exegesis of *Walden*; but one of the distinctive virtues of his study is the analysis of Thoreau's literary style.

MILLER's book is, primarily, an edition of the text of Thoreau's "Lost Journal" of 1840–41, but the notes and commentary to the text have become an established classic of Thoreau scholarship. Miller addresses the biographical circumstances behind the Journal's composition, Thoreau's methods of shaping impressions and experience into literary expression, and his various "stratagems of consciousness" or what we might understand more simply as the articulation of his philosophical and social doctrines. Miller's book has the virtues of clarity and brevity, but it is above all one of the most informed assessments of Thoreau's writing and thinking that is available.

PAUL's book is, arguably, the most thorough study of Thoreau written so far. The full range of Thoreau's writing is discussed: his undergraduate Harvard essays, the journals, the poetry, the essays, the naturalist works, and, of course, *Walden*. The emphasis throughout is on the authenticity and inner coherence of both the life and the thought, but considerable attention is also paid to Thoreau's intellectual relationship with his contemporaries and his indebtedness to other, non-American, traditions of Transcendentalism and Romanticism, notably the influence of Thomas Carlyle, Coleridge, and Goethe. This is essential reading for the student of Thoreau.

HARDING's handbook is essentially a reference document and research tool, intended not "as a substitute for the Thoreau scholarship but as a guide to it". It is divided into five sections, each given over to one category of Thoreau scholarship: his life, his works, his sources, his ideas, and, finally, his fame. Harding offers his own interpretive commentary, and usefully and intelligently summarizes the scholarship and criticism, frequently suggesting new lines of enquiry. Although this book is now nearly 40 years old it remains a valuable aid to research, and can be used profitably alongside Glick's collection (see below).

METZGER's brief book (just over 100 pages) examines what he sees as the shared aesthetic positions of Thoreau and Whitman, arguing that each writer subscribes, in his own way, "to closely related versions of the same transcendental tradition". This tradition is understood as a product of a Protestant religious outlook, which transfers the source of "inward illumination" from God to Nature. Metzger's approach involves a good deal of description and paraphrase, but his subject is an important one, and his account is accurate and detailed.

GLICK's compilation of Thoreau criticism is an extremely useful research tool. Included here are almost all the important essays and reviews available at the time of publication: George Eliot's review of *Walden*, Emerson's 1852 essay, James Russell Lowell's vituperative attack from 1865, Robert Louis Stevenson's essay from the *Cornhill Magazine*, and a broad selection of valuable twentieth-century criticism.

CAVELL's brief monograph on *Walden* is essentially a literary-critical reading, which proposes "that however else one understands Thoreau's topics and projects it is as a writer that he is finally to be known". To this end Cavell is insistent on the semantic and rhetorical effects of Thoreau's prose and is attentive to the ways in which his style impresses his moral and philosophical positions on us. There is no index: Cavell's book has to be read in its entirety to appreciate the force of his understanding of Thoreau's work.

GARBER's is regarded by many scholars as one of the most important studies of Thoreau to appear in the past three decades. His approach is largely through intellectual history, for his interest is in the place Thoreau "occupies in the Romantic movement as a whole" and "the concerns and attitudes" he shares with many of the Anglo-European Romantics. Garber concentrates primarily "on those texts which most clearly illuminate the successes and frustrations of Thoreau's redemptive imagination as it seeks to make a place for the self in American nature" and, as a consequence of this perspective, he offers readings of texts that are frequently disregarded in Thoreau scholarship, notably "Walking", one of his late essays, and "Ktaadn", from *The Maine Woods*. Garber's book is a kind of odyssey through Thoreau's imagination and he is admirably sensitive to nuances of language, tone, and idiom as well as giving us one of the most detailed and informed accounts of what we might call Thoreau's "sensibility". As with Paul's study, this is indispensable reading.

MEYER's book is a study of Thoreau in relation to politics, but not those of the ninteenth-century America in which he lived, but rather of twentieth-century America, which has sought so frequently and assiduously to search in Thoreau's writings for answers to the problems of the modern age. He chooses not "to advance systematically a particular view of Thoreau's politics" and instead takes us from the 1920s to the late 1960s by tracing the various "disguises" in which Thoreau, as "national resource" and "public property", was enlisted in the support of moral, political, and social causes. In effect, as Meyer makes clear in his Introduction, this is a history of Thoreau criticism, but one of great importance for anyone interested in the continuity of Thoreauvian, and Transcendentalist, ideas in the United States. The discussion of Thoreau in relation to the Civil Rights movement in the 1950s is especially recommended.

ROSE's book contains little extended commentary on Thoreau but it is an indispensable study for anyone interested in the interaction between Transcendentalist thinkers and the social and political climate of the United States in the decades immediately before the Civil War. Rose examines the origins of American Transcendentalism, the nature of Transcendentalist ideas (social and economic reform, communitarian experiments, educational theory, theories of marriage and the family, abolitionism, etc.), and draws illuminating connections between the various spokesmen and spokeswomen who articulated the Transcendentalist position. The appendices contain important information about the demographic, economic, and familial circumstances of those associated with the Transcendental "experiment".

RICHARDSON's is an "intellectual biography" of Thoreau "from 1837, when he was twenty and finishing college, to his death in 1862". Richardson's purpose is "to give an account of the development of Thoreau as a writer, a naturalist, and a reader", and greater attention than one finds in Canby is paid to things such as his readings in the classics, the influences of German philosophy (on both him and Transcendental thought more generally) and Hindu mysticism, and his responses to the intellectual, literary, and moral debates of his age. The book is written in a series of numbered sections, which greatly facilitate a reader's use of it as a work of reference.

NEUFELDT addresses Thoreau's place in the economic and social culture of mid-nineteenth-century America, arguing that works such as *Walden* are to be understood as contributing to an on-going discourse about the nature of enterprise. Consequently he stresses what he calls Thoreau's "appropriation and manipulation of economic vernacular". Neufeldt is admirably alert to the populist climate of economic thought, and his reading of *Walden* is contextualized by a familiarity with the contemporary literature of ethical guidebooks and economic success manuals, in relation to which the ironic, parodic, and humourous qualities of Thoreau's work can be appreciated that much more fully.

GOLEMBA's book is significant for its attempt to appropriate Thoreau for some of the more theoretical avenues of contemporary criticism. He sees Thoreau as a writer struggling with the indeterminacy of language and one who articulates a war between language and meaning, notably in his *Journal*. This is a view that many will resist, and Golemba consistently understates the place of the empirical observation of the natural world in Thoreau's writing. But he offers some important challenges to conventional wisdoms, and his book can be recommended for anyone pursuing more literary-theoretical lines of enquiry into Thoreau's writings.

HENRY CLARIDGE

Tolkien, J.R.R. 1892–1973

English novelist

Flieger, Verlyn, *Splintered Light: Logos and Language in Tolkien's World*, Grand Rapids, Michigan: W.B. Eerdmans, 1983
Isaacs, Neil D. and Rose A. Zimbardo (eds.), *Tolkien and the Critics: Essays on J.R.R. Tolkien's "The Lord of the Rings"*, Notre Dame, Indiana: Notre Dame University Press, 1968
Isaacs, Neil D., and Rose A. Zimbardo (eds.), *Tolkien: New Critical Perspectives*, Lexington: University Press of Kentucky, 1981
Kocher, Paul H., *Master of Middle-Earth: The Fiction of J.R.R. Tolkien*, Boston: Houghton Mifflin, 1972; London: Thames & Hudson, 1973
Rosebury, Brian, *Tolkien: A Critical Assessment*, London: Macmillan, 1992; New York: St Martin's Press, 1992
Shippey, T.A., *The Road to Middle-Earth*, London: Allen & Unwin, 1982; Boston: Houghton Mifflin, 1983

Before Isaacs and Zimbardo's first collection there was little critical assessment of Tolkien's works beyond a handful of reviews largely concerned with, and divided by, style and genre: while some of these reviews declared *The Lord of the Rings* a brilliant new kind of imaginative fiction, others condemned it as a pale redeployment of dead forms. With the publication of *The Silmarillion* and other previously unavailable material during the 1970s and 1980s, there was an increase in both the quantity and quality of critical investigation into Tolkien's imaginative fiction and the imaginary world of Middle-Earth.

ISAACS and ZIMBARDO's first collection brings together previously printed material – including pieces by C.S. Lewis and W.H. Auden – and eight original essays. As Isaacs explains in his Introduction, the primary purpose of the collection is to begin serious critical enquiry into Tolkien's images, themes, and motifs without resorting to the simplistic "allegorising" approach of the "fanzines" that sprang up around Tolkien's *oeuvre*, especially in the United States. The papers in this collection offer a wide variety of approaches to Tolkien, among which the archetypal study by Auden, along with Patricia Meyer Spacks' exploration of moral vision and Roger Sale's of heroism, stand out as the most useful. This book is an essential reference source as both the first and most comprehensive collection of serious enquiries into Tolkien's works.

KOCHER provides an overview of Tolkien's aesthetics – his theory of "sub-creation" – and how it is evident in the physical, narrative, and moral structure of Middle-Earth. Like Patricia Meyer Spacks, Kocher examines the nature of good and evil in *The Lord of the Rings* as the battle between free-will and domination, claiming that Middle-Earth is governed by a "natural religion", which Tolkien uses as a subtle critique of the modern age. Kocher's rejection of a Christian gloss of the moral vision leads, ultimately, to his interesting claim that the Man Aragorn "is unquestionably the leading man in *The Lord of the Rings*" instead of, as Roger Sale claims, the Hobbit Frodo. The book also contains chapters that analyse *The Hobbit* as a distinct work (instead of as a prelude) to *The Lord of the Rings*, and Tolkien's seven other short works published before 1962, including the short-story "Leaf by Niggle".

ISAACS and ZIMBARDO's second (1981) collection is as useful as their first. Like their 1968 book, this one combines previously printed material with several new papers. Despite the posthumous publication of *The Silmarillion* in 1977, the editors' emphasis remains *The Lord of the Rings*, and the collection brings together a wide variety of papers to explore the work's many facets. Of particular note are the papers by David L. Jeffrey and Verlyn Flieger, which deal with, respectively, the influence of Old English in the names of several principal characters and the notion of heroism as it is developed by the contrast between the "epic hero" Aragorn and the "fairy-tale hero" Frodo.

SHIPPEY's book is an excellent examination of the role played by Tolkien's lifelong work and research into philology in the creation of his fictions. The book argues that Tolkien's imagination was motivated primarily by his meditations on words and names drawn from the vast array of dead languages and literatures that he both loved and studied. "The essence of Tolkien's belief", Shippey claims, "was that 'the word authenticates the thing'. This was a belief grounded on philology". Convinced that the subtlety of Tolkien's works can only be fully appreciated through an informed examination of the philological roots of many of his characters and events, Shippey examines Tolkien's *oeuvre* (up to, and including, *The Unfinished Tales*) as an expression of his fascination with the history and "allusive meaningfulness" of ancient (or even ancient-sounding) words. Like Kocher, Shippey characterises *The Lord of the Rings* as a modern fable of the universal truth that "absolute power corrupts absolutely", ably defending it against the claims of its detractors that it is little more than juvenile escapism.

FLIEGER was one of the first critics to examine *The Silmarillion* as a necessary prelude to *The Lord of the Rings* and not as a collection of mere background material. She claims that Tolkien's various works should be understood as fragmentary glimpses of a larger narrative, the "governing principles" of which are made explicit in *The Silmarillion*. Flieger focuses on the contrast between light and dark that characterises *The Silmarillion*, and demonstrates how that contrast is mirrored in Tolkien's approach to moral choice, language, and the fragmentation of meaning. She goes on to link her study to both Tolkien's more popular books and his aesthetic theories, claiming finally that Tolkien's "myth" of Middle-Earth is an extended "gloss" of his own devout Christianity. The book includes a useful bibliography, suggested readings and extensive notes.

ROSEBURY evaluates *The Lord of the Rings* as a twentieth-century novel in terms of both its style and content, concluding finally that it has more to offer the modern reader than antiquarian or pseudo-medievalism. While the book's claim to be an overview of Tolkien's *oeuvre* is hindered by an emphasis on *The Lord of the Rings* at the expense of Tolkien's "minor works", the discussion of Tolkien's work as stylistically and psychologically realistic is interesting, as is Rosebury's exploration of Tolkien's work as a commentary on twentieth-century problems, including world war, urban squalor, and political tyranny.

MAC FENWICK

Topographical Poetry

Aubin, Robert Arnold, *Topographical Poetry in XVIII-Century England*, New York: Modern Language Association of America, 1936

Bate, Jonathan, "Wordsworth and the Naming of Places", in *Essays in Criticism*, 39(3), July 1989

Boys, Richard C. (ed.), *Grongar Hill* by John Dyer, Baltimore: Johns Hopkins University Press, 1941

Hamilton, G. Rostrevor, and John Arlott (eds.), *Landmarks: A Book of Topographical Verse for England and Wales*, Cambridge: Cambridge University Press, 1943

Havens, Raymond Dexter, *The Influence of Milton on English Poetry*, Cambridge, Massachusetts: Harvard University Press, 1922; reprinted, New York: Russell & Russell, 1961

Johnston, John H., *The Poet and the City: A Study in Urban Perspectives*, Athens: University of Georgia Press, 1984

Williams, Raymond, *The Country and the City*, London: Chatto & Windus, 1973; New York: Oxford University Press, 1973

At its most general designation, topographical poetry is descriptive poetry about, and usually named for, a particular place. Hence its aliases: "local" poetry; "place" poetry; "loco-descriptive" poetry. In most instances the place is a particular hill which offers the poet a pleasing prospect and a reason to moralize or ruminate. Conventional examples include Sir John Denham's "Cooper's Hill", John Dyer's "Grongar Hill", and Richard Jago's "Edge-Hill". The twentieth century has witnessed fine, though different, examples, such as Dylan Thomas's "Fern Hill". The topographical poem flourished particularly in the late seventeenth and early eighteenth centuries, though by 1788 the *Gentleman's Magazine* complained that readers "have been used to see the Muses labouring up . . . many hills since Cooper's and Grongar, and some gentle Bard reclining on almost every mole-hill".

According to critical opinion, at least since Samuel Johnson's time, the prototypical topographical poem, and the poem which gave definitive form to a hitherto amorphous species of poetry, is Denham's "Cooper's Hill", which first appeared in its authorized form in 1665 though pirated texts began to emerge as early as 1642. Johnson's assessment of "Cooper's Hill" and of topographical or "local" poetry in general has exerted as much authority across the centuries as has the poem itself; in fact the two are inextricable:

> *Cooper's Hill* is the work that confers upon him [Denham] the rank and dignity of an original author. He seems to have been, at least among us, the author of a species of composition that may be denominated *local poetry*, of which the fundamental subject is some particular landscape to be poetically described, with the addition of such embellishments as may be supplied by historical retrospection or incidental meditation.(*Lives of the English Poets*)

Aside from serving as a model for subsequent topographical "hill" poems , the closed pentameter couplets of "Cooper's Hill" anticipate the heroic couplets later employed and so nearly perfected by Alexander Pope, whose "Windsor Forest", also topographical, is indebted to them.

AUBIN's historical survey of eighteenth-century topographical poetry remains standard, if conservative (the topographical poem itself, he says, "is on the whole a conservative genre"), and among its more useful features is a bibliography of some 93 pages listing, by the date of their first appearance, topographical poems from 1641 to 1907. These are classified according to the following categories, which also serve as structural rubrics for Aubin's book: hill-, sea-, mine- (and cave-), estate-, town-, building-, region-, river-, and journey-poems.

Aubin devotes a suitable amount of space to the genre before "Cooper's Hill", noting its sources in Juvenal, Virgil, and Ovid. "The genre", he says, "was present in most of its types among the Romans of the Augustan and late classical periods, maintained a dismal existence through the Middle Ages, and, fostered by interest in learning, travel, and pageantry, blossomed during the Renaissance into a truly European growth". Michael Drayton's *Poly Olbion*, part of which first appeared in 1612–13, "assembled the interests and motifs of earlier topographical poets and passed them on to later ones, virtually establishing their stock-in-trade". Denham then supplied a "convenient mould" for the genre, which included the "incidental meditation" of Johnson's specification. Or, as Aubin remarks: "instruction and description: these form the staple of topographical poetry"; and again: "didactic, descriptive, and topographical: the three types of poetry are . . . inextricably interwoven". Aubin's ensuing critical-historical survey is thorough-going; and as it includes a great many works now (happily) forgotten, it requires some patience.

HAVENS' treatment of topographical poetry is situated in the context of a discussion on "meditative and descriptive poetry", where his particular concern is with the Miltonic influence on such blank verse poems as James Thomson's *The Seasons*, William Cowper's *The Task*, and William Wordsworth's *The Prelude*, each of which may be said to participate in topographical poetry broadly considered. Havens supplies useful evidence of the reappearance of "Miltonisms" in certain eighteenth- and nineteenth-century topographical poems, and although his chief interest is to show the influence of Milton on English poetry in general, he provides a useful list, divided into "hill" and "other" poems from 1642 to 1828, of "loco-descriptive poems not known to be Miltonic".

Aubin's claim that "Grongar Hill" "ranks in next gradation" to "Cooper's Hill", and Havens' claim for the influence of Milton on topographical poetry in general, might serve sufficiently to warrant one's turning to BOYS' critical edition of "Grongar Hill": for there Boys rightly suggests that this somewhat forgotten poem, by reason of its turning from the conventions of English neoclassicism, helped to usher in at the least Wordsworth's particular version of Romanticism. And that turning can be located in Dyer's revising the poem from its original form in heroic couplets into the octosyllables of its final model – Milton's "L'Allegro". The later version, Boys avers, "demonstrates that public taste was not altogether pleased with the use of heroic couplets for descriptive poetry" and that "Dyer's later shift . . . was an expression of this feeling".

As anthologies often participate in the legislation of literary taste and opinion, it is perhaps worthwhile to note that HAMILTON and ARLOTT admit to having compressed the meaning of "topographical" and excluded from it the "incidental meditation" Johnson insisted is one of its chief characteristics; they distinguish it, in other words, from "local poetry". Their anthology of "topographical verse for England and Wales" includes only what they are pleased to call "verse which is truly topographical, that is to say, which is strictly concerned with the spirit or appearance of a particular place or district". The book is an anthology of verses, not whole poems, and their re-defining the genre means the elision, for example, of most of Wordsworth's "Tintern Abbey". Their claim that the "first important figure we meet is that of Drayton, who in his *Poly-Olbion* undertakes to cover single-handedly the same map as our 180 contributors" is accurate enough; Drayton's "deep affection for his native soil" intimates their understanding of the genre: that it relates more to the map than to the mind. Such a conception of topographical poetry would mean barring from inclusion in the genre such candidates as, for example, Matthew Arnold's "Dover Beach".

And yet one must admit that with Wordsworth the genre changes. William Hazlitt observed that Wordsworth "sees all things in himself", that his mind is "conversant only with itself and nature", and that he "is his own subject". These observations accord with BATE, who notes that "Wordsworth's achievement in his naming poems was to develop a highly original sense of specific place and of the relationship between self and place . . . through a new intensity of association between particular places and particular moods or moments".

In contrast to Hamilton and Arlott's compression, and in comparison with Bate's emphasis on the "relationship between self and place", there is a rather fast-moving treatment of the genre in JOHNSTON, who takes his cue from Aubin by beginning with Virgil's *Georgics* (the "classic prototype of the loco-descriptive poem"), who ends by listening to the howl of Allen Ginsberg's disintegrating American cities, and who succinctly concludes that basic "man-and-place relationships . . . lie at the heart of the topographical poem". This intimates the particular strength of Johnston's book – the importance of knowing the long tradition of loco-descriptive poetry if one wishes to know poetry about the modern city. But the discussion is rapid: between Virgil and Ginsberg one encounters no fewer than

22 poets as different as Jonathan Swift and Charles Baudelaire, all in the space of 245 pages. Johnston sees an anticipation of the modern city-poem in Denham, an inversion of georgic human activities in Swift, an anticipation of Carl Sandburg in Richard Jago's "Edge-Hill" (1767), Virgilian concerns in T.S. Eliot's *The Waste Land* and *The Rock*, and an archetypal georgic pattern in William Carlos Williams' "Paterson". These observations constitute what Johnston calls a thesis emerging from "the origin and development of city poetry itself", considered separately from economics or aesthetics, which deal with the city "only in terms of an external thesis".

This "external thesis" of economics constitutes the salient difference between Johnston's and WILLIAMS' books: for Williams, the relations between country and city "are not only of ideas and experiences, but of rent and interest, of situation and power: a wider system". In short, Williams denies that a valid analysis can ever be aloof from these "external" concerns, as Johnston calls them. Thus Johnston accuses Williams of "harshly ideological" readings. The charge is levelled at Williams' estimate of Ben Jonson's panegyric "To Penshurst", which will serve as one suitable example of what Williams is about. The city-country opposition, Williams says, "has been for me a personal issue", particularly because Williams "came from a village to a city" and was close to the ebb of agrarian labor the village was built on. It is just this labor, which is nowhere present in Jonson's "To Penshurst" in spite of the easy consumption the poem presents, that forces Williams to accuse this topographical, more specifically "estate", poem, of an "abuse of language": country life is obscured by social compliment in "the familiar hyperboles of the aristocracy and its attendants". The Edenic curse of labor is removed by the extraction not only of labor but of laborers. Here, then, is a fundamental theoretical disagreement with Johnston on what precisely is the context out of which city poetry emerges.

Williams' critical stance is materialist; he is sometimes a bad reader of poetry. Nevertheless his resistant readings are necessary to our understanding of topographical poetry and the poetry that has emerged from it. His purpose is to describe and analyze the persistent images of country and city and to write about the relationship "explicitly, as a matter of social, intellectual and literary history". The "structure of feeling" (to use one of Williams' favorite idioms) on which his study is constructed might adequately be represented by this observation:

> It is significant, for example, that the common image of the country is now an image of the past, and the common image of the city an image of the future. That leaves, if we isolate them, an undefined present. The pull of the idea of the country is towards old ways, human ways, natural ways. The pull of the idea of the city is towards progress, modernisation, development. In what is then a tension, a present experienced as tension, we use the contrast of country and city to ratify an unresolved division and conflict of impulses, which it might be better to face in its own terms.

Criticism since Johnson's assessment of "Cooper's Hill" has, like topographical poetry itself, shifted noticeably. Among those critics surveyed here, Williams interrogates the poetry in ways least likely during Johnson's time, but his interrogation suggests nonetheless that the shift has been compatible with that "incidental meditation" Johnson initially required of the genre.

JASON R. PETERS

See also **Landscape and Literature**

Tragedy: Theory

Birenbaum, Harvey, *Tragedy and Innocence*, Washington, D.C.: University Press of America, 1983
Draper, R.P., *Tragedy: Developments in Criticism: A Casebook*, London: Macmillan, 1980
Leech, Clifford, *Tragedy*, London and New York: Methuen, 1969
Simon, Ulrich, *Pity and Terror, Christianity and Tragedy*, London: Macmillan, 1989; New York: St Martin's Press, 1989
Steiner, George, *The Death of Tragedy*, London: Faber & Faber, 1961; New York: Knopf, 1961
Williams, Raymond, *Modern Tragedy*, London: Chatto & Windus, 1966; Stanford, California: Stanford University Press, 1966

The definition, application, and implications of the term "tragedy" are highly contested in its classical, medieval, Elizabethan, nineteenth-century, and especially its modern context: Steiner can be read for the case against accepting the notion that there is a form of "Modern" tragedy, while, among many others, Williams can be read for a counter-argument to this view.

STEINER at the outset makes the generally accepted point that the representation of personal suffering and heroism, which we call tragic drama, is a peculiarity of the Western tradition. Violence, grief, ferocity, and death are common to all forms of art, but these should not be confused with the concept of tragedy. After outlining an historical overview, he places the focus on the central dilemma of "modern tragedy", which is identified as a lack of common, shared "mythology" between playwrights and audiences of modern times. Three potential sources of such a common mythology are deemed insufficient for modern needs: a "classic" approach leads to only a dead past, while both Christian and Marxist "mythologies" are essentially anti-tragic in their redemptive and materialist visions respectively: the question arises as to whether or not tragedy is possible in modern literature. In a final chapter, refreshing because of its use of personal recollection, Steiner offers three possible interpretations: tragedy is indeed dead; it continues despite changes in technical form; or, finally, that though dead now it might once more come to life. Bertolt Brecht's *Mother Courage* is held up as an example of the second possibility, while a modern performance by a Chinese agricultural commune is briefly analysed for traces of the elements that gave rise to classic tragedy.

WILLIAMS divides his volume into two parts. In the first part he examines the tradition of tragedy and its historical development, and relates this to the present status of the term in an attempt to "escape the deadlock of the contemporary contrast between 'Tragedy, proper, so-called, as known from the tradition', and the forms and pressures of our own tragic experience". Part Two places the focus on "Modern Tragic Literature". Williams provides a useful overview of the tradition in stating that:

> Greek tragedy has been seen as the concrete embodiment of the conflict between primitive social forms and a new social order. Renaissance tragedy has been seen as the embodiment of the conflict between a dying feudalism and the new individualism. The tragic hero, in . . . Marxist Criticism, is . . . the "world-historical individual" . . .

The essential elements of the traditional concept are defined as "order and accident; the destruction of the hero; the irreparable action and its connections with death; and the emphasis of evil". In the chapter on "Social and Personal Tragedy", he refers to "a loss of belief in the whole experience of life, as men and women can live it. This is certainly the deepest and most characteristic form of tragedy in our century". The counter-argument to Steiner's position on the subject of the possibility of modern tragedy is most cogently stated in the concluding chapters. Williams' comments on the Camus/Sartre quarrel, concerning the distinction between revolt and revolution, are well integrated into the central thrust of his argument that Marxism, Freudianism, and existentialism are, in his view, tragic philosophies. Finally, Williams finds in Brecht's words a precise expression of a new sense of tragedy: "the sufferings of this man appal me, because they are unnecessary".

SIMON pleads the case for the concepts of "Christian tragedy" and "tragic Christianity". Quoting biblical accounts from the Old Testament he seeks to establish tragic elements that will, in Simon's view, inform the concept of Christian tragedy. He states his position at the beginning of Chapter 4:

> Mighty men of heroic stature lie behind the Christian tradition, as any inspection of our great cathedrals will demonstrate. Patriarchs, Moses, judges, kings and prophets pair evangelist, apostles, martyrs, missionaries, rulers. Not all of them suffer or die violently, but their merit is generally weighed in terms of sacrifice, of self-transcendence, of submission to the divine will.

Simon's conclusion is that "Christianity is tragic because of the cross, and tragedy becomes Christian through the Resurrection". If one questions the concept of "Divine Will" or the fundamental basis of Christianity, then Simon makes no sense. On the other hand, if the reader is Christian then this is a most articulate and persuasive argument.

LEECH opens his first chapter with a spatter of quotations on tragedy drawn from a variety of sources, from Aristotle to Polish playwright Sławomir Mrożek. He uses this opening to lead us to the appreciation that "tragedy", as a term, has varied in meaning and application, depending on the specific period in history. Essential terms are explored in passing, and these include "mimesis", "catharsis", "peripeteia", "anagnorisis", and "moira". Concepts of "the tragic hero as scapegoat", "catharsis" again, "the unities", "pathos", and the "chorus" receive particular attention. There is also a useful, but obviously dated, Select Bibliography in three sections, which is fully annotated.

DRAPER presents an excellent selection of extracts from critical commentary on tragedy, the form of which, according to the editor:

> . . . articulates, with subtlety and power, the disturbing resonances of suffering and injustice, and often does so in a way that modulates initial protest into final acceptance, but it stops at the point where philosophy might want to begin. For philosophy could only falsify the experiential effect of tragedy.

This having been stated as an introductory viewpoint, Draper is scrupulous in presenting a highly diverse, and sometimes contradictory, set of views, which nevertheless constitutes, in his opinion, a living tradition. Part Three ("Twentieth-Century Views") will be of particular interest, but the volume as a whole is a valuable reference-source for students and general readers alike.

BIRENBAUM's approach is to place the reader's or spectator's response to tragedy at the centre of his study. Tragedy, he says, "is about the feelings it arouses". Most other authors on the subject subscribe to the view that tragedy is revealed through the interaction of characters, and through the self-revelation of the tragic heroes or heroines. Birenbaum avers that the tragedy is rather the characters' condition: they function not simply as "individuals or as a representative society but as stylized bodies of consciousness". Birenbaum studies tragedy as a phenomenon to be experienced not through logical speculation but through a consciousness of ourselves in relation to the art. This is no dry philosophical text, though; profound shafts of insight shine through a most readable writing style, shot through with wry wit. This holistic approach is highly recommended reading.

D. SCHAUFFER

Tragedy: Renaissance

Aers, David, "A Whisper in the Ears of the Early Modernists", in *Culture and History, 1300–1700*, edited by Aers, London: Harvester Wheatsheaf, 1992

Bamber, Linda, *Comic Women, Tragic Men: A Study of Genre and Gender in Shakespeare*, Stanford, California: Stanford University Press, 1982

Barker, Francis, *The Tremulous Private Body: Essays in Subjection*, London and New York: Methuen, 1984

Barton, Anne, "Shakespeare: His Tragedies" in *English Drama to 1710* (Sphere History of Literature), 2nd edition, edited by Christopher Ricks, Harmondsworth: Penguin, 1987; New York: Frederick Ungar, 1987

Belsey, Catherine, *The Subject of Tragedy: Identity and Difference in Renaissance Drama*, London and New York: Methuen, 1985

Brooke, Nicholas, *Horrid Laughter in Jacobean Tragedy*, London: Open Books, 1979

Butler, Martin, *Theatre and Crisis, 1632–1642*, Cambridge and New York: Cambridge University Press, 1984

Callaghan, Dympna, *Woman and Gender in Renaissance Tragedy: A Study of "King Lear", "Othello", "The Duchess of Malfi", and "The White Devil"*, London: Harvester Wheatsheaf, 1989; Atlantic Highlands, New Jersey: Humanities Press, 1989

Clemen, Wolfgang, *English Tragedy Before Shakespeare: The Development of Dramatic Speech*, translated by T.S. Dorsch, London: Methuen, 1961; New York: Barnes & Noble, 1961

Dollimore, Jonathan, *Radical Tragedy: Religion, Ideology and Power in the Drama of Shakespeare and His Contemporaries*, Brighton, Sussex: Harvester Press, 1984, 2nd edition, 1989; Chicago: University of Chicago Press, 1984

Greenblatt, Stephen J., *Renaissance Self-Fashioning: From More to Shakespeare*, Chicago: University of Chicago Press, 1980

Kernan, Alvin, "The Plays and Playwrights", in *The Revels History of Drama in English, Volume II: 1576–1613*, edited by J. Leeds Barrol *et al.*, London: Methuen, 1986; New York: Barnes & Noble, 1986

McLuskie, Kathleen, "Playwrights and Plays", in *The Revels History of Drama in English, Volume IV: 1613–1660*, edited by Philip Edwards, London: Methuen, 1981; New York: Barnes & Noble, 1981

Sinfield, Alan, *Faultlines: Cultural Materialism and the Politics of Dissident Reading*, Oxford: Clarendon Press, 1992; Berkeley: University of California Press, 1992

Watson, Robert N., "Tragedy", in *The Cambridge Companion to English Renaissance Drama*, edited by A.R. Braunmuller and Michael Hattaway, Cambridge and New York: Cambridge University Press, 1990

Wilson, F.P., *Oxford History of English Literature: English Drama, 1485–1585*, edited by G.K. Hunter, Oxford: Clarendon Press, 1968; New York: Oxford University Press, 1969

Undoubtedly the most influential study of Renaissance tragedy published in the last 20 years has been DOLLIMORE's, which stands against the Hegelian and Bradleyian interpretations of tragedy as the representation of the "ultimate order of things, an order monistic and mystical, beyond the realm of language, rooted in paradox". Dollimore regards this view as ultimately Christian, affirmative, and rooted in a "telos of harmonic integration", features he finds at odds with the sceptical cast of mind that he traces in Renaissance thought, and which obscures the more radical formal and political properties of the drama of the period. Drawing on Bertolt Brecht, recent post-Althusserian Marxist theory, and a broad knowledge of Renaissance philosophy, Dollimore depicts an experimental Renaissance tragedy, formally rooted in contradiction and tension, and intellectually driven by a profound scepticism about the supremacy of man. This leads him to align Renaissance drama with the radical and subversive forces within early-modern culture, and also to argue that the radical theatre of the period "decentres" man. Thus, according to Dollimore, early-modern drama refuses a humanist solution based on individual will and choice. Following Marx's theses on Feuerbach, he associates this refusal with a materialist critique of humanism as a mystification that obscures the ways in which social and economic forces shape consciousness. It is perhaps here that Dollimore is at his most radical, extending Althusserian ideas about subjectivity (the formation of self and consciousness as conditioned by the operations of state power) that inform much critical writing during the 1980s and 1990s. For Dollimore to talk of human will or of consciousness as if they are given entities or ideas is to elide the ways in which power in all its forms – political, economic, and cultural – determines our lives. This study is remarkable for its theoretical drive and ambition, as well as for its knowledge of Renaissance drama and thought. Chapters on neglected writers, such as Fulke Greville, jostle with a fascinating argument about the nature of critical and political praxis in contemporary culture. Without this book much of the critical discourse of the 1980s would simply not have been possible, as Dollimore opens up the fields of cultural materialism, feminism and men's studies, the politics of form, and the study of subjectivity in Renaissance culture.

Against the energy of Dollimore's work many of the contemporary surveys of tragedy appear lacklustre, yet they still offer useful supplementary approaches. WATSON brings out the variety and complexity of tragic form and ethos in the period, while KERNAN emphasises how although "The desire is boundless . . . the act [is] a slave to limit" (*Troilus and Cressida*). Both Kernan and Barton in fact illustrate how many of Dollimore's ideas were already present within the academy, though Dollimore's theoretical agility gave them an additional power and rigour. Although Kernan wishes to recuperate tragedy finally to the Hegelian and Bradleyian providentialist model, his initial premise highlights the Romantic desire for limitlessness, which is constantly frustrated, and whose frustration results in eruptions of fear, anger, and violence. In this account there is an interesting tension between the "iconography of fear", which underpins much Renaissance drama, and Kernan's desire to allow some redemptive properties to the plays: "life does not entirely disappear into chaos, beastliness and meaninglessness". It is as if the evidence (for instance, he notes the "baffling multiplicity, disjunction and absence of absolute truth" in *Hamlet*) actually contradicts his final conclusion. Kernan almost goes as far as Dollimore, although he ultimately rejects contradiction as the aesthetic mode of tragedy. Instead, Kernan delineates a tension between the newer, sceptical, and aspiring modes of thought and poetry, and the harsh reality of the world, just as the plays exploit a tension between tragic models and forms.

A similar pattern underlies BARTON's brief survey of Shakespearean tragedy, for while Kernan emphasises the morality-play elements in Renaissance tragedy, Barton's links are with the history plays, arguing that plays such as *Macbeth* are types of "tragical history", themselves radical rewritings of Elizabethan tragic modes. Kernan advocates a gradual clarification of plot structure as tragedy develops, whereas Barton places greater stress upon the gradual decentring of the tragic protagonist from the play, and traces the slow development of a tragic form that recognises the inaccessibility of the individual interior, offering, in plays such as *Antony and Cleopatra*, a "distant, exterior view" of its heroes. Both Kernan and Barton seem to point towards the Brechtian model, based on a theatre of ideas and symbols rather than characters and emotions, and the alienation that Brecht regarded as the pre-requisite for politically effective drama.

More detailed studies of the origins and development of tragedy can be found in the work of Wilson, Clemen, Butler, and McLuskie. WILSON and CLEMEN present traditional surveys of authors and genres, concentrating on the earlier part of the period. Wilson traces classical and vernacular sources, with a particular emphasis on the connections between early Renaissance tragedy and the "medieval" *de casibus* tradition, and on the influence of Senecanism. Clemen, in contrast, focuses on a narrower period, and upon the development of formal elements, such as metre and rhyme or the dramatic set speech. Although Clemen's book is marred by its emphasis upon a developmental thesis (everything tends towards the superior forms of Shakespearean drama), the discussions of rhetoric and form provide a sound foundation for later studies. Whereas Clemen and Wilson are interested in origins, BUTLER and McLUSKIE consider the later Jacobean and Caroline developments of tragedy. McLuskie briskly surveys the Caroline drama, showing how a highly sophisticated audience, aware of and responsive to conventional elements, developed, and how Caroline theatre therefore manipulated a series of conventions to achieve striking theatrical effects. In contrast, Butler provides a historicised and politicised approach to Caroline theatre, and he articulates valuable critiques of the literary thesis that denigrates Caroline theatre as a decline from the Jacobean "golden age", and the historical thesis that sees all Caroline culture as etiolated and élitist, a sign of the growing cultural rift between court and country in part explaining the Civil War. Butler shows both how theatre was far more various (through the survival of the popular tradition) and how the interaction between court, town, and country was far more complex than earlier critics have suggested. Butler demonstrates, in particular, how serious drama shifted away from tragedy toward tragicomedy as part of an exciting and continued formal experimentation, and how theatre still allowed a range of voices and moods, often engaging with contemporary issues. Although the work lacks the theoretical force of Dollimore's study, the study re-evaluates a grossly neglected part of the dramatic canon, and brings to our attention the manner in which tragedy could be used to debate political and cultural issues, often in a pointed and radical fashion.

Butler's politics are very much the high politics of the court, and he is concerned with how the radical voices outlined by Dollimore responded to particular political situations and issues. Another sort of politics, but one with which Dollimore engaged, can be traced in the feminist accounts of tragedy. BAMBER, for instance, contrasts the apparently pro-feminist comedies with the malevolent women of the tragedies, linking gender and genre. She explains this contradiction in characterisation by seeing the tragedies as a conflict between the masculine self and the feminine "Other", which is subsumed in the benign world of the comic play. The tragedies, because of the form's either/or structure, force women to make choices. Bamber thus argues that representations vary not according to social factors but because of the formal constraints of genre. CALLAGHAN, however, sees tragedy as a site for the exploration of gender politics and the revelation of the "precarious status of phallic power". Tragedy obtains this prominence because of the high regard for the genre in the period (because it was supposed to embody providential justice). In Callaghan's view, gender oppression is the model for a series of analogous political repressions, "crucial social problems [are] presented in relation to a central conflict involving gender oppression", and, because of the basically providentialist nature of Renaissance tragedy, women as victims and agents in both biblical narrative and tragedy are "constructed as simultaneously central and yet tangential to the tragic action". Callaghan rejects Bamber's conclusions about comedy, instead appropriating Dollimore's position to argue that while "tragedy may resist or subvert providential justice . . . it does not suggest that such justice can be transcended". Callaghan suggests that comedy allows inversion (licensed disruption) but tragedy transgresses, that is, in its presentation of women it images an unlicensed, more dangerous disruption of social structures.

Dollimore's book also established, or at least codified, the interest in drama as the site of developing notions of selfhood in the period, and their relation to emergent modern conceptions of subjectivity. Writers such as BARKER and BELSEY consider how the early-modern period experienced a new sense of self, related to modern capitalist individualism, and which the drama articulated. Barker, for example, sees *Hamlet* as the (literally) crucial text, where a new sense of self divided from the exterior world starts to emerge, even if in this instance the new "interior subjectivity" is temporary and transient (or "gestural"). Belsey takes a feminist stance, and argues that such constructions of self are particularly potent in the representation of women, although Belsey actually argues that the very moment the idea of "man" was being constructed in its modern sense was also the moment of a new type of exclusion of femininity. Often the problem with these accounts of the "history of the subject" is not only that they may be challenged historically (see AERS), but that the precise role of tragedy as a *form* is unclear. Indeed, Belsey admits her choice of tragedy is arbitrary, and does not even allow herself the argument permitted by Callaghan of the cultural centrality of tragedy in relation to providentialism.

These trends in criticism are usefully drawn together in SINFIELD's study, which, in its chapter on tragedy, situates the form in the "juxtaposing of overlapping but competing discourses, the foregrounding of contradictions within Christianity, and the relation of such disruptions to the legitimising of secular authority". Sinfield thus draws upon Dollimore's sense of the contradictions within tragedy, but provides a more finely nuanced account, allowing for a complex relation of tragedy to providentialist views, which he also depicts as both internally conflicted and externally in conflict with some aspects of Senecanism. Sinfield argues that the central figures of the plays inhabit the conflicted discursive universe he describes. Thus Macbeth, not the coherent character of earlier criticism, but a type of "character-effect", is located among the divergent discourses, and so must struggle to shape himself, as he is shaped by discursive and cultural forces beyond his control. He stands outside of society (Sinfield calls this "dissidence") not because he manifests a "confident subjectivity choosing to re-orient itself . . . but a radically insecure subjectivity . . . swaying between divergent possible selves and vulnerable to manipulation". Sinfield's approach brings together some of the theoretical power inherent in the cultural-materialist accounts of subjectivity and tragedy, but gives a much more historicised and more open account of the possibilities of both tragedy and selfhood, acting as a useful corrective to some more simplistic readings in recent criticism.

The most striking shift in recent criticism has been the move away from any study of the formal properties of the genre. Most criticism (such as GREENBLATT), brilliant in its assessment of the cultural significance of tragedy as a mediation of cultural violence, avoids any consideration of the centrality of tragedy, or the importance, aesthetic or cultural, of its forms. There has been little work to develop thought on the impact of tragedy upon audiences (although BROOKE provides some interesting pointers) or to recuperate key Aristotelian notions, such as *catharsis* and the emotional response to tragedy, either through the drama's protagonists or its rhetoric. It is to be hoped that a reassessment of tragic form in the light of the exciting new approaches offered by feminism and cultural materialism will soon appear.

JAMES D. KNOWLES

Tragedy: Restoration

Cannan, Paul D., "New Directions in Serious Drama on the London Stage, 1675–1678", in *Philological Quarterly*, 73(2), 1994

Chase, Lewis N., *The English Heroic Play: A Critical Description of the Rhymed Tragedy of the Restoration*, New York: Columbia University Press, 1903

Deane, Cecil V., *Dramatic Theory and the Rhymed Heroic Play*, London: Oxford University Press, 1931

Dobrée, Bonamy, *Restoration Tragedy 1660–1720*, Oxford: Clarendon Press, 1929

Hughes, Derek, *Dryden's Heroic Plays*, London: Macmillan, 1981

Maguire, Nancy Klein, *Regicide and Restoration: English Tragicomedy, 1660–1671*, Cambridge and New York: Cambridge University Press, 1992

Marshall, Geoffrey, *Restoration Serious Drama*, Norman: University of Oklahoma Press, 1975

Rothstein, Eric, *Restoration Tragedy: Form and the Process of Change*, Madison: University of Wisconsin Press, 1967

The tragedy of the Restoration has received fewer wide-ranging studies than the comedy, and these have often concentrated on the heroic play, which was initially treated as an aesthetically aberrant display of ranting and escapist idealism, though critics gradually began to suggest that Dryden, at least, treated the heroic with some scepticism.

CHASE's book has the virtues of very wide coverage, and extensively documents the ideals and conflicts portrayed in the heroic play. Some would still follow him in seeing all the plays as uncritically celebratory, but few would now accept his historical methodology, for he is insensitive to evolution and change, and uninterested in intellectual and political context. He treats heroic drama as a stable, monolithic genre, displaying diversity (in, for example, the variable value placed on chastity) but not chronological development. He does not substantially distinguish the early efforts of William D'Avenant and Roger Boyle, Earl of Orrery from the very different kind of drama introduced by John Dryden, and even yokes John Crowne's *Caligula* (1698), a Whig celebration of the Glorious Revolution, with the royalist plays of the 1660s.

DOBRÉE's study does not provide the broad or historically ordered treatment that its title seems to promise (though such treatment had been provided in Allardyce Nicoll's *A History of Restoration Drama 1660–1700*, 1923). Rather, he muses on four dramatists and two supernumerary plays, with little attention to their contemporaries, context, or even sequence: the first play to be discussed is Dryden's *All for Love* (1677), which is seen only in relation to pre-Restoration Antony-and-Cleopatra plays. His chief interest is in the subjective evaluation of dramatic verse, and he is less comfortable with historical specifics than with hazy universals (the heroic play is seen as a recrudescence of the romantic impulse). The popularity of heroic drama is circularly explained by postulating a hunger for heroism, for which he trivially accounts by imagining one's disillusionment on meeting General Monck the morning after the night before.

DEANE is a far more careful scholar, and he does attempt to document the intellectual background of the drama, though his emphasis on the Cartesian theory of the passions now seems misguided. Unlike Chase, he sees that the heroic play changed over time, with Dryden and Boyle representing different stages in its development. He also has a rudimentary sense of theatrical context, though he generally uses this for pejorative ends, oddly regretting that dramatists should have tailored their parts to the talents of particular actors. There are useful summaries of French and English critical opinions, but the analyses of particular plays do little more than quantify their conformity to neoclassical precepts.

Although good, and still useful articles on individual plays started to appear in the mid-1950s, the entire corpus of Restoration tragedy did not receive intellectually distinguished treatment until ROTHSTEIN's book. Like Deane, Rothstein takes neoclassical theory as his starting point; but, where Deane summarizes, Rothstein analyses. He traces a shift from fabulist to affective theories of drama: that is, from theories that define drama as a decoratively embellished moral fable to those that emphasize excitation – rather than purgation – of the emotions, with consequent emphasis on local emotional effect rather than total aesthetic and providential order. In consequence, he postulates an inexorable movement from a heroic drama of public men to one of greater subjectivity, in which the qualities of events and images fluctuate according to the mental state of the protagonist. Inevitably, later scholarship has modified some of Rothstein's findings; but, after nearly 30 years, his book remains an essential work.

By contrast, MARSHALL's book is disappointing. He shares Chase's blindness to historical development, lumping together plays of greatly differing period and outlook as parallel illustrations of all-embracing generalizations. Texts are constrained to fit schematic ethical commonplaces, such as the necessity of self-control, and moral clichés, which the plays test and find wanting, are quoted out of context as representing their essential outlook. There are also some inaccuracies: in the discussion of John Banks's *The Unhappy Favourite*, for example, a speech by the Countess of Nottingham describing the people's contempt for the Earl of Essex is attributed to Burleigh, and read as a description of the Earl's ecstatic reception by the public.

Some critics (most extensively Bruce King, in *Dryden's Major Plays*, 1966) have seen the rodomontades of Dryden's heroes as designedly ludicrous. In my book (HUGHES) I largely disagree, though I do argue that Dryden's characters are at times baffled by the limitations of language, and I do see his attitude to heroism as being largely sceptical, in contrast to the affirmative idealism of Boyle and D'Avenant. There is a regular disparity between the heroes' professions and their actions, and between the rigid, constricting demands of ideal codes and the ambiguous demands of life. Whereas Boyle celebrates paragons of rational sociability, Dryden creates extensive and subtle parallels between the careers of his heroes and villains, not to equate the two, but to suggest that the anarchic passions, which reign unchecked in the villains, remain a contaminating and ineradicable presence in the noblest characters.

MAGUIRE also analyses the complexity of early Restoration serious drama, seeing in it a conflict between the obsessive, guilt-ridden cult of the martyred king and the royalists' "serious disillusionment with the Stuart myth", fostered by the conduct of Charles II. There is perceptive study of the deconsecration of kingship in Dryden, and of Boyle's divided sympathies, caught as he was "between two kinds of monarchy, actively participating in a new political world while remaining emotionally in the old".

CANNAN's article concentrates on what has generally been seen as a transitional phase of Restoration tragedy, as the heroic play dwindled to extinction through what Rothstein has termed "formal exhaustion". While not disputing that a change took place, Cannan denies that there was any exhaustion: taking his lead from Robert D. Hume's magisterial *The Development of English Drama in the Late Seventeenth Century* (1976), he documents the vitality and variety of experimentation in tragedy of the mid-1670s, with careful attention to the distinctive features of particular seasons, showing the inadmissibility of cramping the plays within a single catch-all generic label. By now the steady-state theory of Chase has been left far behind.

DEREK HUGHES

Tragicomedy

Herrick, Marvin T., *Tragicomedy: Its Origin and Development in Italy, France, and England*, Urbana: University of Illinois Press, 1955

Hirst, David L., *Tragicomedy*, London and New York: Methuen, 1984

Hoy, Cyrus, *The Hyacinth Room: An Investigation into the Nature of Comedy, Tragedy, and Tragicomedy*, New York: Knopf, 1964; London: Chatto & Windus, 1964

Maguire, Nancy Klein (ed.), *Renaissance Tragicomedy: Explorations in Genre and Politics*, New York: AMS Press, 1987

Orr, John, *Tragicomedy and Contemporary Culture: Play and Performance from Beckett to Shepard*, London: Macmillan, 1991

Ristine, Frank Humphrey, *English Tragicomedy: Its Origin and History*, New York: Columbia University Press, 1910; reprinted, New York: Russell & Russell, 1963

Although tragicomedy was treated disdainfully as a hybrid genre as early as the Renaissance (Sir Philip Sidney called it "mungrell Tragy-comedie"), it remained a popular dramatic form with playwrights and audiences, and by the twentieth century became a prevalent one.

RISTINE's classic work begins by confronting difficult problems of definition and then traces the genre's ancient and medieval beginnings on the Continent. Much of his book deals with sixteenth- and seventeenth-century England – the tentative manifestations of tragicomedy in the developing Elizabethan drama and its flowering in the plays of Francis Beaumont and John Fletcher. His focus throughout is on recurrent themes, plots, and character types, and he concludes with a discussion of tragicomedy's "last feeble flickerings at the close of the seventeenth century" and its death in the eighteenth. A useful appendix documents almost 250 extant and lost tragicomedies up to the nineteenth century.

HERRICK's standard study also demonstrates that tragicomedy in England had many Continental forebears, as far back as Plautus. He considers Beaumont and Fletcher to represent its highest degree of development, though their work is highly derivative, and discusses the plays of such contemporaries as Shakespeare, George Chapman, and John Webster that have elements of the genre. Herrick ends this definitive and indispensable history by describing tragicomedy as "the backbone of the modern drama", at the same time expressing his belief that the term has outlived its usefulness.

HOY takes his title from August Strindberg's *The Ghost Sonata*, one of the many plays he presents as examples of tragicomedies in this essential study of dramatic genres, which shows not only the parameters of comedy and tragedy, but also the veritable necessity of the third form. While making clear the thematic and stylistic relationships among the three, he proposes that in the most profound of comic drama, the incongruities of human fate are probed so deeply that the plays verge upon, but are not quite, tragic. Such dramas, "too critical in spirit and tone to be tragic, and too intensely managed to be entirely comic", he labels tragicomedies. Among these plays that dramatize "the equivocal nature of truth, the deceptive quality of appearance, the irresolution of the human will" are Shakespeare's *Measure for Measure* (Hoy considers Angelo a fully developed tragicomic protagonist), Molière's *Le Misanthrope*, Henrik Ibsen's *The Wild Duck*, Anton Chekhov's *Uncle Vanya*, Samuel Beckett's *Waiting for Godot*, and Eugène Ionesco's *The Killer*.

HIRST's brief book, in Methuen's "Critical Idiom" series, reviews tragicomedy from the sixteenth century to the 1980s, taking as its starting point Giambattista Guarini's 1601 essay *Compendio della poesia tragicomica* (the first analysis of the genre). Because of his expansive scope, Hirst has two central points of reference to provide unity: first, a comparison of neoclassical romance and satire in the context of Guarini; and second, the twentieth-century conflict between Romanticism and realism. The survey of previously explored territory, while lucid and concise, echoes those of Hirst's predecessors; more useful is his examination of nineteenth-century melodrama and of how Chekhov and George Bernard Shaw took its basic formula and, by fusing realism and romance, transformed that genre into their versions of tragicomedy. Also valuable is his consideration of the increasing importance of tragicomedy during the twentieth century. In this regard, he focuses on such playwrights as Bertolt Brecht, Luigi Pirandello, Beckett, Edward Bond, Peter Nichols, and Peter Barnes; and because naturalism "seeks to convey the multiplicity of human experience", he concludes that the dramas of Simon Gray, John Osborne, and David Storey must be labeled tragicomedies.

MAGUIRE believes that tragicomedy is neither a hybrid of comedy and tragedy nor a "decadent mixture" of the two, but "a genre in its own right, full of generic implication and significance". The articles in this volume, which elaborate on this thesis, are concerned with definition and practice. Reflecting 1980s' critical theory (and also recalling John F. Danby's important *Poets on Fortune's Hill: Studies in Sidney, Shakespeare, Beaumont and Fletcher*, 1952), most of the essayists focus on the linkage between tragicomic practice and politics of the age. John T. Shawcross's opening piece is far-ranging in its geographical and chronological coverage as he moves toward his definition: "tragicomedy, then, is a comedy with such attributes as movement through the potentially tragic, an interference of a dramatic movement in terms of Henri Bergson's geometric concepts, and a happy resolution". Subsequent essays focus on Fletcher, John Ford, and Shakespeare, with a concluding piece by Maguire on Restoration tragicomedy as a reflection of the chaotic, contradictory duality of the period, in particular the transitional 1660s.

ORR, like Hirst, sees tragicomedy as a major dramatic genre in the second half of the twentieth century, departing from "the realistic dramas of bourgeois conscience" and signalling "the final breakdown of the classical separation of high and low styles". Balancing "comic repetition against tragic downfall" and demonstrating "the coexistence of amusement and pity, terror, and laughter", it spawns a new kind of play, which (starting with Pirandello) "calls into question the conventions of the theatre itself". Close examinations of representative Beckett and Eugene O'Neill dramas lay the basis for chapters devoted to Harold Pinter (and his theatre of "dislocation", a reflection of the loss of empire) and Sam Shepard (a modernist whose tragicomedies lament a loss of innocence while positing a new mythology). Of special interest and value are Orr's references to examples of tragicomedy in film and fiction.

GERALD H. STRAUSS

Traherne, Thomas 1637–1674

English poet and essayist

Allchin, Arthur M., Anne M. Ridler, and Julia Smith, *Profitable Wonders: Aspects of Thomas Traherne*, Oxford: Amate Press, 1989; Harrisburg, Pennsylvania: Morehouse, 1989

Dickson, Donald R., *The Fountain of Living Waters: The Typology of the Waters of Life in Herbert, Vaughan, and Traherne*, Columbia: University of Missouri Press, 1987

Iredale, Queenie, *Thomas Traherne*, Oxford: Blackwell, 1935

Martz, Louis L., *The Paradise Within: Studies in Vaughan, Traherne, and Milton*, New Haven, Connecticut, and London: Yale University Press, 1964

Salter, Keith W., *Thomas Traherne: Mystic and Poet*, London: Edward Arnold, 1964

Seelig, Sharon C., *The Shadow of Eternity: Belief and Structure in Herbert, Vaughan, and Traherne*, Lexington: University Press of Kentucky, 1981

Wade, Gladys I., *Thomas Traherne*, Princeton, New Jersey: Princeton University Press, 1944

Until 1903, Thomas Traherne was known only as the author of the Protestant polemic *Roman Forgeries* and *Christian Ethics*, a well-written but basically conventional manual of morality. The first edition of his *Poems* was published by Bertram Dobell in 1903. His prose *Centuries of Meditations* appeared in 1908, followed by his *Poems of Felicity*, from a manuscript transcribed by his brother Philip, in 1910. Since then, the Traherne canon has been sporadically increased, by the acquisition of printed works and manuscripts not previously ascribed to him, and by a dramatic fresh discovery (see Allchin *et al.*, below). He is now acknowledged as one of the greatest metaphysical writers of the seventeenth century. Although Traherne is largely a twentieth-century discovery, the first critical priority is to remember that the most successful readings are those which set him most firmly into historical context.

IREDALE's general introduction to Traherne's life and works is brief, lucid and (by contemporary standards) comprehensive. She claims Traherne is "one of the few great English mystics, a poet who can rise occasionally to heights of rare beauty, and a master of pure English prose". She believes love of Nature was the central inspiration of Traherne's works, but that it was "at times overlaid" by abstract theory: "if Traherne had been a less earnest student of philosophy, he might have been a greater poet". Iredale occasionally attributes to Traherne's mystic vision a timelessness that later readers might find anachronistic: her observation that Traherne resembles William Wordsworth in his capacity for capturing childhood recollections hardly justifies using Wordsworth's poetry to describe Traherne's experiences; nor is it easy to believe her claim that Traherne was "unaffected" by the Civil War.

WADE's extensively researched critical biography redresses the balance. Hard facts, judicious conjectures, and literal readings of the autobiographical passages in his works produce a Traherne who was no naive dreamer, but an intelligent observer, often painfully aware of his surroundings: "he suffered as only the sensitive can". He became "for some six years a member of a great political household in London". Yet he "found the secret of happiness". The keenness of his terrestrial perceptions measures the extent of his spiritual transcendence. Wade's account of twentieth-century bibliographical discoveries shows how Traherne scholarship, too, is involved with historical contingencies.

MARTZ places Traherne's *Centuries* at the centre of a study beginning with Henry Vaughan's collection of lyrics, *Silex Scintillans*, and ending with Milton's *Paradise Lost* and *Paradise Regained*. His theme is the Augustinian concept of interior "illumination", the "indwelling Teacher" enabling Christians to find Paradise within their own souls. Traherne emerges as a radiant champion of the positive way. Martz admits Traherne's use of repetition can produce "mental fatigue"; nevertheless, he ranks the *Centuries* (with *Paradise Lost*) as one of "the two greatest representations of Paradise in English literature". This book has been widely acclaimed as a critical masterpiece, not only for its subtle insights, but also for its original structure. Martz has shown how literary works that differ widely in form can be brought together to reveal important connections. The frequency with which later critics have adopted this technique should not obscure the magnitude of his achievement.

SALTER's primary aim is not to produce a work of literary criticism, but to point out those features of Traherne's work that may be "of use to a reader in our present times". Traherne's recorded experiences are analysed according to the doctrines and classifications of recognized mystics, from St John of the Cross and St Bernard of Clairvaux to Evelyn Underhill. Salter argues, with commendable precision, that Traherne achieved illumination, but never knew the dark night of the soul that precedes ultimate union with the Absolute.

SEELIG argues that metaphysical poetry "turns on the precarious balance between the divided and distinguished world" of matter and spirit: "the metaphysical conceit is not only a discovery about reality: it is a claim about the nature of reality. Such claims were made boldly by Donne, confidently by Herbert, as a last hope by Vaughan, and, in a shift that marks the end of the line, without any sense of difficulty by Traherne". She writes on Herbert's *The Temple*, Vaughan's *Silex Scintillans*, and Traherne's Dobell *Poems* and *Poems of Felicitie*. Her concentration on Traherne's poetry marks a turning-point. She argues that if a critic as perceptive as Martz finds the *Centuries* fatiguing, a revaluation of the respective merits of Traherne's verse and prose may be at hand.

DICKSON, too, focuses on Traherne's verse, using the *Centuries* to illustrate his argument. His study of the water of life as an image in *The Temple*, *Silex Scintillans*, and the Dobell *Poems*, is scholarly, original, deftly handled, and beautifully presented, with informative illustrations. His accounts of seventeenth-century theories about the water-cycle and various modes of typological exegesis are exemplary in their clarity.

ALLCHIN, RIDLER, and SMITH respond to Traherne with an impressive fusion of enthusiasm, critical sensitivity, and academic rigour. Ridler endorses Martz's interpretation of the *Centuries* as "a counterbalance to the distrust of the body (and especially the sexual instincts) prevalent in much Christian teaching". Allchin's study of the unpublished *Church's Year Book* reveals Traherne as "a true and balanced representative of the Anglican teaching of his time". Smith writes on the manuscript *Commentaries of Heaven*, an alphabetical encyclopedia designed to reveal "The Mysteries of Felicitie", starting with "abhorrence" and breaking off at "Bastard", which demonstrates Traherne's "receptiveness to new ideas". It was "rescued from a burning rubbish tip in South Lancashire" in 1967, and identified as Traherne's in 1982. While the discovery of Traherne's texts is a phenomenon of the twentieth century, their complete publication and evaluation are tasks reserved for the twenty-first.

CAROLYN D. WILLIAMS

Transcendentalism *see* Romanticism and Transcendentalism in America

Translation in the Middle Ages and Renaissance

Beer, Jeanette (ed.), *Medieval Translators and Their Craft*, Kalamazoo: Western Michigan University (Medieval Institute Publications), 1989

Conley, Tom, "Institutionalizing Translation: On Florio's Montaigne", in *Demarcating the Disciplines: Philosophy, Literature, Art*, edited by Samuel Weber, Minneapolis: University of Minnesota Press, 1986

Copeland, Rita, *Rhetoric, Hermeneutics, and Translation in the Middle Ages: Academic Traditions and Vernacular Texts*, Cambridge and New York: Cambridge University Press, 1991

Ellis, Roger, "The Choices of the Translator in the Late Middle English Period", in *The Medieval Mystical Tradition in England*, edited by Marion Glasscoe, Exeter, Devon: University of Exeter Press, 1982

Ellis, Roger (ed.), *The Medieval Translator: The Theory and Practice of Translation in the Middle Ages*, Cambridge: D.S. Brewer, 1989

Hermans, Theo, "Images of Translation: Metaphor and Imagery in the Renaissance Discourse on Translation", in his *The Manipulation of Literature: Studies in Literary Translation*, London and Sydney: Croom Helm, 1985

Kelly, Louis G., *The True Interpreter: A History of Translation Theory and Practice in the West*, Oxford: Blackwell, 1979

Kushner, Eva, and Paul Chavy (eds.), "Translation in the Renaissance/La Traduction à la Renaissance", special issue of *Canadian Review of Comparative Literature*, 8(2), 1981

Rener, Frederick M., *Interpretatio: Language and Translation from Cicero to Tytler*, Amsterdam and Atlanta, Georgia: Rodopi, 1989

Two truisms characterise discussion of the literature of the Middle Ages and Renaissance (and the difficulty of defining the temporal limits of each period must be acknowledged): firstly, that most of the writing in Europe during this time consisted of translations, customarily considered secondary works; secondly, that the period lacked any coherent theory of translation. Critics now fully concede the autonomous status of translated texts in the period, and have challenged the second truism, either by distilling theory from translators' prefaces or extrapolating it from translators' practices.

Much scholarship, however, has adopted a rather hackneyed evaluative approach, which has been concerned with local and specific examples. Rener, though, offers a universal model, and Copeland contests the empiricist assumptions of other critics.

KELLY's technical and scholarly book is an account of how theory and practice have evolved from the classical period to the present day. It is not concerned with establishing a comprehensive theory of translation, rather viewing literary, linguistic, and hermeneutic approaches to language as complementary. It is, however, informed by modern linguistic translation theory, favouring the Geneva School's *stylistique comparée*. The organisation of the material thematically, rather than chronologically, makes it difficult for readers to locate specific and coherent discussion of the periods in question, but its sophistication and breadth of reference are valuable.

ELLIS's seminal 1982 article attempts to put the study of medieval translation, for so long left out of the histories or dealt with in an *ad hoc* way, on a more systematic footing. Ellis's organising concept is that of "translator's choice". Focusing on a corpus of medieval mystical writings, he classifies the translator's role in shaping the work according to various choices: base text, form, the translation of details of the original, style, and medium. Ellis proposes that translators' practices can be characterised according to a fourfold schema, as literal, close, free, or erroneous. Despite offering a set of heuristic categories, Ellis's approach is empiricist rather than theoretical, but he analyses interesting material that is largely neglected by mainstream medievalists.

KUSHNER and CHAVY edit an impressive multilingual volume, largely on the Renaissance, containing six essays in English. It ranges widely, with articles on humanist translation theory; on Renaissance translation as a locus of loss, but also of conquest; on Chaucer and Edmund Spenser from a medieval sign-theory perspective; on Sir Thomas Wyatt as translator of Petrarch; on the role of translations in the emergence of the newly-confident European vernaculars; and on the cultural importance of Renaissance mythographic translations. The elegant writing and breadth of interesting topics, as well as the scholarship and sophistication with which issues are tackled, make this a valuable collection.

HERMANS considers the ideological status of translation as a literary activity in the Renaissance by focusing on the differential relationship between "imitation" (vigorously emulative) and "translation" (weakly derivative). Through a systematic examination of previously unexplored analogies, metaphors, and images in translational meta-texts (prefaces, dedications) of the period, Hermans traces a shift in attitudes towards translation and its relationship with models of imitation. As a result of the vogue in France and England for the so-called "new way of translating", norms of translating changed in the middle of the seventeenth century. The traditional servility of the translator was rejected as the market grew and translation came to perform a public function. Richly detailed and conscious of the cultural politics of translation, this is an essential study.

ELLIS's 1989 collection brings together the work of scholars in Middle English, and one in Old English. Ellis's helpful Introduction includes useful comments on various Middle English meanings of "translation". Most of the essays concentrate on evaluating the linguistic choices made by individual author-translators. Several, however, are to some extent concerned with broader questions of late medieval translation (Barratt's, for example, draws attention to a newly-discovered fifteenth-century female translator), but there is no interest in modern translation models (such as Roman Jakobson's) or wider theoretical issues. Terms such as "author", "text", "original", and "copy" are under-theorised. Copeland's paper – later to become the first chapter of her book – is the only one to address theory. However, this is a landmark volume, attesting both to the range of translation activity in the Middle Ages and to a sophisticated and scholarly interest in it.

BEER's collection differs from Ellis's in featuring work by scholars in a variety of disciplines: Old French, Middle Low German, as well as Middle and Old English. Like Ellis's volume, its emphasis is mainly philological, and its key concepts are unproblematised. However, Beer's Introduction rightly insists on "the complexity of the translative process in the Middle Ages". Many of her contributors favour the comparative approach, deriving theoretical principles empirically from detailed comparison of translations with their originals. However, they also address questions of the place and role of the European vernaculars, and issues such as patronage, the shaping role of audiences, intra-vernacular translation, and generic considerations. The range of texts and languages discussed, as well as the historical specificity of analysis, make this a useful volume.

CONLEY's witty and rigorously textual reading avoids "evaluating" John Florio's translation of Montaigne's *Essais*. Instead, Conley argues that the collision of Florio's English and Montaigne's French reveals "the existence of an unconscious *langue* formed of many tongues visibly embedded in both texts", contesting critical commonplaces that privilege "original" over "copy", and that view translation as a site of loss. This argument is inter-articulated with a re-reading of the place of translation in the historical moment of early-modern Europe. Deliberately provocative, the essay is important as a different kind of translation study, taking account of new developments in poststructuralist theory.

RENER's compendious volume represents an effort to deal systematically and rigorously, as never before, with the theory and practice of translation in Western Europe. Rener identifies a stable system, unified by "a common theory of language and communication and an equally jointly shared idea of translation". In its eliding of difference and its exclusions, such an argument is problematic. The volume is also relatively difficult to use because of its organisation. Covering the period from classical antiquity to the end of the eighteenth century, the analysis is subsumed under two main headings: grammar (structure) and rhetoric (ornamentation). The reader cannot easily obtain information on specific periods, texts, or theories, because such information is scattered through the volume. Despite its broad historical sweep, Rener is most interested in the Renaissance, and medieval theorising is largely by-passed. The value of the book lies in its original research, particularly in its recovery of little-known Renaissance material.

COPELAND's impressive book represents a major scholarly attempt to redraw the map of the field by redirecting the project of medieval translation study towards an understanding of larger discursive and institutional frames:

> A theoretical history of translation in the Western Middle Ages cannot be written as if translation represents a semi-autonomous development of stylistics. Considered in this way, medieval vernacular translation is little more than a collection of disparate practices, united by a few inherited commonplaces which center on the distinction between word for word and sense for sense, and useful for diachronic source study, stylistic analysis, or the study of particular literary or historical relationships. But the earliest theories of translation which the Latin West received from Cicero, Horace, and Quintilian did not emerge as critically transparent and historically portable reflections on practice. These theories of translation were formulated at Rome within a certain academic environment and in response to a certain disciplinary agenda.

Demonstrating that translation in the Roman period was the site for a disciplinary contest between rhetoric and grammar, Copeland argues that the Middle Ages borrowed the classical terminology, but directed it towards a very different theory of translation. Jerome is no Ciceronian. His early Latin patristic model was not at all concerned with the aggressive *displacement* of the biblical source but with serving a meaning that lay beyond the text. Yet Jerome's model is inadequate as an explanation of the nature of later medieval vernacular translation. This, however, does draw on the Roman theory of translation as displacement: it is a process of simultaneous replication and substitution, developed out of the commentary tradition, which itself depended on the relative status of the disciplines of hermeneutics and rhetoric. Writers like Chaucer and Gower sought both to replicate the authority of their sources and to substitute in their place their own authoritative texts. Despite its debt to a non-traditional theoretical framework, the book concentrates (male) high-culture writers who appropriated *auctoritas* through vernacular translation. Often repetitive and unnecessarily abstruse, the book nevertheless puts the *cultural* issue of vernacularity firmly on the agenda, and must be considered the most important paradigm-shifting study to have appeared in the field so far.

RUTH EVANS

Travel Literature: General

Adams, Percy G., *Travellers and Travel Liars: 1600–1800*, Berkeley: University of California Press, 1962; London: Cambridge University Press, 1962

Adams, Percy G., *Travel Literature and the Evolution of the Novel*, Lexington: University Press of Kentucky, 1983

Batten, Charles, Jr., *Pleasurable Instruction: Form and Convention in Eighteenth Century Travel Literature*, Berkeley: University of California Press, 1978

Blunt, Alison, *Travel, Gender and Imperialism*, New York: Guilford Press, 1994

Dodd, Philip (ed.), *The Art of Travel: Essays on Travel Writing*, London and Totowa, New Jersey: Frank Cass, 1982

Fussell, Paul, *Abroad: British Literary Travelling Between the Wars*, Oxford and New York: Oxford University Press, 1980

Mills, Sara, *Discourses of Difference: An Analysis of Women's Travel Writing and Colonialism*, London and New York: Routledge, 1991, revised 1993

Pratt, Mary Louise, *Imperial Eyes: Studies in Travel Writing and Transculturation*, London and New York: Routledge, 1992

Robinson, Jane, *Wayward Women: A Guide to Women Travellers*, Oxford and New York: Oxford University Press, 1990

Said, Edward, *Orientalism*, New York: Pantheon, 1978; London: Routledge & Kegan Paul, 1978

Travel writing has been studied as a genre in its own right in recent years. Early critical accounts of travel writing focused primarily on the formal or aesthetic qualities of the texts. More recent accounts have built on this rhetorical concern, while stressing more the relation of travel writing to the context in which it appears. In this recent critical writing, there has been much interest in travel writing within the British colonial period. The following discussion will deal with this formal analysis of travel writing before moving on to the more theorised accounts.

ADAMS (1983) investigates the relationship between novels and travel writing, exploring the complex interaction between the two genres in the eighteenth century. He makes interesting comparisons between "factual" narratives and canonical fictional accounts. In his work on travel writing and truthfulness (ADAMS, 1962), he analyses the problems that have consistently occurred in travel writing in relation to assertions of fact: he describes the difficult history of travellers' tales and the way that authors were often forced to provide proofs of their exploits within the texts themselves or after publication. FUSSELL was one of the first critics to analyse the literary qualities of travel writing. He focuses on the narrative strategies used in travel texts. His work is primarily concerned with evaluating texts and claiming literary status for those which he considers display aesthetic qualities. BATTEN, as well as giving an account of the conventions of eighteenth-century travel writing, examines the manuals that gave advice to prospective travellers, and which may have determined the conventions of travel writing. He also charts the changes that took place in the conventions governing what was appropriate for writers to describe. He notes that by the nineteenth century a division had developed in travel writing, resulting in travel books that were essentially "factual" and others that were primarily "fictional"; texts written before this period had mixed elements from both literary and factual modes.

DODD's collection of essays treats travel writing as a literary genre, focusing mainly on canonical writers such as D.H. Lawrence, Tobias Smollett, Samuel Johnson, Evelyn Waugh, and V.S. Naipaul. Mezciems' essay in this collection goes some way to explaining the appeal of the form of travel writing where the narrator figure of the travel text is "the powerfully mysterious alien who attracts readers by recounting experiences none can share and whose authority is that of an individual in possession of a reality unique to himself and in his gift to others". This quotation exemplifies some of the problems of this type of formal, literary analysis, since the texts are seen to be simply the products of exceptional authors. While this type of account of travel writing is very productive in encouraging the reader to consider the conventions governing the construction of non-fictional texts, for many this formalist concern has been seen as leading to the socio-historical contexts of travel writing being ignored.

Since many travel texts were written at a time of colonial involvement, it has seemed necessary to consider the relation between travel writing and imperialism. SAID's work has been very influential, stressing as it does the importance of travel writing in creating a sense of colonised countries as "Other", in contrast to a supposedly civilised West. Using a synthesis of the theoretical work of Antonio Gramsci and Michel Foucault, he develops a model of analysis for a wide range of texts within what he terms "colonial discourse". While his work has been criticised, principally because of his tendency to make global statements about a range of disparate texts, his rhetorical analysis has made it possible to combine a formal approach to travel writing with a concern with socio-historical context and power relations. PRATT has analysed a wide range of travel writing, primarily in South America, and has developed a theoretical framework based on the notion of the "contact zone" – the zone of mutual influence created in colonial encounters, where both "natives" and colonisers are transformed through their contact with each other's culture.

While colonial discourse theorists have produced a form of analysis that is more theoretically sensitive to context, they have generally not considered the gender of the writers, and it has only been in recent years that the texts of women travellers have been subject to scrutiny. ROBINSON has produced a book consisting of brief biographical entries on British women travellers. It is often difficult to find accounts by Victorian women travellers, since very few of them are currently in print (despite the efforts of feminist publishers Virago, who have reissued many texts). My own study (MILLS's) makes use of Foucault's discourse theory to describe the tension between discourses of femininity and discourses of imperialism in women's travel writing during the colonial period. BLUNT, while concentrating mainly on the analysis of Mary Kingsley, a nineteenth-century travel writer, has also attempted to provide an overall theoretical framework for the analysis of women's travel writing within a colonial context.

SARA MILLS

Travel Literature: British – 18th and 19th Centuries

Birkett, Dea, *Spinsters Abroad: Victorian Lady Explorers*, Oxford and New York: Blackwell, 1989

Brantlinger, Patrick, *Rule of Darkness: British Literature and Imperialism 1830–1914*, Ithaca, New York: Cornell University Press, 1988

Foster, Shirley, *Across New Worlds: Nineteenth-Century Women Travellers and Their Writings*, London: Harvester Wheatsheaf, 1990

Hulme, Peter, *Colonial Encounters: Europe and the Native Caribbean, 1492–1797*, London and New York: Methuen, 1976

Melman, Billie, *Women's Orients: English Women and the Middle East, 1718–1918: Sexuality, Religion and Work*, Ann Arbor: University of Michigan Press, 1992; London: Macmillan, 1992

Mills, Sara, *Discourses of Difference: An Analysis of Women's Travel Writing and Colonialism*, London and New York: Routledge, 1991

Porter, Dennis, *Haunted Journeys: Desire and Transgression in European Travel Writing*, Princeton, New Jersey: Princeton University Press, 1991

Pratt, Mary Louise, *Imperial Eyes: Travel Writing and Transculturation*, London and New York: Routledge, 1992

White, Andrea, *Joseph Conrad and the Adventure Tradition: Constructing and Deconstructing the Imperial Subject*, Cambridge and New York: Cambridge University Press, 1993

Youngs, Tim, *Travellers in Africa: British Travelogues 1850–1900*, Manchester: Manchester University Press, 1994

The academic study of travel writing becomes, in many ways, a multi-disciplinary task. Different approaches to this period of expanding empire might encompass literary, geographical, historical, cultural, anthropological, ethnographic, social, philosophical, and psychological perspectives, and so the following selection shows a range of these approaches.

PORTER begins his book by focusing on the eighteenth century, and emphasises the importance of travel writing in the Enlightenment. The grand tour was seen as a fundamental educational journey. Writers and thinkers such as James Boswell, Daniel Defoe, Jonathan Swift, Samuel Johnson, Henry Fielding, Tobias Smollett, and Laurence Sterne are all cited for their predominant interest in travel writing. Porter concentrates on male travel writing as he utilises Freudian psychology to explore the father/son relationship: this particular use of psychoanalysis, Porter points out, cannot therefore analyse the travel writing of women. Porter includes some interesting debates about the work of Edward Said and Michel Foucault. The investigation also includes post eighteenth-century travel writers, such as D.H. Lawrence, T.E. Lawrence, Captain Cook, and Charles Darwin. Concluding with the eighteenth century, HULME's study situates texts within a colonial context, for example contrasting Shakespeare's Prospero and Caliban in *The Tempest* with Defoe's Friday in *Robinson Crusoe*, both works being seen as "colonial encounters".

BRANTLINGER's wide-ranging study makes an analysis of British literature and British imperialism in the period 1830–1914, inevitably covering travel writers of the time. His evidence of the interrelationship of literature and history/politics incorporates the works of Captain Marryat, William Makepeace Thackeray, Robert Southey, Sir Richard Burton, and Rudyard Kipling as examples, while one chapter considers critical approaches to Joseph Conrad's *Heart of Darkness*.

Conrad is also highlighted in Youngs' and White's studies. YOUNGS seeks to develop a socio-cultural and socio-historical approach via interdisciplinary work on travellers to Africa in the period 1850–1900. He discusses the use of psychoanalytic analysis of travel texts, acknowledges some usefulness in such an approach, but finds its attention to the individual somewhat stultifying. Youngs instead makes a strong case for an interdisciplinary approach, and introduces some original research in this area. The first chapter deals specifically with Abyssinia, and examines travels here in the context of social events in Britain. Another chapter investigates the expedition of Henry Morton Stanley to Africa, and contrasts this with *Heart of Darkness*. A useful bibliography is provided. WHITE's main focus is Joseph Conrad in the context of the "adventure tradition", but she also provides an analysis of Burton, Dr Livingstone, John Hanning Speke, and Stanley, and their travels to Africa. White discusses the prevailing discourses of the period (acknowledging Foucault's influence in discourse theory). She also draws attention to the importance of the quasi-scientific approaches to travel writing common in the nineteenth century, and exemplified by Gobineau.

PRATT's book endeavours to "show how travel writing has produced 'the rest of the world' for European readerships". The study is approached using two methodologies, the one to place travel writing in its historical context, and the other to develop a "concept of transculturation". This concept "is used to introduce questions about the ways in which modes of representation from [the] metropolis are received and appropriated by groups on the periphery". The book spans the period 1750–1980 and deals mainly with travel writers who were visitors to America and Africa.

An increasing number of studies in recent years have devoted attention to eighteenth- and nineteenth-century women travel writers, often seen as a neglected group. MELMAN acknowledges the work of Edward Said's *Orientalism* (1978) as a seminal to study of travel writing, in particular of the representation of the East in the West, and in considering gender and class in the period 1718–1918 she analyses the ways in which these informed the representation of foreign cultures. The study involves both eighteenth- and nineteenth-century women travellers, such as Mary Wortley Montagu, Lucy Duff-Gordon, Isabel Burton, and Amelia Edwards' journey to study archaeology and Egyptology. The appendix provides a list of women travel writers, and the book contains a generous bibliography. BIRKETT concentrates on nineteenth-century women who travelled worldwide and recorded their experiences, seeing these women as escaping the constraints of their roles in British society, though not all becoming attractive heroines: Birkett acknowledges their often ambivalent stances as feminist role models. The volume includes Mary Kingsley, Gertrude Bell, Isabella Bird, Mary Gaunt, Marianne North, and others, and contains historical and biographical background to the lives discussed. FOSTER confines her study to those women who travelled to Italy, North America, Japan, and Tibet. Chapter 1 gives general background information on women as travellers, and includes some research on nineteenth-century reviews of their work. She points out that women travellers had access to kinds of travel experience different from those of their male counterparts: for example, women were allowed into the harem, an aspect of "Middle Eastern culture which would have otherwise remained relatively unknown". MILLS engages a Foucauldian perspective in analysing the constraints placed upon both the production and reception of women's texts. There is a section on colonial discourse, with discussions on the influence of the theorists Said, Mary Louise Pratt, and Gayatri Spivak. Individual case studies are of Alexandra David-Neel and her journey to Llasa, Mary Kingsley and her travels to West Africa, and Nina Mazuchelli travelling across the Alps. A generous bibliography is provided.

MARJORIE TOONE

See also **Exploration Literature**

Trollope, Anthony 1815–1882

English novelist and essayist

apRoberts, Ruth, *The Moral Trollope: Artist and Moralist*, Athens: Ohio University Press, 1971; as *Trollope: Artist and Moralist*, London: Chatto & Windus, 1971

Booth, Bradford A., *Anthony Trollope: Aspects of His Life and Work*, Bloomington: Indiana University Press, 1958; London: Edward Hulton, 1959

Cockshut, A.O.J., *Anthony Trollope: A Critical Study*, London: Collins, 1955; New York: New York University Press, 1968

Hall, N. John, *Trollope: A Biography*, Oxford: Clarendon Press, 1991; New York: Oxford University Press, 1991

Kincaid, James R., *The Novels of Anthony Trollope*, Oxford: Clarendon Press, 1977

Letwin, Shirley, *The Gentleman in Trollope: Individuality and Moral Conduct*, London: Macmillan, 1982

Polhemus, Robert M., *The Changing World of Anthony Trollope*, Berkeley: University of California Press, 1968

Sadleir, Michael, *Trollope: A Commentary*, London: Constable, 1927

Wall, Stephen, *Trollope and Character*, London: Faber & Faber, 1988

The history of Trollope criticism would have been enjoyed by Samuel Johnson, because it is a notable example of the triumph of the common reader over the professional critic. Not merely his popularity (which might be consistent with inferior or meretricious talents), but also his enduring appeal to intelligent people and discriminating readers revealed, for several decades, a yawning hole in academic criticism. People said he was crude and obvious, when they meant he was subtle, hard to analyze, and curiously resistant to fashionable interpretation of the novel as poetry or symbol. Henry James has been notably ambivalent, speaking dismissively of "a complete appreciation of the usual", but admitting to being haunted by scenes like the "Casalunga" chapter of *He Knew He Was Right*. Hilaire Belloc and Maurice Baring, intelligent lovers of books, who were immune to literary fashion, admired him in the early years of the twentieth century; and Belloc in a memorable phrase, which well captures the slow unfolding of inexorable consequences in his plots, said: "his gods have woollen feet". HALL's biography is full and informative about Trollope's writing habits, his relations with publishers, and his changing appeal to his public. The critical effort does not go much beyond plot summaries.

Modern Trollope criticism begins with SADLEIR, a patient researcher of very wide reading, who suffered from two handicaps; he took too seriously the silly "debunking" of the Victorians by some of the Bloomsbury circle, and he thought that Trollope was "the voice of an epoch". It did not occur to him to ask how, in that case, he could be so utterly different from the real idols of the mid-Victorians, Tennyson and Dickens. Trollope's failure to like Dickens, almost unique in that age, should have given a clue. Later, and more perceptively, Asa Briggs was to compare Trollope to Walter Bagehot, and see both as oblique to their age, and therefore all the shrewder in their criticism of it. But if Sadleir seems too apologetic, even grudging, he did thoroughly know and love the Trollope canon, and must have encouraged many to read Trollope for the first time, and many more to rate as a much higher literary experience the enjoyment they already had. His account of John Eames as an authorial self-portrait is perceptive; he uses the *Autobiography* to good effect, but in the end, following that limiting self-portrait, presents only the solid masculine side of his subject.

My own book (COCKSHUT) was an attempt to take Trollope seriously as an artist. As several later critics have correctly pointed out, it exaggerated the strangeness and pessimism of the later work, and, because I was irritated by the general assumption that the Barsetshire series was the only vintage Trollope, belittled its real merits. Perhaps the best section is the study of death scenes in contrast to those of contemporary novelists.

Bradford BOOTH's account is full and sensible, but somewhat uncritical, with detailed plot summaries. Polhemus enters a sturdy defence of the ordinariness of Trollope's subject-matter, rebuking David Cecil for talking about the "dross of reality", and asserting that the very use of such a phrase shows inability to appreciate his artistic imagination. He says shrewdly: "Trollope's great rhetorical trick is to make us think he is simply reporting the truth about the privileged-class Victorians", and castigates those weak romantics who dream that a murderer or prostitute must be more interesting than a bureaucrat or housewife. For him, Trollope is at his best when, as in *Orley Farm*, a flavour of moral ambiguity remains to the end; a balanced study of the struggle between the Duke and his sons and prospective son-in-law (in *The Duke's Children*) is characteristic of his method at its best.

In an original and interesting work, apROBERTS confronts the peculiar critical difficulties which Trollope presents. He is "least served by our old theories". She shrewdly accuses Sadleir and others of belittling critically what they really admire. ("Nothing is suggested, or connoted, or invoked or adumbrated".) While others complain of Trollope's easy, talkative style, when speaking *in propria persona*, she finds its value in a series of subtle contrasts with the language of characters as various as Lady Glencora and Mr Chaffanbrass. Trollope's religion (a neglected subject) receives full treatment in the chapter "The Novelist as Anglican"; perhaps wisely, she does not attempt to explain how Trollope might have reconciled his Christian ethics with the gentlemanly ideal he so often praises. She develops Briggs's comparison of Trollope with Bagehot – two writers free from cant in an age much given to literary sentimentality. She finds, as many recent readers have done, the peak of Trollope's achievement in the political series; but her judgement that "Palliser fails as Prime Minister precisely because of his goodness" may be more plausible than accurate.

KINCAID takes issue with apRoberts, seeing Trollope as more careless and less consistent than the latter does. He complains that Trollope "seems clearly to be granting too much to the public taste he had no wish to transcend". He finds a maddening vagueness in the gentlemanly code, perhaps seeing it too exclusively as an inadequate ethical system (which it is) and too little as a characteristic class statement by the élite mid-Victorian middle class against the aristocracy they were superseding. One of the best things in the book is a careful reading of *The Duke's Children*. The book is marked by strong, intelligent insights, but also by occasional failures of balanced judgement, owing, perhaps, to lack of historical background.

LETWIN's attempt to find a master-key to Trollope in the idea of the gentleman is an unwilling tribute to his elusiveness. The Trollope "gentleman" is neither an exclusively ethical, nor a merely social, idea; attempts to generalize would require a list of exceptions so long as to be unworkable. And what about feminine behaviour? The "lady" is not a perfect parallel to the "gentleman", as Trollope signals when he tells us that Lady Glencora was not a perfect lady, but would have been a perfect gentleman. And what about inconsistencies that must be deliberate, as when the poor, proud gentleman, Dr Thorne, very aware of his ancient lineage, marries a vulgar *nouveau riche*, who has shown herself an excellent moral mentor to a young gentleman (Frank Gresham), who has been incited to marry her for her money? And why does the same Dr Thorne regard his illegitimate niece as too good for almost any suitor? *Mr Scarborough's Family*, too, is full of pitfalls. Is this persistent liar a gentleman? The author makes it almost impossible to answer either "yes" or "no". But Letwin may well be right in her main thesis that Trollope's morality "denies that human beings are divided between reason and passion". This, however, leaves us with many subtle shades of difference between Trollope's gentlemanly classes: the Duke of St Bungay cannot understand the young Duke of Omnium's scruples about traditional corrupt Whig ways of awarding honours, and the final gentlemanly reconciliation of Grantley and Crawley leaves a moral gulf which Trollope lovingly analyzes.

WALL's book is one of the best treatments of Trollope, because it is neither over-schematic nor defeated by the multiplicity of examples. His choice of topics – "Recurring Situations", "Vacillation and Indecision", "Inheritance and Guilt", and "Obstinacy and Insanity" – is acute both in its inclusiveness and in its implied rebuke to those who find Trollope's world humdrum. Sometimes he achieves phrases that encapsulate the mystery of complex characters, as when he calls Sir Thomas Underwood (in "Ralph the Heir") a "hypersensitive and recessed nature". He makes a robust protest against the moralism of some critics, who make the characters "seem like refugees from 'The Faerie Queen'". His analysis of Plantaganet Palliser's complex grief at the start of *The Duke's Children* is particularly searching. Everywhere he stresses mixed feelings, inconsistent motives, unsuspected half-shades.

Trollope may have become something of an academic industry, which entails the production of much inferior work; but the best has been good. Like an earlier generation of critics of Dickens, critics here have shown that the reading experience is infinitely more complex than literary text-book writers dreamed.

A.O.J. Cockshut

Twain, Mark 1835–1910

American novelist, essayist, and short-story writer

Bellamy, Gladys, *Mark Twain as a Literary Artist*, Norman: University of Oklahoma Press, 1950

Bloom, Harold (ed.), *Huck Finn*, New York: Chelsea House, 1990

Brooks, Van Wyck, *The Ordeal of Mark Twain*, New York: Dutton, 1920, revised 1933; London: Heinemann, 1922; revised edition, London: Dent & Sons, 1934

Budd, Louis J., *Mark Twain: Social Philosopher*, Bloomington: Indiana University Press, 1962

Budd, Louis J., and Edwin H. Cady (eds.), *On Mark Twain: The Best from "American Literature"*, Durham, North Carolina: Duke University Press, 1987

Cardwell, Guy, *The Man Who Was Twain: Images and Ideologies,* New Haven, Connecticut, and London: Yale University Press, 1991

Cox, James, *Mark Twain: The Fate of Humor*, Princeton, New Jersey: Princeton University Press, 1966

De Voto, Bernard, *Mark Twain's America*, Boston: Houghton Mifflin, 1932

Doyno, Victor A., *Writing Huck Finn: Mark Twain's Creative Process*, Philadelphia: University of Pennsylvania Press, 1991

Marx, Leo, "Mr Eliot, Mr Trilling, and Huckleberry Finn", in *American Scholar*, 22, Autumn 1953

Sewell, David R., *Mark Twain's Languages: Discourse, Dialogue, and Linguistic Variety*, Berkeley: University of California Press, 1987

Sloane, David E., *Mark Twain as a Literary Comedian*, Baton Rouge: Louisiana State University, 1978

Smith, Henry Nash, *Mark Twain: The Development of a Writer*, Cambridge, Massachusetts: Belknap Press of Harvard University Press, 1962

Smith, Henry Nash (ed.), *Mark Twain: A Collection of Critical Essays*, Englewood Cliffs, New Jersey: Prentice-Hall, 1963

Tanner, Tony, "Mark Twain", in his *The Reign of Wonder: Naivety and Reality in American Literature*, Cambridge: Cambridge University Press, 1965

Following early tributes, including that by his friend and first literary editor of the Mark Twain Estate, Albert Biglow Paine (*Mark Twain, A Biography: The Personal and Literary Life of Samuel Langhorne Clemens*, 1912), Twain's writing became the focus for a protracted and often ill-tempered debate between Van Wyck Brooks and Bernard De Voto that set the critical agenda for the next three decades. Neither doubted the significance of the so-called "frontier qualities" in Twain's work, but whether this constituted a positive or a negative verdict on native culture became contentious.

The whole debate is voluminously described in Lewis Leary's *A Casebook on Mark Twain's Wound,* 1962, which welcomed "a recent move in criticism towards a more formalist approach – concern with what a man wrote rather than why he wrote it". Subsequent criticism tended to favour De Voto, acknowledging the emergence of an original genius, the author of what H.L. Mencken called "one of the great masterpieces of the world", *The Adventures of Huckleberry Finn.*

Having explored Twain as a humorous writer and satirist, later criticism focused on the ideas behind his work, his debt to Calvinism, and the moral and political allegiances that framed his outlook. Interest in Twain the man continues, however, and several recent studies have adopted a biographical approach in order to reinterpret Twain's representative status or to distinguish the man (Clemens) from his persona (Twain). In keeping with its earliest practice, Twain biography continues to provoke controversy, and a current debate over Clemens's sexual orientation (see for instance, Andrew J. Hoffman's "Mark Twain and Homosexuality", in *American Literature,* March 1995) is no exception.

BROOKS's study was written to prove a thesis: that Twain was an example of a writer who yielded to the "iron hand of convention" in order to retain his popularity. As a potential artist and satirist he was "thwarted", having been obliged to conform to a commercial-industrial America and its prudish late nineteenth-century taboos, operating through both his mother and his wife. For Brooks, Twain's western frontier was "a desert of human sand! – the barrenest spot in all Christendom, surely, for the seed of genius to fall in". Limiting though this view is, it helped to show that Twain was more than a comic writer, and acknowledged in part some of the positive effects of the frontier on his work, in particular the craft of oral storytelling.

DE VOTO's reply, subtitled "An Essay in the Correction of Ideas", set out to refute Brooks. Far from being stranded in a cultural desert, Twain was the beneficiary of a rich frontier culture. His literary intelligence was "shaped by the life of the frontier and found expression in the themes and forms developed by the humor of the frontier". De Voto placed Twain alongside other frontier writers, like A.B. Longstreet, G.W. Harris, J.G. Baldwin, and T.B. Thorpe. Though extremely perceptive on works where the frontier is clearly evoked, De Voto is less illuminating on non-frontier works like *A Connecticut Yankee in King Arthur's Court* and *Joan of Arc*, which he described as "chaotic" and "mediocre or worse". His characterisation of Twain as "the frontier itself" makes him as guilty as Brooks of misleading oversimplification.

BELLAMY's study arises from her conviction that Twain was a far more deliberate craftsman than was then believed. Taking issue with critics like Constance Rourke, who had stated unequivocally that "he was never the conscious artist, always the improviser" (*American Humor*, 1931), Bellamy examines the way Twain employed various devices to distance himself from his subject in order to achieve "a measure of the serenity that art demands". By adopting the vernacular voice, by setting his narratives in remote historical locations, or by employing the dream as an escape from the constraints of reality, Twain was able to keep his growing pessimism at bay.

His later artistic failure arose from an inability to sense "the dignity in human life . . . [or] to invent any technical devices to replace this lack within himself".

MARX's essay, despite limiting itself to Twain's masterpiece *The Adventures of Huckleberry Finn*, represents part of a broader and more far-reaching critical shift. Reacting to essays by T.S. Eliot and Lionel Trilling (in introductions to the 1948 and 1950 editions of the novel), Marx attacks their claim that *Huck Finn's* ending represents a formal unity. Instead he argues that the novel's so called "evasion chapters" signify a wholly illegitimate attempt by Twain to bring the novel to a satisfactory conclusion. From the debate generated over this issue, which focuses on questions of form rather than on elements outside the text, a new era of Twain criticism was ushered in.

SMITH's 1962 study considers the long series of vernacular characters culminating in Huckleberry Finn. Accounting for Twain's later pessimism, Smith devotes an entire chapter to *A Connecticut Yankee in King Arthur's Court* (to which he returned in *Mark Twain's Fable of Progress*, 1964). Analysing the literary techniques involved in the composition of this pivotal work, Smith momentously concludes that "[the] writing of this fable coincided with and perhaps precipitated in Mark Twain something like a negative conversion, a loss of faith in progress and human perfectibility which all but paralysed his powers of imagination and condemned him to the relative sterility of his last twenty years.

BUDD's study is an extremely useful survey of Twain's socio-political views, as revealed chiefly in *The Gilded Age* and *A Connecticut Yankee in King Arthur's Court*, which dealt with current political doings. He demonstrates that Twain was less radical than had previously been thought (by Philip Foner, for instance, in *Mark Twain: Social Critic*, 1958) and more consistently conservative – slanting his writing towards a Republican point of view until he assumed the stance of an aloof observer in supporting Cleveland. Twain's social criticism, according to Budd, fell mostly within "the allowable range of dissent and did not mean to interfere with business as usual".

SMITH's 1963 collection embraces a welcome variety of critical essays, including chapters from Brooks's *Ordeal* and De Voto's *Mark Twain at Work* (1942), as well as useful essays by Walter Blair (on *The Adventures of Tom Sawyer*), W.H. Auden (on Huck and Oliver Twist), and Leslie Fiedler (on *Pudd'nhead Wilson*). Smith himself, in his Introduction, is keen to point out that both the narrative "I" of Twain's fiction and the apparently biographical "I" of his personal books are best treated as fictions. With this confusion overcome, Smith concludes that "Mark Twain criticism has begun to attain the penetration and richness of themes that subject deserves".

TANNER's examination comprises an 86-page section in his influential study, whose subtitle is *Naivety and Reality in American Literature*. Pursuing the vernacular figure through American literature, Tanner argues that "the deliberately constructed naive point of view . . . entails the abandonment of the framework of civilization which is concurrently operative". This subversive voice is present right through early works like *Innocents Abroad, Roughing It,* and *A Tramp Abroad,* and is fully realised in *The Adventures of Huckleberry Finn.* Throughout Twain's successful writing, Tanner concludes, the vernacular supplanted official rhetoric, and the naive "outlaw" represented the author's attempt to find an escape from the compromised language and point of view of convention.

COX takes an *a priori* approach, and is much concerned with the genres of humour and satire. Twain's fate and genius, as Cox views him, was to project "the world as entertainment" by invading the "citadel of seriousness" and converting it to pleasure and laughter. This is essentially a Freudian approach to humour. For Twain, feelings of anger, indignation, shame, and guilt were discharged into the writing, where they yielded "a gain of pleasure". If Cox's thesis leads him to dismiss the merits of important texts like *A Connecticut Yankee in King Arthur's Court,* his illumination of a major aspect of Twain's genius in relation to most of the major works is eminently readable.

SLOANE's study is best read as a complement to, and partial corrective of, earlier analyses of Twain's humour (in, for instance, Walter Blair's *Native American Humor*, 1937, revised 1960, and Kenneth Lynn's *Mark Twain and Southwestern Humor*, 1960). Taking issue with those who may have overestimated the role of southwestern humour as a key source in Twain's writing, Sloane argues that Twain's major debt was to nineteenth-century literary comedians like Artemus Ward. He itemises in great detail all the borrowings in Twain's major works, and demonstrates that in American literary comedy we can find Twain's pragmatic and egalitarian stance, his sympathy for the outcast, his ethical intention, and favourite targets – vanity, power, and "religiosity".

BUDD and CADY have selected what they consider to be the best articles on Twain from the journal *American Literature* between 1929 and 1985. The collection contains many heavyweight names of the past (Leo Marx on "Landscape Conventions and the Style of Huckleberry Finn"; Albert E. Stone on *Joan of Arc*; Fred W. Larch on Twain's 1868–69 lecture tour) and is useful for the way it charts the changes in emphasis of Twain scholarship up to, but not including, more recent language-based studies.

SEWELL's study, as its subtitle suggests, is a rigorous but very readable application of socio-linguistics, which moves fluently between theory and close readings of primary texts, letters, essays, and notebooks. Sewell begins by charting Twain's lifelong preoccupation with language, prescriptive grammar, and nineteenth-century rhetorical theory to show that Twain anticipated much subsequent language theory, in particular that of Mikhail Bakhtin.

BLOOM has collected what he calls "a representative selection of the best criticism of Mark Twain's Huck Finn as a literary character". This is an authoritative and comprehensive series, which gathers early "Critical Extracts" from most of the leading (non-biographical) commentators on Twain and a range of full length "Critical Essays" from 1966 to 1987. In practice these "essays" are really chapters from more general studies of American literature – including contributions by Richard Poirier (on Mark Twain and Jane Austen), Roger Asselineau (on Huck Finn as Transcendentalist), Nancy Walker (on women and virtue), and Harold Beaver (on the way Huck takes after Pap in deliberately "going to hell"). Bloom himself contributes a short Introduction, which attempts to apply the principles of his essay "The Analysis of Character" (reprinted here) to *Huckleberry Finn* in order to show "the senses in which Huck incarnates the American religion of reliance upon what is best and oldest in the self . . . an earlier Orphic existence . . . that he himself cannot know".

DOYNO devotes an entire book to *The Adventures of Huckleberry Finn* in order to document the development of Twain's key text. This is the first full-length work to concentrate on Twain's composition process and to demonstrate how he revised his manuscript to create specific meaning, a procedure known as "genetic criticism". Drawing on Twain's correspondence, notebooks, and biography, Doyno analyses the novel's structure in minute detail under the broad headings "Stylistics", "Thematics", and "The Question of Unity". Interestingly, Doyno concludes in this last section that the novel is "cyclic in structure and aesthetically unified – to a surprising degree". This is a fascinating analysis of relatively unstudied resources which manages to shed new light on this central text.

CARDWELL's book returns to the subject of Twain as an emblematic figure, often taken to be "the robust and genial representative of America's mythic frontier past". Following Justin Kaplan's *Mr Clemens and Mark Twain* (1966) and Hamlin Hill's *Mark Twain: God's Fool* (1973), Cardwell's biography not only redraws the diverging portraits of public figure and private man, but attempts to explore the ideological biases that shaped the Twain iconography. Depicting Twain as both creator and creation of American culture, Cardwell finally constructs his own icon: Twain was the prototype of "the overstrung exploitatively individualistic modern American".

SIMON STEVENS

U

Updike, John 1932–

American novelist, poet, essayist, and short-story writer

Detweiler, Robert, *John Updike*, New York: Twayne, 1972, revised (Boston) 1984

Greiner, Donald J., *The Other John Updike: Poems/Short Stories/Prose/Plays*, Athens: Ohio University Press, 1981

Greiner, Donald J., *John Updike's Novels*, Athens: Ohio University Press, 1984

Hamilton, Alice, and Kenneth Hamilton, *The Elements of John Updike*, Grand Rapids, Michigan: William B. Eerdmans, 1970

Hunt, George, *John Updike and the Three Great Secret Things: Sex, Religion, and Art*, Grand Rapids, Michigan: William B. Eerdmans, 1980

Markle, Joyce B., *Fighters and Lovers: Theme in the Novels of John Updike*, New York: New York University Press, 1973

Newman, Judie, *John Updike*, London: Macmillan, 1988; New York: St Martin's Press, 1988

Schiff, James A., *Updike's Version: Rewriting "The Scarlet Letter"*, Columbia: University of Missouri Press, 1992

Tallent, Elizabeth, *Married Men and Magic Tricks: John Updike's Erotic Heroes*, Berkeley, California: Creative Arts, 1982

Taylor, Larry E., *Pastoral and Anti-Pastoral Patterns in John Updike's Fiction*, Carbondale: Southern Illinois University Press, 1971

Uphaus, Suzanne Henning, *John Updike*, New York: Frederick Ungar, 1980

John Updike, popular among general readers and academics alike, has based his fame on a series of apparent contradictions. Notoriously frank in his treatments of sex, and especially adultery, he is a profoundly religious author, as interesting to those concerned with the theological as with the salacious. A realist, he graces his descriptions with a style so lyrical as to be, at times, distracting. Drawn to writing stories of the suburban professional classes, he has kept in touch with more proletarian issues in his tetralogy focused on Harry "Rabbit" Angstrom, a character whose fortunes ultimately take him into loftier economic realms. At times restrictively middle-class American in his thematic concerns, Updike has made regular exceptions to what is perceived as his dominant style by writing novels on topics as diverse as a modern African dictatorship (*The Coup*) and economic transformations in South America (*Brazil*).

The HAMILTONS' early study responded to Updike's moral and theological concerns even as *Couples*, his most recent novel at the time, was enjoying a somewhat scandalous success. Not just here but in all Updike's novels (and especially his integrated groupings of short stories about growing up in small-town Pennsylvania, and establishing a married life in New York City, then suburban Massachusetts) the critics see religious implications that can be explicated by studying parallel issues in the teachings of Kierkegaard and Karl Barth. TAYLOR looks to secular elements in Updike's work, especially the author's implied contrast between the pastoral (figured as "Olinger", the fictive Pennsylvania region reminiscent of Updike's boyhood) and the urban. *The Centaur* is Updike's novel where pastoral elegy and epic combine to retell the Chiron myth, in which the author examines his own artistic career, young as it was at this point. DETWEILER synthesizes early trends in scholarship by unifying mythic and social concerns, basing his understanding on wide-ranging but consistent image patterns in the fiction; it is the orderliness of these patterns that prevents the disorder Updike portrays from descending into chaos.

More than one early critic perceived Updike's dependence on ritual; taking her lead from the author's own essays collected in his *Assorted Prose*, MARKLE uses Denis de Rougemont's *Love in the Western World* as indicative of attitudes prevalent in Updike's novels from *The Poorhouse Fair* through *Rabbit Redux*, a progression that follows the author's struggle with death as a notion defeatable only by love. But with HUNT's re-emphasis of Kierkegaard and Barth as more profound influences, criticism was redirected to considering Updike's major talent as one dealing with not just sexuality, but also art's transforming power in facing fundamentally religious issues. A good appraisal of the author's status as of *The Coup*, *Too Far to Go*, and *Problems* (1978–79) is provided by UPHAUS, who is able to defend Updike's technical virtuosity without making undue claims for either religion or ritual: it is his "mastery of language" and "rare verbal talent" that generates his "profound sympathy" for characters who, on the face of things, might not merit such loving attention. How these qualities may lead to a privileging of the heroic is explored by TALLENT; to her, Updike's male protagonists seem forever poised as "capable of altering the fixed course of a woman's life, truly able to pose the erotic dilemma in all its formidable richness".

In his two major studies (1981 and 1984) GREINER establishes the first truly canonical reading of Updike's work, including the poetry and his closet drama *Buchanan Dying*. The poems, even those in light verse, are central to his fictive style in terms of their appreciation of language's play; the short stories have matured from nostalgia to a more seasoned irony; the novels, grouped according to theme, trace Harry "Rabbit" Angstrom's fortunes in relation to America's perceived misfortunes and (apart from the Rabbit tetralogy) anticipate a growing interest in the traditions of novel and romance as established by Henry James and Nathaniel Hawthorne (where the author's own characters have neither Hawthorne's moral perspective or James's social contract as guides).

More heavily thematic than Greiner, NEWMAN takes a somewhat broader survey of Updike's career. Here, Updike's early interest in the functions of social and working groups yields for a time to concern for aesthetics and religion, only to be replaced by a fascination with "imagination interrogating its own status" in *The Coup* and *The Witches of Eastwick*. Socio-political sources for the first period are William H. Whyte, Erich Fromm, and Herbert Marcuse, while Kierkegaard (as usual) is cited for Updike's most heavily religious phase. Like Greiner, Newman sees Hawthorne as a major presence in such later works as *Roger's Version* and *S.*

SCHIFF updates the most recent interest in Updike by outlining just what Hawthorne's influence provides. Surprisingly, it is the making of a postmodern Updike, one who experiments with narrative modes and self-reflexive texts, yet drawing on a depth that some critics have claimed the author lacks. Hawthorne's "metaphysical darkening" is indeed something new for Updike, yet in *A Month of Sundays*, *Roger's Version*, and *S.* the author alters the American myth by transforming it from the "bad conscience of a nation" into an "affirming corporeal impulse and thus reconciling body and soul".

JEROME KLINKOWITZ

Utopian Literature

Amis, Kingsley, *New Maps of Hell: A Survey of Science Fiction*, New York: Harcourt Brace, 1960; London: Victor Gollancz, 1961

Barr, Marleen, and Nicholas D. Smith (eds.), *Women and Utopia: Critical Interpretations*, Lanham, Maryland: University Press of America, 1983

Bartkowski, Frances, *Feminist Utopias*, Lincoln: University of Nebraska Press, 1989

Berghahn, Klaus L., and Reinhold Grimm (eds.), *Utopian Vision: Technological Innovation and Poetic Imagination*, Heidelberg: Winter, 1990

Berneri, Marie Louise, *Journey Through Utopia*, London: Routledge & Kegan Paul, 1950; reprinted, New York: Schocken Books, 1971

Davis, J.C., *Utopia and the Ideal Society: A Study of English Utopian Writing 1516–1700*, Cambridge and New York: Cambridge University Press, 1981

Donawerth, Jane L., and Carol A. Kolmerten (eds.), *Utopian and Science Fiction by Women: Worlds of Difference*, Liverpool: Liverpool University Press, 1994; Syracuse, New York: Syracuse University Press, 1994

Elliott, Robert C., *The Shape of Utopia: Studies in a Literary Genre*, Chicago: University of Chicago Press, 1970

Ferguson, John, *Utopias of the Classical World*, London: Thames & Hudson, 1975; Ithaca, New York: Cornell University Press, 1975

Frye, Northrop, "Varieties of Literary Utopias", in *Utopias and Utopian Thought*, edited by Frank E. Manuel, Boston: Houghton Mifflin, 1966; London: Souvenir Press, 1973; reprinted in *The Stubborn Structure: Essays on Criticism and Society*, London: Methuen, 1970

Jones, Libby Falk, and Sarah Webster Goodwin (eds.), *Feminism, Utopia, and Narrative*, Knoxville: University of Tennessee Press, 1990

Manuel, Frank E., and Fritzie P. Manuel (eds.), *Utopian Thought in the Western World*, Oxford: Blackwell, 1979; Cambridge, Massachusetts: Belknap Press of Harvard University Press, 1979

Morton, A.L., *The English Utopia*, London: Lawrence & Wishart, 1952

Moylan, Tom, *Demand the Impossible: Science Fiction and the Utopian Imagination*, New York and London: Methuen, 1986

Mumford, Lewis, *The Story of Utopias: Ideal Commonwealths and Social Myths*, New York: Boni & Liveright, 1922; London: Harrap, 1923

Negley, Glenn, *Utopian Literature: A Bibliography*, Lawrence: Regents Press of Kansas, 1977

Negley, Glenn, and J. Max Patrick (eds.), *The Quest for Utopia: An Anthology of Imaginary Societies*, New York: Henry Schuman, 1952; reprinted, College Park, Maryland: McGrath, 1971

Ruppert, Peter, *Reader in a Strange Land: The Activity of Reading Literary Utopias*, Athens: University of Georgia Press, 1986

Sargent, Lyman Tower, *British and American Utopian Literature, 1516–1985: An Annotated, Chronological Bibliography*, New York: Garland, 1988

Walsh, Chad, *From Utopia to Nightmare*, London: Geoffrey Bles, 1962; New York: Harper & Row, 1962

Williams, Raymond, "Utopia and Science Fiction", in his *Problems in Materialism and Culture: Selected Essays*, London and New York: Verso, 1980

Utopian literature – writing that projects imaginatively (whether positively or negatively) some kind of ideal society or community – emerges at the beginning of the Western tradition. Hence, an awareness of its place in antiquity is important, especially since many modern utopian fictions show affinities (conscious or not) with classical or mythic prototypes, most notably Greek ones, Plato's *Republic* above all. (The word "utopia" itself is punningly formed from classical Greek.) FERGUSON's survey covers the ground from Homer to Augustine, and treats the topic fully and informatively, if rather drily, adopting a wide focus, considering religion, philosophy, and literature. The associated problems of defining "utopia" and of distinguishing and separating utopian *literature* from more general utopian discourses (religious, philosophical, and especially political) are apparent here as throughout criticism of the subject.

NEGLEY's bibliography of over 1,600 items, ordered alphabetically and a useful aid to research, explicitly seeks to define literary utopianism and restricts its ambit accordingly. It also purposely excludes classical literature, but covers material fairly fully though not comprehensively, from the Renaissance onward, listing primary works mainly (but not exclusively) in English, and tracing in outline the genre's historical development. SARGENT's latest bibliography, more focused and more substantial (nearly double Negley's number of entries), is the fullest listing of English utopias available, though still admittedly incomplete. It seeks to be widely inclusive, however, covering works with a utopian element as well as full-blown utopian literature, from Thomas More to the present (over two-thirds on the twentieth century), annotating entries helpfully. Author- and title-indexes enable cross-referencing.

There are several wide-ranging historical surveys of the genre, both critical and anthologising. Among the latter the compilation of excerpts (deliberately favouring less accessible texts) by NEGLEY and PATRICK is selective but helpfully eclectic, and includes a brief survey of the classical period, though its main focus is divided between the modern (from 1850) and the early-modern (1500–1850). Again there is an attempt at definition, with utopian literature seen as fictional, utopia "a world of *as if*" rendered in terms of social and political structure, imaginatively produced, but infused with some degree of realism. Usually, moreover, it includes its dialectical antithesis, the anti-utopia or dystopia, which becomes more prevalent later in the tradition, especially in twentieth-century literature. Clearly, though, the term's degree of inclusiveness remains debatable, and deciding its scope in relation to other genres, such as romance or science fiction, may be difficult.

MANUEL and MANUEL's massive critical and historical survey, the fruit of 25 years' joint research, traces the utopian idea in its widest sense, including associated conceptions of the ideal world, from its beginnings to the present, with reference to religion, philosophy, science, political thought, and architecture, as well as literature. Still selective (it would be "utopian" to imagine including all versions of utopia), it is, perhaps questionably, broad and intentionally "ecumenical" in approach, as comprehensive as one could reasonably expect from a single volume – a useful source of general reference, with selected bibliography and full name-index.

Among earlier historical surveys, MUMFORD's pioneering book, significantly emergent, like other studies of utopia, out of the catastrophe of world war, still has value. Though outdated and oversimplifying in many respects, and with some predilection for rather complacent and superficial philosophising, it offers an urbanely informative chronological treatment of central features of the subject, with its main focus on literature.

MORTON's study, a minor classic in British Marxist criticism, contributes to a major strain in utopian thinking, aligning utopianism firmly with socialism, with dystopias generally seen as reactionary responses. Focusing mainly on British literature, his survey moves chronologically from the popular medieval fantasy of Cokayne, through More, Francis Bacon, and seventeenth- and eighteenth-century learned utopian fiction, then William Blake and Percy Bysshe Shelley, before discussing the nineteenth century, notably William Morris, and concluding with twentieth-century writers, including H.G. Wells, Aldous Huxley, and George Orwell, who are mostly criticised as utopians (or dystopians) of false consciousness. Central is the claim that the utopian imagination is stimulated, even produced, by the disturbing pressures of capitalist and bourgeois society's inexorable advance. Morton's critical evaluation is strongly, indeed fervently, Marxist, naive, sometimes crude (especially his dismissal of Orwell), and doctrinaire perhaps, from our disillusioned perspective, yet often also vigorous, trenchant, and perceptive.

BERNERI adopts a much wider perspective than Morton, surveying the genre from antiquity to the twentieth century, and selecting from the whole Western tradition of utopian writing. More balanced, too, she measures the progressive and sometimes revolutionary force of utopian discourse (earlier versions particularly) against its totalitarian implications, enlightenment against intolerance, with a shrewd sense of the ambivalence, indeed contradictoriness, of utopianism's large ideas. "Utopia" is generously defined, and the survey of selected material is clear, informative, and judicious. Not quite a critical anthology, the book nonetheless quotes extensively from the texts considered.

ELLIOTT offers "interpretive studies of individual literary utopias and genre studies of the utopian mode itself", making no claim to provide a historical survey. He asserts "genetic" relations among utopia, satire, and other versions of ideal places or conditions, and explores their links and contrasts, noting the dual nature of utopian fiction as both negative satire and positive encomium. This perception is applied to a number of literary utopias, English and American for the most part, from More to Huxley, and elaborated in productive and perceptive ways. Wide-ranging but concise, this is a shrewd and lucid engagement with the topic.

DAVIS treats the early-modern period, dealing in detail with various sixteenth- and seventeenth-century British writers, beginning inevitably with More. His thorough, scholarly critique seeks "to clarify our understanding of utopian and other ideal-society forms", and asserts utopia's importance as an imagined rationalisation of government for the growth of the modern Leviathan, the "comprehensive, collective state", seen as dominating social and political evolution throughout modern times. He notes the confusing breadth of definition given to utopia, claiming that his differentiation of the utopian from other ideal-society forms (Cokayne, Arcadia, perfect moral commonwealth, millennium) enables more precise and detailed assessments. Through close readings of the texts, concerned primarily with the political and social rather than literary aspects of utopian thought, he achieves a substantial and finely nuanced critical account of this flourishing period of utopian writing.

Other studies concentrate substantially or entirely on modern, largely twentieth-century utopian literature, where two important related topics, science fiction and feminism, also come into play. WALSH's lively, accessible study focuses on the shift from utopian dream to dystopian nightmare or "inverted utopia" in twentieth-century fiction, with its "unequalled production of imaginary societies" reflecting deep and prescient anxiety or ambivalence about progress. Brief definitions and a swift, cursory survey of the utopian tradition from Plato onward are followed by consideration of dystopian devices and themes, illustrated in Huxley, Evelyn Waugh, Orwell, and others: principal in this consideration is the ironic "Law of Reverse Effect", whereby progressive intentions ensure damaging or evil effects. The monitory force of the dystopia is emphasised from Walsh's Christian-humanist standpoint, with the conclusion that utopian optimism and dystopian pessimism should form a continuing dialectic.

MOYLAN, sympathetic to Morton's analysis, takes a more sophisticated radical stance, welcoming, in the aftermath of the dystopian literature reviewed by Walsh, a more recent revival of the utopian imagination, articulated through science fiction, experimental narrative, and fantasy, expressive of hope and desire, oppositional and subversive, confronting or undermining the ersatz utopias of late twentieth-century capitalism and consumerism. His general analysis, which is broadly neo-Marxist, distinguishing but also relating ideology and utopia, and clarifying aspects of the utopian genre and form, introduces the contemporary "critical utopia", whose principle is activity not systematisation. This is illustrated in four 1970s' novels, all American, underscoring America's significance as both producer and paradigm of modern and contemporary utopianism. For Moylan, they significantly transform and emancipate the utopian genre, presenting imaginatively powerful and disturbing visions of alternative societies and values, affirming deconstructive principles of openness and difference, and reflecting concerns such as ecology and feminism.

The selection of essays edited by BERGHAHN and GRIMM, a German-American collaboration with a European slant, is more welcoming to the scientific spirit, seeking to reconcile it with the utopian (not simply dystopian) imagination in terms of an optimistic vision or intention, affirming harmonious perfectibility rather than the idealising blueprint with its totalitarian implications. The predictive, scientific, instrumental consciousness and the imaginative, fiction-making, even fantasising powers of the mind are linked, it is claimed, and the technological utopia can be poetically, imaginatively validated. The liberating value of imaginative utopian thought, illustrated in a variety of writings from the Renaissance on, is consequently affirmed.

AMIS's book, though earlier and shunning academic solemnity, remains nonetheless among the most substantial investigations of the utopian qualities of science fiction – concealing under its easy, even rollicking approach, wide reading and thoughtful discriminations. Science fiction's concern with verisimilitude and willed transformation allies it with utopian literature, particularly the satirical or dystopian kind, and distinguishes it from fantasy. The "admonitory utopia" is categorised as the chief form of contemporary science fiction, working mainly through dystopian features, and accordingly science fiction's utopian role as "an instrument of social diagnosis and warning" is zestfully explored in a wealth of examples of varying literary merit. The potential for science fiction as a serious literary form, welcomed by Amis, is linked to its utopian capacities.

The utopianism in feminist thinking and approaches to literature, especially women's literature, has long been implicit, but more recent criticism has given it much greater attention and salience. BARR and SMITH's collection of essays focuses largely, though not exclusively, on contemporary utopian fictions by women (Doris Lessing features importantly), in order to raise questions about gender, culture, and sexual difference. Strong on particularised analysis of their chosen texts, the essays perhaps lack wider and more searching insights.

BARTKOWSKI defines the feminist utopia firmly as contemporary, illustrated in ten novels (mostly North American and all written by women), which she groups in pairs in order to interrogate notions of duality and opposition, especially in respect of gender and power relations, and to affirm dialectic as the utopian modal principle. Making unobtrusive use of critical theory, both politically and psychoanalytically oriented, her study investigates this fiction's diversely imaginative representations of "feminist desires", hopeful and speculative; the novels are seen as didactic but inventive critiques of patriarchy and masculinism.

In contrast, JONES and GOODWIN's collection ranges ambitiously in subject matter, from medieval monasticism to postmodern fiction, though with most attention paid to nineteenth- and twentieth-century writing. The relation between utopian and feminist thinking and the narrative expression of this relation are the central and conjoined issues. Both relation and expression are seen as often ambiguously and problematically, rather than programmatically, realised. A stimulating variety of readings results.

DONAWERTH and KOLMERTEN's collection neatly sutures science fiction and feminism, treating various narratives from seventeenth-century utopian fictions through to contemporary science-fiction stories, with texts and treatment all, significantly, by women. The editors claim that these fictions, articulating the woman's view, estranged from the dominant masculine, form a continuous though variegated post-Renaissance tradition previously neglected but now being recovered, which expresses utopian awareness and hope. The individual essays, without compromising the specificity of their topics, generally bear this out, though the degree of continuity remains debatable. A useful bibliography is supplied.

RUPPERT considers the reader's relation to utopian literature, using contemporary reception theory, and argues for the imaginatively stimulating qualities of the literary utopia, which, being no mere reductive or escapist idealisation (as generally thought), is complex and experimental, encouraging critical reaction through defamiliarisation, and frequently arousing creatively uncertain and ambivalent responses. Organised as dialogue, utopian literature "invites the dialectical involvement of its readers" (a dialectic of fictive possibility and factual necessity) and is thus open to active and variable, even conflicting, interpretation, and excited by the dissonance between ideal and reality, dream and fact. Various ways of reading utopian fiction (itself very diverse) are accordingly discussed (the central example is More's *Utopia*), with the emphasis consistently, indeed insistently and somewhat tendentiously, on reading as interrogative activity producing "open" texts.

For concise attempts at general definition one may consult two important essays which provide succinct and cogently discriminating accounts of the utopia as literary genre and form. The first is concerned more with the traditional type, the second with the modern.

With wit and commanding ease and range of reference, FRYE identifies features of the literary utopia (both the "serious" or positive ideal and the "satirical" or dystopian type) and ways in which these are historically related and determined. Serious utopian thought is, he claims, imaginative rather than predictive or instrumental, "less concerned with achieving ends than with visualizing possibilities", salutary and culturally beneficial, and it finds appropriately literary expression. The classical utopia is essentially societal, "a *speculative* myth" envisioning a collective *telos* in relation to current social experience, contrasting imperfect anarchic reality and imagined ordered ideal, satirising the former and valorising the latter. Its typical embodiment is the "orderly city", the rational social system, distinguished from pastoral or Arcadian simplicity. Emphasis rests either on legal and political structures or on technology: the former tends toward socio-political theory, the latter toward science fiction. Modern utopias extend these features globally, often with dystopian emphasis. Future utopias will be more individualistic, provisional, in order to remain true to utopian transcendence. As with any heroically simplifying argument, qualifications can be entered, but Frye's capacity for wide-ranging and deeply intelligent analysis is indisputable.

WILLIAMS, who might justifiably be termed (in a positive sense) the foremost utopian critic in English of the later twentieth century, provides, in this brief analysis of the complex relations between utopian literature and science fiction, definitions of the utopian as the "willed" or more specifically "technological" transformation of the world by human endeavour, in a rational or scientific spirit, toward an evidently better or allegedly ideal condition, and of utopian literature as the imaginative representation of that transformation, as process or achievement or both. The dystopian embodies the same transformation, but "negatively valued". Avoiding loose identification of utopian literature with science fiction, and stressing the variability of both categories, Williams examines briefly but illuminatingly their links and differences in selected nineteenth- and twentieth-century fictions.

In conclusion, it may be observed that criticism of utopian writings has shifted from more descriptive and affirmative accounts (utopia as achievement, notably of social order and justice) toward more analytic and interrogative treatments (utopia as process, animated by desire for betterment), a change to some extent paralleling developments in the history of utopian literature itself.

JEREMY LANE

See also **Fantasy Literature, Science Fiction**

V

Vaughan, Henry 1621/22–1695

English poet and prose writer

Calhoun, Thomas, *Henry Vaughan: The Achievement of "Silex Scintillans"*, Newark: University of Delaware Press, 1981

Pettet, E.C., *Of Paradise and Light: A Study of Vaughan's "Silex Scintillans"*, Cambridge: Cambridge University Press, 1960

Post, Jonathan, *Henry Vaughan: The Unfolding Vision*, Princeton, New Jersey: Princeton University Press, 1982

Post, Jonathan (ed.), Henry Vaughan issue of the *George Herbert Journal*, 7, 1983–84

Rudrum, Alan (ed.), *Essential Articles for the Study of Henry Vaughan*, Hamden, Connecticut: Archon Books, 1987

Simmonds, James, *Masques of God: Form and Theme in the Poetry of Henry Vaughan*, Pittsburgh: University of Pittsburgh Press, 1972; London: Henry M. Snyder, 1972

Henry Vaughan's life has always attracted attention, and many critical articles focus on his experiences during the Civil War, his relationship with his brothers, and, most contentiously, his conversion from secular to sacred poetry. The belief that Vaughan's "best" poetry was inspired by a biographical crisis – a spiritual awakening, which transformed him and his verse – informed much early criticism, and led to a concentration on the religious poetry of *Silex Scintillans*, almost to the complete exclusion of Vaughan's other writings. The tendency for writing along these lines to become an industry was halted by Frank Kermode with an iconoclastic article, in which he asserted that "something happened, something to do with poetry and not with prayer". Of course, as critics quickly pointed out, the two are not mutually exclusive, but the long-term effect of Kermode's intervention has been to restore a certain balance. More recently, critics have attempted to account for the whole body of Vaughan's poetry, arguing for the continuity of his secular and sacred verse.

PETTET's study is the most useful to come out of the "conversionist school". His Introduction interrogates "the mystery of Vaughan's sudden poetic flowering" and advances a hypothesis about Vaughan's regeneration in the light of what inspired and shaped his (religious) poetry. An inevitably partial view of Vaughan achievements results, but in the course of this argument Pettet offers some highly perceptive analyses of individual poems, notably "Regeneration", "The Morning-Watch", "The Night", and "They are all gone into the world of light". He is also usefully attentive to sequences, clusters of images, and large structural patterns, which connect Parts One and Two of *Silex Scintillans*.

SIMMONDS provides a sustained attack on the "conversionist" school as well as the most energetic defence of Vaughan's secular poetry. Downplaying the importance of a conversion of any kind, Simmonds argues for the distinctive merits of a secular Vaughan whose career can be interpreted not as radically disjunctive but as a continuous creative effort. The study focuses on previously neglected verse, and produces many insightful analyses of individual poems. However, while Simmonds' study provides a useful counterbalance to Pettet's, his concentration on the secular verse at the expense of the religious means that his view of Vaughan's achievements is equally, if differently partial. Finally, Simmonds fails to account for many of the impulses that went into the making of *Silex Scintillans*.

CALHOUN pays lip service to the importance of reading Vaughan's poetry as a whole, and the book does include a discussion of *Poems*, but the main thrust of the study is pitched towards interpreting the religious verse. He attributes the distinctive merits of this verse to Vaughan's interests in hermeticism and his possible Rosicrucian affiliations. His argument is sustained by some interesting work on the social and historical context of *Silex Scintillans*, but is unfortunately marred by Calhoun's stress on the influence of Henry's brother, Thomas, and his use of rather dubious biographical evidence.

POST's excellent 1982 study provides a comprehensive, integrating view of the whole body of work, and uniquely manages to emphasise the importance of the poet's relationship to George Herbert without turning Vaughan into a derivative epigone. Arguing that we have no way of understanding Vaughan's "conversion" except literarily, Post places it in the larger context of the poet's other writings and the Civil War. Steering a middle course between Pettet and Simmonds, Post describes the development of Vaughan's career as:

> . . . neither simply continuous nor radically disjunctive but involving, instead, a progressively deeper commitment to the offices of the poet during a time when everything else seemed to be falling apart. Always a revisionist, Vaughan expanded by contracting: he moved forward by seeming to repudiate what he had accomplished or was in the process of accomplishing; and his conversion to religious verse was only the most dramatic

act, initiated in *Poems* and carried on in *Olor*, of continuing to question the appropriate direction for poetry in the midst of what the author came increasingly to view as "the last gasp of time".

Post includes a lengthy discussion of the secular poetry, which supports his contention that it is "more often formidable than bad", and interestingly includes a full chapter on *Thalia Rediviva*, a collection usually given only the briefest of notice in studies of Vaughan.

The Henry Vaughan issue of the *George Herbert Journal* edited by POST has the distinction of being the most up-to-date collection of criticism. Broadly historicist approaches are adopted to examine a variety of topics, such as Vaughan's verification, politics and the self, and the problem of authority. Several essays deal with neglected poems and prose including unusual readings of "*Daphnis*: An Elegiac *Eclogue*" and *Flores Solitudinis*, by Cedric Brown and Mary Jane Doherty.

Finally, RUDRUM has brought together 21 essays (not all reprinted in full) charting the major developments in Vaughan criticism over the last 50 years. The result is a substantial book of criticism whose range and accessibility make it an ideal introduction to the field.

RAMONA WRAY

Victorian Literature: General

Altick, Richard D., *The Presence of the Present: Topics of the Day in the Victorian Novel*, Columbus: Ohio State University Press, 1991

Gilbert, Sandra M., and Susan Gubar, *The Madwoman in the Attic: The Woman Writer and the Nineteenth-Century Literary Imagination*, New Haven, Connecticut, and London: Yale University Press, 1979

Gilmour, Robin, *The Victorian Period: The Intellectual and Cultural Context of English Literature 1830–90*, London and New York: Longman, 1993

Harrison, Antony H., and Beverly Taylor (eds.), *Gender and Discourse in Victorian Literature and Art*, DeKalb: Northern Illinois University Press 1992

Helsinger, Elizabeth K., Robin Lauterbach Sheets, and William Veder, *The Woman Question*, (3 vols., *Defining Voices*, *Social Issues*, *Literary Issues*), Manchester: Manchester University Press, 1983

Henkle, Robert B., *Comedy and Culture: England 1820–1900*, Princeton, New Jersey: Princeton University Press, 1980

Jenkyns, Richard, *The Victorians and Ancient Greece*, Oxford and Cambridge, Massachusetts: Blackwell, 1980

Miller, J. Hillis, *The Disappearance of God: Five Nineteenth-Century Writers*, Cambridge, Massachusetts: Belknap Press of Harvard University Press, 1963

Morse, David, *High Victorian Culture*, New York: New York University Press, 1993; London: Macmillan, 1993

Reed, John R., *Victorian Conventions*, Athens: Ohio State University Press,1976

Small, Ian, *Conditions for Criticism: Authority, Knowledge, and Literature in the Late Nineteenth Century*, Oxford: Clarendon Press, 1991

Timko, Michael, "The Victorianism of Victorian Literature", in *New Literary History*, 6, 1975

With a field as large and as variegated as the Victorian period, it is perhaps not surprising that very few studies attempt the titanic task of providing a comprehensive overview. Instead, general surveys tend to concentrate on sizeable aspects of Victorian culture, often taking these as paradigmatic in some way of the larger picture. ALTICK provides an exception to this rule, and the sheer bulk of his book demonstrates the problems of providing anything that resembles complete coverage. Its 854 pages, packed with details about everyday Victorian culture and common knowledge, do provide a very full context to the literature of the period (mostly, but not exclusively, the novel); but the sheer length of this study also makes for rather heavy reading.

REED opens his book with a claim that "this study is not meant to be exhaustive". Nonetheless, he covers a tremendous amount of ground detailing the literary conventions that most often characterise the various sorts of writings of the Victorian period. On plot devices (with chapters on "Coincidence", "The Return", "Inheritance", and the like) he is straightforward and useful; his treatment of character types ("Women", "Male Types", "The Orphan", "Gypsies") could be more sophisticated; but he really comes into his own on recurring themes and emblems ("Duelling", "Madness", "Disguise", and "The Occult").

GILMOUR's study is an excellent introductory overview of the period, with chapters on "Victorian historiography", "Religious Thought", "Science", "Politics", and the "Visual Arts". Gilmour's prose is never less than lucid, and he manages to accumulate a impressive amount of material without letting it swamp his text. Above all, his concision is both remarkable and praiseworthy. This text represents one of the best starting points for the budding Victorian scholar.

Aside from these more comprehensive studies, there are a number of wide-ranging examinations of the period that focus on more specific aspects of nineteenth-century culture. MILLER's influential and thought-provoking work is one example. This is not the later Miller of rigorous deconstructive fame, and his thesis in this study – that the sense of the withdrawal of God from the world acts as a sort of paradigmatic mood that influences virtually all the important writers of the period – can be attacked for its totalizing tendencies. Nonetheless, he makes a great many excellent points, and his book remains vital.

On a smaller scale, TIMKO's article is still setting the critical terms of debate on what constitutes "Victorianism". Timko sees a shift from Romantic to Victorian as a movement away from the metaphysical or transcendent towards engagement with epistemological issues. In particular, and like Miller, Timko sees a recurring "epistemological despair", a radical doubt about knowledge and man's ability to know, which goes hand in hand with an increasingly scientific attempt to ground knowledge.

Gender studies have been a particularly fertile area of enquiry for the nineteenth century. HELSINGER *et al.* provide a detailed source for students who wish to examine the fuller context of the question, although social history, rather than literature, is the main thrust of their three-volume study. HARRISON's collection of essays examines a variety of issues connected with gender in the nineteeth century, with contributions grouped into the three sections "Poetry", "Fiction", and "Visual Arts". What makes this collection so good is both its range and the subtlety with which many of the essays explore the multifaceted aspects of Victorian attitudes to women. GILBERT and GUBAR also deserve mention, although their large-scale examination of the role and representation of women in the nineteenth century sometimes comes over as a little one-dimensional. Nonetheless, their resurrection of Rochester's mad wife, Bertha, confined to the attic in *Jane Eyre*, as a type for the marginalised status of women in the Victorian period remains compelling.

Comedy, although of central importance to a great deal of nineteenth-century literature, has received surprisingly little critical attention. One exception to this rule is HENKLE, whose approach to the subject aims to avoid the sort of "profitless generalisations" that he sees in most criticism of comedy. He goes about this by grounding his study in the asserting that "the receptivity of the Victorian age to comedy raises issues of comedy's social workings" and by subsequent explorations of the way comedy "expresses middle-class concerns and anxieties". Charles Dickens is treated in depth, but a wide variety of other figures are read in the context of comedy's relationship to the totality of cultural production.

Despite its title's allusion to "culture", MORSE's book is actually a well-balanced study of mainstream Victorian literature. Locating literary production in a sense of Victorian Englishness, which depends on the two concepts of "trade" and "tradition", Morse examines the intellectual continuities between such diverse figures as the Chartists and Thomas Carlyle, taking in Dickens, the Brontës, William Makepeace Thackeray, and Thomas Hardy. Tennyson's *In Memoriam* is read in the context of the Oxford Movement and Victorian worries about the unity of the Church, and the chapter on "Victorian Intellectuals and Their Dilemmas" is particularly good. Morse's book is lucid and accessible, and while it does not engage with modern critico-theoretical debates, it nevertheless represents a sophisticated and impressive contribution to the field.

JENKYNS reveals the extent to which Victorian culture was pervaded by the ancient world, and Ancient Greece in particular. He examines the ways in which Victorian thinkers and writers turned to the classics for inspiration in poetry, the novel, fine art and architecture, theories of education, and other areas. This wide-ranging study is engagingly written, and provides an illuminating overview of the Victorian period. The book also has the (perhaps surprising) virtue of not having been written by a Victorian specialist. Jenkyns, originally a classicist, avoids the oppressive detail that the period expert often feels behoven to produce; yet, at the same time his book is readable and penetrating.

SMALL's work deals primarily with essays and other prose writing, from the 1860s to the end of the century, but he provides valuable insights into the way increasing industrial and social sophistication resulted in the fragmentation of knowledge, such that specialisation became the order of the day and the amateur status of the critic (which had prevailed from Philip Sidney to John Ruskin and Matthew Arnold) was gradually replaced by a sense of the critic as a professional. Walter Pater and Oscar Wilde are central to his argument, but his conclusions range far more widely, and this is an excellent and thought-provoking book.

ADAM ROBERTS

Victorian Literature and the City

Bernstein, Carol, *The Celebration of Scandal: Toward the Sublime in Victorian Urban Fiction*, University Park: State University of Pennsylvania Press, 1991

Cazamian, Louis, *The Social Novel in England, 1830–1850: Dickens, Disraeli, Mrs Gaskell, Kingsley*, translated by Martin Fido, London and Boston: Routledge & Kegan Paul, 1973 (original French edition, 1903)

Flint, Kate (ed.), *The Victorian Novelist: Social Problems and Social Change*, London: Croom Helm, 1987; New York: Croom Helm/Methuen, 1987

Keating, P.J., *The Working Classes in Victorian Fiction*, London: Routledge & Kegan Paul, 1971

Keating, P.J. (ed.), *Into Unknown England, 1866–1913: Selections from the Social Explorers*, Manchester: Manchester University Press, 1976; Totowa, New Jersey: Rowman & Littlefield, 1976

Klaus, H. Gustav (ed.), *The Rise of Socialist Fiction 1880–1914*, Brighton, Sussex: Harvester Press, 1987; New York: St Martin's Press, 1987

Wheeler, Michael, *English Fiction of the Victorian Period 1830–1890*, London: Longman, 1985

Williams, Raymond, *The English Novel from Dickens to Lawrence*, London: Chatto & Windus, 1970; New York: Oxford University Press, 1970

Williams, Raymond, *The Country and the City*, London: Chatto & Windus, 1973; New York: Oxford University Press, 1973

There is no simple or straightforward way to investigate the relationship between the Victorian city and literature, although its images dominate the writing of the period. There are crucial changes of perspective between the mid- and late-century periods, between the north and south of England, and between provincial and metropolitan concerns. In addition, literary-critical approaches rarely consider the city as a single idea. Recurrent motifs discussed in general works can be identified as the working classes and relationships between the classes, and industrial and urban conditions and fears of social instability. However, because of the length and diversity of the period, many important aspects of the city and its literary motifs are explored in relation to specific authors who drew on the city for their material, notably Elizabeth Gaskell, Charles Dickens, Benjamin Disraeli, Charles Kingsley, George Gissing, and H.G. Wells.

The close interaction of fiction and documentary writing makes the reading of some contextual works more than usually important. Relevant contemporary starting points, which also make fascinating reading, are: Friedrich Engels' *The Condition of the Working Classes in England in 1844* (Penguin edition, 1994), which covers the early industrial cities; Henry Mayhew's *Selections*, a mid-century survey of London's poor (Penguin edition, 1994), and Andrew Mearns's *The Bitter Cry of Outcast London*, a plea for better housing in late century London (Leicester University Press edition, 1970). Two collections of similar material are discussed below in more detail. Modern historical and sociological approaches, in particular Asa Briggs's edited *Victorian Cities* (Penguin, 1963), F.H. Dyos and M. Wolff's edited *The Victorian City Images and Realities*, Volumes 1 and 2, (Routledge & Kegan Paul, 1973), and G. Stedman Jones's *Outcast London: A Study of the Relationship Between Classes in Victorian Society* (Oxford University Press, 1971) are also very helpful.

Discussions of the novel dominate the critical literature, because it was the literary form which concerned itself most directly with urban and industrial subject matter. Poetry, with some notable exceptions such as James Thomson's "The City of Dreadful Night" (1880), drew on history, romance, and myth for its material (see Raymond Williams, below, and, for a brief but useful overview, Bernard Richards' "The City" in *English Poetry of the Victorian Period, 1830–1890*, London: Longman, 1988). Drama did not draw on this kind of subject matter until late in the century, but although dramatists such as Oscar Wilde and George Bernard Shaw were deeply concerned with social and urban issues, critics have not singled out for discussion the idea of the city in their works.

Despite considerable cultural and sociological work done by feminists on women and the city, there is currently a scarcity of feminist literary criticism addressing this issue. The city as a space for women to move across is considered by John Goode in his discussion of Gissing's *The Odd Women* (1891) in *George Gissing: Ideology and Fiction* (London: Vision Press, 1988). This book is also useful for its introductory, general discussion about the transformation of urban structures into fiction. Images of fallen women, the New Woman, and working women, important and recurring elements of the fictional urban landscape, are usually considered as part of broader issues of female identity and representation. Elizabeth Wilson's *The Sphinx in the City: Urban Life, the Control of Disorder, and Women* (London: Virago, 1991) is a pioneering work in this respect. She constructs a convincing argument for the city as escape from patriarchal authority (see Chapter 3, "Cesspool City: London", in particular).

CAZAMIAN's book is a pioneering work, an overview of the early Victorian period which examines the major novelists and the popular political, religious, and social movements that formed the context of their work. Cazamian attempts to convey the broad sweep of the intellectual movements that linked one work to another, and to establish a sense of development and coherence in the history of Victorian fiction. Although this book was written at the turn of the century, and some of the critical work on individual novelists may seem unimaginative, this remains a very useful survey of the early period. Its most important contribution is its exploration of the close relationship of fiction to social concerns and its endorsement of the popular contemporary phrase "novels with a purpose" as a critical category. The acceptance of the interaction between literature and society informs all but the most recent critical approaches. "Social conscience was born in England around 1840", Cazamian claims, and points forward to the persistence of this attitude among novelists "as the novel again became the favourite form of expression between 1880 and 1890".

WILLIAMS's work has arguably made the most influential contribution of modern criticism to Victorian studies. Considered together, his books form a philosophical and cultural continuity. Two of them, however, are particularly relevant to a consideration of the Victorian city. The earlier of these (1970) argues the close connection between the emergence of a "new and major *generation* of writers" in the 1840s and the sociological fact that by this time "the English were the first predominantly urban people". Williams assesses the impact of urbanisation on some of the major novelists of the period – Dickens, the Brontës, George Eliot, Thomas Hardy, and Joseph Conrad – through the concept of the "knowable community". He argues that the city cannot be considered simply as a physical phenomenon, not "only a matter of physical expansion and complication. It is also and primarily a problem of viewpoint and consciousness". In the chapter "Alone in the City" Williams discusses, through the work of William Blake, William Wordsworth, Gaskell, Gissing, and others, how the urban experience has changed traditional patterns of observation. He anticipates the modernist mode of James Joyce in his assertion that "the buildings, the noises, the sights and the smells of the city [are] parts of this single and racing consciousness".

WILLIAMS's 1973 study develops his ideas about the nature of urban experience through contrasting it with rural experience and analysing the transformation and function of both in literature. This discussion has a philosophically and historically broad sweep, beginning with classical literature, concluding with an analysis of the modern world, and moving backwards and forwards across the city/country borderland. The opening two chapters set the context for the argument, and chapters 15–20 deal with the issues in Victorian fiction and poetry. Williams resists setting arbitrary period (or territorial) boundaries, showing constructively the movement of eighteenth-century thought into the nineteenth century and the persistence of the rural idyll for city dwellers. Wordsworth's, Blake's, Dickens's, George Eliot's, Hardy's, and Gissing's works are historicised as part of the physical, political, and psychological struggle for identity in the expanding cities, where "the cultural centralisation of England was already at this time [1880] more marked, at every level, than in any comparable society. Even to oppose and reject the city, men came to the city; there was no other ready way".

KEATING's 1971 survey is indispensable to a reader interested in industrial and urban concerns in the Victorian period. Although he concentrates on the latter part of the century, the two introductory chapters cover the earlier period. The chapter "Walter Besant and the 'Discovery' of the East End" deals specifically with the representation of London in fiction, but Keating's identification of urban and industrial fictional motifs and his clear and perceptive discussions of literary strategies of representation make this book more than just a survey. He covers a wide diversity of novels, and many previously unfamiliar texts are introduced with useful contextual discussions.

KEATING has also made an important editorial contribution in his 1976 selection from contemporary works of journalism and sociology, which had a profound impact on society in their time. Among them are extracts from: the journalist George Sims; the sociologist Charles Booth; the founder of the Salvation Army William Booth; and the social commentator C.F.G. Masterman. Keating's excellent Introduction stresses the close relationship of these writings with contemporary novels, and defines broad common categories other than the obvious subject matter, including common literary devices and metaphors around the idea of urban "exploration". "There is barely an area of nineteenth-century fictional and nonfictional prose", he argues, "in which the central attitudes and terminology of social exploration do not appear". FLINT's book serves a similar function, and is part of a series of contextual material collections for students of literature. The Introduction is, however, less helpful in pointing the reader towards literary connections, and the selections are less directly related to urban concerns in fictional material. They cover the broader theme of "social change", as the title indicates, providing a diversity of short political, legal, and sociological extracts as a framework for a broader understanding of the forces that informed the worlds of Victorian novelists. There is also a bibliography of relevant novels.

WHEELER's survey is a straightforward and comprehensive overview of the Victorian period, the end of which he defines as 1890. Although this demarcation cuts off some important writing on the city, notably Gissing, Wells, and Arthur Morrison, this is still useful background reading, particularly for the discussions of the Newgate novel, Dickens, and Gaskell in the first half. Particularly useful for the study of a literature so closely related to history are a date-table of major works and related historical events, and thorough and accessible bibliographies of general and author-specific works.

The collection of essays edited by KLAUS builds on the foundations of his earlier collection *The Socialist Novel in Britain: Towards the Recovery of a Tradition* (1982). The essays all deal with some aspect of socialist engagement with the late nineteenth-century city, and are informed by a conviction of the political function of novels. Most of the writers who are discussed in this collection are unknown or unfamilar, but are presented in a helpful, informative way. The topics, such as literature about strikes, anarchism, and political women writers, reflect the belief that the city is a manifestation of determining political structures. This collection also usefully acknowledges "a significant shift away from an exclusive concentration on the slum fiction of the metropolis ... [to] a less well-known range of fiction exploring the working class environment and poverty in the provincial cities".

BERNSTEIN pursues a structuralist approach to the Victorian novel in a book that is representative of a significant strand of current opinion, more widely held in the USA than in Britain, that the social and moral intentions of the Victorian novel and its realist strategies are limiting and transparent. Although the clarity of her argument is often obscured by an over-zealous use of critical terminology drawn from Michel Foucault and Roland Barthes, and the approach should be treated with respectful caution, the perspectives she brings to her discussions of particular texts are refreshing and a salutary reminder that the realist Victorians were as formally and linguistically inventive as their modernist successors. In emphasising the fictionalising of the city (rather than the historicising of it), Bernstein opens up the possibility of constructive re-readings of textual detail: the city is considered as a "site of mystery" in Dickens's *Bleak House* and Henry James's *Princess Casamassima* (1886); the extended object descriptions in Dickens's *Our Mutual Friend* (1865) and Gissing's *The Whirlpool* (1896) are read as sign systems; the dramatic opening description of the River Thames in *Our Mutual Friend* reveals "the problematics of the visible", while those aspects of the city that deliberately invite the eye, such as the advertisements in Gissing's *In the Year of Jubilee* (1894), "gull the public through their invitations to misread, but they invite the reader of the novel to view the city as a peculiarly physical text".

LYNNE HAPGOOD

Victorian Literature and Religion

Baker, J.E., *The Novel and the Oxford Movement*, Princeton, New Jersey: Princeton University Press, 1932
Ball, Patricia M., *The Heart's Events: The Victorian Poetry of Relationships*, London: Athlone Press, 1976
Chapman, Raymond, *Faith and Revolt: Studies in the Literary Influence of the Oxford Movement*, London: Weidenfeld & Nicolson, 1970
Cockshut, A.O.J., *Anglican Attitudes: A Study of Victorian Religious Controversies*, London: Collins, 1959
Fraser, Hilary, *Beauty and Belief: Aesthetics and Religion in Victorian Literature*, Cambridge and New York: Cambridge University Press, 1986
Jay, Elizabeth, *The Religion of the Heart: Anglican Evangelicalism and the Nineteenth-Century Novel*, Oxford: Clarendon Press, 1979; New York: Oxford University Press, 1979
Maison, M.M., *Search Your Soul, Eustace: A Survey of the Religious Novel in the Victorian Age*, London and New York: Sheed & Ward, 1961
Tennyson, G.B., *Victorian Devotional Poetry: The Tractarian Mode*, Cambridge, Massachusetts: Harvard University Press, 1981
Willey, Basil, *More Nineteenth-Century Studies: A Group of Honest Doubters*, London: Chatto & Windus, 1956; New York: Columbia University Press, 1956

It has been difficult for critics to focus this subject in a satisfactory way, because, though most great Victorian writers were in some sense Christian, the literary vision of many was secular, and the theology of some, great in other ways, feeble and contradictory. Thus, while justice has been done to the profound Christian inspiration of a few, notably John Henry Newman and Gerard Manley Hopkins, others, like Tennyson and Robert Browning, have been valued more for talents oblique to their faith.

BAKER's aim was to "let the fiction throw light on the Oxford Movement", and to allow minor writings to assist us in understanding greater ones. He is skilful in balancing internal views, like those of Charlotte Yonge, with external (Anthony Trollope). He was perhaps the first to analyze Trollope's conflation of periods of time, so that Trollope's

Reverend Arabin, who has experienced Newman's influence, is contemporary with the old High-and-dry thinking, which flourished before the Reform Bill.

WILLEY's book, a sequel to his *Nineteenth-Century Studies* (1949), is subtitled "*A Group of Honest Doubters*". It presents Francis Newman (in a notably sympathetic portrait), Tennyson, and others confronted by an Anglican Church "Romish in its liturgy, Protestant in its articles, Erastian in its government, and committed to an untenable bibliolatry". Tennyson he sees as more simply religious than Christian, while in R.H. Froude and John Morley he analyzes the destructive influence of Thomas Carlyle. *Essays and Reviews* he sees with tolerant liberal hindsight, as shocking the orthodox with opinions which would later become commonplaces, underrating perhaps the note of nihilistic scepticism, which made them true precursors of the ordained atheists of the 1990s.

In my book (COCKSHUT) I studied several controversies over Reverend Cornelius Gorham, *Essays and Reviews*, and John Colenso, in an attempt to discover what they revealed about Anglican conceptions of authority. The stress was on the incompatibility of the principles of parties that existed side by side in the Church, the irritable, yet often feeble, interference of secular authorities, and the bland assumption of each party that it alone represented the true tradition of a Church which had never made up its mind on fundamental points.

MAISON's book is a spirited guide to religious and antireligious fiction. It covers a wide area, and is thus necessarily sketchy when any author who requires close analysis is under discussion. It is most useful as a guide to minor writers who have been neglected by other critics. She concludes with a study of writers whose attitudes, near the end of the century, were more greatly detached and secular than earlier figures, though still concerned with religious practice.

BALL's excellent study is focused on the point where religion and personal feeling meet. This is an approach that proves fruitful especially in the cases of Tennyson and Coventry Patmore, and yields insights also into Matthew Arnold, Arthur Hugh Clough, and others. Her work is marked by close attention to the text, and a healthy respect for the poetic talents of her authors.

CHAPMAN says of the Tractarians, "they stressed a wider and longer view which could sometimes ease the pressures of the here and now". He notes, as others have done in relation to the Evangelicals, the unfairness of many of the novelists. He deals shrewdly with the main difficulty of his subject, that the Tractarian novelists were either minor writers, like Joseph Shorthouse and Charlotte Yonge, or major writers who were only amateurs as novelists, like Newman. He is especially sympathetic to Shorthouse, and gives what is perhaps the best account of *John Inglesant*.

JAY's work is marked by a theological literacy that shows up some better-known critics. To her, different types of Evangelical are never to be covered by a vague generalizing phrase, and the difference between Calvinist and Arminian is palpable. She shows that some novelists who wrote of Evangelicals (like Mrs Trollope in *The Vicar of Wrexhill*) exaggerated the influence of Calvinism because it offered an easier satirical target; and she brings into prominence interesting and forgotten works, like Emma Warboise's answer to *Jane Eyre*, *Thornycroft Hall*.

TENNYSON makes a sensitive study, both critical and historical, of High Church and Catholic poetry. It is interesting and surprising to find that there were 95 editions of John Keeble's *The Christian Year* before its author's death in 1866. Newman's contributions to *Lyra Apostolica* are characterized as "urgent, intense, confident and purposeful", and he links Newman's poetry convincingly with two crises in his life, in 1833 and 1865. He also makes a plea for the merits of the almost forgotten Isaac Williams.

FRASER shows the interrelation of the aesthetic with the theological in a procession of writers from Newman to Walter Pater and Oscar Wilde, in whom she finds the "full implications of romantic tendencies to secularize and personalize Christianity", so that Christ himself is appropriated to a personal myth. Her study of Hopkins is eloquent and strongly felt. It is a skilful study, though perhaps she succumbs at times to the historian's temptation to see too clear a pattern in disparate events.

A.O.J. Cockshut

Victorian Literature and Society

Altick, Richard D., *The English Common Reader: A Social History of the Mass Reading Public 1800–1900*, Chicago: University of Chicago Press, 1957
Altick, Richard D., *Victorian People and Ideas*, New York: Norton, 1973; London: Dent, 1974
Altick, Richard D., *The Presence of the Present: Topics of the Day in the Victorian Novel*, Columbus: Ohio State University Press, 1991
Armstrong, Isobel, *Victorian Poetry: Poetry, Poetics and Politics*, London and New York: Routledge, 1993
Beer, Gillian, *Darwin's Plots: Evolutionary Narrative in Darwin, George Eliot, and Nineteenth-Century Fiction*, London: Routledge & Kegan Paul, 1983
Brantlinger, Patrick, *Rule of Darkness: British Literature and Imperialism, 1830–1914*, Ithaca, New York: Cornell University Press, 1988
Dyos, H.J., and Michael Wolff (eds.), *The Victorian City: Images and Realities*, 2 vols., London and Boston: Routledge & Kegan Paul, 1973
Gallagher, Catherine, *The Industrial Reformation of English Fiction: Social Discourse and Narrative Form, 1832–1867*, Chicago: University of Chicago Press, 1985
Houghton, Walter, *The Victorian Frame of Mind: 1830–1870*, New Haven, Connecticut: Yale University Press, 1957
Hughes, Linda K., and Michael Lund, *The Victorian Serial*, Charlottesville: University Press of Virginia, 1991
Levine, George, *Darwin and the Novelists: Patterns of Science in Victorian Fiction*, Cambridge, Massachusetts: Harvard University Press, 1988
Marcus, Steven, *The Other Victorians: A Study of Sexuality and Pornography in Mid-Nineteenth Century England*, New York: Basic Books, 1966, with new Introduction, 1975; London: Weidenfeld & Nicolson, 1966

Mitchell, Sally, *et al.* (eds.), *Victorian Britain: An Encyclopaedia*, New York: Garland, 1988; London: St James Press, 1991
Showalter, Elaine, *A Literature of Their Own: British Women Novelists from Brontë to Lessing*, Princeton, New Jersey: Princeton University Press, 1977; London: Virago, 1978, revised 1982
Vicinus, Martha, *The Industrial Muse: A Study of Nineteenth Century British Working-Class Literature*, London: Croom Helm, 1974; New York: Barnes & Noble, 1975
Weeks, Jeffrey, *Sex, Politics and Society: The Regulation of Sexuality since 1800*, London: Longman, 1981, 2nd edition, 1989
Wheeler, Michael, *Death and the Future Life in Victorian Literature and Theology*, Cambridge and New York: Cambridge University Press, 1990

The scholarship on Victorian literature is both massive and rich. Keeping in view the intended function of this essay – providing a manageable introductory review – the following discussion is limited to wide-ranging surveys, which discuss literature in a broad historical context. However, the books recommended here should, both in their texts and bibliographies, provide the reader with background and direction enough to continue their reading beyond the scope of this list.

For the reader very new to Victorian literature and culture, two surveys have long stood as the most suitable. ALTICK's *Victorian People and Ideas* is brief, highly readable, and relates the key political, legal, and scientific issues of Victorian culture to the canonical literature of the day. HOUGHTON's book is longer, and somewhat harder going, but also provides greater detail. He breaks down the period into three sets of "attitudes" – emotional, intellectual, and moral – and within those three categories covers subjects ranging from religion, to science, to fashion.

ALTICK's *The Presence of the Present*, although as beautifully readable as all his work, is not intended for the reader unacquainted with the basics of Victorian culture. Instead, this sizeable book concerns itself with reading beyond the major issues of the day for traces of the ephemeral, fashionable, *au courant*, and even trivial concerns of Victorians deeply engaged in their own identities as moderns. Altick cites both canonical and non-canonical works here: the range of references is both delightful and dizzying. He demonstrates that Victorian novels were marked by a particular concern with their own present, which is evidenced both thematically and structurally.

Among the most significant literary developments of this period is the large-scale emergence of women as professional authors. SHOWALTER's groundbreaking book is very valuable for an understanding of British women's literary history, in its discussion of a female literary aesthetics and thematics of the novel in this period, which evolves into a more self-aware, "female" consciousness, as distinguished from earlier "feminine" and "feminist" stages. Showalter is generally less concerned with popular and more with canonical authors, yet her work still brings many authors to notice who had been almost forgotten. In addition, her biographical appendix, filled with short entries on a range of authors, is an excellent place to start working on popular Victorian women writers.

VICINUS provides a survey of working-class literature through the period, including radical Chartist literature, religious and propagandist literature, and the writings of working-class authors who did not define their work primarily in terms of class identification. This is a rich source on a little-understood body of texts, and offers also a sense of the context in which these writings were produced and disseminated.

ARMSTRONG is not for the beginning student of the period. However, she does provide an excellent overview, both of the canonical poetry of the period and of its criticism up to now. The reading of Victorian poetry as "post-Kantian, post-revolutionary, post-industrial and post-teleological" is both an extremely demanding and highly productive one.

ALTICK's *English Common Reader* is the classic study of readership and reading, which gives historical background from the time of William Caxton, but which focuses principally on the nineteenth century, when reading did indeed become "common". It covers several aspects of readership and reading, including educational movements, circulating libraries, and the vicissitudes of the book trade. Those who wish to press on in this area should also read HUGHES and LUND's excellent study of the Victorian serial, a form of publication particularly characteristic of the period. Their detailed, historically precise study is organized thematically, and examines the unique role of serial publication in both expressing and shaping public attitudes.

WHEELER's is an excellent study of a subject central to Victorian consciousness: religion. The book is divided into two parts, each of which is subdivided into four. The first half deals with "Last Things" – death, judgment, heaven, and hell. Wheeler's treatment of these subjects is illustrated with a wide-ranging sample from Victorian literature and culture. The second half of the book is devoted to four authors – Tennyson, Charles Dickens, John Henry Newman, and Gerard Manley Hopkins. Although this is not written for the beginning student, it is worth the effort needed to read it. The bibliography also provides excellent support.

GALLAGHER traces three phases of the "Condition of England" debate and its influence on narrative form in novels. Although also not written for the beginning student, this carefully nuanced study still provides a good overview of Victorian attitudes toward industrialization and their representation in, and effects on, the novel in this period.

The impact of science, especially Darwin, on Victorian culture and literature is LEVINE's subject. He covers the novelists Jane Austen, Dickens, Anthony Trollope, and Joseph Conrad in some depth, but also discusses several other authors, including George Eliot and Sir Walter Scott, and other scientists (most notably William Whewell) besides Darwin. For those particularly interested in Darwin, Levine should be read in conversation with BEER's classic study of Darwin and evolutionary narratives. Beer focuses too much on a single author (George Eliot) to serve as a survey, but hers is the foundational study of the influence of Darwin on Victorian narrative.

BRANTLINGER offers a good overview of the British perspective on the colonies as it appeared in literature from Frederick Marryat to Joseph Conrad. He traces both attitudes toward real historical events, like the Indian Mutiny, and the mobilization of colonial stereotypes and metaphors generally. Brantlinger pays particular attention to India and Africa; there is no coverage, however, of colonial authors, or of Ireland.

DYOS and WOLFF's two-volume collection of essays, although not as strictly literary as the other books discussed here, contains enough literary information to justify its inclusion. Additionally, this excellent collection is the best survey of work connected with the very important issues of urbanization (and industrialization) available. Ranging from studies of health and mortality to the representation of an emerging metropolitan sensibility and aesthetic, the collection offers a balance between comprehensiveness and depth.

MARCUS's work on pornography is foundational both for Victorian studies and studies of erotic fiction. His analysis of pornography as a form that is, in some sense, connate with the novel itself is an important one. Marcus's work is, however, somewhat outdated and should be read with a good overview, like WEEKS's, which, though it does not focus on literature, gives an excellent and up-to-date survey of the history of sexuality in Britain from 1800.

Finally, of relevance to the period as a whole, MITCHELL's encyclopedia is a good source for succinct information on particular movements, persons, inventions, or laws. An entry typically provides a brief summary and often a short bibliography; in addition, a "Guide to Research" is appended. As might be expected of such a large undertaking, coverage is rather uneven. Aids for the reader are provided in the helpful index and useful cross-references.

PAMELA K. GILBERT

Victorian Literature, Science, and Evolutionary Theory

Beer, Gillian, *Darwin's Plots: Evolutionary Narrative in Darwin, George Eliot and Nineteenth-Century Fiction*, London and Boston: Routledge & Kegan Paul, 1983

Henkin, Leo J., *Darwinism in the English Novel, 1860–1910: The Impact of Evolution on Victorian Fiction*, New York: Corporate Press 1940; reprinted, New York: Russell & Russell, 1963

Jordanova, L.J. (ed.), *Languages of Nature: Critical Essays on Science and Literature*, London: Free Association Books, 1986; New Brunswick, New Jersey: Rutgers University Press, 1986

Levine, George, *Darwin and the Novelists: Patterns of Science in Victorian Fiction*, Cambridge, Massachusetts: Harvard University Press, 1988

Morton, Peter, *The Vital Science: Biology and the Literary Imagination, 1860–1900*, London and Boston: Allen & Unwin, 1984

Stevenson, Lionel, *Darwin among the Poets*, Chicago: University of Chicago Press, 1932; reprinted, New York: Russell & Russell, 1963

Critical studies on Victorian literature and science focus almost exclusively on evolutionary theory, tracing its influence on the fiction and poetry of the period. Recent studies treat the writings of Victorian scientists as literary texts, even suggesting that literary models can inform scientific theory.

STEVENSON's opening chapter provides a useful survey of pre-Darwinian evolutionism. He explains how the evolutionary theories of classical philosophers influenced the poetry of Tennyson and Robert Browning, enabling them to reconcile evolution with their religious beliefs. Stevenson then refers to the work of George Meredith and Thomas Hardy, contrasting their responses to scientific discovery. He argues that Meredith's poetry urges a stoic submission to the laws of nature, perceiving physical evolution to imply the possibility for spiritual progress. Conversely, the poetry of Hardy rejects any spiritual deduction from evolution, emphasising the blind workings of chance in the physical world. Stevenson refers to a good range of works by each poet, linking this with illuminating biographical detail.

HENKIN's opening chapters discuss satires on evolutionary theory. He contrasts the satirical approaches of writers such as Richard Blackmore, Marie Corelli, May Kendall, and John Davidson, emphasising the varying sophistication of their arguments against evolution. After outlining the conflict between science and the Church, Henkin praises the reconciliation of religious and scientific viewpoints in the writings of Charles Kingsley. He concludes by exploring the theme of degeneration ("regressive evolution") in novels by Hardy and George Gissing, discussing its more sensational depiction in the science fiction of H.G. Wells. Henkin's book is particularly useful for its reference to lesser-known authors and works.

BEER begins with a detailed analysis of Darwin's prose. She argues that Darwin's use of metaphor and analogy is integral to the evaluative process itself, becoming a "fundamental means of initiating discovery". After outlining Darwin's tastes in literature, she discusses the possible influence of literary texts on his scientific approach. In her chapters on the writings of George Eliot, she explains how the findings of contemporary science informed both the plots and formal organisation of the novels. Beer challenges readings of Hardy as a pessimist, prizing his Darwinian capacity to accommodate human imperfection and identify with other forms of life. This is an excellent and highly influential book, offering sensitive accounts of both the literary and scientific writings.

MORTON begins with a detailed history of post-Darwinian and extra-Darwinian biology up to the year 1900, emphasising how popular misinterpretations of Darwin's theory led to its transformation into "a soft-textured subject where imagination could run riot". W.H. Hudson's futuristic novel *A Crystal Age* (1887) typifies the "soft-textured" evolutionism that results from this transformation, affirming the universal inevitability of progress and the biological perfection of humanity in a future utopia. Wells's science fiction reflected, in Morton's view, the growing awareness among Darwinians that the theory of natural selection implied the possible regression and extinction of humanity. He traces Wells's move towards eugenics in *The First Men in the Moon*, offering an overview of the eugenic theories of W.R. Greg, Francis Galton, and Karl Pearson. Morton concludes with a comparison of Samuel Butler's *The Way of All Flesh* and Hardy's *Tess of the d'Urbervilles*, considering both novels to exemplify late Victorian concepts of heredity. The book offers an excellent account of the scientific background, tracing the major developments of Victorian biology and offering an insight into the complexities of evolutionary thought.

JORDANOVA has brought together essays that represent an interdisciplinary approach to the subject, each emphasising the common ground between literature and science in cultural and social history. Sally Shuttleworth explores the connection between personal identity and social environment in George Eliot's *Silas Marner*. She argues that Eliot's ideas on psychological development stem from her interest in the type of organicist social theory expounded by her close associates George Henry Lewes and Herbert Spencer. Maureen McNeil writes on the poetry of Erasmus Darwin, providing a useful background to Beer's essay on the prose of his grandson's *The Origin of the Species*. Jordanova gives a useful outline of the content of each essay, typifying the clarity of what is, overall, a highly ambitious and stimulating book.

LEVINE argues that Victorian "realist" narratives invoke the authority of Charles Darwin's scientific methodology in their detached methods of narration, emphasis on the ordinary, and gradual development of plot into complexity. He refers chiefly to works by Jane Austen, Charles Dickens, and Anthony Trollope, supporting his argument with close reference to the writings of Darwin himself. Levine traces the development of Darwinian biology out of the "natural theology" of William Whewell, arguing that Darwin's theory of evolution shared many empirical and methodological strategies with the "teleological creationism" of Whewell, and can only be properly understood in the light of this connection. In Levine's view, the social order depicted in Austen's *Mansfield Park* reflects elements of Whewell's creationist science, and represents a pre-Darwinian response to the increasing secularisation of knowledge. He shows how, in their autobiographies, both Darwin and Trollope applied principles of evolutionary gradualism and uniformitarianism to their own identities, creating an "egalitarian" world where any individual can achieve great things through continued application over long periods of time. Levine's book provides an important account of the scientific and theological background to Darwinian evolution, balancing this with detailed references to a good range of literary texts.

ANDREW HAGIIOANNU

Vidal, Gore 1925–

American novelist, essayist, screenwriter, playwright, and short-story writer

Dick, Bernard F., *The Apostate Angel: A Critical Study of Gore Vidal*, New York: Random House, 1974
Kiernan, Robert F., *Gore Vidal*, New York: Frederick Ungar, 1982
Parini, Jay (ed.), *Gore Vidal: Writer Against the Grain*, New York: Columbia University Press, 1992
Stanton, Robert J. (ed.), *Gore Vidal: A Primary and Secondary Bibliography*, Boston: G.K. Hall, 1978
White, Ray Lewis, *Gore Vidal*, New York: Twayne, 1968

As Stanton's comprehensive bibliography illustrates, a great deal has been written about Gore Vidal throughout a literary career that now spans half a century. However, the relative paucity of extended critiques published thus far is indicative of Vidal's problematic status within American letters.

Although now out-dated, STANTON's bibliography remains an invaluable resource for the serious student of Vidal's *oeuvre*. In a substantial introduction, Stanton recounts the critical history of Vidal's various works, remarking at one point on Vidal's "many voices", and likening him as a satirist to Jonathan Swift. A list of writings by Vidal up to 1978 is arranged according to genre. This is followed by a chronologically ordered list of writings about Vidal, from 1946 to March 1978.

WHITE's was the first monograph on Vidal, describing and assessing ten novels, four plays, and seven short stories. The book relies heavily on Vidal's own words, taken from newspaper interviews, book reviews, and essays. White presents Vidal as a writer hitherto undervalued, because of his refusal to endorse or believe in "absolute values", which marked him as out of tune with his time and an object of suspicion in his country.

The tongue-in-cheek title of DICK's critique, equating Vidal with Milton's Satan, signals Dick's more ludic approach. Nevertheless, this remains the most insightful and interesting of the three monographs. Beneath its quirky manner, the book offers a serious attempt to analyse Vidal as "man of letters", demonstrating meticulous research into the literary and other influences on its subject. Dick examines Vidal's career as a whole, rather than just the fiction. He represents Vidal as a classicist, predicting that he will not forever be dismissed by the academy as "just a popular novelist".

KIERNAN's study, a volume in Ungar's "Modern Literature" series, is a curiously grudging assessment of Vidal's output. While apparently sharing the other critics' admiration of Vidal's versatility, Kiernan repeatedly asserts that Vidal's talent is "for the small scene, not the large design", "for the quick effect, not the sustained technique". Although he rates *Myra Breckinridge* and *Myron* as the best of Vidal's novels, his own best chapter is probably that which deals with *Washington, D.C.*, *Burr*, and *1876*. Discussing Vidal's essays, Kiernan states that "Vidal is not really a profound thinker on politics", and his concluding evaluation of Vidal is that he is "an artist of the middle rank".

Originally conceived as a *Festschrift* for the 65th anniversary of Vidal's birthday, the collection edited by PARINI offers an even balance between previously published material (ten essays, book chapters, and reviews) and new pieces (nine essays, as well as Parini's overview of Vidal's career and its critics, and his own interview with Vidal). Besides a selection from each of Dick's, Kiernan's and White's books, Parini has also included among the previously published material a personal response to Vidal's career by Italo Calvino, and Claude J. Summers' analysis of *The City and The Pillar*. Harold Bloom's review of *Lincoln* and Richard Poirier's of *Empire* are significant responses to Vidal's historical fiction. Among the new essays, James Tatum usefully examines Vidal's fascination with ancient Rome, the essayist Samuel F. Pickering discusses Vidal as essayist, Donald E. Pease lucidly argues a relationship between the New Historicism and Vidal's novels about American politics, and my own (Neilson's) and Alan Cheuse's essays on *Messiah* implicitly challenge Kiernan's relegation of this novel to the category of Vidal's "Minor Works". Parini has attempted to address the whole of Vidal's writing career, the commissioned essays including David Price's discussion of *Williwaw*, Vidal's first novel, Catherine R. Stimpson's response to *Myra Breckinridge*, and William H. Pritchard's engagement with Vidal's "satiric voices".

In recent years, Vidal has alluded to himself, *perhaps* wishfully, as a "growth industry". He has a high profile in the United States and England, and there has been, of late, a quantifiable increase in responses to his *oeuvre* from within the academy. Nevertheless, at this point he remains, in Richard Ohmann's term, "pre-canonical".

HEATHER L.E. NEILSON

Vietnam War Literature

Hellmann, John, *American Myth and the Legacy of Vietnam*, New York: Columbia University Press, 1986

Jason, Philip K., *Fourteen Landing Zones: Approaches to Vietnam War Literature*, Iowa City: University of Iowa Press, 1991

Jeffords, Susan, *The Remasculinization of America: Gender and the Vietnam War*, Bloomington: Indiana University Press, 1989

Melling, Philip H., *Vietnam in American Literature*, Boston: Twayne, 1990

Myers, Thomas, *Walking Point: American Narratives of Vietnam*, New York and Oxford: Oxford University Press, 1988

Walsh, Jeffrey, *American War Literature 1914 to Vietnam*, New York: St Martin's Press, 1982; London: Macmillan, 1982

After an initial critical silence following the United States' defeat in Vietnam, the War has become a major commercial staple of the publishing and media industries in the 1980s and 1990s.

WALSH's study is one of the earliest books to address the literature of the Vietnam War in any sustained way. His method develops in three unfolding stages: historical development, formal exegesis, personal judgement. Special attention is given to the writings of America's World-War-I poets, the fiction of Ernest Hemingway and E.E. Cummings, Laurence Stalling's *Plumes*, and John Dos Passos' *Three Soldiers*, American Spanish-Civil-War literature, World-War-II poetry and fiction, and the literature produced by, and as a result of, the Vietnam War, especially Michael Herr's *Dispatches*, Philip Caputo's *A Rumor of War*, and, incidentally, Joseph Heller's *Catch-22*. Vietnam War literature proves to be this study's capstone, not only because the War represented a unique literary event (the merger of New Journalism with traditional literary techniques), but also because there was a radical new structuring of the American metaphor of war. Walsh is particularly acute in his analysis of *Dispatches*, revealing that book's preoccupation with representing a war that was already coded as a media event.

HELLMANN continues this preoccupation with the problems of describing a war that challenged traditional modes of representation. He argues that Vietnam proved unable to validate the myth of American exceptionalism; neither could it confirm the correlative image of a mythic hero, at home in the wilderness but capable of bringing order to it. Beginning with William J. Lederer and Eugene Burdick's *The Ugly American*, Hellmann traces the erosion of that myth to the perceived moral decline that accompanied post-World-War-II affluence and materialism. The attempt to recapture the image of the frontier hero found an idealised projection in the Green Berets and in President Kennedy, whose New Frontier embodied the American self-concept. As American involvement in Vietnam deepened, however, these symbolic figures gave way to an anti-myth. Hellmann examines this reversal of values in a series of memoirs and novels ranging from the "postmodern" journalism of Michael Herr, Susan Sontag, and Mary McCarthy to the often hallucinatory fiction of Norman Mailer, Robert Stone, and Tim O'Brien, in which the descent into nature is seen as a nightmare. In the least persuasive section of the book, Hellmann finds in George Lucas's *Star Wars* trilogy the most successful transformation of utopian pastoral into technological society. However, Hellmann's concentration on myth and symbol leads him to ignore the always troubling contradictions in the American pastoral myth. Despite its limitations, this complex discussion of a pivotal era in American history sharply illuminates the confusions that Vietnam precipitated in the American psyche.

MELLING's analysis is also concerned with the effects of Vietnam on American myth. Linking literary narratives to the texts of the New England Puritans, an enclosed community whose members expressed their righteousness through "good works" and "the rooting out of sin", Melling argues that Vietnam War writings have, with rare exceptions, been based on easy and self-congratulatory assumptions reflecting the legacy of this Puritan self-absorbtion. He punctures the "appalling credentialism" with which veterans have claimed a privileged authority, when their personal narratives suggest that few have been "able to escape the belief that the wilderness is a waste land and that it functions as an analogue of the human mind, redolent with the possibilities of good and evil". Likewise, Melling has little time for the "postmodern" assumptions underlying such books as Herr's *Dispatches*, which work, he states, to dehistoricise the war and transform it into a purely American event. As such, Melling's book provides a corrective to Americo-centric visions of Vietnam. It's surely no accident that Melling goes outside American narratives to Englishman Mark Frankland's novel *The Mother-of-Pearl Men* to show what a work incorporating Vietnamese perspectives can achieve.

MYERS attempts to draw larger meaning out of the emergent American literature of the Vietnam War. He intelligently discusses memoirs and fiction within the framework of the American war novel and the narrative meaning for Americans of "Vietnam". For Myers, the literature is problematic, comprising "clusters of small aberrant narratives", apparently a "secret history" of that which did not make sense by established criteria. The project of the critic, Myers maintains, is to explore this "secret history" with the aid of those literary "point-men" as embodied in the personal and literary experiences of the Vietnam veterans.

JEFFORDS's feminist analysis of Vietnam literature and film seems less willing to put any faith in such encoded masculine experiences. For this critic, Vietnam representation became "the springboard for a general remasculinization of American culture". Jeffords shows that, despite the historical fact of defeat and disillusionment, various popular representations of the War have come to signify neither the destabilisation of the ideal of the male soldier nor the undermining of war's construction of masculinity, but rather the reinstallation of both as fundamentally opposed to women and to femininity in general. Although her analysis is at times reductive, Jeffords succeeds in illustrating the connections between war and sexual difference in American culture.

JASON's anthology consists of a number of essays that vary considerably in scope and quality. The book is marked by a lack of sophisticated critical engagement with the texts under discussion; instead, many offer moderately informative thematic studies which do, at least, help convey the subjects of the literature. So Maria S. Bonn comments on the dream of homecoming, Owen Gilman on the notion of community, and Kali Tal on the writer's presentation of atrocities in an urge to bear witness. Gender is one of the main preoccupations in a number of essays. Jacqueline E. Lawson denies the self-justifying argument that the War increased misogyny, but shows that the military played on recruits' fears of losing their masculinity in order to institutionalise violence against women. Katherine Kinney's analysis of Bobbie Ann Mason's *In Country* shows how childbirth and combat function as reciprocal metaphors.

A motif running through all these collections is the proposition that Vietnam was a new kind of war. J.C. Pratt documents examples of Heller's *Catch-22* being literally confirmed by events. If this novel becomes, as he suggests, a major reference-point for the War, it also has presented novelists with a difficulty: how to convey the absurdity of the War without simply replicating Heller's methods? Pratt goes on to examine how a number of novelists manoeuvred around this problem. Pratt's own novel, *The Laotian Fragments*, is analyzed shrewdly by James Aubrey, showing the numerous parallels between it and Joseph Conrad's *Heart of Darkness*, illustrating how the former novel must be read in a more complex way than as a simple elegy.

FRANK PIEKARCZYK

Visual Arts and Literature

Hagstrum, Jean H., *The Sister Arts: The Tradition of Literary Pictorialism and English Poetry from Dryden to Gray*, Chicago: University of Chicago Press, 1958

Hunt, John Dixon (ed.), *Encounters: Essays on Literature and the Visual Arts*, London: Studio Vista, 1971; New York: Norton, 1971

Meyers, Jeffrey, *Painting and the Novel*, Manchester: Manchester University Press, 1975; New York: Barnes & Noble, 1975

Paulson, Ronald, *Book and Painting: Shakespeare, Milton, and the Bible: Literary Texts and the Emergence of English Painting*, Knoxville: University of Tennessee Press, 1982

Praz, Mario, *Mnemosyne: The Parallel Between Literature and the Visual Arts*, Princeton, New Jersey: Princeton University Press, 1970; London: Oxford University Press, 1970

Steiner, Wendy, *The Colors of Rhetoric: Problems in the Relationship Between Modern Literature and Painting*, Chicago: University of Chicago Press, 1982

Torgovnick, Marianna, *The Visual Arts, Pictorialism, and the Novel: James, Lawrence, and Woolf*, Princeton, New Jersey: Princeton University Press, 1985

Wendorf, Richard (ed.), *Articulate Images: The Sister Arts from Hogarth to Tennyson*, Minneapolis: University of Minnesota Press, 1983

The relationship between painting and the visual arts is one that fluctuates from period to period – historically, artistically, and critically. More often than not, the term "visual arts" usually implies painting. Furthermore, painting and literature are frequently referred to as "the sister arts". Historically, painting and literature frequently competed for the role of the most influential art form, depending on the period: this tussle began in the Renaissance, laying a critical foundation that is often confusing. However, current thinking has acknowledged that the comparison of techniques is critically impossible, and scholars prefer instead to concentrate on overlaps of artistic aims and styles. A writer can be said to employ a visual artist's techniques, and vice versa, but there is no simple correlation. Readers should also be aware that critics distinguish between painting and literature on the one hand, and pictorialism in literature on the other, as outlined by Jean Hagstrum. Moreover, early critics relied on the idea of the *Zeitgeist* – the notion that the spirit of the age is exemplified in the culture of the time – to provide a theoretical basis for interdisciplinary study between the two art forms. Such critical discussions provide useful analogies between the two arts, but are limited by their generalities about specific artistic periods.

HAGSTRUM's book is instrumental in the defining literary pictorialism in literature, and his definition is still one of the most influential ones:

> In order to be called "pictorial" a description or an image must be, in its essentials, capable of translation into painting or some other visual art. It need not resemble a particular painting or even a school of painting. But its leading details and their manner and order of presentation must be imaginable as a painting or a sculpture.

From a literary-historical perspective, Hagstrum examines pictorial images and relates them to the texts' meaning and purpose, particularly with the neoclassical pictorial images in the works of John Dryden, Alexander Pope, and Thomas Gray. Recently, Hagstrum's theories have been challenged by critics such as Torgovnick (see below), who point out that Hagstrum neglects to account for readers' imaginations and prior knowledge of art. However, Hagstrum's is still one of the seminal books on the topic.

PRAZ's book is another early, influential examination of the relationship between literature and the visual arts. Although some scholars consider Praz's theories to be vague in their critical analyses because of their reliance on emotional and philosophical responses rather than critical calculations, his is an important work because of its historical scope. Praz summarizes the entire historical visual arts'literature relationship from the classical period to the modern. Within each period, Praz locates the elements common to all artists in an effort to show "that there is a latent or manifest unity in the productions of the same artist in whatever field he tries his hand".

Each essay in HUNT's volume offers its own specific critical methodology in relation to a specific literary movement. The result is both limiting and liberating. The diversity of topics does provide the student of literature with a broader perspective on the cultural production of a text; but it also inhibits any unifying critical analysis of painting and literature. The book is best utilized for general reading on specific periods – from the medieval to the modern.

MEYER's approach to the "sister arts" is concerned with determining connections between a specific literary work and the painterly influences upon it. He clearly states his theoretical purpose in the Introduction:

> . . . by reproducing the paintings visually, by describing them verbally, by interpreting them iconographically, by looking at them with the same attention and intensity as the novelists, we can attempt to see what they saw and make that ideal correspondence between their visual images while writing and those in our minds while reading.

The chapters are confined to early modernist writers and their influences, including the painter Giotto's influence on E.M. Forster's *A Room with a View*, Mark Gertler's on D.H. Lawrence's *Women in Love*, and Albrecht Dürer's on Thomas Mann's *Doctor Faustus*. Such details are very useful, particularly when examining, for example, how much a character like Loerke in *Women in Love* was based on Gertler's life, and how Gertler's *Merry-Go-Round* painting influenced Lawrence's literary style.

Unlike most other texts examining literature and the visual arts, which focus on the effect of painting on literature, PAULSON's book looks at the role literature played in the development of English painting between 1700 and the early nineteenth century. Paulson claims that English painting is distinguished by its ability to ask "verbal questions", a condition arising out of the superiority of English verse in the nineteenth century. Indeed, Paulson states that English poetry – particularly the works of Shakespeare and Milton's *Paradise Lost* – dictated the direction of English painters, beginning with the paintings of William Hogarth.

TORGOVNICK is a sophisticated writer who is concerned primarily with modernism's relationship to painting and literature, with the intention to illuminate the study of literature rather than the study of painting. She also concentrates on only three authors – Henry James, D.H. Lawrence, and Virginia Woolf. Torgovnick's Introduction contains one of the best critical summaries of literature and the visual arts. She succinctly analyses previous types of interdisciplinary studies, while providing a description of her own critical vocabulary adopted in the rest of the book. By detailing each text's decorative, biographical, ideological, and interpretive uses of the visual arts, the author offers visual metaphor as a continuum to "provide a way to distinguish and compare uses typical of certain novelists or certain periods in the history of the novel with those of other novelists or other periods".

STEINER's study is another rewarding but theoretically complex examination of the modernist period. Stating that structuralism and semiotics have provided "the basis for an organized framework for all the arts", she then argues that painters and writers alike have produced interactive "non-sense". Her third chapter is the most interesting, suggesting a connection between cubist painting, modern writing, and contemporary ideas about history and periodization. With this foundation in place, the author suggests that "cubism" is the main aesthetic principle guiding the arts in the twentieth century.

WENDORF's collection of essays is a continuation of the ideas presented in Hagstrum (see above). The book is intended both as a homage to what the editor considers one of the most influential books on literature and the visual arts, and a critical update of the methods that Hagstrum originated, with focus on the Augustan to early Victorian periods. Of note is W.J.T. Mitchell's essay, "Metamorphoses of the Vortex: Hogarth, Turner, and Blake", in which Mitchell outlines his theory of the "vortex" – the notion that images evolve "not just as representations of objects, but as the underlying forms or constitutive structures in which particular images achieve intelligibility".

PHILIP MINGAY

See also **Pre-Raphaelitism**

Vonnegut, Kurt, Jr. 1922–

American novelist and short-story writer

Allen, William Rodney, *Understanding Kurt Vonnegut*, Columbia: University of South Carolina Press, 1991

Broer, Lawrence R., *Sanity Plea: Schizophrenia in the Novels of Kurt Vonnegut*, Ann Arbor, Michigan: UMI Research Press, 1989

Klinkowitz, Jerome, *Kurt Vonnegut*, London and New York: Methuen, 1982

Lundquist, James, *Kurt Vonnegut*, New York: Frederick Ungar, 1977

Merrill, Robert (ed.), *Critical Essays on Kurt Vonnegut*, Boston: G.K. Hall, 1990

Mustazza, Leonard, *Forever Pursuing Genesis: The Myth of Eden in the Novels of Kurt Vonnegut*, Lewisburg, Pennsylvania: Bucknell University Press, 1990

Schatt, Stanley, *Kurt Vonnegut*, Boston: Twayne, 1976

Kurt Vonnegut is considered by most commentators to be a major contemporary American novelist, this verdict coming despite the critical shuffling of analysis devoted to his work. He reached his critical popularity in the five or so years following the publication of *Slaughterhouse-Five* (1969), and, despite the decline in the number of critical studies devoted to his works that followed, he has experienced a revival of thoughtful, less frenetic evaluations during the last six or seven years. Vonnegut also suffers because, more than any other recent American author, he has been pigeonholed and therefore fragmented: he has been depicted as a dark humorist, a science-fiction writer, a guru for rebellious youth, a social gadfly, a pessimist, a verbal cartoonist, a dystopian author, a postmodernist – and the list goes on.

LUNDQUIST's book is definitely meant for the general reader. Though short on literary analysis, it contains helpful comments on such topics as the nature of science and of science fiction, and effectively interweaves data of Vonnegut's personal life with his works up through *Slapstick* (1976). In typically jaunty style, Lundquist says that Vonnegut is "an enthusiast of sentimental detachment, a Pinball Wizard of cosmic cool". SCHATT's Vonnegut volume in the Twayne series explores at greater length points taken up by Lundquist, but the book contains errors and an overabundance of plot summary.

KLINKOWITZ, arguably the foremost authority on Vonnegut, provides a concise, lucid introduction to his works through *Jailbird* (1979). His wealth of knowledge about Vonnegut the man illuminates several passages from the novels. A central theme in Klinkowitz's book is Vonnegut's "shift, both in form and reputation, from a genre writer to a modern experimentalist". Emphasizing the formative influences on Vonnegut of his midwest heritage and the Great Depression era, Klinkowitz finds in his subject "an offbeat hero of the intellectual élite expressing the most homely sentiments". One flaw in this solid introduction is that Klinkowitz avoids negative criticism of Vonnegut's weaker works, such as *Slapstick*.

Discussing 30 years of Vonnegut's writing, BROER, though admitting that Vonnegut's characters are severely "traumatized and emotionally damaged", rescues him from the clutches of those critics who view him as a glib pessimist with a facile message. Rather, the "purpose of this study", Broer writes, "is to plumb the buried tensions of [his] . . . chilling Kafkaesque underworld". Broer maintains that Vonnegut employs outer space to explore the inner space of his "psychically maimed heroes", who are the products of massive twentieth-century destructive forces. To examine the true meaning of the psychoanalytic elements that lurk just beneath the surface of Vonnegut's works, Broer discusses such image patterns as spirals, clocks, and mirrors, as he traces in each novel the thin line between sanity and psychosis and Vonnegut's constant dual vision of understandable helplessness and the need to resist despair. In his chapter "Oedipus as Galapagos", Broer presents an "overview of Vonnegut's work as an autobiographical psychodrama – a career-long process of cleansing and renewal". In *Slaughterhouse-Five*, Vonnegut rejects the defeatism of Billy Pilgrim and the Tralfamadorians, seeing himself rather in Lot's wife: "Vonnegut shored up his own sanity by facing directly into the fires of Dresden".

ALLEN's book is part of the "Understanding Contemporary American Literature" series; but despite the admonition of the series editor, Matthew J. Bruccoli, that the entries in the series are "aimed at a level of general accessibility", Allen's basic study of the 12 Vonnegut novels through *Bluebeard* (1987) provides not only a readable but also an often insightful introduction to Vonnegut's work. Allen discusses such divergent topics as Vonnegut's stylistic combination of surface simplicity with meta-fictional resonance, his recurrent characters (who form a modernistic, Faulkner-like Yoknapatawpha County), and the personal problems that led to the inferior *Breakfast of Champions* (1973) and *Slapstick*, "an embarrassment". Allen finds that *Jailbird* marks a renaissance in Vonnegut's life and work, with his "abandonment of science fiction in favor of social realism".

MUSTAZZA traces the Eden-Genesis myth in Vonnegut's first 12 novels, through *Bluebeard*, finding in this work that "the author [is] still in pursuit of Genesis". Vonnegut's use of the Genesis myth is counter-cultural, with his "escapist-Edenic vision, his reinvented universes" bearing little resemblance to the nineteenth-century adaptation of the creation account. Mustazza's close focus on a thesis, though it leads to several fresh insights into Vonnegut's thought processes, precludes extensive literary analysis, and judgments such as his belief that the Genesis message is more "brilliantly conveyed" in *Galápagos* (1985) and *Bluebeard* than it is in *Deadeye Dick* (1983) are perforce infrequent.

MERRILL's excellent introduction to this varied collection of comments on Vonnegut's work, including those by such notable twentieth-century figures as John Updike, Tony Tanner, and Robert Scholes, provides an effective assessment of both previous criticism on Vonnegut and a clear statement about the varied reception of the author's books. Writing after the publication of *Bluebeard*, Merrill found that "Vonnegut's critical reputation is now unstable", but thought the dearth of current (late 1980s') critical assessment of Vonnegut no surprise, "for its earlier fluctuations are among the most pronounced in American literary history". Merrill's prediction of a revival of critical interest in Vonnegut began to come true in 1990, and the author believes that Vonnegut, despite the vagaries of the critical canon, remains the "one postmodern American novelist who really matters".

EDWARD A. KOPPER JR.

W

Walcott, Derek 1930–

St Lucian poet and dramatist

Baugh, Edward, *Derek Walcott: Memory as Vision: "Another Life"*, London: Longman, 1978

Brown, Stewart (ed.), *The Art of Derek Walcott*, Bridgend, Glamorgan: Seren Books, 1991: Chester Springs, Pennsylvania: Dufour Editions, 1991

Goldstraw, Irma E. (ed.), *Derek Walcott: A Bibliography of Published Poems, 1944–1979*, St Augustine, Trinidad: University of the West Indies, 1979

Goldstraw, Irma E., *Derek Walcott: An Annotated Bibliography of His Works*, New York: Garland, 1984

Hamner, Robert, *Derek Walcott*, Boston: Twayne, 1981

Hamner, Robert (ed.), *Critical Perspectives on Derek Walcott*, Washington, D.C.: Three Continents Press, 1993

Terada, Rei, *Derek Walcott's Poetry: American Mimicry*, Boston: Northeastern University Press, 1992

Thomas, Ned, *Derek Walcott: Poet of the Islands/Derek Walcott: Bardd yr Ynysoedd*, Cardiff: Welsh Arts Council, 1980

Although Derek Walcott's first published volumes of verses appeared in the late 1940s, it was not until 30 years later that his poetry and plays became the subject of book-length studies. Prior to this, critical articles on his work had frequently focused on his endeavour to develop a personal literary tradition appropriate to his Caribbean origins, sometimes contrasting his incorporation of European influences with Edward Kamau Brathwaite's exploration of African retentions in Caribbean society (e.g. Pat Ismond, "Walcott versus Brathwaite", *Caribbean Quarterly*, 17(3–4), 1971). Other essays had discussed his dedication to naming the hitherto "unnamed" landscape of his native St Lucia (e.g., Michel Fabre, "Adam's Task of Giving Things Their Names: The Poetry of Derek Walcott", *New Letters*, 41(1, 1974). The award of the Nobel Prize for Literature to Walcott in 1992 predictably occasioned an upsurge of critical interest in his work.

BAUGH's short study offers a detailed, section-by-section analysis of Walcott's poetic autobiography, *Another Life*, locating it within the specifics of his St Lucian upbringing, and demonstrating how "memory, the actual and the literal, has transcended itself and become vision". Baugh shows how the formative influences of Walcott's childhood influenced the poem, how his youthful ambition to be a painter was replaced by his realisation that "poetry, metaphor, seemed more appropriate to his instinct for obliquity" and would provide an equally valid means of realising his desire to record his "virginal, unpainted world". Baugh also shows how *Another Life* attempts to move "beyond history", offering the possibility of a pristine "historyless" Caribbean predicament, a "nothing out of which something can be made".

THOMAS's bilingual (English and Welsh) monograph, published to commemorate the award of the Welsh Arts Council's International Writers Prize to Walcott in 1980, stresses the distinctively Caribbean quality of Walcott's poetry, arguing that while it is accessible to the non-Caribbean reader, it demands engagement with particular landscapes and seascapes and "poetic vocabularies", not just "a West Indian background, but a certain set of West Indian poetic vocabularies". Thomas offers readings of "Ruins of a Great House" and sections of *Another Life* and "The Schooner Flight", and pursues parallels with Anglo-Welsh and Australian writers.

HAMNER's 1981 book is a general introduction to Walcott's life and work up to 1980, notable for being the first study to attempt extended consideration of his plays and for offering a chapter on Walcott's expository writing, which includes discussion of his best-known essays published prior to 1980 and his more fugitive prose writing, mostly produced as arts reviewer for the *Trinidad Guardian* in the 1960s. It is particularly good on the development of Walcott's imagination after his "apprenticeship years" (1948–58), demonstrating how his period in New York as a Rockefeller Fellow in 1958 influenced both his own drama and his work as director of the Trinidad Workshop Theatre, which he founded in 1959. Like Thomas, Hamner ponders the paradoxes of Walcott's self-avowed "assimilation", arguing that it does not involve imitativeness, but an approach inspired by being "fed by multiple tributaries". Hamner achieves flexibility within the constraints of the Twayne series format, producing a study that is fully researched, and which remains the most informative, if not the most critically incisive, single-author book on Walcott to have appeared so far.

BROWN's collection comprises 12 new essays on specific aspects of Walcott's work. His contributors include Caribbean poets Mervyn Morris, Fred D'Aguiar, and John Figueroa, and critics from the Caribbean, Africa, America, and Britain. Most of the essays concern themselves with particular volumes of Walcott's verse from *25 Poems* (1948) to *Omeros* (1990), but the collection also includes essays on Walcott's early and later plays and a fascinating essay, by Clara Rosa de Lima, on Walcott's identification with Vincent Van Gogh. The book comes with a bibliography of primary and secondary works, which is particularly valuable for its listings of interviews with Walcott and critical books and essays on his work.

TERADA takes criticism of Walcott's poetry into new territory in offering a study, grounded in the poststructuralist interrogation of "the idea of a cultural or geographic centre and the idea of originality". For Terada, Walcott's American "mimicry ... replaces mimesis as the ground of representation". Terada eschews any attempt at providing an introduction to Walcott's poetry in favour of "a kind of compendium of problems for readers of Walcott to consider". The result is an illuminating analysis of Walcott's remapping of his cultural and geographical horizons, which sees him as a type of the American poet, and argues that his new cartography constructs New and Old Worlds in "a mutually constitutive relation".

Uneven though it is in quality, HAMNER's 1993 collection is the most useful book on Walcott to have appeared to date. It brings together eight pieces of Walcott's own critical writing, including the previously unavailable "The Figure of Crusoe", two interviews, and more than 40 essays and reviews, among them several of the most significant previously published critical articles on his work. The critical material is divided into four sections, which follow a chronological arrangement in grouping together commentary on his "juvenilia" and his writing of the 1960s–80s, with the last section being extended by a year to allow for the inclusion of two short pieces on *Omeros*. Hamner's very full, partially annotated bibliography is the definitive bibliography of secondary material on Walcott, complementing GOLDSTRAW's equally definitive bibliographies of Walcott's own publications.

JOHN THIEME

Walker, Alice 1944–

American novelist, poet, short-story writer, and essayist

Alice Walker issue of *Callaloo*, 12, Spring 1989

Banks, Erma Davis, and Keth Byerman, *Alice Walker: An Annotated Bibliography, 1968–1986*, New York: Garland, 1989

Bloom, Harold (ed.), *Alice Walker*, New York: Chelsea House, 1989

Butler-Evans, Elliott, *Race, Gender and Desire: Narrative Strategies in the Fiction of Toni Cade Bambara, Toni Morrison and Alice Walker*, Philadelphia: Temple University Press, 1989.

Howard, Lillie P. (ed.), *Alice Walker and Zora Neale Hurston: The Common Bond*, Westport, Connecticut: Greenwood Press, 1993

The journal *Callaloo* has published a number of essays in a special section devoted to Alice Walker. Theodore O. Mason, Jr. discusses *The Third Life of Grange Copeland* in terms of the imagery of enclosure that has been used by black writers since Harriet Jacobs and Frederick Douglass to express the experience of marginalization and domination; Joseph A. Brown, Jr., analyzes *Meridian* from the perspective of the title character who, he argues, undertakes a mystical journey, which conforms in outline to the African-American religious tradition of inner growth; Keith Byerman uses a theoretical perspective borrowed from Jacques Lacan to identify the "womanist" characteristics of Walker's narratives, and to determine whether, in her attempts to deconstruct the patriarchal order, Walker does not become complicit in the perpetuation of that very order; Jacqueline Bobo documents the controversy aroused by *The Color Purple* – both the novel and the film; and Keith Byerman and Erma Banks have compiled a very useful short bibliography of books and stories by Walker and criticism of her work, which complements their 1989 book-length bibliography (see below) and that compiled by Louis H. Pratt and Darnell D. Pratt (*Alice Malsenior Walker: An Annotated Bibliography*, 1988).

BLOOM's collection of essays was published in the same year and provides a similar overview of approaches to Walker , though here set out in a useful chronological sequence. Peter Erickson describes the theme of the family and, especially, mother-daughter relationships; Thadious M. Davis explores Walker's representation of the self; Barbara Christian discusses Walker in relation to the role of the black woman artist; Byerman describes the trend towards polemic in Walker's writing and the consequences of this for the aesthetic value of her work; Mae G. Henderson also discusses the relationship between polemic and aesthetics: she focuses on *The Color Purple* and the extent to which this text represents a revision of the Eurocentric male values that inform the traditional epistolary novel; Susan Willis considers the relationship between Walker's involvement in the Southern Civil Rights movement and her agenda as a revolutionary writer; and W. Lawrence Hogue shows how *The Third Life of Grange Copeland* is informed by 1970s' feminist discourse. The concept of literary influence is raised by Harold Bloom in his Introduction, and this issue is explored further by Dianne F. Sadoff, who investigates the influence of Zora Neale Hurston on Walker's work, and Deborah E. McDowell, who places Walker within a broader context of black women novelists and the creation of a black female aesthetic. The creation of narrative voice in Walker's fiction is addressed by John F. Callahan's account of *Meridian* and Tamar Katz's discussion of didacticism in *The Color Purple*. Marianne Hirsch analyses the interplay of anger and love in Walker's representation of maternal subjectivity, while Bell Hook's incisive account of the interplay of conservatism and potentially liberating elements in *The Color Purple* concludes the volume.

The essays collected by HOWARD explore one of the most contentious aspects of Walker's relationship with African-American literary history – the influence she herself describes, which derives from the work and the precedent of Zora Neale Hurston. These essays seek to elucidate just what this influence means, and how it is expressed in Walker's work. The essays are organized into three sections: "The Call and the Response", which deals with the concept of influence and its literary representations; "[Hurston's] *Their Eyes Were Watching God* and [Walker's] *The Color Purple*", which looks to the relationships between these key texts; and "'The Humming': Expanding the Connections to Other Works by Walker and Hurston", where Hurston's *Jonah's Gourd Vine* is treated in more detail, and such Walker novels as *The Third Life of*

Grange Copeland, *The Temple of My Familiar*, and *Possessing the Secret of Joy* provide a more comprehensive context for the relationship between these two writers. Such issues as characterisation, narrative structure and voice, cultural context, and thematic preoccupations are explored by the 12 writers, who include Walker herself: "Zora Neale Hurston: A Cautionary Tale and a Partisan View", Walker's foreword to Robert Hemenway's *Zora Neale Hurston: A Literary Biography* (1977), is reproduced here.

The most extensive bibliographical study of Walker's work is that compiled by BANKS and BYERMAN. This annotated bibliography lists all work by Walker, including interviews, to 1986, and all critical work, including reviews, essays, and articles in books and monographs. Very usefully, Banks and Byerman include reviews and other responses to the Spielberg film version of *The Color Purple*. The entries are numbered to allow easy access to the information. Though this bibliography does not offer a guide to critical opinion concerning Walker's more recent publications, the intelligent annotations offer a fascinating insight into the early reception of Walker's work and the developing trends within the body of critical work devoted to her.

BUTLER-EVANS discusses together *The Third Life of Grange Copeland* and *Meridian*; *The Color Purple* is considered in terms of a comparison with Toni Morrison's *Tar Baby* and Toni Cade Bambara's *The Salt Eaters* as revisionary texts, in which each of these writers seeks, from the perspective of the 1980s, to rewrite their earlier work. Butler-Evans sees Walker's first two novels as marked by ambivalence, ambiguity, and irresolution; *The Color Purple* departs from these texts by offering a more radical treatment of the issues of race and gender oppression, and by engaging more closely in narrative practices that are identified with postmodernism. The intellectual context that Butler-Evans uses to analyze the complex narrative structuring of Walker's fiction is derived from narratology, feminist cultural theory, semiotics, and neo-Marxist concepts of ideology: these concepts are used to identify Walker's often conflicting inscriptions of race and gender in her fiction, and they enable Butler-Evans to highlight the often opposing expressions of desire that motivate and structure the narratives. The comparisons with Morrison and Bambara are instructive, and they indicate clearly the diversity of literary response to cultural pressures represented by contemporary African-American women. This is a dense and difficult book, but the analyses of Walker's fiction provide a degree of theoretical sophistication that is found in few of the many assessments of Walker's achievement.

DEBORAH L. MADSEN

Walpole, Horace 1717–1797

English novelist and prose writer

Judd, Gerrit P., IV, *Horace Walpole's Memoirs*, New York: Bookman, 1959

Lewis, Wilmarth S., *et al.* (eds.), *Horace Walpole's Correspondence*, 48 vols., New Haven, Connecticut: Yale University Press, 1937–1983

Lewis, Wilmarth S., *Horace Walpole*, New York: Pantheon, 1961; London: Rupert Hart-Davis, 1961

Mehrotra, Kewal Krishna, *Horace Walpole and the English Novel: A Study of the Influence of "The Castle of Otranto", 1764–1820*, Oxford: Blackwell, 1934; reprinted, New York: Russell & Russell, 1970

Redford, Bruce. "Horace Walpole: The Letter-Writer as Chameleon", in his *The Converse of the Pen: Acts of Intimacy in the Eighteenth-Century Familiar Letter*, Chicago: University of Chicago Press, 1986

Sabor, Peter (ed.), *Horace Walpole: The Critical Heritage*, London and New York: Routledge, 1987

Though his contemporaries knew him best for his literary and political writings, Horace Walpole's present status rests primarily on his skill as a letter-writer. While some twentieth-century critics have focused on the influence Walpole and *The Castle of Otranto* had on the emerging gothic genre, the majority of critical works concerning Walpole concentrate accordingly on his status as the premier and most proficient letter- and memoir-writer in the English language.

MEHROTRA's study attempts to clarify the origins of the gothic novel in order "to estimate the real significance of *The Castle of Otranto*". To accomplish this, Mehrotra looks at the prevailing mode of eighteenth-century realistic fiction and concludes that, ironically, its imaginative limitations may have contributed to gothic literature's eventual success. His study goes on to trace the first stirrings of critical praise for the gothic novel, if not *Otranto* itself, and concludes that *Otranto*'s influence died out in 1797, when the production of better models, by authors like Ann Radcliffe, made it obsolete. One weakness of Mehrotra's study lies in his assertion that the real inspiration for *The Castle of Otranto* lies in a dream associated with the pseudo-gothic castle, Strawberry Hill, and the atmosphere of Strawberry Hill itself. Mehrotra does not explore other influences on Walpole or his writing of *Otranto*, concluding, rather sophomorically, that it was natural for a man like Walpole living in a place like Strawberry Hill to write the first gothic novel.

JUDD looks at Walpole's memoirs as an historical source, focusing on their accuracy, Walpole's style of writing, his reasons for choosing the memoir form, and his philosophy of history. Judd concludes that, whatever their inaccuracies and the conflicting critical opinion, the memoirs present "in miniature the apprehensions, prejudices, fictions, ethical standards, and political ideals" of the English Whig aristocracy, allowing for a greater understanding of the impact politics had on Walpole's generation. In discussing Walpole's philosophy of history, Judd concludes that he had little idea of the importance of economic and social pressures as historical determinants. Instead, he focused on the conflicts between individuals, believing that history consisted of a series of mechanical events caused by men. To understand history, one simply needed an understanding of the actions and personalities of the people involved, making it unnecessary to look past the human factor in events. Ultimately, Walpole concluded that "history is a romance that is believed; romance, a history that is not believed".

SABOR's study looks at the changing critical view of Walpole and his works, including *The Castle of Otranto* (1764), *The*

Mysterious Mother (1768), *Anecdotes of Painting in England* (1762–80), *A Catalogue of Engravers* (1764), and his letters and memoirs. Sabor, in an attempt to present a balanced view of Walpole and his works, presents passages from both his supporters and critics (as well as from those who, for one reason or another, changed sides) and from Walpole himself. The fact that many critics – and Walpole – changed their opinions repeatedly about the man and his work characterizes the critical dilemma surrounding Walpole. It is, according to Sabor, a situation full of indecision and paradox. "Walpole both is and is not a major writer; he is at once trivial and significant, innovative and merely *avant-garde*, original and jejune".

REDFORD's essay looks at Walpole's letters on four subjects (his health, the coronation of George III, his trip to Paris in 1765, and the Gordon riots of 1780) to analyze differences in his handling of the same subject matter for vastly different audiences. While analyzing his writing style and Walpole's doctrine of "epistolary decorum", Redford concludes that Walpole's greatest strength, his ability to assume a distinctly different persona for each audience, is also his greatest fault, as the mask he assumes makes it difficult ever really to know Walpole from his letters. According to Redford, the author of the letters is so dictated by the intended reader that the "chameleon" merges completely with his background.

One of the most useful works on Horace Walpole, LEWIS's 1961 study "concentrates on explaining the contradictions and complexities of character, behavior, and achievement" that make up Walpole the man. While admitting that objectivity is difficult for someone so closely involved with an historical figure, Lewis presents in book form what was originally six lectures in the A.W. Mellon lecture series. The result is an informative and informal look at Walpole, his relationships, and his time. What might possibly be lacking in objectivity and scholarly citations is balanced by insights into Walpole the man from his biographer and chief collector and critic.

The greatest commentator on Walpole's life, work, and times remains Walpole himself. He wrote over 4,000 letters dealing with politics, literature, and society. Though published for a select few in his lifetime, his letters received no wide circulation until after his death; now, as noted, they are generally viewed as his principal literary achievement. According to their editor LEWIS, widely regarded as the expert in Walpole studies, Walpole retrieved hundreds of his letters and annotated them for posterity, apparently aware that the recognition he craved would come primarily from them and his ability to "accumulate and arrange the chronicles of his own time and to present them in an entertaining way". The Yale edition, in addition to containing Walpole's own letters in unaltered and fully annotated form, also contains many of those written to Walpole by the people he chose to correspond with. It is an exhaustive and extremely useful and revealing source for studying Walpole and his age.

LESLIE K. POURTEAU

War and Literature

Bergonzi, Bernard, *Heroes' Twilight: A Study of the Literature of the Great War*, London: Constable, 1965; New York: Coward-McCann, 1966; 2nd edition, London: Macmillan, 1980

Bergonzi, Bernard, *Wartime and Aftermath: English Literature and Its Background 1939–1960*, Oxford and New York: Oxford University Press, 1993

Bevan, David (ed.), *Literature and War*, Amsterdam and Atlanta, Georgia: Rodopi, 1989

Craig, David, and Michael Egan, *Extreme Situations: Literature and Crisis from the Great War to the Atom Bomb*, London: Macmillan, 1979

Fussell, Paul, *The Great War and Modern Memory*, New York and London: Oxford University Press, 1975

Greicus, M.S., *Prose Writers of World War I*, London: Longman, 1974

Healy, Thomas, and Jonathan Sawday (eds.), *Literature and the English Civil War*, Cambridge and New York: Cambridge University Press, 1990

Klein, Holger (ed.), *The First World War in Fiction: A Collection of Critical Essays*, London: Macmillan, 1976

Klein, Holger, John Flower, and Eric Homberger (eds.), *The Second World War in Fiction*, London: Macmillan, 1984

Melling, Philip H., *Vietnam in American Literature*, Boston: Twayne, 1990

Munton, Alan, *English Fiction of the Second World War*, London and Boston: Faber & Faber, 1989

Onions, John, *English Fiction and Drama of the Great War, 1918–39*, London: Macmillan, 1990

Rutherford, Andrew, *The Literature of War: Five Studies in Heroic Virtue*, London: Macmillan, 1978, revised 1989

Wilson, Edmund, *Patriotic Gore: Studies in the Literature of the American Civil War*, New York: Oxford University Press, 1962

"War Literature" is an almost tautological term, since from the beginning of civilisation war and literature have existed in a near-symbiotic relation. From Homer's epics to the postmodern novel *à la* Thomas Pynchon, it would be difficult to find a literary era or genre that is not deeply permeated by war. Nonetheless, war has usually been regarded as a mere backdrop of literary works, at best as a theme or a decisive historic influence. Only recently have studies begun to focus on the structural analogies of war and literary aesthetics. The bias of the following selection in favour of studies dealing with twentieth-century wars is obvious: books on the literature of earlier wars rarely provide readings that transcend limited historical interest in the direction of a more theoretical connection of literature and war. More recent studies, beginning with those of the Vietnam War, on the other hand, have started to leave the realm of literature in order to focus on the wider area of war and the media.

An exemplary collection that demonstrates the fertile affinities between contemporary theory and war literature is BEVAN's. It contains 14 essays, which are theoretically informed and original in their choice of literary texts and approaches. The first one by James Knibb sets the tone with a balanced and sophisticated analysis of "Literary Strategies of War, Strategies of Literary War". It questions both the simplistic reliance on a "reality" of war and structuralist models, which stress its complete constructedness, and argues for a careful critical balancing of both. Other essays tackle texts not commonly associated with war literature, such as Joyce's *Ulysses*, or aspects of twentieth-century war writing little known to Anglo-American readers, such as the texts of the French Resistance, Portuguese colonial war literature, and contemporary Uruguayan writings. There is still room for well-known epochs, such as the two World Wars, the Spanish Civil War, and Vietnam, and authors such as Katherine Mansfield, Jean Giraudoux, Ernst Jünger, André Malraux, and T.E. Lawrence.

RUTHERFORD's study is more traditional, yet far from uncontroversial. It is both the work of a literary scholar of the Leavisite persuasion who searches in literature for the truths that help us to become better persons and a study that is firmly based on a small canon of very English literature, which revels in the masculine virtues of the superhuman in the average (white and Western) man. "Realism prefers the commonplace, if not the sordid or aberrant", Rutherford states in his Introduction, and this sets the tone for a curious evaluation of war literature through the eyes of Rudyard Kipling, the famous World-War-I writers, T.E. Lawrence, Evelyn Waugh, and John le Carré. Setting out to oppose the "anti-heroic bias of so many modern readers", he aims at supplementing the "bourgeois-domestic version of reality", which offers no place for heroism, with selected examples of the latter. Although he claims to find his motivation in the heroic mythology of modern urban man (which, incidentally, is American rather than British), he wants to pursue it in a "world of literary art" based on the "British national experience" – which he apparently sees embodied in the figures of the subaltern, the intellectual, the common man, the Christian, and the spy.

Although CRAIG and EGAN proclaim in their Introduction that they do not intend to write a study of socialist literature from 1914 to 1945, their approach is clearly a Marxist one. Their study regards war as an extreme manifestation of culturally created crisis, and consequently contains chapters on upheavals and revolutions, too. This leads to an unusual and often interesting focusing on the class structures underlying the wars of the twentieth century. Yet it also produces a reductive view of "true" representations of war versus the "false" ones of official propaganda and élitist artistic production. Through the backdoor, their study is paradoxically invaded by the very liberal humanist values that they attack as hypocritical – especially when they discuss the "meaning" of World War I as the "obliteration of humanity" and its "values". Despite their problematic evaluative approach, their emphasis on often ignored aspects of war literature, such as soldiers' songs, or on those aspects unfamiliar to Western minds, for instance writings about the Russian Revolution and Stalinism, makes their book worthwhile reading.

FUSSELL's study is certainly the most influential attempt to outline the structural analogies between the experience of war and literary conventions. He uses World War I as a starting point, since he rightly claims that it is the first war in history in which the participants had sufficient common grounding in the culture and literature of their age. His major claim is a strong one: the extremities of war can only be rationalised and narrated in established literary models. He traces this literarisation of experience in the choice of terms of war testimonies, poems, and fiction, but also in the very selection of narrated impressions. Special attention is paid to ironic modes of detachment, the analogies of war narratives and myth, ritual and romance, as well as arcadian and homoerotic fantasies. As the title of his book indicates, Fussell's overall aim is to portray war as a decisive factor in the creation of modern cultural memory.

GREICUS's booklet, published in a British Council series, is an early attempt to shift the emphasis from the poets of World War I to the prose writers. Despite its concise format, his book provides both a glimpse of the circumstances from which the writing results and useful introductions to more than 20 authors and their works, some of which are almost forgotten. He also describes the "anti-war boom", the vogue for critical books on World War I between 1928 and 1932. His final chapter summarises the manifold forms of World-War-I prose, from the romantic to the experimental.

BERGONZI's *Heroes' Twilight* is another traditional attempt at portraying World-War-I literature from a combined historical and biographical angle. Its point of departure, the critique of heroism at the basis of many war writings, seems more realistic than Rutherford's attempt to rescue the heroic. Bergonzi also points to the many cracks in the surface of pre-war England, and thereby avoids the presentation of World War I as an inexplicable catastrophe. By linking war literature with the modernist avant-garde movements, such as Vorticism, he contradicts the notion of World War I as an isolated artistic era. His portraits of individual authors appear slightly conventional, yet underneath biographical readings they contain interesting insights, for instance into the problems of representing horror and death. Implicitly, Bergonzi's study traces the literary transformation of war from its idealisation in Rupert Brooke, via its demystification by the likes of Robert Graves, Edmund Blunden, and Siegfried Sassoon, to its renewed integrity, first in the symbolism of Isaac Rosenberg and Wilfred Owen, then in a complex mythical shape in David Jones.

Another study focusing on the issue of heroism is ONIONS's. It assumes a middle ground between Rutherford's reappraisal of heroism and Bergonzi's dismissal. The changing shapes of the hero are outlined from Homer and Shakespeare onwards, via the nineteenth century, Kipling, and Joseph Conrad, to the famous writers of World War I, but also in the rarely discussed drama of the era, such as the plays of Alan Monkhouse. Onion sees a transformation of the hero in the irony of Richard Aldington and Henry Williamson, his isolation in the writings of Forrest Reid, R.C. Sherriff, and W. Somerset Maugham, and a more historic treatment in R.H. Mottram, H.M. Tomlinson, and Ford Madox Ford, and believes that the heroic culminates in what he considers the detached existentialism of Frederic Manning.

KLEIN brings together a number of close readings of individual texts with some comparative studies of motifs and themes. The particular merit of his collection is its comparative presentation of British, American, French, Italian, German, and Austrian-Hungarian authors. In contrast to Fussell's aesthetic approach, Klein's book is characterised by a more mimetic attitude, which sees the particularity of World War I in its material and political circumstances and regards literature as an attempt to come to terms with these external factors. The questions of the study are therefore those of adequate or truthful representation versus lies and propaganda, rather than broader ones concerning the possibility of representing war in fiction. Not much attention is paid to the interference of war and the literary strategies of the analysed authors (the only exception is Jonathan Dale's essay on "Drieu La Rochelle: The War as 'Comedy'"). Neither is there much consideration of the impact of literary conventions on the perception of this gruesome reality. Altogether, despite its often brilliant essays, the volume remains within the boundaries of genre- and motif-studies.

KLEIN, FLOWER, and HOMBERGER's collection is in some ways the successor of Klein's book on World-War-I fiction. The two wars, however, have produced radically different literary responses – and the criticism to match. World War II lacked the relatively unified scenario of the trenches. Consequently, this collection has chapters on Britain, France, Germany, the Soviet Union, the United States, and Japan. The geographic dislocation and simultaneous ubiquity of the war also erased the difference between battlefield and home. Spies and saboteurs therefore became important literary themes. The changed nature of warfare, which no longer knew the stifling immobilisation in the trenches, but was characterised by continual movement, is also reflected in different literary strategies. Still, as Klein remarks in his section on Britain, the continuing popularity of the topic has produced mainly trivial works, such as successful comics and the rehashing of stereotypes in pulp fiction, film, and television. Klein deals with an impressive amount of texts, analysing the recurring themes as well as the limitations of formulas. He also extends his view into the 1970s and 1980s and speculates about the reasons for the continuing fascination with World War II (which he sees in a variety of postwar disappointments) and possible directions of war fiction, such as the tendency to glamorise violence.

MUNTON's study is another attempt to rescue the literature of World War II from the "Orwellian black hole" to which it has been consigned by the prominence of the earlier modernists and the postwar writers. Unfortunately, Munton's adoption of Angus Calder's view that World War II was a "People's War" makes him focus rather narrowly on the social aspects of war writing. He is especially interested in the role of ordinary human relations, including eroticism and sexuality, but also work and boredom in war, an angle that sometimes produces questionable statements, such as "killing is, after all, only work". The apparent one-sidedness of this claim reflects the bias of Munton's approach to both the background of the time – which he attempts to portray in great detail, but with little coherence – and his textual analyses. He covers interesting and almost forgotten texts, but often presents them through a mixture of amateur psychology and generalisations.

Although starting from an original perspective – that wars do not end with an armistice, but a period of recovery in which war remains a decisive cultural influence – BERGONZI's 1993 book on English literature from 1939 to the 1960s remains a conventional mixture of literary history and biographically inspired textual criticism. Not surprisingly, it shows the growing prominence of war in late 1930s' and early 1940s' writings. In a similar vein it demonstrates the resonances of war events, such as the bombing of London, in a variety of texts. The result does not move much beyond a historically informed listing of authors and texts – often with the implicit intention of reclaiming them as war writers and writings. The more interesting sections deal with the internalisation of war in postwar literature, where it leads to critical and often destructive evaluations of Britishness, for instance by Edmund Wilson, Patrick Hamilton, Angus Wilson, and George Orwell. Bergonzi also reminds us how much even writers like Philip Larkin were still looking back to war rather than forward. The later sections of his book, however, seem to be oblivious of the war in its title and merely present a history of 1950s' literature with a very sweeping glance at the 1960s.

MELLING's book begins with an interesting, if somewhat strained, premise: Vietnam War narratives follow the tradition of Puritan public testimonies. This seems a rather homogenising approach to a war that was, after all, fought by Americans of very distinct ethnic groups, by no means all subscribers to Puritan ethics. Melling's attempt to link the personal narrative with wider theoretical implications, such as colonial history, highlights the solipsistic American view of the Vietnam war – whose representations hardly ever feature the Vietnamese. He considers the broad social, economic, and ideological background of the war and also provides an index of its history. Yet tied to his Puritan model, his analyses tend to return to critical commonplaces, such as the motifs of survival and errand. Melling ultimately falls into the very trap he hopes to avoid, that of seeing war as a personal experience. Not even his later sections, which discuss film and the themes of secular and divine mission, break out of this subjectivist view. The perspective of his conclusion is equally regressive: war continues elsewhere – in Latin America, for instance – but still merely re-enacts Puritan obsessions.

WILSON's book would be of mere curiosity value if it did not provide an interesting example of a study that draws a detailed tableau of voices both from within the war experience and surrounding it, and is thus an early and unconscious acknowledgment of the blurred boundaries of war and normality. Some of his authors, such as Harriet Beecher Stowe, are well known; others are hardly ever heard of outside the United States. The enjoyment of Wilson's mainly historical and biographical essays is somewhat diminished by an Introduction that attempts not only a very sweeping history of modern wars, but indeed proposes its own anthropological explanation for the existence of war – drawing on experts as qualified as Walt Disney.

HEALY and SAWDAY's collection seems geared towards specialists at first glance, since it deals with a more remote historical epoch – the English Civil War. However, the essays of the book assess their topic from a variety of interesting theoretical positions. They include evaluations of the role of language in historical representation and the construction of concepts of order and disorder. They tackle myth and escapism – both in the form of anachronism and that of devotion. Finally they discuss confinement and dislocation with reference to women's writing of the period. The overall aim is to question the "truth" embodied by the tropes of militancy and war – and thus to tackle the crucial questions concerning the possibility and dangers of representing war in literature.

RAINER EMIG

The War Poets

Caesar, Adrian, *Taking It Like a Man: Suffering, Sexuality and the War Poets: Brooke, Sassoon, Owen, Graves*, Manchester: Manchester University Press, 1993

Fussell, Paul, *The Great War and Modern Memory*, New York and London: Oxford University Press, 1975

Gilbert, Sandra M., "Soldier's Heart: Literary Men, Literary Women, and the Great War", in *No Man's Land: The Place of the Woman Writer in the Twentieth Century: Sexchanges*, by Gilbert and Susan Gubar, New Haven, Connecticut, and London: Yale University Press, 1989

Khan, Nosheen, *Women's Poetry of the First World War*, Brighton, Sussex: Harvester Press, 1988; Lexington: University Press of Kentucky, 1988

Parfitt, George, *English Poetry of the First World War: Contexts and Themes*, Hemel Hempstead, Hertfordshire: Harvester Wheatsheaf, 1990

Showalter, Elaine, "Male Hysteria: W.H.R. Rivers and the Lessons of Shell Shock", in her *The Female Malady: Women, Madness, and English Culture, 1830–1980*, New York: Pantheon, 1985; London: Virago, 1987

Criticism of the War poets over the last 20 years is marked by a striking double-shift, largely resulting from the impact of feminist criticism. On the one hand, critics have sought to look beyond the "élite" corps of familiar male writers (Wilfred Owen, Siegfried Sassoon, Rupert Brooke) and toward the work of women poets. On the other hand, they have endeavoured to step outside the constraints of a narrow formalism and toward a particular concern with questions of gender as they are inscribed within the war poetry of men and women alike.

FUSSELL's study is a brilliant and indispensable analysis of the British experience on the Western Front during World War I and "some of the literary means by which it has been remembered, conventionalized, and mythologized". It is meticulously researched (invoking personal memoirs, letters, official documents, newspapers, poetry and other literary forms) and displays an astute grasp of the ways in which representations of the War help to determine what Northrop Frye, cited by Fussell, has called "the total cultural form of our present life". The book is of particular interest, additionally, because of its demonstration of the reciprocities and points of intersection between the "trench experience", on the one hand, and literature, on the other: "life", as Fussell puts it, "feeds materials to literature while literature returns the favor by conferring forms upon life". Packed with information and insight, and extremely readable, this is one of the most important treatments of the "war-experience" to have been produced in the last 20 years. The book defines the context, implicit or explicit, for much of the work that comes after it.

Poetry of the War, according to PARFITT, is in danger of being subsumed beneath a "comfortable stereotype". Characteristically it is seen as solely the product of "a handsome young officer who writes either about country and heroism (Rupert Brooke) or about the horrors of trench and bombardment (Wilfred Owen, Siegfried Sassoon)". Parfitt combats and displaces such a restricting view, in this lucid and intelligent book, by focusing on the wider national, cultural, and literary contexts in which the work of these well-known poets is situated. He thus recovers for the reader a sense of the range of poetic responses to the War – from patriots and propagandists to the non-commissioned, civilians, and women. The "understated" achievement of Robert Graves as a poet of the War also receives an exclusive and informative discussion in Chapter 7. The book concludes by making a strong case for a cultural-materialist approach to the poetry of the War rather than one based on pseudo-objective criteria of "literary value".

CAESAR's book controversially explores the "psychological and cultural complexities" frequently elided in accounts of the poetry of the War and readers' responses to it. Such poetry not only communicates the sense that war is "wasteful" and "horrific" but also entails a "celebration of war as a vehicle of pain and suffering" in which, whether consciously or not, readers are also implicated. The elements of "sado-masochism" in the "life and work of Brooke, Owen, Sassoon and Graves" are not seen as intra-psychic "perversions", however. Rather they emerge as symptoms of the cultural traditions – Christianity, empire, Romanticism – which these poets share and which turn, Caesar argues, upon a shared obsession with the ideology of self-sacrifice. The readings in this book are detailed and largely persuasive, constituting a useful contribution to, and extension of, existing analyses of the field.

Thematic in structure, KHAN's book illustrates the breadth of female poetic responses to the War from "the fervently romantic and heroic to deeply realized expressions of revulsion and outrage". Topics covered include the ways in which women poets draw upon "the vocabularies . . . of religion and nature to interpret war" and how their poetry negotiates and inscribes forms of suffering (as wives, mothers, sisters, and lovers), which "can be considered as the female equivalent of the agony of the trenches". Khan is especially concerned, in a chapter on "The War at Home", to challenge the negative image (widely circulated both during and after the War) of the "insensibility" of women on the "Home Front" to the "true nature of war". In more general terms her book is an important intervention, correcting the impression created by most studies (including Fussell's) that poetry of World War I, and indeed the War itself, were exclusively male phenomena.

GILBERT offers a powerful reading of the ways in which the War compounded and accelerated a destabilization of traditional gender-roles already under way in the 1890s. Covering a range of War poems written mainly by women (as well as a number of key postwar texts by men and women), the essay is a critical tour de force which poses and explores a set of questions about "the relations between the sexes during [and in the wake of] this war of wars":

> What part . . . did women play in the Great War? How did men perceive that role? . . . what connections might there be between the wartime activities of women and the sense of sexual wounding that haunts so many male modernist texts? Most importantly, did women themselves experience the wound of the war in the same way that their sons and lovers did?

SHOWALTER also examines connections between war and gender, analysing the "shell shock" experienced by thousands of soldiers as a phenomenon that eroded conventional notions of gender difference. This condition is more properly seen, she argues, as a male version of the hysteria invariably associated, by early psychoanalytic theory, with women. It is, moreover, not just a psychic disorder but a form of (unconscious) political protest and resistance, a "body language of masculine complaint . . . not only against the War but against the concept of 'manliness' itself". From these general points Showalter goes on to consider the "case" of Sassoon and the history of his relationship with the psychotherapist W.H.R. Rivers at Craiglockhart War Hospital in 1917. The success of Rivers's treatment of Sassoon's "'anti-war' complex" is brought about, Showalter demonstrates, by means of Rivers' exploitation of Sassoon's anxieties about his own masculinity. Together with Gilbert's, this essay provides a sophisticated and important feminist perspective on World War I. Both essays are essential reading for all students and scholars concerned with the poetry and literature of the War, and the cultural politics that attend them.

CARL PLASA

Warren, Robert Penn 1905–1989

American novelist, poet, and critic

Bohner, Charles H., *Robert Penn Warren*, New York: Twayne, 1964

Casper, Leonard, *Robert Penn Warren: The Dark and Bloody Ground*, Seattle: University of Washington Press, 1960

Justus, James H., *The Achievement of Robert Penn Warren*, Baton Rouge: Louisiana State University Press, 1981

Longley, John Lewis, Jr.(ed.), *Robert Penn Warren: A Collection of Critical Essays*, New York: New York University Press, 1965; reprinted, Westport, Connecticut: Greenwood Press, 1979

Nakadate, Neil (ed.), *Robert Penn Warren: Critical Perspectives*, Lexington: University Press of Kentucky, 1981

Strandberg, Victor H., *The Poetic Vision of Robert Penn Warren*, Lexington: University Press of Kentucky, 1977

Watkins, Floyd C., *Then and Now: The Personal Past in the Poetry of Robert Penn Warren*, Lexington: University Press of Kentucky, 1982

West, Paul, *Robert Penn Warren*, Minneapolis: University of Minnesota Press, 1964

Robert Penn Warren distinguished himself in a variety of literary fields, but the criticism of his work has, understandably, tended to focus on the fiction and the poetry. Both genres have been read for their place in the Southern literary tradition, and, like many of his Southern contemporaries, Warren has been understood as a writer with a "double vision", belonging at one and the same time to a "homogeneous" South and a "heterogeneous" America. Equally, however, he has been seen as a writer with affinities with the great European novelists, notably Dostoevsky and Joseph Conrad, in the dark, brooding, philosophical intelligence to be found in much of his major fiction. Warren's critical work on other writers, especially those by whom he was influenced such as Conrad and William Faulkner, often offers valuable insights into his own work.

CASPER's was the first book-length study of Warren, and though it obviously can take no account of works published after 1960 it still contains much to recommend it. The opening chapters discuss Warren in his critical and intellectual contexts, as a major practitioner of the New Criticism and as a writer whose ideas about art and its place in the Southern tradition were shaped by the conservative agrarianism of the Fugitives, that group of Southern writers based at Vanderbilt University in Tennessee, in the 1920s. Subsequent chapters consider the poetry, emphasising its religious significance and its "hieratic imagery", and the fiction and biography (notably the biography of John Brown). Warren is viewed as a writer seeking to "heal the division between content and form" and attempting "to resolve paradoxes by redefining their terms at a level superior to semantics".

WEST's brief study (in the University of Minnesota "Pamphlets on American Writers" series) is an intelligent introduction to Warren's writing. A short biographical overview is followed by a more extensive account of the poetry and the fiction, the former read for its mastery of "literate paradox", the latter for its contributions to the genre of the philosophical novel, Warren's "existential perplexity" and the "self-probings" of his major characters being seen as essential constituents of his fictional signature. Considerations of space mean that there is very little on the non-fictional prose, but this is an excellent starting-point for the student of Warren.

BOHNER's book (in the Twayne "United States Authors" series), like West's, is introductory, but the greater length means that there is more attention here to the critical and historical writings. An introductory biographical chapter, "Southern Man of Letters", is followed by a chapter on the early poetry, and three chapters on the major fiction, particularly *All the King's Men*, *At Heaven's Gate*, *Night Rider* and *World Enough and Time*, and the verse-novel *Brother to Dragons*; the final chapter assesses the later poems, especially those in *Promises: Poems 1954–1956* and *You, Emperors, and Others: Poems 1957–1960*, and the novel *The Cave*. Bohner concludes that Warren "very nearly fulfills our idea of the romantic genius" who "exercises his verbal gifts for the sheer magic of the effects he can produce".

LONGLEY's is an excellent collection of critical essays on Warren, some 17 in number, and addressing, in one way or another, all those various guises in which Warren has contributed to American literature. The emphasis is on the fiction, with the poetry "given far fewer pages than it deserves . . . for reasons of space". Included here are Warren's own essay on the genesis of *All the King's Men* and the interview Warren did for *The Paris Review* with Ralph Ellison and Eugene Walter, an interview which, as Longley points out, "is the most extensive commentary by Mr Warren yet to appear on his own working habits, attitudes, and theories". All but two of the essays collected here had appeared previously, but this remains an ideal place to begin a critical assessment of Warren's achievement. The bibliography is admirably thorough up to the date of publication.

JUSTUS's approach is to establish Warren's place both his immediate Southern literary tradition and within the larger context of the American literary tradition as a whole; the former has been much commented on, the latter less so, and

Justus's account of the affinities that Warren's work has with that of Ralph Waldo Emerson, Nathaniel Hawthorne, and Herman Melville is one of the more illuminating aspects of his book. Justus discusses the fiction and poetry at some length, and, to a lesser extent, the criticism and other non-fictional prose. The opening chapter, "Repudiations and Repetitions: A Cycle of Themes", intelligently establishes the thematic concerns of Warren's writings, the most enduring of which he sees as self-knowledge and "the synecdochic recognition of the common frailty of man caught in webs of deceit, delusion, ignorance, and a murderous innocence that believes that the abstract ideal or the governing idea must be translated into act at whatever cost." Justus's book is exhaustive and, as a result, unnecessarily long; but it must be considered the best study of Warren.

NAKADATE draws together a balanced collection of essays on Warren, 12 on the fiction and ten on the poetry, and since there is only minimal overlap with those in Longley this is a valuable supplement to the earlier volume. Included here are two essays by Warren himself, explorations, we might call them, of the geneses of *All the King's Men* and *Brother to Dragons*, though both are anecdotal accounts in a way that suggests disinclination to offer anything that might substitute for criticism. Four essays are devoted to *All the King's Men*, among them Simone Vauthier's theoretical reading (drawn, in part, from the critical vocabularies of Gérard Genette and Gerald Prince) of the place of the "narratee" and the "interlocutor" in the novel, and Ladell Payne's reconsideration of the relationship between the fictional Willie Stark and the "real" Huey Long. This is a collection that is well worth consulting, and it carries a very useful selective bibliography, though unfortunately has no index.

STRANDBERG's second book on Warren's poetry (his first study, *A Colder Fire: The Poetry of Robert Penn Warren*, appeared in 1965) assesses both his vision and his achievement: the first Strandberg sees as, in part, philosophical, and he emphasises Warren's indebtedness to the writings of William James; the second he thinks considerable, though in his reading of the poetry he contends that "The Ballad of Billie Potts" marks a high point in Warren's poetic career that was not to be challenged until the appearance of *Brother to Dragons* (in 1953), which is read as a study of the undiscovered self. Strandberg is kinder to the violence and the temptations towards caricature in "Billie Potts" than are many other critics, but he intelligently draws our attention to the formal and linguistic virtues of this poem and many others. His book is, arguably, the best full-length study of the poetry yet to appear.

WATKINS's book is devoted entirely to the poetry, which here is read largely as verse autobiography. His study constitutes a species of genetic detective work: interviews with Warren himself, members of his family, and friends and contemporaries are analysed for their echoes in the poetry – so much so that Watkins steadily builds up a picture of Warren's childhood, his family's history, and the landscapes of his Kentucky background. There is little in the way of sophisticated criticism, and a good deal of redundant detail; but the book can be profitably consulted as supplementary material to the existing biographical accounts.

HENRY CLARIDGE

Waugh, Evelyn 1903–1966

English novelist and travel writer

Blayac, Alain (ed.), *Evelyn Waugh: New Directions*, London: Macmillan, 1992
Carens, James F. (ed.), *Critical Essays on Evelyn Waugh*, Boston: G.K. Hall, 1987
Heath, Jeffrey, *The Picturesque Prison: Evelyn Waugh and His Writing*, London: Weidenfeld & Nicolson, 1982; Montreal and Kingston, Ontario: McGill-Queen's University Press, 1982
McCartney, George, *Confused Roaring: Evelyn Waugh and the Modernist Tradition*, Bloomington: Indiana University Press, 1987
McDonnell, Jacqueline, *Waugh on Women*, London: Duckworth, 1985; New York: St Martin's Press, 1985
McDonnell, Jacqueline, *Evelyn Waugh*, London: Macmillan, 1988
Morriss, Margaret, and D.J. Dooley (eds.), *Evelyn Waugh: A Reference Guide*, Boston: G.K. Hall, 1984
Myers, William, *Evelyn Waugh and the Problem of Evil*, London and Boston: Faber & Faber, 1991

There is a persistent tendency in Waugh criticism to read the novels through his biography, fostered by Waugh's habit of drawing on his social acquaintances and even using real names. Recently there has been a move in a more formal direction, to consider Waugh's relation to literary tradition, isolating the distinctive innovations of his style from his powerful personality still resonant in letters, diaries, interviews. The selection discussed here aims to balance these critical preferences and provide starting-points for the general reader.

MORRISS and DOOLEY offer a bibliography of Waugh's works and a year-by-year list of writings about Waugh from 1919 to 1983, enabling the tracing of developments in reputation. This is an invaluable aid in tracking down more obscure references and reviews and still a useful supplement to computer searches.

McDONNELL (1988) is an accessible survey of both life and writings, with interesting sections on Waugh's craft and influences, such as P.G. Wodehouse and the cinema. She discusses Waugh's innovations in the use of telephone dialogue, and deals with issues of snobbery and class hatred. There is a straightforward attempt to put Waugh's social prejudices and pre-war political sympathies into historical context in this ideal introduction.

CARENS' collection has the merit of printing extracts from full-length critical works, so giving the reader a chance to sample them. Particularly useful is Terry Eagleton's Marxist analysis of *Brideshead Revisited* and Carens' Introduction, which is a sustained critical survey of the novels, strong on structure and form. The book is divided into general essays and those on individual novels, and contains less-accessible material, such as Orwell's succinct notes, which encapsulate many opinions about Waugh, and J.B. Priestley's analysis of *The Ordeal of Gilbert Pinfold* (with Waugh's fabulously satiric response). There is a helpful group of essays on the sometimes neglected War Trilogy.

HEATH takes for his critical narrative of Waugh's fictions the thesis of Waugh's need for seclusion, withdrawal from modernity in both life and work. In early novels, the secular refuge "looks like a Camelot but turns out to be a jail", with *Brideshead Revisited* proving a turning point. Here the extravagant prison of Brideshead is a necessary forerunner to the right kind of imprisonment, the discipline provided by the Church. While this narrative does not take account of some modernist ambiguities in Waugh's novels, it contains acute speculations about Waugh's psychology, and his fears of his own potential for riot, and is strong on the aesthetic debates within *Brideshead*. Drawing together Waugh's artistic and religious senses in the theme of vocation proves an effective method of examining his writings as a whole. There is also an interesting chronicle of Waugh's relations with his critics.

McCARTNEY takes his title from the hooliganism of the Bollinger Club in *Decline and Fall* to stand for Waugh's attitude to modernity itself; yet this critical work is devoted to detecting a readiness for modernist experiment in the fictions, likening Waugh to T.S. Eliot and locating Nietzschean themes in *Decline and Fall*. He offers a detailed study of philosophical influences, such as Henri Bergson on *Vile Bodies*, and argues that Waugh applied modernist techniques without modernist ideology. McCartney particularly deals with Waugh's fracturing of characterisation and verisimilitude, temporal dislocation, and abandonment of normal laws of logic, pointing out that Waugh's characters have to gain identity from physical or spiritual structures – hence the importance of architecture. This is a valuable work to counteract the tendency to perceive the novels solely through biography.

BLAYAC's stated aim is to draw together new biographical research on relevant and controversial aspects of Waugh's life with critical approaches from an international community of scholars. The result is a stimulating collection of valuable additional material, which does not pretend to be an overview or introductory study. Biographical essays on Waugh and the BBC, and his Vatican divorce enable convincing conclusions about these difficult areas, while Leslek S. Kolek's semiotic approach to *Black Mischief* provides a striking model. Blayac's own essay, "Evelyn Waugh and Humour", gives a Gallic perspective on the early novels, and places Waugh in an English tradition stemming from Ben Jonson.

McDONNELL (1986) has an intriguing and relatively unexplored subject in Waugh's women, but focuses her interpretation almost exclusively through biographical material and chooses not to take any formal or theoretical approach to gender. This work is useful for its additional research on Waugh's relationships with women and for meticulous examination and cross-referencing of the novels.

MYERS' Introduction declares that he will place Waugh in the context of imperialist ideology and Catholic thinking of 1870–1960; yet Myers also tends to take Waugh on his own terms and in a biographical context. There is effective analysis of social taboo and of the metaphysical relations between form and authorial position in the early novels, which leads on to Waugh's later religious stance. Particularly useful is the analysis of the often neglected *Put Out More Flags*, with an intuitive reading of the unusually well-developed moral status of Angela Lyne and Ambrose Silk. There is more perceptive comment on *Brideshead Revisited*, where Myers sees Catholicism presented as both naive story and ally of imperialist conquest: he blends biographical detail and theology to account for the difficulties surrounding the romance and eschatology of the novel. This is a penetrating book for those interested in the wider ideological context.

Susan Rowland

Webster, John c.1580–c.1633

English dramatist

Bliss, Lee, *The World's Perspective: John Webster and the Jacobean Drama*, Brighton, Sussex: Harvester Press, 1989

Bogard, Travis, *The Tragic Satire of John Webster*, Berkeley: University of California Press, 1955

Bradbrook, Muriel C., *John Webster, Citizen and Dramatist*, London: Weidenfeld & Nicolson, 1980; New York: Columbia University Press, 1980

Forker, Charles, *The Skull Beneath the Skin: The Achievement of John Webster*, Carbondale: Southern Illinois University Press, 1986

Hunter, G.K., and S.K. Hunter (eds.), *John Webster: A Critical Anthology*, Harmondsworth, Middlesex, and Baltimore: Penguin, 1969

McLuskie, Kathleen, and Jennifer Uglow (eds.), *The Duchess of Malfi* (Plays in Performance series), Bristol: Bristol Classical Press, 1989

Pearson, Jacqueline, *Tragedy and Tragicomedy in the Plays of John Webster*, Manchester: Manchester University Press, 1980; New York: Barnes & Noble, 1980

The earliest of these studies, BOGARD, avoids the standard comparison many critics have made between Webster and Shakespeare. Instead, more helpfully, his comparisons are with the didactic tragedy of George Chapman and the satiric drama of John Marston. His Webster blends tragedy and satire, with tragic actions given satirical counterpoints, or developed with an imagery that runs counter to the dominant tone. Webster, in Bogard's view, "saw the world with both pity and contempt" and remained true to this vision by "blending the almost incompatible genres, tragedy and satire".

The Penguin *Critical Anthology* edited by HUNTER and HUNTER inaugurated a series of author-related critical anthologies, thus evidencing the dramatist's surprisingly high critical standing at the time. The comments of contemporaries, extracts from Romantic and Victorian critics ("The Developing Debate") and "Modern Views" (from T.S. Eliot, via *Scrutiny* essayists to an array of scholars writing in the 1950s and 1960s) are included. The usual topics and methods of discussion are well represented: Webster and morality (Jack, Bradbrook), Webster and genres (Bogard), imagery (Price), and the use of ritual in his dramaturgy (Ekeblad, Calderwood). With analytic introductions to its three sections by the editors, this is a useful and representative selection of criticism up to its date.

BRADBROOK's volume on Webster came late in her long and productive academic career. Published 45 years after the hard opinions, quotable and illuminating, of her *Themes and Conventions of Elizabethan Tragedy*, this work allows an imaginative response to the dramatist. Three "London legends" are recounted (the careers of the poet John Davies, Penelope

Rich, and the spy Antonio Perez) as a means towards a "re-entry into Webster's world". While inherently interesting, the "legends" supply only cloudy contexts for Webster's characters (Penelope Rich as a "bad woman, the great lady insolent in her power" remotely inspiring Vittoria Corombona). Life and art begin to blur: Professor Bradbrook repeatedly refers to the Duchess of Malfi as Giovanna Bologna, the historical original of the character. On the plays, the discussion is impressionistic, and the connections offered between the art of the tragedies and that of the court masque compare chalk and cheese by asking the reader to imagine one of them in an unrecognisable form ("inverted"). This may be summed up as an imaginative and rather self-indulgent study by an eminent critic of long standing.

PEARSON first presents a case for Jacobean tragicomedy as an important genre in its own right, suggesting that it establishes a particularly rich and close relationship between audience and play, and that the self-conscious mixed-genre play was the pervasive type in Webster's theatre. The effect of laughter in *The White Devil* is examined, as is the generic blurring it produces, while *The Duchess of Malfi* is seen as a four-act tragedy taken over in Act V by anti-tragic forces, so that "tragedy falls apart into satire, self-deception, despair and madness". Pearson is good on the pronounced theatrical self-consciousness of Webster's final scenes, but her account of "warring genres" tends to make tragedy into too monolithically simple a genre in the discussion of *The Duchess of Malfi*.

FORKER's heroic-sized volume (531 pages, and notes) attempts to be a "more detailed study of all Webster's writings than has been attempted before". All the works, dramatic and non-dramatic, and all attributions are examined, there is a lengthy biographical section, and an examination of Webster's later influence, extending into the late seventeenth-century drama. On the major plays Forker is just and sensible; but other parts of the work seem over-accumulative (e.g., a long excursus on coaches, this being the Webster family business) or critically naive (the chapter on love and death in Renaissance drama, which ushers in the discussion of the major plays). In such an accretive volume, valuable suggestions abound – on the professional connection of the Websters to public funerals, for instance; but the book is distended, swollen by its own products of decay.

BLISS reads Webster's tragedies in a context supplied by the theatrical innovations made in a group of ironic tragicomedies written around 1604. Webster's major tragedies are related both to these plays and to another group of somewhat later heroic tragedies. She looks at the manipulators in the tragicomedies, "happy with their engineered endings, although we are not", and the protagonists of the heroic tragedies, seen as passing from self-assertion to recognition of "passionate involvement with others" and attaining briefly an ideal of compassionate humanity. Bliss's "generic cross-references" mobilise (for her purposes) these other texts very effectively as a lead up to Webster, though other critical accounts of the interaction of genres might be imagined. When she comes to Webster, Flamineo and Bosola are seen as manipulators who come (she uses Robert Heilman's words) "to accept the burden of being human". But her study perhaps can show more convincingly the egoism and self-interest than the "fundamental values" purportedly attained.

The edition of *The Duchess of Malfi* edited by McLUSKIE and UGLOW presents a full, typographically compressed plain text, with facing annotation on a range of actors' vocal interpretations, gestures, blocking, stage directions, and cuts, as gathered from playhouse texts, reviews, and witnesses of performances from the eighteenth century to, theoretically, 1985. There is a long Introduction on the stage history, and a selection of rather murkily reproduced photographs. While being in general a valuable corrective to the dramatically theoretical interpretations of academics, this account of actual theatre practice can only supply a limited amount of information in its format. For instance, precision about how many actors playing Bosola have actually entered fully disguised as an old man in Act IV, ii, would have been valuable.

ROY J. BOOTH

Wells, H.G. 1866–1946

English novelist, short-story writer, and prose writer

Bergonzi, Bernard, *The Early H.G. Wells: A Study of the Scientific Romances*, Manchester: Manchester University Press, 1961

Huntington, John, *The Logic of Fantasy: Science Fiction and H.G. Wells*, New York: Columbia University Press, 1982

Reed, John R., *The Natural History of H.G. Wells*, Athens: Ohio University Press, 1982

Scheick, William J., *The Splintering Frame: The Later Fiction of H.G. Wells*, Victoria, British Columbia: University of Victoria Press, 1984

Smith, David C., *H.G. Wells: Desperately Mortal: A Biography*, New Haven, Connecticut, and London: Yale University Press, 1986

Suvin, Darko (ed.), *H.G. Wells and Modern Science Fiction*, Lewisburg, Pennsylvania: Bucknell University Press, 1977

The critical response to H.G. Wells during his lifetime started with surprise and ended with disappointment. Since his death his reputation as a writer has wavered among critics, although his popularity among readers has been steady. His work has struck many critics as slight, more journalistic than literary. Bernard Bergonzi's major challenge to this assessment opened the way to many subsequent explorations and defenses of Wells's fiction. Although a few scholars have tried to revitalize interest in Wells's neglected later fiction, critics and readers alike overwhelmingly prefer the early romances. Oddly, however, Wells's short stories, well regarded in their day, have not received much attention. In recent years the number of biographies of Wells has surpassed the number of critical books.

BERGONZI traces *fin-de-siècle* influences on Wells's early fiction, especially the pervasive ambivalence of that time toward the new century. The tensions Wells felt are often objectified as contesting dualities in his work, and this collision of opposites is a structural device in much of his work. Bergonzi also addresses the critical reception of, and the allegorical meanings in, these early productions. His study is very outdated now, after the advent of more sophisticated and varied critical approaches to Wells, but it still remains the best introduction to Wells's early career.

SUVIN's anthology emphasizes Wells's early fiction as works worthy of attention because of their formative position in relation to the genre of science fiction. The essays in Suvin's collection are at their best when discussing Wells's use of nature imagery and Wells's influence on Yevgeny Zamyatin, George Orwell, and Jorge Luis Borges. There is also a thoughtful structuralist reading of *The Time Machine*. The collection falters, however, in its unwitting deference to established readings of Wells's career, which amounts to a failure to achieve the editorially announced goal of establishing a new frontier for Wellsian studies.

HUNTINGTON critiques previous attempts, like Bergonzi's, to define a consistent point of view in Wells's early fiction. Wells's early work focuses on critical issues concerning the future of civilization, but no single or consistent solution emerges. On the contrary, these writings evidence undirected thought, an on-going dialogism, which Wells later resolves in the directed thought of his disappointing later novels. If not altogether satisfactory as an approach to Wells, Huntington's book provides a correct caution about deducing the meanings of Wells's early writings.

REED, implicitly disagreeing with Huntington, identifies several types of coherence and consistency in Wellsian thought, even though this thought is divided between idealist and pragmatic impulses. Wells's views on liberation, progress, organization, writing, nature, race, self, and will are not original, Reed concludes, but they are presented in original ways. Reed's book is a valuable reservoir of detail, a rich discussion of the various sources and contemporary forces evident in Wells's work.

My own (SCHEICK's) monograph features the literary strategies used by Wells in his undervalued later fiction, specifically the revisionist manner he fashioned to awaken his readers to an emergent new reality. By means of the structural technique of the splintering frame, Wells idiosyncratically appropriated certain fictional conventions, which he redesigned to frustrate his readers' expectations associated with these conventions, to draw his readers' attention to the arbitrariness of the ideology informing them – and finally to direct his readers' thoughts away from the text in hand toward the text of their readers' minds and world.

SMITH's life-and-times biography divides Wells's experience into four periods: his studies from the 1860s to the 1890s, his struggle to become an author from the 1890s to 1918, his role as a teacher during the 1920s and 1930s, and his place as prophet during the 1940s. Each of these periods is characterized by various tensions combined with great literary productivity. Smith, who passionately defends Wells, is particularly good in broadening our knowledge of the world of the author's personal associates, including his negotiations with literary agents and publishers. Smith tends, however, to reduce Wells's work into simplistic morals or themes, as if Huntington had never written his book, to denigrate Wells's later fiction, and to misrepresent the controversial nature of his work throughout his career.

WILLIAM J. SCHEICK

Welsh Literature

Conran, Anthony, *The Cost of Strangeness: Essays on the English Poets of Wales*, Llandysul, Dyfed: Gower Press, 1982

Curtis, Tony (ed.), *Wales: The Imagined Nation: Studies in Cultural and National Identity*, Bridgend, Glamorgan: Poetry Wales Press, 1986

Garlick, Raymond, *An Introduction to Anglo-Welsh Literature*, Cardiff: University Wales Press, 1970

Jones, Glyn, *The Dragon Has Two Tongues: Essays on Anglo-Welsh Writers and Writing*, London: Dent, 1968

Jones, Gwyn, *Background to Dylan Thomas and Other Explorations*, Oxford and New York: Oxford University Press, 1992

Mathias, Roland, *A Ride Through the Wood: Essays on Anglo-Welsh Literature*, Bridgend, Glamorgan: Poetry Wales Press, 1985

Mathias, Roland, *Anglo-Welsh Literature: An Illustrated History*, Bridgend, Glamorgan: Poetry Wales Press, 1987

Stephens, Meic (ed.), *The Oxford Companion to the Literature of Wales*, Oxford and New York: Oxford University Press, 1986

Thomas, M. Wynn, *Internal Difference: Twentieth Century Writing in Wales*, Cardiff: University of Wales Press, 1992

The term "Anglo-Welsh" was coined by H. Idris Bell in 1922, and first applied consistently to literature as recently as 1957 in Gwyn Jones's essay "Anglo-Welsh Literature: The First Forty Years". Since then it has generated considerable controversy within and without Wales. This ranges over disagreements concerning its precise meaning, which authors represent "the tradition", its continual demise and/or rebirth, and its standing as a regional, provincial, or postcolonial literature. Some of the debates have been notably intense (especially between nationalist and British critics), leading one to suspect that those whom the gods wish to destroy they first afflict with a language problem.

Glyn JONES's celebrated book is more useful for its wealth of autobiographical and historical material than for its critical acumen. As well as some fairly general introductory chapters on poetry, fiction, and the short story, he focuses on six writers well-known to him personally: Caradoc Evans, Jack Jones, Gwyn Thomas (prose), and Huw Menai, Idris Davies, and Dylan Thomas (poetry). The Evans and Dylan Thomas sections are deservedly well known, and have done much to entrench the often controversial reputations of those two writers, not least because of Jones's affectionate and congenial memories of them. His thesis is that an Anglo-Welsh writer emerges when "a radical, nonconformist, Welsh-speaking family begins to speak English". Therefore what such writers have in common is not style, subject matter, or attitude, but background. This assertion presumes that the "Welshness" of Anglo-Welsh writing is doomed to disappear, and has proved understandably contentious.

GARLICK's argument is more vigorously academic, possessing something of a missionary zeal in its desire to determine a "canon" of Anglo-Welsh writers, which can be taught in schools and colleges. He locates the genesis of this tradition as early as the fifteenth century, but is hampered by the fact that the majority of those whom he discusses are unpublished, inaccessible, and often just plain bad (which, to Garlick's credit, he frequently admits). At its best, his survey serves to emphasise the talent of modern inter-war Anglo-Welsh writing, and the paucity of worthy material elsewhere.

CONRAN's unjustly neglected collection of essays charts the interconnection between Anglo-Welsh poets from the turn of the century to 1980. He perceives Welsh-language and Anglo-Welsh poetry to be interdependent: "what I have called 'seepage' took place on all cultural levels . . . and 'seepage' is one of the reasons why Anglo-Welsh poetry belongs to the people of Wales, and is not simply interesting but minor English verse". His most interesting discovery is that of a unifying theme in both languages – praise poetry. A corollary of this is his stress on the social function of the poet, which suits some poets rather better than others. R.S. Thomas and his acolytes fit such an argument extremely well, while Dylan Thomas and those influenced by him are correspondingly downgraded.

MATHIAS's rival collection of essays, largely devoted to poetry, and covering the same period, is a more disparate, less coherent read. As the most pre-eminent editor of Anglo-Welsh periodicals of his generation, Mathias's scope and influence has been enormous, and his insights into Vernon Watkins and Alun Lewis, to name but two, are acute. However, with no authorial overview of these reprinted essays, the effect is frequently to freeze the writers in time, especially those like R.S. Thomas and Emyr Humphreys, who have gone on to produce work that sheds new light on their earlier efforts.

The title of CURTIS's book is apt for a series of literary and cultural essays, which tries to fathom how a geographical area becomes an idea. His excellent Introduction assesses "life in Wales as it is reflected, distorted, and created in the arts and media", a bold enterprise usually matched by the high standard of the subsequent articles. The cultural essays catalogue the failure of Welsh art, theatre, television, and cinema to strike an original or distinctive note. Interesting are Stead's withering analysis of film, and Tighe's dissection of stage drama; but the most provocative item is Beddoe's onslaught on the inadequate portrayal of women in Welsh history and literature. The literary essays are similarly original, particularly Davies's discussion of Dylan Thomas's urban middle-classness, and Bianchi's R.S. Thomas piece, which identifies the processes by which Thomas has simultaneously engaged and yet excluded his "Anglo-Welsh readers" from a discourse about Welsh identity.

If the non-Welsh reader were to choose one indispensable book to inform, instruct, and entertain them about the "literature of Wales" (as in its diplomatic title), then that selection should unquestionably be STEPHENS's book. Its 2,825 entries are the work of 222 contributors, almost half devoted to authors or specific books. Most of its evident learning is lightly worn, ranging over saints and soldiers, patriots and politicians, Patagonia to Cymdeithas yr Iaith, and "Welsh Rabbit" to Max Boyce. For the more literary inclined there are suggestions for further reading and some decent attempts at cross-referencing, as well as entries on Waldo Williams, Gwennalt, and Saunders Lewis, invaluable for the non-Welsh-speaking reader. Although the cultural nationalist sympathies of the editor do occasionally emerge (most obviously in a rather patronising discussion of the Anglo-Welsh short story), the book is precisely what its title suggests – not a reference work, survey, or gazetteer, but a "companion".

A similar, shorter, glossier version of Stephens's gargantuan effort is MATHIAS's useful survey. Given the hopelessness of the task – to cover five centuries in 100 pages, including photographs and a bibliography – most critics would have achieved little more than a coffee-table book. Despite the format-dictated brevity of many sections, Mathias though manages to include important details concerning: religious dissent and literary achievement; the dismal contribution of the Anglo-Welsh gentry and bourgeoisie to the arts; and the vital role played by the Welsh Arts Council in funding postwar Anglo-Welsh writing. The final section contains some surprisingly dismissive remarks about contemporary poets and their lack of "Welsh commitment", but otherwise this is an exemplary attempt to produce something better than the sum of its parts.

THOMAS's book is the first critical study of Anglo-Welsh texts to rely centrally on the values of Welsh-language culture. As challengingly radical as it is brilliantly succinct, he shifts the focus of debate from the south to the north and west of Wales. He dismisses the term "Anglo-Welsh" in favour of "Welsh writer in English", and proceeds by concentrating on literature in its social context rather than the stasis of the aesthetic moment. In addition to essays on J.O. Francis, Alun Lewis, and the Glamorgan writers (drama, poetry, and fiction respectively), Thomas's primary interests come to the fore in two chapters each on Emyr Humphreys and R.S. Thomas. He demonstrates how Humphreys' novels relocate the region as the central point of the fiction, and identifies themes of Kierkegaardian resistance and familial dislocation in R.S. Thomas's poetry. It is a *tour de force* of modern Welsh literary scholarship, the only book to bear comparison with similar much-publicised trends in Scottish and Irish criticism.

Gwyn JONES's selection of essays brings together the diverse concerns of the most productive postwar Welsh "man-of-letters". He mixes autobiographical reminiscence with enormous literary erudition, covering Welsh, European, and Norse subjects with equal verve. His belief that the Anglo-Welsh literary identity was born as a reaction to puritanical Methodism is argued through the works of Caradoc Evans and Dylan Thomas, and he draws on his own novels and translations to elucidate a fine essay on the nature of artistic inspiration. Much concerned to justify his place in the "Anglo-Welsh" tradition, which he believes, rightly, that he has done much to establish, his essays are proof of Montale's famous proposition that it isn't the man who wants to continue a tradition who succeeds, but the man who can.

SIMON BAKER

Welty, Eudora 1909–

American short-story writer, novelist, and essayist

Champion, Laurie (ed.), *The Critical Response to Eudora Welty's Fiction*, Westport, Connecticut: Greenwood Press, 1994

Gygax, Franziska, *Serious Daring from Within: Female Narrative Strategies in Eudora Welty's Novels*, Westport, Connecticut: Greenwood Press, 1990
Howard, Zelma Turner, *The Rhetoric of Eudora Welty's Short Stories*, Jackson: University Press of Mississippi, 1973
Manning, Carol S., *With Ears Opening Like Morning Glories: Eudora Welty and the Love of Storytelling*, Westport, Connecticut: Greenwood Press, 1985
Mortimer, Gail L., *Daughter of the Swan: Love and Knowledge in Eudora Welty's Fiction*, Athens: University of Georgia Press, 1994
Schmidt, Peter, *The Heart of the Story: Eudora Welty's Short Fiction*, Jackson: University Press of Mississippi, 1991
Vande Kieft, Ruth M., *Eudora Welty*, New York: Twayne, 1962, revised (Boston) 1987

Since the 1940s, Eudora Welty's fiction has been the constant subject of reviews and critical essays. Although the earliest comments on Welty dealt with her role as a Southern writer, interest in more diverse topics soon began to grow. Fairly early on, critics began to take note of her re-workings of classical mythology, her interest in the issues of alienation and isolation, and her portrayal of the conflicts between innocence and experience. Book-length studies of her work began to appear slowly in the 1960s and 1970s, and the number of books has increased rapidly since the beginning of the 1980s. Today, many critical studies of Welty's fiction are available to scholars.

VANDE KIEFT's original study (1962) was the first book-length critical work to be published on Welty. The 1987 edition revised the original text, and added chapters on works that Welty published after 1962. This book is divided into sections addressing each of Welty's novels and short-story collections; Vande Kieft performs careful and complete close readings of Welty's writing rather than taking any one critical approach. Her discussions of the works focus on such themes as sense of place, universals represented in the works, and Welty's narrative technique. Most scholars still consider Vande Kieft's work to be the best introduction to Welty, a book particularly useful to any student examining her fiction for the first time.

HOWARD, in an early critical study, applies Wayne Booth's terms from *The Rhetoric of Fiction* to three collections of Welty's short stories: *A Curtain of Green*, *"The Wide Net" and Other Stories*, and *The Golden Apples*. Her analysis of the stories focuses on four major rhetorical devices – variations in narrative voice, use of archetypes and naming, language choice, and use of time – which, Howard argues, "express [Welty's] meaning and suggest her attitude toward the behavior of her characters". While this approach may seem old-fashioned today, the book is important because it was the earliest to take one critical method and apply it consistently to Welty's work.

MANNING examines Welty's emphasis on storytelling in her novels and stories. She discusses Welty's stylistic links to various oral traditions that draw on memory and imagination: myths, legends, and folk- and fairy-tales. Manning goes on to argue that Welty's use of storytelling techniques is representative of specifically Southern cultural and literary traditions, and uses Welty's published interviews and autobiographical essays to reinforce this view.

GYGAX offers one of the earliest extended feminist treatments of Welty's fiction. Her interest lies in the issue of narrative and its relationship to the concept of *écriture féminine* – how women writers appropriate the dominant discourse to create a uniquely female type of writing. In her Introduction, she makes a lucid argument for her theory in response to Welty's well-known comments that her work is in no way about "the women's movement". Gygax argues that Welty, although not arguing for feminist ideas, writes "a fiction that reflects a specifically female appropriation of traditional narrative structures". Gygax provides analysis of double-voiced discourse in *Delta Wedding*, *The Golden Apples*, *Losing Battles*, and *The Optimist's Daughter*. She focuses on issues of female narration, Welty's female-oriented revisions of myths, female protagonists interacting with the dominant community, and memory as a female experience that creates a "matrilinear narrative". Gygax presents straightforward and lucid readings in her discussion of female narrative strategies.

SCHMIDT's book is an ambitious study, almost exclusively devoted to the short stories. Schmidt believes that the stories are Welty's greatest works, and argues that they "impress because of their volatile, decentering energy . . . and [that] her critiques of social stereotyping – particularly as it involves the shaping of women's identities – have never appeared more timely or more daring". Schmidt is interested in the "historical context and social engagement" of Welty's work. He uses a feminist approach to examine gender issues in the stories, such as the expression of gender roles through the image of the madwoman, the themes of imprisonment and release, and "comedy" and "tragedy" as gendered literary genres. He then turns to New-Historicist methods to discuss the cultural, historical, and literary contexts of the stories. Schmidt discusses Welty's work in relation to that of earlier American writers, especially women writers, and argues that doing so can help us not only to re-read Welty's work, but also to re-interpret the writers who came before.

MORTIMER examines relationships in Welty's fiction, and discusses their effect on her depiction of knowledge. Basing her discussion on Nancy Chodorow's psychoanalytic object-relations theory, Mortimer examines issues of self-definition, human consciousness, and the development of knowledge in Welty's fiction and essays. She argues that Welty's own upbringing and her parents' concept of "protective love" profoundly affected her life and writing, and that this is expressed in the works through a search for knowledge of self and the world. Mortimer discusses many of Welty's works in relation to these issues; her treatment of *The Optimist's Daughter* as a text that draws her ideas together is particularly convincing.

The collection of essays edited by CHAMPION is not the only such work available; several fine collections of Welty criticism have been published during the past 20 years. However, Champion's is the most recent. This volume of nearly 50 essays spans Welty's career and treats her entire *oeuvre*. Champion includes several critical pieces on each major work, usually providing a range from early reviews to recent articles; in so doing, Champion gives the reader an idea of the variety of response to Welty's writing throughout her career. In addition to the articles collected here, Champion provides as an Introduction a complete survey of Welty criticism, in which she discusses close to 200 reviews, articles, and books. This bibliographical essay is by far the most thorough available on Welty to date, and makes this book the most useful collection of essays on Welty's work available at this time.

SUSANNAH MILNER

West, Nathanael 1903–1940

American novelist and screenwriter

Bloom, Harold (ed.), *Nathanael West*, New York: Chelsea House, 1986
Comerchero, Victor, *Nathanael West: The Ironic Prophet*, Syracuse, New York: Syracuse University Press, 1964
Hyman, Stanley Edgar, *Nathanael West*, Minneapolis: University of Minnesota Press, 1962
Jackson, Thomas H. (ed.), *Twentieth Century Interpretations of "Miss Lonelyhearts": A Collection of Critical Essays*, Englewood Cliffs, New Jersey: Prentice-Hall, 1971
Light, James F., *Nathanael West: An Interpretive Study*, Evanston, Illinois: Northwestern University Press, 1961, 2nd edition, 1971
Long, Robert Emmet, *Nathanael West*, New York: Frederick Ungar, 1985
Madden, David (ed.), *Nathanael West: The Cheaters and the Cheated: A Collection of Critical Essays*, De Land, Florida: Everett/Edwards, 1973
Martin, Jay, *Nathanael West: The Art of His Life*, New York: Farrar, Straus, Giroux, 1970; London: Secker & Warburg, 1970
Martin, Jay (ed.), *Nathanael West: A Collection of Critical Essays*, Englewood Cliffs, New Jersey: Prentice-Hall, 1971
Reid, Randall, *The Fiction of Nathanael West: No Redeemer, No Promised Land*, Chicago: University of Chicago Press, 1967
Widmer, Kingsley, *Nathanael West*, Boston: Twayne, 1982
Wisker, Alistair, *The Writings of Nathanael West*, London: Macmillan, 1990

Largely neglected in his own time, the 1930s, Nathanael West died 17 years before interest in his work began to match his achievement. The West "revival" was sparked by the publication of the mistitled *Complete Works of Nathanael West* in 1957, which included only West's four slim novels, and none of his shorter writings or Hollywood screenplays. Interest in West peaked in the early 1970s. Since then this master of comic grotesquerie has again become what he once was, one of American literature's most undervalued and under-discussed writers.

BLOOM's is the most recent of the four collections of essays devoted to West's work. Leading off with a stimulating Introduction, which places West in the tradition of Jewish gnosticism, Bloom reprints all of Hyman (West's "most useful critic") as well as a chapter from Martin's biography. The other 12 essays cover a broad range of topics, and include W.H. Auden's seminal discussion of "West's Disease" and studies of West's fiction in relation to Dada, satire, black humor, 1930s' politics, "messianic sexuality", and the American Dream. John Keyes's discussion of *Day of the Locust* as "a generic blend" of traditional and industrial folklore is especially noteworthy.

The other three collections appeared more than a decade earlier but remain useful. JACKSON reprints longer selections from Light and Hyman, as well as Robert J. Andreach's fine study of literary sources and Edmond L. Volpes' analysis of *Miss Lonelyhearts* as West's response to Eliot's *The Waste Land*, along with many brief excerpts. Jackson's detailed chronology situates West's life and works in relation to the times. MARTIN's 1971 collection is also brief, but broader in scope. It includes reviews and appreciations by West's contemporaries, discussions of influences and revisions, and is especially valuable for reprinting West's published "Notes" on violence and on *Miss Lonelyhearts* and an early version of part of *Day of the Locust*.

MADDEN's collection is the longest and most comprehensive, as well as the most uneven. Donald T. Torchiana's discussion of *Day of the Locust* and grotesque painting and Helen Taylor's annotated bibliography are especially noteworthy. Lawrence W. DiStasi's reading of *Miss Lonelyhearts* in relation to Freud's *Civilization and Its Discontents*, Kingsley Widmer on the Hollywood novel sub-genre, T.R. Steiner on *A Cool Million* and the American Dream, and James Bowden's on a world without judgment or reward are also worth reading.

LIGHT's unpretentiously titled early study, originally published in 1961, remains remarkably useful. Nicely integrating West's life, writings, and influences, Light emphasizes West's status as a second-generation Jew confronting the problem of identity, a problem translated into the quest theme in West's fiction. West's universe is, Light maintains, limited and even repellent, peopled not with characters but with grotesques who are more pathetic than tragic, and driven by "a desperate need for something worth believing in and searching for".

Appearing just one year after the first edition of Light's study, HYMAN's pamphlet is qualified both by its brevity and by its author's then fashionable Freudian approach. In general, however, Hyman provides considerable insight into the art of the writer he praises for finding "objective correlatives for our sickness and fears" and "convincing present-day forms of the great myths: the Quest, the Scapegoat, the Holy Fool, the Dance of Death".

Often dismissed for following Hyman's Freudian lead, COMERCHERO's reading of West as a modern Jeremiah and his novels as "visionary nightmares" is far better than certain later critics have been willing to admit. According to Comerchero, West's characters are not characters at all; they are "stereotyped personalities", whose "grotesque obsessions" reveal the author's own neuroses, and whose actions represent a "peculiarly modern neurotic response to the twentieth-century spiritual malaise". West's interest in this response is, Comerchero argues, as much sociological as it is psychological.

REID lays similar stress on the psychological and sociological dimensions of this "curious figure" whose works, once out of fashion, now risk "being taken for granted". Reid's study is especially valuable for its excellent and detailed study of West's sources and use of parody as a "diagnostic instrument".

No less important is Reid's summing up of the major contradictions at the heart of West's art: "he repudiated social realism but focused on sociological themes, dismissed psychological novels but was an acute literary psychologist, laughed at art but was a conscious and dedicated artist ... a dandy with proletarian sympathies, a comic writer who specialized in unfunny jokes".

Faulted by some for writing too long a book for so short a life, MARTIN's biography provides a compelling and richly detailed account of West and his works in the context of the main social, political, intellectual, and artistic currents of his times (with particular emphasis on Dada, surrealism, leftist ideas, and popular culture). Martin portrays West as a deeply divided man, and calls special attention to "his passive ability to understand experience and his lack of capacity for deeply active engagement in it". Martin judges West's chief literary achievement to be the invention of "new literary forms and attitudes" with which "to express, for the modern sensibility, moral indignation without righteousness, and a tragic sense without a vision of redemption".

WIDMER, building on his own earlier work, offers a convincing reading of West as "a secularized prophet of doom" and as "both a masquerader and a masquerade breaker, wildly fantasizing and sardonically attacking fantasies". Situating West in the context of Jewish assimilation and Jewish-American fiction, Widmer concludes that West is both "the ancient mocking prophet" and "the energetically modern yearning American".

LONG's study is not nearly as original or coherent as Widmer's, but it is far more comprehensive and objective. Densely packed yet highly readable, it provides an excellent overview of virtually all aspects of West's achievement as a novelist. Long summarizes each of the novels, and comments knowledgeably, and at length, on the critical response, composition, sources and influences, aesthetic techniques, correspondences between text and author's life, and impact on later writers. In general, Long views West as a satirist and fantasist whose major theme is "loss of identity" and whose works constitute a comedy of nonexistence, a "poetry of cruelty".

Finally, WISKER's reading of West as an "ethically engaged" fantasist, whose works are grounded in empirical reality and which operate in the "schism between rational and absurd", relies too heavily on quotation to be either convincing or particularly useful. Yet even Wisker's volume merits attention, less for the chapters on the critical response to West, on literary influences, and on each of the four novels, than for Wisker's inclusion (as appendices) of 14 previously unpublished and/or uncollected pieces by West.

ROBERT A. MORACE

West, Rebecca 1892–1983

English novelist and prose writer

Deakin, Motley F., *Rebecca West*, Boston: Twayne, 1980
Glendinning, Victoria, *Rebecca West: A Life*, London: Weidenfeld & Nicolson, 1987; New York: Knopf, 1987
Hammond, J.R., *H.G. Wells and Rebecca West*, London: Harvester Wheatsheaf, 1991
Orel, Harold, *The Literary Achievement of Rebecca West*, London: Macmillan, 1986
Ray, Gordon N., *H.G. Wells and Rebecca West*, New Haven, Connecticut: Yale University Press, 1974; London: Macmillan, 1974
Weldon, Fay, *Rebecca West*, London and New York: Viking Press, 1985
Wolfe, Peter, *Rebecca West: Artist and Thinker*, Carbondale: Southern Illinois University Press, 1971; London: Feffer & Simons, 1971

The sheer range of Rebecca West's output – fiction, literary criticism, journalism, travel writing – appears to have made critical appraisal of her work problematic. The woman *Time* magazine once hailed as "indisputably the world's No. 1 woman writer" (as quoted in Glendinning, 1987), has attracted surprisingly little serious critical commentary, although much attention has been focused on her relationship with H.G. Wells and her position as an unmarried mother. Early studies rate her non-fiction more highly than her novels, but feminist reassessments draw attention to her strong female characters and craftsmanship, as well as her witty polemic. Although divided in their attempts to define the principles that characterise her work as a whole, critics tend to concentrate on her fascination with theological doctrine and her dualistic view of the world.

WOLFE identifies the Augustine doctrine of Original Sin as the unifying core of West's writing, and uses this as a framework within which to consider her "conservative scepticism". He also stresses her belief in the importance of "process" – the interchange between organism and surroundings – which, he argues, reconciles her dualism and brings together male and female principles. Discussing the non-fiction works at length, particularly her biography of St Augustine and *Black Lamb and Grey Falcon*, Wolfe presents West as a conceptualist, a theorizer fascinated by ideas. He devotes less space to her fiction, calling her early work "a litter of brilliant fragments", and criticising her prose as over-stylised and verbose.

RAY's account of the relationship between West and Wells, which had West's co-operation, started the trend of considering the two writers in tandem. Concentrating on the years 1913–23, its interest for the literary critic lies in its extensive use of Wells' letters to West (often containing comments on West's work) and its biographical readings of West's early fiction.

DEAKIN's book is structured on the belief that West's work can be divided into chronological periods, each dominated by one of her major interests – feminism, literary criticism, history and treason. Each of these subjects was first explored in West's non-fiction writings, Deakin argues, and her fiction was then an attempt to distil her thoughts into a more imaginative and personal form. He sees her writing as being, above all, motivated by a drive to understand, and he stresses her concern with the interrelationship between art and the social and political. Refreshingly clear of the obsession with Wells that dogs so much criticism of West, Deakin provides an informative account of her early career as feminist journalist and reviewer. Attempting to clarify her complex treatment of theological doctrines, he concludes:

> Dame Rebecca's concept of man's nature swings between two heresies, Pelagianism and Manichaeanism, that serve as magnets to which her observations can be pulled. . . . The brightness of the Pelagian perfect free will delighted her, but all her experience told her that it was a dangerous illusion. More often she was drawn by the evidence of circumstance and observation to the dark uncertainties of Manichaeanism.

Like most early critics, however, Deakin argues that "Rebecca West's literary genius is not basically fictive", and his treatment of the novels suffers accordingly.

OREL's study is the most comprehensive attempt so far to assess West's entire achievement, including her literary criticism, which he sees as curiously underrated and uses to draw out the influences on her work. Regarding her as a stylist who very early developed "formidable rhetorical skills and a mature, occasionally Jamesian prose style", Orel acknowledges the difficulty in classifying her, but stresses that her work must be considered as a whole. Attempting to define the controlling principles in her work, he argues that "her passion for order and justice unified her work from the beginning. She was always convinced that a writer has a duty to his society as well as to himself or to his art". Orel traces through her work continuing preoccupations with theological doctrine, with the duties owed to God and to the state, and with the differences between male and female. His treatment of the novels, however, lacks the discussion of gender issues needed to make sense of novels like *The Return of the Soldier* and *The Judge*.

GLENDINNING's sympathetic biography includes brief but useful assessments of West's work, drawing out autobiographical elements in the novels, and arguing that *Black Lamb and Grey Falcon* synthesizes West's thought on dualities and the balance of gender power. West's belief in the primacy of the sentence over the word, in Glendinning's view, gives her prose at its best "its incomparable rhythmic fluidity". Glendinning has also contributed informed introductions to several Virago reprints of West's novels.

HAMMOND explores the complex and influential relationship between West and Wells as writers. He draws out the contrast between Wells' belief that the novel could be a medium for the discussion of social and moral problems and West's Jamesian view of it as a high art form. Unlike earlier critics, Hammond believes West's literary reputation will rest on her novels, which "encapsulate fundamental human truths. They are concerned with life and love, happiness and anguish, and the dichotomy between the search for contentment and the eternal quest for romance".

WELDON's idiosyncratic short Life takes the form of a letter to West, as West recovers from the birth of her son. With the benefit of hindsight, Weldon brings a feminist awareness to her exploration of the social, moral, and literary influences that formed West as a writer. The result is a very readable introduction to West's life and work.

DIANA WALLACE

West Indian Literature *see* Caribbean Literature

The Western *see* Frontier and Western Literature

Wharton, Edith 1862–1937

American novelist, short-story writer, and travel writer

Ammons, Elizabeth, *Edith Wharton's Argument with America*, Athens: University of Georgia Press, 1980
Benstock, Shari, *No Gifts from Chance: A Biography of Edith Wharton*, New York: Charles Scribner's Sons, 1994; London: Hamish Hamilton, 1994
Howe, Irving (ed.), *Edith Wharton: A Collection of Critical Essays*, Englewood Cliffs, New Jersey: Prentice-Hall, 1962
Lewis, R.W.B., *Edith Wharton: A Biography*, New York: Harper & Row, 1975; London: Constable, 1975
Wershoven, Carol, *The Female Intruder in the Novels of Edith Wharton*, Rutherford, New Jersey: Fairleigh Dickinson University Press, 1982; London: Associated University Presses, 1982
Wolff, Cynthia Griffin, *A Feast of Words: The Triumph of Edith Wharton*, New York: Oxford University Press, 1977; 2nd edition, Reading, Massachusetts: Addison-Wesley, 1995

Early criticism of Wharton considered her primarily in the shadow of Henry James, whose most talented disciple she was said to be. Early characterizations of Wharton's work emphasized her role as an aristocratic chronicler of late nineteenth-century New York high society – an image that was reinforced by Wharton's autobiography (*A Backward Glance*) and by Percy Lubbock's memoir of her. As a result, for several decades after her death Wharton was considered interesting and important, but by no means among the first ranks of American novelists. An important biography and a flurry of new criticism in the 1970s challenged older assessments, and since then the body of criticism on Wharton's work has grown and diversified, offering more considered assessments of the entire corpus.

HOWE's collection of essays provides a representative selection of early material. Written by prominent critics, these essays span the years 1915–62 and represent the major strands of early criticism on Wharton. On the question of Wharton's relationship to James, opinions in this collection are mixed. Howe and others challenge the notion that Wharton should be considered primarily as a disciple of James. However, many of the other essays agree with Q.D. Leavis, who labels Wharton "Henry James's Heiress". The other major detraction from Wharton's literary reputation is also represented in this volume: Vernon Parrington criticizes Wharton as a writer solely of, and for, the upper classes. In Parrington's judgment, although Wharton's command of technique was excellent, her writing was at bottom irrelevant. While later scholarship has challenged the claim of irrelevancy, the point of Parrington's essay is an important one: the limits of Wharton's class sympathies ought not to be forgotten. Overall, the essays in this volume generally agree on Wharton's status within the canon of American literature: Wharton was "not a great writer but an exceptional one" (Q.D. Leavis).

In the 1970s, new work on Wharton made a re-evaluation of her works and her status inevitable. LEWIS's biography was one important impetus for this re-evaluation. Using archival materials previously unavailable, Lewis's absorbing biography effectively counters the view of Wharton as an aloof aristocrat and a withdrawn, frigid woman. Lewis details Wharton's relations with family and friends, including her affair with Morton Fullerton, her divorce, and her close friendships with Henry James and Walter Berry. Lewis also sheds light on Wharton's uncertain beginnings as a writer in a family and a social set that discouraged her artistic leanings, beginning in early childhood. Lewis chronicles the genesis of individual novels and stories, and interprets them in relation to the life. He also provides an invaluable service by printing the sexually explicit fragment of "Beatrice Palmato", an unfinished story about incest, which is interesting because it touches on a theme important in many of Wharton's works. Lewis's biography has recently been skillfully challenged and complemented by BENSTOCK, who had access to letters and papers not available to Lewis. Benstock settles some factual matters, dispelling, for example, the oft-repeated story that Wharton underwent S. Weir Mitchell's famous rest treatment, and that Mitchell suggested writing as a therapy for Wharton. Benstock also provides valuable new information on Wharton's relationships with women friends.

WOLFF acknowledges indebtedness to Lewis in her psychoanalytical study. Wolff claims that Wharton was emotionally deprived as a child and that she used her writing to overcome the fears and emotional dependency that she developed in her childhood. This seemingly mundane psychological claim becomes the basis for impressive readings of many of Wharton's works. In Wolff's reading, for example, *The House of Mirth* is Wharton's first successful attempt to deal with her emotional dilemmas; it chronicles "the psychological disfigurement of any woman who chooses to accept society's definition of her as a beautiful object and nothing more; and . . . the novel justifiably bores down into that core of Wharton's own childhood rage". *Ethan Frome* is the culmination of the first period of Wharton's career, in which "her central figures had been swayed and bent by the fortunes that beset them". In Wharton's second period (from *The Reef* to *The Age of Innocence*) her "main characters proclaim an almost muscular need to meet the forces that would shape their lives" – but Wharton never became so optimistic as to write novels about characters mastering their fates. Wolff's interpretation of Wharton's life and work is a significant one.

AMMONS has written a fascinating study of Wharton in relationship to the Progressive Era's notion of the New Woman. As Ammons points out, Wharton's vision of women differed sharply from the prevailing notion that celebrated the liberation of the New Woman: "typical women in her view – no matter how privileged . . . were not free to control their own lives, and that conviction became the foundation of her argument with American optimism for more than twenty years". The early novels depict the repression and economic dependence of women, while the novels of the middle period conduct a more thorough political analysis. Ammons's analysis of Wharton's last work in terms of its turn toward motherhood and matriarchy is an intriguing account of this problematic period of Wharton's writing career.

WERSHOVEN attempts to counter claims that Wharton only critiqued social mores and did not offer an alternative vision of life. She claims that a character type, the "female intruder", functions in many Wharton novels to critique her society, destroy the complacency of some representative of the status quo, and sometimes introduce a model for a better way of life. These intruders are outsiders because of their backgrounds, social statuses, or violations of social taboos, and they embody values of compassion and emotional openness opposed to the repression and intolerance of the society they critique. Intruders, however, are not always sympathetic characters; the grasping Undine Spragg, for example, is seen as an intruder who makes the same critique as Lily Bart: "through their battles in a mercenary world, they expose it as a place where all relationships are at bottom financial transactions, and where great wealth is the only virtue that matters". This is an interesting attempt to reclaim Wharton as having a positive social vision.

ANGELA VIETTO

White, Patrick 1912–1990

Australian novelist, dramatist, and poet

Beatson, Peter, *The Eye in the Mandala: Patrick White: A Vision of Man and God*, London: Paul Elek, 1976; New York: Barnes & Noble, 1976
Bliss, Carolyn, *Patrick White's Fiction: The Paradox of Fortunate Failure*, London: Macmillan, 1986; New York: St Martin's Press, 1986
Edgecombe, Rodney Stenning, *Vision and Style in Patrick White: A Study of Five Novels*, Tuscaloosa: University of Alabama Press, 1989
Marr, David, *Patrick White: A Life*, London: Jonathan Cape, 1991; New York: Knopf, 1991
Tacey, David J., *Patrick White: Fiction and the Unconscious*, Melbourne, Oxford, and New York: Oxford University Press, 1988
Weigel, John A., *Patrick White*, Boston: Twayne, 1983

Until 1973, when he received the Nobel Prize for Literature, Patrick White was relatively unknown outside Australia, and a controversial figure within. Most studies that appeared during the 1970s were universalist, and saw White as striving for a vision of unity, mystically Jungian, or psychologically nuanced. Australian critics sometimes saw his relationship with his own country as deeply problematic. After 1973, White became a much more public figure, and now there is likely to be a shift in the kind of criticism he receives, particularly since the publication of David Marr's biography.

WEIGEL's survey is a volume in the Twayne "World Authors" series, and therefore an introductory overview. Weigel characterizes White as a "visionary with a sense of humor". He offers no all-embracing thesis, while somewhat privileging the most popular view of White as visionary, mystic, religious – but not Christian – seeker. Weigel introduces

White's work from its culmination in the memoir/self-portrait *Flaws in the Glass* (1981), drawing on that work for the biographical first chapter. Particularly useful features of this study are its comprehensiveness (Weigel includes some discussion of the often neglected stories and plays), its coherent chronological table, and an annotated bibliography.

BLISS also believes that White, in his fiction, is a religious seeker, but she argues that he presents this view from a negative standpoint, from White's apparent conviction of the inevitability of failure in human experience: God is present in his absence. In her first chapter, Bliss relates this to a powerful strand in the way Australians have constructed an image for themselves. The historian Manning Clark attributed a characteristically Australian belief in failure to the country's climate and environment, the endless aridity of its daunting Outback. Bliss argues that White's strong-willed characters must experience failure in order to comprehend that the universe is ultimately a moral and spiritual one. Thus they stumble into abjectness and die in failure of one kind or another, yet they dissolve into an apprehension of mystic unity. Dealing with all the novels in a series of subtle and detailed interpretations, Bliss concludes by demonstrating that White communicates failure not only thematically, but also in the novels' very structure, style, and imagery.

TACEY's study is the most thorough of those that have interpreted White in the light of Jungian depth psychology and archetypal theory. Its strength lies in the comprehensive attention Tacey gives both to White's fiction and Jungian and related schema. Its weakness is that it is reductive and judgmental, and Tacey has no problem applying what he sees as the psychological obtuseness of the novels' characters to White himself. Tacey sees White's novels as becoming increasingly tainted after *The Solid Mandala* (1966) – "the most significant of all White's novels". After that novel, Tacey argues, White's fiction enters into decadence and, in archetypal terms, its author is swallowed up by the Great Mother, succumbing to matriarchalism. Tacey accuses White of misogyny, perhaps because his own thesis seems both misogynist and homophobic. In offering the fullest and most doctrinaire of psychological studies on a significant body of fiction, he seems to speak for the several Australian critics who have found Patrick White a very uncongenial novelist.

BEATSON's earlier work on White's spirituality, Jungian archetypalism, and associated insights from depth psychology differs from Tacey's in its unabashed enthusiasm and explicit disclaiming of any judgmental stance. Beatson aims at a direct, thematic treatment, made possible by laying a systematic schema over the work. In terms of the limitations he himself announces, Beatson offers a reading of White the mystic that will be helpful to any reader who responds to those powerful elements in the novels.

EDGECOMBE provides a careful reading of five of the novels from White's middle period – *Voss*, *Riders in the Chariot*, *The Solid Mandala*, *The Vivisector*, and *The Eye of the Storm*. His starting point is the perceived, sometimes unnecessary, ornateness of White's style, which Edgecombe defends as fully integrated with the novelist's moral vision. Rigorous analysis reveals a style answerable to the characters' approach to community and transcendence in a universe that seems stubbornly material. Edgecombe finds that White's style – at any rate after the early novels – tracks his characters' fundamental quests precisely by attending to objects, details, and particulars. This volume, then, is one of strenuously focused analyses yielding important thematic insights, while demonstrating the necessary relation between theme and style. Edgecombe contends that the writing of White's middle period is his best; what preceded and followed is, by comparison, flawed.

MARR's very complete and substantial biography, possible because of White's co-operation in his last years, throws much light on White's fiction. Marr painstakingly constructs the important contexts for the novels: the matriarchal family and English public (i.e., private) schools, which, making White conscious that he did not fully "belong", helped him to elect the role of independent watcher of people and events; his voluntary exile from Australia, and service in World War II, including his meeting with his life-long companion, Manoly Lascaris; his identification with Greece and the Levant; and his return to settled life in Sydney. In showing how White's ambivalent relation to Australia and its discourses, and his discreetly lived homosexuality, made his work fraught for Australian critics, Marr has opened up significant spaces for further approaches to the novelist's work.

PATRICK HOLLAND

Whitman, Walt 1819–1892

American poet, essayist, and journalist

Allen, Gay Wilson, *The Solitary Singer: A Critical Biography of Walt Whitman*, New York: Macmillan, 1955
Allen, Gay Wilson, *The New Walt Whitman Handbook*, New York: New York University Press, 1975
Ceniza, Sherry, "Walt Whitman and Abby Price", in *Walt Whitman Quarterly Review*, 7, 1989
Chase, Richard, *Walt Whitman Reconsidered*, New York: William Sloane, 1955
Kummings, Donald D. (ed.), *Approaches to Teaching Whitman's "Leaves of Grass"*, New York: Modern Language Association of America, 1990
Larson, Kerry C., *Whitman's Drama of Consensus*, Chicago: University of Chicago Press, 1988
Martin, Robert K. (ed.), *The Continuing Presence of Walt Whitman: The Life after the Life*, Iowa City: University of Iowa Press, 1992
Matthiessen, F.O., *American Renaissance: Art and Expression in the Age of Emerson and Whitman*, London and New York: Oxford University Press, 1941
Miller, Edwin Haviland, *Walt Whitman's Poetry: A Psychological Journey*, Boston: Houghton Mifflin, 1968
Miller, Edwin Haviland, *Walt Whitman's "Song of Myself": A Mosaic of Interpretations*, Iowa City: University of Iowa Press, 1989
Miller, James E., Jr., *A Critical Guide to "Leaves of Grass"*, Chicago: University of Chicago Press, 1957
Moon, Michael, *Disseminating Whitman: Revision and Corporeality in "Leaves of Grass"*, Cambridge, Massachusetts: Harvard University Press, 1991

Reynolds, David S., *Walt Whitman's America: A Cultural Biography*, New York: Knopf, 1995
Woodress, James (ed.), *Critical Essays on Walt Whitman*, Boston: G.K. Hall, 1983

Since the publication of *Leaves of Grass* (first edition, 1855), Walt Whitman has inspired criticism – favorable and adverse – from a variety of schools. A massive amount of secondary scholarship and criticism is available for those willing to devote considerable time and effort to its perusal. The major themes running through the secondary scholarship are Whitman's devotion to democratic ideals, his sexual orientation, his concerns for feminism, his alleged "racism", his poetic technique, his literary sources, and the sources of inspiration for his poetry. The sources cited below therefore constitute a small sample of the scholarship and criticism available for the interested reader.

ALLEN's 1975 volume is a revision of the original handbook, first published in 1946. All students of Whitman, scholars and initiates alike, can benefit from consulting this important source compiled by the most distinguished Whitman scholar of the twentieth century. Each chapter in the book contains ample bibliographies and suggestions for further research, along with a brief history of scholarship and criticism in the field. Specific chapters are "The Growth of Whitman Biography", "The Growth of *Leaves of Grass*", "The Realm of Whitman's Ideas", "Literary Technique in *Leaves of Grass*", and "Walt Whitman and World Literature". This is the place to begin for anyone aspiring to knowledge of Walt Whitman's literary works.

MATTHIESSEN's monumental study of America's golden age of literature has continued to be influential in Whitman studies. Whitman is placed in a cultural setting wherein painters, sculptors, musicians, politicians, and popular artists of the period all aimed to re-create American culture. This work remains one of the best means of getting to know American culture – as well as the background for *Leaves of Grass* – during the period from 1840 to 1860. It is Whitman the aesthetic genius, not the ideologue, who is presented in the relevant sections of this work.

CHASE's study is valuable for its lengthy and interesting discussion of "Song of Myself", one of Whitman's most important lyrics in *Leaves of Grass*, and perhaps the most revealing for its insights into Whitman's comic outlook – a subject neglected in previous criticism because of the tacit assumption that Whitman was not in any way a humorist. Concentrating on Whitman as "the comic poet, the radical realist, and the profound elegist", the book attempts to correct the unjustified devaluation of Whitman that has been characteristic of élitist scholarship. The book contains, in addition, an excellent discussion of Whitman's prose work *Democratic Vistas*.

ALLEN's 1955 volume remains the definitive critical biography of Whitman, despite the appearance over the years of numerous biographical studies. Of special value is the author's attempt to relate biographical fact to the poetry itself; thus readers are enabled to better understand the interworkings of the poet's life and artistic output. Rigorous scholarship and sound critical ability make this work crucial for all subsequent biographical and critical study of Whitman. Some critics have faulted Allen, however, for his determined caution in taking a stand on such issues as Whitman's sexual orientation; nevertheless, this biography establishes the facts of Whitman's life and engages in a discussion of various disputed issues.

James E. MILLER's study is often said to be the best single source of critical information on Whitman's *Leaves of Grass* for the student who knows nothing about Whitman or his literary works. This work is a close reading (from the period of the New Criticism), section by section, poem by poem, of Whitman's poetry. *Leaves of Grass* is shown to be highly unified in overall structure, theme, and imagery. The seminal essay in the book, "'Song of Myself' As Inverted Mystical Experience", has been influential for both teachers and critics. The emphasis of the book is *structure*, a topic difficult for both established scholars and students to deal with in Whitman studies.

Edwin Haviland MILLER's *Walt Whitman's Poetry: A Psychological Journey* is widely known as the best single Freudian/psychoanalytical study of *Leaves of Grass* and of the poet's unusual personality. Miller emphasizes the first (1855) edition of the poetic masterpiece, but is careful to explain important later revisions in the poetry. Miller explains his intentions in his Preface:

> This "inner drama" that Whitman unfolds – which is our inner drama as well – cannot be approached from the outside, that is, by discussion of genres, traditional structure, rhetoric, and so forth. The poetry must . . . be approached on its own terms. Hence I have been concerned with latent and manifest content, compulsive repetitions of words and situations, psychic dynamics, narcissism, orgiastic rhythms, and the like.

WOODRESS's collection publishes the most important reprinted criticism on Whitman along with original essays, interviews, bibliographies, letters, manuscript sections, and other materials brought to public attention for the first time. The book contains not only reprinted essays and comments by such notable figures as Ralph Waldo Emerson, Henry James, Ezra Pound, and D.H. Lawrence, but original articles by distinguished Whitman scholars and critics. This collection is perhaps the best of the many available gatherings of scholarship and criticism relating to Whitman and his works.

LARSON's study, a major reinterpretation of Whitman and his literary works, establishes the notion of consensus as the shaping force central to the poet's achievement. Larson shows how this notion not only informs Whitman's more didactic pronouncements on the goals of his democratic aesthetic, but also animates its most basic assumptions and procedures. According to Larson, Whitman's songs offer themselves as the catalyst for social integration – the means through which an irreducible "common ground" of unanimity may be secured. Whitman emerges more strongly than before as America's national poet and the bard of democracy.

CENIZA's essay is cited here because it is the strongest argument to date for a profound "feminist" content within the text of *Leaves of Grass*; her analysis of Whitman's friendships, reading, and associations with important agitators (including Abby Price) in the nineteenth-century feminist movement bolsters her view that Whitman was an important cultural influence in the development of American feminism.

Edwin Haviland MILLER's *Walt Whitman's "Song of Myself": A Mosaic of Interpretations* is an important summary and synthesis of all the important scholarship and criticism published on "Song of Myself". As the absolute master of the secondary scholarship, Miller clearly establishes general lines of interpretation, important critical/scholarly controversies, and textual bibliography. This work is indispensable for anyone contemplating serious study of "Song of Myself." The excellent bibliography of all important published scholarship on "Song of Myself" is most useful. One caveat is that Miller emphasizes the importance of the first (1855) edition of the poem above all subsequent editions, believing that Whitman was at his most creative and dynamic in that first edition; nevertheless, Miller provides an Introduction and summary of scholarship for all editions of the poem.

KUMMINGS, the distinguished Whitman bibliographer, has edited this collection ostensibly as a means of assisting teachers who need help in presenting Whitman to undergraduates. As it turns out, this series of essays has proven helpful even to Whitman scholars and critics; certainly it will be of use to anyone approaching Whitman's literary works for the first time. Important sections of the book, all composed by distinguished Whitman scholars, are those on "Materials" (editions, anthologies, background reading) and "Approaches" (to "Song of Myself" and other major works). Excellent bibliographies are included. Kummings has sought to include most of the most recent critical approaches to literary texts, i.e., feminist, psychoanalytical, deconstructionist, gender-studies, linguistic, as well as prosodic-studies, and close textual readings.

MOON's analysis shows how Whitman's continual modifications of his work intersect with the representations of male homosexual desire throughout his writing. As one of the few scholarly books that deal with Whitman's massive revisions of *Leaves of Grass*, this study has already proved quite useful to Whitman scholars and critics of all stripes. Moon and Robert K. Martin have established themselves as the major spokesmen for a "homotextuality" in Whitman's poetry.

MARTIN, a well-known critic of American poetry, who has been a pioneer in gay studies and is known as the author of *The Homosexual Tradition in American Poetry*, has in this collection of essays shown how the best readers of Whitman have not allowed themselves to be evasive or timid about such matters as Whitman's sexuality, poetics, and politics. Whitman's sexual orientation, especially, is candidly discussed by several of the contributors. The collection demonstrates clearly that Whitman, as the central figure of American poetic history, has been a formative presence in the work of black writers in America and Europe, in the development of a women's poetry that has learned from him to celebrate the body, and of course in the emergence of the gay literary tradition – all of which can be linked to movements of political change.

REYNOLDS's book is a restatement of a major theme in Whitman criticism – his treatment of democracy. As a contribution to the field of cultural studies, Reynolds digs beneath the roots of *Leaves of Grass* and systematically explores the popular culture from which they draw their sap. Whitman is set vividly against the popular culture, the politics, and the mores of his time, and emerges with new definition and amplitude. In the process, Whitman is seen to be much more democratic than even his supporters have contended. Readers will find a systematic treatment of the popular culture that made Whitman what he was, and that finally blossomed in *Leaves of Grass*. The period covered is the profoundly rich one, dating from the Era of Good Feelings (which collapsed in the panic of 1819, the year of Whitman's birth) through the Gilded Age, in which Whitman's life came to a close in 1892. Reynolds highlights the many interests and contradictions in the life of Whitman, and he carefully demonstrates how knowledge of these can assist in interpreting the poetry. Readers interested in such diverse subjects as the evolution theory, phrenology, water cures, the nudist movement, Transcendentalism, printing, photography – and more – will find this book truly engaging.

JAMES T. F. TANNER

Wilde, Oscar 1854–1900

Irish dramatist, novelist, poet, children's writer, and essayist

Bird, Alan, *The Plays of Oscar Wilde*, London: Vision Press, 1977; New York: Barnes & Noble, 1977
Croft-Cooke, Rupert, *The Unrecorded Life of Oscar Wilde*, London: W.H. Allen, 1972
Ellmann, Richard, *Oscar Wilde*, London: Hamish Hamilton, 1987; New York: Knopf, 1988
Gagnier, Regenia (ed.), *Critical Essays on Oscar Wilde*, New York: G.K. Hall, 1991
Miller, Robert Keith, *Oscar Wilde*, New York: Frederick Ungar, 1982
Nassaar, Christopher S., *Into the Demon Universe: A Literary Exploration of Oscar Wilde*, New Haven, Connecticut: Yale University Press, 1974
Pearson, Hesketh, *The Life of Oscar Wilde*, London: Methuen, 1946; New York: Harper, 1946
Small, Ian, *Oscar Wilde Revalued: An Essay on New Materials and Methods of Research*, Greenboro, North Carolina: ELT Press, 1993
Symons, Arthur, *A Study of Oscar Wilde*, London: C.J. Sawyer, 1930

For 50 years after his death, Wilde's reputation was mainly that of a sprightly wit and haughty homosexual. Many critics tended to dismiss him as not fully worthy of all the attention he commanded. Given the public nature of his career, trials, and imprisonment, Wilde could hardly be ignored. His works and personality continue to captivate serious readers and dedicated scholars, proof of which can be found in 15,000 articles and books devoted to Wilde's life, poetry, fiction, essays, and dramas. Not many writers have had so much ink spilled on their behalf, and few, it could be argued, treated so badly. More importantly, a "demythologizing" of Wilde got under way in the 1960s. The change came about with a sudden increase in the availability of scholarly materials, which in turn provided the beginnings of corrective biographical studies. The Wilde that emerges from this new scholarship is that of a professional writer at the turn of the century who persevered in negotiations with publishers, cultivated potential reviewers, and continually sought to perfect his craft. Today, he can be viewed as an author more concerned with the aesthetic and intellectual issues of the 1890s than with the dandyism and Decadence of the decade.

SYMONS's study is a mosaic of memories, articles, and reviews, which he wrote over a period of some 30 years. His views are of special interest, for he was actually involved in most of the events he describes: moreover, he echoes representative contemporary reactions. In his attempt to be fair-minded, Symons shifts between adulation and condemnation. Symons discusses in some detail each of Wilde's works. *The Picture of Dorian Gray*, he agreed with Walter Pater, was a vivid story exposing the corruption of a soul, a tale with a very plain moral: "vice and crime make people coarse and ugly". In *Salomé*, the playwright made manifest his gift for dialogue; he also revealed his own sexual weakness, "his womanish side ... evident ... swollen, puffed out, bloated and sinister". Because of their personal experiences and minute observations, *The Ballad of Reading Gaol* and W.E. Henley's *In Hospital* are compared with one another. In Symons's view, Wilde's brilliant comedies best revealed his genius, but ironically, his desire was to write romantic tragedies in verse.

PEARSON can be credited with producing the first balanced, discerning, compassionate biography of Wilde, one devoid of the sensationalism and tendentiousness that marred previous accounts written by friends and foes. Having no special case to defend or victims to roast, Pearson, in the main, let the facts speak for themselves. Though his work has several gaps, numerous lapses in judgement, and questionable conclusions, it is still reasonably fair and temperate. Written with vigour and gusto, it depicts its subject at times through anecdotes, quotations, and reminiscences. Pearson covers Wilde from his earliest days in Dublin, through his schooling at Trinity and Oxford, to his lecture tour in the United States and return to London to concentrate on a literary career. He gives a good account of Wilde the poet and the reasons why he turned to fiction and drama. *The Picture of Dorian Gray* and *Salomé*, Pearson suggests, are illustrative of "Wilde's boy-like enjoyment of scandalizing the bourgeoisie by a ritualistic indulgence in bizarrerie and devilry". A master of the comedic and satiric, Wilde was his best in *The Importance of Being Earnest*. *The Ballad of Reading Goal* succeeds because when he wrote it Wilde "understood the sufferings of others, far more than his own". Pearson dismisses *De Profundis* as "emotionally unconvincing, simply because Wilde, whenever he became serious about himself, became theatrical". Pearson's comments on Wilde's work are provocative, but his focus is on the man.

CROFT-COOKE claims that his book is the result of a lifetime of study. One would expect, therefore, that it would be a model of accuracy; for not only did he devote much time to his subject, but over the years he had opportunities to verify facts with Lord Alfred Douglas, Frank Harris, Vyvyan Holland, and other prominent figures in the Wilde circle. Croft-Cooke knows his facts well; his interpretations, though, are troublesome. In the opening chapter, he takes all of Wilde's early biographers to task: Robert Sherard (*The Life of Oscar Wilde*, 1906) he dubs "an honest fool", and Frank Harris (*Oscar Wilde: His Life and Confessions*, 1916) "a clever rogue". Implicit in his attacks is his swollen opinion that he alone has mastered the subject and can put everyone and everything straight. The portrait that he produces is closer to the leprous canvas of *Dorian Gray* than to the better-known depictions of Wilde as one of London's most brilliant wits and admired playwrights, who, because of his own folly and insolence, brought about his downfall. Wilde the author comes off no better than Wilde the man, being "not a supremely important writer". His poetry is "derivative", his miscellaneous prose "undistinguished", his short stories "were written with self-conscious bravura", his *Picture of Dorian Gray* "novelettish, vulgar, primed with stagey melodrama", *The Ballad of Reading Gaol* little more than "a mixture of Coleridge, Poe, and self-pity", *The Importance of Being Earnest* the "the only play which is something better than a cleverly constructed but old-fashioned 'society' drama, salted with aphorisms". Croft-Cooke wanted to get at the real Wilde, to paint him warts and all: but his study is cactaceous and prurient, devoid of wit, sympathy, and understanding.

NASSAAR contends that Wilde's fascination with the demonic aspects of human nature made him the writer he became. Had Wilde put aside his pen before 1886, his writings up to that time could easily be ignored. His early poetry, Nassaar claims, is second-rate, his early plays, *Vera* (1880) and *The Duchess of Padua* (1883), experimental failures. Nassaar does not attempt an exhaustive analysis of Wilde's later "vision of evil", but he emphasizes that Wilde underwent a psychological and aesthetic transformation in 1886 when he became a Decadent and created a cosmos of evil, guilt, sin, and atonement. A chronological examination of his work that followed reveals a shift away from the early childlike innocence of his fairy-tales to the destructive nature of evil found in *The Picture of Dorian Gray*. In *Salomé* Wilde went on the delve into the compelling glorification of the iniquitous. With *The Importance of Being Earnest* he produced a self-parody. The solipsistic *Ballad of Reading Gaol* is a prolonged wail of despair from one who finds himself damned. *De Profundis* conveys the anguish of personal defeat and lack of regeneration.

BIRD begins his study by disputing claims that Wilde's life is more interesting than his work, and that only one of his plays, *The Importance of Being Earnest*, is worthy of consideration. He covers Wilde's entire dramatic output, their performances, and the critical attention individual plays merited in their time. As for their plots, the plays are "less sentimental and more socially critical than is generally admitted". He devotes a chapter to each one of them, and concludes with a section on such unfinished dramatic projects as *A Florentine Tragedy* and *La Sainte Courtisane*. This volume, one of the first to concentrate on Wilde as dramatist, contains a proper understanding and perceptive appreciation of its subject: it parts company with the legend of Wilde as a literary trifler and depicts him as a serious playwright whose powers grew from play to play.

MILLER's short book of less than 200 pages is a well-researched, useful distillation of so much that has been written about Wilde. The opening chapter provides the biographical considerations; the basic facts, events, vicissitudes of Wilde's life are discussed insofar as they help to fathom his creativity. Biography assumes a supportive role in the chapters that follow as they try to bring the man of letters into focus. Miller glosses over Wilde's letters, lectures, and poetry, but he does present a probing analysis of *The Picture of Dorian Gray* in his second chapter. Though a "very readable novel ... much more than merely entertaining", it is still the work of a writer who had yet to find himself. *Dorian Gray* "has plot and it has wit; but is intellectually and stylistically immature". The third and fourth chapters are penetrating discussions of Wilde's dramatic efforts: *An Ideal Husband* is the most serious of Wilde's dramas, but, lacking the brilliant dialogue of the other comedies, it has substance seldom credited; the melodramatic *A Woman of No Importance* is less successful than *Lady Windermere's Fan*, but in the former is found the first glimmer of the black humour Wilde would perfect in *The Importance of Being Earnest*. The fifth chapter delves into his fairy-tales, "slighted . . . because they offer inconvenient evidence that Wilde is more complex than he looks at first glance". The sixth chapter adversely criticizes *De Profundis*, yet enthusiastically lauds *The Ballad of Reading Gaol*. The final chapter dispassionately examines Wilde's essays, and concludes with an acerbic evaluation of the aesthete and author as "a major talent of minor accomplishment".

ELLMANN aimed to do for Wilde what he had done so successfully for W.B. Yeats and James Joyce: produce the definitive biography. With admirable facility he unfolds Wilde's life as a "tragedy", his scandals and trials as a "fall" occasioned by the hubris of a too-active socialite. Holding that the child is father of the man, he covers Wilde's early years in more detail than previous biographers have, and then attempts to portray his career as a continuous development. Along the way he discusses Wilde's admiration for Pater, Henry James, and a host of French writers who gave his life and works direction. Despite several errors in fact and judgement, most critics concurred that Ellmann had written a superior biography. To what degree Wilde's homosexuality fired his creativity remains matter for dispute, but there is no debate, Ellmann holds, that among writers of the 1890s Wilde is "the only one whom everyone still reads". Ellmann judges that: *The Picture of Dorian Gray* serves as "a critique of aestheticism", and readers of the novel are "won by Dorian's beauty and regretful . . . of his waste of it, so that he has something of the glamour of a Faust . . . "; *The Importance of Being Earnest* crowned Wilde's career; and his other comedies, especially *Lady Windermere's Fan* and *An Ideal Husband* are "ingenious" in structure and characterization. Ellmann covers the controversies surrounding *Salomé* in great detail, but avoids a critique of the work. He notes that Wilde hoped his *Ballad of Reading Gaol* would be regarded as a "masterpiece" though critics expressed reservations, and W.E. Henley summed up the poem best, perhaps, when he labelled it "a jumble of excellence and rubbish". *De Profundis* Ellmann interprets as "a kind of dramatic monologue" and "elegy for lost greatness"; after designating it as "regenerative", he dilates on its central theme: "to mistreat the guilty, as to mistreat the innocent, was contrary to the canons of art as expressed by Christ the supreme artist and Wilde his prophet".

GAGNIER's volume is meant to pay tribute to one of Ireland's greatest verbal artists through a judicious selection of essays reflective of contemporary criticism. The 16 essays chosen constitute an assessment of what Wilde's work means at this junction of literary history and social theory. There has been substantial scholarship on Wilde and the 1890s, but much of it has been textual, eminently valuable but not of theoretical or critical interest. This volume spans a wide realm of thought subsumed under four major categories, which Gagnier discusses in a long Introduction. They are: Wilde and society; Wilde on wit – *The Importance of Being Earnest*; Wildean critique; and Wilde and suffering, or universality. Some of the essays, such as Jonathan Dollimore's "Different Desires", are politically oriented and aspire to intervene in broader cultural life. Others want platforms for personal style, brilliancy, ingenuity, representing the *outré* so admired in Wilde's works; Patrice Hanrion's "Aesthetic Criticism, Useless Art" is one such essay. Still others make a persuasive case for Wilde's connections and philosophical syntheses, such as Philip E. Smith's "Protoplasmic Hierarchy and Philosophical Harmony: Science and Hegelian Aesthetics in Oscar Wilde's Notebooks". Included are essays Gagnier describes as far from her own perspectives: one, for example, considers the relationship between the author of *A Rebours* and the author of *Dorian Gray* (James Winchell's "Wilde and Huysmans: Autonomy, Reference, and the Myth of Expiation"); another is intended to provide material for the monastic exercise of *lectio*, which leads to meditation, prayer, and contemplation (Brother John Albert's "The Christ of Oscar Wilde"). Among the better-known contributors are Camille Paglia ("Oscar Wilde and the English Epicene"), Kerry Powell ("Algernon's Other Brothers"), and Ian Small (Semiotics and Oscar Wilde's Accounts of Art").

SMALL's own publication is essentially a review of the most significant research on Wilde's life and work. It counteracts biographical inaccuracies and supplies an up-to-date census and description of manuscript materials. Chapter 1 leads off with "The Myth of Wilde". The chapters that follow focus successively on "Biography Reconsidered", "Letters", "Literary Histories", "Major Critical Studies", "Editions", and "Bibliographies". All this research, especially that of the last 35 years, portrays a figure quite different from the tragic egoist that Richard Ellmann wrote about. Of special value are the almost 600 articles and books listed in the "General Bibliography".

G.A. CEVASCO

Wilder, Thornton 1897–1975

American novelist and dramatist

Burbank, Rex, *Thornton Wilder*, New York: Twayne, 1961
Castronovo, David, *Thornton Wilder*, New York: Frederick Ungar, 1986
Haberman, Donald C., *The Plays of Thornton Wilder: A Critical Study*, Middletown, Connecticut: Wesleyan University Press, 1967
Papajewski, Helmut, *Thornton Wilder*, translated by John Conway, New York: Frederick Ungar, 1968
Williams, Mary Ellen, *A Vast Landscape: Time in the Novels of Thornton Wilder*, Pocatello: Idaho State University Press, 1979

Despite popular acclaim for his plays and novels, and the award of such literary honours as the Pulitzer Prize, the National Institute of Arts and Letters Gold Medal, and the Presidential Medal, Thornton Wilder has fallen into neglect. This is rather mysterious in view of the philosophical interests and the narrative innovations of Wilder's fiction – characteristics that would seem to invite theoretical consideration.

CASTRONOVO explains the contemporary lack of interest in Wilder's work as the result of his protean nature: because his works do not fall easily into a single category or conform to a single literary description, because his styles and settings vary, because he is both novelist and playwright, essentially because he represents no coherent vision of the world, Wilder has been neglected in favour of his more accessible contemporaries. But here again emerges a problem, for while Wilder moved in literary circles broadly labelled "modernist", his major works cover the period from 1922 to 1973, and as a result Wilder again eludes the easy description of "modernist" or even "postmodernist". Castronovo makes a compelling case for the significance of Wilder's literary achievement. His analyses of the texts follow patterns of thematic or stylistic coherence rather than a strict chronological organization. So *The Cabala*, *The Bridge of San Luis Rey*, and *The Woman of Andros* are treated in terms of the theme of isolation; this is followed by discussion of Wilder's one-act plays; *Our Town*, *The Merchant of Yonkers*, and *The Skin of Our Teeth* are viewed in the context of Wilder's exploration of what survival means; and *Heaven's My Destination* and *Theophilus North* are considered as picaresque novels, and *The Ides of March* and *The Eighth Day* are discussed as philosophical novels. The kind of unity Castronovo seeks in Wilder's writing is based on Wilder's changing attitudes towards art and, especially, his responses to the European influences that marked all his work.

Where Castronovo seeks unity in the diversity of Wilder's writing, WILLIAMS explores the representation in his novels of Wilder's own quest for coherence within the diversity of lived experience. She argues that the effort to transcend linear historical time in order to represent a transcendent consciousness motivates Wilder's fiction, and links his efforts to those of contemporaries such as James Joyce, William Faulkner, Gertrude Stein, and others. Williams emphasises the mystical nature of Wilder's vision and relates this vision to his recreation of the "eternal present" in his novels. Her analysis of the texts is very competent, and her identification of influences and points of similarity with a range of texts from the European and American literary traditions is very informative. Together, Castronovo and Williams present a convincing case for re-evaluating Thornton Wilder.

Castronovo and Williams both write after Wilder's death and so they have before them a complete canon with which to work. This was not the case for earlier critics, and perhaps explains the relative lack of interest in identifying the unity or coherence of Wilder's writing among them. BURBANK's was the first book-length study of Wilder's work. He begins with a short account of the vicissitudes of Wilder's critical reputation, before setting himself the task of evaluating Wilder's achievement on literary grounds alone. Burbank sets out to clear away the false impressions that have adhered to Wilder and to place his work within the American literary tradition. Burbank emphasises the mystical or religious dimension of the writings, Wilder's interest in classical civilization, and his extensive experience of travel, and it is the parallel between the work and the life that lends Burbank's study its own unity of intention.

PAPAJEWSKI writes more an appreciation than a critical analysis of Wilder's writings. He seeks points of continuity among the texts of Wilder's increasing output, identifying changes of emphasis, patterns of response or reaction to earlier works. So Papajewski pursues a structure of evolution within Wilder's canon. While the discussion is detailed and subtle, the approach does tend towards repetition of the stories, with a consequent weakening of the analytical force of the study as a whole.

HABERMAN deals solely with Wilder's plays, but he provides a comprehensive account which places the drama firstly in the context of Wilder's life and his literary career and then elucidates the particular themes that Wilder explores in dramatic form, as well as the characteristics of that dramatic form itself – characterisation, narration, and the "American" use of language. In the concluding chapter, Haberman situates Wilder's achievement in the context of world literature. This is a sensitive and articulate account, which provides more than simply an introduction to the plays.

DEBORAH L. MADSEN

Williams, Tennessee 1911–1983

American dramatist, screenwriter, and short-story writer

Bigsby, C.W.E., *A Critical Introduction to Twentieth Century American Drama, Volume 2: Williams, Miller, Albee*, Cambridge and New York: Cambridge University Press, 1984

Boxill, Roger, *Tennessee Williams*, London: Macmillan, 1987; New York: St Martin's Press, 1987

Falk, Signi L., *Tennessee Williams*, New York: Twayne, 1962, revised (Boston) 1978

Hirsch, Foster, *A Portrait of the Artist: The Plays of Tenessee Williams*, Port Washington, New York: Kennikat Press, 1979

Kolin, Philip C. (ed.), *Confronting Tennessee Williams's "A Streetcar Named Desire": Essays in Critical Pluralism*, Westport, Connecticut: Greenwood Press, 1993

Londré, Felicia Hardison, *Tennessee Williams*, New York: Frederick Ungar, 1979

Murphy, Brenda, *Tennessee Williams and Elia Kazan: A Collaboration in the Theatre*, Cambridge and New York: Cambridge University Press, 1992

Phillips, Gene D., *The Films of Tennessee Williams*, Philadelphia: Art Alliance Press, 1980; London: Associated University Presses, 1980

Savran, David, *Communists, Cowboys, and Queers: The Politics of Masculinity in the Work of Arthur Miller and Tennessee Williams*, Minneapolis: University of Minnesota Press, 1992

Schroeder, Patricia, *The Presence of the Past in Modern American Drama*, Rutherford, New Jersey: Fairleigh Dickinson University Press, 1989

Tischler, Nancy M., *Tennessee Williams: Rebellious Puritan*, New York: Citadel Press, 1961
Tischler, Nancy M., *Tennessee Williams*, Austin, Texas: Steck-Vaughan, 1969
Thompson, Judith J., *Tennessee Williams' Plays: Memory, Myth, and Symbol*, New York: Peter Lang, 1987
Yacowar, Maurice, *Tennessee Williams and Film*, New York: Frederick Ungar, 1977

Tennessee Williams's early reputation was founded on the Broadway success of *The Glass Menagerie* in 1945, and confirmed by what is arguably the most central play in the modern American canon, *A Streetcar Named Desire* (1947), followed by *Cat on a Hot Tin Roof* (1955), *Suddenly Last Summer* (1958), and *Sweet Bird of Youth* (1959). If his later work marked a falling off from the high accomplishment of these plays, he has remained in the public domain through revivals of his great plays and through film versions of his work. Criticism has frequently centred on the way his plays explore the gap between myths of the South and the reality of the lives of his characters. Much of the best writing on him is in theatre reviews and journal articles; there are good book-length studies of him, but fewer than one would expect, a circumstance conditioned by the relative poverty of theatre criticism until recently. This discussion is largely concerned with studies that have appeared since the late 1970s.

TISCHLER's two books are interesting for their discussion of Williams unburdened by the problem of his homosexuality, which became a public issue in the 1970s. She concentrates on the relationship of the plays to Williams's early years, and his experience of psychoanalysis in the 1960s. She reads much of the work as determined by his Puritan upbringing, his intense relationship with his mother, and his various psychoses engendered by illnesses real or imagined. The nub of her work lies in the view that Williams's drama exposes a persistent conflict between opposing forces, as in those between the flesh and the spirit, reality and dreams, and the sense of the brutality of common life as against idealised expectations of it.

FALK's study follows the format of the Twayne series it comes in, a standard life-and-works treatment, with chapters on all Williams's work including his prose and poetry. Her thematic readings of the plays centre on character analysis, in which she categorises the major protagonists into formulaic types: his women are either protesting gentlewomen enshrined in Southern views of ideal womanhood, or their erotic and divisive alter egos, while his principle male characters are seen as failed heroes.

BOXILL's short study is intended for the uninitiated reader, and provides a good general introduction to the work. He has single chapters on all the major plays and treats the remaining works under three headings, "Wanderer Plays", "Reversal Plays", and "Late Plays". The rather loose categorisations of the first two of these headings focus on recurrent character-types in Williams, the first exemplified by the figure of Val Xavier in *Orpheus Descending*, and the second by the figure of Blanche Dubois as representative of the type of wounded Southern belle. This is a good book to go to for a statement of Williams's concerns, his technical accomplishment, and his overall achievement.

HIRSCH takes the view that all Williams's plays are homosexual fantasies, in which Williams is constrained by the homophobic milieu of the 1940s and 1950s. Hirsch covers all the plays in pursuit of these arguments, and goes as far as reading Blanche Du Bois as "an effeminate male" and a "guilt-ridden gay"; but how this squares with Blanche's response to the discovery of her young husband's homosexuality is a difficulty. He reads *Suddenly Last Summer* as Williams's "ultimate homophile fantasy", and argues that no play is "written on the pattern of the traditional heterosexual chase", generally a tenable view but difficult to sustain in relation to *Orpheus Descending*. Hirsch's book is of interest precisely for his foregrounding of the problematic representation of homosexuality in the plays, and the view that the failure of the late plays is a consequence of Williams's writing "more to explore his own problems than to entertain audiences".

BIGSBY's analysis of the ways in which Williams developed a theatre of poetic symbolism in the early major plays is very persuasive, for though he sees this lyricism as a form of self-conscious poeticism, he sees it as "equally capable of rising to genuine eloquence", and Bigsby writes particularly well on *The Glass Menagerie*, the first of Williams's so-called "memory plays", which has a "fluidity of style that Williams came to value both as a theatrical mode and a personal strategy". Bigsby does not allow biographical materials to impede his discussion of the plays in this sustained critique, which represents one of the most intelligent commentaries on Williams currently available, though his treatment of the work after *The Night of the Iguana* is relatively cursory, because he sees it as unconsciously parodic of the earlier plays.

LONDRÉ, however, concentrates on the plays of the 1960s and 1970s, and provides a synopsis, some critical commentary, and notes about production issues for each play, and establishes lines of connections to the other works. She discusses film and television productions of these works, and compares interpretations by directors and actors. This is a helpful study of an area of Williams's work generally less highly regarded than his earlier work.

KOLIN's edition of essays on *A Streetcar Named Desire* offers an attempt to reflect ways of writing about this central play from a variety of contemporary theoretical perspectives, and accomplishes this mission with some success. The result offers feminist, Marxist, and reader-response readings, mythology-based readings, cultural studies, chaos and anti-chaos theory, film aesthetics, translation theory, and formalist criticism. Some notable contributions include: William Kleb's discussion of the play's confrontation with sexuality, looked at from Michael Foucault's writings on sex; Calvin Bedient's discourse on Blanche Dubois as the embodiment of a "poetics of grief"; June Schlueter's discussion of history and the authority of narrative voice. My own (Kelly's) discussion of the vexed issue of ethnicity and the desire for American identity in the play, polarized by the conflict between Blanche and Stanley Kowalski, is also included.

MURPHY's account of the creative relationship between Williams and his finest director, Elia Kazan, is based on researches into the production history of four plays Kazan directed on Broadway – *A Streetcar Named Desire*, *Camino Real*, *Cat on a Hot Tin Roof*, and *Sweet Bird of Youth* – developing in the process a production idiom, which came to be known as "the American style" in the theatre of the 1950s. Murphy describes this style as one of "subjective realism", a way of making Williams's poetic and symbolic plays acceptable to the tastes of Broadway audiences. Murphy shows that the boundary lines between writer and director were submerged by the intensely interactive part they played in each other's domain throughout these productions, a situation that led some contemporary critics to claim that Kazan was effectively a "co-author" of *A Streetcar Named Desire*, a charge repudiated by both Williams and Kazan. This is one of the best recent books on Williams, and Murphy's recovery of the production processes of these major plays makes for absorbing reading.

Savaran and Schroeder both place Williams next to his contemporary dramatists. SAVRAN's sophisticated comparative study of Miller and Williams has a theoretical grounding unusual in theatre criticism. He makes use of late Marxist theory, psychoanalysis, deconstruction, feminism, and gay studies in this endeavour to define Miller's and Williams's work, which he reads as deeply ingrained in the complex historical forces that underlay the social and demographic upheavals of late-1940s' and 1950s' United States. His achievement is to situate the anxiety about gender positions, especially for men, as central to the dynamics of their plays. In Miller's work Savran reads the failure of his male subjects to adhere to a coherent model of masculinity as that which induces crises of identity throughout all Miller's male-centred texts. Savran's work on Williams is more innovatory and convincing, partly because he sees Williams's radical negotiation of these issues as open-ended and challenging, and responds to the late experimental plays and to Williams's own homophobia in a way that makes Savran one of the acutest critics of Williams for many years. In particular, he sees Williams's use of poetic and symbolic experimentation in his plays as an inspired way of expanding the conventions of realist theatre in order to challenge the conventional representation of heterosexual masculinity.

SCHROEDER looks at Williams, Eugene O'Neill, Thornton Wilder, and Miller to see how they respond to the sense of the past. Her primary interest is in the technical devices they use to manipulate drama's "unique relationship to time", and argues that they transpose the expository elements of their plays to the centre of the present action, rather than prior to it, as is conventional. Schroeder's attention to these technical issues rather limits her analysis of the plays themselves, and in Williams's case we are given not much more than the sense that his characters are indeed bound by the dreams of a romance world the present can never live up to. The scope of this study is too ambitious for its abbreviated scale, though the central idea of it is a good one.

THOMPSON offers a Jungian reading of Williams, seeing recurrent structural patterns in all the plays, which give organic unity to their use of memory, myth, and symbol. She proposes that these patterns are based on the narration of a past event in the memory of a protagonist, a telling that invests both tale and teller with mythic significance, followed by a dramatization of this memory, or its re-enactment, in a "demythicized" and consequently ironized version. Further, the nature and content of this mythicized memory determines a play's symbolic characterization, mythical allusions, and archetypal images, while its demythicized re-enactment decides its dramatic outcome, theme, and mode. In a conventional way, Thompson privileges the eight plays from *The Glass Menagerie* through to *The Night of the Iguana*, and the late plays are given very brief attention.

Two studies here concentrate on Williams's film work. YACOWAR provides a wealth of documentation about the films, listing directors, producers, screenwriters, and so on, and gives a bibliography of articles about Williams in film books and journals. In his commentary he discusses the problems of adapting plays for film, and shares the widely credited theory of adaptation, as it applies to films of novels, that absolute fidelity to the original text is much less important than the way in which the changes made to it "serve the intention and thrust of the original". This leads him to value the film versions of *The Night of the Iguana* and *Boom!* as the best adaptations, "because in both there is the energy and freedom of original creativity", as is also true of the film of *A Streetcar Named Desire*.

PHILLIPS gives a very internalised view of the film industry's treatment of the plays, responding to the film versions by way of commentary on them from Williams himself, the directors, performers, and designers, and covers all the technical aspects of film-making from the conception of the screenplay through to issues of film censorship. Phillips honours the *auteur* theory of film-making by organising his book in chapters on the directors of the films. This is an excellent study – detailed, informative, and largely non-judgemental.

LIONEL KELLY

Williams, William Carlos 1883–1963

American poet, dramatist, short-story writer, and essayist

Ahearn, Barry, *William Carlos Williams and Alterity: The Early Poetry*, Cambridge and New York: Cambridge University Press, 1994

Callan, Ron, *William Carlos Williams and Transcendentalism: Fitting the Crab in a Box*, London: Macmillan, 1992

Conrad, Bryce, *Refiguring America: A Study of William Carlos Williams' "In the American Grain*, Urbana: Illinois University Press, 1990

Cushman, Stephen, *William Carlos Williams and the Meanings of Measure*, New Haven, Connecticut, and London: Yale University Press, 1985

Diggory, Terence, *William Carlos Williams and the Ethics of Painting*, Princeton, New Jersey: Princeton University Press, 1991

Driscoll, Kerry, *William Carlos Williams and the Maternal Muse*, Ann Arbor, Michigan: UMI Research Press, 1987

Duffey, Bernard, *A Poetry of Presence: The Writing of William Carlos Williams*, Madison: University of Wisconsin Press, 1986

Frail, David, *The Early Politics and Poetics of William Carlos Williams*, Ann Arbor, Michigan: UMI Research Press, 1988

Kallet, Marilyn, *Honest Simplicity in William Carlos Williams' "Asphodel, That Greeny Flower"*, Baton Rouge: Louisiana State University Press, 1985
Rapp, Carl, *William Carlos Williams and Romantic Idealism*, Hanover, New Hampshire: University Press of New England, 1984
Sayre, Henry M., *The Visual Text of William Carlos Williams*, Urbana: University of Illinois Press, 1984
Schmidt, Peter, *William Carlos Williams, the Arts, and Literary Tradition*, Baton Rouge: Louisiana State University Press, 1988
Tapscott, Stephen, *American Beauty: William Carlos Williams and the Modernist Whitman*, New York: Columbia University Press, 1984
Tomlinson, Charles (ed.), *William Carlos Williams: A Critical Anthology*, Harmondsworth, Middlesex: Penguin, 1972
Weaver, Mike, *William Carlos Williams: The American Background*, Cambridge: Cambridge University Press, 1971

As a poet Williams celebrated locality and community against the high cultural imperialism of Ezra Pound and T.S. Eliot, though he was a life-long friend of Pound. He responded bitterly to the publication of Eliot's *The Waste Land* for the way the poem seemed to sever connections with its human audience because of Eliot's learned allusive method and his impersonal poetics. Williams wanted an American poetry that would speak for the particularity of the American experience of civilization and culture in a language accessible to everyone, a position celebrated in his programmatic rallying call that there are "no ideas but in things". Commentators on his work address the following major concerns: his early and late use of the visual arts, especially painting, as an instigation for his poems; his explorations into poetic structure in his theories of rhythm, measure, and form to find ways of writing against the grain of conventional metrics and prosody, and to make a language faithfully expressive of the native idioms of American speech; his five-part epic poem *Paterson*, centred on a particular American place through a specific history; his novels and prose writings, especially *In the American Grain* , his "alternative" celebration of American history; and his attitude to women, an issue which has come more into focus in recent years. In addition there remains the complex problem of Williams's relation to Romanticism and modernism. The recent publication of an authoritative two-volume edition of the *Complete Poems* (1987–88), edited by A. Walton Litz and Christopher MacGowan, and MacGowan's authoritative edition of *Paterson* has provided much-needed improvements in the textual status of Williams's poetry.

WEAVER's study of the American context of Williams's work remains absolutely indispensable. Invariably cited in all subsequent accounts of Williams, Weaver is especially interesting on *Paterson*, and provides a wealth of detailed information about the sources Williams went to in composing the poem. Weaver has chapters on every important aspect of Williams, his relations with other poets and painters, his technical experiments with prosody and form, his endeavour to write in a genuinely American idiom, and the nature of Williams's ideas of the national and civic responsibilities of the writer.

TOMLINSON's Penguin anthology of Williams criticism is an unrivalled bargain, and it is very irritating that Penguin has allowed this brilliant critical series to lapse. Tomlinson, a British poet and academic of great distinction, guides us through the various sections of the anthology, arranged chronologically, in a way that gives a clear shape to the entire arc of Williams's creative career. It is difficult to isolate the best of many fine essays herein, but my choices are A. Kingsley Weatherhead's indispensable "William Carlos Williams: Prose, Form and Measure", one of the best things ever written on Williams, Ruth Grogan's "The Influence of Painting on William Carlos Williams", and the critical essays by R.P. Blackmur, Denis Donoghue, Albert Cook, and Hugh Kenner. This collection includes important commentary by Williams's fellow poets Pound, Wallace Stevens, Louis Zukofsky, Marianne Moore, Robert Lowell, and others, materials central to our understanding of Williams in relation to American modernism and to the power of his example for his contemporaries and successor poets.

DUFFEY's book takes on the whole corpus of Williams's work, considered as an "interrelated and interdependent web". Duffey works with a series of defining categories of aesthetic practice derived from the work of the American theorist Kenneth Burke, in which the central concepts are those of "scene", "person" "agency" "purpose", and "action" – terms that describe for Burke the totality of the writer's "dramatic engagement" with his or her field of reference. In this application of Burkeian terminology, Duffey reads *In the American Grain* and Williams's novels as reflective of the imperative of scene; *Kora in Hell*, *Paterson*, and the late sequence of poems, *Pictures from Brueghel*, as examples of poetic person; the shorter poems as poetic agency; and so on, through Burke's categories. This ambitious totalizing view of Williams's work is not for beginners but for initiates who know the work well.

Three books discussed here – by Rapp, Callan, and Tapscott – consider Williams in the context of nineteenth-century poetic traditions.

RAPP sees Williams as the embodiment of a modern version of Ralph Waldo Emerson's idea of the poet, indeed the one who fulfils this idea better than anyone since Emerson. Williams is said to share Emerson's belief in the work of art as an instrument of mental and spiritual power, one whose experiments with forms and language represent an endeavour to regain "an original vitality or innocence" lost to the present. Thus, Williams's objectivist poetry, his concern with "measure", and his search for American speech rhythms reflect activities defined by Rapp as "Thinking as Salvation". The value of this study lies in its challenge to modernist readings of Williams, and in the authority of Rapp's version of an Emersonian Williams.

CALLAN offers a controversial study of Williams's attitude to the figure of metaphor. Against the orthodox view that Williams distrusted metaphors because he was primarily interested in the world of particulars ("no ideas but in things"), Callan argues that the poet began his writing career "with a profound sense of the relatedness of things" and that this sense sustained his work throughout, so that at the end of his life he was still concerned with "the activity of relating, always the conditions of metaphor". In addition, Callan also places Williams in the tradition of American Transcendentalism, and sees him as the fullest embodiment of Emerson's prescriptive definition of the true poet as a "reconciler". An unusual aspect of this study lies in Callan's use of the poet's novels as the "laboratory" of his experiments with ideas of relatedness. This provocative and passionate book is more accessible than this summary account of it will suggest.

TAPSCOTT's interest is both in Williams as a poet in the tradition founded by Walt Whitman, and in modernist ways of reading Whitman. This comparative study reads Williams's objectivist poetry as an endeavour to unite his imperative concern with the local and particular to a "visionary idea of a new language". This complex book is therefore concerned both with the subjects of Williams's poetry and the experiments with line and form that complicate his representation of those subjects.

AHEARN takes the view that Williams's critics have paid insufficient attention to the paradoxes and contradictions of his work and here proposes that the poet exploited "alterity", the spirit and practice of contradiction, as a creative strategy. The restless, unsettled condition of his early poems, which he constantly revised, and the persistent innovation of his verse and prose books, each of them disruptive of the conventions of kind or genre, reflect the work of a man who used anxiety, conflict, and crisis as creative opportunities to determine the conditions and appearance of his work. This is the kind of argument about Williams that works best in relation to his early work – the focus of Ahearn's study – and is less applicable to the more stable products of his late years.

CONRAD has written a powerful revisionary study of *In the American Grain*, where he opens up "the historical and structural elements of the book", relating Williams's text to its sources in order to express a view of it as "anarchically disruptive of systematic thought". Much of Conrad's well-researched study is based on a belief in Williams's sympathy with a modernist, if not postmodernist, view of the fictionality of all writing of history as opposed to the conventional historians' view of the uses of history as a means to securing an objective view of the events of the past. Conrad's account of Williams's reading for this book, his strategies of composition, his editorial interventions in the materials he culled from, and the exploitative uses he made of historical texts set against each other is very impressive, and he provides a mine of information about how this seminal work was put together.

CUSHMAN's book is valuable as one of the more extended accounts of Williams's experiments with metre and prosody, what Williams called "measure". Cushman rightly reads these concerns as an aspect both of technique and of the poet's "vision", his way of representing his world. Cushman works through close analysis of particular poems, examining their "measure" and Williams's taste for innovatory forms of versification and typographical variety. Cushman discusses Williams's attitude to "free verse", a form which entailed "warring elements of freedom and discipline", and from this leads into an account of Williams's theories of the "variable foot", a theory of prosody that few writers on Williams have ever been comfortable with. The rather technical preoccupations of Cushman's study are an inescapable feature of serious engagement with Williams's poetry, and this book is one of the most helpful accounts of these matters.

DIGGORY'S short but difficult book challenges poststructuralist and deconstructive readings of Williams in order to shift the debate about his work from epistemology, or theories of knowledge, to ethics. To do this, Diggory analyses Williams's use of Pieter Brueghel's painting "The Adoration of the Kings", and from this disputes Michel Foucault and Jacques Derrida's belief that violence is inseparable from writing. In turning to the poet's concern with the art of painting Diggory discovers "a critical practice that successfully resists violence". He calls on Julia Kristeva's psychoanalytic and linguistic model of an ethical imperative, which he holds to be close to Williams's beliefs, especially in the investigation of the structure of relationships explored in the Brueghel painting. Finally Diggory wants to see Williams's preoccupation with Brueghel's work as a means of formulating his ideas about the relations between reader and text, self and other, and viewer and object. Diggory's intention is to show that the fundamental imperative of Williams's work is with the ethics and conditions of being and otherness.

Several studies take recourse to biographical sources. DRISCOLL explores the thesis that Williams and his mother "comprise an imaginative universe, the 'he and she of it', spinning in perpetual orbit about one another, seeking coalescence", and that his mother was his primary muse, the spiritual source of his creativity. Driscoll notes the repeated figurations of women in Williams's work and the "generic appeal" of women to him, but argues that his grandmother, mother, and wife were central to him not only because of the intimacy and duration of their relationship to him, but also for the "powerful influences they exerted on his imagination", and that of these three his mother was the most central. In this reading, Williams's neglected book *Yes, Mrs. Williams* assumes a significance otherwise denied it, and is here treated as his "failed magnum opus", an unrealized counterpart to *Paterson*. Driscoll is very persuasive on all these issues, especially in her account of the way in which Elena Williams influenced her son to embrace the idea of an ethnically varied demotic American vocabulary and speech, even if in public he sought to obscure the origins of his own language.

FRAIL offers a biography of Williams's early politics in relation to his practice as a poet, in which Williams's political convictions led to an acceptance of the ideal of liberal democratic service offset against the insistent individualism of his life as an artist, a conflict defined by Frail as the opposition between "poetic radicalism and political nostalgia". The best parts of this book are the last two chapters in which Frail establishes an analogy between Williams's politics of localism and his poetics of presence, where Frail can show a fusion between the poet's broad political commitment to community in relation to his endeavour to realise or speak for that community in his poetry. This is a very well-researched study, which makes a substantial contribution to our understanding of the first phase of Williams's career as a poet.

KALLET wants an uncomplicated reading of Williams's famous late love poem to his wife, *Asphodel, That Greeny Flower*, one of the longer poems that always finds a ready audience because of its nature and ambition. Kallet argues for a synthesis between the lyrical impulse of the poem and Williams's attempt to improvise within it in "a disciplined manner". The confluence of these terms suggests the difficulties of this enterprise, and Kallet should be credited for making so much out of an extremely difficult task, for arguing with considerable conviction for a synthesis of programme and realisation in a poem where contradiction between purpose and effect remain in evidence.

There has been a recent wealth of critical commentary on Williams and the visual arts. SAYRE's book is one of the better examples of this approach. He is both an art historian and a literary critic, which gives him an advantage in this respect. In this scholarly book, Sayres places Williams within the frame of the aesthetics of modern painting, from cubism to abstract expressionism, and argues that Williams's imagination is essentially visual rather than aural. This view contends with that which sees Williams as the primary modernist poet of the spoken word and organic form. Ultimately, Sayre sees Williams's poetry as the creation of a "new poetic space", where the visual and the aural "unendingly compete".

SCHMIDT's study of Williams and the visual arts in relation to literary tradition is also impressive. It offers a finely detailed exposition of the variety of visual and verbal contexts and traditions of Williams's engagement with the visual arts, and considerably extends our understanding of the impact of cubism and Dadaism on him. Schmidt reads *Paterson* as the sum of the visually inspired aesthetic that Williams found in Precisionist, cubist, and Dadaist aesthetics, developed from 1913 through to the making of *Paterson*, and considers the literary tradition that lies behind *Paterson*. Schmidt argues for the poem as an endeavour to renew the American Edenic myth in a way that can accommodate America's urban and technological conquests, while relating the poem to an American transcendental imperative. Schmidt then argues for *Paterson*'s relation to Wordsworth's autobiographical epic *The Prelude*, suggesting that Williams shared with Wordsworth a sense of the necessary incompleteness of all modern epic quests of self-realisation, where the "lacunae and fissures" written into their texts are not signs of creative failure but "badges of honour".

LIONEL KELLY

Wilson, Angus 1913–1991

English novelist, critic, and essayist

Angus Wilson issue of *Twentieth-Century Literature*, 29(2), 1983

Bergonzi, Bernard, *The Situation of the Novel*, London: Macmillan, 1970, 2nd edition, 1979

Cox, C.B., "Angus Wilson: Studies in Depression", in his *The Free Spirit: A Study of Liberal Humanism in the Novels of George Eliot, Henry James, E.M. Forster, Virginia Woolf, Angus Wilson*, London and New York: Oxford University Press, 1963

Faulkner, Peter, *Angus Wilson: Mimic and Moralist*, London: Secker & Warburg, 1980

Gardner, Averil, *Angus Wilson*, Boston: Twayne, 1985

Gindin, James, "Angus Wilson's Qualified Nationalism", in his *Post-War British Fiction: New Accents and Attitudes*, Berkeley: University of California Press, 1961; London: Cambridge University Press, 1962

Gindin, James, *The Harvest of a Quiet Eye: The Novel of Compassion*, Bloomington: Indiana University Press, 1971

Gransden, K.W., *Angus Wilson*, London: Longman, 1969

Halio, Jay L., *Angus Wilson*, Edinburgh: Oliver & Boyd, 1964

Halio, Jay L. (ed.), *Critical Essays on Angus Wilson*, Boston: G.K. Hall, 1985

McSweeney, Kerry, "Angus Wilson: Diversity, Depth, and Obsessive Energy", in his *Four Contemporary Novelists: Angus Wilson, Brian Moore, John Fowles, V.S. Naipaul*, Montreal: McGill-Queen's University Press, 1983; London: Scolar Press, 1983

Mander, John, "The Short Stories of Angus Wilson", in his *The Writer and Commitment*, London: Secker & Warburg, 1961; Westport, Connecticut: Greenwood Press, 1975

Rabinovitz, Rubin, *The Reaction Against Experiment in the English Novel, 1950–1960*, New York: Columbia University Press, 1967

Swinden, Patrick, *The English Novel of History and Society, 1940–80: Richard Hughes, Henry Green, Anthony Powell, Angus Wilson, Kingsley Amis, V.S. Naipaul*, London: Macmillan, 1984

Criticism of Wilson centres on two associated concerns – his treatment of the problems of liberal humanism in postwar Britain and the mixture in his work of more traditional and more experimental fictional modes. It is broadly divided between studies devoted exclusively to him and those in which he appears alongside other, mainly contemporary, novelists.

Among the latter kind, MANDER's book analyses the short fiction, discerning an awkward relation between often superficial social documentary and more serious, intensive psychological scrutiny, a contradictory mix of Marx and Freud. In the best stories, however, a dialectical balance obtains where social and psychological concerns blend productively, revealing Wilson's commitment to a socialist humanism modified by liberalism.

A short chapter in GINDIN's 1963 book places Wilson foremost among contemporary British novelists, relishing the "malice" of the early stories but centring on the greater complexity and thoughtfulness discerned in the novels, which are competently if cursorily discussed. The chapter in GINDIN's later and broader study (1971) offers a more developed and reflective criticism, covering more of Wilson's work, stressing the ironising complexity and ambiguity of the later fiction, which articulates a quieter, more finely nuanced humane awareness.

COX places Wilson at the pessimistic tail-end of the liberal-humanist tradition, whose complex and changing evocation in fiction his book delineates, particularly its fictional projection in the character of the "free spirit". In a thoughtful discussion, Cox concludes that uncertainty, even distrust, with regard to the promise or possibility of liberal-humanist solutions to modernity's problems characterise Wilson's fictions.

RABINOVITZ identifies Wilson, alongside others, with a traditionalist reaction against modernist experiment. The claim that Wilson's style is "Victorian" seems excessive, but the recognition of his debt to nineteenth-century novelists is fair, albeit rather doggedly catalogued, and Rabinovitz shows some awareness of Wilson's later, more subtle and ambiguous responses, both to experimental writing and to traditional novelistic virtues.

BERGONZI's survey of the postwar British novel includes some perceptive pages on Wilson, relating him to the pattern of nostalgic recollection with dystopian anxiety characteristic of much mid-century fiction, criticising his conservatism, his failure or reluctance to experiment and innovate, and the resulting risk of parochialism, though welcoming a developing breadth and ambition in his more recent writing.

HALIO's 1964 volume was the first (though brief) book-length study of Wilson, appearing relatively early in the novelist's relatively belated career, and accordingly incomplete. A short biographical sketch precedes a mainly chronological treatment of the fiction (with additional chapters on plays and criticism). Shrewdly appreciative, noting the "histrionic sensibility" and humaneness apparent in the short stories, with the deeper questioning of humanism in the novels, it provides a helpful critical introduction.

GRANSDEN's essay, covering the earlier half of Wilson's career, notes reflections of the writer's life – especially his uneasy family background – in his work, especially the stories. It effectively analyses Wilson's satirical critique of postwar British society, his skill in social documentary producing a world mingling the louche and the fragilely respectable, where realism edges into "farce, hysteria or violence". It also traces, competently if rather limitedly, his development into the broader and more complex achievements of the novels.

FAULKNER's full-length study assesses Wilson's achievement towards the end of his career, and provides the most substantial and detailed treatment available to date. Defining itself as more formal than biographical or psychological, Faulkner's critique deals more subtly than most with the question of Wilson's traditionalism, claiming a degree of innovation, recognising an interplay of realism and artifice in the fiction, and elucidating an underlying constitutive tension between comic and serious in his art. Working chronologically it perceptively registers Wilson's development, providing quietly lucid and sympathetically astute appraisals of the stories and novels, while focusing, as its title indicates, on the varying blend in them of witty, extensive, and accurate social mimicry with increasingly complex and questioning, even sombre, humanistic concern.

McSWEENEY also discerns in Wilson a fruitful combination of more traditionally realist commitment to the novel, as social and moral document, and the novelist as humanist with a questioning of realism's complacencies. Wilson's diversity and capacity for artistic self-renewal without loss of fundamental consistency are praised, as is the blend of realist breadth and modernist depth in his fiction. Within this general perspective, measured appraisals of the novels are provided, with some reference to Wilson's critical writing.

SWINDEN, in his insightful if partisan study, relates Wilson to the revival of the historical and social novel he discerns and welcomes, following what he considers the unhappy postwar alternatives of tired provincial realism or largely sterile, narcissistic experimentalism. Detecting a disturbing animus, even sadism, in Wilson's investigation and exposure of psychological and familial conditions, Swinden connects this to the theme of evil and the equivocal humanist response portrayed with increasing complexity and breadth in the novels. Central ambiguities are teased out through close reading and through tactful linking of writer and work, in subtle, probing, and stimulating ways.

GARDNER's basically chronological study covers the novelist's whole career, relating the writing to the life (and, more explicitly than other critics, to Wilson's homosexuality) and, like others, noting the writer's ambiguous stance as both innovator and traditionalist. Critical expositions of the short stories are followed by concise treatments of the novels. Clear and informative, Gardner provides a judicious overview, more cursory than Faulkner's but nonetheless both shrewd and generous, affirming Wilson's importance as a writer of ambition and wide scope.

Twentieth-Century Literature's special issue, a *Festschrift* for Wilson's 70th birthday, contains brief recollections by various fellow writers, with brief essays on various aspects of his writing. HALIO's 1985 collection includes some early reviews, a couple of interviews, and a selection of criticism, including excerpts from some of the critical works summarised here. A balanced editorial Introduction provides a helpful survey of Wilson's career (effectively complete by this time), and a selected bibliography rounds off a useful compilation.

JEREMY LANE

Wilson, Edmund 1895–1972

American critic, novelist, poet, and dramatist

Berthoff, Warner, *Edmund Wilson*, Minneapolis: University of Minnesota Press, 1968
Castronovo, David, *Edmund Wilson*, New York: Frederick Ungar, 1984
Douglas, George H., *Edmund Wilson's America*, Lexington: University Press of Kentucky, 1983
Groth, Janet, *Edmund Wilson: A Critic for Our Time*, Athens: Ohio University Press, 1989
Paul, Sherman, *Edmund Wilson: A Study of Literary Vocation in Our Time*, Urbana: University of Illinois Press, 1965
Wain, John (ed.), *Edmund Wilson: A Celebration*, Oxford: Phaidon Press, 1978; as *Edmund Wilson: The Man and His Work*, New York: New York University Press, 1978

Critical discussion of Edmund Wilson has, understandably, tended to concentrate on his literary criticism and journalism, and there has been, regrettably, little in the way of good work on his many other literary "guises". One particular obstacle most critics have found insurmountable is the simple fact that Wilson's prose is so lucid and direct that much of the commentary amounts to little more than paraphrase.

PAUL's study, however, is a significant contribution to the intellectual and cultural history of twentieth-century America, using Wilson as one of its representative voices. He traces Wilson's work through three distinct phases – the period 1912–29, the 1930s, and from 1940 to the early 1960s. He sees Wilson as America's pre-eminent contemporary man of letters, and he pays particular attention to the influences that came to bear on Wilson's work at critical stages of his intellectual growth and his continuing debate with major movements in the history of ideas, notably with communism, the New Humanism, and literary modernism. The book is part biography, part narrative of ideas, and it remains the best single-author study of its subject.

BERTHOFF's brief guide, in the "Pamphlets on American Writers" series, is a very serviceable introduction, appended with a useful bibliography of primary and secondary works. Berthoff discusses the range of Wilson's writing, though again the primary emphasis is on the literary criticism. Only the first four pages are biographical, and readers with an interest in the life are advised to look elsewhere.

DOUGLAS is more narrowly concerned with Wilson's views of America and American civilisation; thus *Apologies to the Iroquois* is accorded fairly extensive treatment, and Wilson's most important work of historical scholarship, *To the Finland Station*, is read not for its account of the development of European socialism but for its implicit commentary on economic and social conditions in the United States of the 1930s. The particular value of Douglas's study lies in the 23 pages devoted to the reading of *Memoirs of Hecate County*.

CASTRONOVO's study assesses Wilson's life and work from literary, cultural, and psychological perspectives, and is, essentially, a record of the progress of Wilson's mind. His implicit belief that there is some defining pattern to Wilson's writing is, arguably, a weakness; but among recent single-author studies this has the particular virtue of seeking to address the full range of Wilson's *oeuvre*, notably the very good chapter devoted to his novels.

GROTH's book is devoted entirely to Wilson's literary criticism, particularly to what we might call the major critical essays: six of the 12 chapters are given over to consideration of the essays on W.B. Yeats and Marcel Proust from *Axel's Castle* (1931), the important essay on Dickens ("Dickens: The Two Scrooges") from *The Wound and the Bow* (1941), "The Ambiguity of Henry James" (the pioneering essay on James's *The Turn of the Screw*) from *The Triple Thinkers* (1938), the chapters on Harriet Beecher Stowe in *Patriotic Gore* (1962), and, finally, the controversy surrounding Wilson's review of Vladimir Nabokov's translation of Pushkin's *Eugene Onegin* and the ensuing critical debate (largely in correspondence) between Nabokov and Wilson. Groth sees Wilson's criticism as part of a broad, humanistic critical tradition, which extends back to Matthew Arnold, Sainte-Beuve, and Hippolyte Taine.

WAIN's collection of essays usefully draws together biographical and critical pieces. Notable among the former is Angus Wilson's brief essay detailing the encouragement Edmund Wilson gave him when he was embarking on a career as a writer and the way in which Wilson shaped his view of modern literature, and, among the latter, Larzer Ziff's "The Man by the Fire: Edmund Wilson and American Literature", which intelligently discusses the significance of his contribution to an understanding of his native literature. Two concluding essays, one by Clive James, the other by John Updike, assess Wilson as a creative writer, James dealing with the poetry, Updike with the fiction.

HENRY CLARIDGE

Wolfe, Thomas 1900–1938

American novelist

Donald, David Herbert, *Look Homeward: A Life of Thomas Wolfe*, Boston: Little Brown, 1987; London: Bloomsbury, 1987

Field, Leslie (ed.), *Thomas Wolfe: Three Decades of Criticism*, New York: New York University Press, 1968; London: London University Press, 1969

Geismar, Maxwell, "Thomas Wolfe: The Unfound Door", in his *Writers in Crisis: The American Novel, 1925–1940*, Boston: Houghton Mifflin, 1942; London: Secker & Warburg, 1947

Gurko, Leo, *Thomas Wolfe: Beyond the Romantic Ego*, New York: Thomas Crowell, 1975

Kazin, Alfred, "The Rhetoric and the Agony", in his *On Native Grounds: An Interpretation of Modern American Prose Literature*, New York: Harcourt, Brace & Co., and Reynal & Hitchcock, both 1942; London: Jonathan Cape, 1943

Holman, C. Hugh (ed.), *The World of Thomas Wolfe*, New York: Charles Scribner's Sons, 1962

McElderry, Bruce R., Jr., *Thomas Wolfe*, New York: Twayne, 1964

Muller, Herbert J., *Thomas Wolfe*, Norfolk, Connecticut: New Directions, 1947

Phillipson, John S. (ed.), *Critical Essays on Thomas Wolfe*, Boston: G.K. Hall, 1985

Reeves, Paschal (ed.), *Thomas Wolfe: The Critical Reception*, New York: David Lewis, 1974

Snyder, William U., *Thomas Wolfe: Ulysses and Narcissus*, Athens: Ohio University Press, 1972

Walser, Richard Gaither, *Thomas Wolfe: An Introduction and Interpretation*, New York: Barnes & Noble, 1961

Wolfe's prolixity, the sheer scale of his major novels and their attendant ambitiousness, has always made him seem something of an oddity in a generation that, under the influence of F. Scott Fitzgerald and Ernest Hemingway, had so assiduously fought for brevity, precision, and selection in fictional style. In many ways Wolfe has become something of a "marginal" figure in modern American literature, being infrequently read and studied, infrequently discussed, and offering little in the way of an influence on other writers of a kind that might make for scholarly inquiry. Most of the criticism is serviceable rather than trenchant or profound; a great deal of it explores the fiction, particularly the four major novels, as a form of autobiographical record.

KAZIN's essay remains a seminal piece of Wolfe criticism. The chapter as a whole pairs Wolfe with William Faulkner as writers who, different as they are, sound a "common note . . . of pure terror", and whose rhetoric, "a mountainous verbal splendor", is a "very American rhetoric". For Kazin, that "Wolfe proved himself the most self-centered and most inclusive novelist of his day is . . . no paradox", since his imagination derived from a tension "between his devotion to himself and his devotion to his self's interests and symbolism". Kazin describes him as "the most alert and most brilliant novelist of depression America, and an extraordinarily imaginative analyst of American types and the social disorganization of the thirties". These are large claims for Wolfe's importance, and they remain at odds with much of what one might call the "critical consensus" that has gathered around him; but Kazin's position is forcefully argued, and no better case has ever been made for Wolfe's "universal" significance as a novelist.

GEISMAR's essay is an early, and influential, account of Wolfe's work. Wolfe, he suggests, was not writing "ordinary" novels, and his ambitiousness as a writer, his commitment to writing on a large scale, frequently results in errors on a similarly "gigantic" scale; "for Wolfe, in fact, the blank page was an everlasting temptation". Geismar sees Wolfe as a writer who replicates much of America's boundless energy and its "fabulous plenty", though it is only rarely that these energies are given artistic shape and coherence, perhaps most recognizably in *You Can't Go Home Again*, which Geismar sees as a "wonderful blending of satiric and affectionate elements". Geismar's is one of the few essays on Wolfe that, while pointing to his obvious deficiencies as an imaginative artist, simultaneously makes his achievement both heroic and compelling. As such, it is indispensable reading.

MULLER's early study (in "The Makers of Modern Literature" series) attempts a serious critical case for Wolfe, seeing him as neither a "romantic" nor "freakish figure" but as one who is important "because he grappled with the fundamental issues of modern life and literature". Muller's reading (of both the life and the work) is heavily indebted to contemporary myth-criticism, and he insists on the "comprehensive and realistic" version of the "native myth" of America that emerges from Wolfe's fiction. The four major novels (*Look Homeward, Angel*; *Of Time and the River*; *The Web and the Rock*; and *You Can't Go Home Again*) are each given extended consideration, and a concluding chapter seeks to locate Wolfe's position within a larger, American tradition, with Muller pointing to his affinities with Ralph Waldo Emerson, Herman Melville, Walt Whitman, and Willa Cather, among others. This is not the most sophisticated criticism, and Muller is frequently rather vague about what he takes to be Wolfe's virtues; but it remains an acceptable "starting-point" for the student.

WALSER's is another introductory study, which combines biography (the chapter on the life is detailed and informative) with chapters on the four major novels as well as some consideration of the "other writings", notably the short stories and *A Western Journal*. Walser suggests that Wolfe is a writer who resists easy categorization, though he reads the novels as "immense *romans à clef*, with an autobiographical hero at their center". He sees the style as one which, in its innocence and exuberance, is "poetic", though the poetry, "when it lost its lyric overtones, exposed itself as rhetoric". The rhetoric and poetry, he argues, tie Wolfe to Southern writing, and explain his "exploitation" of his folk heritage. Again, Walser's book lacks critical sophistication, but it is a useful introductory guide, and the biographical chapter is especially recommended.

HOLMAN's anthology of criticism contains a number of important essays and reviews. The opening section reprints some of Wolfe's own critical writings, notably *The Story of a Novel*, and the subsequent section contains valuable first-hand accounts of Wolfe's working methods. Early, and frequently influential, reviews of the major fiction are reprinted, including those by Basil Davenport and Pamela Hansford Johnson. Another section is devoted to essays on Wolfe's style, and the concluding section offers a variety of critical "reactions" to Wolfe, notably from Bernard DeVoto, John Peale Bishop, Maxwell Geismar, Henry Steele Commager, Malcolm Cowley, and J.B. Priestley. All in all this is a very useful anthology.

McELDERRY's book (in Twayne's "United States Authors" series) is, like Walser's, biographical and critical. He attempts a "revision" of Wolfe's reputation, what he calls a "more just perspective on Wolfe's qualities and defects". To this end he emphasises the selectiveness of Wolfe's treatment of his essentially autobiographical materials, and he tries to demonstrate "not only the parallels between Wolfe's life and fiction, but also the omissions and the shifts of emphasis". The opening chapter is biographical, while the second chapter is one of the few extended discussions we have of the dramatic writings. *Look Homeward, Angel* and *Of Time and the River* are dealt with in separate chapters, as are "The Webber Novels" and the short stories; the concluding chapters provide overviews of "The Man" and "The Writer".

FIELD's anthology usefully draws together reviews and critical essays in such a way that we see the changing shape of Wolfe's critical reputation. This is, in some ways, a more thorough collection than Holman's, and there is inevitably some overlap between the two anthologies, though Field is to be recommended for his coverage of the early criticism.

SNYDER's is a psychological account, predicated on the proposition that Wolfe "was probably the most autobiographical novelist of the century". Snyder speaks of having attempted to "direct upon the writings by and about Thomas Wolfe the insights into personality of a professional clinical psychologist, and to describe the personality which becomes evident". The approach Snyder uses is markedly Freudian in character; thus Wolfe's relationship with his editor, Maxwell Perkins, is construed as one of father and son (Perkins is the "father-figure"), and his sister Mabel is a woman through whom Wolfe "shaped much of his image of his sexual ideal", Snyder pointing out that "the women with whom he formed sexual relationships of some durability were strikingly similar to Mabel". Because the life (especially the "inner" life) is the centre of Snyder's preoccupations, this study says rather less about the fiction than might be desired; but because the life was so frequently, and transparently, re-enacted in the fiction, Snyder's book is worth consulting. It has to be said, however, that the psychology is occasionally naive and simplistic, and the whole book rather clumsily written.

REEVES's anthology of criticism is exclusively of reviews of book-length works by Wolfe, and while there is some overlap with earlier anthologies this collection largely supersedes them. The emphasis is on reviews in American national magazines and newspapers, but there is a generous sampling of British reactions to Wolfe and of small-town newspaper reviews. Little that Reeves reprints offers anything in the way of extended commentary, but for insights into how Wolfe was understood by his contemporaries this is invaluable.

GURKO's is an introductory study aimed at the younger reader, and in order to elicit the interest of a new readership he "reconstructs" Wolfe as a kind of romantic hero, one who belongs as much to the mythologies of popular culture as high culture. Though the book is aimed at a high-school and undergraduate readership, it is occasionally demanding reading.

One particular feature of Gurko's approach is its insistence on Wolfe as someone who is "more" than the author of *Look Homeward, Angel*, the novel with which he is most familiarly identified.

PHILLIPSON's collection reprints essays from *The Thomas Wolfe Review*, many of them on rather narrow and specialized topics. One or two essays discuss questions of composition and reception, notably in relation to *Look Homeward, Angel*, but others have a broader remit, and Larry Rubin's essay, in particular, on Wolfe's treatment of time, both intelligently addresses a complex issue and is of interest to anyone studying chronological and temporal patterns in American (especially modernist) works of the period. John Boone Trotti's essay on Wolfe's familial and religious background is one of the best accounts of how a Presbyterian moral landscape shaped Wolfe's fiction.

DONALD's highly acclaimed biography is quite simply the best book we have on Wolfe's life and times, and is a considerable advance on the biographies by Elizabeth Nowell (1960) and Andrew Turnbull (1967). Donald was given complete access to the Wolfe papers, and his account of the life has a scholarly exactitude of detail that not only surpasses anything written before, but is also lively and readable. Donald sees him as "at once complex and simple, suspicious and withdrawn but open and affectionate, humorlessly self-absorbed but with a superb sense of humor, tragically limited and brilliantly gifted". He offers a highly informed account of Wolfe's reading, showing how consciously literary he was, and how those whom he read shaped his art; he analyses Wolfe's experimentalism, relating it intelligently to that of contemporaries such as John Dos Passos and Faulkner; and in his description of the professional relationship between Wolfe and his publisher, Perkins, he draws attention to "the ambivalent relationship that necessarily exists between authors and their publishers". This is indispensable reading for the student of Wolfe.

HENRY CLARIDGE

Wollstonecraft, Mary 1759–1797

English prose writer and novelist

Ferguson, Moira, and Janet Todd, *Mary Wollstonecraft*, Boston: Twayne, 1984

Kelly, Gary, *Revolutionary Feminism: The Mind and Career of Mary Wollstonecraft*, London: Macmillan, 1992; New York: St Martin's Press, 1992

Lorch, Jennifer, *Mary Wollstonecraft: The Making of a Radical Feminist*, Oxford: Berg, 1990; New York: St Martin's Press, 1990

Maurer, Shawn Lisa, "The Female (As) Reader: Sex, Sensibility, and the Maternal in Wollstonecraft's Fictions", in *Essays in Literature*, 19(1), 1992

Poovey, Mary, *The Proper Lady and the Woman Writer: Ideology as Style in the Works of Mary Wollstonecraft, Mary Shelley, and Jane Austen*, Chicago: University of Chicago Press, 1984

Todd, Janet (ed.), *A Wollstonecraft Anthology*, Bloomington: Indiana University Press, 1977; Cambridge: Polity Press, 1989

Tomalin, Claire, *The Life and Death of Mary Wollstonecraft*, London: Weidenfeld & Nicolson, 1974; New York: Harcourt Brace Jovanovich, 1974; revised edition, Harmondsworth, Middlesex: Penguin, 1992

The revival of interest in Mary Wollstonecraft began in the 1960s, as the women's liberation movement achieved social and cultural prominence. Scholars were greatly interested in recovering texts by women writers and seeking out works by "pioneer theorists of feminism" (as remarked by Ferguson and Todd). Thus Wollstonecraft, with such writings as *Thoughts on the Education of Daughters* (1786) and *A Vindication of the Rights of Woman* (1792), was a rediscovery of great value. A look at Wollstonecraft criticism reveals that those writing about her tend to be equally interested in her life and her work. Typically, the revivalist trend in Wollstonecraft scholarship can be traced from a new edition of *A Vindication of the Rights of Woman* published in the late 1960s, through numerous biographies written in the 1970s, to more current feminist and New-Historicist assessments of her life and works. Fascination with Wollstonecraft shows no sign of abating. Even a "bodice-ripper"-style fictionalized account of her life entitled *Vindication* (New York: Farrar, Straus, Giroux), by Frances Sherwood, appeared in 1993. Scholarly interest in Wollstonecraft's works also continues to flourish, with new considerations of her views on colonization and slavery and of her place in women's literary history appearing frequently.

TODD, in her introduction to this anthology, presents Wollstonecraft's works chronologically while discussing background information on her personal life and political views. As she synthesizes these elements, Todd argues that "clearly, Wollstonecraft came to her ideas on women's sorry situation from her own experiences as a dependent and independent woman". Todd's book covers a broad selection of Wollstonecraft's writings, some of them in excerpt form, and she also provides a useful bibliography. This anthology is a good starting point for the scholar new to Wollstonecraft.

TOMALIN's biography reconstructs Wollstonecraft's life in an engaging manner that brings to life lively depictions of Wollstonecraft, her family, and the colorful political and literary circles in which she moved. Tomalin emphasizes biographical influences on Wollstonecraft's writing, discussing the works throughout her text. The book also includes several pages of portraits of Wollstonecraft and many signficant figures in her life.

FERGUSON and TODD's study is an introduction to Wollstonecraft, which aims to acquaint the reader with her personal life, family history, and major works. They trace the development of her philosophy through her career, noting the influence of John Locke, William Cowper, Richard Price, and many others, as well as her opposition to the ideas of Edmund Burke and Jean-Jacques Rousseau. Additionally, they provide historical background on the state of women's writing and publishing at the time.

KELLY argues that "in her life and writing, Mary Wollstonecraft addressed the problematic relation of subjectivity and society, 'mind' and the state, ideology and culture, especially for women", and, in doing so, she created a feminism for her age. Kelly presents his book as a reading of Wollstonecraft's "mind" and career "in relation to the cultural revolution that founded the modern state in late eighteenth-century Britain", and he explores how the atmosphere and tenets of revolution in general affected and inspired Wollstonecraft's theories. He refutes the view of some that her writing may be seen as incompetent and inartistic, suggesting that it may *appear* thus because of the ways it challenges the traditional "gendered order of writing". The book is especially valuable for its assessment of the history of revolutionary feminism and Wollstonecraft's place in the movement.

LORCH's book is a short work with a dual approach to Wollstonecraft's biography and works. Part One traces Wollstonecraft's life from her experience in Bath as a lady's companion to her death in childbirth, 19 years later. This portion of the narrative is organized around the motifs of Wollstonecraft's "search for independence and her yearning for wholeness or integrity". Part Two traces the development of her thought from "a prim radicalism" in her early writings to a combination of "feminism and proto-socialism" in *Maria, or The Wrongs of Woman.* Additionally, Lorch pays homage to Ralph Wardle in this study, citing his work with Wollstonecraft's letters (*Collected Letters of Mary Wollstonecraft*, Ithaca, New York: Cornell University Press, 1979; *Godwin and Mary, Letters*, Lawrence: University of Kansas Press, 1967, and London: Constable, 1967) as invaluable resources for her analysis of the complexity of Wollstonecraft's character. The book also contains a useful Select Bibliography, which includes Wollstonecraft's works published during her lifetime, facsimile reproductions, and later editions, along with secondary sources on her life and works.

POOVEY explores the cultural, political, and social backgrounds regarding women in the eighteenth century. Two chapters in this book, "Man's Discourse, Woman's Heart: Mary Wollstonecraft's Two Vindications" and "Love's Skirmishes and the Triumph of Ideology" are specifically devoted to Wollstonecraft. Poovey argues that Wollstonecraft "tried to confront directly and aggressively the political inequalities perpetuated in the name of propriety", and illustrates the idea by showing how Wollstonecraft's works raise "the questions that late eighteenth-century intellectuals implicitly posed to the normative definition of woman". Poovey suggests that the early stage of Wollstonecraft's life and writing is "characterized by the persistence of two conflicting desires": the traditional emotional rewards for women of "love, gratitude, and a sense of being necessary to someone else's happiness", and "a fierce determination to be independent" – a dichotomy she analyzes in *A Vindication of the Rights of Men* and *A Vindication of the Rights of Woman.* Next, Poovey turns to the *Letters Written During a Short Residence in Sweden, Norway, and Denmark,* and discusses them in comparison with *Maria, or The Wrongs of Woman*, suggesting that in these later works, Wollstonecraft "grants subjectivity and personal experiences the authority she had previously reserved for the objective 'clear truths' of reason". Poovey's essays provide a valuable comparative analysis of Wollstonecraft's early and later works.

MAURER posits that "Wollstonecraft promotes the expression of female subjectivity through and within motherhood because she recognizes that the conditions of her society mitigate the possibility of rational and reciprocal relations between women and men". Maurer pursues this thesis through a comparative study of the unfinished novel, *Maria, or The Wrongs of Woman* and *Mary, A Fiction*, suggesting that although the two novels are driven by relationships between mothers and daughters, they differ significantly "in each heroine's enactment of the maternal role". She also discusses *Thoughts on the Education of Daughters* and *A Vindication of the Rights of Woman* in relation to Wollstonecraft's fiction, and provides an overview of current Wollstonecraft criticism.

JULIE D. CAMPBELL

Women Writers: General

Abel, Elizabeth, Marianne Hirsch, and Elizabeth Langland (eds.), *The Voyage In: Fictions of Female Development*, Hanover, New Hampshire: University Press of New England, 1983

Blain, Virginia, Patricia Clements, and Isobel Grundy (eds.), *The Feminist Companion to Literature in English: Women Writers from the Middle Ages to the Present*, London: Batsford, 1990; New Haven, Connecticut: Yale University Press, 1990

Delany, Sheila, *Writing Woman: Women Writers and Women in Literature, Medieval to Modern*, New York: Schocken Books, 1983

Gilbert, Sandra M., and Susan Gubar, *The Madwoman in the Attic: The Woman Writer and the Nineteenth-Century Imagination*, New Haven, Connecticut, and London: Yale University Press, 1979

Jacobus, Mary (ed.), *Women Writing and Writing About Women*, London: Croom Helm, 1979; Totowa, New Jersey: Barnes & Noble, 1979

Moers, Ellen, *Literary Women*, New York: Doubleday, 1976; London: W. H. Allen, 1977

Monteith, Moira (ed.), *Women's Writing: A Challenge to Theory*, Brighton, Sussex: Harvester Press, 1986; New York: St Martin' s Press, 1986

Pratt, Annis, Barbara White, Andrea Lowenstein, and Mary Wyer, *Archetypal Patterns in Women's Fiction*, Bloomington: Indiana University Press, 1981; Brighton, Sussex: Harvester Press, 1981

Roe, Sue (ed.), *Women Reading Women's Writing*, Brighton, Sussex: Harvester Press, 1987; New York: St Martin's Press, 1987

Sherry, Ruth, *Studying Women's Writing: An Introduction*, London: Edward Arnold, 1988

Todd, Janet (ed.), *A Dictionary of British and American Women Writers, 1660–1800*, London: Methuen, 1984; Totowa, New Jersey: Rowman & Allanheld, 1985

Yaegar, Patricia S., *Honey-Mad Women: Emancipatory Strategies in Women's Writing*, New York: Columbia University Press, 1988

Early general studies of women writers tended to look for commonalities across linguistic and national boundaries, in order to delineate a coherent "female tradition" of writing, whereas later accounts have been less uneasy with the notion of difference, and less keen to assert universal patterns and concerns.

Ellen MOERS's study takes as its focus the work of generally well-known women writers, such as George Eliot, Jane Austen, Emily Brontë and Emily Dickinson, but offers a reassessment of their work by seeing them specifically as women writers. This is an impressively wide survey, which takes in English, French, and American writers. Organised thematically, the volume is split into two parts: Part I deals with "History and Tradition", and has a chapter on the relationship between the lives of women writers and their art, a chapter organised chronologically as a sample of how the history of women's literature might be read, and further chapters on women's literary traditions, the female gothic, and women writers' thematic and practical concerns with money. Part II is entitled "Heroinism" and includes several chapters examining the woman writer as "heroine" and the depiction of female protagonists. The book ends with detailed notes on the authors examined, their literary works, their writing careers, and various secondary sources. The notes are, however, of limited usefulness as they provide selective rather than complete information.

The collection edited by JACOBUS includes several well-known feminist critics, and when first published marked the way for many later collections of essays on women writers. Jacobus notes, in her useful introductory chapter, that the principle of difference is a structuring feature of the collection: "the aim of the essays . . . is not to present a unified manifesto, but rather to bring together a spectrum of approaches and positions". Certainly there is a wide variety of approaches represented here, and the collection's interdisciplinarity again set a pattern for later studies. There are nine essays in all, plus Jacobus's Introduction. Elaine Showalter's classic "Towards a Feminist Poetics" seeks to delineate some of the directions that may be taken by the feminist critic and some of the dangers and divisions that may beset her. Cora Kaplan writes about the way in which fantasy allowed Victorian poets like Christina Rossetti and Emily Dickinson to represent alien psychic states and censored eroticism. Laura Mulvey's essay is a particularly interesting discussion of feminism, film, and feminist film theory. Other contributors include Elaine Feinstein, Anne Stevenson, and Inga-Stina Ewbank, treating subjects as diverse as Russian women poets, the relationship between real experience and women's poetry, and Henrik Ibsen and his representation of women.

GILBERT and GUBAR's classic of feminist literary criticism perhaps most forcefully of all the surveys of women's writing demonstrates in its own stylistic innovations the potential creativity of feminist criticism, and through its argument asserts most emphatically the existence of a female literary tradition. Revising the Bloomian theory of the "anxiety of influence", the authors detect a common basis of authorial anxiety as the root of the nineteenth-century female literary tradition: "images of enclosure and escape, fantasies in which maddened doubles function as asocial surrogates for docile selves, metaphors of physical discomfort manifested in frozen landscapes and fiery exteriors – such patterns recurred throughout this tradition, along with obsessive depictions of diseases like anorexia, agoraphobia, and claustrophobia". The dominant theme of the study is confinement: women writers, the authors argue, were enclosed in the structures of a patriarchal society and trapped in the textual structures of patriarchal literature. Hence the common impulse shared by nineteenth-century women was the desire to struggle free from social and literary constraints through strategic redefinitions of identity, literary practice, and social structures. The work of Charlotte Brontë, particularly *Jane Eyre*, is a central focus of the study, but other writers examined include Jane Austen, Mary Shelley, George Eliot, and Emily Dickinson.

The drive to find coherence and continuity in women's writing across the centuries is strongly evident in PRATT's study of women's fiction over the last 300 years, which she sees as "self-contained entity" with "its own organic principles". Deliberately wide in scope, the book concentrates less on the major novelists than the minor ones, seeking evidence of archetypal narrative patterns, which, says Pratt, "endure through the centuries because of the perennial dilemmas they express". Pratt demonstrates how women's writing inscribes different narrative patterns to that of men because of, she argues, their different social roles, and she argues that the rape-trauma archetype – the narrative represented by Apollo and Daphne – recurs as one of the most frequent plot structures in women's fiction. Generic narrative patterns, such as the novel of development, of marriage, of social protest, and of rebirth and transformation, are treated in separate chapters ranging across a large number of writers and texts. Such patterns, says Pratt, "have made of the woman's novel a pathway to the authentic self, to the roots of our selves beneath consciousness of self, and to our inner-most being".

The first words of DELANY's study set the mood for her examination of woman as "artifact": "socially, individually, in every way but biologically, woman is made, not born". Woman, whether as a representation within literature or a producer of literature, is, she says, "laboriously worked up, pieced together, written and rewritten". This initial premise leads to a fruitful analysis of women writers ranging from Margery Kempe to Rosa Luxemburg, Charlotte Perkins Gilman to Marge Piercy, Christine de Pizan to Virginia Woolf. The manner in which women have been inscribed in literature is also addressed. Delany discusses bourgeois women in medieval life and letters; womanliness, marriage and misogyny in Chaucer; sex and politics in Alexander Pope's *The Rape of the Lock*; the feminist utopias of Gilman and Piercy; and the place of writing in de Pizan and Woolf. Eclectic in range and scope, the analysis is held together through its consistent attention to the oppression of women and to the sexual politics involved when women write and men write about women.

The desire to outline a female tradition is again evident in ABEL's collection of critical essays, which all address female stories of development. A range of women writers from Britain, USA, Continental Europe, and Latin America provides a cross-cultural context in which to explore commonalities of technique and experience. The essays are arranged according to three historical stages: nineteenth-century novels that redefine the tradition of the male *Bildungsroman*, twentieth-century works that articulate a specifically female tradition, and contemporary narratives that expose similar tensions and oppositions to those found in the previous chapters.

Again, a characteristic breadth of scope and variety of approach is visible in MONTEITH's collection of essays, which reassesses feminist theory through the reading of women writers. Some familiar names (Jean Rhys, Doris Lessing, Woolf, Edith Wharton, Angela Carter) rub shoulders with less well-known writers, such as Winifred Holtby, Phyllis Bentley, Naomi Mitchison, and Rosamond Lehmann. The essays are all motivated by the fundamental assumption that "a theory or practice of writing based on realism has an indirectly sinister (and in the long run, debilitating) effect; it denies the real forces that go into making literature, the social and psychological pressures that function alongside the craft of the individual writer". Consequently, all the essays are concerned with the relationship of female experience to the process of writing, and they challenge the view that literature functions as a realistic representation of women's lives. Instead, they all, implicitly or explicitly, assume that literature inevitably distorts and refracts lived experience. Nicole Ward Jouve examines her own bilingual writing practices and finds that the act of translating words from one language to another reduces the sense of an "authoritative" version. Marion Shaw looks at British women writers between the wars, who, she argues, no longer had to write like men to be taken seriously. The essay demonstrates that two different approaches were taken: the more experimental writers (Rhys, Dorothy Richardson, Lehmann) were pessimistic in their representations of female protagonists, whereas those who carried on in the realist tradition (Bentley, Mitchison, Holtby) wrote detailed and well-documented historical novels, claiming a part for women in history. Shirley Foster considers three books written by Wharton, Kate Chopin, and Willa Cather, and finds evidence of ambivalence in all three writers concerning women's status, role and opportunities. She demonstrates that although they employ conventional literary forms, they nevertheless challenged traditional assumptions about the female protagonist and her aspirations. Other contributors include Lorna Sage, Michelene Wandor, Maggie Humm, and Emma Tennant, and other issues addressed include textual space, identity in women's biography, nationalism, and feminist criticism.

ROE's collection follows in the tradition originated by critics like Moers, in that it too focuses on well-known women writers, but offers reassessment of their work. She says: "we hope in this volume to suggest possibilities for the creative, complicated and potentially exhilarating development of feminist criticism". What is original about this collection is that it emphasises the role of the woman reader, examining how writing as a woman can release the woman critic into a more creative and revealing encounter with the text, the writer, and herself. Each contributor describes her experience of reading a particular woman writer, and by so doing implicitly and explicitly reflects on the role of the feminist critic. Kate Fullbrook's essay on Jane Austen argues that she subverted existing literary forms in order to satirise the economics of social life. Virginia Woolf, argues Gillian Beer, explores the relationship between self and other, and the reader of Woolf's work risks losing perspectival distance. Isobel Armstrong's impressive essay on Christina Rossetti asks how it might be possible to look back at the work of a nineteenth-century woman writer to address critically neglected issues. In questioning critical practice itself, Armstrong asserts the need for a gendered account of pleasure. Diana Collecott continues this theme in her essay on H.D., where she argues that conventional critical thinking is challenged by reading women writers. The other essays, on Rebecca West, George Eliot, Jean Rhys, and Angela Carter all address this issue, both thematically and in their own critical form.

The study by Ruth SHERRY is a small but invaluable introduction to women's writing and the issues that can be raised by reading it. In the process of asking such questions as: does it make sense to talk about "women's writing"? do women write about particular subjects or treat them distinctively? is women's literature the same thing as feminist literature? Sherry covers all the major figures such as Austen, the Brontës, and Virginia Woolf, as well as more recent writers such as Tillie Olsen, Antonia White, and Doris Lessing. There are chapters on "Poetry", Fiction", "Drama", and "Other Genres". With a background in feminist literary criticism and literary theory, this book provides a useful and user-friendly introduction to women writers and ways of reading them.

YAEGAR's book asks the fundamental question of how do women speak about their desires. Theoretically sophisticated in approach, the study seeks to refute, through close reading of a range of women writers, the feminist view that women are estranged and alienated from language. Yaegar challenges the validity of this attitude towards women's writing, and aims to delineate a countertradition of invention and reclamation. Her introduction provides an interesting critique of French feminist writings, and she proceeds to examine the emancipatory strategies evident in the work of a wide range of women writers, including Mary Oliver, Adrienne Rich, Eudora Welty, Charlotte Brontë, Elizabeth Bishop, Mary Wollstonecraft, Tillie Olsen, Emily Brontë, Emily Dickinson, Héléne Cixous, and Lucille Clifton. Her own critical approach mirrors her message: that women writers have found language empowering, playful, and emancipatory.

TODD's invaluable reference volume makes a significant contribution to the process of retrieving women's work and women's literary history. It admirably carries out its two stated purposes: to make visible again those writers who have been forgotten, and to represent the major or accepted writers in the light of new scholarship and new ways of thinking about them. The existence of published works is not necessarily the criteria for inclusion in this volume, because it covers a period when some women felt it a disgrace to publish. Recognition of the legitimacy and importance of private writings such as letters has enabled a wide inclusivity. Indeed, Todd says: "a kind of affirmative action has operated; a higher proportion of minorities than of majorities is represented, of Americans than of the far more numerous British, and of peasant poets than of middle-class sentimental writers". A useful introduction provides background information on the material circumstances in which women wrote, together with an overview of their work.

BLAIN's wide and general survey begins with a happy assertion of failure: "the editors of this book have become acutely aware, in the years in which we have been preparing it, of a field far fuller, richer and more various than we could have dreamed at the outset of this work". Its scope is ambitious: it includes women "writing from the beginning to the present", women writing in English from not only Britain but many other national traditions, and including under-researched genres such as diaries, letters, writing for children, medical writing, slave narratives, theology, and popular literary forms. The volume's procedure reflects a scrupulous feminist methodology and a refusal to accept ideological sedimentations: lesser-known figures are given generous space in order to "defer rather than assist the gradual emergence of a canon of writing by women". A rigorous self-consciousness about methods of representation is evident throughout, and feminist theory informs all facets of procedure, from the naming of writers' mothers, to the sensitivity to difference reflected in its international scope.

VAL GOUGH

Women Writers: 20th Century

Breen, Jennifer, *In Her Own Write: Twentieth Century Women's Fiction*, London: Macmillan, 1990; New York: St Martin's Press, 1990

Gilbert, Sandra M. and Susan Gubar, *No Man's Land: The Place of the Woman Writer in the Twentieth Century*, 3 vols. (*The War of the Words*, *Sexchanges*, *Letters from the Front*), New Haven, Connecticut, and London: Yale University Press, 1988–94

Jump, Harriet Devine (ed.), *Diverse Voices: Essays on Twentieth-Century Women Writers in English*, Hemel Hempstead, Hertfordshire: Harvester Wheatsheaf, 1991; New York: St Martin's Press, 1991

Staley, Thomas F. (ed.), *Twentieth-Century Women Novelists*, London: Macmillan, 1982; New York: Barnes & Noble, 1982

Any survey of criticism of twentieth-century women writers cannot fail to take account of the massive three-volume contribution of two well-known critics working in collaboration: Sandra Gilbert and Susan Gubar. Their work has set high standards of scholarly accuracy coupled with readability. Other critical works have tended to be collections of essays, representing a variety of approaches to what is now firmly recognised as a highly significant and diverse body of women's writing.

GILBERT and GUBAR's first volume in their examination of twentieth-century women writers, *The War of the Words*, seeks to place twentieth-century writers in relation to their nineteenth-century precursors. Examining a range of female modernists, the authors argue that modernism is inflected differently for male writers and for female writers. Their thesis is that "both women and men engendered words and works which continually sought to come to terms with, and find terms for, an ongoing battle of the sexes that was set in motion by the late nineteenth-century rise of feminism and the fall of Victorian concepts of 'femininity'". Indeed, the authors argue that modernism was a product of the "battle of the sexes" they use as their dominant critical motif. The book examines an impressive range of texts as groundwork for their following two volumes.

Sexchanges, their second volume, is meticulously researched and highly readable, and focuses on Olive Schreiner, Charlotte Perkins Gilman, Kate Chopin, Willa Cather, Edith Wharton, and other writers associated with World War I and with lesbian writing. In their third volume, *Letters from the Front*, Gilbert and Gubar examine what they see as the "flowering of feminist modernism" in Virginia Woolf, Marianne Moore, Zora Neale Hurston, H.D., and Edna St Vincent Millay. In particular, the authors focus on writers who look forward to the future, in order to analyse their visions and assess their techniques.

STALEY's collection is unusual in that its editor and several contributors are male, for most critical work on modern women writers is still done by female scholars. The volume focuses on women writers for whom stylistic experimentation is not their first priority, but who have challenged the limitations of their genre through exploration of new or taboo themes. While Staley's Introduction tends to treat texts as mirrors of life, some of his contributors are more aware of issues of textuality. Shari Benstock, for example, examines how Jennifer Johnston's work is deeply concerned with form and narrative technique. Other writers examined include Doris Lessing, Iris Murdoch, Olivia Manning, Barbara Pym, Margaret Drabble, and Edna O'Brien.

BREEN's book flags itself as "general guide to what novels have been written by women over the last ninety years", and it does indeed cover a wide range of writers, from famous names like Woolf and Alice Walker to lesser-known authors such as Jill Miller and Joan Riley. Nevertheless, as Breen herself points out, it cannot be considered an exhaustive survey of women's twentieth-century fiction, since the texts under discussion have been selected to illustrate her method of reading. Breen argues that within any work of fiction, the skilled reader can discern a central voice – not necessarily that of the narrator or author – which reflects a construction of the distinctive point of view of the world in that work of fiction. Her aim is to discover subversive meanings in the given fiction through a deconstructive process, which identifies gaps, silences, contradictions, and blind spots, as well as novelty, revelation, and seditious departures in the world-view of each work. She uses the insights of psychoanalytic theory, and in so doing assesses the usefulness of one of its key ideas, the theory of the repressed "Other". Chapters are organised thematically under headings such as "Sexuality and Marriage", "Politics and War", and "Mothers and Children". Breen provides not only an entertaining and useful account of women's fiction, but also a vision, and a version, of feminist reading as a political and subversive activity.

With an Introduction by Julia Briggs, JUMP's collection of critical essays on an eclectic range of women writers makes a useful contribution to feminist criticism, and characteristically reflects a diversity of approaches, including psychoanalytic theory, deconstruction, and feminist theories of autobiography, language, and subjectivity. Of the nine essays, five are concerned with American writers including some black American poets (Audre Lorde, Alice Walker, Maya Angelou, Ntozake Shange, June Jordan). The rest are concerned with writers from Canada, Australia, Africa, and Ireland. As such, the volume represents a usefully international and cross-cultural perspective. Clare Brant's discussion of Gertrude Stein uses French feminist theories of *écriture féminine* to analyse Stein's subversion of linguistic functions. Julia Briggs writes on Willa Cather and the uneasy dialectic in her work between domesticity and creativity. Dianne Chisholm's account of H.D.

("H.D.'s *Autre*Biography") examines the writer's quest for her inner "other" in autobiography. Other essays focus on Margaret Atwood, Eudora Welty, Christina Stead, Bessie Head, and Ama Ata Aidoo. The collection is refreshing in its emphasis on relatively lesser-known women writers from a variety of cultures, and achieves its stated aim of generating "that productive and friendly disagreement which we like to think of as characteristic of the state of feminist criticism today".

VAL GOUGH

Women Writers: Contemporary

Fullbrook, Kate, *Free Women: Ethics and Aesthetics in Twentieth-Century Women's Fiction*, London: Harvester Wheatsheaf, 1990; Philadelphia: Temple University Press, 1990

Kenyon, Olga, *Writing Women: Contemporary Women Novelists*, London: Pluto Press, 1991

Pearlman, Mickey, and Katherine Usher Henderson (eds.), *Inter/View: Talks with America's Writing Women*, Lexington: University Press of Kentucky, 1990

Rainwater, Catherine, and William J. Scheick (eds.), *Contemporary American Women Writers: Narrative Strategies*, Lexington: University Press of Kentucky, 1985

Walden, Daniel, and Miriyam Glazer (eds.), "Contemporary Women Writers" issue of *Studies in American Jewish Literature*, 1992

Walker, Nancy A., *Feminist Alternatives: Irony and Fantasy in the Contemporary Novel by Women*, Jackson: University Press of Mississippi, 1990

Wyatt, Jean, *Reconstructing Desire: The Role of the Unconscious in Women's Reading and Writing*, Chapel Hill: University of North Carolina Press, 1990

Contemporary women writers in English tend to be regarded, for critical purposes, as forming something of a group, despite national or historical differences, or they are discussed according to the genres in which they write. Several of the studies below reflect such an international perspective, while others, though ostensibly dealing with North American women's writing – arguably the most fertile section of the contemporary field – engage with issues very relevant to discussions of modern women writers generally.

FULLBROOK's account of women's writing has chapters on: Edith Wharton; Willa Cather and Zora Neale Hurston; Gertrude Stein; Virginia Woolf; Dorothy Richardson, Djuna Barnes, and Christina Stead; Doris Lessing; Margaret Atwood; and Toni Morrison. In exploring how women use fiction to restructure ethical vision, she analyses, among other things, Atwood's writing in relation to responsibility, and Morrison's in terms of freedom, justice, and moral responsibility. What emerges from Fullbrook's compelling study is the sense of a dynamic yet coherent women's fictional tradition.

WYATT shares this concern with the power of literature to affect our lives, and uses psychoanalytic theory as a context for her discussion of the potential for change: she asks whether women can alter, through reading, the unconscious structures of fantasy that govern desire. In the work of Alice Walker (*The Color Purple*) and Morrison (*Beloved*) she finds images of female autonomy and alternatives to patriarchal social structures, which can, she feels, act as catalysts for real change. She also gives significant attention to: Kate Chopin (*The Awakening* and *The Waterfall*); Marilynne Robinson (*Housekeeping*), in the chapter on "The Impossible Poetry of the Preoedipal"; Gail Godwin (*Violet Clay*); Margaret Drabble (*The Middle Ground*); and Lessing (*The Golden Notebook*) in the chapter on "Sexual Politics of the Unconscious".

For KENYON, women's literary tradition is characterised by diversity – a rich variety of styles, voices, and forms. This account is embedded in contemporary feminist literary theory, and in a lucid Introduction Kenyon describes the various approaches that now go by the name of "feminism", and she links the theoretical issues highlighted in the Introduction to the emergence of women's writing as a vital aspect of contemporary culture. In a lengthy section on black women novelists, Kenyon analyses the work of Maya Angelou, Alice Walker, and Toni Morrison, with the emphasis on their ethnic and gender identities. Other chapters are devoted to: Angela Carter; Michelene Wandor, Bernice Rubens, and Elaine Feinstein, under the heading "Jewish Writing in Britain"; "Caribbean Women Writers"; and "Buchi Emecheta and Black Immigrant Experience in Britain".

WALKER's study addresses fictions in which women have written their own lives and imagined the lives of other women by creating "unacceptable fantasies" of autonomy, freedom, and power. The narrative strategy by which these fantasies are represented, in a patriarchal culture, is irony – the expression of an arbitrarily constructed social self that is distinct from authentic selfhood. Walker, Marge Piercy, Gail Godwin, Erica Jong, and Maxine Hong Kingston are among the novelists treated in detail in this compelling and engaging study.

In a valuable contribution to the field, PEARLMAN and HENDERSON have gathered a collection of entertaining and informative interviews with 28 writers. Though they are all Americans, they offer an image of the diversity of contemporary women's writing by encompassing a range of differences in terms of race, religion, ethnicity, sexual preference, marital status, age, and geographical situation. Included are both very well-known writers, like Joyce Carol Oates, Godwin, and Alison Lurie, as well as writers who are beginning their careers, like Amy Tan and Elizabeth Winthrop. The interviews are presented not in question-and-answer format but as short essays with lengthy quotations from the writers, with many of the writers commenting on the difference between the kinds of questions asked of men in interviews and those asked of women.

The essays collected by WALDEN and GLAZER deal with contemporary American Jewish writers, a group in which there are a number of influential and prominent women: Tillie Olsen, Grace Paley, Cynthia Ozick, and Piercy are among the major figures discussed. Barbara Cantalupo explores Olsen's articulation of feminine/feminist issues in *Yonnondio: From the Thirties*; Gloria L. Cronin writes of the theme of survival – identified in the Introduction as a prominent concern in American Jewish women's writing – in Paley's fiction; S. Lillian Kremer discusses the representation of the Holocaust by four women writers; Susanne Klingenstein considers mother-daughter relationships in fiction by Ozick, Norma Rosen, and Rebecca Goldstein; Lewis Fried writes of the relationship between the sacred and the profane in Anne Roiphe's *Lovingkindness*; Sanford Pinsker discusses the interplay of satire, social realism, and moral seriousness in the work of Allegra Goodman; Ellen Serlen Uffen considers the detective fiction of Faye Kellerman; and Sarah Blacher Cohen writes engagingly of her own play, *The Ladies Locker Room*.

RAINWATER and SCHEICK have compiled an extremely useful volume, which combines acute critical interpretations of the work of key women writers with extensive bibliographical listings of their work. The various strategies adopted by women who seek to revise and transform generic norms, literary language, and narrative structures are analysed in terms of the examples set by the chosen writers as they appropriate "the master's voice" for the articulation of women's experience. Most of the essays deal with the range of each writer's work; while some analyze in detail a specific text, such as Catherine Rainwater's investigation of Anne Redmon's *Music and Silence*, Elizabeth Fifer's reading of Walker's *The Color Purple*, and Elaine Tuttle Hansen's discussion of Piercy's *Small Changes*. Other writers discussed include Ann Beattie, Annie Dillard, Maxine Hong Kingston, Morrison, Ozick, Paley, and Anne Tyler. This volume provides evidence of both the sophistication and diversity of contemporary women's writing, and the wide range of theoretical and literary approaches taken to contemporary women's issues.

DEBORAH L. MADSEN

Women Writers: British – General

Bell, Maureen, George Parfitt, and Simon Shepherd, *A Biographical Dictionary of English Women Writers 1580–1720*, London: Harvester Wheatsheaf, 1990

Blain, Virginia, Patricia Clements, and Isobel Grundy, *The Feminist Companion to Literature in English: Women Writers from the Middle Ages to the Present*, London: Batsford, 1990; New Haven, Connecticut: Yale University Press, 1990

Ferguson, Moira, *Subject to Others: British Women Writers and Colonial Slavery, 1670–1834*, London and New York: Routledge, 1992

Johnson, R. Brimley, *The Women Novelists*, London: Collins, 1918; reprinted, Freeport, New York: Books for Libraries, 1967

Poovey, Mary, *The Proper Lady and the Woman Writer: Ideology as Style in the Works of Mary Wollstonecraft, Mary Shelley and Jane Austen*, Chicago: University of Chicago Press, 1984

Schlueter, Paul, and June Schlueter (eds.), *An Encyclopedia of British Women Writers*, New York: Garland, 1988; London: St James Press, 1990

Shattock, Joanne, *The Oxford Guide to British Women Writers*, Oxford and New York: Oxford University Press, 1993

Showalter, Elaine, *A Literature of Their Own: British Women Novelists from Brontë to Lessing*, Princeton, New Jersey: Princeton University Press, 1977; London: Virago, 1978, revised 1982

Spencer, Jane, *The Rise of the Woman Novelist: From Aphra Behn to Jane Austen*, Oxford and New York: Blackwell, 1986

Spender, Dale, *Mothers of the Novel: 100 Good Women Writers Before Jane Austen*, London: Pandora, 1986; New York: Routledge & Kegan Paul, 1986

Todd, Janet (ed.), *Dictionary of British Women Writers*, London: Routledge, 1989

Todd, Janet, *Gender, Art and Death*, Cambridge: Polity Press, 1993; New York: Continuum, 1993

Woolf, Virginia, *A Room of One's Own*, London: Hogarth Press, 1929; New York: Fountain Press, 1929; several subsequent reprints

This topic's title itself poses a critical question, since there is no equivalent category for "men writers". Recent criticism of women as writers has focused in various ways on this anomaly. The feminist movement of the last 20 years has considered the definition of the woman writer as "Other", the position of women in the literary canon, the need to rescue a lost heritage, and questions of "difference". Interestingly, several of the most influential studies, while departing quite radically from what is seen as a patriarchal scholarly tradition, yet derive their initial impetus from a reassessment of a writer located firmly within the "Great Tradition", namely Jane Austen.

Apart from critical discussions, a number of dictionaries have been devoted specifically to women writers because they are under-represented in standard reference books. The introductions to the five described here explain the respective compilers' criteria for selection and inclusion. The definition of "British" is problematic since some writers born in Britain spent much of their working lives abroad, and others born abroad chose to live in Britain. The dictionaries take slightly different positions on this in relation to individuals. All interpret the notion of "writer" broadly, but again may make different decisions on whether or not to devote space to a particular woman. The following descriptions indicate the scope of, and general principles behind, each work. All the works are useful in offering a starting point for study of women outside the canon.

The SCHLUETERS' encyclopedia was American in origin, and the contributors list reflects this. "British" includes some Irish-American and Commonwealth writers long resident in Britain. There are some 400 entries, and the editors claim to have included as many medieval and Renaissance writers as possible, and in the later period to lay emphasis on the twentieth century, contacting living writers for authoritative information. The Index includes cross-referenced pseudonyms and variants, genres and topics. The policy of including titles of a writer's works, while useful, means that the entry on Barbara Cartland takes three pages as compared to Austen's two.

TODD's 1989 selection of between 400 and 500 British writers includes women "who have worked in less prestigious areas such as poetry for children or the public letter of advice" as well as canonical names. Some are chosen because they were innovators or representative of groups such as "working-class women". Living writers are not excluded, and there are entries on Isabel Colegate, Ruth Rendell, Penelope Lively, and Molly

Keane among others. Articles, all of which are signed by contributors, include brief critical assessments of writers' work, as well as biographies, and listings of selected publications and references. The dictionary proper is preceded by an alphabetical listing of authors with dates. The Index covers topics touched on in the biographical entries, as well as names and pseudonyms.

BELL deals in detail with the early-modern period. Though the dictionary section, listing several hundred writers by name, forms the major part of this work, substantial critical appendices contextualise the listings and invite consideration of such topics as letter-writing, Quaker publications, petitions, and men as "gatekeepers". "Writers" is interpreted very broadly to include diarists, propagandists, letter-writers, writers in translation, etc.

BLAIN offers 2,700 entries, but covers women of many nationalities writing in English. Entries are alphabetical by surname. Indices give cross-references to married names and pseudonyms, and group writers by date of birth, though not by nationality. There are also entries covering genres and topics, particularly those of feminist interest. The feminist slant influences the selection of women and affects some of the more general topics. The one on "Magazines", for example, gives particular emphasis to political and feminist journals. The contributors' method has been to draw afresh on their own knowledge of the writings of their subjects, and on other primary sources, rather than on standard reference books. Entries are restricted in length, with canonical writers treated briefly and "minor" figures relatively generously.

SHATTOCK's guide (covering over 400 individuals) is aimed at the general reader and student. Focusing on each writer's life and major publications, she also pays some attention to the contemporary context, and includes suggestions for further reading. Since a secondary aim of the guide is to "indicate some of the important critical, theoretical and scholarly work which has been produced on these writers" space is devoted to the provision of a general bibliography on women writers. A few entries cover specific topics, such as "Women Writers' Suffrage League", "Time and Tide", or "Victorian Magazine". There is no index, but the entries are cross-referenced.

Interest in the phenomenon of the female writer, and the sex's particular contribution to literature, has certainly not been confined to recent scholarship; it has been debated by critics over the past three centuries.

JOHNSON's book is interesting as an early twentieth-century view of women's particular contribution to literature. She argues that though "in the beginning" women writers "copied men and saw through men's eyes" there was a period between the publication of Fanny Burney's *Evelina* and George Eliot's *Daniel Deronda* when women novelists "found themselves" and developed their art along lines of their own. A group of earlier writers, notably Aphra Behn, are briefly considered as individual pioneers, but the book focuses particularly on Burney, Jane Austen, George Eliot, and Charlotte Brontë, "The Great Four", all of whom are seen in different ways as innovators. Emily Brontë, Elizabeth Gaskell, and Maria Edgeworth are among other novelists discussed and admired – Edgeworth is credited with the invention of the "national novel" – and a further 22 minor writers are given brief entries in an appendix. Though the argument inevitably seems somewhat dated, it still offers interesting insights: Thackeray and Dickens in many ways followed women's lead; women developed and perfected the realistic novel, created the "domestic novel", and showed the novel to be more persuasive than the pulpit; and women's "revelation of feminity" (the woman's viewpoint) is seen as the outstanding achievement.

WOOLF's slim volume is perhaps even more influential today than when first published in 1929. It originated from papers read to societies at Newnham and Girton colleges, Oxford. Asked to speak on "Women and Fiction" she chose instead to argue in her imaginative, inimitable way that "a woman must have money and a room of her own if she is to write fiction". She thus addresses the central problem of how women can become professional writers in a patriarchal society. Woolf posits a scenario in which Shakespeare has a wonderfully gifted sister, Judith, and traces her life, devoid of proper education, forced to run away from home to escape an unwelcome marriage, unable to earn her living in the theatre, eventually committing suicide, and never managing to write. This is the starting-point for her argument that while male writers often faced great difficulties, women faced greater ones, including the hostility of men. Woolf's account draws on a range of writers, including Lady Winchilsea, the Duchess of Newcastle, Dorothy Osborne, and Aphra Behn. She attributes nineteenth-century women's predilection for fiction to the constraints of their social situation, and regards their work as hampered by their lack of a female tradition and intellectual freedom. She suggests also that women and men naturally write in different styles. These ideas have been explored by later generations of critics.

SPENDER's study argues against the then orthodox scholarly view of the novel form as originating in the eighteenth century, with its founding fathers being Daniel Defoe, Henry Fielding, Samuel Richardson, Tobias Smollett, and Laurence Sterne, a view encapsulated in Ian Watt's influential book *The Rise of the Novel* (1957). Spender's survey of women's fiction from the end of the seventeenth century to the emergence of Jane Austen seeks to demonstrate that it was women, not men, who made the greater contribution to the development of the novel. She argues for the reinstatement in the canon of the women novelists who have "been edited out of the literary records and removed from consciousness" yet who in their own day were acclaimed "the esteemed majority". Though polemical in tone this stimulating book is never strident, and the argument is supported both by documentation of the work of over 100 women whose tradition Jane Austen inherited, and more detailed case studies of some of them.

SPENCER's book also contextualises Jane Austen. She deals with the conditions in which the eighteenth-century critical establishment permitted women's fiction to flourish, and through a detailed examination of a range of works by different novelists, focusing particularly on the treatment of the heroine, charts the ways in which certain themes were dealt with by women in ways significantly different from those of their male counterparts. Though the emphasis is on the eighteenth-century novel, Spencer's examples also include autobiography, drama, polemical writing, and poetry, and she views the seventeenth-century debate about the "proper and improper" woman-writer in relation to later developments. There is thus some assessment of, for example, Katherine Philips, Margaret Cavendish, and Delarivier Manley. This is a good, accessible introduction to the subject.

POOVEY's study of how three women struggled to create professional indentities as writers, against contemporary ideals of femininity, straddles the eighteenth and nineteenth centuries. Introductory chapters draw on a range of eighteenth-century texts to delineate the idea of "The Proper Lady". Writing from a feminist perspective Poovey regards Jane Austen as concerning herself with many of the same issues as the other two subjects, and through her artistry completing Mary Wollstonecraft's "analysis of female inhibition" and perfecting "[Mary] Shelley's attempt to make propriety accommodate female desire". For Poovey, the lives of the three women, despite the difference in circumstance, "were all shaped by the dynamics of the ideological situation that, as women" they shared.

In her acclaimed and influential book, first published in 1978, SHOWALTER aims "to construct a more reliable map from which to explore the achievements of English women novelists" born after 1800 to the present. She argues for a discrete female tradition, and a distinct female subculture is posited. Her analysis of the lives and work of both the canonical writers and others largely forgotten draws on an impressive array of contemporary reviews and memoirs, as well as the novels themselves. Women's achievements are set within their social and cultural contexts, so that, for example, the feminist movement, the professionalising of the woman novelist, and attempts to break "the male monopoly of publishing" are accorded due attention. Both the biographical appendix, listing some 213 women writers and activists born after 1800, and bibliography remain extremely useful.

TODD's lively collection of essays (1993) spans the period from the Restoration to Romanticism, and all but one take women's writing as their subject, covering Behn, Wollstonecraft, Austen, Virginia Woolf's criticism, and a group of autobiographical narratives that each achieved a *succès de scandale* in its day. The essays are linked by the notion of women's "staging of the self", and exemplify a sensitivity to, and cognisance of, the historical and cultural context of the writings discussed. Thus Behn's work is seen in the context of Restoration theatre and the role of the actress, Jane Austen's motivation as a writer viewed against contemporary understandings of "sensibility", and Wollstonecraft's view of suicide within the framework of both revolutionary ideals and eighteenth-century attitudes to self-slaughter. Issues of feminist criticism and New Historicism are also addressed.

A number of recent studies focus on particular topics: FERGUSON's book is an example of such. Her argument is that anti-slavery protest in prose and poetry by Anglo-Saxon female authors contributed to the development of feminism over a two-hundred-year period, but in doing so misrepresented the African-Caribbean slaves whose freedom they advocated. Whether or not the reader is convinced by Ferguson's thesis, the book is valuable in drawing attention to women's voices in the abolitionist movement, and to interesting, often little-known, texts by some 30 women from Aphra Behn to Harriet Martineau. Their writings range across the genres from tracts to poetry, novels, and drama. There is an extensive bibliography.

BARBARA M. ONSLOW

Women Writers: Renaissance

Beilin, Elaine V., *Redeeming Eve: Women Writers of the English Renaissance*, Princeton, New Jersey: Princeton University Press, 1987

Haselkorn, Anne M., and Betty S. Travitsky (eds.), *The Renaissance Englishwoman in Print: Counterbalancing the Canon*, Amherst: University of Massachusetts Press, 1990

Jones, Ann Rosalind, *The Currency of Eros: Women's Love Lyrics in Europe, 1540–1620*, Bloomington: Indiana University Press, 1990

Krontiris, Tina, *Oppositional Voices: Women as Writers and Translators of Literature in the English Renaissance*, London and New York: Routledge, 1992

Travitsky, Betty S., and Adele F. Seeff, *Attending to Women in Early Modern England*, Newark: University of Delaware Press, 1994; London: Associated University Presses, 1994

Woodbridge, Linda, *Women and the English Renaissance: Literature and the Nature of Womankind 1540–1620*, Brighton, Sussex: Harvester Press, 1984; Urbana: University of Illinois Press, 1986

The critical tradition of women writers of the English Renaissance begins with Virginia Woolf asking "why women did not write poetry in the Elizabethan age" (*A Room of One's Own*, 1929). This proved a crucial question for the ensuing decades as scholars discovered that Woolf had been both right to ask, because so many women writers of the sixteenth and seventeenth centuries had been completely overlooked, and wrong because a great many women had written poetry as well as other works. Although "Shakespeare's sister", as Woolf called her imaginary poet, has not been found, scholars now have available a growing body of literature by women to study and to teach both as a literary tradition in its own right and in relation to male authors. Most prominent among these women writers are the poets Anne Askew, Isabella Whitney, Mary Sidney Herbert, Elizabeth I, Aemilia Lanyer, Mary Sidney Wroth, and Katherine Philips; prose writers Margaret More Roper, Catherine Parr, Anne Clifford, Arbella Stuart, Rachel Speght, and Bathsua Makin; and dramatists Elizabeth Cary, Aphra Behn, and Margaret Cavendish. Since the study of women writers of the English Renaissance is relatively new, and texts are constantly being discovered and published, many of the texts and the criticism of these texts have not yet appeared in book form. Two comprehensive bibliographies of book- and article-length studies of individual authors, which include previous bibliographies, appear in *English Literary Renaissance*, 24(1), Winter 1994 – Georgianna M. Ziegler's "Recent Studies in Women Writers of Tudor England 1485–1603", covering 1990 to mid-1993, and Sara Jayne Steen's "Recent Studies in Women Writers of the Seventeenth Century, 1604–1674, also covering 1990 to mid-1993.

BEILIN divides her study of women writers from 1523 to 1630 into three parts. The first discusses the pious writings of early sixteenth-century authors Roper, Askew, and others as the means to discuss the relation between religious conceptions of the "virtuous woman" and the development of both literary personae and distinctive female imagery. The second part examines seventeenth-century authors Mary Sidney Herbert, Mary Sidney Wroth, Elizabeth Cary, and Aemilia Lanyer, who more boldly manipulated the ideal of the "virtuous woman" through experimentation with poetic form, genre, and characterization. The third part focuses on defenses of women, to argue that during this 100-year period, crucial changes occurred in the conceptualization of women, a change in which women participated. This book was germinal both in its treatment of several women writers never before discussed and in the interconnections it constructed among them.

HASELKORN and TRAVITSKY have collected 17 essays, which provide intellectual and historical contexts for understanding women writers, especially Herbert and Wroth. The volume correlates writings by men and women because "many of the gendered assumptions of the English Renaissance are highlighted by this counterbalancing of representations of Renaissance women by contemporary men with writings (on related topics) by Renaissance women". The result is a volume that provides important perspectives on the relationships between male and female authors during the period.

JONES provides sophisticated textual, historicist, and theoretical comparisons between women writers from England, France, and Italy, pairing them "according to parallels between their social situations and the forms of negotiation they invent to win over their publics". The book's development of the term "negotiation", in the sense of "a range of interpretative positions through which subordinated groups respond to the assumptions encoded into dominant cultural forms and systems of representation", is especially useful, since it sets up discussions of the strategies that Whitney, Wroth, Catherine des Roches, and others employed in order to enter the predominantly male discursive realm of love poetry.

KRONTIRIS divides women writers from the 1560s through the 1620s by class, considering Whitney and Margaret Tyler as "Servant Girls Claiming Male Domain," Herbert and Cary as "Noblewomen Dramatizing the Husband-Wife Conflict," and Lanyer and Wroth as "Women of the Jacobean Court Defending Their Sex" – to use her chapter headings. Since her "principal purpose" is to determine the opposition of these women "to contemporary dominant ideologies", the book examines a number of theoretical issues in relation to historical issues in order to talk about the extent to which these women authors might be considered aware of the limitations imposed on them as women in society as well as the ways that women countered or accepted these limitations.

TRAVITSKY and SEEFF collected a group of essays and summaries of workshops from the first "Attending to Women in Early Modern England Conference" held at the University of Maryland in November 1990. The volume presents a wide range of interdisciplinary issues currently under consideration in women's studies, and which bear on women writers, including relations among gender, race, and class, the visibility of women in art and material culture, and pedagogy.

The connections between Renaissance literature and life are discussed by WOODBRIDGE in order to examine the place of women in both. Focusing on the period between 1540 and 1620, she argues for care in reading literary texts as historical documents and for recognizing distinctions between life and literature. The book emphasizes that literary conventions, such as the "stage misogynist", as well as the staging of female characters reveal the complex attitudes toward women in the English Renaissance. While not specifically about women writers, Woodbridge's distinctions proved crucial for current critical discussions of both female characters and historical women, and thus particularly for women writers, who existed not only as historical entities, but who constructed themselves through their writing as fictional entities.

SUSAN FRYE

Women Writers: Restoration and 18th Century

Ballaster, Ros, *Seductive Forms: Women's Amatory Fiction from 1684–1740*, Oxford: Clarendon Press, 1992; New York: Oxford University Press, 1992
Landry, Donna, *The Muses of Resistance: Laboring-Class Women's Poetry in Britain 1739–1796*, Cambridge and New York: Cambridge University Press, 1990
Myers, Sylvia Harcstark, *The Bluestocking Circle: Friendship and the Life of the Mind in Eighteenth-Century England*, Oxford: Clarendon Press, 1990; New York: Oxford University Press, 1990
Pearson, Jacqueline, *The Prostituted Muse: Images of Women and Women Dramatists 1642–1737*, London: Harvester Wheatsheaf, 1988; New York: St Martin's Press, 1988
Spencer, Jane, *The Rise of the Woman Novelist: From Aphra Behn to Jane Austen*, Oxford and New York: Blackwell, 1986
Todd, Janet, *The Sign of Angellica: Women, Writing and Fiction, 1660–1800*, London: Virago Press, 1989; New York: Columbia University Press, 1989

PEARSON's survey is a solid introduction to the study of women dramatists in the seventeenth and early eighteenth centuries. The first part of the book discusses the literary context in which women wrote and explores the role that women played in the theatrical world, not only as writers, but also as actresses, managers, and members of the audience. She is arguing against the view that women had to write like men to succeed in the period, and instead concentrates on a "female tradition" by locating similarities in dramatic themes, images of women, sexual politics, marriage, education, chastity, and virtue in plays by women. These themes are compared with contemporaneous plays by male dramatists, and between women writing in the Restoration period and those writing in the early eighteenth century. The second part of the book concentrates more specifically on individual dramatists, such as Aphra Behn, Susanna Centlivre, Mary Pix, Catherine Trotter and Delarivier Manley, as well as "minor" dramatists such as Eliza Haywood and Mary Davys. Pearson's book provides a wealth of detail, biographical and textual, and to those unfamiliar to the subject the appended "List of Plays by Women Dramatists" and the secondary references should prove invaluable as a base for further study.

SPENCER's influential study is a comprehensive and stimulating exploration of female contribution to the "rise" of the novel. The first part of the book assesses the formation of women's literary authority as writers in the seventeenth and early eighteenth centuries and investigates the movement towards morality in the novel, from which women writers were to gain (conditional) acceptance as professional authors. In the second section of the book, Spencer is concerned with how writers negotiated their special position as "women writers" and she charts the responses to this position by using the linked themes of "protest", "conformity", and "escape", which are expressed in fiction through the figures of the seduced heroine, the reformed heroine, and the romance heroine respectively. This thematic approach allows for an extensive survey of fiction written by a range of women writers and provides a sustained and coherent survey of the developments and continuities between the roles of women writers and the fiction they produced. Spencer's claim that the entry of women writers into public discourse in the eighteenth century was negated to some extent by the increasingly restrictive expectations placed upon them as women supports her argument that their success as writers was not necessarily a "simple gain" in feminist terms. This paradox has become a central feature in contemporary criticism of eighteenth-century fiction written by women, and Spencer's account is the most clear and concise exploration of this phenomenon.

TODD takes as her starting point a sign that the prostitute, Angellica, in Aphra Behn's play *The Rover*, displays herself to attract customers. This "sign" comes to signify Todd's concern with the various strategies that women writers from 1660 to 1800 employed to negotiate their roles as public and professional authors. Todd explores how this "constructed nature of femininity" was formed in the fiction written by women in the period. She traces the development of these self-representations both by writers of fictions (including here memoirists and autobiographiers) and in the fiction itself. The representation of the woman writer is seen to move from the relatively "frank" expression of the Restoration, through to an emphasis in the mid-century on sensibility and sentimentalism. The last section of the book describes the contradictory reactions to this new respectable image, yet Todd also stresses the gains for later writers of the creation of a female literary authority based on morality. The readings of work by individual authors, such as Delarivier Manley, Sarah Fielding, Fanny Burney, and Ann Radcliffe, are intermingled with a historical account of the social, political, and economic conditions in which they wrote, to provide a context for the achievements of particular writers. Todd describes her work as an "overview", and it is successful and informative on this level. However, the volume of material included can be overwhelming and tends to obscure the finer points of her theoretical approach.

BALLASTER's study places a welcome emphasis on women's novelistic writing "prior to the rise of the sentimental myth inaugurated by Richardson's *Pamela*". By reassessing various theoretical explanations for the development of the novel as a form, Ballaster argues that the continuing appeal of non-realistic forms (such as the seventeenth-century French romance) and the particular contribution of women writers to novelistic discourse had a specific and instrumental role in the development of the novel. Ballaster stresses the need for a more sophisticated analysis of the narratives that focus on the themes of love or seduction by placing "seductive forms" in a party-political context, and by viewing seduction as a metaphor for the literary power of the woman writer over her "seduced" reader. The second section of the book provides a detailed exploration of the fiction of Behn, Manley, and Haywood in the light of this revisionary context.

MYERS examines the term "bluestocking" as it developed from a description of intellectual men who showed an interest in the conversation and acquaintance of women to its usage as an ambiguous term denoting women who aspired to "the life of the mind" through literature and learning. Myers' approach is primarily biographical. She traces the lives, marriages, social circumstances, and writings of Elizabeth Carter, Elizabeth Montagu, Catharine Talbot, and Hester Chapone, among others, in an attempt to convey a measure of their accomplishments and of their acknowledgement of the inevitable limitations placed on female education. Myers places great emphasis on the importance of female friendship in this literary group. She characterises these friendships as "supportive", dedicated to creating a communal image of virtue and chastity, which helped to establish the "bluestocking" women as respectable and useful members of society. This concentration on the personal biographical details of the writers under discussion does not lend itself easily to a theoretical context, and Myers' attempts to incorporate feminist theory into her thesis often seem rather forced. Nevertheless, Myers provides a detailed and fascinating account of an immensely significant aspect of the history of the woman writer.

As with all the critical works discussed here, LANDRY's book constitutes a challenge to the traditional (male) eighteenth-century literary canon. However, Landry stresses that feminist literary history must not only be content to "rediscover" texts by women, but must address issues of class, race, and nationality, as well as gender. The objects of her study are what she terms "laboring-class" women poets, in opposition to a clearly defined "working-class" movement usually associated with the nineteenth century. Landry emphasises the necessity of a Marxist, feminist, and New-Historicist approach in which she grounds her readings of the poetry of, for example, Mary Collier, Mary Leapor, Phillis Wheatley, and Ann Yearsley. The insights that such an approach provides are often productive, as with her reassessments of Mary Wollstonecraft and Hannah More, but the theoretical language she employs could be seen as potentially alienating or too dense. The major significance of this book is that it forces the student of eighteenth-century women's writing into the realisation that the history we study is largely that of middle-class women. By widening her discursive field to include other considerations apart from gender, Landry not only provides insight into a largely neglected area of eighteenth-century women's poetry, but also provides a different perspective from which to view, for example, the "bluestocking" women of Myers' study.

SARAH PRESCOTT

Women Writers: British – 19th Century

1. General

Bald, Marjory A., *Women Writers of the Nineteenth Century*, Cambridge: Cambridge University Press, 1923; reprinted, New York: Russell & Russell, 1963
Black, Helen, *Notable Women Authors of the Day*, Glasgow: David Bryce & Son, 1893
Clarke, Norma, *Ambitious Heights: Writing, Friendship, Love – the Jewsbury Sisters, Felicia Hemans, and Jane Welsh Carlyle*, London and New York: Routledge, 1990
Colby, Vineta, *The Singular Anomaly: Women Novelists of the Nineteenth Century*, New York: New York University Press, 1970; London: University of London Press, 1970
Gilbert, Sandra M., and Susan Gubar, *The Madwoman in the Attic: The Woman Writer and the Nineteenth-Century Literary Imagination*, New Haven, Connecticut, and London: Yale University Press, 1979
Leighton, Angela, *Victorian Women Poets: Writing Against the Heart*, Hemel Hempstead, Hertfordshire: Harvester Wheatsheaf, 1992; Charlottesville: University Press of Virginia, 1992
Oliphant, Mrs, *et al.*, *Women Novelists of Queen Victoria's Reign: A Book of Appreciations*, London: Hurst & Blackett, 1897

Several nineteenth-century books celebrated the achievements of women authors. BLACK's 26 interviews "at home" are adulatory in tone and dwell as much on the decor of her subjects' charming houses as on their achievements. She nevertheless gives some intriguing insights into the personalities and working methods of such writers as Eliza Linton, Rhoda Broughton, Mrs Alexander, and Jean Ingelow. The publisher Hurst & Blackett commissioned a group of living women novelists, including OLIPHANT, to write essays on "leading Women Novelists of the Victorian Era" in celebration of "the longest reign". No writers then still living were included because "in the case of living lady fictionists, it is too early to assess the merit or forecast the future of their works". The selection is itself of interest. Alongside writers now firmly established in the literary canon are names such as Caroline Clive, Hesba Stretton, and Anne Manning. But the collection is perhaps chiefly known for two particular essays: firstly, Oliphant's discussion of the Brontës, in which she credits Charlotte with expressing for the first time, and to the consternation of her contemporaries, a woman's grievance at being denied the right to express her love and seek her mate; secondly, Eliza Linton's review of George Eliot, in which she acknowledges both her genius and high critical reputation, and praises much in the novels, though she snipes at Eliot's personal life.

BALD's collection of studies is an interesting example of early twentieth-century criticism of women writers by a female scholar. Her book does not, she writes, "profess to be in any sense a 'feminist treatise' or to "determine what the woman of letters should be like". She sees the eight women whose work she discusses (Jane Austen, the Brontës, Elizabeth Gaskell, George Eliot, Elizabeth Browning, and Christina Rossetti) as both "remarkable women" and "remarkable human beings". Yet throughout her very readable and often perceptive and sensitive, if conservative, discussions, Bald remains constantly aware that they *were* women, and the subheadings within her chapters include such aspects as "Treatment of Her Own Sex" and "The Woman's Point of View". She concludes that all the writers had to fight to establish the normality of being both writers and women, and that all shared in some degree "feminine characteristics" as writers. Modern critics may find her somewhat patronising dismissals of Anne Brontë and Elizabeth Browning controversial to say the least. Interestingly, Gaskell is accorded by far the most extended treatment.

GILBERT's substantial work, now recognised as a seminal feminist text on women's writing, draws particularly on the lives and works of Austen, Elizabeth Barrett Browning, the Brontës, George Eliot, and Christina Rossetti. Charlotte Brontë is a pivotal figure, and her novels are given detailed treatment. Nineteenth-century women are seen as trapped within literary constructs created by men, and what unites them is an impulse to break these constraints, and redefine self, art, and society. This thesis draws on the writers' minor works and juvenilia as well as well-known texts.

Though "The Singular Anomaly" of COLBY's study of work in the last decades of the nineteenth and early years of the twentieth centuries is that all her subjects are women, she sees the genre of the novel, as a vehicle for expressing and disseminating ideas, as more important than the fact that the writers are women. Nevertheless, as she admits, and as her studies of five novelists reveal, their work was influenced in both "the circumstances of its composition, and its reception" by their sex. In different circumstances, with more channels of influence and varied means of earning a living open to them, they might not all have turned to writing novels. Indeed, Colby's study, both in its biographical elements and in its critical commentary, considers drama and other writings by her subjects. Covering Eliza Linton, Olive Schreiner, Mary Ward, Pearl Craigie, and Vernon Lee, the book discusses – usefully within one volume – novels that mostly receive little critical attention.

CLARKE's critical analysis of the relationships between the Jewsbury sisters, Felicia Hemans, and Jane Carlyle centres on the ambivalences in nineteenth-century women writers' sense of identity. All four women she regards as living "lives in which the business of literary production was an organizing principle"; but their literary ambitions were circumscribed by the domestic ideology to which they subscribed. From a feminist standpoint Clarke discusses the constraints on female friendship in a patriarchal society, and suggests reasons why literary history has accorded their work so low a status, and why they deserve greater scholarly attention. In the course of her thesis Clarke draws on and examines an interesting selection of their work. Each chapter is fully annotated and there is an additional useful short reading list of mainly recent scholarly studies.

While recent criticism of nineteenth-century women's writing in general, as opposed to assessment of individuals, has emphasised the novel, one good recent study that redresses the balance is LEIGHTON's collection of essays on eight women who viewed themselves as professional poets (Hemans, L.E.L. [Letitia Landon], Elizabeth Browning, Christina Rossetti, Augusta Webster, "Michael Field" [Katherine Bradley and

Edith Cooper], Alice Meynell, and Charlotte Mew). Though the emphasis is on the later decades of the century, Hemans and L.E.L. are included as "the true originators of a line of poetry which can be distinguished from the Romantics, on the one hand, and the modernists on the other". Leighton views this poetry as growing from and struggling with contemporary cultural notions of women's sensibility, and her concern throughout the book to acknowledge that "the socio-political reality of women's lives remains embedded in the figures even of the most fantastical of their dream poems" makes for an interesting balance of biographical and historical context, and critical analysis of individual poems. The recovery of less well-known poets and the bibliography add to the book's usefulness.

BARBARA M. ONSLOW

2. Romantic Era

Favret, Mary A., *Romantic Correspondence: Women, Politics and the Fiction of Letters*, Cambridge and New York: Cambridge University Press, 1993

Favret, Mary A., and Nicola J. Watson (eds.), *At the Limits of Romanticism: Essays in Cultural, Feminist, and Materialist Criticism*, Bloomington: Indiana University Press, 1994

Homans, Margaret, *Women Writers and Poetic Identity: Dorothy Wordsworth, Emily Brontë, and Emily Dickinson*, Princeton, New Jersey: Princeton University Press, 1980

Landry, Donna, *The Muses of Resistance: Labouring-Class Women's Poetry in Britain 1739–1796*, Cambridge and New York: Cambridge University Press, 1990

Mellor, Anne K. (ed.), *Romanticism and Feminism*, Bloomington: Indiana University Press, 1988; Oxford: Blackwell, 1988

Richardson, Alan, *Literature, Education and Romanticism: Reading as Social Practice 1780–1832*, Cambridge and New York: Cambridge University Press, 1994

Ross, Marlon B., *The Contours of Masculine Desire: Romanticism and the Rise of Women's Poetry*, New York and Oxford: Oxford University Press, 1989

Spender, Dale, *Mothers of the Novel: 100 Good Women Writers Before Jane Austen*, London: Pandora, 1986; New York: Routledge & Kegan Paul, 1986

Wilson, Carol Shiner, and Joel Haefner (eds.), *Revisioning Romanticism: British Women Writers 1776–1837*, Philadelphia: University of Pennsylvania Press, 1994

Critical studies of women's writing within the cultural field of Romanticism have tended to centre on fiction, usually in the genre characterised as "gothic romance". The interest of women novelists in the gothic conventions of mysterious and supernatural occurrences in exotic and remote settings has been the subject of many excellent studies, including ones Janet Todd, Eve Kosofsky-Sedgwick, and more recently Emma Clery. A useful place to start, however, is the wide-ranging survey by SPENDER of women fiction-writers before Jane Austen. An entire chapter is devoted to Ann Radcliffe, the best known of the women gothic novelists, but equal attention is accorded to writings less well known to us today but nonetheless justly celebrated in their time: the "political fictions" of Lady Morgan, the autobiographical novels of Mary Hays, Amelia Opie's "novel of ideas", and Charlotte Smith's fictional investigations into "real life". It is Fanny Burney and Maria Edgeworth who, for Spender, attain the "height of achievement" in women's fiction during the early Romantic period, and theirs are the works that provide "incontrovertible evidence that women had forged a full, fascinating – and fantastic – literary tradition".

In recent years, more attention has been devoted to women's poetry. Feminist revisionary readings of the Romantic poetic tradition have ensured that the canon can no longer be thought to be comprised solely of the so-called "big six" male poets (Coleridge, Wordsworth, Keats, Shelley, Blake, Byron). The publication of the collection edited by MELLOR was a significant contribution to this reappraisal. Mellor introduces studies of previously unheard, or rather, under-heard, voices, for as Stuart Curran points out, the poetry of Joanna Baillie, Charlotte Smith, and Felicia Hemans was more highly regarded than any of the "big six" (except Byron) by contemporary critics and purchasers alike. Concentrating on Smith, Curran points out that her work in the 1780s anticipates many of the thematic and formal concerns of later writers. Curran has recently edited the first new edition of Smith's complete poems for over a century, and a return to critical and perhaps popular favour is certainly overdue. Other Romantic writers studied in this volume include Mary Wollstonecraft, Mary Lamb, and Mary Robinson, but more familiar topics are reinflected. The relation of William and Dorothy Wordsworth, for instance, is again central: this vexed question is discussed in economic terms by Kurt Heinzelman, who examines the two writers' differing ideas of the domestic, and by Susan Wolfson, who reads Dorothy's prose works as encoded rejections of some of her brother's ideas of the ideal relation between individuality and community.

If Mellor's volume has been the most influential of the revisionary studies, then among the earliest is that of HOMANS, whose book discusses in some depth the poetry of Dorothy Wordsworth, Charlotte Brontë, and Emily Dickinson. For any reader of Dorothy Wordsworth's poetry, the available material is extremely thin: only around 20 poems survive, most of which were left unfinished and unpublished. Like many subsequent readers of Dorothy's writing, including Heinzelman and Wolfson, Homans appears to feel unable to study the poetry outside the parameters of a life inextricably linked to her brother's. Powerful as Homans' critique of William's suppression of Dorothy's writing is, a more radical gesture might have been to read the poetry independently of its author's life-story. This book nevertheless offers a useful introduction for any student of women in Romanticism, and is throughout quite conscious of the difficulties of reading women's Romantic poetry in isolation from the male tradition. The opening chapter is particularly helpful, a succinct study of how a masculine poetics is naturalised and women's writing apostrophised in the ancient Greek and Hebraic traditions, since Plato and the Book of Genesis. This study is also sensitive to the difficulties – social and epistemological – of Romantic writing for women. Homans is attentive to these problems as they are reflected in the work of the three main writers under discussion, but also in two twentieth-century poets who have continued a broad Romantic women's tradition. The final chapter details the roles of Anne Sexton and Sylvia Plath in this movement, pointing out the continuities of their work with Dickinson's project in particular.

Perhaps the most theoretically-minded work to emerge in the feminist reappraisal of Romanticism is that of ROSS, whose long and thorough study contentiously suggests the impossibility of a woman writer possessing an authentic Romantic voice. The Romantic, he argues, was and still is an inherently masculine mode predicated on the excision or co-option of the female. This need not devalue the work of Mary Shelley or Dorothy Wordsworth and others, so long as we recognise that they cannot express a Romantic epistemology. Instead, Ross attempts to recover a "cultural space" for a "feminine poetics of affection", which can express "a community of shared desire". What makes the women poets un-Romantic is their refusal of masculine traits of solitary quest and conquest in favour of a feminine form of desire based on sympathy and community. Ross traces the lineage of female poetry from the later eighteenth to the early nineteenth centuries, to show how the work of Hemans, Baillie, and Letitia Landon (L.E.L.) completes the project of earlier "bluestocking" and "sentimental" poets in attempting to locate a cultural space outside masculinity by embracing and extending "the traditional feminine role".

Ross also contributes to the collection of essays edited by WILSON and HAEFNER, offering an article on a dissenting tradition among British women writers which, together with the essay by Jane Aaron on religion and gender in Anglo-Welsh Romantic writing, invites readers of Romanticism to question the pre-eminence of secularised quasi-mystic spirituality in the male tradition, especially Blake and Wordsworth. We have failed to study such popular and re-worked Romantic modes as the hymn in favour of the lyric and epic, while also greatly overlooking the dissenting tradition to which Anna Barbauld, Lucy Aiken, and Hannah More belong. The editors suggest that the 1990s will see a "revisioning of romanticism" as a series of Romantic*isms*, a non-homogenous and diverse network of cultural practices. To this end, some unfamiliar writers are rehabilitated: Mary Robinson, Hemans, and Smith are each accorded two studies, and Elizabeth Inchbald, Mary Lamb, and Jane Taylor are also read. Women scientists and the cultural significance of needlework are also scrutinised, as is the theoretical work on drama by Baillie, whose plays were frequently compared to Shakespeare in the early nineteenth century.

LANDRY is concerned with the poetry of labouring-class women, following Mary Collier's critique of Stephen Duck in 1739, and the discursive conditions that enabled women's poetry to be patronised, published, and widely and genuinely admired. Many of the writers discussed here are certainly pre-Romantic in their poetic assumptions and practices, but Ann Yearsley, a milkwoman from Bristol, is reclaimed by Landry as an important voice in early Romantic writing. Her first collection of poetry appeared in 1785, her third and last in 1796, and between these she produced a historical tragedy play, a successful gothic novel, and several long political poems. As well as offering a sensitive reading of the poetry, which at its best subtly yet radically feminises a range of male landscapes and genres, Landry suggests that Yearsley's life story – which included near death from starvation and a furious public argument with her celebrated patron, Hannah More – offers a "parable" for feminist revisionist critics and historians. The parable consists not so much in setting up Yearsley's courageous stand against her patron, who withheld her sales earnings as an act of class resistance, but in drawing attention to the class and gender subtleties that a working-class writer can effect in her writing. Landry's book is a superb delineation of a tradition that has been too often relegated to the margins of Romantic culture.

RICHARDSON offers a brief discussion of Yearsley and other so-called "peasant poets" in terms of working-class literacy. However, this book is of interest to more general students of women's place in Romantic culture. The period saw an intensification of the debate on the reading matter appropriate for polite women. The question of reading is of course a central preoccupation of much women's writing in the Romantic period, from Hannah More to Radcliffe and Austen. Lucinda Cole and Richard Swartz, in their contribution to the collection of essays edited by FAVRET and WATSON, have followed Richardson in discussing Yearsley's work in terms of cultural literacy, comparing her work with Dorothy Wordsworth's more formally-trained writing. The quest for an appropriate public voice, given the cultural sanctions placed on the right to utterance of the poor, is seen as forcing the woman poet into deferential articulations, as in Yearsley's early work. Again, this collection of essays contains much of interest to all students of women in Romanticism. Other highlights include Favret's article on the poetry of domesticity; Sonia Hofkosh's article on "Sexual Politics and Literary History", which focuses on Sarah Hazlitt's *Journal*; and Nanora Sweet's study of the cultural value of Felicia Hemans' long-neglected poetry in "the post-Napoleonic moment".

While the study of Romantic poetry by women is beginning to rival gothic fiction in terms of critical attention, another important form of women's writing is the subject of FAVRET's 1993 book, which contends that the letter form was, as previously, a predominantly female pursuit but increasingly became a public and political form in the Romantic period. Favret discusses a range of letters, from Jane Austen's personal correspondence to the political missives from 1790s' France by Helen Maria Williams, Wollstonecraft's travel writings in Scandinavia, and Mary Shelley's *Frankenstein*, a rare example of epistolary fiction in the period. Her opening chapter examines the duplicitous letter sent by Marat's assassin Charlotte Corday to her victim, depicted in David's painting *The Death of Marat*. Corday's letter, often ignored by art historians, is a request for an audience with Marat to discuss the possibility of becoming a double agent; for Favret, this politicisation of the private and "secret" stands as a figure for the project of correspondence in the period. For instance, Wollstonecraft's *Letters Written . . . In Sweden, Norway, and Denmark* betray, to the historicist scholar, a similarly "duplicitous" motive. Wollstonecraft's ostensible travel writings screen another purpose, to deal with entrepreneurs and government "agents" to assist her correspondent Gilbert Imlay's illegal business of cargo-running between England and France. In their posthumous published form, the author's husband William Godwin significantly excised the personal, sometimes suicidal, aspects of the letters in order to present a singularly public voice.

Favret's fascinating historical reconstruction of these letters confirms her book as a further important contribution to the overdue feminist reappraisal of Romantic Studies.

TIM BURKE

3. Victorian

Armstrong, Isobel, *Victorian Poetry: Poetry, Poetics and Politics*, London and New York: Routledge, 1993
Clarke, Norma, *Ambitious Heights: Writing, Friendship, Love – the Jewsbury Sisters, Felicia Hemans, and Jane Welsh Carlyle*, London and New York: Routledge, 1990
Gilbert, Sandra M., and Susan Gubar, *The Madwoman in the Attic: The Woman Writer and the Nineteenth-Century Literary Imagination*, New Haven, Connecticut, and London: Yale University Press, 1979
Homans, Margaret, *Bearing the Word: Language and Female Experience in Nineteenth-Century Women's Writing*, Chicago: University of Chicago Press, 1986
Leighton, Angela, *Victorian Women Poets: Writing Against the Heart*, Hemel Hempstead, Hertfordshire: Harvester Wheatsheaf, 1992; Charlottesville: University Press of Virginia, 1992
Michie, Helena, *The Flesh Made Word: Female Figures and Women's Bodies*, New York: Oxford University Press, 1987
Moers, Ellen, *Literary Women*, Garden City, New York: Doubleday, 1976; London: W.H. Allen, 1977
Showalter, Elaine, *A Literature of Their Own: British Women Novelists from Brontë to Lessing*, Princeton, New Jersey: Princeton University Press, 1977; London: Virago, 1978, revised 1982

Victorian women's writing as a discrete area of study has emerged in parallel with feminist criticism. This has meant not only the rediscovery of forgotten writers and their work, but also energetic revaluations of those who never disappeared. The Victorian heroine and the Victorian woman writer herself offer perfect images of the struggles of all women caught in patriarchal structures, be they social, linguistic, or literary.

MOERS' pioneering book sets the agenda for much later criticism. It ranges from the eighteenth to the twentieth centuries, although certain nineteenth-century women are central – George Sand, the Brontës, Emily Dickinson, Christina Rossetti, Elizabeth Barrett Browning, Harriet Beecher Stowe, and George Eliot. She rediscovers neglected women writers, tracing relationships and influences among them. She is illuminating on the female literary tradition, for instance Dickinson's debt to Barrett Browning. Thematically arranged chapters cover topics such as money in women's fiction, the female gothic tradition, and the evolution of Victorian women's love poetry. Although at times historically very broad, Moers remains an informative basis for further study.

Although she also considers twentieth-century writers, SHOWALTER focuses on Victorian women novelists, arguing that the enforced production of "feminine" work (novels internalising the patriarchal conventions of the time) paradoxically created innovative and compelling texts. She claims that cultural pressures, like the need for male pseudonyms, the critical double standard, and the tension between womanhood and authorship, stimulated Charlotte Brontë, Elizabeth Gaskell, and George Eliot to write intense, symbolic novels. The concentration on writers publishing between the 1840s and the 1860s leads to some undervaluing of later Victorian writers, but Showalter remains essential reading.

Like Moers and Showalter, GILBERT and GUBAR's monumental work comes from the heroic early stages of feminist criticism. They see women writers as suffering an "anxiety of authorship" in patriarchal culture, and want to liberate from the Victorian text its submerged meanings – the madwoman in literature's attic who articulates the rage and resistance concealed there. The work of the Brontës, in particular *Jane Eyre* with its dispossessed "sister" Bertha Mason, is central to their attempt at a feminist poetics. Their argument is less powerfully sustained on George Eliot and on poetry in general, although *Aurora Leigh* and *Goblin Market* are recognised for the significant texts they are.

HOMANS draws on psycholinguistic theories to characterise the Victorian woman writer as a figure caught between a "literal" mother-daughter language and the desire to enter the "symbolic" realm of literary language, between the conflicting processes of bearing a child and bearing the word. Persuasive readings support her thesis: for example, both Nature as mother in *Jane Eyre* and the "outlawed" mother of *Wuthering Heights* must be betrayed by the acceptance-seeking woman writer. A full treatment of Elizabeth Gaskell, using diaries and letters beside canonical texts, establishes her as a paradigmatically successful exponent of both literal and figurative language.

MICHIE looks at the cultural construction of the female body in a range of novels, poetry, painting, and non-fictional prose, such as etiquette books and sex manuals by men as well as women. She reads what the text excludes as well as what it includes, arguing that Victorian writing's elaborately coded exclusions of women's bodies actually render them more visible. Activities such as work, eating, or prostitution are seen to be marginal to the literature yet present in its metaphoric subtexts; her overall thesis, however, lacks the sustained textual support in Homans.

CLARKE uses the friendship between Geraldine Jewsbury (a woman with a strong identity as a writer) and Jane Carlyle (whose "writing self" was silenced by marriage) to discuss the contradictions of the Victorian woman writer. She examines both published and private writing – Jewsburys' novels *Zoe* and *The Half Sisters*, as well as Carlyle's letters – and includes as a parallel the relationship between Maria Jane Jewsbury and the poet Felicia Hemans. Clarke's concerns are familiar: the silencing of women in Victorian culture; the guilt of the woman writer at her apparent rejection of conventional female roles; and the conflict between work and womanliness. The strength of the book comes from the relative unfamiliarity of the material, and her interweaving of biography, textual analysis, and the wider cultural context.

The aesthetic and formal configurations of poetry are less susceptible to the politicised readings that have been so fruitful for novels by women: "gender has tended to eclipse genre". However, both Leighton and Armstrong redress this imbalance.

LEIGHTON devotes a chapter each to eight poets (Felicia Hemans, L.E.L. [Letitia Landon], Elizabeth Barrett

Browning, Christina Rossetti, Augusta Webster, "Michael Field" [Katharine Bradley and Edith Cooper], Alice Meynell, and Charlotte Mew), all "Victorian" in sensibility and style. She provides useful biographical information, but discusses her "recuperated" poets on primarily aesthetic grounds. The argument connecting Leighton's excellent chapters is that these women used various objectifying techniques (for example, the self-distancing dramatic monologue of Webster, or the "wintriness" of Rossetti's imagination) to evade the poetry of unmediated feeling and write "against the heart".

In one chapter of a long general study, ARMSTRONG deals briefly with such Victorian poets as Adelaide Anne Procter, Dora Greenwell, Jean Ingelow, and Mathilde Blind, as well as Elizabeth Barrett Browning and Christina Rossetti. As the perhaps deliberately awkward chapter title indicates, Armstrong problematises "Women's Poetry" and refuses a pat definition of this tricky category. Reluctant to read all women's poetry in political terms, as to do so loses the particularity of individual poems, she also acknowledges that the conventional view of it as simple, pious, and effective did at least give the woman poet an accepted space in Victorian culture. Her remarks indicate that the debates about Victorian women's writing, particularly poetry, are still active and unresolved.

CATHERINE WELLS COLE

Women Writers: British – 20th Century

see **Women Writers: 20th Century, Women Writers: Contemporary**

Women Writers: American – General

Ammons, Elizabeth, *Conflicting Stories: American Women Writers at the Turn into the Twentieth Century*, New York and Oxford: Oxford University Press, 1991, revised 1993

Baym, Nina, *Feminism and American Literary History: Essays*, New Brunswick: Rutgers University Press, 1992

Berg, Temma F. (ed.), *Engendering the Word: Feminist Essays in Psychosexual Poetics*, Urbana: University of Illinois Press, 1989

Dearborn, Mary V., *Pocahontas's Daughters: Gender and Ethnicity in American Culture*, New York and Oxford: Oxford University Press, 1986

Gelfant, Blanche H., *Women Writing in America: Voices in Collage*, Hanover, New Hampshire: University Press of New England, 1984

Huf, Linda, *A Portrait of the Artist as a Young Woman: The Writer as Heroine in American Literature*, New York: Frederick Ungar, 1983

McClave, Heather (ed.), *Women Writers of the Short Story: A Collection of Critical Essays*, Englewood Cliffs, New Jersey: Prentice-Hall, 1980

McNall, Sally Allen, *Who is in the House? A Psychological Study of Two Centuries of Women's Fiction in America, 1795 to the Present*, New York: Elsevier, 1981.

Romines, Ann, *The Home Plot: Women, Writing and Domestic Ritual*, Amherst: University of Massachusetts Press, 1992

Showalter, Elaine, *Sister's Choice: Tradition and Change in American Women's Writing*, Oxford: Clarendon Press, 1991; New York: Oxford University Press, 1991

Showalter, Elaine (ed.), *Modern American Women Writers*, New York: Charles Scribner's Sons, 1991

Most critical works on American women writers tend to be grouped according to historical period. Those that are not, incline either toward specific thematic topics or toward essay collections which address a disparate and sometimes idiosyncratic collection of authors. A reader will find general surveys on American women writers most useful if pursuing information on an individual author or a specific trope in women's fiction generally.

McCLAVE's collection of essays adopts a traditional approach to late nineteenth- and twentieth-century American women short-story writers, among them Sarah Orne Jewett, Edith Wharton, Willa Cather, Katherine Anne Porter, Eudora Welty, and Flannery O'Connor. In her Introduction, McClave argues that "all of these writers tend to minimize sexual identity and sexual problems, concentrating instead on such issues as the power and value of tradition; moral qualities and tests of character; self-fulfillment and its limits in relation to the world; emotional bonds and deprivation". In keeping with this humanist, rather than theoretical focus, McClave offers general and introductory essays, written by such respected critics as Warner Betrhoff, R.W.B. Lewis, Robert Penn Warren, Robert Fitzgerald, and Joyce Carol Oates. This collection represents some of the earliest and, in many ways, foundational work on American women writers, which later critics have both revised and expanded significantly.

McNALL's study is psychoanalytic in focus, and takes as its topic the romance novel in America as it has been written by women from the eighteenth through the twentieth centuries. McNall concerns herself with one prominent and recurring theme – "the young woman's ambivalence about growing up to be a woman". Her critical premise is that "character, setting, and plot in popular women's fiction in America illustrate again and again some element in the early crisis of separation-individuation". Employing ideas of the "collective unconscious" drawn from Carl Jung, as well as precepts from the object-relations school embodied in the work of Melanie Klein, McNall investigates the ways in which popular American romance novels replicate unconscious emotional processes. McNall does not propose a theory of continuous historical development; rather, she focuses specific chapters – the sentimental gothic novel in the early national period, the nineteenth-century cult of domestic fiction, twentieth-century romantic fiction produced between the world wars, and the rise of women's fiction during the 1950s – on the historical interplay between family and fictional structures embedded in the popular literature she examines.

HUF's study organizes itself around the crucial differences between male and female protagonists of the *Künstlerroman*, a genre chronicling the growth and development of the artist. She outlines five salient differences between women heroes and their male counterparts. The first is in temperament: whereas male artist protagonists are usually "passive, sensitive, and shy", female artist figures tend to be resilient, capable, courageous, and intrepid. Huf's second difference is located in what she terms "the protagonist's ruling conflict", a self-division that in women manifests itself as a tension "not only between life and art but, more specifically, between her role as a woman, demanding selfless devotion to others, and her aspirations as an artist, requiring exclusive commitment to work". Women's *Künstlerromane* also differ from men's in that their female protagonists are often pitted "against a sexually conventional foil. This frivolous friend or enemy, who embodies excessive devotion to the female role, serves to make the aspiring artist look not unwomanly, but heroic by contrast". Women artists are also distinguished from men in their lack of a muse and, Huf contends, the novels in which they appear express an untempered radicalism toward gender liberation. Huf traces her argument through separate readings of three nineteenth-century writers and three twentieth-century ones, and her work in general is a useful introduction to the permutations this trope can encompass in narratives.

GELFANT's eclectic collection of essays on mostly non-canonical women writers (Grace Paley, Meridel Le Sueur, Jean Stafford, Harriet Wilson, Harriet Beattie, Tillie Olsen, and Willa Cather) embodies the collage motif of its subtitle, and expresses Gelfant's "preference for criticism that is open-ended, capable of surprise, and subversive of traditional standards and forms". Her brilliant and persuasive feminist investigation of these writers turns its attention to various themes, which she sees as potentially representative of American women's fiction in general. For instance, Gelfant argues that violence is a recurring theme, which "American women writers plant in their fiction and then conceal by various narrative strategies". Gelfant also self-consciously seeks out spaces where American motifs intersect with "themes pertinent to women: female patterns of development, mother-daughter relationships, romance and marriage, conflicts between caring for others and the self, response to a demand for passivity, and (disguised) forms of rebellion". Gelfant's readings are incisive and illuminating throughout the collection, and her two chapters on Cather, in particular, stand as formative essays in the field.

DEARBORN begins her argument with the premise that all ethnic literature is American literature, rather than some marginalized category of "other". Such an assumption allows her to pose the question crucial to her endeavor: "why is it, in fact, that there seems to be no ethnic female literary tradition?". Dearborn argues that there is, indeed, a viable tradition of ethnic literature written by women, though she believes authorship in general to be a rather "tenuous condition" for women. Focusing on literature produced by Native American, African-American, and Jewish-American women, Dearborn pursues the question of cultural mediation for women writers, as well as "the meanings of the ethnic woman's acculturation and her 'conversion' to the American self". She also examines how women writers have responded to what she terms "one of America's most ideologically potent myths: that of the mixed marriage between a native-born white male and an eroticized and exoticized ethnic woman". Dearborn's analysis is both far-ranging and interdisciplinary, and her work stands alone as the single most important treatment of ethnicity in American women's writing.

BERG's edition of essays collected from the first feminist seminar at the School of Criticism and Theory focuses broadly on "the relationship between gender and genre, between sexuality and textuality", and on the ways in which "such relationships get dramatized in poems and historicized in the lives of poets". In particular, the essays uniformly turn their attention to the differences between masculine and feminine linguistic subjects. Divided into three areas of investigation, the collection begins by exploring how "theories of psychosexuality – theories about the nature and origin of sexual identity – help us understand the grounds of *poesis*". Part Two includes essays on contemporary women's fiction, while Part Three refocuses its attention on the poetics of Emily Dickinson, Marianne Moore, and H.D., emphasizing "women's linguistic generativity by investigating the connections between womanly power and voice". Many of the essays in this collection are both theoretically dense and critically sophisticated; they represent a welcome addition to the discourse about the intersections of gender and textuality.

AMMONS' study, spanning the turn from the nineteenth century into the twentieth, seems at first to be more historically specific than other more general examinations of American women's writing. Yet Ammons' focus on this diverse and rich period of writing raises broader questions for the study of American literature. Her purpose, she writes, is:

> . . . to pull together the work of writers who were contemporaries but who are in the criticism almost always treated singly or at best as couples or small clusters. . . . The book joins the deepening critical discussion of the disjunction for many women writers between gender and high art . . . and provokes a number of questions about the relationship between political and social history and the production of art by women. The inquiry as a whole asserts the central and imperative need of bringing together into one account the work of white women writers and women of color.

Exploring literary productions that are "social, adult, topical", Ammons examines issues of silence, form and difference, freedom, art, and plot as they appear in fictions produced by a racially and ethnically diverse group of women writers. Combining history and biography with trenchant close readings of the texts, Ammons offers an important contribution to a much neglected period, which formulates many of the twentieth-century preoccupations shared by later writers.

Though best known for her pioneering work on nineteenth-century British women writers, SHOWALTER has also contributed two works to the study of American women writers. The more wide-ranging of the two, *Modern American Women Writers* is a reference guide to all major American women writers of the nineteenth and twentieth centuries. Combining biography with brief synopses of the major fiction or poems, each entry situates a writer in her cultural milieu and offers an extensive bibliography of both primary and secondary works. SHOWALTER's other study, *Sister's Choice*, is more an extended meditation on the role and place of American women's fiction within the literary canon, or what Showalter calls "the meaning and practice of gynocriticism with reference to American women's writing". Drawn from the Clarendon lectures, Showalter ranges across topics and authors, "from women's rewriting of *The Tempest* to the genre of Female Gothic to the history of the patchwork quilt itself".

Among the essays in this collection, Showalter's piece, "The Death of the Lady (Novelist): Wharton's *House of Mirth*", is one of the best known and most widely respected.

BAYM's work collects most of her major essays from the past decade and exhibits her characteristic concerns with revisionary efforts in American literary history. The first part of her collection (containing her much anthologized essay "Melodrama of Beset Manhood: How Theories of American Fiction Exclude Women Authors") is composed of "forays into the center of national literary history that focus on material ignored in or suppressed by that center". Baym explores a variety of critical methodologies in this section, including close reading, literary contextualization, author biography, and an "analysis of larger schemes by which disparate texts and authors have conventionally been connected in a nationalist literary-historical narrative: the romance-novel distinction, the self-in-the-wilderness myth, the myth of New England origins". The second part of this collection attempts to revise the narrative of pre-Civil-War white women's fiction as one defined solely by domestic sentimentality. In this section Baym explores the historical and political writing of this period in an effort to enlarge our "understanding of American women's literary discourse before the Civil War". In the final part of her collection, she addresses issues pertaining to feminist writing and to feminist pedagogy, arguing that in both our own critical work and in our classrooms we must remain ever vigilant to the structures of silencing and stereotyping that shape our construction of self in a male-centred world.

ROMINES builds on two decades of feminist scholarship in her study of how domestic ritual – in particular, the traditions of housekeeping handed down from mothers to daughters – has shaped some of the major fiction produced by American women writers of the nineteenth and twentieth centuries. Examining what she terms the domestic codes in the works of Harriet Beecher Stowe, Jewett, Mary E. Freeman, Cather, and Welty, Romines argues that these writers self-consciously experiment with, and incorporate, tropes of domesticity as telling markers of female worlds and of female fiction. Reading domestic ritual as a gendered language, Romines suggests that the trivialization and devaluation of domesticity and practices of housekeeping is both ignorant and distorting. Her elegant, subtle, and intelligent readings of the function of domesticity in specific novels stands as an important contribution in the reclaiming of women's work (both literary and domestic) as valuable.

DEBORAH CARLIN

Women Writers: American – to 1900

Baym, Nina, *Woman's Fiction: A Guide to Novels by and about Women in America, 1820–1870*, Ithaca, New York: Cornell University Press, 1978; 2nd edition, Urbana: University of Illinois Press, 1993

Davidson, Cathy N., *Revolution and the Word: The Rise of the Novel in America*, New York and Oxford: Oxford University Press, 1986

Foster, Frances Smith, *Written By Herself: Literary Production by African American Women, 1746–1892*, Bloomington: Indiana University Press, 1993

Harris, Susan K., *Nineteenth-Century American Women's Novels: Interpretative Strategies*, Cambridge and New York: Cambridge University Press, 1990

Kelley, Mary, *Private Woman, Public Stage: Literary Domesticity in Nineteenth-Century America*, New York: Oxford University Press, 1984

Tompkins, Jane, *Sensational Designs: The Cultural Work of American Fiction, 1790–1860*, New York and Oxford: Oxford University Press, 1985

Warren, Joyce W. (ed.), *The Other American Traditions: Nineteenth-Century Women Writers*, New Brunswick, New Jersey: Rutgers University Press, 1993

White, Barbara A., *American Women's Fiction, 1790–1870: A Reference Guide*, New York: Garland, 1990

Starting in the late 1970s, feminist critics started drawing attention to the neglected writings of early American women writers. The enterprise of rediscovery was originally conducted mainly by white scholars, and the writers being re-evaluated were almost exclusively elite white women. More recently, however, African-American women writers have also been extensively studied, and there are indications that the field will expand to include other ethnic groups as well. Despite the explosion of critical interest in the field, most of the attention has been directed to writers of fiction, and a comprehensive scholarly work on women's poetry is still awaited.

WHITE's bibliography is a full and accurate guide to sources on early American women's fiction. It lists and carefully annotates secondary works on women novelists, ranging from nineteenth-century biographical dictionaries to recent criticism. The major shortcoming of White's book is that it stops at 1985, and thus does not review the most recent critical contributions to the field. Yet, it is broad-ranging, precise, and easy to consult – an obligatory first step in the study of any early American woman novelist.

BAYM was the first scholar to analyze nineteenth-century women's novels as worthy literary artifacts. Although she is, at times, apologetic about her subject, which suggests her entrapment in the same traditional critical conventions she intends to criticize, Baym's study remains useful as a guide to the works of an extraordinary number of writers. The student in the field will find detailed plot summaries of novels that, in most cases, are still unavailable in modern reprints and relatively unknown. Baym's thesis is also still valid. She maintains that all the novels participate in one basic overplot, the story of a young girl who is left destitute, needs to struggle for subsistence, and in the process learns self-reliance. Though marriages often put an end to the heroine's adventures, the novels still emphasize female self-reliance throughout. The book also contains a bibliography of recent literary and cultural studies on nineteenth-century women writers, which adds to its value as a reference tool.

DAVIDSON devotes a large section of her brilliant study of American fiction to 1820 to the sentimental novel, a genre most commonly written and read by women. She is especially concerned with the effect of sentimental fiction on its audience: she argues that by staging the disastrous outcomes of their heroines' unfortunate romantic choices, sentimental novelists aimed at enabling their women readers, who would lose all property and legal rights to their husbands, to make judicious marital choices. In Davidson's hands, moreover, seemingly traditional plots of female sexual crime and well-deserved punishment reveal unsuspected radical elements, in that they depict fallen women as victims rather than offenders, as in Susanna Rowson's *Charlotte Temple*, or denounce the powerlessness of women within marriage, as in Hannah Webster Foster's *The Coquette*. With its sophisticated combination of literary and cultural analysis, Davidson's book is essential reading for those interested in eighteenth-century American women novelists.

KELLEY's exploration of the writings of 12 major women writers of the mid-nineteenth century resembles Davidson's book on earlier novelists in that she reaches beyond the purely literary to examine the cultural context in which these women wrote – for instance, in the publishing industry that made writing a profitable enterprise. Her thesis is that nineteenth-century women authors, whom she calls "literary domestics", were very uneasy about the publicity they had acquired as successful writers of fiction. Because woman's socially mandated sphere was the home, public writing seemed to these authors an indecorous and unbecoming activity. According to Kelley, the writers' apprehension and ambivalence emerged in their choice to publish anonymously, or under pseudonyms, their insistence that they were writing only to support their families, and their constant praise for women's domestic lives and belittling of their own literary efforts.

Although TOMPKINS's book is only in part about nineteenth-century women writers, it is the first study that fully addressed the issue of their exclusion from the canon and tried to redress it on a theoretical basis as well as by recovering their works. Tompkins denies that the canonic status of accepted classics arises from their intrinsic literary value, and argues instead that literary reputation is the result of a complex set of circumstances, which make a text visible when it is first published and maintain it in its position of pre-eminence afterwards. Moreover, she perceives literary texts as embedded in history rather than external to it, and the study of literature as an investigation of its impact on the social order rather than of its formal properties. Harriet Beecher Stowe's *Uncle Tom's Cabin* and Susan Warner *The Wide, Wide World* can then be read precisely *because* they are steeped in the evangelical tradition of their times – not in spite of that.

HARRIS's study offers theoretically informed, extensive readings of lesser-known novels, from Augusta Evans Wilson's *St Elmo* to Elisabeth Stuart Phelps's *The Silent Partner*. Harris's thesis is that mid-nineteenth-century women's fiction was characterized by a conventional cover-plot of female dependence and a subversive underplot of female independence. Influenced by recent theories of gender-based reading strategies, Harris maintains that women readers would perceive the novels' radical messages and dwell on them, discarding instead the conservative cover story. Despite her controversial assessment of eighteenth-century women's novels as advocating conventional female behavior, Harris's theoretically ambitious book is a milestone in the criticism on the subject.

The excellent collection of essays edited by WARREN evaluates the work of recovery of primary materials done so far, and suggests new directions of investigation. Thus, while some essays examine how the introduction of women's sentimental fiction into the canon has changed our understanding of the nature of nineteenth-century American literature, others analyze the writings of African-American and Jewish women, who had been previously neglected by scholars in the field. The collection is also original in that several essays examine non-literary as well as literary texts, from reform-minded journalism to travel writing and historical narratives. The book closes with a useful essay on the pedagogy of women's literature.

FOSTER's important study charts the territory of African-American women's writing from the earliest known works in the eighteenth century to the explosion of literary activity around 1892. The book offers both careful close readings of often newly recovered materials and a detailed recreation of their historical context. Foster demonstrates that early black women writers were mostly free-born, middle-class northerners who wrote without the aid of white patrons, thus correcting the traditional view of antebellum African-American literature as constituted by narratives of slavery co-written by whites. Her thesis is that black women's writings were argumentative and community-oriented, that is, that they sought to demonstrate the fundamental humanity of African Americans and advocate their right to full citizenship in the American Republic.

PAOLA GEMME

Women Writers: American – 1900 to the Present

Ammons, Elizabeth, *Conflicting Stories: American Women Writers at the Turn into the Twentieth Century*, New York and Oxford: Oxford University Press, 1991, revised 1993

Huf, Linda, *A Portrait of the Artist as a Young Woman: The Writer as Heroine in American Literature*, New York: Frederick Ungar, 1985

Moers, Ellen, *Literary Women*, Garden City, New York: Doubleday, 1976; London: W.H. Allen, 1977

Rabinowitz, Paula, *Labour and Desire: Women's Revolutionary Fiction in Depression America*, Chapel Hill: University of North Carolina Press, 1991

Showalter, Elaine, *Sister's Choice: Tradition and Change in American Women's Writing*, Oxford: Clarendon Press, 1991; New York: Oxford University Press, 1991

Walker, Alice, *In Search of Our Mother's Gardens: Womanist Prose*, New York: Harcourt Brace Jovanovich, 1983; London: Women's Press, 1983

Writing that deals specifically with American women writers of the twentieth century is a growing body of criticism, in which American feminist critical theory has, in some respects, given ground to the contemporary movement towards gender studies. Contemporary questions about the validity of American literary history in terms of "Americanness" and post-modernist cultural expression have also been made more complex by the debates surrounding race, class, gynocriticism, female sexual and social identity, and subjectivity within feminist discourse. The following works are suggested as starting points.

MOERS' investigation of "literary women" has been recognised as a major contribution to the field. It covers mainly English and American women writers, and although for a 1990s' reader its limitations are evident, it is significant as part of the initiative that generated the interest in women's writing, feminist literary criticism, publishing, and culture in the 1970s. It remains an important text for understanding the complexities of women's literary production, creativity, and the re-writing of a female literary history.

SHOWALTER's many contributions to American literary criticism are all valuable, and selection for this entry has not been an easy task. The scope of analysis in this book is wide, and the initial thematic chapters include a range of writers from varied backgrounds. Subsequent selection for in-depth analysis of Louisa May Alcott, Kate Chopin, and Edith Wharton constructs a bridge between the past and present. Questioning the history, traditions, and contradictions of American women's writing and, importantly, challenging the idea that monolithic national identity is possible within a multi-cultural reality like America, this critical analysis also looks beyond its own textual analysis.

AMMONS writes with authority of the "turn of the century" as an important time for American women writers. Usual critical concentrations which "scatter" or "ignore" women writers from 1890 to 1920 are discarded, as is the practice of separating white and black women writers. This "New Historical" critical work, concentrating on little-studied writers, identifies the pioneer women writers of the period and demonstrates a diverse and yet cohesive body of work, which illuminates the struggle women writers faced as artists and as women. The Introduction also allows insights into contemporary criticism, and, as Ammons states, the whole is meant to be "suggestive, a beginning", not definitive.

HUF also chooses to discuss both nineteenth- and twentieth-century writers in her study of the *Künstlerromane* (novels about artists) of American women authors. Taking six women's texts in chronological order, she investigates the character and conflict of the author-character exposing herself to a world. The study develops through analysis of the images by which each constructs her individuality as artist. In the process Huf traces images that recur in women's texts – monsters, entrapment, flight in the context of the struggle for artistic expression within a world that elevates male self-absorbtion and rebellion, while condemning those attributes in the female artist. The work is also valuable because it addresses issues in contemporary literary-critical discourse (through the work of Sylvia Plath).

RABINOWITZ offers a rare investigation into 1930s' revolutionary fiction by American women, and is based on two sets of revisions – firstly the revision of prevailing scholarship, and secondly the reconsideration of neglected or disparaged texts by women writers. The novels selected provide access to the study of an area of women's writing ignored by the critical canon. The view of the 1930s as irrelevant to feminist issues because of the dominance of class issues is overturned, as this critical analysis reads gender and class as "mutually sustaining discursive systems", through which narrative becomes the arena for an understanding of "new histories and new theories about women, literature and politics in 1930s America".

WALKER's collection of essays is the starting point for an understanding of the negation of, and struggle for, black female literary authority. The relationship to history, and the consequent ancestral inspiration from which the black woman's literary tradition evolves are subjects of many of the essays in this text. Stressing the importance of the female ancestral heritage, which forms a bridge from the past to the present and future, allows for an "outsider-within" stance. Exemplifying the dual negatives of whiteness and femaleness, and blackness and maleness in critical discourse, Walker's text promotes her personal view of loneliness as a "gift" which leads to "radical vision". By seeking out her own tradition in this way Walker opposes the dominant literary values, exposing the heterosexism and racism of both the women's movement and the critical canon.

MARGARET E. ROBERTS

Women Writers: African-American

Baker, Houston A., Jr., *Workings of the Spirit: The Poetics of Afro-American Women's Writing*, Chicago: University of Chicago Press, 1991

Carby, Hazel V., *Reconstructing Womanhood: The Emergence of the Afro-American Woman Novelist*, New York and Oxford: Oxford University Press, 1987

Christian, Barbara, *Black Feminist Criticism: Perspectives on Black Women Writers*, New York: Pergamon Press, 1985

Pryse, Marjorie, and Hortense J. Spillers (eds.), *Conjuring: Black Women, Fiction, and Literary Tradition*, Bloomington: Indiana University Press, 1985

Shockley, Ann Allen, *Afro-American Women Writers, 1746–1933: An Anthology and Critical Guide*, Boston: G.K. Hall, 1988

Wall, Cheryl (ed.), *Changing Our Own Words: Essays on Criticism, Theory, and Writing by Black Women*, New Brunswick, New Jersey: Rutgers University Press, 1989; London: Routledge, 1990

Willis, Susan, *Specifying: Black Women Writing the American Experience*, Madison: University of Wisconsin Press, 1987; London: Routledge, 1990

Criticism that examines the works of African-American women writers is both a recent phenomenon (produced primarily within the last two decades) and one devoted to the incorporation of a diversity of texts and writers into a literary canon from which African-American women's literature has hitherto been excluded.

CHRISTIAN's collection of essays addresses itself precisely to the task of documenting the historical process of invention, which she believes has shaped African-American women's literature through two centuries. Her essays chronicle the political necessity for African-American women writers to construct alternative and revisionary representations in order to counter "the images, primarily negative, of black people that predominated in the minds of white Americans". Much more heavily weighted toward contemporary African-American women's fiction (with multiple essays on Alice Walker, Toni Morrison, Paule Marshall, and Audre Lorde), Christian's study also includes three historical summaries of African-American women's poetry, the transformation from stereotype to character in literary representation of African-American peoples, and an examination of Frances E.W. Harper's important nineteenth-century novel, *Iola Leroy*. Though brief and often elliptic, Christian's essays raise insightful issues and articulate suggestive readings of selected African-American women's writings.

PRYSE and SPILLERS's collection of essays extends Christian's project of literary restoration by offering essays that attend to the breadth and depth of, primarily, twentieth-century literature of African-American women. The acknowledged project of this study is "to raise questions about individual writers and works, and about the aggregate significance of their fiction, that will move us closer to assessing the influence and writing the literary history of black women novelists". Two essays in the collection address nineteenth-century autobiography and slave narratives, and excellent readings of Ann Petry's influential 1946 novel *The Street* are offered by Bernard W. Bell and Marjorie Pryse. Other writers addressed in the collection are Morrison, Marshall, Octavia Butler, Toni Cade Bambara, Jessie Fauset, Pauline Hopkins, Walker, and Zora Neale Hurston. Four more general theoretical essays, which address themselves to different traditions within African-American women's fiction (interracial friendship, self-definition, cross-currents, and "ancient" power), round out this provocative and useful compilation.

WILLIS's study also groups contemporary women writers (Hurston, Marshall, Morrison, Walker, Bambara) under the loosely defined rubric of history. But:

> . . . the relationship of black women to history is twofold. As mothers, the reproducers of the labor force, black women have had a keen awareness of history as change. In their hope for their children's future, black women have learned to be attentive to moments of historical transition, and many have struggled for social change. In their role as producers, black women have known the present; then, in relation to the economics of reproduction, they have envisioned and strived for the future. As workers, they have sustained their families; as mothers, they have borne the oral histories from their grandmothers to their children. For all these reasons, today's black women writers understand history both as period and as process.

Willis's study throughout is characterized by such generalized and even abstract formulations. As she reads each author's *oeuvre* she touches on issues such as specifying (name-calling), folk tradition, the urban environment, and the relation of sexuality to history. Though she raises interesting details about individual works, the obscurity of her focus results in a less than coherent argument about African-American women's fiction in general.

CARBY's study, conversely, represents one of the most thoroughly historically grounded and intellectually sophisticated analyses of African-American women's literature within the critical tradition. Her project "works within the theoretical premises of societies 'structured in dominance' by class, by race, and by gender and is a materialist account of the cultural production of black women intellectuals within the social relations that inscribed them". Providing trenchant interpretations of the writing of Harriet Jacobs, Frances E.W. Harper, Anna Julia Cooper, Pauline Hopkins, and Nella Larsen, Carby's study analyzes the development of African-American women's fiction as a forum for political and cultural reconstruction, bound within certain literary conventions shaped by the prevailing sexual ideologies of the time. Carby's work remains a milestone in the criticism of African-American women's literature, for its intelligent and ground-breaking combination of literary analysis and cultural history.

SHOCKLEY's anthology chronicles the work and biographies of African-American writers from the eighteenth through the early twentieth-century. She divides her project into four sections: the colonial period to the Civil War, 1742–1862; Reconstruction to the turn of the century, 1868–99; the progressive era through World War I, 1900–23; and what Shockley terms the "New Negro" Movement, now commonly referred to as the Harlem Renaissance, 1924–33. Introductions to each section summarize the social, historical, racial, and political climate of the time, and are accompanied by a chronological listing of publications within each period, and by brief biographical sketches of the authors represented. Shockley's study is a valuable resource for lesser-known eighteenth- and nineteenth-century African-American writers, and it situates brief excerpts of literary works within their historical and cultural milieux.

WALL's edition of essays by various well-known African-American women critics is based on a conference held at Rutgers University, whose title the book reflects. Its project, broadly stated, "was how to bring the terms *criticism*, *theory*, and *writing by black women* into conjunction". While some essays in the collection approach individual literary works or genres specifically (Gloria T. Hull on Audre Lorde; Claudia Tate on nineteenth-century sentimental narratives; Abena P. Busia on Paule Marshall), the best essays focus on the relationship between African-American male and female critics, and on the sexual politics of critical inquiry as they are played out in the academy. Of particular note are the essays by Valerie Smith and Deborah E. McDowell, both of which examine the historical tensions between black feminist and black male critics who have taken issue with the attention paid to African-American women's writing (often, they feel, at the exclusion of work by African-American male writers) and with the representation of African-American men in that literature. Smith's and McDowell's essays cannily trace the debate about such alleged privileges and misrepresentations by examining who wrote what and when, outlining the story of academic infighting from a feminist perspective. This is an intelligent collection of essays and necessary reading for anyone interested in the politics of literary representation and criticism.

BAKER's work is an extended reply to critics such as Smith and McDowell, in which he attempts to position himself as a sympathetic critical traveler on the road of African-American women's writing. Baker claims at the outset, however, that resistance to theory (in his eyes what African-American literature deserves and needs articulated within academic discourse) has come largely "from the community of Afro-American women scholars, writers, and critics themselves". Baker characterizes a political debate – between feminist critics, who practice primarily historical analyses of African-American women's literature, and male critics (of whom he and Henry Louis Gates, Jr. are the most prominent), who practice non-historical, poststructuralist criticism. In a deft slight-of-hand, Baker manages to conflate contemporary African-American women critics with the literature they investigate. His project, conversely, he believes to be the examination of African-American women's literature through what he considers to be the critically rigorous lens of poststructuralist theory. Through this lens Baker hopes to restore the discursive modernity of African-American literature; the examples he cites throughout his study "serve to adumbrate a lineage of autobiographical, metalevel negotiations that constitute Afro-American discourse in its most cogent form". While Baker's analyses of individual works and passages are uniformly provocative and regularly brilliant, his broader argument would be better served by choosing an alternative construction on which to base itself than the subtle repudiation of African-American feminist criticism.

DEBORAH CARLIN

Woolf, Virginia 1882–1941

English novelist, short-story writer, and essayist

Abel, Elizabeth, *Virginia Woolf and the Fictions of Psychoanalysis*, Chicago: University of Chicago Press, 1990

Beer, Gillian, *Arguing with the Past: Essays in Narrative from Woolf to Sidney*, London and New York: Routledge, 1989

Bennett, Joan, *Virginia Woolf: Her Art as a Novelist*, Cambridge: Cambridge University Press, 1945, 2nd edition, 1964

Bowlby, Rachel, *Virginia Woolf: Feminist Destinations*, Oxford: Blackwell, 1988

Bowlby, Rachel (ed.), *Virginia Woolf*, London: Longman, 1992

Caughie, Pamela, *Virginia Woolf and Postmodernism: Literature in Quest and Question of Itself*, Urbana: University of Illinois Press, 1991

Guiguet, Jean, *Virginia Woolf and Her Works*, London: Hogarth Press, 1965; New York: Harcourt Brace & World, 1966

Homans, Margaret (ed.), *Virginia Woolf: A Collection of Critical Essays*, Englewood Cliffs, New Jersey: Prentice-Hall, 1993

London, Bette, *The Appropriated Voice: Narrative Authority in Conrad, Forster and Woolf*, Ann Arbor: University of Michigan Press, 1990

Marcus, Jane (ed.), *New Feminist Essays on Virginia Woolf*, Lincoln: University of Nebraska Press, 1981; London: Macmillan, 1981

Minow-Pinkney, Makiko, *Virginia Woolf and the Problem of the Subject: Feminine Writing in the Major Novels*, Brighton, Sussex: Harvester Press, 1987; New Brunswick, New Jersey: Rutgers University Press, 1987

Zwerdling, Alex, *Virginia Woolf and the Real World*, Berkeley: University of California Press, 1986

The canon of criticism on Virginia Woolf is so huge that any selection is, to a degree, idiosyncratic. Studies of her life, letters, and literature proliferate, while the recent release of her copyright has heralded the publication of several new annotated editions of her novels. As Rachel Bowlby points out, "Woolf's texts provide ample support for almost any position" (*Virginia Woolf: Feminist Destinations*, 1988) and the enormous changes in critical debate over the last three decades are reflected in the different periods of Woolf scholarship.

In 1942 E.M. Forster suggested that readers should dismiss Woolf's image as the "Invalid Lady of Bloomsbury" (*Virginia Woolf*, 1942). In the criticism of the 1940s–60s such an image had little influence. The body of the writer did not precede and determine that of the writing. However, there is a notable difference between the critical works written before and after the stories of her life and, more significantly, her death, began to be told. In the wake of the publication of both Quentin Bell's authorised two-volume biography and of Woolf's letters and diaries, Forster's image predominated. However, since the publication of Toril Moi's influential *Sexual/Textual Politics* in 1985, in which she argues that it is Woolf's textual practice, not her life, that needs reading, criticism of Woolf seems to have changed in line with Moi's position. The decision to exclude more overtly biographical readings of Woolf's texts is an attempt to highlight the shift away from such approaches, which has taken place in the last decade.

BENNETT'S study, published in 1945 and reprinted in 1964 with two new chapters on Woolf's diary and essays, is one of the first full-length critiques of the novels. Focusing on the specificity of Woolf's vision, Bennett argues that Woolf makes a textual shift from outside experience to inside experience: "the moral, social, economic and religious problems which play so large a part in the novels of the nineteenth century are important in her books too, but we are made aware of them only as they colour the world for the people she presents and form part of what life feels like to them". Not only does Bennett's work provide comprehensive analyses, which continue to be of interest, but, since she stresses that though Woolf's "genius was not autobiographical, she was not preponderantly interested in herself", it provides a cogent and lucid example of pre-Bell biographical criticism.

GUIGUET's study, originally published in French in 1962 as *Virginia Woolf et son oeuvre*, focuses on the whole of Woolf's writing. His systematic and thorough approach considers every novel, in sequence, and assigns each equal attention, thus avoiding the production of a hierarchy of "major" and "minor" texts. In a similar fashion, Guiguet also analyses both Woolf's diary and essays as texts in themselves, rather than treating them as keys to understanding the novels. The examination of the fiction is preceded by a discussion of the "ambiance" that produced it – Woolf's "constant contact with the literary production of the time" as well as the

Bloomsbury Group. Guiguet argues that "to define the world in which she developed and wrote, and to define it in relation to herself, will be a way of getting near her and sharing her point of view". This is an accessible classic, which contains a useful, and rare, overview of Woolf criticism, in both French and English, from 1930 to 1960.

MARCUS's 1981 collection on Woolf is a good introduction to the radical feminist perspective that she advocates. The essays are wide-ranging in their approach and focus, and they provide a comprehensive survey of the Woolf criticism of the early 1980s. Several now-classic articles appear, including Marcus's "Thinking Back through Our Mothers", Jane Lilienfeld's "Where the Spear Plants Grew: the Ramsays' Marriage in *To the Lighthouse*", and Judy Little's "*Jacob's Room* as Comedy: Woolf's Parodic *Bildungsroman*". It is a historically significant and critically useful book.

ZWERDLING's book concentrates on the "complex relationship, represented in Woolf's novels, between the interior life and the life of society". He accounts for the terms in this relationship as follows:

> By the "interior life" I mean the thoughts, feelings, needs, and fantasies that constitute the core of the self, whether or not they find expression in action or speech. By the life of society I mean the whole range of external forces that may be said to influence our behaviour: familial ideals, societal expectations, institutional demands, significant historical events or movements that affect our lives.

The latter term becomes "real world" in the title "not because it is more real than the interior life but . . . because its force must inevitably be taken into account". Zwerdling examines how Woolf's novels represent and analyse the "power relationship" between the two and their "relative strengths" at different historical periods, in this interesting and thorough book.

MINOW-PINKNEY employs Julia Kristeva's theories of subjectivity and poetic language and Freudian and Lacanian psychoanalysis in her analysis of Woolf's novels. She considers that Woolf's modernism and feminism are "the two faces of a single project", constituting a "single awareness and concern": the questioning of phallocentricism. Woolf's notion of androgyny is the mediator, linking "aesthetic innovation and feminist conviction". Minow-Pinkney's chapter on *Orlando* and Freud's *Jokes and Their Relation to the Unconscious* is especially helpful. This is a lucid and cogently argued book.

BOWLBY's book, in the informative and helpful "Rereading Literature" series, is probably the ideal introduction to post-structuralist readings of Woolf's writing. It is accessible, engaging, informative, and well-written. Focusing on how Woolf is the "only twentieth-century British woman writer" to be "taken seriously by critics of all casts", Bowlby challenges the possibility of fitting Woolf's writing in to any one critical category. Using the metaphor of trains throughout the study, she suggests that Woolf's texts constantly refuse, and question, the sexual and textual politics of being allocated to one "compartment".

ABEL's study is not concerned with influence but with "intertextuality" between Freud's work and Woolf's writing. Her project is to "dislodge the binary construction of the encounter not only between Woolf and psychoanalysis but also between literature and psychoanalysis as criticism habitually couples them". Woolf's relationship to Freud and Melanie Klein, argues Abel, moves in the course of her literary career from an emphasis on "maternal to paternal genealogies", and it is the "signal moments" in that shift which are analysed. This is an advanced study, both useful and perceptive.

BEER's study of narrative and its relationship to history includes four chapters that concentrate on Woolf. Warning against a "presentist mode of argument" in literary criticism, which "takes *now* as the source of authority, the only real place", she foregrounds the necessity of encountering "the otherness of earlier literature" in order to question the critical and social assumptions of one's own historical position. In the course of the four essays, Beer considers the following: the relationship of Woolf's writing to late nineteenth-century and early twentieth-century deterministic organisations of experience; Woolf's language as new, and yet descended from Victorian writing; the kinship of prehistory and present history in *Between the Acts* and *The Voyage Out*; and, finally, the "consonances" between *To the Lighthouse*, the writing of Woolf's father, and Hume. Beer's book must be considered invaluable.

LONDON's study of the novels of Joseph Conrad, E.M. Forster, and Virginia Woolf focuses on voice, which, she argues, has frequently been read in modernist writing, and the criticism which surrounds it, as a site of authenticity. By analysing critical moves to produce a stable and whole voice for an author, or an author's style, London suggests that voice is not so much "the modern novel's given – or even its supreme achievement" but rather it is "the question the novel sets itself". London's approach, which she calls "reading interestedly", employs contemporary theory to question the politics of seeking out a single position from which to speak. Although more difficult than Bowlby's (1988) or Minow-Pinkney's arguments, London's work on Woolf's "characteristic circumventions" is innovative.

CAUGHIE's argument springs from a desire to change the "dominant tradition in literature", which produces categories and binary oppositions in texts, writers, and schools of thought, without replacing it with yet another, equally limiting tradition. Her approach, based on Wittgenstein's linguistic philosophy and pragmatics, aims to shift the emphasis from discerning a text's meaning to considering its language and function. Despite the fact that Caughie's own argument often relies on the very binary oppositions she aims to question, her analysis of both Woolf criticism and Woolf's writing is still refreshing and challenging, especially in the discussions of *Flush*, *Orlando*, and *The Voyage Out*.

BOWLBY's 1992 collection, like Homans's, includes Erich Auerbach's analysis of *To the Lighthouse* (from his *Mimesis*) and Elizabeth Abel's psychoanalytic study of *Mrs Dalloway*. However, these are the only articles the two books have in common. Focusing on the diversity of criticism that surrounds Woolf's writing, and the lack of consensus therein, Bowlby has chosen several significant articles by critics renowned for their feminist critical praxes, as much as for their knowledge of Woolf. For example, Gillian Beer's historical and textual analysis, in "The Island and the Aeroplane: The Case of Virginia Woolf", is included, as is Mary Jacobus's persuasive psychoanalytic approach in "The Third Stroke: Reading Woolf with Freud". Articles by Tony Inglis and Françoise Defromont, previously only available in French, appear in translation for the first time. This is an ideal overview.

HOMANS's collection of essays ranges from 1945 to 1992, and thus provides a necessary and compact overview of Woolf scholarship. A wide variety of different readings is included. She stresses that:

> . . . the selection is slightly weighted toward approaches that take Woolf seriously as an innovative political writer, but . . . also find Woolf's political analysis first and foremost in her writing . . . in the very qualities of beauty and plangency that have convinced other readers that she is above politics.

Classics such as Auerbach's "The Brown Stocking" and Geoffrey Hartman's "Virginia's Web" are accompanied by more recent and unusual work, especially on *The Voyage Out* and *Night and Day*, by Rachel Blau DuPlessis and Christine Froula. This is an excellent survey.

LOUISE TUCKER

Wordsworth, William 1770–1850

English poet

Abrams, M.H., *Natural Supernaturalism: Tradition and Revolution in Romantic Literature*, New York: Norton, 1971; Oxford: Oxford University Press, 1971

Bate, Jonathan, *Romantic Ecology: Wordsworth and the Environmental Tradition*, London and New York: Routledge, 1991

Bewell, Alan, *Wordsworth and the Enlightenment: Nature, Man, and Society in the Experimental Poetry*, New Haven, Connecticut: Yale University Press, 1989

Chandler, James K., *Wordsworth's Second Nature: A Study of the Poetry and Politics*, Chicago: University of Chicago Press, 1984

Gill, Stephen, *William Wordsworth: A Life*, Oxford: Clarendon Press, 1989; New York: Oxford University Press, 1989

Glen, Heather, *Vision and Disenchantment: Blake's Songs and Wordsworth's Lyrical Ballads*, Cambridge and New York: Cambridge University Press, 1983

Hartman, Geoffrey H., *Wordsworth's Poetry, 1787–1814*, New Haven, Connecticut: Yale University Press, 1964, revised 1971

Jacobus, Mary, *Romanticism, Writing, and Sexual Difference: Essays on "The Prelude"*, Oxford: Clarendon Press, 1989; New York: Oxford University Press, 1989

Johnston, Kenneth R., *Wordsworth and "The Recluse"*, New Haven, Connecticut: Yale University Press, 1984

Kelley, Theresa M., *Wordsworth's Revisionary Aesthetics*, Cambridge and New York: Cambridge University Press, 1988

Levinson, Marjorie, *Wordsworth's Great Period Poems: Four Essays*, Cambridge and New York: Cambridge University Press, 1986

Lindenberger, Herbert, *On Wordsworth's "Prelude"*, Princeton, New Jersey: Princeton University Press, 1963

Liu, Alan, *Wordsworth: The Sense of History*, Stanford, California: Stanford University Press, 1989

Reed, Mark L., *Wordsworth: The Chronology of the Early Years, 1770–1799*, Cambridge, Massachusetts: Harvard University Press, 1967

Reed, Mark L., *Wordsworth: The Chronology of the Middle Years, 1800–1815*, Cambridge, Massachusetts: Harvard University Press, 1975

Simpson, David, *Wordsworth's Historical Imagination: The Poetry of Displacement*, London and New York: Methuen, 1987

As Matthew Arnold once said, Wordsworth has been good to his critics. This and sheer volume make a short list of the best recent criticism problematic. The present listing strives to include a range of viewpoints, but important exclusions are inevitable, and to some degree arbitrary. Modern readers should keep in mind that early Wordsworth criticism, not listed here, remains well worth consulting, beginning with Coleridge's *Biographia*, Keats's letters, and essays by William Hazlitt, Thomas De Quincey, and Arnold.

Moreover, the most important recent critical developments are arguably embodied in basic reference works, which cannot be fully listed here – new editions of the poetry, prose, and letters, biographies, chronologies, and catalogs of Wordsworth's reading and verse forms. Especially noteworthy are the Cornell Wordsworth editions (1975–): reversing the traditional preference for the poet's latest, heavily revised, texts, they make most of his poetry available in its earliest complete versions (or, in the case of frequently revised works like *The Prelude*, in multiple versions). In the process, they give immensely detailed records of the poetry's composition and revision (including photographic reproductions and meticulous transcriptions of the manuscripts). These editions may affect Wordsworth studies more in the long run than any other twentieth-century development.

GILL's critical biography assimilates the discoveries and emphases of recent criticism and scholarship, especially the textual scholarship that has recovered so many of the earliest texts and moved unfinished poems such as *The Recluse* toward center stage. Gill's care in assessing Wordsworth's own account of his life in *The Prelude* constitutes an important advance on his predecessor, Mary Moorman, though her *William Wordsworth: A Biography* (2 vols., Oxford University Press, 1957–65) is more detailed and remains useful. REED's two chronologies, cornerstones for subsequent scholarship, give the best and handiest possible record of the Wordsworths' daily activities, including the composition dates of individual works, while scrupulously distinguishing between facts, probabilities, and conjectures. Appendices include valuable essays on more complex and conjectural matters.

HARTMAN has been the most influential critic of Wordsworth, at least until, and arguably notwithstanding, the recent rise in New-Historical approaches. With complex, sensitive, and provocative readings of the early and major verse, Hartman presents Wordsworth's "consciousness of consciousness" as his predominant theme, focuses on the dialectic between his transcendent impulses and his loyalty to this world, and reads him as laboring to "humanize" his "otherworldly power of imagination". ABRAMS' influential study, to which the Wordsworth of the Prospectus to *The Recluse* and *The Prelude* is central, sees Romanticism's coherence in its secularization of "theological ideas and ways of thinking". Developing a tradition derived from A.C. Bradley's Oxford Lectures of 1903, Abrams emphasizes Wordsworth's transcendental or "visionary style" and his naturalization of Christian, especially Miltonic, theodicy.

JACOBUS' volume comprises the essays of a decade (1979–89) on the 1805 *Prelude*, especially remarkable for their mobility of viewpoint: in psychoanalytic and deconstructionist essays, Jacobus examines Wordsworth's production of a unified autobiographical subject despite his awareness of self-difference in the self and in writing; in New-Historicist essays, she relates *The Prelude*'s anxiety of imagination to contemporary "anti-theatrical prejudice", or ponders its determined silence about the slave trade; and in essays on sexual difference, she considers problems of gender and genre in "Vaudracour and Julia", relates the figure of the prostitute to that of personification in Book 7, and re-examines Romantic pedagogy in the light of Wordsworth's and Rousseau's representations of sexual difference. All of Jacobus's essays share a comparative bent, considering Wordsworth's poetics in relation to predecessors and contemporaries, especially De Quincey, Coleridge, Hazlitt, and Charles Lamb. LINDENBERGER's book, pursuing several "ways to look at *The Prelude*" rather than a single thesis, is still a very useful introduction to the poem. Beginning by situating *The Prelude* in relation to "the older rhetoric", Lindenberger compares both traditional epics and later long poems, explores tensions between personal and communal, spontaneity and decorum, lyric and epic, and illuminates major themes including "interaction" and "time-consciousness". LIU's massive study combines New Historicism with what has been called "new formalism". Emphasizing the displacement or "burial" of history in Wordsworth's writing ("*Sense of*" receives the emphasis in Liu's subtitle), it correlates this movement with a generic progression in the early Wordsworth – in broad terms, the eclipse of narrative and the development of the characteristic lyric and autobiographical modes. Thus Liu's argument culminates in a study of the lyric and autobiographical bent of the French Revolution books of *The Prelude*, though his conclusion moves on to consider the re-historicizing movement of the poet's later works and arrangements, especially the "tour" series.

Of books concentrating on the other poetry, GLEN juxtaposes *Lyrical Ballads* with Blake's *Songs* in a materialist perspective – with attention to the poets' social positions, audiences, forums, and markets – to see how their apparent "simplicity" engaged and revolutionized contemporary expectations. Glen's readings illuminate the subtle complexities of Wordsworth's verse. LEVINSON gives provocative revisionary readings to the Immortality Ode, "Tintern Abbey", "Michael", and "Elegiac Stanzas". Her deliberately iconoclastic title reflects her New-Historicist argument: precisely the poems that seem most to transcend history are "period poems", if the period be taken as one that idealized transcendence; they are likewise the poems that most demand historical treatment if their "displacements" or "identifiably absented signifiers" are to be appreciated. JOHNSTON treats Wordsworth's *Recluse* not as an unrealized conception but as a grand, though fragmentary, accomplishment, with stimulating readings of the component or related parts, especially "Home at Grasmere", the 1805 *Prelude*, and *The Excursion*.

BATE, partly in reaction to recent "red" or Marxist criticism, including the New Historicism, and partly in apologetics for a "green" alternative, seeks to steer Wordsworth studies back to their traditional emphasis on nature-appreciation, as exemplified by Hazlitt and John Ruskin. Beyond its polemicism, this book is a valuable guide to the ecological tradition beginning with Wordsworth (especially *The Excursion* and *Guide to the Lakes*) and continuing through the Victorians to the present.

Wordsworth's contexts – political, philosophical, aesthetic, etc. – are examined in a number of studies. BEWELL's book is among the best guides to Wordsworth's relation to the philosophy and science of his period, viewing his major poetry in the context of anthropology's development out of eighteenth-century moral philosophy. Formally, Bewell presents the short poems as essays related to *The Recluse* project much as diverse essays were related to the encyclopedic ambitions of moral philosophy. Historically, his recontextualization shows how Wordsworth's poetic encounters with marginal figures responded to an emergent intellectual program that considered alternative cultures as "experiments" illuminating European prehistory. CHANDLER's study of the politics contrasts Wordsworth with Jean-Jacques Rousseau and emphasizes his compatibility with Edmund Burke's traditionalism, especially in the valorization of custom and habit as "second nature". Chandler locates Wordsworth's conservative turn in the late 1790s, considerably earlier than is sometimes thought, and gives much attention to Wordsworth's educational conceptions in *The Prelude* and elsewhere. SIMPSON's study is useful for those interested in Wordsworth's peculiarly difficult shifting of subject-positions, or *personae*, as well as for those concerned with his historical-political bearings. With keen readings of a handful of exemplary works, Simpson stresses Wordsworth's social "displacement" or betweenness as a poet who idealized agrarian life but wrote for those who were replacing it, and the ensuing contradictions and ambiguities of his writings. KELLEY responds to recent critical preoccupations with Wordsworth's "egotistical sublime", as Keats called it, by emphasizing the resistance to egotism and commitment to community implicit in his revision of the Burkean and Kantian sublimes, and particularly in his cultivation of the beautiful as "containment" or "domestication" of the sublime. Reading the major (and some later) poetry through the topographical and aesthetic writings, Kelley charts a progression from sublime to beautiful, but also stresses Wordsworth's very early ambivalence to sublimity and his usual practice of "aesthetic revision" toward beauty.

MARK JONES

Wright, Judith 1915–

Australian poet, essayist, and children's writer

Dowling, David, "Judith Wright's Delicate Balance", in *Australian Literary Studies*, 9(3), 1980
Scott, W.N., *Focus on Judith Wright*, St Lucia: University of Queensland Press, 1967
Thomson, A.K. (ed.), *Critical Essays on Judith Wright*, Brisbane: Jacaranda Press, 1968
Walker, Shirley, *Judith Wright*, Melbourne: Oxford University Press, 1981
Walker, Shirley, *Flame and Shadow: A Study of Judith Wright's Poetry*, St Lucia: University of Queensland Press, 1991

The criticism of Judith Wright's poetry should be more extensive, and is not, generally, of a high standard, with exceptions such as Dowling's essay and Walker's study.

SCOTT's book is a deceptively simple introduction to the poetry. It was intended as an appreciation rather than literary criticism: "poetry is not to be understood by the examination of its mechanics, it must be recognized in part by the gooseflesh on the thighs, the prickling of the nape of the neck, the singing in the mind and spirit". Despite this disclaimer, it picked up on the main themes that would dominate the criticism of the Australian poet for the next 20 years: the extermination of the Aborigines, the historical context of World War II, the Korean and projected nuclear war, the country's landscape, gender politics, environmental issues, and literary movements such as the Jindyworobaks. The text includes material from Scott's interview with Wright, and is complemented by photographs and a copy of one of her manuscripts. The "appreciative" nature of the writing does become overbearing at times, as in the grand claim for Wright as "one of the greatest women poets ever to write in English".

THOMSON collects 11 critical essays and reviews on Wright written between 1946 and 1966, and includes a bibliography. The standard of criticism is not good: for example, Thomson himself argues that the critic's job is to understand and contextualise a poem in the rest of the writer's work and life (is that really all?). There are essays on "Judith Wright's World-View", which examines the "universals" of love, birth, and death in the poetry, "The Quest of Judith Wright", which focuses on her metaphysics, and R.F. Brissenden's review of *Five Senses*. Vincent Buckley's essay ("The Poetry of Judith Wright") is the most useful introduction to her work. He tackles her "modernism", her gender politics, the Aboriginal presence, the label "nature poet", and the way in which critics have overestimated her value. Wright's poetry has a "brilliance of image", and he acknowledges two of her best poems, "Bullocky" and "Train Journey", but the poetry can also be unoriginal, confused, pessimistic, awkward and vapidly symbolist.

DOWLING takes issue, in his essay published 12 years after Thomson's collection, with much of the previous criticism of Wright. He attacks it for focusing too much on the autobiographical, and "masculine" and "feminine" elements of the poetry, and its supposed universality. In contrast, he produces a short but packed introduction to her work. He covers the main themes of the poetry via her "complexity of vision": her poems are an "evolving series of exhaustive intellectual and emotional exercises, directed at reconciling the basic dichotomies of human existence into paradox or harmony". He splits the texts into four dualities: "man v. environment", "man v. man", "soul v. flesh" and "world v. world". In the first, Wright is not just a "descriptive" poet, but attuned to her status as a settler and the guilt of her colonising forefathers; the failure of white Australians to identify with the environment is presented as the tragedy of the country's recent history. In the second and third, love is the answer to the binaries: Dowling believes this poetry of human relationships is her best. In the fourth, Wright is frustrated with language because she senses some form of experience beyond it.

WALKER's (1981) bibliography is now 15 years out of date, but it remains one of the most comprehensive listings (with 2,500 items) of Wright's work (both published and unpublished), references about her, theses, manuscripts, magazines, newspapers and radio broadcasts, from 1925 to 1979. It is split into two sections – writing by and about Wright; the critical material is composed of "Books", "Theses", "General Articles, Lecture and Verse", "Shorter References", "Brief Notes", and "Specific Reviews"; and there are two indexes – one to Wright and the other to editors, reviewers, illustrators etc. The most useful section is the one on manuscript material in libraries and archives.

WALKER's study is the definitive introduction to the poetry. It updates her first book on Wright (*The Poetry of Judith Wright: A Search for Unity*, 1980), and provides a comprehensive chronology and bibliography, in which she includes articles absent from Thomson's list. She breaks from traditional approaches in the preface by arguing that Wright's later texts need to be appreciated, whereas critics have tended to focus on the earlier, canonical pieces, such as "South of My Days". Walker reworks the major issues of 1960s' criticism (the destructiveness of time, the celebration of sexual love, the loss of faith in language, philosophical questioning [influenced by Susanne Langer and Ernst Cassirer]), and adds the concepts of understatement and laconic tone in the later collections. The canonical texts are out of date because they "assume the notion of progress in [Australia], and the heroic nature of the pastoral conquest of the land". She re-evaluates the poems in the second collection as a frank response to female sexuality, and then traces recurring symbols in the poetry, such as the cave, blade, sun, and mandala. The chapter on aesthetics is particularly illuminating, as it develops Dowling's thesis and argues that Wright aims for a fusion of binaries, the main one being the "fundamental" opposition between the subject and object.

ANTONY ROWLAND

Wright, Richard 1908–1960

American novelist and essayist

Fabre, Michel, *The Unfinished Quest of Richard Wright*, translated by Isabel Barzun, New York: William Morrow, 1973
Gates, Henry Louis, Jr., and K.A. Appiah (eds.), *Richard Wright: Critical Perspectives Past and Present*, New York: Amistad Press, 1993

Gayle, Addison, *Richard Wright: Ordeal of a Native Son*, Garden City, New York: Anchor Press/Doubleday, 1980
Kinnamon, Keneth, *The Emergence of Richard Wright: A Study in Literature and Society*, Urbana: University of Illinois Press, 1972
Kinnamon, Keneth (ed.), *New Essays on "Native Son"*, Cambridge and New York: Cambridge University Press, 1990
McCall, Dan, *The Example of Richard Wright*, New York: Harcourt Brace Jovanovich, 1969
Walker, Margaret, *Richard Wright, Daemonic Genius: A Portrait of the Man; A Critical Look at His Work*, revised edition, New York: Warner Books, 1988
Webb, Constance, *Richard Wright: A Biography*, New York: Putnam, 1968

Spurred on, in part, by the social and political upheavals in the United States during the 1960s, academic and critical interest in Richard Wright developed rapidly during this period, beginning with the publication of Webb's biography, and has continued apace since that time.

WEBB draws on her intimate knowledge of many figures associated with Wright's circle (she was once married to C.L.R. James, the notable Trotskyist, Pan-African writer, and political activist) to create the first, full-length portrait of Wright. A combination of personal reminiscences, interviews with Wright's wife Ellen, scholarly research, and literary analysis, Webb's biography has sometimes been criticized for the literary license she takes with her subject, as well as for factual accuracy; but it is still a useful introduction to the man and his work.

McCALL's interpretative study is concerned primarily with examining the social meanings and contemporary relevance of Wright. In the social and political context of the 1960s, McCall assesses Wright's major literary work from the vantage point of his position as both a left-wing polemicist and a black spokesman. His study remains an important pioneering investigation of Wright's achievement.

KINNAMON's 1972 study is a meticulously researched examination of the life, social milieu, and literary career of Wright from his birth through the publication of *Native Son* in 1940. Kinnamon moves fluidly across the boundaries of biography, literary analysis, and social history, judiciously balancing the claims of literary and social criticism. As a study of the social, aesthetic, and ideological underpinnings of Wright's literary achievements, Kinnamon's work is indispensable.

FABRE's is rightly regarded as the standard biography of Wright, a monumental accomplishment unlikely to be superseded. The product of more than a decade's research, it fulfills impressively its aim of tracing Wright's life in detail and placing his work in literary and historical perspective. Fabre's rebuke of Webb in his Introduction signals his intention to put Wright scholarship on a much firmer basis than that of her pioneering biography, a task that he completes admirably. It is not an overstatement to say that Wright scholarship, from the mid-1970s onward, owes a tremendous debt to Fabre's work.

GAYLE's biography is distinguished by his investigation, made possible by the Freedom of Information Act, of previously classified government documents pertaining to Wright. Encouraged by the persistent references to government harassment, which are rife in Wright's biographies, Gayle revisits the familiar terrain of Wright's life and re-examines it through the lens of American social and political culture, at home and abroad, from the 1930s through the 1960s. At the very least, Gayle's study sheds greater light on this one important source of the tensions that plagued Wright's later life. Other conclusions, as Gayle points out, are more difficult to arrive at.

WALKER's biographical and critical study is unique in several important respects: the first biography of Wright by one of his contemporaries (Walker first met Wright in Chicago in 1936), it is also a critical biography written by another accomplished African-American writer and scholar. Both eyewitness account and critique, Walker's study proposes to examine Wright in the context of the social, sexual, political, and literary forces that shaped him. The result is a combination of personal reminiscence, scholarly research, social and literary critique, and polemic – all designed to illustrate Wright's "daemonic genius", the obsessions that drove him to write the way he did. An often highly personal and idiosyncratic study, Walker's book nevertheless sheds important light on aspects of Wright's life and work unexamined by other critics and biographers.

KINNAMON's 1990 collection brings together the work of five leading African-Americanists to examine the enduring legacy of Wright's masterpiece. Kinnamon, John Reilly, Trudier Harris, Houston A. Baker, Jr., and Craig Werner attest to the continuing fascination of *Native Son*, and move beyond standard interpretations of, and debates about, the novel by offering critical commentary often informed by new theory and recent perspectives. Kinnamon analyzes manuscripts, letters, and other documents to explore the interaction between Wright's imagination and external forces in the composition of the novel; Reilly shows how Wright subverts conventional racial discourse to create the space for the emergence of Bigger Thomas's voice at the end of the novel; Harris analyzes Wright's unfavorable representation of black female characters in the novel; Baker examines patterns and characterization in *Native Son* against the backdrop of the view of African-American history he proposes in *12 Million Black Voices*; and Werner links *Native Son* to a modernist tradition that shares important affinities with the African-American blues tradition.

GATES and APPIAH have compiled selected reviews – many of them by Wright's colleagues and contemporaries – of all Wright's major works, and linked them with 22 essays by present-day scholars, from the late 1960s to the present. The result is a fascinating cross-section of critical opinion on Wright by many of the key commentators in the field.

JAMES A. MILLER

Wyatt, Sir Thomas 1503–1542

English poet

Baldi, Sergio, *Sir Thomas Wyatt*, translated by F.T. Prince, London: Longmans, Green & Co., 1961

Harrier, Richard, *The Canon of Sir Thomas Wyatt's Poetry*, Cambridge, Massachusetts: Harvard University Press, 1975

Jentoft, Clyde W., *Sir Thomas Wyatt and Henry Howard, Earl of Surrey: A Reference Guide*, Boston: G.K. Hall, 1980

Mason, H.A., *Humanism and Poetry in the Early Tudor Period: An Essay*, London: Routledge & Kegan Paul, 1959; New York: Barnes & Noble, 1960

Mason, H.A., *Editing Wyatt: An Examination of the Collected Poems of Sir Thomas Wyatt*, Cambridge: Cambridge Quarterly Publications, 1972

Mason, H.A., *Sir Thomas Wyatt: A Literary Portrait; Selected Poems*, Bristol: Bristol Classical Press, 1986

Muir, Kenneth, *Life and Letters of Sir Thomas Wyatt*, Liverpool: Liverpool University Press, 1963

Southall, Raymond, *The Courtly Maker: An Essay on the Poetry of Wyatt and His Contemporaries*, Oxford: Blackwell, 1964; New York: Barnes & Noble, 1964

Thomson, Patricia, *Sir Thomas Wyatt and His Background*, London: Routledge & Kegan Paul, 1964; Stanford, California: Stanford University Press, 1964

Thomson, Patricia (ed.), *Wyatt: The Critical Heritage*, London and Boston: Routledge & Kegan Paul, 1974

Long overshadowed by his younger contemporary the Earl of Surrey, Sir Thomas Wyatt came to be recognised in the early part of the twentieth century as perhaps the most significant English poet in the period after Chaucer. Earlier criticism tended to concentrate on his lyric writing, but more recent studies acknowledge the variety and versatility of his work, ranging beyond the lyrics into his satires and translations.

Although there is no general collection of critical essays on Wyatt, THOMSON's 1974 collection brings together a selective range of early responses to the poet, both in prose and verse, including the important comments by Surrey and George Puttenham. Significantly, editorial commentary is well represented, with extracts from Nott, Foxwell, and Tillyard. The collection concludes with C.S. Lewis's somewhat unsympathetic account of Wyatt. A comprehensive and annotated account of Wyatt criticism up to 1978 can be found in JENTOFT, together with a useful introduction examining the evolution of the critical response to the poet.

While certain areas of Wyatt's biography – such as his precise relation to Anne Boleyn – still remain in obscurity, MUIR, the major editor of Wyatt's poetry, provides in his biography what information there is, together with a complete collection of Wyatt's letters. The biography surveys in particular Wyatt's career as a courtier at the court of Henry VIII, and discusses the important occasions when he was arrested and imprisoned.

BALDI, in a shorter version of an earlier Italian text, gives a succinct and still useful introduction to Wyatt's work, concentrating on the better-known sonnets and the lyrics. Although relatively simple, the work is sensible and wide-ranging. This still remains perhaps the best short introduction to Wyatt's work. But MASON (1959) was the first serious study of Wyatt's work, and did much to relocate interest in the translations rather than the lyrics. Mason expresses a degree of scepticism as to the attribution of many of Wyatt's poems – a scepticism that increases in his later writing on Wyatt – seeing many of the lyrics contained in the Devonshire manuscript (and attributed to Wyatt) as simply part of the popular tradition of court poetry. Mason focuses instead on Wyatt's translations as the centre of his work, seeing these as part of the larger humanist movement of the early sixteenth century, and provides, in particular, a compelling reading of Wyatt's translations of the Penitential Psalms. THOMSON's 1964 work is the most thorough study in English of Wyatt's use of his sources, both native and foreign, and is particularly useful in demonstrating in detail Wyatt's transformations of his Italian originals in his sonnets. Some of this work was later incorporated in her edition (with Muir) of Wyatt's poems, but this work still remains the broadest discussion of Wyatt in terms of his Italian originals.

Probably the most rounded of the studies of Wyatt, SOUTHALL provides both a powerful social reading of the poems and a study of their construction. Of all the writers under consideration, Southall is the most plausible in siting Wyatt in his social and artistic context. This work also contains useful appendices on the Egerton and Devonshire manuscripts, drawing on Southall's earlier unpublished transcriptions of them.

MASON (1972), in the aftermath of the publication of Muir and Thomson's edition of the poems by Liverpool University Press in 1969, calls into question the accuracy of the texts represented in the various editions to date. His work provides an exhaustive account of what he sees as misreadings of the manuscripts in the various editions. More doubtful are his suggestions as to possible emendations of accepted readings on the grounds of metrical regularity. HARRIER provides what is essential for a study of Wyatt, a diplomatic transcript of the Egerton manuscript, partly fulfilling the demands made by Mason (1972). His transcript is an essential supplement to the published editions of the poems, and, in his presentation of the changes made in certain poems, allows the reader to follow Wyatt's process of revision.

MASON (1986), in an idiosyncratic conclusion to his studies of Wyatt, provides powerful and relevant contextual readings of several of Wyatt's poems; but the editorial procedure, particularly with regard to "They flee from me", is marred by his suspicion of the Egerton manuscript. While fascinating and illuminating, many of Mason's conclusions in this work should be treated with a degree of scepticism.

ROBIN HAMILTON

Wycherley, William 1641–1715

English dramatist and poet

Chadwick, W.R., *The Four Plays of William Wycherley: A Study in the Development of a Dramatist*, The Hague: Mouton, 1975

Holland, Norman N., *The First Modern Comedies: The Significance of Etherege, Wycherley, and Congreve*, Cambridge, Massachusetts: Harvard University Press, 1959

McCarthy, B. Eugene, *William Wycherley: A Biography*, Athens: Ohio University Press, 1979

Markley, Robert, *Two-Edg'd Weapons: Style and Ideology in the Comedies of Etherege, Wycherley and Congreve*, Oxford: Clarendon Press, 1988; New York: Oxford University Press, 1988

Palmer, John, *The Comedy of Manners*, London: Bell & Sons, 1913; reprinted, New York: Russell & Russell, 1962

Rogers, Katharine M., *William Wycherley*, New York: Twayne, 1972

Thompson, James, *Language in Wycherley's Plays: Seventeenth-Century Language Theory and Drama*, University: University of Alabama Press, 1984

Zimbardo, Rose, *Wycherley's Drama: A Link in the Development of English Satire*, New Haven, Connecticut, and London: Yale University Press, 1965

Before the 1960s, most studies of Wycherley appeared in books about Restoration comedy generally. And even the more recent studies that focus on Wycherley tend to do so in the context of a general thesis about Restoration comedy.

PALMER provided an important, highly influential counter to Victorian moral condemnation of Restoration comedy. He argues that the plays are worthy of study and performance as accurate reflections of their society. The typical "comedy of manners" portrays its society uncritically. Wycherley is the exception. Eschewing delicacy and fineness of style, he is the satirist whose "honourable misanthropy" gives him licence to indulge in the "moral ferocity" that, for Palmer, spoils large parts of all Wycherley's plays except *The Country Wife*, that "most perfect farce in English dramatic literature – a whirlwind of inspired buffoonery".

HOLLAND also begins by asserting that Restoration comedies give pleasure by representing reality. They are true to the society they represent; they are not, therefore, immoral. The plays are informed by a "dialectic between inner desires and outward appearance", that is, between "the nature of things" as we understand them and what "we perceive by our senses" and "let the world at large see". This dialectic provides a bridge from the Restoration to the present, since it remains a central one for people in the twentieth century. Holland reads each of Wycherley's plays through the theme of "appearance" and "nature", and its inevitable simile of "right" and "wrong".

ZIMBARDO wrote the first important critical study of Wycherley's plays. She takes Wycherley as seriously as the Victorian moralists did, seeing in his plays the "brutal, disgusting, and shocking obscenity" that they found. Her argument is that the Victorians (and their successors, the "manners critics") mistook the purpose of that obscenity: to attack "bestial human behavior". Wycherley is, for Zimbardo, not a comic writer but a satirist, exposing the moral corruption of vice in the tradition of Roman and Elizabethan satire, the tradition of Juvenal, Ben Jonson, and John Marston. He provides the link between that earlier satire and the Augustans. The readings of the plays are full of valuable insights, but Zimbardo drives her thesis so hard that it diminishes the value of her study as a whole.

ROGERS' volume follows the standard format of the Twayne series: a biographical sketch is followed by chapters on the literary works. Wycherley's plays are distinguished by a moral concern that "deepens his comedy and gives it a substance wanting in the airier creations of his contemporaries". Rogers' readings of the plays synthesize the results of the most important critical debates through the 1960s: the result remains a sound, useful introduction to Wycherley. CHADWICK complements Rogers in providing an alternative, equally sound introduction to the plays, written at roughly the same time. His study consists entirely of readings of each of the plays with a brief conclusion. Rogers' readings are highly literary, whereas Chadwick looks at Wycherley's plays as "stage pieces, to suggest what sort of plays they are and why they took the form they did, and finally to trace and account for the development of Wycherley's thought and dramatic technique". His readings are, thus, always with an eye to production. Chadwick joins other critics in seeing Wycherley as "the most complete satiric dramatist of his period"; he refines their view by tracing "a significant development through the four plays, from relative optimism to a pessimism that seems gradually to have embraced most facets of the society in which he lived".

McCARTHY's is the most accurate and reliable biography of Wycherley to date. His central chapter, "The Playwright", looks at the genesis of the plays, especially their literary and dramatic sources, and "their conscious manifestation or reflection of contemporary political, social, moral, and philosophical ideas and trends, and as well at the more concrete topical details". In other words, the plays are read as part of a traditional, literary-intellectual biography.

THOMPSON approaches Wycherley the moralist through seventeenth-century language theory. That theory is primarily semantic theory, and "meaning and signification . . . tend to expand from language to morality to religion and on to politics". People are judged by their use of words, since speech was believed "to reveal the essence of men, not just their social grace". Thompson's Wycherley is a political, moral, and religious conservative, sharing the views of the ruling class of his age, an ideology asserting "a fundamental homology among providentialist theology, authoritarian and monarchical government, feudal economics, aristocratic social structure", and what he calls "the rectitude of language". Wycherley's commitment to this ideology tempers his satire: "however savage his satire may be, his plays always include some exemplar of right conduct; however corrupt and immoral contemporary society and speech may be made to appear, standards for right speech remain intact". Thompson's, then, is a more positive, less ambiguous portrait of Wycherley than most. Two chapters outlining seventeenth-century language theory are followed by chapters on each of the plays.

MARKLEY, too, focuses on the language of the drama. His examination of seventeenth-century language theory also sees it as concerned more with "the ideology of privilege" than "a theory of style". But, following Mikhail Bakhtin, he sees ideology as "an activity created by the contradictions and conflicts within and among social utterances"; his playwrights use language not to assert or fix values but "to register the ironies of fashionable existence in the late seventeenth century". The playwrights do not share a single ideology. Wycherley's plays are distinguished by:

> . . . a complex and profoundly ironic attempt to accommodate a radical practice to a conservative ideology; they exhibit an insistent, embattled anti-authoritarianism that questions the ability of any discourse – including the playwright's own – to stabilize moral, social, and ideological values.

Markley's readings of the plays emphasize their subversive qualities; the language of wit is turned against itself so that "comedy can function as vehicle for a serious criticism of the ways of an imperfect world".

BRIAN CORMAN

Y

Yeats, W.B. 1865–1939

Irish poet, dramatist, and essayist

Bloom, Harold, *Yeats*, Oxford and New York: Oxford University Press, 1970

Clark, David R., with Rosalind Clark, *W.B. Yeats and the Theatre of Desolate Reality*, Dublin: Dolmen Press, 1965; revised edition, Washington, D.C.: Catholic University of America Press, 1993

Cullingford, Elizabeth, *Yeats, Ireland and Fascism*, London: Macmillan, 1981; New York: New York University Press, 1981

Cullingford, Elizabeth, *Gender and History in Yeats's Love Poetry*, Cambridge and New York: Cambridge University Press, 1993

Dorn, Karen, *Players and Painted Stage: The Theatre of W.B. Yeats*, Brighton, Sussex: Harvester Press, 1984

Engelberg, Edward, *The Vast Design: Patterns in W.B. Yeats's Aesthetic*, Toronto: University of Toronto Press, 1964; revised edition, Washington, D.C.: Catholic University of America Press, 1988

Good, Maeve, *W.B. Yeats and the Creation of a Tragic Universe*, London: Macmillan, 1987; Totawa, New Jersey: Barnes & Noble, 1987

Hall, James, and Martin Steinmann, *The Permanence of Yeats: Selected Criticism*, New York: Macmillan, 1950

Harris, Daniel Arthur, *Yeats: Coole Park and Ballylee*, Baltimore: Johns Hopkins University Press, 1974

Henn, Thomas Rice, *The Lonely Tower: Studies in the Poetry of W.B. Yeats*, London: Methuen, 1950, 2nd edition, 1966

Keane, Patrick J., *Yeats's Interactions with Tradition*, Columbia: University of Missouri Press, 1987

Kermode, Frank, *Romantic Image*, London: Routledge & Kegan Paul, 1957; New York: Macmillan, 1958

Knowland, A.S., *W.B. Yeats: Dramatist of Vision*, Gerrards Cross, Buckinghamshire: Colin Smythe, 1983; Totowa, New Jersey: Barnes & Noble, 1983

O'Brien, Conor Cruise, "Passion and Cunning: An Essay on the Politics", in *In Excited Reverie: A Centenary Tribute to William Butler Yeats, 1865–1939*, edited by A. Norman Jeffares and K.G.W. Cross, London: Macmillan, 1965; New York: St Martin's Press, 1965

Rajan, Balachandra, *W.B.Yeats: A Critical Introduction*, London: Hutchinson, 1965, 2nd edition, 1969

Skene, Reg, *The Cuchulain Plays of W.B. Yeats: A Study*, New York: Columbia University Press, 1974

Snukal, Robert, *High Talk: The Philosophical Poetry of W.B.Yeats*, Cambridge: Cambridge University Press, 1973

Torchiana, Donald T., *W.B. Yeats and Georgian Ireland*, Evanston, Illinois: Northwestern University Press, 1966; London: Oxford University Press, 1966; new edition, Washington, D.C.: Catholic University of America Press, 1992

Ure, Peter, *Yeats the Playwright: A Commentary on Character and Design in the Major Plays*, London: Routledge & Kegan Paul, 1963

Vendler, Helen Hennessy, *Yeats's Vision and the Later Plays*, Cambridge, Massachusetts: Harvard University Press, 1963

Whitaker, Thomas Russell, *Swan and Shadow: Yeats's Dialogue with History*, Chapel Hill: University of North Carolina Press, 1964; new edition, Washington, D.C.: Catholic University of America Press, 1991

Worth, Katharine, *The Irish Drama of Europe from Yeats to Beckett*, London: Athlone Press, 1978

Poetry

W.B. Yeats, who began his publishing career as a late Victorian, was already an established poet before Ezra Pound and T.S. Eliot brought about the modernist revolution in poetry (1910–22). Their work had a direct and beneficial effect on the development of Yeats's mature style in the longest and greatest phase of his career (1914–39), but their influential doctrines – particularly Eliot's theory of impersonality and his defense of a tradition that was principally European and Christian – accounted for the harshness of much of the early academic reception of Yeats. As a poet with a heightened poetic style, autobiographical subject-matter, and a range of esoteric sources from spiritualism to Rosicrucianism, he breached many of the credos of Eliot's academic admirers.

HALL and STEINMANN's outstanding collection brings together the best early criticism of Yeats (with essays written by the leading poet-critics of the period, including Eliot himself). These essays (which give an important insight into Yeats's effect on the poets and critics of the mid-century) speculate on the nature and possibility of poetry in the modern period. Individual judgements – both sympathetic and unsympathetic – tell us as much about an author's relationship to Eliot as about his relationship to Yeats. The collection contains an exhaustive bibliography of material on Yeats up to 1950.

HENN's pioneering study marked a break from these judgmental preoccupations. He was one of the first to draw attention to Yeats's Irish background and to describe his poetic and historical system (both in his theory of the self and anti-self and in his *A Vision*) not as an eccentric hotchpotch but as a source of intelligence and power. Henn's treatment of women in Yeats's poetry, and his exploration of the influence of painting on his poetry, also marked out other important areas of interest many later scholars would pursue.

Many followed Henn's lead. TORCHIANA, taking as his starting-point Yeats's anomalous position as a Protestant-born writer in a Catholic society, explored his relationship to the writers and institutions of the Anglo-Irish Ascendancy from the eighteenth century (Jonathan Swift, Edmund Burke, George Berkeley, and Oliver Goldsmith) to the twentieth (the Gregorys and Coole Park). Yeats's position vacillated between rebellion against this tradition and glorification of it. WHITAKER, who also produced two important chapters on Yeats's Anglo-Irish background, examined his view of history in the course of a detailed analysis of his *A Vision*. History, Whitaker suggested, was a mysterious interlocutor with whom the poet came into dialogue. In this study, he explicated very convincingly Yeats's most difficult and unusual text.

These studies treated Yeats as a major and important modern poet. In what remains the best introductory study, RAJAN did the same by placing Yeats in the mainstream of English poetry. He summarised and explicated both his poetry and drama, with insight into its driving force as "the assertion of man's creative power against the strength of circumstance". The human self remained throughout Yeats's work a place of struggle and conflict.

ENGELBERG, in a much more extensive account, suggested that Yeats was the last great European writer, with a scope derived from Goethe, Balzac, and Nietzsche. His aesthetic was founded on a philosophy of history derived from the discussion of Greek and Renaissance art and culture in Walter Pater. In order to achieve (as had been the case in the greatest periods of European art) epic grandeur with lyric intensity and dramatic tension, Yeats attempted to reconcile the three great elements of European literature: epic, drama, and lyric. Engelberg's study not only distinguished Yeats's aesthetic principles from the modernists, but also examined his self-identification as a "single poet". "The single poet, still creating the whole of a nation's traditions, 'the race', and 'the reality', that was Yeats's great aim as an artist", he argued with Yeatsian fervour. "To help stabilise the equilibrium of the European mind was for Yeats the responsibility of the modern poet".

Engelberg's book did justice to Yeats's undoubted range both as a lyric poet and a poetic dramatist, but failed to address the disquiet raised by others about the anti-democratic impetus of such singularity. In a subtle and widely admired account, KERMODE had defined the common root of Romantic and modernist notions of the image and symbol and focused on the isolation and estrangement implicit in these notions. Such detachment from ordinary experience had, as he showed in a brilliant reading of "An Irish Airman Foresees His Death", questionable political consequences. O'BRIEN's provocative essay was more direct. Yeats's poetry was never detached from his politics and were opportunistic, ambiguous and, in the proto-fascist writings of the 1930s, authoritarian. This remains the single most influential essay on the topic. Even BLOOM, who inserted Yeats within the Romantic line of vision (William Blake and Percy Bysshe Shelley) he had set up in response to Eliot's anti-Romantic tradition, found him, in a scintillating and strenuous reading, to be the last representative and betrayer of that tradition. When judged against the achievements of his Romantic precursors, Yeats's achievement has been over-rated. The fact, however, that Yeats was being judged by a leading Romantic scholar as a late Romantic represented an important (and still important) transformation in his reception.

SNUKAL's demanding but deeply rewarding study of Yeats's indebtedness to Kant marked a less polemical phase in Yeats studies. He argued that the theory of imagination Yeats had developed from Kant provided a key to his ideas about history, philosophy, art, and the phenomenal world itself. HARRIS, too, in one of the most thoughtful and subtle analyses of Yeats, explored his knowing dependence on his own personal and cultural fictions. He discussed the poetry Yeats wrote about Coole Park and Ballylee, set it in the context of his preoccupations with the ideas of Georgian Anglo-Ireland, and examined his dual debt to the Irish tradition and the Renaissance literature of Baldassarre Castiglione and Ben Jonson. "Because Byzantium could never be possessed, it could never be lost: a safe utopia. With Coole Park and Thoor Ballylee, Yeats attempted something more difficult: his territory was an incipient Eden, perpetually awaiting redemption, perpetually endangered by chaos". The twin myths of paradise lost and paradise regained went hand in hand, in the midst of rebellion and civil war, to produce the emotion of tragic joy.

CULLINGFORD (1981) took up the issues raised in O'Brien's essay, examining the links between Yeats's poetic and political vision, with particular attention to his relations in the 1930s with Irish and European fascism. This was a meticulously researched account which has not been superseded. Even those who admired her rigour, however, were not always convinced by an argument that not only exonerated Yeats but made him an advocate of diversity.

KEANE, in the most substantial recent account, accepts the continuing need to locate Yeats's poetry and drama – which he describes as principally a poetry and drama of ideas – very specifically in its historical context. In a masterly interweaving of textual, literary, cultural, and political histories, he not only enters into an informed and informative dialogue with Yeats's major interpreters, but also considers the processes involved in Yeats's poetic and intellectual interactions with his literary, philosophical, and esoteric sources. He sympathetically explicates Yeats's Nietzschean self-dramatisations in the context of Irish and European history and, through an analysis of Yeats's use of Greek tragedy, discusses (in one of the most perceptive sections of a consistently searching and incisive account) his poetic representation of women.

CULLINGFORD (revised 1993), in an equally rich combination of biography, social history, critical theory, and close reading, draws on an extensive range of feminist discourses to discuss Yeats as a love poet. "Yeats's tenuous and intermittent identification with traditional models of masculinity resulted in an oblique relationship to the canonical genre of the love lyric". This makes him, she argues, a much more sympathetic subject than the misogynist modernists. The merit of her study is that, by drawing both on literary and art history, and social and cultural history, it examines questions of female representation as fully as the question of the male speaking subject. The volume as a whole stands as an important contribution not only to Yeats studies but also to modernist studies.

ALISTAIR DAVIES

Drama

During Yeats's lifetime, his plays appealed mainly to the coterie audience he so much valued, and were regarded by critics as more or less interesting appendages to the poetry. In the early 1960s, there was a new acceptance of Yeats the *playwright*, and more recent specialist commentaries place him high in the ranks of twentieth-century dramatists. Outside Ireland, the plays are now only performed by university groups, though one hopes that the enthusiastic advocacy of such critics as Knowland and Worth will tempt professional directors, actors, designers, and composers, towards a Yeats revival. Students of Yeats the *poet* should also find that these studies will enhance their appreciation of the dramatic elements in his lyric poetry.

URE was one of the first critics to give serious attention to Yeats's drama as something separate from the poetry. He approaches a selection of the plays heuristically, without, as he says, "a dominant theory". The result is an uneven book. He offers a strong reading of *Purgatory*, for example, but spends too much time "puzzling through" more obscure pieces such as *The Herne's Egg*; and his commentary on the other plays in the "Dante trilogy" – *The Dreaming of the Bones*, *The Words upon a Window Pane*, and *Purgatory* – lacks authority beside Clark's. Nor, despite the challenge implicit in Ure's title, does he reveal much sense of how the plays might work in the theatre. This is a pioneering and often-quoted study, but it can no longer be recommended as the standard work on Yeats's plays. VENDLER believes that Yeats's plays are "not really stageworthy". Her discussion of *A Vision* is interesting, but her sense of the late plays as "settings for lyrics" is extremely limiting. This is one of the best-known works of Yeatsian scholarship, but it now seems curiously dated and eccentric as a reading of the late plays.

CLARK bases his approach to the plays on Francis Fergusson's theory of the tragic rhythm of action (*The Idea of a Theater*, 1949); the author believes that "although Yeats's theatre contains implicitly the whole tragic rhythm, there is only one movement explicit to and central to most of his plays – the movement from passion to perception". The highlight of this study is a fine structuralist interpretation of the "Dante trilogy", enhanced by insights into the powerful sense of place in these dramas. This expanded edition contains two previously unpublished pieces by Yeats – his first play, *Vivien and Time*, and *The Poet and the Actress*, a dialogue – as well as a previously uncollected address on the Irish National Theatre.

SKENE argues persuasively that the five Cuchulain plays – *At the Hawk's Well*, *The Green Helmet*, *On Baile's Strand*, *The Only Jealousy of Emer*, and *The Death of Cuchulain* – make up a unified dramatic cycle. In the first part of his book, he traces the development of a Yeatsian "ritual theatre" through the paths of Celtic mysticism and mythology, the lunar phases in *A Vision*, the dramatist's relationship with Maud Gonne, and the influence of Craig. In the second, he demonstrates the individual unity of each play in the cycle. In this regard, his reading of *On Baile's Strand* is exemplary, with a strong analysis of the Shakespearean interweaving of comic and tragic plots.

GOOD's premise – that Yeats's tragic *landscape* is the West of Ireland, "its barren terrain, stunted trees, storm-beaten towers" – brings the plays at once to fresh life in the reader's mind. Her discussion of his tragic universe, which involves a relatively routine dialogue with Vendler's analysis of *A Vision*, is less impressive, but she recovers with unflinchingly dark readings of *The Dreaming of the Bones* and *The Words Upon a Window-Pane*. One can only regret that this author does not really capitalize on her initial evocation of the Irish landscape.

DORN's short but valuable study demonstrates how Yeats's growth as a dramatist was indebted to his "continual refinement of dramatic language and form". Each chapter links a play or group of plays with a significant theatrical movement, which influenced this process of refinement: *Deirdre* with the Irish "National Argument" and the early days of the Abbey Theatre; *The Hour-Glass* with Edward Gordon Craig's revolutionary lighting and stage design; *At the Hawk's Well* and *The Only Jealousy of Emer* with the Noh play; the Sophocles adaptations with the Greek theatre movement; and the last plays with the new dance drama, and the art of Ninette de Valois. The author makes skilful use of some well chosen black-and-white photographs, especially those of Craig's models and designs. Her book is written primarily for students and practitioners of the theatre, but her commentary on the connection between word, movement, and image in Yeats's plays also recommends itself to the more general reader.

Also setting Yeats in the company of other writers, WORTH has him as the central figure in a tradition of symbolist drama, which originates with Maurice Maeterlinck, and runs through John Millington Synge, T.S. Eliot, Samuel Beckett, and Harold Pinter. Her study is unique in its placing of Yeats in this international context, and she charts the development of an Irish-European "drama of the interior" with considerable authority. What makes her book especially valuable for students of Yeats is that he is not simply given a separate chapter, but is an ever-present point of reference. Her interpretations of *The Dreaming of the Bones*, *Purgatory*, and *The Death of Cuchulain*, are among the best available, and her work as a whole profits from reference to productions, on stage and video, which she has seen or directed.

The strength of KNOWLAND's study stems from his wish to keep all discussion of the plays' meaning related to their effect in performance. He divides Yeats's dramatic output usefully into four stages, with *Deirdre* and *On Baile's Strand* marking the transition from apprenticeship to maturity, and the plays from *At the Hawk's Well* to *A Full Moon in March* as his central achievement. The author is particularly good at relating meaning to stage space and the actor's movements.

He demonstrates how, in *On Baile's Strand*, for example, Cuchulain's tragically divided personality is evident in his vacillation between the threshold and the sea. This book can be recommended as a perceptive, thorough, and clear introduction to the plays.

JOHN LINGARD

Yonge, Charlotte 1823–1901

English novelist, prose writer, and children's writer

Battiscombe, Georgina, and Marghanita Laski (eds.), *A Chaplet for Charlotte Yonge*, London: Cresset Press, 1965

Dennis, Barbara, *Charlotte Yonge (1823–1901), Novelist of the Oxford Movement: A Literature of Victorian Culture and Society*, Lewiston, New York, and Lampeter, Dyfed: Edwin Mellen Press, 1992

Mare, Margaret Laura, and Alicia Constance Percival, *Victorian Best Seller: The World of Charlotte M. Yonge*, London: Harrap, 1947

Sandbach-Dahlström, Catherine, *Be Good, Sweet Maid: Charlotte Yonge's Domestic Fiction: A Study in Dogmatic Purpose and Fictional Form*, Stockholm: Almqvist & Wiksell International, 1984

Known as the key novelist of the Oxford Movement, Charlotte Mary Yonge, immensely popular in her own day, has been less so subsequently, perhaps in part because her fiction is written to illustrate religious principles which no longer widely command a strong interest. Regardless of her fall from popular grace, she has had a steady, if small, following among critics, scholars, and general readers, and in recent years, with the revision of the canon, she has gained an interested following among many scholars of the nineteenth century, especially of women writers. She has long been regarded as a "minor" novelist, one who subordinates the artistry of the story to her "dogmatic" concerns, and much criticism, early and late, has concerned itself with apologies for her style, defenses of the critic's enthusiasm for her work, and the like. Her many biographies often contain only minimal literary criticism, and, to the extent that they do, tend simply to link her writing with events and persons in her life. (Biographers have been hampered even in this by the actions of Christabel Coleridge, her first biographer, who burned all Yonge's personal documents.) It is perhaps only in the last few years that the apparatus of New Historicism and cultural studies has provided critics with the means to read her work on its own merits and, crucially, in its own context.

SANDBACH-DAHLSTRÖM provides close readings of six of Yonge's most widely read novels in the light of Yonge's religious beliefs and "dogmatic purpose". Although she seems initially to fall into a traditional stance, describing Yonge as a "minor" literary talent, the author does address some of the most persistent aesthetic issues in reception of Yonge's work. Specifically, she looks at the demands of realism and their conflicts and collaborations with Yonge's religious purposes in writing. She also attempts to come to terms with the other key issue in current readings of Yonge's work – her status as a religious conservative and its impact on her view of women's roles. She arrives at the predictable conclusion that although Yonge's views of women's roles were highly influenced by the dominant ideology, there is some ambivalence displayed in the actual novels, particularly when Yonge attempts the task of producing a female *Bildungsroman*. Sandbach-Dahlström's work represents an important effort to revise the aesthetic misprision of Yonge, and to read her novels "on their own premises". It should be read for this, and for the close readings of the novels she chooses; as a treatment of the feminist theme of ambivalence and women's roles, however, it lacks sophistication.

DENNIS situates Yonge's work in her biography, with the additional benefit of having gained access to some materials that the Coleridge conflagration missed. Dennis gives the most detailed treatment of the Oxford Movement and its impact on the larger Victorian cultural and religious scene. She reads the novels in the light of the Movement's emphasis on religion, missionary work, and social service, and Yonge's later work as an unwavering champion of conservative religious values in the face of what she saw as a growing tendency toward apostasy.

BATTISCOMBE and LASKI's volume includes some short pieces by Yonge herself, and a bibliography of her work and early criticism, as well as several critical essays. This is a publication by the Charlotte Yonge Society, founded in 1961 by a group of critics and scholars. Their enthusiasm for Yonge comes through clearly, in essays ranging from source studies to discussions of the dramatic in Yonge's novels and a treatment of Yonge as a critic herself. The essays are well written, although they generally lack an appeal to the critical methods most often used today. Perhaps most interesting is the overall perspective this volume can offer. Poised on the verge of the 1960s' sexual revolution, these critics give a sense of the decisive changes in values that have made Yonge's concerns all but incomprehensible to the historically "naive" reader of today.

MARE and PERCIVAL are largely interested in Yonge from a biographical standpoint, and tend to interpret her fiction in that light. However, they offer the advantage over other biographies by situating Yonge in a broader historical perspective. To that end they offer historical material on poverty, dress, religious beliefs, and other themes, which they relate to Yonge's fiction. The approach is somewhat uncritical, in that the authors take the view that Yonge's work is simply illustrative of Victorian life, and the depth of detail they offer in the historical treatment will be found wanting by scholars of the period. However, students and general readers will be attracted by the book's engaging prose and manageable content.

PAMELA K. GILBERT

INDEXES

BOOKLIST INDEX

Books and articles discussed in the entries are listed here by author/editor name. The page numbers refer to the lists themselves, where full publication information is given. Journal articles and essays from collections are indicated by the word "article" in parenthesis.

GENERAL INDEX

Page numbers in **bold** indicate writers with their own entries in the *Reader's Guide*.

NOTES ON ADVISERS AND CONTRIBUTORS

Abramson, Edward A. Head of American Studies Department, University of Hull. Author of *The Immigrant Experience in American Literature* (1982), *Chaim Potok* (1986), and *Bernard Malamud Revisited* (1993). **Essays:** Jewish-American Writers; Malamud; Singer.

Ackerley, Chris. Senior Lecturer, English Department, University of Otago, Dunedin, New Zealand. Author of *A Companion to "Under the Volcano"* (with Lawrence J. Clipper, 1984) and *The Bridging of Troy* (1986). Contributor to *The Journal of Beckett Studies*, *Nabokov Studies*, and *The Malcolm Lowry Review* (also editorial consultant). **Essays:** Beckett; T.S. Eliot; Graham Greene; Lowry; Pound.

Allen, Rosamund S. Reader, School of English and Drama, Queen Mary and Westfield College, University of London. Editor of *King Horn* (1984). Editor and translator of *Richard Rolle: The English Writings* (1988), and *Laȝamon: Brut* (1992). **Essays:** Allegory; Chronicle Literature; Mystical Literature.

Anderson, Misty G. Teaching Fellow, Department of English, Vanderbilt University, Nashville, Tennessee. Contributor to *Jane Austen and Discourses of Feminism* edited by Devoney Looser (1995), *Gender and Popular Culture* edited by Susan Rollins (1995), and the journal *The Eighteenth Century: Theory and Representation*. **Essay:** Burney.

Armstrong, Katherine A. Lecturer, Department of English Literature, Chester College, Chester. **Essays:** Defoe; Novel: 18th Century.

Arseneau, Mary. Assistant Professor, Department of English, University of Ottawa. Contributor to *Victorian Poetry*, *Victorian Newsletter*, *English Language Notes*, and *Journal of Canadian Poetry*. **Essay:** Christina Rossetti.

Ashburn, Gwen McNeill. Assistant Professor, Department of English, University of North Carolina at Asheville. Contributor to *The Arts Journal*. **Essay:** Southern United States Literature: General.

Ashley, Bob. Head of Media and Cultural Studies, Department of English and Media Studies, Nottingham Trent University. Editor of *The Study of Popular Fiction: A Source Book* (1989). **Essays:** Horror Literature; Popular Fiction: General.

Baker, Simon. Lecturer, Department of English, Unversity College of Wales, Swansea. Contributor to *Writing Region and Nation* edited by J.A. Davies and Glyn Pursglove (1994), *Reference Guide to Short Fiction* edited by Noelle Watson (1994), and the journals *The Anglo-Welsh Review*, *Welsh Book News*, *The New Welsh Review*, *Planet*, *Welsh Academy Journal*, and *The Swansea Review* (also short-story editor). **Essays:** Short Fiction: British; Dylan Thomas; R.S. Thomas; Welsh Literature.

Bazin, Victoria. Researcher and lecturer, University of Northumbria, Newcastle-upon-Tyne. **Essays:** Millay; Marianne Moore; Rich.

Bell, Sandra J. Researcher, Queen's University of Belfast, Northern Ireland. Contributor to *Dictionary of Literary Biography 121* (1992). **Essay:** Scottish Literature: Medieval and Renaissance.

Belsey, Catherine. (Adviser). Professor, Centre for Critical and Cultural Theory, University College of Wales, Cardiff. Author of *Critical Practice* (1980, revised 1988), *The Subject of Tragedy* (1985), *John Milton: Language, Gender, Power* (1988), and *Desire: Love Stories in Western Culture* (1994). Editor of *The Feminist Reader* (1989).

Bending, Stephen. Lecturer, School of English, University of Leeds. Contributor to *Serials and Their Readers 1620-1914* edited by Robin Myers and Michael Harris (1993), *Journal of Garden History*, *Huntington Library Quarterly*, and *Journal of the Warburg and Courtauld Institutes*. **Essays:** Cowper; Landscape and Literature.

Berkove, Lawrence I. Professor, Department of English, University of Michigan-Dearborn. Editor of *Ambrose Bierce: Selected Journalism, 1898–1901* (1986); also editor of *Dives and Lazarus* (1988), *The Gnomes of the Dead Rivers* (1990), and *The Fighting Horse of Stanislaus: Stories and Essays* (1990), all by Dan DeQuille. Contributor to *American Literary Realism*, *Mark Twain Journal*, and *CEA Critic*. **Essay:** Bierce.

Bernau, Anke. Researcher, Department of English, University College of Wales, Cardiff. **Essay:** Dream-Vision Literature.

Bird, Delys. M.Phil Co-ordinator, Australian Studies and Women's Studies, University of Western Australia, Nedlands.

Author of *Killing Women: Rewriting Detective Fiction*, 1993. Editor of *Elizabeth Jolley: New Critical Essays* (with Brenda Walker, 1991), *Whose Place? A Study of Sally Morgan's "My Place"* (with Dennis Haskell, 1992), *Off the Air: Elizabeth Jolley's Radio Plays* (1995), and the journal *Westerly*. **Essay:** Jolley.

Blair, David. Chairman, Board of Studies in English and American Literature, University of Kent, Canterbury. Contributor to *Reading the Victorian Novel: Detail into Form* edited by Ian Gregor (1980) and the journals *Essays in Criticism* and *The Dickensian*. **Essays:** Marvell; Novel: Romantic Era; Scott; The Sonnet.

Blake, Christine. Researcher, Department of English, University of Sussex, Brighton. **Essay:** Parker.

Bone, J.D. Vice Principal for External Affairs, University of Glasgow. Contributor to *Imagination in England and German Romanticism* edited by J. Klein and F. Burwick (1994), *Questioning Romanticism* edited by John Beer (1995), and journals including *Literaria Pragensia* and *Wordsworth Circle*. Editor of *The Byron Journal* 1978–88 and co-editor of *Romanticism* (with Nick Roe and Tim Webb). **Essay:** Byron.

Booth, Howard J. Researcher and part-time lecturer in English Studies, University of Kent, Canterbury. Contributor to *Wasafari*. **Essay:** Isherwood.

Booth, Roy J. Lecturer, Department of English, Royal Holloway, University of London. Editor of *The Love Poems of D.H. Lawrence* (1993), *The Love Poetry of Shakespeare* (1994), and *Elizabethan Sonnets* (revised edition, 1994). Contributor to *English*. **Essays:** Donne; Herbert; Metaphysical Poetry; Poetry: Renaissance; Webster.

Bowen, Deborah C. Sessional Professor, Department of English, University of Ottawa. Contributor to *Canadian Literature*, *Studies in Canadian Literature*, *World Literature Written in English*, *Mosaic*, *ADE Bulletin*, and *English Studies in Canada*. **Essays:** Canadian Literature: Recent and Contemporary; MacLennan; Realism: General.

Bradbury, Malcolm. (Adviser). Professor Emeritus, School of English and American Studies, University of East Anglia. Author of *Evelyn Waugh* (1964), *What is a Novel?* (1969), *The Social Context of Modern English Literature* (1971), *Possibilities* (1973), *The Outland Dart: American Writers and European Modernism* (1978), *The Expatriate Tradition in American Literature* (1982), *Saul Bellow* (1983), *The Modern American Novel* (1983, revised 1991), *My Strange Quest for Mensonge: Structuralism's Hidden Hero* (1987), *No, Not Bloomsbury* (1987), *The Modern World: Ten Great Writers* (1989), *From Puritanism to Postmodernism: The Story of American Literature* (with Richard Ruland, 1991), and *The Modern British Novel* (1993), and several novels, plays, and radio dramas. Editor of essay and short-story collections.

Bradbury, Nicola. Lecturer, Department of English, University of Reading, Berkshire. Author of *Henry James: The Later Novels* (1979), *An Annotated Critical Bibliography of Henry James* (1987), and *Charles Dickens's "Great Expectations"*. Editor of *The Portrait of a Lady* by James (1995) and *The Yearbook of English Studies*. **Essay:** Henry James.

Brady, Kevin P. Adjunct Instructor, Department of English, Rider University, Lawrenceville, New Jersey. Contributor to *New Jersey Review of Literature*, *The Rectangle*, and *The Highlander: Journal of Scottish America*. **Essay:** Muir.

Brake, Laurel. (Adviser). Senior Lecturer in Literature, Centre for Extra-Mural Studies, Birkbeck College, University of London. Author of *Walter Pater* (1994) and *Subjugated Knowledges: Journalism, Gender, and Literature in the Nineteenth Century* (1994). Editor of *Investigating Victorian Journalism* (1990) and *Pater in the 1990s* (with Ian Small, 1991).Editor of *Year's Work in English Studies* for several years and co-editor of *Pater Newsletter*.

Brittan, Simon. Tutor, School of English and American Studies, University of East Anglia. Contributor to *Times Literary Supplement* and *Thumbscrew*. Editor of *New Poetry Quarterly*. **Essays:** The Erotic in Literature; Religion and Literature.

Brown, Stephen W. Professor, Department of English, Trent University, Peterborough, Ontario. Editor of *The Manuscript Papers of William Smellie* (1995) and *"The Characteristical Lives" and Other Essays of William Smellie* (1996). Contributor to *The Blackwell Companion to the Enlightenment* edited by John W. Yolton (1992), *Dictionary of Literary Biography: The British Literary Booktrade* edited by James Bracken and Joel Silver (1995), and journals including *Dalhousie Review*, *Studies on Voltaire*, *Eighteenth-Century Scotland*, and *Brick: A Literary Review*. **Essays:** British Literature: 18th Century; Fiction: Theory; Fiction: Australian; Poetry: American – 20th Century, General; Scottish Literature: 18th and 19th Centuries; Sterne.

Burgass, Catherine. Researcher, Department of English, University of Leicester. Contributor to *Postmodern Surroundings* edited by Steven Earnshaw (1994). **Essays:** Murdoch; Postmodernist Literary Theory.

Burke, Tim. Researcher, School of English, University of Leeds. **Essays:** Literary Aesthetics: Romantic; Popular Literature in Britain; Women Writers: British – 19th Century, Romantic Era.

Burnett, Mark Thornton. Lecturer, Department of English, Queen's University of Belfast, Northern Ireland. Co-editor of *New Essays on "Hamlet"* (with John Manning, 1994). Contributor to *Studies in Philology*, *CIEFL Bulletin*, and *Criticism*. **Essays:** Comedy: Renaissance; Drama: Renaissance, General.

Campbell, Julie D. Researcher and teaching assistant, Department of English, Texas A & M University, College Station. Contributor to *Seventeenth-Century News*. **Essays:** Porter; Wollstonecraft.

Carlin, Deborah. Associate Professor, Department of English, University of Massachusetts, Amherst. Author of *Cather, Canon and the Politics of Reading* (1992). Contributor to several essay collections and the journals *Texas Studies in Language and Literature* and *MELUS* (also member, editorial board). Guest editor, *Legacy: A Journal of American Women Writers*, 9(1), 1992. **Essays:** African-American Writers: General; African-American Writers: 20th Century; Women Writers: American – General; Women Writers: African-American.

Cevasco, G.A. Associate Professor, English Department, St John's University, Jamaica, New York. Author of *Oscar Wilde: British Author, Poet and Wit* (1972), *The Population Problem* (1973), *J.-K. Huysmans: A Reference Guide* (1980), *John Gray* (1982), *The Sitwells* (1987), *Three Decadent Poets: Ernest Dowson, John Gray and Lionel Johnson: An Annotated Bibliography* (1990), and several books on the English language. Editor of *The 1890s: An Encyclopedia of British Literature, Art and Culture* (1993). Contributor to *English Literature in Transition*, *Research Studies*, *Studies in Drama*, *Yearbook of English Studies*, and *Journal of Aesthetics and Art Criticism*. **Essays:** The Sitwells; Wilde.

Chow, Karen Har-Yen. Researcher, Department of English, University of California at Santa Barbara. Contributor to *Encyclopedia of Multiculturalism* edited by Susan Auerbach (1994), *Reference Guide to American Literature* (3rd edition, edited by Jim Kamp, 1994), and *Journal of Popular Culture*. Editorial assistant, *Asian America: Journal of Culture and the Arts*. **Essays:** Asian-American Literature; Hurston.

Christie, Christine. Lecturer, Department of English and Drama, Loughborough University, Leicestershire. Contributor to *Gendering the Reader* edited by Sara Mills (1994). **Essays:** Irony; Richards.

Claridge, Henry. (Adviser). Lecturer, English and American Studies, University of Kent, Canterbury. Editor of *F. Scott Fitzgerald: Critical Assessments* (4 vols., 1991). Contributor to *Yearbook of English Studies*. **Essays:** Anderson; Dos Passos; Dreiser; Fiction: American – 20th Century, Before World War II; Hawkes; Hellman; Howells; London; Norris; Poetry: American – 19th Century; Thoreau; Warren; Edmund Wilson; Wolfe.

Coates, Carole. Senior Lecturer, Department of English, University College of St Martin, Lancaster. Contributor to *John Cowper Powys's "Wolf Solent": Critical Studies* edited by Belinda Humfrey (1990) and journals including *Orbis*, *Outposts*, and *Rialto*. **Essay:** Powys.

Coates, John. Lecturer, Department of English, University of Hull. Author of *Chesterton and the Edwardian Crisis* (1984) and *Combative Styles: Romantic Writing and Ideology* (with Bruce Woodcock, 1994). Contributor to *Journal of the History of Ideas*, *Shakespeare Survey*, *Mosaic*, *Yearbook of English Studies*, *Modern Language Review*, and *Renascence*. **Essay:** Chesterton.

Cockin, Katharine Mary. Researcher and part-time lecturer, Leicester and De Montfort Universities, both Leicester. Contributor to *International Dictionary of Theatre 1: Plays* edited by Mark Hawkins-Dady (1992), *Difference in View: Women in Modernism* edited by Gabriele Griffin (1994), *Victorian Periodicals Review*, and *Theatre Notebook*. **Essays:** Atwood; Gender and Literature.

Cockshut, A.O.J. G.M. Young Lecturer in Nineteenth-Century English Literature, University of Oxford. Author of *Anthony Trollope* (1955), *Anglican Attitudes* (1959), *The Imagination of Charles Dickens* (1961), *The Unbelievers: English Agnostic Thought 1840–1890* (1964), *George Eliot: Middlemarch* (1966), *The Achievement of Walter Scott* (1969), *Truth to Life: The Art of Biography in the Nineteenth Century* (1974), *Man and Woman: A Study of Love and the Novel* (1977), and *The Art of Autobiography in 19th and 20th Century England* (1984). Editor of *Religious Controversies of the Nineteenth Century: Selected Documents* (1966). **Essays:** Biography and Autobiography: Victorian; George Eliot; Newman; Trollope; Victorian Literature and Religion.

Cole, Catherine Wells. Senior Lecturer, Department of English, Roehampton Institute, London. **Essays:** Romance Fiction; Women Writers: 19th Century, Victorian.

Collins, Fiona M. Senior Lecturer, Department of Education, Roehampton Institute, London. Contributor to *The Power of the Page: Children's Books and Their Readers* edited by Pat Pinsent (1993) and *Contemporary Juvenile Reading Habits* (with other members of the Children's Literature Research Centre, 1994). **Essay:** Children's Literature: 20th Century.

Cooper, Caroline M. Senior Lecturer, School of Literary and Media Studies, University of North London. Contributor to *Literature/Film Quarterly*, and *European Studies*. Translator of *Abstract Art since 1945* (1971) and *Figurative Art since 1945* (1971), both edited by Jean Leymarie. **Essay:** Film and Literature.

Cordle, Daniel. Researcher, Department of English, University of Leicester. **Essay:** Science and Literature.

Corker, D.T. Lecturer, School of English and American Studies, University of East Anglia. **Essays:** American Renaissance; Drama: American – 20th Century, Before World War II; Realism in American Literature.

Corman, Brian. Professor, Department of English, University of Toronto. Author of *Genre and Generic Change in English Comedy 1660–1710* (1993) and articles on Restoration and 18th-century literature. **Essays:** Etherege; Wycherley.

Crane, Ralph J. Lecturer, Department of English, University of Waikato, Hamilton, New Zealand. Author of *Inventing India: A History of India in English-Language Fiction* (1992) and *Ruth Pràwer Jhabvala* (1992). Editor of *Passages to Ruth Prawer Jhabavla* (1991). Co-editor of journal *SPAN*. **Essays:** Anand; Narayan; Rao.

Cutmore, Jonathan. Researcher, Department of English, University of Toronto. **Essay:** Southey.

Daly, Macdonald. Lecturer, Department of English Studies, University of Nottingham. Editor of *D.H. Lawrence: Sons and Lovers* (1994), *Elizabeth Gaskell: Mary Barton* (1995), *H.G. Wells: The Invisible Man* (1995), and *D.H. Lawrence: Kangaroo* (1996). Contributor to *Modern Language Review*, *English Studies*, *The Edinburgh Review*, *Critique*, *Durham University Journal*, *British Journal of Eighteenth-Century Studies*, and *British Journalism Review*. **Essays:** Fowles; Nabokov; Postmodern Literature; Scottish Literature: 20th Century.

Davenport, Tony. Professor, Department of English, Royal Holloway, University of London. Author of *The Art of the Gawain-Poet* (1978), *Fifteenth-Century English Drama* (1982), *Chaucer, Complaint and Narrative* (1988). **Essay:** Butler.

Davies, Alistair. Lecturer, Department of English, University of Sussex. Author of *An Annotated Critical Bibliography of Modernism* (1982). **Essays:** Modernism: Fiction; Yeats: Poetry

Davies, Paul. Lecturer, Department of English, University of Ulster, Coleraine. Author of *The Ideal Real: Beckett's Fiction and Imagination* (1994). Contributor to *The Cambridge Companion to Beckett* edited by John Pilling (1994) and the journal *TEMENOS*. Co-editor of *Writing Ulster* 1–3. **Essays:** Coleridge; Romanticism: British.

Davis, Lloyd. Lecturer, Department of English, University of Queensland, St Lucia, Australia. Author of *Sexuality and Textuality in Henry James* (1988), *Guise and Disguise: Rhetoric and Characterization in the English Renaissance* (1993), and *Tools for Cultural Studies: An Introduction* (with Tony Thwaites, 1994). Editor of *Virginal Sexuality and Textuality in Victorian Literature* (1993). Contributor to journals including *Literature in North Queensland* (*LiNQ*), *AUMLA*, and *Southern Review*. **Essay:** Postcolonial Theory.

Day, Brian J. Researcher, Queen's University, Kingston, Ontario. Contributor to *Yeats: An Annual*. **Essay:** Morris.

DePasquale, Paul W. Researcher and lecturer, Department of English, University of Alberta. Edmonton; also creative-writing instructor, Grant MacEwan Community College, Edmonton. **Essays:** New England Literature; Ralegh.

Draper, R.P. Regius Chalmers Professor, Department of English, University of Aberdeen. Author of *A Midsummer Night's Dream* (1980), *Cymbeline* (1980), *Lyric Tragedy* (1985), *The Winter's Tale: Text and Performance* (1985), *Sons and Lovers* (1986), *Twelfth Night* (1988), *An Annotated Critical Bibliography of Thomas Hardy* (1989). Editor of *Hardy: The Tragic Novels: A Casebook* (1975, revised 1991), *"The Mill on the Floss" and "Silas Marner": A Casebook* (1977), *Tragedy: Developments in Criticism: A Casebook* (1980), *Hardy: Three Pastoral Novels: A Casebook* (1987), *The Literature of Region and Nation* (1989), *The Epic: Developments in Criticism: A Casebook* (1990), *A Spacious Vision: Essays on Thomas Hardy* (with Phillip V. Mallett, 1994). **Essays:** Auden; Hardy; Housman; Ted Hughes; Larkin; Poetry: British – 20th Century, General; Poetry: British – 20th Century, Postwar.

Duncan, Dawn E. Assistant Professor, Department of English, Concordia College, Moorhead, Minnesota. Contributor to *1941: Texas Goes to War* edited by James Ward Lee *et al.* (1991) and Brian Friel issue of *Working Papers in Irish Studies*, 94(3), (1994). **Essays:** Drama: Irish; Melodrama; Shaw.

Earnshaw, Steven. Tutor, Department of English, University of Leicester, and Bedford College of Higher Education. Editor of *Postmodern Surroundings* (1994). Contributor to *Cambridge Quarterly*. **Essays:** Carroll; Novel: 20th Century; Pynchon; The Thirties Generation.

Echard, Siân. Assistant Professor, Department of English, University of British Columbia, Vancouver. Co-translator (with Claire Fanger) of *The Latin Verses in the "Confessio Amantis"* (1991). Contributor to *Journal of Medieval Latin* (1994). **Essays:** British Literature: Medieval; Gawain-Poet; Gower; Malory; Poetry: Middle English; Romance.

Edwards, Colin J. Senior Lecturer in English, Faculty of Humanities, Bath College of Higher Education, Avon. Contributor to *The Cambridge Guide to Literature in English* edited by Ian Ousby (1988) and the journals *Agenda* and *Wyndham Lewis Annual*. **Essay:** Ford Madox Ford.

Emig, Rainer. Lecturer, School of English Studies, Communication and Philosophy, University College of Wales, Cardiff. Author of *Modernism in Poetry: Motivations, Structures and Limits* (1995). **Essay:** War and Literature.

Evans, Ruth. Lecturer, School of English Studies, Communication and Philosophy, University College of Wales, Cardiff. Co-editor of *Feminist Readings in Middle English Literature* (with Lesley Johnson, 1994) and *The Medieval Translator 4* with Roger Ellis (1994). **Essays:** Drama: Medieval, Cycle Plays; Kempe; Prose: Old English; Translation in the Middle Ages and Renaissance.

Fairley, Ian. Lecturer, School of English, University of Leeds. Translator and editor, *The Evolution of Modern Drama* by Georg Lukács (1996). Contributor to *Comparative Criticism* and *Hungarian Studies*. **Essays:** Decadence, Aestheticism, and the 1890s; Pater.

Fennell, Francis L. Professor, Department of English, Loyola University, Chicago. Author of *Dante Gabriel Rossetti: An Annotated Bibliography* (1982). Editor of *The Rossetti-Leyland Letters* (1978) and *The Fine Delight: Centenary Essays on Gerald Manley Hopkins* (1989). **Essays:** Robert Browning; Hopkins; Dante Gabriel Rossetti.

Fenwick, Mac. Researcher, Department of English, Queen's University, Kingston, Ontario. **Essay:** Tolkien.

Filewod, Alan. Professor, Department of Drama, University of Guelph, Ontario. Author of *Collective Encounters: Docu-*

mentary Theatre in English Canada (1987). Editor of *New Canadian Drama 5: Political Drama* (1991) and *The CTR Anthology: 15 Plays* (1993). Contributor to *Aboriginal Voices: Amerindian, Inuit and Sami Theater* edited by Per Brask and William Morgan (1992), *Imperialism and Theatre* edited by J. Ellen Gainor (1995), *Contemporary Issues in Canadian Theatre and Drama* edited by Per Brask (1995), *World Encyclopedia of Contemporary Theatre 2: The Americas* edited by Don Rubin (1996), and the journals *Canadian Theatre Review*, *Theatre Journal*, *Theatre Research in Canada*, *Essays in Theatre*, *Australasian Drama Studies*, and *Modern Drama*. **Essay:** Drama: Canadian.

Fremantle, Susan. Visiting Lecturer, Department of Education, Roehampton Institute, London. Contributor to *The Power of the Page: Children's Books and Their Readers* edited by Pat Pinsent (1993). **Essay:** Children's Literature: 20th Century.

Frye, Susan. Associate Professor, Department of English, University of Wyoming, Laramie. Author of *Elizabeth I: The Competition for Representation* (1993). Contributor to *Sixteenth-Century Journal*, *Signs*, and *Literature and History*. Member, editorial boards of *English Language Notes* and *Medieval Feminist Newsletter*. **Essay:** Women Writers: Renaissance.

Fung, Eileen Chia-Ching. Researcher, University of California at Santa Barbara. **Essay:** Julian of Norwich.

Gardner, Elizabeth. Instructor, Department of English, Rutgers University, New Brunswick, New Jersey. **Essay:** Music and Literature.

Gasper, Julia. Researcher and writer. Author of *The Dragon and the Dove: The Plays of Thomas Dekker* (1990). Contributor to *Theatre and Government under the Early Stuarts* edited by J.R. Mulryne and Margaret Shewring (1993) and *Durham University Journal*. **Essay:** Dekker.

Gavioli, Davida. Visiting Associate Professor, Department of Romance Languages, Oberlin College, Ohio. Contributor to *Gendered Contexts: New Perspectives in Italian Cultural Studies* edited by Laura Benedetti, Julia L. Hairston, and Silvia M. Ross (1995) and the journal *Présence Francophone*. **Essay:** Oates.

Gemme, Paola. Researcher, Department of English, Pennsylvania State University, University Park. Contributor to *Legacy: A Journal of American Women Writers*, *Prospects*,*Proceedings of the XI International Biennial AISNA Conference*, and *Quaderni di Lingue e Letterature Straniere Moderne dell'Università di Genova*. **Essay:** Women Writers: American – to 1900.

Gilbert, Pamela K. Assistant Professor, Department of English, University of Wisconsin, Parkside. Contributor to *Victorian Newsletter* and *English*. **Essays:** Madness and Literature; Popular Fiction for Women; Schreiner; Victorian Literature and Society; Yonge.

Gillespie, Stuart. Lecturer, Department of English, University of Glasgow. Editor of *The Poets on the Classics: An Anthology* (1988). Contributor to *Review of English Studies*, *Year's Work in English Studies*, *Notes & Queries*, *Cambridge Quarterly*, *Literature and Theology*, and *Restoration*. **Essays:** British Literature: Restoration; Dryden; Poetry: 18th Century; Rochester.

Goodridge, John. Senior Lecturer, Department of English and Media Studies, Nottingham Trent University. Author of *Rural Life in Eighteenth-Century English Poetry* (1995). Editor of *The Independent Spirit: John Clare and the Self-Taught Tradition* (1994), and *The John Clare Society Journal* since 1992. **Essay:** Clare.

Gough, Val. Lecturer, Department of English, University of Liverpool. Contributor to *Anticipations: Essays on Early Science Fiction and Its Precursors* edited by David Seed (1994) and *Virginia Woolf: Emerging Perspectives* edited by M. Hussey and V. Nemerow (1994). Member, editorial boards of *Woolf Studies Annual* and *Liverpool Studies in Language and Discourse*. **Essays:** The Bloomsbury Group; Gilman; Women Writers: General; Women Writers: 20th Century.

Griffiths, Trevor R. Professor, School of Literary and Media Studies, University of North London. Author of *Stagecraft* (1982; US edition as *Practical Theater*, 1982), *Guide to Shakespeare Quotations* (with T.A. Joscelyne, 1985; as *Shakespeare's Quotations*, 1992), *Theatre Guide* (with Carole Woddis, 1988, revised 1991). Co-editor of *British and Irish Women Dramatists since 1958* (with Margaret Llewellyn-Jones, 1993). Contributor to *Theatre Notebook*, *Shakespeare Quarterly*, *Yearbook of English Studies*, and *Year's Work in English Studies*. Associate editor of Drama Classics series, Nick Hern Books. **Essays:** Drama: British – 20th Century, General; Drama: British – 20th Century, Postwar; Drama: British – 20th Century, Recent and Contemporary; Pinter.

Hadfield, Andrew. Lecturer, Department of English, University College of Wales, Aberystwyth. Author of *Literature, Politics and National Identity: Reformation to Renaissance* (1994). Co-editor of *Representing Ireland: Literature and the Origins of Conflict, 1534–1660* (with Brendan Bradshaw *et al.*, 1993) and *"Strangers to That Land": British Perceptions of Ireland from the Reformation to the Famine* (with John McVeagh, 1994). **Essays:** Bale; Jonson; Literary Aesthetics: Renaissance; New Criticism; Pastoral Literature; Spenser.

Hagiioannu, Andrew. Researcher, Department of English, University of Leicester. **Essays:** Kipling; Victorian Literature, Science, and Evolutionary Theory.

Halliwell, Martin. Researcher, Department of English Studies, University of Nottingham; part-time lecturer, De Montfort University, Leicester. Contributor to *Journal of American Studies*. **Essays:** Fiction: British – 20th Century, General; Fiction: British – 20th Century, Before World War II; Fiction: British – 20th Century, Postwar; Peacock.

Hamilton, Robin. Lecturer, Department of English and Drama, Loughborough University, Leicestershire. Author of several volumes of poetry, including *The Lost Jockey: Collected Poems 1966–1982* (1983). Editor of *John Donne: Collected Poems* (1994). **Essays:** Dunbar; Wyatt.

Hancock, Susan. Academic assistant, Children's Literature Research Centre, Roehampton Institute, London. Contributor to *Contemporary Juvenile Reading Habits* (with other members of the Children's Literature Research Centre, 1993). **Essay:** Children's Literature: British – General.

Hapgood, Lynne. Principal Lecturer, Department of English and Media Studies, Nottingham Trent University. Contributor to *Cultural Politics at the Fin de Siècle* edited by Sally Ledger and Scott McCracken (1994) and *Transforming Genres: British Fiction of the 1890s* edited by Meri-Jane Rochelson and Lee Manos (1994). **Essays:** Gissing; Victorian Literature and the City.

Harris, Margaret. Professor and Chair, Department of English, University of Sydney. Editor of *One of Our Conquerors* (1975), *Beauchamp's Career* (1988), and *The Egoist* (1992), all by George Meredith. Co-editor of *The Notebooks of George Meredith* (with Gillian Beer, 1983) and *Reconnoitres: Essays in Australian Literature* (with Elizabeth Webby, 1992). **Essays:** Meredith; Stead.

Harris, Oliver. Lecturer, Department of American Studies, Keele University, Staffordshire. Editor of *The Letters of William S. Burroughs 1945–1959* (1993). **Essays:** Beat Generation; Burroughs.

Hassler, Donald M. Professor, Department of English, Kent State University, Ohio. Author of *Erasmus Darwin* (1973), *Comic Tones in Science Fiction* (1982), *Hal Clement* (1982), *Patterns of the Fantastic* (2 vols., 1983–85), *Death and the Serpent* (1985), and *Isaac Asimov* (1991). Co-editor of *Arthur Machen and Montgomery Evans: Letters* (with Sue S. Hassler, 1994). Editor of the journal *Extrapolation* since 1990. **Essay:** Science Fiction.

Hathaway, Heather A. Assistant Professor, Department of English, Marquette University, Milwaukee. Contributor to *Refiguring the Father: New Feminist Readings of Patriarchy* edited by Patricia Yaeger and Beth Kowaleski-Wallace (1989) and *The Oxford Companion to Women's Writing in the United States* edited by Cathy N. Davidson and Linda Wagner-Martin (1994). **Essay:** Langston Hughes.

Herbert, Michael. Lecturer, School of English, University of St Andrews, Fife. Editor, *D.H. Lawrence: "Reflections on the Death of a Porcupine" and Other Essays* (1988). **Essay:** Lawrence.

Hobbs, Michael. Assistant Professor, Department of English, Northwest Missouri State University, Maryville. Contributor to *Henry James Review*, *Studies in Short Fiction*, *American Literary Realism*, *Western American Literature*, and *The Wallace Stevens Journal*. **Essays:** Native American Literature; Stevens.

Hobsbaum, Philip. Professor, Department of English, University of Glasgow. Author of *A Theory of Criticism* (1970), *A Theory of Communication* (1970), *A Reader's Guide to Charles Dickens* (1973), *Tradition and Experiment in English Poetry* (1979), *A Reader's Guide to D.H. Lawrence* (1981), *Essentials of Literary Criticism* (1983), *A Reader's Guide to Robert Lowell* (1988), *Metre, Rhythm and Verse Form* (1996), and several volumes of poetry. Editor of *A Group Anthology* (with Edward Lucie-Smith, 1963), *Ten Elizabethan Poets* (1969), and *Wordsworth: Selected Poetry and Prose* (1989). **Essay:** Leavis.

Holland, Patrick. Associate Professor, Department of English, University of Guelph, Ontario. Co-editor of *Images of Louis Riel in Canadian Culture* (with Ramon Hathorn, 1992). Associate editor of the journal *World Literature Written in English* 1989–93. **Essays:** Canadian Literature: General; Conrad; Exploration Literature; Fiction: Canadian; Findley; Hazlitt; Hearn; Laurence; Munro; Poetry: Canadian; Ross; White.

Holloway, David. Part-time lecturer in American literature, University of Derby and The Open University. Contributor to *Journal of American Studies* and *Over Here*. **Essays:** Du Bois; Fiction: American – General; Sinclair Lewis; Sinclair.

Houlahan, Mark. Lecturer, Department of English, University of Waikato, Hamilton, New Zealand. Contributor to *International Dictionary of Theatre 1: Plays* edited by Mark Hawkins-Dady (1992) and the journals *Milton Studies*, *Extrapolation*, *Landfall*, and *1650–1850: Ideas, Aesthetics and Enquiries in the Early Modern Era*. **Essays:** Apocalyptic Literature; Comedy: Renaissance, City Comedy; Farquhar; John Ford; The Grotesque; Massinger; New Historicism; Pepys.

Hughes, Derek. Senior Lecturer, Department of English, University of Warwick, Coventry. Author of *Dryden's Heroic Plays* (1981). Contributor to *University of Toronto Quarterly*, *Studies in English Literature*, *Comparative Drama*, *Yearbook of English Studies*, *Philological Quarterly*, *Studies in Philology*, *Modern Language Review*, *Modern Language Quarterly*, *Durham University Journal*, and *Review of English Studies*. Member, editorial board of *Restoration*. **Essays:** Congreve; Tragedy: Restoration.

Hunt, Peter. (Adviser). Senior Lecturer, School of English Studies, Communication and Philosophy, University College of Wales, Cardiff. Author of *Criticism, Theory and Children's Literature* (1991), *Arthur Ransome* (1991, as *Approaching Arthur Ransome*, 1992), *An Introduction to Children's Literature* (1994), *Masterworks of Children's Literature* (1994), and several volumes of fiction. Editor of *Children's Book Research in Britain* (1977, revised 1982), *Further Approaches to Research in Children's Literature* (1982), *Bevis* by Richard Jeffries (1989), *Children's Literature: The Development of Criticism* (1990), *Literature for Children: Contemporary Criticism* (1992), and *Children's Literature: An Illustrated History* (1995). **Essay:** Children's Literature: General.

Hunt, Philippa. Senior Lecturer, Department of Education, Roehampton Institute, London. Contributor to *The Power of the Page: Children's Books and Their Readers* edited by Pat Pinsent (1993) and several publications for teachers. **Essay:** Children's Literature: British – 1900 to the Present.

Jansson, Siv. Researcher and part-time tutor, Department of English, Royal Holloway, University of London; also part-time tutor, University of North London. Contributor to *Year's Work in English Studies* (Romantic Novel section), *Modern Language Review*, *Journal of Gender Studies*, *Studies on Women* (abstracts), and *Baetyl: The Journal of Women's Literature*. **Essay:** Drama: American – 20th Century, Postwar.

Jarvis, Brian. Lecturer, Department of English and Drama, Loughborough University, Leicestershire. Contributor to *Journal of American Studies* and *Studies in Women* (abstracts). **Essays:** Douglass; Ellison; Gaddis; Poe.

Johanyak, Debra. Assistant Professor of English, Wayne College, University of Akron, Orrville, Ohio. Contributor to *Pennsylvania English*, *College Language Association Journal* (*CLAJ*), and *Mississippi Quarterly*. **Essays:** Cooper; Fiction: American – 19th Century.

Jones, Lawrence. Associate Professor, English Department, University of Otago, Dunedin, New Zealand. Author of *Barbed Wire and Mirrors: Essays on New Zealand Prose* (1987). Contributor to *The Oxford History of New Zealand Literature* edited by Terry Sturm (1991). Co-editor of *Journal of New Zealand Literature*. **Essays:** Fiction: New Zealand; Frame; New Zealand Literature.

Jones, Mark. Associate Professor, Department of English, Queen's University, Kingston, Ontario. Author of *Wordsworth Scholarship and Criticism, 1972–1984: An Annotated Bibliography* (with Karl Kroeber, 1985) and *The "Lucy Poems": A Case Study in Literary Knowledge* (1995). Contributor to *PMLA*, *Studies in Romanticism*, *Journal of English and Germanic Philology*, and *Boundary 2: A Journal of Postmodern Literature and Culture*. **Essay:** Wordsworth.

Jowitt, Penelope. Researcher, St Hilda's College, University of Oxford; also teacher. **Essay:** Lessing.

Kaston, Andrea J. Researcher, Department of English, University of Wisconsin, Madison. **Essay:** Children's Literature: American.

Kehler, Dorothea. Professor, Department of English and Comparative Literature, San Diego State University, California. Author of *Problems in Literary Research: A Guide to Selected Reference Works* (1975, revised 1981, 1987). Co-editor of *In Another Country: Feminist Perspectives on Renaissance Drama* (with Susan Baker, 1991). Contributor to journals including *English Language Notes*, *Milton Newsletter*, *American Notes & Queries*, *Rocky Mountain Review*, *The English Record*, *Renaissance Papers*, *The Explicator*, *Shakespeare-Jahrbuch*. **Essays:** Shakespeare: History of Criticism; Shakespeare: Tragedies; Shakespeare: Problem Plays.

Kelly, Lionel. Senior Lecturer (and Director of American Studies 1989–95), Department of English, University of Reading, Berkshire. Editor of *Tobias Smollett: The Critical Heritage* (1987) and *Richard Aldington: Papers from the Reading Symposium* (1987). Contributor to *Ezra Pound and History* edited by M. Korn (1985), *Re-Reading the Short Story* edited by Clare Hanson (1989), *Sir James Frazer and the Literary Imagination* edited by Robert Fraser (1990), *The Ideal Core of the Onion: Reading Beckett Archives* edited by John Pilling and Mary Bryden (1992), *Confronting Tennessee Williams: Essays in Critical Pluralism* edited by Philip C. Kolin (1993), and the journal *Yearbook in English Studies*. **Essays:** Berryman; Chopin; Hart Crane; Dickinson; Emerson; Fugitives and Agrarians; Hemingway; Jeffers; Lowell; Mamet; Poetry: American – General; Poetry: American – 20th Century, Postwar; Poetry: American – 20th Century, Recent and Contemporary; Robinson; Tennessee Williams; William Carlos Williams.

Kelly, Philippa. Lecturer, Department of English, Australian Defence Force Academy, Sydney. Author of *Shakespeare's "King Lear"* (1993). Contributor to *Meridian*, *Southerly*, *Literature in North Queensland* (*LiNQ*), *Southern Review*, and *SPAN*. **Essay:** Postcolonial Theory.

Kennedy, Ruth. Lecturer, Department of English, Royal Holloway, University of London. Contributor to *Medieval Literature and Antiquities: Studies in Honour of Basil Cottle* edited by Myra Stokes and T.L. Burton (1987). **Essay:** Alliterative Tradition.

Keymer, Tom. Lecturer, Department of English, Royal Holloway, University of London. Author of *Richardson's "Clarissa" and the Eighteenth-Century Reader* (1992) and various articles. Editor of *Laurence Sterne: "A Sentimental Journey" and Other Writings* (1994). **Essays:** Boswell; Epistolary Novel; Macpherson; Samuel Richardson; Smart; Smollett.

King, Pamela M. Head of Department of English, University College of St Martin, Lancaster. Co-editor of *York Mystery Plays: A Selection in Modern Spelling* (with Richard Beadle, 1984) and *London and Europe in the Middle Ages* (with Julia Boffey, 1994). Contributor to *Chaucer and Fifteenth-Century Poetry* edited by Julia Boffey and Janet Cowan (1991), *Comedy: A Festschrift for Peter Dixon* edited by E. Maslen (1993), *The Cambridge Companion to Medieval English Theatre c.1350–1520* edited by Richard Beadle (1994), and the journals *Themes in Drama*, *Medieval English Theatre*, and *Archiv*. **Essays:** British Literature: 15th Century; Drama: Medieval, General; Lyric in Medieval Literature.

Klinkowitz, Jerome. Professor, Department of English, University of Northern Iowa, Cedar Falls. Author of *Kurt Vonnegut Jr.: A Descriptive Bibliography* (with Asa B. Pieratt Jr., 1974), *Literary Disruptions* (1975, revised 1980), *The Life of Fiction* (1977), *Donald Barthelme: A Comprehensive Bibliography* (1977), *The Practice of Fiction in America* (1980), *The American 1960s* (1980), *Kurt Vonnegut* (1982), *Peter Handke and the Postmodern Transformation* (with James

Knowlton, 1983), *The Self-Apparent Word* (1984), *Literary Subversions* (1985), *The New American Novel of Manners* (1986), *Kurt Vonnegut: A Comprehensive Bibliography* (with Judie Huffman-Klinkowitz, 1987), *Rosenberg/Barthes/Hassan: The Postmodern Habit of Thought* (1988), *"A Short Season" and Other Stories* (1988), *Their Finest Hours* (1989), *Slaughterhouse-Five: Reinventing the Novel and the World* (1990), *Listen, Gerry Mulligan* (1989), *Donald Barthelme: An Exhibition* (1991), and *Structuring the Void* (1992). Editor of *Innovative Fiction* (with John Somers, 1972), *The Vonnegut Statement* (with Somers, 1973), *Vonnegut in America* (with Donald L. Lawler, 1977), *Writing under Fire: Stories of the Vietnam War* (with Somers, 1978), *The Diaries of Willard Motley* (1979), *Nathaniel Hawthorne* (1984), and *Writing Baseball* (1991). **Essays:** Barthelme; Updike.

Knowles, James D. Lecturer, Department of English, University of Newcastle-upon-Tyne. Contributor to *Theatre and Government under the Early Stuarts* edited by J.R. Mulryne and Margaret Shewring (1993) and the journal *English Manuscript Studies*. **Essays:** Drama: Renaissance, Elizabethan; The Masque; Shakespeare: Middle Comedies; Tragedy: Renaissance.

Kopper, Edward A., Jr. Professor, Department of English, Slippery Rock University, Pennsylvania. Author of *Lady Isabella Persse Gregory* (1976) and several articles. Editor of *James Joyce: New Glances* (1980), *A J.M. Synge Literary Companion* (1988), *Synge: A Review of the Criticism* (1990), and *Lady Gregory: A Review of the Criticism* (1991). Editor of *Modern British Literature* 1976–80 and *Notes on Modern Irish Literature* since 1989. **Essay:** Vonnegut.

Kuhlmann, Elizabeth. Researcher, Department of English, Indiana University, Bloomington. **Essay:** Deconstruction.

Lane, Jeremy. Lecturer, Department of English, University of Sussex, Brighton. Contributor to *The Modern English Novel* (edited by Gabriel Josipovici, 1976), and the journals *History of European Ideas*, *Granta*, *Universities Poetry*, and *South East Arts Review*. **Essays:** Burgess; Durrell; Short Fiction: General; Utopian Literature; Angus Wilson.

Lathey, Gillian. Senior Lecturer, Department of Education, Roehampton Institute, London. Contributor to *Looking at Language in the Primary School* (edited by C. Mills and L. Timson, 1988), *Shared Reading, Shared Writing* (CLPE, 1990), *Contemporary Juvenile Reading Habits* (with other members of the Children's Literature Research Centre, 1994), and the journals *English in Education* and *Early Child Development and Care*. **Essay:** Children's Literature: 20th Century.

Lee, A. Robert. Reader in American Literature, University of Kent, Canterbury. Author of *Black American Fiction since Richard Wright* (1983). Editor of *Moby-Dick* by Herman Melville (1973), *Black Fiction: New Studies in the Afro-American Novel since 1945* (1980), *Nathaniel Hawthorne: New Critical Essays* (1982), *Herman Melville: Reassessments* (1984), *Nineteenth-Century American Poetry* (1985), *The Nineteenth-Century American Short Story* (1985), *Edgar Allan Poe: The Design of Order* (1985), *First-Person Singular: Studies in American Autobiography* (1988), *Scott Fitzgerald: The Promises of Life* (1989), *The Modern American Novella* (1989), *William Faulkner: The Yoknapatawpha Fiction* (1990), *Tensions and Transitions (1869–1990): The Mediating Imagination* (1990), *Typee* by Melville (1993), *"Billy Budd, Sailor" and Other Stories* by Melville (1993), *A Permanent Etcetera: Cross Cultural Perspectives on Post-War America* (1993), *Shadow Distance: A Gerald Vizenor Reader* (1994), *Other Britain, Other British: Contemporary Multicultural Fiction* (1995), and *Making America, Making American Literature: Franklin to Cooper* (with W.M. Verhoeven, 1994). **Essays:** African-American Writers: Recent and Contemporary; Latino Writers.

Lerner, Laurence. Formerly Professor of English at Sussex (Brighton) and Vanderbilt (Nashville, Tennessee) universities. Author of *An Introduction to English Poetry: Fifteen Poems* (1975), *Thomas Hardy's "The Mayor of Casterbridge": Tragedy or Social History?* (1975), *Love and Marriage: Literature and Its Social Context* (1979), *The Literary Imagination* (1982), *The Frontiers of Literature* (1988), and ten volumes of poetry. Editor of *The Contexts of English Literature: The Victorians* (1978), *Shakespeare's Tragedies* (1982), *Reconstructing Literature* (1983), *Poems* (by Milton, 1985), and *On Modern Poetry* (with Vereen Bell, 1988). **Essay:** Dickens.

Lingard, John. Assistant Professor, Department of English, University of Western Ontario, London, Canada. Contributor to *Dalhousie Review*, *Pinter Review*, *Dictionary of Literary Biography*, *Scandinavian Studies*, *Scandinavian-Canadian Studies*, and *Essays in Theatre*. Translator of plays by Ibsen and Strindberg. **Essays:** Drama: British – 20th Century, Before World War II; Osborne; Yeats: Drama.

Llewellyn-Jones, Margaret L. Senior Lecturer, School of Literary and Media Studies, University of North London. Editor of *British and Irish Dramatists since 1958* (with Trevor R. Griffiths, 1993) and *Contemporary Theatre Review* special issue on "Spectacle, Silence and Subversion: Women's Performance Languages and Strategies" (1994). **Essays:** Churchill; Drama: Theory; O'Casey; Synge.

Lockyer, Judith. Associate Professor, Department of English, Albion College, Michigan. Author of *Ordered by Words: Language and Narration in the Novels of William Faulkner* (1991). Contributor to *Arizona Quarterly* and *Michigan Historical Review*. **Essays:** Faulkner; Southern United States Literature: 20th Century.

Londry, Michael. Researcher, Department of English, University of Alberta, Edmonton. Textual editor of *Norna, or, The Witch's Curse* (by Louisa May Alcott, 1994). Contributor to journals including *U.C. Review*, *WestWord*, and *Other Voices*. **Essay:** Ashbery

Longstaffe, Stephen. Lecturer, Department of English, University College of St Martin, Lancaster. **Essays:** Robert Greene; Historical Drama; Philips; Shakespeare: Histories.

Lord, Bruce R.A. Teaching Assistant, Department of English, University of Western Ontario, London, Canada. Contributor to *(Sa)Fire/Works: More Works in Progress by Students of Feminism* (1994). **Essays:** Literary Theory: General; Owen.

Lyle, A.W. Formerly Lecturer, Department of English Literature, University of Sheffield. **Essays:** Comedy: Theory; Narrative Theory; Parody; Reader-Response Theory; Satire: General; Semiotics; Structuralism.

McCarron, Kevin. Lecturer, Department of English, Roehampton Institute, London. Author of *William Golding* (1994) and *The Coincidence of Opposites: William Golding's Later Fiction* (1994). Editor of *Critical Survey* since 1994. **Essays:** Baxter; Golding.

McCormick, I.D. Lecturer in English, Nene College, Northampton. **Essays:** Fielding; Locke; Satire: 18th Century.

McGowan, Philip. Researcher, Department of English, Trinity College, Dublin. **Essays:** Stephen Crane; Crime Fiction; Frontier and Western Literature.

Madsen, Deborah L. Senior Tutor for American Studies, Department of English, University of Leicester. Author of *The Postmodernist Allegories of Thomas Pynchon* (1991), *Rereading Allegory: A Narrative Approach to Genre* (1994). Editor of *Visions of America since 1492* (1994). Contributor to journals including *Southern Review*, *Over Here*, *American Studies*, *Journal of American Studies*, *Journal of Narrative Technique*, and *Science and Culture*. Executive editor of *Year's Work in English Studies* 1990–93. **Essays:** American Literature: General; American Literature: 20th Century; Fiction: American – 20th Century, General; Fiction: American – 20th Century, Postwar and Contemporary; Hawthorne; Heller; Morrison; Walker; Wilder; Women Writers: Contemporary.

Maley, Willy. Lecturer, Department of English, University of Glasgow. Author of *A Spenser Chronology* (1994). Co-editor of *Representing Ireland: Literature and the Origins of Conflict, 1534–1660* (1993). **Essay:** Miller.

Mangum, Bryant. Professor, Department of English, Virginia Commonwealth University, Richmond. Author of *A Fortune Yet: Money in the Art of F. Scott Fitzgerald's Short Stories* (1991). Contributor to *Critical Survey of Short Fiction* edited by Frank Magill (1983), *Fifty Caribbean Writers* edited by Daryl Cumber Dance (1986), *New Essays on F. Scott Fitzgerald* edited by Jackson R. Bryer (1996), and the journals *American Literary Realism*, *American Notes & Queries*, *Fitzgerald/Hemingway Annual*, *Notes on Contemporary Literature*, and *Lost Generation Journal*. **Essay:** Fitzgerald.

Marriott, D.S. Lecturer, School of English and Drama, Queen Mary and Westfield College, University of London. Contributor to *Fragmente*, *Culture and Critical Form*, and *Parataxis*. **Essays:** African Literature: General; Baldwin; Black Mountain Poets; Poetry: Theory; Poetry: Recent and Contemporary: Poetry: British – 20th Century, Recent and Contemporary.

Matthews, Brian. (Adviser). Professor and Head of Sir Robert Menzies Centre for Australian Studies, Institute of Commonwealth Studies, London. Author of *The Receding Wave: A Study of Henry Lawson's Prose* (1972), *Louisa: A Diary, a Life* (1986), *Romantics and Mavericks: The Australian Short Story* (1987), *Oval Dreams* (1991), and *"Quickening" and Other Stories*. Editor of *Selected Stories of Henry Lawson* (1972).

Matthews, Steven. Lecturer, School of English, University of Leeds. Contributor to *Poetry Durham*, *Times Literary Supplement*, and *The Swansea Review*. **Essays:** British Literature: 20th Century; Poetry: 20th Century.

May, Krista L. Researcher, Department of English, Texas A & M University, College Station; editorial assistant and reviewer, *South Central Review*. Contributor to *Sir Thomas Malory: Views and Re-Views* edited by D. Thomas Hanks Jr. (1992). **Essays:** Erdrich; Stein.

Mazzeno, Laurence W. Vice President for Academic Affairs and Academic Dean, Ursuline College, Pepper Pike, Ohio. Author of *Victorian Poetry: A Bibliography of Criticism* (1989), *The Victorian Novel: A Bibliography of Criticism* (1994), *Herman Wouk* (1994). Managing Editor, *Arnoldian Review*, 1980–84; editor/managing editor of *Nineteenth-Century Prose*, 1986–92. **Essays:** British Literature: 19th Century; The Essay; Historical Fiction; Novel: General; Poetry: Victorian; Swift.

Meer, Sarah. Keasby Research Fellow, Selwyn College, University of Cambridge. **Essays:** Southern United States Literature: 19th Century; Stowe.

Meyer, Bruce. Instructor, Department of English, University of Toronto. Author of *The Open Room* (1989), *Lives and Works* (1992), *Radio Silence* (1992), and *Goodbye Mr Spalding* (1995). Editor of *In Their Words: Interviews with Fourteen Canadian Writers* (with Brian O'Riordan, 1985), *Arrivals: Canadian Poetry in the Eighties* (1986), and *The Selected Poems of Frank Prewett* (1987). Contributor to *The Oxford Companion to Canadian Literature* edited by Philip Toye (1983) and *Contemporary Poets* (also adviser) edited by Tracy Chevalier (5th edition, 1991). **Essay:** Reaney.

Miller, James A. Professor of English and Director of African-American Studies Program, University of South Carolina, Columbia. Contributor to *The Year Left: 2* edited by Fred Pfeil (1987), *Reimagining America* edited by Mark O'Brien and Craig Little (1990), *Revisioning the 30s* edited by Sherry Linkon and William Mullen (1996), and the journals *Callaloo*, *Journal of American Studies*, and *Children's Literature*. **Essays:** Baraka; Proletarian Literature in America; Richard Wright.

Mills, Sara. Senior Lecturer, Department of English and Drama, Loughborough University, Leicestershire. Author of *Feminist Readings/Feminists Reading* (with others, 1989), *Discourses of Difference: Analysis of Women's Travel Writing and Colonialism* (1991), and *Feminist Strategies* (1994). Editor of *Gendering the Reader* (1994). **Essays:** Feminist Literary Theory; Travel Literature.

Milner, Susannah. Researcher, Department of English, Pennsylvania State University, University Park. Contributor to *Philological Quarterly*. **Essays:** Stevenson; Welty.

Mingay, Philip. Researcher, Department of English, University of Alberta, Edmonton. Contributor to *Commonwealth Novel in English*. **Essays:** Davies; Visual Arts and Literature.

Mohanram, Radhika. Lecturer, Department of Women's Studies, University of Waikato, Hamilton, New Zealand. Co-editor of *Postcolonial Discourse and Changing Cultural Contexts* (with Gita Rajan, 1995). Contributor to *New Zealand Women's Studies Journal*. Co-editor of journal *SPAN*. **Essays:** Fiction: Indian; Indian Literature; Psychoanalytic Literary Theory.

Morace, Robert A. Associate Professor, Department of English, Daemen College, Amherst, New York. Author of *John Gardner: An Annotated Secondary Bibliography* (1984) and *The Dialogic Novels of Malcolm Bradbury and David Lodge* (1989). Co-editor of *John Gardner: Critical Perspectives* (with Kathryn Van Spanckeren, 1982). Consulting editor of *Critique* since 1982. **Essays:** Roth; Nathanael West.

Moseley, Merritt. Professor, Department of Literature and Language, University of North Carolina at Asheville. Author of *David Lodge* (1991) and *Understanding Kingsley Amis* (1993). Contributor to *The Encyclopedia of American Humorists* edited by Steven H. Gale (1988) and other books and journals. **Essays:** American Humor; Amis.

Mullaney, Julie. Researcher, School of English, University of Leeds. **Essay:** Malouf.

Nattrass, Leonora. Lecturer, Department of Literary and Media Studies, Nottingham Trent University. Author of *William Cobbett: The Politics of Style* (1995). Contributor to *The Independent Spirit: John Clare and the Self-Taught Tradition* edited by John Goodridge (1994). **Essay:** Prose and Journalism: Romantic – Historical and Political.

Neilson, Heather L.E. Lecturer, Department of English, Australian Defence Force Academy, Sydney. Contributor to *Literature in Context* edited by Richard Jordan (1983), *Gore Vidal: Writer Against the Grain* edited by Jay Parini (1992), and the journals *Sydney Studies in English*, *Antithesis*, and *Literature in Northern Queensland* (*LiNQ*). **Essay:** Vidal.

Newman, Judie. Reader in American and Postcolonial Literature, School of English, University of Newcastle-upon-Tyne. Author of *Saul Bellow and History* (1984), *John Updike* (1988), *Nadine Gordimer* (1988), and several articles. Editor of *Dred: A Tale of the Great Dismal Swamp* by Harriet Beecher Stowe (1992). **Essays:** Bellow; Coetzee; Gordimer; Jhabvala; Naipaul.

Newton, K.M. Professor, Department of English, University of Dundee. Author of *George Eliot: Romantic Humanist* (1981), *In Defence of Literary Interpretation* (1986), *Barchester Towers* (1987), and *Interpreting the Text* (1990). Editor of *Twentieth-Century Literary Theory: A Reader* (1988), *George Eliot* (1991), and *Theory into Practice: A Reader* (1992). Co-editor of journal *English*. **Essays:** Literary Theory: Postwar Approaches; Marxist Literary Theory.

Nichols, Shannon L. Researcher, Department of English, Pennsylvania State University, University Park. Managing Editor of *Legacy: A Journal of American Women Writers* since 1993. **Essays:** Alcott; Simms.

Norvig, Gerda S. Visiting Professor, Department of English, University of Colorado, Boulder. Author of *Dark Figures in the Desired Country: Blake's Illustrations to "The Pilgrim's Progress"* (1993). Contributor to *Studies in Romanticism*, *Blake: An Illustrated Quarterly*, *Philosophy and Literature*, and *The Massachusetts Review*. Member, editorial board of *English Language Notes*. **Essay:** Blake.

Nunn, Jacqueline. Senior Lecturer, Department of Education, Roehampton Institute, London. Contributor to *The Power of the Page: Children's Books and Their Readers* edited by Pat Pinsent (1993). **Essay:** Children's Literature: British – 1900 to the Present.

O'Brien, George. Associate Professor, Department of English, Georgetown University, Washington, D.C. Author of *The Village of Longing* (1987), *Dancehall Days* (1988), *Brian Friel* (1989), and *Brian Friel: A Reference Guide* (1995). **Essays:** Edgeworth; Heaney; Irish Literature: General; Irish Literature: Literary Revival to the Present; Joyce; George Moore.

O'Driscoll, Michael J. Researcher, Department of English, University of Western Ontario, London, Canada. **Essays:** Poetry: American – 20th Century, Before World War II; Sandburg.

Oh, Seiwoong. Assistant Professor, Department of English, Rider University, Lawrenceville, New Jersey. Contributor to *MELUS*, *Conference of College Teachers of English of Texas Proceedings* (*CCTEP*), *The Explicator*, and *English in Texas*. **Essays:** British Literature: General; Chapman.

Okonkwo, Chidi. Lecturer, Department of English, Chester College, Cheshire. Contributor to *The Routledge Encyclopedia of Post-Colonial Literatures* edited by Eugene Benson and L.W. Conolly (2 vols., 1994), *Post-Colonial Literatures: Achebe, Ngugi, Walcott and Desai* edited by Michael Parker and Roger Starkey (1994), and the journal *Textual Practice*. **Essays:** African Literature: West; Fiction: African; New Literatures: General; South African Literature: Black Writers; Soyinka.

Onslow, Barbara M. Lecturer, Department of English, University of Reading, Berkshire. Contributor to *Victorian Poetry* and *Victorian Periodicals Review*. **Essays:** Journalism and Literature in Britain; Martineau; Novel: British – General; Popular Literature in Britain: Grub Street; Prose and Journalism: Victorian; Women Writers: British – General; Women Writers: British – 19th Century, General.

Page, Norman. Emeritus Professor of Modern English Literature, University of Nottingham. Author of many books, including *The Language of Jane Austen* (1972), *Speech in the English Novel* (1973, revised 1987), *Thomas Hardy* (1977), *E.M Forster's Posthumous Fiction* (1977), *A.E. Housman: A Critical Biography* (1983), *A Dickens Companion* (1983), *A Kipling Companion* (1984), *A Conrad Companion* (1986), *Muriel Spark* (1990), *Tennyson: An Illustrated Life* (1992), and several volumes in the Macmillan "Author Chronologies" and "Masterguides" series. Editor of *Dickens: "Hard Times", "Great Expectations", "Our Mutual Friend": A Casebook* (1979), *The Language of Literature: A Casebook* (1984), *The Literature of Place* (with Peter Preston, 1993), and several volumes in the "Interviews and Recollections" series. Former editor of *Thomas Hardy Journal* and *Thomas Hardy Annual*. **Essays:** Austen; Forster.

Peacock, Noel. Assistant Professor, Department of English, University of Western Ontario, London, Canada. **Essay:** le Carré.

Pearce, Brian. Lecturer, Department of Drama, Technikon Natal, Durban. Contributor to *International Dictionary of Theatre 1: Plays* edited by Mark Hawkins-Dady (1992), *Twentieth-Century Britain: An Encyclopedia* edited by F.M. Leventhal (1995), and the journals *Shakespeare in Southern Africa* and *New Theatre Quarterly*. Board member, Durban Theatre Workshop Company. **Essays:** Fugard; Shakespeare: Performance History; Shakespeare: Late Comedies (Romances).

Peck, John. Lecturer, School of English Studies, Communication and Philosophy, University College of Wales, Cardiff. Author of *How to Study a Novel* (1983, revised 1995), *Literary Terms and Criticism* (with Martin Coyle, 1984, revised 1993), *How to Study a Shakespeare Play* (with Martin Coyle, 1985, revised 1995), *How to Study a Thomas Hardy Novel* (1987), *How to Read an English Novel* (1987), *How to Study a Poet* (1989), and *Practical Criticism* (with Martin Coyle, 1995). Editor of *Encyclopedia of Literature and Criticism* (with M. Coyle, P. Garside, and M. Kelsall), *Middlemarch: A New Casebook* (1992), and *"David Copperfield" and "Hard Times": A New Casebook* (1995). Contributor to *Journal of the Eighteen Nineties Society*, *Ariel*, *English Literature in Transition*, *English Dionysos*, and *English Studies*. Joint general editor of "How to Study Literature" and "New Casebook" series. **Essay:** Thackeray.

Peters, Jason R. Visiting Assistant Professor, Department of English, Roanoke College, Virginia. Contributor to *St. James Guide to Biography* edited by Paul E. Schellinger (1991). **Essay:** Topographical Poetry.

Peterson, Craig G. Researcher, Department of English, Queen's University, Kingston, Ontario. **Essay:** Prose and Journalism: 18th Century.

Piekarczyk, Frank. Researcher, Department of English Studies, University of Nottingham. Contributor to *Over Here* and *Social History Society* journal. Member, editorial board of *Over Here*. **Essays:** American Literary Naturalism; Vietnam War Literature.

Pilditch, Jan. Senior Lecturer, Department of English, University of Waikato, Hamilton, New Zealand. Editor of *The Critical Response to Katherine Mansfield* (1996). Contributor to *The Stow Debate* edited by Mason Lowance Jr. (1994) and *The Inward Sun: A Tribute to Janet Frame* edited by Elizabeth Alley (1994).Contributor to journals including *Australasian Journal of American Studies*, *Philosophy and Literature*, and *Landfall*. **Essay:** Mansfield.

Pinsent, Pat. Principal Lecturer, Department of English, Roehampton Institute, London. Editor of *Language, Culture and Young Children* (1992) and *The Power of the Page: Children's Books and Their Readers* (1993). Contributor to journals including *The School Librarian*, *Children's Literature in Education*, *Reading*, and *Early Childhood Development and Care*. Former editor of *Network*, 1984–94. **Essay:** C.S. Lewis.

Plasa, Carl. Lecturer, Centre for Critical and Cultural Theory, University College of Wales, Cardiff. Co-editor of *The Discourse of Slavery: Apha Behn to Toni Morrison* (with Betty J. Ring, 1994). Contributor to *Victorian Poetry*, *Prose Studies*, *English*, and *Gulliver*. **Essays:** Elegy and Poetry of Death; Novel: Victorian; Poetry: British – 20th Century, Before World War II; Tennyson; The War Poets.

Plastow, Jane. Lecturer, Theatre Workshop (School of English), University of Leeds. Contributor to *The Cambridge Guide to African and Caribbean Theatre* edited by Martin Banham, Errol Hill, and George Woodyard (1994) and the journal *Africa Events*. **Essays:** Achebe; African Literature: General; African Literature: East and Central; Ngugi.

Pooley, Roger. Lecturer, Department of English, Keele University, Staffordshire. Author of *English Prose of the Seventeenth Century* (1992). Editor of *The Green Knight: Selected Poetry and Prose of George Gascoigne* (1982) and *The Lord of the Journey: A Reader in Christian Spirituality* (with Philip Seddon, 1986). **Essays:** The Bible and Literature; Bunyan; Hobbes; Prose: Renaissance; Puritan Literature: British.

Pourteau, Chris. Assistant Research Editor, Texas Transportation Institute. Contributor to *Shakespeare Quarterly*, *Journal of Popular Culture*, and compiler of bibliographical information for the Folger Shakespeare Library's *Cumulative Shakespeare Bibliography*. **Essays:** American Civil-War Literature; Irving.

Pourteau, Leslie K. Researcher and teaching assistant, Department of English, Texas A & M University, College Station. Contributor to *Proceedings of the Philological Association of Louisiana*. **Essays:** Radcliffe; Walpole.

Prescott, Sarah. Researcher, Department of English, University of Exeter, Devon. Contributor to the journals *Women's Writing: The Elizabethan to the Victorian Period* and *Baetyl: The Journal of Women's Literature*. **Essay:** Women Writers: Restoration and 18th Century.

Price, Joanna. Lecturer in American Studies, School of Media, Critical, and Creative Arts, John Moore's University, Liverpool. Contributor to *Journal of American Studies*. **Essay:** McCullers.

Pritchard, R.E. Lecturer, Department of English, Keele University, Staffordshire. Author of *D.H. Lawrence: Body of Darkness* (1971). Editor of *English Women's Poetry: Elizabethan to Victorian* (1990) and *Mary Sidney, Countess of Pembroke, and Sir Philip Sidney: The Sidney Psalms* (1992). Contributor to journals including *Year's Work in English Studies* (also associate editor, 1979–95). **Essays:** British Literature: Renaissance, Tudor and Elizabethan; Green.

Quinn, Patrick J.M. Senior Lecturer in English, Nene College, Northampton. Author of *The Good English Manual* (1989), *The Great War and the Missing Muse* (1993), and *Re-Charting the Thirties: The Early Writings of Robert Graves and Siegfried Sassoon* (1995). Editor of *Robert Graves: Complete Short Stories* (1995) and *Robert Graves: The Centenary: Selected Poems* (1995). Contributor to *Yearbook of English Studies* and *Deus Loci: The Lawrence Durrell Quarterly*. Editor of the journal *Focus on Robert Graves and His Contemporaries* since 1987; advisory editor, *The European English Messenger*. **Essays:** Bennett; Georgian Poetry; Graves.

Radice, William. Lecturer in Bengali, School of Oriental and African Studies, University of London. Author of *Teach Yourself Bengali* (1994) and several volumes of poetry. Editor of *The Translator's Art: Essays in Honour of Betty Radice* (with Barbara Reynolds, 1987). Translator of *Rabindranath Tagore: Selected Poems* (1985, revised 1987), *Rabindranath Tagore: Selected Short Stories* (1991, revised 1994), and several libretti and other Bengali works. **Essay:** Tagore.

Rae, Patricia. Assistant Professor, Department of English, Queen's University, Kingston, Ontario. Contributor to *Comparative Literature*, *English Literary History*, *Southern Review*, *Queen's Quarterly*, and *English Studies in Canada*. **Essay:** William James.

Raines, Gay. Formerly Lecturer in English and American Literature, University of Kent, Canterbury. Contributor to *The Cambridge Guide to Literature in English* edited by Ian Ousby (revised edition, 1993), *Return in Post-Colonial Writing: A Cultural Labyrinth* edited by Vera Mihailovich-Dickman (1994), *Other Britain, Other British* edited by A. Robert Lee (1995), and the journals *Year's Work in English Studies* (Australian section), *Australian Studies* (guest editor, Volume 9), *Antipodes*, and *Australian Literary Studies*. Secretary of British Australian Studies Association (BASA) 1991–94. **Essays:** Australian Literature: General; Drama: Australian.

Reddell, Trace. Researcher, Department of English, University of Colorado, Boulder. Contributor to *Science Fiction Eye*, *American Book Review*. Author of short fiction for various anthologies and periodicals. **Essay:** Lovecraft.

Reedy, Penelope. Founding editor and publisher, The Redneck Press and *The Redneck Review of Literature*. Author of volumes of poetry. Contributor to *Western American Literature* and *Texas Books in Review*. **Essay:** Frontier and Western Literature.

Rees, Emma L.E. Part-time lecturer, School of English and American Studies, University of East Anglia. Contributor to *The Guinness Encyclopedia of Popular Music* (1991) and *Baetyl: The Journal of Women's Literature*. **Essays:** Behn; Drama: Restoration; Fiction to 1700.

Reeve, N.H. Lecturer, Department of English, University College of Wales, Swansea. Author of *The Novels of Rex Warner* (1989), *Nearly Too Much: The Poetry of J.H. Prynne* (1995), and various articles. Editor of *The Swansea Review* 1986–90. **Essay:** Huxley.

Reynolds, Kimberley. Senior Lecturer, Department of English, Roehampton Institute, London. Author of *Illustrated Dictionary of Art Terms* (with Richard Seddon, 1987), *Girls Only? Gender and Popular Children's Fiction in Britain 1880–1910* (1990), *Victorian Heroines: Representations of Femininity in Nineteenth-Century Literature and Art* (with Nicola Humble, 1993), and *Children's Literature in the 1890s and the 1990s* (1994). Associate editor, *The Artist*. **Essay:** Children's Literature: British – to 1900.

Riach, Alan. Lecturer, Department of English, University of Waikato, Hamilton, New Zealand. Author of *Hugh MacDiarmid's Epic Poetry* (1991) and two volumes of poetry. Editor of *The Radical Imagination: Lectures and Talks by Wilson Harris* (1992), *Selected Poetry of Hugh MacDiarmid* (with Michael Grieve, 1992), *Selected Prose of MacDiarmid* (1992), *Scottish Eccentrics: Hugh MacDiarmid* (1993), *Lucky Pet: An Autobiography* by MacDiarmid (1994), and *Contemporary Scottish Studies: Hugh MacDiarmid* (1995). Contributor to journals including *The Edinburgh Review*, *Verse*, *Landfall*, *Sport*, *Callaloo*, *Lines Review*, *Scottish Literary Journal*, and *Journal of New Zealand Literature*. **Essays:** Burns; Harris; MacDiarmid; Melville; Olson.

Rigby, Nigel. Researcher, English and American Studies, University of Kent, Canterbury. **Essay:** New Zealand and South Pacific Literatures: South Pacific.

Righelato, Pat. Lecturer, Department of English, University of Reading, Berkshire. Contributor of 20th-Century American section to *Year's Work in English Studies* since 1991. **Essays:** Bishop; Frost; Fuller.

Roberts, Adam. Lecturer, Department of English, Royal Holloway, University of London. Contributor to *Victorian Poetry*, *Browning Society Notes*, *Studies in English Literature*, *The Dickensian*, and *Notes & Queries*. **Essays:** Arnold; Poetry: Romantic; Percy Bysshe Shelley; Swinburne; Victorian Literature: General.

Roberts, Margaret E. Tutor, Department of American and Commonwealth Arts, University of Exeter, Devon. **Essays:** Irish Literature: Women Writers; Rhys; Women Writers: American – 1900 to the Present.

Roberts, Marie Mulvey. Senior Lecturer in Literary Studies, University of the West of England, Bristol. Author of *British Poets and Secret Societies* (1986) and *Gothic Immortals: The Fiction of the Brotherhood of the Rosy Cross* (1990). Co-editor of *Explorations in Medicine 1* (with David Lamb and Teifion Davies, 1987), *Literature and Medicine During the Eighteenth Century* (with Roy Porter, 1993), *Out of the Night: Writings from Death Row* (with Benjamin Zephaniah, 1994), *Perspectives on the History of British Feminism* (with Tamae Mizuta, 1994), *Secret Texts: The Literature of Secret Societies* (with Hugh Ormsby-Lennon, 1995), and the journal *Women's Writing* (with Janet Todd). **Essays:** Gothic Fiction; Medicine and Literature; Mary Shelley.

Robertson, Elizabeth. (Adviser). Associate Professor, Department of English, University of Colorado, Boulder. Author of *Early Devotional Prose and the Female Audience* (1990). Co-editor of *Chaucer's Religious Tales* (with C. David Benson, 1991). Contributor to *Seeking the Woman in Medieval and Renaissance Texts* edited by Sheila Fisher and Janet E. Halley (1989), *Images of Sainthood in Medieval Europe* edited by Renate Blumenfeld-Kosinski and Timea Szell (1991) and *Feminist Approaches to the Body in the Middle Ages* edited by Linda Lomperis and Sarah Stanbury (1993). Founding editor of *The Medieval Feminist Newsletter*. **Essay:** Chaucer.

Robinson, Danny L. Associate Professor, Department of English, Bloomsburg University, Pennsylvania. **Essays:** Cummings; Ondaatje; Styron.

Robinson, Jeffrey C. Professor, Department of English, University of Colorado, Boulder. Author of *Radical Literary Education: A Classroom Experiment with Wordsworth's "Ode"* (1987), *The Walk: Notes on a Romantic Image* (1989), *The Current of Romantic Passion* (1991), and *Romantic Presences: Living Images from the Age of Wordsworth and Shelley* (1995). Editor and reviser of *Keats: The Myth of the Hero* by Dorothy Van Ghent (1983). **Essay:** Keats.

Robson, Mark. Researcher and teaching assistant, School of English, University of Leeds. Contributor to *Modern Language Review*. **Essays:** Biography: General; Biography: Renaissance; More.

Rombes, Nicholas. Lecturer, Department of English, University of Detroit, Mercy. Contributor to *The Heath Anthology of American Literature* (edited by Paul Lauter, 1990, and revised edition, 1993), *Making America, Making American Literature: Franklin to Cooper* edited by A. Robert Lee and W.M. Verhoeven (1994) and the journal *Studies in American Fiction*. Managing editor, *Resources for American Literary Study* 1991–92 (and guest editor, Fall 1993). **Essays:** Brown; Jefferson.

Ross, Robert L. Research Associate, Edward A. Clark Center for Australian Studies, University of Texas, Austin. Editor of *Research: An Introduction* (1974), *Australian Literary Criticism 1945–1988* (1989), *International Literature in English: Essays on the Major Writers* (1991), and the journal *Antipodes: A North American Journal of Australian Literature* since 1987. Contributor to *Journal of Commonwealth and Postcolonial Studies*, *World Literature Today*, *South Asian Review*, *South African Theatre Journal*, *The Literary Criterion*, *Review of Contemporary Fiction*, *Commonwealth Novel in English*, and several essay collections. **Essays:** Australian Literature: Recent and Contemporary; Poetry: Australian; Henry Handel Richardson.

Rowland, Antony. Researcher and tutor, School of English, University of Leeds. Contributor to *English*, *Cascando*, *Psychopoetica*, and *Torch*. Editor of *Poetry and Audience* since 1992. **Essays:** The Movement; Poetry: General; Judith Wright.

Rowland, Susan. Lecturer, Department of English, University of Liverpool. Contributor to *Saul Bellow Journal* and *Literature and Theology*. **Essay:** Waugh.

Royle, Nicholas. Lecturer, Department of English Studies, University of Stirling. Author of *Telepathy and Literature: Essays on the Reading Mind* (1990), *Elizabeth Bowen and the Dissolution of the Novel* (with Andrew Bennett, 1994), and *After Derrida* (1995). Editor, *Afterwords* (1992). Joint editor, *Oxford Literary Review*; co-editor, *The Bowen Newsletter*. **Essay:** Bowen.

Rusinko, Susan. Professor Emeritus, Bloomsburg University, Pennsylvania. Author of *Terence Rattigan* (1983), *Tom Stoppard* (1986), *A Critical History of British Drama, 1950 to the Present* (1989), *The Plays of Benn Levy: Between Shaw and Coward* (1994), and *Joe Orton* (1995). Contributor to *Shaw Review*, *Modern Drama*, *World Literature Today*, and several essay collections and reference works. **Essays:** O'Neill; Stoppard.

St-Jacques, Raymond. Professor, Department of English, University of Ottawa. Contributor to *Traditio*, *Notes & Queries*, *Studies in Medieval Culture*, *English Studies in Canada*, *Mosaic*, *Neophilologus*, *Yearbook of Langland Studies*, *The Explicator*, and *Florilegium*. **Essays:** Beowulf; Langland.

Schauffer, D. Professor, Department of Drama, University of Durban-Westville. Contributor to *Pageant Theatre Quarterly*, *South African Theatre Journal* (also member of advisory board), and *Tabs*. Editor of *Association of Drama Departments of South Africa Newsletter* since 1990. **Essay:** Tragedy: Theory.

Scheick, William J. J.R. Millikan Centennial Professor, Department of English, University of Texas, Austin. Author of *The Will and the Word: The Poetry of Edward Taylor* (1974), *The Writings of Jonathan Edwards* (1975), *Seventeenth-Century Poetry: A Reference Guide* (with JoElla Doggett, 1977), *The Slender Human Word: Emerson's Artistry in Prose* (1978), *The Half-Blood: A Cultural Symbol* (1979), *The Splintering Frame: The Later Fiction of H.G. Wells* (1984), *H.G. Wells: A Reference Guide* (with J. Randolph Cox, 1988), *Fictional Structure and Ethics* (1990), *Design in Puritan American Literature* (1992), *Paine, Scripture, and Authority* (with Edward H. Davidson, 1994), and *The Ethos of Romance at the Turn of the Century* (1994). Editor of *Critical Essays* *on Jonathan Edwards* (1979), *Contemporary American Women Writers: Narrative Strategies* (1985), *Two Mather Biographies* (1989), and *The Critical Response to H.G. Wells*, 1995. **Essays:** American Literature: Early Period; Bradstreet; Edwards; Puritan Literature: American; Taylor; Wells.

Scragg, Leah. Senior Lecturer, Department of English, University of Manchester. Author of *The Metamorphosis of "Gallathea"* (1982), *Discovering Shakespeare's Meaning* (1988, revised 1994), *Shakespeare's Mouldy Tales: Recurrent Plot Motifs* (1992). Contributor to journals including *Shakespeare Survey* (also resident reviewer), *Review of English Studies*, *Notes & Queries*, and *English Language Notes*. **Essay:** Lyly.

Seed, David. Senior Lecturer, Department of English, University of Liverpool. Author of *The Fictional Labyrinths of Thomas Pynchon* (1988), *The Fiction of Joseph Heller* (1989), *Rudolph Wurlitzer* (1991), and *James Joyce's "A Portrait of the Artist as a Young Man"* (1992). Editor of *"The Handling of Words" and Other Studies in Literary Psychology* by Vernon Lee (1992) and *Anticipations: Essays on Early Science Fiction and Its Precursors* (1995). General editor, Liverpool University Press "Science Fiction Texts and Studies" series. **Essays:** Chandler; Wyndham Lewis; Mailer; Salinger.

Smith, Peter J. Lecturer, Department of English and Media Studies, Nottingham Trent University. Author of *Social Shakespeare* (1995). Editor of *The Jew of Malta* by Christopher Marlowe (1994) and *Hamlet: Theory in Practice* (with Nigel Wood, 1996). Associate editor, *Cahiers Elisabéthains*. **Essay:** Shakespeare: *Hamlet*.

Solomon, Rakesh H. Associate Professor, Department of Theatre and Drama, Indiana University, Bloomington. Contributor to *Alan Ayckbourn: A Casebook* edited by Bernard F. Dukore (1991), *The Drama Review*, *Theatre Journal*, *Journal of Performance Studies*, *Theatre Survey*, *American Drama*, *Beckett Circle*, and *Forum for Modern Languages*. **Essay:** Albee.

Speer, Clara Elizabeth. Instructor, Department of English, Albuquerque T-VI Community College. Editorial assistant, *World Shakespeare Bibliography* project. **Essays:** Adams; Burke; Franklin; Godwin; Paine; Prose in America: 19th Century; Steinbeck.

Spivack, Charlotte. Professor, Department of English, University of Massachusetts, Amherst. Author of *George Chapman* (1967), *The Comedy of Evil on Shakespeare's Stage* (1978), *Ursula K. Le Guin* (1984), *Merlin's Daughters: Contemporary Women Writers of Fantasy* (1987), *Merlin: A Thousand Heroes with One Face* (1994), *The Company of Camelot: Arthurian Characters in Romance and Fantasy* (with Roberta Lynne Staples, 1994). Editor of *Merlin versus Faust: Contending Archetypes in Western Culture* (1992). **Essays:** Drama: Medieval, Morality Plays; Drama: Renaissance, Jacobean and Caroline; Fantasy Literature; Middleton.

Stabler, Jane. Teaching Fellow, School of English, University of St Andrews, Fife. Contributor to *Reading Douglas Dunn* edited by Robert Crawford and David Kinlach (1992) and the journal *Translation and Literature*. **Essays:** De Quincey; Lamb.

Stephens, John Russell. Senior Lecturer, Department of English, University College of Wales, Swansea. Author of *The Censorship of English Drama 1824–1901* (1980) and *The Profession of the Playwright: British Theatre 1800–1900* (1992). Contributor to *The Cambridge Guide to Theatre* edited by Martin Banham (1988, revised 1992) and the journals *Theatre Notebook*, *Nineteenth Century Theatre*, and *Notes & Queries*. **Essays:** Dramatic Censorship; Drama: British – 19th Century.

Stevens, Simon. Part-time lecturer, Wakefield College, Yorkshire. Contributor to *The Cambridge Guide to Literature in English* edited by Ian Ousby (1988) and the journal *Cambridge Quarterly*. **Essay:** Twain.

Stewart, Alan. Lecturer, Department of English, Birkbeck College, University of London. Contributor to *The Works of Francis Bacon: 6* edited by Graham Rees (1996) and the journals *Representations* and *Medieval English Theatre*. **Essays:** Bacon; Drayton; Gay and Lesbian Literature; Marston; Shakespeare: Recent and Contemporary Approaches; Shakespeare: Early Comedies.

Stone, Marjorie. Associate Professor, Department of English, Dalhousie University, Halifax, Nova Scotia. Author of *Elizabeth Barrett Browning* (1994). Contributor to *Victorian Studies*, *Victorian Literature and Culture*, *Victorian Poetry*, *Dickens Studies Annual*, *Browning Studies*, and *The Dalhousie Review*. Member, editorial boards of *English Studies in Canada* and *Victorian Review*. **Essays:** Elizabeth Barrett Browning; Dramatic Monologue.

Strauss, Gerald H. Professor Emeritus of English, Bloomsburg University, Pennsylvania. Contributor to the *Dictionary of Literary Biography* series, *Critical Survey of Drama* edited by Frank Magill (6 vols., 1985, revised 1994), and *Magill's Literary Annual*. **Essays:** Fletcher; Tragicomedy.

Striff, Erin. Researcher, School of English Studies, Communication and Philosophy, University College of Wales, Cardiff. **Essay:** Drama: American – 20th Century, Recent and Contemporary.

Tanner, James T.F. Professor, Department of English, University of North Texas, Denton. Author of *Walt Whitman: A Supplemental Bibliography* (1969) and *The Texas Legacy of Katherine Anne Porter* (1991). Contributor to *Studies in American Humor*. Editor, *American Periodicals* since 1991. **Essays:** American Literature: 19th Century; Romanticism and Transcendentalism in America; Whitman.

Thieme, John. Professor of New Literatures, Department of English, University of Hull. Author of *V.S. Naipaul: The Mimic Men* (1985) and *The Web of Tradition: Uses of Allusion in V.S. Naipaul's Fiction* (1987). Contributor to journals including *Modern Fiction Studies*, *Ariel*, *World Literature Written in English*, *Kunapipi*, *Journal of Commonwealth Literature* (also co-editor), and *Prose Studies*. Editor, "Contemporary World Writers" series. **Essays:** Caribbean Literature; Walcott.

Thoms, Peter. Assistant Professor, Department of English, University of Western Ontario, London, Canada. Author of *The Windings of the Labyrinth: Quest and Structure in the Major Novels of Wilkie Collins* (1992). **Essay:** Collins.

Tobias, Richard C. Professor, Department of English, University of Pittsburgh, Pennsylvania. Author of *The Art of James Thurber* (1969), *T.E. Brown* (1978), and *Bibliographies of Victorian Studies* (1991). Editor of *Shakespeare's Late Plays* (with Paul G. Zolbrod, 1974), *Guide to the Year's Work in Victorian Poetry and Prose* (1974), and *Victorian Poetry*. **Essay:** Macaulay.

Toone, Marjorie. Lecturer, School of Applied Arts and Design, De Montfort University, Leicester. Contributor to *Gulliver* and *Postcolonial Studies*. **Essay:** Travel Literature: British – 18th and 19th Centuries.

Tressider, George A. Tutor, Department of English, University College of Wales, Aberystwyth. Contributor to *British Journal of Eighteenth-Century Studies*. **Essay:** Crabbe.

Tripp, Anna. Lecturer, Department of English, University of Hertfordshire, Watford. Contributor to *The English Review* and *Women: A Cultural Review*. **Essay:** Plath.

Trussler, Michael. Assistant Professor, Department of English, University of Toronto. Contributor to *Critical Essays on Donald Barthelme* edited by Richard F. Patteson (1992), *Studies in Short Fiction*, and *Wascana Review*. **Essays:** Carver; O'Connor; Short Fiction: American.

Tucker, Louise. Visiting Assistant Professor, Department of English, University of Maryland, Baltimore. Contributor to *The Bowen Newsletter*, *New Comparisons*, and *Times Higher Education Supplement*. Editorial assistant, *Textual Practice*. **Essays:** Dorothy Richardson; Woolf.

Turner, Elizabeth A. Lecturer, Department of English, University of Nebraska, Lincoln. Contributor to *Legacy: A Journal of American Women Writers*. **Essay:** Cather.

Veitch, Jonathan. Assistant Professor, Department of English, University of Wisconsin, Madison. Contributor to *Contemporary Literature* (also assistant editor), *American Quarterly*, and *Prospects*. **Essay:** Harlem Renaissance.

Vietto, Angela. Researcher, Department of English, Pennsylvania State University, University Park. **Essays:** Politics and Literature; Prose in America: Historical and Political; Roethke; Wharton.

Voss, Tony. Professor, Department of English, University of Natal, Durban. Contributor to *English in Africa*, *English Studies in Africa*, and *African Studies*. **Essay:** South African Literature: General.

Vulpe, Nicola. Professor of English, Departamento de Filologia Moderna, Universidad de Las Palmas de Gran Canaria, Canary Islands. Editor of *Sealed in Struggle: Canadian Poetry and the Spanish Civil War – An Anthology* (1995). Contributor to *Atlantis*, *Canadian Literature*, *Journal of Canadian Poetry*, *Journal of Near Eastern Studies*, and *Revista Española de Estudios Canadienses* (also advisory board member). **Essay:** Pratt.

Wallace, Diana. Researcher, Department of English and Drama, Loughborough University, Leicestershire. **Essays:** Spark; Rebecca West.

Watson, Elizabeth Porges. Lecturer, Department of English Studies, University of Nottingham. Author of *Spenser* (1967). Editor of *Cranford* by Elizabeth Gaskell (1972) and *Spenser: Selected Writings* (1992). Contributor to journals including *Renaissance and Modern Studies*, *New University Quarterly*, *Cosmos*, *Leeds Studies in English*, *Reinardus*, and *Explorations*. **Essays:** Gaskell; Sidney; Skelton.

Watt, Diane. Lecturer, Department of English, University College of Wales, Aberystwyth. Contributor to *Dear Sister: Medieval Women and the Epistolary Genre*, edited by Karen Cherewatuk and Ulrike Wiethaus (1993) and the journals *Parergon* and *Renaissance Quarterly*. **Essay:** Poetry: Old English.

Weber, Diane Looms. Teaching assistant, Department of English, Texas A & M University, College Station. **Essay:** Doyle.

Wells, Lynn S. Researcher, Department of English, University of Western Ontario, London, Canada. **Essays:** Fiction: British – 20th Century, Recent and Contemporary; Rushdie.

Williams, Carolyn D. Lecturer, Department of English, University of Reading, Berkshire. Author of *Pope, Homer and Manliness: Some Aspects of Eighteenth-Century Classical Learning* (1993). Contributor to journals including *British Journal of Eighteenth-Century Studies*, *Essays in Criticism*, *The Scriblerian*, *Studies in English Literature*, and *Cauda Pavonis*. **Essays:** Addison; Ballad; Comedy: Restoration; Drama: British – General; Drama: 18th Century; Gibbon; Goldsmith; Sentimentalism; Sheridan; Steele; Traherne.

Wilmeth, Don B. Professor, Department of Theatre, Speech and Dance, Brown University, Providence, Rhode Island. Author of *The American Stage to World War I: A Guide to Information Sources* (1978), *American and English Popular Entertainment: A Guide to Information Sources* (1980), *George Frederick Cooke* (1980), *The Language of American Popular Entertainment: A Glossary* (1981), and *Variety Entertainment and Outdoor Amusements: A Reference Guide* (1982). Editor of *Plays by William Hooker Gillette* (with Rosemary Cullen, 1983), *Plays by Augustin Daly* (with Rosemary Cullen, 1984), and *The Cambridge Guide to American Theater* (with Tice L. Miller, 1993). **Essays:** Drama: American – General; Drama: American – 19th Century.

Winans, Amy E. Researcher, Department of English, Pennsylvania State University, University Park. Contributor to *Resources for American Literary Study*. **Essays:** Equiano; Jacobs.

Winnifrith, T.J. Senior Lecturer, Department of English, University of Warwick, Coventry. Author of *The Brontës and Their Background* (1973), *The Brontës* (1977), *Brontë Facts and Problems* (with Edward Chitham, 1983), *A New Life of Charlotte Brontë* (1987), and *Fallen Women in the Nineteenth-Century Novel* (1994). Editor of *The Poems of Branwell Brontë* (1983), *The Poems of Charlotte Brontë* (1984), and *The Philosophy of Literature* (with others, 1989). **Essays:** Charlottë Bronte; Emily Brontë; Kingsley; Novel: Victorian Novel of Social Conscience; Orwell.

Wood, Derek N.C. Professor, Department of English, St Francis Xavier University, Antigonish, Nova Scotia. Contributor to *The Spenser Encyclopedia* edited by A.C. Hamilton (1990) and journals including *Neophilologus*, *Cahiers Elisabéthains*, *Milton Quarterly*, *English Studies in Canada*, and *English Language Notes*. **Essays:** Milton; Shakespeare: Poetry.

Woodman, Thomas. Lecturer, Department of English, University of Reading, Berkshire. Author of *Thomas Parnell* (1985), *Politeness and Poetry in the Age of Pope* (1989), *Faithful Fictions: The Catholic Novel in British Literature* (1991), and *A Preface to Samuel Richardson* (1993). **Essays:** Johnson; Pope.

Woods, Tim S. Lecturer, Department of English, University College of Wales, Aberystwyth. Contributor to *Beyond the Red Notebook: Essays on Paul Auster* edited by Dennis Barone (1995) and the journals *Parataxis*, *Fragmente*, and *Textual Studies*. **Essays:** Barth; Doolittle [H.D.]; Ginsberg; Imagism; Kerouac; Literary Theory: Contemporary Approaches; MacNeice; Modernism: Poetry; Novel: Recent and Contemporary; Poetry: British – General.

Wray, Ramona. Researcher, Department of English, Trinity College, Dublin. **Essays:** Autobiography; British Literature: Renaissance; Vaughan.

Wright, Charlotte M. Editor, University of North Texas Press, Denton. Contributor to *The Oxford Companion to Twentieth-Century Poetry in English* edited by Ian Hamilton (1995), the *Dictionary of Literary Biography* series, and the journals *Western American Literature* and *New Mexico Humanities Review*. **Essay:** Shepard.

Zemka, Sue. Assistant Professor, Department of English, University of Colorado, Boulder. Contributor to *Macropolitics of Nineteenth-Century Literature* edited by Jonathan Arac and Harriet Ritvo (1989) and the journals *Nineteenth-Century Literature* and *Victorian Studies*. **Essays:** Carlyle; Pre-Raphaelitism; Ruskin.

Zunder, William. Lecturer, Department of English, University of Hull. Author of *The Poetry of John Donne* (1982), *Elizabethan Marlowe: Writing and Culture in the English Renaissance* (1994), and *Writing and the English Renaissance* (with Suzanne Trill, 1996). Contributor to *Jacobean Poetry and Prose: Rhetoric, Representation and the Popular Imagination* (1988) and the journals *English Studies* and *Literature and History*. **Essays:** Marlowe; Shakespeare: *King Lear*.